THE READER'S ENCYCLOPEDIA

*

An Encyclopedia of
World Literature and the Arts

*

Edited by
WILLIAM ROSE BENÉT

THOMAS Y. CROWELL COMPANY * NEW YORK

Manufactured in the United States of America

Preface

At the end of the nineteenth century there died an English schoolmaster and clergyman whose life had spanned most of it. He was born in 1810. Two books in my father's library made me familiar, at an early age, with the Englishman's name. They were Brewer's *A Dictionary of Phrase and Fable* and Brewer's *The Reader's Handbook*. His full name was Ebenezer Cobham Brewer. Years later, when I was asked to edit a *Reader's Encyclopedia,* using *Crowell's Handbook for Readers and Writers* as nucleus, I discovered that according to the preface of the first editor of that volume, it had originally owed much to the fascinating books of Dr. Brewer. (I always imagined him with a delightful beard—something like Edward Lear's—in which nested all the oddities of learning. Alas, I can boast no such receptaculum!) However, the *Handbook for Readers and Writers* had given his material extremely detailed revision, to say nothing of supplying a great deal that was new, relating to the Victorian era and to subsequent years, with especial attention to American literature and allusion. Since that time, of course, almost as many changes in taste, viewpoint, and interest have occurred as the handbook's editor found to have taken place between 1897 (when Dr. Brewer died) and 1925 (when the *Crowell Handbook* appeared). Twenty or more recent years have shown as many alterations as the previous thirty. And now, in the midst of the new Atomic Age, there are changes that even a modern editor could not have anticipated several years ago!

I wish immediately to acknowledge my indebtedness, not only to the editor of *Crowell's Handbook for Readers and Writers,* Miss Henrietta Gerwig, but also to an intermediate reviser, Miss Irene Hendry, whose knowledge of modern literature has proved indispensable to the present volume. Miss Gerwig's handbook was designed as "a dictionary of famous characters and plots in legend, fiction, drama, opera, and poetry, together with dates and principal works of important authors, literary and journalistic terms and familiar allusions." Miss Hendry's work, never before appearing in print, is incorporated here. But the original handbook is only one of several ancestors of the present work. Since the handbook's publication, so many people have contributed ideas and suggestions that the present volume has, in a sense, been composed for you by inquiring readers from all parts of the country. It is no mere revision, but veritably a new book.

Original entries on established authors of the past have been enlarged, with modern treatment. Full advantage has been taken of all the most modern reference books. (A complete list of all books consulted will be found below.) More attention has been given to obscure works and figures in literature both of the distant and recent past. And, in line with the methodological advance in literary criticism of the past fifteen years or so, "whereby an author is interpreted not only in terms of the literal content of his works and the facts of his biography, but also in terms of the general intellectual forces of his time," entries have been chosen of significant figures, movements, and terms in aesthetics, science, philosophy, economics, and politics. Freud, Jung, Karl Marx, Lenin, The New Deal, the stream-of-consciousness tendency in fiction, and even futurism and surrealism have received due consideration. The fields of art and music are now extensively covered, incorporating important twentieth-century additions.

Such is the nature of an encyclopedia of this kind that one could go on almost indefinitely adding new information to that already accumulated. The limitations of such a volume are hard to establish. What is it that intelligent readers and writers do *not* wish to know? One simply has to set a term, and mark boundaries. Therefore, for this new book, much more grist has actually been gathered than has come through the mill. At that, it deserves to be called a one-volume literary encyclopedia.

I have endeavored carefully to check over what was already amassed, to expand, to fill up gaps, to carry on what was unfinished; to add biographical, historical, and other data that unfolding world events made obligatory; to comb for word, phrase, and allusion, such reference works as had been searched either superficially or not at all; to discard the obsolete; to bring to light the overlooked; and to play, in general, the role of Argus-eyed modernizer. I am bound to have made errors both of omission and commission. But, with the able assistance of Dr. Alexander Gode and the invaluable final rechecking of that brilliant literary detective, Earle F. Walbridge, I believe that this encyclopedia will now prove one of the most complete and practicable in existence. It will be found to cover an unusual range of information, to provide a reference to most allusions occurring in your reading, to give all the important myths and legends and a great many of the most important themes and characters in fiction old and new, to include references that constantly crop up in the critical writing of yesterday and today, to furnish information as to literary schools, trends, and movements past and present and biographical data on most "people of importance." Likewise it will prove a real aid to the vocabulary and allusiveness of writers, as well as providing them with a genuine source book of ideas. As for cross-word puzzlers, they will, of course, discover it to be a necessity!

The curious mind inevitably stores up what it has sometimes characterized as "much useless information." Yet, in literature, it is often these peculiar bits of learning that serve most to adorn and give flavor to a style. I have, however, endeavored to rid the book of all that is merely archaic. I have tried to maintain balance and proportion between the modern world and the world of antiquity. People used to speak of "dead languages." Yet, in English derivations, the dead languages still live. In the same way, the mythology of the past constantly reappears in the poetry of the present; and the classics may furnish groundwork for the most modern fiction. (One has only to think of *Ulysses*.) All of this such a book as the one before you must comprehend. It must also show itself thoroughly familiar with modern literature and thought of all kinds, with modern invention and science, with new art media, with the continuity of history.

Either my memory is at fault or there is one essay that neither Charles Lamb,

William Hazlitt, or Christopher Morley ever wrote: one on Reference Books. The phrase for them, now cliché, has been "mines of information." But a mine, at best, is a rather dark and dreary excavation—not to say *dank*, at times. I prefer to think of the book before you as a cave like the famous one stumbled upon by Aladdin. I might go on from there to describe its revelation of treasure of so many varieties and kinds, yet each in its own particular bin. For the office of a reference book is, after all, to bring some sort of order out of chaos. But it is also to present to you a well-organized supplementary memory, in one volume. The delights of such a memory may be inexhaustible; the safaris of research it can initiate, endless; the urge to literary creation which it can supply, present on every page. And remember, that to enter this domain of learning and imagination you have not even to use that mysterious phrase, "Open Sesame!"

WILLIAM ROSE BENÉT

Of the many books consulted from time to time in the compilation of this encyclopedia, special acknowledgment is due to the following: *Baker's Biographical Dictionary of Musicians;* Thomas Bulfinch, *Mythology* (Dictionary and Index); *The Cambridge History of American Literature; The Cambridge History of English Literature;* Lewis Copeland, *The Handy Encyclopedia of Useful Information;* John Colin Dunlop, *History of Prose Fiction;* Bessie Graham, *The Bookman's Manual; Heroes and Heroines of Fiction;* Albert M. Hyamson, *A Dictionary of English Phrases;* Helen L. Kaufmann, *The Stories of One Hundred Great Composers;* Helen Rex Keller, *The Reader's Digest of Books;* Stanley J. Kunitz and Howard Haycraft, *American Authors: 1600–1900;* Stanley J. Kunitz and Howard Haycraft, *British Authors of the Nineteenth Century;* Stanley J. Kunitz and Howard Haycraft, *Twentieth Century Authors;* George G. Loane, *A Short Handbook of Literary Terms;* J. Walker McSpadden, *Opera Synopses;* J. Walker McSpadden, *Shakespearean Synopses; The New Modern Encyclopedia; The Oxford Companion to American Literature; The Oxford Companion to English Literature;* H. A. Reason, *The Road to Modern Science;* Bertrand Russell, *The History of Western Philosophy;* Joseph T. Shipley, *Dictionary of World Literature;* Benjamin H. Smith, *The Century Cyclopedia of Names;* Bernard Sobel, *The Theatre Handbook and Digest of Plays;* Carl Van Doren, *The American Novel;* Carl Van Doren, *Contemporary American Novelists;* William S. Walsh, *Modern Prose and Poetry;* Webster's *New International Dictionary;* Webster's *Biographical Dictionary;* William A. Wheeler, *A Dictionary of the Noted Names in Fiction; The World at War; Who's Who in America; World Almanac;* and many others.

Note to the User: All the abbreviations used in this book are self-explanatory. Words or phrases printed in SMALL CAPITALS refer to special entries elsewhere in the book. So do references of the type, "See THE MARRIAGE OF WILLIAM ASHE." A reference of the type, "Cf. the novel, *The Marriage of William Ashe,* by Mrs. Humphry Ward," however, would not refer to a special entry but to the work itself. Definite and indefinite articles are disregarded for purposes of alphabetization.

A

A, as a brand or mark, was used as the initial letter of Adulterer or Adulteress. Cf. *The Scarlet Letter* by Nathaniel Hawthorne, in which Hester Prynne wore a "rag of scarlet cloth" on the breast of her gown that "assumed the shape of a letter. It was the capital letter A."

A1 means first-rate—the very best. In Lloyd's Register of British and Foreign Shipping, the character of the ship's hull is designated by letters, and that of the anchors, cables, and stores by figures. A1 means hull first-rate, and also anchors, cables, and stores: A2, hull first-rate, but fittings second-rate. Vessels of an inferior character are classified under the letters AE, E and I.

Aagesen, Svend (ca. 1185). First historian of Denmark, author of COMPENDIOSA HISTORIA REGUM DANIAE (300 to 1185 A. D.).

Aani. In Egyptian mythology, the dog-headed ape sacred to the god Thoth.

Aaron. In the Old Testament, brother of MOSES with whom he was associated in the calling down of the Ten Plagues and the leading of the Children of Israel out of Egypt (ca. 1200 B. C.). As high priest Aaron was responsible for the making of the Golden Calf which the Israelites worshiped in the wilderness while Moses was receiving the Ten Commandments from Jehovah.

Aaron's Beard. The popular name of many wild plants, including Great St. John's Wort (Rose of Sharon), the Ivy-leaved Toadflax, Meadowsweet, Saxifrage Sarmentosa, etc.

Aaron's Rod. The name given (with reference to *Num.* xvii. 8 where a rod is mentioned which blossomed miraculously and bore almonds) to various flowering plants, including Golden Rod, Great Mullein, and others. It is also the title of a novel by D. H. Lawrence.

Aaron's Serpent. (1) Something so powerful as to eliminate minor powers. The allusion is to *Exod.* vii. 10–12.

(2) A Moor, beloved by Tamora, queen of the Goths, in the tragedy of *Titus Andronicus,* published amongst the plays of Shakespeare.

Aaru. In Egyptian mythology, the fields of Aaru are the abode of the blessed dead and of the gods and goddesses.

Aasen, Ivar Andreas (1813–1896). Norwegian philologist, who made from various dialects a Norwegian literary language called New Norwegian or *Landsmaal* in contrast to the Dano-Norwegian *Rigsmaal.*

Abaddon. The angel of the bottomless pit (*Rev.* ix. 11), from Hebrew *abad,* "he perished." Milton uses the name for the bottomless pit itself.

abalone. A univalve mollusk concerning which the California poet George STERLING composed a famous song that is now a part of American folklore. When pounded, shredded, and cooked, it makes a gourmet's dish. The first stanza of Sterling's song goes,

> In Carmel Bay, the people say,
> We feed the Lazzaroni
> On caramels and cockleshells
> And hunks of abalone.

Sinclair LEWIS added several stanzas to the original song, one of which runs,

> He wanders free beside the sea
> Where every crab's a crony.
> He flaps his wings and madly sings,
> The plaintive abalone.

Abaris. A mythical Greek sage of the 6th century B. C. (surnamed "the Hyperborean") mentioned by Herodotus, Pindar, etc. Apollo gave him a magic arrow which rendered him invisible, cured diseases, gave oracles, and on which he could ride through the air. Abaris gave it to Pythagoras, who, in return, taught him philosophy. Hence *the dart of Abaris.*

Abbadona. One of the most interesting figures in Klopstock's epic poem, THE MESSIAH (Ger. *Der Messias,* 1748–1773), an angel who is drawn into the rebellion of Satan half unwillingly. In hell he constantly bewails his fall and reproves Satan for his pride and blasphemy; and during the crucifixion he lingers about the cross with repentance, hope and fear. His ultimate fate we are not told, but his redemption is implied.

Abbassides. A dynasty of thirty-seven caliphs who reigned over the Mohammedan Empire from 750 to 1258. They were descended from Abbas, uncle of Mahomet. Haroun al Raschid (b. 765, reigned 786–808), of the ARABIAN NIGHTS, was one of their number.

Abbey, Edwin Austin (1852–1911). American painter. His illustrations for *Old Songs* (1889) caused Joseph Pennell to call him "the greatest living illustrator." He also illustrated *Selections from the Poetry of Robert Herrick* and executed panels illustrating the *Quest of the Holy Grail* for the Boston Public Library (1890–1902).

Abbé Constantin, L. A novel by Ludovic Halévy (*Fr.* 1834–1908), in which the kindly old village priest who bears the title rôle plays something of the matchmaker.

Abbot, The. A novel (1820) by Sir Walter SCOTT. The Abbot, Father AMBROSE, plays a subordinate part. The hero is Roland Graeme, a foundling brought up by Lady Avenel as a kind of page. He later becomes page to Mary Queen of Scots, who plays a prominent rôle in the novel.

Abbot of Misrule, see KING OF MISRULE.

Abbot of Unreason, see KING OF MISRULE.

Abbotsford. The name given by Sir Walter Scott to Clarty Hole, on the south bank of the Tweed, after it became his residence in 1812.

Abbott, George (1889–). American playwright, producer, and director. Co-author of *Three Men on a Horse; Coquette; The Boys from Syracuse;* etc.

Abbott, Jacob (1803–1879). American clergyman. Author of the *Rollo* books, histories, biographies for the young, etc.

Abbott, Lyman (1835–1922). Congregational minister, author and editor. Retired (1899) to devote himself to editorship of the famous weekly *The Outlook*. Wrote a life of Henry Ward Beecher and other books.

A.B.C. An abbreviation having a number of meanings that can be decided only by the context. Thus, "So-and-so doesn't know his A B C" means that he is intensely ignorant; "he doesn't understand the A B C of engineering" means that he has not mastered its rudiments. So, an *A B C Book* or *Absey Book*, is a primer which used to be used as a child's first lesson book and contained merely the alphabet and a few rudimentary lessons often set in catechism form, as is evident from Shakespeare's lines:

> That is question now;
> And then comes answer like an Absey book.
> *King John*, i. 1.

A. B. C. Nations. Argentina, Brazil and Chile; or recently by extension of the term, all Latin America.

Abdaldar. A magician in Southey's THALABA THE DESTROYER.

Abdera, Abderitan. Abdera was a maritime city of Thrace whose inhabitants were proverbial in ancient times for their stupidity.

Abderitan laughter. Scoffing laughter, incessant laughter. So called because Abdera was the birthplace of Democritus, the laughing philosopher.

Abdiel (*Arab.*, "the servant of God"). In Milton's *Paradise Lost* (v. 805, 896, etc.) the faithful seraph who withstands Satan when he urges the angels to revolt.

Abdul-Baha. The title of Abbas Effendi (1892–1921), head of the Bahai movement. See BAHAISM.

Abdulla. A powerful Malay trader who appears in Conrad's OUTCAST OF THE ISLANDS and ALMAYER'S FOLLY.

Abdullah, Achmed. Pseudonym **A. A. Nadir** (1881–1945). British novelist and playwright, specializing in romance and adventure. He was born at Yalta in the Crimea of mixed Russian and Afghan ancestry, and educated at Eton and Oxford.

Abdul the Bul Bul Ameer. Also **Abdul the Bulbul Ameer; Abdul Abulbul Amir;** etc. A character in a famous comic song of that title, vastly popular in American colleges and extant in many variants. Cf., e.g., Carl Sandburg's *American Songbag*. The subject of the song is an epic contest between Abdul and one variously called Ivan Petrosky Skivar, Ivan Skavinsky Skivah, etc.

The song may have been suggested by the Crimean War. It begins in this fashion:

> The sons of the Prophet are hardy and bold,
> And quite unaccustomed to fear;
> But of all the most reckless of life or of limb
> Was Abdul the Bul Bul Ameer . . .

abecedarian. One who is learning the alphabet; hence, a tyro. An *abecedarian poem* is a poem having verses beginning with the successive letters of the alphabet, as the 119th Psalm in Hebrew.

Abednego, see SHADRACH.

Abel. In the Old Testament, the son of Adam and Eve, murdered by his brother Cain because his sacrifice was more acceptable to Jehovah than Cain's (*Gen.* IV). For his rôle in Mohammedan legend and in Byron's *Cain, a Mystery* (1821), see *Cain.*

Abel, Mr. The hero and narrator of W. H. Hudson's GREEN MANSIONS.

Abélard, Pierre (1079–1142). Medieval Christian theologian and philosopher, a brilliant and popular lecturer at the cathedral school of Notre Dame in Paris, whose pupils included many men later famous in their own right. In the controversy between Realism and Nominalism he took a middle stand, based on Aristotle's teaching, maintaining that universals are concepts of the mind and thus are real without being material. He was attacked as a heretic by ST. BERNARD and condemned by a church council, and was also involved in a tragic love affair with the celebrated HÉLOISE.

Abe Lincoln in Illinois. A play by Robert E. SHERWOOD, produced in 1938 and awarded the Pulitzer prize in 1939. It deals with the life of Lincoln up to his election to the presidency, and the dialogue contains selections from a number of Lincoln's own writings and speeches.

Abencerrages. A family of Moors in Granada in the fifteenth century, famous in romance for their feud with the family of the Zegris.

Abercrombie, Lascelles (1881–1938). English poet and critic, author of *Interludes and Poems* (1908); *Emblems of Love* (1912); *Thomas Hardy: A Critical Study* (1912), and other books of poetry and prose. He is associated with those English poets before World War I who are known as the "Georgians."

Abide With Me. A hymn (1847) by Henry F. Lyte.

Abie's Irish Rose. A popular American comedy by Anne Nichols, produced in 1924, which had one of the longest records of performance (2,327) in the history of the theater. Surpassed by *Tobacco Road* and *Life With Father*. See Caldwell, Erskine, and Day, Clarence.

Abigail. A lady's maid. *Abigail,* wife of Nabal and afterwards of David, is a well-known Scripture heroine (1 *Sam.* xxv. 3). Marlowe called the daughter of *Barabas,* his *Jew of Malta,* by this name, and it was given by Beaumont and Fletcher to the "waiting gentlewoman" in *The Scornful Lady.* Swift, Fielding, and other novelists of the period employ it in their novels, and it was further popularized by the notoriety of Abigail Hill, better known as Mrs. Masham, the waiting-woman to Queen Anne.

Abigor. In medieval demonology, the Grand Duke of Hell.

Abington, Fanny. English character actress with David Garrick at the Drury Lane (1764–1782). She created the part of Lady Teazle (1777).

Able McLaughlins, The. A novel by Margaret Wilson (*Am.,* 1923), the story of a family of hardy Scotch settlers in Iowa. The book was awarded the Pulitzer prize as the best novel of the year.

Abnaki. An Indian of the confederacy of thirteen Algonquian tribes occupying Maine and parts of New Brunswick and Quebec. The Abnaki were allies of the French.

abolitionists. Those who advocated the abolition of slavery, especially members of the American Anti-Slavery Society, organized in 1833. William Lloyd Garrison and John Brown were among the most active abolitionists.

Abomination of Desolation, The. Mentioned in *Dan.* (chs. ix, xi, and xii), and in *Matt.* xxiv. 15, probably refers to some statue set up in the Temple by either the heathen or the Romans. The phrase is used for anything very hateful or destructive.

Abou Ben Adhem. A short poem by Leigh Hunt. Because Abou begged to be written as "one who loves his fellowmen" his angel visitor

> . . showed the names whom love of God had blest
> And lo! Ben Adhem's name led all the rest.

Abou Hassan. Young merchant of Bagdad, hero of the tale called *The Sleeper Awakened* in the *Arabian Nights' Entertainments.* While Abou Hassan is asleep he is conveyed to the palace of Haroun al Raschid, and the attendants are ordered to do everything they can to make him fancy himself the Caliph. He subsequently becomes the Caliph's favorite. See also Sly, Christopher.

Abra. A favorite concubine of Solomon. In his poem *Solomon on the Vanity of the World* (1718), Matthew Prior describes her devotion in the celebrated lines:

> Abra was ready ere I called her name,
> And though I called another, Abra came.

abracadabra. A cabalistic charm, said to be made up from the initials of the Hebrew words Ab (Father), Ben (Son) and Ruach ACadsch (Holy Spirit) and formerly used as a powerful antidote against ague, flux, toothache, etc. Hence a charm; also any meaningless jargon. The word was written on parchment, and suspended from the neck by a linen thread, in the following form:

A B R A C A D A B R A
A B R A C A D A B R
A B R A C A D A B
A B R A C A D A
A B R A C A D
A B R A C A
A B R A C
A B R A
A B R
A B
A

Abraham. The founder of the Hebrew nation and its first patriarch. With his wife Sarai and his nephew Lot he migrated from Ur of Chaldees into the Land of Canaan, where he settled and prospered. To test his faith Jehovah commanded him to offer up his son Isaac as a burnt offering, but when he was about to draw the knife, a ram was provided instead. The story of Abraham is told in *Gen.* xii–xiii and in various Mohammedan legends, which relate that at the age of fifteen months Abraham was equal in size to a lad of fifteen, and was so wise that his father introduced him to the court of King Nimrod; that Abraham and his son "Ismail" rebuilt for the fourth time the Kaaba over the sacred stone at Mecca; and that Abraham destroyed the idols manufactured and worshiped by his father, Terah. See also *Sarai, Hagar, Isaac, Sodom and Gomorrah.*

Abraham's bosom. The repose of the happy in death (*Luke* xvi. 22).

Abrahamic covenant. (1) The covenant made by God with Abraham, that Messiah should spring from his seed. This promise was given to Abraham, because he left his country and father's house to live in a strange land, as God told him. (2) The rite of circumcision.

sham Abraham. See Abraham-man.

Abraham Lincoln. A biography of the American president by Carl Sandburg. The first part, entitled *Abraham Lincoln: The Prairie Years,* was published in two volumes in 1926, and the second part, *Abraham Lincoln: The War Years,* was published in four volumes in 1939. It is Sandburg's chief work, research and its preparation having occupied many years of the poet's life.

Abraham-man or **Abraham cove.** A pretended maniac who, in Tudor and early Stuart times, wandered about the country as a begging impostor; a TOM O' BEDLAM; hence the phrase, *to sham Abraham,* meaning to pretend illness or distress, in order to get off work.

Inmates of BEDLAM who were not dangerously mad were kept in the "Abraham Ward," were allowed out from time to time in a distinctive dress, and were permitted to supplement their scanty rations by begging. This gave an opportunity to impostors, and large numbers availed themselves of it. Says *The Canting Academy* (Richd. Head, 1674), they

> used to array themselves with party-coloured ribbons, tape in their hats, a fox-tail hanging down, a long stick with streamers, and beg alms; but for all their seeming madness, they had wit enough to steal as they went along.

There is a good picture of them in *King Lear* ii. 3; and cf. also Beaumont and Fletcher's *Beggars Bush,* ii. i.

> Come, princes of the ragged regiment
> And these, what name or title e'er they bear,
> *Jarkman* or *Pat'rico, Cranke* or *Clapper-dudgeon,*
> *Frater* or *Abram-man,* I speak to all
> That stand in fair election for the title
> Of King of Beggars.

Abraham Newland. A bank-note, so called from the name of the chief cashier at the Bank of England from 1782 to 1807, without whose signature no Bank of England notes were genuine.

abraxas. A cabalistic word used by the Gnostics to denote the Supreme Being, the source of 365 emanations, the sum of the numbers represented by the Greek letters of the word totaling 365. It was frequently engraved on gems (hence known as *abraxas stones*) that were used as amulets or talismans. By some authorities the name is given as that of one of the horses of Aurora.

Absalom. In the Old Testament (2 *Sam.* xviii), the handsome but rebellious son of David who "stole the hearts of the men of Israel" and plotted to become king in his father's stead. In the battle in which the issue was decided, Absalom, who rode on a mule, was caught by his head in an oak tree; and one of David's army, finding him so suspended, killed him in spite of the previous commands of the King. David's lament, "O my son Absalom, my son, my son Absalom! would God I had died for thee," has become a classic expression of paternal grief.

Absalom, Absalom. See FAULKNER, WILLIAM.

Absalom and Achitophel. A famous political satire in verse published in 1681, the first part by Dryden and the second by Nahum Tate and revised by Dryden. The general scheme is to show the rebellious character of the Puritans, who insisted on the exclusion of the Duke of York from the succession, on account of his being a pronounced Catholic, and the determination of the King to resist this interference with his royal prerogative, even at the cost of a civil war. Of the principal characters, David stands for Charles II; Absalom for his natural son James, Duke of Monmouth (handsome and rebellious); Achitophel for Lord Shaftesbury; Zimri for the Duke of Buckingham; and Abdael for Monk. The accommodation of the biblical narrative to contemporary history is so skilfully made that the story of David seems to repeat itself. Of Absalom, Dryden says (Part i):

> Whate'er he did was done with so much ease.
> In him alone 'twas natural to please;
> His motions all accompanied with grace,
> And paradise was opened in his face.

Absent-minded Beggar. The title of one of Kipling's poems (1900), hence applied to an English private, a TOMMY ATKINS.

Absentee, The. A novel by Maria Edgeworth (1812). The "Absentee," Lord Clonbrony, allows his foolish wife to persuade him to leave his estate in Ireland and try to force a way into fashionable London society.

absey book. See *A. B. C.*

Absolon. A priggish parish clerk in *The Miller's Tale* in Chaucer's *Canterbury Tales.* His hair is curled, his shoes slashed, his hose red. He can let blood, cut hair, and shave, can dance, and play either on the ribible or the gittern. This gay spark pays his addresses to Mistress ALISON, the young wife of John, a wealthy aged carpenter.

Absolute, Sir Anthony. One of the most popular characters in all English comedy, a testy, but warm-hearted old gentleman in Sheridan's RIVALS, who imagines that he possesses a most angelic temper and when he quarrels with his son, the captain, fancies it is the son who is out of sorts, and not himself.

Captain Absolute. The clever and gallant son of Sir Anthony, in love with Lydia Languish, the heiress, to whom he is known only as Ensign Beverley. Bob Acres, his neighbor, is his rival, and sends a challenge to the unknown ensign; but when he finds that Ensign Beverley is Captain Absolute, he declines to fight, and resigns all further claim to the lady's hand.

Absyrtus. In Greek mythology, the young brother of MEDEA. She cut his body to pieces and scattered it (*membra disjecta*) along her way to delay her father, Aeëtes, in his pursuit of her when she escaped from Colchis with JASON.

Abt Vogler. A dramatic monologue by Robert Browning in his volume *Dramatis Personae* (1864). The speaker is Abt Vogler, "after he has been extemporizing upon the musical instrument of his invention."

Abydos. In the legend of HERO and LEANDER, a city on the Hellespont. See also SESTOS; BRIDE OF ABYDOS.

Abyla. A promontory in Morocco, near Ceuta, now called Jebel Musa or Ape's Hill, forming the northwestern extremity of the African coast opposite Gibraltar. It is one of the PILLARS OF HERCULES, the other being the promontory of Calpe. Also referred to as *Abyla Mons* and *Abyla Columna.*

academe. A place of study and instruction; specifically, *Academe,* the Academy of Plato.

> See there the olive grove of Academe . . .
> Milton, *Paradise Regained.*

Academus. A Greek hero who told Castor and Pollux where Theseus had hidden Helen.

Academy. The Greek school of philosophy founded by Plato, so called from a garden planted by Academus where Plato taught his followers.

French Academy (*Académie française*) was formally established in 1635 by Cardinal Richelieu, its principal function being:

> To labor with all the care and diligence possible, to give exact rules to our language, to render it capable of treating the arts and sciences.

Its forty members, "the Forty Immortals," are supposed to be the most distinguished living men of letters.

Académie Goncourt. A French literary society founded in 1900, consisting of ten members. It awards the Prix Goncourt.

The English *Royal Academy of Arts* was founded in 1768 by George III for the establishment of an art school and the holding of annual exhibitions of works by living artists.

The Royal Spanish Academy was founded at Madrid in 1713 for purposes similar to those of the French Academy.

The American Academy of Arts and Letters was founded in 1904 with a like purpose. Its membership is limited to fifty. They are chosen from the National Institute of Arts and Letters.

There is also a *Royal Academy of Science* at Berlin (founded 1700), at Stockholm (the *Royal Swedish Academy,* founded 1739), and at Copenhagen (founded 1742).

The Imperial Academy of Sciences at Petrograd was established by Catherine I in 1725.

Academy figures. Drawings in black and white chalk, on tinted paper, usually about half life-size and from the nude.

Academy headache. A headache as a result of attending art exhibitions. The phrase was popularized in 1885 with reference to the Royal Academy Exhibit.

Acadia. The old name for Nova Scotia, so called by the French from the river *Shubenacadie.* In 1621 Acadia was given to the Scotchman, Sir William Alexander, and its name changed; and in 1755 the old French settlers were driven into exile by George II. Longfellow has made this the subject of a poem in hexameter verse, called EVANGELINE.

Accoramboni, Vittoria (1557?–1585). Her husband was murdered so that she might marry the Duke of Bracciano. After Bracciano's death in 1585 she was murdered by assassins hired by a relative of his. John WEBSTER used her story in his play *The White Devil or Vittoria Corombona* (ca. 1610).

aceldama. A battlefield, a place where much blood has been shed. So called from the field purchased by the priests with the blood-money thrown down by Judas, and appropriated as a cemetery for strangers (*Matt.* xxvii. 8; *Acts* i. 19).

Acestes. In a trial of skill described in Virgil's *Aeneid,* Acestes, the Sicilian, discharged his arrow with such force that it took fire from the friction of the air. He was the son of a river god and a Trojan woman.

Achates. In Virgil's *Aeneid,* the chosen and ubiquitous companion of the hero in adventures of all kinds. Hence a *fidus Achates,* a faithful companion, a bosom friend.

Acheloüs. In Greek mythology, the god of rivers. Represented as a bull with a human head. Also the name of the largest river in Greece.

Acheron. A Greek word meaning "the River of Sorrows"; the river of the infernal regions into which Phlegethon and Cocytus flow: also, the lower world (Hades) itself. See STYX.

> They pass the bitter waves of Acheron
> Where many souls sit wailing woefully.
> Spenser, *Faërie Queene,* I. v, 33.

food for Acheron. A dead body.

Achilles. In Greek legend, the son of Peleus and the Nereid Thetis, and king of the Myrmidons, a Thessalian tribe. He is the hero of Homer's ILIAD and became the prototype of the Greeks' conception of manly valor and beauty. He took part in the Trojan War on the side of the Greeks as their most illustrious warrior, and slew the Trojan hero HECTOR. Achilles had been dipped in the Styx by his mother, which rendered him invulnerable except in the heel by which she held him and where he was fatally wounded by an arrow shot by Paris, Hector's younger brother, or, according to another version of the story, by the god Apollo who had assumed Paris' shape.

heel of Achilles. The vulnerable or weak point in a man's character or in a nation.

Achilles' spear, see PELIAN SPEAR.

Achilles of England. (1) John Talbot, first Earl of Shrewsbury (1373–1453); (2) the Duke of Wellington (1769–1852).

Achilles of Germany. Albert, elector of Brandenburg (1414–1486).

Achilles of Lombardy. Brother of Sforza and Palamedes in Tasso's *Jerusalem Delivered.* This was not a complimentary title, but a proper name.

Achilles of Rome. Lucius Sicinius Dentatus, the Roman tribune; also called the *Second Achilles.* Put to death 450 B. C.

Achilles of the West. Roland the Paladin.

Achitophel. In the Old Testament, David's traitorous counsellor, who deserted to Absalom. (2 *Sam.* xv.) The Achitophel of Dryden's satire (see ABSALOM AND ACHITOPHEL) was the Earl of Shaftesbury.

Of these the rebel the false Achitophel was first;
A name to all succeeding ages curst;
For close designs and crooked counsels fit;
Sagacious, bold, and turbulent of wit;
Restless, unfix'd in principles and place;
In power unpleased, impatient in disgrace.
I. 150.

Acis. In Greek legend, a handsome Sicilian youth, son of Faunus and the naiad Symaethis, lover of Galatea, who was killed by his rival, the Cyclops Polyphemus. The blood flowing forth from Acis' body changed into water and formed the river Acis.

Acrasia. In Book II of Spenser's FAËRIE QUEENE, Intemperance personified. Spenser says she is an enchantress living in the "Bower of Bliss," in "Wandering Island." She had the power of transforming her lovers into monstrous shapes; but Sir Guyon (Temperance), having caught her in a net and bound her, broke down her bower and burnt it to ashes.

acre. O. E. *aecer,* is akin to the Lat. *ager* and Ger. *acker* (a field). *God's Acre,* a cemetery or churchyard. Longfellow calls this an "ancient Saxon phrase," but as a matter of fact it is a modern borrowing from Germany.

three acres and a cow. A small plot for gardening or farming; a phrase used by British radicals in the political campaign of 1885.

Acre, St. Jean d'. Seaport on the Palestine coast, captured by the forces of the Third Crusade, among whom RICHARD CŒUR DE LION was prominent, in 1191. The last stronghold of the Christians on the mainland, it fell to the Moslems again in 1291.

Acres, Bob. In Sheridan's comedy THE RIVALS, a country gentleman, the rival of Ensign Beverley, *alias* Captain Absolute, for the hand and heart of Lydia Languish, the heiress. He tries to ape the man of fashion, gets himself up as a loud swell, and uses "sentimental oaths," *i.e.* oaths bearing on the subject. Thus if duels are spoken of he says, *ods triggers and flints;* if ladies, *ods blushes and blooms.* Bob Acres is a great blusterer, but when put to the push "his courage always oozed out of his fingers' ends." Hence a "regular Bob Acres" is a coward.

Acrisius. In Greek mythology, the father of Danaë. An oracle declared that Danaë would give birth to a son who would kill him, so Acrisius kept his daughter shut up in a brazen tower. Here she became the mother of Perseus, by Zeus in the form of a shower of gold. The King of Argos now ordered his daughter and her infant to be put into a chest, and cast adrift on the sea, but they were rescued by Dictys, a fisherman. When grown to manhood, Perseus accidentally struck the foot of Acrisius with a quoit, and the blow caused his death, thus fulfilling the oracle. This tale is told by William Morris in *The Earthly Paradise: April.*

acrostic. A composition, often inverse, where one or more sets of letters, initial, middle, or final, form a word or a sentence when taken in order. See also DOUBLE CROSTIC.

across lots. By a short cut. The threat of the Mormon leader, Brigham Young, "We'll send them [the Gentiles] across lots" gave the phrase a new and obvious significance.

Actaeon. In Grecian mythology a huntsman who, having surprised Diana bathing, was changed by her into a stag and torn to pieces by his own hounds. A stag being a horned animal, he became a representative of men whose wives are unfaithful.

Actian games. The games celebrated at Actium in honor of Apollo. They were reinstituted by Augustus to celebrate his naval victory over Antony, 31 B. C., and were held every five years.

Action at Aquila. See ALLEN, WILLIAM HERVEY.

Act of Settlement. An act passed during the reign of William III in 1701 in England, limiting the crown after Anne's succession to members of the House of Hanover, provided they were Protestant. This began the reign of the Four Georges.

Actors' Equity. A voluntary association for the protection of actors' rights, organized in New York City (March 26, 1913). An annual performance is given for the benefit of the association.

Acts and Monuments. A history of religious persecution and Christian Reformers, especially in England, by John Foxe, better known as *The Book of Martyrs,* published in 1563 by John DAY.

Acunha, Teresa d'. The Spanish maid of the Countess of Glenallan in Scott's novel THE ANTIQUARY, of whom it is said, "If ever there was a fiend on earth in human form, that woman was ane."

Adah. In Byron's CAIN, A MYSTERY, the wife of Cain. After Cain has been conducted by Lucifer through the realms of space, he is restored to the home of his wife and child, where all is gentleness and love. Adah is also the name of Cain's wife in Rabbinical tradition.

Adam. In Shakespeare's *As You Like It,* a faithful retainer in the family of Sir Rowland de Boys. At the age of four score, he voluntarily accompanies his young master Orlando into exile, and offers to give him his little savings. He has given rise to the phrase "a faithful Adam" with reference to a manservant.

Adam and Eve. In the Old Testament, the first man and woman. The familiar story of their creation, sin and expulsion from the Garden of Eden is told in the first chapters of *Genesis* and forms the basis for Milton's *Paradise Lost.*

Mohammedan legends add to the Bible story the tradition that—

> God sent Gabriel, Michael, and Israfel one after the other to fetch seven handfuls of earth from different depths and of different colors for the creation of Adam (thereby accounting for the varying colors of mankind) but they returned empty-handed because Earth foresaw that the creature to be made from her would rebel against God and draw down his curse on her, whereupon Azrael was sent. He executed the commission, and for that reason was appointed to separate the souls from the bodies and hence became the Angel of Death. The earth he had taken was carried into Arabia to a place between Mecca and Tayef, where it was kneaded by the angels, fashioned into human form by God, and left to dry for either forty days or forty years. It is also said that while the clay was being endowed with life and a soul, when the breath breathed by God into the nostrils had reached as far as the navel, the only half-living Adam tried to rise up and got an ugly fall for his pains.

old as Adam. Generally used as a reproof for stating as news something well known. "That's as old as Adam," it was known as far back as the days of Adam.

the old Adam. The offending Adam, etc.

> Consideration, like an angel, came
> And whipped the offending Adam out of him.
> Shakespeare, *Henry V,* i, 1

Adam, as the head of unredeemed man, stands for "original sin," or "man without regenerating grace."

the second Adam. The new Adam, etc. Jesus Christ is so called.

Adam's ale. Water; because the first man had nothing else to drink. In Scotland sometimes called *Adam's Wine.*

Adam's apple. The protuberance in the forepart of the throat, the anterior extremity of the thyroid cartilage of the larynx; so called from the superstition that a piece of the forbidden fruit stuck in Adam's throat.

Adam's Diary. A humorous book by Mark Twain; also *Eve's Diary.*

Adam's needle. Gen. iii. 7, tells us that Adam and Eve "sewed fig leaves together"; needles were (presumably) not then obtainable, but certain plants furnish needle-like spines, and to some of these the name has been given. The chief is the Yucca, a native of Mexico and Central America.

Adam's Peak. A mountain in Ceylon where, according to Mohammedan legend, Adam bewailed his expulsion from Paradise, standing on one foot for two hundred years to expiate his crime; Gabriel than took him to Mount Arafath, where he found Eve.

Adam's profession. Gardening or agriculture is sometimes so called—for obvious reasons.

Adam, Juliette, *née* **Lamber.** Pen names **Juliette Lamber; La Messine;** and **Comte Paul Vasili** (1836–1936). French writer; founded (1879) and edited *La Nouvelle Revue.* (Note her life span!)

Adamastor. (1) The spirit of the stormy Cape (Good Hope), described by Camoëns in the *Lusiad* as a hideous phantom that appears to Vasco da Gama and prophesies disaster to all seeking to make the voyage to India.

(2) Title of a book of poems by Roy Campbell (1930).

Adam Bede. A novel by George Eliot (1859). It tells of a young carpenter, Adam Bede; his love for the pretty and superficial Hetty Sorrel who murders her illegitimate child by Arthur Donnithorne, a young country squire, and is sentenced to life transportation in punishment; and his eventual marriage to Dinah Morris, a Methodist preacher. The character of the hero was drawn from George Eliot's father, Robert Evans.

Adam Bell. Hero of a ballad of that name included in Percy's *Reliques* (I. ii. 1), a wild, north-country outlaw, noted, like Robin Hood, for his skill in archery.

Adam Blair, a Story of Scottish Life. A novel by J. G. Lockhart (1822).

Adamic, Louis (1899–). Author, born in Yugoslavia, who wrote of life in his native country and in the U.S. His best-known books are *Dynamite: The Story of Class Violence in America* (1931); *The Native's Return* (1934); *Cradle of Life* (1936); *My America* (1938); *From Many Lands* (1940); and *Two-Way Passage* (1941).

Adamites. The name given to various heretical sects who supposed themselves to attain to primitive innocence by rejecting marriage and clothing. There was such a sect in

North Africa in the 2nd century; the *Abelites* were similar; the heresy reappeared in Savoy in the 14th century, and spread over Bohemia and Moravia in the 15th and 16th. One Picard, of Bohemia, was leader in 1400, and styled himself "Adam, son of God." There are references to the sect in James Shirley's comedy *Hyde Park* (1632), and in *The Guardian,* No. 134 (1713).

Adams, Alice, see ALICE ADAMS.

Adams, Charles Francis (1807–1886). American lawyer, diplomat, and author. Minister to Great Britain through the Civil War, he helped settle the ALABAMA CLAIMS. He edited the *Memoirs* of John Quincy Adams (his father) in 12 volumes. His son, **Charles Francis Adams** (1835–1915), was a lawyer, railroad expert, and historian. He was president of the Union Pacific (1884) and was forced out by Jay GOULD. He exposed the looting of the Erie Railroad by Gould in *Chapters of Erie* (1871); wrote a life of his father, a biography of Richard Henry Dana, and *Railroads: Their Origins and Problems* (1878).

Adams, Franklin Pierce. Signs his work **F. P. A.** (1881–). Popular American newspaper columnist and author, best known for his humorous column, "The Conning Tower." He was associated with a number of newspapers, including the Chicago *Journal,* New York *Evening Mail,* New York *World,* New York *Herald-Tribune,* and New York *Post.* In 1938 he became a member of the cast of INFORMATION PLEASE, a popular radio "quiz" program.

Adams, Hannah (1755–1831). The first professional woman writer in the U.S., author of books on history and religion, including *A Summary History of New England* (1799), used as a textbook in the schools.

Adams, Henry Brooks (1838–1918). American man of letters, historian, scholar, and critic of his age, a member of the famous Adams family of American statesmen. Most of his life was spent in a quest for order and integration in a world which he considered to be in the process of disintegration. His best known works are *History of the United States during the Administrations of Jefferson and Madison, 1801–1817* (1889–1891); MONT-SAINT-MICHEL AND CHARTRES (1904); *Life of George Cabot Lodge* (1911); THE EDUCATION OF HENRY ADAMS (1906, awarded the Pulitzer prize in 1919); THE DEGRADATION OF THE DEMOCRATIC DOGMA (1919).

Adams, James Truslow (1878–). American historian, author of *The Founding of New England* (1921), awarded the Pulitzer prize in 1922; *Revolutionary New England* (1923); *New England in the Republic* (1926); *The Epic of America* (1931); *The March of Democracy* (1932–1933); *Building the British Empire* (1938); *Empire on the Seven Seas* (1940); and other works.

Adams, John (1735–1826). Second president of the U.S. Joined Jay and Franklin in Paris (1782) to negotiate treaty of peace with Great Britain. Envoy to Great Britain. Elected vice-president (1788; 1792) and president (1796); defeated for presidency by Jefferson (1800). He was also a signer of the Declaration of Independence. He wrote *Thoughts on Government* (1776), *Defence of the Constitutions of the United States of America against the Attack of Mr. Turgot* (1787), and *Discourses on Davila* (1791) but the letters to Abigail, his wife, and the correspondence with Jefferson are famous.

Adams, John Quincy (1767–1848). Sixth president of the U.S. One of the negotiators of peace after the War of 1812. Minister to Great Britain, secretary of state; elected president (1825–29); defeated by Jackson for second term. Representative in Congress (1831–1848). Writer: *Dermot MacMorrogh* (1832); *Poems* (1848); *Poems of Religion and Society* (1859), and voluminous *Diaries.*

Adams, Léonie Fuller (1899–). American poet whose work is marked by symbols chosen from nature to express an intense personal emotion. Many of her lyrics are considered akin to those of William Butler YEATS. Published volumes of her verse are *Those Not Elect* (1925); *High Falcon* (1929); *This Measure* (1933).

Adams, Maude (1872–). American actress, known for her performances in plays by Sir James M. BARRIE, notably PETER PAN, THE LITTLE MINISTER, QUALITY STREET, WHAT EVERY WOMAN KNOWS, and *A Kiss for Cinderella.* Her real name was **Maude Kiskadden,** and she adopted her mother's maiden name, Adams, as her stage name. She was also notable in Rostand's *L'Aiglon* and *Chantecler.* Teacher of dramatics at Stephens College, Columbia, Mo. (since 1937).

Adams, Parson. A leading character in Fielding's *Joseph Andrews* (1742), often taken as the type of the simple-minded, hard-working, and learned country curate who is totally ignorant of "the ways of the world." He was drawn from Fielding's friend, the Rev. William Young, who edited Ainsworth's *Latin Dictionary* (1752).

Adams, Samuel (1722–1803). American pamphleteer and political writer, active in arousing public opinion against England in the early days of the American Revolution. He was a member of the Continental Congress from 1774 to 1782 and was the author of many state papers. Wrote with Joseph Warren *Rights of the Colonies.*

Adams, Samuel Hopkins (1871–). American novelist and journalist. *Revelry* (a novel about the Harding administration; 1926); *The Flagrant Years* (1929); *The Gorgeous Hussy* (1934); the motion picture *It Happened One Night* (1934); *Maiden Effort* (1937); *The Incredible Era* (1939); another motion picture, *The Harvey Girls* (1942); etc. He also wrote a biography of Alexander WOOLLCOTT (1945).

Adams, Will (1575?–1620). Japanese title, **Anjin Sama**, i.e., "Mr. Pilot." The first Englishman to visit Japan (1600). His life was spared, and because of his knowledge of ships, ship-building, navigation, etc., he was held by the Shoguns as adviser for twenty years. He married a Japanese woman and was given an estate.

Adams, William T. Pseudonym **Oliver Optic** (1822–1897). Author of various series of books for boys. Editor of the journal *Our Boys and Girls,* founded in 1867 as a weekly, subsequently a monthly.

Addams, Jane (1860–1935). American leader in social work and the peace and woman suffrage movements. She is best known for her settlement work at Hull House, Chicago, which she founded in 1889. In 1931 she shared the Nobel peace prize with Nicholas Murray BUTLER. She wrote a number of books and articles on sociology and world peace, including *Twenty Years at Hull House* (1910); *Peace and Bread in Time of War* (1922); and *The Second Twenty Years at Hull House* (1931).

Adding Machine, The. A play by Elmer RICE, produced in 1923. It is written in an expressionistic vein (see EXPRESSIONISM), satirically depicting the enslavement of man by the machine.

Addison, Joseph (1672–1719). English essayist, famous for his contributions to the TATLER and SPECTATOR, which established and perfected the essay as a literary type, and laid the foundations of the novel. Addison produced a tragedy, *Cato* (1713) an enormously popular play which portrayed the last of the Roman republicans making a last stand for liberty.

Addison of the North. A sobriquet of Henry Mackenzie (1745–1831), author of *The Man of Feeling.*

Addisonian Termination. The name given by Bishop Hurd to the construction which closes a sentence with a preposition, such as—"which the prophet took a distinct view of." Named, of course, from Joseph Addison, who frequently employed it.

Addled Parliament. See PARLIAMENTS.

Ade, George (1866–1944). American humorist and playwright, best known for ARTIE (1896); *Fables in Slang* (1899); and *The College Widow* (1904).

Adelphi (Gr. *adelphoi,* "brothers"). A quarter of London, built in the 18th century by the brothers Adam, with literary and historical associations. Also, a theater on the Strand, London, noted in the 19th century for its melodramas.

Adler, Alfred (1870–1937). Austrian psychoanalyst, disciple of Sigmund FREUD, who later rebelled against his master's teachings and held to a system of "individual psychology." In this he maintained that psychological differences among individuals—in behavior, attitude, etc.—were due to the differences in their means of attaining a feeling of superiority in their relations with society. See COMPLEX; INFERIORITY; SUPERIORITY. See biography by Phyllis BOTTOME.

Adler, Felix (1851–1933). American philosopher. Founder of the Ethical Culture movement. In 1908, Theodore Roosevelt appointed him exchange professor at the University of Berlin.

Adler, Mortimer Jerome (1902–). American college professor and author, writing chiefly on Thomistic philosophy (see ST. THOMAS AQUINAS) and aesthetics. In 1940 his *How to Read a Book* became a best seller.

Admetus. In Greek mythology, a king of Thessaly, husband of ALCESTIS, who consented to die in his stead. Apollo, being condemned by Jupiter to serve a mortal for twelve months for slaying a Cyclops, once entered the service of Admetus. James Russell LOWELL has a poem on the subject, called *The Shepherd of King Admetus.*

Admirable, the. Abraham ben Meir ben Ezra, a celebrated Spanish Jew (about 1090–1168) was so called. He was noted as a mathematician, philologist, poet, astronomer, and commentator on the Bible. Browning has a poem entitled RABBI BEN EZRA.

the Admirable Crichton. James Crichton (1560–1585?), Scottish traveler, scholar, and swordsman. So called by Sir Thomas Urquhart. (See also next item for Barrie's play by this name.)

Admirable Doctor. See under DOCTOR.

Admirable Crichton, The. A dramatic fantasy by J. M Barrie (1902). The Earl of Loam, his family and one or two friends are wrecked on a desert island, where the butler, the "Admirable Crichton" proves himself a man of infinite resource and power, far superior to the rest of the party. Barrie took the name of his play but nothing else from the original *Admirable Crichton.*

Admiral. English admirals used to be of three classes, according to the color of their flag. *Admiral of the Red* used to hold the center in an engagement, *Admiral of the White,* the van, *Admiral of the Blue,* the rear. The distinction was abolished in 1864; now all admirals carry the white flag. It has, however, given rise to a number of humorous allusions.

Admiral of the Blue. (1) A butcher who dresses in blue to conceal blood-stains; (2) A tapster from his blue apron.

Admiral of the Red. A punning term applied to a wine-bibber whose face and nose are very red.

Admiral of the Red, White and Blue. A beadle; hall-porter; etc. From their gorgeous uniforms.

Admiral of the White. (1) A coward. (2) A fainting person.

Admission Day. A legal holiday commemorating the day of the admission of a state into the United States of America.

Adonai. Hebrew name for God, translated in the Old Testament as "Lord." See TETRAGRAMMATON.

Adonais. The poetical name given by Shelley to Keats in his elegy on the death of the latter (1821), probably in allusion to the mourning for Adonis. *Adonais* is considered one of the greatest elegies in the English language.

Adonbeck al Hakim. A doctor in Scott's *Talisman* who is really Saladin in disguise.

Adonic verse. A verse consisting of a dactyl and a spondee or trochee, probably so called after the Adonia, the festival of ADONIS.

Adonis. In Greek mythology, a beautiful youth, beloved by Venus and Proserpina, who quarreled about the possession of him. Jupiter, to settle the dispute, decided that the boy should spend six months with Venus in the upper world, and six with Proserpina in the lower. Adonis was gored to death by a wild boar in a hunt.

Shakespeare has a long poem called *Venus and Adonis.* Shelley calls his elegy on the poet Keats *Adonais,* under the idea that the untimely death of Keats resembled that of Adonis. The word *Adonis* is used, often ironically, for any beautiful young man. In one famous instance Leigh Hunt was sent to prison for libeling George IV when Regent, and calling him "a corpulent Adonis of 50."

Adonis' Garden. A worthless toy; a very perishable good. The allusion is to the baskets or pots of earth used at the annual festival of Adonis, in which quick-growing plants were sown, tended for eight days, allowed to wither, and then thrown into the sea or river with images of the dead Adonis.

Adosinda. In Southey's epic poem *Roderick, the Last of the Goths* (1814), the daughter of the Gothic governor of Auria in Spain.

Adramelech. One of the fallen angels. Milton has him overthrown by Uriel and Raphael (*Paradise Lost,* vi. 365). KLOPSTOCK introduces him into *The Messiah,* and represents him as surpassing Satan in malice and guile, ambition and mischief. He is made to hate every one, even Satan, of whose rank he is jealous.

Adraste. The hero of Molière's comedy *Le Sicilien ou l'amour peintre* (1667), a French gentleman who enveigles a Greek slave named Isidore from her master Don Pedre. He is introduced as a portrait-painter, and thus imparts to Isidore his love.

Adrastea. In Greek mythology, the goddess of inevitable fate; later NEMESIS.

Adrastus. (1) A mythical Greek king of Argos, leader of the expedition of the "Seven Against Thebes." See under THEBES.

(2) In Tasso's JERUSALEM DELIVERED, an Indian prince who aids the King of Egypt against the Crusaders. He is slain by Rinaldo.

Adrian IV. Also **Hadrian.** Real name **Nicholas Breakspear.** Pope (1154–1159). The only English pope; born near St. Albans. Gave Ireland to Henry II of England (1154). In conflict with Emperor Frederick I through his adherence to the policies of GREGORY VII.

Adrian, Dr. Adrian Van Welche in Couperus' SMALL SOULS and its sequels.

Adriana. In Shakespeare's COMEDY OF ERRORS, a wealthy Ephesian lady, who marries Antipholus, twin-brother of Antipholus of Syracuse.

Adriano de Armado, Don. See under ARMADO.

Adriatic, Marriage of the. See BRIDE OF THE SEA.

Adullam. A cave in which David took refuge when he fled from King Saul; and thither resorted to him "every one that was in distress, and every one that was in debt, and every one that was discontented" (1 *Sam.* xxii. 1, 2).

Adulterous Bible. See BIBLE, SPECIALLY NAMED.

ad usum Delphini (*Lat.*). For the use of the dauphin. See *Grand Dauphin* under DAUPHIN. The phrase now often signifies "arranged—i.e., expurgated, etc.—for the use of children or young people."

ad valorem (*Lat.*). According to the price charged. A commercial term used in imposing customs duties according to the value of the goods imported. Thus, if teas pay duty *ad* *valorem,* the high priced tea will pay more duty per pound than the lower priced tea.

Advancement of Learning, The. A treatise on philosophy by Francis BACON, published in 1605 in English. It contains a criticism of the traditional methods of increasing knowledge, characteristic of the change in thought taking place in the 17th century under the influence of new scientific discoveries. Later, it formed the first part of his *Instauratio Magna.*

Advent (Lat. *adventus,* the coming to). The four weeks immediately preceding Christmas, commemorating the first and second coming of Christ; the first to redeem, and the second to judge the world. The season begins on St. Andrew's Day (Nov. 30th), or the Sunday nearest to it.

Adventists. Christian religious sects believing that the Second Coming of Christ and the End of the World are near at hand.

Adventures. For novels beginning with this word, as *The Adventures of Tom Sawyer, The Adventures of Sherlock Holmes, The Adventures of Philip,* etc., see under *Tom Sawyer, Sherlock Holmes, Philip* and other proper names of heroes or heroines.

Adversary, the. A name frequently given in English literature to the Devil (from 1 *Pet.* v. 8).

Advice to the Privileged Orders. A prose tract by Joel BARLOW, published in 1792 and pleading for justice, political equality, and democratic rights. It aroused a great deal of discussion and unfavorable criticism in England and was the subject of debate in the House of Commons.

adytum. The innermost sanctuary in ancient temples, open only to the priests.

Æ or **A. E.** Pseudonym of **George William Russell** (1867–1935). Irish poet, known for his mystic verse. Among his works are DEIRDRE (1902), a drama; *The Divine Vision* (1904); *By Still Waters* (1906); *The Renewal of Youth* (1911); *Imaginations and Reveries* (1915); *The Candle of Vision* (1919); *The Interpreters* (1922); *Midsummer Eve* (1928); *Enchantment, and Other Poems* (1930); and *The Living Torch* (1937), a posthumous collection of table-talk.

Aeacus. In classic legend, King of Oenopia, a man of such integrity and piety that he was made at death one of the three judges of Hades. The other two were Minos and Rhadamanthus. He was the ruler of the Myrmidons whom Zeus had created for him out of ants to people his island after it had been stricken by the plague. His son Peleus became the father of ACHILLES.

A. E. F. The American Expeditionary Force which was sent overseas for service in World War I.

Aegeon. (1) In classic legend, a huge monster with 100 arms and 50 heads, who with his brothers, Cottus and Gyges, conquered the Titans by hurling at them 300 rocks at once. Some authorities say he inhabited the Aegean Sea; others make him one of the gods who stormed Olympus.

(2) A merchant of Syracuse in Shakespeare's *Comedy of Errors.*

Aegeus. A fabulous king of Athens who gave the name to the Aegean Sea. His son, Theseus, went to Crete to deliver Athens from the tribute exacted by Minos. Theseus said, if he succeeded he would hoist a white sail on his home-voyage, as a signal of his safety. This he neglected to do, and Aegeus, who watched the ship from a rock, thinking his son had perished, threw himself into the sea.

Aegipan. The god Pan, whose horns, ears and legs were goatlike. Literally, goat Pan.

Aegis. The shield of Jupiter made by Vulcan was so called, and symbolized divine protection. The shield of Minerva was called an *aegis* also.

I throw my aegis over you. I give you my protection.

Aegisthus. In Greek legend the seducer of Clytemnestra, wife of AGAMEMNON.

Aegle (*Gr.* "radiance"). The mother of the Graces.

Aegyptus. In classic myth the father of fifty sons who were married to the fifty daughters of his twin brother Danaus and all except one of whom were murdered by their brides on the wedding night. See DANAIDES.

A.E.I.O.U. The device adopted by Frederick V, archduke of Austria, on becoming the Emperor Frederick III in 1440. It had been used by his predecessor, Albert II, and then stood for—

Albertus Electus Imperator Optimus Vivat.

The meaning that Frederick gave them was—

Archidux Electus Imperator Optime Vivat.

Many other versions are known, including—

Austriae Est Imperare Orbi Universo.
Alles Erdreich Ist Oesterreich Unterthan.
Austria's Empire Is Overall Universal.

To which wags added after the war of 1866—

Austria's Emperor Is Ousted Utterly.

Frederick the Great is said to have translated the motto thus:

Austria Erit In Orbe Ultima (*Austria will be lowest in the world*).

Aelfric (955?–?1025). Anglo-Saxon teacher and churchman, educated at the famous monastery at Winchester. He wrote numerous homilies, treatises, and commentaries. In prose style, he followed classical Latin literature as a model.

Aelia Laelia. An insoluble riddle. From the title of a Latin inscription discovered at Bologna.

Aemilia. In Shakespeare's COMEDY OF ERRORS, the wife of Aegeon the Syracusan merchant, the mother of the twins called Antipholus.

Aemilius. A Roman noble in Shakespeare's *Titus Andronicus.*

Aeneas. The hero of Virgil's epic, the AENEID, son of Anchises, king of Dardanus, and Aphrodite. According to Homer, he fought against the Greeks in the Trojan War and after the sack of Troy reigned in the Troad. Later legends tell how he carried his father Anchises on his shoulders from the flames of Troy, and after roaming about for many years, came to Italy, where he founded a colony which the Romans claim as their origin. The epithet applied to him is *pius,* meaning "dutiful." He is revered as the ancestral hero of the Romans.

Aeneas Silvius. *Italian* **Enea Silvio Piccolomini** (1405–1464). Humanist, Pope (under the title of Pius II, 1458–1464), patron of letters, historian, and long an agitator for a crusade against the Turks. He was the author of *Eurialus and Lucretia,* which has been described as a novel in the style of Boccaccio, as well as Latin pastoral poetry, some of which was translated by Alexander BARCLAY in 1548.

Aeneid. The epic poem of Virgil, in twelve books. When Troy is taken by the Greeks and set on fire, Aeneas with his father, son and wife, takes flight, with the intention of going to Italy, the original birthplace of the family. The wife is lost, and the old father dies on the way; but after numerous perils by sea and land, Aeneas and his son Ascanius reach Italy. Here Latinus, the reigning king, receives the exiles hospitably, and promises his daughter Lavinia in marriage to Aeneas; but she has been already betrothed by her mother to Prince Turnus, son of Daunus, king of the Rutuli, and Turnus will not forego his claim. Latinus, in this dilemma, says the rivals must settle the dispute by an appeal to arms. Turnus is slain, Aeneas marries Lavinia, and soon succeeds his father-in-law on the throne.

Book I. The escape from Troy; Aeneas and his son, driven by a tempest on the shores of Carthage, are hospitably entertained by Queen Dido.

II. Aeneas tells Dido the tale of the wooden horse, the burning of Troy and his flight with his father, wife and son. The wife was lost and died.

III. The narrative continued; he recounts the perils he met with on his way, and the death of his father.

IV. Dido falls in love with Aeneas; but he steals away from Carthage, and Dido, on a funeral pyre, puts an end to her life.

V. Aeneas reaches Sicily, and witnesses there the annual games. This book corresponds to the *Iliad* xxiii.

VI. Aeneas visits the infernal regions. This book corresponds to *Odyssey* xi.

VII. Latinus, king of Italy, entertains Aeneas, and promises to him Lavinia (his daughter) in marriage; but Prince Turnus had been already betrothed to her by the mother, and raises an army to resist Aeneas.

VIII. Preparations on both sides for a general war.

IX. Turnus, during the absence of Aeneas, fires the ships and assaults the camp. The episode of NISUS AND EURYALUS.

X. The war between Turnus and Aeneas. Episode of Mezentius and LAUSUS.

XI. The battle continued.

XII. Turnus challenges Aeneas to single combat, and is killed.

Aeolus. In classic mythology, god of the winds, which he kept imprisoned in a cave in the Aeolian Islands, and let free as he wished or as the over-gods commanded.

the breath of Aeolus. Scandal.

Aeon (Gr. *aion*). An age of the universe, an immeasurable length of time; hence the personification of an age, a god, any being that is eternal. Basilides reckons there have been 365 such Aeons, or gods, but Valentinius restricts the number to 30.

Aeschylus (525–456 B.C.). The father of the Greek tragic drama. Titles of seventy-two of his plays are known, but only seven are now extant. They are the *Supplices, Persae, Septem, Prometheus, Agamemnon, Choephori* and *Eumenides,* the last three comprising the trilogy known as the *Oresteia.*

Aeschylus of France. Prosper Jolyot de Crébillon (1674–1762).

Aesculapius. The Latin form of the Greek Asklepios, god of medicine and of healing. Now used for "a medical practitioner." The usual offering to him was a cock, hence the phrase "to sacrifice a cock to Aesculapius"—to return thanks (or pay the doctor's bill) after recovery from an illness.

Aesir. The collective name of the celestial gods of Scandinavia, who lived in ASGARD. We are told that there were twelve gods and twenty-six goddesses, but it would be hard to determine who they were, for, like Arthur's knights, the number seems variable. The following may be mentioned: (1) Odin, the chief; (2) Thor (his eldest son, god of thunder); (3) Tiu (another son, god of wisdom); (4) Balder (another son, Scandinavian Apollo); (5) Bragi (god of poetry); (6) Vidar (god of silence); (7) Hoder the blind (slayer of Balder); (8) Hermoder (Odin's son and messenger); (9) Hoenir (a minor god); (10) Odnir (husband of Freya, the Scandinavian Venus); (11) Loki (the god of mischief); (12) Vali (Odin's youngest son).

wives of the Aesir. Odin's wife was Frigga; Thor's wife was Sif (beauty); Balder's wife was Nanna (daring); Bragi's wife was Iduna; Loki's wife was Siguna.

The important deities mentioned above are more fully treated under their several names. See also VANIR.

Aeson. In Greek mythology, the father of Jason. He was restored to youth by Medea, who infused into his veins the juice of certain herbs.

Aesop's Fables, written in Greek prose, are traditionally ascribed to Aesop, a deformed Phrygian slave of the 6th century B.C.; but many of them are far older, some having been discovered on Egyptian papyri of 800 or 1000 years earlier.

Aesop of Arabia. Lokman; and Nasser (5th century).

Aesop of England. John GAY (1688–1732).

Aesop of France. Jean de LAFONTAINE (1621–1695).

Aesop of Germany. Gotthold Ephraim LESSING (1729–1781).

Aesop of India. Bidpai or PILPAI.

aesthetics. The branch of philosophy dealing with art and beauty. The term was first used by the German philosopher Alexander Baumgarten (1714–1762), though the problems of aesthetics were of course studied much earlier. Occidental preoccupation with them goes back to the Greeks of the fourth century B.C.

Aetion. In Spenser's poem COLIN CLOUT'S COME HOME AGAIN, a "shepherd" thought by many critics to be meant for Shakespeare.

a fortiori (*Lat.,* "by a stronger reason"). An *a fortiori* argument is one in which the conclusion is considered to be established by the proof of another proposition, analogous to the first or including it, which has seemed more improbable.

Afreet, Afrit. In Mohammedan mythology the most powerful but one (Marids) of the five classes of Jinn, or devils. They are of gigantic stature, very malicious, and inspire great dread. Solomon, we are told, once tamed an Afreet, and made it submissive to his will.

Africa, Out of. See BLIXEN.

Africaine, L'. An opera by Meyerbeer (1865) (libretto by Scribe) dealing with the adventures of the Portuguese explorer, Vasco da Gama.

African magician, the. In the *Arabian Nights,* the pretended uncle of ALADDIN who sent the lad to fetch the "wonderful lamp" from an underground cavern. After sundry adventures Aladdin caused him to be poisoned in a draught of wine.

Afrika Korps. A German military division in World War II, which made history with brilliant tank forays in Africa under Field Marshal Erwin Rommel. Specially equipped for desert fighting. After two years the British 8th Army won the Battle of El Alamein where General Thoma, Commander of the Afrika Korps was captured. The Afrika Korps finally, after a long retreat, established a perimeter defense of Northern Tunisia. Surrendered in May, 1943.

After Many a Summer Dies the Swan. See HUXLEY, ALDOUS.

Afternoon of a Faun, The. See L'APRÈS-MIDI D'UN FAUNE.

After Strange Gods. See ELIOT, THOMAS STEARNS.

After Such Pleasures. See PARKER, DOROTHY.

Agadir incident. An international crisis (1911) brought on by sending the German gunboat Panther to Agadir, South Morocco, to maintain German economic interests in Morocco.

Against the Grain. The title of the English translation of **A Rebours,** a novel by Joris-Karl HUYSMANS. It concerns the quest of the hero, DES ESSEINTES, for the rare, the unusual, and the perverse in sensation, which he attempts to find in perfume, jewels, music, paintings, foods, the love of circus acrobats, and Latin literature of the Middle Ages. It had an influence on Oscar WILDE and others associated with him in the "aesthetic" group of writers in late Victorian England, and is one of the clearest expressions of the DECADENT movement in literature.

Aga Khan I. Real name **Hasan Ali Shah** (1800–1881). Head of an important sect of British Indian Mohammedans. For checking fanatic frontier tribes for the British Government in India, he was granted a large pension and the title, "His Highness the Aga Khan."

Agamedes. In classic legend, the brother of Trophonius. Together they built the temple of Apollo at Delphi and a treasury for king Hyrieus. Agamedes was caught stealing part of the king's treasure and killed by his brother who feared being discovered as an accomplice.

Agamemnon. In Greek legend the King of Mycenae, son of Atreus, and leader of the Greeks at the siege of Troy. Homer makes him ruler over all Argos. He was the brother of Menelaus, the theft of whose wife Helen by Paris brought on the Trojan War. Before the expedition against Troy could sail, Agamemnon's daughter Iphigenia was sacrificed to Diana to appease that goddess for a sacred stag Agamemnon had killed. At Troy, Agamemnon's quarrel with ACHILLES cost the Greeks many lives and delayed the end of the war. After the sack of Troy, Agamemnon returned home only to be murdered by his wife Clytemnestra, who was living as the paramour of Aegisthus. For the tragic vengeance which his son Orestes and his daughter Electra took for their father's death, see under those entries. Agamemnon is the principal figure in Aeschylus' trilogy, the *Agamemnon, Choephori* and *Eumenides,* and is prominent in many plays on the fate of IPHIGENIA.

Aganippe. Fountain of the Muses, at the foot of Mount Helicon, in Boeotia.

Agapemone. A 19th-century Communistic establishment of men and women in England, suspected of free-love practices; hence, any free-love institution.

Agapida, Fray Antonio. The imaginary chronicler of *The Conquest of Granada* (1829) by Washington IRVING.

Agar, Herbert Sebastian (1897–). American author and editor. Among his books are *The People's Choice* (1933, winner of the Pulitzer prize in 1934); *What is America?* (1936); *Pursuit of Happiness* (1938); *Beyond German Victory* (1940), with Helen Hill.

Agassiz, Jean Louis Rodolphe (1807–1873). Scientist and educator, trained in Switzerland and Germany, who came to the U.S. and exerted wide influence as a member of the faculty of Harvard University. He made important contributions in the fields of geology and biology.

Agastya. In Hindu mythology a dwarf who drank the sea dry. As he was walking one day with Vishnu, the insolent ocean asked the god who the pigmy was that strutted by his side. Vishnu replied it was the patriarch Agastya, who was going to restore earth to its true balance. Ocean, in contempt, spat its spray in the pigmy's face, and the sage, in revenge of this affront, drank the waters of the ocean, leaving the bed quite dry.

Agate, James Evershed (1877–1947). English dramatic critic. On staff of Manchester GUARDIAN, SATURDAY REVIEW, Sunday TIMES.

Agatha. The daughter of Cuno, and the betrothed of Max, in Weber's opera of DER FREISCHÜTZ.

Agatha, St. See under SAINTS.

Agathocles (361–289 B.C.). Tyrant of Sicily (316–304 B.C.). He was the son of a potter, and raised himself from the ranks to become general of the army. There is a story that he always kept an earthen pot at hand in memory of his origin; hence *Agathocles' pot* signifies a poor relation. When he attacked the Carthaginians, he "carried the war into Africa" and "burned his ships behind him" that his soldiers might feel assured they must either conquer or die. Agathocles died of poison administered by his grandson. He is the hero of an English tragedy by Richard Perrington, a French tragedy by Voltaire and a German novel by Caroline Pichler, all called by his name.

agathodaemon. A Greek deity of good fortune in the form of a shepherd.

Agave. In classic mythology daughter of Cadmus and mother of Pentheus whom she tore to pieces in a mad fury under the illusion that he was a wild beast. This episode forms a part of Euripides' drama THE BACCHAE.

age. A word used of a long but more or less indefinite period of history, human and pre-human, distinguished by certain real or mythical characteristics and usually named from these characteristics or from persons connected with them, as the GOLDEN AGE, the MIDDLE AGES, the DARK AGES, the *Age of the Antonines* (from Antoninus Pius, 138, to Marcus Aurelius, 180), the *Prehistoric Age,* etc. Thus, Hallam calls the 9th century the *Age of the Bishops,* and the 12th, the *Age of the Popes.*

Varro (*Fragments,* 1623) recognizes three ages:

> From the beginning of mankind to the Deluge, a time wholly unknown.
> From the Deluge to the First Olympiad, called the mythical period.
> From the First Olympiad to the present time, called the historic period.

Shakespeare's passage on the seven ages of man (*As You Like It,* ii. 7) is well known; and Titian symbolized the three ages of man thus:

> An infant in a cradle.
> A shepherd playing a flute.
> An old man meditating on two skulls.

According to Lucretius also there are three ages, distinguished by the materials employed in implements (v. 1282), viz.:

> *The age of stone,* when celts or implements of stone were employed.
> *The age of bronze,* when implements were made of copper or brass.
> *The age of iron,* when implements were made of iron, as at present.

Hesiod names five ages, viz.:

The *Golden* or patriarchal, under the care of Saturn.
The *Silver* or voluptuous, under the care of Jupiter.
The *Brazen* or warlike, under the care of Neptune.
The *Heroic* or renaissant, under the care of Mars.
The *Iron* or present, under the care of Pluto.

Fichte names five ages also:

The antediluvian, post-diluvian, Christian, satanic and millennian.

Aged or **Aged P.** In Dickens' novel *Great Expectations,* WEMMICK's father.

Age of Innocence, The. A novel by Edith WHARTON (1920), depicting the social life of the New York of fifty years previous. The hero, Newland Archer, marries an affectionate, pretty girl of the circumscribed social sphere of the élite to which he is born, and is loyal to her, but is torn by love for his vivid, warm-blooded, unconventional cousin, Ellen Olenska, and impatience at the petty conventions that make up his world. This novel was awarded the Pulitzer prize in 1921. The title is from a famous painting of a child by Sir Joshua Reynolds.

Age of Reason. A controversial treatise by the American pamphleteer, Thomas PAINE (1795) on the subject of revealed religion.

Agib. (1) The Third CALENDER of the *Arabian Nights.* He was wrecked on the loadstone mountain, lived for a year in the palace of the forty princesses, and lost an eye for his curiosity.

(2) The Prince of Tartary in one of the *Bab Ballads* by W. S. Gilbert.

Agincourt, Battle of (October 25, 1415). In this battle Henry V of England defeated a French army of cavalry superior in numbers to his own while invading France to claim the throne. Shakespeare's drama *Henry V* concerns this invasion, and the English poet Michael DRAYTON wrote a poem entitled *Agincourt* in ballad style.

Aglaia. (1) One of the three Graces of classic mythology.

(2) In Dostoyevski's novel THE IDIOT, the fiancée of Prince Myshkin.

Aglaos. A poor Arcadian peasant called by the Delphic oracle "happier than King Gyges of Lydia," because he was contented.

Aglauros. The wife or daughter of Cecrops, King of Athens. Also, a goddess presiding over agricultural fertility.

Agnes. In Molière's L'ÉCOLE DES FEMMES, the girl on whom Arnolphe tries his pet experiment of education, so as to turn out for himself a "model wife." She has been brought up in a country convent and kept in entire ignorance of the difference of sex, conventional proprieties, the mysteries of marriage, and so on. When removed from the convent, she treats men like school-girls, plays with them and kisses them.

An *Agnes* is therefore any naïve and innocent young girl. The French have a proverb *Elle fait l'Agnès,* that is, she pretends to be wholly unsophisticated and ingenuous.

Agni. The Hindu god of fire and of sunlight and lightning. He is one of the more important deities described in the Vedas.

agnostic (Gr. *a,* "not," *gignoskein,* "to know"). A term coined by Professor Huxley in 1869 (with allusion to St. Paul's mention of an altar to "the Unknown God") to indicate the mental attitude of those who withhold their assent to whatever is incapable of proof, such as an unseen world, a First Cause, etc. Agnostics neither dogmatically accept nor reject such matters, but simply say *agnosco*—I do not know—they are not capable of proof.

agony column. A column in a newspaper containing advertisements of missing relatives and friends, or other messages of a confidential nature. The practice originated with the London *Times.* It is also the title of a novel by Earl Derr Biggers.

Agramant. In ORLANDO INNAMORATO by Boiardo and ORLANDO FURIOSO by Ariosto, the king of Africa who carried the war against Charlemagne into France. In an encounter with Oliver he was seriously wounded.

Agrarians. A group of American writers of Southern origin, including Allen TATE, John Crowe RANSOM, and Robert Penn WARREN, who favor an economic base of agriculture for the South and a return to the aristocratic culture once made possible by such a society. *I'll Take My Stand* (1932) expresses their views.

Agrawain or **Agraivain, Sir.** In Arthurian romance, a knight of the Round Table who aided his half-brother Modred to spy upon Launcelot.

Agreement of the People. A proposed constitution submitted by John Lilburne and the LEVELERS in October, 1647, but not accepted by Cromwell.

Agricane. In Carlovingian legend, the famous King of Tartary who besieges Angelica in the castle of Albracca and is slain in combat by Orlando. He brought into the field 2,200,000 men, according to the account in Boiardo's ORLANDO INNAMORATO.

Agricola, Johannes. Real name **Johannes Sneider** (1494?–1566). German reformer of the 16th century, alleged founder of the sect of Antinomians. Cf. Browning's poem, *Johannes Agricola.*

Agricultural Adjustment Administration (AAA). An agency of the NEW DEAL (1933) which sought to reduce overproduction in agriculture and equalize the farmer's return with that of the businessman. Its chief feature was payment in compensation for a prescribed annual crop reduction.

Agrippa. In the New Testament, one of the rulers before whom Paul was tried. His comment "Almost thou persuadest me to become a Christian" is often quoted.

Agrivain. One of King Arthur's knights, brother of Sir Gawain, who betrayed Sir Launcelot and the queen to the king. His other brothers were Gahariet and Gareth.

Aguecheek, Sir Andrew. In Shakespeare's TWELFTH NIGHT, a silly old fop with "3000 ducats a year," very fond of the table, but with a shrewd understanding that "beef had done harm to his wit." Sir Andrew thinks himself "old in nothing but in understanding," and boasts that he can "cut a caper, dance the coranto, walk a jig, and take delight in masques," like a young man.

Aguinaldo, General Emilio (1870?–). Leader of a Filipino insurrection against the Spaniards in 1896 and later (1899) against American forces when the Philippine Islands were taken over by the U.S. after the Spanish-American War. He was finally captured (1901) and took the oath of allegiance to the U.S.

Agur's wish (*Prov.* xxx. 8). "Give me neither poverty nor riches."

Ahab. A king of Israel whose name has become a byword for wickedness. He is remembered especially for his hostility to the prophet Elijah and his seizure of Naboth's vineyard at the instigation of his wife JEZEBEL. His story is told 1 *Kings* xvi–xxii.

Ahab, Captain. The whaler who pursues MOBY DICK in Herman Melville's famous American novel of that name. In his passionate soliloquies and the violence of his quest for revenge, this character has been compared with the heroes of Elizabethan tragedy.

Ahasuerus. (1) In the Old Testament, king of the Medes and Persians. His story is related in the book of ESTHER.

(2) In medieval legend, the name of the WANDERING JEW.

Ahi. In Vedic myth, the sky dragon that releases the rain when INDRA's thunderbolt is hurled.

Ahmed, Prince. A character in the *Arabian Nights,* noted for the tent given him by the fairy Paribanou, which would cover a whole army, but might be carried in one's pocket, and for the apple of Samarkand, which would cure all diseases.

Aholah and **Aholibah** (*Ezek.* xxiii). Personifications of prostitution. Used by the prophet to signify religious adultery or running after false faiths. These Hebrew names signify "she in whom are tents," and have reference to the worship at the high places. Swinburne has a poem *Aholibah* (*Poems and Ballads, 1st Series*), in which occurs the verse:

> God called thy name Aholibah,
> His tabernacle being in thee,
> A witness through waste Asia:
> Thou wert a tent sown cunningly
> With gold and colours of the sea.

Aholibamah. In the Bible, the name of one of Esau's wives (*Gen.* xxxvi. 2) and of a "duke" that came of Esau (*Gen.* xxxvi. 41), but in Byron's HEAVEN AND EARTH, daughter of Cain's son, loved by the seraph Samiasa. She is a proud, ambitious, queen-like beauty a female type of Cain. When the flood came, her angel-lover carried her off to "a brighter world than this."

Ahriman or **Ahrimanes.** In the dual system of Zoroaster, the spiritual enemy of mankind, also called *Angra Mainyu,* and *Druj* (deceit). He has existed since the beginning of the world, and is in eternal conflict with Ahura Mazda or ORMUZD.

Ah Sin. Bret Harte's HEATHEN CHINEE in the poem usually known by that name but first published as *Plain Language from Truthful James* (1870). In 1880 Bret Harte and Mark Twain made this popular innocent-appearing coolie villain the central figure in a play called *Ah Sin.*

Ah! Wilderness. See O'NEILL, EUGENE.

Aïda. An opera by VERDI (libretto by Ghislanzoni from the French of Camille du Locle) generally considered his masterpiece (1871). The scene is laid in Egypt in the time of the Pharaohs. The Egyptian general Rhadames is in love with Aïda, a slave who is in reality the daughter of Amonasro, ruler of Ethiopia. She returns his passion, but he is also beloved by Amneris, daughter of the king of Egypt, whose hand is formally bestowed upon him by his sovereign. The exigencies of the war between Egypt and Ethiopia make King Amonasro a captive of the victorious Rhadames, but his true rank is not known. Urged by her father's fiery words, Aïda endeavors to persuade Rhadames to flee with them and give his support to Ethiopia. Rhadames holds back but involuntarily betrays the place of attack planned for the morrow Amneris and the chief priest interrupt the scene; Amonasro and Aïda flee and Rhadames, who gives himself up, is condemned to be buried alive for treason. While the remorseful Amneris prays in the temple above, Aïda joins him and perishes with him in the crypt.

Aidenn. So Poe calls Eden in THE RAVEN.

> Tell this soul, with sorrow laden,
> If within the distant Aidenn,
> It shall clasp a sainted maiden,
> Whom the angels name Lenore.

Aïdes, also **Aïdoneus.** Hades, the god.

Aiglemont, Julie d'. Titular heroine of Balzac's novel, *A Woman of Thirty* (*La femme de trente ans*). After marriage she resists one lover, who dies of pneumonia contracted in the effort to save her from being compromised, but yields to another, the Marquis de Vandenesse. She devotes herself to her daughter Moina, who does not return her affection and whose unkind taunts bring about her death.

Aiglon, L'. A drama by Edmond ROSTAND (1900), based on the tragic career of the son and heir of Napoleon, whom Victor Hugo had called *l'Aiglon* (the eaglet). The young hero knows little or nothing of his father's story for years. When he learns the truth he escapes from the Austrian court, but his attempt at conspiracy is doomed to utter failure and he dies in Vienna.

Aiken, Conrad Potter (1889–). American poet and novelist, whose work is marked by a strong interest in psychoanalysis. Poetry: *The Jig of Forslin* (1916); *The House of Dust* (1920); *Priapus and the Pool* (1922); *The Pilgrimage of Festus* (1923); *Serlin* (1925); *Time in the Rock* (1936); *And in the Human Heart* (1940). Fiction: *Blue Voyage* (1927); *Costumes by Eros* (short stories, 1928); *Great Circle* (1933); *King Coffin* (1935); *Conversation* (1940).

ailanthus. The tree of heaven or Chinese sumach. Silkworms feed on its leaves. Imported to New York City for an unsuccessful silk industry, and is now a characteristic tree there. The tree in *A Tree Grows in Brooklyn.*

Aimwell, Viscount Thomas. An impoverished gentleman who succeeds in redressing his fortunes by paying his addresses to Dorinda, daughter of Lady Bountiful. He and Archer are the two beaux of THE BEAUX' STRATAGEM, a comedy by George Farquhar (1705).

Ainsworth, William Harrison (1805–1882). English historical novelist and editor of *Bentley's Miscellany* and *Ainsworth's Magazine.* Wrote 39 novels, including *Rookwood* (1834); *Jack Sheppard* (1839); *Old St. Paul's* (1841); *Windsor Castle* (1843); *The Flitch of Bacon* (1854); etc.

Ainu. A hairy, primitive member of an indigenous race of Japan, living on Hokkaido and Karafuto.

Airavata. In Hindu myth, the elephant upon which INDRA rides.

Air Raid. See under MACLEISH, ARCHIBALD.

Airways, Inc. See DOS PASSOS, JOHN.

Aïssa. In Conrad's OUTCAST OF THE ISLANDS, the daughter of the one-eyed native Babalatchi, loved by Willems.

Ajax. The most famous hero of the Trojan War after Achilles; King of Salamis, a man of giant stature, daring, and self-confident, son of Telamon. When the armor of Hector was awarded to Ulysses instead of to himself, he turned mad from vexation and stabbed himself. His deeds are narrated by Homer and later poets. Sophocles has a tragedy called *Ajax,* in which "the madman" scourges a ram he mistakes for Ulysses. His encounter with a flock of sheep, which he fancied in his madness to be the sons of Atreus, has been mentioned at greater or less length by several Greek and Roman poets. This Ajax is introduced by Shakespeare in his drama called *Troilus and Cressida.*

Ajax the Less. In Greek legend son of Oileus, king of Locris. The night Troy was taken, he offered violence to Cassandra, the prophetic daughter of Priam; in consequence of which his ship was driven on a rock, and he perished at sea.

Akeley, Carl Ethan (1864–1926). American taxidermist, sculptor, naturalist, explorer. Made trips for Field Museum and American Museum of Natural History. Died in Africa.

à Kempis, St. Thomas. See under SAINTS.

Akenside, Mark (1721–1770). English poet and physician to the queen (1761). He is the author of *Pleasures of the Imagination* (1744), a book of verse.

Akins, Zoë (1886–). American playwright, best known for *The Greeks Had a Word for It* (1930), a comedy, and *The Old Maid* (1934), which was adapted from a novelette of the same title by Edith WHARTON and received the Pulitzer prize for drama in 1935.

Al. For *Al Araf, Al Borak* and similar entries of Mohammedan legend, see under ARAF, BORAK, etc.

Alabama Claims, the. A Confederate warship, the *Alabama,* was built in England for use against Union shipping during the American Civil War. It was the subject of an international diplomatic incident because it had been permitted to sail from a British port, and the Union government was awarded heavy damages in payment for Great Britain's violation of neutrality.

Aladdin. One of the most celebrated characters in the *Arabian Nights,* the son of Mustafa a poor tailor, of China, "obstinate, disobedient, and mischievous," wholly abandoned "to indolence and licentiousness." One day an African magician accosts him, pretending to be his uncle, and sends him to bring up the "wonderful lamp," at the same time giving him a "ring of safety." Aladdin secures the lamp, but will not hand it to the magician till he is out of the cave; whereupon the magician shuts him up in the cave, and departs for Africa. Aladdin, wringing his hands in despair, happens to rub the magic ring. The genius of the ring appears before him, and asks his commands. Aladdin asks to be delivered from the cave, and he returns home. By means of this lamp, he obtains untold wealth, builds a superb palace, and marries Badroulboudour, the sultan's daughter. After a time, the African magician gets possession of the lamp, and causes the palace, with all its contents, to be transported into Africa. Ultimately Aladdin poisons the magician, regains the lamp, and has his palace retored to its original place in China.

Aladdin's lamp. The source of wealth and good fortune.

Aladdin's ring, given him by the African magician, was a "preservative against every evil."

Aladdin's window. To finish Aladdin's window—i.e., to attempt to complete something begun by a great genius, but left imperfect. The palace built by the genius of the lamp had twenty-four windows, all but one being set in frames of precious stones; the last was left for the sultan to finish; but after exhausting his treasures, the sultan was obliged to abandon the task as hopeless.

Alamo, The. A fort in San Antonio, Texas, formerly a Roman Catholic mission and in 1836 the scene of a siege and the slaughter of its American defenders by a Mexican army. "Remember the Alamo!" was a favorite battle slogan of the Mexican War (1846–1848).

Alan-a-Dale or **Alin-a-Dale,** see ALLAN-A-DALE.

Alan Breck Stewart. In Stevenson's DAVID BALFOUR.

Alarcón, Pedro Antonio de (1833–1891). Spanish writer, statesman, and radical journalist. Author of short stories and sketches of Spanish rustic life, including *El Sombrero de Tres Picos* (1874) and *El Niño de la Bola* (1880).

Alarcón y Mendoza, Juan Ruiz de (1580?–1639). Spanish dramatist, a leading representative of the Golden Age. One of his plays, LA VERDAD SOSPECHOSA, was imitated by CORNEILLE in *Le Menteur*. Author of *El Semejante de Sí Mismo; Las Paredes Oyen; El Tejedor de Segovia;* etc.

A la Recherche du temps perdu, see REMEMBRANCE OF THINGS PAST.

Alaric (370?–410). Gothic king and conqueror. Invaded Greece as king of the Visigoths (395–396) and plundered Rome (410).

Alaric Cottin or Cotin. A nickname which Voltaire gave Frederick the Great, from the Visigoth conqueror Alaric (c. 376–410), and Charles Cotin (1604–1682), a French poet of small merit.

Alasnam, Prince Zeyn. A character in the ARABIAN NIGHTS who possessed eight statues, each a single diamond on a gold pedestal, but had to go in search of a ninth, more valuable than them all. This ninth was a lady, the most beautiful and virtuous of women, "more precious than rubies," who became his wife.

Alasnam's mirror. When Alasnam was in search of his ninth statue, the king of the genii gave him a test-mirror, in which he was to look when he saw a beautiful girl. If the glass remained pure and unsullied, the damsel would be the same, but if not, the damsel would not be wholly pure in body and in mind. This mirror was called "the touchstone of virtue."

Alastor. The evil genius of a house; a Nemesis, which haunts and torments a family.

Alastor or *The Spirit of Solitude.* A poem in blank verse by Percy Bysshe Shelley (1815). The poet wanders over the world admiring the wonderful works which he cannot help seeing, but finds no solution to satisfy his inquisitive mind, and nothing in sympathy with himself.

Albania, Albany, Albion. A poetical name for Scotland or North Scotland. ALBION is also the oldest name of the island occupied by England, Scotland, and Wales.

> In that nook-shotten isle of Albion.
> Shakespeare.

Albany regency. The name given to an American political group, with headquarters at Albany, that exerted considerable influence about 1820–1850.

albatross. The largest of web-footed birds, called by sailors the *Cape Sheep,* from its frequenting the Cape of Good Hope. Many fables are told of the albatross; it is said to sleep in the air, because its flight is a gliding without any apparent motion of its long wings, and sailors say that it is fatal to shoot one. Coleridge's *Ancient Mariner* is founded on this superstition.

Alberich. In Scandinavian legend, the dwarf who guards the treasure of the Nibelungs, owner of a magic ring. He plays a prominent part in both the *Völsunga Saga* and the *Nibelungenlied*. In Wagner's music-drama, *Der Ring des Nibelungen,* Loki and Wotan steal the ring and treasure, and Alberich's curse follows the ring wherever it goes.

Albert. A character in Goethe's romance THE SORROWS OF WERTHER, drawn from his friend Kestner. He is a young German farmer, who married Charlotte Buff (called "Lotte" in the novel), with whom Goethe was in love. Goethe represents himself as Werther.

Albert of Geierstein, Count. In Scott's ANNE OF GEIERSTEIN.

Albertine. A character in REMEMBRANCE OF THINGS PAST, by Marcel Proust, object of the love and intense jealousy of the narrator, Marcel, and concerned in much of his introspective analysis.

Albertus Magnus. Albert the Great (1193–1280). Medieval German scholar, teacher, and churchman, who wrote commentaries on Aristotle and many treatises on natural science. He was an early empiricist in his philosophical attitude, insisting always on testing authority by the lessons of experience. St. Thomas Aquinas (see, under SAINTS) was one of his pupils.

Albigenses. A common name for a number of anti-sacerdotal sects in southern France during the 13th century; so called from the Albigeois, inhabitants of the district which now is the department of the Tarn, the capital of which was Albi, Languedoc.

Albigensian Crusade, The. A military campaign to suppress the heretical ALBIGENSES which began in 1209 under Pope Innocent III and soon became a war of feudal conquest.

Albino (from Lat. *albus* "white"). A term originally applied by the Portuguese to those Negroes who were mottled with white spots; but now to those who, owing to the congenital absence of coloring pigment, are born with red eyes and white hair and skin. Albinos are found among white people as well as among Negroes. The term is also applied to beasts and plants, and even, occasionally, in a purely figurative way: thus, Oliver Wendell Holmes, in the AUTOCRAT OF THE BREAKFAST TABLE (ch. viii), speaks of Kirke White as one of the "sweet Albino poets," whose "plaintive song" he admires, apparently implying some deficiency of virility, and possibly playing upon the name.

Albion. An ancient and poetical name for Great Britain: thought to have been so called from the white (Lat. *albus*) cliffs that face Gaul, but possibly from the Celtic *alp, ailp,* a rock, cliff, mountain. It was Napoleon who called England *Perfide Albion.*

Albracca. In Boiardo's famous epic, ORLANDO INNAMORATO, a castle of Cathay (China), to which Angelica retires in grief when she finds her love for Rinaldo is not reciprocated. Here she is besieged by Agricane, king of Tartary, who is resolved to win her, and here many of the adventurous paladins of Charlemagne's court follow her to join in the fray.

Alcaic verse or ALCAICS. A Greek lyrical metre, so called from *Alcoeus,* a lyric poet, who is said to have invented it. Alcaic measure is little more than a curiosity in English poetry; probably the best example is Tennyson's:

O migh|ty-mouthed | in|ventor of | harmonies,
O skilled | to sing | of | Time or E|ternity.
God-gift|ed or|gan-voice | of Eng|land,
Milton, a | name to re|sound for | ages.

Alcatraz. An American federal penitentiary for particularly dangerous criminals, located on an island in San Francisco Bay, formerly a fort and a military prison.

Alceste. The hero of Molière's comedy *Le Misanthrope* (1666). Alceste is disgusted with society. Courtesy seems to him the vice of fops, —and the usages of civilized life no better than hypocrisy. He is in love with Célimène, a coquette who produces caustic "portraits" of her friends behind their backs and embodies all the qualities of which he is most impatient.

Alcestis, Alceste, or **Alcestes.** In Greek legend daughter of Pelias and wife of Admetus. On his wedding day Admetus neglected to offer sacrifice to Diana, but Apollo induced the Fates to spare his life, if he could find a voluntary substitute. His bride consented to die for him, but Hercules brought her back from the world of shadows.

Euripides has a Greek tragedy on the subject (*Alcestis*); Gluck has an opera (*Alceste*), libretto by Calzabigi (1765); Philippi Quinault produced a French tragedy entitled *Alceste,* in 1674; and Lagrange-Chancel in 1694 produced a French tragedy on the same subject. The story is told by William MORRIS in his *Earthly Paradise* (*April*).

Alchemist, The. The last of the three great comedies of Ben Jonson (1610). The other two are *Volpone* (1605), and *The Silent Woman* (1609). The object of *The Alchemist* is to ridicule the belief in the philosopher's stone and the elixir of life. The alchemist is Subtle, a mere quack: and Sir Epicure Mammon is the chief dupe, who supplies money, etc., for the "transmutation of metal." Abel Drugger, a tobacconist, and Dapper, a lawyer's clerk, are two other dupes. Captain Face, *alias* Jeremy, the house-servant of Lovewit, and Dol Common are his allies. The whole thing is blown up by the unexpected return of Lovewit.

Alcibiades. A brilliant but traitorous Athenian general (450–404 B.C.). Being banished by the senate, he marched against the city, and the senate, unable to offer resistance, opened the gates to him. This incident is introduced in *Timon of Athens.* Alcibiades was a favorite pupil of Socrates and pupil and master are depicted in Plato's dialogue *Phaedo.* He is caricatured in Aristophanes' comedy THE CLOUDS under the name Pheidippides.

Alcides. HERCULES, son of Alcaeus; hence any strong and valiant hero. But see *Alcmene.*

Alcina. In the Italian epics dealing with the adventures of ORLANDO, Carnal Pleasure personified. In Boiardo's *Orlando Innamorato* she is a fairy, who carries off Astolpho. In Ariosto's *Orlando Furioso* she reappears as a kind of Circe, whose garden is a scene of enchantment. Alcina enjoys her lovers for a season, and then converts them into trees, stones, wild beasts and so on, as her fancy dictates.

Alcinous. In classic legend, ruler of the Phaeacians and father of Nausicaä. The shipwrecked Odysseus was hospitably received and feasted in his palace and responded by unfolding the tale of his adventures on the way home from Troy.

Alciphron. (1) A Greek rhetorician of the 2nd or 3rd century, author of fictitious letters giving details of domestic life and manners of his time.

(2) The hero of T. MOORE's romance *The Epicurean.*

Alciphron or The Minute Philosopher. The title of a work by Bishop BERKELEY. So called from the name of the chief speaker, a freethinker. The object of this work is to expose the weakness of infidelity.

Alcmaeon. Leader of the sons of the defeated Seven Against Thebes who, thirty years later, conquered and destroyed that city. He was driven mad by the Erinyes for killing his mother Eriphyle.

Alcman. A celebrated Dorian lyric poet of Sparta, first half of 7th century B. C.

Alcmena or Alcmene. In classic legend, wife of AMPHITRYON and mother of Hercules by Jupiter. She is a leading character in the comedies of Plautus, Molière and Dryden (all entitled *Amphitryon*) founded on the story of Jupiter's deceitful amour.

Alcofribas. The pseudonym assumed by Rabelais in his *Gargantua and Pantagruel.* Alcofribas Nasier is an anagram of "François Rabelais."

Alcoran. The KORAN.

Alcott, Amos Bronson (1799–1888). American educator, author, mystic, transcendentalist. An early pioneer in educational reform, he was condemned for his experiments, and tried in vain to establish a cooperative community, Fruitlands, near Harvard. Alcott aspired to be an American Plato and had great influence on EMERSON, THOREAU, HAWTHORNE, and CHANNING. He is suggested in the character of the father in LITTLE WOMEN, a popular novel by his daughter, Louisa May ALCOTT.

Alcott, Louisa May (1832–1888). American author and reformer, daughter of Amos Bronson ALCOTT. She took part in the temperance and woman suffrage movements of 19th-century America, and wrote immensely popular fiction for children. The best-known of her books are LITTLE WOMEN (1869); *An Old-Fashioned Girl* (1870); *Little Men* (1871); *Eight Cousins* (1875); and *Rose in Bloom* (1876).

Alcuin. Sometimes called **Albinus** (753–804). Christian theologian and teacher, born at York, who spent most of his life as director of Charlemagne's famous Palace School and led in reform of texts and calligraphy.

Alcyone or Halcyone, see HALCYON.

Aldanov, M. A. Pseudonym of **Mark A. Landau** (1889–). Russian novelist. Author of the extremely controversial novel *The Fifth Seal* (translated, 1943).

Aldebaran. A red star of the first magnitude, in the eye of Taurus.

> For I have seen red Aldebaran,
> The star of hate in Taurus' horn.
> Belloc.

The brightest star in the "watery Hyades."

Aldegonde, Lord St. In Disraeli's political novel LOTHAIR, the son and heir of a duke, but "a republican of the deepest dye . . . opposed to all privileges and all orders of men except dukes, who were a necessity." He is witty and good-natured, but thoroughly bored with life.

Alden, John. The young man loved by the Puritan maiden, Priscilla, in Longfellow's COURTSHIP OF MILES STANDISH.

Alden, Oliver. Hero of THE LAST PURITAN, novel by George SANTAYANA.

Aldiborontephoscophornio. A courtier in Henry Carey's burlesque, *Chrononhotonthologos* (1734). Sir Walter Scott called his printer and personal friend James Ballantyne by this name.

Aldine editions. Editions of the Greek and Latin classics, published and printed under the superintendence of Aldo Manuzio (Aldus Minutius), his father-in-law Andrea of Asolo, and his son Paolo, from 1490 to 1597. Most of them are in small octavo, and all are noted for their accuracy. The father invented the type called *italics,* once called *Aldine,* and first used in printing *Virgil,* 1501.

Aldingar, Sir. The story of Sir Aldingar is told in Percy's *Reliques.* He is steward to a Queen Eleanor, wife of King Henry. He impeached her fidelity, and submitted to a combat to substantiate his charge; but an angel, in the shape of a child, established the Queen's innocence. The story is common to the ballad literature of most European countries.

Aldington, Richard (1892–). English novelist and poet, at one time married to the American poet Hilda DOOLITTLE. Member of the group that introduced Imagism. A poetic pioneer. *Collected Poems* (1928). After World War I, he wrote several striking and bitter novels, including *Death of a Hero* (1929); *All Men Are Enemies* (1933); *Very Heaven* (1937); and *Rejected Guest* (1939). He compiled the *Viking Book of Poetry of the English Speaking World* (1941).

Aldrich, Bess Streeter (1881–). American novelist who wrote chiefly of pioneer life in Iowa and Nebraska. *Lantern in Her Hand* (1928); *White Bird Flying* (1931); and *Song of Years* (1939) are her best-known books.

Aldrich, Henry. Small-boy hero of a popular radio "soap opera," *The Aldrich Family,* written by Clifford Henshaw Goldsmith. The series originated from Mr. Goldsmith's play *What a Life* (1938)—later made into a moving picture—in which Ezra Stone and Betty Field created the roles of Henry Aldrich and Barbara Pearson.

Aldrich, Thomas Bailey (1836–1907). American man of letters, best known for his *Story of a Bad Boy* (1868), *Marjorie Daw* (1873), and his verse. See GENTEEL TRADITION.

Aldrick. The Jesuit confessor of Charlotte, countess of Derby, in Scott's *Peveril of the Peak.*

Alecto. In classic myth, one of the three FURIES.

Alectryon. A Greek youth changed by Ares into a cock.

Alembert, Jean Le Rond d' (1717?–1783). French mathematician and philosopher. Son of Mme de Tencin. Associate of Diderot in editing the *Encyclopédie.*

alembic. An apparatus for distilling, hence anything that distils.

> The alembic of a great poet's imagination.
> Brimley

Alessandro. The American Indian hero of Helen Hunt Jackson's RAMONA.

Alessio. The lover of Liza, in Bellini's opera LA SONNAMBULA.

Alexander. So PARIS, son of Priam, was called by the shepherds who brought him up.

Alexander VI. Real name **Rodrigo Lanzol y Borgia** (1431?–1503). Famous Borgia Pope, father of Cesare and Lucretia BORGIA. A great patron of the arts. Among his protégés were Bramante, Raphael, and Michelangelo.

Alexander, Sir Harold Rupert Leofric George (1891–). British general in charge of evacuation of British army from Dunkirk in World War II, commander in Middle East, North Africa, and Italy. His Chief of Staff accepted surrender of Germans in Italy, May 2, 1945.

Alexander, John White (1856–1915). American painter celebrated for his portraits of famous contemporaries.

Alexander, Sir William, Earl of Sterling, (ca. 1567–1640). Scotch poet in the retinue of King JAMES I of England. His best-known work is *Doomsday* (1614), an epic poem in twelve books.

Alexander of Hales (?–1245). English Franciscan theologian and philosopher, surnamed *Doctor Irrefragabilis.* Author of *Summa Theologiae* (printed 1475). Initiated the work of correlating the Christian system with the divergent metaphysical views of the newly introduced writings of Aristotle and the Arab commentators.

Alexander's Feast or The Power of Music. A Pindaric ode by DRYDEN (1694), in honor of St. Cecilia's Day. St. Cecilia was a Roman lady who, it is said, suffered martyrdom in 230, and was regarded as the patroness of music. See under SAINTS.

Alexander the Corrector. The self-assumed nickname of Alexander Cruden (1701–1770), compiler of the *Concordance to the Bible.* After being, on more than one occasion, confined in a lunatic asylum he became a reader for the Press, and later developed a mania for going about constantly with a sponge to wipe out the licentious, coarse, and profane chalk scrawls which met his eye.

Alexander the Great, King of Macedonia (356, 336–323 B.C.), and conqueror of the East. Many medieval romances were built about his career, notably the *Romance of Alexander* (Fr. *Roman d' Alexandre*) by Lambert-li-Cort and the *Lay of Alexander* (Ger. *Alexander Lied*) by Lambrecht, both written in the 12th century. Alexander's life is the subject of a tragedy by Racine (1665), of Lyly's *Alexander and Campaspe* (1581) and *Alexander the Great or the Rival Queens* (see *Statira*) by Nathaniel Lee (1667). See also *Diogenes.*

Alexander's beard. A smooth chin, or very small beard. Alexander had no perceptible beard, and hence is said to have had "an Amazonian chin."

the Albanian Alexander. George Castriot (*Scanderbeg* or *Iscander beg,* 1404–1467).

the English Alexander. Henry V. (1388, 1413–1422).

Alexander of the North. Charles XII of Sweden (1682–1718).

the Persian Alexander. Sandjar (1117–1158).

Alexandre, Jeanne. The school girl kidnaped by the kindly old scholar, Sylvestre

Bonnard, in Anatole France's CRIME OF SYLVESTRE BONNARD.

Alexandrian. Anything from the East was so called by the old chroniclers and romancers, because Alexandria was the depot from which Eastern stores reached Europe.

Alexandrian library. Founded by Ptolemy Soter, in Alexandria, in Egypt. The tale is that it was burnt and partly consumed in 391; but when the city fell into the hands of the caliph Omar, in 642, the Arabs found books sufficient to "heat the baths of the city for six months." It is said that it contained 700,000 volumes, and the reason given by the Mohammedan destroyer for the destruction of the library was that the books were unnecessary in any case, for all knowledge that was necessary to man was contained in the Koran, and any knowledge contained in the library that was not in the Koran must be pernicious.

Alexandrian school. An academy of learning founded about 310 B. C. by Ptolemy Soter, son of Lagus, and Demetrius of Phaleron, especially famous for its grammarians and mathematicians.

Alexandrine. In prosody, an iambic or trochaic line of twelve syllables or six feet with, usually, a caesura (break) at the sixth syllable. So called either from the 12th century French metrical romance, *Alexander the Great* (commenced by Lambert-li-Cort and continued by Alexandre de Bernay), or from the old Castilian verse chronicle, *Poema de Alexandro Magno,* both of which are written in this meter. It is the standard line of French poetry, holding much the same place as the iambic pentameter line in English poetry. The final line of the Spenserian stanza is an Alexandrine.

> A needless Alexandrine ends the song,
> Which, like a wounded snake,—drags its slow length along.
>
> Pope, *Essay on Criticism,* ii, 356.

Alexandrine Age. From about 323 to 640 A. D., when Alexandria, in Egypt, was the center of science, philosophy, and literature.

Alex D'Urberville. In Thomas Hardy's TESS OF THE D'URBERVILLES.

Alexis, St. See under SAINT.

Alexius Comnenus (1048–1118). First of the Comneni dynasty of Byzantine emperors, whose appeal for help from the West against the Turkish invaders gave impetus to the Crusades.

Alfheim. One of the heavenly mansions in Scandinavian mythology. It is inhabited by Frey and the light elves.

Alfieri, Conte Vittorio (1749–1803). Italian tragic dramatist. Author of nineteen tragedies classical in form, sonnets, odes. His love of freedom revived the national spirit of Italy.

Alfio. Husband of Lola in Mascagni's opera, CAVALLERIA RUSTICANA.

Alfonso XI. In Donizetti's opera, LA FAVORITA, the monarch of Castile, whose "favorite" was Leonora de Guzman.

Alfred's jewel. A gold plaque with a portrait in enamel of Anglo-Saxon workmanship found in 1693 at Athelney, site of a monastery on an island.

Alfred's scholars. When Alfred the Great set about the restoration of letters in England he founded a school and gathered around him learned men from all parts. These became known as "Alfred's scholars"; the chief among them are: Werfrith, Bishop of Worcester; Ethelstan and Werwulf, two Mercian priests; Plegmund (a Mercian), afterwards Archbishop of Canterbury; Asser, a Welshman; Grimbald, a French scholar from St. Omer, and John the Old Saxon.

Alfred the Great (870–901). English king who finally concluded peace with the raiding Danes, united the English people in a spirit of determination which eventually brought defeat to the invaders, and encouraged the intellectual growth of his nation. He translated works by Gregory the Great, Orosius, St. Augustine, Boethius, and the Venerable BEDE.

Algarsife. In Chaucer's unfinished *Squire's Tale,* in the *Canterbury Tales* (1388), the son of Cambuscan, and brother of Camballo, who "won Theodora to wife."

> This noble king, this Tartre Cambuscan,
> Had two sones by Elfeta his wife,—
> Of which the eldest sone highte Algarsife,
> That other was ycleped Camballo.
> A doghter had this worthy king also,
> That youngest was, and highte Canace.

Alger, Horatio, Jr. (1832–1899). The author of the innumerable *Alger Books* for boys, most of which are built around the formula of a poor but worthy hero who enters life as a bootblack or newsboy, surmounts impossible obstacles and achieves the heights of success. *Struggling Upward and Other Works,* was edited with an introduction by Russel Crouse, 1945.

Algerine Captive, The. An early American novel by Royall Tyler (1797) recounting the adventures of the hero, Updike Underhill, in his native New England backwoods, in Philadelphia where he meets Franklin, in London where he sees Tom Paine, and finally as a captive among the Algerines. The book is famed chiefly for its preface, which contained the first significant plea for native American fiction.

Algonquin. A family of American Indian tribes in various eastern and middle states and parts of Canada. Also the name of a hotel in New York City (see CASE AND WAYWARD INN) famous for its hospitality to actors and writers

Alhambra. The citadel and palace built at Granada by the Moorish kings in the 13th century. The word is the Arabic *al-hamra,* or at full length *kal'-at al hamra* (the red castle). Washington Irving called one of his best-known volumes of sketches and tales *The Alhambra* (1812) because it dealt with this famous palace and with legends of the Moors.

Ali. Cousin and son-in-law of Mahomet, the beauty of whose eyes is with the Persians proverbial; insomuch that the highest term they employ to express beauty is *Ayn Hali* (eyes of Ali). See SHIAH.

Alianora. In James Branch Cabell's FIGURES OF EARTH the Unattainable Princess, who travels in the appearance of a swan. Manuel loves and is loved by her, but she marries the King of England.

Ali Baba and the Forty Thieves. One of the best-known stories in the *Arabian Nights.* The forty thieves lived in a vast cave, the door of which opened and shut at the words, "Open, Sesame!" "Shut, Sesame!" One day, Ali Baba, a woodmonger, accidentally discovers the secret, and makes himself rich by carrying off gold from the stolen hoards. The captain tries several schemes to discover the thief, but is always outwitted by Morgiana, the wood-cutter's female slave, who, with boiling oil, poured into the jars where they have hidden themselves, kills the whole band, and at length stabs the captain himself with his own dagger.

Alice. (1) The heroine of Bulwer Lytton's novel ERNEST MALTRAVERS and its sequel *Alice or the Mysteries.*

(2) In Meyerbeer's opera ROBERT LE DIABLE the foster sister of Robert.

(3) The heroine of Tennyson's poem *The Miller's Daughter.*

See also below.

Alice, sweet. The charming but oversensitive heroine of the song BEN BOLT.

Who wept with delight when you gave her a smile
And trembled with fear at your frown.

Alice Adams. A novel by Booth TARKINGTON (1921). Alice Adams, the engaging young heroine, sees herself always in a romantic role; she sets her cap at the most eligible man in sight and almost deceives herself into believing that the fanciful explanations which she finds for the crudities of her hopelessly shabby middle-class family are true.

Alice-for-Short. A novel by William De Morgan (1907).

Alice in Wonderland. A whimsical story by Lewis Carroll (C. L. DODGSON) (Full title: *Alice's Adventures in Wonderland*). (1865.) A sequel, *Through the Looking-Glass,* appeared in 1871. In the former Alice falls down a well into a strange country where she becomes a giantess or a pigmy by partaking of alternate bites of cake and has remarkable adventures with the White Rabbit, the Cheshire Cat, the Mad Hatter, the March Hare, the Duchess, and other strange characters. (See under those entries.) In the sequel Alice manages to slip through a mirror into another strange country, where the inhabitants are chessmen.

Alice of Old Vincennes. A popular historical novel by Maurice Thompson (Am. 1900) dealing with the life of the Northwest in Revolutionary times.

Alice-Sit-by-the-Fire. A comedy by J. M. Barrie (1905).

Alice W———n. The old love conjured up by Charles LAMB in his *Dream Children, a Reverie* as the mother of his imaginary children. She has been identified as the actress Frances Maria Kelly.

Alien and Sedition Laws. Three Congressional acts passed in 1798, which gave the president power to deport or imprison any alien considered dangerous to the nation, and to punish any person engaging in treasonable acts or issuing writings considered to be seditious. These measures were directed by the Federalists against French revolutionary propagandists and the Republican party in the U.S.

Alifanfaron. Don Quixote in Cervantes' romance of that name, once attacked a flock of sheep, and declared them to be the army of the giant Alifanfaron.

Aliris. Sultan of Lower Bucharia and hero of Moore's LALLA ROOKH.

Alison. In THE MILLER'S TALE, one of Chaucer's *Canterbury Tales,* the young wife of John, a rich old miserly carpenter and in love with a poor scholar named Nicholas, lodging in her husband's house. She had a roguish eye, small eyebrows and was more "pleasant to look on than a flowering pear tree." For the tale see NICHOLAS.

Alison's House. See GLASPELL, SUSAN.

Alkahest or the House of Claës. The English title of Balzac's novel, *La Recherche de l'absolu.* See *Claës.*

al Kaswa, see KASWA AL.

Alla, King, see ELLA.

Allah. The Arabic name of the Supreme Being, from *al,* the, *illah,* god. *Allah il Allah,* the Mohammedan war-cry, and also the first clause of the confession of faith, is a corruption of *la illah illa allah,* meaning "there is no God but the God."

The Garden of Allah. A popular novel by Robert Hichens (1904), the title of which refers to a region of the Sahara Desert, south of the town of Beni Mora.

Allan-a-Dale, Allin-a-Dale or **Allen-a-Dale.** A minstrel in the Robin Hood ballads, who appears also in Scott's *Ivanhoe.* He is assisted by Robin Hood in carrying off his bride when she is on the point of being married against her will to a rich old knight.

allegory. A systematic symbolism, by which abstractions are represented as accurately as possible by concrete characters, plots, and situations, often with identifying tag-names. Spenser's THE FAËRIE QUEENE is the best-known literary allegory in English.

Allegro, L', see L'ALLEGRO.

Allen, Barbara. See BARBARA ALLEN.

Allen, Mr. Benjamin. A young surgeon in Dickens' PICKWICK PAPERS, the roommate and friend of Bob Sawyer.

Allen, Ethan. (1738–1789). American Revolutionary soldier. A hero of early Vermont. His story is told in Thompson's GREEN MOUNTAIN BOYS.

Allen, Frederick Lewis (1890–). American author, on the editorial staffs successively of *The Atlantic Monthly, The Century,* and *Harper's Monthly.* He is best known for his lively social histories, *Only Yesterday* (1931), an account of the period of the 1920's in the U.S., and *Since Yesterday* (1940), a similar treatment of the 1930's.

Allen, James Lane (1849–1925). American novelist and short-story writer of Kentucky scenes. His books include *The Blue Grass Region of Kentucky* (1892); *A Kentucky Cardinal* (1895); *The Last Christmas Tree* (1914); and *The Landmark* (1925).

Allen, Josiah. See JOSIAH ALLEN'S WIFE.

Allen, Mrs. A character in Jane Austen's NORTHANGER ABBEY.

Allen, Ralph. A celebrated friend of Pope, and benefactor of Fielding. Fielding depicted him in *Tom Jones* as ALLWORTHY and Pope wrote of him:

> Let humble Allen, with an awkward shame,
> Do good by stealth, and blush to find it fame.

Allen, William Hervey (1889–). American novelist, poet, and biographer, author of *Israfel* (1926), a biography of Edgar Allan Poe; the novel ANTHONY ADVERSE (1933); *Action at Aquila* (1938); and other books.

Allenby, Edmund Henry Hynman, 1st Viscount (1861–1936). English field marshal, famous in World War I. His biography was written by Field Marshal Sir Archibald Wavell (1940).

All for Love or A Sinner Well Saved. A poem in nine parts, in the form of a ballad, by Southey (1829).

All for Love or The World Well Lost. A tragedy by Dryden (1678) based on the story of Antony and Cleopatra. See ANTONY.

All God's Chillun Got Wings. A play by Eugene O'NEILL, produced in 1924, a dramatic psychological study of a Negro-white marriage.

All-Hallows' Day. All Saints' Day (Nov. 1st), "hallows" being the Old English *halig,* a holy (man), hence, a saint. The French call it *Toussaint.*

All-Hallows' Eve. Many old folklore customs are connected with Halloween or All Hallows' Eve (Oct. 31st), such as bobbing for apples, cracking nuts, finding by various "tests" whether one's lover is true, etc. Burns' *Halloween* gives a good picture of Scottish customs. There is a tradition in Scotland that those born on All Hallows' Eve have the gift of double sight, and commanding powers over spirits. Mary Avenel, on this supposition, is made to see the White Lady, invisible to less gifted visions.

> Christ and the Mother of Christ and all His Hallows.
> Masefield.

Allingham, William (1824–1889). Irish poet. Editor, *Fraser's Magazine* (1874–1879). Famous for the fairy poem beginning:

> Up the airy mountain,
> Down the rushy glen,
> We daren't go a-hunting
> For fear of little men. . . .

alliteration. The rhetorical device of commencing adjacent accented syllables with the same letter or sound, as in Quince's ridicule of it in *Midsummer Night's Dream* (v. 1):

> With *b*lade, with *b*loody *b*lameful *b*lade,
> He *b*ravely *b*roached his *b*oiling *b*loody *b*reast.

Alliteration was almost a *sine qua non* in Anglo-Saxon and early English poetry, and in modern poetry it is frequently used with great effect, as in Coleridge's:

> The fair *b*reeze *b*lew, the white *f*oam *f*lew.
> The *f*urrow *f*ollowed *f*ree.
> *Ancient Mariner.*

And Tennyson's:

> The *m*oan of doves in i*mm*e*m*orial el*m*s,
> And *m*ur*m*uring of innu*m*erable bees.
> *Princess,* vii.

Many fantastic examples of excessive alliteration are extant, and a good example from a parody by Swinburne will be found under the heading *Amphigouri.*

Allmers, Mr. and Mrs. The chief characters in Ibsen's drama, LITTLE EYOLF.

All Quiet on the Western Front. A novel by Erich Maria REMARQUE, published in the U.S. in 1929. It is the best-known of the antiwar literature written during the period 1920–1939, expressing the horror and futility of war as it was recognized by a whole generation of disillusioned youth in Europe and America.

All Saints' Day, or All-Hallows. Between 603 and 610 the Pope (Boniface IV) changed the heathen Pantheon into a Christian church, and dedicated it to the honor of all the martyrs. The festival of All Saints was first held on May 1st, but in the year 834 it was changed to November 1st.

All Sorts and Conditions of Men. A novel by Walter Besant (1882) notable as one of the first to deal with modern social reform.

All Souls' Day. The 2nd of November, so called because Catholics on that day seek by prayer and almsgiving to alleviate the sufferings of souls in purgatory. It was instituted in the monastery of Cluny in 993.

According to tradition, a pilgrim, returning from the Holy Land, was compelled by a storm to land on a rocky island, where he found a hermit, who told him that among the cliffs was an opening into the infernal regions through which huge flames ascended, and where the groans of the tormented were distinctly audible. The pilgrim told Odilo, abbot of Cluny, of this; and the abbot appointed the day following, which was November 2nd, to be set apart for the benefit of souls in purgatory.

All's Well that Ends Well. A comedy by Shakespeare (about 1598). The plot is taken from Boccaccio's *Decameron* ix. 3. The heroine, Helena, only daughter of a famous physician, cures the king of an illness and in consequence is allowed to choose her own husband. She is married to Bertram, son of the Countess of Rousillon, but he hates her and leaves the country almost immediately, stating in a letter that he will never see her more till she can get the ring from off his finger. Helena goes on a pilgrimage, passes herself off as a young girl of Florence with whom Bertram is in love and by subterfuge gains the ring, so all ends well.

All-the-Talents Ministry. See under TALENTS.

Allworthy, Squire. In Fielding's *Tom Jones* (1750), a man of sturdy rectitude, modesty, and untiring philanthropy, with an utter disregard of money or fame. Fielding's friend, Ralph ALLEN, was the academy figure of this character.

Bridget Allworthy. In the same novel, the unmarried sister of Squire Allworthy. It develops that she was the mother of Tom Jones.

Ally Sloper. A grotesque character invented by the English humorist W. G. BAXTER. *Ally Sloper's Holiday* is the title of an English comic weekly (founded, 1884).

Alma. In Spenser's *Faërie Queene,* Queen of "Body Castle," the soul personified, beset by enemies for seven years. The besiegers are a rabble rout of evil desires, foul imaginations, and silly conceits. Matthew Prior has a poem called *Alma.*

Almack's. Assembly rooms on King Street in London, built 1764 by William Almack. Scene of 19th-century balls. Also, a London Club on St. James Street, formerly famous as a gambling place, founded before 1763 by Almack, renamed the *Whig Club,* and later *Brooks's.*

Almagest (*Arab.* article *al,* Gr. *megistē,* "greatest"). Astronomical treatise by the 2nd century Alexandrian scholar PTOLEMY, a work extensively used during the Middle Ages in an Arabic translation.

Almahide. Heroine of Mlle. de Scudéry's historical romance *Almahide or the Captive Queen* (1660–1663) and of Dryden's drama *Almanzor and Almahide, or the Conquest of Granada* (1672). Both works deal with the history of Granada.

Alma Mater. A collegian so calls the university of which he is a member. The words are Latin for "fostering mother," and in ancient Rome the title was given to several goddesses, especially Ceres and Cybele.

Almanach de Gotha. A periodical publication in Germany, founded in 1763, giving data on all royal or titled European families.

Almanack, Poor Richard's, see POOR RICHARD'S ALMANACK.

Almanzor and Almahide or The Conquest of Granada. A tragedy by Dryden (1672), dealing with the history of Granada. The bombastic warrior Almanzor, who makes love to Queen Almahide and finally wins her after the death of her royal husband Boabdelin, was caricatured in the DRAWCANSIR of Buckingham's burlesque, *The Rehearsal,* which was staged the same year.

Almaviva, Count and Countess. Leading characters in Beaumarchais' comedy *The Barber of Seville,* in *The Marriage of Figaro* and the operas based upon the two plays. See FIGARO.

Almayer's Folly. A novel by Joseph Conrad (1895).

Almerio. The peasant hero of Sardou's drama GISMONDA and of Fevrier's opera of the same name.

Almesbury. It was in a sanctuary at Almesbury that Queen Guinevere, according to Malory, took refuge, after her adulterous passion for Launcelot was revealed to the king (Arthur). Here she died; but her body was buried at Glastonbury.

almighty dollar. Washington Irving seems to have been the first to use this expression which has become a byword for American materialism.

The almighty dollar, that great object of universal devotion throughout our land. . . .
W. Irving, *Wolfert's Roost, Creole Village* (1837).

B. E. Woolf was the author of a successful comedy called *The Mighty Dollar* (*Am.* 1875), which helped to popularize the expression.

Alnaschar. In the *Arabian Nights,* the dreamer, the "barber's fifth brother." He invests all his money in a basket of glassware, on which he is to gain so much, and then to invest again and again, till he grows so rich that he can marry the vizier's daughter and live in grandeur; but, being angry with his supposed wife, he gives a kick with his foot and smashes all the ware which has given birth to his dream of wealth. Hence an *Alnaschar dream* is counting one's chickens before they are hatched.

Aloadin. In Southey's THALABA THE DESTROYER, a sorcerer, who made for himself a palace and garden in Arabia called "The Earthly Paradise." Thalaba slew him with a club, and the scene of enchantment disappeared.

Alonzo the Brave. The name of a famous ballad by M. G. Lewis (1775–1818). The fair Imogen was betrothed to Alonzo, but, during his absence in the wars, became the bride of another. At the wedding feast Alonzo's ghost sat beside the bride, and, after rebuking her for her infidelity, carried her off to the grave.

Alp. The leading character in Byron's *Siege of Corinth.* He is a renegade who forswore the Christian faith to become a commander in the Turkish army, and was shot during the siege. He loved the daughter of the governor of Corinth, but she died of a broken heart because he was a traitor and apostate.

Alph. In Coleridge's poem *Kubla Khan,* the sacred river in Xanadu, which ran "through caverns measureless to man." It is probably a shortened form of ALPHEUS.

alpha. *"I am Alpha and Omega, the first and the last"* (*Rev.* i. 8). "Alpha" is the first, and "omega" the last letter of the Greek alphabet.

Alpheus and Arethusa. The Greek legend is that a youthful hunter named Alpheus was in love with the nymph Arethusa; she fled from him to the island of Ortygia on the Sicilian coast and he was turned into a river of Arcadia in the Peloponnesus. Alpheus pursued her under the sea, and, rising in Ortygia, he and she became one in the fountain hereafter called Arethusa. The myth seems to be designed for the purpose of accounting for the fact that the course of the Alpheus is for some considerable distance underground.

Alquife. A famous enchanter, introduced into the old romances, especially those relating to Amadis of Gaul.

Al Raschid, Haroun, see HAROUN AL RASCHID.

Alroy, David. A half-mythical Jewish medieval prince, local governor of his people under Moslem rule, with the title "Prince of the Captivity." He is the hero of Disraeli's prose romance *The Wondrous Tale of Alroy.*

alruna-wife. The Alrunes were the Lares or Penates of the ancient Germans. An alruna-wife was the household goddess of a German family.

Alsatia. The Whitefriars district of London, which from early times till the abolition of all privileges in 1697 was a sanctuary for debtors and law-breakers. It was bounded on the north and south by Fleet Street and the Thames, on the east and west by the Fleet River (now New Bridge Street) and the Temple; and was so called from the old Latin name of Alsace, which was for centuries a debatable frontier ground and a refuge of the disaffected. Scott, in his *Fortunes of Nigel,* described the life and state of this rookery; he borrowed largely from *The Squire of Alsatia* (1688), a comedy by Shadwell, who had been the first to use the name in literature.

Alsop, Richard (1761–1815). American author, a member of the group known as the HARTFORD WITS.

Altamira. Site near Santander, Spain, of a cave decorated with paleolithic mural paintings discovered in 1879.

Altamont, Colonel Jack (also known as J. Amory and Johnny Armstrong). In Thackeray's *Pendennis* (1849), the disreputable father of Blanche Amory and first husband of Lady Clavering.

Altar of the Dead, The. A volume of short stories by Henry JAMES, published in 1909. Nearly all have touches of the supernatural, used in special symbolic sense by the author.

Alte Fritz, der. Old Fritz. The nickname given by the Prussians to Frederick the Great.

alter ego. (*Lat.,* "other I, other self"). One's double; one's intimate and thoroughly trusted friend; one who has full powers to act for another.

Althaea's brand. A fatal contingency. Althaea's son, Meleager, was to live as long as a log of wood, then on the fire, remained unconsumed. With her care it lasted for many years, but being angry one day with Meleager, she pushed it into the midst of the fire; it was consumed in a few minutes and Meleager died in great agony at the same time. Cf. *Atalanta in Calydon* by Algernon Charles Swinburne.

Althea. The divine Althea of Richard Lovelace was Lucy Sacheverell, also called by the poet, "Lucasta."

When Love with unconfinëd wings
Hovers within my gates,
And my divine Althea brings
To whisper at the grates.

Lovelace was thrown into prison by the Long Parliament for his petition in favor of the King; hence the grates referred to.

Altisidora. In Cervantes' *Don Quixote,* one of the duchess' servants, who pretends to be in love with Don Quixote, and serenades him.

Alton Locke, Tailor and Poet. A novel by the Rev. Charles Kingsley (1850). This novel won for the author the title of "The Chartist Clergyman" because of its picture of Alton Locke and his radical Chartist friends. It was one of the first English novels to present a study of industrial conditions.

Altruria. The imaginary country from which Mr. Homos, the "Traveller from Altruria" in W. D. Howells' story of that title (1894) arrives, to make his embarrassing comments on American life as compared with the ideal conditions of his native land. He is the guest of Mr. Twelvemough, a conservative novelist, at a summer resort hotel.

Altsheler, Joseph Alexander (1862–1919). Writer of immensely popular juvenile stories. One or two are historical romances worth adult reading.

Alva, Duke of (1508?–1583). Ill-famed for his bloody suppression and persecution of the Dutch in Holland when sent there by Philip II of Spain.

Alvan, Dr. Sigismund. The name under which George Meredith portrays Ferdinand Lassalle in the novel THE TRAGIC COMEDIANS of which he is the hero.

Alvarado, Pedro de (1495?–1541). Soldier under Cortez, famed for saving his own life by a famous leap during "la noche triste."

Alvaro, Don. (1) The lover of Leonora in Verdi's opera FORZA DEL DESTINO and the name of the drama by the Duke of Rivas on which the opera is based.

(2) In Le Sage's *Gil Blas,* the husband of MENCIA OF MOSQUERA.

Alving, Oswald. The principal character in Ibsen's drama *Ghosts* (1881), a neurotic and dissipated young man who reaps the harvest sown by his worthless father and becomes insane from inherited disease.

Mrs. Alving. In the same drama, Oswald's widowed mother. Embittered by her experience, she is in revolt against a society where such conditions exist.

Alviss. In Norse mythology, especially in the *Edda,* a dwarf who demands Thor's daughter in marriage. Thor detains him till dawn which is fatal to dwarfs.

Alyosha. In *The Brothers Karamazov.* See KARAMAZOV, ALEXEY FYODOROVITCH.

Alzire. Titular heroine of a tragedy by Voltaire (1736), the scene of which is laid in Peru. Under the impression that her lover Zamore has been killed, she marries a German conqueror.

A.M. The academic degree, Master of Arts, the same as *M.A.* In America it is conferred upon the successful completion of one year of postgraduate work or its equivalent. When the Latin form is intended the A comes first, as *Artium Magister:* but where the English form is meant the M precedes, as *Master of Arts.*

The abbreviation "A.M." also stands for *ante meridiem* (*Lat.* before noon) and *anno mundi* (*Lat.,* "in the year of the world").

Amadis of Gaul. The hero of a prose romance of the same title, supposed to have been written by the Portuguese, Vasco de Lobeira (d. 1403), with additions by the Spaniard Montalvo, and by many subsequent romancers, who added exploits and adventures of other knights and thus swelled the romance to fourteen books. The romance was referred to as early as 1350; it was first printed in 1508, became immensely popular, and exerted a wide influence on literature far into the 17th century. It is the work responsible for DON QUIXOTE's madness.

Amadis, called the "Lion-knight," from the device on his shield, and "Beltenebros" (*darkly beautiful*), from his personal appearance, was a love-child of Perion, king of Gaula (which is Wales), and Elizena, princess of Brittany. He was cast away at birth and becomes known as the *Child of the Sea,* and after many adventures, including wars with the race of Giants, a war for the hand of his lady-love, Oriana, daughter of the king of Greece, the Ordeal of the Forbidden Chamber, etc., he and the heroine, Oriana, are wed. He is represented as a poet and musician, a linguist and a gallant, a knight-errant and a king, the very model of chivalry.

Other names by which Amadis was called were the *Lovely Obscure,* the *Knight of the Green Sword,* the *Knight of the Dwarf,* etc. The name means literally Love of God and is a variant of Amadeus, the name of a great angel.

Amadis of Greece. A Spanish continuation of the seventh book of AMADIS OF GAUL, supposed to be by Feliciano de Silva. It tells the story of Lisuarte of Greece, a grandson of Amadis.

Amaimon. One of the chief devils in medieval demonology; king of the eastern portion of hell. Asmodeus is his chief officer. He might be bound or restrained from doing hurt from the third hour till noon, and from the ninth hour till evening.

Amalthea. (1) In Greek mythology, the nurse of Zeus.

Amalthea's Horn. The cornucopia or "HORN OF PLENTY." The infant Zeus was fed with goats' milk by Amalthea, one of the daughters of Melisseus, king of Crete. Zeus, in gratitude, broke off one of the goat's horns, and gave it to Amalthea, promising that the possessor should always have in abundance everything desired.

(2) In Roman legend Amalthea is the name of the Sibyl who sold the SIBYLLINE BOOKS to Tarquin.

Amanda. The victim of Peregrine Pickle's seduction, in Smollett's novel, *Peregrine Pickle* (1751).

Amarant. A cruel giant slain in the Holy Land by Guy of Warwick. Cf. *Guy and Amarant,* in Percy's *Reliques.*

Amaryllis. A rustic sweetheart. The name is borrowed from a shepherdess in the pastorals of Theocritus and Virgil. In Spenser's *Colin Clout's Come Home Again,* Amaryllis is intended for Alice Spenser, countess of Derby.

> To sport with Amaryllis in the shade.
> Milton.

Amasis, ring of. Herodotus tells us (iii. 40) that Polycrates, tyrant of Samos, was so fortunate in everything that Amasis, king of Egypt, fearing such unprecedented luck boded ill, advised him to part with something which he highly prized. Polycrates accordingly threw into the sea a ring of great value. A few days afterwards, a fish was presented to the tyrant, in which the ring was found. Amasis now renounced friendship with Polycrates, as a man doomed by the gods; and not long afterwards, a satrap put the too fortunate despot to death by crucifixion.

Owen Meredith (E. R. Bulwer LYTTON) gave the title *The Ring of Amasis* to a romance. T. Sturge Moore has a well-known poem on the story in the *Oxford Book of English Verse.*

Amaterasu. The central deity of Japanese Shinto, ancestress of the imperial house. Cf. *The East I Know* by Paul Claudel.

amateur. See under DILETTANTE.

Amaurote (*Gr.,* "the shadowy or unknown place"). The chief city of UTOPIA in the political romance of that name by Sir Thomas More. Rabelais, in his *Pantagruel,* introduces Utopia and "the great city of the Amaurots" (Bk. II, ch. xxiii).

Amazing Marriage, The. A novel by George Meredith (1895).

Amazon. A Greek word meaning without breast, or rather, "deprived of pap." According to Herodotus there was a race of female warriors, or *Amazons,* living in Scythia, and other Greek stories speak of a nation of women in Africa of a very warlike character. There were no men in the nation; and if a boy was born, it was either killed or sent to its father, who lived in some neighboring state. The girls had their right breasts burnt off, that they might the better draw the bow. The term is now applied to any strong, brawny woman of masculine habits.

PINERO has a play called *The Amazons* (1893).

Ambassadors, The. A novel by Henry JAMES (1902–1903). The central character, Lambert Strether, goes to Paris at the instigation of Mrs. Newscome, a wealthy widow whom he plans to marry, in order to persuade her son Chad to come home. Chad is very much engaged in an affair with a charming French woman, the Countess de Vionnet, and the novel deals chiefly with Strether's gradual conversion to the idea that life in Paris may hold more of real meaning for Chad than in Woollett, Mass. After the arrival of a second ambassador, Chad's New England sister, Strether decides to return to Woollett, but Chad remains in Paris. Henry James once pointed out Strether's remark, "Live all you can; it's a mistake not to," as the essence of the novel.

Ambersons. The family whose story forms the subject matter of Booth Tarkington's novel, THE MAGNIFICENT AMBERSONS.

Amber Witch, The (Die Bernstein Hexe). A romance by J. W. Meinhold (*Ger.,* 1843), interesting chiefly because it was for years considered as a genuine chronicle of events in Pomerania in the early 17th century.

Ambitious Guest, The. One of the best known sketches in Hawthorne's *Twice Told Tales,* built around the incident of a mountain slide which buried a cottage at the foot of the mountain.

Ambree, Mary. An English heroine, immortalized by her valor at the siege of Ghent in 1584. See the ballad in Percy's *Reliques:*

> When captains couragious, whom death cold not daunte,
> Did march to the siege of the citty of Gaunt,
> They mustred their souldiers by two and by three,
> And the formost in battle was Mary Ambree.

Her name is proverbial for a woman of heroic spirit. Also cited in Elizabethan literature as a typical virago.

Ambrose. The tavern keeper whose name suggested the title for the celebrated NOCTES AMBROSIANAE, a series of imaginary conversations chiefly by Christopher North (John Wilson) published in *Blackwood's Magazine.* The blue parlor of Ambrose's Hotel in Edinburgh was in reality a rendezvous for Wilson and his friends, although the Ambrosian Nights were largely imaginary.

Ambrose, Father. "THE ABBOT" in Scott's novel of that title. He is the abbot of Kennaquhair, in reality Edward Glendinning, brother of Sir Halbert Glendinning, the knight of Avenel, but he appears at Kinross disguised as a nobleman's retainer.

Ambrose, St. See under SAINTS.

ambrosia (Gr. *a,* privative, *brotos,* "mortal"). The food of the gods, so called because it made them immortal. Anything delicious to the taste or fragrant in perfume is so called from the notion that whatever is used by the celestials must be excellent.

Ambrosio. The hero of M. G. Lewis' once famous novel, THE MONK.

Ameer, Amir. See RULERS, TITLES OF.

Amelia. A model of conjugal affection, in Fielding's novel of that name (1751). It is said that the character is intended for his own wife. Amelia is tried to the utmost by the vagaries of her wilful, profligate husband, Captain Booth, but remains both lovable and loving under the severest tests.

Amelia Sedley. In Thackeray's *Vanity Fair.* See SEDLEY, AMELIA.

Amen Corner, at the west end of Paternoster Row, London, is where the monks used to finish the *Pater Noster* as they went in procession to St. Paul's Cathedral on Corpus Christi Day. They began in *Paternoster* Row with the Lord's Prayer in Latin, which was continued to the end of the street; then said *Amen,* at the corner or bottom of the Row; then turning down *Ave Maria* Lane, commenced chanting the "Hail, Mary!" then crossing Ludgate, they entered *Creed* Lane chanting the *Credo.*

Amen-Ra, see AMMON.

America. Designation for both North and South America, although loose usage applies it chiefly to the U.S. Its origin is the name of Amerigo VESPUCCI (1451–1512), a Florentine merchant and traveler who claimed to have made a voyage in 1497 during which he discovered what is now the mainland of South America. His claim, although never proven, was perpetuated in the name given to the new continent in the West.

America. A novel by Franz KAFKA, published in the U.S. in 1941. It describes the humorous and pathetic adventures of a European lad, who is akin to Voltaire's *Candide,* in a fantastic land called America. This book is less marked by religious symbolism than Kafka's other novels and is lighter in tone.

America: A Prophecy. A poem by William BLAKE, dated 1793, in the poet's apocalyptic vein.

America Comes of Age. See SIEGFRIED, ANDRÉ.

America in Midpassage. See BEARD, CHARLES AUSTIN.

American. For *The American Sappho* and similar entries, see under SAPPHO, etc.

American, The. A novel by Henry James (1877) which shows a "robust compatriot" of comparatively simple, genuine nature in contact with the subtleties of European civilization. Christopher Newman, "the American" who at the age of thirty-five has made his own fortune, hopes to marry Claire de Cintré, a widowed daughter of the De Bellegardes, but that aristocratic old French family finally succeeds in circumventing him. Newman then plans to take revenge by publishing proof which he has discovered that Claire's mother and brother were the virtual murderers of her father, the Marquis, but decides to give up the plan because revenge is "really not his game."

American Academy of Arts and Letters. A society formed in 1904, modeled on the French Academy and limited to fifty members chosen from its parent organization, the National Institute of Arts and Letters, which has a larger membership.

American Caravan. An annual publication of American poetry and fiction, founded in 1927 by a group of critics including Lewis MUMFORD and Van Wyck BROOKS and issued irregularly thereafter. A number of well-known writers were represented in its pages.

American Crisis, The. An essay written by Thomas PAINE in 1776. It contains a stirring appeal to the American colonists to struggle against the tyranny of Great Britain, and was ordered by Washington to be read to his soldiers on the eve of the battle of Trenton.

American Federation of Labor (A.F. of L.). An organization of American trade unions, founded in 1881 and based on the principle of organization by craft rather than by industry. It was later opposed by the CONGRESS OF INDUSTRIAL ORGANIZATIONS.

American Institute of Public Opinion. A research organization, founded in 1935 under the direction of Dr. George Gallup, devoted to scientifically conducted surveys of public sentiment on questions of current interest. It featured house-to-house interviews in selected areas and came into prominence through its accurate prediction of the outcome of the

American presidential election of 1936. The surveys were popularly known as the Gallup Poll.

Americanism. The term seems to have been used for the first time in 1781 by John Witherspoon, President of Princeton University.

American Language, The. A popular study of the language spoken in the U.S. as a distinct and individual national tongue, written by H. L. MENCKEN and first published in 1919. *Supplement I* was published in 1945; *Supplement II* in 1948.

American Legion. An organization of former members of the American Expeditionary Force and others in army service in World War I. It was formed in 1919 to "perpetuate a one hundred per cent Americanism" and "promote peace and good will on earth," among other aims.

American Mercury. An iconoclastic magazine founded by H. L. MENCKEN and George Jean NATHAN in 1924. During the 1920's, many of the best-known American authors served as contributors. Nathan left the staff in 1930. After Mencken resigned his editorship in 1934, the character of the publication underwent a change.

American Notes. A volume of travel sketches by Charles Dickens (1842). The book was well received in England, but gave great offence in America.

American plan. The system of paying a fixed price for room and regular meals at a hotel in contrast to the *European Plan* of paying for room only with meals optional at additional cost.

American Scene, The. A volume of sketches by Henry James written after revisiting America (1907).

American Scholar, The. An address by Ralph Waldo Emerson (delivered before the Phi Beta Kappa Society at Cambridge, 1837) which has been called "the intellectual declaration of American independence." The title became the name of the Phi Beta Kappa magazine.

American Songbag, The. A collection of native American songs and folk ballads (1927), gathered and edited by Carl SANDBURG.

American Tragedy, An. A novel by Theodore DREISER, published in 1925. It recounts the story of a young man who tries to escape the poverty and emptiness of his Midwestern family background, only to be swept off his feet by contact with unaccustomed wealth and glitter. He commits murder and is sentenced to death. This novel aroused much public controversy because of the nature of its theme. A dramatization by Patrick Kearney was produced in New York, Oct. 11, 1926.

America's Coming of Age. See BROOKS, VAN WYCK.

America the Beautiful. The popular title of a national song by Katharine Lee Bates, set to music by Horatio Parker, and sung also to the tune *Materna.* It begins, "O beautiful for spacious skies . . ."

Amerigo Vespucci. *Lat.* Americus Vespucius. See VESPUCCI.

Amethyst Ring, The. A novel by Anatole France. See under BERGERET.

Amfortas. In medieval legend, keeper of the Holy Grail, the grandson of Titurel from whom he received his sacred charge. For his neglect he was wounded by the lance of Longinus and could be cured only by a guileless fool who should ask the cause of his pain. He is one of the leading characters in Wagner's opera PARSIFAL, which tells of his cure. See also FISHERMAN, KING.

Amgiad and Assad. One of the stories of the *Arabian Nights,* a tale of two half-brothers who were forced to leave home and wandered about encountering many strange adventures.

Amhara. The kingdom in northern Abyssinia in which was located the famous HAPPY VALLEY described in Samuel Johnson's *Rasselas* (1759).

Amiel, Henri Frederic. A Swiss professor (1821–1881) whose *Journal* has become one of the classic autobiographies. It was translated by Mrs. Humphry Ward (1899).

Amina. Heroine of Bellini's opera, LA SONNAMBULA.

Amine. In the Arabian Nights, wife of Sidi Nouman, who ate her rice with a bodkin, and was in fact a ghoul. "She was so hardhearted that she led about her three sisters like a leash of greyhounds."

Aminta. Heroine of Meredith's novel LORD ORMONT AND HIS AMINTA.

Aminte. In Molière's *Précieuses Ridicules* the name assumed by CATHOS.

Amintor. A character in Beaumont and Fletcher's *The Maid's Tragedy* who sacrificed his loyalty to his betrothed to his King.

Amis, see AMYS.

Amish. The Amish Mennonites, a strict sect of the 17th century, named from Jacob Ammann or Amen, a Swiss MENNONITE bishop.

Ammers-Küller, Johanna van (1884–). Dutch novelist. Her best-known novel is *The Rebel Generation* (1925), which was a best seller in Holland and widely translated.

Ammon, Amun or **Amen-Ra.** The supreme King of the Gods among the ancient

Egyptians, usually figured as a man with two long plumes rising straight above his head, but sometimes with a ram's head, the ram being sacred to him. He was the patron of Thebes. His oracle was at the oasis of Jupiter Ammon, and he was identified by the Greeks with Zeus. Ammon was originally the local deity of Thebes, but by the time his name was joined with that of Ra, the sun god, he reigned supreme above all other deities.

Amneris. In Verdi's opera AÏDA, the daughter of the king of Egypt.

Amonasro. In Verdi's opera AÏDA, the father of Aïda.

Amores. The collective title of a series of love poems in elegiac verse by OVID, written in three books in 13 B. C.

Amoret, in Spenser's *Faërie Queene,* is the daughter of Chrysogone, sister of Belphoebe, wife of Scudamore, and was brought up by Venus in the courts of love. In her relations with Timias (typifying Raleigh) she stands for Elizabeth Throgmorton. She falls a prey to Corflambo (sensual passion) but is rescued by Timias and Belphoebe.

Amoretti. A sonnet sequence by Edmund Spenser, published in 1595 together with EPITHALAMION. Both works were addressed to his wife, Elizabeth Boyle.

Amory, Blanche. In Thackeray's *Pendennis* (1849) the daughter of Lady Clavering and the disreputable Colonel Altamont *alias* J. Amory.

Amos. One of the Minor Prophets of the Old Testament. His pleas for social righteousness are to be found in the book of *Amos.*

Amos Barton, The Sad Fortunes of the Reverend. A story by George Eliot, one of her *Scenes of Clerical Life* (1857).

Amos 'n' Andy. Two Negro characters, taxi-drivers in HARLEM, in a comic radio serial named for them, at its height of popularity in the U.S. in the early 1930's.

Amour médecin, l' (The Love Doctor). A comedy by Molière (1665). The heroine is LUCINDE.

amour propre (Fr.). One's self-love, vanity, or opinion of what is due to self. *To wound one's amour-propre,* is to gall his good opinion of himself—to wound his vanity.

Ampère, André Marie (1775–1836.) French scientist. Discovered important principles in field of magnetism and electricity; formulated Ampère's law which is the basis of study of electrodynamics. The *ampère,* the unit of intensity of an electric current, is named in his honor.

Amphiaraus. In classic legend, the soothsayer of Argos who foretold calamity for the famous expedition of the "Seven against Thebes" but accompanied Adrastus in spite of his misgivings. He was pursued by his enemies and, due to Jupiter's intervention, was swallowed up by the earth. He also took part in the Calydonian boar hunt and the expedition of the Seven against THEBES.

amphigouri. A verse composition which, while sounding well, contains no sense or meaning. A good example is Swinburne's well-known parody of his own style, *Nephelidia,* the opening lines of which are:

From the depth of the dreamy decline of the dawn through a notable nimbus of nebulous moonshine.
Pallid and pink as the palm of the flag-flower that flickers with fear of the flies as they float,
Are they looks of our lovers that lustrously lean from a marvel of mystic miraculous moonshine.
These that we feel in the blood of our blushes that thicken and threaten with throbs through the throat?

Amphion. The son of Zeus and Antiope who, according to Greek legend, built Thebes by the music of his lute, which was so melodious that the stones danced into walls and houses of their own accord. Tennyson has a poem called *Amphion,* a skit and rhyming *jeu d'esprit.*

Amphitrite. In classic mythology, the goddess of the sea; wife of Poseidon, daughter of Nereus and Doris. (Gr. *amphi-trio* for *tribo,* rubbing or wearing away [the shore] on all sides.)

Amphitryon. *Le véritable Amphitryon est l'Amphitryon ou l'on dîne* (Molière). That is, the person who *provides the feast* (whether master of the house or not) is the real host. The tale is that Jupiter assumed the likeness of Amphitryon for the purpose of visiting his wife, ALCMENA, and gave a banquet at his house; but Amphitryon came home, and claimed the honor of being the master of the house. As far as the servants and guests were concerned, the dispute was soon decided—"he who gave the feast was to them the host." Alcmena was by Jupiter the mother of Hercules. This legend is the subject of three famous comedies by Plautus, Molière and Dryden, all entitled *Amphitryon.* In 1929 there appeared a play entitled *Amphitryon 38,* meaning that it was the thirty-eighth treatment of the famous theme, by the French dramatist Jean Giraudoux (1882–), later produced on the New York stage. See also BEHRMAN, S. N.

amrita or **amreeta** (*Sans.*). In Hindu mythology, the elixir of immortality, the soma-juice, corresponding to the AMBROSIA of classical mythology.

Amun, see AMMON.

Amundsen, Roald (1872–1928). Famous Norwegian polar explorer. Flew across North Pole with Lincoln Ellsworth (1926). Disappeared (June, 1928) on flight to rescue the Italian explorer Nobile, who was lost returning from the North Pole.

Amyclaean silence. Amyclae was a Laconian town in the south of Sparta, ruled by the mythical Tyndareus. The inhabitants had so often been alarmed by false rumors of the approach of the Spartans that they made a decree forbidding mention of the subject. When the Spartans actually came no one dared give warning, and the town was taken. Hence the proverb, *more silent than Amyclae.*

Castor and Pollux were born at Amyclae and are hence sometimes referred to as the *Amyclaean brothers.*

Amys and **Amylion.** A French romance of the 13th century telling the story of the friendship between two heroes of the Carlovingian wars, the Pylades and Orestes of medieval story. The story culminates in Amylion's sacrifice of his children to save his friend. It is of Greek or Oriental origin.

Anabasis. The expedition of the younger Cyrus against his brother Artaxerxes, and the retreat of his "ten thousand" Greeks, described by Xenophon the Greek historian. Literally *anabasis* means a journey upward. The French poet Léger, under the pseudonym of St.-T. Perse, wrote a long poem *Anabase,* a series of images of migration, etc.

Anacharsis, Le Voyage du jeune. A once celebrated historical romance by Barthélemy (1788). It is a description of Greece in the time of Pericles and Philip. The original Anacharsis the Scythian, a historical character of princely rank, left his native country to travel in pursuit of knowledge. He reached Athens, about 594 B. C. Barthélemy's romance is not a translation of the Scythian's book, but an original work.

anachorism (Gr. *ana choros,* "out of place"). A thing geographically out of place—in contrast to anachronism, a misplacing in the order of time.

anachronism (Gr. *ana chronos,* "out of time"). An event placed at a wrong date; as when Shakespeare, in *Troilus and Cressida,* makes Nestor quote Aristotle.

Anacreon. A Greek lyric poet, who wrote chiefly in praise of love and wine (about 563–478 B. C.).

Anacreon of the Twelfth Century. Walter Mapes (about 1140–1210), also called "The Jovial Toper." His best-known piece is the famous drinking-song, *Meum est propositum in taberna mori,* translated by Leigh Hunt.

Anacreon Moore. Thomas Moore (1779–1852), who not only translated Anacreon into English, but also wrote original poems in the same style.

Anacreon of Painters. Francesco Albano, a famous painter of beautiful women (1578–1660).

Anacreon of the Guillotine. Bertrand Barère de Vieuzac (1755–1841), president of the National Convention; so called from the flowery language and convivial jests used by him towards his miserable victims.

Anacreon of the Temple. Guillaume Amfrye (1639–1720), abbe de Chaulieu; the "Tom Moore" of France.

the French Anacreon. Pontus de Thiard, one of the Pleiad poets (1521–1605); also P. Laujon (1727–1811).

the Persian Anacreon. Hafiz (d. about 1390).

the Scotch Anacreon. Alexander Scot, who flourished about 1550.

the Sicilian Anacreon. Giovanni Meli (1740–1815).

Anadyomene. An epithet of Aphrodite, alluding to her rising from the sea at birth.

anagoge. An elevation of mind to things celestial. The mystical or spiritual meaning and application of words. Interpretation of the Bible in the mystical sense. See Four Senses.

anagram (Gr. *ana graphein,* "to write over again"). A word or phrase formed by transposing and writing over again the letters of some other word or phrase. Among the many famous examples are:

Dame Eleanor Davies (prophetess in the reign of Charles I.) = *Never so mad a lady.*
Gustavus = *Augustus.*
Horatio Nelson = *Honor est a Nilo.*
Queen Victoria's Jubilee Year = *I require love in a subject.*
Quid est Veritas (*John* xviii, 38)? = *Vir est qui adest.*
Marie Touchet (mistress of Charles IX, of France) = *Je charme tout* (made by Henri IV).
Voltaire is an anagram of *Arouet l(e) j(eune).*

These are interchangeable words:

Alcuinus and Calvinus; Amor and Roma; Eros and Rose; Evil and Live; and many more.

Anah. In Byron's Heaven and Earth, a tender-hearted, pious creature, granddaughter of Cain, and sister of Aholibamah.

Anak. In the Old Testament, a giant of Palestine, whose descendants were terrible for their gigantic stature. The Hebrew spies said that they themselves were mere grasshoppers compared with the Anakim.

analogy. Similarity of relations, congruence, resemblance. The analogy between *sleep* and *death* lies in passivity and apparent repose. It is a device used extensively in literature.

analects. Remnants gathered from a feast. Miscellaneous passages collected from works of authors, as *Analects of Confucius.* See Four Books.

Ananias. A liar. Ananias and Sapphira, his wife, were struck dead for lying about the price of a piece of land which they had sold in order to give the proceeds to the early church (*Acts* V).

Ananias club. A hypothetical organization to which Theodore Roosevelt, president of the United States 1901–1909, made frequent reference. The allusion is obvious.

anapest. In prosody an anapest is a poetic foot consisting of two short syllables followed by a long one, as contravene, acquiesce, importune. Anapestic verse is verse based on anapests. The following is a good example of anapestic trimeter.

> I am mo|narch of all|I survey,
> My right|there is none|to dispute;
> From the center all round to the sea,
> I am lord of the fowl and the brute,
> Cowper, *Alexander Selkirk.*

anarchist. One who believes that society should not be governed by any constituted authority. The theory that all government is evil was advanced by PROUDHON, who was often called the "Father of Anarchism," as a political theory. At its best, it recommends a society in which everyone produces according to his powers and receives according to his needs. A "philosophical anarchist" is one who believes in such a society but takes no direct action to bring it about.

Anarchiad, The. An American satirical epic poem, published in the New Haven Gazette in 1786–1787, in twelve installments. The five HARTFORD WITS collaborated in its composition. It was chiefly an attack on French philosophy and the condescending attitude of Europeans toward America.

anathema. A denunciation or curse. The word is Greek, and means "a thing devoted"—originally, a thing devoted to any purpose, e.g., to the gods, but later only a thing devoted to evil, hence, an accursed thing. It has allusion to the custom of hanging in the temple of a patron god something devoted to him. Thus Gordius hung up his yoke and beam; the shipwrecked hung up their wet clothes; retired workmen hung up their tools; cured cripples their crutches, etc.

Anatol. The best known drama of Arthur SCHNITZLER (1893), a series of "seven vignettes connected only by the fact that they present seven different scenes out of the love adventures of the same idle worldling."

Anatomy of Melancholy, The. A famous prose work by Robert Burton (1621) which treats of all phases of melancholy with an abundance of illustrative material from classic sources.

Anatomy of the World, An. An elegiac poem by John DONNE.

Anaxagoras (500?–428 B.C.). An early Greek philosopher, who asserted *nous,* or "mind," to be the source of all motion and creation in the world. *Nous* acts upon masses of extremely small particles, or atoms, of which all natural objects are composed. He taught for thirty years in Athens, his pupils including Pericles, Euripides, and possibly Socrates. Later, he was charged with impiety, and banished from Athens for life.

Anaxarete. In Greek legend, a noble lady of Cyprus who treated her lover Iphis with such haughtiness that he hanged himself at her door. The gods punished her by changing her body into stone. She was kept as a statue in the temple of Venus at Salamis.

Anaximander (fl. 547 B.C.). An early Greek philosopher, of the MILESIAN SCHOOL, who interpreted motion and separation as the cause of plurality and variety in the universe, asserting that the primary substance is eternal and indestructible matter, containing within itself all contradictory elements. He also introduced the sundial and invented geographical maps. See also ANAXIMENES.

Anaximenes (died ca. 525 B.C.). An early Greek philosopher, of the MILESIAN SCHOOL, who regarded air as the primary substance from which the universe was formed. See also ANAXIMANDER.

Anchises. In classic legend, the father of Aeneas by Venus, who had fallen in love with him on account of his beauty. When Troy fell, Aeneas carried his aged father out of the burning city on his shoulders.

ancien régime (*Fr.*). The old order of things; a phrase used during the French Revolution for the old Bourbon monarchy, or the system of government, with all its virtues and vices, which existed prior to that great change.

Ancient Mariner, Rime of the. A poem by Coleridge (about 1796). It deals with the supernatural punishment and penance of a seaman who had shot an albatross, a bird of good omen, in the Arctic regions. The story is told by the Ancient Mariner himself who stops a wedding guest and holds him with his "skinny hand" and "glittering eye," and finally with the mystery and horror of his tale.

Ancient of Days. A scriptural title of the Deity (*Dan.* vii. 9).

Andersen, Hans Christian (1805–1875). Danish poet, novelist, and dramatist. In English he is best known as the author of *Andersen's Fairy Tales,* a series the first group of which was published in 1835. These are stories of folk and legendary origin, often invested with moral and symbolic significance in their retelling, which have become popular in books for children.

Anderson, Charley. A character in *U. S. A.*, trilogy by John Dos PASSOS. Of a poor North Dakota family, he is interested in socialism for a while as a boy, joins World War I, and becomes a war hero. After the armistice he returns to the U.S. and turns airplane manufacturer. In spite of himself he becomes involved in the stock manipulations and illegal financial ventures of the 1920's and escapes only by death in an automobile accident.

Anderson, Mary Antoinette (1859–1940). American actress, chiefly known for her Shakespearean roles.

Anderson, Maxwell (1888–). American playwright, best known for his experiments in verse drama. Among his plays are WHAT PRICE GLORY? (1924) written with Laurence Stallings; *Saturday's Children* (1927); *Elizabeth the Queen* (1932); *Mary of Scotland* (1933); *Both Your Houses* (1933), winner of the Pulitzer prize in 1934; WINTERSET (1935); *The Star Wagon* (1937); *High Tor* (1937); *Journey to Jerusalem* (1940); *Candle in the Wind* (1941). *The Feast of the Ortolans* (1938) is a radio play.

Anderson, Sherwood (1876–1941). American author, associated with the "Chicago group" of writers which included Theodore DREISER, Carl SANDBURG, Floyd DELL, Ben HECHT and others in the period immediately preceding and following World War I. He became known for his realistic portrayal of life in the small towns of the American Middle West. Novels: POOR WHITE (1920); *Many Marriages* (1923); DARK LAUGHTER (1925); *Beyond Desire* (1933); *Kit Brandon* (1936). Short stories: *Winesburg,* OHIO (1919); *The Triumph of the Egg* (1921); *Windy McPherson's Son* (1922); *Horses and Men* (1923); *Death in the Woods* (1933). Essays: *Sherwood Anderson's Notebook* (1926); *A New Testament* (1927); *Perhaps Women* (1931); *No Swank* (1934); *Puzzled America* (1935); *Home Town* (1940). *A Story-Teller's Story* (1924) and *Tar* (1927) were autobiographical works. *Sherwood Anderson's Memoirs* was published posthumously in 1942.

André, Major John. The British officer to whom Benedict Arnold delivered the plans for the betrayal of West Point during the American Revolution. He was caught and executed as a spy in 1780. His remains were later transferred to Westminster Abbey. He is the hero of several early American dramas of which the best is by Dunlap (1798). Over a century later, Clyde FITCH made him the hero of his play, *Major André.*

Andrea del Sarto. The title of a poem by Robert Browning in which Andrea del Sarto, known as "the Faultless Painter" (1487–1531), tells of the consuming passion for his beautiful, unscrupulous wife, Lucrezia, that weakened him and kept him from real attainment.

Andrea Ferrara. A sword, also called, from the same cause, an *Andrew* and a *Ferrera.* So called from a famous 16th century sword-maker of the name.

Andreas Capellanus. Chaplain to Marie de Champagne, daughter of ELEANOR OF AQUITAINE and an early patroness of the TROUBADOURS. At her behest he wrote *De Arte Honeste Amandi* (*Concerning the Art of Loving Honestly*), a treatise on the art of love in the tradition of Ovid's ARS AMORIS. It later became a handbook in the practice of the highly stylized convention of COURTLY LOVE.

André Chénier. An opera by Umberto Giordano (first produced, 1896), dealing with the French Revolution.

Andreiev, Leonid (1871–1919). Russian dramatist and novelist, and short-story writer. He is best known for *The Red Laugh* (1904); THE LIFE OF MAN (1906), a symbolic drama; *The Seven That Were Hanged* (1908), an attack on capital punishment; and *He Who Gets Slapped* (1916), a play.

Andret. In medieval romance a dishonorable knight who spied upon Tristram and Ysolde (or Isoude) and aroused King Mark's suspicions of their mutual passion.

Andrew, St. See under SAINTS.

Andrewes, Lancelot (1555–1626). An Anglo-Catholic churchman, Bishop of Winchester and author of numerous sermons, devotions, and religious commentaries, who was known as one of the greatest preachers of his day. Interest in him in the 20th century was awakened by the essays of T. S. ELIOT.

Andrews, Joseph. Hero of Fielding's novel JOSEPH ANDREWS.

Andrews, Pamela. Heroine of Richardson's novel PAMELA.

Androcles and the Lion. An oriental apologue on the benefits to be expected as a result of gratitude; told in Aesop, by Aulus Gellius, in the *Gesta Romanorum,* etc., but of unknown antiquity. Androcles was a runaway slave who took refuge in a cavern. A lion entered, and instead of tearing him to pieces, lifted up his fore paw that Androcles might extract from it a thorn. The slave, being subsequently captured, was doomed to fight with a lion in the Roman arena. It so happened that the same lion was let out against him, and recognizing his benefactor, showed towards him every demonstration of love and gratitude.

Androcles and the Lion is the title of a play by Bernard Shaw (1912), in which he treats the early Christian faith in satirical vein. Androcles appears as a Christian eager for martyrdom, but the lion circumvents his desire.

Andromache. In Greek legend, the heroic and devoted wife of HECTOR and mother of Astyanax. After Hector's death and the fall of Troy she was allotted to Neoptolemus of Epirus, but eventually became the wife of Hector's brother Helenus. She is the subject of Euripides' tragedy *Andromache* (B. C. 420), of Racine's *Andromaque* (1667) and of an English adaptation of the latter by Ambrose Phillips called *The Distressed Mother* (1712).

Andromeda. In Greek mythology, daughter of Cepheus and Cassiopeia. Her mother boasted that the beauty of Andromeda surpassed that of the Nereids; so the Nereids induced Neptune to send a sea-monster on the country, and an oracle declared that Andromeda must be given up to it. She was accordingly chained to a rock, but was delivered by Perseus, who married her and, at the wedding, slew Phineus, to whom she had been previously promised, with all his companions. After death she was placed among the stars.

Andronicus, Titus, see TITUS ANDRONICUS.

Andvari. In northern myth, especially in the *Edda* and the *Völsunga Saga,* a dwarf whom Loki robs of his treasure and a ring. See also ALBERICH.

Andy, Handy, see HANDY ANDY.

Anet, Claude, see SCHOPFER, J.

Anelida and Arcite. A poem by CHAUCER, written during his early period.

Angel. (1) From Greek *angelos* 'messenger.' In post-canonical and apocalyptic literature angels are grouped in varying orders, and the hierarchy thus constructed was adapted to Church uses by the early Christian Fathers. In his *De Hierarchia Celesti* the pseudo-Dionysius (early 5th century) gives the names of the nine orders; they are taken from the Old Testament, *Eph.* i. 21, and *Col.* i. 16, and are as follows:

(i) Seraphim, Cherubim, and Thrones, in the first circle.

(ii) Dominions, Virtues, and Powers, in the second circle.

(iii) Principalities, Archangels, and Angels, in the third circle.

The seven holy angels are—Michael, Gabriel, Raphael, Uriel, Chamuel, Jophiel, and Zadkiel. Michael and Gabriel are mentioned in the Bible, Raphael in the Apocrypha, and all in the apocryphal book of *Enoch* (viii. 2).

Milton (*Paradise Lost,* Bk. i. 392) gives a list of the fallen angels.

Mohammedans say that angels were created from pure, bright *gems;* the genii, of *fire;* and man, of *clay.*

(2) An obsolete English coin, current from the time of Edward IV to that of Charles I, bearing the figure of the archangel Michael slaying the dragon. Its value varied from 6s. 8d. in 1465 (when first coined) to 10s. under Edward VI. It was the coin presented to persons touched for the KING'S EVIL.

Angel of the Schools. St. Thomas Aquinas. See under DOCTOR.

Angel Arms. See FEARING, KENNETH.

Angel Clare. In Hardy's TESS OF THE D'URBERVILLES.

Angelica. (1) The fascinating heroine of the Italian epic poems dealing with the adventures of ORLANDO and other famous paladins of Charlemagne's court. She appears in Biardo's ORLANDO INNAMORATO and Ariosto's ORLANDO FURIOSO as the daughter of Galaphron, king of Cathay.

(2) The heroine of Congreve's comedy *Love for Love* (1695), an heiress whom the debtor-hero Valentine Legend courts and finally marries.

(3) The bad-tempered heroine of Thackeray's THE ROSE AND THE RING.

Angélique. (1) In Molière's comedy *Le Malade imaginaire,* daughter of ARGAN, the *malade imaginaire.*

(2) In Molière's GEORGE DANDIN the aristocratic wife of George Dandin, a French commoner. She has a liaison with a M. Clitandre, but always contrives to turn the tables on her husband.

Angell, Sir **Norman.** Originally **Ralph Norman Angell Lane** (1874–). English economist and peace advocate. *The Great Illusion* (1933) was published in eleven countries, translated into fifteen languages.

Angelo. (1) In Shakespeare's comedy of *Measure for Measure,* lord-deputy of Vienna in the absence of Vincentio, the duke. His betrothed lady is Mariana. Lord Angelo conceives a base passion for Isabella, sister of Claudio; but his designs are foiled by the Duke, who compels him to marry Mariana.

(2) The name of a goldsmith in Shakespeare's *Comedy of Errors.*

Angels and Earthly Creatures. See WYLIE, Elinor.

Angel Street. Long-run (1295 performances) mystery play by Patrick Hamilton.

Angelus. A Roman Catholic devotion in honor of the Incarnation, consisting of three texts, each said as versicle and response and followed by the Ave Maria, and a prayer. So called from the first words, "Angelus Domini" (The angel of the Lord, etc.).

The prayer is recited three times a day at 6 A. M., noon, and 6 P. M., at the sound of a bell called the *Angelus*. Millet has a well-known painting with this title.

Angevin, Angevine. Member of this famous ruling family of France, whose power was founded by the marriage of Geoffrey, heir to the County of Anjou, to Matilda, daughter of Henry I of England, in 1128, and the subsequent conquest of much territory in France. Also a designation of the PLANTAGENETS.

Angiolina. In Byron's MARINO FALIERO, the daughter of Loredano, and the young wife of Marino Faliero, the doge of Venice.

Angles. A people, first located in what is now Schleswig-Holstein, who, with the Saxons and Jutes, came to conquer England in the 5th century. From their name come the words *England* and *English*.

Anglin, Margaret Mary (1876–). Well-known American actress.

Anglo-Saxon Chronicle, The. The source-book for much of the early history of England, said to have been begun at the instigation of King Alfred. The early material is compiled in a great measure from the VENERABLE BEDE, who died in 901. It ends with the accession of Henry II in 1154.

Angurvadel. Frithiof's sword, inscribed with runic letters, which blazed in time of war, but gleamed with a dim light in time of peace.

Anider for Anyder (Gr. *ana udor*, "without water"). The chief river of Sir Thomas More's *Utopia*.

animal.

animals in heaven. According to Mohammedan legend the following ten animals have been allowed to enter paradise:

(1) Jonah's *whale;* (2) Solomon's *ant;* (3) the *ram* caught by Abraham and sacrificed instead of Isaac; (4) the *lapwing* of Balkis; (5) the *camel* of the prophet Saleh; (6) Balaam's *ass;* (7) the *ox* of Moses; (8) the *dog* Kratim or Katmir of the Seven Sleepers; (9) Al Borak, Mahomet's *ass;* and (10) Noah's *dove.*

animals in art. Some animals are appropriated to certain saints: as the calf or ox to *St. Luke;* the cock to *St. Peter;* the eagle to *St. John the Divine;* the lion to *St. Mark;* the raven to *St. Benedict,* etc.

animals sacred to special deities. To Apollo, the *wolf,* the *griffon,* and the *crow;* to Bacchus, the *dragon* and the *panther;* to Diana, the *stag;* to Aesculapius, the *serpent;* to Hercules, the *deer;* to Isis, the *heifer;* to Jupiter, the *eagle;* to Juno, the *peacock* and the *lamb;* to the Lares, the *dog;* to Mars, the *horse* and the *vulture;* to Mercury, the *cock;* to Minerva, the *owl;* to Neptune, the *bull;* to Tethys, the *halcyon;* to Venus, the *dove,* the *swan,* and the *sparrow;* to Vulcan, the *lion,* etc.

animals in symbolism. The lamb, the pelican, and the unicorn, are symbols of Christ.

The dragon, serpent, and swine, symbolize Satan and his crew.

The ant symbolizes *frugality* and *prevision;* ape, *uncleanness, malice, lust,* and *cunning;* ass, *stupidity;* bantam cock, *pluckiness, priggishness;* bat, *blindness;* bear, *ill-temper, uncouthness;* bee, *industry;* beetle, *blindness;* bull, *strength, straight-forwardness;* bull-dog, *pertinacity;* butterfly, *sportiveness, living in pleasure;* camel, *submission;* cat, *deceit;* calf, *lumpishness, cowardice;* cicada, *poetry;* cock, *vigilance, overbearing insolence;* crow, *longevity;* crocodile, *hypocrisy;* cuckoo, *cuckoldom;* dog, *fidelity, dirty habits;* dove, *innocence, harmlessness;* duck, *deceit* (French, *canard,* a hoax); eagle, *majesty, inspiration;* elephant, *sagacity, ponderosity;* fly, *feebleness, insignificance;* fox, *cunning, artifice;* frog and toad, *inspiration;* goat, *lasciviousness;* goose, *conceit, folly;* grasshopper, *old age;* gull, *gullibility;* hare, *timidity;* hawk, *rapacity, penetration;* hen, *maternal care;* hog, *impurity;* horse, *speed, grace;* jackdaw, *vain assumption, empty conceit;* jay, *senseless chatter;* kitten, *playfulness;* lamb, *innocence, sacrifice;* lark, *cheerfulness;* leopard, *sin;* lion, *noble courage;* lynx, *suspicious vigilance;* magpie, *garrulity;* mole, *blindness, obtuseness;* monkey, *tricks;* mule, *obstinacy;* nightingale, *forlornness;* ostrich, *stupidity;* ox, *patience, strength,* and *pride;* owl, *wisdom;* parrot, *mocking verbosity;* peacock, *pride;* pigeon, *cowardice* (pigeon-livered); pig, *obstinacy, dirtiness;* puppy, *empty-headed conceit;* rabbit, *fecundity;* raven, *ill luck;* robin redbreast, *confiding trust;* serpent, *wisdom;* sheep, *silliness, timidity;* sparrow, *lasciviousness;* spider, *wiliness;* stag, *cuckoldom;* swallow, *a sunshine friend;* swan, *grace;* swine, *filthiness, greed;* tiger, *ferocity;* tortoise, *chastity;* turkey-cock, *official insolence;* turtle-dove, *conjugal fidelity;* vulture, *rapine;* wolf, *cruelty, savage ferocity,* and *rapine;* worm, *cringing;* etc.

Animal Kingdom, The. See BARRY, PHILIP.

Anitra. An Oriental enchantress in Ibsen's PEER GYNT.

Anker Larsen, Johannes (1874–). Danish novelist. His *The Philosopher's Stone* (English translation, 1924) won the Gyldendal prize of 70,000 Kroner.

ankh. A tau cross with a loop on top, symbolizing life; a sacred emblem, also called *crux ansata.*

Ann, Mother. Ann Lee (1736–1784) the founder and "spiritual mother" of the SHAKERS.

Annabel Lee. A poem by Edgar Allan Poe (1849).

Anna Christie. A drama by Eugene O'Neill (1922). Anna Christie is the daughter of Chris Christopherson, a Swedish bosun who has come to regard all evil and misfortune as the work of "dat ol' devil sea." He had sent her away to be brought up in Minnesota, but in the play she turns up in port and falls in love both with the sea and with a brawny Irish seaman named Mat Burke. When she confesses to a shameful past in St. Paul, both her father and lover repudiate her. In the end, however, she is forgiven by them both. *Anna Christie* was awarded the Pulitzer prize in 1922.

Anna Comnena (1083–?1148). Daughter of the Byzantine emperor ALEXIUS COMNENUS, who wrote a history of her father's career entitled the *Alexiad*.

Anna Karénina. A novel by Tolstoi (1873–1876). The heroine, Anna Karénina, is a young and beautiful woman of noble birth and sensitive, passionate nature. Her husband, Alexis Karenin, who is much older, she finds vain and tiresome. The novel deals with the mutual love of Anna and Count Vronski, an ardent, talented young officer; with her struggle and surrender and its desperate, tragic outcome. Anna at last commits suicide as the only way out of her despair.

Anna Livia Plurabelle. In James Joyce's monumental novel FINNEGAN'S WAKE, the personification of the Irish river Liffey, which flows through Dublin, and in general symbolic of the feminine principle in the universe, as Humphrey Chimpden EARWICKER generally represents the masculine principle. Anna Livia is frequently invoked throughout the book by her identifying initials, ALP.

Anna Matilda. An ultra-sentimental girl. Mrs. Hannah Cowley used this pen-name in her responses in the *World* to "Della Crusca." See DELLA CRUSCANS.

Anna of the Five Towns. A novel by Arnold Bennett (1902).

Annapolis. The United States naval academy at Annapolis, Md., where all regular officers of the American navy are trained.

Anne, Sister. In the old fairy tale, the sister of Fatima, the seventh and last wife of BLUEBEARD. Fatima, having disobeyed her lord by looking into the locked chamber, is allowed a sort of respite before execution. Sister Anne ascends the high tower of the castle, with the hope of seeing her brothers, who are expected to arrive every moment. Fatima, in her agony, keeps asking "Sister Anne" if she sees them, and Bluebeard keeps crying out for Fatima to use greater dispatch. As the patience of both is well-nigh exhausted, the brothers come and Fatima is rescued from death.

Anne of Cleves (1515–1557). Fourth wife of Henry VIII of England. The marriage was declared null and void at his request, but she was pensioned and not beheaded as was his wont with other wives.

Anne of Geierstein. A novel by Sir Walter Scott (1829), based on the conquest of Charles the Bad, Duke of Burgundy, by the Swiss in the 14th century.

Anne of Green Gables. A widely read book for girls by L. M. Montgomery.

Annie, Little Orphant, see LITTLE ORPHANT ANNIE.

Annie Kilburn. A novel by W. D. Howells (1888). After eleven years in Italy, Annie Kilburn returns to New England open to modern ideas and desirous of doing good with her wealth. The hero of the book is Rev. Mr. Peck, a young clergyman afire with social service ideals and extremely impatient of the old-fashioned snobbish charity carried on by the local "Social Union."

Annie Laurie was eldest of the three daughters of Sir Robert Laurie, of Maxwellton. William Douglas, of Fingland (Kirkcudbright), wrote the popular song, but Annie married, in 1709, James Fergusson, of Craigdarroch, and was the grandmother of Alexander Fergusson, the hero of Burns' song called *The Whistle*.

Annie Oakley. See under OAKLEY, ANNIE.

anno Domini (*Lat.*). In the Year of our Lord; *i.e.*, in the year since the Nativity: generally abbreviated to "A.D." It was Dionysius Exiguus who fixed the date of the Nativity; he lived in the early 6th century, and his computation is probably late by some three to six years. The custom of determining dates on this basis is said to be the result of the work of the VENERABLE BEDE.

Annual Register, The. A summary of the chief historic events of the year, first published by John Dodsley in 1758. It is still issued annually in England.

Annunciation, The Day of the. The 25th of March, also called *Lady Day,* on which the angel announced to the Virgin Mary that she would be the mother of the Messiah.

ORDER OF THE ANNUNCIATION. An Italian order of military knights, founded as the Order of the Collar by Amadeus VI of Savoy in 1362, and dating under its present name from 1518.

Annunzio, Gabriele D', see D'ANNUNZIO, GABRIELE.

annus mirabilis. The year of wonders, 1666, memorable for the great fire of London and the English successes over the Dutch.

Dryden wrote a poem with this title, in which he described both these events.

Ann Veronica. A novel by H. G. WELLS (1909), dealing with the struggle for independence made by a girl of the middle class.

Another Time. See under AUDEN, WYSTAN HUGH.

ansate cross. The *crux ansata.* See ANKH.

Anschauung (*Ger.*). Intuitive apprehension. **Weltanschauung,** literally, "world view." A philosophical apprehension of the universe.

Anschluss (*Ger.*). Union. Specifically, the proposed political and economic attachment between the Austrian republic and the German Reich after World War I.

Anselm, St. See under SAINTS.

Anselme. In Molière's *L'Avare,* an old man who wishes to marry the daughter of HARPAGON.

Anselmo. Hero of an episode called FATAL CURIOSITY told in Cervantes' *Don Quixote.*

Anstey, F. Pseudonym of Thomas Anstey GUTHRIE (1856–1934).

Antaeus. In Greek mythology, a gigantic wrestler (son of Earth and Sea, Ge and Poseidon), whose strength was invincible as long as he touched the earth; and when he was lifted from it, it was renewed by touching it again. It was Hercules who succeeded in killing this charmed giant by lifting him up from the earth and squeezing him to death.

Antelope State. Nebraska. See under STATES.

Antenor. In Homer's *Iliad,* a Trojan who advises that Helen return to Menelaus. He appears also in Chaucer's *Troilus and Criseyde* and in Shakespeare's *Troilus and Cressida.*

Anteros. In classic mythology, the brother of Eros, the avenger of unreturned love; or according to some authorities the opponent of Eros.

Antheil, George (1900–). Modern American concert pianist and composer, famous for his *Ballet-Mécanique* (1925). Has written an autobiography, *Bad Boy of Music.*

Anthony, Captain Roderick. Hero of Conrad's novel, CHANCE.

Anthony, John. Head of the Trenartha Tin Plate Works and the chief representative of capital in Galsworthy's drama STRIFE. His son Edgar Anthony also plays a prominent part.

Anthony, Katharine Susan (1877–). Descendant of Susan B. ANTHONY. American biographer. Author of *Margaret Fuller* (1920); *Catherine the Great* (1925); *Queen Elizabeth* (1929); *Marie Antoinette* (1932); *Louisa May Alcott* (1937); etc.

Anthony, St. See under SAINTS.

Anthony, Susan Brownell (1820–1906). Famous American leader in the cause of woman suffrage. She also participated in the Abolitionist and Temperance movements.

Anthony Adverse. Best-selling historical novel of the Napoleonic period, written by Hervey ALLEN and published in 1933.

Antic Hay. See HUXLEY, ALDOUS.

antipope. A pope chosen or nominated by temporal authority in opposition to one canonically elected by the cardinals; or one who usurps the popedom: the term is particularly applied (by the opposite party) to those popes who resided at Avignon during the Great Schism of the West, 1309–1376.

antichrist. The many legends connected with Antichrist, or the *Man of Sin,* expected by some to precede the second coming of Christ, that were so popular in the Middle Ages are chiefly founded on 2 *Thess.* ii. 1–12, and *Rev.* xiii. In ancient times Antichrist was identified with Caligula, Nero, etc., and there is little doubt that in 2 *Thess.* ii. 7, St. Paul was referring to the Roman Empire. Mahomet was also called Antichrist, and the name has been given to many disturbers of the world's peace. It has been applied, often as a figure of speech but often also in sincere conviction, to Napoleon, William II of Germany, Stalin, and Hitler. The Mohammedans have a legend that Christ will slay the Antichrist at the gate of the church at Lydda, in Palestine.

anticlimax. An event or statement which instead of being more important than the series leading up to it, is of decidedly less importance, as, for instance, the judge's charge to the jury in a larceny case, "For forty centuries the thunders of Sinai have echoed through the world 'Thou shalt not steal.' It is also a principle of the common law and a rule of equity." Anticlimax is frequently made use of to good effect in humorous writing but is considered very weakening in serious work.

Antigone. In classic legend, daughter of Oedipus by his mother Jocasta, famed for her heroic attachment to her father and brothers. When Oedipus had blinded himself, and was obliged to quit Thebes, Antigone accompanied him, and remained with him till his death, after which she returned to Thebes. Creon, the king, had forbidden any one to bury Polynices, her brother, who had been slain by his elder brother in battle (see *Seven Against Thebes* under THEBES); but Antigone, in defiance of this prohibition, buried the dead body. Creon shut her up in a vault under ground, where, according to the usual version, she killed herself. Haeman, her lover, killed himself also by her side. She is the heroine of Sophocles' drama *Antigone* and of Euripides' *Suppliants.*

The modern Antigone. Marie Therese Charlotte, duchesse d'Angoulême, the sister of Louis XVII.

Antigonus. In Shakespeare's *Winter's Tale,* a Sicilian lord, commanded by King Leontes to take his infant daughter to a desert shore and leave her to perish.

Antilochus. In Greek legend, the son of Nestor and friend of ACHILLES. He was chosen to break to Achilles the news of Patroclus' death. Antilochus himself was killed by Memnon, the son of Aurora and Tithonus. The three friends, Antilochus, Achilles, and Patroclus were buried in the same mound. Ulysses saw them walking together in the underworld.

antimacassar. A tidy for use on the back of chairs, sofas, etc. Macassar oil used to be a favorite hair oil.

Antinous. A model of manly beauty. He was the page of Hadrian, the Roman emperor.

Antiope. (1) In classic myth, Queen of Thebes and mother of AMPHION. See THESEUS.

(2) In Fénelon's TÉLÉMAQUE, an accomplished maiden loved by Télémaque.

Antipholus. In Shakespeare's COMEDY OF ERRORS, the name of two brothers, twins, the sons of Aegeon, a merchant of Syracuse.

Antiquary, The. A novel by Sir Walter Scott (1816), the story of the love and eventual marriage of William Lovel and the daughter of Sir Arthur Wardour, in the period of George III.

Anti-Saloon League. A temperance organization, founded in 1893, active in the passage of the Eighteenth Amendment to the American Constitution (1919, repealed in 1933) which prohibited the sale of intoxicating liquor. See also PROHIBITION.

anti-Semitism. A movement of agitation against and persecution of the Jewish people.

antithesis. A placing of things in opposition to heighten their effect by contrast, as "I will talk of things *heavenly* or things *earthly;* things *moral* or things *evangelical,* things *sacred* or things *profane,* things *past* or things *to come,* things *foreign* or things *at home,* things more *essential* or things *circumstantial,* provided that all be done to our profit (Bunyan's *Pilgrim's Progress*)." See also BALANCED SENTENCE.

Antoinette, Marie, see MARIE ANTOINETTE.

Antoinette de Langeais, see LANGEAIS, *Antoinette de.*

Ántonia. Heroine of Willa Cather's novel MY ÁNTONIA.

Antonio. (1) The "MERCHANT OF VENICE" in Shakespeare's drama so called.

(2) The usurping Duke of Milan, brother of Prospero, the rightful heir, in Shakespeare's TEMPEST.

(3) Father of Proteus and suitor of Julia in Shakespeare's TWO GENTLEMEN OF VERONA.

(4) An old fisherman in Cooper's novel, *The Bravo.*

(5) The monk killed by Donatello in Hawthorne's MARBLE FAUN.

Antony. Titular hero of a tragedy by Dumas (1831). This proud and sensitive misanthrope wins Adele away from her husband Colonel d'Hervey but with disastrous results.

Antony, Mark (83–31 B. C.). A Roman who came into power after the assassination of Julius Caesar, through his successful efforts to defeat the conspirators responsible for Caesar's death. He is one of the chief characters of Shakespeare's JULIUS CAESAR and hero of Shakespeare's *Antony and Cleopatra* (1608) and Dryden's *All for Love or the World Well Lost* (1678).

The first-mentioned play portrays his skilfully organized opposition to the conspirators, Brutus and Cassius, launched by the famous oration over Caesar's dead body and ending in victory at Philippi. The other plays deal with his love for Cleopatra, queen of Egypt, and consequent neglect of his duties as one of the triumvirate ruling the vast Roman empire. He is recalled to Rome and induced to marry Octavia, the sister of Octavius Caesar, but when he returns to Egypt he falls again under Cleopatra's spell, and Caesar proclaims war against him. Upon his defeat at the battle of Actium, he falls on his own sword and Cleopatra kills herself with the poisonous bite of an asp. For names of other dramas see CLEOPATRA.

Anubis. In Egyptian mythology, a deity similar to the Hermes of Greece, whose office it was to take the souls of the dead before the judge of the infernal regions. Anubis was the son of Osiris the judge, and is represented with a human body and jackal's head.

Anville, Evelina. Heroine of Fanny Burney's novel EVELINA.

anxious bench. At Methodist and other religious revivals in America the anxious benches used to be set aside for those members of the congregation who had repented of their previous life and desired to be admitted to the Church. Hence *on the anxious bench,* in a state of great difficulty or depression.

Anzac. Originally, a member of the Australian and New Zealand Army Corps engaged, during World War I, in the fighting at Gallipoli. The word was formed from the initials of the corps name. Loosely, any Australian or New Zealand soldier serving abroad or even a civilian from those parts of the British empire.

Aonian. Pertaining to Aonia, the region of Mts. Helicon and Cithaeron, in Ancient Boeotia. The MUSES were supposed to live there.

Aonian fount. The fountain of Aganippe at the foot of Mt. Helicon.

Aouda. In Verne's romance, AROUND THE WORLD IN EIGHTY DAYS, the Hindu widow rescued from SUTTEE.

Apache. The name of a tribe of North American Indians, given to—or adopted by—the hooligans and roughs of Paris about the opening of the last century.

ape. lead apes in Hell. Said of old maids, from the medieval legend that women married neither to God nor to man will be given to apes in the next world.

play the sedulous ape. See SEDULOUS.

Apelles. Greek painter of the 4th century B.C. Regarded as the greatest painter of antiquity.

Apemantus. In the drama *Timon of Athens,* attributed to Shakespeare, a churlish Athenian philosopher, who snarls at men systematically, but shows his cynicism to be mere affectation when Timon attacks him with his own weapons.

aphorism. A concise definition, a pithy, compendious sentence, a maxim.

Aphrodite (Gr. *aphros,* foam). The Greek VENUS; so called because she sprang from the foam of the sea.

Aphrodite's girdle. The cestus. Whoever wore it immediately became the object of love.

Apicius. An epicure in the time of Tiberius. He wrote a book on the ways of provoking an appetite. Having spent a fortune in supplying the delicacies of the table, and having only ten million sesterces (about $400,000) left, he hanged himself, not thinking it possible to exist on such a wretched pittance. *Apicia,* however, became a stock name for certain cakes and sauces, and his name is still proverbial in all matters of gastronomy.

Apis. In Egyptian mythology, the bull of Memphis, sacred to Osiris of whose soul it was supposed to be the image. The sacred bull had to have natural spots on the forehead forming a triangle, and a half-moon on the breast. It was not suffered to live more than twenty-five years, after which it was sacrificed and buried with great pomp. Cambyses, king of Persia (529–522 B.C.), and conqueror of Egypt, slew the sacred bull of Memphis with his own hands, and is said to have become mad in consequence.

Apley, George. A pompous, convention-bound Bostonian, hero of THE LATE GEORGE APLEY, by J. P. MARQUAND.

Apocalypse. The *Revelation* which constitutes the last book of the New Testament; any revelation. See also LAWRENCE, D. H. and THE FOUR HORSEMEN OF THE APOCALYPSE.

apocalyptic number. The mystic number 666 (*Rev.* xiii. 18.). See THE BEAST.

Apocrypha (Gr. *apokrupto,* hidden; hence, of unknown authorship). Those books included in the Septuagint and Vulgate versions of the Old Testament, but which, at the Reformation, were excluded from the Sacred Canon by the Protestants, mainly on the grounds that they were not originally written in Hebrew and were not looked upon as genuine by the Jews. They are not printed in Protestant Bibles in ordinary circulation, but in the Authorized Version, as printed in 1611, they are given immediately after the Old Testament. The books are as follows:

1 and 2 Esdras
Tobit
Judith
The rest of Esther
Wisdom
Ecclesiasticus
Baruch, with the Epistle of Jeremiah
The Song of the Three Children
The Story of Susanna
The Idol Bel and the Dragon
1 and 2 Maccabees

The New Testament also has a large number of apocryphal books more or less attached to it. These consist of later gospels and epistles, apocalypses, etc., as well as such recently discovered fragments as the *Logia* (sayings of Jesus) of the Oxyrhynchus papyrus. The best known books of the New Testament apocrypha are:

Protevangelium, or the Book of James
Gospel of Nicodemus, or the Acts of Pilate
The Ascents of James
The Acts of Paul and Thecla
Letters of Abgarus to Christ
Epistles of Paul to the Laodiceans, and to the Alexandrines, and the Third Epistle to the Corinthians
The Teaching of the Apostles (Didaché)
The three Books of the Shepherd of Hermas

Apollinaire, Guillaume. Pseudonym of **Wilhelm Kostrowitzki** (1880–1918). French poet, short story writer, and art critic, of Polish origin. A colorful personality, he was among the leaders of *avant-garde* movements in the painting and literature of the early 20th century. His writing was marked by mystery and eroticism, his last works anticipating many of the elements of SURREALISM. His best-known works are *Le Bestiaire ou le cortège d'Orphee* (1911); *Alcoöls* (1913); *Le poète assassiné* (1916), translated into English as *The Poet Assassinated* (1923); *Les Mamelles de Tirésias* (1917), described as a "super-realist" drama; and *Calligrames* (1918).

Apollo. In Greek and Roman mythology, son of Zeus and Leto (Latona), one of the great gods of Olympus, typifying the sun in its light- and life-giving as well as in its destroying power; often identified with Helios, the sun-god. He was god of music, poetry and the healing art, the latter of which he bestowed on his son, Aesculapius. He is represented in art as the perfection of youthful manhood.

a perfect Apollo. A model of manly beauty, referring to the Apollo Belvedere.

Apollo of Portugal. Luis Camoëns (c. 1524–1580), author of the *Lusiad.*

Apollo Belvedere. An ancient marble statue, supposed to be a Roman-Greek copy of a bronze votive statue set up at Delphi in commemoration of the repulsion of an attack by the Gauls on the shrine of Apollo in 279 B. C.

Apollonius of Tyana. Greek philosopher of the 1st century A. D. Traveled in India. Regarded as a magician and miracle worker by his contemporaries.

Apollyon. The Greek name of ABADDON, king of hell and angel of the bottomless pit. (*Rev.* ix. 11). His introduction by Bunyan into PILGRIM'S PROGRESS has made his name familiar.

Apologia pro Vita Sua. A famous autobiographical treatise in which the English Cardinal John Henry NEWMAN defends his conversion from the Anglican to the Roman Catholic Church.

Apology for Poetry, An. Essay written by Sir Philip SIDNEY in 1580 in answer to an attack on poetry by Stephen Gosson in *The School for Abuse.* In it, Sidney maintains that the purpose of poetry is to teach under the guise of entertainment.

Apophis. In Egyptian mythology, the power of darkness in the form of a serpent against whom the sun, as Ra, waged daily war.

aposiopesis. An abrupt breaking off in the middle of a sentence for effect, as, for example, "And if it bear fruit—but if not, cut it down." The best-known instance in literature is probably Virgil's QUOS EGO.

a posteriori (*Lat.* from the latter). An *a posteriori* argument is proving the cause from the effect. Thus, if we see a watch we conclude there was a watchmaker. Robinson Crusoe inferred there was another human being on the desert island, because he saw a human footprint in the wet sand. It is thus the existence and character of Deity is inferred from His works. See also A PRIORI.

apostles (Literally, one sent forth). A name used with reference to the original twelve disciples of Jesus, sometimes with the addition of Matthias and Paul; also used in a general sense for the missionaries of the early church whose deeds are related in *The Acts of the Apostles.*

The badges or symbols of the fourteen apostles:

Andrew, *a cross,* because he was crucified on a cross shaped like the letter x.

Bartholomew, *a knife,* because he was flayed with a knife.

James the Greater, *a scallop-shell, a pilgrim's staff,* or *a gourd bottle,* because he is the patron saint of pilgrims.

James the Less, *a fuller's pole,* because he was killed by a blow on the head with a pole, dealt him by Simeon the fuller.

John, *a cup with a winged serpent flying out of it,* in allusion to the tradition about Aristodemos, priest of Diana, who challenged John to drink a cup of poison. John made the sign of a cross on the cup, Satan like a dragon flew from it, and John then drank the cup, which was quite innocuous.

Judas Iscariot, *a bag,* because he had the bag and "bare what was put therein." (*John* xii. 6).

Jude, *a club,* because he was martyred with a club.

Matthew, *a hatchet* or *halbert,* because he was slain at Nadabar with a halbert.

Matthias, *a battle-axe,* because he was first stoned, and then beheaded with a battle-axe.

Paul, *a sword,* because his head was cut off with a sword. The convent of La Lisla, in Spain, boasts of possessing the very instrument.

Peter, *a bunch of keys,* because Christ gave him the "keys of the kingdom of heaven." *A cock,* because he went out and wept bitterly when he heard the cock crow. (*Matt.* xxvi. 75.)

Philip, *a long staff surmounted with a cross,* because he suffered death by being suspended by the neck to a tall pillar.

Simon, *a saw,* because he was sawn to death, according to tradition.

Thomas, *a lance,* because he was pierced through the body, at Meliapour, with a lance.

Apostles of

Abyssinians, St. Frumentius. (4th century.)
Alps, Felix Neff. (1798–1829.)
Andalusia, Juan de Avila. (1500–1569.)
Ardennes, St. Hubert. (656–727.)
Armenians, Gregory of Armenia, "The Illuminator." (256–331.)
Brazil, José de Anchieta, a Jesuit missionary. (1533–1597.)
English, St. Augustine. (Died 604.) St. George.
Ethiopia. See *Abyssinians.*
Free Trade, Richard Cobden. (1804–1865.)
French, St. Denis. (3rd century.)
Frisians, St. Willibrord. (657–738.)
Gauls, St. Irenaeus (130–200); St. Martin of Tours (338–401).
Gentiles, St. Paul.
Germany, St. Boniface. (680–755.)
Highlanders, St. Columba. (521–597.)
Hungary, St. Anastatius. (954–1044.)
Indians (American), Bartolomé de Las Casas (1474–1566); John Eliot (1604–1690).
Indies (East), St. Francis Xavier. (1506–1552.)
Infidelity, Voltaire. (1694–1778.)
Ireland, St. Patrick. (373–463.)
Iroquois, François Piquet (1708–1781).
Liberty. Henry Clay.
North, St. Ansgar or Anscarius (801–864); Bernard Gilpin. (1517–1583.)
Peak, The. William Bagshaw. (1628–1702.)
Peru, Alonzo de Barcena. (1528–1598.)
Picts, St. Ninian. (5th century.)
Scottish Reformers, John Knox. (1505–1572.)
Slavs, St. Cyril. (c. 820–869.)
The Sword, Mahomet. (570–632.)
Temperance, Father Mathew. (1790–1856.)

Apostolic Fathers. Christian authors born in the 1st century, when the apostles lived. John is supposed to have died about 99 A. D., and Polycarp, the last of the Apostolic Fathers, born about 69, was his disciple. The *Five Apostolic Fathers* most referred to are Clement of Rome, Barnabas, Hermas, Ignatius, and Polycarp.

apostolic succession. Theological doctrine enunciated by Irenaeus (fl. 190), maintaining that since the bishops of the church were direct spiritual descendants of Christ through the Apostles, authority on questions of orthodoxy should reside with them.

apostrophe. A figure of speech in which something absent is addressed in the second person as if present; for example, "O death, where is thy sting?" "Milton, thou shouldst be living at this hour," "But come, thou Goddess fair and free."

Appian Way (Lat. *Via Appia*). The oldest and best of all the Roman roads, leading from Rome to Brundisium (Brindisi) by way of Capua. This "queen of roads" was commenced by Appius Claudius, the decemvir, 313 B. C.

Appius Claudius. A Roman decemvir (ruled 451–449 B. C.) whose passion for Virginia, a beautiful plebeian girl whom he managed by a mock trial to make his slave, caused her father to kill her in the forum. For the use made of this famous legend in drama, see VIRGINIA.

apple.

Newton and the apple. The well-known story is that the great scientist Newton, seeing an apple fall, was led into the train of thought which resulted in his establishment of the law of gravitation (1685).

When Newton saw an apple fall, he found,
In that slight startle from his contemplation, . . .
A mode of proving that the earth turned round,
In a most natural whirl called gravitation.
Byron: *Don Juan*, x. 1.

apple of discord. A cause of dispute; something to contend about. At the marriage of Thetis and Peleus where all the gods and goddesses met together, Discord (Eris), who had not been invited, threw on the table a golden apple "for the most beautiful." Juno, Minerva, and Venus put in their separate claims; the point was referred to PARIS, who gave judgment in favor of Venus. This brought upon him the vengeance of Juno and Minerva, to whose spite the fall of Troy is attributed.

The "apple" appears more than once in Greek story; see ATALANTA'S RACE; HESPERIDES.

Of course, the story of Eve and the apple will be familiar to every reader, but it is a mistake to suppose that the apple is mentioned in the Bible story. We have no further particulars than that it was "the fruit of that forbidden tree," and the Mohammedans leave the matter equally vague, though their commentators hazard the guess that it may have been an ear of wheat, or the fruit of the vine or the fig. The apple is a comparatively late conjecture.

For the story of William Tell and the apple, see TELL.

Prince Ahmed's apple or the *apple of Samarkand.* In the *Arabian Nights* story of Prince Ahmed, a cure for every disorder. The prince purchased it at Samarkand.

apples of Istakhar are "all sweetness on one side, and all bitterness on the other."

apples of Paradise, according to tradition, had a bite on one side, to commemorate the bite given by Eve.

apples of perpetual youth. In Scandinavian mythology, the golden apples of perpetual youth, in the keeping of Idhunn, daughter of the dwarf Svald and wife of Bragi. It is by tasting them that the gods preserve their youth.

apples of Pyban, says Sir John Mandeville, fed the pigmies with their odor only.

apples of Sodom. Thevenot says—"There are apple-trees on the sides of the Dead Sea which bear lovely fruit, but within are full of ashes." Josephus, Strabo, Tacitus, and others speak of these apples, and are probably referring to the gall-nuts produced by the insect *Cynips insana.* The phrase is used figuratively for anything disappointing.

apple of the eye. The pupil, because it was anciently supposed to be a round solid ball like an apple. Figuratively applied to anything extremely dear or extremely sensitive.

apple-pie order. Prim and precise order.

The origin of this phrase is still doubtful. Some suggest *cap-à-pie,* like a knight in complete armor. Some tell us that apples made into a pie are quartered and methodically arranged when the cores have been taken out. Perhaps the suggestion of *nap-pe-pli* (Fr. *nappes pliées,* folded linen, neat as folded linen) is nearer the mark. It has also been suggested that it may be a corruption of *alpha, beta,* meaning as orderly as the letters of the alphabet; and another guess is that it is connected with the old alphabet rhyme, "A was an apple pie," etc., the letters of the alphabet being there all "in apple-pie order."

Appreciations. See PATER, WALTER.

Après-midi d'un faune, L'. *The Afternoon of a Faun,* a poem by the French poet Stephane MALLARMÉ, published in 1876. It presents the wandering thoughts of a faun on a drowsy summer afternoon. Claude DEBUSSY, the French Impressionist composer, set it to music in a tone poem of the same title (1891), and it became one of the most popular ballets in the repertoire of the Russian Ballet when introduced in 1912 by the famous dancer NIJINSKI. It is best known in its musical and choreographic form.

Aprile. In Browning's PARACELSUS, the Italian poet who exalts love as Paracelsus exalts knowledge.

April Fools' Day. April 1st, when practical jokes are in order. An April *Fool* is called line, king of Britain. He was banished, and stole away, out of revenge, the King's two infant sons, Guiderius and Arviragus.

Belasco, David (1859–1931). American playwright and theatrical producer. Known for the stars he managed, his stage effects, *Madame Butterfly, The Girl of the Golden West* and *The Return of Peter Grimm*.

Belch, Sir Toby. A reckless, roistering, jolly fellow; from the knight of that name in Shakespeare's *Twelfth Night*.

beldam. An ugly old woman. According to its etymology the word ought to mean "fair lady."

bel-esprit (*Fr.*). Literally, fine mind, means, in English, a vivacious wit; one of quick and lively parts, ready at repartee (*pl.* beaux-esprits).

Belford. A friend of Lovelace in Richardson's CLARISSA HARLOWE. These "friends" made a covenant to pardon every sort of liberty which they took with each other.

Belgravia. A fashionable residence district in the West End of London. Type name for the world of aristocratic fashion.

Belial (Heb.). The worthless or lawless one, *i.e.*, the devil.

> What concord hath Christ with Belial?
> 2 *Cor.* vi. 15.

Milton, in his pandemonium, makes him a very high and distinguished prince of darkness.

> Belial came last—than whom a spirit more lewd
> Fell not from heaven, or more gross to love
> Vice for itself
> *Paradise Lost*, bk. i. 490.

sons of Belial. Lawless, worthless rebellious people.

> Now the sons of Eli were sons of Belial.
> 1 *Sam.* ii. 12.

Believe me, if all those endearing young charms. A famous song by the English poet Thomas MOORE.

Belinda. (1) The heroine of Pope's mock heroic poem, THE RAPE OF THE LOCK.

(2) Title and heroine of a novel by Maria Edgeworth (1803).

Beline. The wife of ARGAN in Molière's comedy, *Le Malade Imaginaire*.

Belisarius (d. 565). The greatest of Justinian's generals. Being accused of conspiring against the life of the emperor, was deprived of all his property. The tale is that his eyes were put out, and that when living as a beggar in Constantinople he fastened a bag to his roadside hut, with the inscription, "Give an obolus to poor old Belisarius." This tradition is of no historic value.

Belise. In Molière's FEMMES SAVANTES, sister of Philaminte, and, like her, a *femme savante*. She imagines that everyone is in love with her.

bell.

bear the bell. To be first fiddle; to carry off the palm; to be the best. Before cups were presented to winners of horse-races, etc., a little gold or silver bell used to be given for the prize.

who is to bell the cat? Who will risk his own life to save his neighbors? Anyone who encounters great personal hazard for the sake of others undertakes to *bell the cat*. The allusion is to the fable of the cunning old mouse, who suggested that they should hang a bell on the cat's neck to give notice to all mice of her approach. Archibald Douglas, Earl of Angus, was called *Bell-the-Cat*. James III made favorites of architects and masons; one mason, named Cochrane, he created Earl of Mar. The Scotch nobles held a council in the church of Lauder for the purpose of putting down these upstarts, and Lord Gray asked, "Who will bell the cat?" "That will I," said Douglas, and he fearlessly put to death, in the King's presence, the obnoxious minions.

ban with bell, book, and candle. A solemn form of excommunication used in the medieval church.

Bell, Acton, Ellis, and Currer. The pseudonyms adopted by Anne, Emily and Charlotte BRONTË respectively. In 1846 they published a volume entitled *Poems by Currer, Ellis, and Acton Bell*.

Bell, Adam, see ADAM BELL.

Bell, Alexander Graham (1847–1922). Scottish-American scientist and inventor of the telephone. In 1871 he came from Scotland to the U.S. as teacher of a system of speech for the deaf.

Bell, Babie, see BABIE BELL.

Bell, Bessie, see BESSIE BELL.

Bell, Clive (1881–). English art critic. Married Vanessa Stephen, sister of Virginia Woolf. "Bloomsbury Group." Chevalier of the Legion of Honor (1936). Critical articles a feature of the *New Statesman and Nation*. Believes in the complete separation of Art from Life. His son, Julian, a modern poet, was fatally wounded driving ambulance for Loyalists in war of the Spanish people against Fascism.

Bell, Gertrude Margaret Lowthian (1868–1926). English traveler and writer on travel. An authority on Arabia.

Bell, J. J. (1871–1934). Scottish journalist and author. Creator of *Wee Macgreegor*.

Bell, Laura or more accurately, *Helen Laura*. The heroine of Thackeray's PENDENNIS. As Mrs. Arthur Pendennis she appears also in *The Newcomes* and *Philip*.

Bell, Peter, see PETER BELL.

Bellamy, Edward (1850–1898). American author, best known for his popular Utopian novel, LOOKING BACKWARD (1887).

Bellario, Dr. In Shakespeare's *Merchant of Venice,* the lawyer whose letter Portia produces in the famous trial scene. He does not appear on the stage.

Bellaston, Lady. In Fielding's TOM JONES, a profligate, from whom Tom Jones accepts support.

Bellay, Joachim du (ca. 1525–1560). French poet, member of the school of the PLÉIADE. He wrote sonnets in the Italian neo-Platonic tradition (see NEO-PLATONISM) and a series, inspired by a visit to Rome (1553–1558), which consisted of *Antiquités de Rome, Regrets,* and *Jeux rustiques.* He is best known for his DÉFENSE ET ILLUSTRATION DE LA LANGUE FRANÇAISE (1549), an important critical treatise.

belle (*Fr.*). A beauty.

the belle of the room. The most beautiful lady present.

belle amie (*Fr.*). Fair friend; mistress.

la belle France. Beautiful France. A common French phrase applied to France.

la belle sauvage. A name for POCAHONTAS.

Belleau Wood. Forested tract east of Paris where American troops stopped the German offensive in 1918. Beginning June 6, two weeks' fighting cost the U.S. 285 officers and 7,585 men killed, wounded or missing.

Belle Dame sans Merci, La. A poem by John Keats (1819), the title and general theme of which are taken from an earlier poetic dialogue "between a gentleman and a gentlewoman, who finding no mercy at her hand dieth for sorrow." The earlier poem was once considered a translation by Chaucer from Alain Chartier (1385?–after 1433).

Bellefontaine, Benedict. In Longfellow's *Evangeline,* a wealthy farmer of Grand Pré (Nova Scotia) and father of Evangeline. When the inhabitants of his village are driven into exile, Benedict dies of a broken heart as he is about to embark, and is buried on the seashore.

Bellegarde, De. The name of the old French family in Henry James' novel THE AMERICAN who opposes Christopher Newman's efforts to marry their widowed daughter, Claire de Cintré.

belle-mère (*Fr.*). Mother-in-law; stepmother. Kathleen Norris used the phrase as the title of one of her novels.

Bellenden, Lady Margaret. In Scott's OLD MORTALITY, an old lady, mistress of the Tower of Tillietudlem, and devoted to the house of Stuart.

Miss Edith Bellenden. Heroine of Scott's OLD MORTALITY, granddaughter of Lady Margaret, betrothed to Lord Evendale, of the King's army, but in love with Morton, a leader of the Covenanters, and the hero of the novel.

Bellerus. A giant, the fabled guardian of Land's End, England.

> Sleep'st by the fable of Bellerus old.
> Milton, *Lycidas.*

belles-lettres. Polite literature; poetry, and standard literary works which are not scientific or technical: the study or pursuit of such literature. The term—which, of course, is French—has given birth to the words *belle-letrist* and *belletristic.*

Bellerophon. The Joseph of Greek mythology; Antaea, the wife of Proetus, being "Potiphar's wife" who tempted him, and afterwards falsely accused him. Her husband, Proetus, sent Bellerophon with a letter to Iobates, the king of Lycia, his wife's father, recounting the charge, and praying that the bearer might be put to death. Iobates, unwilling to slay him himself, gave him many hazardous tasks (including the killing of the CHIMAERA), but as he was successful in all of them, Iobates made him his heir. Later Bellerophon is fabled to have attempted to fly to heaven on the winged horse Pegasus, but Zeus sent a gadfly to sting the horse, and the rider was overthrown. See also URIAH.

Bellerophontic letters. Letters containing the bearer's death warrant, as the letter which Bellerophon brought from the jealous Proetus to king Iobates of Lycia.

Bellew, Harold Kyrle (1855–1911). Well-known actor on English and American stage. Son of one of England's foremost preachers. An English actress is named Kyrle Bellew.

Bellicent. Daughter of Gorloise and Igerna, half-sister of King Arthur. According to Tennyson, she was the wife of Lot, King of Orkney; but in *Le Morte d'Arthur* Lot's wife is Margause.

Bellin. The ram in the tale of *Reynard the Fox.* His wife was Olewey.

Bellini, Giovanni (ca. 1430–1516). Venetian painter, of a famous Venetian family of painters, influenced by MANTEGNA and DONATELLO. He is best known for his altar-pieces.

Bellini, Vincenzo (1802–1835). Composer of the operas LA SONNAMBULA, NORMA and I PURITANI.

Bellisant. The mother of Valentine and Orson in the romance of that name, sister to King Pepin of France, wife of Alexander, emperor of Constantinople. Being accused of infidelity, she was banished by the Emperor.

Bellman, the. Character in Lewis Carroll's *The Hunting of the Snark.*

Bellman of London, The. A prose pamphlet by Thomas DEKKER, written in 1608 and an example of Elizabethan "ROGUE LITERATURE."

bell mare. A mare wearing a bell to lead a mule herd, or pack-animals. Cf. BELLWETHER, used contemptuously for the leader of a (human) herd.

Belloc, Joseph Hilaire Pierre (1870–). English writer, born in France, author of light verse, travel books, history, biography, essays, and fiction. His works include: *The Bad Child's Book of Beasts* (1896); a series of essays, *On Nothing, On Everything, On Anything, On Something, On* (1908–1911, 1923); *Book of the Bayeux Tapestry* (1914); *History of England* (1925–1927); biographies of ROBESPIERRE, JAMES II, RICHELIEU, and Cardinal WOLSEY (1927–1930). Like G. K. CHESTERTON, a firm Roman Catholic in his beliefs.

Belloc Lowndes, see LOWNDES.

Bellona. In Roman mythology, goddess of war and wife of Mars.

Bellona's handmaids. Blood, fire and famine.

Bellona's bridegroom. Mars, and hence, war.

Belloni, Sandra, see SANDRA BELLONI

Bellows, George Wesley (1882–1925). American painter and lithographer best known for his scenes of prizefights.

Bells, The. A famous onomatopoetic poem by Edgar Allan POE.

Bells and Pomegranates. A series of pamphlets containing poems by Robert BROWNING, issued (1841–1846) in an effort by his publishers to popularize his work.

Bells of Basle, The. See ARAGON, LOUIS.

bellwether of the flock. A jocose and rather deprecatory term applied to the leader of a party. Of course the allusion is to the wether or sheep which leads the flock with a bell fastened to its neck.

beloved disciple. John, to whom the Fourth Gospel is attributed (*John* xiii. 23, etc.).

beloved physician. Supposedly Luke the evangelist (*Col.* iv. 14).

Beloved Returns, The. English translation of *Lotte in Weimar,* a novel by Thomas MANN, published in the U.S. in 1941. It tells of an imagined visit to GOETHE in his honored old age at WEIMAR by Charlotte BUFF, the reputed original of the heroine in his first important work, *The Sorrows of Werther* (see WERTHER). The book gives an ironic portrait of a Romantic poet grown old and overshadowed by his greatness, and contains numerous philosophic conversations on art and the rôle of the artist in society in the author's familiar vein.

Beloved Vagabond, The. A novel by W. J. Locke (*Eng.* 1906). The "Beloved Vagabond" is Paragot, a Bohemian philosopher and violinist who, with the adopted stray, Anticot (who tells the story), and Blanquette, a homeless country girl whom he has befriended, wanders about Europe as a tramp musician.

Belphegor. The Assyrian form of "Baal-Peor" (see BAAL), the Moabitish god to whom the Israelites became attached in Shittim (*Numb.* xxv. 3).

The name was given in a medieval Latin legend to a demon who was sent into the world from the infernal regions by his fellows to test the truth of certain rumors that had reached them concerning the happiness—and otherwise—of married life on earth. After a thorough trial, the details of which are told with great intimacy, he fled in horror and dismay to the happy regions where female society and companionship were nonexistent. Hence, the term is applied both to a misanthrope and to a nasty, licentious, obscene fellow.

The story is found in Machiavelli's works and became very popular. Its first appearance in English is in Barnabe Rich's *Farewell to the Military Profession* (1581); and it either forms the main source of. or furnishes incidents to, many plays including *Grim, the Collier of Croydon* (1600), Jonson's *The Devil is an Ass* (1616), and John Wilson's *Belphegor, or the Marriage of the Devil* (1691)

Belphoebe. The huntress-goddess in Spenser's FAËRIE QUEENE, daughter of Chrysogone and sister of Amoret with whom she is contrasted. Belphoebe, who was brought up by Diana, as Amoret by Venus, typifies Queen Elizabeth as a model of chastity. She was of the Diana type; cold as an icicle, passionless, immovable, and, like a moonbeam, had light without warmth.

Belshazzar. King of Babylon when it was taken by Cyrus 539 B. C. Son of Nebuchadnezzar and the last of the Chaldaean dynasty. Cf. *Dan.* 30. The name means "may Bel protect the king."

Belsize, The Honorable Charles. In Thackeray's NEWCOMES, a gay young nobleman known as Jack, who later becomes Lord Highgate.

Beltane. The May-day festival, originally connected with sun or fire worship, celebrated with bonfires. Druids drove their cattle between two fires at Beltane to prevent the murrain.

Belus. Dido's father, king of Tyre.

Belvawney, Miss. In Dickens' NICHOLAS NICKLEBY, an actress of the Portsmouth Theater.

Belvidera. The heroine of Otway's *Venice Preserved* (1682).

Bembo, Pietro (1470–1547). Italian writer and ecclesiastic. Restored classic tradition in Italian language and literature.

Bemelmans, Ludwig (1898–). Austrian-born writer and illustrator, a naturalized American citizen, known for the humor and whimsical charm of his stories and paintings. His books for children are *Hansi* (1934); *Castle Number Nine* (1937); *Quito Express* (1938); *Madeline* (1939). His other books, chiefly autobiographical, include *The Golden Basket* (1936); *My War with the United States* (1937); *Life Class* (1938); *Hotel Splendide* (1941); *The Donkey Inside* (1941).

Benares. City on the Ganges in India. Birthplace of the Hindu religion.

Benassis, Dr. The hero of Balzac's COUNTRY DOCTOR (*Le Médecin de campagne*), one of Balzac's most admirable characters. His kindly spirit and his indefatigable efforts on behalf of all the people of his little French town make him universally beloved.

Benavente y Martínez, Jacinto (1866–). Spanish playwright. Nobel Prize winner 1922. During World War I Benavente ranged himself on the side of Germany, but during the Franco rebellion in Spain which preceded World War II, he stood by the Loyalists. His technique in dramatic writing has been called analogous to Bernard Shaw's.

Ben Bolt. A popular song of the 19th century, published for the first time in 1843 in the New York *Mirror*. See also SWEET ALICE.

bench. Properly, a long wooden seat, hence the official seat of judges in Court, bishops in the House of Lords, aldermen in the council chamber, etc.; hence, by extension, judges, bishops, etc., collectively, the court or place where they administer justice or sit officially, the dignity of holding such an official status, etc. Hence *Bench of bishops*. The whole body of prelates, who sit in the House of Lords. The word *bench* appears in French as *banc,* in Italian as *banca.* Both words were taken into English as *bank.*

be raised to the bench. To be made a judge.

be raised to the Episcopal bench. To be made a bishop.

bench and bar. Judges and barristers.

Benchley, Robert Charles (1889–1945). American humorist and dramatic critic, contributor to leading New York periodicals, especially THE NEW YORKER, and also a radio and motion-picture performer. His humor revolves about the difficulties of the average middle-class American man in contact with the complexities of 20th-century social and mechanical life, presented in whimsical satire. Among his books are *20,000 Leagues under the Sea or David Copperfield* (1928); *The Treasurer's Report* (1930); *My Ten Years in a Quandary* (1936); *After 1903—What?* (1938); *Inside Benchley* (1941).

bench show. An exhibition of small animals, especially dogs.

bend. In heraldry, an ordinary formed by two parallel lines drawn across the shield from the dexter chief (*i.e.* the top left-hand corner when looking at the shield) to the sinister base point (*i.e.* the opposite corner). It is said to represent the sword-belt.

bend sinister. A bend running across the shield in the opposite direction, *i.e.* from right to left. It is taken as an indication of bastardy (see BAR SINISTER); hence the phrase *"he has a bend sinister,"* he was not born in lawful wedlock.

Benda, Julien (1867–). French novelist and critic, author of *Dialogue d'Éleuthère* (1911); *L' Ordination* (1912), a novel; *Le Bergsonisme ou une philosophie de la mobilité* (1912), a criticism of the philosophy of Henri BERGSON; Belphégor (1919), an analytical essay on the tendencies of French thought in his day; *La Trahison des clercs* (1927), translated as *The Treason of the Intellectuals,* an attack on scholars with political ambitions. His writings in general denounce emotionalism and uphold the principle of rationality.

Benda, Wladyslaw Theodor (1873–). Polish-American painter and illustrator. Creator of the Benda masks.

Ben Day process. After Benjamin Day (1838–1916), New York printer. Mechanical method of making a shaded, stippled background on a line plate by means of the Ben Day shading machine.

Bender, Harold Herman (1882–). American philologist. Special editor for etymology and philology, *Webster's New International Dictionary, Second Edition.*

Bendix, Vincent (1881–). American industrialist. Head of a large corporation manufacturing self-starters (of his development), brakes, carburetors, etc. for automobiles. Also president of Bendix Aviation Corporation.

Bendy, Old, see OLD BENDY.

benedicite. The 2nd pers. pl. imperative of the Latin verb, *benedicere,* meaning "bless you," or "may you be blessed." In the first given sense it is the opening word of many old graces ("Bless ye the Lord," etc.); hence, a grace, or a blessing. The second sense accounts for its use as an interjection or expression of astonishment, as in Chaucer's

> The god of love, A benedicite,
> How myghty and how great a lord is he!
> *Knight's Tale,* 927.

Benedick. A sworn bachelor caught in the snares of matrimony: from Benedick the hero of Shakespeare's MUCH ADO ABOUT NOTHING.

Benedick and Benedict are used indiscriminately, but the distinction should be observed.

Benedict. A bachelor, not necessarily one pledged to celibacy, but simply a man of marriageable age, not married. St. Benedict was a most uncompromising stickler for celibacy.

Benedictines. Monks who follow the rule of St. Benedict, implicit obedience, celibacy, abstaining from laughter, spare diet, poverty, the exercise of hospitality, observance of canonical hours, feasts, and fasts, and unremitting industry. They are known as the "Black Monks" (the Dominicans being the *Black Friars*). The Order was founded by St. Benedict at Subiaco and Monte Cassino, Italy, about 530, and its members have from the earliest times been renowned for their learning.

benefice. Under medieval European feudalism, land owned by one person and granted by him to another for cultivation and use, often as a means of payment or in return for the performance of certain services. The practice originated in the surrender by small property owners of title to their holdings in exchange for the right to live and farm on their land, and for protection by the lord who received the title. In time, the rendering of military service came to be one of the conditions of obtaining a benefice. The Roman Catholic Church in the Middle Ages extensively granted benefices.

Benefield, John Barry (1880–). American short-story writer and novelist. Best-known novel, made into motion picture, *Valiant is the Word for Carrie* (1935).

benefit of clergy. Originally, the privilege of exemption from trial by a secular court enjoyed by the clergy if arrested for felony. In time it comprehended not only the ordained clergy, but all who, being able to write and read, were capable of entering into holy orders. It was finally abolished in the reign of George IV (1827).

Kipling called one of his best-known stories *Without Benefit of the Clergy,* meaning by the phrase, without the religious rites of matrimony. It deals with the love of an Englishman and a native Indian woman.

Benelli, Sem (1877–). Italian dramatist known especially for his *La Cena Delle Beffe* (1909) produced in New York as *The Jest* (1919), with John and Lionel Barrymore.

Benengali, Cid Hamet, see CID HAMET BENENGALI.

Beneš, Eduard (1884–). Modern Czechoslovak statesman. President of Czechoslovakia 1935–1938, 1946–1948. Author of works on political problems.

Benét, Stephen Vincent (1898–1943). American poet, novelist, and short-story writer, interested in fantasy and American themes. His best-known works are *John Brown's Body* (1928), a narrative poem of the American Civil War, awarded the Pulitzer prize in 1929, and *The Devil and Daniel Webster,* a short story first published in the SATURDAY EVENING POST which became very popular and was later made into a one-act opera, with libretto by the author and music by Douglas Moore, and into a motion picture. It appears in *Thirteen O'Clock: Stories of Several Worlds* (1937). Benét's poetry includes *A Ballad of William Sycamore* (1923); *Tiger Joy* (1925); *The Barefoot Saint* (1929); *Ballads and Poems, 1915–1930* (1931); *A Book of Americans* (1933), written with Rosemary Benét; *Burning City* (1936); *Johnny Pye and the Fool-Killer* (1938); *The Ballad of the Duke's Mercy* (1939). Among his novels are: *Young People's Pride* (1922); *Jean Huguenot* (1923); and *Spanish Bayonet* (1926).

Benét, William Rose (1886–). American poet and critic. His poetry includes *Merchants from Cathay* (1913); *The Falconer of God* (1914); *The Burglar of the Zodiac* (1918); *Moons of Grandeur* (1920); *Man Possessed* (1927); *Rip Tide* (1932), a novel in verse; *Starry Harness* (1933); *The Dust Which Is God* (1941; Pulitzer prize 1942); *Day of Deliverance; A Book of Poems in Wartime* (1944); *The Stairway of Surprise* (1947). He has edited a number of books, including the works of Elinor WYLIE, his wife; with Norman Pearson, *The Oxford Anthology of American Literature;* with Norman Cousins, *The Poetry of Freedom; Anthology of Famous English Poetry,* etc.

Bengodi. A "land of COCKAIGNE" mentioned in Boccaccio's *Decameron* (viii. 3), where "they tie the vines with sausages, where you may buy a fat goose for a penny and have a gosling into the bargain; where there is also a mountain of grated Parmesan cheese, and people do nothing but make cheesecakes and macaroons."

Benham, William. The hero of Wells' RESEARCH MAGNIFICENT.

Ben Hur, A Tale of the Christ. A best-selling historical novel by Lew Wallace (*Am.* 1880). The hero is Judah Ben Hur, heir of a rich Jewish family, by accident responsible for injury to the new Roman governor by a falling tile. His quondam friend Messala accuses him of treason and he is sent to the galleys. It is years before he escapes. In the course of the novel John the Baptist and Jesus are introduced. The most famous of the many adventuresome episodes of the book is the chariot race in which Ben Hur defeats his old friend and enemy Messala. *Ben Hur* was dramatized on stage and screen with great success.

Benicia Boy. John C. Heenan, the American pugilist, who challenged and fought Tom Sayers for "the belt" in 1860; so called from Benicia in California, his birthplace.

Benjamin. The pet, the youngest; in allusion to Benjamin, the youngest son of Jacob (*Gen.* xxxv. 18). When Jacob sent his sons down from Canaan to buy bread during the famine, he refused to let Benjamin go "lest peradventure harm befall him." Jacob's son Joseph who was in charge over the granaries of Egypt, without revealing his identity, told his brothers that they must bring Benjamin with them if they returned for more corn. When they finally did so, Joseph feasted them and gave them grain, but sent word after them that his silver cup was missing; and when search was made, "the cup was found in Benjamin's sack" where it had been placed by Joseph's orders. He then disclosed his identity.

Benjamin's mess. The largest share. The allusion is to the banquet given by Joseph, viceroy of Egypt, to his brethren. "Benjamin's mess was five times so much as any of theirs" (*Gen.* xliii. 34).

Benjamin, René (1885–). French novelist, best known for *Gaspard* (1915), a novel of a Paris street urchin become soldier in World War I; *Les Plaisirs du hazard* (1922); *La Prodigieuse vie de H. de Balzac* (1925).

Bennet, Elizabeth. Heroine of Jane Austen's PRIDE AND PREJUDICE.

Mrs. Bennet. In the same novel, the type of a fussy, match-making mother. *Jane Bennet, Lydia* and *Mr. Bennet* are also prominent characters.

Bennett, Enoch Arnold (1867–1931). English journalist, novelist, and playwright. He is best known for THE OLD WIVES' TALE (1908), and the novels in the "CLAYHANGER" series—*Clayhanger* (1910), *Hilda Lessways* (1911), *These Twain* (1916), and *The Clayhanger Family* (1925), an omnibus volume. Bennett was also the author of *Buried Alive* (1908); *Denry the Audacious* (1911); *The Matador of the Five Towns* (1912), short stories; *Mr. Prohack* (1922); RICEYMAN STEPS (1923); *Lord Raingo* (1926); *The Vanguard* (1927); *Accident* (1929); IMPERIAL PALACE (1930). See also FIVE TOWNS.

Bennett, Floyd (1890–1928). American aviator. With Commander Byrd in flight over North Pole (1926). Was to be second in command of Byrd's South Pole exploration, but died of pneumonia. Had received Congressional Medal of Honor.

Bennett, James Gordon (1795–1872). American journalist and editor. Born in Scotland. Started New York *Herald* (May 6, 1835). His son of same name (1841–1918) became famous; sent Stanley to Africa to find Livingstone; financed North West passage and Arctic expeditions; established Paris edition of New York *Herald* (1887); with John W. Mackay in Commercial Cable Co. laid transatlantic cables and broke Gould monopoly. Resident of Paris (from 1877). Established James Gordon Bennett trophies in yachting and automobile and aeroplane racing.

Benoît, Pierre (1886–). French novelist whose *L'Atlantide* (1919) won him the Grand Prix du Roman of the Académie Française.

Benoît de Sainte-Maure (fl. 12th cent.). Medieval French poet, author of the *Roman de Troie* (ca. 1165), written in honor of ELEANOR OF POITOU. This was one of the metamorphoses of the TROILUS and Cressida story, which culminated in the famous romance by Chaucer. Benoît contributed to the traditional theme the atmosphere of feudal luxury and the conventions of COURTLY LOVE.

Benserade, Isaac de (1613–1691). French poet and naturalist. His sonnet, "Job," as rivaling Voiture's sonnet "Uranie," started literary war of the two poets at court. Their factions called Jobelins and Uranins.

Benshee, see BANSHEE.

Benson, Arthur Christopher (1862–1925), Edward Frederic (1867–1940), and Robert Hugh (1871–1914). Three sons of **Edward White Benson** (1829–1896) archbishop of Canterbury. Arthur Christopher wrote a biography of his father, and monographs and essays; Edward Frederic, a novelist, captured society with the sensational *Dodo;* Robert Hugh, as a Catholic priest, wrote interesting historical fiction from the Catholic viewpoint.

Benson, Sir **Frank Robert** (1858–1939). English actor-manager; founded touring repertory company. Produced many of Shakespeare's plays.

Benson, Frank Weston (1862–). American painter. Excels in painting women and children, often in outdoor scenes of brilliant light and color. Murals in Congressional Library, Washington, D.C.

Benson, Sally (1900–). American short-story writer, best known for the biting wit and irony of her character sketches of women, published chiefly in THE NEW YORKER. Collections of her stories are *People Are Fascinating* (1936); *Emily* (1938); *Junior Miss* (1941); *Meet Me in St. Louis* (1942). The last two volumes are series of stories grouped about a single set of characters, written in a gentler mood than the author's characteristic work. *Junior Miss* was a best-seller, and was adapted as a successful play in 1941.

Benson, Stella (1892–1933). English novelist, whose witty and original books include: *Living Alone* (1919); *The Poor Man* (1922); *Goodbye, Stranger* (1926); *The Faraway Bride* (1930); *Hope Against Hope, And Other Stories* (1931); *Collected Short Stories* (1936); *Mundos* (1935), a novel left unfinished at her death.

Bentham, Jeremy (1748–1832). English philosopher of the Utilitarian school (see UTILITARIANISM. His social and philosophical ideas are to be found in his *Fragment on Government* (1776) and *Introduction to Principles of Morals and Legislation* (1789). His watchword was "the greatest good for the greatest number," and he tried to work out scientifically on a quantitative scale the values of pleasure and pain in moral motivation.

Bentinck, William. 1st Earl of Portland (1649?–1709). Trusted agent and intimate friend of William III of England. Arranged Treaty of Ryswick (1697).

Bentley, Edmund Clerihew (1875–). English writer of detective fiction and originator of a kind of pseudo-biographical verse known as clerihews. *Trent's Last Case* (1912) is his best and best-known book.

Bentley, Richard (1662–1742). English clergyman and scholar. In controversy (1697–1679) with Charles Boyle proved spuriousness of *Epistles of Phalaris.* This controversy gave rise to *The Battle of the Books* by Jonathan Swift.

Benton, Thomas Hart (1889–). American painter, known for his pictures of life in the U.S., particularly in the Middle West. Grandnephew of **Thomas Hart Benton** (1782–1858), the American political leader whose daughter Jessie married John Charles FRÉMONT.

ben trovato (*Ital.*). Well found, well invented; a happy discovery or invention. The full phrase is *se non è vero, è ben trovato,* if it is not true it is well invented: said of a plausible story.

Bent Twig, The. A novel by Dorothy Canfield FISHER (1915). The scene is laid in a middle-western University town where the heroine, Sylvia Marshall, grows up to maturity. The novel deals with the problems of her youth.

Benu. Egyptian prototype of Greek phoenix. A bird, the embodiment of Ra, sacred to Osiris.

Benvolio. Nephew to Montague in Shakespeare's *Romeo and Juliet;* a testy, litigious gentleman, who would "quarrel with a man that had a hair more or a hair less in his beard than he had."

Beowulf. The hero of the ancient Anglo-Saxon epic poem of the same name, of unknown original date and authorship, but certainly written before the coming of the Saxons to England, and modified subsequent to the introduction of Christianity.

The scene is laid in Denmark or Sweden: the hall (Heorot) of King Hrothgar is raided nightly by GRENDEL, whom Beowulf mortally wounds after a fierce fight. Grendel's dam comes next night to avenge his death. Beowulf pursues her to her lair under the water and ultimately slays her with a magic sword. Beowulf in time becomes king, and fifty years later meets his death in combat with a dragon, the guardian of an immense hoard, his faithful Wiglaf being his only follower at the end.

The version of the epic that we know dates from the 8th century, but it probably represents a gradual growth which existed in many successive versions. In any case, it is not only the oldest epic in English, but one of the oldest in the whole Teutonic group of languages.

Beppo. A contraction of Giuseppe, and therefore equal to our Joe. In Byron's poem of this name (1818), Beppo is husband of Laura, a Venetian lady. He is taken captive in Troy, becomes a Turk, joins a band of pirates, grows rich, and, after several years' absence, returns to his native land, where he discovers his wife at a carnival ball with her *cavaliero servente.* He makes himself known to her, and they live together again as man and wife.

Béranger, Pierre Jean de (1780–1857). French lyric poet. Author of popular songs, gay and ribald, patriotic and topical, and sentimental. He frequently celebrated Napoleon, and is considered to have crystallized the popular feeling of his time in his work, although it is not distinguished by much literary merit.

Bérard, Victor (1864–1931). French scholar and publicist. Translator of the *Odyssey.*

Berchta, see PERCHTA.

Berchtesgaden. One of the sites of the legendary sleep of the German emperor, Frederick BARBAROSSA, in a mountain cave until the day when he is destined to awake and leave his resting place to restore unity, power, and peace to Germany. Berchtesgaden, in Bavaria, came into prominence in the third decade of the 20th century as the mountain retreat of Adolf HITLER who, as Führer of the National Socialist government of Germany, promised to restore unity and power to the nation. In September 1938, Berchtesgaden was the scene of a visit to Hitler made by Neville CHAMBERLAIN, Prime Minister of England, during the MUNICH CRISIS.

Bercovici, Konrad (1882–). American author, born in Roumania, whose writings are concerned with the East Side section of New York City, travel, and life among the Balkan gypsies. Among his works are *Crimes of Charity* (1917); *Dust of New York* (1919); *Ghitza* (1921); *The Marriage Guest* (1925); *The Volga Boatman* (1926); *Peasants* (1928); *Story of the Gypsies* (1928); *The Incredible Balkans* (1933); *It's the Gypsy in Me* (1941), an autobiography.

Berdyaev, Nikolai Aleksandrovich (1874–1948). A widely read Russian philosophical writer. He was expelled by the Bolsheviks in 1922 as an upholder of religion. In 1934 he directed the Academy of the Philosophy of Religion in Paris. He acknowledged Dostoievsky as playing a decisive part in his spiritual life. Wrote *The Bourgeois Mind; Dostoievsky: An Interpretation; The Origin of Russian Communism,* etc.

Berengaria. Queen-consort of Richard Cœur de Lion, introduced in Scott's novel, THE TALISMAN. Berengaria died in 1230.

Berenger, Eveline. Heroine of Scott's novel, THE BETROTHED.

Berenice. The sister-wife of Ptolemy Euergetes, king of Egypt (247–222 B. C.). She vowed to sacrifice her hair to the gods if her husband returned home the vanquisher of Asia. She suspended her hair in the temple of Arsinoë at Zephyrium, but it was stolen the first night, and Conon of Samos told the king that the winds had wafted it to heaven, where it still forms the seven stars near the tail of Leo, called *Coma Berenices.*

Berenson, Bernhard (1865–). American art critic, born in Lithuania of a poor Jewish family. Recognized as the greatest living connoisseur of Italian Renaissance art. Collectors rely implicitly on his judgment. Member of the American Academy of Arts and Letters.

Beresford, John Davys (1873–1947). English novelist, author of *Jacob Stahl* (see STAHL) (1911); *God's Counterpoint* (1919); *The Monkey Puzzle* (1925); *Love's Illusion* (1930).

Berezina. A river in White Russia which flows into the Dnieper. Here the Russians in retreat halted the Germans for almost a week, July 3–8, 1941, and here the Russian First Baltic Army crossed in return on July 4, 1944. In 1812 the retreating *Grande Armée* of Napoleon forced the crossing of the Berezina with enormous losses.

Bergamasca (*Ital.*). A type of dance, originating in Bergamo, Italy, referred to in Shakespeare's *Midsummer Night's Dream.* In the 17th century it became a form of instrumental music. Debussy has written a *Suite Bergamasque.* Cf. *Chaconne; Passacaglia.*

Bergelmir. One of the frost-giants of *Scandinavian mythology.* When Ymir was slain by Odin and others, and the whole race of frost-giants was drowned in his blood, Bergelmir alone escaped, and he thereupon founded a second dynasty of giants.

Bergen, Edgar John (1903–). American ventriloquist who achieved success on radio and in motion pictures with his famous dummy, "Charlie McCarthy" (first radio appearance, Dec. 17, 1936), and, later, "Mortimer Snerd."

Bergerac, Cyrano de (1619–1655). French soldier and author, best known as the hero of a successful play written over three centuries after his death by Edmond ROSTAND (see CYRANO DE BERGERAC). An adventure tale of unknown authorship, *Cyrano de Bergerac's Voyage to the Moon and the Sun,* was widely read in France and England during the 17th century.

Bergeret, Monsieur. The central figure in the four novels that comprise Anatole France's *Histoire Contemporaine* (1897–1900)—*The Elm Tree on the Mall* (*L'Orme du Mail*), *The Wicker-Work Woman* (*Le Mannequin d'osier*), *The Amethyst Ring* (*L'Anneau d'améthyste*) and *M. Bergert à Paris.* In the first volumes M. Bergeret holds an official position in one of the provincial universities of France; in the last two he is divorced from his wife and lives in Paris. The four novels deal very largely with the famous DREYFUS case and Bergeret is said to be a vehicle for much of France's own feelings and convictions on the subject.

Berghof, Haus, see HAUS BERGHOF.

Bergson, Henri (1859–1941). French philosopher, of wide influence and popularity in the years immediately preceding World War I, awarded the Nobel Prize for literature in 1927. His intellectual system, which tends toward the anti-rational and the mystical, favors direct intuition as a means of attaining knowledge, rather than the experimental and rationalistic methods of science. It also regards change or movement as the source of all reality (see also HERACLITUS) and time as a continuous flow, or duration, in which the past and present are inseparable to consciousness and the memory. These views, particularly as they apply to memory and time, appear prominently in the pattern of Marcel Proust's long novel, REMEMBRANCE OF THINGS PAST. Bergson's most famous work is *L'Evolution créatrice* (1907), translated as CREATIVE EVOLUTION in 1911. Among his other important works are: *Matière et mémoire* (1896), translated as *Matter and Memory; Le Rire* (1900), translated as *Laughter; L'Énergie spirituelle* (1919), translated as *Mind-Energy; Durée et simultanéité* (1922). In 1940, after the defeat of France in World War II, Bergson renounced all of his honors and his posts in France as a protest against hostile legislation passed by the VICHY GOVERNMENT against the Jews, of whom he was one.

Bergsonism. The intuitive, anti-rational, and highly poetic philosophy of Henri BERGSON, part of the movement of reaction against the mechanistic conceptions of 19th-century science which arose in a number of intellectual quarters at the beginning of the 20th century.

Berkeley, George (1685–1753). English churchman and philosopher, born in Ireland, one of the earliest and most important thinkers of the philosophic school of IDEALISM. He maintained that the objects of sense perception are only ideas in our minds, with no independent existence outside of the perceiving mind, and that the whole of reality consists only of ideas in the mind of God. His chief works are ESSAY TOWARDS A NEW THEORY OF VISION (1709); *Principles of Human Knowledge* (1710); THREE DIALOGUES BETWEEN HYLAS AND PHILONUS (1713); ALCIPHRON (1732), pseudo-Platonic dialogues; *Theory of Vision* (1733); SIRIS (1744). He was active in attacking the opinions of free-thinkers, and was associated with a number of well-known 18th-century literary figures, including Addison, Pope, and Swift. From 1729 to 1732 he lived in the colony of Rhode Island in America, where he wrote *Alciphron* and founded a Literary and Philosophical Society.

Berkeley, Sir William (1606–1677). English governor of the colony of Virginia (1642–1652 and 1660–1677). His dictatorial policy of government led to BACON'S REBELLION and became even harsher after the death of the leader of the revolt, Nathaniel Bacon.

Berlin, Irving (Israel Baline) (1888–). American composer of popular songs and lyrics for musical shows. Born in Russia. His *Alexander's Ragtime Band* (1911) was one of the first and most successful examples of JAZZ. His later compositions were of a sentimental and patriotic nature, such as *White Christmas* and *God Bless America*.

Berlin Conference. (1) November 15, 1884, to January 30, 1885. By the Berlin Act it recognized the International Association of the Congo of King Leopold, regulated commerce in that region and tried to partition Africa.

(2) The Berlin Conference of 1945 settled areas in Germany assigned to management by Britain, U.S., Russia, and France.

Berlin decree. A decree issued at Berlin by Napoleon I in November, 1806, forbidding any of the nations of Europe to trade with Great Britain, proclaiming her to be in a state of blockade, declaring all English property forfeit, and all Englishmen on French soil prisoners of war.

Berlin Diary. A best-selling book by William L. Shirer, published in 1941. It contains selections from a diary kept by the author while he was an American newspaper correspondent and radio news commentator in Berlin just preceding and during the first years of World War II. Its informal, first-hand impressions of the war and the Nazi régime in Germany made it extremely popular.

Berling, Gösta, see GÖSTA BERLING.

Berlioz, Louis Hector (1803–1869). French composer, known for the typically Romantic quality of his music, much of which was written on literary subjects. The work for which he is most famous, the SYMPHONIE FANTASTIQUE (*Fantastic Symphony*) (1830), subtitled *Épisode de la vie d'un artiste,* was the first piece of sustained narrative music (see TONE POEM), a form later used notably by Richard STRAUSS. Others of Berlioz's best-known works are *Waverley* (1827–1828), *Les Francs-Juges* (1827–1828), *Le Roi Lear* (1831), and *Le Carnaval romain* (1844), all overtures; *Harold en Italie* (1834) and *Roméo et Juliette* (1838–1839), dramatic symphonies; *Benvenuto Cellini* (1838), an opera; and *La Damnation de Faust* (1846), a "concert opera." The composer also wrote essays and criticism on music, and a volume of memoirs (1870); his correspondence was published after his death. See also RECIO, MARIE.

Berma. In Marcel Proust's REMEMBRANCE OF THINGS PAST, a famous actress whose art is an object of the narrator's youthful admiration. The character is considered to represent Sarah BERNHARDT.

Bermoothes. The name of the island in the *Tempest,* feigned by Shakespeare to be enchanted and inhabited by witches and devils.

> From the still-vexed Bermoothes, there she's hid.
> Shakespeare, *The Tempest*, i. 2.

Shakespeare almost certainly had the recently discovered Bermudas in his mind, but a case has also been made out for the island of Lampedusa between Malta and the coast of Tunis.

Bermudas. An old slang name for a district of London—thought to have been the narrow alleys in the neighborhood of Covent Garden, St. Martin's Lane, and the Strand—which was an ALSATIA, where the residents had certain privileges against arrest. Hence, *to live in the Bermudas,* to skulk in some out-of-the-way place for cheapness or safety.

Bernadette of Lourdes, St. See under SAINT. *The Song of Bernadette,* a novel by Franz WERFEL (1890–1945) became a successful moving picture.

Bernard, Rosine, see BERNHARDT, SARAH.

Bernard de Ventadour (fl. 12th cent.). TROUBADOUR of ELEANOR OF AQUITAINE and considered one of the greatest of the group of love poets who wrote in the convention of COURTLY LOVE.

Bernardo. In Shakespeare's *Hamlet,* an officer in Denmark to whom the ghost of the murdered King appeared during the night-watch at the royal castle.

Bernardo del Carpio. A semi-mythical Spanish hero of the 9th century, and a favorite subject of the minstrels, and of Lope de Vega, who wrote many plays around his exploits. He is credited with having defeated Roland (or Orlando) at Roncesvalles.

Bernard of Clairvaux, St. (1091–1153). French ecclesiastic known as "Thaumaturgus of the West." Founder and first abbé of the Cistercian Monastery of Clairvaux. See also under SAINTS.

Bernard of Cluny or **Morlaix.** 12th century Benedictine monk; author of Latin poem *De Contemptu Mundi,* the beginning of which was translated by John Mason Neale into three hymns: *Jerusalem the Golden, The World is Very Evil,* and *For Thee, O Dear, Dear Country.*

Berners, Isopel. A gypsy girl in George BORROW's *Lavengro.*

Berners, 2nd Baron. **John Bourchier** (1467–1533). English author and statesman, who was in attendance to Henry VIII at the FIELD OF THE CLOTH OF GOLD. He translated a number of French and Spanish works, including the *Chronicles* of FROISSART (1523–1525) and the romance, HUON OF BORDEAUX.

bernesque poetry. Serio-comic poetry; so called from Francesco Berni (1498–1535), of Tuscany, who greatly excelled in it. Byron's *Beppo* is a good example of English bernesque.

Bernhardi, Friedrich von (1849–1930). Prussian general and military writer. Fought in World War I on eastern front (1915) and on western front (1918). Author of *Germany and the Next War* (1911). Disciple of von Treitschke, calling war a biological necessity.

Bernhardi, Professor, see PROFESSOR BERNHARDI.

Bernhardt, Sarah (1845–1923). Originally Rosine Bernard. Famous French actress, noted for her performances in plays by Victor HUGO, Victorien SARDOU, and Edmond ROSTAND, and especially in Racine's PHÈDRE. See also BERMA.

Bernini, Giovanni Lorenzo (1598–1680). Italian sculptor, architect, painter. Dominant influence for over a century on European sculpture. Created the Berninesque style.

Bernstein, Baroness. The name under which the Beatrix ESMOND of *Henry Esmond* appears, as an old woman, in Thackeray's *Virginians.*

Bernstein, Henry (1876–). French dramatist, writer of violent realistic melodrama, noted duelist. His plays have been successful in U.S.

Bernstorff, Count **Johann-Heinrich von** (1682–1939). German diplomat. Tried without his government's support, to help President Wilson's mediation attempts prior to America's entry into World War I. Later chairman of the German League-of-Nations Union.

Béroul (fl. 12th cent.). Medieval French poet, author of an early version of the famous romance of TRISTAN and Isolt. See also THOMAS.

Berry, Bessie. Richard's good-hearted old nurse in Meredith's RICHARD FEVEREL.

Bersagliere. Member of an infantry corps organized in 1850 by Victor Immanuel II of Italy as riflemen. The *Bersaglieri* wore hats decorated with cock's feathers. They were in World War I and in Albania in World War II.

berserker. In Scandinavian mythology, a wild, ferocious, warlike being who was at times possessed of supernatural strength and fury. The origin of the name is doubtful; one account says that it was that of the grandson of the eight-handed Starkader and the beautiful Alfhilde, who was called *boer-serce* (bare of mail) because he went into battle unharnessed. Hence, any man with the fighting fever on him.

Another disregards this altogether and holds that the name means simply "men who have assumed the form of bears." It is used in English both as an adjective denoting excessive fury and a noun denoting one possessed of such.

> Let no man awaken it, this same Berserker rage!
> Carlyle, *Chartism.*

> You say that I am berserker. And . . . baresark I go to-morrow to the war.
> Kingsley, *Hereward the Wake.*

Bertha, Big, see BIG BERTHA.

Bertha, Frau. A German impersonation of the Epiphany, corresponding to the Italian BEFANA. Represented as a white lady, who steals softly into nurseries and rocks infants asleep in the absence of negligent nurses, she is, however, the terror of all naughty children. Her feet are very large, and she has an iron nose.

Berthe au Grand Pied (Bertha with the large foot). Mother of Charlemagne, and great-granddaughter of Charles Martel: so called because she had a clubfoot. She is a prominent character in the medieval romances dealing with Charlemagne and his court, and is in particular the heroine of a 13th-century romance by a minstrel named Adenés which was immensely popular.

Bertillon, Alphonse (1853–1914). As chief of identification bureau of Paris police established an identification system adopted throughout Europe. It was based on physical measurements, markings, deformities, color, impression of thumb lines. Modern fingerprinting has superseded this system.

Bertoldo. A famous clown of popular Italian legend. The tales of his witty pranks were collected in a *Life of Bertoldo* (*Vita di Bertoldo*) by Giulio Caesare Croce in the 16th century; and in the two centuries that followed, his exploits and those of his son Bertoldina and grandson Cacasenno, both of whom were supposed to have succeeded to his post of court jester, formed the subject matter of many tales and poems.

imperturbable as Bertoldo, i.e. not to be taken by surprise, thrown off your guard, or disconcerted at anything.

Bertram. (1) The hero of Shakespeare's ALL'S WELL THAT ENDS WELL.

(2) In Meyerbeer's opera ROBERT LE DIABLE, the fiend father of Robert.

Bertram, Edmund, also **Maria Bertram** and Sir **Thomas Bertram.** Characters in Jane Austen's novel MANSFIELD PARK.

Bertram, Harry. Hero of Scott's GUY MANNERING, *alias* Captain Vanbeest Brown, *alias* Dawson, *alias* Dudley, son of the laird, and heir to Ellangowan. The character was suggested by James Annesley, Esq., rightful heir of the earldom of Anglesey, of which he was dispossessed by his uncle Richard. He died in 1743.

Bertran de Born (1140?–1215). One of the poets of medieval Provence (see TROUBADOURS), who was best known for his songs of war. He is to be found in Dante's INFERNO because he allegedly stirred up hostility between Henry II of England and his sons.

Berzelius, Baron **Jöns Jakob** (1779–1848). Swedish chemist. Author of the system of chemical symbols. Discovered *selenium* and *thorium*. Experimented in electrolysis. His name was used as the name of one of the senior societies of the Sheffield Scientific School of Yale University. A passage in his writings dealing with *elective affinities* in chemistry became the nucleus of GOETHE's famous novel of that title (*Die Wahlverwandtschaften*).

Bes. Egyptian god of pleasure.

Besant, Mrs. **Annie Wood** (1847–1933). English theosophist. First became an active Free Thinker with Charles Bradlaugh. Did much for wayward children and homeless girls. W. T. Stead introduced her to the work of Mme. Blavatsky. She became her right-hand helper in 1891 and succeeded her as head of the Esoteric School. Went to India 1894. President of Theosophical Society 1907. Discovered a "New Messiah" in Krishnamurti. Died at Madras. Wrote at least seventeen principal works.

Besant, Sir Walter (1836–1901). English novelist. Co-author with James Rice of a series of novels. Sole author of novels on social conditions such as *All Sorts and Conditions of Men* (1882).

Beside the Bonnie Briar Bush. A narrative of Scotch life by Ian Maclaren (1894), relating simple incidents in the little village of Drumtochty.

Besier, Rudolf. See THE BARRETTS OF WIMPOLE STREET.

Bess, Good Queen. Queen Elizabeth (1533–1603).

Bess o' Bedlam. A female lunatic vagrant. See BEDLAM.

Bess of Hardwick. Elizabeth Talbot, Countess of Shrewsbury (1518–1608) to whose charge, in 1569, Mary Queen of Scots was committed. The Countess treated the captive Queen with great harshness, being jealous of the earl her husband. Bess of Hardwick married four times: Robert Barlow (when she was only fourteen); Sir William Cavendish; Sir William St. Loe, Captain of Queen Elizabeth's Guard; and lastly, George sixth Earl of Shrewsbury. She built Hardwick Hall, and founded the wealth and dignity of the Cavendish family.

Bessee, the beggar's daughter of Bednall (Bethnal) Green, the heroine of an old ballad given in Percy's *Reliques,* and introduced by Chettle and Day into their play *The Blind Beggar of Bednal Green* (1600). Sheridan Knowles also has a play on the story (1834). Bessee is very beautiful, and is courted by four suitors at once—a knight, a gentleman of fortune, a London merchant, and the son of the innkeeper at Romford. She tells them that they must obtain the consent of her father, the poor blind beggar of Bethnal Green. When they hear, they all slink off except the knight, who goes to ask the beggar's leave to wed the "pretty Bessee." The beggar gives her £3,000 for her dower, and £100 to buy her wedding gown. At the wedding feast he explains to the guests that he is Henry, son and heir of Sir Simon de Montfort, and has only assumed the garb of a beggar to escape the vigilance of King Henry's spies because of his participation in the battle of Evesham on the barons' side.

Bessie, Alvah Cecil (1904–). American story-writer, novelist, and essayist. Served in the Lincoln Battalion in Spain for the Loyalists (1937) continuously at the front till end of the war. *Men in Battle* (1939).

Bessie Bell and Mary Gray. A ballad by Allan Ramsey, relating how two young ladies of Perth, to avoid the plague of 1666, retire to a rural retreat called the Burnbraes, near Lynedock, the residence of Mary Gray. A young man, in love with both, carries them provisions, and they all die of the plague and are buried at Dornock Hough.

Bessus. In BEAUMONT AND FLETCHER'S *King and No King,* a cowardly, bragging captain, a sort of BOBADIL.

bestiaries. Books very popular in the 11th, 12th, and 13th centuries, containing accounts of the supposed habits and peculiarities of animals, which, with the legendary lore connected with them, served as texts for devotional homilies. They were founded on the old *Physiologi,* and those in English were, for the most part, translations of continental originals. The *Bestiaires* of Philippe de Thaon, Guillaume le Clerc, and *Le Bestiaire d'amour,* by Richard de Fournival, were among the most popular.

Beston, Henry (1888–). A distinguished American naturalist and writer, of mixed Irish and French extraction, married to the poet, Elizabeth Coatsworth. His *American Memory* (1937) is the first study of our history to give a proper perspective to the rôle of the American Indian.

best seller. Loosely, a book that sells better than others; also its author. Originally a phrase not essentially different from "good seller, excellent seller," etc., the term has been crystallized since about 1910 and is often but mistakenly thought to be a technical term for books selling a stipulated minimum number of copies. Weekly lists of best sellers were started by *Publishers' Weekly* and are now a feature of several newspaper book supplements. Perennial best sellers include the *Bible;* Post's *Etiquette; Uncle Tom's Cabin;* etc. Cf. F. L. Mott's GOLDEN MULTITUDES (1947).

bête noire (*Fr.* black beast). The thorn in the side, the bitter in the cup, the spoke in the wheel, the black sheep, the object of aversion. A black sheep has always been considered an eyesore in a flock, and its wool is really less valuable. In times of superstition it was looked on as bearing the devil's mark.

Bethany. Town of Palestine on the Mount of Olives that was the home of Lazarus, whose sisters were Mary and Martha, and whom Christ raised from the dead.

Bethesda, pool of. A spring in Jerusalem which was supposed to possess healing powers "when the water is troubled." Jesus here cured a sick man who had waited thirty-eight years, but had always been set aside by others.

Beth Gelert or the Grave of the Greyhound. A ballad by the Hon. William Robert Spencer. The tale is that one day Llewellyn returns from hunting, when his favorite hound, covered with gore, runs to meet him. The chieftain runs to see if anything has happened to his infant son, finds the cradle overturned and sprinkled with blood. Thinking the hound has eaten the child, he stabs it to the heart. Afterwards he finds the babe quite safe, and a huge wolf under the bed, dead; Gelert has killed the wolf and saved the child. The story is of very old origin and very widespread: with variations it is found in Sanskrit and in most ancient literatures.

It is told of Tsar Piras of Russia and in the *Gesta Romanorum,* of Folliculus a knight, but instead of a wolf the dog is said to have killed a serpent. The story occurs again in the *Seven Wise Masters.* In the Sanskrit version the dog is called an ichneumon and the wolf a "black snake." In the *Hitopadesa* (iv. 3) the dog is an otter; in the Arabic a weasel; in the Mongolian a polecat; in the Persian a cat, etc.

Bethlehem. (1) Town in Judaea where Christ was born.

(2) Town in Pennsylvania where war ordnance is manufactured by a huge steel company, and where the Bach Festival is held every year. Founded by Moravians.

Bethmann-Hollweg, Theobald von (1856–1921). Prussian who succeeded von Bülow as chancellor of German empire (1909–1917). Referred to Belgian neutrality treaty as a "scrap of paper" (1914). Forced out of office by Hindenburg and Ludendorff (1917) after having tried to restrict submarine warfare.

Bethulia, Judith of. A poem by Thomas Bailey Aldrich.

Betrothed, The. A novel by Sir Walter Scott (1825), dealing with the times of Henry II of England.

Betsy Ross, see Ross.

Bett, Lulu, see MISS LULU BETT.

Betterton, Thomas (1635–1710). Famous English actor who excelled in Shakespeare's characters.

Bettina. The name taken by Elisabeth Brentano, Countess von Arnim (1785–1859), in her publication, *Letters to a Child,* in 1835. The letters purported to be her correspondence with Goethe (1807–1811).

Betty. A name of contempt given to a man who interferes with the duties of female servants, or occupies himself in female pursuits. See also MOLLY. Also burglar's slang for a skeleton key (the servant of a picklock), and sometimes for a jimmy.

Betty, Cousin. In Balzac's *Cousin Betty.* See FISCHER, LISBETH.

Beulah, see LAND OF BEULAH.

Bevan, Mr. In Dickens' MARTIN CHUZZLEWIT, an American physician, who befriends Martin Chuzzlewit and Mark Tapley in many ways during their stay in the New World.

Beveridge, Albert Jeremiah (1862–1927). American historian and statesman. Famous for his two-volume *Life of John Marshall* (1916, 1919).

Beveridge, Sir **William Henry** (1879–). English economist, famous for the Beveridge Plan, making recommendations as to postwar social security in Great Britain. It was developed by Beveridge as chairman of the Inter-Departmental Committee on Social Insurance and Allied Services (1941) and is much in advance of anything so far considered in the U.S.

Beverley, Cecilia. Heroine of Fanny Burney's novel CECILIA.

Beverley, Ensign. The name assumed by CAPTAIN ABSOLUTE in Sheridan's *School for Scandal.*

Beverly, Robert (1675–1716). American historian of the Virginia colony. His chief work is *History of the Present State of Virginia,* published in 1705, which gives a clear picture of life in the colony in its early days.

Beverly of Graustark, see GRAUSTARK.

Bevis. (1) Marmion's horse in Scott's narrative poem *Marmion.*

(2) The faithful mastiff of Sir Harry Lee in Scott's novel *Woodstock.* See next entry.

Bevis of Hamtown or **Southampton,** Sir. A very well known medieval chivalric romance, slightly connected with the Charlemagne cycle, which (in the English version given in Drayton's *Polyolbion*) tells how the father of Bevis is slain by the mother, and how, when Bevis tries to avenge the murder, she sells him into slavery to Eastern merchants. After many adventures he converts and carries off Josian, daughter of the Soldan, returns to England and gets his revenge, and all ends happily. See ASCAPART.

bevy. See under COVEY.

Bewick, Thomas (1753–1828). Founder of modern school of English wood engraving. His *History of British Quadrupeds* and his *British Birds* are famous.

Bey. See RULERS, TITLES OF.

Beyle, Henri, see STENDHAL.

Beyond Life. A narrative, or more properly a series of essays by James Branch CABELL (1919). The supposed author is John CHARTERIS who appears in other Cabell novels and is frequently Cabell's mouthpiece.

Beyond the Horizon. A drama by Eugene O'NEILL (1920). Robert Mayo, a romantic dreamer, has always wanted to seek adventure "beyond the horizon" but has given up his dreams to marry the girl he loves and stay on the New England farm. Instead his prosaic brother Andrew, who has also loved Ruth, the girl, is the one to go adventuring over seven seas and come home with strange tales. Robert's life is embittered by the fact that Ruth comes to despise him as a failure and to idealize Andrew, and finally disease takes away all hope. *Beyond the Horizon* was awarded the Pulitzer prize in 1920.

bezonian. A new recruit; applied originally in derision to young soldiers sent from Spain to Italy, who landed both ill-accoutred and in want of everything (Ital. *besogni,* from *bisogno,* need; Fr. *besoin*).

Bhagavadgita. A very early Hindu poem of religious and philosophical import "sung by the holy one," that is by KRISHNA. It is paraphrased in Edwin Arnold's *Song Celestial.*

Bianca. (1) In Shakespeare's TAMING OF THE SHREW the younger daughter of Baptista of Padua, as gentle and meek as her sister Katherine was violent and irritable.

(2) A courtesan in Shakespeare's *Othello.*

Bianca among the Nightingales. A poem by Elizabeth Barrett Browning. The Italian Bianca, forsaken by her English lover, pours out her grief and her hatred of the England in which she is living.

Bianchi. The political faction in Tuscany to which Dante belonged. It and the Neri (Whites and Blacks), both being branches of the Guelph family, engaged in a feud shortly before 1300 which became very violent in Florence and the neighboring cities, and eventually the Bianchi joined the Ghibellines, the opponents of the Guelphs. In 1301 the Bianchi, including Dante, were exiled from Florence.

Bianchi, Martha Dickinson (1866–1943). Niece of Emily Dickinson. Author of poems and translator of Slavic and other poetry. Introduction to *The Single Hound* by Emily Dickinson (1914); editor of *The Life and Letters of Emily Dickinson* (1924), *The Poems of Emily Dickinson* (1930; centenary edition), *Unpublished Poems of Emily Dickinson* (1935; with Alfred Leete Hampson), *Poems of Emily Dickinson* (with preface by Alfred Leete Hampson). Also *Further Poems of Emily Dickinson Withheld From Publication By Her Sister Lavinia* (with Alfred Leete Hampson).

Bianchon, Horace. A tolerant and charitable Parisian physician who appears in many of the novels of Balzac's COMÉDIE HUMAINE. He is a member of the CÉNACLE.

Bianco, Margery Williams (1881–1944). Writer of fiction for children, as *The Velveteen Rabbit* (1922), mother of Pamela Bianco, child prodigy and remarkable artist and illustrator.

Biathanatos, a Declaration of that Paradox or Thesis that Self-Homicide Is not so Naturally Sin that It May Never Be Otherwise. A defense of suicide, published in 1644, by John DONNE.

Biberius Caldius Mero. The punning nickname of Tiberius Claudius Nero (the Roman Emperor, Tiberius, who reigned from 14 to 37 A. D.). Biberius [Tiberius], drink-loving. Caldius Mero [Claudius Nero], by metathesis for *calidus mero,* hot with wine.

Bibesco, Princess **Marthe Lucie** (1887–). Rumanian novelist and essayist. Her work has been praised by Anatole France and Marcel Proust. Her travel book, *The Eight Paradises,* which she published at the age of eighteen, was crowned by the French Academy.

Bible.

(1) *English versions.* The principal versions of the English Bible are:

American Revised Version. A separate version published in 1901, the work of the American Committee on the Revised Version. It differs in a few particulars from the REVISED VERSION.

Authorized Version. This, the version in general use in England, was made by a body of scholars working at the command of King James I (hence sometimes called "King James' Bible") from 1604 to 1611, and was published in 1611. The modern "Authorized Version" is, however, by no means an exact reprint of that authorized by King James; a large number of typographical errors which occurred in the first edition have been corrected, the orthography, punctuation, etc., has been modernized, and the use of italics, capital letters, etc., varied. The BISHOPS' BIBLE was used as the basis of the text, but Tyndale's, Matthew's, Coverdale's, and the Geneva translations were also followed when they agreed better with the original.

Bishops' Bible. A version made at the instigation of Archbishop Parker (hence also called "Matthew Parker's Bible"), to which most of the Anglican bishops were contributors. It was a revision of the GREAT BIBLE, first appeared in 1568, and by 1602 had reached its eighteenth edition. It is this edition that forms the basis of our Authorized Version. See TREACLE BIBLE.

Coverdale's Bible. The first complete English Bible to be printed, published in 1535 as a translation out of Douche (i.e., German) and Latin by Miles Coverdale. It consists of Tyndale's translation of the Pentateuch and New Testament, with translations from the Vulgate, a Latin version (1527–1528) by the Italian Catholic theologian, Sanctes Pegninus, Luther's German version (1534) and the Swiss-German version of Zwingli and Leo Juda (Zurich, 1527–1529). The first edition was printed at Antwerp, but the second (Southwark, 1537) was the first Bible printed in England. MATTHEW'S BIBLE is largely based on Coverdale's. See BUG BIBLE.

Cranmer's Bible. The name given to the GREAT BIBLE of 1540. It, and later issues, contained a prologue by Cranmer, and on the wood-cut title-page (by Holbein) Henry VIII is shown seated while Cranmer and Cromwell distribute copies to the people.

Cromwell's Bible. The GREAT BIBLE of 1539. The title-page (see CRANMER'S BIBLE) includes a portrait of Cromwell.

Douai Bible. A translation of the Vulgate, made by English Catholic scholars in France for the use of English boys designed for the Catholic priesthood. The New Testament was published at Rheims in 1582, and the Old Testament at Douai in 1609; hence sometimes called the Rheims-Douai version. See ROSIN BIBLE; also DOUAI.

Geneva Bible. A revision of great importance in the history of the English Bible, undertaken by English exiles at Geneva during the Marian persecutions and first published in 1560. It was the work of William Whittingham, assisted by Anthony Gilby and Thomas Sampson. Whittingham had previously (1557) published a translation of the New Testament. The Genevan version was the first English Bible to be printed in roman type instead of black letter, the first in which the chapters are divided into verses (taken by Whittingham from Robert Stephen's Greek-Latin Testament of 1537), and the first in which italics are used for explanatory and connective words and phrases (taken from Beza's New Testament of 1556). It was immensely popular; from 1560 to 1616 no year passed without a new edition, and at least two hundred are known. In every edition the word "breeches" occurs in *Gen.* iii. 7; hence the Geneva Bible is popularly known as the "Breeches Bible." See GOOSE BIBLE, PLACEMAKERS' BIBLE.

Great Bible. Coverdale's revision of his own Bible of 1535 (see COVERDALE'S BIBLE), collated with Tyndale's and Matthew's, printed in Paris by Regnault, and published by Grafton and Whitchurch in 1539. It is a large folio, and a splendid specimen of typography. It is sometimes called "Cromwell's Bible," as it was undertaken at his direction, and it was made compulsory for all parish churches to purchase a copy. The Prayer Book version of the Psalms comes from the November, 1540, edition of the Great Bible. See also CRANMER'S BIBLE.

King James' Bible. The AUTHORIZED VERSION.

Matthew Parker's Bible. The BISHOPS' BIBLE.

Matthew's Bible. A pronouncedly Protestant version published in 1537 as having been "truly and purely translated into English by Thomas Matthew," which was a pseudonym, adopted for purposes of safety, of John Rogers, an assistant of Tyndale. It was probably printed at Antwerp, and the text is made up of the Pentateuch from Tyndale's version together with his hitherto unprinted translation of Joshua to 2 Chronicles inclusive and his revised edition of the New Testament, with Coverdale's version of the rest of the Old Testament and the Apocrypha. It was quickly superseded by the GREAT BIBLE, but it is of importance as it formed the starting-point for the revisions which culminated in the Authorized Version. See BUG BIBLE.

Revised Version. A revision of the Authorized Version commenced under a resolution passed by both Houses of Convocation in 1870 by a body of twenty-five English scholars (assisted and advised by an American Committee), the New Testament published in 1881, the complete Bible in 1885, and the Apocrypha in 1895.

Rheims-Douai Version. See DOUAI BIBLE.

Taverner's Bible. An independent translation by a Greek scholar, Richard Taverner, printed in 1539 (the same year as the first Great Bible) by T. Petit for T. Berthelet. It had no influence on the Authorized Version, but is remarkable for its vigorous, idiomatic English, and for being the first English Bible to include a third Book of Maccabees in the Apocrypha.

Tyndale's Bible. This consists of the New Testament (printed at Cologne, 1525), the Pentateuch (Marburg, Hesse, 1530 or 1531), Jonah, Old Testament lessons appointed to be read in place of the Epistles, and a MS. translation of the Old Testament to the end of Chronicles which was afterwards used in MATTHEW'S BIBLE. His revisions of the New Testament were issued in 1534 and 1535. Tyndale's principal authority was Erasmus' edition of the Greek Testament, but he also used Erasmus' Latin translation of the same, the Vulgate, and Luther's German version. Tyndale's version fixed the style and tone of the English Bible, and subsequent Protestant versions of the books on which he worked should—with one or two minor exceptions—be looked upon as revisions of his, and not as independent translations.

Wyclif's Bible. The name given to two translations of the Vulgate, one completed in 1380 and the other a few years later, in neither of which was Wyclif concerned as a translator. Nicholas of Hereford made the first version as far as Baruch iii. 20; who was responsible for the remainder is unknown. The second version has been ascribed to John Purvey, a follower of Wyclif. The Bible of 1380 was the first complete version in English; as a whole it remained unprinted until 1850, when the monumental edition of the two versions by Forshall and Madden appeared, but in 1810 an edition of the New Testament was published by H. H. Baber, an assistant librarian at the British Museum.

(2) *specially named editions.* The following Bibles are named either from typographical errors or archaic words that they contain, or from some special circumstance in connection with them:

Adulterous Bible. The "WICKED BIBLE."

Bamberg Bible. The "THIRTY-SIX LINE BIBLE."

Bear Bible. The Spanish Protestant version printed at Basle in 1569; so called because the woodcut device on the title-page is a bear.

Bedell's Bible. A translation of the Authorized Version into Irish carried out under the direction of Bedell (d. 1642), Bishop of Kilmore and Ardagh.

Breeches Bible. The GENEVAN BIBLE was popularly so called because in it *Gen.* iii. 7, was rendered, "The eyes of them bothe were opened . . . and they sowed figge-tree leaves together, and made themselves breeches." This reading occurs in every edition of the Genevan Bible, but not in any other version, though it is given in the then unprinted Wyclif MS. ("ya sewiden ye levis of a fige tre and madin brechis"), and also in the translation of the Pentateuch given in Caxton's edition of Voragine's *Golden Legend* (1483).

Brothers' Bible. The "KRALITZ BIBLE."

Bug Bible. COVERDALE'S BIBLE of 1535, is so called because *Ps.* xci. 5, is translated, "Thou shalt not nede to be afrayed for eny bugges by night." The same reading occurs in MATTHEW'S BIBLE and its reprints; the Authorized and Revised Versions both read "terror."

Complutensian Polyglot. The great edition, in six folio volumes, containing the Hebrew and Greek texts, the Septuagint, the Vulgate, and the Chaldee paraphrase of the Pentateuch with a Latin translation, together with Greek and Hebrew grammars and a Hebrew Dictionary, prepared and printed at the expense of Cardinal Ximenes, and published at Alcala (the ancient Complutum) near Madrid, 1513–1517.

Discharge Bible. An edition printed in

1806 containing *discharge* for *charge* in 1 *Tim.* v. 21: "I *dis*charge thee before God, . . that thou observe these things, etc."

Ears to Ear Bible. An edition of 1810, in which *Matt.* xiii. 43, reads: "Who hath ears to *ear,* let him hear."

Ferrara Bible. The first Spanish edition of the Old Testament, translated from the Hebrew in 1553 for the use of the Spanish Jews. A second edition was published in the same year for Christians.

Forty-two Line Bible. The "MAZARIN BIBLE."

Goose Bible. The editions of the GENEVAN BIBLE printed at Dort; the Dort press had a goose as its device.

Gutenberg's Bible. The "MAZARIN BIBLE."

He Bible. In the two earliest editions of the Authorized Version (both 1611) in the first (now known as "the He Bible") *Ruth* iii. 15, reads: "and *he* went into the city"; the other (known as "the She Bible") has the variant *"she."* "He" is the correct translation of the Hebrew, but nearly all modern editions—with the exception of the Revised Version—perpetuate the confusion and print "she."

Idle Bible. An edition of 1809 in which "the idole shepherd" (*Zech.* xi. 17) is printed "the idle shepherd." In the Revised Version the translation is "the worthless shepherd."

Kralitz Bible. The Bible published by the United Brethren of Moravia (hence known also as the *Brothers' Bible*) at Kralitz, 1579–1593.

Leda Bible. The third edition (second folio) of the BISHOPS' BIBLE published in 1572, and so called because the decoration to the initial at the *Epistle to the Hebrews* is a startling and incongruous woodcut of Jupiter visiting Leda in the guise of a swan. This, and several other decorations in the New Testament of this edition, were from an edition of Ovid's *Metamorphoses;* they created such a storm of protest that they were never afterwards used.

Leopolita Bible. A Polish translation of the Vulgate by John of Lemberg (anc. Leopolis) published in 1561 at Cracow.

Mazarin Bible. The first printed Bible (an edition of the Vulgate), and the first large book to be printed from movable metal type. It contains no date, but was printed probably in 1455, and was certainly on sale by the middle of 1456. It was printed at Mainz, probably by Fust and Schoeffer, but as it was for long credited to Gutenberg—and it is not yet agreed that he was not responsible—it is frequently called the *Gutenberg Bible.* By bibliographers it is usually known as the *Forty-two Line Bible* (it having 42 lines to the page), to differentiate it from the Bamberg Bible of 36 lines. Its popular name is due to the fact that the copy discovered in the Mazarin Library, Paris, in 1760, was the first to be known and described.

Murderers' Bible. An edition of 1801 in which the misprint *murderers* for *murmurers* makes *Jude* 16, read: "These are murderers, complainers, walking after their own lusts, etc."

Old Cracow Bible. The "LEOPOLITA BIBLE."

Ostrog Bible. The first complete Slavonic edition; printed at Ostrog, Volhynia, Russia, in 1581.

Pfister's Bible. The "THIRTY-SIX LINE BIBLE."

Place-makers' Bible. The second edition of the GENEVA BIBLE, 1562; so called from a printer's error in *Matt.* v. 9, "Blessed are the placemakers [peacemakers], for they shall be called the children of God." It has also been called the "Whig Bible."

Printers' Bible. An edition of about 1702 which makes David pathetically complain that "printers [princes] have persecuted me without a cause" (*Ps.* cxix. 161).

Proof Bible (*Probe-Bible*). The revised version of the first impression of Luther's German Bible. A final revised edition appeared in 1892.

Rebecca's Camels Bible. An edition printed in 1823 in which *Gen.* xxiv. 61 tells us that "Rebecca arose, and her camels," instead of "her damsels."

Rosin Bible. The DOUAI BIBLE, 1609, is sometimes so called, because it has in *Jer.* viii. 22: "Is there noe rosin in Galaad." The Authorized Version translates the word by "balm," but gives "rosin" in the margin as an alternative. See TREACLE BIBLE.

Sacy's Bible. A French translation, so called from Louis Isaac le Maistre de Sacy, director of Port Royal, 1650–1679. He was imprisoned for three years in the Bastille for his Jansenist opinions, and there translated, 1667, completing the Bible a few years later, after his release.

Schelhorn's Bible. A name sometimes given to the "THIRTY-SIX LINE BIBLE."

September Bible. Luther's German translation of the New Testament, published anonymously at Wittenberg in September, 1522.

She Bible. See HE BIBLE.

Standing Fishes Bible. An edition of 1806 in which *Ezek.* xlvii. 10, reads: "And it shall come to pass that the fishes (instead of *fishers*) shall stand upon it, etc."

Thirty-Six Line Bible. A Latin Bible of 36 lines to the column, probably printed by A. Pfister at Bamberg in 1460. It is also known as the Bamberg, and Pfister's, Bible, and sometimes as Schelhorn's, as it was first described by the German bibliographer J. G. Schelhorn, in 1760.

To-remain Bible. In a Bible printed at Cambridge in 1805 *Gal.* iv. 29, reads: "Persecuted him that was born after the spirit to remain, even so it is now." The words "to remain" were added in error by the compositor, the editor having answered a proofreader's query as to the comma after "spirit" with the penciled reply "to remain" in the margin. The mistake was repeated in the first 8vo edition published by the Bible Society (1805), and again in their 12mo edition dated 1819.

Treacle Bible. A popular name for the BISHOPS' BIBLE, 1568, because in it *Jer.* viii. 22, reads: "Is there no tryacle in Gilead, is there no phisition there?" See ROSIN BIBLE. In the same Bible "tryacle" is also given for "balm" in *Jer.* xlvi. 11, and *Ezek.* xxvii. 17. Coverdale's Bible (1535) also uses the word "triacle."

Unrighteous Bible. An edition printed at Cambridge in 1653, containing the printer's error, "Know ye not that the unrighteous shall inherit [for "shall not inherit"] the Kingdom of God?" (1 *Cor.* vi. 9). The same edition gave *Rom.* vi. 13, as: "Neither yield ye your members as instruments of righteousness unto sin," in place of "*un*righteousness." This is also sometimes known as the "Wicked Bible."

Wicked Bible. So called because the word *not* is omitted in the seventh commandment, making it, "Thou shalt commit adultery." Printed at London by Barker and Lucas, 1632. The "UNRIGHTEOUS BIBLE" is also sometimes called by this name.

Wife-hater Bible. An edition of 1810 in which the word "life" in *Luke* xiv. 26, is printed "wife."

Wuyck's Bible. The Polish Bible authorized by the Roman Catholics and printed at Cracow in 1599. The translation was made by the Jesuit, Jacob Wuyck.

Zurich Bible. A German version of 1530 composed of Luther's translation of the New Testament and portions of the Old, with the remainder and the Apocrypha by other translators.

Bible in Spain, The. An account of a journey through Spain by George BORROW, published in 1843 and one of the best-known books of travel in English. It was written while the author was touring Spain as an agent of the British and Foreign Bible Society.

Biblia Pauperum, *the poor man's Bible.* A picture-book, widely used by the illiterate in the Middle Ages in place of the Bible. It was designed to illustrate the leading events in the salvation of man, and later MSS. as a rule had a Latin inscription to each picture. These *Biblia* were probably the earliest books to be printed, first from blocks and later with movable type.

bibliography. (1) The history, or better historiography, of books.

(2) A list of books compiled for a specific purpose, as a list of references to sources or on a specific topic, as a list of works dealing with Shakespeare. A critical bibliography is one in which the merits of the individual items are evaluated.

bibliomancy. Practice of prophecy by interpreting the first passage one happens on in a random opening of some book, especially the Bible.

Bibulus. Colleague of Julius Caesar, a mere cipher in office, whence his name has become proverbial for one in office who is a mere nonentity.

Bickerstaff, Isaac. A pseudonym assumed by Dean Swift, in his violent burlesque paper-war with Partridge, the almanac-maker and astrologer (1709). This Isaac Bickerstaff, entering into competition with the astrologer in his own field, solemnly predicted his death at a particular moment and afterwards announced the details of the demise. Partridge insisted that he was still very much alive, but Bickerstaff continued to argue to the contrary, and the joke was taken up and played upon for months. So popular was it that Richard Steele, editor of *The Tatler,* entitled his periodical "The Lucubrations of Isaac Bickerstaff, Esq., Astrologer" (1709–1711) and continued to write for *The Tatler* under that pseudonym. Later a real Isaac Bickerstaffe (1735?–1812?) won fame as a dramatist.

Bickerstaffe-Drew, Monsignor Count **Francis Browning Drew** (1858–1928). English Roman Catholic clergyman and author under pseudonym of John Ayscough of twenty novels.

Bicorne. A mythical beast, fabled by the early French romancers to grow very fat and well-favored through living on good and enduring husbands. It was the antitype to CHICHEVACHE.

> Chichevache (or *lean cow*) was said to live on good women; and a world of sarcasm was conveyed in always representing Chichevache as very poor,—all ribs, in fact—her food being so scarce as to keep her in a wretched state of famine. Bycorne, on the contrary, was a monster who lived on good men: and he was always bursting with fatness, like a prize pig.
> Sidney Lanier, *Shakespeare and his Forerunners,* ch. vi.

Biddle, Francis (1886–   ). American lawyer and novelist. Attorney General of U.S. 1941. His brother **George Biddle** (1885–   )

distinguished American painter and sculptor. See also CHAPIN, KATHERINE GARRISON.

Biddle, Nicholas (1786–1844). Philadelphia financier, President of Bank of United States 1819. Center of attack by Jackson against bank. Secured state charter and bank became "The Bank of the United States of Pennsylvania" (1836). Resigned in 1839.

Biddy (*i.e.* Bridget). A heroic name for an Irish servant-maid, as Mike is for an Irish laborer. These generic names are very common: for example, Tom Tug, a waterman; Jack Pudding, a buffoon; Cousin Jonathan, a citizen of the United States; Cousin Michel, a German; John Bull, an Englishman; Moll and Betty, English female servants of the lower order; Colin Tompon, a Swiss; Nic Frog, a Dutchman; Mossoo, a Frenchman; John Chinaman, and many others.

Bidpay, Bilpay, see PILPAY.

Biedermeier. After Gottlieb Biedermeier, an imaginary Philistine and author of poems written by Ludwig Eichrodt (1827–1892). A style of German furniture resembling French EMPIRE. Also applied to literature and the arts.

Bienville, Jean Baptiste Lemoyne (1680–1768). Son of Charles Lemoyne. Explorer of lower Mississippi and Red River (1699). Lieutenant of the King in Louisiana (1700); governor of the colony (1701–1712, 1718–1726, 1733–1743).

Bierce, Ambrose Gwinett (1842–1914?). American journalist and short-story writer. His best-known books are *The Fiend's Delight* (1871); *Tales of Soldiers and Civilians* (1891; later published as *In the Midst of Life*, 1898); *Can Such Things Be?* (1894); *Black Beetles in Amber* (1895); *Shapes of Clay* (1910). Bierce, with Stephen CRANE, was one of the earliest of the realists in American fiction, although the element of horror is also strong in his work.

Bifrost (Icel. *bifa,* "tremble," *rost,* "path"). In Scandinavian mythology, the bridge between heaven and earth, Asgard and Midgard; the rainbow may be considered to be this bridge, and its various colors are the reflections of its precious stones. The keeper of the bridge is HEIMDALL. At Ragnarok it will collapse under the weight of the onrushing sons of Muspelheim.

Big Apple, the. A popular American ballroom dance of the year 1937, based on the old-fashioned SQUARE DANCE.

Bigart, Homer (1907–). American journalist. In World War II he covered for the New York *Herald Tribune* London and North Africa; then, in the Pacific theater, the invasion of Leyte and the campaigns of Iwo and Okinawa. He filed the last eyewitness story of the war with Japan after returning from a bombing run over Kumagaya. Received one of the four Pulitzer Prizes for reporting (1946).

Big Ben. The name given to the large bell in the Clock Tower (or St. Stephen's Tower) at the Houses of Parliament. It weighs 13½ tons, and is named after Sir Benjamin Hall, Chief Commissioner of Works in 1856, when it was cast. *Big Ben* and *Baby Ben* are trademark names of alarm clocks on the market.

Big Bend State. Tennessee. See under STATES.

Big Bertha. A German gun in World War I with a very large bore, so called from Frau Berta (or Bertha) Krupp von Bohlen und Halbach of the huge Krupp steel and munition works in Germany. See also FRAU BERTHA, BERTHE.

Bigelow, John (1817–1911). American writer and diplomat. Co-owner with William Cullen Bryant of New York *Evening Post* (1848–1861). Author of *Life of Benjamin Franklin* (1874).

Bigelow, Poulteney (1855–). American traveler, journalist and author. Personal friend of emperor William II of Germany.

Big-endians. In Swift's GULLIVER'S TRAVELS a party in the empire of Lilliput, who make it a matter of conscience to break their eggs at the *big end*. They are looked on as heretics by the orthodox party, who break theirs at the *little end*. The BIG-ENDIANS typify the Catholics, and the LITTLE-ENDIANS the Protestants.

Big Fiddle. A story by Kay BOYLE, published in a collection entitled *The Crazy Hunter* (1940). It is a psychological study of a member of an American jazz band in England, obsessed with the memory of a prison sentence and the charge on which he was convicted.

Big Five. (1) At the Paris Peace Conference in 1919, Clemenceau for France, Lloyd George for England, Orlando for Italy, Makino for Japan, and President Wilson for the U.S.

(2) The BIG THREE (U.S., Britain, Russia) plus China and France after World War II.

Biggers, Earl Derr (1884–1933). Popular American novelist and playwright, known for *Seven Keys to Baldpate* (1913), later made into a melodrama for the stage and the motion pictures, and for Charlie Chan, a clever Chinese detective, leading character in a series of detective stories which includes: *The Chinese Parrot* (1926); *Behind That Curtain* (1928); *The Black Camel* (1929). A large number of the books in this series were made into motion pictures also, starring the late Warner Oland and the late Sidney Toler.

Biglow Papers, The. A series of satires, chiefly in verse, written in the New England vernacular by James Russell LOWELL (1846–1848; second series, 1867). The original series, published during the Mexican War, was extremely popular throughout the North, where the general feeling was that the southern states were supporting the war merely to gain more slave territory. Three typical Yankee characters, created by Lowell, express their views in the *Biglow Papers:*—Hosea Biglow, a shrewd and sensible New England farmer with a deal of wit of the homely variety and a genuine enthusiasm for the cause of freedom; Birdofredum Sawin, a good-for-nothing fellow villager who goes off to the war and becomes an unconvincing advocate of the Southern cause; and Rev. Homer Wilber, an earnest but somewhat pompous and over-scholarly country minister. The second series tells how Birdofredum Sawin married and settled in the South.

Big Money, The. A novel by John Dos PASSOS, published in 1936 and the last volume in his trilogy entitled U.S.A. It follows the pattern of the two preceding volumes in the series, THE 42ND PARALLEL and *1919,* with the same set of characters. The extravagance, abandon, and corruption of the era of the 1920's are here portrayed, culminating in the stock market crash of 1929 and the personal tragedy or moral defeat of several of the leading characters. Short biographies of representative people in the public eye at the time are included, presenting Henry FORD, Thorstein VEBLEN, Isadora DUNCAN, Frank Lloyd WRIGHT, William Randolph HEARST, the WRIGHT brothers, Samuel INSULL, and Rudolph VALENTINO.

Big Parade, The. A popular motion picture dealing with World War I, released in 1925, and written by Laurence Stallings.

big stick. A phrase popularized by Theodore Roosevelt (1858–1919), president of the United States, denoting threats with some show of warlike attitude to back them up; pressure that may be brought to bear upon recalcitrant individuals, trusts, or nations who persist in alleged wrong-doing.

Big Three. (1) In Britain, an alliance (formed in 1919) of the miners' federation, the national transport workers federation, and the national union of railway men.

(2) Since the days of World War II, Great Britain, the U.S., and Russia; often also Churchill, Roosevelt, and Stalin.

bigwig. A person in authority, a "nob." Of course, the term arises from the custom of judges, bishops, and so on, wearing large wigs.

Bikini Atoll (Marshall Islands). Scene of underwater atomic bomb test by U.S. Navy, July 1, 1946.

bill.

true bill. Under the old judicial system before a case went to the criminal Assizes it was examined by the Grand Jury whose duty it was to decide whether or not there was sufficient evidence to justify a trial. If they decided that there *was* they were said "to find a true bill"; if, on the other hand, they decided there was *not* sufficient evidence they were said "to ignore the bill." Hence *to find a true bill* is a colloquial way of saying that after proper examination one can assert that such and such a thing is true.

bill of attainder. A legislative Act, introduced and passed exactly like any other Bill, declaring a person or persons attainted. It was originally used only against offenders who fled from justice, but was soon perverted to the destruction of political opponents, etc. The last Bill of Attainder in England was that passed in 1697 for the attainting and execution of Sir John Fenwick for participation in the Assassination plot.

bill of exchange. An order transferring a named sum of money at a given date from the debtor ("drawee") to the creditor ("drawer"). The drawee having signed the bill becomes the "acceptor," and the document is then negotiable in commercial circles just as is money itself.

bill of fare. A list of the dishes provided, or which may be ordered, at a restaurant, etc.; a menu.

bill of health. A document, duly signed by the proper authorities, to certify that when the ship set sail no infectious disorder existed in the place. This is a *clean* bill of health, and the term is frequently used figuratively. A *foul bill of health* is a document to show that the place was suffering from some infection when the ship set sail. If a captain cannot show a *clean bill,* he is supposed to have a foul one.

bill of lading. A document signed by the master of a ship in acknowledgment of goods laden in his vessel. In this document he binds himself to deliver the articles in good condition to the persons named in the bill, certain exceptions being duly provided for. These bills are generally in triplicate—one for the sender, one for the receiver, and one for the master of the vessel.

bill of pains and penalties. A legislative Act imposing punishment (less than capital) upon a person charged with treason or other high crimes. It is like a BILL OF ATTAINDER, differing from it in that the punishment is never capital and the children are not affected.

bill of quantities. An abstract of the probable cost of a building, etc.

Bill of Rights. The declaration delivered to the Prince of Orange on his election to the British throne, and accepted by him, confirming the rights and privileges of the people (February 13, 1689).

(2) The first ten amendments to the Constitution of the U.S., passed in 1791 and containing guarantees of freedom of speech, press, assembly, and religion, and protection in legal matters.

bill of sale. When a person borrows money and delivers goods as security, he gives the lender a "bill of sale," that is, permission to sell the goods if the money is not returned on a stated day.

Billings, Josh. The literary name of Henry Wheeler Shaw (1818–1885), an extremely popular American humorist. For many years he published an annual known as *Josh Billings' Farmers' Allminax.*

Billingsgate. The site of an old passage through that part of the city wall that protected London on the river side: so called from the Billings, who were the royal race of the Varini, an ancient tribe mentioned by Tacitus. Billingsgate has been the site of a fish-market for many centuries, and its porters, etc., were famous for their foul and abusive language at least three hundred years ago.

> Parnassus spoke the cant of Billingsgate.
> Dryden, *Art of Poetry,* c. 1.

talk Billingsgate. To talk slang; to use foul, abusive language; to scold in a vulgar, coarse style.

Billy Barlow. A street droll, a merry-andrew; so called from a half-idiot of the name, who fancied himself some great personage. He was well known in the East of London in the early half of the 19th century, and died in Whitechapel workhouse. Some of his sayings were really witty, and some of his attitudes really droll.

bi-metallism. The employment for coinage of two metals, silver and gold, which would be of fixed relative value. Gold was the only standard metal in England and some other countries; silver coins, like copper, were mere tokens; but a gold sovereign was always of one fixed legal value. The object was to minimize the fluctuations in the value of money.

Bimini. A legendary island of the Bahama group where the FOUNTAIN OF YOUTH conferred eternal youth on all who drank its waters. Many journeys were made in search of it. There is an island called Bimini or Bemini from this legend.

Binet test, Binet-Simon test, see SIMON-BINET TEST.

Bingen, bishop of. See under HATTO.

Bingham, Alfred Mitchell (1905–). American economist and journalist. Son of Hiram Bingham, American explorer and politician. The younger Bingham founded a journal, *Common Sense,* in 1932 with Selden Rodman. His writings include *Insurgent America, Man's Estate, The United States of Europe,* etc.

Binnie, James. In Thackeray's NEWCOMES, an amiable Scotch bachelor of the Indian Civil Service who lives for a time with Colonel Newcome in London.

Binns, Archie (1899–). American novelist, author of *Lightship* (1934); *The Laurels Are Cut Down* (1937); *The Land Is Bright* (1939); and other books dealing with the Northwest.

Binyon, Laurence (1860–1943). English poet and art historian. In charge of Oriental prints and drawings, British Museum (1913–1932). Author of works on Chinese, Japanese, and East Indian art; translated Dante. *Collected Poems* (1931).

Biographia Literaria. Volume of essays on literary criticism and aesthetics by COLERIDGE, published in 1817. The poetic theory expressed by the author here was found particularly interesting by the 20th-century English critic I. A. RICHARDS and publicized in his own aesthetic studies.

Biography. See BEHRMAN, S. N.

Bion. Greek pastoral poet of Smyrna, 3rd or 2nd century B.C. A contemporary of THEOCRITUS. Best known for *Lament for Adonis.*

Biondello. In Shakespeare's *Taming of the Shrew,* one of the servants of Lucentio, the future husband of Bianca.

Birch, Harvey. The patriotic peddler hero of Cooper's novel THE SPY.

Birch, Reginald (1856–1943). English-born American illustrator, first famous for a depiction of Frances Hodgson Burnett's LITTLE LORD FAUNTLEROY. Illustrator for magazines and many books. Noted for pen-and-ink work of great delicacy and charm.

Birches. A poem by Robert FROST (1916).

Birchin Lane. *I must send you to Birchin Lane, i.e.* whip you. The play is on *birch* (a rod).

a suit in Birchin Lane. Birchin Lane was once famous for all sorts of apparel; references to second-hand clothes in Birchin Lane are common enough in Elizabethan books.

Passing through Birchin Lane amidst a camp-royal of hose and doublets, I took . . . occasion to slip into a captain's suit—a valiant buff doublet stuffed with points and a pair of velvet slops scored thick with lace.

Middleton, *Black Book* (1604).

bird. This is the Middle English and Anglo-Saxon *brid* (occasionally *byrde* in M.E.), which meant only the *young* of feathered flying animals, *foul, foule,* or *fowel* being the M.E. corresponding to the modern *bird.* Cf. German *Vogel* "bird." An endearing name for a girl.

And by my word, your bonnie bird
In danger shall not tarry;
So, though the waves are raging white,
I'll row you o'er the ferry.
Campbell, *Lord Ullin's Daughter.*

This use of the word is probably connected with BURD, a poetic word for a lady which has long been obsolete, except in ballads.

a bird in the hand is worth two in the bush. Possession is better than expectation.

bird of passage. A person who shifts from place to place; a temporary visitant, like a cuckoo, the swallows, starlings, etc.

bird of Juno. The peacock.

bird of Washington. The American eagle.

Arabian bird. The phoenix.

birds of Diomedes. Swans.

The Blue Bird. See under BLUE.

Bird in Space. See BRANCUSI, CONSTANTIN.

Birds, The. A famous comedy by Aristophanes (414 B. C.) in which "the birds" construct a cloud city (see CLOUD CUCKOO LAND) in midair and enter into friendly relations with the gods.

Birds and Poets. See BURROUGHS, JOHN.

Birds, Beasts, and Flowers. See LAWRENCE, D. H.

Birds' Christmas Carol, The. A Christmas tale by Kate Douglas Wiggin (*Am.* 1888).

Birmingham, George A. Pseudonym of James Owen HANNAY.

Birmingham Poet. John Freeth, who died at the age of seventy-eight in 1808. He was wit, poet, and publican, who not only wrote the words and tunes of songs, but sang them also, and sang them well.

Biron. In Shakespeare's LOVE'S LABOUR'S LOST, a merry mad-cap young lord, in attendance on Ferdinand, king of Navarre. Biron promises to spend three years with the King in study, during which time no woman is to approach his court; but no sooner has he signed the compact than he falls in love with Rosaline.

Birotteau, César. The hero of Balzac's novel, *César Birotteau* (*L'Histoire de la grandeur et de la décadence de César Birotteau*), a dealer in perfumes who is allied with the militant royalists. When he is admitted into the Legion of Honor, he gives a great ball in honor of the occasion. The necessary changes in his apartments, together with unfortunate speculations, ruin him completely. He now devotes himself to the task of paying off his creditors and succeeds within three years, but dies soon afterward.

Birrell, Augustine (1850–1933). English essayist and statesman. Author of *Obiter Dicta.*

birth control. Control, usually limitation, of the number of children born, by conscious regulation of impregnation. Many books have been written concerning birth control, including those by Margaret SANGER. Opposition to birth control on religious grounds argues that the birth of a child is considerably more than purely a matter of biology.

Birthmark, The. An allegory by HAWTHORNE published in 1845 in *Mosses from an Old Manse.* It tells of Aylmer, a scientist with a passion for perfection, who kills his beautiful wife Georgiana by removing a small birthmark from her cheek, the one flaw in her beauty.

Birth of a Nation, The. A motion picture dealing with the Civil War period in the South, produced in 1915 by D. W. GRIFFITH and the first of the gigantic screen "epics" for which Hollywood later became famous.

bisexual. Of both sexes. Hermaphroditic. This state of nature, frequent in flowers, not rare in animals, is now recognized as a compelling force in human psychology and hence in certain areas of literature.

bishop.

bishop Barnaby. The Maybug, lady-bird, etc.

Bishop of Chester. The wealth of the Bishopric of Chester in the 15th century was proverbial; hence the satiric expression *as poor as the Bishop of Chester.*

Bishop of Hippo. St. Augustine (354–430) is often so referred to. He held the See for many years.

Bishop's Bible. See under BIBLE.

Age of the Bishops. See AGE.

Bishop, Bridget. One of the women accused by Cotton MATHER of witchcraft during the celebrated trials in Massachusetts at the end of the 17th century. She is mentioned in Mather's WONDERS OF THE INVISIBLE WORLD.

Bishop, Isabel (1902–). American artist, instructor of life painting and composition at the Art Students League, New York City (1936–1937); represented in Whitney Museum, Metropolitan Museum, Corcoran Art Galleries, etc. Member of National Institute of Arts and Letters.

Bishop, John Peale (1891–1944). American poet and novelist. His poetry includes *The*

Undertaker's Garland (1922) (with Edmund Wilson); *Now With His Love* (1933); *Minute Particulars* (1935). He was also the author of *Many Thousands Gone* (1931), stories, and *Act of Darkness* (1935).

Bishop Blougram's Apology. A dramatic monologue by Browning in his *Men and Women* (1885). The speaker is Sylvester Blougram, a bishop who confesses to intellectual scepticism yet continues to stand before the world as an exponent of doctrines he no longer holds. He justifies his position to Gigadibs, a young poet.

Bismarck, in full Prince **Otto Eduard Leopold von Bismarck-Schönhausen** (1815–1898). Prussian statesman who brought about the foundation of the German Reich in 1871 at the end of the Franco-Prussian war. Called the "Iron Chancellor" of Germany (1871–1890). The event of his resignation, precipitated by his disagreement with Emperor William II, was interpreted by the London *Punch* in a famous cartoon, "Dropping the Pilot," in which the young emperor watches his dejected Chancellor leaving the ship, where he remains in sole command.

Bismarck of Asia. Li Hung Chang (1823–1901), the Chinese statesman; so called after Otto von BISMARCK.

Bitter Sweet. (1) A long narrative poem by J. G. HOLLAND (1858), at one time widely read. Its characters are Israel, a good old New England farmer, and his numerous children and grandchildren, gathered together in the old homestead for Thanksgiving Day.

(2) An operetta by Noel COWARD (1929).

Bixion, Jean-Jacques. A keen-witted cartoonist and humorist who appears in many of the novels of Balzac's *Comédie humaine*. He was one of the lesser officials of the Civil Service, where he exercised his talent for caricature and practical jokes in unofficial moments.

Bizet, Alexandre César Léopold, called *Georges* (1838–1875). French composer, best known for his suite of incidental music to Alphonse DAUDET's play, *L'Arlésienne* (1872), and for his opera CARMEN (1875). The latter was NIETZSCHE's favorite opera after he had turned his back on WAGNER's music.

Björkman, Edwin August (1866–). Swedish-American novelist and critic. Editor of the Modern Drama series which introduced Strindberg, Björnson, and Schnitzler to an American audience. Translated Georg Brandes' *Jesus, A Myth* (1926).

Bjørnson, Bjørnstjerne (1832–1910). Norwegian dramatist, known for his plays of his native country. His works include *Between the Battles* (1852); *Lame Hulda* (1858); *Sigurd Slembe* (1862); *Mary Stuart in Scotland* (1864); *The Newly Married* (1868); *The Editor* (1874); *The King* (1877); *A Gauntlet* (1883); *Beyond Our Power* (1883); *Geography and Love* (1885); *Paul Lange and Tora Parsburg* (1898); *Laboremus* (1901); *Dayland* (1904); *When the New Wine Blooms* (1909).

black. In blazonry, the symbol of prudence, wisdom, and constancy. In art, it represents evil and error, and as a mortuary color, grief and death; by extension of the latter, it is the church decoration for Good Friday. See under COLORS for other information on symbolism and usage.

black and blue. Bruised.

in black and white. In plain writing, the paper being white and the ink black.

swear black is white. To persist in an obvious untruth.

Blacks. (1) Mutes at funerals. (2) An Italian faction of the 14th century. See NERI.

Black and Tan. Member of the irregular force enlisted in 1920 for service in Ireland as auxiliaries to the Royal Irish Constabulary. So called because their original uniform was the army khaki with the black leather accouterments of the R.I.C.

black art. The art practiced by conjurors, wizards, and others who professed to have dealings with the devil; so called from the idea that necromancy was connected with the Lat. *niger,* black.

Black Assize. July 6, 1577, when a putrid pestilence broke out at Oxford during the time of assize.

be in one's black books. In bad odor; in disgrace; out of favor. A *black book* is a book recording the names of those who are in disgrace or have merited punishment. Amherst, in his *Terrae Filius, or the Secret History of the Universities of Oxford* (1726), speaks of the Proctor's black book, and tells us that no one can proceed to a degree whose name is found there.

Black Code. Legislation regulating the treatment of Negroes in the southern part of the United States before the emancipation of the slaves. Properly, the *Code Noir* or Black Code, introduced by Bienville, the French governor of Louisiana, about 1723.

Black Death. A plague which ravaged Europe in 1348–1351; a putrid typhus, in which the body rapidly turned black.

black diamond. Coal. Coal and diamonds are both forms of carbon.

Black Douglas. William Douglas, lord of Nithsdale (d. 1390).

black flag. The banner of a pirate ship; hence a symbol of defiance to the law. The pirate flag was usually decorated with skull and cross-bones and known as the "Jolly Roger." The name *Black Flag* has been given to (1) Moslem soldiers, from the black banner of the Abbasides; (2) Chinese sea pirates who opposed the French in Tonquin.

Black Friars. The Dominican monks; so called from their black cloaks. The district of this name in the City of London is the site of a large monastery of Dominicans who used to possess rights of sanctuary, etc.

Black Friday. (1) May 11, 1866, the date of the failure of Overend and Gurney, the Glasgow bankers, which led to a financial panic.

(2) Dec. 6, 1745, the day on which the news reached London that the Young Pretender had reached Derby.

(3) In the United States Sept. 24, 1869, and Sept. 18, 1873, days of financial panic in New York.

(4) Good Friday, on account of the black vestments worn in the Roman Catholic Church.

black gown. A parson, collegian, or other learned man, in allusion to the uniform of the two former classes.

Black Hand. A secret organization, especially among Italians, with the object of blackmail or lawlessness. The name comes from a former society in Spain with anarchistic aims.

Black Hawk War (1831–1832). A war of the U.S. against the Sac and Fox Indians whose leader was Black Hawk.

black hole. The lock-up in military barracks. It was the official British term until 1868. The allusion is to the so-called *Black Hole of Calcutta,* a dark, small, suffocating cell into which Suraja Dowlah thrust 146 British prisoners (1756), only twenty-three of whom survived.

Black Jack. (1) A nickname given to the American general, John Alexander Logan (1826–1886), on account of his complexion and hair.

(2) A nickname of General John J. Pershing (1860–   ), commander-in-chief of the A.E.F. in World War I. See also BLACKJACK.

black letter. The heavy Gothic type used generally by the early printers in England. Hence, *black-letter dogs* are literary antiquaries who pry into every corner to find out black-letter copies of books.

black-letter day. An unlucky day; one to be recalled with regret. The Romans marked their unlucky days with a piece of black charcoal, and their lucky ones with white chalk.

black list. A list of persons in disgrace, or who have incurred censure or punishment; a list of bankrupts for the private guidance of the mercantile community.

black looks. Looks of displeasure. *To look black.* To look displeased. The figure is from black clouds indicative of foul weather.

Black Maria. The van which conveys prisoners from the police courts to jail. There is an unsupported tradition that the term originated in America. Maria Lee, a Negress of great size and strength, kept a sailors' boarding house in Boston, and when constables required help it was a common thing to send for "Black Maria," who soon collared the refractory men and led them to the lock-up.

During World War I *Black Maria* was one of the names given to large enemy shells that emitted dense smoke on bursting.

Black Man. The Evil One.

Black Monday. Easter Monday, April 14, 1360, was so called. Edward III was with his army lying before Paris, and the day was so dark, with mist and hail, so bitterly cold and so windy, that many of his horses and men died. Monday after Easter holidays is called "Black Monday," in allusion to this fatal day.

> It was not for nothing that my nose fell a-bleeding on Black Monday last, at six o'clock i' the morning.
> Shakespeare, *Merchant of Venice,* ii. 5.

February 27, 1865, was so called in Melbourne from a terrible sirocco from the N.N.W., which produced dreadful havoc between Sandhurst and Castlemain; the schoolboys give the name to the first Monday after the holidays are over, when lessons begin again.

Black Prince. Edward, Prince of Wales (1330–1376), eldest son of Edward III. Froissart says he was "styled black by terror of his arms." The appellation is sometimes thought to refer to the color of his armor, but usually to his martial deeds.

Black Republic. Hayti; a West Indian state formed for the most part of Negroes.

Black Republicans. Republican opponents of slavery, during the period which preceded the American Civil War.

Black Rod. The short title of an English Court official, who is styled fully "Gentleman Usher of the Black Rod," so called from his staff of office—a black wand surmounted by a golden lion.

Black Saturday. Aug. 4, 1621; so called in Scotland, because a violent storm occurred at the very moment the Parliament was sitting to enforce episcopacy on the people.

black sheep. A disgrace to the family or community. Black sheep are looked on with dislike by some shepherds, and are not so valuable as white ones. See also BÊTE NOIRE.

Black Shirt. One of the Italian Fascisti under Mussolini. The black shirt was the distinctive part of their uniforms.

black swan. A very rare thing.

Black Thursday. Feb. 6, 1851, is so called

in the colony of Victoria, from a terrible bush fire which occurred on that day.

Blackacre, Widow. In Wycherley's comedy, *The Plain Dealer* (1677), a masculine, litigious, pettifogging, headstrong woman. She is considered the best of Wycherley's comic characters.

blackamoor. A Negro, especially one from Africa. Hence the phrase *wash the blackamoor white—i.e.,* be engaged upon a hopeless and useless task. The allusion is to one of Aesop's fables.

Black April. See PETERKIN, JULIA.

Black Armour. See WYLIE, ELINOR.

blackballed. Excluded from a club. In voting by ballot, those who accept the person proposed used to drop a white or red ball into the box, but those who would exclude the candidate a black one.

Black Bands (Fr. *Bandes Noires*). 16th century infantry distinguished by their famous leader, Giovanni delle Bande Nere, Italian General.

Black Beauty, his Grooms and Companions. An imaginary autobiography of the horse, Black Beauty, by Anna Sewall, pleading for kindness in the treatment of animals.

black bottom. A popular American dance of the jazz period (ca. 1925), violent and acrobatic, of Negro origin. See JAZZ. The title refers to the deposits of black soil on the banks of the Mississippi River.

Black Cat, The. A horror tale by Edgar Allan POE, published in 1845.

Black Crook, The. A play with music and dancing, by Charles M. Barras, produced in 1866. It was the first successful American revue (produced at Niblo's Garden), and brought nearly a million dollars to its producer. Revived by Christopher Morley in Hoboken in a carefully planned mélange of all the versions from Barras to the version of 1891, the text was that of the original version "with some small mischievous editing." Harry Wagstaff Gribble directed this revival and Cleon Throckmorton made the sets.

Black Dwarf, The. A novel by Sir Walter Scott (1816). The Black Dwarf (see also DWARF) is called Elshander the Recluse or Cannie Elshie, the Wise Wight of Mucklestane Moor, but is in reality Sir Edward MAULEY. Embittered by his deformity and his own experience, he lives a solitary existence, but gives help to many who seek him out and finally declares his identity in order to prevent a forced marriage between Isabella Vere and Sir Frederick Langley. The character of the Black Dwarf is said to have been drawn from David Ritchie, whose cottage was on Manor Water in the county of Peebles.

blackjack. (1) A large leather bottle tarred on the outside.

(2) A pirate flag.

Black Masters, The. An allegorical play by Leonid ANDREYEV, produced in 1908. The black masters are evil thoughts assailing and overwhelming the human soul.

Blackmore, Richard Doddridge (1825–1900). English novelist, author of LORNA DOONE.

Blackmur, Richard P. (1904–). American literary critic and poet, known for his interpretations and analyses of the work of such 20th-century poets as E. E. CUMMINGS, Hart CRANE, and Wallace STEVENS. His books include *The Double Agent: Essays in Craft and Elucidation* (1935); *From Jordan's Delight* (1937), poems; and *The Expense of Greatness* (1940), a collection of criticism.

Black Oxen. A novel by Gertrude ATHERTON (1923), built around a current fad of the time of rejuvenation by the transfer of animal glands to human bodies.

Black Riders, The, and Other Lines. A book of poetry in free verse by Stephen CRANE, published in 1895 and considered to be a forerunner of the IMAGIST style.

Blackstick, Fairy. The fairy of Thackeray's ROSE AND THE RING.

Blackstone, Sir William (1723–1780). An English jurist, author of the famous *Commentaries* bearing his name which are fundamental in any study of English law. Hence Blackstone is synonymous with the law.

Black Tulip, The. A historical romance by Alexander DUMAS (1895), dealing with 17th century Dutch history, particularly the struggle between the patriotic De Witt brothers and their enemies, who gained the support of William of Orange. The novel treats also of the famous Haarlem tulip craze; hence the name.

Black Watch. A Highland regiment, originating in the 18th century, now territorials known as the Royal Highlanders, wearing kilts of dark tartan.

Blackwell, Alice Stone (1857–). The daughter of Lucy STONE and a great organizer of woman suffrage. A translator of much foreign poetry.

Blackwood, Algernon (1869–). English novelist and short story writer of the supernatural and mystical. One of his best books is *John Silence,* a series of stories about a psychical detective.

Blackwood's Magazine. An English literary periodical, started in 1817. J. G. LOCKHART and James HOGG were members of its staff. Its political sympathies were Tory, and it was violently opposed to the "COCKNEY SCHOOL" of poets. Its attack on Keats in this connection was considered by some of his friends to have been responsible for his death.

Blair, Adam, see ADAM BLAIR.

Blake, George (1893–). Scottish editor and novelist.

Blake, Goody, see GOODY BLAKE.

Blake, Nicholas. Pseudonym of Cecil DAY LEWIS.

Blake, William (1757–1827). Famous English poet and engraver, known for his mysticism, humanitarianism, sentiment, and complex symbolism. His works, in which both text and illustrations were engraved, include POETICAL SKETCHES (1783); SONGS OF INNOCENCE (1787); SONGS OF EXPERIENCE (1794); and the volumes in his series of so-called "Prophetic Books"—THE BOOK OF THEL (1787), THE MARRIAGE OF HEAVEN AND HELL (1790), THE GATES OF PARADISE (1793), THE VISION OF THE DAUGHTERS OF ALBION (1793), JERUSALEM (1804), THE EMANATION OF THE GIANT ALBION (1804), and MILTON (1804). For a discussion of Blake's symbolism, cf. *William Blake: His Philosophy and Symbols,* by S. Foster Damon.

Blake, William. Pseudonym and adaptation of **William James Blech** (1894–). American author, husband of Christina STEAD. *The World is Mine: The Story of a Modern Monte Cristo* (1938); *An American Looks at Karl Marx* (1939); *The Copperheads* (1941), etc.

Blakelock, Ralph Albert (1847–1919). American landscape painter. After years of struggle and neglect, recognized by the National Academy.

Blanchard, Jenny and **Emmy.** The principal characters in Frank Swinnerton's NOCTURNE.

Blancheflor. The heroine of the Old French metrical romance, *Floris et Blancheflor,* which was used by BOCCACCIO as the basis of his prose romance, *Il Filocopo.* The old story tells of a young Christian prince who falls in love with the Saracen slavegirl with whom he has been brought up. They are parted, but after many adventures he rescues her unharmed from the harem of the Emir of Babylon. It is a widespread story, and is substantially the same as that of Dorigen and Aurelius by CHAUCER, and that of Dianora and Ansaldo in the *Decameron.* See DORIGEN.

Blancove, Edward. The seducer of Dahlia Fleming in Meredith's novel, RHODA FLEMING.

Blandish, Serena. Title of a book by Enid BAGNOLD (Lady Jones).

Blane, Neil. The landlord of the Howf in Scott's OLD MORTALITY, also the town piper.

blank verse. Rhymeless verse. In English prosody the term refers to unrhymed iambic pentameter. Shakespeare and Milton wrote almost entirely in blank verse.

> The qua | lity | of mer | cy is | not strained
> It drop | peth as | the gen | tle dew | from heaven
> Upon | the place | beneath; | it is | twice blessed.
> Shakespeare, *Merchant of Venice.*

blanket.

wet blanket. A discouragement; hence a marplot or spoil-sport. A person is a wet blanket who discourages a proposed scheme. "A wet blanket influence" etc. A wet blanket is used to smother fire, or to prevent one escaping from a fire from being burnt.

the wrong side of the blanket. An illegitimate child is said to come of the wrong side of the blanket.

> He grew up to be a fine waule fallow, like mony ane that comes o' the wrang side o' the blanket.
> Scott, *The Antiquary,* ch. xxiv.

Blanketeers. The name given to a body of some 5,000 working men out of employment who assembled on St. Peter's Field, Manchester, March 10, 1817, and provided themselves with blankets intending to march to London, to lay before the Prince Regent a petition of grievances. Only six got as far as Ashbourne Bridge, when the expedition collapsed.

In more recent times journalists have applied the name to similar bodies of unemployed, both in Great Britain and in America.

blarney. Soft, wheedling speeches to gain some end; flattery, or lying, with unblushing effrontery. Blarney is a village near Cork. Legend has it that Cormac McCarthy held its castle in 1602, and concluded an armistice with Carew, the Lord President, on condition of surrendering the fort to the English garrison. Day after day his lordship looked for the fulfillment of the terms, but received nothing but soft speeches, till he became the laughing-stock of Elizabeth's ministers, and the dupe of the Lord of Blarney.

Blarney Stone. In the wall of the castle at Blarney, about twenty feet from the top and difficult of access, is a triangular stone containing this inscription: "Cormac McCarthy *fortis me fieri fecit, A.D.* 1446." Tradition says that to whomever can kiss this is given the power of being able to obtain all his desires by cajolery. As it is almost impossible to reach, a substitute has been provided by the custodians of the castle, and it is said that this is in every way as efficacious as the original.

Blas, Gil, see GIL BLAS.

Blasco Ibáñez, Vicente (1867–1928). Spanish novelist, author of internationally best-selling books with life in Spain as a background for their melodramatic plots. Well known among the English-speaking public are: *The Shadow of the Cathedral* (*La Catedral;* 1903); *Blood and Sand* (*Sangre y Arena;*

1908); THE FOUR HORSEMEN OF THE APOCALYPSE (*Los Cuatro Jinetes del Apocalipsis;* 1916); MARE NOSTRUM (Our Sea; 1918). The last three were made into successful American motion pictures during the 1920's. As an ardent republican he finally fled to South America and died in exile at Mentone, France.

Blashfield, Edwin Howland (1848–1936). American painter, especially of murals. Decorated central dome in the Library of Congress, Washington, D.C.

Blatant Beast. In Spenser's *Faërie Queene* "a dreadful fiend of gods and men, ydrad"; the type of calumny or slander. He was begotten of Cerberus and Chimaera, and has a hundred tongues and a sting; with his tongues he speaks things "most shameful, most unrighteous, most untrue"; and with his sting "steeps them in poison." Sir Artegal pursues him and Sir Calidore muzzles the monster, and draws him with a chain to Faërie Land. The beast breaks his chain and regains his liberty. The word "blatant" seems to have been coined by Spenser, and he never uses it except as an epithet for this monster, who is not mentioned till the twelfth canto of the fifth book. It is probably derived from the provincial word *blate,* meaning to bellow or roar.

Blathers and Duff. In Dickens' OLIVER TWIST, detectives who investigate the burglary in which Bill Sikes had a hand.

Blaue Reiter. German school of painting, founded in 1912 and located near Munich. The name is derived from the title of a manifesto of the group, *Der Blaue Reiter* (*The Blue Knight*), published in 1912. The chief influence on the group came from folk art, the religious art of the Middle Ages, and children's drawings. Subjects were principally farm landscapes and animals. Vassily KANDINSKY, Franz Marc, and Heinrich Campendonck were among the members of the school. See also BRÜCKE.

Blavatsky, Helena Petrovna (1831–1891). A famous spiritualist and theosophist, who toured Europe, the U.S., Egypt, and India, preaching her doctrines and engaging in wild adventures. She is generally referred to as Mme. Blavatsky.

Bleak House. A novel by Dickens (1852). The heroine is Esther SUMMERSON or rather Esther Hawdon, the illegitimate child of Lady Dedlock and Captain Hawdon. Esther, whom Lady Dedlock believes dead, is the ward of Mr. Jarndyce of the interminable case of Jarndyce and JARNDYCE in Chancery Court, and lives with him at Bleak House. Lord Dedlock's lawyer, Mr. Tulkinghorn, gets wind of Lady Dedlock's secret past; and when Tulkinghorn is murdered, Lady Dedlock is suspected, disappears and is later found dead.

Blefuscu. In Swift's *Gulliver's Travels,* an island inhabited by pigmies. It is situated northeast of Lilliput, from which it is separated by a channel 800 yards wide. It is supposed to represent France.

Blenheim, Battle of. See under BATTLES, FIFTEEN DECISIVE. Robert SOUTHEY wrote a ballad of this title and on this event in 1798.

Blenheim Steps. There was an anatomical school, over which Sir Astley Cooper presided at Blenheim Steps, Bond Street. Here "resurrectionists" were sure to find a ready mart for their gruesome wares, for which they received sums of money varying from £3 to £10, and sometimes more. Hence, *going to Blenheim Steps,* going to be dissected, or unearthed from one's grave.

Blennerhassett (1901). A novel by Charles Felton Pidgin (1844–1923) concerning the wealthy ostracized Englishman, Harman Blennerhassett (1765–1831), who gave financial aid to Aaron Burr's conspiracy. Many other works have been written about Blennerhassett and the Burr conspiracy. Cf., e.g., Rupert Sargent Holland's (1878–) *Secret of Blennerhassett* (1941) and William Henry Venable's (1836–1920) *A Dream of Empire.*

Blessed Damozel, The. A poem by Dante Gabriel Rossetti (1850) giving expression to the longing of the "blessed damozel" in heaven for her lover on earth.

> The blesséd damozel leaned out
> From the gold bar of Heaven;
> Her eyes were deeper than the depth
> Of waters stilled at even;
> She had three lilies in her hand,
> And the stars in her hair were seven.

Blessington, Countess of, *née* **Marguerite Power** (1789–1849). Irish woman of letters. Literary salon. Author of personal reminiscences, including *Conversations with Lord Byron* (1834). Subject of Michael Sadleir's *The Strange Life of Lady Blessington* (1933).

Blifil. A noted character in Fielding's TOM JONES. He pretends to be Tom Jones' friend, but is in reality a hypocritical villain of the deepest dye.

Bligh, Captain. Captain of H.M.S. BOUNTY during the voyage when the famous mutiny took place in 1789. He was seized by Fletcher CHRISTIAN and others and set adrift in an open boat with 18 of the loyal crew. See HALL, JAMES NORMAN and NORDHOFF, CHARLES.

blighter. Slightly contemptuous but good-natured British slang for a man, a fellow; generally with the implication that he is a bit of a scamp or, at the moment, somewhat obnoxious.

Blighty. Soldiers' slang for the homeland. It came into popular use during World War I, but was well known to soldiers who had served in India long before. It is the Urdu Vilayati or Bilati, an adjective meaning provincial, removed at some distance; hence adopted by the military for England.

Blimber, Dr. In Dickens' novel DOMBEY AND SON, head of a school for the sons of gentlemen, at Brighton.

Cornelia Blimber. Daughter of Dr. Blimber, a slim young lady, who keeps her hair short and wears spectacles. Miss Blimber has "no nonsense about her," but has grown "dry and sandy with working in the graves of dead languages." She marries Mr. Feeder, B.A., Dr. Blimber's usher.

Blimp, Colonel. Imaginary British officer, fussy and mossbound.

Blind, The (*Les Aveugles*). A symbolic play by Maurice MAETERLINCK, produced in 1890. In the figures of blind men and women, guided by a returned dead priest, is represented confused mankind, led by outworn doctrines.

blind alley. A *cul de sac,* an alley with no outlet; hence a state or condition affording no opportunity for progress. Similar metaphors are *blind nettle, blind siding, blind stitch* etc.

blind bard or **poet, the.** Homer. The tradition of Homer's blindness may be related to the fact that the precious stones which Greek sculptors used in their statues as eyes have generally been removed. Byron in his *Bride of Abydos* calls Homer the Blind old Man of Scio's rocky Isle.

Blind Beggar of Bethnal Green. See under BESSEE.

Blind Bow-Boy. A novel (1923) by Carl VAN VECHTEN.

Blind Boy. Cupid. Love is blind or supposed to be.

blind department. In British Post Office parlance, that department where letters with insufficient, or illegible addresses are examined. The clerk so employed is called "the blind man."

Blind Fireworks. See MACNEICE, LOUIS.

blind harper, the. John Parry, who died in 1739.

Blind Harry. A Scotch minstrel of the 15th century. His epic of *Sir William Wallace* runs to 11,861 lines.

blind leaders of the blind. An allusion to pharisees (*Matt.* xv. 14). Cf. Brueghel the Younger's painting of *Blind Leaders of the Blind.*

blindman's buff. A very old and well-known children's game. "Buff" here is short for "buffet," and is an allusion to the three buffs or pats which the "blind man" gets when he has caught a player.

blindman's holiday. The hour of dusk, when it is too dark to work, and too soon to light candles.

Blind Raftery. See DONN-BYRNE.

Bliss. One of the best known and most characteristic of the short stories of Katherine MANSFIELD, published in 1920. It depicts the sudden disintegration of a woman's happiness on discovering that her husband is unfaithful.

Blithedale Romance, The. A novel by Nathaniel HAWTHORNE, published in 1852 and based on the community of BROOK FARM. It tells of the relations among the people Miles COVERDALE, a writer, encounters at Blithedale, an experimental community near Boston. See ZENOBIA; PRISCILLA; HOLLINGSWORTH.

Blitzstein, Marc (1905–). American playwright and composer, of proletarian sympathies, best known for *The Cradle Will Rock* (1937), an experimental play with music on a capital-*vs.*-labor theme.

Bliven, Bruce (1889–). American journalist. Member of editorial board of *The New Republic,* 1923–1946; editorial director from 1946. Author of *Men Who Make the Future* (1942).

Blixen, Karen Dinesen, Baronesse (1883–). See DINESEN, ISAK.

Blizzard State. South Dakota. See under STATES.

Bloch, Ernest (1880–). Swiss-born composer, living in the U.S., known for the Hebraic flavor of his music and his frequent use of ancient Hebrew themes. He wrote chamber music, symphonic poems, music for voice and orchestra, and five symphonies, including *Israel* (1912–1915) and one entitled *America* (1927).

Bloch, Jean-Richard (1884–1947). French novelist, playwright, poet, critic, and social thinker.

block book. A book printed from engraved wood blocks, in a technique in sporadic use before the time of the invention of movable letters by Gutenberg.

Blok, Aleksandr Aleksandrovich (1880–1921). Russian poet. Author, in *The Twelve,* of a poem reflecting the initial phase of the bolshevik revolution "with quintessential succinctness." One of the great post-revolutionary Russian poets.

Blondel de Nesle. A troubadour who appears in Scott's TALISMAN.

Blondie. Heroine of a popular series of newspaper comics, radio sketches, and motion pictures (ca. 1940). She and her husband Dagwood are typical in their lives and problems of young American married couples of the "white collar" class. Played in the movies by Penny Singleton, with Arthur Lake as Dagwood.

Blondin, Charles (1824–1897). Pseudonym for Jean François Gravelet, French tight-rope walker famous in his time. Crossed Niagara Falls on tight-rope in 1855, 1859, 1860.

blood. (1) Family descent. (2) A buck, an aristocratic rowdy. A term taken from blood horses.

blood is thicker than water. Relationship has a claim which is generally acknowledged.

a Prince of the Blood. One of the Royal Family.

bad blood. Anger, ill-feeling and contention.

blue blood. See under BLUE.

young blood. Fresh members; as, "To bring young blood into the concern."

in cold blood. Deliberately; not in the excitement of passion or of battle.

it makes one's blood boil. It provokes indignation and anger.

it runs in the blood. It is inherited or exists in the family race.

one's own flesh and blood. One's own children, brothers, sisters or other near kindred.

field of blood. ACELDAMA. Cf. *Acts* i, 19.

the Man of Blood. Charles I; so called by the Puritans on account of his armed opposition to them.

blood-and-iron policy. A relentless policy of war. The phrase was popularized though not coined by the German statesman, Otto von BISMARCK, in a speech before the Budget Commission of the Prussian House of Delegates in 1862. Hence Bismarck is known as *the man of blood and iron.*

blood and thunder. Cheap sensationalism and violence, such as characterizes melodrama.

blood brother. One who is bound by a blood bond, either by birth or as the result of a ceremonial mingling of blood. It is not customary to speak of *blood* sisters.

blood money. Money paid to a person for giving such evidence as shall lead to the conviction of another; money paid to the next of kin to induce him to forgo his "right" of seeking blood for blood, or (formerly) as compensation for the murder of his relative; money paid to a person for betraying another, as Judas was paid blood money for his betrayal of the Savior.

blood of the Grograms. Taffety gentility; make-believe aristocratic blood. Grogram is a coarse silk taffety stiffened with gum (Fr., *gros-grain*).

See also the FIVE BLOODS OF IRELAND.

Blood, Captain. Chivalrous pirate, in romance of that name by Rafael Sabatini (1922).

Blood, Captain Thomas. A villainous historical character (1628–1680) who appears in Scott's *Peveril of the Peak*. He was "a robber from his cradle, a murderer since he could hold a knife."

Blood, Lydia. Heroine of W. D. Howells' LADY OF THE AROOSTOOK.

Blood Council or **Council of Blood.** Supreme tribunal established 1567 in Netherlands by the Duke of ALVA to punish the enemies of Spanish rule and the Roman church.

blood pudding. A kind of sausage made of blood and flour, almost black in color. Fry it in lard.

Bloody Angle. A section of the battlefield of Spottsylvania Court House, Virginia, where on May 11 and 12, 1864, the armies of Grant and Lee fought one of the bloodiest battles of the American Civil War.

> Fallen down like stars to spangle
> Earth, upon the Bloody Angle.
> Elinor Wylie, *Miranda's Supper.*

Bloody Assizes. Conducted in 1685 by Lord Chief Justice JEFFREYS of hated memory, after the collapse of Monmouth's Rebellion. An example of relentless cruelty.

Bloody Brook. A brook near South Deerfield, Mass., in Franklin County. So called because it was the scene of an Indian massacre in 1675.

bloody hand. A term in old Forest Law denoting a man whose hand was bloody, and was therefore presumed to be the person guilty of killing the deer shot or otherwise slain. In *heraldry,* the "bloody hand" is the badge of a baronet, and the armorial device of Ulster.

Bloody Mary. Queen Mary of England, daughter of Henry VIII and elder half-sister of Queen Elizabeth. So called on account of the sanguinary persecutions carried on against the Protestants in her short reign (1553–1558).

bloody shirt. The blood-stained shirt of a slain man used to incite to vengeance. Hence any symbol used to inflame retaliation. Used after the Civil War in the phrase, "to wave the bloody shirt."

Bloody Tenent, The. A famous tract pleading for religious toleration, written by Roger Williams and published in 1644, as part of a controversy with John COTTON. Its full title is *The Bloody Tenent of Persecution for Cause of Conscience Discussed in a Conference between Truth and Peace,* and it urges freedom of belief for Catholics, Jews, pagans, and nonbelievers as well as for Christians. Cotton wrote an answer to it entitled *The Bloody Tenent Washed and Made White in the Blood of the Lamb* (1647), and Williams in turn wrote another tract, reaffirming the ideas of his first work, which he called *The Bloody Tenent Yet More Bloody by Mr. Cotton's Endeavour to Wash It White in the Blood of the Lamb;* this was published in 1652. Both writings are considered among the most forceful and eloquent prose written in the American colonies in the 17th century.

Bloody Wedding. The massacre of St. Bartholomew in 1572 is so called because it took place during the marriage feast of Henri (afterwards Henri IV) and Marguerite (daughter of Catherine de Medici).

Bloody Week. The week ending on Sunday, May 28, 1871, when Paris was set on fire by the Communists.

Bloom, Leopold. Chief character in James Joyce's novel ULYSSES, an advertising solicitor of Jewish origin, living in Dublin, whose thoughts, feelings, and sense perceptions while he engages in a typical day's activities constitute the principal subject of the book. He is the average man raised to mythological level —coarse, sensual, half-educated, sentimental, but possessed of a questing intelligence and a persistent, yearning love for his lost son Rudy, dead in infancy, whom he believes for a while he has found in the person of Stephen Dedalus. Variously throughout the novel he is also made to symbolize figures in history, mythology, and religion with whom the situations of the day make him comparable—Ulysses, the Wandering Jew, and even Christ. Leopold Bloom is considered one of the greatest character creations in literature.

Bloom, Milly. In James Joyce's ULYSSES, the young daughter of Leopold and Molly BLOOM.

Bloom, Molly. A character in James Joyce's novel ULYSSES, wife of Leopold BLOOM, to whom she is unfaithful. A sardonic counterpart of Penelope, she is a sensual woman, direct, elemental, and devoid of complexity in personality, mythologized by the author to an even greater degree than her husband, until she becomes more a symbol of a universal feminine principle than an individual woman. Although often referred to throughout the book, she herself does not appear until the last section, which is a stream-of-consciousness soliloquy presenting her thoughts as she goes to sleep, written in a single, uninterrupted sentence.

bloomer. A female costume consisting of a short skirt and loose trousers gathered closely round the ankles, so called from Mrs. Amelia Bloomer, of New York, who tried in 1849 to introduce the fashion. In the plural form "bloomers," the term came to be applied only to the trousers portion of the outfit.

Bloor, Ella Reeve, called **Mother Bloor** (1862–). American Communist leader and writer. Active in many strikes for betterment of labor conditions. After the Russian Revolution of 1917, she became identified with international socialist workers.

Blot on the 'Scutcheon, A. A poetic drama by Robert Browning (1843). The chief character is Thorold, earl of Tresham, head of a noble family whose boast is that no blot has ever stained their 'scutcheon. Henry, earl of Mertoun, Thorold's neighbor, whose lands adjoin, asks permission to marry Thorold's young sister Mildred, and Thorold, unaware of the fact that Mertoun had seduced Mildred, consents. When he learns the truth, he is beside himself with fury and shame. He kills Mertoun and poisons himself, and Mildred dies soon after.

Blougram, Bishop Sylvester. See BISHOP BLOUGRAM'S APOLOGY.

blow.

blow the gaff. In sailors' slang, to let out a secret.

"blow the man down." Refrain of an anchor shanty.

Blowzelinda. A country maiden in Gay's pastoral called *The Shepherd's Week.*

B. L. T. The initials of Bert Leston Taylor (*Am.* 1866–1921) with which he signed his popular humorous column in the Chicago *Tribune.*

blubber. Fat of whales and other sea mammals. It is eaten by Eskimos and other connoisseurs.

blucher. A shoe named after the Prussian general Blücher.

Bludsoe, Jim, see *Jim Bludsoe.*

Bludyer, Mr. In Thackeray's PENDENNIS, a cruel literary critic who "had a certain notoriety in his profession and reputation for savage humor."

blue is the symbol of divine eternity and human immortality. Consequently, it is a mortuary color used in covering the coffins of young persons. When used for the garment of an angel, it signifies faith and fidelity. As the dress of the Virgin, it indicates modesty. In *blazonry,* it signifies chastity, loyalty, fidelity, and a spotless reputation, and seems frequently to represent silver; thus we have the *Blue Boar* of Richard III, the *Blue Lion* of the Earl of Mortimer, the *Blue Swan* of Henry IV, the *Blue Dragon,* etc.

The *Covenanters* wore blue as their badge, in opposition to the scarlet of royalty. They based their choice on *Numb.* xv. 38, "Speak unto the children of Israel, and bid them that they make them fringes in the borders of their garments . . . and that they put upon the fringe . . . a *ribband of blue*."

See also under COLORS.

a blue or *a staunch blue* descriptive of political opinions, for the most part means a Tory, for in most counties the Conservative color is blue. A *blue* is also a BLUE STOCKING.

a dark blue. An Oxford man or Harrow boy.

a light blue. A Cambridge man or Eton boy.

an old blue. One who has taken part in any of the English University athletic contests.

true blue. This is a Spanish phrase. See BLUE BLOOD.

true as Coventry blue. The reference is to a blue cloth and blue thread made at Coventry, noted for its permanent dye.

Presbyterian true blue. The allusion is to the blue apron which some of the Presbyterian preachers used to throw over their preaching-tub before they began to address the people.

blue-apron statesman. A lay politician, a tradesman who interferes with the affairs of the nation. The reference is to the blue apron once worn by almost all tradesmen.

hoist the blue flag. To turn publican or fishmonger, in allusion to the blue apron still worn to some extent by English tradesmen.

once in a blue moon. Very rarely indeed.

shout blue murder. An expression indicative more of terror or alarm than of real danger.

blue beans. Bullets, because lead is blue.

Bluebeard (*Barbe Bleue*). A famous ogre, hero of one of the *Contes* of Charles Perrault (1697). The Chevalier Raoul is a merciless tyrant, with a blue beard. His young wife is entrusted with all the keys of the castle, with strict injunctions on pain of death not to open one special room. During the absence of her lord the "forbidden fruit" is too tempting to be resisted, the door is opened, and the young wife finds the floor covered with the dead bodies of her husband's former wives. She drops the key in her terror, and can by no means obliterate from it the stain of blood. Bluebeard, on his return, commands her to prepare for death, but Sister Anne watches from the tower and at last, by the timely arrival of her brothers, her life is saved and Bluebeard put to death.

The Bluebeard story has been widely adapted into English literature. Among the burlesques and plays on the subject are those by George Colman, Jr. (1798), J. R. Planché (1839), H. J. Byron (1860), F. C. Burnand (1883). Maeterlinck made it the subject of his *Ariane et Barbe Bleue.*

Bluebeard's key. When the blood stain of this key was rubbed out on one side, it appeared on the opposite side; so prodigality being overcome will appear in the form of meanness; and friends, over-fond, will often become enemies.

Blue Bird, The (*L'Oiseau bleu*). A drama by Maurice MAETERLINCK (1909), dealing with the search for the Blue Bird of Happiness undertaken at the behest of the old Fairy Berylune by the woodcutter's children, Tyltyl and Mytyl. With the aid of a green cap with a magic diamond that can be turned at will, Tyltyl and his little sister bring to life the personalities of the familiar things about them, such as Fire, Water, the Hours and the animals, Cat and Dog; visit the Land of Memory, the Palace of Night, the Garden of Happiness, and the Kingdom of the Future, but return without the Blue Bird. Next morning they discover that their pet dove, which they are sending to a little sick friend, is blue, but when the child brings the bird back, it makes its escape.

Blue Birds. The junior organization of the Camp Fire Girls, for girls from eight to ten years of age.

blue blood. High or noble birth or descent; it is a Spanish phrase, and refers to the fact that the veins shown in the skin of the pure-blooded Spanish aristocrat, whose race had suffered no Moorish or other admixture, were more blue than those of persons of mixed, and therefore inferior, ancestry.

Blue Blouse. One who belongs to one of the numerous amateur theatrical groups in Soviet Russia which are organized for communistic education.

bluebottle. A beadsman, a policeman; so called from the color of his dress.

bluebonnets. The Highlanders of Scotland, or the Scots generally. So called from the blue woolen cap at one time in very general use in Scotland, and still far from uncommon.

blue books. In England, parliamentary reports and official publications presented by the Crown to both Houses of Parliament. Each volume is in folio, and is covered with a blue wrapper.

In America a *Blue Book* is a list of persons or places of special prestige. The *New York Blue Book* is an exclusive social register, and the *Automobile Blue Book* a list of specially recommended hotels and restaurants for tourists.

Blue Boy, The. A famous painting by Thomas Gainsborough (1728–1788).

blue devils, or a fit of the blues. A fit of spleen, low spirits.

Blue Eagle. Insignia, printed in red, white, and blue, and featuring an American eagle, given to merchants, industrialists, and the like, to testify their compliance with the provisions of the NATIONAL INDUSTRIAL RECOVERY ACT, first important legislation of the NEW DEAL program in the U.S.

Blue Flag in the Bog, The. Title of a poem by Edna St. Vincent MILLAY.

blue gown. (1) a harlot, from the blue gown worn in the English House of Correction.

(2) A Scottish bedesman or beggar licensed by the King, so called from his blue cloak.

Bluegrass State. Kentucky. See under STATES.

Blue Grotto. A beautiful cavern on the north shore of Capri, Italy, noted for the dazzling blue light inside. It is entered from the sea. It was discovered accidentally by the German poet, August Kopisch (1799–1853).

Blue Hen's Chickens. The nickname for inhabitants of the State of Delaware. It is said that in the Revolutionary War a certain Captain Caldwell commanded, and brought to a high state of efficiency, a Delaware regiment. He used to say that no cock could be truly game whose mother was not a blue hen. Hence the Delaware regiment became known as "Blue Hen's Chickens," and the name was transferred to the inhabitants of the State generally. Also title of book of poems by Vincent MCHUGH (1947).

Blue Juniata. See COWLEY, MALCOLM.

blue laws. Puritanical laws from the extremely rigid codes passed at various times and places in the 17th and 18th centuries in America, especially those passed in 1732, at New Haven, Connecticut. Their object was to stamp out "heresy," enforce a strict observance of the Sunday, and regulate even kissing between husbands and wives. Connecticut is sometimes called the *Blue Law State.*

Connecticut *blue laws* of about 1650 included the following: "Common fowlers, tobacco-takers, and other persons who could give no good account of how they spent their time" were to be put in jail. No one was allowed to give lodging to a Quaker. It was forbidden to bring musical instruments into the colony, except drums, trumpets, and jew's harps.

Blue Monday. The Monday before Lent, spent in dissipation; the dreary Monday spent at work after a weekend devoted to pleasure.

Bluenoses. The Nova Scotians, supposedly from the name of a variety of potato.

> " 'Pray, sir,' said one of my fellow-passengers, 'can you tell me the reason why the Nova Scotians are called "Blue-noses"?'
>
> " 'It is the name of a potato,' said I, 'which they produce in the greatest perfection, and boast to be the best in the world. The Americans have in consequence, given them the nickname of *Blue Noses.*' "
>
> Haliburton, *Sam Slick.*

blue peter. A flag with a blue ground and white square in the center, hoisted as a signal that the ship is about to sail. Peter is a corruption of the French *partir* (leave or notice of departure). Hence, *to hoist the blue peter,* to leave.

In whist, *blue peter* is a "call for trumps"; that is, laying on your partner's card a higher one than is required.

blue ribbon. The Garter, the badge of the highest and most coveted Order of Knighthood in the gift of the British Crown; hence the term is used to denote the highest honor attainable in any profession, walk of life, etc. *The blue ribbon of the turf,* the Derby.

blue ribbon army. A total abstinence society founded in the early eighties of the last century by Richard Booth in the United States. The members were distinguished by wearing a piece of narrow blue ribbon in the buttonhole of the coat. From this symbol the phrase *blue ribbon army* came in time to be applied to the body of teetotalers generally, whether connected with the original society or not.

blues. Songs expressing sorrow, usually for a lost lover or sweetheart, in pronounced rhythm. They were of Negro origin and were at the height of their popularity during the 1920's. The first of the cycle, and considered to be the most authentic, was *St. Louis Blues* (1914), by W. C. Handy. Other famous "blues" were *Beale Street Blues, Limehouse Blues, Memphis Blues,* and *St. James Infirmary Blues.* This popular jazz form was raised to the level of symphonic music in *Rhapsody in Blue* (1927), by George GERSHWIN.

Blue Saltire. The flag of Scotland. A cross on it is formed of a bend dexter and a bend sinister crossing in the middle. It is St. Andrew's cross.

Blues and Grays. In the American Civil War, the Union and Confederate forces respectively, from the color of their uniforms.

bluestocking, or **bas bleu.** A female pedant, a woman of pretentious intellectual or literary interests. The term Blue Stocking originated about 1750 in allusion to the frequenters of the salon of Mrs. Elizabeth Montagu in London. The usual derivation goes back to 1400 when a society of ladies and gentlemen was formed at Venice, distinguished by the color of their stockings and called *della calza.* In 1590 a similar movement was the rage among the lady *savantes* of Paris. Another theory has it that the term Blue Stocking was in allusion to Mr. Benjamin Stillingfleet, a prominent member of Mrs. Montagu's clique who always wore blue worsted stockings instead of the customary black silk.

Blue-Tailed Fly, The. An old American song.

Blue Voyage. See AIKEN, CONRAD.

Bluff, Captain Noll. In Congreve's *Old Bachelor* (1693), a swaggering bully and boaster. He says, "I think that fighting for fighting's sake is sufficient cause for fighting. Fighting, to me, is religion and the laws."

Bluff King Hal. Henry VIII of England (1491–1547).

Blum, Léon (1872–). French political leader of Socialist party, then of Popular Front. Premier of France (June 4, 1936–June 21, 1937); carried through radical reforms affecting banking, labor, agriculture. Arrested after defeat of France (1940), and imprisoned. Released by Allies.

Blumine. The "Rose Goddess," heroine of Carlyle's SARTOR RESARTUS beloved by Teufelsdröckh, whom she makes "immortal by a kiss." She marries another and more eligible suitor and leaves him to despair.

Blunden, Edmund Charles (1896–). English poet and critic. Received Military Cross in World War I. Received Arthur Benson Medal of Royal Society of Literature (of which he was made a fellow) in 1930. Essentially a nature writer. Has a long list of books in verse and prose to his credit.

Blunderbore. A nursery-tale giant, brother of Cormoran, who puts Jack the Giant Killer to bed, intending to kill him. Jack thrusts a billet of wood into the bed, and creeps under the bedstead. Blunderbore comes with his club and breaks the billet to pieces, but is much amazed at seeing Jack next morning at breakfast-time.

Blunt, Sir James. In Shakespeare's *Richard III*.

Blunt, Sir Walter. In Shakespeare's 1 *Henry IV*.

Blunt, Wilfrid Scawen (1840–1922). English poet, author, diplomat, and explorer, opposed to the 19th-century British policies of imperialism. His writings include *The Future of Islam* (1882); *Ideas about India* (1885); *Atrocities of Justice under British Rule in Egypt* (1907); *Secret History of the English Occupation of Egypt* (1907); *India under Ripon* (1909); *Gordon at Khartoum* (1911); *The Land War in Ireland* (1912); *My Diaries, 1888–1914* (1919–1920). *Wind and the Whirlwind* (1883) and *Satan Absolved* (1899) are political poems. Blunt's translations of Oriental poetry, especially Persian, did much to arouse English interest in Eastern literature.

blurb. Any highly inflated publicity, particularly that got out by publishers with reference to new books and printed on the book jacket and elsewhere. The term was invented by Gelett BURGESS in his *Burgess Unabridged* (1914) and has become common usage. The French call it "juice," the Germans "laundry slip."

Bly, Nelly. A character in Grundy and Solomon's operetta, *The Vicar of Bray* (1882). Also the assumed name of a New York woman journalist who attracted note in 1890 by touring the world to rival the feat accomplished by Phileas Fogg in Jules Verne's romance, AROUND THE WORLD IN EIGHTY DAYS.

B'nai B'rith. From Hebrew, "the sons of the covenant." A Jewish fraternity founded in New York City in 1843, and since extended over the U.S., various countries of Europe, Palestine and Egypt. No dogma or ceremony.

Boadicea. In legendary British history, a queen contemporary with Nero who rebelled against Roman rule. See also BONDUCA.

Boanerges. A name given to James and John, the sons of Zebedee, because they wanted to call down "fire from heaven," to consume the Samaritans for not "receiving" the Lord Jesus. It is said in the Bible to signify "sons of thunder," but "sons of tumult" would probably be nearer its meaning (*Luke* ix. 54; see *Mark* iii. 17).

boar.

the bristled Baptist boar. So Dryden denominates the Anabaptists in his *Hind and Panther*.

> The bristled Baptist boar, impure as he [*the ape*],
> But whitened with the foam of sanctity,
> With fat pollutions filled the sacred place,
> And mountains levelled in his furious race.
>
> Pt. i. 43.

the Calydonian boar. In Greek legend, Aeneus, king of Calydon, in Aetolia, having neglected to sacrifice to Artemis, was punished by the goddess sending a ferocious boar to ravage his lands. A band of heroes collected to hunt the boar, who was eventually slain by Meleager after he had been first wounded by Atalanta.

the wild boar of the Ardennes. Guillaume, Comte de la Marck (1485), so called because he was fierce as the wild boar, which he delighted to hunt. He is introduced by Scott in QUENTIN DURWARD.

Boar's Head. The Old English custom of serving this as a Christmas dish is said to derive from Scandinavian mythology. Freyr, the god of peace and plenty, used to ride on the boar Gullinbursti; his festival was held at Yuletide (*winter solstice*), when a boar was sacrificed to his honor.

The head was carried into the banqueting hall, decked with bays and rosemary on a gold or silver dish, to a flourish of trumpets and the songs of the minstrels. Many of these carols are still extant and the following is the first verse of that sung before Prince Henry at St. John's College, Oxford, at Christmas, 1607:

> The Boar is dead,
> So, here is his head;
> What man could have done more
> Than his head off to strike,
> Meleager like
> And bring it as I do before?

the Boar's Head Tavern. Made immortal by Shakespeare, this used to stand in Eastcheap, on the site of the present statue of William IV. The sign was the cognizance of the Gordon clan, the progenitor of which slew in the forest of Huntley a wild boar, the terror of all the Merse (1093).

Boar, the. Richard III.

> The wretched, bloody, and usurping boar
> That spoiled your summer fields and fruitful vines:
> . . . This foul swine . . . lies now . . .
> Near to the town of Leicester, as we learn.
> Shakespeare, *Richard III,* v. 3.

Boardman, Mabel Thorn (1861–1946). National secretary of the American Red Cross (from 1919); all in all, a leader (without pay) of that organization for more than forty years. During World War I she had a former German ship put into commission for the Red Cross for relief trips to Europe.

Boas, Franz (1858–). American anthropologist and scholar, born in Germany, best known for his studies of the American Indian. His books for the general public include *The Mind of Primitive Man* (1911); *Primitive Art* (1927); *Anthropology and Modern Life* (1932).

Boat, The Open. A story by Stephen CRANE.

Boat of Longing, The. See RÖLVAAG, O. E.

Boatswain. The name of Byron's favorite dog, buried in Newstead Abbey garden. According to Byron's inscription on the monument over his grave he "had all the Virtues of Man without his Vices."

> To mark a friend's remains, these stones arise;
> I never knew but one,—and here he lies.

Bobadil, Captain. A military braggart of the first water. He is a character in Ben Jonson's *Every Man in his Humor* (1598), an ignorant, clever, shallow bully, thoroughly cowardly, but thought by his dupes to be an amazing hero. The name was probably suggested by Bobadilla, first governor of Cuba, who sent Columbus home in chains.

bobby. An English policeman. This slang word is either derived from Sir Robert Peel, or became popular through his having in 1828 remodeled the London Metropolitan Police Force.

Bobby Shaftoe. Character in an old song.

> Bobby Shaftoe's gone to sea,
> Silver buckles on his knee,
> He'll come back and marry me,
> Pretty Bobby Shaftoe.

Bob, Son of Battle. A novel by Alfred Ollivant (*Eng.* 1898), the first novel of any note to have a dog for its hero.

Boccaccio, Giovanni (1313?–1375). Italian poet and humanist, friend of DANTE and PETRARCH in Florence. He is most famous for his DECAMERON (1471), which he repudiated in his old age for its licentiousness. In his youth, he wrote a number of romances and long poems in Italian which reflect events in his life at the time (see MARIA D'AQUINO). These include *Il Filocolo* (1472) (see BLANCHEFLEUR); IL FILOSTRATO (1480?), which was used by Chaucer for his version of the TROILUS story; *Il Teseide* (1475), which became Chaucer's KNIGHT'S TALE; *Ameto* (1478); *L'Amorosa Visione* (1521); *L'Amorosa Fiammetta* (1472) (see FIAMMETTA); *Ninfale Fiesolano* (1471); and *Il Corbaccio* (1487), a satire. He also wrote a "life" of Dante (1477) and a number of Latin encyclopedic works in his later days as a scholar. Among these are: *De Casibus Virorum Illustrium, De Claris Mulieribus; De Genealogiis Deorum.* Boccaccio acted as benefactor to one of the first Greek scholars to come to Italy in the Renaissance, and sponsored him until he had finished a translation of a Greek manuscript of Homer.

boche. An insulting name for a German which came into use during World War I. It may be derived from German *bursch*, a lad, or from *bürschen,* to shoot (with a rifle). Another derivation given is from *les alboches,* a contemptuous nickname given by French printers to Germans in the same trade in the sixties of the last century, and itself derived from the colloquial *boche* coined in France about 1860 to designate a worthless person.

A somewhat more appealing etymology bases the frequent combination *les sales boches,* "the dirty boches," on *les allemands,* "the Germans," which some punster may well have corrupted into *les sales mands.*

Still another derivation is from the French *caboche,* "head," implying in the new word something of the meaning of blockhead.

bodacious. American slang. A PORTMANTEAU contraction of bold and audacious.

Bodanzky, Artur (1877–1939). Conducted the Wagner répertoire at Metropolitan Opera Co., New York City, 1915–1939.

bodega. Spanish. A wine-shop or cellar. The same word as French *boutique.* Both are related to "apothecary." Title of novel by Vicente BLASCO IBÁÑEZ.

Bodenheim, Maxwell (1892–). American poet and novelist, known for the sardonic and iconoclastic nature of his writings and one of the most typical of the Bohemians of GREENWICH VILLAGE during the 1920's. His poetic works include *Minna and Myself* (1918); *Introducing Irony* (1922); *Against This Age* (1923); *Returning to Emotion* (1927); *The King of Spain and Other Poems* (1928); *Bringing Jazz* (1930). Among his novels are: *Crazy Man* (1924), *Replenishing Jessica* (1925); *Sixty Seconds* (1929); *Naked on Roller Skates* (1931). *Lights in the Valley* (1942) expresses his later proletarian sympathies.

bodhisattva or **bodhisat.** In Buddhism, one who has entered on the path of Buddhahood and will, in a future incarnation, become a Buddha.

bodies seven. In alchemy, the metals corresponding to the seven planets.

Sol gold is, and Luna silver we threpe [assert to be]
Mars yren [iron], Mercurie quicksilver we clepe [call]
Saturnus lead, and Jupiter is tin, and Venus coper.
Chaucer.

Bodleian library. The celebrated library projected by Sir Thomas Bodly in 1598 and opened at Oxford in 1602. Full of rare books and valuable manuscripts.

Bodoni. From the name of the Italian printer, Giambattista Bodoni (1740–1813). A style of type.

Body of Liberties. A code of laws for the government of the Massachusetts colony, the first to be established in New England, adopted in 1641. It was a forerunner of the BILL OF RIGHTS and was prepared by a committee in which Nathaniel WARD was the most active.

Body of This Death. See BOGAN, LOUISE.

body-snatcher. One who snatches or purloins bodies, newly buried, to sell them to surgeons for dissection. The first instance on record was in 1777, when the body of Mrs. Jane Sainsbury was "resurrected" from the burial ground near Gray's Inn Lane. The "RESURRECTION MEN" were imprisoned for six months.

By a play on the words, a bumbailiff was so called, because his duty was to snatch or capture the body of a delinquent.

Boehme, Jakob, see BÖHME.

Boeotian. A rude, unlettered person, a dull blockhead. The ancient Boeotians loved agricultural and pastoral pursuits, so the Athenians used to say they were dull and thick as their own atmosphere; yet Hesiod, Pindar, Corinna, Plutarch, Pelopidas, and Epaminondas, were all Boeotians.

Boeotian ears. Ears unable to appreciate music or rhetoric.

Boer. A South African of Dutch or Huguenot descent. The word is Dutch and means "farmer."

Boethius, Anicius Manlius Severinus (470?–525). Roman philosopher, for a time a consul under Theodoric, the Ostrogothic king. He translated into Latin the *Categories* and *On Interpretation* of Aristotle, and an introduction to the *Categories* which had been written by the neo-Platonist philosopher PORPHYRY (see also NEO-PLATONISM). His translations supplied the form in which the Aristotelian treatises were known to centuries of medieval scholars, and in his commentary on the selection from Porphyry he first formulated the problem of universals, which was to prove so vexing in the endless medieval dispute between NOMINALISM and REALISM. He is best known, however, for his *De Consolatione Philosophiae* or CONSOLATION OF PHILOSOPHY, which was later translated by King ALFRED, Chaucer, and Queen Elizabeth, among others.

Bœuf, Front de, see FRONT DE BŒUF.

Boffin, Nicodemus. In Dickens' novel OUR MUTUAL FRIEND, "the golden dustman," foreman of old John Harmon, dustman and miser. Being residuary legatee of John Harmon, dustman, he comes in for £100,000.

Mrs. Boffin. Wife of Nicodemus Boffin, and the daughter of a cat's-meat man. After Mr. Boffin comes into his fortune she becomes "a high flyer at fashion," wears black velvet and sable, but retains her kindness of heart and love for her husband.

Bogan, Louise (1897–). American poet. Published volumes of her work are *Body of This Death* (1923); *Dark Summer* (1929); *The Sleeping Fury* (1937); *Poems and New Poems* (1941). Poetry reviewer for the *New Yorker*.

Bogart, Humphrey (1899–). American moving picture actor, chiefly appearing in "tough" rôles. Married Lauren Bacall, moving picture actress (1945). First wife was Helen Menken, actress.

bogey. A goblin, a bugbear. Sometimes called boggart or bogey-man. A Scotch bogle is more of a specter. The word *bogey* appeared only in the early 19th century.

Bogey or **Colonel Bogey.** A name given in golf to an imaginary player whose score for each hole is settled by the committee of the particular club and is supposed to be the lowest that a good average player could do it in. *Beating Bogey* or *the Colonel,* is playing the hole in a fewer number of strokes.

Boh Da Thone. The *Ballad of Boh Da Thone* by Rudyard KIPLING relates the rather bloody story of how—during the Burma War (1883–1885)—Captain O'Neil of the Black

Tyrone was finally brought the head of his old enemy, "a Pretender to Theebaw's Throne" and a warrior of India who raided and ravaged, and of how the "Boh" (as the raider was known) was accidentally done to death by Babu Harendra (Gomashta), Head Clerk of the Government Bullock Train. Like much of Kipling's work, the scales are heavily weighted on the side of the English, but in its climactic passages the ballad has the extraordinary vivacity and immediacy of Kipling at his best.

Bohème, La. An opera by Puccini (1896) based upon Henri Murger's *Vie de Bohème* (1848). The story deals with the love affair of Rudolph, a poet, and Mimi, a Paris flower girl; also with Rudolph's penniless Bohemian friends and the ups and downs of artist life in the Latin Quarter. Mimi is ill and finally dies.

Bohemia. Any locality frequented by journalists, artists, actors, opera-singers and other similar characters. See next entry.

Bohemian. A term applied to literary men and artists of loose and unconventional habits, living by what they can pick up by their wits. Originally the name was applied to the gipsies, from the belief that before they appeared in western Europe they had been denizens of Bohemia, or because the first that arrived in France came by way of Bohemia (1427). When they presented themselves before the gates of Paris they were not allowed to enter the city, but were lodged at La Chapelle, St. Denis. The French nickname for gipsies is *cagoux* (unsociables).

Bohemian Girl, The. A light opera by M. W. Balfe (1843), libretto by Bunn. The plot centers about the kidnaping of Arline, the little daughter of the Governor of Presburg, by Devilshoof and his gipsy band. With the gipsies is Thaddeus, a Polish exile from justice, who falls in love with Arline. The Gipsy Queen is jealous and makes trouble, but after many difficulties Arline is restored to her father and marries Thaddeus, whose identity is finally revealed.

Böhme, Jakob. Also **Behmen** (1575–1624). German shoemaker and mystic, a believer in the creative value of the conflict of opposites, which he saw producing a new unity, and in the will of God as a basic universal force. He also regarded the universe as the manifestation of God, and evil as God's wrath. Denounced as heretical by the clergy of his time, he wrote numerous treatises expounding his beliefs, including *Aurora, oder die Morgenröte im Aufgang* (*Aurora, or Morning Redness*) (1612) and *Der Weg zu Christo* (*The Way to Christ*) (1624). One of his best-known single works is *The Signature of Things* (*Signatura Rerum*), concerning symbolism. In England in the 17th century he had a number of followers, called Behmenists, who later became Quakers

Bohn, Henry George (1796–1884). English publisher and translator of German extraction, whose "library" of republications of standard works at cheap prices has become famous

Bohort, Sir. A knight of Arthur's Round Table, brother of Sir Lionel, and nephew of Launcelot of the Lake, also called Sir Bors.

Boiardo or **Bojardo, Matteo Maria** (1434–1494). Italian poet, famous for his epic, ORLANDO INNAMORATO.

Boileau, Nicolas (Despréaux) (1636–1711). French poet and critic, one of the earliest and most characteristic of the neo-Classicists, who urged always prudence, moderation, common sense, and obedience to authority in the writing of literature. In his *Satires* he imitated Horace and Juvenal and attacked the social and literary foibles of his day, while his *Le Lutrin* is a mock-epic in the manner of Pope's THE RAPE OF THE LOCK. His chief work is his ART POÉTIQUE (1674), in which he formulated in verse the literary principles of neo-Classicism which were dominant throughout the 18th century. Boileau was called the *législateur du Parnasse* ("legislator of Parnassus"), and he greatly influenced RACINE, MOLIÈRE, and LA FONTAINE, his friends and literary associates.

Boisbrûlé (*Fr.* "burnt wood"). A Canadian halfbreed, particularly French and Indian, so called because of his dark complexion.

Bois de Boulogne. A large park containing the famous race tracks of Longchamp and Anteuil, west of Paris, France. Parisians call it simply *le Bois*

Bois-Guilbert, Sir Brian de. In Scott's IVANHOE, a preceptor of the Knights Templars. He offers insult to Rebecca, and she threatens to cast herself from the battlements if he touches her. When the castle is set on fire by the sibyl, Sir Brian carries off Rebecca from the flames. Later, the Grand-Master of the Knights Templars charges Rebecca with sorcery, and she demands a trial by combat. Sir Brian de Bois-Guilbert is appointed to sustain the charge against her, and Ivanhoe is her champion. Sir Brian is found dead in the lists, and Rebecca is declared innocent.

Boissevain, Mrs. Eugen Jan. Married name of Edna St. Vincent MILLAY.

Bojer, Johan (1872–). Norwegian novelist. Many works available in English, including his most widely known novel, *The Great Hunger* (1919). His French biographer has said, "Bojer is of the family of great writer-philosophers."

Bok, Edward William (1863–1930). Widely known American editor of the *Ladies' Home Journal.*

Bokardo. Name of a poem and character in it by Edwin Arlington ROBINSON.

Boker, George Henry (1823–1890). American playwright and diplomat, author of several verse dramas including *Calaynos* (1849); *Leonor de Guzmán* (1853); and *Francesca da Rimini* (1855). The last-named is his best-known work and deals with the PAOLO AND FRANCESCA theme.

bola, also **bolas.** Spanish. A missile consisting of two or three balls of stone or iron attached to a cord. The GAUCHOS of South America hurl the *bola* to entangle game.

boldface. Any "face" or type of type that is "bold" in the sense of thick, heavy.

Boldrewood, Rolf. Pseudonym of Thomas Alexander Browne (1826–1915). Australian novelist. His *Robbery Under Arms* is a tale of the bushranger.

Boldwood, William. A character in Hardy's FAR FROM THE MADDING CROWD.

Bolerium. In ancient geography, LAND'S END.

bolero. A Spanish dance, performed in triple time to the accompaniment of castanets. The best-known concert version of the bolero is the popular one by Maurice RAVEL (1928). The composer himself is said to have later scorned this most widely played of his works.

Bolingbroke, Henry, Duke of Hertford, later **Henry IV.** Character in Shakespeare's *Richard II, 1 Henry IV, 2 Henry IV.* The name comes from the castle in which he was born.

Bolitho, William (1891–1930). Pen name of **William Bolitho Ryall.** British journalist and author. London correspondent for *Manchester Guardian* and *New York World.* Wrote, among other books, *Twelve Against the Gods.*

Bolívar, Simón (1783–1830). South American soldier, statesman, and revolutionary leader. Won victory for Venezuela, freed Peru from Spain, organized a new republic named after him, Bolivia. He is known as *El Libertador,* "The Liberator."

Bollweevil Song, the. An American folk-song popularized by Carl Sandburg.

Bolshevik or **Bolshevist.** Properly, a member of the Russian revolutionary party that seized power under LENIN in 1917, declared war on capitalism and the *bourgeoisie* in all lands, and aimed at the establishment of supreme rule by the proletariat. The history of the term goes back to the congress of the Russian Social Democratic Labor Party in London (1903) where it was adopted by the faction, headed by Lenin, which professed to act in the name of the majority (*bolshe* is the comparative of the adjective *bolshoi,* big, large). In 1918, when the Menshevik group, representing the 1903 minority, was finally liquidated, the party of the Bolsheviks assumed the name of the Communist party. In England, America, and elsewhere the name *Bolshevik* came to be applied to those suspected of wishing to overthrow the *status quo.* The form "Bolsheviki" is the Russian plural.

Bolton, Fanny. In Thackeray's PENDENNIS, the pretty sentimental daughter of a London porter, with whom Pen is madly in love for a short time.

Bolton, Guy (1884–). Playwright, especially musical comedy, *Sally, Lady Be Good,* etc., and moving picture scenarios. Collaborated on *Polly with a Past, Rio Rita,* etc.

Boltrope. A seaman in Cooper's PILOT.

Bombastes Furioso. One who talks big or in an ultra-bombastic way. From the hero of a burlesque opera so called by William Barnes Rhodes, produced in 1810 in parody of ORLANDO FURIOSO. *Bombastes Furioso* is the general of Artaxaminous, king of Utopia. He is plighted to Distaffina, but Artaxaminous promises her "half-a-crown" if she will forsake the general for the King. When Bombastes sees himself flouted, he goes mad, and hangs his boots on a tree, with this label duly displayed:

> Who dares this pair of boots displace,
> Must meet Bombastes face to face.

The King, coming up, cuts down the boots, and Bombastes "kills him." Fusbos, seeing the King fallen, "kills" the general; but at the close of the farce the dead men rise one by one, and join the dance, promising, if the audience likes, "to die again to-morrow."

In ORLANDO FURIOSO, the hero, Orlando, goes mad, and hangs up his armor on a tree, with this distich attached thereto:

> Orlando's arms let none displace,
> But such who'll meet him face to face.

Bonacieux, Constance. In DUMAS' *The Three Musketeers,* the young wife of the aged landlord, whose protector d'Artagnan became.

Bona Dea. An ancient Roman goddess of fertility, fruitfulness and chastity of women. Sister of Faunus; also called *Fauna.*

bona fide (*Lat.*). In good faith; hence without subterfuge or deception; really and truly. *To produce one's bona fides* is to produce one's credentials, to give proof that one is what he appears to be or can perform that which he says he can.

bonanza. A stroke of luck, from the Bonanza silver-mine in Nevada which was at first considered a failure and produced suddenly immense wealth. The Spanish word *bonanza,* which explains the name of the Bonanza mine, means 'calm, fair weather, prosperity.'

Bonanza State. Montana. See under STATES.

Bonaparte. See NAPOLEON; BONEY.

Bonaventura, St. See under SAINT.

bonaventure. The sail hoisted on the fourth mast of a vessel in the Middle Ages. The word means 'good luck.'

Bond, Carrie Jacobs (1862–1947). Popular American song writer (*A Perfect Day,* etc.). Also wrote books for children and an autobiography.

Bonduca. One of the many forms of the name of the British Queen, which in Latin was frequently (and in English is now usually) written BOADICEA, but which should properly be *Bonduca.* Fletcher wrote a fine tragedy with this name (1616), the principal characters being Caractacus and Bonduca.

bone.

have a bone to pick with one. To have an unpleasant matter to discuss and settle. Two dogs and one bone invariably forms an excellent basis for a fight. Hence *a bone of contention.*

make no bones about it. To do it, say it, etc., without hesitation; to offer no opposition, present no difficulty or scruple. Dice are called "bones," and the Fr. *flatter le dé* (to mince the matter) is the opposite of our expression. To make no bones of a thing is not to flatter, or "make much of," or humor the dice in order to show favor. Hence, *without more bones.* Without further scruple or objection.

Bone, Sir **Muirhead** (1876–). Scottish etcher and painter. His brother, **David William Bone** (1874–), is a master mariner and novelist. A third brother is an editor of the *Manchester Guardian.*

Boney. A familiar contradiction of BONAPARTE used by the English in the early part of the 19th century by way of depreciation. Thus Thomas Moore speaks of "the infidel Boney."

Bon Gaultier Ballads. Parodies of contemporary poetry by W. E. Aytoun and Sir Theodore Martin. They first appeared in *Tait's, Fraser's,* and *Blackwood's Magazines* in the 'forties, and were published in volume form in 1855.

Bonheur, Rosa (1822–1899). French painter, known for her popular studies of horses.

Bonhomme. A French peasant. See JACQUES BONHOMME.

Bonhomme Richard. The French form of Benjamin Franklin's pseudonym, Richard Saunders. Also the name of Paul Jones's famous man-of-war in naval battles off England (1779).

Boniface, Father. In Scott's novel THE MONASTERY, the successor of the Abbot Ingelram, as Superior of St. Mary's Convent. In its sequel THE ABBOT he has retired, still in search of the peace and quiet which, due to the pressure of contemporary events, he has failed to find in the cloister. In this second novel he first appears under the name of Blinkhoodie in the character of gardener at Kinross, and afterwards as the old gardener at Dundrennan.

Boniface, St. See under SAINTS.

Boniface, Will. A famous character in Farquhar's comedy *The Beaux' Stratagem* (1707), landlord of the inn at Lichfield, in league with the highwaymen. This sleek, jolly publican is fond of the cant phrase, "as the saying is." Thus, "I'm old Will Boniface; pretty well known upon this road, as the saying is." He has lived at Lichfield "man and boy above eight and fifty years, and not consumed eight and fifty ounces of meat," for, says he, "I have fed purely upon ale. I have eat my ale, drank my ale, and I always sleep upon my ale." Hence *Boniface* has become a common term for a publican or tavern keeper.

Bon Marché. A noted department store in Paris. The phrase *bon marché* means "good bargain." Cf. *à bon marché* "inexpensive(ly)."

bon mot (*Fr.*). A good or witty saying; a pun; a clever repartee.

Bonnard, Abel (1883–). French poet and novelist. His two volumes of travel sketches *En Chine* (1923) won him the Grand Prix de Littérature from the French Academy (1924).

Bonnard, Sylvestre. Hero of THE CRIME OF SYLVESTRE BONNARD by Anatole FRANCE.

Bonnet, Kate. Novel about a female pirate by Frank R. STOCKTON.

bonnet rouge. The red cap of liberty worn by the leaders of the French revolution. It is the emblem of Red Republicanism.

Bonneville, Adventures of Captain, by Washington Irving, concerned with the actual Benjamin L. E. Bonneville, who explored the northwest (1832–1835).

Bonnicastle, Arthur. Hero of J. G. HOLLAND's *Arthur Bonnicastle.*

Bonnie Dundee. John Graham of Claverhouse, Viscount Dundee. Born about 1649, he became a noted soldier in the Stuart cause, and was killed at the Battle of Killiecrankie in 1689.

Bonnie Lesley. A lyric by Robert Burns. The heroine of this song, in real life, was Miss Leslie Baillie.

> O saw ye bonnie Lesley
> As she gaed o'er the border?
> She's gane like Alexander,
> To spread her conquests farther.

Bonnivard, François de. A historical character (1495–1570) who appears in idealized form as the hero of Byron's *Prisoner of Chillon*. See CHILLON.

Bonsels, Waldemar (1881–). German author of somewhat precious novels and nature stories. Best known for *The Adventures of Maya the Bee*.

Bontemps, Roger. A fat, cheery, optimistic companion, the personification of "Never say die." The character is from a famous popular song by Pierre Jean de BÉRANGER (1814).

bonus. A grant of money in excess of stipulated pay, particularly prominent during the 1920's and early 1930's in connection with the demands of the American veterans of World War I for additional compensation for their services abroad. A World War Adjusted Compensation Act was passed in 1925, with payment promised in 1945. It was made in 1936 as a result of pressure by veterans' groups, including the AMERICAN LEGION, which had acted as a powerful lobby in obtaining passage of the bill. See also BONUS ARMY.

Bonus Army or **Bonus Expeditionary Force.** Journalistic term used to describe an "army" of American veterans of World War I who came to Washington, in the spring of 1932, to try to persuade Congress to vote them immediate payment of the promised "BONUS." These men, many with wives and children, camped in shacks near the Capitol, picketed the Congressional buildings, and were finally dispersed with tear-gas bombs.

bon vivant (*Fr.*). A free liver; one who indulges in the "good things of the table." *Bon viveur* means much the same, but is rather stronger, suggesting one who makes a pursuit of other pleasures besides those of the table.

bonze. The name given by Europeans to the Buddhist clergy of the Far East, particularly of Japan. In China the name is given to the priests of the Fohists.

Booby, Lady. In Fielding's novel, JOSEPH ANDREWS, a vulgar upstart who tries to seduce her footman, Joseph Andrews. Parson ADAMS reproves her for laughing in church. Lady Booby is a caricature of Richardson's Pamela.

Boojum. In Lewis Carroll's *Hunting of the Snark*, a kind of snark whose hunters "softly and silently vanish away."

book.

the Book of Books. The Bible; also called simply "the Book," or "the good Book."

the book of life, or of fate. In Bible language, a register of the names of those who are to inherit eternal life (*Phil.* iv. 3; *Rev.* xx. 12).

For *black, blue, red* and *yellow book*, see under respective colors.

Battle of the Books. See under BATTLE.

bell, book and candle. See under BELL.

Book of Americans, A. See BENÉT, STEPHEN VINCENT.

Book of Kells. A famous Irish illuminated manuscript of the four Gospels, considered to have been written in the 8th century and to be one of the best examples of the art of manuscript illumination. It was named for a monastery famed for its scholarship.

Book of Marriage, The. A symposium on the subject of marriage with Count Hermann Alexander KEYSERLING as editor and chief contributor (1926). George Bernard Shaw declined to participate because he felt that no man can tell the truth about marriage while his wife is alive.

Book of Martyrs, The, see ACTS AND MONUMENTS.

Book of Mormon. The sacred scriptures of the Mormon church, first published in 1830.

Book of Nonsense. A well-known volume of humorous verse by Edward LEAR (1846). See LIMERICK.

Book of Snobs, The. A series of papers by Thackeray (1846–1847) portraying a variety of typical English snobs.

Book of the Dead. A collection of magic incantations, used in the religion of ancient Egypt as a guide for liberated souls on their journey to the land of the dead.

Book of the Duchess, The. An allegorical poem by CHAUCER (1369), mourning the death of Blanche, first wife of John of GAUNT, who was the author's patron. It is in the form of a dream-vision.

Book of Thel, The. The first of William Blake's mystical writings known as his PROPHETIC BOOKS, published in 1787. Its theme is death, redemption, and eternity.

Book-of-the-Month Club. See SUBSCRIPTION BOOK.

bookworm. One always poring over books; so called in allusion to the maggot that eats holes in books, and lives both in and on its leaves. Modern book cloth protects books against the latter kind of worm.

Boone, Daniel (1734–1820). American frontiersman, known for his exploration and settlement of Kentucky and celebrated by a number of American and English writers, including AUDUBON, and Byron in DON JUAN, as well as in American folklore.

Boötes. Greek for "the ploughman"; the name of the constellation which contains the bright star, ARCTURUS. See also ICARIUS. According to ancient mythology, Boötes invented the plough, to which he yoked two oxen, and at death, being taken to heaven with his plough and oxen, was made a constellation. Homer calls it "the wagoner," *i.e.* the wagoner of "Charles' Wain," the Great Bear.

Booth, Amelia. Heroine of Fielding's novel AMELIA.

Booth, Captain. In Fielding's novel AMELIA, the husband of Amelia, said to be a drawing of the author's own character and experiences. He has all the vices of Tom Jones, with an additional share of meanness.

Booth, Edwin Thomas (1833–1893). American actor, son of Junius Brutus BOOTH and one of the most noted of Shakespearean performers.

Booth, John Wilkes (1838–1865). American actor, son of Junius Brutus BOOTH and brother of Edwin BOOTH, who assassinated Abraham Lincoln, April 14, 1865, in Ford's Theatre, Washington, D.C.

Booth, Junius Brutus (1796–1852). English actor, most famous for his performances in the U.S.

Booth, William (1829–1912). English Methodist preacher, founder of the SALVATION ARMY in 1865. He is the subject of a well-known poem by Vachel LINDSAY, GENERAL BOOTH ENTERS HEAVEN.

Boothe, Clare (1903–). American playwright and journalist, wife of Henry LUCE and the author of popular plays of malicious wit as well as magazine articles on travel and World War II. Her plays are *The Women* (1937); *Kiss the Boys Goodbye* (1938); and *Margin for Error* (1939). The first two are merciless satires on the foibles and deceits of women. She also wrote *Stuffed Shirts* (1933) and *Europe in the Spring* (1940), the latter an account of the invasion of France, Holland, and Belgium by Germany in World War II. Member of Congress, 1943–1947.

bootleggers. In American slang, traders in legally prohibited liquor, especially during the Prohibition era in the U.S. during the 1920's. See PROHIBITION. GANGSTERS and racketeers organized bootlegging as a great industry at this time, became wealthy and powerful, and often terrorized the communities where they operated. Traders in other prohibited goods, such as products under rationing restrictions during wartime, are also called bootleggers. The word *bootleg* meant originally to carry something concealed in the leg of one's boots.

Boots at the Holly-tree Inn. A story by Charles Dickens (1855). The "boots" in his own picturesque language glibly tells the story of a boy, eight years old, eloping to Gretna Green with a girl of seven.

Bopeep. The heroine of a nursery rhyme:

> Little Bopeep has lost her sheep
> And can't tell where to find them
> Leave them alone and they'll come home,
> Bringing their tails behind them.

Bor. See BORR.

Bor, General. Assumed name of Lieutenant General Tadeusz Komorowski, who led Polish patriots and held Warsaw for 63 days in World War II.

Borachio. In Shakespeare's *Much Ado About Nothing,* a follower of Don John of Aragon. He is a great villain, engaged to Margaret, the waiting-woman of Hero.

Borah, William Edgar (1865–1940). U.S. Senator from Idaho who strongly opposed World Court and entrance of United States into League of Nations; advocated disarmament conference (1920–1921).

Borak or **Al Borak** (the lightning). The animal brought by Gabriel to carry Mahomet to the seventh heaven, and itself received into Paradise. It had the face of a man, but the cheeks of a horse; its eyes were like jacinths, but brilliant as the stars; it had the wings of an eagle, spoke with the voice of a man, and glittered all over with radiant light.

Bordeaux, Henry (1870–). French novelist and member of the French Academy since 1919. He has published 100 volumes in all, including travel books, biographies, and dramatic criticism.

Borden, Lizzie (Andrew). Principal in a celebrated murder case in the U.S. in 1892, in which she was accused of having killed her father and stepmother with an axe. She became the heroine of many popular ballads of the time, and attracted the interest of a number of literary men in the 1920's and 1930's, notably Edmund PEARSON and Alexander WOOLLCOTT.

Borden, Mary (1886–). Anglo-American novelist, born in Chicago but for long an English subject. Her novels reveal a quiet but devastating wit.

Border, the. The frontier of England and Scotland, which, from the 11th to the 15th century, was the field of constant forays, and a most fertile source of ill blood between North and South Britain.

Border minstrel. Sir Walter Scott (1771–1832) because he sang of the Border.

Border-thief school. A term applied by Thomas CARLYLE, in his SARTOR RESARTUS, to Walter Scott and others, who celebrated the achievements of free-booters, etc., like Rob Roy.

Border Eagle State. Mississippi. See STATES.

Border State. See under STATE.

Borderers, The. A drama by William WORDSWORTH, written in 1795–1796. It is set in the time of Henry III.

border ruffian. A pro-slavery Missourian who would cross the border into Kansas and Nebraska to vote illegally or intimidate anti-slavery settlers.

Boreas. In Greek mythology, the god of the north wind, and the north wind itself. He was the son of Astraeus, a Titan, and Eos, the morning, and lived in a cave of Mount Haemus, in Thrace. He loved the nymph Orithyia and tried to be gentle with her. Since he could not speak soothingly or sigh softly, he carried her off true to his real character. He was by her the father of Zetes and Calais who both took part in the Argonauts' expedition.

Borgese, Guiseppe Antonio (1882–). Italo-American novelist, scholar, and critic. *The March of Fascism* (1937).

Borgia, Cesare (1476–1507). Notorious Italian military leader, son of Pope Alexander VI (see BORGIA, RODRIGO) and known for his ruthlessness and his crimes. He sought to unify Italy into a single, sovereign state and is considered to be the model of the ideal leader depicted in Machiavelli's *Il Principe* (THE PRINCE).

Borgia, Lucrezia. A famous or rather infamous historical personage (1480–1519), daughter of Pope Alexander VI, and sister of Cesare BORGIA. She was thrice married, her last husband being Alfonso, duke of Ferrara. Another, Alfonso of Aragon, was murdered by her brother. She had a natural son named Gennaro, who was brought up by a Neapolitan fisherman. When grown to manhood, Gennaro had a commission given him in the army, and in the battle of Rimini he saved the life of Orsini. In Venice he declaimed freely against the vices of Lucrezia di Borgia, and on one occasion he mutilated the escutcheon of the Duke by knocking off the B, thus converting Borgia into Orgia. Lucrezia insisted that the perpetrator of this insult should suffer death by poison, but when she discovered that the offender was her own son, she gave him an antidote, and released him from jail. Scarcely, however was he liberated, than he was poisoned at a banquet given by the Princess Negroni. Lucrezia now told Gennaro that he was her own son, and died as he breathed his last. Victor Hugo's drama *Lucrèce Borgia,* which embodies this story, is the basis of Donizetti's opera, *Lucrezia Borgia* (1834).

Borgia, Rodrigo (1431–1503). Father of Cesare and Lucrezia BORGIA who, as the Spanish-born Pope Alexander VI, devoted most of his efforts to extending the power of his family. The crimes of the Borgias have become legendary.

Borglum, John Gutzon de la Mothe (1871–1941). American sculptor, whose work is represented in a number of public buildings and monuments in the U.S. His most famous undertaking was the carving of the faces of Washington, Jefferson, Lincoln, and Theodore Roosevelt in gigantic scale on Mount Rushmore, South Dakota.

Bori, Lucrezia (1888–). Spanish lyric soprano; with Metropolitan Opera Co., N.Y. 1913–1936.

Boris Godounoff. An opera by MOUSSORGSKY (1874) based on Pushkin's historical drama of the same title. The action is laid in Russia and deals with the last years of Boris Godounoff (c. 1551–1605), czar of Russia. He was suspected of having murdered the Czarevitch Dimitri, son of Ivan the Terrible, in order to secure the throne. A pretender, a monk named Gregory who claimed to be Dimitri, headed an uprising against him and was acclaimed by the people. Boris, half insane, died in the midst of the excitement.

Borkman, John Gabriel. See *John Gabriel Borkman.*

Borodin, Alexander Porphyrievich (1833–1887). Russian composer, with a reputation also as a chemist, one of "THE FIVE." He made use of Russian folk-themes in much of his music and is considered to have influenced Debussy, Ravel, Stravinsky, and Sibelius. He wrote operas, symphonies, chamber music, and numerous songs. His best-known works are: *In the Steppes of Central Asia* (1880), a tone poem, and the *Polovtsian Dances* from *Prince Igor,* an unfinished opera later completed by RIMSKY-KORSAKOV and Alexander Glazunov.

Borr. In Scandinavian mythology, the son of Buri (see AUDHUMLA) and father of Odin, Ville, Ve, and Hertha or Earth. The priests claimed descent from him.

Borrioboola-Gha. In *Bleak House* by Dickens, an imaginary place in Africa, the subject of Mrs. Jellyby's missionary zeal.

Borrow, George (1803–1881). English author of books on travel and adventure, based on his own experiences while touring Europe as a Bible agent and a newspaper correspondent. His best-known works, part autobiography and part fiction, are THE BIBLE IN SPAIN (1843); LAVENGRO (1851); and THE ROMANY RYE (1857).

Bors. In Arthurian legend, a King of Gaul and uncle of Lancelot.

Boru, Brian, see BRIAN.

Bosch, Jerome or **Bos, Hieronymus** (1450?–1516). Dutch painter born in Hertogenbosch. Hence his traditional name. His real name is **Hieronymus van Aeken** or **Aken.** He is best known for his scenes of fantastic and nightmarish tortures in hell at the hands of weird monsters. He also did religious pictures, allegories, and satirical *genre* pieces.

Bosinney, Philip. An architect in Galsworthy's FORSYTE SAGA.

boss (Dut. *baas,* head of the household). Hence the great man, chief, overseer. The word has been widely applied in business and in the political field. In the latter case it generally has a derogatory meaning, implying the use of dubious methods of control. Hence *boss-rule* and the verb *to boss.* See next entry.

Boss, The. A drama of politics and business by Edward Sheldon (*Am.* 1886–1945).

Bossuet, Jacques-Bénigne (1627–1704). French churchman, attached to the court of King Louis XIV as tutor to the Dauphin. He was famous for his sermon oratory and his controversies with Protestants and heretics of his day. The most important of his writings is *Discours sur l'histoire universelle* (1679), a treatise on history from the standpoint of religion.

Boston. A novel by Upton SINCLAIR (1928), dealing with the SACCO-VANZETTI case.

Boston Evening Transcript. An American newspaper, founded in 1830 and suspended in 1941, representing conservative aristocratic opinion in New England. T. S. ELIOT wrote a poem named for the newspaper and satirizing what he regarded as the withered, empty lives of its readers.

Bostonians, The. A novel by Henry JAMES (1886), a study of the New England temperament and feminism as combined in the strong-minded but none too lovable heroine, Olive Chancellor.

Boston News-Letter. The first newspaper published in the American colonies to have a permanent life. The first issue appeared on April 20, 1704. See also BOSTON PUBLIC OCCURRENCES.

Boston Public Occurrences. The first newspaper to be published in the American colonies, appearing in 1690. It lasted only one day. See also BOSTON NEWS-LETTER.

Boston Tea Party, the. The destruction in Boston Harbor (Dec. 16th, 1773) of a number of chests of tea by disguised citizens as a protest against the British proposal to tax the American colonists.

Boswell, James (1740–1795). The biographer of Dr. Samuel JOHNSON. His work, *Life of Samuel Johnson* (1791), is considered one of the greatest of all biographies. Boswell's tirelessness in gathering intimate first-hand material during Dr. Johnson's lifetime and his unbounded admiration for Johnson are proverbial; hence, *Boswellian.*

Bosworth, Battle of. The concluding battle of the Wars of the Roses, 1485, in which RICHARD III was killed by the Earl of Richmond, later Henry VII.

Botany Bay. Harbor on east coast of Australia; proposed site of English convict settlement. So called from the number of new plants found there in 1770 by Captain Cook.

Bothwell, Francis Stewart, Earl of. A historic character, known as the Bastard Earl (d. 1624). He appears in Scott's FORTUNES OF NIGEL.

Bothwell, James Hepburn, Earl of (ca. 1536–1578). The husband of MARY QUEEN OF SCOTS. He is the hero of Swinburne's tragedy *Bothwell* (1874), one of a trilogy on the unhappy Queen.

Bothwell, Sergeant, *alias* Francis Stewart. An officer in the royal army in Scott's *Old Mortality.*

Both Your Houses. See ANDERSON, MAXWELL.

bo tree. The pipal tree, or *Ficus religiosa,* of India, allied to the banyan, and so called from Pali *Bodhi,* perfect knowledge, because it is under one of these trees that Gautama attained enlightenment and so became the Buddha.

Botticelli, Sandro (Alessandro di Mariano Filipepi) (1444–1510). Famous Italian painter, pupil of FRA LIPPO LIPPI. He is known for the freshness, charm, and sentiment of his studies of classical and religious subjects. His most celebrated works are *Spring* (ca. 1477) and *The Birth of Venus* (ca. 1485). He painted for the famous MEDICI family, and was a follower of the religious reformer SAVONAROLA.

Bottle, Oracle of the Holy. See under ORACLE.

Bottle Imp, The. A story by Robert Louis STEVENSON.

bottle-washer. Chief agent; the principal man employed by another; a factotum The full phrase—which usually is applied more or less sarcastically—is "chief cook and bottle-washer."

Bottom, the Weaver. A character in Shakespeare's MIDSUMMER NIGHT'S DREAM, a man who fancies he can do everything, and do it better than anyone else. Shakespeare has drawn him as profoundly ignorant, brawny, mock heroic, and with an overflow of self-conceit. When the play of *Pyramus and Thisbe* is cast, Bottom covets every part; the lion, Thisbe, Pyramus, all have charms for him. He is in one part of the drama represented with an ass' head, and Titania, queen of the fairies, under a spell, caresses him as an Adonis.

Bottome, Phyllis (1884–). English novelist. Her *The Mortal Storm* deals with the workings of the Nazi régime.

bottomless pit, The. Hell is so called in the book of *Revelation.* The expression had previously been used by Coverdale in his translation of *Job* xxxvi. 16.

William Pitt was humorously called *the bottomless Pitt,* in allusion to his remarkable thinness.

Bottomley, Gordon (1874–). English poet and poetic dramatist. He revived English verse drama.

Bottomley, Horatio William (1860–1933). Established the rabidly patriotic weekly, *John Bull.* Imprisoned for five years for misappropriation of funds.

Boucher, François (1703–1770). French painter, best known for his decorative panels and tapestries on classical subjects, which he designed for the royal buildings at Versailles and elsewhere.

Boucicault, Dion Lardner (1822–1890). Irish author of plays, especially melodrama. He is best known for THE OCTOROON, OR LIFE IN LOUISIANA (1859), *The Colleen Bawn* (1859), *Arrah-na-Pogue* (1864), and *The Shaughraun* (1875).

Bouguereau, Adolphe William (1825–1905). Popular French decorative and religious painter.

bouillabaisse. A French fish chowder. Thackeray extols it in *The Ballad of Bouillabaisse* which is quoted from in Du Maurier's *Trilby.*

Boulangism. The principles of a French political movement (1886–1890). Identified with General Georges Ernest Jean Marie Boulanger (1837–1891) who advocated militarism and revenge on Germany. He was called "Man on Horseback" because he often appeared mounted before Paris crowds. He is the subject of a biography called *Brave General* (1942) by Herbert S. GORMAN.

Boule de Suif (*Fr.* "Suet Ball"). The heroine of De MAUPASSANT's first novelette, with that title, 1880. A prostitute who patriotically plies her trade in the Franco-Prussian War of 1870.

Boulle or Boule, Charles André (in English **Buhle**) (1642–1732). Established in Louvre palace as cabinet-maker to Louis XIV. Is famous for furniture inlaid with metals, tortoise-shell, and mother-of-pearl, on ebony, a style called buhlework.

Bound East for Cardiff. A one-act play by Eugene O'NEILL, produced in 1916 and concerned with tragedy among seamen on a tramp steamer.

bounds, beating the. An old custom, still kept up in many English parishes, of going round the parish boundaries on Holy Thursday, or Ascension Day. The schoolchildren, accompanied by the clergymen and parish officers, walked through their parish from end to end; the boys were switched with willow wands all along the lines of boundary, the idea being to teach them to know the bounds of their parish.

Many practical jokes were played even during the first quarter of the nineteenth century, to make the boys remember the delimitations: such as "pumping them," pouring water clandestinely on them from house windows, beating them with thin rods, etc.

Beating the bounds was called in Scotland *riding the marches* (bounds), and in England the day is sometimes called *gang-day.*

Bountiful, Lady. A famous character in Farquhar's comedy *The Beaux' Stratagem* (1705), the widow of Sir Charles Bountiful. Her delight is curing the parish sick and relieving the indigent. Hence a *Lady Bountiful* is a gracious dispenser of charity.

Bounty, H.M.S. The ship in a famous English case of mutiny during a voyage from Tahiti to the West Indies in 1789. It was first celebrated by Sir J. Barrow in his *The Mutiny and Piratical Seizure of H.M.S. Bounty,* published in 1831. Byron's poem THE ISLAND was based on events following the mutiny, and a best-selling trilogy of novels (see MUTINY ON THE BOUNTY) was written on the case by the American authors Charles Nordhoff and James Norman Hall in the 1930's. See also BLIGH, CAPTAIN; CHRISTIAN, FLETCHER; PITCAIRN ISLAND.

bounty jumper. In the latter part of the American Civil War, one who enlisted to get a money gift from the government and then deserted.

Bourbon. The Bourbon Kings of France were Henry IV, Louis XIII, XIV, XV and XVI (1589–1793). This royal family, it was said, "learned nothing and forgot nothing"; hence a *Bourbon* is anyone who fails to learn by experience. The name was given to the American Democratic party by its opponents.

Bourgeois Gentilhomme, Le. A comedy by Molière (1670). The hero is M. Jourdain, a rich tradesman who sets up as a gentleman.

bourgeoisie (*Fr.*). The merchants, manufacturers, and entrepreneurs considered as a class. The term came into special prominence in the economic theories of Karl MARX and his disciples in the 19th and 20th centuries, which presented the bourgeoisie as the ruling class under the capitalist system of society, from whose hands ownership of the means of production and distribution must be removed in order that socialism might be established. The Russian revolution in 1917 transferred ownership of capital property in that country from the bourgeoisie to the state, which was professedly acting in the interests of the PROLETARIAT. In the ideology and the governmental policies of both Fascism and NAZISM, the bourgeoisie was also subject to taxation and gradual expropriation, although in their early years both movements were encouraged and financed by large industrialists who hoped to protect themselves thereby against Communist revolution. Originally, the bourgeoisie belonged to the THIRD ESTATE of feudalism, and are considered to have furnished the direction for the French Revolution.

The term *bourgeois* is often used as a synonym of Philistine. Hence the French phrase, dear to Latin Quarter geniuses, *épater le bourgeois* "bowl over the bourgeois."

Bourget, Paul Charles Joseph (1852–1935). French novelist and critic, who developed from the society and psychological novel, the latter of which he helped popularize, to political conservatism and an interest in Catholicism. His criticism was marked by psychological analysis. Among his novels are *Cruelle Enigme* (1885); *Le Disciple* (1889); *Cosmopolis* (1893); *L'Etape* (1902); *Le Démon de Midi* (1914). His critical works include *Etudes et Portraits* (1888) and *Pages de Doctrine et de Critique* (1912).

Bourgh, Lady Catherine de. A patronizing and overbearing "great lady" in Jane Austen's PRIDE AND PREJUDICE.

Bourke, Chevalier. An Irish character in Stevenson's MASTER OF BALLANTRAE, devoted to the Master.

Bourke-White, Margaret (1906–). American photographer, former wife of Erskine CALDWELL and known for her photographic studies of industry, social and economic conditions, news personalities, foreign countries, and the like. Her work includes *Eyes on Russia* (1931) and *Red Republic* (1934), motion-picture travelogues; *U.S.S.R.: A Portfolio of Photographs* (1934); YOU HAVE SEEN THEIR FACES (1937), *North of the Danube* (1939), and *Say! Is This the U.S.A.?* (1941), books of text and photographs prepared in collaboration with her husband; and *Shooting the Russian War* (1942). She was associated with FORTUNE, LIFE, and *PM* as editor and photographer.

Bourne, Randolph Silliman (1886–1918). American literary critic and essayist, a radical in political thought and a pacifist during World War I. He contributed to the leading "advanced" periodicals of the day, including THE DIAL, THE NEW REPUBLIC, THE MASSES, and SEVEN ARTS. Chief among his collections of essays are *Youth and Life* (1913); *Towards an Enduring Peace* (1916); *Untimely Papers* (1919); and *The History of a Literary Radical* (1920). The last two books were brought out posthumously.

Bourne, Reuben. The chief character in Hawthorne's ROGER MALVIN'S FUNERAL.

Bourrienne, Louis Antoine Fauvelet de (1769–1834). French diplomat. Author of *Mémoires sur Napoléon* (1829).

Boutet de Monvel, Louis Maurice (1851–1913). French painter and illustrator. Known for his illustrations of children's books, *Chansons de France, Jeanne d'Arc,* etc.

bouts-rimés (*Fr.* rhymed-endings). A parlor game which, in the 18th century, had a considerable vogue in literary circles as a test of skill. A list of words that rhyme with one another is drawn up; this is handed to the competitors, and they must make a poem to the rhymes, each rhyme-word being kept in its place on the list.

Bovary, Charles. In Flaubert's MADAME BOVARY, the husband of the heroine, Emma BOVARY. He is a conscientious but slow-moving, crude, and unimaginative provincial doctor.

Bovary, Emma. The heroine of Flaubert's MADAME BOVARY, a young country woman whose wistful dreams of romantic love are frustrated in her relations with her husband, Charles BOVARY, and who tries to realize them in extra-marital love-affairs. Hence bovarysm, when a woman is possessed by a romantic conception of herself.

Bow bells. The bells of Bow Church. Hence *born within the sound of Bow bells,* born in the vicinity of Bow Church or St. Mary-le-bow, nearly in the center of London. See COCKNEY.

Bow-boy, The Blind. See VAN VECHTEN, CARL.

bowdlerize. To expurgate a book. Thomas Bowdler, in 1818, gave to the world an edition of Shakespeare's works "in which nothing is added to the original text; but those words and expressions are omitted which cannot with propriety be read aloud in a family." This was in ten volumes. Bowdler subsequently treated Gibbon's *Decline and Fall* in the same way. Hence the words bowdlerist, bowdlerizer, bowdlerism, bowdlerization, etc.

Bowen, Elizabeth (1899–). Distinguished Anglo-Irish novelist. Writes of the upper middle class. One of her best books is *The Hotel.*

Bowen, Marjorie. See under LONG, GABRIELLE MARGARET VERE.

Bower, Bertha Muzzy (1871–1940). American woman writer of "Westerns." Her first and best-liked romance of this type was *Chip of the Flying U.*

Bower of Bliss. A beautiful and enchanting place of temptation. (1) In Tasso's JERUSALEM DELIVERED, a garden belonging to the enchantress ARMIDA. It abounds in everything that can contribute to earthly pleasure. Here

Rinaldo spends some time with ARMIDA but he ultimately breaks from the enchantress and rejoins the war.

(2) In Spenser's *Faërie Queene* the residence of the witch ACRASIA, a beautiful and most fascinating woman. This lovely garden is situated on a floating island filled with everything to enchant the senses and "wrap the spirit in forgetfulness."

Bowers, Claude Gernade (1878–). American journalist, historian, diplomat. *Jefferson and Hamilton* (1925), *The Tragic Era* (1929); etc.

Bowery. The "tough" district of New York City; the slums. Bowery or *bouwerij* is the old Dutch word for farm; and Bowery Lane received its name because it led out to the farm of Peter Stuyvesant, one of the Dutch governors of colonial days. It was for a long time the height of fashion to live on Bowery Lane, but with the growth of the city the character of the district underwent a radical change, becoming the site of dance halls and gambling resorts. *The Bowery,* a popular song by Charles H. Hoyt, gives an indication of the reputation of the district at the close of the 19th century. Hence *Bowery boy,* a toughie of the neighborhood.

Bowes, Major Edward (1874–1946). Master of ceremonies of an extremely popular American radio program, *Major Bowes' Amateur Hour* (ca. 1935), which featured the introduction and supposedly extemporaneous performance of talented "amateur" singers, musicians, impersonators, and the like, accompanied by "human-interest" biographies.

Bowes-Lyon. Family name of Queen ELIZABETH of England (b. 1900).

Bowie State. Arkansas. See under STATES.

Bowling, Lt. Tom. The immortal type of a brave and hardy sailor; from the character of that name in Smollett's RODERICK RANDOM. He is the uncle of Random; a man too frankly the product of the sea to be anything but ill at ease and careless of the niceties of life ashore.

In a famous sea-song Captain Thomas Dibdin is commemorated by his brother Charles Dibdin under the name of Tom Bowling.

> Here a sheer hulk lies poor Tom Bowling
> The darling of the crew.

Bowman, Isaiah (1878–). American geographer. Authority on physiography and political geography. President of Johns Hopkins University.

Bow Street. A street near Covent Garden in London which contains the principal police court. Bow Street Runners were early police officers.

bowwow theory. A theory, now abandoned, going back to the philologist MAX MÜLLER, according to which language originated in the sounds made by animals. The *poohpooh theory* had language originate in interjections and the *dingdong theory* in acoustic reflexes.

Box and Cox. A farce by J. M. Morton (1847) the principal characters of which are Box and Cox. It has been called "the best farce for three characters in the English language." The third character is the thrifty landlady who rents the same rooms to Box and Cox (one of whom is employed by night, the other by day) in the vain hope that her two tenants will remain ignorant of each other's existence. Hence a *Box and Cox arrangement.*

Boxers. A secret society in China which took a prominent part in the rising against foreigners in 1900 which was suppressed by joint European action. The Chinese name was *gee ho chuan,* signifying "righteousness, harmony, and fists," and implying training as in athletics, for the purpose of developing righteousness and harmony.

Boxing Day. In England the first weekday after Christmas, a legal holiday on which Christmas boxes are given to postmen, etc.

box the compass. To name the 32 points of the compass in their order. Figuratively speaking, to make a complete turnabout or reversal.

Boy and the Mantle. A ballad in Percy's *Reliques.* See MANTLE OF FIDELITY.

Boy Bishop. St. Nicholas of Bari was called "the Boy Bishop" because from his cradle he manifested marvelous indications of piety. The custom of choosing a boy from the cathedral choir, etc., on his day (December 6th), as a mock bishop, is very ancient. The boy possessed episcopal honor for three weeks, and the rest of the choir were his prebendaries. If he died during his time of office he was buried *in pontificalibus.* Probably the reference is to Jesus Christ sitting in the Temple among the doctors while He was a boy. The custom was abolished in the reign of Henry VIII.

boycott. To refuse to deal with a person, to take any notice of him, or even to sell to him. The term arose in 1881, when Captain Boycott, an Irish landlord, was thus ostracized by the Irish agrarian insurgents.

Boyd, Ernest (1887–1946). Irish literary critic, who lived in the U.S. His chief critical works are *Appreciations and Depreciations* (1918); *Ireland's Literary Renaissance* (1922); *Portraits, Real and Imaginary* (1924); *Literary Blasphemies* (1927).

Boyd, James (1888–1944). American novelist, living for many years at Southern Pines, North Carolina. Author of *Drums* (1925), *Marching On* (1927), *Long Hunt* (1930), etc.

His poems were published posthumously. His novels all deal with different periods in American history.

Boyd, Nancy. Pseudonym of Edna St. Vincent MILLAY as a writer of short stories in the early years of her career.

Boyd, Thomas (1898–1935). American novelist and short story writer. First came into prominence by writing a novel about World War I, *Through the Wheat,* at the age of 25, after his discharge from the Army where he had won the Croix de Guerre. His historical studies deal with such American characters as Simon Girty, the White Savage, Mad Anthony Wayne, and John Fitch, inventor of the steamboat.

Boyg, The. A mysterious and invisible but powerful force, an animistic representation of Norwegian folklore found in Ibsen's PEER GYNT.

Boy in the Bush, The. See LAWRENCE, DAVID HERBERT.

Boylan, "Blazes." A character in James Joyce's ULYSSES, lover of Molly BLOOM at the time of the novel's action.

Boyle, Elizabeth. Wife of Edmund Spenser. See AMORETTI.

Boyle, Kay (1903–). American novelist and short-story writer, an expatriate resident of France for many years until World War II, known for the stylistic precision of her work and her penetrating psychological studies of character. Her published collections of short stories are *Wedding Day* (1930); *First Lover* (1933); *The White Horses of Vienna* (1936); THE CRAZY HUNTER (1940). Her novels include *Plagued by the Nightingale* (1931); *Year Before Last* (1932); *Gentlemen, I Address You Privately* (1933); *My Next Bride* (1934); *Death of a Man* (1936); *Monday Night* (1938); *The Youngest Camel* (1939). *A Glad Day* (1938) is a volume of poetry.

Boyle, Robert (1627–1691). Famous British physicist and chemist. Boyle's law states that when a gas is subjected to compression, and kept at a constant temperature, the product of the pressure and the volume is a constant quality, the volume is inversely proportioned to the pressure.

Boyle controversy. A book-battle between Charles Boyle, fourth Earl of Orrery, and the famous Bentley, respecting the *Epistles of Phalaris,* which were edited by Boyle in 1695. Swift's BATTLE OF THE BOOKS was one result of the controversy.

Boylesve, René (1867–1926). French novelist. A master of irony. Member of the French Academy since 1919.

Boynton, Dr. A leading character in Howells' UNDISCOVERED COUNTRY. His daughter Egeria is also prominent.

Boynton, Henry Walcott (1869–1947). American critic and biographer. Author of lives of Washington Irving, Bret Harte, and James Fenimore Cooper.

Boynton, Percy Holmes (1875–1946). Brother of the above. American scholar and critic. *America in Contemporary Fiction* (1940).

Boy Orator or **Boy Orator of the Platte.** William Jennings BRYAN of Nebraska.

Boys from Syracuse, The. An American musical comedy adapted freely from Shakespeare's A COMEDY OF ERRORS, with music by Richard Rodgers and Lorenz Hart, produced in 1938.

Boy Scouts. An organization of boys for civic duty, camping, etc., founded in England in 1908 by Sir Robert Stephenson Smyth (now Baron) Baden-Powell.

Boythorn, Laurence. In Dickens' BLEAK HOUSE, a robust gentleman with the voice of a Stentor, a friend of Mr. Jarndyce. He would utter the most ferocious sentiments, while at the same time he fondled a pet canary on his finger. Once on a time he had been in love with Miss Barbary, Lady Dedlock's sister. The character is supposed to have been drawn from Walter Savage Landor, the noted poet.

Boyville, The Court of. A book by William Allen WHITE.

Boz. Charles Dickens (1812–1870). His *Sketches by Boz* (two series) appeared in 1836. "Boz, my signature in the *Morning Chronicle,*" he tells us, "was the nickname of a pet child, a younger brother, whom I had dubbed Moses, in honor of the *Vicar of Wakefield,* which, being pronounced *Bozes,* got shortened into *Boz.*"

Bozzaris, Marco. See MARCO BOZZARIS.

Bozzy. James Boswell, the biographer of Dr. Johnson (1740–1795).

Brabançonne. The national anthem of Belgium, composed by Van Campenhout in the revolution of 1830, and so named from Brabant, of which Brussels is the chief city.

Brabantio. In Shakespeare's *Othello,* a senator of Venice, father of Desdemona. He thought the "insolence" of Othello in marrying his daughter unpardonable, and that Desdemona must have been drugged with love-potions so to degrade herself.

Braccio. In Browning's poetical drama, LURIA, the commissary of the republic of Florence, employed in picking up every item of scandal he could find against Luria.

Bracebridge Hall. A volume of sketches by Washington IRVING (1822). Many of them deal with the comfortable country home and the family concerns of Squire Bracebridge, a delightfully typical old English gentleman whose whims and customs give Irving opportunity for some of his most pertinent comments on English life.

Bracegirdle, Anne (1663?–1748). English actress closely associated with plays of Congreve.

Brackenridge, Hugh Henry (1748–1816). American novelist, one of the first to seek to write of the native American scene as valid literature. He collaborated with Philip FRENEAU on *The Rising Glory of America* (1772), a commencement oration at Princeton, and also wrote *The Battle of Bunker's Hill* (1776) and *The Death of General Montgomery* (1777), blank verse dramas in the 18th-century style. His most important work is MODERN CHIVALRY, OR THE ADVENTURES OF CAPTAIN JOHN FARRAGO AND TEAGUE O'REGAN HIS SERVANT (1792–1815).

Bracy, Sir Maurice de. In Scott's IVANHOE, a follower of Prince John. He sues the Lady Rowena to become his bride, and threatens to kill both Cedric and Ivanhoe if she refuses. The interview is intercepted, and at the close of the novel Rowena marries Ivanhoe.

Bradamant. In Carlovingian legend, a celebrated female warrior, prominent in both Boiardo's *Orlando Innamorato* and Ariosto's ORLANDO FURIOSO. She is the sister of Rinaldo and niece of Charlemagne and is known as the "Virgin Knight." She wears white armor and a white plume and possesses an irresistible spear which unhorses any knight at a touch. Although she is in love with Rogero the Moor, she refuses to marry him until he is baptized. Her marriage and Rogero's victory over Rodomont form the subject of the last book of ORLANDO FURIOSO.

Braddock, Edward (1695–1755). British General, leader of ill-fated expedition against Fort Duquesne. Lost half his force from obstinacy, against the French and Indians. Died of wounds a few days after a surprise attack. Washington was one of his junior officers.

Braddon, Mary Elizabeth (1837–1915). Author of *Lady Audley's Secret* (1862) and some 80 other novels. She was, says G. B. Shaw, "what we now call a lowbrow; but . . . her style would overawe us now as classical." Mother of W. B. MAXWELL, also a novelist.

Bradford, Andrew (1686–1742). American printer and publisher. Brought out the first newspaper of Pennsylvania: *American Weekly Mercury* (Philadelphia, from December 1719). For eleven years (1712–1723) Bradford was the only printer in Pennsylvania.

Bradford, Gamaliel (1863–1932). American biographer, known for his psychological studies of literary and historical figures. DAMAGED SOULS (1923) is his best known work. Others are *Confederate Portraits* (1914); *Portraits of Women* (1916); *American Portraits* (1922); *Wives* (1925); *Daughters of Eve* (1930); and *The Quick and the Dead* (1931). *Life and I* (1928) is autobiographical. His *Journal* was published posthumously in 1933.

Bradford, Roark (1896–). American author of books of pseudo-Negro folklore, especially stories of the Bible. The best-known are *Ol' Man Adam an' His Chillun* (1928), from which the play THE GREEN PASTURES was adapted; *This Side Jordan* (1929); *Ol' King David an' the Philistine Boys* (1930); *John Henry* (1931).

Bradford, William (1588–1657). Leader in the founding of Plymouth, governor of the colony from 1621 to his death, except for five years during which he refused election. He was one of the authors of an account of the settlement of Plymouth known as MOURT'S RELATION, published in 1622, and is best known for his *History of Plymouth Plantation,* a chronicle of events in the colony from 1620 to 1646, which was not discovered and published until 1856.

Bradlaugh, Charles (1833–1891). English social and political reformer. Free-thought lecturer. When prosecuted with Mrs. Annie BESANT in 1876 for republishing Malthusian *Fruits of Philosophy,* his acquittal helped remove existing restrictions on freedom of the press. Barred from Parliament, though elected M.P. for six years, because as a free-thinker he refused to swear on the Bible and instead wished to affirm. Finally championed a bill that made such affirmation legal.

Bradley, Edward. Pseudonym **Cuthbert Bede** (1827–1889). English clergyman, author and illustrator of *Adventures of Mr. Verdant Green, an Oxford Freshman* (1853–1856); *Little Mr. Bouncer,* etc. Illustrated his own verse and prose.

Bradley, Francis Herbert (1846–1924). English philosopher of the school of Idealism, his thought being related particularly to that of Hegel. In ethics, he attacked Herbert SPENCER and the Utilitarians (see UTILITARIANISM), asserting that the individual must integrate his efforts with a larger whole in order to attain self-realization. In metaphysics, he maintained that nature is only appearance, an imperfect manifestation of the Absolute, which is a self-sufficient spirit, requiring nothing outside itself for its completion. His chief work is *Appearance and Reality* (1893), which aroused a great deal of discussion. Other works include *Ethi-*

cal Studies (1876); *The Principles of Logic* (1883); *Essays on Truth and Reality* (1914).

Bradley, Omar Nelson (1893-). American general in World War II. In command of U.S. Second Corps in Tunisia and of the Allied Twelfth Army Group in Western Europe. After the war in charge of the Veterans' Administration. Attacked by commander of American Legion but vigorously defended by President Truman, General Eisenhower, and others. Highly praised in *Top Secret* (1946) by Ralph Ingersoll. Appointed Chief of Staff in November 1947.

Bradstreet, Anne (1612?–1672). American poet of the Massachusetts Bay Colony, writing of religious subjects according to the Puritan outlook and under the general influence of George HERBERT, Francis QUARLES, and Guillaume DU BARTAS. THE TENTH MUSE LATELY SPRUNG UP IN AMERICA is a collection of her poems, published in 1650 and the first volume of original verse to be written in New England. She also wrote *Religious Experiences,* an autobiographical sketch, and *Meditations Divine and Moral,* a collection of aphorisms for the instruction of her son.

Bradwardine, Como Cosmyne, Baron of. One of Scott's most famous characters, described by him in WAVERLEY as "the very model of the old Scottish cavalier, with all his excellencies and peculiarities." He is a scholar, full of pedantry and vanity, but very gallant and lovable.

In Thackeray's *Book of Snobs* ii, the *Baron of Bradwardine,* described as "the most famous man in Haggisland," is meant for Sir Walter Scott.

Bradwardine, Rose. Daughter of Baron BRADWARDINE and heroine of WAVERLEY.

Brady, Cyrus Townsend (1861–1920). American clergyman and author of many books for boys and historical stories, biographies of Paul Jones, Andrew Jackson, etc.

Brady, Mathew B. (ca. 1823–1896). American photographer, the first significant representative of his profession in the U.S. He is best known for his record of the Civil War in photographs, *National Photographic Collection of War Views* (1869).

Brady, William A. (1863-). American theatrical producer and manager. Also managed the prizefighters, James J. Corbett and James J. Jeffries. Married the actress Grace George. The daughter of a former marriage, the late Alice Brady, became a star of stage and screen.

Braes of Yarrow, see YARROW.

Brag, Jack, see JACK BRAG.

Bragdon, Claude (1866–1946). American theosophist and architect. Author of books on both theosophy and architecture.

Bragelonne, The Vicomte de. See THREE MUSKETEERS.

Bragg, Braxton (1817–1876). U.S.M.A. 1837. Confederate general in U.S. Civil War. Won battle of Chickamauga.

Braggadochio. A braggart; one who is valiant with his tongue but a great coward at heart. The character is from Spenser's *Faërie Queene,* and a type of the "Intemperance of the Tongue." After a time, like the jackdaw in borrowed plumes, Braggadochio is stripped of all his glories: his shield is claimed by Sir Marinell; his lady is proved by the golden girdle to be the false Florimel; his horse is claimed by Sir Guyon; Talus shaves off his beard and scourges his squire; and the pretender sneaks off amidst the jeers of everyone. It is thought that the poet had the Duke d'Alençon, a suitor of Queen Elizabeth, in his eye when he drew this character. Others believe it was drawn from Philip II of Spain.

Bragi. In Scandinavian mythology the son of Odin and Frigga, and the god of poetry; represented as an old man with a long white beard. His wife was Iduna.

Bragi's apples were an instant cure of weariness, decay of power, ill temper, and failing health; the supply was inexhaustible, for immediately one was eaten another took its place.

Bragi's cup. To each new king before he ascended the high-seat of his fathers Bragi's cup was handed, and he had to make a pledge by it and drain it.

Bragi's story. A lengthy but interesting tale.

Bragmardo, Janotus de. In Rabelais' *Gargantua,* a sophister who seeks to recover from Gargantua the great bells of Notre Dame and windily exhorts him.

Brahe, Tycho (1546–1601). Danish astronomer, who tried to establish a middle ground between the PTOLEMAIC and COPERNICAN systems of astronomy, maintaining that the earth was motionless, but that the five planets revolved around the sun, which circled the earth once every year. He also discovered the celebrated "new star" in Cassiopeia, the first in a world previously considered fixed for eternity, on November 11, 1572. His account of it, *De Nova Stella,* was published in 1573. He wrote a number of treatises on astronomy in Latin, the most important being *Astronomiae Instauratae Progymnasmata* (1602–1603), edited by KEPLER.

Brahma. In Hinduism, Brahma, properly speaking, is the Absolute, or God conceived as entirely impersonal. The theological abstraction was endowed with personality, and became the Creator of the universe, the first in the divine Triad, of which the other partners were Vishnu, the Maintainer, and Siva (or Shiva), the Destroyer. The Brahmins claim Brahma as the founder of their religious system.

Brahmin. A worshiper of Brahma, a member of the highest caste in the system of Hinduism, and of the priestly order. Also a satirical term for a member of the New England aristocracy, a group known for its emphasis on class differences. See CASTE.

Brahmo Samaj (*Sans.*, the Society of Believers in the One God). A monotheistic sect of Brahmins, founded in 1818 in Calcutta by Ramohun Roy (1744–1833), a wealthy and well educated Brahmin who wished to purify his religion and found a National Church which should be free from idolatry and superstition. In 1844 the Church was reorganized by Debendro Nath Tagore, and since that time its reforming zeal and influence have gained it many adherents. The Brahmo Samaj became more and more political, until it was looked upon as one of the chief factors in the movement for complete nationalization and autonomy.

Brahms, Johannes (1833–1897). German composer, known for the combined strength and sentiment of his music and regarded by many as the heir and successor or again a mere epigonus of BEETHOVEN. A pet abomination of Romain ROLLAND. His works include four symphonies, concertos, chamber music, and numerous *lieder*. The *First* (1876) and the *Fourth* (1885) are the most popular of Brahms' symphonies.

Braid, James (1870–). Famous professional golfer. Born in Fifeshire not far from St. Andrews, the great Mecca of the game. Three times Open Champion (1901, 1905, 1906). With Taylor and Harry Vardon, one of the great names in golf. Author of *Advanced Golf*, etc.

Braille. An alphabetic system of raised points by which the blind are enabled to read and write, invented by Louis Braille (1809–1852), a Frenchman, in 1829.

Brailsford, Henry Noel (1873–). British journalist. Author of *Shelley, Godwin, and their Circle* (1913), *How the Soviet Works* (1927), *Rebel India* (1932), *Voltaire* (1935).

Brainworm. In Ben Jonson's comedy *Every Man in His Humor* (1598), the servant of Knowell, a man of infinite shifts, and a veritable Proteus in his metamorphoses. He appears first as Brainworm; afterwards as Fitz-Sword; then as a reformed soldier whom Knowell takes into his service; then as Justice Clement's man; and lastly as valet to the courts of law, by which devices he plays upon the same clique of some half-dozen men of average intelligence.

Braithwaite, William Stanley (1878–). Negro poet and compiler for many years of the *Anthology of Magazine Verse and Year Book of American Poetry*, in seventeen volumes.

Bramble, Matthew. The chief character of Smollett's EXPEDITION OF HUMPHREY CLINKER, an "odd kind of humorist," "always on the fret," dyspeptic, and afflicted with the gout, but benevolent, generous, and kind-hearted. With his sister Tabitha and her maid he goes on a "family tour" which furnishes the chief interest of the book.

Miss Tabitha Bramble. In the same book, the maiden sister of Matthew Bramble, of some forty-five years of age, noted for her bad spelling. She is starch, vain, prim, and ridiculous; soured in temper, prying and uncharitable. She contrives at last to marry Captain Lismahago, who is content to take her for the sake of her £4000.

Bramine and **Bramin.** Mrs. Elizabeth Draper and the English novelist Laurence Sterne. Ten of Sterne's letters to Mrs. Draper are published, and called *Letters to Eliza.* The fact that Sterne was a clergyman and that Mrs. Draper had been born in India suggested the names.

Bran. In MACPHERSON's poem Temora, Fingal's dog, a mighty favorite. Hence the phrase, *if not Bran, it is Bran's brother.* If not the real "Simon Pure," it is just as good. A complimentary expression.

Bran, son of Febal. Hero of THE VOYAGE OF BRAN, an early Irish tale.

Branch, Anna Hempstead (1874–1937). American lyric and mystical poet. Among her works are *The Heart of the Road* (1901); *The Shoes that Danced* (1906); *Rose of the Wind* (1910); *Rose of the Lock Box* (1929); *Last Poems,* edited with a Foreword by Ridgely Torrence (1944). Her long poem *Nimrod* is one of the most extraordinarily sustained poems written by a woman.

Brancusi, Constantin (1876–). Roumanian sculptor, known for his use of abstract forms, executed in wood, glass, steel, stone, bronze, etc. His best-known single work is *Bird in Space* (1925).

Brand. A drama by Henrik IBSEN (*Nor.* 1866). The hero is an idealistic peasant priest in violent revolt against the pettiness and evil of conventional society. He perishes at last in the ruins of his ice-church under an avalanche.

The dramatist wrote of him "Brand is myself in my best moments."

Brand, Ethan, see ETHAN BRAND.

Brand, Max (1892–1944). Pseudonym of Frederick Faust, tremendously successful American writer of Western stories. He was also the author of the "Dr. Kildare" motion pictures. He began as a poet, but none of his listed eighty-five books is of poetry.

Brand, Millen (1906–). American novelist. Author of the successful *The Outward Room*.

Brandan or **Brendan, St.** See under SAINT.

Brandeis, Louis Dembitz (1856–1941). Distinguished American jurist and legal light. Up to his retirement, associate justice of the U.S. Supreme Court (1916–1939).

Brandenburg Concertos. A series of six concertos, written by J. S. BACH and sent to the Margrave of Brandenburg in 1721, whose name has been given to them. They are among the most widely played of the composer's works.

Brandes, Georg Morris (1842–1927). Danish literary critic. Chief Scandinavian advocate of the non-historicity theory of Jesus. Introduced feminism into Denmark. Took all literature for his province. His original surname was Cohen.

Brandon, Charles, Duke of Suffolk. The hero of Major's historical romance, WHEN KNIGHTHOOD WAS IN FLOWER.

Brandt, Margaret. The heroine of Reade's historical novel, *The Cloister and the Hearth,* the mother of Erasmus. Her father. Peter Brandt, is a prominent character.

Branghtons. Vulgar, malicious, jealous people, from a family of that name in Fanny Burney's EVELINA. They are cousins of the heroine, Evelina, and put her to endless embarrassment and shame by their vulgarity and their habit of making use of her friends for their own purposes, but she is too well bred to make them feel their own lack of breeding.

Brangwaine. In the TRISTAN legend, the maid of Iseult.

Brann, William Cowper (1855–1898). Known as Brann the Iconoclast. Founded *The Iconoclast* (1891; Waco, Tex.) Killed in a pistol fight on streets of Waco.

Brant, Joseph (1742–1807). Mohawk Indian Chief, with Tories under the Butlers and Johnsons ravaged the Mohawk Valley.

Brant, Sebastian (1457–1521). German humanist and satirist, author of the allegory *Das Narrenschiff* (SHIP OF FOOLS, 1494), a modern American translation of which was published by Prof. Zeydel in 1944.

Bran the Blessed. In Celtic mythology, god of the underworld and son of LLYR

Brantôme, Pierre de Bourdeilles, Seigneur de (1535?–1614). French chronicler His *Mémoires,* published in 1665–1666, are full of interesting gossip about important people of the times.

Branwen. In Welsh legend, the daughter of King Llyr of Britain and wife of Matholch, king of Ireland.

Brangwyn, Frank (1867–). Famous British painter and mural decorator. Known for richness of color.

Braque, Georges (1882–). French painter, associated with Pablo PICASSO in founding the school of CUBISM. He was influenced by CÉZANNE and his subjects were chiefly still lifes.

Brass. See NORRIS, CHARLES G.

Brass Check, The. A book by Upton SINCLAIR, published in 1919 and attacking abuses in the newspapers of the time.

Brass, Sampson. In Dickens' OLD CURIOSITY SHOP, a knavish, servile attorney, affecting great sympathy with his clients but in reality fleecing them without mercy.

Sally Brass. Sampson's sister, and an exaggerated edition of her brother.

Brassbound, Captain. Hero of Shaw's CAPTAIN BRASSBOUND'S CONVERSION.

Brassbounder, The. A nautical novel by David W. BONE.

Brave New World. A novel by Aldous HUXLEY, published in 1932, which gives a satirical picture of a future world in which science has solved all human problems.

Braves. In American baseball parlance, a nickname for the Boston Nationals. See BASEBALL TEAMS.

Bravo, The. A novel by James Fenimore COOPER (1831), dealing with the intrigues of 16th-century Venice. The "bravo," Jacopo, revolts against his trade of spying and murdering and assists a pair of young lovers to escape their enemies, but pays for his act with his life.

brazen age. The age of war and violence. See also under *age*.

Brazen Head. The legend of the wonderful head of brass that could speak and was omniscient is common property to early romances, and is of Eastern origin. In *Valentine and Orson,* for instance, we hear of a gigantic head kept in the castle of the giant FERRAGUS, of Portugal. It told those who consulted it whatever they required to know, past, present, or to come; but the most famous in English legend is that fabled to have been made by the great Roger BACON.

It was said if Bacon heard it speak he would succeed in his projects; if not, he would fail. His familiar, Miles, was set to watch, and while Bacon slept the Head spoke thrice: "Time is"; half an hour later it said, "Time was." In another half-hour it said, "Time's past," fell down, and was broken to atoms. Byron refers to this legend.

> Like Friar Bacon's brazen head, I've spoken,
> "Time is," "Time was," "Time's past."
> *Don Juan,* i. 217.

References to Bacon's Brazen Head are frequent in literature; among them may be mentioned:

> Bacon trembled for his brazen head.
> Pope, *Dunciad,* iii, 104.
> Quoth he, "My head's not made of brass,
> As Friar Bacon's noddle was."
> Butler, *Hudibras,* ii. 2.

Brazenhead the Great. A novel by Maurice HEWLETT.

Bread. See NORRIS, CHARLES G.

Breadwinners, The. A novel by John HAY (1883) dealing with labor problems and presenting an unsympathetic portrait of a union organizer, Offitt. The hero, Alfred Farnham, organizes a body of volunteer policemen to preserve order during a strike. The novel, which was first published anonymously, aroused much discussion.

Break, Break, Break. A poem by TENNYSON (1842), one of those inspired by the death of his friend Arthur HALLAM. See also IN MEMORIAM.

Breasted, James Henry (1865–1935). American orientalist, archaeologist, and historian. Also university professor. Wrote *A History of Egypt* (1905), *Ancient Times: A History of the Early World* (1916). In 1919 he became director of the New Oriental Institute at the University of Chicago. Member National Academy of Sciences. Did much exploration on the Nile.

Breath of Life, The. See BURROUGHS, JOHN.

Brebœuf and His Brethren. A narrative poem by E. J. PRATT, leading Canadian poet, dealing with the Jesuit missionaries in Canada in the 17th century. Brebœuf was killed by the Iroquois. He was beatified in 1925 by the Church.

Brecht, Bertold (1898–). German revolutionary poet, playwright and novelist. Left Germany in 1935. In the U.S. since 1941. The most significant of his short dramas is the one-act, *Señora Carrar's Rifles* (1938), dealing with the Spanish war.

Breck, Alan. An adventurer in Stevenson's KIDNAPPED and DAVID BALFOUR, whose full name is Alan Breck Stewart.

Breeches Bible, the. See under BIBLE, SPECIALLY NAMED.

Breen, Grace. The heroine of Howells' novel, DR. BREEN'S PROFESSION.

Breitmann, Hans. A "Pennsylvania Dutchman" of picturesque speech and jovial habits, created by Charles Godfrey Leland. He first appeared in *Hans Breitmann's Party* in 1856, and in 1868 his adventures were collected into book form in the *Breitmann Ballads.* He is typical of the German immigrants of 1848 and thereabouts.

Bremond, Henri (1855–1933). French literary critic and historian.

Brendan or **Brandan, St.** See under SAINT.

Brenn or **Brenhin.** See under RULERS, TITLES OF.

Brenner Pass. Lowest pass over the Tyrolean Alps. The route from Central Germany to Italy where, following the formation of the Rome-Berlin Axis, the two dictators, Hitler and Mussolini, frequently met.

Brentano, Clemens Maria (1778–1842). German romantic poet, brother of BETTINA. With his friend and brother-in-law Achim von Arnim he tried to do in *Des Knaben Wunderhorn* for the German folksong what the GRIMM brothers did for the folktale. Brentano's work is voluminous and includes a record of the nun Anna Katharina Emmerich's visions, written after his return to the Church.

Brentano, Lujo (1844–1931). German political economist, nephew of Clemens Brentano. Championed working class. Winner of Nobel peace prize in 1927.

Brentford, the two kings of. In the Duke of Buckingham's farce called *The Rehearsal* (1671), the two kings of Brentford enter hand-in-hand, dance together, sing together, walk arm-in-arm, and to heighten the absurdity, the actors represent them as smelling at the same nosegay (Act ii. 2). Some say this was a skit on Charles II and James (afterwards James II). Others think the persons meant were Boabdelin and Abdalla, the two contending kings of Granada in Dryden's tragedy, *The Conquest of Granada.* See ALMANZOR AND ALMAHIDE.

Brer Rabbit, Brer Fox, etc. Animal characters, heroes of the stories in UNCLE REMUS by Joel Chandler Harris.

Breshkovsky, Catherine. *Russian* **Ekaterina Breshko-Breskovskaya** (1844–1934). Called "Babushka" and "Grandmother of the Russian Revolution." Of a wealthy and noble family, devoted her life to the welfare of the Russian peasants. Imprisoned, exiled, released several times. Forced to flee after Bolsheviks came to power. Lectured in U.S. 1919. Spent last years in Czechoslovakia.

Brest-Litovsk. Former Polish town 100 miles east of Warsaw. The Treaty of Brest-

Litovsk, ending Russian participation in World War I, was signed there March 3, 1918. In 1919 the Treaty of Versailles recognized the Republic of Poland, and Brest-Litovsk became a Polish city. In 1939 it was captured by Germany and later in that year, when Poland was partitioned for the fourth time, became a part of Russia.

Brethren, Plymouth. Members of a Calvinistic sect which arose at Plymouth, England, about 1830.

Brethren Church. Conservative branch of the Dunkers or Dunkards, German Baptist Brethren in Pennsylvania.

Brethren of the Coast. French, English, and Dutch marauders in the West Indies late in the 16th century.

Brethren of the Common Life. A group of mystics in Germany and the Low Countries during the 14th and 15th centuries, founded by Gerard Groote (1340–1389), a Dutchman. The Brethren lived together communally and through their schools assisted greatly in establishing reforms in education and religion. ERASMUS and Martin LUTHER were at one time their pupils, and the IMITATION OF CHRIST was one of the products of the influence of the sect's brand of mysticism.

Breton, André (1896–). French poet and critic, one of the founders and leaders of the movement of SURREALISM and its predecessor, DADAISM, living in the U.S. after the defeat of France by Germany in World War II. His works, consisting of both examples of Surrealism and expositions of it, include *Manifeste du surréalisme: Poisson soluble* (1924); *Point du jour* (1934), essays; *Position politique du surréalisme* (1935); *Qu'est-ce que le surréalisme?* (1934), translated as *What Is Surrealism?* (1936); *L'Amour fou* (1937). *Fata Morgana* (1942), a long poem, was forbidden publication in France in 1940 by the censors of the Vichy government. It appears in NEW DIRECTIONS, 1941 edition.

Breton, Nicholas (1545?–1626). English poet, author of numerous prose pamphlets, moral, religious, and lyric verse. He is best known as a pastoral poet, and is represented in THE ARBOR OF AMOROUS DEVICES (1597) and ENGLAND'S HELICON (1600). Breton's name is to be found on the title page of the former work, and *Breton's Bower of Delights* (1591), another collection of lyrics, was also assigned to him by the printers of the book, although other authors are represented.

Breton's Bower of Delights. See BRETON, NICHOLAS.

Brett, Dorothy. A friend of Katherine MANSFIELD and D. H. LAWRENCE, author of a book about the latter. She is mentioned frequently in Lawrence's correspondence.

Bretwalda. See under RULERS, TITLES OF.

Breugnon, Colas, see COLAS BREUGNON.

brevet rank. Titular rank without the pay that usually goes with it. A brevet major has the title of major, but the pay of captain, or whatever his *substantive* rank happens to be. (Fr. *brevet,* dim. of *bref,* a letter, a document.)

Brewster, Margaret. The heroine of Whittier's poem *In the Old South Church,* versifying an incident of July, 1677, when the Quaker, Margaret Brewster, came to church in Puritan Boston in sackcloth and ashes. She was whipped through the town by way of punishment.

Brian Boru (926–1014). King of Ireland. Son of the King of Munster. Broke the Danish power in Ireland for all time at Clontarf (April 23, 1014), and was slain in the battle.

Briand-Kellogg Pact, see PACT OF PARIS.

Briareus, or **Aegeon.** In Greek mythology a giant with fifty heads and a hundred hands. Homer says the gods called him Briareus, but men called him Aegeon (*Iliad,* i. 403). He was the offspring of Heaven and Earth and was of the race of the Titans, with whom he fought in the war against Zeus.

Brice, Stephen. The hero of Winston Churchill's THE CRISIS.

Brice. Bishop of Tours, died in 444. St. Brice's day is November 13. In Arthurian legend, he is the sustainer of Arthur when elected king.

brick.

a regular brick. A jolly good fellow; perhaps because a brick is solid, four-square, plain, and reliable.

make bricks without straw. To attempt to do something without having the necessary material supplied. The allusion is to the Israelites in Egypt, who were commanded by their taskmasters so to do (*Ex.* v. 7).

Brick, Jefferson. In Dickens' MARTIN CHUZZLEWIT, a very weak, pale young man, the war correspondent of the *New York Rowdy Journal,* of which Colonel Diver is editor.

Bricklayer, the. A nickname for Ben JONSON from his stepfather's trade.

Bricks Without Straw. A novel by Albion W. TOURGEE, published in 1880 and dealing with the period of Reconstruction and the early freedom of the Negro in the South after the Civil War.

Brideau, Philippe. An unscrupulous villain who appears in several of the novels of Balzac's COMÉDIE HUMAINE, notably *Scenes from a Courtesan's Life* (*Les Splendeurs et* *misères des courtesanes*). He was originally in the army, but was forced to find other means of livelihood after being involved in a military plot. He then became a ruthless plunderer, robbed his aunt, his brother and his mother, and even disowned the latter, in spite of her unfailing devotion, because he thought she stood in the way of his social success.

Joseph Brideau. Philippe's brother, a talented artist and one of the members of the club known as the Cénacle.

Agatha Brideau. The affectionate, devoted mother of the scoundrel Philippe and his brother.

Bridehead, Sue. The chief female character in Hardy's novel, JUDE THE OBSCURE.

Bride of Abydos, The. A poem by Byron (1813). The heroine is Zuleika, daughter of Giaffer, pasha of Abydos. She is the trothplight bride of Selim; but Giaffer shoots the lover, and Zuleika dies of a broken heart.

Bride of Lammermoor. A historical novel by Sir Walter Scott (1819), laid in the time of William III. The titular heroine is Lucy Ashton, daughter of Sir William Ashton, lord-keeper of Scotland. She is in love with Edgar, master of Ravenswood. The lovers plight their troth at the "Mermaid's Fountain," but Lucy is compelled to marry Frank Hayston, laird of Bucklaw. In a fit of insanity, the bride attempts to murder the bridegroom, and dies in convulsions. Bucklaw recovers, and goes abroad. Colonel Ashton appoints a hostile meeting with Edgar; but on his way to the place appointed young Ravenswood is lost in the quicksands of Kelpies Flow, in accordance with an ancient prophecy.

In Donizetti's opera of LUCIA DI LAMMERMOOR, Bucklaw dies of the wound inflicted by the bride, and Edgar, heartbroken, comes on the stage and kills himself.

Bride of the Sea. Venice; so called from the ancient ceremony of the wedding of the sea by the doge, who threw a ring into the Adriatic, saying, "We wed thee, O sea, in token of perpetual domination." This took place each year on Ascension Day, and was enjoined upon the Venetians in 1177 by Pope Alexander III, who gave the doge a gold ring from his own finger in token of the victory achieved by the Venetian fleet at Istria over Frederick Barbarossa, in defense of the pope's quarrel. See BUCENTAUR.

Bridewell. A generic term for a house of correction, or prison, so called from the London Bridewell, Bridge Street, Blackfriars, which was built as a hospital on the site of a former royal palace over a holy well of medical water, called St. Bride's (Bridget's) Well.

Bridge, The. Most important work of the American poet Hart CRANE, published in 1930, in which he attempted to synthesize a picture of modern America by the use of symbols from its past and present, centered about BROOKLYN BRIDGE as chief symbol of man's aspiration and achievement.

Bridge of San Luis Rey, The. A novel by Thornton WILDER, published in 1927 and a Pulitzer Prize winner. It deals with the collapse of a bridge near Lima, Peru, in the early 18th century, and the lives of the five people killed thereby: the Marquesa de Montemayor; Pepita, her companion-maid; Uncle Pio; his young charge, Jaime, son of a famous actress, La Périchole; and Esteban, grief-stricken by the recent death of his twin brother, Manuel. Brother Juniper, a friar, is the supposed author of the account of the accident. In structure this novel is reminiscent of the Italian *novelle*.

Bridge of Sighs. Over this bridge, which connects the palace of the doge with the state prisons of Venice, prisoners were conveyed from the judgment hall to the place of execution.

> I stood in Venice on the Bridge of Sighs,
> A palace and a prison on each hand.
> Byron, *Childe Harold's Pilgrimage*, iv. 1.

Waterloo Bridge, in London, used, some years ago, when suicides were frequent there, to be called *the Bridge of Sighs,* and Thomas HOOD gave the name to one of his most pathetic poems.

Bridger, James (1806–1881). American trader and explorer. Known as the "Daniel Boone of the Rocky Mountains."

Bridges, Harry Renton (1900–). American labor leader on Pacific Coast. Native of Australia. Subject to long wrangles and various decisions as to deportation. Cf. *Men Who Lead Labor* and *Harry Bridges on Trial* (Modern Age books).

Bridges, Robert Seymour (1844–1930). English poet, appointed poet laureate in 1913 and best known for his work in metrics. In addition to a number of short lyrics, his works include: *Prometheus, the Firegiver* (1884); *Eros and Psyche* (1894); *Eden* (1891), an oratorio; *The Testament of Beauty* (1929). He also wrote plays, chiefly on classical subjects, was the author of critical essays on such figures as Milton and Keats, was interested in church music, spelling and phonetics, and edited several volumes, including the poetry of Gerard Manley HOPKINS.

Bridget Allworthy. In Fielding's *Tom Jones*. See ALLWORTHY.

Bridlegoose, Judge. The anglicized form given to Taiel de Bridoison (or *Juge Bridoie*), a judge in Rabelais' GARGANTUA AND PANTAGRUEL, who decided the causes brought before him, not by weighing the merits of the case, but by the more simple process of throwing dice. BEAUMARCHAIS, in his *Marriage of Figaro* (1784), has introduced this judge under the name of "Bridoison." The person satirized by Rabelais is said to be Chancellor Poyet (1474–1548) who served as chancellor of France under Francis I.

Bridlegoose, The Verdict of. Essays by T. F. POWYS.

Bridoison. See BRIDLEGOOSE, JUDGE.

Brie cheese. A soft French cheese, from the district of Brie in France, ripened by mold. Connoisseurs claim that there is something poetic about it.

Brief Candles. See HUXLEY, ALDOUS.

Brief Moment. See BEHRMAN, S. N.

Brieux, Eugène (1858–1932). French playwright, sponsored by Bernard Shaw. Famous for *Damaged Goods.* Commander of the Legion of Honor and member of the French Academy.

Briffault, Robert Stephen (1876–). English surgeon, anthropologist, philosopher and novelist. *The Mothers* probably the most notable work in its field since Sir James Frazer's *The Golden Bough.* His novel *Europa* was widely read.

brig. Place of confinement aboard ship in the U.S. Navy. The word has nothing to do with *brig,* a two-masted, square-rigged vessel.

brigantine. A word used variously for a piratical vessel or a specific sailing vessel differing from a *brig* in not carrying a square mainsail.

Brigard, Gilberte. The heroine of FROU-FROU, a drama by Meilhac and Halévy.

Briggs, Clare A. (1875–1930). American cartoonist. Among his creations *Skin-nay, The Days of Real Sport, When a Feller Needs a Friend, Mr. and Mrs.,* etc.

Briggs, Le Baron Russell (1855–1934). Dean of Harvard (1902–1925). Trained in his select composition course many well-known poets and authors.

Briggs, Mr. An ardent but very poor amateur sportsman whose blundering adventures at hunting and fishing were depicted in the London *Punch* in serial form. Mr. Briggs was the invention of John Leech.

Bright, John (1811–1889). English orator, member of Parliament and official in the governments under GLADSTONE, an outstanding spokesman for the industrialists of Great Britain and opponent of the CORN LAWS.

Bright Shawl, The. See HERGESHEIMER, JOSEPH.

Bright Star! Would I Were Steadfast as Thou Art. A sonnet by Keats (1820), the last before his death, written in a volume of poems by Shakespeare and presented to his friend Severn on his departure to Italy.

Brigit. The Vesta or Minerva of the heathen Irish, inspirer of poetry and wisdom. Christian saint of same name called the Patroness of Ireland and the Mary of the Gael.

Brigliadaro. In Boiardo's ORLANDO INNAMORATO, the name of Orlando's horse. It means literally "golden bridle."

Brillat-Savarin, Anthelme (1755–1826). French politician and gourmet. His *Physiologie du goût* is a famous work on gastronomy.

Brimming Cup, The. A novel by Dorothy Canfield FISHER (1920), the story of how the heroine, Marise, chose to resist the attractions of an ardent, sophisticated and wealthy lover from the great world outside and remain in her little Vermont village, faithful to her husband and children. *Rough Hewn* (1922) relates the early life and love affair of Marise and her husband Neale.

Brinig, Myron (1900–). American novelist, best known for *The Sisters* (1937), author also of *Madonna Without Child* (1929), *Out of Life* (1935), *All of Their Lives* (1941), *The Family Way* (1942).

Brinvilliers, Marquise **Marie Madeleine de** (1630?–1676). Notorious French poisoner much written about; beheaded.

Brisbane, Arthur (1864–1936). Sensational American journalist and editorial writer for Hearst. The son of a radical economist. He was called "a master of the commonplace" and said to have written "down to the mass mind."

Briseida. Heroine of the *Roman de Troie* by BENOÎT DE SAINTE-MAURE. In the hands of BOCCACCIO this character became Criseida and was adopted by Chaucer in his Middle English version of the legend of TROILUS and Cressida. The name Briseida is similar to BRISEIS, but the characters themselves are unlike.

Briseis. The patronymic name of Hippodamia, daughter of Briseus. She was the cause of the quarrel in the *Iliad* between Agamemnon and Achilles, and when the former robbed Achilles of her, Achilles refused any longer to go to battle, and the Greeks lost ground daily.

Brisingamen. In Norse mythology, the necklace of Freya. *Brisingr* means "fire" and *men* "necklace."

Bristol Boy, the. Thomas CHATTERTON, the poet (1752–1770).

> The marvellous boy,
> The sleepless soul that perished in his pride.
> Wordsworth, *Resolution and Independence.*

Britannia. A personification of the British Empire. The first known representation of Britannia as a female figure sitting on a globe, leaning with one arm on a shield, and grasping a spear in the other hand, is on a Roman coin of Antoninus Pius, who died 161 A. D. The figure reappeared on the English copper coin in the reign of Charles II, 1665, and the model was Frances Stewart, afterwards created Duchess of Richmond. The engraver was Philip Roetier, 1665.

Britannicus (41–55 A.D.). Son of Emperor Claudius and Messalina. Set aside by Agrippina in favor of her son, Nero. Poisoned by Nero. Subject of a tragedy by RACINE.

British Broadcasting Corporation (*B.B.C.*). Government-owned radio broadcasting body of Great Britain, established in 1927.

British Commonwealth of Nations. Great Britain and the British Dominions, with reference to the greater autonomy (self-government) of the dominions resulting from the Imperial Conferences, particularly in 1926, and from the Statute of Westminster in 1931. There are advocates of an expansion of the British Commonwealth of Nations to make it include the countries of Western Europe and others.

British lion, the. The pugnacity of the British nation, as opposed to the *John Bull,* which symbolizes the substantiality, solidity, and obstinacy of the people, with all their prejudices and national peculiarities. "Never," said an inspired broadcaster, "will the British lion be forced to retire into its shell and pull in its horns."

to rouse the British lion is to flourish a red flag in the face of John Bull; to provoke him to resistance even to the point of war.

to twist the tail of the British lion used to be a favorite phrase in America for attempting to annoy the British people and government by abuse and vituperation.

British Museum in London, containing science, literature, and art. Originally in Montague House in Great Russell Street, Bloomsbury. Opened to the public in 1759. During 1823–1847 the present building erected. The library contains over four million printed volumes. In the museum proper are the Elgin Marbles, the Egyptian Book of the Dead, and the Rosetta Stone. The Museum was badly damaged by air attack September 1940.

Britling, Mr. See MR. BRITLING SEES IT THROUGH.

Britomart. In Spenser's *Faërie Queene,* a female knight, daughter of King Ryence of Wales. She is the impersonation of chastity and purity; encounters the "savage, fierce bandit and mountaineer," without injury, and is assailed by "hag and unlaid ghost, goblin, and swart fairy of the mine," but "dashes their brute violence into sudden adoration and blank awe." She finally marries Artegal.

Spenser got the name, which means "sweet maiden," from Britomartis, a Cretan nymph of Greek mythology, who was very fond of the chase. King Minos fell in love with her, and persisted in his advances for nine months. She finally threw herself into the sea.

Brittain, Vera Mary (1893?–). English essayist and novelist. *The Dark Tide* (1923); etc. Her autobiographical *Testament of Youth* (1933) was very popular. Her *Testament of Friendship* (1940) is a tribute to Winifred HOLTBY.

Broad Highway, The. A historical novel by Jeffrey Farnol (Am. 1911) concerning the England of the early 18th century.

broadhorn. A kind of flatboat used especially on the Mississippi. An immense oar placed on roof, or on either side near bow making it look as though the boat had horns.

Broadhurst, George H. (1866–). Anglo-American dramatist. His *The Man of the Hour* (1907), a play about corrupt politics, and his *Bought and Paid For* (1913) were both successes.

broadside ballads. Popular songs and poems, written in doggerel, which were printed in BLACK LETTER on a single sheet of paper, decorated with woodcuts, with the name of the tune to which the ballads in question were to be sung, and sold for a penny or two on the street-corners of England in the late 16th and early 17th centuries. Their subject-matter was taken from political events, battles or wars, murders, strange happenings, executions, freakish births, domestic quarrels, and the like, and also included moral exhortations and religious propaganda during the Protestant-Catholic controversies. Thomas DELONEY was a ballad-writer, and peddlers of broadside ballads are introduced in Jonson's BARTHOLOMEW FAIR and in Shakespeare's character of AUTOLYCUS.

Broadway. A term synonymous with the American theater, from Broadway, the street on or near which the theaters of New York City are to be found. In a more general sense it denotes the gay night life of the American metropolis in an almost legendary conception.

Broadwood and Sons, John. Cooperated with Americus Bockers, Dutch piano maker, in manufacturing the first grand piano in England. See Kipling's reference to this make of piano in "The Song of the Banjo."

Brobdingnag. In Swift's GULLIVER'S TRAVELS the country of gigantic giants, to whom Gulliver is a pigmy "not half so big as a round little worm plucked from the lazy finger of a maid." Hence the adjective, *Brobdingnagian,* colossal, gigantic.

Broceliande. In Arthurian legend a magic forest in Brittany, where Merlin was enchanted by Vivian. Poem by Alan SEEGER.

Broch, Hermann (1886–). Austrian novelist, connected with Princeton University. Known as the author of *The Sleepwalker* until publication of *Der Tod des Vergil* (*Death of Virgil*) (1945), a work which aroused a good deal of controversy in that some held it to outdo Joyce and Thomas Mann in a positive sense while others interpreted the comparison as a crushing verdict of artificiality and mannerism.

Brocken. The highest peak of the Harz range in Saxony. On the eve of May Day, i.e., the feast of Walburga (Walpurgis) or Walpurgis Night the Brocken was the scene of a witches' Sabbath.

the specter of the Brocken is an optical illusion, first observed on the Brocken, in which shadows of the spectators, greatly magnified, are projected on the mists about the summit of the mountain opposite. In one of DE QUINCEY's opium-dreams there is a powerful description of the Brocken specter.

Brocken, Henry. A novel by Walter DE LA MARE.

Brodie, Steve. American celebrity of the saloons and dance halls of New York City during the 1880's, reputed to have jumped from BROOKLYN BRIDGE into the East River in 1886.

Broken Stowage. A collection of sea sketches (1915) by David Bone.

Broken Tower, The. A poem by Hart CRANE, written in 1932, the last important work before his death by suicide. It uses bells and a bell-tower to symbolize the destruction of the physical body by the imagination.

Brom Bones. The nickname of Brom Van Brunt, Ichabod Crane's rival in Irving's LEGEND OF SLEEPY HOLLOW. "He was always ready for either a fight or a frolic."

Brome, Alexander (1620–1666). English poet, of Royalist sympathies during the English civil war, who wrote rousing songs for the Cavaliers. He is believed to be the author of *Rump Songs* (1662), a book of Royalist lyrics.

Bromfield, Louis (1896–). American novelist and short-story writer. Chief among his books are *The Green Bay Tree* (1924); *Possession* (1925); *Early Autumn* (1926), winner of the Pulitzer Prize; *A Good Woman* (1927); THE STRANGE CASE OF MISS ANNIE SPRAGG (1928); *Twenty-Four Hours* (1930); *Awake and Rehearse* (1929); *A Modern Hero* (1932); *The Farm* (1933); *The Rains Came* (1937); *Night in Bombay* (1940); *Wild Is the River* (1941); *Until the Day Break* (1942).

bromide and **sulphite.** Words coined by Gelett BURGESS in his humorous essay, *Are You a Bromide, or The Sulphitic Theory* (1906), which explain "the terms 'bromide' and 'sulphite' as applied to psychological rather than chemical analysis." The bromide, according to Burgess, "does his thinking by syndicate. He follows the main-traveled roads, he goes with the crowd." The sulphite, on the other hand, is unconventional, original, everything that the bromide is not.

Broncho, The, that would not be broken of Dancing. Poem by Vachel LINDSAY.

Bronstein, Lev Davidovitch. See TROTSKY, LEON.

Brontë, Anne (1820–1849). Sister of Charlotte and Emily BRONTË, author with them of poems and novels under the pseudonym of BELL. Her novels were *Agnes Grey* (1847) and *The Tenant of Wildfell Hall* (1848), which she published under the name of Acton Bell. See also BRONTË, PATRICK BRANWELL.

Brontë, Charlotte (1816–1855). English novelist, most famous of the three Brontë sisters (see BRONTË, ANNE and BRONTË, EMILY) and author with her sisters of poems and novels under the name of BELL. Her best-known and most successful novel is JANE EYRE (1847). Her other works are SHIRLEY (1849); *Villette* (1853); and *Emma,* a fragment published in 1860. She wrote under the pseudonym of Currer Bell. See also BRONTË, PATRICK BRANWELL.

Brontë, Emily (1818–1848). English novelist and poet, sister of Anne and Charlotte BRONTË, with whom she wrote poems and novels under the name of BELL, her pseudonym being Ellis Bell. The best of the poetry in *Poems by Currer, Ellis, and Acton Bell* (1846) was admitted to be hers. She is most famous for her novel *Wuthering Heights* (1848). Her work is notable for the spirit of passion and rebellion that it reveals. See also BRONTË, PATRICK BRANWELL.

Brontë, Patrick Branwell (1817–1848). Brother of Anne, Charlotte, and Emily BRONTË and tutor to them, shown to have been neurotic, tubercular, and addicted to opium.

Bronx, the. A borough of New York City, mainly residential and middle class, with a large Jewish population, frequently chosen as the scene of action by proletarian and humorous authors, among whom are Clifford ODETS and Arthur KOBER. Bronx and Manhattan are also cocktails.

Brook, Alexander (1898–). Distinguished American painter. Married Peggy Bacon 1920. Divorced 1940. Member National Institute of Arts and Letters, etc.

Brook Farm. A famous literary and economic community of a somewhat Utopian nature, more formally known as the Brook Farm Institute of Agriculture and Education, which was established in 1841 at West Roxbury, nine miles from Boston. Its members shared equally in work, benefits, and remuneration. It was disbanded in 1846. Its founder was the Rev. George Ripley and among its interested visitors of note were Emerson, Alcott, Theodore Parker, Margaret Fuller, and other Transcendentalists. Hawthorne's BLITHEDALE ROMANCE gives a picture of Brook Farm.

Brook Kerith, The. A historical novel by George MOORE (1915), a presentation of the life of Jesus. The author follows the customary account as far as the Crucifixion, but later, according to the novel, JOSEPH OF ARIMATHEA finds Jesus still alive. For thirty years afterward he lives as a shepherd by the Brook Kerith. He is utterly disillusioned concerning his early belief in himself, which he considers blasphemy, and when finally he meets Paul the Apostle and hears his version of the story, he is horrified and plans to go to Jerusalem to confess. Paul, however, considers him mad, and he is forced to admit that his story would not be believed.

The ravens fed Elijah by this brook of Palestine, called in the Biblical narrative Cherith.

Brook, Master. In Shakespeare's MERRY WIVES OF WINDSOR, the name assumed by Ford when Sir John Falstaff makes love to his wife. Sir John, not knowing him, confides to him every item of his amour.

Brooke, Dorothea. The heroine of George Eliot's MIDDLEMARCH. Her sister Celia and their uncle, Squire Brooke, with whom they live, are also prominent characters.

Brooke, Rupert (1887–1915). English poet. His best-known poems are *Grantchester, The Great Lover* and his series of war sonnets entitled *1914*. He died of sunstroke in service in the World War. ST. JOHN ERVINE is said to have drawn the hero of his novel *Changing Winds* from Rupert Brooke.

Brookfield, Jack. A professional gambler, one of the chief characters in the play, THE WITCHING HOUR by Augustus Thomas.

Brooklyn. A borough of New York City, manufacturing and residential, located on Long Island and separated from Manhattan by the East River. It was an independent city until 1898. Walt WHITMAN, Hart CRANE, and Thomas WOLFE are among the literary men who have written of Brooklyn. See CROSSING BROOKLYN FERRY, THE BRIDGE, and ONLY THE DEAD KNOW BROOKLYN.

Brooklyn Bridge. The first bridge built to connect BROOKLYN with Manhattan Island, started in 1869 and finished in 1883. Its designer was J. A. Roebling. Brooklyn Bridge is used as a symbol of man's achievement in Hart Crane's poem THE BRIDGE.

Brooklyn Dodgers. A local baseball club of the borough of BROOKLYN, popularized among the rest of the nation by the enthusiasm of its fans. It participated in the WORLD SERIES of 1941 and 1947, in which it was defeated by the New York Yankees. See BASEBALL TEAMS.

Brooks, Cleanth (1906–). American literary critic, associated with the Southern group of poets and critics, including John Crowe RANSOM, Allan TATE, and Robert Penn WARREN, who in the late 1930's and the 1940's sought to give 20th-century literature the status in scholarship occupied by the older and better-established literatures. In *Modern Poetry and the Tradition* (1939) Brooks emphasizes the technical continuity between traditional English poetry and the poetry of the 20th century

Brooks, Phillips (1835–1893). American Episcopal bishop. Author of the hymn *O Little Town of Bethlehem*.

Brooks, Van Wyck (1886–). American critic, best known for his interpretations of New England literature and literary figures. In his early critical writings he attacked the narrowness and insularity of the Puritan tradition and urged a broader, more unified cultural ideal for the nation. Chief among his works are *The Wine of the Puritans* (1909); *America's Coming of Age* (1915); *The Ordeal of Mark Twain* (1920); *The Pilgrimage of Henry James* (1925); *Sketches in Criticism* (1932); *The Life of Emerson* (1932); *Three Essays on America* (1934); THE FLOWERING OF NEW ENGLAND (1936); NEW ENGLAND: INDIAN SUMMER (1940); *Opinions of Oliver Allston* (1941); *The World of Washington Irving* (1944); *The Times of Melville and Whitman* (1947).

Brooks of Sheffield. A name used in place of that of an actual person, from an imaginary individual mentioned in *David Copperfield* to put little David off the scent that he was being referred to:

> "Quinnion," said Mr. Murdstone, "take care, if you please. Somebody's sharp."
> "Who is?" asked the gentleman, laughing.
> I looked up quickly; being curious to know.
> "Only Brooks of Sheffield," said Mr. Murdstone.
> I was quite relieved to find it was only Brooks of Sheffield; for, at first, I really thought it was I. (Ch. ii.)

See HARRIS, MRS.

Brother, Can You Spare a Dime? American popular song of 1932, expressing an appeal for charity and testifying to the poverty and unemployment that followed the stock market crash of 1929 and the depression years of the early 1930's.

Brother Jonathan. Generic name for a New Englander, hence for Americans and America. One account of its origin tells how, when Washington was in want of ammunition, he called a council of officers, but no practical suggestion could be offered. "We must consult Brother Jonathan," said the general, meaning His Excellency Jonathan Trumbull, governor of the State of Connecticut. This was done, and the difficulty was remedied. "To consult Brother Jonathan" then became a set phrase, and Brother Jonathan became a name for the typical shrewd Yankee. He appears as a character in THE CONTRAST (1787), a play by Royall TYLER.

Brother Juniper. (1) See BRIDGE OF SAN LUIS REY, THE.

(2) One of St. Francis' early disciples.

Brothers' Bible. See BIBLE, SPECIALLY NAMED.

Brothers Karamazov, The. A novel by Fyodor DOSTOYEVSKY (1879–1880), a story of three brothers. The oldest, Dmitri, quarrels violently with his father over money matters and over a woman, and when the father is found murdered, he is accused of the crime. In reality the old man has been killed by Smerdyakov, a fourth and illegitimate son who is a servant, subject to epilepsy. Ivan, the second son, discovers he has all unconsciously suggested the crime to Smerdyakov by his cynical philosophy. Smerdyokov commits suicide and Ivan tries in vain to save his brother Dmitri. There is a third brother, Alyosha, who also plays a prominent part in the novel. This is the author's best-known work, marked by the passionate introspection, argumentation, and intense social, political, and psychological analysis of all of Dostoyevsky's books. The three brothers represent three distinct types of the Russian national character during the 19th century—the soldier, the intellectual, and the religious mystic. See entries under KARAMAZOV.

Broun, (Matthew) Heywood Campbell (1888–1939). American newspaperman, known for his liberal sympathies and his firm opposition to social injustice. He wrote columns, articles, and dramatic criticism for the New York *Tribune, World,* and *World-Telegram,* the Scripps-Howard newspaper chain, THE NATION, and THE NEW REPUBLIC, was a radio commentator for a time, and once ran unsuccessfully for election as Congressman from New York City. Among his books are *The A. E. F.* (1918), an account of his service as a correspondent during World War I; *Seeing Things at Night* (1921), dramatic criticism; *Pieces of Hate, And Other Enthusiasms* (1922) and *Sitting on the World* (1924), both collections of pieces from his columns; *Anthony Comstock* (1927), a biography with Margaret Leech; and *Christians Only* (1931), dealing with ANTI-SEMITISM and written in collaboration with George Britt. In 1941 a posthumous volume of his collected writings was published. Mr. Broun liked to have his name pronounced *Broon* and not *Brown.*

Browdie, John. In Dickens' NICHOLAS NICKLEBY, a brawny, big-made Yorkshire corn-factor, bluff, honest, and kind-hearted. He befriends poor Smike, and is much attached to Nicholas Nickleby. John Browdie marries Matilda Price, a miller's daughter.

Brown, Alice (1857–). American novelist and dramatist. In 1914 won the Winthrop Ames prize for her play *Children of Earth.* The last of the traditional New England story writers. A poet and friend of Louise Imogen Guiney.

brown study. Absence of mind; apparent thought, but real vacuity. The corresponding French expression explains it—*sombre rêverie. Sombre* "somber" and *brun* "brown" both mean sad, melancholy, gloomy, dull.

Bruckner, Anton (1824–1896). Austrian composer of church and symphonic music, a friend of Richard WAGNER. His best-known composition is his Fourth, or "Romantic," Symphony. His work is considered to be rich in spiritual content.

Brown, Buster, see BUSTER BROWN.

Brown, Captain. A likable character in Mrs. Gaskell's CRANFORD.

Brown, Charles Brockden (1771–1810). American novelist, writing in the tradition of the GOTHIC NOVEL. His works include: WIELAND, OR THE TRANSFORMATION (1798); *Ormond, Or the Secret Witness* (1799); *Arthur Mervyn, Or Memoirs of the Year 1793* (1799–1800); *Edgar Huntley, Or Memoirs of a Sleep Walker* (1799); *Clara Howard, in a Series of Letters* (1801); and *Jane Talbot* (1801). He also wrote political tracts under the influence of the writings of William GODWIN.

Brown, Ford Madox (1821–1893). English painter, Romantic in tendency, who specialized in historical, religious, and literary subjects. His work served as inspiration to the PRE-RAPHAELITE BROTHERHOOD.

Brown, John (1800–1859). Famous American abolitionist, fanatically devoted to his cause and known for his attack on Harpers Ferry in Virginia, October 16, 1859, when he and his men captured an armory and planned to free the Negro slaves by force. He was seized, tried, and hanged, and became a martyr in the eyes of his fellow abolitionists. The famous Union song of the Civil War, JOHN BROWN'S BODY, made him a legend. A number of authors, including WHITTIER, THOREAU,

Edmund Clarence STEDMAN, and Stephen Vincent BENÉT, have written of John Brown and his exploit.

Brown, John (1810–1882). Scottish physician and friend of Thackeray and Ruskin. Wrote an immortal essay on the ten-year-old prodigy and pet of Sir Walter Scott, Marjorie FLEMING.

Brown, John Mason (1900–). American dramatic critic. Served in Navy in World War II and wrote *To All Hands: An Amphibious Adventure,* foreword by Rear Admiral Alan G. Kirk, USN (1943), and *Many a Watchful Night* (1944). Among his other books are *Upstage: The American Theater in Performance* (1930); *The Art of Playgoing* (1936); *Two On The Aisle* (1938); *Broadway in Review* (1940). Cf. also his weekly dramatic department, "Seeing Things," in the *Saturday Review of Literature.*

Brown, Jones, and Robinson. The typification of middle-class Englishmen; from the adventures of three Continental tourists of these names which were told and illustrated in *Punch* in the 1870's by Richard Doyle. They hold up to ridicule the gaucherie, insular ideas, vulgarity, extravagance, conceit, and snobbism that too often characterize the class.

Brown, Rollo Walter (1880–). American novelist and essayist. Has traveled widely as a lecturer.

Brown, Tom, see TOM BROWN.

Brown, Vanbeest. In Scott's GUY MANNERING, lieutenant of Dirk Hatteraick, the smuggler and mate of his vessel. Under this same name of Vanbeest Brown, the young Harry Bertram, the missing heir of Ellangowan, grows up believing that the "lieutenant" is his father.

Brown, Mrs. **Zenith Jones,** pseudonyms Leslie Ford, David Frome (1898–). Popular American writer of detective fiction.

brown Bess. The early British flintlock smoothbore musket with bronzed barrel.

Browne, Charles Farrar. See WARD, ARTEMUS.

Browne, Lewis (1897–). Popular historian and biographer. Wrote *This Believing World, That Man Heine,* and edited *The Graphic Bible.*

Browne, Sir **Thomas** (1605–1682). English physician, scholar, and author, famous for his wide and eccentric learning and his quaint, exotic prose style. His works are RELIGIO MEDICI (1643); PSEUDODOXIA EPIDEMICA (1646), which was also called *Vulgar Errors;* HYDROTAPHIA OR URN BURIAL, published with THE GARDEN OF CYRUS in 1658; and CHRISTIAN MORALS, edited in 1756 by Samuel JOHNSON.

Browne, William (ca. 1591–1643?). English poet, one of the Spenserian pastoral school of the early 17th century which also included George WITHER and John DAVIES of Hereford. He was the author of *Two Elegies* on the death of Prince Henry (1613) and *Britannia's Pastorals* (1613 and 1616) His poems were also published in *The Shepherd's Pipe* (1614), a book of eclogues in which Wither and Davies of Hereford were also represented.

Brownell, William Crary (1851–1928). American literary critic, writing in the tradition of Matthew ARNOLD. Among his works are *French Traits* (1889); *Victorian Prose Masters* (1901); *Standards* (1917); *The Genius of Style* (1924); *Democratic Distinction in America* (1927).

brownie. The house spirit in Scottish superstition. At night he is supposed to busy himself in doing little jobs for the family over which he presides. Farms are his favorite abode. Brownies are brown or tawny spirits, in opposition to fairies, which are fair ones. In America the adventures of the Brownies were popularized by a series of *Brownie Books* by Palmer Cox.

Browning, Edward W. (*"Daddy"*). New York real estate man, involved in a sensational suit for separation in the 1920's, brought by his wife, Frances Heenan ("Peaches") Browning, who at one time had been adopted by him. It achieved unsavory notoriety in the tabloid newspapers of the time. The case is considered to be satirically referred to in James Joyce's FINNEGANS WAKE, part I, third section:

> . . . Old grum has his gel number two (bravevow, our Grum!) and he would like to canoodle her too some part of the time for he is downright fond of his number one but O he's fair mashed on peaches number two . . .

Browning, Elizabeth Barrett (1806–1861). English poet, wife of Robert BROWNING, who was unknown when she was at the height of her popularity. Her work is marked by scholarship and humanitarian sympathies. She is best known for her SONNETS FROM THE PORTUGUESE (1850), a sequence of love sonnets addressed to her husband. Her other works are *Essay on Mind, With Other Poems* (1826); a translation of *Prometheus Bound* (1833), the drama by Aeschylus; *The Seraphim And Other Poems* (1838); *Poems* (1844); *Casa Guidi Windows* (1851); AURORA LEIGH (1857), a romance in blank verse; *Poems Before Congress* (1860); and *Last Poems* (1862). The Brownings were among the most celebrated of literary lovers. See also THE CRY OF THE CHILDREN, LADY GERALDINE'S COURTSHIP, and THE BARRETTS OF WIMPOLE STREET.

Browning, John Moses (1855–1926). American designer of firearms. Son of a gunsmith. Inventor of Browning automatic pistol, model of 1911; Browning machine gun, model of 1917; Browning automatic rifle, model of 1918, used in World War I.

Browning, Robert (1812–1889). English poet, husband of Elizabeth Barrett BROWNING. His poetry is distinguished by its learning, its psychological analyses of character, and its use of the dramatic MONOLOGUE; at the time of its first publication, much of it was considered obscure and "difficult." THE RING AND THE BOOK (1868–1869) is his most famous and most ambitious work. His other works include PARACELSUS (1835); STRAFFORD (1836), a play; SORDELLO (1840); BELLS AND POMEGRANATES (1841–1846); CHRISTMAS EVE AND EASTER DAY (1850); COLOMBE'S BIRTHDAY (1853); MEN AND WOMEN (1855); BALAUSTION'S ADVENTURE (1871); DRAMATIC IDYLS (1879–1880); JOCOSERIA (1883); and ASOLANDO (1889), published on the day he died. Among the single poems for which he is best known are PIPPA PASSES; A BLOT IN THE 'SCUTCHEON; MY LAST DUCHESS; HOW THEY BROUGHT THE GOOD NEWS FROM GHENT TO AIX; THE LOST LEADER; SAUL; CALIBAN UPON SETEBOS; FRA LIPPO LIPPI; THE PIED PIPER OF HAMELIN; THE GLOVE; ANDREA DEL SARTO; A GRAMMARIAN'S FUNERAL. Browning was particularly fond of Italian Renaissance subjects.

Brownism. The teachings of Robert Browne (1550?–1633), an English divine, who first formulated the principles of Congregationalism.

Browns, the. In American baseball parlance, a nickname for the St. Louis Americans. See under BASEBALL TEAMS.

Brownyng. One of the names given to the bear in Caxton's version of REYNARD THE FOX. See also BRUIN.

Brozovich, Josip. See TITO, MARSHAL.

Bruce. The Scottish national hero, Robert Bruce, who became king in 1314, is a prominent character in Jane Porter's SCOTTISH CHIEFS.

Bruce and the Spider, see under SPIDER.

Brücke. A German school of painting, founded in 1906 and located near Dresden. It was influenced by the art of Africa and the South Seas, primitive German religious art, and the drawings of children. Characteristic paintings were violent and melodramatic scenes from the theater and religion. Outstanding members of the group were Emil Nolde, Otto Mueller, Maurice Vlaminck, Heckel, and Pechstein. See BLAUE REITER.

Brueghel, also **Bruegel** or **Breughel, Pieter** the Elder (1525–1569). Flemish painter, known for his fresh and humorous scenes of robust peasant life, executed in brilliant colors. He also painted religious pictures, amusing, moralizing subjects, and scenes of fantasy and witchcraft. He had two sons who were also painters: Pieter the Younger (1564?–?1638), known as "Hell Brueghel" because of his fondness for painting scenes of devils, hell, and purgatory; and Jan, called "Velvet Brueghel" (1568–1625).

Bruere, Robert Walther (1876–) and **Martha Bensley,** his wife. American industrial researchers, joint authors of *Increasing Home Efficiency.*

Bruin. In Butler's HUDIBRAS, one of the leaders arrayed against the hero. His prototype in real life was Talgol, a Newgate butcher who obtained a captaincy for valor at Naseby. He marched next Orsin (Joshua Gosling, landlord of the bear-gardens at Southwark).

Sir Bruin. The bear in the famous German beast-epic, REYNARD THE FOX. See also BROWNYNG.

Brumaire. The month in the French Republican Calendar from October 23rd to November 21st. It was named from *brume* fog (Lat. *bruma,* winter). The celebrated 18th Brumaire (November 9th, 1799) was the day on which the Directory was overthrown and Napoleon established his supremacy.

Brummagem. Worthless or very inferior metallic articles made in imitation of better ones. The word is a local form of the name *Birmingham,* which is the great mart and manufactory of gilt toys, cheap jewelry, imitation gems, and the like.

Brummel, Beau, see BEAU BRUMMEL.

Brunelleschi (Filippo di Ser Brunelesco) (1377–1446). Florentine architect, sculptor, and engineer, friend of DONATELLO. Among the edifices that he built are: the great dome of the Cathedral of Florence (1420–1434); the Pazzi Chapel (1429); the Ospedale dei Innocenti (1419); and San Lorenzo, the church of the MEDICI family. He is said to have been the first artist of the Renaissance to rediscover perspective.

Brunetière, Vincent de Paul Marie Ferdinand (1849–1906). French literary critic, conservative and neoclassical in his tastes, known for his attempts to apply the principles of Darwinian evolution to the interpretation of literature and for his strong opposition to the school of NATURALISM. Among his most important works are: *Le Roman Naturaliste* (1883); *Études critiques sur la littérature française* (1880–1907); *Évolution des genres* (1890–1894); and *Histoire de la littérature française classique* (1904–), left incomplete at the time of his death.

Brunetto Latini (1212?–?1294). Florentine scholar, called "master" by DANTE Alighieri but nevertheless, because of his vices, placed among the tortured in Dante's *Inferno* (Canto XV), in the region reserved for those who have been violent against themselves, against art, against life, or against God and man. Brunetto Latini was the author of the *Livre du trésor* (1265), a work written in French.

Brunhild. A heroine of Teutonic and Scandinavian legend. In the NIBELUNGENLIED she is the Queen of Issland, who makes a vow that none shall win her who cannot surpass her in three trials of skill and strength: (1) hurling a spear; (2) throwing a stone; and (3) jumping. Gunther, king of Burgundy, undertakes the three contests, and by the aid of Siegfried, who is clad in his invisible cloak, succeeds in winning the martial Queen. After marriage Brunhild is so obstreperous that the King again applied to Siegfried, who succeeds in depriving her of her ring and girdle, after which she became a very submissive wife. In the VOLSUNGA SAGA, the Scandinavian version of the *Nibelungenlied,* Brunhild is a Valkyrie who becomes a mortal, and Wagner follows this version in his *Nibelungen Ring.* Brunhild plays a leading rôle in *Die Walküre, Siegfried* and *Gotterdämmerung,* three of the four operas of the Ring. For the story, see NIBELUNGEN RING.

Bruno, Giordano (ca. 1548–1600). Italian philosopher, a lecturer in Switzerland, Germany, France, and England. He was a critic of the Christianity of his day, and in his thought upheld a mystical philosophy of pantheism, derived largely from NEO-PLATONISM, which saw God as the unifying force in an infinite, varied, and complex universe, itself a manifestation of God, and the soul of man as a self-existent universe in miniature, contemplating divine unity. For these beliefs and for his support of the COPERNICAN system of astronomy, Bruno was imprisoned, excommunicated, and burned at the stake by the Inquisition. He wrote a number of metaphysical treatises in Latin and Italian, including *Della Causa, Principio, ed Uno; Del' Infinito, Universo, e Mondi; De Triplici Minimo et Mensura; De Monade, Numero, et Figura; De Immenso et Innumerabilibus.* The first two were written in 1583; the latter three were published in 1590. Among his other works are *Il Candelajo,* a satirical comedy; *Cena de la Ceneri,* containing a criticism of English life as he observed it during his stay at Oxford in 1583; *Gli Heroici Furori, Cabala del Cavallo Pegaseo,* and *Spaccio della Bestia Trionfante,* mystical and allegorical poems. Edmund Spenser's FOUR HYMNS TO LOVE AND BEAUTY are considered by some critics to show the influence of Bruno. James JOYCE was another admirer of the Italian and his philosophy, and Bruno is alluded to throughout FINNEGANS WAKE under a number of epithets, including "Nolan," which refers to his birthplace near Nola, in Italy.

Brush, George de Forest (1855–1941). American figure and portrait painter.

Brush, Katherine (1902–). American author of best-selling books of love, marriage, and adultery, often in an atmosphere of metropolitan "GLAMOR." These include *Young Man of Manhattan* (1930); *Red-Headed Woman* (1931); *Other Women* (1933). Several were made into successful motion pictures.

Brushwood Boy, The. A famous dream story by Rudyard KIPLING (1898).

Brut. A chronicle of British history beginning with the mythical BRUT, and so named from him. Wace's *Le Roman de Brut,* or *Brut d'Angleterre,* written in French about 1150, is a rhythmical version of GEOFFREY OF MONMOUTH's *Historia Regüm Britanniae* with additional legends. It is here that first mention is made of Arthur's Round Table. Wace's work formed the basis of Layamon's *Brut* (early 13th century), a history of England from the fall of Troy to 689 A. D. Layamon's poem, written in alliterative verse with occasional rhymes, contains 32,250 lines: Wace's has over 14,000. See also ARTHUR.

Brut or **Brutus.** In the mythological history of England, the first king of the Britons, son of Sylvius (grandson of Ascanius and great-grandson of Aeneas). Having inadvertently killed his father, he first takes refuge in Greece and then in Britain. In remembrance of Troy, he calls the capital of his kingdom TROYNOVANT, the later London. His tale is told at length in the *Chronicles* of Geoffrey of Monmouth, in the first song of Drayton's *Polyolbion,* and in Spenser's *Faërie Queene,* ii.

Brutus, Lucius Junius. In legend, the first consul of Rome, fabled to have held office about 509 B. C. He condemned to death his own two sons for joining a conspiracy to restore to the throne the banished Tarquin. He was—

> The public father who the private quelled,
> And on the dread tribunal sternly sat.
>
> Thomson, *Winter.*

This subject was dramatized by N. Lee (1679) and John H. Payne, under the title of *Brutus, or The Fall of Tarquin* (1820). Alfieri, in 1783, wrote an Italian tragedy on the same subject. In French we have the tragedies of Arnault (1792) and Ponsard (1843) both entitled *Lucrèce.* See LUCRETIA.

The Spanish Brutus. Alonso Pérez de Guzmán (1258–1320). While he was governor, Castile was besieged by Don Juan, who had revolted from his brother, Sancho IV. Juan, who held in captivity one of the sons of Guzmán, threatened to cut his throat unless Guzmán surrendered the city. Guzmán replied, "Sooner than be a traitor, I would myself lend you a sword to slay him," and he threw a sword over the city wall. The son, we are told, was slain by the father's sword before his eyes.

Brutus, Marcus (85–42 B.C.) Caesar's friend, who joined the conspirators to murder him because he made himself a dictator. This Brutus is the real hero of Shakespeare's tragedy of *Julius Caesar,* and the poet endows him with every quality of a true patriot. He loves Caesar much, but he loves Rome more.

et tu, Brute. What! Does my own familiar friend lift up his hand against me? The reference is to the exclamation of Julius Caesar when he saw that his old friend was one of the conspirators against him.

Bruyère, Jean de La, see LA BRUYÈRE.

Bryan, Bryan, Bryan, Bryan! A poem by Vachel LINDSAY.

Bryan, William Jennings (1860–1925). American lawyer, Democratic candidate for the presidency of the U.S. in 1896, 1900, and 1908, Secretary of State in the Cabinet of Woodrow WILSON from 1913 to 1915. He was famous for his "Cross of Gold" speech in 1896 (see CROSS OF GOLD, THE), and was a prominent CHAUTAUQUA lecturer and a leader in the PROHIBITION movement. He was last in the public eye in 1925, when he took part in the notorious SCOPES TRIAL. See also DARWINISM and DARROW, CLARENCE.

Bryant, William Cullen (1794–1878). American poet, among the first of any genuine talent to be produced by the U.S., author mainly of nature poetry, in which he was influenced by WORDSWORTH. He is best known for THANATOPSIS (1817), considered by some critics to be the first great poem written by an American. Other well-known single poems are *To a Waterfowl; To the Fringed Gentian; A Forest Hymn; Rizpah.* Published volumes of his poems include *Poems* (1821); *Poems* (1832); *The Fountain* (1842); *Thirty Poems* (1864); *The Little People of the Snow* (1873); and *The Flood of Years* (1878). Bryant also wrote essays and speeches, represented in *Letters of a Traveler* (1850, 1859), and was editor of the New York EVENING POST from 1829 until his death.

Bryce, James (1838–1922). English author and statesman, ambassador to the U.S. from 1907 to 1913. He is best known for *The Holy Roman Empire* (1864) and *The American Commonwealth* (1888), both studies in history and political science. He wrote a number of other books also, on travel, biography, jurisprudence, and political science.

Brynhild. The Valkyrie awakened by Sigurd in the Scandinavian VOLSUNGA SAGA. See BRUNHILD.

B's, three. In music, BACH, BEETHOVEN, and BRAHMS, so designated by many critics as a trinity of great composers. In French literature, also, this term has been applied to the writers BARRÈS, BOURGET, and BRUNETIÈRE, who became Catholics or Conservatives in reaction against the school of NATURALISM.

B.S. degree. Bachelor of science; the degree conferred upon the completion of a four years' college course or its equivalent, with major work in scientific studies. See also A.B.

Bubastis. (1) Greek name of Bast, or Pasht, the Diana of Egyptian mythology. She was daughter of Isis and sister of Horus, and her sacred animal was the cat.

(2) An ancient Egyptian city.

bubble, or **bubble scheme.** A project or scheme of no sterling worth and of very ephemeral duration—as worthless and frail as a bubble. See MISSISSIPPI; SOUTH SEA.

Bubble Act. An Act of George I, passed in 1719, its object being to punish the promoters of bubble schemes. It was repealed in 1825.

bucentaur. A gaily ornamented ship or barge, from the name of the Venetian state-galley employed by the Doge when he went on Ascension Day to wed the Adriatic. The word is Gr. *bous,* ox, and *centauros,* centaur; and the original galley was probably ornamented with a man-headed ox. It. *bucentoro.*

Bucephalus (Gr. *boukephalos* "bull-headed"). A horse. Strictly speaking, the favorite charger of Alexander the Great. By taming him Alexander fulfilled an oracle as to the succession to the throne of Macedon.

Buchan, John, 1st Baron **Tweedsmuir** (1875–1940). Scottish novelist, biographer, historian, diplomat, in 1935 Governor-General of Canada. His *Cromwell* is a fine biography. His romantic fiction, of which *The Thirty-Nine Steps* became an outstanding motion picture, is above average. He wrote *A History of the Great War* in four volumes.

Buchanan, James (1791–1868). Fifteenth President of the U.S. during years just preceding Civil War (1857–1861).

Buchanan, Robert Williams (1841–1901). British poet and novelist. Attacked Swinburne in *Spectator* (1866), and Pre-Raphaelites in *The Fleshly School of Poetry; Contemporary Review* (1871).

Buck. The dog hero of Jack London's CALL OF THE WILD, the offspring of a St. Bernard father and a Scotch shepherd dog.

Buck, Paul Herman (1899–). American historian and university professor. Received the Pulitzer Prize for History (1938) for his book on post-Civil War reconstruction, *The Road to Reunion: 1865–1900.*

Buck, Pearl Sydenstricker (1892–). American novelist, raised in China and best known for her books on Chinese life, for which she won the Nobel Prize in 1938. Her most famous novel is THE GOOD EARTH (1931), awarded the Pulitzer Prize in 1932 and made into a play and a motion picture. Among her other books are *East Wind: West Wind* (1930); *The Young Revolutionist* (1932); *Sons* (1932); *The First Wife, And Other Stories* (1933); *The Mother* (1934); *A House Divided* (1935), which, with *The Good Earth* and *Sons,* was published as a trilogy, *The House of Earth* (1935); *The Exile* (1936); *This Proud Heart* (1938); *The Patriot* (1939); *Other Gods* (1940); *Today and Forever* (1941), short stories. She also translated the Chinese classic, *Shui Hu Chuan,* a picaresque novel, as *All Men Are Brothers* (1933).

Bucket, Mr. In Dickens' *Bleak House,* a shrewd detective officer, who cleverly discovers that Hortense, the French maidservant of Lady Dedlock, was the murderer of Mr. Tulkinghorn, and not Lady Dedlock who was charged with the deed by Hortense. Swinburne, speaking of the detectives of fiction, calls Bucket "that matchless master of them all," and "the incomparable Mr. Bucket."

Buck-eye State. Ohio. See under STATES.

Buckingham, George Villiers, 1st Duke of (1592–1628). The profligate favorite of James I, who because of his beauty called him "Steenie," a pet corruption of Stephen, whose face at martyrdom was "as the face of an angel." This was the duke who was assassinated by Fenton (1592–1628). He is introduced by Walter Scott in THE FORTUNES OF NIGEL and by Dumas in his THREE MUSKETEERS.

George Villiers, second duke of *Buckingham.* Son of the preceding, and favorite of Charles II. He made the "whole body of vice his study." His name furnishes the third letter of the famous anagram *"Cabal."* This was the Duke who wrote *The Rehearsal.* He is introduced by Walter Scott in WOODSTOCK and PEVERIL OF THE PEAK, and by Dryden in his ABSALOM AND ACHITOPHEL, where he is called ZIMRI.

Off with his head! so much for Buckingham! A famous line, often searched for in vain in Shakespeare's *Richard III.* It is not to be found there, but is in Act iv, Sc. iii, of Colley Cibber's *The Tragical History of Richard III,* altered from Shakespeare (1700).

Buck in the Snow, The. A volume of poems by Edna St. Vincent MILLAY.

Bucklaw, Laird of. Frank Hayston. Lucy's suitor in Scott's BRIDE OF LAMMERMOOR.

Buckle, Henry Thomas (1821–1862). English historian, known for his theories of the influence of climate and soil on history and civilization. He planned a large work on this subject, but only the first two volumes, *History of Civilization in England* (1857, 1861), which were intended as an introduction, were completed at the time of his death.

Buck-tail. A member of the American Democratic-Republican Party. It originally referred to TAMMANY.

bucolic. A term referring to shepherds or herdsmen. Virgil's pastoral poems are called *Bucolics.* See IDYLL.

Buddenbrook, Hanno. In BUDDENBROOKS, by Thomas Mann, the son of Thomas Buddenbrooks and the last of the declining family. He is frail and sickly, fond of the music of Richard WAGNER and possesssed of an aesthetic yearning which is considered to be symbolic of the family's material decay, since in Mann's novels pure aestheticism is often synonymous with death. See TONIO KRÖGER.

Buddenbrooks. An early novel by Thomas MANN, first published as *Buddenbrooks: Verfall einer Familie* (1901) and brought out in an American translation in 1924. It deals with the decline and dissolution of a prosperous, conservative, and honored German family of merchants in the 18th and 19th centuries. The family's loss of money and commercial power is paralleled by an increase in its members' interest in art and learning and a growing dominance of the Swiss and French strains in its blood. The leading characters include Johann Buddenbrook, patriarch of the family at the time the novel opens; Consul Buddenbrook, his son; Antonie, Christian, and Thomas, children of the Consul; and Hanno BUDDENBROOK, Thomas' son.

Buddha (*Sans.* "the enlightened"). The title given to Prince Siddhartha or GAUTAMA, also called (from the name of his tribe, the Sakhyas) Sakya muni, the founder of Buddhism, who lived in the 6th century B.C.

Buddhism. The system of religion inaugurated by the Buddha in India in the 6th century B.C.

The four sublime verities of Buddhism, i.e., the "Four Aryan *or* Noble Truths," are as follows:

(1) Pain exists.
(2) The cause of pain is "birth sin." The Buddhist supposes that man has passed through many previous existences, and all the heaped-up sins accumulated in these previous states constitute man's "birth sin."
(3) Pain is ended only by Nirvana.

(4) The way that leads to Nirvana is the "Eightfold Path"—right faith, right judgment, right language, right purpose, right practice, right obedience, right memory, and right meditation (eight in all).

The abstract nature of the religion, together with the overgrowth of its monastic system and the superior vitality and energy of Brahminism, caused it to decline in India itself; but it spread rapidly in the surrounding countries and took so permanent a hold that it is computed that at the present time it has some 140,000,000 adherents, of whom ten and three-fourths millions are in India, and the rest principally in Ceylon, Tibet, China, and Japan.

Esoteric Buddhism. See THEOSOPHY.

Budënny, Semën Mikhailovich (1883–). Russian general. Active in Revolution of 1917; joined Red Army 1918; cavalry leader against Denikin and Wrangel; marshal of Soviet Union from 1935; member of Central Committee of Communist Party from 1939; first vice-commissar of defense 1940; in command of southern front July–November 1941.

Bufano, Remo. American puppeteer. *Pinocchio for the Stage in Four Short Plays* (1929); *The Show Book of Remo Bufano: Seven Plays for Marionettes and People* (1929); *Be a Puppet Showman* (1933); *Magic Strings, Marionette Plays* (1939).

Buffalo Bill. A venturesome pony-express rider and scout, the name under which the daredevil exploits of Col. William F. CODY attained dime-novel fame.

buffalo soldiers. Colored soldiers serving in the west. The Indians called them so because their woolly heads looked like the matted wool between a bison's horns.

buffer state. A small, self-governing state separating two larger states, and thus tending to prevent hostilities between the two. The term seems to have originated on the northwest frontiers of India.

Buffon, Georges-Louis Leclerc, Comte de (1707–1788). French naturalist, best known for his *Histoire naturelle* (1749–1788), *Époques de la nature,* appearing after 1774, and his *Théorie de la terre.* These works deal with the earth, minerals, the animals, and man. Buffon helped lay the foundations for 19th-century work in natural science, especially zoölogy, and was the first to write a history of the earth as a series of successive geological stages. His style is vivid and eloquent.

Buford, Chad. The hero of THE LITTLE SHEPHERD OF KINGDOM COME by John Fox.

bug. An old word for goblin, sprite, bogy; probably from Welsh *bwg,* a ghost. The word is used in Coverdale's Bible, which was afterwards known as the "Bug Bible" (see BIBLE, SPECIALLY NAMED), and survives in *bogle, bogy,* and in *bugaboo,* a monster or goblin, introduced into the tales of the old Italian romancers, and *bugbear,* a scarecrow, or sort of hobgoblin in the form of a bear.

big bug. A person of importance—especially in his own eyes; a swell; a pompous or conceited man. There is an old adjective *bug,* meaning pompous, proud.

buhlwork. See BOULLE.

Builders, The. See GLASGOW, ELLEN.

Building of the Ship, The. Poem (1870) by Longfellow. Quoted from by Franklin D. Roosevelt to Winston Churchill during World War II.

Bukharin, Nikolai Ivanovich (1888–1938). Russian Communist leader and editor. Edited 1916 *Novy Mir* (*The New World*) in New York City. Head of Third International (1926–1929); expelled from Communist Party, again admitted, suspected of support of Trotsky; arrested, tried, executed with other Bolshevist leaders (1938); wrote several works on Communism.

Bulba, Taras, see TARAS BULBA.

Bulbo, Prince. A character in Thackeray's ROSE AND THE RING.

Bulfinch, Thomas (1796–1867). American scholar and popularizer of mythology, author of *The Age of Fable* (1855), *The Age of Chivalry, Legends of Charlemagne,* etc., based upon classical, Oriental and medieval legends.

bull. A blunder, or inadvertent contradiction of terms, for which the Irish are proverbial.

In astronomy, the English name of the northern constellation (Lat. *Taurus*) which contains Aldebaran and the Pleiades; also the sign of the zodiac that the sun enters about April 22nd and leaves a month later. It is between Aries and Gemini. The time for ploughing, which in the East was performed by oxen or bulls.

Papal bull. An edict or mandate issued by the Pope, so called from the heavy laden seal (Lat. *bulla*) appended to the document. See GOLDEN BULL.

a bull in a china shop. A maladroit hand interfering with a delicate business; one who produces reckless destruction.

take the bull by the horns. To attack or encounter a threatened danger fearlessly; to go forth boldly to meet a difficulty.

John Bull, see JOHN BULL.

Bull, Ole Bornemann (1810–1880). Norwegian violinist. Toured as virtuoso through Europe and five times through North America. Spent last years of life in Cambridge, Mass.

bulla. In Roman antiquity, a small case of metal or leather containing amulets and suspended by a cord around the neck.

it is long
Since Time was first a fledgeling:
Yet thou may'st be but as a pendant bulla
Against his stripling bosom swung.
Francis Thompson, *Anthem of Earth.*

Bullard, Arthur. Pseudonym Albert Edwards (1879–1929). American foreign correspondent; in State Department's Russian division. Wrote *Comrade Yetta,* a novel of Socialism, etc.

bulldozer. One who bulldozes, i.e., intimidates by threats of violence. Hence, in World War II a heavy wheeled machine with a driver used to flatten the terrain.

Bullen, Frank Thomas (1857–1915). English writer of sea stories. Wrote *The Cruise of the "Cachalot"* (1898).

Bullion State. Missouri. See under STATES.

Bullitt, William Christian (1891–). American diplomat. U.S. ambassador to Russia (1933–1936), to France (1936–1940). Special assistant to Secretary of Navy, June 1942.

Bull Moose Party. Formed by Theodore Roosevelt in presidential campaign of 1912. Said to have originated from a remark made by him that he "felt like a bull moose." The Progressive Party.

Bülow, Hans Guido, Freiherr von (1830–1894). Celebrated German pianist and orchestral conductor. His wife, Cosima LISZT, after a divorce, became the wife of Richard WAGNER.

Bulwer-Lytton, see LYTTON.

Bumble. In Dickens' *Oliver Twist,* beadle of the workhouse where Oliver Twist was born and brought up, stout, consequential, hard-hearted, fussy official, with mighty ideas of his own importance. This character has given to the language the word *bumbledom,* the officious arrogance and bumptious conceit of a parish authority or petty dignitary. After marriage with Mrs. Corney, the high and mighty beadle is sadly henpecked and reduced to a Jerry Sneak.

Bumboat Woman, The. Heroine of one of the most popular of Sir William Gilbert's BAB BALLADS. Her name is Poll Pineapple, and she sails in seaman's clothes with Lieutenant Belaye in the *Hot Cross-Bun*. Jack tars generally greet each other with "Messmate, ho! what cheer?" but the greeting on the *Hot Cross-Bun* is always, "How do you do, my dear?" and never is any oath more naughty than "Dear me!" One day, Lieutenant Belaye comes on board and says to his crew, "Here, messmates, is my wife, for I have just come from church." Thereupon they all faint and it is found that the crew consists of young women only, who have dressed like sailors to follow the fate of the handsome lieutenant.

bumping race. An English rowing race in which boats start at a fixed distance from each other and each tries to overtake and bump the boat ahead of it, taking its place in the next race if it does so.

Bumppo, Natty. The central figure of Cooper's Leatherstocking series, better known as LEATHERSTOCKING.

Bunch, Mother. A noted London alewife of the late Elizabethan period, on whose name have been fathered many jests and anecdotes, and who is mentioned more than once in Elizabethan drama, *e.g.*:

Now, now, mother Bunch, how dost thou? What, dost frowne, Queene Gwyniver, dost wrinckle?
Dekker, *Satiromastix,* III. i.

In 1604 was published *Pasquil's Jests, mixed with Mother Bunches Merriments* and in the "Epistle to the Merrie Reader" is given a humorous description of her:

. . . She spent most of her time in telling of tales, and when she laughed, she was heard from Aldgate to the Monuments at Westminster, and all Southwarke stood in amazement, the Lyons in the Tower, and the Bulls and Beares of Parish Garden roar'd louder than the great roaring Megge . . . She dwelt in Cornhill, neere the Exchange, and sold strong Ale . . . and lived an hundreth, seventy and five yeares, two dayes and a quarter, and halfe a minute.

Other books were named after her, such, for instance, as *Mother Bunch's Closet newly Broke Open,* "containing rare secrets of art and nature, tried and experienced by learned philosophers, and recommended to all ingenious young men and maids, teaching them how to get good wives and husbands."

Buncombe, bunkum. Claptrap. The story is that a representative at Washington being asked why he made such a flowery speech, so wholly uncalled for, made answer, "I was not speaking to the House, but to Buncombe," the county in North Carolina which he represented.

bundling. Occupying the same bed without undressing—a custom prevailing in courtship in the less sophisticated portions of New England, New York, New Jersey, and Pennsylvania. Probably a survival from pioneering days when the importance of courtship was recognized but could not lay claim to a heated room.

Bungay. In Thackeray's *Pendennis,* bookseller and publisher of the *Pall Mall Gazette,* edited by Captain Shannon. He publishes Arthur's novel.

Bungay or Bongay, Friar. A famous necromancer of the 15th century, whose story is much overlaid with legend. It is said that he "raised mists and vapors which befriended Edward IV at the battle of Barnet." In the old prose romance, *The Famous History of Friar Bacon,* and in Greene's *Honourable History of Friar Bacon and Friar Bungay* (acted 1591), he appears as the assistant to Roger Bacon (d. 1292) in his diabolical scientific experiments, and he is also in Bulwer-Lytton's LAST OF THE BARONS.

Bunin, Ivan Alexeyevich (1870–). Russian poet and novelist who won the Nobel Prize for Literature in 1933. Reported destitute in Unoccupied France in 1941.

Bunker Hill, Bunker Hill Day. See under CHARLESTOWN, MASS.

Bunner, Henry Cuyler (1855–1896). American journalist and short-story writer, one of the first to write of simple people in the great cities of the nation, a forerunner of O. HENRY. Among the collections of his stories are *Short Sixes* (1890); *The Runaway Browns* (1892); *More Short Sixes* (1894); *Love in Old Cloathes* (1896).

Bunsby, Captain John or Jack. In Dickens' DOMBEY AND SON, the owner of the *Cautious Clara.* Captain Cuttle considers him "a philosopher, and quite an oracle." Captain Bunsby has one "stationary and one revolving eye," and a very red face, and is extremely taciturn. The Captain is trapped by Mrs. McStinger, the termagant landlady of his friend, Captain Cuttle, into marrying her.

Bunsen burner. Used for heating purposes in every chemical laboratory. Invented by Robert Wilhelm Eberhard Bunsen, German chemist (1811–1899).

Bunthorne, Reginald. The hero of Gilbert and Sullivan's comic opera PATIENCE, the subtitle of which is *Bunthorne's Bride.* He is reputed to be a caricature of Oscar WILDE.

Buntline, Ned. Pseudonym of Edward Z. C. JUDSON.

Bunyan, John (1628–1688). English prose writer, a non-conformist lay preacher, twice imprisoned under the Stuart restoration for his beliefs, who became famous for his religious allegories. The most celebrated of his works, in many quarters almost as widely read as the Bible, is THE PILGRIM'S PROGRESS FROM THIS WORLD TO THAT WHICH IS TO COME (1678), written during an imprisonment of six months. His other writings, all religious in character, most of them allegorical, are: *The Holy City, Or the New Jerusalem* (1665); *Grace Abounding to the Chief of Sinners* (1666); *A Confession of My Faith and a Reason of My Practice* (1672); *The Life and Death of Mr. Badman* (1680); *The Holy War* (1682). (See separate entries.) Bunyan's only literary influence was the Bible, and his style is simple, vigorous, and concrete, highly praised by critics.

Bunyan, Paul. A legendary hero of the lumber camps of the American Northwest. Many tales are told of his feats in a sort of chapbook called *Paul Bunyan Comes West.* The dragging of his pick behind him cuts out the Grand Canyon of the Colorado. When he builds a hotel he has "the last seven stories put on hinges so's they could be swung back for to let the moon go by." Innumerable stories of the prowess of this remarkable Paul Bunyan have been invented by the lumbermen for their own amusement.

Burbage, James (d. 1597). English actor, who, in 1576, built the first theatre in England specifically intended for stage performances. Moved to a different site, the building became the Globe Theatre in 1598, later the scene of the presentation of many of Shakespeare's plays. See also BURBAGE, RICHARD.

Burbage, Richard (1567?–1619). English actor, son of James BURBAGE. He performed in plays by Shakespeare, Ben Jonson, and Beaumont and Fletcher, being particularly celebrated for his rôles in tragedy. He was a member of the Lord CHAMBERLAIN's Men, and was also a painter of some note. The Felton portrait of Shakespeare has been attributed to him.

Burbank, Luther (1849–1926). American scientist, known for his experiments in plant-breeding. He improved a number of varieties of plants, including the potato, citrus fruits, corn, tomatoes, berries, cacti, and the like.

Burbon. In Spenser's *Faërie Queene* (Bk. v) the lover of Fleurdelis (France), typifying Henry of Navarre. He is assailed by a rabble rout, who batter his shield to pieces, and compel him to cast it aside. The rabble rout is the Roman Catholic party that tried to throw him off; the shield he is compelled to abandon is Protestantism; his carrying off Fleurdelis is his obtaining the kingdom by a *coup* after his renunciation of the Protestant cause.

Burchell, Mr. The name assumed by Sir William THORNHILL in Goldsmith's VICAR OF WAKEFIELD.

Burckhardt, Jakob Christoph (1818–1897). Swiss historian of art and culture, best known for his monumental work, *Die Kultur der Renaissance in Italien* (*The Civilization of the Renaissance in Italy*) (1885). Teacher of NIETZSCHE.

Burchfield, Charles Ephraim (1893–). American landscape painter.

Burd, Helen, see HELEN BURD.

Bureau of Internal Revenue. A bureau of the Treasury Department, collecting taxes and revenue leveled within the country.

Bureau of Standards. A bureau of the Commerce Department. In its care are all standards of weights and measures used in the U.S.

burgee. A swallow-tailed or triangular flag used as a pennant by yachts and merchant vessels.

Burgess, Frank Gelett (1866–). American humorist, author of *Goops and How to Be Them* (1900), *Are you a Bromide* (1906), etc. See GOOP; BROMIDE; BLURB.

Burgess, Thornton Waldo (1874–). American author of *Bedtime Stories,* a syndicated series of animal stories for children, beginning in 1912 and appearing daily in numerous newspapers throughout the U.S. He also published a large number of his stories in book-form.

Burglar of the Zodiac, The. See BENÉT, WILLIAM ROSE.

Burgoyne, John (1722–1792). British army officer and dramatist. Forced to surrender to the Americans at Saratoga in 1777. Participated in impeachment of Warren HASTINGS. Garrick produced his *The Maid of the Oaks* (1775) and *The Heiress* was played in 1786.

Burgundy, Charles the Bold, duke of. A historical personage introduced by Scott in his *Quentin Durward* and in *Anne of Geierstein.* The latter novel contains an account of the Duke's defeat at Nancy, and his death.

Buridan's ass. A man of indecision; like one "on double business bound, who stands in pause where he should first begin and both neglects." Buridan is reputed by differing authorities to be either a Greek sophist or a French scholastic philosopher who died about 1360. He is credited with inventing the well-known sophism:

> If a hungry ass were placed exactly between two haystacks in every respect equal, it would starve to death, because there would be no motive why it should go to one rather than to the other.

Buried Alive. See BENNETT, ENOCH ARNOLD.

Burke, Edmund (1729–1797). English statesman and author, born in Ireland, known for his orations as a member of Parliament. He was sympathetic toward the American colonies and the Irish Catholics, and was a strong enemy of the French Revolution. Among his most famous speeches are ON AMERICAN TAXATION (1774); ON CONCILIATION WITH THE COLONIES (1775); *On the Nabob of Arcot's Private Debts* (1785). His published works include: *A Vindication of Natural Society* (1756); A PHILOSOPHICAL INQUIRY INTO THE ORIGIN OF OUR IDEAS OF THE SUBLIME AND BEAUTIFUL (1756), his most ambitious work; *Observations on the Present State of the Nation* (1769); *Letter to the Sheriffs of Bristol* (1777); REFLECTIONS ON THE FRENCH REVOLUTION (1790); *Letters on a Regicide Peace* (1795–1797). He was associated with the literary groups of the 18th century. His influence on early 19th century German national economists is particularly pronounced.

Burke, Kenneth Duva (1897–). American literary critic and author. His works include *The White Oxen* (1924), short stories; *Counterstatement* (1931), criticism; *Permanence and Change* (1935), a study of the evolution of ethics; *Attitudes toward History* (1937), a psychological study of history; *The Philosophy of Literary Form* (1941), aesthetics.

Burke, Tom, see TOM BURKE.

Burke, Thomas (1886–1945). English novelist and essayist. He told exciting melodramatic stories of the Limehouse district of London, the best-known of which, perhaps, is *Broken Blossoms.*

burlesque. Stage entertainment featuring low comedy, obscene humor, lewd dancing, and an exploitation of nakedness. It was introduced in the U.S. during the 1860's, after the first appearance of women's tights in the performances of Lydia Thompson, Adah Isaacs Menken, and THE BLACK CROOK. During the latter part of the 19th century, attendance at burlesque shows was often surreptitious and under the threat of a police raid, and was considered an exciting adventure. By the 1930's, however, burlesque had declined greatly in popularity because of competition by the musical-comedy and revue stage and the motion pictures, and because its increasing license had brought about legal restrictions against it. The word comes ultimately from Italian *burla* "joke, jest."

Burlingame, William Roger (1889–). Author, grandson of Anson Burlingame, American lawyer and diplomat. Wrote *March of the Iron Men* (1938), *Engines of Democracy* (1940).

Burman, Ben Lucien (1895–). American author. Wrote *Steamboat Round the Bend* (1933), filmed with Will Rogers as star (1935).

Burnand, Sir **Francis Cowley** (1836–1917). English playwright and editor of *Punch* (1880–1906). Author of many burlesques including *Cox and Box* with music by Sir Arthur Sullivan (1867). *Happy Thoughts,* originally a series in *Punch* has been widely read.

Burne-Jones, Sir **Edward Coley** (1833–1898). English painter, member of the PRE-RAPHAELITE BROTHERHOOD, accorded wide public adulation. He painted classical, religious, medieval, literary, and symbolic scenes, marked by mysticism, emotion, and exotic decoration.

Burnet, Gilbert (1643–1715). English bishop and historian. Counseled William and Mary. Author of a *History of the Reformation* in three volumes (1679–1714) and the *History of my Own Times* in two volumes (1723–1734).

Burnett, Frances Eliza Hodgson (1849–1924). English-born American author of popular romances and books for children, including LITTLE LORD FAUNTLEROY (1886); *Sara Crewe* (1888); and *The Secret Garden* (1911).

Burnett, Whit (1899–). With Martha Foley, founded and edited the magazine *Story* for the discovery of new short-story talent. Has edited the anthologies *This is my Best* and *The Seas of God*.

Burnett, William Riley (1899–). Author of fast-paced fiction with mature technique of the hard-boiled school. His *Little Caesar* was his first published work and made a star of Edward G. Robinson in the movie hit.

Burney, Fanny (Madame d'Arblay) (1752–1840). English author known for her diaries and letters and her two novels EVELINA (1778) and CECILIA (1782). She was one of the first novelists to deal with the experiences of a young girl coming in contact with the social world.

Burning Babe, The. A mystical religious poem by Robert SOUTHWELL.

burning bush. A bush out of which the voice of God spoke to Moses, "and behold the bush burned with fire, and the bush was not consumed."

Burning Bush, The. See UNDSET, SIGRID.

Burning Cactus. See SPENDER, STEPHEN.

Burning City. See BENÉT, STEPHEN VINCENT.

burning ghat. See under GHAT.

Burning Wheel, The. See HUXLEY, ALDOUS.

Burns, Helen. A character in Charlotte Brontë's novel, JANE EYRE.

Burns, Robert (1759–1796). Scotch poet, the greatest of his nation, a plowboy who became a social and literary sensation. He is best known for his dialect lyrics on nature, love, patriotism, humanitarianism, and humble peasant life. Among the most famous of these are TO A MOUSE; TO A MOUNTAIN DAISY; SWEET AFTON; MY LUVE IS LIKE A RED, RED ROSE; SCOTS, WHA HAE; JOHN ANDERSON, MY JO; A MAN'S A MAN FOR A' THAT; TO MARY IN HEAVEN; AULD LANG SYNE. THE COTTER'S SATURDAY NIGHT (1787), TAM O' SHANTER (1791), and THE JOLLY BEGGARS (1799) are longer poems. Editions of Burns's poetry were published in 1786 and 1787.

Burnside, Ambrose Everett (1824–1881). American army commander. West Point 1847. In command of Army of Potomac Oct. 1862. Unsuccessful in Fredericksburg and Petersburg campaigns and resigned commission in 1865. Governor of Rhode Island and then U.S. Senator 1875–1881. His type of side whiskers gave us the word "burnsides," now often amusingly inverted as "sideburns."

Burnt Njal. Hero of one of the best known of the early Icelandic sagas, *The Story of Burnt Njal*. The plot concerns the grim blood-feud between the families of two well-to-do landowners, Njal and Gunnar, who are personal friends. Hallgerda, the spiteful and selfish wife of Gunnar, is the instigator of the feud, which progresses with a regular alternation of murders between the two sides, until it culminates in the firing of Njal's home and the burning to death of Njal within it.

Burnt Norton. See ELIOT, THOMAS STEARNS.

Burr, Aaron (1756–1836). American politician, once New York State Attorney General, U.S. Senator, defeated candidate for governor of New York State, and Vice President of the U.S. under Thomas Jefferson, by whom he was defeated in the presidential election of 1800. Burr is best known for his enmity with Alexander HAMILTON, whom he killed in a famous duel. He was later tried on a charge of treason in connection with an alleged plot to set up an empire in the Southwest. A number of romantic novels have appropriated Burr as a character, including Gertrude Atherton's THE CONQUEROR.

Burroughs, Edgar Rice (1875–). See TARZAN.

Burroughs, John (1837–1921). American scientist and essayist on nature subjects. His books include *Wake-Robin* (1871); *Birds and Poets* (1877); *Locusts and Wild Honey* (1879); *Squirrels and Other Fur-Bearers* (1900); *The Breath of Life* (1915); *Accepting the Universe* (1920). He was influenced by EMERSON and THOREAU and was a friend of Walt Whitman, and his later thoughts tend toward their mysticism.

Burt, Maxwell Struthers (1882–). American novelist and short-story writer. His books include *The Interpreter's House* (1924); *The Diary of a Dude Wrangler* (1924), autobiographical; *The Delectable Mountains* (1927); and *Festival* (1931). His wife, **Katharine Newlin Burt,** is a novelist in her own right, having eighteen books to her credit, most of them "Westerns."

Burton, Sir **Richard Francis** (1821–1890). English traveler and author, best known for his translation of the ARABIAN NIGHTS (1885–1888). He also published books on travel in Africa, India, and America, and was one of the first Englishmen to visit MECCA.

Burton, Robert (1577–1640). English churchman and prose writer, known for his wide and curious learning as represented in his most famous work, THE ANATOMY OF MELANCHOLY (1621).

Burwell Papers. Accounts of BACON'S REBELLION, named for the Burwell family of Virginia, which released them publicly a century after the events they describe. They consist of three separate accounts *The Beginning, Progress, and Conclusion of Bacon's Rebellion in Virginia in the Years 1675 and 1676,* by "T. M."; *An Account of Our Late Troubles in Virginia,* by "Mrs. An. Cotton of Q. Creek"; and *A Narrative of the Indian and Civil Wars in Virginia,* by an anonymous author. "T. M." identifies himself in his work as a planter and a member of the Virginia Assembly in 1676, but nothing is known of the other two authors.

Bury Me Not on the Lone Prairie. An American folk-ballad of the West, better known in its more popular version of *Carry Me Back to the Lone Prairie.*

Bury the Dead. A one-act play by Irwin SHAW, produced in 1936, a re-written version of an earlier drama, *Miracle at Verdun* (1931), by Hans Chlumberg, Austrian playwright. In it, soldiers killed during one of the catastrophic wars of the 20th century refuse to be buried, resist all attempts to persuade them to become passive, and incite the living army to rebellion.

busby. A tall headdress worn in British army by hussars, artillerymen, engineers. Of fur, with a bag of same color as facings of the regiment hanging from the top on the right.

Busch, Wilhelm (1832–1908). German humorous illustrator and poet. His bitter satire against bourgeois pettiness is generally missed by the bourgeois himself who adores Busch's work. *Max und Moritz* is available in Pennsylvania Dutch. From 1859–1871 Busch worked for the Munich *Fliegende Blätter.*

bush. Rural districts as opposed to town or city; the "sticks," as in the baseball term "bush league." In Australia, large tracts of scrub-covered country as distinguished from cultivated areas.

Bush, Ishmael. A rough, ferocious squatter in Cooper's novel THE PRAIRIE, whose story, with that of his family, comprises much of the action of the novel.

bushel. The expression, *to put one's light under a bushel,* is an allusion to Matthew v. 15; Mark iv. 21; Luke xi. 33.

business. A.S. *bisigness,* from *bisigian,* to occupy, to worry, to fatigue. In theatrical parlance "business" or "biz" means by-play. Thus, Hamlet trifling with Ophelia's fan, Lord Dundreary's hop, and so on, are the special "business" of the actor of the part. As a rule, the "business" is invented by the actor who creates the part, or by the director or producer, and it is handed down by tradition.

business to-morrow. When the Spartans seized upon Thebes they placed Archias over the garrison. Pelopidas, with eleven others, banded together to put Archias to the sword. A letter containing full details of the plot was given to the Spartan polemarch at the banquet table; but Archias thrust the letter under his cushion, saying, "Business to-morrow." But long ere that sun arose he was numbered with the dead.

business as usual. An expression meaning that the everyday routine must be carried on as usual to preserve morale in a crisis. It was much in use during World War I. During World War II it came to have in the U.S. a derogatory meaning, in reproach to those manufacturers who neglected to devote their total plant facilities to aiding in the war effort but tried to continue their peacetime consumer production.

mean business. To be determined to carry out one's project; to be in earnest.

Busirane. An enchanter bound by Britomart in Spenser's *Faërie Queene* (Bk. iii). He is the typification of unrestrained amorous passion.

Busiris. A mythical king of Egypt who, in order to avert a famine, used to sacrifice to the gods all strangers who set foot on his shores. Hercules was seized by him; and would have fallen a victim, but he broke his chain, and slew the inhospitable king. He is the titular hero of a blood-and-thunder tragedy by Edward Young (1718).

buskin. A sort of half-boot. The Greek tragic actors used to wear a sandal some two or three inches thick, to elevate their stature. To this sole was attached a very elegant buskin, and the whole was called *cothurnus.* Hence *buskin-cothurnus.*

Busqueue, Lord. In Rabelais' *Gargantua and Pantagruel,* plaintiff in the great Pantagruelian lawsuit known as "Lord Busqueue *vs.* Lord Suckfist." See SUCKFIST.

Bussy D'Ambois. A historical tragedy by George Chapman (1607). The hero wins for himself a position of influence at the French court of Henry III, but his downfall is brought about by his enemies through their exposure of his clandestine love affair with the Countess Tamyra.

Buster Brown. A young imp of the American comic supplement, the invention of R. F. Outcault. He was very popular as the titular hero of a comedy, and Buster Brown suits, dresses and collars, so named from his mode of dress, were fashionable for children in the early years of the 20th century. Only Buster Brown shoes have survived.

Butler, Ellis Parker (1869–1937). American humorist. Creator of the classic *Pigs Is Pigs.*

Butler, Nicholas Murray (1862–1947). American educator, president of Columbia University in New York City 1902–1945, and active in public affairs. Among his writings are *Education in the United States* (1910); *A World in Ferment* (1918); *The Faith of a Liberal* (1924); *The Path to Peace* (1930); and *Across the Busy Years* (1939, 1940), volumes one and two of an autobiography.

Butler, Rhett. Leading character in GONE WITH THE WIND, hero to Scarlett O'HARA.

Butler, Samuel (1612–1680). English poet, most famous for HUDIBRAS (1663, 1664, 1678), a mock-epic satirizing the Puritans. He also wrote a set of *Characters* in the manner of THEOPHRASTUS and THE ELEPHANT IN THE MOON, a satire in verse on the ROYAL SOCIETY. Butler's *Genuine Remains in Verse and Prose* were published in 1759.

Butler, Samuel (1835–1902). English author, best known for his novel THE WAY OF ALL FLESH (1903), a bitter and realistic study of bigotry, narrowness, and hypocrisy in the Victorian PONTIFEX family. He wrote also EREWHON (1872), a satire on the England of his day in the manner of SWIFT, and a number of controversial scientific studies attacking Darwinism. The latter include *Life and Habit* (1877); *God the Known and God the Unknown* (1879); *Unconscious Memory* (1880); *Luck or Cunning* (1887). The remainder of his works consists of satires on religious orthodoxy, books of travel, literary studies, and translations of the ODYSSEY and the ILIAD. *Erewhon Revisited* was published in 1901, and *The Notebooks of Samuel Butler,* in 1912.

Buttercup, Little. In Gilbert and Sullivan's comic opera, *H. M. S. Pinafore* (1877), a "bumboat woman." She interchanged the babies who afterwards became Ralph Rackstraw and the Captain of the *Pinafore.*

Butterfly, Madame, see MADAME BUTTERFLY.

Butterworth, Elias Baptist. The hero of George Eliot's poem *A Minor Prophet;* an American "vegetarian seer."

button-molder, the. In Ibsen's *Peer Gynt,* the appearance of Destiny or Death.

Buzfuz, Serjeant. In Dickens' PICKWICK PAPERS, the pleader retained by Dodson and Fogg for the plaintiff in the celebrated case of "Bardell *v.* Pickwick." Serjeant Buzfuz is an able orator, who proves that Mr. Pickwick's note about "chops and tomato sauce" is a declaration of love; and that his reminder "not to forget the warming-pan" is only a flimsy cover to express the ardor of his affection.

Buzzards. The inhabitants of Georgia, so called from the wild turkeys in that state.

bwana. In African stories, master or boss. The word comes from the African trade language Swahili.

Bycorne, see BICORNE.

Byliny. Epic poems of the Russian peasantry in song form. A number of specific heroes reappear throughout these songs, among the best known of whom are Mikula, Ilya of Murom, Dobrynya, Alyosha Popovich, Churilo Plenkovich, and Dyuk Stepanovich. Their feats are fantastic and often engagingly ingenuous. Many of the byliny are divided into cycles, such as the cycle of Kiev, the cycle of Novgorod, the cycle of Ivan the Terrible, etc., and they range in time from the earliest mythological periods to the 18th century.

Bynner, (Harold) Witter (1881–). American poet, author of *Grenstone Poems* (1917); *A Canticle of Pan* (1920); *The Jade Mountain* (1929), a translation of Chinese poetry; *Indian Earth* (1929); and *Against the Cold* (1940).

Byrd, Richard Evelyn (1888–). American aviator and explorer, a descendant of the Virginia planter William BYRD. He made an airplane flight across the North Pole in 1926 and the Atlantic Ocean in 1927, and led two expeditions to the Antarctic region in 1929 and 1934. Books in which he describes his adventures are *Skyward* (1928); *Little America* (1930); and *Alone* (1938).

Byrd, William (1543?–1623). English composer, known at home and in 16th-century Europe as the "Father of Music." He wrote much church music, including three masses, chamber and instrumental music, and a number of songs and madrigals on texts by Sir Philip Sidney, Ovid, Ariosto, and other famous poets. He is considered to have originated the solo song with string accompaniment. Although he wrote music for the Anglican Church, Byrd remained a devout Catholic.

Byrd, William (1674–1744). American historian of the Virginia colony, scholar, explorer, and member of the English ROYAL SOCIETY. His best-known works are *The History of the Dividing Line,* which concerns the dispute over the boundary between Virginia and North Carolina; *A Journey to the Land of Eden; A Progress to the Mines;* and *An Essay on Balk Tobacco.* They are included in collections of his papers, known as the Westover Manuscripts, which were published in 1841, 1866, and 1901. A diary which Byrd kept in shorthand as a hobby for several years was discovered nearly two hundred years after his death and published as *The Secret Diary of William Byrd of Westover* in 1940.

Byrne, Donn (1889–1928). Irish-American novelist. Born Brian Oswald Donn Byrne. Married Dorothea Cadogan, co-author of the successful play, *Enter Madame*. In 1920 his *Messer Marco Polo* was a *succès d'estime*. Wrote many other novels and stories.

Byron, George Noel Gordon, Lord (1788–1824). English poet, internationally the most famous of the English Romantic writers and the one who exerted the widest influence. He created the "Byronic hero," who reappears throughout his work—a sad and melancholy young man, brooding in a melodramatic manner upon something mysterious and evil in his background which he never explains. Byron's poetry is marked by fluent and rhetorical verse, frequent satire in the manner of the 18th century, and a choice of exotic and adventurous Oriental subjects in his narrative poems. The latter include CHILDE HAROLD (1812, 1816, 1817) the poem which made him famous; THE GIAOUR (1813); THE BRIDE OF ABYDOS (1813); THE CORSAIR (1814); LARA (1814); THE SIEGE OF CORINTH (1816); PARISINA (1816); THE PRISONER OF CHILLON. Among his poetic dramas are MANFRED (1817); CAIN, A MYSTERY (1821); MARINO FALIERI (1820); HEAVEN AND EARTH (1822); WERNER (1823); and THE DEFORMED TRANSFORMED (1824), left unfinished at the time of his death. His satires are ENGLISH BARDS AND SCOTCH REVIEWERS (1809); BEPPO (1818); THE VISION OF JUDGMENT (1822); THE AGE OF BRONZE (1823); and DON JUAN, his most important work, begun in 1818 and left incomplete at his death. Byron was a constant rebel against convention and encouraged the legend of wildness, evil, and debauchery that grew up about his name, to which his wife, Anne MILLBANKE, contributed by her suspicions of incest. See also Teresa GUICCIOLI, Augusta LEIGH.

the French Byron. Alfred de MUSSET (1810–1857).

the Oregon Byron. Joaquin Miller.

the Polish Byron. Adam Mickiewicz (1798–1855).

the Russian Byron. Alexander Sergeivitch PUSHKIN (1799–1837).

Byron, Harriet. In Richardson's *Sir Charles Grandison,* a beautiful and accomplished woman of high rank, devotedly attached to Sir Charles Grandison, whom ultimately she marries.

Byrsa. The citadel of Carthage, built, according to legend, by Dido, on the basis of a bargain with the natives, within the limits of a piece of land that could be enclosed with a bull's hide. The bull's hide, which had been cut up into strips, gave the place its name (Gr. *byrsa,* "hide"). Historically, the name comes from a Phoenician word meaning "citadel."

Byzantine (from Byzantium, the ancient name of Constantinople). In art, the symbolical system which was developed by the early Greek or Byzantine artists out of the Christian symbolism. Its chief features are the circle, dome, and round arch; and its chief symbols the lily, cross, vesica, and nimbus. St. Sophia, at Constantinople, and St. Mark, at Venice, are excellent examples of Byzantine architecture and decoration, and the Roman Catholic Cathedral at Westminster is a development of the same.

Byzantine Empire. The Eastern or Greek Empire, which lasted from the separation of the Eastern and Western Empires on the death of Theodosius in 395 A. D., till the capture of Constantinople by the Turks in 1453.

C

Caaba, al Caaba, see KAABA.

cabal. A JUNTO or council of intriguers. One of the Ministries of Charles II was called a "cabal" (1670), because the initial letters of its members formed the word: **C**lifford, **A**shley, **B**uckingham, **A**rlington, and **L**auderdale. This accident may have popularized the word, but it was in use in England many years before this, and is the Hebrew *qabbalah.* See CABALA.

These ministers were emphatically called the Cabal, and they soon made the appellation so infamous that it has never since . . . been used except as a term of reproach.—Macaulay, *England,* I, ii.

Conway Cabal. A faction organized by Gen. Thomas Conway, of the American Revolutionary army, to supersede Washington and make Gen. Gates commander-in-chief. This was in 1777–1778.

cabala. The oral traditions of the Jews, said to have been delivered by Moses to the rabbis and from them handed down through the centuries from father to son by word of mouth. In medieval times the term included the occult philosophy of the rabbis, and the *cabala* and its guardians, the *cabalists,* were feared as possessing secrets of magical power. The word is the Heb. *qabbalah,* accepted tradition.

Cabala, The. See WILDER, THORNTON.

Caballero, Francisco Largo, see LARGO CABALLERO.

cabaret. A restaurant where customers are entertained by performers. The French and generally continental equivalent of the American night club.

Cabbages and Kings. A volume of short stories by O. Henry (1862–1910). The title is taken from Lewis Carroll's ballad on the Walrus and the Carpenter in *Through the Looking-Glass.*

The time has come, the walrus said,
To talk of many things,
Of shoes, and ships and sealing wax
And cabbages and kings.

Cabell, James Branch (1879–). American novelist, known for his series of novels collectively entitled *Biography of Manuel,* dealing with the history of the family of Dom MANUEL, imaginary medieval count of an imaginary medieval country called POICTESME, from the Middle Ages to 20th-century America. The characters are often symbolic and satiric. Cabell's works include GALLANTRY (1907); CHIVALRY (1909); THE CORDS OF VANITY (1909); THE SOUL OF MELICENT (1913); THE RIVET IN GRANDFATHER'S NECK: A COMEDY OF LIMITATIONS (1915); THE CREAM OF THE JEST: A COMEDY OF EVASIONS (1917); BEYOND LIFE (1919); JURGEN: A COMEDY OF JUSTICE (1919); DOMNEI: A COMEDY OF WOMAN-WORSHIP (1920); FIGURES OF EARTH: A COMEDY OF APPEARANCES (1921); THE HIGH PLACE: A COMEDY OF DISENCHANTMENT (1923); THE EAGLE'S SHADOW: A COMEDY OF PURSE-STRINGS (1923); THE MUSIC FROM BEHIND THE MOON (1926); THE SILVER STALLION: A COMEDY OF REDEMPTION (1926); SOMETHING ABOUT EVE: A COMEDY OF FIG LEAVES (1927); THE WHITE ROBE (1928); WAY OF ECBEN (1929); SMIRT: AN URBANE NIGHTMARE (1934); SMITH: A SYLVAN INTERLUDE (1935); LADIES AND GENTLEMEN (1936), essays; SMIRE: AN ACCEPTANCE IN THE THIRD PERSON (1937); THE KING WAS IN HIS COUNTING-HOUSE: A COMEDY OF COMMON SENSE (1938); HAMLET HAD AN UNCLE: A COMEDY OF HONOR (1940); THE FIRST GENTLEMAN OF AMERICA: A COMEDY OF CONQUEST (1942). Cabell's novels were the subject of considerable literary controversy during the early 1920's, and the suppression of *Jurgen* for a time caused a sensation. Mr. Cabell's name is pronounced to rhyme with rabble.

Cabestaing, or Cabestan, Guillaume de. Late 12th-century Provençal troubadour. According to legend loved Marguerite, wife of Raymond of Château Roussillon, slain by the husband who cooked Cabestaing's heart and served it to his wife, who when she learned she had eaten it committed suicide by starvation. Richard Aldington wrote a poem about this, *The Eaten Heart.*

Cabeza de Vaca, Álvar Núñez (1490?–?1557). Spanish explorer of northern Mexico and Brazil, anticipating the expedition of Coronado (1540–1542).

Cable, George Washington (1844–1925). American author of stories and romances of the Creoles (see *Creole*) of Louisiana, including *Old Creole Days* (1879); THE GRANDISSIMES (1880); *Madame Delphine* (1881); *The Creoles of Louisiana* (1884); DR. SEVIER (1885); *Bonaventure* (1888); *Strong Hearts* (1899); *The Cavalier* (1901); *Posson Jone and Père Raphael* (1909); *Lovers of Louisiana* (1918).

Cabot, John (1450–1498) and **Sebastian** (1476?–1557) his son. Italian navigators and explorers. The former reached Baffin Land and Newfoundland, explored coast south to 38th parallel; the latter founded, and was made governor of, Company of Merchant Adventurers of London (1551) and searched for northeast passage. The Italian form of their name is Caboto.

ca' canny. A Scots expression meaning "go easily," "don't exert yourself." It is used in trade union slang, and the method of "ca' canny" is adopted by workmen for the purpose of bringing pressure on the employers when, in the workmen's opinion, a strike would be hardly justifiable, expedient, or possible. *Ca'* is Scots *caw,* to drive or impel. Cf. the more modern slowdown strike.

cachet (*Fr.*). Literally a seal, as of a letter. Hence *lettre de cachet,* a sealed letter, especially from a sovereign. Before the French Revolution arbitrary orders of arrest were often issued in the form of royal *lettres de cachet.*

Cacique. See RULERS, TITLES OF.

cacodaemon. An evil spirit (Gr. *kakos daimon*). Astrologers give this name to the Twelfth House of Heaven, from which only evil prognostics proceed.

> Hie thee to hell for shame, and leave the world,
> Thou cacodemon.
> Shakespeare, *Richard III*, i. 3.

Cacus. In classical mythology, a famous robber, represented as three-headed, and vomiting flames. He lived in Italy, and was strangled by Hercules.

caddie, caddy. An 18th-century Edinburgh attendant. Today one who carries a golf-player's clubs. From *cadet.*

Cade, Jack. An Irishman, who headed about 20,000 armed men, chiefly of Kent, "to procure redress of grievances" (1450). One of the most successful dramas of the American stage of the 19th century was Conrad's *Jack Cade* (1832). See also CADE'S REBELLION.

Cadenus. A name for Dean Swift in *Cadenus and Vanessa,* a poem. The word is simply de-ca-nus ("a dean") with the first two syllables transposed (ca-de-nus). See VANESSA.

Cade's Rebellion. Uprising of the men of Kent in 1450 under Jack Cade, in protest against heavy taxation and other abuses. London was seized but the insurgents were soon dispersed and Cade was killed.

Cadi. Arabic for a town magistrate or inferior judge.

Cadignan, Diane de. The Duchess of Maufrigneuse, afterwards Princess of Cadignan, one of Balzac's most heartless, brilliant and accomplished women, the mistress in turn of many of the men who appear in the novels of his *Comédie Humaine.* Her great achievement is perhaps her affair with the high-minded Daniel d'Arthez who was the best friend of her dead lover. Diane considers herself the friend of the Marquise d'Espard and her rival in social leadership. She is the heroine of *The Secrets of a Princess* (*Les Secrets de la Princesse de Cadignan*) (1839).

Cadman, Charles Wakefield (1881–1947). American composer, best known for his songs and instrumental and orchestral pieces on American Indian themes. One of the most popular of his songs in this vein is *From the Land of the Sky-Blue Water,* from *Four Indian Songs* (1909).

Cadmus. In Greek mythology, the son of Agenor, king of Phoenicia, and Telephassa; founder of Thebes (Boeotia) and the introducer of the alphabet into Greece. The name is Semitic for "the man of the East." Legend says that, having slain the dragon which guarded the fountain of Dirce, in Boeotia, he sowed its teeth, and a number of armed men sprang up surrounding Cadmus with intent to kill him. By the counsel of Minerva, he threw a precious stone among the men, who, striving for it, killed one another.

Cadmean letters. The Greek alphabet.

Cadmean victory. A very costly victory.

caduceus. A white wand carried by Roman heralds when they went to treat for peace; the wand placed in the hands of Mercury, the herald of the gods, of which poets feign that he could therewith give sleep to whomsoever he chose; wherefore Milton styles it "his opiate rod" in *Paradise Lost,* xi, 133. It is generally pictured with two serpents twined about it (a symbol thought to have originated in Egypt), and—with reference to the serpents of Aesculapius—it was adopted as the badge of the Royal Army Medical Corps and later of the Medical Corps of the U.S. Army.

> So with his dread caduceus Hermes led
> From the dark regions of the imprisoned dead;
> Or drove in silent shoals the lingering train
> To Night's dull shore and Pluto's dreary reign.
> Darwin, *Loves of the Plants,* ii. 291.

Cadwal. In Shakespeare's CYMBELINE, Arviragus, son of Cymbeline, was so called while he lived in the woods with Belarius.

Cadwallader, Rev. Mr. and **Mrs.** The rector and his wife in George Eliot's *Middlemarch.* The rector was kindly disposed toward everyone, but his wife had a sharp tongue on occasion.

Cadwallon. In Scott's novel, THE BETROTHED, the favorite bard of Prince Gwenwyn. He enters the service of Sir Hugo de Lacy, disguised, under the assumed name of Renault Vidal.

Cady, (Walter) Harrison (1877–). American artist and illustrator. For years did comic drawings for J. A. Mitchell's *Life* and other magazines. Illustrated books by Frances Hodgson Burnett, Robert W. Chambers, Thornton W. Burgess; generally known for his regular Sunday feature of Peter Rabbit in the New York *Herald Tribune.* Has exhibited paintings in many exhibitions and won several awards. Author of *The Bug Book* (1913); *Caleb Cottontail* (1921); etc.

Caedmon (fl. 675). Anglo-Saxon poet of conjectural existence. A series of Christian epics, called the "Caedmonian cycle," have been attributed to him or to followers of him, and are found in a single manuscript but in several handwritings. They consist of the poems *Genesis, Exodus, Daniel,* and *Christ and Satan.* See CYNEWULF. According to Bede, Caedmon was an ignorant man and knew nothing of poetry until one night, when sleeping in the byre, he was miraculously commanded by an angel to sing the Creation and the beginning of created things. His metrical paraphrase of *Genesis* some regard as the germ of Milton's PARADISE LOST.

Caerleon (literally, "the city of legions," from caer, Welsh for "city," and leon, a Welsh contraction of "legion"). A town in Monmouthshire, England, on the river Usk, the seat of King Arthur's court. It was also his habitual residence where he lived in splendid state, surrounded by the knights of his ROUND TABLE. See also CAMELOT.

Caesar, Caius Julius (100–44 B. C.). Roman general and administrator. He made himself master of the Roman world by defeating Pompey and ruled supreme until he was assassinated by a group of conspirators headed by Brutus and Cassius. Caesar appears in many historical dramas, notably in Shakespeare's *Julius Caesar* (ca. 1601) and G. B. Shaw's *Caesar and Cleopatra* (1898). In JULIUS CAESAR, although he plays the title rôle, Caesar is in reality a subordinate figure and something of a weakling and braggart, and the characterization has often been criticized as untrue to history. Shaw, who is quoted as saying that Shakespeare's character is "the *reductio ad absurdum* of the real Julius Caesar," wrote his *Caesar and Cleopatra* as "a simple return to nature and history." Caesar's own account of his *Gallic Wars* is still regarded as a Latin classic. The name Caesar survives in the words *Kaiser* and *Czar.*

Caesar's famous despatch, *"Veni, vidi, vici* (I came, I saw, I conquered)," was written to the senate to announce his overthrow of Pharnaces, king of Pontus.

Caesar's wife must be above suspicion. The name of Pompeia having been mixed up with an accusation against P. Clodius, Caesar divorced her; not because he believed her guilty, but because the wife of Caesar must not even be suspected of crime.

aut Caesar aut nullus (*Lat.* either Caesar or no one), everything or nothing; all or not at all.

the City of the Caesars. See under *city.*

Caesar, Irving (1895–). American librettist. Wrote lyrics for George White's *Scandals* and for musical comedies.

Caesarean operation. Also **Caesarian section.** Delivery of a child by cutting through the walls of abdomen and uterus. Caesar was believed to have been so delivered.

Caesura. In modern, especially English prosody a rhythmic break or pause which occurs naturally about the middle of a line of any length, but may be varied with different effects. It is usually a sense pause. The classical caesura was the division of a foot between two words.

Caf. See *Kaf.*

café-au-lait. Like the color of coffee with milk. From French *café au lait,* hot coffee and hot milk poured in equal portions simultaneously from two pots.

café chantant (*Fr.*). A café where singers or musicians entertain patrons. Note that the expression means literally "a singing café."

café dansant. A café where the patrons can dance.

café parfait. A coffee-flavored frozen dessert of whipped cream and eggs.

cafeteria. With a stress on the "i," the word came from Mexico, where it meant "coffee shop," to the Western U.S., where the stress moved up one syllable. After the American self-service feature had been added, the thing and the word spread all over the U.S. and also back to Mexico.

caftan. A Levantine garment. Long gown with extra long sleeves. The word comes from Turkish. Its association with the Jews took place in Western minds.

Cagliostro, Count **Alessandro Di.** Real name Giuseppe Balsamo (1743–1795). Famous Italian impostor who posed as alchemist and was the founder of a kind of freemasonry. Traveled all over Europe. Was involved in the famous affair of the DIAMOND NECKLACE in France. Modern students feel that the complete story of Cagliostro remains to be cleared up. GOETHE was greatly interested in his case and visited his family at Palermo.

Cagots. A sort of gipsy race living in the Middle Ages in Gascony and Bearne, supposed to be descendants of the Visigoths, and shunned as something loathsome. In modern French, a hypocrite or an ultra-devout person is called a *cagot.*

Cagoulard. A member of the French secret terroristic organization, the Comité Secret d'Action Révolutionnaire. From *cagoule* "a sort of hood."

Cahan, Abraham (1860–). Russian-American novelist. Editor of *Jewish Daily Forward,* New York City. Best-known novel, *The Rise of David Levinsky.*

Cahill, Marie (1874–1933). American actress. Starred in *The Wild Rose* (1902); *Sally in Our Alley* (1902); *Nancy Brown* (1903), etc.

Caiaphas. In the New Testament, a high priest, before whom Jesus was brought for trial.

Caillaux, Joseph (1863–1945). Premier of France (1911–1912) and twice minister of finance. Editor of *Le Figaro*. Gaston Calmette accused him of peculation and Caillaux's wife afterward shot and killed Calmette (1914).

Cain. In the Old Testament, the son of Adam and Eve and murderer of his brother Abel. After the murder, which was committed out of jealousy because Abel's sacrifice was more acceptable to Jehovah than Cain's, Jehovah cursed Cain and made him "a fugitive and a wanderer in the earth." Cain and Abel are called in the *Koran* "Kabil and Habil."

The Mohammedan tradition is this: Cain was born with a twin sister who was named Aclima, and Abel with a twin sister named Jumella. Adam wished Cain to marry Abel's twin sister, and Abel to marry Cain's. Cain would not consent to this arrangement, and Adam proposed to refer the question to God by means of a sacrifice. God rejected Cain's sacrifice to signify his disapproval of his marriage with Aclima, his twin sister, and Cain slew his brother in a fit of jealousy.

Byron's dramatic poem *Cain, a Mystery* (1821) is based largely on the Biblical narrative. Cain's wife he calls Adah, and Abel's wife he calls Zillah. Coleridge wrote a prose poem called *The Wanderings of Cain* (1798).

brand of Cain. The stigma of an outlaw from society (*Gen.* iv. 15).

curse of Cain. Continual wandering.

Cain-colored beard. Yellowish, or sandy red, symbolic of treason. In the ancient tapestries Cain and Judas are represented with yellow beards; but it is well to note that in the extract below the word, in some editions, is printed "*cane*-colored."

> He hath but a little wee face, with a little yellow beard, a Cain-coloured beard.
> Shakespeare, *Merry Wives of Windsor,* i. 4.

Cain, James Mallahan (1892–). American novelist of the hard-boiled school, known for *The Postman Always Rings Twice, Serenade,* etc.

Caine, Sir **Hall** (1853–1931). Manx novelist. A vigorous Christian Socialist. Friend and guest (until 1882) of D. G. Rossetti. After early poverty his books attained sales comparable with those of Marie Corelli. Several of his most widely read novels were *The Deemster* (1887); *The Christian* (1897); *The Eternal City* (1901); *The Woman Thou Gavest Me* (1913); etc.

Cainites. An heretical sect of the 2nd century. They renounced the New Testament in favor of *The Gospel of Judas,* which justified the false disciple and the crucifixion of Jesus; and they maintained that heaven and earth were created by the evil principle, and that Cain with his descendants were the persecuted party.

Ça Ira (*Fr.* it will go). The name, and refrain, of a popular patriotic song in France which became the *Carillon National* of the French Revolution (1790). It went to the tune of the *Carillon National,* which Marie Antoinette was for ever strumming on her harpsichord.

The rallying cry was borrowed from Benjamin Franklin of America, who used to say, in reference to the American revolution, "*Ah! ah! ça ira, ça ira!*" ('twill be sure to do).

The refrain of the French revolutionary version was:

> Ah! ça ira, ça ira, ça ira,
> Les aristocrates à la lanterne.

Caissons, The, Go Rolling Along. Artillery song. Caisson, a four-wheeled ammunition or gun carriage, consisting of two parts, body and limber, joined together.

Caius. (1) In Shakespeare's KING LEAR, the assumed name of the Earl of Kent when he attended on King Lear, after Goneril and Regan refused to entertain their aged father with his suite.

(2) In Shakespeare's MERRY WIVES OF WINDSOR, Dr. Caius is a French physician, whose servants are Rugby and Mrs. Quickly.

cake.

take the cake. To carry off the prize. The allusion is to the CAKE-WALK of the Southern Negroes of the United States, but cakes were prizes for competitions even in ancient times. Cf. the expression, *bring home the bacon.* See under BACON.

you cannot eat your cake and have it too. You cannot spend your money and yet keep it. You cannot serve God and Mammon.

my cake is dough. My project has failed.

cakes and ale. Luxuries.

Land of Cakes. Scotland, from its oatmeal cakes.

why don't they eat cake? A question Marie Antoinette is supposed to have asked when she was told that the poor had no bread.

Cake. A play by Witter Bynner (1926).

Cakes and Ale. A novel by W. Somerset MAUGHAM, published in 1930, considered to be a satirical presentation of Thomas HARDY and Hugh WALPOLE.

cake-walk. A popular American dance (ca. 1900), involving strutting and prancing, solo or in couples. This was the first dance of Negro origin to become popular in the ballroom. See also *jazz; ragtime.*

Calainos. The most ancient of Spanish ballads. Calainos the Moor asks a damsel to be his wife; she consents, on condition that he bring her the heads of the three paladins of Charlemagne—Rinaldo, Roland, and Olivier. Calainos goes to Paris and challenges the paladins. First Sir Baldwin, the youngest knight, accepts the challenge and is overthrown; then his uncle, Roland, goes against the Moor and smites him.

Calamus. A section in the 2nd Edition of Walt Whitman's *Leaves of Grass* which contains the remarkable, "I Saw in Louisiana a Live-Oak Growing." Not capitalized, also a root, the sweet flag, used as a medicine, frequently mentioned in the stories of *Uncle Remus* by Joel Chandler HARRIS. The word means reed and in association with classical antiquity it stands for a writing tool, a pen.

Calamity Jane. One who is always predicting misfortune; one who puts the worst possible interpretation on any turn of events. Sobriquet of Martha Jane Burke (1852?–1903), frontier character, portrayed in *Deadwood Dick on Deck,* or *Calamity Jane the Heroine of Whoop Up,* a popular dime novel by Edward J. Wheeler.

Calandrino. A typical simpleton frequently introduced in Boccaccio's DECAMERON; expressly made to be befooled and played upon.

Calchas. In Greek mythology, a celebrated soothsayer among the Greeks at Troy. In some versions of the TROILUS legend he is the father of CRESSIDA.

Calas. One wrongly condemned. The reference is to Jean Calas (1698–1762), a Calvinist of Toulouse who was cruelly executed on a false charge of murder.

Calaveras County, The Celebrated Jumping Frog of. See CELEBRATED JUMPING FROG.

Calaynos. See BOKER, GEORGE HENRY.

calculus. From Latin. Literally, a pebble. Hence a medical term for "stone," as in "biliary calculi." As a mathematical term, *calculus* owes its use to the fact that reckoning was done by means of pebbles. Differential calculus and integral calculus are methods of mathematical exploration.

Caldecott, Randolph (1846–1886). English artist and illustrator. Illustrated Washington Irving and many books for children; contributed to *Punch.* See also under GREENAWAY, CATHERINE.

Calderón de la Barca, Pedro (1600–1681). Famous early Spanish dramatist. His best-known work is *La Vida Es Sueño* (*Life Is a Dream*). He wrote approximately 120 plays and numerous AUTOS, or dramatic religious ceremonials concerning the Mystery of the Eucharist. A number of English writers, including DRYDEN and SHELLEY admired his works and wrote dramas under his influence.

Caldwell, Erskine Preston (1903–). American novelist and short-story writer, noted for his realistic studies, either earthy or starkly tragic, of life among the Southern SHARECROPPERS and of Negro-white conflicts in the South. Several of his books were attacked as immoral, and he was denounced by Southern critics. His best-known novel is TOBACCO ROAD (1932), dramatized as a phenomenally successful play in 1933 (3182 performances). Other novels are *God's Little Acre* (1933); JOURNEYMAN (1935); TROUBLE IN JULY (1940). Collections of his short stories include *American Earth* (1931); *We Are the Living* (1933); *Kneel to the Rising Sun* (1935); *Southways* (1938); *Jackpot* (1940). *Some American People* (1935) is a documentary study of various sections of the U.S. YOU HAVE SEEN THEIR FACES (1937), *North of the Danube* (1939), dealing with a trip through Czechoslovakia, and *Say! Is This the U.S.A.?* (1941), another documentary account of America, are books of photographs and running commentary, done in collaboration with Margaret BOURKE-WHITE, Caldwell's wife (now divorced). *All Out on the Road to Smolensk* (1942) is a book describing the Russian resistance to invasion by Germany during World War II.

Caleb. (1) In the Old Testament, one of the twelve spies who were sent by the Israelites to investigate the land of Canaan. He and JOSHUA were the only ones who reported favorably; hence they were the only ones of their generation permitted to enter the Promised Land.

(2) In Dryden's satire of *Absalom and Achitophel,* Caleb is meant for Lord Grey of Wark (Northumbe land), one of the adherents of the Duke of Monmouth.

> And, therefore, in the name of dulness, be
> The well-hung Balaam [Earl of Huntingdon] and old Caleb free.
> *Lines* 512–513.

Caleb Williams. A novel by William GODWIN (1794). The central character is Falkland, an aristocrat who values his good name above everything else. Under great provocation, he is goaded on to commit murder, but is honorably acquitted, and another person is executed for the crime. Caleb Williams, a lad in Falkland's service, accidentally becomes acquainted with these secret facts and is made to swear a solemn oath of secrecy. Finally unable to live in the house under the suspicious eyes of Falkland, he runs away. Falkland tracks him from place to place, like a bloodhound, and at length arrests him for robbery. The true statement now comes out, and Falkland dies of shame and a broken spirit. This tale was dramatized by G. Colman, under the title of *The Iron Chest;* Falkland is called Sir Edward Mortimer, and Caleb Williams is called Wilford.

Caledonia. Scotland; the ancient Roman name, now used only in poetry and in a few special connections, such as the *Caledonian Railway,* the *Caledonian Canal,* etc.

Calendar.

Julian Calendar. See JULIAN.

Gregorian Calendar. A modification of the Julian, introduced in 1582 by Pope Gregory XIII, and adopted in Great Britain in 1752. This is called "the New Style." See *Gregorian Year.*

Mohammedan calendar, used in Mohammedan countries, dates from July 16, 622, the day of the HEGIRA. It consists of 12 lunar months of 29 days 12 hours, 44 minutes each; consequently the Mohammedan year consists of only 354 or 355 days. A cycle is 30 years.

French Revolutionary calendar, adopted on October 5, 1793, retrospectively as from September 22, 1792, and in force in France till January 1, 1806, consisted of 12 months of 30 days each, with 5 intercalary days, called Sansculottides at the end. It was devised by Gilbert Romme (1750–1795), the names of the months having been given by the poet, Fabre d'Eglantine (1755–1794).

Newgate Calendar. See NEWGATE.

calender (From Persian *galandar*). A member of a begging order of dervishes, founded in the 13th century by Qalandar Yusuf al-Andalusi, a native of Spain, with the obligation on its members of perpetual wandering. This feature has made the calenders prominent in Eastern romance; the story of the Three Calenders in the *Arabian Nights* is well known. They are three royal princes, disguised as begging dervishes, each of whom has lost his right eye.

Tale of the First Calender. No names are given. This calender was the son of a king, and nephew of another king. While on a visit to his uncle, his father died, and the vizier usurped the throne. When the prince returned, he was seized, and the usurper pulled out his right eye. The uncle died, and the usurping vizier made himself master of this kingdom also. So the hapless young prince assumed the garb of a calender, wandered to Bagdad, and being received into the house of "the three sisters," tells his tale in the hearing of the Caliph Haroun al Raschid.

Tale of the Second Calender. No names given. This calender, like the first, was the son of a king. On his way to India he was attacked by robbers, and though he contrived to escape, he lost all his effects. In his flight he came to a large city, where he encountered a tailor, who gave him food and lodging. In order to earn a living, he turned woodman for the nonce, and accidentally discovered an underground palace, in which lived a beautiful lady, confined there by an evil genius. With a view of liberating her, he kicked down the talisman; the genius killed the lady and turned the prince into an ape. As an ape he was taken on board ship, and transported to a large commercial city, where his penmanship recommended him to the sultan, who made him his vizier. The sultan's daughter undertook to disenchant him and restore him to his proper form; but to accomplish this she had to fight with the malignant genius. She succeeded in killing the genius, and restoring the enchanted prince; but received such severe injuries in the struggle that she died, and a spark of fire which flew into the right eye of the prince, destroyed it. The sultan was so heart-broken at the death of his only child, that he insisted on the prince's quitting the kingdom without delay. So he assumed the garb of a calender, and being received into the hospitable house of "the three sisters," tells his tale in the hearing of the Caliph Haroun al Raschid.

Tale of the Third Calender. This calender, King Agib, was wrecked on the loadstone mountain, which drew all the nails and iron bolts from his ship; but he overthrew the bronze statue on the mountaintop, the cause of the mischief. Agib then visited ten young men, each of whom had lost his right eye, and was carried by a roc to the palace of forty princesses, with whom he tarried a year. The princesses were then obliged to leave for forty days, but entrusted him with the keys of the palace, with free permission to enter every room but one. On the fortieth day curiosity finally induced him to open this room, where he saw a horse, which he mounted, and was carried through the air to Bagdad. The horse then deposited him, and knocked out his right eye with a whisk of its tail, as it had done the ten young men whom he had previously met.

calends. The first day of the Roman month. Varro says the term originated in the practice of *calling together* or assembling the people on the first day of the month, when the pontifex informed them of the time of the new moon, the day of the nones, with the festivals and sacred days to be observed. The custom continued till *A.U.C.* 450, when the *fasti* or *calendar* was posted in public places.

Greek calends. Never; because there are no Greek Calends.

calf.

kill the fatted calf. To welcome with the best of everything. The phrase is taken from the parable of the prodigal son (*Luke* xv. 30).

the golden calf. We all worship the golden calf, i.e., money. The reference is to the golden calf made by Aaron when Moses was absent on Mount Sinai. (*Exod.* xxxii.)

calf-love. Youthful fancy as opposed to lasting attachment.

calf-skin. Fools and jesters used to wear a calf-skin coat buttoned down the back; hence a fool.

Calhoun, John Caldwell (1782–1850). South Carolinian, Vice-President U.S. (1825–1832). U.S. Senator and Secretary of State. Orator and champion of slavery and Southern cause in Senate debates.

Caliban. Rude, uncouth, unknown; as a Caliban style, a Caliban language. The allusion is to Shakespeare's Caliban in THE TEMPEST, the deformed, half-human son of a devil and a witch, slave to Prospero. Browning's poem *Caliban upon Setebos, or Natural Theology in the Island* is an attempt to express for such a creature as Caliban his crude philosophy of God and the universe. Percy MacKaye wrote a poetic drama called *Caliban* (*Am.* 1916), showing the regeneration of Caliban through love for Miranda.

Caliburn. Same as EXCALIBAR, the famous sword of King Arthur.

Calico Cat. See GINGHAM DOG AND CALICO CAT.

Calidore, Sir. In Spenser's *Faërie Queene* (Bk. vi) the type of courtesy, and the lover of "fair Pastorella." He is described as the most courteous of all knights, and is entitled the "all-beloved." It is said that he typifies Sir Philip Sidney. His adventure is against the Blatant Beast, whom he muzzles, chains, and drags to Faërie Land. *Calidore* is also the name of a poetical fragment by KEATS.

California widow, see under WIDOW.

Caligula. The Roman Emperor Gaius Caesar (37–41), called Caligula from wearing in his youth the *caligae,* that is, the heavy military shoes worn by soldiers of all ranks up to the centurions. He was a cruel tyrant and incestuous epileptic.

calipash and **calipee.** The carapace and the plastron of a turtle. Both contain a substance which is considered a delicacy by those who care for that sort of thing.

Calista. The heroine of Rowe's tragedy *The Fair Penitent* (1703), the fierce and haughty daughter of Sciolto, a proud Genoese nobleman. She yields to the seduction of Lothario, but promises to marry Altamont, a young lord who loves her dearly. On the wedding day a letter is picked up which proves her guilt, and she is subsequently seen by Altamont conversing with Lothario. A duel ensues, in which Lothario falls. In a street-row Sciolto receives his death-wound, and Calista stabs herself.

Calkins, (Marion) Clinch. American woman sociologist, poet, dramatist and story writer. *Spy Overhead* (1937).

Callaghan, Morley (1903–). Canadian novelist and short-story writer, known for his realism and his studies of human experience. Collections of his short stories are *A Native Argosy* (1929); *No Man's Meat* (1931); *Now That April's Here* (1936). His novels, dealing with such people as bootleggers, the relatives of a murderer, ex-prisoners, and average men and women beset by the depression, are *Strange Fugitive* (1928); *It's Never Over* (1930); *A Broken Journey* (1932); *Such Is My Beloved* (1934); *They Shall Inherit the Earth* (1935); *More Joy in Heaven* (1937).

Calligrames. See *Apollinaire, Guillaume.*

Callimachus. (1) Greek sculptor of 5th century B.C., reputed to have been the first to use a running drill in order to cut drapery folds and other depressions in marble. See also CORINTHIAN ORDER.

(2) Greek scholar of 3rd century B.C., head of a school in Alexandria, and chief librarian at Alexandria. Of about 800 works ascribed to him there are only 6 hymns, 64 epigrams, and a few fragments extant.

Calliope (*Gr.* beautiful voice). Chief of the nine MUSES; the muse of epic or heroic poetry, and of poetic inspiration and eloquence. Her emblems are a stylus and wax tablets. See also KALLYOPE.

Callirrhoe. The lady-love of Chaereas, in Chariton's Greek romance entitled the *Loves of Chaereas and Callirrhoë,* probably written in the 6th century A.D.

Callista, a Sketch of the Third Century. A historical romance by Cardinal NEWMAN (1855). The Greek heroine, Callista, is loved by the Christian Agellius, becomes converted, and suffers martyrdom.

Callisto and Arcas. Callisto was an Arcadian nymph metamorphosed into a she-bear by Jupiter. Her son Arcas having met her in the chase, would have killed her, but Jupiter converted him into a he-bear, and placed them both in the heavens, where they are recognized as the Great and Little Bear.

Call of the Wild, The. A novel by Jack LONDON (1903), usually considered his best. The dog hero, Buck, is stolen from his comfortable home and pressed into service as a sledge dog in the Klondike. At first he is abused by both men and dogs, but he learns to fight ruthlessly and finally finds in John Thornton a master whom he can respect and love. When Thornton is murdered, he breaks away to the wilds and becomes the leader of a pack of wolves.

Calmette, Gaston (1858–1914). See under CAILLAUX, JOSEPH.

Calpe. Gibraltar, one of the Pillars of Hercules, the other, the opposite promontory in Africa (modern Jebel Musa, or Apes' Hill), being anciently called *Abyla.* According to one account, these two were originally one mountain, which Hercules tore asunder; but some say he piled up each mountain separately, and poured the sea between them.

Calpurnia. Wife of Julius Caesar (from 59 B.C.). Tried to dissuade him from attending the senate the day he was assassinated.

calumet. This name for the tobacco-pipe of the North American Indians, used as a symbol of peace and amity, is the Norman form of Fr. *chalumeau* (from Lat. *calamus,* a reed), and was given by the French-Canadians to certain plants used by the natives as pipe-stems, and hence to the pipe itself.

The calumet, or "pipe of peace," is about two and a half feet long, the bowl is made of highly polished red marble, and the stem of a reed, which is decorated with eagles' quills, women's hair, and so on.

To present the calumet to a stranger is a mark of hospitality and good will; to refuse the offer is an act of hostile defiance.

Calvary. The Latin translation of the Gr. GOLGOTHA, which is a transliteration of the Hebrew word for "a skull." The name given to the place of Jesus' crucifixion; hence a place of martyrdom. Legend has it that the skull of Adam was preserved here, but the name is probably due to some real or fancied resemblance in the configuration of the ground to the shape of a skull.

Calvé, Emma. Stage name of Emma de Roquer (1862?–1942). French operatic soprano. Sang in many countries. Especially successful in *Cavalleria Rusticana, Sapho,* and *Carmen.*

Calverley, Charles Stuart (1831–1884). English author of light verse and parodies, including *Verses and Translations* (1862); *Theocritus Translated into English Verse* (1869); and *Fly Leaves* (1872).

Calverley's. A poem by Edwin Arlington ROBINSON.

Calverton, Victor Francis (1900–1940). American editor and literary critic of Marxist persuasion, author of books on social problems, anthropology, and literature as viewed from a sociological standpoint. His works include *The Newer Spirit: A Sociological Criticism of Literature* (1925); *The Bankruptcy of Marriage* (1928); *Sex in Civilization* (1929), of which he was editor; *The New Generation* (1930); *Three Strange Lovers* (1930), stories; *For Revolution* (1932); *The Liberation of American Literature* (1932); *The Passing of the Gods* (1934), on religion and sociology; *The Man Inside: Being the Record of the Strange Adventures of Allen Steele Among the Xulus* (1936); *The Awakening of America* (1939); *Where Angels Dared to Tread* (1941), a study of Socialist and Communist Utopian colonies established in the U.S. Calverton was editor of *The Modern Quarterly: A Journal of Radical Opinion,* which was founded in 1923 and later became *The Modern Monthly.*

Calvin, John. Adapted form of **Jean Cauvin** (1509–1564). French Protestant reformer, whose theological doctrines had tremendous influence, particularly through their incorporation in the Puritan religion of England and later America. Calvin had an early background of HUMANISM, being a student of Latin and Greek and familiar with the writings of Plato, Seneca, and St. Augustine. His great work is *Institution de la religion chrétienne* (INSTITUTES OF THE CHRISTIAN RELIGION), published in an early Latin version in 1536 and in the complete, better-known version in French in 1541; it was the first theological treatise to be published in French. Because of the radical Protestant views expressed in a public speech he wrote in 1533 to be delivered at an inaugural ceremony at the University of Paris, Calvin was forced to flee the capital and soon France as well. He took up headquarters in Geneva, where eventually he became an absolute dictator, strictly enforcing his theological doctrines and rules of conduct.

Calvinism as a religious system recognized only the Bible as a source of knowledge and an authority in questions of belief. Its chief principles were: (1) the total depravity of mankind as a result of Adam's fall; (2) the absolute power of the will of God; (3) the superiority of faith to good works, since man has no free will of his own; (4) salvation by grace from God rather than by any act of the will of man; and (5) the divine predestination of those to be saved, or the Elect, although, since no one can tell whether he is a member of the Elect, all must lead holy and pious lives, acknowledging God's supreme power and obeying His commands. Outstanding exponents of the doctrines of Calvinism were John MILTON, John BUNYAN, and Jonathan EDWARDS.

Calvo, Baldassare. In George Eliot's ROMOLA, the wealthy scholar who brings up Tito Melema as a son.

Calydonian boar. In Greek legend, Oeneus, king of Calydon, in Aetolia, having neglected to sacrifice to Artemis, was punished by the goddess' sending a ferocious boar to ravage his lands. A band of heroes collected to hunt the boar, who was eventually slain by Meleager after he had been first wounded by Atalanta. A dispute over the boar's head led to a war between the Curetes and the Calydonians.

Calypso. (1) In classical mythology, the queen of the island Ogygia on which Ulysses was wrecked. She kept him there for seven years, and promised him perpetual youth and immortality if he would remain with her for ever. Ogygia is generally identified with Gozo, near Malta. In TÉLÉMAQUE, a prose epic by Fénelon, *Calypso* is said to be meant for Mme de Montespan. In ULYSSES by James Joyce, she is represented by Martha CLIFFORD.

(2) A long, rambling, topical song, originated by Trinidad Negroes.

Cam and Isis. The universities of Cambridge and Oxford; so called from the rivers on which they stand.

> May you, my Cam and Isis, preach it long,
> "The right divine of kings to govern wrong."
> Pope, *Dunciad,* iv. 187.

Cama, see KAMA.

Camacho. In Cervantes' *Don Quixote,* the "richest of men," who makes grand preparations for this wedding with Quiteria, "fairest of women"; but as the bridal party are on their way, Basilius cheats him of his bride. Hence *Camacho's wedding* has become a byword for vast but futile expenditures of time or money.

Camaralzaman, Prince. In the *Arabian Nights,* the lover of BADOURA.

Camargue, Horses of the. A poem by Roy Campbell. La Camargue is a marshy delta of the Rhone River in France, where wild horses run.

Camarína. A lake in Sicily. It was a source of malaria to the inhabitants, who, when they consulted Apollo about draining it, received the reply, "Do not disturb it." Nevertheless, they drained it, and ere long the enemy marched over the bed of the lake and plundered the city. The proverb *Ne moveas Camarinam* (Don't meddle with Camarina) is applied to those who remove one evil, but thus give place to a greater—leave well alone. The application is very extensive, as: Don't kill the small birds, or you will be devoured by insects; one pest may be a safeguard against a greater one.

A similar Latin pharse is *Anagyrin movere.*

> When the laird of Ellangowan drove the gipsies from the neighbourhood, though they had been allowed to remain there undisturbed hitherto, Dominie Sampson warned him of the danger by quoting the proverb *"Ne moveas Camarinam."*
> Scott, *Guy Mannering,* ch. vii.

Cambalo's Ring. Cambalo was the second son of CAMBUSCAN in Chaucer's unfinished *Squire's Tale.* He is introduced, as CAMBEL, in Spenser's *Faërie Queene* (Bk. iv). The ring, which was given him by his sister CANACE, had the virtue of healing wounds.

> Well mote ye wonder, how that noble knight,
> After he had so often wounded been,
> Could stand on foot now to renew the fight . . .
> All was through virtue of the ring he wore;
> The which, not only did not from him let
> One drop of blood to fall, but did restore
> His weakened powers, and dulled spirits whet.
> Spenser, *Faërie Queene,* IV. iii. 23–24.

Cambalu. The chief city of Cathay, described in the *Voyages* of MARCO POLO. It is identified with Peking.

Cambel. The name given by Spenser in his sequel to Chaucer's *Squire's Tale* (*Faërie Queene,* Bk. iv) to Cambalo, brother of CANACE. He challenges every suitor to his sister's hand, and overthrows all except Triamond, who marries her.

Camber. In British legend, the second son of BRUTE. Wales fell to his portion; this may be one source of its ancient name of CAMBRIA.

Cambremer, Mme de. In Marcel Proust's REMEMBRANCE OF THINGS PAST, a fashionable lady who frequents the Wednesday evening salons of the VERDURINS and who makes an elaborate fetish of her interests in literature, art, and music.

Cambria. The ancient name of Wales, the land of the Cimbri or Cymry. Cf. *Camber.*

Cambuscan. In Chaucer's unfinished *Squire's Tale,* the King of Sarra, in Tartary, model of all royal virtues. His wife is Elfeta; his two sons, ALGARSIFE and Cambalo; and his daughter, CANACE. On her birthday (October 15) the King of Arabia and India send Cambuscan a "steed of brass, which, between sunrise and sunset, would carry its rider to any spot on the earth." All that is required is to whisper the name of the place in the horse's ear, mount upon his back, and turn a pin set in his ear. When the rider has arrived at the place required, he must turn another pin. The horse instantly descends, and, with another screw of the pin, vanishes till it is again required. Milton refers to the story in *Il Penseroso.*

Cambyses. King of Persia (529–522 B. C.). In drama he appears as a pompous, ranting character in Preston's tragedy, *Cambyses, King of Persia* (1569); and his name has become proverbial for bombastic language, because of Falstaff's speech (*1 Henry IV.* ii. 4).

> Give me a cup of sack, to make mine eyes look red; for I must speak in passion, and I will do it in King Cambyses' vein.

camel.

break the camel's back. To pile on one thing after another till at last the limit is reached and a catastrophe or break-down caused. The proverb is, "It is the last straw that breaks the camel's back."

the Camel Driver of Mecca. Mahomet.

Camel, The Song of the. In *The Admiral's Caravan* by Charles E. Carryl.

Camelot. In British fable, the legendary spot where King Arthur held his court. It has been tentatively located at various places—in Somerset, near Winchester, in Wales, and even in Scotland.

Camembert. A soft unpressed cheese, originally made in Camembert, France. In its felt-like rind it ripens toward the center and should not be eaten before it is soft all the way through.

camera eye. The device used by John Dos Passos in his trilogy *U.S.A.* to give perspective to his kaleidoscopic narrative. In contrast to the NEWSREEL, the camera eye makes use of the subjective sense impressions, memories of childhood, random thoughts, etc., of a spectator with whom the reader may identify himself. It is an outgrowth of James Joyce's "STREAM-OF-CONSCIOUSNESS" technique.

Cameron, Margaret, see MARGARET CAMERON KILVERT.

Camilla. (1) In Roman legend a virgin queen of the Volscians. Virgil (*Aeneid,* vii. 809) says she was so swift that she could run over a field of corn without bending a single blade, or make her way over the sea without even wetting her feet. She aided Turnus against Aeneas.

(2) One of the principal characters of *The Fatal Curiosity,* an episode in Cervantes' DON QUIXOTE.

Camille. (1) The name under which the French *Dame aux Camélias* (*The Lady of the Camellias*), a novel and later a drama by Alexandre DUMAS *fils,* was produced on the American stage. The play was enormously successful, both in France (1852) and in its various American adaptations which appeared in 1853, 1857 and 1874. Its heroine is a beautiful courtesan who gives up the one man she has come to love genuinely because she does not want to ruin his life, and goes back to her old round of frivolity. The character was drawn from the French courtesan, Madeleine du Plessis. In the French novel and drama she is known as Marguerite Gauthier, in the American versions as Camille and in Verdi's opera, *La Traviata,* founded on the story, she becomes Violetta Valery.

(2) In Corneille's historical tragedy, *Les Horaces,* the name of the daughter of HORATIUS, heroine of the drama.

Camillo. In Shakespeare's WINTER'S TALE, a lord in the Sicilian court, and a very good man. Being commanded by King Leontes to poison Polixenes, instead of doing so he gave him warning, and fled with him to Bohemia.

Camisards. In French history, the Protestant insurgents of the Cevennes, who resisted the violence of the dragonnades, after the revocation of the edict of Nantes (1685), and so called from the white shirts (*camisards*) worn by the peasants. Their leader was Cavalier, afterwards governor of Jersey.

Camlan, Battle of. In Arthurian legend the battle which put an end to the Knights of the Round Table, and at which Arthur received his death wound from the hand of his nephew Modred, who was also slain. It took place about 537 A. D., but its site (traditionally placed in Cornwall) is as conjectural as that of CAMELOT.

Cammaerts, Émile (1878–). Belgian poet and patriot. Settled in England (1908) but remained a Belgian subject. His volumes of poetry written during World War I and translated from the French into English by his wife include *Belgian Poems; Messines and Other Poems* and *Through the Iron Bars.*

Camoëns, Luis de (1524–1579). The most famous of Portuguese poets. His masterpiece is the epic poem THE LUSIAD.

Camorra. A lawless, secret society of Naples, Italy, organized early in the 19th century. It claimed the right of settling disputes, etc., and was so named from the blouse (Ital. *camorra*) worn by its members, the *Camorrists.* The term came to be used for any secret society with lawless or revolutionary aims.

camouflage (*Fr.*). Disguise. The term was introduced during World War I in connection with military disguise and was popularized by application to blinds and disguises of every sort.

Campagna. In full **Campagna di Roma.** Territory of Old Latium surrounding Rome, about thirty by one hundred miles in extent.

Campagna, Two in the. A poem by Robert Browning.

Campaign, The. A poem by Joseph ADDISON, written in 1704 and praising the Duke of Marlborough, who had become a hero as the result of his victories during the War of the Spanish Succession.

Campaigner, The old. Mrs. Mackenzie, mother of Rosa, in Thackeray's novel, *The Newcomes* (1855).

Campaspe. A beautiful woman, the favorite concubine of Alexander the Great. Apelles, it is said, modeled his Venus Anadyomene from her. According to Pliny, Alexander gave her up to Apelles, who had fallen in love with her while painting her likeness.

John Lyly produced, in 1583, a drama, *Alex-*

ander and Campaspe, in which is the well-known lyric—

> Cupid and my Campaspe played
> At cards for kisses: Cupid paid.

Campbell, Joseph (1881–). Irish poet. Under his Gaelic name, Seosamh MacCathmhaoil, published *The Rushlight,* 1906, and *The Mountainy Singer,* 1909, etc.

Campbell, Mary. One of the women loved by Robert BURNS. She died of fever in 1788, and the poem *To Mary in Heaven* was written on the anniversary of her death.

Campbell, Mrs. **Patrick.** *Née* **Beatrice Stella Tanner** (1865–1940). English actress who played important rôles beginning with title rôle in Pinero's *The Second Mrs. Tanqueray* (1893).

Campbell, Roy (1901–). Brilliant South African poet. Wrote *The Flaming Terrapin* in a fisherman's cabin in Wild Wales after marrying on nothing a year. About 1935 Campbell became a Roman Catholic convert and fought for Franco in Spain. His first youthful volume remains his masterpiece.

Campbell, Thomas (1777–1844). Scotch poet, best known for his literary ballads, the most popular of which was GERTRUDE OF WYOMING (1809). Others include *Hohenlinden* (1802); LORD ULLIN'S DAUGHTER (1809); *The Battle of the Baltic* (1809).

Campbell, Viola. One of the chief characters in THE WITCHING HOUR by Augustus Thomas.

Campbell, William Wilfred (1860–1919). Canadian poet, edited *Oxford Book of Canadian Verse* (1906).

Campbeller. Religious follower of Rev. Alex Campbell (1788–1866), a Baptist minister of Bethany, Va. Cf. the poem by Vachel Lindsay.

Campbells are coming, The. A famous song composed in 1715, when the Earl of Mar raised the standard for the Stuarts against George I. John Campbell was commander-in-chief of his Majesty's forces and the rebellion was quashed.

Campeachy wood. Logwood from Campeche on S.W. part of Gulf of Mexico. It is used for dyeing. Cf. the poem by John Masefield, *Campeachy Picture.*

Campeador (*Sp.* "Champion"). Surname of the CID.

Campendonck, Heinrich. See under *Blaue Reiter.*

Camperdown, Ballad of the, by Rudyard KIPLING.

Camp Fire Girls of America, The. An organization for girls (aged 12–20) founded in 1912 by Dr. and Mrs. Luther H. Gulick. It corresponds to the Boy Scout organization in idea and ideal.

Campion, Thomas (1567–1620). English poet and musician. *A Book of Airs* (1601), *Two Books of Airs* (ca. 1613), and *The Third and Fourth Books of Airs* (ca. 1617) are volumes of lyrics, both words and music of which were written by Campion. He was also the author of *Observations in the Art of English Poesy* (1602), a critical treatise in which he argued for the use of classical, quantitative meters in English verse. There had long been a controversy at Cambridge University as to whether the classical meter or rimed and accentual verse were better suited for the English language, and Samuel DANIEL wrote an answer to Campion.

Campus Esquilinus. The burial place for the lowest classes just outside the Servian Wall of Rome.

Campus **Martius.** The field of Mars. A grassy plain along the east bank of the Tiber in ancient Rome, used for elections, martial exercises, public games, etc. Cf. the *Champs de Mars* in Paris.

Camus. Personification of the river Cam. Cf. Milton's *Lycidas,* line 103.

Camus, Albert (1913–). Ship broker, journalist, and social reformer in Algiers, who moved to France in 1940, when many Frenchmen were leaving for North Africa. Founded the clandestine newspaper *Combat* to countercheck the Nazi and Vichy censors. Wrote clear and forceful editorials. After the liberation his newspaper became the most vigorous in Paris. Camus was spokesman for the "pure *résistance*" group. Although a friend of SARTRE, he was an independent who stood against "EXISTENTIALISM" and represented the recognition of the absurdity of human life, which nevertheless did not affect his drive for a better world. His novel *L'Étranger* (1942), translated (1946) as *The Stranger,* is reminiscent of KAFKA. His philosophical essay, *Le Mythe de Sisyphe* (1942), holds his concept of the absurd, recommending living lucidly within it. He published two plays (1944), illustrating the same point of view of the absurd. His *Caligula* appeared in 1938, and a series of letters to German friends and an essay on revolt in 1945. In the latter he summarizes his views in the statement: "I am pessimistic in everything that concerns the nature of man, but obstinately optimistic in all that concerns human action."

Canaan. The Biblical "Promised Land"; hence any land of promise.

The Conquest of Canaan. See under CONQUEST, also TARKINGTON, BOOTH.

Canace. In Chaucer's *Squire's Tale,* a paragon of women, daughter of CAMBUSCAN, to whom the King of Arabia and India sends as a present a mirror and a ring. The mirror will tell the lady if any man on whom she sets her heart will prove true or false, and the ring (which is to be worn on her thumb) will enable her to understand the language of birds and to converse with them. It will also give the wearer perfect knowledge of the medicinal properties of all roots.

Chaucer never finished the tale. Spenser, however, continued it in the *Faërie Queene* (Bk. iv), and here Canace is courted by a crowd of suitors, but her brother Cambel (see *Cambalo*) insists that anyone who pretends to her hand must encounter *him* in single combat and overthrow him. She ultimately marries Triamond, son of the fairy Agape.

Canal Boy. James A. Garfield (1831–1881), president of the United States, so called from his early occupation on a canal boat.

Canale, Antonio, see CANALETTO.

Canaletto, Antonio. Originally Canale (1697–1768). Venetian painter, known for his paintings of scenes in Venice and his effects of mists and sunlight.

Canallers, Mostly. See Walter D. EDMONDS.

Canal Zone. Strip of territory extending 5 miles on each side of the Panama Canal, leased in perpetuity to the U.S. by the Republic of Panama 1903.

canard. A fabricated statement or story designed to delude; a hoax. Generally in connection with newspapers. The word means "duck" but the connection is obscure.

canary-bird. A jail-bird. At one time certain desperate convicts were dressed in yellow; and jail was the cage of these "canaries."

Canby, Henry Seidel (1878–). American literary critic, college professor, and chairman, editorial board, SATURDAY REVIEW OF LITERATURE, which he founded with Christopher MORLEY and William Rose BENÉT in 1924. *Thoreau: A Biography* (1939); *Walt Whitman* (1943); *American Memoir* (autobiography, 1947), etc.

cancan (*Fr.*). A type of dance, popular in France in the latter half of the 19th century, and once considered both daring and vulgar. Jacques OFFENBACH made use of it in his light opera *Orpheus in the Underworld* (*Orphée aux Enfers*) (1874). His music and the dance itself were revived by the Ballet Russe de Monte Carlo in the popular ballet *Gaité Parisienne* (*Parisian Gaiety*) (1938).

Cancer. One of the twelve signs of the zodiac (the Crab). It appears when the sun has reached its highest northern limit, and begins to go backward towards the south; but, like a crab, the return is sideways (June 21st to July 23rd).

According to fable, Juno sent Cancer against Hercules when he combated the Hydra of Lerne. It bit the hero's foot, but Hercules killed the creature, and Juno took it up to heaven.

Candace. (1) A title applied to several queens of Ethiopia.

(2) Title of a poem by Herbert S. GORMAN.

Candaules. King of Lydia about 710–668 B.C. Legend relates that he exposed the charms of his wife to Gyges, whereupon the queen compelled him to assassinate her husband, after which she married the murderer, who became king, and reigned twenty-eight years.

Candelabra. See GALSWORTHY, JOHN.

Candelajo, Il. See BRUNO, GIORDANO.

Candida. A drama by George Bernard SHAW (1897). The heroine, Candida, is the wife of the Rev. James Morell, but is loved by Eugene Marchbanks, a sensitive and visionary young poet who thinks Morell nothing but a "moralist and windbag." According to agreement between the two men, Candida is to make her choice, and when she demands that they bid for her, Morell offers his strength, Eugene his weakness. She chooses Morell, not, however, because of his strength but because of his need for her love.

Candide. The hero of Voltaire's philosophical novel, *Candide, ou L'Optimisme* (1759), written to satirize the optimistic creed that "All is for the best in this best of all possible worlds." Candide's tutor, the philosophic Dr. Pangloss, is the embodiment of this theory, maintaining it through thick and thin, in spite of the most blatant evidences to the contrary. He is considered to satirize the philosopher LEIBNITZ. Misadventures begin when the young Candide is kicked out of the castle of Thunder-ten-tronckh for making love to the Baron's daughter, Cunagonde; and thereafter he and Pangloss and Cunagonde, sometimes together, more often apart, in various far quarters of the earth, endure a long succession of the most unfair and appalling calamities conceivable. Eventually they settle down together on a little farm, Candide marries Cunagonde, now alas grown ugly, and tells himself often, *"Il faut cultiver notre jardin,"* "We must cultivate our garden."

Canebrake, The Cat in the. See Frederick Stuart GREENE.

candle.

he is not fit to hold the candle to him. He is very inferior. The allusion is to link-boys who held candles in theaters and other places of night amusement.

the game is not worth the candle. The effort is not worth making; the result will not pay for the trouble, even the cost of the candle that lights the players.

burn the candle at both ends. To overdo in expenditure of either time or money. See also under BURN.

vow a candle to the devil. To propitiate the devil by a bribe, as some seek to propitiate the saints in glory by a votive candle.

bell, book and candle. See under BELL.

candle-holder. An abettor. The reference is to the practice of holding a candle in the Catholic Church for the reader, and in ordinary life to light a workman when he requires more light.

Candle in the Wilderness, A. See BACHELLER, IRVING.

Candlemas Day. February 2nd, the feast of the Purification of the Virgin Mary, when Christ was presented by her in the Temple; one of the quarter days in Scotland. In Roman Catholic churches all the candles which will be needed in the church during the year are consecrated on this day; they symbolize Jesus Christ, called "the light of the world," and "a light to lighten the Gentiles." The Romans had a custom of burning candles to scare away evil spirits. There is also a weather-legend associated with Candlemas Day. See GROUNDHOG DAY.

> If Candlemas Day be dry and fair,
> The half o' winter's come and mair;
> If Candlemas Day be wet and foul,
> The half o' winter was gane at Youl.
> *Scotch Proverb.*

> The badger peeps out of his hole on Candlemas Day, and, if he finds snow, walks abroad; but if he sees the sun shining he draws back into his hole.
> *German Proverb.*

Candle of Vision, The. See A. E.

Candour, Mrs. In Sheridan's SCHOOL FOR SCANDAL, the *beau idéal* of female backbiters.

Canfield, Dorothy. See FISHER, DOROTHY CANFIELD.

Can Grande's Castle. See LOWELL, AMY; also SCALA.

Canidia. A Neapolitan, beloved by the poet Horace. When she deserted him, he held her up to contempt in certain of his *Epodes* as an old sorceress who could by a rhomb unsphere the moon. Hence any witch.

Canio. The showman in Leoncavallo's opera, I PAGLIACCI.

Cannae. The place where Hannibal defeated the Romans under Varro and L. Aemilius Paulus with great slaughter in 216 B.C. Any fatal battle that is the turning point of a great general's prosperity may be called his Cannae. Thus Moscow was the Cannae of Napoleon.

Cannan, Gilbert (1884–). English novelist. Translated Rolland's *Jean Christophe.* Love of his life really the drama. Wrote many books.

Canning, George (1770–1827). British statesman. Fostered liberal and nationalist movements in Europe. Prime Minister of England. Shielded Greece against Turkish aggression (1825–1827).

Cannon, George. In Arnold Bennett's CLAYHANGER, the bigamist to whom Hilda Lessways believes she is married.

Cannon, Joseph Gurney (1836–1926). Called "Uncle Joe." American politician. Leader of reactionary Republicans. Autocratic Speaker of the House for many years.

Cano, Juan Sebastián del (1460?–1526). Spanish navigator. Commander of the *Concepción* on MAGELLAN's expedition. Succeeded Magellan as first in command after the latter's death (1521) and completed the first circumnavigation of the globe by sailing westward. Died during a second voyage along the same route.

canon. From *Lat.* and *Gr.*, a carpenter's rule, a rule, hence a standard (as "the canons of criticism"), a model, an ordinance, as in Shakespeare's—

> Or that the Everlasting had not fixed
> His canon 'gainst self-slaughter.
> *Hamlet,* i. 2.

In sculpture, a *canon* signifies the "correct," i.e., the conventionally accepted proportions of a statue, as those of an athlete embodied in the DORYPHORUS by POLYCLITES.

In music, a *canon* is a type of vocal FUGUE, named from its 16th-century Latin designation of *fuga per canonem* (fugue according to the rule). In it, one voice, called the subject, *dux* (leader), or *vox antecedens* (antecedent voice), starts to sing a melody and is imitated note for note by a second voice, called the answer, *comes* (companion), or *vox consequens* (consequent voice). If more than two voices are required, two may be "in canon," or exactly imitating each other, while the others may make use of free counterpoint. See COUNTERPOINT. Rounds, of the sort represented by *Three Blind Mice,* are canons known as "circular" or "infinite" canons, because they return to their starting-point without breaking off. SUMER IS ICUMEN IN is an example of a 13th-century canon.

the canon. Canon law. Also, the body of the books in the Bible which are accepted by the Christian Church generally as genuine and inspired; the whole Bible from *Genesis* to *Revelation,* excluding the Apocrypha. Called also the *sacred canon* and the *canonical books.*

Canon law. A collection of ecclesiastical laws which serve as the rule of church government. The professors or students of canon law are known as *canonists.*

Canongate. The lower part of the Royal Mile in Edinburgh, running from Holyrood Palace to the Castle.

Canon Yeoman's Tale, The. One of Chaucer's *Canterbury Tales* (1388), known in the old spelling as *The Chanouns Yemannes Tale,* that is, a yeman's tale about a chanoun or canon. (A "yeman" is a bailiff.) This is a tale in ridicule of alchemy. A canon deceives a priest by pretending to convert rubbish into gold. With a film of wax he conceals in a stick a small lot of thin gold. The priest stirs the boiling water with the stick, and the thin pieces of gold, as the wax melts, drops into the pot. The priest gives the canon a large sum for the recipe; and the crafty alchemist is never seen by him afterwards.

Canossa. Canossa, in the duchy of Modena, is where, in January, 1077, the Emperor, Henry IV, went to humble himself before Pope GREGORY VII (Hildebrand). Hence, *go to Canossa* means to eat humble pie; to submit oneself to a superior after having refused to do so.

Canova Antonio (1757–1822). Italian sculptor. Marks transition from baroque to the classicism of THORVALDSEN.

Can Such Things Be? See BIERCE, AMBROSE.

cantata (*Ital.*). A musical work, dramatic or narrative, sung by a chorus and soloists, with orchestral accompaniment and without scenery or costumes. The cantata began as a concert form, the *cantata da camera,* and in the 17th century developed into a form for church performance as well, the *cantata da chiesa.* J. S. BACH is the best-known composer of cantatas, having written 295 in his lifetime. Among the most familiar of these are the *Coffee Cantata* and the *Peasant Cantata.* Scarlatti, Couperin, Handel, Haydn, Mozart, and Beethoven also wrote cantatas.

canteen. Sutler's shop in U.S. Army. Now called Post Exchange. Also places for meals and entertainment for service men opened in large cities during World War II.

cante hondo. Literally, "deep song." An Andalusian form of folk singing. See under GARCÍA LORCA, FEDERIGO.

Canterbury Tales, The. The great work of the poet CHAUCER (1388) consisting of twenty-four tales told by a company of pilgrims going to visit the shrine of St. Thomas à Becket at Canterbury. The party first assembles at the Tabard, an inn in Southwark, and there agrees to tell one tale each both going and returning; the person who tells the best tale is to be treated by the rest to a supper at the Tabard on the homeward journey. The party consists of twenty-nine pilgrims, so that the whole budget of tales should have been fifty-eight; but only twenty-three and the fragment of another (Sir Thopas) were told. In the Prologue Chaucer aptly and wittily describes each of his fellow pilgrims. As individual characters the most celebrated of these are probably the Clerk, Knight, Man of Law, Parson, Prioress, Squire and Wife of Bath. See under those entries.

Among the tales almost all the types of narrative of the Middle Ages are represented: romance, *fabliau,* Saint's life, beast epic, *exemplum,* etc. The tales are as follows:

Canon Yeoman's Tale (*Chanouns Yemannes Tale*). The transmutation of metals. See under CANON.

Clerk's Tale (*Clerkes Tale*). Patient GRISELDA.

Cook's Tale (*Cokes Tale*). GAMELYN.

Franklin's Tale (*Frankeleyns Tale*). DORIGEN and Arviragus.

Friar's Tale (*Freres Tale*). A compact with the devil. See under FRIAR.

Host's Tale. MELIBEUS.

Knight's Tale (*Knightes Tale*). PALEMON and Arcite.

Man of Law's Tale (*Mannes Tale of Lawe*). King Ella and CUNSTANCE.

Manciple's Tale (*Maunciples Tale*). The tell-tale crow turned black. See under MANCIPLE.

Merchant's Tale (*Marchantes Tale*). JANUARY and May.

Miller's Tale (*Milleres Tale*). NICHOLAS and Alison.

Monk's Tale (*Monkes Tale*). The mutability of fortune. See under MONK.

Nun's Priest's Tale (*Nonne Prestes Tale*). CHANTICLEER and the Fox.

Pardoner's Tale (*Pardoneres Tale*). The devil and the proctor. See under PARDONER.

Parson's Tale (*Persones Tale*). A kind of Pilgrim's Progress. See under *Parson.*

Physician's Tale (*Phisiciens Tale*). VIRGINIA.

Prioress' Tale (*Prioresses Tale*). The singing boy. See under PRIORESS.

Reeve's Tale (*Reves Tale*). Simon and the Miller of Trompington. See under REEVE.

Second Nun's Tale (*Seconde Nonnes Tale*). St. Cecily. See under SECOND.

Shipman's Tale (*Shipmannes Tale*). The merchant and the monk. See under *Shipman.*

Squire's Tale (*Squyeres Tale*). Cambuscan.

Summoner's Tale (*Somnours Tale*). The begging friar. See under SUMMONER.

Thopas, Sir. Told by Chaucer, but cut short by the host. See THOPAS.

Wife of Bath's Tale (*Wyf of Bathes Tale*). What a woman likes best. See under WIFE.

Canterbury Pilgrims, The. A drama by Percy MacKaye (*Am.* 1909), based on Chaucer's *Canterbury Tales,* and later produced as an opera with music by Reginald De Koven. The plot centers about a rivalry between the shy, gentle Prioress and the Wife of Bath over the attentions of Chaucer, the poet. The Wife of Bath makes a bet that she will get a certain bracelet from the Prioress, and Chaucer is to become her much-desired sixth husband if she does. She wins by trickery, but King Richard rules that she must marry the Miller instead.

Canticle of Pan, A. See Bynner, Harold Witter.

Canton, William (1846–1926). English poet and journalist. Author of a series of books for his daughter, Winifred Vida, including the charming *W. V. Her Book.*

cantonment. Military term used for a district where troops are quartered. Large camp in World War I. From French *cantonnement.*

Cantor, Eddie (1893–). American comedian, real name Israel Iskowitz. In vaudeville, burlesque, musical comedy, motion pictures, radio. Interested in charitable causes as the fight against tuberculosis, racial intolerance, etc.

Cantos. Fragments of a proposed long poem by Ezra Pound, published in separate volumes: *A Draft of XXX Cantos* (1930); *Eleven New Cantos* (1934); *The Fifth Decad of Cantos* (1937). Composed of quotations from a wide selection of literary and historical documents, especially of the ancient Greeks, the medieval Provençal poets, the Italian Renaissance, and the U.S. of the Jeffersonian period, these poems present a vivid and immediate, impressionistic picture of mankind throughout the ages. For a fuller analysis and critical discussion, cf. *The Double Agent,* by R. P. Blackmur.

Cantwell, Dr. In Bickerstaffe's comedy *The Hypocrite* (1768), the English representative of Molière's Tartuffe. He makes religious cant the instrument of gain, luxurious living and sensual indulgence. His dishonorable conduct towards Lady Lambert and her daughter is thoroughly exposed, and at last he is arrested as a swindler. *The Hypocrite* was adapted from Colley Cibber's *Non-Juror* (1717) which was in turn founded very largely on Molière's Tartuffe.

Cantwell, Robert (1908–). American novelist of the "proletarian" school. His short stories have appeared in several editions of *American Caravan.* Since 1938 an associate editor of *Time.*

Canty, Tom. The beggar boy who changes places with Prince Edward in Mark Twain's Prince and the Pauper.

Canucks. The name given in the United States to Canadians generally, but in Canada itself to Canadians of French descent. The origin is uncertain.

Canute, or Knut. Danish king, a leader of the regular Norse invading forces of England, who actually reigned as king of England (1016–1035). He is the Canute of ancient legend who is reported to have commanded the waves to stand still as a proof of his power.

cap.

cap and bells. The insignia of a professional fool or jester.

cap and feather days. The time of childhood.

cap and gown. The full academical costume of a university student or professor.

cap of liberty. The sign of freedom. When a slave was manumitted by the Romans, a small Phrygian cap, usually of red felt, called *pilëus,* was placed on his head, he was termed *libertinus* (a freedman), and his name was registered in the city tribes. When Saturninus, in 100 B. C., possessed himself of the Capitol, he hoisted a similar cap on the top of his spear, to indicate that all slaves who joined his standard should be free; Marius employed the same symbol against Sulla; and when Caesar was murdered, the conspirators marched forth in a body, with a cap elevated on a spear, in token of liberty.

In the French Revolution the cap of liberty (*bonnet rouge*) was adopted by the revolutionists as an emblem of their freedom from royal authority.

cap of maintenance. A cap of dignity anciently belonging to the rank of duke; the fur cap of the Lord Mayor of London, worn on days of state; a cap carried before the British sovereigns at their coronation.

a feather in one's cap. An achievement to be proud of; something creditable.

I must put on my considering cap. I must think about the matter before I give a final answer. The allusion is to the official cap of a judge, formerly donned when passing any sentence, but now only when passing sentence of death.

if the cap fits, wear it. If the remark applies to you, apply it yourself.

setting her cap for him. Trying to catch him for a sweetheart or a husband. In the days when ladies habitually wore caps they would naturally put on the most becoming, to attract the attention and admiration of the favored gentleman.

Capablanca y Granperra, José Raoul (1888–1942). Cuban chess master. First place in masters' tournament of 1911.

Capaneus. In Greek mythology, one of the seven heroes who marched against Thebes. He was struck dead by a thunderbolt for declaring that not Jupiter himself should prevent his scaling the city walls. Evadne, his wife, threw herself into the flames while his body was burning.

Capatez de Cargadores. See NOSTROMO.

Cape-Horner. A vessel that has sailed around Cape Horn. Cf., for instance, *Two Years Before the Mast* by Richard Henry Dana.

Čapek, Karel (1890–1938). Czechoslovakian playwright, best known for his play *R. U. R.* (1923). His other plays include *The Makroupolos Secret* (1925), dealing with the scientific prolongation of life; *Adam the Creator* (1930); *The Life of the Insects* (produced in New York as *The World We Live In*) (1922), a satire; *Power and Glory* (1938); *The Mother* (1939). *Money and Other Stories* (1929) is a collection of short stories; *The First Rescue Party* (1939) and *The Cheat* (1941) are novels.

Capes, the. (1) Cape Charles and Cape Henry, Virginia.

(2) Cape Ann and Cape Cod, Mass.

Capet. A famous ruling family of France, which furnished the kings of France from 987 to 1328. Odo, the first Capetian king, was elected in 888, while Hugh Capet, crowned in 987, began the uninterrupted succession. The feudal domain of the Capetian family was Île de France, compact and centrally located, which assisted consolidation of power and administration. The Valois and Bourbon dynasties of France were descendants of the Capetians.

capital. (1) In architecture, the upper part of a column, supporting the weight of the arch or roof. It may be a simple slab, or an ornate piece of sculpture. In ancient Egypt the capital was often in the shape of a lotus flower. In Persia, it was sometimes adorned with crouching bulls, while in Greece the Corinthian capital (see CORINTHIAN ORDER) was based on the design of the acanthus leaf. See also DORIC ORDER; IONIC ORDER.

(2) In economics, wealth which is used to produce more wealth, such as money, machinery, buildings, tools, raw materials, etc.

Capital (Das Kapital). Famous economic treatise by Karl MARX. The first volume was published in 1869 and 1873, and the second and third volumes, edited by Friedrich ENGELS from unpublished manuscripts, were published between 1885 and 1894. The work contains the author's analysis of economics and the formulation of his own economic theories, based on modifications of the theories of Adam SMITH and RICARDO by the German Idealistic philosophy of HEGEL and the writings of revolutionary thinkers of the 19th century, including Bruno Bauer, Arnold Ruge, and Ludwig Feuerbach. It is considered one of the most influential books of all time.

capitalism. Economic system whose characteristics are: a money exchange; private ownership of the means of industrial production (or CAPITAL); production for the purpose of obtaining a profit; competition among private manufacturers or "businessmen" in the sale of goods or services, at prices set by the producers to bring in a profit over the original investment; and private control over the return from the sale of goods or services. Capitalism came into being at the end of the Middle Ages, with the break-up of the system of FEUDALISM. Typical capitalists are bankers, industrial manufacturers, merchants, and "businessmen" of various sorts. The earliest period of capitalism, during the Renaissance and early part of the 17th century, is considered to have been marked by an accumulation of capital, and the next stage, during the 18th century, by the development of large industries held in individual hands. From the 19th century to the World Wars of the 20th century, capitalism came to be distinguished more and more by a development from individual to corporate ownership, reduction in competition through monopoly and centralized control, and separation of ownership and management.

capital punishment. Punishment by death for crime. The word *capital* signifies here "main, supreme," but it is interesting to connect it with its ultimate origin in Latin *caput,* the head.

Capitoline. The smallest of the seven hills of Rome.

capitulation. Special agreement under which Westerners in certain non-Christian countries are exempted from local jurisdiction and held subject instead to their own consuls. Basically a capitulation is the drawing up of an agreement under specific heads (Lat. *caput,* head). The military use of the term is not very old.

capon. A cock castrated to improve its flesh. Also a castrated rabbit and, in archaic or humorous usage, a eunuch.

Caponsacchi, Giuseppe. In Browning's RING AND THE BOOK, the young priest under whose protection Pompilia flees from her husband to Rome.

Caporetto. Scene of a military disaster sustained by the Italians under General Cadorna (Oct. 24–Nov. 9, 1917), at the hands of Germans and Austrians under Otto von Buelow. North of Gorizia a general retreat was forced to the Piave. It is graphically described in Hemingway's *A Farewell to Arms.*

Capote, Truman (1923?–). American novelist. *Other Voices, Other Rooms* (1948).

Capra, Frank (1897–). Moving picture director. *It Happened One Night* (1934); *Mr. Deeds Goes to Town* (1936); *Lost Horizon* (1938); etc. Received Motion Picture Academy award for 1934, 1936, 1938.

Capricorn. Called by James THOMSON, in his *Winter,* "the centaur archer." Anciently, the winter solstice occurred on the entry of the sun into Capricorn, *i.e.* the Goat: but the stars, having advanced a whole sign to the east, the winter solstice now falls at the sun's entrance into Sagittarius (the centaur archer), so that the poet is exactly right, though we commonly retain the ancient classical manner of speaking. Capricorn is the tenth, or, strictly speaking, the eleventh, sign of the zodiac (December 21–January 20). According to classic mythology, Capricorn was Pan, who, from fear of the great Typhon, changed himself into a goat, and was made by Jupiter one of the signs of the zodiac.

Caproni, Gianni (1886–). Italian airplane builder. Constructed biplane bomber during World War I. Developed bombers used in World War II.

captain. For captains in fiction and drama, see under their respective names; also below for titles beginning with *Captain.*

the Great Captain (*El Gran Capitano*). (1) Gonzalvo di Cordova (1453–1515).

(2) Manuel Comnenus of Trebizond (1120, 1143–1180).

Captain Cauf's tail. The commander-in-chief of the mummers of Plough Monday.

Captain Copperthorne's crew. All masters and no men.

Captain Podd. A showman. So called from "Captain" Podd, a famous puppet-showman in the time of Ben Jonson.

Captain Rock. A fictitious name assumed by the leader of certain Irish insurgents in 1822, etc. All notices, summonses, and so on, were signed by this name.

come Captain Stiff over one. To treat one with cold formality.

Captain Blood. The title of a romantic novel by Rafael SABATINI.

Captain Brassbound's Conversion. A comedy by George Bernard SHAW (1900). Captain Brassbound is a pirate, out for revenge at any cost and feeling quite justified until the heroine, Lady Cicely Waynflete, disarms and "converts" him by a unique method.

Captain Craig. A book of poems by Edwin Arlington ROBINSON.

Captain Fracasse (Le Capitaine Fracasse). A novel by Théophile GAUTIER (1863), presenting a picture of Bohemian life in the France of Louis XIII. The young and poverty-stricken Baron de Sicognac entertains a group of vagabond players, falls in love with Isabella, one of their number, and for a time joins them as Captain Fracasse, a member of the troupe.

Captain Jinks of the Horse Marines. A ballad written by T. MacLagan and brought into vogue by William Lingard, an overwhelmingly popular music hall singer, in 1869. It recalls the play of the same title by Clyde Fitch in which the remarkable American actress, Ethel BARRYMORE, made her début. The refrain of the song is:

> I'm Captain Jinks of the Horse Marines,
> I give my horse good corn and beans;
> Of course, 'tis quite beyond my means,
> Though a Captain in the army.

Captain, My Captain, O. A short and very well-known poem by Walt WHITMAN (1865) on the death of Abraham Lincoln.

Captains Courageous. A story by Rudyard KIPLING (1897). The boy hero is an American millionaire's son, Harvey Cheyne. This spoiled youngster falls overboard, is picked up by a fishing dory and against his will is hired by Disko Troop, the skipper, at ten dollars a month. By the time the fishing season is over, he has a different and much more healthy attitude toward life.

Captain's Doll, The. See LAWRENCE, DAVID HERBERT.

Captain Singleton. See DEFOE, DANIEL.

Captain Traprock, see CHAPPELL, GEORGE S.

caption. The heading or title of a document, section, chapter, etc. Also the legend or title of a picture or illustration. The word stood originally for that which captivates one's attention but got associated with the idea of Latin *caput* "head, heading."

Captures. See GALSWORTHY, JOHN.

Capua. Once the most luxurious city in Italy.

Capua corrupted Hannibal. Luxury and self-indulgence will ruin anyone. Hannibal was everywhere victorious over the Romans till he took up his winter quarters at Capua. When he left Capua, his star began to wane, and, ere long, Carthage was in ruins and himself an exile.

Capulet. A noble house in Verona, the rival of that of Montague. In Shakespeare's ROMEO AND JULIET, Juliet is of the former, and Romeo of the latter. Lady Capulet is the *beau idéal* of a proud Italian matron of the 15th century. The expression, "the tomb of all the Capulets," is from Burke; he uses it in his

Reflections on the *Revolution in France* (vol. iii. p. 349), and again in his *Letter to Matthew Smith*, where he says:

I would rather sleep in the southern corner of a country churchyard than in the tomb of the Capulets.

caput mortuum (*Lat.* dead head). An alchemist's term, used to designate the residuum left after exhaustive distillation or sublimation; hence, anything from which all that rendered it valuable has been taken away. Thus, a learned scholar paralyzed is a mere *caput mortuum* of his former self. The French Directory, towards its close, was a mere *caput mortuum* of a governing body.

Carabas, Marquis de. (1) An ultra-conservative nobleman, of unbounded pretensions and vanity, who would restore the slavish foolery of the reign of Louis XIV; one with Fortunatus' purse, which was never empty. The character is taken from Perrault's tale of *Puss in Boots,* where he is Puss's master; but it is BÉRANGER's song (1816) which has given the word its present meaning.

Prêtres que nous vengeons
Levez la dime et partageons;
Et toi, peuple animal,
Porte encor le bât féodal. . . .
Chapeau bas! Chapeau bas!
Gloire au marquis de Carabas!

(2) The *Marquis of Carabas* in Disraeli's VIVIAN GREY is said to be intended for the Marquis of Clanricarde.

Caracalla. Real name **Marcus Aurelius Antoninus** (188–217). Roman emperor nicknamed from a long hooded tunic worn by Gauls which he introduced. Cruel and treacherous. The Baths (Thermae) of Caracalla and the Arch of Septimius Severus (his father) erected by Roman senate (205–207) in his honor. He was assassinated.

Caractacus or Caradoc. In legendary history, a king of the Silures in Britain who withstood the Roman arms for nine years, but was finally betrayed by Carthismandu, queen of the Brigantes, and led captive to Rome 51 A. D. He is a prominent figure in the Welsh *Triads* and in Drayton's POLYOLBION.

Caravaggio, Michelangelo Amerighi da (1569–1609). Italian painter of the reaction against MANNERISM. He painted religious subjects in a dramatic and realistic manner, and is known best for his lighting effects, in which light and shadow are violently contrasted. See CHIAROSCURO.

Caravan. See GALSWORTHY, JOHN; also AMERICAN CARAVAN.

caravel. The type of vessel Columbus sailed to the New World. Small, with broad bows, high narrow poop, three or four masts, and lateen sails on two or three of them. Columbus' caravels were the *Niña,* the *Pinta,* and the *Santa María.* A faithful reconstruction of the last-named was built by the North German Lloyd at the time of the launching of the liner *Columbus.*

Carbonari. This name, assumed by a secret political society in Italy (organized 1808–1814), means *charcoal burners.* The singular is hardly in use. It would be *Carbonaro.* The *Carbonari* called their place of muster a "hut": its inside "the place for selling charcoal"; and the outside, the "forest." Their political opponents they called "wolves." Their object was to convert the kingdom of Naples into a republic.

Carco, Francis (1886–). French poet and novelist. Grand Prix of the French Academy for *L'Homme Traqué* (1927; *The Hounded Man*). Received into the Académie Goncourt (1937).

Cárdenas, Lázaro (1895–). President of Mexico (1934–1940). Expropriation (1938) of foreign-owned oil properties. Succeeded 1940 by General Ávila Camacho. Placed in command of all Mexican forces on Pacific Coast in 1941.

cardigan. A warm jacket of knit worsted, named after the 7th Earl of CARDIGAN.

Cardigan, 7th Earl of. **James Thomas Brudenell** (1797–1868). Commander of cavalry, led the "Six Hundred" in the famous charge of the Light Brigade at Balaclava in Crimean War (1854). Cf. Tennyson's poem.

cardinal. The Lat. *cardo* means a hinge: its adjective, *cardinalis* (from which we get cardinal), meant originally "pertaining to a hinge," hence "that on which something turns or depends," hence "the principal, the chief." Hence, in Christian Rome, a "cardinal church" (*ecclesia cardinalis*) was a principal or parish church as distinguished from an oratory attached to such, and the chief priest (*presbyter cardinalis*) was the "cardinal," the body (or "College") of cardinals forming the Council of the Pope, and electing the Pope from their own number. This did not become a stabilized regulation until after the third Lateran Council (1173); since then the College of Cardinals consisted of six cardinal bishops, fifty cardinal priests, and fourteen cardinal deacons. From the thirteenth century on the majority of the cardinals were Italians. In 1945 this tradition was broken by the Pope's nomination of a number of additional cardinals.

The cardinals' "red hat" was made part of the official vestments by Innocent IV (1245) "in token of their being ready to lay down their life for the gospel."

cardinal humors. An obsolete medical term for the four principal humors or liquids of the body: blood, phlegm, yellow bile and black bile. In the old conception these correspond to the four principal temperaments: the sanguine, the phlegmatic, the choleric, and the melancholic. Albrecht DÜRER is said to have thought of the four temperaments and humors in connection with his paintings of the four evangelists.

cardinal numbers. The natural, primitive numbers, which answer the question "how many?", such as 1, 2, 3, etc. 1st, 2nd, 3rd, etc., are *ordinal* numbers.

cardinal points of the compass. Due north, west, east, and south. So called because they are the points on which the intermediate ones, such as N.E., N.W., N.N.E., etc., hinge or hang. (Lat. *cardo,* a hinge.)

The poles, being the points upon which the earth turns, were called in Latin *cardines* (*cardo,* a hinge, see CARDINAL above), and the *cardinal points* are those which lie in the direction of the poles and of the sunrise and sunset. Thus, also, the winds that blow due East, West, North, and South are known as the *cardinal winds.* It is probably from the fact that the cardinal points are *four* in number that the cardinal humors, virtues, etc., are also *four.*

cardinal signs (of the zodiac). The two equinoctial and the two solstitial signs, Aries and Libra, Cancer and Capricorn.

cardinal virtues. Justice, prudence, temperance, and fortitude, on which all other virtues hang or depend. A term of the Schoolmen, to distinguish the "natural" virtues from the "theological" virtues (faith, hope, and charity).

cardinal winds. See CARDINAL POINTS above.

Cardinals. In American baseball parlance, the nickname of the St. Louis Nationals. Cf. BASEBALL TEAMS.

Carducci, Giosuè (1835–1907). Italian poet, awarded Nobel prize for literature (1906). Considered national poet of modern Italy. Also author of historical studies in literary criticism.

Cardozo, Benjamin Nathan (1870–1938). Eminent American jurist. Associate justice of the U.S. Supreme Court (1932). Author of several books on law.

Carew, Thomas (1594 or 1595–1639?). English poet, one of the "sons of Ben," or poets influenced by the style of Ben JONSON. He was a courtier for Charles I, and was noted for his tact. An anecdote tells of one occasion when, as Gentleman of the Privy Chamber, he was lighting the King to bed and found the Queen in a compromising situation with another courtier. Carew is reported to have stumbled and extinguished the light so that the King saw nothing. Carew wrote love poems, epitaphs and elegies in the style of Jonson and also of John DONNE. His *Poems* were published in 1640.

Carey, Henry (d. 1743). English poet and composer; wrote farces, burlesques, songs, and often the accompanying music for the stage, as for instance "Sally in our Alley." There was a rumor that he was also the author of "God Save the King."

Carey, Matthew (1760–1839). English-born American editor and author, founder of the *American Museum* (1787) which, together with the COLUMBIAN MAGAZINE, also edited for a time by Carey, was the first successful American magazine. He is best known for his *A Plum Pudding for the Humane, Chaste, and Enlightened Peter Porcupine* (1799), which is a bitter and violent attack upon William COBBETT for the latter's criticism of America. The *Porcupiad* (1799) is a satiric poem in the same vein as the *Plum Pudding.* Carey also wrote a *History of the Yellow Fever* (1793), *Miscellaneous Trifles* (1796), a collection of short stories, and a number of political articles.

Carey, Mother. See MOTHER CAREY'S CHICKENS.

Carey, Philip. Hero of W. Somerset Maugham's novel OF HUMAN BONDAGE. He is a sensitive young English lad of more than average intelligence and talent, living in the care of an uncle and aunt, his loneliness as an orphan aggravated by the self-consciousness and sense of isolation he feels because of a club-foot. He aspires to a career as a painter and to a true love, but is ironically frustrated by his passion for a waitress named Mildred.

Carey, Rosa Nouchette (1840–1909). English writer of stories for girls.

Cargadores, Capatez de. A powerful Italian, nicknamed "NOSTROMO" in Joseph Conrad's novel of that title.

Cargill, Rev. Josiah. In Scott's ST. RONAN'S WELL, minister of St. Ronan's Well, tutor of the Hon. Augustus Bidmore and the suitor of Miss Augusta Bidmore, his pupil's sister.

Cargoes. A popular poem by John MASEFIELD.

carillon. A set or chime of fixed bells originally four, hence the name, now normally tuned to the chromatic scale.

Carinthia Jane Kirby. In Meredith's AMAZING MARRIAGE.

Carker, James. In Dickens' DOMBEY AND SON, manager in the house of Mr. Dombey, merchant. Carker is a man of forty of a florid complexion, with very glistening white teeth, which show conspicuously when he speaks. His smile is like "the snarl of a cat." He is the Alastor of the house of Dombey, for he not only brings the firm to bankruptcy, but he seduces Alice Marwood (cousin of Edith, Dombey's second wife) and also induces Edith to elope with him. Edith leaves him at Dijon, and Carker, returning to England, is run over by a railway train and killed.

John Carker. The elder brother, a junior clerk in the same firm. He twice robs it and is forgiven.

Harriet Carker. A gentle, beautiful young woman, who marries Mr. Morfin, one of the employés in the house of Mr. Dombey, merchant. When her elder brother John falls into disgrace by robbing his employer, Harriet leaves the house of her brother James to live with and cheer her disgraced brother John.

Carleton, Will (1843–1912). Homespun American poet. Author of *Farm Ballads* (1873), *City Ballads* (1875). Best-known poem "Over the Hill to the Poor House."

carline. An old woman, used disparagingly. Scotch. The word is related to *churl.*

> As he rode down the sanctified
> bends of the Bow,
> Ilka carline was flyting and shaking her
> pow.
>
> Sir Walter Scott, "The Bonnets of Bonnie Dundee."

Carlisle, Lady. In Browning's historical tragedy, STRAFFORD, a character introduced to supply a love element. She is not a historical personage.

Carlson, Evans Fordyce (1896–1947). American officer and writer. Traveled two thousand miles with the Chinese Eighth Route Army (1937–1939). Resigned from U.S. army and wrote *Twin Stars of China* and *The Chinese Army* (1940). In 1941 he was recommissioned in the marines, and, as a lieutenant colonel, organized and led a guerrilla unit called "Carlson's Raiders" which scored brilliant successes against the Japanese.

Carlyle, Thomas (1795–1881). Scotch-born English prose writer, known for his explosive attacks on sham, hypocrisy, and excessive materialism, his distrust of democracy, and his belief in the power of the individual, especially a strong, heroic leader. He was influenced in his early career by German literature and thought, being a particular admirer of SCHILLER and GOETHE. His best-known book is his *History of the French Revolution* (1837). Of his public lectures, the most famous and those best expressing his particular cult of the leader are ON HEROES, HERO-WORSHIP, AND THE HEROIC IN HISTORY, which were delivered in 1840 and published in 1841. Carlyle's views on economics, including a hatred of LAISSEZ-FAIRE policies, attacks on the destruction of human personality by the machines of industrialism, and a distrust of social legislation, are to be found in the essays *Chartism* (1839), *Past and Present* (1843), and *Latter Day Pamphlets* (1850). Among his biographies are *Life of Schiller* (1823–1824); *Cromwell* (1845); *The Life of Sterling* (1851); *History of Frederick II of Prussia, Called Frederick the Great* (1858–1865). SARTOR RESARTUS (1833–1834), called a "spiritual biography," is one of the author's most characteristic works and aroused a storm of violent protest when it was published. Carlyle's style is savage, violent, and apocalyptic, marked by unusual words and figures of speech and expressions influenced by the German language. See also BLUMINE; CRAIGENPUTTOCK; WELSH, JANE.

carmagnole. (1) Costume of French Revolutionists: wide-collared jacket, wide black pantaloons, red cap, and scarlet or tricolored waistcoat (adopted from workmen of Carmagnola in the Piedmont).

(2) A Red Republican song and dance of the time of the first French Revolution with the refrain

> Dansons la Carmagnole,—Vive le sou, vive le sou,—
> Dansons la Carmagnole,—Vive le sou du canon!

Carman, William Bliss (1861–1929). Canadian poet and journalist, founder of the magazine *The Chap-Book.* He is best known as collaborator with Richard HOVEY on *Songs from Vagabondia* (1894), *More Songs from Vagabondia* (1896), and *Last Songs from Vagabondia* (1900), extremely popular books of verse on the joys of travel and the outdoors. He also wrote *Pipes of Pan I* (1902); *Pipes of Pan II* (1903); *The Poetry of Life* (1904); *The Rough Rider* (1909); *Echoes from Vagabondia* (1912); *Far Horizons* (1925). See GENTEEL TRADITION.

Carmelites. Order of mendicant friars, founded at Mt. Carmel by the Crusader Berthold in the 12th Century. Expelled from Holy Land by Saracens in the 13th Century, came to Europe. The order of Carmelite nuns dates from 15th Century, the greatest of these being the Spanish mystic, Saint Teresa of Ávila, who organized the austere branch of the discalced Carmelites in contrast to the traditional Carmelites of the mitigated rule.

Carmen. An opera by Georges BIZET (1875) based on Mérimée's novel of the same name. Carmen, a gypsy coquette, piqued at the indifference of the young Spanish officer Don José, succeeds in winning his interest, and a moment later, when she has stabbed another girl in the cigarette factory where she is employed, he allows her to escape her bonds. She now persuades him to desert and cast in his lot with the gypsies. His love grows stronger as hers cools; she soon has eyes only for Escamillo, the famous toreador. José allows himself to be led home to the bedside of his dying mother by Michaela, a peasant girl who loves him, but returns to find Carmen entering the arena for the bull fight. She refuses to return to him, and he stabs her.

Carmen Deo Nostro (Song to Our Lord). See CRASHAW, RICHARD.

Carmen Sylva. Pseudonym of the poetess Elizabeth, Queen of Rumania, *née* **Pauline Elisabeth Ottilie Luise,** princess of **Wied** (1843–1916). She was a patroness of arts and letters and wrote practically all her own works (some 20 books) in German.

Carmer, Carl Lamson (1893–). American poet, novelist, and folklorist. Taught at Hamilton College, Univ. of Rochester, Univ. of Alabama. First success *Stars Fell on Alabama* (1934). Wrote *Listen for a Lonesome Drum* (1936), *The Hurricane's Children, Genesee Fever* (1941), and *The Hudson* (1939).

Carmilhan. A legendary phantom ship of the Baltic. The captain of this ship swore he would double the Cape, whether God willed it or not. For this impious vow he was doomed to abide for ever and ever captain in the same vessel, which always appears near the Cape, but never doubles it. The kobold of the phantom ship, named Klaboterman, helps sailors at their work, but beats those who are idle. When a vessel is doomed, the kobold appears smoking a short pipe, dressed in yellow, and wearing a night-cap. See also FLYING DUTCHMAN.

Carnal, Grandma Called It. See DAMON, BERTHA FOSTER.

Carnegie, Andrew (1835–1919). American steelmaster from Dunfermline, Scotland. Worked up from bobbin-boy at Pittsburgh and amassed one of the great American fortunes. Adopted the Bessemer process for his mills. Bought up or crowded out his rivals. His labor policy was stern. He devoted his later years to redispersing his wealth by making many public benefactions, including the endowment of public libraries and the Carnegie Institute of Technology.

Carnegie, Dale (1888–). American teacher of public-speaking, lecturer, and author of inspirational "self-help" books. He is best known for *How to Win Friends and Influence People* (1937), a book of phenomenal sales purporting to give rules for the achievement of professional and personal success. Its title became a national catch-phrase.

Caroline. Queen-consort of George II, introduced by Walter Scott in THE HEART OF MIDLOTHIAN. Jeanie Deans has an interview with her in the gardens at Richmond, and Her Majesty promises to intercede with the King for Effie Deans' pardon.

Carolingians. The early ruling family of France and Germany to which CHARLEMAGNE belonged and which was named for him. The first important members of the family were *Pepin of Landen* and *Pepin of Heristal,* Austrasian counts who became mayors of the palace under the feeble Merovingian kings. *Charles* MARTEL (Charles the Hammer) was the true founder of the Carolingian house, serving as mayor of the palace for the whole kingdom of the Franks and consolidating his power against the feudal nobles. His son *Pepin the Short* was elected king in 751, and his grandson *Charlemagne* (Carolus Magnus, or Charles the Great), Pepin's son, came to the throne in 771, ruling until 814. Charlemagne fought wars constantly and gradually enlarged the Frankish state until, on Christmas Day, 800, he was crowned Emperor of the Romans by Pope Leo III, and the Holy Roman Empire came into being. Upon his death his realm was divided and in course of time gave rise to the distinct kingdoms of Germany and France.

The *Carolingian Renaissance* was a revival of interest in scholarship, education, literature, and philosophy, which took place under Charlemagne's empire, when the threat of Mohammedan and Norse invasions was over for awhile. Monastic schools and libraries were established, an effort was made to determine correct and authoritative texts of known works, a reform in manuscript handwriting was made with the introduction of the clear minuscule hand, which is that used in the best manuscripts that have been preserved, and a school was conducted at the palace itself by leading scholars. Connected with the palace school were ALCUIN of York, the most important single figure of the Carolingian Renaissance; EINHARD, Charlemagne's biographer; THEODULF, the leading poet of the group; and later, the Irish philosopher JOHN SCOTUS ERIGENA.

Caron, Pierre Augustin, see BEAUMARCHAIS.

Carpaccio, Vittore (1460?–1526?). Venetian painter who influenced Bellini. Noted for dramatic representations of sacred subjects.

Carpenter, John Alden (1876–). American composer, best known for his orchestral suite *Adventures in a Perambulator* (1915), portraying the impressions of a baby as it is wheeled along the street by its nurse. His ballet KRAZY KAT (1922), based on the popular comic strip of that name, is an attempt to make use of JAZZ in serious music. *Skyscrapers* (1926) is another ballet, presenting impressions in sound of a great American city.

Carpenter, Edward (1844–1929). English writer, interested in socialist movements. Lecturer on socialism. His most famous book is *Love's Coming of Age* (1896).

Carpentier, Georges (1894–). Famous French pugilist, light-heavyweight champion of the world (1920); defeated by Dempsey for heavyweight championship (1921). In 1922 lost light-heavyweight crown to Battling Siki.

carpet.

magic carpet. The carpet which, to all appearances, is worthless, but which, if anyone sits thereon, will transport him instantaneously to the place he wishes to go, is one of the stock properties of Eastern wonder-tales and romance. It is sometimes termed *Prince Housain's carpet,* because of the popularity of the *Story of Prince Ahmed* in *The Arabian Nights,* where it supplies one of the principal incidents; but the chief magic carpet is that of King Solomon, which, according to the Mohammedan legend related in the Koran, was of green silk. His throne was placed on it when he traveled, and it was large enough for all his forces to stand upon, the men and women on his right hand, and the spirits on his left. When all were arranged in order, Solomon told the wind where he wished to go, and the carpet, with all its contents, rose in the air and alighted at the place indicated. In order to screen the party from the sun, the birds of the air with outspread wings formed a canopy over the whole party.

be on the carpet, or *be carpeted.* To be reprimanded.

bring a question on the carpet. To bring it up for consideration: a translation of Fr. *sur le tapis* (on the tablecloth)—*i.e.* before the House, under consideration.

carpetbagger. The name given in the United States to the Northern political adventurers, who sought a career in the southern states after the Civil War of 1865. Their only "property qualification" was in the personal baggage they brought with them, and they were looked upon with great suspicion.

carpet knight. One dubbed at Court by favor, not having won his spurs by military service in the field. Perhaps because mayors, lawyers, and civilians generally are knighted as they kneel *on a carpet* before their sovereign in contradistinction to those knighthoods that used to be conferred on the actual field of battle; but more probably with allusion to the preference shown by non-martial knights for the carpeted drawing-room over the tented field.

Carpio, Bernardo del, see BERNARDO DEL CARPIO.

Carr, John Dickson (1905–). American-English writer of detective fiction, also known under the pseudonyms of Carter Dickson and Carr Dickson. J. B. Priestley finds his work above average.

Carr, Private. In James Joyce's ULYSSES, the English soldier who, with his companion Private Compton, starts a fight with Stephen DEDALUS at the establishment of Bella COHEN. The incident is believed to be a personal satirical attack directed by the author against one Carr, an attaché at the British Consulate at Zürich during World War I, with whom Joyce had an argument and litigation over a pair of trousers for an amateur performance of THE IMPORTANCE OF BEING EARNEST.

Carraci. A famous Italian family of painters of the late 16th and early 17th centuries. It consisted of *Agostino* (1557?–1602) and *Annibale* (1560?–1609), brothers; *Antonio* (1583–1618), son of Agostino; and *Ludovico* (1555–1619), cousin of Agostino and Annibale. Ludovico led his cousins in a movement of revolt against MANNERISM, establishing the Carraci Academy in 1585, called "Accademia dei Desiderosi" or "Accademia degli Incamminati." Here an eclectic style was taught which sought to combine the best elements of the individual styles of the great artists of the Italian Renaissance. The movement became known as Eclecticism. Ludovico, Annibale, and Agostino often collaborated in painting pictures for churches and for secular palaces, although the brothers together and singly had a better professional reputation than Ludovico.

Carranza, Venustiano (1859–1920). Mexican president. Associate of Francisco Madero in the revolution of 1910. Embroiled with U.S. in 1916 over border raids of Pancho Villa. In April 1920 he was driven out and slain by his own followers.

Carrel, Alexis (1873–1944). French scientist, best known for his experiments in keeping organs alive outside the bodies of animals. *Man, the Unknown* (1935) is a book by Carrel on the contributions and social potentialities of science, written for the layman.

Carrie, Sister, see SISTER CARRIE.

Carrion Crow, Old Adam the. Song by Thomas Lovell Beddoes in *Death's Jest Book*. There is also a nursery rhyme, "The Carrion Crow."

Carroll, Charles, of Carrollton (1737–1832). A signer of the Declaration of Independence. The Carrolls are a famous Maryland family.

Carroll, Gladys Hasty (1904–). New England novelist whose work carries on the New England tradition of Sarah Orne Jewett and Mary E. Wilkins Freeman and supplements the novels of the Maine seacoast by Mary Ellen CHASE and Rachel FIELD.

Carroll, Lewis. Pseudonym of **Charles Lutwidge Dodgson** (1832–1898). English mathematician, famous for his whimsical fantasies, ALICE IN WONDERLAND (1865) and its sequel, *Through the Looking-Glass* (1871). These were written for a child, Alice Liddell, but became popular among adult readers; theorists of SURREALISM in the 20th century seriously interpreted Carroll's works as early embodiments of their own principles. Other examples of Carroll's fantasy, together with satires and parodies on a number of respected and popular English writers of his day, are *The Hunting of the Snark* (1876) and *Sylvie and Bruno* (1889–1893). Under his own name of Dodgson he wrote *An Elementary Treatise on Determinants* (1867) and *Symbolic Logic* (1896). See also FATHER WILLIAM; JABBERWOCKY; THE WHITE KNIGHT'S BALLAD.

Carroll, Paul Vincent (1900–). Irish dramatist. Received the Drama Critics' Circle award for best foreign play of 1938 for his *Shadow and Substance*. The Abbey Theatre refused his *The White Steed* but it was produced in America.

Carryl, Charles Edward (1842–1920). New York financier and writer of children's books of a type reminiscent of Lewis CARROLL, as *Davy and the Goblin* (1886); *The Admiral's Caravan* (1892). They are now classics and contain some brilliant NONSENSE verse.

Carryl, Guy Wetmore (1873–1904). Son of Charles Edward CARRYL. Writer of brilliant humorous verse, serious poetry, short stories and novels. *Fables for the Frivolous* (1899), a book of verse; *Mother Goose for Grown-Ups* (1900) and *Grimm Tales Made Gay* (1903), two more books of verse; *Zut and Other Parisians* (1903), a volume of short stories; *The Lieutenant-Governor* (1903), a novel.

Carson, Kit (1809–1868). A famous trapper and guide of the American West. In his poem *Kit Carson's Ride,* Joaquin Miller tells how the scout and his bride and his friend Revels ride desperately before a prairie fire on his wedding day and finally come to safety. Kit Carson attained additional fame through the dime novels of the Beadle Library in such thrillers as *Kit Carson, King of the Guides.*

Carstone, Richard. In Dickens' BLEAK HOUSE, cousin of Ada Clare, both being wards in chancery, interested in the great suit of "Jarndyce *v.* Jarndyce." Richard Carstone is a "handsome youth, about nineteen, of ingenuous face, and with a most engaging laugh." He marries his cousin Ada, and lives in hope that the suit will soon terminate and make him rich.

Carswell, Mrs. **Catherine** (1879–). Her biography of D. H. Lawrence (1932), a close friend who had encouraged her work, was called a libel by J. Middleton Murry, and suppressed, but is said to be "the most illuminating book about Lawrence."

Cartaphilus. One of the names of the WANDERING JEW. The story of Cartaphilus is taken from the *Book of the Chronicles of the Abbey of St. Albans,* which contains the earliest account of the Wandering Jew (1228).

Carte, Richard D'Oyly (1844–1901). English stage producer, known for his productions of GILBERT AND SULLIVAN operas at his Savoy Theater in London. The D'Oyly Carte companies became those most closely associated with performances of Gilbert and Sullivan works.

carte blanche (*Fr.* white card). A paper with only the signature written on it, so that the person to whom it is given may write his terms knowing that they will be accepted. It was originally a military phrase, referring to capitulation at discretion; but it is now used entirely in a figurative sense, conferring absolute freedom of action on one to whom it is given.

cartel. An association of business competitors in the same field, formed with the object of controlling the market and creating a monopoly. From German *Kartell,* corresponding to the American pool.

Carter, Colonel George Fairfax, see COLONEL CARTER OF CARTERSVILLE.

Carter, Hodding (1907–). Editor of the *Delta Democrat-Times* of Greenville, Mississippi. Associated with STARS AND STRIPES in World War II. Author of *The Winds of Fear* and *Lower Mississippi.* In 1946 he received the Pulitzer Prize for editorial writing.

Carter, Howard (1873–1939). Famous English Egyptologist. Discovered the tomb of Tutankhamen (ca. 1350 B.C.).

Carter, John Franklin (1897–). American political journalist and writer of detective fiction. Better known under the pseudonyms of "Jay Franklin" and "Diplomat."

Carter, Nick. The pseudonym under which Frederick Van Rensselaer Dey (1861–1922) produced his popular dime novels. The character of Nick Carter was reputedly invented by John R. Coryell (1848–1924), American writer of popular fiction and turned over by him to Dey and to Thomas Chalmers Harbaugh (1849–1924). The first Nick Carter novel appeared in 1890 with the title *Nick Carter, Detective,* by "a Celebrated Author." The series was continued as *The Nick Carter Weekly* by Nick Carter. It is said that Dey wrote no less than 1076 stories, or about forty million words, in the person of the adventurous Nick. Together with Harbaugh he is also said to have written some of the novels appearing under the pseudonym of Bertha M. CLAY.

Carteret, Philip (1639–1682). Colonial governor of America: of New Jersey (1664–1676), of East New Jersey (1676–1682). In conflict with Andros, governor of New York, over collection of customs.

Cartesianism. The philosophical system of René DESCARTES, Latinized as Cartesius. See also COGITO ERGO SUM.

Carthage. Famous city of the ancient world in North Africa.

delenda est Carthago. Lat. "Carthage must be destroyed." These are the words with which Cato the Elder concluded every speech in the Senate when Carthage was a menace to the power of Rome. They are now proverbial, and mean, "That which stands in the way of our greatness must be removed at all hazards."

Carthage of the north. Lübeck was so called when head of the Hanseatic League.

Carthaginian faith. Treachery.

Carthaginian peace. A peace treaty implying the virtual annihilation of the vanquished.

Carthon: A Poem. One of the supposed translations from the poetry of OSSIAN by James MACPHERSON, published in *Fragments of Ancient Poetry Collected in the Highlands* (1760). It is written in highly poetic prose and tells of Carthon, a Celtic hero, who is unknowingly killed in single combat by his father Clessámor. Clessámor had been forced to flee for his life, leaving his wife Moina, and so was not aware of his son's name or existence. The theme is of the frequent and ancient SOHRAB AND RUSTUM type.

Carthusians. From *Chartreuse,* near Grenoble in France. Order of monks founded in 1084 by St. Bruno. Vowed to perpetual silence, continuous wearing of hair shirts, and eating of only one meal a day.

Cartier, Jacques (1494–1557). French navigator. Discovered St. Lawrence River in 1536.

Carton, Sydney. The hero of Dickens' TALE OF TWO CITIES, a dissipated young man whose temperament is in distinct contrast to that of Charles Darnay, whom he personally resembles. Sydney Carton loves Lucie Manette, but, knowing of her attachment to Darnay, never attempts to win her. Her friendship, however, calls out his good qualities, and he dies on the guillotine instead of Darnay.

cartouche. In Egyptology, an oval or oblong figure as on monuments, containing a sovereign's name.

Cartwright, William (1611–1643). English scholar, teacher of metaphysics at Oxford, poet, and author of plays successfully presented at the university. He was one of the "sons of Ben," or poets influenced by Ben JONSON. *Comedies, Tragi-Comedies, with Other Poems* was published in 1651.

Carus, Paul (1852–1919). German-American philosopher. Editor of *Open Court* and *The Monist.* Translated and edited Kant.

Caruso, Enrico (1873–1921). Italian operatic tenor of world-wide popularity, best known for his performances in AÏDA, PAGLIACCI, and RIGOLETTO.

Carvel, Richard, see RICHARD CARVEL.

Carvel, Virginia. The heroine of Churchill's CRISIS.

Carver, George Washington (1864–1943). American Negro botanist. Teacher at Tuskegee Institute from 1896. Bureau of Plant Industry, U.S. Dept. of Agriculture from 1895. Known for researches on industrial uses of the peanut, sweet potato and soy-bean. Subject of a widely sold biography by Rackham Holt.

Carver, John (1575–1621). First governor of Plymouth Colony.

caryatids. Figures of women in Greek costume, used in architecture to support entablatures. Caryae, in Laconia, sided with the Persians at Thermopylae, in consequence of which the victorious Greeks destroyed the city, slew the men, and made the women slaves. Praxiteles, to perpetuate the disgrace, employed figures of these women, instead of columns. See ATLANTES.

Casabianca. A well-known poem by Felicia Hemans (1794–1835) celebrating the heroic death of Giacomo Jocante Casabianca, the little son of a French naval captain. The boy was set by his father on watch. The ship caught fire, and his father was burnt to death. As the flames spread, the boy called to his father, but stood by his post until the ship blew up.

Casablanca Conference. Meeting of Churchill and Roosevelt, January 14–26, 1943, together with their Chiefs of Staff. Premier Stalin and Generalissimo Chiang Kai-shek did not attend but were kept informed of progress of discussions. General de Gaulle of the Fighting French and General Giraud, High Commissioner of French Africa, were brought together to unite France against Hitler. The entire field of war was surveyed.

Casa Guidi Windows. A long poem by Elizabeth Barrett Browning (1851), written on behalf of the national aspirations of the Florentines.

Casamassima, Princess, see PRINCESS CASAMASSIMA.

Casanova de Seingalt, Giovanni Jacopo (1725–1798). Italian adventurer, whose *Memoirs*—a record of rogueries and amours—are of great value and interest—not only for the historian.

Casas, Bartolomé de las, see LAS CASAS.

Casaubon, Isaac (1559–1614). French theologian, and with Scaliger and Lipsius, member of renowned triumvirate of the 16th century classical scholars.

Casaubon, Rev. Mr. In George Eliot's MIDDLEMARCH, the elderly scholar whom Dorothea Brooke marries.

Casca. In Shakespeare's *Julius Caesar*, a blunt, violent conspirator, in the faction of Brutus. When Caesar is slain, Antony says, "See what a rent the envious Casca made!"

case knife. A knife carried in a sheath or case. Such knives were formerly used at table. Hence the occasional use of the word for "table knife."

Casey, Mr. In James Joyce's A PORTRAIT OF THE ARTIST AS A YOUNG MAN, a friend of the family of Stephen Dedalus. He figures prominently in a childhood incident remembered by Stephen, a quarrel during a Christmas dinner with Mrs. RIORDAN about PARNELL, of whom he is an admirer.

Casey Jones. John Luther Jones, an American railroad engineer who worked on the Illinois Central's famous "Cannonball." Jones, noted for his skill, daring, and resourcefulness, died in a train wreck in 1900, and was found with one hand still on the whistle and the other on the airbrake lever. Wallace Saunders, his Negro engine wiper and close friend, created the BALLAD which has made Jones an almost legendary figure. The nickname Casey was derived from the town of Cayce, Kentucky, near which Jones was born. A play entitled *Casey Jones* was produced by the Group Theater.

Casket Letters, The. Letters supposed to have been written between Mary Queen of Scots and Bothwell, at least one of which was held to prove the complicity of the Queen in the murder of her husband, Darnley. They were kept in a casket which fell into the hands of the Earl of Morton (1567); they were examined and used as evidence, though denounced as forgeries by the Queen, who was never allowed to see them. They disappeared after the execution of the Regent, the Earl of Gowrie (1584), in whose custody they had last been. They have never been recovered, and their authenticity is still a matter of dispute.

Caslon, William (1692–1766). English type-founder. Designed a highly legible type called after him.

Casper Milquetoast. A character, created by the American cartoonist H. T. Webster, of a painfully timid man.

Cass, Godfrey and Dunstan. Two brothers who play an important part in George Eliot's SILAS MARNER.

Cassandra. A prophetess. In Greek legend the daughter of Priam and Hecuba, gifted with the power of prophecy; but Apollo, whose advances she had refused, brought it to pass that no one believed her predictions, although they were invariably correct. She appears in Shakespeare's *Troilus and Cressida.* See under TROILUS.

Cassatt, Mary (1845–1926). American painter, resident most of her life in France, where she was associated with the Impressionists. See IMPRESSIONISM. She is known for her numerous mother-and-child studies, in which she is considered to have been influenced by DÉGAS. Sister of American railroad executive and president of the Pennsylvania Railroad, Alexander Johnston Cassatt (1839–1906).

Casseres, Benjamin de, see DE CASSERES.

Cassibelan. Uncle to Cymbeline, mentioned in Shakespeare's play of that name. He is the historical Cassivellaunus, a British prince who ruled over the Catrivellauni (in Herts, Bucks, and Berks), about 50 B. C., and was conquered by Caesar.

> When Julius Caesar . . . was in this Britain
> And conquer'd it, Cassibelan, thine uncle, . . . for him
> And his succession granted Rome a tribute,
> Yearly three thousand pounds; which by thee lately
> Is left untender'd. *Cymbeline,* iii. 1.

Shakespeare drew his particulars from HOLINSHED, where it is Guiderius, not Cymbeline, who refuses to pay the tribute.

Cassim Baba, see BABA.

Cassino. In World War II a key position in the German Gustav line in Italy. In 1944 the Allies tried to land at Anzio in order to turn the Gustav Line and also to cut through it beyond Cassino with a view of taking Rome. The battle for Cassino itself began February 1. It was not taken until May 17. In the process the Benedictine Monastery of Monte Cassino was finally destroyed by bombing.

Cassio, Michael. In Shakespeare's OTHELLO, a Florentine, lieutenant in the Venetian army under the command of Othello. He engages in a street-brawl, for which he is suspended by Othello, but Desdemona pleads for his restoration. Iago makes capital of this intercession to rouse the jealousy of the Moor.

Cassiopeia. In Greek mythology, the wife of Cepheus, king of Ethiopia, and mother of ANDROMEDA. In consequence of her boasting of the beauty of her daughter, she was sent to the heavens as the constellation Cassiopeia, the chief stars of which form the outline of a lady seated in a chair and holding up both arms in supplication.

Cassius. In Shakespeare's JULIUS CAESAR, a Roman general, the instigator of the conspiracy against Julius Caesar, and friend of Brutus.

Brutus. The last of all the Romans, fare thee well!
It is impossible that ever Rome
Should breed thy fellow. Friends, I owe more tears
To this dead man than you shall see me pay.
I shall find time, Cassius, I shall find time.
Act v. Sc. 3.

Castaigne, André (1861–). Illustrator and author. Did much work in early days for *Century* magazine; many historical drawings. Wrote *Fata Morgana* (1904); *The Bill-Toppers* (1909).

Castalia, or **Castaly.** A fountain of Parnassus sacred to the Muses. Its waters had the power of inspiring with the gift of poetry those who drank of them.

castanets. Span. *castañeta.* Spoon-shaped shells of wood or ivory looped to the thumb and beaten together by middle finger as accompaniment to dance. So called for their resemblance to chestnuts.

Castaway, The. The last poem by William COWPER, written in 1799 and published in 1803. It was based on an incident described in *A Voyage Round the World* (1748), by Admiral George Anson (1697–1762), a celebrated English seaman of the 18th century. It tells of a lonely death at sea and compares this with the poet's own in a mood of despairing prophecy.

caste (Port. *casta,* race). One of the hereditary classes of society in India; hence any hereditary or exclusive class, or the class system generally. The four great Hindu castes are *Brahmins* (the priestly order), *Shatriya* or *Kshatriya* (soldiers and rulers), *Vaisya* (husbandmen and merchants), *Sudra* (agricultural laborers and mechanics). The first issued from the mouth of Brahma, the second from his arms, the third from his thighs, and the fourth from his feet. Below these come the Outcastes to whom the Vedas are sealed, and who are held cursed in this world and without hope.

lose caste. To lose position in society. To get degraded from one caste to an inferior one.

Castiglione, Baldassare de (1478–1529). Italian humanist, best known for *Il Libro d'Oro,* popularly known as *Il Cortegiano* (*The Courtier;* 1528), a prose dialogue which establishes the characteristics of the ideal aristocratic gentleman in dress, bearing, pastimes, conversation, behavior, ethics, culture, intellectual attainments, and the like. This work was translated into English in 1561 by Sir Thomas Hoby and had a wide influence in Elizabethan England, particularly in the life and personality of Sir Philip SIDNEY and the concepts embodied in Spenser's *Faërie Queene.* Many of the attributes of the ideal courtier are considered similar to those grouped under the term Magnificence in Aristotle's *Nicomachean Ethics.*

Castle, The (*Das Schloss*). A symbolic novel by Franz KAFKA, published in the U.S. in 1931. The hero, known as K., the Land Surveyor, comes to the little peasant village of Madeleinegasse in the Bohemian countryside. His aim is to enter the great, lonely castle of the Count West-West that stands on the side of a hill outside the town, but he discovers that entrance is forbidden him. Although he solicits the aid of the townspeople, seeking out the ostracized family of AMALIA because her brother Barnabas serves as a messenger from the Castle, and ingratiating himself with the mistress of one of the administrative officials, the bureaucracy attached to the Castle frustrates his efforts at every turn. He is, however, permitted to use the local schoolroom as living-quarters, and the Assistants, a strange, pathetic pair of men who do absurd and comical things, are assigned to serve him in any way he wishes. He fills out a questionnaire supplied by the village secretary as the only means of approach to Klamm, an official of the Castle whom he is particularly anxious to see, but is assured that in spite of this he will never gain an interview with Klamm. The novel was left incomplete. In the author's plan of the final chapters, however, K. receives permission at last to live and work in the village, if not to enter the Castle, although the permission comes while he is on his deathbed, after having already lived in the village for a number of years!

The Castle contains the ideas on the relationship between God and man which occur in nearly all of Kafka's writings. It has been interpreted as the symbol of divine grace, sought by average mankind (represented by K.); the bureaucracy which frustrates the seeker's efforts has in its turn been interpreted as the body of religious tradition, ritual, and law which, with conflicting interpretations and misapprehensions of it on the part of the human mind itself, intervenes between God and man. In this novel, as in his other writings on the same theme, the author could see only misery, frustration, and ironic defeat for man. Cf. THE TRIAL. See also FRIEDA; OLGA; SORTINI.

Castle, Egerton (1858–1920). Wrote in collaboration with his wife Agnes (d. 1922) a series of popular romantic novels, *The Pride of Jennico* being perhaps best remembered.

Castle, Vernon and **Irene.** American team of ballroom dancers, famous in the U.S. (ca. 1914) for their performances of popular dances of the time, especially the TANGO.

Castle Dangerous. A novel by Scott (1831). "Castle Dangerous" or "the Perilous Castle of Douglas" was so called because it was taken from the English three times between 1306 and

1307. In the novel Black DOUGLAS promises to release his prisoner, Lady Augusta, if the castle is surrendered to him. Sir John de Walton consents, gives up the castle and marries the lady.

Castle Garden. Large circular building at the Battery, New York City, built as a fort in 1807. Later a concert hall where Jenny Lind sang. Then an immigrant station; last an aquarium. Now torn down.

Castlemaine. See Barbara VILLIERS.

Castlemon, Harry. Pseudonym of **Charles Austin Fosdick** (1842–1915), who wrote boys' books, including *Frank on the Lower Mississippi* (1869) and *Frank Nelson in the Forecastle* (1904).

Castle Number Nine. See BEMELMANS, LUDWIG.

Castle of Indolence. In Thomson's poem of this name (1748), the Castle is situated in the land of Drowsiness, where every sense is steeped in enervating delights. The owner is an enchanter, who deprives all who enter his domains of their energy and free will.

Castle of Otranto. A famous novel of the mystery and terror school, by Horace WALPOLE (1764). After his son Conrad, who has been on the point of marrying Isabella, daughter of the Marquis of Vicenza, is found dead by mysterious means in the castle court, Manfred, prince of Otranto, decides to marry Isabella himself. His grandfather's portrait descends from the wall for an interview with Manfred, and meantime Isabella escapes, aided by the peasant Theodore. One supernatural horror now follows another, until finally the castle falls and the statue of an ancestor, towering out of the ruins, cries "Behold in Theodore the true heir of Alphonse."

Castle Perilous, see PERILOUS CASTLE.

Castle Rackrent. An Irish story by Maria EDGEWORTH (1799), illustrating the evils of absenteeism. The old steward, Thady Quirk, tells of the various masters he has served under in the old castle—Sir Patrick, Sir Murtagh, Sir Kit and Sir Condy—and of the decline of the family fortunes.

Castles in the Air. Visionary projects, daydreams, splendid imaginings which have no real existence. In fairy tales we often have these castles built at a word, and vanishing as soon, like that built for Aladdin by the Genius of the Lamp. These air-castles are called by the French *châteaux d' Espagne* or *châteaux en Asie.*

Castlewood, Lady. In Thackeray's HENRY ESMOND, Rachel Esmond, the wife of Francis Esmond (Lord Castlewood), and later of Henry Esmond.

Castor and Pollux. In Roman mythology, the twin sons of Jupiter and Leda. Jupiter is said to have visited Leda in the form of a swan. She produced two eggs, from one of which sprang Castor and Clytemnestra, and from the other Pollux and Helen. Castor and Pollux, also known as the Dioscuri, had many adventures, were worshiped as gods, and were finally placed among the constellations.

Their name used to be given by sailors to the ST. ELMO'S FIRE or Corposant. If only one flame showed itself, the Romans called it *Helen,* and said that it portended that the worst of the storm was yet to come; but two or more luminous flames they called *Castor and Pollux,* and said that they boded the termination of the storm.

Castorp, Hans. Hero of THE MAGIC MOUNTAIN by Thomas MANN. He is a young engineer of mediocre mind and talents, the son of a Hamburg merchant family. His only original aesthetic tendency is a dreamy susceptibility to music, but his fascination by the atmosphere of disease and death of the mountain sanatorium, the recondite conversations with SETTEMBRINI, and the voluptuous beauty of Claudia CHAUCHAT, and his final contraction of tuberculosis himself, have been interpreted as symbolic of a gradual yielding to the excesses of pure aestheticism. Castorp himself is considered by many critics to symbolize the artist, especially the German Romantic artist, torn by a conflict between the insidiously dreamy lassitude of pure art, always perilously close to death, and the necessity for social action. His dreamy singing of a Schubert song as he goes into battle at the end of the novel ironically symbolizes the imperfect compromise he has made. Hans Castorp is akin to numerous other characters of Mann's who symbolize the artist, including GUSTAVE ASCHENBACH, TONIO KRÖGER, and the Biblical JOSEPH.

Castriota, George. See Scanderbeg, hero of a poem by Longfellow with that title, in which he is also called Castriot.

Castruccio Castracino's sword. See under SWORD.

Casuals of the Sea. A novel by William McFEE (1916), dealing with the Goodrich family, chiefly Minnie Goodrich, the hard, selfish daughter who becomes a courtesan because she can achieve her own ambitions best in that fashion, and her brother Hannibal, a blundering dreamer, whose sense of achievement, such as it is, comes from leaving the tobacconist's counter for the more rigorous life of a trimmer on a steamship.

Casuarina Tree, The. A story by W. Somerset MAUGHAM (1926), dramatized with wide success as *The Letter* (1927).

cat. Called a "familiar," from the medieval superstition that Satan's favorite form was a black cat. Hence witches were said to have a cat as their familiar.

In ancient Rome the cat was a symbol of liberty. The goddess of Liberty was represented as holding a cup in one hand, a broken scepter in the other, and with a cat lying at her feet. No animal is so great an enemy to all constraint as a cat.

In Egypt the cat was sacred to Isis, or the moon. It was held in great veneration, and was worshiped with great ceremony as a symbol of the moon, not only because it is more active after sunset, but from the dilation and contraction of its pupil, symbolical of waxing and waning. The goddess Bast (*Bubastis*), representative of the life-giving solar heat, was portrayed as having the head of a cat, probably because that animal likes to bask in the sun. Diodorus tells us that whoever killed a cat, even by accident, was by the Egyptians punished by death, and according to Egyptian tradition, Diana assumed the form of a cat, and thus excited the fury of the giants.

grin like a Cheshire cat. An old simile, popularized by Lewis CARROLL—

> "Please would you tell me," said Alice a little timidly, . . . "why your cat grins like that?" "It's a Cheshire cat," said the Duchess, "and that's why."—*Alice in Wonderland* (1865).

The phrase is applied to persons who show their teeth and gums when they laugh.

let the cat out of the bag. To disclose a secret. It was formerly a trick among country folk to substitute a cat for a sucking-pig, and bring it in a bag to market.

live a cat and dog life. To be always snarling and quarreling, as a cat and dog, whose aversion to each other is intense.

play cat and mouse with one. "To have him on a string"; while he is in your power to pretend constantly to let him go, but not actually to do so.

be made a cat's paw of, i.e. the tool of another, the medium of doing another's dirty work. The allusion is to the fable of the monkey who wanted to get some roasted chestnuts from the fire, and used the paw of his friend, the cat, for the purpose.

bell the cat. See under BELL.

fight like Kilkenny cats. To fight till both sides have lost their all; to fight with the utmost determination and pertinacity. The story is that during the Irish rebellion of 1798 Kilkenny was garrisoned by a troop of Hessian soldiers, who amused themselves by tying two cats together by their tails and throwing them across a clothes-line to fight. The authorities resolved to put a stop to the "sport," but, on the officer on duty approaching, one of the troopers cut the two tails with a sword, and the cats made off. When the officer inquired the meaning of the bleeding tails, he was told that two cats had been fighting and had devoured each other all but the tails.

waitin' for the cat to die. Waiting for a rope swing to come to a gradual standstill. James Whitcomb RILEY wrote a poem so entitled.

catachresis. Wrong use of one word for another, or a forced trope or mixed metaphor —the latter very popular with modern poets. *Example:* the British lion will never pull in its horns.

catacomb. A subterranean gallery for the burial of the dead, especially at Rome. The origin of the word is unknown. It is found on a very early calendar which appoints a feast at *San Sebastian in Catacumbas.* Here it is still part of a proper name, that of the cemetery of St. Sebastian on the Appian Way. From about the 5th century on, the term seems to have been in general use in the modern meaning.

Cataian. A native of Cathay or China; hence, a thief, liar, or scoundrel, because the Chinese had the reputation of being such.

> I will not believe such a Cataian, though the priest of the town commended him for a true man.
> Shakespeare, *Merry Wives,* ii. 1.

Catalan. A native of Catalonia in Spain. The Catalan language, spoken in Catalonia, adjacent parts of Southern France, and by immigration in Cuba and Argentina, is a Romance language related to Provençal and Spanish.

catch.

first catch your hare. It is generally believed that "Mrs. Glasse," in the *Art of Cookery,* gave this direction; but the exact words are, "Take your hare when it is cased, and make a pudding . . . etc." To "case" means to take off the skin, as in *All's Well,* iii. 6, "We'll make you some sport with the fox ere we case him." "First catch your hare," however, is a very old phrase, and in the 13th century Bracton (Bk. iv. tit. i. ch. xxi. sec. 4) has these words:

> Vulgariter dicitur, quod primo oportet cervum capere, et postea, cum captus fuerit, illum excoriare (it is vulgarly said that you must first catch your deer, and then, when it is caught, skin it).

"Mrs. Glasse" was the pen-name of Dr. John Hill (1716–1775), who published *The Art of Cookery Made Plain and Easy* in 1747 as *by a Lady;* the pseudonym was added later.

catch a crab. In rowing, to be struck with the handle of one's oar; to fall backwards. This occurs when the rower leaves his oar too long in the water before repeating the stroke.

catch a Tartar. Said of the biter bit. Grose says an Irish soldier in the Imperial service, in a battle against the Turks, shouted to his comrade that he had caught a Tartar. "Bring him along, then," said his mate. "But he won't come," cried Paddy. "Then come along yourself," said his comrade. "Arrah!" replied Paddy, "I wish I could, but he won't let me."

catchword. A cue word, or a phrase used as significant by one having really little knowledge of a subject. Technically, a catchword is a word so placed in print that it "catches" the reader's attention, as in dictionaries over the columns, or formerly in many books at the foot of every page taking up the first word of the following page.

Câteau-Cambrésis, Treaty of. See DISASTROUS PEACE.

categorical imperative. In the philosophy of KANT, a universal rule for ethical conduct: "Act only on that maxim whereby thou canst at the same time will that it should become a universal law." In non-philosophical language, the categorical imperative corresponds to the GOLDEN RULE.

catharsis. Purification of the emotions through artistic expression. Aristotle used it in a phrase about tragedy purging the emotions through pity and terror. The problem is analyzed in detail in Lessing's LAOCOÖN.

Cathay. Marco Polo's name for a country in eastern Asia, roughly identical with northern China; from *Ki-tah,* the name of the ruling race in those parts in the 10th century.

Cathay, Merchants from. See BENÉT, William Rose.

Cathédrale, la. See HUYSMANS, JORIS-KARL.

Cather, Willa Sibert (1876–1947). American novelist and short-story writer, editor of *McClure's Magazine* (1906–1912), known for her studies of character and her stories of life in the Middle West. Her best-known novels are O PIONEERS! (1913); MY ÁNTONIA (1918); and DEATH COMES FOR THE ARCHBISHOP (1927). Among her other novels are *Alexander's Bridge* (1912); THE SONG OF THE LARK (1915); *One of Ours* (1922), winner of the Pulitzer prize; *A Lost Lady* (1923); *The Professor's House* (1925); *My Mortal Enemy* (1926); SHADOWS ON THE ROCK (1931); *Lucy Gayheart* (1935); *Sapphira and the Slave Girl* (1940). Her collections of short stories include *The Troll Garden* (1905); *Youth and the Bright Medusa* (1920); *Obscure Destinies* (1932). *April Twilights* (1903) is a book of poems, and *Not Under Forty* (1936) is a volume of essays.

Catherine. A story by Thackeray, written as a satire on the then popular romances idealizing criminals. The heroine, Catherine Hall (after her marriage, Catherine Hayes), is an unscrupulous murderess and is portrayed in anything but ideal terms.

Catherick, Anne. "THE WOMAN IN WHITE" in Wilkie Collins' novel of that title.

Catherine, St. See under SAINT.

Catherine de Médicis (1519–1589). Italian name **Caterina de' Medici.** Daughter of Lorenzo de' Medici, Queen of France, mother of three kings. Provoked civil and religious wars and is held responsible for the Massacre of St. Bartholomew (1572).

Catherine of Russia. The heroine of Shaw's historical drama *Great Catherine* (1913) which presents a picture of the 18th century Russian court.

Catherine wheel, Catherine tresses, etc. See under SAINT CATHERINE.

Catholic League. A confederacy of Catholics formed in 1614 to counterbalance the EVANGELIC LEAGUE of Bohemia. The two Leagues kept Germany in perpetual disturbance, and ultimately led to the Thirty Years' War (1618–1648).

Catholic Majesty. In Spanish, **Católica Majestad.** The special title of the Kings of Spain. It was first given to King Recared (590) in the third Council of Toledo, for his zeal in rooting out the "Arian heresy." But it was not until 1500 when Pope Alexander VI gave the title to Ferdinand V, king of Aragon and Castile, that it became annexed to the Spanish crown.

Cathos. One of the two titular heroines of Molière's comedy, LES PRÉCIEUSES RIDICULES.

Catiline. A Roman patrician, who headed a conspiracy to overthrow the government, and obtain for himself and his followers all places of power and trust. The conspiracy was discovered by Cicero, who exposed it in his four eloquent orations *In Catilinum,* which have become classics of oratory. Catiline escaped and put himself at the head of his army, but fell in battle 62 B.C. Voltaire, in his *Rome sauvée* (1752), introduced the conspiracy and death of Catiline.

Catlin, George (1796–1872). American artist who devoted himself to the study of American Indians. A series of his Indian portraits are in the National Museum, Washington, D.C. Author of *Life Among the Indians* (1867) etc.

Cato. (1) A man of simple life, severe morals, blunt speech, but undoubted patriotism, like the Roman censor of that name (234–149 B.C.). Cato the Censor, also known as Cato the Elder, is the man who concluded all his speeches in the Senate by insisting *Ceterum censeo Carthaginem esse delendam,* "For the rest I vote that Carthage should be destroyed."

(2) Grandson of Cato the censor, the titular hero of a tragedy by Addison (1713). Disgusted with Caesar, Cato retires to Utica, where he sets up a small republic; but Caesar resolves to reduce Utica as he has done the rest

of Africa, and Cato, finding resistance hopeless, falls on his own sword.

cat-o'-nine-tails. A whip with nine lashes, used for punishing offenders, briefly called *a cat;* probably so called because it can be said to "scratch" the back as a cat might.

Catt, Carrie Chapman (1859–1947). American feminist leader.

cattle kingdom. The grasslands of the American West from the Rio Grande to the northern frontier and from Kansas and Nebraska into the Rocky Mountains. Here millions of buffaloes became extinct in two decades, their place being taken by Texas longhorns and Montana steers. The cowmen's commonwealth was a romantic phase of American life. For an account of this time and the coming of the "nesters," cf. *The Sea of Grass* by Conrad RICHTER (1937).

Catullus, Gaius Valerius (84?–54 B.C.). One of the greatest Roman lyric poets. Many of his poems are addressed to "Lesbia," identified as the sister of Clodius.

Caudine Forks. A narrow pass in the mountains near Capua, now called the Valley of Arpaia. It was here that the Roman army, under the consuls T. Veturius Calvinus and Sp. Postumius, fell into the hands of the Samnites (321 B.C.), and were made to pass under the yoke. Hence, the term means an ignominious defeat.

Caudle lecture. A curtain lecture. The term is derived from a series of papers by Douglas Jerrold, which were published in *Punch* (1846). These papers represent Job Caudle as a patient sufferer of the lectures of his nagging wife, Margaret, after they had gone to bed and the curtains were drawn. If he replied, she pronounced him insufferably rude, and if he did not, he was insufferably sulky.

caul. An investing membrane. Specifically, the membrane covering the fetus. A child "born with a caul," that is, with part of the fetal membrane covering its head, is supposed to be lucky, or to possess second-sight.

Cauld-lad, The, of Hilton Hall. A house-spirit, who moved about the furniture during the night. Being resolved to banish him, the inmates left for him a green cloak and hood, before the kitchen-fire, which so delighted him that he never troubled the house any more; but sometimes he might be heard singing—

> Here's a cloak, and here's a hood,
> The cauld-lad of Hilton will do no more good.

Cauline or **Cawline, Sir.** The hero of one of the ballads in Percy's *Reliques*. He lives in the palace of the king of Ireland, and "used to serve the wine." He falls in love with Christabelle, the King's daughter, who secretly plights her troth to him, but the King discovers the lovers in a bower, and banishes Sir Cauline. He, however, returns just in time to slay a "Soldain" who is seeking the lady's hand, but dies of the wounds received in the combat; and the fair Christabelle dies of grief, having "burst her gentle hearte in twayne."

Cautionary Tales. See BELLOC, HILAIRE.

Cauvin, Jean, see CALVIN, JOHN.

Cavalcade. See COWARD, NOEL PIERCE.

Cavalcanti, Guido (ca. 1250–1300). Leading Florentine poet before Dante who called him his "first friend."

Cavalier Poets. English lyric poets associated with the court of Charles I, chief of whom were HERRICK, CAREW, SUCKLING, LOVELACE.

Cavalieri, Lina (1874–1944). Italian operatic soprano. Sang in many leading European cities and in U.S. Killed in a bombing raid in World War II.

Cavalleria Rusticana (Rustic Chivalry). An opera by Mascagni (1890) based on a story by Giovanni Verga. The characters are all simple village folk. Turiddu's old love, Lola, has married Alfio, a carrier, but Turiddu, after dallying with the affections of the too-willing Santuzza, returns to Lola. Santuzza arouses Alfio's suspicions, a duel is fought and Turiddu is killed.

Cavallini, Madame. The heroine of Edward Sheldon's drama, ROMANCE.

Cavaradossi, Mario. Tosca's artist lover in Puccini's opera, LA TOSCA.

cave of Adullam, see ADULLAM.

caveat. (*Lat.,* let him beware). A notice directing the recipient to refrain from some act pending the decision of the Court. Hence, *enter a caveat.* To give legal notice that the opponent is not to proceed with the suit in hand until the party giving the notice has been heard; to give a warning or admonition.

caveat emptor. Lat., "let the purchaser beware"; *i.e.* the buyer must keep his eyes open, for the bargain he agrees to is binding.

Cavell, Edith Louisa (1872–1915). Heroic English nurse. Enabled many Allied soldiers to escape to Holland. Executed by the Germans Oct. 12, 1915. Cf. the painting by George Bellows.

Cavender's House. See ROBINSON, EDWIN ARLINGTON.

Cavendish, Margaret, Duchess of Newcastle (ca. 1625–1673). English noblewoman, one of the few outstanding writers of her sex in the 17th century, known for her eccentricity of dress and behavior. She wrote prolifically on a variety of subjects and in a variety of forms, producing thirteen printed books. Her best-known work is her *Sociable Letters* (1664), presenting a vivid picture of her times. She also wrote a biography of her husband, the Duke of Newcastle, who had been a devoted follower of Charles I and Charles II. In his celebrated diary, Samuel PEPYS refers to the Duchess as "a mad, conceited, ridiculous woman."

Cavendish, Thomas (1555?–1592). Third circumnavigator of the globe. Died at sea.

caviar. The roe of the sturgeon, pickled, salted, and prepared for use as a relish. Caviar is an acquired taste; hence, Shakespeare's *caviar to the general* (*Hamlet,* ii. 2) which means, above the taste or comprehension of ordinary people.

Cavour, Conte **Camillo Benso di** (1810–1861). Famous Italian statesman. Founded with Count Cesare Balbo *Il Risorgimento,* organ for Italian National Movement (1847). Aided Garibaldi (1860). Secured union of Central and Southern Italy to Piedmont through plebiscites.

Cawdor. See JEFFERS, ROBINSON.

Cawein, Madison Julius (1865–1914). American southern poet. *Kentucky Poems* (1902), etc.

Caxton, William (1422–1491). The first English printer, also a well-known translator. While in the household of the Duchess of Burgundy, a sister of Edward IV of England, (1471–1476), Caxton learned the art of printing. In 1474 he printed his own translation of a French romance, *Le Recueil des histories de Troyes,* as *Recuyell of the Histories of Troy,* and in 1475, another translation from the French, *The Game and Playe of Chess.* When he returned to England, he set up a press at Westminster and from 1477 to 1491 printed nearly eighty books, many of which were translations he himself had made from the French.

Caxtons, The. A novel by BULWER-LYTTON (1849) which with its sequels *My Novel* (1853) and *What Will He Do with It* (1858), narrates the history of an upper middle-class English family. The story is supposed to be written by Pisistratus Caxton. His father, Austin Caxton, is an impractical philosopher and scholar, lost in vague dreams and plans for his proposed masterpiece on "The History of Human Error." The launching of this *magnum opus* is finally made possible by the money which Pisistratus brings back from Australia. Other of the Caxtons are the gay, irresponsible Uncle Jack, who is an inveterate and not too lucky promoter; the fine old soldier, Captain Roland, also an uncle of Pisistratus, and Roland's son Herbert a wild young man with gypsy blood in his veins, who dies a heroic death in India.

Cayley, Charles. The man with whom Christina ROSSETTI was in love but whom she was reported by her brother, W. M. Rossetti, to have refused to marry because of his liberal attitude in matters of religion.

Cazamian, Louis (1877–). French scholar and authority on English literature. His *Histoire de la littérature anglaise* (1924), written in collaboration with Émile Legouis, is in many respects superior to English books of a comparable scope.

Cazique. See RULERS, TITLES OF.

Ceca to Mecca, from. From one end of the world to the other; from pillar to post. Ceca and Mecca are two places visited by Mohammedan pilgrims. Cf. *Dan to Beersheba;* and *Land's End to John o' Groat's.*

Cecil. English family from which have come many famous statesmen, among them **William Cecil,** 1st Baron **Burghley** (1520–1598), director of Queen Elizabeth's policy. The youngest, **Edward Christian David Cecil** (1902–) is a biographer. Cf. his *The Young Melbourne* (1939).

Cecilia, or Memoirs of an Heiress. A novel by Fanny BURNEY (1782). The heroine, Cecilia Beverley, is an heiress of somewhat inferior birth, who must, to keep her fortune, marry a husband who will adopt her name. The hero, Mortimer Delville, loves her, but numerous obstacles keep them apart for a long time, particularly the schemes and prejudices of people who wish to make use of her for their own advantage.

Čech, Svatopluk (1846–1908). Czech epic and satiric national poet.

Cecilia, St. See under SAINT.

Cecily, St. The heroine of the SECOND NUN'S TALE in Chaucer's *Canterbury Tales.*

Cecrops. Traditional founder of Athens and first King of Attica. Supposed to have sprung from the ground and was represented as half man, half dragon.

Cedar Creek, in the Shenandoah, where Early surprised Sheridan's Army (Oct. 19, 1864). Sheridan mustered a victorious countercharge that broke the Confederates' command of the Valley for incursions northward.

cedilla. Literally, a "little z (or zeta)." A diacritical mark placed under a "c" (as in façade) to assign to it the sound value of "s" rather than of "k." The form *ç* is a development from an older *cz.* It is used in French and Portuguese, formerly also in Spanish.

Cedric. In Scott's IVANHOE, a thane of Rotherwood surnamed "the Saxon." He is the father of the hero, and the guardian of Rowena, the heroine.

Celadon. A general name for a lover. In D'Urfé's ASTRÉE he is the shepherd lover of Astrée; in Thomson's SEASONS the shepherd lover of Amelia.

Celandine, To the Small. Poem by William WORDSWORTH. The celandine is a herb whose yellow flowers resemble buttercups. Less poetically it is called pilewort, a specific.

Celebrated Jumping Frog of Calaveras County, The. A sketch by Mark TWAIN, based on an old American "tall tale" and first published in 1865. It was the first of the author's works to bring him fame as a humorist.

celesta. A keyboard instrument having a piano-like action. Its tone is similar to that of the glockenspiel. It is occasionally demanded in modern orchestral scores.

Celestial City. Heaven is so called by John Bunyan, in his *Pilgrim's Progress* (1678). Peking, in China, was so called also.

Celestial Empire. China; a translation of the Chinese *Tien Chao,* literally "heavenly dynasty," alluding to the belief that the old emperors were in direct descent from the gods. Hence, the Chinese themselves are sometimes spoken of as *Celestials.*

Celeus. In Greek legend, husband of Metanira. He sheltered Demeter when she was seeking Persephone. His son Triptolemus was in gratitude made by the goddess the teacher of men in the use of the plough.

Celia. (1) Rosalind's cousin in Shakespeare's AS YOU LIKE IT. She marries Oliver de Boys.

(2) In English lyrics of the Elizabethan and Stuart periods, a poetic name for any lady-love, as, "Would you know my Celia's charms?"

Célimène. In Molière's MISANTHROPE, a coquette courted by Alceste the "misanthrope"; hence any flagrant coquette. For the plot, see ALCESTE.

Celine, Louis Ferdinand, see DESTOUCHES.

Cellini, Benvenuto (1500–1571). Florentine sculptor, famous for his work as a goldsmith and his *Autobiography of Benvenuto Cellini,* which was written between 1558 and 1562 and first published in 1730. It is one of the most celebrated autobiographies of history, giving an intimate and lively picture of the life of the times and of the author's vivid and arrogant personality. GOETHE was so fascinated by it that he translated it into German. Cellini was a pupil of MICHELANGELO and for a time was attached to the court of FRANCIS I of France, for whom he made his best-known piece, a gold salt-cellar.

An overture called *Benvenuto Cellini* was written by the French Romantic composer BERLIOZ.

celt. (*Welsh* cellt, flint). Prehistoric implement, one of man's most primitive tools, chisel-shaped, an elongated stone. Progenitor of the axe, hoe, and chisel. See also FOLSOM POINT.

Cénacle, the. A club or group of men of letters and affairs prominent in many of the novels of Balzac's *Comédie Humaine.* The leader is Daniel d'Arthez and among the most active members are Henri de Marsay, Horace Bianchon and Joseph Brideau.

Cena de la Ceneri. See BRUNO, GIORDANO.

Cena delle Beffe, La. See BENELLI, SEM.

Cenci, Beatrice. A historical character (1577–1599) known as the "Beautiful Parricide" from a famous portrait in the Barberini Palace at Rome attributed to Guido Reni. She was the daughter of Francesco Cenci, a dissipated and passionate Roman nobleman, and, with her brothers, plotted the death of her father because of his unmitigated cruelty to his wife and children. She was executed in 1599, and at the trial her counsel, with the view of still further gaining popular sympathy for his client, accused the father, probably without foundation, of having attempted to commit incest with her. Her story has been a favorite theme in poetry and art; Shelley's tragedy *The Cenci* (1819) is particularly noteworthy.

Cendrars, Blaise (1887–). French novelist and poet. *Sutter's Gold* (1926) is his best-known work in English. John Dos PASSOS has translated his *Panama, or the Adventures of my Seven Uncles* (1931).

cenobite. As opposed to *anchorite,* "a hermit," one of a religious order dwelling in a convent community.

centaurs. In classic mythology, a set of beings who were half horse and half man. They fought with the Lapithae at the marriage feast of Pirithous, were expelled from their country, and took refuge on Mount Pindus. Chiron was the most famous of the centaurs.

Centennial Exposition. At Philadelphia (1876). See under EXPOSITION.

Centennial State. Colorado. See under STATES.

center party. In politics, a party occupying a place between two extremes: the *left center* is the more radical wing, and the *right center* the more conservative. In the French Revolution *the Center* of the Legislative Assembly included the friends of order.

In the Fenian rebellion (1866) the chief movers were called *Head Centers,* and their subordinates *Centers.*

Centlivre, Susanna (1667?–1723). English dramatist and actress. A widow at 17, she began to write plays. In 1706 she married Joseph Centlivre, the chief cook to Queen Anne. Among her comedies are *The Gamester* (1705), and *A Bold Stroke for a Wife* (1718), in which one of the characters is SIMON PURE.

Cent nouvelles nouvelles (1462). An early work of French literature akin to Boccaccio's *Decameron* or Poggio's *Facetiae*. It uses everyday French of the period. The authorship is in doubt.

cento (*Lat.*, a patchwork). Poetry made up of lines borrowed from established authors. It was an art freely practised in the decadent period of Greece and Rome, and Ausonius, who has a nuptial idyll composed from verses selected from Virgil, composed rules governing their manufacture. Among well-known examples are the *Homerocentones,* the *Cento Virgilianus* by Proba Falconia (4th century), and the hymns made by Metellus out of the Odes of Horace. Of modern centos the following portion of a Shakespearean cento that appeared in *English,* November, 1919, may serve as an example:

Let fame that all hunt after in their lives
Among the buzzing pleasèd multitude
For present comfort and for future good,
Taint not thy mind; nor let thy soul contrive
With all the fierce endeavour of your wit
To woo a maid in way of marriage,
As it is common for the younger sort,
The lunatic, the lover, and the poet:
Thus bad begins, and worse remains behind.
I see a man's life is a tedious one,
For it appears, by manifest proceeding,
There's nothing serious in mortality.
Life's but a walking shadow, a poor player,
And one man in his time plays many parts,
As an unperfect actor on the stage.

In many passages, T. S. Eliot's poem THE WASTELAND might be called a cento, since the author juxtaposes quotations from great works of the past with tawdry modern popular songs in order to show the contrast between two civilizations. Ezra Pound's CANTOS often are characterized by this device also.

Central Powers. In World War I, Austria-Hungary and Germany, so called because of their geographical position. Sometimes including their allies Bulgaria and Turkey.

Century of Progress. Official subtitle of the Chicago World's Fair of 1933, held in celebration of the centenary of the city's founding.

Century Was Young, The. Title of the English translation of *Les Voyages de l'impériale* (1940) a novel by Louis ARAGON. It is one of a series designed to present a sociological portrait of twentieth-century France in the manner of Balzac. It tells of Pierre Mercadier, a provincial history teacher of modest means, who becomes a secret gambler on the stock exchange and eventually deserts his family and ruins himself in the pursuit of his vain goal of winning a fortune.

cephalic index. A number obtained by dividing the maximum breadth of the cranium by its maximum length and multiplying by 100. When measured on skeletons it is called **cranial index.** Used to classify racial types.

Cephalus and Procris. Made familiar to us by an allusion in the MIDSUMMER NIGHT'S DREAM. In classic legend, Cephalus was husband of Procris, who, out of jealousy, deserted him. He went in search of her, and rested awhile under a tree. Procris, knowing of his whereabouts, crept through some bushes to ascertain if a rival was with him; and he, hearing the noise and thinking it to be made by some wild beast, hurled his javelin into the bushes and slew her. When the unhappy man discovered what he had done, he slew himself in anguish of spirit with the same javelin.

the unerring dart of Procris. Diana gave Procris a dart which never missed its aim, and after being discharged returned back to the shooter.

Cepola. See DEVICES OF CEPOLA.

Cerberus. A grim, watchful keeper, house-porter, guardian, etc. Cerberus, according to Roman mythology, is the three-headed dog that keeps the entrance of the infernal regions. Hercules dragged the monster to earth, and then let him go again. Orpheus lulled Cerberus to sleep with his lyre, and the Sibyl who conducted Aeneas through the Inferno, also threw the dog into a profound sleep with a cake seasoned with poppies and honey.

give a sop to Cerberus. To give a bribe, to quiet a troublesome customer. When persons died, the Greeks and Romans used to put a cake in their hands as a sop to Cerberus, to allow them to pass without molestation.

Ceres. The Roman name of *Mother Earth,* the protectress of agriculture and of all the fruits of the earth; later identified with the Greek DEMETER. She is the personification of the fruits of the harvest. See PROSERPINE.

Cerf, Bennett Alfred (1898–). American publisher and anthologist. *Try and Stop Me* (1944), etc.

Cervantes Saavedra, Miguel de (1547–1616). Spanish novelist, famous for DON QUIJOTE, his great satire on chivalry, the first part of which was published in 1605 and the second, in 1615. He wrote a number of plays as well, most of which are now lost. *Novelas Ejemplares,* a collection of short tales, and *Persiles y Sigismunda,* an adventure tale, are also included among his works.

Cervera y Topete, Marqués **de Santa Ana** (1839–1909). Spanish naval commander whose squadron was blockaded and defeated in Spanish-American war in harbor of Santiago de Cuba (July 3, 1898).

César Birotteau, see BIROTTEAU, CÉSAR.

cesarevitch. See under CZAREVITCH.

Cesario. In Shakespeare's *Twelfth Night,* the name assumed by Viola when disguised as a boy.

Cestius, Pyramid of. Tomb of the Roman *Praetor* Gaius Cestius in Rome. Keats and Shelley are buried nearby.

Cestre, Charles (1871–). French critic. *An Introduction to Edwin Arlington Robinson* (1929).

cestus. (1) The girdle of Venus, made by her husband Vulcan. When she wantoned with Mars it fell off and was left on the "Acidalian mount." It was reputed to possess magical power to move to ardent love. By a poetical fiction, all women of irresistible attraction are supposed to be wearers of Aphrodite's girdle, or the cestus. It is introduced by Spenser in the *Faërie Queene* as the girdle of FLORIMEL; it gave to those who could wear it "the virtue of chaste love and wifehood true," but if any woman not chaste and faithful put it on, it "loosed or tore asunder."

(2) In Greek and Roman games the covering for the hands of boxers of leather bands, often loaded with lead or iron.

The girdle and the glove are etymologically not related.

Cézanne, Paul (1839–1906). Famous French painter, a leader of the Post-Impressionist movement (see POST-IMPRESSIONISM) and known for his emphasis on the geometric forms in nature. He painted chiefly still lifes and landscapes, which were misunderstood and regarded as ugly by many people of his time. During most of his life he was unknown, but he had an important influence on the painters of CUBISM and soon came to be regarded as a modern classic. Cézanne is considered to have been in the mind of ZOLA, his life-long friend, during the composition of *L'Œuvre,* a novel dealing with painting.

chaconne (*Fr.*), **ciacona** (*Ital.*), **chacona** (*Span.*) From Basque *chocuna,* pretty. A lively folk dance, considered to have been of Mexican Indian origin, adopted in Spain and popular in the 17th century. Later it came to be used in orchestral suites. Cf. *Bergamasca; Passacaglia.*

Chadband, The Rev. Mr. In Dickens' BLEAK HOUSE, a famous type of a canting hypocrite "in the ministry." He calls himself "a vessel," is much admired by his dupes, and pretends to despise the "carnal world," but nevertheless loves dearly its "good things," and is most self-indulgent.

Chadwick, James (1891–). English physicist. Director of radioactive research, Cavendish Laboratory, Cambridge. Discovered the neutron (1932). Nobel Prize for physics (1935).

Chagall, Marc (1887–). Russian painter; studied under BAKST. Identified with impressionism and cubism. Known for scenes of Russian life and illustrations for La Fontaine's *Fables.*

Chaillu, Paul Belloni Du, see DU CHAILLU, PAUL BELLONI.

Chain Gang, I was a Member of A Georgia. Moving picture in which Paul MUNI scored a sensation.

chaise (*Fr.* chair). A two-wheeled carriage for one or two persons with a calash top and body hung on leather straps. Usually a one horse affair. Corrupted in America to Shay. See ONE HOSS SHAY.

Chaliapin, Feodor Ivanovich (1873–1938). Russian basso. Sang in several Moscow opera companies. Great success in London and U.S.

Challenger, Professor. Sir Arthur CONAN DOYLE thought him the most amusing character he ever invented. He appears in *The Lost World* (1912); *The Poison Belt* (1913); *The Land of Mist* (1926); *The Maracot Deep* (1928).

Chalons, Battle of. See BATTLES, FIFTEEN DECISIVE.

cham [pronounce *k*-]. The sovereign prince of Tartary, now written "khan."

> Fetch you a hair off the great Cham's beard.
> Shakespeare, *Much Ado About Nothing,* ii. 1.

the Great Cham of Literature. Dr. Samuel JOHNSON (1709–1784).

Chambered Nautilus, The. Poem by Dr. Oliver Wendell HOLMES (1858).

Chamberlain, John Rensselaer (1903–). American critic writing for *New York Times, Saturday Review of Literature, Fortune* (as editor), *Scribner's* and *Harper's Magazine.* Has written four books, among them *The American Stakes* (1940).

Chamberlain, Neville (1869–1940). English statesman, Conservative in politics and holder of numerous offices in the British government, including those of Chancellor of the Exchequer (1923–1924, 1931–1937) and Prime Minister (1937–1940). He is best known for his rôle in the MUNICH CRISIS of September 1938, which brought him into wide public disfavor. For a time, his name became synonymous with betrayal in the writings of Marxists and Liberals, who considered that he had delivered Czechoslovakia into the hands of Adolf HITLER. Chamberlain made the official declaration of war against Germany on September 3, 1939, at the outset of World War II, but his war policies were not satisfactory to the British public, who preferred his successor, Winston Churchill. See CHURCHILL, WINSTON LEONARD SPENCER.

chamber music. Instrumental music designed for performance by a small orchestra in a moderate-sized room. Originally it referred to music performed for a nobleman in his own home as distinguished from music in a church or theater. It began about the year 1600 in Italy and England. William BYRD, Alessandro SCARLATTI, HAYDN, MOZART, and BEETHOVEN were outstanding composers of chamber music, which is chiefly represented by the string quartet.

Chamber Music. A volume of poems by James JOYCE, published in 1907 and consisting of lyrics showing the influence of the Elizabethan poets.

Chambers, Charles Haddon (1860–1921). Australian playwright. His best comedy *The Tyranny of Tears* produced by Charles Wyndham.

Chambers, Robert (1802–1871). Scottish publisher of the celebrated *Chambers' Encyclopaedia* in ten volumes (1859–1868). His brother William (1800–1883) started *Chambers' Edinburgh Journal.*

Chambers, Robert William (1865–1933). Enormously prolific and popular American novelist. Some good work, such as *The King in Yellow* (1893) and *Cardigan* (1901), hidden under a mass of trash.

chameleon. A small lizard that changes its color according to mood and surroundings. Hence a person whose attitude and opinions so change.

Chaminade, Cécile Louise Stéphanie (1861–1944). French salon composer and pianist. Most popular works are *The Flatterer* and *Scarf Dance.*

Chamisso, Adelbert von (1781–1838). German romantic writer, best known for his tale of the man who sold his shadow, PETER SCHLEMIHL. Chamisso was born in France and is one of the very few Frenchmen who achieved literary fame in German after having learned that language as a second tongue. In his earlier years he was the botanist of the Romanzov expedition to Oceania and the Arctic. See also Otto von KOTZEBUE.

Champion of England. A person whose office it is to ride up Westminster Hall on a Coronation Day, and challenge anyone who disputes the right of succession. The office was established by William the Conqueror, and was given to Marmion and his male descendants, with the manor of "broad Scrivelsby." De Ludlow received the office and manor through the female line; and at the Coronation of Richard II Sir John Dymoke succeeded through the female line also. Since then the office has continued in the Dymoke family, but the actual riding and challenge were discontinued after the coronation of Queen Victoria.

Champlain, Lake. Site of an American naval victory over a slightly superior British fleet (1814) which thus failed in its task to cover an invasion of the U.S. by land.

Champlain, Samuel de (1570–1635). French explorer who in 1608 founded the colony of Quebec. He discovered Lake Champlain, between the present New York and Vermont.

Champollion, Jean François (1790–1832). Famous French Egyptologist. From his study of the ROSETTA STONE he obtained a clue for deciphering Egyptian hieroglyphics.

Champs Élysées. Literally, Elysian Fields. A beautiful avenue in Paris.

Chamson, André (1900–). French novelist and essayist. Simple and austere.

Chan, Charlie. See BIGGERS, EARL DERR.

Chan, Marse, see MARSE CHAN.

Chance. A novel by Joseph CONRAD (1914). In the home of his sister, Mrs. Fyne, Captain Roderick Anthony, master of the *Ferndale,* meets and falls in love with Flora de Barral, the daughter of a once wealthy man now serving a prison sentence for his frauds. Flora is poor and utterly wretched and imagines that Anthony is marrying her out of pity; he, on his part, begins to fear that she has accepted him merely from the necessity of providing for herself and her father, who emerges from prison and is taken on board the *Ferndale* by the newly married pair. The hatred which the old man conceives for his daughter's husband serves to intensify the misunderstanding which the isolation of life on shipboard makes all the more painful. Finally De Barral's attempt to poison Anthony, discovered and thwarted by mere "chance" clears the situation. Most of the story is told by MARLOW.

Chance Acquaintance, A. A novel by W. D. Howells (*Am.* 1873), dealing with the short-lived steamboat romance of Miles Arbuton and Kitty Ellison. See ARBUTON, MILES.

Chancellor, Lord or **Lord High.** The highest judicial functionary of England, who ranks above all peers, except princes of the blood and the Archbishop of Canterbury. He is "Keeper of the Great Seal," is called "Keeper of His (or Her) Majesty's Conscience," and presides on the Woolsack in the House of Lords, and in the Chancery Division of the Supreme Court.

Chancellor, Olive. A New England feminist, the leading character in Henry James' novel THE BOSTONIANS.

Chancellorsville, Battle of. In American Civil War (May 1–3, 1863). Defeat of Union Army under Hooker by Confederate Army under Lee.

chancery. The highest division of the High Court of Justice in the English judicial system, comprising a court of common law and a court of equity.

get a man's head into chancery is to get it under your arm, where you can pummel it as long as you like, and he cannot get it free without great difficulty. The allusion is to the long and exhausting nature of a Chancery suit. If a man once gets his head there, the lawyers punish him to their hearts' content.

In Chancery is the title of a novel by Galsworthy, one of the novels in the FORSYTE SAGA.

Channel Islands, The. The islands of Jersey, Guernsey, Alderney, and Sark in the English Channel. Held by the Germans in World War II.

Channing, Edward (1856–1931). American historian. Won Pulitzer Prize for history (1926) with the final volume (on the Civil War) of his large *A History of the United States*.

Channing, William Ellery (1780–1842). American Transcendentalist (see TRANSCENDENTALISM) and Unitarian clergyman, the friend of Emerson, Hawthorne, and Thoreau. He was involved in many religious controversies, being especially opposed to Calvin's doctrine of the total depravity of mankind. See CALVINISM. Channing was also a pioneer in the opposition to slavery and to war, and urged improvements in the working conditions of laborers.

Chanouns Yemannes Tale, see CANON YEOMAN'S TALE.

chanson de geste (*Fr.* song of deeds, from Lat. *gesta,* deeds). A type of early French epic poems of the 11th and 12th centuries, celebrating the heroic deeds in battle of fictional and historical knights. The *chanson de geste* was a forerunner of the medieval romance, although it lacked the rich feudal trappings and the importance of women in the plot that was a leading characteristic of the romance. The form of the *chanson* consisted of stanzas, called *laisses,* of unequal length, written in ten-syllable lines and marked by assonance or a single rhyme; it was set to music and sung by minstrels or *jongleurs,* who arranged the *chansons* in cycles, the name of some ancestor at the head of each. Most of the *chansons de geste* were written about CHARLEMAGNE and heroes of Charlemagne's time, the best-known being the *Chanson de Roland* (see ROLAND), which William of MALMESBURY, the medieval English chronicler, asserts was sung during the Battle of HASTINGS in 1066. Another cycle was of the Crusades, containing the *Chanson de Jérusalem* and the *Chanson d'Antioche*.

Chantecler. A drama by ROSTAND (1910). The hero, the lord of the barnyard, believes that his Cock-a-doodle-doo brings the Dawn. When the owls and the cat, his enemies, stir up trouble for him with the hens, he wins back supremacy by defending them from a hawk. He later goes off into the woods with a hen-pheasant, and one day, in her jealousy of the Dawn, she covers his eyes and he learns that Dawn can come without him. Although this is a severe shock, he recovers and returns to the barnyard, confident that his crowing will be of some comfort on gray mornings.

Chanticleer (*Fr. chanter,* to sing, *clairment, i.e.* distinctly). A cock. Chanticleer plays a prominent rôle in the medieval beast-epic REYNARD THE FOX and is the hero of Chaucer's *Nun's Priest's* (*Nonne Prestes*) *Tale,* one of the *Canterbury Tales* (1388). The latter tells of how one day, Dan Russell, the fox, comes into the poultry-yard, and tells Master Chanticleer he cannot resist the pleasure of hearing him sing, for his voice is divinely ravishing. The cock, pleased with this flattery, shuts his eyes, and begins to crow most lustily; whereupon Dan Russell seizes him by the throat, and runs off with him. When they get to the wood, the cock says to the fox, "I would recommend you to eat me at once, for I think I can hear your pursuers." "I am going to do so," says the fox; but when he opens his mouth to reply, out flies the cock into a tree, and while the fox is deliberating how he may regain his prey, up come the farmer and his men with scythes, flails, and pitchforks, with which they despatch the fox without mercy.

chant royal. In old French poetry an elaborate form of ballade. Five stanzas of eleven lines and an envoy of eight lines, and five rhymes. The most frequent rhyme-scheme is *ababccddede*.

chantry. Chapel founded for the constant chanting of masses. The word might be rendered by "singery."

Chanute, Octave (1832–1910). Aviation pioneer. Wright brothers paid tribute to his experiments and designs.

Chaos. In Greek mythology, the original confusion in which earth, sea, and air were mixed up together. It was personified by the Greeks as the most ancient of the gods. The egg of Nyx, the daughter of Chaos, was floating on Chaos and from it arose the world.

chapbook. Originally one of the books carried about for sale by *chapmen* ("tradesmen," *chap* meaning purchase or bargain). Hence, any book of a similar nature, a tract, small collection of ballads, or the like.

The Chap-Book was a distinguished LITTLE MAGAZINE, published by Stone and Kimball in Chicago (1894–1898).

chapeau bras (*Fr.* literally "arm hat"). Three-cornered hat in use in 18th-century France. So called because it could be compressed and carried under the arm. Still occasionally seen at French state and naval functions.

Chapelain, Jean (1595–1674). A French critic who attempted epic verse with indifferent success but was important in forming the classical doctrine. "Between Malherbe and Boileau the notable name in criticism is that of Chapelain."

chaplet. A garland. Cf. *The Chaplet,* an early poem by Witter Bynner. In the Catholic Church, a third of the rosary.

Chaplin, Charlie. In full **Charles Spencer Chaplin** (1889–). English-born American motion-picture comedian, perhaps the most famous film actor in the world. He became known for his skill at pantomime and for the combined humor and pathos of the little tramp character who appears in all his pictures, dressed in a costume said to have been inspired by the shabby-genteel clothes of ill-paid London clerks. Chaplin's best-known films, written, acted, and directed by him, are *The Kid* (1920); *The Gold Rush* (1925); *City Lights* (1932); *Modern Times* (1936), a satire on the mechanical civilization of the 20th century; *The Great Dictator* (1940), a satire on Adolf Hitler; and *Monsieur Verdoux* (1947). Chaplin's art has frequently been praised by serious critics, and in *Chaplinesque,* a poem by Hart CRANE, his famous screen character is used as a symbol of the average, unimportant man of the 20th century.

Chapman, Frank Michler (1865–1945). American ornithologist, the "most influential since AUDUBON." For thirty-four years curator of birds at the American Museum of Natural History. Built up one of the finest collections of birds in the world. He also is known as the father of the bird-sanctuary system in the United States.

Chapman, George (1559?–1634). English poet and scholar, best known for his translations of the works of Homer, beginning in 1598 and extending to 1624. He made additions of his own and very nearly rewrote Homer from an Elizabethan standpoint. His translation was praised by Lamb and Coleridge, and Keats paid a tribute to it in his sonnet *On First Looking into Chapman's Homer.* Chapman also completed HERO AND LEANDER, which had been left unfinished on the death of Christopher Marlowe; it was published in 1598. Other works of Chapman include *The Shadow of Night* (1594); *Ovid's Banquet of Sense* (1595), with which was also published a sonnet sequence, *A Coronet for his Mistress Philosophy; The Memorable Mask of the Middle Temple and Lincoln's Inn* (1613); and a play, BUSSY D'AMBOIS (1607).

Chapman, John (1775?–1847), see JOHNNY APPLESEED.

Chapman, John Jay (1862–1933). American man of letters. Edmund Wilson calls him the best writer on literature of his generation. He was also the best letter-writer of his time.

Chapman, Maristan (1895–). Pen-name of two American novelists, authors of books on the life and people of the Tennessee Mountains. The best known are *The Happy Mountain* (1928) and *Homeplace* (1929).

Chappell, George Shepard (1877–1946). American humorist. Wrote, as Captain Traprock, *The Cruise of the Kawa* (1921), *My Northern Exposure: The Kawa at the Pole* (1922) etc.

Chapter on Ears, A. A whimsical essay by Charles LAMB, appearing in *Essays of Elia* (1823).

Chapultepec. Ancient residence of the kings of Mexico. The Mexicans were heavily defeated there by General Winfield Scott (1786–1866) in 1847.

Characteristics of Shakespeare's Dramas. Lecture by Samuel Taylor COLERIDGE (1818).

characterizer, the complete. Phrase used for a series of epigrams by "F.P.A." (Franklin P. Adams) and others in the newspaper column "The Conning Tower."

Characters, The. See OVERBURY, Sir THOMAS.

Characters of Shakespeare's Plays, The. See HAZLITT, WILLIAM.

Characters of Virtues and Vices. See HALL, JOSEPH.

character writers. A school of English prose writers in the first half of the 17th century who wrote sketches of men and women, either individuals or types, in descriptive, analytical, or satirical form, as observed in the life of their time. Many of them were influenced by the work of the Athenian Peripatetic philosopher Theophrastus (373–284 B.C.), who wrote studies of thirty ethical types of mankind under the title of *Characters.* The best-known English character writers are Joseph HALL, Sir Thomas OVERBURY, John EARLE, and Owen FELTHAM.

Chardin, Jean Baptiste Siméon (1699–1779). French painter, known for his still lifes and domestic scenes, and his luminous color effects.

chargé d'affaires. The proxy of an ambassador, or the diplomatic agent where none higher has been appointed.

Charge of the Light Brigade. A poem by TENNYSON based on the fatal "death charge of the 600" at Balaclava in the Crimea, Sept. 20th, 1854.

> When can their glory fade?
> O the wild charge they made!
> All the world wonder'd.
> Honor the charge they made
> Honor the Light Brigade
> Noble six hundred!

Charicleia. The lady-love of Theagenës in the exquisite erotic Greek romance called *The Loves of Theagenës and Charicleia* by Heliodoros, Bishop of Tricca, in Thessaly, in the 4th century.

Charing Cross. South of Trafalgar Square in London, triangular space of roadway, named for a Gothic cross erected there in the formerly independent village of Cherringe. South of it is Whitehall guarded by the Statue of King Charles I. Cf. Lionel Johnson's poem "On the Statue of King Charles" and Francis Thompson's poem "In No Strange Land" containing the lines:

> Shall shine the traffic of Jacob's ladder
> Pitched between Heaven and Charing Cross.

Charis. In the *Iliad* the wife of Hephaestus or Vulcan. In later times any one of the three Graces.

Charity. See COWPER, WILLIAM.

charivari. A mock serenade of discordant noise, a disorderly demonstration after a wedding in the west. Also **chivaree, shivaree.** *The London Charivari,* meaning a medley of jest, is the subtitle of *Punch,* the famous English comic paper.

Charlemagne. Charles the Great, King of the Franks and Emperor of the West (742–814). Historically Charlemagne is a very distinct figure of whose deeds and characteristics there is a definite record; but there grew up during the Middle Ages tales of a quite different and mythical Charlemagne, the center of a cycle of romances concerned with wars against the Saracens. The principal source of the early Carolingian legends is a chronicle which was long falsely attributed to Archbishop TURPIN, a contemporary of Charlemagne, and which relates the heroic deeds of Charlemagne's famous Twelve Paladins. For the most important of these legends, see under *Paladins* and separate entries for individual names. The Carolingian legends form the subject matter of the famous French *Chanson de Roland* and of the Italian epic poems *Orlando Innamorato* and *Orlando Furioso,* by Boiardo and Ariosto respectively (see ROLAND), as well as of a host of lesser romances. See also CAROLINGIAN.

Charles I and **Charles II** of England. See STUART.

Charles d'Orléans (1391–1465). Son of Louis of Orleans and Valentina of Milan. Inherited love of art and letters. Captured by the English in 1415, he was in captivity for a quarter of a century. His best poetry was written at that time. It suggests both Petrarch and Heine. It was not printed in any amount until the 17th Century.

Charles Edward. See YOUNG PRETENDER.

Charles Emmanuel. Son of Victor Amadeus, king of Sardinia. Robert BROWNING wrote a poem called "King Victor and King Charles." See under VICTOR.

Charles Martel, i.e., Charles the Hammer. Founder of the power of the CAROLINGIANS in the Frankish state, known for his wars to drive the invading Mohammedans out of France and his victory over them at the Battle of Tours in 732. See BATTLES, FIFTEEN DECISIVE. He began the alliance with the papacy which was one of the important factors in the success of his grandson Charlemagne.

Charles the Great. See CAROLINGIANS; CHARLEMAGNE.

Charleston. An extremely popular American ballroom dance, in four-four time, Negro in origin, introduced in 1922. Cf. BLACK BOTTOM.

Charleston School. A group of American literary men of the South in the years before the Civil War, centered in Charleston, S.C. It included Paul Hamilton HAYNE, William Gillmore SIMMS, and Henry TIMROD.

Charlestown, Mass., with Bunker Hill. First great battle of American Revolution; actually fought on Breed's Hill nearby June 17, 1775. The anniversary of the battle is celebrated as *Bunker Hill Day.*

Charles's Wain, Charles' Wain. An old popular name for the Great Bear. The constellation forms the rough outline of a wheelbarrow or rustic wagon, and the "Charles" stands for "CHARLEMAGNE," probably owing to the similarity of the names *Arcturus* and *Arturus* (*Lat.* for Arthur), and the confusion in the popular mind between the legendary cycles of romance connected with King Arthur and Charlemagne, respectively.

Charley, plu. Charleys. An old watchman or "night guardian," before the reorganization of the English police force in 1829. See *Bobby.* So called from Charles I, who extended and improved the English police system.

Charley's Aunt. An immensely popular comedy by Brandon Thomas (1892), revived on the American stage with José Ferrer in the principal rôle.

Charlot, André Eugène Maurice (1882–). British theatrical manager and producer born in Paris and well known for *Charlot's Revue.*

Charlotte. (1) A character in Goethe's novel, WERTHER. See THE BELOVED RETURNS.

(2) In Dickens' *Oliver Twist,* a dishonest, rough servant girl, who ill-treats Oliver Twist, and robs her master, Sowerberry.

Charlotte Baynes, see BAYNES, CHARLOTTE.

Charlotte Elisabeth of Bavaria (1652–1722). Daughter of Charles Louis, Elector Palatine.

Second wife of Philippe d'Orléans, brother of Louis XIV. Her *Letters,* translated 1855, 1880, are full of delightful gossip. In Germany her healthy common sense and habit of calling a spade a spade endeared her to the people who remember her even now as *Liselotte von der Pfalz.* At the court of Versailles she was something like a bull in a china shop.

Charlottesville, Virginia. Site of the University of Virginia, founded in 1819.

Charlotte Temple. An early American novel by Susannah Haswell Rowson (published in England, 1790; America, 1794) which has run through more than a hundred editions and is still occasionally read. The heroine is lured from her English home and deserted in New York by a British officer named Montrésor. She was a real person, probably Charlotte Stanley, but her tomb in Trinity Churchyard, New York, bears the name *Charlotte Temple.*

Charlus, Palamède, Baron de. One of the leading characters in Marcel Proust's REMEMBRANCE OF THINGS PAST. He is an aristocrat, a member of the ancient family of de GUERMANTES and uncle of Robert SAINT-LOUP, a friend of the narrator, MARCEL. In society, the Baron is proud and imperious, doing all he can to conceal the fact that in secret taste and practice he is a depraved homosexual, verging on insanity as he grows older. CITIES OF THE PLAIN, Book IV of the series, gives a full account of the Baron's character and his vices. De Charlus is regarded as one of Proust's masterly creations, and is considered by some critics to have been drawn in large part from Robert de Montesquiou, an actual personage with whom the author was friendly in his youth.

Charmian. In Shakespeare's *Antony and Cleopatra* and Dryden's ALL FOR LOVE, a kindhearted, simple-minded attendant on Cleopatra. After the Queen's death, she applies one of the asps to her own arm; and when the Roman soldiers enter the room, falls down dead. Rider Haggard in his romance *Cleopatra* represents her as in love with HARMACHIS.

Charnwood, 1st Baron. **Godfrey Rathbone Benson** (1864–1945). English biographer chiefly known in the U.S. for his *Abraham Lincoln* (1916).

Charon. In classic myth, the ferryman of the STYX.

Charon's toll. A coin, about equal to a penny, placed in the mouth or hand of the dead by the ancient Greeks to pay Charon for ferrying the spirit across the river Styx to the Elysian fields.

Charon's staircase. In the Greek theater, a flight of steps from mid-stage to the orchestra.

Charpentier, Gustave (1860–). French composer whose opera *Louise* is widely known.

Charter, the Atlantic, see ATLANTIC CHARTER.

Charteris, John. In the contemporary novels of James Branch CABELL, a novelist, the supposed author of the series of essays entitled *Beyond Life* (1919). Charteris is prominent in CORDS OF VANITY in which he is depicted as the hero of almost as many illicit amatory episodes as his young friend Robert Townsend, the hero of the novel.

Charteris, Leslie (1907–). English writer of stories of crime and adventure. Noted for creation of "the Saint," a latter-day Raffles. Charteris' real name is Leslie Charles Bowyer Lin. His father was a Chinese surgeon, his mother an Englishwoman.

Charter Oak. Oak tree in Hartford, Conn. where the Charter of Connecticut, rescued from Governor Andros in 1687, is said to have been concealed. It was blown down in August, 1856.

Chartier, Alain (1385?– after 1433). Called the "father of French letters," but remembered mainly for his poetry, particularly *La Belle dame sans merci* (a title later used by Keats). His prose, however, modeled on Seneca made him a classic to the 16th Century.

Chartism. The political system of the English Chartists, who, in 1838, demanded the *People's Charter,* consisting of five principles: universal suffrage, annual parliaments, stipendiary members, vote by ballot, and electoral districts. They disappeared as a party about 1849.

the Chartist Clergyman. Charles KINGSLEY (1819–1875) because of his novel, ALTON LOCKE.

Chartres, Cathedral of. Famous Gothic cathedral at Chartres, France. Several churches were built on its site throughout the Middle Ages and subsequently destroyed by fire, but the main building as it appears today was erected between 1194 and 1220, with additions later. Chartres is particularly celebrated for its stained-glass windows. In MONT-SAINT-MICHEL AND CHARTRES, by Henry ADAMS, the cathedral of Chartres serves as a symbol of the spirit of unity of the Middle Ages.

chartreuse. A liqueur of complex composition. Also a color, called green or yellow according to brilliance. Named after LA GRANDE CHARTREUSE, the home of the CARTHUSIANS, where chartreuse was originally distilled.

Charudatta. The hero of the old Sanskrit drama known as THE LITTLE CLAY CART.

Charybdis. A whirlpool on the coast of Sicily. SCYLLA and Charybdis are employed to signify two equal dangers. Thus Horace says an author trying to avoid Scylla, drifts into Charybdis, *i.e.* seeking to avoid one fault, falls into another.

The Homeric account says that Charybdis dwelt under an immense fig tree on the rock, and that thrice every day he swallowed the waters of the sea and thrice threw them up again; but later legends have it that he stole the oxen of Hercules, was killed by lightning, and changed into the gulf.

Chase, Mary Ellen (1887–). American educator and novelist. Her best-known novel is *Mary Peters.* Her locale is boat-building and fisherman's Maine north of the farmland of which Gladys Hasty CARROLL writes.

Chase, Salmon Portland (1808–1873). American statesman. Prominent in defending fugitive slaves, active in free-soil movement. Chief justice, U.S. Supreme Court (1864–1873). As Lincoln's Secretary of Treasury (1861–1864), originated national banking system.

Chase, Stuart (1888–). American economist and author of popular books on governmental control and liberal reform. His works include *The Tragedy of Waste* (1925), dealing with conservation of natural power and resources; *Your Money's Worth* (1927), advice to the consumer; *Mexico: A Study of Two Americas* (1931); *A New Deal* (1932), a book on economic reform whose title became the name of the reform program of President Franklin D. ROOSEVELT (see NEW DEAL); *Rich Land, Poor Land* (1936), on conservation; and *The Tyranny of Words* (1938), a popular study of SEMANTICS.

Chase, William Merritt (1849–1916). Leading American painter. Landscapes, portraits, still lifes.

Chastelard. In Swinburne's tragedy of that name (1865), a gentleman of Dauphiny, who falls in love with Mary, Queen of Scots. He is discovered in the Queen's bedroom. Chastelard was a historical personage who atoned for his sin on the scaffold. Swinburne's drama shows Mary Beaton, one of the Queen's ladies, in love with him, but to little avail. The tragedy is the first of a trilogy. See MARY QUEEN OF SCOTS.

château (*Fr.*). A feudal castle, especially in France. Hence the fact that the names of a good many wines, grown on the estates belonging to such castles, have the word *château* as the first part of their names. Cf. *Château Lafite, Château d'Yquem,* etc.

Chateaubriand, François René de (1768–1848). French novelist, a forerunner of the Romantic movement in France, whose work is marked by the characteristic Romantic qualities of melancholy, impassioned emotion, individualism, a fondness for wild nature, primitive tribes, and distant, exotic countries, and a strong attraction to the Catholicism of the Middle Ages. He had a stormy career and was prominent in the politics of his time, favoring the Bourbon monarchy, under which he served as ambassador to England, Italy, and Germany, and as Minister of Foreign Affairs. Chateaubriand is most famous for his fictional portrayals of America and the Orient. ATALA (1801), RENÉ (1802), and LES NATCHEZ (1826) are novels dealing with North America and the North American Indians; LES MARTYRS (1809) and L'ITINÉRAIRE DE PARIS À JÉRUSALEM ET DE JÉRUSALEM À PARIS (1811) are concerned with Greece, the Holy Land, and the Near East. Others of Chateaubriand's works are LE GÉNIE DU CHRISTIANISME (*The Genius of Christianity*) (1802) and MÉMOIRES D'OUTRE-TOMBE (*Memoirs from Beyond the Tomb*) (1848–1850). He had a great influence on the writers of the French Romantic school, among whom are considered to be LAMARTINE, George SAND, FLAUBERT in *Salammbô,* and Pierre LOTI.

Château-Thierry. In France on Marne River. During World War I American troops won their first success here against the Germans. On August 27, 28, 1944, the American Third Army drove through it again and went 22 miles beyond to take Soissons.

Châtelet, Marquise **du. Gabrielle Émilie Le Tonnelier de Breteuil** (1706–1749). Among the finest female minds of her time. Mistress of Voltaire, living with him at Montjeu and at Château de Cirey. The connection lasted 14 years until her death. The Marquise had an intense interest in mathematics and the theories of Leibnitz and Newton. Wrote *Traité sur le Bonheur* and *Traduction des Principes de Newton.*

Chatfield-Taylor, Hobart Chatfield (1865–1945). Wealthy American writer of Chicago.

Chatham, Lord. William Pitt (1708–1778). British statesman. Used his influence on behalf of the American colonies though unwilling to recognize their independence from England.

Chatrian, Alexandre. See under ERCKMANN-CHATRIAN.

Chatterley, Lady. See LADY CHATTERLEY'S LOVER.

Chatterton, Edward Keble (1878–1944). English journalist, author of many books on ships, as *Sailing Ships* (1907), *Ship Models* (1923). In 1940 he published *The Epic of Dunkirk.*

Chatterton, Thomas (1752–1770). English poet, known for his literary frauds distinguished by poetic genius. He wrote a number of poems which he pretended were the work of one Thomas Rowley, a non-existent monk of the 15th century. His deception was successful for awhile, although it was exposed in 1777. He also wrote *Apostate Will* (1764), a satire, and *The Revenge* (1770), a successful burlesque opera. In despair at his poverty in London, he committed suicide by poison at the age of seventeen. A volume of his "collected works" was published in 1803, but many of his poems are said to be still in manuscript, being considered too obscene to publish. Chatterton was a favorite figure in the writings of the English Romantic poets. Cf. also the drama *Chatterton* by Alfred de Vigny (1835).

Chaucer, Geoffrey (ca. 1343–1400). Middle English poet, considered the greatest literary figure of his age and one of the most important of English poets. He lived an extremely active life, having been a soldier in the English army in France, a commercial agent for the English government in Italy, a customs comptroller of hides and skins and wines, a country justice of the peace, a member of Parliament, Clerk of the King's Works, and a deputy forester for the crown. He was associated with John of Gaunt, Duke of LANCASTER, who at one time was his patron, and was an important public figure of his time. Chaucer's work is usually divided into three literary periods: (1) the French period (1355?–1370), when he was influenced by the French poets of the day, including FROISSART, Eustace Deschamps, Guillaume Machaut, Guillaume Deguilleville, etc.; (2) the Italian period (1370–1385), when he was influenced by the Italian literature he encountered on his trip to Italy, especially by the works of BOCCACCIO; and (3) the English period (1385–1400), when he did his best work. Chaucer's most famous and greatest work is THE CANTERBURY TALES, begun about 1386. His version of the famous TROILUS story, *Troilus and Criseyde* (ca. 1385), is his next best-known work. Other works, on which, as on all of Chaucer's writings, there is much scholarly debate as to date of composition and source, include THE BOOK OF THE DUCHESS; THE HOUSE OF FAME; ANELIDA AND ARCITE; THE PARLIAMENT OF FOWLS; BOECE (*Boethius*); THE LEGEND OF GOOD WOMEN; a fragmentary translation of THE ROMANCE OF THE ROSE; A TREATISE ON THE ASTROLABE; and a number of shorter poems, some of which are only doubtfully attributed to him. In his work, Chaucer summed up the ideas, attitudes, and literary themes and forms of the Middle Ages, as well as stamping upon it, for the first time in English literature, the mark of a definite personality. He is known for his humor, his realism, his psychological insight, the accuracy of his observation, and the grace and technical excellence of his style. The poets of the 15th century in England, notably Spenser, looked on Chaucer as their literary master. The Middle English dialect in which he wrote, that of London, became the basis for the standard English language of today.

Chaucer of France. Clément Marot (1496–1544).

Chaucer of Painting. Albrecht Dürer of Nuremberg (1471–1528).

Chauchat, Claudia. In Thomas Mann's THE MAGIC MOUNTAIN, a beautiful Russian patient at the HAUS BERGHOF. She has red hair, bites her fingernails, dresses carelessly, and slams doors. She has a powerful and mysterious attraction for Hans CASTORP, the hero, who is unable to leave the mountain while she is there. She has the qualities of a mythological enchantress, and has been compared to such figures as VENUS and ASTARTE.

Chauncey, Charles (1705–1787). American churchman, known for his opposition to the preachings of Jonathan EDWARDS. His best-known writings are those in which he sought to refute the genuineness of the violent conversions that accompanied the GREAT AWAKENING: *The New Creature Described, and Considered as the Sure Characteristic of a Man's Being in Christ* (1741), *The Out-Pouring of the Holy Ghost* (1742), and *Enthusiasm Described and Cautioned Against* (1742), all three sermons; and *Seasonable Thoughts on the State of Religion in New England* (1743), a book in reply to Edwards' *Some Thoughts Concerning the Present Revival of Religion in New England.* Chauncey was a liberal in his views on both religion and politics, and was well known in America and Great Britain. His political writings include: the *Massachusetts Election Sermon* (1747), which warns the British governors that all government originates in God and they must not exceed the bounds of their power; *A Discourse on the Good News from a Far Country* (1766), dealing with the Stamp Act; *Trust in God the Duty of a People in a Day of Trouble* (1770); *A Letter to a Friend, Giving a Concise but Just Representation of the Hardships and Sufferings the Town of Boston Is Exposed to . . . in Consequence of the Late Act of the British Parliament* (1774); and *The Accursed Thing Must Be Taken Away from the People* (1778). The *Massachusetts Election Sermon* aroused so much opposition among the Boston Tories that for a time it was not permitted publication.

Chautauqua. An institution which offers a popular program of lectures, entertainments, etc. The original or mother Chautauqua is a summer resort on Lake Chautauqua, N.Y., but the name has been popularized by traveling *Chautauquas* which go from place to place presenting a week's program, usually in a big tent.

Chauve Souris. The entertainment offered by a group of Russian comedians, under the direction of Nikita Balieff. The group took their name from the Russian word for "bat," in French, *Chauve Souris.* "The Bat" was a Moscow institution before World War I; after the war it was reorganized in Paris and later came to New York.

chauvinism. Blind and pugnacious patriotism of an exaggerated kind; unreasoning jingoism. Nicholas Chauvin, a soldier of the French Republic and Empire, was madly devoted to Napoleon and his cause. He was introduced as a type of exaggerated bellicose patriotism into a number of plays. Scribe's *Le Soldat laboureur,* Cogniard's *La Cocarde tricolore,* 1831, Bayard and Dumanoir's *Les Aides de camps,* Charet's *Conscrit Chauvin,* are some of them. The term *chauvinism* spread quickly into a great number of languages.

Cheeryble Brothers. In Dickens' novel NICHOLAS NICKLEBY, brother Ned and brother Charles, the incarnations of all that is warm-hearted, generous and kind. They were once homeless boys running about the streets barefooted; and, when they grew to be wealthy London merchants, were ever ready to stretch forth a helping hand to those struggling against the buffets of fortune.

Cheese, Rev. Cream. In *The Potiphar Papers,* a series of satires on New York life by G. W. Curtis (*Am.* 1856), a high church Episcopalian minister. He gives Mrs. Potiphar solemn advice on the proper color for her prayer-book cover and other important religious matters. He was very popular in the dramatized version.

Chavez, Carlos (1899–). Mexican orchestra leader and composer of operatic ballet *H.P.* presented in Philadelphia by Leopold Stokowski.

Cheapside. Anciently **The Cheap.** London street running east from St. Paul's Churchyard, formerly noted for its shops. Before the Great Fire of 1666, it was an open square, where markets and fairs were held.

Cheka. In Soviet government, secret police acting against counter-revolutionary movements. From *che* and *ka,* the initial Russian letters of the words for "extraordinary commission." In 1922 succeeded by the Gay-Pay-Oo (OGPU).

Chekhov, Anton Pavlovich (1860–1904). Russian dramatist, novelist, and short-story writer, known for the irony and pathos of his studies of frustrated middle-class lives in the Russian provinces, and for his skillful and penetrating delineation of character. His best-known play is THE CHERRY ORCHARD (1904); and other works for the theater include *Ivanov* (1887), *The Seagull, Uncle Vanya,* and *The Three Sisters. The Peasants, My Life,* and *Ward No. 6* are among his novels. Chekhov's short stories are considered among the most distinguished examples of the form, and influenced a number of the leading authors of short stories in the 20th century, including James JOYCE and Katherine MANSFIELD.

chela. In India, a disciple. Cf. *Kim,* by Rudyard Kipling.

Chelsea Rooming House. See GREGORY, HORACE.

Cheltenham. A style of type.

Cheney, Sheldon Warren (1886–). American writer on art and the theatre. Author of *Modern Art and the Theatre* (1921), *A World History of Art* (1937), etc.

Chénier, André Marie de (1762–1794). French poet, sympathetic with the French Revolution in its first years, although he later attacked Robespierre and was guillotined. His chief poems were written in a classical manner, by which he sought to recapture the outlook of the original Greeks. He also wrote 18th-century neo-Classical verse, political poems and satires, and philosophical poetry celebrating the science of his day. His best-known poem and also his last is *La Jeune captive,* written in prison about a fellow victim.

Chennault, Claire Lee (1891–). American general and aviator. Demonstrated the use of parachute troops (1926). Resigned from U.S. Army (1937). Subsequent to Japanese invasion of China became air adviser to Chiang Kai-shek and formed the volunteer air corps, the "Flying Tigers" to aid China, superseded by the U.S. Fourteenth Air Force under General Chennault (1943). Protected Burma Road against superior Japanese air forces (1941). Commanded U.S. Army air forces in China. Made Major General in 1943.

Cheops. See under PYRAMID.

Chequers. The official country seat of the prime ministers of England. It is an historic Tudor house, thirty-five miles northwest of London, which was presented to the government in 1917 by Lord and Lady Lee of Fareham.

Cherokee strip. A narrow strip of land along the Southern border of what is now the State of Kansas, ceded by the Cherokee Indians to the U.S. in 1866.

Cherry Fair. A sort of passing show that will not last. Gower says of this world, "Alle is but a cherye-fayre," a phrase frequently met with. The phrase comes from the Cherry Fairs, held in Worcestershire and elsewhere. They may have been held in cherry orchards, but another explanation is that they were "cheery" fairs—*i.e.* gay or merry-making occasions.

Cherry Orchard, The. A play by Anton CHEKHOV (1904). The estate of Madame Ranievskaya is about to be sold for debt. She and her brother and daughter turn a deaf and horrified ear to the plan of Lopachin, a rich neighbor of serf ancestry, who suggests that they cut down the orchard and turn it into suburban lots. They talk excitedly and at length but do nothing, and when the sale comes, Lopachin buys the estate and carries out the plan himself. Bernard Shaw presented an adaptation of this play in his HEARTBREAK HOUSE.

chersonese. A peninsula. The Cimbrian Chersonese is Jutland; the Tauric Chersonese, the Crimea; the Thracian Chersonese, Gallipoli; the Golden Chersonese, the Malay peninsula; etc.

Cherubic Doctor. St. Thomas Aquinas. See under SAINT.

Cherubim, Don. The titular hero of Le Sage's BACHELOR OF SALAMANCA.

Cherubini, Maria Luigi Carlo Zenobio Salvatore (1760–1842). Italian composer. *Ifigenia in Aulide* (1787).

Chery and Fair-star. One of the best known of Countess d'Aulnoy's *Fairy Tales* (*Fr.* 1682). Prince Chery (*Chéri*) and his cousin Princess Fair-star are set adrift in infancy, but after numerous adventures find their way back to their own kingdom. The tale is remembered chiefly for the three magic gifts which Chery secures for Fair-star: (1) *the dancing water,* which has the gift of imparting beauty; (2) *the singing apple,* which has the gift of imparting wit; and (3) *the green bird,* which can reveal all secrets. By this bird the story of their birth is made known, and Fair-star marries Chery.

Cheshire cat. In *Alice in Wonderland* by Lewis Carroll. When it vanished, its grin vanished last of all. Hence the phrase, *to grin like a Cheshire cat.*

Cheshire Cheese. A famous inn on Wine Office Court, Fleet Street, London, where Dr. Johnson used to dine. *Cheshire cheese* is a kind of hard cheese, originally made in Cheshire county, England.

Chesnutt, Charles Waddell (1858–1932). The first American Negro novelist. *The Conjure Woman* (1899), etc. Praised by William Dean Howells. Awarded the Spingarn Gold Medal for pioneer work as a literary artist in depicting the Negro (1928).

Chester, George Randolph (1869–1924). American novelist and short-story writer, creator of the character Get-Rich-Quick Wallingford.

Chester, Sir John. In Dickens' BARNABY RUDGE, a plausible, foppish villain, the sworn enemy of Geoffrey Haredale, by whom he is killed in a duel as a result of his effort to put an end to the match between Emma Haredale and his son Edward.

Chester Cycle. A series of twenty-four MYSTERY PLAYS performed by the guilds of Chester at Whitsuntide (13th to 16th centuries).

Chesterfield, Lord (1694–1773). The author of a famous series of *Letters* to his son, chiefly regarding the manner in which a gentleman should conduct himself in all the affairs of life. Hence, *Chesterfieldian,* an adjective applied to manners and dress of gentlemanly correctness.

Chesterton, Gilbert Keith (1874–1936). English journalist and author of biography, history, fiction, essays, and plays. His books include *The Man Who Was Thursday* (1908), a novel; a series of detective stories beginning in 1911 and dealing with the adventures of FATHER BROWN, a priest; *A Short History of England* (1917); *The Everlasting Man* (1925), an outline of history; *Come to Think of It* (1930) and *As I Was Saying* (1936), essays; *Autobiography* (1936). Chesterton was converted to Catholicism in 1922 and, like Hilaire BELLOC, frequently expressed his religious views in his writings.

chestnut. A stale joke. The term is said to have been popularized in America by a Boston actor named Warren, who, on a certain apposite occasion, quoted from *The Broken Sword,* a forgotten melodrama by William Dimond, which was first produced in 1816 at Covent Garden. Captain Xavier, a principal character, is for ever repeating the same yarns, with variations. He is telling about one of his exploits connected with a cork tree, when Pablo corrects him, "A chestnut-tree, you mean, captain." "Bah!" replies the captain, "I say a cork-tree." "A chestnut-tree," insists Pablo. "I must know better than you," says the captain, "it was a cork-tree, I say." "A chestnut," persists Pablo. "I have heard you tell the joke twenty-seven times, and it was always a chestnut before."

Chettam, Sir James. In George Eliot's MIDDLEMARCH, the lover who wins Dorothea Brooke's sister Celia.

Chettle, Henry (1560?–?1607). English dramatist. Wrote or collaborated on some forty-eight Elizabethan plays. Author of an elegy on Queen Elizabeth.

chevalier.

the Chevalier or *Chevalier de St. George.* James Stuart (1688–1766), the Old Pretender.

the Young Chevalier. Charles Edward Stuart (1720–1788), the Young Pretender.

le Chevalier sans peur et sans reproche. The French hero, BAYARD (1473–1524).

Chevalier, Maurice (1889–). French actor and singer in variety and moving pictures.

Chevalier de Maison Rouge, Le (The Knight of the Red House). A romance by Alexandre DUMAS. The titular hero attempts to rescue Marie Antoinette from the Tower, but succeeds only in unwittingly preventing her rescue by others and is killed by his rival conspirators. The novel has a basis in the career of A. D. J. Gonze de Rougeville, but presents a highly idealized version of his story.

Chevy Chase. A celebrated ancient ballad with a Scottish version earlier than 1549. There is evidence to indicate that it has grown out of the traditions of the Battle of Otterbourne (1388).

Chew, Samuel Claggett (1888–). Professor at Bryn Mawr; writer on Byron, Swinburne, etc.

Cheyne, Harvey. The boy hero of Kipling's CAPTAINS COURAGEOUS.

Chiang Kai-shek (1888–). Generalissimo of the Chinese Army and President of the Executive Yuan. First became protégé of Sun Yat-sen who sent him to Russia to study Soviet military methods. On Sun Yat-sen's death he became the leader of the Nationalist movement. In 1926 he broke with Russian communists to get the support of Shanghai bankers. Fought against communistic elements in China. Was kidnaped by one of his own allies who demanded that he unite with communists against Japan. Freed, he formed a so-called united China. When the United Nations organized in 1942, he was made Commander-in-Chief of the Chinese theater of war. For Mme Chiang Kai-shek, see CHIANG MEI-LING.

Chiang Mei-ling (1898–). American-educated, Christian Chinese wife of Generalissimo Chiang Kai-shek, commander-in-chief of the armies of China in their war against the invading Japanese (1932–1945). She became known throughout the world for her activities in the administration of the national affairs of her country, for her constructive influence on the policies of her husband, and for her importation of Western ideas and methods into China. *China Fights for Her Life* (1938), *China in Peace and War* (1940), and *This Is Our China* (1940) are books by Mme. Chiang, written in English.

chiaroscuro (Ital.). "A method of painting with deep shadows emphasizing the modelling and atmosphere, thus creating a pictorial design through light and dark areas." (*Harper's Encyclopedia of Art.*) CARAVAGGIO and REMBRANDT were outstanding painters of chiaroscuro effects.

Chibiabos. The musician in Longfellow's *Hiawatha;* the harmony of nature personified. He teaches the birds to sing and the brooks to warble as they flow. "All the many sounds of nature borrow sweetness from his singing."

Chicago. A poem in free verse by Carl SANDBURG, celebrating the Midwestern American city for its vitality amid its evil and brutality. It appears in CHICAGO POEMS.

Chicago Group. A group of American writers, living in Chicago and dealing with Middle Western subjects in their works, which flourished from about 1912 to about 1925. It included Sherwood ANDERSON, Floyd DELL, Theodore DREISER, Ben HECHT, and Carl SANDBURG. POETRY: A MAGAZINE OF VERSE and THE LITTLE REVIEW were the leading magazines of the group.

Chicago Poems. A volume of poetry by Carl SANDBURG, published in 1916 and dealing with the Middle West. It served to establish his reputation as a poet.

Chichen-Itza. Ancient city of Yucatan, Mexico, founded in 530 A.D., with well-preserved ruins of the MAYAN civilization.

Chichikov. The rascally hero of Gogol's DEAD SOULS.

Chichivache. A fabulous animal that lived only on good women, and was hence all skin and bone, because its food was so extremely scarce; the antitype to BICORNE. Chaucer introduced the word into English from French; but in doing so he changed *chichifache* (thin or ugly face) into *chichivache* (lean or meager-looking cow), and hence the animal was pictured as a kind of bovine monstrosity.

> O noble wyves, ful of heigh prudence,
> Let noon humilitie your tonges nayle:
> Ne lat no clerk have cause or diligence
> To write of you a story of such mervayle
> As of Griseldes, pacient and kynde,
> Lest Chichivache you swolwe in hir entraile.
> Chaucer, *Envoy to the Clerk's Tale.*

Chicken, The Game. In Dickens' DOMBEY AND SON, a low fellow, to be heard of at the bar of the Black Badger. Mr. Toots selects this man as his instructor in fencing, betting, and self-defense. The Chicken has short hair, a low forehead, a broken nose, and "a considerable tract of bare and sterile country behind each ear."

Chickweed, Conkey. In Dickens' OLIVER TWIST, the famous character who robs himself. He is a licensed victualer on the point of failing, and announces that he has been robbed of 327 guineas "by a tall man with a black patch over his eye." He is much pitied, and numerous subscriptions are made on his behalf. A detective is sent to inquire into the "robbery," and Chickweed cries out, "There he is!" and runs after the hypothetical thief for a considerable distance, then losing sight of him. He is caught at the trick at last.

Chigi, Agostino (1465?–1520). Banker, born in Siena, who used his great wealth to encourage leading artists, as Peruzzi, Perugino, Sebastiano del Piombo, and especially Raphael.

Chikamatsu Monzaemon (1653–?1724). Japanese romantic dramatist. Sometimes called "the Shakespeare of Japan." Created new type of drama. Composed nearly one hundred five-act plays, half of which are still produced or read.

Child, Francis James (1825–1896). American philologist. Authority on the ballad. *English and Scottish Popular Ballads* (5 vols., 1883–1898). See also George Lyman KITTREDGE.

Child, Richard Washburn (1881–1935). American writer and diplomat. U.S. Ambassador to Italy (1921–1924). Wrote many romances and several factual works.

Child, Lydia Maria (1802–1880). American author and reformer, an active worker for the abolition of slavery and the emancipation of women. She wrote historical novels and anti-slavery tracts, including *Anti-Slavery Catechism* (1836) and *The Evils of Slavery and the Cure of Slavery* (1836).

Childe. In *Childe Harold, Childe Roland, Childe Tristram,* etc., "Childe" is a title of honor, like the Spanish *infante* and *infanta.* In the times of chivalry, noble youths who were candidates for knighthood were, during their time of probation, called *infans, valets, damoysels, bacheliers,* and *childe.*

Childe Harold. Byron's poem which depicts a man sated of the world, who roams from place to place to flee from himself. The "Childe" is, in fact, Lord Byron himself, who was only twenty-one when he began, and twenty-eight when he finished the poem. In canto I (1809), he visits Portugal and Spain; in canto II (1810), Turkey in Europe; in canto III (1816), Belgium and Switzerland; and in canto IV (1817), Venice, Rome, and Florence. The French composer BERLIOZ based his overture *Harold en Italie* on Byron's poem.

Childe or **Gil Morrice.** The hero of an old Scottish ballad, natural son of an earl and the wife of Lord Barnard, and brought up "in the gude grene wode." Lord Barnard, thinking the Childe to be his wife's lover, slays him with a broadsword, and setting his head on a spear gives it to "the meanest man in a' his train" to carry to the lady. When she sees it she says to the baron, "Wi' that same spear, O pierce my heart, and put me out o' pain"; but the baron replies, "Enouch of blood by me's bin spilt, sair, sair I rew the deid," adding—

> I'll ay lament for Gil Morice,
> As gin he were mine ain;
> I'll neir forget the dreiry day
> On which the youth was slain.
>
> Percy's *Reliques,* ser. iii. 1.

Percy says this pathetic tale suggested to Home the plot of his tragedy, *Douglas.*

Childe Roland (sometimes spelled *Rowland*). Youngest brother of the "fair burd Helen" in the old Scottish ballad. Guided by Merlin, he undertakes to bring back his sister from Elf-land, whither the fairies have carried her, and succeeds in his perilous exploit.

> Childe Roland to the dark tower came;
> His word was still "Fie, foh, and fum,
> I smell the blood of a Britishman."
>
> Shakespeare, *King Lear,* iii. 4.

Browning's poem, *Childe Roland to the Dark Tower Came,* in title suggested by the Shakespeare passage above, is not connected in any way (except by the first line) with the old ballad.

Childers, Erskine (1870–1922). Anglo-Irish writer and politician. Wrote a history of the Boer War, and a curiously prophetic novel, *The Riddle of the Sands* (1903), concerning a carefully planned invasion of England by Germany. The second edition of this remarkable book was published, at the insistence of Christopher Morley, in November 1940 when the Luftwaffe attack over London was at its peak. Though Childers received promotion and the D.S.C. in World War I, he devoted the rest of his life to securing Irish independence. On establishment of the Irish Free State government, Childers joined the Republican Army. He was shot by a firing squad of Free State soldiers, after shaking hands with them all, on Nov. 24, 1922.

Childers, Haveth, Everywhere. One of the several excerpts from Joyce's *Finnegans Wake,* published separately in 1931, the other separate parts published being *Anna Livia Plurabelle* (1932); *Two Tales of Shem and Shaun* (1932); and *The Mime of Mick, Nick and the Maggies* (1934).

Childe Waters. The hero of a ballad in Percy's *Reliques.* He is cruel to his love, the fair Ellen who accompanies him on his travels as his foot-page, but finally relents and marries her.

Child in the House, The. A study by Walter PATER (1894) of his own childhood.

Children and Fools. See MANN, THOMAS.

Children in the Wood. A ballad in Percy's *Reliques* III. ii. 18. The story is, shortly, as follows: The master of Wayland Hall, Norfolk, leaves a little son and daughter to the care of his wife's brother; both are to have money, but if the children die first the uncle is to become the heir. After twelve months the uncle hires two ruffians to murder the babes; one of the ruffians relents and kills his fellow, leaving the children in a wood; they die during the night, and "Robin Redbreast" covers them over with leaves. All things go ill with the wicked uncle; his sons die, his barns are fired, his cattle die, and he himself perishes in jail. After seven years the ruffian is taken up for highway robbery, and confesses the whole affair. An old melodrama by Robert Farrington (1599) also embodied the tale.

children of Ler. In Irish legend the children of Ler, the Celtic Neptune, were transformed by his second wife into swans, with power to speak and to sing for thrice three hundred years.

Children of the Earth. A drama of New England life by Alice Brown (Am. 1915) which was awarded the prize of $10,000 offered by Winthrop Ames, director of the Little Theater of New York, for the best American play by an American author.

Children of the Mist. In Scott's *Legend of Montrose,* a branch of the clan MacGregor, a band of Highland outlaws.

Children of the Soil. A novel by H. Sienkiewicz (*Pol.* 1894). The hero is Pan Stanislas Polanyetski, and the heroine, whom he finally marries, Maryina Plaritski. The book gives a vivid and comprehensive picture of Polish life.

Children of the Sun. The ancient people who erected megaliths.

Children's Crusade. A crusade of about fifty thousand unarmed children, which set out in 1212 from France and Germany to recover the Holy Sepulcher. It was a complete failure, but the naive purity of faith which inspired it has remained a beautiful symbol of medieval civilization.

Children's Hour, The. A poem by Longfellow (1859). Also a play by Lillian Hellman (1934), based on a case described in William ROUGHEAD's *Bad Companions* (1931).

Childs, Marquis William (1903–). American journalist. Author of *Sweden—The Middle Way* (1936), *I Write from Washington* (1942), etc.

Child's Garden of Verses, A. See STEVENSON, ROBERT LOUIS.

Chillingly, Kenelm, see KENELM CHILLINGLY.

Chillingworth, Roger. In Hawthorne's SCARLET LETTER the name assumed by Hester Prynne's physician husband in order to work his cruel revenge on Arthur Dimmesdale, the clergyman who is the father of Hester's child.

Chillingworth, William (1602–1644). English Protestant prose writer, at one time a Roman Catholic in belief. He is known for his work entitled *The Religion of the Protestants a Safe Way to Salvation* (1638).

Chillon, Prisoner of. François de Bonnivard (d. about 1570), a Genevan prelate and politician. In his poem of that title, Byron makes him one of six brothers, all of whom suffer for their opinions. The father and two sons die on the battlefield; one is burnt at the stake; three are incarcerated in the dungeon of Chillon, on the edge of the Lake of Geneva. Of these, two die, and François, who has been imprisoned for "republican principles" by the Duke-Bishop of Savoy, is set at liberty by "the Bearnais." Although Bonnivard was an actual prisoner at Chillon, the rest of the tale and the idealized character of the man seem to have been Byron's own invention.

Chills and Fever. A volume of poems by John Crowe RANSOM.

Chiltern Hundreds. In British history, a hundred is a division of a county. The Chiltern hundreds are Stoke, Desborough, and Burnham, in Buckinghamshire. At one time the Chilterns, i.e., the hills between Bedford and Hertford, etc., were much frequented by robbers, so a steward was appointed by the Crown to put them down. The necessity has long since ceased, but the office remains; and, since 1740, when a Member of Parliament wishes to vacate his seat, one way of doing so is by applying for the stewardship of the Chiltern Hundreds; for no member of Parliament may resign his seat, but if he accepts an office of profit under the Crown he is obliged to be re-elected if he wishes to remain a member. The Stewardship of the Manor of Northstead (Yorks) is used in the same way. The gift of both is in the hands of the Chancellor of the Exchequer; it was refused to a member for Reading in 1842.

The Stewardships of Old Sarum (Sussex), East Hendred (Berks), Poynings (Sussex), Hempholwic (Yorks), were formerly used for the same purpose, as were (till 1838) the Escheatorships of Munster and Ulster.

Chilton, Eleanor Carroll (1898–). American novelist, poet and playwright. Wrote *Shadows Waiting, The Burning Fountain,* and, in collaboration with her former husband Herbert Agar, *The Garment of Praise.* She is a fastidious artist.

Chimborazo.

> Chimborazo, Cotopaxi,
> They had stolen my soul away!

Last lines of a well-known poem by the Australian poet, W. J. Turner (1889–). Chimborazo and Cotopaxi are peaks in the South American Andes.

Chimaera (*Gr. chimaira,* a "she-goat"). A fabulous monster of Greek mythology, described by Homer as a monster with a goat's body, a lion's head, and a dragon's tail. It was born in Lycia, and was slain by Bellerophon. Hence the term *chimera* is used in English for an illusory fancy, a wild, incongruous scheme.

Chimes, The. A Christmas story by Dickens (1844). It is about some bells which ring the old year out and the new year in. Trotty Veck, a little old London ticket-porter and messenger hears the Christmas chimes, and receives from them both comfort and encouragement.

Chimney-Sweeper, The. One of William BLAKE's early humanitarian poems, appearing in *Songs of Experience.*

Chinaman, John, see JOHN CHINAMAN.

Chinatown. That section of an American city, particularly of San Francisco or New York, inhabited by Chinese. In both of the above-mentioned cities, Chinatown was formerly notorious for vice, opium and gambling dens and the like and many horrible tales of conditions are still told. Chinatown is now a commercially exploited show place, but is still the scene of *tong* feuds between the different *tongs* or secret associations and of occasional murders as a result.

Chinee, The Heathen, see HEATHEN CHINEE.

Chinese Gordon. General Gordon (killed at Khartoum in 1885), who in 1863 was placed in command of the EVER-VICTORIOUS ARMY and in the following year succeeded, after thirty-three engagements, in putting down the Taëping rebellion, which had broken out in 1851.

Chinese Parrot, The. See BIGGERS, EARL DERR.

Chingachgook. The Indian chief, friend of LEATHERSTOCKING in four of the novels of Cooper's Leatherstocking series: *The Deerslayer, The Pathfinder, The Last of the Mohicans* and *The Pioneers.* He is known as *Le Gros Serpent* (*the Great Serpent*) because of his cunning and stealth. Cooper's portrayal of Chingachgook and his son UNCAS was greatly criticized as an over-idealized conception of the American Indian.

chinook. A warm, moist southwest wind on the coast of Oregon and Washington. Called so by white settlers of Astoria because it came from the direction of a camp of Flathead Indians, i.e., Chinookans.

Chinook. Also called **Chinook jargon** or **Oregon jargon.** A mixed trade language of Chinook, other Indian, English and French elements. It was the equivalent of Pidgin English in the northwestern U.S. and neighboring Canada.

Chios, the man of. Homer, who lived at Chios, near the Aegean Sea.

Chippendale. Furniture by or in the style of Thomas Chippendale, English cabinetmaker (1718?–1779). Graceful outline with rococo ornamentation. Experts distinguish French, Chinese, and Gothic Chippendale.

Chips, Goodbye Mr. Popular novel and moving picture by James HILTON. Mr. Chips was an English schoolmaster.

Chirico, Giorgio de (1888–). Italian painter, an early leader of and an important influence on the movement of SURREALISM. He was influenced first by the Italian Renaissance painters, and is best known for his early landscapes, done before the founding of Surrealism and marked by ruins of massive classical architecture, long perspectives, deep shadows, and a sense of barrenness and immense space. Many of the paintings of Salvador DALI resemble those of de Chirico in these respects. During the 1920's, when de Chirico was definitely associated with Surrealism, he often painted faceless figures suggestive of dummies or mannequins in his characteristic landscapes.

Chiron. The centaur who taught Achilles and many other heroes music, medicine, and hunting. Jupiter placed him in heaven among the stars as Sagittarius (*the Archer*).

In the INFERNO Dante gives the name to the keeper of the lake of boiling blood, in the seventh circle of hell.

chiton. The garment worn next to the skin by both sexes in classic times. A single piece of cloth, folded, pinned, and girdled; or a loose linen gown sewed. The former is Dorian, the latter Ionian.

Chitra. A play by Sir Rabindranath TAGORE.

Chitterlings, The. See RABELAIS.

chivalry. The system of customs and conventions connected with knighthood in the Middle Ages. It included the curriculum of training the young knight to fight, hunt, serve his lord, and govern his own vassals, the system of values of the feudal aristocracy, the ceremonies connected with the knighting of the squire, and the cult of gallantry and veneration of women. See COURTLY LOVE.

Chivers, Thomas Holley (1809–1858). American poet. Associated with Edgar Allan POE (1843–1849). When accused of plagiarism from Poe (1850), he retorted by charging that Poe plagiarized from him. Made unusual experiments in metres.

Chkalov, Valeri Pavlovich (1904–1938). Soviet aviator. Order of Lenin 1935. Piloted nonstop flight (5400 miles) from Moscow over North Pole to Vancouver, Washington, in 1937.

chlamys. In classical Greece, a short mantle usually fastened by a clasp on the shoulder. It was a horseman's cloak that became the ordinary outdoor garment for young men.

Chloe. (1) The shepherdess beloved by Daphnis in the pastoral romance of Longus, entitled *Daphnis and Chloe,* and hence a generic name among romance writers and pastoral poets for a rustic maiden—not always of the artless variety.

(2) In Pope's *Moral Essays* (ii) Chloe is intended for Lady Suffolk, mistress of George II, "Content to dwell in decencies for ever." Matthew PRIOR uses the name for Mrs. Centlivre.

Chloe, Aunt. In Harriet Beecher Stowe's UNCLE TOM'S CABIN, the wife of Uncle Tom.

Chloris. The ancient Greek name of FLORA.

Choate, Rufus (1799–1859). Eminent American jury lawyer and orator. House of Representatives (1831–1834), Senate (1841–1845).

Chocano, José Santos (1875–1934). "The poetic trumpeter of the South American continent."—Alice Stone Blackwell. His *Alma América* is his masterpiece.

Chocolate Soldier, The. A character in Shaw's ARMS AND THE MAN and the name of the popular comic opera by Oscar Straus which was founded on the drama; hence, a soldier more remarkable for his faculty of appearing to good effect in uniform than for his fighting ability.

Choir Invisible, The. A novel by James Lane ALLEN (1897). John Gray, an idealistic school teacher, falls in love with Mrs. Falconer, but because of her marriage ties, she keeps their relationship that of friendliness only. When years later she writes that she is free and has always loved Gray, he has incurred other obligations. The title is borrowed from the first line and title of George Eliot's poem, *O May I Join the Choir Invisible.*

Choke, General. In Dickens' MARTIN CHUZZLEWIT, a lank North American gentleman, "one of the most remarkable men in the century." He is editor of *The Watertoast Gazette,* and a member of the "EDEN Land Corporation." It is General Choke who induces Martin Chuzzlewit to stake his all in the Eden swindle.

Cholmondeley (pronounce Chumley) **Mary** (1859–1925). English novelist. Her *Red Pottage* (1899) was "a minor literary scandal" because it satirized the pretentious complacency of the English middle class. Her niece was the novelist Stella Benson.

Chomette, René, see CLAIR, RENÉ.

Chopin, Frédéric François (1810–1849). Composer of the Romantic school, son of a French father and Polish mother, born near Warsaw but resident for most of his career in France. Famous for his compositions for the piano, on which he was also a gifted performer. His work, which includes dance forms, concertos, sonatas, songs, and solo pieces, is marked by delicacy, technical precision, grace, and sentiment. Chopin was a close friend of the painter DELACROIX and was admired by the pianist SCHUMANN. For several years he was associated with George SAND, the novelist, in an unhappy affair which ended in a quarrel and estrangement. Chopin died of tuberculosis of the larynx, a disease which caused him much weakness and physical suffering throughout his life. See also GLADKOWSKA, CONSTANTIA; WODZINSKA, MARIE; WOJCIECHOWSKI, TITUS.

Chopin, Kate O'Flaherty (1851–1904). American author of stories of Creole life in Louisiana. *Bayou Folk* (1894) and *A Night in Arcadia* (1897) are two collections of such stories.

choragus. In Greek antiquity a chorus leader.

Choral Symphony. Subtitle by which Beethoven's Ninth Symphony (1824) is popularly known. It refers to the chorus and soloists used in the last movement of the symphony to sing Schiller's *Ode to Joy.*

choreography. A system of notation in signs to indicate the steps, gestures, attitudes, etc., to be used in a dance, especially a ballet. The practice is said to have begun in the 15th century with Margaret of Austria, and to have been given its present name in 1699.

Chorus for Survival. See GREGORY, HORACE.

chosen people. The Jews, so called because of the divine promises of special protection recorded in the Biblical narrative.

Chotzinoff, Samuel (1889–). American pianist and music critic. Accompanist for Zimbalist, Alma Gluck, and others. Critic New York *World* (1925–1930); New York *Post* (1934–1940).

Chouans, The (Les Chouans). A historical novel by BALZAC (1829). The heroine is the beautiful spy, Marie de VERNEUIL and the hero the Marquis de Montauran, a Royalist leader. The Chouans are French insurgents of the Royalist party during the Revolution. Jean Cottereau is their leader, nicknamed *Chouan* (a corruption of Fr. *chathuant,* a screech-owl), because he is accustomed to warn his companions of danger by imitating the screech of an owl. They are also known as "Companions of JEHU."

Chou En-lai (1898?–). Chinese communist leader. A founder of the party. Joined Sun Yat-sen (1924); became active in Chinese Red Army (1931); its political leader, second only to Mao Tse-tung. Communist representative at kidnaping of CHIANG KAI-SHEK in 1936.

Chrétien de Troyes (fl. second half of 12th century). Leading French author of medieval romances, known for his psychological insight and his attempts in his writings to prove that love and marriage, considered mutually exclusive in the code of COURTLY LOVE, could be reconciled. His most important romances are *Lancelot, Ou le chevalier de la charette* (*Lancelot, Or the Knight of the Cart*), dealing with the adventures of the LANCELOT of Arthurian legend; and the *Conte del Graal,* or *Perceval,* left incomplete at his death, the earliest literary version of the celebrated legend of the Holy GRAIL. He also wrote *Erec et Enide, Cligés,* and *Yvain, Ou le chevalier au lion* (*Yvain, Or the Knight of the Lion*). *Guillaume d'Angleterre,* a version of the life of St. Eustace, has been attributed to him by some scholars. Marie de Champagne, daughter of ELEANOR OF AQUITAINE and Philip of Flanders were patrons of Chrétien de Troyes.

Chriemhilda, see KRIEMHILD.

Christabel. The heroine of a fragmentary poem of the same title by COLERIDGE (1816), known for its interesting metrical form and its distinctive effects of the supernatural, which are often compared with those of THE RIME OF THE ANCIENT MARINER. Her purity and innocence are threatened by the wicked enchantress, Lady Geraldine.

Christabelle. In Percy's *Reliques* I. i. 4, daughter of "a bonnie king of Ireland," beloved by Sir CAULINE.

Christian. (1) A follower of Christ. So called first at Antioch (*Acts* xi. 26).

most Christian Doctor. John Charlier de Gerson (1363–1429).

most Christian King. The title of the King of France. Pepin le Bref was so styled by Pope Stephen III (714–768). After 1469, when it was conferred upon Louis XI, it was regularly used.

founder of Christian eloquence. Louis Bordaloue, the French preacher (1632–1704).

For *the Christian Cicero, the Christian Virgil,* etc., see under CICERO, VIRGIL, etc.

(2) The hero of Bunyan's PILGRIM'S PROGRESS; the "pilgrim" of the title, whose journey from the City of Destruction to the Celestial City forms the substance of Part i.

Christian, The. A novel by Hall Caine (*Eng.* 1897). "The Christian" is John Storm, first a clergyman and later a member of a monastic brotherhood, but his love for the music-hall singer and actress, Glory Quayle, a woman very much of this world, finally breaks down his faith and resolution.

Christian II. King of Illyria in Daudet's KINGS IN EXILE. He is meant for Francis II, king of Naples, who abdicated in 1860.

Christian, Edward. In Scott's PEVERIL OF THE PEAK, a conspirator who has two *aliases,* "Richard Ganlesse" and "Simon Canter."

Colonel William Christian. In the same work, Edward's brother, shot for insurrection.

Christian, Fletcher. In the famous mutiny case on H.M.S. BOUNTY, the ringleader of the rebellious crew. With eight other men, Christian eventually reached the South Sea island called Pitcairn Island and founded a settlement there, where their half-white, half-Polynesian descendants live today under British rule. A poem by Byron, "The Island," drew upon their adventure.

Christiana. The wife of Christian in Pt. ii. of Bunyan's PILGRIM'S PROGRESS, who starts with her children and Mercy from the City of Destruction long after her husband. She is placed under the guidance of Mr. Great-Heart, and goes, therefore, in "silver slippers" along the thorny road.

Christian Endeavor, Young People's Society of. Religious association for promoting Christian faith founded in Portland, Maine, in 1881.

Christian Front. An American anti-Semitic, pro-Fascist organization (ca. 1938–1940), with which Father Charles E. COUGHLIN was associated. In 1940 several of its members were arrested on a charge of conspiring to overthrow the U.S. government by force.

Christian Hero, The. A didactic pamphlet by Richard STEELE (1701), written while the author was in the British army. It was praised by King William III but was the cause of a duel between Steele and one of his fellow-soldiers, who was seriously wounded. After this incident, Steele was opposed to the custom of dueling.

Christiania or **Christiania turn.** Also **Christy.** In skiing a Norwegian swinging turn. Upward spring from a forward crouch, inward leaning—of several kinds, as *pure, jerked,* or *stem.*

Christian Science. A religious movement whose basic principles are healing by spiritual means rather than by surgery or medicine, optimism in the face of disaster, and a belief in God as a universal, impersonal, infinite Mind. Christian Science was founded by Mary Baker EDDY in Massachusetts in 1866 and spread to the rest of the U.S., to the British Empire, and to Germany. The name of the movement is believed to have been used for the first time by P. P. Quimby, a physician and mesmerist in Portland, Maine, of whom Mrs. Eddy was once a patient. The official name of the organization is Church of Christ, Scientist.

Christians Only. See BROWN, HEYWOOD CAMPBELL.

Christie, Agatha Miller (189?–). English detective story writer, a consistent best seller. Her invented Belgian detective, Hercule Poirot, is nearest to being a successor in popularity to Sherlock Holmes. The best-known of her books is *The Murder of Roger Ackroyd* (1926).

Christie, Anna, see ANNA CHRISTIE.

Christie Johnstone. A novel by Charles READE (1855), the story of a Scots fishergirl and her artist lover, Charles Gatty. Gatty's mother opposes the match, but when Christie saves his life, her opposition is removed. The Viscount Ipsden, whose health has been impaired by his cousin Barbara Sinclair's refusal to marry him, meets Christie in the course of following his physician's prescription to mingle with humble folk and "relieve one fellow creature a day." Eventually Barbara relents and marries the Viscount.

Christina (1626–1689). Queen of Sweden, daughter of Gustavus Adolphus (1594–1632) who was given the education of a man and who made her court a center of intellectual activity to which she invited distinguished foreign scholars, artists, and philosophers. The French philosopher DESCARTES died while in Christina's employ as tutor. Before she came of age, the affairs of state, troubled by the Thirty Years' War, were conducted by Axel Oxenstierna. She herself reigned for ten years (1644–1654) and abdicated in favor of her cousin Charles X. She embraced Roman Catholicism (1655) and died in poverty in Rome.

Christina de Pisan (1364–1430). Italian-born French poet, one of the few women authors of her time. She wrote lyrics, marked by a strong personal touch and the influence of classical reading, and three longer, philosophical poems: the *Chemin de long estude* (*The Road of Long Study*), the *Mutacion de fortune* (*The Mutation of Fortune*), and *Avision* (*Advice*). "She died . . . shortly after celebrating in song Joan of Arc, whose triumph she had lived to see."

Christ in China. Title of a poem by Witter Bynner and another by Arthur Davison Ficke.

Christ in Hades. Title of a poem by Stephen Phillips.

Christ in the Tyrol. See LAWRENCE, DAVID HERBERT.

Christmas Carol. A Christmas story in prose by Dickens (1843). The subject is the conversion of SCROOGE, "a grasping old sinner," to generous good temper, by a series of dreams.

There is a story by Kate Douglas Wiggin, THE BIRDS' CHRISTMAS CAROL.

Christmas Day. December 25th. Also called *the Nativity* (*of Christ*), *Noel, Yule.* Before the 5th century there was no consensus of opinion as to when Christmas should come in the calendar. In Britain, December 25 was a festival in pre-Christian times. BEDE says: "The ancient peoples of the Angli began the year on December 25 when we now celebrate the birthday of the Lord; and the very night which is now so holy to us, they called in their tongue *modranecht,* that is, the mothers' night." In 1644 Christmas was forbidden in England. Charles II revived it.

Christmas Eve and Easter Day. See BROWNING, ROBERT.

Christophe, Henri (1767–1820). Negro King of Haiti (1811–1820). Lieutenant to TOUSSAINT L'OUVERTURE in the revolution against the French (1791). See also DESSALINES.

Christophe, Jean. See ROLLAND, ROMAIN.

Christy, Howard Chandler (1873–). American illustrator and creator of a type of American girl on magazine covers. Also has done portraits of prominent people and the large *Signing the Constitution* in Capitol building, Washington D.C.

Christy Minstrels. A troupe of Negro minstrels organized in New York (ca. 1860) by Edwin P. Christy (1815–1862).

Christopher, St. See under SAINT.

chromatic scale. In music, a scale of twelve semitones or half-steps within an octave, the more usual diatonic scale plus five additional steps. It is used for rich, colorful, emotionally expressive effects and is notably to be found in the works of the musical Impressionists (see IMPRESSIONISM), particularly DEBUSSY and RAVEL.

Chronicle, Anglo-Saxon, see ANGLO-SAXON CHRONICLE.

Chronicle of Charlemagne. See under TURPIN, ARCHBISHOP.

Chronicle of the Kings of England. See WILLIAM OF MALMESBURY.

Chronicle Play. A play with purely historical theme, consisting of scenes more or less loosely connected by a thread of history. Cf., e.g., Shakespeare's *Henry VI.*

Chronicles. Two canonical books of the Old Testament following 2 Kings.

Chronicles of England, Scotland, and Ireland. The famous history by Raphael HOLINSHED, published in 1578. The section concerning the history of Scotland is said to be chiefly a translation of *Scotorum Historiae* (1527), by Hector Boece. In 1587 a second edition was published, but parts of it did not please Queen Elizabeth, and she tried to have it suppressed. The *Chronicles* was the source of much of the material used in Shakespeare's *Cymbeline, King Lear,* and *Macbeth.*

Chronicles of the Popes. See WILLIAM OF MALMESBURY.

Chroniques de la grande guerre. See BARRÈS, MAURICE.

Chronon-hoton-thologos. A burlesque pomposo, King of Queerummania, in Henry Carey's farce of the same name—"the most tragical tragedy ever tragedized"—(1734). The name is used for any bombastic person who delivers an inflated address. See ALDIBORONTEPHOSCOPHORNIO.

Chrysale. In Molière's comedy, LES FEMMES SAVANTES, a simple-minded, henpecked French tradesman, whose wife Philaminte neglects her house for the learned languages, women's rights, and the aristocracy of mind.

chryselephantine. From the Greek words for gold and ivory. In their chryselephantine statues the Greeks used ivory for the flesh and gold, generally decorated with color, for hair and clothing.

Chryseis. In Homer's *Iliad,* daughter of Chryses, priest of Apollo, famed for her beauty. During the Trojan War Chryseis was taken captive and allotted to Agamemnon, king of Argos, and when he refused to accept ransom for her, Chryses called down a plague, so that Agamemnon was forced to let her go.

Chrysostom, John, St., see ST. JOHN CHRYSOSTOM.

Chubb, Thomas Caldecot (1899–). American poet and biographer. *The Life of Giovanni Boccaccio* (1930); *Ships and Lovers* (1933), *Cliff Pace and Other Poems* (1936), two volumes of poetry; *Aretino: Scourge of Princes* (1940); *A Time to Speak* (1943), another volume of poetry; etc.

Chucks. An amusing boatswain who serves under Captain Savage in Marryat's *Peter Simple* (1833).

Church, Benjamin (1639–1718). American soldier and author, known as one of the outstanding fighters in the wars between the New England colonists and the Indians. He wrote *Entertaining Passages Relating to Philip's War* (1716), an account of his experiences in the various Indian wars of the period.

Church, Richard (1893–). English poet, novelist, critic. His novel, *The Porch,* won the *Femina Vie-Heureuse* Prize for 1937.

Churchill, John, 1st Duke of **Marlborough** (1650–1722). Great English military commander; nicknamed "Corporal John"; son of the impoverished Royalist Sir Winston. Assisted in advancing his fortunes by his sister Arabella, who was the mistress of the Duke of York, the later James II. Defeated the French at Blenheim, Ramillies, Oudenarde, and Malplaquet. His wife, the famous Duchess of Marlborough, was Queen Anne's closest friend for some years until she was dismissed. See also MALBROUK.

Churchill, Winston (1871–1947). American novelist, writing chiefly on political and historical subjects. His works include *Richard Carvel* (1899); THE CRISIS (1901); THE CROSSING (1904); CONISTON (1906); *Mr. Crewe's Career* (1908); *The Inside of the Cup* (1913); *A Far Country* (1915); *The Dwelling Place of Light* (1917); *Dr. Jonathan* (1919).

Churchill, Winston Leonard Spencer (1874–). English author and statesman, Conservative in political affiliation and holder of a number of British governmental offices, including those of First Lord of the Admiralty (1911–1915, 1939–1940), Chancellor of the Exchequer (1924–1929), and Prime Minister (1940–1945). Churchill was unpopular during World War I because of his conduct of naval affairs in his position as First Lord of the Admiralty, and in the period preceding World War II because of his Conservative policies. During World War II, however, as Prime Minister in succession to Neville CHAMBERLAIN, he became very popular both in England and the U.S. because of his personality and the confidence and encouragement of his speeches. Books by Churchill include *The World Crisis* (1923–1929), dealing with World War I; *Marlborough* (1933–1938), a biography of an earlier English statesman, the author's ancestor; *Blood, Sweat, and Tears* (1940), and *War Memoirs* (1948).

Churchyard, Thomas (ca. 1520–1604). English poet, for several years a soldier in the Low Countries, France, Ireland, and Scotland. His poems appeared in several of the popular Elizabethan miscellanies (see TOTTEL'S MISCELLANY). He was the author of the accounts of Jane Shore and Cardinal Wolsey in THE MIRROR FOR MAGISTRATES, editions of 1563 and 1587, respectively. SHORE'S WIFE is considered his best work. His poetry appears in a series of volumes exemplified by *Churchyard's Challenge* (1593) and continuing with *Churchyard's Chips, Churchyard's Chance,*

Churchyard's Charge, Churchyard's Good Will, etc.

Chute, The. A novel by Albert HALPER, published in 1937 and dealing with the mail-order business as seen through the eyes of a minor employee.

Chuzzlewit, Martin. The hero of Dickens' MARTIN CHUZZLEWIT. At first he is both selfish and exacting; but the hardships he undergoes in America completely transform him, and he becomes worthy of Mary Graham, whom he marries.

Martin Chuzzlewit, senior. Grandfather to the hero of the same name, a stern old man, whose kind heart has been turned to gall by the selfishness of his relations. He goes to live in Pecksniff's house, and pretends to be weak in intellect, but keeps his eyes open, and is able to expose the canting scoundrel.

Jonas Chuzzlewit. Son of Anthony, of the "firm of Anthony Chuzzlewit and Son, Manchester warehousemen." A consummate villain. He attempts to poison his old father, murders Montague Tigg, who knows his secret, marries Mercy Pecksniff, his cousin, and leads her a life of utter misery. He poisons himself to save his neck from the gallows.

> This fine young man had all the inclination of a profligate of the first water, and only lacked the one good trait in the common catalogue of debauched vices—open-handedness—to be a notable vagabond. But there his griping and penurious habits stepped in.—Chap. xi.

Anthony Chuzzlewit. The cousin of Martin Chuzzlewit, the grandfather. Anthony is an avaricious old man, proud of having brought up his son Jonas to be as mean and grasping as himself.

Ciacco. In Dante's *Inferno,* a glutton, spoken to by Dante, in the third circle of hell, the place to which gluttons are consigned to endless woe. The word means "a pig," and is not a proper name, but only a symbolical one. He is introduced into Boccaccio's *Decameron* ix. 8.

Ciano, Conte **Galeazzo** (1903–1944). Married the daughter of Benito Mussolini, and became prominent in Italian Fascism. Member of the Fascist Supreme Council. Executed by order of Mussolini. His diaries, published in 1946 with an introduction by Sumner Wells, reveal him as "the creature of his times and the times in which he had his being are the least admirable mankind has known for many centuries."

Cibber, Colley (1671–1757). English actor, dramatist, and poet. Brought out 30 dramatic pieces between 1697 and 1748. Appointed poet laureate in 1730. Depreciated by Pope and Johnson, and attacked by Fielding for style, language, and mutilation of Shakespeare.

Cicero, Marcus Tullius (106–43 B.C.). Great Roman orator, philosopher, and statesman. He is often referred to as Tully. His essays on *Friendship* (*De Amicitia*) and *Old Age* (*De Senectute*) are Latin classics, as are his orations against the conspirator CATILINE.

la bouche de Ciceron (*Cicero's mouth*). Philippe Pot, prime minister of Louis XI. (1428–1494).

Cicero of France. Jean Baptiste Massillon (1663–1742).

Cicero of Germany. Johann III, elector of Brandenburg (1455–1499).

Cicero of the British Senate. George Canning (1770–1827).

British Cicero. William Pitt, Earl of Chatham (1708–1778).

Christian Cicero. Lucius Coelius Lactantius, a Christian father, who died 330.

German Cicero. Johann Sturm, printer and scholar (1507–1589).

cicerone. A sight-seers' guide in Italy. Hence any guide. The term is an allusion to the proverbial talkativeness of guides which reminds ironically of the Roman orator CICERO.

Cid. A corruption of *seyyid,* Arabic for lord. The title was given to Roderigo or Ruy Diaz de Bivar (ca. 1040–1099), also called El Campeador, the national hero of Spain and champion of Christianity against the Moors. His exploits, real and legendary, form the basis of many Spanish romances and chronicles, as well as Corneille's tragedy, *Le Cid* (1636).

the Cid's horse. Babieca.

the Cid's sword. Colada. The sword taken by him from King Bucar was called Tizona.

Cid Hamet Benengeli. The supposititious author upon whom CERVANTES fathered the adventures of DON QUIXOTE.

Spanish commentators have discovered this pseudonym to be only an Arabian version of Señor Cervantes: Cid, "Señor"; Hamet, a Moorish prefix; and Ben-en-geli, meaning "son of a stag." So *cervato* "a young stag" is the basis of the name Cervantes.

Cimabue, Cenni di Pepo (fl. 1301–1302). Florentine painter, known chiefly through his reputation among his contemporaries. He executed mosaic work at Pisa and painted religious scenes and figures for other churches in Florence and Assisi. He is mentioned by Dante in *The Divine Comedy.*

Cimmerian darkness. Intense darkness. Homer places the legendary Cimmerians beyond Oceanus, in a land of never-ending gloom. Immediately after Cimmeria he places the empire of Hades. Pliny (*Historia Naturalis,* vi. 14) places Cimmeria near the lake

Avernus, in Italy, where "the sun never penetrates."

Cimourdean. A character in Victor Hugo's NINETY-THREE.

Cincinnatus (ca. 500–430 B. C.). A legendary Roman hero who, after having been consul years before, was called from his plough to be Dictator. After he had conquered the Aequians and delivered his country from danger, he laid down his office and returned to his plough. The name has been assumed as a pen name by political columnists, particularly in Europe.

Cincinnatus of the Americans. George Washington (1732–1799).

Cincinnatus of the West. William Henry Harrison (1773–1841), President of the United States.

Cinderella. In French *Cendrillon* and in German *Aschenbrötel.* Literally, the little cinder girl. Heroine of a fairy tale of very ancient, probably Eastern, origin, mentioned in German literature in the 16th century and popularized by Perrault's *Contes de ma mère l'oye* (1697). Cinderella is drudge of the house, dirty with housework, while her elder sisters go to fine balls. At length a fairy enables her to go to the prince's ball; the prince falls in love with her, and she is discovered by means of a glass slipper which she drops, and which will fit no foot but her own.

J. M. BARRIE wrote a play entitled *A Kiss for Cinderella* (1916). The heroine is "Miss Thing, the Penny Friend," who keeps a day-nursery for war babies and, like Cinderella, has her dreams, which finally come true.

Cinna. A drama on Roman history by Pierre CORNEILLE (1640), revolving about the struggle in the mind of Augustus between revenge and mercy with regard to the conspirators against his life. He finally chooses to be merciful.

Cinq-Mars, Henri, Marquis de (1620–1642). A French nobleman who plotted against Richelieu when the latter opposed his love for Marie de Gonzague. Alfred de Vigny made him the hero of a historical novel, *Cinq-Mars ou une conjuration sur Louis XIII* (1826), which was later the basis of an opera by Gounod (1877).

cinquain. A five-line stanza, particularly the form invented by Adelaide CRAPSEY, a minor American poet. It is based on the Japanese HOKKU.

> Just now,
> Out of the strange
> Still dusk—as strange, as still—
> A white moth flew. Why am I grown
> So cold?
>
> Adelaide Crapsey, *The Warning.*

cinquecento. Literally, five hundred. The Italian name for the *sixteenth* century, that is, the century with years in the names of which 500 occurs, applied as an epithet to art and literature with much the same significance as *Renaissance* or *Elizabethan.* The great men of the period included Ariosto, Tasso, Raphael, Titian and MICHELANGELO. It was the revival of the classical or antique, but is often used as a derogatory term, implying debased or inferior art.

Cinque Ports. Originally the five seaports, Hastings, Sandwich, Dover, Romney, and Hythe, which were granted special privileges from the 13th to the 17th centuries, and even later, in consideration of their providing ships and men for the defense of the Channel. Subsequently Winchelsea and Rye were added.

Cintré, Claire de. In Henry James' AMERICAN, the widow with whom Christopher Newman falls in love.

CIOPW. See CUMMINGS, EDWARD ESTLIN.

Cipango or **Zipango.** A marvelous island described in the *Voyages* of MARCO POLO, the Venetian traveler. He described it as lying some 1500 miles from land. This island was an object of diligent search by Columbus and other early navigators; but it belongs to that wonderful chart which contains the *El Dorado* of Sir Walter Raleigh, the *Utopia* of Sir Thomas More, the *Atlantis* of Lord Bacon, the *Laputa* of Dean Swift, and other places better known in story than in geography.

Circe. A sorceress in Greek mythology, who lived in the island of Aeaea. When Ulysses landed there, Circe turned his companions into swine, but Ulysses resisted this metamorphosis by virtue of a herb called MOLY, given him by Mercury.

Circensian. Having to do with the Circus in Rome. The Circensian games (Lat. *Ludi Circenses*) were held in the Circus Maximus.

circuit rider. A pioneer preacher assigned to a circuit, particularly on the frontier. Had to ride on horseback. In 1874 Edward Eggleston wrote *The Circuit Rider,* and in 1910 Corra Harris wrote *A Circuit Rider's Wife.*

Circumlocution Office. A term applied in ridicule by Dickens in LITTLE DORRIT to public offices in England, because each person tries to shuffle off every act to someone else; and before anything is done it has to pass through so many departments and so much time elapses that it is hardly worth having bothered about it.

> Whatever was required to be done, the Circumlocution Office was beforehand with all the public departments in the art of perceiving—How not to do it.
>
> Dickens, *Little Dorrit,* ch. x.

Hence, routine, formality, red tape.

Cistercians. A monastic order, founded at Cistercium, or Cîteaux, by Robert, abbot of Molême, in Burgundy, in 1098, as a branch of the Benedictines. The monks are known also as *Bernardines,* owing to the patronage of St. Bernard (see under SAINT), who entered Citeaux in 1112 and in 1115 became abbot of a daughter monastery at Clairveaux. In 1664 the order was reformed on an excessively strict basis by Jean le Boutillier de Rance.

Cithaeron. In ancient geography, a mountain range between Attica and Boeotia. It was the scene of the Bacchic festival at which king Pentheus of Thebes was torn to pieces by his frenzied mother and aunts. It was also the place where the usurping King Lycus of Thebes exposed Amphion and Zethus, the sons of Queen Antiope.

Cities of the Plain. English translation of *Sodome et Gomorrhe* (1921–1922), Book IV of Marcel Proust's long novel, REMEMBRANCE OF THINGS PAST. Presenting the characters who appear in the rest of the series, this book is devoted chiefly to a careful and objective exposition of the unnatural vices and the sexual perversions practiced by the decadent French aristocrats with whom the narrator, Marcel, associates. Outstanding among these is the Baron de CHARLUS. *Cities of the Plain* was first published in English in 1928. See also under CITY.

Citizen King, The. Louis Philippe (1773–1850), the first elective king of France (1830 to abdication in 1849).

Citizen of the World, The. A series of satires by Oliver GOLDSMITH (1762), published with the subtitle *Letters from a Chinese Philosopher Residing in London to his Friends in the East.* Lien Chi Altangi, the "Chinese philosopher," Beau TIBBS and the "Man in Black" who is Lien's companion at the theater are entertaining personalities, through whom the author makes his comments on contemporary English life.

Citroën. A low-priced French automobile, named for the maker. Paris sightseers of the twenties will always remember the Citroën advertisement on the Eiffel Tower.

city. Strictly speaking, a *large* town with a corporation and cathedral; but any large town is so called in ordinary speech. In the Bible it means a town having walls and gates.

City of a Hundred Towers. Pavia, in Italy; famous for its towers and steeples.

City of Bells. Strasburg.

City of Brotherly Love. A nickname of Philadelphia. (Gr. *philadelphia* means "brotherly love").

City of David. Jerusalem. So called in compliment to King David (2 *Sam.* v. 7, 9).

City of Destruction. In Bunyan's PILGRIM'S PROGRESS, the world of the unconverted. Bunyan makes CHRISTIAN flee from it and journey to the "Celestial City," thereby showing the "walk of a Christian" from conversion to death.

City of God. The Church, or whole body of believers; the kingdom of Christ, in contradistinction to the City of Destruction. The phrase is that of St. Augustine; one of his chief works bears that title.

City of Lanterns. A supposititious city in Lucian's *Verae Historiae,* situated somewhere beyond the zodiac. See LANTERN-LAND.

City of Legions. Caerleon-on-Usk, where King Arthur held his court.

City of Lilies. Florence.

City of Magnificent Distances. Washington; famous for its wide avenues and splendid vistas.

City of Palaces. Agrippa, in the reign of Augustus, converted Rome from "a city of brick huts to one of marble palaces." Calcutta is also called the *city of palaces.*

city of refuge. Moses, at the command of God, set apart three cities on the east of Jordan, and Joshua added three others on the west, whither any person might flee for refuge who had killed a human creature inadvertently. The three on the east of Jordan were Bezer, Ramoth, and Golan; the three on the west were Hebron, Shechem, and Kedesh (*Deut.* iv. 43; *Josh.* xx. 1–8).

By Mohammedans, Medina, in Arabia, where Mahomet took refuge when driven by conspirators from Mecca, is known as the *city of refuge.* He entered not as a fugitive, but in triumph 622 A. D. Also called the *city of the Prophet.*

city of St. Michael. Dumfries, of which city St. Michael is the patron saint.

City of Saints. Montreal, in Canada, is so named because all the streets are named after saints. Salt Lake City, Utah, U.S.A., also is known as the *city of the saints,* from the Mormons who inhabit it.

Cities of the Plain. Sodom and Gomorrah.

> Abram dwelled in the land of Canaan, and Lot dwelled in the cities of the plain, and pitched his tent toward Sodom.—*Gen.* xiii, 12.

City of the Golden Gate. San Francisco. See GOLDEN GATE.

City of the Prophet. Medina. See CITY OF REFUGE.

City of the Seven Hills. Rome, built on seven hills (*urbs septacollis*). The hills are the Aventine, Caelian, Capitoline, Esquiline, Palatine, Quirinal, and Viminal.

City of the Sun. Baalbec, Rhodes, and Heliopolis, which had the sun for tutelary deity, were so called. It is also the name of a treatise on the Ideal Republic by the Dominican friar Campanella (1568–1639), similar to the *Republic* of Plato, *Utopia* of Sir Thomas More, and *Atlantis* of Bacon.

City of the Three Kings. Cologne; the reputed burial-place of the MAGI.

City of the Tribes. Galway; because it was anciently the home of the thirteen "tribes" or chief families, who settled there in 1232 with Richard de Burgh.

City of the Violated Treaty. Limerick; because of the way in which the Pacification of Limerick (1691) was broken by England.

City of the Violet Crown. Athens is so called by Aristophanes.

Celestial City. See under CELESTIAL.

Cream City. Milwaukee is sometimes so called from its numerous cream-colored brick houses.

Crescent City. New Orleans, from its location on the curving Mississippi River.

Elm City. New Haven, Conn., so called from its magnificent elm trees.

Empire City. New York City, so called from its commercial importance and because it is the metropolis of New York, the *Empire State.*

Eternal City. Rome. See also under ETERNAL.

Forest City. Cleveland, Ohio, has been so called.

Heavenly City. The New Jerusalem; paradise.

Holy City. See under HOLY.

Imperial City. Rome, the seat of empire.

Marsh City. Leningrad, from its low-lying situation and frequent floods.

Monumental City. Baltimore, U.S., is so called because it abounds in monuments.

Nameless City. Ancient Rome, so called from a superstition that anyone who uttered its mystical name would perish.

Puritan City. Boston, Mass., the metropolis of the Puritan settlements of New England.

Quaker City. Philadelphia, so called from its Quaker founders.

Railroad City. Indianapolis, Ind., has been so called because of its importance as a railroad center.

Smoky City. Pittsburgh, so called from the dirt and smoke of its industries.

Twin Cities. Minneapolis and St. Paul, two cities of about equal importance across the Mississippi River from each other near its head in Minnesota.

Windy City. Chicago is so called from its stiff lake breezes.

City of Dreadful Night, The. A long poem by the Victorian poet James THOMSON, published in *The City of Dreadful Night, And Other Poems* (1880). It describes an imaginary city of misery and horror created out of the author's own sense of despair as, afflicted with insomnia, he walked at night through the streets of London.

City of God. Latin title **De Civitate Dei.** The most famous work of St. Augustine (see under SAINT, written after the sack of Rome by the Visigoths (410 A. D.) in order to disprove the charges then being made that Christianity was to blame for the collapse of the Roman Empire. Augustine asserts that all history is a conflict between good, represented by the City of God (*Civitas Dei*), which includes all pious Christians—in other words, the Church which later became the Roman Catholic Church, and evil, represented by the Earthly City (*Civitas Terrena*), including pagans and unfaithful Christians, or the Roman Empire. This conflict is leading, through the will of God, which is supreme, to the Last Judgment, when the people in the City of God will win immortality, and the Earthly City will be destroyed; the Church, therefore, is more important than the state, since it is destined for triumph, and should be given support.

civet cat. An African animal which produces most of the civet (used as a perfume) for commerce. In Elizabethan times the appellation was passed about as a term of opprobrium.

civic crown. Also **civic wreath.** In ancient Rome, a garland of oak leaves bestowed upon a soldier who had saved the life of a citizen.

Civilian Conservation Corps (C.C.C.). An agency of the NEW DEAL, established in 1933 and terminated in 1942. Under it, unemployed American youths were enlisted in an "army" to aid in reforestation and lived in camps under semi-military discipline.

Civil Code. See CODE NAPOLÉON.

Civil Works Administration (C.W.A.). An agency of the American NEW DEAL, established in 1933 to provide Federal work RELIEF for the nation's unemployed. It provided for the building of bridges, roads, and other public projects. It was abandoned in 1934 and replaced by the WORKS PROGRESS ADMINISTRATION (W.P.A.) in 1935.

Civitate Dei, De, see CITY OF GOD.

Claës-Molina, Balthazar. In Balzac's novel, *The Quest of the Absolute* (*La Recherche de l'absolu*) (1834) a chemist who spends a huge fortune and neglects his family completely in the "quest" of the secret of chemical affinity. He dies crying "Eureka."

Claflin, Victoria (1838–1927), and **Claflin, Tennessee Celeste** (1846–1923). Victoria married Dr. Canning Woodhull (1853) and is hence also known as Victoria Woodhull. American sisters, who traveled as children with a "medicine show." Later opened brokerage offices under the wing of Cornelius Vanderbilt. In 1870 founded *Woodhull and*

Claflin's Weekly in which they advocated women's rights, free love, and the like.

Claimant, The American (1892). Novel by Mark TWAIN.

Claimant, The Tichborne. See ORTON.

Clair, René. Real name **René Chomette** (1898–). French motion-picture director, known for the wit, social satire, and sophisticated fantasy of his films. He is best known in the U.S. for *Sous les toits de Paris* (*Under the Roofs of Paris*) (1930); *Le Million* (*The Million*) (1931); and *À Nous la liberté* (*Liberty for Us*) (1932).

clairaudience. Term formed by analogy with clairvoyance. The power of hearing significant distant or future sounds.

Clairmont, Clara Mary Jane, usually **Claire** (1798–1879). Stepdaughter of William Godwin and mother of Lord Byron's daughter Allegra; friend of the Shelleys.

clairvoyance. The power of seeing significant distant or future objects or scenes.

Clan-na-Gael. An Irish Fenian organization founded in Philadelphia in 1881, and known in secret as the United Brotherhood; its avowed object being to secure "the complete and absolute independence of Ireland from Great Britain, and the complete severance of all political connection between the two countries, to be effected by unceasing preparation for armed insurrection in Ireland."

claque (*Fr.*). (1) Paid applauders at a theatrical performance. Hence any trucklers. (2) A collapsible opera hat.

Clärchen. The heroine of Goethe's historical drama EGMONT, noted for her constancy and devotion.

Clare. In the Roman Catholic Church, a nun of the order founded by St. Clare (see under SAINTS) as the equivalent for women of the Franciscan friars minor. The nuns of this order are known as Poor Clares.

Clare, Ada. In Dickens's *Bleak House,* John Jarndyce's ward, who marries Richard Carstone.

Clare, Angel. A leading character in Hardy's TESS OF THE D'URBERVILLES.

Clare, John (1793–1864). The "Northamptonshire peasant poet." Wrote *The Shepherd's Calendar* (1827), *Rural Muse* (1835). Confined in a lunatic asylum.

Clarence. A play by Booth TARKINGTON.

Clarendon Press. A printing establishment connected with the university of Oxford, England. It was founded partly with the profits from Edward Hyde, 1st Earl of Clarendon's (1609–1674) *History of the Rebellion* (published from transcript, 1702–1704; from original manuscript, 1826).

Claretie, Jules (1840–1913). French journalist and writer. Director of the Comédie Française (1885). Many novels and historical works.

Clari. An opera by J. Howard Payne and Sir Henry Bishop (1823), with the subtitle *The Maid of Milan.* It is remembered chiefly because of the famous song *Home, Sweet Home,* which was one of its melodies.

Clarinda. The name which Mrs. M'Lehose used in her correspondence with Robert Burns.

Clarissa Harlowe. A novel by Samuel RICHARDSON (1749), the full title of which is *The History of Clarissa Harlowe.* As one of the earliest English novels it exercised a marked influence on the development of fiction. It is constructed as a series of letters to Clarissa's friend, Miss Howe. To avoid a marriage to which her heart cannot consent, but to which she is urged by her parents, Clarissa casts herself on the protection of a lover, named Lovelace, who abuses the confidence reposed in him. He afterwards proposes marriage; but she rejects his proposal, and retires to a solitary dwelling, where she pines to death with grief and shame. See also HARLOWE.

Clark, Badger (1883–). American poet, author of the famous singing ballad "High Chin Bob" or "Way up high in the Mokiones."

Clark, Barrett Harper (1890–). Dramatic teacher and editor of many books on the drama.

Clark, Champ. In full **James Beauchamp** (1850–1921). Well-known American political leader. Speaker of the House of Representatives (1911–1919). Defeated as candidate for President (1912) when Bryant supported Woodrow Wilson.

Clark, George Rogers (1752–1818). American Revolutionary frontier leader. Fought British and Indians (1779–1783).

Clark, Mark Wayne (1896–). American army man. As lieutenant-general he commanded the Fifth Army which made the principal assault on the Italian mainland in World War II (Sept. 9, 1943).

Clark, William (1770–1838). American explorer. Crossed continent with Capt. Meriwether Lewis finding route to Pacific Ocean (1804–1805).

Clarke, Austin (1896–). Irish poet. National award for poetry at Tailtean Games (1932). Also author of verse plays and novels. *The Vengeance of Fionn* (1917), *The Cattle-drive in Connaught* (1925), etc.

Clarke, Charles Cowden (1787–1877). English Shakespearean scholar. Taught Keats his letters. Friend of Hunt, Shelley, Hazlitt,

Charles and Mary Lamb. His wife, Mary, compiled *The Complete Concordance to Shakespeare.*

Clarke, Micah, see MICAH CLARKE.

Clark's Field. A novel by Robert Herrick (*Am.* 1914). Ardelle Clark, an orphan, is heir to a huge fortune from the sale of "Clark's Field," which has remained vacant in the midst of a great industrial district. She marries Archie Davis, a shiftless art student, and they squander the inheritance freely. Among the workmen on their great estate in California is a mason named Tom Clark who, Adele discovers, is a distant cousin and, as she believes, an equal heir to the estate. After his brave but unsuccessful effort to save her child from fire, she decides to recognize his claim; and when this decision cannot be legally carried out, she asks his assistance in using the money for the welfare of the industrial community in which "Clark's Field" was located.

classical. (1) Usually, a term referring to the CLASSICS, or to the period of greatest power among the Greeks and Romans, as "classical culture."

(2) In literature and art in general, a term used to express, with reference to a single work as well as to an entire age, dominance of form over content, technical precision over emotional expressiveness, clarity, restraint, and rationality over wildness, bombast, and imaginative excess; opposed to ROMANTIC. See also NEO-CLASSICAL.

(3) In music, specifically referring to the period of the 18th century, which was marked by the development of the symphony and the rise of such composers as HANDEL, HAYDN, and MOZART. "Classical music" also means, in loose usage, generally among those opposed to it or unfamiliar with it, all music not included in the category of "popular"—in other words, music other than folk-tunes, the songs of TIN PAN ALLEY composers and their successors, and music produced on a mass-scale for ballroom dancing.

Classical Symphony. A symphony by Serge PROKOFIEV (1917). In this, the composer announced, he tried to capture the spirit of Mozart's music and to write as Mozart might have written if he were living in the 20th century.

classics. The Romans were divided by Servius into five classes. Any citizen who belonged to the highest class was called *classicus,* all the rest were said to be *infra classem* (unclassed). From this the best authors were termed *classici auctores* (classic authors), *i.e.* authors of the best or first class. The high esteem in which Greek and Latin were held at the revival of letters obtained for these authors the name of classics; and when other first-rate works are intended some distinctive name is added, as the English, French, Spanish, etc., classics.

Claudel, Paul (1868–). French poet, playwright, and diplomat. Was once French ambassador to Japan and wrote *The East I Know.* He is a mystical Catholic poet. His plays owe a debt to Aeschylus. *The Tidings Brought to Mary* (1916) is among his most notable works.

Claude Lorrain, see LORRAIN.

Claudine. See COLETTE.

Claudio. (1) In Shakespeare's MEASURE FOR MEASURE, brother of Isabella and the suitor of Juliet. He is imprisoned by Lord Angelo for the seduction of Juliet, and his sister Isabella pleads for his release.

(2) In Shakespeare's MUCH ADO ABOUT NOTHING, Lord Claudio of Florence is a friend of Don Pedro, prince of Aragon, and engaged to Hero.

Claudius. In Shakespeare's HAMLET, Hamlet's uncle, who poisons his brother, marries the widow, and usurps the throne.

Claudius the God. See GRAVES, ROBERT.

Claus, Peter, see KLAUS, PETER.

Claus, Santa, see SANTA CLAUS.

Clausewitz, Karl von (1780–1831). Prussian army officer whose books on the science of war, notably *Vom Kriege* (3 vols.; 1833), are classics in their field.

Clavering, Sir Francis. In Thackeray's PENDENNIS, a dissipated baronet who marries the rich mother of BLANCHE AMORY, only to discover that her scoundrelly first husband is still alive and eager for blackmail. See ALTAMONT; AMORY.

Claverings, The. A novel by Anthony Trollope (1867). The hero is Harry Clavering, a rector's son and a somewhat fickle but likable young man.

clavichord. A keyboard instrument, precursor of the piano by which it was superseded. The distinct charms have brought it back into use, especially for the performance of works composed before the piano was developed.

> While you sat and played Toccatas,
> Stately at the clavichord.
>
> Robert Browning, "A Toccata of Galuppi's."

Clavigo. A drama by Goethe (1774) based on the career of Don José Clavijo y Foxardo (1730–1806). This Spanish official seduced a sister of BEAUMARCHAIS and suffered consequent disgrace. Beaumarchais wrote his drama *Eugénie* around the same episode.

Clavileno. In DON QUIXOTE (II, iii. 4 and 5), the wooden horse on which the Don mounts in order to disenchant the Infanta

Antonomasia and her husband, who are shut up in the tomb of Queen Maguncia of Candaya. It is the very horse on which Peter of Provence carried off the fair Magalona; it was constructed by Merlin, and is governed by a wooden pin in the forehead. The word means *Wooden Peg.* See also CAMBUSCAN.

Clay, Bertha M. Pseudonym of **Charlotte Monica Braeme** (1836–1884). English author of a flood of romantic novels. See also CARTER, NICK.

Clay, Henry (1777–1852). Famous American statesman. Senator; Speaker of the House; Secretary of State. From the Missouri Compromise (1820) he derives his nickname "The Great Pacificator." He lived up to his reputation in the so-called Compromise of 1850 by which he sought to avoid civil war.

Clay, Robert. The hero of SOLDIERS OF FORTUNE by Richard Harding DAVIS.

Clayhanger. A novel by Arnold BENNETT (Eng. 1910). Under the domination of his old father Darius, the hero, Edwin Clayhanger, is forced into the family printing business. He falls in love with Hilda Lessways, who is visiting in town, but learns that Hilda is the wife of George Cannon. Much later he finds her living in wretched quarters and learns that Cannon is a bigamist and the marriage void. His old father dies, and Edwin marries Hilda.

In *Hilda Lessways* the same events are narrated from Hilda's point of view. *These Twain* continues the study of the two temperaments into their married life, and *The Roll Call* (1919) carries their story still further. In all four books, Hilda's son George plays an important part. As a boy of ten he does much to bring Edwin and Hilda together and after their marriage his experiences are the leading element.

Clayton Act or **Clayton Antitrust Act.** An act passed by the 63rd Congress (Oct. 14, 1914) as a supplement to the Sherman Antitrust Act (1890). It is directed against agreements between banks and large corporations, as far as these are designed "to substantially lessen competition." Its provisions are enforced by the Federal Trade Commission.

Cléante. A favorite name with Molière: (1) In his *Malade imaginaire,* the lover of Angélique, the daughter of ARGAN. (2) In *L'Avare,* the son of HARPAGON. (3) In TARTUFFE, the brother-in-law of Orgon.

clearing house. An agency set up by banks, railroads, buyers and sellers, etc. for the purpose of adjusting their accounts with each other. Hence, any agency functioning in a comparable manner. As, "the office of the cultural attaché is to be a clearing house for matters of non-political importance concerning the two countries."

Cleave, Richard. The hero of Mary Johnston's LONG ROLL.

clef. A character used in musical notation to determine the pitches to be represented by the lines and spaces of the staff.

> The clefs are three:
> C, F, and G.

The shape of the clefs grew out of the letters by which they are named. The word is French and means "key."

clef, romans à. See *Romans à clef.*

Clegg, Jane, see JANE CLEGG.

Cleghorn, Sarah Norcliffe (1876–). American poet with a passion for social justice. A typical New Englander, a native of Vermont, she has allied herself with many causes and also written beautifully of New England.

Cleishbotham, Jedediah. The imaginary editor, schoolmaster and parish clerk of Gandercleuch, who is supposed to have employed his assistant teacher, Peter Pattieson, to write down THE TALES OF MY LANDLORD. Of course the real author is Sir Walter SCOTT. Jedediah Cleishbotham is also introduced in the preface to *The Black Dwarf.*

Clelia or **Cloelia.** In the legendary history of Rome, a Roman maiden, one of the hostages given to Porsena. She made her escape from the Etruscan camp by swimming across the Tiber. She was sent back by the Romans, but Porsena not only set her at liberty for her gallant deed, but allowed her to take with her a part of the hostages. Mlle. de Scudéry took this story as the framework for her celebrated romance *Clélie,* published in ten volumes (*Fr.* 1654–1660). Like her CYRUS, it deals with contemporary French life under the thin disguise of other times and other scenes.

Clélie. A novel by Mlle. de Scudéry. See CLELIA.

Clemenceau, Georges (1841–1929). French journalist and statesman. Correspondent in U.S. with Grant's army (1865). Premier of France (1906–1909, 1917). Head of French delegation to Peace Conference at Versailles (1919). Both his looks and attitudes are responsible for his nickname "the Tiger."

Clement, St. See under SAINT.

Clementina, The lady. In Richardson's novel *Sir Charles Grandison,* an amiable, accomplished, but unfortunate woman, deeply in love with Sir Charles Grandison. Sir Charles, however, married Harriet Byron.

Clementine, O my Darling. An old song, beginning

> In a cavern, in a cavern,
> Excavating for a mine,
> Lived a miner—Forty-niner—
> And his daughter, Clementine.

Clendening, Logan (1884–1945). Physician and author. *The Human Body* (1927) is his most popular book.

Cleofas, Don. The hero of a novel by Le Sage, entitled *Le Diable boiteux* (*The Devil on Two Sticks*). He is a fiery young Spaniard, proud, high-spirited and revengeful, noted for gallantry, and not without generous sentiments. His guide is the fiend ASMODEUS.

Cleombrotos. A philosopher who so admired Plato's discourse on the immortality of the soul (in the *Phaedo*) that he jumped into the sea in order to exchange this life for a better. He was called *Ambraciota,* from *Ambracia,* in Epirus, the place of his birth.

Cleon. In Browning's poem of this name the writer is supposed to be one of the poets alluded to by St. Paul in *Acts* xvii. 28 ("As certain also of your own poets have said"). Cleon believes in Zeus under the attributes of the one God, but sees nothing in his belief to warrant the hope of immortality, which disconcerts him. The poem is a protest against the inadequacy of the earthly life.

Cleopatra. Queen of Egypt, wife of Ptolemy Dionysius. She was driven from her throne, but re-established by Julius Caesar, 47 B.C. Antony, captivated by her, repudiated his wife, Octavia, to live with the fascinating Egyptian. After the loss of the battle of Actium, Cleopatra killed herself by an asp. She is the heroine of many tragedies, of which the most notable in English are Shakespeare's *Antony and Cleopatra* (1608) Dryden's *All for Love or the World Well Lost* (1682) and Shaw's *Caesar and Cleopatra* (1908). There is an Italian tragedy by Alfieri (1773), and French tragedies by E. Jodelle, *Cléopatre captive* (1550); Jean Mairet, *Cléopatre* (1630); Isaac de Benserade (1670), J. F. Marmontel (1750), and Mde. de Girardin (1847). Rider Haggard has a romance called *Cleopatra* (1889). See HARMACHIS.

Cleopatra and her pearl. It is said that Cleopatra made a banquet for Antony, the costliness of which excited his astonishment; and, when Antony expressed his surprise, Cleopatra took a pearl ear-drop, which she dissolved in a strong acid, and drank to the health of the Roman triumvir, saying, "My draught to Antony shall far exceed it."

Cleopatra's Needle. The obelisk so called, now in London on the Thames Embankment, was brought there in 1878 from Alexandria, whither it and its fellow (now in Central Park, New York) had been moved from Heliopolis by Augustus about 9 B.C. It has no connection with Cleopatra, and it has carved on it hieroglyphics that tell of its erection by Thothmes III, a Pharaoh of the 18th dynasty who lived many centuries before her time.

Cleopatra's nose. It was Blaise Pascal (d. 1662) who said, "If the nose of Cleopatra had been shorter, the whole face of the earth would have been changed" (*Pensées* viii. 29); the allusion, of course, being to the tremendous results brought about by her enslavement through her charm and beauty, first of Julius Caesar and then of Mark Antony.

clerihew. See BENTLEY, EDMUND CLERIHEW.

Clerk-Maxwell, James, see MAXWELL, JAMES CLERK.

Clerk's or Clerkes Tale. In Chaucer's *Canterbury Tales.* See GRISELDA. The Clerk is probably best described in the following well-known lines:

> A Clerk ther was of Oxenford also
> That unto logik hadde longe y-go . . .
> For him was lever have at his beddes heed
> Twenty bokes, clad in blak or red
> Of Aristotle and his philosophye
> Than robes riche, or fithele, or gay sautrye . . .
> Souninge in moral vertu was his speche,
> And gladly wolde he lerne and gladly teche.
>
> *Prologue.*

Clermont, The. The first American steamboat built by Robert Fulton (1765–1815). It made a trial trip from New York to Albany (150 miles) in 32 hours (August 11, 1807). It was popularly called Fulton's Folly.

Clery, Emma. In James Joyce's A PORTRAIT OF THE ARTIST AS A YOUNG MAN, a girl with whom Stephen DEDALUS attends a Gaelic class and who is the object of his adolescent love. She is the "E—— C——" to whom he addresses a sentimental poem.

Cléry, Lucile: A Woman of Intrigue (1932), reprinted as **The Strange Case of Lucile Cléry** (1941), by Joseph Shearing, pseudonym of Mrs. Gabrielle M. V. Campbell Long. It was based on the actual murder of the Duchesse de Praslin in Paris (1847). In the real story the actual governess, after coming to America, married the great-uncle of Rachel FIELD, American novelist, and in 1938 Miss Field published a novel, *All This, and Heaven Too,* dealing with the same case, which became a most successful motion picture.

Cleveland, Duchess of, see VILLIERS, BARBARA.

Cleveland, (Stephen) Grover (1837–1908). 22nd and 24th President of the United States. Democrat. 1st election 1884. Re-elected 1892. Second term noted for vigorous handling of national credit and firm foreign policy. Under the name of Peter Stirling he is the hero of Paul Leicester Ford's HONORABLE PETER STIRLING (1894).

Cleveland, John (1613–1658). English poet, a reader in rhetoric at Cambridge and a Royalist during the English Civil War, serving both as a soldier and a verse and prose satirist against the Puritans. His poetry is marked by fantastic conceits (see CONCEIT) carried to an extreme of ornamentation. He was very popular in his day and was imitated by numerous lesser poets. Among his works are *Jonsonus Virbius* (1638) and *Poems* (1653).

cliché. Literally, a stereotype plate; hence, a stereotyped expression, a stock phrase, such as "few and far between," "ever and anon," "at the eleventh hour."

Cliff Dwellers, The. A novel by Henry Fuller (*Am.* 1893), concerning a heterogeneous group of characters of varying social backgrounds, all of whom work in a huge office building in Chicago. The term came to be often used with reference to modern city life.

Cliffe, Geoffrey. A character in Mrs. Humphry Ward's MARRIAGE OF WILLIAM ASHE.

Clifford, Lady. **Mrs. Henry de la Pasture.** English novelist and playwright. Second marriage to Sir Hugh Clifford. Mother of Elizabeth Monica Dashwood whose pen-name, E. M. Delafield, is an Anglicized form of de la Pasture.

Clifford, Mrs. Lucy Lane (d. 1929). English novelist and playwright. Robert Browning said he should like to have written her first novel, *Mrs. Keith's Crime* (1885), which was also admired by Hardy. Kipling commented on her good literary judgment, and Henry James remembered her in his will.

Clifford, Martha. A character in James Joyce's ULYSSES, a stenographer with whom Leopold BLOOM is carrying on a clandestine affair. She addresses love-letters to him as Henry Flower. In the novel's parallel with the *Odyssey,* she represents CALYPSO.

Clifford, Paul, see PAUL CLIFFORD.

Cligés. See CHRÉTIEN DE TROYES.

Clim of the Clough, see CLYM.

climax. (*Lat., Gr.* a ladder.) The rhetorical figure in which the sense rises gradually in a series of images, each exceeding its predecessor in force or dignity. Popularly, the word is used to denote the last step in the gradation, the point of highest development.

Clinker, Humphrey, see HUMPHREY CLINKER.

Clinton, Sir Henry (1738?–1795). English general at Bunker Hill. In 1778 commander-in-Chief of all British forces in America. Captured Charleston, S.C., but could not prevent Cornwallis's surrender at Yorktown, Va.

Clinton's Ditch. The Erie Canal. Begun in 1817 through the efforts of Governor DeWitt Clinton (1769–1828). Formally opened in 1825 at the beginning of Clinton's second term.

Clio. In classic mythology, one of the nine Muses, the inventor of historical and heroic poetry.

ADDISON adopted the name as a pseudonym, perhaps because many of his papers in the *Spectator* are signed by one of the four letters in this word, probably the initial letters of Chelsea, London, Islington, Office.

clipper or **clipper ship.** The type of full-rigged ship developed by American builders about 1840. Fine lines, overhanging bow, tall raking masts, large sail area. Sailed in the tea and china trade. Cf. *Java Head* by Joseph Hergesheimer.

Clive, Kitty. *Nee* **Catherine Raftor** (1801–1873). British comedy actress of Irish extraction. Played for Colley Cibber at Drury Lane. Married a relative of Robert CLIVE. An original member of Garrick's Drury Lane Company (1746–1769).

Clive, Robert. Baron **Clive of Plassey** (1725–1774). Founder of the empire of British India. Governor and Commander-in-Chief of Bengal (1764). Obtained for East India Company sovereignty over whole province. On return to England (1767) met storm of obloquy and inquiries into his actions and committed suicide.

Clitandre. In Molière's comedy, LES FEMMES SAVANTES, a wealthy bourgeois, in love with Henriette, "the thorough woman," by whom he is beloved. Her elder sister Armande also loves him.

cloak-and-sword plays. Swashbuckling plays, full of fighting and adventure. The name comes from the Spanish comedies of the 16th century dramatists, Lope de Vega and Calderón—the COMEDIA DE CAPA Y ESPADA. With them it signified merely a drama of domestic intrigue and was named from the rank of the chief characters, in France—and, through French influence, in England—it was applied as above.

Clockmaker, The. See SLICK, SAM.

Clod and the Pebble, The. Short mystical lyric by William BLAKE, occurring in *Songs of Experience.*

Cloe, see CHLOE.

Cloete, Stuart (1897–). South African novelist. Born in Paris, educated in England, "half ex-Coldstream Guards officer and half Dutch ex-farmer." His *The Turning Wheels* (1937) was highly successful.

Cloelia. A maiden in Roman legend who was given as a hostage to Porsena and escaped by swimming the Tiber.

Cloister and the Hearth, The. A historical novel by Charles Reade (1861). The action takes place on the Continent in the latter years of the 15th century; and among the historical characters of note introduced are Froissart, Gringoire, Deschamps, Luther, Villon and the child Erasmus. The interest centers in the love story of Erasmus' parents—Gerard, a talented young writer, and the red-haired Margaret, daughter of Peter Brandt. A forged letter convinces Gerard of Margaret's death and he becomes a monk, but after many misadventures, the pair meet again at last.

Cloisters, The. See BARNARD, GEORGE GREY.

Clonbrony, Lord and **Lady.** The chief characters in Maria Edgeworth's ABSENTEE.

Clongowes Wood College. In A PORTRAIT OF THE ARTIST AS A YOUNG MAN by James JOYCE, an Irish Jesuit school attended by Stephen DEDALUS as a boy.

Clootie, Auld, see AULD CLOOTIE.

Clorinda. The pagan heroine whose praises are sung in Tasso's JERUSALEM DELIVERED, daughter of Senapus of Ethiopia, a Christian. Because she was born white, her mother changes her for a black child. The eunuch Arsetes is entrusted with the infant Clorinda, and as he is going through a forest, he sees a tiger, drops the child, and seeks safety in a tree. The tiger takes the babe and suckles it, after which the eunuch carries the child to Egypt. In the siege of Jerusalem by the Crusaders, Clorinda is a leader of the pagan forces. TANCRED falls in love with her, but slays her unknowingly in a night attack. Before she expires she receives Christian baptism at the hands of Tancred, who greatly mourns her death.

Clorinda Walks in Heaven. See COPPARD, ALFRED EDGAR.

Cloten. In Shakespeare's CYMBELINE, a vindictive lout, son of the second wife of Cymbeline by a former husband. He is noted for "his unmeaning frown, his shuffling gait, his burst of voice, his bustling insignificance, his fever-and-ague fits of valor, his froward tetchiness, his unprincipled malice, and occasional gleams of good sense." Cloten is the rejected lover of Imogen.

Clotho (Gr. *klôtho,* to draw thread from a distaff.). One of the Three Fates in classic mythology. She presided over birth, and drew from her distaff the thread of life; Atropos presided over death and cut the thread of life; and Lachesis spun the fate of life between birth and death.

Cloud, The. A famous poem by P. B. SHELLEY (1820), in which the cloud recounts its cyclical journey from the sky to the earth and back once more to the sky. It expresses the poet's ideas of resurrection and recurrence and his pantheism.

Cloud-cuckoo-Land (Gr. *Nephelo-Coccygia*). An idealistic plan to reform the world; any visionary scheme. So called from the city in the clouds in Aristophanes' comedy, THE BIRDS.

Cloudesley, William of, see WILLIAM OF CLOUDESLEY.

Clouds, The. The best-known comedy of Aristophanes (422 B.C.), a satire on Socrates and the Sophists. The young Athenian, Pheidippides, is a caricature of the Alcibiades of history. Under Socrates' instruction he becomes so bereft of common virtues and so adept in proving that black is white that his irate father sets fire to Socrates' house.

Clouet. Family of Flemish-French painters of the 15th and 16th centuries.

Clough, Arthur Hugh (1819–1861). English poet, known for the expression of his melancholy and his religious conflicts in his works. These include *The Bothie of Tober-na-Vuolich* (1848), a love story written in hexameter verse; *Amours de Voyage,* written in 1849 and published in 1858; *Mari Magno,* written in 1849 and published in 1862, a series of narratives in verse; and *Dipsychus,* written in 1849 and published in 1862 also, a series of dialogues between a Faustian hero and a Satan-like spirit. Matthew ARNOLD, a friend of Clough, wrote the elegy THYRSIS (1866) in his memory.

Clovis *Ger.* **Chlodwig** (d. 511 A.D.). King of the Salian Franks, who after his succession in 481 A.D. led his people in a series of systematic conquests and migrations until they occupied the remainder of the Roman Empire in Gaul and the territory of other German tribes, including the Alemanni and the Visigoths. Clovis was converted to the orthodox Christianity of the Western Church and ordered all his people baptized as well, thus securing the important co-operation of the clergy. The Frankish kingdom of Clovis, who has been called the greatest figure in political history between CAESAR and CHARLEMAGNE, is considered to be the foundation of modern Western Europe. It lasted in Germany until 911 and in France until 987.

Clout, Colin, see COLIN CLOUT.

Clown's House. See SITWELL, EDITH.

Club of Queer Trades, The by Gilbert K. CHESTERTON.

Cluny. A Benedictine monastery founded in Burgundy in 910 by William, Count of Auvergne and Duke of Aquitaine. It became the center of monastic reform, assuming a centralized control over old monasteries and founding new, subordinate houses, enforcing celibacy among the monks and secular clergy, and insisting that the power to appoint members of the clergy be in the hands of ecclesiastical authorities rather than of kings and feudal lords. After 1046, Cluniac reform was handled by Hildebrand, later Pope GREGORY VII.

cluricaune. In Irish folklore, an elf, particularly one guarding secret treasures.

Clutterbuck, Captain. The hypothetical editor of some of Sir Walter Scott's novels, as *The Monastery* and THE FORTUNES OF NIGEL. Captain Clutterbuck is a retired officer, who employs himself in antiquarian researches, idle literary pursuits. THE ABBOT is dedicated by the "author of *Waverley*" to "Captain Clutterbuck," late of His Majesty's —— infantry regiment.

Clutton-Brock, Arthur (1868–1924). English essayist and critic. Known particularly for his studies of SHELLEY and William MORRIS. Became a FABIAN Socialist in 1909.

Clymene. In Greek mythology, the daughter of Oceanus, mother of Atlas and Prometheus.

Clym of the Clough. A noted archer and outlaw, supposed to have lived shortly before Robin Hood, who, with Adam BELL and William of Cloudesly, forms the subject of one of the ballads in Percy's *Reliques*. The three became as famous in the north of England as Robin Hood and Little John in the midland counties. Their place of resort was in Englewood Forest, near Carlisle. Clym of the Clough means Clement of the Cliff. He is mentioned in Ben Jonson's *Alchemist* (I. ii. 46).

Clytemnestra. In Greek legend, the wife of AGAMEMNON, whom she and her paramour Aegisthus murders after his return from Troy. She is slain by her son ORESTES.

Clytie. In classical mythology, an ocean nymph, in love with Apollo. Meeting with no return, she was changed into the heliotrope, or sunflower, which, traditionally, still turns to the sun, following him through his daily course.

coalition government. A government formed by various parties by a mutual surrender of principles; such as the Ministry of the Duke of Portland which included Lord North and Fox in 1783, and fell to pieces in a few months, and that of Lord Salisbury with the old Whig Party headed by Lord Hartington in 1886. The most famous Coalition in British history, however, is that formed in May, 1915, by Mr. Asquith, when Mr. Bonar Law with the Unionist and Conservative parties joined the Liberals—the whole being under Mr. Asquith—for the better conduct of World War I which had then been in progress for nearly ten months. In spite of a General Election at the end of the War in 1918 and many changes of Government—Mr. Lloyd George succeeded Mr. Asquith as Premier in December, 1916—the Coalition lasted till October, 1922.

coals.

carry coals to Newcastle. To do what is superfluous; to take something where it is already plentiful. Newcastle, of course, is a great coal port. The French say, "porter de l'eau à la rivière" (to carry water to the river). There are a great many phrases expressing this same idea, as, to carry owls to Athens, teach fishes to swim, kill the slain, teach one's grandmother to suck eggs, etc.

heap coals of fire on one's head. To melt down his animosity by deeds of kindness; to repay bad treatment with good. (Prov. xxv. 21, 22).

coalsack. One of the black spaces in the Milky Way.

coaster. A coasting vessel. Cf. "The Coasters," a poem by Thomas Fleming Day in E. C. Stedman's *American Anthology*.

Coates, Robert Myron (1897–). Author of *The Eater of Darkness*, the first Dada novel in English. His *The Outlaw Years* is valuable Americana. Associated with *The New Yorker* as art critic.

Coatsworth, Elizabeth (1893–). American poet and juvenile writer. Her poetry is vivid, her children's books popular.

Cobb, Humphrey (1899–1944). American novelist known for his *Paths of Glory* (1935), one of the post-war novels of the school of Remarque, later made into a successful play by Sidney Howard.

Cobb, Irvin Shrewsbury (1876–1944). American humorist, journalist, and short-story writer. He was on the staffs of the New York *Sun* and the New York WORLD. His books, a number of which are collections of local-color stories of Kentucky, include *Back Home* (1912); *Old Judge Priest* (1915) (see PRIEST, JUDGE); *Speaking of Operations* (1916); *The Thunders of Silence* (1918); *Snake Doctor* (1923); *Ladies and Gentlemen* (1927); *To Be Taken Before Sailing* (1930); *Faith, Hope, and Charity* (1934); *Judge Priest Turns Detective* (1937); *Exit Laughing* (1941), an autobiography.

Cobb, Ty (Tyrus Raymond) (1886–). American professional baseball player. Detroit (1904–1926); Philadelphia (1926–1930).

Cobbett, William (1762–1835). English author and journalist, best known for his pro-British pamphlets, written in the U.S. under the pseudonym of Peter Porcupine, and his newspaper, *Cobbett's Political Register*, published in England beginning in 1802. He was later an M.P. and wrote a number of books, including *Rural Rides* (1830), descriptions of life and agricultural conditions in the English countryside. Cobbett was attacked by Matthew CAREY for his criticisms of America.

Cobden, Richard (1804–1865). English statesman and economist, known as the Apostle of Free Trade. Attacked doctrine of balance of power in Europe. With John Bright a leader of national Anti-Corn-Law League (1838–1846). See CORN LAWS. Shared unpopularity with Bright for opposing Crimean War. Came out in favor of the North in American Civil War.

Cobden-Sanderson, Thomas James (1840–1922). English bookbinder and printer. Established, with Emery Walker, the Doves Press. Designed a new font of type. Printed, among other books, an English Bible (1903–1905) and edition of Milton (1905).

Coburn, Charles Douville (1877–). American actor (stage and screen) and manager. Organized the Coburn Players (1906).

Cocagne or Cocaigne, see COCKAIGNE.

Cochet, Henri (1901–). French lawn tennis player. Member of the Davis Cup Team that won (1927) and successfully defended the cup (1928–1930). Professional since 1933.

Cochran, Jacqueline. Well-known American aviatrix. Winner of Bendix Transcontinental Air Race (1938) and holder of national and international speed records. Also businesswoman running a chain of beauty parlors and a cosmetics factory.

cock.

cock of the walk. The dominant bully or master spirit. The place where barndoor fowls are fed is *the walk,* and if there is more than one cock they will fight for the supremacy of this domain.

cock-and-bull story. A far-fetched tale with little foundation in fact. The derivation is obscure.

Cockade State. Maryland. See under STATES.

Cockaigne, The Land of. An imaginary land of pleasure, wealth, luxury, and idleness. London is so called, and Boileau applies the word to Paris. This mythical Utopia (spelled also *Cokayne* and *Cocagne*) was the subject of many mock-serious poems of the Middle Ages. According to a typical account of the 13th century, the houses were made of barley-sugar and cakes, the streets were paved with pastry, and the shops supplied goods without requiring money in payment. James Branch CABELL makes JURGEN visit Cocaigne in his satiric romance *Jurgen* and describes it as a land of curious delights, presided over by ANAÏTIS.

cockatrice. A fabulous and heraldic monster with the wings of a fowl, tail of a dragon, and head of a cock. It was so called because it was said to be produced from a cock's egg hatched by a serpent. According to legend, the very look of this monster would cause instant death. In consequence of the *crest* with which the head is crowned, the creature is called a BASILISK. Isaiah says, "The weaned child shall put his hand on the cockatrice' den" (xi, 8), to signify that the most obnoxious animal should not hurt the most feeble of God's creatures.

Figuratively, it means an insidious, treacherous person bent on mischief.

> They will kill one another by the look, like cockatrices.
>
> Shakespeare, *Twelfth Night,* iii. 4.

Cock Lane ghost. A tale of terror without truth; an imaginary tale of horrors. In Cock Lane, Smithfield (1762), certain knockings were heard, which Mr. Parsons, the owner, declared proceeded from the ghost of Fanny Kent, who died suddenly, and Parsons wished people to suppose that she had been murdered by her husband. All London was agog with this story; but it was found out that the knockings were produced by Parsons' daughter (a girl twelve years of age) rapping on a board which she took into her bed. Parsons was condemned to stand in the pillory. Cf. Dr. Johnson's account in *Gentleman's Magazine,* vol. xxxii, pp. 43 and 81.

Cock Lorel or Cocklorel. Titular hero of the satirical poem *Cocke Lorelles Bote* (ca. 1515) which tells the story of a ship filled with merry renegades and rascals. The poem is one of many imitations of Sebastian BRANT's *Narrenschiff* (SHIP OF FOOLS, 1494).

cockney. The origin of this word is obscure. The most picturesque explanation which deserves to be preserved runs as follows. *Cockney* is the M.E. *cokeney,* meaning "a cock's egg"; *-ey* = A.S. aeg, an egg. This is a small egg with no yolk that is occasionally laid by hens; hence it was applied originally to a foolish, spoiled, cockered child:

> I made thee a wanton and thou hast made me a fool, I brought thee up like a cockney and thou hast handled me like a cock's-comb, I made more of thee than became a father and thou less of me than beseemed a child.
>
> Lyly, *Euphues* (1578).

From this the word came to signify a foolish or effeminate person; hence, by the country-dwellers—the majority of the population—it was applied to townsmen generally, and finally became restricted to its present meaning, one born within sound of Bow Bells, London; one possessing London peculiarities of speech, etc.; one who, hence, is—or is supposed to be—wholly ignorant of country sports, country life, farm animals, plants, and so on.

> As Frenchmen love to be bold, Flemings to be drunk, Welchmen to be called Britons, and Irishmen to be costermongers; so cockneys, especially she cock-

neys, love not aqua-vitae when 'tis good for them.
Dekker Webster, *Westward Hoe*, II, ii. (1607).

Shakespeare uses the word for a squeamish woman:

Cry to it, nuncle, as the cockney did to the eels, when she put them into the paste alive.—*King Lear*, ii. 4.

Cockney School. A nickname given by Lockhart (see quotation below) to the group of writers including Leigh HUNT, HAZLITT, SHELLEY, and KEATS, most of whom were Londoners or lived in London. Lockhart was a strong partisan of the LAKE SCHOOL and had great animosity against writers with other aims or principles. Hunt he called "the Cockney Homer," Hazlitt "the Cockney Aristotle," and Haydon "the Cockney Raphael."

If I may be permitted to have the honour of christening it, it may be henceforth referred to by the designation of the "Cockney School"—Lockhart, *Blackwood's Magazine*, Oct., 1817.

king of cockneys. A master of the revels chosen by students of Lincoln's Inn on Childermas Day (December 28).

Cockpit of Europe. Belgium has for long been so called because it has been the site of more European battles than any other country. From *cockpit* in the sense of "pit for fighting cocks."

Cock Robin. The hero of a nursery rhyme beginning, "Who killed Cock Robin?"

Cockton, Henry (1807–1853). English humorist. His novels include *Valentine Vox, the Ventriloquist* (1840), and *Sylvester Sound, the Somnambulist* (1844).

Cocles, Horatius, see HORATIUS COCLES.

Cocteau, Jean (1891–). French poet, playwright, and novelist, known for his iconoclastic writings and conduct and his association with the movement of SURREALISM. His works include *Discours du grand sommeil,* poems of World War I; *Poésies* (1920); *Plain-chant* (1923); *Le Rappel a l'ordre* (1926), essays; *Grand écart* (1925), *Thomas the Impostor* (1925), and *Enfants terribles* (1930), novels; *Parade, Les Mariés de la Tour Eiffel,* and *Le Bœuf sur le toit,* ballets; *La Machine infernale* (*The Infernal Machine,* 1936), a play. Cocteau served as the literary spokesman for the group of musicians known as "Les Six" ("THE SIX"). *Le Sang d'un poète* (THE BLOOD OF A POET, 1932) is a Surrealist motion picture written and produced by Cocteau.

Cocytus. One of the five rivers of hell in Greek mythology. The word means the "river of lamentation." The unburied were doomed to wander about its banks for 100 years. It flows into the river Acheron.

coda. In music, a concluding, rounding-out passage, the use of which was extended by BEETHOVEN. The word is Italian and means "tail."

Code Napoléon. The French law as embodied in the "Five Codes" (enacted 1804 to 1810), or, more commonly, the *Code Civil des Français* (enacted 1804). It was enforced in the conquered countries, and traces of it are found in the modern laws of Belgium, the Netherlands, Spain, Switzerland, Quebec, Louisiana, South America.

Cody, William Frederick, see BUFFALO BILL.

Coelebs' Wife. A bachelor's ideal of a model wife. Coelebs is the hero of a novel by Mrs. Hannah More, entitled *Coelebs in Search of a Wife* (1809).

Coelum Britannicum. See CAREW, THOMAS.

Cœur de Lion. (1) Richard I of England (1157–1199). So called from the prodigies of personal valor performed by him in the Holy Land.

(2) Louis VIII of France (1187–1226). Also called **le Lion.**

Coffee Cantata. See CANTATA.

Coffin, Long Tom. A famous sailor in Cooper's sea novel, THE PILOT. Of Nantucket origin, Long Tom loves the sea with passionate devotion and hates land as passionately. As an ex-whaler he flourishes a harpoon even on board a man-of-war. His simple, hardy virtues and his thorough professional skill have caused him to be regarded as a Leatherstocking of the sea, and he rivals the famous scout for first place in popularity among Cooper's characters.

Coffin, Robert Peter Tristram (1892–). American poet. Pulitzer prize for Poetry (1936) for *Strange Holiness.* Also a biographer with *Laud* (1930) and *The Dukes of Buckingham* (1931). Lecturer and essayist. *Collected Poems* (1939) with a preface on poetry.

Coghlan, Rose (1853–1932). English-born American actress. Leading lady in Wallack's company (1880–1889).

cogito ergo sum. The axiom formulated by DESCARTES as the starting-place of his system of philosophy. It means "I think, therefore I exist." Descartes, at the beginning, provisionally doubted everything, but he could not doubt the existence of the *ego,* for the mere fact that *I* doubt presupposes the existence of the *I;* in other words, the *doubt* could not exist without the *I.* The phrase lends itself to adaptation and parody: *dubito ergo sum* ("I doubt, therefore I exist"); I sneeze, therefore I exist; etc.

Cohan, George Michael (1878–1942). American actor, playwright, producer and composer of popular songs, notably *Over There.* The "Yankee Doodle Boy," because of his song "I'm a Yankee Doodle Dandy." Also a serious and charming playwright in *Pigeons and People.* A huge popular success in musical comedy. James Cagney has acted in the biographical moving picture made of his life.

Cohen, Bella. In James Joyce's ULYSSES, the proprietress of a Dublin house of prostitution which is visited near the climax of the novel by STEPHEN DEDALUS and to which LEOPOLD BLOOM also comes in order to protect Stephen. Bella Cohen corresponds to CIRCE in the Homeric legend, because under her influence men are turned into swine. It is at her establishment that the famous "witches' sabbath" episode of the novel takes place.

Cohen, Mirah. In George Eliot's DANIEL DERONDA, the beautiful Jewess whom Deronda marries. She is also known as Mirah Lapidoth.

Mordecai Cohen. Mirah's lost brother Ezra; an idealistic Jew, on fire with plans for the advancement of the race. The character is said to have been drawn from a Jewish journeyman watchmaker named Cohn or Kohn.

> A man steeped in poverty and obscurity, weakened by disease, consciously within the shadow of advancing death, but living an intense life in an invisible past and future, careless of his personal lot, except for its possibly making some obstruction to a conceived good which he would never share except as a brief inward vision—a day afar off, whose sun would never warm him, but into which he threw his soul's desire, with a passion often wanting to the personal motives of healthy youth.—Ch. xliii.

Cohen, Morris Raphael (1880–). American philosopher. *Reason and Nature* (1931), *Law and the Social Order* (1933), *An Introduction to Logic and Scientific Method* (1934). Harold J. Laski called him "the most penetrating and creative United States philosopher since William James."

Cohen, Octavus Roy (1891–). Writer of popular detective fiction and Negro stories that created the characters of Florian Slappey and Epic Peters.

Coignard, Jerome. An irreverent, licentious abbé, who is nevertheless something of the philosopher and saint. He is the chief character in Anatole France's novels *At the Sign of the Reine Pédauque* (*La Rôtisserie de la Reine Pédauque*) (1893) and its sequel, *The Opinions of Monsieur Jerome Coignard.* Coignard is one of France's most popular characters and is said to be a mouthpiece for many of the author's opinions.

Coke, Sir **Edward** (1552–1634). Famous English jurist. Best known for his four *Institutes* (1628–1644). The first of these is currently called *Coke upon Littleton.*

Cokes or Cook's Tale. In Chaucer's CANTERBURY TALES. See GAMELYN.

Colas Breugnon, Burgundian. A romance of 16th century Burgundy by Romain Rolland (*Fr.* 1919). The hero and supposed narrator is an old craftsman, who indulges in delightful reminiscences.

Colbert, Jean Baptiste (1619–1683). French statesman. Made controller general of finance by Louis XIV (1665). A great financial reformer. Because of his coldness of temperament Mme de Sévigné called him *le Nord.* Patron of men of letters and academies.

Colby, Frank Moore (1865–1925). American essayist. *The Colby Essays* were edited by Clarence Day, Jr. after his death.

Colcord, Lincoln Ross (1883–1947). American poet and author of sea stories. Born aboard ship, off Cape Horn. Collaborated with O. E. Rölvaag in translating the latter's *Giants in the Earth* (1927).

Cole, George Douglas Howard (1880–). English economist of socialist leanings and, in collaboration with his wife, writer of numerous detective stories. Author of a series of studies, from *World of Labour* (1913) to *Socialism in Evolution* (1938). He also has written a life of William Cobbett.

Cole, King, see KING COLE.

Cole, Timothy (1852–1931). British-born American wood engraver. Employed by *Scribner's Magazine* from 1875 and its successor the *Century Magazine.* Sent to Europe to engrave old masters. After his return, continued the same sort of work in American collections.

Coleridge, Samuel Taylor (1772–1834). English poet, essayist, and literary critic, known for the brilliance of his intellect and his great, if never fully realized, talent, which was defeated by his procrastinating nature and his addiction to opium. He was an early crusader for UNITARIANISM, and was associated with Robert SOUTHEY in plans for the PANTISOCRACY settlement and with William WORDSWORTH in the publication of LYRICAL BALLADS. He also became a keen student of German philosophy and literature, lectured extensively, was a brilliant conversationalist, and was interested in a wide variety of subjects, including politics, the drama, and the history of the Christian religion. His most famous poems are THE RIME OF THE ANCIENT MARINER, published in LYRICAL BALLADS (1798), and the fragments CHRISTABEL and KUBLA KHAN, written in 1797 and 1800, and in 1798, respectively. In the realm of literary criticism, in which no other prose writer of the English Romantic period was a significant rival, his best-known work is BIOGRAPHIA LITERARIA (1817). Among his other works are *The Fall of Robespierre* (1794), *Zapolya* (1817), *Osorio* (ca. 1798, performed as *Remorse* in 1813), all plays; *Lay Sermons* (1816); and *Aids to Reflection* (1825). Well-known minor poems include *France: An Ode* (1798); *Ode to Dejection* (1802); and *Youth and Age* (1828–1832). Coleridge's three greatest poems, which are sharply different from his others in conception, imagery, style, and versification, are marked by subtlety of meter, imagination, powerfully evocative qualities of mystery and the supernatural, and a sophistication of symbolism not generally found in poetry until much later. His prose is distinguished by its accomplishments in metaphysics, psychology, and aesthetics beyond the usual attainments of the time. For a study of the operation of Coleridge's imagination on the source-materials of *The Rime of the Ancient Mariner* and *Kubla Khan,* consult *The Road to Xanadu,* by J. L. Lowes.

Coleridge-Taylor, Samuel (1875–1912). English composer. Won acclaim with his choral work in the trilogy, *Hiawatha's Wedding Feast* (1898), in *Death of Minnehaha* (1899), and *A Tale of Old Japan* (1911).

Colet, John (1467?–1519). English scholar and theologian. Accompanied Erasmus on his pilgrimage to Canterbury (1514). Dean of St. Paul's 1504–1519.

Colette. Pen-name of **Sidonie Gabrielle Claudine Colette** (1873–). French writer of semi-autobiographical stories, the main character being Claudine. Has also written short stories, essays, and a few plays.

Colette Baudoche. See BARRÈS, MAURICE.

Coligny, Gaspard de (1519–1572). Admiral of France and, after his conversion to Protestantism, leader of the Huguenots. Killed in the Massacre of St. Bartholomew (1572). His brothers, cardinal **Odet de Coligny** (1517–1571) and **François de Coligny** (1521–1569), also broke with the Church of Rome, but both died a natural death.

Colin Clout. A name which Spenser assumes in THE SHEPHERD'S CALENDAR, and in other pastoral poems, particularly *Colin Clout's Come Home Again,* which represents his return from a visit to England (1589–1591) to Sir Walter Raleigh, "the Shepherd of the Ocean" and allegorically praises Queen Elizabeth and attacks the intrigues at her court. SKELTON previously (about 1520) used the name as the title of a satire directed against the abuses of the Church.

Colin Tampon. See NICKNAMES OF NATIONALITIES.

Collar, The. Famous religious poem by George HERBERT (1633), in which an ox-yoke is used as a symbol of spiritual authority and restraint and obedience to God.

Collean, May. The heroine of a Scotch ballad, which relates how "fause Sir John" carried her to a rock for the purpose of throwing her down into the sea; but May outwitted him, and subjected him to the fate he had designed for her.

Colleen Bawn, The. See BOUCICAULT, DION.

Collegians, The. An Irish novel by Gerald GRIFFIN.

Colleoni, Bartolommeo (1400–1475). Venetian soldier. Foremost tactician of the 15th century.

Collier, Jeremy (1650–1726). English clergyman, known for his *Short View of the Immorality and Profaneness of the English Stage* (1698), an attack on the license of the Restoration drama.

Collier, John (1901–). His first book, a fantastic novel, *His Monkey Wife,* is a frivolous masterpiece. His short stories are unrivaled in the fantastic vein. His early verse received *This Quarter's* prize for English poetry in 1922.

Collier, John Payne (1789–1833). English Critic. Brought out texts of Shakespeare based on forged marginal corrections but was exposed in 1859. Editor of Spenser's works (1862) and compiler of a critical bibliography of the rarest English books (1865).

Collier, Old Cap. A character of dime-novel fame. The *Old Cap Collier Library* was published by the house of Munro during the latter part of the 19th century. Irvin S. COBB wrote, in the Captain's defense, *A Plea for Old Cap Collier* (1921), a sketch of the dime novel.

Collier, William (Willie) (1866–1944). American comedian and playwright. Very popular in his day.

Collin, Jacques. The most consummate villain and criminal of Balzac's COMÉDIE HUMAINE, playing a part in many of the novels. In *Father Goriot* (*Le Père Goriot;* see GORIOT), under the name and disguise of Vautrin he makes love to the landlady whose cheap scanty fare he eats, until the spiteful Mlle. Michonneau gives him up to the police. He appears in *Scenes from a Courtesan's Life* (*Les Splendeurs et misères des courtisanes*) and *The Last Incarnation of Vautrin* (*La Dernière incarnation de Vautrin*) as a Spanish priest and philosopher. In this guise he befriends the discouraged Lucien de Rubempré and makes use of Lucien's love affair with Esther Van Gobseck to secure money from Esther's wealthy admirer, Nucingen. Finally both Lucien and Collin are given over to justice, but Collin, by placing his knowledge of the criminal world at the service of the police, wins for himself safety.

Collins, Michael (1890–1922). Irish revolutionary leader. Commander of the army of the Irish Free State and minister of finance in the Sinn Fein ministry. Killed in the civil war of 1922.

Collins, Mr. In Jane Austen's PRIDE AND PREJUDICE, a self-important clergyman, very much the toady and the prig. Elizabeth Bennet refuses him, and he marries Charlotte Lucas. A "bread and butter letter" is sometimes called a Collins, from him.

Collins, William (1721–1759). English poet, one of the pre-Romantics of the 18th century. He wrote only a small quantity of poetry, consisting chiefly of odes on nature subjects in a quiet, melancholy vein, distinguished by their smoothness and their skillful use of sound-effects. His best-known poems are *Ode to Evening* (1746); *How Sleep the Brave* (1746); and a dirge for Shakespeare's *Cymbeline* (1744). Others are *Ode to Simplicity* (1746); *The Passions: An Ode for Music* (1746); *Ode to Fear; On the Poetical Character; On the Popular Superstitions of the Highlands* (1749). All his life Collins suffered from poverty and illness, and he was insane before his death.

Collins, William Wilkie (1824–1889). English novelist, best known as the author of THE WOMAN IN WHITE (1860) and THE MOONSTONE (1868). He wrote numerous other works similar to these two, and is considered by some to have been the first English author of *bona fide* "detective" and "mystery" novels. Collins and Charles DICKENS collaborated on several stories for periodicals of the time.

Colloquy on the Occupations. A Latin work by AELFRIC in the form of a dialogue between master and pupil and consisting of questions and answers on the trades and occupations of Anglo-Saxon England.

cologne, cologne water, eau de cologne. Perfumed toilet water, originally made in Cologne. The most famous brands are "4711" (read: forty-seven eleven) and "Johanna Maria Farina." The former got its name from the number of the house (before street names were in general use) in which it was manufactured; the latter from its Italian originator.

Cologne. French name of the German city of Köln. Founded by the Romans as *Colonia Agrippina* in honor of a wife of Claudius (50 A.D.).

the three kings of Cologne. The three Wise Men of the East, the MAGI, Gaspar, Melchior, and Balthazar, whose bones, according to tradition, were deposited in Cologne Cathedral.

Colombe's Birthday. See BROWNING, ROBERT.

Colonel Carter of Cartersville. A novel of Southern life by F. Hopkinson Smith (*Am.* 1891). Colonel Carter is a typical Virginia gentleman of the old school. A dramatic version won popular favor in 1892 and he reappeared in *Colonel Carter's Christmas* (1903).

Colonel Jack. See DEFOE, DANIEL.

Colonna, Guido. The Pisan commander, husband of MONNA VANNA in Maeterlinck's drama of that name.

colophon. The end of a book; the statement containing information about the date, place, printer, and edition which, in the early days of printing, was given at the end of the book but which now appears on the title page. It is derived from Gr. *kolophon,* the top or summit, a word which, according to Strabo, is from Colophon, a city of Ionia, the inhabitants of which were such excellent horsemen that they would turn the scale of battle to the side on which they fought. *The Colophon* (1928–1940; 1948–) is an American literary quarterly.

Color.

complementary colors. Colors which, in combination, produce white light. Red and green, orange and blue, violet and yellow are complementary.

> The color transmitted is always complementary to the one reflected.—Brewster, *Optics*, xii.

fundamental colors. The seven colors of the spectrum: violet, indigo, blue, green, yellow, orange, and red. Or red, yellow, blue, also called *primary* or *simple* colors.

secondary colors. Those which result from the mixture of two or more primary or simple colors, such as green, which is a blend of blue and yellow.

national colors:

Great Britain	*red, white, and blue.*
Argentina	*blue and white.*
Austria	*red, white, and red.*
Belgium	*black, yellow, and red.*
Bolivia	*red, yellow, and green.*
Brazil	*green and yellow.*
Bulgaria	*white, green, and red.*
Chili	*white, blue, and red.*
China	*yellow ochre.*
Colombia	*yellow, blue, and red.*
Costa Rica	*blue, white, red, white, and blue.*
Cuba	*five horizontal stripes, blue and white.*
Denmark	*red, with white cross.*
Ecuador	*three horizontal stripes, yellow, blue, and red, the yellow being twice the width of the others.*
France	*blue, white and red, vertical stripes.*
Germany	*black, red and white* (Imperial and Third Reich); *black, red and gold* (Republican).
Greece	*nine horizontal stripes, blue and white.*
Guatemala	*blue, white and blue, vertical stripes.*
Hayti	*blue and red.*
Honduras	*blue, white, and blue, horizontal stripes.*
Irish Free State	*orange, white and green.*
Italy	*green, white, and red, vertical stripes.*
Japan	*white, with red disk in center, from which spring sixteen red rays to edge.*
Liberia	*eleven horizontal stripes, red and white.*
Luxemburg	*red, white, and blue.*
Morocco	*red.*
Mexico	*green, white, and red, vertical stripes.*

Monaco	*red and white, horizontal.*
Netherlands	*red, white, and blue, horizontal stripes.*
Nicaragua	*blue, white, and blue, horizontal stripes.*
Norway	*red, with blue cross bordered with white.*
Panama	*blue, white, red.*
Paraguay	*red, white, blue, in horizontal stripes.*
Peru	*red, white and red, vertical stripes.*
Persia	*white, top edge green, bottom edge red.*
Portugal	*blue and white.*
Roumania	*blue, yellow, and red, vertical stripes.*
Russia	*white, with blue St. Andrew's cross.*
Salvador	*nine horizontal stripes, blue and white.*
Serbia	*red, blue, and white.*
Siam	*red, with a white elephant.*
Sweden	*blue, with yellow cross.*
Switzerland	*red, with white cross.*
Turkey	*green and red.*
Uruguay	*nine horizontal stripes, blue and white.*
United States	*stars on blue, white with red stripes.*
Venezuela	*yellow, blue, and red, horizontal stripes.*

colors in symbolism, ecclesiastical use, etc.

Black:

In blazonry, sable, signifying prudence, wisdom, and constancy; it is engraved by perpendicular and horizontal lines crossing each other at right angles.
In art, signifying evil, falsehood, and error.
In Church decoration it is used for Good Friday.
As a mortuary color, signifying grief, despair, death. (In the Catholic Church violet may be substituted for black.)
In metals it is represented by lead.
In precious stones it is represented by the diamond.
In planets it stands for Saturn.

Blue:

Hope, love of divine works; (in dresses) divine contemplation, piety, sincerity.
In blazonry, azure, signifying chastity, loyalty, fidelity; it is engraved by horizontal lines.
In art (as an angel's robe) it signifies fidelity and faith (as the robe of the Virgin Mary), modesty and (in the Catholic Church) humility and expiation.
In Church decoration, blue and green are used indifferently for ordinary Sundays, and blue for all weekdays after Trinity Sunday.
As a mortuary color it signifies eternity (applied to Deity), immortality (applied to man).
In metals it is represented by tin.
In precious stones it is represented by sapphire.
In planets it stands for Jupiter.

Pale Blue:

Peace, Christian prudence, love of good works, a serene conscience.

Green:

Faith, gladness, immortality, the resurrection of the just; (in dresses) the gladness of the faithful.
In blazonry, vert, signifying love, joy, abundance; it is engraved from left to right.
In art, signifying hope, joy, youth, spring (among the Greeks and Moors it signifies victory).
In Church decoration it signifies God's bounty, mirth, gladness, the resurrection, and is used indifferently with blue for ordinary Sundays.
In metals it is represented by copper.
In precious stones it is represented by the emerald.
In planets it stands for Venus.

Pale Green:

Baptism.

Purple:

Justice, royalty.
In blazonry, purpure, signifying temperance; it is engraved by lines slanting from right to left.
In art, signifying royalty.
In metals it is represented by quicksilver.
In precious stones it is represented by amethyst.
In planets it stands for Mercury.

Red:

Martyrdom for faith, charity; (in dresses) divine love.
In blazonry, gules; blood-red is called sanguine. The former signifies magnanimity and the latter fortitude; it is engraved by perpendicular lines.
In Church decorations it is used for martyrs, for Ash Wednesday, for the last three days of Holy Week, and for Whit Sunday.

Colosseum. The great Flavian amphitheater of ancient Rome, said to be so named from the colossal statue of Nero that stood close by in the Via Sacra. It was begun by Vespasian in 72 A. D., and, for 400 years, was the scene of the gladiatorial contests. The ruins remaining are still colossal and extensive, but quite two-thirds of the original building have been taken away at different times and used for building material.

Byron, adapting the exclamation of the 8th-century pilgrims (and adopting a bad spelling), says:

> While stands the Coliseum, Rome shall stand;
> When falls the Coliseum, Rome shall fall;
> And when Rome falls—the world.
> *Childe Harold,* IV. cxlv.

The name has since been applied to other amphitheaters and places of amusement.

Colossians, Epistle to the. One of the books of the New Testament, written by "Paul the apostle" to the people of Colossae, in Asia Minor, during his imprisonment at Rome.

Colossus or **Colossos** (*Lat.* and *Gr.* a gigantic statue). The Colossus of Rhodes, completed probably about 280 B. C., was a representation of the sun-god, Helios, and commemorated the successful defense of Rhodes against Demetrius Poliorcetes in 304 B. C. It was one of the Seven Wonders of the World; it stood 105 feet high, and is said to have been made from the warlike engines abandoned by Demetrius by the Rhodian sculptor Chares, a pupil of Lysippus. The story that it was built striding across the harbor and that ships could pass in full sail between its legs, rose in the 16th century. There is nothing to support it; neither Strabo nor Pliny makes mention of it, though both describe the statue minutely.

Colossus of Maroussi, The. See MILLER, HENRY.

Colton, Arthur Willis (1868–1943). American poet and story writer. *The Delectable Mountains* (1901); *The Belted Seas* (1905); *Harps Hung Up in Babylon* (1907), poems. Colton's fine qualities as a writer have been too little appreciated.

Colum, Mary Gunning (Maguire). Irish-American literary critic and writer of short stories. Wife of Padraic COLUM. *From These Roots* (1937) traces the historical background of modern criticism. *Life and the Dream* (1947) is her distinguished and fascinating autobiography.

Colum, Padraic (1881–). Irish writer, associated as playwright with the IRISH RENAISSANCE and the Irish National Theater, in company with A. E., W. B. YEATS, and Lady GREGORY. His works include *Wild Earth* (1907), poems; *The Boy Who Knew What the Birds Said* (1918); *Dramatic Legends And Other Poems* (1922); *Castle Conquer* (1923); *Balloon* (1929), a comedy; *The Big Tree of Bunlahy* (1933), stories; *The Story of Lowry Maen* (1937), a narrative poem; and numerous books on travel and folklore.

Columban, St., see ST. COLUMBAN.

Columbia. (1) A poetic name for America, or for the United States of America, from Christopher Columbus, the discoverer of the New World. It is in common use in patriotic songs and pageants. Columbia is usually personified as a woman in white flowing garments, draped with an American flag.

(2) An American revolutionary poem by Timothy DWIGHT, published in 1777. It hails the coming greatness of the U.S. and is considered to be Dwight's best work.

Columbiad, The. An epic poem (1807) by Joel BARLOW first published in briefer form as *The Vision of Columbus* (1787) and of interest chiefly as a specimen of early American literature. Columbus is taken by Hesper, the spirit of the Western World, to the Mount of Vision and there foresees the history of the North American continent up to the times of the poet.

Columbian Magazine. One of the first two successful magazines in the U.S., founded in 1786 by a group of editors that included Matthew CAREY. It was published until 1792, although its title was changed in 1790. See also AMERICAN MUSEUM.

Columbine. A stock character in old Italian comedy, where she first appeared about 1560 and thence was transplanted to English pantomime. She is the daughter of PANTALOON, and the sweetheart of HARLEQUIN, and, like him, is supposed to be invisible to mortal eyes. *Columbina* in Italian is a pet name for a ladylove, and means dove-like. See also PIERROT.

Columbus Day. October 12, an American holiday in commemoration of the discovery of America, October 12, 1492.

column or (humorously) **colyum.** A popular newspaper feature which became something of an American institution in the period between World Wars I and II. It appears daily and contains a heterogeneous mixture of prose and poetry, humor and satire, gossip and prediction, narrative and comment, much of the material being supplied by contributors. See ADAMS, FRANKLIN PIERCE; BROUN, HEYWOOD CAMPBELL; WINCHELL, WALTER. Many well-known humorous characters were created by American columnists, notably DULCY, ARCHY THE COCKROACH, HERMIONE, and the OLD SOAK.

Colvin, Sir Sidney (1845–1927). British critic of art and literature. Friend of Robert Louis Stevenson. Keeper of department of prints, British Museum (1884–1912). Edited Stevenson's letters to him from Samoa as *Vailima Letters* (1895). His *John Keats, His Life and Poetry* (1917) is authoritative.

Combe, William, see DR. SYNTAX.

Combray. In Marcel Proust's REMEMBRANCE OF THINGS PAST, a French village where the narrator, Marcel, spent his childhood, and where the country homes of his mother, Charles SWANN, and the de GUERMANTES family are located. It plays a prominent part in Marcel's memories of the past.

Comédie Française. French national theater in Paris. Founded in 1681 by the union of several theatrical companies—MOLIÈRE's among them—; renamed *Théâtre Français* in 1791.

Comédie humaine, La (The Human Comedy). The name given (1841) by Honoré de BALZAC to his great project of representing in his novels a complete social history of France in his own day through the portrayal, in separate panels, of the lives of typical individuals of the various classes. In the preface of *The Cat and the Racket* Balzac discusses the scope of the *Comédie humaine*. It comprises three main divisions, Studies of Manners, Studies of Philosophy, and Studies of Marriage. The first group subdivided into Scenes of Private Life, of Provincial Life, of Parisian Life, of Country Life, of Political Life, and of Military Life. Some of the projected novels were not completed, but there are no less than ninety-two in the series as it stands today. Some of the best-known titles include *Les Chouans* (*The Chouans*, 1829), the first of the series; *Eugénie Grandet*, 1833; LE PÈRE GORIOT (*Father Goriot*, 1834); LA RECHERCHE DE L'ABSOLU (*The Quest of the Absolute*); CÉSAR BIROTTEAU (1837); ILLUSIONS PERDUES (*Lost Illusions*); LE MÉDECIN DE CAMPAGNE (*The Country Doctor*); LE CURÉ DE VILLAGE (*The Village Priest*, 1837); LE COUSIN PONS (*Cousin Pons*, 1847); LA COUSINE BETTE (*Cousin Betty*, 1847). Many of the characters appear in several novels.

La Comédie humaine is considered the first work of Realism in French literature, and had tremendous influence upon French novelists of the 19th and 20th centuries, from the GON-

COURT brothers down to Marcel PROUST and Jules ROMAINS.

Comedy of Errors, A. A drama by Shakespeare (ca. 1591). Aemilia, wife of Aegeon, has twin sons, both named Antipholus, who are shipwrecked in infancy and carried, one to Syracuse, the other to Ephesus. The play represents Antipholus of Syracuse going in search of his brother; and to make the confusion of identities more absurd, the brothers each have a slave named Dromio and the Dromios are also indistinguishable twins. Adriana, the wife of the Ephesian, mistakes the Syracusan for her husband and later has her real husband arrested as a madman. Great confusion results, but ultimately the matter is brought into court, and not only do the brothers recognize each other at last, but their mother Aemilia, an abbess in whose priory the Syracusan had taken refuge during the excitement, and their father Aegeon, who had come to Ephesus in search for his son, appear in court and the entire family is reunited. The source of the plot is the *Menoechmi* of Plautus. THE BOYS FROM SYRACUSE (1938), an American musical comedy, was based on *A Comedy of Errors.*

Comedy, The Divine, see DIVINE COMEDY.

Comedy, The Human, see COMÉDIE HUMAINE, LA.

Come Hither. An anthology of verse and prose compiled by Walter DE LA MARE.

Come into the Garden, Maud. A well-known lyric from the romance *Maud* by TENNYSON.

Come out of the Kitchen. A story by Alice Duer MILLER.

Comfort, Will Levington (1878–1932). American novelist and war correspondent. *Routledge Rides Alone* (1910), his best-known novel, based on his experiences during the Russo-Japanese war, was circulated by peace societies as anti-war propaganda.

comic relief. The relaxation of the listener's tension by means of an interpolated comic episode in a serious play. Its function is to permit a stronger renewal of the emotional surge. Best-known example: the grave diggers in HAMLET. Some critics hold that the function of such scenes is not relief but increased tension through senseless and ironical juxtaposition of opposites. "The bitter smile with which we greet the comic interlude is almost the grin of the death's head."—Philo Buck, *The Golden Thread.*

comic spirit. Invoked by George Meredith as the attitude that regards human problems and complications as conducive to "thoughtful laughter."

comic strip. A strip of drawn panels telling a comic story, entirely without or with a clearly subordinated text. Comic-strip magazines have become very popular. Educators and publishers have begun to investigate the applicability of the comic-strip technic to serious subjects. Cf. Biblical stories in picture continuities, etc.

comic supplement. The cartoon section of an American newspaper, 1900 and thereafter; particularly those series of cartoons (COMIC STRIPS) which present the adventures of certain humorous characters whose story is carried on from day to day. Among the most popular characters of the comic supplement, whose names have been adopted into common speech are BARNEY GOOGLE, BLONDIE, BUSTER BROWN, the GUMPS, JIGGS AND MAGGIE, the KATZENJAMMER KIDS, Little Abner, MUTT AND JEFF, and Moon Mullins. See also TOONERVILLE TROLLEY.

Comines or **Commines, Philippe de** (1447?–?1511). French chronicler. His *Mémoires* are a classic of medieval historiography.

Coming of Arthur, The. A narrative on the Arthurian legend (see ARTHUR) included in Tennyson's IDYLLS OF THE KING.

Coming Race, The. A satiric romance by Bulwer LYTTON (1870), in which an American discovers a Utopia inhabited by a strange race of beings called "Vrilya" or "Ana" who are far ahead of mankind in their scientific attainments. They are scornful of democracy, which they call Koombosh, or government of the ignorant.

Coming Struggle for Power, The. Chief work of John STRACHEY, published in 1932 and predicting a close and final conflict between capitalism and Communism, and the doom of capitalism.

Coming through the Rye. A Scottish poem, partly composed or revised by Robert BURNS.

Comintern. The Third or *Com*munist *Intern*ational of Moscow. Officially dissolved May 15, 1943. See also COMMUNISM.

comitatus (*Lat.,* from *comes* "companion"). Among the early Germanic tribes, a band of warriors gathered about a specific chief to whom they pledged themselves by a personal oath, with whom they lived, and whom they served in battle. This institution had an important influence on later feudalism, especially in the relationship between lord and vassal. The Anglo-Saxon epic BEOWULF contains an excellent illustration. Cf. modern German *Gefolgschaft* which is a loan translation of *comitatus.*

comitia and Comitium. In ancient Rome the *comitia* were assemblies of the people which had the authority to act on certain matters submitted to them through official channels. They met at the foot of the Capitol at a place called *Comitium*.

Commander of the Faithful. A title of the Caliphs, first assumed by Omar I. (581, 634–644).

Commandments, the Ten. The Decalogue; the laws given to Moses on tables of stone at Mount Sinai (*Ex.* xx. 1–18).

commandos. In World War II, British shock troops specially trained for lightning attacks on enemy key positions. The term *commando* had been in use with about the same meaning in South Africa. It was adapted from Dutch which in turn had taken it from Portuguese.

commedia dell'arte (*It.*, not to be rendered by "art theater" but by "theater of professionals"). Italian comedy as performed by guilds of professional actors who were trained to embroider improvised lines and business on a written plot. The rôles were fairly fixed, representing such typical figures as *Pantalone,* a Venetian merchant; *Pulcinella,* a wag of Apulia; *Arlecchino,* a clown; and so on. The *commedia dell'arte* flourished from about 1560 to 1625. It influenced the Elizabethan drama. Without it certain features of the modern opera, ballet, musical revue, and circus could not be explained.

Commemoration, Ode recited at the Harvard. Poem by James Russell LOWELL.

Commentaries on the Gallic War. *Lat.* **De bello Gallico.** Julius CAESAR's account of his wars in Gaul, written by him in seven books about 51 B. C.

commissar. In Soviet Russia, one of the *people's commissars,* that is, the head of a governmental department (called commissariat) in one of the republics of the U.S.S.R. Through Arthur Koestler's *The Yogi and the Commissar* (1945), the term has come to stand for the typical 20th-century man of aggressive efficiency.

Commodus, Lucius Aelius Aurelius (161–192 A. D.). Roman emperor (180–192). Prided himself on his gladiatorial skill and was strangled by an athlete in a conspiracy.

Common. The name of the principal public park in Boston, so called because it was originally the "common," or public cow pasture.

Common, Doll. A young woman in Ben Jonson's comedy THE ALCHEMIST, in league with Subtle the alchemist, and with Face his ally.

Commoner, The Great. The elder William Pitt (1708–1778), afterwards Earl of Chatham.

common-law marriage. A marriage concluded without ecclesiastical or civil ceremony, simply by mutual consent of the partners. Not recognized in all jurisdictions.

common sense. A general sense assumed as the medium of perception in cases where none of the five traditional senses seems to fit. This "general" common sense is often called the sixth sense. It is viewed as having the entire body as its organ or as not being in need of a special organ at all. Its name is a translation of Latin *sensus communis.* The signification "good sense, horse sense" is a more recent development. It seems to imply, on the basis of eighteenth century philosophy, that what is common to all human beings must be sound.

Common Sense. A political treatise by Thomas PAINE (1776) largely influential in bringing about the American Declaration of Independence.

commonwealths, ideal. The most famous ideal, or imaginary, commonwealths in which equity and wisdom rule, are those sketched by Plato in the *Republic* (from which all the others derive), by Cicero in his DE REPUBLICA, by St. Augustine in his *De Civitate Dei* (THE CITY OF GOD), by Dante in his *De Monarchia,* by Sir Thomas More in *Utopia* (1516), by Bacon in the NEW ATLANTIS (a fragment, 1616), by Campanella, a Dominican friar (about 1630), and Samuel Butler's EREWHON (1872).

To these some would add Johnson's *Rasselas* (1759), Lytton's *Coming Race* (1871), Bellamy's *Looking Backward* (1888), Wm. Morris' *News from Nowhere* (1891), and some of H. G. Wells' romances, such as *In the Days of the Comet* (1906) and *The World Set Free* (1914). See also COMMUNISM.

Commune of Paris, the. The government established in Paris in 1792 by the representatives of the communes and leading up to the period called "The Reign of Terror." More commonly the term is applied to the insurrectionary government that took possession of Paris, March 18 to May 28, 1871, after the withdrawal of the Prussian troops.

communism (from Lat. *communis,* common). A form of SOCIALISM characterized by the principle of control by society of all economic activities, especially the common ownership of property, personal as well as productive. It differs from socialism in a strict sense in that the latter aims at the social ownership only of property used for production, not of personal property. The term "communism" was coined (ca. 1840) by the French revolutionary societies, and thereafter came to mean more specifically a doctrine advocating the overthrow of capitalist society (see CAPITALISM), while socialism was used in connection with a program of peaceable reform.

Revolutionary violence was the popular implication of communism especially after the BOLSHEVIK Revolution of 1917 in Russia.

Communism, in one form or another, based on anti-materialistic doctrines and humanitarian sympathies, was for centuries an ideal among philosophers such as Plato, ZENO the Stoic, Sir Thomas MORE, and others. See COMMONWEALTHS, IDEAL. It was also an intermittent practice among various Christian monastic sects, Jesus Himself having urged charity, benevolence, and common ownership of goods. During the 19th century, a number of experimental communities were established which practiced communism, especially in America. See BROOK FARM; OWEN, ROBERT; PANTISOCRACY.

By combining traditional humanitarian ideals and the philosophical ideas of HEGEL with a scientific theory of economics, Karl MARX gave great impetus to the communist movement, strengthening it both in its principles and objectives and in its practical program. After his death, however, and in the 20th century the movement was considerably weakened by factional disputes on doctrine and method. See also BABEUF, GRACCHUS; GOLDEN AGE; MARXISM; TROTSKY, LEON.

Communist Manifesto. A pamphlet, published in 1848 by Karl MARX and Friedrich ENGELS under the title of *Manifest der Kommunisten.* It contains a survey of the history of the working classes in modern times, written on the basis of the materialist conception of history, and leading up to the conclusion that social and political changes of a revolutionary nature are to be foreseen with absolute certainty. Its principles account for much of the driving force behind the Communism of Nikolai Lenin and modern Russia.

Communist parties. Political organizations designed to put into practice the principles of Marxist Communism, their aim being revolution, the abolition of capitalist economy (see CAPITALISM), and the establishment of a "dictatorship of the proletariat," the model for which became the Soviet Union of Russia. Lenin did much to influence the form of the Communist parties, in accordance with his modifications of Marx's theory, which were attacked by the Socialists. The first Communist Party was formed in Russia in 1918 by the BOLSHEVIK faction of the Social Democratic Party, and the first outside Russia, in Germany in 1919. Within the next few years, in accordance with the program of the Third, or Communist, INTERNATIONAL, Communist parties were established in over fifty countries. They were very strong in a number of European countries during the first ten years after World War I, especially in Germany, France, and Czechoslovakia. The policies of the various Communist parties consistently followed those of the Soviet Union, and their original revolutionary aims were considerably modified by the rise of FASCISM. See also TROTSKYISM; POPULAR FRONT; FELLOW TRAVELERS.

Communist Party of the U.S.A. Established in 1919 as the Communist Party of America and the Communist Labor Party by the radical faction of the Socialist Party, which were combined in 1920 as the United Communist Party. After being called next the Worker's Party (1921), it acquired the name of Communist Party of the U.S.A. in 1928. After the dissolution of the COMINTERN it became the Communist Political Association (May 20, 1944). It had its greatest influence during the 1930's, under the secretaryship of Earl BROWDER; then, because of the effects of the widespread economic depression of the time, numerous college students, intellectuals, and members of the unemployed either joined the Party or became sympathetic "FELLOW TRAVELERS." Among certain of the educated classes, Communist leanings were often little more than conformity with a fad of the period. At this time, the American Communist party devoted itself prominently to labor organization and defense of civil liberties and the rights of the Negro, and showed a resemblance to the indigenous American reform movements of the 19th century, such as Abolitionism and POPULISM. Its general policies, however, continued to follow those of the Soviet Union of Russia. See also COMMUNISM; DAILY WORKER; MARXISM; MASSES; NEW MASSES; PROLETARIAN LITERATURE.

Companionate Marriage, The. A treatise by Benjamin Barr Lindsey and Wainwright Evans (1927), proposing a form of marriage which childless couples would be allowed to dissolve by mutual consent and without ensuing legality of economic or financial claims of one of the partners on the other.

Companions of Jehu. The CHOUANS were so called, from a fanciful analogy between their self-imposed task and that appointed to Jehu, on being set over the kingdom of Israel. Jehu was to cut off Ahab and Jezebel, with all their house, and all the priests of Baal. The Chouans were to cut off all who assassinated Louis XVI, and see that his brother (*Jehu*) was placed on the throne.

Company of Jesus, see JESUITS.

Compensation. One of the best-known and most characteristic essays of Ralph Waldo EMERSON (1841). Compensation is "the cosmic process" by which "each thing is a half, and suggests another to make it whole. . . . What we call retribution is the universal necessity by which the whole appears wherever a part appears . . . Every act rewards itself."

Compiègne. French town on Oise river where Joan of Arc was captured by the English in 1430. In the forest of Compiègne the Armistice of Nov. 11, 1918, ending World War I was signed in a railroad car. This car was preserved in a near-by museum. On June 21, 1940, Hitler made use of it to re-enact the scene of the signing of the armistice with changed parts.

Compleat Angler, The. A famous volume on fishing by Izaak Walton (1653). It has the subtitle *Contemplative Man's Recreation,* being "a Discourse on Rivers, Fish-ponds, Fish and Fishing."

complex. One of the more popular terms of PSYCHOANALYSIS; in general terms, any deeply rooted, subconscious association of ideas with a strong emotional tone, so functioning that reference to a minor idea on the fringe of the main association or even slightly connected with it, tends to bring to the fore the entire feeling-tone and so prevent rational thought or action. According to the FREUDIANS, such complexes may be resolved or sublimated through psychoanalysis. The specific nature of a complex will be more evident from the following specially named complexes which were popularized by the psychoanalytic craze of the years immediately following World War I.

inferiority complex. A feeling of being inferior to other people, usually deeply rooted in subconscious childhood associations that operate to prevent normal mental activity. Technically it is always the negative partner of a repressed superiority complex. See also ADLER, ALFRED.

Messiah complex. A delusion that one is born to do great things, to be a sort of Messiah.

Narcissism. The term given by the Freudians to the complex of self-love, with obvious allusion to NARCISSUS who fell in love with his own reflection.

Oedipus complex. Any undue or unhealthful attachment of a child for his mother, which, according to the Freudians, is apt to be morbidly suppressed and to cause great mental distress through illogically remote manifestations in later years. The allusion to the involuntary incest of the Greek hero OEDIPUS is obvious.

Complutensian Polyglot. See BIBLE, SPECIALLY NAMED.

Compromise, Missouri. See MISSOURI.

Compton, Ben. In Dos Passos' trilogy U.S.A., a young Jewish Communist who becomes the lover for awhile of Mary FRENCH.

Compton, Private. In James Joyce's *Ulysses.* See under CARR, PRIVATE.

Comsomol (Russ. *Komsomol: Kommunisticheskii* "communist" + *soyuz* "union" + *molodezh* "youth"). The youth organization of the Russian Communist Party.

Comstock, Anthony (1844–1915). An American reformer spokesman for the New York Society for the Suppression of Vice. His name came to be frequently used as a synonym for a strait-laced and narrow-minded Puritan.

Comstock lode. A famous gold and silver lode discovered in 1859 in Storey County, Nevada, near the site of what is now Virginia City. Owing to the Comstock lode Nevada ceased to be a transit area for gold seekers and became instead their most popular goal. Virginia City was for a time the most famous mining camp of the Far West.

Comte, Auguste (1798–1857). French philosopher, known for his philosophy of POSITIVISM, by which he planned to apply the methods and findings of science to philosophy, social science, and even religion and thereby achieve true social reform. His ideas are to be found in *Cours de philosophie positive* (1839–1842). Comte had an important influence on the thought of his time, John Stuart MILL and Hippolyte TAINE showing the effect of his ideas in their own writings. Comte's socio-ethical religion is summed up in the principle *"vivre pour autrui"* (to live for one's neighbor).

Comus. In Milton's masque of this name (1634) Comus is the god of sensual pleasure, son of Bacchus and Circe. The name is from the Gr. *komos,* carousal.

In the masque the elder brother is meant for Viscount Brackley, the younger brother is Mr. Thomas Egerton, and the lady is Lady Alice Egerton, children of the Earl of Bridgewater, at whose castle in Ludlow it was first presented. The lady is left in the woods by her two brothers, who go in search of "cooling fruit" for her. She falls into the hands of Comus, but the brothers come to her rescue just as the god is offering his captive a magic potion; and SABRINA is invoked to break the spell.

Conachar. In Scott's FAIR MAID OF PERTH the Highland apprentice of Simon Glover, the old glover of Perth. Conachar is in love with his master's daughter, Catharine, called "the fair maid of Perth"; but Catharine loves and ultimately marries Henry Smith, the armorer. Conachar is at a later period Ian Eachin M'Ian, chief of the clan Quhele.

Conan. The Thersites of *Fingal* in Macpherson's OSSIAN; brave even to rashness.

Blow for blow, or *claw for claw, as Conan said.* Conan makes a vow never to take a blow without returning it; when he descends into the infernal regions, the arch fiend gives him a cuff, which Conan instantly returns, saying "Claw for claw."

Conan Doyle, see DOYLE.

Conant, James Bryant (1893–). American educator and teacher of chemistry. President of Harvard University since 1933.

conceit. A poetic device of extended metaphor, by which an object, a scene, person, situation, or emotion is presented by means of comparison with a simpler analogue, usually chosen from nature or a context familiar to author and reader alike. The conceit was developed in the poetry of PETRARCH and his followers, and spread to Elizabethan England, where it became almost an institution in the poetry of the day.

The following is an excellent example:

> My galley charged with forgetfulness
> Through sharp seas, in winter nights, doth pass
> 'Tween rock and rock; and eke my foe, alas,
> That is my lord, steereth with cruelness;
> And every oar a thought in readiness,
> As though that death were light in such a case.
> And endless wind doth tear the sail apace,
> Of forced sighs and trusty fearfulness;
> A rain of tears, a cloud of dark disdain,
> Have done the wearied cords great hinderance;
> Wreathed with error and with ignorance,
> The stars be hid that led me to this pain;
> Drowned is reason, that should be my comfort,
> And I remain despairing of the port.
>
> Sir Thomas WYATT, an adaptation of *Petrarch's Sonnet 159.*

concerto. A musical composition in which there is one solo instrument, usually a violin or piano, accompanied by a full orchestra. The concerto began as music for voices and organ in the early 17th century and then developed into a chamber orchestra in the 18th century. MOZART is considered to have fixed the form of the modern concerto.

concert of Europe. The European powers, as they existed in the past, insofar as they were bound by agreement or understanding to concerted action in questions of common interest, especially with reference to the Balkan States and the Near East.

concerto grosso. An early form of concerto in which several solo instruments, usually strings, appear with a full orchestra. CORELLI (1653–1713), HANDEL, and J. S. BACH were composers of *concerti grossi.* Bach's BRANDENBURG CONCERTOS are examples of this form.

conchy, see CONSCIENTIOUS OBJECTOR.

conclamatio. Among the ancient Romans, the loud cry raised by those standing round a death-bed at the moment of death. It probably had its origin in the idea of calling back the departed spirit, and was similar to the Irish howl over the dead. "One not howled over" (*corpus nondum conclamatum*) meant one at the point of death; and "one howled for" was one given up for dead or really deceased. Hence the phrase *conclamatum est,* he is dead past all hope, he has been called and gives no sign. Virgil makes the palace ring with howls when Dido burns herself to death.

> Lamentis, gemituque, et foemineo ululato,
> Texta fremunt. *Aeneid,* iv. 667.

concordance. An index of words (also often of subjects), showing their various occurrences (with indication of context) in a work or a collection of works. The term is often used as a *pars pro toto* instead of "Bible concordance."

concordat. An agreement made between a ruler and the Pope. Concordats of outstanding historical importance are the Concordat of 1801 between Napoleon and Pius VII; the Concordat of 1516 between François I and Leo X to abolish the "pragmatic sanction"; and the Germanic Concordat of 1448 between Frederick III and Nicholas V.

Concord Hymn. A poem by Ralph Waldo EMERSON, sung at the completion of the Bunker Hill Monument in 1836. It contains the much-quoted lines

> Here once the embattled farmers stood
> And fired the shot heard round the world.

concubinage. From Lat. *con* "together" and *cubare* "to lie down." A form of marriage considered inferior by the Romans because the absence of legal bonds excluded the offspring from the *potestas* of the father. The partners in such a union were called concubines (in Lat. *concubinus* and *concubina*). In modern usage the term *concubine* stands only for the woman and is little more than a euphemism for "kept mistress."

Conder, Charles (1868–1909). English artist. His *The Hot Wind* (1890) was painted in Australia. Especially known for his technique of water-color decorations on white silk.

Condon, Linda, see LINDA CONDON.

Condor, Legion, see LEGION KONDOR.

Condorcet, Marquis de (1743–1794). French philosopher and mathematician. Protagonist of the theory of the "infinite perfectibility of man" in his *Esquisse d'un tableau historique des progrès de l'esprit humain* (1794). Arrested as a member of the Girondist faction, he died in prison.

condottieri (*It.*). Leaders of mercenaries and military adventurers, particularly from about the 14th to 16th centuries. The most noted of these brigand chiefs in Italy were Guarnieri, Lando, Francesco of Carmagnola, and Francesco Sforza. The singular is *condottiere.*

Conestoga wagon or wain. A great white-topped covered wagon, boat-shaped, as much as 16 ft. long and 6 ft. deep. Used by the pioneers and designed for travel in soft soil and on prairies. First manufactured at Conestoga, Lancaster Co., Pa.

Confederate flag, see STARS AND BARS.

Confederate States, see under STATES.

Confessio Amantis (The Lover's Confession). A Latin work by the medieval English author John GOWER (ca. 1386–1390), in the story-within-a-frame tradition. In it, a young man confesses the sins he has committed against love—love here being the convention of COURTLY LOVE. To illustrate each one he tells a story, usually from the Bible or from classical literature. The stories of Jason, Narcissus, Gideon, Tobias, and Appollonius of Tyre are included.

confession. As a literary term, a form of autobiography, in which the true or manipulated account of the author's life serves some sort of didactic purpose. In this sense, confessions constitute a literary *genre* which took its start in the CONFESSIONS OF ST. AUGUSTINE. They reached the height of their development in the era of romanticism when they began to show symptoms of narcissistic decadence. See ROUSSEAU, DE QUINCEY, MUSSET, CHATEAUBRIAND.

Confession of Golias. A famous medieval Latin poem by the ARCHPOET, addressed to the Archbishop of Cologne, which sums up the pursuits and the general attitude of the wandering scholars of the Middle Ages. See GOLIAS.

Confession of My Faith and a Reason of My Practice, A. See BUNYAN, JOHN.

Confessions. Famous autobiography of Jean Jacques ROUSSEAU, in which he frankly reveals the details of his erratic and rebellious life.

Confessions of an English Opium-Eater. The most famous work of Thomas DE QUINCEY, published in 1822. It gives an account of the poet's early life and describes the growth and effects of his habit of taking opium.

Confessions of a Thug. See TAYLOR, M.

Confessions of St. Augustine. Autobiography of St. Augustine (see under SAINT), written after 390 A.D. in order to reveal to the world the circumstances of his conversion to Christianity. The work gives an excellent picture of Augustine's mind and personality, and of the life and conflicting philosophies and religions current in the last days of the Roman Empire.

Confraternità della Misericordia. Brotherhood of Mercy. An organization established in Florence, Italy, in 1244 to give help to the sick and bury the dead. It is still active.

Confucius. Latinized form of Chinese **Kung Fu-tzu,** literally "the philosopher Kungx" (ca. 551–479 B.C.). Great Chinese teacher of ethics who called himself a "transmitter, not an originator." His function of strengthening the native Chinese religion has been exaggerated to a point where Confucianism is considered a full-fledged religious system on a par with the other Chinese religions of Taoism and Buddhism. In essence, however, the system of Confucius is concerned with mundane ethics, and endeavors to regulate the five relationships of life, that is, the relationships of prince and subject, parent and child, brother and brother, husband and wife, and friend and friend.

Congo, The: A Study of the Negro Race. A poem by Vachel LINDSAY, published in 1914 in *The Congo And Other Poems.* It is an attempt to represent African and Negro RAGTIME rhythms in verse by means of various verbal effects.

Congregationalist. A member of the Congregational Church whose doctrines, known as evangelical or orthodox, include autonomy tempered by co-operation and fellowship of the individual congregations. Hence the name.

Congress of Industrial Organizations (C.I.O.). An American organization of labor unions, founded by John L. LEWIS in 1935 and first known as the Committee for Industrial Organization. It split away from the AMERICAN FEDERATION OF LABOR, favoring union organization on the basis of the type of industry in which its prospective members might be employed rather than on their individual crafts.

Congreve, William (1670–1729). The most prominent English dramatist of the Restoration period, known for his witty contributions to the comedy of manners of his time. His best-known comedies are *The Double Dealer* (1694), *Love for Love* (1695) and THE WAY OF THE WORLD (1700). Congreve was one of the playwrights attacked for lewdness by Jeremy COLLIER. He was a friend of SWIFT, STEELE, and POPE.

Coningsby or the New Generation. A political novel by DISRAELI (1844). The hero, Harry Coningsby, is the mouthpiece of the political group known as YOUNG ENGLAND; and in sharp contrast to him is his grandfather, the Marquis of Monmouth, a shrewd and worldly representative of the old school. Coningsby's love affair with the daughter of a self-made man named Millbank is kept distinctly subordinate to the political interest. A noteworthy character is the Jew, Sidonia, said to have been drawn partly from Baron Alfred de Rothschild and partly from the author himself. He has wealth, strength of body and of intellect and unswerving devotion to high ideals. In *Coningsby* Disraeli introduced many prominent figures of contemporary affairs in thinly veiled disguise and much of its popularity may be credited to the interest of identification. Gladstone is said to be depicted as Oswald Millbank; the Marquis of Hertford as the Marquis of Monmouth; and as for the hero, Coningsby, he has been variously identified as Lord Littleton, Lord Lincoln or George Smythe.

The characters are supposed to be as follows: *Croker* is Rigby; *Monmouth* is Lord Howard; *Eskdale,* Lowther; *Urmsby,* Irving; *Lucretia* is Mde. Zichy; the countess *Colonna* is Lady Strachan; *Sidonia* is baron A. de Rothschild; *Henry Sidney* is Lord John Manners; *Belvoir,* the duke of Rutland. —*Notes and Queries,* March 6, 1875.

Coniston. A political novel by Winston CHURCHILL (1906), narrating the career of Jethro Bass, the local "boss." His corrupt political practices separate him from the girl he loves and later from her daughter, whom he has taken to live with him.

Conkey Chickweed, see CHICKWEED, CONKEY.

Conkling, Grace Hazard (1878?–). American poet. Teacher of English, Smith College. Her daughter Hilda (1910–) was a phenomenal child poet.

Conmee, Father. In James Joyce's A PORTRAIT OF THE ARTIST AS A YOUNG MAN, the elegant rector of CLONGOWES WOOD COLLEGE, to whom Stephen DEDALUS appeals when he is unjustly punished by Father DOLAN. Father Conmee also appears briefly in ULYSSES, when Leopold BLOOM observes him taking a walk in Dublin.

Connally Resolution. Nov. 5, 1943, in favor of international organization. The House of Representatives had adopted the Fulbright Resolution, Sept. 21, 1943, by a vote of 360 to 29, in favor of American participation in "the creation of appropriate international machinery with power adequate to establish and maintain a just and lasting peace." The U.S. Senate adopted the language of the Moscow Conference in passing the Connally Resolution.

Connecticut Yankee in King Arthur's Court, A. A satirical romance by Mark TWAIN (1889), narrating the imaginary adventures of a 19th century Yankee who suddenly wakes up in a court of medieval chivalry. His knowledge of modern inventions, together with his native shrewdness, gives him many an opportunity to impress and outwit the valorous but slow-moving knights of King Arthur.

Connell, Richard Edward (1893–). American novelist and short-story writer. Has also made motion pictures. *Apes and Angels* (1924) is a characteristic collection of short stories.

Connelly, Marcus Cook (1890–). American playwright, best known for his comedies written in collaboration with George KAUFMAN, including *Dulcy* (1921); *Beggar on Horseback* (1924); *Merton of the Movies* (1925). Connelly also dramatized THE GREEN PASTURES (1929) from *Ol' Man Adam an' His Chillun* by Roark BRADFORD. Winner of the O. Henry Memorial award (1930) for his short story, "Coroner's Inquest."

Conning Tower, The. See ADAMS, FRANKLIN P.; COLUMNS.

Connolly, James Brendan (1868?–). Well-known American writer of sea stories, knowing all that concerns sea-going fishermen. Has written *Out of Gloucester* (1902), *Steel Decks* (1925), *American Fishermen* (1940), and *Canton Captain* (1942), as well as many other books.

Connor, Ralph, see GORDON, C. W.

Conqueror, The. A historical novel by Gertrude ATHERTON (1902), based on the career of Alexander Hamilton (1757–1804).

Conqueror, the. An epithet applied to leading warriors of history, including the following:

Alfonso I (ca. 1109–1185). King of Portugal.
Aurungzebe the Great (1619, 1659–1707). The most powerful of the Moguls.
James I (1206, 1213–1276). King of Aragon.
Mohammed II (1430–1481). Sultan of Turkey.
Othman or *Osman I* (1259, 1299–1326). Founder of the Turkish power.
Francisco Pizarro (1475–1541). Called *el Conquistador* because he conquered Peru.
William, Duke of Normandy (1027, 1066–1087). Called "the Conqueror" because he obtained England by conquest.

Conquest of Canaan, The. A poem by Timothy DWIGHT (1785) based on the Old Testament book of *Joshua* and called by its author "the first American epic." Joshua was the leader under whom the Jews entered the Promised Land of Canaan and defeated the inhabitants.

The phrase was taken as the title of a novel by Booth TARKINGTON (1905), dealing with small-town politics. The hero is Joe Louden, a young lawyer who finally becomes mayor of his town.

Conquest of Granada, The. A mock serious history by Washington IRVING (1829), purporting to be written by the priest Fray Agapida. This book, which gives an account of the conflict between Spanish Christians and Moors in the days of Ferdinand, was Irving's favorite among his own works.

For Dryden's tragedy *Almanzor and Almahide, or The Conquest of Granada,* see under ALMANZOR.

Conquest of Mexico, The. One of the two principal works of the American historian William Hickling PRESCOTT (1843). The other chief work of the author, written in a similar pattern, is *The Conquest of Peru* (1847). *The Conquest of Mexico* is known for its dramatic sweep and its centering of the historic conflict between native Mexicans and invading Spaniards in the heroic figures of Hernando CORTÉS and MONTEZUMA.

Conquistador. A narrative poem in TERZA RIMA by Archibald MACLEISH, published in 1932, winner of the Pulitzer Prize for poetry in 1933. It is based on an eye-witness account of the Spanish expedition to Mexico (1519–1520) led by Hernando CORTÉS, as told by one of Cortés' soldiers, Bernal Díaz. It is heroic and realistic in flavor.

Conrad. Hero of Byron's poem, THE CORSAIR. He was afterwards called LARA in the poem of that title.

Conrad, Joseph (1857–1924). English novelist, of Polish parentage and upbringing. Original name **Teodor Józef Konrad Korzeniowski.** He worked at sea on British merchant ships from 1878 to 1894, and is known for his studies of character against a background of life at sea. His novels include ALMAYER'S FOLLY (1895); AN OUTCAST OF THE ISLANDS (1896); THE NIGGER OF THE NARCISSUS (1898); LORD JIM (1900); NOSTROMO (1904); ROMANCE (1903), with Ford Madox Hueffer (see FORD, FORD MADOX); UNDER WESTERN EYES (1911); CHANCE (1914); VICTORY (1915); THE ARROW OF GOLD (1919); THE RESCUE (1920). Conrad wrote an autobiographical volume entitled *A Personal Record.*

Conrad in Quest of His Youth. A novel by Leonard MERRICK.

Conroy, Gabriel, see GABRIEL CONROY.

Conscience, Hendrik (1812–1883). Flemish novelist. *In't Wonderjaer 1566* (*In the Year of Marvels 1566*), published in 1837, was his first novel and the first book to be published in modern Flemish. *De Leeuw van Vlanderen* (*The Lion of Flanders*) of 1838 is the one of his more than 100 books that will continue to be read.

conscience clause. A clause in an Act of Parliament to relieve persons with conscientious scruples from certain requirements in it. It generally has reference to religious matters, but it came into wider prominence in connection with the English Compulsory Vaccination Act of 1898.

conscience money. Money paid anonymously to a local or national government by persons who have defrauded the revenue, or who have understated their income to the income-tax assessors; also any money secretly refunded on the dictates of conscience.

conscientious objector. One who takes advantage of a CONSCIENCE CLAUSE, and so does not have to comply with some particular requirement of the law in question. In England, the name used to be applied specially to those who would swear legally that they had a conscientious objection to vaccination; but during the recruiting campaigns of World War I it was given—usually with contempt—to those who refused to fight in the army because they found war incompatible with their religious beliefs. They were also known as *Conchies* and *C.O.'s.*

Conscious Lovers, The. See STEELE, RICHARD.

conscript fathers (Lat. *Patres conscripti*). The Roman senate. Romulus instituted a senate consisting of a hundred elders, called *Patres* (Fathers). After the Sabines joined the State, another hundred were added. Tarquinius Priscus, the fifth king, added a third hundred, called *Patres Minorum Gentium.* When Tarquinius Superbus, the seventh and last king of Rome, was banished, several of the senate followed him, and the vacancies were filled up by Junius Brutus, the first consul. The new members were enrolled in the senatorial register, and called *Conscripti;* the entire body was then addressed as *Patres [et] Conscripti* or *Patres conscripti.*

Consolation of Philosophy, The (De Consolatione Philosophiae). Best-known work of the Christian philosopher BOETHIUS, written while he was in prison after being condemned to death by the Emperor Theodoric. In it, the Lady Philosophy comes to comfort the author in his cell, and they discuss various philosophical issues of the time, including riches, honor, love, fate, free will, and the like. Lady Philosophy expresses a modified STOIC attitude throughout. *The Consolation of Philosophy* was extremely popular during the Middle Ages, having been translated by King Alfred, Chaucer, and Queen Elizabeth, among others.

consols, i.e., consolidated annuities. In 1751, several public securities forming part of the debt of Great Britain were consolidated into one fund and became popularly known as "consols." Securities of this type constituted at times more than half of the country's national debt.

Conspiracy of Pontiac, The. A book by Francis PARKMAN.

constable. From Latin *comes stabuli,* count of the stable. In the monarchial establishments of the Middle Ages the constables were originally chief grooms and later chief officials in the palace, the army, and the like. Hence the titles *Constable of France, Lord High Constable of England, Constable of Scotland,* etc.

Constable, Henry (1562–1613). English poet of Catholic faith. He wrote sonnets and pastoral poems which are represented in the first edition of Sir Philip Sidney's APOLOGY FOR POETRY, in the *Poetical Exercises* (1591) of King JAMES I, and in ENGLAND'S HELICON (1600). He also wrote a sonnet sequence, *Diana,* published in 1592 and 1594, and a series of religious sonnets, *Spiritual Sonnets to the Honor of God and His Saints,* not published until 1815 because they were Catholic in flavor.

Constable, John (1776–1837). English painter, known for his rural landscapes and his effects of light and color. He influenced the BARBIZON SCHOOL.

Constance. Mother of Prince Arthur and widow of Geoffrey Plantagenet portrayed in Shakespeare's *King John* (1598). See also CUNSTANCE.

Constance of Beverley. In Scott's MARMION, a Benedictine nun, who falls in love with Marmion, and, escaping from the convent, lives with him as a page. Marmion proves faithless; and Constance, falling into the hands of the Benedictines, is tried for violating her vows and immured in the convent wall.

Constant, Benjamin (1845–1902). French romantic painter. Algerian scenes and portraits. Among the latter *Queen Victoria, Leconte de Lisle,* etc.

Constant de Rebecque, Benjamin (1767–1830). French author and politician. Friend of Mme de Staël. His *Adolphe: anecdote trouvée dans les papiers d'un inconnu* (1816) is a psychological novel of lasting interest.

Constantin, L'Abbé, see ABBÉ CONSTANTIN, L'.

Constantine, Lady Viviette. Heroine of Hardy's TWO ON A TOWER.

Constantine the Great. Roman emperor (306–337). Became sole emperor of the West (312) after defeating Maxentius in the battle at the Milvian Bridge, where a cross appeared to him in the sky, bearing the famous words, *in hoc signo vinces,* "by this sign you will conquer." Adopted Christianity (313). Defeated Licinius (323) and became sole emperor of the Roman world. Called Council of Nicaea (325) where Nicene Creed was adopted. Chose Byzantium as his new capital, calling it after himself Constantinople (The City of Constantine).

Constitution. A 44-gun frigate, U.S. Navy, launched in 1797. When, under Jefferson, the United States resisted at last the Barbary corsairs after this country had paid them a tribute of two million dollars, the *Constitution* was one of the ships taking part in the expedition known as the Tripolitan War (1801–1805). Later, in the War of 1812, under the command of Isaac Hull (1773–1843), she forced the surrender of the British frigate *Guerrière* off Cape Race, Newfoundland (August 19, 1812). When the *Constitution* was ordered dismantled (1830), Oliver Wendell HOLMES wrote the poem, OLD IRONSIDES, that caused her rebuilding.

Constitution of the United States of America. Fundamental law adopted in 1787 and in effect since March 1789, supplanting the articles of confederation signed in 1781. See CONTINENTAL CONGRESS. Up to 1942, 21 amendments to the original instrument had been adopted. The 21st amendment repealed the 18th or Prohibition amendment in 1933. The Constitution established a republican form of government for the United States, with separate executive, legislative, and judicial branches.

Consul Bibulus, see under BIBULUS.

Consuelo. One of the best known of George SAND's novels (1844), which, together with its sequel *The Countess of Rudolstadt* (LA COMTESSE DE RUDOLSTADT), relates the adventures of the beautiful Venetian singer Consuelo. She grows up in the streets, but is given a musical education by Porporo, a maestro who becomes interested in her gifts. After she has made her début in opera, she visits the castle of the Rudolstadts in Bohemia and there marries Count Albert of Rudolstadt on his deathbed. Albert is a firm believer in the occult and expects to be reborn, but instead he comes to life after burial, having been in a deep trance. In the sequel Consuelo and her husband go on together through life affirming a sort of occult gospel that brings them great satisfaction.

Conte del Graal. See CHRÉTIEN DE TROYES; GRAIL.

Contentment, Adventures in. See BAKER, RAY STANNARD.

Contes de fées. Fairy tales in French prose by Claude Perrault (1697), a source book for many old tales and nursery rhymes. They have been translated into English.

Contes de ma mère l'oye. See MOTHER GOOSE.

Contes Drôlatiques (Droll Stories), by Honoré de BALZAC (1832, 1833, 1837). A collection of stories, written in the style of Rabelais "for the diversion of the Pantagruelists and no others."

Continental Congress. The congress of deputies from the British colonies of North America meeting to consider their common interests. The First Continental Congress met in Philadelphia, Sept. 5 to Oct. 26, 1774; the

Second May 10, 1775 to Dec. 12, 1776; the Third in Baltimore Dec. 20, 1776. Others followed till March 1, 1781.

Continental system. A name given to Napoleon's plan for shutting out Great Britain from all commerce with the continent of Europe. He forbade under pain of war any nation of Europe to receive British exports, or to send imports to any of the British dominions. It began November 21, 1806.

continuity. In motion picture and radio, a technical term for that which assures the continuity of the performance, that is, the scenario of a film or the interpolated remarks by the announcer which serve to connect the various selections of the broadcast.

contraception. See BIRTH CONTROL.

Contrast, The. The first native American comedy, written by Royall TYLER and produced in New York in 1787. It concerns the contrast between Colonel Manly, representing dignified simplicity, and Dimple, Charlotte, and Letitia, who represent the social frivolities of the time. One of the leading characters is Jonathan, the Colonel's servant, who is the typical Yankee. See BROTHER JONATHAN. *The Contrast* was a great success.

contredanse, see COUNTRY-DANCE.

Convent Threshold, The. A poem by Christina ROSSETTI (1862), presenting the thoughts of a girl about to go into a convent as she ponders on a past love and repentance and a mystic dream.

Conversation at Midnight. A long poem by Edna St. Vincent MILLAY, published in 1937, in which a group of men, representing varying shades of interest and opinion, discuss controversial social, political, and aesthetic issues of the time. The characters are presented satirically.

Converse, Florence (1871–). American poet. *Collected Poems* (1937). Also wrote *Long Will,* an historical novel concerning William Langland, author of PIERS PLOWMAN, which is a classic in *Everyman's Library.*

Converse, Frederick Shepherd (1871–1940). American musician and composer who wrote in *Pipe of Desire* (1910) the first opera by an American composer ever performed by the Metropolitan Opera Company of New York City.

Convivio. See DANTE ALIGHIERI.

convoy. Fleet of merchant vessels voyaging under protection of one or more warships. The formation of convoys was found, during World War I, to be an effective defense against U-boat attacks. The method was further developed during World War II.

Conway, Moncure Daniel (1832–1907). An American abolitionist clergyman. Noted as biographer of Thomas PAINE, and for works on CARLYLE, EMERSON, and HAWTHORNE.

Conway Cabal. See under CABAL.

Cook, George Cram (1873–1924). American novelist, poet, and playwright. He figures in Floyd Dell's novel *Moon-Calf* as Tom Alden. He wrote *The Chasm,* a socialistic novel, in 1911. He married Susan Glaspell and organized with her the Provincetown Players "in an old fish-house which Mrs. Wilbur Daniel Steele had taken for a studio, at the end of Mary Heaton Vorse's wharf." In 1915 Cook established the Playwrights' Theatre in New York City. In 1921 he sailed for Greece where he entered into the peasant life and died at sixty. His daughter Nilla is a disciple of Gandhi and published her autobiography in 1939.

Cook, James (1728–1779). English navigator and explorer. Discovered New Caledonia and Sandwich Islands. Was murdered by Sandwich Islanders in revenge for a flogging administered to one of them for stealing a boat.

Cooke, Jay (1821–1905). American banker. After the Civil War, financed construction of western railroads and made a fortune from mining investments in Utah.

Cooke, Rose Terry (1827–1892). American poet and author of local-color stories dealing with New England. Her works include *Poems* (1860); *Happy Dodd, Or She Hath Done What She Could* (1878); *Somebody's Neighbors* (1881); *The Sphinx's Children and Other People's* (1886); *Huckleberries Gathered from New England Hills* (1891).

Cook's or **Cokes Tale.** In Chaucer's CANTERBURY TALES. See GAMELYN.

Coolidge, Calvin (1872–1933). Thirtieth president of the U.S. (1923–1929). Elected vice-president in 1921, he succeeded president Harding after the latter's death. Re-elected in 1924.

Coolidge, Dane (1873–1940). American naturalist. Also author of western stories.

Coomaraswamy, Ananda Kentish (1877–1947). East Indian scholar. Author of books on Buddhism and Indian art and literature. Resident (from 1917) in Boston.

Cooper, Courtney Ryley (1886–1940). Versatile American author. Once press agent for Buffalo Bill. Wrote on the circus, on crime, and 750 stories besides many books of a wandering life. *Wild Cargo* and *The Plainsman;* also moving pictures.

Cooper, James Fenimore (1789–1851). American novelist, the first to achieve substantial fame outside the U.S. He is best known for his historical novels of romance and adventure, dealing with the native American scene, which are best represented by the LEATHERSTOCKING TALES. These include THE PIONEERS (1823); THE LAST OF THE MOHICANS (1826); THE PRAIRIE (1827); THE PATHFINDER (1840); and THE DEERSLAYER (1841). Among his other works are THE SPY (1821); THE PILOT (1823); THE RED ROVER (1827); THE BRAVO (1831); several scholarly and biographical studies; volumes of social criticism expressing Cooper's own conservatism and his political theories; and the Littlepage Manuscripts, a trilogy of historical novels on the relations between American economic classes, consisting of SATANSTOE (1845), THE CHAINBEARER (1845), and THE REDSKINS (1846).

Cooper, Peter (1791–1883). American industrialist and humanitarian. Owner of a Baltimore iron works. Founder of Cooper Union (1857–) in New York City, dedicated to the "advancement of science and art," and offering free courses and lectures in a variety of (chiefly practical) subjects.

Cooper, Samuel (1724–1783). American clergyman of New England, known for his revolutionary writings against British rule in the colonies. He was the author of sermons, pamphlets, and articles for the Boston GAZETTE. His most famous work is *The Crisis* (1754), a pamphlet attacking the currently proposed bill for excise taxes on America. Cooper also worked prominently in support of the alliance with France made by Benjamin Franklin.

Cooper's Hill. See DENHAM, SIR JOHN.

Copernicus Nicolaus. Latinized form of **Niklas Koppernigk** (1473–1543). Polish astronomer, famous as the proponent of the theory that the earth and planets revolve around the sun, in radical opposition to the widely held theory of PTOLEMY, which was one of the pillars of medieval cosmology. "The Copernican revolution dethroned man as the center and lord of Creation."

Cophetua, a King. Anyone who marries far below his station. From a mythical king of Africa, of great wealth, who fell in love with a beggar-girl, Penelophon (Zenelophon in Shakespeare's *Love's Labour's Lost,* IV, I.), and married her. He is the hero of a ballad in Percy's *Reliques,* and Tennyson versified the tale in *The Beggar-Maid.*

Copland, Aaron (1900–). American composer of ballet music, symphonies, chamber music, and orchestral and choral works, mostly in the dissonant 20th-century idiom, and adaptations of jazz. See DISSONANCE, JAZZ. His *Dance Symphony* (1930) won the RCA-Victor Company award of that year. One of the best known of his works is *El Salón Méjico* (1936). A number of his compositions were written for motion pictures and radio, and *Billy the Kid* (1941) is an attempt in the manner of American folk music, being based on cowboy songs.

Copley, John Singleton (1738–1815). American painter, resident of England from 1774 until his death. He is best known for his portraits.

Coppard, Alfred Edgar (1878–). English short-story writer and poet, known for the pathos and quiet irony of his work. His volumes of short stories include *Adam and Eve and Pinch Me* (1921); *Clorinda Walks in Heaven* (1922); *The Black Dog* (1923); *The Field of Mustard* (1926); *Count Stefan* (1928); *The Gollan* (1929); *Pink Furniture* (1929); *Rummy* (1930); *Easter Day* (1931); *Ring the Bells of Heaven* (1933); *Emergency Exit* (1934); *The Ninepenny Flute* (1937). Among his books of poems are: *Hips and Haws* (1922); *A Yokohama Garland* (1926); *Collected Poems* (1928).

Coppée, François Édouard Joachim (1842–1908). French poet and playwright. Contributor to the PARNASSE CONTEMPORAIN (1866).

Copper Captain, A. A poseur, a masquerader, from the famous character so called in Beaumont and Fletcher's *Rule a Wife and Have a Wife* (1624). The *Copper Captain* is Michael Perez, a captain without money, but with a plentiful stock of pretense, who seeks to make a market of his person and commission by marrying an heiress. He is caught in his own trap, for he marries Estifania, a woman of intrigue, fancying her to be the heiress Margaritta. His wife says to him—

> Here's a goodly jewel . . .
> Did you not win this at Goletta, captain . . .
> See how it sparkles, like an old lady's eyes . . .
> And here's a chain of whitings' eyes for pearls . . .
> Your clothes are parallels to these, all counterfeits.
> Put these and them on, you're a man of copper,
> A copper . . . copper captain.
>
> Fletcher, *Rule a Wife and Have a Wife.*

Copperfield, David, see DAVID COPPERFIELD.

Copperheads. The copperhead is a poisonous snake of North America (*Trigonocephalus contortrix*), which, unlike the rattlesnake, gives no warning of its attack. Hence the name *Copperheads* was applied by the early colonists to the Indians, then to the Dutch (cf. Washington Irving's *History of New York*), and, finally, in the Civil War to the pro-Southerners among the Northerners, the covert friends of the Confederates.

Copts. The Jacobite Christians of Egypt who, since the Council of Chalcedon in 451, have been in possession of the patriarchal chair of Alexandria. The word is probably derived from Coptos, the metropolis of the Thebaid. These Christians conduct their worship in a dead language called "Coptic" (language of the Copts). St. Anthony (ca. 250–350), the founder of Christian monachism, was a Copt.

copyright. The exclusive right of multiplying for sale copies of works of literature, art, etc., or substantial parts thereof, allowed to the author or his assignees.

United States copyrights may be secured under the Act of March 4, 1909 (as amended), for a period of twenty-eight years and a twenty-eight-year renewal is allowed, making the entire period of possible copyright, fifty-six years. Serial rights, motion picture rights, etc., are often disposed of separately and the matter is an intricate one. International copyright was established in 1891, but is regarded as inadequate and a matter for agitation.

The first Copyright Act in England is that of 1709; modifications and additions to it were made at various times, and in 1842 a new Act was passed granting copyright for forty-two years after publication or until the expiration of seven years from the death of the author, whichever should be the longer.

This Act was superseded by the Copyright Act of 1911, under which the period of protection was extended to fifty years after the death of the author, irrespective of the date of publication of the book. This Act deals also with the copyright in photographs, engravings, architectural designs, musical compositions, gramophone records, etc. See also PIRACY.

Coq d'or, Le (*Fr.* literally, the golden cockerel). A satirical opera (1909) by Rimsky-Korsakov, flaying the foibles of royalty.

Coquelin, Benoît Constant (1841–1909). Famous French actor and actor-manager. Mainly remembered as having created the rôle of Cyrano in Edmond ROSTAND's *Cyrano de Bergerac.*

Coquette, The. An early American novel by Hannah Webster Foster (1797) which ran through thirty editions in forty years, but is now forgotten. It was based on the tragic story of Elizabeth Whitman of Hartford.

coquillard (*Fr.,* from *coquille* "cockle, shell"). In medieval France, a beggar pretending to be on a pilgrimage, and wearing or selling cockles supposedly coming from Santiago de Compostela. See St. James under SAINTS.

Cora Munroe. In Cooper's LAST OF THE MOHICANS.

Corbaccio, Il. See BOCCACCIO, GIOVANNI.

Corbet, Richard, Bishop of Oxford and Norwich (1582–1635). English churchman and poet, known for his joviality. An old story tells how once, on seeing a vender of broadside ballads (see BALLADS; BROADSIDE) unable to sell his wares at a marketplace, the bishop took off his gown, put on the other man's jacket, and began hawking the ballads in a loud voice until they were all sold. Corbet was a friend of Ben JONSON and was popular at the MERMAID TAVERN because of his skill at extemporizing poetry. His best-known poem is *Iter Boreale,* an account of a vagabonding trip he once took.

Corbett, James J. (1866–1933). American professional boxer, popularly known as "Gentleman Jim." Knocked out world champion John L. Sullivan on Sept. 7, 1892 and held title till March 17, 1897, when he lost it to Robert Fitzsimmons.

Corbière, Jean Antoine (1793–1875). French naval officer, known as author of sea tales. **Édouard Joachim Corbière** (1845–1875), the son of Jean Antoine, made a name for himself as a poet of the SYMBOLIST group.

Corbin, Alice. See HENDERSON.

Corbin, John (1870–). American author and dramatic critic. Member of the National Institute of Arts and Letters.

Corbino, Jon (1905–). Italian-American painter whose work is represented in the Pennsylvania Academy of Art and the Toledo Museum of Art. Member of the National Institute of Arts and Letters.

Corbusier, Le, see LE CORBUSIER.

Corceca. The typification of blindness of heart (Lat. *cor,* heart, *caecus,* blind) in Spenser's *Faërie Queene* (I, iii). She is a blind old woman, mother of Abessa (Superstition) and is often regarded as a personification of Romanism.

Corcoran Art Gallery at Washington, D.C. Founded and endowed for maintenance by William Wilson Corcoran, American financier and humanitarian (1798–1888).

Corday, Charlotte (1768–1793). French patriot who stabbed MARAT, a leader of the Terrorists, to death in his bath. Guillotined July 17, 1793. She was an adherent of the Revolution but felt repelled by the excesses of the REIGN OF TERROR. Cf. Joseph Shearing's *The Angel of the Assassination.*

Cordelia. In Shakespeare's KING LEAR, the youngest of Lear's three daughters, and the only one who loves him. Hence the expression *Cordelia's gift,* a "voice ever soft, gentle and low, an excellent thing in woman."

Cordelier, *i.e.* "cord-wearer." A FRANCISCAN friar of the strict rule, an Observantin. In the Middle Ages they distinguished themselves in philosophy and theology. DUNS SCOTUS was one of their most distinguished members. The tale is that in the reign of St. Louis these Minorites repulsed an army of infidels, and the king asked who those *gens de cordelics* (corded people) were. From this they received their appellation.

There is a French proverb, *Il ne faut pas parler latin devant les Cordeliers,* "don't talk Latin before the Cordeliers," which means that one should be careful what one says on a subject before those who are masters of it.

In the French Revolution the name *Club des Cordeliers* was given to a political club, because it held its meetings in an old convent of Cordeliers. The Cordeliers were the rivals of the Jacobins, and numbered among their members Paré (the president), Danton, MARAT, Camille Desmoulins, Hébert, Chaumette, Dufournoy de Villiers, Fabre d'Eglantine, and others.

cordillera (*Span.,* a mountain range, from *cuerda* "a rope"). Originally applied to the Andes. Now often used loosely, as in "the western cordillera of the U.S.," which includes the Rocky Mountains, the Sierra Nevada, and the Coast and Cascade ranges.

cordon (*Fr.*). A ribbon or cord; especially the ribbon of an order of chivalry: also, a line of sentries or military posts enclosing some position; hence, an encircling line.

cordon bleu. A knight of the ancient order of the *St. Esprit* (Holy Ghost); so called because the decoration is suspended on a blue ribbon. It was at one time the highest order in the kingdom of France.

The title is also given, as a facetious compliment, to a good cook; and to a member of the "BLUE RIBBON ARMY," *i.e.* a teetotaler.

cordon noir. A knight of the Order of St. Michael, distinguished by a black ribbon.

Cords of Vanity. A novel of 20th-century life by James Branch CABELL (1905), a story, chiefly, of the numerous love affairs of Robert Etheridge Townsend, a rising young author. John CHARTERIS is also a prominent character.

Corelli, Marie. Pseudonym of **Mary Mackay** (1855–1924). English romantic novelist. *The Sorrows of Satan* (1895), *The Master Christian* (1900), etc. George Meredith encouraged her as a musician but not as a writer. A pretty little blonde woman who wrote torrentially and died of her 28th novel in her 70th year.

Corey, Bromfield. An aristocratic Bostonian art connoisseur who appears in Howells' *Rise of Silas Lapham* and THE MINISTER'S CHARGE. He is considered one of Howells' most amiable and delightful characters.

Corey, Giles, see GILES COREY.

Corey, Lewis (1894–). American free-lance economist. *The House of Morgan: A Social Biography of the Masters of Money* (1930), *The Decline of American Capitalism* (1934), *The Crisis of the Middle Class* (1935), etc.

Corey, Tom. A character in Howells' RISE OF SILAS LAPHAM.

Corinne or Italy. A novel by Madame de STAËL (1807). Corinne's lover, Oswald, marries her younger sister Lucile instead and Corinne's consequent suffering brings about her death. The book is famed for its descriptions of Italy; and Corinne, whose mother was Italian, represents the ideal qualities of Italy as her sister does those of England.

Corinthian. A licentious libertine; also a gentleman sportsman who rides his own horses on the turf, or sails his own yacht. The immorality of Corinth was proverbial both in Greece and Rome. The sporting rake in Pierce Egan's *Life in London* (1821) was known as "Corinthian Tom," and in Shakespeare's day a "Corinthian" was the "fast man" of the period. See also EPHESIAN.

> I am no proud Jack, like Falstaff; but a Corinthian, a lad of mettle, a good boy.—1 *Henry IV,* ii. 4.

Corinthian brass. An alloy made of a variety of metals (said to be gold, silver, and copper) melted at the conflagration of Corinth in 146 B.C., when the city was burnt to the ground by the consul Mummius. Vases and other ornaments, made by the Romans of this metal, were of greater value than if they had been silver or gold.

> I think it may be of Corinthian brass,
> Which was a mixture of all metals, but
> The brazen uppermost.
> Byron, *Don Juan,* vi. 56

Corinthian order. A type of Greek architecture, of later date than the DORIC and IONIC orders. It was used less frequently than the other two, appearing chiefly in the CAPITAL, where the ornamentation was based on the design of the acanthus leaf. An unfounded legend traces the origin of this to a basket of playthings placed on the grave of a little girl of Corinth by her nurse and weighted with a tile. The following spring an acanthus plant was discovered to have twined its leaves about the basket. CALLIMACHUS, the sculptor, is said to have seen it and been inspired to imitate in a metal capital.

Coriolanus, Caius Marcius. A legendary Roman general called Coriolanus from his victory over the Volscians at Corioli. Shakespeare wrote a drama *Coriolanus* (ca. 1608–1610). Returning to Rome in triumph he is elected consul, but opposes the plebeian interests and is shortly afterwards banished. He joins his former enemies the Volscians against Rome, but is finally persuaded to give up the siege by the entreaties of his wife and mother. In the classic sources his mother was Veturia, not Volumnia, and his wife Volumnia, not Virgilia, as Shakespeare has called them.

Corkery, Daniel (1878–). Irish playwright, short story writer, novelist. Among his best known books is one of short stories, *The Hounds of Banba.*

Corleone. One of the novels of F. Marion CRAWFORD'S SARACINESCA series.

Corley, Donald. American writer who illustrated his own fantastic stories, *The House of Lost Identity* (1927), *The Fifth Son of the Shoemaker* (1929), etc.

Cormoran. The Cornish giant who, in the nursery tale, fell into a pit dug by Jack the Giant-killer. For this doughty achievement Jack received a belt from King Arthur, with this inscription—

> This is the valiant Cornish man
> That slew the giant Cormoran.
> *Jack the Giant-killer.*

Corn Cracker State. Kentucky. See under STATES.

Corneille, Pierre (1606–1684). Famous French dramatist of the early neo-Classical period, author of tragi-comedies and tragedies dealing chiefly with psychological conflicts of mind and will in reference to honor, patriotism, duty, etc. His best-known plays are LE CID (1636); CINNA (1640); HORACE (1640); and POLYEUCTE (ca. 1641). His other works include MÉLITE (1629); MÉDÉE (1634); LA MORTE DE POMPÉE (1643); LE MENTEUR (1644); RODOGUNE (1645); NICOMÈDE (1650); ANDROMÈDE (1650); PERTHARITE (1652); OEDIPE (1659); OTHON (1664); TITE ET BÉRÉNICE (1669). RACINE was Corneille's rival and successor.

Cornelia. In Roman history, wife of Titus Sempronius Gracchus, and mother of the two tribunes, Tiberius and Caius. She was almost idolized by the Romans, who erected a statue in her honor, with this inscription, *Cornelia, Mother of the Gracchi.*

Cornelia's jewels. One day a lady from Campania called upon Cornelia, the mother of the Gracchi, and after showing her jewels, requested in return to see those belonging to the famous mother-in-law of Africanus. Cornelia sent for her two sons, and said to the lady, "These are my jewels, in which alone I delight."

Cornell, Katharine (1898–). American actress, best known for her performances in THE GREEN HAT (1925), THE LETTER (1927), and THE BARRETTS OF WIMPOLE STREET (1931).

Cornford, Frances Crofts (1886–). English poet; wife of the English philospher Francis Macdonald Cornford (1874–). Outstanding among her volumes of poetry is *Spring Morning.*

Cornhusker State. Nebraska. See under STATES.

Cornish, N.H. Abode of a number of poets and artists, as Augustus St. Gaudens, Percy MacKaye, William Vaughn Moody, Maxfield Parrish, etc.

corn laws. Laws passed at various times in English history to prevent first the export and later the import of grain. The most controversial Corn Laws were those of the 19th century, which levied a high duty on imports and raised domestic prices, causing great suffering among the poor of England, especially in the manufacturing districts. An Anti-Corn Law League was formed to bring about repeal of the laws, and John BRIGHT was one of the orators who worked toward this end. The grain tariff was reduced in 1849 and entirely abolished in 1862.

cornucopia. The horn of plenty or the horn of Amalthaea. According to one Greek legend, it was broken off the goat Amalthaea by the infant JUPITER, who endowed it with the magic power of becoming filled with whatever its owner wished, and gave it to his nurses.

Cornwallis, Charles, 1st Marquis (1738–1805). English major general in American Revolution; defeated Greene but was forced to surrender shortly thereafter (1781). Viceroy of Ireland (1798–1801). Died as governor general of India.

Cornwell, Dean (1892–). American artist. Illustrated Blasco IBÁÑEZ, Somerset MAUGHAM, etc. Murals in General Motors Building at World's Fair (1939) and elsewhere.

Corombona, Vittoria, see ACCORAMBONI.

coronach. See under BALLAD.

Coronado, Francisco Vásquez (1510–1554). Spanish explorer in America. In search of famed Quivira. (See poem "Quivira" by Arthur Guiterman.) Followed course of Rio Grande and went north across what is now the Texas Panhandle and Oklahoma into eastern Kansas.

Coronet for his Mistress Philosophy, A. See CHAPMAN, GEORGE.

Corot, Jean Baptiste Camille (1796–1875). French painter associated with the BARBIZON SCHOOL. He is known for his landscapes, often containing classical figures and representing classical scenes, marked by Romantic feeling and tremulous effects of mist and sunlight.

Corporal, the little. Napoleon Bonaparte, so called after the battle of Lodi (1796). During his exile at Elba Napoleon was called *Corporal Violet* because his adherents wished for his return with the violets of Spring.

Corporal John. John CHURCHILL, the duke of Marlborough (1650–1722).

Corporal Trim. Uncle Toby's attendant in STERNE'S *Tristram Shandy.*

corporation. In commerce, etc., a body of persons considered, with legal authorization, as an individual.

> A corporation is an artificial being, invisible, intangible, and existing only in contemplation of law.
> *Dartmouth College Case* (17. *U.S.* 518, 636).

In their names, corporations are often identified by the abbreviation *Inc.,* meaning "incorporated."

corposant. The ST. ELMO'S FIRE or "Castor and Pollux" of the Romans; the ball of fire which is sometimes seen playing round the masts of ships in a storm. So called from Span. *corpo santo,* holy body. Sometimes known as *comazant.*

Corpus Christi. A festival of the Church, kept on the Thursday after Trinity Sunday, in honor of the Eucharist. It was instituted by Urban IV in 1264, and was the regular time for the performance of religious dramas by the trade guilds. In England many of the Corpus Christi plays of York, Coventry, and Chester are still extant.

Corpus Christi College at Cambridge was founded in 1352, and the College of the same name at Oxford in 1516.

Correggio, Antonio Allegri da (1494–1534). Italian painter, known for the grace and sensuous charm of his classical landscapes, and their effects of color, light, and shade.

Corrigan, Douglas. American airplane pilot, object of a flurry of publicity in the summer of 1938 when he made a flight from New York to Ireland. He claimed that he believed he was flying to California, and he was known in the newspapers for awhile as "Wrong-way" Corrigan.

Corsair (Ital. *corsaro;* Fr. *corsaire;* ultimately from Lat. *cursus,* "a chase, run"). Properly "one who gives chase," applied to the pirates of the northern coast of Africa.

The Corsair is the title of a narrative poem in three cantos by BYRON (1814). The hero is Conrad, chief of the pirates, afterwards known as Lara in the poem of that title which relates his last adventures. He enters the palace of the Sultan Seyd in the disguise of a dervish but is discovered and thrown into a dungeon. Gulnare, queen of the harem, releases him and follows him from the palace disguised as a page. Upon returning to the Pirates Isle, he finds that Medora, his true love, has died during his absence, so he returns to his native land, heads a rebellion and is shot. On his death his page Kaled is discovered to be Gulnare in disguise. Byron is said to have based *The Corsair* and *Lara* on the career of Lafitte, a notorious American buccaneer, pardoned by General Jackson for services rendered in 1815 during the attack of the British on New Orleans.

Corsican, the. Napoleon Bonaparte who was born in Ajaccio on the island of Corsica.

Cortegiano, Il. See CASTIGLIONE, BALDASSARE DE.

Cortes. The Spanish or Portuguese parliament. The word means "courts," that is, "court officers." The Portuguese name in full is *Cortes Gerais* "general courts."

Cortés, Hernán. More commonly **Hernando Cortes** (1485–1547). Spanish conqueror of Mexico (1519–1521). He is an important figure in THE FAIR GOD, by Lew Wallace, and the story of his conquest is told in Prescott's CONQUEST OF MEXICO and Archibald MacLeish's poem CONQUISTADOR, both of which were based on records of the Spanish expedition left by Bernal Díaz, one of its members.

Cortesi, Arnaldo (1897–). American journalist. New York *Times* correspondent from Rome (1921–1938), Mexico, Argentina. In 1946 he won one of four Pulitzer prizes for reporting for his dispatches from Buenos Aires.

Cortissoz, Royal (1869–). American art critic and journalist. Wrote studies of Augustus St. Gaudens (1907) and John La Farge (1911).

Corvo, Baron, see ROLFE.

Corwin, Norman (1910–). Widely known American writer of radio scripts, as *Ten by Corwin, More by Corwin, On a Note of Triumph.* His scripts approach poetry in their rhythmic and dramatic qualities.

Cory, William Johnson (1823–1892). English lyric poet. Author of *Ionica* (1858), and the famous translation, "They told me, Heraclitus, they told me you were dead."

Coryate or **Coryat, Thomas** (1577?–1617). English traveler and buffoon at court. *Coryate's Crudities* (1611) are an account of his travels through Germany, Switzerland, and the Netherlands.

Corybantes. The Phrygian priests of Cybele, whose worship was celebrated with orgiastic dances and loud, wild music. Hence, a wild, unrestrained dancer is sometimes called a *corybant.*

Corydon. A conventional name for a rustic, a shepherd; a brainless, love-sick youth; derived from the shepherd in Virgil's *Eclogue* VII, and in Theocritus.

Coryell, John R. See CARTER, NICK.

coryphaeus. The leader and speaker of the chorus in Greek dramas; hence, figuratively, the leader generally, the most active member of a board, company, expedition, etc.

Coryphaeus of German literature. GOETHE (1749–1832).

Coryphaeus of Grammarians. Aristarchus (220–143 B.C.).

coryphée. A leading ballerina, formerly also her male equivalent. Hence in American colloquial usage, a chorus-girl.

Cosette. In Victor Hugo's LES MISÉRABLES, the daughter of Fantine. While she is still a little girl, Jean Valjean rescues her from a wretched existence and becomes the most devoted of fathers. Eventually she falls in love with Marius and marries him.

Così Fan Tutte (*It.* Thus Do They All). An opera buffa by MOZART (1790).

Cosima. Wife of Richard WAGNER. See LISZT, COSIMA.

Cosme, St. See under SAINT.

Cosmological Eye, The. See MILLER, HENRY.

Cosmopolis. See BOURGET, PAUL.

cosmos (Gr. *kosmos* "order, harmony"). The universe as an organic whole. Hence any independent organic entity. Cf. *microcosm,* "a small cosmos," as applied for instance to the human individual in contrast to *macrocosm,* "the world at large."

Costard. In Shakespeare's LOVE'S LABOUR'S LOST, a clown who apes the court wits of Queen Elizabeth's time. He uses the word "honorificabilitudinitatibus," and some of his blunders are very ridiculous, as "ad dunghill, at the fingers' ends, as they say."

Coster, Charles de (1827–1879). Belgian writer, whose best-known work, *La Légende de Thyl Ulenspiegel et de Lamme Goedzak* (1868), succeeds in making of TYLL EULENSPIEGEL a delightful incarnation of the Flemish folk spirit.

Costigan, Captain. The father of Miss Fotheringay, in Thackeray's PENDENNIS. He is a happy-go-lucky Irishman, an ex-army officer, usually known as "Cos" to his companions. Though he is none too particular about his own reputation, he has always an eye out for his daughter's good name and fortune. When he learns that Pen has no special prospects financially, he makes his daughter break her engagement.

Emily Costigan. The Captain's daughter, an actress engaged, for a time, to Pen. She is better known under her stage name of The Fotheringay.

Cottard, Dr. In Marcel Proust's REMEMBRANCE OF THINGS PAST, an eminent physician with snobbish ambitions in the social world who attends the Wednesday evening salons of M. and Mme VERDURIN, neglects his practice, and insultingly reprimands his meek wife in public for being dowdy or graceless.

Cotter's Saturday Night, The. A poem by Robert BURNS (1787) famous for its description of Scottish peasant life.

Cottle, Joseph (1770–1853). English bookseller, publisher, and poet. He brought out some of the first works of SOUTHEY, COLERIDGE, and WORDSWORTH. Author of *Early Recollections, chiefly relating to Samuel Taylor Coleridge* (1837). His poetic efforts are remembered as having won the distinction of Byron's sarcastic scorn.

Cotton, Charles (1630–1687). English poet and first translator of Montaigne's *Essays* (1685). He also brought out various burlesques of Virgil, Lucian, etc., and a second part to the fifth edition of Walton's *Compleat Angler* (1676).

Cotton, John (1585–1652). Puritan divine, who fled from England to New England and became one of the most powerful and influential men in the American colony, successor to Thomas HOOKER. He was known for his tireless scholarship and religious fanaticism. He was the author of sermons, religious treatises, and pamphlets. His works include *The Keys of the Kingdom of Heaven* (1644); *The Way of the Churches of Christ in New England* (1645); *Milk for Babes, Drawn Out of the Breasts of Both Testaments* (1646), a children's catechism; *The Bloody Tenent Washed and Made White in the Blood of the Lamb* (1647), part of a celebrated controversy on religious toleration which took place between Cotton and Roger Williams (see BLOODY TENENT, THE); *The Way of the Congregational Churches Cleared* (1648); *A Survey of the Sum of Church Discipline* (1648). Increase MATHER was his son-in-law.

Cotton, Sir **Robert Bruce** (1571–1631). English antiquary, collector of books, manuscripts, coins, medals, and the like. He was the founder of the famous Cottonian Library, which contained many otherwise unobtainable manuscripts saved from destroyed monasteries, including those of BEOWULF, THE PEARL, and GAWAIN AND THE GREEN KNIGHT. The titles of the manuscripts were derived from the busts of Roman emperors which adorned the bookcases in these collections; thus the *Beowulf* manuscript is called Cotton Vitellius A XV, from the Emperor Vitellius, and the manuscript of *The Pearl* is known as Cotton Nero A X, from the Emperor Nero. Cotton allowed the free use of his library to leading scholars of his time and presented manuscripts from his collection to the Bodleian Library when it was founded. His library was bequeathed to the English nation on the death of his grandson in 1701.

Cotton Plantation State. Alabama. See under STATES.

Cotytto. The Thracian goddess of immodesty, worshiped at Athens with licentious rites. See BAPTES.

> Hail! goddess of nocturnal sport,
> Dark-veiled Cotytto.
> Milton, *Comus*, 129, 130.

Couch, Sir **Arthur Quiller-,** see QUILLER-COUCH.

Coughlin, Father Charles Edward (1891–). Canadian-born American Roman Catholic priest, known for a series of Sunday afternoon radio sermons which he delivered from his church, the Shrine of the Little Flower, at Royal Oak, Michigan (ca. 1930–1940). In these he criticized contemporary events and forcefully presented economic and political platforms of his own devising, in which he urged nationalization of natural resources and banking functions and attacked Wall Street, Communism, and the Jews. At first he supported the NEW DEAL, but later became a strong enemy of it and President Franklin D. ROOSEVELT. During the depression years of the 1930's Coughlin commanded a tremendous following among his radio audience, the members of his National Union for Social Justice, and the readers of his newspaper *Social Justice,* which was devoted chiefly to the propagation of anti-Semitism. He was opposed to the entry of the U.S. into World War II. The similarity of his ideas to those of Fascism was frequently pointed out. Cf. AMERICA FIRST COMMITTEE; CHRISTIAN FRONT; LONG, HUEY; TOWNSEND, DR. FRANCIS E. TOMMY GALLAGHER'S CRUSADE by James T. FARRELL portrays the type of person to whom sentiments like those expressed by Father Coughlin make their greatest appeal.

Coulin. A British giant mentioned by Spenser (*Faërie Queene,* II, x. 11); he is pursued by Debon until he comes to a chasm, and, after leaping it, he slips on the opposite side, falls back, and is killed.

Council of Clermont. A church council, held in 1095, at which Pope Urban II made a powerful speech urging the knights of medieval Europe to join in a Crusade to the Holy Land, to assist the Byzantine emperor ALEXIUS COMNENUS in his war against the Turks, to rescue the Holy Sepulcher from Moslem hands, and to reach the lands of the East where there was greater wealth and a greater abundance of food. The First Crusade was a direct outcome of the Pope's skillful pleading.

Counter-Attack. A book of poems by Siegfried SASSOON, published in 1918, denouncing and satirizing war.

countercheck quarrelsome. "Sir, how dare you utter such a falsehood? Sir, you know that it is not true." This, in TOUCHSTONE's classification (Shakespeare's *As You Like It,* v. 4), is the third remove from the lie direct; or rather, the lie direct in the third degree.

The reproof valiant, the countercheck quarrelsome, the lie circumstantial, and the lie direct, are not clearly defined by Touchstone; but *that* is not true; how *dare* you utter such a falsehood; *if* you say so, you are a liar; you lie, or are a liar, seem to fit the four degrees.

Counterfeiters, The (Les Faux-monnayeurs). A novel by André GIDE (1925; English translation, 1927). According to Gide, it was the first novel he ever wrote. It deals with the family relationships and social experiences of Bernard Profitendieu, an adolescent French youth who runs away from his home on discovering what he regards as evidence of his illegitimate birth. Édouard, uncle of Olivier Molinier, a friend of Bernard, is introduced as the supposed author of the novel, and his journal, commenting on the characters and the progress of the action, is interspersed among the chapters of the novel itself. The "counterfeiters" of the title are teachers of what Gide regards as false morals.

Counterpane, The Land of. A poem in *A Child's Garden of Verse* by Robert Louis Stevenson.

Counterparts. A story in DUBLINERS by James Joyce, in which a clerk is reprimanded by his employer and, to salve his wounded pride, becomes drunk and beats his small son.

counterpoint (from It. *contrappunto*). In music, the term for the combining of two or more melodies in simultaneous rendition, first used in the 14th century as *punctus contra punctus* (Lat.), "note for note." One melody, called the *cantus firmus,* at first taken from a Gregorian plain-song, remains fixed, and other, independent melodies accompany it. *Strict* counterpoint is counterpoint written according to the established rules of its early usage; *free* counterpoint permits variation and greater scope. Counterpoint was at first vocal, used in religious music, and in the 17th century it became instrumental. J. S. BACH is considered the greatest writer of counterpoint since the 17th century. Aldous HUXLEY wrote a novel *Point Counter Point* (1928).

Countess Kathleen, The. See YEATS, WILLIAM BUTLER.

Count of Monte Cristo, The. A romance by Alexandre DUMAS (1844). When the story opens, the young hero, Edmond Dantes, is on the point of becoming captain of his vessel and of marrying his sweetheart, Mercedes. On a false charge of political intrigue made by jealous rivals, he is sentenced to life imprisonment in the Château d'If. He digs a passageway through the thick walls of the Château with infinite labor and finally makes his escape. A half-mad fellow prisoner, a Catholic Abbé with whom he had established communications, had told him of a buried treasure on the island of Monte Cristo. With this treasure he becomes a powerful and mysterious figure and eventually exacts a fearful revenge from all those who have wronged him.

Count Robert of Paris. A novel by Sir Walter SCOTT (1831), relating the adventures of Count Robert and his wife Brenhilda, who set out together on the First Crusade (1096–1099). Vying in interest with Robert is Hereward the Saxon, one of the Varangian guard of the Emperor ALEXIUS COMNENUS. Hereward enlists under the Count's banner and discovers in Brenhilda's maid Bertha his old Saxon sweetheart.

Country, Father of his. See under FATHER.

country-dance. An English dance of popular origin, viewed by Nicolas Slonimsky as the ancestor of several modern ballroom dances.

The English *Country-dance* became the *Contredanse* in France, and this in turn was called *Contradanza* in Spain, or later, simply *Danza*. When imported by the Spaniards into Cuba, it became the *Danza Habanera*, that is, the dance of Havana, and then was reintroduced into Spain as *Habanera*. During the Spanish-American War, a popular dance called *Habanera del Café* appeared, which was the prototype of the *Tango*.

Country Doctor, The (Le Médecin de campagne). A novel by BALZAC (1833). The principal character is Dr. BENASSIS.

coup (*Fr.*). Properly a blow or stroke, but used both in French and English in a large number of ways, as for a clap of thunder, a draught of liquids, a piece of play in a game (a move in chess, etc.), a stroke of policy or of luck, a trick, etc.

a good coup. A good hit or haul.

coup d'essai. A trial-piece; a piece of work serving for practice.

coup d'état. A state stroke; the term is applied to a bold measure taken by a government to prevent a supposed or actual danger, as when a large body of men are arrested suddenly for fear they should overturn the government. It also applies to deliberate action to seize power undertaken by a group of relatively minor authority.

The famous *coup d'état,* by which Louis Napoleon became possessed of absolute power, took place on December 2, 1851.

coup de grâce. The finishing stroke; the stroke of mercy. When a criminal was tortured by the wheel or otherwise, the executioner gave him a *coup de grâce,* or blow on the head or breast, to put him out of his misery.

coup de main. A sudden stroke, a stratagem whereby something is effected suddenly.

coup d'œil. A view, glance, prospect; the effect of things at the first glance; literally "a stroke of the eye."

coup de pied de l'âne. Literally, a kick from the ass's foot; figuratively, a blow given to a vanquished or fallen man; a cowardly blow; an insult offered to one who has not the power of returning or avenging it. The allusion is to the fable of the sick lion kicked by the ass.

coup de soleil. A sunstroke, any malady produced by exposure to the sun.

coup de théâtre. An unforeseen or unexpected turn in a drama producing a sensational effect; a piece of claptrap, something planned for effect.

coup manqué. A false stroke, a miss, a failure.

Couperus, Louis Marie Anne (1863–1923). Dutch novelist. *The Small Souls* (1914), one of his more than thirty novels, is an example of his best work.

couplet. In versification, a pair of lines whose end-words rhyme. The best-known example of the form is the *heroic couplet,* so named because it was used in the composition of epic poetry in the 17th and 18th centuries. It was written in iambic pentameter measure, and in neo-Classical usage the two lines were required to express a complete thought, with a subordinate pause at the end of the first line. Pope was the most skillful writer of heroic couplets, which were often used for epigrams:

You beat your pate, and fancy wit will come.
Knock as you please—there's nobody at home.
Pope

Ill fares the land, to hastening ills a prey,
Where wealth accumulates, and men decay.
Goldsmith

By the time of the Romantic period the thought was carried beyond the two rhyming lines of the couplet, which was then known as *open* or *run-on,* in contrast with the former example, or *closed* couplet:

A thing of beauty is a joy forever:
Its loveliness increases; it will never
Pass into nothingness; but still will keep
A bower quiet for us, and a sleep.
Keats

Courageous, Captains, see CAPTAINS COURAGEOUS.

Courbet, Gustave (1819–1877). French painter, initiator of the movement against the painters of historical and pseudo-classical subjects of the school of DAVID and INGRES. He painted realistic pictures of men and women, sometimes on autobiographical events, animal scenes, and landscapes. During his entire career, Courbet's work was attacked by hostile critics, and his association with the Communists in the Revolution of 1871 added further to his misfortunes, causing him to be sentenced to a term in prison and to the payment of heavy fines in money.

Cournos, John (1881–). Russian-American novelist. Author of *The Mask* (1919), *The Wall* (1921), *The New Candide* (1924), etc.

Cours de Philosophie Positive. See COMTE, AUGUSTE.

Courtier, The. See CASTIGLIONE, BALDASSARE DE.

courtly love (Fr. *amour courtois*). A widespread convention of the Middle Ages, according to which the knight regarded the lady with whom he was in love with deep veneration and unquestioning devotion. This was accompanied by exaggerated gallantry of conduct and violent physical effects—such as fainting, loss of sleep and appetite, and the like—when he came into her presence or brooded upon her indifference. The convention originated in the Provençe, the south of France, during the late 11th century or early 12th century, and was at its height at the court of ELEANOR OF AQUITAINE; from there it spread to the north of France and to Germany. See MINNESÄNGER. Eleanor employed Andreas CAPELLANUS to draw up an elaborate list of rules for the courtly lover in his treatise *De Arte Honeste Amandi* (*Concerning the Art of Loving Honestly*). This includes an enumeration of the virtues required of the knight who aspired to be a lover, and announces as an outstanding tenet of the cult of Courtly Love the incompatibility of love with marriage, although the lady in question was nearly always married to someone other than her lover and often to his overlord. "Courts of Love" were held, and theoretical problems of love were proposed on which Eleanor and her ladies passed judgment in accordance with the rules of Andreas.

The TROUBADOURS expressed the convention in their poetry, and through their influence it reached Italy, where it was adopted by a group of poets associated with the Sicilian court of the Emperor FREDERICK II and by the school of IL DOLCE STIL NUOVO. Here the exaggerated worship of women acquired religious overtones and was identified with the cult of worship of the Virgin Mary. Through DANTE and PETRARCH, the convention finally reached the Elizabethan writers of lyrics and love-sonnets and became a permanent part of the literary concept of love until the 19th century.

Scholars disagree on the origin of the cult of Courtly Love, but some maintain it grew out of the influence of the Near Eastern goddess-cults or the strongly Platonized literature of the Arabs in Spain. The principles of the convention are embodied in a number of medieval romances, particularly the cycles dealing with King ARTHUR, TRISTAN and Isolt, and TROILUS and Cressida. Outstanding single works exemplifying it are *Lancelot, ou le chevalier de la charette* (*Lancelot, Or the Knight of the Cart*) (see LANCELOT), by CHRÉTIEN DE TROYES; THE ROMANCE OF THE ROSE; and Chaucer's *Troilus and Criseyde*.

Courtrai, Battle of, see BATTLE OF SPURS.

Courtship of Miles Standish, The. A narrative poem by LONGFELLOW (1858), based on the early history of the PILGRIM FATHERS. Miles Standish, the bluff middle-aged soldier of the colony, wishes to marry the Puritan maid, Priscilla, but instead of presenting his own cause, he sends his young friend, John Alden. Priscilla's answer is, "Why don't you speak for yourself, John?"; and although John is too loyal to speak for himself at once, eventually all ends happily for the two lovers.

Courvoisier, Eugen. The hero of Jessie Fothergill's FIRST VIOLIN.

Cousin, Victor (1792–1867). French philosopher. Studied German philosophy. Met Hegel and Schelling. Leader of the Eclectic School and first to formulate ECLECTICISM as a method. Wrote histories of philosophy in the 18th Century and studies of Pascal and Kant.

Cousin Betty (La Cousine Bette). A novel by BALZAC (1846). See FISCHER, LISBETH.

Cousin Jacky or Jan. A Cornishman.

Cousin Michel or Michael. The nickname of a German. See NICKNAMES OF NATIONALITIES.

Cousin Pons. A novel by BALZAC (1847). See PONS.

Cousins, Norman (1910?–). Editor *Saturday Review of Literature*. Author of *Modern Man is Obsolete* (1945), an essay concerning the release of atomic energy; also *The Good Inheritance: The Democratic Chance* (1942); etc. Co-editor with William Rose Benét of *The Poetry of Freedom* (1945).

couvade (from Fr. *couver*, to hatch). The name given by anthropologists to the custom prevalent among some primitive races by which the father of a newly born infant makes a pretense of going through the same experiences as the mother, lies up for a time, abstains from certain foods, etc., as though he, too, were physically affected by the birth. The custom has been observed by travelers in Guiana and other parts of South America, among some African tribes, in parts of China, Borneo, etc., and it was noted by the ancients as occurring in Corsica and among the Celtiberians.

Covarrubias, Miguel (1902–). Mexican artist and illustrator. Did much work for *Vanity Fair* and illustrated many American books, mainly in a style of grotesque characterization.

Covenanters. A term applied, during the English civil wars, to the Scotch Presbyterians, who, in 1643, united by "SOLEMN league and covenant" to resist the encroachments of Charles I on religious liberty.

Coventry. A town in England of historic associations. During World War II it was laid in complete ruin by bombing attacks from the air. Worst raid, November 14, 1940.

Coventry Mysteries or *Plays.* One of the important series of English MYSTERY PLAYS, so called because they were supposedly acted at Coventry.

send one to Coventry. To take no notice of him; to make him feel that he is in disgrace by having no dealings with him. Cf. also BOYCOTT. It is said that the citizens of Coventry had at one time so great a dislike to soldiers that a woman seen speaking to one was instantly tabooed; hence, when a soldier was sent to Coventry he was cut off from all social intercourse.

Hutton, in his *History of Birmingham,* gives a different version. He says that Coventry was a stronghold of the parliamentary party in the civil wars, and that troublesome and refractory royalist prisoners were sent there for safe custody.

Peeping Tom of Coventry. See under GODIVA.

Coverdale, Miles (1) (1488–1568). English priest, converted to Lutheranism and reputed to be the translator of the first complete Bible in English (1535). See under BIBLE, THE ENGLISH.

(2) The narrator of Hawthorne's BLITHEDALE ROMANCE and a leading character in the story.

Coverley, Sir Roger de. (1) A member of an hypothetical club in the SPECTATOR, "who lived in Soho Square when he was in town." Sir Roger is the type of an English squire in the reign of Queen Anne. He figures in thirty papers of the *Spectator.*

Who can be insensible to his unpretending virtues and amiable weaknesses; his modesty, generosity, hospitality, and eccentric whims; the respect for his neighbors, and the affection of his domestics?—Hazlitt.

(2) A well-known country dance was known by this name (also *Roger of Coverly*) many years before Addison's time. Its American form is the *Virginia reel.*

covey. An assemblage of birds, specifically of partridges. There are numerous terms in English signifying group, assemblage, etc., restricted by usage to certain creatures and hence in extension to certain metaphoric situations. Some of them are: *flock* (of sheep, geese, goats, and hence of believers), *herd* (of cattle or swine and hence of vulgar, unreasoning people), *pack* (of hounds and wolves, and hence of pursuers), *drove* (of cattle and hence of docile fools), *bevy* (of quails, larks), *flight* (of birds and hence of girls or women), *swarm* (of insects and hence numberless insignificant individuals), *shoal* (of fish). Cf. also *skein, gaggle,* etc.

Coward, Noel Pierce (1899–). English actor, composer, and playwright, known for his witty, brittle, and sophisticated comedies of the English "leisure class." His works for the theater, in addition to musical revues, include *The Vortex* (1923), a serious drama; *Bitter Sweet* (1929), an operetta; *Private Lives* (1931), his most successful comedy; *Cavalcade* (1931), a patriotic play on the British Victorian tradition in the history of a single family; and *Blithe Spirit* (1941). *Present Indicative* (1937) is an autobiography.

Cowboy. An American cattle herder on the Western plains, hero of folk-ballads, tall tales, dime novels, motion-picture melodramas, radio serials, and the games of small boys. The name originally was applied to Tory raiders during the American Revolution, who plundered neutral land.

Popular representatives and portrayers of the cowboy have been BUFFALO BILL, KIT CARSON, WILLIAM S. HART, TOM MIX, and the LONE RANGER.

Cowden-Clarke, see CLARKE.

Cowl, Jane (1884–). Original surname Cowles. American actress. Starred in *Within the Law, Common Clay, Lilac Time, Romeo and Juliet, The Road to Rome,* etc.

Cowley, Abraham (1618–1667). English poet and essayist, a Royalist in sympathies during the English Civil War. His CONCEITS were fantastic and extreme, popular in his own day but regarded with disfavor by the time of DRYDEN. His best-known poem is the DAVIDEIS (1656). His other works include *Poetical Blossoms* (1636) and *The Works of Mr. Abraham Cowley* (1668). *The English Writings* of Cowley were published in 1905–1906.

Cowley, Malcolm (1898–). American literary critic and poet, an editor of THE NEW REPUBLIC. His poetry, marked by satirical wit and sharp impressions in a disillusioned picture of his age, appears in *Blue Juniata* (1929) and *The Dry Season* (1942). *The Lost Generation* (1931) is a critical study of the neurotic and disillusioned intellectuals of the years following World War I, and *Exile's Return:*

A Narrative of Ideas (1934) is concerned with a similar subject, autobiographical in part.

Cowper, William (1731–1800). English poet of the pre-Romantic school of the 18th century. From his twenty-fourth year on he suffered from a morbid religious mania which manifested itself in a sense of overwhelming guilt and despair and intermittent attacks of insanity. His poetic activity began late in life, with the production of hymns, didactic verse, and nature lyrics, and intense, introspective religious poetry. His most famous poem is THE TASK (1785). Other poems of Cowper's which are well known are *Truth, The Progress of Error, Expostulation, Hope, Charity, Conversation,* and *Retirement,* all published in 1782, and THE DIVERTING HISTORY OF JOHN GILPIN, a humorous ballad, published with *The Task*. A collection of his hymns appears in *Olney Hymns* (1779). He also translated Homer and Milton and on his death left letters and introspective autobiographical writings. See also AUSTEN, LADY; CASTAWAY, THE; OLNEY; UNWIN, MRS. MARY; STRICKEN DEER.

Cowperwood, Frank. The central figure of Theodore DREISER's novels *The Financier* (1912), *The Titan* (1914) and *The Stoic* (1947). Cowperwood is a ruthlessly dominating Philadelphia financier who finally receives a prison sentence for illegal dealings. In *The Titan* he puts his prison life behind him and builds up another great fortune in Chicago. He marries his former mistress, but continues to indulge in innumerable affairs with women. The novels are said to be in some respects based on the career of Charles T. Yerkes.

Cox, Anthony Berkeley (1893–). English author of detective and psychological crime fiction. Writes under the pseudonyms of Anthony Berkeley and Francis Iles.

Cox, Kenyon (1856–1919). American painter and writer on art. Portrait of Saint Gaudens in Metropolitan Museum of Art, murals in Library of Congress, etc. *The Fine Arts* (1911), *Concerning Painting* (1917).

Cox, Palmer (1840–1924). Illustrator and author. Best-known for series of "Brownie" books for children.

Coxey's Army. An "army" of several hundred unemployed, led by the business man and politician Jacob Sechler Coxey (1854–), on a march on Washington, D.C. (1894 and 1914) to demonstrate in favor of legislation to produce emergency work for the unemployed. Coxey's demands anticipated the plans of the W.P.A.

Coyle, Kathleen. Irish novelist. *A Flock of Birds,* a novel about the Irish revolution, is her own choice among her sensitive novels. In *Immortal Ease* (1939), the character Victoria Rising is supposed to be based on Elinor WYLIE.

Cozzens, James Gould (1903–). American novelist. The first of his novels to attract wide attention was based on the Vestris disaster and called *S.S. San Pedro* (1931). *The Just and the Unjust* (1942) is a novel concerning a trial in a country town.

Crabbe, George (1754–1832). English poet, associated with Samuel JOHNSON and Edmund BURKE, considered to be a transitional figure between neo-Classicism and Romanticism. He was humanitarian in his sympathies but realistic and opposed to sentimentality; he wrote in the heroic couplet. His best-known poem is THE VILLAGE (1783), a satirical answer to Goldsmith's THE DESERTED VILLAGE. Other poems by Crabbe, similar in theme to *The Village,* include *The Newspaper* (1785); *The Parish Register* (1809); *The Borough* (1810); *Tales of the Hall* (1819).

Crabbed Age and Youth. (1) An anonymous Elizabethan lyric (1599), presenting a series of antitheses between youth and age.

(2) An essay (1878) by Robert Louis STEVENSON, appearing in a collection entitled *Virginibus Puerisque* (*To Girls and Boys*) (1881).

Crabshaw, Timothy. A servant in Smollett's ADVENTURES OF SIR LAUNCELOT GREAVES (1760).

Crabtree, Lotta (1847–1924). American actress, excelling in burlesque. Subject of *Troupers of the Gold Coast: or the Rise of Lotta Crabtree* by Constance Rourke.

Cracker State. Georgia. See under STATES.

cracklings. Usually **cracklins.** Dialect. Meat tissue from which fat has been fried.

> . . . the smell of hot cracklin and of young roast pork.
>
> Thomas Wolfe

Hence *cracklin bread,* corn bread containing little fatty leftovers from lard making.

Crack-up, The. Title of Edmund Wilson's edition of the literary remains of F. Scott Fitzgerald.

Craddock, Charles Egbert. Pseudonym of **Mary Noailles Murfree** (1850–1922). American author of local-color novels and stories dealing with life in the Tennessee Mountains, including *In the Tennessee Mountains* (1884); *Down the Ravine* (1885); *The Prophet of the Great Smoky Mountains* (1885); *The Mystery of Witch-Face Mountain* (1895); *The Young Mountaineers* (1897).

Cradle of Liberty. Faneuil Hall in Boston is so called from its use as a meeting-place for the American patriots during the Revolutionary era.

Cradle Will Rock, The. See BLITZSTEIN, MARC.

Craig (Edward) Gordon (1872–). English actor, stage designer, producer, and writer on subjects related to the theater. He organized and published a journal, *The Mask* (1908), and founded a theatrical school at the Arena Goldoni in Florence, Italy. Son of Ellen Terry and Edward Godwin.

Craigenputtock. The lonely farm owned by Jane WELSH, the wife of Thomas CARLYLE who lived and wrote there from 1826 to 1834.

Craigie, Pearle Mary Teresa. Pseudonym **John Oliver Hobbes** (1867–1906). English novelist and dramatist of American birth. Became a Roman Catholic in 1892. One of her best-known novels is *The Herb Moon* (1896).

Crais-Billon, see CRÉBILLON.

Cram, Ralph Adams (1863–1942). American architect, known for his use of English Gothic architecture in churches, schools, and colleges, from which it came to be called "collegiate Gothic."

Crampart. In the medieval beast epic *Reynard the Fox,* the king who makes a wooden horse which will travel 100 miles an hour.

swifter than Crampart's horse. Quick as lightning; quick as thought.

Cranach, Lucas (1472–1553). German painter and engraver. His fame rests firmly on his portraits of Martin LUTHER and Philip MELANCHTHON, both of whom were his personal friends. His son **Lucas Cranach** the Younger (1515–1585) painted portraits and historical subjects.

Crane, Harold Hart (1899–1932). American poet, one of the first to attempt to express the spirit of a mechanized 20th century in valid and appropriate poetic terms. He was influenced mainly by T. S. ELIOT and the Elizabethan and 17th-century poets, and his poetry is marked by dramatic rhetoric reminiscent of the Elizabethans and extremely complex, compact imagery which is often obscure and fantastic in the manner of the METAPHYSICALS. He used blank verse and conventional stanza forms. Denounced as unintelligible by many readers, Crane influenced a number of younger American poets. His published works are *White Buildings* (1926), chiefly lyrics; THE BRIDGE (1930), an attempt at an epic poem on America, left incomplete; and *Collected Poems* (1933). See also GREENBERG MANUSCRIPTS. For full analysis of some of Crane's characteristic poems, cf. *The Double Agent,* by R. P. Blackmur.

Crane, Ichabod. The gawky and timorous schoolmaster in Washington IRVING'S *Legend of Sleepy Hollow.* "He was tall, but exceedingly lank, with narrow shoulders, long arms and legs, hands that dangled a mile out of his sleeves, feet that might have served for shovels, and his whole frame most loosely hung together . . . He was, in fact, an odd mixture of small shrewdness and simple credulity." Ichabod is one of the best-known characters in all American literature. For the tale, see SLEEPY HOLLOW.

Crane, Nathalia Clara Ruth (1913–). American poet, celebrated during the 1920's for the precocious lyric poetry she wrote as a child, first published in *The Janitor's Boy* (1924). Her other books of verse include *Lava Lane* (1925), *The Singing Crow* (1926), *Venus Invisible* (1928), and as adult volumes, *Swear by the Night* (1936), *The Ark and the Alphabet* (1939), and *The Death of Poetry* (1942).

Crane, Stephen (1871–1900). American novelist and short-story writer, one of the first realists in American fiction, influenced by the 19th-century Russian novelists and the French writers of the school of NATURALISM. His best-known novel is THE RED BADGE OF COURAGE (1895). His other works include MAGGIE: A GIRL OF THE STREETS (1892), regarded as the first Naturalistic novel of the U.S.; *The Black Riders* (1895), a volume of poems influenced by Walt Whitman and Emily DICKINSON; *The Little Regiment* (1896); *The Open Boat* (1898), a short story; *Active Service* (1899); *The Monster* (1899); *War is Kind* (1899); *Wounds in the Rain* (1900), sketches of the Spanish-American War; *The O'Ruddy* (1903), completed after his death by Robert Barr. Crane's reputation was repeatedly attacked by people hostile to his works, although he was defended by such figures as Hamlin GARLAND, W. D. HOWELLS, and James HUNEKER.

Crane, Walter (1845–1915). English painter and illustrator. Leader and typical representative of the romantic movement in decorative art. Excelled in imaginative illustrations, particularly for children's books. Cf. also his illustrations for Spenser's *Faërie Queene* (1894–1896). He was associated with William Morris in the contemporary Socialist movement.

Cranford. A story by Mrs. GASKELL (1853) dealing with the life of the peaceful little English village of Cranford, inhabited chiefly by old ladies who practice "elegant economy" and a quaint social decorum, under the leadership of the Honorable Mrs. Jamieson. The chief characters are the two Miss Jenkyns. Miss Deborah, the elder, is a great admirer of the involved sentences of Samuel Johnson and very firm as to the proprieties; Miss Mattie is her gentle, lovable, timid sister. After Deborah's death and the failure of the bank, Miss Mattie is forced to open a little shop, but soon afterward her brother Peter, who ran away from home as a boy, returns from India with a considerable fortune. One of the most interesting episodes of the book is concerned with the noisy and likable Captain Brown, a bull in a china shop among the old ladies of Cranford—disapproved of because he prefers Dickens to Dr. Johnson and speaks aloud of his poverty, but greatly mourned when he sacrifices his life to save a child from being run over by a train.

cranial index. See under CEPHALIC INDEX.

Cranmer, Thomas (1489–1556). Archbishop of Canterbury (1533). Resourceful adviser to Henry VIII in his marital troubles. Gained the king's confidence by suggesting a way of repudiating Catherine of Aragon without Papal dispensation. The king summoned him (1529) in these terms: "Let him be sent for out of hand. This man, I trow, has got the right sow by the ear." On accession of Queen Mary, he was degraded, condemned, and burned at the stake. Cranmer's constructive work for the church was remarkable (promotion of Bible translation, revision of Prayer Book, etc.). He was one of those extraordinary characters who seem to have remained limited to the 16th century. His seemingly devious actions gain in consistency when one remembers that Church and State to him were one and that he held that their joint sovereignty should rest in the hands of the king.

Cranmer's Bible. See under BIBLE, THE ENGLISH.

Crapaud or **Johnny Crapaud.** A Frenchman; according to Guillim's *Display of Heraldry* (1611), so called from a device of the ancient kings of France, "three toads (Fr. *crapauds*) erect, saltant."

craps.

shoot craps. To take part in a gambling game played with two dice in which the dice are exhorted in a particular lingo. A losing throw of 2, 3, 12 is called *crap, craps, crap-out;* 7 or 11 is *natural, nick;* 3 is *little trey;* 4 *Little Joe;* 5 *fever in the South* (*and no doctor*), *Phoebe, Little Phoebe;* 6 *Captain Hicks, Captain Jimmy Hicks of the Horse Marines;* 8 *Ada Ross the stable hoss, eighter from Decatur;* 9 *quinine* (*the bitter dose*), *Carolina nine;* 10 *Big Dick from Boston;* 12 *boxcars;* etc. Negroes are particularly fond of this game.

> Wild crap-shooters with a whoop and call.
> Vachel Lindsay, *The Congo.*

Crapsey, Adelaide (1878–1914). American poet. Her brief, compact lyrics, predominantly in a form called CINQUAIN, resemble the work of the Imagists (see IMAGISM). They are few in number and were published after her death in a volume entitled *Verse* (1915). Her father was **Algernon Sidney Crapsey** (1847–1927), American Episcopal clergyman, convicted of heresy in 1906, author of *The Last of the Heretics* (1924).

Crashaw, Richard (1612–1649). English poet, a convert to Catholicism. His poetry is marked by passionate religious emotion and mysticism, and lush, sensuous imagery and ornate CONCEITS in the manner of the Italian poetry of the 16th and early 17th centuries. His works include *Epigrammatum Sacrorum Liber* (1634); *Steps to the Temple* (1648); and *Carmen Deo Nostro* (1652). From the beginning of the English Civil War until his death he lived in Italy, attached to the household of Cardinal Palotto and to the shrine of Loretto.

Crassus, Marcus Licinius. Surnamed **Dives,** i.e. "the Rich" (115?–53 B.C.). Roman financier and politician. After the bloody rivalry of Marius and Sulla, contending leaders, as Lucullus, Pompey the Great, Crassus, and Julius Caesar dominated the Roman affairs. Crassus defeated SPARTACUS in 73 B.C. when the latter led a great insurrection of slaves and gladiators. Through speculation he amassed a vast fortune; joined Pompey and Caesar in organizing the First Triumvirate; was finally killed at Carrhoe by the Parthians.

Cratchit, Bob. In Dickens' CHRISTMAS CAROL, clerk of Ebenezer Scrooge, stockbroker. Though Bob Cratchit has to maintain nine persons on 15*s.* a week, he has a happier home and spends a merrier Christmas than his master, with all his wealth and selfishness.

Tiny Tim Cratchit. The little lame son of Bob Cratchit, the Benjamin of the family, the most helpless and most beloved of all. Tim does not die, but Ebenezer Scrooge, after his change of character, makes him his special care.

Craven, Frank (1875?–1945). American actor and playwright. Notable success in the rôle of commentator in Thornton Wilder's *Our Town;* author of *Too Many Cooks* and *The First Year.*

Craven, Thomas (1889–). American art critic and popular writer. *Men of Art* (1931); *A Treasury of Art Masterpieces* (1939); etc.

Crawford, Francis Marion (1854–1909). American novelist, best known for his popular romances set against a background of history or a glamorous depiction of life in cosmopolitan society. His books include MR. ISAACS: A TALE OF MODERN INDIA (1882); the *Saracinesca* series, consisting of SARACINESCA (1887), SANT' ILARIO (1889), DON ORSINO (1892), and CORLEONE (1896); VIA CRUCIS (1898); THE WHITE SISTER (1909); and numerous other historical and romantic novels.

Crawford, Mary and Henry. Characters in Jane Austen's novel, MANSFIELD PARK.

Crawford, Nelson Antrim (1888–). American author and poet. *A Man of Learning* (1928), *Unhappy Wind* (1930), *We Liberals* (1936). Editor of *The Household Magazine* (from 1928).

Crawley, Captain Rawdon. The husband of Becky Sharp in Thackeray's VANITY FAIR. He is separated from his wife and ends his days as governor of Coventry Island.

Sir Pitt Crawley. Rawdon's father, a rich, vulgar baronet, "a philosopher with a taste for low life." On the death of his second wife Sir Pitt proposes to Becky Sharp, but she has already married his son.

Mr. Pitt Crawley. Sir Pitt's eldest son. He inherits fortunes from his father and from the aunt who disowned Crawley for his marriage to Becky.

Mr. and Mrs. Bute Crawley. A "tall, stately, jolly, shovel-hatted rector," brother of Sir Pitt, and his politic little wife.

Crawley or **Crawley brook.** A river in Bedfordshire. That part called the brook, which runs into the Ouse, is so crooked that a boat would have to go eighty miles in order to make a progress direct of eighteen. Hence the phrase, *crooked as Crawley* or *Crawley brook.*

Crawley, Rev. Josiah. In Trollope's *Last Chronicle of Barset* (see BARSETSHIRE), a proud and sensitive country clergyman, driven almost out of his mind by financial pressure. He is accused of having stolen a check, and in spite of his absolute integrity, has hard work to allay suspicion because of his unpleasant and formidable manner, which keeps even his best friends at a distance.

Crayant. The name given to one of the daughters of Chanticleer, the Cock, in Caxton's version of *Reynard the Fox.* Her sisters were Coppen and Cantart.

Crayon, Geoffrey, Esq. A pseudonym of Washington IRVING.

Crazy Horse. Indian name **Tashunca-Uitco** (1849?–1877). American Indian chief of the Oglala Sioux. Surrendered after the battle of Little Big Horn (1876), in which Custer was killed and was killed himself when he refused to submit to imprisonment. Cf. Longfellow's poem, "The Year of a Hundred Years," and John G. Neihardt, *Songs of the Indian Wars.*

Crazy Hunter, The. A short novel by Kay BOYLE (1940), in which a lonely young girl devotes herself to the training of a blind horse, with which she identifies herself in her unhappiness and isolation, until he is able to carry her as easily as he did before he lost his sight.

Creakle. In Dickens' DAVID COPPERFIELD, a hard, vulgar schoolmaster, to whose charge David is entrusted, and in whose school he first makes the acquaintance of Steerforth.

> The circumstance about him which impressed me most was that he had no voice, but spoke in a whisper.
> Dickens, *David Copperfield,* vi.

Cream City. Milwaukee. See under CITY.

Cream of the Jest, The. A novel by James Branch CABELL (1917). The hero, Felix Kennaston, is a rather unattractive American author of forty or thereabouts who lives a prosaic enough existence in a little Virginia town by day; but by night he visits the magic realm of POICTESME, where he loves the elusive, beautiful Ettare.

Creasy, Sir Edward Shepherd (1812–1878). English historian and author of *Fifteen Decisive Battles of the World* (1851). See under BATTLES.

Creation, The. An oratorio by HANDEL, produced in 1798 at Vienna under the title of *Die Schöpfung.*

Creative Evolution (L'Évolution créatrice). Chief work of Henri BERGSON (1911). In it he explains how intuition penetrates to the essence of the soul—the *élan vital,* vital impulse or energy—where science cannot extend, and how the individual participates in all his perceptions and actions and responses in the actual processes of evolution, which are taking place continually by dissociation, change, and constant movement. By intensity of feeling and knowledge of the self, the individual can direct the continual evolutionary energy of life into the channels he chooses and achieve progress. The introduction of the irrational concept of the *élan vital* into modern philosophy marks to some people the bankruptcy of positivistic science and re-establishes the claim to serious consideration of traditional "mystico-romantic" ideas like the *vital force, vis vitae* or *vitalis,* etc.

creature comfort. Not the comfort of God's creatures but their animal needs, as food, drink, clothing, without which they cannot be comfortable.

Crébillon. Originally in full **Prosper Jolyot,** Sieur **de Crais-Billon** (1674–1762). French tragic poet and member of the *Académie Française. Idoménée* (1705), *Atrée et Thyeste* (1707), *Rhadamiste et Zénobie* (1711). His son **Claude Prosper Jolyot de Crébillon** (1707–1777) is remembered for his novels in which he portrayed the corruption of contemporary society.

credence. A kind of sideboard, or buffet, generally associated with the Renaissance. Originally, the table on which the food was placed before serving to be tasted by a servant to guard against poisoning. The tasting itself was also called credence because it proved that credence could be given to the wholesome nature of the food.

credo. A creed or confession of faith. *Credo* is Latin for "I believe" and is the first word of several creeds. The Protestant creeds are felt to be authoritative only in subordination to the Bible. In the Catholic Churches the creeds have equal authority with the Bible. The more important historical Christian creeds are the *Apostles' Creed* and the *Nicene Creed* (4th century), the *Athanasian Creed* (5th century), the *Decrees of the Council of Trent* (1563), the *Augsburg Confession* (1530), the *Westminster Confession of Faith* (1647), etc.

Creel, George (1876–). American journalist. Chairman of the Committee on Public Information (1917–1919) and of the national advisory board, W.P.A. (1935). Author of *Tom Paine—Liberty Bell* (1931), etc.

creese, kris. A heavy dagger, used among the Malays, with a waved blade and a handle forming an oblique angle with it. In George Du Maurier's novel *Peter Ibbetson* (1891) the hero's uncle used a creese when Peter fought with him and killed him.

Creevey, Thomas (1768–1838). English diarist of the Georgian era. His journals and correspondence covering a period of 36 years were published in 1903 as the *Creevey Papers.*

Cremona. A violin of the greatest excellence; so called from Cremona, in Lombardy, where in the 17th and early 18th centuries lived violin makers of world-wide notoriety, such as Andrea Amati and Antonio his son, Antonius Stradivarius his pupil, and Giuseppe Guarnerius the pupil of Stradivarius.

Creole (from Span. *criadillo,* diminutive of *criado,* bred, brought up, native to the locality). A descendant of white people, born in Mexico, South America, and the West Indies. Also, a descendant of French and Spanish settlers of the southern U.S., especially in Louisiana. Hence, anything "native" and therefore superior may be called *Creole.* The phrase *creole negro* is used in the West Indies to distinguish native Negroes from immigrants.

Creole Sketches. See HEARN, LAFCADIO.

Crescent, The. Turkey, from the crescent moon on its flag.

Crescent City. New Orleans. See under CITY.

Cressida or Criseyde. See TROILUS AND CRESSIDA.

Cresswell, Madame. A woman of infamous character who bequeathed £10 for a funeral sermon, in which nothing ill should be said of her. The Duke of Buckingham wrote the sermon, which was as follows: "All I shall say of her is this—she was born *well,* she married *well,* lived *well,* and died *well;* for she was born at Shadwell, married Cresswell, lived at Clerken-well, and died in Bridewell."

cretin. A person showing striking mental deficiency. The word has developed from a French dialectal form meaning "Christian," not because the French thought that Christians were mentally deficient but because the word for Christian had become synonymous with human being and the mentally deficient were referred to, as it were, as "that (poor) human being" or "that (poor) creature."

Creusa. In classic myth, the daughter of Priam and wife of Aeneas.

Crèvecœur, Michel Guillaume Jean de (1735–1813). Pseudonym **J. Hector St. John.** French author and traveler, a resident of America from 1754 to 1780. He lived for some time on a farm in the colony of New York with his American wife, Mahetable Tiffet, and their three children, after having traveled through Canada, the Great Lakes region, and Pennsylvania. He is best known for his *Letters from an American Farmer,* an extremely popular series of essay-letters, published in London in 1782, in Paris in 1784, and in Philadelphia in 1793. Crèvecœur returned to the U.S. as a French consul in 1783, but found his wife dead and his family scattered. He also wrote *Voyage dans la haute Pennsylvanie et dans l'état de New York, par un membre adoptif de la nation Onéida* (1801), an account of his early travels and of the American Indians, which he pretended to have translated from an original manuscript.

Crewe, Sara, or What Happened at Miss Minchin's. A book by Frances Hodgson BURNETT.

Crews, Laura Hope (1880–1942). American actress on stage and screen. In 1906 she created the role of Polly Jordan in William Vaughn MOODY's *The Great Divide* (1906).

Cribb, Tom (1781–1848). English champion pugilist whose claim to fame rests on the fact that he lost but one fight in his entire professional career.

Crichton, Admirable, see ADMIRABLE CRICHTON.

Crichton, Kyle (1896–). American journalist. A college graduate with experience as a coal miner and steel worker. Under the pseudonym of Robert Forsythe he contributed biting articles to the *New Masses* and the *Daily Worker.* Associate editor of *Collier's Weekly. Redder Than The Rose* is a collection of his Leftist articles.

Cricket on the Hearth, The. A Christmas tale by Charles Dickens (1845). See PEERYBINGLE.

crickey, crikey. An exclamation; a mild oath; originally one of the numerous euphemistic modifications of *Christ.* Others are *crickets, jeepers, Christopher Columbus, cheeses, gee-my-knee.* The supply is inexhaustible.

Crillon, Louis Balbis de Berton de (1541–1615). One of the greatest captains of the 16th century. He fought at the battle of Ivry (1590), and was entitled by Henri IV *"le brave des braves."* He is also known as *l'homme sans peur* (the man without fear).

Henry IV, after the battle of Argives (1589), wrote to Crillon: *"Prend-toi, brave Crillon, nous avons vaincu à Arques, et tu n'y étais pas."* This letter has become proverbial.

where wert thou, Crillon? Crillon, surnamed *the Brave,* in his old age went to church, and listened intently to the story of the Crucifixion. In the middle of the narrative he grew excited, and, unable to contain himself, cried out, *"Où étais-tu, Crillon?"* (What were you about, Crillon, to allow of such things as these?)

Crime and Punishment. A novel by Fyodor DOSTOYEVSKY (1866). The student Raskolnikov, almost out of his mind with poverty and depression, murders an old woman money-lender. Tormented by his thoughts, he finds a friend in Sonia, a girl who is attempting by prostitution to save her family from starving. After she reads aloud to him the story of Lazarus, he feels sure of her sincerity. He confesses his crime and is sentenced to seven years in Siberia, but looks forward hopefully to the future. This novel, an intense psychological study, is marked by the introspective analysis of the author's other novels. It was dramatized as a play and repeatedly as a motion picture.

Crimean War (1854–1856). Turkey and its allies (England, France and Sardinia) fought Russia and succeeded for the time being in shattering their adversary's ambitions of leadership in southeastern Europe. The chief battles were at Alma, Balaklava, Inkerman, and the famous siege of Sevastapol. The result was the Treaty and Declaration of Paris (1856), in which the integrity of Turkey was guaranteed, the Black Sea neutralized and Danubian navigation declared free.

Crime of Sylvestre Bonnard, The (Le Crime de Sylvestre Bonnard). A novel by Anatole FRANCE (1881). Sylvestre Bonnard is a delightfully kind-hearted, absent-minded old archeologist whose immense learning has served only to make him more lovable. His simple wants are cared for by his vigilant and devoted servant Thérèse. This old scholar commits the "crime" of kidnaping a minor, Jeanne Alexandre, the orphaned daughter of the only love of his bygone youth, from a miserable school where she is abused and unhappy. Many threatening complications result, but when it is discovered that Jeanne's guardian is an embezzler, she is made the legal ward of M. Bonnard.

Crimes of Charity. See BERCOVICI, KONRAD.

Cripps, Sir **Richard Stafford** (1889–). Youngest son of **Charles Alfred Cripps,** 1st Baron **Parmoor** (1852–1941). Lawyer and socialist. King's council; solicitor general; Labor M.P.; etc. Ambassador to Russia (1940); special envoy to India (March–April 1942); Chancellor of the Exchequer, Nov. 1947–. Wrote *Why This Socialism* (1934), *Democracy Up-to-date* (1940), etc.

Crishna, see KRISHNA.

Crisis, The. (1) A novel of Civil War times by Winston CHURCHILL (1901). The hero is Stephen Brice, a young New England lawyer in the South; the heroine Virginia Carvel, a loyal daughter of the courtly old Southerner, Colonel Carvel. Of course the lovers are estranged by the conflict, but after many adventures, come together at last. The novel introduces Lincoln and Grant and contains, among other interesting types, the characters of Eliphalet Hopper, the carpet bagger, and Judge Whipple, the abolitionist.

(2) See COOPER, SAMUEL.

Crispin. A sort of HARLEQUIN in early French comedy. He is a blustering valet, apparently copied from an Italian model around 1650.

Crispin, St. See under SAINTS.

Battle on St. Crispin's Day. Cf. in Shakespeare's *King Henry V,* the king's speech beginning "This day is called the feast of Crispin" and ending "That fought with us upon Saint Crispin's day."

Criterion, The. A quarterly literary review (1922–1939), edited in London by T. S. ELIOT and reflecting the opinions of Eliot.

Critic, The. A famous comedy by Richard Brinsley SHERIDAN (1779), a satire on the contemporary stage, with the subtitle *A Tragedy Rehearsed.* The principal characters are Sir Fretful Plagiary, the author, Dangle, the critic, and Puff, the promoter. The burlesque tragedy which is rehearsed is entitled *The Spanish Armada.* In it are introduced the Governor of Tilbury Fort, his daughter Tilburnia and her lover Whiskerandos.

criticaster. An inferior critic.

The rancorous and reptile crew of poeticules, who decompose into criticasters.

Swinburne

Critique of Pure Reason. A famous philosophical treatise by Immanuel KANT (1781) in which the power of pure reason as an instrument for the attainment of metaphysical truth is "criticized," that is, examined and defined in its limitations. The **Critique of Practical Reason** (1788) and the **Critique of Judgment** (1790) complete the trilogy of Kant's major works which are responsible for the term *critical philosophy* in its meaning of Kantianism.

Crito (fl. late 5th century B. C.). The friend and disciple of Socrates who tried to arrange for his escape from prison. Socrates' last words were, "Crito, I owe a cock to Aesculapius." Plato immortalized him in the dialogue *Crito.*

Croaker. A famous character in Goldsmith's *Good-Natured Man* (1768), guardian to Miss Richland. Croaker is never so happy as when he imagines himself a martyr. He loves a funeral better than a festival, and delights to think that the world is going to rack and ruin. His favorite phrase is "Maybe not."

> A poor, fretful soul, that has a new distress for every hour of the four and twenty.—Act i. 1.

Mrs. Croaker. The very reverse of her husband. She is mirthful, light-hearted, and cheerful as a lark.

Leontine Croaker. Son of Mr. Croaker. Being sent to Paris to fetch his sister, he falls in love with Olivia Woodville, whom he brings home instead, introduces her to Croaker as his daughter, and ultimately marries her.

Croaker Papers, The. A series of satires on contemporary American life (1819) by Fitz-Greene Halleck and Joseph Rodman Drake.

Croatan. An island off the North Carolina coast, on which Sir Walter Raleigh left a colony of about 140 people (1587), was the scene of the "Lost Colony." None of them was ever seen again. Some may have intermarried with Indians. On the trunk of a tree one word was roughly cut, *Croatan.* An historical novel by Mary Johnston has that title.

Croce, Benedetto (1860–). Italian philosopher and literary critic, best known for his *Estetica Come Scienza dell' Espressione e Linguistica Generale* (*Aesthetics as Science of Expression and General Linguistics*) (1902), a study of aesthetics, in which art is considered as the expression of imagination. His other works include *Logica Come Scienza del Concetto Puro* (*Logic as the Science of the Pure Concept*) (1905), *Filosofia della Practica, Economica, ed Etica* (*Philosophy of the Practical, Economic, and Ethical*) (1908), and *Teoria e Storia della Storiografia* (*Theory and History of Historiography*) (1916), all three of which, with the *Estetica,* constitute his *Filosofia Come Scienza dello Spirito* (*Philosophy As Science of the Spirit*); *Historical Materialism and Marxian Economy* (1914); *The Poetry of Dante* (1922); *The Conduct of Life* (1924); *Autobiography* (1927); *History of Italy from 1871 to 1915* (1928); *Moral Aspects of Political Life* (1930); *History as the Story of Liberty* (1941).

Crockett, David (1786–1836). A celebrated American frontiersman. His autobiography (1834) was very popular. He became a member of Congress from Tennessee, was one of the six survivors of the ALAMO but was executed on March 6. Famous as a humorist and marksman. He is the hero of a drama by Frank Murdock (*Am.* 1874) entitled *Davy Crockett.*

Crockett, Samuel Rutherford (1860–1914). Scottish romantic novelist and clergyman. Member of the KAILYARD school of writers. He wrote *The Stickit Minister* (1893) and many fine and exciting historical novels.

crocodile. A symbol of deity among the Egyptians, because, says Plutarch, it is the only aquatic animal which has its eyes covered with a thin transparent membrane, by reason of which it sees and is not seen, as God sees all, Himself not being seen. To this he subsequently adds another reason, saying, "The Egyptians worship God symbolically in the crocodile, that being the only animal without a tongue, like the Divine Logos, which standeth not in need of speech." (*De Iside et Osiride,* vol. ii. p. 381.)

Achilles Tatius says, "The number of its teeth equals the number of days in a year." Another tradition is, that during the seven days held sacred to Apis, the crocodile will harm no one.

crocodile's tears. Hypocritical tears. The tale is, that crocodiles moan and sigh like a person in deep distress, to allure travelers to the spot, and even shed tears over their prey while in the act of devouring it.

> As the mournful crocodile
> With sorrow snares relenting passengers.
> Shakespeare, *2 Henry VI,* iii. 1.

Crocus. In classic legend, a young man enamored of the nymph Smilax, who did not return his love. The gods changed him into the crocus flower, to signify unrequited love.

Croesus, the king of Lydia (560–546 B. C.) was so rich and powerful that all the wise men of Greece were drawn to his court, and his name became proverbial for wealth. Hence the expression, *rich as Croesus.*

Croftangry, Mr. Chrystal. The pretended editor of Scott's two novels, *The Highland Widow* (1827) and THE FAIR MAID OF PERTH. Lockhart tells us that Mr. Croftangry is meant for Sir Walter Scott's father, and that "the fretful patient at the death-bed" is a living picture.

Crofts, Freeman Wills (1879–). Anglo-Irish author of detective stories and creator of "Inspector French."

Croix de Feu (*Fr.* fiery cross). A French fascist organization headed by Colonel François de la Rocque; disbanded in 1936 and reorganized as the French social party.

Croix de guerre (*Fr.* war cross). A French war decoration, a cross of bronze, suspended by a green ribbon with red stripes. It was instituted during World War I, April 19, 1915, and is awarded for gallantry in action.

Cro-Magnon race. A prehistoric people, remains of whom have been found in the Cro-Magnon cave in Dordogne, France, in 1868. They are regarded as belonging to the same species as modern man. Some anthropologists hold that their descendants can be identified among the races now living in Europe.

Crome Yellow. A novel by Aldous HUXLEY.

cromlech. An ancient sepulchral monument, a circle of stones around a DOLMEN. Also the dolmen itself.

Crommyonian sow. In Greek mythology, a dangerous wild pig that roamed the land of Crommyon on the Isthmus of Corinth. THESEUS killed it.

Cromwell, Oliver (1599–1658). Lord protector that is, chief executive, of the Commonwealth of England, Scotland, and Ireland (1653–1658). Nicknamed Old Noll by the Cavaliers. In the great Civil War in England in 1642 he raised a famous troop of cavalry called the Ironsides. In 1644 he decided the battle of Marston Moor and, under Fairfax, led the army to victory at Naseby in 1645. As commander in chief and lord lieutenant of Ireland he massacred the garrisons of Drogheda and Wexford. His protectorate was characterized by religious toleration, advantageous commercial treaties with foreign powers, and several successful wars. He died of tertian ague. His eldest surviving son, Richard, trained to be his successor, fell between the Army and Parliament and was dismissed in 1659.

Cromwell, Thomas (1485?–1540). English statesman. Son of a blacksmith who rose to the earlship of Essex. In the employ of Cardinal Wolsey after whose death he became Lord Great Chamberlain (1539). Convicted of treason, he died on the scaffold in the Catholic faith. In Shakespeare's Henry VIII, he appears as a servant to Cardinal Wolsey.

Cromwell's Bible. See BIBLE, THE ENGLISH.

Cronin, Archibald Joseph (1896–). Scotch novelist and physician, author of best-selling works of fiction, often dealing with the medical profession. His books include *Hatter's Castle* (1931); *Three Loves* (1932); *Grand Canary* (1933); *The Stars Look Down* (1935); *Jupiter Laughs* (1940), a play; *The Keys of the Kingdom* (1941); *The Green Years* (1944). *The Citadel* and *The Keys of the Kingdom* were the most popular.

Cronus. One of the Titans of Greek mythology, son of Uranus and Ge, father (by Rhea) of Hestia, Demeter, Hera, Hades, Poseidon, and Zeus. He dethroned his father as ruler of the world, and was in turn dethroned by his son, Zeus. By the Romans he was identified with SATURN.

Crook, George (1829–1890). American army officer who served during the Civil War and took part in various campaigns against the Indians. Major general in 1888. Cf. General Charles King, *Campaigning with Crook*.

Crooked Dick. Richard III of England (1452, 1483–1485). Also nicknamed "the Crouchback."

Crookes, Sir William (1832–1919). English physicist, chemist, and inventor. Studied radium. Engaged in psychical research. His name is perpetuated in several technical terms as *Crookes glass, crookesite, Crookes layer, Crookes space, Crookes tube, Crookes vacuum.*

Croppy Boy, The. Famous Irish poem of revolutionary times.

Crosby, Jane. The heroine of Owen Davis' play, ICEBOUND.

Crosby, Percy. American cartoonist. Created the popular small-boy character of *Skippy*.

Crosley rating. The rating in popularity of a radio performer. Called after the organizer of the Crosley Radio Corporation (1921).

Crosman, Henrietta (1870–1944). American actress. Connected with Charles Frohman's company (1892–1894). Later starred in many plays.

cross. The cross is not solely a Christian symbol, originating with the crucifixion of the Redeemer. In Carthage it was used for ornamental purposes; runic crosses were set up by the Scandinavians as boundary marks, and were erected over the graves of kings and heroes; Cicero tells us (*De Divinatione*, ii. 27, and 80, 81) that the augur's staff with which they marked out the heaven was a cross; the Egyptians employed the same as a sacred symbol, and two buns marked with the cross were discovered at Herculaneum. It was a sacred symbol among the Aztecs long before the landing of Cortez; in Cozumel it was an object of worship; in Tabasco it symbolized the god of rain; and in Palinque it is sculptured on the walls with a child held up adoring it.

> The cross is not only a Christian symbol, it was also a Mexican symbol. It was one of the emblems of Quetzalcoatl, as lord of the four cardinal points, and the four winds that blow therefrom.—Fiske, *Discovery of America*, vol. ii. ch. viii.

The cross of the crucifixion is legendarily said to have been made of four sorts of wood (palm, cedar, olive, and cypress), to signify the four quarters of the globe.

Ligna crucis palma, cedrus, cupressus, oliva.

In his *Monasteries of the Levant* (1849) Curzon gives the legend that Solomon cut down a cedar and buried it on the spot where the pool of Bethesda stood later. A few days before the crucifixion, this cedar floated to the surface of the pool, and was employed as the upright of the Savior's cross.

It is said that CONSTANTINE, on his march to Rome, saw a luminous cross in the sky, in the shape and with the motto *In hoc vinces,* by this [*sign*] conquer. In the night before the battle of Saxa Rubra (312) a vision appeared to the Emperor in his sleep, commanding him to inscribe the cross and the motto on the shields of his soldiers. He obeyed the voice of the vision, and prevailed. The monogram is XPιστος (Christ). Cf. Gibbon's *Decline and Fall,* ch. xx.

This may be called a standing legend; for, besides St. Andrew's cross, and the Danneborg, there is the story concerning Don Alonzo before the battle of Ourique in 1139, when the figure of a cross appeared in the eastern sky; Christ, suspended on it, promised the Christian king a complete victory, and the Moors were totally routed. This legend is commemorated by Alonzo's device, in a field argent five escutcheons azure, in the form of a cross, each escutcheon being charged with five bezants, in memory of the five wounds of Christ. *See* LABARUM.

In heraldry, as many as 285 varieties of cross have been recognized, but the twelve in ordinary use, and from which the others are derived, are: (1) The ordinary cross; (2) the cross humetté, or couped; (3) the cross urdé, or pointed; (4) the cross potent; (5) the cross crosslet; (6) the cross botonné, or treflé; (7) the cross moline; (8) the cross potence; (9) the cross fleury; (10) the cross paté; (11) the Maltese cross (or eight-pointed cross); (12) the cross cleché and fitché.

As a mystic symbol the number of crosses may be reduced to four:

the Greek cross (✢), found on Assyrian tablets, Egyptian and Persian monuments, and on Etruscan pottery.

the crux decussata (**X**), generally called St. Andrew's cross. Quite common in ancient sculpture.

the Latin cross (†), or *crux immissa.* This symbol is found on coins, monuments, and medals long before the Christian era.

the tau cross (T), or *crux commissa.* Very ancient indeed, and supposed to be a phallic emblem.

The tau cross with a handle (☥), or *crux ansata,* is common to several Egyptian deities, as Isis, Osiris, etc.; and is the emblem of immortality and life generally. The circle signifies the eternal preserver of the world, and the T is the monogram of Thoth, the Egyptian Mercury, meaning wisdom.

Invention of the Cross. A church festival held on May 3, in commemoration of the discovery (Lat. *invenire,* to discover) of the Cross (326) by St. Helena. At her direction, after a long and difficult search in the neighborhood of the Holy Sepulcher (which had been overbuilt with heathen temples), the remains of the three buried crosses were found. These were applied to a sick woman, and that which effected her cure was declared to be the True Cross. The Empress had this enclosed in a silver shrine (after having carried a large piece to Rome), and deposited in a church that was built on the spot for the purpose.

Cross, Wilbur Lucius (1862–). American educator and Governor of Connecticut. An authority on Henry Fielding. Founded *Yale Review* (1911). Wrote *Life and Times of Laurence Sterne* (1909); *History of Henry Fielding* (1918); and several other works on the English novel.

cross and ball. The orb of royalty is a sphere or ball surmounted by a cross, an emblem of empire introduced in representations of our Savior. The cross stands *above* the ball, to signify that the spiritual power is above the temporal.

Cross Creek. See RAWLINGS, MARJORIE.

Crossing, The. A historical novel by Winston CHURCHILL (1901), dealing with the ending of the Revolution and the Clark expedition westward. George Rogers Clark is a prominent character. Among the other historical personages introduced are Daniel Boone and Andrew Jackson. The hero is David Ritchie, leader of the Kentucky pioneers who accompany the expedition.

Crossing the Bar. A pious religious poem by TENNYSON, written in 1889, which the author before his death gave instructions to his publishers to insert at the end of each edition of his works.

Cross of Gold, The. A famous speech delivered by William Jennings BRYAN at the Democratic national convention in Chicago in 1896. In it, Bryan, advocating the unlimited free coinage of silver, charged that the nation was being "crucified on a cross of gold," referring to the gold standard.

crossword puzzle. A forerunner of the crossword puzzle was the word square, letters arranged in a square so that vertical and horizontal reading yields the same words, as

B I R D S
I D I O T
R I F L E
D O L O R
S T E R N

In the crossword puzzle proper, the square is a checkerboard pattern in which the letters of words in vertical and horizontal arrangement are to be filled in, with the known number of spaces and a definition of the word as guides. Crossword puzzles are so popular that special dictionaries have been published in which, in contrast to ordinary dictionaries, the definitions are alphabetized and precede the terms they define. Cf. Andrew Swanfeldt, *Crossword Puzzle Dictionary*, 568 pages.

Crotalus. A poem about the rattlesnake by Bret HARTE.

Crotchet Castle. A novel by T. L. PEACOCK (1831) relating the sayings and doings, but chiefly the sayings, of the eccentric guests of Mr. Crotchet of Crotchet Castle.

Crothers, Rachel (1878–). American playwright. *When Ladies Meet* (1932), *Susan and God* (1937), etc.

Crothers, Samuel McChord (1857–1927). American clergyman and essayist. Author of *The Gentle Reader* (1903) and other collections.

Crotona or **Croton.** The ancient **Cotrone** on the Ionian Sea, where Pythagoras of Samos passed the chief portion of his life. In 510 B. C. the city of Sybaris, which was celebrated among the more important cities of Magna Graecia for luxury and effeminacy, was conquered and destroyed by an army under the leadership of the Crotonian athlete Milo. Crotona was colonized by the Romans in 194 B. C.

Crouse, Russel (1893–). American journalist, playwright and theatrical producer. Author of *Mr. Currier and Mr. Ives* (1930) and other books, of librettos for musical comedies, scenarios for motion pictures, and collaborator in the stage adaptation of Clarence DAY'S *Life with Father* (1939). With Howard Lindsay he won the Pulitzer Prize for drama (1946) for the play *State of the Union*. Mrs. Crouse is the daughter of John ERSKINE.

crow.

as the crow flies. The shortest route between two given places.

I must pluck a crow with you; I have a crow to pick with you. I am displeased with you, and must call you to account. I have a small complaint to make against you.

crow over one. To exult over a vanquished or abased person. The allusion is to cocks, who always crow when they have vanquished an adversary.

eat crow. To take back what one has said.

Crow, Carl (1883–1945). American journalist and writer on the Orient. His *Four Hundred Million Customers* discusses the potentialities of the Chinese market.

Crow, Jim, see JIM CROW.

Crowdero. In Butler's poem HUDIBRAS, one of the rabble leaders encountered by Hudibras at a bear-baiting. The original was one Jackson or Jephson, a milliner, of the New Exchange, Strand.

Crowe, Captain. In Smollett's ADVENTURES OF SIR LAUNCELOT GREAVES (1760) the attendant of Sir Launcelot Greaves in his peregrinations to reform society. Sir Launcelot is a modern Don Quixote, and Captain Crowe is his Sancho Panza.

> Captain Crowe had commanded a merchant-ship in the Mediterranean trade for many years, and saved some money by dint of frugality and traffic. He was an excellent seaman, brave, active, friendly in his way, and scrupulously honest, but as little acquainted with the world as a sucking child; whimsical, impatient, and so impetuous that he could not help breaking in upon the conversation, whatever it might be, with repeated interruptions. . . . When he himself attempted to speak, he never finished his period.—Smollett, *The Adventures of Sir Launcelot Greaves.*

Crowfield, Christopher. A pseudonym of Mrs. Harriet Beecher STOWE.

crown. In heraldry, nine crowns are recognized: the oriental, the triumphal or imperial, the diadem, the obsidional crown, the civic, the crown vallery, the mural crown, the naval and the crown celestial. In ancient Egypt, there were two crowns, one of Upper and another of Lower Egypt. Together they formed the head-dress of the pharaohs and were called the *pschent.* The crown of Upper Egypt was a tall red cap whereto was bound that of Lower Egypt, of stiff white linen.

Among the Romans of the Republic and Empire crowns of various patterns formed marks of distinction for different services; the principal ones were:

> *The blockade crown* (*corona obsidionalis*), presented to the general who liberated a beleaguered army. This was made of grass and wild flowers gathered from the spot.—*A camp crown* (*corona castrenses*) was given to him who first forced his way into the enemy's camp. It was made of gold, and decorated with palisades.—*A civic crown* to one who saved a *civis* or Roman citizen in battle. It was of oak leaves, and bore the inscription, H.O.C.S.—*i.e. hostem occidit, civem servavit* (*a foe he slew, a citizen saved*).—*A mural crown* was given to that man who first scaled the wall of a besieged town. It was made of gold and decorated with battlements.—*A naval crown,* of gold, decorated with the beaks of ships, was given to him who won a naval victory.—*An olive crown* was given to those who distinguished themselves in battle in some way not specially mentioned.—*An ovation crown* (*corona ovatio*) was by the Romans given to a general in the case of a lesser victory. It was made of myrtle.—*A triumphal crown* was by the Romans given to the general who obtained a triumph. It was made of laurel or bay leaves. Sometimes a massive gold crown was given to a victorious general.

The *iron crown of Lombardy* is the crown of the ancient Longobardic kings. It was used at the coronation of Agilulph, King of Lombardy, in 591, and among others that have since been crowned with it are CHARLEMAGNE, as King of Italy (774), Henry of Luxemburg (the Emperor Henry VII), as King of Lombardy (1311), Frederick IV (1452), Charles V (1530); in 1805 Napoleon put it on his head with his own hands.

In 1866, at the conclusion of peace, it was given up by Austria to Italy and was replaced in the cathedral at Monza, where Charlemagne had been crowned, and whence it had been taken in 1859. The crown is so called from a narrow band of iron about three-eighths of an inch broad, and one-tenth of an inch in thickness, within it, said to be beaten out of one of the nails used at the Crucifixion. According to tradition, the nail was given to CONSTANTINE by his mother, St. HELENA, who discovered the cross. The outer circlet is of beaten gold, and set with precious stones.

The *crown,* in English coinage, is a five-shilling piece, and is so named from the French *denier à la couronne,* a gold coin issued by Philip of Valois (1339) bearing a large crown on the obverse. The English crown was a gold coin of about 43½ grs. till the end of Elizabeth's reign, except for a silver crown which was issued in the last coinage of Henry VIII and one other of Edward VI.

Crowninshield, Francis Welch (1872–1947). American editor and collector of modern art. Publisher of *The Bookman* (1895–1900) and editor of several magazines, among them *Vanity Fair* (1914–1935).

Croy, Homer (1883–). American novelist. Wrote *West of the Water Tower* (1923), etc.

Croy, Kate. One of the chief characters of Henry James' WINGS OF A DOVE.

Croye, Isabelle, Countess of. A ward of Charles "the bold," duke of Burgundy in Scott's QUENTIN DURWARD. She first appears at the turret window in Plessis les Tours, disguised as Jacqueline. Her marriage with Quentin Durward concludes the novel.

Cruden, Alexander (1701–1770). Scottish bookseller in London, who compiled and brought out one of the best-known Biblical CONCORDANCES (1737).

Cruikshank, George (1792–1878). English illustrator and caricaturist. Famous illustrator of DICKENS (*Sketches by Boz* and *Oliver Twist* only) and SCOTT and satirist of his time.

Cruise of the Snark, The. A book by Jack LONDON (1911) recording a Pacific voyage.

Crummles, Mr. Vincent. In Dickens' NICHOLAS NICKLEBY (1838) the eccentric but kind-hearted manager of the Portsmouth Theater.

Mrs. Crummles. Wife of Mr. Vincent Crummles, a stout, ponderous, tragedy-queen sort of a lady. She walks or rather stalks like Lady Macbeth, and always speaks theatrically. Like her husband, she is full of kindness, and always willing to help the needy.

Miss Ninetta Crummles. Daughter of the manager, and called in the play-bills "the infant phenomenon."

Cruncher, Jerry. In Dickens' TALE OF TWO CITIES, an odd-job man in Tellson's bank. His wife is continually saying her prayers, which Jerry terms "flopping." He is a "RESURRECTION MAN."

Crusades. Wars undertaken in late medieval times by Christians against the Turks and Saracens for the recovery of the Holy Land and, nominally at least, for the honor of the cross. The word is ultimately derived from *Lat.* crux "cross."

The seven principal Crusades are:

(1) 1096–1100. Preached up by Peter the Hermit. Led by Godfrey of Bouillon, who took Jerusalem and founded a Christian kingdom in Palestine, himself becoming King of Jerusalem.
(2) 1147–1149. At the instigation of St. Bernard. Led by Louis VII and the Emperor Conrad. It was a failure.
(3) 1189–1193. Led by Richard *Lionheart,* Frederick Barbarossa, and Philip Augustus. It did not succeed in recapturing Jerusalem, which the Mohammedans had taken in 1187.
(4) 1202–1204. Led by Baldwin of Flanders and the Doge of Venice. It established a Latin Empire at Constantinople.
(5) 1228–1229. Led by Frederick II. Palestine was ceded to Frederick, who was crowned king of Jerusalem.
(6) 1248–1254 and (7) 1268–1270. Unsuccessful expeditions undertaken by St. Louis, Louis IX of France.

See also CHILDREN'S CRUSADE.

cruse. A jar for water, oil, honey, etc. For the story of the widow's cruse, cf. 1 *Kings* xvi. 10 ff.

Crusoe. A solitary man; the only inhabitant of a place. From the tale of Daniel DEFOE, which describes ROBINSON CRUSOE as cast on a desert island.

Crutched Friars. A Catholic order of monks in England, whose members bore the sign of the cross on their staves and habits (13th to 17th centuries).

crux ansata. (1) In Egyptian *ankh* means life, prosperity. A tau CROSS with a loop at the top, signifying life and called *ankh* or *crux ansata,* is used by the Church as a sacred emblem.

(2) The title of a book by H. G. Wells on the Roman Catholic Church, an indictment.

Cruze, James. In full **James Cruze Bosen** (1884–1942). Famous moving-picture director: *Old Ironsides* (1925), *The Covered Wagon, Merton of the Movies, Ruggles of Red Gap, I Cover the Waterfront, Sutter's Gold,* etc. Twice named as one of the best ten directors.

Cry of the Children, The. A humanitarian poem by Elizabeth Barrett BROWNING (1843), expressing intense sympathy for the victims of child labor in the English mines and factories of her day and indignantly indicting those who were responsible for their exploitation.

wolf. The phrase *cry wolf* means to give alarm without occasion by allusion to the fable in which the warning, "the wolf is coming," was given in vain so often that nobody paid attention to it when the wolf finally did come.

Ctesiphon. An ancient city of Mesopotamia, whose site is now occupied by ruins.

Cuba (from Lat. *cubo,* to lie down in bed). The Roman deity who kept guard over infants in their cribs and sent them to sleep. Note: The island of Cuba has nothing to do with the old deity. It got its name because of its shape, Spanish *cuba* meaning "vat."

Cubism. A movement in painting, begun about 1910 in reaction against IMPRESSIONISM. It involved the reduction of figures, objects, and occasionally landscapes to their fundamental geometric forms, and the abstraction and resynthesis of these forms into new designs from which naturalistic subject considerations and literary "meaning" were banished. The culmination of the development of Cubism, which tended more and more toward the simple and geometrically "abstract," is considered to be found in the colored squares of Piet MONDRIAN (ca. 1925). Georges BRAQUE and Pablo PICASSO were the founders of Cubism and also its most outstanding representatives, the work of one often being indistinguishable from that of the other. They derived an important influence from the work of Paul CÉZANNE. Cubism was regarded with bewilderment and hostility by many people, and had a sensational vogue in the years immediately preceding and following World War I.

Cubs. In American baseball parlance, the Chicago Americans. Cf. under BASEBALL TEAMS.

cucking stool, see under DUCKING STOOL.

cuckold. The husband of an adulterous wife; so called from *cuckoo,* the chief characteristic of this bird being to deposit its eggs in other birds' nests. Johnson says "it was usual to alarm a husband at the approach of an adulterer by calling out 'Cuckoo,' which by mistake was applied in time to the person warned." Greene calls the cuckoo "the cuckold's quirister" (*Quip for an Upstart Courtier,* 1592), and the Romans used to call an adulterer a "cuckoo," as *"Te cuculum uxor ex lustris rapit"* (Plautus: *Asinaria,* v. 3). See also ACTOEON; HORN.

Cudahy, Michael (1841–1910). Well-known Irish-American meat packer, originally with Armour & Co. and then (1890–1910) president of his own, the Cudahy Packing Co.

cuddy. Aboardship a small cabin or the galley or pantry of a small vessel. In a house, a small room; also a cupboard or closet. The name *Cuddy* which Edmund Spenser gave to a rustic swain in his *Shepheardes Calendar* is a variant of *Cuthbert.*

Cuffy. A Negro; both a generic word and proper name; possibly from the English slang term "cove."

> Sambo and Cuffey expand under every sky.—Harriet Beecher Stowe, *Uncle Tom's Cabin.*

Cui, César Antonovich (1835–1918). Russian composer, engineer, and music critic, author of operas, songs, piano pieces, etc. He was a member of the group known as "THE FIVE."

cui bono? (*Lat.*) Who is benefited thereby? To whom is it a gain? A common, but quite erroneous meaning attached to the words is, What good will it do? For what good purpose? It was the question of the Roman judge L. Cassius Pedanius. Cf. Cicero, *Rosc. Am.,* xxx. 84.

> Cato, that great and grave philosopher, did commonly demand, when any new project was propounded unto him, *cui bono,* what good will ensue in case the same is effected?—Fuller, *Worthies* (The Design, i.).

Culbertson, Ely (1893–). American authority on contract bridge. Also protagonist of a scheme for world co-operation.

cul-de-sac (*Fr.* bottom of a bag). A blind alley, or alley blocked up at one end like a sack. Figuratively, an argument, etc., that leads to nothing.

Culebra Cut (From Span. *culebra* "snake"). Earlier name of the **Gaillard Cut,** the deeply excavated part of the Panama Canal, about 10 miles northwest of Panama, 6.97 miles long. It was renamed after David Du Bose Gaillard (1859–1913), the American army engineer in charge of the Culebra Cut excavations (1907).

Cullen, Countée (1903–1946). American Negro poet, known for his poetry on Negro themes. His books include *Color* (1925); *Copper Sun* (1927); *The Ballad of the Brown Girl* (1927); *The Black Christ* (1929); *One Way to Heaven* (1932); *The Medea And Some Poems* (1935), which contains a translation of Euripides' *Medea; The Lost Zoo* (1940), for children; *My Lives and How I Lost Them* (1942), stories supposedly by "Christopher Cat."

Cullinan diamond. The largest diamond ever known. It was discovered in 1905 at the Premier Mine in South Africa, and when found weighed 3,025¾ carats (about 1 lb. 6 oz.), as against the 186¹⁄₁₆ carats of the famous KOH-I-NUR in its uncut state. It was purchased by the South African Government for £150,000 and presented to Edward VII, and now forms part of the Crown Jewels, its estimated value being over £1,000,000. It was cut into a number of stones, of which the two largest weigh over 516 and 309 carats respectively. It was named after Sir T. M. Cullinan, South African mineowner (1862– .) at the time of its discovery.

Culloden, or Drummossie Moor. A heath in Scotland where the Duke of Cumberland defeated Prince Charles Edward Stuart (the Young Pretender) on April 27, 1746. "Drummossie Moor, Drummossie Day!" begins the old Scots ballad of Culloden.

Culprit Fay, The. A nature fantasy and fairy tale in verse by Joseph Rodman Drake (*Am.* 1795–1820), published posthumously in 1835.

Cult of Unintelligibility, The. An essay by Max EASTMAN, appearing in *The Literary Mind* (1931). It denounces 20th-century authors—including E. E. CUMMINGS, T. S. ELIOT, James JOYCE, Gertrude STEIN, and Edith SITWELL—for the private character of their allusions and what Eastman regards as the general uncommunicativeness of their writing. The title of this essay came to be applied to the writers in question as a generic designation by hostile critics.

Culture and Anarchy. A collection of essays on political and social conditions by Matthew ARNOLD, published in 1869. In these are found some of his most famous utterances. The collection includes the famous essay on HEBRAISM AND HELLENISM.

Cumberland Road. The first main road to the American West, begun in 1811 and built for the most part with Federal money. It ran from Cumberland, Md., over the mountains to Wheeling and Zanesville on the Ohio and finally to Vandalia, Illinois. When completed it was about 600 miles long, sixty feet wide, and had a paved strip twenty feet wide in the middle. Over this "National Pike" ran the Western mails.

cum laude (*Lat.*). With praise. Used on diplomas and the like. A distinction is made between *magna cum laude* "with great praise," *insigne cum laude* "with notable praise," and *summa cum laude* "with the highest praise."

cummerbund. In India, a sash worn around the waist. Adapted to men's evening dress in England and America.

Cummings, Bruce Frederick. Pseudonym **W. N. P. Barbellion** (1889–1919). Biologist in Natural History Museum, South Kensington. His book, *The Journal of a Disappointed Man* (1919), has been called one of the great autobiographies of all time.

Cummings, Edward Estlin (1894–). American poet, known for the eccentricity of his typography and punctuation, employed in order to indicate the rhythm of the poem immediately to the eye of the reader. His work consists of love poems, often treated in a romantic and even sentimental manner, humorous character sketches, and bitter satires on the foibles and institutions of his time. "Tough" characters of the type well publicized in the U.S. in the 1920's—gangsters, prize-fighters, night-club singers, and the like—frequently appear in his poems, along with contemporary slang and "tough" dialect and the rhythms of jazz. Some critics consider Cummings' cynicism and "toughness" an attempt to suppress a natural poetic tendency toward lyric sentiment. His books of poetry are *Tulips and Chimneys* (1923); *XLI Poems* (1925); *&* (1925); *is 5* (1926); *ViVa* (1931); *No Thanks* (1935); *Collected Poems* (1938). Among his other works are THE ENORMOUS ROOM (1922), a prose account of experiences during World War I; *him* (1927), a play in prose and verse; EIMI (1933), an account of a trip to Russia, written in prose and verse; *CIOPW* (1931), a collection of drawings and paintings, so named because the artwork is done in charcoal, ink, oil, pencil, and watercolor; *Tom* (1935), a satirical ballet from UNCLE TOM'S CABIN.

cumulative story. A type of story found in the folklore of all peoples, having many forms and varying details. It assumes that all things are equally possessed of intelligence. The more civilized the version, the more it has degenerated into a nursery tale or jingle. Most famous is the story of the old woman who fears that she won't get home before dark because her pig will not go under the fence. She appeals to a dog to bite the pig; but "dog won't bite pig." She appeals to a stick; but "stick won't beat dog." And *cumulatively,* "fire won't burn stick, water won't quench fire, ox won't drink water, butcher won't kill ox, rope won't hang butcher, rat won't gnaw rope, cat won't kill rat," until finally the cat is given some milk and attacks the rat. "The rat begins to gnaw the rope, the rope begins to hang the butcher," etc., each object doing as requested, until the dog bites the pig, the pig goes under the fence, and the old woman gets home before dark.

Cunctator (*Lat.* the delayer). Quintus Fabius Maximus (d. 203 B.C.), the Roman general who baffled Hannibal by avoiding direct engagements, and wearing him out by marches, countermarches, and skirmishes from a distance. This was the policy by which Du Guesclin forced the English to abandon their French possessions in the reign of Charles V. Cf. FABIAN.

Cunégonde. In Voltaire's CANDIDE, the Baron's daughter beloved through long years by the hero. See KUNIGUNDE.

cuneiform. Wedge-shaped. The cuneiform inscriptions of ancient Assyria, Babylonia, Persia, etc. were made with wooden styles on blocks of soft clay which were baked when permanent records were required.

Cunha. See TRISTAN DA CUNHA.

Cunizza. Heroine of Browning's SORDELLO, called Palma until the end of the poem. Dante refers to her in his *Paradiso* ix. 32 as in paradise. She was the sister of Ezzelino III.

Cunningham, Alison. The nurse of Robert Louis STEVENSON during his childhood. *A Child's Garden of Verses* is dedicated to her.

Cunningham, Allan (1784–1842). Scottish author, who wrote many songs, as "A Wet Sheet and a Flowing Sea" (1825), several novels, biographies, etc. Best known for his *Lives of the Most Eminent British Painters, Sculptors, and Architects* (6 vols., 1829–1833) and as an editor of Burns's works (1834).

Cunningham, Sir Andrew (1883–), and **Cunningham, Sir John.** British admirals. Sir Andrew commanded the Mediterranean Fleet in 1943 in World War II. Following the Teheran Conference and the reorganization of the Mediterranean theater, Sir John remained in command of all Mediterranean naval forces.

Cunningham, Martin. A character in James Joyce's DUBLINERS and ULYSSES. At one point in the latter work he is said to represent the mythological character of SISYPHUS, since he continually sets up a home for his wife, who is habitually intoxicated, only to find that she has pawned the furniture in order to buy liquor. His hopelessly repeated effort is thus a parallel to Sisyphus' rolling a rock uphill forever.

Cunninghame Graham, Robert Bontine (1852–1936). Scottish traveler, writer, and historian. His grandmother was Spanish. He himself spoke Spanish fluently. He lived in Argentina on a large cattle ranch, steeping himself in the life of South America. Back in England, he became a Labor M.P. and organized the Scottish Labor Party. He was a close friend of W. H. HUDSON, Joseph CONRAD, and Bernard SHAW. He was a rover and an eccentric, a great horseman, and always a fine writer. Among his many books, cf. especially *Thirteen Stories* (1900) and *Rodeo* (1936).

Cunstance. In *The Man of Law's Tale,* one of Chaucer's CANTERBURY TALES, a model of resignation, daughter of the Emperor of Rome. The Sultan of Syria, in order to marry her, turns Christian, whereupon his mother murders him, and sets Cunstance adrift on a raft. The raft is stranded on a rock near Northumberland, Cunstance is rescued, and eventually, after having been falsely accused of murder and proved innocent, marries King Ella or Alla. She presents him with a son Maurice, but during the King's absence Ella's mother, angry with Cunstance for introducing Christianity into the land, puts her on a raft with her baby. They are rescued by a senator and taken to Rome, whither Ella, having put his mother to death, goes on pilgrimage to atone for his crime. Here he meets his wife, who returns with him to Northumberland, and lives in peace and happiness the rest of her life.

Cupid (Lat. *cupido,* desire, passion). The god of love in Roman mythology identified with the Greek Eros; son of Mercury and Venus. He is usually represented as a beautiful winged boy, blindfolded, and carrying a bow and arrows, and one legend says that he wets with blood the grindstone on which he sharpens his arrows.

> Ferus et Cupido,
> Semper ardentes acuens sagittas.
> Horace, *2 Odes,* viii. 14, 15.

Cupid and Psyche. An exquisite episode in the GOLDEN Ass of Apuleius. It is an allegory representing the progress of the soul to perfection. William Morris retells the story in his *Earthly Paradise* (*May*) and it occurs also in Walter Pater's *Marius the Epicurean.* See PSYCHE.

Cupid and Campaspe. A well-known lyric by John Lyly that appeared first in his drama *Alexander and Campaspe* (1586).

> Cupid and my Campaspe play'd
> At cards for kisses; Cupid paid.

Cupid's golden arrow. Virtuous love.
Cupid's leaden arrow. Sensual passion.

Cuppy, Will (1884–). American humorist. *How to Be a Hermit* (1929); *How to Tell Your Friends from the Apes* (1931), *How to Become Extinct* (1941). Critic for over 20 years of detective fiction for the New York *Herald Tribune.*

Curan. A courtier in Shakespeare's tragedy of KING LEAR.

Curate of Meudon. RABELAIS, who had for a time (1550–1552) the parish of Meudon.

Curé de Meudon, see CURATE OF MEUDON.

Curetes. A mythical people of Crete, to whom the infant Zeus was entrusted by his mother Rhea. By clashing their shields they drowned the cries of the infant, to prevent its father (Cronus) from finding the place where the babe was hid.

curfew bell. A bell that announces curfew (from Fr. *couvre-feu* "cover fire"), that is, the time at which lights and fires are to be extinguished; especially the bell rung in the reigns of William I and II at sunset in summer and at eight o'clock in winter for this purpose.

> The curfew tolls the knell of parting day.
> Gray, *Elegy.*

Curiatii, the. In Roman legendary history, the three brothers who engaged in combat against the three Horatii. See HORATIUS.

Curie, Marie Sklodowska (1867–1934). Polish scientist, best known for her discovery, with her husband, Pierre Curie, of the important cancer cure, radium. She was a winner of the Nobel Prize for chemistry in 1911. *Madame Curie* (1937) was a best-selling biography, written by her daughter, Eve Curie. It was later made into a moving picture.

Curious Myths of the Middle Ages. See BARING-GOULD, SABINE.

Curle, Richard Henry Parnell (1883–). English writer and traveler. Known as the author of books on the life of his friend Joseph CONRAD.

Curlicism. Literary indecency. From Edmund Curle (1675–1747), English bookseller notorious for publication of *A Nun in her Frock* and similar books for which he was convicted and fined in 1728. Satirized by Alexander Pope in the DUNCIAD.

Curlylocks. The heroine of a familiar nursery rhyme:

> Curlylocks, Curlylocks, wilt thou be mine,
> Thou shalt not wash the dishes nor yet feed the swine
> But sit on a cushion and sew a fine seam
> And feed upon strawberries, sugar and cream.

Curran, John Philpot (1750–1817). Irish orator and judge. Famous for his defense of the leaders of the Irish insurrection of 1798.

Currier and Ives prints. A series of popular lithographs published by the firm of Currier & Ives in New York from 1857 to about 1900. The partners were Nathaniel Currier (1813–1888), who had started the publication of prints in 1835, and James M. Ives (1824–1895), who joined the firm in 1857. The subjects of the prints were contemporary American political, social, and sporting events and figures. Cf. Russel Crouse, *Mr. Currier and Mr. Ives* (1930).

Curry, John Steuart (1897–1946). American painter, known for his portrayals of Midwestern farm life, especially of the state of Kansas.

curse.

curses, like chickens, come home to roost. Curses fall on the head of the curser, as chickens which stray during the day return to their roost at night.

cursing by bell, book, and candle. See under BELL.

curse of Cain. One who is always on the move and has no abiding place is said to be "cursed with the curse of Cain." The allusion is to God's judgment on Cain after he had slain his brother Abel:

> And now art thou cursed from the earth, . . . a fugitive and a vagabond shalt thou be in the earth.—*Gen.* iv. 11–12.

curse of Scotland. The nine of diamonds. The two most plausible explanations are these: (1) The nine of diamonds in the game of *Pope Joan* is called the Pope, the Antichrist of the Scotch reformers. (2) In the game of *comette,* introduced by Queen Mary, it is the great winning card, and the game was the curse of Scotland because it was the ruin of so many families.

cursive. Said of script and print in which the strokes of the letters run on. The oldest cursive Roman writing goes back to the first century. From it all modern European scripts have developed and also the so-called ITALIC printing face.

Cursor Mundi. A Middle English work, written in the Northern dialect about 1300, of unknown authorship. It is a history in rhymed couplets of the Hebrew and Christian world, based on various Biblical sources.

curtain.

curtain lecture. The nagging of a wife after she and her husband are in bed. See CAUDLE LECTURE.

curtain raiser, see LEVER DE RIDEAU.

ring down the curtain. To bring a matter to an end. A theatrical term. When the play is over, the bell rings and the curtain comes down.

Curtain, The. A London theater in Shoreditch (1576–1625).

Curtana. The sword of mercy borne before the English kings at their coronation; it has no point and is hence *shortened* (O. Fr. *curt,* Lat. *curtus*). It is called the sword of Edward the Confessor, which, having no point, was the emblem of mercy. The royal sword of England was so called to the reign of Henry III.

> But when Curtana will not do the deed
> You lay the pointless clergy-weapon by,
> And to the laws, your sword of justice fly.
> Dryden, *Hind and Panther,* Pt. ii. 419.

Curt-hose or **Courte-Heuse** (*Fr.* short-hose). A surname of Robert II (1054?–1134), duke of Normandy, eldest son of William the Conqueror.

Curtin, Jeremiah (1840?–1906). American folklorist and translator of Tolstoy, Sienkiewicz, etc.

Curtis, Cyrus Hermann Kotzschmar (1850–1933). Head of the Curtis Publishing Co., publishers of *Ladies' Home Journal* (which Cyrus Curtis established in 1876), *The Country Gentleman, Saturday Evening Post.*

Curtis, George William (1824–1892). American author and journalist. Member of Brook Farm community (1842–1843); editorial writer for *Harper's Magazine* and editor of *Harper's Weekly.* Author of *Potiphar Papers* (1853), *Prue and I* (1857), etc.

Curtiss, Glenn Hammond (1878–1930). American inventor and aviator. Winner of trophy in first public airplane flight of a mile in U.S. (1908) and New York *World's* $10,000 prize (1910) for flight from Albany to New York. Founded schools of aviation at Hammondsport, San Diego, Buffalo, Miami, and elsewhere. The Navy-Curtiss (NC) flying boat, known as the "Wasp," that made the first Atlantic crossing (1919), and a variety of other air and water speedcraft were developed by him.

Curtius, Marcus. Roman hero of fourth century B. C. who, according to legend, leaped in full armor on horseback into a chasm that had been opened in the Forum at Rome by an earthquake, because a soothsayer had proclaimed that the sacrifice of Rome's chief treasure, which Curtius interpreted to mean a brave man, would close the fissure. It did.

Curtmantle, Courtmantle. Surname of Henry II of England, from the short Anjou *court mantle* he wore.

Curwood, James Oliver (1878–1927). American popular "he-man" novelist. Lived much in Canada and the Hudson Bay country. Wrote 26 books in 19 years.

Curzon Line, the. Proposed in 1919 by the Allies, on ethnic grounds, as the boundary between Russia and Poland. The Russo-Polish peace treaty of 1921 (treaty of Riga), however, moved the boundary farther east. In 1939 Poland east of the Curzon line was incorporated into the Soviet Union. The name of the boundary line comes from Lord Curzon of Kedleston, Foreign Secretary in Lloyd George's cabinet.

Cusack, Michael. In James Joyce's ULYSSES, the Dublin "citizen" with whom Leopold BLOOM has an altercation in the saloon of Barney Kiernan. Cusack sneers at Bloom for being a Jew and throws a biscuit box at him, at which Bloom hurriedly leaves in order to avoid a fight, while "Garryowen," Cusack's dog, snarls at his heels. In FINNEGANS WAKE, Michael Cusack is referred to as "Micholas de Cusack," his name being combined with that of NICHOLAS OF CUSA.

Custance, see CUNSTANCE.

Custer, George Armstrong (1839–1876). American general. Renowned as an Indian fighter. Destroyed with his entire force by the Oglalla Sioux in the battle of the Little Big Horn (June 25, 1876).

Custom of the Country, The. A novel by Edith WHARTON (1913), dealing with divorce. The heroine, Undine Spragg, a crude, ambitious Western girl of great physical attractions, is divorced three times before she finally finds her own level and marries the youth from her home town who has become a millionaire.

Cutcliffe Hyne, see HYNE.

Cuthbert. In England, a name given in contempt during World War I to fit and healthy men of military age who, particularly in government offices, were not "combed out" to go into the army; also, to one who actually avoided military service. It was coined by "Poy," the cartoonist of the *Evening News,* who represented these civilians as frightened-looking rabbits. See also under CUDDY.

Cuthbert, St. See under SAINT.

cutlass. Heavy, curved sword with bowl-shaped guard, used by seamen in battle.

cutpurse. Now called "pickpocket." The two words are of historical value. When purses were worn suspended from a girdle, thieves cut the string by which the purse was attached; but when pockets were adopted, and purses were no longer hung on the girdle, the thief was no longer a cutpurse, but became a pickpocket.

> To have an open ear, a quick eye, and a nimble hand, is necessary for a cutpurse.—Shakespeare, *Winter's Tale,* 14. 3.

Moll Cutpurse. The familiar name of Mary Frith (ca. 1585–1660), a woman of masculine vigor, who not unfrequently assumed man's attire. She was a notorious thief and once attacked General Fairfax on Hounslow Heath, for which she was sent to Newgate. She escaped by bribery, and died at last of dropsy in the seventy-fifth year of her age. Middleton's and Dekker's play, *The Roaring Girl* (1611) is founded on her doings.

Cuttle, Captain. An eccentric, kind-hearted sailor in Dickens' DOMBEY AND SON; simple as a child, credulous of every tale, and generous as the sun. Captain Cuttle was a skipper, has a hook instead of a right hand, and always wears a very hard glazed hat. He is in the habit of quoting, and desiring those to whom he spoke "to overhaul the catechism till they found it"; but, he adds, "When found, make a note of."

Cutty Sark. (1) A character in Robert Burns' *Tam O'Shanter's Ride.*

(2) The name of a late 19th century American clipper ship which became famous for establishing a speed record on the run from China to England.

Cuvier, Baron **Georges Léopold Chrétien Fréderic Dagobert** (1769–1832). French naturalist. Educated in France and Germany. Considered by many the founder of comparative anatomy and of paleontology.

Cuzco. Famous Peruvian city of the Incas. Said to have been founded by Manco Capac (early 11th century), the son of the son-god of the Incas. Pizarro desired its treasures.

Cybele. In classic myth (but originally in Phrygia), the wife of Cronus, mother of the gods of Olympus, identified with RHEA. In Rome she became known as the Great Mother of the Gods (*Magna Deum Mater*), and was one of the most important deities of the Empire.

Cyclades. A group of islands in the Grecian Archipelago. So called because of the belief that they formed a ring or *cycle* around Delos. One is Andros; cf. Thornton Wilder, *The Woman of Andros* (1930). Another is Naxos, where Bacchus wooed Ariadne.

Cyclic poets. Epic poets who, on the death of Homer, caught the contagion of his poems, and wrote continuations, illustrations, or additions thereto. These poets wrote between 800 and 550 B. C., and were called *cyclic* because they confined themselves to the cycle of the Trojan War. The chief were Agias, Arctinos, Eugamon, Lesches, and Strasinos.

Cyclops (*Gr.*, "circular-eye"). One of a group of giants that, according to legend, inhabited Thrace. They had only one eye, and that in the center of their forehead, and their work was to forge iron for Vulcan.

> Roused with the sound, the mighty family
> Of one-eyed brothers hasten to the shore
> And gather round the bellowing Polypheme.
> Addison, *Milton Imitated.*

Cyclopean Masonry. The old Pelasgic ruins of Greece, Asia Minor, and Italy, such as the Gallery of Tiryns, the Gate of Lions at Mycenae, the Treasury of Athens, and the Tombs of Phoroneus and Danaos. They are composed of huge blocks fitted together without mortar, with marvelous nicety, and are fabled to be the work of the Cyclops. The term is also applied to similar structures in many parts of the world.

Cylix. In Greek and Roman antiquity, a drinking cup with a two-handled shallow bowl and a short sturdy stem.

Cyllenius. Mercury. So called from Mount Cyllenë, in Peloponnesus, where he was born.

Cymbeline. A mythical prince of Britain. When Caesar invaded the British island, he forced the Britons to pay tribute and took Cymbeline with him as a hostage. Cymbeline was brought up in Rome as a Roman. When he became king of Britain, he lived peacefully with the Romans. After his death his sons Guiderius and Arviragus refused to pay tribute and a new Roman invasion ensued.

Cymbeline. A drama by Shakespeare (ca. 1610). Posthumus, who secretly married Imogen, the daughter of Cymbeline, king of Britain, is banished by the King when he hears of the marriage, and goes to Rome. Here he meets Iachimo, an Italian libertine, and the two, conversing of the fidelity of wives, make a wager concerning Imogen's faithfulness. Iachimo by craftiness secures access to Imogen's bedroom, steals a bracelet from her while she is asleep and convinces Posthumus that he has won the wager. Posthumus orders his servant to put Imogen to death, but instead she escapes in boy's clothing. In a hut in the forest she discovers her two long-lost brothers who had been abducted by Belarius years before. Eventually Iachimo's villainy is exposed, Cymbeline welcomes back his two sons, his daughter and her repentant husband and all ends happily. The plot of *Cymbeline* is from the DECAMERON of Boccaccio (Day ii. 9).

Cymochles. In Spenser's *Faërie Queene* (II, iv, v, vi, and viii), a man of prodigious might, brother of Pyrochles, son of Acrates and Despite, and husband of Acrasia, the enchantress. He sets out to encounter Sir Guyon, but is ferried over the idle lake by Phaedria and forgets himself; he is slain by King Arthur.

Cymodoce. A sea nymph and companion of Venus in Virgil's *Georgics* (iv, 338) and *Aeneid* (v. 826). In Spenser's *Faërie Queene* (III, iv and IV, xii), she is a daughter of Nereus and mother of Marinell by Dumarin. She frees Florimel from the power of Proteus. The word means "wave-receiving."

Garden of Cymodoce. Sark, one of the Channel Islands. It is the title of a poem by Swinburne in his *Songs of the Springtides.*

Cymry. A collective term for the Gauls; often, but incorrectly, also the Brythonic Celts, that is, the Welsh.

Cynara. The lady to whom the best-known poem of Ernest DOWSON is addressed. Each stanza closes, "I have been faithful to thee, Cynara, in my fashion." The poem has a Latin title: *Non sum qualis eram bonae sub regno Cynarae.*

Cynewulf (750?–825?) Anglo-Saxon poet, whose existence is conjectured on a manuscript signature in ancient Germanic runic characters (see RUNES) forming the name "Cynewulf." Attributed to his authorship are four poems: a life of St. Juliana (see under SAINT); *Elene,* concerning St. Helena (see under SAINT); *Christ,* consisting of three separate poems on the Incarnation, the Ascension, and the Last Judgment; and *The Fates of the Apostles.* THE DREAM OF THE ROOD has also been assigned to Cynewulf by some scholars. These poems are said to belong to the "Cynewulfian cycle" of Anglo-Saxon verse. Cf. CAEDMON.

cynic. The ancient school of Greek philosophers known as the *Cynics* was founded by Antisthenes, a pupil of Socrates, and made famous by his pupil, DIOGENES. They were ostentatiously contemptuous of ease, luxury, or wealth, and were given their name because Antisthenes held his school in the Gymnasium, *Cynosarges* (white dog), so called because a white dog once carried away part of a victim which Diomeos was there offering to Hercules. Hence the term has come to be applied to the sort of person who seems to make it his business to despise everything and to have faith in nothing.

Cynic Tub. The tub from which Diogenes lectured. Similarly we speak of the "PORCH," meaning Stoic philosophy; the "GARDEN," Epicurean philosophy; the "ACADEMY," Platonic philosophy; and the "Colonnade," meaning Aristotelian philosophy.

> [They] fetch their doctrines from the Cynic tub.
> Milton, *Comus*, line 708.

Cynosure (*Gr.* dog's tail). The Pole star; hence, the observed of all observers. It is applied to the constellation called *Ursa Minor*. As seamen guide their ships by the north star, and observe it well, the word "cynosure" is used for whatever attracts attention, as "The cynosure of neighboring eyes" (*Milton*), especially for guidance in some doubtful matter.

Cynthia. The moon: a surname of Artemis or Diana. The Roman Diana, who represented the moon, was called Cynthia from Mount Cynthus in Delos, where she was born. Pope, speaking of the inconstant character of woman, "matter too soft a lasting mark to bear," says—

> Come, then, the colors and the ground prepare
> Dip in the rainbow, trick her off in air;
> Choose a firm cloud, before it fall, and in it
> Catch, ere she change, the Cynthia of the minute.
> *Epistle*, ii. 17–20.

By Elizabethan poets—Spenser, Phineas Fletcher, Raleigh, Ben Jonson, and others—the name was one of the many that were applied to Queen Elizabeth.

Cynthia's Revels. See JONSON, BEN.

Cyprian. Cyprus was formerly famous for the worship of Venus; hence the adjective has been applied to lewd or profligate persons and prostitutes.

Cyprian, St., see ST. CYPRIAN.

Cyrano de Bergerac. A drama by Edmond Rostand (*Fr.* 1897). The hero, Cyrano de BERGERAC was a real character, a 17th-century French poet contemporary with Molière. In the drama he is valiant and romantic in the extreme, but desperately sensitive regarding the size of his nose. Although he adores the beautiful Roxane, he wins her love, through his ardent, poetical letters, not for himself but for the handsome and stupid Christian de Neuvillette, whom he also prompts to eloquence under Roxane's balcony at night. Christian and Roxane marry and though Christian is killed in battle almost immediately, Cyrano keeps his secret and feeds her love for the dead man by his friendly visits for long years until at last, when he is dying, the truth is disclosed.

Cyrus the Great (d. 529 B.C.). Founder of the Persian empire. He is the ostensible hero of Mlle de Scudéry's long pastoral romance *Artamene ou le Grand Cyrus*, published in ten volumes (1648–1653). Cyrus is brought up by shepherds under the name of Artamenes, but after a long series of adventures finally gains his rightful position on the throne. Most of the characters are slightly disguised portraits of the author's contemporaries in 17th century France; Cyrus is Louis XIV, and Sappho, Mlle de Scudéry herself. In spite of its length, the romance enjoyed great prestige. It was the source for Dryden's dramas, *Secret Love, Marriage à la Mode* and *Aurengzebe*, and for Banks' *Cyrus the Great*.

The historical Cyrus overthrew Croesus and his kingdom of Lydia (547–546), made a successful conquest of Babylon (540–539), delivered the Jews from their captivity and allowed them to return to Palestine, and was killed in battle.

Cyrus the Younger (424?–410 B.C.) was a Persian prince and satrap of Asia Minor who led a great army against his brother, Artaxerxes, and was defeated and killed. Following the battle came the famous retreat of the Ten Thousand Greeks that XENOPHON, their leader, immortalized.

Cytherea. (1) A name for Venus; so called from Cythera (now Cerigo), a mountainous island of Laconia noted for the worship of Aphrodite (or Venus). The tale is that Venus and Mars, having formed an illicit affection for each other, were caught in a delicate net made by Vulcan, and exposed to the ridicule of the court of Olympus.

(2) A novel by Joseph Hergesheimer (1922).

Czar. See RULERS, TITLES OF.

czardas. A Hungarian dance, in 2/4 or 4/4 measure, in which there is a slow, somewhat pensive introduction, called the *Lassu*, and then a main section, spirited and wild, which is called the *Friss*.

czarevitch. A son of a Czar of Russia but not the title of the eldest son or heir to the throne, which was cesarevitch. Czarevitch, originally a title, was afterward replaced by Grand Duke.

Czerlaski, Countess. A character in George Eliot's AMOS BARTON.

czigany, tzigany. Hungarian. A gypsy.

Czolgosz, Leon. Assassin of President McKinley at the Pan-American Exposition in Buffalo, N.Y. (Sept. 1901). Czolgosz was executed at the end of October.

D

Dacier, Percy. A brilliant young politician in Meredith's novel, Diana of the Crossways.

dacoit. In India and Burma, a robber and murderer of the kind operating in gangs.

dactyl. In prosody a dactyl is a poetic foot consisting of a long syllable followed by two short ones, as possible, wonderful, laborer. Dactylic verse is verse based on dactyls. Longfellow's Evangeline is a well-known example of dactylic hexameter. The Greek word *daktylos* means "finger." The syllables of the dactylic foot are arranged like the joints of a finger.

> This is the forest primaeval, the murmuring pines and the hemlocks.
>
> Longfellow, *Evangeline I.i.*

Dactyls. Mythic beings connected with the worship of Cybele, in Crete, to whom is ascribed the discovery of iron. Their number was originally three—the Smelter, the Hammer, and the Anvil; but was afterwards increased to five males and five females, whence their name Dactyls or Fingers.

Dadaism. A European movement in art and literature, founded in Zürich in 1916 with an admittedly destructive intent—to mock, pervert, and demolish all the tenets of painting, music, poetry, philosophy, logic, and even reason itself and set up a pretended madness instead, in protest against what the leaders of the movement regarded as the insane and vicious destruction of civilization, life, and thought taking place in the trenches of World War I. Successive manifestoes were issued in which the nihilistic principles of Dadaism were expounded, and mass meetings were held which usually turned into riots. During the meetings, someone would read poetry which would be drowned out by discordant music, chairmen would be elected from the audience, and poems would be composed by the chance selection of words written on separate slips of paper and tossed into a hat. Dadaism was a phenomenon of the war years and lost its force with the signing of the armistice in 1918. It became less violent and bitter and turned to deriding itself, finally dying "of cheerfulness" in the comparatively "cheerful" year of 1920. In Germany, where the movement had been more political than aesthetic, it was absorbed into the Communist movement (see Communism); in France it took the form of Surrealism. Among the originators and leaders of Dadaism were Hans Arp, Richard Hullsenbeck, Hugo Ball, and Tristan Tzara, several of whom later became leaders in the Surrealist movement.

Daddy-Long-Legs. A very successful novel by Jean Webster (1912).

Daedalus. Literally, "the cunning worker." In Greek legend, a personification of skill in the mechanical art; the patron of artists' and craftsmen's guilds. As the hero of legends and tales, Daedalus was an inventive Athenian, son of Metion and grandson of Erechtheus, who originated axes, awls, bevels, and the like. He was the architect who built the labyrinth for king Minos of Crete. Imprisoned in it himself, Daedalus fashioned wings for himself and his son Icarus and escaped to Sicily. Icarus fell into the sea, but his father reached Sicily safely. Daedalus also had a nephew, Perdix, of whose skill he was envious. He tried to kill him by pushing him off a tower, but Minerva intervened, saving the boy's life by changing him into a partridge. His name is perpetuated in the words *daedal,* skilful, fertile of invention, *daedalian,* labyrinthine or ingenious, etc.

daemon. A supernatural power intermediary between gods and men and never thought of as clearly personified. Hence, the driving power of the creative genius considered simultaneously as demonic and tutelary. In modern usage, *daemon* absorbs also the meaning of *daimonion,* a term used by Socrates to designate a certain power that warned him against one course of action and made him pursue another.

daeva. One of certain malignant demons of Persian mythology, ferocious and gigantic spirits under the sovereignty of Eblis. Also *deva,* deev, etc.

> At Lahore, in the Mogul's palace, are pictures of Dews and Dives with long horns, staring eyes, shaggy hair, great fangs, ugly paws, long tails, and such horrible deformity, that I wonder the poor women are not frightened.—William Finch, *Purchas' Pilgrims,* vol. i.

Dafoe, Dr. Allan Roy (1883–1943). Canadian physician. *Dr. Dafoe's Guide Book for Mothers* (1936) owed its success to the fact that its author had delivered the Dionne quintuplets (May 28, 1934).

Daffodil Fields, The. A narrative poem by John Masefield.

Daffodils, The. A famous nature poem by William Wordsworth, characteristic of English Romanticism in its appreciation of an object of nature for its own sake.

Dagda. Chief god of the pagan Irish, who defeated the Tuatha De Danann (the other gods) and as their king assumed the rank of a Jupiter of the Gaels. His name signifies literally the good god.

Dagnan-Bouveret, Pascal Adolphe Jean (1852–1929). Once popular French painter.

Dago. American nickname for a foreigner of one of the Latin nationalities: From the Spanish proper name *Diego;* hence, originally, a Spaniard. Now generally restricted again and applied, chiefly in contempt, to an Italian.

Dagobert, see KING DAGOBERT AND ST. ELOI.

Dagon. A god of the Philistines, supposed —from very uncertain etymological and mythological indications—to have been symbolized as half man and half fish.

> Dagon his name; sea-monster, upward man
> And downward fish; yet had his temple high
> Rear'd in Azotus, dreaded through the coast
> Of Palestine, in Gath and Ascalon,
> And Accaron and Gaza's frontier bounds.
> Milton, *Paradise Lost, i. 462.*

Dagonet, Sir. The fool of King Arthur in the Arthurian legends. He was knighted by the King himself.

daguerreotype. A photograph of the kind brought into general use (1839) by the French painter Louis Jacques Mandé Daguerre (1789–1851). The silver plate, on which the exposure was taken, represented the one and only copy of the finished picture. The calotype or talbotype, invented by the Englishman William Henry Fox Talbot (1800–1877), permitted the taking of prints from a "film" of translucent paper (patented 1841).

Dagwood. See BLONDIE.

Dahak. The Satan of Persia. According to Persian mythology, the ages of the world are divided into periods of 1,000 years. When the cycle of "chiliasms" (1,000-year periods) is complete, the reign of Ormuzd will begin, and men will be all good and all happy; but this event will be preceded by the loosing of Dahak, the serpent king, who will break his chain and fall upon the world, and bring on man the most dreadful calamities.

Dahlgren gun. A cast-iron smooth-bore, 11-inch gun, devised in 1851 by the American Lieutenant John A. Dahlgren, much used by the Navy during the Civil War. Lieutenant (later Admiral) Dahlgren (1809–1870) wrote several books on naval ordnance.

> Dumb are the dahlgrens and mortars.
> H. H. Brownell, *The Bay Fight.*

Daibutsu. A colossal image of Buddha. The most famous one is at Kamakura. Cf. the poem by Kipling. Cast in bronze, it is 58 ft. tall and 98 ft. around.

Daikoku. One of the seven gods of Good Fortune in the Japanese pantheon. He is invoked specially by artisans. He sits on a ball of rice, holding a magic mallet, each stroke of which confers wealth, and is usually accompanied by a rat. He is one of the most popular of the Japanese gods.

Dail Eireann or **Dail.** The lower house of the legislature of the Irish Free State. Its membership is fixed on the basis of population; its sessions continue for four years unless dissolved.

daimio or **daimyo** (Chinese *dai myo,* great name). A Japanese nobleman.

Daimler, Gottlieb (1834–1900). German inventor. Produced the Mercedes and Daimler-Benz automobiles. The Daimler engine (patented in 1887) marked an important step forward in the development of the automobile.

Dai Nippon (*Japanese* Great Nippon). Japan, so called by the Japanese. Cf. *Great Britain,* also *Grossdeutschland.*

Dain Maroola. In Conrad's LORD JIM, the son of Chief Doramin and Jim's best friend in Patusan.

Daisy, Solomon. The parish clerk in Dickens' BARNABY RUDGE.

Daisy Miller. A short story by Henry JAMES (1878), a pathetic tale of an unsophisticated, "strikingly, admirably pretty" girl from Schenectady who runs athwart European conventions. With her complacent mother and ill-mannered little brother Randolph, she travels about Europe with tragic results.

Dakin's solution, Carrel-Dakin solution. Antiseptic solutions developed during World War I for the treatment of wounds. Named after the English chemist Henry Drysdale Dakin (1880–) and the French surgeon Alexis CARREL (1873–1944).

Daladier, Édouard (1884–). Premier of France (1933, 1934, 1938–1940), who with Prime Minister Neville Chamberlain of England was responsible for the Munich pact with Hitler. Arrested after collapse of French defense in 1940. Daladier's premiership of 1934 lasted eleven days.

Dalai Lama. The Grand Lama, pope of the Lamaists, who has his seat at Lhasa, the Buddhist sacred city of Thibet. See LAMAISM.

Dalcroze, see JAQUES-DALCROZE.

Dale, Sir Henry Hallett (1875–). English physiologist. Investigated, in collaboration with the German pharmacologist Otto Loewi (1873–) the chemistry of the transmission of nerve impulses. Shared with Loewi 1936 Nobel prize for physiology.

Dale, Laetitia. A character in George Meredith's novel, THE EGOIST.

Dalgarno, Lord Malcolm of. In Scott's FORTUNES OF NIGEL, a profligate young nobleman. It was for striking Dalgarno with his sword that Nigel was obliged to seek refuge in Alsatia. Dalgarno's villainy to the Lady Hermione excites the displeasure of King James, but he wins forgiveness by marrying her. He is finally shot by Captain Colepepper.

Dalgetty, Dugald. The Laird of Drumthwacket in Scott's LEGEND OF MONTROSE, a soldier of fortune in the service of the Earl of Monteith. He is a pedant and a braggart, one of Scott's most celebrated characters. The original was probably a certain Munro who wrote an account of the campaigns of Scotch and English auxiliaries in the island of Swinemunde in 1630.

Dali, Salvador (1904–). Spanish painter. Ultramodernist, associated with futurism, constructivism, cubism, abstract irrationalism and surrealism. Has collaborated in scenarios of two surrealist moving pictures and written several books including his autobiography. Is noted for foregrounds containing incongruous objects and anatomical curiosities with beautifully painted delicate backgrounds. A master draughtsman, who exploits the irrational.

Dalloway, Mrs. See MRS. DALLOWAY.

Dalmatian or **Dalmatian dog.** A dog of a large breed with white coat and black or brown spots; also called *coach dog* from its habit of running between the wheels of a carriage at the heels of the horse. A favorite with Fire Departments.

Daly, Arnold (1875–1927). American actor. Produced Shaw's *Candida* (1903) and thereafter appeared exclusively in Shaw's dramas. His arrest, trial, and acquittal after the first performance of *Mrs. Warren's Profession* (1905) is a famous case.

Daly, Augustin (1838–1899). Famous American theatrical manager and playwright. Established Daly's Theater (1879) and assembled a new company including John Drew, Ada Rehan, Otis Skinner, etc.

Daly, Thomas Augustine (1871–). American poet best known for his Italian dialect poems and sometimes called the "laureate of the dago." *Canzoni* (1906); *Carmina* (1909); *Madrigali* (1912); *McAroni Ballads* (1919); etc. See MACARONIC.

Damaged Souls. A collection of biographical sketches by Gamaliel BRADFORD (1923), presenting analyses of P. T. BARNUM, Aaron BURR, Thomas PAINE, and others.

Damascus. A city in Syria on the edge of the desert, famous for its silks and steel. It is referred to in the Old Testament, *Gen.* xiv. 15, xv. 2. For the rôle it played in the history of Paul, cf. *Acts* ix.

Damascus, The Gates of. A poem by James Elroy FLECKER.

Damayanti. A heroine of Hindu legend. See NALA.

Dame. A title, corresponding to *knight*, accorded in England to women appointed to the 1st or 2nd class of the Order of the British Empire.

Dame aux camélias, La. See CAMILLE.

Dame Care (Frau Sorge). A novel by Hermann Sudermann (*Ger.* 1888). The hero is Paul Meyerhofer, a boy whose struggles against poverty and sordid family difficulties are attended always by Dame Care. At length his prospective marriage to his only love, Elsbeth Douglas, opens up a way of escape.

Damien de Veuster, Joseph. Known as **Father Damien** (1840–1889). Belgian Roman Catholic missionary noted for his work with the lepers in a government hospital on Molokai Island in the Hawaiian group. Contracted leprosy and died. Cf. the famous essay by Robert Louis Stevenson, *Father Damien: An Open Letter to the Rev. Dr. Hyde* (1890).

Damnation of Faust, The. See FAUST.

Damnation of Theron Ware, The. A novel by Harold FREDERIC (1896). It describes the development of the character of Theron Ware, an earnest young Methodist clergyman, who is thrown into emotional conflict on discovering the weaknesses and deficiencies of the church and himself. After being unhappily in love with Celia Madden, a rich Catholic, who rejects him, he finds salvation in association with Sister Soulsby, a religious revivalist.

Damocles' Sword. Evil foreboded or dreaded. Damocles, a sycophant of Dionysius the Elder, of Syracuse, was invited by the tyrant to try the felicity he so much envied. Accepting, he was set down to a sumptuous banquet, but overhead was a sword suspended by a hair. Damocles was afraid to stir, and the banquet was a tantalizing torment to him.

Damoetas. A herdsman. Theocritus and Virgil use the name in their pastorals.

> And old Damoetas loved to hear our song.
> Milton: *Lycidas.*

Damon. The name of a goatherd in Virgil's *Eclogues*, and hence used by pastoral poets for rustic swains.

Damon, Samuel Foster (1893–). American poet, literary biographer, and university professor. Best-known for his *William Blake: His Philosophy and Symbols* (1924), (the first edition is now very rare) and his definitive life of Amy Lowell (1935). His poetry is collected in *Astrolabe* (1927) and *Tilted Moons* (1929).

Damon and Pythias. Inseparable friends. They were Syracusans of the first half of the 4th century B. C. Pythias, condemned to death by Dionysius the tyrant, obtained leave to go home to arrange his affairs on condition that Damon agree to take his place and be executed should Pythias not return. Pythias was delayed, Damon was led to execution, but his friend arrived just in time to save him. Dionysius was so struck with this honorable friendship that he pardoned both of them.

> Spenser fables that in the temple of Venus, Hercules and Hylas, Jonathan and David, Theseus and Pirithous, Pylades and Orestes, Titus and Gesippus, Damon and Pythias whom death could not sever:
> All these and all that ever had been tyde
> In bands of friendship, there did live for ever.
> *Faërie Queene,* IV. x. 27.

Dampier, William (1652–1715). English navigator and buccaneer. Gave his name to Dampier Archipelago and Dampier Strait. Piloted the expedition which rescued Alexander Selkirk, the prototype of ROBINSON CRUSOE (1709). Among the accounts of his voyages *A New Voyage Round the World* (1697) is the best-known.

Damrosch, Walter Johannes (1862–). Son of Leopold Damrosch (1832–1885), a famous German conductor, and brother of Frank Heino Damrosch (1859–1937), well-known chorus-master. German-born director of New York Symphony Orchestra (1903–1927); founder and conductor of educational orchestral radio concerts, composer of several operas. American Academy of Arts and Letters.

Dan.

from Dan to Beersheba. From one end of the kingdom to the other; all over the world; everywhere. The phrase is Scriptural, Dan being the most northern and Beersheba the most southern city of the Holy Land.

Dana, Charles Anderson (1819–1897). One of America's greatest journalists. Managing editor New York *Tribune* (1847–1861), editor Chicago *Republican* (1866–1868), editor and chief proprietor New York *Sun* (1868–1897).

Dana, John Cotton (1857–1929). American librarian, Denver, Colo.; Springfield, Mass.; Newark, N.J.

Dana, Richard Henry (1815–1882). American lawyer and author, best known for Two YEARS BEFORE THE MAST (1840), a realistic account of a sea-voyage which had an important influence on later sea-stories. He was active in giving legal help to sailors and escaped slaves, and wrote on international law. His father, **Richard Henry Dana**, Sr. (1787–1879), was a literary critic and one of the founders of the NORTH AMERICAN REVIEW.

Danaë. An Argive princess, daughter of Acrisius, King of Argos. He, told that his daughter's son would put him to death, resolved that Danaë should never marry, and accordingly locked her up in an inaccessible tower. Zeus foiled the king by changing himself into a shower of gold, under which guise he readily found access to the fair prisoner, and she thus became the mother of Perseus.

Danaides. The fifty daughters of Danaus, King of Argos. They married the fifty sons of Aegyptus, and all but Hypermnestra, wife of Lynceus, at the command of their father murdered their husbands on their wedding night. They were punished in Hades by having to draw water everlastingly in sieves from a deep well. Hence *Danaid's work* is endless and purposeless labor.

Dance, A Time to. A book of poems by Cecil DAY-LEWIS.

dance of death. An allegorical representation of death leading all sorts and conditions of men in a dance to the grave, originating in Germany in the 14th century as a kind of morality play, quickly becoming popular in France and England, and surviving later principally by means of pictorial representations, the best-known example of which is in Basel, Switzerland, and in the folksong. There is a series of woodcuts, said to be by Hans HOLBEIN (1538), representing death dancing after all sorts of persons, beginning with Adam and Eve. He is beside the judge on his bench, the priest in the pulpit, the nun in her cell, the doctor in his study, the bride and the beggar, the king and the infant; but is "swallowed up at last."

The 20th-century English poet, W. H. AUDEN entitled a satiric poetic drama on the "decline of the English middle class" *The Dance of Death.*

Dancing Chancellor. Sir Christopher Hatton (1540–1591). So called because he had attracted Queen Elizabeth's attention by his dancing at a court masque.

Dandie Dinmont. In Scott's GUY MANNERING, a border farmer. He owns two terriers, Mustard and Pepper, reputedly the progenitors of the Dandie Dinmont terriers.

Dandin, George, see GEORGE DANDIN.

Dandolo, Enrico (1108?–1205). Doge of Venice. One of the leaders of the Fourth CRUSADE and said to have been the first to mount the walls of Constantinople when it was captured by the Christians.

Dane, Clemence. Pseudonym, taken from the church of St. Clements Dane in London, of **Winifred Ashton.** Leading English novelist, dramatist, and poet. Her best-known play, *A Bill of Divorcement* (1921) made the reputation of Katharine Cornell; her best-known novels, *Regiment of Women* (1917) and *Broome Stages* (1931), about a theatrical family whose history parallels that of the Plantagenet family.

Danegeld, Danegelt. A special tax imposed in early medieval England to buy off the Danish invaders or to raise a force against them. Not leveled under this name after 1163.

Danelaw. The Danish law in force in the northeastern part of England while it was held by the Danes.

Dangeau, Marquis de. Philippe de Courcillon (1638–1720). French favorite of Louis XIV. His *Mémoires,* covering the years 1684–1720, are a valuable source of historical detail.

Dangle. In SHERIDAN's comedy *The Critic* (1779), a gentleman bitten with the theatrical mania, who annoys a manager with impertinent flattery and advice. It is said that Thomas Vaughan, a playwright of small reputation, was the original of this character.

Daniel. A hero of the Old Testament whose deeds and prophecies are recorded in the book of *Daniel.* He was cast into a den of lions for continuing to pray to his own God while in captivity in Babylon, but was found unhurt the following morning. Daniel was famed as the interpreter of two dreams of Nebuchadnezzar and of the Handwriting on the WALL. *A Daniel come to Judgment* is an impartial judge. The phrase is first used by Shylock, in Shakespeare's *Merchant of Venice,* when he thinks Portia is deciding in his favor, and later by Gratiano to mock the defeated Jew.

Daniel, Arnaud. 12th-century Provençal poet, called by Petrarch *gran maestro d'amore,* "the great master of love." Inventor of the SESTINA, used by Dante and Petrarch.

Daniel, Samuel (ca. 1562–1619). English poet, known for the purity of his diction—he was called "well-languaged Daniel" by his contemporaries—and for his use of historical material in his verse. His works include: an edition of his sonnets (1592); *Complaint of Rosamund* (1592), based on the type of legend in the *Mirror for Magistrates; Civil Wars* (1595), dealing with English history; *Defense of Rhyme* (1602), a critical essay in answer to the attack by Thomas CAMPION on rhyme; *The Vision of the Twelve Goddesses* (1604), the first masque written for the new court of Queen Anne.

Daniel Deronda. A novel by George Eliot (1868). The heroine, Gwendolyn Harleth, finds in Daniel Deronda the only man she knows who is indifferent to her charms; and in her efforts to win his regard, especially after her unhappy marriage to the rich but tyrannical Henleigh Grandcourt, she gradually develops her finer qualities. When Grandcourt drowns in the moment of delay before Gwendolyn throws him a rope, she blames herself bitterly and finds comfort only in Deronda's sympathetic advice. Deronda is a man of the highest ideals, who has been brought up by his rich guardian, Sir Hugo Mallinger in the belief that he is a Christian, but learns that he is a Jew. He marries Mirah Cohen (or Lapidoth), a beautiful Jewess whom he had saved from suicide, and in the idealistic Mordecai, who turns out to be Mirah's lost brother Ezra, he finds a friend who inspires him with the cause of Jewish nationalism. After Mordecai's death, he and Mirah go to Palestine to live.

For the character of the hero, see under DERONDA.

Daniels, Jonathan Worth (1902–). Son of **Josephus Daniels** (1862–1948), secretary of the navy under President Wilson. Himself secretary to Franklin D. Roosevelt, after being assistant director of the Office of Civilian Defense. A journalist and writer on the South whose work is valuable as source material.

Danite. A descendant of Dan (*Judges* xiii. 2.). Hence, one of an alleged secret association of MORMONS, the **Danite Band** (1837).

Dannebrog or **Danebrog.** The national flag of Denmark (*brog* is Old Danish for cloth). The tradition is that Waldemar II of Denmark saw in the heavens a fiery cross which betokened his victory over the Esthonians (1219).

order of Danebrog. The second of the Danish orders of knighthood; instituted in 1219 by Waldemar II, restored by Christian V in 1671, and several times modified since.

D'Annunzio, Gabriele (1863–1938). Italian poet, novelist, dramatist, and aviator. His best-known works are LA GIOCONDA (1898); IL FUOCO (*The Flame of Life*) (1900) a novel detailing his liaison with Eleonora DUSE; *Francesca da Rimini* (1901); *Forse Che Si, Forse Che No* (1910). Lost an eye in aerial combat during World War I; in 1919 led an expedition into the city of Fiume and held it for fifteen months, in defiance of the treaty obligations of Italy. Cf. Leonard Bacon's long poem *The Furioso,* in which D'Annunzio is dissected.

Danny Deever. A well-known ballad by Rudyard KIPLING (1892), dealing with the military hanging of Danny Deever, a soldier in the British army who "shot a comrade sleepin'."

Dansker. A Dane. Denmark used to be called Danskë. Hence Polonius says to Reynaldo, "Inquire me first what Danskers are in Paris." (*Hamlet,* ii. 1.)

Dante (short for **Durante**) **Alighieri** (b. at Florence in 1265, d. at Ravenna in exile in 1321) may be considered the incarnation of the greatest poetical power known in the history of the human mind. Carlyle said of the Italian poet that "he gave a voice to ten silent centuries." The work in which Dante effected this achievement is his "Comedía," known as *La Divina Commedia,* "THE DIVINE COMEDY" (ca. 1300)—the epithet "Divine" being attached to the poem in the 16th century. The

Divine Comedy, consisting of 100 cantos in TERZA RIMA, reveals a scheme of the universe, a comprehensive moral, religious, and political system, a visionary journey through Hell, Purgatory, and Paradise, and at the same time the way of an individual soul from sin to purification. Between Plato's *Dialogues* and Shakespeare's Plays the *Divine Comedy* is, apart from the New Testament, the only exemplar of deeply humane and immediate relationship on every level between soul and soul.

The entire structure of the religious, moral, and political world of the Middle Ages has found its adequate representation in a threefold way: in philosophy, in the all-embracing encyclopedias (*summae*) of the German Albertus Magnus and the Italian Thomas Aquinas; in art, in the French cathedrals of the 12th and 13th centuries; in poetry, in the *Divine Comedy.*

The vast encyclopedia of human and divine knowledge embodied in the *Divine Comedy* has, as if by metamorphosis, been transfigured into unalloyed poetry. There is no English translation which transmits the poetical magic of the poem adequately, or even approximately, whereas Dante's early relation, in verse and commenting prose, of his love for Beatrice, LA VITA NUOVA (*The New Life;* 1291) has found an almost ideal translator in Dante Gabriel ROSSETTI. In the *Divine Comedy* Beatrice, in whom the earthly woman is indissolubly merged with the allegory of Grace and divine Theology, leads the Poet through the Heavens. The cantos devoted to Beatrice's praise are the greatest homage ever paid to a mortal woman.

Dante was a friend of PETRARCH and BOCCACCIO. In addition to the works mentioned, he wrote the *Convivio* (*Banquet;* ca. 1300), a philosophical treatise; *De Vulgari Eloquentia,* a Latin treatise on language and metrics, urging the literary use of the vernacular language; and *De Monarchia,* a Latin treatise on political theory and the relations between Pope and emperor, favoring strong rule by the emperor. The Tuscan dialect used by Dante in his vernacular writings later became the standard language of Italy.

Dantes, Edmond. The titular hero of Dumas' COUNT OF MONTE CRISTO.

Danton, Georges Jacques (1759–1794). French revolutionary leader. Minister of justice (August 1792); implicated in September massacres (1792). He overthrew Hébert in a joint action with Robespierre by whom he was in turn overthrown himself. Victim of the Reign of Terror. Cf. the dramatic poem *Dantons Tod* (*Danton's Death*) by Georg Büchner (*Ger.* 1835). In a speech (September 2, 1792) inspired by the dangers of the European alliance against revolutionary France, Danton uttered the famous words: "De l'audace, encore de l'audace, et toujours de l'audace."

Danzig, Free City of. The city of Danzig (*Ger.*), Gdansk (*Pol.*), or Gedanum (Lithuanian) near the mouth of the Vistula is mentioned as early as 997; it came under the rule of the Teutonic Order (ca. 1310), was a Hanseatic city, fell to Poland (1466) and finally to Prussia (1793). In the 19th century it was Germany's most important Baltic port. Under the Versailles treaty it was established as a free city, which satisfied neither Poland nor Germany. Its severance from the Reich was an important factor in the propagandistic preparation of World War II carried on by the Nazis. The slogan, "Why should we die for Danzig?" has become a symbol of Western, especially French, apathy in the face of the territorial ambitions of the THIRD REICH.

Daphnaida. An elegy by Spenser (1591) on Douglas Howard Gorges, the only daughter of Lord Bindon. In general design and several details it is indebted to Chaucer's BOOK OF THE DUCHESS.

Daphne. In Greek mythology, daughter of a river-god, loved by Apollo. She fled from the amorous god, and escaped by being changed into a laurel, thenceforth the favorite tree of the sun-god.

Daphnis. In Greek mythology, a Sicilian shepherd who invented pastoral poetry. He was a son of Mercury and a Sicilian nymph, was protected by Diana, and was taught by Pan and the Muses.

Daphnis and Chloë. Title of a Greek pastoral, generally ascribed to the sophist Longus (4th or 5th century A. D.). It tells the story of the tender love of Daphnis and Chloë, the children of a goatherd and a shepherd. It owes its fame in modern times to the French version by Amyot (1559). Major works in its later tradition are Tasso's *Aminta,* Montemayor's *Diana,* St. Pierre's *Paul et Virginie,* etc.

Dapper. In Ben Jonson's ALCHEMIST, a lawyer's clerk, who goes to Subtle "the alchemist," to be supplied with a familiar to make him win in horse-racing, cards, and all games of chance. Dapper is told to prepare himself for an interview with the fairy queen by taking "three drops of vinegar in at the nose, two at the mouth, and one at either ear," "to cry *hum* thrice and *buzz* as often."

Dapple. The donkey ridden by Sancho Panza, in Cervantes' romance of DON QUIXOTE.

Darby and Joan. The type of loving, old-fashioned, virtuous couples. The names belong to a ballad called *The Happy Old Couple,* probably written by Henry Woodfall, and the characters are said to be of John Darby, of Bartholomew Close, who died in 1730, and his wife. Woodfall served his apprenticeship as a printer to John Darby. Some authorities attribute the ballad to Matthew Prior.

Darcy. The hero of Jane Austen's PRIDE AND PREJUDICE.

D'Arcy, Bartell. An Irish tenor who appears briefly in both THE DEAD and ULYSSES by James Joyce.

Dardanelles. The ancient Hellespont, a strait between Europe and Asiatic Turkey. During World War I the Allies attacked the Turks here, and suffered defeat. In 1941 it was the gateway to Russia from the Mediterranean but Turkey, as neutral, refused passage of it. Its fortifications were so strong that no attempt on it was made by sea. Russia's traditional ambitions to gain control over the Dardanelles are inspired by the country's need for free access to ice-free waters.

Dare, Virginia (1587– ?). First American-born child of English colonists on Roanoke Island, Virginia (now North Carolina). In 1591, when relief reached the island, all traces of the settlers had vanished.

Dares Phrygius. Author of an early version of the TROILUS legend in Latin prose, written about the 6th century A. D. The account is preceded by a forged letter from Cornelius Nepos, claiming to have discovered the manuscript, written in Phrygian characters, in Athens. It purports to be the story of Troy told by a supposed eye-witness, and is biased in favor of the Trojan point of view. Odd quirks are given to the story, including the endowment of Paris with effeminate characteristics and of BRISEIDA, as in later versions, with joined eyebrows. Although now regarded as a literary forgery, the account of Dares was one of the versions by which the story of Troy was known to the Middle Ages. Cf. DICTYS CRETENSIS.

Dargan, Olive Tilford. American poet and novelist. Some of her best work is in the ballad and the poetic drama. Wrote two proletarian novels under the pseudonym of Fielding Burke, *Call Home the Heart* (1932) and *A Stone Came Rolling* (1935).

Darien. The Isthmus of Darien is the place from which, according to Keats, "Stout Cortez" first viewed the Pacific. Actually it was Balboa at Darien who stood "silent, upon a peak" first viewing what he called "el mar del sur."

Darío, Rubén (1867–1916). Nicaraguan poet. Outstanding in South American literature. Aristocratic and in many respects rather European than American.

Darius. A Greek form of Persian *dara,* a king, or of Sanskrit *darj,* the maintainer. Gushtasp or Kishtasp assumed the title on ascending the throne in 521 B. C., and is generally known as Darius the Great.

Legend relates that seven Persian princes agreed that he should be king whose horse neighed first; and the horse of Darius was the first to neigh.

It is said that Darius III (Codomannus), the last king of Persia, who was conquered by Alexander the Great (331 B. C.), when Alexander succeeded to the throne, sent to him for the tribute of golden eggs, but the Macedonian answered, "The bird which laid them is flown to the other world, where Darius must seek them." The Persian King then sent him a bat and ball, in ridicule of his youth; but Alexander told the messengers, with the bat he would beat the ball of power from their master's hand. Lastly, Darius sent him a bitter melon as emblem of the grief in store for him; but the Macedonian declared that he would make the Shah eat his own fruit.

dark.

the Dark Ages. The earlier centuries of the Middle Ages; roughly, the era between the death of Charlemagne and the close of the Carolingian dynasty; so called because of the intellectual darkness supposedly characteristic of the period. Nowadays few writers dare to use the term without the qualification "so-called."

the Dark and Bloody Ground. A name for the State of Kentucky, either (1) from the early warfare with the Indians, or (2) a translation of the Indian name of the State.

the Dark Continent. Africa; concerning which the world was so long "in the dark," and which, also, is the land of dark races.

dark horse. A racing term for a horse of good pretensions, but of which nothing is positively known by the general public. Its merits are kept dark from betters and bookmakers. The term is widely used in the political field for a candidate brought forward at the last minute.

Dark Flower, The. A novel by John GALSWORTHY (1913) relating the love affairs of Mark Lennan. The "dark flower" is passion.

dark lady of the sonnets. The mysterious person to whom Shakespeare addressed his sonnets. She has been the subject of much interesting speculation. George Bernard SHAW wrote a play entitled *The Dark Lady of the Sonnets* (1910).

Dark Laughter. A novel by Sherwood ANDERSON (1925). It deals with the escape of John Stockton, a Chicago newspaperman, from a life he regards as sterile and oppressive, ruled by the machine. He travels by boat down the Mississippi River and eventually takes a job as a laborer, under the name of Bruce Dudley, in a factory in his former hometown in Indiana. There he and Aline Grey, the wife of his employer and a woman similarly dissatisfied with the mechanical civilization of the time, fall in love and elope. The title refers to the animal joy of the Negroes, symbolic of simple, happy, and uninhibited living.

Darley, George (1795–1846). Irish poet. Author of several enduring lyrics, the fairy opera, *Sylvia* (1827), etc.

Darley Arabian. About 1700 a Mr. Darley, of Yorkshire, imported into England from Aleppo three thoroughbred Arabian stallions which became the founders of the line of thoroughbreds in England. *Darley Arabian,* the sire of *Flying Childers,* and great-great-grandsire of *Eclipse,* was one; the others were *Byerby Turk* and *Godolphin Barb.* From the first comes the Herod breed, and from the second the Matchem.

Darling, Grace Horsley (1815–1842). The Farne Islands, off Northumberland county, England, were the scene of the shipwreck of the *Forfarshire* (1838) and the heroic rescue of nine survivors by young Grace Darling and her father, the keeper of the lighthouse.

Darling, Jay Norwood (1876–). Well-known American cartoonist. Also active in preservation of wild life. His signature reads **Ding.**

Darling, Wendy, Michael and **John.** In Barrie's PETER PAN, the children whom Peter teaches to fly with him to Never-Never Land.

Darling of the Graces. (1) Aristophanes (444–380 B.C.).

(2) Heinrich Heine (1789–1856).

Darlington, Lord. In Oscar Wilde's play LADY WINDERMERE'S FAN, the lover of Lady Windermere.

Darmesteter, Agnes Mary Frances, *nee* **Robinson** (1857–). English poet and novelist. Wife of the French Orientalist **James Darmesteter** (1849–1894) and sister-in-law of the lexicographer **Arsène Darmesteter** (1846–1888) whose *Dictionnaire Général de la Langue Française* (in collaboration with Adolphe Hatzfeld and Antoine Thomas) came out posthumously (1890–1900) and stands, through the precision of its definitions, as a monument to the proverbial clarity of French thought. Now Mme Duclaux.

Darnay, Charles. In Dickens' TALE OF TWO CITIES, the lover and afterwards the husband of Lucie Manette. He bears a strong likeness to Sydney CARTON.

Darnel, Aurelia. A character in Smollett's novel, THE ADVENTURES OF SIR LAUNCELOT GREAVES (1760).

Darnley, Lord. Henry Stuart (1545–1567). Second husband of MARY, QUEEN OF SCOTS. Took part in the murder of Rizzio (1566). Himself murdered, at Kirk o'Field, a solitary house near Edinburgh, which was blown up with gunpowder, possibly with Mary's knowledge.

Darrel of the Blessed Isles. A novel by Irving BACHELLER (1903), concerning an old clock-maker who dwells in the "Blessed Isles" of the imagination.

Darrow, Clarence Seward (1857–1938). American criminal lawyer, humanitarian and author of *Crime: Its Cause and Treatment* (1922), *The Story of My Life* (1932), etc. Among his famous cases were his winning of an acquittal for Eugene V. Debs in the American Railway Union strike (1894); another for "Big Bill" Haywood and two other Western Federation of Miners officials; his plea for mitigating circumstances of insanity for Loeb and Leopold (1924); his victory over William Jennings Bryan in the SCOPES case (1925), though he lost the jury verdict in that Tennessee controversy on evolution; and the Negroes in the Scottsboro case (1932). He was a confirmed pessimist and agnostic but also a brave, kindly, and simple man.

D'Artagnan. See THREE MUSKETEERS, THE.

Dartle, Rosa. In Dickens' DAVID COPPERFIELD, companion of Mrs. Steerforth. She loves Mrs. Steerforth's son, but her love is not reciprocated. Miss Dartle is a vindictive woman, noted for a scar on her lip, which tells tales when her temper is aroused. This scar is from a wound given her by young Steerforth, who struck her on the lip when a boy.

Dartmoor. Short for **Dartmoor prison,** a famous English prison on a table land in South Devonshire.

Dartmouth College. A nonsectarian American college in Hanover, N.H. founded in 1769 by Eleazer Wheelock. Over two thousand students; over two hundred teachers.

Darwin, Charles Robert (1809–1882). Great English naturalist, grandson of Erasmus Darwin. Participated as naturalist in the surveying expedition on the Beagle to South America and Australasia (1831–1836); published *Zoology of the Voyage of the Beagle* (1840). Published his own and Alfred Russel Wallace's theories of natural selection together (1857). Author of *On the Origin of Species by Means of Natural Selection* (1859); and *The Descent of Man* (1871), in which the human race is considered to have descended from an animal of the anthropoids; etc. Buried in

Westminster Abbey. The essence of Darwin's theories, often referred to as Darwinism, consists in the idea that, because offspring can vary from the parents and because nature tolerates only *the survival of the fittest,* the principle of *natural selection* can explain the *evolution* of a higher species from a lower one. In its unqualified form, Darwinism is no longer tenable, but Darwin's historical importance remains tremendous. He was a great scientific pioneer and his ideas affected the 19th- and 20th-century faith in universal and continued progress. See also SCOPES TRIAL; MISSING LINK.

Darwin, Erasmus (1731–1802). English physician, botanist, and author of *The Botanic Garden* (1789 and 1791), a didactic poem in heroic couplets discoursing on plants and flowers according to the theories of LINNAEUS. Darwin's *Zoönomia* (1794–1796) is a treatise on evolutionary development, not, however, in the sense which Erasmus Darwin's grandson, Charles Robert DARWIN, was to assign to that term.

Dashwood, Elinor and **Marianne.** Joint heroines of Jane Austen's SENSE AND SENSIBILITY.

date line. A hypothetical line, fixed by convention approximately on the meridian 180° from Greenwich as the place where each calendar day *first* begins. It is deflected in several places to avoid the inconvenience of different day-reckoning between places in close proximity. Vessels crossing the line to the westward set the date forward by one day. Vessels crossing to the eastward set it back by a day.

Dauber. Title and hero of a narrative poem (1912) by John MASEFIELD, the tragic story of an artist-sailor who is the butt of all his companions' jokes.

Daudet, Alphonse (1840–1897). French novelist of the Naturalist school (see NATURALISM), known for his keen observation and his rendering of characters and incidents, most of which were autobiographical or belonged to the biographies of people he knew. His novels deal with life in Provence, his birthplace, and with the social classes of Paris, both wealthy and poor. The Provençal stories, vigorous and good-humored, include *Lettres de mon moulin* (1866); *Tartarin de Tarascon* (1872), *Tartarin sur les Alpes* (1885), and *Port-Tarascon* (1890), belonging to the TARTARIN series. Daudet's novels of Parisian manners include THE NABOB (*le Nabob*) (1877); *Numa Roumestan* (1881); KINGS IN EXILE (*Les Rois en exil* (1879); SAPHO (1884); *L'Immortel* (1888). Other novels deal with the humbler classes of the metropolitan population in a manner sometimes compared with that of DICKENS. Among these are *Fromont jeune et Risler aîné* (1874), *Jack* (1876), and *L'Évangeliste.* Like the other novelists of the Naturalist group, Daudet often worked fifteen hours a day on his books, and his health was impaired by overwork. His writings are considered to be less somber and less bookish than those of the other Naturalists. His son, **Léon Daudet** (1867–1942), was a French journalist and writer of novels, books on psychology and medicine, political works and books of literary criticism. He founded with Charles Maurras the royalist journal, *L'Action Française* (1907).

daughter of Heth. An alien woman. Cf. *Gen.* xxvi. 34–35. Title of a novel by William Black.

daughter of Jezebel. See JEZEBEL.

Daughter of the Middle Border. See MIDDLE BORDER.

Daughters of the American Revolution (D.A.R.). A patriotic society of American women organized at Washington, D.C. (1890) to preserve in memory those active in achieving American Independence. It has become an extremely conservative and in some respects intolerant organization with emphasis on the social privilege of membership. Cf. Grant Wood's devastating portrayal *Daughters of Revolution.*

Daumier, Honoré (1808–1879). Famous French caricaturist. Political and bourgeois subjects. On staff of *La Caricature* and *Charivari.* His serious work is less well-known.

dauphin. The heir of the French crown under the Valois and Bourbon dynasties. Guy VIII, count of Vienne, was the first so styled, apparently because he wore *a dolphin* as his cognizance. The title descended in the family till 1349, when Humbert III ceded his seigneurie, the Dauphiné, to Philippe VI (de Valois), one condition being that the heir of France assume the title of *le dauphin.* The first French prince so called was Jean, who succeeded Philippe; and the last was the Duc d'Angoulême, son of Charles X, who renounced the title in 1830.

Grand Dauphin. Louis, Duc de Bourgogne (1661–1711), eldest son of Louis XIV, for whose use was published the so-called Delphin Latin classics entitled *ad usum Delphini.*

Second or *Little Dauphin.* Louis, son of the Grand Dauphin (1682–1712).

Davenport, Griffith. See GRIFFITH DAVENPORT.

Davenport, Marcia (1903–). Daughter of Alma GLUCK. Married to Russell W. DAVENPORT. Author of a biography of Mozart and of the novels *Of Lena Geyer* (1936), *The Valley of Decision* (1942), etc.

Davenport, Russell W. (1899–). American author and editor. Served overseas in World War I and was twice awarded the Croix de Guerre. Joined *Fortune* magazine (1930) and became managing editor. Chief editorial writer, *Life* magazine (1942–1944). Author of *My Country: A Poem of America* (1944) which aroused considerable controversy and had a wide sale. Davenport is a progressive Republican who worked for Wendell WILLKIE as president before and after his nomination.

David. The shepherd king of the Old Testament (1 *Sam.* xvi–1 *Kings* ii), the reputed author of many of the Psalms. He was the youngest son of Jesse, "ruddy and withal of a beautiful countenance and goodly to look upon." David was secretly anointed king by the prophet Samuel while Saul was still on the throne and the stories of his early life are concerned with his immortal friendship for Saul's son Jonathan and Saul's growing jealousy. He killed Goliath, the huge champion of the Philistines, when no one else would venture to respond to the giant's challenge; and with his harp he charmed away the black moods of King Saul. For many years, however, he was forced to flee from Saul's anger.

After the death of Saul and Jonathan, David became king of Israel. His latter years were concerned with his guilty love for BATHSHEBA and his grief over the revolt of his son ABSALOM.

David is the hero of Peele's drama *David and Bethsabe* (1598), of Drayton's narrative poem *David and Goliath* (1630), and of two long poems entitled *Davideis,* one by Abraham Cowley, the other by Thomas Elwood. Stephen Phillips (Eng. 1868–1915) wrote a poetic drama entitled *The Sin of David*. Elmer Davis has a novel, *Giant Killer* (1928).

David, in Dryden's satire of *Absalom and Achitophel,* is meant for Charles II. As David's beloved son Absalom is against him, so the Duke of Monmouth rebels against his father Charles II. As Achitophel is a traitorous counsellor to David, so was the Earl of Shaftesbury to Charles II. As Hushai outwits Achitophel, so Hyde (Duke of Rochester) outwitted the Earl of Shaftesbury, etc.

Auspicious prince,
Thy longing country's darling and desire,
Their cloudy pillar, and their guardian fire . . .
The people's prayer, the glad diviner's theme
The young men's vision, and the old men's dream.
Dryden, *Absalom and Achitophel*, i. 231–240.

David, Jacques Louis (1748–1825). French painter, "founder of the French classical school." Court painter to Louis XVI. He sympathized with the French Revolution and was connected with Robespierre. After 1804, court painter to Napoleon. At Restoration, exiled to Brussels (1815).

David Balfour, Being Memoirs of His Adventures at Home and Abroad. A novel by Robert Louis STEVENSON (1893), a sequel to KIDNAPPED. It concerns David's efforts to bring about the escape of his Jacobite friend Alan Breck Stewart and his brother, and the love and eventual marriage of David and Catriona Drummond.

David Copperfield. A novel by Charles DICKENS, admittedly largely autobiographical. As a mere boy, after his mother's death David is sent by his harsh stepfather, Mr. Murdstone, to London, where he pastes labels on bottles in a warehouse by day and is the single lodger of the poverty-stricken hopeful MICAWBERS. He finally runs away to his great-aunt Betsy Trotwood at Dover, where he finds a genuine welcome. After a period of school life, he settles down to work with Mr. Wickfield, a lawyer, and finds a warm friend in Wickfield's daughter Agnes. He marries Dora Spenlow, a "child-wife," but after her death he marries Agnes Wickfield. See also PEGGOTTY, STEERFORTH, HEEP.

Davideis. (1) An epic poem in four books by Abraham Cowley (1656) describing the troubles of King David.

(2) A sacred poem by Thomas Elwood (1712).

David Harum. A novel by E. N. Westcott (*Am.* 1898). The humorous flavor for which the book is noted comes from its chief character, David Harum, the shrewd if unlettered philosopher of the New York country town of Homeville. David is a country banker whose chief recreation is that of horse-trading. A love story is interwoven, the principals of which are Mary Blake and John Lenox, the latter a young man of good antecedents who takes a position in David Harum's bank.

David Levinsky, The Rise of. A novel by Abraham Cahan (*Am.* 1917) telling the story of a Russian Jew who emigrates to America and becomes, finally, the chief figure in the New York cloak and suit trade.

Davidson, Jo (1883–). American sculptor. His best works are sculptures of Woodrow Wilson, Anatole France, Marshal Foch, General Pershing, Will Rogers, Walt Whitman; and portrait busts of Franklin D. Roosevelt, Rabindranath Tagore, Clemenceau, etc. He is represented in the Luxembourg, Paris, and in the rotunda of the Capitol, Washington, D.C.

Davidson, John (1857–1909). Scottish poet and playwright. Did his best work in the era of the nineties. His *Fleet Street Eclogues* and several volumes of *Ballads* were well-known at the time. His pessimistic philosophy is in his *Testaments* and *The Man Forbid*. Several of his poems have evinced endurance, notably the *Ballad of Hell* and *A Runnable Stag*.

Davidson, Lawrence H. Pseudonym under which David Herbert LAWRENCE published *Movements in European History* (1921).

Davies, Sir **John** (1569–1626). English poet, author of epigrammatic and ingenious poetry and treatises in verse, known for the vigor and intelligence of his writing. Among his works are *Orchestra* (1594), a treatment in poetry of the dance; *Epigrams and Elegies* (1596); *Hymns of Astraea* (1599), a collection of acrostic hymns praising Queen Elizabeth; *Nosce Teipsum* (1599), a philosophical poem on the immortality of the soul; *Twelve Wonders of the World* (1608), a collection of epigrams.

Davies, Joseph Edward (1876–). American ambassador to Russia (1936–1938). Author of *Mission to Moscow* (1941), one of the most important gestures of friendship toward the Soviet Union during World War II, later made into a moving picture, sharply criticized for bias and distortion of facts.

Davies, Rhys (1903–). Remarkable Welsh novelist. *Withered Root* (1928) and many others.

Davies, William Henry (1871–1940). Welsh-born English poet, author of lyrics on nature and love in traditional manner and form, known for their simplicity and feeling. Until he was over thirty, he was a hobo and peddler from choice. His books include *Collected Poems* (1916, 1923, 1929); *Forty-Nine Poems* (1929); *Love Poems* (1935); *The Birth of Song* (1936). Davies owes his reputation, however, to his *Autobiography of a Super-Tramp* (1907) with its "splendid, rough, simple, direct prose."

Dávila y Padilla, Agustín (1562–1604). Mexican historian, prior of the Dominican convent at Pueblo de los Angeles, known as the "Chronicler of the Indies." His principal work, the *Historia de la provincia de Santiago de Mejico* (published at Madrid, 1596), was commissioned by the Mexican government.

Davis, Clyde Brion (1894–). American novelist, who wrote the epic of all average American newspaper men in *"The Great American Novel—"* (1938). He is one of our best Western writers of realistic and humorous fiction. He claims that his hobbies are "hypochondria and weed-culture."

Davis, Elmer Holmes (1890–). American journalist, essayist, novelist, publicist, radio news commentator. Head of the Office of War Information during World War II. Author of *Friends of Mr. Sweeney* (1925), *Love Among the Ruins* (1935) (short stories); *Not to Mention the War* (essays, 1940), etc.

Davis, Fannie Stearns, see GIFFORD, FANNIE STEARNS DAVIS.

Davis, Harold Lenoir (1896–). American poet and novelist. Winner of Harper and Pulitzer prizes for *Honey in the Horn* (1935). Writer of uproarious folktales. Owns a cattle ranch.

Davis, Jefferson (1808–1889). President of the Confederate States of America during the American Civil War. Native of Kentucky. Graduate of U.S.M.A., West Point (1828). Frontier army service. House of Representatives (1845–1846). Served in Mexican War. Secretary of War under Pierce; U.S. Senator (1857–1861). Defender of South and the institution of slavery.

Davis, Owen (1874–). American playwright, author of numerous popular melodramas, the most celebrated being NELLIE, THE BEAUTIFUL CLOAK MODEL. He also wrote serious plays, including *Detour* (1921) and *Icebound* (1923), a winner of the Pulitzer prize in 1923.

Davis, Rebecca Blaine Harding (1831–1910). American author, mother of Richard Harding DAVIS, known for her attempts to deal in fiction with the life of industrial workers, the Negro problem, and political corruption. Her works include: *Margaret Howth* (1862), *Waiting for the Verdict* (1868), and *John Andross* (1874), novels, and *Silhouettes of American Life* (1892), a collection of short stories. See also *Life in the Iron Mills*.

Davis, Richard Harding (1864–1916). American journalist, war correspondent, and author of numerous popular novels, short stories, plays, and accounts of his adventures. He was on the staff of the New York *Sun* (1889–1890), contributed short stories to *Scribner's,* and was managing editor of *Harper's Weekly* for awhile. Davis was an extremely popular personality of his time, reporting the Spanish-American War, the Boer War, the Russo-Japanese War, and World War I. His news stories were vivid and dramatic, but his fiction is considered to be journalistic, slick, and superficial. He is best known as a short-story writer for GALLEGHER first published in *Scribner's* and appearing in book-form in *Gallegher And Other Stories* (1891), and his VAN BIBBER stories, in *Van Bibber and Others* (1892). He was the son of Rebecca H. DAVIS, and is regarded as a typical personality of the American GILDED AGE.

Davis, Thomas Osborne (1814–1845). Irish poet. Founded, with John Blake Dillon and Charles Gavan Duffy, *The Nation* (1842). One of the leaders of Young Ireland party.

Davis, William Stearns (1877–1930). American historical novelist and professor of history. Author of *A Friend of Caesar* (1900); *Life on a Mediaeval Barony* (1923); *The Whirlwind* (1929); etc.

Davis cup. An international lawn tennis challenge cup, presented in 1900 by Dwight F. Davis, now representing world team championship. Cup ties are to be played every year in two zones (America and Europe), with the challenge round following in the country that holds the cup.

Davus. A plain, uncouth servitor. A common name for a slave in Greek and Roman plays, as in the *Andria* of Terence.

> His face made of brass, like a vice in a game,
> His gesture like Davus, whom Terence doth name.
> Tusser, *Five Hundred Points of Good Husbandry,* liv. (1557).

Davus sum, non Oedipus. I am a homely man, and do not understand hints, innuendoes, and riddles, like OEDIPUS. The proverb is used by Terence, *Andria,* I, 2, 23.

Davy. In Shakespeare's 2 *Henry II,* the varlet of Justice Shallow, who so identifies himself with his master that he considers himself half host, half varlet. Thus when he seats Bardolph and Page at table, he tells them they must take "his" good will for their assurance of welcome.

Davy, Sir **Humphry** (1778–1829). English chemist. Among many experiments and discoveries he demonstrated that chlorine is an element, that the diamond is carbon, advanced the electrical theory of chemical affinity, and invented the miner's safety lamp, known as Davy lamp. Published *Elements of Chemical Philosophy* (1812), *Elements of Agricultural Chemistry,* etc. In his nontechnical works, *Salmonia* (1827) and *The Last Days of a Philosopher* (1830) Davy displayed unusual descriptive powers and a rich poetical imagination. It has been said of him that "God meant him to be a poet but the world harnessed his talents to science."

Davy Jones. A sailor's name for the evil spirit of the sea. The term seems to be a corruption of *Duffy* or *Duppy Jonah,* the word *duffy* or *duppy* standing, among the Negroes of the West Indies, for "a haunting spirit or ghost." Jones is a corruption of Jonah, the prophet who was thrown into the sea.

He's gone to Davy Jones' locker is the nautical way of saying that a messmate is dead and has been buried at sea.

Daw, Marjorie, see MARJORIE DAW.

Dawes Plan. A plan evolved by the commission of which General Charles Gates Dawes (1865–), American lawyer, financier, and politician, was chairman, to investigate possibilities as to German payment of reparations after World War I (1923). The plan was put into effect September 1, 1924. The Dawes Plan involved balancing the budget and stabilizing the currency of Germany and had as special features a five-year sliding scale of payments up to 2500 million marks, covered by a mortgage on German industries, etc.

Dawkins, Jack. A character in Dickens' OLIVER TWIST, better known by the sobriquet of the "ARTFUL DODGER."

Dawn Man. See PILTDOWN MAN.

Dawn O'Hara. First novel by Edna FERBER (1911).

Dawson, Coningsby William (1883–). Anglo-American poet and novelist, his best-known novel being *The Garden Without Walls* (1913).

Day, Clarence Shepard (1874–1935). American author, best known for his humorous autobiographical sketches, *God and My Father* (1932), *Life with Father* (1935), *Life with Mother* (1937), and *Father and I* (1940), first published in *The New Yorker.* They portray life in a typical American upper-middle-class family of the 19th century. In 1939, *Life with Father* was dramatized as a successful comedy, with a record-breaking 3183 performances. From middle age he was crippled by arthritis. His uncle, **Benjamin Day** (1838–1916), New York printer, invented the BEN DAY process for shading in printed illustrations.

Day, Fancy. Heroine of Thomas Hardy's UNDER THE GREENWOOD TREE.

Day, Holman Francis (1865–1935). American novelist and writer of verse. Specialized in Maine types. Wrote the saga of logging and timber-cutting in his best novels, a series begun in *King Spruce* (1910). *Pine Tree Ballads* (1902) and *Kin o' Ktaadn* (1904) contain some of his best doggerel verse.

Day, John (1522–1584). English printer who printed the first church music book in English and the first English edition of John Foxe's ACTS AND MONUMENTS (1563). His name has been taken as the company name of a New York publishing house.

Day or **Daye, Stephen** (1594?–1668). Printer of the *Bay Psalm Book* (1640), the first book in English printed in America. The town of Cambridge, Mass., granted him 300 acres of land for "being the first that sett upon printing."

Day-Lewis, Cecil (1904–). Irish-born English poet, a descendant of Oliver GOLDSMITH and associated with W. H. AUDEN and Stephen SPENDER in writing poetry reflecting

Marxist convictions during the 1930's. His work makes use of traditional lyric forms to preach the decadence of the bourgeois English society of his time and the promise of a Socialist society. It is chiefly didactic and makes use of 20th-century social and industrial symbols, as does the poetry of Auden and Spender. Critics say, however, that Day-Lewis' work lacks the virtuosity and satirical brilliance of the former and the emotional intensity of the latter. His books of poetry are *Transitional Poem* (1929); *From Feathers to Iron* (1931); *The Magnetic Mountain* (1933); *A Time to Dance* (1935); *Noah and the Waters* (1936); *Overtures to Death* (1938). He was also author of *A Hope for Poetry* (1934), a critical essay on the aims and techniques of the English Marxist poets, and *The Friendly Tree* (1936) and *Starting Point* (1938), novels. Under the pseudonym of Nicholas Blake he wrote detective stories and children's books. Day-Lewis was an active member of the Communist Party in England. He signs his name commonly as Cecil Day Lewis.

Day of Atonement. See YOM KIPPUR.

Day of Doom, The. A celebrated and popular poem by Michael WIGGLESWORTH, published in 1662. It describes the judicial sentencing to punishment in Hell of sinners and infants who died before baptism, as it takes place on Judgment Day. The work was widely read in New England as a theological treatise for a century after publication, being second only to the Bible in popularity. It is reported to have been published in New York as late as 1867.

Day of the Rabblement, The. An attack upon the Irish national theater movement (see IRISH RENAISSANCE) written by James JOYCE (1901). It marked the beginning of life-long hostility between Joyce and the leading figures of the Irish literary Renaissance.

Day's Work, The. A volume of short stories by Rudyard KIPLING (1898).

Dayton trial, see SCOPES TRIAL.

De, de. For such foreign names as De Barrel, De Bracy, etc., see also under BARREL, BRACY, etc.

Deacon's Masterpiece, The. See ONE HOSS SHAY.

Dead, The. A story by James JOYCE in DUBLINERS. It concerns Gabriel Conroy, an Irish school-teacher and author of occasional book reviews who is rapidly approaching middle age, and his wife Gretta. After a party, Gretta tells him of Michael Furey, a young man, now dead, who once was in love with her and who has been recalled to her memory by a song delivered for their entertainment earlier in the evening. Conroy feels suddenly shut out of his wife's life on hearing this revelation. He becomes more and more aware of the power of the dead as snow, the symbol of death, falls silently outside. This story is analyzed in *After Strange Gods,* a book of lectures on literary criticism by T. S. ELIOT.

Dead End. A play by Sidney Kingsley (1935), depicting life in New York's slums by means of typical scenes taking place in a dead-end street. The children playing various roles in the stage performance were used in the film version of the play and later in a number of less valuable productions. They came to be known as **Dead End Kids,** a term now often used for slum urchins reminiscent of the original play.

Deadeye, Dick. In Gilbert and Sullivan's comic opera, PINAFORE, a terrible villain.

dead language. A language no longer used in social intercourse. Greek and classical Latin are dead languages. Hebrew is an interesting example of a dead language that has come to life again.

deadly sins, see SEVEN DEADLY SINS.

Dead Pan. See under PAN.

Dead Sea fruit. The Apple of Sodom. See also under APPLE. The *Dead Sea* is the Lake of Palestine.

Dead Souls. A humorous novel by N. V. GOGOL (1846). The hero, Chichikov, in order to obtain a large tract of colonization land in southern Russia (the size of the tract offered being dependent on the number of serfs to till it), goes about Russia buying up "dead souls"—that is, serfs (souls) who have died since the last census and are therefore not yet officially dead. His travels and adventures give the author opportunity for portrayal of all classes of Russian society. The schemer is detected and put in prison, but escapes and settles down as a country gentleman.

Deadwood Dick. A hero of dime-novel fame created by Edward L. Wheeler. His adventures appeared in *Beadle's Half-Dime Pocket Library* from 1884 on, with such titles as *Deadwood Dick on Deck, or Calamity Jane, the Heroine of Whoop Up, The Double Daggers or Deadwood Dick's Defiance,* etc. He is said to have had a prototype in Robert Dickey (1840–1912), a trapper and fur merchant of the American West, many of whose adventures furnished plots for Wheeler's thrillers.

De Amicitia. Concerning friendship. An essay by Cicero written in the form of a dialogue. The chief interlocutor is Gaius Laelius Sapiens. Hence the essay is also known under the name of Laelius.

Deans, Douce Davie. In Scott's HEART OF MIDLOTHIAN, a cowherd at Edinburgh, full of eccentricities, but affectionate and kind. He is immovable where his devotion to his religious convictions is concerned.

Jeanie Deans. Daughter of Douce Davie, one of Scott's most famous characters. She had a prototype in Helen Walker, to whose memory Sir Walter Scott erected a tombstone in Irongray Churchyard.

Effie Deans. Jeanie's half sister, betrayed by George Staunton and imprisoned for child murder.

Dear Brutus. A comedy by Sir James M. BARRIE (1917). Title from Shakespeare's *Julius Caesar* I, ii.

Deasy, Mr. In James Joyce's ULYSSES, headmaster of the school at which Stephen DEDALUS teaches and from which he resigns in the early sections of the novel.

Death Angel. Azrael, the angel who, in Jewish and Mohammedan angelology, watches for the coming of death to take the soul away from the body.

Death Comes for the Archbishop. A novel by Willa CATHER, published in 1927. It describes the careers of the French bishop Jean LATOUR and his vicar, Father Joseph VAILLANT, in establishing a diocese in pioneer New Mexico. They have difficulties with the indifferent Indians, the climate, and the Spanish clergy, but at last triumph and win the affection and respect of the natives. The novel is founded on the lives of Bishop Lamy of Santa Fé and his vicar general, Father Machebeuf.

Death in the Afternoon. See HEMINGWAY, ERNEST.

Death in Venice. A famous short story by Thomas MANN, published in 1912. Gustave ASCHENBACH, a German author, gives up his family and his career in order to be near a beautiful Polish boy, Tadzio, whom he encounters while on a visit to Venice and who symbolizes unattainable beauty and pure art as it is sought by the artist. The city is afflicted with plague, but Aschenbach chooses to remain and die of the fever rather than desert his ideal. This story was one of the first to embody the ideas of pure art, the artist, and society which later filled Mann's writings.

Death of the Hired Man, The. A long poem by Robert FROST, describing the death of Silas, a proud but defeated old New Englander who returns to his former employers in his last hours.

deathwatch. Small black beetle that strikes its head on woodwork in old houses at regular intervals, possibly to attract the attention of its mate. The resultant hollow noise, according to popular belief, presages death.

debacle. Breakdown, collapse. From French *débâcle,* which in turn seems to come from a Dutch word and might be rendered literally as *"unbaking."* Originally applied to the breaking up of ice in a stream.

Débâcle, La. A novel by Émile ZOLA (1892), one of the ROUGON-MACQUART series. It deals realistically with the Franco-Prussian War.

debatable land. A tract of land between the Esk and Sark, claimed by both England and Scotland, and for a long time the subject of dispute. It was the haunt of thieves and vagabonds.

debate. A literary form popular in the Middle Ages, in which a dialogue takes place between two persons representing two differing points of view on the subject of philosophy, theology, love (see COURTLY LOVE), religious dogma, the virtues of a soldier or student or the country versus the town, or even a simple, commonplace topic. In Middle English, two of the best-known debates are THE OWL AND THE NIGHTINGALE (12th or 13th century) and *The Debate of the Body and the Soul* (between 1250 and 1275). In the latter poem, the soul and the body of a dead man destined for punishment in Hell argue spiritedly with each other over which is responsible for the plight of the unfortunate sinner.

De bello Gallico, see COMMENTARIES ON THE GALLIC WAR.

Debonair (Le Débonnaire). Louis I of France (778, 814–840), also called *The Pious,* son and successor of Charlemagne; a man of courteous manners, cheerful temper, but effeminate and deficient in moral energy.

Deborah. In the Old Testament (*Judges* iv, v), a Hebrew prophetess who went with Barak to battle against Sisera and afterwards celebrated the victory in a famous song. She was one of the judges of Israel. See also JAEL.

Debrett, John (1752–1822). London publisher and original compiler of the *Peerage of England, Scotland, and Ireland* (1802), and the *Baronetage of England* (1808).

Debs, Eugene Victor (1855–1926). American socialist leader who began his career as a locomotive fireman. A Hoosier who helped lead the Pullman strike in Chicago in 1894; was arrested and imprisoned for six months. Organized the Social Democratic Party of America (1897). Five times socialist candidate for U.S. presidency (1900–1920). Indicted and sentenced for violation of Espionage Act in 1918 but released by President Harding in 1921. A lovable and sincere friend of the people and a courageous fighter for his principles.

Debussy, Achille Claude (1862–1918). French composer and for a while leader of the musical vanguard in France. His best-known works include *L'Enfant prodigue* (cantata, 1884), *Printemps* (symphonic suite),

L'Après-midi d'un faune (symphonic poem, 1902), *Pelléas et Mélisande* (opera, 1902; see also MAETERLINCK), nocturnes, piano compositions, etc.

decadents. Narrowly, the group of poets following the lead of Paul VERLAINE, among them Arthur RIMBAUD and Francis Jammes; see also PARNASSIANS; SYMBOLISM. Broadly, and more popularly, the term decadents is applied to the poets and prose writers, chiefly French, of the post-Romantic period of the 19th century, and their followers and successors. They were characterized by morbid and perverse tastes, unconventional and often sensational social behavior, dissolute and frequently perverted morals, hyperaesthetic and neurasthenic temperaments, intense introspection, an attraction to the Roman Catholic religion and the Middle Ages, an interest in esoteric, fantastic, and erotic lore, an emphasis in their writing upon form rather than content and upon the ideal of "pure" art, and a pervading sense of restlessness, boredom, and maladjustment to their environment. BAUDELAIRE, J. K. HUYSMANS, VILLIERS DE L'ISLE ADAM, Verlaine, and Rimbaud were outstanding decadents, and the typical decadent characteristics are well exemplified in DES ESSEINTES, hero of Huysmans' novel *Against the Grain*. The term probably originated in allusion to the decadence of the Roman Empire. Oscar WILDE and his group brought the movement to England.

Decameron (Gr. *deka,* ten, *hēmera,* day). The collection of 100 tales by BOCCACCIO (1353) represented as having been told in ten days during the plague at Florence in 1348. The storytellers are also ten (seven ladies and three gentlemen) and they each tell a tale on each day. The stories are chiefly FABLIAUX and fairy-tales, with ancient analogues in the legendary literatures of Europe and the Orient. The *Decameron* was widely read in English and other European languages, and its plots were widely imitated; CHAUCER used several in his CANTERBURY TALES, the framework of which is similar to that of Boccaccio's work. Boccaccio himself repudiated the *Decameron* in his old age as immoral. See also NOVELLA; NOVELLE.

De Casseres, Benjamin (1873–1945). American poet and essayist of SEPHARDIC stock. Disciple of Schopenhauer, Nietzsche, Spinoza. A militant radical individualist; a fantasist of wild dreams.

Decatur, Stephen (1779–1820). American naval officer commanding the squadron which sailed to Algeria in 1815 to force upon the British a peace on American terms. On his return he uttered at a banquet the famous toast: "Our country! In her intercourse with foreign nations may she always be in the right; but our country, right or wrong!"

Decembrist. In Russian history, a member of the group conspiring for constitutional government against the new Emperor Nicholas in December 1825.

Dechartre. A sculptor in THE RED LILY by Anatole France.

De civitate Dei, see CITY OF GOD.

Declaration of Independence, The. The public act by which the Second Continental Congress on July 4, 1776, declared the thirteen North American colonies to be free and independent of Great Britain. New York alone did not ratify the act until July 9. It was signed August 2, 1776, by the representatives of all thirteen colonies. The document was nominally the work of a drafting committee, but actually one of its members, Thomas Jefferson, wrote it practically in its entirety.

Decline and Fall of the Roman Empire, The. Famous historical work by GIBBON, volume I of which was published in 1776, volumes II and III in 1781, and the last three volumes in 1788. It covers the periods from the reign of the Emperor Trajan to the disintegration of the western Empire, from the age of Justinian in the East to that of Charlemagne in the West, and thence to the capture of Constantinople by the Turks in 1453. It discusses Christianity, the Germanic tribes, the conquests of Moslem, and the Crusades. Although newer information has supplanted much of this work, it is considered to be the first great contribution to modern historical knowledge. Gibbon's attitude in writing his study was that history consists chiefly of crime and folly.

Decoration Day. A day originally set apart in the United States for decorating the graves of those who fell in the Civil War (1861–1865); now extended to include also the dead of the Spanish-American and the World Wars. It is a legal holiday in most states and is celebrated on May 30th with the following deviations: April 26 in Alabama, Florida, Georgia, Mississippi; May 10 in Kentucky, North Carolina; June 3 in Louisiana, Tennessee.

De Corona (*Lat.*), **Peri Stephanou** (*Gr.*). On the Crown. Title of a model speech by Demosthenes.

decorum. The chief literary principle of the neo-Classical period of the latter 17th century and the 18th century. See NEO-CLASSICISM. In accordance with it, literature, especially poetry, was required to be polished, dignified, clear, rational, moderate, conventional, and "elevated," with a tendency toward Latinized diction and toward generality and abstraction in figurative language in order to achieve elegance. The prevailing use of the EPITHET was a direct example of the preference for the general rather than the specific in the tenets of "decorum." Leading exponents of the principle were BOILEAU, POPE, and Samuel JOHNSON. The history of the principle goes back to Greece and Rome. With Cicero it was the "all-embracing critical doctrine characteristic of the Latin genius." A fine, though negative, formulation occurs in Goldsmith (*The Bee,* Oct. 6, 1759): "What must be the entire perversion of scenical decorum, when . . . we see an actress . . . unwieldy with fat endeavoring to convince the audience that she is dying with hunger."

Decoud. A young journalist in Conrad's NOSTROMO.

De Coverley Papers, see SIR ROGER DE COVERLEY PAPERS.

decretals. The name given by ecclesiastical historians to the second part of the canon law, which contains the decrees and decisions of the early popes on disputed points.

The **false** or **forged decretals** were designed to support the claim of the popes to temporal as well as spiritual authority, and purport to be the decisions of some thirty popes of the first three centuries. The **Isidorian decretals,** which form part of them, were compiled in the 9th century, and assigned to Isidore of Seville, who died in 636. They comprise nearly a hundred letters written in the names of the early popes, as Clement and Anacletus, as well as letters from their supposed correspondents and acts of fictitious councils.

The 9th-century forgery known as the *Donation of Constantine* is also among the false decretals. This purports to relate how Constantine the Great, when he retired to the Bosporus in 330, conferred all his rights, honors, and property as Emperor of the West on the Pope of Rome and his successors. It is said, also, to have been confirmed by Charlemagne.

Dedalus, Stephen. The hero of James Joyce's novel, A PORTRAIT OF THE ARTIST AS A YOUNG MAN, and second most important character in ULYSSES, regarded as having been based on the character of the author himself. The name is perhaps symbolic of the creative artist. See DAEDALUS. Dedalus is a proud, sensitive, and talented young man, embittered by the poverty and religious orthodoxy of his family, the narrowness of his Roman Catholic upbringing, and the cultural aridness of his native Ireland, wishing to escape, doubting everything but longing to believe. In *Ulysses* he is brooding upon his mother's death, fighting against a feeling of guilt for having denied her deathbed request that he kneel and pray, thereby reacknowledging the religion he had rebelled against. Estranged from his own father, he corresponds to TELEMACHUS in the *Odyssey* in his search for a spiritual father, whom he finds for awhile at the climax of the novel in Leopold BLOOM.

Simon Dedalus. Father of Stephen, gay, irresponsible, fond of drinking and singing, with a tendency to neglect his family. He is an admirer of PARNELL.

Dilly Dedalus. Stephen's young sister.

May Goulding Dedalus. Stephen's mother, a frail, sickly woman, who believes staunchly in the teachings of the Roman Catholic Church and is heart-broken at her son's defection. Both Simon and she are considered to be fictional portraits of Joyce's own parents. The deathbed incident in which she figures in *Ulysses* appears in modified form in Joyce's play *Exiles.*

Dedannans, see TUATHA DE DANANN.

Dedlock, Sir Leicester, Bart. A personage in Dickens' BLEAK HOUSE who has a general opinion that the world might get on without hills, but would be "totally done up" without Dedlocks. He loves Lady Dedlock, and believes in her implicitly. Sir Leicester is honorable but intensely prejudiced, and proud as "county" can make a man. His pride has a most dreadful fall when the guilt of Lady Dedlock becomes known.

Lady Dedlock. Wife of Sir Leicester, beautiful, cold, and apparently heartless, but she is weighed down with a terrible secret, that before marriage she had had a daughter by Captain Hawdon. This daughter is Esther [Summerson], the heroine of the novel.

deductive method. A method of scientific reasoning by which inferences concerning the parts of a whole are made to depend on one's previous knowledge of the whole. It is a method that proceeds from general principles to specific truths in contrast to the INDUCTIVE METHOD which is favored by the exact sciences of modern times. The conclusion that man must have an intermaxillary bone because he is a mammal is deductive. The conclusion that he is a mammal because all the characteristics of mammals have been observed in him is inductive.

Dee, John (1527–1608). English mathematician and astrologer. Prosecuted and acquitted on charge of sorcery against Queen Mary (about 1555). Practiced magic at various courts in Bohemia, Poland, etc. Favored by Queen Elizabeth whom he instructed in astrology (1564). Advocated adoption of Gregorian calendar in England. Subject of a novel by Marjorie BOWEN.

Deemster, The. A novel by Hall CAINE. One of two common-law justices on the Isle of Man.

Deeping, George Warwick (1877–). Popular English novelist; best-known for *Sorrell and Son* (1925), a product of the author's experiences in World War I. His success has a good deal to do with his healthy common sense and simple optimism. "A negative cynicism seems to me to be a form of cowardice."

Deerfield massacre. See BLOODY BROOK.

Deerslayer, The. A historical novel by COOPER (1841) one of the Leatherstocking series. See also LEATHERSTOCKING. It treats of Natty Bumppo, or Leatherstocking, as a young hunter of twenty, of his warm friendship for the Indian Chingachgook, and his blighted love affair with Judith Hutter, a girl who shows the same taint of the settlements that embitters the scout's life under many guises.

Deever, Danny, see DANNY DEEVER.

Defarge. In Charles Dickens' TALE OF TWO CITIES, a revolutionist, keeper of a wineshop in the Faubourg St. Antoine, in Paris. He is a bull-necked, implacable-looking man.

Mme. Defarge. His wife, a dangerous woman, with great force of character; everlastingly knitting.

Defender of the Faith (Fidei Defensor). A title given by Pope Leo X to Henry VIII of England, in 1521, for a Latin treatise *On the Seven Sacraments.* Many previous kings, and even subjects, had been termed "defenders of the Catholic faith," "defenders of the Church," and so on, but no one had borne it as a title. The sovereign of Spain is entitled *Catholic,* and of France *Most Christian.*

Richard II, in a writ to the sheriffs, uses these words: *"Ecclesia cujus nos defensor sumus,"* and Henry VII, in the Black Book, was styled *Defender of the Faith.*

Defenestration of Prague. (1) The throwing from the windows of the city hall at Prague of the burgomaster and others by the Hussites in 1419.

(2) The throwing of some Bohemian officials from the windows of the palace at Prague in May, 1618. The victims are said to have landed on a dung heap, but the action became the immediate (farcical) occasion of the THIRTY YEARS' WAR.

Défense et illustration de la langue française. A critical treatise by Joachim du BELLAY, written in 1549. It urges the use of French as the language of literary expression instead of Latin, and proposes a number of reforms in poetry, including the use of rhyme, varied meters, and more varied syntax and construction, as well as the deliberate choice of dialect words, archaic words, and terms from the various trades and professions. This treatise had a wide influence, both at home and in England, where the principle of using dialect and archaic words and technical terms was applied enthusiastically in much English poetry of the latter 16th century, culminating in the Metaphysical school. See METAPHYSICAL POETS. As a plea for the vernacular language as a literary vehicle, it ranks with the *De Vulgari Eloquentia* of *Dante.*

Defence of Poesie, The. Title first used for one of the unauthorized editions of Sir Philip Sidney's *Apologie for Poetrie* 1595.

Deffand, Marquise **du** (1697–1780). Witty and cynical French noblewoman, leader in Parisian social life and literary and philosophical circles. Corresponded with Voltaire, Montesquieu, Horace Walpole, etc.

Deficit, Madame. Marie Antoinette; so called because she was always demanding money of her ministers, and never had any. According to the Revolutionary song:

> La Boulangère a des écus,
> Qui ne lui content guère.

See also under BAKER.

Defoe, Daniel (1659–1731). English novelist and journalist, one of the first outstanding figures in both the English novel and English journalism. He is known for his frank and dramatic realism in fiction, and the accuracy of observation, vigor, and lucidity of his journalism. He is best known for ROBINSON CRUSOE (1719) and THE FORTUNES AND MISFORTUNES OF MOLL FLANDERS (1722), novels, and his semi-factual JOURNAL OF THE PLAGUE YEAR (1722). Others of his works are: *The True-Born Englishman* (1701), a satirical poem on English opposition to King William III because of William's foreign birth; *An Essay on Projects* (1698), a prose collection of suggestions for reform in education, banking, road conditions, the treatment of sailors, and the like, in which Defoe advocates education of women; *The Shortest Way with Dissenters* (1702), a satire on the Church of England for which he was imprisoned; and several novels other than his most famous, including *Memoirs of a Cavalier* (1720), *Captain Singleton* (1720), *The History of Colonel Jack* (1722), and *Roxana, Or the Fortunate Mistress* (1724). Defoe edited a political newspaper, *The Review* (1704–1713), which anticipated THE TATLER and THE SPECTATOR. He supported King William III and was later an agent of the Tory party. Defoe was also the first author of ghost-stories in modern English literature, an example of which is *The Apparition of Mrs. Veal* (1706).

Deformed Transformed, The. A drama by Lord BYRON (1824). The hero, Arnold, hates life because he is horribly deformed, but when he is by magic transformed into the shape of his own choice, he goes forth a young Achilles, on adventure bent. He joins the besieging army of Bourbon at Rome, and attempts to rescue the beautiful but disdainful Olimpia, but here the drama breaks off.

de Gaulle, Charles André Joseph Marie (1890–). French general who first made a name for himself by his advocacy of a highly mechanized army. After the French débâcle in World War II he rallied his countrymen to the cause of a Free France, refusing to accept the terms of the armistice with Germany. He was court-martialed in absentia and condemned to death (Aug. 2, 1940). Leader of France after Germany's surrender. President of the fourth French Republic (which took the place of PÉTAIN's French State) until his withdrawal from the political scene, after a series of brawls with the parties of the left, in January, 1946.

Degeneration. A work by the German physician Max Simon NORDAU (2 vols., 1892–1893), in which an attempt is made to connect genius and degeneracy. Cf. the idea that illness and creative power are related and particularly its importance in the work of Thomas MANN.

Degradation of the Democratic Dogma, The. A volume expressing the "dynamic theory of history" held by Henry ADAMS, published in 1920 by his brother, Brooks Adams. It contains *A Letter to American Teachers of History,* in which Adams applies the second law of thermodynamics, which asserts a continual dissipation of mechanical energy in the universe, to history and finds a growing, universal decrease in spiritual and intellectual energy, making social progress in the future impossible. In another section of the book, entitled *The Rule of Phase Applied to History,* Adams discusses the rule of phase in physics, first enunciated by Willard GIBBS, and uses it to interpret history as the passing of human thought from one phase to another, under the influence of attraction, acceleration, and volume, as the equilibrium of a chemical substances changes according to pressure, temperature, and physical volume. Adams concludes that only a physicist can properly produce a theory of history, since only he can devise the correct scientific formulae.

Deianira. Wife of Hercules, and the inadvertent cause of his death. NESSUS told her that anyone to whom she gave a shirt steeped in his blood, would love her with undying love. She gave it to her husband, and it caused him such agony that he burnt himself to death on a funeral pile. Deianira killed herself for grief.

Dei judicium (*Lat.,* judgment of God). The judgment by ORDEALS was so called, because it was taken as certain that God would deal rightly with the appellants.

De Imitatione Christi. See IMITATION OF CHRIST and THOMAS À KEMPIS.

Deiphobus. In classic legend, one of the sons of Priam, and, next to Hector, the bravest and boldest of all the Trojans. On the death of his brother Paris, he married Helen; but Helen betrayed him to her first husband, Menelaus, who slew him. He appears in the *Iliad* and *Aeneid,* and also in Shakespeare's TROILUS AND CRESSIDA.

Dei plenus. Full of the god. Inspired, or possessed by frenzy as the MAENADS in Greco-Roman mythology, who celebrated the orgiastic rites of DIONYSUS or the CORYBANTES dancing to CYBELE. See these names.

Deirdre. Heroine of the ancient Irish legend called *The Sons of Usnach.* She was the daughter of Fedlimid, the harper of King Conchobar of Ulster, and she was raised in seclusion, because the king wished to make her his wife and it had been prophesied that her beauty would bring about disaster. She fell in love with Naoise, the son of Usnach, and was kidnaped by him and his brothers to Scotland. Conchobar eventually slew them, and Deirdre killed herself in sorrow and remorse. She is the heroine of dramas by A. E., YEATS, and SYNGE.

Deism. Belief in a personal God who created the world and will judge mankind but takes no interest and does not participate in any way in the temporal course of events. He does not reveal Himself either in nature or in history and religious experience. "The world is a clock which God made and wound. Then He left and will be back when the clock is run down." The rationalistic movement known as English Deism started in the seventeenth century and lasted almost to the end of the eighteenth. Lord Herbert (1583–1648) is often referred to as "the Father of Deism."

Dekker, Thomas (1570?–1641?). English playwright and pamphleteer. He had a checkered career against the Bohemian and underworld background of Elizabethan London, and earned his living by miscellaneous writings. He is best known for THE SHOEMAKER'S HOLIDAY (1599). Among his other dramas, of which he wrote nearly forty, are *Old Fortunatus* (1600); *The Honest Whore* (1604), dealing rather sentimentally with the reform of a prostitute; THE ROARING GIRL (1610), in collaboration with Thomas MIDDLETON; *The Virgin Martyr* (ca. 1620), a tragedy written with Philip MASSINGER; and *The Witch of Edmonton* (1621), a murder melodrama, written with Ford and Rowley. Dekker also wrote a number of pamphlets, the best-known of which is THE GULL'S HORNBOOK (1609). Others are *The Wonderful Year* (1603), a description of the plague in London (see also THE JOURNAL OF THE PLAGUE YEAR); *The Seven Deadly Sins of London* (1606), a moral allegory, and *The Bellman of London* (1608). Dekker is known for his vivid, humorous, and realistic pictures of life among the thieves, harlots, craftsmen, and lower middle-class shopkeepers of his time.

De Koven, Reginald (1859–1920). American composer of light operas (as *The Begum,* 1887; *Robin Hood,* 1890; *Student King,* 1906) and the grand opera *Canterbury Pilgrims* (1917; with a libretto by Percy MACKAYE). Also known for his musical setting for Kipling's *Recessional.*

de Kruif, Paul (1890–). American bacteriologist and popularizer of scientific subjects. Bacteriologist for Rockefeller Institute (1920–1922). Provided background of science and medicine for Sinclair Lewis's *Arrowsmith.* Lost position with Institute because of *Our Medicine Men* (1922). Wrote *Microbe Hunters* (1926), *Hunger Fighters* (1928), *Men Against Death* (1932), *Yellow Jack* (a play with Sidney Howard, 1934), etc.

Delacroix, Ferdinand Victor Eugène (1799–1863). French painter; identified as the leader of the romantic school. His great murals are in the library of the Chamber of Deputies, in the Louvre, in the Library of the Luxembourg, and in the Salon de la Paix of the Hôtel de Ville in Paris. His best-known canvases include *Dante et Virgile* (1822), *Massacre de Scio* (1824), *Femmes d'Alger* (1834), *Prise de Constantinople* (1841).

Delafield, E. M. (1890–1943). Pen-name of Elizabeth Monica Dashwood, English novelist, *née* **de la Pasture,** of which the name Delafield is an English adaptation. Daughter of Mrs. Henry de la Pasture (Lady Clifford) who wrote numerous novels, and Count Henry de la Pasture of a family that came from France to England after the French Revolution. Her childhood French governesses were models for the *Mademoiselle* of her delightful *Diary of a Provincial Lady* (1931). She wrote some twenty books, lectured in America, and her short stories and plays vied with the success of her brilliant novels of manners.

De la Mare, Walter (1873–). English poet, author of sensitive, imaginative lyrics in traditional form, many of them expressing nostalgia for the past. His works include *The Return* (1910); *Peacock Pie* (1913); *Motley And Other Poems* (1918); *Collected Poems, 1910–1918* (1920); *Memoirs of a Midget* (1921), a novel; *The Veil And Other Poems* (1921); *Broomsticks* (1925); *On the Edge* (1930).

Deland, Margaret Ware (1857–1946). American novelist and short-story writer. Established her reputation with a volume of poems, *The Old Garden* (1887). In the novel, *John Ward, Preacher* (1888), she made a vigorous attack on the fundamentalist doctrine of eternal damnation. Her other works include *Philip and his Wife* (1894); *The Awakening of Helena Richie* (1906); several volumes of Old Chester stories; and the autobiography *Golden Yesterdays* (1941). As a young girl she had moved from Pennsylvania to Boston and soon became "more Bostonian than the natives."

de la Pasture, see DELAFIELD.

De la Roche, Mazo (1885–). Canadian novelist, author of a popular series of books dealing with the fortunes and the history of a vigorous Canadian family. These include: *Jalna* (1927); *Whiteoaks of Jalna* (1929); *Finch's Fortune* (1931); *The Master of Jalna* (1933); *Young Renny* (1935); *Whiteoak Harvest* (1936); and *Whiteoak Heritage* (1940). In 1936 *Jalna* was dramatized as *Whiteoaks.*

Delaroche, Paul (1797–1856). French historical and portrait painter who founded the Eclectic school to unite the art of design as it was cultivated by the Classic school with the coloration and choice of subject matter of the Romantic school. Great mural in hall of École des Beaux-Arts in Paris.

Delectable Duchy. Cornwall. So called after the novel *The Delectable Duchy* (1893) by Sir Arthur Thomas Quiller-Couch (1863–1944), a native of Cornwall.

Delectable Mountains. In Bunyan's PILGRIM'S PROGRESS, a range of hills from the summits of which the Celestial City can be seen. These mountains are beautiful with woods, vineyards, fruits of all sorts, flowers, springs and fountains, etc.

> Now there were on the tops of these mountains shepherds feeding their flocks. The pilgrims, therefore, went to them, and leaning on their staffs . . . they asked, "Whose delectable mountains are these, and whose be the sheep that feed upon them?" The shepherds answered, "These mountains are Emmanuel's land, . . . and the sheep are His, and He laid down His life for them."—Bunyan, *Pilgrim's Progress,* i.

Deledda, Grazia (1872–1936). Italian novelist. Nobel prize for literature (1926). Member of Italian Academy of Immortals. Born on Sardinia, the scene of almost all her books, very few of which are available in English.

delf. A variant of delft. Blue china made in Delft, formerly Delf, in Holland. The word is much used in poetry as a very appropriate rhyme for "shelf."

Delia. Any female sweetheart; one of Virgil's shepherdesses; the lady to whom the sonnets by Samuel DANIEL were addressed; the lady-love of Tibullus. The Delia of Pope's *Satires* (i. 81) is the second Lady Deloraine of Ledwell Park.

Delias. The Delian ship (*i.e.* the ship of Delos) that Theseus made and on which he went to Crete when he slew the Minotaur. In memory of this it was sent every fourth year with a solemn deputation to the Delian Apollo. During the festival, which lasted thirty days, no Athenian could be put to death, and as Socrates was condemned during this period his death was deferred till the return of the sacred vessel. The ship had been so often repaired that not a stick of the original vessel remained at that time.

Delight of Mankind. Surname of Titus Flavius Sabinus Vespasianus (40?–81 A. D.), Roman Emperor (79–81), whose reign was marked by great beneficence.

Delilah. In the Old Testament (*Judges* xvi), the woman of the Philistines who betrayed SAMSON; hence any fascinating and deceitful woman.

Delineator, The. The most popular of American women's magazines, founded in 1873 and featuring fashion news, fiction, and articles on problems of interest to women, as well as a definite editorial outlook at times with regard to the contemporary scene. It reached a circulation of over 2,000,000. In 1937, it merged with the magazine *Pictorial Review*.

Delisle, see LECONTE DE LISLE; ROUGET DE LISLE; VILLIERS DE L'ISLE-ADAM.

Dell, Ethel M. (?–1939). English romantic novelist. *The Way of an Eagle* (1912), *Sown Among Thorns* (1939), etc.

Dell, Floyd (1887–). American novelist and journalist, a member of the "CHICAGO GROUP" of writers and first celebrated as a radical during the period of World War I. He was an editor of THE MASSES and *The Liberator,* and in 1917 was tried for sedition with Max EASTMAN and John REED because of pacifist writings. He later became known for a number of novels dealing with post-war disillusion, youth in the JAZZ AGE, and the Bohemian life current at the time in GREENWICH VILLAGE. The most popular and most representative of these is MOON-CALF (1920). *The Briary-Bush* (1921) is a sequel, and *Janet March* (1923) and *Runaway* (1925) are other novels of the same type. Dell also wrote *Intellectual Vagabondage—An Apology for the Intelligentsia* (1926); *The Outline of Marriage* (1926); *An Unmarried Father* (1927), dramatized in 1928 as a successful comedy, *Little Accident; Love in the Machine Age* (1930); and *Homecoming* (1933), an autobiography.

Della-Cruscans or **Della-Cruscan School.** A school of poetry started by some young Englishmen at Florence in the latter part of the 18th century. Their silly, sentimental affectations, which appeared in the *World* and the *Oracle,* created for a time quite a furore, but were mercilessly gibbeted in the *Baviad* and *Maeviad* of Gifford (1794 and 1795). The clique took its name from the famous Academia della Crusca (literally, Academy of Chaff) which was founded in Florence in 1582 with the object of purifying the Italian language—sifting away its "chaff"—and which (in 1611) published an important dictionary. Robert Merry, who signed himself *Della Crusca,* James Cobb a farce-writer, James Boswell (biographer of Dr. Johnson), O'Keefe, Morton, Reynolds, Holcroft, Sheridan, Colman, the younger, Mrs. H. Cowley, and Mrs. Robinson were the best-known exponents of the school.

Della Robbia ware. Majolicalike enameled reliefs produced in Florence by Luca della Robbia and his family in the fifteenth century.

Delmar, Viña. See BAD GIRL.

Delmare, Colonel. In George Sand's INDIANA, the old husband of the heroine.

Delmonico's. Famous New York restaurant established about 1834 by Lorenzo Delmonico (1813–1881), a Swiss who came to the United States in 1832. Delmonico potatoes, a kind of scalloped potatoes, and the Delmonico steak, a club steak, perpetuate Lorenzo's fame.

Delobelle. An actor in DAUDET's *Fromont jeune et Risler aîné* (1874). His deformed daughter *Desirée Delobelle* is the pathetic heroine of the tale.

Deloney, Thomas (1543?–1600?). English prose writer, a silk-weaver and author of numerous BROADSIDE BALLADS. He is best known for his vivid tales of life among the craftsmen and laborers of London. The most famous of these is THE GENTLE CRAFT (1597).

Delorme, Marion. See MARION DELORME.

Delos. A floating island, according to Greek legend, ultimately made fast to the bottom of the sea by Poseidon. Apollo having become possessor of it by exchange made it his favorite retreat. It is the smallest of the Cyclades.

Delphi or **Delphos.** A town of Phocis at the foot of Mount Parnassus (the modern Kastri), famous for a temple of Apollo and for an oracle which was silenced only in the 4th century A. D. by Theodosius, and was celebrated in every age and country.

Delphin Classics. See under DAUPHIN.

Delphine. A novel by Madame de STAËL (1802), the tale of a girl whose lover is faithless and who dies of a broken heart.

Madame Delphine. A story by G. W. CABLE.

delta. A Greek letter corresponding to the Roman D. Also an alluvial tract at the mouth of a river, which frequently has the shape of the letter delta; first used in this sense for the delta of the Nile.

Deluge, The. (1) The second of a Polish historic trilogy by SIENKIEWICZ. See WITH FIRE AND SWORD.

(2) In the Old Testament, the Flood that destroyed all living creatures but those in NOAH's Ark.

The French phrase *après nous le déluge,* after us the Flood, means roughly, "let's enjoy the hour and the devil may take care of the future."

Delville, Mortimer. The hero of Fanny Burney's CECILIA.

Demeter. One of the great Olympian deities of ancient Greece, identified with the Roman CERES. She was the goddess of fruits, crops, and vegetation generally, and the protectress of marriage. Persephone (PROSERPINE) was her daughter. See ELEUSINIAN MYSTERIES.

Demetrios. In James Branch Cabell's DOMNEI, Perion's rival, who keeps Melicent captive for years.

Demetrius. In Shakespeare's MIDSUMMER NIGHT'S DREAM, a young Athenian in love with Hermia. After the fairies have done their work, he is content to marry his old love, Helena.

De Mille, Henry Churchill (1853–1893). American playwright and collaborator with David BELASCO. Father of **William Churchill De Mille** (1878–   ), playwright, and of **Cecil Blount De Mille** (1881–   ), moving picture producer, who as president of Cecil B. De Mille Productions, Inc. produced *The Ten Commandments, The King of Kings, The Crusades, The Plainsman,* etc.

demimonde (*Fr.,* adapted in English as "half-world"). The class of women depicted in DUMAS' play LE DEMI-MONDE. So called because they belong only half to the *monde,* i.e., polite society. The term seems to have been originated by Dumas. Its usefulness is attested by its spread into many other languages. Hence *demi-mondaine,* a woman of the *demimonde.*

Demi-monde, Le. A comedy by Alexandre DUMAS fils (1855), dealing with a class of women in good circumstances but cut off from virtuous society by public scandal.

Demiurge. Any power or personality that creates a world, real or imaginary. From the Greek for "worker of the people." The modern meaning goes back to PLATO's use of the word for the inferior god who created the world.

Democracy: An American Novel. A novel by Henry ADAMS, published anonymously in 1880. It deals with political and social intrigue in Washington. President Hayes is said to be portrayed in the novel in the character of "Old Granite," a simple lawyer from the Middle West who is elected to the presidency and is forced to yield power to Senator Ratcliffe, a political boss.

Democritus. The laughing philosopher of Abdera (ca. 460–357 B.C.). He should rather be termed the *deriding* philosopher, because he derided or laughed at people's folly or vanity. It is said that he put out his eyes that he might think more deeply.

> Democritus, dear droll, revisit earth,
> And with our follies glut thy heightened mirth.
> Prior.

Democritus Junior. Pseudonym of Robert Burton (1577–1640) author of THE ANATOMY OF MELANCHOLY.

Demodocus. A minstrel who, according to Homer (*Odyss.* viii), sang the amours of Mars and Venus in the court of Alcinous while Ulysses was a guest there.

> Such as the wise Demodicos once told
> In solemn songs at King Alcinous' feast,
> While sad Ulysses' soul and all the rest
> Are held, with his melodious harmony,
> In willing chains and sweet captivity.
> Milton, *Vacation Exercise* (1627).

Demogorgon. A terrible deity, whose very name was capable of producing the most horrible effects. He is first mentioned by the 4th century Christian writer, Lactantius, who, in so doing, is believed to have broken the spell of a mystery, for *Demogorgon* is supposed to be identical with the infernal Power of the ancients, the very mention of whose name brought death and disaster, to whom reference is made by Lucan and others:

> Must I call your master to my aid,
> At whose dread name the trembling furies quake,
> Hell stands abashed, and earth's foundations shake?
> Rowe, *Lucan's Pharsalia,* vi.

Hence Milton speaks of "the dreaded name of Demogorgon" (*Paradise Lost,* ii. 965). According to Ariosto, Demogorgon was a king of the elves and fays who lived on the Himalayas, and once in five years summoned all his subjects before him to give an account of their stewardship. Spenser (*Faërie Queene,* IV. ii. 47) says that he dwells in the deep abyss with the three fatal sisters. Shelley so calls eternity in *Prometheus Unbound.*

De Morgan, William (1839–1917). English novelist. His best-known novels are JOSEPH VANCE (1906), ALICE-FOR-SHORT (1907) and IT CAN NEVER HAPPEN AGAIN (1909). De Morgan was frequently called "the modern Dickens."

Demosthenes (385?–322 B. C.). Athenian statesman; commonly regarded as the greatest of the Greek orators. Tradition has it that he would walk by the sea shore with pebbles in his mouth to strengthen his voice by trying to make himself heard above the roar of the sea. The name of his three PHILIPPICS, scathing orations attacking Philip of Macedon (351, 344, 341), has become proverbial. He died after taking poison to escape capture by his enemies. There is a portrait-statue of him in the Vatican.

demotic writing. An Egyptian script in the fifth century B. C., employed by the priests of Isis as late as 452 A. D. It was a simplified form of the HIERATIC letters and was written from right to left in horizontal lines.

Dempsey, William Harrison. Known as **Jack** (1895–). American heavyweight boxer, born in Manassa, Colo., and hence often called the Manassa Mauler. Defeated Jess Willard for heavyweight championship in Toledo (July 4, 1919); lost title to Gene Tunney at Philadelphia (Sept. 23, 1926).

Dempster, Arthur Jeffrey (1886–). Canadian-born physicist, naturalized U.S. citizen (1918). Discovered the existence of U-235 (uranium 235) by means of an "atomic microscope" at the physics laboratory of the University of Chicago. See DUNNING, JOHN RAY. Professor at the University of Chicago (since 1937). Research in positive ray analysis of chemical elements, excitation of light and electrical discharge in gases.

Dempster, Janet. The heroine of George Eliot's JANET'S REPENTANCE. Her husband, **Robert Dempster,** is also a prominent character.

Dendin, Peter. In Rabelais' GARGANTUA AND PANTAGRUEL, an old man, who has settled more disputes than all the magistrates of Poitiers, though he is no judge. His plan is to wait till the litigants are thoroughly sick of their contention, and long to end their disputes; then he interposes, and his judgment never fails to be acceptable.

Tenot Dendin. Son of the above. Unlike his father, he always tries to crush quarrels in the bud; consequently, he never succeeds in settling a single dispute submitted to his judgment.

Racine has introduced the same name in his comedy called *Les Plaideurs* (1669), and Lafontaine in his *Fables* (1668).

Denham, Ruth. Heroine of T. B. Aldrich's QUEEN OF SHEBA.

Denham, Sir **John** (1615–1669). English poet, a Royalist during the English Civil War and for a time Surveyor General of Works, in charge of architecture, with the young Christopher WREN as his assistant. Denham was famous in his own day for *The Sophy,* a melodramatic tragedy, and *Cooper's Hill* (1642), a didactic poem. The latter work was praised by Dryden, and Pope imitated it in WINDSOR FOREST.

Denikin, Anton Ivanovich (1872–). Russian general during World War I. After the Russian Revolution of 1917, he fled to the Caucasus, where he assisted Alekseev and Kornilov in raising a force to fight the Bolsheviki. Set up a South Russian government (1919). Was defeated by Bolshevik troops under Budënny (1920). Lived in France from 1926.

Denis, Duval. Titular hero of a novel by THACKERAY (1864). Left unfinished at the author's death.

Denis, St. See under SAINTS.

Denis of Burgundy. In Charles Reade's *The Cloister and The Hearth,* an arbalester whom Gerard meets on journey to Italy. They become close friends. "Courage, mon ami, le diable est mort!" is his favorite expression.

Dennis, Father. The lovable, hot-tempered, Roman Catholic chaplain of an Irish regiment in India, who appears in Kipling's *Mutiny of the Mavericks* and other of his stories.

Dennis, Geoffrey Pomeroy (1892–). English novelist and essayist whose fantasy *The End of the World* (1930) won the Hawthornden prize. The first and best of his novels is *Mary Lee* (1922). His *Coronation Commentary* (1937), written at the time of the accession of George VI, which was a violent condemnation of the Duke of Windsor, caused a sensation. It had to be withdrawn when the Duke threatened to sue Dennis for libel.

dénouement (Fr. *dénouer,* to untie). The untying of a plot; the winding-up of a novel or play.

Densher, Merton. In Henry James' WINGS OF A DOVE, the young journalist who is engaged to Kate Croy but at Kate's urging marries the wealthy Milly Theale.

Denys, St. See under SAINTS.

Deodars, Under The. Tales by Rudyard Kipling (1888). A deodar is a species of evergreen found in the mountains of India. It resembles the cedar of Lebanon.

Deor's Lament. An ancient Anglo-Saxon poem, in which a wandering bard laments his having been cast off by his former lord and seeks consolation in the thought of the greater misfortunes of legendary Germanic heroes and heroines. It is divided into uneven stanzas by a refrain, translated as: "Yet his trouble passed; so can mine."

Depew, Chauncey M. (1834–1928). American lawyer known for his oratory. Secretary of State (1863–1865); general counsel for the Vanderbilt railways (1875); unsuccessful candidate for the Republican presidential nomination (1888); Senator (1899–1911). Notable after-dinner speaker.

de profundis (*Lat.*). Out of the deep; hence, an extremely bitter cry of wretchedness. *Ps.* 130 is so called from the first two words in the Latin version. It forms part of the Roman Catholic burial service. Oscar Wilde's personal essay of confession and reminiscence written in prison bore the title of *De Profundis* (1905).

De Quincey, Thomas (1785–1859). English critic and essayist, for a time a resident of the LAKE COUNTRY and an associate of WORDSWORTH and COLERIDGE. He wrote numerous essays on politics, philosophy, and literature, as well as personal essays, for BLACKWOOD'S MAGAZINE, and he is known for his polished style and what he himself called his "impassioned prose." His most famous work is his CONFESSIONS OF AN ENGLISH OPIUM EATER (1821). Well-known single essays are *The English Mail-Coach, Murder Considered as One of the Fine Arts,* and *Joan of Arc.*

Derby stakes. Started by Edward Stanley, the twelfth Earl of Derby, in 1780, the year after his establishment of the OAKS STAKES.

Derby Day is the day when the Derby stakes are run for, during the great Epsom Summer Meeting; it is usually either the Wednesday before or the second Wednesday after Whit Sunday. The Derby, known as the "Blue Ribbon of the Turf," is for colts and fillies of three years old only; consequently, no horse can win it twice. The name of the race is pronounced *Darby,* that of the town and county *Durby.* See also CLASSIC RACES.

De rerum natura (Of the Nature of Things). A didactic poem in six books by LUCRETIUS, developing the doctrines of EPICURUS and DEMOCRITUS and treating of physics, psychology, and ethics. First published in 1486. Cf. SANTAYANA, *Three Philosophical Poets.*

Derleth, August William (1909–). American regional poet and writer of weird tales, and novels about his native Wisconsin. He has projected a Sac Prairie Saga which is to include fifty books of all kinds, ultimately constituting a sort of HUMAN COMEDY of Sac Prairie, Wis.

Deronda, Daniel. The hero of George Eliot's DANIEL DERONDA.

> His eyes had a peculiarity which has drawn many men into trouble; they were of a dark yet mild intensity, which seemed to express a special interest in every one on whom he fixed them, and might easily help to bring on him those claims which ardently sympathetic people are often creating in the minds of those who need help.—Ch. xxix.

Déroulède, Paul (1846–1914). French writer, politician, and author of patriotic verse. *Chants du Paysan* (1894). Also a playwright.

Desborough, Colonel. In Scott's WOODSTOCK, one of the parliamentary commissioners.

Desborough, Lucy. Heroine of Meredith's novel, RICHARD FEVEREL.

Descartes, René. Latinized as **Renatus Cartesius** (1595–1650). French mathematician and philosopher, founder of Cartesianism and father of the modern science of thought through his belief in the possibility of mathematical exactitude in metaphysical reasoning. His *Discours de la méthode* (Leyden, 1639) is but a short treatise but constitutes a cornerstone of modern philosophy.

Descent of Man, The. The scientific volume, published in 1871, which, together with his earlier *Origin of Species,* embodies the evolutionary theories of Charles DARWIN, the naturalist.

descent to the underworld. The motif of numerous stories occurring in the mythology and folklore of all peoples, expressing the human belief that death can be overcome and that the dead may return. Invariably the descent is made to rescue someone either abducted or rightfully dead, to find the answer to a question or discover a secret from the ruler of the underworld, or to seize some treasure. To partake of the food of the dead (or of fairyland in later folklore) prevents the visitor from ever returning. Among the most famous descent stories are the Greek myths of Orpheus and Eurydice, Ceres and Persephone, and Hercules' bringing of Cerberus up from Hades; also well-known are the Babylonian story of Ishtar's descent to rescue Tammuz, the Norse myth of Hermod's journey to Hel to bring back Balder. There are similar tales in Hindu, Chinese, and Japanese writings, and among the Ainus, Melanesians, North American Indians, and Eskimos. Descents to Hell are common also in early Christian literature.

Deschamps, Eustache (1340?–1405). French poet, a friend of CHAUCER, who imitated his work. Deschamps is best known for his *Miroir de mariage,* a satire on women and the world of the court which he found less stimulating than the taverns he frequented. He also wrote *Art de dictier et fere chansons,* a critical treatise, called the first of its type in French to be preserved. Among his shorter pieces there are 1175 (!) BALLADES.

Desdemona. Heroine of Shakespeare's OTHELLO.

The soft simplicity of Desdemona, confident of merit and conscious of innocence, her artless perseverance in her suit, and her slowness to suspect that she can be suspected, are proofs of Shakespeare's skill in human nature.—Dr. Johnson.

De senectute. Essay in dialogue form in praise of old age. Also known as **Cato Major** after Cato the censor, one of the interlocutors.

Deserted Village, The. A famous descriptive poem by Oliver GOLDSMITH (1770). See AUBURN.

Des Esseintes. Hero of AGAINST THE GRAIN by J. K. HUYSMANS. He is the typical DECADENT hero—hypersensitive, capricious, irresolute, introspective, constantly restless and depressed, highly neurasthenic and seeking always new and perverse sensations to relieve himself of the burdensome *ennui* of living. He is believed to have been drawn from Comte Robert de MONTESQUIOU.

de Seversky, Alexander Procofieff (1894–). Russian-born American aviator and aeronautical engineer. President Seversky Aircraft Corporation (1931–1939). Inventor, among other airplane devices, of a bombsight. Author of *Victory Through Air Power* (1942) in which the thesis implied in the title is presented from an extremist point of view.

Desgenais. A character who appeared in Alfred de MUSSET's CONFESSIONS OF A CHILD OF THE AGE and whose name and general character were taken over by Barrière in his *Marble Heart* (originally *Les Filles de marbre*) (1853), in *The Parisians of the Decadence* and other plays. He is a cynical philosopher and moralist, who preaches virtue from a sort of enlightened self interest but is convinced of the futility of all moralizing.

Désirée's Baby. A short story by Kate CHOPIN, published in *Bayou Folk* (1894). It tells of the birth of a child to Désirée, wife of the aristocratic Creole Armand Aubigny, and the discovery that the child gives evidence of Negro blood. Armand accuses his wife of being half black, and heart-broken, she decides to return with the child to her mother. Instead, however, she kills herself and her baby. Later Armand, while burning his wife's effects, discovers a letter which reveals that his own mother was of Negro blood.

Desire Under the Elms. A play by Eugene O'NEILL, produced in 1924. It deals with intrigue, greed, family hate, crime, and adultery on a Puritan New England farm in 1850. Abbie Putnam, the young third wife of miserly old Ephraim Cabot, plots to win her husband's wealth and to do so, seduces his rebellious son Eben. After numerous dramatic complications, Eben and Abbie are arrested for the murder of their illegitimate child.

Desmarets, Nicolas, see MARETS, NICOLAS DES.

Desmond, Shaw (1877–). Irish journalist, novelist, poet. Author of *Democracy* (1919), *The Drama of Sinn Fein* (1923), *Reincarnation for Everyman* (1939), etc. In 1934 he founded the International Institute for Psychical Research.

Desmoulins, Camille (1760–1794). Prominent pamphleteer during the French Revolution. Called *Procureur de la lanterne,* i.e., agent of the lantern, for his antiaristocratic pamphlet *Le Discours de la lanterne aux Parisiens.* See *Ça Ira.* Deputy to the Convention (1792); he was executed with DANTON by ROBESPIERRE.

de Soto, Hernando (1500?–1542). Spanish explorer in America. Explored country north and west of Florida, and was buried in the Mississippi River, which he had discovered (1541). Note: the mouth of the Mississippi had been discovered by Alonso de Pineda (1519) who had named the river Espirito Santo.

Despair, Giant. In Bunyan's PILGRIM'S PROGRESS, a giant who lives in Doubting Castle. He takes Christian and Hopeful captives for sleeping on his grounds, and locks them in a dark dungeon from Wednesday to Saturday, without "one bit of bread, or drop of drink, or ray of light." By the advice of his wife, Diffidence, the giant beats them soundly "with a crab-tree cudgel." On Saturday night Christian remembers he has a key in his bosom, called "Promise," which will open any lock in Doubting Castle. So he opens the dungeon door and they both make their escape with speed.

Despréaux, see BOILEAU, NICOLAS.

Desportes, Philippe (1545–1606). French poet, court poet to Henry III. He wrote both worldly and religious devotional verse, chiefly characterized by exaggerated CONCEITS in the Italian tradition. Desportes belonged to a group of poets which was an offshoot of the PLÉIADE.

Dessalle, Jeanne. The heroine of Fogazzaro's novels, *The Sinner* and *The Saint.* See MAIRONI, PIERO.

Dessalines, Jean Jacques (1758–1806). Leader of insurgent slaves in Haiti; founder of republic (1804); emperor of Haiti (1804–1806). See TOUSSAINT L'OUVERTURE. Assassinated by Christophe and Pétion. His name was taken from his French master.

Destinn, Emmy (1878–1930). Bohemian operatic soprano. Created leading roles in Puccini's *Madame Butterfly* and Richard Strauss's *Salome* in London and Paris respectively. Member Metropolitan Opera Co., New York City (1908–1916).

Destiny, the Man of. Napoleon Bonaparte. See under MAN.

Destouches, Louis Ferdinand (1894–). French physician and novelist who signs his works **Louis-Ferdinand Céline.** Wrote *Journey to the End of the Night* (1934), *Death on the Installment Plan* (1938), etc. Represents a new wave of disillusionment and decadence in French letters. A powerful writer who violates his language as he violates all codes in order to achieve his DALI-esque results.

Destroying Angels. The members of the DANITE Band.

Destruction of Sennacherib, The. A well-known poem by Lord BYRON (1815) describing an invasion of Palestine by the Assyrian king Sennacherib (7th century B.C.): "The Assyrian came down like a wolf on the fold." The story is taken from 2 *Kings*, 18 ff.

Detailles, Jean Baptiste Édouard (1848–1912). French painter noted for battle and military subjects.

Deterding, Sir **Henri** (1865–1939). Dutch oil magnate. Became a supporter of the Nazi movement in Germany, possibly because his claims to Russian oil interests had been repudiated by the Soviets.

Deucalion's Flood. The Deluge, of Greek legend. Deucalion was son of Prometheus and Clymene, and was king of Phthia, in Thessaly. When Zeus sent the deluge Deucalion built a ship, and he and his wife, Pyrrha, were the only mortals saved. The ship at last rested on Mount Parnassus, and Deucalion was told by the oracle at Themis that to restore the human race he must cast the bones of his mother behind him. His interpretation of this was the stones of his mother Earth, so the two cast these as directed and those thrown by Deucalion became men, and those thrown by his wife became women.

Bayard TAYLOR has a lyrical drama entitled *Prince Deukalion* (1878), in which he takes Deukalion and Pyrrha over all the earth and through all ages of history.

Deuceace, Hon. Algernon Percy. One of Thackeray's characters, a worthless rascal who is the hero of THE AMOURS OF MR. DEUCEACE, and appears in THE SHABBY GENTEEL STORY, VANITY FAIR, PENDENNIS and THE RAVEN'S WING. In the first-mentioned, he fleeces an acquaintance out of a huge sum, but is himself fooled into marrying an heiress who loses her wealth by eloping without consent.

Deukalion, see DEUCALION.

deus (*Lat.*). God.

deus ex machina. The intervention of some unlikely event in order to extricate one from difficulties; such as, in a novel, a forced incident, like the arrival of a rich uncle from the Indies to help a young couple in their pecuniary embarrassments. Literally, it means "a god (let down upon the stage) from the machine," the "machine" being part of the furniture of the stage in an ancient Greek theater.

Deus vobiscum. God be with you.

Deus vult. God wills it. Specifically, the rallying cry of the First Crusade.

Deuteronomy. The Greek name of the fifth book of the Old Testament. The word means, "the law repeated." So called because it contains a repetition of the law of Moses.

Deutsch, Babette (1895–). (Mrs. Avrahm Yarmolinsky). American poet. Once secretary to Thorstein Veblen. Has given courses on poetry, and has translated from the Russian and German with her husband who is Chief of the Slavonic Division of the New York Public Library. She has written several novels and a book about Walt Whitman. Her poetry, through five or six volumes has steadily gathered strength and definition.

Deutschland. German submarine merchant vessel, first of its class to cross Atlantic. Won fame in World War I for carrying cargoes through Allied blockade.

Deutschland über alles (*Ger.* "Germany above all"). An expression of German patriotism, taken from the national anthem as written by HOFFMANN VON FALLERSLEBEN in 1841 on Helgoland (then belonging to Great Britain) and sung to the tune (by Haydn; 1797) of the Austrian anthem. The text shows clearly its dependence on a poem by WALTHER VON DER VOGELWEIDE (13th century).

deva, see DAEVA.

Deval, Jacques (1893–). French playwright and novelist. Script writer for Hollywood. *Tovarich* (1937) his most successful comedy.

de Valera, Eamon (1882–). Irish statesman, born in New York of a Spanish father and Irish mother. President of Sinn Fein (1917–1926). Led Fianna Fail into Free State parliament (August 1927). President of executive council and minister for external affairs (1932–1948).

de Vere, Aubrey Thomas (1814–1902). Irish poet, writing Irish bardic lore and ecclesiastic medievalism. Convert to Catholicism (1851). Friend of Browning and Tennyson.

devices of Cepola. Quips of law, so called from Bartolommeo Cepola, a fifteenth-century Italian lawyer, whose law-quirks, teaching how to elude the most express law, and to perpetuate lawsuits *ad infinitum,* have been frequently reprinted. They were printed once in 8vo, in black letter, by John Petit (1503).

devil. The name usually given to the chief of devils, known as *The Devil,* is Satan. He is also called LUCIFER and MEPHISTOPHELES, and is popularly referred to as AULD (or Old) NICK, HORNIE, CLOOTIE, HANGIE, the AULD ANE, etc. See those entries for individualized legendary conceptions and use in literature, also ASMODEUS, ASTAROTTE, BEELZEBUB, SAMAEL.

The devil is frequently represented with a cloven foot, because by the Rabbinical writers he is called *seirizzim* (a goat). As the goat is a type of uncleanness, the prince of unclean spirits is aptly represented under this emblem.

Printer's devil. A printer's message boy; formerly, the boy who took the printed sheets from the tympan of the press. Moxon says (1683): "They do commonly so black and bedaub themselves that the workmen do jocosely call them devils." The black slave employed by Aldo Manuzio, Venetian printer, was thought to be an imp. Hence the following proclamation:

> I, Aldo Manuzio, printer to the Doge, have this day made public exposure of the printer's devil. All who think he is not flesh and blood may come and pinch him.—*Proclamation of Aldo Manuzio,* 1490.

the devil's advocate. A carping or adverse critic. From the *advocatus diaboli,* the person appointed to contest the claims of a candidate for canonization before a papal court. He advances all he can against the candidate, and is opposed by the *advocatus Dei* (God's Advocate), who says all he can in support of the proposal.

devil may care. Wildly reckless; also a reckless fellow.

devil on two sticks. The English name of Le Sage's novel *Le Diable boiteux* (1707) in which ASMODEUS plays an important part. It was dramatized by Foote in 1768. As slang the term is applied to a crusty old cripple.

devil's apple. The mandrake; also the thorn apple.

devil's Bible. See DEVIL'S BOOKS below.

devil's bones. Dice, which are made of bones and lead to ruin.

devil's books, or *devil's picture-book.* Playing cards. A Presbyterian phrase used in reproof of the term King's Books, applied to a pack of cards, from the Fr. *livre des quatre rois* (the book of the four kings). Also called the *devil's Bible.*

Devil Dick. A nickname of Richard Porson (1759–1808), the great English Greek scholar.

Robert the Devil, see ROBERT LE DIABLE.

the French Devil. Jean Bart (1651–1702), an intrepid French sailor, born at Dunkirk.

the devil's missionary. A nickname given to Voltaire (1694–1778), and very likely to others.

son of the devil. Ezzelino (1194–1259), the noted Ghibelline leader and Governor of Vicenza; so called for his infamous cruelties.

the White Devil of Wallachia. Scanderbeg, or George Castriota (1403–1468), was so called by the Turks.

Devil and Daniel Webster, The. A popular short story by Stephen Vincent BENÉT, first published in the SATURDAY EVENING POST, collected in *Thirteen O'Clock* (1937), and adapted as a one-act opera and a motion picture, *All That Money Can Buy* (the title was later changed). In it, a New England farmer, Jabez Stone, sells his soul to the Devil for material prosperity, but is saved from paying his debt by the oratorical eloquence of Daniel Webster before a demonic jury.

devil dog. A U.S. marine. Supposedly an adaptation of German *Teufelshund,* a term of abuse applied by German sailors to the marines in World War I.

Devilshoof. The chief of the gipsy band in Balfe's opera, THE BOHEMIAN GIRL.

De Vinne, Theodore Low (1828–1914). American printer, known as head of The De Vinne Press. Responsible for great improvements in American typography. Author of books on printing and typography, especially *The Practice of Typography* (4 vols., 1900, 1901, 1902, 1904).

De Voto, Bernard Augustine (1897–). American critic, novelist, and editor. Born in Ogden, Utah, of partly Italian, partly Mormon descent. On teaching staff of Harvard University (1929–1936). Editor of "The Easy Chair" in *Harper's Magazine* (since 1935), editor of the *Saturday Review of Literature* (1936–1938). Author of *Mark Twain's America* (1932), opposing the views of Van Wyck Brooks; *The Year of Decision,* etc.

De Vulgari Eloquentia. See DANTE ALIGHIERI.

Dewey, George (1837–1917). American admiral. Hero of the Battle of Manila Bay in the American-Spanish War (1898).

Dewey, John (1859–). American philosopher and educator. Adherent of Jamesian pragmatism, "the philosophy of the common man." Father of the Progressive School movement in education. A fighter for civil and academic freedom. In the words of Will Durant: "He sees man as an organism in an environment, remaking as well as made." The influence of Dewey's thought upon American philosophy and education has been very great. As a writer his language is unfortunately pedantic.

Dewey, Melvil (1851–1931). American librarian. The "Father of Library Science" in the U.S. Founder of the first library school

(Columbia University, 1887). Published *Decimal Classification and Relativ Index* (1876–1929). Ardent advocate of simplified spelling. The "Dewey Decimal System" of library classification is in use in 85% of U.S. libraries. (The Library of Congress system for unusually large collections takes care of another 10%).

Dewey, Thomas Edmund (1902–). American lawyer who came into prominence through his prosecution in the investigation of organized crime in New York in 1935–1937. District Attorney of New York county (1937–1938); governor of New York State (1942). Running for President in 1944, he was defeated by Franklin Delano ROOSEVELT who thus secured a fourth term.

Dewey Decimal System. See under DEWEY, MELVIL.

Dewy, Dick. Hero of Hardy's UNDER THE GREENWOOD TREE.

Dexter, Timothy (1743–1806). American merchant and eccentric of Newburyport, Mass. Called himself "Lord." Cf. *Lord Timothy Dexter* (1925) by John P. MARQUAND.

Dey. See under RULERS, TITLES OF.

de Young, Michel Harry (1849–1925). American newspaper man. With his brother, **Charles de Young** (1847–1880) founder and (from 1880) sole owner and editor-in-chief of the San Francisco *Chronicle*.

Dhu, Roderick. A Highland chieftain and outlaw in Scott's "The Lady of the Lake."

diacritical mark. A "distinguishing" conventional mark added to a letter to modify its phonetic value. The more important diacritical marks are the DIAERESIS in English, the TILDE in Spanish, the CEDILLA in French and Portuguese, the UMLAUT in German, and the various accent marks (´, `, ˆ, ˇ) used in common orthographies and in phonetic transcription.

diaeresis. A DIACRITICAL MARK, consisting of two dots, placed over a vowel to indicate its independence from the preceding syllable. Thus Chloë, the Greek proper name, does not rhyme with either *shoe* or *doe,* but is pronounced in two syllables.

Diafoirus, Thomas. In Molière's comedy, LE MALADE IMAGINAIRE, two pompous doctors, father and son, caricatures of the medical men of the period. The younger Dr. Diafoirus is a suitor for the hand of Angelique, but loses her to Cléante.

Diaghilev, Sergei Pavlovich (1872–1929). Russian ballet producer and art critic. Member of the Imperial Russian Theater in Moscow (since 1899), where he collaborated with FOKINE and Léon Bakst in developing the Russian ballet. Through him Rimski-Korsakov's *Schéhérazade* and Debussy's *L'Après-midi d'un faune* were used for choreographic purposes. Collaborated with Stravinsky on *The Firebird* and *Pétrouchka.* Organized the Ballet Russe in Paris (1909). See also NIJINSKY.

Dial, The. (1) American quarterly magazine, founded in 1840 as the organ of the movement of TRANSCENDENTALISM. Margaret FULLER was editor until 1842, and EMERSON from 1842 until publication ceased in 1844. Essays and articles on literature, religion, and philosophy, expressing Transcendentalist ideas, were published, and contributors included THOREAU, Bronson ALCOTT, Theodore PARKER, EMERSON, Miss FULLER, LOWELL, W. H. CHANNING, and Jones VERY. The magazine was attacked by the press for its "obscurity."

(2) American literary magazine, founded in 1880 in Chicago, conservative in policy until 1916, when it moved to New York and became the outstanding literary review of its time. Until 1920, under the editorship of Conrad AIKEN, Randolph BOURNE, and Van Wyck BROOKS, it published articles by leading American radicals, including John DEWEY and Thorstein VEBLEN. After 1920, it was devoted to the encouragement of *avant-garde* authors. Marianne MOORE was editor beginning in 1926. It ceased publication in 1929.

dialectical materialism. The theory that human phenomena, historical, social, economic or psychological, should be interpreted in terms of physical or material causes, arrived at by critical examination of logical consequences springing from natural causes, and by the discrimination of truth from error, with no belief in the supernatural. It is the result of a materialistic application of HEGEL's dialectic with its progression from thesis and antithesis to synthesis.

Dialogues in Limbo. A collection of philosophic discourses, written by George Santayana and published in 1926. In it, the ghosts of six philosophers of the past, among them Democritus, Aristippus, Socrates, and Avicenna, discuss problems of ethics, aesthetics, metaphysics, and political theory.

diamond (Gr. *a damao,* what cannot be subdued). A corruption of *adamant.* So called because the diamond, which cuts other substances, can be cut or polished with no substance but itself.

In Spenser's *Faërie Queene* (Bk. iv), Diamond is one of the three sons of Agape. He was slain by Cambalo. See also TRIAMOND.

a diamond of the first water. A specially fine diamond, one of the greatest value for its size. The color or luster of a diamond is called its "water." Hence, figuratively, "a man of the first water" is a man of the highest merit.

a rough diamond. An uncultivated genius; a person of excellent parts, but without society manners.

the diamond jousts. Jousts instituted by King Arthur, "who by that name had named them, since a diamond was the prize." The story, as embroidered by Tennyson in his *Launcelot and Elaine* from Malory (Bk. xviii, ch. 9–20) is that Arthur found nine diamonds from the crown of a slain knight and offered them as the prize of nine jousts in successive years. Launcelot had won them all, but when he laid them before the queen, Guinevere, in a fit of jealousy—the result of believing false rumors about Launcelot and Elaine—flung them into the river a moment before the corpse of Elaine passed in the barge.

Diamond Necklace Affair. A famous incident of French history (1783–1785) which centers round Marie Antoinette. Cardinal de Rohan, a profligate churchman, entertained (partly for political reasons) a passion for the queen, and an adventuress, the "Countess" de Lamotte, partly by means of the Queen's signatures, which were forged, induced him to purchase for the Queen, for about £85,000, a diamond necklace, originally made for Mme Dubarry. The cardinal handed the necklace to the countess, who sold parts of it to an English jeweler and kept the money. After futile attempts to recover his money from Rohan, Boehmer, the jeweler, sent his bill in to the Queen, who denied all knowledge of the matter. A nine months' trial ensued which created immense scandal and has been considered one of the proximate causes of the French Revolution.

Diamond Pitt. Thomas Pitt (1653–1726), owner of the famous Pitt Diamond and grandfather of the Earl of Chatham, was so known.

Diamond. The little dog belonging to Sir Isaac Newton. One winter's morning he upset a candle on his master's desk, by which papers containing minutes of many years' experiments were destroyed. On perceiving this terrible catastrophe Newton exclaimed: "Oh, Diamond, Diamond, thou little knowest the mischief thou hast done!" and at once set to work to repair the loss.

Diamond State. Delaware. See under STATES.

Diana. (1) An ancient Italian and Roman divinity, later identified with the Olympian goddess Artemis, who was daughter of Zeus and Leto, and twin-sister of Apollo. She was the goddess of the moon and of hunting, protectress of women, and—in earlier times at least—the great mother goddess or nature goddess. See SELENE. The temple of Diana at Ephesus, built by Dinochares, was set on fire by Erostratus for the sake of perpetuating his name. The Ionians decreed that anyone who mentioned his name should be put to death, but this very decree gave it immortality. The temple was one of the Seven Wonders of the World.

Diana of Ephesus. This statue, a cone surmounted by a bust covered with breasts, we are told, fell from heaven. If so, it was an aerolite; but Minucius (2nd century A.D.), who says he saw it, describes it as a wooden statue, and Pliny, a contemporary, tells us it was made of ebony.

great is Diana of the Ephesians. A phrase sometimes used to signify that self-interest blinds the eyes, from the story told in *Acts* xix. 24–28 of Demetrius, the Ephesian silversmith who made shrines for the temple of Diana.

tree of Diana. See *philosopher's tree* under TREE.

(2) The heroine and title of a pastoral by Montemayor, imitated from the *Daphnis and Chloe* of Longos. Although by a Portuguese author, it was written in Spanish (1560).

Diana à la biche, Diana of the Hind. An antique sculpture in the Louvre at Paris.

Diana of the Crossways. A novel by George MEREDITH (1885). Diana, the witty and charming if somewhat capricious Irish heroine, marries Warwick, but soon finds that he is uncongenial. Hearing her name unpleasantly coupled with that of Lord Dannisburgh, one of the cabinet members, Warwick sues for divorce, but Diana successfully opposes the suit, leaves her husband and becomes celebrated for her novels and her salon. She has an affair with the brilliant young politician Percy Dacier and on one occasion all but elopes with him; later in an impetuous moment she sells to a newspaper a political secret which he has told her in confidence. Although Warwick dies a few days later, her chance of happiness with Dacier is gone, and she finally marries Thomas Redworth, the faithful and worthy suitor who has extricated her from numerous difficulties and has persistently "believed in the soul of Diana."

This novel was based on the career of Caroline Norton, but in his second edition Meredith cautioned his readers against applying its incidents to any individual in a literal fashion.

Diane de Lys. A novel by Alexandre DUMAS *fils* (1851), dramatized two years later under the same title. It centers about a love affair between the titular heroine and the ardent young sculptor, Paul Aubrey, with Diane's neglectful husband as the third character of importance.

Diane de Poitiers (1499–1566). Very influential mistress of Henry II of France.

Dianora. In Boccaccio's DECAMERON (x. 5), the wife of Gilberto of Friuli, loved by Ansaldo. In order to rid herself of his importunities, she vows never to yield to his suit till he can "make her garden at midwinter as gay with flowers as it was in summer," meaning *never*. Ansaldo, by the aid of a magician, accomplishes the appointed task; but when the lady tells him her husband insists on her keeping her promise, Ansaldo, not to be outdone in generosity, declines to take advantage of his claim, and from that day forth is the firm and honorable friend of Gilberto. The *Franklin's Tale* of Chaucer is substantially the same story. See DORIGEN.

Diary of a Nobody. Humorous novel of London middle-class Victorian life ("hero," Mr. Pooter) by George and Weedon GROSSMITH.

diastole and systole. The rhythmical expansion and contraction of the cavities of the heart, causing the circulation of the blood through the body.

Diavolo, Fra, see FRA DIAVOLO.

Díaz, Porfirio (1830–1915). Mestizo Mexican general and statesman. Fought against MAXIMILIAN and opposed JUAREZ. President for seven terms (1876–1911). Forced to abdicate; died in exile in Paris.

Díaz del Castillo, Bernal. See CONQUISTADOR; CORTÉS, HERNANDO.

Dibdin, Thomas Frognall (1776–1847). Pseudonym **Reginald Wolfe.** Famous bibliographer, nephew of **Charles Dibdin** (1745–1814), dramatist.

Dichtung und Wahrheit (Poetry and Truth). Current title of Goethe's autobiography (1811, 1812, 1814, 1831), which should not suggest that the work is factually unreliable (though in some details it undoubtedly is) but rather that it was intended, and is, a work of art making use of autobiographical data. It is a beautifully conceived psychological and historical novel in which the hero happens to be the author. The full title is *Aus meinem Leben* (From my Life), *Dichtung und Wahrheit.*

Dick, Deadwood, see DEADWOOD DICK.

Dick, Mr. In Dickens' *David Copperfield* (1849), an amiable, half-witted man, devoted to David's great-aunt, Miss Betsey Trotwood, who thinks him a prodigious genius.

Dick, Ragged. One of the boy heroes of the stories of Horatio ALGER, Jr.

Dick Deadeye, see DEADEYE, DICK.

Dickens, Charles (1812–1870). English novelist, of wide popularity, which he won by journalistic use of the popular devices of sentimentality, melodrama, broad humor, and familiar characters and turns of plot. He is known for his creation of striking types, many of which, such as Pecksniff, Uriah Heep, Micawber, etc., have supplied tag-names for the quirks of character they represent, and for the essential realism of his portrayal of life among the poor and the lower middle-class of England. Critics point out, however, that his characters are most often caricatures, and that his realism is largely diluted by sentimentality or strained for conventional comic effects. His best-known works are PICKWICK PAPERS (1836); OLIVER TWIST (1837–1838); THE OLD CURIOSITY SHOP (1840); A CHRISTMAS CAROL (1843); DAVID COPPERFIELD (1849–1850); A TALE OF TWO CITIES (1859). Dickens was a successful journalist and lecturer, editing the weekly periodical *Household Words* (1849–1859) and also *All the Year Round* (1859–1870). In spite of his journalistic, caricaturist's attitude toward his characters, Dickens was regarded highly by DOSTOYEVSKY and TOLSTOY for his portrayals of life among the poor and downtrodden. For other novels by Dickens, see the following entries: NICHOLAS NICKLEBY; BARNABY RUDGE; MARTIN CHUZZLEWIT; THE CHIMES; THE CRICKET ON THE HEARTH; DOMBEY AND SON; BLEAK HOUSE; HARD TIMES; LITTLE DORRIT; GREAT EXPECTATIONS; OUR MUTUAL FRIEND; THE MYSTERY OF EDWIN DROOD.

the modern Dickens. William De Morgan (1839–1917), author of JOSEPH VANCE, ALICE-FOR-SHORT and other novels, was so called because of his Victorian manner and emphasis on character rather than plot.

Dickinson, Emily Elizabeth (1830–1886). American poet, known for her precise and delicate lyrics dealing with personal emotions and states of mind, many mystical in tone. They are considered to have an affinity with the poetry of the Imagists (see IMAGISM), and influenced the women poets of the 1920's, especially Edna St. Vincent MILLAY and Elinor WYLIE. Only two poems were published while the poet was alive, and her work, edited by several different hands over a long period of years, came into prominence only in the 20th century. Volumes published so far include *Poems* (1890); *Poems: Second Series* (1891); *Poems: Third Series* (1896); *The Single Hound* (1914); *Further Poems* (1929); *Unpublished Poems* (1936); *Poems: Centenary Edition* (1930); *Bolts of Melody* (1945). Emily Dickinson lived an uneventful and secluded life, carrying on literary correspondence with several prominent critics and authors of her time; she is considered to have been influenced in part by the ideas of EMERSON. Many speculations have been made with regard to unrevealed details of her biography. She is believed to be portrayed as the titular heroine of Helen Hunt Jackson's novel *Mercy Philbrick's Choice* (1876), and of the play *Alison's House* (1930), by Susan Glaspell.

Dickinson, Goldsworthy Lowes (1862–1932). English essayist. Best-known for *The Greek View of Life* (1896). A gentleman and a scholar and a bachelor to the end.

Dickon. In Percy MacKaye's SCARECROW, a "Yankee improvisation of the Prince of Darkness."

Dick's hatband. The crown of England, so referred to in allusion to the short rule of Richard Cromwell, the weak son of Oliver CROMWELL. "As queer as Dick's hatband" is an expression originally meaning how queer it was that the crown had come to this.

Dickson, Carter, see CARR, JOHN DICKSON.

Dick Turpin, see TURPIN, DICK.

Dictator of Letters. VOLTAIRE (1694–1778), called the *Great Pan.*

Dicte. The cave in the Cretan mountain —center of a prehistoric cult—where the infant Zeus was tended by nymphs. Hence *Dictaean.*

diction. Manner or mode of verbal expression, particularly with regard to clearness, accuracy, etc. Comparable to *style,* which, however, is a matter of structure where diction is a matter of form.

> In the sure and flawless perfection of his rhythm and diction he [Milton] is as admirable as Vergil or Dante.—Matthew Arnold.

Dictys Cretensis. Reputed author of an eye-witness account in Latin of the siege of Troy, which was one of the versions of the TROILUS legend known to the Middle Ages. Both Dictys Cretensis and DARES PHRYGIUS are names mentioned by Homer.

didactic poetry (Gr. *didasko,* I teach). Poetry which uses the beauties of expression, imagination, sentiment, etc., for teaching some moral lesson, as Pope's ESSAY ON MAN, or the principles of some art or science, as Virgil's *Georgics,* Garth's *Dispensary,* or Erasmus Darwin's *Botanic Garden.*

Diderot, Denis. Nicknamed **Pantophile Diderot** (1713–1784). French encyclopedist and philosopher. With d'Alembert and others compiler of the ENCYCLOPÉDIE, OU DICTIONNAIRE RAISONNÉ DES SCIENCES, DES ARTS ET DES MÉTIERS (28 vols.). His best-known play is *Le Fils naturel* (1757), his best-known novel *Le Neveu de Rameau* (posthumous).

Dido. The name given by Virgil to Elissa, founder and queen of Carthage. She fell in love with Aeneas, driven by a storm to her shores, who, after abiding awhile at Carthage, was compelled by Mercury to leave the hospitable queen, Elissa, in grief, burns herself to death on a funeral pile. (*Aeneid,* i. 494–iii. 650.) Dido is really the Phoenician name of Astarte (Artemis), goddess of the moon and protectress of the citadel of Carthage. Ovid, in his *Heroides,* has a letter supposed to be written by Dido to Aeneas, reminding him of all she had done for him, and imploring him to remain. There are several English tragedies on Queen Dido: *Dido, Queen of Carthage,* by Nash and Marlowe (1594); *Dido and Aeneas,* by D'Urfey (1721); the opera of *Dido and Aeneas,* by Purcell (1657); also *Dido,* an opera, by Marmontel (1703) and *Didon Abbandonata,* by Metastasio (1724).

Didymus (*Gr.* the twin). Surname of the apostle Thomas; hence a doubter.

die-hard. In political phraseology *diehards* are the crusted members of any party (particularly the Tories who opposed any reform of the House of Lords, and the Unionists who refused to budge an inch in the direction of Irish Home Rule) who stick to their long-held theories through thick and thin, regardless of the changes that time or a newly awakened conscience may bring.

Diego, San. A modification of Santiago (St. James), champion of the red cross and patron saint of Spain. See under SAINT.

Dies Irae (Lat. *Day of Wrath*). A famous medieval hymn on the last judgment, probably the composition of Thomas of Celano, a native of Abruzzi, who died in 1255. It is derived from the Vulgate version of *Joel* ii. 31, and used by Catholics in the Mass for the Dead and on All Souls' Day. Scott has introduced the opening into his *Lay of the Last Minstrel.*

> Dies irae, dies illa
> Solvet saeclum in favilla,
> Teste David cum Sibylla.

Dietrich of Bern. The name given the German folk epic to Theodoric the Great (454–526), king of the Ostrogoths (Bern = Verona). He appears in many Middle High German poems, especially the NIBELUNGENLIED, where he is one of the liegemen of King Etzel.

Dietz, Howard (1896–). American librettist. *Dear Sir* (with Jerome Kern; 1924); *Merry-Go-Round* (with Morrie Ryskind; 1927) and other comic operas.

digamma. A letter of the original Greek alphabet, standing for about the sound of English *w* and looking somewhat like a capital F, in which the Greeks saw two gammas (Γ) on top of each other. Hence the name.

Digby, Sir **Kenelm** (1603–1665). English philosopher and student of occultism. Discovered the essential function of oxygen in plant life. Among his books are *A Treatise Declar-*

ing the Operations and Nature of Man's Soul (1644) and highly fantastic *Memoirs.*

Digges, Dudley (1880–1947). Irish actor of an old family. A favorite in the United States where he appeared both on the stage and in moving pictures. Most recently played in *The Iceman Cometh,* by Eugene O'NEILL.

Dignam, Paddy. In James Joyce's ULYSSES, a friend of Leopold BLOOM and Simon DEDALUS whose funeral Bloom attends early in the action of the novel, in what is considered to be intended as an analogue of Ulysses' visit to Hades in the Homeric legend. Dignam himself represents ELPENOR.

digraph. Two letters representing one sound, as *th, sh,* etc. Not to be confused with *diphthong,* which is the sound of two vowels connected by a glide, regardless of whether it is represented by one or several letters.

dilettante. From Italian; literally, "one who takes delight in a thing." Like *amateur,* which comes from French and means literally, "one who likes a thing," the term *dilettante* is especially applied with reference to the fine arts. Since mere fondness of an art guarantees neither knowledge nor ability, *amateur* as well as *dilettante* have come to mean "one who dabbles in a given subject."

Dillon, George (1906–). American poet. Pulitzer prize winner in 1931. Translated Baudelaire's *Fleurs du Mal* with Edna St. Vincent MILLAY. Editor of *Poetry: A Magazine of Verse.*

Dimanche, Monsieur. A dun. The term is from Molière's *Don Juan,* and would be in English *Mr. Sunday.*

dimeter. A verse consisting of two metrical feet or of two DIPODIES.

Dimmesdale, Rev. Arthur. In Hawthorne's SCARLET LETTER, the father of Hester Prynne's illegitimate child. After years of cowardly silence he finally makes public confession.

Dimnet, Ernest (1866–). French abbé; lecturer and essayist. Commonly known as Abbé Dimnet. His most popular book, *The Art of Thinking* (1928).

Dinah. In UNCLE TOM'S CABIN by Harriet Beecher STOWE, the cook in St. Clare's household. The name is a common one for a Negro cook or servant. It is a feminine proper name in the Bible.

Dinarzade. Sister of SCHEHERAZADE.

Dindymus. In ancient geography, a mountain range between Phrygia and Galatia, sacred to CYBELE, the Great Mother of the Gods, often also called Dindymene.

Dîners Magny. A restaurant in Paris which was the scene of informal meetings of an "inner circle" of French novelists whose attitudes and aims were in many ways common. Among these novelists were Edmond and Jules de GONCOURT, Théophile GAUTIER, Alphonse DAUDET, Ernest RENAN, and Gustave FLAUBERT, and the critic Charles Augustine SAINTE-BEUVE.

Dinesen, Isak, see BLIXEN.

Ding, see DARLING, JAY NORWOOD.

Ding an sich (*Ger.* thing in itself). In Kantian philosophy, a thing as it is in its own essence, not distorted by subjective interpretation or sense perception. Contrasted with *phenomenon,* which is a thing as it is perceived. If all awareness is due to sense perception, it becomes possible to claim that there are no *Dinge an sich.* The subsequent conclusions to be derived from such a premiss, lead deeply into romantic philosophy and possibly to nihilistic subjectivism.

dingdong theory. See BOWWOW THEORY.

Dingley tariff. A protective tariff in effect from 1897–1909. The Dingley Act governing the tariff was framed by Representative Nelson Dingley of Maine (1832–1899).

Dinmont, Dandie. In Scott's GUY MANNERING, an eccentric and humorous storefarmer at Charlie's Hope. He is called "The Fighting Dinmont of Liddesdale." Dandie Dinmont is considered one of Scott's best-drawn characters.

Dinsmore, Elsie. See ELSIE DINSMORE.

Diocletian, Gaius Aurelius Valerius (245–313). Roman Emperor (284–305 A.D.). Inaugurated the period of the Partnership of Emperors. Ruled Asia and Egypt as one of four associate Caesars. Began a terrible ten year persecution of the Christians (303–313). With Maximian built Baths of Diocletian in Rome (opened 306).

Diogenes. (1) A noted Greek cynic philosopher (about 412–323 B.C.), who, according to Seneca, lived in a tub. Another well-known tale is that he went about in daylight with a lantern, looking for an honest man. When Alexander went to see him, the young King of Macedonia introduced himself with these words: "I am Alexander, surnamed the Great," to which the philosopher replied: "And I am Diogenes, surnamed the Dog." When Alexander asked if he could do the philosopher any favor, Diogenes replied, "Yes, move out of my sunshine," to which Alexander is said to have answered, "If I were not Alexander, I should be Diogenes."

> The whole world was not half so wide
> To Alexander, when he cried
> Because he had but one to subdue,
> As was a paltry narrow tub to Diogenes.
>
> Butler, *Hudibras,* i. 3.

(2) Surname of Romanus IV, Emperor of the East (1067–1071).

Diomedes or **Diomed.** (1) In Greek legend, a hero of the siege of Troy, king of Aetolia, brave and obedient to authority. He survived the siege, but on his return home found his wife living in adultery, and saved his life by living an exile in Italy. His horses were Dinos and Lampon. See HORSE.

(2) In later versions of the TROILUS legend, Diomede is the forthright Greek warrior for whom Cressida betrays her promise to Troilus.

Diomedean swop. An exchange in which all the benefit is on one side. The expression is founded on an incident related by Homer in the *Iliad.* Glaucus recognizes DIOMED on the battlefield, and the friends change armor:

> For Diomed's brass arms, of mean device,
> For which nine oxen paid (a vulgar price),
> He gave his own, of gold divinely wrought,
> An hundred beeves the shining purchase bought.
> Pope, *Iliad,* vi.

Dione. A Titaness; daughter of Oceanus and Tethys, and mother by Jupiter of Venus. The name has been applied to Venus herself, and Julius Caesar, who claimed descent from her, was hence sometimes called *Dionaeus Caesar.*

> So young Dioné, nursed beneath the waves,
> And rocked by Nereids in their coral caves. . . .
> Lisped her sweet tones, and tried her tender smiles.
> Darwin, *Economy of Vegetation,* ii.

Dionne quintuplets. Cécile, Yvonne, Annette, Émilie, and Marie Dionne, born May 28, 1934, to Ovila and Elzire Dionne of Callander, Northern Ontario, Canada. See also DAFOE.

Dionysia. See BACCHANALIA.

Dionysus. The Greek name of BACCHUS.

Dioscuri (Gr. *Dious kouros,* "son of Zeus"). CASTOR AND POLLUX.

Diotima. An Arcadian priestess, probably fictitious, teacher of Socrates, quoted by him in Plato's *Symposium.*

diphthong. Two vowel sounds in one syllable connected by a continuous glide (and regardless of its representation in spelling by one or several letters). The use of the word *diphthong* for DIGRAPH is erroneous.

dipody. In prosody, a measure of two feet.

Dipsas (Gr. *dipsa,* thirst). A serpent, so called because those bitten by it suffered from intolerable thirst. Milton refers to it in *Paradise Lost,* x. 526.

Dipsychus. See CLOUGH, ARTHUR HUGH.

diptych. In Roman antiquity, a two-leaved hinged writing tablet. Hence an altar piece consisting of two painted tablets hinged together. When there are three tablets, the altar piece is called a *triptych.*

Dircaean Swan. Pindar; so called from Dirce, a fountain in the neighborhood of Thebes, the poet's birthplace (518–442 B.C.). The fountain is named from Dirce, who was put to death by the sons of Antiope for her brutal treatment of their mother, and was changed into the spring by Bacchus.

direct discourse. A discourse literally quoted, as: *He says, "I am hungry."* Opposed to indirect discourse in which the quotation is changed by grammatical subordination, as: *He says that he is hungry.*

Directoire. French for DIRECTORY. Used in English as an adjective designating a style of dress prevalent at the time. High waistline, long skirt, low neckline, puffed sleeves.

Director, Our. A musical march by John Philip SOUSA.

Directory, The. In French history, the constitution of 1795, when the executive was vested in five "Directors," one of whom retired every year. After a sickly existence of four years, it came to an end at Napoleon's *coup d'état* of 18 Brumaire (November 9), 1799.

Dis. A name for PLUTO and hence the lower world.

> Proserpine gathering flowers,
> Herself a fairer flower, by gloomy Dis
> Was gathered.
> Milton, *Paradise Lost,* iv. 270.

Disastrous Peace, the (La Paix malheureuse). A name given to the Treaty of Câteau-Cambrésis (1559), which followed the battle of Gravelines. It was signed by France, Spain, and England, and by it France ceded the Low Countries to Spain, and Savoy, Corsicá, and 200 forts to Italy.

Discharge Bible. See under BIBLE, SPECIALLY NAMED.

Discobolus (from *Gr.* a discus thrower). Name of a famous Greek statue by Myron (5th century B.C.), representing a youth about to throw a discus. The original is lost. Restored copies are in the Vatican Museum, the British Museum, and in the Palazzo Lanceolotti. The last of these is now held to be nearest the original.

Samuel Butler introduces the Discobolus in *A Psalm of Montreal* with the amusing refrain, "O God, O Montreal!", claiming to have found it consigned to a lumber room because it is considered indecent.

disestablishment. The act of withdrawing a church from its position or privileges in relation to the state. The Irish Church was disestablished by an act of Parliament in 1869. The Church of England was disestablished in Wales by several acts in 1920.

Dishart, Gavin. The titular hero of Barrie's LITTLE MINISTER. He also appears in *Auld Licht Idylls.*

disjecta membra. Scattered limbs, referring to the MAENADS dismembering Pentheus.

Hence in literature the literary remains of a poet or writer.

Dismas or **Dysmas.** The name usually given, in the apocryphal gospels, to the penitent thief who was crucified with Jesus. The impenitent thief is commonly known as Gesmas or Gestas. Longfellow, in his *Golden Legend,* calls the penitent Titus and his fellow thief Dumachus.

Disney, Walt (1901–). American producer of animated moving-picture cartoons in which he created the immortal characters of Mickey Mouse and Donald Duck. His best-known full-length pictures, also in animated technique and in technicolor, *Snow White and the Seven Dwarfs* (1938), *Pinocchio* (1940), *Fantasia* (1940), *Dumbo* (1941).

dispensation (Lat. *dispensatio,* from *dis-* and *pendere,* to weigh). The system which God chooses to *dispense* or establish between Himself and man. The dispensation of *Adam* was that between Adam and God; the dispensation of *Abraham,* and that of *Moses,* were those imparted to these holy men; the *Gospel* dispensation is that explained in the Gospels.

papal dispensation. Permission given by the Pope to *dispense* with something enjoined; a license to do what is forbidden, or to omit what is commanded by the law of the Church, as distinct from the moral law.

Disraeli, Benjamin, 1st Earl of **Beaconsfield** (1804–1881). English novelist and statesman, Prime Minister of England in 1868 and from 1874 to 1880. His literary works include VIVIAN GREY (1826–1827); *Contarini Fleming* (1832); *The Infernal Marriage* (1834); *Venetia* (1837); CONINGSBY (1844); *Sybil* (1845); TANCRED (1847); *Lothair* (1870); *Endymion* (1880). Disraeli based many of his characters on his contemporaries, and his novels are marked by their presentation of types of persons in the social and political life. He also wrote biography and political studies. Nicknamed Dizzy.

D'Israeli, Isaac (1766–1848). Father of Benjamin DISRAELI and son of Benjamin D'Israeli, a Jewish merchant descended from a family of Spanish refugees who went to England in 1748. Published anonymously *Curiosities of Literature* (6 vols., 1791–1834), *Amenities of Literature* (3 vols., 1841), and other works.

dissenter, Dissenter. In England, a nonconformist Protestant (or Catholic) who disputes the authority of the Church of England.

Dissertation on Roast Pig, A. One of the most famous of the *Essays of Elia* by Charles Lamb. See ELIA.

distaff. The staff for holding flax, tow, or wool to be spun. Since the 15th century an attachment to the spinning wheel but originally constituting the complete spinning apparatus. Hence a woman or the female sex. The phrase **distaff side** or **distaff side of the house** is an old collective for the female members of the family. **Saint Distaff's Day** or **Distaff Day** is January 7, the day after Twelfth Day (January 6), when the women used to resume their normal work after the Christmas holidays.

Distaffina. The heroine of Rhode's burlesque, BOMBASTES FURIOSO.

distemper. In art, a method of painting with the pigments tempered with an emulsion of egg yolk, size or white of egg. Cf. Browning's poem *Pacchiarotto or How he Worked in Distemper.*

distich. A strophic group of two lines. The modern rhymed distich is called a couplet. An elegiac distich, so called because it was in classical times favored as a strophic form for elegies, consists of a hexameter followed by a pentameter. Goethe and Schiller are the principal poets of distichs in modern times. One by Schiller, which is at the same time a characterization of the distich, reads in Coleridge's translation:

In the hexameter rises the fountain's silvery column,
In the pentameter aye falling in melody back.

dithyrambic (Gr., *dithyrambos,* a choric hymn). Dithyrambic poetry was originally a wild, impetuous kind of Dorian lyric in honor of Bacchus, traditionally ascribed to the invention of Arion of Lesbos (about 620 B. C.), who was thereafter called *the father of dithyrambic poetry.*

Ditmars, Raymond Lee (1876–1942). American naturalist. Curator of reptiles, later in charge of department of mammals, in the New York Zoological Park. Author of *The Book of Living Reptiles* (1936), etc.

Ditrichstein, Leo (1865–1928). Hungarian-American actor and playwright. Created the rôle of Zou-Zou in the stage version of Du Maurier's *Trilby* (1895). Successful in adaptations of French and German stage hits.

Ditzen, Rudolf. See FALLADA, HANS.

Diver, Colonel. In Dickens' MARTIN CHUZZLEWIT, editor of the *New York Rowdy Journal,* in America.

Diverting History of John Gilpin, The. See JOHN GILPIN.

Dives (*Lat.,* rich). The name popularly given to the rich man in Jesus' parable of "The Rich Man and Lazarus" (*Luke* xvi. 19–31). It is taken from the Vulgate, where the word *dives* occurs.

divide and govern. An old maxim of politics, now usually associated with MACHIAVELLI's reiteration of it. It implies that if you divide a nation into parties, or set your enemies at loggerheads, you have a better chance of having your own way. It is often quoted in one of these variant Latin forms: *divide et impera; divide ut imperes; divide ut regnes.*

Divine, the. Epithet variously applied to Ariosto (1474–1533), Italian poet; Raphael (1483–1520), the painter; Luis de Morales (1509–1586), a Spanish religious painter; Ferdinand de Herrera (1534–1567), the Spanish lyric poet; Sarah Bernhardt (1844–1923), etc.

Divine Comedy (Divina Commedia). An epic poem in TERZA RIMA by DANTE ALIGHIERI, divided into three parts: *Inferno* (1300), *Purgatory* (1308), and *Paradise* (1311). Dante called it a *comedy,* because the ending is happy and his countrymen added the word *divine* from admiration of the poem. The poet depicts a vision, in which he is conducted, first by Virgil (human reason) through hell and purgatory; and then by Beatrice (revelation) and finally by St. Bernard through the several heavens, where he beholds the Triune God.

Hell or the Inferno is represented as a funnel-shaped hollow, formed of gradually contracting circles, the lowest and smallest of which is the earth's center. Purgatory is a mountain rising solitarily from the ocean on that side of the earth which is opposite to us. It is divided into terraces, and its top is the terrestrial paradise. From this "top" the poet ascends through the seven planetary heavens, the fixed stars, and the "primum mobile," to the empyrean or seat of God.

The *Divine Comedy* is considered the greatest literary production of the Middle Ages, and has been compared to a Gothic cathedral in its scope, its detail, the sublimity of its aspiration, and its character as a monument to the entire culture. As a vision and an account of a living man's visit to Hell, Purgatory, and Heaven, it is in the tradition of a form which had a very wide vogue in the popular religious literature of the medieval period. See ST. PATRICK'S PURGATORY. Much of the Aristotelian philosophy of St. Thomas Aquinas (see under SAINT) is used in the cosmology and the theological and metaphysical concepts embodied in the poem, and many actual historical personages appear, as well as Greek and Latin authors and philosophers admired by Dante and famous legendary figures. Dante's own friends and enemies in his political career are especially to be found in his representation of the Other World, respectively exalted or damned. The characterization, vivid and imaginative visualization, dramatic presentation of individual scenes, and poetic distinction of the poem have made it famous through the centuries. For a full discussion, cf. *Dante,* by T. S. Eliot, and *Mediaeval Culture,* by Karl Vössler.

Divine Doctor. Jean de Ruysbroeck. See under DOCTOR.

Divine Fire, The. A novel by May Sinclair (*Eng.,* 1905), a study of temperamental genius. The hero, Savage Keith Rickman, a young Cockney poet, is said to have been drawn in some measure from the poet Ernest DOWSON.

Divine Pagan. Hypatia (370?–?415), who presided over the neo-Platonic School at Alexandria. See also NEO-PLATONISM.

divine right of kings. The notion that kings reign by direct ordinance of God, quite apart from the will of the people. This phrase was much used in the 17th century on account of the pretensions of the Stuart kings. The idea arose from the Old Testament, where kings are called "God's anointed," because they were God's vicars on earth, when the Jews changed their theocracy for a monarchy.

> The right divine of kings to govern wrong.
> Pope, *Dunciad,* iv. 188.

Divine Sarah, the. Sarah BERNHARDT.

divine speaker. See THEOPHRASTUS.

Divorcement, A Bill of. Title of a play by Clemence DANE.

Dix, Dorothy. Pseudonym of **Elizabeth Meriwether Gilmer** (1870–). American newspaper writer, author of a widely syndicated column of advice on love and domestic problems which was begun in 1896 in the New Orleans *Picayune.*

Dixie or **Dixie's Land.** An ideal country, a sort of Utopia in the southern part of the United States; hence a general term for the states south of the Mason and Dixon line. The term was popularized by the song *Dixie,* written by D. D. Emmett and first sung in public by Bryant's Negro Minstrels in New York in 1859. During the Civil War, the song became a great favorite with the Confederate soldiers.

Originally, however, Dixie referred not to the South, but to Manhattan Island, and this use of the term was said to be current for about fifty years before the song was written. According to the account usually given, Dixie was a slave-holder of Manhattan Island, who removed his slaves to the southern states, where they had to work harder and fare worse, so that they were always sighing for their old home, which they called "Dixie's Land." Imagination and distance soon advanced this island into a sort of Delectable Country or Land of Beulah.

Dixon, Thomas (1864–1946). American Baptist clergyman. Democrat but anti-Communist and opponent of New Deal. Wrote *The Leopard's Spots* (1902), *The Clansman* (1905), etc. The latter painted the Ku Klux Klan as a band of dedicated knights and was the basis of D. W. Griffith's epochal silent film, *The Birth of A Nation* (1914).

Dizzy. A nickname of Benjamin DISRAELI.

Djabal. In Browning's tragedy, THE RETURN OF THE DRUSES, a man who poses as divine from patriotic motives and stabs himself when his scheme is uncovered.

Djinnestan, see JINNISTAN.

Dmitri Fyodorovich, see KARAMAZOV, DMITRI FYODOROVICH.

Dmitri Rudin. A novel by TURGENEV (1860), a keen study of a man whose colossal vanity leads him to think himself a genius, but who is contented with fascinating a few ladies and talking endlessly.

Dobbin, Captain, afterwards **Colonel.** In Thackeray's VANITY FAIR, the faithful friend of George Osborne and lover of Amelia Sedley. He is ungainly and self-effacing; for years he devotes himself to Amelia's welfare without demanding anything in return. At last he is rewarded with her hand. Dobbin's sterling qualities place him in sharp contrast with many of the other, more worldly, self-assertive characters of the book.

Dobell, Bertram (1842–1914). English book-seller and man of letters. Friend of James THOMSON, for the publication of whose *The City of Dreadful Night* (1880) he was responsible. Editor of works of Thomas TRAHERNE.

Dobell, Sydney (1824–1874). English poet and critic. In private life a wine merchant at Cheltenham (1848–1874). Wrote *The Roman* (1850) and *Balder* (1854). Best-known single poem *Keith of Ravelston*. See also under FIRMILIAN.

Dobie, Charles Caldwell (1881–1943). American fiction writer and playwright. He was called "a professional San Franciscan," "a conservative interpreter of San Francisco."

Dobie, J. Frank (1888–). American writer and folklorist. Professor of English, University of Texas. *Apache Gold and Yaqui Silver* (1939) etc.

Döblin, Alfred (1878–). German nerve specialist and writer. His major work, *Berlin Alexanderplatz* (1929), was a valuable experiment in a realistic cinematographic technique undertaken by a man who had learned a good deal as an expressionistic poet. It was translated into five languages.

Doboobie, Dr. Demetrius. In Scott's KENILWORTH, a doctor who taught Wayland SMITH something of his art.

Dobrée, Bonamy (1891–). English authority on Restoration drama. *Restoration Comedy* (1924), *Restoration Tragedy* (1929).

Dobson, Henry Austin (1840–1921). English poet and prose-writer, a scholar of 18th-century literature, which he depicted in prose sketches and biographies. Among his works are *Vignettes in Rhyme* (1873); *Proverbs in Porcelain* (1877); *The Ballad of Beau Brocade* (1892); *The Story of Rosina* (1895); and *Carmina Votiva* (1901).

doctor. A scholastic or honorary title conferred by a university. The word doctor is commonly synonymous with physician, from the degree M.D., Doctor of Medicine. In the medieval universities doctors were advanced students who were usually also teachers. The degree Ph.D., Doctor of Philosophy, is regularly conferred by American universities on the satisfactory completion of the equivalent of about three years' study beyond the BACHELOR's degree including the presentation of an original thesis.

Other doctors' degrees than the Ph.D. such as LL.D., Doctor of Law, Litt.D., Doctor of Literature—are generally honorary and conferred by a university for high distinction in any field, often regardless of whether the recipient has done academic work at that or any other university.

In the Middle Ages, the Schoolmen or theologians who lectured in the cloisters and cathedral schools were called doctors, and many of them became known under special titles, as:

Admirable Doctor (*Doctor Mirabilis*). Roger BACON (1214?–1294), the English medieval philosopher.

Angelic Doctor. Thomas Aquinas (1224–1274), also known as the *Angel of the Schools,* was so called, because he discussed the knotty points in connection with the being and nature of angels.

Authentic Doctor. A title bestowed on the scholastic philosopher, Gregory of Rimini (d. 1358).

Divine Doctor. Jean de Ruysbroeck, also called the ECSTATIC DOCTOR.

Eloquent Doctor. Peter Aureolus (14th century), archbishop of Aix, a schoolman.

Ecstatic Doctor. Jean de Ruysbroeck, the mystic (1294–1381).

Enlightened Doctor. Raymond Lully of Palma (about 1234–1315), a Spaniard, and one of the most distinguished of the 13th century scholastic philosophers.

Evangelic Doctor. John Wyclif (1320–1384), "the morning star of the Reformation."

Illuminated Doctor. (1) Raymond Lully. Also called the ENLIGHTENED DOCTOR.

(2) Johannes Tauler (1294–1361), the German mystic.

Invincible Doctor. William of Occam (d. 1347), or Ockham (a village in Surrey), the scholastic philosopher. He was also called *Doctor Singularis,* and *Princeps Nominalium,* for he was the reviver of NOMINALISM.

Irrefragable Doctor. Alexander Hales (d. 1245), an English Franciscan, author of *Summa Theologiae,* and founder of scholastic theology.

Mellifluous Doctor. St. Bernard (1091–1153), whose writings were called a "river of Paradise."

Profound Doctor. Thomas Bradwardine, Richard Middleton, and other 14th century scholastic philosophers were given this title.

Most Profound Doctor. Aegidius de Columna (d. 1316), a Sicilian schoolman.

Seraphic Doctor. St. Bonaventura, the scholastic philosopher (1221–1274), placed by Dante among the saints of his *Paradiso.*

Singular Doctor. William Occam, *Doctor Singularis et Invincibilis.* See INVINCIBLE DOCTOR.

Subtle Doctor. The Scottish schoolman and Franciscan friar, Duns Scotus (about 1265–1308).

Universal Doctor. Alain de Lille (1114–1203), one of the schoolmen.

Well-founded Doctor. Aegidius de Columna (1247?–1316).

Dr. Faustus, see under FAUST.

Dr. Fell, see FELL.

Doctors' Commons. Site near St. Paul's Churchyard in London, occupied (till 1867) by a group of buildings of the same name. In them were the offices attending to marriage licenses, divorces, and the like. Their name goes back to the time when they were occupied by the Association or College of Doctors of Civil Law. The *commons* of the doctors was originally their common table and then their dining hall.

Doctor of Physic's Tale or Physicians Tale. In Chaucer's *Canterbury Tales.* See VIRGINIA.

Doctors of the Church. Certain early Christian Fathers, especially four in the Greek (or Eastern) Church and four in the Latin (or Western) Church.

(*a*) *Eastern Church.* St. Athanasius of Alexandria (331), who defended the divinity of Christ against the Arians; St. Basil the Great of Caesarea (379) and his co-worker St. Gregory of Nazianzus (376); and the eloquent St. John Chrysostom (398), Archbishop of Constantinople.

(*b*) *Western Church.* St. Jerome (420), translator of the Vulgate; St. Ambrose (397), bishop of Milan; St. Augustine (430), bishop of Hippo; and St. Gregory the Great (604), the pope who sent St. Augustine, the Apostle of the Anglo-Saxons, to England.

Dodd, David. An important character in Charles Reade's *Love Me Little, Love Me Long* (1859) and in its sequel, *Hard Cash* (1864). He is a seaman, completely at home on shipboard but extremely ill at ease on land. The first mentioned novel treats of his successful wooing of Lucy Fountain. In the latter his struggles to bring home a large sum in "hard cash" result in his losing his mind, and as "Silly Billy Thompson" he escapes from a burning lunatic asylum to a frigate and lives through a series of exciting adventures before fate restores to him his reason, his wife and daughter and his bank account of "hard cash." This novel was written as an exposure of conditions in the private lunatic asylums of England and as such aroused much discussion.

Julia Dodd. David's daughter, the exuberant young heroine of *Hard Cash.*

Dodd, Lee Wilson (1879–1933). American poet, playwright, and novelist. *The Changelings* (1923; play), *The Book of Susan* (1920; novel).

Dodd, William Edward (1869–1940). Historian and diplomat. Ambassador to Germany (1933–1937); resigned and returned to lecture against the Nazis. His German diary, *Ambassador Dodd's Diary,* was published in 1941. Wrote *Statesmen of the Old South* (1911), *Woodrow Wilson and His Work* (1920); with Ray Stannard Baker editor of *The Public Papers of Woodrow Wilson* (1924–1926).

Dodd Family Abroad, The. A satiric romance by Charles Lever (1806–1872), ridiculing English travelers in Europe. The Dodds are Anglo-Irish.

Dodge, Esq., Steadfast. In Cooper's novels, HOMEWARD BOUND and HOME AS FOUND, an American journalist typical of all the unpleasant qualities which Cooper saw in his fellow countrymen after his own travels abroad. This character and others of a similar nature did much to involve Cooper in controversies, legal and otherwise, and to dull his popularity.

Dodge, Mabel, see LUHAN, MABEL DODGE.

Dodge, Mary Mapes (1831–1905). American writer and editor of *St. Nicholas Magazine* (1873–1905). Her books for children, *Hans Brinker, or the Silver Skates* (1865) and *Donald and Dorothy* (1883) are classics.

Dodgson, Charles Lutwidge, see CARROLL, LEWIS.

Dodona. A famous oracle in the village of Dodona in Epirus, and the most ancient of Greece. It was dedicated to Zeus, and the oracles were delivered from the tops of oak and other trees, the rustling of the wind in the branches being interpreted by the priests. Also, brazen vessels and plates were suspended from the branches, and these, being struck together when the wind blew, gave various sounds from which responses were concocted. Hence the Greek phrase *Kalkos Dodones* (brass of Dodona), meaning a babbler, or one who talks an infinite deal of nothing.

black pigeons of Dodona. Two black pigeons, we are told, took their flight from Thebes, in Egypt; one flew to Libya, and the other to Dodona. On the spot where the former alighted, the temple of Jupiter Ammon was erected; in the place where the other settled, the oracle of Jupiter was established, and there the responses were made by the black pigeons that inhabited the surrounding groves. This fable is probably based on a pun upon the word *peleiai,* which usually meant "old women," but in the dialect of the Epirots signified pigeons or doves.

Dods, Meg. In Scott's novel, ST. RONAN'S WELL, landlady of the Clachan, or Mowbery Arms inn at St. Ronan's Old Town. The inn was once the manse, and Meg Dods reigns there despotically, but her wines are good and her cuisine excellent. She is considered one of the best low comic characters in the whole range of fiction.

> She had hair of a brindled colour, betwixt black and grey, which was apt to escape in elf-locks from under her mutch when she was thrown into violent agitation, long skinny hands terminated by stout talons, grey eyes, thin lips, a robust person, a broad though fat chest, capital wind, and a voice that could match a choir of fishwomen.—Sir W. Scott, *St. Ronan's Well,* i.

Dodsley, Robert (1703–1764). English poet, playwright, and bookseller. Editor of a collection of *Old Plays* (12 vols., 1744), beginning with a morality play, which went through several revised and enlarged editions.

Dodson and Fogg, Messrs. In Dickens' *Pickwick Papers,* two unprincipled lawyers, who undertake on speculation to bring an action against Mr. Pickwick for "breach of promise," and file accordingly the famous suit of "Bardell *v.* Pickwick." The names *Dodson and Fogg* are frequently used as synonymous with unscrupulous or dishonest solicitors.

Dodsworth. A novel by Sinclair LEWIS, published in 1929 and later dramatized as a play and a motion picture. It tells of Samuel Dodsworth, a rich automobile manufacturer in the Midwestern city of ZENITH, who retires and goes to Europe with his frivolous wife Fran. Fran becomes involved in several love affairs with European adventurers, and Dodsworth, lonely and unhappy, meets Edith Cortright, an American widow who teaches him to appreciate the traditions of Europe. After complications, he leaves his wife for the more mature companionship of Edith. Dodsworth appears briefly in the novel BABBITT, and George F. Babbitt in turn appears briefly in *Dodsworth.*

Doe, John and **Richard Roe.** Any plaintiff and defendant in an action of ejectment. They were sham names used at one time to save certain "niceties of law"; but the clumsy device was abolished in 1852. Any mere imaginary persons, or men of straw are so called.

Doeg. In the satire of ABSALOM AND ACHITOPHEL, by Dryden and Tate, Doeg is meant for Elkanah Settle, a poet who wrote satires upon Dryden, but was no match for his great rival. Doeg in the Biblical narrative was Saul's herdsman, who had charge of his mules and asses. He told Saul that the priests of Nob had provided David with food; whereupon Saul sent him to put them to death, and eighty-five were ruthlessly massacred. (1 *Sam.* xxi. 7; xxii. 18.)

> Doëg, though without knowing how or why,
> Made still a blundering kind of melody . . .
> Let him rail on; let his invective Muse
> Have four-and-twenty letters to abuse,
> Which if he jumbles to one line of sense,
> Indict him of a capital offence.
> *Absalom and Achitophel,* Part ii.

dog. Dogs as the best loved of all animals figure prominently in legend and fiction. In medieval art they symbolize fidelity. A dog is represented as lying at the feet of St. Bernard, St. Benignus, and St. Wendelin; as licking the wounds of St. Roch; as carrying a lighted torch in representations of St. Dominic. In monuments the dog is placed at the feet of women to symbolize affection and fidelity, as a *lion* is placed at the feet of men to signify courage and magnanimity. Many of the Crusaders are represented with their feet on a dog, to show that they followed the standard of the Lord as faithfully as a dog follows the footsteps of his master.

Among the many dogs whose names have become proverbial are ARGUS; Aubry's dog or the Dog of MONTARGIS; BEAUTIFUL JOE; BETH GELERT; BOATSWAIN; BOB SON OF BATTLE; BRAN; BUCK; DIAMOND; JIP KATMIR; and TOBY. See also MAHABHARATA.

a black dog has walked over him. Said of a sullen person. Horace tells us that the sight of a black dog with its pups was an unlucky omen, and the devil has been frequently symbolized by a black dog.

a cat and dog life. See under CAT.

a dead dog. Something utterly worthless. A Biblical phrase (cf. 1 *Sam.* xxiv. 14, "After whom is the king of Israel come out? After a dead dog?"). See also IS THY SERVANT, etc., below. There is no expression in the Bible of the fidelity, love, and watchful care of the dog.

a dog in a doublet. A bold, resolute fellow. In Germany and Flanders the strong dogs employed for hunting the wild boar were dressed in a kind of buff doublet buttoned to their bodies. Rubens and Sneyders have represented several in their pictures. A false friend is called *a dog in one's doublet.*

a dog in the manger. A churlish fellow, who will not use what is wanted by another, nor yet let the other have it to use. The allusion is to the well-known fable of a dog that fixed his place in a manger, and would not allow an ox to come near the hay.

a dog's life. A wretched life or a life of debauchery.

Gingham dog. See under GINGHAM.

a living dog is better than a dead lion. The meanest thing with life in it is better than the noblest without. The saying is from *Eccles.* ix. 4.

between dog and wolf. "*Entre chien et loup.*" The hour of dusk.

I am his Highness' dog at Kew; Pray tell me, sir, whose dog are you? Frederick Prince of Wales had a dog given him by Alexander Pope, and these words are said to have been engraved on his collar. They are still sometimes quoted with reference to an overbearing, bumptious person.

is thy servant a dog, that he should do this thing? Said in contempt when one is asked to do something derogatory or beneath one. The phrase is (slightly altered) from 2 *Kings* viii. 13.

it was the story of the dog and the shadow. A case of one who gives up the substance for its shadow, of one who throws good money after bad, of one who gives *certa pro incertis.* The allusion is to the well known fable of the dog who dropped his bone into the stream because he opened his mouth to seize the reflection of it.

let sleeping dogs lie; don't wake a sleeping dog. Let well alone; if some contemplated course of action is likely to cause trouble or land you in difficulties you had better avoid it.

> It is nought good a sleping hound to wake,
> Nor yeve a wight a cause to devyne.
> Chaucer, *Troilus and Criseyde,* iii. 764.

love me, love my dog. If you love me you must put up with my faults, my little ways, or (sometimes) my friends.

St. Roch and his dog. Two inseparables. See under SAINT.

rain cats and dogs. See under CAT.

wake a sleeping dog. See LET SLEEPING DOGS LIE.

try it on the dog! A jocular phrase used of medicine that is expected to be unpalatable, or of food that is suspected of being not quite fit for human consumption.

Dog Beneath the Skin, The, Or, Where Is Francis? A satiric drama in verse and prose by W. H. AUDEN and Christopher ISHERWOOD (1935). Parodying traditional fairy-tale themes and the technique of the popular 20th-century musical comedy, it concerns the quest for Sir Francis Crewe, the missing heir to the holdings of the Crewe family, typical of the English country gentry. According to the will of old Sir Bingham Crewe, half the family's ancestral possessions and the hand of Iris, the Crewe daughter, are offered for the discovery and return of Francis, a candidate being chosen each year by lottery from among the villages. As the play opens, Alan Norman is chosen for the quest and sets off on his journey accompanied by a dog that is actually the missing Francis himself, in the disguise in which he has spent the ten years of his "absence" circulating about the town and finding out what the people are really like. The credulous Alan and his companion have a number of adventures, in which the authors satirically attack European royalty, Fascism, corrupt finance capitalism, the English public-school system, and the like. Francis eventually is forced to reveal himself to Alan, and the two return to the Crewe manor, only to find a celebration in progress in honor of Iris' forthcoming wedding to someone other than Alan. Francis reveals his identity to the assembled townspeople, denounces Iris and the English middle class in general, and inspires five youths of the village to depart with him and Alan, their goal presumably being a Socialist state: "To each his need: from each his power." Like numerous other poems and verse dramas of Auden's earlier literary period, this play was intended to represent the conversion of younger members of the English middle class to the doctrines of COMMUNISM.

Dogberry and Verges. In Shakespeare's MUCH ADO ABOUT NOTHING, two ignorant conceited constables, who greatly confound their words. Dogberry calls "assembly" *dissembly;* "treason" he calls *perjury;* "calumny" he calls *burglary;* "condemnation," *redemption,* "respect," *suspect.* When Conrade says, "Away! you are an ass"; Dogberry tells the town clerk to write him down "an ass." "Masters," he says to the officials, "remember I am an ass." "Oh that I had been writ down an ass!"

dog days. Days of great heat. The term comes from the Romans, who called the six or eight hottest weeks of the summer *caniculares* *dies.* According to their theory, the DOG STAR or Sirius, rising with the sun, added to its heat, and the dog days (about July 3 to August 11) bore the combined heat of the Dog Star and the sun.

Doge. See RULERS, TITLES OF.

dog fall. A fall in wrestling, when the two combatants touch the ground together.

doggerel. A word of unknown origin, probably not to be connected with *dog*. Originally applied to poetry of loose, irregular measure, like that of HUDIBRAS, but now implying baseness and deficiency. See also KNITTELVERS.

dog grass. Couch grass (*Triticu rempens*), which is eaten by dogs when they have lost their appetite; it acts as an emetic and purgative.

dog head. The part of a gun which bites or holds the flint.

Dohna, Count. See CHRISTINA, QUEEN.

dog Latin. Pretended or mongrel Latin. An excellent example is Stevens' definition of a kitchen:

> As the law classically expresses it, a kitchen is "camera necessaria pro usus cookare; cum saucepannis, stewpannis, scullero, dressero, coalholo stovis, smoakjacko; pro roastandum, boilandum, fryandum et plum-pudding-mixandum. . . ."—*A Law Report* (*Daniel* v. *Dishclout*).

Dog of Montargis. See under MONTARGIS.

Dog Star. Sirius, the brightest star in the firmament, whose influence was anciently supposed to cause great heat, pestilence, etc. It was called Dog Star (Caniculus) because it belongs to the constellation *Canis Major* (larger dog). See DOG DAYS.

Doheny, Edward Laurence (1856–1935). American oil magnate, involved in the TEAPOT DOME scandals; accused (1924) of bribing Senator Fall; was indicted with Fall on charges of conspiracy and bribery; acquitted.

Doherty, Reginald Frank (1872–1911) and **Hugh Laurence Doherty** (1875–1919). Famous early English tennis champions. Authors of *On Lawn Tennis* (1903).

Dolan, Father. In James Joyce's A PORTRAIT OF THE ARTIST AS A YOUNG MAN, the Jesuit at Clongowes Wood College who punishes young Stephen DEDALUS unjustly for not doing his lessons, when the boy has broken his glasses and is unable to see. Stephen appeals to the higher authority of Father CONMEE and is vindicated. Father Dolan is said to have been based on a Father Daly, who punished James Joyce as a child in a similar situation.

dolce stil nuovo, il (*It.* **the sweet new style**). Designation by DANTE of the school of Italian poets of the 13th century which replaced that of the Sicilian poets under Emperor FREDERICK II and carried the tradition of COURTLY LOVE to a higher artistic development. The first great figure of the new school was Guido GUINICELLI (or Guinizelli). Dante himself was a member, his VITA NUOVA being considered to mark the victory of the new movement over the old, and others were his friends, Guido CAVALCANTI, Lapo Gianni, and Cino da Pistoia.

Dolet, Étienne (1509–1546). French renaissance scholar and printer. Issued many remarkable works from his Lyons plant; was accused and found guilty of heresy for printing a translation of Plato; suffered a martyr's death at the stake.

Dollar, The Almighty, see ALMIGHTY DOLLAR.

dollar diplomacy. Diplomacy on a commercial basis between nations, for national gain and aggrandizement. The term was coined for the foreign policy of the U.S. in the early 20th century.

Dollfuss, Engelbert (1892–1934). Austrian statesman. Proclaimed dictatorship (1933) as a last resort to maintain Austrian independence. Killed by National Socialist rebels.

Dolls, Mr. In Dickens' novel OUR MUTUAL FRIEND, a nickname for the drunken old father of Jenny WREN.

Doll's House, A. A drama by Henrik IBSEN (1879). The "doll," Nora Helmer, with a naïve innocence of the realities of life that is the result of her petted existence, commits forgery to secure money for her sick husband. The results of her act awaken her to a new world. When the danger from the law is past, her resentment at being treated as a doll forces her to leave home to learn something about life for herself.

Doll Tearsheet. A coarse, violent-tempered female character in Shakespeare's *King Henry the Fourth.*

Dolly Varden fashions. See VARDEN, DOLLY.

dolmen. A prehistoric monument, probably used as a tomb, consisting of unhewn stones arranged in the form of a chamber. The dolmen known as the Pierre Couverte near Saumur in France is 64 feet long, 14 feet wide and about 6 feet high. See also CROMLECH.

Doltaire. A dashing Frenchman in Gilbert Parker's SEATS OF THE MIGHTY.

Dombey and Son. A novel by Charles DICKENS (1846).

Mr. Dombey. A purse-proud, self-contained London merchant, living in Portland Place, Bryanstone Square, with offices in the City. His god is wealth; and his one ambition is to have a son, that the firm may be known as "Dombey and Son." When Paul is born, his ambition is attained; his whole heart is in the boy, and the loss of the mother is but a small matter. The boy's death turns his heart to stone, and he treats his daughter Florence not only with utter indifference, but as an actual interloper. Mr. Dombey marries a second time, but his wife elopes with his manager, James Carker.

Paul Dombey. Son of Mr. Dombey; a delicate, sensitive little boy, quite unequal to the great things expected of him. He is sent to Dr. Blimber's school, but soon gives way under the strain of school discipline. In his short life he wins the love of all who know him, and his sister Florence is especially attached to him. His death is one of the famous passages of fiction. During his last days he is haunted by the sea, and is always wondering what the wild waves are saying.

Florence Dombey. Mr. Dombey's daughter; a pretty, amiable, motherless child, who incurs her father's hatred because she lives and thrives while her younger brother, Paul, weakens and dies. Florence hungers to be loved, but her father has no love to bestow on her. She marries Walter Gay.

Domdaniel (Lat. *domus,* house or home; *Danielis,* of Daniel). A fabled abode of evil spirits, gnomes, and enchanters, "under the roots of the ocean" off Tunis, or elsewhere. It first appears in Chaves and Cazotte's *Continuation of the Arabian Nights* (1788–1793), was introduced by Southey into his THALABA, and used by Carlyle as synonymous with a den of iniquity.

Domesday Book. The book containing a record of the census or survey of England, giving the ownership, extent, value, etc., of all the different holdings, undertaken by order of William the Conqueror in 1086. It is in Latin, is written on vellum, and consists of two volumes. The value of all estates is given, firstly, as in the time of the Confessor; secondly, when bestowed by the Conqueror; and, thirdly, at the time of the survey. It is also called *The King's Book,* and *The Winchester Roll* because it was kept there. It was printed in facsimile in 1783 and 1816.

The book was so called from A.S. *dōm,* judgment, because every case of dispute was decided by an appeal to these registers. Edgar Lee Masters gave the title to a volume of poetry (1920), a sort of sequel to his SPOON RIVER ANTHOLOGY in which the coroner investigating the mysterious death of Elenor Murray searches out all the remote causes.

Domett, Alfred (1811–1887). English poet and colonial administrator; subject of BROWNING's poem *Waring.*

Domiduca. The Roman deity who presided over infants when they were away from their parents.

Dominic, St. See under SAINT.

Dominicans. An order of preaching friars, instituted by St. Dominic in 1215, and introduced into England (at Oxford) in 1221. They were formerly called in England *Black Friars,* from their black dress, and in France *Jacobins,* because their mother-establishment in Paris was in the Rue St. Jacques.

dominie. A schoolmaster, a pedagogue. Chiefly Scots. As Dominie Sampson in Scott's *Guy Mannering.*

Dominick, Friar or **Father.** The titular hero of Dryden's comedy, THE SPANISH FRIAR, a kind of ecclesiastical Falstaff, a most immoral, licentious Dominican, who for money would prostitute even the Church and Holy Scriptures.

> He is a huge, fat, religious gentleman . . . big enough to be a pope. His gills are as rosy as a turkey-cock's. His big belly walks in state before him, like a harbinger; and his gouty legs come limping after it. Never was such a tun of devotion seen.—Dryden, *The Spanish Fryar,* ii. 3.

Dominion Day. In Canada a legal holiday, July 1, celebrated as the anniversary of the proclamation of the Dominion in 1867.

Domnei, A Comedy of Woman Worship. A novel by James Branch CABELL (1920) originally published, in 1913 under the title *The Soul of Melicent.* It is a story of the unconquerable love of Perion and Melicent, two medieval lovers who are separated by a rival lover, Demetrios of Anatolia, who keeps Melicent captive for long years; but the true lovers win through to happiness at last. The scene is laid in POICTESME and the heroine, Melicent, is the daughter of Count Manuel, the hero of FIGURES OF EARTH.

Domus Aurea (*Lat.*). Golden House. A palace of the emperor Nero at or near the site of the Colosseum; site of many banqueting orgies.

Domus Procerum (*Lat.*). House of Lords.

don. A man of mark, an aristocrat. At the universities the masters, fellows, and noblemen are termed *dons.* The word is the Spanish form of Lat. *dominus.*

Don Adriano de Armado. A pompous Spaniard in LOVE'S LABOUR'S LOST by Shakespeare. He has "a mint of phrases in his brain."

Donald and Dorothy. A famous children's book by Mary Mapes DODGE.

Don Alvaro. The husband of MENCIA OF MOSQUERA in Le Sage's *Gil Blas;* also a character in Verdi's opera, LA FORZA DEL DESTINO.

Donatello. Real name **Donato di Niccolò di Betto Bardi** (1386?–1466). Italian sculptor of early Renaissance. Deserves to be called the founder of modern sculpture on account of his realistic characterization and stress on dynamic action. Associate of Ghiberti and Brunelleschi. His best works are in Florence, others in Padua, Naples, and Siena.

Donatello, Count. The irresponsible faunlike Italian who gives the title to Hawthorne's MARBLE FAUN.

Donati, Gemma. Wife of DANTE ALIGHIERI, married some time before 1298. She is believed to be the "second lady" in LA VITA NUOVA, who takes pity on the poet when BEATRICE dies.

Donation of Constantine. See DECRETALS.

Donati's comet. An unusually brilliant triple-tailed comet discovered in 1858 by G. B. Donati. Its period is about 2,800 years.

Donatus. Short for **Donatus de octibus partibus orationis.** Also known as **Donatus pro puerilis.** The most famous Latin grammar, the only book without pictures issued as a BLOCK BOOK. Named after its author Aelius Donatus, Roman grammarian of the fourth century, who was one of the instructors of St. Jerome. Original title *Ars grammatica.*

Don Carlos. (1) The name of several tragedies, notably one by SCHILLER (1786), based on the life of Don Carlos, son of Philip II of Spain, and dealing with his unhappy love for Elizabeth of Valois, who for reasons of state marries his father, and his fatal connection with the revolt against his father in the Netherlands. There is an opera by Verdi (1867) based on Schiller's tragedy. Other dramas on the same theme include one by Otway in English (1672), by M. de Chénier in French (1789) and by Alfieri in Italian about the same time.

(2) *Don Carlos* (Charles V) is one of the chief characters in Victor Hugo's drama HERNANI and Verdi's opera *Ernani,* founded on the play.

(3) In Verdi's opera LA FORZA DEL DESTINO, Leonora's revengeful brother is named *Don Carlos di Vargas.*

Don César de Bazan. (1) The chivalrous bandit chief in Victor Hugo's *Ruy Blas.* Hero of a French comedy of this name, and of an opera by Massenet.

(2) Title of a French comedy by Dumanoir and D'Ennery (1844).

(3) Title of an opera by Massenet (1872).

Don Florestan, see FLORESTAN.

Don Giovanni. An opera by MOZART (1787), book by Da Ponte. The plot deals with the adventures of the Spanish libertine DON JUAN. After he and his servant Leporello have put through one piece of villainy after another, the statue of a nobleman Don Juan has murdered appears and takes him off to the infernal regions. A second title of the opera is *The Marble Guest.*

Donizetti, Gaetano (1797–1848). Italian composer. His best-known operas are LUCREZIA BORGIA, LUCIA DI LAMMERMOOR and LA FAVORITA.

Don Juan. Don Juan Tenorio, the hero of a large number of plays and poems, as well as of Mozart's opera, DON GIOVANNI, was the son of a leading family of Seville in the 14th century, and killed the commandant of Ulloa after seducing his daughter. To put an end to his debaucheries the Franciscan monks enticed him to their monastery and killed him, telling the people that he had been carried off to hell by the statue of the commandant, which was in the grounds.

His name has become a synonym for a rake, roué or aristocratic libertine, and in Mozart's opera (1787), Don Giovanni's valet, Leporello, says his master has "in Italy 700 mistresses, in Germany 800, in Turkey and France 91, in Spain 1,003." His dissolute life was first dramatized by Gabriel Tellez in the 17th century, then by Molière in his *Don Juan ou le festin de Pierre,* also by Corneille, Shadwell, Grabbe (German), Dumas, and others, and in the 20th century by George Bernard Shaw (third act of *Man and Superman,* 1903), Bataille, and Rostand (*La Dernière nuit de Don Juan*).

In Byron's well-known poem *Don Juan* (1819–1824), when Juan is sixteen years old he gets into trouble with Donna Julia, and is sent by his mother, then a widow, on his travels. His adventures in the Isles of Greece, at the Russian Court, in England, etc., form the story of the poem, which, though it extends to sixteen cantos and nearly 16,000 lines, is incomplete.

Byron's Don Juan is not the legendary character except in name and in the fact that he is a young Spanish aristocrat. His adventures include amatory episodes, but his restless, romantic, gloomy temperament is quite distinct from the gallant frivolity of the traditional Don Juan. See also HAIDEE; DUDU.

Donkin. A Cockney sailor in Conrad's NIGGER OF THE NARCISSUS.

Donn-Byrne, Brian Oswald (1889–1928). Irish-American novelist, writing under the name of Donn Byrne. He was the author of novels and tales marked by imagination and fantasy, including *Messer Marco Polo* (1921); *The Changeling* (1923); *Blind Raftery* (1924); *Hangman's House* (1926); *Destiny Bay* (1928); and *Field of Honor* (1929).

Donne, John (1572–1631). English poet, greatest of the METAPHYSICAL POETS, imitated often with small success by a number of the younger poets of his day. Donne was Roman Catholic in early life, but was converted to Anglicanism in 1614 and ordained in 1615, six years later becoming Dean of St. Paul's. His poetry, including both his early ironic and erotic verse and his later religious poems, is marked by intellectual power, deep learning, and intense emotion. His imagery, to which the adjective "metaphysical" was chiefly applied, is powerful and striking, drawn from Scholastic philosophy (see SCHOLASTICISM), the science of the day, trades and professions, and the simple, commonplace things of everyday life ignored by the Elizabethan lyric poets. His meter is irregular and dramatic, censured by conservative critics but praised by others. His sermons, widely celebrated in their day, show similar characteristics to his poetry.

Donne's poems were published in 1633 and were very popular during the next generation. He was almost unknown, however, during the 18th century and was disapproved of by Samuel JOHNSON. A few of the Romantics liked him, but it was only in the 20th century that interest in him was revived to any considerable extent. Critics publicized his work, among them T. S. ELIOT being the most outstanding, and a number of young poets, notably Hart CRANE and the AGRARIANS, came under his influence. The use of a quotation from one of his sermons in the title of the best-selling novel FOR WHOM THE BELL TOLLS, by Ernest HEMINGWAY (1940) brought Donne to the attention of a new audience. Among his most famous poems are *Go and Catch a Falling Star; Twicknam Garden; The Flea; The Ecstasy; The Relic; Death, Be Not Proud; The Progress of the Soul* (1601), a satire dealing with metempsychosis and heresy, left incomplete; and numerous elegies, epistles, satires, and the like.

Donnerwetter (*Ger.*). Literally, thunderstorm. An exclamation of astonishment. A more emphatic form is *Himmel Herrgott Donnerwetter.*

Donnithorne, Arthur. A prominent character in George Eliot's ADAM BEDE.

Donnybrook Fair. This fair, held in August from the time of King John, till 1855, was noted for its bacchanalian orgies and light-hearted rioting. Hence it is proverbial for a disorderly gathering or a regular rumpus. The village was a mile and a half southeast of Dublin, and is now one of its suburbs.

Donovan, William Joseph (1883–). American army officer, known as "Wild Bill." In World War I, as an infantry colonel, he was awarded the Congressional Medal of Honor. In World War II, he was United States co-ordinator of Information (1941–1942) and head of the Office of Strategic Services. Brigadier general (1943).

Don Pasquale. The title and hero of a comic opera by Donizetti (1845).

Don Q. A fictional Spanish outlaw and *sequestrador,* in stories by Hesketh Prichard (1904, 1906, 1909). Filmed by DOUGLAS FAIRBANKS.

Don Quixote de la Mancha. A satirical novel by CERVANTES, published at Madrid, Pt. i, 1605, Pt. ii, 1615. Don Quixote is a gaunt country gentleman of La Mancha, gentle and dignified, affectionate and simple-minded, but so crazed by reading books of knight-errantry, especially the AMADIS, that he believes himself called upon to redress the wrongs of the whole world, and actually goes forth to avenge the oppressed and run a tilt with their oppressors. Hence, a *Quixotic* man, or a *Don Quixote,* is a dreamy, unpractical, but essentially good, man—one with a "bee in his bonnet."

Don Quixote's lady love is the fair DULCINEA. He engages for his squire Sancho Panza, a middle-aged ignorant rustic, selfish but full of good sense, a gourmand but attached to his master, shrewd but credulous. The knight thinks wind-mills to be giants, flocks of sheep to be armies, inns to be castles, and galley-slaves oppressed gentlemen; but the squire sees them in their true light. Ultimately, the knight is restored to his right mind, and dies like a peaceful Christian. See also WINDMILLS.

> It seemed unto him [Don Quixote] very requisite and behooveful . . . that he himself should become a knight-errant, and go throughout the world, with his horse and armour, to seek adventures, and practise in person all that he had read was used by knights of yore; revenging all kinds of injuries, and offering himself to occasions and dangers, which, being once happily achieved, might gain him eternal renown.—Cervantes, *Don Quixote* (*Shelton's tr.* 1612).

It is generally agreed that Cervantes meant his novel to be a satire on the exaggerated chivalric romances of his time, but some critics have interpreted it as an ironic story of an idealist frustrated and mocked in a materialistic world, a forerunner of Voltaire's CANDIDE, SANCHO PANZA representing the materialist viewpoint.

Don Sebastian. A tragedy by DRYDEN (1690). The hero is Sebastian, king of Portugal, defeated and taken prisoner by the Moors in 1574. See also SEBASTIAN.

Dony. Florimel's dwarf. Cf. Spenser, *Faërie Queene,* III, v. V, ii.

doodlesack (Ger. *Dudelsack,* literally "tootling bag"). The Scotch bagpipe.

Dooley, Mr. A famous humorous personage created by the American journalist, F. P. DUNNE. A middle-aged Irish-American and the presiding genius of a saloon in Archey

Road, Chicago, Mr. Dooley is never at a loss for an occasion or a topic on which to exercise his ready wit and common sense. His friend, Mr. Hennessey, usually meets him half way, and his neighbor, Mr. McKenna, is full of skeptical questions. Mr. Dooley's reputation was made in the newspapers at the time of the Spanish-American War. *Mr. Dooley in Peace and War* appeared in 1898. It was followed by *Mr. Dooley in the Hearts of His Countrymen* (1899), *Mr. Dooley's Philosophy* (1900), *Mr. Dooley's Opinions* (1901), *Observations by Mr. Dooley* (1902), *Mr. Dooley's Dissertations* (1906), *Mr. Dooley Says* (1910) and *Mr. Dooley: On Making a Will and Other Necessary Evils* (1919).

Doolin of Mayence. The hero of a French CHANSON DE GESTE of the 14th century, and of a 15th century prose romance. He was the father of OGIER THE DANE.

Doolin's sword is Merveilleuse (literally, wonderful).

Doolittle. The picturesque, disreputable old dustman in Shaw's drama, PYGMALION.

Doolittle, Hilda, see H. D.

Doolittle, Lt. Gen. **James Harold.** In World War II awarded Congressional Medal of Honor for leading a carrier-based bombing raid over Tokyo on April 18, 1942. At 1500 ft. 16 tons of bombs and incendiaries were dropped. The Japanese were caught completely unaware. Eight of the pilots who did not successfully crash-land in China, were captured and put to death by the Japanese.

Doomsday Book, see DOMESDAY BOOK.

Doon. A river in Ayrshire, Scotland, celebrated in the poems of Robert BURNS.

Doone, Lorna, see LORNA DOONE.

Dop Doctor, The (1910). A novel by Richard Dehan, pseudonym of Clotilde GRAVES (1863–1932). The term *dop doctor,* as used in South Africa, stands for a quack who prescribes brandy for every disease.

Dopey. A lovable character in Walt DISNEY's production of SNOW WHITE AND THE SEVEN DWARFS.

Doppelgänger (*Ger.* doubleganger). A double, especially one of the kind favored by romantic authors like E. T. A. HOFFMANN, in whom the distinction between reality and apparition is blurred.

Dora. (1) The child-wife of David Copperfield. See SPENLOW, DORA.

(2) A narrative poem by TENNYSON (1842).

Dorado, El, see EL DORADO.

Doramin. The old native chief in Conrad's LORD JIM.

Dorante. A name introduced into three of Molière's comedies. In *Les Fâcheux* he is a courtier devoted to the chase. In the play *L'École des femmes* he is a chevalier. In *Le Bourgeois gentilhomme* he is a count in love with the Marchioness Dorimène.

Dorax. In Dryden's tragedy, DON SEBASTIAN, the assumed name of Don Alonzo of Alcazar, when he deserts Sebastian, king of Portugal, turns renegade, and joins the emperor of Barbary.

Dorcas Society. A woman's circle for making clothing for the poor. So called from Dorcas, in *Acts* ix. 39, who made "coats and garments" for widows.

Doré, Paul Gustave (1833–1883). French illustrator of Rabelais, Balzac, *The Divine Comedy, Paradise Lost,* The Bible, etc.

Dorgan, Thomas Aloysius (1877–1929). American cartoonist and sports writer in the San Francisco *Bulletin* and New York *Journal.* Known as Tad.

Doria, Andrea (1468?–1560). Genoese admiral; called "Father of Peace" and "Liberator of Genoa." One of the main characters in SCHILLER'S *Fiesko.*

Dorian Gray, The Picture of. See WILDE, OSCAR.

Dorian mode. One of the four principal modes of ancient Greek music. Its character is bold and grave. See also LYDIAN MODE, PHRYGIAN MODE; MYXOLYDIAN MODE.

Doric. Pertaining to Doris, one of the divisions of ancient Greece, or to its inhabitants, a simple, pastoral people.

Doric dialect. The dialect spoken by the natives of Doris, in Greece. It was broad and hard. Hence, any broad dialect like that of rustics. Bloomfield and Robert Burns are examples of British Doric.

Doric land. Greece, Doris being a part of Greece.

Doric order. The oldest, strongest, and simplest of the Grecian ORDERS of architecture.

the Doric reed. Pastoral poetry. Everything Doric was very plain, but cheerful, chaste and solid.

Dorigen. The heroine of Chaucer's *Franklin's Tale,* which was taken from Boccaccio's DECAMERON (X. v), the original being in the Hindu *Vetála Panchavinsati.* She is married to Arviragus, but was greatly beloved by Aurelius, to whom she has been long known. Aurelius tries to win her, but Dorigen will not listen to him till the rocks round the coast of Britain are removed "and there n'is no stone yseen." Aurelius, by the aid of a magician, causes them all to disappear, and claims his reward. Dorigen is very sad, but her husband insists that she keep her word, and she goes to meet Aurelius, who, when he sees her grief and hears what Arviragus has counseled, says he would rather die than injure so true a wife and noble a gentleman. See DIANORA.

Dorimant. A witty, aristocratic libertine in Etherege's comedy, *The Man of Mode* (1676), said to have been drawn from the Earl of Rochester. See WILMOT, JOHN. The name later came to be used for any gay, unprincipled young man.

Dorimene. In Molière's comedy *Le Mariage Forcé* (1664), a young girl who marries SGANARELLE, an old man of sixty-three. In *Le Cocu imaginaire,* she is Sganarelle's wife.

Dormouse, The. A character in *Alice in Wonderland*. Thrust into a teapot by the Mad Hatter and March Hare.

The word *dormouse* means probably "sleeping mouse" (from Fr. *dormir* "to sleep"). Cf. Ger. *Schlafratte* "sleeping rat" for the same animal.

Dorothea. The heroine of Goethe's poem HERMANN AND DOROTHEA.

Dorothea, St. See under SAINT.

Dorothy la Desirée. In Cabell's JURGEN, the girl whom Jurgen loves as a young man. She jilts him to become a countess, but when he is given his year of renewed youth, he sees once more by magic the young and beautiful girl of his ideals. Dorothy la Desirée is one of the daughters of MANUEL, the hero of FIGURES OF EARTH.

dorp. A hamlet. Rare or poetic.

> No neighbouring dorp, no lodging to be found,
> But bleaky plains, and bare unhospitable ground.
> Dryden, *Hind and Panther.*

As a word of Dutch origin, meaning village, still alive in South Africa.

Dorrit, Amy. Heroine of Dickens' novel, LITTLE DORRIT.

Dorr's Rebellion. A rising in Rhode Island (1842) headed by Thomas Wilson Dorr (1805–1854) seeking to modernize the state constitution, extend suffrage, etc. Dorr was elected governor in 1842. The opposition elected Samuel King and both men were inaugurated. Dorr's attempt to seize the arsenal at Providence was frustrated by King. The Supreme Court sentenced Dorr, but he was released. Cf. the long poem on Dorr by Winfield Townley Scott.

Dorset, Thomas Sackville, Earl of, see SACKVILLE, THOMAS.

Dorsey, George Amos (1868–1931). American anthropologist. Curator at Field Museum, Chicago (1898–1915). Lecturer New School for Social Research, New York (from 1925). Wrote *Why We Behave like Human Beings* (1925), etc.

Dory, John, see JOHN DORY.

Doryphorus (*Gr.,* a spear-bearer). A statue of an athlete bearing a spear by the Greek sculptor Polyclitus (5th century B. C.). It embodies the "correct," i.e., the conventionally accepted proportions, called the CANON, of the athletic type. The best-known replica was found in the palaestra at Pompeii.

do-see-do. In mountain dances, for *dos-à-dos* (*Fr.* back to back). To dance *do-see-do* refers to a figure in which the partners pass back to back.

Dos Passos, John Roderigo (1896–). American novelist and poet, best known for his stylistic and structural experimentation in prose, which is outstandingly exemplified in his trilogy *U.S.A.* (1938), consisting of *The 42nd Parallel* (1930), *1919* (1932), and *The Big Money* (1936). His technique suggests the influence of James JOYCE and achieves an almost poetic stylization in its rigid detachment and the absence of any mediation by the author between his story and his audience. Dos Passos developed from a preoccupation with the conflict between the sensitive individual and the conventions of society, to a broader, sociological outlook, influenced by Marxian and Communist doctrines. (See MARXISM IN LITERATURE; PROLETARIAN LITERATURE.) Later he lost faith in the Communist program. In addition to *U.S.A.,* his works include *One Man's Initiation* (1920) and THREE SOLDIERS (1921), war novels; *A Push-cart at the Curb* (1922), poems; *Rosinante to the Road Again* (1922), essays on Spain; *Streets of Night* (1923) and MANHATTAN TRANSFER (1925), fiction; *Orient Express* (1927), a travel book; *The Garbage Man* (produced as *The Moon Is a Gong*) (1926), *Airways, Inc.* (1929), and *Fortune Heights* (1933), dramas, collected as *Three Plays* (1934); *In All Countries* (1934) and *Journeys Between Wars* (1938), travel books; *Adventures of a Young Man* (1939; see YOUNG MAN, ADVENTURES OF), a novel; and THE GROUND WE STAND ON (1941), historical essays and sketches. Dos Passos is considered one of the most original and most important of 20th-century American novelists.

Dostoyevsky, Fyodor Mikhailovich (1821–1881). Russian novelist, considered one of the greatest European novelists of the 19th century. His books are distinguished by their skillful character studies, especially in the realm of abnormal psychology, their sympathy for the poor and the defeated, their dramatic dialogue and passages of intense introspection, and their penetrating portrayals of life in 19th-century Russia, especially among the intellectual and revolutionary classes. Many of his novels reflect his own experiences, for Dostoyevsky was an epileptic, like several of his best-known characters, and he himself was active in the revolutionary movement in Russia. In 1849 he was condemned to death and was actually standing before the firing squad when his sentence was commuted to hard labor in the Siberian salt mines.

Among Dostoyevsky's works are *Poor Folk* (1846); THE HOUSE OF THE DEAD (1861); *Letters from the Underworld* (1864); CRIME AND PUNISHMENT (1866); *The Insulted and Injured* (1867); THE IDIOT (1868–1869); THE POSSESSED (1871); *A Raw Youth* (1871); *Journal of an Author* (1876–1877); THE BROTHERS KARAMAZOV (1879–1880). His stories, published in various editions, include *The Double, An Honest Thief, White Nights, Nyetochka Nyezhvanov, The Friend of the Family, The Gambler, The Eternal Husband.*

Dostoyevsky was an admirer of Charles DICKENS, and several of his comic, hypocritical, or villainous characters suggest a development of Dickens' method of characterization.

Dot. In Dickens' *Cricket on the Hearth.* See PEERYBINGLE.

Dotheboys Hall. A school in Dickens' NICHOLAS NICKLEBY where boys are taken in and done for by Mr. Wackford Squeers, a puffing, ignorant, overbearing brute, who starves them and teaches them nothing.

It is said that Squeers was a caricature of a Mr. Shaw, a Yorkshire schoolmaster; but Mr. Shaw has been defended as a kind-hearted man, whose boys were well fed, happy, and not ill taught. Like Squeers he had only one eye, and one daughter. The ruthless exposure of this kind of "school" led to the closing or reformation of many of them.

Douai Bible. See also under BIBLE, THE ENGLISH. The English college at Douai was founded by William Allen (afterwards cardinal) in 1568. The Douai Bible translates such words as *repentance* by the word *penance,* etc., and the whole contains notes by Roman Catholic divines.

Doubleday, Abner (1819–1893). American army officer of Huguenot descent. Reputedly inventor, while attending school at Cooperstown, N.Y., of baseball (adoption of diamond-shaped field, assignment of playing positions, etc.). Buried in Arlington National Cemetery.

Double Dealer, The. A comedy by Congreve (1693). The hero is the sinister scoundrel Maskwell whose double-dealing was more than the public was ready to accept in a comedy.

Double Trouble. A novel by Herbert Quick (1905).

Doubting Castle. In Bunyan's PILGRIM'S PROGRESS, the castle of GIANT DESPAIR, into which Christian and Hopeful are thrust, but from which they escape by means of the key called "Promise."

doughboy. An American soldier. The term was in use long before World War I, when it was popularized. Probably—though for no very clear reason—from *doughboy* in the sense of "a boiled dumpling of raised dough" of the kind served in the navy.

Doughty, Charles Montagu (1843–1926). English traveler and author, best known for his *Travels in Arabia Deserta* (1888), in which his curious style combines the archaic English of the Chaucerian and Elizabethan periods with Arabic.

Douglas. A family famed in Scotch history, legend and romance. There were two branches, the *Black Douglases* or senior branch and the *Red Douglases,* who came to the fore later. They are prominent in Scott's novels, notably the following:

(1) Sir *James,* the first of the Black Douglases, hero of CASTLE DANGEROUS known as "the Good Sir James." This was also the Douglas which was such a terror to the English that the women used to frighten their unruly children by saying they would "make the Black Douglas take them." He first appears in *Castle Dangerous* as "Knight of the Tomb." The following nursery rhyme refers to him:

> Hush ye, hush ye, little pet ye;
> Hush ye, hush ye, do not fret ye;
> The Black Douglas shall not get thee.
> Sir W. Scott, *Tales of a Grandfather.*

(2) *Archibald the Grim,* natural son of "the Good Sir James." He is prominent in *The Fair Maid of Perth.*

(3) *James Douglas,* earl *of Morton,* one of the Red Douglases. He figures prominently in THE MONASTERY and THE ABBOT.

(4) *Ellen Douglas.* Heroine of Scott's narrative poem, *The Lady of the Lake.*

the Douglas larder. The flour, meal, wheat, and malt of Douglas Castle, emptied on the floor by good Lord James Douglas, in 1307, when he took the castle from the English garrison. Having staved in all the barrels of food, he next emptied all the wine and ale, and then, having slain the garrison, threw the dead bodies into this disgusting mess, "to eat, drink, and be merry." Scott gives the story in his *Tales of a Grandfather.*

See also BELL THE CAT.

The Douglas Tragedy. A ballad in Scott's *Border Minstrelsy,* telling how Lord William steals away Lady Margaret Douglas and is pursued by her father and two brothers. A fight ensues; the father and his two sons are sore wounded; Lord William, also wounded, creeps to his mother's house and there dies; and the lady dies next morning.

Douglas, Gawain or **Gavin** (1474?–1522). Scottish poet, Bishop of Dunkeld. He was the author of *The Palace of Honor* (1553?) and *King Hart* (first printed in 1786), two allegorical poems, and a translation of the *Aeneid* (1553) which is called the earliest translation of the Latin classics into English. Douglas was a member of the group called the SCOTTISH CHAUCERIANS.

Douglas, George Norman (1868–). English novelist, best-known as the author of SOUTH WIND (1917). His other works include: *They Went* (1921); *Together* (1923); *Fountains in the Sand* (1925); *Experiments* (1925); *Old Calabria* (1928); *Birds and Beasts of the Greek Anthology* (1929); *One Day* (1929); *Three of Them* (1930); *Goodbye to Western Culture* (1930); *Summer Islands* (1931); *Looking Back* (1933), an autobiographical volume; and several treatises on zoölogy, geology, and archeology. His books deal chiefly with the ancient, semi-Greek islands south of Italy in the Mediterranean Sea, Douglas having lived for some time on the island of Capri.

Douglas, Lloyd Cassel (1877–). American Lutheran clergyman, author of best-selling novels of a piously didactic, inspirational character. The best-known are *Magnificent Obsession* (1929), *Green Light* (1935), and *The Robe* (1943), a phenomenal best-seller.

Douglas, Stephen Arnold (1813–1861). American Democratic political leader. Famous for platform debates with Abraham Lincoln on slavery (1858), upholding the doctrine of *squatter sovereignty* in the Territories. Defeated by Lincoln but afterwards faithful supporter of his opponent's administration. Nicknamed "the little giant."

Douglas fir. A tall evergreen, the most important timber tree in the Western U.S., known in the lumber trade as *red fir* or *Oregon pine*. Like the Douglas squirrel, named after the Scottish botanist David Douglas (1798–1834), who discovered it in 1825.

Douglass, Frederick (1817?–1895). American Negro lecturer and writer. Called in consultation by Lincoln. The *Narrative of the Life of Frederick Douglas* (1845) is his autobiography, relating his experiences as the illegitimate son of a white man and a Negro slave and his final escape to freedom.

Dove Cottage. Home of William and Dorothy WORDSWORTH at Grasmere in the English Lake Country from 1799 to 1807.

Dove Dulcet. Literally, the "sweet-sounding dove." A pseudonym used by Christopher Morley for some of his columnar contributions.

Dover Beach. A well-known poem by Matthew ARNOLD (1867), expressing his pessimism with regard to the future of industrial and scientific civilization:

> And we are here as on a darkling plain
> Swept with confused alarms of struggle and flight,
> Where ignorant armies clash by night.

Dove's Nest, The. An unfinished short story by Katherine MANSFIELD, published in 1923. It presents a satirical picture of Mrs. Fawcett and her daughter Mildred, two Englishwomen living together on the French Riviera, who are thrown into a flurry of excitement on the visit of Mr. Walter Prodger, a touring American.

Dowden, Edward (1843–1913). Irish Shakespearean critic. *Shakspere, his Mind and Art* (1875). Also author of a *Life of Shelley* (1886).

Dowel, Dobet, Dobest. Allegorical characters in PIERS PLOWMAN (*passus* ix).

Dowie, John Alexander (1847–1907). American leader of a religious sect, born in Scotland. Built a wooden tabernacle in Chicago in 1890 and attracted a large following through his faith healing. Cf. William Vaughn Moody's play *The Faith Healer* (1909) which may have been inspired by Dowie.

Dowland, John (1563?–?1626), and his son **Robert Dowland** (1585?–?1641). English lutists. Cf. the poem by MILTON to John Dowland.

Dowlas, Mr. A generic name for a linen-draper, who sells dowlas, a coarse linen cloth, so called from Daoulas, in Brittany, where it was manufactured.

> *Mrs. Quickly.* I bought you a dozen of shirts to your back.
> *Falstaff.* Dowlas, filthy dowlas: I have given them away to bakers' wives, and they have made bolters of them.
> *Quick.* Now, as I am true woman, holland of eight shillings an ell.
>
> Shakespeare, 1 *Henry IV*, iii. 3.

Downing Street. A name often given to the heads of the British Government collectively, from No. 10 Downing Street (Westminster), the official town residence of the Prime Minister, where the meetings of the Cabinet are usually held. The street was named in honor of Sir George Downing (d. 1684), a noted Parliamentarian and ambassador, who served under both Cromwell and Charles II.

Down the River. A narrative poem by Roscoe W. Brink (1922), in free verse, divided into short sections, by seasons, and telling a realistic story. It is somewhat like the New England poems of Amy Lowell called *The Overgrown Pasture.*

Dowsabell. A common name for a sweetheart, especially an unsophisticated country girl, in poems of Elizabethan times. It is the Fr. *douce et belle,* sweet and beautiful.

It were not good . . . to cast away as pretty a dowsabell as any could chance to see in a summer's day.—*The London Prodigal,* IV, i (1605).

Drayton wrote a poem, *The Ballad of Dowsabell.*

Dowson, Ernest (1867–1900). English poet, associated with the Aesthetic movement in England during the latter part of the 19th century which was led by Walter PATER and Oscar WILDE. Dowson is best known for his poem CYNARA (1896), properly entitled *Non Sum Qualis Eram . . .* , with the following refrain: "I have been faithful to thee, Cynara, in my fashion."

doxology. A short hymn or psalm expressing praise of God. The greater doxology is the *Gloria in Excelsis.* The lesser doxology is the *Gloria Patri,* or especially the stanza, from the closing lines of two hymns by Bishop Ken (1637–1711):

Praise God from whom all blessings flow!
Praise him all creatures here below!
Praise him above, Ye heavenly host!
Praise Father, Son, and Holy Ghost!

doxy. A mistress or sweetheart. Generally in a bad sense.

Doyle, Sir **Arthur Conan** (1859–1930). English novelist, best known for his series of novels and short stories concerning Sherlock HOLMES and for his historical novels, *Micah Clarke* (1889) and *The White Company* (1891). Doyle was much interested in spiritualism and wrote a *History of Spiritualism* (1926). His Professor CHALLENGER and Brigadier GERARD are also notable creations.

Doyle, John. A pseudonym used by Robert GRAVES in publishing *The Marmosite's Miscellany* (1925), a book of poetry.

D'Oyly Carte, see CARTE, RICHARD D'OYLY.

Dr. For titles beginning with *Dr.,* see also under DOCTOR.

Drachenfels (*Ger.* Dragon-rock). So called from the legend that it was the home of the dragon slain by Siegfried, the hero of the NIBELUNGENLIED.

The castled crag of Drachenfels
Frowns o'er the wide and winding Rhine,
Whose breast of waters broadly swells
Between the banks which bear the vine.
Byron, *Childe Harold.* iii. 55.

Dr. Adrian. A novel by Couperus. See SMALL SOULS.

Draconian code. One very severe Draco was an Athenian law-maker of the 7th century B.C., and the first to produce a written code of laws for Athens. As nearly every violation of his laws was a capital offense, Demades the orator said "that Draco's code was written in blood."

Draft of XXX Cantos, A. See CANTOS.

Draft Riots. Demonstrations in opposition to the draft for the Federal Army, in New York City, July 13–16, 1863. About 1000 people were killed. The property damage was great. Suppressed by police and militia.

dragoman. In the Near East, an interpreter, chiefly one in the employ of an embassy or consulate or hired as a guide by tourists.

dragon. The Greek word *drakon* comes ultimately from a verb meaning "to see," to "look at," and more remotely "to watch" and "to flash."

A dragon is a fabulous winged crocodile, usually represented as of large size, with a serpent's tail; whence the words serpent and dragon are sometimes interchangeable. The word was used in the Middle Ages as the symbol of sin in general and paganism in particular, the metaphor being derived from *Rev.* xii. 9, where Satan is termed "the great dragon" and *Ps.* xci. 13, where it is said that the saints "shall trample the dragon under their feet." Hence, in Christian art the dragon symbolizes Satan or sin, as when represented at the feet of Christ and the Virgin Mary; and St. John the Evangelist is sometimes represented holding a chalice, from which a dragon is issuing.

flying dragon. A meteor.

Chinese dragon. In China, a five-clawed dragon is introduced into pictures and embroidered on state dresses as an amulet. See also DRAGON THRONE.

The Dragon of Wantley. See WANTLEY.

sow dragons' teeth. To foment contentions; to stir up strife or war; especially to do something that is intended to put an end to strife but which brings it about later. See CADMUS.

Among the many saints who are usually pictured with dragons may be mentioned St. Michael, St. George, St. Margaret, Pope Sylvester, St. Samson (Archbishop of Dol), St. Donatus, St. Clement of Metz; St. Romain of Rouen, who destroyed the huge dragon, La Gargouille, which ravaged the Seine; St. Philip the Apostle, who killed another at Hierapolis, in Phrygia; St. Martha, who slew the terrible dragon, Tarasque, at Aix-la-Chapelle; St. Florent, who killed a dragon which haunted the Loire; St. Cado, St. Maudet, and St. Pol, who did similar feats in Brittany; and St. Keyne of Cornwall.

Among the ancient Britons and Welsh the dragon was the national symbol on the war standard; hence the term, PENDRAGON for the *dux bellorum,* or leader in war (*pen* = head or chief).

See also FAFNER; GRENDEL.

Dragon Throne. The imperial throne of China. The dragon (Chinese *lung*) is a symbol of good fortune and hence, as a representation of the beneficent being *yang,* of the emperor.

dragoon. A mounted infantryman. Usually restricted to soldiers of certain regiments. Originally so called after the type of musket, called *dragoon,* with which they were equipped. *Dragoon* is historically a different form of the word *dragon.* The musket was given that name because it spat fire.

Drake, Joseph Rodman (1795–1820). American poet of the early national period. His best-known poem is *The Culprit Fay.*

Drake, an English Epic. A long narrative poem by Alfred Noyes (Eng. 1880–), dealing with the adventures of the famous English sailor and explorer, Sir Francis Drake (1545?–1596).

Drake's drum. A ghostly warning. From a popular legend according to which Sir Francis Drake's drum is heard whenever England is in danger. Immortalized by Sir Henry Newbolt in his poem *Drake's Drum* (1914).

Drama, Father of (French, Spanish, etc.), see under FATHER.

dramatic irony. A theatrical device, consisting in the conscious production by the author of an ironical situation, i.e., a marked incongruity between a character's words and the action; as for instance in Schiller's *Wallenstein* when the hero (not aware of the plot on his life of which the audience has been informed) says before going to bed: "I intend to take a long rest." The understanding of the unintentional play on words imparts to the audience for a moment the rôle of "an omniscient god of the drama."

dramatic unities. See under UNITIES.

dramatis personae. The characters of a drama, novel, or (by extension), of an actual transaction. Often abbreviated to *dram. pers.*

Dramatis Personae is the title of a collection of poems by Robert BROWNING (1864).

dramaturgy. Science or art of dramatic composition or stage performance.

Drang nach Osten (*Ger.* pressure toward the East). The German policy of imperialistic expansion toward the East, much talked of before and during World War I, and also during Germany's rearmament during the 1930's under Adolf HITLER.

Draper, John William (1811–1882). British-born American scientist. Helped found medical school of New York University; renowned for researches in photochemistry, spectrum analysis, etc.; made portrait photography possible through improvements on Daguerre's process.

Drapier's Letters. A series of letters written by Dean SWIFT to the people of Ireland and published in 1724, advising them not to take the copper money coined by William Wood. The patent had been granted to him by George I through the influence of the Duchess of Kendal, the king's mistress, and Wood and the Duchess were to share the profits (40 per cent). These letters, which were signed "M. B. Drapier," crushed the infamous job and the patent was canceled.

Draupadi. A heroine of the great Hindu epic, the MAHABHARATA, the wife won by Arjuna and shared by the five Pandavas.

Draupnir. In Scandinavian mythology, Odin's magic ring, from which every ninth night dropped eight rings equal in size and beauty to itself. It was fashioned by the dwarfs.

Dravot, Daniel. Hero of Kipling's MAN WHO WOULD BE KING.

Drawcansir. A burlesque tyrant in Buckingham's *Rehearsal* (1671); hence, a blustering braggart. The character was a caricature of Dryden's Almanzor in *Conquest of Granada.* Drawcansir's opening speech (he has only three) is:

> He that dares drink, and for that drink dares die,
> And, knowing this, dares yet drink on, am I.
> *Rehearsal,* iv. 1.

which parodies Almanzor's:

> He who dares love, and for that love must die,
> And, knowing this, dares yet love on, am I.
> *Conquest of Granada,* iv. iii.

See also BAYES, BOBADIL.

Drayton, Michael (1563–1631). English poet, considered one of the most representative of the Elizabethan period. His style changed with the changes in taste that took place in his lifetime, and he experimented in all the poetic forms popular in his day, including sonnet, drama, ode, mythological poem, Biblical paraphrase, historical tale, pastoral, and so on. Among his works are *Idea, the Shepherd's Garland* (1593); *Idea's Mirror* (1594); *England's Heroical Epistles* (1597), historical poems modeled on Ovid's *Heroides* which were his most successful poems; *Sonnets to Idea* (1619) (see IDEA); *Polyolbion* (1612, 1622), a topographical poem celebrating the beauty and the heroic glory of England; *Nymphidia* (1627); *The Battle of Agincourt* (1627); and *The Muses' Elysium* (1630).

Dr. Breen's Profession. A novel by W. D. HOWELLS (1881). The heroine, Grace Breen, as the outcome of an unhappy love affair, plunges into the profession of medicine in the effort to make herself of some real service in the world and so find the peace that is otherwise denied her.

dreadnought. Any battleship of the class of the *Dreadnought* which was commissioned by the British navy in 1907.

Dream-Children: A Reverie. One of the best-known essays of Charles LAMB (1822), prompted by the death of the author's brother James. In it, Lamb describes an imaginary conversation held with the children he has never had.

Dreamer, the Immortal. John Bunyan (1628–1688).

dreams, the gates of. There are two, one of ivory and one of horn. Dreams which delude pass through the Ivory Gate, those which come true pass through the Gate of Horn.

> That children dream not the first half-year; that men dream not in some countries, with many more, are unto me sick men's dreams; dreams out of the ivory gate, and visions before midnight.—Sir Thos. Browne, *On Dreams.*

This fancy depends upon two puns: ivory in Greek is *elephas,* and the verb *eliphairo* means "to cheat with empty hopes"; the Greek for horn is *keras,* and the verb *karanoo* means "to accomplish."

Anchises dismisses Aeneas through the ivory gate, on quitting the infernal regions, to indicate the unreality of his vision.

Dream Life. A sequel to Donald G. Mitchell's REVERIES OF A BACHELOR.

Dream of Gerontius, The. Title of a poem by Cardinal Newman. It was set to music in an oratorio by Sir Edward Elgar (1900).

Dream of John Ball, A (1888). A book describing a socialist commonwealth in England, by William Morris. The real John Ball (d. 1381) was an English priest; expounder of the doctrines of Wycliffe; influential in stirring up Wat Tyler's rebellion; executed.

Dream of the Rood, The. An Anglo-Saxon poem, attributed to CYNEWULF in the later years of the 8th century, which describes with intense religious motion a vision seen by the poet of the Crucifixion.

Dream Pedlary. A famous poem by Thomas Lovell BEDDOES.

Dred. A novel by Harriet Beecher STOWE (1856). Dred, the hero, is a runaway slave.

Dred Scott Decision. A famous decision of the U.S. Supreme Court (1856) ruling that a slave was property and had no personal rights. The problem had come up through the fact that Dred Scott, a Negro slave whom his master had taken with him to live on free soil, had sued for his freedom.

Dreikaiser Bund (*Ger.* three Emperors' alliance). Cooperation between the emperors of Germany, Austria and Russia during the years 1872–1879.

Dreiser, Theodore Herman Albert (1871–1945). American novelist and journalist, known for the extreme realism and bitter frankness of his writing, which is in the tradition of NATURALISM. Many critics regard his style as awkward and "muddy." His first novel, SISTER CARRIE (1900), was banned, as was THE 'GENIUS' (1915), because its theme was considered objectionable at the time of publication, and also his most famous novel, AN AMERICAN TRAGEDY (1925), met with the disapproval of the censors and the conservative public. His works include *Jennie Gerhardt* (1911); a "trilogy of desire," designed to illustrate the effects of lust for power and for women and consisting of *The Financier* (1912), *The Titan* (1914) (see COWPERWOOD, FRANK), and THE 'GENIUS'; *Plays of the Natural and Supernatural* (1916) and *The Hand of the Potter* (1919), dramas; *A Hoosier Holiday* (1916), an account of an automobile trip from New York to Indiana; *Free And Other Stories* (1918) and *Twelve Men* (1919), short story collections; *Hey-Rub-a-Dub-Dub!* (1920) and *The Color of a Great City* (1923), essays; *Dreiser Looks at Russia* (1928), an account of a trip to the U.S.S.R.; *A Gallery of Women* (1929), a collection of novelettes; *Fine Furniture* (1930); *Tragic America* (1932), studies of the U.S. during the depression of the time. *Moods* (1926) and *Epitaph* (1930), poetry; *A Traveler at Forty* (1913), *A Book about Myself* (1922), and *Dawn* (1931), autobiographical volumes; *The Bulwark* (1946), a novel, and *The Stoic* (1947), another COWPERWOOD novel. Dreiser was a sensational figure during the 1920's and had a wide influence at that time, inaugurating in *An American Tragedy* the use of actual case-history material in fiction. His brother was **Paul Dresser,** a composer of popular songs of the Tin Pan Alley variety during the first decade of the 20th century. The two collaborated in the composition of *On the Banks of the Wabash Far Away,* a song popular at the time of the Spanish-American War. After Dreiser's death, Howard Mumford Jones wrote in the New York *Times:* "The death of Theodore Dreiser removes from the American scene something primary, brooding and enormous. It is as if a headland crumbled and slid into the sea."

Dreiser Protest. A petition signed by nearly five hundred American writers (1916) protesting the banning by the courts of Dreiser's novel THE 'GENIUS.'

Dresden ware or china. A decorated porcelain made in the former kingdom of Saxony in factories near Dresden and Meissen. Originated by Johann Friedrich Böttger or Böttiger (1682–1719) who, according to a local story, was employed by the Saxon king to make gold.

Dresser, Paul. See under DREISER, THEODORE.

Dressler, Marie (1873–1934), stage name of Leila Koerber, Canadian-born American actress (comédienne). Success on stage and in motion pictures, e.g., *Anna Christie, Tillie's Punctured Romance* (with Charlie Chaplin) and several *Tugboat Annie* films. Made famous a song, "Heaven Will Protect the Working Girl."

Drew, Daniel (1797–1879). American financier. Defeated Cornelius Vanderbilt in the stock-market battle known as the "Erie War" (1866–1868). With James Fisk and Jay Gould he reaped a fortune by raising the price of gold and causing a country-wide depression. Later bankrupt.

Drew, John (1827–1862). Irish-born American actor. On American stage, he gained success as portrayer of Irish rôles, notably as Sir Lucius O'Trigger in Sheridan's *Rivals*. His wife **Louisa Drew** (1820–1897) was also an actress. Their son, **John Drew** (1853–1927), born in Philadelphia, was a notable actor and leading man. Excelled in comedies of manners. Uncle of Ethel, John, and Lionel BARRYMORE.

Dreyfus, Alfred (1859–1935). An officer of the French artillery, of Jewish descent, who was convicted in 1894 on a charge of having betrayed military secrets, degraded and sent to Devil's Island. In 1899 the first trial was annulled. He was brought back to France, retried, and again condemned, but shortly afterwards pardoned, though it was not until 1914 that he was finally and completely rehabilitated. See also BERGERET.

Feeling with regard to the Dreyfus case was strong in France, especially among the intellectuals. Émile ZOLA, the novelist, wrote a pamphlet entitled *J'Accuse* (1898), heatedly attacking the military authorities who had indicted Dreyfus, with the result that Zola himself was sentenced to prison and had to flee to England for a time. Marcel Proust's REMEMBRANCE OF THINGS PAST gives an excellent picture of the alignment of French opinion on the case and of the way in which Dreyfusards and Jews were regarded by the fashionable society of the time.

D'ri and I. A novel by Irving Bacheller (*Am.* 1901). The hero is the hired man, Darius Olin, nicknamed D'ri and the story centers about his adventures and those of his employer's son, Ramon Bell, during the War of 1812.

driver of Europe (cocher de l'Europe). So the Empress of Russia used to call the Duc de Choiseul (1719–1785), minister of Louis XV, because he had spies all over Europe, and thus ruled its political cabals.

Dr. Jekyll and Mr. Hyde, see under JEKYLL.

Dr. Lavendar's People. A volume of stories by Margaret Deland. See under LAVENDAR.

Dr. Luke of the Labrador. A narrative by Norman Duncan based on the career of Sir Wilfred Grenfell, a medical missionary in Labrador.

Dr. Marigold's Prescriptions, Christmas number of *All the Year Round* (1865) by Dickens. Dr. Marigold is an itinerant Cheap Jack, called "doctor" in compliment to the medical man who attended at his birth and would only accept a tea-tray for his fee. The death of little Sophy in her father's arms, while he is convulsing the rustic crowd with his ludicrous speeches, is the central incident of the tale.

Drogheda (the bridge over the ford). In Eire, seaport on the Boyne, 26 miles north of Dublin. Cromwell massacred its garrison in September, 1649.

Dromio of Ephesus and **Dromio of Syracuse.** Two brothers exactly alike, who served two brothers exactly alike. The mistakes of masters and men form the fun of Shakespeare's COMEDY OF ERRORS based on the *Menaechmi* of Plautus.

Drood, Edwin. The hero of a novel called *The Mystery of Edwin Drood*, by DICKENS. Only eight numbers appeared. They were published in 1870, the year of the author's death.

droshky (Russian *drozhky*). Originally a low four-wheeled open carriage used in Russia. Generally, in many European countries, any horse-drawn cab or hackney coach. Cf. German *Droschke,* Swedish *droska,* Danish *Droske,* etc.

drove. See under COVEY.

Dr. Sevier. A story of life in New Orleans (1885) by G. W. Cable (1844–1925). Dr. Sevier is a physician of New Orleans, of high-minded but somewhat severe character and manner.

Dr. Syntax, see SYNTAX.

Dr. Thorne. A novel by Anthony Trollope, one of his *Chronicles of Barsetshire.* See BARSETSHIRE; THORNE.

Drugger, Abel. In Ben Jonson's comedy THE ALCHEMIST, a seller of tobacco; artless and gullible in the extreme. He is building a new house, and comes to Subtle "the alchemist," to know on which side to set the shop-door, how to dispose the shelves so as to ensure most luck, on what days he may trust his customers, and when it will be unlucky for him so to do.

Druid. A member of the ancient Gaulish and British order of priests, teachers of religion, magicians, or sorcerers. The word is the Lat. *druidae* or *druides* (always plural), which was borrowed from the Old Irish *drui* and Gaelic *draoi.* The druidic cult presents many difficulties, and practically our only literary sources of knowledge of it are Pliny and the Commentaries of Caesar, whence we learn that the rites of the Druids were conducted in oak groves and that they regarded the oak and the mistletoe with peculiar veneration; that they studied the stars and nature generally; that they believed in the transmigration of souls, and dealt in "magic." Their distinguishing badge was a serpent's egg (see below), to which very powerful properties were credited. The order seems to have been highly organized, and, according to Strabo, every chief had his druid, and every chief druid was allowed a guard of thirty men.

In Butler's HUDIBRAS* (III. i) there is an allusion to the

> Money by the Druids borrowed,
> In t'other world to be restored.

This refers to a legend recorded by one Patricius (St. Patrick?) to the effect that the Druids were wont to borrow money to be repaid in the life to come. His words are, *"Druidae pecuniam mutuo accipiebant in posteriore vita reddituri."*

The Druids' egg. This wonderful egg was hatched by the joint labor of several serpents, and was buoyed into the air by their hissing. The person who caught it had to ride off at full speed, to avoid being stung to death; but the possessor was sure to prevail in every contest, and to be courted by those in power. Pliny says he had seen one of them, and that it was about as large as a moderate-sized apple.

drum. A popular name in the 18th century —and later—for a crowded evening party, so called from its noise with, perhaps, a side allusion to the tea-*kettle* and *kettle*-drums.

> This is a riotous assembly of fashionable people, of both sexes, at a private house, consisting of some hundreds, not unaptly stiled a drum, from the noise and emptiness of the entertainment.—Smollett, *Advice, a Satire* (1746).

John (or *Jack*) *Drum's entertainment.* Turning an unwelcome guest out of doors.

> O! for the love of laughter, let him fetch his drum; he says he has a stratagem for 't. When your lordship sees the bottom of his success in 't, and to what metal this counterfeit lump of ore will be melted, if you give him not John Drum's entertainment, your inclining cannot be removed.—Shakespeare, *All's Well,* iii. 6.

Marston wrote a comedy with the title *Jack Drum's Entertainment* (1600), in which he is supposed to have satirized Ben Jonson.

drummer. An Americanism for a commercial traveler, his vocation being to collect customers as a recruiting officer "drums up" recruits.

Drummond, William Henry (1854–1907). Irish-born Canadian poet noted for French-Canadian dialect verse, as in the collections *The Habitant* (1897); *Johnny Courteau* (1901), etc.

Drummond of Hawthornden, William (1585–1649). Scotch-born English poet, owner of an extensive library and ardently Royalist in politics. He translated and imitated French and Italian lyric poetry, especially the work of Ronsard, Passerat, and Desportes. He is known for the grace and smoothness of his verse. Friend of Ben Jonson.

Drunken Parliament. See under PARLIAMENTS.

Drury Lane. This famous London street (and, consequently, the theater) is named from Drury House, built in the time of Henry VIII by Sir William Drury. It stood on a site about in the middle of the present Aldwych. The theater is the fourth of the name, the first having been opened in 1663.

Druses. A people and sect of Syria, living about the mountains of Lebanon and Anti-Libanus. Their faith is a mixture of the Pentateuch, the Gospel, the Koran, and Sufism. They offer up their devotions both in mosques and churches, worship the images of saints, and yet observe the fast of Ramadan. Their name is probably from that of their first apostle, Ismail Darazi, or Durzi (11th century A. D.). Browning has a tragedy THE RETURN OF THE DRUSES.

dryad. In classical mythology, a tree-nymph (Gr. *drus,* a tree) who was supposed to live in the trees and die when the trees died. Eurydice, the wife of Orpheus the poet, was a dryad. Also called *hamadryads* (Gr. *hama,* with).

Dryasdust. The name given by Scott to the fictitious "reverend Doctor," a learned pundit, whom he had sign the prefaces, etc., of many of his novels: hence, a heavy plodding author, very prosy, very dull, and very learned; an antiquary.

> The Prussian Dryasdust, otherwise an honest fellow, and not afraid of labor, excels all other Dryasdusts yet known. . . . He writes big books wanting in almo t every quality; and does not even give an *Index* t them.—Carlyle.

Dryden, John (1631–1700). English poet, dramatist, and critic, outstanding figure in letters during the Restoration period and literary dictator of his age. He won official court favor by altering his political and religious views and celebrating in his poetry in turn Oliver Cromwell (by *Heroic Stanzas,* 1659), Charles II (by *Astraea Redux,* 1660), and James II (by *The Hind and the Panther,* 1685). His poetry shows the characteristic restraint and finish of NEO-CLASSICISM, his prose is lucid and simple, and he established the heroic couplet (see COUPLET) as the vehicle for satire and didactic poetry for the next century. Dryden's works include: *The Indian Queen* (1664), *The Indian Emperor* (1665), *Aurengzebe* (1676), ALL FOR LOVE (1678) and *Don Sebastian* (1690), all plays in verse; ABSALOM AND ACHITOPHEL (1681), *The Medal*

(1682), *MacFlecknoe* (1682), *Religio Laici* (1682), and THE HIND AND THE PANTHER (1685), all political, literary, or religious satires; *Annus Mirabilis* (1667), a poem describing the momentous happenings in England in the year 1665–1666, such as the plague, the London fire, the Dutch War, etc.; and such celebrated lyrics as *A Song for St. Cecelia's Day* (1687), the ode *To Mrs. Killigrew,* and *Alexander's Feast* (1697). Dryden had a great influence on Alexander POPE, his disciple. He was made Poet Laureate in 1670 and held numerous royal offices until he refused allegiance to King William III in 1688. Cf. *John Dryden,* by Mark Van Doren.

Dryfoos, Conrad. A leading character in Howells' HAZARD OF NEW FORTUNES. His father and sisters are also prominent in the novel.

Dryope. In Greek legend, sister of Iole and wife of Andraemon. For having plucked inadvertently the lotus into which the nymph Lotis had been changed, Dryope herself was changed into a lotus.

d.t. An abbreviation, used as a euphemism, for *delirium tremens.*

du. For names beginning with the particle *du,* see under the simple form.

dualism. A philosophical theory or religious doctrine which considers the ultimate nature of the universe to be constituted by two mutually irreducible elements as mind and matter, good and evil, etc. Opposed to monism and pluralism. *Manichaeanism* and *Zoroastrianism* are instances of religious dualism.

Duat. In Egyptian mythology, one of the abodes of the dead in the underworld through which the sun passed by night.

Du Barry, Comtesse, **Marie Jeanne Bécu** (1746–1793). Adventuress and mistress of Louis XV from 1768 to his death (1774). Ruled king and court. Famous for her prodigality as a patron of artists and men of letters. Guillotined under Robespierre (December 7, 1793).

Dubliners. A collection of short stories and sketches by James JOYCE, published in 1914. Roughly divided in subject-matter into childhood, adolescence, maturity, and public life, they deal with incidents in the lives of people living in the city of Dublin, in character mean, petty, or tragic. The style is simple and moving, in the manner of Anton CHEKHOV rather than in that of the author's more famous works. Several of the characters later appearing in ULYSSES are introduced in these sketches, among the outstanding of which are COUNTERPARTS, THE DEAD, and IVY-DAY IN THE COMMITTEE ROOM. It has been pointed out that *Dubliners* represents one of the first uses of a short-story technique which was to become standardized later, especially in the magazine THE NEW YORKER. See also WINESBURG, OHIO.

Joyce had difficulty in finding a publisher for this book, and after publication it was severely attacked because the names of actual people and places in Dublin are mentioned in it.

Du Bois, William Edward Burghardt (1868–). American educator and novelist of Negro ancestry. Editor of the *Crisis,* a "Record of the Darker Races" (1910–1932). An official of the National Association for the Advancement of Colored People. Member of the National Institute of Arts and Letters.

Dubuque, The Old Lady from. A phrase coined by THE NEW YORKER magazine meaning "an unintelligent and easily-shocked provincial."

ducat. Name of a number of old coins, the first apparently being the one struck in silver in 1140 by Roger II of Sicily with the motto *"sit tibi, Christe, datus, quem tu regis, iste ducatus"* (let this duchy which thou rulest be dedicated to thee, O Christ).

Du Chaillu, Paul Belloni (1835–1903). French-American explorer of the interior of Equatorial Africa. Author of books on travel and adventure. *Stories of the Gorilla Country* (1868); *The Country of the Dwarfs* (1871); etc.

Duchamp-Villon, Raymond (1876–1918). French Cubist sculptor. His brother, **Marcel Duchamp-Villon** (1887–), Dadaist painter.

Duchess de Langeais, The. A story by BALZAC (1834) usually published as part of *The Thirteen* (*L'Histoire des treize.*) See also under LANGEAIS.

Duchess of Malfi, The. A drama by John WEBSTER (ca. 1618). The Duchess is twin-sister of Ferdinand, Duke of Calabria. She falls in love with Antonio, her steward, and gives thereby mortal offense to her twin-brother Ferdinand, and to her brother the cardinal. She and her children are finally strangled but not before she has been made to endure a series of horrible tortures of mind and body.

duck. In World War II, a soldiers' term for an amphibious landing craft.

a lame duck. See under LAME.

To make ducks and drakes of one's money. To throw it away as stones with which "ducks and drakes" are made on water. The allusion is to the sport of throwing stones to skim over water for the sake of seeing them ricocheting or rebounding.

Mr. Locke Harper found out, a month after his marriage, that somebody had made ducks and drakes of his wife's money.—Dinah M. Craik, *Agatha's Husband,* chap. xxiii.

ducking stool. A chair used for the punishment of common scolds, disorderly women, dishonest apprentices, etc. It was so fastened to a beam projecting over a pond or river that the culprit seated in it could be submerged at will. The term *cucking stool* (from O.E. *cuck,* "to void excrement"), so called because it resembled a closestool, was sometimes used for the same apparatus, but more often for a stool in which dishonest tradesmen were exposed in front of their shops to the pelting and hooting of the mob.

Now, if one cucking-stool was for each scold,
Some towns, I fear, would not their numbers hold.
Poor Robin (1746)

Duckling, Ugly, see UGLY DUCKLING.

Duclos, Charles Pinot (1704–1772). French historian and man of letters. Remembered as author of *Mémoires pour servir à l'histoire des moeurs du XVIIIe siècle* (1751). As secretary of the *Académie Française,* he supervised the publication of its famous dictionary.

Dudley, Robert. 1st Earl of **Leicester** (1532?–1588). English courtier, politician, and general. Chief favorite of Queen Elizabeth. Recalled for incompetence from command of the English army assisting the States-General against Spain (1587), but appointed captain-general of the queen's armies against the Spanish Armada (1588).

Dudu. In Byron's DON JUAN, one of the three beauties of the harem, into which Juan, by the sultana's order, has been admitted in female attire. Next day, the sultana, out of jealousy, orders that both Dudu and Juan be stitched in a sack and cast into the sea; but, by the connivance of Baba, the chief eunuch, they effected their escape.

A kind of sleeping Venus seemed Dudu . . .
But she was pensive more than melancholy . . .
The strangest thing was, beauteous, she was holy,
Unconscious, albeit turned of quick seventeen.
Don Juan, Canto vi. 42–44.

duende (*Span.*). A goblin or house-spirit. CALDERON wrote a comedy called *La Dama Duenda.*

duergar. A Norse name for the dwarfs of Scandinavian mythology; they dwell in rocks and hills, and are noted for their strength, subtlety, magical powers, and skill in metallurgy. According to the *Gylfaginning* they owe their origin to the maggots in the flesh of the first giant, YMIR. Cf. the English word *durgan,* a dialectal variant of "dwarf."

Duessa (Double-mind or Falsehood). In Spenser's *Faërie Queene* (Bk. I) the "scarlet woman," typifying the Roman Catholic Church, and (Bk. V) Mary Queen of Scots. She is the daughter of Deceit and Shame, and assumes divers disguises to beguile the Red Cross Knight. In Bk. I she is stripped of her gorgeous disguise, is found to be a hideous hag, and flees into the wilderness for concealment.

Du Gard, Roger Martin (1881–). French novelist, best known for LES THIBAULTS (1922–1936), ten volumes in length, a characteristic ROMAN-FLEUVE of 20th-century French literature. *The World of the Thibaults* (1941) completes the story of the family. In 1937 Du Gard was awarded the Nobel prize for literature.

Du Guesclin, Bertrand (1320?–1380). French commander who distinguished himself in the campaigns against the English and Pedro the Cruel of Castile. Surnamed "the Eagle of Brittany." He was made marshal of Normandy in 1364 and constable of France in 1369.

Duhamel, Georges (1884–). French author. Pseudonym **Denis Thévenin.** From 1906 worked and wrote for 2 years with a literary group in the "Abbaye," 11 kilometers from Paris. A doctor by profession, became a surgeon at the front in World War I. Emerged after the war as a mature novelist. His *Pasquier Chronicles* (from 1933) are important. Member of French Academy (1936) and Academy of Medicine.

Dujardin, Édouard (1861–). French poet and novelist, associated with the movement of SYMBOLISM and a close friend of Stephane MALLARMÉ. He is best known as the author of the experimental novel *Les Lauriers sont coupés* (1887), published in the U.S. as *We'll to the Woods No More* (1939) and considered to be the first making use of the STREAM-OF-CONSCIOUSNESS technique, although it is perhaps more properly in the form of an INTERIOR MONOLOGUE. Dujardin also experimented in free verse and the verset form—the latter being used by T. S. Eliot in MURDER IN THE CATHEDRAL and THE FAMILY REUNION—and helped publicize in his lectures the theories of the Symbolists.

Duke's Children, The. A novel by Anthony TROLLOPE (1880). See also OMNIUM, DUKE OF.

Dukhobors or, in the Russian form, **Dukhobortsy** (literally, spirit-wrestlers). A fanatical Russian sect founded (1785) by the soldier Procope Loupkin. The Dukhobors hold that their knowledge of the true spirit of Christianity imposes upon them the duty to reject the use of images, rites, and ceremonies, to dispense with an ordained clergy, and to deny the divinity of Christ as well as the authority of Scriptures. Accused of ritual murders and cruelties, they were removed to the Caucasus in 1841; because of continued persecution thousands emigrated to Canada in 1898. They continue to believe in an inner light and several divine incarnations.

Dulcamara, Doctor. A wandering physician in the opera *L'Elisir d'Amore* by Donizetti (1832). He is a typical charlatan and pompous ass.

dulcarnon. The horns of a dilemma (or *syllogismum cornutum*); a puzzling question. From an Arabic word meaning "the possessor of two horns." The 47th proposition of the First Book of Euclid is called the Dulcarnon, as the 5th is the Pons Asinorum, because the two squares which contain the right angle roughly represent horns.

be at dulcarnon. To be in a quandary, or on the horns of a dilemma.

Dulce et Decorum Est. A poem by Wilfred OWEN, published in 1920, bitterly denouncing war. The title is a quotation from Horace (*Odes,* III, 2): *"Dulce et decorum est pro patria mori"* ("It is sweet and fitting to die for one's country").

dulcimer. An old instrument with metal wires over a trapezoidal sounding board, played with two hammers with hard and soft sides held in the hands. It is particularly interesting as a prototype of the modern piano which might be described as a dulcimer with keyboard hammer action. See HARPSICHORD. In the Southern Mountains of the U.S., a "dulcimore" is more like a guitar.

> It was an Abyssinian maid,
> And on her dulcimer she played.
> S. T. Coleridge, *Khubla Khan.*

Dulcinea. A lady-love. Taken from DON QUIXOTE's *amie du coeur.* Her real name is Aldonza Lorenzo, but the knight dubs her Dulcinea del Toboso. "Her flowing hair," says the knight, "is of gold, her forehead the Elysian fields, her eyebrows two celestial arches, her eyes a pair of glorious suns, her cheeks two beds of roses, her lips two coral portals that guard her teeth of Oriental pearl, her neck is alabaster, her hands are polished ivory, and her bosom whiter than the new-fallen snow."

> I must ever have some Dulcinea in my head—it harmonises the soul.—Sterne.

> "Sir," said Don Quixote, "she is not a descendant of the ancient Caii, Curtii, and Scipios of Rome; nor of the modern Colonas and Orsini; nor of the Rebillas and Villanovas of Valencia; neither is she a descendant of the Palafoxes, Newcas, Rocabertis, Corellas, Lunas, Alagones, Ureas, Fozes, and Gurreas of Aragon; neither does the Lady Dulcinea descend from the Cerdas, Manriquez, Mendozas, and Guzmans of Castile; nor from the Alencastros, Pallas, and Menezes of Portugal; but she derives her origin from a family of Toboso, near Mancha." (Bk. ii., ch. v.)

Sancho Panza says she is "a stout-built sturdy wench, who could pitch the bar as well as any young fellow in the parish."

Dulcy. A character created by the columnist F. P. A. and later made the titular heroine of a comedy by George S. KAUFMAN and Marc CONNELLY (1921). In the course of her well-meaning self-appointed task of helping her husband put through an important business deal, Dulcy makes one blunder after another, but is blissfully unaware of her own limitations and gathers in all the credit when the deal goes through.

dulia, see LATRIA.

dulse. A coarse red seaweed used as food in certain northern countries. In Iceland it is stored in casks to be eaten with fish. In Kamchatka a fermented liquor is made from it. Also eaten in Scotland and New England.

Duma, also **Douma.** The Russian Council of State, or Parliament, created by an imperial ukase of August 19, 1905 and dissolved by the Bolshevist revolution in 1917. As a common name, Russian *duma* stands for any council or assembly; it is of Teutonic origin and related to English *doom,* "judgment."

Dumachus. See under DISMAS.

Dumain. In Shakespeare's LOVE'S LABOUR'S LOST, a French lord in attendance on Ferdinand, king of Navarre. He agrees to spend three years with the King in study, during which time no woman is to approach the court. Of course, the compact is broken as soon as it is made, and Dumain falls in love with Katharine.

Dumas, Alexandre, known as **Dumas père** (1802–1870). French novelist and dramatist, best known for his historical romances of the swashbuckling variety. He maintained a corps of collaborators with the assistance of whom he turned out almost three hundred books. He used the works of earlier memoir-writers as sources for his material, and has been accused of altering historical fact to suit his fictional purposes. Critics point out Dumas' excessive melodrama, the over-simplicity of his characters, and his poor style.

Among Dumas' plays, which were very successful and for which he is known in France if not in English-speaking countries, are *Henri III et sa cour* (1829); *Christine* (1830); *Napoléon Bonaparte* (1831); *Antony* (1831); and *La Tour de Nesle* (1832). These are violent and melodramatic, dealing with historical periods and with the adventures of the typical Romantic hero. Of Dumas' historical novels, whose contemporary popularity continues, especially in the theater, the motion picture and the juvenile library, the best known are THE THREE MUSKETEERS (*Les Trois mousquetaires* (1844), THE COUNT OF MONTE CRISTO (1844) and THE BLACK TULIP (1845).

Dumas was the son of a part-Negro general

of the French army and was of a wild and robust nature, alternating between fantastic luxury and heavy debt.

Dumas, Alexandre, known as **Dumas fils** (1824–1895). French dramatist, the natural son of the historical novelist Alexandre DUMAS *père*. His plays are characterized by a realistic technique (see REALISM) and frequent moralizing, dealing chiefly with adultery and intrigue, both sexual and financial, in the higher social classes. The best-known is *La Dame aux Camélias* (1852), translated as CAMILLE. Other plays include *Le Demi-Monde* (1855); *Un Père Prodigue* (1859); *La Question d'Argent* (1857); *Les Idées de Mme Aubray* (1867); *L'Ami des Femmes* (1864). DIANE DE LYS (1851) is a novel.

du Maurier, George Louis Palmella Busson (1834–1896). English novelist and illustrator of a family of French émigrés. Best known as the author and illustrator of *Peter Ibbetson* (1891) and *Trilby* (1894). His granddaughter **Daphne du Maurier** (1907–), daughter of the noted actor Sir Gerald du Maurier (1873–1934), is an extremely successful novelist, author of the bestsellers *Rebecca* (1938; somewhat reminiscent in its theme of *Vera* by ELIZABETH Countess Russell), and *The King's General* (1945).

Dumbiedikes, the old laird of. In Scott's HEART OF MIDLOTHIAN, an exacting landlord, taciturn and obstinate.

> The laird of Dumbiedikes had hitherto been moderate in his exactions . . . but when a stout, active young fellow appeared . . . he began to think so broad a pair of shoulders might bear an additional burden. He regulated, indeed, his management of his dependents as carters do their horses, never failing to clap an additional brace of hundred-weights on a new and willing horse.

the young laird of Dumbiedikes. A bashful young laird, in love with Jeanie Deans. Jeanie marries the Presbyterian minister, Reuben Butler.

Dumb Ox, the. St. Thomas Aquinas (1224–1274), known afterwards as "the Angelic Doctor" or "Angel of the Schools." Albertus Magnus, the tutor of the "dumb ox," said of him: "The dumb ox will one day fill the world with his lowing." The name was given to him by his fellow students at Cologne from his taciturnity and dreaminess.

Dumont, Lewis. The hero of William Gillette's drama, SECRET SERVICE.

dum sola (*Lat.*). While single or unmarried. A legal term applied to women. The phrase **dum sola et casta,** "while single and chaste" occurs as a condition in wills.

dum spiro, spero (*Lat.*). Literally, while I breathe, I hope; while there's life, there's hope. It is the motto of the Viscounts Dillon of the Irish royalist family Dillon.

dum vivimus vivamus (*Lat.*). While we live, let us enjoy life. The motto adopted by Dr. Doddridge (1702–1751), who translated and expanded it into the subjoined epigram:

> "Live, while you live," the epicure would say,
> "And seize the pleasures of the present day."
> "Live, while you live," the sacred preacher cries,
> "And give to God each moment as it flies."
> Lord, in *my* views let each united be;
> I live in pleasure, when I live to thee.

Dunbar, Paul Laurence (1872–1906). American Negro poet, author of verse chiefly on Negro themes and in Negro dialect. Among his books of poetry are *Lyrics of Lowly Life* (1896); *Lyrics of the Hearthside* (1899); *Lyrics of Love and Laughter* (1903); *Lyrics of Sunshine and Shadow* (1905).

Dunbar, William (1465?–1530?). Scottish poet, for a time a Franciscan friar and later a diplomatic agent for James IV of Scotland. His works include *The Thistle and the Rose* (1503), a political allegory; *The Dance of the Seven Deadly Sins* (between 1503 and 1508), a religious dream-vision; *The Golden Targe* (ca. 1508), an allegory in the tradition of the ROMANCE OF THE ROSE; *Lament for the Makers* ("makers" meaning poets) (ca. 1508), an elegy on the death of great poets of the past which has been compared to the poetry of François VILLON; and *The Two Married Women and the Widow* (ca. 1508), a satire on women. Dunbar is considered one of the best of the SCOTTISH CHAUCERIANS.

Duncan. In Shakespeare's tragedy, MACBETH, the King of Scotland, murdered by Macbeth.

Duncan, Isadora (1878–1927). American dancer. Acclaimed in London, Paris, and on the Continent. Established a German school of dancing near Berlin (1904), and later one in Moscow. Wrote autobiography, *My Life* (1926–1927). Rendered compositions by Tchaikovsky and Chopin in the dance. Strangled in an automobile accident when her scarf was caught in a wheel.

Duncan Gray. A ballad by BURNS (1792) with the refrain "Ha, ha! the wooing o't." Duncan woos a young lass called Maggie, but she "coost her head fu' high, looked asklent," and bids him behave himself. "Duncan fleeched, and Duncan prayed," but Meg is deaf to his pleadings; so Duncan takes himself off in dudgeon. This is more than Maggie meant, so she falls sick and seems about to die. As Duncan "could na be her death," he comes back and all ends happily.

Duncan Phyfe. A style of furniture named after the Scottish-born New York City cabinet maker Duncan Phyfe (1768–1854). In the U.S., all Empire styles are so called. In a more restricted sense, it is a modified DIRECTOIRE.

Dunciad. The dunce-epic, a satire by Alexander POPE, first published in 1728 with Theobald figuring as the Poet Laureate of the realm of Dullness, but republished with an added fourth part in 1741 with Colley Cibber in that rôle. His installation is celebrated by games, the most important being the proposal to read, without sleeping, two voluminous works—one in verse and the other in prose; as everyone falls asleep, the games come to an end. The Laureate is later taken to the temple of Dullness, and is lulled to sleep on the lap of the goddess; and, during his slumber, sees in a vision the past, present, and future triumphs of the empire. Finally, the goddess, having destroyed order and science, establishes her kingdom on a firm basis, gives directions to her several agents to prevent thought and keep people to foolish and trifling pursuits, and Night and Chaos are restored, and the poem ends.

Dundreary, Lord. The impersonation of a good-natured, indolent, blundering, empty-headed swell, from the chief character in Tom Taylor's *Our American Cousin* (1858). E. A. Sothern created the character by the genius of his acting and the large additions he made to the original text, in which this English personage had been given only forty-seven lines.

Hence *Dundreary whiskers,* the style of whiskers worn by this character.

Dun Edin. Poetical name of Edinburgh.

Dunkers or **Tunkers** (*Ger.,* "Dippers"). A religious sect akin to the Baptists, founded in Germany in 1708 by Alexander Mack. In 1719 a party of them emigrated to Pennsylvania. They follow Bible teaching as closely as possible and adhere to the simplicity of the primitive Church. They practice immersion; hence their name.

Dunmow flitch, the. The flitch of bacon mentioned below.

eat Dunmow bacon. To live in conjugal amity, without even wishing the marriage knot to be less firmly tied. The allusion is to a custom said to have been instituted by Juga, a noble lady, in 1111, and restored by Robert de Fitzwalter in 1244; which was, that

> any person from any part of England going to Dunmow, in Essex, and humbly kneeling on two stones at the church door, may claim a gammon of bacon, if he can swear that for twelve months and a day he has never had a household brawl or wished himself unmarried.

Between 1244 and 1772 eight claimants were admitted to eat the flitch. Allusions to the custom are very frequent in 17th and 18th century literature; and in the last years of the 19th century it was revived. Later it was removed to Ilford. The oath administered is in doggerel, somewhat as follows:

> You shall swear, by the custom of our confession,
> That you never made any nuptial transgression
> Since you were married man and wife,
> By household brawls or contentious strife;
> Or, since the parish clerk said *"Amen,"*
> Wished yourselves unmarried again;
> Or, in a twelvemonth and a day,
> Repented not in thought any way,
> If to these terms, without all fear,
> Of your own accord you will freely swear,
> A gammon of bacon you shall receive,
> And bear it hence with our good leave.
> For this is our custom at Dunmow well known—
> The sport is ours, but the bacon your own.

Dunne, Finley Peter (1867–1936). American humorist, creator of Mr. DOOLEY.

Dunsany, Lord **Edward John Moreton Drax Plunkett** (1878–). Irish dramatist and writer of short tales, associated with the Abbey Theater (see IRISH RENAISSANCE). He is known for the imaginative fantasy of his writing, in which wit and satire are combined with a romantic, fairy-tale atmosphere. He has been compared with James Branch CABELL. His works include *The Glittering Gate* (1914); *The Gods of Pegana* (1916); *A Dreamer's Tales* (1917); *Plays of Gods and Men* (1917); *Tales of War* (1918); *Nowadays* (1918), an essay on the author's theory of literature; *Unhappy Far-Off Things* (1919); *If, A Play* (1922); *Plays of Near and Far* (1923); *Time and the Gods* (1924); *The Charwoman's Shadow* (1926); *The Blessing of Pan* (1927); *The Travel Tales of Mr. Joseph Jorkens* (1931); *The Curse of the Wise Woman* (1933); *Jorkens Remembers Africa* (1934); *Mr. Faithful, A Play* (1935); *My Talks with Dean Spanley* (1937); and *Rory and Bran* (1937).

Duns Scotus, John (1265?–?1308). Scottish scholastic theologian, born in Duns, Scotland. Known as **Doctor Subtilis** because of his great dialectical skill. He wrote a philosophical grammar, commentaries on the Bible, Aristotle, etc. Founded a scholastic system known as Scotism. It was from the opposition of his followers to the classicism of the Renaissance that his name—in the form of *dunce*—assumed the connotations of sophist and blockhead.

Dunstan, St. See under SAINT.

Dunsterville, Major General **Lionel Charles** (1866–1946). Childhood friend of KIPLING. See STALKY AND CO. In World War I, Dunsterville "bluffed the Turks out of the Baku oil fields with a handful of men."

duodecimo (from Lat. *duodecimus,* twelfth, in the phrase *in duodecimo*). A book whose sheets are folded into twelve leaves each, often called "twelvemo," from the contraction 12mo. The book is naturally a small one, hence the expression is sometimes applied to other things of small size, such as a dwarf.

Dupes, Day of (Fr. *Journée des Dupes*). In French history, November 11, 1630, when

Marie de Medici and Gaston, Duc d'Orléans extorted from Louis XIII a promise that he would dismiss his minister, the Cardinal Richelieu. The cardinal went in all speed to Versailles, the king repented, and Richelieu became more powerful than ever. Marie de Medici and Gaston, the "dupes," had to pay dearly for their short triumph.

Dupin, Aurore, see SAND, GEORGE.

Dupin, C. Auguste. A brilliant amateur detective of Paris who appears in Poe's *Murders in the Rue Morgue, The Mystery of Marie Rogêt* and *The Purloined Letter.* He is said to have been drawn from a real character, a certain C. Auguste Dupont, whose exploits were reported to Poe by a friend.

Du Pont de Nemours, Pierre Samuel (1739–1817). French economist, friend and disciple of the PHYSIOCRAT François Quesnay. Was imprisoned in the French Revolution and emigrated to the U.S. (1799). At Jefferson's request he prepared a scheme for national education which was never adopted in the U.S. but influenced the French educational code. Returned to France (1802–1815) but again emigrated to the U.S. two years before his death. His son **Éleuthère Irénée Du Pont de Nemours** (1771–1834) came to the U.S. in 1799 and founded in Wilmington, Del., the powerful gunpowder and textile firm of E. I. Du Pont de Nemours & Co. (1802–1804).

Durandana or **Durindana.** Orlando's sword, given him by his cousin Malagigi. It once belonged to Hector, was made by the fairies, and could cleave the Pyrenees at a blow.

> Nor plaited shield, nor tempered casque defends,
> Where Durindana's trenchant edge descends.
> *Orlando Furioso,* Bk. v.

Durant, William James. Known as **Will Durant** (1885–). American author and journalist, in his early years associated with Lola RIDGE and Upton SINCLAIR in the Socialist movement. He was active in experimental education and as a lecturer on philosophy and art. He is best known as the author of *The Story of Philosophy* (1926), a popular account of the lives and ideas of the world's great philosophers.

Duranty, Walter (1884–). English-born American journalist, best known for *I Write as I Please* (1935), a best-selling account of his experiences as a newspaperman in Russia, and one of the first books by foreign correspondents to become popular with the public in the days of growing crisis in Europe before World War II. He also wrote *One Life, One Kopek* (1937), a novel, and *Babies Without Tails* (1937), short stories.

Durbeyfield, Tess. Heroine of Hardy's novel, TESS OF THE D'URBERVILLES.

Durdles, Stony. In Dickens' unfinished novel THE MYSTERY OF EDWIN DROOD, a stonemason who is usually intoxicated, but knows the secrets of the cathedral crypt.

Durendal. The sword of Roland, given him by Charlemagne, in legend. Identical with DURANDANA.

Dürer, Albrecht (1471–1528). Famous German painter, engraver and woodcut artist. Traveled in Italy and carried a new conception of his art back over the Alps. Leader of German Renaissance school of painting. Regarded as inventor of etching. His copperplates *Ritter, Tod, und Teufel* (Knight, Death, and Devil) and *Melancholia* are the most popular of his numerous works. Wrote *Von menschlicher Proportion* (On the measurements of the human figure; 1528); a study on *Fortification* (1527); etc.

Durfey, Tom. Originally **Thomas D'Urfey** (1653–1723). English song writer and dramatist of French Huguenot descent. His songs were collected in six volumes as *Wit and Mirth or Pills to Purge Melancholy* (1719–1720).

Durga. One of the names of the Hindu goddess KALI, the wife of Siva.

Durgin, Jeff. The hero of Howells' *The Landlord at Lion's Head* (1898).

Durham, Henrietta. Heroine of Flotow's opera, MARTHA.

Duronceray, Marie Justine Benoîte. See under FAVART.

Durrie, James and **Henry Durrie.** Two brothers, principal characters in Stevenson's MASTER OF BALLANTRAE.

Duruy, Victor (1811–1894). French historian. Author of many school histories, a history of the Roman people in seven volumes and one of Greece in three volumes.

Durward, Quentin, see QUENTIN DURWARD.

Dusantes, The. A sequel to F. R. Stockton's CASTING AWAY OF MRS. LECKS AND MRS. ALESHINE.

Duse, Eleonora (1859–1924). Famous Italian actress. Toured Europe and America. Close friend of Gabriele D'ANNUNZIO till 1899. Interpreted Sardou, Ibsen, Sudermann, D'Annunzio, Maeterlinck.

Dust Bowl. The region, along the western border of the Great Plains, in Colorado, Oklahoma, Texas, Kansas, and New Mexico, where overgrazing or uncontrolled cultivation made it possible for the droughts in the 1930's to bring about complete denudation so that the topsoil was blown away in terrible dust storms. See also OKIES. Cf. the novel by Feike Feikima, *The Golden Bowl.*

dustman. In folklore the genius of sleep, so named because a sleepy child will wink and rub his eyes as though he had dust in them. Also called *sandman.* Cf. French *marchand de sable.*

Dutch. In a number of phrases the adjective Dutch has an opprobrious or humorous application, possibly in consequence of the long struggle for supremacy of the seas waged by England against the Netherlands in the seventeenth century and in part also due to the traditional association of the Dutch with boorishness and lack of polish.

Dutch auction. An *"auction"* in which the bidders *decrease* their bids till they come to the minimum price. Dutch gold is no gold at all; Dutch courage is no real courage; Dutch concert is no music at all, but mere hubbub; and Dutch auction is no *auction,* or increase of bids but quite the contrary.

Dutch comfort. The comfort derivable from the consideration that, however bad the evil which has befallen you may be, a worse evil is at least conceivable.

Dutch concert. A great noise and uproar, like that made by a party of Dutchmen in sundry stages of intoxication, some singing, others quarreling, speechifying, wrangling, and so on. Cf. also *Dutch nightingale,* "a frog."

Dutch courage. The courage excited by drink; pot valor.

Dutch door. A door divided horizontally, so that the lower part can be shut while the upper part is open. A phrase in which, by exception, the word Dutch has no unpleasant connotations. Dutch doors are also found in Ireland.

Dutch treat. Refreshments paid for individually; each one "treats" only himself. Hence *to go Dutch.*

Dutch uncle: I will talk to you like a Dutch uncle, I will reprove you smartly.

Dutch wife. A frame of cane used in the East Indies in hot weather to rest the arms and legs on while trying to keep cool in bed.

Well, I'm a Dutchman! An exclamation of strong incredulity.

Dutch Republic, Rise of the. See under RISE.

Duun, Olav (1876–1939). Norwegian novelist, called "the greatest living spokesman for the peasant mind." His books, among them the series *The People of Juvik* (6 vols.; 1918–1923) are written in the *landsmaal,* the spoken language of Norway, and not in the traditional literary Dano-Norwegian *riksmaal.*

Duval, Claude. A highwayman, famed in legend and ballad. He was hanged at Tyburn in 1670 and provided with an epitaph beginning:

> Here lies Du Vall: Reader, if male thou art
> Look to thy purse, if female, to thy heart.

Duval, Madame. In Fanny Burney's novel EVELINA, the heroine's vulgar old grandmother.

Duvarney, Alixe. The heroine of Gilbert Parker's SEATS OF THE MIGHTY.

Duveen, Joseph, Baron **Duveen of Milbank** (1869–1939). English art connoisseur and dealer. Donor of the gallery housing the Elgin Marbles and benefactor of the National Gallery in London.

Dvořák, Anton (1841–1904). Czech composer; director of the National Conservatory of Music in New York City (1892–1895). Head of the Conservatory in Prague (1901). Wrote many operas and symphonies (among these the *New World Symphony*), symphonic poems, overtures, rhapsodies, nocturnes, scherzos, concertos, and choral works. His piano music includes the widely known *Humoresque.*

dwarf. Dwarfs have figured in the legends and mythology of nearly every race, and Pliny gives particulars of whole races of them, possibly following travelers' reports of African pigmies. Among the Teutonic and Scandinavian peoples dwarfs held an important place in mythology. They generally dwelt in rocks, caves, and recesses of the earth, were the guardians of its mineral wealth and precious stones, and were very skilful in the working of these. They had their own king, as a rule were not inimical to man, but could, on occasion, be intensely vindictive and mischievous. They play an important role in the RING DES NIBELUNGEN.

In England diminutive persons—dwarfs—were popular down to the 18th century as court favorites or household pets; and in later times they have frequently been exhibited as curiosities at circuses, etc.

the black dwarf. A gnome of the most malignant character, once held by the dalesmen of the border as the author of all the mischief that befell their flocks and herds. Scott has a novel so called (1816), in which the name is given to Sir Edward Mauley, *alias* Elshander, the recluse, Cannie Elshie, and the Wise Wight of Mucklestane Moor.

See also ALBERICH; TOM THUMB.

Dwight, Harrison Griswold (1875–). American writer born in Turkey. Special assistant in U.S. Department of State (1920–1925). Wrote *Stamboul Nights* (1916), *Persian Miniatures* (1917), *The Emperor of Elam and Other Stories* (1920), etc.

Dwight, Timothy (1752–1817). American poet and clergyman, a grandson of Jonathan EDWARDS and leader of the HARTFORD WITS. He was a Calvinist in religion and a Federalist in politics. Dwight is best known for several popular poems: THE CONQUEST OF CANAAN (1785); GREENFIELD HILL (1794); *The Triumph of Infidelity* (1788); and a song of the American Revolution, *Columbia,* considered by a few critics to be his best composition from the standpoint of literary value. Dwight's other works in prose include *The True Means of Establishing Public Happiness* (1798); *The Duty of Americans, at the Present Crisis* (1798); *Essay on the Stage* (1824), attacking the theater; and *Theology, Explained and Defended* (1818–1819), a collection of 173 sermons. Dwight was president of Yale University (1805–1826) and helped develop the staff and curricula of the college.

Dyce, Alexander (1798–1869). Scottish dramatic editor. Edited works of Peele, John Webster, Greene, Shirley, Middleton, Beaumont and Fletcher, Marlowe, Richard Bentley and Shakespeare. His reputation is based on his edition of Shakespeare and on his notes on Shakespeare. Author of *Recollections of the Table Talk of Samuel Rogers* (1856).

Dyer, Sir **Edward** (d. 1607). English poet of the Elizabethan period, best known for his lyric beginning "My mind to me a kingdom is."

Dykes, John Bacchus (1823–1876). English musician and theologian. His hymn tunes are regarded as the best in modern music.

Dying Gaul, the. A famous marble statue of the Pergamene school in the Capitoline Museum at Rome. Formerly known as *the Dying Gladiator.*

Dymphna, St. See under SAINT.

Dynamo. A play by Eugene O'NEILL.

Dynasts, The. A dramatic poem of epic scope by Thomas HARDY (published 1903–1908) dealing with the Napoleonic Wars.

Dysmas, see DISMAS.

Dzugashvili, Iosif Vissarionovich, see STALIN, JOSEPH.

E

eagle.

Thy youth is renewed like the eagle's (*Ps.* ciii. 5). This refers to the ancient superstition that every ten years the eagle soars into the "fiery region," and plunges thence into the sea, where, moulting its feathers, it acquires new life. Cf. PHOENIX.

> She saw where he upstarted brave
> Out of the well. . . .
> As eagle fresh out of the ocean wave,
> Where he hath lefte his plumes all hory gray,
> And decks himself with fethers youthly gay.
> Spenser, *Faërie Queene,* I, xi. 34.

the American Eagle. A widely used national symbol. See SPREAD EAGLE.

The *Golden Eagle* and the *Spread Eagle* are commemorative of the crusades; they were the devices of the emperors of the East, and formerly figured as the ensigns of the ancient kings of Babylon and Persia, of the Ptolemies and Seleucides. The Romans adopted the eagle in conjunction with other devices, but Marius made it the ensign of the legion, and confined the other devices to the cohorts. The French under the Empire assumed the same device.

In Christian art, the eagle is emblematic of St. John the Evangelist, because, like that bird, he looked on "the sun of glory."

St. Augustine, St. Gregory the Great, and St. Prisca are also often shown with an eagle. In *heraldry,* it signifies fortitude.

the Eagle. Gaudenzio Ferrari (1481–1549), the Milanese painter.

the Eagle of the doctors of France. Pierre d'Ailly (1350–1420), French cardinal and astrologer, who calculated the horoscope of our Lord, and maintained that the stars foretold the deluge.

Eagle of Brittany. Bertrand du Guesclin (1320–1380), constable of France.

Eagle of Divines. St. Thomas Aquinas (1225–1274).

Eagle of Meaux. Jacques Bénigne Bossuet (1627–1704), Bishop of Meaux, the grandest and most sublime of the pulpit orators of France.

Eagle of the North. Count Axel Oxenstierna (1583–1654), the Swedish statesman, was so called.

two-headed eagle. The German eagle has its head turned to our left hand, and the Roman eagle to our right hand. When Charlemagne was made "Kaiser of the Holy Roman Empire," he joined the two heads together, one looking east and the other west; consequently, the late Austrian Empire, as the direct successor of the Holy Roman Empire, included the *double-headed eagle* in its coat of arms.

In Russia it was Ivan Vasilievitch who first assumed the two-headed eagle, when, in 1472, he married Sophia, daughter of Thomas Palaeologus, and niece of Constantine XIV, the last Emperor of Byzantium. The two heads symbolize the Eastern or Byzantine Empire and the Western or Roman Empire.

Eagle, Solomon, see SOLOMON EAGLE.

Eaker, Ira Clarence (1896–). Major General and head of U.S. army air force in Europe (1943). Pilot of army plane "Question Mark" which set world's endurance record (1929). Made first transcontinental blind flight (1936).

Eakins, Thomas (1844–1916). Noted American painter and sculptor. One of the finest of our American painters. Some of his best works are *Clinic of Dr. Gross, Clinic of Dr. Agnew, The Chess Players,* and *Max Schmitt in a Single Scull.* He did the reliefs on the battle monument in Trenton, N.J.

Earhart, Amelia (1898–1937). Leading American aviatrix. First woman pilot to cross Atlantic Ocean in an airplane (June 17, 1928). Married George Palmer Putnam, the publisher. Author of several books, notably *Last Flight* (1938; edited by her husband). Lost in attempt to fly across the Pacific (July, 1937).

Earle, John (1601?–1665). English prose-writer, one of the CHARACTER WRITERS. His *Microcosmography* (1628) deals with "characters" as seen from an academic point of view, such as "a pretender to learning," "an antiquary," etc.

Early, Stephen (1889–). American journalist and secretary to President Franklin Delano Roosevelt (from 1937).

Earnshaw, Catherine. The heroine of Emily Brontë's WUTHERING HEIGHTS.

Ear of Dionysius. In a quarry of Syracuse, Sicily, an ancient cavern tapered to a hole above where the tyrant Dionysius (d. 367 B.C.) listened to the conversation of prisoners below. Also an invention of Leonardo da Vinci for the same purpose for the tyrant of Milan. Hence the phrase has been used for an ear trumpet.

Ears to Ears Bible. See under BIBLE, SPECIALLY NAMED.

Earthly Paradise, The. In medieval times it was a popular belief that paradise, a land—or island—where everything was beautiful and restful, and where death and decay were unknown, still existed somewhere on earth and was to be found for the searching. It was usually located far away to the east; Cosmas (7th century) placed it beyond the ocean east of China, in 9th century maps it is shown in China itself, and the fictitious letter of PRESTER JOHN to the Emperor Emmanuel Comnenus states that it was within three days' journey of his own territory—a "fact" that is corroborated by Mandeville. The Hereford map (13th century) shows it as a circular island near India, from which it is separated not only by the sea, but also by a battlemented wall. See also BRANDAN, ST.

The *Prologue* to William Morris' collection of narrative poems with this title (1868–1870) tells how a party of adventurers leaves a Scandinavian port during a pestilence to search for the Earthly Paradise. After many misadventures the remnant of the band discovers it, are hospitably received, and regale their hosts each month with versified renderings of old world stories from classical and Scandinavian legend.

Earwicker, Humphrey Chimpden. Protagonist of James Joyce's FINNEGANS WAKE. In his literal metamorphosis, he is a middle-aged keeper of a public-house in Dublin, a Protestant Irishman of Scandinavian descent and hence another of the strangers in Ireland preferred by Joyce as characters. See BLOOM, LEOPOLD. At various times Earwicker is also the following characters: Tim FINNEGAN; Finn MAC COOL; ADAM, LUCIFER, and HUMPTY DUMPTY, because of their legendary falls (see FINNEGAN); Howth Castle, sometimes signified by the Norse name Jarl van Hoother (Earl of Howth); Persse O'Reilly; and in general, the masculine principle of the universe, as opposed to the feminine principle, represented by his wife. See MAGGIE EARWICKER below. Throughout the book the initials HCE, either alone or embodied in names or phrases, serve as a constant LEITMOTIF for Earwicker, as ALP stand in similar usage for Anna Livia Plurabelle, or his wife. During Earwicker's epic dream, there are recurring allusions to and representations of an unknown crime committed by him in PHOENIX PARK and about which he is apparently worried, and to latent, subconscious tendencies toward incest and homosexuality with reference to his children.

Earwicker is supposedly a Scandinavian name, said to be a corruption of *Eirikr,* a poetic form of the name *Erik,* and also, possibly, to mean "dweller in Ireland" (from *Eire,* Ireland, A.S. *wician,* to dwell) according to the technique of popular etymology practiced by Joyce himself. The name in addition contains an allusion to earwigs, which, referred to frequently throughout the book, are interpreted as another symbol of Earwicker himself, because falling (see FINNEGAN, TIM) is a familiar movement of the insects.

Maggie Earwicker. Wife of Humphrey, ultimately the feminine principle of the universe, who chiefly takes the form of ANNA LIVIA PLURABELLE, the personification of the river LIFFEY. In the opening section of *Finnegans Wake,* the courtship of husband and wife is depicted in a series of symbolical episodes, in which the symbols of male and female are, respectively, Howth Castle and the Liffey ("lord of the heights" and "lady of the valley"), a tree and a stone, a cloud and a hill, a river and a city, and so on. Basically, the two are also Adam and Eve, the ancestors of humanity, comprising "the city-building resourcefulness of mankind and the vital fertility of womankind" (Harry Levin, *James Joyce*). The novel closes with a dream-soliloquy by Maggie, or rather, Anna Livia Plurabelle (see ULYSSES; BLOOM, MOLLY), which is broken on the last page in the midst of a sentence and continued in the broken sentence with which the novel opens on page one, so that the structure is circular.

Jerry Earwicker. One of H. C. Earwicker's twin boys, Jerry and Kevin. Jerry appears most frequently as Shem, from the name *Seumas,* or James. He is considered to represent the author himself, since he is the problem-child of the family, continually writing and continually being accused of impiety and a lack of patriotism, as was Joyce throughout his whole career. Jerry is referred to as "Shem the Penman." It is also believed that Jerry, or Shem, is identified with Dean SWIFT, the phrase "Mr. O'Shem the Draper" occurring on one occasion. See DRAPIER'S LETTERS.

Kevin Earwicker. The second of H. C. Earwicker's twin boys, who appears as Shaun (from *Sean*) and is called "Shaun the Post." He seems destined for success in later life, as a statesman, a businessman in America, or a priest. He is interpreted as the man of action ("Jno Citizen"), as opposed to the artist, or the man of feeling ("Jas Pagan"). See ONDT AND THE GRACEHOPER, THE. It is believed that the scenes of battle and the allusions to warfare throughout the novel, especially those associated with the Crimean War, serve to present the brothers in conflict with each other. One Buckley kills a Russian general at one point, an incident interpreted as follows:

> The Russian general, *alias* "General Jinglesome," *alias* "Mr. Jinglejoys" may well be Shem, whose writing is caviar to the general. Buckley, pronounced somewhat like the Gaelic *bouchalleen bawn* ("fair-haired boy") may again be Shaun, taking his stand for young Ireland.
>
> Harry Levin, *James Joyce.*

Ultimately, it is said, Jerry and Kevin, or Shem and Shaun are Cain and Abel, Jacob and Esau, and even their father himself, or mankind struggling against itself in accordance with the principle of DUALISM held by Giordano BRUNO.

Isobel Earwicker. Earwicker's daughter, who appears as Iseult (see TRISTAN AND ISEULT) and is symbolized by CHAPELIZOD, a village on the river Liffey which is the scene of the action in the second section of *Finnegans Wake.* She is regarded as the "second heroine" of the book, the second feminine object of Earwicker's love. Cf. the two Iseults of Tristan. One passage in which Shaun, or Kevin (see above), is presented as preaching a sermon on chastity to twenty-nine young girls is interpreted as a dream-distortion of the lover's manner in which her father subconsciously would like to speak to her. His pet name for her is "PPT," and she and her mother at times may correspond to STELLA and VANESSA, the two women between whom Swift's affections were torn.

Easiest Way, The. A drama by Eugene Walter (*Am.* 1908). The heroine, Laura Murdock, an actress with a past, has been genuinely drawn to John Madison, a reckless, carefree Western newspaper reporter, and has promised to marry him. While Madison, whose love steadies him, is saving money for the venture, Laura goes back to the stage and soon takes to "the easiest way" in spite of her resolves. She attempts to lie to Madison when he comes for her unexpectedly, but he learns the truth and leaves her.

East. Regions and countries lying to the east, specifically:

the Far East. China, Japan and neighboring sections of the Orient.

the Middle East. A term used somewhat loosely to designate the region between the Near and Far East.

the Near East. The countries that were comprised in the Turkish empire before the World War.

From the point of view of, let us say, a Californian, the Far East is nearer than the Near East, unless he insists on getting there traveling east rather than west. The expressions *East, Far East,* etc. originated in Europe.

down East. In New England.

East and West Poems. A volume by Bret HARTE. See PIKE.

Easter. The name was adopted for the Christian Paschal festival from A.S. *eastre,* a heathen festival held at the vernal equinox in honor of the Teutonic goddess of dawn, called by Bede *Eostre* (cognate with Lat. *aurora* and Sanskrit *ushas,* dawn). On the introduction of Christianity it was natural for the name of the heathen festival to be transferred to the Christian, the two falling about the same time.

Easter Sunday is the first Sunday after the Paschal full moon, *i.e.* the full moon that occurs on the day of the vernal equinox (March 21) or on any of the next 28 days. Consequently, Easter Sunday cannot be earlier than March 22, or later than April 25. This was fixed by the Council of Nice, A. D. 325.

It was formerly a common belief that the sun danced on Easter Day.

> But oh, she dances such a way,
> No sun upon an Easter day
> Is half so fine a sight.
> Sir John Suckling, *Ballad upon a Wedding.*

Eastlake, Sir Charles Lock (1793–1865). English painter and art critic. Made sketches of Napoleon as prisoner aboard H.M.S. *Bellerophon* from which he developed two large portraits. Keeper of National Gallery (1843–1847), director (1855). Known for pictures of Italian banditti and several paintings of episodes in the life of Christ.

East Lynne. A novel by Mrs. Henry WOOD (1861) which was immensely popular, particularly in a dramatic version. Its heroine, Lady Isabel Vane, after running off with another man, returns to her remarried husband, completely disguised as a nurse hired to care for her own children, and successfully keeps up the pretense over a considerable period of time. In the end she and her husband are reconciled.

Eastman, Charles Alexander (1858–1939). American physician of Sioux Indian descent. Indian name **Ohiyesa.** Wrote half a dozen books on Indian life. Married the poet Elaine Goodale.

Eastman, George (1854–1932). American inventor and industrialist. Inventor of the portable hand camera known as Kodak (1888). Treasurer and general manager, Eastman Kodak Co. Founded Eastman School of Music, Rochester, N.Y.

Eastman, Max Forrester (1883–). American literary critic, editor, and essayist. His thought showed an early tendency toward radicalism, and he founded the magazine THE MASSES in 1913, editing it until 1917, when he was tried for sedition, along with Floyd DELL and John REED, for anti-war writings. He founded *The Liberator,* another radical periodical, in 1918, editing it until 1922. He was a member of the American COMMUNIST PARTY for a time, but was expelled for being a defender of TROTSKY; his Trotskyist sympathies continued thereafter, although his main interest was literature. Among his works are *Child of the Amazons, And Other Poems* (1913), *Colors of Life* (1918), and *Kinds of Love* (1931), books of poetry; *The Enjoyment of Poetry* (1913), his best-known work; *Journalism versus Art* (1916); *Understanding Germany* (1916); *The Sense of Humor* (1921); *Leon Trotsky* (1925); *Marx and Lenin: The Science of Revolution* (1926); *Venture* (1927), a novel; *The Literary Mind: Its Place in an Age of Science* (1931); *Art and the Life of Action* (1934); *Artists in Uniform* (1934); *The Enjoyment of Laughter* (1936); *The End of Socialism in Russia* (1937); *Heroes I Have Known* (1942) and several translations from the Russian, including *Gabriel* (1929), by PUSHKIN, and three works by Trotsky—*The Real Situation in Russia* (1928), *History of the Russian Revolution* (1932), *Revolution Betrayed* (1937). See also THE CULT OF UNINTELLIGIBILITY.

East Side, the. The East-side tenement districts of Manhattan, inhabited almost entirely by foreigners. Synonymous with the slums. Corresponds to the London East End.

Eatanswill Gazette. A journal of some importance in Dickens' PICKWICK PAPERS, the persistent opponent of the *Eatanswill Independent.*

Eaton, Walter Prichard (1878–). American dramatic critic. Has taught pioneer playwriting classes at Yale, taking over from George Pierce BAKER. (Now retired.) Author of many books of dramatic criticism, nature essays, and juvenile and adult fiction.

Eaton, Wyatt (1849–1896). Canadian American painter, chiefly of portraits. One of the founders of the Society of American Artists (1877).

Ebb Tide, The. A novel by Robert Louis STEVENSON, in collaboration with Lloyd OSBOURNE.

Eben Holden. A novel by Irving BACHELLER (1900). The chief interest of the book lies in the character and quaint sayings of Eben Holden, the sturdy and loyal "hired man." There is a love affair in which the orphaned William and Hope Brower, the daughter of the kindly couple who have given Eben Holden and William a home, are the principals.

Eberhart, Mrs. **Mignon (Good)** (1899–). American detective story writer. Many of her books center around Nurse Sarah Keate, a character of her invention.

Ebert, Friedrich (1871–1925). German Social Democratic leader and first president of the German Reich (1919–1925). Rose from humble beginnings as saddle maker and innkeeper. Suppressed the Kapp Putsch (1920) and the Hitler-Ludendorff attempt to establish a dictatorship in Bavaria (1923).

Ebert, Karl Egon von (1801–1882). Author in German of the Bohemian national heroic poem and epic *Wlasta* (1829).

Eblis. A jinn of Arabian mythology, the ruler of the evil genii, or fallen angels. Before his fall he was called AZAZEL. When Adam was created, God commanded all the angels to worship him; but Eblis replied, "Me thou hast created of smokeless fire, and shall I reverence a creature made of dust?" God was very angry at this insolent answer, and turned the disobedient angel into a Sheytân (devil), and he became the father of devils.

Another Mohammedan tradition has it that before life was breathed into Adam all the angels came to look at the shape of clay, among them Eblis, who, knowing that God intended man to be his superior, vowed never to acknowledge him as such and kicked the figure till it rang.

When he said unto the angels, "Worship Adam," all worshipped him except Eblis.—*Koran*, ii.

Eblis had five sons, viz. (1) *Tir,* author of fatal accidents; (2) *Awar,* the demon of lubricity; (3) *Dasim,* author of discord; (4) *Sut,* father of lies; and (5) *Zalambur,* author of mercantile dishonesty.

Ecbasis cuiusdam Captivi, per Tropologiam (*The Running-Away of a Certain Captive, with Allegorical Significance*), normally called **Ecbasis Captivi.** A medieval Latin allegory in the tradition of the beast-epic (see under REYNARD), composed in the 10th century. It deals with a calf who decides to run away from his stable, does so, and falls into the hands of a wolf, being threatened with mortal danger until rescued by a fox. This is supposed to be connected with the movement of Cluniac reform (see CLUNY), the calf representing an errant monk who breaks his vows and is in danger of committing great sin until rescued by the new disciplinary movement. The enmity of the fox and the wolf in the beast-epics is considered to date from this early version, which contains classical quotations from Horace and Virgil and is believed to have been written by a learned member of the clergy, probably in Germany.

ecce homo (*Lat.,* Behold the man). The name given to many paintings of our Lord crowned with thorns and bound with ropes, as He was shown to the people by Pilate, who said to them, *"Ecce homo!"* (*John* xix. 5), especially those by Correggio, Titian, Guido, Van Dyck, Rembrandt, Poussin, and Albrecht Dürer. In 1865 Sir John Seeley published a survey of the life and work of Christ with the title *Ecce Homo.* This is also the title of an essay by Friedrich NIETZSCHE, describing his life, ideas, and theories of art, and calling himself ANTICHRIST.

Eccles, Robert. A character in Meredith's RHODA FLEMING, weak and dissipated but likable.

Ecclesiastes. One of the books in the Old Testament, formerly ascribed to Solomon, because it says (verse 1), "The words of the Preacher, the son of David, king in Jerusalem," but now generally assigned to an unnamed author of the 3rd century B. C. The Hebrew name is *Koheleth,* which means "the Preacher." The refrain of the book is "Vanity of vanities, all is vanity."

Ecclesiastical History of the English People (Historia Ecclesiastica Gentis Anglorum). A Latin history by the Venerable BEDE, completed in 731. It deals with the period from the invasion of Britain by Julius Caesar, up to the year 731. It was based on the works of Pliny and other Latin authors, and is the best-known source of the famous Anglo-Saxon simile which compares man's life to the flight of a bird out of darkness through a lighted hall and into darkness again.

Ecclesiasticus. One of the books of the Old Testament Apocrypha, traditionally (and probably correctly) ascribed to a Palestinian sage named Ben Sirah, or Jesus, the Son of Sirach.

Echegaray, José (1833–1916). Spanish dramatist. His best-known play is THE GREAT GALEOTO. Echegaray was a recipient of the Nobel prize.

Echidna. A monster of classical mythology, half woman, half serpent. She was mother of the Chimaera, the many-headed dog Orthos, the hundred-headed dragon of the Hesperides, the Colchian dragon, the Sphinx, Cerberus, Scylla, the Gorgons, the Lernaean hydra, the vulture that gnawed away the liver of Prometheus, and the Nemean lion.

Spenser makes her the mother of the BLATANT BEAST.

> Echidna is a Monster direfull dred,
> Whom Gods doe hate, and heavens abhor to see;
> So hideous is her shape, so huge her hed,
> That even the hellish fiends affrighted bee
> At sight thereof, and from her presence flee:
> Yet did her face and former parts professe
> A faire young Mayden full of comely glee;
> But all her hinder parts did plaine expresse
> A monstrous Dragon, full of fearfull uglinesse.
> *Faërie Queene, VI,* vi. 10.

Echo. The Romans say that Echo was a nymph in love with NARCISSUS, but because her love was not returned, she pined away till only her voice remained.

> Sweet Echo, sweetest nymph, that liv'st unseen
> Within thy airy shell,
> By slow Meander's margent green. . . .
> Canst thou not tell me of a gentle pair
> That likest thy Narcissus are?
> Milton, *Comus,* 230.

Eckelied, Das. A Middle High German epic of the theodoric cycle, written toward the end of the thirteenth century and commonly known as *Eckes Ausfahrt.* It was used by Wagner as a secondary source for his RING DES NIBELUNGEN.

Eckermann, Johann Peter (1792–1854). Friend and literary assistant to Goethe. Helped him prepare the *Ausgabe letzter Hand* (final edition) of his works. His *Gespräche mit Goethe* (English edition, *Conversations with Goethe,* in 3 vols., 1836–1848) are daily records of Goethe's personal talks with Eckermann and constitute in their remarkable authenticity a monument to the ideal amanuensis.

Eckhardt. Eckhardt, in German legends, appears on the evening of Maundy Thursday (in the week before Easter) to warn all persons to go home, that they may not be injured by the headless bodies and two-legged horses which traverse the streets on that night, or by Frau Holle or HULDA leading the dead.

Hence the phrase, *a faithful Eckhardt, who warneth everyone.*

Eclectics (from Gr. *ek-legein,* to choose, select). The name given to those who do not attach themselves to any special school (especially philosophers and painters), but pick and choose from various systems, selecting and harmonizing those doctrines, methods, etc., which suit them.

École des beaux-arts (*Fr.,* literally, school of the beautiful arts). Endowed school of fine arts in Paris, founded in 1648.

École des femmes, L' (The School for Wives). A comedy by Molière. For the plot, see AGNES.

École des maris, L' (The School for Husbands). A comedy by Molière (1661). For the plot, see SGANARELLE.

Ecstatic Doctor. See under DOCTOR.

Ector, Sir. In Arthurian romance, the foster-father of King Arthur, and father of Sir Kay. Tennyson gives this rôle to Sir Anton instead.

> The child was delivered unto Merlin, and he bare it forth unto Sir Ector, and made a holy man to christen him, and named him Arthur; and so Sir Ector's wife nourished him with her own pap.—Malory, *Le Morte d'Arthur,* I, iii.

Edda. This name—which may be from *Edda,* the great-grandmother in the Old Norse poem *Rigsthul,* or from the old Norse *odhr,* poetry—is given to two separate works or collections, viz. *The Elder* or *Poetic Edda,* and *The Younger Edda,* or *Prose Edda of Snorri.* The first-named was discovered in 1643 by an Icelandic bishop, and consists of mythological poems dating from the 9th century and supposed to have been collected in the 13th century. They are of unknown authorship, but were erroneously attributed to Saemund Sigfusson (d. 1133), and this has hence sometimes been called *Saemund's Edda.* The *Younger Edda* is a work in prose and verse by Snorri Sturluson (died 1241), and forms a guide to poets and poetry. It consists of the *Gylfaginning* (an epitome of Scandinavian mythology), the *Bragaraeour* or sayings of Bragi, the *Skaldskaparmàl* (a glossary of poetical expressions, etc.), the *Hattatal* (a list of meters, with examples of all known forms of verse), with a preface, history of the origin of poetry, lists of poets, etc.

Eddington, Sir Arthur Stanley (1882–1944). English astrophysicist. His principal fields as an astronomer are relativity, stellar evolution and the motions of stars. Author of many works, the best known non-technical book being *The Nature of the Physical World* (1928).

Eddy, Mary Morse Baker (1821–1910). Founder of the Church of Christ, Scientist (1879). Influenced by Dr. Phineas Parkhurst Quimby of Portland, Me. Disseminated his teachings and practiced the system of healing known as Christian Science. Published *Science and Health* (1875). Founded *The Christian Science Journal* (1883) and the Christian Science Publishing Society (1898) which published *The Christian Science Quarterly* and *The Christian Science Monitor* (1908).

Eddy, Sherwood (1871–). American publicist and Y.M.C.A. official (till 1931) Joined Socialist Party and worked and lectured much among students of Near and Far East. He has been called "a fearless and dynamic writer and speaker."

edelweiss (*Ger.,* literally, "noble white"). A small perennial herb growing in the Alps and Pyrenees. Its blossom is the floral emblem of Switzerland. Coveted by tourists as proof of alpine prowess because it grows principally in situations difficult of access.

Eden. Paradise, the country and garden in which Adam and Eve were placed by God (*Gen.* ii. 15). The word means *delight, pleasure.* It is often used to describe a place of charming scenery. In Dickens' MARTIN CHUZZLEWIT Eden was a dismal swamp somewhere in the United States, the climate of which generally proves fatal to the poor dupes who are induced to settle there through the swindling transactions of General Scadder and General Choke. So dismal and dangerous is the place, that even Mark Tapley is satisfied to have found at last a place where he can "come out jolly with credit."

Eden, Robert Anthony (1897–). English statesman. Resigned as secretary of state for foreign affairs in disagreement with policy of Chamberlain government after Munich conference. Secretary of state for dominions (1939–1940), war secretary (1940), again secretary of state for foreign affairs (1940). Important in Churchill government and England's representative at the San Francisco Conference.

Edman, Irwin (1896–). American philosopher. Professor at Columbia since 1935. His philosophy has been called a blend of Plato, Santayana, and Manhattan. His *Philosopher's Holiday* (1938) is a semi-autobiographical causerie.

Edenhall, Luck of. A goblet which is the property of the Musgrave family of Edenhall in England. It is said to have been left by the little folk at St. Cuthbert's Well. The luck of the family depends on its possession.

> If this cup either break or fall,
> Farewell the luck of Eden Hall.

One of the best-known ballads by UHLAND (*Ger.,* 1787–1862) is called *Das Glück von Edenhall.*

Ederle, Gertrude (1907–). American swimmer. First woman to swim across English Channel (Aug. 6, 1926). Time (from France to England): 14 hrs 31 min.

Edgar. The hero of Scott's BRIDE OF LAMMERMOOR, the master of Ravenswood, son of Allan of Ravenswood, a shabby Scotch nobleman. The story also forms the substance of Donizetti's opera, *Lucia di Lammermoor.* In the novel Edgar perishes in the quicksands at Kelpies Flow, but in the opera he stabs himself.

Edgar Huntley, Or Memoirs of a Sleepwalker. A once-famous detective story by Charles Brockden BROWN (1801).

Edgett, Edwin Francis (1867–1946). For thirty-seven years, literary editor of the Boston *Evening Transcript;* dean of American book editors at the time of his death. Author of an autobiography, *I Speak for Myself;* wrote more than eighty articles for the *Dictionary of American Biography.* Originally joined the *Transcript* staff, upon graduation from Harvard (1894), as dramatic critic and remained always interested in the theater.

Edgeworth, Maria (1767–1849). English novelist, author of CASTLE RACKRENT (1800) and other novels, most dealing with Irish life, among them *Belinda* (1801); THE ABSENTEE (1812); *Ormond* (1817); *Frank* (1822); *Harry and Lucy* (1825).

Edison, Thomas Alva (1847–1931). Famous American inventor. Patented over a thousand inventions, including the incandescent electric lamp, the microphone, the phonograph, the Edison accumulator, etc., etc. In 1913 he produced talking motion pictures. His biography is a typical example of the "story of a poor boy who became famous." At the age of twelve he was a newsboy on the Grand Trunk Line running into Detroit. When he died, his name had become synonymous with "inventive genius." He is said to have defined *genius* as 99% perspiration and 1% inspiration.

Edmonds, Walter Dumaux (1903–). American novelist specializing in stories about his native state of New York. *Rome Haul*

(1929), *Mostly Canallers* (1934), *Drums along the Mohawk* (1936), etc.

Edmund. In Shakespeare's KING LEAR, the natural son of the Earl of Gloucester. Both Goneril and Regan, daughters of King Lear, are in love with him. Regan, on the death of her husband, plans to marry Edmund, but Goneril, out of jealousy, poisons her.

Edricson, Alleyne. Hero of A. Conan Doyle's WHITE COMPANY.

Education of Henry Adams, The. An autobiographical work by Henry ADAMS, privately printed in 1907 and again issued in 1918. It is subtitled *A Study of 20th-Century Multiplicity,* and serves as a companion to MONT-SAINT-MICHEL AND CHARTRES. In it, the author uses his own life as an example of the difficulties of the individual in contact with a hostile and complex world. The book presents a vivid picture of the time in which Adams lived and the places he visited, and gives penetrating analyses of people and events along with the author's subtle, intricate, and thoroughly pessimistic ideas on the course of historical development.

Edward. A famous English folk-BALLAD of the "domestic relations" type, considered one of the best examples of its form. Through a dramatic dialogue structure, the bitter hatred of Edward, a son who has killed his father, is revealed to be directed against his mother, the other person who participates in the dialogue, who has apparently urged him to his deed. A poem by Robinson JEFFERS, *Such Counsels You Gave to Me,* is a modern version of the old ballad.

Edward II. King of England (1284–1327). Christopher MARLOWE's historical drama of this title (1594) is generally considered his masterpiece.

Edward IV. King of England (1442–1483). He is introduced into Shakespeare's historical dramas, 2 and 3 *Henry VI* and *Richard III* and appears in Scott's *Anne of Geierstein.*

Edward VI. King of England (1537–1553). As Prince of Wales he is the "prince" in Mark Twain's story for children, THE PRINCE AND THE PAUPER.

Edwards, Harry Stillwell (1855–1938). American writer and journalist. Awarded Chicago *Record* $10,000 prize (1896) for *Sons and Fathers.* Wrote excellent Negro stories.

Edwards, Jonathan (1703–1758). American philosopher, mystic, and Puritan theologian. In his early youth he was a precociously brilliant scholar, showing a keen interest in scientific observation. His early philosophical thought tended toward IDEALISM under the influence of LOCKE, and many of his ideas resembled those of BERKELEY, whose work he did not at that time know. As a Puritan clergyman, after his conversion to CALVINISM, Edwards was one of the most violent and merciless exponents of the doctrines of predestination and the total depravity of mankind. His famous sermon, *Sinners in the Hands of an Angry God* (1741), is considered the apotheosis of Puritanism in its expression of hatred and contempt for erring humanity. Edwards was prominent in the GREAT AWAKENING and defended it in a series of controversial pamphlets exchanged with critics of the movement. Among his works are *A Faithful Narrative of the Surprising Work of God in the Conversion of Many Hundred Souls in Northampton* (1737); *Discourse on Various Important Subjects* (1738); *The Distinguishing Marks of the Work of the Spirit of God* (1741); *An Inquiry into the Modern Prevailing Notions Respecting that Freedom of the Will Which Is Supposed to be Essential to Moral Agency* (1754); *Dissertation Concerning the End for Which God Created the World* (1765). Edwards is regarded as the greatest intellect of pre-Revolutionary America.

Edwin and Angelina. The hero and heroine of a famous ballad by Oliver Goldsmith (1767), called *The Hermit.* Angelina is the daughter of a wealthy lord "beside the Tyne." Her hand is sought in marriage by many suitors, among whom is Edwin, "who had neither wealth nor power, but he had both wisdom and worth." Angelina loves him, but "trifled with him," and Edwin, in despair, leaves her, and retires from the world. One day, Angelina, in boy's clothes, asks hospitality at a hermit's cell; she is kindly entertained, tells her tale, and the hermit proves to be Edwin. From that hour they never part again.

> A correspondent accuses me of having taken this ballad from *The Friar of Orders Gray* . . . but if there is any resemblance between the two, Mr. Percy's ballad is taken from mine. I read my ballad to Mr. Percy, and he told me afterwards that he had taken my plan to form the fragments of Shakespeare into a ballad of his own.—Signed, O. Goldsmith (1767).

Two familiar lines are from this ballad:

> Man wants but little here below,
> Nor wants that little long.

Edyrn. Son of Nudd; called the "Sparrowhawk," in Tennyson's *Marriage of Geraint* (*Idylls of the King*), which was founded on the story of *Geraint, Son of Erbin,* in Lady Charlotte Guest's translation of the MABINOGION. He ousted Yniol from his earldom, and tried to win Enid, the earl's daughter, but was overthrown by Geraint and sent to the court of King Arthur, where his whole nature was completely changed, and "subdued to that gentleness which, when it weds with manhood, makes a man."

Effendi. A Turkish title, about equal to the English "Mr." or "Esq." but always following the name. It is given to emirs, men of learning, the high priests of mosques, etc.

Efficiency Engineer, The. Title of a long poem by Florence Converse. The duties of an efficiency engineer involve the scientific analysis of business management with a view to its more efficient operation and the elimination of waste.

effigy. An image or representation of a person. The term is used most commonly in phrases like "to burn or hang in effigy." The maltreatment of an image in place of the absent culprit can be linked up with the old belief that a thing is vitally connected with its representation and can be affected through it.

e.g. (Lat. *exempli gratia*). By way of example; for instance. Often read as "example given."

Egan, Maurice Francis (1852–1924). American writer and diplomat and journalist. Created the character of Sexton Maginnis, an Irish-American about whom he wrote a number of stories (1902–1905).

Egan, Pierce (1772–1849). English sports writer, author of the monthly serial *Boxiana or Sketches of Modern Pugilism* (1818–1824); *Book of Sports* (1832); etc.

Egeria. In Roman legend, the nymph who instructed Numa in his wise legislation; hence, a counsellor, adviser; especially a woman advising and influencing a statesman.

Egeus. Father of Hermia in Shakespeare's MIDSUMMER NIGHT'S DREAM.

Eggleston, Edward (1837–1902). American novelist and Methodist minister, known for his novels depicting pioneer life in Indiana in a realistic manner. The most famous is THE HOOSIER SCHOOLMASTER (1871). Others include *The End of the World* (1872); *The Circuit Rider* (1874); *Roxy* (1878); and *The Hoosier Schoolboy* (1883).

Egil. Brother of Wieland or Volund the Vulcan of Northern mythology. Egil was a great archer, and in the Saga of Thidrik there is a tale told of him the exact counterpart of the famous story about William TELL and the apple.

Eglamour. In Shakespeare's TWO GENTLEMEN OF VERONA, the person who aids Silvia, daughter of the Duke of Milan, in her escape.

Eglantine, Madame. The name of the PRIORESS in Chaucer's *Canterbury Tales.*

Egmont. A historical tragedy by GOETHE (1788). The hero is the Count of Egmont (1522–1568), a Flemish general and patriot who was executed for his opposition to Philip II. Goethe has departed from history by making him fall in love with the beautiful but low-born Clärchen.

Egoist, The. A novel by George MEREDITH (1879). The "egoist" is Sir Willoughby Patterne of Patterne Hall, possessed of good looks, wealth and all the virtues except humility and a sense of humor. He invites his fiancée, Clara Middleton, and her father, a clergyman who loves good food and wine, to spend a month at the Hall where he is the idol of his two old aunts. Clara, "a rogue in porcelain" as Mrs. Mountstuart Jenkinson, the clever widow who regulates the social life of the countryside, pronounces her, is soon longing to extricate herself from the attentions of her self-centered lover. She is thankful for the diversion of Patterne's gay Irish guest, De Craye, who makes violent love to her, but gives her confidence to Vernon Whitford, Patterne's cousin and secretary, tutor to the lazy and impish young Crossjay. Patterne, who has had a sad experience previously, is in mortal dread of being jilted by Clara and to preserve his dignity proposes to his former worshiper Laetitia Dale, whom he had made use of for this same purpose before. Many complications arise, but Vernon and Clara finally confess their love and Patterne is forced to plead with the now thoroughly disillusioned Laetitia to become the mistress of Patterne Hall.

Egyptian bondage. Cruel servitude, such as that of the Israelites in Egypt.

Egyptian darkness. Great darkness, from *Exod.* x. 22.

Egyptian disposition. A thieving disposition. *Egyptian,* as used in this phrase, is the same as GYPSY.

Egyptian Solomon. Rameses III (ca. 1200 B.C.) of the 20th Egyptian dynasty.

Ehrenbourg, Ilya (1891–). Russian novelist, poet and journalist. Joined Bolshevist Party in 1906. Best-known for *Out of Chaos* (1934) and his thrilling news dispatches from the front during the Russo-German war. Excels by his wit, his caustic satire, and skill in giving shallow thoughts the appearance of depth. He has been called a modern HEINE. Flew to U.S. (1946) with Konstantin SIMONOV and General Mikhail Galaktionov to be interviewed by American Society of Newspaper Editors.

Ehrlich, Leonard (1905–). American novelist, best known for a fictionalized biography of John Brown called *God's Angry Man* (1932).

eidillion or **eidyllion** (*Gr.*). A short pastoral poem. Also a form of comedy.

Eiffel Tower. An iron tower 984.25 feet high built for the Paris Exposition of 1885 on the Champ de Mars. It was named for the engineer Alexandre Gustave Eiffel (1832–1923) who also built the framework for the Statue of Liberty and designed the locks for the Panama Canal.

Eightfold Path. See BUDDHISM.

eighth wonder of the world. See under WONDER.

Eight Immortals. In Taoist mythology, eight characters who have found the elixir of life.

Eiker, Mathilde (1893–). American novelist. *Mrs. Mason's Daughters* (1925), etc.

Eike von Repgow (13th century). A Saxon noble, compiler of the *Sachsenspiegel,* the first attempt (in Latin) at codifying the German law.

Eikon Basiliké (*Gr.,* "royal likeness"). A book originally published in 1649 (1648?) as by Charles I, purporting to set forth the private meditations, prayers, thoughts on the political situation, etc., of the king during and before his imprisonment. Its authorship was claimed by John Gauden at the time of the Restoration (when he was seeking to obtain a bishopric, and was made Bishop of Worcester), but who was the actual author is still an open question.

> . . . an incomparable picture of a stedfast prince, who acknowledges his weakness yet asserts the purity of his motives, the truth of his political and religious principles, the supremacy of his conscience. Such a dramatic presentment would not be above the ability of Gauden: and it is quite possible that he had before him, when he wrote, actual meditations, prayers and memoranda of the king, which perished when they had been copied and had found their place in the masterly mosaic.—W. H. Hutton, in *Camb. Hist. of Eng. Lit.*, vol. *VII*, ch. vi (1911).

Eilshemius, Louis Michel (1864–1941). Amazingly versatile American painter and writer. Famous only in his later years.

Ein feste Burg (*Ger.* A mighty fortress). Name and first words of a hymnic version of Psalm xlvi by Martin LUTHER.

Einstein, Albert (1879–). Famous European theoretical physicist. Enunciated theory of relativity (1905), etc. Nobel prize for physics (1922). Born in Germany, Swiss citizen at the age of fifteen, re-naturalized German citizen, and finally, as a refugee from Nazi Germany, naturalized American.

Eisenhower, Dwight David (1890–). American army man, native of Texas. Commander-in-Chief of U.S. forces in European theater and Lieutenant General (1942). Commander of allied forces in invasion of Northwest Africa (Nov. 1942). Promoted to general, and named supreme allied commander in North Africa (Feb. 1943). In command of invasion of Sicily and Italy. Transferred from Mediterranean to become Supreme Allied Commander in Western Europe. Organized D-Day invasion of France and Allied landing in Normandy, etc. Chief of Staff (1945). Resigned (1948) to become president of Columbia University.

eisteddfod (*Welsh,* "a sessions," from *eistedd,* to sit.). The meetings of the Welsh bards and others now held annually for the encouragement of Welsh literature and music.

Ekdal, Hjalmer. A character in Ibsen's WILD DUCK. His supposed daughter, Hedwig, is the heroine.

Elaine. In Arthurian romance the name is given to two maidens, both of whom were in love with Launcelot. The first was the daughter of King PELEAS, who wished her to marry Launcelot. When Launcelot refused, Elaine was made by magic to assume the form of Guinevere. She became, through this deception, the mother of Sir Galahad.

The other Elaine is known as the "lily maid of ASTOLAT" who in Tennyson's *Lancelot and Elaine* (*Idylls of the King*), in which he follows Malory (Bk. xviii, ch. 9–20), loved Sir Launcelot "with that love which was her doom." Sir Launcelot's love was bestowed on the queen, and Elaine, realizing the hopelessness of her situation, died. By her request her dead body was placed on a barge; a lily was in her right hand, and a letter avowing her love and showing the innocence of Launcelot in the left. An old servitor rowed, and when the barge stopped at the palace entrance, Arthur ordered the body to be brought in. The letter was read and Arthur directed that the maiden should be buried like a queen, with her sad story blazoned on her tomb. Tennyson has told her story in his *Lady of Shalott* also.

élan vital. See under CREATIVE EVOLUTION.

El Dorado (*Sp.* the gilded). Originally the name given to the supposed King of Manoa, the fabulous city of enormous wealth localized by the early explorers on the Amazon. He was said to be covered with oil and then powdered with gold dust, an operation performed from time to time so that he was permanently, and literally, gilded. Many expeditions, both from Spain and England (two of which were led by Sir Walter Raleigh) tried to discover this king, and the name was later transferred to his supposed territory. Hence any extraordinarily rich region, or vast accumulation of gold, precious stones, or similar wealth.

Edgar Allan POE wrote a poem called *Eldorado* (1849). Voltaire makes Candide visit El Dorado in his satiric romance, CANDIDE, and Milton describes it in *Paradise Lost* vi. 411.

Eleanor Crosses. The crosses erected by Edward I to commemorate his queen, Eleanor, whose body was brought from Nottinghamshire to Westminster for burial. At each of the following places, where the body rested, a cross was set up: Lincoln, Newark, Grantham, Leicester, Stamford, Geddington, Northampton, Stony Stratford, Woburn, Dunstable, St. Albans, Waltham, West Cheap (Cheapside) and Westminster.

Eleanor of Aquitaine (1122?–1204). Queen of Louis VII of France (married 1137, divorced under pretext of consanguinity (1152) and of Henry II of England (1152–1204). Known as "Damsel of Brittany." As heiress of Guienne or Aquitaine, she brought to England one half of Southern France which possession started the contention between France and England that lasted for some four hundred years. Mother of Richard Cœur de Lion, John Lackland and other sons. Backed rebellion of her sons against her unfaithful husband and was held in honorable confinement by her husband for twelve years (1173–1185). Secured succession of Richard and protected his interests from his brother John while Richard was on a crusade. Protected her son King John's interests against her grandson Arthur. Published a compilation of maritime laws called the *Laws of Oléron.*

Elberich. The most famous dwarf of German romance. See ALBERICH.

Elderton, William. A lawyer and actor of the Elizabethan period, known for his composition of BROADSIDE BALLADS. Many jokes were made concerning his red nose.

Elector (Ger. *Kurfürst*). A prince who had a vote in the election of the Emperor of the Holy Roman Empire. In 1806 Napoleon broke up the old Empire, and the College of Electors was dissolved.

the Great Elector. Frederick William of Brandenburg (1620–1688).

Electra. (1) One of the PLEIADES, wife of Dardanus. She is known as "the Lost Pleiad," for it is said that she disappeared a little before the Trojan war, that she might be saved the mortification of seeing the ruin of her beloved city. She showed herself occasionally to mortal eye, but always in the guise of a comet.

(2) Another, better known *Electra* of classic myth is the daughter of Agamemnon and Clytemnestra, sister of Iphigenia and of Orestes. She assisted Orestes in avenging their father's death by slaying their mother, Clytemnestra. For the use of this legend in drama, see ORESTES.

Electra complex. In psychoanalysis, the love of a daughter for her father. The female form of an Oedipus complex.

Eleemon. The hero of Southey's ballad, ALL FOR LOVE OR A SINNER SAVED.

elegiacs. Verse consisting of alternate HEXAMETERS and PENTAMETERS, so called because it was the meter in which the elegies of the Greeks and Romans were usually written. See also DISTICH. In Latin it was commonly used by Ovid, Catullus, Tibullus, and others. The following is a good specimen of English elegiacs:

> Man with inviolate caverns, impregnable holds in his nature,
> Depths no storm can pierce, pierced with a shaft of the sun:
> Man that is galled with his confines, and burdened yet more with his vastness,
> Born too great for his ends, never at peace with his goal.
>
> Sir William Watson, *Hymn to the Sea* (1899)

elegy. A poem of lament over someone who is dead. Among the great English elegies are Milton's LYCIDAS, Shelley's ADONAIS, Tennyson's IN MEMORIAM and Matthew Arnold's THYRSIS. A reflective poem in plaintive or sorrowful mood is also called an elegy. Gray's *Elegy in a Country Churchyard* (1750) is the most celebrated of this latter type.

element. A word of unexplained origin that cannot be traced beyond Latin *elementum*. The most appealing (though probably incorrect) theory derives it from LMN as a name for the alphabet, which agrees nicely with the meaning "rudiments of a thing," quite parallel to the modern ABC, as "the ABC of physics," etc.

The meaning "ultimate constituent" is at the base of the distinction of the four elements fire, water, air, and earth, which were considered by the ancients to constitute the building materials of the universe. From this, modern chemistry derived its use of *element* which, until the breakdown of atoms came about, could be defined as a kind of matter not decomposable into other kinds.

Elena. Heroine of Turgenev's ON THE EVE.

elephant.

King of the White Elephant. The proudest title borne by the old kings of Ava and Siam. In Ava the sacred white elephant bore the title of "lord," and had a minister of high rank to superintend his household.

only an elephant can bear an elephant's load. An Indian proverb: Only a great man can do the work of a great man; also, the burden is more than I can bear; it is a load fit for an elephant.

land of the White Elephant. Siam.

have a white elephant to keep. To have an expensive and unprofitable dignity to support, or some possession the expense or responsibility of which is more than it is worth. The allusion is to the story of a King of Siam who used to make a present of a white elephant to courtiers whom he wished to ruin.

Elephant in the Moon, The. A satire by the 17th-century Samuel BUTLER, directed against the ROYAL SOCIETY. In it, what is apparently an elephant is discovered on the face of the moon as seen through the telescopes of the time, but it is revealed to be only a mouse which was somehow imprisoned in the instrument.

Eleusinian Mysteries. The religious rites in honor of Demeter or Ceres, performed originally at Eleusis, Attica, but later at Athens as part of the state religion. There were *Greater* and *Lesser Eleusinia,* the former being celebrated between harvest and seed-time and the latter in early spring. Little is known about the details, but the rites included sea bathing, processions, religious dramas, etc., and the initiated attained thereby a happy life beyond the grave.

eleven.

at the eleventh hour. Just in time; from the parable in *Matt.* xx.

Eleven Thousand Virgins. See URSULA under SAINT.

elf. Originally a dwarfish being of Teutonic mythology, possessed of magical powers which it used either for the benefit or to the detriment of mankind. Later the name was restricted to a malignant kind of imp, and later still to those airy creatures that dance on the grass in the full moon, have fair golden hair, sweet musical voices, magic harps, etc.

Elgar, Sir **Edward** (1857–1934). English composer. His most notable compositions include the oratorios DREAM OF GERONTIUS (1900); *The Apostles* (1903); *Pomp and Circumstance,* march (1902); *The Kingdom* (1906); *Enigma Variations* (1899). Symphonies, songs, sonatas, etc.

Elgin marbles. A collection of Greek sculptures, mainly of the Phidian School (see PHIDIAS), including the bulk of the surviving plastic decoration of the Parthenon. Removed from Athens (1803–1812) by Lord Elgin and purchased by the British Government (1816). Now in the British Museum, London.

Elia. The assumed name of Charles LAMB, author of the *Essays of Elia,* contributed to the *London Magazine* between 1820 and 1825.

Elidure. A legendary king of Britain, who, according to some accounts, was advanced to the throne in place of his elder brother, Arthgallo (or Artegal), supposed by him to be dead. Arthgallo, after a long exile, returned to his country, and Elidure resigned to him the throne. Wordsworth has a poem on the subject (*Artegal and Elidure*); and Milton (*History of Britain,* Bk. i) says that Elidure had "a mind so noble, and so moderate, as is almost incredible to have been ever found."

Eligius, St. See under SAINTS.

Elihu. In the book of *Job,* the young man who attempts to reason with Job about his troubles after the three false comforters have finished speaking.

Elijah. In the Old Testament, a prophet who lived in the days of Ahab, king of Israel. During a drought which he foretold, he was fed by ravens by the brook Cherith (1 *Kings* xviii. 6). He opposed the prophets of Baal and challenged them to a dramatic contest on Mount Carmel, where two altars were built, one to Baal and one to Jehovah. Baal was deaf to the repeated cries of his prophets, but Jehovah answered Elijah by sending fire from heaven. The story of Elijah's discouragement under the juniper tree is well known. Elijah did not die, but was carried up to heaven in a whirlwind. He cast his mantle on Elisha whom he had anointed prophet in his stead; hence *Elijah's mantle* signifies succession to any office.

Eliot, Charles William (1834–1926). American educator. President of Harvard (1869–1909). Helped establish Radcliffe College for women (1894). Developed elective system of undergraduate courses. Editor of the FIVE-FOOT SHELF of the *Harvard Classics.*

Eliot, George. Pseudonym of **Mary Ann Evans** (1819–1880). English novelist, known for her scholarly accomplishments, her intellectual power, her studies of character, and her treatment of social problems in her novels. Her works include SCENES FROM CLERICAL LIFE (1857); ADAM BEDE (1859); THE MILL ON THE FLOSS (1860); SILAS MARNER (1861); ROMOLA (1863); FELIX HOLT (1866); MIDDLEMARCH (1871–1872); and DANIEL DERONDA (1876). George Eliot was opposed to organized religion, and was widely criticized during her lifetime for her unconventional alliance with George Henry Lewes, a distinguished scholar and critic of her time.

Eliot, George Fielding (1894–). Army officer, serving with an Australian contingent in World War I, writer on military affairs, and radio commentator. Author of *The Ramparts We Watch* (1938), and *Bombs Bursting in Air* (1939).

Eliot, Sir **Thomas,** see ELYOT, Sir THOMAS.

Eliot, Thomas Stearns (1888–). American poet and critic, beginning in 1914 a resident of England, of which he became a naturalized subject in 1927. Descendant of Sir Thomas ELYOT. Because of the disillusionment and despair and the repugnance toward the industrial and materialistic civilization of the 20th century which Eliot expressed in his most famous poems, THE LOVE SONG OF ALFRED J. PRUFROCK, THE WASTE LAND, and THE

HOLLOW MEN, he became the most influential poet of his generation, being considered the spokesman of the young writers disillusioned by World War I and frustrated in their search for culture in the U.S. Eliot became associated with the Anglo-Catholic Church in the late 1920's and began to affirm religious orthodoxy in his writings, announcing himself to be, as well as "an Anglo-Catholic in religion," "a classicist in literature and a royalist in politics." During the period of the 1930's, he was attacked by sociological critics for his religious and academic leanings.

In his poetry Eliot shows the influence of the Elizabethans, the METAPHYSICAL POETS, and the French Symbolists (see SYMBOLISM); in ideas, that of the Harvard Humanists (see HUMANISM), Henry ADAMS, P. E. HULME, the 17th-century English theologians, and DANTE Alighieri. His poetry is marked by irony, trenchancy of phrasing, a dramatic use of symbols (see OBJECTIVE CORRELATIVE), and wide learning, which often takes the form of the abstraction of whole passages from an older source for incorporation into a current poem by the author. Eliot's criticism has been praised for its keenness of analysis and its insight, and especially favors Dryden, Elizabethan drama, early 17th-century figures, and the Middle Ages.

Eliot's volumes of poetry are PRUFROCK, AND OTHER OBSERVATIONS (1917); POEMS (1920); THE WASTE LAND (1922); THE HOLLOW MEN (1925); POEMS, 1909–1925 (1926); ASH WEDNESDAY (1930); SWEENEY AGONISTES; FRAGMENTS OF AN ARISTOPHANIC MELODRAMA (1932); THE ROCK (1934), MURDER IN THE CATHEDRAL (1935), and THE FAMILY REUNION (1939), poetic dramas; COLLECTED POEMS (1936); OLD POSSUM'S BOOK OF PRACTICAL CATS (1939), a collection of humorous verse on cats; EAST COKER (1940); BURNT NORTON (1941); THE DRY SALVAGES (1941). His criticism includes TRADITION AND THE INDIVIDUAL TALENT; *The Sacred Wood* (1920); *Homage to John Dryden* (1924); *Shakespeare and the Stoicism of Seneca* (1928); *For Lancelot Andrewes* (1928); *Dante* (1929); *Thoughts After Lambeth* (1931); *Selected Essays* (1932); *The Use of Poetry and the Use of Criticism* (1933); *After Strange Gods* (1934); *Elizabethan Essays* (1934); *Essays Ancient and Modern* (1936); THE IDEA OF A CHRISTIAN SOCIETY (1939); *Points of View* (1941). Eliot was editor of THE CRITERION for a number of years. For a critical discussion, cf. *The Achievement of T. S. Eliot,* by F. O. Mathiessen, and *The Talent of T. S. Eliot,* by G. Williamson.

Elisha. One of the prophets of the Old Testament, successor to Elijah. He worked many miracles. See NAAMAN, SHUNAMMITE.

Elissa. Step-sister of Medina and Perissa, and mistress of Hudibras in Spenser's *Faërie Queene* (II, ii). She typifies moral deficiency and moroseness; she

> evermore did seeme
> As discontent for want of merth or meat;
> No solace could her Paramour intreat
> Her once to show, ne court nor dalliance,
> But with bent lowring browes, as she would threat,
> She scould, and frownd with froward countenance,
> Unworthy of faire ladies comely governance.
>
> *Faërie Queene*, II, ii, 35.

Elivagar. In Scandinavian mythology, a cold venomous stream which issued from Niflheim, in the abyss called the Ginnunga Gap, and hardened into layer upon layer of ice.

elixir of life. The potion of the alchemists that would prolong life indefinitely. It was imagined sometimes as a dry drug, sometimes as a fluid. *Elixir* (Arabic, a powder for sprinkling on wounds) also meant among alchemists the philosopher's stone, the tincture for transmuting metals, etc., and the name is now given to any sovereign remedy for disease—especially one of a "quack" character.

Eliza. The lady to whom Laurence STERNE addressed his *Letters to Eliza* (1775). She was a Mrs. Draper, wife of a counsellor of Bombay. See also BRAHMINE AND BRAHMIN.

Elizabeth. (1) The heroine of Wagner's opera TANNHÄUSER.

(2) *Queen of England* (1533–1603). Succeeded Mary on the throne, 1558. Signed death warrant of Mary Queen of Scots, saw Spanish Armada defeated, gave her name to one of the greatest literary ages of England.

She is a prominent character in Scott's KENILWORTH. According to Scott her character was "strangely compounded of the strongest masculine sense with those foibles which are chiefly supposed proper to the female sex. Her subjects had the full benefit of her virtues, which far predominated over her weaknesses, but her courtiers and those about her person had often to sustain sudden and embarrassing turns of caprice, and the sallies of a temper which was both jealous and despotic."

In the 20th century there was a resurgence of interest in Queen Elizabeth, marked by such best-selling biographies as *Elizabeth and Essex,* by Lytton STRACHEY, and such popular plays as *Elizabeth the Queen,* by Maxwell ANDERSON. See ELIZABETHAN; VIRGIN QUEEN.

(3) Countess *Russell,* nee *Mary Annette Beauchamp* (1866–1941). English novelist, best known as the author of *Elizabeth and Her German Garden* (1898), a best-selling autobiographical novel in diary form, describing her life in Germany as the wife of the Prussian Count von Arnim. In it, she calls her husband "the Man of Wrath," and her chil-

dren are the "April," "May," and "June" babies. She wrote popular novels, gay and lightly satirical, including *The Pastor's Wife* (1910); *Vera* (1921); *The Enchanted April* (1922), which was dramatized as a successful play; *Love* (1925); and *Father* (1931). "Elizabeth" was a cousin of Katherine MANSFIELD. Her second husband, Francis, second Earl Russell, was a brother of Bertrand RUSSELL.

(4) Queen of Rumania (1843–1916). Writer under the pseudonym of CARMEN SYLVA.

(5) Elizabeth Angela Marguerite Bowes-Lyon (1900–). Full name of Queen of George VI, King of England.

(6) Elizabeth Stuart (1596–1662). Called "Queen of Hearts." Eldest daughter of James I of England. Her marriage to Frederick V of Bohemia commemorated in *Epithalamium* by John Donne. Mother of brilliant children: Elizabeth of Bohemia, abbess of Herford; Prince Rupert of the Rhine; Sophia, electress of Hanover, etc. The son of the last-named was George I of England, 1st of the kings of the House of Hanover. Elizabeth is also celebrated in a poem by Sir Henry Wotton.

Elizabeth or the Exiles of Siberia. A novel by Sophie Cottin (*Fr.* 1805), concerning a Polish family exiled in Siberia for political reasons. Elizabeth made a long and dangerous journey on foot to seek pardon for her parents from the Czar Alexander at the Russian court.

Elizabethan. After the style of things in the reign of Queen Elizabeth (1558–1603). Elizabethan architecture is a mixture of Gothic and Italian, prevalent in the reigns of Elizabeth and James I, and when referring to literature *Elizabethan* is generally held to include the writers of the time of James I. By *Elizabethan drama* is meant the drama of the period from the accession of Queen Elizabeth until the closing of the theaters in 1642.

Ella or Alla, King. The husband of CUNSTANCE in Chaucer's *Man of Law's Tale*, one of the *Canterbury Tales*.

Elle et Lui. A novel by George SAND (1859) depicting the author's relations with Alfred de Musset twenty-five years before. Alfred de Musset had died two years before the publication of this book, but his brother Paul wrote *Lui et Elle* in protest at George Sand's interpretation of her breaking off with De Musset.

Ellida. Heroine of Ibsen's drama, THE LADY FROM THE SEA.

Ellinham, Gertrude. The heroine of Bronson Howard's drama, SHENANDOAH.

Elliot, Anne. The gentle heroine of Jane Austen's PERSUASION.

Elliott, Ebenezer (1781–1849). English poet called the "Corn-Law Rhymer." Active Chartist. Wrote *Corn-Law Rhymes* (1831); *The Splendid Village* (1833–1835); and many miscellaneous poems.

Ellis, Havelock (1859–1939). English author and literary critic, best known for his studies in sexual psychology, a subject to which his contributions were considerable, although he emphasized biology at a time when the clinical methods of the Freudians (see FREUD, SIGMUND) were attracting most attention. Ellis' works include *The New Spirit* (1891), critical literary essays; *Studies in the Psychology of Sex* (6 vols.; 1900–1910); *Man and Woman* (1894); *Affirmations* (1897); *A Study of British Genius* (1904); *The Soul of Spain* (1908); *The Philosophy of Conflict* (1919); *The Dance of Life* (1923), his most popular book, in which the dance is made to symbolize the vital rhythm of the universe; *Sonnets, with Folk-Songs from the Spanish* (1925), poetry; *The World of Dreams* (1926); *Marriage of Today and Tomorrow* (1929); *The Fountain of Life* (1930); *From Rousseau to Proust* (1935); and *My Life* (1939), an autobiography.

Ellison, Kitty. Heroine of W. D. Howells' CHANCE ACQUAINTANCE. She also appears in *Their Wedding Journey*.

Ellsberg, Edward (1891–). American naval officer and sea writer. Director of salvage operations for raising U.S. Submarine S-51 from sea bottom (1926). *On the Bottom* (1929), *Thirty Fathoms Deep* (1930), *Pigboats* (1931; made into the moving picture, *Hell Below*); *Hell on Ice* (1938); *Captain Paul* (1941; see JONES, JOHN PAUL).

Ellsworth, Lincoln (1880–). American polar explorer and writer. Transpolar flight in airship *Norge* with Amundsen and Nobile (1926). Transarctic submarine expedition with Hubert Wilkins (1931). His 2300-mile airplane flight across Antarctic (1935) enabled him to claim 300,000 square miles of previously undiscovered land for the U.S. (roughly one-tenth of present area).

Ellwood, Thomas (1639–1714). English Quaker. Milton's friend and Latin reader. Said to have suggested writing of *Paradise Regained* (1665). Author of several books, among them his autobiography (1714).

Elm City. New Haven. See under CITY.

Elm Tree on the Mall, The. A novel by Anatole FRANCE. See also under BERGERET.

Elohim. The plural form of the Heb. *eloah*, God, sometimes used to denote heathen gods collectively (Chemosh, Dagon, Baal, etc.), but more frequently used as an intensive singular denoting one god, or God Himself.

Elohistic and Jehovistic Scriptures *Elohim* and *Jehovah* (*Jahveh* or *Yahvè*) are two of the most usual of the many names given by the ancient Hebrews to the Deity, and the fact that they are both used with interchangeable senses in the Pentateuch gave rise to the theory, widely held by Hebraists and Biblical critics, that these books were written at two widely different periods. The Elohistic paragraphs, being more simple, more primitive, more narrative, and more pastoral, are held to be the older; while the later Jehovistic paragraphs, which indicate a knowledge of geography and history, seem to exalt the priestly office, and are altogether of a more elaborate character, were subsequently enwoven with these. This theory was originally stated by Jean Astruc, the French scholar, in his *Conjectures sur les mémoires originaux, dont il paroit que Moyse s'est servi pour composer le livre de la Genèse* (1753), a book which formed the starting-point of all modern criticism of the Pentateuch.

Eloi or **Eligius, St.** See under SAINT.

Eloisa. The supposed writer of Pope's *Epistle from Eloisa to Abelard* (1717). She is better known as HÉLOISE.

Elpenor. In the Odyssey, a member of the crew of ULYSSES who falls from a roof and is killed, preceding the others on their visit to Hades. See also DIGNAM, PADDY.

Elsa, princess of Brabant. Bride of LOHENGRIN.

Elshender. Scotch form of *Alexander.* One of the names given to Sir Edward Mauley, hero of Scott's BLACK DWARF and usually known as "the Black Dwarf."

Elsie. The heroine of Longfellow's *Golden Legend,* a farmer's daughter who offers to sacrifice her life to cure Prince Henry of Hoheneck of leprosy but becomes his bride instead. The tale first appeared as a medieval romance called HEINRICH VON AUE.

Elsie Dinsmore. Title of one of the 26 "Elsie Books" by Martha Finley (*Am.;* real name, Martha Farquharson; 1828–1909) dealing with the trials and adventures of Elsie Dinsmore. Elsie is a pious little prig and remains a paragon of all the virtues although she is persecuted by associates, relatives, and even her father. Her story proved so popular with 19th-century girl readers that the series was continued until long after she had become a grandmother.

Elsie Venner. A novel by Oliver Wendell HOLMES (1861). The heroine shows both physical and moral manifestations of a snake-like nature, supposedly caused by a rattler bite from which her mother suffered just before her birth. Stimulated by a love affair she struggles against this nature and eventually conquers it, but dies as a result.

Elsmere, Robert, see ROBERT ELSMERE.

Elssler, Fanny (1810–1884) and her sister, **Therese Elssler** (1808–1878). Austrian ballet dancers. Fanny amassed a fortune and retired from the stage in 1831. Therese contracted a morganatic marriage with prince Adalbert of Prussia and was made baroness von Barnim by king Frederick William IV.

Elsted, Thea. A leading character in Ibsen's HEDDA GABLER.

Elstir. In Marcel Proust's REMEMBRANCE OF THINGS PAST a painter of landscapes, much admired by the narrator MARCEL and frequently referred to throughout the novels. He is believed to have been based in part on the French Impressionist painter (see IMPRESSIONISM) MONET.

Elton, Mr. and Mrs. In Jane Austen's novel EMMA, a young clergyman and his wife.

Elves, see ELF.

Elvino. In Bellini's opera, LA SONNAMBULA, a wealthy farmer, in love with Amina the somnambulist.

Elvira. (1) The heroine of Bellini's opera, I PURITANI.

(2) The heroine of Verdi's opera, ERNANI.

Elyot, Sir Thomas (1499?–1546). English prose writer, at one time during his life ambassador from the English court to the court of the Emperor Charles V. Elyot is best-known for his *Book of the Governor* (1531), a treatise on education and politics of classic influence, regarded as one of the important 16th-century contributions to the development of English prose. He also did a number of translations from Latin and Greek which did much to spread the reading of the classics throughout the educated classes of England. Elyot is said to have been an ancestor of the 20th-century American poet T. S. ELIOT, in whose long poem *East Coker* (1940) some critics have found quotations from and allusions to the work of Sir Thomas.

Elysium. The abode of the blessed in Greek mythology; hence *the Elysian Fields,* the Paradise or Happy Land of the Greek poets. *Elysian* means happy, delightful.

Elzevir. Family of Dutch publishers and printers flourishing in the 17th century. A style of type was named *Elzevir* after this family. Books of their printing are of special value. The best are editions of classical and French authors. The Elzevir imprint is found in 1213 books: 968 Latin, 44 Greek, 126 French, 32 Flemish, 22 Oriental, 11 German, 10 Italian.

em. A unit of measure in printing. The standard is a pica em, and the width of a line is measured by the number of pica m's laid on their sides— E E E —that would equal the measure required. A system was introduced later, the unit of which is a "point" equal to one-seventy-second of an inch; all letters, spaces, rules, etc., are multiples of this "point," and the system is known as the "point system." A pica is 12 point. The point system gradually superseded the older method.

Embla. In Norse mythology, the first woman, created out of an elder by the gods Odin, Vili, and Ve. The first man was Ask.

emblem books. During the Elizabethan period in England, a popular form of literature consisting of books containing a motto, a picture (usually a woodcut), and a short poem, all combining to expound a moral of some sort. The first emblem book was *Emblematus Libellus* (1522), by Andrea Alciati, a Milanese author. The best-known English writers of emblem books were George WITHER and Francis QUARLES.

Emerald Isle. Ireland. This term was first used by Dr. Drennan (1754–1820), in the poem called *Erin*. Of course, it refers to the bright green verdure of the island.

Emerson, Ralph Waldo (1803–1882). American essayist and poet, one of the most influential figures of the 19th century. He was one of the founders of TRANSCENDENTALISM, a movement to which he was introduced by his association with WORDSWORTH, COLERIDGE, and CARLYLE during a visit to Europe in 1832. He was also influenced by NEO-PLATONISM, Oriental religion and philosophy, the English Idealist philosophers, and SWEDENBORG. His own system of thought is a combination of Puritanism and Romanticism and is characterized by an emphasis on pantheism, optimism, a love of nature, mysticism, ethical responsibility, and extreme individualism. His poetic style is simple, plain, compact, and epigrammatic, and has been compared to that of the English METAPHYSICAL POETS.

Emerson's works include NATURE (1836); THE AMERICAN SCHOLAR (1837), an oration; *Essays* (1841 and 1844); *Representative Men* (1850), a series of lectures; *Poems* (1847); *Addresses and Lectures* (1849); *English Traits* (1856), *The Conduct of Life* (1860), and *Society* and *Solitude* (1870), lectures. Among his most famous essays are *Friendship*, COMPENSATION, and THE OVERSOUL. Emerson outstandingly influenced THOREAU, WHITMAN, and Emily DICKINSON.

Émile. A famous educational romance by Jean Jacques ROUSSEAU (1762) describing in loose, story form the bringing-up of the boy Émile according to the so-called principles of nature. It had a notable influence on pedagogical theory. The fifth and last book deals with the education of Sophie, a girl intended for Émile's wife.

Emilia. (1) In Shakespeare's OTHELLO, wife of Iago, the ancient of Othello in the Venetian army. She is induced by Iago to purloin a certain handkerchief given by Othello to Desdemona. Iago then prevails on Othello to ask his wife to show him the handkerchief; but she cannot find it, and Iago tells the Moor she has given it to Cassio as a love-token. At the death of Desdemona, **Emilia**, who till then never suspected the real state of the case, reveals the truth of the matter, and Iago rushes on her and kills her.

(2) The heroine of Chaucer's *Knight's Tale,* beloved by Palamon and Arcite. See *Palamon.*

(3) An attendant in Shakespeare's WINTER'S TALE.

(4) The lady-love of Peregrine Pickle, in *The Adventures of Peregrine Pickle,* by Smollett (1751).

See also SANDRA BELLONI.

Emilia, Dona. The wife of Charles Gould in Conrad's NOSTROMO.

Emilie. The "divine Emilie," to whom Voltaire wrote verses, was the Marquise du Châtelet, with whom he lived at Cirey for some ten years, between 1735 and 1749.

Emir. See under RULERS, TITLES OF.

Em'ly, Little. In Dickens' *David Copperfield.* See under PEGGOTTY.

Emma. A novel by Jane Austen (1816). The heroine, Emma Woodhouse, is wealthy, and with no responsibilities other than her devotion to her invalid father, finds time heavy on her hands. To divert herself she plays with other people's affairs, but makes one well-meaning blunder after another. She encourages Harriet Smith to aspire to the hand of a young clergyman, Mr. Elton, but the latter finally brings home as Mrs. Elton a wife who has been described as "the finished type of a feminine bore." Other moves, notably interference in the love affairs of Jane Fairfax and Frank Churchill, are not much more successful. When Harriet transfers her affections to Emma's brother-in-law Knightly, a middle-aged landowner of frank and generous, if somewhat dictatorial, nature, Emma discovers that her long friendship for Knightly has grown into something stronger and marries him herself. The best-drawn character in *Emma* is the good-hearted, talkative village spinster, Miss Bates.

Emmerich. In James Branch Cabell's novels of medieval POICTESME, the son and successor of Count Manuel.

Emmet, Robert (1778–1803). Irish nationalist; led a rising in Dublin (1803); tried and hanged. His brother **Thomas Addis Emmet** (1764–1827) was released on condition that he would leave the country. Became a lawyer in New York (1804).

empathy. Imaginative and involuntary projection of one's self into an object or being leading to sympathetic understanding or vicarious experience of events witnessed. The theory of empathy tries to account for the observer's expansive mood in viewing wide open spaces, his experience of the "feel" of motion at the sight of a flying sea gull, etc. and is particularly enlightening for the psychology of poetic imagery.

Empedocles. One of Pythagoras' scholars, who threw himself secretly into the crater of Etna, that people might suppose the gods had carried him to heaven; but alas! one of his iron pattens was cast out with the lava, and recognized.

> He who to be deemed
> A god, leaped fondly into Etna flames,
> Empedocles.
> Milton, *Paradise Lost*, iii. 469.

Matthew Arnold published a dramatic poem called *Empedocles on Etna* (1853).

Emperor. See RULERS, TITLES OF.

Emperor Jones. (1) A drama by Eugene O'NEILL (1920). Emperor Jones is a lordly American Negro who has landed by chance in Africa, set up an empire in miniature and made himself rich trading on the superstitions of the natives. The drama shows him making his escape through the dense forest with the terrible drum of the now infuriated savages sounding behind him. As the strain begins to tell on him, layer after layer of his cocksure feeling of civilized superiority is stripped off, until finally he becomes the victim of his own terror.

(2) Opera, based on O'Neill drama, by Louis Gruenberg (1932). Lawrence Tibbett sang the title-rôle.

empiricism. The pursuit of knowledge by observation and experiment. In philosophy, the theory of particular importance, from Locke to Hume, which attributes the origin of all our knowledge to experience, implying that there are no innate conceptions and that the mind is at birth a TABULA RASA.

empirics. An ancient Greek school of medicine founded by Serapion of Alexandria, who contended that it is not necessary to obtain a knowledge of the nature and functions of the body in order to treat diseases, but that experience is the surest and best guide (Gr. *empeiros,* experienced, from *peira,* trial). The empirics were opposed to the dogmatic school founded by Hippocrates, which made certain dogmas or theoretical principles the basis of practice. Hence any quack or pretender to medical skill is called an *empiric.*

empyrean. According to Ptolemy, there are five heavens, the last of which is pure elemental fire and the seat of deity; this fifth heaven is called the empyrean (Gr. *empuros,* fiery); hence, in Christian angelology, as employed, for instance, by DANTE in his DIVINE COMEDY, the abode of God and the angels.

> Now had the Almighty Father from above
> From the pure empyrean where He sits
> High throned above all height, bent down his eye.
> Milton, *Paradise Lost,* iii. 56.

Enceladus. In classic mythology, the most powerful of the hundred-armed giants, sons of Tartarus and Ge, who conspired against Zeus (Jupiter). The king of gods and men cast him down at Phlegra, in Macedonia, and threw Mount Etna over him. The poets say that the flames of the volcano arise from the breath of this giant. Longfellow wrote a poem called *Enceladus.*

> So fierce Enceladus in Phlegra stood.
> Hoole, *Jerusalem Delivered.*

> I tell you, younglings, not Encelados,
> With all his threat'ning band of Typhon's brood . . .
> Shall seize this prey out of his father's hands.
> Shakespeare, *Titus Andronicus,* iv. 2.

encyclopedia (Gr. *enkyklios paideia,* "instruction in the circle of arts and sciences"). A work in which various topics covering a specific field or all fields of knowledge are treated in separate entries, now normally arranged in alphabetical order. The first encyclopedia we know about is that by Marcus Porcius Cato (234–149 B. C.). The oldest encyclopedia entirely extant is the *Historia Naturalis* (37 books) of Pliny the Elder (23–79 A. D.). The modern idea of an encyclopedia goes back to the eighteenth century. See also ENCYCLOPÉDISTES. The *Encyclopedia Britannica,* for instance, began as a "dictionary of arts, sciences, and general literature," first published in Edinburgh from 1768 to 1771.

a walking encyclopedia is a person of inexhaustible factual knowledge, generally somewhat dusty.

Encyclopédie, ou dictionnaire raisonné des sciences, des arts et des métiers ("Methodical Dictionary of the Sciences, Arts, and Trades"). A French ENCYCLOPEDIA, based originally on a French translation of Chambers' *Cyclopaedia,* developed by Diderot, d'Alembert, and the other encyclopédistes into an organ of the most advanced and revolutionary opinions of the time, mirroring the French brand of eighteenth-century skepticism which contributed a large share to the preparation of the French Revolution. Appeared at Paris in 28 volumes (1751–1772) with a supplement of five volumes (1776–1777) and an analytical index in two volumes (1780).

Endicott, John (1589?–1665). First colonial governor of Massachusetts (1628–1630); acted until Governor Winthrop (appointed by the Crown in 1629) arrived to take charge. Continued as assistant and deputy and later was governor again four times. A zealous Puritan. Four Quakers were executed in Boston under his administration.

Endor, witch of. See under WITCH.

Endymion. In Greek mythology, a beautiful youth, sometimes said to be a king and sometimes a shepherd, who, as he slept on Mount Latmus, so moved the cold heart of Selene, the moon goddess, that she came down and kissed him and lay at his side. He woke to find her gone, but the dreams which she gave him were so strong and enthralling that he begged Zeus to give him immortality and allow him to sleep perpetually on Mount Latmus. Other accounts say that Selene herself bound him by enchantment so that she might come and kiss him whenever she liked. Keats used the story as the framework of his long allegory, *Endymion* (1817), and it forms the basis of Lyly's comedy, *Endimion, the Man in the Moone* (1585). Longfellow has a poem so called. Disraeli gave the name *Endymion* to one of his political novels (1835). The hero is Endymion Farrars.

enfant terrible (*Fr.*). Literally, a terrible child. A precocious child; one who says or does awkward things at inconvenient times and "gives his elders away."

en garçon (*Fr.*). As a bachelor. "To take me *en garçon*," without ceremony, as a bachelor fares in ordinary life.

Englander. A name applied, now only humorously or somewhat contemptuously, by foreigners to Englishmen.

Little Englander. One who would rather see England small, contented, and as self-contained as possible than have her the head of a world-wide empire, the possession of which might be a source of trouble and danger to her; the opposite to an Imperialist. The term came into prominence at the time of the South African War of 1899–1902.

England's Helicon. One of the miscellanies (see TOTTEL'S MISCELLANY), or collections of poetry, published in the Elizabethan period. It was published in 1600 and is distinguished by the good taste shown in the selection of its contents. It contains poems by SHAKESPEARE, SIDNEY, SPENSER, DRAYTON, LODGE, and others.

English. (1) The language of the people of England; also the people themselves. *Middle English* is the language as used from about 1150 to 1500; *Old English,* also called *Anglo-Saxon,* is that in use before 1150.

the King's or *Queen's English.* English as it should be spoken; pure, grammatical, or "correct" English. The term is found in Shakespeare (*Merry Wives,* i. 4), but it is older and was evidently common.

> These fine English clerkes wil saih thei speake in their mother tonge, if a manne should charge them for counterfeityng the Kinges Englishe.—Wilson, *Arte of Rhetoricke* (1553).

The notion, if not the term, is found in Chaucer's Prologue:

> God save the king, that is lord of this language.

plain English. Plain, unmistakable terms. To tell a person *in plain English* what you think of him is to give him your very candid opinion without any beating about the bush.

For *the English Rabelais, the English Solomon,* etc., see under RABELAIS, etc.

(2) In printing, a size of type, equivalent to 14-pt. type.

(3) In billiards, a spinning rotary motion given to a ball by striking it to the right or left of its center in order to increase or reduce the angle at which it will rebound upon hitting a cushion or another ball.

Engels, Friedrich (1820–1895). German socialist; collaborated with Moses Hess as editor of *Gesellschaftsspiegel* (Mirror of Society; 1845–1846), with Karl Marx in the *Communist Manifesto* (1847). Was a manufacturer in Manchester, England (1850–1869); edited and published Marx's works. His most important independent contribution is a study of the development of socialism "from Utopia to Science": *Entwicklung des Sozialismus von der Utopie zur Wissenschaft* (ca. 1880).

English, Thomas Dunn (1819–1902). American physician and lawyer; author of novels, plays, and poems. Mainly remembered for his song *Ben Bolt.*

English Bards and Scotch Reviewers. A long satiric poem by Lord BYRON (1809), written in heroic couplets and expressing a neo-Classical attitude. It was occasioned by a harsh review of Byron's first book of poems, *Hours of Idleness,* appearing in BLACKWOOD'S MAGAZINE. In it, Byron attacks his critics, and also attacks the older generation of English Romantic poets, including WORDSWORTH, COLERIDGE, SCOTT, and SOUTHEY. See also EPISTLE TO DR. ARBUTHNOT.

Enid. In Tennyson's *Idylls of the King* the wife of GERAINT.

enjambment (Fr. *enjambement,* "a striding, encroaching"). In prosody, the continuation of the sense and hence the grammatical construction in a phrase beyond the end of a verse or couplet. This *run-on* device, contrasted with *end-stopped,* can be very effective when it is not used as a mere mannerism, as in:

In cock-wattle sunset or grey
Dawn when the dagger
Points again of longing . . .

Enlightened Doctor. See under DOCTOR.

ennead (from Gr. *ennea,* "nine"). A group, system, or the like, of nine units, as, for instance, in Egyptian religion, any one of several groups or cycles of nine gods.

The title **The Enneads** was given to the works of the neo-Platonist PLOTINUS because each of the six books contains nine chapters.

Enniskilleners, also **Inniskillings.** A famous cavalry regiment (6th Dragoons) of the British service, so named because it was first organized from the defenders of Enniskillen (1689) during the armed conflict of the Irish Protestants and Catholics.

Ennius. The earliest of the great epic poets of Rome (about 239–169 B. C.), and chief founder of Latin literature.

the English Ennius. Layamon (fl. about 1200), who made a late Anglo-Saxon paraphrase of Wace's *Roman de Brut,* has been so called, but the title is usually given to Chaucer.

the French Ennius. Guillaume de LORRIS (ca. 1235–1265), author of the *Romance of the Rose.* Sometimes Jean de Meun (ca. 1260–1318), who wrote a continuation of the romance, is so called.

the Spanish Ennius. Juan de Mena (d. 1456), born at Cordova.

Enoch Arden. A narrative poem by TENNYSON (1864). The hero is a seaman who has been wrecked on a desert island, and returning home after an absence of several years, finds his wife married to another. Seeing her both happy and prosperous, he resolves not to make himself known, so he leaves the place, and dies of a broken heart.

Enormous Room, The. An autobiographical volume by E. E. CUMMINGS (1922). It describes a period of imprisonment in a French military concentration camp near Paris (1917–1918), to which the author was sentenced on a mistaken charge of treason. The personalities of the various prisoners are presented, and their individual psychological reactions to their harsh treatment and their squalid surroundings. The structure of the book is modeled on that of PILGRIM'S PROGRESS.

en papillotes (*Fr.*). In a state of undress; literally, in curl-papers. Cutlets with frills on them are *en papillotes.*

en pension (*Fr.*). *Pension* is payment for board and lodging; hence, a boarding-house. "To live *en pension*" is to live at a boarding-house or at a hotel, etc., for a charge that includes board and lodging.

Enquiry Concerning Political Justice. A political treatise by William GODWIN (1793), in which the author examines the systems of government, law, and religion of his day, and concludes that monarchy is corrupt and all government, in fact, an obstacle in the development of mankind. It urges the abolition of all social and political institutions created by man, including government, law, wealth, and marriage, and places total confidence in the fundamental perfectibility of humanity. See J. J. ROUSSEAU. This treatise was regarded with horror by the conservative elements of the day, and had a great influence upon the English Romantic poets, especially P. B. SHELLEY.

En Route. A novel by J. K. HUYSMANS (1895), dealing with the religious experiences of a blasé and dissipated young Parisian named Dortal, who yields to the esthetic spell of Christian mysticism. It is the middle volume of a trilogy.

entablature. In classical architecture, the wall above the columns, supporting the roof (that is, the triangular "pediment" when situated on the front and the roof plate when situated on the flank of the building). It consists normally of three horizontal divisions: the *architrave,* above it the *frieze,* and uppermost the *cornice.*

entelechy (Gr. *telos,* "fulfillment, end"). Aristotle's term for the complete realization or full expression of a function or potentiality; the result of the union of Matter (*potentiality*) and Form (*reality*); e.g., the soul, considered as an end that is attained, is the Entelechy of the body.

In Rabelais' *Gargantua and Pantagruel* (Bk. V, ch. xix), *entelechy* is the name given to the Kingdom of the Lady Quintessence. The argument on the name, whether it is *entelechy* (perfecting and coming into actuality) or *endelechy* (duration) reflects the fierce disputes that took place among the medieval schoolmen on these two words.

entente.

entente cordiale (Fr.). A cordial understanding between nations; not quite amounting to an alliance, but something more than a *rapprochement.* The term is not new, but is now usually applied to the *entente* between England and France that was arranged largely by the personal endeavors of Edward VII in 1906.

Triple Entente. A friendly alliance between Great Britain, France and Russia before World War I. During the war Great Britain, France and Italy were referred to as the *Entente.*

Little Entente. An alliance between Czechoslovakia, Yugoslavia and Rumania entered into after the signing of the Treaty of the Trianon (1920), with the avowed purpose of defeating any Hungarian plan for a restoration of the Hapsburgs.

entomology. The science of insects. The word is ultimately related to *tome,* "a volume," literally "a piece cut off," and is derived from Greek *entomon,* "insect," so called (in Greek as well as in Latin and English) because it is virtually cut in two. The word *entomology* is often confused, erroneously or for a humorous effect, with *etymology,* the science of the derivation of words.

entr'acte or, occasionally, **interact.** The interval between two acts of a play. Also an intermezzo performed during that interval.

eolian harp. See under AEOLIAN.

Eolus, see AEOLUS.

eon, see AEON.

Eothen or Traces of Travel Brought Home from the East. A book by Alexander William Kinglake (1844), considered one of the classics of travel.

Épée, Charles Michel de l' (1712–1789). French abbé and pioneer in ways of communication for the deaf and dumb. His one-hand sign alphabet, still in use, was developed to help his two deaf sisters.

Ephesian letters. Magic characters. The Ephesians were greatly addicted to magic. Magic characters were marked on the crown, cincture, and feet of Diana, and, at the preaching of Paul, in Ephesus, many converts who had used "curious" or magical books burned them. (*Acts* xix. 19.)

Ephesian poet. Hipponax, born at Ephesus in the 6th century B. C.

Ephialtes. A giant, who was deprived of his left eye by Apollo, and of his right eye by Hercules. The Greek word is from a verb meaning "to leap upon" and it used to be given to the supposed demon which caused nightmares.

> [We refer unto sober examination] what natural effects can reasonably be expected, when to prevent the Ephialtes or night-Mare we hang up an hollow stone in our stables, when for amulets against Agues we use the chips of Gallows and places of execution. —Sir Thos. Browne, *Pseudodoxia Epidemica,* V, xxiii.

epic. A poem of dramatic character dealing by means of narration with the history, real or fictitious, of some notable action or series of actions carried out under heroic or supernatural guidance. Epic poetry may be divided into two main classes: (*a*) the popular or national epic, including such works as the Greek *Iliad* and *Odyssey,* the *Sanscrit Mahabharata,* and the Teutonic *Nibelungenlied;* and (*b*) the literary or artificial epic, of which the *Aeneid,* Ariosto's *Orlando Furioso,* Tasso's *Jerusalem Delivered,* and Milton's *Paradise Lost* are examples.

father of epic poetry. See under FATHER.

EPIC. A program with the slogan *End Poverty in California,* advanced by Upton SINCLAIR in 1934, calling for increase of inheritance taxes, seizure of idle factories for operation by the unemployed, etc.

Epicene, or the Silent Woman. One of the comedies of Ben Jonson (1609), produced by Garrick in 1776. For the plot, see MOROSE.

Epictetus. Greek Stoic philosopher, originally a slave. Taught in Rome until 90 A. D., when an edict of Emperor Domitian banished all philosophers. He left no writings, but his philosophy is known through a manual written by his pupil Flavius Arrianus. The essence of his doctrine states that it is wise to desire nothing but freedom and contentment, that evil is only apparent, and that happiness depends only on man's free will with which even Jupiter cannot interfere.

Epicurus. The Greek philosopher (340–270 B. C.) who founded the Epicurean school. His axiom was that "happiness or enjoyment is the *summum bonum* of life." His disciples corrupted his doctrine into "Good living is the object we should all seek." Hence, *epicure,* one devoted to sensual pleasures, especially those of the table; *epicurean,* pertaining to good eating and drinking, etc.

the Epicurus of China. Tao-Tse (6th century B. C.).

Epigoni. See under THEBES.

epigram. A brief, pithy, pointed, often witty saying or poem, popular as a literary form in classic Latin literature and in European and English literature of the Renaissance and the neo-Classical era. See NEO-CLASSICISM. Cf. Coleridge's delightful, though inadequate, definition:

> What is an epigram? A dwarfish whole,
> Its body brevity, and wit its soul.

epilogue. In rhetoric, the last of the five divisions of a typical speech; hence, the final plea of an actor for courteous treatment by critics and audience as practiced on the seventeenth and eighteenth century stage. Also, a last section of any literary work functioning as a summary, and the opposite of preface, introduction, or the like. A free use of the term occurs in Goethe's *Epilogue to Schiller's Bell* (*Epilog zu Schillers Glocke*), written in commemoration of the younger poet's death.

Epimenides. A Cretan poet and philosopher of the 7th century B. C. who, according to Pliny (*Natural History*) fell asleep in a cave when a boy, and did not wake up for fifty-seven years, when he found himself endowed with miraculous wisdom. See also RIP VAN WINKLE.

Epimetheus. In classic myth, the brother of Prometheus and husband of Pandora. The name signifies "afterthought," in contrast to Prometheus, "forethought."

Épinay, Louise Florence Pétronille de la Live d' (1726–1783). French author. Friend of Diderot, d'Alembert, Holbach, Melchior Grimm, and others. For Rousseau she built a cottage in the garden of her château near Montmorency. Voltaire was her guest (1757–1759) in the château itself. Her *Mémoires et correspondance* was published in 1818. SAINTE-BEUVE remarked: "Les mémoires de Mme d' Épinay ne sont pas un ouvrage, ils sont une époque."

Epinicia (*Latin,* from *Greek*). Odes of victory in national games, as the Olympic, Pythian or Delphic, Nemean, and Isthmian games. There are among PINDAR's extant works 44 Epinicia.

Epiphany (Gr. *epiphaneia,* "an appearance, manifestation"). The time of appearance, meaning the period when the star appeared to the wise men of the East. January 6th is the Feast of the Epiphany in commemoration of this event.

Epipsychidion (*Gr.*, literally, "a little poem on the soul"). A poem by Shelley (1821).

episode (*Gr.* coming in besides—i.e., adventitious). Originally, the parts in dialogue which were interpolated between the choric songs in Greek tragedy; hence, an adventitious tale introduced into the main story which can be naturally connected with the framework but which has not necessarily anything to do with it.

In music, an intermediate passage in a fugue, where the subject is for a time suspended.

Epistle to Dr. Arbuthnot. A satirical poem by Alexander POPE (1735) in the form of a dialogue between the poet and Dr. John Arbuthnot (1667–1735), a physician and man of letters who was a friend of Pope. The poem gives a judgment of Pope's work by Pope himself, and attacks his contemporaries, especially ADDISON and Lord John Hervey.

Epistolae obscurorum virorum (1515 and 1517; "letters of unknown men"). A satire in the form of letters supposedly written by uneducated and worthless Roman Catholic priests addressed to the humanist Reuchlin during his feud with the converted Jew Pfefferkorn.

Epithalamion. A lyric poem written by SPENSER (1595) to celebrate his marriage to Elizabeth BOYLE. It has been called his highest poetic achievement. It is quoted and used for ironic contrast in T. S. Eliot's THE WASTE LAND. The word *epithalamion* (Greek) or *epithalamium* (Latinized) signifies "nuptial song." The *Song of Songs* is an epithalamium. Sappho, the Greek poetess, devoted a book to epithalamia.

epithet. A descriptive word or phrase, usually referring to the outstanding quality of a person or thing, as Homer's "rosy-fingered dawn." The epithet was used frequently in classic epics and universally during the neo-Classical period in English literature. There, in compliance with the principle of DECORUM of the time, epithets reached absurd extremes. In order to avoid using the common nouns of the language, which they considered "low" and unworthy of the dignity of their subject-matter, the neo-Classical poets would devise by means of the epithet clumsy and elaborate circumlocutions which they would use instead of the original word. Thus "fish" would be called "the finny tribe," "gun" would become a "leveled tube," and so on.

e pluribus unum (*Lat.*). One unity composed of many parts. The motto of the United States of America; taken from *Moretum* (line 103), a Latin poem attributed to Virgil.

eponym. A personal name, also the person (real or mythical) bearing the name, used to designate a place, era, family, race, etc. Brute is the mythical eponym of Britain; Amerigo the historical one of America.

Epsom Races. English horse races originally instituted by Charles I, and held on Epsom Downs for four days in May. The second day (Wednesday) is "DERBY DAY," and on the fourth the "OAKS" is run.

There are other races held at Epsom besides the great four-day races—for instance, the City and Suburban and the Great Metropolitan (both handicap races).

Epstein, Jacob (1880–). American sculptor of Russo-Polish descent. Settled in London (1905); worked in New York and elsewhere in the U.S. (since 1927). His best-known works include eighteen symbolical figures on the British Medical Association Building in London (1907–1908); the tomb of Oscar Wilde (1909); a marble *Genesis* (1931), and a huge alabaster *Adam* (1939). Most of his portraits are cast in bronze. He is the author of *The Sculptor Speaks* (1931).

Epworth League. A Methodist youth organization, founded in Cleveland, Ohio (1889), and named after the birthplace of John WESLEY, the small town of Epworth in Lincolnshire, England.

Equality State. Wyoming. See under STATES.

equinox. The time of year, recurring twice, when day and night are everywhere of equal length. The two yearly equinoxes (vernal equinox, about March 21; autumnal equinox, September 23) together with the two

SOLSTICES (summer solstice, June 22; winter solstice, December 22) divide the year into four equal parts. The equinoxes are traditionally expected to be ushered in by violent storms and other meteorological excesses.

equivoque. An ambiguous term, a word susceptible of two or several interpretations; often used for puns of the type cultivated by traveling salesmen.

era. (1) A count of years beginning from a specific starting point. The *Christian era* begins with the birth of Christ.

The era of Abraham begins	Oct. 1, 2016 B. C.
the era of Actium,	Jan. 1, 30 B. C.
the era of Alexander the Great,	324 B. C.
the era of American Independence,	July 4, 1776 A. D.
the era of Armenia,	July 9, 552 A. D.
the era of Augustus,	27 B. C.
the era of the Chinese,	2697 B. C.
the era of Diocletian,	Aug. 29, 284 A. D.
the era of the Foundation of Rome,	753 B. C.
the era of the French Republic,	Sept. 22, 1792 A. D.
the era of the Greek Olympiads,	776 B. C.
the era of the Hegira,	July 16, 622 A. D.
the era of the Maccabees,	166 B. C.
the era of Nabonassar,	747 B. C.
the era of the Seleucidae,	45 B. C.
the era of Tyre,	Oct. 19, 125 B. C.
the era of the Yezdegird,	June 16, 632 A. D.

(2) A period of time characterized by some distinctive feature. The *Mundane era*, or the supposed number of years between the Creation and the Nativity is:

according to the modern Greek Calendar,	7,388 years;
according to Josephus,	5,829 years;
according to the ancient Greek Church,	5,508 years;
according to Professor Hales,	5,411 years;
according to *l'Art de vérifier les dates,*	4,968 years;
according to Archbishop Ussher,	4,004 years;
according to Calmet,	4,000 years;
according to the Jews,	3,760 years.

the era of good feeling. A name given to the period between 1817 and 1824 in American history because of the absence of political strife.

Jazz era, see under JAZZ.

See also AGE.

Erasmus, Desiderius. Actual name **Gerhard Gerhards** or **Geert Geerts** (1466?–1536). A noted Dutch scholar and humanist of the Renaissance. The love story of his parents is told in Reade's CLOISTER AND THE HEARTH, and the young Erasmus is introduced in the latter part of the novel. Erasmus favored the Reformation at first, but opposed it when it seemed to develop the characteristics of a revolution. Erasmic aloofness, horror of violence and devotion to quiet scholarship have become proverbial. His most generally known book is the wisely satirical *Praise of Folly* (*Encomium Moriae*), and his most important contribution to scholarship is his edition of the Greek text of the New Testament. The classical refinement of his Latin style (especially in his letters) is admirable, but—ironically—contributed largely to the decline of Latin as a language fit for vernacular use.

Erato. In Greek mythology, one of the nine MUSES; the muse of erotic poetry; usually represented holding or playing a lyre.

Erceldoune, Thomas of, see THOMAS THE RHYMER.

Erckmann-Chatrian. Joint pen-name of **Émile Erckmann** (1822–1899) and **Alexandre Chatrian** (1826–1890). French authors of many historical romances and also of several plays. Their collaboration (begun in 1847) was unusual in that Erckmann did most of the creative writing while Chatrian worked as an editor and also adapted the material for the stage.

Erda. In Wagner's *Ring,* the earth goddess HERTHA.

Erebus. In Greek mythology, the son of Chaos and brother of Night; hence darkness personified. His name was given to the gloomy cavern underground through which the Shades had to walk in the course of their passage to Hades.

Érec et Énide. A medieval chivalric romance by CHRÉTIEN DE TROYES. It tells of Érec, a knight at the court of King ARTHUR, who goes out in search of adventure and stays overnight at a run-down castle, where he meets the beautiful daughter of the baron who is the master of the castle. Érec asks her hand, marries her, and then retires from the active life of a knight to enjoy the pleasures of home life. His reputation soon begins to suffer from this, however, and one day he overhears his wife bemoaning the situation. The knight thereupon blames her for the state of affairs in which they find themselves and sets out once more in search of adventure, forcing the lady to accompany them. They have amazing adventures, in which Érec proves himself to be of prodigious strength and valor, although he is harsh in his treatment of his wife. Eventually she is kidnaped by a robber-baron while the knight lies in an apparent state of death, but he revives in time to rescue her, and at length they are reconciled.

Erechtheum or **Erechtheion.** A temple of the tutelary deities of Athens. It derived its name from King **Erechtheus,** the mythical son of Gaea and Hephaestus (Vulcan), who built the Erechtheum and is also remembered for having invented the four-wheeled chariot. He is the subject of a poetic drama by Swinburne.

Eretrian bull. Menedemus of Eretria, in Euboea, a Greek philosopher of about 350–270 B. C., who founded the Eretrian school, a branch of the Socratic.

Erewhon. The name of the ideal COMMONWEALTH in Samuel BUTLER's philosophical novel of the same name (1872). It is, of course, an anagram on "Nowhere." A sequel, *Erewhon Revisited,* was published in 1901.

Ericson or Ericsson, Leif, that is, *Leif, the son of Eric.* Norse navigator who sailed westward and discovered (ca. 1000) a land which he called VINLAND because of the grapevines he found there. It has been variously identified as Labrador, Newfoundland, New England, etc. At any rate, Leif spent a season there, and it may be claimed that he set foot on American soil some 500 years before Columbus. His father Eric founded a colony (986) on Greenland which was named by him; he became the hero of an Icelandic saga, *Eric the Red.*

Ericsson, John (1803–1889). Swedish-born American engineer. Invented the ironclad *Monitor* (1862) which started a new era of naval engineering. See MERRIMAC.

Erie War. See under DREW, DANIEL.

Erigena, Johannes Scotus (815?–?877). Irish philosopher and theologian, doubtless of Scottish parentage. His major work, *De Divisione Naturae,* teaches a monistic fusion of God and Nature which has been labeled as Neoplatonic.

Erik Dorn. A novel by Ben HECHT published in 1921. The action takes place against a background of radical activities and unconventional Bohemian life in Chicago, New York, and Europe immediately preceding and following World War I. Erik Dorn, the hero, is a cynical and sophisticated journalist. He leaves his wife to live with an artist, Rachel Laskin, is deserted by Rachel, becomes a celebrated author, is involved in revolutionary plots in Germany, and eventually commits murder in self-defense.

Erin. Poetic form of *Eire.* See also under MAVOURNIN.

Erinyes. In Greek mythology, daughters of Ge (Earth), avengers of wrong; the Furies. See EUMENIDES.

Eris. The goddess of discord, sister of Ares or Mars. At the wedding of Peleus and Thetis, Eris, being uninvited, threw into the gathering an apple bearing the inscription "For the Fairest," which was claimed by Juno, Venus, and Minerva. Paris, being called upon for judgment, awarded it to Venus. See also *apple of discord,* under APPLE.

Erisichthon or **Erysichthon.** In classic myth, an impious person who profaned a grove sacred to Ceres by cutting down a great oak. He was punished by terrible, incessant hunger.

Erlanger, Abraham Lincoln (1860–1930). American theatrical manager and producer. The *Theatrical Syndicate,* which he helped form in 1896, had virtual monopoly of American theatrical business.

erlking, *Ger.* **Erlkönig.** In German legend, a malevolent goblin who haunts forests and lures people, especially children, to destruction. His appearance in folklore is secondary to his literary career (a rare and interesting phenomenon). There was a Danish *ellerkonge,* "king of the elves," whose name was mistranslated into German by HERDER as *Erlkönig,* "king of the alders." The idea that alders, especially when looked at through a dense fog, should have folkloristic potentialities, struck GOETHE so forcibly that he created his famous ballad *Der Erlkönig,* in which a father riding home with a delirious and dying child in his arms is pursued by the goblin.

Erlynne, Mrs. In Oscar Wilde's play, LADY WINDERMERE'S FAN, the leading character, mother of Lady Windermere.

Ermeline, Dame. Reynard's wife, in the tale of REYNARD THE FOX.

ermine. Several species of weasels that assume a pure white coat in the winter, except for the end of the tail that remains black. The fur of the ermine (often used with the black tailends inserted at regular intervals), being a favorite material for official and ceremonial garments (e.g., the robes of English judges) has come to be regarded as a symbol of dignity and authority.

> Law and gospel both determine
> All virtues lodge in royal ermine.
> Swift, *On Poetry.*

Erminia. A heroine of Tasso's Italian epic JERUSALEM DELIVERED (1575). She falls in love with Tancred, and when the Christian army besieges Jerusalem, arrays herself in Clorinda's armor to go to him. After certain adventures, she finds him wounded, and nurses him tenderly; but the poet has not told us what is the ultimate lot of this fair Syrian.

Ernani. An opera by Verdi (1844) founded on Victor Hugo's drama HERNANI. In the opera, the heroine is called Donna Elvira instead of Donna Sol, and the hero stabs himself instead of taking poison.

Ernest Maltravers. A novel by Bulwer LYTTON (1837), which, with its sequel, ALICE, OR THE MYSTERIES, relates the story of a talented poet. His first love is Alice, the innocent young daughter of a burglar. After many vicissitudes, including several other love affairs, one of which is with Alice's daughter, Evelyn Cameron, he finds the long-lost Alice and marries her.

Ernst, Morris (1888–). New York lawyer, associated with liberal causes and the combating of censorship. Counsel of Dramatists' Guild and Authors' League of America; attorney for American Newspaper Guild. Author of numerous books: *To the Pure* (1928; with William Seagle); *Censored* (1930; with

Pare Lorentz); *Ultimate Power* (1937); *The Censor Marches On* (1937; with A. Lindey); *Too Big* (1940); etc.

Eroica. BEETHOVEN's Symphony No. 3. Its first title was *Sinfonia grande Napoleon Bonaparte.* In a fit of rage Beethoven changed it to *Sinfonia eroica composta per festiggiare il sovvenire d'un grand' uomo* (*Heroic symphony composed to celebrate the memory of a great man*), when he learned about Napoleon's accession to the imperial throne of France (May 18, 1804). Beethoven's hero had to be a champion of liberty, not of imperial power.

Esarhaddon (d. 669 B. C.). Son of SENNACHERIB. One of the most powerful kings of Assyria and a great builder. He rebuilt Babylon which his father had destroyed. His great palace in Nineveh has been excavated. He abdicated a year before his death in favor of his son Ashurbanipal.

Erskine, John (1879–). American college professor, amateur musician, and author of best-selling, humorous, 20th-century versions of traditional legends, including *The Private Life of Helen of Troy* (1925), *Galahad* (1926), and *Adam and Eve* (1927). See his autobiography, *The Memory of Certain Persons* (1947).

Eros. The Greek god of love, the youngest of all the gods; equivalent to the Roman CUPID.

Erostratus or **Herostratus.** The Ephesian who set fire to the temple of Diana on the day that Alexander the Great happened to be born (356 B. C.). This he did to make his name immortal; and, in order to defeat his object, the Ephesians forbade his name ever to be mentioned.

Erra Pater. The supposititious author of an almanack published about 1535 as *The Pronostycacion for ever of Erra Pater: a Jewe born in Jewery, a Doctour in Astronomye and Physycke.* It is a collection of astrological tables, rules of health, etc., and is arranged for use in any year.

> [He] had got him a suit of durance, that would last longer than one of Erra Pater's almanacks, or a constable's browne bill.—Nash, *Nashe's Lenten Stuffe* (1599).

The almanacks were frequently reprinted, and nearly a hundred years later Butler says of William Lilly, the almanack maker and astrologer:

> In mathematics he was greater
> Than Tycho Brahe or Erra Pater.
> *Hudibras,* i, 1.

Erring, Joe. The hero of E. W. Howe's STORY OF A COUNTRY TOWN.

Error. In Spenser's FAËRIE QUEENE, a monster who lives in a den in "Wandering Wood," and with whom the Red Cross Knight has his first adventure. She has a brood of 1000 young ones of sundry shapes, and these cubs creep into their mother's mouth when alarmed, as young kangaroos creep into their mother's pouch. The knight is nearly killed by the stench which issues from the foul fiend, but he succeeds in "rafting" her head off. Whereupon the brood lap up the blood, and burst with satiety.

> Half like a serpent horribly displayed,
> But th' other half did woman's shape retain . . .
> And as she lay upon the dirty ground,
> Her huge long tail her den all overspread,
> Yet was in knots and many boughts [folds] upwound,
> Pointed with mortal sting.
> Spenser, *Faërie Queene,* i. 1.

Ertz, Susan (1894?–). Anglo-American novelist. *Madame Claire* (1922), *The Proselyte* (1933), *No Hearts to Break* (1937).

Ervine, St. John Greer (1883–). Irish dramatist, critic, and novelist, associated with the Abbey Theater in Dublin. See IRISH RENAISSANCE. His plays include: *Jane Clegg* (1911); *The Magnanimous Lover* (1913); *John Ferguson* (1916); *The Ship* (1922); *Anthony and Anna* (1925); *The First Mrs. Fraser* (1928); *People of Our Class* (1936); *Boyd's Ship* (1936); *Robert's Wife* (1938). Among his novels are: *Mrs. Martin's Man* (1914); *Alice and a Family* (1915); *Changing Winds* (1917); *Foolish Lovers* (1920); *The Wayward Man* (1927); *Sophia* (1941). His novel *Changing Winds* presents a hero supposedly based on Rupert BROOKE.

Erymanthian. Designating a devastating boar which wandered about Mount Erymanthus in Arcadia. Slain by Hercules.

Erymanthian boar. In Greek mythology, a devastating boar which had its haunt on the mountain range of Erymanthus between Arcadia and Achaia. It was finally killed by Hercules.

Erysichthon, see ERISICHTHON.

Erythraean main. Literally, the Red Sea. In ancient geography, the Erythraean Sea was the Indian Ocean including the Red Sea and the Persian Gulf.

Erythynus, have no doings with the, i.e., "don't trust a braggart." This is the thirty-third symbol of the *Protreptics* of Iamblichus. The Erythynus is mentioned by Pliny (ix. 77) as a red fish with a white belly, and Pythagoras used it as a symbol of a braggadocio, who fable says is white-livered.

Esau. In the Old Testament, the son of Isaac, who sold his birthright to his brother JACOB in return for a mess of pottage. Jacob pretended to be Esau and so secured from Isaac the blessing which was intended for his brother. His name is a Hebrew word meaning "rough, covered with hair."

Escamillo. The toreador of Bizet's opera, CARMEN.

eschatology. From Greek *eschatos,* "uttermost, furthest." In theology, the doctrine of the last or final things, as death, resurrection, immortality, the second advent of Christ, Judgment Day, the millennium, and the future state of existence.

Escoffier, Auguste (1847?–1935). One of the most famous chefs; a Parisian.

Escorial. A vast structure, 27 miles northwest of Madrid, Spain, royal palace, mausoleum, church, college and monastery, containing a celebrated library and art collection. It was erected in 1563–1584 by Philip II who had vowed to do so during the battle of St.-Quentin in 1557. It has the general form of a gridiron in memory of the martyrdom of St. Lawrence to whom Philip had made the vow.

Esculapius, see AESCULAPIUS.

Esenin, Sergei Aleksandrovich (1895–1925). Russian poet, founder of the Russian imagist group (1919). His first wife was Isadora Duncan; the second, a granddaughter of Tolstoi. Esenin became insane and committed suicide. He has been called the "poet laureate of the Revolution."

Esmeralda. In Victor Hugo's novel, NOTRE DAME DE PARIS, a beautiful gipsy-girl, who, with tambourine and goat, dances in the square before Notre Dame de Paris, and is looked on as a witch. Quasimodo conceals her for a time in the church, but she is finally gibbeted.

Esmond, Henry or **Harry.** The hero of Thackeray's HENRY ESMOND.

Francis Esmond. The supposed heir to the Castlewood estate, who brings up Henry with his own children but allows him to believe he is an illegitimate son of the dead Viscount to whom the estate belonged.

Rachel Esmond (Lady Castlewood). The wife of Francis. After his death she marries Henry Esmond.

Frank Esmond. Son of Francis and Rachel and, like Henry, an ardent supporter of the Pretender.

Beatrix Esmond. In *Henry Esmond,* a beautiful coquette, the daughter of Francis and Rachel Esmond. After numerous affairs, notably one with James Stuart the Pretender which destroys his chances for the throne, she marries Tusher, her brother's tutor, and succeeds in having him made bishop. "She was imperious," says the author, "she was light-minded, she was flighty, she was false. She had no reverence for character and she was very, very beautiful." In *The Virginians,* she has become Baroness Bernstein, a clever, sharp-tongued and wicked old lady.

esoteric (*Gr.*). Those within, as opposed to *exoteric,* those without. The term originated with Pythagoras, who stood behind a curtain when he gave his lectures. Those who were allowed to attend the lectures, but not to see his face, he called his *exoteric disciples;* but those who were allowed to enter the veil, his *esoterics.*

Aristotle adopted the same terms; those who attended his evening lectures, which were of a popular character, he called his *exoterics;* and those who attended his more abstruse morning lectures, his *esoterics.*

esoteric Buddhism, see THEOSOPHY.

Espard, Marquise de. A despotic coquettish woman of the world who appears in several of the novels of Balzac's COMÉDIE HUMAINE. She is married and separated from her husband early in life; and with a fortune of her own and no warmer emotions than the desire to dominate, she rules the social world from her salon.

Esperanto. A universal language invented (1887) and promoted by *Dr. Esperanto,* in reality Dr. L. Zamenhoff of Poland.

Espionage Act. An act of Congress (June 15, 1917) providing measures and penalties against spying and SABOTAGE. It was amended by a second Sedition Act (May 16, 1918).

Esquemeling, Alexander Olivier (1645?–1707). Dutch buccaneer. His book, *De Americaensche Zeerovers* (*The Buccaneers of America;* 1678), has become an important source for the history of piracy.

Essay Concerning Human Understanding (1690). See LOCKE.

Essay on Man, An. The best-known poem of Alexander POPE (1733), the source of most quotations from the author. Written in heroic couplets (see COUPLET), it is divided into four Epistles which deal respectively with man's relation to the universe, to himself, to society, and to happiness. The poem was suggested to Pope by a friend, Henry St. John, Lord Bolingbroke, and expresses a Deistic philosophy (see DEISM) loosely derived from LEIBNITZ, being intended "to vindicate the ways of God to man." It is optimistic and shows the characteristic neo-Classical faith in reason and respect for tradition and authority.

Essay on Projects, An. See DEFOE, DANIEL.

Essay Towards a New Theory of Vision (1709). See BERKELEY.

Essen. A city in the Prussian Rhine Province, near the Ruhr, 19 miles northeast of Düsseldorf. Its minster, consecrated in 873, was one of the oldest German churches and had a remarkable early-Romanesque cloister. Essen, situated in the center of a large coal-mining district, was the seat of the KRUPP cast-steel works, which were important in World Wars I and II.

Essenes. A sect or order of Jews of Palestine, from 2nd century B. C. to 2nd century A. D. Strictest asceticism on a rigidly communistic basis.

estates of the realm. The powers that have the administration of affairs in their hands. The three estates of the English realm are the Lords Spiritual, the Lords Temporal, and the Commons; popularly speaking, the public press is termed the FOURTH ESTATE.

Estella. The heroine of Dickens' GREAT EXPECTATIONS.

Esterhazy, Marie Charles Ferdinand Walsin (1847–1923). French army officer. Confessed in 1899 that he forged the documents which had led to the conviction of Alfred DREYFUS. After that lived in exile in England.

Esther. A heroine of the Old Testament, whose story is told in the book bearing her name. After the Persian king, Ahasuerus, put away Queen VASHTI, he chose the beautiful Jewish maiden, Esther, as his Queen. Esther kept her nationality secret, on the counsel of her uncle and guardian, Mordecai, until the jealous, evil-minded Haman conceived a plot to destroy all the Jews who were in captivity throughout the kingdom. Then Esther courageously pled for her people with the King; and as a result Haman was hanged on a high gallows which he had made for his enemy Mordecai. This story is the subject of Racine's famous drama *Esther* (1689).

Esther Waters. A novel by George MOORE (1894). Its heroine is an English servant and the novel deals with her long struggle to bring up her illegitimate son. The boy's father, William Latch, who had been footman in the horse-racing household where Esther had her first position, finally turns up as a bookmaker and innkeeper and marries her, but her happy married life is only an interlude in a life of troubles.

Estmere, King. Hero of one of the ballads given in Percy's *Reliques*. He is a king of England who requests permission to pay suit to the daughter of King Adland. He is answered that Bremor, King of Spain, has already proposed to her and been rejected; but when the lady is introduced to the English king she accepts him. King Estmere starts home to prepare for the wedding, but has not proceeded a mile when the king of Spain returns to press his suit, and threatens vengeance if it is not accepted. Estmere is requested to return, and, with his brother, rides into the hall of King Adland in the guise of a harper. Bremor bids them leave their steeds in the stable. A quarrel ensues in which the "sowdan" is slain, and the two brothers thereupon put the retainers to flight.

Estrildis. In Geoffrey of Monmouth's HISTORY OF THE KINGS OF BRITAIN, the daughter of a German king, and handmaid to the mythical King Humber. When Humber is drowned in the river that bears his name, Locrine falls in love with Estrildis, and would have married her, were he not betrothed already to Guendoloena; but he has by her a daughter named Sabrina.

Etchepars. The central figure in Brieux's RED ROBE, a peasant accused of murder and helpless in the coils of the law.

Eteocles and Polynices. The two sons of Oedipus. After the expulsion of their father, these two young princes agreed to reign alternate years in Thebes. Eteocles, being the elder, took the first turn, but at the close of the year refused to resign the scepter to his brother. This incident was the cause of the famous "Seven against Thebes." See under THEBES. The two brothers met in combat, and each was slain by the other's hand.

Eternal, The. God.

the Eternal City. Rome. The epithet occurs in Ovid, Tibullus, etc., and in many official documents of the Empire; also Virgil (*Aeneid*, i. 79) makes Jupiter tell Venus he would give to the Romans *imperium sine fine* (an eternal empire). Hall Caine has taken the phrase as the title of one of his novels, dealing with the establishment of an ideal state, in Rome, based on the principles of human brotherhood.

Ethan Brand. An allegorical tale by HAWTHORNE, published in *The Snow Image* (1851). It presents the hero, Ethan Brand, a lime-burner, who has been guilty of the Unpardonable Sin. This is intellectual pride and, literally, a "heart of stone," for Brand, depressed over his unpopularity with the townspeople, burns himself to death in his lime-furnace, and when his skeleton is found inside, the ribs enclose a piece of marble shaped like a human heart.

Ethan Frome. A short novel by Edith WHARTON (1911). As a young farmer unable to do more than make a scant living, Ethan Frome devotes himself to his old mother, and after her death to his fretful and self-absorbed invalid wife, Zeena. Mattie, a young cousin of Zeena's, delicate and left without means of support, comes to live with them, and as time goes on, Mattie and Ethan find each other's companionship meaning much to them. Zeena on the pretext that a doctor has advised more complete rest and a strong hired girl, now declares that Mattie cannot stay. On the way to the station Mattie and Ethan take one final coast down the long hill, at the foot of which is a great elm, a challenge to skilful steering. In the overwhelming mood of the moment they agree to put an end to things by running into the elm. But long years afterward all three are still living on the barren farm, Mattie a helpless invalid with a broken back, Ethan a taciturn cripple.

Ethelberta. Heroine of Hardy's HAND OF ETHELBERTA.

Etherege, Sir George (1635?–?1691). English dramatist. Began period of Restoration Comedy; invented comedy of intrigue; led the way for the comedy of manners of Congreve and Sheridan. His private life is not without interest. In 1676 he had to leave England after a disgraceful brawl. He had started on a diplomatic career and was sent to The Hague and later to Ratisbon where he disgusted the Germans by his debauchery and libertinage. He fled to Paris where he seems to have died.

Ethiopians. From Greek *aithiops,* either derived from or popularly associated with *aithein,* "to burn" and *ops,* "face." The country of the Ethiopians lay south of Egypt, close to the stream of Ocean. Cepheus, husband of Cassiopeia and father of Andromeda, was one of their kings. Memnon, the son of Aurora and Tithonus, who fell in the Trojan war as an ally of the Trojans, was another.

Ethnic plot. The name Dryden gave in his ABSALOM AND ACHITOPHEL to the POPISH PLOT. Charles II is called David, the Royalists the Jews, and the Papists Gentiles or Ethnoi, whence the name.

> Saw with disdain an Ethnic plot begun . . .
> 'Gainst form and order they their power employ,
> Nothing to build, and all things to destroy.
>
> Pt. i, 518, 532–3.

Ethnogenesis. A poem by HENRY TIMROD, written in 1861 for the meeting of the first Confederate Congress. It celebrates the glories of the South and hails the victorious future of the Confederate nation.

ethos (*Gr.,* "character"). In art and literature, the moral and intellectual tenor of a work as distinguished from transitory emotional or pathetic elements.

Etna. The famous Italian volcano. Virgil (*Aeneid,* iii, 578, etc.) ascribes its eruption to the restlessness of Enceladus, a hundred-headed giant, who lies buried under the mountain, where also the Greek and Latin poets placed the forges of Vulcan and the smithy of the Cyclops.

Eton College. Famous PUBLIC SCHOOL for boys at Eton in Buckinghamshire, England. It was founded in 1440 by Henry VI. The Duke of Wellington said, "The battle of Waterloo was won on the playing fields of Eton."

Ettare. (1) For the story told by Tennyson in his *Pelleas and Ettare,* one of the *Idylls of the King,* see under PELLEAS.

(2) Heroine of Cabell's CREAM OF THE JEST. She is one of the daughters of Count Manuel, the hero of FIGURES OF EARTH.

Ettrick shepherd, the. A name given in the NOCTES AMBROSIANAE to James Hogg, the poet (1772–1835), who was born in the forest of Ettrick, in Selkirkshire, and in early life was a shepherd.

et tu, Brute. According to Suetonius, *Lives of the Caesars,* Julius Caesar, on being stabbed by Brutus, whom he had counted among his trusted friends, exclaimed: *Et tu, Brute filii* (You also, O Brutus, my son). Shakespeare (*Julius Caesar,* III, 1, 77) immeasurably heightened the effect of the passage by adding to it an expression of utter despair at such ingratitude: "Et tu, Brute! Then fall, Caesar!" The phrase is currently used as an expression of amazement at a sudden revelation of treachery or ingratitude.

Etzel. The name given in German heroic legend to Attila (d. 453 A.D.), king of the Huns, a monarch ruling over three kingdoms and more than thirty principalities. In the NIBELUNGENLIED he is made very insignificant, and sees his liegemen, and even his son and heir, struck down without any effort to save them, or avenge their destruction. He marries Kriemhild, the widow of Siegfried, called Gudrun in the VÖLSUNGA SAGA, where Attila figures as *Atli.*

Eucharist. Ultimately from a Greek word meaning thanksgiving. The sacrament of the Lord's Supper.

Eucken, Rudolf Christoph (1846–1926). German philosopher and historian of religion and philosophy. Nobel Prize in literature (1908). His own tenets can be described as representing a metaphysical idealism of ethical activism.

Euclid (fl. 300 B.C.). Greek geometer who lived and taught at Alexandria. *Elements* (of Geometry) in 13 books. Basis of future geometry.

> Euclid alone saw beauty bare.
>
> Edna St. Vincent Millay.

Eugene Aram. A novel by Bulwer LYTTON (1832) founded on a famous murder case. The real Eugene Aram (1704–1759) was a Knaresborough schoolmaster convicted of murdering a shoemaker, Daniel Clarke, to whom he owed money. Bulwer Lytton makes the youthful Aram commit murder to secure money to further his own idealistic purposes. He goes free for a time, falls in love, all unknowingly, with a relative of the murdered man, and is in his wedding clothes when he is accused of the crime.

Eugene of Savoy (1663–1736). Prince and Austrian General. Because of banishment of his mother by Louis XIV, fought for the Austrian Emperor. Fought against the Turks, whom he defeated at Zenta (1697) and forced to accept the treaty of Carlowitz (1699). Active in the coalition against Louis XIV (1689–1697). With Marlborough won Blenheim (1704), Oudenarde (1708), and Malplaquet (1709). "Prinz Eugen, der edle Ritter" (Prince Eugene, the noble knight) is a figure of almost folkloristic import in many Austrian and German songs about the man who saved Vienna and Western Europe from the Turks.

Eugénie Grandet. A novel by BALZAC (1833). See under GRANDET.

Eugénie Marie de Montijo de Guzmán (1826–1920). Married Napoleon III. Empress of the French (1853–1870). Her feminine charm added brilliance to the French court. She became a leader of fashion. In her influence over her husband she showed no interest in liberal and democratic ideas. After the downfall of the Empire, she was befriended by Queen Victoria in England.

Eugenius. The friend and counsellor of Yorick in Sterne's TRISTRAM SHANDY. He is intended for John Hall-Stevenson (1718–1785), author of *Crazy Tales,* and a friend of Sterne.

Eulalie, St. See under SAINT.

Eulenspiegel (i.e., "Owlglass), **Tyll.** A 14th-century villager of Brunswick round whom clustered a large number of popular tales of all sorts of mischievous pranks, first printed in 1515. The work has been attributed (probably erroneously) to Thomas Murner (1475–1530); it was translated into many languages and rapidly achieved wide popularity. Richard STRAUSS based his tone-poem, *Tyl Eulenspiegel's Merry Pranks,* on the adventures of this rogue. See also under Charles de COSTER.

eulogy. An oration in commendation; an encomium or panegyric.

Eumaeus. The slave and swineherd of Ulysses; hence, a swineherd.

Eumenides (*Gr.,* the good-tempered ones). A name given by the Greeks to the Furies, as it would have been ominous and bad policy to call them by their right name, ERINYES.

Eunoe. In Dante's DIVINE COMEDY, a river of Purgatory, a draught of which makes the mind recall all the good deeds and good offices of life. It is a little beyond Lethe or the river of forgetfulness.

> Lo! where Eunoe flows,
> Lead thither; and, as thou art wont, revive
> His fainting virtue.
> Dante, *Purgatory,* xxxiii.

eunuch. From a Greek word meaning chamberlain. Since (in Asia and elsewhere in the Greek empire) chamberlains employed in harems and palaces were generally castrated, the word eunuch developed the meaning of a castrated man. The famous Byzantine general Narses (478?–573) was a eunuch.

euphemism. Word or phrase substituted to soften down offensive expressions. Pope refers to the use of euphemisms in his lines:

> To rest the cushion and soft dean invite,
> Who never mentioned hell to ears polite.
> *Moral Essays,* epist. iv, 49.

"His Satanic majesty"; "light-fingered gentry"; "a gentleman on his travels" (one transported); "she has met with an accident" (has had a child before marriage); "not quite correct" (a falsehood); "an obliquity of vision" (a squint) are common examples. See EUMENIDES above.

euphony. Harmony or beauty of sound. In philology the term has little or no significance. The French do not stick an *l* between *ou* and *on* for reasons of euphony; Italian is not intrinsically more euphonious than Yiddish; etc. In rhetoric, euphony may be said to be conditioned by a functionally well-proportioned pattern of sounds. The implied judgment is subjective.

Euphrasia. (1) Heroine of Beaumont and Fletcher's PHILASTER. She assumes boy's attire and calls herself Bellario in order to serve Philaster as a page.

(2) The heroine of Murphy's *Grecian Daughter* (1772), who nurses her starving father, Evander, king of Syracuse, with milk from her own breast when he is imprisoned by Dionysius the younger. The incident is not historical, but is related of other heroines of legend.

Euphrosyne. In classic mythology, one of the three GRACES.

Euphues. The chief character of John Lyly's *Euphues: Or The Anatomy of Wit* (1579) and *Euphues and his England* (1580). He is an Athenian, who goes to Naples and attempts to win the governor's daughter Lucilla, the fiancée of his friend Philautus. This procedure estranges him from Philautus, but when Lucilla marries a third lover, the two friends are united in their disillusionment regarding all the opposite sex. There is little plot in either romance; the interest lies chiefly in their long philosophic discussions and in the elaborated and affected style that gave rise to the words *Euphuism* and *Euphuist.* The book undoubtedly had a marked influence upon prose style, and for a time Euphuism, or stilted, fine writing was in great vogue. See also GONGORISM.

eureka (*Gr.,* more correctly *heureka,* I have found it). An exclamation of delight at having made a discovery; originally that of Archimedes, the Syracusan philosopher, when he discovered how to test the purity of Hiero's crown. The tale is that Hiero delivered a certain weight of gold to a smith to be made into a votive crown, but, suspecting that the gold had been alloyed with an inferior metal, asked Archimedes to test it. The philosopher did not know how to proceed, but in stepping into his bath, which was quite full, observed that some of the water ran over. It immediately struck him that a body must remove its own bulk of water when it is immersed; silver is lighter than gold, therefore a pound-weight of silver will be more bulky than a pound-weight of gold, and would consequently remove more water. In this way he found that the crown was deficient in gold; and Vitruvius says:

When the idea flashed across his mind, the philosopher jumped out of the bath exclaiming, "Heureka! heureka!" and, without waiting to dress himself, ran home to try the experiment.

Eureka! The motto of California, in allusion to the gold discovered there.

Euripides. Greek playwright of the 5th century B. C., born on the island of Salamis, according to popular tradition, on the day of the great sea battle (Sept. 480 B. C.). Ranked with AESCHYLUS and SOPHOCLES as the greatest of Greek dramatists. He has been characterized as the RACINE of antiquity. Eighteen of his reputed seventy-five plays are extant, among them *Alcestis, Medea, Hippolytus, Hecuba, Andromache, Tion, Iphigenia at Aulis,* and *Bacchae.*

Euroclydon. A tempestuous northeast wind of the Mediterranean. Also called *gregale,* i.e., the wind from Greece. The first part of *Euroclydon* is EURUS, the east wind of classical antiquity. The second part is *clydon,* "a wave." The word occurs Acts xxvii. 14 and may be a popular adaptation of the manuscript variant (now preferred) *Euraquilo,* in which the second part is *Aquilo,* "the north wind."

Europa. In classic myth, a daughter either of Phoenix or of Agenor, famed for her beauty. Jupiter in the form of a white bull carried her off and swam with her to the island of Crete. She was the mother of Minos, Rhadamanthus and Evandros, and, according to some forms of the legend, of the MINOTAUR.

Europeans, The. A novel by Henry JAMES (1878), a study in contrasting cultures. The plot centers about the visit of "the Europeans," Felix Young, a temperamental artist and his sister Eugenia, the morganatically married Baroness Münster, to the farm of their New England relatives, the Wentworths. The Europeans hope to gain much from their American cousins, but find their schemes difficult of attainment because of the New England standards by which they are judged.

Eurus. The southeast or east wind; connected with Gr. *eos* and Lat. *aurora,* the dawn. See also EUROCLYDON.

Eurydice. See ORPHEUS.

Eurylochus. In classic myth, the only companion of Ulysses whom CIRCE was unable to change into a hog.

Eurystheus. The cousin of HERCULES, who, on the urging of Juno, imposed upon that hero his twelve famous labors.

eurythmics. The art of expressive bodily movements, normally exercised in conjunction with music on the basis of a system like that originally devised by JAQUES-DALCROZE.

Eurytion. In Greek legend, the Centaur, who, at the marriage feast of Pirithous with Hippodamia, became intoxicated and offered violence to the bride, thus causing the celebrated battle of the Lapithae and Centaurs. Eurytion was also the name of the giant guarding Geryon's cattle and slain by Hercules.

Eusebio. Hero of CALDERÓN's drama *The Devotion to the Cross* (*La Devoción de la Cruz;* 1634). He is a man of many crimes who nevertheless is saved by his religious devotion.

Eusebius of Caesarea (260?-?340). Theologian. Called "father of ecclesiastical history." Wrote a Christian Church history in ten books and also a universal history.

Eustace Diamonds, The. A novel by Anthony TROLLOPE. The principal character, Lady Elizabeth Eustace, is described in his autobiography as "a cunning little woman of pseudo fashion . . . a second Becky Sharp."

Eutaw. A historic novel by W. G. Simms (1856) dealing with the American Revolution. See KATHERINE WALTON.

Euterpe. One of the nine MUSES; the inventor of the double flute; the muse of Dionysiac music; patroness of joy and pleasure, and of flute-players.

euthanasia. An easy, happy death. The word occurs in the DUNCIAD, and Byron has a poem so called. Euthanasia generally means a harbor of rest and peace after the storms of life. Now applied also to so-called "mercy-killings."

Euxine. The Black Sea. Literally, the hospitable sea.

Eva, Little, see LITTLE EVA.

Evadne. (1) In Greek legend, wife of CAPANEUS. She threw herself on the funeral pile of her husband, and was consumed with him.

(2) One of the principal characters of Beaumont and Fletcher's drama, *The Maid's Tragedy* (1610), the sister of Melantius. Amintor was compelled by the King to marry her, although he was betrothed to Aspasia, the

"maid" whose death forms the tragical event of the drama.

Evander. In classic myth, a son of Mercury and an Arcadian nymph. According to legend he was banished from Arcadia about sixty years before the Trojan war and led a group of colonists into Italy. In the *Aeneid,* this old man welcomes Aeneas to Italy after his escape from Troy.

evangelical. Contained in or relating to the Four Gospels or their record of Christ's life. The term is specifically applied to those Christian denominations that profess to base their tenets only on Scripture and that consequently are primarily concerned with the doctrines of man's corrupt nature, of atonement by Christ, justification by faith, etc.

Evangelic Doctor. See under DOCTOR.

Evangeline. A narrative poem by LONGFELLOW (1847). The subject of the tale is the expulsion of the inhabitants of Acadia (Nova Scotia) from their homes by order of George II. Evangeline is the daughter of Benedict Bellefontaine, the richest farmer of Acadia. At the age of seventeen she is legally betrothed by the notary public to Gabriel, son of Basil, the blacksmith. Next day all the colony is exiled by order of George II, and their houses, cattle, and lands are confiscated. Gabriel and Evangeline are parted, and for years she wanders from place to place to find her betrothed. At length, grown old in this hopeless search, she goes to Pennsylvania and becomes a Sister of Mercy. The plague breaks out in the city, and as she visits the almshouse she sees an old man smitten down with the pestilence. It is Gabriel. He tries to whisper her name, but death closes his lips. He is buried, and then Evangeline lies beside him in the grave.

Evangelists. The four Evangelists, Matthew, Mark, Luke, and John, are usually represented in art as follows:

Matthew. With a pen in his hand, and a scroll before him, looking over his left shoulder at an angel. This Gospel was the first, and the angel represents the Being who dictated it.

Mark. Seated writing, and by his side a couchant winged lion. Mark begins his gospel with the sojourn of Jesus in the wilderness, amidst wild beasts, and the temptation of Satan, "the roaring lion."

Luke. With a pen, looking in deep thought over a scroll, and near him a cow or ox chewing the cud. The latter part refers to the eclectic character of St. Luke's Gospel. He is also frequently shown as painting a picture, from the tradition that he painted a portrait of the Virgin.

John. A young man of great delicacy, with an eagle in the background to denote sublimity.

Evan Harrington. A novel by George MEREDITH (1860). The hero, Evan Harrington, is the son of Melchisedec Harrington, the tailor, "the great Mel." Mel, who is ambitious, has succeeded in marrying his three daughters into good society and with their assistance proposes to make of Evan a gentleman. Through the scheming manipulations of his sister the Countess de Saldar, "the most consummate liar in literature," Evan is introduced under false pretenses among the guests at a house party at the home of the high-born Rose Jocelyn. Evan and Rose fall in love; she half suspects the truth; he tries to confess it. Meantime "the great Mel" has died, leaving huge debts, and the sensible and forthright Mrs. Mel makes every effort to persuade her son to assume the business. The truth comes out at last, but the romance survives the shock.

Evans, Caradoc (1883?–1945). Welsh anti-Welsh novelist, playwright, and journalist. Has been called "the greatest satirist of his own people since Swift."

Evans, Mary Ann. See ELIOT, GEORGE.

Evans, Maurice (1901–). English actor. Has been a success in many Shakespearean rôles. Now an American citizen.

Evans, Robley Danglison (1846–1912). American Admiral, remembered as "Fighting Bob Evans." His ship fired the first gun at the Spaniards at Santiago (1898). Commander in chief of U.S. fleet on its voyage around the world (1907). Wrote *A Sailor's Log* (1901) and *An Admiral's Log* (1910).

Evans, Sir Hugh. In Shakespeare's MERRY WIVES OF WINDSOR, a pedantic Welsh parson and schoolmaster of extraordinary simplicity and native shrewdness.

Evans, William. The giant porter (d. 1632) of Charles I, who carried about in his pocket Sir Jeffrey Hudson, the king's dwarf. He was nearly eight feet high. Fuller speaks of him in his *Worthies,* and Scott introduces him in PEVERIL OF THE PEAK:

> As tall a man as is in London, always excepting the king's porter, Master Evans, that carried you about in his pocket, Sir Geoffrey, as all the world has heard tell.—Ch. xxxiii.

Evarts, Hal George (1887–1934). Popular writer of Western fiction. One of his best books is *Spanish Acres* (1925).

Eve. Literally, "living, life." The first woman; the "mother of all living." An *Eve* is a temptress, so called because Eve persuaded Adam to eat the forbidden fruit. See ADAM AND EVE.

Mark TWAIN has a humorous satire called *Eve's Diary.* There is a well-known poem by Ralph Hodgson entitled *Eve.*

Evelina or The History of A Young Lady's Entrance into the World. A novel by Fanny BURNEY (1778). The heroine, Evelina, is brought up in the country by a guardian. She and her lover, Lord Orville, are kept apart by the mystery surrounding her parentage, by the mortifications caused her by her vulgar cousins, the BRANGHTONS and by numerous misunderstandings; but she turns out to be the daughter of Sir John Belmont and all ends happily.

Evelyn, John (1620–1706). English diarist, contemporary of PEPYS. His *Diary* (1640–1706) is of great historical value although or because it was written by a strong Royalist. He was a prominent member of the Royal Society, at one time its secretary (1672), and author of over thirty works on numismatics, architecture, landscape gardening, etc.

Evelyn Hope. A poem by Browning in his *Men and Women* (1855).

Evelyn Innes. A novel by George MOORE (1898), dealing with the career of a beautiful and talented singer and her struggle between worldly and spiritual attachments. In the sequel, *Saint Theresa* (1901), she has become a nun.

Evening Post. A New York newspaper, founded in 1801 by Federalists. Drake and HALLECK contributed to it the *Croaker Papers.* William Cullen Bryant was its editor from 1829 to 1878, and made it the mouthpiece of Jacksonian Democracy. The Villard family took it over in 1881, and E. L. Godkin and Carl Schurz edited it. The *Post* was always a crusading paper. Mr. Villard sold it in 1918. It was for an interim edited by Edwin F. Gay and then sold to the Curtis Publishing Company. Its name was altered in 1934 to the New York *Post,* and it became the property of Dorothy S. Thackrey. Its columnists include Dorothy Thompson, Edgar Ansel Mowrer, Samuel Grafton, Marquis W. Childs, and others.

Eve of St. Agnes, The. A poem by John KEATS (1819), based on the medieval superstitions surrounding St. Agnes Eve. See under SAINT. It describes the elopement of Madeline, a baron's daughter, with Porphyro, her lover and the enemy of her father. Some of Keats's most striking sensuous imagery is found in this poem.

Eve of St. John, The. A ballad by Sir Walter SCOTT (1799), concerned with the visit made by Sir Richard of Coldinghame, slain in the battle of Ancram Moor (1545) by the Baron of Smaylho'me, to the bower of the Baron's wife, at the lady's urgent invitation. The ghost curses the Baron for murder and the lady for adultery, and the two end their days repentantly as a nun and a monk.

Eve of St. Mark's. An unfinished poem by John KEATS.

Everdene, Bathsheba. Heroine of Hardy's FAR FROM THE MADDING CROWD.

Everglade State. Florida. See under STATES.

Everlasting Mercy, The. A narrative poem by John MASEFIELD (1911), the story of the conversion of Saul Kane, a drunkard.

Ever Victorious Army, the. A force of Chinese, officered by Europeans and Americans, raised in 1861, and placed under the charge of Gordon. See CHINESE GORDON. By 1864 it had stamped out the Taëping rebellion, which had broken out in 1851.

Everyman. An old morality play of about the time of Edward IV, depicting man's progress through life. Everyman is symbolic of humanity, and the characters he meets with are personified vices and virtues. The subtitle reads *A Treatise how the hye Fader of Heven sendeth Dethe to somon every creature to come and gyve a counte of theyr lyves in this Worlde.*

Every Man in His Humor. A comedy by Ben JONSON (1598). For the use of the word *humor* as a peculiarity of temperament, see HUMOR. The persons to whom the title of the drama apply are: Captain Bobadil, whose humor is bragging of his brave deeds and military courage and who is thrashed as a coward by Downright; Kitely, whose humor is jealousy of his wife and who is befooled and cured by a trick played on him by Brainworm; Stephen, whose humor is verdant stupidity and who is played on by everyone; Kno'well, whose humor is suspicion of his son Edward, which turns out to be all moonshine; Dame Kitely, whose humor is jealousy of her husband, but she, like her husband, is cured by a trick devised by Brainworm.

Everyman's Library. A series of books, popularly priced, including among its 1000 items all the best works of the greatest authors of the past. The idea of the Library was conceived by Ernest RHYS. The first fifty items appeared in 1905. It is published by J. M. Dent & Sons in London (original publishers) and E. P. Dutton & Co. in New York.

evil eye. It was anciently believed that the eyes of some persons darted noxious rays on objects which they glared upon. The first morning glance of such eyes was certain destruction to man or beast. Virgil speaks of an evil eye making cattle lean.

Evil May Day. The name given to the serious rioting made on May 1, 1517, by the London apprentices, who fell on the French residents. The riot was put down with difficulty. Sir Thomas MORE, and the Earls of

SHREWSBURY and SURREY were among those who assisted. Two hundred and seventy-eight of the rioters were arrested, of whom fifteen were hanged, drawn, and quartered. The insurrection forms the basis of the anonymous Elizabethan play, *Sir Thomas More*.

Evoe. Pseudonym of Edmund George Valpy KNOX.

Évolution créatrice, L', see CREATIVE EVOLUTION.

Évremond, see SAINT-ÉVREMOND.

Ewald or Evald, Johannes (1743–1781). Danish national lyric poet and dramatist. Author of the first original Danish tragedy *Rolf Krage* (1770) and the national festival drama, *The Fishers* (1779), containing the song, *King Christian Stood by the Lofty Mast,* which has become a Danish national song.

ewe lamb. A single possession greatly prized; in allusion to the story told in 2 *Sam.* xii, 1–14.

Ewing, Juliana Horatia (1841–1885). English writer of children's stories.

exarch. See RULERS, TITLES OF.

Excalibur. The name of Arthur's sword (O.Fr., *Escalibor*), called by Geoffrey of MONMOUTH *Caliburn,* and in the MABINOGION *Caledvwlch.* There was a sword called *Caladbolg* famous in Irish legend, which is thought to have meant "hard-belly," i.e., capable of consuming anything; this and the name *Excalibur* are probably connected.

By virtue of being the one knight who could pull Excalibur from a stone in which it had been magically fixed (from which has been put together another so-called derivation of the name, viz., Lat. *ex cal* [*ce*] *liber* [*are*], to free from the stone) Arthur was acclaimed as "the right born king of all England." After his last battle, when the king lay sore wounded, it was returned at his command by Sir Bedivere to the LADY OF THE LAKE, who, according to some accounts, had given it to him herself. Sir Bedivere threw it into the water and an arm clothed in white samite appeared to receive it.

ex cathedra. With authority. The Pope, speaking *ex cathedra,* is said to speak with an infallible voice—to speak as the successor and representative of St. Peter, and in his pontifical character. The words mean "from the chair"—i.e., the throne of the pontiff—and are applied to all dicta uttered by authority, and ironically to self-sufficient, dogmatic assertions.

excelsior (*Lat.,* "higher"). Aim at higher things still. It is the motto of the United States, and has been made popular by Longfellow's poem so named (1842).

Excelsior State. New York. See also under STATE.

excommunication. (1) The *greater* is exclusion of an individual from the seven sacraments, from every legitimate act, and from all intercourse with the faithful. (2) The *lesser* excommunication is sequestration from the services of the Church only. See also under BELL.

Excursion, The. A long didactic poem in blank verse by WORDSWORTH, forming part of *The Recluse* (1814). It includes discussions of virtue, religious faith, the industrial revolution and its social effects, and the education of children. Wordsworth is sometimes called "the poet (or bard) of *The Excursion.*"

exemplum. In the religious literature of the Middle Ages, a short tale which is used for a didactic purpose, as to illustrate one of the Seven Deadly Sins. Several of Chaucer's CANTERBURY TALES are *exempla.*

Exeter Book. A MS. collection of Anglo-Saxon poetry, presented about 1060 by Bishop Leofric to Exeter Cathedral, and still preserved in the library there. It includes poems and "riddles" by CYNEWULF (8th century), the legends of St. Guthlac and St. Juliana, *Widsith, The Wanderer,* DEOR'S LAMENT, etc.

The EXON or EXETER DOMESDAY is also sometimes called the "Exeter Book."

Exiles. A play by James JOYCE (1918) in the tradition of IBSEN. It concerns Richard Rowan, an Irish writer who has been living in Italy and returns to Ireland to visit his dying mother from whom he has been estranged because of his religious dissidence; his wife, Bertha; Beatrice Justice, a music teacher whom he loved as a young man; and Robert Hand, a journalist and man of action attracted to Bertha. Richard Rowan is considered to be based on the character of the author himself, and the psychological and spiritual problems presented in the play are similar to those treated in THE DEAD, A PORTRAIT OF THE ARTIST AS A YOUNG MAN, and ULYSSES. The spiritual relationship of Beatrice to Richard and its contrast with the relationship implied between Bertha and Robert have caused the play to be interpreted by some as a variation on the story of Dante and Beatrice. See BEATRICE.

existentialism. A somewhat unsystematic system of philosophy in vogue after World War II in France and developed by Jean Paul Sartre on the basis of the teachings of the German philosopher, Heidegger, who in turn owes a great deal to the Dane, Soren Kierkegaard. The basic tenet of existentialism seems to be that "we and things in general exist, and that is all that there is to this absurd business called life." Since Sartre is a novelist and playwright as well, existentialism came to play an important part in French letters after World War II. It proved an ideal vehicle for the basic concept of "absurde" of the new lost generation.

ex libris. Literally, from the (collection of) books. The phrase is written in the books or printed on the bookplate, and is followed by the name of the owner in the genitive. Hence, a bookplate is often called an *ex libris.*

ex luce lucellum. Literally, "Out of light a little profit." Coined by William Pitt in reference to the tax on windows and suggested by Robert Lowe, the Chancellor of the Exchequer, as a motto for match boxes when it was proposed (in 1871) that lucifer matches should be taxed.

Exodus (Gr. *exodos,* a journey out). The second book of the Old Testament, which relates the departure of the Israelites from Egypt under the guidance of Moses; hence, not capitalized, a going out generally, especially a transference of population on a considerable scale.

Exon Domesday. A magnificent MS. on 532 folio vellum leaves, for long preserved among the muniments at Exeter Cathedral, containing the survey of Wilts, Dorset, Somerset, Devon, and Cornwall. In 1816 it was published by Sir Henry Ellis as a supplement to the DOMESDAY BOOK.

Expectation Week. Between the Ascension and Whit Sunday, when the Apostles continued praying "in earnest expectation of the Comforter."

ex pede Herculem. From this sample you can judge of the whole. Plutarch says that Pythagoras calculated the height of Hercules by comparing the length of various stadia in Greece. A stadium was 600 feet in length, but Hercules' stadium at Olympia was much longer; therefore, said the philosopher, the foot of Hercules was proportionately longer than an ordinary foot; and as the foot bears a certain ratio to the height, so the height of Hercules can be easily ascertained. *Ex ungue leonem,* a lion (may be drawn) from its claw, is a similar phrase.

expressionism. A movement in art of about the time of World War I, at its height of influence during the first years of the 1920's. It involves an expression of the author's or artist's state of mind, thoughts, emotions, dreams, and the like, by means of projection through a set of external objects, situations, events, etc., which have a public reference and are not otherwise interrelated. See also OBJECTIVE CORRELATIVE; SYMBOLISM. It originated in painting, was utilized in literature, and was most widely exemplified in the theater, in stage design and dramatic technique, especially in Germany. American expressionistic plays include THE ADDING MACHINE and THE EMPEROR JONES.

expurgate. To divest of objectionable elements. Especially applied to books divested of obscene or morally noxious elements. See also AD USUM DELPHINI; INDEX.

Expurgatory Index. See under INDEX.

Exter. *That's Exter, as the old woman said when she saw Kerton.* A Devonshire saying, meaning "I thought my work was done, but I find much still remains before it is completed." "Exter" is the popular pronunciation of Exeter, and "Kerton" is Crediton. The tradition is that the woman in question was going for the first time to Exeter, and seeing the grand old church of Kerton (Crediton), supposed it to be Exeter Cathedral. "That's Exeter," she said, "and my journey is over"; but alas! she had still eight miles to walk.

extravaganza (*It.*). A musical or dramatic composition characterized by extravagant irregularity. Hence, a caricature, burlesque, etc.

Extreme Unction. (1) One of the seven sacraments of the Catholic Church, founded on *James* v. 14, "Is any sick among you? let him call for the elders of the Church; and let them pray over him, anointing him with oil in the name of the Lord."

(2) Title of a famous poem by Ernest DOWSON.

extrovert or **extravert.** In psychological parlance, one whose interest is centered in external objects and phenomena, in physical rather than mental activities, etc. See also the opposite, INTROVERT; JUNG, CARL GUSTAV.

Eyck, Jan van (1370?–?1440) and his brother **Hubert van** (1366?–1426). Founders of the Flemish School of painting who introduced, according to tradition, a new technique of oil painting with a drying varnish. In their famous altarpiece at Ghent one of the panels is occupied by a picture of St. Anthony in the midst of a group of his monks who follow their master in his adoration of the Lamb of God.

eye.

the eye of a needle. A reference to the words of Christ in *Matt.* xix. 24:

> It is easier for a camel to go through the eye of a needle, than for a rich man to enter into the kingdom of God.

the eye of Greece. Athens.

> Athens, the eye of Greece, mother of arts.
> Milton, *Paradise Regained,* iv. 240.

the eye of the Baltic. Gotland, in the Baltic.

the eye of the storm. An opening between the storm clouds.

almond eyes. The Chinese, from the shape of their eyes.

bull's eye. The center of a target.

evil eye, see EVIL EYE.

eye-opener. Something that furnishes enlightenment, or food for astonishment; also, a strong, mixed drink, especially a morning pick-me-up.

eye-wash. Flattery; soft sawder; fulsome adulation given for the purpose of blinding one to the real state of affairs.

an eye for an eye. Retribution in kind. *Deut.* xix. 21.

in the eye of the wind. Almost directly opposed to the wind.

Eyolf, Little, see LITTLE EYOLF.

Eyre, Jane, see JANE EYRE.

Eyre, Simon. A merry English shoemaker, who built Leadenhall and gave it to the city of London. He had a political career which took him from the position of alderman to that of sheriff and finally to that of Lord Mayor in 1445. His story is told in THE GENTLE CRAFT (1597) by Thomas Deloney, and he also appears in THE SHOEMAKER'S HOLIDAY by Thomas Dekker.

Ezzelin, Sir. In Byron's LARA, the gentleman who recognizes Lara at the table of Lord Otho, and charges him with being Conrad, the corsair. A duel ensues, and Ezzelin is never heard of any more.

F

Fabian. Servant to Olivia in Shakespeare's TWELFTH NIGHT.

Fabian Society. An association of socialists founded in January, 1884, by a small group of middle-class "intellectuals," which included George Bernard SHAW and Sidney WEBB, among others. As announced in its prospectus, it

> aims at "the reorganization of society by the emancipation of land and industrial capital from individual and class ownership, and the vesting of them in the community for the general benefit" . . . and at "the transfer to the community of the administration of such industrial capital as can conveniently be managed socially."

The name is derived from Quintus Fabius (275–203 B.C.), surnamed CUNCTATOR, the Roman general, who won his way against Hannibal by wariness, not by violence, by caution, not by defiance.

Fabius. See CUNCTATOR, and FABIAN SOCIETY above.

the American Fabius. Washington (1732–1799), whose military policy was similar to that of Fabius. He wearied out the English troops by harassing them, without coming to a pitched battle.

Fabius of the French. Anne, Duc de Montmorency, grand constable of France; so called from his success in almost annihilating the imperial army which had invaded Provence, by laying the country waste and prolonging the campaign (1493–1567).

Fable for Critics, A. A satire in verse by James Russell LOWELL, published anonymously in 1848. It contains critical estimates of Lowell's literary contemporaries, including EMERSON, POE, LONGFELLOW, Margaret FULLER, Bronson ALCOTT, THOREAU, and others. Amy LOWELL's *Critical Fable* is a 20th-century imitation of this.

fable. The term means historically a narrative or story. This sense survives in the use of the word as a synonym of falsehood as also of the plot of a play or poem. In the more restricted sense, a fable, i.e., an Aesopic fable is a story conveying a principle of behavior through the analogy of fictitious, though plausible, actions of animals, men, gods, or inanimate objects. In form the typical fable is brief and epigrammatic. It may or may not wind up with an explicit statement of its moral. The most important authors of fables are listed under AESOP.

fabliaux. Ribald and often obscene stories of the Middle Ages, an important part of the literature of the common people. They usually concern sexual intrigue and adultery, women and the clergy most often being the objects of satirical attack, as well as practical jokes and tricks of revenge. See Chaucer's MILLER'S TALE. They are very ancient in origin, many analogues to popular European *fabliaux* having been found in the literature of the Orient, and were transmitted from age to age by oral tradition; a number of 20th-century "smoking-room" stories and off-color vaudeville jokes are direct descendants of medieval stories. Boccaccio's DECAMERON, Chaucer's CANTERBURY TALES, and Balzac's DROLL STORIES contain outstanding representatives of *fabliaux.*

Fabre, Jean Henri (1823–1915). French naturalist; author of *Souvenirs entomologiques* (1879–1907) in 10 volumes, parts of which have appeared in English, translated by A. Teixeira de Mattos and Bernard Miall. His work was crowned by the Institute of France.

Fabricius. A Roman hero (d. ca. 270 B.C.), representative of incorruptibility and honesty. The ancient writers tell of the frugal way in which he lived on his farm, how he refused the rich presents offered him by the Samnite ambassadors, and how at death he left no portion for his daughters, whom the senate provided for.

> Fabricius, scorner of all-conquering gold.
> Thomson, *Seasons* (*Winter*).

Fabulinus. The Roman deity who presided over the speech of infants.

facile (*Fr.*) Easy. Hence, specifically applied to authors, writing with great ease and not always avoiding superficiality. Also in phrases like *a facile pen.*

facsimile. An exact copy of a document. The term is now chiefly used with the implication of photographic identity.

factotum (Lat., *facere totum,* "to do everything required"). One who does for his employer all sorts of services. Sometimes called a *Johannes Factotum.* Formerly the term meant a busybody, or much the same as our "Jack-of-all trades," and it is in this sense that Robert GREENE used it in his famous reference to Shakespeare:

> There is an upstart Crow beautified with our feathers, that with his *Tygers heart wrapt in a Players hide,* supposes he is as well able to bumbast out a blanke verse as the best of you: but being an absolute *Johannes factotum,* is in his owne conceit the onely Shake-scene in a countrie.—*Groatsworth of Wit* (1592).

Fadda. MAHOMET's white mule.

Fadiman, Clifton (1904–). American literary critic, conductor of "Information Please" on the radio (since 1938), receiver of the *Saturday Review of Literature* award (for 1940), editor of *I Believe* (1939) and a prose anthology, *Reading I've Liked* (1941). One of the literary judges of the BOOK-OF-THE-MONTH CLUB.

Fadladeen. In Moore's LALLA ROOKH, the great nazir or chamberlain of Aurungzebe's harem. He criticizes the tales told by a young poet to Lalla Rookh on her way to Delhi, and great is his mortification to find that the poet is the young king, his master.

Fadladeen was a judge of everything, from the pencilling of a Circassian's eyelids to the deepest questions of science and literature; from the mixture of a conserve of rose leaves to the composition of an epic poem.

Faërie Queene, The. An allegorical romance of chivalry by Edmund SPENSER, originally intended to have been in 12 books, each of which was to have portrayed one of the 12 moral virtues. Only six books of twelve cantos each, and part of a seventh, were written (I to III published in 1590, IV to VI in 1596, and the remaining fragments in 1611). It details the adventures of various knights, who personify different virtues, and belong to the court of Gloriana, the Faërie Queene, who sometimes typifies Queen Elizabeth. The poem makes use of much material of ARTHURIAN ROMANCE, in tribute to Elizabeth, whose family, the Tudors, were at the time popularly celebrated as descendants of King Arthur. It also contains attacks on the Roman Catholic Church.

The first book contains the legend of the Red Cross Knight (*the spirit of the Church of England*), and the victory of Holiness over Error.

The second book is the legend of Sir Guyon (*Temperance, or the golden mean*).

The third book is the legend of Britomartis (*Chastity, or love without lust*).

The fourth book tells the story of Cambel and Triamond (*Fidelity*).

The fifth book gives the legend of Artegal (*Justice*).

The sixth book, the legend of Sir Calidore (*Courtesy*).

The fragments of the seventh book—viz. cantos VI and VII, and two stanzas of canto III—have for their subject *Mutability*.

Fafner. In Wagner's RING, one of the giants that built Valhalla for Wotan. He and his brother Fasolt accept Alberich's golden hoard as payment in place of Freya, the price originally agreed upon. Fafner kills Fasolt and transforms himself into a dragon to guard the hoard which is now his. He is killed by Siegfried. In the Norse sources, Fafnir (not Fafner) has no brother and is guarding Andvari's gold as a venom-breathing dragon from the start.

fag. Modern slang for a cigarette. It is said to be short for "fag-end," and the story is that it arose through street-boys asking passing cigarette-smokers to "chuck us the *fag*, guv'nor," meaning the *end*, which is dried, mixed with others, and then made into new cigarettes or smoked in a pipe.

In public schools a fag is a small boy who waits upon a bigger one. Possibly, in this sense, a contracted form of FACTOTUM. See also FAG below.

Fag. In Sheridan's comedy THE RIVALS (1775), the lying servant of Captain Absolute. He "wears his master's wit, as he does his lace, at second hand." He "scruples not to tell a lie at his master's command, but it pains his conscience to be found out."

Fagin. In Dickens' OLIVER TWIST, an old Jew, who employs a gang of thieves, chiefly boys. These boys he teaches to pick pockets and pilfer adroitly. Fagin assumes a most suave and fawning manner but is grasping, and full of cruelty. He is ultimately arrested, tried, and condemned to death.

Faguet, Émile (1847–1916). French literary critic and professor of literature at the Sorbonne. Member of the French Academy (1900). Author of an outstanding *History of French Literature* (1900) and a book on *The Art of Reading* (1912).

Fahrenheit, Gabriel Daniel (1686–1736). German physicist who did most of his work in Holland and Great Britain. He improved the thermometer by the use of mercury (1714) and introduced a scale (still in use in Britain and U.S. but not in Germany) based on an "absolute" zero (the lowest temperature encountered by Fahrenheit) and reaching the freezing point of water at 32, the boiling point at 212 degrees. The abbreviation is *F.* or *Fahr.*

fainéant (*Fr.*, from *faire*, "to do," and *néant*, "nothing"). An idler.

In Scott's Ivanhoe Richard Lionhearted is so called *le noir fainéant* by spectators at the tournament which he attends in disguise.

Clovis II (d. 656) and his ten Merovingian successors on the French throne are known as *les rois fainéants*, "the do-nothing kings." The line came to an end in 751, when Pepin the Short usurped the crown. Louis V (d. 987), the last of the Carlovingians, is also referred to as a *roi fainéant*.

fair. Frequent as a personal epithet, corresponding with French *le Bel, la Belle.*

Edwy, or *Eadwig, the Fair.* King of Wessex (938–98).

Charles IV, King of France, *le Bel* (1294, 1322–1328).

Philippe IV of France, *le Bel* (1268, 1285–1314).

Fair Geraldine, see GERALDINE.

the fair-haired. Harold I, King of Norway (reigned 872–930).

Fair Maid of Anjou. Lady Edith Plantagenet (*fl.* 1200), who married David, Prince Royal of Scotland.

Fair Maid of Brittany. Eleanor (d. 1241),

granddaughter of Henry II, and, after the death of Arthur (1203), the rightful sovereign of England. Her uncle, the usurper King John, imprisoned her in Bristol Castle, where she died. Her father, Geoffrey, John's elder brother, was Count of Brittany.

Fair Maid of Kent. Joan (1328–1385), Countess of Salisbury, wife of the Black Prince, and only daughter of Edmond Plantagenet, Earl of Kent. She had been twice married before she gave her hand to the prince.

Fair Maid of Norway. Margaret (1283–1290), daughter of Eric II of Norway, and granddaughter of Alexander III of Scotland. Being recognized by the states of Scotland as successor to the throne, she set out for her kingdom, but died at sea from sea-sickness.

Fair Maid of Perth. Katie Glover, the most beautiful young woman of Perth. Heroine of Scott's novel of the same name (see below), she is supposed to have lived in the early 15th century, but is not a definite historical character, though her house is still shown at Perth.

Fair Parricide. Beatrice CENCI.

Fair Rosamond, see ROSAMOND.

Fairbanks, Charles Warren (1852–1918). U.S. Senator from Indiana (1897–1905). Vice-president of U.S. (1905–1909).

Fairbanks, Douglas (1883–1939). American actor on the stage and in moving pictures. For many years married to MARY PICKFORD. Famous for athletic, swashbuckling rôles. Father of Douglas Fairbanks, Jr. (1908–), also a moving-picture actor.

Fairchild, Henry Pratt (1880–). American social scientist. Author of *Immigration* (1913), *Elements of Social Science* (1924), *General Sociology* (1934), and *Economics for the Millions* (1940).

Fairchild Family, The History of the (1818). An old-fashioned and once extremely popular story for children by Mrs. Mary Martha Sherwood (1775–1851), which lives up to its subtitle, *The Child's Manual,* by never losing an opportunity for moral instruction. It was reprinted in 1889.

Fairfax, Edward (d. 1635). English author, considered one of the best of Elizabethan translators. He translated Tasso's JERUSALEM DELIVERED as *Godfrey of Bulloigne, Or the Recovery of Jerusalem* (1600), transforming the original into an Elizabethan work by the richness of his language and imagery, of which Ben JONSON disapproved.

Fairfax, Jane. A character in Jane Austen's EMMA.

Fairfax, Thomas (1612–1671). Commander in Chief of the Parliamentary army (1645), defeated Charles I at Naseby. Less able in civilian affairs, he became an instrument in the hands of stronger men as witnessed by his reluctant participation in the condemnation of the king (1649). He was active again in preparing the Restoration, and headed the commission dispatched to Charles II at the Hague (1660).

Fairford, Allan. In Scott's REDGAUNTLET, a young barrister, son of Saunders. He marries Lilias Redgauntlet, sister of Sir Arthur Darsie Redgauntlet, called "Darsie Latimer." Scott's biographer Lockhart says that this character is largely autobiographical.

Fair God, The. A historical novel by Lew WALLACE (1873), dealing with the Spanish conquest of Mexico in the first part of the 16th century. "The Fair God" is Quetzalcoatl, the Aztec god of the air. The Emperor Montezuma, deceived by the Spanish leader Cortez, allows his forces to come in as guests. At the head of the Aztec opposition is Guatamozin, nephew and son-in-law of Montezuma. After a series of dramatic events, the Aztecs finally compel the Spaniards to withdraw, but they themselves are left in a weakened and chaotic state.

Fair Maid of Perth, The. A novel by Sir Walter SCOTT (1828), of the period of Henry IV of England and Robert III of Scotland. The "Fair Maid" is Catherine Glover, daughter of a glover of Perth, who kisses Henry Smith, the armorer, in his sleep on St. Valentine's Day. Smith proposes marriage, and although Catherine refuses at first, at the end of the novel she becomes his wife. The concurrent plot is the amour of Prince James of Scotland, son of Robert III, and Louise the Glee-maiden. The novel is full of intrigue; the Prince quarrels with his father, is arrested and finally secretly murdered. The Glee-maiden then casts herself down from a high precipice.

Fair Penitent, The. A drama by Nicholas ROWE (1703). See LOTHARIO.

Fairservice, Andrew. In Sir Walter SCOTT's *Rob Roy,* a cunning Scottish gardener.

Fair-star. See CHERY AND FAIR-STAR.

fairy. The names of the principal fairies and of groups of similar sprites known to fable and legend are given throughout the *Encyclopedia.* See:

AFREET, ARIEL, BANSHEE, BOGY, BROWNIE, BUG, CAULD LAD, DEEV, DUENDE, DUERGAR, ELF, ESPRIT FOLLET, FATA, GENIUS, GNOME, GOBLIN, HOBGOBLIN, JINN, KELPIE, KOBOLD, LEPRECHAUN, LUTIN, MAB, MONACIELLO, NAIAD, NIX, OBERON, OREAD, PERI, PIGWIGGIN, PIXY, PUCK, ROBIN GOODFELLOW, STROMKARL, SYLPH, TROLL, UNDINE, WHITE LADIES.

fairy darts. Flint arrow-heads.

fairy loaves or *stones.* Fossil sea-urchins, said to be made by the fairies.

fairy money. Found money. Said to be placed by some good fairy at the spot where it was picked up. "Fairy money" is apt to be transformed into leaves.

fairy of the mine. A malevolent GNOME supposed to live in mines, busying itself with cutting ore, turning the windlass, but effecting nothing.

> No goblin, or swart fairy of the mine,
> Hath hurtful power o'er true virginity.
> Milton, *Comus*, 447.

fairy rings. Circles of rank or withered grass, often seen in lawns, meadows, and grass-plots, and popularly supposed to be produced by fairies dancing on the spot. In sober truth, these rings are simply an agaric or fungus below the surface, which has seeded circularly, as many plants do. Where the ring is brown and almost bare, the "spawn" has enveloped the roots and thus prevented their absorbing moisture; but where the grass is rank, the "spawn" itself has died, and served as manure to the young grass.

> You demi-puppets, that
> By moonshine do the green-sour ringlets make,
> Whereof the ewe not bites.
> Shakespeare, *Tempest*, v. 1.

fairy sparks. The phosphoric light from decaying wood, fish, and other substances. Thought at one time to be lights prepared for the fairies at their revels.

Faithful. In Bunyan's PILGRIM'S PROGRESS, a companion of Christian in his walk to the Celestial City. Both are seized at Vanity Fair, and Faithful, being burnt to death, is taken to heaven in a chariot of fire.

Faithful, Father of the. Abraham. See under FATHER.

Faithful, Jacob, see JACOB FAITHFUL.

Faithful Shepherdess, The. A pastoral drama by John FLETCHER (1610). The "faithful shepherdess" is Corin, who remains faithful to her lover although he is dead.

Faith Gartney's Girlhood. Once a widely read story for girls by Mrs. A. D. T. Whitney (*Am.*, 1863).

Faith Healer, The. A drama by William Vaughn MOODY (1909), the study of a prophet, Ulrich Michaelis, in the throes of a struggle between love and what he conceives to be his divine mission.

Faithless Nelly Grey and **Faithless Sally Brown.** Comic poems by Thomas HOOD (1799–1845). Both are full of puns.

fakir. A Mohammedan religious beggar or mendicant. They wear coarse black or brown dresses, and a black turban over which a red handkerchief is tied, and perform menial offices connected with burials, the cleaning of mosques, and so on.

Fakredeen. A gay young emir in Disraeli's TANCRED OR THE NEW CRUSADE who "was fond of his debts; they were the source, indeed, of his only real excitement, and he was grateful to them for their stirring powers."

Fala. The White House dog, which belonged to Franklin D. Roosevelt. A scottie.

Falangist (Span. *falangista,* from *falange,* "phalanx"). A member of a Spanish fascist organization. See FASCISM; also PHALANSTERY.

Falder, William. The leading character in John Galsworthy's drama, JUSTICE.

faldstool. A folding stool or chair used by a bishop. Also a stool or small desk at which one kneels during devotions. The King of England uses a faldstool at his coronation. The word is interesting in that it comes, by way of medieval Latin *faldistolium,* from Old High German *faldstuol,* "folding chair," which was also taken over by French in which language it survives as *fauteuil.*

Falerno. An Italian sweet wine, grown in what the ancients called *Falernus Ager,* a fertile district some 20 miles north of Naples. It was celebrated by HORACE.

Faliero, Marino, see MARINO FALIERO.

Falk. A novel by Joseph CONRAD.

Falkenhayn, Erich von (1861–1922). Prussian general and chief of German general staff in World War I, blamed for failure at Verdun, succeeded by von Hindenburg.

Falkland. The principal character in Godwin's CALEB WILLIAMS.

fall.

in the fall. In the autumn, at the fall of the leaf. Though now commonly classed as an Americanism, the term was formerly in good use in England, and is found in the works of Drayton, Middleton, Raleigh, and other Elizabethans. In England it is now, except in provincial use, practically obsolete.

> What crowds of patients the town doctor kills,
> Or how, last fall, he raised the weekly bills.
> Dryden, *Juvenal.*

the fall of man. The degeneracy of the human race in consequence of the disobedience of Adam. Adam fell from innocence under temptation.

the fall of the drop, in theatrical parlance, means the fall of the drop-curtain at the end of the act or play.

Fall, Albert Bacon (1861–1944). American politician. As U.S. Secretary of the Interior (1921–1923; resigned) he secretly transferred government oil lands (TEAPOT DOME) to Doheny and Sinclair, receiving $100,000 as a "loan," etc. Convicted and imprisoned (1931–1932).

Fallada, Hans. Pseudonym of **Rudolf Ditzen** (1893–1947). German novelist, best known as the author of the best-selling novel *Little Man, What Now?* (*Kleiner Mann, Was Nun?;* 1933), a sympathetic account of the struggles of a commonplace young couple to make a living in Germany in the depression years of the 1920's and 1930's.

Fall of the House of Usher. A short story by Edgar Allan POE in his *Tales of the Grotesque and Arabesque* (1840). The lady Madeline of the house of Usher dies, leaving a single melancholy brother. He is a prey to horrible fears that she has been buried alive, and when she appears in her shroud, he dies of terror. The House of Usher crumbles and falls into the nearby tarn.

Falls of Princes, The. A poem in Middle English by John LYDGATE, written in rhyme royal between 1430 and 1438, first printed in 1494. It depicts the rise to and decline from fame and power by great men, subject to the fluctuations of fortune (see FORTUNA), and was based on Boccaccio's *De Casibus Virorum Illustrium*. See also Chaucer's MONK'S TALE.

Fallopius, Gabriel (1523–1562). Italian anatomist. Known as the discoverer of the function of the oviducts, now called Fallopian tubes.

falsetto (*It.*). The human voice in the upper or head register. Yodeling consists in sudden shifts from chest to head voice or falsetto. The word signifies "sort of false."

Falstaff, Sir John. The most famous comic character of Shakespearean drama, appearing in THE MERRY WIVES OF WINDSOR, and in the two parts of *Henry IV*. In *Henry V* his death is described by Mrs. Quickly, hostess of an inn in Eastcheap. Sir John is represented in the comedy as making love to Mrs. Page, who "fools him to the top of her bent." In the historic plays, he is a soldier and a wit, the boon companion of "Mad-cap Hal," the Prince of Wales. In both cases, he is a mountain of fat, sensual, mendacious, boastful and fond of practical jokes. He is also the chief character in Verdi's opera *Falstaff* (libretto by Boïto founded on *The Merry Wives of Windsor*) and in several less important operas and plays.

> Falstaff, unimitated, inimitable Falstaff, how shall I describe thee? Thou compound of sense and vice: of sense which may be admired, but not esteemed; of vice which may be despised, but hardly detested. "Falstaff" is a character loaded with faults, and with those faults which naturally produce contempt. He is a thief and a glutton, a coward and a boaster, always ready to cheat the weak and prey upon the poor, to terrify the timorous and insult the defenceless. At once obsequious and malignant, yet the man thus corrupt, thus despicable, makes himself necessary to the prince by perpetual gaiety, and by unfailing power of exciting laughter.—Dr. Johnson.

fame.

temple of fame. A PANTHEON where monuments to the famous dead of a nation are erected and the memories honored, especially that at Paris. Hence, *he will have a niche in the temple of fame,* he has done something that will cause his people to honor him and keep his memory green.

> The temple of fame is the shortest passage to riches and preferment.—*Letters of Junius: Letter* lix.

Hall of Fame. The American temple of fame in New York University, devoted to the memory of famous Americans who are chosen every five years as worthy of a place there.

familiar. Bound to service by a supernatural tie, as, the familiar spirit or, simply, the familiar of a witch, generally represented as at its master's beck in the form of a small animal, a cat, mouse, poodle, etc.

Family Reunion, The. A drama in verse by T. S. ELIOT, published in 1939. It deals with the return of Harry, Lord Monchensey, to the home of his family in England, for the birthday of his mother, Amy. He is neurotic and obsessed with the knowledge that he has murdered his wife, a deed which he soon is driven to confess. In a talk with his aunt, Agatha, he learns that his father hated his mother, she having used him merely to obtain what she wanted, and feels that his own situation is in part the result of this. Harry departs in order to complete his atonement, and Amy dies of shock.

fancy. In English Romantic literary criticism, notably that of S. T. COLERIDGE, the clever, playful faculty of mind which combines sensations, observations, impressions, etc., into poems of wit, humor, or whimsy, but does not create or transform its material to produce inspired literature. See also IMAGINATION.

Fancy Day. In Hardy's UNDER THE GREENWOOD TREE.

Fane, Michael and **Stella.** The principal characters in Compton Mackenzie's SINISTER STREET and prominent in other novels of the series. They are brother and sister.

Faneuil Hall. A market house containing an assembly hall in Boston, given in 1742 to his fellow citizens by the merchant Peter Faneuil (1700–1743). After the fire of 1761 it was rebuilt by the city, became the meeting place of American patriots during the Revolution and is now remembered as the "cradle of freedom."

fanfaron (Fr. *fanfare,* a flourish of trumpets). A swaggering bully; a cowardly boaster who blows his own trumpet. Scott uses the word for finery, especially for the gold lace worn by military men.

> "Marry, hang thee, with thy fanfarona about thy neck!" said the falconer.—Scott, *The Abbot,* cxvii.

Hence, *fanfaronade* means swaggering, vain boasting, ostentatious display.

> The bishop copied this proceeding from the fanfaronade of M. Boufflers.—Swift.

Fang. A bullying, insolent magistrate in Dickens' OLIVER TWIST, who would have sent Oliver to prison, on suspicion of theft, if Mr. Brownlow had not interposed on the boy's behalf.

The original of this ill-tempered, bullying magistrate was Mr. Laing, of Hatton Garden, removed from the bench by the home secretary.—Forster, John, *Life of Dickens,* iii. 4.

Fanny. A satirical poem by Fitz-Greene Halleck (*Am.* 1819).

Fanny's First Play. A drama by George Bernard SHAW (1911), which by the device of a "play within a play" satirizes several contemporary critics.

Fanshawe. The title and hero of HAWTHORNE's first novel, anonymously published in 1826.

Fantasia. Title of a DISNEY musical film (1940), representing an attempt to exploit a non-objective color symphony as a surrealist medium of expression.

Fantastic Symphony, see SYMPHONIE FANTASTIQUE.

Fantine. One of the principal characters of Victor Hugo's LES MISÉRABLES, the mother of Little Cosette.

Fantin-Latour, Ignace Henri Joseph Théodore (1826–1904). French painter known for portrait, still-life, and genre paintings.

Faraday, Michael (1791–1867). English chemist and physicist. As a journeyman bookbinder he heard a lecture by Sir Humphry Davy who impressed him so deeply that he turned all his attention to the natural sciences. He became one of the greatest chemists of his time and a pioneer in the young science of electricity. His publications are numerous. His monograph on candles deserves to rank as a classic in popular scientific literature.

Faragoh, Francis Eduardo (1898–). Hungarian-born playwright and stage director. Managing director New Playwrights Theatre, New York City. Worked on scenarios for well-known moving pictures, among them *Frankenstein, Becky Sharp,* and others.

farce. A grotesque and exaggerated kind of comedy, full of ludicrous incidents and expressions. The word is the Old French *farce,* "stuffing" (from Lat. *farcire,* "to stuff"); hence, an interlude stuffed into or inserted in the main piece, such interludes always being of a racy, exaggerated comic character.

Far Country, A. A novel by Winston CHURCHILL (1915). The hero, Hugh Paret, wanders far from his early ideals, but realizes the fact before it is too late. The allusion in the title is to the New Testament story of the PRODIGAL SON who "went into a far country and there wasted his substance in riotous living."

Far East. See under EAST.

Farewell Address. The address delivered by George Washington just before his retirement from the presidency in which he summarized the ideas and principles that had guided him in his actions (Sept. 17, 1796). See FRAUNCES' TAVERN.

Farewell to Arms, A. A novel by Ernest HEMINGWAY, published in 1929. It deals with the romance of Frederic Henry, an American ambulance driver, and Catherine Barkley, an English nurse, in Italy during World War I. She becomes pregnant, and after the retreat from Caporetto with its attendant horrors, Henry deserts, joins Catherine, and escapes with her to Switzerland, where she dies in childbirth. This is one of the best-known novels depicting the tragedy and destruction of World War I. It was dramatized as a play and a motion picture. The title is from the title of a lyric poem addressed to Queen Elizabeth by the English poet George Peele (ca. 1558–ca. 1597).

Far from the Madding Crowd. A novel by Thomas HARDY (1874). Bathsheba Everdene is courted by Gabriel Oak, a young farmer who becomes bailiff of the farm she inherits, by William Boldwood, who owns the neighboring farm, and by Sergeant Troy, a handsome young adventurer. She marries Troy, who spends her money freely. Troy now accidentally meets his old love Fanny Robin and her child in pitiful condition on the way to the workhouse and the next day finds them both dead. The incident brings about a quarrel with Bathsheba and his departure; and he is swept out to sea. Bathsheba, who believes him drowned, becomes engaged to William Boldwood. When Troy reappears in blustering mood, Boldwood kills him and is sentenced to penal servitude for life. Bathsheba now marries Gabriel Oak.

Farigoule, Louis, see ROMAINS, JULES.

Farina, Salvatore (1846–1918). Italian novelist, "the Italian Dickens."

Farinata degli Uberti. A noble Florentine, leader of the Ghibelline faction, and driven from his country in 1250 by the GUELPHS. Some ten years later, by the aid of Mainfroi of Naples, he defeated the Guelphs, and took all the towns of Tuscany and Florence. Dante, in his *Inferno,* represents him as lying in a fiery tomb yet open, and not to be closed till the last judgment day.

Farinelli, Carlo (1705–1782). Called "il Ragazzo." Famous Italian male soprano. Grove wrote of him: "The most remarkable singer, perhaps, who has ever lived."

Farintosh, Marquis of. A conceited young nobleman in Thackeray's novel THE NEW-

COMES. Ethel Newcome refuses to marry him.

Farjeon, Eleanor (1881–). Granddaughter of the actor Joseph Jefferson (1829–1905). English writer famous for her juveniles. Her brother, Joseph Jefferson Farjeon (1883–) is a skilled English mystery story writer.

Farley, James Aloysius (1888–). American politician. Chairman, Democratic National Committee (1932–1940). U.S. postmaster general (1933–1940).

Farman, Henri (1874–). French aviation pioneer and airplane manufacturer. Made first one-kilometer flight back to base; developed the Farman biplane; etc. Holder of various records.

Farmer George. George III (b. 1738, reigned 1760–1820); so called from his farmer-like manners, taste, dress, and amusements.

> A better farmer ne'er brushed dew from lawn.
> Byron, *Vision of Judgment.*

Farnese Hercules. A statue of Hercules, originally in the Farnese Palace, now in the National Museum of Naples. It is the work of Glycon of Athens (1st century B.C.) and represents the demigod naked, with extraordinary muscular development, leaning on his club.

Farnham, Alfred. The hero of John Hay's novel, THE BREADWINNERS.

Farnol, John Jeffery (1878–). English writer of popular historical romances, such as his first, *The Broad Highway* (1910).

Faro. A banking game, formerly called Pharaoh, possibly because the Egyptian monarch appeared on one of the cards. Played with a "layout," that is, a representation on the center of the table of thirteen cards from the ace up to the king in regular order, and a full pack of 52 cards. The betting is done on the cards of the layout and winners are determined by the dealer who removes one card at a time from the pack.

Farquhar, George (1678–1707). Irish-born English playwright of the Restoration period, who wrote with the satire, frivolity, and sophisticated licentiousness of his contemporaries CONGREVE and WYCHERLEY, but is considered to be more moral and tending more to the sentimental than they. His most famous play is THE BEAUX' STRATAGEM (1707). Other comedies are *Love and a Bottle* (1698) and *A Constant Couple* (1699).

Farrago, Captain. Hero of Brackenridge's early American novel, MODERN CHIVALRY.

Farragut, David Glasgow (1801–1870). American admiral. Son of a Spaniard who had joined the Continental army. Famous for action in U.S. Civil War, at Mobile Bay, August 1864. Two grades, Vice-admiral and Admiral, created specially for him by Congress. In American Hall of Fame.

Farrand, Livingston (1867–1939). American anthropologist. Special study of Indian tribes of British Columbia. His brother **Max Farrand** (1869–), historian and director of research at Henry E. Huntington Library (1927).

Farrar, Geraldine (1882–). Famous American dramatic soprano. Chief rôles: Madame Butterfly, Manon, Mignon, Tosca, Juliet, Gilda, Carmen, Zaza. She also played Carmen and Joan of Arc in the silent motion-pictures.

Farrell, Aminta. Heroine of Meredith's LORD ORMONT AND HIS AMINTA.

Farrell, James Thomas (1904–). American novelist, known for his lengthy studies of lower middle-class Irish Catholic life in the South Side slum section of Chicago. They are written in the tradition of NATURALISM, combined with a modification of the STREAM-OF-CONSCIOUSNESS technique of James JOYCE, and present their characters with what is often a sociologist's objectivity in the light of their background. Poverty, religious bigotry and narrowness, economic inequality, individual frustration, sordidness, vice, and the destructive influence of environment are emphasized, with contemporary references appropriate to the period of the 1920's and 1930's. Some critics assert that the dreariness and turgidity of Farrell's style defeat the author's purpose, but others praise the powerful, cumulative effect of personal tragedy that distinguishes Farrell's most famous work, the STUDS LONIGAN trilogy. This comprises *Young Lonigan* (1932), *The Young Manhood of Studs Lonigan* (1934), and *Judgment Day* (1935). Another series of novels, dealing with the life of DANNY O'NEILL, includes *A World I Never Made* (1936), *No Star Is Lost* (1938), and *Father and Son* (1940). Among Farrell's other works are: *Gas-House McGinty* (1933); *Calico Shoes* (1934), *Guillotine Party* (1935), *Can All This Grandeur Perish?* (1937), and *$1000 a Week* (1942), short stories; *A Note on Literary Criticism* (1936), a critical essay of modified Marxist viewpoint; TOMMY GALLAGHER'S CRUSADE (1939); *Ellen Rogers* (1941); *Bernard Clare* (1946), which was banned in Canada. See also PROLETARIAN LITERATURE.

Farwell, Arthur (1872–). American musician; best-known for American Indian songs and melodies. Founder of the Wa-Wan Press at Newton Center, Mass. (1901), aiming "to promote . . . the most progressive works of American composers . . . and to present compositions based on the melodies and folklore of the American Indians." Established at Lansing, Mich., a lithographic hand-press (1936) for the reproduction of his own compositions.

fasces. A bundle of rods, usually of birch, enclosing an axe with its blade projecting, borne by lictors before Roman magistrates as a badge of authority. The symbol and the word are at the base of the derivative "FASCISM."

Fascism. An authoritarian and totalitarian political system which considers the individual in every respect subordinate to the interests of the historical reality of the national state. Its principles were developed by Benito MUSSOLINI (1883–1945) and his followers in the period after 1922. Since the advent of similar movements in Spain (FALANGISM) and Germany (NAZISM) the term came to be applied to any form of nationalistic statism and finally (especially since the end of World War II) signified vaguely nothing but opposition to liberalism, individualism, democracy, and other American ideals.

Fashion. A satiric comedy by Anna C. Mowatt Ritchie (*Am.* 1845), dealing with contemporary New York society. Mrs. Tiffany, "a lady who imagines herself fashionable," attempts to make a match between her daughter Seraphina and Count Jolimaitre, who, alas, is only a valet in disguise. Seraphina has another suitor in the person of Snobson, her father's confidential clerk. Affairs get extremely involved with Count Jolimaitre making ardent love to Gertrude, the governess, on the side, but Gertrude's grandfather, Adam Trueman, a brusque and breezy farmer from out of town, manages to straighten everything out. Several fashionable New York types, such as "a modern poet," "a drawing-room appendage," and the like, make their appearance in Mrs. Tiffany's wake.

Fashion, Sir Brilliant. In Murphy's comedy *The Way to Keep Him* (1760), a man of the world, who "dresses fashionably, lives fashionably, wins your money fashionably, loses his own fashionably, and does everything fashionably." His fashionable asseverations are, "Let me perish, if . . . !" "May fortune eternally frown on me, if . . . !" "May I never hold four by honors, if . . . !" "May the first woman I meet strike me with a supercilious eyebrow, if . . . !" and so on.

Fashion, Tom, or **Young Fashion.** In Vanbrugh's *Relapse* (1697) and Sheridan's adaptation called *A Trip to Scarborough* (1777), the younger brother of Lord FOPPINGTON. As his elder brother does not behave well to him, Tom resolves to outwit him, and to this end introduces himself to Sir Tunbelly Clumsy and his daughter, Miss Hoyden, as Lord Foppington. Between the latter and Miss Hoyden a marriage negotiation has been going on. Tom marries the heiress under his brother's name and explains matters afterward, to every one's satisfaction but his brother's.

Fasolt. In *Das Rheingold,* the first of the four operas of Wagner's RING DES NIBELUNGEN, one of the two chief giants opposed to the gods. See FAFNER.

Fastolfe, Sir John. A character in Shakespeare's 1 *Henry VI.* This is not the "Sir John Falstaff" of huge proportions and facetious wit, but the lieutenant-general of the Duke of Bedford, and a knight of the Garter.

> Here had the conquest fully been sealed up
> If Sir John Fastolfe had not played the coward;
> He being in the vanward . . .
> Cowardly fled, not having struck one stroke.
> Shakespeare, 1 *Henry VI* Act i. sc. 1.

fata (*Ital.,* "a fairy"). Female supernatural being introduced in Italian medieval romance, usually under the sway of DEMOGORGON. In ORLANDO INNAMORATO we meet with the "Fata Morgana" (see MORGAN LE FAY); in Boiardo, with the "Fata Silvanella," and others.

Fata Morgana. (1) A sort of mirage in which objects are reflected in the sea, and sometimes on a kind of aerial screen high above it, occasionally seen in the neighborhood of the Straits of Messina, so named from MORGAN LE FAY who was fabled by the Norman settlers in England to dwell in Calabria. Hence, any mirage or glamorous illusion.

(2) A play by Ernst Vajda, produced by the Theatre Guild (1924) with Emily Stevens.

Fatagaga (*Fabrication de tableaux garantis gazométriques*). One of a series of COLLAGES collaborated upon by a Dadaist group founded by Max Ernst (1919). See DADAISM.

Fatal Curiosity. An epilogue in Cervantes' DON QUIXOTE, Pt. I. iv. 5, 6. The subject of this tale is the trial of a wife's fidelity. Anselmo, a Florentine gentleman, has married Camilla, and, wishing to rejoice over her incorruptible fidelity, induces his friend Lothario to put it to the test. The lady is not trial-proof, but elopes with Lothario. The end is that Anselmo dies of grief, Lothario is slain in battle, and Camilla dies in a convent.

Fat Boy, the. Joseph or Joe, in Dickens' PICKWICK PAPERS, a lad of astounding obesity, whose employment consists of alternate eating and sleeping. Joe is in the service of Mr. Wardle. He was once known to "burst into a horse-laugh," and to defer eating to say to Mary, "How nice you do look!"

> This was said in an admiring manner, and was so far gratifying; but still there was enough of the cannibal in the young gentleman's eyes to render the

compliment doubtful.—Dickens, *Pickwick Papers,* liv.

Fates. The Greeks and Romans supposed there were three *Parcae* or Fates, who arbitrarily controlled the birth, life, and death of every man. They were Clotho (who held the distaff), Lachesis (who spun the thread of life), and Atropos (who cut it off when life was ended), and are called "cruel" because they pay no regard to the wishes of anyone. Clotho is from Gr. *klotho,* to draw thread from a distaff; Lachesis is from *lagchano,* to assign by lot; and *Atropos* = inflexible.

father. The name is given as a title to Catholic priests, especially confessors, superiors of convents, religious teachers, etc.; also to the senior member of a body or profession, as the *Father of the House of Commons,* the *Father of the Bench,* and to the originator or first leader of some movement, school, etc., as the *Father of Comedy* (Aristophanes), the *Father of English Song* (Caedmon). In ancient Rome the title was given to the senators (see also PATRICIAN, CONSCRIPT FATHERS), and in ecclesiastical history to the early church writers and doctors.

Father Abraham. Abraham Lincoln (1809–1865), President of the United States.

Father Adam. Adam, the first man, the father of humanity.

Father Christmas. Santa Claus.

Father Nile. The Nile, personified.

Father of America. Samuel Adams (1722–1803), American statesman.

Father of Angling. Izaak Walton (1593–1683).

Father of Believers. Mahomet.

Father of Botany. Joseph Pittou de Tournefort (1656–1708), French botanist.

Father of British Inland Navigation. Francis Egerton, Duke of Bridgewater (1736–1803), who planned and financed the Bridgewater Canal system.

Father of Business Efficiency. Frederick Winslow Taylor (d. 1915).

Father of Chemistry. Arnauld de Villeneuve (1238–1314).

Father of Comedy. Aristophanes (448–385 B. C.).

Father of Dutch Poetry. Jakob Maerlant (1235–1300).

Father of Ecclesiastical (Church) History. Eusebius of Caesarea (264–349).

Father of English Botany. William Turner (1520–1568).

Father of English Cathedral Music. Thomas Tallis (1510–1585).

Father of English Poetry. Geoffrey Chaucer (1340–1400).

Father of English Printing. William Caxton (1412–1491).

Father of English Prose. (1) Wycliffe (1324–1384); (2) Roger Ascham (1515–1568).

Father of Epic Poetry. Homer (10th century B. C.).

Father of Equity. Heneage Finch, Earl of Nottingham (1621–1682), Lord Chancellor.

Father of French Drama. Etienne Jodelle (1532–1573).

Father of French History. André Duchesne (1584–1640).

Father of French Prose. Geoffroi de Villehardouin (1167–1212).

Father of French Satire. Mathurin Regnier (1573–1613).

Father of French Surgery. Ambrose Paré (1517–1590).

Father of French Tragedy. (1) Rob. Garnier (1545–1600); (2) Pierre Corneille (1606–1684).

Father of Geology. (1) Avicenna (980–1037), Arabic scientist; (2) Nicolas Steno (1631–1687), Danish-Italian geologist; (3) Wm. Smith (1769–1840).

Father of German Literature. Gotthold Ephraim Lessing (1729–1781).

Father of Good Works. The Sultan Mahomet II (1430–1481).

Father of Greek Drama. (1) Aeschylus (525–456 B. C.); (2) Thespis (*fl.* 535 B. C.).

Father of Greek Music. Terpander (*fl.* 676 B. C.).

Father of Greek Prose. Herodotus (ca. 484–424 B. C.).

Father of Greek Tragedy. Aeschylus (525–456 B. C.).

Father of his Country. Cicero was so entitled by the Roman Senate. They offered the same title to Marius, but he refused to accept it. Several of the Caesars were so called—Julius, after quelling the insurrection of Spain; Augustus, etc.

Cosimo de' Medici (1389–1464).

George Washington, the first President of the United States (1732–1799).

Andrea Doria (1468–1560). This sobriquet was inscribed on the base of his statue by his countrymen of Genoa.

Andronicus Palaeologus II assumed the title (ca. 1260–1332).

Cf. also 1 *Chron.* iv. 14.

Father of His People. (1) Louis XII of France (1462–1515); (2) Christian III of Denmark (1503–1559). See also FATHER OF THE PEOPLE below.

Father of Historic Painting. Polygnotos of Thaos (*fl.* 463–435 B. C.).

Father of History. Herodotus (484–408 B. C.), so called by Cicero.

Father of Iambic Verse. (Archilochus of Paros (*fl.* 700 B. C.).

Father of Inductive Philosophy. Francis Bacon, Lord Verulam (1561–1626).

Father of International Law. Hugo Grotius (1583–1645), Dutch jurist.

Father of Italian Prose. Giovanni Boccaccio (1313–1375).

Father of Jests. Joseph Miller (1684–1738), English wit.

Father of Jurisprudence. Ranulph de Glanville (d. 1190), author of *Tractatus de Legibus et Consuetudinibus Angliae* (1181).

Father of Landscape Gardening. André Lenôtre (1613–1700), French architect and landscape gardener.

Father of Letters. Francis I of France (1494–1547), a patron of literature.

Father of Lies. Satan. (*John* viii. 44.)

Father of Medicine. (1) Aretaeos of Cappadocia (*fl.* 70); (2) Hippocrates of Cos (460–357 B. C.).

Father of Modern Oil Painting. Jan van Eyck (1385–1440), Flemish painter.

Father of Modern Prose Fiction. Daniel Defoe (1663–1731).

Father of Modern Scepticism. Pierre Bayle (1647–1706), philosopher.

Father of Moral Philosophy. Thomas Aquinas (1227–1274), Italian scholastic theologian.

Father of Music. Giovanni Pierluigi da Palestrina (1525–1594), Italian composer.

Father of Musicians. Jubal. (*Gen.* iv. 21.).

Father of Navigation. Don Henrique, Duke of Viseo (1394–1460), one of the greatest of Portuguese travelers.

Father Neptune. The ocean. After Neptune, the Roman god of the seas.

Father of Ornithology. George Edwards (1693–1773).

Father of Orthodoxy. Athanasius, Bishop of Alexandria (293–373).

Father of Parody. Hipponax (6th century B. C.), Greek iambic poet.

Father of Peace. Andrea Doria (1466–1560), Genoese admiral and condottiere. Title given to him by the Senate of Genoa.

Father of Philosophy. (1) Roger Bacon (1214–1294), English philosopher and scholar; (2) Albrecht von Haller (1708–1777), Swiss physiologist, anatomist, botanist and poet.

Father of Poetry. (1) Orpheus, a semi-legendary Greek poet; (2) Homer.

Father of Reform. John Cartwright (1740–1824), English radical politician and publicist.

Father of Ridicule. François Rabelais (1490–1553), French satirist.

Father of Rivers. (1) The River Apidanus in Thessaly, so called by Euripides in *Hecuba* (ll. 446–452); (2) the River Lydia in Macedonia, so called by Euripides in *Bacchae* (ll. 571–575).

Father of Roman Philosophy. Cicero (106–43 B. C.).

Father of Roman Satire. Caius Lucilius (180–103 B. C.).

Father of Satire. Archilochus of Paros (*fl.* 700 B. C.).

Father of Scotch Landscape Painting. John Thomson, of Duddington (1778–1840).

Father of Swedish Eloquence. Nordenhjelm.

Father of Symphony. Francis Joseph Haydn (1732–1809).

Father of the Church. One of the writers of the Early Church, whose teachings are accepted as authoritative.

Father of the Faithful. The Patriarch Abraham. (*Rom.* iv.)

Father of the House of Commons. The living member who has sat there continuously for the longest period.

Father of the Human Race. Adam.

Father of the People. (1) a title assumed by the Absolutist kings of Denmark; (2) Gabriel du Pineau (1573–1644), French lawyer. See also FATHER OF HIS PEOPLE above.

Father of the Potteries. Josiah Wedgwood (1730–1795).

Father of the Spanish Drama. Lope Felix de Vega Carpio (1562–1635).

Father of the Vaudeville. Olivier Basselin (ca. 1400–1450) of Van-de-Vire, Normandy.

Father of Tragedy. (1) Aeschylus (525–456 B. C.); (2) Thespis (*fl.* 535 B. C.).

Father of Waters. (1) The Irrawaddy; (2) the Mississippi; (3) the Nile, so called by Samuel Johnson in *Rasselas* (1759).

father on a person. To impute to a person.

Father Thames. The River Thames.

Father, the Thoughtful. Nicholas Catinat (1637–1712), Marshal of France, so called by his soldiers.

Father Tiber. The River Tiber, personified.

Father Time. Time, personified; generally depicted as an old man with a scythe.

Fathers of Christian Doctrine, the Founder of the. Caesar de Bus (1544–1607).

Fathers of the Church. (1) the Apostolic Fathers, contemporaries of the Apostles, *viz.*, Clement of Rome, Barnabas, Hermas, Ignatius and Polycarp; (2) the Primitive Fathers, who lived in the first three centuries of the Christian era, *viz.*, Justin, Theophilus of Antioch, Irenaeus, Clement of Alexandria, Cyprian of Carthage, Origen, Gregory Thaumaturgus, Dionysius of Alexandria, Tertullian; (3) see FATHERS OF THE GREEK CHURCH below.

Fathers of the Greek Church. Eusebius, Athanasius, Basil the Great, Gregory Nazianzenus, Gregory of Nyssa, Cyril of Jerusalem,

Chrysostom, Epiphanius, Cyril of Alexandria, and Ephraim of Edessa.

Fathers of the Latin Church. Origen, Tertullian, Clement of Rome, Ignatius, Justin, Irenaeus, Cyprian, Hilary of Poitiers, Ambrose, Optatus, Jerome, Augustine, Leo the Great, Prosper, Vincent of Lerins, Peter Chrysologus, Caesarius of Arles, Gregory the Great, Isidore of Seville, Bede, Peter Damian, Anselm, Bernard.

Father Goriot, see GORIOT.

Fathers and Sons. A novel by TURGENEV (1861), portraying the conflicting points of view of two generations. Turgenev coined the word "Nihilist" for the chief character, Bazarov, an iconoclastic young radical. He endeavors in vain to convert his father to his theories of a new social order, although the older man makes pathetic efforts to understand him and meet him half way. Part of the action takes place on the family estate of Bazarov's friend, Arcadi Kirsanov, a gentler, less radical "son," and here Kirsanov's father and uncle represent the older generation with whom Bazarov feels himself at war.

Father William. A famous humorous ballad by Lewis CARROLL appearing in *Alice in Wonderland.*

"You are old, Father William," the young man said,
"And your hair has become very white,
And yet you incessantly stand on your head—
Do you think, at your age, it is right?"

It is a parody of *The Old Man's Comforts* (1799), a poem by SOUTHEY.

Fathom, Ferdinand, Count. The hero of Smollett's novel, *The Adventures of Ferdinand, Count Fathom* (1754), a villain who robs his benefactors, pillages everyone, but is finally forgiven and reforms under an assumed name.

Fatima. (1) According to the Koran, daughter of Mahomet, and one of the four perfect women. The other three are Khadijah, the prophet's first wife; Mary, daughter of Imran; and Asia, wife of that Pharaoh who was drowned in the Red Sea.

(2) A female hermit in the *Arabian Nights* who was murdered by the African Magician as a part of his schemes against Aladdin.

(3) The name usually given to the last wife of BLUEBEARD.

faubourg. A suburb of a French city, now also a district within the city, any quarter of a city, chiefly, that is, a quarter that used to be a suburb, as the faubourgs St. Germain, St. Antoine, etc., of Paris. *L'Accent des faubourgs* is still something like a Bronx accent.

Faulconbridge, Philip. In Shakespeare's *King John,* the natural son of King Richard I and Lady Robert Faulconbridge. He is generous and open-hearted, but hates foreigners like a true-born islander. Referred to as "the Bastard."

Faulkland. In Sheridan's comedy THE RIVALS, the over-anxious lover of Julia Melville. He is always fretting and tormenting himself about her whims, spirit, health, etc. Every feature in the sky, every shift of the wind, is a source of anxiety to him. If she is gay, he frets that she should care too little for his absence; if she is low-spirited, he fears she is going to die; if she dances with another, he is jealous; if she doesn't, she is out of sorts.

Faulkner, William Harrison (1897–). American novelist and short-story writer, noted for his studies of decadence and subnormality in the Deep South, in the undertaking of which he was influenced to a large extent by Sherwood ANDERSON. In his style he sometimes made use of the techniques of STREAM-OF-CONSCIOUSNESS and INTERIOR MONOLOGUE. Faulkner's novels include *Soldier's Pay* (1926); *Mosquitoes* (1927); *Sartoris* (1929); THE SOUND AND THE FURY (1929); AS I LAY DYING (1930); SANCTUARY (1931); *Idyll in the Desert* (1931); *Light in August* (1932); *Pylon* (1935); *Absalom, Absalom* (1936); *The Unvanquished* (1938); *The Wild Palms* (1939); *The Hamlet* (1940). Collections of his short stories are: *These Thirteen* (1931); *Miss Zilphia Gant* (1932); *Dr. Martino* (1934); *Go Down, Moses* (1942). *The Marble Faun* (1924), *Salmagundi* (1932), *This Earth* (1932), and *A Green Bough* (1933) are books of poems.

Faultless Painter, the. Andrea del Sarto (1488–1530) was so called. He is the speaker in one of Browning's dramatic monologues, called by his name. See ANDREA DEL SARTO.

faun. In Roman myth, Faunus was a king of Italy who devoted himself to promoting agriculture and religion and after his death became a rural deity. He was in many ways similar to the Greek Pan. Later there grew up the idea of a number of fauns or satyr-like beings with tails, horns, goats' legs and feet and furry pointed ears. Two festivals called *Faunalia* were held on February 13 and December 5.

Hawthorne wrote a novel THE MARBLE FAUN in which the hero, it is hinted, is a faun. It was suggested by the statue of a youthful faun by Praxiteles, now in the Capitoline Museum in Rome.

One of the best-known poems of Stéphane MALLARMÉ is his *L'Après-midi d'un faune* (*Afternoon of a Faun*). DEBUSSY's symphonic tone poem *Prélude à l'après-midi d'un faune* (1892, perf. 1894, publ. 1902) became the firm foundation of its composer's fame. One of DIAGHILEV's best-known ballets was adapted to it, with NIJINSKY dancing the Faun.

Fauntleroy, Little Lord, see under LITTLE.

Faunus. In Roman mythology, a rural deity; son of Picus, grandson of Saturn and father of Acis, the suitor of Galatea, and of Latinus, the father of Lavinia. He, as well as Silvanus, came to be more and more identified with the Greek Pan, with whom he had many traits in common. His priests were the Luperci, his main festival the Lupercalia. When not viewed as an individual, he appeared in the multiformity of the fauns, possibly under the influence of the Greek panes, satyrs, etc. in their relation with Pan.

Faure, Élie (1873–1937). French art critic and historian. In 1905 helped found the Université Populaire, a school of adult education. *History of Art* (1923–1930), his greatest work. *Dance Over Fire and Water* (1926); *The Italian Renaissance* (1929); *The Spirit of Japan* (1930).

Fauré, Gabriel Urbain (1845–1924). French composer. Director (1905–1920) Conservatory of Music, Paris. With Debussy, emancipator of modern French music from German tutelage.

Fauset, Jessie Redmon (1884?–). American Negro novelist. M.A. University of Pennsylvania. Studied at Sorbonne. Zona GALE wrote a preface to her third novel, *The Chinaberry Tree* (1931). Her brother, **Arthur Huff Fauset** (1899–), is an American Negro educator and writer.

Faust. The hero of Marlowe's *Tragical History of Dr. Faustus* (ca. 1589) and Goethe's *Faust* (1790–1833) originated in Dr. Johann Faust, or Faustus, a scoundrelly magician and astrologer, who was born in Wurtemberg and died about 1538. Many tales previously ascribed to other astrologers crystallized about him, he became the popular ideal "of one who sought to sound the depths of this world's knowledge and enjoyment without help from God," and in 1587 he appeared for the first time as the central figure in a book by Johann Spies (published at Frankfort-on-Main), which immediately became popular and was soon translated into English, French, and other languages. Marlowe

> treated the legend as a poet, bringing out with all his power the central thought—man in the pride of knowledge turning from God. The voices of his good and evil angel in the ear of Faustus, the one bidding him repent and hope, the other bidding him despair, were devised by Marlowe himself for the better painting of a soul within the toils of Satan.—Morley, *English Writers,* vol. ix. p. 255.

The basis of the legend is that, in return for twenty-four years of further life during which he is to have every pleasure and all knowledge at his command, Faust sells his soul to the Devil. and the climax is reached when, at the close of the period, the Devil claims him for his own. MEPHISTOPHELES is his evil angel, and the supplier of all his desires.

Faust early became a popular character in the German puppet shows. Marlowe, in his tragedy, follows the German legend and gives Faust as a mistress Helen of Troy, whom Mephistopheles conjures up from the other world. Goethe also follows this tradition in the second part of his *Faust.* In the first part, however, he introduces a distinctly new love element in the tragic story of Gretchen or MARGARET. This episode is the basis of Berlioz' opera, *The Damnation of Faust* (1846), Gounod's opera, *Faust* (1859), and Boito's opera, *Mefistofele* (1868). In Goethe's masterpiece the old Faust legend is given a philosophic content far beyond its original significance, and at the end of his long quest for knowledge, for pleasure, for power, Faust finds his real satisfaction in reclaiming a great swamp for humanity. The two parts of the drama are markedly different in tone, the latter being much more abstract and symbolic. Part I appeared in 1808, Part II was not finished until 1831, a year before Goethe's death.

The Faust legend is also the subject of FESTUS, a dramatic poem by P. J. Bailey (1839) and *Faust* by Stephen Phillips (1868–1915).

See also FUST.

Faust, Frederick, see BRAND, MAX.

Faustina, Annia Galeria. The name of two Roman empresses. Faustina the Elder married the Emperor Antonius Pius, and died 141 A. D. Faustina the Younger, her daughter, married the Emperor Marcus Aurelius, the adopted son and successor of Antonius, and died 175 A. D. Both were famous for their evil lives, though MARCUS AURELIUS professed to believe his wife the best of women. Cf. Swinburne's poem, *Faustine,* written with these empresses in mind.

Fust or **Faust** (d.? 1467). German printer, for a time associate and financial backer of GUTENBERG. Because of his name, he has often been confused with Dr. FAUSTUS, the magician, and appears as the central figure of a story, according to which he was one of the earliest printers of Bibles, and passed off a large number as manuscripts for sixty crowns apiece, the usual price being five hundred crowns. The uniformity of the books, their rapid supply, and their unusual cheapness excited astonishment. Information was laid against him for magic, the brilliant red ink with which his copies were adorned was declared to be his blood; he was charged with dealings with the devil, and condemned to be burnt alive. To save himself, he revealed his secret to the Paris

Parlement, and his invention became the admiration of the world.

Fauvist. One of a group of French artists (Matisse, Rouault, Derain, Dufy, etc.) who revolted (ca. 1906) from current tendencies in academic art, calling themselves aggressively *les Fauves,* "the untamed beasts."

faux pas (*Fr.*). A "false step"; a breach of manners or moral conduct. The sub-standard American variant "foxpaw" is a fine example of folk etymology.

Favart, Charles Simon (1710–1792). French dramatist, author of musical comedies and husband of the singer Marie Justine Benoîte Duronceray (1727–1772).

Faversham, Rev. Michael. The hero of MICHAEL AND HIS LOST ANGEL by H. A. Jones.

Faversham, William (1868–1940). British-born American actor. Leading man in Charles Frohman's company for six years. Popular matinée idol.

Favonius. In Roman mythology, a personification of the west wind. He is a promoter of vegetation, identical with Zephyrus.

Favorita, La (The Favorite). An opera by DONIZETTI (1842). *La Favorita* is Leonora de Guzman, "favorite" of Alfonzo XI of Castile. The time is the year 1340. Ferdinand (Fernando), an idealistic young officer, falls in love with her, and the king, to save himself from excommunication, sanctions the marriage. But when Ferdinand learns that Leonora is the king's mistress, he rejects the alliance with indignation and becomes a monk. Leonora becomes a novice in the same monastery, sees Ferdinand, obtains his forgiveness, and dies.

favorite son. A political candidate who has the cordial support of his own state, but is not well known or highly regarded elsewhere.

Fawcett, Edgar (1847–1904). American poet, novelist, and dramatist, who satirized New York high society.

Fawkes, Guy (1570–1606). English Catholic. Enlisted in the Spanish army in Flanders (1593). Became involved in the GUNPOWDER PLOT (Nov. 5, 1605). Arrested, tried, and executed (Jan. 31, 1606). See also GUY; GUY FAWKES DAY.

Fawley, Jude. The hero of Hardy's JUDE THE OBSCURE.

fay, see FAIRY.

Morgan le Fay, see MORGAN, also FATA.

Faÿ, Bernard (1893–). French historian and biographer specializing in American history. One of his outstanding books is *Franklin, the Apostle of Modern Times* (1929). An active collaborator with the Vichy government during World War II.

F. B. The initials and familiar nickname of Frederick BAYHAM in Thackeray's NEWCOMES.

Fearing, Kenneth (1902–). American poet of proletarian sympathies. He is noted for the jazzed satirical style of his best-known poems, published in the period of the 1930's, in which symbols from motion-pictures, tabloid newspapers, comic strips, the radio, advertising, and the like, presented in free verse in the colloquial idiom of the time, are used to mock and satirize the popularly accepted American faith in success and wealth, which was shaken by the current depression and unemployment. Fearing's books include: *Angel Arms* (1929); *Poems* (1935); *Dead Reckoning* (1938); *Collected Poems* (1940); and a novel, *The Hospital* (1939). Has also written clever mystery novels.

feasts. Anniversary days of joy. They are either immovable or movable. *The chief immovable feasts* in the Christian calendar are the four quarter-days—viz., the Annunciation or Lady Day (March 25), the Nativity of John the Baptist (June 24), Michaelmas Day (September 29), and Christmas Day (December 25). Others are the Circumcision (January 1), Epiphany (January 6), All Saints' (November 1), All Souls' (November 2), and the several Apostles' days.

The movable feasts depend upon Easter Sunday. They are—Palm Sunday: The Sunday next before Easter Sunday; Good Friday: The Friday next before Easter Sunday; Ash Wednesday: The first day of Lent; Sexagesima Sunday: Sixty days before Easter Sunday; Ascension Day or Holy Thursday: Fortieth day after Easter Sunday; Pentecost or Whit Sunday: The seventh Sunday after Easter Sunday; Trinity Sunday: The Sunday next after Pentecost.

feast of reason. Conversation on and discussion of learned and congenial subjects.

> There St. John mingles with my friendly bowl
> The feast of reason and the flow of soul.
>
> Pope, *Imitations of Horace,* ii. 1.

See also LOVE FEAST.

feather.

the white feather. See under WHITE.

that's a feather in your cap. An honor to you. The allusion is to the very general custom in Asia and among the American Indians of adding a new feather to their head-gear for every enemy slain.

he has feathered his nest well. He has made lots of money; has married a rich woman. The allusion is to birds, which line their nests with feathers to make them soft and warm.

Featherstone, Mr. A miser in George Eliot's MIDDLEMARCH.

Feathertop: a Moralized Legend. A well known sketch or tale of Hawthorne's in his MOSSES FROM AN OLD MANSE. It treats of the bringing to life of a scarecrow who passes for a fine gentleman. The sketch gave Percy MacKaye the basis for his drama, THE SCARECROW.

Fedalma. The heroine of George Eliot's narrative poem, THE SPANISH GIPSY.

Federalist, The. A series of eighty-five papers or essays published in 1787–1788 in defense of the American Constitution. Fifty-one of the series are said to have been written by Alexander Hamilton; the others by Madison and Jay. They are considered the best expression of the political temper of the times.

Federal Reserve System. A system of banking established in the U.S. by the Federal Reserve Act (Owen-Glass) of December 23, 1913, concentrating the banking resources of the country and providing an elastic currency. There are twelve mutually independent quasi-public Federal Reserve banks, serving a corresponding number of Federal Reserve Districts, located at Boston, New York, Philadelphia, Richmond, Atlanta, Dallas, Cleveland, Chicago, St. Louis, Minneapolis, Kansas City, and San Francisco. These banks are "bankers' banks." Their stock is owned by the member banks of each district. They deal almost exclusively with other banks, and their functions include the issuing of notes, the holding of reserves for their members, and the buying and selling of government securities. There is a supervisory Federal Reserve Board of eight members.

Fédora. (1) In Balzac's WILD ASS'S SKIN (*Le Peau de Chagrin*), a "woman without a heart" on whom Raphael wastes his love, while the magic skin shrinks away.

(2) Title and heroine of a tragedy by SARDOU (*Fr.*, 1883), in which Sarah BERNHARDT scored great success.

Feeble. The name of a "woman's tailor," brought to Sir John Falstaff as a recruit (Shakespeare, 2 *Henry IV*, iii. 2). He tells Sir John "he will do his good will," and the knight replies, "Well said, courageous Feeble! Thou wilt be as valiant as the wrathful dove, or most magnanimous mouse . . . most forcible Feeble." The phrase, "most forcible Feeble," is sometimes applied to a writer whose language is very "loud," but whose ideas are very jejune.

Feenix. In Dickens' DOMBEY AND SON, nephew of the Hon. Mrs. Skewton (mother of Edith, Mr. Dombey's second wife). Feenix is a very old gentleman, patched up to look as much like a young fop as possible.

> Cousin Feenix was a man about town forty years ago; but he is still so juvenile in figure and manner that strangers are amazed when they discover latent wrinkles in his lordship's face, and crows' feet in his eyes. But Cousin Feenix getting up at half-past seven, is quite another thing from Cousin Feenix got up.—Dickens, *Dombey and Son*, xxxi.

Feignwell, Colonel. In Mrs. CENTLIVRE's comedy, *A Bold Stroke for a Wife* (1718), the poseur who wins an heiress by passing himself off as SIMON PURE.

Feininger, Lyonel (1871–). German-American artist. Caricatures and political cartoons. As a painter influenced by Cubism.

Feisi or **Feiyasi, Abul Feis ibn Mubarak** (1547–1595). Indo-Persian poet and scholar; court poet of Emperor Akbar (1572). Translator of parts of the MAHABHARATA into Persian.

feist. U.S. dialect. A small dog. Also spelled **fice, fyst, fyste, fyce, fist, fiste, fiest, fise, feice, feest, faust, fife,** etc. and used in redundant combinations as **fice dog, faust dog,** etc. *The Bench-legged Fyce* is a dialect poem by Eugene FIELD. It begins:

> Speakin' of dorgs, my bench-legged fyce
> Hed most o' the virtues, an' nary a vice . . .

The description of the dog is:

> His legs wuz so crooked, my bench-legged pup
> Wuz as tall settin' down as he wuz standin' up.

Félibrige. An association of Provençal poets, founded near Avignon (1854) for the cultivation of Provençal as a literary language. Its first leader was Joseph Roumanille. Its membership included Frédéric Mistral. A *Félibre* is a member of the *Félibrige*. The origin of both terms is obscure.

Felician, Father. In Longfellow's poem EVANGELINE, the Catholic priest and schoolmaster of Grand Pré, in Acadia. He accompanies Evangeline in part of her wanderings to find Gabriel, her affianced husband.

Felix. In Longfellow's *Golden Legend* (1851), a monk who listens to the singing of a milk-white bird for a hundred years, which seem to him "but a single hour," so enchanted is he with the song. See also HILDESHEIM.

Felix, Antonius. A Greek freedman; procurator of Judaea (ca. 52–60 A. D.) under whom St. Paul was tried (*Acts* xxiii. 23, 24, xxiv). Succeeded by Festus, before whom St. Paul made his famous "appeal unto Caesar" (*Acts* xxv. 12).

Felix Holt, the Radical. A novel by George ELIOT (1866). The action takes place at the time of the Reform Bill, 1832–1833. The plot, which is somewhat complicated, deals primarily with the affairs of Harold TRANSOME, heir to the Transome estate. Harold horrifies his dominating and conventional-minded mother by running for Parliament as a Radical and in this connection meets Felix HOLT, a young idealist who is making a living as a watchmaker rather than live on proceeds from patent medicine. Felix becomes greatly interested in Esther Lyon, the step-daughter of a lovable, unworldly Independent minister; and although the two young people have diametrically opposite views, they fall in love. It is discovered that Esther is the real heir to the Transome estate and Harold an illegitimate son, the father being the attorney Jermyn. Harold offers to give up the estate to Esther and also proposes marriage. In the meantime Felix, in his effort to prevent riots on Election Day, has accidentally killed a man and is on trial. His trouble brings to Esther the realization that she loves Felix; she gives up her claim to the Transome estate, and after his pardon, becomes his wife.

Felixmarte. The hero of *Felixmarte of Hyrcania,* a Spanish romance of chivalry by Melchior de Orteza Caballero de Ubeda (1566). The curate in DON QUIXOTE condemns this work to the flames.

Fell, Dr.

> I do not like thee, Dr. Fell,
> The reason why I cannot tell;
> But this I know, I know full well,
> I do not like thee, Dr. Fell.

These well-known lines are by the "facetious" Tom Brown (1663–1704), and the person referred to was Dr. Fell, Dean of Christchurch (1625–1686), who expelled him, but said he would remit the sentence if he translated the thirty-third Epigram of Martial:

> Non amo te, Zabidi, nec possum dicere quare;
> Hoc tantum possum dicere non amo te.

The above is the translation, which is said to have been given impromptu.

fellah. Plural **fellahin** or **fellahs.** A race type in modern Egypt, descended from the ancient Egyptians, of mixed Coptic, Arabian, and Nubian stock. The fellahin are heavy of build, broad-faced, thick-lipped, with a brown-red skin.

fellow traveler. A translation of the Russian *popuchiki.* One who merely sympathizes with and furthers the ideals of some organized group but does not actually join it. Used mainly with reference to the Communist party. See also PINK.

felo-de-se. One who kills himself by an act legally ranking as felony. Plural **felones-de-se.**

Feltham, Owen (1602–1668). English prose writer, one of the CHARACTER WRITERS. He was the author of *Resolves: Divine, Moral, and Political* (ca. 1620), a popular series of moralistic "characters."

Felton, John (1595?–1628). English lieutenant under Sir Edward Cecil at Cadiz (1625). He assassinated the Duke of Buckingham who had refused him the command of a company (Aug. 23, 1628) and was hanged at Tyburn. He appears in *The Three Musketeers* by Alexandre DUMAS as a victim of Milady's intrigues.

Felton, Septimus, see SEPTIMUS FELTON.

feme. From Old French, the modern *femme,* "woman, wife." Occurs in several legal terms, as **feme covert,** "a married woman"; **feme sole,** "a single woman"; **feme-sole trader,** a married woman engaging in business on her own account.

feminine ending. An extra, unaccented syllable at the end of an iambic or anapestic line of poetry. It is very common in blank verse.

> To bĕ | or nŏt | to bĕ | —that ĭs | thĕ quĕs | tiŏn.

feminine rhyme. Rhymed feminine endings, also called *double rhyme.* They are common in the heroic couplet.

femmes savantes. Women who go in for women's rights, science and philosophy, to the neglect of domestic duties and wifely amenities. The expression comes from Molière's comedy, *Les Femmes savantes* (1672), in which the "blue-stockings" are Philaminte, the mother of Henriette, who discharges one of her servants because she speaks bad grammar; Armande, sister of Henriette, who advocates platonic love and science; and Bélise, sister of Philaminte, who sides with her in all things, but imagines that everyone is in love with her. Henriette, who has no sympathy with these "lofty flights," is in love with Clitandre, but Philaminte wants her to marry Trissotin, a *bel esprit.* However, the father loses his property through the "savant" proclivities of his wife, Trissotin retires from the affair, and Clitandre marries Henriette, the "perfect" or thorough woman. The comedy is usually known in English translation as *The Learned Ladies.*

Fenella, *alias* **Zarah.** In Scott's PEVERIL OF THE PEAK, daughter of Edward Christian, a pretended deaf-and-dumb, elf-like attendant on the Countess of Derby. She has been brought up to believe that her father was Edward's murdered brother William, and that to secure vengeance is her "first great duty on earth"; hence the pretense of being a deaf-mute in order to spy upon her supposed enemies. Fenella falls in love with Julian Peveril and plays the part of Zarah, a "Moorish sorceress" to rescue him from prison. In her hopeless love as in other characteristics, she is akin to Goethe's MIGNON.

Fénelon, François de Salignac de La Mothe (1651–1715). French churchman and author, attached to the royal court and a tutor to the Dauphin until exiled for his unorthodox advocacy of the mystic doctrines of QUIETISM. He is known for his tolerance and liberalism in political ideas and educational theories. His works include *De l'Éducation des filles* (1687), a short treatise on education for women; *Tél-*

émaque (see TELEMACHUS) (1699), an epic in imitation of the *Aeneid* and the *Odyssey*, giving political advice to the Dauphin and indirectly reproving Louis XIV for his policies; and *Lettre a l'Académie* (1714), literary criticism, in which Fénelon prefers the precepts of the classic Ancients to those of the Moderns. See ANCIENTS AND MODERNS.

fêng-huang, fêng-hwang. In Chinese mythology, a gorgeous bird, phoenix or pheasantlike that appears in time of peace and prosperity.

Fenians. An anti-British secret association of disaffected Irishmen formed simultaneously in Ireland by James Stephens and in New York by John O'Mahony in 1857, with the object of overthrowing the domination of England in Ireland, and making Ireland a republic. The word is from the Old Irish *Fene*, a name of the ancient Irish, confused with *Fianna*, the semi-mythological warriors, led by Finn McCool, who defended Ireland in the time of FINN or FINGAL. Scott, in his fictitious translation from Ossian in THE ANTIQUARY (ch. xxx), uses the term in place of Macpherson's "Fingalians," i.e., the Norse followers of Fionnghal (Fingal): "Do you compare your psalms to the tales of the bare-armed Fenians?" These ancient Fenians are represented as warriors of superhuman size, strength, and courage, and became the nucleus of a large cycle of legends. See also CLAN-NA-GAEL; SINN FEIN.

Fenn, George Manville (1831–1909). English writer of boys' books.

Fenellosa, Ernest Francisco (1853–1908). American Orientalist. Convert to Buddhism. Decorated by the Mikado. Curator of Oriental Art, Boston Museum of Fine Arts (1890–1897); Professor, Imperial Normal School, Tokyo (1897–1900). Ezra POUND, his literary executor, produced three books from his notes, *Cathay* (1915), *Certain Noble Plays of Japan* (1916), *Noh, or Accomplishment* (1917).

Fenrir or **Fenris-wolf.** In Scandinavian mythology, the wolf of LOKI, typifying, perhaps, the goading of a guilty conscience. He was the brother of HEL, and when he gaped one jaw touched earth and the other heaven. This monster was expected to swallow up ODIN at the day of doom. Percy MacKaye wrote a dramatic poem entitled *Fenris the Wolf* (1905).

Fenton. In Shakespeare's MERRY WIVES OF WINDSOR, the lover of Anne Page. Fenton is of good birth, and seeks to marry a fortune to "heal his poverty." In "sweet Anne Page," however, he soon discovers that which makes him love her for herself more than for her money.

Fenton, Robert. The hero of Howells' A WOMAN'S REASON.

Feramorz. In Moore's LALLA ROOKH, the name assumed by the Sultan in his disguise as a young Cashmerian poet who relates poetical tales to Lalla Rookh on her journey from Delhi to Lesser Bucharia.

Ferber, Edna (1887–). American novelist, short-story writer, and playwright, author of numerous best-selling novels and successful plays. Among the best-known novels are *So Big* (1924); *Show Boat* (1926); *Cimarron* (1929); *American Beauty* (1931); *Come and Get It* (1935); *Saratoga Trunk* (1941). Her plays include *The Royal Family* (1927), considered to be a satire on the family of BARRYMORE; *Dinner at Eight* (1932); and *Stage Door* (1936). *A Peculiar Treasure* (1939) is an autobiography. Emma MCCHESNEY, a traveling saleswoman, is her best-known character.

Ferdinand. (1) King of Navarre in Shakespeare's comedy, LOVE'S LABOUR'S LOST. He agrees with three young lords to spend three years in severe study, during which time no woman is to approach his court; but no sooner is the agreement made than he falls in love with the Princess of France.

(2) In Shakespeare's TEMPEST, son of Alonso, king of Naples. He falls in love with Miranda, daughter of Prospero, the exiled duke of Milan.

(3) The hero of Donizetti's opera LA FAVORITA, also called Fernando.

(4) A Spanish bull, famous hero of an American children's book (1936) by Munro Leaf and Robert Lawson which became a best-seller. Ferdinand preferred smelling the flowers to fighting.

Ferdinand, Count Fathom, The Adventures of. A novel by Smollett (1754). See FATHOM.

fere. A mate or companion. Cf. *The Ballad of the Goodly Fere* by Ezra Pound. Historically a *fere* is one with whom one travels (from an old verb *faran*, "to travel"), as a *companion* is one with whom one shares one's bread (from Latin *panis*).

Ferguson. *It's all very fine, Ferguson, but you don't lodge here.* A popular saying about the middle of last century. There is more than one account of its origin. One refers it to a young Scot of the name who got intoxicated at Epsom races and found it impossible to prevail on any hotelkeeper to take him in; another has it that Ferguson was a companion of the notorious Marquis of Waterford. In one of their sprees they got separated; the marquis went to bed at the house of his uncle, the Archbishop of Armagh, Charles Street, St. James' Square. A thundering knock came at the door, and the marquis threw up the window and said, "It is all very fine, Ferguson, but you don't lodge here." Cf. *Notes and Queries,* January 16, 1886, p. 46.

Ferguson, Elizabeth. A leading character in Margaret Deland's IRON WOMAN.

Ferguson, John, see JOHN FERGUSON.

Fergusson, Harvey (1890–). American novelist of New Mexican history and contemporary life. His sister Erna has written interesting books about the Southwest, South America, and Cuba.

Fermi, Enrico (1901–). Italian physicist. Came to United States in 1939. Professor of physics at Columbia University. Awarded Nobel Prize for physics (1938). Worked under Major General Leslie R. Groves on the atomic bomb.

Fernald, Chester Bailey (1869–1938). Though born in Boston, Fernald acquired the material for his best books in San Francisco: *The Cat and the Cherub* (1896) and *Chinatown Stories* (1899). He also wrote *Under the Jack-staff* (1903), stories of the sea, the Spanish-American War, etc. He traveled widely and lived in England after 1907 where he wrote for the stage. His short stories are notable for their humor.

Ferney, the Patriarch or **Philosopher of.** VOLTAIRE is so called, because for the last twenty years of his life he lived at Ferney, a small sequestered village near Geneva, now officially known as Ferney-Voltaire, from which obscure retreat he poured forth his invectives against the French Government, the Church, nobles, nuns, priests, and indeed all classes.

Ferohers. The guardian angels of ancient Persian mythology. They are countless in number, and their chief tasks are for the well-being of man. The winged circular symbol, supposed to represent either them or the sun-god, and found on many Mesopotamian monuments, is also known as the *Feroher.*

Ferracute (i.e., sharp iron). A giant in Turpin's CHRONICLE OF CHARLEMAGNE. He had the strength of forty men, and was thirty-six feet high. Though no lance could pierce his hide, ORLANDO slew him by divine interposition.

Ferragus. The giant of Portugal in VALENTINE AND ORSON. He took Bellisant under his care after she had been divorced by the Emperor of Constantinople. The great "BRAZEN HEAD," that told those who consulted it whatever they required to know, was kept in his castle.

Ferrara. A broadsword or claymore with the name Ferrara inscribed on the blade. Thought to be made by the famous sixteenth-century armorer Andrea Ferrara at Belluno, Italy. Highly esteemed in England and Scotland in the 16th and 17th centuries.

Ferrara Bible, the. See BIBLE, SPECIALLY NAMED.

Ferrars, Edward. In Jane Austen's SENSE AND SENSIBILITY, the lover of Elinor Dashwood.

Ferrars, Endymion. Hero of Disraeli's political novel, *Endymion* (1835).

Ferrau, Ferraute, Ferracute, or **Ferragus.** In Ariosto's ORLANDO FURIOSO, a Saracen, son of Lanfusa. He dropped his helmet in the river, and vowed he would never wear another till he had won that worn by Orlando. Orlando slew him with a wound in the navel, his only vulnerable part.

Ferrero, Guglielmo (1871–1942). Italian historian of Jewish descent. Author of five volumes on *The Greatness and Decline of Rome* (1907–1909), a massive history. Also a novelist. A long list of books to his credit. Advocated Italian participation in World War I on the side of the Allies.

Ferrex and Porrex. Two sons of GORBODUC, a mythical British king, who divided his kingdom between them. Porrex drove his brother from Britain, and when Ferrex returned with an army he was slain, but Porrex was shortly after put to death by his mother. The story is told in Geoffrey of MONMOUTH'S *Historia Regum Britanniae,* and it forms the basis of the first regular English tragedy, *Gorboduc,* or *Ferrex and Porrex,* written by Thomas NORTON and Thomas SACKVILLE, Earl of Dorset, and acted in 1561.

Ferris wheel. A giant power-driven steel wheel, for amusement and observation, with balanced passenger cars, the first one being erected by George Washington Gale Ferris (1859–1896), American engineer, at the World's Columbian Exposition in Chicago in 1893.

Fescennine. Low, scurrilous, obscene. Applied to poetry, especially in the phrase *Fescennine verses,* a genre of licentious poetry of a personal character, extemporized at public meetings, originally in the Etruscan city of Fescennia but later also at Rome.

Feste. In Shakespeare's *Twelfth Night,* Olivia's clown.

Festus. (1) A dramatic poem by Philip J. BAILEY (1839). Like FAUST the hero is conducted by a diabolical companion through the whole of human experience and more, but Lucifer, his guide, is not so much the tempter as the philosopher and theologian.

(2) In Browning's PARACELSUS, a true friend of the hero. He is the husband of Michal.

(3) *Porcius Festus.* A Roman procurator

in Palestine, successor to Antonius FELIX and responsible for St. Paul's journey to Rome.

fetish. An object with magical powers, temporary or permanent seat of a supernatural power. In psychoanalysis or psychopathology, a part of the body, as somebody's foot, or an article of clothing, as a handkerchief of the beloved person, on which erotic interest has become fixed.

Feu, Le, see UNDER FIRE.

Feuchtwanger, Lion (1884–). German novelist, author of best-selling novels dealing with historical and political subjects, especially Jews in positions of power. Among his works are *The Ugly Duchess* (*Die Hässliche Herzogin*) (1923); *Jud Süss* (1926), translated as *Power; Two Anglo-Saxon Plays* (1928), including *The Oil Islands* and *Warren Hastings; Success* (*Erfolg*) (1930); *Der Jüdische Krieg* (1932), translated as *Josephus; Die Geschwister Oppenheim* (1933), translated as *The Oppermanns; The Jew of Rome* (1935); *The Pretender* (1937); *Exil* (1940), translated as *Paris Gazette; Josephus and the Emperor* (1942).

Feuchtwanger's writings were suppressed during World War I because of their revolutionary content, and he was among the authors forced, because of Jewish parentage and the nature of their books, to flee Germany under the repressive policies of the National Socialist government. See NAZISM.

feudalism or **feudal system.** The system of political organization with reference to land tenure and service and allegiance prevalent during the Middle Ages throughout Europe. In its purest form, the feudal system assigns sovereignty over all the land of the realm to the highest feudal lord, i.e., the king, who invests his vassals in exchange for military service and fealty with inheritable fiefs (or divisions of land), which they in turn and under similar conditions distribute by subinfeudation among their subtenants, and so on down the line. The feudal lords holding their fiefs from the king are tenants *in capite;* the subtenants are *mesne lords.*

In its ideal form the feudal system represents an organic hierarchy in which every member carries a balanced burden of obligations and authority. It reached its highest development in the period from the ninth to the fourteenth century. Increasingly adulterated and corrupt elements of it have survived into the nineteenth century. It has been observed that its basic principles still govern the English and American real-property law. The theory of the FÜHRER PRINCIPLE is likewise patterned on it.

Feuerbach, Paul Johann Anselm von (1775–1833). German jurist; reformer of penal legislation. His third son, **Ludwig Andreas von Feuerbach** (1804–1872), was a philosopher; a pupil of Hegel, he abandoned Hegelian idealism for a naturalistic materialism and attacked orthodox religion and immortality, especially in *Das Wesen des Christentums* (*The Nature of Christianity;* 1840). **Anselm von Feuerbach** (1829–1880), a grandson of Paul Johann Anselm by his eldest son Anselm, became a well-known historical and portrait painter, representing a sort of nostalgic and romanticizing classicism.

Feuillet, Octave (1821–1890). French novelist and playwright. His newspaper serials were the first to be called FEUILLETON.

feuilleton. French, from *feuille,* "a leaf," but at the same time a pun on the name of Octave FEUILLET. The part of French newspapers devoted to tales, light literature, etc.; hence, in England a serial story in a newspaper, or the "magazine page" which contains light articles, tit-bits, and so on.

Féval, Paul (1860–). Sea-rover, writer of sailors' songs; used fictional characters of d'Artagnan and Cyrano in several books; one of the founders of the Society of French Novelists. Son of **Paul Henri Corentin Féval** (1817–1887), novelist and playwright; rival of SARDOU and patron of GABORIAU.

Feverel, Richard. Hero of Meredith's novel, THE ORDEAL OF RICHARD FEVEREL.

Sir Austin Feverel in the same novel is the short-sighted father of the hero.

Fezon. In VALENTINE AND ORSON, the daughter of Savary, Duke of Aquitaine, demanded in marriage by a pagan, called the Green Knight. Orson, having overthrown the pagan, was accepted by the lady instead.

Fezziwig. The name of a family of cheerful people in Dickens' *A Christmas Carol.* Of the mother we are told that she was "one vast substantial smile."

F. F. V's. The First Families of Virginia, descended from early settlers.

> Mason wuz F.F.V., though a cheap card to win on,
> But t'other was jes' New York trash to begin on.
> Lowell, *Biglow Papers.*

fiacre. A small four-wheeled carriage for hire. The word comes from the *Hôtel de St. Fiacre* in Paris where the first fiacre station was established about 1650 to accommodate pilgrims on their way to St. Fiacre's shrine in Breuil. This St. Fiacre (d. ?670) had come from Ireland and is a patron saint of gardeners. His day is August 30.

Fiammetta (from Ital. *fiamma,* "flame"). The name under which BOCCACCIO celebrated MARIA D'AQUINO in his works. *L'Amorosa Visione* is dedicated to her by means of an acrostic of the name, and *L'Amorosa Fiammetta* tells her love story in the form of an autobiography, with the lady eventually deserted by her lover and left to weep alone, a reversal of the situation in the author's own life. She is also considered to have been drawn upon for the character of Criseida (in Chaucer, *Criseyde,* and in Shakespeare, *Cressida*), the heroine of *Il Filostrato,* Boccaccio's version of the famous story of TROILUS.

Fianna. See under FENIAN.

Fianna Fail. Literally, Fenians of Ireland. Name of a party of the Irish Free State opposed to the oath of allegiance to Great Britain. See also SINN FEIN.

Fibber McGee and Molly. A radio serial or "soap opera" given by Marian and Jim Jordan, ex-Peoria mailman, which has held first or second place on the top 50 radio programs. It is a Horatio Alger story, rags-to-riches, and became the nation's top radio program in 1941 after 17 years on the air. Given weekly, it has had 20 million or so listeners.

Fichte, Johann Gottlieb (1762–1814). German philosopher and metaphysician, the son of a poor Lusatian weaver. After the Prussian disaster at Jena (1806), he delivered in Berlin his famous patriotic *Reden an die deutsche Nation* (*Addresses to the German Nation;* 1807–1808). At the opening of the Berlin university (1810) he was given a chair of philosophy and became the second rector of that institution. His most important philosophical work, *Grundlage der gesammten Wissenschaftslehre* (*Fundamental Principles of the Whole Theory of Science;* 1794) reveals Fichte as a disciple of KANT in search for a solution of the master's fundamental dilemma, the limitation of pure reason, its inability to arrive at full knowledge of a "thing-in-itself" (the DING AN SICH) and to yield doctrines of morals and rights. Fichte's solution is solipsistic in that it deduces à priori from the Ego not only the categories of our knowledge of nature but also the doctrines of ethical and legal obligations, thus uniting Kant's two critiques (of Practical and Pure Reason) in one epistemological system.

Ficino, Marsilio (1433–1499). Italian philosopher, the earliest Platonist of the Renaissance period, who as a child was taken into the household of Cosimo de' Medici to be trained specifically as a philosopher and student of the theories of PLATO. He was a leader of the Platonic Academy established at Florence by the Medici with which PICO DELLA MIRANDOLA and Angelo POLIZIANO were also associated. Ficino made translations of works by Plato, PLOTINUS, and DIONYSIUS THE AREOPAGITE, and wrote numerous essays and treatises in which he sought to harmonize Platonism with Christianity. His work was widely known during his time and, like most of that studied and produced by the Florentine Academy, was more in accordance with the teachings of the neo-Platonists (see NEO-PLATONISM) than with those of Plato himself.

Ficke, Arthur Davison (1883–1945). American poet, married the painter Gladys Brown. An authority on Japanese prints. Wrote some twenty books, mostly poetry, among the best-known of which is his *Sonnets of a Portrait Painter* (1914). Perpetrated with Witter Bynner under assumed names the literary hoax of the volume *Spectra* (1916), purporting to be the product of a new faction of the imagist school of poetry. Ficke was actually a classical poet of fine achievement.

Fiddler's Green. The ELYSIUM of sailors; a land flowing with rum and lime-juice; a land of perpetual music, mirth, dancing, drinking, and tobacco; a sort of Dixie Land or land of the leal.

Fidei Defensor, see DEFENDER OF THE FAITH.

Fidele. In Shakespeare's CYMBELINE, the name assumed by Imogen, when, attired in boy's clothes, she starts for Milford Haven to meet her husband, Posthumus.

Fidelio. An opera by BEETHOVEN (1805), based on Bouilly's *Leonore.* The hero is Don Fernando Florestan, a state prisoner in Spain, and the heroine his faithful wife LEONORE, who disguises herself as a man and under the name Fidelio becomes the jailer's servant in order to protect her husband and bring about his release.

Fidessa. In Spenser's *Faërie Queene* a name assumed by DUESSA.

field.

Field of Blood. ACELDAMA. The battle of Cannae is so called.

Field of the Cloth of Gold. The plain, near Guisnes, where Henry VIII had his interview with Francis I in 1520; so called from the splendor and magnificence displayed there on the occasion.

Field of the Forty Footsteps. At the back of the British Museum, once called Southampton Fields, near the extreme north-east of the present Upper Montagu Street. The tradition is that at the time of the Duke of Monmouth's rebellion two brothers fought each other here till both were killed, and for many years forty impressions of their feet remained on the field, and no grass would grow there. The scene was built upon about 1800.

Field, Cyrus West (1819–1892). American financier. Promoter of a variety of adventurous and progressive schemes, among them the first submarine telegraph cable between America and Europe (1854 to 1866) and the

New York elevated railroad (from 1877). Made and lost several fortunes.

Field, Eugene (1850–1895). American poet and journalist. Best-known as poet of childhood, many of his verses in this vein being famous. *With Trumpet and Drum* (1892), etc.

Field, Marshall (1835–1906). American merchant. In 1881 he founded Marshall Field and Co., in Chicago, which became one of the largest department stores in the world. Gave the site of the University of Chicago, the Field Museum of Natural History in Chicago, etc.

Field, Michael. Pseudonym of **Katharine Harris Bradley** (1846–1914) and **Edith Emma Cooper** (1862–1913), English authors collaborating (from 1884) on lyric poetry and poetic dramas.

Field, Rachel Lyman (1894–1942). American novelist and writer for children. Her father was a nephew of Cyrus West FIELD. Her *Hitty,* the story of a doll (1929), was awarded the Newbery Medal for the most distinguished work of children's literature of the year and was a turning point in her career. In 1938 she achieved her greatest popular success with the adult novel *All This, and Heaven Too,* based on the life story of a great-aunt, Henriette Deluzy-Desportes, central figure of a famous *cause célèbre.* The same real-life plot was used by Joseph SHEARING in *The Strange Case of Lucile Cléry* (see CLÉRY, Lucille).

Field, Sara Bard (1882–). American poet and leader in the Woman Suffrage movement. The widow of the distinguished American poet and satirist Charles Erskine Scott Wood (1852–1944). Her *Barabbas* (1932) is a partially historical long dramatic poem. She is also a fine lyricist.

Fielding, Henry (1701–1754). English novelist, burlesque playwright, and journalist, known for the wit, satire, realism, and character delineation of his picaresque novels. His works include JOSEPH ANDREWS (1742), a satire on Richardson's PAMELA; JONATHAN WILD (1743); TOM JONES (1749); and AMELIA (1751). Fielding is considered to be the founder of the novel of incident and to have broadened the novel form by his development of character along with plot.

Fielding, Mrs. A character in Dickens' CRICKET ON THE HEARTH, a little querulous old lady with a peevish face, who, in consequence of once having been better off, or of laboring under the impression that she might have been if something in the indigo trade had happened differently, is very genteel and patronizing indeed.

May Fielding. Her daughter, very pretty and innocent. She was engaged to Edward Plummer, but hears that he has died in South America, and consents to marry Tackleton, the toy merchant. A few days before the day fixed for the wedding, Edward Plummer returns and May Fielding marries him. Tackleton gives them as a present the cake he ordered for his own wedding feast.

Fields, Lew, in full **Lewis Maurice** (1867–1941). With **Joseph Weber** (1867–1942), as Weber and Fields, a famous American team of comedians and theatrical managers.

Fierabras or **Ferumbras, Sir.** One of Charlemagne's paladins, and a leading figure in many of the romances. He was the son of BALAN, king of Spain, and for height of stature, breadth of shoulder, and hardness of muscle he never had an equal. He possessed all Babylon to the Red Sea; was seigneur of Russia, Lord of Cologne, master of Jerusalem, and even of the Holy Sepulcher. He carried away the crown of thorns, and the balsam which embalmed the body of our Lord, one drop of which would cure any sickness, or heal any wound in a moment. One of his chief exploits was to slay the "fearful huge giant that guarded the bridge Mantible," famous for its thirty arches of black marble. His pride was laid low by Olivier, he became a Christian, was accepted by Charlemagne as a paladin, and ended his days in the odor of sanctity, "meek as a lamb and humble as a chidden slave." Sir Fierabras, or Ferumbras, figures in several medieval romances, and is allegorized as Sin overcome by the Cross.

Of the famous **balsam of Fierabras,** DON QUIXOTE says

> It is a balsam of balsams; it not only heals all wounds, but even defies death itself. If thou should'st see my body cut in two, friend Sancho, by some unlucky backstroke, you must carefully pick up that half of me which falls on the ground, and clap it upon the other half before the blood congeals, then give me a draught of the balsam of Fierabras, and you will presently see me as sound as an orange.—Cervantes, *Don Quixote,* I. ii. 2.

Fiesole, Giovanni da. Originally **Guido di Pietro.** Known as **Fra Angelico** (1387–1455). Italian Dominican friar and painter of religious subjects. Among his most famous works are the frescoes at Orvieto (1447).

Fifteen, the. The Jacobite rebellion of 1715, when James Edward Stuart, "the Old Pretender," with the Earl of Mar, made a half-hearted and unsuccessful attempt to gain the throne.

Fifteen decisive battles. See under BATTLES OF THE WORLD, FIFTEEN DECISIVE.

fifteener. In collectors' parlance, a book printed in the fifteenth century, i.e., an INCUNABULUM.

Fifth Avenue. A phrase synonymous with wealth and luxury, from Fifth Avenue in

New York City, a street of fashionable retail shops and expensive dwellings. "Park Avenue" is now used with the same connotation for the same reasons.

fifth column. Term applied during World War II to a systematic organization of spies penetrating the civilian life of the enemy country to acquire information, obstruct military preparations, alarm, confuse, and divide the populace, and assist or join the invading army. It was also applied to citizens who were enemy sympathizers. The term was first used during the Spanish Civil War (1936–1939), by General Mola who stated in a broadcast that he had four columns of soldiers advancing on Madrid and a fifth column of sympathizers within the city that would arise to attack the defenders from the rear. It was popularized by Ernest HEMINGWAY in a play of the same title dealing with the Spanish conflict, and came into wide use with the German invasion of Holland, Belgium, Luxembourg, and France in 1940, when "fifth columnists" were active. The fifth column, in fact and rhetoric, is the equivalent of the Trojan horse of the past.

Fifth Monarchy Men. A fanatical sect of millenarians in England at the time of the Commonwealth, who maintained that the fifth monarchy, when Christ should reign on earth a thousand years, was near at hand and that they must establish it by force. They listed Assyria, Persia, Greece, and Rome as the preceding four monarchies. Their uprisings (1657 and 1661) failed.

Figaro. The rascally hero of two comedies by BEAUMARCHAIS and several operas. In Beaumarchais' *Barber of Séville* (*Le Barbier de Séville;* 1775) Figaro appears as a cunning scamp who, in connection with his duties as barber, manages time after time to thwart Rosina's guardian, Dr. Bartolo, who wishes to marry his ward, and promote her love affair with Count Almaviva. The latter appears in one scene as a drunken soldier; in another, disguised as a music master, he is shaved by Figaro in accord with the suspicious doctor's instructions. In the second comedy, *The Marriage of Figaro* (*Le Mariage de Figaro*), Count Almaviva, having won his lady-love, proves a fickle husband. Figaro, who is now in the Count's service, succeeds after much difficulty in marrying Susanna, a ward of the Countess. Several operas have been founded on these two comedies, notably Rossini's *Barber of Seville* (*Il Barbiere di Siviglia;* 1816) and Mozart's *Marriage of Figaro* (*Le Nozze di Figaro;* 1786).

Fight at Finnsburgh or Finnsburh, The. Fragment of an Anglo-Saxon epic, dealing with the story of Finn and Hildeburh sung by the minstrel in BEOWULF. It was discovered in the 18th century by the Saxon scholar George Hickes (1642–1715).

Fighting France (France Combattante). The movement of French soldiers and sympathizers, led by General Charles de Gaulle, in opposition to the Vichy government of Marshal Pétain. Organized under the name of *France Libre* (*Free French*) in 1940 when France was defeated and forced to collaborate with the Axis. The Free French fought for the liberation of Syria from Vichy in 1941. On Bastille Day (July 14) 1942, the name was changed to *Fighting France.* After the Allied invasion of Europe the Fighting French helped greatly to bring about the final collapse of the German army.

Fighting Prelate. Henry Spencer, bishop of Norwich, who greatly distinguished himself in the rebellion of Wat TYLER. He met the rebels in the field, with the temporal sword, then absolved them, and sent them to the gibbet.

Figueroa, Francisco de (1536?–1620). Spanish poet and soldier; master of blank verse.

Figures of Earth, A Comedy of Appearances. A satiric romance by James Branch CABELL (1921), the scene of which is medieval POICTESME. The hero is Count Manuel, who begins by following after his own thinking and his own desires but is soon diverted into doing what is expected of him, which includes the redemption and governing of Poictesme. His mother has laid on him a *geas* to cut a fine figure in the world, and at various stages of his career he models images or "figures of earth" but never to his own satisfaction. See SESPHRA. For his love affairs with Suskind, with Niafer who becomes his wife, with Freydis, and with Alianora of Provence, see those entries. Manuel's daughter Melicent, who appears in this book, is the heroine of DOMNEI.

Fildes, Sir Luke (1844–1927). Well-known English genre and portrait painter.

filibuster. Use of dilatory tactics in Congress (or a similar body) to prevent presentation or passage of a bill, such as speaking merely to consume time. The connection with the original sense of freebooter, buccaneer, pirate lies in the noncooperative anti-social character of the practice of filibustering. The word traveled from Dutch (*vrijbuiter*) by way of French (*fribustier, flibustier*) into Spanish (*filibustero*) from where it was taken into American English.

Filicaia, Vincenzo da (1642–1707). Italian lyric poet and jurist. Especially remembered for his odes and sonnets.

Filioque Controversy. An argument that long disturbed the Eastern and Western Churches, and the difference of opinion concerning which still forms one of the principal barriers to their fusion. The point was: Did the Holy Ghost proceed from the Father *and* the Son (*filio-que*), or from the Father only? The Western Church maintains the former and the Eastern the latter dogma. The *filioque* was recognized by the Council of Toledo, 589.

The gist of the Western argument is this: If the Son is one with the Father, whatever proceeds from the Father must proceed from the Son also. This is technically called "The Procession of the Holy Ghost."

Filippo Lippi, Fra, see FRA LIPPO LIPPI; LIPPI, Fra FILIPPO.

Fillmore, Millard (1800–1874). Thirteenth president of the U.S.A. Succeeded to presidency in 1850 on the death of President Zachary Taylor. Defeated as Whig candidate in 1852.

Fillpot, Toby. Hero of a famous English drinking song by Rev. Francis Fawkes (1721–1777), entitled *The Brown Jug*. Toby was a thirsty old soul, who "among jolly topers bore off the bell." It chanced as in dog days he sat boozing in his arbor, that he died "full as big as a Dorchester butt." His body turned to clay, and out of the clay a brown jug was made, sacred to friendship, mirth, and mild ale:

His body, when long in the ground it had lain,
And time into clay had resolved it again,
A potter found out in its covert so snug,
And with part of fat Toby he formed this brown jug.
Now sacred to friendship, to mirth, and mild ale.
So here's to my lovely sweet Nan of the vale.
Rev. F. Fawkes.

Filocolo, Il, see BLANCHEFLEUR.

Filomena, St. See under SAINTS.

Filostrato, Il. A poem in *ottava rima* by BOCCACCIO, dealing with the TROILUS AND CRESSIDA story. It was the direct source of Chaucer's famous version of the legend in his *Troilus and Criseyde*. See also GUIDO DELLE COLONNE.

Finality Men. A term of derision applied by antislavery men in the years 1850 to 1860 to those Northerners, who, wishing to avoid agitation of the slavery question, considered the Compromise of 1850 as a final settlement.

John Finality was a nickname given to Lord John Russell because he habitually referred to the Reform Bill of 1831 as a finality.

Financier, The. A novel by Theodore DREISER. See also COWPERWOOD, FRANK.

Finch, Anne (1666–1720), Countess of Winchilsea. Author of occasional verse. In her long Pindaric ode, *The Spleen* (1701), she wrote a couplet echoed in Pope's *Essay on Man* and Shelley's *Epipsychidion*. She was celebrated by Pope under the name of Ardelia.

Finch, Francis Miles (1827–1907). American poet. Author of *The Blue and the Gray* (1867).

Finchley, Sondra. In Theodore Dreiser's AN AMERICAN TRAGEDY, a small-town society girl with whom Clyde GRIFFITHS falls in love and for whom he contrives to rid himself of Roberta ALDEN.

fin de siècle (*Fr.,* "end of the century"). Pertaining to or characteristic of the end of the 19th century. The term originated in the title of a French play by Micard and De Jouvenot (1888). There is an implication of decadence in the allusion, due to its association with the literature of the period and doubtless also because of the possibility of a poetic mistranslation as "end of the saeculum or end of the world." See also DECADENTS.

Fineman, Irving (1893–). American novelist. Served as engineer officer in Navy in World War I. Won Longmans, Green Prize (1930) with *This Pure Young Man* and has since devoted himself to novel-writing.

Fingal, Finn, or **Fionn.** The great Gaelic semi-mythological hero (see FENIAN), father of OSSIAN who was purported by MACPHERSON to have been the original author of the long epic poem *Fingal* (1762), which narrates the hero's adventures. He was the son of Comhal, an enormous giant, who could place his feet on two mountains, and then stoop and drink from a stream in the valley between.

Finger, Charles Joseph (1871–1941). Anglo-American writer on travel and adventure. Short stories, novels, juveniles. Thirty-two books. Won Newbery medal in 1925.

Finley, John Huston (1863–1940). American educator, editor, and poet. Editor-in-chief of the New York *Times* (1937–1938).

Finn. In James Joyce's FINNEGANS WAKE, Finn is one of the characters with whom the hero, H. C. EARWICKER is identified. References to Finn's legendary pursuit of Dermont and Grania (Diarmuid and GRAINME), and to other events in which he is involved in surviving literature occur throughout the novel. According to one of the legends, Finn was to return someday to be the savior of Ireland, in a kind of "resurrection" of which Joyce takes advantage to identify the ancient hero also with Tim FINNEGAN.

Finn, Huckleberry. Titular hero of Mark Twain's novel, HUCKLEBERRY FINN.

Finn, Phineas, see PHINEAS FINN.

Finnegan, Tim. Subject of an Irish-American music-hall ballad, which was the source of the title of James Joyce's novel FINNEGANS WAKE. In the ballad, Finnegan is a stonemason who is killed in a fall but miraculously revives during the wake held to mourn him:

"Och, he revives. See how he raises."
And Timothy, jumping from the bed,
Cried, while he lathered around like blazes,
"Bad luck to your sowls. D'ye think I'm dead?"
Whack, Hurroo. Now dance to your partners,
Welt the flure, your trotters shake;
Isn't it all the truth I've told ye,
Lots of fun at Finnegan's wake?
Quoted by Harry Levin, *James Joyce*, p. 154.

Because of his return to life, Finnegan serves in the novel as a symbol of resurrection and renewal, principles of the theories of Giambattista VICO followed extensively by Joyce, and is an *alter ego* of H. C. EARWICKER. He is also considered to stand for the Irish hero FINN or FINGAL, because of his name (Finnegan = Finn-again), and perhaps, through his trade, for the artist as a craftsman. See DAEDALUS; DEDALUS, STEPHEN. In addition, Finnegan is on occasion synonymous with Adam, Lucifer, and Humpty-Dumpty, because they, too, had epic falls. Throughout the book references to Finnegan, his fall, and his return to life are found again and again, in various forms and various verbal disguises.

Finnegans Wake. The last and most important novel by James JOYCE, regarded as his masterpiece, begun in 1922 and completed in 1939, when it was published. Most literally, it presents the dreams and nightmares of H. C. Earwicker, the keeper of a public-house called the Bristol in Dublin, Ireland, and his family (see under EARWICKER), as they lie asleep at night, the events of the day just past and their anxieties, secret thoughts, and unexpressed desires recurring in their minds. Simultaneously, it describes the topography, atmosphere, and characteristic scenes of Dublin and its vicinity, gives an account of the development of civilization and the whole history of the human race, and dramatizes the problem of original sin, the fall of man, and redemption. The title refers to both the history of mankind and the religious problem, being taken from a music-hall ballad telling of the fall and miraculous resurrection of one Tim FINNEGAN, who is a leading symbol throughout the book.

The plan and structure of the novel are based on several theories followed by various schools of thought during the author's lifetime. Among the well-known figures whose ideas are embodied in *Finnegans Wake* are the following: Sigmund FREUD (theories of sex, dreams, and the unconscious); Sir James G. FRAZER (studies of comparative folklore, mythology, and religion); LÉVY-BRUHL (anthropology); Giambattista VICO (cyclical repetition in history and successive stages in the development of civilization); Giordano BRUNO (dualism and the universal conflict of opposites). Bruno and Vico are referred to constantly throughout the book under a variety of names, variants on the originals, the most frequent being perhaps "Nolan" and "Vicus" or "Jean Baptister Vickar."

In order to maintain his four simultaneous levels of meaning in his novel—analogous to the four levels of meaning (literal, allegorical, anagogical, and moral) frequent in the art, literature, and Biblical exegesis of the Middle Ages and explained by Dante in a famous letter addressed to Can Grande della Scala—Joyce uses an elaborate language of his own devising. It is made up of numerous puns, portmanteau words, malapropisms, and the like, with endless philological variations, such as assimilation, dissimilation, metathesis, etc., words from foreign languages, ancient and modern; literary, historical, and philosophical allusions; snatches of church liturgy; echoes of popular songs; current slang; newspaper headlines; advertising slogans; place-names of Dublin and its vicinity; names of individuals, business firms, and government officials of Dublin; Irish heroes of the present and the near and remote past; titles of books and magazines, references to paintings and statues; references to local occurrences, private anecdotes, and neighborhood gossip; names of Joyce's friends, enemies, and literary contemporaries, Roman Catholic saints, sport celebrities, American motion-picture stars, and so on, almost actually *ad infinitum*. To the unprepared reader, this welter of bizarre language and unfamiliar allusion is bewildering, but it is a clever device by which the distortions and illogicality of dreams can be approximated and several ideas and associations can be conveyed at once. Among the personages most often referred to are: TRISTAN, JOHN PEEL, Finnegan, ISOLT, Bruno, Vico, the DUKE OF WELLINGTON, PARNELL, ST. LAWRENCE O'TOOLE, ST. PATRICK, ADAM, LUCIFER, Finn, and Jonathan SWIFT.

Finnegans Wake is divided into four sections, the first three of which consist of several episodes apiece, each section taking place in a different part of Dublin. The following is an approximate summary:

Section I takes place in PHOENIX PARK.

Episode 1 is a general introduction, presenting a description of Dublin and Phoenix Park, and a dialogue between Mutt and Jute, a kind of vaudeville team.

In Episode 2, charges of an unknown crime committed in Phoenix Park are made against Humphrey Earwicker through THE BALLAD OF PERSSE O'REILLY, sung by a reveler in Earwicker's "pub."

Episode 3 continues the charges after the tavern has closed for the night.

Episode 4 presents the trial of Earwicker.

Episode 5 concerns a lost letter from another world, which, literally, is probably a gossipy letter to Maggie Earwicker from a woman in Boston, Massachusetts, which appears on a dunghill but is carried away by a neighbor's hen. The "letter" may also be the profession of letters, or literature; the Biblical "handwriting on the wall," or a similar prophecy in hieroglyphics; or history itself.

Episode 6 consists of questions and answers dealing with the Earwicker family, their household, their business, twelve patrons of their tavern, Vico's theory of history, Swift's theory of love, and the theory of time and space—the latter being illustrated by the fable of the MOOKSE and the GRIPES.

Episode 7 is an allegorical debate between Shem and Shaun in the persons of Justius and Mercius, with Shem as the villain; this leads into

Episode 8—the famous *Anna Livia Plurabelle* episode, in which the rhythm of the river Liffey is expressed in the rhythm of the sentences, and the names of various rivers of the world are woven into the querulous, gossiping speech of washwomen at their work on the banks of the river.

Section II takes place in CHAPELIZOD.

Episode 1 presents a play, THE MIME OF MICK, NICK, AND THE MAGGIES, with the program, cast, and credits and a synopsis announced in a sprightly manner.

In Episode 2, a thunderstorm breaks up a picnic, and the party seeks refuge in the "book of childhood."

Episode 3 deals with a voyage of discovery, with patrons of the "pub" appearing as Viking sailors, perhaps in reference to Earwicker's supposed Norse ancestry.

Episode 4 presents the romance of Tristan and Isolt (see TRISTAN), with four old men eavesdropping.

Section III takes place on the hill of HOWTH.

Episode 1 is the fable of the ONDT and the GRACEHOPER, told by Shaun.

In Episode 2, Shaun preaches a sermon on chastity to an audience of young girls.

Episode 3 presents a lamentation over the barrow, or primitive tomb, of the hero.

Episode 4 contains a survey of the household, its members, and appurtenances (cf. the question-and-answer inventory near the closing section of ULYSSES), as the family half-awakens. This episode supplies the best clues to the literal aspects of the novel.

Section IV presents a salute to dawn and a lyrical soliloquy by Maggie Earwicker (cf. the soliloquy by Molly BLOOM, at the close of ULYSSES), or Anna Livia Plurabelle, as the river Liffey flows down to the sea, her "cold father." The final sentence is cut off in the middle and completed by the broken sentence which opens the first episode of section I, so that the structure of the whole book is circular, in keeping with the theories of Vico.

As with all of Joyce's works, opinion was sharply divided on *Finnegans Wake* at its publication. Some reviewers found it a hopeless *tour de force* or a mass of unintelligible gibberish, but serious critics who made a study of it presented interpretations which clarified the author's intention and method, expressing high praise for the book's humor and lively, robust spirit and its frequent passages of distinguished lyric quality. These critics tended to place *Finnegans Wake* among such works of unique personality as Dante's DIVINE COMEDY, Rabelais' GARGANTUA AND PANTAGRUEL, Browne's RELIGIO MEDICI, Burton's ANATOMY OF MELANCHOLY, and Sterne's TRISTRAM SHANDY.

During the seventeen years of its composition, *Finnegans Wake* was known as *Work in Progress,* and several parts of it were published separately as they were completed, although they were later revised for final publication. These are: TALES TOLD OF SHEM AND SHAUN (1929); HAVETH CHILDERS EVERYWHERE (1931); ANNA LIVIA PLURABELLE (1932); TWO TALES FROM SHEM AND SHAUN (1932); THE MIME OF MICK, NICK, AND THE MAGGIES (1934); STORYELLA AS SHE IS SYUNG (1938). Joyce himself made a phonograph recording of a reading of a passage from the *Anna Livia Plurabelle* episode.

For further entries in this *Encyclopedia* dealing with *Finnegans Wake,* see HOSTY; PHIL THE FLUTER'S BALL; PRANKQUEAN. For full analysis and interpretation, consult the appropriate chapter in *The Wound and the Bow,* by Edmund Wilson, and, especially, *James Joyce,* by Harry Levin. For the analysis of *Finnegans Wake* and its characters presented above and elsewhere, this *Encyclopedia* is indebted to Mr. Levin's study.

Finney, Charles Grandison (1905–). Outré novelist. Proofreader on the *Arizona Daily Star,* Tucson, Arizona. Wrote *The Circus of Dr. Lao* (1935); *The Unholy City* (1937); *Past the End of the Pavement* (1939). His first novel was awarded the American Bookseller's Association prize as "the most original novel" of its year.

Fion. Another form of the name *Finn,* or FINGAL.

Fionnuala. The daughter of Lir in old Irish legend, who was transformed into a swan, and condemned to wander over the lakes and rivers of Ireland till the introduction of Christianity into that island. Moore has a poem on the subject in his *Irish Melodies.*

Fiorelli, Tiberio (d. 1694). Italian actor who introduced the stock character of the Italian COMMEDIA DELL'ARTE, the boastful SCARAMUCCIA as SCARAMOUCHE on the French stage (ca. 1640).

Firbank, Ronald (1886–1926). Outré English writer. Author of *The Flower Beneath the Foot* (1922), *Prancing Nigger* (1924), etc. He was a "precious" character. Converted to Catholicism in 1908.

Firbolgs. Literally, "skin-boat men." In Irish legendary history, a dark-haired people of small stature and slender limbs, probably representing the Iberian race which preceded the Celtic. According to one account, they were defeated by the Fomorians and escaped to Greece where they fell into slavery. They created the great stone forts found in Ireland.

Firdausi, Firdusi, or **Firdousi.** Real name, **Abul Qasim Mansur** or **Hasan** (940?–?1020). Persian epic poet. Wrote the great epic SHAH NAMAH and the long poem, *Yusuf and Zuleikha,* based on the Koranic version of the story of Joseph and Potiphar's wife.

fire-eaters. Persons ready to quarrel for anything. The allusion is to the jugglers who "eat" flaming tow, pour melted lead down their throats, and hold red-hot metal between their teeth. Richardson, in the 17th century, Signora Josephine Girardelli (the original Salamander), in the early part of the 19th century, and Chaubert, a Frenchman, of the 20th century, were the most noted of these exhibitors.

Firestone, Harvey Samuel (1868–1938). American industrialist in rubber business. Planted 60,000 acres of rubber trees on leased land in Liberia (up to 1936).

firmament. The vault of heaven viewed as a fortress. The word is hence also used interchangeably with fastness. The Hebrew *rakia* (suggesting expansion) is rendered in Greek by *stereoma* and in Latin by *firmamentum* (both suggesting solidity; cf. related words like *stereotype, firm,* etc.).

> And God made the firmament and divided the waters which were under the firmament from the waters which were above the firmament.
>
> *Gen.* i, 7.

Cf. the use of the idea of a solid firmament in THE GREEN PASTURES.

Firmilian. Title of "a spasmodic tragedy" (1854) by Professor W. E. Aytoun, who parodied in it the "spasmodic school" of the poets George Gilfillan, Philip James Bailey, Alexander Smith, Sydney Thompson DOBELL, and others.

Firmin, Philip. Hero of Thackeray's novel *The Adventures of* PHILIP. His father, Dr. George Brandon Firmin, who had appeared as George Brandon in *A Shabby-Genteel Story,* is also a prominent character in its sequel, *Philip.*

First Folio. The first collected edition of Shakespeare's works, a famous and valued collector's item, published in folio in 1623. It contains fourteen comedies, ten histories, and twelve tragedies. With the addition of *Pericles,* another comedy, in the 1664 edition (third folio), this group forms the canon of generally accepted Shakespearean plays, 37 in number.

First Gentleman of Europe. A nickname given to George IV. Louis d'Artois was so called also.

First Grenadier of France. A title given by Napoleon to Latour d'Auvergne (1743–1800).

First Violin, The. A musical novel by Jessie Fothergill (*Am.,* 1877). The heroine is May Wedderburn, an English girl studying music in Germany, and the hero Eugen Courvoisier, the first violin in the orchestra.

Fischer, Lisbeth. The envious heroine of Balzac's *Cousin Betty* (*La Cousine Bette;* 1846), better known as the Cousin Betty of the title. She is brought up to feel inferior to her cousin, Adeline, who marries Baron HULOT. The latter dubs Lisbeth "the Nanny Goat" because of her brusqueness and apparent hatred of men. This harsh old maid, whose employment with a firm of embroiderers gives her independence, makes a protégé of the young Polish sculptor, Wenceslas Steinbock, a poor and desperate fellow-lodger whom she finds attempting suicide; and upon him she lavishes all her interest and care. Wenceslas now falls madly in love with the charming young Hortense Hulot, Cousin Adeline's daughter. Out of pure spite and malice Lisbeth introduces both Wenceslas and Adeline's scapegrace husband, the Baron, to her friend Mme Valérie Marneffe, the worst of heartless coquettes, and untold mischief results. Lisbeth's relatives, however, remain under the delusion that she is concerned only for their welfare and is "the angel of the family."

Fischer, Louis (1896–). American journalist. European correspondent of *The Nation,* author of *Men and Politics* (1941), etc.

Fischer, Theodor. The narrator in Mark Twain's MYSTERIOUS STRANGER.

fish. The fish was used as a symbol of Christ by the early Christians because the letters of its Greek name—ICHTHUS—formed a monogram of the words Jesus Christ, Son of God, Savior.

a fish out of water. Said of a person who is out of his usual environment and so feels awkward and in the way; also of one who is without his usual occupation and is restless in consequence.

I have other fish to fry. I am busy and cannot attend to anything else just now; I have more important matters on hand.

neither fish, flesh, nor fowl; or *neither fish, flesh, nor good red herring.* Suitable to no class of people; fit for neither one thing nor another. Not fish (food for the monk), not flesh (food for the people generally), nor yet red herring (food for paupers).

a pretty kettle of fish, see KETTLE.

Fish, Hamilton (1808–1893; 1849–1926; 1888–). Grandfather, father, and son. (1) American statesmen; negotiated "Alabama Claims" with Great Britain. (2) Lawyer and politician. (3) Politician; member, House of Representatives (1920–1944).

Fishback, Margaret (1904–). American author of light verse, as *Out of My Head, One to a Customer,* etc.

Fishbein, Morris (1889–). American physician. Editor of the *Journal of the American Medical Association* (from 1924). Author of books on medicine and health.

Fisher, Dorothy Canfield (1879–). American novelist, author of novels dealing largely with domestic problems. Her works include THE SQUIRREL CAGE (1912); THE BENT TWIG (1915); THE BRIMMING CUP (1921); ROUGH-HEWN (1922); HER SON'S WIFE (1926); THE DEEPENING STREAM (1930); BONFIRE (1933); SEASONED TIMBER (1939).

Fisher, Harrison (1877–1934). American illustrator, famous for magazine covers displaying the "typical" American girl.

Fisher, Herbert Albert Laurens (1865–1940). English historian. Member of Parliament. Author of *A History of Europe* (1935) in three volumes and other works.

Fisher, Irving (1867–1947). American economist and professor at Yale. Author of many books on monetary questions, including *100% Money* (1935).

Fisher, Mahlon Leonard (1874–). American poet, specializing in the sonnet.

Fisher, Vardis Alvero (1895–). American author, best known for his series of novels dealing with the life of Vridar Hunter, an autobiographical hero who is carried through childhood, adolescence, and maturity and portrayed in the turmoil of sex, war, and a quest for the meaning of life. These novels are *In Tragic Life* (1932); *Passions Spin the Plot* (1934); *We are Betrayed* (1935); and *No Villain Need Be* (1936). Among other works by Fisher are *Sonnets to an Imaginary Madonna* (1927), poetry; *Toilers of the Hills* (1928); *Dark Bridwell* (1931); *The Neurotic Nightingale* (1935), essays; *April: A Fable of Love* (1937); *Forgive Us Our Virtues* (1938); *Children of God* (1939); and *City of Illusion* (1941).

Fisher Maiden, The. A novel by Björnstjerne BJÖRNSON (1868). The heroine, Petra, grows up in a fishing village and later becomes an actress. The book gives a vivid picture of Norwegian village life.

Fisherman's ring. A gold signet ring which the Pope uses to attest papal briefs. It bears his name encircling a figure of Peter, the fisherman and first bishop of the Roman Church.

Fisk, James (1834–1872). American stock-market speculator and wrecker of the Erie Railroad, from which he made a fortune. Caused a country-wide depression by rigging the gold market with Daniel Drew and Jay Gould. Was shot in a quarrel over a woman, Josie Mansfield.

Fiske, Bradley Allen (1854–1942). American rear admiral (1911); inventor of naval electrical devices including a system of wireless control of moving vessels.

Fiske, John (1842–1901). American historical writer and philosopher. Successful lecturer. Many historical works and books on religion and the impact of modern knowledge on its basic tenets. His original name was **Edmund Fisk Green.** He had it changed legally to **John Fisk** (1855) and later adopted the form *Fiske* (ca. 1860).

Fiske, Minnie Maddern (1865–1932). Famous American actress. In collaboration with her husband, the theatrical manager Harrison Grey Fiske (1861–1944), she helped popularize Ibsen's plays in the U.S. Also excelled as a comedienne. Cf. *Mrs. Fiske,* by Alexander Woollcott.

fit, see FYTTE.

Fitch, Clyde William (1865–1909). American playwright, author of numerous popular works for the theater, many of which were written specifically for various outstanding actors of the time. Among his best-known plays are BEAU BRUMMEL (1890); BARBARA FRIETCHIE (1899); NATHAN HALE (1899); *The Climbers* (1901); *Captain Jinks of the Horse Marines* (1901); *The Girl with the Green Eyes* (1902); *Her Great Match* (1905); THE TRUTH (1906).

Fitch, John (1743–1798). American inventor. Launched his first steamboat on the Delaware River Aug. 22, 1787. Received U.S. patent on third boat Aug. 26, 1791. Committed suicide when the wrecking of his fourth boat discouraged financial backers. Life written by Thomas BYRD (1935).

fitchew. The pole-cat of Europe; also its fur.

To be a dog, a mule, a cat, a fitchew, a toad, . . .
I would not care; but to be Menelaus, I would conspire against destiny.
Shakespeare, *Troilus and Cressida*, v. 1.

Fitz Boodle Papers, The. A series of sketches and tales by THACKERAY. The principal character is a lazy young nobleman named George Savage Fitz Boodle, with a flair for Bohemian life.

FitzGerald, Edward (1809–1883). English man of letters, famous for his free rendition of the RUBAIYAT OF OMAR KHAYYAM.

Fitzgerald, Francis Scott Key (1896–1940). American novelist, known for his studies of youth in the JAZZ AGE, presenting its cynicism, confusion, and eventual tragedy. His works include *This Side of Paradise* (1920); *The Beautiful and Damned* (1922); THE GREAT GATSBY (1925); *Tender Is the Night* (1934); and several collections of short stories—*Flappers and Philosophers* (1920), *Tales of the Jazz Age* (1922), *All the Sad Young Men* (1926), and *Taps at Reveille* (1935). *The Vegetable, Or From President to Postman* (1923) is a satirical play. See also under FLAPPER.

Fitzmaurice-Kelly, James (1857–1923). English authority on Spanish literature. Author of authoritative works in his field and editor of *The Oxford Book of Spanish Verse* (1913).

Fitzsimmons, Robert Prometheus (1862–1917). English-born New Zealand pugilist. World's middle weight champion (1891), heavyweight (1897). Lost championship to James J. Jeffries at Coney Island (June 9, 1899).

Fitzurse, Lord Waldemar. In Scott's IVANHOE, a baron in the suite of Prince John of Anjou, brother of Richard Cœur de Lion.

Fiume. Seaport on the Adriatic. The name is developed from Latin *Fanum Sancti Viti ad Flumen*, "Church of Saint Vitus of the River." Annexed by the Hapsburgs in the fifteenth century (1471), Fiume passed to Hungary in the eighteenth (1779). After World War I, D'ANNUNZIO settled the Italo-Yugoslav dispute over the important seaport by seizing it. The treaty of Rapallo (1920) made of it a free city and D'Annunzio was ejected. In 1924 Italy and Yugoslavia reached an agreement which gave Fiume to Italy.

Five Blessings. The five beatitudes desired by the Chinese: long life, wealth, tranquillity, love of virtue, and a peaceful end.

five bloods of Ireland, the. (1) The O'Neils of Ulster; (2) the O'Connors of Connaught; (3) the O'Briens of Thomond; (4) the O'Lachlands of Meath; and (5) the M'Murroughs of Leinster. These are the five principal septs or families of Ireland, and all not belonging to one of these five septs were (even down to the reign of Elizabeth) accounted aliens or enemies, and could "neither sue nor be sued."

Five Classics. The Confucian canon of five books, comprising the *I Ching* (Book of Changes), the *Shu Ching* (Book of History), the *Shih Ching* (Book of Odes), the *Li Chi* (Book of Rites), and the *Ch'un Ch'iu* (Spring and Autumn Annals).

Ranking second to the *Five Classics* are the **Four Books** comprising the *Lun Yü* (Analects of Confucius), the *Mêng Tsu* (Book of Mencius), the *Ta Hsüeh* (a treatise on practical wisdom), and the *Chung Yung* (Doctrine of the Mean).

Five Dynasties. Short dynasties of China (907–960 A. D.) between the T'ang and Sung dynasties: the Later Liang (907–923), the Later T'ang (923–936), the Later Chin (936–947), the Later Han (947–950), and the Later Chou (951–960). During this period there were numerous rulers, mostly Turkish and Uigur invaders.

Five-Foot Shelf. A popular name for the HARVARD CLASSICS.

Five Nations. (1) The five confederated Indian tribes, viz., the Mohawks, Oneidas, Onondagas, Cayugas, and Senecas, known as the *Iroquois Confederacy*. (2) The five component parts of the British Empire, used in this sense by Rudyard KIPLING as the title of a volume of poems, *The Five Nations*, published in 1903. (3) The **Five Civilized Nations** or **Tribes** are the Cherokee, Chickasaw, Choctaw, Creek, and Seminole Nations of Oklahoma in the former "Indian Territory."

Five Points. A region in the lower part of the city of New York, at the intersection of Baxter, Park, and Worth streets, formerly notorious as a center of crime, poverty, and vice.

five senses. Sight, hearing, smell, taste and touch. See also COMMON SENSE.

Five Towns, the. An industrial district in northern Staffordshire, England, noted as the scene of most of Arnold BENNETT's novels and stories, notably *Anna of the Five Towns, The Old Wives' Tale, Tales of the Five Towns*, etc. The district is known as the Potteries from its chief industry; Bennett calls the towns Turnhill (actually it is Tunstall), Bursley (Burslem) Hanbridge (Hanley), Knype (Stoke) and Longshaw (Longton). The Five Towns have now united with a sixth to form a single borough, Stoke-on-Trent. Bennett says of the district:

It seems to me the most English piece of England that I ever came across. With extraordinary clearness I see it as ridiculously, splendidly English! All the English characteristics are quite remarkably exaggerated in the Potteries.

five wits. The five senses; also five faculties: (1) Common wit, (2) imagination, (3) fantasy, (4) estimation, and (5) memory.

Flaccus, Quintus Horatius, see HORACE.

flag. For the colors of national flags, see COLORS, NATIONAL.

On the *railways,* a *white* flag denotes that the line is clear and the driver can go ahead, the *red* is the danger signal and means "no advance," and the *green* signifies "go slow."

> White is all right; Red is all wrong;
> Green is go cautiously bowling along.
> *Mnemonic Rhyme for Signalmen.*

a black flag is the emblem of piracy or of no quarter. See BLACK.

a red flag. To display a red flag is to defy or dare to battle. Red is the signal of "danger ahead," the emblem of blood and of revolution. A red flag is therefore commonly used by rebels and revolutionists, and *The Red Flag* is the battle song of advanced socialists.

a white flag is the flag of truce or surrender; hence, *to hang out the white flag* is to sue for quarter, to give in.

a yellow flag signals contagious disease on board ship, and all vessels in quarantine or having contagious disease aboard are obliged to fly it.

to hang the flag half-mast high is in token of mourning or distress.

to lower one's flag. To eat humble pie; to eat the leek; to confess oneself in the wrong; to eat one's own words.

Flag Day. June 14, celebrated in America as the anniversary of the formal adoption of the Stars and Stripes in 1777.

Flagellants. Members of religious associations who hold that the wrath of God can only be appeased by self-flagellation. The first wave of this heresy spread over Europe, starting from Italy, about the year 1260. Scenes of public processions with the exhibition of bloody self-castigation were repeated on a larger scale at the time of the plague called the "black death" (about 1348). Religious groups with similar tenets continue to exist in Colorado and New Mexico.

Flagg, James Montgomery (1877–). American illustrator and author.

Flagler, Henry Morrison (1830–1913). American oil magnate who organized Florida East Coast Railway (1886) and built a number of hotels at Florida resorts.

Flagstad, Kirsten (1895–). Norwegian operatic soprano. Member of Metropolitan Opera Company, New York. Wagnerian rôles. Went to Norway in 1940 to join her husband, a Nazi sympathizer, and returned after the war to find herself the center of a controversy.

Flamborough, Solomon. In Goldsmith's VICAR OF WAKEFIELD, a farmer, a talkative neighbor of Dr. Primrose, vicar of Wakefield. Moses Primrose marries one of his daughters.

the Misses Flamborough. Daughters of the farmer. Their homeliness contrasts well with the flashy pretenders to fashion introduced by Squire Thornhill.

Flame of Life, The (Il Fuoco). A novel by Gabriele D'ANNUNZIO (1899) dealing with the love affair of La Foscarina, a great tragic actress in her prime, and Stelio, a young poet. It is said to be, to some extent, the story of the author and Eleonora DUSE.

Flanagan, Betty. A humorous Irish-woman in Cooper's novel, THE SPY, one of Cooper's few well-drawn women. Maria Edgeworth said of her that no Irish author could draw her better. She appears in THE PIONEERS as the wife of the innkeeper Sergeant Hollister.

Flanders, Moll, see MOLL FLANDERS.

Flandrau, Charles Macomb (1871–1938). American writer, especially remembered for *The Diary of a Freshman* (1901) and *Viva Mexico* (1908). His sister-in-law, **Grace C. (Hodgson) Flandrau** is a well-known novelist.

flapper. Slang term applied to the typical young woman of the JAZZ AGE in the U.S., who wore short skirts, bobbed her hair, painted her face, smoked cigarettes, danced the CHARLESTON or BLACK BOTTOM, and in general defied the conventions upheld by her parents. The novelist F. Scott FITZGERALD and the illustrator John HELD, Jr. portrayed the flapper most effectively in their work. This meaning of the word is doubtless derived from the *flapper* which is a young bird when first trying its wings, especially a young duck. When Theodore Roosevelt, *Hunting Trips* (p. 54), wrote, "A good bag can be made at [the flappers] in the fall," he meant ducks.

Flash, Sandy. A highwayman in Bayard TAYLOR's *Story of Kennett.* The real name of this outlaw, notorious in Chester County, Pennsylvania, was Fitzpatrick.

flashback. Strictly, a short cutback, but usually used in lieu of the older term. In a story or moving picture, the device of interrupting the course of the topical action by interpolating an account of previous events, as scenes of a person's childhood related as part of the account of his death.

Flaubert, Gustave (1821–1880). French novelist, associated with, although not representative of, the movement of NATURALISM and known as one of the greatest Realists of 19th-century France. Beset by ill-health, personal misfortune, and a frustration of what many critics consider his naturally Romantic tendencies, he devoted his life to long hours and heavy toil over literature. See also BALZAC, DAUDET, GONCOURT BROTHERS. His work is marked by exactness and accuracy of observation, extreme impersonality and objectivity of treatment, and precision and expressiveness in style, or the principle of the MOT JUSTE. His works are *The Temptation of St. Anthony* (*Tentation de Saint-Antoine*) (see under SAINT) (1849 and 1874); MADAME BOVARY (1857), his most famous novel; SALAMMBÔ (1862); SENTIMENTAL EDUCATION (*L'Éducation sentimentale*) (1869); *Trois contes* (*Three Stories*) (1877); and the unfinished *Bouvard et Pécuchet* (1881), a novel dealing with two retired clerks engaged in hobbies unsuited to them. Flaubert was one of the most distinguished and influential writers of his time.

Flavian Amphitheater. The Colosseum in Rome. So called after the **Flavian Emperors** or CAESARS, Vespasian (69–79) and his sons Titus (79–81) and Domitian (81–96) who belonged to the house of Flavius and, although they had little else in common, made of the period known as Flavian an architectural landmark in the history of Rome. The Colosseum, the Arch of Titus, the Amphitheater at Verona are all Flavian works.

Flavin, Martin (1883–). American dramatist and novelist.

Flavius. (1) In TIMON OF ATHENS, attributed to Shakespeare, the faithful, honest steward of Timon the misanthrope.

(2) See under FLAVIAN.

Flaxman, John (1755–1826). English sculptor and draftsman. Drawings for *Iliad, Odyssey,* and *Divine Comedy.* Statues of Burns and Kemble in Westminster Abbey. CANOVA wrote of him:

> You come to Rome, and admire my works, while you possess, in your own country, in Flaxman, an artist whose designs excel in classical grace all that I am acquainted with in modern art.

Fleance. In Shakespeare's MACBETH the son of Banquo. After the assassination of his father, he escapes to Wales. From him, according to legend, proceeded in a direct line the Stuarts of Scotland, a royal line which gave James VI of Scotland and I of England.

Flecker, James Elroy (1884–1915). English poet and dramatist, known for his iconoclastic manner, his interest in Greece and the Orient, and the pictorial richness of his writing. His works include *The Bridge of Fire* (1908), *The Golden Journey to Samarkand* (1913), *The Burial in England* (1915), and *Collected Poems* (1916), books of poetry; *The King of Alsander* (1914), a novel; and *Hassan* (1922) and *Don Juan* (1925), the former of which was widely celebrated on its posthumous production in the theater. Flecker was called by some "the last of the PARNASSIANS."

Flecknoe, Richard. An Irish priest who printed a host of poems, letters, and travels, and died about 1678. As a poet, his name, like the names of Maevius and Bavius among the Romans, is proverbial for vileness. Dryden says he—

> Reigned without dispute
> Through all the realms of nonsense absolute.
> Dryden, *MacFlecknoe.*

Fleece, Golden, see GOLDEN FLEECE.

Fleet-book evidence. No evidence at all. The books of the old Fleet prison, where prior to 1753 clandestine marriages were concluded, are not admissible as evidence in British courts.

Fleet marriages. Clandestine marriages, at one time performed without banns or license by needy chaplains, in Fleet Prison, London. As many as thirty marriages a day were sometimes celebrated in this manner; Malcolm tells us that 2,954 were registered in the four months ending February 12, 1705. This practice was suppressed and declared null and void in 1774. *The Chaplain of the Fleet,* by Besant and Rice, contains a good account of the evils connected with Fleet marriages.

Fleet Street (London). Now synonymous with journalism and newspaperdom, Fleet Street was a famous thoroughfare centuries before the first newspaper was published there at the close of the 18th century. It takes its name from the old Fleet River.

Fleetwood, Lord. One of the partners to "the amazing marriage" in Meredith's novel of that name. See AMAZING MARRIAGE.

Fleming, Henry. The hero of Stephen Crane's RED BADGE OF COURAGE.

Fleming, Rhoda. Titular heroine of Meredith's novel RHODA FLEMING. *Dahlia Fleming* is an important character in the same novel.

Flemish account. A sum less than that expected. In Antwerp accounts were kept in *livres, sols,* and *pence;* but the *livre* or pound was only 12s.; hence, an account of 100 livres Flemish was worth £60 only, instead of £100, to the English creditor.

Fleshly School, The. In the *Contemporary Review* for October, 1871, Robert Buchanan published a violent attack on the poetry and literary methods of the Pre-Raphaelites (see PRE-RAPHAELITE BROTHERHOOD), including Swinburne, Rossetti, Morris, O'Shaughnessy, John Payne, and one or two others under the heading *The Fleshly School of Poetry,* and over the signature "Thomas Maitland." The incident created a literary sensation. Buchanan at first denied the authorship but was soon obliged to admit it, and some years later was reconciled to Rossetti, his chief victim. Swinburne's very trenchant reply is to be found in his *Under the Microscope* (1872).

Flestrin, Quinbus, see QUINBUS FLESTRIN.

Fletcher, Giles. Called *the younger* (ca. 1588–1623). English poet, son of Giles Fletcher, the elder (1549?–1611), an early writer of sonnet-sequences (ca. 1593). Giles, the younger, is best known for *Christ's Victory over and after Death* (1610), a religious poem modeled on the work of duBARTAS and SPENSER, which is considered to have had a great influence on Milton's *Paradise Regained.* See under PARADISE LOST.

Fletcher, John (1579–1625). English dramatist. See BEAUMONT AND FLETCHER.

Fletcher, John Gould (1886–). American poet, first associated with the Imagist movement (see IMAGISM) and later (after 1933) with the AGRARIANS. His poetry includes: *Irradiations* (1915); *Goblins and Pagodas* (1916); *Breakers and Granite* (1921); *Branches of Adam* (1926); *The Black Rock* (1928); *XXIV Elegies* (1935); *The Epic of Arkansas* (1936); *Selected Poems* (1938). In prose he has written *Paul Gauguin* (1921); *John Smith—Also Pocahontas* (1928); *The Two Frontiers* (1930), dealing with the U.S. and the U.S.S.R.; *The Crisis of the Film* (1929); and *Life Is My Song* (1937), an autobiography.

Fletcher, Joseph Smith (1863–1935). English antiquarian and writer of mystery and detective fiction. *The Middle Temple Murder* (1918), etc. His output is exceeded only by that of Edgar Wallace.

Fletcher, Phineas (1582–1650). Brother of Giles FLETCHER, the younger, and also a follower and imitator of SPENSER. He is best known for *The Purple Island* (1633), an allegorical poem on man in terms of the topography and settlement of an island. Among his other works are: *Locustae* (1627), an anti-Jesuit poem in Latin, with a paraphrase in English called *The Apollyonists; Britain's Idea* (1627), a mythological poem in the manner of Spenser and first published as the work of Spenser; *Piscatory Eclogues and Other Poetical Miscellanies* (1633). Milton's LUCIFER is believed to have been suggested by *The Apollyonists.*

Fletcher, Phineas. An important character in Craik's JOHN HALIFAX, GENTLEMAN.

Fletcherize. To chew one's food long and carefully. The term was popularized in the early years of the 20th century by the lectures of the American nutritionist Horace Fletcher (1849–1919), who maintained that such a habit would do away with any dyspeptic tendency, go far toward insuring perfect health, and reduce the world's needs of foodstuffs to a fraction.

fleur-de-lis (*Fr.*) Half-translated as *flower-de-lis* or *flower-de-luce.* Literally, flower of the lily. The iris. In heraldry, a conventionalized flower, possibly suggested by the iris, possibly also by the head of a lance, of unknown origin and familiar through its representation in the coat of arms of ancient France (since 1179). England bore the *lilies of France* from 1340 to 1801.

Fleurs du mal, Les (Flowers of Evil). A book of poems by Charles BAUDELAIRE published in 1857. The poems deal with Catholic mysticism, debauchery, and imaginative descriptions of horrors, perverse sensations, and the fantastic creations of the author's mind. In form, his poetry is Classical, with striking images and epithets.

Flexner, Simon (1863–1946). American pathologist. His brother **Abraham Flexner** (1866–), educator, director of Institute for Advanced Study at Princeton (1930). Abraham's wife **Anne Crawford** is a well-known playwright.

Flibbertigibbet. One of the five fiends that possess "poor Tom" in KING LEAR. Shakespeare got the name from Harsnet's *Declaration of Egregious Popish Impostures* (1603), where we are told of forty fiends which the Jesuits cast out, and among the number was "Fliberdigibet," a name which had previously been used by Latimer and others for a mischievous gossip. Shakespeare says he "is the fiend of mopping and mowing, who possesses chambermaids and waiting women" (*Lear,* iv); and, again, that he "begins at curfew and walks till the first cock," where he seems to identify him with the will o' the wisp, giving men pins and needles, squint eyes, harelips, and so on (*Lear,* iii. 4). Elsewhere the name is apparently a synonym for Puck.

flight. See under COVEY.

Flint, F[rancis] S[tuart] (1885–). British imagist poet and translator. A remarkable linguist. At one time held an important position in the Ministry of Labor.

Flint, Trueman. In M. S. Cummins' LAMPLIGHTER, the old lamplighter who brought up the heroine as his daughter.

Flirt, The. A novel by Booth TARKINGTON (1913) analyzing the schemes and maneuvers of the titular heroine, Cora Madison, and their ruinous effect on her gentle lovable sister and on the entire family.

flitch of Dunmow, see DUNMOW FLITCH.

Flite, Miss. In Dickens' *Bleak House,* a pathetic little old woman; demented because of the delay of her suit in chancery.

flock. See under COVEY.

Flodden, Battle of. A bloody battle in Northumberland (Sept. 9, 1513), in which James IV of Scotland was defeated and killed by the forces of the Earl of Surrey, who was in charge of the action in the absence of Henry VIII. The English were 32,000, the Scots 30,000 strong. The losses are variously given as 3,000 to 4,000 for the English, 5,000 to 12,000 for the Scots.

Flora. In Greek mythology, goddess of flowers. Hence, in natural history all the flowers and vegetable productions of a country or locality are called its *flora.*

Flora's dial. A fanciful or imaginary dial supposed to be formed by flowers which open or close at stated hours.

I. Dial of flowers which open at approximately the time given—

(*a*) The first twelve hours.

a.m.
1. (*Scandinavian Sowthistle closes.*)
2. Yellow Goat's-beard.
3. Common Ox-tongue.
4. Hawkweed: Late-flowering Dandelion; and Wild Succory.
5. White Water-lily: Naked-stalked Poppy; and Smooth Sowthistle.
6. Shrubby Hawkweed and Spotted Cat's-ears.
7. White Water-lily: Garden Lettuce; and African Marigold.
8. Scarlet Pimpernel: Mouse-ear Hawkweed: and Proliferous Pink.
9. Field Marigold.
10. Red Sandwort.
11. Star of Bethlehem.

Noon. Ice Plant.

(*b*) The second twelve hours.

p. m.
1. Common Purslane.
2. (*Purple Sandwort closes.*)
3. (*Dandelion closes.*)
4. (*White Spiderwort closes.*)
5. Julap.
6. Dark Crane's-bill.
7. (*Naked-stalked Poppy closes.*)
8. (*Orange Day-lily closes.*)
9. Cactus Opuntia.
10. Purple Bindweed.
11. Night-blooming Catch-fly.

Midnight. (*Late-flowering Dandelion closes.*)

II. Dial of flowers that close at the approximate hours.

(*a*) The first twelve hours.

a.m.
1. Scandinavian Sowthistle.
2. (*Yellow Goat's-beard opens.*)
3. (*Common Ox-tongue opens.*)
4. (*Wild Succory opens.*)
5. (*Several Sowthistles open.*)
6. (*Spotted Cat's-ear opens.*)
7. Night-flowering Catch-fly.
8. Evening Primrose.
9. Purple Bindweed.
10. Yellow Goat's-beard.
11. Bethlehem Star (*la dame d'onze heures*).

Noon. Field Sowthistle.

(*b*) The second twelve hours.

p.m.
1. Red or Proliferous Pink.
2. Purple Sandwort.
3. Dandelion or Field Marigold.
4. White Spadewort and Field Bindwort.
5. Common Cat's-ears.
6. White Water-lily.
7. Naked-stalked Poppy.
8. Orange Day-lily and Wild Succory.
9. Convolvulus Linnaeus and Chickweed.
10. Common Nipple-wort.
11. Smooth Sowthistle.

Midnight. Creeping Mallow and Late Dandelion.

Florac, Comte de. In Thackeray's novel THE NEWCOMES, a French emigrant, courteous, extravagant, light-hearted and vain. He is the son of a gentle Catholic lady with whom Colonel Newcome once was in love.

Flore, Flores or **Floris.** See under BLANCHEFLOR.

Florent or **Florentius.** In Gower's CONFESSIO AMANTIS, a knight who promises to wed a hag if she will teach him to expound a riddle, and thus save his life. See also WIFE OF BATH'S TALE.

> Be she foul as was Florentius' lover.—Shakespeare, *Taming of the Shrew,* Act. i. 2.

Florestan, Don Fernando. The hero of Beethoven's opera, FIDELIO.

Florestan, Prince. A character in DISRAELI's political novel *Endymion,* said to be meant for Napoleon III.

Florian, St., see under SAINTS.

Floriani, Lucrezia, see LUCREZIA FLORIANI.

Florimel. A character in Spenser's FAËRIE QUEENE said to typify the complete charm of womanhood. She is fair and chaste and bears the name of *Florimel the Fair.* Although she is courted by Sir Satyrane, Sir Peridure, and Sir Calidore, her love for Marinel is not returned until after much tribulation and her seizure by Proteus and imprisonment in a submarine cell. One day, Marinel and his mother go to a banquet given by Proteus to the sea-gods, and as Marinel is loitering about, he hears the captive bemoaning her hard fate, and all "for love of Marinel." His heart is touched; he resolves to release the prisoner, and obtains from his mother a warrant of release, signed by Neptune himself. Proteus does not dare to disobey, so the lady is released, and becomes the happy bride of her liberator. She is the possessor of the CESTUS of Venus, the prize of a tournament in which Sir Salgrane and several others take part, which can be worn only by the chaste, and when the False Florimel (who has been made out of wax by a witch to simulate the true one) tries to put it on, she melts away.

Florinda. In Southey's RODERICK, THE LAST OF THE GOTHS, daughter of Count Julian, one of the high lords in the Gothic court of Spain. She is violated by King Roderick, and the count, in his indignation, renounces the Christian religion and calls over the Moors, who come to Spain in large numbers and drive Roderick from the throne. Florinda appears in other literary versions of the story.

Florio, John (1553?–1625). English lexicographer. Son of an Italian Protestant refugee. Compiled an Italian-English dictionary, *A Worlde of Words* (1598), revised as *Queen Ann's New World of Words* (1611). Also translated MONTAIGNE'S *Essays* (1603).

Floris. See under BLANCHEFLOR.

Florisel of Nicea. A knight whose exploits and adventures form a supplemental part of the Spanish version of AMADIS OF GAUL.

Florismart. One of Charlemagne's paladins, and the bosom friend of ROLAND.

Florizel. Son of Polixenes, king of Bohemia in Shakespeare's WINTER'S TALE. In a hunting expedition, he sees Perdita, the supposed daughter of a shepherd, falls in love with her, and courts her under the assumed name of Doricles. Afterwards he learns she is a king's daughter, and the pair are happily married.

Flosshilda. In Wagner's *Ring* (not in actual mythology), one of the three Rhine-daughters guarding the Nibelungen Hoard.

Flotow, Friedrich von (1812–1883). German composer of light opera. Famous for MARTHA (1847). Also ballets and songs.

Flower and the Leaf, The. A late Middle English allegorical poem in RHYME ROYAL, of unknown authorship, once attributed to Chaucer.

Flowering of New England, The. A book of literary history by Van Wyck BROOKS, published in 1936. It gives an impressionistic account of places, personalities, and writings in New England in the first half of the 19th century, seeking to present a picture of the period rather than a study of literary development.

Flower of Chivalry. (1) Sir William Douglas, knight of Liddesdale (1300?–1353); (2) Sir Philip Sidney, statesman, poet, and soldier (1554–1586); (3) The Chevalier de Bayard, *le Chevalier sans Peur et sans Reproche* (1476–1524).

Flowery Kingdom, the. China. The Chinese called their kingdom *Hwa Kwoh,* which means "The Flowery Kingdom."

Flowery State. Florida. See under STATES.

Fluellen. A Welsh captain and great pedant in Shakespeare's HENRY V, who, among other learned quiddities, attempts to draw a parallel between Henry V and Alexander the Great, but when he has said that one was born at Monmouth and the other at Macedon, both beginning with the same letter, and that there is a river in both cities, he has exhausted his parallelisms.

> His parallel is, in all essential circumstances, as incorrect as that which Fluellen drew between Macedon and Monmouth.—Lord Macaulay.

Flute. In Shakespeare's MIDSUMMER NIGHT'S DREAM, the bellows-mender, who in the travesty of *Pyramus and Thisbe* is assigned to take the part of Thisbe.

> *Flute:* What is Thisbe? a wandering knight?
> *Quince:* It is the lady Pyramus must love.
> *Flute:* Nay, faith, let not me play a woman; I have a beard coming.—Act i. sc. 1.

Flute, The Magic, see MAGIC FLUTE.

fly. It is said that no fly was ever seen in Solomon's temple; and according to Mohammedan legend, all flies shall perish except one, and that is the bee-fly.

the god or *lord of flies.* In the temple of Actium the Greeks used annually to sacrifice an ox to Zeus, who, in this capacity, was surnamed Apomyios, the averter of flies. Pliny tells us that at Rome sacrifice was offered to flies in the temple of Hercules Victor, and the Syrians offered sacrifice to the same tiny tormentors.

flies in amber. Insects, small leaves, etc. are often preserved in amber; hence, such phrases as "preserved for all time in the imperishable amber of his genius."

> Pretty! in amber, to observe the forms
> Of hairs, or straws, or dirt, or grubs or worms,
> The things, we know, are neither rich nor rare,
> But wonder how the devil they got there.
> Pope, *Ep. to Arbuthnot,* 169–72.

the fly in the ointment. The trifling cause that spoils everything; a Biblical phrase.

> Dead flies cause the ointment of the apothecary to send forth a stinking savour; so doth a little folly him that is in reputation for wisdom and honour. —*Eccles.* x. 1.

the fly on the coach-wheel. One who fancies himself of mighty importance, but who is in reality of none at all. The allusion is to Aesop's fable of a fly sitting on a chariot-wheel and saying, "See what a dust I make!" Cf. also La Fontaine's *Fables,* vii. 9

there are no flies on him. He's all right; he's very alert.

fly-by-night. One who defrauds his creditors by decamping at night-time; also the early name of a sedan-chair, and later a horsed vehicle (hence *fly,* a cab) designed in 1809 for speed.

Flying Dutchman. A legendary spectral ship, supposed to be seen in stormy weather off the Cape of Good Hope, and considered ominous of ill-luck. Scott, in his note to ROKEBY, ii. 11, says she was originally a vessel laden with precious metal, but a horrible murder having been committed aboard, the plague broke out among the crew, and no port would allow the vessel to enter. The ill-fated ship still wanders about like a ghost, doomed to be sea-tossed, but never more to enjoy rest. Captain Marryat's novel *The Phantom Ship* (1839) tells of Philip Vanderdecken's successful but disastrous search for his father, the captain of the *Flying Dutchman.* WAGNER has an opera called *The Flying Dutchman* (*Der*

Fliegende Holländer; 1843). According to the legend it embodies, the old Dutch captain, in the midst of a struggle with the elements, had sworn an impious oath to round the Cape even if it took an eternity to do it. The curse which is laid on him for centuries will be lifted if he finds a wife willing to sacrifice everything for his sake; and the opera deals with the lifting of the curse by the Norwegian maiden, Senta.

Flying Island. See LAPUTA.

Flying Tigers. See under CHENNAULT.

Flynn, John Thomas (1882–). American journalist. "One of the best-known living pathologists of capital." Conducted a column called "Other People's Money" for the *New Republic.* Wrote in *God's Gold* (1932) a searching biography of John D. Rockefeller, Sr.

Flynt, Josiah. Pseudonym of Josiah FLYNT WILLARD.

Foch, Ferdinand (1851–1929). Marshal of France and supreme commander of all Allied Armies (1918). Had planned the strategy by which Joffre defeated the Germans on the Marne (1914). Carried the 1918 offensive to triumphant conclusion.

fo'c'sle, see FORECASTLE.

Foerster, Norman (1887–). American critic and educator. Professor of English, University of Iowa (1930). In accord with the HUMANISM of Irving BABBITT. Modern Language Association. Editor of many textbooks.

Fogarty, Phil. Hero of a burlesque of Lever's military novels by Thackeray, entitled PHIL FOGARTY, A TALE OF THE ONETY-ONETH.

Fogazzaro, Antonio (1842–1911). Italian novelist representative of liberal Catholicism. His *Il Santo* (1905) was called heretical by the censors of the Index. He attempted to reconcile the traditional Church dogma with modern science. Se also MAIRONI, PIETRO.

Fogg. In Dickens' *Pickwick Papers.* See DODSON AND FOGG.

Fogg, Phileas. Hero of Jules Verne's AROUND THE WORLD IN EIGHTY DAYS.

Fo-hi. A hero of ancient Chinese legend. His mother, Moyë, was walking one day along a river bank, when she became suddenly encircled by a rainbow, and at the end of twelve years gave birth to Fo-hi. During gestation she dreamed that she was pregnant with a white elephant; hence, according to some accounts, the honors paid to this beast throughout the East.

Foix, Gaston de (1489–1512). Duc de Nemours. Called "the Thunderbolt of Italy"; French soldier, nephew of Louis XII; commanded French army in Italy; noted for the rapidity of his maneuvers. Killed at Ravenna. His sister was Queen of Aragon and Naples.

Foker, Henry. In Thackeray's PENDENNIS, the son of Lady Foker. He marries Blanche AMORY.

Fokine, Michel (1880–1942). Russian choreographer. Created modern ballet. Influenced by Isadora DUNCAN. Became an American citizen in 1932. His wife, Vera Fokina, well-known dancer and choreographer.

Fokker, Anthony Herman Gerard (1890–1939). Dutch designer and builder of aircraft. Born in Java. First factory in Johannesthal, Germany. Came to America (1922) where he established the Fokker Aircraft Corporation of America. Naturalized. His planes were used by the Germans in both World Wars.

Földes, Jolán, Anglicized as **Yolanda** (1903–). Hungarian novelist, permanently established in London. *The Street of The Fishing Cat* was awarded the All-Nations Novel prize in 1936.

folio. A book made of sheets each folded only once (four pages to a sheet). Hence, a book of a large size, fixed by the American Library Association at more than 30 cm in height. The size of a folio (in the original sense) depends of course on the size of the sheets used. The variants formerly in current were (with sizes of untrimmed leaves): pott folio (7½ x 12½ inches), foolscap folio (8 x 12½), flat-cap folio (8½ x 14), crown *or* post folio (9½ x 15), demy folio (10½ x 16); medium folio (12 x 19), royal folio (12½ x 20), superroyal folio (14 x 22), imperial folio (16 x 22), elephant folio (14 x 23), atlas folio (16½ x 26), columbier folio (17½ x 24), double-elephant folio (20 x 27), antiquarian folio (26½ x 31). In printers' language the term *folio* also stands for page number.

folk etymology. A term adapted in linguistics from German *Volksetymologie.* The changing of an unfamiliar word into one of satisfactorily clear component parts, frequent in the language of uneducated but imaginative speakers. Instances listed in Wentworth's *American Dialect Dictionary* include ally waiter (elevator), brown kitties (bronchitis), peculiar or curious ointment (mercurial ointment), our beauties (arbutus), high-bred (hybrid), penny ciders (appendicitis), summer stop (thermostat), very coarse veins (varicose veins), glow shoes (goloshes), lie bill (libel), Queen Ann (quinine), red heater (radiator), sparrowgrass (asparagus), etc.

Follett, Wilson (1887–). American writer and editor. Author of *The Modern Novel* (1918), etc.

Follies. See under ZIEGFELD.

Folsom point. A stone point of the kind found near Folsom, N. Mex., in 1925. Believed to have been used as a javelin and the like by Stone Age people (called Folsom men) of North America. Cf. Frank C. Hibben, *The Lost Americans.*

Fomorians. In Celtic mythology, a race of sea robbers raiding ancient Ireland to keep her under tribute. It has been suggested that they were originally gods representing the powers of evil.

Fonck, René (1894–). French aviator in World War I, credited with the destruction of seventy-five enemy planes.

fons Bandusiae. The spring at Bandusia, near the birthplace of Horace, celebrated by him in one of his *Odes* (III, xiii), "O Fons Bandusiae." Hence, a source of inspiration.

Fontaine, Jean de La, see LA FONTAINE, JEAN DE.

Fontainebleau. A town in the department of Seine-et-Marne, 37 miles southeast of Paris. Its palace was from the Middle Ages a favorite residence of the royal families of France. Among the treaties signed there is the Peace of Fontainebleau (Nov. 8, 1785) between the emperor and the Dutch. The forest of Fontainebleau is considered the most beautiful in France. It was the resort of the BARBIZON school of painters, also known as the Fontainebleau or Fontainebleau-Barbizon school.

Fontanne, Lynn (1887?–). British-American actress, married Alfred LUNT (1922). Co-starred with her husband in many plays.

Fontenelle, Bernard de (1657–1757). French author, conversationalist, and popularizer of science. His works include *Dialogues des morts* (1683), a series of imaginary witty dialogues between historical figures on philosophical subjects; *Entretiens sur la pluralité des mondes* (1686), the best-known of Fontenelle's writings, discussing the solar system in terms easily understood by a lay audience, particularly one composed of aristocratic ladies; *Histoire des oracles* (1686), subtly attacking religious orthodoxy and blind obedience to authority while ostensibly disproving the pagan belief in oracles and upholding the scientific method; and *Digressions sur les anciens et les modernes* (1688), in which he takes the side of the Moderns in the quarrel between the ANCIENTS AND MODERNS and predicts unlimited progress in both arts and sciences.

fool.

a fool's paradise. To be in a fool's paradise is to be in a state of contentment or happiness that rests only on unreal, fanciful foundations; to believe and behave as though one were in better circumstances than one is. See also LIMBUS FATUORUM.

the Feast of Fools. A kind of Saturnalia, popular in the Middle Ages. Its chief object was to honor the ass on which our Lord made His triumphant entry into Jerusalem. This blasphemous mummery was held on the Feast of the Circumcision (Jan. 1). The office of the day was chanted in travesty, then a procession was formed and all sorts of foolery was indulged in. An ass was an essential feature, and from time to time the whole procession imitated braying, especially in the place of "Amen."

The wisest fool in Christendom. James I was so called by Henri IV of France, who learned the phrase of Sully.

court fools. From medieval times till the 17th century licensed fools or jesters were commonly kept at court, and frequently in the retinue of wealthy nobles. Thus we are told that the regent Morton had a fool, Patrick Bonny; Holbein painted Sir Thomas More's jester, Patison, in his picture of the chancellor; and as late as 1728 Swift wrote an epitaph on Dickie Pearce, the fool of the Earl of Suffolk, who died at the age of 63 and is buried in Berkeley Churchyard, Gloucestershire. Dagonet, the fool of King Arthur, is also remembered.

Among the most celebrated court fools are: Rayère, of Henry I; Scogan, of Edward IV; Thomas Killigrew, called "King Charles' jester" (1611–1682); Archie Armstrong (d. 1672), and Thomas Derrie, jesters in the court of James I, James Geddes, to Mary Queen of Scots; his predecessor was Jenny Colquhoun; Patch, the court fool of Elizabeth, wife of Henry VII; Will Somers (d. 1560), Henry VIII's jester, and Patche, presented to that monarch by Cardinal Wolsey; and Robert Grene, jester in the court of Queen Elizabeth.

The fools of Charles V of France were Mitton and Thévenin de St. Léger; Haincelin Coq belonged to Charles VI, and Guillaume Louel to Charles VII. Triboulet was the jester of Louis XII and Francis I (1487–1536); Brusquet, of whom Brantôme says "he never had his equal in repartee," of Henri II; Sibilot and Chicot, of Henri III and IV; and l'Angély, of Louis XIII.

The guild "fools" of medieval times played an important part in the spread of literature and education. They formed a branch of the Troubadour organization—a force which permeated Europe.

foot. In prosody, a division in verse consisting of a certain number of syllables or pauses, one of which is stressed. The term, which comes from Greece, refers to beating time with the foot. The most common varieties of poetic foot are IAMBUS, ANAPEST, TROCHEE, DACTYL and SPONDEE. See also SCANSION.

Foote, Mary Hallock (1847–1938). American writer. Her novels, illustrated by herself, were laid in the Far West. Among them are *The Led-Horse Claim; John Bodewin's Testimony;* etc.

Foppington, Lord. An empty coxcomb in Vanbrugh's *Relapse* (1677), of which Sheridan's *Trip to Scarborough* (1777) is a modified version. He appears also in Cibber's *Careless Husband* (1704).

The shoemaker in the *Relapse* tells Lord Foppington that his lordship is mistaken in supposing that his shoe pinches.—Lord Macaulay.

Forain, Jean Louis (1852–1931). French painter and illustrator. Noted for his deeply ironic drawings. On the staffs of many Paris journals.

Forbes, Esther (1894?–). American novelist. Her biographical study *Paul Revere and the World He Lived In* (1942) is much acclaimed and was awarded the Pulitzer prize. Other works include *O Genteel Lady!* (1926); *A Mirror for Witches* (1928); *Paradise* (1937), which reconstructs a Colonial town; *The General's Lady* (1938), based on the case of Bathsheba Spooner, the murderess. *The Running of the Tide* (1948), another historical novel, won the Metro-Goldwyn-Meyer prize of $150,000.

Forbes-Robertson, Sir Johnston (1853–1937). English actor. Member of leading English companies. Achieved success in *Othello* and *Hamlet.* One of his daughters, **Jean Forbes-Robertson** (1905–), made her début on the London stage in 1925. Another, **Diana Forbes-Robertson,** married Vincent SHEEAN (now divorced).

Forbidden City. The city of Lhasa in Tibet, so called because of the hostility of the lamas to visitors other than pilgrims. Also the section of Peiping (Peking) with the Imperial palace which was formerly closed to the general public.

forbidden fruit. Figuratively, unlawful indulgence, from the fruit eaten by Adam and Eve in disobedience of God's commands. According to Mohammedan tradition the forbidden fruit partaken of by Eve and Adam was the banana or Indian fig, because fig-leaves were employed to cover the disobedient pair when they felt shame as the result of sin.

forbidden land. Tibet, which still excludes foreigners. See also FORBIDDEN CITY.

Ford. In Shakespeare's MERRY WIVES OF WINDSOR, a gentleman of fortune living at Windsor. FALSTAFF makes love to his wife, but is the dupe of the situation.

Mrs. Ford. Wife of Mr. Ford. Sir John Falstaff pays court to her, and she pretends to accept his protestations of love, in order to expose and punish him. Her husband assumes for the nonce the name of Brook, and Sir John tell him from time to time the progress of his suit, and how he succeeds in duping her fool of a husband.

Ford, Ford Madox. Original surname **Hueffer** (1873–1939). English novelist, editor, and literary critic, grandson of Ford Madox BROWN, the Pre-Raphaelite painter, and nephew of William ROSSETTI. He edited the *English Review,* beginning in 1908, and the *Transatlantic Review* (ca. 1924), to both of which a number of well-known 20th-century English authors contributed, including Joseph CONRAD, Thomas HARDY, W. H. HUDSON, and John GALSWORTHY. Ford was also among the first to recognize the talents of James JOYCE and D. H. LAWRENCE. His works include *The Inheritors* (1901) and *Romance* (1903), novels written in collaboration with Joseph Conrad; *Some Do Not* (1924); *No More Parades* (1925); *A Man Could Stand Up* (1926); *The Last Post* (1928); *No Enemy* (1929), an autobiographical volume; *When the Wicked Man* (1931); *Return to Yesterday* (1932), memoirs; *It Was the Nightingale* (1933), autobiographical; *The Rash Act* (1933); *Henry for Hugh* (1934); *Mightier than the Sword* (1938), critical essays.

Ford, Henry (1863–1947). American automobile manufacturer; founder and president of the Ford Motor Co. (1903). Largest automobile manufacturer in the world. During World War I Ford organized the unsuccessful mission of his *Peace Ship,* and has been known for other peculiarities. Introduced a profit-sharing plan in the Ford Motor Company (1914) but managed by no means to solve the problems of labor-management relations more successfully than his competitors. Built a hospital and a museum. His program to build cheap automobiles within the reach of practically everyone caught the American imagination. He and his early *Model T* became virtually elements of American folklore. No other automobile is known by more nicknames in American slang than the Ford: Baby Lincoln, bouncing Betty, dehorn, flivver, Henrietta, Henry's go-cart, Michigan Mistake, perpetual pest, Spirit of Detroit, Model T-pot, tin Lizzie, tin lizzard, etc.

Ford, John (fl. 1602–1638). English playwright of the Elizabethan period, known for his portrayals of sorrow and despair. His works include *The Witch of Edmonton* (1621), written in collaboration with DEKKER and Rowley; *Lover's Melancholy* (1629); *Love's Sacrifice* (1633); *'Tis Pity She's a Whore* (1633); *The Broken Heart* (1633); *Perkin Warbeck* (1634); *The Ladies' Trial* (1638).

Ford, John. Real name **Sean O'Feeney** (1895–). American moving-picture director. Did *Arrowsmith, The Informer, Grapes of Wrath, Tobacco Road,* etc.

Ford, Leslie. Pseudonym of Zenith Jones BROWN.

Ford, Paul Leicester (1865–1902). American novelist and historian; brother of Worthington Chauncey FORD; best known for THE HONORABLE PETER STIRLING (1894) and JANICE MEREDITH (1899). He also compiled editions of Americana, including *The Writings of Thomas Jefferson* (1892–1894) and *The True George Washington* (1896).

Ford, Worthington Chauncey (1858–1941). American bibliographer, historian, statistician; brother of Paul Leicester FORD. Library of Congress (1902–1909). Collected, just before the outbreak of World War II, foreign manuscripts for deposit in Library of Congress.

Fordney-McCumber Tariff. The tariff law of September 21, 1922, sponsored by U.S. Representative Joseph Warren Fordney (1853–1932) and U.S. Senator Porter James McCumber (1858–1933). It increased the duties on many articles; in it was introduced for the first time the principle of the flexible tariff which authorized the President to raise or lower rates within definite limits.

A *protective tariff* is a rate of duty imposed on imports with the sole purpose of raising their price for the consumer to a level which makes it impossible for them to compete with domestic products. Justified at times by the necessity of encouraging young industries or of maintaining employment, wages, standard of living, etc. Harmful when carried to extremes which interfere with international trade. After World War I, U.S. tariff walls were very high. See FORDNEY-MCCUMBER TARIFF; HAWLEY-SMOOT TARIFF. Opponents of protective tariffs point out that only a policy of FREE TRADE would have enabled foreign debtors of the U.S. to meet their obligations without disturbing the balance of international trade and bringing about the worldwide post-war depression. Great Britain broke with a tradition of eighty years by the adoption (in 1932) of a system of protective tariffs.

Ford's Theater. The theater in Washington, D.C., where John Wilkes Booth assassinated President Lincoln (Apr. 14, 1865). It was used later on to house the record division of the War Department. In June, 1893, it collapsed and again several lives were lost.

forecastle. A short upper deck forward in a vessel, or that forward part of the vessel where the sailors live. In agreement with sailors' pronunciation often spelled *fo'c'sle.*

Foregone Conclusion, A. A novel by W. D. HOWELLS' (1875). The scene is laid in Venice. The "foregone conclusion" is a tragic end to the love of the Venetian priest-inventor Don Ippolito for the young American girl, Florida Vervain, to whom he acts for a time as tutor. Ippolito is tormented by a scepticism and by his love for this reserved and haughty girl who can at times give way to violent emotion. The priest's confidant is Ferris, the United States consul, a man of honor, but himself secretly in love with Florida.

foreign word. A word from one language used without adaptation in another, as French *chic, cliché,* etc. in English. Distinguished from LOAN WORD.

Forel, Auguste Henri (1848–1931). Swiss psychiatrist, noted for work on the anatomy of the brain; also an authority on insects, specializing in the study of the behavior and psychology of ants, and a pioneer in sex hygiene.

Forest City. Cleveland. See under CITY.

Forester, Cecil Scott (1899–). English novelist, whose first novel, the murder story *Payment Deferred* (1924), was a success in its later adaptation for stage and screen. His stories of Captain Horatio Hornblower (later Commodore and Lord Hornblower) won prizes and were extremely popular.

Forest Lovers, The. A romance by Maurice HEWLETT (1898). The hero, Prosper le Gai, marries out of pity a waif who turns out to be Countess Isoult of Morgraunt.

forgotten man. A term popularly used to refer to the typical man of low economic status, especialy if unemployed, during the depression period in the U.S. in the early 1930's. It was popularized in 1932 by Franklin D. ROOSEVELT during a campaign speech when he was running for the presidency, and thereafter became a national catchword. Its origin seems to go back to William Graham Sumner's (1840–1910) posthumous volume *The Forgotten Man and Other Essays* (1919).

forlorn hope. Not "a lost hope" but "a lost heap," that is a body of soldiers selected for some desperate or very dangerous enterprise. An adaptation of Dutch *verloren hoop,* rendered in French as *enfants perdus,* "lost children," in German as *verlorene Posten,* "lost post or assignment."

Forman, Harry Buxton (1842–1917). British critic and editor. Held high position in postal service. Responsible for painstaking editions of Keats and Shelley, and associated with the literary forger Thomas James WISE.

Forrest, Nathan Bedford (1821–1877). Confederate general; famous for his cavalry raids in the U.S. Civil War. Surrendered May

9, 1865. His slogan, perhaps apocryphal, was "to get thar fustest with the mostest men."

Forrestal, James Vincent (1892–). U.S. Undersecretary of the Navy (1940) and Secretary of the Navy in the cabinet of President Truman (1945). Appointed Secretary of Defense (1947).

Forsaken Merman, The. A poem by Matthew ARNOLD, relating the story of a merman whose human wife, Margaret, leaves him and her children to go back to pray in church and never returns.

Fors Clavigera. Literally, Fortune the club-bearer. A phrase coined by John RUSKIN as the title of a serial work, published at irregular intervals, consisting of 96 open letters to British workmen on remedies for poverty and destitution (1871–1884).

Forster, Edward Morgan (1879–). English novelist, known for the quiet irony of his writing and his satirical studies of the English middle class. His best-known and most highly praised novel is *A Passage to India* (1924). Other works include *Where Angels Fear to Tread* (1905); *The Longest Journey* (1907); *A Room with a View* (1908); *Howards End* (1910). *Aspects of the Novel* (1927) is a book of literary criticism.

Förster-Nietzsche, Elisabeth (1846–1935). Sister of Friedrich NIETZSCHE; married to Bernhard Förster, after whose death (1889) she dedicated her entire life to the service of her brother. She wrote a number of books on him, among them a biography.

Forsyte Saga, The. Two series of novels by John GALSWORTHY, dealing with the fortunes of the Forsytes, a family of the English upper middle-class. The five books in the first group appeared separately but were later published in one volume (1922). These are *The Man of Property* (1906), *In Chancery* (1920) and *To Let* (1921), with two "interludes," *The Indian Summer of a Forsyte* (1920) and *The Awakening* (1921).

The "man of property" and the chief character of the entire Saga is Soames Forsyte, the son of the eldest of six Forsyte brothers who are prosperously settled about the London parks. Soames plans to build himself a suitable house and employs Philip Bosinney, a brilliant young architect who is engaged to June Forsyte, the daughter of Soames' uncle, who is always spoken of in family circles as "Young Jolyon." Desperate at being considered, like everything else in Soames' life, as his "property" to do with as he will, his young wife Irene falls in love with Bosinney. When the two run off together, Soames' rage over his thwarted sense of ownership knows no bounds, and he employs all the means that money and power can give to punish them. Bosinney is killed. Years later, Irene marries Young Jolyon, the only one of the Forsytes who shows any real understanding of other attitudes toward life than that assumed by the Forsytes.

The Indian Summer of a Forsyte is an episode in the life of Old Jolyon, then a very old man; and *The Awakening* presents a simple story of the childhood of one of the new generation of Forsytes. *To Let* also is a story of the younger generation. Soames has married a French woman and his latter life is taken up with his devotion to his engaging young daughter, Fleur. To his utter horror, Fleur falls in love with her cousin Jon, the son of Young Jolyon and Irene. Both young people have been kept in ignorance of the past, and when the truth comes out, Jon chooses to give Fleur up and remain loyal to his mother.

Perhaps the best expression of the Forsyte attitude toward life is given by Young Jolyon when he ironically warns the artistic young Bosinney of the new world he is about to enter when he plans to marry June:

> Art, literature, religion survive by virtue of the few cranks who really believe in such things and the many Forsytes who make a commercial use of them. The Forsytes are the middlemen, the commercials, the pillars of society, the corner-stones of convention, everything that is admirable . . . My people are not very extreme, and they have their own private peculiarities like every other family, but they possess in a remarkable degree those two qualities which are the real tests of a Forsyte—the power of never being able to give yourself up to anything soul and body, and the "sense of property."

Of Soames, Galsworthy says in his *Preface* to *The Forsyte Saga:*

> He, too [the author] pities Soames, the tragedy of whose life is the very simple, uncontrollable tragedy of being unlovable without quite a thick enough skin to be thoroughly unconscious of the fact.

A second series of novels dealing with the Forsytes began with *The White Monkey* (1924) and includes *The Silver Spoon* (1926); *Swan Song* (1928); *On Forsyte 'Change* (1930); and *Forsytes, Pendyces, and Others* (1935). The two "interludes" in this series are *The Silent Wooing* (1925) and *Passersby* (1927).

Fort, Charles Hoy (1874–1932). American critic of science; held bizarre but documented theories on scientific phenomena, expressed in an apocalyptic prose. The Fortean Society, founded by Tiffany THAYER (1931), was joined by men like Booth TARKINGTON, Theodore DREISER, Alexander WOOLLCOTT. Fort's books, *The Book of the Damned* (1919), *New Lands* (1923), *Lo!* (1931), *Wild Talents* (1932), were reissued in one volume (1941).

Fort, Paul (1872–). Distinguished French poet, "prince des poètes." More than thirty volumes of charmingly popular *Bal-*

lades françaises. Produced unexpected effects by printing verses of classical perfection in normal prose style: "Je me tenais debout entre les genêts d'or, dans le soir où Dieu jette un grand cri de lumière, et je levais tremblant la palme de mon corps vers cette grande voix qui rhythme l'Univers." Founder of the Théâtre des Arts (1890) and editor of the magazine *Vers et Prose* (1905–1914).

Fortinbras. Prince of Norway in Shakespeare's HAMLET.

Fort Sumter. A fort in Charleston Harbor, S.C. On April 12–13, 1861, the Confederates bombarded it. This was the first engagement of the U.S. Civil War. When General Beauregard surrendered on April 13, no casualties had occurred on either side. The fort was held by the Confederates until February 17, 1865.

Fortuna. In classic mythology, the goddess of good fortune or chance. She was blind and was depicted with a wheel. The *wheel of Fortune* was a widely used symbol in medieval art and literature, forming the concept on which Lydgate's FALLS OF PRINCES, Chaucer's MONK'S TALE, and THE MIRROR FOR MAGISTRATES were based.

Fortunate Islands. Also **Islands of the Blessed** or the **Happy Islands.** Originally, imaginary islands in the western ocean where the souls of the good lived in eternal bliss. Later applied to Canary and Madeira Islands.

Fortunatus. A hero of medieval legend from Eastern sources who possessed an inexhaustible purse, a wishing cap, etc. He appears as a man on the brink of starvation, on whom Fortune offers to bestow either wisdom, strength, riches, health, beauty, or long life. He chooses riches, and she gives him an inexhaustible purse, but his gifts prove the ruin, both of himself and his sons. He appears in a German *Volksbuch* of 1509, Hans Sachs dramatized the story in 1553, and at Christmas, 1599, Dekker's *Pleasant Comedy of Old Fortunatus* was played before Queen Elizabeth. See also PETER SCHLEMIL.

you have found Fortunatus' purse. You are in luck's way.

Fortune. A monthly magazine, founded in 1930, dealing with business, industry, and finance in a "glamorizing" fashion, and featuring detailed articles, photography, and maps, with an appeal similar to that of LIFE and TIME magazines published by the same organization, Time, Inc. See also LUCE, HENRY R.

Fortunes of Nigel, The. A novel by Sir Walter SCOTT (1822), a story of the period of James I, introducing King James himself. The hero is Lord Nigel Olifaunt, a young man whose estates are very heavily mortgaged. James I gives his sign-manual for their release, but when Nigel strikes Lord Dalgarno for insulting him and is forced to flee to ALSATIA, the sign-manual is stolen. Nigel is arrested and sent to the Tower for treason, but eventually the mortgage is paid for him by Moniplies, a quondam serving-man of his who has gained possession of the treasures of the old miser who stole the sign-manual. Nigel is set free and marries Margaret Ramsay, a watchmaker's daughter, with whom he has been in love.

Fortuny y Carbó, Mariano (1838–1874). Spanish genre painter and aquafortist; known chiefly for his rococo paintings.

forty. A number of frequent occurrence in Scripture, and hence formerly treated as, in a manner, sacrosanct. Moses was forty days in the mount; Elijah was forty days fed by ravens; the rain of the flood fell forty days, and another forty days expired before Noah opened the window of the ark; forty days was the period of embalming; Nineveh had forty days to repent; our Lord fasted forty days; He was seen forty days after His resurrection, etc.

St. Swithin betokens forty days' rain or dry weather; a quarantine extends to forty days; forty days, in the Old English law, was the limit for the payment of the fine for manslaughter; the privilege of sanctuary was for forty days; the widow was allowed to remain in her husband's house for forty days after his decease; a knight enjoined forty days' service of his tenant; a stranger, at the expiration of forty days, was compelled to be enrolled in some tithing; Members of Parliament were protected from arrest forty days after the prorogation of the House, and forty days before the House was convened; a new-made burgess had to forfeit forty pence unless he built a house within forty days, etc., etc.

The ancient physicians ascribe many strange changes to the period of forty; the alchemists looked on forty days as the charmed period when the philosopher's stone and elixir of life were to appear.

forty stripes save one. The Jews were forbidden by the Mosaic law to inflict more than forty stripes on an offender, and for fear of breaking the law they stopped short of the number. If the scourge contained three lashes, thirteen strokes would equal "forty save one." The Thirty-nine Articles of the Anglican Church used sometimes to be called "the forty stripes save one" by irreverent young theological students.

forty winks. A short nap.

the Forty. A name given to the Venetian Senate.

the Forty Immortals or simply *the Forty.* The members of the French Academy, who number forty; sometimes applied also to the members of the English Royal Academy.

the hungry 'forties. The period just before and about the middle of the 19th century, when, largely owing to the high import duties on corn, bread and food generally were very dear.

the roaring forties. The Atlantic Ocean between 40° and 50° north latitude; well known for its rough and stormy character.

Forty Days Court. In English history, the "woodmote," i.e., forest *court of attachments,* which, as stipulated in the *Charta Forestae* or Charter of the Forests (1217), was to be held every forty days to deal with trespasses in the forests.

forty-eightmo. A book composed of sheets so folded that each sheet yields 48 leaves or 96 pages, the page being usually about 2¼ x 4 inches. Also 48mo.

forty-five, or '45, the. The second JACOBITE rebellion which occurred in 1745. See also the FIFTEEEN.

forty-niners. A name popularly given to the Easterners rushing to California to mine gold in the period immediately following the discovery of gold in California in 1849.

42nd Parallel, The. A novel by John Dos PASSOS, published in 1930, the first of the author's famous trilogy U.S.A. It serves to introduce several of the characters who appear in all three novels, and presents a picture of the U.S. on the eve of its entrance into World War I. Short biographies of Eugene Debs, Luther Burbank, William Jennings Bryan, Andrew Carnegie, Edison, Steinmetz, La Follette, and others are included.

Forty-seven Ronin, see RONIN.

47 Workshop or **Harvard 47,** see HARVARD WORKSHOP.

Forty Thieves, see ALI BABA AND THE FORTY THIEVES.

Forty-two Line Bible, see BIBLE, SPECIALLY NAMED.

Forwards, Marshal. The Prussian field marshal Blücher (1742–1819) was called *Marschall Vorwärts,* from his constant exhortation to his soldiers in the campaigns preceding the great battle of Waterloo, "*Vorwärts!*"

For Whom the Bell Tolls. A best-selling novel by Ernest HEMINGWAY, published in 1940, which deals with an incident in the Spanish Civil War (1936–1939). Robert Jordan, an idealistic college instructor, has come to Spain to fight with the Republican army and has been assigned to join a band of guerrillas led by Pilar, a powerful peasant woman, and blow up a bridge of strategic importance. He falls in love with MARIA, a young Spanish girl who has been raped by the Fascists, and during the three days they are together they try to forget the impending event in their passion for each other. There is jealousy and distrust among the peasant members of the guerrilla company, several are killed, and the inefficiency and jealousies of the Communist leaders are revealed, but Jordan carries out his mission. He blows up the bridge successfully, but is wounded and left on the hillside to die.

The title of the novel refers to a quotation from one of the *Devotions,* Number XVII, of John DONNE:

> No man is an Iland, intire of it selfe; . . . any man's death diminishes me, because I am involved in Mankinde; and therefore never send to know for whom the bell tolls; It tolls for thee.

Forza del Destino, La (The Force of Destiny). An opera by Giuseppe VERDI (1862), based on the drama, *Don Alvaro,* by the Duke of Rivas. Don Alvaro, the valiant lover of Leonora, accidentally kills her father, the Marquis of Calatrava, when the latter attempts to prevent the pair from eloping. Leonora's brother, Don Carlos di Vargas, vows vengeance; and although the two dons swear fast friendship when they meet as strangers in the same army, Don Carlos eventually learns the truth and twice attacks Don Alvaro. Don Carlos is mortally wounded, but kills his sister before he dies. In one version Alvaro leaps from a precipice.

Foscarina, La. The actress heroine of D'Annunzio's FLAME OF LIFE (*Il Fuoco*).

Fosco, Count. A villainous Italian in Wilkie Collins' WOMAN IN WHITE.

Fosdick, Harry Emerson (1878–). American clergyman. Author of many religious books including *A Guide to Understanding the Bible* (1938). Pastor, Riverside Church, New York City (now retired). See also MODERNISTS AND FUNDAMENTALISTS.

Foss, Sam Walter (1858–1911). American editor and humorist. Wrote homely light verse.

Foster, Mrs. **Laurence** (1907?–). Pseudonym **Rumer Godden.** English novelist. *Black Narcissus* (1939), *Breakfast with the Nikolides* (1941).

Foster, Stephen Collins (1826–1864). American song writer and popular composer. Several of his best-known songs are *My Old Kentucky Home; Massa's in the Cold, Cold Ground; Old Folks at Home; Nelly was a Lady; Old Black Joe;* etc. His *Oh! Susanna* appeared in 1848 and, becoming extremely popular with the gold-rush "forty-niners," established his success. Many of his songs were used by the Negro minstrel troupes popular at the time and have become genuine American folk-songs. Foster died, almost destitute, in the charity ward of Bellevue Hospital in New York. On June 2, 1937, the Stephen Foster Memorial hall was dedicated at the University of Pittsburgh. It houses the collection of Fosteriana owned by Josiah Kirby Lilly.

Fothergill. In Trollope's Parliamentary novels, the managing man of the Duke of Omnium.

Fotheringay. The site of the English Castle where Mary Queen of Scots was imprisoned, tried, and executed. Her son, James I of England, had the castle demolished.

Fotheringay, Miss. In Thackeray's PENDENNIS, an actress whose real name is Costigan.

Fouché, Joseph (1763–1820). French statesman; past-master of political intrigue; renowned for his spy systems. In turn minister of police, senator, minister of the interior, and again minister of police. Napoleon made him duke of Otranto. Exiled from France in 1816. Cf. Stefan ZWEIG's biographical study, *Joseph Fouché* (1930).

Fountain, Lucy. Heroine of Charles Reade's *Love Me Little, Love Me Long* (1859). She marries David DODD.

Fountain of Life. ALEXANDER OF HALES, "the Irrefragible Doctor" (d. ca. 1245), was so called.

Fountain of Youth. In popular folk tales, a fountain supposed to possess the power of restoring youth. Expeditions were fitted out in search of it, and at one time it was supposed to be in one of the Bahama Islands. See also PONCE DE LEÓN.

Fouqué. See LA MOTTE-FOUQUÉ.

Fouquet or **Foucquet, Nicolas** (1615–1680). French official under Cardinal Mazarin; superintendent of finance (1653); arrested by order of Louis XIV (1661) and tried and convicted for peculation. Died in prison at Pignerol, Piedmont. Identified by some as the MAN IN THE IRON MASK. His grandson was the **Charles Louis Auguste Fouquet,** duc **de Belle-Isle** (1684–1761), Marshal of France.

Fouquier-Tinville, Antoine Quentin (1746–1795). French revolutionist; public accuser before Revolutionary Tribunal (March 1793–July 1794). Guillotined (May 7, 1795). Author of articles of accusation against Marie Antoinette and Robespierre, once his benefactor.

Four Aryan Truths. See BUDDHISM.

Fourberies de Scapin, les. A comedy by Molière (1671). See under SCAPIN.

Four Books. See under FIVE CLASSICS.

Four Elements, Four Constitutions, Four Ages of Man, Four Seasons and **Four Monarchies.** The titles of the pretentious poems published by Anne BRADSTREET in her *Tenth Muse Lately Sprung up in America* (London, 1650), the first volume of American poetry. They were, as is indicated by the titles, all-inclusive in their scope, covering the whole of history, geography, and so on. The volume also included a *Dialogue between Old England and New.*

Four Freedoms. The chief objectives of American and United Nations' policy, as proposed by President Franklin D. Roosevelt in his message to Congress (January 6, 1941) with the stipulation that they should prevail "everywhere in the world." 1. Freedom of speech and expression; 2. freedom of every person to worship God in his own way; 3. freedom from want, economic understandings, which will secure to every nation a healthy peace-time life for its inhabitants; 4. freedom from fear, world-wide reduction of armaments. etc. A popular series of paintings by Norman ROCKWELL illustrated these.

Four Georges, The. A study of England's four Hanoverian Kings by W. M. THACKERAY (1855).

Four Horsemen of the Apocalypse, the. Conquest, Slaughter, Famine and Death who appear in the Apocalypse (*Revelation*) on white, red, black and pale horses respectively. They typify the evils of war. The Spanish novelist Vicente BLASCO IBÁÑEZ wrote a novel of World War I, entitled *The Four Horsemen of the Apocalypse* (*Los cuatro jinetes del apocalipsis;* 1916). It was made into a successful American motion picture.

Four Hundred. The inner circle of New York society; the élite. The term originated in 1892, when only 400 guests could be invited to a party given by Mrs. William ASTOR since her ballroom had space for only that number.

Four Hymns to Love and Beauty. A set of poems by Edmund SPENSER, published in 1596. The first two, *A Hymn in Honor of Love* and *A Hymn in Honor of Beauty,* which show evidence of influence by Platonic and neo-Platonic doctrines, were written in the author's youth, as he announces in an introductory note. The second two, *A Hymn of Heavenly Love* and *A Hymn of Heavenly Beauty,* more pious in tone, were written later in an effort to correct the impression of the others.

Fourierism. A Communistic system (see COMMUNISM), so called from François Marie Charles Fourier (1772–1837), of Besançon. All the world was to be grouped into "phalansteries," consisting each of 400 families or 1,800 individuals, who were to live in a common edifice, furnished with workshops, studios, and all sources of amusement. The several groups were at the same time to be associated together under a unitary government like the cantons of Switzerland or the United States. Only one language was to be admitted; all profits were to go to the common purse; talent and industry were to be rewarded; and no one was to be suffered to remain indigent, or without the enjoyment of certain luxuries and public amusement.

Four Kings, The History of the (Livre des quatre rois). A pack of cards. In a French pack the four kings are Charlemagne, David, Alexander, and Caesar, representatives of the Franco-German, Jewish or Christian, Macedonian and Roman monarchies.

Four Masters, The Annals of the. The name usually given to a collection of old Irish chronicles published in 1632–1636 as *Annals of the Kingdom of Ireland*. The Four Masters (authors or compilers) were Michael O'Clery (1575–1643), Conaire, his brother, his cousin Cucoigcriche O'Clery (d. 1664), and Fearfeasa O'Mulconry.

Four Million, The. A volume of short stories by O. Henry (1906). The title refers to the population of New York City. See also FOUR HUNDRED.

Four P's, The. A play by John HEYWOOD (1569). It is a contention as to which of the four can tell the greatest lie, and the Palmer, who asserts that he never saw a woman out of temper, wins the prize. The other three P's are the Pardoner, the Poticary, and the Pedlar.

fourragère. A French military decoration (a braided cord worn around the left shoulder-seam) presented to all the men of a unit to be honored for distinguished service or gallantry in action.

Four Saints in Three Acts. An opera by Gertrude STEIN, with music by Virgil THOMSON, produced in the U.S. in 1934. In it, a libretto uses words for their effects of sound and suggestion, in the author's usual manner, instead of for conventional meaning. ("Pigeons in the grass alas," etc.) In its presentation on the stage, the opera was sung by a cast of Negroes in vivid costumes, portraying Saints Ignatius, Chavez, Vincent, Gallo, Therese, and others. Some critics found it delightful, but others called it ridiculous. The text has been published.

four senses. The four varieties of Scriptural interpretation: 1. historical or literal, 2. allegorical, 3. moral, 4. anagogical. "Jerusalem is *literally* a city in Palestine, *allegorically* the Church, *morally* the believing soul, *anagogically* the heavenly Jerusalem."

Four Sons of Aymon. See under AYMON.

fourteener. In prosody, an iambic line of fourteen syllables or seven feet, also called "poulter's measure" as in

> And every guard allowed
> Fifty stout men, by whom their horse ate oats and hard white corn,
> And all | did wish | fully | expect | the sil | ver-thron | ed morn.
>
> Chapman, Translation of Homer's *Iliad.*

It was widely used in English poetry about the middle of the 16th century.

fourteen hundred. The cry raised on the London Stock Exchange to give notice that a stranger has entered the "House." The term is said to have been in use in Defoe's time, and to have originated at a time when, for a considerable period, the number of members had remained stationary at 1399.

Fourteen Points or Fourteen Peace Points. A famous statement of Allied war aims during World War I made by Woodrow WILSON, president of the United States, in an address to Congress on Jan. 8, 1918. Briefly, abridged from the address, the fourteen points are as follows:

(1) Open covenants of peace, openly arrived at.

(2) Freedom of navigation upon the seas, except by international action.

(3) Removal of economic barriers; establishment of equality of trade conditions.

(4) Adequate guarantees of reduction of national armaments to the lowest point consistent with domestic safety.

(5) An impartial adjustment of all colonial claims with fair consideration for the interests of populations and governments concerned.

(6) Full coöperation in obtaining for Russia an unhampered opportunity for the independent determination of her own political development.

(7) The evacuation of Belgium.

(8) The restoration of Alsace-Lorraine to France.

(9) The readjustment of Italian frontiers on clearly recognized lines of nationality.

(10) Autonomous development for the peoples of Austria Hungary.

(11) The relations of the Balkan States to be determined along historically established lines of allegiance and nationality.

(12) Autonomous development for other nationalities under Turkish rule; freedom of the Dardanelles.

(13) The establishment of an independent Polish state.

(14) The establishment of a general association of nations for the purpose of affording mutual guarantees of political and territorial integrity to great and small alike.

An attempt was made to put the provisions of the Fourteen Points into effect during the framing of the Treaty of Versailles in 1919, especially in the drawing of boundaries according to ethnological lines, but dissatisfactions and injustices were not removed and the outbreak of World War II in 1939 could not be prevented.

fourth dimension. The three dimensions of space universally recognized by mathematicians are length, breadth, and thickness. A line has only one dimension, length; a surface has two, length and breadth; a solid, and space generally, three, length, breadth, and thickness. The so-called "fourth dimension" is an extension hypothesized by mathematicians with the object of explaining equations of the fourth degree in analytical geometry. The term was adopted by many psychical investigators to explain certain apparently supernormal phenomena otherwise inexplicable, and achieved a semi-popular inaccurate usage thereby. The relationship of the fourth to the other three dimensions is assumed to be analogous to that borne by any one of these to the other two, i.e., it is a property that is to volume what volume is to area.

When *time* is considered the fourth dimension, the object is no longer space as such but rather the so-called *time-space continuum* in which every point can be fixed by four co-ordinates.

fourth estate of the realm. The daily Press, reputed to be the most powerful of all, the others (see ESTATES) being the Lords Spiritual, the Lords Temporal, and the Commons. Edmund BURKE, referring to the Reporters' Gallery, is credited with having said, "Yonder sits the fourth estate, more important than them all," but it does not appear in his published works.

Fourth of July. An American national holiday celebrating the signing of the Declaration of Independence, July 4, 1776, which declared the thirteen colonies free and independent and absolved from all allegiance to Great Britain. It is also called *Independence Day.*

Fowler, Gene (1890–). American novelist, biographer, playwright, and scenarist. *The Great Magoo* (1931; play, with Ben Hecht); *Timberline* (biography; 1933); *Mighty Barnum* (with Ben Meredyth; 1935); *Good Night, Sweet Prince* (biography of John Barrymore) (1944) etc. Cf. H. A. Smith, *Low Man on a Totem Pole.*

Fowler, Henry Watson (1858–1933). English lexicographer. Co-author with his brother, **F. G. Fowler** (1870–1918) of *The King's English* (1906). Compiled a number of dictionaries based on the great *Oxford English Dictionary,* and *A Dictionary of Modern English Usage* (1926). This latter work is remarkably useful and has served as the model for H. W. Horwill's *Dictionary of Modern American Usage* (1935).

Fownes, Charles. Hero of P. L. Ford's JANICE MEREDITH.

Fox, Charles James (1749–1806). Celebrated English statesman and orator. Tory member of Parliament at the age of twenty (1768); junior Lord of the Admiralty under Lord North; removed at the insistence of King George III who disliked him for personal reasons and on account of the dissoluteness of his life; led opposition to North's coercive measures against the American colonies; foreign secretary (1782–1783) in Rockingham's and Portland's coalition ministry, which latter was defeated by the king's intervention against Fox's India reform bill; kept out of office by the king till 1806 when Pitt died and he again held the portfolio of foreign secretary in the All-Talents ministry during the last year before his own death. Fox once gave a toast, "Our Sovereign, the people." He urged abolition of slavery. He favored the French revolution and objected to the French wars.

Fox, George (1624–1691). Son of a weaver, itinerant lay preacher, and founder of the Society of Friends (ca. 1650). See QUAKER. Missionary journeys to Scotland (1657), Ireland (1669), West Indies and North America (1671–1672), etc.

Fox, John William. Normally called **John Fox, Jr.** (1863–1919). American novelist; roughrider and war correspondent in Spanish-American war (1898); married Fritzi SCHEFF. Wrote *Little Shepherd of Kingdom Come* (1903); *The Trail of the Lonesome Pine* (1908); etc.

Fox, Ralph Winston (1900–1937). Promising Anglo-Canadian novelist and political writer, killed in action with the Spanish Loyalists. Wrote on Lenin, British Colonial policy, the class struggle in Britain, communism, etc. Also *The Novel and the People* (1937).

Fox and the Wolf, The. A Middle English beast-epic (see REYNARD), written between 1250 and 1275. It tells of a hungry fox who is caught in a well and by a trick escapes and imprisons his equally hungry friend the wolf in his place. Chaucer's *Nun's Priest's Tale* (see CHANTICLEER) is the only other beast-epic in Middle English.

Foxe, John (1516–1587). English martyrologist. His Latin history of religious persecution and the Reformers in England, translated by himself, appeared in English as *Actes and Monuments* (1563) and is popularly known as *The Book of Martyrs.*

Fra Angelico, see Giovanni da FIESOLE.

Fracasse, Captain, see CAPTAIN FRACASSE.

Fra Diavolo (*It.*, Brother Devil). Auber's opera of this name (1830) is founded on the exploits of Michele Pezza (1771?–1806), a celebrated brigand and renegade monk, who evaded pursuit for many years amidst the mountains of Calabria. The libretto is by Scribe.

Fradubio (the Doubter). In Spenser's FAËRIE QUEENE (I. ii. 28 ff.), the lover of Fraelissa (Frailty). DUESSA turns his mistress into a tree and bewitches him into loving her; but when he accidentally discovers the foul deformities of the hag, and shows by his manner that he has done so, she turns him into a tree also.

Fra Elbertus, see Elbert HUBBARD.

Fragonard, Jean Honoré (1732–1806). French painter and engraver. Decorated a pavilion for Mme du Barry, a series of paintings now known as *Romance of Love and Youth.* His rococo style is reflected in the names of his canvases: *Longed-for Moment; Pastoral Hour; Oath of Love;* etc.

Fra Lippo Lippi. (1) See under LIPPI.

(2) The title of a dramatic monologue by Robert BROWNING (1855), in which the painter, speaking to the street guards of Florence who have come upon him in the midst of a night adventure, gives his biography and his ideas on life and art.

frame of reference. In physics, a set of axes with reference to which the position or movement of a body is described. The term has been taken over into the terminology of literary criticism where it signifies the axiomatic tenets or the viewpoint by which an argument or a judgment is justified.

Framley Parsonage, The. A novel by Anthony TROLLOPE, one of his *Chronicles of Barsetshire.* See BARSETSHIRE.

France, Anatole. Real name **Jacques Anatole François Thibault** (1844–1924). French novelist, known for his taste for the classics, his early fondness for legends and fairy-tales, and his later wit and irony. His works include: THE CRIME OF SYLVESTRE BONNARD (1881); THAÏS (1890); *L'Étui de Nacre* (1892), tales and legends; *At the Sign of the Reine Pédauque* (*La Rôtisserie de la Reine Pédauque;* 1893). See under REINE PÉDAUQUE. *Les Opinions de M. Jérôme Coignard* (1893). See COIGNARD. THE RED LILY (*Le Lys Rouge;* 1894); *Le Jardin d'Épicure* (1894), essays; *Histoire Contemporaine* (see BERGERET, MONSIEUR) (1897–1900); *La Vie de Jeanne D'Arc* (1908); PENGUIN ISLAND (*L'Ile des Pingouins;* 1908); THE GODS ARE ATHIRST (*Les Dieux Ont Soif;* 1912); THE REVOLT OF THE ANGELS (*La Révolte des Anges;* 1914); LITTLE PIERRE (*Le Petit Pierre;* 1918); and *La Vie en Fleur* (1922). France was a strong DREYFUSARD and held Socialist sympathies. He is considered to have contributed largely to the character of BERGOTTE in Proust's *Remembrance of Things Past.*

Francesca da Rimini. Daughter of Guido da Polenta, Lord of Ravenna. Her story is told in Dante's INFERNO (canto v). She was married to Giovanni Malatesta, lord of Rimini, but her guilty love for his younger brother, Paolo, was discovered, and both were put to death by him about 1289. Leigh Hunt has a poem on the subject, entitled *The Story of Rimini* (1816); and Gabriele D'ANNUNZIO's tragedy, *Francesca da Rimini* (1901), and Stephen Phillips' *Paola and Francesca* (*Eng.*, 1897), in addition to the less well known tragedies by G. H. Boker (*Am.*, 1855) and Marion Crawford (*Am.*, 1902), are based on the story of the unhappy lovers.

Franceschini, Guido. See RING AND THE BOOK.

Francia, José Gaspar Rodríguez. Known as **Dr. Francia** (1761?–1840). Paraguayan lawyer and statesman. Dictator for three years in 1814, for life in 1817. Governed with absolute power over the life and death of his subjects and carried his isolationism to the extreme of virtually surrounding his country with a Chinese wall. He avoided all foreign entanglements and during his entire rule Paraguay was at peace.

Francis I (1494–1547). King of France (1515–1547). Conquered Milan by his victory at Marignano (1515). Was unsuccessful as candidate for the imperial dignity (1519). Waged four wars against his victorious rival Charles V, who advanced claims to the French duchy of Burgundy and also to Milan. The first war (1521–1525) came to an end when Francis was defeated and taken prisoner at Pavia. In the second war (1527–1529) he lost his hold on Italy by the peace of Cambrai, concluded for him by his mother Louise of Savoy and known as the *Paix des Dames.* The third war (1536–1538) led to a truce. The fourth war (1542–1544) was terminated with the peace of Crespy which left Francis in possession of Burgundy while Charles retained Milan. Francis' reign is marked by the Renaissance in France. He himself was a patron of the arts. His sister was the celebrated MARGARET OF NAVARRE.

Francis, St., see under SAINTS.

Franciscans. A religious order consisting of friars, novices, and lay brothers founded by St. Francis of Assisi (see under SAINTS) in 1206 and confirmed by Innocent III in 1210. By their rules they are bound to poverty, but the *Conventual Franciscans* (which branched off in 1230 and wear a black habit instead of grey) are allowed to possess revenues. The Franciscans are known as *Minors* or *Minorites* in token of their humility, and as the *Greyfriars* from the original color of their habit.

Francis Ferdinand (1863–1914). Nephew of Emperor Francis Joseph; Archduke of Austria. Assassinated with his wife (June 28, 1914) at Sarajevo, Bosnia, by the Serbian student Gavrilo Princip (1893–1918). Through the death of Crown Prince RUDOLF (1889) and of his own father (1896), Francis Ferdinand had become heir apparent of the crown and his assassination precipitated the first World War.

Francis Joseph I. German form **Franz Josef** (1830–1916). Emperor of Austria (1848–1916). A great "imperial civil servant," uninspired and stubbornly devoted, the last symbolic embodiment of the principle of a nonnational empire by the grace of God. Condemned to witness during his long reign the slow dissolution of the great Danubian monarchy. Succeeded to the throne after the abdication of his uncle Ferdinand I during the "year of revolutions" 1848; forced to abandon Lombardy to a French-Sardinian coalition; assisted Prussia against Denmark (1864) but in the ensuing wrangle over the spoils was defeated by the Prussians at Sadowa (1866) and Austria was expelled from the German Confederation; had to accept the Hungarian *Ausgleich* (1867) which reconstituted the monarchy on a dualistic basis; entered with Russia and Germany into the Dreikaiserbund (1872) but lost the good will of the Czars and concluded the Triple Alliance with Germany and Italy (1883). His only son RUDOLF committed suicide (1889). The assassination of the heir apparent, Archduke FRANCIS FERDINAND (1914) precipitated the first World War which brought about the collapse of Francis Joseph's realm. He died before the end.

Franck, César Auguste (1822–1890). Belgian-French organist and composer of great influence on modern French instrumental music. Among his students were Vidal, Chapuis, Marty, Guilmant, d'Indy, Bordes, etc. The last three founded the *Schola Cantorum* (1894) to perpetuate the master's influence and methods. His works include oratorios, symphonic poems, symphonies, etc.

Franck, Harry Alverson (1881–). American travel author. *A Vagabond in Sovietland* (1935), etc.

Francke, Kuno (1855–1930). German-born American historian and educator, founder and curator of the Germanic Museum at Harvard. Author of *A German-American's Confession of Faith,* etc.

Franco, Francisco (1892–). Dictator of Spain. Chief of staff of the Spanish army at the beginning of the Civil War (1936–1939), Franco became the leader of the insurgents after the death of generals José Sanjurjo and Goded. With the help of Germany and Italy, favored by British and American "nonintervention," he consolidated his position and assumed dictatorial powers shortly after the fall of Madrid (March 28, 1939).

François, The Adventures of. A historical novel by S. Weir MITCHELL (1898) dealing with the period of the French Revolution. The hero, François, who tells his own story, is a happy-go-lucky stray who lives most of his life on the streets. He was a real person and, according to the subtitle of the novel was *Foundling, Thief, Juggler and Fencing Master during the French Revolution.*

Françoise. In Marcel Proust's REMEMBRANCE OF THINGS PAST, the cook in the family home of Marcel, the narrator. She is a simple, shrewd peasant woman, whose idiosyncrasies of speech, reasoning, and behavior are minutely portrayed by the author throughout the novel.

franc-tireur. Literally, "free-shooter." A French partisan soldier. Franc-tireurs were first organized in 1792 and played an important part in the war of 1870–1871. Also a guerrilla or sniper. The French speak of franc-tireurs of journalism, "free-lance journalists."

Frank, Bruno (1887–1945). German novelist. Close friend of FEUCHTWANGER. His historical novels are extremely accurate in detail. The Theater Guild has produced several of his plays. *A Man Called Cervantes* (1934), etc.

Frank, Florence Kiper (1886?–). American poet and playwright. *Three Plays for a Children's Theater* (1926).

Frank, Leonhard (1882–). German novelist, short story writer, playwright. His novelette, *Carl and Anna* (1926; English translation, 1929), caused his election to the German Academy of Letters.

Frank, Waldo David (1889–). American novelist and critic, whose work combines mysticism and political liberalism, sometimes tending toward Marxism, written in a poetic style. Among his novels are *The Unwelcome Man* (1917); *The Dark Mother* (1920); *Rahab* (1922); *City Block* (1922); *Holiday* (1923); *Chalk Face* (1924); *The Death and Birth of David Markand* (1934), describing the spiritual regeneration of a commonplace American businessman; *The Bridegroom Cometh* (1939), dealing with the religious satisfaction found by a worker for social reform. Other works—essays, sociological studies, travel sketches, and the like—include *Our America* (1919); *Salvos* (1924); *Virgin Spain* (1926); *The Rediscovery of America* (1928); *America Hispaña* (1931); *Dawn in Russia* (1932); *In the American Jungle* (1937); *Chart for Rough Water* (1940), a proposal for American world leadership toward an idealistic goal.

Frank was one of the founders of the magazine THE SEVEN ARTS.

Frankau, Gilbert (1884–). English novelist. *World Without End* (1943). His daughter, **Pamela Frankau** (1908–) is also a novelist and short-story writer.

Franken, Rose, maiden name **Lewin** (1895–). American playwright and novelist. Produces a serial every year. Her plays, *Another Language* (1934) and *Claudia* (1941), have been popular.

Frankenstein. The young student in Mrs. SHELLEY's romance of that name (1818). He makes a soulless monster out of corpses from churchyards and dissecting-rooms, and embues it with life by galvanism. The tale shows how the creature longs for sympathy, but is shunned by everyone. It is only animal life, a parody on the creature man, bent on evil, and later the instrument of dreadful retribution to the student who usurped the prerogative of the Creator. Several moving pictures have been based on the novel.

Mrs. Shelley gave no name to the monster, and therefore he is not infrequently called "Frankenstein" when alluded to. This, of course, is an error.

> I believe it would be impossible to control the Frankenstein we should have ourselves created.—Lord Avebury, (*Speech,* 1886).

Frankfurter, Felix (1882–). Austrian-born American jurist; Associate Justice of U.S. Supreme Court (from 1939).

Frankie and Johnny. Popular old American ballad with numerous versions and verses. It tells how the girl Frankie shot unfaithful Johnny "with a forty-four gun." The refrain is, "He was her man, but he done her wrong."

Franklin, Benjamin (1706–1790). American statesman, author of an *Autobiography* that is a classic in its field, also of POOR RICHARD'S ALMANACK. Irving BACHELLER introduced him into a novel entitled *In the Days of Poor Richard* (1922). He is said to have been "more universal than Newton or Voltaire," to have "invented the Hoax, the Lightning-Rod, and the Republic," to say nothing of bi-focal spectacles. Cf. Carl Van Doren, *Benjamin Franklin* (1938).

Franklin, Fabian (1853–1939). American mathematician and writer. Author of *People and Problems* (1908); *Plain Talks on Economics* (1924); etc.

Franklin's or **Frankeleyns Tale.** One of Chaucer's *Canterbury Tales.* See DORIGEN.

Frank Mildmay, or The Naval Officer. A novel of the sea by Captain MARRYAT (1829). It is said that Frank Mildmay represents the author himself.

Fraser, James Earle (1876–). American sculptor. Portrait busts of Ulysses Grant, Theodore Roosevelt, etc. Designed U.S. five-cent piece with Indian head and buffalo (1913); also Victory Medal (1919).

Fratelli della Misericordia. Members of the CONFRATERNITÀ DELLA MISERICORDIA.

Frateretto. In Shakespeare's KING LEAR, a fiend, who told Edgar that Nero was an angler in the Lake of Darkness.

Fraternity. A novel by John GALSWORTHY (1909). An old professor, Sylvanus Stone, is lost in writing a masterpiece to be known as the "Book of Brotherhood," but the modern young people in whose house he lives, his artist daughter Bianca, her husband, Hillary Dallison, and Bianca's model, Ivy Barton, who types the professor's manuscript, are meantime enacting a drama that throws into ironic contrast the theories of the benevolent old man.

Fraunces' Tavern. Ancient building in lower New York City (at Broadway and Pearl Street) in which George Washington delivered his FAREWELL ADDRESS to his officers (Dec. 4, 1783).

Fraunhofer lines. The dark lines in the solar SPECTRUM, named after their first observer, the Bavarian physicist Joseph von Fraunhofer (1787–1826).

Frau Sorge, see DAME CARE.

fravashi. In Persian religion, a spiritual protector or guardian angel of each individual, especially of the believer. It is the pre-existing archetype of every man in the presence of ORMAZD and corresponds to the Roman GENIUS.

Frazer, Sir **James George** (1854–1941). English scholar and anthropologist, best known for his famous work THE GOLDEN BOUGH (1890–1915), which is noted for its important contributions to the study of folklore and anthropology. Other works include *Totemism* (1887); *Pausanias and Other Greek Sketches* (1900); *Letters of William Cowper* (1912); and a translation of the *Fasti of Ovid* (1929).

Fredegund. French **Frédégonde** (d. 597 A.D.). Queen of the Franks. She married Chilperic I of Neustria, having caused his wife Galeswintha to be killed. Later caused death of Galeswintha's sons and probably of Chilperic himself.

Frederic, Harold (1856–1898). American novelist, known for his attempts at realistic depictions of American small-town and rural life. His best-known work is THE DAMNATION OF THERON WARE (1896). Others include: *Seth's Brother's Wife* (1887); *The Lawton Girl* (1890); *The Return of the O'Mahoney* (1892); *The Copperhead* (1893).

Frederick. In Shakespeare's AS YOU LIKE IT, the usurping Duke, father of Celia and uncle of Rosalind. He is about to make war upon his banished brother when he encounters a hermit and is so completely changed that he not only restores his brother to his dukedom, but retires to a religious house, to pass the rest of his life in penitence and acts of devotion.

Frederick II. Known as **Frederick the Great** (1712–1786). King of Prussia (1740–1786). Son of King Frederick William I and Sophia Dorothea (daughter of George I of England and sister of George II). Started Prussia on its rise to German leadership; enlarged its territory and withstood the combined forces of Austria, Russia and Saxony in the Seven Years War. Joined Russia in first partition of Poland (1772). Notable patron of literature, music, and art. Built the palace of Sans Souci near Potsdam (1745–1747) and invited Voltaire to live at his court. Voluminous writer, almost exclusively in French. His early rebellion against his father (trial, condemnation, pardon) and later acceptance of the idea of unconditional devotion to the state, even at the expense of personal unhappiness, have become favorite motives in literature. He countered Louis XIV of France's motto, *I am the State,* by the principle, "The prince is the first servant of the State." His personal isolation made of him a legendary figure. As *der alte Fritz* he is the protagonist of innumerable stories and anecdotes. See the MILLER OF SANS SOUCI.

Fredericksburg. Town in Spotsylvania County, Va. Scene of a battle in the U.S. Civil War (Dec. 13, 1862), in which the Confederates under General Lee defeated the Federals under Burnside. Cf. the sonnet *Fredericksburg* by Thomas Bailey Aldrich.

freebooter. A pirate. See also FILIBUSTER.

freedom of the press, see LIBERTY OF THE PRESS.

freedom of the seas. The right of every nation to navigate the seas beyond a certain limit, usually three miles from the coast, free from control or molestation by any other nation, upheld as a traditional doctrine by the U.S. from colonial times. It was the violation of the freedom of the seas by Germany that caused the United States to enter World War I.

Free French. See under FIGHTING FRANCE.

Free Kirk. The church organized by those who, in 1843, left the national Church of Scotland (thereafter often referred to as the Auld Kirk), in order to be free from state control in spiritual matters. In 1929 the United Free Church of Scotland was reunited with the established Church of Scotland thus bringing together the large majority of all Scottish Presbyterians.

free lance. One who acts on his own judgment, and not from party motives; a journalist or writer who is not definitely attached to, or on the salaried staff of, any one paper or publishing house. The reference is to the Free Companies of the Middle Ages, called in Italy *condottieri,* and in France *compagnies grandes,* which were free and willing to sell themselves to any master and any cause, good or bad.

free love. The doctrine of the rightfulness of free choice in sexual matters without recourse to religious or legal sanction. The doctrine is old. The term, however, was introduced in America.

Freeman, Douglas Southall (1886–). American historian. Monumental life of *Robert E. Lee* in four volumes won Pulitzer prize in biography (1934).

Freeman, Harold Webber (1899–). English regional novelist. *Joseph and His Brethren* (1928).

Freeman, John (1880–1929). English poet and critic. *Collected Poems* (1928).

Freeman, Joseph (1897–). Russian-born American poet, editor, critic, Bohemian and revolutionary. Among the founders of the magazine *New Masses* (1926). His books include *The Soviet Worker* (1932); *An American Testament* (1936); etc.

Freeman, Mary Eleanor Wilkins (1852–1930). American novelist and short-story writer of the local-color school, who dealt chiefly with New England. She is known for her use of dialect and her character studies of the frustrated and decadent descendants of the Puritans. Among the collections of her short stories, which are considered to be her best work, are *A Humble Romance* (1887); A NEW ENGLAND NUN (1891); *The Wind in the Rose Bush* (ghost stories) (1903). Her novels include: *Jane Field* (1893); *Pembroke* (1894); *Jerome, A Poor Man* (1897); *The Heart's Highway* (1900); *The Portion of Labor* (1901).

Freeman, Richard Austin (1862–1943). English scientific detective-story writer, creator of Dr. Thorndyke. Physician by profession.

Freeman, The. A literary and political weekly published in New York City (1920–1924). Editors: Francis Neilson and Albert Jay Nock. One of the associate editors was Van Wyck BROOKS.

Freemasons. It is only in the realm of fable, not even in that of tradition, that modern Freemasonry can be traced to Hiram of Tyre and the Temple of Solomon; the modern secret fraternity had its origin in England in the 17th century, and its connection with masons—the workers in stone—arises from the fact that the founders adopted many of the practices of the old masonic guilds as being most suitable to their purpose. These medieval guilds consisted of workmen who, by the nature of their calling, had to move from place to place, and their secret passwords, ritual, etc., were adopted so that when on their travels they could prove without difficulty that they were actually "Free and Accepted Masons," and so obtain the comradeship of their brother masons as well as get employment. In each district where cathedrals and churches were being built "lodges" were created, much as a branch of a trade union would be today, and these had their masters, wardens, and other officials.

the Lady Freemason. Women are not admitted into freemasonry, but there is a story that a lady was initiated in the early 18th century. She was the Hon. Elizabeth St. Leger, daughter of Lord Doneraile, who hid herself in an empty clock-case when the lodge was held in her father's house, and witnessed the proceedings. She was discovered, and compelled to submit to initiation as a member of the craft. The story is fairly well authenticated.

Freeport, Sir **Andrew.** A London merchant, industrious, generous, and of sound good sense, one of the members of the hypothetical club under whose auspices the SPECTATOR was launched.

Free-Soil party. An American political party opposed to slavery. It became a part of the Republican party in 1854.

Freestone State. Connecticut. See under STATES.

free trade. Interchange of commodities between countries politically independent, without obstacles specifically intended to restrict their free flow. The theory of free traders is that all taxes on imports have ultimately an adverse effect on exports. Adam Smith in his *Wealth of Nations* (1775) influenced England's free trade policy of trading in articles that could not be produced at home. This policy was initiated by the repeal of the Corn Laws in 1846. A basic British policy for more than eighty years, it was abrogated by the reintroduction of PROTECTIVE TARIFFS after World War I.

The term free trader signified "smuggler" in the time of Sir Walter Scott. Cf., e.g., *Guy Mannering.*

free verse (Fr. vers libre). Poetry that does not follow a conventional pattern of meter and rhyme but depends upon other devices, such as assonance, alliteration, and cadence, for its rhythmic effects. It was first officially employed by French poets of the Symbolist movement (see SYMBOLISM), but unofficially it is as ancient as Anglo-Saxon verse and that of other early European languages. Walt WHITMAN was a prominent user of free verse in the 19th century, his work serving to influence later poets. Under the influence of Whitman and the Symbolists, free verse became the prevailing poetic form of the period of the 1920's and 1930's, especially in the U.S., although during the 1930's it began to be replaced by more formal verse making use of a modified system of rhyme, meter, and stanza, appropriate to the new subject matter of intellectual rather than wholly sensuous appeal.

Poets whose work outstandingly makes use of free verse and is most representative of the form at its height of popularity are: Amy LOWELL and the other Imagists (see IMAGISM), Carl SANDBURG, and Edgar Lee MASTERS. The following is a typical free-verse poem:

Out of me unworthy and unknown
The vibrations of deathless music
"With malice toward none, with charity for all,"
Out of me the forgiveness of millions toward millions
And the beneficent face of a nation
Shining with justice and truth.
I am Anne Rutledge who sleep beneath these weeds,
Beloved in life of Abraham Lincoln,
Wedded to him, not through union,
But through separation,
Bloom forever, O Republic,
From the dust of my bosom.

Edgar Lee Masters, *Anne Rutledge* from *The Spoon River Anthology.*

Freischütz (*Ger.*, literally, the free-shooter). A legendary German marksman in league with the Devil, who gave him seven balls, six of which were to hit infallibly whatever the marksman aimed at, and the seventh was to be directed as the Devil wished. F. Kind wrote the libretto of, and Carl Maria von WEBER set to music, the opera based on the legend called *Der Freischütz* (1820). In the opera the ranger, Max, makes his bargain with the Devil in order to win a sharp-shooting contest and with it the hand of his sweetheart Agnes. His seventh bullet, aimed at a dove, wounds his bride, but a wreath blessed by a hermit has turned the bullet aside, so that he finds her still alive.

Freki and **Geri.** The two wolves of ODIN.

Frémont, John Charles (1813–1890). American explorer and general, called the "pathfinder." Governor of California territory and senator when it became a state (1850). Ascended highest peak of the Wind River Mountains, now called Fremont's Peak. His wife **Jessie Frémont** (1824–1902) made a name for herself as a writer and succeeded in saving her husband from complete poverty when he had lost his fortune in railroad ventures (1870).

Fremstad, Olive (1870?–). Dramatic soprano; born in Stockholm, Sweden. Interpreter of Wagnerian rôles for the Metropolitan Opera Company in New York City. Original of Thea Kronborg in Willa CATHER's novel, *The Song of the Lark* (1915).

Freneau, Philip Morin (1752–1832). Early American poet, known as "the Poet of the American Revolution."

French, Alice. See THANET, OCTAVE.

French, Daniel Chester (1850–1931). American sculptor. *The Minute Man of Concord,* at Concord (see MINUTE MAN); *John Harvard,* Harvard University yard, etc.

French, Mary. In Dos Passos' U.S.A., a character who is prominent in the last volume, THE BIG MONEY. She is a Vassar student, daughter of a doctor in Colorado, who develops in college an interest in social reform and comes to take part in trade union organizational work. For awhile she is the mistress of G. H. BARROW and of an ardent Communist, Ben COMPTON, but is disillusioned in all her love affairs.

French and Indian War (1754–1763). The last, most decisive conflict in the 150 years' struggle between France and England for the possession of the North American continent. It was the American phase of the SEVEN YEARS WAR and ended with the cession of Canada to Great Britain.

French leave. The expression "to take French leave" has its origin in the eighteenth-century convention in French society to leave a party without taking leave from host or hostess. It is translated into French as "filer à l'anglaise."

French Revolution, The. A history in three parts, by Thomas CARLYLE (1837), one of his most famous works.

Freneau, Philip Morin (1752–1832). American poet, one of the first to achieve renown for his verse in the U.S., employed variously as teacher, clerk, shipmaster, and editor. He is best known for his political poems, most of which were written at the time of the American Revolution. Among these are: *The Rising Glory of America* (1771), which he wrote in collaboration with Hugh Henry BRACKENRIDGE on their graduation from Princeton; *General Gage's Soliloquy* (1775); *General Gage's Confession* (1775); and *The British Prison Ship* (1781), an account of his experiences as a British prisoner of war after capture at sea near the West Indies. He also wrote poems on nature, animals and insects, and the American Indian, including: *The Wild Honeysuckle* (1786); *The Indian Burying Ground* (1788); *On a Honey-Bee Drinking from a Glass of Wine* (1809).

Freneau was anti-Federalist in his opinions and edited the *National Gazette* from 1791 to 1793, especially attacking Alexander HAMILTON. He was admired by Jefferson.

Frenssen, Gustav (1863–). German writer of novels and stories of peasant life in north Germany, the epic poem *Bismarck* (1914), and plays.

Frere, John Hookham (1769–1846). English diplomat and one of the founders of the QUARTERLY REVIEW.

Fresh the American. A comedy (1881) by Archibald C. Gunter, (*Eng.-Am.,* 1847–1907), presenting the European adventures of F. N. Fresh, a self-made American millionaire who is not a whit in awe of anything European, and in spite of his crudities, manages to play a hero's part.

Freuchen, Peter (1886–). Danish explorer, autobiographer and travel writer. Began writing when an accident forced him to abandon his home in the Arctic and return to Denmark.

Freud, Sigmund (1856–1939). Austrian psycho-analyst, regarded as the founder of the science of psycho-analysis, which grew out of his experiences in treating sufferers from hysteria and neurosis. He is famous for his therapeutic methods and his revolutionary theories of sex, many of which show the influence of German romantic philosophy and make use of literary and classical allusions. The leading principles of these theories are: the primacy of sex as a motivating factor in human psychology and social behavior; the existence of elements of strong sexuality among children and of abnormality and inversion in normal sexual psychology; the repressive influence of social and individual inhibitions on sex, resulting in neuroses and "complexes" (see COMPLEX); the rôle of the unconscious as the repository of repressed sexual desires, tendencies, memories, anxieties, and the like; the embodiment of sexual repressions in symbolic form in dreams, art, literature, wit and humor, and religion and folk-lore. The typical psycho-analytical treatment was to release the inhibition by persuading the patient to talk to the physician with absolute freedom and frankness, and by the analysis of the patient's dreams. Freud's most important works include *Three Contributions to the Theory of Sex* (1910); *The Interpretation of Dreams* (*Die Traumdeutung;* 1909); *The Psycho-pathology of Everyday Life* (1914); *Wit and Its Relation to the Unconscious* (1916); *Leonardo da Vinci: A Psycho-*

sexual Study of an Infantile Reminiscence (1916); *Totem and Taboo* (1918); *Beyond the Pleasure Principle* (1922); *The Ego and the Id* (1927); *Civilization and Its Discontents* (1930); *Moses and Monotheism* (1939).

Freud's theories achieved wide notoriety in Europe and the U.S. during the years immediately preceding and immediately following World War I, and psycho-analysis was extremely popular during the 1920's, particularly among the wealthy. His system was violently attacked by conservative elements and the clergy and seriously criticized by his fellow scientists, including his own early disciples (see ADLER; JUNG), but in its social, intellectual, and literary and artistic influence it is among the most important developments of 20th-century thought. Freudian theories were adopted by the movement of SURREALISM and are outstandingly embodied in the novels of Thomas MANN and in FINNEGANS WAKE by James Joyce. For a study of Freud from a literary standpoint, cf. Thomas Mann's *Freud, Goethe, and Wagner.*

In 1938, when the German National Socialist government (see NAZISM) seized power in Austria, Freud was among the eminent authors, scholars, and scientists forced to flee because of Jewish parentage. He died in exile in London.

Frey or **Freyr.** Son of NJÖRD, originally one of the Vanir, but received among the Aesir after the war between the two. He was the Scandinavian god of fertility and peace, the dispenser of rain, and the patron god of Sweden and Iceland. His wife was GERDA, and among his treasures were: *Blodighofi* (Bloodyhoof), his horse; a golden helmet with the crest of a wild-boar, *Gullinbursti* (*i.e.* with gold bristles); and the magic ship *Skithblathnir,* which could be folded up like a tent.

Freya. In Scandinavian mythology, the sister of Frey and wife of Odin, who deserted her for FRIGGA because she loved finery better than her husband. (See *Brisingamen.*) She is the fairest of the goddesses, goddess of youth and love and also of the dead. One account says that she flies through the air with the wings of a falcon, another that she rides in a chariot drawn by two cats. She is also known as *Frea, Frija, Frigg, Frige,* etc., and it is from her that our *Friday* is named. In Teutonic mythology Freya and Frigga are the same goddess.

The chief legends concerning Freya have to do with the efforts of the giants to carry her off. In one instance, THOR dressed as a veiled bride, impersonates Freya in order to recover his hammer from the giant Thrym. In Wagner's NIBELUNGEN RING, Freya is given to the giants as payment for their construction of Valhalla, and her return involves the transfer of the magic ring.

Freyberg, Bernard Cyril (1890–). New Zealand army officer; in World War II, major general in command of the 2nd New Zealand Expeditionary Force. Veteran of World War I.

Freydis. In Cabell's FIGURES OF EARTH, the dread high Queen of Audela who becomes a human woman for love of Manuel, and by her magic gives life to his images, among them SESPHRA.

Freytag, Gustav (1816–1895). German novelist, playwright, and critic. His historical panorama in six volumes, *Die Ahnen* (*The Ancestors*), added to his popular fame and brought him the accusation of being an author of PROFESSORENROMANE.

friar (Lat. *frater,* "brother"). A monk, especially one belonging to one of the four great mendicant orders, i.e., FRANCISCANS, DOMINICANS, AUGUSTINIANS, and CARMELITES.

In printer's slang a *friar* is a part of the sheet which has failed to receive the ink properly, and is therefore paler than the rest. As William CAXTON set up his press in Westminster Abbey, it is but natural that monks and friars should give foundation to some of the printer's slang.

For friars famed in fable and story, see under each respective name or pseudonym.

Friar Lawrence. A Franciscan who marries the lovers in Shakespeare's ROMEO AND JULIET.

Friar Rush. *Ger.* **Bruder Rausch.** A late medieval mythical personage originating in German popular legend; a devil disguised as a friar, corrupting monks and friars by all sorts of devious and generally amusing devices. Several English tales and plays were written about him.

Friars Major (Lat. *fratres majores*). The Dominicans.

Friars Minor (Lat. *fratres minores*). The Franciscans.

Friar's or **Freres Tale.** In the CANTERBURY TALES (1388), a tale throwing discredit on summoners. CHAUCER obtained it from the Latin collection *Promptuarium Exemplorum.* It tells how a rascally "sumpnour" or summoner meets the Devil disguised as a yeoman, swears eternal friendship, and agrees to share whatever they may get. They meet a carter in difficulties, crying, "The Devil take it, both horse and cart and hay!" When the summoner urges his companion to obey, the Devil refuses, because it is clear that the wish is not intended literally. Later, the summoner declares that he will squeeze twelve pence out of a poor old woman for a crime that she never committed. She pleads poverty and implores mercy, and finally, her entreaties being in vain, consigns him to the Devil. The seeming yeoman questions her and, finding that she was completely in earnest, seizes the summoner and carries him off.

Friar Tuck. A fat and jovial vagabond friar; the father-confessor to ROBIN HOOD in the Robin Hood ballads and legends. He appears in Sir Walter SCOTT's *Ivanhoe* as the "holy clerk of Copmanhurst."

Fribble. In David GARRICK's *Miss in Her Teens* (1747), a mollycoddle, troubled with weak nerves. He "speaks like a lady for all the world, and never swears. . . . He wears nice white gloves, and tells his lady-love what ribbons become her complexion, where to stick her patches" and all such matters. There had been a *Fribble* in Shadwell's comedy, *Epsom Wells,* before Garrick's day.

Frick, Henry Clay (1849–1919). American industrialist. Chairman, Carnegie Steel Co. (1889–1900). His home in New York, 1 East 70th Street, housing a remarkable art collection, was given by him to the public and endowed as the *Frick Collection.*

Fricka. In Wagner's NIBELUNGEN RING, the goddess of marriage. See also under FRIGGA.

Fricker, Sarah. A "milliner of Bath" who became the wife of S. T. COLERIDGE, to whom she was ill-matched. Her sister, Edith, married the poet SOUTHEY. In DON JUAN (canto ii) Byron makes fun of these marriages.

Friday. The sixth day of the week named for the goddess FREYA. In the Romance languages it is named for the corresponding Roman goddess *Venus.* Friday is considered the day when Adam was created, when he was expelled from paradise, when he repented, when he died, when Christ was crucified, when the dead will rise for the last judgment. In many Christian churches Friday is a fast day. To spill salt on Friday is a bad omen. It used to be the day for the execution of capital punishment and is often called hangman's day.

Good Friday, see GOOD FRIDAY.

Man Friday. In Defoe's ROBINSON CRUSOE, the young savage found by Crusoe on a Friday, and kept as his servant and companion on the desert island; hence, a faithful and willing attendant, ready to turn his hand to anything.

Frideswide, Saint. An English abbess of the early eighth century, patroness of the city and university of Oxford. According to legend, she was a royal princess who fled from the importunities of her lover to Oxford where she founded a monastery which became Christ Church College.

Fried, George (1877–). Captain of the "President Roosevelt," widely known for his rescue of the crew of the British steamer "Antinoe" in an Atlantic storm (Jan. 1926) and subsequent sea rescues. Cf. the narrative poem by E. J. PRATT, "The Roosevelt and the Antinoe."

Friend. A QUAKER, i.e., a member of the Society of Friends; also, one's second in a duel, as "Name your friend," "Captain B. acted as his friend."

Friendship Village. A small town which is the scene of numerous short stories by Zona GALE, notably those of *Friendship Village* (1908) and *Peace in Friendship Village* (1919).

Frietchie, Barbara, see BARBARA FRIETCHIE.

Friganza, Trixie. Real name **Delia O'Callahan** (1870–). American actress and singer.

Frigga or Frigg. In Scandinavian mythology, the supreme goddess, wife of ODIN. She presides over marriages, and may be called the Juno of Asgard. In Teutonic mythology she is identified with FREYA.

Frithiof. A hero of Icelandic myth who married Ingeborg, daughter of a petty king of Norway, and widow of Hring, to whose dominions he succeeded. His adventures are recorded in the saga which bears his name, and which was written about the close of the 13th century. The name signifies "the peacemaker."

Fritz. A nickname for a German soldier.

unser Fritz (*Ger.,* "our Fritz"). The German Emperor Frederick III (1831–1888) when he was crown prince of Prussia.

der alte Fritz. See under FREDERICK THE GREAT.

The term *Fritz* was also applied to certain kinds of German shells and battle-planes during World War I.

Frobisher, Sir Martin (1535?–1594). English navigator; commanded expedition in search of Northwest Passage (1576) and discovered Frobisher Bay. One of his sailors having found a piece of ore which seemed to contain gold, Frobisher was sent out on two further (but futile) expeditions in search of gold. Vice-Admiral under Drake in West Indian expedition (1586). Fought with distinction against the Spanish Armada. Knighted (1588).

Fröding, Gustaf (1860–1911). Swedish poet of lyric and religious verse.

Froebel system. A system of kindergarten or elementary education introduced by the German educator Froebel (1782–1852).

the Italian Froebel. Antonio Rosmini-Serbati (1797–1855).

frog. A frog and mouse agreed to settle by single combat their claims to a marsh; but, while they fought, a kite carried them both off. (Aesop, *Fables,* clxviii.) See also *Battle of the Frogs and Mice* under BATTLE.

> Old Aesop's fable, where he told
> What fate unto the mouse and frog befel.
> Cary, *Dante,* cxxiii.

In Ovid's *Metamorphoses* (vi. 4) we are told that the Lycian shepherds were changed into frogs for mocking Latona.

> As when those hinds that were transformed to frogs
> Railed at Latona's twin-born progeny.
> Milton, *Sonnet,* vii.

Frog, Nic. A Dutchman. In Arbuthnot's JOHN BULL Nic Frog is a Dutchman; and frogs are called "Dutch Nightingales." As the French have the reputation of feeding on frogs, the word has sometimes also been transferred to them. See also BIDDY, NATIONALITIES, NICKNAMES OF.

Frogs, The. A satiric comedy by ARISTOPHANES (405 B.C.). The principal scene is laid in Hades where Aeschylus and Euripides compete for the honor of accompanying Dionysus back to Athens as the chief tragic poet.

Frohman, Charles (1860–1915). American theatrical manager. Nicknamed "the Napoleon of the Drama." In 1895 he took charge of the Empire Theater, New York City, and two years later organized his famous and influential theatrical company. He presented John Drew, Maude Adams, Julia Marlowe, and was one of the first American managers to produce American plays in London. He lost his life on the torpedoed *Lusitania.* His brother, **Daniel Frohman** (1851–1940), managed Fifth Avenue Theater, Madison Square Theater, and Lyceum Theater.

Froissart, Jean (1333?–?1404). French poet and historian, associated with the English court under the patronage of Queen Philippa, holding the position of royal historiographer. In England he became acquainted with the great figures of the day, including CHAUCER. Froissart is best known for his *Chronicles,* begun in 1373 when he was sent back to France, and completed about 1400. This work deals with the period in western Europe beginning in 1325 and graphically depicts the events of the Hundred Years' War. Froissart wrote the first book according to the English viewpoint, later revising it to attack the English. In the realm of poetry, he is known for his allegory, *Paradis d'Amour,* imitated by Chaucer, for *Méliador,* an Arthurian romance (see ARTHUR), and graceful lyrics in a light vein.

Frollo, Claude. The villain of Hugo's NOTRE DAME DE PARIS, an archdeacon, absorbed by a search after the philosopher's stone. He has a great reputation for sanctity, but entertains a base passion for Esmeralda, the beautiful gipsy girl. QUASIMODO flings him into the air from the top of Notre Dame and dashes him to death.

Frome, David. Pseudonym of Zenith Jones BROWN.

Fromentin, Eugène (1820–1876). French genre painter, known for his scenes of life in Algiers. Author of the successful romance *Domenique.*

Fronde. A political party during the ministry of Cardinal MAZARIN, in the minority of Louis XIV (1648–1653). Its members, who were opposed to the court party, were called *Frondeurs* from *fronde,* "a sling," they being likened to boys who sling stones about the streets and scamper away the moment anyone in authority approaches.

> It was already true that the French government was a despotism . . . and as speeches and lampoons were launched by persons who tried to hide after they had shot their dart, some one compared them to children with a sling (*fronde*), who let fly a stone and run away.—C. M. Yonge, *History of France,* Ch. viii.

Front de Boeuf, Sir Reginald. In Scott's IVANHOE, a follower of Prince John of Anjou, and one of the knight's challengers. He tries to extort money from Isaac the Jew, and bids two slaves to chain him to the bars of a slow fire, but they are disturbed in this diabolical plot by the bugle's sound. It is in his castle of Torquilstone that Cedric and his party are confined, and Front de Boeuf dies as a result of the attack on the castle which the bugle heralds.

Frontenac, Comte **de Palluau et de. Louis de Buade** (1620–1698). Governor of New France, the French possessions in North America (1672–1682 and 1689–1698). Forced the British to lift the siege of Quebec (1690) and fought the Iroquois. Encouraged explorations and has been called "a sure breeder of storms in time of peace, but in time of calamity and danger a tower of strength."

Frontoni, Jacopo. Hero of Cooper's novel, THE BRAVO.

Front Page, The. A famous American play about newspapermen by Ben HECHT and Charles MACARTHUR (1928).

Frost, Frances (1905–). American novelist and poet. *Innocent Summer* (1936), etc.

Frost, Robert Lee (1875–). American poet, known for his verse dealing with New England life and characters. His style is simple, plain, and colloquial, often in the form of blank verse dramatic monologues in which Yankee people speak for themselves, concrete, everyday experiences being used to symbolize more generalized conclusions and observations. Books of his poems include *A Boy's Will* (1913); *North of Boston* (1914); *Mountain Interval* (1916); *New Hampshire* (1923), winner of the Pulitzer prize in 1924; *West-Running Brook* (1928); *Collected Poems* (1930), winner of the Pulitzer prize in 1931; *A Further Range* (1936), winner of the Pulitzer prize in 1937; and *A Witness Tree* (1942). Well-known individual poems are: BIRCHES; THE DEATH OF THE HIRED MAN; *A Servant to Servants; Putting in the Seed.*

Froth, Lord and **Lady.** A couple in Congreve's comedy, *The Double Dealer* (1700). He is a gentleman of fashion, she a lady of letters, who writes songs, elegies, satires, lampoons, and even plays.

Froth, Master. In Shakespeare's MEASURE FOR MEASURE, a foolish gentleman, too shallow for a great crime and too light for virtue.

Froude, James Anthony (1818–1894). English historian. Author of a history of England in twelve volumes. As literary executor of CARLYLE he wrote *Reminiscences of Carlyle* (1881) and a *Life of Thomas Carlyle* (1882).

Frou-Frou (*Fr.,* of imitative origin, meaning rustling of garments). A play by Henri Meilhac and Ludovic Halévy (*Fr.,* 1869, subsequently produced in several European languages). The nickname had been used previously for a character in Charles Yriarte's PARISIAN LIFE (*La Vie Parisienne*). In the drama the shallow, light-hearted coquette nicknamed Frou-Frou is Gilberte Brigard. She marries M. de Sartoris with whom her older sister Louise had secretly been in love, neglects her home and child for social gayety, and allows Louise to assume charge of the household. Finally she becomes violently jealous of Louise and goes off with a lover. The lover is killed by Sartoris and Frou-Frou, somewhat melodramatically, repents of her sins and dies.

Frowde, Henry (1841–1927). English publisher of CLARENDON PRESS books; official publisher for the University of Oxford (1882–1913).

frozen music. Architecture. So called by Friedrich von SCHLEGEL in his *Philosophie der Kunst.*

Fruitlands. An experimental co-operative community founded by Bronson ALCOTT at Harvard, Massachusetts, in 1842. Its plan included vegetarianism, farming, and teaching. The experiment ended in 1843. *Transcendental Wild Oats,* by Alcott's daughter Louisa May ALCOTT, is based on the Fruitlands community.

Frundsberg, Georg von (1473–1528). Called "father of the German LANDSKNECHTE." Won distinction at battle of Pavia (1525). Great fighter in wars of that period.

Fry, Elizabeth (1780–1845). English Quaker philanthropist, noted as promoter of prison reform. Founded an order of nursing sisters. Cf. her biography by Janet WHITNEY.

Fry, Roger Eliot (1866–1934). English art critic and painter. For a few years curator of paintings at the Metropolitan Museum in New York. Editor of Sir Joshua Reynolds' *Discourses* (1905); author of monographs on Bellini (1899), Cézanne, Matisse, etc. Also *Vision and Design* (1920), *Transformations* (1926), *Last Lectures* (published posthumously, 1939).

Fryatt, Charles Algernon (1872–1916). British captain in the merchant marine. Captured by the Germans in World War I and shot as a "FRANC-TIREUR" (July 26, 1916) on the charge of having attempted to ram a U-boat.

Fudge Family. A family whose adventures are related in Thomas Moore's poetical *Fudge Family Abroad* (1818). It consists of Phil Fudge, Esq., his son Robert, his daughter Biddy, and a poor relation named Phelim Connor (an ardent Bonapartist and Irish patriot) acting as bear-leader to Bob. These four write letters to their friends in England. The skit is meant to satirize the *parvenu* English abroad.

Fuertes, Louis Agassiz (1874–1927). American ornithological expert and illustrator. Named for the famous naturalist AGASSIZ. His series of eight important books of bird illustrations was begun in 1897 with *Song Birds and Water Fowl* and concluded in 1910 with *Birds of New York.*

Fugitive Slave Law. Statutes passed by Congress from 1793–1850, providing for the return of slaves who escaped from one state into another or into the territories. The law of 1850 placed reclamation of slaves in the hands of the federal authorities, but resulted in political dissension culminating in the secession of 1861 and the Civil War. The law was repealed in 1864.

fugleman (Ger. *Flügelmann,* a file leader; literally, a wingman). Formerly, a file leader in front of a military company; hence a leader in politics, a model, example, etc.

fugue (*Fr.,* from It. *fuga;* literally, "a flight"). A polyphonic musical composition, developed from one or several themes, which are enunciated in turn by the several parts and gradually built up according to strict contrapuntal rules into a complex form of distinct divisions and a marked final climax. The fugue has been called "the consummate form of the polyphonic style of composition requiring a mastery of all the devices of counterpoint and a high grade of inventive and constructive genius." The greatest masters of the fugue are BACH (1685–1750) and HANDEL (1685–1759).

Führer (*Ger.*) or **Fuehrer.** A leader, guide, etc. Hence **der Führer,** the Chancellor of the THIRD REICH, Adolf HITLER, as supreme leader of the National Socialist Party (and the entire German people); also the head of any subdivision or unit within the party structure.

Führer principle (Ger. *Führerprinzip*). The hierarchic principle of organization derived by the German National Socialists from FEUDALISM and early Teutonic history, partly in imitation of the Italian Fascist organization (see DUCE), and applied by them to all phases of social and political life in the THIRD REICH. Under the Führer principle in its historical perfection, every member of the national hierarchy wills obedience to a trusted leader and receives obedience from faithful followers. In theory, the Führer principle is a democratic ideal; in corrupt application, it spells regimentation and dictatorship.

Fu Hsi. The first of the five legendary emperors of China (his dates given as 2953–2838 B.C.). Inventor of the Chinese system of writing and a variety of useful arts.

Fujiyama. More correctly **Fuji-no-Yama** (literally, sacred mountain). The highest mountain of Japan, in the province of Suruga, sixty miles west of Tokyo. Height 12,395 feet. It is a snow-capped volcano, inactive since 1707, a resort of pilgrims and prominent in Japanese art.

Fulkerson. In Howells' A HAZARD OF NEW FORTUNES, an energetic Westerner, a born promoter, responsible for the launching of the periodical, *Every Other Week*.

Fuller, Henry Blake (1857–1929). American novelist, known for his realistic studies of life in Chicago and his fanciful romances of Europe. In the first form, his works include THE CLIFF-DWELLERS (1893); *With the Procession* (1895); *Under the Skylights* (1901); *On the Stairs* (1918); *Bertram Cope's Year* (1919); *Not on the Screen* (1930). His books in the second form include: *The Chevalier of Pensieri-Vani* (1890); *The Châtelaine of La Trinité* (1892); *The Last Refuge* (1900); *Waldo Trench and Others* (1908); *Gardens of This World* (1929).

Fuller, Sarah Margaret (1810–1850). American author and literary critic, associated with the movement of TRANSCENDENTALISM, editor of THE DIAL from 1840 to 1842, and one of the most important Feminist leaders of her time. Her personality and keen critical sense made her one of the best-known literary figures in the U.S. She visited Europe, became an intense admirer of MAZZINI in Italy, and married one of his followers, the Marquis Angelo Ossoli. Her works include: *Woman in the Nineteenth Century* (1845); *Summer on the Lakes* (1843); *Literature and Art* (1869). The character of ZENOBIA in Hawthorne's BLITHEDALE ROMANCE is said to have been inspired by Margaret Fuller, as was ELSIE VENNER.

Fuller, Thomas (1608–1661). English prose-writer, a CHARACTER WRITER and didactic essayist. Among his works are: *The Holy State and the Profane State* (1642), a series of character sketches; *History of the Holy War* (1643), an account of the mediaeval Crusades; *Good Thoughts in Bad Times* (1645), essays on the religious conflicts of his time; *The Worthies of England* (1662), a collection of biographical sketches.

Fülöp-Miller, René (1891–). Hungarian author, writing in German. His father was of Alsatian Huguenot descent, his mother a Serb. Student of cultural subjects; characterized by occult leanings and an uncanny flair for the expressive and concrete detail or anecdote. Naturalized American citizen. *Lenin and Gandhi* (1927), *Rasputin the Holy Devil* (1927), *The Power and Secret of the Jesuits* (1929), *The Saints that Moved the World* (1945), a great autobiographical novel (1947), works on Bolshevism (1926), the Russian and American theater, etc., etc. The first part of his name is the Hungarian form of Philip.

Fulton's Folly. See under CLERMONT.

Fulvia (d. 40 B.C.). A Roman matron married successively to Clodius Pulcher the demagogue (so called for his beauty), Curio, and Mark Antony. When Cicero was murdered by Antony's orders, his head was brought to Fulvia who drove a needle through his tongue in revenge for the things he had said against her husband in his famous *Philippics*.

Fum or **Fung-hwang.** The PHOENIX of Chinese legend, one of the four symbolical animals presiding over the destinies of China. It originated from fire, was born in the Hill of the Sun's Halo, and has its body inscribed with the five cardinal virtues. One account says it has the forepart of a goose, the hindquarters of a stag, the neck of a snake, the tail of a fish, the forehead of a fowl, the down of a duck, the marks of a dragon, the back of a tortoise, the face of a swallow, the beak of a cock, is about six cubits high, and perches only on the woo-tung tree. It is this curious creature that is embroidered on the dresses of certain mandarins.

functionalism. Any doctrine or practice that lays stress upon function or adaptation to practical use. In art, notably architecture, the principle that aesthetic satisfaction cannot be derived from a work or an element in it, which does not convey the idea of its indispensability. A column which has nothing to support is ugly. So is an ornament which has nothing to express. Extreme functionalism often rules out the fact that practically superfluous objects can very well have a rationally less apparent function. VOLTAIRE formulated this point strikingly: "Le superflu, chose si nécessaire."

fundamentalists. See under MODERNISTS AND FUNDAMENTALISTS.

Fung-hwang, see FUM.

Funk, Peter. A fake bidder at an auction, to whom articles are sold when the price fails to go up sufficiently, and by whom the price is often artificially boosted.

Furies, the. The Roman name (*Furiae*) for the Greek ERINYES, said by Hesiod to have been the daughters of Ge (the earth) and to have sprung from the blood of Uranus, and by other accounts to be daughters of night and darkness. They were three in number, Tisiphone (the Avenger of blood), Alecto (Implacable), and Megaera (Disputatious).

Furioso, see BOMBASTES FURIOSO; ORLANDO FURIOSO.

Furious Host. See under WILD HUNT.

Furness, Horace Howard (1833–1912). American Shakespearean scholar and legal writer. Edited *Variorum Shakespeare* (from 1871), carried to completion by his son **Horace Howard Furness** (1865–1930).

Furniss, Harry (1854–1925). British illustrator and caricaturist. *Sylvie and Bruno* by Lewis Carroll, editions of Dickens and Thackeray, etc.

Furnivall, Frederick James (1825–1910). English philologist. Founder of Early English Text Society (1864), Chaucer Society, Ballad Society (1868), New Shakespeare Society (1873), Browning Society (1881), Wyclif Society (1882), Shelley Society (1885). Editor of *Six-Text Print of Chaucer's Canterbury Tales* (1868–1875). Began a dictionary for the Philological Society which developed into the *Oxford English Dictionary.* Enthusiastic oarsman throughout his life. Built the first English narrow wager boats (1845), etc.

Furor. In Spenser's FAËRIE QUEENE (Bk. ii) the personification of mad anger. He is son of Occasion, an old hag, and Sir Guyon binds him "with a hundred iron chains and a hundred knots."

Furuseth, Andrew (1854–1938). Norwegian-born American labor leader. President, International Seamen's Union of America (1908–1938).

Fury (plural **Furies**). The Furies, in Greek Erinyes or euphemistically Eumenides, were avenging spirits of retributive justice. Their names, when in course of time their number had come to be fixed as three, were Alecto, Megaera, and Tisiphone. Their task was to punish crimes not within the reach of human justice. Through Aeschylus the tradition developed that after the time when they had intervened in the case of Orestes, their functions no longer covered cases of "guiltiness" free from moral guilt. In spite of their inexorable sternness, they wept when they heard ORPHEUS implore the deities of the underworld to restore Eurydice to life.

fustian. A coarse twilled cotton cloth with a velvety pile, probably so called from Fustat, a suburb of Cairo. It is chiefly used now in its figurative sense meaning inflated or pompous talk, clap-trap, bombast, pretentious words.

Futrelle, Jacques (1875–1912). American writer of detective fiction. *The Thinking Machine* (1907), etc. Tragic death in *Titanic* catastrophe.

futurism. A movement in Italian painting of the period of World War I, a development of CUBISM, in which the aim was to portray dynamic movement within a two dimensional medium. A favorite device was the presentation of a moving object in successive stages of motion, as in a motion-picture film. The later "stream-lined" effects in industrial design are considered to be in part an outgrowth of futurism.

Fuzzy Wuzzy. Title and hero of one of Kipling's BARRACK-ROOM BALLADS (1892).

> So 'ere's *to* you, Fuzzy Wuzzy, at your 'ome in the Soudan;
> You're a pore benighted 'eathen but a first-class fightin' man
> An' 'ere's *to* you, Fuzzy Wuzzy, with your 'ayrick 'ead of 'air—
> You big black boundin' beggar—for you broke a British square.

fylfot. The SWASTIKA. Literally, either "four-foot" (because of its shape) or "fill-foot" (because of its ornamental use to fill the lower part of a painted window).

Fyne, Mrs. The best friend of Flora de Barrel in Conrad's CHANCE.

fyrd. In English history before the Norman Conquest, the national military land force.

fytte, also **fit**. A division of a poem or song; a canto or the like.

> Poems sweet
> Like separate souls shall fly from it,
> Each to an immortal fytte.
> Elizabeth Barrett Browning, *Isobel's Child.*

G

Gabbara. The giant who, according to Rabelais, was "the first inventor of the drinking of healths." See GEMMAGOG.

gabelle. A salt tax, as levied in France for several centuries prior to 1790 and in China up to modern times. The word is ultimately of Arabic origin.

gaberdine or **gabardine.** The Jewish gown or mantle of the Middle Ages. The word seems to come ultimately from German *Wallfahrt*, "pilgrimage."

Gabler, Hedda, see HEDDA GABLER.

Gaboriau, Émile (1835–1873). Famous French detective-story writer. Creator of Monsieur Lecoq and Père Tabaret.

Gabriel. Literally, man of God. One of the archangels of Hebrew mythology, sometimes regarded as the angel of death, the prince of fire and thunder, but more frequently as one of the Deity's chief messengers, and traditionally said to be the only angel that can speak Syriac and Chaldee. The Mohammedans call him the chief of the four favored angels, and the spirit of truth. In medieval romance he is the second of the seven spirits that stand before the throne of God (*Jerusalem Delivered*, Bk. i), and Milton makes him chief of the angelic guards placed over Paradise:

> Betwixt these rocky pillars Gabriel sat,
> Chief of the angelic guards.
> *Paradise Lost*, iv. 549.

Longfellow, in his GOLDEN LEGEND, calls him the angel of the moon, and says he brings to man the gift of hope.

In the TALMUD he appears as the destroyer of the hosts of Sennacherib, as the man who showed Joseph the way (*Gen.* xxxvii. 15), and as one of the angels who buried Moses (*Deut.* xxxiv. 6).

It was Gabriel who (we are told in the Koran) took Mahomet to heaven on AL-BORAK, and revealed to him his "prophetic lore." In the Old Testament Gabriel is said to have explained to Daniel certain visions; in the New Testament he announced to Zacharias the future birth of John the Baptist, and appeared to Mary, the mother of Jesus. (*Luke* i. 26, etc.) He is expected to blow the trumpet on the Day of Judgment.

Gabriel's hounds. Wild geese. According to legend they are unbaptized souls, doomed to wander until Judgment Day.

Gabriel Conroy. A novel by Bret HARTE (1876) dealing with the adventures of a party lost in the snow in the California Sierras in the early days of the settlement of California. The heroine is Grace Conroy, Gabriel's sister, and the hero Arthur Poinsett, who is traveling under the name of Philip Ashley. The professional gambler Jack HAMLIN is introduced, as are many other typical western characters.

Gabrielle, La Belle (1571–1599). Daughter of Antoine d'Estrées, grand-master of artillery, and governor of the Ile de France. Henri IV, toward the close of 1590, happened to sojourn for a night at the Château de Coeuvres, and fell in love with her. To throw a flimsy veil over his intrigue, he married her to Liancourt-Damerval, created her Duchess de Beaufort, and took her to live with him at court.

Gabrilówitsch, Ossip (1878–1936). Russian pianist and orchestral director. Married Mark Twain's daughter, Clara Clemens.

gadfly. A fly that bites or annoys cattle. In Greek mythology Juno sent a gadfly to torment the white-horned cow in whose shape Jupiter tried to protect his beloved Io from his wife's jealousy.

Gadsden Purchase. A strip of land (45,535 square miles) negotiated for and purchased for $10,000,000 from Mexico (1853) by James Gadsden (1788–1858), then U.S. Minister to Mexico. It is situated in what is now New Mexico and Arizona.

Gadshill. A companion of Sir John Falstaff in Shakespeare's 1 *Henry IV*. This thief receives his name from a place called Gadshill, on the Kentish road, notorious for the many robberies committed there.

Gaea, see GE.

Gaekwar, see RULERS, TITLES OF.

Gág, Wanda (1893–1946). American painter; author and illustrator of children's books. *Millions of Cats* (1928), etc. Cf. also her autobiography, *Growing Pains* (1940).

Gaheris. A knight of the ROUND TABLE, brother of Gawain and nephew of KING ARTHUR. He slew his mother Morganse for adultery.

Gaillard, David Du Bose (1859–1913). American army officer and engineer in charge (1908) of excavation at Culebra Cut, Panama Canal, renamed *Gaillard Cut* in his honor.

Gainsborough, Thomas (1727–1788). Famous English painter. Son of a wool manufacturer. One of the original 36 members of the Royal Academy. 300 pictures; 220 portraits. Eight poses of George III; several pictures known as *Blue Boy*, etc.

Galahad, Sir. In the Arthurian legends, the purest and noblest knight of the Round Table. He is a late addition and was invented by Walter Map in his *Quest of the San Graal.* He was the son of Launcelot and Elaine. At the institution of the Round Table one seat (the *Siege Perilous*) was left unoccupied, and could be occupied only by the knight who could succeed in the Quest, all others who attempted it being swallowed by the earth.

When Sir Galahad sat there it was discovered that it had been left for him. See Malory's MORTE D'ARTHUR; Tennyson's IDYLLS OF THE KING (*The Holy Grail*), etc.

> There Galahad sat, with manly grace,
> Yet maiden meekness in his face.
> Sir W. Scott, *Bridal of Triermain*, ii. 13.

After divers adventures, Sir Galahad came to Sarras, where he was made king, was shown the Grail by Joseph of Arimathea, and even "took the Lord's body between his hands," and died. Then suddenly "a great multitude of angels did bear his soul up to heaven," and "sithence was never no man that could say he had seen the sangreal." See also ELAINE; GRAIL; GALEOTO.

Galapagos Islands. An archipelago of volcanic islands on the equator, west of Ecuador. Formerly noted for large tortoises (Span. *galápago*, "tortoise"). Investigated by Darwin during his voyage in the Beagle, later by William BEEBE.

Galatea. (1) A sea-nymph, beloved by Polypheme, but herself in love with Acis. Acis was crushed under a huge rock by the jealous giant, and Galatea threw herself into the sea, where she joined her sister nymphs. Handel has an opera entitled *Acis and Galatea*. (2) A statue made by Pygmalion, which became animated, caused much mischief by her want of worldly knowledge, and returned to her original state. For modern versions of this legend, see PYGMALION.

Galba (5 B.C.?–69 A.D.). Roman emperor (68–69 A.D.). Made emperor after Nero's death by the Praetorian guard. Killed after a few months when unwilling to fulfill the expectations of his followers.

Gale, Roger. The central figure of Ernest Poole's novel HIS FAMILY. His three daughters are prominent in the novel.

Gale, Zona (1874–1938). American novelist and short-story writer, at one time a reporter on the New York *World*, whose books deal chiefly with small-town life in the Middle West, in the local color tradition, often presented realistically. Her works include: FRIENDSHIP VILLAGE (1908), *Yellow Gentians and Blue* (1927), and *Bridal Pond* (1930), short stories; *When I Was a Little Girl* (1913) and *Portage, Wisconsin* (1928), autobiographical accounts; MISS LULU BETT (1920), in its dramatic form a winner of the Pulitzer Prize in 1921; *Birth* (1918), dramatized in 1924 as *Mr. Pitt; Faint Perfume* (1923); *Preface to a Life* (1926); *Borgia* (1929); *Papa La Fleur* (1933); and *Magna* (1939).

Galen. A very famous Greek physician and philosopher of the 2nd century A.D. For centuries he was the supreme authority in medicine; hence, any physician.

> *Galen says "Nay" and Hippocrates "Yea."*

The doctors disagree, and who is to decide? Hippocrates—a native of Cos, born 460 B.C.—was also a celebrated physician.

Galeoto or **Galeotto.** The Italian name of Gallehault, one of the forms of GALAHAD, which has attached to itself a quite divergent meaning. Its modern connotations come from a passage in Dante's INFERNO telling how Paolo and Francesca read of a guilty kiss between Launcelot and Guinevere and yielded to the suggestion. Gallehault was the knight who had brought Launcelot and the Queen together, and he performed the same office for Paolo and Francesca for "Galeoto was the book and he who wrote it. That day we read no more." Hence, though far from the character of Galahad, Galeoto has become a term for a panderer in Italy and Spain.

José Echegaray has a modern tragedy (*Sp.*, 1881) called *The Great Galeoto* (*El gran Galeoto*), in which spiteful gossip is the "Galeoto" of the title. An adaptation by C. F. Nirdlinger was produced in America under the title, *The World and His Wife*. The heroine is suspected by the spying public and finally by her husband, Julian, of improper relations with his young secretary, Ernest. They are innocent, but are powerless to convince Julian, who dies from a wound received in a duel fought for his wife's honor. Ernest says—

> "This woman is mine. The world has so decreed, and I accept the world's decision. It has driven her to my arms. You cast her forth. We obey you. But should anybody ask who was the go-between in this business, you should say 'Ourselves, all unwilling and the stupid chatter of gossip.' "

Galeotti, Martius. Louis XI's Italian astrologer.

> "Can thy pretended skill ascertain the hour of thine own death?"
> "Only by referring to the fate of another," said Galeotti.
> "I understand not thine answer," said Louis.
> "Know then, O king," said Martius, "that this only I can tell with certainty concerning mine own death, that it shall take place exactly twenty-four hours before your majesty's."
> Scott, *Quentin Durward*, ch. xxix.

Thrasullus, the soothsayer to Tiberius, made the same diplomatic answer to the same question, and in each case it had the effect of making the ruler protect the life of the prophet.

Galiana. A Moorish princess, whose father, King Gadalfe of Toledo, according to Spanish tradition, built for her a palace on the Tagus so splendid that the phrase "a palace of Galiana" became proverbial in Spain.

Galignani. Name of a family of British publishers of Italian descent in Paris. *Galignani's Messenger* (1814) and continental reprints of British books. Stopped by copyright treaty of 1852.

Galileo Galilei. Commonly known as **Galileo** (1564–1642). Italian astronomer and physicist. Discovered isochronism of the pendulum (1583), hydrostatic balance (1586), Jupiter's satellites (1610), sun spots (1610), moon's libration (1637), etc. Advocated Copernican system. His doctrines were condemned by Rome (1616), and after the publication of his *Dialogo ai due massimi Sistemi* (*Dialogue on the Two Chief Systems*, 1632), he was forced by the Inquisition to recant in public. In doing so he is said to have whispered *Eppur si muove* (*And yet it moves*)! The story is not true, but it illustrates the typically modern attitude of the man of science who has faith in the final victory of truth and sees no reason why he should sacrifice himself for it in stubborn heroism.

gall. Bile; the very bitter fluid secreted by the liver; hence, used figuratively as a symbol for anything of extreme bitterness.

gall and wormwood. Extremely disagreeable and annoying.

And I said, My strength and my hope is perished from the Lord: Remembering my affliction and my misery, the wormwood and the gall.—*Lam.* iii. 18, 19.

the gall of bitterness. The bitterest grief; extreme affliction. The ancients taught that grief and joy were subject to the gall as affection was to the heart, knowledge to the kidneys, and the gall of bitterness means the bitter center of bitterness, as the heart of heart means the innermost recesses of the heart or affections. In the *Acts* it is used to signify "the sinfulness of sin," which leads to the bitterest grief.

I perceive thou art in the gall of bitterness, and in the bond of iniquity.—*Acts* viii, 23.

the gall of pigeons. The story goes that pigeons have no gall, because the dove sent from the ark by Noah burst its gall out of grief, and none of the pigeon family has had a gall ever since.

For sin' the Flood of Noah
The dow she had nae ga'.
Jamieson, *Popular Ballads* (*Lord of Rorlin's Daughter*).

Gall, Franz (1758–1828). German brain anatomist. Remembered especially as the founder of phrenology, a system of character reading based on the theory that there is a relation between mental faculties and the shape of the brain and (hence) the skull. It is a typical product of an age which refused to admit the possibility of external phenomena devoid of internal significance.

Gallagher, Tommy. See TOMMY GALLAGHER'S CRUSADE.

Gallaudet, Thomas Hopkins (1787–1851). Founder of the first American institution for the instruction of the deaf and dumb at Hartford, Conn. (1817). Gallaudet College (Washington, D.C.) was named after him. His son **Thomas Gallaudet** (1822–1902) founded in New York a church for deaf-mutes (1859).

Gallegher. A short story by Richard Harding DAVIS (1891). Gallegher, the Irish-American office boy of a daily newspaper, succeeds, after exciting adventures, in bringing in the much desired "story" of a private secretary who had murdered his employer and absconded with securities.

Gallehault. The name for GALAHAD in the old French romance, *Lancelot du Lac.* See also GALEOTO.

galley. A large one-decked sea-going vessel, propelled by both oars and sails. In use from antiquity to the seventeenth century. The oars were manned by mercenaries, slaves, prisoners of war, and, especially in France, by convicts. Also the cookroom of a vessel.

The *printers' galley* is an oblong shallow tray of metal or, formerly, wood designed to hold type which has been set. A *galley proof* is a proof pulled from type not yet made up into pages.

galliambus. Also **galliambic.** A kind of Ionic verse consisting of two IAMBIC dimeters CATALECTIC, the last of which lacks the final syllable. So called in Greek antiquity in association with the *Galli* (singular *Gallus*), the priests of Cybele, whose traditional ravings were reminiscent of the fable that the waters of the river Gallus had maddening virtues.

Gallicism. A phrase or sentence constructed after the French idiom; as, "when you *shall have returned* home you will find a letter on your table." Government documents are especially guilty of this fault. In *Matt.* xv. 32, is a Gallicism: "I have compassion on the multitude, because *they continue* with me now three days, and have nothing to eat." Cf. also *Mark* viii. 2. Intentional Gallicisms are also often used to give a literary passage the tone and feeling of the French language, as "it is to laugh" for *c'est à rire.*

Galli-Curci, Amelita (1889–). Operatic coloratura soprano. Joined Metropolitan Opera Company, New York, in 1920. Sang Lakmé (in *Lakmé*), Violetta (in *La Traviata*), Gilda (in *Rigoletto*), Juliette (in *Roméo et Juliette*), Lucia (in *Lucia di Lammermoor*), Mimi (in *La Bohème*), Elvira (in *I Puritani*), etc.

Gallieni, Joseph Simon (1849–1916). In World War I, the "Savior of Paris." As military governor of Paris he rushed 80,000 reserves in taxis and automobiles to the front (1914) thus enabling General MAUNOURY to repulse von KLUCK at the Marne.

Galligantus. One of the giants of nursery-lore slain by Jack the Giant Killer. Arrayed in his cap, which renders him invisible, Jack goes to the castle and reads the inscription: "Whoever can this trumpet blow, will cause the giant's overthrow." He seizes the trumpet, blows a loud blast, the castle falls down, Jack slays the giant, and is married soon after to a duke's daughter, whom he finds there and rescues.

Gallipoli. Title of a collection of prose sketches (1916) by John Masefield giving a full account of the unsuccessful Dardanelles campaign by which British and French troops under the direction of Winston CHURCHILL attempted to break Turkish resistance and invade the citadel of the Central Powers through a backdoor.

galloglass or **gallowglass.** A cateran or kern, that is, an armed Irish foot-soldier.

Gallomania. A *furor* for everything French, generally applied to that imitation of French literature and customs which prevailed in Germany in the time of FREDERICK II of Prussia.

Gallup, George Horace (1901–). American statistician. Founder of the Gallup polls (1935) which endeavor to measure public interest and opinion in various matters.

Galsworthy, John (1867–1933). English novelist and dramatist, known for his portrayals of the British upper classes. His most famous work is THE FORSYTE SAGA, consisting of two series of novels written over his entire career, which deal with the fortunes of the Forsyte family. Other novels are: *Jocelyn* (1899) and *Villa Rubein* (1900), published under the pseudonym of John Sinjohn; *The Island Pharisees* (1904); FRATERNITY (1909); *The Patrician* (1911); *The Dark Flower* (1913); *One More River* (1933). His plays include: STRIFE (1909); JUSTICE (1910); *The Mob* (1915); *The Skin Game* (1920); *The Family Man* (1921); *Loyalties* (1922); *Windows* (1922); *Old English* (1924); *The Show* (1925); *Escape* (1926); *The Roof* (1931). Collections of short stories include: *A Sheaf* (1916); *Another Sheaf* (1919); *Five Tales* (1919); *The Burning Spear* (1923); *Captures* (1923); *Caravan* (1925). Galsworthy's work combines sentimentalism with social observation and a sense of character.

Galton, Sir **Francis** (1822–1911). English scientist and African traveler. Best known for his work in the study of heredity. Founder of the science of eugenics. Devised a system of fingerprint identification. *Hereditary Genius* (1869); *Record of Family Faculties* (1883); etc.

Galuppi, Baldassare (1706–1798). Italian composer of comic operas. Cf. the poem *A Toccata of Galuppi's* by Robert BROWNING.

Galvani, Luigi (1737–1798). Italian physician and physicist. Interpreted the twitchings of frogs' legs in contact with metals as due to "animal electricity," a form of energy which he hoped could be shown to be instrumental in all muscular movements. VOLTA corrected his interpretation, but the phenomenon as such proved so important in the study of direct electric currents that this entire branch of physics is justly called *galvanism*.

Galway jury. An independent jury, neither to be browbeaten nor led by the nose. In 1635, certain trials were held in Ireland respecting the right of the Crown to the counties of Ireland. Leitrim, Roscommon, Sligo and Mayo gave judgment in favor of the Crown, but Galway stood out, whereupon each of the jury was fined £4000.

Gama, Vasco da. One of the greatest of the early Portuguese navigators (d. 1524), the first European to round the Cape of Good Hope. He is the hero of Camoëns' LUSIAD (1572), where he is represented as sagacious, intrepid, tenderhearted, pious, fond of his country, and holding his temper in full command. He is also the hero of Meyerbeer's posthumous opera L'AFRICAINE.

> Gama, captain of the venturous band,
> Of bold emprise, and born for high command,
> Whose martial fires, with prudence close allied,
> Ensured the smiles of fortune on his side.
>
> Camoëns, *Lusiad*, Bk. i.

Gambetta, Léon (1838–1882). French lawyer and statesman. Opposed to Napoleon III. Made spectacular escape from Prussian-besieged Paris by balloon (Oct. 8, 1870) in a futile attempt to organize national resistance. President, Chamber of Deputies (1879–1881); premier of France (1881–1882).

Gambrinus or **Gambrivius.** A hero of folklore, famed as the legendary inventor of beer or ale. The legend exists in many countries with numerous variations.

Game Chicken, the. A prize fighter in Dickens' DOMBEY AND SON. See also under CHICKEN.

Gamelin, Evariste. The hero of the historical novel THE GODS ARE ATHIRST by Anatole France.

Gamelin, Maurice Gustave (1872–). French professional soldier. Succeeded General WEYGAND as inspector general of the army and vice-president of the Higher Council of War (1935). After the defeat of the French armies in World War II (1940), he was relieved of his command. Replaced by General Weygand (May 19, 1940). Of "MAGINOT" mentality. He was one of the defendants at Riom in a trial for treason and in 1943 was put into a German prison.

Gamelyn, The Tale of. A Middle English metrical romance, found among the Chaucer mss., and supposed to have been intended by him to form the basis of one of the unwritten CANTERBURY TALES. It was formerly attributed to Chaucer and is usually known as *The Coke's [Cook's] Tale of Gamelyn.* Gamelyn is a younger son to whom a large share of property had been bequeathed by the father. He is kept in servitude and tyrannically used by his elder brother until he is old enough effectually to rebel. After many adventures, during which he becomes a leader of outlaws in the woods, he comes to his own again with the help of the king, and justice is meted out to the elder brother and those who aided him. Thomas Lodge made the story into a novel—*Rosalynde, or Euphues' Golden Legacie* (1590)—and from this Shakespeare drew a large part of his AS YOU LIKE IT. The defeat of the wrestler, the loyalty of Adam Spencer, the outlaws, the free life of the greenwood, are common to the *Tale* and the play; and, as has been said, "The *Tale of Gamelyn* is *As You Like It* without Rosalind or Celia."

Gammer Gurton's Needle. The earliest English comedy with the exception of RALPH ROISTER DOISTER. It was first acted at Christ's College, Cambridge, in 1552, and printed in 1575. It was published as "By Mr. S. Mr. of Art," and has been assigned to Bishop Still and with more probability to William Stevenson. The comedy is coarse and vigorous; it closes with the painful but farcical discovery of Gammer Gurton's missing needle in the seat of Hodge's breeches.

Gamp, Sarah (usually called "Sairey"). A disreputable monthly nurse in Dickens' MARTIN CHUZZLEWIT, famous for her bulky umbrella and perpetual reference to Mrs. Harris, a purely imaginary person, whose opinions always confirm her own. She is fond of strong tea and other stimulants.

Hence, "a regular Gamp" came to signify a low-class, drink-sodden, uncertificated maternity nurse, and an umbrella, especially a large, badly rolled cotton one, came to be called a "gamp."

Gamut, David. A Yankee singing teacher in Cooper's LAST OF THE MOHICANS. He is an uncouth and incongruous figure, the butt of many remarks from the scornful Hawkeye, but his simple heroism as he pours out psalm-tune after psalm-tune in the midst of the massacre at Fort William Henry in the attempt to protect Cora and Alice from the Indians, wins even their respect.

Gandercleugh (folly-cliff). That mysterious place where a person makes a goose of himself. Jedediah Cleishbotham, the hypothetical editor of Sir Walter Scott's TALES OF MY LANDLORD, lived at Gandercleugh.

Gandhi, Mohandas Karamchand, called **Mahatma** (great-souled) **Gandhi** (1869–1948). Hindu nationalist leader. Studied law in London, practiced in India. Went to South Africa (1893), where, in support of his defense of Asiatic immigrants, he instituted his first campaign of "passive resistance." Returned to India (1914). Organized the Satyagraha (1919), a politico-religious movement of non-cooperation with the British and was imprisoned for "civil disobedience." President of Indian National Congress (1925). Attended Round Table Conference in London (1931). Urged boycott of British goods (1932) and advocated social reforms. Began his "fast unto death" (1932) in protest against the official treatment of the "untouchables" and won his point after six days. Resigned presidency of Indian National Congress (1934). From 1937 less active but again arrested (1942) for activities against Great Britain. Assassinated (shot) by a Hindu Nationalist, Nathuran Vinaak Godse, at New Delhi, Jan. 30, 1948. Among Gandhi's books are *Indian Home Rule; Young India;* etc. Outstanding among the numerous works on Gandhi is Romain Rolland's *Mahatma Gandhi* (1926).

Ganelon or **Gan.** One of the famous characters of Carolingian legend, a type of black-hearted treachery, figuring in Dante's *Inferno* and grouped by Chaucer (*Nun's Priest's Tale,* 407) with Judas Iscariot and "Greek Sinon, that broghtest Troye al outrely to sorwe." He was Count of Mayence, one of Charlemagne's paladins. Jealousy of Roland made him a traitor; and in order to destroy his rival, he planned with Marsilius, the Moorish king, the attack of Roncesvalles where the Christians were defeated by the Moslems. Sir Ganelon was six feet and a half in height, had large glaring eyes, and fiery red hair. He was very taciturn and morose, and the name has become a byword for a false and faithless friend.

Ganem, the Slave of Love. The hero and title of one of the ARABIAN NIGHTS tales. As a result of accidental curiosity Ganem rescues Fetnab, the caliph's favorite, who has been buried alive by order of the sultana, out of jealousy. When the caliph hears of the incident, he is extremely jealous of the young merchant, and orders him to be put to death. Ganem makes his escape in the guise of a waiter, and lies concealed till the angry fit of the caliph subsides.

Ganesh or **Ganesa.** The god of wisdom or prudence in Hindu mythology. He was the son of Siva and Parvati. He is propitiated at the commencement of important work, at the beginning of sacred writings, etc., and is one of the most popular of all Hindu deities. Ganesh is always represented with an elephant's head.

Ganges. The sacred river of India. Rising in the Himalayas, it flows about 1500 miles to empty into the Bay of Bengal by many mouths. According to Hindu legend its source lies at the feet of Brahma, which makes it imperative for adherents of the Hindu faith to bathe in it on certain days.

gangster. Member of a gang of roughs, hireling criminals, etc. Gangsterism is on the whole restricted to big cities. It flourished during the era of Prohibition in Chicago, New York, etc. Its history is however much older. Cf. Herbert ASBURY, *The Gangs of New York* (1928). The term *gangster* is a colloquial derivative from *gang* on the model of *teamster,* etc.

Gann, Caroline. A prominent character in Thackeray's *Shabby Genteel Story* and its sequel PHILIP.

Gannett, Lewis (1891–). American critic and book-columnist for the New York *Herald Tribune.* Long a combative liberal of the *Nation.* Periodically goes on transcontinental auto trips; after the first of these he wrote *Sweet Land* (1934).

Ganor, Ganora, Geneura, Ginevra, Genievre, Guinevere, Guenever, are different ways of spelling the name of Arthur's wife. She is called by Geoffrey of Monmouth, Guanhumara or Guanhumar, but Tennyson made GUINEVERE the popular English form.

Gant, Eugene. Hero of LOOK HOMEWARD, ANGEL and its sequel, *Of Time and the River,* novels by Thomas WOLFE, considered to represent the author himself. Eugene is a young man of robust energies, intense emotion, a feeling of being "different" from others, and vast, romantic yearnings toward love, adventure, personal achievement, and a semi-mystical, unknown goal which carries him on a virtual pilgrimage through the U.S. and Europe.

Oliver Gant. Eugene's father, a stonecutter of tremendous, sensual passions and a fondness for inflated rhetoric in his speech, sprinkled with quotations from Shakespeare and Milton. He has a great influence on the character of his son.

Eliza Gant. Eugene's mother, frugal, sharp-tongued, exasperated by her husband's irresponsibility. After violent quarrels, she leaves him and goes away with the child Eugene to open a boarding-house.

Ben Gant. Eugene's elder brother, quiet, mature, and dependable, friend and confidant of the younger during their childhood and adolescence. His death is a memorable scene in the first novel.

Steve, Daisy, Helen, and *Luke* are other brothers and sisters of Eugene, all older than he.

Gantry, Elmer. The title hero of a novel by Sinclair LEWIS (1927). A venal evangelist, he represents a definitely American type of religious racketeer. The Rev. L. M. Birkhead of Kansas helped the author with his preparatory research; a minister in Virginia, after reading the book, invited him to visit his state and be lynched.

Ganymede. In Greek mythology, the cup-bearer of Zeus, successor to Hebe, and the type of youthful male beauty. Originally a Trojan youth, he was taken up to Olympus and made immortal. Hence, a cup-bearer generally.

the birds of Ganymede. Eagles. Ganymede rode to Olympus on an eagle's back.

Garagantua. A misspelling of GARGANTUA, originated by Pope in his edition of Shakespeare (*As You Like It,* iii. 2).

Garamond. Name applied to several Roman styles of type going back to that produced about 1540 by the French designer and founder Claude Garamond (died 1561) to replace the Gothic then still in general use.

García Lorca, Federigo, see under LORCA.

Garcias, the soul of Pedro. Money. The story told in the Preface of Le Sage's romance *Gil Blas,* is that two scholars of Salamanca discovered a tombstone with this inscription: "Here lies the soul of the licentiate Pedro Garcias." On searching they found a purse with a hundred golden ducats.

Garcilaso de la Vega (1503–1536). Called "the Spanish Petrarch," poet and soldier. Killed in battle. Wrote pastorals, sonnets, canciones, elegies, and a blank verse epistle. Another **Garcilaso de la Vega** (1539?–1617) was a Peruvian historian writing on the conquest of Peru and the history of the Incas; hence often called **el Inca.**

Garda. Novel of fantasy by Rose O'NEILL.

Garda, Lago di. The largest and one of the most beautiful lakes in Italy. It borders on Tyrol, is 37 miles long, was called *Lacus Benacus* by the Romans, and is noted for its storms.

Gardarike. So Russia is called in the EDDAS.

garden.

Garden City. A name given to Norwich, and to Chicago; also, as a generic name, to model suburbs and townships that have been planned with a special view to the provision of plenty of gardens, open spaces, and wide roads.

the Garden or *Garden Sect.* The disciples of Epicurus, who taught in his own private garden.

the Garden of Eden. See EDEN. The name as applied to Mesopotamia, with its vast sandy deserts, is nowadays somewhat ironical, but it is traditionally supposed to be its "original site."

Garden of Allah. See ALLAH.

Garden of Argentine. Tucuman.

Garden of Cymodoce. In SWINBURNE'S poem of that title, the island of Sark. See also under CYMODOCE.

Garden of England. Kent and Worcestershire are both so called.

Garden of Erin. Carlow.

Garden of Europe. (1) Italy; (2) Belgium.

Garden of France. Amboise, in the department of Indre-et-Loire; also Touraine.

Garden of India. Oude.

Garden of Ireland. Carlow.

Garden of Italy. The island of Sicily.

Garden of South Wales. The southern division of Glamorganshire.

Garden of Switzerland. Thurgau.

Garden of Spain. Andalusia.

Garden of the Gods. A region of about 500 acres near Colorado Springs, U.S., where there are many strange rock formations of red and white sandstones, is so called.

Garden of the Hesperides. See HESPERIDES.

Garden of the Sun. The East Indian or Malayan Archipelago.

Garden of the West. Illinois; Kansas ("the Garden State") is also so called.

Garden of the World. The region of the Mississippi.

Garden, Mary (1877–). Operatic soprano. Debut at Opéra Comique, Paris (1900), as title heroine in *Louise;* in New York (1907) in *Thaïs.* With Chicago Civic Opera Company (from 1910). Chief rôles beside above: Marguerite, Mélisande, Salome, Sappho, Fiora (in *L'Amore dei Tre Re*).

Garden Party, The. A short story by Katherine MANSFIELD, published in 1922. It describes the festive preparations of a well-to-do woman and her daughters for a garden party, and the sudden and violent intrusion of reality in the form of a death by accident which occurs in a neighboring poor family.

Garden State. New Jersey. See under STATES.

Gardner, Erle Stanley (1889–). American detective-story writer. His books have been called "top-notchers in the time-killer division of the mystery field." Most of them have titles beginning *The Case of the—* and feature the lawyer Perry Mason who somewhat resembles the author.

Gareth. In Malory's MORTE D'ARTHUR, the youngest son of Lot, king of Orkney and Morgawse, Arthur's half-sister. His mother, to deter him from entering Arthur's court, says jestingly, she will consent to his doing so if he conceals his name and goes as a scullion for twelve months. To this he agrees and Sir Kay, the king's steward, nicknames him "Beaumains," because his hands are unusually large. At the end of the year he is knighted, and obtains the quest of Linet (Lynette), who begs the aid of some knight to liberate her sister Liones (Lyonors) held prisoner by Sir Ironside in Castle Perilous. Linet treats Sir Gareth with great contempt, calling him a washer of dishes and a kitchen knave, but he overthrows five knights and frees the lady, whom he marries. Tennyson retells the story in *Gareth and Lynette* (*Idylls of the King*), making Gareth the son of Lot and Bellicent, and concluding with his marriage to Lynette instead of her sister:

> He that told the tale in olden times
> Says that Sir Gareth wedded Lyonors;
> But he that told it later says Lynette.

He was the brother of Gahariet, Gawain, and AGRIVAIN, siding with the first two against Agrivain when he decided to betray Launcelot and the queen to King Arthur.

Garfield, James Abram (1831–1881). Twentieth president of the United States. Elected in 1880, inaugurated in 1881, shot by Charles J. Guiteau, a disappointed office-seeker, in the Washington railroad station (July 2, 1881).

Gargamelle. In Rabelais' satire GARGANTUA AND PANTAGRUEL, daughter of the king of the Parpaillons (*butterflies*), wife of Grangousier, and mother of GARGANTUA. On the day that she gives birth to him she eats sixteen quarters, two bushels, three pecks, and a pipkin of *dirt,* the mere remains left in the tripe which she had for supper; for, as the proverb says—

> Scrape tripe as clean as e'er you can,
> A tithe of filth will still remain.

She is said to be meant either for Anne of Brittany, or Catherine de Foix, queen of Navarre.

Gargantua (from Sp. *garganta,* "gullet"). A giant of medieval (perhaps Celtic) legend famous for his enormous appetite, adopted by Rabelais in his great satire *Gargantua and Pantagruel* (1532), and made the father of Pantagruel. One of his exploits is to swallow five pilgrims with their staves and all in a salad. He is the subject of a number of chapbooks, and became proverbial as a voracious and insatiable guzzler.

> You must borrow me Gargantua's mouth first [before I can utter so long a word]; 'tis a word too great for any mouth of this age's size.—Shakespeare, *As You Like It,* iii. 2.

In some cases Rabelais seems to have been satirizing Francis I under this name. According to Rabelais, Gargantua is the son of Gangousier and Gargamelle. Immediately he is born he cries out lustily "Drink, drink!", whereupon his royal father exclaims *"Que grand tu as!"* which, being the first words he uttered after the birth of the child, are accepted as its name. 17,913 cows are needed to supply the babe with milk. When he goes to Paris to finish his education, he rides on a mare as big as six elephants, and takes the bells of Notre Dame to hang on his mare's neck as jingles. After being fired at on his way home he combs his hair with a comb 900 feet long, and at every "rake" seven bullets fall. Many other stories are told of him. In honor of his great victory over Picrochole at the rock Clermond he founds and endows the Abbey of THELEME.

Gargantua's mare. Attempts have been made to identify all the persons, incidents, and even many of the animals mentioned by Rabelais with historical characters, and Gargantua's "great mare" has been held to stand for Mme d'Estampes, and to depict the wilfulness and extravagance of court mistresses. Motteux, Rabelais' earliest English translator, who looks upon the romance as a satire on the Reform party, merely says, "It is some lady." Rabelais says—

"She was as big as six elephants, and had her feet cloven into fingers. She was of a burnt-sorrel hue, with a little mixture of dapple-grey; but, above all, she had a terrible tail, for it was every whit as great as the steeple pillar of St. Mark." When the beast got to Orléans, and the wasps assaulted her, she switched about her tail so furiously that she knocked down all the trees that grew in the vicinity, and Gargantua, delighted, exclaimed, *"Je trouve beau ce!"* wherefore the locality has been called "Beauce" ever since.

Gargantuan. Enormous, inordinate, great beyond all limits. 900 ells of Châtelleraut linen are needed to make the body of Gargantua's shirt, and 200 more for the gussets; for his shoes, 406 ells of blue and crimson velvet are required, and 1100 cow-hides for the soles. He can play 207 different games, picks his teeth with an elephant's tusk, and does everything in the same "large way."

a Gargantuan course of studies. A course including all languages, as well ancient as modern, all the sciences, all the -ologies and -onomies, with calisthenics, athletic sports, etc. etc. etc. so called from Gargantua's famous advice to his son PANTAGRUEL on educational matters.

gargoyle. A grotesquely carved waterspout of the kind projecting from roof gutters and other upper parts of Gothic buildings, especially of the thirteenth to sixteenth centuries. See NOTRE DAME DE PARIS. The word is related to "gargle."

Garibaldi, Giuseppe (1807–1882). Italian patriot. Associated with MAZZINI. Exiled for political reasons (1834), he lived in South America (1836–1848) until the short-lived Roman Republic permitted him to return. After its abolition, he went to the U.S. (1850–1854) where he became naturalized and earned his living as a candle-maker on Staten Island. In the war of Sardinia and France against Austria, he was back in Europe and organized, after its conclusion, an expedition of "Redshirts" against the Two Sicilies in order to bring about a complete union of Italy. He became dictator of Sicily, expelled Francis II from Naples, and, after the union of the Two Sicilies and Sardinia, and the proclamation (1861) of Victor Emmanuel of Sardinia as king of Italy, settled down as a farmer in Caprera. In 1862 and 1867 he undertook unsuccessful expeditions against Rome. In 1870 he commanded a French force in the war against the Prussians and was instrumental in the transfer of the Italian capital from Florence to Rome (1870). Elected deputy for Rome in Italian Parliament (1874). On his statue on the Janiculum overlooking Rome is engraved his famous cry: *Roma o Morte* (Rome or Death)! His son, **Menotti Garibaldi** (1840–1903), born in Brazil, fought with him, entered the Italian Parliament and joined the party of the extreme left. Menotti's brother, **Ricciotti Garibaldi** (1847–1924), born in Uruguay, organized the Garibaldi Legion to fight for France in World War I. He hailed MUSSOLINI's Black Shirts as continuing the tradition of Garibaldi's Redshirts.

Garland, Hannibal Hamlin (1860–1940). American novelist and short-story writer, known for his realistic studies of the hardships and frustrations of Middle Western farm life. His best-known books are *Main-Traveled Roads* (1891), and *Other Main-Traveled Roads* (1910), collections of short stories; and *A Son of the Middle Border* (1917) and *A Daughter of the Middle Border* (1921; winner of the Pulitzer Prize in 1922) (see MIDDLE BORDER), volumes of autobiography. His novels include: *Jason Edwards: An Average Man* (1892), setting forth the single-tax ideas of Henry GEORGE; *A Spoil of Office* (1892), exposing the corruption of politics; *A Member of the Third House* (1892), on railroad lobbying; *A Little Norsk* (1892) and *Rose of Dutcher's Coolly* (1895), dealing with the barren lives of farm girls; *The Captain of the Gray-Horse Troop* (1902), on injustice to the Indian; and *Cavanagh, Forest Ranger* (1910). Garland at the end of his life wrote other volumes of memoirs, rather marred by a querulous self-pity, and books on spiritualism.

Garm: A Hostage. Title of a story by Rudyard Kipling. Garm, in Norse mythology, is Hel's watchdog who, at RAGNAROK, slays, and is slain by, Tyr.

Garnett, David (1892–). English novelist. Son of Edward GARNETT. Started a bookshop in Gerrard Street, Soho, with Francis Birrell, a descendant of Augustine Birrell (1919). Garnett's *Lady Into Fox* (1922) won the Hawthornden Prize and the James Tait Black Memorial Prize. Other pleasant novels followed. Adviser to Francis Meynell on Nonesuch Press for ten years. Flight lieutenant R.A.F.V.R. and staff officer in Intelligence in World War II. Wrote *War in the Air* (1941); etc.

Garnett, Edward (1868–1937). English critic, biographer, and essayist, the best-esteemed publisher's reader in London. His wife, **Constance Garnett** (1862–1946), was renowned for her translations of Dostoevski and other Russian authors.

Garnett, Porter (1871–). American writer and printer. Founded the Laboratory Press at Carnegie Tech. (1923), specializing in hand-press printing.

Garnett, Richard (1835–1906). On staff of British Museum (from 1857). Keeper of Printed Books (1890–1899). Published *Relics of Shelley* (1862); *The Twilight of the Gods* (1888); *History of Italian Literature* (1897); and a number of biographies. His son was Edward GARNETT. His father, **Richard Garnett** (1789–1850), was also on the staff of the British Museum.

Garratt, the mayor of. Garratt is near Earlsfield, Wimbledon; the first "mayor" was elected in 1778. He was really merely the chairman of an association of villagers formed to put a stop to encroachments on the common, and as his election coincided with a general election, the society made it a law that a new "mayor" should be chosen at every general election. The addresses of these mayors, written by Garrick, Wilkes, and others, are satires on the corruption of electors and political squibs. The first mayor of Garratt was "Sir" John Harper, a retailer of brickdust; and the last was "Sir" Harry Dimsdale, muffinseller, in 1796. Foote has a farce entitled *The Mayor of Garratt.*

Garrick, David (1716–1779). English actor. Began his career as a wine merchant. Made reputation in rôle of *Richard III* (Oct. 19, 1741). Continued Shakespearean success. Comanager of Drury Lane Theater (1747). Successful in large repertory. One of the circle around Dr. Samuel JOHNSON. Retired with a considerable fortune to Hampton and wrote comedies and farces and adaptations of older plays.

Garrish, Mr. An ultra-conventional character in Howells' *Annie Kilburn* (1889) and *The Quality of Mercy* (1892), who protests against the modern social ideals of the Rev. Mr. Peck, in the former book, and is in general a champion of the established order.

Garrison, William Lloyd (1805–1879). American leader of the ABOLITIONIST movement, a radical agitator for the immediate freeing of the slaves. He caused a split in the ranks of the Anti-Slavery Society and advocated secession from the Union because the Constitution upheld slavery. In 1831 he founded *The Liberator,* a magazine which he edited until 1865.

Garstin, Crosbie (1877–). English novelist and poet. Author of *The Mud Larks* (1918); *The Coasts of Romance* (1922), *The Owls' House* (1924), *The Ballad of the Royal Ann* (poems; 1922); etc.

Garter, the Most Noble Order of the. The highest order of knighthood in Great Britain and in the world, traditionally instituted by King Edward III about 1348, and later reconstituted in 1805 and 1831. The popular legend is that Joan, Countess of Salisbury, accidentally slipped her garter at a court ball. It was picked up by the king, who gallantly diverted the attention of the guests from the lady by binding the blue band round his own knee, saying as he did so, *"Honi soit qui mal y pense."* The order is limited to the Sovereign, the Prince of Wales, and other members of the Royal Family with twenty-five Knights, and such foreign royalties as may be admitted by statute. Queen Mary and Queen Alexandra were Ladies of the Garter; until, in 1912, Viscount Grey (then Sir Edward Grey) was admitted to the order, no commoner for centuries had been able to put "K.G." after his name.

Garth, Caleb. A builder in George Eliot's MIDDLEMARCH, said to have been drawn, in part at least, from the author's carpenter father.

> A large amount of painful experience had not sufficed to make Caleb Garth cautious about his own affairs or distrustful of his fellow men when they had not proved themselves untrustworthy . . . He was one of those rare men who are rigid to themselves and indulgent to others. He had a certain shame about his neighbor's errors and never spoke of them willingly.—Ch. xxiii.

Mary Garth. Caleb's daughter, who marries Fred Vincy.

> Advancing womanhood had tempered her plainness, which was of a good human sort, such as the mothers of our race have very commonly worn in all latitudes under a more or less becoming headgear. Rembrandt would have painted her with pleasure, and would have made her broad features look out of the canvas with intelligent honesty. For honesty, truth-telling fairness, was Mary's reigning virtue: she neither tried to create illusions, nor indulged in them for her own behoof, and when she was in a good mood, she had humor enough in her to laugh at herself.—Ch. xii.

Garth, Sir **Samuel** (1661–1719). English physician who wrote occasional verse, including mock-heroic *The Dispensary* (1699). Member of the KIT-CAT CLUB.

Gartney, Faith, see FAITH GARTNEY.

Garuda. In Hindu mythology, a supernatural being, half man and half bird, with golden body and red wings, on which VISHNU rides.

Gary Plan or **System.** A system of vocational education which divides the pupil's time between academic studies in school and supervised trade work in actual factories, etc., under normal working conditions; so called from the town of Gary, Ind., where it was first extensively carried out.

Gas, Charlatan. A garrulous and self-important politician in Disraeli's VIVIAN GREY.

Gascoigne, George (1525?–1577). English poet, soldier, and adventurer, one of the leading men of letters in the period before Spenser and after Wyatt and Surrey. His works include: *Supposes* (1566), a translation of a play by Ariosto and the first prose comedy in English; *A Hundred Sundry Flowers* (1573), a collection of poems; *The Glass of Government* (1575), a moral comedy; *Certain Notes of Instruction* (1575), called the earliest treatise on English prosody; *The Steel Glass* (1576), one of the first true satires in English; *The Complaint of Philomene* (1576), a narrative poem; *The Grief of Joy* (1577), a collection of elegies presented to Queen Elizabeth. Gascoigne was the step-father of Nicholas BRETON.

Gascoigne, Sir William (1350?–1419). Lord Chief Justice of England in the reigns of Henry IV and Henry V. Shakespeare introduces him into 2 *Henry IV*. There is a tradition, referred to by Shakespeare, that Prince Hal "struck the chief justice in the open court"; but it does not appear from history that any blow was given. A more likely account is the following:

> One of the gay companions of the prince being committed for felony, the prince demanded his release; but sir William told him the only way of obtaining a release would be to get from the king a free pardon. Prince Henry now tried to rescue the prisoner by force, when the judge ordered him out of court. In a towering fury, the prince flew to the judgment-seat, and all thought he was about to slay the judge; but sir William said very firmly and quietly, "Syr, remember yourselfe. I kepe here the place of the kynge, your sovereigne lorde and father, to whom you owe double obedience; wherefore I charge you in his name to desyste of your wylfulnes. . . . And nowe for your contempte goe you to the prysona of the Kynges Benche, whereunto I commytte you, and remayne ye there prisoner untyll the pleasure of the kynge be further known." With which words, the prince being abashed, the noble prisoner departed and went to the King's Bench.—Sir T. Elyot, *The Governour* (1531).

Gasconade. Talk like that of a Gascon—absurd boasting, vainglorious braggadocio. The Dictionary of the French Academy gives us the following specimen: "A Gascon, in proof of his ancient nobility, asserted that they used in his father's house no other fuel than the bâtons of the family marshals."

Gas House McGinty. Title of a novel by James T. FARRELL (1933).

Gaskell, Elizabeth Cleghorn (1810–1865). English novelist, known for her pictures of English country life and her studies of conflicts between capital and labor in Victorian industrialism. Her works include: MARY BARTON (1848); CRANFORD (1853); *Ruth* (1853); *North and South* (1855); *Life of Charlotte Brontë* (1857); *Wives and Daughters* (1866), left unfinished at her death. She wrote frequently for HOUSEHOLD WORDS.

Gasoline Alley. See SKEEZIX.

Gaspar or **Caspar** (the white one). One of the three MAGI or Kings of Cologne. His offering to the infant Jesus was *frankincense*, in token of divinity.

Gastibelza. The hero of a ballad by Victor HUGO published in his volume *Les Rayons et les ombres* (1840). It tells of the despair of Gastibelza, the "Madman of Toledo" over the treachery of Donna Sabine. It became enormously popular, and an opera, *Gastibelza*, by Maillart, with libretto by Dennery and Corman founded on the ballad, was produced in 1847.

Gaston de Foix, see FOIX, GASTON DE.

gate of horn and ivory gate. In Greek mythology, the two gates of the abode of Sleep through which dreams come forth. Those passing through the gate of horn are true.

Gate of Tears. The passage into the Red Sea. So called by the Arabs (*Bab-el-mandeb*) from the number of shipwrecks that took place there.

Gate of the Lions. The gate leading from the ancient Greek city of Mycenae in Argolis to the acropolis. It is about ten feet high and wide, has monolithic jambs and a huge lintel. Above the lintel is a great slab with a relief of two affronted rampant lions which account for the name. It was built in the Mycenaean era (1400–1100 B. C.).

Gates, Eleanor (1875–). American playwright. *Poor Little Rich Girl* (1913; play and novel); etc.

Gates, Horatio (1728?–1806). American revolutionary general. Repulsed Burgoyne's army from the North. Lost disastrous battle of Camden. Served Washington loyally.

Gath. In Dryden's ABSALOM AND ACHITOPHEL, it means Brussels, where Charles II long resided while in exile.

> Had thus old David [Charles II] . . .
> Not dared, when fortune called him, to be king,
> At Gath an exile he might still remain

tell it not in Gath. Don't let your enemies

hear it. Gath was famous as being the birthplace of the giant Goliath.

Tell it not in Gath, publish it not in the streets of Askelon; lest the daughters of the Philistines rejoice, lest the daughters of the uncircumcised triumph.—2 *Sam.* i. 20.

Gatti-Casazza, Giulio (1869–1940). Italian-born operatic manager. Director of the SCALA at Milan (1898–1908) and General Manager of the Metropolitan Opera House in New York (1908–1935). Married Frances Alda (divorced); second wife, Rosina Galli.

Gatty, Harold (1903–). With Wiley Post, flew around the world as navigator in the monoplane *Winnie May* (1931) in 8 days, 15 hours, 51 minutes. Wrote *The Raft Book; Lore of Sea and Sky* (1943); issued in envelope with folded chart and folded "date and time tape," for the benefit of flyers or others lost at sea.

Gaucho. A cowboy or herdsman of the pampas, of mixed Spanish and Indian descent. Cf. the Argentinian epic, *The Departure of Martin Fierro,* by José Hernández, translated by Walter Owen. The word is probably of Araucan origin.

gaudeamus ("Let us rejoice"). Title and first word of a Latin student song of German origin and popular in the U.S. Original version 1267; present version 1781.

Gaudier-Brzeska, Henri (1891–1915). French sculptor. Identified with the post-impressionist movement known as vorticism, the theory of which calls for the exploitation on the part of the artist of the aesthetic potentialities of modern machines.

Gauguin, Eugène Henri Paul (1848–1903). French painter. Cofounder of the symbolist school of Pont-Aveu. Went to Tahiti (1890) and painted brilliantly native types and scenes. Cf. *The Moon and Sixpence* (1919) by W. Somerset Maugham for a fictionized version of his life.

Gaul. In classical geography, the country inhabited by the Gauls; hence, in modern use, France. *Cisalpine Gaul* lay south and east of the Alps, in what is now northern Italy. *Transalpine Gaul* was north and northwest of the Alps, and included Narbonensis, Aquitania, Lugdunensis, and Belgica. It was inhabited by Franks, Germans, Burgundians, etc., and Celts, as well as by Gauls.

Insulting Gaul has roused the world to war.
Thomson, *Autumn.*

Shall haughty Gaul invasion threat?—Burns.

Gaumont, Léon Ernest (1864–). French motion-picture inventor; introduced sound and color. Gaumont films named for him.

Gaunt, Griffith, see GRIFFITH GAUNT.

Gaunt, John of, see JOHN OF GAUNT.

Gauntlet, to run the. To be attacked on all sides, to be severely criticized. The word came into English at the time of the Thirty Years' War as *gantlope,* meaning the passage between two files of soldiers, and is the Swedish *gata,* a way, passage and *lopp* (connected with our *leap*), a course. The reference is to a punishment formerly common among soldiers and sailors; the company or crew, provided with rope ends, were drawn up in two rows facing each other, and the delinquent had to run between them, while every man dealt him as severe a chastisement as he could.

to throw down the gauntlet. To challenge. The custom in the Middle Ages, when one knight challenged another, was for the challenger to throw his gauntlet on the ground, and if the challenge was accepted the person to whom it was thrown picked it up.

Gauss, Christian (1878–). Dean of Princeton (since 1925). Writer on educational subjects.

Gautama. The family name of BUDDHA. His personal name was Siddhartha, his father's name Suddhodana, and his mother's Maya. *Buddha* means "The Enlightened," "The One Who Knows," and he assumed this title at about the age of 36, when, after seven years of seclusion and spiritual struggle, he believed himself to have attained to perfect truth.

Gauthier, Marguerite. Heroine of the novel *La Dame aux Camélias* (novel 1848; play 1852) by Dumas *fils,* dramatized in France under the same title and in America as CAMILLE.

Gautier, Théophile (1811–1872). French poet and novelist, known for the pictorial and jewel-like effects of his later poems, and the fantasy and *macabre* quality of his prose tales and early poems. In the morbidity and violence of the latter he has been compared to Baudelaire, and in the sense of perfection of form in the former he has been compared to the PARNASSIANS. Gautier's poetry includes: *Poésies* (1830); *Albertus* (1832), a fantastic narrative poem; *La Comédie de la Mort* (1833), another long poem, dealing with the sensual and the ideal; and *Emaux et Camées* (1852), considered the best example of his pure, minutely chiseled style. Among his novels and tales are: *Les Jeunes France* (1833); MLLE. DE MAUPIN (1835); *La Jettatura* (1856); CAPTAIN FRACASSE (1861–1863). Gautier was one of the first official exponents of the doctrine of *l'art pour l'art* ("ART FOR ART'S SAKE"). He studied painting early in his career and applied its methods of observation to his poetry. See also GONCOURT BROTHERS.

Gautier et Garguille. A proverbial expression in France for "all the world and his wife."

Gauvain. A character in Victor Hugo's NINETY-THREE.

Gauvaine. The French form of the name GAWAIN.

Gavarni. Pseudonym of **Sulpice Guillaume Chevalier** (1804–1866). French illustrator and caricaturist. Best known for his studies of social contrasts between extreme luxury and poverty of Parisian life in *L'Illustration*.

Gavroche. In Victor Hugo's LES MISÉRABLES, a happy-go-lucky little Parisian street Arab who gives a good account of himself in the fighting on the Day of the Barricades and goes gaily to meet his death.

Gawain. One of the most famous of the Arthurian knights, nephew of King Arthur, and probably the original hero of the Grail quest. He appears in the Welsh *Triads* and the MABINOGION as Gwalchmei, and in the Arthurian cycle is the center of many episodes and poems. He is known as "the Courteous" and is first represented as the flower of chivalrous knighthood, but later writers (including Malory in his *Morte d'Arthur*) degraded him, probably on account of his connection with the Grail and to leave the literary field clear for Percival, until Tennyson, in *The Passing of Arthur,* makes Sir Bedivere brand him as "light in life and light in death." The Middle English poem (about 1360), *Sir Gawain and the Green Knight,* is a weird romance telling how Gawain beheads the Green Knight in single combat after having promised to meet him for a return stroke twelve months later at the Green Chapel. On the appointed day Gawain is there, and so is the Green Knight: Gawain's honor is, by arrangement, severely but successfully tested by the wife of the knight, and as he has proved himself true he escapes unharmed.

Gawrey. In Pultock's PETER WILKINS, a flying woman, whose wings served the double purpose of flying and dress. Youwarkee, the heroine, is one of these strange beings.

gay.

a gay deceiver. A LOTHARIO; a libertine.

> I immediately quitted the precincts of the castle, and posted myself on the high road, where the gay deceiver was sure to be intercepted on his return.—Le Sage, *Gil Blas,* vii, i, 3 (*Smollett's translation,* 1749).

the Gay Science. A translation of *gai saber,* the old Provençal name for the art of poetry. See also COURTLY LOVE; TROUBADORS. E. S. Dallas used it (1866) as the title for a treatise on Criticism. In explanation he says:

> Why the Gay Science, however? The light-hearted minstrels of Provence insisted on the joyfulness of their art. . . . Neither need anyone be repelled if this doctrine of pleasure strike the key-note, and suggest the title of the present work, in which an attempt will be made to show that a science of criticism is possible, and that it must of necessity be the science of the laws of pleasure, the joy science, the Gay Science.—*Preface.*

A guild formed at Toulouse in 1323 with the object of keeping in existence the dying Provençal language and culture was called the *Gai Saber.* Its full title was "The Very Gay Company of the Seven Troubadors of Toulouse."

Gay, John (1688–1732). English poet and playwright, a friend of POPE, known for his sprightly satire and contemporary realism, especially in his treatments of city life. Among his works are: *Rural Sports* (1713), a poem dedicated to Pope; *The Shepherd's Week* (1714), six pastorals parodying the artificial literary pastorals of Ambrose Philips; TRIVIA, OR THE ART OF WALKING THE STREETS OF LONDON (1716), a long poem picturing life in 18th-century London; *Poems on Several Occasions* (1720); THE BEGGAR'S OPERA (1728), a forerunner of the 20th-century musical-comedy form and Gay's best-known work, satirizing Sir Robert Walpole, British prime minister of the time, and the court of George II; and *Polly* (1729), a sequel to *The Beggar's Opera,* suppressed because of its political satire.

Gay, Walter. In Dickens' novel DOMBEY AND SON, a member of the firm of that name, an honest, frank, ingenuous youth, who loves Florence Dombey, and comforts her in her early troubles. Walter Gay is sent in the merchantman called *The Son and Heir,* as junior partner, to the Barbadoes, and survives a shipwreck. After his return from the Barbadoes, he marries Florence.

Gayarré, Charles Étienne Arthur (1805–1895). New Orleans lawyer and historian of Louisiana, writing both French and English.

Gayda, Virginio (1885–1944). Italian journalist; as director of the *Giornale d'Italia* (1926–1944), the mouthpiece of Italian Fascism.

Gaylord, Marcia. The heroine of Howells' MODERN INSTANCE. Her father, **Squire Gaylord,** is a prominent character in the same novel.

Gay Lord Quex, The. A drama by PINERO (1899). The hero, Lord Quex, is about to reform and settle down with the charming heroine Muriel, but he must first lay numerous ghosts. The plot centers about the effort of Sophie Fullgarney, Muriel's foster sister, to save her from Quex. She fails, or rather is convinced of his sincerity at last.

Gay-Lussac, Joseph Louis (1778–1850). French scientist. Made first balloon ascent for scientific investigation (1804). Discovered hydrosulphuric and oxychloride acids. His name remains associated with Gay-Lussac's law which he enunciated regarding the proportions in which gases combine.

gazogene. A portable apparatus for making gases, used to carbonate liquids, etc. Cf. the stories of Sherlock HOLMES, where the gasogene and tantalus are often in use.

Ge or **Gaea.** In Greek mythology, the personification of the Earth. She sprang from Chaos and gave birth to Uranus (Heaven) and Pontus (Sea). She is identified with the Roman Tellus.

Geb. In Egyptian religion, the father of Osiris. He is the god of the earth and is represented in human form with a goose on his head.

Geber or **Jabir** (*Arab.*, **Jābir ibn-Hayyān**) (*fl.* 721–776). An Arabian alchemist, born at Thous, in Persia. He wrote several treatises on the "art of making gold," in the usual mystical jargon of the period; hence, by imitation of his name, our word *gibberish* (senseless jargon).

> This art the Arabian Geber taught . . .
> The Elixir of Perpetual Youth
> Longfellow, *The Golden Legend.*

Gebir. A narrative poem by Walter Savage LANDOR (1797). The hero, Gebir, ruler of Iberia, has sworn to avenge ancient wrongs by conquering Egypt, but he falls madly in love with the enemy queen, Charoba. On the day of his marriage to her, he is killed by a poisoned shirt. See also *Nessus*. Throughout the poem the warlike Gebir is in sharp contrast with his peaceful shepherd brother Tamar.

Geddes, Norman Bel (1893–). American stage designer and architect. Remembered chiefly for his work for the Metropolitan Opera Company in New York. As an industrial designer he was largely responsible for the popularization of streamlined furniture and utensils.

Geddes, Sir Patrick (1854–1932). Scottish biologist and sociologist. Once HUXLEY's assistant. Has been called "one of the fathers of modern geography, and of much in modern psychology and biology." Lewis MUMFORD was among his students. Cf. A. D. Defries, *Pioneers of Science.*

Geddes, Virgil (1897–). American playwright and poet. First play produced in New York, *The Earth Between*, by Provincetown Players (1929) with Bette Davis (her first appearance). Directed Brookfield Players. Many of his plays have caused considerable controversy, notably *Native Ground* (1932) with its theme of incest.

Gedye, George Eric Rowe (1890–). English journalist. *Betrayal in Central Europe* (1939), etc.

geese. For the legend of *Rome saved by geese*, see under GOOSE.

Gehenna. The place of eternal torment. Strictly speaking, it means simply the Valley of Hinnom (*Ge-Hinnom*), where sacrifices to Baal and Moloch were offered (*Jer.* xix. 6, etc.), and where refuse of all sorts was subsequently cast, for the consumption of which fires were kept constantly burning.

> And made his grove
> The pleasant valley of Hinnom, Tophet thence
> And black Gehenna called, the type of hell.
> Milton, *Paradise Lost*, Bk. i, 403.

Geierstein, Anne of, see ANNE OF GEIERSTEIN.

Geijerstam, Gösta af (1888–). Swedish novelist and painter. Settled in Norway (since 1906). Stories of Norwegian family life.

Geisel, Theodor Seuss. Pseudonym **Dr. Seuss** (1904–). American comic draughtsman and writer and illustrator of humorous children's books. *The Seven Lady Godivas* (1939); etc.

geisha. A Japanese professional singing and dancing girl. Hence, especially in Western misconception, a licensed prostitute.

Gelert. Llewellyn's dog. See BETH GELERT.

Gellatly, Davie. In Scott's WAVERLEY, the idiot servant of the Baron of Bradwardine, described as "a crack-brained knave, who could execute very well any commission which jumped with his own humor, and made his folly a plea for avoiding every other."

Gemara (*Aramaic,* "complement"). The second part of the TALMUD, consisting of annotations, discussions, and amplifications of the *Mishna,* which is the first part. The *Mishna* is the interpretation of the written law, the *Gemara* the interpretation of the *Mishna.* There is the Babylonian *Gemara* and the Jerusalem *Gemara.* The former, which is the more complete, is by the academies of Babylon, and was completed about 500 A. D.; the latter is written by those of Palestine, completed toward the close of the 4th or during the 5th century A. D.

Gemini (the twins). CASTOR AND POLLUX; the name of a constellation.

Gemmagog. According to Rabelais in GARGANTUA AND PANTAGRUEL (Bk. ii, ch. i), son of the giant Oromedon, and inventor of the Poulan shoes—i.e., shoes with a spur behind, and turned-up toes fastened to the knees. These shoes were forbidden by Charles V of France in 1365, but the fashion revived again.

The same authority says giants were great inventors: Erix invented tricks of thimble-rigging; Gabara, drinking healths; Hapmouche, drying and smoking neats' tongues; Morgan "was the first in this World who played at Dice with Spectacles"; Galehault, the inventor of flagons; etc. etc. They were all direct ancestors of Gargantua and Pantagruel.

General, Mrs. In Dickens' LITTLE DORRIT, the widow who teaches Little Dorrit, among other matters of etiquette, to say Papa, prunes and prisms. She explains—

"Father is rather vulgar, my dear. The word Papa, besides, gives a pretty form to the lips. Papa, potatoes, poultry, prunes and prism are all very good words for the lips, especially prunes and prism. You will find it serviceable in the formation of a demeanor if you sometimes say to yourself in Company—on entering a room, for instance—Papa, potatoes, poultry, prunes and prism, prunes and prisms."

General William Booth Enters Into Heaven. A poem by Vachel LINDSAY, published in 1913. It is written in the rhythm of drum-beats as sounded by a Salvation Army band and, meant to be sung to the music of *Washed in the Blood of the Lamb,* the Salvation Army hymn, it describes the triumphant entry of General William BOOTH into Paradise.

Genesee Fever. Title of a novel by Carl CARMER (1941).

Genesis. The Greek name for the first book of the Old Testament. The Jews call it "In the beginning," from the first words.

Genêt, Edmond Charles Édouard (1763–1834). French diplomat in U.S. Endeavored to draw U.S. into France's war against Great Britain and Spain. Attacked Washington for his policy of neutrality. Sought to force the President to change his attitude by popular agitation and commissioned privateers in American ports to prey upon British commerce. Superseded at Washington's request but stayed in U.S. and became naturalized American citizen. Known as "Citizen Genêt." Janet Flanner, American journalist, signs her work Genêt.

Geneva. The capital of the Swiss canton of Geneva. Center of the Reformation under CALVIN (1536–1564). Birthplace of Jean Jacques ROUSSEAU. Seat of the LEAGUE OF NATIONS after World War I.

Geneva bands. See BANDS.

the Geneva Bible. See BIBLE, THE ENGLISH.

the Geneva bull. A nickname given to Stephen Marshall (d. 1655), a Presbyterian divine, and one of the authors of *Smectymnuus,* because he was a disciple of John Calvin of Geneva, and, when preaching, roared like a "bull of Bashan."

Geneva convention. An agreement made by the European powers at Geneva (1864; supplemented 1868), establishing humane regulations for the treatment of disabled soldiers in war. Revised and brought into accord with modern methods of warfare (1906). Now ratified by almost every country.

Geneva courage. Pot valor; the braggadocio which is the effect of having drunk too much gin, or geneva. See also DUTCH COURAGE. The word *Geneva,* punning on Calvinism and gin, is frequent in old allusions to drink. Thus Scott has:

"You have been reading Geneva print this morning already."
"I have been reading the Litany," said John, shaking his head with a look of drunken gravity.
Old Mortality, ch. xi.

Geneva Cross. See RED CROSS.

Geneva doctrines. Calvinism.

Geneva gown. Loose, black gown introduced as a vestment for preaching by the Calvinists and adopted by many other protestant denominations.

Genevieve. A ballad by Coleridge and also the name of the heroine in his poem *Love.*

And so I won my Genevieve
My bright and beauteous bride.

Geneviève, see GENOVEFA; also under SAINTS.

Genghis Khan (1167–1227). Mongol conqueror. He plundered northern India and subdued what is now Iran, Iraq, and part of Russia. A military genius. His original name was **Temujin.** His surname signifies "the greatest lord." One of his descendants was TAMERLANE.

Génie du Christianisme, Le (*The Genius of Christianity*). A book of criticism by CHATEAUBRIAND (1802), considered to mark a revolution in critical literary taste in France, since it is unfriendly to the 18th-century tradition, chooses the Middle Ages over the Renaissance, establishes the individual "self" as the source of artistic inspiration, and exalts Christianity as the great force for developing the soul of man. This book is regarded as the origin of the "aesthetic" view of religion that dominated French literature in the later 19th century.

genii or **ginn,** see JINN.

Genius (pl., Genii). In Roman mythology the tutelary spirits that attended one from his cradle to his grave, and that governed his fortunes, determined his character, and so on. The Eastern genii were the JINN, entirely different from the Roman, not guardian or attendant spirits, but fallen angels, dwelling in Djinnistan, under the dominion of Eblis. The Roman were very similar to the guardian angels spoken of in *Matt.* xviii. 10, and in this sense Mephistopheles is spoken of as the *evil genius* (the "familiar" of Faust.) The Romans maintained that two genii attended every man from birth to death—one good and the other evil. Good luck was brought about by the agency of his "good genius," and ill luck by that of his "evil genius."

"Genius," The. A novel by Theodore DREISER (1915), relating the numerous love affairs of an artist, Eugene Witla, who attains some note as an illustrator and some fortune as a director of advertising art. His marriage to Angela is one incident in his amatory life.

Genji, The Tale of. See Murasaki.

Gennaro. In Donizetti's opera, Lucrezia Borgia, the natural son of Lucrezia Borgia before her marriage with Alfonso, Duke of Ferrara.

Genovefa. The heroine of an old German folk-tale, which relates that she was the wife of a Count Palatine Siegfried of Brabant, in the time of Charles Martel. Being suspected of infidelity, she is driven into the forest of Ardennes, where she gives birth to a son, who is nourished by a white doe. In time, Siegfried discovers his error, and restores his wife and child to their home. The name is another form of Geneviève or Genevieve.

genre painter. A painter of domestic, rural, or village scenes, such as *A Village Wedding, The Young Recruit, Blind Man's Buff, The Village Politician,* etc. Wilkie, Ostade, Gerard, Dow, Pieter de Hooch, Jan Steen, Franz Hals, and, on occasion, Rembrandt and Vermeer, belonged to this class. In the drama, Victor Hugo introduced the genre system in lieu of the stilted, unnatural style of Louis XIV's era.

Genseric or Gaiseric (d. 477 A. D.) King of the Vandals of Arian creed. Invaded Africa from Spain (429). Captured Carthage and made it his capital. The town of Hippo fell into his hands a few days after the death of St. Augustine. Sacked Rome (455).

Genteel Tradition, The. Term applied to a group of American writers and men of letters of the latter part of the 19th century whose literary standards were correct and conventional, tending toward the academic, and whose poetry was for the most part correct and conventional also, sentimental, and far removed from the contemporary American scene. Leading representatives of the Genteel Tradition were: Richard Henry Stoddard, Bayard Taylor, Edmund Clarence Stedman, Thomas Bailey Aldrich, and Edward Rowland Sill.

Gentle Craft, The. A tale by Thomas Deloney (1597), in which he celebrates shoemakers and their craft. Part I deals with St. Hugh, the patron saint of cobblers, and St. Winifred (see under Saint). Part II tells of St. Crispin (see under Saint) and St. Crispinian, also patron saints of cobblers. Part III, the best-known section of the story, gives an account of the life of Simon Eyre, the shoemaker Lord Mayor of London.

Gentle Grafter, The. A volume of short stories by O. Henry.

Gentleman from Indiana, The. A novel by Booth Tarkington (1899). The hero is John Harkless, the young editor of a country newspaper in Indiana. His courageous struggles, particularly against the lawless White Caps, bring him enemies, and when he vanishes after an attack upon him, he is given up for dead. However, he reappears, and the novel ends with his marriage to the charming girl who has run his paper in his absence and so made possible his nomination to Congress.

Gentleman Usher of the Black Rod. See Black Rod.

Gentleman's Magazine, The. An English periodical, founded in 1731, the first to call itself a "magazine" in the later widespread sense. Samuel Johnson at one time was a regular contributor. The publication was issued until 1914.

Gentlemen Prefer Blondes. A best-selling novel by Anita Loos (1925), satirizing the "flappers" and "gold-diggers" of the Jazz Age.

Gentle Shepherd, The. The title and chief character of a pastoral drama by Allan Ramsay (1725).

Geoffrey of Monmouth (1100?–1154) Medieval English historian, believed to have been a churchman of the Benedictine order. He is famous for his *History of the Kings of Britain* (*Historia Regum Britanniae*), an important source of the legend of King Arthur. He is considered to be the creator of the heroic characteristics of Arthur, and to have used his imagination liberally in his history, "Nennius," the source he acknowledges, being regarded as a fictional name.

geopolitics (from German *Geopolitik*). A science dealing with the significance of geographical factors for the attitude of a people in domestic and foreign policies. See Haushofer.

George.

let George do it. A popular phrase meaning "Let somebody else do it." The allusion is to a popular comic supplement feature of that title by the American cartoonist George McManus.

as good as George-a-Green. Resolute minded; one who will do his duty come what may. George-a-Green was the mythical *Pinder* (Pinner or Pindar) or pound-keeper of Wakefield, who resisted Robin Hood, Will Scarlet and Little John single-handed when they attempted to commit a trespass in Wakefield.

> Were ye bold as George-a-Green,
> I shall make bold to turn again.
>
> Butler, *Hudibras*

Robert Greene wrote a comedy (published 1599) called *George-a-Greene, or the Pinner of Wakefield.*

George, Henry (1839–1897). American writer and lecturer on political economy known for his study of the problems of pov erty and his attempts at remedy, a field in which he was one of the first leaders to arise in the U.S. His most famous theory is that of the "single tax," or a tax on land, which was the most important form of wealth in his day, set forth most persuasively in *Progress and Poverty* (1879). Other works are: *The Irish Land Question* (1881); *Social Problems* (1884); *Protection and Free Trade* (1886); *Science of Political Economy* (1897). The FABIAN SOCIETY in England and the later movements for economic reform in the U.S. were influenced by George's theories.

George, St., see under SAINTS.

George, Stefan Anton (1868–1933). German poet; the "embodiment of Roman culture on Rhenish soil." Master of all Latin tongues; associate or translator of the French symbolists in MALLARMÉ's group and the Pre-Raphaelites of England. From neo-romantic beginnings his poetry, in content and form, developed more and more toward a "rigidly exclusive, static, and statuelike classicism." In his conception the poet is the priest and prophet of his nation while of necessity his "heroic virility" removes him from all possible contact with the masses. All attempts to translate George's poems have failed. His work is extremely difficult of access and is made more so by artifices of spelling, punctuation, and typography. It has never been widely read or understood, but its influence has been tremendous due to the immediate and mediate members of his group. George has been called a "Napoleon at the court of the Muses."

George, Walter Lionel (1882–1926). English novelist, born and reared in France. Immediate success of his first novel, *A Bed of Roses* (1911). His work has great vitality. *The Second Blooming* (1914), *The Strangers' Wedding* (1916), etc. He has been characterized as having "wit but no humor, conscience but no taste," but was a genuine liberal.

George Dandin. A comedy by MOLIÈRE (1668). The principal character, George Dandin, is a rich French tradesman, who marries Angelique, the daughter of M. de Sotenville, and has the "privilege" of paying off the family debts, maintaining his wife's noble parents and being snubbed on all occasions to his heart's content. He constantly said to himself, in self-rebuke, *"Vous l'avez voulu, vous l'avez voulu, George Dandin!"* (You have no one to blame but yourself! you brought it on yourself, George Dandin!) Hence his name is used with reference to one who brings trouble upon his own head; also to one who marries above his station.

George Junior Republic. An industrial community under a form of self-government founded near Ithaca, N.Y., by the American businessman and philanthropist William Reuben George (1866–1933), designed to give delinquent and neglected children a chance to prove their worth in a wholesome environment.

Georgianna. (1) The heroine of James Lane Allen's KENTUCKY CARDINAL and its sequel *Aftermath.*

(2) Heroine of Hawthorne's tale THE BIRTHMARK.

Geraint. In Arthurian legend, a tributary prince of Devon, and one of the knights of the Round Table. In the MABINOGION story he is the son of Erbin, as he is in the French original, Chrestien de Troyes' *Eric et Enide,* from which Tennyson drew his *Geraint and Enid* in the *Idylls of the King.* In the latter, Geraint, overhearing part of Enid's words, fancied she was faithless to him and treated her for a time very harshly; but Enid nursed him so carefully when he was wounded that he saw his error, "nor did he doubt her more, but rested in her fealty, till he crowned a happy life with a fair death."

Gerald, a Portrait. By Daphne DU MAURIER (1934). A biography of her father, the noted actor Sir Gerald du Maurier (1873–1934).

Geraldine, the Fair. Lady Elizabeth Fitzgerald (d. 1589) is so called in the Earl of Surrey's poems. She was the youngest daughter of the Earl of Kildare.

Lady Geraldine's Courtship. A poem by Mrs. Browning (1844). The lady falls in love with a peasant-poet, whom she marries.

Gerard. The father of Erasmus, whose love story is told in Charles Reade's CLOISTER AND THE HEARTH.

Gerard, Brigadier. An egotistical, swashbuckling, braggart Napoleonic soldier, hero of a series of tales (1896) by Sir Arthur Conan DOYLE.

Gerda, Gerdr, or **Gerdhr.** In Scandinavian mythology (the *Skírnismál*), a young giantess, wife of Frey, and daughter of the frost giant Gymer. She is so beautiful that the brightness of her naked arms illumines both air and sea. According to the myth, Frey (the god of fruitfulness) married Gerda (the frozen earth), and she became the mother of children.

Gerhardi, William Alexander (1895–). English novelist and short-story writer. Born in St. Petersburg, Russia. Military attaché at British embassy in Petrograd (1917–1918). Observed Russian Revolution and Allied Intervention at first-hand. Wrote Chekhov's biography. Has a strong vein of satire. *Futility* (1922); *The Polyglots* (1925); *The Romanovs* (1939).

Germ, The. A "little magazine" published by the PRE-RAPHAELITE BROTHERHOOD from January to April, 1850. It contained expositions of the Brotherhood's artistic ideas, poems, and reproductions of their paintings. Its subtitle was *Thoughts Towards Nature in Poetry, Literature, and Art.*

Germanicus Caesar (15 B.C.–19 A.D.). Roman general; nephew and adopted son of Emperor Tiberius. Father of Emperor Caligula and, by his daughter Agrippina, grandfather of Nero. In his campaign against the Germans (11–16 A.D.) he defeated ARMINIUS but was recalled through the emperor's jealousy.

Germinal. A novel by Emile ZOLA, published in 1885. It is a study of workers in the French mines.

Germinie Lacerteux. A novel by the GONCOURT brothers, published in 1869, and considered the first representative of NATURALISM to deal with the more sordid aspects of life. It was based on the life of the Goncourts' own servant.

Gerolstein, Rudolph, Grand Duke of. In Eugene Sue's MYSTERIES OF PARIS a powerful young prince who loves to go about "playing Providence" in disguise, meting out punishment, as well as rewards where he believes they are most fitting.

Gérôme, Jean Léon (1824–1904). French historical painter in the classical manner. Student of Paul DELAROCHE. Professor at École des Beaux-Arts, Paris (1863).

Geronimo. Indian name **Goyathlay,** "One Who Yawns" (1829–1909). American Apache chieftain. Led sensational campaign of the Chiricahua band against the whites (1885–1886). Captured by General Cook. Escaped, was recaptured, settled at Fort Sill, and later became a member of the Dutch Reformed Church (1903). Dictated the story of his life (1906).

Géronte. (1) In Molière's *Médécin Malgré Lui,* the father of LUCINDE. (2) In Molière's *Fourberies de Scapin,* father of Léandre and Hyacinthe. See SCAPIN. The name is common in French comedy as that of a father of a family.

Gerontius, The Dream of. A poem by Cardinal NEWMAN in which Gerontius makes his last journey to God, carried by his guardian angel through a world of good and evil spirits. *The Dream of Gerontius* has been set to music in the form of an oratorio by Sir Edward ELGAR (1900).

Gerould, Katharine Fullerton (1879–1944). American novelist, essayist, and short-story writer, wife of G. H. Gerould. "A fictional artist of subtle power and distinguished skill" (especially in *Vain Oblations*), also, sometimes, accused of snobbishness.

gerrymander. So to divide a county or nation into representative districts as to give one special political party undue advantage over others. The word is derived from Elbridge Gerry, who adopted the scheme in Massachusetts when he was governor. Gilbert Stuart, the artist, looking at the map of the new distribution, with a little invention converted it into a salamander. "No, no!" said Russell, when shown it, "not a Salamander, Stuart, call it a Gerry-mander."

Hence, to *gerrymander* means also to hocus-pocus statistics, election results, etc., so as to make them appear to give other than their true result, or so as to affect the balance.

Gershwin, George (1898–1937). American composer, often associated with the development of JAZZ, especially in symphonic orchestration. *Rhapsody in Blue* (1923); *Piano Concerto in F* (1925). His musical comedy, *Of Thee I Sing* (1931), was awarded the Pulitzer Prize. His brother **Ira Gershwin** (1896–) wrote the lyrics for many of his musical comedies. His most ambitious score was that for the folk-opera *Porgy and Bess* (for which Du Bose HEYWARD wrote the book based on his play PORGY).

Gerson, Jean (1363–1429). French theologian and court preacher to Charles VI, known for his sermons in French and Latin. He was one of the leading opponents of the *Romance of the Rose* (see under ROSE), which he condemned to be burned (1399) as a threat to morality. In 1402 he wrote an allegorical "vision," *Tractatus contra Romantium de Rosa,* attacking it.

Gertrude. In Shakespeare's HAMLET Hamlet's mother. In SAXO GRAMMATICUS she is called Geruth.

Gertrude of Wyoming. A poem by Thomas CAMPBELL (1809). The setting is in the wilds of the Wyoming Valley in Pennsylvania. The heroine, Gertrude, is the daughter of the patriarch Albert; the hero is Henry Waldegrave, who as a boy spends three years in the patriarch's home and later returns to marry Gertrude. The settlement is attacked by a mixed army of Indians and British and both Albert and Gertrude are shot. Henry then joins the army of Washington.

Gertrude, St. See under SAINTS.

Gerund or **Gerundio, Friar.** Hero of a satirical romance, *Fray Gerundio de Campazas* (*Sp.,* 1758), ridiculing the wandering friars of Spain and their pretentious sermons.

Gervaise. One of the principal characters in the novels of Zola's ROUGON MACQUART series.

Geryon. In Greek mythology, a monster with three bodies and three heads, whose oxen ate human flesh, and were guarded by Orthros, a two-headed dog. Hercules slew both Geryon and the dog.

Geryoneo. In Spenser's FAËRIE QUEENE (V. xi), a giant with three bodies typifying Philip II of Spain (master of three kingdoms), the Spanish rule in the Netherlands, or sometimes the Inquisition. He is the son of Geryon.

Gesmas. The impenitent thief crucified with our Lord. In the apocryphal *Gospel of Nicodemus,* he is called Gestas. The penitent thief was Dismas, Dysmas, Demas, or Dumacus.

Gessler. The tyrannical Austrian governor of the three forest cantons of Switzerland who figures in the WILLIAM TELL legend.

Gestalt psychology. The term is an adaptation of Ger. *Gestaltpsychologie,* which is often rendered more literally as "configuration psychology." The basic principle of *Gestalt* psychology, as developed by Kurt Koffka (1886–1941), Wolfgang Köhler (1887–), and others, maintains that perception and memory are always concerned with "wholes" which determine the significance of their "parts." In a naïve formula: Salt in soup is not just salt. In other words: A whole is more than the sum of its parts.

Gestapo. Abbreviated from Ger. *Geheime Staatspolizei,* "secret state police." Organized under the Nazi régime for operation particularly against political offenders; corresponded to the Russian CHEKA and Gay-Pay-Oo.

Gesta Romanorum. A pseudo-devotional compilation of popular tales in Latin (many from Oriental sources), each with an arbitrary "moral" attached for the use of preachers, assigned—in its collected form—to about the end of the 14th century. The name, meaning "The Acts of the Romans," is merely fanciful. It was first printed at Utrecht about 1472. Shakespeare drew the plot of PERICLES from the *Gesta Romanorum,* as well as the incident of the three caskets in the MERCHANT OF VENICE; and many other English poets, from CHAUCER to William MORRIS, have drawn material from it.

Gestas. The traditional name of the impenitent thief. See DYSMAS.

Gettysburg Address. President Lincoln's address (Nov. 19, 1863) at the dedication of the National Cemetery at Gettysburg, Pa. It has been called "the only great prose poem of classical perfection in modern English." Cf. also *The Perfect Tribute* (1906), a "sentimental footnote to history" by Mary Raymond Shipman Andrews.

Gezelle, Guido (1830–1899). The mystical poet of Flanders who has been called "the soul of Flanders, a natural and a national poet."

Ghent, Stephen. The hero of Moody's drama THE GREAT DIVIDE.

ghetto. The Jewish quarter of a city, in some cases a district to which Jews are restricted. Israel ZANGWILL wrote a book of sketches and tales entitled *Children of the Ghetto* (1892).

Ghibellines. The imperial and aristocratic faction in Italy in the Middle Ages, opposed to the Guelphs. See GUELPHS AND GHIBELLINES. The name was the war cry of the followers of the Emperor Conrad at the battle of Weinsberg (1140) and is the Italian form of Ger. *Waiblingen,* an estate in Württemberg then belonging to the Emperor's family, the House of Hohenstaufen. See also GOBLIN.

Ghiberti, Lorenzo (1378–1455). Florentine goldsmith, painter, sculptor. Constructed famous bronze doors of baptistery of San Giovanni, Florence. Worked on one, with the assistance of twenty artists, for twenty-one years; on the other for twenty-three.

Ghirlandajo. Pseudonym of **Domenico di Tommaso Bigordi** (1449–1498). Florentine painter and mosaicist; best-known for his frescoes in the Palazzo Vecchio and the church of the Innocenti in Florence. His masterpiece is the frescoes in the choir of Santa Maria Novella (1485–1488), also in Florence. He contributed to the decoration of the Sistine Chapel at the Vatican (1483).

Ghismonda. Daughter of Tancred in Boccaccio's *Decameron* IV. 1. For her story, see SIGISMONDA.

Ghosts. A play by Henrik IBSEN (1881). Its subject is the haunting malice of nature in transmitting evil traits by heredity. See also ALVING.

Giafar, or Jaffar the Barmecide. Vizier of the Caliph Haroun al Raschid and companion of his adventures. He appears frequently in the ARABIAN NIGHTS.

Giaffir. In Byron's BRIDE OF ABYDOS, pasha of Abydos, and father of ZULEIKA.

Giall. The Styx of Scandinavian mythology, the river on the frontiers of Niflheim, or hell. Over it the doomed pass on a golden bridge.

Giallarhorn, see GJALLARHORN.

Giamschid, see JAMSHID.

Gian ben Gian. In Arabic legend, a king of the Jinn and founder of the Pyramids. He was overthrown by Azazael or Lucifer.

giants, i.e., persons well above the average height and size, are by no means uncommon as "sports" or "freaks of nature"; but the widespread belief in pre-existing races or individual instances of giants among primitive peoples is due partly to the ingrained idea that the present generation is invariably a degeneration—

"There were giants in the earth in those days" (*Gen.* vi. 4)—and partly to the existence from remote antiquity of cyclopean buildings, gigantic sarcophagi, etc., and to the discovery from time to time in pre-scientific days of the bones of extinct monsters which were taken to be those of men.

The giants of Greek mythology were, for the most part, sons of TARTARUS and GE. When they attempted to storm heaven, they were hurled to earth by the aid of Hercules, and buried under Mount Etna. Those of Scandinavian mythology were evil genii, dwelling in Jotunheim (*giantland*), who had terrible and superhuman powers, could appear and disappear, reduce and extend their stature at will, etc. See FAFNER, FASOLT.

For the principal giants known to legend see: ADAMASTOR, AEEGAEON, ALIFANFARON, AMERANT, ANTEUS, ASCAPART, ATLAS, BALAN, BLUNDERBORE, BRIAREUS, BROBDINGNAG, CACUS, ST. CHRISTOPHER, CORFLAMBO, CORMORAN, CYCLOPS, ENCELADUS, EPHIALTES, FERRAGUS, FIERABRAS, FINN, GALLIGANTUS, GARGANTUA, GERYONEO, GOG AND MAGOG, GRANGOUSIER, GRANTORTO, GUY OF WARWICK, GYGES, JOTUN, MAUGIS or MALEGIGI, ORGOGLIO, ORION, PANTAGRUEL, POLYPHEMUS, the SEVEN CHAMPIONS, SKRYMIR, the TITANS, TITYUS, TYPHOEUS, TYPHON.

Giants. The nickname of New York Nationals. See BASEBALL TEAMS.

Giants in the Earth: A saga of the Prairie. A novel by O. E. RÖLVAAG, published in Norway in 1924–1925 and in English translation in the U.S. in 1927. It deals with the hardships, both mental and physical, of a small group of Norwegian farmers from Minnesota who set out with their families in 1873 to settle in the then unopened Dakota Territory.

giaour. Among Mohammedans, one who is not an adherent of their faith, especially a Christian; generally used with a contemptuous or insulting implication. In Byron's poem *The Giaour* (1813), Leilah, the beautiful concubine of the Caliph Hassan, falls in love with a Giaour, flees from the seraglio, is overtaken, put to death, and cast into the sea. The Giaour cleaves Hassan's skull, flees for his life, and becomes a monk. Six years afterwards he tells his history to his father confessor on his deathbed, and prays him to "lay his body with the humblest dead, and not even to inscribe his name on his tomb." Accordingly, he is called "the Giaour," and is known by no other name.

Gibbie, Goose. In Scott's OLD MORTALITY, a half-witted lad, first entrusted to "keep the turkeys," but afterwards "advanced to the more important office of minding the cows." He is in the service of Lady Bellenden.

Gibbon, Edward (1737–1794). English historian and member of parliament, famous for his DECLINE AND FALL OF THE ROMAN EMPIRE (1776–1788).

Gibbon, John Murray (1875–). Canadian publicist; worked for the protection of Canadian authors by adequate copyright laws. Also known as an expert in Canadian history and folk literature.

Gibbon, Perceval (1879–1926). British journalist, war correspondent, novelist, and writer of short-stories, of which *The Second Class Passenger* is the most famous.

Gibbons, Floyd Phillips (1886–1939). American journalist and war correspondent. Covered strife on Mexican border (1915). See VILLA. During World War I he lost an eye in the battle of Château-Thierry.

Gibbons, Grinling (1648–1720). English woodcarver and sculptor. Employed by Sir Christopher Wren to carve stalls in St. Paul's Cathedral and other churches; did work at Windsor, Whitehall, Kensington. Excelled in flowers, fruit, game, and other decorative elements.

Gibbons, James Sloan (1810–1892). American abolitionist banker. Wrote the famous Civil War Song, *We are coming, Father Abraham, three hundred thousand Strong.* During the draft riot in 1863, his house was sacked by a New York mob.

Gibbs, Arthur Hamilton (1888–). English novelist, author of best-selling novels including *Soundings* (1925); *Labels* (1926); *Harness* (1928); and *Chances* (1930).

His brothers, Sir **Philip Hamilton Gibbs** (1877–) and **Cosmo Hamilton Gibbs** (1879–1942) were also authors.

Gibbs, Josiah Willard (1839–1903). American physicist, son of philologist of same name (1790–1861). Professor of mathematical physics at Yale (1871–1903). Cf. his biography, *Willard Gibbs: American Genius* (1942) by Muriel RUKEYSER.

Gibeonite. A slave's slave, a workman's laborer, a farmer's understrapper, or Jack-of-all-work. The Gibeonites were made "hewers of wood and drawers of water" to the Israelites (*Josh.* ix. 27).

Gibraltar. Famous rock fortress at the western entrance to the Mediterranean Sea.

the Gibraltar of America or *of the New World.* Quebec; more properly Cape Diamond, Quebec.

Gibran, Kahlil (1883–1931). Well-known Syrian-American symbolist poet and painter. *The Prophet* (1923); *Jesus the Son of Man* (1928), etc.

Gibson, Charles Dana (1867–1944). American illustrator. Created the "Gibson Girl," a type of American girl representative of the fashions and manners of the gay nineties.

Gibson, Wilfrid Wilson (1878?–). English poet. One of the founders of the "Georgian" magazine of poetry, *New Numbers* (with Abercrombie, Brooke and Drinkwater). His work is often grim, usually strong of structure and telling. He writes simply and directly and has been called "the poet of the industrial poor." *Daily Bread* (1910); *Borderlands and Thoroughfares* (1914); *Collected Poems* (1926); etc.

Gide, André Paul Guillaume (1869–). French novelist and critic, known for his satire, attacks on "Puritanism," and apologies for homosexuality, chiefly in the form of autobiography and semi-autobiography. His works include: *Les Cahiers d'André Walter* (*The Notebooks of André Walter;* 1891) (see under WALTER ANDRÉ); THE IMMORALIST (*L'Immoraliste*) (1902); *La Porte étroite* (1907), translated as *Strait is the Gate; Les Caves du Vatican* (1914), translated as *The Vatican Swindle; La Symphonie pastorale* (1919); *Si le Grain ne Meurt* (1921), a revealing autobiography, translated as *If It Die;* THE COUNTERFEITERS (*Les Faux-Monnayeurs;* 1925); *Dostoyevsky* (1926); *Travels in the Congo* (*Voyage au Congo*) (1928); *Geneviève* (1936); *Return from the U.S.S.R.* (*Retour de l' U.R.S.S.*) (1936); *Afterthoughts on the U.S.S.R.* (*Retouches à mon retour de l' U.R.S.S.*) (1938).

Early in his career Gide was a member of the Symbolist groups (see SYMBOLISM), although he soon repudiated the movement. He later became associated with the literary periodical *Nouvelle Revue Française,* and was a leader of young French writers during the 1920's. For a time, he professed Socialist sympathies. He was awarded the Nobel prize for literature in 1947.

Giddings, Franklin Henry (1855–1931). American sociologist; professor at Columbia (from 1894). *The Scientific Study of Human Society* (1924), etc.

Gideon. In the Old Testament, one of the judges of Israel. With a company of only three hundred men, he delivered his people from the Midianites. The army was purposely reduced to three hundred by eliminating all who were afraid and all who drank from a stream instead of lapping the water from their hands. They made a great noise by breaking pitchers and blowing trumpets, to give the impression of a huge army (*Judges* vii. 16–20).

Gielgud, Arthur John (1904–). English actor. In *The Constant Nymph, Richard of Bordeaux, Hamlet, The Importance of Being Earnest,* etc.

Gifford, Fannie Stearns, *née* **Davis** (1884–). American poet. *Myself and I* (1913), *The Ancient Beautiful Things* (1923), etc.

Gifford, William (1756–1826). English literary critic and poet, chiefly famous for his attack on Keats's *Endymion* in the *Quarterly Review* (1818). Edited Elizabethan plays.

gift-horse. *Don't look a gift-horse in the the mouth.* When a present is made, do not inquire too minutely into its intrinsic value.

Latin: *Noli equi dentes inspicere donati. Si quis det mannos ne quaere in dentibus annos.* (*Monkish.*)

Italian: *A cavallo dato non guardar in bocca.*

French: *À cheval donné il ne faut pas regarder aux dents.*

Spanish: *A caballo dado no le mire el diente.*

German: *Einem geschenkten Gaul schaut man nicht ins Maul.*

Gigadibs. A young poet in Browning's poem BISHOP BLOUGRAM'S APOLOGY.

Giglamps. Nickname for Verdant Green in BRADLEY'S *Adventures of Mr. Verdant Green, an Oxford Freshman* (1853–1856). A gig is a one-horse, two-wheeled vehicle with lamps on either side in front. The term "gig lamps" is slang for spectacles.

Giglio, Prince. A character in Thackeray's ROSE AND THE RING.

Gilbert, Cass (1859–1934). American architect of U.S. Custom House and Woolworth Building, New York City; Minnesota capitol at St. Paul, Detroit Public Library, St. Louis Central Public Library, etc.

Gilbert, Henry Franklin Belknap (1868–1928). American composer. *Negro Rhapsody* (1912); *Nocturne, from Whitman* (1925), etc.

Gilbert, Sir **Humphrey** (1539?–1583). English navigator. Half brother of Sir Walter Raleigh. Established first British colony in North America at St. John's, Newfoundland (August 5, 1583). On the return voyage his good ship, the *Squirrel,* foundered and he drowned off the Azores, his last words being the famous "We are as near to heaven by sea as by land."

Gilbert, Sir **William Schwenck** (1836–1911). English author of parodies and humorous "nonsense" verse, collaborator with Sir Arthur Seymour SULLIVAN (1842–1900) in the writing of the famous Gilbert and Sullivan light operas. Among these are TRIAL BY JURY (1875); H.M.S. PINAFORE (1878); THE PIRATES OF PENZANCE (1879); PATIENCE (1881); IOLANTHE (1884); THE MIKADO (1885); RUDDICORE (1887); THE YEOMAN OF THE GUARD (1888); and THE GONDOLIERS (1889). Gilbert is known for his whimsicality, his gift for satire, and his facility in versifying, first shown in his humorous poems, *The Bab Ballads.*

Gilberte. In Marcel Proust's REMEMBRANCE OF THINGS PAST, the daughter of Charles SWANN and his wife Odette, known to the narrator Marcel when both are children, and the first object of his love. She later becomes the wife of Robert SAINT-LOUP.

Gilbert Go-Ahead, The Travels and Adventures of. A humorous volume by Peter PARLEY, narrating the adventures of a Yankee engaged in selling clocks the world over. See also SLICK, SAM.

Gilbert with the White Hand. One of the companions of Robin Hood, mentioned often in *The Lyttell Geste of Robyn Hode* (fytte v. and vii).

> Thair saw I Maitlaind upon auld Beird Gray,
> Robene Hude, and Gilbert "with the quhite hand,"
> Quhom Hay of Nauchton slew in Madin-land.
> *Scottish Poems,* i. 122.

Gil Blas. A famous picaresque romance by LE SAGE (1715). The hero, Gil Blas, is a merry rogue brought up by his uncle, Canon Gil Perez. During his brief sojourn at Dr. Godinez' school of Oviedo, he obtains the reputation of being a great scholar. He becomes a valet and later a secretary, and as he changes his master frequently and scrutinizes his world with keen interest, his story becomes a good-humored exposure of the weaknesses and foibles of human nature.

Gilda. The heroine of Verdi's opera RIGOLETTO.

Gildas (516?–?570). British monk and historian, known as "Saint Gildas the Wise." Author of *De Excidio Britanniae,* a history of Britain from the earliest times, first printed by Polydore Vergil (London, 1525).

Gilded Age, The. A novel by Mark TWAIN and Charles Dudley WARNER (1873), relating the adventures of Col. Mulberry Sellers, an incurable optimist. According to Mark Twain's own statement he was drawn from his mother's cousin James Lampton, "a pathetic and beautiful spirit." The novel was successfully dramatized in 1874. Its title came to be used as a descriptive term for the post-Civil War period in the U.S., in the last quarter of the 19th century.

Gilder, Richard Watson (1844–1909). American poet and editor of *Century Magazine* (1881–1909); his brother, **William Henry Gilder** (1838–1900), a journalist and explorer; their sister, **Jeannette Leonard Gilder** (1849–1916), a journalist and literary agent.

Gilderoy. A famous cattle-stealer and highwayman of Perthshire, who is said to have robbed Cardinal Richelieu in the presence of the king, picked Oliver Cromwell's pocket, and hanged a judge. He was hanged in 1636. There are ballads on him in Percy's *Reliques,* Ritson's collection, etc., and a modern one by Campbell. Some authorities say there were two robbers by this name, both handsome and both Scotch.

to be hung higher than Gilderoy's kite is to be punished more severely than the very worst criminal. The greater the crime, the higher the gallows, was at one time a practical legal axiom. The gallows of Montrose was 30 feet high. The ballad says:

> Of Gilderoy sae fraid they were
> They bound him mickle strong,
> Tull Edenburrow they led him thair
> And on a gallows hong;
> They hong him high aboon the rest,
> He was so trim a boy. . . .

Giles. A mildly humorous generic name for a farmer. From the French form of Latin Aegidius.

Giles Corey. The title of one of Longfellow's *New England Tragedies* and of a drama by Mary E. Wilkins Freeman. Giles Corey was an inhabitant of Salem, Massachusetts, who at the age of eighty was condemned as a wizard in the Salem witchcraft trials and pressed to death. He met his death so stoically that he was called "the Man of Iron." His ghost, according to legend, appears from time to time on the site of his death.

Giles, St. See under SAINTS.

Gilfil, Maynard. The hero of George Eliot's MR. GILFIL'S LOVE STORY.

Gilgamesh. A legendary king of the Babylonian Gilgamesh Epic. Cf. translation by William Ellery LEONARD.

Gill, Eric (1882–1940). English sculptor and engraver. Also author of *Christianity and Art* (1927) and *Money and Morals* (1934).

Gill, Harry. See GOODY BLAKE AND HARRY GILL.

Gillray, James (1757–1815). English political caricaturist, famous for his reflections on the king, "Farmer George." He died in a state of imbecility.

Gilpatric, Guy (1896–). American novelist and short-story writer. Creator of "Muster" Colin Glencannon, chief engineer of the freighter "S.S. Inchcliffe Castle," undoubtedly "the biggest, drunkenest, fightenest blackguard in either steam or sail, on any ocean."

Gilpin, Charles Sidney (1878–1930). American Negro actor. Especially remembered as Brutus Jones in Eugene O'Neill's *Emperor Jones* (1920–1924). Received Drama League Award and Spingarn Medal (both 1921).

Gilpin, John, see JOHN GILPIN.

Ginevra. (1) *Ginevra dei Benci.* The young Italian bride who hid in a trunk with a spring-lock. The lid fell upon her, and she was not discovered till the body had become a skeleton. This legend was popularized in Rogers' poem *Italy* (1822).

Be the cause what it might, from his offer she shrunk,
And Ginevra-like, shut herself up in a trunk.—
Lowell.

(2) *Ginevra degli Amieri.* A Florentine heroine who was in love with Antonio Rondinelli, and, when forced to marry another, fell into a trance which was taken for death. She was buried in the family vault, but managed to make her escape to Rondinelli. She is the heroine of Shelley's *Story of Ginevra* (1821), Leigh Hunt's *Legend of Florence* (1847) and Scribe's *Guido et Ginevra.*

(3) In Ariosto's ORLANDO FURIOSO, Ginevra is the lady love of the absent Ariodantes, falsely accused and doomed to die unless she finds within an appointed time a champion. Rinoldo makes her cause his own, slays her accuser and restores her to her lover.

Gingerbread. Brummagem wares, showy but worthless. The allusion is to the gingerbread cakes fashioned like men, animals, etc., and profusely decorated with gold leaf or Dutch leaf, which looked like gold, commonly sold at fairs up to the middle of the 19th century.

to take the gilt off the gingerbread. To destroy the illusion; to appropriate all the fun or profit and leave the *caput mortuum* behind.

Giles Gingerbread. The hero of an old nursery tale.

Ginn, Edwin (1838–1914). American publisher. Founder of the firm now known as Ginn & Co. (Boston, 1867). Especially successful with text books.

Ginnunga Gap. In Scandinavian mythology, the abyss between Niflheim (the region of fog) and Muspelheim (the region of heat). It existed before either land or sea, heaven or earth, as a chaotic whirlpool.

ginseng. A Chinese herb, valued as a medicine. Its root, often forked, explains why it corresponds in Chinese folklore to the Western MANDRAKE.

Ginx's Baby. A satiric novel by John Edward Jenkins published anonymously in London in 1871. Ginx is about to drown his baby, the thirteenth to arrive in a poverty-stricken household, when it is rescued by the Sisters of Mercy. Passed from one charitable society to another and back to Ginx, because of antagonisms, lack of funds, etc., in the organizations, the "baby" becomes a thief and finally jumps over the bridge at the same spot where his father was prevented from drowning him.

Gioconda, La. (1) A drama by Gabriele D'ANNUNZIO (1898). Gioconda is the model of the brilliant young sculptor, Lucio Settala. Although he struggles to resist the fascination she exercises over him, out of loyalty to his devoted wife Silvia, he feels that Gioconda is the real inspiration of his art. During the sculptor's illness Gioconda refuses to give up the key of the studio to anyone but Lucio, and Silvia, who goes to plead her own cause, arouses the model's fury and is horribly maimed in the act of protecting Lucio's most prized statue. Nevertheless Lucio and Gioconda go off together and Silvia is left to her misery.

(2) An opera by Ponchielli (1876) based on Victor Hugo's tragedy *Angelo the Tyrant of Padua.* The scene is laid in 17th-century Venice, and the complex plot deals with the loves and jealousies of the street singer, La Gioconda; Enzo Grimaldo, a nobleman beloved by Gioconda; Alvise Badoero, the inquisitor; his wife Laura, who is engaged in an affair with Enzo; and the spy Barnaba. La Gioconda saves her rival Laura and stabs herself.

(3) A famous portrait of Mona Lisa Gioconda by Leonardo da VINCI. See MONA LISA.

Giocondo. Hero of an episode in Ariosto's ORLANDO FURIOSO, better known in its French paraphrase JOCONDE.

Giono, Jean (1895–). French novelist, known for the mysticism, the love of nature, and the exaltation of simple people engaged in semi-primitive agricultural pursuits, which mark his books, the scene of most of which is laid in Provence. His works include *Un des Baumurges* (1929), translated as *Lovers Are Never Losers; Harvest* (1930; *Regain*); *Colline* (1929), translated as *Hill of Destiny; Le Grand troupeau* (1931); *Jean le Bleu* (1932), translated as *Blue Boy* (1946); *Solitude de la pitié* (1932), short stories; *Song of the World* (*Le Chant du monde;* 1934); *Que ma joie demeure* (1935), translated as *Joy of Man's Desiring; Refus d'obéissance* (1937), accounts of World War I; *Lettre aux paysans sur la pauvreté et la paix* (1938); *Batailles dans la montagne* (1937); *Le Serpent d'étoiles* (1938); *Précisions* (1939), essays on European politics. Two French motion pictures highly praised by American critics, *Harvest* (1937) and *The Baker's Wife* (1938), were based respectively on *Harvest* and *Jean le Bleu.*

At the outbreak of World War II Giono was imprisoned as a pacifist. It has been said of him that he "is a great prose poet of nature, as pagan as a faun."

Giorgione, Il. Real name, **Giorgio Barbarelli** (1478?–1511). Venetian painter. Pupil of Giovanni Bellini and chief master of the Venetian school of his time. Traces of his influence are said to be apparent in the works of many of his contemporaries, including Titian. His pictures of secured authenticity are rare.

Giotto. Full name **Giotto di Bondone** (1276?–?1337). Florentine painter, architect, and sculptor; chief Italian pre-Renaissance painter; pupil of Cimabue; friend of DANTE. Many fresco series. Designed campanile and façade of the Florence Duomo. Florence dates its supremacy in Tuscan painting from Giotto. He broke the rigid traditional forms of the Byzantine school and through his introduction of individuality of treatment on the basis of observation became the father of portraiture in the modern sense.

round as Giotto's O. Said of work that is perfect and complete, but done with little labor. The story is that the Pope, wishing for an artist to undertake some special decorations, sent to Giotto for a specimen of his work, and the artist in front of the messenger and with his unaided hand drew a circle with red paint. The messenger, in amazement, asked Giotto if that were all. Giotto replied, "Send it, and we shall see if His Holiness understands the hint."

> I saw . . . that the practical teaching of the masters of Art was summed up by the O of Giotto.—Ruskin, *Queen of the Air*, iii.

Giovanni, Don, see DON JUAN.

Giovannitti, Arturo (1884–). Italian-American poet of hymns to labor in unrhymed verse. Socialist. Jailed after textile mill strike at Lawrence, Mass. Cf. his personal "prison-document" poem, *The Walker,* which has been compared with Wilde's THE BALLAD OF READING GAOL. In 1917 he wrote *When the Cock Crows,* a poem inspired by the lynching of the labor leader Frank Little. His principal collection of verse is *Arrows in the Gale* (1914).

Gipsy, see GYPSY.

Giraldus Cambrensis (1146?–?1220). Welsh ecclesiastic, geographer, and historian. His chief work is the *Itinerarium Cambriae,* a description and natural history of Wales.

Girard, Stephen (1750–1831). French-born American businessman and philanthropist. Founder of a banking house in Philadelphia. Aided in financing the War of 1812, and in establishing the Second Bank of the United States (1816). Left funds for the establishment of a college (Girard College) in Philadelphia for "poor, white, male orphans" with the explicit stipulation that "no ecclesiastic, missionary, or minister of any sect whatever" should be permitted to "hold or exercise any station or duty" in it, or even to be admitted as a visitor.

Giraud, Henri Honoré (1879–). French general. In World War II, escaped from Germany (1942) to unoccupied France and cooperated in Algeria with the Allies by organizing a French colonial army. Succeeded DARLAN as high commissioner of French North and West Africa. Commander in chief of French forces in North Africa. Joined Free French. Co-president with General De Gaulle of the French Committee of National Liberation (1943). Had escaped from a German war-prisoners' camp once before (1914).

Giraudoux, Jean (1882–). French novelist and playwright, holder of several important diplomatic positions after World War I. His works include *Provinciales* (1909); *L'École des Indifférents* (1911); *Campaigns and Intervals* (1918), an account of experiences during World War I; *Simon le Pathétique* (1918); *Adorable Clio* (1920); *Suzanne and the Pacific* (*Suzanne et le Pacifique*) (1921); *Siegfried et le Limousin* (1922), translated as *My Friend from Limousin; Bella* (1926); *Eglantine* (1927); AMPHITRYON 38 (1929), *Judith* (1932), *Intermezzo* (1933), and *Cantique des Cantiques* (1939), plays; *Choix des Elues* (1939).

Girl of the Golden West, The. An opera by PUCCINI (1910) based on a drama of that title by Belasco. The scene is laid in a California mining camp of the early days, where Minnie, the titular heroine, presides over the bar room and is courted by the local sheriff, Jack Rance, and Ramarrez, an outlaw known to her as Johnson. She loves Johnson, conceals him from justice, gambles with Rance for his life, and upon his promise to reform, accompanies him to a new life in another state.

Girl Scouts. An American national organization of girls over ten, patterned after the BOY SCOUTS, and established by Juliette Low in Savannah, Georgia, in 1912, at first under the name of "Girl Guides." See also CAMP FIRE GIRLS.

Girondists or the Gironde. The moderate republicans in the first French Revolution (1791–1793). So called from the department of Gironde, which chose for the Legislative Assembly five men who greatly distinguished themselves for their oratory, and formed a political party. They were subsequently joined by Brissot (and were hence sometimes called the *Brissotins*), Condorcet, and the adherents of Roland.

Girty, Simon (1741–1818). Known as "The Great Renegade." American soldier who turned against the Americans (1778) and became a leader of British and Indian raiding expeditions. Cf. Elinor WYLIE's poem, *Simon Girty.* He also appears in S. V. Benét's *The Devil and Daniel Webster.* Subject of a biography by Thomas BOYD.

Giselle. One of the most famous of ballets; one of great rôles of Alicia MARKOVA.

Gish, Lillian (1896?–). American stage and screen actress. First success in *Birth of a Nation.* Played, in films, *The Scarlet Letter, Broken Blossoms, Orphans of the Storm,* etc.; on stage, *Camille, Uncle Vanya, The Star*

Wagon, etc. Her sister Dorothy is also well-known as an actress, and appeared with her in several pictures.

Gismonda. A drama by SARDOU, later made into an opera by Fevrier (1919). Gismonda, duchess of Athens, has agreed to marry the man who will save her small son from a tiger's pit where he has been thrown by intriguers, but when the peasant falconer, Almerio, does so, she repents of her bargain and says she will pay her debt by a visit to his cottage. He must, however, give up all other claims. At the cottage she is spied upon by Zacario, the conspirator, and kills him. Almerio assumes the blame, to protect the Duchess, but she relents and marries him.

Gissing, George Robert (1857–1903). English novelist, one of the first exponents of NATURALISM in English fiction. As a result of his poverty and unhappy experiences in London and America, and his study of the philosophy of SCHOPENHAUER in Germany, his work is marked by pessimism, realism, and introspective analysis. His books include: *Workers of the Dawn* (1880); *Demos* (1886); *The Nether World* (1889); NEW GRUB STREET (1891); and THE PRIVATE PAPERS OF HENRY RYECROFT (1903).

Gizelle. A girl loved by NOSTROMO in CONRAD's novel of that title.

Gjallarhorn. In Norse mythology, the horn sounded by Heimdall, the warder of Asgard, to assemble the gods and heroes for the contest of RAGNAROK, the "twilight of the gods," at Vigrid.

Gjellerup, Karl (1857–1919). Danish writer long resident in Germany. Jointly with Henrik Pontoppidan he received the Nobel prize for literature in 1917. His later works were written in German.

Glad Game, The. See POLLYANNA.

Gladkowska, Constantia. Polish singer, with whom the composer CHOPIN was vainly in love for a time in his youth.

Gladstone, William Ewart (1809–1898). British statesman. Chancellor of the exchequer (1852–1855). Leader of Liberal party (1867). Prime minister (1868–1874; 1880–1885; 1886; 1892–1894). Milestones of his career are the disestablishment of the Irish Church, the denunciation of Turkish atrocities in Bulgaria, the reform of the Irish government by a new land bill and a home-rule bill (defeated 1886 and 1893), etc. The Gladstones (earlier form, Gledstones) are an old Scottish family. The word signifies "hawk-stone."

Gladstone wine is a humorous term for any of the cheaper French wines, duties on which were reduced by W. E. Gladstone (1860).

Glanvill, Joseph (1636–1680). English clergyman and philosopher; defended preexistence of souls and belief in witchcraft. Mentioned in Matthew Arnold's poem, *The Scholar Gipsy.* In one of his numerous books, *The Vanity of Dogmatizing* (1661), he is thought to have anticipated the electric telegraph.

Glasgow, Ellen Anderson Gholson (1874–1945). American novelist, known for her studies of social change and contrasting social classes in the South, presented both realistically and satirically. Her works include: *The Descendant* (1897); *The Voice of the People* (1900); *The Battle-Ground* (1902); *The Deliverance* (1904); *The Wheel of Life* (1906); *The Ancient Law* (1908); *The Romance of a Plain Man* (1909); *Virginia* (1913); *Life and Gabriella* (1916); *The Builders* (1919); *One Man in His Time* (1922); *Barren Ground* (1925); *The Romantic Comedians* (1926); *They Stooped to Folly* (1929); *The Sheltered Life* (1932); *Vein of Iron* (1935); *In This Our Life* (1941).

Glaspell, Susan (1882–). American playwright, one of the founders of the Provincetown Players. Her plays include: *Suppressed Desires* (1914); *A Woman's Honor* (1918); *Bernice* (1919); *The Inheritors* (1921); *The Verge* (1921); *Alison's House* (1930), winner of the Pulitzer Prize in 1931, supposedly based on the life of Emily DICKINSON. She also wrote novels and short stories.

Glass, Carter (1858–1946). American statesman. U.S. secretary of the treasury (1918–1920). U.S. senator from Virginia (from 1920).

Glass, Montague Marsden (1877–1934). American fiction writer and playwright. Creator of POTASH AND PERLMUTTER (1910).

Glasse, Mrs. Hannah. The author of a cookery-book, immortalized by the saying, "First catch [skin] your hare, then cook it." Mrs. Glasse is the assumed name of Dr. John Hill (1716–1775).

Glass Houses: *Those who live in glass houses should not throw stones.* Those who are open to criticism should be very careful how they criticize others. This is an old proverb found in varying forms from the time of Chaucer at least. Cf. TROILUS AND CRISEYDE, Bk. ii; also *Matt.* vii. 1–4.

Glastonbury. An ancient town in Somerset, dating from Roman times, and famous in the Arthurian and Grail cycles as the place to which Joseph of Arimathea came and as the burial place of King Arthur (see *Avalon*). It was here that Joseph planted his staff—the famous *Glastonbury Thorn*—which took root and burst into leaf every Christmas Eve.

Glaucus. The name of a number of heroes in classical legend, including:

(1) A fisherman of Boeotia, who became a sea-god endowed with the gift of prophecy and who instructed Apollo in the art of soothsaying.

(2) A son of Sisyphus who would not allow his horses to breed. The goddess of Love so infuriated them that they killed him. Hence, the name is given to one who is so overfond of horses that he is ruined by them.

(3) A commander of the Lycians in the War of Troy (*Iliad,* Bk. vi.) who was connected by ties of ancient family friendship with his enemy Diomed. When they met in battle they not only refrained from fighting but exchanged arms in token of amity. As the armor of the Lycian was of gold, and that of the Greek of brass, it was like bartering precious stones for French paste. Hence the phrase *a Glaucus swap,* of which the story of Moses, in Goldsmith's VICAR OF WAKEFIELD, and his bargain with the spectacle-seller is a good example.

Glaucus is also the name of the hero in Bulwer Lytton's LAST DAYS OF POMPEII.

Gleaners, The. A famous painting of women gleaning in a harvest field by Jean François MILLET.

Glee-maiden, Louise the. One of the most prominent characters in Scott's FAIR MAID OF PERTH.

Glegg, Mrs. or **Aunt.** In George Eliot's MILL ON THE FLOSS, an aunt of Tom and Maggie Tulliver, conspicuous for her family loyalty and her domineering methods of compelling it in others. She has "a very comely face and figure, though Tom and Maggie considered their Aunt Glegg as a type of ugliness."

Gleipnir (*Old Norse,* "the fetter"). In Scandinavian legend, the chain by which the wolf Fenris is bound. It is extremely light, and made of the noise made by the footfalls of a cat, the roots of the mountains, the sinews of bears, the breath of fishes, the beards of women, and the spittle of birds. When the chain breaks, the wolf will be free and the end of the world will be at hand.

Glencoe, the massacre of. The treacherous massacre of the Macdonalds of Glencoe on February 13, 1692. Pardon had been offered to all Jacobites who submitted on or before December 31, 1691. Mac-Ian, chief of the Macdonalds of Glencoe, delayed till the last minute, and, on account of the state of the roads, did not make his submission before January 6. The Master of Stair (Sir John Dalrymple) obtained the king's permission "to extirpate the set of thieves." Accordingly on February 1, 120 soldiers, led by a Captain Campbell, marched to Glencoe, told the clan they were come as friends, and lived peaceably among them for twelve days; but on the morning of the 13th, the glenmen, to the number of thirty-eight, were scandalously murdered, their huts set on fire and their flocks and herds driven off as plunder. CAMPBELL and SCOTT have written poems, Talfourd a play, and Marjorie BOWEN a romance, on the subject.

Glendinning, Edward. A prominent character in Scott's MONASTERY and its sequel THE ABBOT, in which he is called Father AMBROSE.

Glendower, Owen. In Shakespeare's 1 *Henry IV,* a Welsh nobleman, descended from Llewellyn (last of the Welsh kings). Sir Edmund Mortimer marries one of his daughters. Shakespeare makes him a wizard, but very highly accomplished.

Glenn, Isa (1888–). American novelist. One of her cousins was James McNeill Whistler. Married General Schindler of the U.S. Army. Wrote *Heat* (1926); *Southern Charm* (1928); *Transport* (1929); *The Little Candle's Beam* (1935); *According to Mac Tavish* (1938).

Glinka, Mikhail Ivanovich (1803–1857). Russian composer. *A Life for The Czar* (first Russian national opera; 1836); *Russlan and Ludmilla* (after a poem by Pushkin; 1842), overtures, symphonies, orchestral suites, etc.

globaloney. A word coined by Representative Clare BOOTHE LUCE to ridicule what she considered excessive emphasis on the *global* interrelation of world affairs in the days after World War II.

Globe, The. A London theater located on the Bankside, Southwark, famous for the first production of plays by Shakespeare, Jonson, Beaumont and Fletcher, etc. Built in 1599, it was burned in 1613, was immediately rebuilt and finally pulled down by the Puritans in 1644. A modern theater by the same name was built in Wych street in 1868.

Gloriana. Spenser's name in his FAËRIE QUEENE for Queen Elizabeth. She holds an annual feast for twelve days, during which adventurers appear before her to undertake whatever task she chooses to impose upon them. On one occasion twelve knights present themselves before her, and their exploits form the scheme of Spenser's allegory.

> By Gloriana I mean [true] Glory in my general intention, but in my particular I conceive the most excellent and glorious person of our sovereign the queen [Elizabeth] and her kingdom is Faerye-land. —Spenser, *Introduction to the Faërie Queene* (1590).

gloss. An interpretation, the rendering of an obscure expression, especially in the form of a marginal or interlinear note, of the kind abounding in medieval literature where Latin,

Greek, or Hebrew words had to be rendered in the vernacular Teutonic, Celtic, and Romanic tongues. These special glosses are philologically very important and represent the oldest rudiments of bi-lingual dictionaries.

Glossin, Gilbert. In Scott's GUY MANNERING, a knavish lawyer, who purchases the Ellangowan estate, and is convicted by Pleydell of kidnaping Henry Bertram, the heir. Both Glossin and Dirk Hatteraick, his accomplice, are sent to prison; and in the night Hatteraick first strangles the lawyer and then hangs himself.

Glove, The. A long poem in octosyllabic couplets by Robert BROWNING (1845), in which the French poet Pierre de RONSARD supposedly tells the story of a lady at the court of FRANCIS I of France who tests her lover's devotion by dropping her glove before a dangerous captive lion, for the lover to rescue. Cf. also Schiller's ballad *Der Handschuh* (*The Glove*). One version ends:

> He threw the glove, but not with love,
> Right in the lady's face.

Glover, Catherine. Heroine of Scott's FAIR MAID OF PERTH.

Glover, Richard (1712–1785). English poet, author of the ballad *Hosier's Ghost*, which was published in PERCY'S *Reliques*. His chief work, *Leonidas* (1737; enlarged in 1770), is an epic poem which was translated into French and German and owed its success in part to the use Walpole's opponents could make of it.

Glubdubdrib. In Swift's GULLIVER'S TRAVELS, the land of sorcerers and magicians, where Gulliver is shown many of the great men of antiquity.

Gluck, Christoph Willibald (1714–1787). German composer who revolutionized opera through the dramatic intensity of his music. His major works are *Orfeo ed Euridice* (1762; see ORPHEUS); *Iphigénie en Aulide* (1774); *Armide* (1777); and *Iphigénie en Tauride* (1779). See also GLUCKISTS and PICCINI, NICCOLO.

Gluckists. A foolish rivalry excited in Paris (1774–1780) between the admirers of GLUCK and those of PICCINI—the former a German composer, and the latter an Italian. Marie Antoinette was a Gluckist, and consequently Young France favored the rival claimant. In the streets, coffee-houses, private houses, and even schools, the merits of Gluck and Piccini were canvassed, and all Paris was ranged on one side or the other. This was, in fact, a contention between the relative merits of the German and Italian schools of music.

Glumdalclitch. In Swift's GULLIVER'S TRAVELS, a girl, nine years old, and only forty feet high, who has charge of Gulliver in Brobdingnag.

Glyn, Elinor (Sutherland) (1865?–1943). Canadian-born English novelist, known for her best-selling novels dealing sentimentally, and what was considered daringly, with adultery themes. Among the best-known were: *Three Weeks* (1907); *Six Days* (1924); *It* (1927); *Romantic Adventure: The Autobiography of Elinor Glyn* (1936); *The Third Eye* (1940). Several of her books were used successfully as motion picture scenarios.

gnome. According to the Rosicrucian system, a misshapen elemental spirit, dwelling in the bowels of the earth, and guarding the mines and quarries. The word seems to have been first used (perhaps invented) by Paracelsus, and to be derived from Gr. *ge-nomos*, earth-dweller. See also SALAMANDER.

> The four elements are inhabited by spirits called sylphs, gnomes, nymphs, and salamanders. The gnomes or demons of the earth, delight in mischief. —Pope, *Pref. Letter to the Rape of the Lock.*

Gnomic poets. Greek poets, as Theognis of Megara and Solon, the lawgiver, whose writings are gnomic or aphoristic, containing maxims.

Gnostics (Gr. *gnosticos*). The *knowers*, as opposed to *believers*, various sects in the first six centuries of the Christian era, which tried to accommodate Christianity to the speculations of PYTHAGORAS, PLATO, and other Greek and Oriental philosophers. They taught that knowledge, rather than mere faith, is the true key of salvation. In the Gnostic creed Christ is esteemed merely as an eon or divine attribute personified, like Mind, Truth, Logos, Church, etc., the whole of which eons made up this divine pleroma or fullness. St. Paul, in several of his epistles, speaks of this "fullness (pleroma) of God."

goat. From very early times the *goat* has been connected with the idea of sin (see SCAPEGOAT) and associated with devil-lore. It is an old superstition in England and Scotland that a goat is never seen during the whole of a twenty-four hours, because once every day it pays a visit to the devil to have its beard combed. Formerly the devil himself was frequently depicted as a goat; and the animal is also a type of lust and lechery.

to be the goat. To get the worst of an affair; to be given the blame for others' misdeeds. The allusion is to the Jewish SCAPEGOAT.

to get one's goat. An Americanism for annoying one, making him wild, as, "It gets my goat to see a man knocking his wife about."

to separate the sheep from the goats. To divide the worthy from the unworthy, part the good from the evil. A Biblical phrase, the allusion being to *Matt.* xxv. 32, 33:

And before him shall be gathered all nations; and he shall separate them one from another, as a shepherd divideth his sheep from the goats.
And he shall set the sheep on his right hand, but the goats on the left.

Gobbo, Old. In Shakespeare's MERCHANT OF VENICE, the father of Launcelot. He is stone blind.

Launcelot Gobbo. Son of Old Gobbo. He leaves the service of Shylock the Jew for that of Bassanio, a Christian. Launcelot Gobbo is one of the famous clowns of Shakespeare, and more amusing than most of them.

Gobineau, Comte **Joseph Arthur de** (1816–1882). French diplomat, Orientalist, and writer. His most important work, the sociological treatise *Essai sur l'inégalité des races humaines* (1854, 1884), advanced an early form of the theory of Nordic racial superiority. He also wrote on the Italian renaissance and Oriental religions and philosophies.

goblin. A familiar demon, dwelling, according to popular belief, in private houses and chinks of trees; in many parts miners attribute those strange noises heard in mines to them. The word is the Fr. *gobelin,* probably a diminutive of the surname *Gobel,* but perhaps connected with Gr. *kobalos,* an impudent rogue, a mischievous sprite, or with the Ger. KOBOLD. As a specimen of forced etymology, it may be mentioned that Johnson, in his *Dictionary,* records that

this word some derive from the *Gibellines,* a faction in Italy; so that *elfe* and *goblin* is *Guelph* and *Gibelline* because the children of either party were terrified by their nurses with the name of the other (!)

Gobseck, Jean Esther Van. A famous old miser, titular hero of Balzac's GOBSECK (1830), and appearing in other of the novels of the COMÉDIE HUMAINE. He was a cabin boy and pirate before he devotes himself to the pursuit of wealth, and even as a miser he loves to lose himself in a game of dominoes.

Esther Van Gobseck. A courtesan prominent in Balzac's SCENES FROM A COURTESAN'S LIFE (*Les Splendeurs et misères des courtisanes*) and other novels; the great-grandniece of the old miser Gobseck. She and young Lucien de Rubempré fall in love and both are used as tools by the criminal, Jacques COLLIN, who wishes to secure a hold over the financier Nucingen, an admirer of Esther. When this scheme comes to a violent end, involving Rubempré's suicide in prison, Esther swallows poison and dies unconscious of the fact that she has inherited old Gobseck's millions.

Goddard, Henry Herbert (1866–). American psychologist. Ohio State University (from 1922). *The Kallikak Family* (1912), a study not unlike that of the "Jukes family" by R. L. Dugdale (1877). *Feeble-Mindedness* (1914), *The Criminal Imbecile* (1915).

Godden, Rumer, see Laurence FOSTER.

Godey, Louis Antoine (1804–1878). Founder, with Charles Alexander, of the first American periodical for women (1830). Originally named *Lady's Book,* it came to be known later on as *Godey's Lady's Book.*

Godfrey de Bouillon. The principal character of Tasso's epic poem JERUSALEM DELIVERED, which was published in 1575, and translated into English with the title *Godfrey of Bullogne* or *Boulogne* by Carew (1594) and FAIRFAX (1600). Godfrey, Duke of Lorraine, was the chosen chief of the allied Crusaders and was proclaimed king of Jerusalem at one time when the city was in their hands. He appears also in Scott's COUNT ROBERT OF PARIS.

Godiva, Lady. Patroness of Coventry. In 1040, Leofric, Earl of Mercia and Lord of Coventry, imposed certain exactions on his tenants, which his lady besought him to remove. He said he would do so if she would ride naked through the town at midday. Lady Godiva took him at his word, and the Earl faithfully kept his promise. According to legend, everyone kept indoors at the time, but a certain tailor peeped through his window to see the lady pass and was struck blind in consequence. He has ever since been called "Peeping Tom of Coventry." The incident of Lady Godiva's ride is still annually commemorated at Coventry by a procession in which Lady Godiva plays a leading part. The story is told in Tennyson's *Godiva, a Tale of Coventry* (1842). The American humorist, "Dr. Seuss," has written *The Seven Lady Godivas* (1939).

Godkin, Edwin Laurence (1831–1902). Editor and author. Founder and editor of the magazine *Nation* (1863) which merged into the New York *Evening Post* (1881) and became its weekly edition. Editor in chief of the *Evening Post* (1883–1900).

Gododin, The. A poem by Aneurin, the sixth-century Welsh bard, on the battle of Cattraeth (603), in which the tribe of the Gododin (Latin *Otadini*) was defeated by the Saxons.

Godolphin, Sidney (1645–1712). First Earl of **Godolphin** (from 1706). Lord high treasurer of England, and supporter of the Marlborough (1702–1710). Dismissed from office by Queen Anne at the fall of the Marlboroughs (1710), but allowed a pension for life.

gods. Legends of the principal gods of various mythologies will be found under their several names. For convenience names of the chief deities are given below.

Classical mythology. Greek and Roman gods were divided into *Dii Majores* and *Dii*

Minores, the greater and the lesser. The Dii Majores were twelve in number:

Latin	*Greek*
Jupiter (King)	Zeus
Apollo (*the sun*)	Phoebus
Mars (*war*)	Ares
Mercury (*messenger*)	Hermes
Neptune (*ocean*)	Poseidon
Vulcan (*smith*)	Hephaistus
Juno (Queen)	Hera
Ceres (*tillage*)	Demeter
Diana (*moon, hunting*)	Artemis
Minerva (*wisdom*)	Athena
Venus (*love and beauty*)	Aphrodite
Vesta (*home-life*)	Hestia

Their blood was *ichor,* their food was *ambrosia,* their drink *nectar.*

Four other deities often referred to are:

Bacchus (*wine*)	Dionysus
Cupid (*the lad Love*)	Eros
Pluto (*of the Inferno*)	Pluton
Saturn (*time*)	Kronus

Of these, Proserpine (Latin) or Persephone (Greek) was the wife of Pluto, Cybele was the wife of Saturn and Rhea of Kronus.

In Hesiod's time, the number of gods was 30,000, and that none might be omitted, the Greeks observed a *Feast of the Unknown Gods.*

Scandinavian mythology. For names of the principal deities, see AESIR, VANIR.

Egyptian mythology. The chief deities are Amon (or Ammon), Osiris and his wife Isis, Anubis, Horus or Harpocrates, and Typhon.

Hindu mythology. The Hindu triad or Trimurti comprises BRAHMA the Creator, VISHNU the Preserver, and SIVA the Destroyer. Other important deities are INDRA, AGNI, YAMA, SURYA, KAMA, GANESH, KUBERA, HANUMAN and DURGA (Kali). See also AVATAR; KRISHNA.

God's acre, see under ACRE.

Gods Are Athirst, The (*Les Dieux ont soif.*) A historical novel by Anatole FRANCE (1912) dealing with the French Revolution. The hero is a young artist, Evariste Gamelin, who becomes a member of the Revolutionary Tribunal, but is himself at last a victim of the guillotine.

Godwin, William (1756–1836). English prose-writer, a leading radical of the 18th century, advocating a complete overthrow of the existing systems of government, religion, the family, and accumulated private property as they existed in his day. He was influenced by the ideas of J. J. ROUSSEAU and the French ENCYCLOPEDISTS, and in turn had a great influence on the English Romantics, especially WORDSWORTH, COLERIDGE, SHELLEY, and BYRON; Shelley's *Preface* to his REVOLT OF ISLAM is an excellent exposition of Godwin's ideas. Among Godwin's works are AN ENQUIRY CONCERNING POLITICAL JUSTICE (1793); CALEB WILLIAMS (1794), a novel; *St. Leon* (1799), another novel; and a *History of the Commonwealth* (1824–1828).

Godwin's wife was **Mary Wollstonecraft, a** pioneer in the movement of FEMINISM, and their daughter **Mary** was the second wife of SHELLEY, her unconventional arrangement with the poet enraging the professedly radical father.

Goethals, George Washington (1858–1928). American army officer (Major General) and head of consulting engineering firm (1923–1928). Completed the Panama Canal (1914).

Goethe, Johann Wolfgang von (1749–1832). German poet, dramatist, and novelist, one of the most famous of German authors and a leading figure in the movement of ROMANTICISM. He held a number of government positions in Weimar, studied painting during most of his career, and carried on scientific research, the most outstanding result of which was the formulation of a theory of light, expounded in a treatise entitled *Farbenlehre* (1810). Among Goethe's works are *Goetz von Berlichingen* (1771), a drama; *The Sorrows of Werther* (1774), an autobiographical novel in the form of letters (see WERTHER); IPHIGENIA (1787), a drama; EGMONT (1788); HERMANN AND DOROTHEA (1797), a narrative poem; WILHELM MEISTER, a novel; and FAUST (1790–1833). Goethe is a leading figure in the novel THE BELOVED RETURNS, by Thomas Mann, and also in Mann's studies of FREUD, GOETHE, AND WAGNER. See also BUFF, CHARLOTTE; VULPIUS, CHRISTIANE. In a sense Goethe was the last *uomo universale* of Western civilization. His science pervades his poetry and vice versa. The unconsciously constant query and leitmotiv of his work are most concisely stated in the little botanical essay *On the Metamorphosis of Plants.* Without having recourse to the crude idea of material descent, Goethe endeavored to visualize varying forms in each other and thus to reduce their multiplicity to a limited number of type phenomena which can be seen and experienced but must be accepted without further philosophical analysis. The modern school of anthroposophism propagates a Goethean philosophy. Goethe's contribution is a universal humanism of German origin rather than a German humanism of universal impact.

Gog and Magog. In British legend, the sole survivors of a monstrous brood, the offspring of the thirty-three infamous daughters of the Emperor Diocletian, who murdered their husbands, and, being set adrift in a ship, reached Albion, where they fell in with a number of demons. Their descendants, a race of giants, were extirpated by Brute and his companions, with the exception of Gog and Magog, who were brought in chains to London and were made to do duty as porters at the royal palace, on the site of the London Guildhall, where their effigies have been at least since the reign of Henry V. The old giants were destroyed in the Great Fire, and the present ones, fourteen feet high, were carved in 1708 by Richard Saunders.

In the Bible, Magog is spoken of as a son of Japhet (*Gen.* x. 2), in the *Revelation* Gog and Magog symbolize all future enemies of the kingdom of God; and in *Ezekiel,* Gog is a prince of Magog, a terrible ruler of a country in the north, probably Scythia or Armenia. By rabbinical writers of the 7th century A. D. Gog was identified with Antichrist.

Gogarty, Oliver St. John (1878–). Irish physician and author, said to be the original of Malachi ("Buck") MULLIGAN in ULYSSES by James JOYCE, an early friend of Gogarty. He was the author of several exuberant books of memoirs, including *As I Was Going Down Sackville Street* (1937) and *I Follow St. Patrick* (1939).

Gogh, Vincent van (1853–1890). Dutch painter, etcher, lithographer of postimpressionist tendencies. Committed suicide in a state of mental aberration. Some of his notable canvases are *The Potato Eaters; The Restaurant on Montmartre; L'Arlésienne; Berceuse; Mairie au 14 Juillet;* etc.

Gogol, Nikolai Vasilievich (1809–1852). Russian novelist and playwright; best-known as the author of TARAS BULBA (1842), a historical novel telling of the Cossack struggles with Tartars and Poles in the 16th century, and DEAD SOULS (1837), a social satire. His plays include *The Inspector General* (1836), a biting satire on the corruption and the pettiness of Russian government officials. Gogol is considered the "father of realism" in Russian literature.

Golconda. An ancient kingdom and city in India (west of Hyderabad), famous and powerful up to the early 17th century. The name is emblematic of great wealth, particularly of diamonds. There never were diamond mines in Golconda, however, they were merely cut and polished there.

gold.

gold of Nibelungen. Unlucky wealth. See NIBELUNGENLIED.

gold of Tolosa. Ill gains, which never prosper. The reference is to Caepio, the Roman consul, who, on his march to Gallia Narbonensis, stole from Tolosa (Toulouse) the gold and silver consecrated by the Cimbrian Druids to their gods. He was utterly defeated by the Cimbrians, and some 112,000 Romans were left dead on the field of battle (106 B. C.).

Gold, Michael. Pseudonym of **Irving Granich** (1894–). American novelist, playwright, journalist; for many years contributor to the official Communist newspaper, the *Daily Worker*. His potentialities as a writer were long nearly submerged in political journalism. *John Brown* (1923); *Jews Without Money* (1930); *Battle Hymn* (1936; a play); etc.

Goldberg, Isaac (1887–1938). American biographer, philologist, and miscellaneous writer. A pioneer writer on Spanish-American literature. Author of *The Wonder of Words* (1939), and a biography of H. L. MENCKEN.

Gold Bug, The. A famous short story by Edgar Allan POE (1843). William Le Grand discovers by pure accident that the parchment which he had snatched up from the ground to catch a strange beetle, is covered with invisible writing that the heat of the fire brings to light. He unravels its mysterious directions and, with the aid of his awed Negro servant Jupiter, drops the beetle, or "gold bug," through one eye of the skull that he finds in a tree, and unearths at last a considerable treasure.

Goldemar, King. In German folklore, name of a KOBOLD who can be touched but not seen.

Golden.

golden age. An age in the history of peoples of real or (more often) imaginary happiness, when everything was as it should be, or when the nation was at its summit of power, glory, and reputation; the best age, as the golden age of innocence, the golden age of literature. See also AGE; the *golden ages* of the various nations are usually given as follows:

Ancient Nations

Assyria. From the reign of Esarhaddon, third son of Sennacherib, to the fall of Nineveh (about 700 to 600 B. C.).

Chaldaeo-Babylonian Empire. From the reign of Nabopolassar to that of Belshazzar (about 606–538 B. C.).

China. The reign of Tae-tsong (618–626), and the era of the Tang dynasty (626–684).

Egypt. The reigns of Sethos I and Rameses II (about 1350–1273 B. C.), the XIXth Dynasty.

Media. The reign of Cyaxares (about 634–594 B. C.).

Persia. From the reign of Khosru, or Chosroes, I, to that of Khosru II (about 531–628 A. D.).

Modern Nations

England. The reign of Elizabeth (1558–1603).

France. Part of the reigns of Louis XIV and XV (1640–1740).

Germany. The reign of Charles V (1519–1558).

Portugal. From John I to the close of Sebastian's reign (1383–1578).

Prussia. The reign of Frederick the Great (1740–1786).

Russia. The reign of Peter the Great (1672–1725).

Spain. The reign of Ferdinand and Isabella, when the crowns of Castile and Aragon were united (1474–1516).

Sweden. From Gustavus Vasa to the close of the reign of Gustavus Adolphus (1523–1632).

golden apples. See APPLE OF DISCORD; ATALANTA'S RACE; HESPERIDES.

Golden Bull. An edict by the Emperor Charles IV, issued at the Diet of Nuremberg in 1356, for the purpose of fixing how the German emperors were to be elected. It was sealed with a golden *bulla.*

golden calf. Money. The reference is to the golden calf made by Aaron when Moses was absent on Mount Sinai (*Exod.* xxxii) and worshiped by the people.

Golden Fleece. The old Greek story is that Ino persuaded her husband, Athamas, that his son Phryxus was the cause of a famine which desolated the land. Phryxus was thereupon ordered to be sacrificed, but, being apprised of this, he made his escape over sea on the winged ram, Chrysomallus, which had a golden fleece. When he arrived at Colchis, he sacrificed the ram to Zeus, and gave the fleece to King Aeetes, who hung it on a sacred oak. It later formed the quest of Jason's celebrated Argonautic expedition, and was stolen by him. See ARGO: JASON.

Golden Fleece, the Order of the (Fr. *l'Ordre de la toison d'or*). An order of knighthood common to Spain and Austria, instituted in 1429 for the protection of the Church by Philip the Good, Duke of Burgundy, on his marriage with the Infanta Isabella of Portugal. Its badge is a golden sheepskin with head and feet attached, and its motto *Pretium laborum non vile.*

Australia has been called *the Land of the Golden Fleece,* because of the quantity of wool produced there.

Golden Gate. The name given by Sir Francis Drake to the strait connecting San Francisco Bay with the Pacific. San Francisco is hence called *the City of the Golden Gate.*

Golden Horn. The inlet of the Bosphorus on which Constantinople stands; so called from its shape and beauty.

Golden Legend. See below.

golden mean. "Nothing to excess."

to keep the golden mean. To practice moderation in all things. The wise saw of Cleobulos, king of Rhodes (about 630–559 B. C.):

> Distant alike from each, to neither lean,
> But ever keep the happy Golden Mean.
> Rowe, *The Golden Verses.*

golden number. The number of the year in the Metonic Cycle. As this consists of nineteen years it may be any number from 1 to 19, and in the ancient Roman and Alexandria calendars this number was marked in gold, hence the name. The rule for finding the golden number is:

> Add one to the number of years and divide by nineteen; the quotient gives the number of cycles since 1 B. C. and the remainder the golden number, 19 being the golden number when there is no remainder.

It is used in determining the Epact and the date of Easter.

Golden Rule. "Do as you would be done by."

> Whatsoever ye would that men should do to you, do ye even so to them: for this is the law and the prophets.—*Matt.* vii. 12.

Golden State. California. See STATES.

golden wedding. The fiftieth anniversary of one's wedding, husband and wife being both alive.

Golden, John (1874–   ). American playwright and producer of plays and musical comedies. Also composer of songs.

Golden Ass, The. A common alternative title of the *Metamorphoses,* a satirical romance by APULEIUS, written in the 2nd century A. D., and called *golden* because of its excellency. It tells the adventures of Lucian, a young man who, being accidentally metamorphosed into an ass while sojourning in Thessaly, falls into the hands of robbers, eunuchs, magistrates, and so on, by whom he is ill-treated, but ultimately he recovers his human form. Boccaccio borrowed largely from it, as also did LE SAGE, for GIL BLAS, and others. It also contains the story of Cupid and Psyche, the latest-born of the myths.

Golden Bough, The. A famous work on comparative folk-lore, mythology, and religion by Sir James G. FRAZER in 12 volumes, the first being published in 1890 and the last in 1915. The title refers to the branch broken from a sacred tree by AENEAS before descending to the underworld. (Cf. *Aeneid,* vi, 136.) This work was an outstanding influence in the conception of FINNEGANS WAKE by James Joyce.

Golden Bowl, The. A novel by Henry JAMES (1904). The heroine, Maggie Verver, an American millionaire's daughter, marries a poverty-stricken Italian prince, and then, to keep her adored father from being lonely, brings about his marriage to her old school friend Charlotte. She is unaware of the fact that Charlotte and the prince had previously been in love. The two couples live in close intimacy until eventually Adam Verver discovers the truth and solves the problem by giving up his companionship with Maggie and taking his wife far away.

Golden Horde. A body of Mongol Tartars that overran eastern Europe in the 13th century. So called from the magnificent tent of Batu Kahn, grandson of GENGHIS KHAN. The kingdom of the Golden Horde at its height reached from the Dniester to central Asia. It was overthrown by Ivan III of Russia (1480), and broke up into a number of smaller khanats with that of Astrakhan representing the Golden Horde.

Golden Legend, The (Lat. *Legenda Aurea*). A collection of so-called lives of the saints made by Jacobus de Voragine in the 13th century. It is valuable for the picture it gives of medieval manners, customs, and thought. Jortin says that the "lives" were written by young students of religious houses to exercise their talents by accommodating the narratives of heathen writers to Christian saints.

Longfellow has a dramatic poem entitled *The Golden Legend* (1851). It is based on a story by Hartmann von der Aue, a German minnesinger of the 12th century. See HEINRICH VON AUE.

Golden Mount. The Janiculum in Rome; formerly so called for its yellow sand. The name survives in that of the church on its summit, *S. Pietro in Montorio*.

Golden Multitudes. Full-length history of best sellers from Colonial times to the present, by Frank Luther Mott (1947).

Golden Treasury of Songs and Lyrics, The. A celebrated anthology by Francis Turner PALGRAVE. The first edition was published in 1861, a second series in 1897.

Golden Yardarm. The three stars in the belt of Orion; called also *Ell and Yard; Yard and Ell; Jacob's Staff;* etc.

Goldilocks. The heroine of the well-known nursery tale concerning the Three Bears of varying size, who had three bowls of porridge, three chairs and three beds. Goldilocks, who tried them all on a day when the Bears were not at home, found them to be of varying degrees of satisfaction. The middle-sized bowl and chair and bed were, however, "just right" and when the Bears came home, they found their visitor fast asleep on the middle-sized bed, which belonged to the Mother Bear.

Goldman, Emma (1869–1940). Famous Russian-born American anarchist. Delegate to two anarchist congresses. Wrote *Anarchism and Other Essays* (1910) and the autobiography *Living my Life* (1931).

Goldoni, Carlo (1707–1793). Italian dramatist. Started out with unsuccessful tragedies. Wrote more than 120 comedies through which he became the creator of the modern Italian character comedy in the style of MOLIÈRE, superseding the conventional COMMEDIA DELL' ARTE.

Goldsmith, Oliver (1728–1774). Irish-born English poet and man of letters, of lighthearted and irresponsible behavior and character. His work is marked by humor, whimsy, neo-Classical forms, and occasional sentimentality. His works include: THE CITIZEN OF THE WORLD (1762), a series of satirical essays; *The Traveler* (1764), a philosophical poem, praised by Samuel JOHNSON; THE VICAR OF WAKEFIELD (1766), a novel; *The Good-Natured Man* (1768), a comedy; THE DESERTED VILLAGE (1770); SHE STOOPS TO CONQUER (1773); and *Retaliation* (1774), a series of caricatures of contemporaries. Goldsmith was always heavily in debt and for a long time did hackwork to support himself.

Goldy. The pet name given by Dr. Johnson to Oliver GOLDSMITH. Garrick said of him, "He wrote like an angel and talked like poor Poll."

Golgotha (the place of a skull). The place of Jesus' crucifixion. A small elevated spot northwest of Jerusalem, where criminals used to be executed. In modern poetry it stands for a battle-field or place of great slaughter.

> Except they meant to bathe in reeking wounds,
> Or memorize another Golgotha.
> Shakespeare, *Macbeth,* act. i. sc. 2.

Golias, Bishop. Mythical patron of the Latin student poets of the Middle Ages, celebrated in their gay and often licentious verse for his intemperance and immorality. From his name, these poets came to be called Goliards, and their poetry Goliardic. See also ARCHPOET; CONFESSION OF GOLIAS, THE.

Goliath. The Philistine giant, slain by the stripling David with a small stone hurled from a sling. (1 *Sam.* xvii, 23–54.)

golliwog. A grotesque person reminding one of the "golliwog dolls" created by the portrait painter and illustrator Florence Upton (–1922) in *The Golliwog Series* (1895). The word is a free invention, possibly suggested by polliwog.

Gollomb, Joseph (1881–). Russian-American novelist and writer on criminology, politics, etc. While teaching school (1902–1912) he wrote a number of books for boys.

Gómez, Máximo (1826–1905). Cuban patriot and general. Served in the Spanish Army; joined the Cuban insurrection (1868); rose from private to general and became a prominent leader in the war of 1895–1898. Aided in reconstruction of Cuba. Wrote several books.

Gómez de la Serna, Ramón (1891–). Spanish writer, known as Ramón. Throughout his career a literary rebel. In 1910, he launched a "futurist" manifesto. He dealt with the breakup of society, especially in his "new genre" of *greguerías,* metaphoric maxims and aphorisms in prose and verse which, as Christopher Morley says, are worthy to stand beside Chekhov's *Notebook*. His fantasy, *La Viuda*

Blanco y Negro (1917), has been highly praised. In sympathy with Republican Spain, he went to live in Buenos Aires, a voluntary exile.

Gompers, Samuel (1850–1924). British-born American labor leader. President, A.F. of L. (1886–1924, except 1895). Member, Council of National Defense (1917); member, Commission on International Labor Legislation at Peace Conference after World War I (1919).

Goncourt, Edmond (1822–1896) and **Jules de** (1830–1870). French novelists, brothers, early leaders in the movement of NATURALISM, who lived together and devoted their lives to their writing. See also BALZAC, DAUDET, FLAUBERT. Their work is marked by accuracy of detail and documentation, studies of pathological and "low-life" subjects, impersonality of treatment, a preference for separate scenes rather than a formal plot construction, and a hypersensitive, impressionistic style ("l'écriture artiste"). *Germinie Lacerteux* (1869), a novel on which both brothers collaborated, dealing with the life of a servant-girl, is regarded as the first example of naturalism of the sort associated later with ZOLA. *Manette Salomon* (1867) and *Madame Gervaisais* (1869) are also novels writtten in collaboration. Works by Edmond alone include *La Fille Elisa* (1877) which deals with prostitution. Their *Journal* presents vivid contemporary portraits.

The Goncourt brothers often used their own experiences or those of their friends in their novels, studied hospitals first-hand in search of "material," and applied the methods of painting, which they studied early in their careers (see GAUTIER), to their fiction. They wrote several studies of 18th-century society, costumes, art, furniture, and the like, and are believed to have introduced Japanese art into France. Their work was known to only a few people. See DINERS MAGNY; also PRIX GONCOURT.

Goneril. In Shakespeare's tragedy, KING LEAR, eldest daughter of King Lear, and wife of the Duke of Albany. Her name is proverbial for filial ingratitude. She treated her aged father with such scant courtesy that he could not live under her roof, and she induced her sister Regan to follow her example.

Gone With the Wind. A best-selling novel by Margaret Mitchell (*Am.,* 1936), awarded the Pulitzer Prize in 1937 and later dramatized as a record-breaking motion-picture spectacle. It deals with the adventures of Scarlett O'Hara, a beautiful, selfish, headstrong, fiery-tempered Southern belle, during the Civil War, especially her establishment of a successful business in war-ruined Atlanta and her tempestuous marriage to Rhett Butler, whose character matches her own. This was one of the first of the oversized, "escapist" historical novels popular in the U.S. during the 1930's and 1940's.

Gongorism. Extremely stilted, artificial preciosity in the poetry of Spain in the 16th century; named from the Spanish poet Luis de Góngora y Argote (1561–1627). It was paralleled in Italy by Marinism (see MARINO, GIOVANNI BATTISTA), in France by the *précieux* movement, and in England by Euphuism (see EUPHUES), and in its later forms was called CULTISM.

Gonne, Maud (1866–). A beautiful Irish revolutionist, loved by W. B. YEATS and the subject of a number of his poems. See *Life and the Dream,* by Mary COLUM.

Gonzalo. In Shakespeare's TEMPEST, an honest old counsellor of Alonso, King of Naples.

Goodbye, Mr. Chips. A best-selling novelette by James HILTON, published in 1934 and later dramatized (1938) as a successful motion picture. It deals sentimentally with the life of a popular teacher in an English public school who has been known to several generations of boys as "Mr. Chips."

Good Earth, The. A best-selling novel by Pearl BUCK, published in 1931, awarded the Pulitzer Prize in 1932, and later dramatized as a play and a motion picture. It describes the rise of Wang Lung, a Chinese peasant, from poverty to the position of a rich landowner, helped by his patient wife O-lan. Their vigor, fortitude, persistence, and enduring love of the soil are emphasized throughout.

Goodenough, Dr. A physician who attends Pen in Thackeray's PENDENNIS and is the friend of Caroline BRANDON in THE ADVENTURES OF PHILIP. He is also mentioned in THE NEWCOMES.

Good Friday. The Friday preceding Easter Day, held as the anniversary of the Crucifixion. "Good" here means *holy;* Christmas, as well as Shrove Tuesday, used to be called "the good tide." John MASEFIELD has a poem so called.

born on Good Friday. According to old superstition, those born on Christmas Day or Good Friday have the power of seeing and commanding spirits.

Goodhue, Bertram Grosvenor (1869–1924). American architect. Designed buildings at U.S. Military Academy, West Point; St. Thomas' and St. Bartholomew's Churches, New York City; Academy of Sciences, Washington, D.C.; etc.

Goodman, James or, in the original French, **Jacques Bonhomme.** A peasant nickname implying slight contempt. From it is derived the term *Jacquerie,* originally the French peasant revolt of 1358 and later any similar uprising.

Good-natured Man, The. A comedy by Oliver GOLDSMITH (1768). See also CROAKER.

Good Parliament. See under PARLIAMENTS.

Good Queen Anne. Anne of Bohemia (1366–1394), wife of Richard II of England.

Good Queen Bess. Queen ELIZABETH of England.

Goodrich, Arthur Frederick (1878–1941). American playwright. Awarded Theatre Club Gold Medal for the best play of the year for *Caponsacchi* (1926), made from Browning's masterpiece, *The Ring and The Book*. Also author of the libretto for the grand opera *Tragedy in Arezzo* (1932), later renamed *Caponsacchi*.

Goodrich, Hannibal and **Minnie.** The chief characters in William McFee's novel, CASUALS OF THE SEA.

goods.

I carry all my goods with me (*Omnia mea mecum porto*). Said by Bias, one of the SEVEN SAGES, when Priene was besieged and the inhabitants were preparing for flight.

that fellow's the goods. He's all right, just the man for the job.

to deliver the goods. To fulfill promises or come up to expectations.

Good Samaritan, see SAMARITAN.

Goodwin, Nat. Full name **Nathaniel Carll Goodwin** (1857–1919). Popular American actor. Married Maxine ELLIOTT, and several other women.

Goody Blake and Harry Gill. A poem by WORDSWORTH (1798). Harry Gill is a farmer, who forbids old Goody Blake to carry home a few sticks, which she has picked up from his land, to light a wee fire to warm herself by. Old Goody Blake curses him for his meanness, saying he would never from that moment cease from shivering with cold, and from that hour, a-bed or up, summer or winter, at home or abroad, his teeth go "chatter, chatter, chatter still."

Goodyear, Charles (1800–1860). American inventor. Patented vulcanization process, the basic patent of the rubber manufacturing industry. One of his sons, **William Henry Goodyear** (1846–1923), was an art-museum curator and historian.

Goody Two-shoes. This nursery tale first appeared in 1765. It was written for Newbery, as it is said, by Oliver GOLDSMITH. Goody Two-shoes is a very poor child, whose delight at having a *pair* of shoes is so unbounded that she cannot forbear telling everyone she meets that she has "two shoes"; whence her name. She acquires knowledge and becomes wealthy. The title-page states that the tale is for the benefit of those—

> Who from a state of rags and care,
> And having shoes but half a pair,
> Their fortune and their fame should fix,
> And gallop in a coach and six.

Googe, Barnabe (1540–1594). English poet and translator, best known for his volume of *Eclogues, Epitaphs,* and *Sonnets* (1563), regarded as containing some of the earliest examples of pastoral poetry in English. His work is considered to be typical of the type of English poetry between the period of WYATT and SURREY and that of SPENSER. It is particularly marked by alliteration and the use of the "FOURTEENER."

Google, Barney, see BARNEY GOOGLE.

Gookin, Daniel (1612–1687). American Puritan author, holder of public offices in Massachusetts and known for his humanitarian interest in the Indians. He wrote *Historical Collection of the Indians in New England* (1792) and *An Historical Account of the Doings and Sufferings of the Christian Indians* (1836), both posthumously published.

goon. Probably a PORTMANTEAU WORD from *go*rilla and babo*on,* introduced by E. C. Segar (1894–1938) for certain subhuman creatures in one of his comic strips. Hence, in slang, a slugger, bomber, incendiary, etc., hired by racketeers for purposes of terrorization.

Goops. A strange set of beings invented by Gelett BURGESS for the edification and delight of juvenile readers. Their unmannerly pranks form the subject of *Goops and How to be Them* (1900), *More Goops and How Not to be Them* (1903), *Goop Tales* (1904), *The Goop Directory* (1913), *The Goop Encyclopedia* (1916).

goose.

the Goose Bible. See BIBLE, SPECIALLY NAMED.

goose fair. A fair formerly held in many English towns about the time of MICHAELMAS, when geese were plentiful. That at Nottingham, still held, was the most important.

the goose step. A step formerly *de rigueur* in the Prussian army for ceremonial purposes, "marching past," and so on. At each pace the thigh had to be brought to a right-angle with the erect body. It was supposed to look extremely dignified when carried out by a well drilled body of men, but it was unmercifully ridiculed by the Allies during World War I.

Also, balancing on one foot and moving the other back and forwards; preliminary exercise for recruits.

he killed the goose to get the eggs. He grasped at what was more than his due, and lost an excellent customer. The Greek fable says a countryman had a goose that laid golden eggs; thinking to make himself rich, he killed the goose to get the whole stock of eggs at once, but lost everything.

he steals a goose and gives the giblets in alms. He amasses wealth by overreaching, and salves his conscience by giving small sums in charity.

I'll cook your goose for you. I'll pay you out. It is said that Eric, king of Sweden, coming to a certain town with very few soldiers, the enemy, in mockery, hung out a goose for him to shoot at. Finding, however, that the king meant business, and that it would be no laughing matter for them, they sent heralds to ask him what he wanted. "To cook your goose for you," he facetiously replied.

Michaelmas goose. See MICHAELMAS.

the old woman is plucking her goose. A children's way of saying, it is snowing.

the older the goose, the harder to pluck. Old men are unwilling to part with their money.

the Royal Game of Goose. The game referred to by GOLDSMITH (*Deserted Village,* 232) as being present in the ale-house—

> The pictures placed for ornament and use,
> The twelve good rules, the royal game of goose—

was a game of compartments through which the player progressed according to the cast of the dice. At certain divisions a goose was depicted, and if the player fell into one of these he doubled the number of his last throw and moved forward accordingly.

what's sauce for the goose is sauce for the gander. See GANDER.

geese save the capitol. The tradition is that when the Gauls invaded Rome a detachment in single file clambered up the hill of the capitol so silently that the foremost man reached the top without being challenged; but when he was striding over the rampart, some sacred geese, disturbed by the noise, began to cackle, and awoke the garrison. Marcus Manlius rushed to the wall and hurled the fellow over the precipice. To commemorate this event (390 B.C.) the Romans carried a golden goose in procession to the capitol every year.

> Those consecrated geese in orders,
> That to the capitol were warders,
> And being then upon patrol,
> With noise alone beat off the Gaul.
>
> Butler, *Hudibras,* ii 3.

Goose, Mother. A mythical character famous as giving the name to *Mother Goose's Nursery Rhymes,* which seems to have been first used in *Songs for the Nursery, Or Mother Goose's Melodies for Children,* published by T. Fleet in Boston, Mass., in 1719. The story goes that Fleet married Elizabeth Goose, whose mother used to sing the rhymes to her grandson, but this explanation of the name is discounted by the fact that Perrault's *Contes de ma mère l'oye* (Tales of my Mother Goose) had appeared in 1697.

gooseberry.

the big gooseberry season. In England, the dull time in journalism when Parliament is not sitting, the Law Courts are up, and "nobody" is in town, when the old-fashioned editor will publish accounts of giant gooseberries, sea-serpents, vegetable marrows, sweet peas, just to fill up; the "silly season."

to play gooseberry. To act as chaperon: to go about with two lovers for appearance' sake. The person "who plays propriety" is expected to hear, see, and say nothing. A chaperon was perhaps so called because one performing this duty would turn to anything convenient, such as gooseberry picking, to give the young people a chance.

Gopher Prairie. The small town in Minnesota which is the scene of Sinclair Lewis' novel, MAIN STREET. It quickly became a synonym for a small town of petty, self-centered interests, and prejudices.

Gopher State. Minnesota. See under STATES.

gorblimey. From *God blind me.* A British vulgarism expressing surprise.

Gorboduc. The first historical play and first tragedy in the English language (1562), by Thomas SACKVILLE and Thomas NORTON. Gorboduc is a mythical British king, who has two sons, FERREX AND PORREX. Ferrex is driven by his brother out of the kingdom, and on attempting to return with a large army, is defeated by him and slain. Soon afterwards, Porrex himself is murdered in his bed by his own mother, who loved Ferrex the better.

Gordian knot. A great difficulty. Gordius, a peasant, being chosen king of Phrygia, dedicated his wagon to Jupiter, and fastened the yoke to a beam with a rope of bark so ingeniously that no one could untie it. Alexander was told that "whoever undid the knot would reign over the whole East." "Well then," said the conqueror, "it is thus I perform the task," and, so saying, he cut the knot in twain with his sword. Hence, *to cut the Gordian knot* is to get out of a difficult or awkward position by one decisive step, to solve a problem by a single brilliant stroke.

Gordon, Caroline (1895–). American novelist. Wife of the poet Allen TATE. Once a reporter on the Chattanooga *News.* Ford Madox Ford hailed her work as "a classical phenomenon." Her first and best-known novel is *Penhally* (1931).

Gordon, Charles George (1833–1885). Known as **Chinese Gordon** or **Gordon Pasha.** English soldier. Commander of a Chinese force, called the Ever Victorious Army, against the Taiping rebels (1863). In the service of the Khedive of Egypt (1874–1876). As governor of the Sudan and the Equatorial Provinces (1877–1879), he suppressed the slave trade. Sent by the British government (1884) to rescue Egyptian garrisons in their struggle against the Mahdi, he evacuated 2500 women, children, and wounded from Khartoum, held the place for ten months and was killed when it was forced to surrender.

Gordon, Charles William (1860–1937). Pseudonym **Ralph Connor.** Canadian Presbyterian clergyman and novelist; best-known for *Black Rock* (1898), *The Sky Pilot* (1899), and *Glengarry School Days* (1902).

Gordon or **No-Popery Riots.** Riots in 1780, headed by Lord George Gordon, to compel the House of Commons to repeal the bill passed in 1778 for the relief of Roman Catholics. Gordon was of unsound mind, and he died in 1793, a proselyte to Judaism. Dickens has given a very vivid description of the Gordon riots in BARNABY RUDGE.

Gorgas, William Crawford (1854–1920). American army surgeon; freed Havana of yellow fever. Chief sanitary officer, Panama Canal Commission (1904–1913). Brigadier general as surgeon general, U.S. Army (1914). See REED, WALTER.

Gorgibus. (1) In Molière's PRÉCIEUSES RIDICULES, an honest, simple-minded citizen of middle life, father of Madelon and uncle of Cathos. (2) Father of Célie in Molière's SGANARELLE.

Gorgon. Anything unusually hideous, particularly a hideous or terrifying woman. In classical mythology, there were three Gorgons, with serpents on their heads instead of hair. MEDUSA was the chief, and the only one that was mortal, but so hideous was her face that whoever set eyes on it was instantly turned to stone. She was slain by Perseus, and her head placed on the shield of Minerva.

What was that snaky-headed Gorgon shield
That wise Minerva wore, unconquered virgin.
Wherewith she freezed her foes to congealed stone?
But rigid looks of chaste austerity,
And noble grace, that dashed brute violence
With sudden adoration and blank awe.
Milton, *Comus*, 458.

Goriot, Father. The titular hero of BALZAC's novel *Father Goriot* (*Le Père Goriot;* 1835), an old man whose consuming passion it is to deprive himself of everything, self-respect included, for the sake of his two ungrateful daughters, Mme de Nucingen and Mme de Restaud (Delphine and Anastasie). The two sisters are married to wealthy men of position, but both, though ashamed and intolerant of the bourgeois manners of the ex-vermicelli-manufacturer, expect him to extricate them from financial difficulties. Goriot allows himself to be shamefully abused, lives in a state of utter shabbiness and poverty in a cheap boarding house, and after he has sacrificed his last silver plate, dies of apoplexy. The two daughters send empty carriages to the funeral.

Gorki, Maxim. Pseudonym of **Alexey Maximovich Peshkov** (1868–1936). Russian short-story writer and dramatist, associated with LENIN in the Russian revolution of 1917 and widely honored in the U.S.S.R. He is best known for his early short stories dealing with underworld characters, vagabonds, and social outcasts. Among his works are *Foma Gordeyev* (1901); *Orloff and His Wife* (1901), tales; *Twenty-six and One* (1902); *The Outcasts, And Other Stories* (1905); *A Night's Lodging* (1905); *Mother* (1907); *Creatures That Once Were Men* (1906); *The Spy* (1908); THE LOWER DEPTHS (1912), his most famous play; *Submerged* (1915), a play; *The Confession* (1916); *My Childhood* (1915), *In the World* (1923), and *My University Days* (1923), autobiography; *Stories of the Steppe* (1918); *The Judge* (1924), a play; *Days with Lenin* (1932).

Gorlois. In Arthurian legend, Duke of Cornwall and husband of YGERNE. On the night that he is slain through the enchantments of Merlin, Uther Pendragon comes to Ygerne in the likeness of Gorlois and makes her the mother of King Arthur. Before the child is born Uther Pendragon marries her.

Gorman, Herbert Sherman (1893–). American writer. *Notations for a Chimaera* (poems; 1926); *The Place Called Dagon* (novel; 1927); *The Incredible Marquis* (biography; 1929); *James Joyce: a Biography* (1940), etc.

Gosling, Giles. In Scott's KENILWORTH, landlord of the Black Bear Inn, near Cumnor Place.

Cicely Gosling. Daughter of Giles.

Gosnold, Bartholomew (d. 1607). English navigator. Second in command of expedition carrying settlers to Jamestown, Va. (1606–1607).

Gosse, Sir **Edmund William** (1849–1928). English poet, critic, essayist, and biographer. Noted for introducing Scandinavian literature to English readers. Also keenly interested in French literature. His autobiographical *Father and Son* (1907) is a fine human document. A friend of many English authors of note, especially R. L. STEVENSON. His somewhat feline disposition, notable in his *Letters*, also made him some enemies.

Gossips, Prince of, see PRINCE.

Gösta Berling, The Story of. A novel of Swedish life by Selma LAGERLÖF (1894), for which she was awarded the Nobel Prize in

1909. It relates the adventures of the impulsive and temperamental young hero, whose magnetic personality inevitably draws people, particularly women, to him, and whose turbulent passions just as inevitably involve him and them in misfortune. Eventually he marries the Countess Elizabeth, whose husband, Hendrik Dohna, has divorced her, and through Elizabeth's influence and his own effort enters upon a life that more nearly approximates his own ideals.

Goth. One of an ancient tribe of Teutons which swept down upon and devastated large portions of southern Europe in the 3rd to 5th centuries, establishing kingdoms in Italy, southern France, and Spain. They were looked on by the civilized Romans as merely destroying barbarians; hence the name came to be applied to any rude, uncultured, destructive people.

The Goths were divided by the Dnieper into East Goths (Ostrogoths), and West Goths (Visigoths), and were the most cultured of the German peoples.—Baring-Gould, *Story of Germany*, p. 37.

the last of the Goths. See RODERICK.

Gotham, wise men of. Fools, wiseacres. The legend is that King John, on his way to Lynn Regis, intended to pass through Gotham, in Nottinghamshire, with his army, and sent heralds to prepare his way. The men of Gotham were resolved, if possible, to prevent this expense and depredation, so they resolved to play the fool. Some raked the moon out of the pond, some made a ring to hedge in a bird, some did other equally foolish things. The king then abandoned his intention, and the "wise men" of the village cunningly remarked, "We ween there are more fools pass through Gotham than remain in it." A collection of popular tales of stupidity was published in the reign of Henry VIII as *Merie Tales of the Mad Men of Gotham, gathered together by A. B. of Phisike, Doctour,* and since that date many other tales have been attached to the inhabitants of Gotham. The old nursery rhyme is well known—

Three wise men of Gotham
Went to sea in a bowl;
If the bowl had been stronger
My story had been longer.

The name *Gotham* was given to New York City by Washington Irving in his satirical *Salmagundi Papers* (1807) and has remained in current use.

Gothic. An adjective used often in reference to the Middle Ages, especially during the neo-Classical period of the 18th century, when it meant wild, uncivilized, unrestrained, and had a derogatory connotation.

Gothic architecture. A style of medieval architecture of northern and western Europe (about 1150 to 1500). It developed from the Romanesque. Examples of it are stone-vaulted churches with three to five aisles, the middle aisle being loftier than the others. Its decoration is allegorical and symbolic, often with grotesque carvings of birds, beasts, GARGOYLES, human figures. It used the pointed arch which allowed for larger windows. Such cathedrals as those at Chartres, Paris, Rheims, Cologne, York, Glasgow and Westminster Abbey are examples.

Gothic novel. A type of novel popular in England in the latter half of the 18th century, later spreading to the U.S. and Europe, especially Germany. It is characterized by horror, terror, supernatural effects, murder, violence, and taste for the medieval, usually set against a background of Gothic architecture, especially a gloomy and isolated castle. Horace Walpole's CASTLE OF OTRANTO (1764), Beckford's VATHEK (1786), Lewis's THE MONK (1795), and Mrs. Radcliffe's THE MYSTERIES OF UDOLPHO (1795) are the outstanding English representatives of the Gothic novel. American authors of novels in the Gothic tradition were Charles Brockden BROWN, Nathaniel HAWTHORNE, and Edgar Allan POE. The movement of SURREALISM claimed the Gothic novel as one of its forerunners, and the 20th-century "mystery story" featured in lending-libraries and drug-stores was a descendant of this *genre*.

Gothland, The Queen of. A poem by Herbert FRENCH.

Gottfried von Strassburg (*fl.* 13th century). Medieval German poet, best known for his treatments in Middle High German of the *Parzival* and *Tristam* legends. See GRAIL; PERCIVAL; PARSIFAL.

Gottlieb, Max. In Sinclair Lewis' ARROWSMITH, a kindly German doctor who teaches young Martin Arrowsmith the qualities required of a scientist.

Götz von Berlichingen. A romantic drama (1773) by GOETHE, based on the autobiography of the sixteenth-century knight of that name.

gouache. A method of painting with water colors made opaque by the addition of white and mixed with a gum preparation. Also a picture so painted, or the pigment used.

Goudy, Frederic William (1865–1947). American printer and type designer. Produced over ninety type faces. Established the Village Press, now near Marlborough, N.Y.

Goujon, Jean (1510?–?1568). The greatest sculptor of the French Renaissance. With Pierre LESCOT restored the church of St. Germain l'Auxerrois in Paris. Assisted Lescot in work on the Louvre, notably the musician's gallery. According to tradition he was shot on his scaffold in the court of the Louvre during the massacre of St. Bartholomew (1572).

Gould, Charles. In Conrad's NOSTROMO, the head of the Gould silver mines.

Dona Emilia Gould. Gould's gentle and beautiful wife.

Gould, Jay (1836–1892). American financier. With James Fisk and Daniel Drew ruined Erie Railroad and looted its treasury (1868). Attempted to corner gold, causing panic of Black Friday (Sept. 24, 1869). His son, **George Jay Gould** (1864–1923), inherited vast railroad interests which he lost to Kuhn, Loeb and Co., and E. H. Harriman.

Gounod, Charles François (1818–1893). French composer. His best-known operas are *Faust* (1859) and *Roméo et Juliette* (1867). He at first wrote sacred music; among his songs is the famous *Ave Maria* based on Bach's first prelude of the *Well Tempered Clavichord.* At one time he had thought of entering the Church.

gourmand and **gourmet** (*Fr.*). The *gourmand* is one whose chief pleasure is eating; but a *gourmet* is a connoisseur of food and wines. The *gourmand* regards quantity more than quality; the *gourmet,* quality more than quantity. See APICIUS.

> In former times [in France] *gourmand* meant a judge of eating, and *gourmet* a judge of wine . . . Gourmet is now universally understood to refer to eating, and not to drinking.—Hamerton, *French and English,* Pt. v, ch. iv.

the gourmand's prayer. "O Philoxenos, Philoxenos, why were you not Prometheus?" Prometheus was the mythological creator of man, and Philoxenos was a great epicure, whose great and constant wish was to have the neck of a crane, that he might enjoy the taste of his food longer before it was swallowed into his stomach. (Aristotle, *Ethics,* iii. 10.)

Gourmont, Rémy de (1858–1915). French critic, novelist, and poet, whose work is marked by fantasy, irony, and an emphasis on sensuality, in his early career associated with the Symbolist (see SYMBOLISM) group. Among his works of fiction, short stories, letters, and the like, are: *Sixtine* (1890); *Histoires Magiques* (1894); *Les Chevaux de Diomède* (*The Horses of Diomede;* 1897); *Le Songe d'une Femme* (1899); A *Night at the Luxembourg* (*Une Nuit au Luxembourg;* 1906); *The Virgin Heart* (*Un Coeur Virginal;* 1907); *Couleurs* (1908); *Lettres à l'Amazone* (1914); *Lettres Intime à l'Amazone* (1927). His essays and critical prose include: *The Book of Masques* (*Le Livre des Masques;* 1896–1898); *L'Esthétique de la Langue Française* (1899); *Le Problème du Style* (1902); *Physiology of Love* (*Physique de l'Amour;* 1903); *Promenades Littéraires* (1904–1913).

During a large part of his life, Gourmont's face was disfigured by an unsightly growth. He lived in seclusion in stuffy, dusty rooms, dressed in the robes of a Trappist monk. A number of his articles were written under the name of Richard de Bury. See also BARNEY, NATALIE.

Gower, John (1330?–1408). English poet, a friend and contemporary of CHAUCER, author of moral and didactic allegorical poems of the type popular at the time. His best-known works are: MIROIR DE L'HOMME (*Speculum Meditantis;* ca. 1382), written in Norman French; VOX CLAMANTIS (ca. 1382), written in Latin; and CONFESSIO AMANTIS (1390?) in Middle English.

Go West, Young Man! Horace GREELEY'S recipe for success.

Gowk-thrapple, Maister. In Scott's WAVERLEY, a covenanting preacher.

> A man of coarse, mechanical, perhaps rather intrinsically feeble intellect, with the vehemence of some pulpit-drumming Gowk-thrapple.—Carlyle.

gown and town row. In university towns, a scrimmage between the students of different colleges and the townsmen. These feuds go back at least to the reign of King John, when 3,000 students left Oxford for Reading, owing to a quarrel with the men of the town.

Goya y Lucientes, Francisco José de (1746–1828). Spanish master painter, etcher, and lithographer. He designed cartoons for tapestries for the Prado in Madrid, and was the chief painter to the Spanish King. He is widely known for his ferocious depiction of the stark realities of war, and for his realistic portrayal of contemporary life in Spain, Spanish customs, bullfights, etc. He died in voluntary political exile in Bordeaux, France. The best modern book about Goya is *In the Blazing Light* by Max White, a novel concerning the lusty life of the painter.

Gozzoli, Benozzo (1420–1498). Florentine painter and goldsmith; helped GHIBERTI on one of the bronze doors of the Florence baptistery; chiefly known for his narrational murals in the Campo Santo, Pisa.

Gracae. In Greek mythology, sentinels for the Gorgons, daughters of the sea deity Phorcus. They were Deino, Enyo, and Pephredo.

Gracchi, mother of the. CORNELIA.

Grace Abounding to the Chief of Sinners. An autobiography of John BUNYAN (1666), written in prison and describing his religious experiences and the development of his spiritual convictions.

grace. In music, an embellishment which is not a necessary part of the melody or harmony; an appoggiatura, a trill, a turn, etc. The execution and allocation of graces, especially in the eighteenth century, was often left to the discretion of the performer.

Graces, the three. In classical mythology, the goddesses who bestowed beauty and charm and were themselves the embodiment of both. They were the sisters Aglaia, Thalia, and Euphrosyne.

> They are the daughters of sky-ruling Jove,
> By him begot of faire Eurynome, . . .
> The first of them hight mylde Euphrosyne,
> Next faire Aglaia, last Thalia merry;
> Sweete Goddesses all three, which me in mirth do cherry
> Spenser, *Faërie Queene,* VI, x, 22.

Andrea Appiani (1754–1817), the Italian fresco artist, was known as *the Painter of the Graces.*

Gracioso. The interlocutor, a stock character in the Spanish *drame romantique.* He thrusts himself forward on all occasions, ever and anon directing his gibes to the audience.

Gradgrind, Thomas. A character in Dickens' Hard Times, typical of a man who measures everything with rule and compass, allows nothing for the weakness of human nature, and deals with men and women as a mathematician with his figures. Everything about him is square; his forehead is square, and so is his forefinger, with which he emphasizes all he says. Formerly he was in the wholesale hardware line. In his greatness he becomes M.P. for Coketown, and he lives at Stone Lodge, a mile or so from town. He prides himself on being eminently practical, and, though not a bad man at heart, he blights his children by his hard, practical way of bringing them up.

Gradus. Short for **Gradus ad Parnassum,** literally, "steps to Parnassus." A dictionary of prosody, poetical phrases, etc., of the kind once used in English schools as an aid to Latin versification. Also the title of a Latin work on counterpoint by Johann Joseph Fux (1725) and a name used for similar works on the other arts.

Graeme, Roland. In Scott's Abbot the foundling heir of Avenel. He first appears as page to the Lady of Avenel, then as page to Mary, Queen of Scots.

Graemes, the. A clan of freebooters who inhabited the Debatable Land, and were transported to Ireland at the beginning of the 17th century.

graffiti, sing. **graffito.** In archeology, rude scribblings found on rocks, walls, vases, etc. Valuable to archaeologists and historians for information concerning the habits and modes of thought of the ancients.

Graham, Stephen (1884–). English writer and authority on Russian literature and history. Tramped the American Far West with Vachel Lindsay (1921). Traveled extensively and regularly wrote books of competent journalism.

Grahame, Kenneth (1859–1932). British author. Wrote a masterpiece of fantasy, The Wind in the Willows (1908), for his son Alastair (who died in an accident at twenty). *The Golden Age* (1895) and *Dream Days* (1898) are permanent literature, written about children, "the only really living people."

Grahame-White, Claude (1879–). English aviator and aeronautical engineer. Founded at Pau in France the first British school of aviation (1909). First flight by night. Won Gordon Bennett trophy. Established Grahame-White Aviation Co.

Graham of Claverhouse, John. 1st Viscount **Dundee.** Known as **Bloody Claverse** or **Bonny Dundee** (1649?–1689). Scottish Royalist and Jacobite. Under Marquis of Montrose employed in repression of conventicles in favor of episcopacy in Scotland. Persecuted the Covenanters. In 1689 raised a body of Highlanders to fight for James II, won the battle of Killiecrankie but was mortally wounded.

Grail, Holy Grail, or **Sangreal (Sangraal).** The cup or chalice traditionally used by Christ at the Last Supper, and the center round which a huge *corpus* of medieval legend, romance, and allegory revolves.

According to one account, Joseph of Arimathea preserved the Grail, and received into it some of the blood of the Savior at the Crucifixion. He brought it to England, but it disappeared. According to others, it was brought by angels from heaven and entrusted to a body of knights who guarded it on top of a mountain. When approached by anyone not of perfect purity, it disappeared from sight, and its quest became the source of most of the adventures of the Knights of the Round Table. See also Perceforest.

The mass of literature concerning the Grail cycle, both ancient and modern, is enormous. The chief sources of the principal groups of legends are: the *Peredur* (Welsh, given in the Mabinogion), which is one of the most archaic forms of the Quest story; the unfinished *Conte del Graal* by Chrétien de Troyes, in which the Grail is a hollow dish, accompanied in a procession by a bleeding spear; Wolfram von Eschenbach's Parzifal (ca. 1210), the best example of the story as transformed by ecclesiastical influence; a chivalric version by Gottfried von Strassburg; the 13th-century French Percival le Gallois (founded on earlier English and Celtic legends which had no connection with the Grail), showing Percival in his later rôle as an ascetic hero, translated by Dr. Sebastian Evans (1893), as *The High History of the Holy Grail;* and the *Quête du St. Graal,* which, in its English dress, forms Bks. 13–18 of Malory's Morte d'Arthur. See Galahad. It was the French poet, Robert de BORON (*fl.* ca. 1215), who, in his *Joseph d'Arimathie or Le Saint Graal,* first definitely attached the history of the Grail to the Arthurian cycle and first mentioned the Grail as a container for the Host. The framework of Tennyson's *Holy Grail,* IDYLLS OF THE KING, is taken from Malory.

A second conception of the Grail is that it was not a cup, but the dish out of which Christ and his disciples ate the Paschal lamb at the Last Supper. The following passages from the *Morte d'Arthur* are illustrative of Malory's treatment of the Grail legend:

> Then anon they heard cracking and crying of thunder. . . . In the midst of the blast entered a sunbeam more clear by seven times than the day, and all they were alighted of the grace of the Holy Ghost. . . . Then there entered into the hall the Holy Grale covered with white samite, but there was none that could see it, nor who bare it, but the whole hall was full filled with good odours, and every knight had such meat and drink as he best loved in the world, and when the Holy Grale had been borne through the hall, then the holy vessel departed suddenly, and they wist not where it became.—Ch. 35.
>
> Then looked they and saw a man come out of the holy vessel, that had all the signs of the passion of Christ, and he said . . . "This is the holy dish wherein I ate the lamb on Sher-Thursday, and now hast thou seen it . . . yet hast thou not seen it so openly as thou shalt see it in the city of Sarras . . . therefore thou must go hence and bear with thee this holy vessel, for this night it shall depart from the realm of Logris . . . and take with thee . . . sir Percivale and sir Bors."—Ch. 101.
>
> So departed sir Galahad, and sir Percivale and sir Bors with him. And so they rode three days, and came to a river, and found a ship . . . and when on board, they found in the midst the table of silver and the Sancgreall covered with white samite. . . . Then sir Galahad laid him down and slept . . . and when he woke . . . he saw the city of Sarras (Ch. 103). . . . At the year's end, . . . he saw before him the holy vessel, and a man kneeling upon his knees in the likeness of the bishop, which had about him a great fellowship of angels, as it had been Christ Himself . . . and when he came to the sakering of the Mass, and had done, anon he called sir Galahad, and said unto him, "Come forth, . . . and thou shalt see that which thou hast much desired to see" . . . and he beheld spiritual things . . .—Ch. 104.

It is also believed by some that the Grail was originally, in pre-Christian times, a female sexual symbol which, with the bleeding spear appearing in Chrétien de Troyes' early account, was used in fertility rites. For a further discussion of this interesting theory, cf. *From Ritual to Romance,* by Jessica L. Weston, a source used by T. S. ELIOT in his poem THE WASTE LAND, where the Grail theme occurs in a similarly symbolic form.

Grainne. A heroine of ancient Irish legend, a daughter of King Cormac and beloved by Finn. See under FINGAL. She was, however, in love with Finn's nephew Diarmuid or Dermot, and the two eloped, pursued at length and through many adventures by Finn, until Diarmuid was at last killed. See also DEIRDRE. Diarmuid and Grainne are among the Irish legendary characters invoked by James Joyce in his novel FINNEGANS WAKE.

Gram. In the *Völsunga Saga,* the sword which Odin thrusts into a tree. It is pulled out by Siegmund, father of Siegfried. In the Nibelungenlied, it is Siegfried's sword, called BALMUNG.

Grammarian's Funeral, A. A poem (1855) by Robert BROWNING.

Gramont, Comte **Philibert de** (1621?–1707). A French nobleman at Louis XIV's court until 1662 when he was banished because of an affair with one of the king's mistresses and settled at the court of Charles II of England. The *Mémoires du Comte de Gramont* were written by his brother-in-law Anthony Hamilton.

Granada, Archbishop of, see under ARCHBISHOP.

Granada, conquest of, see under CONQUEST.

grand, le.

le Grand Bâtard. Antoine de Bourgogne (d. 1504), a natural son of Philip the Good, famous for his deeds of prowess.

le Grand Corneille. Pierre Corneille, the French dramatist (1606–1684).

le Grand Dauphin. Louis, son of Louis XIV (1661–1711).

la Grand Mademoiselle. The Duchesse de Montpensier (1627–1693), daughter of Gaston, Duc d'Orleans, and cousin of Louis XIV.

le Grand Monarque. Louis XIV, King of France (b. 1638, reigned 1643–1715).

le Grand Pan. Voltaire (1694–1778).

Monsieur le Grand. The Grand Equerry of France in the reign of Louis XIV.

Grand Army of the Republic. A secret association organized in 1866 of veterans who had served in the Union Army or Navy during the Civil War. Abbreviation G.A.R. Its first "post" was organized at Decatur, Illinois. The annual meetings were called encampments.

Grand Canal. The chief water thoroughfare of Venice, Italy. It is shaped like an S and runs from the railroad station to Santa Maria del Salute.

Grandcourt, Henleigh. In George Eliot's DANIEL DERONDA a wealthy man of middle age who married GWENDOLYN HARLETH.

Grandet, Félix. One of BALZAC's well known characters, a type of greed and domestic tyranny. When his daughter Eugénie, who loves her cousin Charles Grandet, opposes the miser in his schemes to cheat Charles of his inheritance, he locks her up and becomes so violent that he alarms the town. But in general his greed is of the cold, methodical variety.

Eugénie Grandet. Daughter of the above and heroine of Balzac's novel called by her name. See EUGÉNIE GRANDET. Her cousin Charles whom she loves goes to India and returns with a wife who has both wealth and title. Eugénie then marries the elderly Cruchot de Bonfons, who has long been her suitor. Upon his death, she devotes herself to charity.

Grandfather's Chair, The Whole History of. A volume of children's stories by HAWTHORNE (1840–1842). The tales include episodes in early American history, chiefly stories of persons who might have sat in the chair given to Lady Arabella Johnson by her father, the Earl of Lincoln.

Grandgent, Charles Hall (1862–1939). American educator. Head of Department of Romance languages at Harvard (1899–1911). Author of many textbooks and an authority on Dante.

Grand Guignol. A small theater in the Rue Chaptal, Montmartre, Paris, specializing in brief horror plays. From *guignol,* a puppet or puppet show, after *Guignol,* the town "character" of Lyon where a theater of the kind later named after him was established in 1795.

Grandison, Mrs. Caroline. In Meredith's RICHARD FEVEREL, a "colorless lady of an unequivocal character, living upon drugs and governing her husband and the world from her sofa."

Grandison, Sir Charles, see SIR CHARLES GRANDISON.

Grandissimes, The. A novel by G. W. CABLE (1880). The setting is New Orleans in the period of the Louisiana Purchase. The central plot of the book has to do with the enmity of two powerful families, the Grandissimes and the De Grapions, and their final reconciliation through a pair of lovers. A powerful character in the novel is the African king Bras Coupé, who allows himself to be tortured to death rather than be a slave. See also NANCANOU.

Grand Pré. The scene of much of Longfellow's EVANGELINE, a village of Acadia (now Nova Scotia), inhabited by a colony from Normandy, of very primitive manners, preserving the very costume of their old Norman forefathers. They had no locks to their doors nor bolts to their windows. There "the richest man was poor, and the poorest lived in abundance."

Grand Prix de Rome. French Government Prize to French artists, giving the most successful competitor in painting, sculpture, engraving, architecture, or music a four-year stipend at the French Academy of Fine Arts at Rome (founded by Louis XIV in 1666) and exemption from military service for the period of attendance.

Grand Remonstrance. In English history, the protest passed by the House of Commons against the tyrannical acts of King Charles I (November, 1641).

grangerize. Chiefly a British expression, meaning to "extra-illustrate" a book; to supplement it by the addition of illustrations, portraits, autograph letters, caricatures, prints, broadsheets, biographical sketches, anecdotes, scandals, press notices, parallel passages, and any other sort of matter directly or indirectly bearing on the subject. So called from James Granger (1723–1776) who, in 1769, started the craze by publishing a *Biographical History of England* with blank pages for the insertion of extra illustrations, etc.

Grangousier. In Rabelais' satire, GARGANTUA AND PANTAGRUEL, a king of Utopia, who marries, in "the vigor of his old age," Gargamelle, daughter of the King of the Parpaillons, and becomes the father of Gargantua. Some say he is meant for Louis XII, but Motteux thinks the "academy figure" of this old Priam was John d'Albret, King of Navarre.

Grani. In old Norse hero legends, the gray charger of Siegfried or Sigurd, whose swiftness exceeded that of the winds. Gunnar borrowed him from Siegfried and fruitlessly attempted to ride him through the flames to rescue Brunhild, but as soon as Siegfried himself mounted, Grani recognized his master's spur and dashed through the fire.

Granite City or **Capital.** Aberdeen. See under CITY.

Granite State. New Hampshire. See STATES.

Granjon, Robert. A sixteenth-century French type founder, engraver, and printer in Paris (1551) and Lyon (1558). His *caractères de civilité* were based on French handwriting. Modifications of his italic and roman types are still in use. In musical notation his name is associated with the introduction of round notes.

Grant, Gordon (1875–). American painter and illustrator. Made a name for himself especially through his pictures of ships.

Grant, Percy Stickney (1860–1927). American Protestant Episcopal minister, pastor of Church of the Ascension in New York City (till resignation, 1924). Advocate of socialism and founder of a forum on social problems. Involved in a dispute with Bishop Manning on questions of church doctrine.

Grant, Robert (1852–1940). American lawyer, essayist, novelist. Advocated more liberal divorce laws in the 1920's. He was a member of Governor Fuller's Advisory Committee which sealed the death sentence of Sacco and Vanzetti (1927). His best-known novel is *Unleavened Bread* (1900).

Grant, Ulysses Simpson (1822–1885). U.S. Civil War General. Carried command under Lincoln of all armies of U.S. Eighteenth (Republican) President of the United States (elected 1868; re-elected 1872). Though personally honest, major scandals (as the Crédit Mobilier, the Whisky Ring, the attempt of speculators to corner the gold market, etc.) discredited his administration. His *Memoirs* were published in two volumes (1885–1886). His tomb in New York City suffers as a monument in his honor through the comparison with that of Napoleon which it invites.

Grantly, Archdeacon. In Trollope's *Chronicles of Barsetshire* (see BARSETSHIRE) an archdeacon, one of the best known of Trollope's clerical characters.

Grantorto (great wrong). In Spenser's FAËRIE QUEENE (V. xi. xii), a giant who withholds the inheritance of Irena (*Ireland*). He typifies rebellion. He is slain by Sir Artegal.

Granville-Barker, Harley Granville (1877–1946). English actor, manager, playwright. Wrote *The Voysey Inheritance* (1905), *The Madras House* (1910), and made adaptations of SCHNITZLER, GUITRY, and ROMAINS; etc.

grapes.
the grapes are sour. You disparage it because it is beyond your reach. The allusion is to Aesop's well known fable of the fox, which tried in vain to get at some grapes, and, when he found they were beyond his reach, went away saying, "I see they are sour."

There, economy was always "elegant," and money-spending always "vulgar" and ostentatious—a sort of sour grapeism, which made us very peaceful and satisfied.—Mrs. Gaskell, *Cranford*, ch. i.

Grapes of Wrath, The. A best-selling novel of the proletarian type by John STEINBECK, published in 1939, awarded the Pulitzer Prize in 1940, and soon afterwards dramatized as a successful motion picture. It tells of the hardships of the JOAD family, farmers who are leaving the Oklahoma Dust Bowl region where it is no longer possible to raise crops to drive to California in search of work as migrant fruit-pickers. The grandparents die on the way, and on arrival the others are beset by the police, starvation, and strike conflicts, during one of which Tom, the Joad son, kills a man. At the conclusion of the novel, throughout which descriptive and philosophical passages alternate with narrative portions, the family is defeated but still resolute. See also PROLETARIAN LITERATURE.

graphology. The science and practice of character reading based on a person's handwriting. The axiom of graphology is that a person's handwriting is a form of behavior and, just as any other human product or action, must bear the imprint of his personality. The difficulties of practical application of this axiom have brought graphology into disrepute and opened the doors wide to all sorts of charlatanism.

Gratiano. In Shakespeare's MERCHANT OF VENICE, one of Antonio's friends. He "talked an infinite deal of nothing, more than any man in all Venice." Gratiano marries Nerissa, the waiting-gentlewoman of Portia.

Grattan, Henry (1746–1820). Irish orator and statesman. Persistent advocate of Irish independence and Catholic emancipation. Cf. *Memoirs of the Life and Times of Henry Grattan, by his son Henry Grattan* (1839–1846).

Grau, Maurice (1849–1907). Austrian-born operatic manager. Managed Salvini, Irving, Terry, Réjane, Bernhardt. Business manager Metropolitan Opera House, N.Y. Head of Maurice Grau Opera Company.

Graustark. An imaginary petty kingdom of Europe, the scene of George Barr McCutcheon's adventure tales, *Graustark* (*Am.*, 1901) and *Beverly of Graustark*. It is frequently referred to in literary criticism as typical of impossibly melodramatic fiction.

Graves, Alfred Perceval (1846–1931). Irish man of letters and poet. Leader in Irish literary renascence. *Songs of Killarney* (1872); *Irish Songs and Ballads* (1879). Father of Robert GRAVES.

Graves, Clotilde Inez Mary (1863–1932). Pseudonym **Richard Dehan.** Irish novelist. *The Dop Doctor* (1910), etc. Also playwright.

Graves, Robert (1895–). English poet and novelist, first known for his poetry protesting against the horrors of World War I. His collections of verse include: *Over the Brazier* (1916); *Goliath and David* (1916); *Fairies and Fusiliers* (1917); *The Treasure Box* (1919); *Country Sentiment* (1920); *The Pier Glass* (1921); *Whipperginny* (1923); *The Feather Bed* (1923); *Mock Beggar Hall* (1924); *Welshman's Hose* (1925); *The Marmosite's Miscellany* (1925), this being published under the pseudonym of John Doyle. Among his later works, chiefly scholarly and critical, are: *The Meaning of Dreams* (1924); *My Head! My Head!* (1925); *John Skelton* (1927); *Mrs. Fisher* (1928); *The Shout* (1929); *The Real David Copperfield* (1933); *Antigua Penny Puce* (1936); *T. E. Lawrence to his Biographer* (1937). *Goodbye to All That* (1929) is an autobiography, dealing chiefly with the author's experiences during the war; *I Claudius* (1934) and *Claudius the God* (1934) are unusual historical novels with a psychological approach to their subject.

graveyard school. A pre-Romantic movement in English poetry of the 18th century, composed chiefly of followers and imitators of Edward YOUNG and so named because of the meditative, melancholy tone of the characteristic verse of the school, the scene of much of which was laid in graveyards and cemeteries.

Gray, Alice. The heroine of Barrie's ALICE-SIT-BY-THE-FIRE.

Gray, Asa (1810–1888). Leading American botanist of his time. Author of *Flora of North America* (1838–1843) etc., etc. Professor of Natural History at Harvard. Member of Hall of Fame.

Gray, Auld Robin, see AULD ROBIN GRAY.

Gray, Duncan, see DUNCAN GRAY.

Gray, Jacquelin. The hero of Page's novel RED ROCK.

Gray, John. The hero of J. L. Allen's CHOIR INVISIBLE.

Gray, Mary. See BESSIE BELL AND MARY GRAY.

Gray, Thomas (1716–1771). English poet, a friend of Horace WALPOLE and one of the forerunners of the romantic movement in England. His work is marked by love of nature, melancholy reflection, and imagination. His poetry includes: *Ode to Spring, Hymn to Adversity,* and *Ode on a Distant Prospect of Eton College* (1742); *Ode on the Death of a Favorite Cat* (1748), light verse in the neo-Classical manner; *Elegy in a Country Churchyard* (1751), his most famous work; *The Progress of Poesy* and THE BARD (1757); *The Fatal Sisters* and *The Descent of Odin* (1761). Cf. *Two Quiet Lives* (1947), by David CECIL.

Grayson, David. See BAKER, RAY STANNARD.

Great, the. The following rulers were called "the Great":

Abbas I, Shah of Persia. (1557, reigned 1585–1628.)
Albertus Magnus, the schoolman. (*d.* 1280.)
Alexander, of Macedon. (356, 340–323 B. C.)
Alfonso III, King of Asturias and Leon. (848, 866–912.)
Alfred, of England. (849, 871–901.)
St. Basil, Bishop of Caesarea. (4th cent.)
Canute, of England and Denmark. (995, 1014–1035.)
Casimir III, of Poland. (1309, 1333–1370.)
Charles, King of the Franks and Emperor of the Romans, called *Charlemagne.* (742, 764–814.)
Charles III, Duke of Lorraine. (1543–1608.)
Charles Emmanuel I, Duke of Savoy. (1562–1630.)
Clovis, King of the Franks. (466–511.)
Condé. See *Louis II,* below.
Constantine I, Emperor of Rome. (272, 306–337.)
Cyrus, founder of the Persian Empire. (*d.* 529 B. C.)
Darius, King of Persia. (*d.* 485 B. C.)
Douglas (*Archibald, the great Earl of Angus,* also called *Bell-the-Cat*).
Ferdinand I, of Castile and Leon. (Reigned 1034–1065.)
Frederick William, Elector of Brandenburg, surnamed *The Great Elector.* (1620–1688.)
Frederick II, of Prussia. (1712, 1740–1786.)
Gregory I, Pope. (544, 590–604.)
Gustavus Adolphus, of Sweden. (1594, 1611–1632.)
Henri IV, of France. (1553, 1589–1610.)
Herod I, King of Judea. (73–3 B. C.)
John I, of Portugal. (1357, 1385–1433.)
Justinian I, Emperor of the East. (483, 527–565.)
Leo I, Pope. (440–461.)
Leo I, Emperor of the East. (457–474.)
Leopold I, of Germany. (1640–1705.)
Lewis I, of Hungary. (1326, 1342–1383.)
Louis II, de Bourbon, Prince of Condé, Duc d'Enghien (1621–1686), always known as *The Great Condé.*
Louis XIV, called *Le Grand Monarque.* (1638, 1643–1714.)
Mahomet II, Sultan of the Turks. (1430, 1451–1481.)
Maximilian, Duke of Bavaria, victor of Prague. (1573–1651.)
Cosmo di' Medici, first Grand Duke of Tuscany. (1519, 1537–1574.)
Gonzales Pedro de Mendoza, great Cardinal of Spain, statesman and scholar. (1428–1495.)
Nicholas I, Pope (was Pope from 858–867).
Otho I, Emperor of the Romans. (912, 936–973.)
Peter I, of Russia. (1672, 1689–1725.)
Pierre III, of Aragon. (1239, 1276–1285.)
Sancho III, King of Navarre. (ca. 965–1035.)
Sapor III, King of Persia. (*d.* 380.)
Sforza (*Giacomo*), the Italian general. (1369–1424.)
Sigismund II, King of Poland. (1467, 1506–1548.)
Theodoric, King of the Ostrogoths. (454, 475–526.)
Theodosius I, Emperor. (346, 378–395.)
Matteo Visconti, Lord of Milan. (1252, 1295–1323.)
Vladimir, Grand Duke of Russia. (973–1015.)
Waldemar I, of Denmark. (1131, 1157–1182.)

Great Bear. See BEAR.

Great Bible. See BIBLE, THE ENGLISH.

Great Bullet-head. George Cadoudal (1771–1804), leader of the CHOUANS, born at Brech, in Morbihan.

Great Captain. See CAPITANO, EL GRAN.

Great Cham of Literature. So Smollett calls Dr. Johnson (1709–1784).

Great Commoner. William Pitt (1759–1806).

Great Dauphin. See GRAND.

Great Elector. Frederick William, Elector of Brandenburg (1620, 1640–1688).

Great Galeoto. See GALEOTO.

Great Magician or *the Great Magician of the North.* Sir Walter Scott. So called first by Professor John Wilson (1771–1832).

Great Mogul. The title of the chief of the Mogul Empire; hence any self-important person.

Great Unknown. Sir Walter Scott (1771–1832), who published his WAVERLEY NOVELS anonymously.

Great Unwashed. The artisan class. Burke first used the compound, but Sir Walter Scott popularized it.

Great Awakening, The. A religious revivalist movement which swept through the American colonies (1739–1740) and was marked by violent and sensational public repentance and conversion. It began in Massachusetts under the influence of the preaching of Jonathan EDWARDS and of the English evangelist George Whitefield. Controversies arose because of it between Edwards and Charles CHAUNCEY, and Edwards eventually came to lose his popularity in his own congregation. Unitarianism grew up out of the liberal faction under Chauncey.

Great Dictator, The. See CHAPLIN, CHARLES SPENCER.

Great Divide, The. A drama by William Vaughn MOODY (1906). The New England heroine, Ruth Jordan, alone on an Arizona ranch and suddenly menaced by three men, promises to marry Stephen Ghent, a Westerner, if he will save her. The interest lies in the subsequent effort of the two principal characters to bridge the gap between the ideals and standards of New England and the West.

Great Expectations. A novel by DICKENS (1860) in the form of an autobiography. A fine moving-picture version was made in England (1946). The hero is Pip, who is reared by his sister and her husband, Joe Gargery, the blacksmith. Later he is informed that he is to be reared as a gentleman of "great expectations," as an unknown person has provided money for his education and expects to make him his heir. This patron is Magwitch, a runaway convict to whom the boy Pip had once been of great assistance. Magwitch has made a fortune in New South Wales, but when he secretly returns to England, he is arrested as a returned convict and all his money is confiscated. Pip's love affair is a similar "great expectation." He falls in love with Estella, the adopted daughter of the rich Miss Havisham, but Estella marries Bentley Drummle.

Great Gatsby, The. A novel by F. Scott FITZGERALD, published in 1925 and later dramatized on the stage and screen. It deals with sexual intrigue between Jay Gatsby, wealthy through bootlegging and racketeering, and Daisy Buchanan, wife of a wealthy boor who keeps as a mistress the wife of a local garageman. The latter woman is accidentally run over by Daisy, whose husband seeks revenge upon Gatsby by telling the garageman that it was Gatsby who killed the woman. The garageman thereupon shoots Gatsby. This novel is considered to typify the life of the boom period of the 1920's. See also BIG MONEY, THE.

Great God Brown, The. A play by Eugene O'NEILL, produced in 1926, in which masks are used to symbolize the varying personalities of the characters as they are and as they appear to other people. "The Great God Brown" is a wealthy man, devoid of inner character or spiritual resources, who takes the mask of Dion Anthony, a frustrated artist who dies, and wearing it, is accepted as Dion by Dion's wife, for she has known and loved only her husband's mask, not his true self.

Great Meadow, The. A novel by Elizabeth Madox ROBERTS (1930), dealing with the settlement of Kentucky by Virginia pioneers in the 18th century and their hardships in protecting themselves against the raiding Indians.

Great Mother. Nature goddess of ancient Anatolia. Her names and appellations include Cybele, Earth Mother, Mountain Mother, Idaean Mother, etc. In Greek mythology, the goddess Demeter is called the Great Mother.

Great Pacificator. A nickname given to Henry CLAY for his skill as a compromiser.

great Scott or **Scot!** An exclamation of surprise, wonder, admiration, indignation, etc. It seems to have originated in America about the late 1860's perhaps in memory of Gen. Winfield Scott (d. 1866), an unsuccessful candidate for the Presidency in 1852, or, more likely perhaps, as a euphemism for *Great God* (like *by gosh* for *by God,* etc.), the initial letter of the Ger. *Gott* being changed into *Sc.*

Great Stone Face, The. A story by Nathaniel HAWTHORNE. The title refers to the "Old Man of the Mountain," also known as the "Profile," a natural rock formation on Profile Mountain in the Franconia Range, N.H., which, looked at from a certain direction, bears a striking resemblance to a human face.

Great White Father, The. A title of honor sometimes given to the President of the U.S. by the Indians.

Great White Way. That part of Broadway in New York City which centers about Times Square and is brightly illuminated due to a concentration there of theaters and other places of entertainment.

Greaves, Sir Launceot, see LAUNCELOT GREAVES.

Greco, El, i.e. *the Greek.* Greek name **Kyriakos Theotokopoulos.** Spanish name **Domingo Teotocópuli.** Italian name **Domenico Teotocopulo** (1548?–?1614 or ?1625). Painter. Pupil of Titian. Foremost painter of the Castilian school of the 16th century. Leading exponent of the mysticism of the baroque. Rediscovered in his importance for modern painting by Meier-Graefe.

Greek. See also under DOUBLE DUTCH.

a merry Greek. See GRIG.

all Greek to me. Quite unintelligible; an unknown tongue or language. Casca says, "For mine own part, it was all Greek to me." (Shakespeare, *Julius Caesar,* i. 2.)

last of the Greeks. Philopoemen, of Megalopolis, whose great object was to infuse into the Acheans a military spirit, and establish their independence (252–183 B.C.).

to play the Greek. To indulge in one's cups. The Greeks were considered a luxurious race, fond of creature comforts.

when Greek meets Greek, then is the tug of

war. When two men or armies of undoubted courage fight, the contest will be very severe. The line is slightly altered from a 17th-century play, and the reference is to the obstinate resistance of the Greek cities to Philip and Alexander, the Macedonian kings.

When Greeks joined Greeks, then was the tug of war.
Nathaniel Lee, *The Rival Queens,* IV, ii.

Greek calends. Never. See CALENDS.

Greek fire. A combustible composition used for setting fire to an enemy's ships, fortifications, etc., of niter, sulphur, and naphtha. Tow steeped in the mixture was hurled in a blazing state through tubes, or tied to arrows. The invention is ascribed to Callinicos, of Heliopolis, 668 A. D., and it was first used by the Greeks at Constantinople.

Greek gift. A treacherous gift. The reference is to the Wooden Horse said to be a gift or offering to the gods for a safe return from Troy, but in reality a ruse for the destruction of the city.

"Timeo Danaos et dona ferentes."
Virgil, *Aeneid,* ii. 49.

Greek trust. *"Graeca fides"* was with the Romans no faith at all.

Greek Anthology, The. A collection of several thousand poems, songs, gravestone inscriptions, epigrams, epitaphs, and the like, by numerous Greek writers, known and anonymous, from the 5th century B. C. to the 6th century A. D. Its original form was a collection called the *Garland of Meleager* (ca. 60 B. C.), to which continuous additions were made. A number of the poems in the Greek Anthology have become very famous. The Elizabethan poetic "miscellany" (see TOTTEL'S MISCELLANY) was a spiritual descendant of the Greek Anthology.

Greeley, Horace (1811–1872). American journalist, author, politician. Founder of the successful and influential New York *Tribune* (1841). Promoter of antislavery sentiment and, after the Civil War, of the principles of universal amnesty and universal suffrage. Member of Congress from New York (1848–1849) and unsuccessful presidential nominee in the election of 1872. Greeley Square in New York City is named after him.

Greely, Adolphus Washington (1844–1935). American major general. Commanded U.S. arctic expedition of 1881, attained the most northerly point reached up to that time, 83° 24′ N., and discovered new land north of Greenland. In charge of relief operations in San Francisco fire and earthquake (1906). Wrote books on polar expeditions. *Three years of Arctic Service* (1885); etc.

green. Young, fresh, as *green cheese,* cream cheese, which is eaten fresh; *a green old age,* an old age in which the faculties are not impaired and the spirits are still youthful; *green goose,* a young or midsummer goose.

If you would fat green geese, shut them up when they are about a month old.—Mortimer, *Husbandry.*

Immature in age or judgment, inexperienced, young.

My salad days
When I was green in judgment!
Shakespeare, *Antony and Cleopatra,* i, 5.

The text is old, the orator too green.
Shakespeare, *Venus and Adonis,* 806.

Simple, raw, easily imposed upon; the characteristic GREENHORN.

"He is so jolly green," said Charley.—Dickens, *Oliver Twist,* ch. iv.

Jealous. See GREEN-EYED MONSTER below. See also COLORS for its symbolisms.

green room. The common waiting-room beyond the stage at a theater for the performers; so called because at one time the walls were colored green to relieve the eyes affected by the glare of the stage lights.

green-eyed monster. So Shakespeare called jealousy:

Iago. O! beware, my lord, of jealousy;
It is the green-ey'd monster which doth mock
The meat it feeds on.
Othello, iii, 3.

A greenish complexion was formerly held to be indicative of jealousy; and as cats, lions, tigers, and all the green-eyed tribe "mock the meat they feed on," so jealousy mocks its victim by loving and loathing it at the same time.

Gawain and the Green Knight. See GAWAIN.

The Wearing of the Green. An Irish patriotic and revolutionary song, dating from 1798. Green was the emblematic color adopted by Irish Nationalists.

They're hanging men and women for the wearing of the green.

Green, Anna Katharine (1846–1935). American writer of detective fiction, beginning with *The Leavenworth Case* (1878).

Green, Anne (1899–) and **Julien** (1900–). Brother and sister, novelists of American parentage, resident for most of their lives in Paris, which is the scene of most of their books. Anne Green is known chiefly as the author of witty, satirical stories and character studies, including *The Selbys* (1930); *Reader, I Married Him* (1931); *Fools Rush In* (1934); *16 Rue Cortambert* (1937); *The Silent Duchess* (1939); and *The Delamer Curse* (1940). Julien Green is best known for his psychological studies, written in French and then translated into English, of people who are the prey of suppressed emotions. Among these are: *The Pilgrim on the Earth* (1929); *The Dark Journey* (1929); *The Strange River* (1932); *The Dreamer* (1934); *Midnight* (1936); *Then Shall the Dust Return* (1941).

Green, Paul Eliot (1894–). American playwright, best known for his dramas dealing with the southern Negroes, many being one act in length and written in Negro dialect. His full-length plays include: *In Abraham's Bosom* (1924 and 1927), awarded the Pulitzer Prize; *The Field God* (1927), concerning poor whites; *The House of Connelly* (1932), dealing with the decadence of an old Southern family; *Roll, Sweet Chariot* (1934); *Johnny Johnson* (1937), a musical satire on war; and *The Lost Colony* (1937), an historical pageant dealing with the first settlement on Roanoke Island.

Green, Verdant, see VERDANT GREEN.

Greenaway, Catherine (1846–1901). English illustrator and painter. Renowned for children's books among which *Under the Window* (1879) was outstanding and is still in print. Kate Greenaway, as she is generally called, and Randolph CALDECOTT, partly thanks to their common publisher, Edmund Evans, mark a turning point in the history of children's books, which, in the words of Robert Lawson, "here for the first time were given a true dignity and importance. Here, for the first time, children were regarded as real, intelligent human beings, worthy of the very best of draughtsmanship, imagination and publishing integrity. With these three, children's books began their career gloriously."

greenback. A popular name for a U.S. note with devices on back printed in green, a form of fiat paper currency issued in 1862 to aid in financing the Civil War.

The *Greenback party* was a minor party in elections from 1876 to 1884 demanding the continued issuance of fiat money as one of the points of its program.

Greenberg Manuscripts. A collection of poems marked by strange imagery and frequent flights of intense imagination, together with a neglect of form and technical polish, by Samuel D. Greenberg, a young Jewish-American poet of poverty-bound background, who died of tuberculosis in 1917. Hart CRANE "discovered" Greenberg's work and enthusiastically regarded the dead youth as a genius. Much of Crane's own poetry is believed to have been influenced by Greenberg's, and even whole passages to have been incorporated in his poems with little alteration. A selection from the Greenberg Manuscripts was published in 1939 under that title.

Green Carnation, The. A novel by Robert S. HICHENS (1894) satirizing the decadence of the period at the end of the 19th century, and intended as a lampoon on Oscar WILDE. The "green carnation" of the title is "the arsenic flower of an exquisite life." The hero, Lord Reginald Hastings, "too modern to be reticent" is put in his place by a heroine who, when he complains that she is almost ordinary, replies that she is glad of it and flatly refuses to marry him.

Greene, Graham (1904–). English writer of novels of action dealing with peculiarities of sinister psychology. A master of suspense. *This Gun for Hire* (1936), successfully filmed. *Brighton Rock* (1938); *The Power and the Glory* (in America: *The Labyrinthine Ways;* 1940), Hawthornden Prize. Has also been filmed.

Greene, Robert (1560?–1592). English dramatist, poet, and prose-writer, known for his wild and dissolute Bohemian life as scholar, vagabond, and "university wit," holder of the M.A. degree from both Oxford and Cambridge. He wrote heroic and historical plays, artificial romances in the manner of John LYLY, and realistic prose pamphlets denouncing the roguery of London and revealing conditions in the contemporary underworld of the city. His plays include: *Orlando Furioso* (1588?), taken from Ariosto's work of the same title; *Alphonsus, King of Aragon* (1588), suggested by Christopher Marlowe's TAMBURLAINE; FRIAR BACON AND FRIAR BUNGAY (1589), said to have been suggested by Marlowe's *Dr. Faustus* (see FAUST); and *James IV*. Among his romances are: *Euphues' Censure to Philautus* (1587); *Pandosto* (1588), used in part by Shakespeare as the basis for THE WINTER'S TALE; and *Menaphon* (1589). These contain several well-known lyrics, such as "Weep Not, My Wanton" in the last named. Greene's "rogue" pamphlets, many of them autobiographical and serving as personal documents of repentance and confession, include: *The Mourning Garment* (1590); *A Groatsworth of Wit Bought with a Million of Repentance* (1592); *The Repentance of Robert Greene* (1592); *A Quip for an Upstart Courtier* (1592); and his various "cony-catching" pamphlets (1591–1592), among the best-known of which are *A Defense of Cony-Catching, Disputation between a He-Cony-Catcher and a She-Cony-Catcher,* and *The Black Book's Messenger.*

Green Hat, The. A novel, published in 1924, by Michael ARLEN. Phenomenally successful, it was one of the many best-selling books of the 1920's dealing sentimentally with license among the wealthy. Its heroine, Iris MARCH, was portrayed on the stage by Katharine CORNELL and in the films by Greta Garbo.

Green Mansions. A romance of the South American tropics by W. H. HUDSON (1916). The hero, Mr. Abel, tells the tragic story of his love for Rima, the "bird girl" who understands the language of nature.

Green Mountain Boys, The. A novel by Daniel Pierce Thompson (1839), with the Vermont hero Ethan Allen as its central figure. It gives a vivid picture of pre-Revolutionary and Revolutionary times in Vermont. The book went through fifty editions before the Civil War, and remains a favorite with boys.

There was also a popular comedy entitled *The Green Mountain Boy* by J. S. Jones (*Am.*, 1833), famed chiefly because of the character of Jedediah Homebred, a Yankee man-of-all-work.

Green Mountain State. Vermont. See under STATES.

Green Pastures, The. A play by Marc CONNELLY, produced in 1930 and a winner of the Pulitzer Prize. It was based on *Ol' Man Adam an' His Chillun,* a book of sketches by Roark BRADFORD. It presents humorous versions of Old Testament stories as they are told by an old Southern Negro preacher in terms of the lives of his congregation.

Greenwich Village or **the Village.** A section of New York City west of Washington Square, noted during the early 20th century and the years immediately preceding and following World War I as being the haunt of Bohemian artists, writers and radicals, who originally chose it as a place to live because of its cheapness. In former days it was a quaint, small village reached from the city in lower Manhattan by stage coach.

By the time of the 1930's, Greenwich Village was chiefly a residential district for young business and professional couples, who could pay higher rents than their predecessors the Bohemians, and the artists and writers had moved to Brooklyn or to the Connecticut suburbs. Among the well-known personalities who lived and worked in Greenwich Village at one time or another are: Floyd DELL, Gelett BURGESS, Max EASTMAN, Emma GOLDMAN, William Vaughn MOODY, Eugene O'NEILL, Edna St. Vincent MILLAY; among the "little magazines" published there were THE LITTLE REVIEW, THE MASSES, and THE SEVEN ARTS. Several novels by Floyd Dell deal with life in Greenwich Village in its heyday.

Gregorian. Of or pertaining to any of the Popes named Gregory and their various periods.

Gregorian calendar, see CALENDAR.

Gregorian chant. The ritual plain song, or *cantus firmus,* a kind of unisonorous music in the eight church modes, a collection of which, edited by Pope Gregory I, has come down to us. It is still used in the services of the Roman and Greek Catholic Churches. See also PLAIN SONG; MODES.

Gregorian epoch. The epoch or day on which the Gregorian calendar commenced—March, 1582.

Gregorian year. The civil year, according to the correction introduced by Pope Gregory XIII in 1582. See CALENDAR. The equinox, which occurred on March 25 in the time of Julius Caesar, fell on March 11 in the year 1582. This was because the Julian calculation of 365¼ days to a year was 11 min. 10 sec. too much. Gregory suppressed ten days, so as to make the equinox fall on March 21, as it did at the Council of Nice, and, by some simple arrangements, prevented the recurrence in future of a similar error.

The New Style, as it was called, was adopted in England in 1752, when Wednesday, September 2, was followed by Thursday, September 14.

This has given rise to a double computation, as Lady Day, March 25, Old Lady Day, April 6; Midsummer Day, June 24, Old Midsummer Day, July 6; Michaelmas Day, September 29, Old Michaelmas Day, October 11; Christmas Day, December 25, Old Christmas Day, January 6.

Gregory. The pretended Dmitri in Moussorgsky's opera BORIS GODOUNOFF.

Gregory I, called **Gregory the Great** (540?–604). Benedictine monk on the Papal throne (590–604). Reformed monastic discipline; enforced celibacy; sent missionaries to Britain. Through him the Roman patriarchate assumed supremacy over all others and was transformed into the papal system which has endured to the present. His name is associated (possibly incorrectly) with the arrangement of the so-called Gregorian mode or chant.

Gregory VII. Original name **Hildebrand** (1020?–1085). Pope (1073–1085). Aimed to establish supremacy of papacy within the church and of the church over the state. Excommunicated Emperor Henry IV in the famous struggle over lay investitures, but received him in penance at Canossa (1077) where the emperor had to wait outside the castle for three days and three nights, barefoot and dressed in nothing but a thin shirt. Gregory again excommunicated Henry, was driven from Rome and displaced by Guibert as Clement III. He died in exile.

Gregory, Horace Victor (1898–). American poet and literary critic, associated with the school of American poets of Marxist convictions in the 1930's. Much of his poetry criticizes middle-class life and presents dramatic monologues or character studies of petty racketeers and gangsters and people of the city slums. His books of poems include: *Chelsea Rooming House* (1930); *The Poems of Catullus* (1931), translations from the Latin;

No Retreat (1933); *Chorus for Survival* (1935); *Poems: 1930–1940* (1941). *Pilgrim of the Apocalypse* (1933) is a study of D. H. LAWRENCE. In 1925 Gregory married Marya ZATURENSKA, with whom he wrote *A History of American Poetry, 1900–1940.*

Gregory, Lady Augusta, *née* **Isabella Augusta Persse** (1852–1932). Irish playwright and producer, associated with W. B. YEATS in founding and managing the Abbey Theater. See IRISH RENAISSANCE. She is known for her studies of Irish folk-lore, her collections and translations of old Irish legends, and her plays dealing with the life and people of the Irish countryside. Her works include: *Cuchulain of Muirthemne* (1902); *Gods and Fighting Men* (1904); *Seven Short Plays* (1909); *Visions and Beliefs in the West of Ireland* (1920); *Irish Folk-History Plays* (1922); *The Image, And Other Plays* (1922); *The Story Brought by Brigit* (1924). Her best-known one act plays are *The Rising of the Moon, Spreading the News, The Workhouse Ward,* published with others in the volume entitled *Seven Short Plays.*

Gremio. In Shakespeare's TAMING OF THE SHREW, an old man who wishes to marry Bianca, but the lady prefers Lucentio, a young man.

Grendel. In the Anglo-Saxon epic BEOWULF, the monster from which Beowulf delivers Hrothgar, king of Denmark. It is half monster, half man, a beast whose haunt is the marshes among "a monster race." Night after night it creeps stealthily into the palace called Heorot, and slays sometimes as many as thirty of the inmates. At length both Grendel and Grendel's mother, another murdering monster, are slain by Beowulf.

Grenville, Sir **Richard.** The commander of the *Revenge,* in the reign of Queen Elizabeth and the hero of Tennyson's poem *The Revenge* which celebrates his gallant fight with the Spanish against overwhelming odds.

Gresham, Frank. The hero of Trollope's novel *Doctor Thorne* (1858), a pleasant young man in love with Mary Thorne but urged by his mother, Lady Arabella Gresham, to marry for money. He remains true in spite of insidious pressure.

Gresham's law. Also **Gresham's theorem.** Popularly formulated: "Bad money drives out good." That is, when two coins of equal debt-paying power but of unequal intrinsic value are simultaneously in circulation, the coin of superior intrinsic value will be hoarded leaving the field to the intrinsically less valuable coin. The "law" is named after Sir Thomas Gresham (1519?–1579), English financier and adviser to Henry VIII and Elizabeth, but it had been known centuries before by Dutch bankers.

Gretchen. A German diminutive of Margaret; the heroine of Goethe's FAUST. See MARGARET. The name has come to typify blond and blue-eyed innocence.

Gretel. See HÄNSEL AND GRETEL.

Gretna Green marriages. Runaway matches. In Scotland, all that was required of contracting parties was a mutual declaration before witnesses of their willingness to marry, so that elopers reaching Gretna, a hamlet near the village of Springfield, Dumfriesshire, 8 miles N.W. of Carlisle, and just across the border, could (up to 1856), get legally married without either license, banns, or priest. The declaration was generally made to a blacksmith.

CRABBE has a metrical tale called *Gretna Green,* and a *Gretna Green marriage* has formed the motive, or an incident, of countless romances, stories, and ballads.

Grettir the Strong. The titular hero of one of the English translations of a series of Icelandic sagas written and published (from 1890) by William MORRIS.

Greuze, Jean-Baptiste (1725–1805). French portrait and genre painter of typical rococo charm. Amassed a fortune under the *ancien régime* but died in misery.

Greville, Sir **Fulke.** 1st Baron **Brooke** (1554–1628). English courtier and author, known as the friend of Sir Philip SIDNEY. He wrote a large number of poems, chiefly philosophical, and a *Life of Sir Philip Sidney,* first published in 1652.

Grew, Joseph Clark (1880–). American diplomat. Ambassador to Turkey (1927–1932), and Japan (1932–1941). Author of *Report from Tokyo* (1942) and *Ten Years in Japan* (1944).

Grey, Sir **Edward.** Viscount **Grey of Fallodon** (1862–1933). British statesman. Consolidated the Triple Entente of Great Britain, France, and Russia as secretary of state for foreign affairs (1905–1916); British Ambassador to U.S. (1919); Chancellor of Oxford (1928). In 1914, he made an historic speech in the House of Commons, after which, looking at night from his room in the Foreign Office, he is quoted as saying to a friend, "The lamps are going out all over Europe; we shall not see them lit again in our life-time."

Grey, Lady **Jane** (1537–1554). A great-granddaughter of Henry VII of England. At fifteen she was proficient in Greek, Latin, Italian, French, German. At sixteen she was married against her will to Lord Guildford Dudley as part of a plot to change the succession of the crown from the Tudors to the Dudleys.

After the death of Edward VI, she was proclaimed queen; nine days later, after the defeat of her father-in-law's troops, she was imprisoned. When her father participated in WYATT'S REBELLION, she and her husband were executed on Tower Hill. She is the subject of tragedies by Rowe (1715), Laplace (1745), Madame de Staël (1800), Tennyson (1876) and many others.

Grey, Vivian, see VIVIAN GREY.

Grey, Zane (1875–1939). Writer of American stories of adventure in the West. *Riders of the Purple Sage* (1912), and many other best-sellers. Began his career as a dentist in New York. Wrote also extensively on his hobby, fishing.

Grey Friars. FRANCISCANS. Black Friars are Dominicans, and White Friars Carmelites.

Gridley, Professor. In O. W. Holmes' GUARDIAN ANGEL, the "guardian angel" of the heroine, Myrtle Hazard.

Grieg, Edvard (1843–1907). Norwegian composer. *Humoresken* (for piano), *Peer Gynt* suites, a very popular piano concerto, operas, choral works, dances, folksongs, etc.

Grierson, Francis (1848–1927). Author's name of **Benjamin Henry Jesse Francis Shepard,** American musician and essayist. After a fabulously successful career as a pianist under the name of Francis Shepard, he began writing (ca. 1880) under the name of Francis Grierson lest his literary efforts be considered a mere musician's whim. *Modern Mysticism* (1899); *The Celtic Temperament and Other Essays* (1901); *The Valley of Shadows* (1909; reissued by the History Book Club, 1948).

Grieux, le Chevalier des. Hero of Provost's MANON LESCAUT.

Grieve, Christopher Murray, see McDIARMID, HUGH.

griffin. A mythical monster, also called *griffon, gryphon,* etc., fabled to be the offspring of the lion and eagle. Its legs and all from the shoulder to the head are like an eagle, the rest of the body is that of a lion. This creature was sacred to the sun, and kept guard over hidden treasures. The griffins were in perpetual strife with the Arimaspians, a people of Scythia, who rifled the gold mines for the adornment of their hair.

> As when a gryphon thro' the wilderness,
> With winged course, o'er hill or moory dale,
> Pursues the Arimaspian, who, by stealth,
> Had from his wakeful custody purloined
> The guarded gold.
>
> Milton, *Paradise Lost,* ii. 943, etc.

> [The griffin is] an Emblem of valour and magnanimity, as being compounded of the Eagle and Lion, the noblest Animals in their kinds; and so is it appliable unto Princes, Presidents, Generals, and all heroick Commanders; and so is it also born in the Coat-arms of many noble Families of *Europe*.—Sir Thos. Browne, *Pseudodoxia Epidemica,* III, xi.

Among Anglo-Indians a newcomer, a GREENHORN, is called a *griffin.* The residue of a contract feast, taken away by the contractor, half the buyer's and half the seller's, is known in the trade as *griffins.*

Griffin, Vielé, see VIELÉ-GRIFFIN.

Griffith, Arthur (1872–1922). Irish political leader, printer by trade. Founded SINN FEIN (about 1905). While in prison, elected vice president of the "Irish Republic" (1918). Was acting head while DE VALERA was in U.S. (1919–1920). Elected president of the DAIL EIREANN (1922).

Griffith, David Lewelyn Wark (1880–). American motion-picture producer. *The Birth of a Nation, Intolerance, Hearts of the World, Broken Blossoms,* etc.

Griffith Davenport, The Rev. Title and hero of a Civil War drama by James A. Herne (*Am.,* 1898). Griffith Davenport is a southern circuit rider to whom the war brings conflicting duties.

Griffith Gaunt. A novel by Charles READE (1867), later dramatized under the title *Jealousy.* The titular hero, jealous of his wife's spiritual adviser, is found dead near the house after a terrible scene. She is accused of his murder, but the murdered man turns out to be a half-brother and physical double whom he had impersonated in a false marriage with another woman.

Griffiths, Clyde. Hero of Theodore Dreiser's novel, AN AMERICAN TRAGEDY.

Grig, merry as a. A grig is a cricket, or grasshopper, but it is by no means certain that the animal is referred to in this phrase, which is at least as old as the mid-sixteenth century. *Grig* here may be a corruption of GREEK, as in "merry as a Greek," which dates from about the same time. Shakespeare has: "Then she's a merry Greek"; and again, "Cressid 'mongst the merry Greeks" (*Troilus and Cressida,* i. 2; iv. 4). Among the Romans, *graecari* signified "to play the reveller."

Grillparzer, Franz (1791–1872). Austrian writer, outstanding as a dramatist. Has been called a "classicist of romantic training in an age of realism." His most important work is the trilogy *Das goldene Vlies* (1822), including *Der Gastfreund, Die Argonauten,* and *Medea.* Embittered by lack of tangible success during the era of Metternich censorship. Considerable influence in France, also through his critical and aesthetic writings.

Grim, Giant. In Bunyan's PILGRIM'S PROGRESS, a huge giant who tries to stop pilgrims on their way to the Celestial City. He is slain by Mr. Greatheart.

Grimald, Nicholas (1519–1562). English poet, scholar, and clergyman, best known for forty poems of his which were published (1557) in the first edition of TOTTEL's MISCELLANY. He also wrote two Latin plays and translated Cicero's *De Officiis*.

Grimaldi, Joseph (1779–1837). English comic actor, pantomimist, clown. It is through him that the term *Joey* came to signify "circus clown" in slang.

Grimaldo, Enzo. A nobleman in Ponchielli's opera, LA GIOCONDA.

Grimalkin. A cat, the spirit of a witch. Any witch was permitted to assume the body of a cat nine times. When the "first Witch" in Shakespeare's MACBETH hears a cat mew, she says, "I come, Grimalkin."

Grimm, Jacob Ludwig Carl (1785–1863) and **Wilhelm Carl** (1786–1859). Brothers, German philologists and scholars of folk-lore, best known for their collections of *Märchen,* or fairy tales, published 1812–1815 as *Kinder- und Hausmärchen,* and their investigations into the origins of other examples of myth and legend.

Grimm's law. The law of the permutation of consonants in the principal Aryan languages, first formulated by Jacob GRIMM in his *Deutsche Grammatik* (1822). Thus, what is *p* in Greek, Latin, or Sanskrit, becomes *f* in Gothic, and *b* or *f* in the Old High German; what is *t* in Greek, Latin, or Sanskrit becomes *th* in Gothic, and *d* in Old High German; etc. For example, changing *p* into *f,* and *t* into *th,* "pater" becomes "father."

Grimm, Peter. The central figure of Belasco's RETURN OF PETER GRIMM.

gringo. Among Spanish Americans, a foreigner, especially one speaking English. Chiefly contemptuous. The word means gibberish and is probably a corruption of *griego,* "Greek." Cf. our expression, "That's all Greek to me."

Grip. The clever raven of Barnaby RUDGE in Dickens' novel of that name. During the Gordon riots it learns the cry of "No Popery!" Other of its phrases are "I'm a devil!", "Never say die!" and "Polly, put the kettle on!", etc.

Grisaille. A method of decorative painting in gray monochrome of various shades designed to attain representation of objects as if in relief. In English the term is generally used with reference to stained-glass windows.

grisette. A French girl of the working class of lively and free manners. The term is derived from *gris,* "gray," and stood originally for a kind of coarse woollen fabric often worn by the "grisettes."

Grisi, Giuditta (1805–1840) and her sister, **Giulia** (1811?–1869). Italian opera singers.

Grisilda or **Griselda.** The model of enduring patience and obedience, often spoken of as "Patient Grisel or Grizel." She is the heroine of the last tale in BOCCACCIO's DECAMERON, obtained by him from an old French story, *Parlement des Femmes.* It was translated from Boccaccio by Petrarch, and thence used by Chaucer for his *Clerk's Tale* in the *Canterbury Tales.*

Grisilda is the daughter of a charcoal-burner, but becomes the wife of Walter, Marquis of Saluzzo. Her husband tries her, as God tried Job. He takes away her two children and tells her they are murdered, and finally divorces her and sends her home, saying he is about to marry another. Finally, however, her patience has its full reward. The trials to which the flinty-hearted marquis subjects his innocent wife are almost as unbelievable as the fortitude with which she is credited to have borne them, and perhaps it is just as well that, as Chaucer says in his own "Envoy" to the *Clerk's Tale:*—

> Grisilde is dead, and eke her pacience,
> And both at once buried in Italie.

Grizel. A variant—like *Grissel*—of GRISILDA. Octavia, wife of Mark Antony and sister of Augustus Caesar, is called the "patient Grizel" of Roman story. Also an appealing character in *Sentimental Tommy* and *Tommy and Grizel,* by J. M. BARRIE.

Grizzly Bear State. California. See STATES.

Groatsworth of Wit Bought with a Million of Repentance. A posthumous tract by Robert GREENE (1592). In part a confession. It attacks MARLOWE and PEELE and is thought to refer to SHAKESPEARE as an "upstart crow."

grog. A strong drink, originally a mixture of spirit and water (two-water grog, three-water grog, etc.) served to British sailors in compliance with an order issued in 1740 by Admiral Edward Vernon. The word is taken from the admiral's nickname. He was called Old Grog because he wore "a grogram cloak in foul weather." Grogram (French *gros grain*) is a coarse fabric.

Grogan, Tom, see TOM GROGAN.

Grolier de Servières, Jean (1479–1565). French bibliophile; treasurer general of France under Francis I. His passion for fine books regarded alike subject, binding, printing, paper. Designed many of his ornaments himself. The **Grolier Club** of New York (founded in 1884, incorporated in 1888) was named after him. Its object is "the encouragement and promotion of bookmaking as an art, and the occasional publication of works designed to advance and illustrate that art."

Groote, Gerard (1340–1384). Dutch reformer and founder of the society of BRETHREN OF THE COMMON LIFE.

Gropius, Walter (1883–). German architect, founder of the famous BAUHAUS art school, of which he was director (1919–1928). Later he came to the U.S. and taught at Harvard University.

Grosseteste, Robert. Nicknamed **Greathead** (?–1253). English divine and scholar. Chancellor of Oxford. Bishop of Lincoln (1235–1253). Vigorously defended his rights and privileges against the Pope and King Henry III. Had the courage to refuse (1253), on the ground of unfitness, the induction into a canonry of the Pope's nephew Frederick di Lavagna; etc. "A man of spotless orthodoxy" and a voluminous writer.

Grossmith, George (1847–1912). English comedian; singer in many Gilbert and Sullivan operas. His son, **George Grossmith** (1874–1935), is said to have introduced the *revue* in England; successful in moving pictures (from 1932).

Grosz, George (1893–). German painter of radical views in art and politics. Hater of bourgeoisie and capitalism. Protagonist of *Neue Sachlichkeit* (New Objectivity). Voluntary exile (since 1932) in U.S. Studio near New York.

Grote, George (1794–1871). English historian, banker by profession. *History of Greece* (8 vols., 1846–1856), etc.

Grotius, Hugo. Latinized form of **Huig de Groot** (1583–1645). Dutch jurist and statesman. His *De Jure Belli et Pacis* (1625) written after his escape to France as leader of Remonstrants, is regarded as the real beginning of the science of international law. His voluminous writings include a number of tragedies.

ground-hog day. February 2. On that day, according to popular legend, the groundhog emerges from his hole, but if he sees his shadow, goes back for six weeks more of winter sleep. See CANDLEMAS DAY.

Ground We Stand On, The. A book of biographical sketches and essays on democracy and the early leaders in democratic thought, by John Dos PASSOS (1941). The biographical narrative method in this book is a development of that used in the celebrated biographical sections of U.S.A.

Grove, Sir **George** (1820–1900). British editor of the standard *Dictionary of Music and Musicians* (1879–1886). Engineer by profession. Built the first iron lighthouse at Jamaica (1841); etc. Director of the Royal College of Music, Kensington (1882–1894).

Growth of the Soil. A novel by Knut HAMSUN, the story of an elemental existence in the rough open country of Norway. Isak and Inger, the man and woman of the novel, are individuals, yet have a simple, hardy vitality that makes them types of pioneer life. Hamsun was awarded the Nobel Prize in 1920 for this novel.

Grub Street. The former name of a London street (now Milton Street), which, says Dr. Johnson, was "Much inhabited by writers of small histories, dictionaries, and temporary poems; whence any mean production is called *grubstreet*." The word is used allusively for needy authors, literary hacks, and their work. George GISSING has a novel entitled NEW GRUB STREET.

gruel, ***to give him his.*** To give him severe punishment; properly, to kill him. The allusion is to the practice in 16th-century France of giving poisoned possets—an art brought to perfection by Catherine de Medici and her Italian advisers.

Grumbo. A giant in the nursery tale of TOM THUMB. A raven drops Tom at the giant's castle; he creeps up Grumbo's sleeve, and the giant shakes him into the sea, where a fish swallows him. The fish, having been caught and brought to Arthur's table, is the means of introducing Tom to the British king, by whom he is knighted.

Grumio. One of the servants of Petruchio in Shakespeare's TAMING OF THE SHREW.

Grundy, Mrs. *What will Mrs. Grundy say?* What will our very proper and strait-laced neighbors say? The phrase is from Tom Morton's *Speed the Plough* (1798). In the first scene Mrs. Ashfield shows herself very jealous of neighbor Grundy, and farmer Ashfield says to her: "Be quiet, wull ye? Always ding, dinging Dame Grundy into my ears. What will Mrs. Grundy zay? What will Mrs. Grundy think? . . ."

> They eat, and drink, and scheme, and plod,
> They go to church on Sunday;
> And many are afraid of God,
> And more of Mrs. Grundy.
> Locker Lampson, *London Lyrics.*

One story has it that the original Mrs. Grundy was the wife of the Hon. Felix Grundy, of Tennessee, who ruled aristocratic society in Washington with a rod of iron. Her edicts were law, her presence was essential to the success of a fashionable gathering, and such an authority she became on social topics that the phrase, "Mrs. Grundy says so-and-so," long outlived her.

Grünewald, Matthias (fl. 1500–1530). German painter. Climax of the Gothic tradition mastered by means of an amazingly modern technique. His altar of Isenheim (now in Colmar) is the painted counterpart of Dante's *Divine Comedy.*

Gryll. *Let Gryll be Gryll, and have his hoggish mind* (Spenser, *Faërie Queene,* II, xii, 87). Don't attempt to wash a blackamoor white; the leopard will never change his spots. Gryll is the Gr. *grullos,* a hog. When Sir Guyon disenchants the forms in the BOWER OF BLISS some are exceedingly angry, and Gryll, who had been metamorphosed by Acrasia into a hog, abuses him most roundly.

Gryll Grange. A novel (1860) by Thomas Love PEACOCK.

gryphon, see GRIFFIN.

guano. A substance found on some coasts and islands, chiefly in Peruvian waters, frequented by seafowl. It consists chiefly of their partially decomposed excrement and is found in layers from 50 to 60 feet thick. It is rich in phosphate, nitrogen, etc., and is used for fertilizer (since 1841).

Guardian Angel, The. A novel by O. W. HOLMES (1867). The heroine is Myrtle Hazard, and the novel deals with her struggle to make some peaceful adjustment between the different racial strains in her blood. She was born in India and finds life difficult in the New England village where she lives with her aunt from the age of fifteen on. Through her "Guardian Angel," Professor Gridley, and her life as a nurse in the Civil War, she finds herself at last. She marries Clement Lindsay, a young sculptor who rescued her from drowning on one occasion when, disguised as a boy, she ran away from home.

Guarinos. One of Charlemagne's paladins, taken captive at Roncesvalles. Refusing to become a Moslem, he was cast into a dungeon, where he lay for seven years. A joust was then held, and Guarinos was allowed to try his hand at a target. He knelt before the Moor, stabbed him to the heart, and then vaulted on his gray horse Trebozond, and escaped to France.

Guarnieri. Family of Italian violin makers, including **Andrea Guarnieri** (1626–1698) born in Cremona, his sons, a grandson, and a nephew.

Guatamozin. In THE FAIR GOD, a historical romance by Lew Wallace, the leader of the Aztec forces against Cortez.

Gudrun. (1) The heroine of the great popular German epic poem, *Gudrun*, or *Kudrun*, written about 1210. She was the daughter of Hetel, king of Ireland, and was betrothed to Herwig of Seeland, but Hartmut, the king of Norway, carried her off captive. As she would not marry him he put her to all sorts of menial work, such as washing the dirty linen. Thirteen years later her brother and lover appeared on the scene with an army; they laid waste the country, razed the castle, released the prisoners, carried Hartmut off captive, and Gudrun and Herwig were married—to live happy ever after. Gudrun is the German type of wifely loyalty and love.

(2) In the Scandinavian VÖLSUNGA SAGA, the sister of Gunther, who marries first Sigurd (the Siegfried of Teutonic legend) and, after his death, King Atli. She plays a prominent part in the old legends, but is better known as the Kriemhild of the NIBELUNGENLIED or the Gutrune of the operas of Wagner's NIBELUNGEN RING.

(3) Heroine of the Icelandic LAXDALE SAGA, a selfish, independent, forceful woman, married successively to Thorwald, Thord, and Bolli, and in love with KJARTAN, whose death she causes.

(4) One of the two leading women characters in D. H. Lawrence's novel *Women in Love*. She is believed to have been based on Katherine MANSFIELD.

Gudule, St., see under SAINTS.

Guebres or **Ghebers.** Followers of the ancient Persian religion, reformed by Zoroaster; fire-worshipers; Parsees. The name, which was bestowed upon them by their Arabian conquerors, is now applied to fire-worshipers generally.

Guedalla, Philip (1889–1944). English historian and essayist. "A liberal, a sceptic, a Zionist, and the fine quintessence of Balliol." Shared with Lytton Strachey the reputation of revivifying the writing of history and biography. *The Second Empire* (1922); *Wellington* (1931); *The Hundred Days* (1934); *The Hundredth Year* (1940); *Mr. Churchill* (1941); etc.

Guelphs and **Ghibellines.** Two great parties whose conflicts made much of the history of Italy and Germany in the 12th, 13th, and 14th centuries. The Guelphs were the papal and popular party in Italy; their name is the Italian form of *Welfe,* as Ghibelline is that of *Waiblingen,* and the origin of these two words is this: At the battle of Weinsburg, in Suabia (1140), Conrad, Duke of Franconia, rallied his followers with the war-cry *Hie Waiblingen* (his family estate), while Henry the Lion, Duke of Saxony, used the cry of *Hie Welfe* (the family name). The Ghibellines supported in Italy the side of the German emperors; the Guelphs opposed it, and supported the cause of the Pope. See also BIANCHI.

Guendoloena. According to GEOFFREY OF MONMOUTH, daughter of Corineus and wife of Locrine, son of Brute, the legendary king of Britain. She was divorced, and Locrine married Estrildis, by whom he already had a daughter named Sabrina. Guendoloena, greatly indignant, got together a large army, and near the river Stour a battle was fought, in which Locrine was slain. Guendoloena now assumed the government, and one of her first acts was to throw both Estrildis and Sabrina into the river Severn.

Guenever, see GUINEVERE.

Guenn. A novel by Blanche Willis HOWARD (Teufel) (1884) telling of an American painter's life in a Breton village. Guenn, the heroine, is a fisher girl whom the artist secures as a model. She breaks her heart in futile love for him.

Guérard, Albert Léon (1880–). Franco-American historian and critic. Various studies of French civilization. Professor of General Literature at Stanford University. Stanch supporter of the principle of an auxiliary world language.

Guérin, Georges Maurice de (1810–1839). French poet. His *Le Centaur* was published posthumously by George Sand in *Revue des Deux Mondes* (1840). His sister **Eugénie Guérin** (1805–1848) is famous for her *Journal,* a posthumously published diary.

Guerin, Jules (1866–). American painter; best-known for his murals. Lincoln Memorial Building, Washington, D.C.; Pennsylvania Railroad Station, New York; Civic Opera Building, Chicago; etc.

Guermantes, de. In Marcel Proust's REMEMBRANCE OF THINGS PAST a French noble family of ancient lineage, the leading representatives of the aristocratic class in the novel. They are portrayed with merciless thoroughness, shown to be devoid of culture or vital intelligence, preoccupied solely with maintaining their position as members of an ancient aristocracy, although they know little of the actual history and traditions of their own family. Leading representatives of the de Guermantes family in the novel are:

Duc de Guermantes (Basin). Courteous and socially affable, although underneath his agreeable veneer he is contemptuous of all who are not of the de Guermantes clan.

Duchesse de Guermantes (Oriane). Wife of Basin, a beautiful woman who is the object of distant and romantic adoration by the narrator Marcel during his adolescence.

Prince de Guermantes. Cousin of the Duc and Duchesse de Guermantes, a man of cold and arrogant manner who takes no pains to conceal his contempt for non-aristocrats.

Princesse de Guermantes. His wife.

Baron de Charlus. Brother of the Prince and cousin of the Duc de Guermantes. See CHARLUS.

Robert Saint-Loup. Nephew of the de Guermantes. See SAINT-LOUP.

See also entry below.

Guermantes Way, The (*Le Coté de Guermantes*). Book III of REMEMBRANCE OF THINGS PAST by Marcel Proust, published 1920–1921. It deals exhaustively with personalities, places, balls, dinners, and entertainments, gossip and conversation, family history, jealousies and animosities, social and political intrigue, duplicity, adultery, and sexual inversion in the aristocratic circle of the de GUERMANTES family. The subject matter is continued in CITIES OF THE PLAIN. The title, *The Guermantes Way,* refers to one of the two paths usually taken by the narrator Marcel during childhood walks at COMBRAY—the one which led past the Guermantes property. See also SWANN'S WAY.

Guernsey. One of the Channel Islands. Jersey, Alderney, and Sark are the other important ones. The name signifies "green isle." Famous for its cows and as the residence (1855–1870) of the French poet Victor HUGO.

Guest, Lady Charlotte Elizabeth (1812–1895). Welsh writer. Published *Mabinogion* (1838–1849) from old Welsh manuscripts with translations. Cf. Bulfinch's *Mythology.*

Guest, Edgar Albert (1881–). English-born author of homely, sentimental, and moralistic doggerel verse, extremely popular and widely syndicated in newspapers of the U.S. *A Heap o' Livin'* (1916), *Just Folks* (1917), and *Life's Highway* (1933) are collections of it.

Guggenheim. A family dominating copper industry in U.S. Philanthropy on a large scale. The Daniel and Florence Guggenheim Foundation for the promotion of "the well-being of mankind" (1924); the School of Aeronautics at N.Y. University (1925); the Daniel Guggenheim Foundation for the Promotion of Aeronautics (1926–1930); the John Simon Guggenheim Memorial Foundation for the provision of annual fellowships to scientists, artists, writers, and musicians.

Guicciardini, Francesco (1483–1540). Florentine historian and statesman in pontifical and Medicean service. Author of *Storia d'Italia,* principal historical work of the 16th century (20 books, 1561–1564).

Guiccioli, Teresa, Countess. Young wife of an old Italian nobleman, with whom Lord BYRON had an officially recognized *liaison* and under whose steadying influence the poet's writing increased in skill and facility during the years he was in Italy.

Guiderius. The elder son of CYMBELINE, a legendary king of Britain during the reign of Augustus Caesar. In Shakespeare's CYMBELINE Guiderius and his brother Arviragus are stolen in infancy by Belarius, a banished nobleman, out of revenge, and are brought up by him in a cave.

GEOFFREY OF MONMOUTH says that Guiderius succeeded his father, and was slain by Hamo.

Guido, surnamed the Savage. In ORLANDO FURIOSO, son of Constantia and Amon, therefore younger brother of Rinaldo. He is also Astolpho's kinsman. Being wrecked on the coast of the Amazons, he is doomed to fight their ten male champions. He slays them all, and is then compelled to marry ten of the Amazons. He makes his escape with Aleria, his favorite wife, and joins the army of Charlemagne.

Guido d'Arezzo or **Guido Aretino.** Also known as **Fra Guittone** (995?–?1050). Italian Benedictine monk and reformer of musical notation and vocal instruction. He introduced the staff of four lines and added new lines above or below to do away with all uncertainty of pitch. It is probable that he invented the system of solmization. Other reforms ascribed to him are more doubtful.

Guido delle Colonne (*fl.* ca. 1285). Italian writer, known for his *Historia Troiana* (ca. 1285), a Latin work embodying in it the TROILUS story, adapted from the *Roman de Troie* of BENOÎT DE ST. MORE. Guido is considered to have been the source of Boccaccio's IL FILOSTRATO. He was one of the poets of the Sicilian School (see COURTLY LOVE) and visited England in the retinue of Edward I when the latter returned from the Crusades.

Guido Franceschini. The nobleman in Browning's RING AND THE BOOK who tries to repair his fortune by marrying Pompilia, the putative child of Pietro and Violante.

Guido Reni, see RENI.

Guignol. The principal character in a popular French puppet-show similar to "Punch and Judy" dating from the 18th century. As the performance comprised *macabre* and gruesome incidents, the name came to be attached to short plays of this nature; hence GRAND GUIGNOL, a series of such plays, or the theater in which they are performed, in Paris and other places, as London.

Guildenstern. In Shakespeare's HAMLET, one of Hamlet's companions, employed by the King and Queen to divert him, if possible, from his strange and wayward ways.

> Rosencrantz and Guildenstern are favourite samples of the thorough-paced time-serving court knave . . . ticketed and to be hired for any hard or dirty work.—Crowden Clarke.

Guillaume de Lorris (*fl.* ca. 1230). French poet, author of the first part of the ROMANCE OF THE ROSE, which he is believed to have written between 1225 and 1230. The sections of the poem of his authorship emphasize the psychology of COURTLY LOVE from the aristocratic standpoint. See also JEAN DE MEUN.

Guillaume de Machaut (ca. 1300–1377). French poet, the founder of the 14th-century French school of lyric poetry which includes Eustache DESCHAMPS and Jean FROISSART. He is best known for his compositions in the forms of the *ballade, rondel, chant royal,* and the *lai,* and for his alliance of poetry and music. Chaucer is considered to have imitated Guillaume de Machaut in his BOOK OF THE DUCHESS.

guillotine. A machine for beheading persons, much used in the French revolution. Joseph Ignace Guillotin (1738–1814), a French physician, first proposed its use in 1789, recommending it reputedly because of the "voluptuously pleasant sensation" produced by the contact of its blade with the neck.

Guinevere (Geoffrey of Monmouth's *Guanhumara,* the Welsh *Gwenhwyvar,* meaning "the white ghost"). In the Arthurian legends, the wife of King Arthur. According to Malory (who spells the name Guenever), she was the daughter of Leodegrance, king of the land of Cameliard. She entertains a guilty passion for Sir Launcelot of the Lake, one of the knights of the Round Table, but during the absence of King Arthur in his expedition against Leo, king of the Romans, she is seduced by Modred, her husband's nephew, who has usurped the kingdom. Arthur hastens back, Guinevere flees, and a desperate battle is fought, in which Modred is slain and Arthur mortally wounded. Guinevere takes the veil at Almesbury, where later she dies. She is buried at Glastonbury, and has left her name as a synonym for a beautiful, faithless, but repentant wife. Tennyson, in his IDYLLS OF THE KING makes Guinevere guilty only in her passion for Launcelot, and not a party to Modred's treachery.

James Branch Cabell introduces Guinevere into his JURGEN as the heroine of a love episode with Jurgen.

For variant spellings of Guinevere, see GANOR.

Guiney, Louise Imogen (1861–1920). American Catholic poet and essayist whose later life was spent in England. A generous and romantic nature steeped in the past. "Only at ease," said Sir Edmund GROSSE, "in a chivalrous and antique dreamland." *Songs at the Start* (1884); *Patrins* (essays), 1897; *Happy Ending* (1909); etc.

Guinicelli or **Guinizelli, Guido** (*fl.* ca. 1274). Italian medieval poet, considered the greatest Italian poet before Dante, who praises him in various of his works, including his DIVINE COMEDY. Guinicelli wrote in the tradition of COURTLY LOVE, and his *Canzone Of the Gentle Heart* (*Al Cor Gentil*), found as an influence throughout Dante's VITA NUOVA is regarded as the inauguration of "the sweet new style" (IL DOLCE STIL NUOVO).

Guiscard, Robert (1015?–1085). Norman leader. Founder of the state of the Two Sicilies. He is the hero of a powerful dramatic fragment left by Heinrich von Kleist (1777–1811).

Guiscardo. The son of AYMON and squire of Tancred of Salerno. In Dryden's *Sigis-*

monda and Guiscardo, translated from Boccaccio, he secretly marries Tancred's daughter and is strangled.

Guise's motto. *"À chacun son tour,"* on the standards of the Duc de Guise, who put himself at the head of the Catholic League in the 16th century, meant, "My turn will come."

Guiterman, Arthur (1871–1943). American poet and light versifier born in Vienna of American parents. Initiated *Rhymed Reviews* in the magazine *Life.* Adopted Molière's *L'Ecole des maris* in English rhymed verse, successfully produced by Theatre Guild (1933). Wrote libretto and lyrics for *The Man Without a Country* by Walter Damrosch, produced by the Metropolitan Opera Company in New York (1937).

Guitry, Sacha (1885–). French actor and dramatist; writer and producer of moving pictures. The "quintessence of Gallicism." His father, the actor **Lucien Germain Guitry** (1860–1925), appeared in a number of his plays.

Guizot, François Pierre Guillaume (1787–1874). French historian and statesman. Minister in various capacities throughout the reign of citizen king Louis Philippe (1830–1848). His voluminous writings include beside his major historical works a number of Shakespeare translations.

Gulbeyas. The sultana in Byron's DON JUAN. Having seen Juan amongst Lambro's captives, "passing on his way to sale," she causes him to be purchased, and introduces him into the harem in female attire. On discovering that he prefers Dudu, one of the attendant beauties, to herself, she commands both to be stitched up in a sack and cast into the Bosphorus. They contrive, however, to make their escape.

Gulbrannsen, Trygve (1894–). Norwegian novelist. Chronicles of an aristocratic Norwegian family living on their huge hill estates. Has been compared with both Knut HAMSUN and Sigrid UNDSET.

Gulf Stream. The great, warm ocean current which flows out of the Gulf of Mexico (whence its name) and, passing by the eastern coasts of the United States, is, near the banks of Newfoundland, deflected across the Atlantic to modify the climate of Western Europe as far north as Spitzbergen and Nova Zembla. It washes the shores of the British Isles.

Gulf States, see STATES.

Gulistan (*Pers.,* "the garden of roses"). The famous *recueil* of moral sentences by Sadi (ca. 1190–1291), the most celebrated of Persian poets except, perhaps, Omar Khayyam. It consists of sections on kings, dervishes, contentment, love, youth, old age, social duties, etc., with many stories and philosophical sayings.

Gullah. One of a group of Negroes, descendants of West African slaves, occupying the sea islands and coast districts of South Carolina, Georgia, and a section of northeastern Florida. Also their dialect, the modern form of which is a corruption of English. For its use in literature, cf. *Porgy* by DuBose HEYWARD.

Gulliver, Lemuel. The hero of the famous *Travels into Several Remote Nations of the World, by Lemuel Gulliver, first a Surgeon, and then a Captain of several ships,* written by Jonathan SWIFT (1726). Gulliver first gets wrecked on the coast of Lilliput, a country of pygmies. Subsequently he is thrown among the people of Brobdingnag, giants of tremendous size. In his next voyage he is driven to Laputa, an empire of quack pretenders to science and knavish projectors; and in his fourth voyage he visits the Houyhnhnms, where horses are the dominant powers.

Gulliver's Travels, frequently looked upon as a mere children's book, is in reality a biting social and political satire.

> Whether we read it, as children do, for the story or as historians, for the political allusions, or as men of the world, for the satire and philosophy, we have to acknowledge that it is one of the wonderful and unique books of the world's literature.—Edmund Gosse, *History of English Literature.*

Gull's Hornbook, The. A prose satire by Thomas DEKKER (1609), in the form of a mock "hornbook," or primer, for the guidance of wealthy young gallants, called "gulls," who came to London for adventure and experience. It tells them how to behave at the theater, the tavern, the gambling-house, and so on.

Gulnare. In Byron's CORSAIR, queen of the harem, and the most beautiful of all the slaves of Seyd. She is rescued by Conrad the corsair from the flames of the palace, and, when Conrad is imprisoned, she goes to his dungeon, confesses her love, and proposes that he murder the sultan and flee. As Conrad refuses to assassinate Seyd, she herself does it, and then flees with Conrad to the "Pirate's Isle." The rest of the tale is continued in LARA, in which Gulnare assumes the name of Kaled, and appears as a page.

Gummere, Francis Barton (1855–1919). American university professor and authority on popular ballads. *Old English Ballads* (1894); *Democracy and Poetry* (1911); etc. His theory of the origin of English and Scottish ballads in group dancing is indebted to HERDER and GRIMM. It is presented in some detail in *The Popular Ballad* (1907).

Gummidge, Mrs. In Dickens' DAVID COPPERFIELD the widow of Dan'el Peggotty's partner. She keeps house for Dan'el, who is a bachelor. Old Mrs. Gummidge has a deep-rooted conviction that she is neglected and uncared for, a waif in the wide world, of no use to anyone. She is always talking of herself as "a poor lone lorn cretur."

Gump, Andy and **Min.** Two popular characters of the American comic supplement in the 1920's, created by the cartoonist Sidney Smith. Andy Gump is a long, chinless individual, full of foibles, particularly a habit of bragging that always ends in trouble and a frantic call for his faithful wife Min. In the election of 1924 Andy Gump ran for Congress and was even unofficially nominated for president.

Gundy, Solomon, see SWAP, SOLOMON.

Gunga Din. One of Kipling's *Barrack-Room Ballads* (1892) in praise of a Hindu water carrier for a British regiment.

> An' for all 'is dirty 'ide
> 'E was white, clear white, inside
> When 'e went to tend the wounded under fire!
> It was "Din, Din, Din!"
> With the bullets kickin' dust-spores on the green
> When the cartridges ran out
> You could hear the front-ranks shout,
> "Hi! ammunition-mules an' Gunga Din!' "

Gunnar. In the Icelandic saga of BURNT NJAL, friend of Njal and husband of the trouble-making HALLGERDA. Because of her quarrels and misadventures, and the feud caused between the two men through her vengefulness, Gunnar is declared an outlaw. He refuses to leave Iceland, which makes it possible for his enemies to kill him without payment of the WERGELD.

Gunnarsson, Gunnar (1889–). Icelandic novelist. His four-volume "Borg" series covers three generations of an Icelandic farm family. Among his books available in English are *Guest the One-Eyed* (1930); *Seven Days' Darkness* (1930); *The Good Shepherd* (1940); etc.

Gunpowder Plot. The project of a few Roman Catholics to destroy James I with the Lords and Commons assembled in the Houses of Parliament, on November 5, 1605. It was to be done by means of gunpowder when the king went in person to open Parliament. Robert CATESBY originated the plot, and Guy FAWKES undertook to fire the gunpowder. The plot was betrayed, and Guy Fawkes was arrested the night before it was to have been put into execution. November 5 is still celebrated in England and parts of the Empire as Guy Fawkes Day.

> Please to remember the fifth of November
> The gunpowder treason and plot.

See also GUY.

Gunther. In the NIBELUNGENLIED, a Burgundian king, brother of Kriemhild, the wife of Siegfried. He resolved to wed the martial queen BRUNHILD, who had made a vow to marry only the man who could ride through the flames that encircled her castle. Gunther failed (see GRANI), but Siegfried did so in his likeness and remained with the Queen for three nights, his sword being between them all the time. Gunther then married Brunhild, but when Kriemhild later told Brunhild that it was Siegfried who had ridden through the fire, jealousy sprang up between the families. Gunther, with unpardonable ingratitude, was privy to the murder of his friend and brother-in-law, and was himself slain in the dungeon of Etzel's palace by his sister Kriemhild. Gundicarius, a Burgundian king who, with his whole tribe, perished at the sword of the Huns in 437, is supposed to be the historical character round whom these legends collected. In the VÖLSUNGA SAGA, the Scandinavian version of the same legend, Gunther figures prominently, as also in the operas of Wagner's NIBELUNGEN RING.

Gunther, John (1901–). American newspaper correspondent, known for his accounts of European and Asiatic affairs during the period from 1926 to 1939. He is the author of best-selling books of informal contemporary history and prediction, extremely popular during the period of crisis immediately preceding World War II: *Inside Europe* (1936); *Inside Asia* (1939); *Inside Latin America* (1941); *Inside U.S.A.* (1947). See also DURANTY, WALTER; SHEEAN, VINCENT.

Guppy, William. In Dickens's *Bleak House,* a vulgar young law clerk, hopelessly in love with Esther Summerson.

Gurth. In Scott's IVANHOE, the swineherd and thrall of Cedric of Rotherwood.

Gurton, Gammer, see GAMMER GURTON.

Gustavus II. Known as **Gustavus Adolphus** (1594–1632). King of Sweden. Called "Lion of the North," also "Snow King." Supported Protestant cause in Thirty Years' War (1630–1632). Won the great battle of Lützen against Wallenstein, but was mortally wounded. One of the greatest generals of all times. Saved Protestantism in Germany. His death left Sweden under a regency with his six-year-old daughter CHRISTINA as nominal queen.

Gutenberg's Bible. See BIBLE, SPECIALLY NAMED.

Guthlac, St. See under SAINTS.

Guthrie, Thomas Anstey, pseudonym **F. Anstey** (1856–1934). English humorist, fantasist and playwright. *Vice-Versâ or a Lesson to Fathers* (1882); *The Tinted Venus* (1885), adapted by Ogden NASH as *One Touch of Venus,* popular musical comedy (1944); *The Brass Bottle* (1900); etc. Long on the staff of *Punch.*

Gutrune. In *Götterdämmerung,* the last of the four operas of Wagner's NIBELUNGEN RING, the sister of Gunther, courted and won by Siegfried. She is the GUDRUN of the VÖLSUNGA SAGA and the KRIEMHILD of the NIBELUNGENLIED.

guy. An effigy of a man, stuffed with combustibles and supposed to represent Guy FAWKES, carried round in procession and finally burned on November 5, in memory of GUNPOWDER PLOT; hence, any dowdy, fantastic figure, a "fright." In America the word, as applied to a person, has a wide significance, and can mean almost anyone. "A good guy" is a term of approval.

Guy Mannering. A novel by Sir Walter SCOTT (1815), a tale of the period of George III. Because of the antagonism which his magistrate father had aroused among the gypsies, Harry Bertram, the hero, heir to the Ellengowan estate, is kidnaped by a lawyer named Glossin, who secures the estate. Harry's sister Lucy, who is forced to leave her home, is hospitably entertained by Guy Mannering and his daughter Julia. The gypsy, Meg Merrilies, befriends Harry Bertram, aids his escape and afterwards tells him he is the rightful heir of the Ellengowan estate. Glossin is then sent to prison, where he enters the cell of Dirk Hatteraick, a Dutch smuggler, and is strangled by him. Eventually Harry Bertram marries Julia Mannering. The book is noted not so much for its plot as for the famous characters of Dandie DINMONT, PLEYDELL, HATTERAICK, Dominie SAMPSON and Meg MERRILIES.

Guy of Warwick. An English hero of legend and romance, whose exploits were first written down by some Anglo-Norman poet of the 12th century and were, by the 14th century, accepted as quite authentic history.

To obtain Phelis (Felice) as his wife he undertook many knightly deeds. He rescued the daughter of the Emperor of Germany, and went to fight against the Saracens, slaying the doughty Coldran, Elmaye King of Tyre, and the soldan himself. Then he returned and wedded Phelis, but in forty days went back to the Holy Land, where he slew the giant Amarant, and many others. Having achieved all this and numerous other adventures, he now became a hermit near Warwick. Daily he went in disguise to his own castle and begged bread of his wife Phelis; but on his death-bed he sent her a ring, by which she recognized her lord, and went to close his dying eyes.

Guyon, Sir (from Sp. *guía,* "a guide"). The knightly hero of Spenser's FAËRIE QUEENE, Bk. II, typical of Temperance or Self-government. He destroys the witch Acrasia, and her BOWER OF BLISS. The Palmer, typifying Prudence and Sobriety, is his companion, and Brigador ("bridle of gold") his horse.

Guy Rivers. A novel by William Gilmore SIMMS (1834). The scene is laid in Georgia, and the hero and a romantic border bandit contend for the heroine.

Guzmán de Alfarache, The Life and Adventures of. A famous picaresque romance by Mateo Alemán in two parts (*Sp.*, pt. I, 1599; pt. II, 1604).

Guzmán, Leonora de, see LEONORA.

Gwalchmei. The name under which GAWAIN appears in the Welsh *Mabinogion.*

Gwyn, Nell (1652–1687). An actress, and one of the mistresses of Charles II. She was a great favorite with the public. Scott mentions her in PEVERIL OF THE PEAK.

Gwynplaine. The hero of Victor Hugo's romance THE MAN WHO LAUGHS (*L'Homme qui rit*).

Gyas and Cloanthus. In Virgil's AENEID, two companions of Aeneas, generally mentioned together as *"fortis Gyas fortisque Cloanthus."* The phrase has become proverbial for two very similar characters.

Gyges. A king of Lydia of the 7th century B.C., who founded a new dynasty, warred against Asurbanipal of Assyria, and is memorable in legend for his ring and his prodigious wealth.

According to Plato, Gyges descended into a chasm of the earth, where he found a brazen horse. Opening the sides of the animal, he found the carcass of a man, from whose finger he drew off a brazen ring which rendered him invisible.

> Why, did you think that you had Gyges ring,
> Or the herb that gives invisibility [fern-seed]?
> Beaumont and Fletcher, *Fair Maid of the Inn,* i, 1.

It was by the aid of the ring that he obtained possession of the wife of CANDAULES and, through her, of his kingdom.

gymkhana. A word of Anglo-Indian origin, the first syllable being from English *gymnastics.* A meeting for athletic contests, as racing, swimming, etc.

Gynt, Peer, see PEER GYNT.

Gypsy. A member of a dark-skinned nomadic race which first appeared in England about the beginning of the 16th century, and, as they were thought to have come from Egypt, were named *Egyptians,* which soon became corrupted to *Gypcians,* and so to its present form. They call themselves *Romany* (from Gypsy *rom,* a man, husband), which is also the name of their language—a debased Hindu dialect with large additions of words from Persian, Armenian, and many European languages.

The name of the largest group of European gypsies is *Atzigan;* this, in Turkey and Greece, became *Tshingian,* in the Balkans and Roumania *Tsigan,* in Hungary *Czigany,* in Germany *Zigeuner,* in Italy *Zingari,* in Portugal *Cigano,* and in Spain *Gitano.* The original name is said to mean "dark man." See also BOHEMIAN.

There is a legend that the gypsies are waifs and strays on the earth because they refused to shelter the Virgin and her child in their flight to Egypt.

H

Habakkuk. A Hebrew prophet whose book of prophecies (3 chapters) holds the eighth place among the minor prophets of the Old Testament. Nothing is known about his life, and he has become the subject of many legends. Both his dialogue with Jehovah and his hymn on promised deliverance exhibit poetical genius of high order.

habeas corpus (*Lat.,* "that you have the body."). The Habeas Corpus Act was passed in 1679, and defined a provision of similar character in the Magna Charta, to which also it added certain details. Its chief purpose was to prohibit any judge, under severe penalties, from refusing to issue to a prisoner a writ of habeas corpus by which the jailer was obliged to produce the prisoner in court in person and to certify the cause of imprisonment, thus preventing people's being imprisoned on mere suspicion, and making it illegal for one to be left in prison an indefinite time without trial.

It further provides that every accused person shall have the question of his guilt decided by a jury of twelve, and not by a Government agent or nominee; that no prisoner can be tried a second time on the same charge; that every prisoner may insist on being examined within twenty days of his arrest, and tried at the next session; and that no one may be sent to prison beyond the seas, either within or without the British dominions.

The Habeas Corpus Act has been suspended in times of political and social disturbance, and its provisions have been more than once amended and extended.

Habington, William (1605–1654). English poet; author of the lyrical collection *Castara* (1634).

Hachette, Louis Christophe François (1800–1864). French publisher, founder of the Paris firm of Hachette et Cie. (1826.)

hack. Originally, short for "hackney." A horse let out for hire; hence, one who hires himself out for literary work. LOWELL wrote: "Dryden, like Lessing, was a hack writer . . ."

Hacker, Louis Morton (1899–). American historian, following in the tradition of the great historical sociologists, Marx, Sombart, Weber, etc. *The Triumph of American Capitalism* (1940); etc.

Hackett, Francis (1883–). Irish-American critic, biographer, and novelist. *Henry the Eighth; A Personal History* (1929); *Francis the First* (1934); *Queen Anne Boleyn* (1938), a novel.

Hades. In HOMER, the name of the god (Pluto) who reigns over the dead; in later classical mythology, the abode of the departed spirits, a place of gloom but not necessarily like the Christian *Hell,* a place of punishment and torture. As the state or abode of the dead it corresponds to the Hebrew *Sheol,* a word which, in the authorized version, has frequently been translated by the misleading *Hell.* Hence *Hades* is sometimes vulgarly used as a euphemism for *Hell.*

Hadith (Arab., *hadīth,* "a saying or tradition"). The traditions about the prophet Mahomet's sayings and doings. This compilation, which was made in the 10th century by the Moslem jurists Moshin and Bokhari, forms a supplement to the Koran as the Talmud to the Jewish Scriptures. Like the Jewish *Gemara,* the Hadith was not allowed originally to be committed to writing, but the danger of the traditions being perverted or forgotten led to their being placed on record.

hadji. A pilgrim; specifically, a Moslem having completed the required pilgrimage or HADJ to Mecca. The word is often prefixed to a name as an epithet of honor. A delightful instance is that of *Hadji Halef Omar ben Hadji Abbul Abbas ibn Hadji David al Gossarah* in Karl MAY's stories. Here *ben* stands for "son of," and *ibn* for "grandson of."

Hadley, Arthur Twining (1856–1930). American economist. President of Yale University (1899–1921).

Hadleyburg, The Man that Corrupted. See under MAN.

Hadrian. Latin **Publius Aelius Hadrianus** (76–138 A.D.). Roman emperor (117–138). Established the Euphrates as the eastern boundary of the Roman empire as part of his policy of consolidation and of renouncing conquest. Caused construction in Britain of Hadrian's Wall (120–123) from Solway Firth to mouth of Tyne as a protection against the Picts and Scots.

Haeckel, Ernst Heinrich (1834–1919). Well-known German biologist and monistic philosopher. Supposed to have carried the logic of pure positivistic science to the sarcastic conclusion: "God is invisible; man is an image of God. Ergo, God is a gaseous mammal." Formulated the basic law of biogenetics: "The development of the individual recapitulates the evolution of the species." His best-known popular work is *Riddles of the Universe* (*Welträtsel,* 1899).

Hafed. In *The Fire-Worshippers,* the third tale in Moore's LALLA ROOKH, a Gheber, or fire-worshiper, in love with Hinda, the emir's daughter. He is the leader of a band sworn to free their country or die in the attempt. His rendezvous is betrayed, but when the Moslem comes to arrest him, he throws himself into the sacred fire and is burnt to death.

Hafiz. Real name **Shams ud-din Mohammed** (*fl.* 14th century). The great Persian poet and one of the greatest poets of the world. His *ghazels* (i.e., songs, odes) tell of love and wine, nightingales, flowers, the instability of all things human, of Allah and the Prophet, etc. His tomb at Shiraz is still the resort of pilgrims. The name *Hafiz* is Arabic for "one who knows the KORAN and HADITH by heart."

Hagan or **Hagen.** In the NIBELUNGENLIED and the old Norse sagas (where he is called Hogni), a prominent character, son of a mortal and a sea-goblin. In the *Nibelungenlied,* Hagan kills Siegfried, then seizes the Nibelung hoard, and buries it in the Rhine, intending to appropriate it. Kriemhild, after her marriage with Etzel, king of the Huns, invites him to the court of her husband, and cuts off his head. He is described as "well grown, strongly built, with long sinewy legs, deep broad chest, hair slightly grey, of terrible visage, and of lordly gait." There are other versions of the story, many of them quite contradictory, and the rough and treacherous Hagan appears in many legends. He is a prominent character in *Götterdämmerung* (The Dusk of the Gods), the last of the four operas of Wagner's NIBELUNGEN RING.

Hagar. In the Old Testament, the servant of Abraham's wife Sarai, who became the mother of ISHMAEL. After the birth of Isaac, Hagar and Ishmael were cast out into the wilderness at the instigation of Sarai. On one occasion, when they were perishing of thirst, an angel spoke to Hagar and showed her a well of water.

Hagedorn, Hermann (1882–). American poet. Great friend of Theodore ROOSEVELT. Biographer of Edwin Arlington ROBINSON.

Hagenbeck, Karl (1844–1913). German wild-animal dealer. Established animal park near Hamburg (1907), famous for its successful reproduction of natural habitats.

Haggadah. The portion of the MIDRASH which contains rabbinical interpretations of the historical and legendary, ethical, parabolic, and speculative parts of the Hebrew Scriptures; the portion devoted to law, practice, and doctrine is called the *Halachah.* They were commenced in the 2nd century A. D. and completed by the 11th.

Haggard, Sir **Henry Rider** (1856–1925). English romancer. Author of *King Solomon's Mines* (1885); *She* (1887); *Allan Quatermain* (1887); *Ayesha* (1905), etc.

Hague Tribunal. An international court of arbitration meeting at The Hague. It arose out of the Hague Congress on disarmament in 1899 and has been superseded by the PERMANENT COURT OF INTERNATIONAL JUSTICE.

Hahn, Emily (1905–). American writer. Author of *Seductio ad Absurdum* (1927); *Congo Solo* (1933); *The Soong Sisters* (1941); *China to Me* (1945); *Raffles of Singapore* (1946), and numerous short stories about her life in China mostly appearing in the *New Yorker.* Cf. the collection *Mr. Pan* (1942).

Haidee. In Byron's DON JUAN (ii–iv) the beautiful Greek girl who finds Don Juan when he is cast ashore and restores him to animation. "Her hair was auburn, and her eyes were black as death." Her mother, a Moor, is dead, and her father, Lambro, a rich Greek pirate, is living on one of the Cyclades. She and Juan fall in love with each other during the absence of Lambro from the island. On his return Juan is sent from the island; Haidee goes mad and, after a lingering illness, dies. There is also a *Haidee* who figures in Dumas' COUNT OF MONTE CRISTO.

haikai. A kind of brief Japanese composition cultivated in later feudal ages. The HOKKU is its poetic variety.

Hail and Farewell. An autobiography by the Irish author, George MOORE, in three volumes: *Ave, Salve and Vale* (1911–1914).

Hail Columbia. An American national hymn by Joseph Hopkinson (1798), beginning:

> Hail, Columbia! happy land!
> Hail, ye heroes! heaven-born band
> Who fought and bled in Freedom's cause.

Haile Selassie (1891–). Name assumed upon coronation by Ras **Tafari,** emperor of Ethiopia (1930). Called the "Lion of Judah." Driven from Ethiopia by Italian conquest (1936–1941). Restored to his throne in 1941.

Hairy Ape, The. An expressionistic (see EXPRESSIONISM) drama by Eugene O'NEILL (1922). The hero, Yank, is a great, crude stoker on a huge ocean liner. He is sustained by his feeling that the man who works somehow "belongs," until he suddenly becomes wild with fury at the look on the face of a society girl who inspects him at his task.

Hajar-al-Aswad. The famous black stone in the northeast corner of the KAABA. It is an irregular oval, about 7 inches in breadth, and is surrounded with a circle of gold. The legend is that when Abraham wished to build the Kaaba, the stones came to him of their own accord, and the patriarch commanded all the faithful to kiss this one.

The stone is probably an aerolite, and it was worshiped long before Mahomet's day, for in the 2nd century A. D. Maximus Tyrius spoke of the Arabians paying homage to it, and Persian legend states that it was an emblem of Saturn.

Ibn Abbas reports that the Prophet said that when it came from Paradise it was whiter than milk, and that it had become black through the sins of the millions that had kissed it. On the Day of the Resurrection it is to have two eyes, by which it will recognize all those who have kissed it, and a tongue with which it will bear witness to Allah.

Hajji Baba of Ispahan, The Adventures of. A picaresque romance by James MORIER (1824), dealing with life in Persia. The hero is a sort of Persian Gil Blas whose roguery takes him into all spheres of Persian society. In a sequel, *Hajji Baba in England* (1828), he visits England as a government official.

Hakim, Adonbec el. In Scott's TALISMAN, Saladin in the disguise of a physician. He visits Richard Coeur de Lion in sickness, and gives him a medicine in which the "talisman" has been dipped, and the sick king recovers from his fever.

Hajji Khalfah. Original name **Mustafa ibn-Abdallah** (1600?–1658). Turkish historian and bibliographer. Compiled a bibliographical lexicon, with memoirs of the authors, of over 25,000 books in Arabic, Turkish, and Persian.

Hakim Ibn Allah. Known as the "veiled prophet" in the 8th century. Led a serious revolt against the Calif Mahdi in Bagdad. His story is told in *Lalla Rookh* (1817) by Thomas MOORE.

Hakluyt, Richard (1553–1616). English scholar and diplomat, famous for his collection of accounts of travel and adventures written by miscellaneous seamen and explorers during the reign of Queen Elizabeth. The first edition appeared in 1589 and the full title is *The Principal Navigations, Voyages, Traffics, and Discoveries of the English Nation, Made by Sea or over Land to the Remote and Farthest Distant Quarters of the Earth at Any Time within the Compass of These 1500 Years.*

Hakluyt Society. An organization "for the publication of rare and valuable voyages, travels, and geographical records," instituted in 1846.

Hal, Bluff King. A nickname for Henry VIII of England, also called *Bluff Harry.*

Prince Hal. The nickname of Henry, prince of Wales, afterwards Henry V. He is introduced in Shakespeare's, 1 *Henry IV* and 2 *Henry IV.*

Halachah. The division of the MIDRASH that deals with the interpretation of the law, points of doctrine, etc. See also HAGGADAH; GEMARA; MISHNA.

> The halachah . . . had even greater authority than the Scriptures of the Old Testament, since it explained and applied them.—Edersheim, *Life of Jesus the Messiah,* vol. i, bk. i, ch. i.

halcyon days. A time of happiness and prosperity. Halcyon is the Greek for a kingfisher, compounded of *hals,* "the sea," and *kuo,* "to brood on." The ancient Sicilians believed that the kingfisher laid its eggs and incubated for fourteen days, before the winter solstice, on the surface of the sea, during which time the waves of the sea were always unruffled.

> "Amidst our arms as quiet you shall be
> As halcyon brooding on a winter's sea."
> Dryden.

Haldane, John Burdon Sanderson (1892–). English biologist, whose forebears were philosophers, scientists, and statesmen. Worked in fields of human physiology and genetics. In 1933, disgusted with the Chamberlain policy in England, he entered the political field. Became a Marxist. A "burly, tweedy, shaggy man." Many academic distinctions. Research in genetics. Author of *Daedalus: or Science and the Future* (1924); *The Marxist Philosophy and the Sciences* (1938), etc.

Haldin. An anarchist in Conrad's UNDER WESTERN EYES.

Nathalie Haldin. His sister, the heroine of the novel.

Hale, Edward Everett (1822–1909). American Unitarian clergyman and popular author, best known for his story THE MAN WITHOUT A COUNTRY (1863). He also wrote whimsical tales, historical romances, and autobiographical and scholarly works, including: *Sybaris and Other Homes* (1869); *Ten Times One is Ten* (1871); *The Fortunes of Rachel* (1884); *East and West* (1892); *Franklin in France* (1887–1888); *A New England Boyhood* (1893).

Hale, George Ellery (1868–1938). American astronomer. Organizer and director of Mount Wilson Observatory under the Carnegie Institution (1904–1923).

Hale, Nancy (1908–). American short-story writer and novelist. Daughter of Philip Leslie Hale. Her short stories—cf. the collection *Between the Dark and the Daylight* (1943)—have been reprinted in some twenty anthologies. Her best-known novel is *The Prodigal Women* (1942).

Hale, Nathan (1755–1776). American hero of the Revolutionary War. He was sentenced by the British to be hanged as a spy and went to his death with the words, "I only regret that I have but one life to lose for my country." He is the hero of a drama by Clyde FITCH entitled *Nathan Hale* (1898).

Hale, William Harlan (1911?–). American writer and journalist. Founded at Yale University with Selden Rodman *The Harkness Hoot* (1930–1932), a periodical published irregularly during the college year. Editor of *Common Sense.* Author of *Challenge to Defeat: Modern Man in Goethe's World and Spengler's Century* (1932); *Hannibal Hooker, His Death and Adventures* (1939); etc.

Halévy, Ludovic (1834–1908). French dramatist and novelist. Wrote librettos for many operas including Bizet's *Carmen.* Wrote the drama *Frou-Frou,* and the novel *L'Abbé Constantin.*

Half Moon. Ship of Hendrik Hudson in voyage of discovery on Hudson River (1609).

Haliburton, Thomas Chandler (1796–1865). Canadian jurist who created in his humorous writings the character of **Sam Slick,** alter ego and pseudonym of the author.

Halicarnassian, The. HERODOTUS.

Halifax.

Halifax Law. By this law, whoever committed theft in the liberty of Halifax was to be executed on the Halifax gibbet, a kind of guillotine. Hence the expression *go to Halifax.*

> At Hallifax the law so sharpe doth deale,
> That whoso more than thirteen pence doth steale.
> They have a jyn that wondrous quick and well
> Sends thieves all headless into heaven or hell
> Taylor (the Water Poet), *Works* ii. (1630).

Hull, Hell, and Halifax. An old beggars' and vagabonds' "prayer," as quoted by Taylor, the Water Poet (early 17th century), was:

> From Hull, Hell, and Halifax,
> Good Lord, deliver us.

"Hell" was probably the least feared as being farthest from them; "Hull" was to be avoided because it was so well governed that beggars had little chance of getting anything without doing hard labor for it; and "Halifax," because anyone caught stealing cloth in that town was beheaded without intermediate proceedings.

Halifax, John, see JOHN HALIFAX, GENTLEMAN.

Hall, Catherine. The heroine of Thackeray's satiric romance CATHERINE. After marriage she becomes Catherine Hayes.

Hall, Granville Stanley (1844–1924). American psychologist and educator. President Clark University (1889–1919). A leader in the "new" psychology. *Adolescence* (1904).

Hall, Holwortly. Pseudonym of Harold Everett PORTER.

Hall, James Norman (1887–). American novelist. Flier in the Lafayette Flying Corps in World War I. Co-author with Charles Bernard NORDHOFF of *The Lafayette Flying Corps* (1920); a trilogy of romances narrating the story of the ship BOUNTY, and of other popular books.

Hall, Joseph (1574–1656). English prose writer, one of the CHARACTER WRITERS, a bishop of Exeter and Norwich. He is known for his *Characters of Virtues and Vices* (1608), a study of mental and ethical "characters" in the direct tradition of THEOPHRASTUS.

Hall, Radclyffe (188?–1943). English novelist and short-story writer, best-known for *The Well of Loneliness* (1928), a book which caused a sensation because of its theme of sexual inversion among women and was banned in England, as well as being temporarily suppressed in the U.S. See also DREISER, THEODORE; JURGEN; LADY CHATTERLEY'S LOVER; ULYSSES.) Her other works include: *The Unlit Lamp* (1924); *The Forge* (1924); *A Saturday Life* (1925); *Adam's Breed* (1926); *Miss Ogilvy Finds Herself* (1934), short stories; *The Sixth Beatitude* (1936).

Hallam, Arthur Henry (1811–1833). A close friend of the poet TENNYSON in his youth and the fiancé of the poet's sister Emily. Hallam's death in Vienna in 1833 was a profound shock to Tennyson and was the direct cause of the conflict between doubt and faith in the poet's life. The elegy IN MEMORIAM was dedicated to Hallam's memory.

Halleck, Fitz-Greene (1790–1867). American poet. Clerk in John Jacob Astor's office (1832–1849). *Poetical Works* (1847). Best-known for his *Marco Bozzaris,* first appearing in New York *Review* (1825), and his memorial verses on his friend Joseph Rodman DRAKE, *Green be the turf above thee.*

Hallelujah (Heb., *halelu-Jah,* "praise ye Jehovah"). An exclamation used in songs of praise and thanksgiving, meaning, "praise ye the Lord."

Hallelujah lass. A name given, with a humorously contemptuous import, to female members of the Salvation Army in the early days of that movement.

Hallelujah victory. A victory said to have been gained by some newly baptized Britons over the Picts and Scots near Mold, Flintshire, in 429. They were led by Germanus, Bishop of Auxerre, and commenced the battle with loud shouts of "Hallelujah!"

Halley, Edmund (1656–1742). English astronomer. A friend of NEWTON whose *Principia* he published (1687) at his own expense. Predicted accurately the return of a comet, which is now known as Halley's Comet. Several expeditions to the southern hemisphere.

Hallgerda. In the Icelandic saga of BURNT NJAL, the wife of GUNNAR, a beautiful, willful, and selfish woman who quarrels with Bergthora, wife of Gunnar's friend Njal, and keeps up the bitter feud between the two families which ends in tragedy for both. When Gunnar is besieged by his enemies in his house, he begs Hallgerda for a lock of her golden hair to make a new bowstring. She, however, reminds him of an occasion in the past when he slapped her for stealing some cheese and says spitefully, "I think I shall not cut off my hair."

Halliburton, Richard (1900–1939). American traveler and adventurer, author of best-selling books describing his spectacular feats in various parts of the world, which included swimming the Hellespont and the Panama Canal and following the legendary routes of Ulysses, Cortes, and Alexander the Great. Among his books are: *The Royal Road to Romance* (1925); *The Glorious Adventure* (1927); *New Worlds to Conquer* (1929); *The Flying Carpet* (1932); and *Seven League Boots* (1935). He disappeared in 1939 while attempting to sail a Chinese junk from China to San Francisco, and was declared legally dead.

Halliwell, or later, having assumed his wife's surname, **Halliwell-Phillipps, James Orchard** (1820–1889). English librarian and Shakespearean scholar.

Hall of Fame. See under FAME.

Hallowe'en. October 31, which in the old Celtic calendar was the last day of the old year, its night being the time when all the witches and warlocks were abroad and held their wicked revels. On the introduction of Christianity it was taken over as the Eve of All Hallows, or All Saints. It is still devoted to all sorts of games in which the old superstitions can be traced. Cf. Burns' poem *Hallowe'en.*

Hallowell, Robert (1886–1939). American painter. One of the founders and later the publisher of the *New Republic* (1914–1925). Friend of John REED, whose portrait he painted.

Halper, Albert (1904–). American novelist and short-story writer on proletarian subjects (see PROLETARIAN LITERATURE), known for his studies of life and workers in the large industry of the U.S. and of people without money living in city slums, especially in the city of Chicago, where Halper was born. His books include: *Union Square* (1933), concerning New York radicals and their activities; *On the Shore* (1934); *The Foundry* (1934), with an electrotyping plant as its background; *The Chute* (1937), set in a large mail-order house; *Sons of the Fathers* (1940), dealing with Jewish immigrants and World War I; and *The Little People* (1942), of life in a Chicago department store. Most of Halper's work is autobiographical in whole or in part.

Hals, Franz (1580?–1666). Dutch portrait and genre painter, ranking with REMBRANDT, RUBENS, and VANDYKE. Has been called a gay pessimist, the first great painter of his century and country.

Halsey, Margaret Frances (1910–). American humorous writer. *With Malice Toward Some* (1938), etc.

Halsey, William Frederick (1882–). American admiral. Commander of Allied naval forces in South Pacific (Oct., 1942). Defeated Japanese in three-day naval and air battle off Solomon Islands (Nov., 1942).

Ham. In the Old Testament one of the three sons of Noah. The other two were Shem and Japheth. According to legend Ham's descendants populated Africa; hence, a *son of Ham,* a Negro.

hamadryads, see DRYAD.

Haman. In the Old Testament, a conspirator against the Jews, whose purposes were defeated by Mordecai and ESTHER and who was hanged on the gallows that he had prepared for his enemy Mordecai.

Hambidge, Jay (1867–1924). Originator of the theory of dynamic symmetry, a system of proportions and balances observed in ancient Greek art, especially striking in vase decorations.

Hamelin. A town in Brunswick on the Weser in Germany. The medieval legend of *The Pied Piper of Hamelin* is generally known through the poem of that title by Robert BROWNING.

Hamerton, Philip Gilbert (1834–1894). English artist and essayist. Author of *Etching and Etchers* (1866); *The Intellectual Life* (1873), etc.

Hamet, Cid Hamet or **Cid Hamet Benengeli,** see under CID.

Hamilcar Barca (270?–228 B. C.). Father of Hannibal. Carthaginian general who began the reduction of Spain to a Carthaginian province. Killed in action.

Hamilton, Alexander (1753? or 1757–1804). American statesman, known as the chief author of the *Federalist* essays (1787–1788), urging a strong central government. He is the hero of Gertrude Atherton's historical novel, THE CONQUEROR (1902). Died in a duel with Aaron BURR.

Hamilton, Cosmo, see GIBBS, COSMO HAMILTON.

Hamilton, Lady **Emma,** *née* **Lyon** (1761?–1815). Wife of Sir William Hamilton, mistress of Nelson. Of humble birth, illiterate, and of loose character. Before the time of her social success, she posed as the Goddess of Health in a quack doctor's exhibition. She became an intimate friend of Queen Maria Carolina of Naples and played an important part in Anglo-Neapolitan political intrigues. Mother of Nelson's daughter Horatia (1801). Arrested for debt in 1813 but released in 1814. Painted by ROMNEY. Cf. *The Divine Lady* (1924), by "E. Barrington" (L. Adams BECK).

Hamlet. A tragedy by Shakespeare (ca. 1600). Hamlet, Prince of Denmark, learns to his horror that Claudius, his uncle, and Gertrude, his mother, now reigning together as king and queen, have been responsible for the death of his royal father. Although he is in love with the fair Ophelia, he puts her roughly aside and pretends madness in order to devote himself to revenge. But he cannot bring himself to the point of taking action. While he is vacillating, Laertes, the brother of Ophelia, who has gone mad and drowned herself, challenges him to a supposedly friendly duel, but, encouraged by the King, uses a poisoned sword. The swords are exchanged by accident and both Hamlet and Laertes receive their death wounds. On learning of the treachery, the dying Hamlet at last kills the King.

The play is based on a crude story told by the 13th-century Saxo Grammaticus, a Danish chronicler, in his *Historia Danica* (first printed 1514), which found a place in Pierre de Belleforest's *Histoires Tragiques* (1570), a French miscellany of translated legend and romance.

"The whole play," says SCHLEGEL, "is intended to show that calculating consideration exhausts . . . the power of action." GOETHE is of the same opinion, and says that "Hamlet is a noble nature, without the strength of nerve which forms a hero. He sinks beneath a burden which he cannot bear, and cannot cast aside."

As a result of the literary criticism of the romantic period, Hamlet came to be regarded as the prototype of the modern introspective man, the first outstanding representative of this psychological phenomenon in a development which culminated in the 19th-century DECADENTS.

it's Hamlet without the Prince. Said when the person who was to have taken the principal place at some function is absent.

Hamlin, Jack or John. A professional gambler in Bret Harte's GABRIEL CONROY and a number of his shorter tales, a man of gay, courteous manners and a melancholy turn of mind far removed from the previous types of the desperado in fiction. See also JOHN OAKHURST.

hammer and sickle. Insignia of U.S.S.R. Adopted in 1923 as a symbol of the union of industrial and farm labor.

Hammer of the Scots. Edward I, King of England (1272–1307).

Hammerstein, Oscar (1895–). Playwright, librettist of *Show Boat* (1927), *Oklahoma!* (1945), and, in collaboration, of many other light operas. Nephew of **Oscar Hammerstein** (1847?–1919), German-born theatrical manager.

Hammett, Dashiell (1894–). American founder of the "hard-boiled" school of detective fiction. *The Maltese Falcon* (1930); *The Thin Man* (1932), which became a very popular moving picture series.

Hammurabi (ca. 1955–1913 B. C. or one or two hundred years earlier). Greatest king of the first Babylonian dynasty. Called the founder of the Babylonian empire which survived for almost 2000 years. Great war lord and builder of roads and canals. The codification of his laws and edicts on a block of black diorite was discovered in 1901.

Hampden, John (1594–1643). British statesman. Resisted the collection of the obsolete tax of ship-money and became a symbol of British freedom. At the outbreak of the English civil war, he raised a regiment for the Parliamentary army. Mortally wounded at Chalgrove Field.

Hampden, Walter (1879–). Professional name of Walter Hampden Dougherty. American actor in Shakespearian rôles and other plays, as *The Servant in the House, Cyrano de Bergerac, Richelieu,* etc.

Hampton Court Conference. A conference held under James I at Hampton Court in January, 1604, to settle the disputes between the Church party and the Puritans. It lasted three days. Its chief result was a few slight alterations in the Book of Common Prayer, but it is here that the first suggestion was made for the official re-translation of the Bible which resulted in the "Authorized Version" of 1611.

Hamsun, Knut Pedersen (1859–). Norwegian novelist, resident for a number of years in the U.S., known for the grim realism of his portrayals of life among farmers and laborers. GROWTH OF THE SOIL (1920) is his best-known novel. Among others are: *Hunger* (1920); *Shallow Soil* (1914); *Children of the Age* (1924); *In the Grip of Life* (1924); *Benoni* (1925); *Rosa* (1926); *Mysteries* (1927); *Women at the Pump* (1928); *Chapter the Last* (1929); *August* (1930); *The Road Leads On* (1934); *The Ring is Closed* (1937); *Look Back on Happiness* (1940).

Han, Sons of. The Chinese; so called from Hân, the village in which Lieou-pang was chief. Lieou-pang conquered all who opposed him, seized the supreme power, assumed the name of Kao-hoângtee, and the dynasty, which lasted 422 years, was "the fifth imperial dynasty, or that of Hân." With his dynasty the modern history of China begins (202 B. C.–220 A. D.).

Hanafites. One of the four sects of SUNNITES.

Hanbalites. One of the four sects of SUNNITES.

Hancock, John (1737–1793). American Revolutionary statesman. President, Continental Congress (1775–1777). First signer of Declaration of Independence. From the legibility of his handwriting there developed the expression a *John Hancock*, "an autograph signature."

Handel, Georg Friedrich (1685–1759). German composer. Naturalized British subject (1726). First opera, *Almira* (1705). Composed more than 40 operas, 23 oratorios, odes, songs, church and chamber music. *Esther* (1720); *Saul* (1739); *The Messiah* (1742); *Judas Maccabaeus* (1746); etc. Rose to fame only after he was fifty and first partially and then completely blinded. British opposition to him during his earlier years gave rise to John Byrom's epigram which ends:

> Strange all this difference should be
> 'Twixt Tweedledum and Tweedledee!

Handlyng Synne (*M.E.*, "handbook, or manual, of sins"). A Middle English religious treatise in rhymed couplets, written in the Northeast-Midland dialect by Robert Manning (ca. 1260–ca. 1340). It is a translation of a French work, *Manuel des Pechiez*, by William of Waddington, and deals with the seven sins, the seven sacraments, the requisites of confession, and the twelve resulting graces. Several *exempla* (see EXEMPLUM) are introduced during the course of the work.

Hand of Ethelberta, The. A novel by Thomas HARDY (1876), narrating the adventures of Ethelberta, the daughter of a butler, who is in turn governess, companion, poet and public entertainer. She loses her first husband, but finally marries a wealthy lord.

Handsel Monday. The first Monday after New Year's, when in Scotland and elsewhere people give presents (that is, handsels) to servants, children, etc.

handwriting on the wall. An announcement of some coming calamity, or the imminent fulfilment of some doom. The allusion is to the handwriting on Belshazzar's palace wall announcing the loss of his kingdom (*Dan.* v. 5–31).

Handy Andy. A novel by Samuel Lover (1842). The Irish hero Andy Rooney "had the most singularly ingenious knack of doing everything the wrong way." Despite his blunders Handy Andy finally wins his cousin, Oonah, and is declared heir to Lord Scatterbrain's title and wealth.

Hanfstaengl, Franz (1804–1877). German lithographer and photographer; founded a printing establishment for art reproductions in Munich. Copied in lithographs canvases of Dresden gallery (till 1852). **Ernst Frank Sedgwick Hanfstaengel,** known as "Putzi," was a piano-playing crony of HITLER.

Hanging Gardens of Babylon. A square garden (according to Diodorus Siculus), 400 ft. each way, rising in a series of terraces from the river in the northern part of Babylon, and provided with earth to a sufficient depth to accommodate trees of a great size. These famous gardens were one of the Seven Wonders of the World, and according to tradition were constructed by Nebuchadnezzar to gratify his wife Amytis, who felt weary of the flat plains of Babylon, and longed for something to remind her of her native Median hills.

Hanks, Nancy (1783–1818). Mother of Abraham Lincoln. Married Thomas Lincoln (1806).

Hanna, Marcus Alonzo, known as **Mark Hanna** (1837–1904). American businessman and politician. Influential presidential adviser to McKINLEY. Cf. *Hanna* by Thomas BEER.

Hannah. In the Old Testament, the mother of SAMUEL, because of whose vow he was given to the service of the temple as a child.

Hannah Thurston. A novel by Bayard TAYLOR (1864), dealing with life in a small town. The heroine is a Quaker and an advocate of woman's rights. She finally gives up her independence to marry Maxwell Woodberry.

Hannibal (249–183 B. C.). Carthaginian general, son of HAMILCAR BARCA. Swore eternal enmity to Rome. Invaded Italy from Spain, crossing the Alps with elephants by way of the Little St. Bernard, and plunged Rome into immediate danger through his victory at Cannae (216). Hence the proverbial rallying cry in the face of desperate danger, *Hannibal ante portas*, "Hannibal at the gates." Defeated by Scipio Africanus and recalled to Africa. Escaped extradition to Rome by committing suicide.

Hanno. Carthaginian navigator who led a colonizing expedition down the west coast of Africa (5th century B. C.).

Hanno the Great. Carthaginian politician of 3rd century B. C. Favored peaceful relations with Rome in opposition to HAMILCAR BARCA and HANNIBAL.

Han of Iceland (*Han d'Islande*). A romance by Victor HUGO (1823). The hero is a wild and blood-thirsty individual boasting descent from the monster, Ingulph the Exterminator. His career is a long succession of crimes and horrors. After the loss of his son, he becomes even more venomous but at last gives himself up to justice, being "tired of life since it cannot be a lesson and an example to a successor."

Hanotaux, Gabriel (1853–1944). French historian and statesman. *Histoire illustrée de la guerre de 1914* (17 vols., 1915–1926); etc.

Hanover, House of. Electoral house of Germany descended from the Welf (GUELPH) family, which gave the four Georges to England as kings of England. The House of Hanover was succeeded by royal houses of Saxe-Coburg and Gotha, and Windsor (George V).

Hansards. Official reports of parliamentary proceedings in England, named after the printer of the House of Commons journals (from 1774), Luke Hansard (1752–1828).

Hans Brinker or The Silver Skates. A well-known story for children by Mary Mapes DODGE (*Am.,* 1865). The hero is a Dutch boy, and the book gives an interesting picture of life in Holland.

Hanseatic League. The confederacy, first established in 1239, between certain cities of northern Germany for their mutual prosperity and protection. The diet which used to be held every three years was called the *Hansa* (Old High German for *Association*), and the members of it *Hansards.* The league in its prosperity comprised eighty-five towns; it declined rapidly in the Thirty Years War; in 1669 only six cities were represented; and the last three members of the league (Hamburg, Lübeck, and Bremen) joined the German Customs Union in 1889.

Hänsel and Gretel. A light opera by HUMPERDINCK (1893) based on the well-known fairy tale by the Brothers GRIMM. It portrays the adventures of Hänsel and Gretel, the broom-maker's children, with the Sand Man, the Dew Man and the terrible Crunch Witch.

Hanuman. A monkey-god of Hindu mythology. In the RAMAYANA, he and his monkeys construct a bridge across the straits to Ceylon to assist Rama in rescuing his wife Sita from the demon-king of Ceylon.

Hapgood, Hutchins (1869–1944). American novelist, essayist, and newspaperman. *The Autobiography of a Thief* (1903); *The Spirit of Labor* (1907); *A Victorian in the Modern World* (autobiography; 1939).

Happy Valley, the. The home of the Prince of Abyssinia in Dr. Johnson's tale of RASSELAS. It is placed in the kingdom of Amhara, and is inaccessible except in one spot through a cave in a rock. It is a Garden of Peace, completely isolated from the world, and replete with every luxury, but life there is so monotonous that the philsopher, Imlac, and the prince, Rasselas, are glad to escape. Afterwards they idealize it and after many experiences in less pleasant places, make their way back at last.

Happy Warrior, The Character of the. Famous poem (1807) by William WORDSWORTH.

Hapsburg. A princely German family whose name is derived from the Habsburg (Hawk's Castle) in what is now Switzerland. Counts of Hapsburg, known as early as the 11th century, figured as rulers of Germany, Austria, Hungary, Bohemia, Spain, etc. and as Emperors of the Holy Roman Empire of German Nationality. The protruding lip, observed in eighteen generations of Hapsburgs, explains the current expression, "a Hapsburg lip."

hara-kiri (Jap. *hara,* "the belly," *kiri,* "to cut"). A method of suicide by disemboweling practiced by Japanese military officials, daimios, etc., when in serious disgrace or liable to be sentenced to death. The first recorded instance of *hara-kiri,* or *Happy Dispatch,* as it is also called, is that of Tametomo, brother of Sutoku, an ex-Emperor in the 12th century, after a defeat at which most of his followers were slain.

Harbor, The. A novel of New York City by Ernest POOLE (*Am.,* 1915). The hero, who tells the story, has by nature the would-be author's tendency to see life from the artist's point of view, and his Manhattan boyhood, his college life and his Bohemian days in Paris all encourage this disposition, but his wife's father, Dillon, a scientific engineer, and his college friend, Joe Kramer, who becomes a radical labor leader, introduce him to other attitudes toward life, reflected always, to his imaginative mind, in the changing perspectives of the Harbor.

Hard Cash. A novel by Charles READE (1863), written to expose abuses in private lunatic asylums. See DODD.

Hardcastle, Squire. In Goldsmith's comedy, SHE STOOPS TO CONQUER, a jovial, prosy, but hospitable country gentleman of the old school. He loves to tell his long-winded stories about Prince Eugene and the Duke of Marlborough. He says, "I love everything that's old—old friends, old times, old manners, old books, old wine."

Mrs. Hardcastle. A very "genteel" lady indeed. Mr. Hardcastle is her second husband, and Tony LUMPKIN her son by her former husband. She is fond of "genteel" society, and the latest fashions.

Miss Hardcastle. The pretty, bright-eyed, lively daughter of Squire Hardcastle. She is in love with young Marlow, and "stoops" to a pardonable deceit "to conquer" his bashfulness and win him.

Harden, Maximilian Felix Ernst. Real surname **Witkowski** (1861–1927). German journalist and brother of the historian of literature **Georg Witkowski** (1863–1939). During World War I, Harden often attacked German government policies. Wrote, among other books *Deutschland, Frankreich, England* (1923).

Hardenberg, Friedrich Leopold von, see NOVALIS.

Hardie, Keir James (1856–1915). British Socialist and labor leader. First leader of Labor Party in Parliament (1906–1907).

Harding, Rev. Septimus. One of the clergymen in Trollope's *Chronicles of Barsetshire* (see BARSETSHIRE), described as "a good man without guile, believing humbly in the religion he has striven to teach and guided by the precepts which he has striven to learn."

Harding, Warren Gamaliel (1865–1923). Twenty-ninth president of the United States (1921–1923), whose administration was the most corrupt in American history. Cf. the novel *Revelry* (1926) by Samuel Hopkins Adams.

Hardmuth, Frank. The assistant district attorney in THE WITCHING HOUR, a play by Augustus THOMAS.

Hardouin, Jean (1646–1729). A learned Jesuit, chronologer, and numismatist, and librarian to Louis le Grand. He was so skeptical that he doubted the truth of all received history, denied the authenticity of the *Aeneid* of Virgil, the *Odes* of Horace, etc., placed little faith in deductions drawn from medals and coins, regarded all councils before that of Trent as chimerical, etc. Thus he became typical of the doubting philosopher.

> Even Père Hardouin would not enter his protest against such a collection.—Dr. A. Clarke, *Essay.*

hardshell. A term used in American politics for an "out-and-outer," one prepared, and anxious, to "go the whole hog." It was originally applied to a very strict and rigid sect of Baptists, their somewhat weaker brethren being known as *softshells.*

Hard Times. A novel by DICKENS (1854), dramatized in 1867, and called *Under the Earth,* or *The Sons of Toil.* Josiah Bounderby, a street Arab who has raised himself to banker and cotton prince, proposes marriage to Louisa, daughter of Thomas Gradgrind, Esq., and is accepted. One night the bank is robbed of £150, and Bounderby believes Stephen Blackpool to be the thief, because he dismissed him, as obnoxious to the mill hands; but the culprit is Tom Gradgrind, the banker's brother-in-law, who lies in hiding for a while, and then escapes out of the country.

Hardwick, Nan. The heroine of Masefield's TRAGEDY OF NAN.

Hardy, Thomas (1840–1928). English novelist, short-story writer, and poet, known for the pessimism of his ideas, the bareness and strength of his style, and his powerful, realistic studies of life in the bleak English countryside, in which individuals are defeated in their struggle against their physical and social environment and the caprices of chance. Hardy divided his prose work into three groups: novels of character and environment; romances and fantasies; and novels of ingenuity, stressing turns of plot. In the first group are UNDER THE GREENWOOD TREE (1872); FAR FROM THE MADDING CROWD (1874); THE RETURN OF THE NATIVE (1878); THE MAYOR OF CASTERBRIDGE (1886); THE WOODLANDERS (1887); TESS OF THE D'URBERVILLES (1891); JUDE THE OBSCURE (1896). The second group includes: A PAIR OF BLUE EYES (1873); THE TRUMPET-MAJOR (1880); TWO ON A TOWER (1882); THE WELL BELOVED (1897). Those of the last group are DESPERATE REMEDIES (1871); THE HAND OF ETHELBERTA (1876); A LAODICEAN (1882). See also WESSEX. Hardy's outstanding work in poetry is THE DYNASTS (1903, 1906, 1908). Other poetry includes: *Wessex Poems, And Other Verses* (1898); *Poems of the Past and the Present* (1902); *Time's Laughingstocks, And Other Verses* (1909); *Satires of Circumstance* (1911–1914). *The Queen of Cornwall,* a play, was produced in 1923. Thomas Hardy is considered one of the most important figures in the English revolt at the end of the 19th century against the Victorian tradition.

hare. It is unlucky for a hare to cross your path, because witches were said to transform themselves into hares.

> A witch is a kind of hare
> And marks the weather
> As the hare doth.
> Ben Jonson, *Sad Shepherd,* ii, 2.

According to medieval "science," the hare was a most melancholy beast, and ate wild succory in the hope of curing itself; its flesh, of course, was supposed to generate melancholy in any who partook of it.

Another superstition was that hares are sexless, or that they change their sex every year. And among the Hindus the hare is sacred to the moon because, as they affirm, the outline of a hare is distinctly visible in the full disk.

first catch your hare. See under CATCH.

mad as a March hare. Hares are unusually shy and wild in March, which is their rutting season.

Erasmus says "Mad as a marsh hare," and adds, "hares are wilder in marshes from the absence of hedges and cover."

the hare and the tortoise. Everyone knows the fable of the race between the hare and the tortoise, won by the latter, and the moral, "Slow and steady wins the race." The French equivalent is *Pas à pas le boeuf prend le lièvre.*

Hare, James H. (1856–1946). British-born American war correspondent and news photographer. In the Spanish-American War (for *Collier's*) he pierced the Spanish lines and found the Cuban leader, General Gómez. Covered Russo-Japanese War, World War I, etc. Figures by name in the works of Stephen Crane, Richard Harding Davis, Frederick Palmer, Gelett Burgess, Fairfax Downey, etc. Outstanding contributions to the development of aerial photography.

Harewood, Earls of. See LASCELLES.

Hargreaves, James (died 1778). English mechanic and reputed inventor of the spinning jenny (1764).

Hark! The Herald Angels Sing. A hymn by Charles WESLEY (1739).

Harkless, John. The hero of Booth Tarkington's GENTLEMAN FROM INDIANA.

Harkness, Edward Stephen (1874–1940). American capitalist; trustee of Metropolitan Museum of Art and Presbyterian Hospital, N.Y. Large benefactor to Harvard, as his mother and wife were to Yale.

Harkness, Helen. The heroine of Howells' A WOMAN'S REASON.

Harland, Marion. See under TERHUNE.

Harleian. Of or pertaining to Robert Harley (1661–1724) and his son Edward (1689–1741) or their celebrated collections of books, pamphlets, etc. The Harleian manuscripts were acquired by the British government for the British Museum. A selection of Harleian pamphlets was published as *The Harleian Miscellany* (1744–1746).

Harlem. A section of New York City inhabited largely by Negroes and Latin Americans, popular among intellectuals and "society" people of the 1920's because of its cabarets and SPEAKEASIES and its JAZZ. During the latter 1930's it also became a center of attraction for devotees of "SWING" and "BOOGIE-WOOGIE" music. Harlem is the scene of *Naked on Roller Skates,* by Maxwell BODENHEIM, *All God's Chillun Got Wings,* by Eugene O'NEILL, and *Nigger Heaven,* by Carl VAN VECHTEN. The character of its residents is depicted in the works of such Negro writers as Countée CULLEN, Langston HUGHES, W. E. DUBOIS, and Ann Petry (author of *The Street* [1946]).

Harlequin. In the British pantomime, a sprite supposed to be invisible to all eyes but those of his faithful COLUMBINE. His office is to dance through the world and frustrate all the knavish tricks of the Clown, who is supposed to be in love with Columbine. He derives from *Arlecchino,* a stock character of Italian comedy (like Pantaloon and Scaramouch), whose name was in origin probably that of a sprite or hobgoblin. See also PIERROT.

Harlequin. So Charles Quint (1500–1558) was called by François I of France.

Harleth, Gwendolyn. The self-centered heroine whose gradual regeneration is depicted in George Eliot's DANIEL DERONDA.

Harley. The titular hero of Mackenzie's MAN OF FEELING.

> The principal object of Mackenzie is . . . to reach and sustain a tone of moral pathos by representing the effect of incidents . . . upon the human mind . . . especially those which are just, honourable, and intelligent.—Sir W. Scott.

Harley, Robert. See under HARLEIAN.

Harley Street. A street in London. There are many specialist physicians' and surgeons' offices on Harley Street.

Harlowe, Clarissa, see CLARISSA HARLOWE.

Harmachis. The supposed narrator of Rider Haggard's romance *Cleopatra* (1889), a priest and magician who plots to seize the throne from Cleopatra but is prevented by his love for her. She encourages him for her own ends until Antony appears on the scene. The Queen's favorite, Charmian, is desperately in love with Harmachis.

Harman, Sir Isaac. One of the principals in Wells' novel, THE WIFE OF SIR ISAAC HARMAN.

Harmon, John, *alias* **John Rokesmith.** In Dickens' novel, OUR MUTUAL FRIEND, Mr. Boffin's secretary. He lodges with the Wilfers, and ultimately marries Bella Wilfer. He is described as "a dark gentleman, thirty at the utmost, with an expressive, one might say, a handsome face."

Harmonia's Necklace. An unlucky possession, something that brings evil to all who possess it. In classic mythology, Harmonia was the daughter of Mars and Venus. On her marriage with King Cadmus, she received a necklace which proved fatal to all who possessed it.

On the same occasion Vulcan, to avenge the infidelity of her mother, made the bride a present of a robe dyed in all sorts of crimes, which infused wickedness and impiety into all her offspring. See NESSUS. Both Harmonia and Cadmus, after having suffered many misfortunes, and seen their children a sorrow to them, were changed into serpents.

Harmonious Blacksmith, The. A well-known air written by HANDEL, or, rather, based by him on an earlier air. The grave of the blacksmith, the ringing of whose hammer set Handel to work on it, is still to be seen in the little churchyard at Whitchurch—where Handel was organist—near Edgware, Middlesex.

Harmsworth. Family of British publishers and politicians including several brothers, notably **Alfred Charles William Harmsworth** (1865–1922), later Viscount **Northcliffe,** and his brother **Harold Sidney Harmsworth** (1868–1940), later Viscount **Rothermere,** who set up together a general publishing business in London (1887). The older Harmsworth founded the *Daily Mail,* a half-penny morning newspaper for busy men (1896), and the *Daily Mirror* (1903), an illustrated morning paper.

Harold (1022–1066). He is the hero of Bulwer Lytton's romance, *Harold, the Last of the Saxons* (1848), containing an account of the battle of Hastings, where this last of the Saxon Kings was slain, and William the Norman succeeded to the crown of England. Tennyson wrote a dramatic poem on the same subject (1876).

Harold, Childe, see CHILDE HAROLD.

Haroot and **Maroot.** Angels in medieval angelology, who, in consequence of their want of compassion to man, were susceptible to human passions, and were sent upon earth to be tempted. They were kings of Babel, and teachers of magic and the black arts.

Harpagon. A miser; from the miser of that name in Molière's *L'Avare* (1668). He is the father of Cléante and Elise. Both Harpagon and his son desire to marry Mariane; but the father, having lost a casket of money, is asked which he prefers—his casket or Mariane. As the miser prefers the money, Cléante marries the lady. Harpagon imagines that everyone is going to rob him, and when he loses his casket, seizes his own arm in the frenzy of passion. He proposes to give his daughter in marriage to an old man named Anselme, because no *dot* will be required. When Valère, who is Elise's lover, urges reason after reason against the unnatural alliance, the miser makes but one reply, *"sans dot."* Harpagon, at another time, solicits Jacques to tell him what folks say of him; but when told that he is called a miser and a skinflint, he towers with rage, and beats Jacques in his uncontrolled passion.

Harpagus. A Median general of the sixth century B. C. According to legend, the Median king Astyages chose him to expose the infant Cyrus. He gave the task to a herdsman who kept the infant alive. Astyages punished Harpagus by serving to him at a banquet the flesh of his own son. Harpagus afterwards became Cyrus's most trusted general. Cf. the poem by Thomas Lovell BEDDOES.

Harper. The name under which Cooper represents George Washington in his SPY.

Harpers Ferry. A town in West Virginia. The arsenal of Harpers Ferry was raided Oct. 16, 1859, by John BROWN, the abolitionist. Lee took it from a large Union force Sept. 15, 1862.

Harper's Magazine. American magazine, founded in 1850 as *Harper's New Monthly Magazine,* called *Harper's Monthly Magazine* after 1900 and *Harper's Magazine* after 1925. During the 19th century it was devoted to literature, but later expanded to include articles on politics and current problems. William Dean HOWELLS, E. S. MARTIN, and Bernard DE VOTO have conducted the department of comment known as the *Editor's Easy Chair.*

Harpocrates. The Greek form of the Egyptian Heru-P-Khart (Horus the Child), who is represented as a youth, and, as he has one finger pointing to his mouth, was adopted by them as the god of silence.

harpsichord. A musical instrument, immediate precursor of the piano, in vogue during the 16th, 17th, and 18th centuries. The harpsichord has all the essential characteristics of the piano except one: it is a plucking instrument without hammers and has a tinkling sound which cannot be modulated.

harpy. In classical mythology, a winged monster with the head and breasts of a woman, very fierce, starved-looking, and loathsome, living in an atmosphere of filth and stench, and contaminating everything which she came near. Homer mentions but *one* harpy. Hesiod gives *two,* and later writers *three.* Their names, Ocypeta (*rapid*), Celeno (*blackness*), and Aëllo (*storm*), indicate that these monsters were personifications of whirlwinds and storms.

he is a regular harpy. One who wants to appropriate everything; one who sponges on another without mercy.

Harraden, Beatrice (1864–1936). English novelist whose greatest success was *Ships That Pass in the Night* (1893) which sold over a million copies. The setting of the story is a winter resort for consumptive patients. Thomas MANN later used a similar setting in THE MAGIC MOUNTAIN. Miss Harraden was a leader in the Woman Suffrage movement in England.

Harriman, Edward Henry (1848–1909). American railroad magnate and "Robber Baron." Lost in the struggle with James J. Hill for control of the Northern Pacific which precipitated the stock market panic of May 9, 1901.

Harrington. A novel by Maria EDGEWORTH (1811). The titular hero is a Jew, and the novel was one of the first deliberate attempts to portray a Jew in fiction in a favorable light. As such it is worthy of note, but the character of Harrington is generally dismissed as wooden and over-sentimentalized.

Harrington, Evan. Titular hero of Meredith's novel EVAN HARRINGTON.

Harris, Frank (1856–1931). Irish-born American short-story writer and literary biographer; a naturalized citizen of the U.S. but later a resident of England and the European continent. He is known for the frankness of his revelations of intimate, scandalous (and often apocryphal) secrets in the lives of the subjects of his biographical studies. Among these are: *The Man Shakespeare* (1909); *The Women of Shakespeare* (1911); *Contemporary Portraits* (1915–1923); *Oscar Wilde* (1916); *Latest Contemporary Portraits* (1927). *Elder Conklin* (1894), *Unpath'd Waters* (1913), *The Veil of Isis* (1915), and *A Mad Love* (1920), are collections of short stories. *Great Days* (1914) and *Love in Youth* (1916) are novels; *My Reminiscences as a Cowboy* (1930), memoirs. *My Life and Loves* is scabrous autobiography.

Harris, George and **Eliza.** Two slaves, husband and wife, in Harriet Beecher Stowe's UNCLE TOM'S CABIN.

Harris, Joel Chandler (1848–1908). American journalist and author, best known for his humorous adaptations of native Negro folk-legends in his *Uncle Remus* stories, marked by authentic approximations of Negro dialect. Among the collections of these tales, dealing chiefly with animals and directed toward an audience of children, are *Uncle Remus: His Songs and His Sayings* (1880); *Nights with Uncle Remus* (1883); *Mr. Rabbit at Home* (1895); *The Tar-Baby, And Other Rhymes of Uncle Remus* (1904); *Uncle Remus and Br'er Rabbit* (1906). Harris also wrote local-color stories of the South, including *Mingo, And Other Sketches in Black and White* (1884); *Free Joe, And Other Georgian Sketches* (1887); *Tales of the Home Folks in Peace and War* (1898); and *Gabriel Tolliver: A Story of Reconstruction* (1902), a novel.

Harris, Mrs. In Dickens' MARTIN CHUZZLEWIT, a purely imaginary character, existing only in the brain of Mrs. Sarah GAMP, and brought forth on all occasions to corroborate the opinions and trumpet the praises of Mrs. Gamp, the monthly nurse.

> "'Mrs. Harris,' I says to her, . . . 'if I could afford to lay out all my fellow-creeturs for nothink, I would gladly do it; sich is the love I bears 'em.'" Again: "What!" said Mrs. Gamp, "you bage creetur! Have I know'd Mrs. Harris five and thirty year, to be told at last that there an't no sich a person livin'? Have I stood her friend in all her troubles, great and small, for it to come to sich a end as this, with her own sweet picter hanging up afore you all the time, to shame your Bragian words? Go along with you!"
> —Dickens, *Martin Chuzzlewit*, xlix. (1843.)

Harris, Roy (1898–). American composer of orchestral works, symphonies, among them a *Folk-Song Symphony*, chamber music, and choral works. Member National Institute of Arts and Letters.

Harris, Sam Henry (1872–1941). American theatrical producer. Co-founder of the firm of Cohan and Harris (1904). *Music Box Revues, Rain, Animal Crackers, Of Thee I Sing, Dinner at Eight, You Can't Take it With You, Of Mice and Men,* etc.

Harris, William Torrey (1835–1909). American philosopher and educator. Leading American Hegelian; interpreter of German philosophical thought to America. Founder of *Journal of Speculative Philosophy* (1867). Editor in chief, Webster's *New International Dictionary,* first edition (1909).

Harrison, Benjamin (1833–1901). Twenty-third president of the United States (1889–1893). Grandson of William Henry HARRISON.

Harrison, Dr. In Fielding's AMELIA, a clergyman, in general the model of benevolence, who nevertheless on one occasion takes in execution the goods and person of his friend Booth, because Booth, while pleading poverty, is buying expensive and needless jewelry.

Harrison, Gabriel. The name under which Charles Craven, governor of the Carolinas in 1715, is depicted in Simms' historical novel, THE YEMASSEE.

Harrison, Henry Sydnor (1880–1930). American novelist, author of *Queed* (1911), V. V.'s EYES (1913), and books on social problems.

Harrison, Mrs. **Mary St. Leger** (1852–1931). Pseudonym **Lucas Malet.** A daughter of Charles Kingsley, novelist and Catholic. *Sir Richard Calmady* (1901), etc.

Harrison, William Henry (1773–1841). Ninth president of the United States (1840). Died of pneumonia after having served only one month in 1841. Grandfather of Benjamin HARRISON. See also under TECUMSEH.

Harrovian. Of or pertaining to Harrow, the boys' public school in England, founded by John Lyon (1571).

Harry.

Harry of the West. So Henry Clay (1777–1852), American statesman, was called.

Old Harry, see under OLD.

Harry Lorrequer, The Confessions of. A novel by Charles Lever (1839), dealing with the scrapes and adventures of the high-spirited young Irish hero, Harry Lorrequer. The first part of the book is concerned wtih his part in Wellington's campaigns.

Harry the Minstrel. Also known as **Blind Harry** and **Henry the Minstrel** (fl. 1470–1492). Scottish bard. Author of a poem on William Wallace.

Hart, Liddell, see LIDDELL HART.

Hart, Moss (1904–). American librettist and playwright. Collaborated with Irving BERLIN and George S. KAUFMAN. *You Can't Take it With You* (Pulitzer prize, 1936); *The Man Who Came to Dinner* (1939), etc. Alone, wrote *Lady in the Dark* (1941), etc.

Harte, Bret (Francis Brett Harte) (1836–1902). American journalist and short-story writer, known for his popular local-color tales of the Far West, especially of the California mining camps during the Gold Rush days. His work is marked by humor, sentimentality, and a fondness for showing thieves, vagabonds, and miners as more admirable than conventional, moral, and law abiding people. He is best known for his stories THE LUCK OF ROARING CAMP and *The Outcasts of Poker Flat,* and his poem THE HEATHEN CHINEE. His works include: *The Luck of Roaring Camp, And Other Sketches* (1870); *Mrs. Skaggs's Husbands* (1873); *An Heiress of Red Dog, And Other Sketches* (1878); *Colonel Starbottle's Client, And Some Other People* (1892); GABRIEL CONROY, *M'liss: An Idyll of Red Mountain* (1873), and *Jeff Briggs' Love Story* (1880), novels; *Two Men of Sandy Bar* (1876) and *Ah Sin* (1877), plays, the latter written with Mark TWAIN. Harte had a spectacular success for a while, but it soon declined.

Hartford Wits, the. Name given to an important group of Revolutionary poets known first as the "Connecticut Wits," and later as above, although the leaders, John TRUMBULL, TIMOTHY DWIGHT, and Joel BARLOW were Yale College (New Haven) men. They were authors respectively of M'FINGAL (1775), THE CONQUEST OF CANAAN, and THE COLUMBIAD (1807). Other members of the group were: Lemuel Hopkins, David Humphries, Richard Alsop, Theodore Dwight. Their work is now considered richer in patriotic fervor than in poetic imagination. See also ANARCHIAD, THE.

Hartmann, Carl Sadakichi (1869–1944). American playwright, poet and art connoisseur, born in Japan of a German father and a Japanese mother; naturalized U.S. citizen (1894). Among his well-known plays are *Christ* (1893); *Buddha* (1897); *Moses* (1934). His poetry includes *Drifting Flowers of the Sea* (1906); *My Rubaiyat* (1926), *Tanka and Haikai* (1926); etc.

Harum, David, see DAVID HARUM.

Harun-al-Rashid or **Haroun-al-Raschid,** that is, *Aaron the Upright* (764?–809). Fifth Abbasside Caliph of Arabia (785–809). He entertained friendly relations with Charlemagne. The two great rulers were not unlike each other in their patronage of the arts and learning, and it is curious to note that both were idealized in popular tradition: the one in the legends of the cycle of Charlemagne, the other as the splendid caliph of the ARABIAN NIGHTS, in which everything curious, romantic, and wonderful is associated with his name and his reign.

Harvard, John (1607–1638). English clergyman, son of a butcher. He settled at Charlestown, Mass., and became the first benefactor of the college at "New Towne," bequeathing to it his library of 300 volumes and half his estate, valued at £800. The college was renamed Harvard College in his honor in the year of his death, the third year of its existence.

Harvard Classics, The. A set of books, known also from its physical make-up as the "Five-Foot Shelf," which contains such selections from the literature of the world as to constitute "the essentials of a liberal education." The contents, which were chosen by Dr. Charles W. Eliot, President Emeritus of Harvard University, comprise 418 masterpieces.

Harvard Workshop. A name popularly given to the course in drama construction taught at Harvard University by Prof. George P. BAKER (resigned from Harvard, 1925). The course is also widely known by its catalogue number "English 47" and as the "47 Workshop" or "Harvard 47." A number of successful productions were the work of playwrights who studied at the Harvard Workshop, notably Edward SHELDON, Josephine Preston PEABODY, Eugene O'NEILL, Philip BARRY, S. N. BEHRMAN, Sidney HOWARD, etc.

Harvey. A long-run (1944–), fantastic play about an invisible rabbit or POOKA by Mary Coyle Chase. Won Pulitzer prize.

Harvey, Gabriel (1545?–1630). English scholar and author, a friend of Edmund SPENSER, whom he influenced. He wrote satires against the court and such contemporary literary men as Robert GREENE and Thomas NASHE, was the author of a Latin treatise on rhetoric, and tried to introduce the meters of classical poetry into English. See also HOBBINOL.

Harvey, George Brinton McClellan (1864–1928). American journalist. Owner and editor *North American Review* (1899–1926). President, Harper and Brothers (1900–1915); Editor *Harper's Weekly* (1901–1913), *Harvey's Weekly* (1918–1921). Supported Wilson's nomination (1912). Helped select Harding as Republican candidate (1920). U.S. ambassador to Great Britain (1921–1923).

Harvey, William (1578–1657). English physician, physiologist, and anatomist. Discoverer of the circulation of the blood. *Exercitatio de motu cordis et sanguinis* (*Essay on the Motion of the Heart and the Blood,* 1628).

Hašek, Jaroslav (1883–1923). Czech novelist and short-story writer. His major work, *The Good Soldier: Schweik* (English translation, 1930), is a satire in four volumes (planned as six), which has been compared with the creations of Rabelais and Cervantes.

Hashimura Togo. Name of a fictional Japanese schoolboy created by Wallace IRWIN.

Hassam, Childe (1859–1935). American painter and etcher. One of the foremost exponents of impressionism in America.

Hassan. A play (1922) by James Elroy FLECKER.

Hastings, Battle of. Oct. 14, 1066, at Senlac Hill, Sussex, England. William the Norman (William I of England, William the Conqueror) defeated the English army under Harold who was killed. This was the only battle in the Norman conquest. It is listed as one of the "Fifteen Decisive BATTLES OF THE WORLD."

Hastings, Lord Reginald. The hero of Hichens' GREEN CARNATION.

Hastings, Warren (1732–1818). English statesman in the East India service. Impeached (1788) for corruption and cruelty chiefly in his conduct in reference to Chait Singh (the zamindar of Benares, deposed by him) and the begum of Oudh (part of whose treasures he had confiscated). He was prosecuted among others by Burke and Sheridan, but the trial resulted in an acquittal (1795).

Hasty Pudding. A mock-heroic poem by the American poet and diplomat Joel BARLOW (1792), describing the making and eating of the celebrated New England dish. It was one of the most popular of Barlow's works.

hatchet, bury the. Let bygones be bygones. The "Great Spirit" commanded the North American Indians, when they smoked the calumet, or peacepipe, to bury their hatchets, scalping-knives, and war-clubs, that all thought of hostility might be put out of sight.

> Buried was the bloody hatchet;
> Buried was the dreadful war-club;
> Buried were all warlike weapons,
> And the war-cry was forgotten;
> Then was peace among the nations.
> Longfellow, *Hiawatha*, xiii.

Hatchway, Lieutenant Jack. In Smollett's PEREGRINE PICKLE (1751), a retired naval officer on half-pay, living with Commodore Trunnion as a companion.

Hathaway, Anne. The wife of William SHAKESPEARE, by unauthenticated tradition considered to have been a shrew who made life difficult for the poet.

Hathor. In Egyptian mythology, the goddess of love, mirth, and social joy, corresponding to the Greek Aphrodite and related through many common epithets to Isis.

Hatim, generous as. An Arabian expression. Hatim was a Bedouin chief famous for his warlike deeds and boundless generosity. His son was contemporary with Mahomet.

Hatshepsut. Egyptian queen of the XVIIIth dynasty. Sister and wife of Thutmose III. Built magnificent temple near Thebes with representations of an expedition to the land of Punt; erected two obelisks at Karnak; and generally preferred the arts of peace to war and conquest.

Hatteraick, Dirk, *alias* **Jans Janson.** In Scott's GUY MANNERING, a Dutch smuggler-captain, the accomplice of Glossin in kidnaping Harry Bertram. He hangs himself in prison.

Hatto. A 10th-century archbishop of Mainz, a noted statesman and councillor of Otho the Great, proverbial for his perfidy, who, according to tradition (preserved in the *Magdeburg Centuries*), was devoured by mice. The story says that in 970 there was a great famine in Germany, and Hatto, that there might be better store for the rich, assembled the poor in a barn, and burnt them to death, saying: "They are like mice, only good to devour the corn." By and by an army of mice came against the archbishop, who, to escape the plague, removed to a tower on the Rhine. But hither came the mouse-army by hundreds and thousands, and ate him up. The tower is still called MOUSE-TOWER.

> And in at the windows and in at the door,
> And through the walls by thousands they pour,
> And down through the ceiling, and up through the floor
> From the right and the left, from behind and before,
> From within and without, from above and below.
> And all at once to the bishop they go.
> They have whetted their teeth against the stones.
> And now they are picking the bishop's bones;
> They gnawed the flesh from every limb,
> For they were sent to do judgment on him.
> Southey, *Bishop Hatto.*

Hatton, Sir **Christopher** (1540–1591), see DANCING CHANCELLOR.

Hauksbee, Mrs. Lucy. A clever little woman who appears in many of KIPLING's stories, notably in *Three and—an Extra.* She is essentially good-hearted, but so full of schemes and intrigues and so happy in feeling her power that she invariably makes trouble.

Hauptmann, Gerhart Johann (1862–1946). German dramatist, at first a sculptor, known for his plays of social protest, dealing realistically with conditions of the working class. Among these, which aroused great criticism at the time of their first presentation, are *Before Dawn* (*Vor Sonnenaufgang;* 1889); *The Weavers* (*Die Weber;* 1892), the most famous of his works; *Der Biberpelz* (*The Beaver Cape;* 1893); *Der Rote Hahn* (*The Red Cock;* 1901); *Rose Bernd* (1903); *Die Ratten* (*The Rats;* 1910). *Hanneles Himmelfahrt* (1893), THE SUNKEN BELL (*Die Versunkene Glocke;* 1896), and *Der Arme Heinrich* (see under HEINRICH VON AUE; 1902), are romantic examples of poetic mysticism in the drama. Later plays of Hauptmann are *Veland* (1925); *Dorothea Angermann* (1926); and *Vor Sonnen-*

untergang (*Before Sunset;* 1932), a symbolic counterpart of Vor Sonnenaufgang. He won the Nobel prize for literature in 1912.

Having developed from naturalistic beginnings through a stage of symbolic mysticism, Hauptmann slowly but surely became "the patriarch of modern German literature." He was tolerated or courted by, and to a degree was a mouthpiece of, the various phases of Germany's subsequent history. Shortly before his death he accepted a Soviet invitation to go to Berlin. This versatility of his has been condemned as opportunism, explained as aloofness, or praised as evidence of the ever-progressing contemporaneity of his work.

Haus Berghof. In THE MAGIC MOUNTAIN by Thomas Mann, a luxurious mountain sanatorium for tuberculosis patients, located in Davos, Switzerland. It is considered to be in the novel a symbol of isolated and sterile aestheticism.

Hauser, Heinrich (1901–). German traveler, journalist, and novelist. Awarded Gerhart Hauptmann prize (1929) for his novel *Brackwasser* (1928; *Bitter Waters,* 1929). Settled in U.S. during World War II. His political testament, *The German Talks Back* (1945), showed him as a man of passionate convictions and no mellow wisdom.

Hauser, Kaspar (1812?–1833). German foundling who appeared as a youth of about sixteen in Nuremberg. He showed no signs of ever having been in contact with other humans but displayed normal intelligence. His case gave rise to many popular stories. He is the subject of the novel *Caspar Hauser* (1909) by Jakob WASSERMANN.

Haussmann, Baron **Georges Eugène** (1809–1891). French prefect of the Seine (1853–1870) who carried through huge municipal works for the sanitation and embellishment of Paris, including the creation of new wide boulevards, one of which is named in his honor.

havelock. After Sir Henry Havelock (1795–1857), English general in the Sepoy mutiny, 1857. A light cloth cap-cover hanging over the neck, worn by soldiers when exposed to the sun in hot climates.

Havelok the Dane. A hero of medieval romance. He is the orphan son of Birkabegn, King of Denmark and is exposed at sea through the treachery of his guardians. The raft drifts to the coast of Lincolnshire. Here a fisherman named Grim finds the young prince, and brings him up as his own son. In time it so happens that an English princess stands in the way of certain ambitious nobles, who resolve to degrade her by uniting her to a peasant, and select the young foundling for the purpose; but Havelok, having learned the story of his birth, obtains the aid of an army of Danes to recover his wife's possessions. In due time he becomes King of Denmark and part of England.

Havergal, Frances Ridley (1836–1879). English author of hymns and other religious verse. *The Ministry of Song* (1870); etc.

Havergal, Luke, see LUKE HAVERGAL.

Haveth Childers Everywhere. A fragment of James Joyce's FINNEGANS WAKE, published separately in 1933. The title is one of the many forms by which the name of the hero of the novel, Humphrey Chimpden EARWICKER, is disguised.

Havisham, Miss. In Dickens' GREAT EXPECTATIONS, an old spinster who lives in Satis House, the daughter of a rich brewer. She was engaged to be married to a man named Compeyson, who threw her over on the wedding morn. From this moment she has always worn her wedding-dress, with a lace veil from head to foot, white satin shoes, bridal flowers in her hair, jewels round her neck and on her fingers. She adopts a little girl, three years old, who eventually marries and leaves her. She somehow sets fire to herself, and, though Pip succeeds in saving her, she soon dies from the shock. Satis House was pulled down.

Estella Havisham. The adopted child of Miss Havisham, by whom she is brought up. She is proud, handsome, and self-possessed. Pip loves her, and probably she reciprocates his love, but she marries Bentley Drummle, who ill-treats her, and dies, leaving her a young widow. The tale ends with these words—

> I [Pip] took her hand in mine, and we went out of the ruined place. As the morning mists had risen . . . when I first left the forge, so the evening were rising now; and . . . I saw no shadow of another parting from her.—Dickens, *Great Expectations.*

Haward, Marmaduke. The hero of Mary Johnston's AUDREY.

Hawes, Stephen (d. ca. 1523). English poet in the tradition of CHAUCER, author of *Pastime of Pleasure* (1509) and *Example of Virtue* (1512), poetic allegories, both of which were printed by Wynkyn de WORDE. See also SCOTTISH CHAUCERIANS.

Haw Haw, Lord. Nickname for William Joyce, British traitor claiming American birth, prosecuted for broadcasting Nazi propaganda during the Second World War. Executed January, 1946.

Hawk, Sir Mulberry. In Dickens' NICHOLAS NICKLEBY, the bear-leader of Lord Frederick Verisopht. He is a most unprincipled *roué,* who sponges on his lordship, snubs him, and despises him. "Sir Mulberry was remarkable for his tact in ruining young gentlemen of fortune."

Hawke, Edward. 1st Baron **Hawke** (1705–1781). Famous English admiral. Defeated the

French off Belle-Île (1747) and at Quiberon Bay (1759).

Hawkeye. The name under which Natty Bumppo or LEATHERSTOCKING appears in THE LAST OF THE MOHICANS, one of Cooper's Leatherstocking series.

Hawk Eye State. Iowa. See STATES.

Hawkins, Sir **Anthony Hope.** Pseudonym **Anthony Hope** (1863–1933). English romantic novelist. In 1894 he published *The Dolly Dialogues* (light and humorous, admired by George Meredith) and *The Prisoner of Zenda* (concerning a mythical kingdom) which was a huge success. Both *The Prisoner of Zenda* and its sequel, *Rupert of Hentzau* (1898), made long-run plays, and the former was filmed with Ronald Colman in the lead.

Hawkins, Sir **John** (1532–1595). Elizabethan naval hero. Engaged in West Indian slave trade in violation of Spanish laws. Attacked and defeated by a Spanish fleet in the harbor of Vera Cruz (1568). Rear admiral who helped defeat the Spanish Armada (1588). Died while second in command under Drake on an expedition to the West Indies (1595).

Hawley-Smoot Tariff. The tariff law of June 17, 1930. It established the highest rates in American PROTECTIVE-TARIFF history, tempered only by the principle of tariff flexibility which authorized the President to initiate reductions for reciprocal trade agreements and the like. Sponsored by U.S. Representative Willis Chatman Hawley (1864–1941) and U.S. Senator Reed Smoot (1862–1941).

Hawthorne, Julian (1846–1934). American novelist. Only son of Nathaniel HAWTHORNE. Wrote also on his father. His daughter, **Hildegarde Hawthorne (Oskisson),** wrote children's books.

Hawthorne, Nathaniel (1804–1864). American novelist and short-story writer, considered one of the greatest American literary figures of the 19th century. His work is marked by the use of symbolism and allegory, frequent supernatural themes, a rhetorical style compared to that of the 18th century, psychological insight, pessimism and introspection, a preoccupation with moral issues, and an outlook composed of both Puritan and Romantic elements. He is noted for his portrayals of New England Puritanism. Hawthorne's works include: FANSHAWE (1828), published anonymously; TWICE-TOLD TALES (1837, 1842); MOSSES FROM AN OLD MANSE (1846); THE SCARLET LETTER (1850); THE HOUSE OF THE SEVEN GABLES (1851); THE BLITHEDALE ROMANCE (1852); *The Snow-Image, And Other Twice-Told Tales* (1852); A WONDER BOOK (1852); TANGLEWOOD TALES (1853); THE MARBLE FAUN (1860). *Septimius Felton* (1871), *The Dolliver Romance* (1876), *Dr. Grimshawe's Secret* (1883), and *The Ancestral Footstep* (1883) are posthumously published fragments of unfinished romances. Famous single tales are: *The Maypole of Merry Mount; The Minister's Black Veil; Young Goodman Brown;* THE BIRTHMARK; *The Snow-Image;* and ETHAN BRAND.

Hawthorne was solitary in his habits, sensitive, and retiring. He worked as Surveyor of the Port of Salem, was associated with the BROOK FARM experiment, and was in the consular service in England. Henry JAMES is considered to have been strongly influenced by Hawthorne, especially in his supernatural themes. For a study of Hawthorne and his works, cf. *American Renaissance,* by F. O. Mathiessen.

hay. A rustic dance. The word, of uncertain origin, has nothing to do with cut and dried grass. Cf. *Antic Hay* (1923), title of a novel by Aldous HUXLEY.

Hay, Ian, see BEITH, JOHN HAY.

Hay, John Milton (1838–1905). American statesman and author, assistant secretary to Abraham Lincoln, Assistant Secretary of State under President Hayes, ambassador to Great Britain under McKinley, and Secretary of State under McKinley and Theodore ROOSEVELT. He is known for his *Pike County Ballads* (see PIKE; JIM BLUDSOE) (1871), frontier poems in dialect, and THE BREADWINNERS (1884), a novel published anonymously. Hay was instrumental in establishing the Open Door policy in China and in bringing about the Hay-Pauncefote Treaty (1901), which made the Panama Canal possible.

Hay, Sara Henderson (1906–). American poet and critic. Wife of Raymond HOLDEN. *Field of Honor* (1933); *This My Letter* (1939).

Haydn, Joseph (1732–1809). Austrian composer. Kapellmeister of the Esterhazy family at Eisenstadt in Hungary (1760–1790), where he wrote some of his greatest music, operas, masses, piano sonatas, symphonies, an oratorio, etc. In England (1791–1792; 1794–1795) he wrote and conducted twelve symphonies. In Vienna (from 1795), he wrote his last eight masses, his finest chamber music, the Austrian national anthem and the two great oratorios, *The Creation* and *The Seasons.* His friendship with Mozart helped him to attain complete mastery of orchestral effects in his later symphonies.

Haydon, Benjamin Robert (1786–1846). A noted English historical painter. *Lectures on Painting and Design* (1844–1846). Died by his own hand. Wordsworth and Keats addressed sonnets to him.

Hayes, Catherine. The married name of the heroine of Thackeray's CATHERINE.

Hayes, Helen (1900–). American actress. Married (1928) the playwright Charles MACARTHUR. Starred in many plays and motion pictures. *Victoria Regina, Mary of Scotland*, etc.

Hay Fever. A comedy by Noel COWARD (1925).

Haymarket. A street in London between Pall Mall and Piccadilly Circus. Like New York's Broadway, famous as a theater center.

Hayne, Paul Hamilton (1830–1886). American lyric poet of the South, a friend of Henry TIMROD and associated with Timrod and W. G. Simms in the CHARLESTON SCHOOL. His volumes of verse include: *Avolio: A Legend of the Island of Cos* (1860); *Legends and Lyrics* (1872); and *The Mountain of Lovers* (1875).

Hays, Will H. (1879–). American politician. Chairman, Republican National Committee (1918–1921). Postmaster General (1921–1922). President, Motion Picture Producers and Distributors of America (1922–1945). The "Hays office" (taken over by Eric Johnston) censored moving pictures for the trade.

Hayston, Frank. In Scott's novel THE BRIDE OF LAMMERMOOR, the laird of Bucklaw to whom Lucy Ashton is unwillingly betrothed. In the opera, LUCIA DI LAMMERMOOR, based on the novel, he is known as Arthur Bucklaw.

Hazard, Caroline (1856–1945). American educator. President, Wellesley College (1899–1910). Wrote poetry and essays.

Hazard, Myrtle. The heroine of O. W. Holmes' GUARDIAN ANGEL. She is one of the first characters in fiction analyzed from the standpoint of a mixed racial inheritance.

Hazard of New Fortunes, A. A novel by W. D. HOWELLS (1890), in which Howells' old favorites, Mr. and Mrs. MARCH, are brought to New York, he to become the editor of *Every Other Week*, a journal published by a Pennsylvania Dutch capitalist named Dryfoos. Dryfoos' daughters, who are battering at the doors of New York society, inherit his vulgarity, but his son Conrad is a gentler, more intellectual type, a radical whose sympathies with labor bring about his death by a chance shot during a strike. The old German socialist Lindau is a prominent character.

Hazel Kirke. A drama by Steele MacKaye (*Am.*, 1879). The rather complicated plot turns on parental plans for having each of the two lovers pay an old debt by marrying without love, but the chief appeal of the play lies in the rôle of Dunstan Kirke, Hazel's old father, who turns her out when she marries against his wishes, but cannot be happy without her. Eventually all turns out well and Hazel and her father are reconciled.

Hazlitt, Henry (1894–). American financial writer, editor, critic, author. *The Anatomy of Criticism* (1933); etc.

Hazlitt, William (1778–1830). English essayist and literary critic, at first dedicated to a career as a philosopher and a painter. He became known for his studies and lectures on the Elizabethan playwrights (see COLERIDGE, HUNT, LAMB, DE QUINCEY), and for his radical political ideas, which caused him to receive harsh treatment at the hands of the reviewers. His works include: *Essay on Principles of Human Action* (1807); *The Characters of Shakespeare's Plays* (1817); *Table Talk* (1821); *The Spirit of the Age* (1825); *Life of Napoleon* (1828–1830). He was associated with Leigh HUNT, serving as a contributor to THE EXAMINER.

HCE, see EARWICKER, HUMPHREY CHIMPDEN.

H. D., i.e., **Hilda Doolittle** (1886–). American poet, resident for most of her life abroad, considered by some critics the most accomplished of the Imagist poets. See IMAGISM. Her work shows the influence of the Greek classics and is marked by simple, clear, and precise visualizations of scenes, images, and objects, chiefly on Greek subjects. Her books of poetry are: *Sea Garden* (1916); *Hymen* (1921); *Heliodora, And Other Poems* (1924); and *Hippolytus Temporizes* (1927). *Palimpsest* (1926), *Hedylus* (1928), and *The Hedgehog* (1936) are books of fiction; in 1937 she made a translation of the *Ion* of Euripides. She married Richard ALDINGTON, English Imagist poet and novelist (now divorced).

Headlong Hall. A novel by T. L. PEACOCK (1816). There is little plot; the interest lies chiefly in the pleasant, witty conversation of the guests of the Squire of Headlong Hall. See also CROTCHET CASTLE.

Headrigg, Cuddie. In Scott's OLD MORTALITY, a ploughman in Lady Bellenden's service described as a blending of "apparent dulness with occasional sparkles which indicated the craft so often found in the clouted shoe."

Heard, Gerald (full name, Henry FitzGerald) (1889–). English writer, now living in California. *The Ascent of Humanity* (1929) was given the Henrietta Hertz award by the British Academy. Popular science commentator for British Broadcasting Corporation. His contributions to the mystery field as H. F. Heard have been *A Taste for Honey* (1941), and *Reply Paid* (1942), both resurrecting

SHERLOCK HOLMES. His mystical philosophy has greatly influenced Aldous HUXLEY.

Hearn, Lafcadio (1850–1904). American journalist and author, of Greek and English-Irish parentage, born in the Ionian Islands. He is known for his exotic and fantastic tales, many dealing with New Orleans and the West Indies, his poetic prose style, and his sketches and studies of Japan, of which he became a citizen in 1893 under the name of Koizumi Yakumo and where he taught English literature in the Imperial University of Tokyo from 1894 to 1903. His works include: *One of Cleopatra's Nights* (1882), translations of stories by Théophile GAUTIER; *Stray Leaves from Strange Literatures* (1884); *Gombo Zhèbes* (1885), proverbs in Negro-French dialect; *Some Chinese Ghosts* (1887); *Chita* (1887), a novel; *Two Years in the French West Indies* (1890); *Youma* (1890), a novel of Martinique; *Glimpses of Unfamiliar Japan* (1894); *Out of the East* (1895); *Kokoro* (1896); *In Ghostly Japan* (1899); *Kotto* (1902); *Japanese Fairy Tales* (1903); *Japan: An Attempt at Interpretation* (1904); *Creole Sketches* (1904).

Hearst, William Randolph (1863–). American newspaper publisher, owning a chain of newspapers including the San Francisco *Examiner*, the Chicago *American*, the Boston *American*, the New York *American*, the New York *Mirror*, and of magazines, including *Cosmopolitan, Good Housekeeping, Harper's Bazaar*, etc. The term "Hearst paper" is often used with the implied connotation of yellow journalism. Cf. the moving picture by Orson Welles, *Citizen Kane*.

Heartbreak House. A play by George Bernard SHAW (1917), the scene of which is laid during World War I, dealing with the problems, weaknesses, and failures of 20th-century civilization by means of a representative group of characters. It is considered among the greatest of 20th-century dramas. See also CHERRY ORCHARD, THE.

Heart of England. A name given to Warwickshire from its central position.

Heart of Midlothian, The. A novel by Sir Walter Scott (1817). The allusion of the title is to the old jail of Edinburgh. The plot is briefly as follows. Effie Deans, the daughter of the Scotch cow-feeder affectionately known to his friends as Doucie Davie, is seduced by George Staunton, son of the rector of Willingham, and is brought to trial and sentenced to death for child murder. Her loyal and plucky half sister, Jeanie Deans, determines to go to London to ask George II for a pardon and in spite of all the obstacles in her way, actually accomplishes her task. Effie and Staunton marry, but shortly afterwards he is shot by a gipsy boy who is in reality his illegitimate son. Jeanie Deans marries Reuben Butler, the Presbyterian minister. The novel is based on fact.

Heath, Charles. The hero of De Morgan's ALICE-FOR-SHORT.

Heathcliffe. The fierce and brooding hero of Emily Brontë's novel, WUTHERING HEIGHTS.

Heathen Chinee, The. A humorous poem by Bret HARTE (1870) first published under the title *Plain Language from Truthful James*. It later furnished the germ for a play by Bret Harte and Mark Twain in which the *Heathen Chinee* was known as Ah Sin. The poem begins:

> Which I wish to remark,
> And my language is plain,
> That for ways that are dark,
> And for tricks that are vain,
> The heathen Chinee is peculiar.
> Which the same I would rise to explain.

heaven (A.S. *heofon*). The word properly denotes the abode of the Deity and His angels —"heaven is My throne" (*Is.* lxvi. 1, and *Matt.* v. 34)—but it is also used in the Bible and elsewhere for the air, the upper heights as "the fowls of heaven," "the dew of heaven," "the clouds of heaven"; "the cities are walled up to heaven" (*Deut.* i. 28); and a tower whose top should "reach unto heaven" (*Gen.* xi. 4); the starry firmament, as, "Let there be lights in the firmament of heaven" (*Gen.* i. 14).

In the Ptolemaic system the heavens were the successive spheres of space enclosing the central earth at different distances and revolving round it at different speeds. The first seven were those of the so-called Planets, viz., the Moon, Mercury, Venus, the Sun, Mars, Jupiter, and Saturn; the eighth was the firmament of heaven containing all the fixed stars; the ninth was the crystalline sphere, invented by Hipparchus (2nd cent. B.C.), to account for the precession of the equinoxes. These were known as *The Nine Heavens* (see *Nine Spheres*); the tenth—added much later—was the primum mobile.

> Sometimes she deemed that Mars had from above
> Left his fifth heaven, the powers of men to prove.
> Hoole, *Orlando Furioso*, Bk. xiii.

The Seven Heavens of the Mohammedans:

The first heaven is of pure silver, and here the stars, each with its angel warder, are hung out like lamps on golden chains. It is the abode of Adam and Eve.

The second heaven is of pure gold and is the domain of John the Baptist and Jesus.

The third heaven is of pearl, and is allotted to Joseph. Here Azrael, the angel of death, is stationed, and is for ever writing in a large book or blotting words out. The former are the names of persons born, the latter those of the newly dead.

The fourth heaven is of white gold, and is Enoch's. Here dwells the Angel of Tears, whose height is "500 days' journey," and he sheds ceaseless tears for the sins of man.

The fifth heaven is of silver and is Aaron's. Here dwells the Avenging Angel, who presides over elemental fire.

The sixth heaven is composed of ruby and garnet, and is presided over by Moses. Here dwells the Guardian Angel of heaven and earth, half-snow and half-fire.

The seventh heaven is formed of divine light beyond the power of tongue to describe, and is ruled by Abraham. Each inhabitant is bigger than the whole earth, and has 70,000 heads, each head 70,000 mouths, each mouth 70,000 tongues and each tongue speaks 70,000 languages, all for ever employed in chanting the praises of the Most High.

to be in the seventh heaven. Supremely happy. The Cabbalists maintained that there are seven heavens, each rising in happiness above the other, the seventh being the abode of God and the highest class of angels. See also PARADISE.

Heaven and Earth, A Mystery. A dramatic poem by Lord BYRON (1822), founded on the text—

> And it came to pass . . . that the sons of God saw the daughters of men, that they were fair; and they took them wives of all whom they chose.—*Gen.* vi. 2.

Heavenly City, see under CITY.

Hebe. In Greek mythology, goddess of youth, and cup-bearer of the immortals before GANYMEDE superseded her. She was the wife of Hercules, and had the power of making the aged young again.

Heber, Reginald (1783–1826). English prelate and hymn-writer. Bishop of Calcutta (1823). *From Greenland's Icy Mountains; Brightest and Best; Holy, Holy, Holy, Lord God Almighty;* etc. In *Hymns written and adapted to the Weekly Church Service of the Year,* 58 are by Reginald Heber.

He Bible. See BIBLE, SPECIALLY NAMED.

Hebraism and Hellenism. A well-known essay by Matthew ARNOLD, appearing in the collection *Culture and Anarchy* (1869). It analyzes and contrasts the Hebraic and the Hellenic cultures, the most influential upon British culture, and asserts the "uppermost idea" of Hellenism is "to see things as they really are," while that of Hebraism is "conduct and obedience."

Hecate. One of the Titans of Greek mythology, and the only one that retained her power under the rule of Zeus. She was the daughter of Perses and Asteria, and became a deity of the lower world after taking part in the search for Persephone. She taught witchcraft and sorcery, and was a goddess of the dead, and as she combined the attributes of, and became identified with, Selene, Artemis, and Persephone, she was represented as a triple goddess and was sometimes described as having three heads—one of a horse, one of a dog, and one of a lion. Her offerings consisted of dogs, honey, and black lambs, which were sacrificed to her at cross-roads. Shakespeare, in his tragedy of MACBETH, calls her queen of the witches.

Hecate County, Memoirs of. See WILSON, EDMUND.

Hecht, Ben (1894–). American novelist, short-story writer, and playwright, early in his career a member of the CHICAGO GROUP and known for his eroticism, iconoclasm, and flamboyant Bohemianism, variously influenced by GAUTIER, HUYSMANS, and DOSTOYEVSKY. His novels include: *Erik Dorn* (1921); *Fantazius Mallare* (1922); *The Florentine Dagger* (1923); *Humpty Dumpty* (1924); *The Kingdom of Evil* (1924); *Count Bruga* (1926); and *A Jew in Love* (1931). Collections of short stories are: *Gargoyles* (1922); *1001 Afternoons in Chicago* (1922); *Tales of Chicago Streets* (1924); *Broken Necks* (1924); *The Champion from Far Away* (1931); and *A Book of Miracles* (1939). At this time he was a friend of Maxwell BODENHEIM, with whom he wrote several plays. Later Hecht became famous for his successful Broadway plays and motion-picture scripts written with Charles MacArthur, including: *The Front Page* (1928); *20th Century* (1932); and *Ladies and Gentlemen* (1939). Passionate defender of Jews in Palestine.

Hector. Eldest son of Priam, the noblest and most magnanimous of all the Trojan chieftains in Homer's ILIAD. After holding out for ten years, he was slain by Achilles, who lashed him to his chariot, and dragged the dead body in triumph thrice round the walls of Troy. The *Iliad* concludes with the funeral obsequies of Hector and Patroclus.

In modern times his name has somewhat deteriorated, for it is used today for a swaggering bully, and "to hector" means to browbeat, bully, bluster.

the Hector of Germany. Joachim II, Elector of Brandenburg (1514–1571).

you wear Hector's cloak. You are paid off for trying to deceive another. You are paid in your own coin. When Thomas Percy, Earl of Northumberland, in 1569, was routed, he hid himself in the house of Hector Armstrong, of Harlaw. This villain betrayed his guest for the reward offered, but never after did anything go well with him; he went down, down, down, till at last he died a beggar in rags on the roadside.

Hecuba. In Homer's ILIAD, second wife of Priam, and mother of nineteen children, including Hector. When Troy was taken by the Greeks she fell to the lot of Ulysses. She was afterwards metamorphosed into a dog, and threw herself into the sea. Her story has furnished the material for a host of Greek tragedies.

on to Hecuba. To the main point.

Hedda Gabler. A drama by Henrik IBSEN (1890). Hedda has married a professor who bores her. A former lover, Lövborg, is now tutor to the step-children of Thea Elvsted, and under Thea's steadying influence reforms and writes a book that wins him fame. In a jealous determination to show her power, Hedda lures him back to dissipation, and when by accident she gets possession of the manuscript of a second book, she burns it secretly, gives Lövborg a pistol and urges him to "die beautifully." He does die, in a brawl, and Hedda, who is threatened with exposure by a man who recognizes the pistol, shoots herself.

Hedin, Sven Anders (1865–). Swedish geographer and explorer in Asia. *The Silk Road* (1936); *Chiang Kai-shek, Marshal of China* (1940), etc. Also wrote in German *Germany and World Peace* (1937).

hedonism (Gr. *hedone,* "pleasure"). The doctrine of Aristippus that pleasure or happiness is the chief good and end of man.

Hedwig. The heroine of Ibsen's WILD DUCK.

Heep, Uriah. In Dickens' DAVID COPPERFIELD, a detestable sneak, who is everlastingly forcing on one's attention that he is *'umble.* Uriah is Mr. Wickfield's clerk, and, with all his ostentatious 'umility, is most designing and malignant. His infamy is dragged to light by Mr. Micawber.

> "I am well aware that I am the 'umblest person going, let the other be who he may. My mother is likewise a very 'umble person. We live in an 'umble abode, Master Copperfield, but have much to be thankful for. My father's former calling was 'umble —he was a sexton."—Dickens, *David Copperfield,* xvi.

Hegel, Georg Wilhelm Friedrich (1770–1831). German philosopher. Hegelianism is a philosophy of the absolute and was the leading system of metaphysics throughout the second quarter of the nineteenth century. It is an attempt to harmonize Greek ontology with Kantian psychology. It is Hegel who developed the dialectic method of progression from thesis and antithesis to synthesis which proved so important for Marxism. Hegel's system as a whole is hard to understand. It has been said that all the books dealing with the secret of Hegel have managed to keep it.

hegira (Arab. *hejira,* the departure). The epoch of the flight of Mahomet from Mecca to Medina when he was expelled by the magistrates, July 15, 622. The Mohammedan calendar starts from this event.

Heidegger, Martin (1889–). German philosopher. Most important inspiration of the French EXISTENTIALISTS.

Heidenstam, Verner von (1859–1940). Swedish poet and novelist. Began as a painter. The publication of his *Nya Dikter* (1915; *New Poems*) gave him the reputation of being the greatest of Sweden's contemporary lyricists. His work won him the Nobel Prize for Literature (1916).

Heidi. A children's story of life in the Swiss Alps by Johanna Spyri (*Swiss,* d. 1891).

Heifetz, Jascha (1901–). Russian Jewish violinist, born at Vilna. Studied under Leopold Auer. Gave his first concert at the age of nine, but continued his career as a distinguished violinist instead of becoming a child prodigy. Considered the outstanding violinist of this century.

Heil dir im Siegerkranz. The Prussian national anthem. Originally written by Heinrich Harries (1790) to the tune of "God save Great George the King" as a birthday song for King Christian VII of Denmark. Arranged for Prussia (1793) by B. G. Schumacher.

Heimdall. One of the gods of Scandinavian mythology, son of the nine virgins, daughters of Aegir, and in many attributes identical with Tiw. He was called the "White God with the Golden Teeth," and, as the watchman or sentinel of ASGARD, dwelt on the edge of heaven, guarded the bridge Bifrost (the rainbow), and possessed a mighty horn whose blast could be heard throughout the universe. He could see for a hundred miles by day or night, slept less than a bird, and heard the grass grow, and even the wool on a lamb's back. At the end of the world he is to wake the gods with his horn.

Heimdall. In Norse mythology, the guardian against the giants of the bridge of the gods, at the end of which he dwells in Himinbjörg. At Baldur's obsequies he appears on his horse Gulltopp, and when Ragnarok, the twilight of the gods, comes, he will sound his Gjallarhorn to assemble the gods and heroes.

Heimskringla. An important collection of sixteen sagas containing an account of the history of Norway—sketched through the medium of biography—and a compendium of ancient Scandinavian mythology and poetry. It is probably by Snorri Sturluson (d. 1241). See EDDA.

Heine, Heinrich (1797–1856). German poet, famous for his lyrics and his wit and irony. He was born of Jewish parentage but was baptized a Christian in 1825 and lived in

Paris after 1830. Politically he was a radical and hoped to see a liberal government established in Germany, although his hopes were not realized. His works include: *Das Buch der Lieder* (*The Book of Songs*) (1827), a collection of poems; *Reisebilder* (*Travel Sketches*) (1826–1831), notes on his travels; *Philosophie und Literatur in Deutschland* (*Philosophy and Literature in Germany*) (1834) and *Die Romantische Schule* (*The Romantic School*) (1836), criticism; *Atta Troll* (1847); *Romancero* (1851); *Neueste Gedichte* (*Latest Poems*) (1853–1854). Heine wrote frequently in French as well as in German and was much interested in philosophy. Cf. Louis Untermeyer's *Heinrich Heine*.

Heinemann, William (1863–1920). British publisher of German descent. His firm (established 1890) came to be regarded as one of the most distinguished publishing houses in England.

Heinrich. The hero of Hauptmann's drama THE SUNKEN BELL.

Heinrich von Aue. The hero of a medieval romance *Poor Heinrich* (*Der Arme Heinrich*) told, ostensibly from family records, by the Minnesinger Hartmann von der Aue (*Ger.*, 1210). Heinrich is a rich nobleman, who is afflicted with leprosy, and is told he will not recover till a virgin of spotless purity is willing to die on his behalf. As Heinrich neither hopes nor even wishes for such a sacrifice, he gives the main part of his possessions to the poor, and goes to live with a poor tenant farmer, who is one of his vassals. The daughter of this farmer hears by accident on what the cure of the leper depends, and goes to Salerno to offer herself as the victim. No sooner is the offer made than the lord is cured, and the damsel becomes his wife. This tale forms the subject of Longfellow's *Golden Legend* (1851). Heinrich is there called Prince Henry of Hoheneck. Gerhart HAUPTMANN also used this legend as the basis for his drama *Der arme Heinrich* (1902).

Heinrich von Ofterdingen. One of the German MINNESINGERS of the 13th century. In legend, he appears as one of the contestants at the BATTLE OF WARTBURG. Failing in one contest, he returned for another with the magician Klingsor who saved him from defeat, but was not able to wrest victory from his rival WOLFRAM VON ESCHENBACH.

Heinsius, Daniel (1580–1655). Dutch classical philologist and poet.

Heir at Law, The. A comedy by George COLMAN the younger (1797; printed 1808). Prominent characters in it are Dr. PANGLOSS, a satire on the mercenary private tutors of the period, and Zekiel and Cicely HOMESPUN, among the earliest "country jakes" appearing on the English stage.

Heiser, Victor George (1873–). American physician and public health authority. *An American Doctor's Odyssey* (1936); etc.

Hel or **Hela.** The name, in late Scandinavian mythology, of the queen of the dead; also, of her place of abode, which was the home of the spirits of those who had died in their beds, as distinguished from Valhalla, the abode of heroes slain in battle. She dwelt beneath the roots of the sacred ash (Yggdrasil), and was the daughter of LOKI.

> Down the yawning steep he rode
> That led to Hela's drear abode
> Gray, *Descent of Odin.*

Held, John (1889–). American cartoonist, illustrator, and writer. Created a type of boy and girl in the Jazz Age. Author of *Grim Youth* (1930); *A Bowl of Cherries* (1933); etc.

Heldar, Dick. The hero of Kipling's LIGHT THAT FAILED.

Heldenbuch. *Ger.*, Book of Heroes. Name of several collections of medieval epics. (1) *Dresdner Heldenbuch,* manuscript of 1472; (2) a printed collection of 1477; (3) *Ambraser Heldenbuch,* compiled early in the 16th century at the request of Emperor Maximilian; (4) (5) two 19th-century translations by Simrock; *Das grosse Heldenbuch, Das kleine Heldenbuch;* (6) *Deutsches Heldenbuch,* a scholarly edition by Prof. Müllenhof and others, 1866ff.

Helen. (1) The title of two poems by Edgar Allan POE. The first, a short lyric written at the age of fourteen and published in 1831, was addressed to Mrs. Jane Stanard. It contains the frequently quoted lines:

> To the glory that was Greece
> And the grandeur that was Rome.

The second poem is in blank verse and is addressed to the poetess, Sarah Helen Whitman.

(2) Heroine of a ballad by D. G. Rossetti called *Sister Helen* (1870), a tale of a forsaken maiden who makes use of sorcery for a terrible, relentless revenge on the body and soul of her lover.

See also following entries.

Helen, Burd. In Scotch legend, a sister of CHILDE ROWLAND rescued by him from the fairies who had shut her up in a castle in Elfland.

Helen of Kirconnell. A famous Scotch ballad. The story is that Helen, a Scotch lady, is the lady-love of Adam Flemming. One day, while they are standing on the banks of a river, a rival suitor points his gun at Adam. Helen throws herself before him and is shot.

The two rivals then fight, and the murderer falls and is slain. Wordsworth embodies the same story in his *Ellen Irwin*.

Helen of Troy. The immortal type of the beautiful woman. In Greek legend she was the daughter of Zeus and Leda, and wife of Menelaus, king of Sparta. She eloped with Paris, and thus brought about the siege and destruction of Troy which forms the subject of Homer's ILIAD and the first books of Virgil's AENEID.

After the Trojan War, Helen returned to Menelaus. Later legends (given by Herodotus, Stesichorus, etc.) state that Helen did not accompany Paris all the way to Troy, but was detained in Egypt (see PALINODE); thus Euripides in his *Helena* makes the real Helen stay in Egypt, while a ghostly Helen lives through the Trojan War in Troy. According to one account, she marries Achilles after the death of Menelaus.

Centuries later, Helen of Troy came to play a prominent part in the legend of FAUST. According to the generally accepted tale, embodied in both Marlowe's *Dr. Faustus* and Goethe's *Faust,* she was called up from the world of spirits by Faust, to whom she bore a son. Marlowe's apostrophe to her is famous:

> Was this the face that launched a thousand ships
> And burnt the topless towers of Ilium?
> Sweet Helen, make me immortal with a kiss;
> Her lips suck forth my soul, see where it flies!
> Marlowe, *Dr. Faustus* V, iii.

> For which men all the life they here enjoy
> Still fight, as for the Helena of their Troy.
> Lord Brooke, *Treatie of Humane Learning.*

> She moves a goddess and she looks a queen.
> Pope, *Homer's Iliad,* iii.

Sara TEASDALE published a volume called *Helen of Troy, And Other Poems* (1911). In his satiric romance, JURGEN (1919) James Branch Cabell introduces Helen of Troy as the immortal wife of Achilles, living in Pseudopolis, a country at war with Philistia. A best-selling novel, *The Private Life of Helen of Troy,* by John Erskine (1925), shows Helen at home with Menelaus, after the Trojan Wars.

Helena. (1) In Shakespeare's MIDSUMMER NIGHT'S DREAM, a young Athenian lady in love with Demetrius.

(2) One of the chief characters of Shakespeare's ALL'S WELL THAT ENDS WELL.

(3) The name under which HELEN OF TROY appears in Goethe's *Faust.*

Helenus. In Virgil's *Aeneid,* the prophet, the only son of Priam who survives the fall of Troy. He falls to the share of Pyrrhus when the captives are awarded. Because he saved the life of the young Grecian, he is allowed to marry Andromache, his brother Hector's widow. In some versions of the legend he is said to have deserted the Trojan cause for the Greek.

Helice. A Cretan nymph, one of the nurses of the infant Zeus.

Helicon. The home of the Muses, a part of the Parnassus, a mountain range in Greece. It contained the fountains of Aganippe and Hippocrene, connected by "Helicon's harmonious stream." The name is used allusively of poetic inspiration.

Heliogabalus. Original name **Varius Avitus Bassianus** (204–222). Roman emperor (218–222). Began as priest in temple of sun god Elagabalus (hence his name as emperor). Put forward as son of Caracalla and proclaimed emperor by soldiers. Gave himself up to infamous debauchery, leaving affairs of state to his mother. Killed by PRAETORIANS. Title of a play by H. L. MENCKEN and George Jean NATHAN.

Helios. The Greek sun-god, who rode to his palace in Colchis every night in a golden boat furnished with wings. He is called Hyperion by Homer, and, in later times, Apollo.

heliotrope (*Gr.,* "turn-to-sun"). Apollo loved CLYTIE, but forsook her for her sister Leucothoe. On discovering this, Clytie pined away; and Apollo changed her at death to a flower, which, always turning towards the sun, is called "heliotrope."

The bloodstone, a greenish quartz with veins and spots of red, used to be called "heliotrope," the story being that if thrown into a bucket of water it turned the rays of the sun to blood-color. This stone also had the power of rendering its bearer invisible.

> No hope had they of crevice where to hide,
> Or heliotrope to charm them out of view.
> Dante, *Inferno,* xxiv.

> The other stone is heliotrope, which renders those who have it invisible.—Boccaccio, *The Decameron,* Novel iii, Eighth day.

Hell. See GEHENNA, HADES, INFERNO, JOHANNUM, NARAKA, NASTROND, SHEOL, TARTARUS.

Helle. See under HELLESPONT.

Hellen. In Greek legend, a king of Phthia, EPONYM of the Hellenic race.

Hellespont. The "sea of Helle" so called because Helle, the sister of Phryxus, was drowned there. She was fleeing with her brother through the air to Colchis on the golden ram to escape from Ino, her mother-in-law, who most cruelly oppressed her, but turning giddy, she fell into the sea. It is the ancient name of the Dardanelles. Leander used to swim across the Hellespont to visit HERO, a priestess of Sestos. Lord Byron was proud of having repeated the feat.

> He could, perhaps, have passed the Hellespont,
> As once (a feat on which ourselves we prided)
> Leander, Mr. Ekenhead, and I did.
> Byron, *Don Juan,* ii. 105 (1819).

Hell Gate. A dangerous passage between Great Barn Island and Long Island, N.Y. The

Dutch settlers of New York called it Hoellgat (whirling-gut), corrupted into Hell Gate.

Hellman, Lillian (1905–). American writer of plays and scenarios for moving pictures. Author of *The Children's Hour* (1934); *The Little Foxes* (1939); *Watch on the Rhine* (1941) which was granted the award of the New York Drama Critics Circle, etc.

Hell's Kitchen. A district on the lower west side of Manhattan. So called because it was formerly notorious for gunmen and thieves.

Hellzapoppin. Long-run (1404 performances) American musical revue by Olsen and Johnson.

Helmer, Nora. The heroine of Ibsen's DOLL'S HOUSE.

Helmholtz, Hermann Ludwig Ferdinand von (1821–1894). German physicist, anatomist, and physiologist. One of the founders of the principle of the conservation of energy (1847). Many other investigations and contributions to science, as the invention of the ophthalmoscope (1850), the development of a theory of color vision, etc. Helmholtz was born with internal hydrocephalus and after an operation developed into a prodigy and genius of science.

Héloïse. Niece of the medieval Canon Fulbert of Notre Dame Cathedral, a beautiful and learned woman famous as the beloved of the philosopher Pierre ABÉLARD, who served as her tutor. They were married secretly after she gave birth to a son, although she begged that the marriage not take place, in order that his career might not be ruined. The outcome of the affair was tragic, with Héloïse entering a nunnery and Abélard emasculated by the enraged Fulbert. After the death of both lovers, their bodies were laid in the same tomb. The tender and passionate love-letters written by Héloïse to Abélard while she was a nun and he a monk are famous. It is said by some that Héloïse is one of the three outstanding women of the Middle Ages, the other two being ROSWITHA and MARIE DE FRANCE.

Helot. One of the lowest class of the people of ancient Sparta. They were serfs, bound to the soil, but owned by the state and not to be sold. They were possibly descendants of the original population conquered by the Dorian Spartiates.

Helvetia. Switzerland. So called from the Helvetii, a powerful Celtic people who dwelt thereabouts.

Hemans, Felicia Dorothea, *née* **Browne** (1793–1835), English poet, best known in the U.S. for her lyrics, *The Pilgrim Fathers* and CASABIANCA.

Hemingway, Ernest Miller (1898–). American novelist and short-story writer, early in his career a newspaperman and foreign correspondent. He first attracted attention as an American expatriate writer in Paris, a representative member of the "LOST GENERATION" in the circle of Gertrude STEIN. His books expressed the disillusionment that was widespread after World War I—in which he had volunteered and served with the Italian army—and dealt with drinking, physical sensation, sexual promiscuity, frequent sentimental broodings on the past, and violent death. He became famous for his style—clipped and staccato, colloquial, with short sentences and monosyllabic words, often repeated in a free-verse effect, and an extremely simple, detached, "hard-boiled" narrative technique, in which he is considered to have been influenced by Miss Stein. For awhile Hemingway, regarded as one of the novelists best portraying the spirit of the post-war JAZZ AGE, devoted himself to writing essays celebrating sports involving danger and physical violence. In the 1930's he became interested in the radical social and political reform movements of the time and went to Spain as a war correspondent during the Spanish Civil War, in which his sympathies were with the Loyalist government and with which his writings then began to deal. Hemingway's works include: *Three Stories and Ten Poems* (1923), *In Our Time* (1924), *Men Without Women* (1927), *Winner Take Nothing* (1933), and *The Fifth Column and the First Forty-Nine Stories* (1938), collections of short stories; *The Torrents of Spring* (1926); THE SUN ALSO RISES (1926); FAREWELL TO ARMS (1929), his best-known novel; *Death in the Afternoon* (1932), essays glorifying bullfighting; *The Green Hills of Africa* (1935), a book on big-game hunting; TO HAVE AND HAVE NOT (1937); FOR WHOM THE BELL TOLLS (1940), his most successful novel. Among his short stories, THE KILLERS is the most famous. See also FIFTH COLUMN. He also edited an anthology, *Men at War* (1942).

Hémon, Louis (1880–1913). French novelist, best-known for *Maria Chapdelaine* (1916), a novel of farm life in the Canadian province of Quebec, which he was inspired to write by his stay on the farm of a French-Canadian named Samuel Bédard, and which became very popular after its posthumous publication. Other books by Hémon are: *Blind Man's Buff* (1925) and *Monsieur Ripois and Nemesis* (1925), novels; *My Fair Lady* (1923), short stories; and *The Journal of Louis Hémon* (1924). The author died penniless, killed by a train while he was walking along a railroad track in Canada on his way to a new locality in search of work.

hemophilia. A morbid condition, usually hereditary, characterized by a tendency to bleed profusely and uncontrollably from the slightest wounds. Some royal families are prone to it, especially the former Spanish royal house. It is often latent in women and always acute in men.

Henchard, Michael. Titular hero of Hardy's MAYOR OF CASTERBRIDGE.

hendecasyllable. A metrical line of eleven syllables.

O you chorus of indolent reviewers.
Tennyson.

Henderson, Alice Corbin (1881–). American poet. Associate Editor of *Poetry: A Magazine of Verse* (1912–1916) with Harriet MONROE. Compiler (with Miss Monroe) of the *The New Poetry, an Anthology* (1917).

Henderson, Archibald (1877–). American educator. Head of mathematics department (from 1920) of University of North Carolina. Author of *George Bernard Shaw, His Life and Works* (1911); etc. Official biographer of Shaw.

Henderson, Arthur (1863–1935). British Labor party leader and statesman. Awarded Nobel peace prize (1934).

Henderson, Leon (1895–). American economist. Member, National Industrial Recovery Board (1934–1935); administrator, Office of Price Administration; holder of several other important government posts in World War II.

Henderson, William James (1855–1937). American music critic and author. His books on singers and the art of singing are authoritative works in the field. Author of *The Story of Music* (1889); *Richard Wagner* (1901); *Early History of Singing* (1921); etc. Associate editor, *The Standard Dictionary* (1892–1894).

hendiadys. The use of a pair of nouns joined by "and" where one has the force of an adjective, as Tennyson's "waving to him white hands and courtesy," i.e., courteous white hands.

Hendrick, Burton Jesse (1871–). American magazine and newspaper writer. Co-author (with William S. Sims) of *The Victory at Sea* (Pulitzer Prize for history, 1920); author of *The Training of an American* (Pulitzer Prize for biography, 1928); etc.

Hengist and **Horsa.** The semi-legendary leaders of the Jutes, who landed in England at Ebbsfleet, Kent, in 449. Horsa is said to have been slain at the battle of Aylesford, about 455, and Hengist to have ruled in Kent till his death in 488.

Henley. The Henley Regatta, an annual event (since 1839) at Henley-on-Thames, in Oxfordshire, 36 miles west of London, England.

Henley, William Ernest (1849–1903). English poet and editor, a friend of Robert Louis STEVENSON. He was an advocate of individuality and novelty, and is known for the vigor of his verse and the vividness of some of his impressionistic sketches. The most outstanding of the latter are found in the volume called *In Hospital* (1888), a collection of poems written while Henley was a tubercular patient in the Edinburgh Infirmary; his best-known poem, INVICTUS, is contained therein. Other books of poetry are: *A Book of Verse* (1888); *The Song of the Sword* (1893), later known as *London Voluntaries; Poems* (1898); *Hawthorn and Lavender* (1901). He wrote several plays, three in collaboration with Stevenson. As editor of the magazine *National Observer* in Edinburgh he advocated imperialistic policies for Britain (see IMPERIALISM), publishing the *Barrack-Room Ballads* of Rudyard KIPLING.

Hennepin, Father **Louis** (1640–?1701). Flemish Roman Catholic friar of the order of Récollects of St. Francis and explorer in America. Accompanied La Salle through Great Lakes (1679); with exploring party in upper Mississippi region (1680). Published *Description de la Louisiane* (1683); etc. While a captive of the Sioux (1680), he discovered the Falls of St. Anthony. His claim to have descended to the mouth of the Mississippi has been shown to be false.

Hennessey, Mr. The friend and crony of Mr. DOOLEY.

Henriade, The. A historical poem in ten chants, by VOLTAIRE (1724). The subject is the struggle of Henri IV of France (1553–1610) with the Holy League.

Henrietta Anne, Duchesse **d'Orléans** (1644–1670). Fifth daughter of Charles I of England. Popular at Charles II's Court; married brother of Louis XIV, and was the latter's intermediary with Charles II. Died of poisoning (?). Cf. *Royal Fluster: The Story of Minette* by Margaret Irwin.

Henrietta Maria (1609–1669). Queen consort (1625–1649) of Charles I of England. Daughter of Henry IV of France. Roman Catholic. Forced to flee to France (1644). Permitted to return to England after the Restoration. Mother of CHARLES II, JAMES II, HENRIETTA ANNE, etc.

Henriette. In Molière's comedy LES FEMMES SAVANTES, daughter of Chrysale and Philaminte. She is in love with Clitandre, and ultimately becomes his wife. Her mother and sister believe that Henriette ought to devote her life to science and philosophy; but Henriette loves woman's work far better, and thinks that her natural province is domestic life, with wifely and motherly duties. The French call Henriette "the type of a perfect woman."

Henriot, Émile. Pseudonym of **Émile Maigrot** (1889–). French poet and novelist. Awarded Grand Prix of French Academy (1924) for *Aricie Brun.*

Henriques, Robert David Quixano (1905–). English novelist. *No Arms No Armour* (1939); *The Voice of the Trumpet* (1942), etc. As a soldier in World War II, he organized British commandos.

Henry II (1133–1189). King of England. He is introduced by Walter SCOTT in both *The Betrothed* and *The Talisman.*

Henry IV. Also called **Henry of Navarre** and **Henry the Great** (1553–1610). King of France (1589–1610). Brought up as a Calvinist. Sided with Huguenots. Married Margaret of Valois, sister of Charles IX (1572). Escaped massacre of St. Bartholomew. Became king at death of Henry III. Formally renounced Protestantism (1593). Signed Edict of Nantes (1598). His final years were a period of recovery from wars and of prosperity for France. Assassinated by the Roman Catholic fanatic Ravaillac. See also THE HENRIADE by Voltaire. When Henry was crowned King of France, he made his famous promise (reminiscent of Herbert Hoover): "Je veux que le dimanche chaque paysan ait sa poule au pot."

Henry IV (1366–1413). King of England, hero of Shakespeare's 1 and 2 *Henry IV.* He appears as Bolingbroke in *Richard II,* which deals with the period previous to his reign. 1 *Henry IV* treats of English history from the deposition of Richard II to the defeat and death of Henry Percy (Hotspur) at the battle of Shrewsbury, July 23, 1403. 2 *Henry IV* continues the history from the battle of Shrewsbury to the death of the King. The two plays date from about 1598. Much of their interest depends on the famous comic character, Sir John FALSTAFF.

Henry V (1387–1422). King of England and the central figure in Shakespeare's *Henry V.* The action covers the period from the opening of Parliament in 1414 to the preparation for Henry's marriage with Katherine in 1420.

Henry VI (1421–1471). King of England and hero of Shakespeare's 1, 2 and 3 *Henry VI.* 1 *Henry VI* covers the twenty-three-year period from the accession of Henry VI to his marriage with Margaret of Anjou. It opens with the funeral procession of Henry V. This part contains the victories of Joan of Arc, the restitution of France to Charles, the Dauphin (nominally the viceroy of Henry VI, but really an independent king), and the loss of France to the English scepter by right of conquest.

2 *Henry VI* begins with the marriage of the king to Margaret of Anjou, and terminates with the battle of St. Albans, in May, 1455, in which Richard, duke of York, took the King prisoner. This part contains the commencement of the wars of the White and Red Roses, the death of the good Duke Humphrey, and the rebellion of Jack Cade.

3 *Henry VI.* This part ends with the accession of Edward IV, who sends Margaret of Anjou, the queen consort of Henry VI, back to France.

Henry VIII (1491–1547). The last of the English Tudor kings, hero of the historical play *Henry VIII* attributed to Shakespeare. The play treats of the divorce of Katharine, marriage of the King to Anne Boleyn, and birth of Elizabeth.

Henry, Frederic. An American ambulance driver in Italy during World War I, hero of Ernest Hemingway's A FAREWELL TO ARMS.

Henry, John. Negro hero of a cycle of American BALLADS and TALL TALES, originating in the last quarter of the 19th century. John Henry is a man of prodigious strength who sometimes appears as a railroad steel-driller and others as a roustabout on Mississippi River boats. In one well-known version of the tales he dies from over-exertion after taking part in a contest of drilling against a steam-drill and winning out over the machine. Roark BRADFORD wrote a synthesis of the various tales in *John Henry* (1931). See also *Bunyan, Paul.*

Henry, Joseph (1797–1878). American physicist. While a teacher at the Albany Academy (1827) made first demonstration before the Albany Institute of a magnet with doubled lift due to insulation. As a professor of natural philosophy at Princeton, he established induction theories that were of great use to Samuel F. B. MORSE in inventing the telegraph. He became the first secretary of the Smithsonian Institution (1846). The name *henry* was adopted in his honor for the unit of inductance by the International Electrical Congress at Chicago (1893).

Henry, O. Pen name of **William Sydney Porter** (1862–1910). American short-story writer, noted for his extremely popular stories dealing chiefly with the lives of modest people in great cities, marked by sentimentality, semi-realism, and a surprise ending which came to be known as the "O. Henry ending" and was widely imitated in commercial fiction. Collections of his stories include: *Cabbages and Kings* (1904); THE FOUR MILLION (1906); *The Trimmed Lamp* (1907); *The Heart of the West* (1907); *The Voice of the City* (1908);

The Gentle Grafter (1908); *Roads of Destiny* (1909); *Strictly Business* (1910); *Sixes and Sevens* (1911); *Rolling Stones* (1913); *Waifs and Strays* (1917). *The Gift of the Magi* is his most famous single story. O. Henry had a contract with the New York *World* to produce a story a week at the rate of $100 a story—a contract which the author fulfilled. In his early career he was a newspaperman and bank-clerk, and served a prison term in Ohio (1898–1901) for embezzlement, although it is said that inefficient methods in use by the bank were responsible for the shortages of funds for which he was blamed.

O. Henry Memorial Award Prize Stories. A collection of American short stories chosen annually by the Society of Arts and Sciences. The first volume was issued in 1919.

Henry, Patrick (1736–1799). American statesman and orator. Revolutionary leader from Virginia. As member of the Virginia House of Burgesses, he offered a series of resolutions declaring the Stamp Act unconstitutional. Prominent member of the Continental Congress (1774). Governor of Virginia (1776–1779; 1784–1786). Famous passages from his speeches include:

I am not a Virginian, but an American (Continental Congress, Sept. 5, 1774).

I have but one lamp by which my feet are guided, and that is the lamp of experience (Virginia House of Delegates, March 23, 1775).

It is natural to man to indulge in the illusions of hope. We are apt to shut our eyes against a painful truth, and listen to the song of that siren, till she transforms us into beasts (ditto).

Is life so dear or peace so sweet as to be purchased at the price of chains and slavery? Forbid it, Almighty God! I know not what course others may take; but as for me, give me liberty, or give me death! (ditto).

I know of no way of judging the future but by the past (Virginia Convention, March, 1775).

Caesar had his Brutus; Charles the First, his Cromwell; and George the Third—*may profit by their example*. If *this* be treason, make the most of it (Virginia Convention, 1765).

Henry Esmond, The History of. A historical novel by THACKERAY (1852) written in the first person, supposedly by Henry Esmond. He is brought up by Francis Esmond, heir to the Castlewood estate with Francis' own children, Beatrix and Frank, and grows up in the belief that he is the illegitimate son of Thomas Esmond, the deceased viscount of Castlewood. On his deathbed Francis confesses to Harry that he is the lawful heir, but Harry keeps the information secret. He and Frank Esmond are ardent supporters of James the Pretender, who, however, falls in love with Beatrix and ruins his chances for the throne. Beatrix joins the Prince abroad, and Harry, who has been in love with her, renounces the Pretender, marries her mother Rachel, Lady Castlewood, instead, and takes her to America.

Henry Ryecroft, The Private Papers of, see under PRIVATE.

Henryson, Robert (1430?–1506). Scotch poet, one of the group of SCOTTISH CHAUCERIANS. His works include: *Tale of Orpheus* (1508); *Testament of Cressid* (1593), a treatment of the TROILUS legend, attributed to Chaucer until the 18th century; *Moral Fables of Aesop the Phrygian* (1621).

Henty, George Alfred (1832–1902). English writer of many books for boys laid in various historical periods.

Hepburn. Family name of the earls of BOTHWELL.

Hepburn, Katharine (1909–). American actress on stage and screen. Received award of Academy of Motion Picture Arts and Sciences (1934) for her performance in *Morning Glory*. Success in Philip Barry's *The Philadelphia Story* (1939).

Hephaestus. The Greek name for VULCAN.

Hepplewhite, George (d. 1786). English cabinetmaker. Famous for light and elegant design of furniture, not basically different from SHERATON.

Heptameron, The (Greek, *hepta,* "seven," *hemera,* "day"). A collection of Italian and medieval stories, many of them of a somewhat licentious nature, written by—or at any rate ascribed to—Marguerite of Angoulême, Queen of Navarre (1492–1549), and published posthumously in 1558. They were supposed to have been related in seven days, hence the title. See also DECAMERON.

heptarchy (*Gr.,* "seven governments"). A government consisting of seven persons, or a group of seven countries or districts each under its own ruler, but allied and friendly toward each other.

Anglo-Saxon heptarchy. The division of England into seven parts, Kent, Sussex, Wessex, Essex, East Anglia, Mercia, and Northumbria. Their alliance flourished in various periods from the 6th to the 9th centuries under a BRETWALDA, but it seldom consisted of exactly seven members, and the names and divisions were constantly changing.

Hera (*Gr.,* "the chosen one," from *haireo,* "I choose"). The Greek JUNO, the wife of Zeus.

Heraclitus (ca. 540–475 B.C.). Greek philosopher in Ephesus, known as "The Weeping Philosopher." One of the earliest metaphysicians.

Herald. A New York newspaper, founded as a penny daily by James Gordon BENNETT. Before the Civil War it was a Tammany organ of reaction, but during the Civil War it was strongly pro-Union. In 1872 the younger James Gordon Bennett succeeded his father as editor. It was he who founded in France the

Paris *Herald* (1887). The news coverage of the *Herald* was its main feature. Frank Munsey purchased it in 1920 and merged it temporarily with the *Sun*. Ogden Reid bought it in 1924 and combined it with the New York *Tribune*. As the *Herald Tribune* it became a Republican daily morning paper, its chief columnist being Walter Lippmann.

heraldry. The herald (O.Fr. *heralt, heraut*) was an officer whose duty it was to proclaim war or peace, carry challenges to battle, and messages between sovereigns, etc. Nowadays war or peace is still proclaimed by the heralds, but their chief duty as court functionaries is to superintend state ceremonies such as coronations, installations, etc., and also to grant arms, trace genealogies, attend to matters of precedence, honors, etc.

There are nine *points* on the *shield* or *escutcheon*, distinguished by the first nine letters of the alphabet: three at top, A, B, C; three down the middle, D, E, F; and three at the bottom, G, H, I. The first three are *chiefs;* the middle three are the *collar point, fess point,* and *nombril* or *navel point;* the bottom three are the *base* points.

The *colors,* or *tinctures,* used in heraldry are:

Or, gold.	*Sable,* black.
Argent, silver.	*Vert,* green.
Gules, red.	*Purpure,* purple.
Azure, blue.	

Besides these there are the different furs, as *ermine, vair,* and their arrangements as *erminois, erminites, pean, potent, verry,* etc.

In blazoning the arms of royalties the old heralds frequently used the names of the planets for the tinctures, and in noblemen's arms the names of precious stones, the equivalents being:

Sol—topaz—*or.*
Luna—pearl—*argent.*
Saturn—diamond—*sable.*
Mars—ruby—*gules.*
Jupiter—sapphire—*azure.*
Venus—emerald—*vert.*
Mercury—amethyst—*purpure.*

The heraldic terms denoting the positions of beasts shown in coats of arms, as crests, etc., are:

couchant, lying down (emblematic of sovereignty);
counter-passant, moving in opposite directions;
coward or *coué,* with tail hanging between the legs;
dormant, sleeping;
gardant, full-faced;
hauriant, standing on its tail (of fishes);
issuant, rising from the top or bottom of an ordinary;
lodged, reposing (of stags, etc.);
naiant, swimming (of fishes);
nascent, rising out of the middle of an ordinary;
passant, walking, the face in profile (emblematic of resolution);
passant gardant, walking, with full face (emblematic of resolution and prudence);
passant regardant, walking and looking behind;
rampant, rearing, with face in profile (emblematic of magnanimity);
rampant gardant, erect on the hind legs; full face (emblematic of prudence);
rampant regardant, erect on the hind legs; side face looking behind (emblematic of circumspection);
regardant, looking back (emblematic of circumspection);
salient, springing (emblematic of valor).
sejant, seated (emblematic of counsel);
statant, standing still;
trippant, running (of stags, etc.);
volant, flying.

Herbert, Alan Patrick (1890–). English journalist and writer. Wounded at Gallipoli in World War I. Regular contributor to *Punch.* His novel *The Water Gipsies* (1930) served to footnote his fight for freedom of the Thames to non-commercial craft. Also secured, as an M.P., passage of the Matrimonial Causes Bill (1937), modifying the outmoded English divorce laws. (His novel, *Holy Deadlock* [1934] was helpful here). A great after-dinner speaker. Has written much light verse and some successful comic operas.

Herbert, George (1593–1633). English poet of the Metaphysical school. See METAPHYSICAL POETS. A clergyman and one-time Public Orator of Cambridge University, he wrote poetry marked by religious piety, striking, colloquial rhythms, simple diction, and the use of symbols and arresting images from ecclesiastical ritual, farming, the trades, science, and everyday household pursuits; the poems themselves were often arranged on the page in strange shapes, such as altars, crosses, and the like. His best-known group of poems are those contained in *The Temple* (1633).

Edward, Lord Herbert of Cherbury (1583–1648), his brother, was a well-known courtier, adventurer, and philosopher, in the last capacity arguing for rationalism in religion and attacking the clergy. He also wrote poetry in the Metaphysical vein which is reputed to have been too obscure and complex for the members of the Metaphysical school themselves.

Herbert, Victor (1859–1924). Irish-American conductor and composer. Wrote light operas, *The Wizard of the Nile* (1893); *Babes in Toyland* (1903); *Mlle. Modiste* (1905);

The Red Mill (1906); *Naughty Marietta* (1910); etc. Also two grand operas and musical scores for the Ziegfeld Follies.

Herbst, Josephine Frey (1897–). American novelist. Three of her novels—*Pity is not Enough* (1933); *The Executioner Waits* (1934); *Rope of Gold* (1939)—were designed as a trilogy to portray the decay of capitalistic society and "the upthrust of a new group society."

Hercules. A hero of ancient Greek myth, who was possessed of superhuman physical strength and vigor. He is represented as brawny, muscular, short-necked, and of huge proportions. The Pythian told him if he would serve Eurystheus for twelve years he should become immortal; accordingly he bound himself to the Argive king, who imposed upon him twelve tasks of great difficulty and danger known as the *Labors of Hercules:*

(1) To slay the Nemean lion.
(2) To kill the Lernean hydra.
(3) To catch and retain the Arcadian stag.
(4) To destroy the Erymanthian boar.
(5) To cleanse the stables of King Augeas.
(6) To destroy the cannibal birds of the Lake Stymphalis.
(7) To take captive the Cretan bull.
(8) To catch the horses of the Thracian Diomedes.
(9) To get possession of the girdle of Hippolyta, Queen of the Amazons.
(10) To take captive the oxen of the monster Geryon.
(11) To get possession of the apples of the Hesperides.
(12) To bring up from the infernal regions the three-headed dog Cerberus.

For the story of Hercules' madness and death, see NESSUS. He is the hero of a tragedy, *Hercules Furens,* by Euripides, and another by Seneca.

After death Hercules took his place in the heavens as a constellation, and is still to be seen between Lyra and Corona Borealis.

Hercules' choice. Immortality, the reward of toil in preference to pleasure.

Hercules' labor. Very great toil.

Hercules' Pillars, see PILLARS.

the Attic Hercules. Theseus, who went about like Hercules, destroying robbers and achieving wondrous exploits.

the Jewish Hercules. SAMSON.

the Hercules of the North American Indians. KWASIND.

the Persian Hercules. RUSTUM.

the Hercules of Music. Christoph Willibald von Gluck (1714–1787).

Hercules Secundus. Commodus, the Roman emperor (b. 161, reigned 180–192) gave himself this title.

Herculean knot. A snaky complication on the rod, or caduceus, of Mercury, adopted by the Grecian brides as the fastening of their woolen girdles, which only the bridegroom was allowed to untie. As he did so he invoked Juno to render his marriage as fruitful as that of Hercules, whose numerous wives all had families, amongst them being the fifty daughters of Thestius, each of whom conceived in one night.

herd. See under COVEY.

Herder, Johann Gottfried (1744–1803). German poet and literary critic, of wide influence during the romantic period in Germany, interested in classic Greece, German folk-lore, and philosophy. See ROMANTICISM; STURM UND DRANG.

Heredia, José María de (1842–1905). Cuban-born French poet of the group called PARNASSIANS, a pupil of Leconte de LISLE and known for the richness of his imagery, the sonority, cadence, and rhythm of his language, and the evocative character of his historical impressions. His one book is *Les Trophées* (1893), consisting chiefly of sonnets and dealing with conquest through the ages, especially in Greece, Rome, the Middle Ages, the Renaissance, and the Orient.

heretoga. Among the Anglo-Saxons, the leader or commander of an army. The word survives in German as *Herzog* and was translated by the Romans as *dux.* HENGIST AND HORSA were two "heretogas."

Hereward. An important character in Scott's COUNT ROBERT OF PARIS.

Hereward the Wake. A historical novel by Charles KINGSLEY (1865). The titular hero is a reckless young Saxon who for a time successfully opposes the Norman conquest. He plunders and burns the abbey of Peterborough, establishes his camp in the Isle of Ely where he is joined by Earl Morcar, is blockaded for three months by William I, but makes his escape with some of his followers.

Herford, Oliver (1863–1935). Writer and illustrator. Drew for *Life, Harper's Weekly,* and other magazines. Wrote and illustrated about fifty books of artistic nonsense. Some of his work comes close to greatness.

> The bubble winked at me, and said,
> "You'll miss me, brother, when you're dead."

Hergesheimer, Joseph (1880–). American novelist and short-story writer, author of popular studies of upper-class American families and picturesque romances in colorful settings. His books include: *The Lay Anthony* (1914); THE THREE BLACK PENNYS (1917); JAVA HEAD (1919); *The Happy End* (1919), short stories, among them his best known story, *Tol'able David,* which was dramatized as a popular motion picture; LINDA CONDON (1919); *Cytherea* (1922); *The Bright Shawl* (1922); *Tampico* (1926); *Swords and Roses* (1929); *The Limestone Tree* (1931); *The Foolscap Rose* (1934).

Heriot, George (1563–1624). Scottish goldsmith. Jeweler to James VI (James I of England); founder of Heriot's Hospital at Edinburgh (1659). As Geordie he is a prominent figure in Scott's *Fortunes of Nigel.*

Hermann and Dorothea. A narrative pastoral poem by GOETHE (1797). The hero, Hermann, son of a well-to-do German farmer, falls in love with one of a band of refugees from the horrors of the French Revolution, Dorothea by name. For a time she becomes a servant in his father's household. Eventually, after certain painful misunderstandings have been cleared away, the lovers are betrothed.

hermaphrodite. A human body having both sexes; a vehicle combining the structure of a wagon and cart; a flower containing both the male and female organs of reproduction. The word is derived from the fable of Hermaphroditus, son of Hermes and Aphrodite as told in Ovid's *Metamorphoses.* The nymph Salmacis became enamored of him, and prayed that she might be so closely united that "the twain might become one flesh." Her prayer being heard, the nymph and boy became one body.

Hermes. The same as MERCURY, applied both to the god and to the metal.

Hermia. In Shakespeare's MIDSUMMER NIGHT'S DREAM, daughter of Egeus of Athens, and promised by him in marriage to Demetrius but herself in love with Lysander.

Hermione. (1) In Greek legend, only daughter of Menelaus and Helen. She became the wife of Pyrrhus or Neoptolemus, son of Achilles; but Orestes assassinated Pyrrhus and married Hermione, who had already been betrothed to him.

(2) The heroine of Shakespeare's WINTER'S TALE, wife of King Leontes of Sicily.

(3) The self-important heroine of Don Marquis' humorous volume *Hermione and Her Little Group of Serious Thinkers* (*Am.,* 1916). Hermione made her first appearance in the columns of the New York *Evening Sun.* She is devoted to a number of "causes" of the day, which prove too much for her feeble intellect, though she is quite unaware of the fact, and give ample opportunity for contemporary satire.

Hermit, The. A ballad by Oliver GOLDSMITH (1766). The hero and heroine are EDWIN AND ANGELINA. It contains the well-known lines—

> Man wants but little here below,
> Nor wants that little long.

Hermit Nation or Hermit Kingdom. Korea, so called because of its seclusion before it came under Japanese influence.

Hermod or Hermodr. In Scandinavian mythology, the son of Odin who journeyed to HEL and made the unsuccessful attempt to recall Balder to the Upper World. It is he who, with Bragi, receives and welcomes to VALHALLA all heroes who fall in battle.

Hernani. The title and hero of a tragedy by Victor HUGO (1830). As the first drama of note to be produced by the romantic school, it attracted great attention and had much the same effect on the French theater that *The Sorrows of Werther* had on German fiction. See WERTHER. Hernani is a bandit, in love with Donna Sol, the betrothed of Don Ruy Gomez, an old Spanish grandee who is her guardian. Don Carlos (Charles V) also falls in love with the lady, complicating the situation greatly, for one or another of these romantic gentlemen is time after time forced by the rites of chivalry to protect his rival from the third suitor. Thus Carlos saves Hernani from Ruy Gomez, Hernani returns the compliment by saving the King, and still later Carlos is thwarted in his hot pursuit of the bandit by Ruy Gomez' interposed protection. In return for this generous assistance, Hernani now presents Ruy Gomez with a horn, saying that when the horn sounds, he will forfeit his life. Just as he is about to marry Donna Sol in the last act, Ruy Gomez blows the horn, the lovers take poison and Ruy Gomez stabs himself. Verdi has an opera, *Ernani* (1844), founded on the drama.

Herndon, William Henry (1818–1891). American lawyer. Entered into law partnership with Abraham Lincoln (1843), which continued in form until the latter's death. Author, with Jesse W. Weik, of *Herndon's Lincoln: The True Story of a Great Life* (3 vols., 1889). His letters and papers relating to Lincoln were edited by Emmanuel Hertz as *The Hidden Lincoln* (1938).

Herne, James A. (1839–1901). American dramatist and actor. His best-known plays are MARGARET FLEMING (1890), SHORE ACRES (1892) and GRIFFITH DAVENPORT (1898). His daughter Chrystal is a well-known actress.

Hero. In Shakespeare's MUCH ADO ABOUT NOTHING, the greatly maligned daughter of Leonato, governor of Messina. She is of a quiet, serious disposition, and forms a good contrast to the gay, witty, rattle-pate Beatrice, her cousin.

Hero and Leander. The old Greek tale is that Hero, a priestess of Venus, fell in love with Leander who swam across the Hellespont every night to visit her. One night he was drowned, and heartbroken Hero drowned herself in the same sea. The story is told in one of the poems of Musaeus, and in Marlowe's *Hero and Leander* (1598), left unfinished at Marlowe's death and completed by George CHAPMAN.

Lord Byron and Lieutenant Ekenhead repeated the experiment of Leander and accomplished it in 1 hour 10 minutes. (See also HALLIBURTON, RICHARD.) The distance, allowing for drifting, would be about four miles. In DON JUAN, Byron says of his hero:

> A better swimmer you could scarce see ever,
> He could, perhaps, have pass'd the Hellespont,
> As once (a feat on which ourselves we prided)
> Leander, Mr. Ekenhead, and I did.
> *Canto,* II. cv.

Herod. There are two rulers of this name famed in history and legend.

(1) *Herod the Great* (73?–4 B. C.). Ruler over Judea under the Roman régime. For the tragic story of Herod and his wife Mariamne, and its use in dramatic literature, see MARIAMNE.

The birth of Christ took place in the last year of this Herod's reign (4 B. C.—an error in chronology first assigned it to 1 A. D.) and it was he who ordered the MASSACRE OF THE INNOCENTS.

to out-herod Herod. To outdo in wickedness, violence, or rant, the worst of tyrants. The Herod who destroyed the babes of Bethlehem (*Matt.* ii. 16), was made (in the ancient mysteries) a ranting, roaring tyrant, the extravagance of his rant being the measure of his bloody-mindedness. See also PILATE.

> Oh, it offends me to the soul to hear a robustious, periwig-pated fellow tear a passion to tatters, to very rags, to split the ears of the groundings . . . it outherods Herod.—Shakespeare, *Hamlet* iii. 2.

(2) *Herod Antipater.* Son of Herod the Great and tetrarch of Galilee from 4 B. C. to 39 A. D. It was this Herod who married his brother's wife Herodias and at the request of his step-daughter SALOME presented her with the head of John the Baptist on a platter.

Hérodiade. A dramatic poem by Stéphane MALLARMÉ in which the heroine, a woman of white and ice-like beauty, soliloquizes upon the deliberate isolation and sterility of her life. She is interpreted as a symbol of the aesthetic coldness and sterility celebrated in another poem of Mallarmé's, THE SWAN.

Herodias (1) (14? B. C.–after 40 A. D.). Daughter of Aristobulus and sister of Herod Agrippa I; married her uncle Herod Philip, whom she left to marry his brother, Herod Antipas as his second wife; mother of Salome (*Matt.* xiv, 3–12; *Mark* iv, 17–29).

(2) In Sue's WANDERING JEW the half-sister of Ahasuerus, like him condemned to eternal wandering.

Herodotus (484–432 B. C.). Famous Greek historian. Known as "The Halicarnassian" after his birthplace Halicarnassus. His great work, a history of the Greco-Persian wars from 500 to 479 B. C., brought him the surname of "Father of History." It consists of nine books, named after the nine Muses, and was first printed in Greek by Aldus Manutius (1502).

Heroes and Hero Worship. A famous series of lectures by Thomas CARLYLE (1840).

heroic verse. That verse in which epic poetry is generally written, so called because it is employed to celebrate heroic exploits. In Greek and Latin it is *hexameter* verse; in English it is ten-syllable iambic verse, either in rhymes or not; in Italian it is the *ottava rima.*

The English heroic verse becomes the *heroic couplet* (see under COUPLET) when used in rhymed pairs of lines. The 18th-century poets, particularly Dryden and Pope, brought its use to a high degree of perfection.

Herostratus, see EROSTRATUS.

Herrera, Fernando de. Called **el Divino** (1534?–1597). Head of Sevilian school of lyric poetry; friend of Cervantes; disciple of GARCILASO DE LA VEGA. Known particularly for his classicistic poems in Italian style. Also wrote a life of Thomas More, *Vida y Muerte de Tomas Moro* (1592).

Herrick, Robert. A brilliant degenerate in Stevenson's romance, EBB TIDE (1894).

Herrick, Robert (1591–1674). English poet, one of the "Sons of Ben," or poets who followed in the tradition of Ben JONSON. Herrick's poetry is graceful, lyrical, and charming, marked by delicate, pictorial imagery culled from nature, rustic scenes, and court life, broadly influenced by the Latin classic poets. He was a country vicar in Devonshire until 1647, when he was ejected by the Puritans for his royalist principles. *Hesperides, or the Works both Human and Divine of Robert Herrick, Esq.* (1648).

Herrick, Robert (1868–1938). American novelist and teacher. The center of his activity was Chicago, "the characteristic American metropolis." He desired his novels to contribute to an understanding of modern American life. A writer of careful prose and a pioneer realist. *The Common Lot* (1904); *The Master of the Inn* (1908); *Together* (1908); *Clark's Field* (1914); *The End of Desire* (1931); etc.

Herries Novels. By Hugh WALPOLE, a series of chronicles of English social history: *Rogue Herries* (1930); *Judith Paris* (1931); *The Fortress* (1932); *Vanessa* (1933); *The Bright Pavilions* (1940); *Katherine Christian* (1943).

herring-pond, the. A name humorously given to various dividing seas, especially to the

Atlantic, which separates America from the British Isles. The English Channel, the North Sea, and the seas between Australasia and the United Kingdom are also so called.

Herrings, Battle of. See under BATTLE.

Herriot, Édouard (1872–). French statesman. Radical Socialist leader; premier of France (1924–1925; 1932); minister of state; president, Chamber of Deputies; under arrest after the fall of France.

Herschel, Sir **William.** Originally **Friedrich Wilhelm Herschel** (1738–1822). English astronomer, born in Hanover. Discovered a new planet (1781) which he called *Georgium Sidus* in honor of King George III. It is now known as Uranus. Also discovered moons of Saturn and Uranus. In his earlier years he attained considerable success as a violinist and organist. The *Dictionary of National Biography* writes: "In nearly every branch of modern physical astronomy he was a pioneer. He was the virtual founder of sidereal science. As an explorer of the heavens he had but one rival—his son." Cf. the poem by Alfred Noyes, "Sir William Herschel Conducts," in *The Watchers of the Skies* (1937). His studies were continued by his son Sir **John Frederick William Herschel** (1792–1871). Also two of his grandsons achieved renown as astronomers.

Herse. A Greek deity of the fertilizing dew. According to legend, she and her sister Aglauros opened a box given them by Athena. In it was a snake, and Herse and Aglauros hurled themselves from the Acropolis.

Hertha, see NERTHUS.

Hertz, Emanuel (1870–1940). Lawyer and writer on Abraham Lincoln. Made special study of Lincoln's life. See also under HERNDON.

Hertz, Heinrich Rudolph (1857–1894). German physicist. Demonstrated the existence of electric or electromagnetic waves, called also "hertzian waves." His further investigations of them led to the development of wireless telegraphy.

Hervé Riel. A Breton sailor, who saved the French squadron when beaten at Cape la Hogue and flying before the English, by piloting it into the harbor of St. Malo (May 31, 1692). He was so unconscious of the service he had rendered that, when desired to name his reward, he begged for a whole day's holiday to see his wife. Browning has a poem called *Hervé Riel* (1867).

Hervey, John. Baron **Hervey of Ickworth** (1696–1743). English politician. Lord Privy Seal (1740–1742). Author of *Memoirs of the Court of George II.* Attacked by Alexander POPE, because of his effeminacy, as "Lord Fanny."

Herzog, Émile Salomon Wilhelm. See MAUROIS, ANDRÉ.

Hesiod. Greek poet of 8th century B.C. "Father of Greek didactic poetry." The most important works ascribed to him are *Works and Days* and *Theogony.* The one consists of moral maxims and rural precepts. The other is an account of the origin of the world and the gods.

Hesione. In Greek legend, daughter of Laomedon, king of Troy, and sister to Priam. Her father exposed her to a sea-monster in order to appease the wrath of Apollo and Poseidon, but she was rescued by Hercules, who made the stipulation that he should receive a certain reward. Laomedon did not keep his promise, so Hercules slew him, took Troy, and gave Hesione to Telamon, by whom she became the mother of Teucer. The refusal of the Greeks to give her up to Priam is given as one of the causes of the Trojan War.

Hesperia. From Greek *hesperos,* "evening." Italy was so called by the Greeks, because it was to them the land of the setting sun and the evening star. The Romans, for a similar reason, transferred the name to Spain.

Hesperides. Three sisters who guarded the golden apples which Hera received as a marriage gift. They were assisted by the dragon Ladon. Hercules, as the last of his "twelve labors," slew the dragon and carried some of the apples to Eurystheus. Many poets call the place where these golden apples grew the *garden of the Hesperides.*

Hesperus. (1) The evening star.

(2) Longfellow wrote a poem of a shipwreck called *The Wreck of the Hesperus* (1842).

Hess, Rudolf (1894–). German politician. Born in Alexandria, hence nicknamed the "Egyptian." Intimate friend of HITLER (since 1921). Took down and influenced dictation of *Mein Kampf.* Third deputy Führer, after Göring (1939). Created world sensation by solo flight (May, 1941) to Scotland. Held as prisoner of war. One of the German leaders tried as WAR CRIMINALS in Nuremberg, where he was sentenced to life imprisonment.

Hesse, Hermann (1877–). German novelist, poet and essayist, resident of Switzerland. Cultivated writer little known in America. Also noteworthy as an aquarellist.

Hessian. One whose services in politics or war can be easily bought; so called from the Hessian mercenaries who fought for England in the American Revolution.

Hestia. A Greek goddess, later identified with VESTA, the Roman goddess of the hearth.

Hesychasts (from Gr. *hesychos,* "still, calm"). A sect of mystics or quietists in the

Eastern Church, who lived on Mount Athos in the 14th century. They aimed to attain by contemplating their navel perfect serenity and supernatural insight which enabled them to feel, diffused through them, an uncreated but communicable divine light, the same which shone on Mt. Tabor at the transfiguration of Christ.

hetaera. Literally, a female companion or comrade. In ancient Greece, a mistress of the better class. Some hetaeras were freed women or even women of free birth. LAIS and PHRYNE are the most famous ones.

Hetman (Ger. *hauptmann,* "chief man"). A general or commander-in-chief. The chief of the Cossacks of the Don used to be so called. He was elected by the people, and the mode of choice was thus: The voters threw their fur caps at the candidate they voted for, and he who had the largest number of caps at his feet was the successful candidate. The last elected Hetman was Count Platoff (1812–1814). See MAZEPPA.

> After the peace, all Europe hailed their hetman, Platoff, as the hero of the war.—J. S. Mosby, *War Reminiscences,* ch. xi.

Hewlett, Maurice (1861–1923). English novelist. His best-known novels are historical; they include THE FOREST LOVERS (1898), RICHARD YEA-AND-NAY (1900), *The Queen's Quair* (1904), and BENDISH (1913). See also MARY, QUEEN OF SCOTS.

Hexam, Lizzie. The heroine of DICKENS' novel *Our Mutual Friend.* She is the daughter of Jesse ("Gaffer") Hexam, a Thames waterman, and finally marries Eugene Wrayburn.

hexameron. Six days taken as one continuous period; especially the six days of the Creation.

hexameter. In prosody, a six-foot line. The word is, however, usually reserved for dactylic hexameter, consisting of dactyls and spondees. This is the meter in which the Greek and Latin epics were written, and has been more or less imitated in English in such poems as Longfellow's *Evangeline,* Clough's *Bothie,* Kingsley's *Andromeda.*

The line consists, says Professor Saintsbury (*Manual of English Prosody,* iv, 1):

> of six feet, dactyls or spondees at choice for the first four, but normally always a dactyl in the fifth and always a spondee in the sixth—the latter foot being by special license sometimes allowed in the fifth also (in which case the line is called spondaic), but never a dactyl in the sixth. To this metre, and to the attempts to imitate it in English, the term should be strictly confined, and never applied to the Alexandrine or iambic trimeter.

Verse consisting of alternate hexameters and PENTAMETERS is known as ELEGIAC. Coleridge illustrates this in his:

> In the hexameter rises the fountain's silvery column;
> In the pentameter aye falling in melody back.

The Authorized Version of the Bible furnishes a number of examples of "accidental" hexameter lines; the following are well known:

> How art thou fallen from Heaven, O Lucifer son of the Morning.
> Why do the heathen rage and the people imagine a vain thing?
> God is gone up with a shout, the Lord with the sound of the trumpet.

Hexapla (*Gr.,* "sixfold"). The collection of Old Testament texts collated by Origen (3rd century A. D.), and containing in parallel columns the Hebrew text in Hebrew and in Greek characters, the Septuagint (with emendations), and the versions of Aquila, Theodotion, and Symmachus.

Hexateuch. The first six books of the Old Testament, that is, the PENTATEUCH plus Joshua, relating the final settlement of the Jews in the promised land.

Heyse, Paul (1830–1914). German poet and novelist. Nobel Prize for Literature (1910). Especially celebrated for his NOVELLEN.

Heyst, Axel. The hero of Conrad's VICTORY.

Heyward, Du Bose (1885–1940). American novelist and dramatist, and poet. Best known for *Porgy* (1925) and *Mamba's Daughters* (1929) both made into successful plays and the former also into an opera. See GERSHWIN. His widow, Dorothy Hartzell *née* Kuhns is also a playwright and novelist.

Heywood, John (1497?–?1580). English poet, a friend of Sir Thomas MORE and a court musician and entertainer under Henry VIII, Edward VI, and Queen Mary. He made popular the court interludes (see INTERLUDE) that later became an important part of entertainment for royalty and the nobility in Elizabethan and Jacobean times. He also wrote epigrams and a satirical allegory on religion, *The Spider and the Fly* (1556). See also FOUR P'S, THE, a typical interlude of Heywood's. He was possibly author of *The Pardoner and the Frere.*

Heywood, Thomas (d. 1650?). English dramatist and poet, connected with the Lord Admiral's company of actors and the queen's company, and attached to the Earl of Southampton's retinue. His plays include: *A Woman Killed with Kindness* (1603); *The Four Prentices of London* (ca. 1600), considered to be the object of satire in Beaumont's and Fletcher's KNIGHT OF THE BURNING PESTLE; *Edward IV* (1604 and 1605); *The Rape of Lucrece* (1608); *The Captives* (1624); *The Fair Maid of the West* (1631). He is said to have written a total of 220 plays, as well as masques and pageants. He also wrote several compilations and translations, such as *Pleasant Dialogues and Dramas* (1637); *Troia Britannica* (1609), an historical poem; and *The Hierarchy of Blessed Angels* (1635), a didactic poem.

Hezekiah. In the Old Testament, one of the kings of Judah, noted for his efforts to abolish idolatry and establish the worship of Jehovah. The famous destruction of the Assyrian army under SENNACHERIB took place during his reign.

Hiawatha. The Iroquois name of a hero of miraculous birth who came (under a variety of names) among the North American Indian tribes to bring peace and goodwill to man. In Longfellow's poem of that title (1855) he is an Ojibway, son of Mudjekeewis (the west wind) and Wenonah. His mother dies in his infancy, and Hiawatha is brought up by his grandmother, Nokomis, daughter of the Moon. He represents the progress of civilization among the American Indians. He first wrestles with Mondamin (Indian maize), whom he subdues and gives to man bread-corn. He then teaches man navigation; then he subdues the Mishe-Nahma or sturgeon, and tells the people to "bring all their pots and kettles and make oil for winter." His next adventure is against Megissogwon, the magician, "who sent the fiery fever on man; sent the white fog from the fen-lands; sent disease and death among us"; he slays the terrible monster, and teaches man the science of medicine. He next marries Minnehaha (Laughing Water), setting the people an example to follow. Lastly, he teaches the people picture-writing. When the white man lands and teaches the Indians the faith of Jesus, Hiawatha exhorts them to receive the words of wisdom, to reverence the missionaries who have come so far to see them, and departs "to the kingdom of Ponemah, the land of the Hereafter."

Hiawatha's mittens. "Magic mittens made of deer-skin; when upon his hands he wore them, he could smite the rocks asunder."

Hiawatha's moccasins. Enchanted shoes made of deer-skin. "When he bound them round his ankles, at each stride a mile he measured."

Hibben, Paxton Pattison (1880–1928). American diplomat and journalist. During his army career (from 1917) he became twice the subject of investigation by a U.S. military tribunal because of his sympathies with the Russian revolution.

Hichens, Robert Smythe (1864–). English popular novelist. Chiefly known as the author of *The Garden of Allah* (1905) of which 800,000 copies have been sold. His other works include *Bella Donna* (1909); *The Paradine Case* (1933); *A New Way of Life* (1942); etc. He also collaborated on a number of plays, among them an adaptation of his masterpiece. The GREEN CARNATION (1894), a novel, satirizes Oscar Wilde.

hic jacets. Tombstones, so called from the first two words of their inscriptions; "Here lies . . ."

> By the cold *Hic Jacets* of the dead.
> Tennyson, *Idylls of the King* (*Vivien*).

Hickok, James Butler. Known as **Wild Bill Hickok** (1837–1876). American scout and U.S. marshal. On tour with Buffalo Bill (1872–1873). Murdered.

hickory.

Old Hickory. General Andrew Jackson (1767–1845), President of the United States, 1829–1837. He was first called "tough," from his great powers of endurance, then "tough as hickory," and lastly, "Old Hickory."

Young Hickory. Martin Van Buren (1782–1862), President of the United States, was so-called from his relation to Jackson, whose policies he carried on.

Hicks, Granville (1901–). American author and literary critic, best known for his criticisms and interpretations of literature and social problems during the 1930's from a Marxian standpoint. See MARXISM IN LITERATURE. His works from this period are: *The Great Tradition* (1933), on American literature; *John Reed* (1936), a biography; *I Like America* (1938); and *Figures of Transition* (1939), on late 19th-century British literature. In 1939, after the pact of friendship between the U.S.S.R. and the National Socialist government of Germany, Hicks resigned from the Communist party. *The First to Awaken* (1940) written in collaboration with R. M. Bennett is a Utopian romance similar to LOOKING BACKWARD of Edward Bellamy, and *Only One Storm* (1942) is a novel celebrating the practices of democracy in a New England small town. *Small Town* (1947) is a sociological study.

hieratic. Consecrated to sacred uses, as, hieratic chants, etc. The Greeks applied the term to a cursive form of hieroglyphic writing which, though originally used for all literature, came to be reserved for religious texts when DEMOTIC writing was adopted for secular use.

Hieronimo. The chief character of Thomas KYD's drama in two parts, the first part being called *Hieronimo,* and the second part, *The Spanish Tragedy, or Hieronimo is Mad Again* (1588). In the latter play, Horatio, only son of Hieronimo, sitting with Belimperia in an alcove, is murdered by his rival Balthazar and the lady's brother Lorenzo. The murderers hang the dead body on a tree in the garden, and Hieronimo, aroused by the screams of Belimperia, rushing into the garden, sees the dead body of his son, and goes raving mad.

Higginson, Thomas Wentworth Storrow (1823–1911). American author. Prominent as an opponent of slavery. In Unitarian ministry (1847–1881). Colonel of the first colored regiment of the Civil War (1862–1864). Biographer. Friend of Emily DICKINSON.

high.

High Church. The High Church party in the Church of England is distinguished by its maintenance of sacerdotal claims, by the very great and preponderating efficacy with which it endows the sacraments, and by the apparent importance which it attaches to ritual and outward forms and ceremonies.

high days. Festivals. *On high days and holidays.* Here "high" means grand or great; as, *un grand jour.*

high hand: with a high hand. Arrogantly. To carry things with a high hand in French would be: *Faire une chose haut la main.*

High Heels and *Low Heels.* The names of two factions in Swift's tale of Lilliput (*Gulliver's Travels*), satirizing the High and Low Church parties.

high places, in Scripture language, means elevated spots where sacrifices were offered. Idolatrous worship was much carried on in high places. Some were evidently artificial mounds, for the faithful are frequently ordered to remove or destroy them. Hezekiah removed the high places (2 *Kings* xviii. 4), so did Asa (2 *Chron.* xiv. 3), Jehoshaphat (2 *Chron.* xvii. 6), Josiah, and others. On the other hand, Jehoram and Ahaz made high places for idolatrous worship.

high seas. All the sea which is not the property of a particular country. The sea three miles out from the coast belongs to the country, and is called "territorial waters." High seas, like high-ways, means for the public use. In both cases the word *high* means "chief," "principal." (Lat. *altum,* "the main sea"; *altus,* "high.")

high tea. A meal served about the usual teatime which includes, besides tea, fish, cold meats, pastry, etc.

> A well understood "high tea" should have cold roast beef at the top of the table, a cold Yorkshire pie at the bottom, a mighty ham in the middle. The side dishes will comprise soused mackerel, pickled salmon (in due season), sausages and potatoes, etc., etc. Rivers of tea, coffee, and ale, with dry and buttered toast, sally-lunns, scones, muffins and crumpets, jams and marmalade.—*Daily Telegraph* May 9, 1893.

high words. Angry words.

high-brow. A superior person, especially one who, in his own estimation at least, is intellectually superior; one who takes an academic view of things; also, in general, a term popularly applied to intellectual interests and pursuits, or to people of intellectual interests and pursuits, by non-intellectuals. The expression is of American origin. Its opposite, *lowbrow,* is also in use.

higher criticism. The name given to modern textual criticism of the Bible with regard to problems of dates of composition, authorship, authenticity, etc. By those who accept the doctrine of the literal inspiration of the Bible it is used with a derogatory connotation. The first use of the phrase was in 1787 in Eichhorn's *Einleitung in das Alte Testament.* See also ELOHISTIC AND JEHOVISTIC SCRIPTURES.

Higher Pantheism, The. A poem by TENNYSON, written in 1869, in which the poet urges a belief that God not only is found in the world (pantheism) but also that He transcends it. A. C. SWINBURNE wrote a parody of this in *The Higher Pantheism in a Nutshell.*

Highgate. A North London suburb, so called from a gate set up there about 400 years ago to receive tolls for the bishop of London, when the old miry road from Gray's Inn Lane to Barnet was turned through the bishop's park. The village being perched on a hill explains the first part of the name.

sworn at Highgate. A custom anciently prevailed at the public-houses in Highgate to administer a ludicrous oath to all travelers who stopped there. The party was sworn on a pair of horns fastened to a stick—

(1) Never to kiss the maid when he can kiss the mistress.

(2) Never to eat brown bread when he can get white.

(3) Never to drink small beer when he can get strong—unless he prefers it.

Highland Mary. The most shadowy of Robert BURNS' sweethearts, but the one to whom he addressed some of his finest poetry, including *My Highland Lassie, O, Highland Mary* (*Ye banks and braes and streams around the castle o' Montgomery*), *Thou Ling'ring Star* and—perhaps— *Will ye go to the Indies my Mary?* She is believed to have been Mary CAMPBELL.

Hilary, St. See under SAINTS.

Hilda. A New England art student in Rome, one of the leading characters of Hawthorne's MARBLE FAUN.

Hilda, St. See under SAINTS.

Hilda Lessways. A novel by Arnold Bennett. See CLAYHANGER.

Hildebrand. (1) The Nestor of German romance. His story is told in the *Hildebrandslied,* an Old High German poem, and he also appears in the *Nibelungenlied, Dietrich von Bern,* etc. Like Maugis among the heroes of Charlemagne, he was a magician as well as champion.

(2) Pope GREGORY VII. Hence a *Hildebrand* one resembling Gregory VII, noted for sub

jugating the power of the German emperors, and specially detested by the early reformers for his ultra-pontifical views.

Hildesheim. Legend relates that a monk of Hildesheim, an old city of Hanover, doubting how with God a thousand years could be as one day, listened to the singing of a bird in a wood, as he thought for three minutes, but found the time had been three hundred years. Longfellow introduced this tale in his GOLDEN LEGEND, calling the monk Felix.

Hill, Frank Ernest (1888–). American poet. *The Westward Star* (1934); etc. Collaborator with Joseph AUSLANDER on *The Winged Horse,* an anthology of poetry (1927).

Hill, George Birkbeck Norman (1835–1903). English educator and authority on Doctor Johnson. Editor of Johnson's letters (1892); *Lives of the English Poets,* etc.

Hill, Grace Livingston (1865–1947). Popular and voluminous American novelist. Some three million copies of her output have been absorbed.

Hill, James Jerome (1838–1916). American railroad promoter and financier. A "robber baron." Developed Great Northern and Northern Pacific systems. Rival of E. H. HARRIMAN. Co-responsible for stock-market panic of 1901.

Hill Difficulty, the. One of the obstacles met by Christian on his way to the Celestial Country in Bunyan's *Pilgrim's Progress.*

hill folk. So Scott calls the Cameronian Scotch Covenanters, who met clandestinely among the hills. Sometimes the Covenanters generally are so called.

A class of beings in Scandinavian tradition between the elves and the human race were known as "hill folk" or "hill people." They were supposed to dwell in caves and small hills, and to be bent on receiving the benefits of man's redemption.

Hillman, Sidney (1887–1946). Lithuanian-born American labor leader. President, Amalgamated Clothing Workers of America (from 1915); vice-president, CIO; with William S. Knudsen co-director, Office of Production Management (1941); head of labor division, War Production Board (1942); etc. Cf. *Sidney Hillman, Labor Statesman* by George Henry SOULE.

Hillquit, Morris (1869–1933). Riga-born lawyer and Socialist leader. Author of *History of Socialism in the United States* (1903), etc.

Hilton, James (1900–). English novelist, best known for his widely popular and extremely successful novelette GOODBYE, MR. CHIPS (1935). Other books by the same author, marked by sentimental or adventurous appeal, are: *And Now Goodbye* (1931); *Rage in Heaven* (1932); *Lost Horizon* (1933); *Contango* (1934); *Catherine Herself* (1935); *Knight Without Armour* (1935); *We Are Not Alone* (1937). *Goodbye, Mr. Chips, Lost Horizon,* and *We Are Not Alone* and others were dramatized as motion pictures. See also SHANGRI-LA.

himation. In Greek antiquity, a garment for both sexes consisting of a rectangular cloth about five feet wide and ten feet long, draped about the body in various ways according to the taste of the wearer. It was often lavishly embroidered and could be worn over the tunic or as the sole garment.

Himmler, Heinrich (1900–1945). German Nazi leader. Party member since 1925. As Reich director of propaganda (1926–1930), predecessor of GOEBBELS. Leader of the *Schutzstaffel* (250,000 strong). As chief of the GESTAPO (from 1936) responsible to Hitler alone. After the collapse of the Nazi regime, committed suicide in prison by swallowing poison hidden in a vial in his mouth.

hinc illae lacrymae (*Lat.* "hence those tears"). (Terence, *Andria,* I. i. 99.) This was the real offense; this was the true secret of the annoyance; this, *entre nous,* was the real source of the vexation.

Hind and Panther, The. A poem by DRYDEN (1687) in defense of the Catholic religion. The hind is the Latin Church, and the panther is the Church of England. James II is the lion which protects the hind from the bear (Independents), the wolf (Presbyterians), the hare (Quakers), the ape (Freethinkers), the boar (Anabaptists), and the fox (Arians).

Hindemith, Paul (1895–). German violist and composer. Associated with the "Musikalische JUGENDBEWEGUNG." Identified with the modern ideal of "Gebrauchsmusik" (functional everyday music). *Wir bauen eine Stadt* (*We are building a town;* children's opera, 1930); *Der Plöner Musiktag* (a work written while studied by the performing group); etc. In most of his work a representative of the ultramodern school of composition. Attacked in Third Reich as "cultural bolshevik." In U.S. (since 1933).

Hindenburg, Paul von (1847–1934). German general and elected Reich President (1925; re-elected, 1932). Remembered as victor over the Russians at Tannenberg (1914) and as having yielded to Nazi pressure by appointing Hitler as chancellor (1933). Memoirs, *Aus meinem Leben* (1920). Buried in the National War Memorial at Tannenberg.

Hindenburg line. In World War I, a strong line of defense established by the Germans under General von HINDENBURG (1916) across northeastern France from Lille through St.-

Gobain to Rethel, later to Vougiers and Metz. It was set up after von Falkenhayn's failure at Verdun when Hindenburg took his place as chief of general staff of German army.

Hind Horn. An English ballad dealing with an incident from the medieval romance KING HORN—the return of Horn, disguised as a palmer, to Rymenhild. This is considered to be a ballad written by a minstrel, rather than a genuine folk-ballad. See also BALLAD.

Hindu calendar. The year is divided into twelve months. An intercalary month occurs after every month in which there are two new moons, which is once in every three years. This inserted month takes the name of the month preceding it. The months, the first of which begins about April 11, are *Baisakh, Jeth, Asarh, Sawan, Bhadon, Asin* (*Kuar*), *Katik, Aghan, Pus, Magh, Phagun* (Phalgun), and *Chait.*

Hinduism. The religious and social system of India. Hinduism stresses birth and conduct, and has no founder or creed. On the social side it involves matters of caste. Belief in *karma* or the principle of cause as affecting a future existence, in *samsara,* or transmigration of souls, and in *nirvana,* or an ultimate state of salvation, is combined with image-worship, pilgrimage, YOGA, ascetic practices, and respect for some especial religious teacher or *guru.* Hinduism has a great number of sects, and their monistic or pantheistic philosophy is derived from the Vedanta or Upanishads which were organized by the philosopher Shankara. See VEDA.

Hindus, Maurice Gerschon (1891–). Russian-American writer. Author of *The Russian Peasant and the Revolution* (1920); *Humanity Uprooted* (1929); *Red Bread* (1931); *Green Worlds* (autobiography; 1938); *Hitler Cannot Conquer Russia* (1941); etc. In 1922 Hindus spent some time among the DUKHOBORS of Canada and wrote several articles about them.

Hinkle, Beatrice (1874–). First woman physician to hold a public health position. Opened in New York first psychotherapeutic clinic in America (1908). Author of *Re-creating the Individual.*

Hinkson, Mrs. **Katherine,** see TYNAN, K.

Hippe, Pribislav. In THE MAGIC MOUNTAIN by Thomas MANN, a boy of exotic appearance from whom the hero Hans CASTORP once borrowed a pencil in his schooldays and by whom he was oddly fascinated. When Castorp first encounters Clavdia CHAUCHAT, he is strangely reminded of Pribislav.

hippocampus. In Greek mythology, a fabulous sea horse; head and forequarters of a horse and tail of a dolphin. Represented as attached to chariots of Neptune and the tritons. Paintings of hippocampi were found in Pompeii.

hippocras. A highly spiced cordial much in favor in Europe during the Middle Ages. So called because it was strained through a linen bag known as HIPPOCRATES' sleeve.

Hippocrates (460?–?377 B.C.). Greek physician born on the island of Cos; known as "Father of Medicine." According to tradition, devised a code of medical ethics which imposed on his disciples the oath still administered to men about to enter medical practice and known as the HIPPOCRATIC OATH. Eighty-seven treatises are attributed to him. Some of his most famous aphorisms are:

> Life is short and the art is long.
> By opposites opposites are cured.
> Everything in excess is opposed to nature.

Hippocratic oath. An oath of allegiance to ethical professional standards administered to M.D. candidates at each commencement at Columbia, Cornell, and other universities. Its original version is attributed to HIPPOCRATES. The form now commonly used is:

> I do solemnly swear by that which I hold most sacred:
> That I will be loyal to the profession of medicine and just and generous to its members;
> That I will lead my life and practise my art in uprightness and honor;
> That into whatsoever house I shall enter, it shall be for the good of the sick to the utmost of my power, I holding myself aloof from wrong, from corruption, and from the temptation of others to vice;
> That I will exercise my art solely for the cure of my patients, and will give no drug, perform no operation for a criminal purpose, even if solicited, far less suggest it.
> That whatsoever I shall see or hear of the lives of men which is not fitting to be spoken, I will keep inviolably secret.
> These things I do promise, and in proportion as I am faithful to this my oath may happiness and good repute be ever mine—the opposite if I shall be forsworn.

Hippocrene (Gr. *hippos,* horse; *krene,* fountain). The fountain of the Muses on Mount Helicon, produced by a stroke of the hoof of Pegasus; hence, poetic inspiration.

Hippodamia. In classical mythology, is a daughter of Oenomaus and wife of Pelops. Pelops won her in a chariot race against Oenomaus, she having bribed a charioteer to remove a spoke from her father's chariot.

Hippogriff (Gr. *hippos,* "a horse"; *gryphos,* "a griffin"). The winged horse, whose father was a griffin and mother a filly. He is described in Ariosto's ORLANDO FURIOSO, where he carries Rogero away from his beloved Bradamant and into many strange adventures.

> So saying, he caught him up, and without wing
> Of hippogrif, bore through the air sublime,
> Over the wilderness and o'er the plain.
> Milton, *Paradise Regained,* iv, 541–3.

Hippolyta. In classic legend, Queen of the Amazons, and daughter of Mars. She was famous for a girdle given her by the war-god, which Hercules had to obtain possession of, as one of his twelve labors. Shakespeare has introduced Hippolyta in his MIDSUMMER

NIGHT'S DREAM, and betroths her to THESEUS, Duke of Athens; but according to most versions of the classic fable, it was her sister Antiope who married Theseus.

Hippolytus. In Greek myth, a son of Theseus. He provoked the anger of Venus by disregarding her love, and Venus, in revenge, made PHAEDRA, his step-mother, fall in love with him. When Hippolytus repulsed her advances she accused him to her husband of seeking to dishonor her. Theseus prayed Neptune to punish the young man, and the sea-god, while the young man was driving in his chariot, scared the horses with sea-calves. Hippolytus was thrown from the chariot and killed. This legend is the subject of tragedies by Euripides, Seneca and Racine, as well as by a number of lesser dramatists.

Hippomenes. In Greek legend, a prince who outstripped ATALANTA in a foot race, by dropping three golden apples, which she stopped to pick up. By this conquest he won Atalanta to wife.

Hiren. A strumpet. She was a character in Greene's lost play *The Turkish Mahomet and Hyren the Fair Greek* (ca. 1594), and is frequently referred to by Elizabethan dramatists.

Hirohito. Reign name **Showa** (1901–). Emperor of Japan (1926–), 124th in direct lineage. During his reign, the influence of the military became supreme and precipitated war with the United States.

Hiroshige, Ando (1797–1858). Japanese landscape painter; influenced Whistler in his moonlight scenes.

Hiroshima. Japanese city destroyed (1945) by first atomic bomb used in warfare. Title of book by John Hersey.

His Family. A novel by Ernest Poole (*Am.*, 1916), a story of Roger Gale, a man of fifty odd and his three daughters of diverse temperaments. The scene is laid in New York City. This novel was awarded the Pulitzer Prize in 1918.

Historia Regum Britanniae (History of the Kings of Britain) by Geoffrey of Monmouth (ca. 1100–1134), the chief source of Arthurian romance.

Histriomastix. An old play satirizing the stage, probably revised by MARSTON in 1599. In the same year it was satirized by Jonson in his *Every Man out of his Humour*. First printed in 1610.

Hitchcock, Alfred Joseph (1899–). British-born American motion-picture director. Began as a junior technician (1920). As director (from 1925), he produced among other pictures *The Lodger* (1925); *Juno and the Paycock* (1932); *The 39 Steps* (1935); *The Woman Alone* (1937); *The Lady Vanishes* (1938); *Rebecca* (1940); *Saboteur* (1942); *Lifeboat* (1943); etc., etc. A master of suspense, shock, and tension, who established a school of superior screen melodrama.

Hitchcock, Curtice (1892–1946). One of the most liberal and best liked of American publishers. Formerly with Macmillan and the Century Company, he formed with Eugene Reynal, in 1933, his own firm of Reynal and Hitchcock. This firm has published many outstanding books among which are the books of Saint-Exupéry, *The Century of the Common Man* by Henry A. Wallace, the poetry of Karl Shapiro, and *Strange Fruit* by Lillian Smith. Mr. Hitchcock believed in book publication being the testing ground for ideas.

Hitler, Adolf (1889–?1945). German chancellor and FÜHRER (1933–1945). Veteran of World War I. Founder of National Socialist German Workers party. Editor, *Der Völkische Beobachter* (1922). Unsuccessful *Beer Hall Putsch* (1923). Sentenced to five years' imprisonment. Wrote *Mein Kampf* at the fortress of Landau. Released after nine months. By 1933 his party was strong enough to force President von Hindenburg to appoint him chancellor. After von Hindenburg's death he combined the president's and the chancellor's powers in his own person with the title of *Führer*. His anti-Semitism and aggressive policies (designed to undo the treaty of Versailles) precipitated World War II. The data regarding his suicide at the time of the collapse of the Reich are not absolutely clear. His demonic power over his followers tallies with myth-forming elements in his career as also with his own superstitious nature. He was born in Braunau, married Eva Braun, chose brown as the color of his party, etc., etc.

Hit the Deck. A musical comedy (1927) by Herbert Fields, lyrics by Leo Robin and Clifford Guy, music by Vincent Youmans. Based on *Shore Leave* by Hubert Osborne.

H.M.S. His or Her Majesty's service or ship, as H.M.S. *Wellington.*

Hoare, Sir Samuel John Gurney (1880–). English statesman. Secretary of state for home affairs (1937–1939), Lord Privy Seal (1939–1940); ambassador to Spain (1940–1944).

Hobart, George Vere (1867–1926). Humorous writer on Baltimore *American*. Wrote "Dinkelspiel" papers; *The John Henry Books*, fifteen volumes of humorous stories; etc.

Hobbema, Meindert (1638–1709). Dutch landscape painter. Influenced by Ruisdael. The figures in some of his pictures are not by him. *The Hermitage, St. Petersburg* (1663) is in the collection of the New York Historical Society. *Avenue of Trees, Middleharnis,* is a popular painting.

Hobbes, Thomas (1588–1679). English philosopher. Friend of Harvey, Ben Jonson, Cowley, Sidney Godolphin, Selden, etc. His best-known work is *Leviathan, or the Matter, Form, and Power of a Commonwealth, Ecclesiastical and Civil* (1651), which contains his famous social contract theory. Hobbes was a forerunner of associational psychology and a leader of modern rationalism, insisting upon complete separation of philosophy and theology.

Hobbididance. In Shakespeare's tragedy KING LEAR, the prince of dumbness, and one of the five fiends that possessed "poor Tom." See MODU.

This name is taken from Harsnett's *Declaration of Egregious Popish Impostures* (1561–1631).

Hobbinol. The shepherd in Spenser's SHEPHERD'S CALENDAR who sings in praise of Eliza, queen of shepherds (Queen Elizabeth). He typifies Spenser's friend and correspondent, Gabriel HARVEY.

hobbyhorse. In medieval revels, notably the MORRIS DANCE, a person with a light framework suggesting the shape of a horse, so fixed around him that he appeared to be riding.

hobgoblin. An impish, ugly, and mischievous sprite, particularly Puck or ROBIN GOODFELLOW. The word is a variant of *Rob-Goblin*—i.e., the goblin Robin, just as Hodge is the nickname of Roger.

> Those that Hobgoblin call you, and sweet Puck,
> You do their work, and they shall have good luck.
> Shakespeare, *Midsummer Night's Dream*, ii, 1.

Hobhouse, John Cam. Baron **Broughton de Gyfford** (1786–1869). British administrator and writer. Byron's friend and executor, who advised destruction of his *Memoirs* (1824). Wrote Bonapartist account of the Hundred Days (1816); etc. In 1819 he was arrested for an anonymous pamphlet, *A Trifling Mistake in Thomas, Lord Erskine's recent Preface* . . . , in which the House of Commons saw a breach of privilege.

Hobson, Richmond Pearson (1870–1937). American naval officer who sank the collier *Merrimac* in Santiago harbor in an attempt to bottle up the Spanish fleet (1898). Resigned from Navy and entered House of Representatives. Congressional Medal of Honor (1933).

Hobson's choice. This or none; "take it or leave it." Tobias Hobson was a carrier and innkeeper at Cambridge in the 17th century, who erected the handsome conduit there, and settled "seven lays" of pasture ground towards its maintenance. "He kept a stable of forty good cattle, always ready and fit for travelling; but when a man came for a horse he was led into the stable, where there was great choice, but he obliged him to take the horse which stood nearest to the stable door; so that every customer was alike well served, according to his chance, and every horse ridden with the same justice." (*Spectator*, No. 509.)

Milton wrote two quibbling epitaphs upon this eccentric character.

Hoccleve, Thomas, see OCCLEVE, THOMAS.

hockamore or **hock.** Corrupted or short form of German *Hochheimer,* a fine Rhine wine, product of the "Hochheimer Domdekanei."

hocus pocus. The words formerly uttered by conjurers when performing a trick; hence, the trick or deception itself, also the juggler himself.

The phrase dates from the early 17th century, and is the opening of a ridiculous string of mock Latin used by some well-known performer: *hocus pocus, toutus talontus, vade celerita jubes.* The first two words may have been intended as a parody of *hoc est corpus,* occurring in the Roman communion service, while the whole was reeled off merely to occupy the attention of the audience.

Our word *hoax* is probably a contraction of *hocus pocus,* which also supplies the verb *to hocus,* to cheat, bamboozle, tamper with.

Hoder. The Scandinavian god of darkness, typical of night. He is called the blind old god. Balder is the god of light, typical of day. According to fable, Hoder killed Balder with an arrow made of mistletoe, but the gods restored him to life again.

> Hodur, the blind old god,
> Whose feet are shod with silence.
> Longfellow, *Tegner's Death.*

Hodge, Mr., and Mr. Hazard. A novel by Elinor WYLIE (1928).

Hodges, Courtney H. (1887–). American army officer. Rose through the ranks to brigadier general (1940). Chief of infantry and major general (1941–1943). Lieutenant general in command of 3rd Army (1943). After D-Day took BRADLEY's place as commander of 1st Army.

Hodgson, Ralph (1871–). English "Georgian" poet. Famous for his poems *Eve, The Bull,* and a few others which bid fair to become fixtures in all future anthologies of English verse.

Hodgson, William Hope (1877–1918). English writer of fantastic mysteries and sea stories. *The Ghost Pirates* (1909), *Men of the Deep Waters* (1914), *Captain Gault* (1917).

Hoffenstein, Samuel Goodman (1890–1947). Lithuanian-born American poet and humorist. Best known for his *Poems in Praise of Practically Nothing* (1928).

Hoffmann, August Heinrich, known as **Hoffmann von Fallersleben** (1798–1874). German poet, philologist, and historian of literature. As a political refugee in British Helgoland he wrote "Deutschland, Deutschland über alles" (1841). About this song, the poet's great-granddaughter, Ursula S. Lamb, wrote: "In it he admonished the Germans to make justice and liberty the basis for a united Germany as against the oppression then existing in some 300-odd German principalities. The song remained in official disgrace under the later German emperors until President Ebert recognized it as the German national anthem of the Weimar Republic in 1919. The first line of the first stanza referred to the hope Hoffmann held in 1841 for a united Germany above (über) all the many reactionary German states. The misunderstanding of those words has led to continued abuse of the hymn, especially in translation, which means doing an injustice to its origin and to its meaning."

Hoffman, Ernst Theodor Amadeus (1776–1822). German author, known for his popular romances in the GOTHIC tradition. Among them are *Phantasiestücke* (1814–1815); *Elixire des Teufels* (1815–1816); *Serapionsbrüder* (1819–1821); *Kater Murr* (1821–1822). See also TALES OF HOFFMAN.

Hoffmann, Malvina (1887–). American sculptor. Awarded 1st prize in Paris (1911) for her *Russian Dancers.* Author of *Heads and Tales* (1930), an autobiography, the title of which alludes to the fact that she had been commissioned to execute 101 racial types in bronze for the Field Museum in Chicago.

Hofmannsthal, Hugo von (1874–1929). Austrian romantic-symbolic poet and dramatist. Descendant of a Spanish-Jewish family. Close collaborator with Richard Strauss, the composer. Wrote words for *Salome, Elektra, Der Rosenkavalier,* etc. A brilliant classical scholar. It has been said of his work that it follows the leitmotiv of Calderon's *"La vida es sueño, sueños vida son."* In it dreams are a higher form of reality, and realities are the foil of a true dream.

Hofmann, Josef (1876–). Polish pianist. Infant prodigy. Since 1901, a favorite concert pianist in the U.S. Also a composer. Author of *Piano-Playing with Piano-Questions Answered* (1907) and other textbooks.

hog. In slang use, a *hog* is a gluttonous, greedy, or unmannered person, and motorists who, caring nothing for the rights or convenience of other travelers, drive in a selfish and reckless manner, wanting the whole road to themselves, are called *road-hogs.*

to go the whole hog. To do the thing completely and thoroughly, without compromise or reservation; to go the whole way. Hence the expression *whole-hogger,* one who will see the thing through to the bitter end, and "damn the consequences." At the time of Mr. Joseph Chamberlain's great agitation on behalf of Protection (1903, *et seq.*) those who advocated a complete tariff of protective duties regardless of possible "reciprocity" were called the *whole-hoggers.*

Hogarth, William (1697–1764). English painter and engraver. His reputation was established through the plates for Butler's *Hudibras* (1726). His best-known series are *The Harlot's Progress* (1732) and *The Rake's Progress* (1735). He secured the passage of an act, known as Hogarth's Act (1735), which protects designers from piracy. Portraits, historical pictures. Supreme pictorial satirist and great social force. His object was "to show vice her own feature, scorn her own image." Author of *The Analysis of Beauty.*

Hogben, Lancelot Thomas (1895–). English writer. *Mathematics for the Million* (1936); *Science for the Citizen* (1938); etc. Other more or less alliterative titles of his are *Nature and Nurture* (1933); *Retreat from Reason* (1936); and *Dangerous Thoughts* (1939). Cf. his *Author in Transit* (1940).

Hogen-Mogen. A High Mightiness, originally of the Netherlands States-General; hence, the Dutch or a Dutchman. The term is a corruption of Dutch *hoogmogend,* "high in might." Colloquially it means strong and can be applied to liquor.

Hogg, James (1770–1835). English poet, called the ETTRICK SHEPHERD because he was self-educated and inherited the occupation of shepherd from his family. He is known for his celebrations in dialect verse of Scotch rural scenes and rural pursuits, and his treatments of the Celtic fork-lore tradition. He was encouraged by Sir Walter SCOTT and in his later life was associated with BLACKWOOD'S MAGAZINE. See also NOCTES AMBROSIANAE.

Hogg, Thomas Jefferson (1792–1862). English lawyer and intimate friend of Shelley. Author of two volumes of a biography of Shelley (1858).

Hogni, see HAGEN.

Hohensteil Schwangau, Prince. The speaker in Browning's poem *Prince Hohensteil Schwangau, the Savior of Society* (1872) in which the Prince reviews his past life. The character is usually regarded as drawn from Napoleon III.

Hohenzollern. German princely family, deriving its name from the Swabian castle of Zollern, later Hohenzollern, first mentioned in the eleventh century. It furnished the dukes of Brandenburg (from 1415), the kings of

Prussia (from 1701), and the German emperors (from 1871).

hoi polloi (*Gr.* The commonalty, the many). In English University slang the "poll men," or those who take degrees without "honors."

hokku. A form of Japanese poetry, stating in three lines (5, 7, 5 syllables) a complete picture, mood, etc. An example by Masaoka Shiki (1867–1902) reads:

Kumo no mine
shiraho minami ni
muragareri.

Mountain-peaks of cloud;
White sails, in the south,
Crowded together.

The hokku looks accidentally like a truncated TANKA, but it is a complete form in itself.

Hokusai (1760–1849). Japanese artist. His drawings and prints exerted a lasting influence on the art of other countries. *The Mangwa* or *Ten Thousand Sketches* is a huge collection, published (till 1836) in fifteen volumes. His best-known work are *The Hundred Views of Mount Fuji* (1835).

Holbein, Hans, the Younger (1497?–1543). German portrait and historical painter, and wood engraver. Court painter to Henry VIII of England. Portraits of Erasmus, Sir Thomas More, Anne of Cleves, Henry VIII, etc. Best-known for his series of woodcuts, *The Dance of Death* (first published in 1538). Also religious paintings.

Holda, see HULDA.

Holden, Eben, see EBEN HOLDEN.

Holden, Raymond Peckham (1894–). American poet and novelist. Author of mystery novels under the pseudonym of Richard Peckham. First wife, Louise BOGAN (divorced); second wife, Sara Henderson HAY. Holden's best work in poetry is in *The Arrow in the Heel* (1940); in prose, in *Chance Has a Whip* (1935).

Hölderlin, Friedrich (1770–1843). German poet, author of *Hyperion,* a romance in the form of letters (2 vols.; 1797, 1799). His poetry has been called the last and most perfect flower of the Greek tradition. Like all supreme poetry, it can only be approximated in translation. The last forty years of Hölderlin's life were spent in mental disequilibrium.

hole. *A better 'ole.* Any situation that is preferable to that occupied at present. The phrase came into being during World War I, and the allusion is to an incident—pictured by Captain Bruce Bairnsfather—in which a soldier, Old Bill, "taking cover" in a shell-hole objects to leaving it until a "better 'ole" is provided.

Holger Danske. The Danish name of OGIER THE DANE, one of the most venturesome of Charlemagne's paladins.

Holgrave. The young daguerreotypist who marries Phoebe in Hawthorne's HOUSE OF THE SEVEN GABLES.

Holinshed, Raphael (d. ca. 1582). English clergyman and historian, known for his CHRONICLES OF ENGLAND, SCOTLAND, AND IRELAND (1578).

Holland, Josiah Gilbert (1819–1881). American writer, author of *Timothy Titcomb's Letters* (1858), *Arthur Bonnicastle,* and the metrical narrative BITTER SWEET (1858). Many of his early writings appeared under the pseudonym of Timothy TITCOMB.

Hollar, Wenceslaus or **Wenzel** (1607–1677). Bohemian engraver. Pupil of Matthäus Merian at Frankfort. Stayed in England (from 1635). Illustrated Dugdale's *History of St. Paul's Cathedral* and designed a map of London after the great fire (1666); etc.

Hollingsworth. The ardent but ruthless social reformer who plays a leading part in Hawthorne's BLITHEDALE ROMANCE.

Holloway, Emory (1885–). American educator and Whitman authority. Pulitzer prize for biography (1927) for *Whitman—An Interpretation in Narrative.*

Hollow Men, The. Poem by T. S. ELIOT, depicting the spiritual emptiness and doom of the 20th century as he saw it through the symbol of a scarecrow.

Hollywood. A word sometimes used as synonymous with the American motion-picture industry, from Hollywood, Cal., a suburb of Los Angeles where many of the large motion-picture studios are located.

Holm, Saxe. See JACKSON, HELEN HUNT.

Holmes, Oliver Wendell (1809–1894). American author, man of letters, and lecturer, a professor of anatomy and physiology at Harvard (1847–1882) and a leader in the Unitarian movement against CALVINISM. See UNITARIANISM. He is known for the humor and satire of his essays and verses. His works include: THE AUTOCRAT OF THE BREAKFAST TABLE (1858), a famous series of essays, imitated by *The Professor at the Breakfast Table* (1860), *The Poet at the Breakfast Table* (1872), and *Over the Teacups* (1891); ELSIE VENNER (1861), THE GUARDIAN ANGEL (1867), and *A Mortal Antipathy* (1885), novels; *Soundings from the Atlantic* (1864) and *Pages from an Old Volume of Life* (1883), essays; *Songs in Many Keys* (1862), *The Iron Gate* (1880), and *Before the Curfew* (1888), collections of essays. He also wrote biographies, lectures, and numerous public addresses, as well as regular contributions to the ATLANTIC MONTHLY, which he named. Holmes' best-known single poems are: OLD IRONSIDES (1830); *The Chamber'd Nautilus;* and *The Deacon's Masterpiece* (1858), see ONE-HOSS SHAY.

Oliver Wendell Holmes (1841–1935), his son, was a law professor at Harvard and later Associate Justice of the U.S. Supreme Court (1902–1932), known for his learning and his liberal opinions.

Holmes, Sherlock. The most famous detective of fiction; a creation of Sir Arthur Conan DOYLE, who introduced him first in his *Study in Scarlet* (1887). His adventures are continued in *The Sign of the Four* (1889), *The Adventures of Sherlock Holmes* (1891), *The Memoirs of Sherlock Holmes* (1894), *The Hound of the Baskervilles* (1902), *The Return of Sherlock Holmes* (1905), *The Valley of Fear* (1915); *His Last Bow* (1917); and *The Case Book of Sherlock Holmes* (1927). Although only an amateur, Sherlock Holmes has such brilliant analytical faculties and such indefatigable interest in any detective problem as such, that he frequently puts Scotland Yard to shame. He is abrupt in manner, a victim of the cocaine habit and otherwise very much a law unto himself. His admiring friend, Dr. Watson, usually records his triumphs. It is said that Dr. Joseph Bell, a physician and instructor of Conan Doyle, was the original model from which the figure of Sherlock Holmes was elaborated. In the 20th century, Sherlock Holmes became a popular detective character in motion pictures and radio also. A club of New York enthusiasts, The Baker Street Irregulars, publishes a quarterly, *The Baker Street Journal.*

Holofernes. (1) In Shakespeare's LOVE'S LABOUR'S LOST, a pedantic schoolmaster, who speaks like a dictionary. The character has been considered by some students as a caricature of John Florio, a teacher of Italian in London and famous translator of MONTAIGNE, who published, in 1598, a dictionary called *A World of Words.* He may have provoked the retort by condemning wholesale the English dramas, which, he said, were "neither right comedies, nor right tragedies, but perverted histories without decorum." *Holofernes* is, according to this speculation, an imperfect anagram of "Joh'nes Florio," the first and last letters being omitted. According to another theory the character may have been suggested by the pedantic tutor *Holoferne* in Rabelais' GARGANTUA AND PANTAGRUEL. The following sentence is a specimen of the style in which Holofernes talked:

> The deer was . . . in *sanguis* (blood), ripe as a pomewater who now hangeth like a jewel in the ear of *caelo* (the sky, the welkin, the heaven); and anon falleth like a crab on the face of *terra* (the soil, the land, the earth).—Shakespeare, *Love's Labour's Lost,* act iv. sc. 2.

(2) The name of the general slain by the Jewish heroine JUDITH.

Holt, Felix. The hero of George Eliot's FELIX HOLT, THE RADICAL, described as a "shaggy headed, strong limbed person . . . a peculiar-looking person but not insignificant."

> His strong health, his renunciation of selfish claims, his habitual preoccupation with large thoughts and with purposes independent of everyday casualties, secured him a fine and even temper, free from moodiness or irritability. He was full of longsuffering toward his unwise mother.—Ch. xxx.

Holt, Henry (1840–1926). American publisher and novelist. Organized firm of Henry Holt and Co. (1873).

Holtby, Winifred (1898–1935). English novelist who died just as her powers were maturing. *South Riding* (1936), her "magnificent epitaph." Cf. *Testament of Friendship* by Vera BRITTAIN.

holy.

Holy Alliance. A league formed by Russia, Austria, and Prussia in 1815 to regulate the affairs of Europe after the fall of Napoleon "by the principles of Christian charity"—meaning that every endeavor would be made to stabilize the existing dynasties and to resist all change. It lasted until 1830, and was joined by all the European sovereigns except those of England and Turkey, and the Pope.

Holy City. That city which the religious consider most especially connected with their religious faith, thus:

> *Allahabad* is the Holy City of the Mohammedans of India.
> *Benares,* of the Hindus.
> *Cuzco,* of the ancient Incas.
> *Fez,* of the Western Arabs.
> *Jerusalem,* of the Jews and Christians.
> *Kairwan,* near Tunis. It contains the Okbar Mosque in which is the tomb of the prophet's barber.
> *Mecca* and *Medina,* of the Mohammedans.
> *Moscow* and *Kiev,* of the Russians, the latter being the cradle of Christianity in Russia.

Holy Cross or *Holy Rood Day.* September 14, the day of the Feast of the Exaltation of the Cross, called by the Anglo-Saxons "Rood-mass-day," and kept in honor of the exposition of a portion of the true Cross in the basilica erected at Jerusalem by the Empress Helen (ca. 326). Another event connected with it is the recovery of the piece of the Cross, which had been stolen from Jerusalem in 614 by Chosroes, king of Persia, by Heraclius in 629.

Holy Family. The infant Savior and his attendants, as Joseph, Mary, Elizabeth, Anne, the mother of Mary, and John the Baptist. All the five figures are not always introduced in pictures of the Holy Family.

Holy Ghost. The third Person of the Trinity, the Divine Spirit, represented in art as a dove.

The seven gifts of the Holy Ghost are: (1) counsel, (2) the fear of the Lord, (3) fortitude, (4) piety, (5) understanding, (6) wisdom, and (7) knowledge.

Holy Land.

(1) Christians call *Palestine* the Holy Land, because it was the site of Christ's birth, ministry, and death.

(2) Mohammedans call *Mecca* the Holy Land, because Mahomet was born there.

(3) The Chinese Buddhists call *India* the Holy Land, because it was the native land of Sakya-muni, the BUDDHA.

(4) The Greek considered *Elis* as Holy Land, from the temple of Olympian Zeus and the sacred festival held there every four years.

Holy League. A combination formed by Pope Julius II in 1511 with Venice, Maximilian of Germany, Ferdinand III of Spain, and various Italian princes, to drive the French out of Italy.

Other leagues have been called by the same name, particularly that formed in the reign of Henri III of France (1576), under the auspices of Henri de Guise, "for the defence of the Holy Catholic Church against the encroachments of the reformers," i.e., for annihilating the Huguenots.

Holy of Holies. The innermost apartment of the Jewish temple, in which the ark of the covenant was kept, and into which only the high priest was allowed to enter, and that but once a year—the Day of Atonement. Hence, a private apartment, a *sanctum sanctorum.*

Holy Roman Empire. The name given to the often very nebulous confederation of Central European States that subsisted, either in fact or in theory, from 800 A. D., when Charlemagne was crowned Emperor of the West, until the abdication of Francis II (Francis I of Austria) in 1806. It was first called "Holy" by BARBAROSSA, in allusion both to its reputed divine appointment, and to the interdependence of Empire and Church. It comprised the German-speaking peoples of Central Europe, and was ruled by an elected Emperor, who claimed to be the representative of the ancient Roman Emperors.

The name has been sometimes brought forward as an excellent instance of contradiction in terms, the confederation not properly being entitled to any one of the three epithets—"Holy," "Roman," or "Empire."

Holy Thursday. ASCENSION DAY, i.e., the Thursday but one before Whitsun, is what is generally meant by this among Anglicans; but by Roman Catholics and others MAUNDY THURSDAY, i.e., the Thursday before Good Friday, is sometimes called Holy Thursday.

Holy War. A war in which religious fanaticism plays, or purports to play, a considerable part. The Crusades, the Thirty Years War, the wars against the Albigenses, etc., were so called. A holy war launched by Mohammedans against Christians is called a *jehad.*

Holy Week. PASSION WEEK, the last week in Lent. It begins on Palm Sunday; the fourth day is called "Spy Wednesday"; the fifth is "Maundy Thursday"; the sixth is "Good Friday"; and the last "Holy Saturday" or the "Great Sabbath."

Holy Week has been called *Hebdomada Muta* (Silent Week); *Hebdomada Inofficiosa* (Vacant Week); *Hebdomada Penitentialis; Hebdomada Indulgentiae; Hebdomada Luctuosa; Hebdomada Nigra;* and *Hebdomada Ultima.*

Holy Writ. The Bible.

> Trifles light as air
> Are to the jealous confirmations strong
> As proofs of holy writ.
>
> Shakespeare, *Othello,* iii. 3.

Holy Bottle. See under BACBUC.

Holy Living and Dying. A famous religious work by Jeremy TAYLOR (1650).

Holy Moses. Not only an exclamation but also, in World War II, a high-velocity aircraft rocket weighing about 140 pounds.

Holy Roman Empire or **Heiliges Römisches Reich Deutscher Nation.** The medieval empire, which, from the time of Charlemagne, came to be regarded as the Christian heir of the ancient empire of Rome and at the same time as the secular counterpart of the Church. In the ideal conception it was the *imperium Dei* and hence indivisible and universal. It survived till 1806. The Third Reich of Hitler can be understood as a perverted reincarnation of it.

Holyrood Palace. An ancient royal palace in Edinburgh, Scotland, developed from what was originally **Holyrood Abbey** (founded 1128). At one time occupied by Mary Queen of Scots. It suffered at the hands of the English in 1544 and was completely destroyed by a Protestant mob in 1688.

Holy War, The. An allegory by John BUNYAN (1682), depicting the capture of the city of Mansoul (man's soul, or soul of mankind) by Diabolus, its siege and rescue by an army led by Emmanuel, son of the builder of the city, its weakening and falling into evil, and the second assault by Diabolus, who is ultimately defeated by Emmanuel. Bunyan's experiences in the English Civil War contributed to this work.

Holywell Street. An old London street that used to run parallel with the Strand, from St. Dunstan's Church to St. Clement Danes, and was thrown into the Strand itself by the improvements that took place in that quarter in the closing years of the 19th century, and that resulted in the formation of Kingsway and Aldwych. It was commonly known as "Booksellers' Row," from the large number of second-hand booksellers who had their shops there. (This name has since been transferred to Charing Cross Road, to which many of the booksellers migrated.)

Holy Willie. A religious hypocrite. From the poem *Holy Willie's Prayer* by Robert Burns.

Home, Daniel Dunglas (1833–1886). Scottish spiritualist medium. Subject of Robert Browning's poem, *Sludge the Medium* (1864). Séances at courts and in public in U.S., England, France, Prussia, etc. Author of *Incidents of my Life* (1863); etc.

Homebred, Jedediah. A Yankee man-of-all-work in the play *The Green Mountain Boy* written by J. S. Jones (*Am.,* 1833) for the actor George Hill.

Home of Lost Causes. Oxford University, so called by Matthew ARNOLD.

Home, Sweet Home. This popular English song first appears in the opera *Clari, the Maid of Milan* (Covent Garden, 1823). The words are by John Howard Payne, an American, and the music by Sir Henry Bishop, who professed to have founded it on a Sicilian air. Cf. *Long, Long Ago,* by Alexander WOOLLCOTT.

> Mid pleasures and palaces though we may roam
> Be it ever so humble, there's no place like home.

Homer. The name given to the entirely unknown poet—or group of poets perhaps—to whom is assigned the authorship of the ILIAD and the ODYSSEY, the greatest monuments of ancient or modern epic poetry. It is much doubted whether any such person ever existed, but the name rests on very ancient tradition, and the date at which the poems are thought to have received their final shape is conjecturally put at anywhere between the 12th and the 9th century B. C.

Homer's birthplace is quite unknown. The old rhyme, founded on an epigram preserved by Aulus Gellius, says,

> Seven cities warred for Homer being dead,
> Who living had no roof to shroud his head.
> Heywood, *Hierarchie of the Blessed Angels* (1635).

the "seven cities" being Smyrna, Rhodes, Colophon, Salamis, Chios, Argos, and Athens.

Homer sometimes nods. Even the best of us is liable to make mistakes. The line is from Horace's *De Arte Poetica,* 359:

> Quandoque bonus dormitat Homerus!
> Verum operi longo fas es obrepere somnum.
> (Sometimes good Homer himself even nods; but in so long a work it is allowable if there should be a drowsy interval or so.)

the British Homer. Milton (1608–1674).

the Celtic Homer. Ossian, son of Fingal, King of Morven.

the Homer of dramatic poets. SHAKESPEARE is so called by Dryden (1564–1616).

> "Shakespeare was the Homer of our dramatic poets; Jonson was the Virgil. I admire rare Ben, but I love Shakespeare."—Dryden.

Homer of Ferrara. ARIOSTO is so called by TASSO.

Homer of the Franks. Charlemagne called Angilbert (d. 814) his *Homer.*

the Oriental Homer. Firdusi (940–1020), the Persian poet, who wrote the *Shah Nameh* (1010), a history of the Persian kings. It contains 120,000 verses, and was the work of over thirty years.

the Homer of philosophers. Plato (429–347 B. C.).

the prose Homer of human nature. Henry FIELDING, so called by BYRON.

the Scottish Homer. William WILKIE, author of *The Epigoniad.*

Homeric laughter. "Laughter unquenchable," like that of the gods.

Homeric verse. Hexameter.

Homer, Winslow (1836–1910). American painter, notably of marines. *The Gulf Stream; North Easter; Cannon Rock; Maine Coast* and twelve fine water colors now in the Metropolitan Museum of Art, New York City. Paintings in various galleries including Corcoran Art Gallery, Washington, D.C., and Luxembourg Museum, Paris, France.

home rule. Local autonomy of an integral part of a state or empire. Fought for for years in Ireland, in her long and bloody struggle for independence from Britain. The term is applicable to the form of government adopted successfully by Canada, Australia, and the Union of South Africa as integral parts of the British Empire.

Homespun, Zekiel. In George Colman's comedy THE HEIR AT LAW (1808), a farmer of Castleton who goes to London to seek his fortune. He was one of the first "country jakes" on the English stage.

Cicely Homespun. The sister of Zekiel, an innocent country girl betrothed to Dick Dowlas.

Homunculus. In the second part of Goethe's FAUST, a small human being created artificially by Faust's famulus, Wagner.

Hone, Philip (1780–1851). American businessman. From 1828 to 1851 he kept a *Diary* which is a valuable source of information on New York local life and the beginnings of the Whig Party.

Honegger, Arthur (1892–). Eminent French composer, leader of *Les Six,* a group of futurist French musicians including Auric, Durey, Milhaud, Poulenc and Taillefere. He appeared in the U.S. (1929) as conductor of his own works, including the symphonic poem, *Pastorale d'été,* and the tone poem, *Pacific 231,* which "impersonates" a modern locomotive.

Honeycomb, Will. In the SPECTATOR, a fine gentleman, and great authority on the fashions of the day. He was one of the members of the imaginary club from which the *Spectator* issued.

Honeyman, Charles. In Thackeray's novel, THE NEWCOMES, a free-and-easy clergyman, of social habits and fluent speech.

Miss Honeyman. The likable old sister of Rev. Charles Honeyman and aunt of Clive Newcome. She keeps lodgers in Steyne Gardens and is known by admiring tradespeople as "the Duchess."

Honeywood. The titular hero of GOLDSMITH's comedy *The Good-Natured Man* (1767), a young man whose motto is "universal benevolence." He is taken advantage of continuously, until his uncle, Sir William Honeywood, allows him to be arrested for endorsing a bill for an absconder. After this wholesome experience he decides to mend his ways and confesses, "though inclined to the right, I had not courage to condemn the wrong. My charity was but injustice, my benevolence but weakness and my friendship but credulity." He marries Miss Richland, who had been instrumental in his reform. Honeywood is considered in some respects a self-portrait of the author.

Honorable Peter Stirling, The. A novel by Paul Leicester FORD (1894) dealing with ward politics. Its hero, Peter Stirling, is said to represent the young Grover Cleveland. After his graduation from Harvard, he settles in New York, takes an active and genuine interest in the lives of the people in his East Side ward and rises to eminence from the anomalous position of political boss.

Honoria. The heroine of Dryden's THEODORE AND HONORIA.

honorificabilitudinitatibus. A made up word on the Lat. *honorificabilitudo,* honorableness, which frequently occurs in Elizabethan plays as an instance of sesquipedalian pomposity, etc.

Hooch, Pieter de (1629–after 1677). Dutch genre painter.

Hood, Thomas (1799–1845). English poet, known for his humorous and humanitarian poems, the most outstanding of which are *The Song of the Shirt* (1843), dealing with the wretched conditions of London workers, and THE BRIDGE OF SIGHS (1844).

Hook, Captain. In Barrie's PETER PAN, Peter's terrible one-handed enemy with a hook for his missing hand.

Hook, Theodore Edward (1788–1841). English humorist and novelist. Editor of *John Bull* (from 1820) and *New Monthly Magazine* (1836–1841). Wrote under several pseudonyms. He was the original of Mr. Wagg in Thackeray's *Vanity Fair.*

Hooker, Richard (1554?–1600). English scholar and theologian, author of *The Laws of Ecclesiastical Polity* (1594–1597), a famous prose defense of the Church of England.

Hooker, Thomas (1586?–1647). Congregational clergyman in England. Migrated to Connecticut. Active in framing what became a constitution for Connecticut (1639). Favored a confederation of New England settlements, as realized (1643) in the "United Colonies of New England." Author (with John Cotton) of *Survey of the Summe of Church Discipline* (1648).

Hooker, (William) Brian (1880–). American poet and writer of period stories. His opera *Mona* was awarded the prize in the Metropolitan Opera Company competition (1911). His opera *Fairyland* won the prize of the American Opera Association (1915). He also wrote *Morven and the Grail* (1915), and a commemoration poem, *A. D. 1919,* with music by Horatio Parker; etc.

hooligan. A violent young rough. The term originated in the last years of the 19th century from the name of one of this class. From it is derived the substantive *hooliganism.*

The original *Hooligans* were a spirited Irish family of that name whose proceedings enlivened the drab monotony of life in Southwark towards the end of the 19th century. The word is younger than the Australian *larrikin,* of doubtful origin, but older than Fr. *apache*—Ernest Weekley, *Romance of Words* (1912).

Hoosier.

Hoosier State. Indiana. See STATES. A native of the state is called a *Hoosier.*

Hoosier poet. James Whitcomb RILEY (1853–1916), so called because he was a native of Indiana.

Hoosier Schoolmaster, The. The title of a widely read story of frontier life in the Middle West by Edward EGGLESTON (1871), which deals with the life of the schoolmaster, Ralph Hartsook, in the days before the Civil War. It was followed by *The Hoosier Schoolboy.* Meredith Nicholson was the author of *A Hoosier Chronicle* (*Am.,* 1912).

Hoother, Jarl van. See EARWICKER, HUMPHREY CHIMPDEN; HOWTH CASTLE.

Hoover, Herbert Clark (1874–). Thirty-first president of the United States (1929–1933). Republican. Food and relief administrator in various capacities during and after World War I and after World War II.

Hope, Anthony, see HAWKINS, Sir ANTHONY HOPE.

Hope, Bard of. See under BARD.

Hope, Evelyn, see EVELYN HOPE.

Hope, Laurence. Real name **Adela Florence Cory** (1865–1904). English poet. Married

Colonel Nicolson of the Bengal army; poisoned herself after his death. *The Garden of Kama* (1901); *Stars of the Desert* (1903); *Indian Love* (1905); *Songs from the Garden of Kama* (1908).

Hopeful. In Bunyan's PILGRIM'S PROGRESS, a companion of Christian after the death of Faithful at Vanity Fair.

Hopkins, don't hurry. A satirical reproof to those who are not prompt in their payments. It is said that one Hopkins, of Kentucky, gave a creditor a promissory note on which was this memorandum, "The said Hopkins is not to be hurried in paying the above."

Hopkins, Arthur Melancthon (1878–). American theatrical producer of plays by IBSEN, O'NEILL, etc.

Hopkins, Gerard Manley (1844–1889). English poet, at Oxford a student of Walter PATER and Jowett, later converted to Roman Catholicism (1866) and inducted into the Jesuit order (1868), after which he became a follower of Cardinal NEWMAN. He is known for the power and striking originality of his lyrics, which deal with nature and religion and show the influence of the METAPHYSICAL POETS in many respects, especially that of George HERBERT. His poetry is distinguished by an intricate type of rhythm which he called "SPRUNG RHYTHM," and by an extremely individual technique of elliptical phrasing and compound metaphor capable of great concentration of meaning. His work, contained in a single volume entitled *Poems* and published in 1918, influenced in varying degrees a number of 20th-century British and American poets, notably W. H. AUDEN. Hopkins became a professor of Greek in Dublin University in 1884, and was a friend of Robert BRIDGES and Coventry PATMORE, the former serving as editor of his poems. Volumes of Hopkins' correspondence were published in 1935 and 1938, and his *Notebooks and Papers* in 1937.

Hopkins, Harry Lloyd (1890–1946). American administrator and politician. Special assistant to President Franklin D. ROOSEVELT (1942); etc.

Hopkins, Johns (1795–1873). American financier and philanthropist. Gave a free hospital to the city of Baltimore, Md., and over three million dollars to found Johns Hopkins University.

Hopkins, Mark (1802–1887). American educator. President, Williams College (1836–1872). Inspired teacher and lecturer. Author of many books on moral and religious subjects. Member, American Hall of Fame.

Hopkinson, Francis (1737–1791). American politician and writer. Signer of Declaration of Independence. Had an important part in designing the American flag (1777). Wrote a famous satire in verse, *The Battle of the Kegs* (1778).

Hop-o'-my-Thumb. A pigmy or midget. The name has been given to several dwarfs, as well as being commonly used as a generic term. Tom Thumb in the well known nursery tale is quite another character. He was the son of peasants, knighted by King Arthur, and killed by a spider.

Horace. Short English form of *Quintus Horatius Flaccus* (65–8 B. C.). Roman lyricist and satirist. Under patronage of MAECENAS. Extant among his works are two books of satires, one of epodes, four of odes, two of epistles, and the *Ars Poetica.*

Horace of England. (1) Ben Jonson (1574–1637), nicknamed Horace by Dekker in the so-called "War of the Theaters";

(2) Cowley (1618–1667), called by the Duke of Buckingham "the Pindar, Horace and Virgil of England."

Horace of France. (1) Jean Macrinus or Salmon (1490–1557).

(2) Pierre Jean de Béranger (1780–1857), also called the *French Burns.*

the Portuguese Horace. A. Ferreira (1528–1569).

the Spanish Horace. Both Lupercio Argensola and his brother Bartolome are so called.

Horace. (1) A famous tragedy by Corneille. See HORATIUS.

(2) The lover of AGNES in Molière's *École des femmes.*

Horae. In classic myth, the Hours, goddesses of change in the seasons and the works of men. They were the daughters of JUPITER and Themis.

Horatii, the Three. See under HORATIUS.

Horatio. In Shakespeare's HAMLET, the intimate friend of Hamlet.

Horatius. A legendary hero of ancient Rome, the subject of Corneille's tragedy *Horace* (1639), and Whitehead's *Roman Father* (1741) adapted from the French play. The tragedies are based on the well-known legend of the pitched battle between the three Roman Horatii and the three Albanian Curiatii. Horace, "the Roman father," shows only pride that his sons have been chosen to uphold the honor of Rome, but his daughter Horatia (in Corneille's drama, *Camille*), who is the betrothed of Caius Curiatus, is more human. When her lover is slain, she so provokes her single surviving brother by her taunts that he kills her. Horatius sternly gives up his son to justice, but the people refuse to have him killed.

Horatius Cocles (Horatius, the One-eyed). The hero of one of the best known of Macaulay's *Lays of Ancient Rome* (1842). He and two other Romans hold the bridge against the advancing Etruscan army led by Lars Porsena until his comrades on the Roman bank succeed in breaking down the bridge. He orders his two companions to make good their escape, and they have just crossed the bridge when it falls in with a crash. Horatius then throws himself into the Tiber and swims safely to shore amid the applauding shouts of both armies.

Hore-Belisha, Leslie (1898–). English political leader. As secretary for war (1937–1940) wrought reforms in British army.

horn.

the Horn Gate. See DREAMS, GATE OF.

horn of fidelity. MORGAN LE FAY sends a horn to King Arthur, which has the following "virtue": No lady can drink out of it who is not "to her husband true"; all others who attempt to drink are sure to spill what it contains. This horn is carried to King Mark, and "his queene with a hundred ladies more" tries the experiment, but only four manage to "drinke cleane." Ariosto's *enchanted cup* possesses a similar spell. See also MANTLE OF FIDELITY.

horn of plenty. AMALTHEA'S HORN, the cornucopia, an emblem of plenty.

Ceres is represented with a ram's horn in her left arm, filled with fruits and flowers; sometimes they are being poured on the earth, and sometimes they are piled high in the horn as in a basket. Diodorus (iii. 68) says the horn is one from the head of the goat by which Jupiter was suckled.

Moses' Horns, see MOSES.

to come or *be squeezed out at the little end of the horn.* To come off badly in some affair; get the worst of it; fail conspicuously.

to draw in one's horns. To retract, or mitigate, a pronounced opinion; to restrain pride. In French, *rentrer les cornes.* The allusion is to the snail.

to put to the horn. To denounce as a rebel, or pronounce a person an outlaw, for not answering to a summons. In Scotland the messenger-at-arms used to go to the Cross of Edinburgh and give three blasts with a horn before he proclaimed judgment of outlawry.

to the horns of the altar. (Lat. *usque ad aras amicus.*) Your friend even to the horns of the altar—i.e., through thick and thin. In swearing, the ancient Romans held the horns of the altar, and one who did so in testimony of friendship could not break his oath without calling on himself the vengeance of the angry gods.

(The altar in Solomon's temple had a projection at each of the four corners called "horns"; these were regarded as specially sacred, and probably typified the great might of God.)

> Upon Thine altar's horn of gold
> Help me to lay my trembling hold.
> Keble, *Christian Year; 1st Sun. aft. Easter.*

to wear the horns. To be a cuckold.

Horn, Alfred Aloysius (1861?–1931). Known as "Trader Horn." See under Ethelreda LEWIS.

Horn, King. The hero of a French metrical romance of the 13th century, and the original of our *Horne Childe,* generally called *The Geste of Kyng Horn.* The nominal author is a certain Mestre Thomas.

Horn's father, Murry, king of Suddene, is killed by invading Saracens, and Horn is set adrift in a boat. He lands at Westernesse, is welcomed by the King, and falls in love with the King's daughter, Rymenhild. This attachment causes his banishment, but after seven years, filled with the usual adventures, he returns just in time to save Rymenhild from a forced marriage and to marry her himself. Horn then leaves to recover his father's kingdom, and having done so comes back for his wife, arriving just in time to save her from a traitorous friend. Horn then takes Rymenhild to his own country, where they reign as king and queen. See also HIND HORN.

Hornaday, William Temple (1854–1937). American zoologist. Advocated game preserves and promoted laws for the protection of wild life. Wrote many books about wild animals.

Horne, Doc. A humorous character invented by George ADE, who made his first appearance in the columns of the Chicago *Record* and later became the hero of the volume *Doc Horne* (1899).

Horner, Jack, see JACK HORNER.

Hornie, Auld, see AULD HORNIE.

Hornung, Ernest William (1866–1921). English novelist and short-story writer; inventor of Raffles, the Gentleman Cracksman, Stingaree, the Australian bushwhacker, etc. Brother-in-law of Sir Arthur Conan DOYLE.

horoscope. The scheme of the twelve houses by which astrologers tell your fortune. See HOUSES, ASTROLOGICAL. The word (Greek) means the "hour-scrutinized," because it is the disposition of the heavens at the exact hour of birth which is examined.

horse.

Banks' horse. See MAROCCO, below.

brazen horse. See CAMBUSCAN.

dark horse. See DARK.

gift horse. See GIFT.

Seian horse. A possession which invariably brought ill luck with it. Hence the Latin proverb *Ille homo habet equum Seianum.* Cneius

Seius had an Argive horse, of the breed of DIOMED, of a bay color and surpassing beauty, but it was fatal to its possessor. Seius was put to death by Mark Antony. Its next owner, Cornelius Dolabella, who bought it for 100,000 sesterces, was killed in Syria during the civil wars. Caius Cassius, who next took possession of it, perished after the battle of Philippi by the very sword which stabbed Caesar. Antony had the horse next, and after the battle of Actium slew himself.

Like the gold of Tolosa and Hermione's necklace, the Seian or Sejan horse was a fatal possession.

wooden horse. An enchanted horse of the old romance that could be directed by a peg turned by the rider and could fly through the air. CAMBUSCAN had such a horse, but his was of brass. See also CLAVILENO.

> This very day may be seen in the king's armoury the identical peg with which Peter of Provence turned his Wooden Horse, which carried him through the air. It is rather bigger than the pole of a coach, and stands near Babieca's saddle.—*Don Quixote,* pt. i, bk. iv. 19.

wooden horse of Troy. Virgil tells us that Ulysses had a monster wooden horse made after the death of Hector, and gave out that it was an offering to the gods to secure a prosperous voyage back to Greece. The Trojans dragged the horse within their city, but it was full of Grecian soldiers, who at night stole out of their place of concealment, slew the Trojan guards, opened the city gates, and set fire to Troy. Menelaus was one of the Greeks shut up in it. It was made by Epeios.

the Pale Horse. Death. *Rev.* vi. 8.

famous steeds of legend and fiction are the following:

Aligero Clavileno. The "wooden-pin wing-horse" which Don Quixote and his squire mounted to achieve the deliverance of Dolorida and her companions.

Arion (martial). Hercules' horse, given to Adrastus. Also, the horse of Neptune, brought out of the earth by striking it with his trident. Its right feet were those of a man, it spoke with a human voice, and ran with incredible swiftness.

Arundel. The horse of Bevis of Southampton. The word means swift as a swallow (Fr. *hirondelle*).

Bajardo (the same name as *Bayard* below). Rinaldo's horse, of a bright bay color, once the property of Amadis of Gaul. He was found by Malagigi, the wizard, in a cave guarded by a dragon, which the wizard slew. According to tradition he is still alive, but flees at the approach of man, so that no one can ever hope to catch him. See also ORLANDO FURIOSO.

Bavieca (*Span.,* a simpleton). The Cid's horse. He survived his master two years and a half, during which time no one was allowed to mount him; and when he died he was buried before the gate of the monastery at Valencia, and two elms were planted to mark the site. It is so called because, when Rodrigo in his youth was given the choice of a horse, he passed by the most esteemed ones and selected a rough colt; whereupon his godfather called the lad *bavieca,* and Rodrigo transferred the appellation to his horse.

Borak, Al. The "horse" which conveyed Mahomet from earth to the seventh heaven. It was milk-white, had the wings of an eagle and a human face, with horse's cheeks. Every pace it took was equal to the farthest range of human sight. The word is Arabic for "the lightning."

Brigadore or *Brigliadore* (golden bridle). Sir Guyon's horse, in Spenser's FAËRIE QUEENE (V. ii, etc.). It had a distinguishing black spot in its mouth, like a horseshoe. Orlando's famous charger, second only to Bajardo in swiftness and wonderful powers, had the same name —*Brigliadoro.*

Bucephalus (ox-head). The celebrated charger of Alexander the Great. Alexander was the only person who could mount him, and he always knelt down to take up his master. He was thirty years old at death, and Alexander built a city for his mausoleum, which he called Bucephala.

Bayard (bay colored). The horse of the four sons of Aymon, which grew larger or smaller as one or more of the four sons mounted it. According to tradition one of the footprints may still be seen in the forest of Soignes, and another on a rock near Dinant. Also the same as *Bajardo* above.

Barbary, see ROAN BARBARY.

Bevis. Marmion's horse, in Scott's poem. The word is Norse, and means swift.

Black Beauty. The horse hero of a story called BLACK BEAUTY.

Black Bess. The famous mare ridden by the highwayman Dick Turpin, which, tradition says, carried him from London to York.

Dapple. Sancho Panza's ass in *Don Quixote.* So called from its color.

Fadda. Mahomet's white mule.

Grani (gray-colored). Siegfried's horse, of marvelous swiftness.

Marocco. Banks' performing horse, famous in the late Elizabethan period, and frequently mentioned by the dramatists. Its shoes were of silver, and one of its exploits was to mount the steeple of St. Paul's.

Pegasus ("born near the *pege* or source of the ocean"). The winged horse of Apollo and the Muses. Perseus rode him when he rescued Andromeda.

Rabicano or *Rabican.* Argalia's horse in

Orlando Innamorato, and Astolpho's horse in *Orlando Furioso.* Its dam was Fire, its sire Wind; it fed on unearthly food. The word means a horse with a "dark tail but with some white hairs."

Reksh. In Persian legend, Rustam's horse.

Roan Barbary. The favorite horse of Richard II.

> When Bolingbroke rode on Roan Barbary
> That horse that thou so often has bestrid.
> Shakespeare, *Richard II,* v, 5.

Rosinante ("formerly a hack"). Don Quixote's horse, all skin and bone.

Sleipnir. Odin's grey horse, which had eight legs and could traverse either land or sea. The horse typifies the wind which blows over land and water from eight principal points.

Xanthus (golden-hued). One of the horses of Achilles, who announced to the hero his approaching death when unjustly chidden by him.

Horse-Shoe Robinson. A romance (1835) of the American Revolution by J. P. Kennedy (*Am.,* 1795–1870; better known under pseudonym *Mark Littleton*). The titular hero, who receives his nickname from his former trade of blacksmith, is a man of Herculean physique and courage. He has ample opportunity to use all his strength, and a supply of native wit besides, in the series of exciting adventures in which he gets the better of his British and Tory enemies. The scene is laid in Virginia. There was a popular dramatic version.

Hortense. In Dickens' BLEAK HOUSE, the vindictive French maidservant of Lady Dedlock. In revenge for the partiality shown by Lady Dedlock to Rosa, the village beauty, Hortense murdered Mr. Tulkinghorn, and tried to throw the suspicion of the crime on Lady Dedlock. Said to have been drawn from Marie Manning, a murderess, who made black satin unpopular by electing to be hanged in it.

Hortensio. In Shakespeare's TAMING OF THE SHREW, a suitor to Bianca, the younger sister of Katharina "the Shrew."

Horthy, Miklós von Nagybánya (1868–). Hungarian regent (from 1920). Had been commander in chief of Austro-Hungarian fleet in World War I and leader of anti-Bolshevik Hungarian troops after the collapse of the dual monarchy. In 1941 Horthy conferred with Hitler on Hungary's share in defeated Yugoslavia.

Horus. One of the major gods of the ancient Egyptians, a blending of Horus the Elder, the sun-god (corresponding to the Greek Apollo), and Horus the Child (see HARPOCRATES), the son of Osiris and Isis. He is the god of silence. He was represented in hieroglyphics by a hawk, which bird was sacred to him, or as a hawk-headed man; and his emblem was the winged sun-disk. In many of the myths he is hardly distinguishable from RA.

Horvendile. A strange youth who appears in Cabell's novels of medieval POICTESME, particularly in THE CREAM OF THE JEST. In FIGURES OF EARTH, he confesses to Manuel that he is, perhaps, insane, for "all of you appear to me to be persons I have imagined: and all the living in this world appears to me to be only a notion of mine."

Hosier's Ghost, Admiral. A ballad by Richard GLOVER (1739). Admiral Hosier is sent with twenty sail to the Spanish West Indies, to block up the galleons of that country. He arrives at the Bastimentos, near Portobello, but has strict orders not to attack the foe. His men perish by disease, but not in fight, and the admiral himself dies of a broken heart. After Vernon's victory, Hosier and his 3,000 men rise, "all in dreary hammocks shrouded, which for winding-sheets they wore," and lament the cruel orders that forbade them to attack the foe, for "with twenty ships he surely could have achieved what Vernon did with only six."

Hospitalers of St. John of Jerusalem, Order of the. A body of military monks, organized in the 12th century on the basis of an older order, founded (1048) in Jerusalem to minister to the poor and strangers in the Holy Land. The knights of the order are also known—after subsequent headquarters—as Knights of Rhodes and Knights of Malta.

Jean Parisot de la Valette (1494–1568) was a famous French grand master of the Knights of Malta or HOSPITALERS. He defended Malta successfully against the Turks (1565). The Maltese capital which he built is named after him, VALETTA.

Host (from Lat. *hostia,* a sheep when offered in sacrifice). The consecrated bread of the Eucharist is so called in the Latin Church because it is regarded as a real victim consisting of flesh, blood, and spirit, offered up in sacrifice. At the Benediction it is exposed for adoration or carried in procession in a transparent vessel called a *monstrance.*

the elevation of the Host. The celebrant lifting up the consecrated wafers above his head, that the people may see the paten and adore the Host while his back is turned to the congregation.

Host's Tale. (In Chaucer's *Canterbury Tales.*) See MELIBEUS. The Host is to be the judge of the tales told by the pilgrims. He is the proprietor of the Tabard Inn (see CANTERBURY TALES) and is perhaps best described in the following lines:

A semely man our hoste was with-alle
For to hav been a marshal in an halle;
A large man he was with eyen stepe
A fairer burgeys is there noon in Chepe
Bold of his speche, and wys, and wel y-taught
And of manhood him lakkede right naught
Eek therto he was right a mery man.
Chaucer, *Prologue to the Canterbury Tales.*

Hosty. In James Joyce's FINNEGANS WAKE, a cricketer, one of the characters in which the hero, H. C. EARWICKER, is represented. The name contains a reference to the HOST of Roman Catholicism.

Hotel Universe. A play by Philip BARRY, produced in 1930. It deals with a group of frustrated and unhappy people assembled as week-end guests at the home of Ann Field, an American woman living in southern France. Stephen Field, Ann's father, who believes in a triple system of worlds—of fact, imagination, and fact plus imagination after death—analyzes the problems of each guest in turn and reveals the past causes of their present distress. Their difficulties are solved as the old man dies.

hotspur. A fiery person who has no control over his temper. Harry Percy (d. 1403), son of the first Earl of Northumberland (cf. Shakespeare; 1 *Henry IV*), was so called. He is introduced in both parts of *Henry IV*. Lord Derby (d. 1879), the Prime Minister, was sometimes called the *"hotspur of debate."*

Houdin, Jean Eugène Robert (1805–1871). French watchmaker and magician, who took delight in explaining the mechanics of his tricks and in exposing the pretense of "fakes." On a government mission to Algeria he proved to the natives that French "magic" was superior to theirs. Author of books on magic and of an autobiography.

Houdini, Harry. Real name **Erich Weiss** (1874–1926). Famous American magician, who took his professional name from HOUDIN. Especially known for his ability to extricate himself from handcuffs and sealed containers.

Houdon, Jean Antoine (1741–1828). French sculptor remembered for some two hundred portrait busts of famous people. Came to America with Franklin and modeled a bust of Washington from which he made afterward his Richmond statue.

Hough, Emerson (1857–1923). American writer who worked for the preservation of wild life and the establishment of national parks. Wrote *Story of the Cowboy* (1897); *The Mississippi Bubble* (1902); and *The Covered Wagon* (1922) which became "a gold mine in the moving pictures."

Houghton, Claude, see OLDFIELD, C. H.

Houghton, William Stanley (1881–1913). English dramatist. Fame and fortune from *Hindle Wakes* (1912). Within a year of first performance in London, the play had been acted 2,000 times in London, Manchester, New York, and Chicago. It dealt with the cotton mill districts of Lancashire. Houghton had begun his career in the business of his father who was a cotton merchant.

Hound and Horn. A literary magazine founded at Harvard University in 1927, later moving to New York. Until it ceased publication in 1934 it published the work of the leading poets and prose writers of the time, many of whom were unknown when they first appeared in its pages. Among these are T. S. ELIOT, Gertrude STEIN, Allen TATE, Ezra POUND, and Kenneth BURKE.

Hound of Heaven, The. Best-known poem of Francis THOMPSON, published in 1893. Mystical and revelatory in character, it portrays the eternal pursuit of reluctant mankind by the grace and redemption of God, symbolized in the chase of a hare by a hound.

houri. The black-eyed damsels of the Mohammedan Paradise, possessed of perpetual youth and beauty, whose virginity is renewable at pleasure; hence, in English use, any dark-eyed and attractive beauty.

Every believer will have seventy-two of these *houris* in Paradise, and, according to the Koran, his intercourse with them will be fruitful or otherwise, according to his wish. If an offspring is desired, it will grow to full estate in an hour.

Hours of Idleness. The first series of poems published, in 1807, by Lord BYRON. The severe criticism in the *Edinburgh Review* brought forth the satire called *English Bards and Scotch Reviewers* (1809).

House, Edward Mandell (1858–1938). American diplomat. Personal representative of President Wilson in Europe (1914–1916). Appointed to act for U.S. in negotiating armistice with Central Powers (1918). With Charles SEYMOUR (later president of Yale), author of *What Really Happened at Paris.* Known as "Colonel House" in accordance with the rank he had once held on the staff of Governor Culberson of Texas.

Household Words. A weekly periodical (1850–1857) published by Charles DICKENS; it gave place to *Once a Week,* which, after 1859, was called *All the Year Round.*

House of Life, The. A sonnet sequence by Dante Gabriel ROSSETTI, written during the period between 1848 and 1881, chiefly autobiographical and inspired by Elizabeth SIDDALL, the author's wife. The title refers to the "house of human life" in astrology (see HOUSES, ASTROLOGICAL), which is classed as the most important.

House of Mirth, The. A novel by Edith WHARTON (1905). Lily Bart, an orphan who has beauty, social connections, and expensive tastes but little money, is courted by a number of men. One, Lawrence Seldon, she loves, but his lack of a fortune makes him ineligible; another, Simon Rosedale, a wealthy Jew, she cannot quite force herself to marry. Meantime she puts herself under great obligations to Gus Trenor, a married friend who keeps up the pretext of giving her returns from her investments until she refuses to allow his attentions. Lily's fortunes gradually go from bad to worse until, shunned and snubbed by her friends, she goes to live in a third-rate boarding house, tries to learn millinery and at last, in despair, takes an overdose of chloral. Before her death she manages to discharge her debt to Trenor.

House of the Dead, The. An account of prison life in Siberia during the 19th century by Fyodor DOSTOYEVSKY, published in 1861. It was based on the author's own experiences in the land to which Russian prisoners, especially political prisoners, were sent in exile.

House of the Seven Gables, The. A novel by Nathaniel HAWTHORNE (1851). The story has to do with the slow relentless working out of a curse on the Pyncheon family of Salem, who have inhabited the House of the Seven Gables for generations. The ancestral Colonel Pyncheon whose portrait on the wall still rules the house, built on the property of a man named Maule who was executed for witchcraft largely through Pyncheon's efforts. As Maule stood with the halter round his neck he cursed his enemy, saying, "God will give him blood to drink." The book deals, in passing, with the effect of the curse upon the early Pyncheons, particularly the death of the Colonel, the disappearance of the deed to rich Maine lands (hid away by Maule's carpenter son in a nook of the Pyncheon house itself) and the hypnotizing of the proud and beautiful Alice Pyncheon by Maule's carpenter grandson. The story proper, however, concerns the few surviving Pyncheons two centuries after the building of the house. The principal characters are the gaunt old maid, Hepzibah Pyncheon, and her brother Clifford, both well past middle age. Hepzibah is desperately poor and finally forces her pride to the point of opening a little cent-shop. Clifford comes home to the old house weak and embittered from thirty years' unjust imprisonment as the supposed murderer of his uncle. His suffering was the fault of his hypocritical cousin Judge Jaffrey Pyncheon, now the most distinguished member of the old house, and prosperous from an inheritance that should have been Clifford's. In contrast to these elderly characters, steeped in the traditions of the past, are the young and pretty cousin, Phoebe, and Holgrave, the radical and adventuresome daguerreotypist (in reality the descendant of Maule), who rents a gable of the old house, falls in love with Phoebe and marries her. The death of the old Judge by apoplexy brings a fortune to make life easier for the old brother and sister and the young lovers.

houses, astrological. In judicial astrology the whole heaven is divided into twelve portions by means of great circles crossing the north and south points of the horizon, through which the heavenly bodies pass every twenty-four hours. Each of these divisions is called a *house;* and in casting a HOROSCOPE the whole is divided into two parts beginning from the east, six above and six below the horizon. The eastern ones are called the *ascendant,* because they are about to rise; the other six are the *descendant,* because they have already passed the zenith. The twelve houses each have their special functions—(1) the house of life; (2) fortune and riches; (3) brethren; (4) parents and relatives; (5) children; (6) health; (7) marriage; (8) death; (9) religion; (10) dignities; (11) friends and benefactors; (12) enemies.

Three houses were assigned to each of the four ages of the person whose horoscope was to be cast, and his lot in life was governed by the ascendancy or descendancy of these at the various periods, and by the stars which ruled in the particular "houses."

Housman, Alfred Edward (1859–1936). English Latin scholar and poet, known for his small quantity of lyrics showing the influence of traditional English ballads and classical verse, set against a background of the English countryside. They are marked by economy, directness, and dramatic simplicity in style, and a spirit of irony and fatalism, finding disillusionment and betrayal in love, patriotism, and sin alike. Housman was reluctant to publish his poetry, and for years was known only for his first book, *A Shropshire Lad* (1896). *Last Poems* appeared in 1922, and *More Poems,* selections made from his manuscripts, in 1936, after his death.

Housman, Lawrence (1865–). English dramatist, novelist and illustrator; brother of A. E. HOUSMAN. His first—almost his only—popular success came by accident. He published anonymously *An Englishwoman's Love Letters* (1900). The public thought them genuine! With thirty-two of his plays censored in one way or another, he has been called "England's most censored playwright," but his *Victoria Regina,* with Helen Hayes, was an enormous success in America. He is brilliantly versatile, a beautiful draughtsman, a fine poet, a delightful writer of fantastic stories. *The Phoenix and the Carpet,* by E. NESBIT, is based on a suggestion of his.

Houssain. Brother of Prince Ahmed in one of the ARABIAN NIGHTS stories. He possesses a piece of carpet or tapestry of such wonderful power that anyone has only to sit upon it and it will transport him in a moment to any place to which he desires to go.

Houston, Samuel (1793–1863). Known as **Sam Houston.** American general and statesman. Native of Virginia. As commander in chief of the Texans defeated the Mexicans at San Jacinto (1836). President of Texas (1836–1838; 1841–1844) and, after its admission to the Union (1845), U.S. senator (1846–1859) and governor (1859–1861) of Texas. Deposed for opposition to the Confederacy.

Houyhnhnms (*whinms,* or *whinhims*). A race of horses endowed with reason and all the finer characteristics of man, introduced with caustically satirical effect by Swift in his GULLIVER'S TRAVELS. They are the rulers of the YAHOOS. The name was the author's invention, coined in imitation of the "whinny" of a horse.

Hovey, Richard (1869–1900). American poet, best known for the *Songs from Vagabondia* which he and Bliss CARMAN published in collaboration. Among his well-known lyrics are *The Sea Gipsy* and *Comrades.*

Howard, Henry, Earl of **Surrey,** see SURREY, HENRY HOWARD, EARL OF.

Howard, Leslie (1893–1943). English actor, popular on New York stage and in moving pictures from 1930. Lost in airplane accident (his plane was probably shot down) during World War II. Played in *Berkeley Square, Hamlet, The Petrified Forest,* etc.

Howard, Sidney Coe (1891–1939). One of the best of modern American playwrights. *They Knew What They Wanted* (1925), awarded Pulitzer Prize; *Yellow Jack* (1928); *The Late Christopher Bean* (1933); *Dodsworth* (with Sinclair Lewis; 1934); *Paths of Glory* (with Humphrey Cobb; 1935); also adapted plays and novels for moving pictures, *Bulldog Drummond,* etc.

Howe, Edgar Watson (1853–1937). American newspaper and magazine editor and novelist, known for his first novel, THE STORY OF A COUNTRY TOWN (1883), one of the early examples of realism in American fiction. His other works, less powerful in character, include *A Man Story* (1889); *An Ante-Mortem Statement* (1891); *Country Town Sayings* (1911); *Ventures in Common Sense* (1919); *The Anthology of Another Town* (1920); and *Plain People* (1929), an autobiography. See KIRKLAND, JOSEPH; also LOCAL COLOR; NATURALISM.

Howe, Elias (1819–1867). American inventor. Completed the first sewing machine in 1845. Member, Hall of Fame.

Howe, Julia Ward (1819–1910). American poet, author, and reformer, active particularly in the anti-slavery and woman suffrage movements. She is best known as the author of *The Battle Hymn of the Republic* (1862), set to the music of *John Brown's Body* and sung by the Union forces during the American Civil War. She also wrote *Sex and Education* (1874), *Modern Society* (1881), and a biography of Margaret FULLER (1883).

Howe, Mark Antony DeWolfe (1864–). Vice-president, Atlantic Monthly Co. (1911–1929); director, Boston Athenaeum (from 1933). Author of *Barrett Wendell and His Letters* (Pulitzer prize for biography, 1924); *Yankee Ballads* (1930); etc. His father, **Mark Antony DeWolfe Howe** (1808–1895), was the Episcopal bishop of Central Pennsylvania.

Howe, Miss. In Richardson's CLARISSA HARLOWE, the friend of Clarissa Harlowe, to whom she presents a strong contrast. In questions of doubt, Miss Howe suggests some practical solution, while Clarissa dreams of hypothetical contingencies. She is a girl of high spirit, disinterested friendship, and sound common sense.

Howell, James (1594?–1666). English man of letters. Historiographer royal of Restoration (1661). Best-known for his *Epistolae Ho-elianae: Familiar Letters,* most of which were written while he was in prison as a royalist sympathizer during the Civil War (1643–1651). His chief lexicographical contribution is the *Lexicon Tetraglotton* (1660), a polyglot dictionary of English, French, Italian, and Spanish.

Howells, William Dean (1837–1920). American journalist, editor, and novelist, known for his realistic character studies, his interest in social, economic, and ethical problems of his time, and his insistence on truthfulness and didacticism in fiction. His works include: *Their Wedding Journey* (1872); *A Chance Acquaintance* (1873); *A Foregone Conclusion* (1875); *The Lady of the Aroostook* (1879); *Dr. Breen's Practice* (1881); *A Modern Instance* (1882); *The Rise of Silas Lapham* (1885); *Indian Summer* (1886); *The Minister's Charge* (1887); *April Hopes* (1888); *Annie Kilburn* (1889); *A Hazard of New Fortunes* (1890); *A Traveler from Altruria* (1894); *The Kentons* (1902). (See separate entries.) *My Literary Passions* (1895), *Literary Friends and Acquaintance* (1900), and *Literature and Life* (1902) are books of criticism. Howells also wrote a number of other novels, short stories, 31 plays, autobiographical works, and poetry. He was editor of the ATLANTIC

MONTHLY for several years beginning in 1871, and later conducted the department in HARPER'S MAGAZINE called *The Editor's Easy Chair*. He was widely honored as the leading American man of letters during the latter part of his career and encouraged a number of younger writers, including Stephen CRANE, Hamlin GARLAND, and Frank NORRIS. He was a friend of Mark TWAIN.

Howlegas or Owleglass. A name given to Tyl EULENSPIEGEL.

Howth Castle. A castle surmounting the hill of Howth, which is located on a peninsula overlooking the harbor of Dublin, in Ireland. It is the background for a love scene between Molly and Leopold Bloom in ULYSSES, and appears prominently in FINNEGANS WAKE, both novels by James JOYCE. In the opening sections of FINNEGANS WAKE there is a scene in which tourists are shown the ancient relics in Howth Castle. It is said that Dubliners like to picture the hill as the head of a sleeping giant whose body is the peninsula, and this may account for the role of Howth in FINNEGANS WAKE as one of the metamorphoses of the sleeping H. C. EARWICKER. One of Earwicker's names is *Jarl van Hoother*, a pseudo-Dutch form for "Earl of Howth."

How They Brought the Good News from Ghent. A ballad by Robert BROWNING (1845), noted for its onomatopoetic effects. It describes a purely imaginary incident.

Hoyle, Edmond (1672–1769). English writer on card games. His whist laws remained in effect for a century (1760–1864). Cf. the phrase, "according to Hoyle."

Hrotsvitha, see ROSWITHA.

Hrothgar. In the Anglo-Saxon epic BEOWULF, King of Denmark, whom Beowulf delivers from the monster GRENDEL.

Huang Ti. A legendary emperor of China (about 2600 B. C.) credited with the invention of bricks, carts, musical instruments, etc. His name means "yellow emperor."

huaca. Among the ancient Peruvians, a local spirit or tribal god, as distinguished from the major Inca divinities.

Huayna Capac (1450?–1525). Eleventh Inca ruler of Peru. During his reign of 42 (or 33) years the Inca empire attained its greatest splendor and extent (3000 miles long and 400 miles wide). At his death he divided it between his sons ATAHUALPA and Huáscar. His capital was Cuzco.

hub. The nave of a wheel; a boss. Boston, Massachusetts, has been called *the hub of the solar system;* i.e., the center round which everything revolves and is dependent. This phrase and the similar one, *the hub of the universe,* have also been applied to numerous other cities.

> Boston State-house is the hub of the solar system. You couldn't pry that out of a Boston man, if you had the tire of all creation straightened out for a crowbar.
> —Holmes, *Autocrat of the Breakfast Table,* vi, 143.

Hubbard, Bartley. The chief character in Howells' MODERN INSTANCE.

Hubbard, Elbert (1859–1915). Successful American businessman who retired at the age of 35 to seek culture, established the Roycroft Press in imitation of the KELMSCOTT PRESS of William MORRIS, although not as a communal venture, and himself wrote the majority of the material published there. This included two pseudo-artistic magazines, the *Philistine* and *The Fra,* and a series of 170 *Little Journeys* to the homes of famous men. Hubbard is best-known for A MESSAGE TO GARCIA (1899), an exhortation to fidelity and enterprise which became enormously popular among businessmen, who distributed copies of it among their employees as "inspiration." Hubbard died when the S. S. *Lusitania* was sunk in the Irish Sea by a German submarine.

Hubbard, Mother. An old lady of nursery rhyme fame whose whole time and attention were taken up by her dog.

> The dame made a curtsey, the dog made a bow,
> The dame said, "Your servant!" the dog said, "Bow, wow!"
> *A Nursery Tale in Rhyme.*

A woman's loose coatlike wrapper is called a *Mother Hubbard* from this familiar character.

Hubberd, Mother. The supposed narrator of a tale called *The Fox and the Ape,* related to the poet SPENSER in his *Prosopopoia, Or Mother Hubberd's Tale* (1591), to beguile the weary hours of sickness. Several persons told him tales, but

> Amongst the rest a good old woman was
> Hight Mother Hubberd, who did far surpass
> The rest in honest mirth that seemed her well;
> She, when her turn was come her tale to tell,
> Told of a strange adventure that betided
> Betwixt a fox and ape by him misguided;
> The which, for that my sense it greatly pleased, . .
> I'll write it as she the same did say.
> Spenser.

Hubert. In Shakespeare's KING JOHN, chamberlain to King John, and "keeper" of young Prince Arthur. King John conspires with him to murder the young prince, and Hubert actually employs two ruffians to burn out both the boy's eyes with red-hot irons. Arthur pleads so with Hubert to spare his eyes that he relents. However, the lad is found dead soon afterwards, either by accident or foul play. This *Hubert* was Hubert de Burgh, justice of England and Earl of Kent.

Hubert, St., see under SAINT.

Hubscher, Caterina, see MADAME SANS GÊNE.

Huckleberry Finn, The Adventures of. A story by Mark TWAIN (1884), sequel to TOM

SAWYER. After the first few chapters in his home town, the vagabond Huck with his raft and his faithful friend, Jim the Negro, drifts down the Mississippi into innumerable adventures.

Hudibras. A satirical poem in three parts and nine cantos (1663–1678) by Samuel BUTLER, so named from its hero, who is variously said to be drawn from Sir Samuel Luke, Colonel Rolle of Devonshire, or Sir Henry Roswell. Hudibras is a Presbyterian justice in the Commonwealth, who sets out with his squire, Ralpho, an Independent, to reform abuses, and enforce the observance of the laws for the suppression of popular sports and amusements. He is humpbacked and potbellied with a long untidy yellow-red beard. Among several other features of the poem that are reminiscent of DON QUIXOTE may be mentioned the half-blind old horse on which Hudibras rides forth on his crusade. This satiric poem against the Puritans gave rise to the adjective *hudibrastic* meaning mock-heroic, or in the style of *Hudibras.*

There are two characters of this name in Spenser's FAËRIE QUEENE: (1) the lover of Elissa (II. ii), typifying rashness, and (2) a legendary king of Britain (II. x. 25).

Hudson, Sir **Jeffrey** (1619–1682). A famous dwarf, at one time page to Queen Henrietta Maria. When he was thirty years old he was 18 in. high, but he later reached 3 ft. 6 in. or 3 ft. 9 in. He was a captain of horse in the Civil War. Afterwards he was captured by pirates and sold as a slave in Barbary, but managed to escape. Scott introduces him in his PEVERIL OF THE PEAK, ch. xxxiv; Vandyke immortalized him by his brush; and his clothes are said to be preserved in Sir Hans Sloane's museum.

Hudson, Roderick, see RODERICK HUDSON.

Hudson, Stephen. Pseudonym of **Sidney Schiff.** English novelist; adamant about letting nothing be known of his private life. Started writing after he was fifty. Close personal friend of Marcel PROUST. Translated a volume of *A la Recherche du temps perdu.* Also intimate friend of Katherine MANSFIELD. "His is a condensed, eliminative, almost taciturn art."

Hudson, William Henry (1841–1922). English naturalist and novelist, born in Argentina of American parentage, naturalized as a British subject in 1900. He is best known for his writings on nature subjects, especially those with an Argentine background. His books include: *The Purple Land* (1885); *Argentine Ornithology* (1888–1889); *Fan* (1892), published under the name of Henry Harford; *Birds in a Village* (1893); *Nature in Downland* (1900); *El Ombú* (1902); *Hampshire Days* (1903); GREEN MANSIONS (1904); *A Little Boy Lost* (1905); *A Crystal Age* (1906); *A Shepherd's Life* (1910); *Far Away and Long Ago* (1918), autobiographical; *The Book of a Naturalist* (1919); *A Hind in Richmond Park* (1922).

Hudson River school. A group of 19th-century American painters—among others Thomas Cole, A. B. Durand, F. E. Church, and Albert Bierstadt—for whom the scenery of the Hudson River Valley was the main source of subject matter and inspiration.

Hudson's Bay Company. A joint stock company chartered in 1670 by Charles II for the purpose of purchasing furs from the Indians. Its territory, the Hudson's Bay Territory or Rupert's Land, included all the streams flowing into Hudson Bay. It was sold to the British government (1869) and incorporated with the Dominion of Canada (1870).

Huggins and Muggins. Two characters of popular legend who personify vulgarity and false pretensions. They were frequently introduced in comic literature of the 19th century. The phrase may be a corruption of the Dutch *Hooge en Mogende* (high and mighty) or may possibly be derived from Hugin and Munin, Odin's two ravens of Scandinavian myth.

Hughes, Charles Evans (1862–). American jurist. Unsuccessful presidential candidate against Wilson (1916). Chief justice of the U.S. Supreme Court (1930). Retired (1941).

Hughes, David Edward (1831–1900). English-born American inventor of the printing telegraph 1850. Resident of London (from 1877). Gold Medal of Royal Society (1885).

Hughes, Hatcher (1886?–1945). American dramatist and university professor. *Hell-Bent for Heaven* (1922), Pulitzer prize for drama (1924); etc. National Institute of Arts and Letters.

Hughes, James Langston (1902–). American Negro poet, whose work is marked by bitter clowning and the use of the rhythms of Negro folk-music and JAZZ. Books of poems are *The Weary Blues* (1926); *Dear Lovely Death* (1931); *The Negro Mother* (1931); *The Dream Keeper* (1932); *A New Song* (1938); etc. *Scottsboro Limited* (1932) is a collection of poems and a play. *Troubled Island* and *Mulatto* (1936) are plays; *Not Without Laughter* (1930), a novel; *The Ways of White Folks* (1934), a collection of short stories; *The Big Sea* (1940), an autobiography. Poems by Hughes have been translated into German, French, Spanish, Russian, Yiddish, and Czech. Many of them have been set to music.

Hughes, John Ceiriog (1832–1887). Welsh poet. Author of hundreds of songs; called the "Welsh Burns."

Hughes, Richard Arthur Warren (1900–). Welsh novelist, poet, and dramatist. Bernard Shaw called his *The Sisters' Tragedy* (1924) "the finest one-act play ever written." His novel *High Wind in Jamaica* (in America, *The Innocent Voyage;* 1929), an amazing story of children, has been also successful as a play.

Hughes, Rupert (1872–). American novelist, dramatist, biographer, vastly successful magazine writer. His work varies from trash to a biography of George Washington showing great research. At his best, Hughes writes with great vigor.

Hughes, Thomas (1822–1896). English jurist, reformer, and author of *Tom Brown's School Days* (1857), and *Tom Brown at Oxford* (1861); etc. Associated with *Christian Socialism,* a movement for the improvement of the conditions of the poor.

Hugues of Saxe-Gotha, Master. A poem by Robert BROWNING.

Huitzilopochtli. The war god of the Aztecs. He was extremely sanguinary and great numbers of captives were periodically sacrificed before him. His great festival was the December solstice. At that time his image, made of bread, was ceremonially eaten.

Hugh of Lincoln. It is said that the Jews of Lincoln in 1255 stole a boy of 8 years named Hugh, whom they tortured for ten days and then crucified or drowned in a well. Eighteen of the richest Jews of Lincoln were hanged for taking part in this affair, and more would have been put to death had it not been for the intercession of the Franciscans. The boy was buried in state. This is the subject of *The Prioress's Tale* of Chaucer; it is also given in *Alphonsus of Lincoln* (1459), etc., and was modernized by Wordsworth. See also WILLIAM OF NORWICH.

Hugh Wynne, Free Quaker. A novel by S. Weir Mitchell (*Am.,* 1897), dealing with the Philadelphia of Revolutionary times. The hero, who is also the narrator, is the son of a once light-hearted French mother and the strictest and most intolerant of Quaker fathers. The plot centers about his adventures during the Revolution as a spy and member of Lafayette's and Washington's staffs and his love for the charming Darthea Peniston. Darthea is also loved by Hugh's best friend, Jack Warder, and his rascally cousin, Arthur Wynne, but eventually gives her heart and hand to Hugh. The novel was illustrated by Howard PYLE.

Hugin and Munin. In Scandinavian mythology, the two ravens that sit on the shoulders of Odin. They typify *thought* and *memory.*

Hugo, Victor Marie (1802–1885). French poet, novelist, and dramatist, an early leader of French Romanticism and the most famous and most influential figure in 19th-century French literature. He is best-known to the English-speaking public for his historical novels, marked by tremendous sweep, violent melodrama, rhetorical and colorful style, and a frequent humanitarian interest in the problems and sufferings of the proletariat. Among his most popular novels are: *Han of Iceland* (*Han d'Islande*) (1823); *The Hunchback of Notre Dame* (NOTRE-DAME DE PARIS; 1831); LES MISÉRABLES (1862); TOILERS OF THE SEA (*Les Travailleurs de la mer;* 1866); THE MAN WHO LAUGHS (*L'Homme qui rit;* 1869); and NINETY-THREE (*Quatre-Vingt Treize;* 1874).

In the drama, Hugo was a leader in establishing the Romantic drama in place of the Classical, introducing such innovations as a mixture of the comic and the tragic in the same play, by realistic touches, both colloquial and extravagantly rhetorical dialogue, new freedom in meter, and violation of the old principle of unity of action. His best-known plays, chiefly historical and melodramatic, include: *Cromwell* (1827); HERNANI (1830), his most famous dramatic work; *Marion Delorme* (1831); *Ruy Blas* (1838); *Les Burgraves* (1843). Hugo also wrote numerous volumes of poetry throughout his life, dealing with nature subjects, the Orient and Spain, political satire and invective, and history, all marked by intense imagination, excessively rich figures, and violent and apocalyptic rhetoric. Outstanding volumes are: *Les Orientales* (1829); *Les Chants du Crépuscule* (1835); *Les Châtiments* (1853), an attack on Napoleon III and a prediction of the triumph of the forces of good; and *La Légende des Siècles* (1859–1883), an account of history through the ages including Biblical lore, mythology, and legend.

Hugo is said to have been inordinately vain and egotistical in his personal life. He opposed Napoleon III and was exiled (1852–1870), living in the Channel Islands.

Huguenots. The French Protestants (Calvinists) of the 16th and 17th centuries. The name was first applied to the revolutionaries of Geneva by the adherents of the Duke of Savoy, about 1560, and is probably an adaptation of the Ger. *Eidgenossen,* confederates.

Philippe de Mornay (1549–1623), the great supporter of the French Protestants, was nicknamed *the Huguenot Pope.*

The Huguenots (*Les Huguenots*) is the title of an opera by MEYERBEER (1836) which is brought to its tragic end by the Massacre of St. Bartholomew's Day (1572). The heroine is

Valentine, a Catholic; the hero Raoul de Nangis, a Huguenot. Political intrigues and personal jealousies separate them and they are united at last only to go to their death.

Hulda. The old German goddess of marriage and fecundity, who sent bridegrooms to maidens and children to the married. The name means "the Benignant," and is a euphemistic appellation.

Hulda is making her bed. It snows.

Hull, Cordell (1871–). U.S. secretary of state (1933–1944). Negotiated various reciprocal trade agreements especially with Latin-American countries.

Hull, Edith Maude. English novelist. Best known for *The Sheik* (1921) which was made into a silent moving picture for Rudolph Valentino. A preposterous story that made a semi-scandalous sensation.

Hull House. A famous settlement house in Chicago. It is widely known through Jane ADDAMS' autobiographical volumes *Twenty Years at Hull House* (1910) and *The Second Twenty Years at Hull House* (1931).

Hulme, Thomas Ernest (1883–1917). English author and philosopher, known for his forceful personality, his championing of abstract art, and his influence on the ideas of his contemporaries, especially Ezra POUND and T. S. ELIOT. He was an early leader in the movement of IMAGISM, founding a group of enthusiasts which met weekly for the writing of free-verse poems and himself composing a number of such pieces. He never wrote a complete book, although he prepared many notes for a series of intended works on 20th-century art and medieval philosophy, and attacks on romanticism and post-Renaissance humanist views. These notes are collected in *Speculations* (1924), and *Notes on Language and Style* (1929). Hulme was influenced by Remy de GOURMONT, Henri BERGSON, and Georges SOREL, translating the works of the latter two authors. He was enthusiastic about World War I, wrote articles defending militarism, and was killed in battle.

Hulot. In Balzac's novels, notably in THE CHOUANS (*Les Chouans*), an honorable and distinguished soldier, the elder of two brothers. His concern over his brother's misdeeds hastens his death.

Baron Hector Hulot d'Ervy. Brother of the above, a worthless character whose gradual degeneration is traced in Balzac's *Cousin Betty* (*La Cousine Bette*). See FISCHER, LISBETH. After a brilliant start in life, he becomes involved in disgraceful speculations and in numerous affairs with women. When his wife finally dies, he marries a kitchen maid. He is known under various names, to disguise his misdoings.

Baroness Hulot d'Ervy. Wife of the disreputable Hulot. She endures with infinite patience the shame which the Baron brings upon her, and for her children's sake makes every effort to hold the family together.

Hortense Hulot. The Baron's daughter, beloved by Wenceslas Steinbock, the young and talented protégé of Cousin Betty.

Huma. A fabulous Oriental bird which never alights, but is always on the wing. It is said that every head which it overshadows will wear a crown. The bird suspended over the throne of Tippoo Sahib at Seringapatam represented this poetical fancy. In the first chapter of the *Autocrat of the Breakfast-Table* a certain popular lecturer is made to compare himself, in allusion to his many wanderings, to this bird:

> "Yes, I am like the Huma, the bird that never lights; being always in the cars, as the Huma is always on the wing."

Human Comedy, The, see COMÉDIE HUMAINE.

Human Understanding, An Essay concerning. A famous essay by John LOCKE, published in 1690, against the dogma of innate ideas, and in proof that experience is the key of knowledge.

Humanism, or **the New Humanism.** A movement in philosophy and criticism, centered at Harvard University in the period following World War I and led by Irving BABBITT and Paul Elmer MORE. The movement sought to avoid the extremes of both religion and science and stressed the importance of human reason and freedom of will in ethical, intellectual, and artistic considerations. Its chief values were harmony and restraint, resulting from the "inner check" of free and enlightened reason. Romanticism in thought and literature was particularly frowned on by the Humanists, whose ideas are summed up in the symposium *Humanism and America* (1930). George Santayana's *The Genteel Tradition at Bay* (1931) is a criticism of the movement.

Humanism is considered to have had a strong influence on the ideas of T. S. ELIOT, but he adapted it according to his own aims and purposes.

Humanism is a term also applied in general to the attitude of mind which grew up with the Renaissance and which laid emphasis on the individual and the secular world, rather than on feudal group relations and the world to come as in the Middle Ages, with the rediscovered literature of Greece and Rome as an inspiration and a model. The "humanists" were classical scholars and men of letters and often, especially in the early part of the Renaissance period, lived riotous and corrupt lives. The Italian humanists were the most famous, including PETRARCH, BOCCACCIO, Lorenzo VALLA, Pietro ARETINO, Marsilio FICINO, Pico della MIRANDOLA, POGGIO, and Angelo POLIZIANO. Humanists of northern Europe were: John REUCHLIN, Philip MELANCHTHON, John COLET, Sir Thomas MORE, William BUDÉ, and ERASMUS.

Humanities or **Humanity studies.** Grammar, rhetoric, and poetry, with Greek and Latin (*literae humaniores*); in contradistinction to divinity (*literae divinae*).

humble pie, to eat. To come down from a position you have assumed; to be obliged to take "a lower room." Here "humble" is a pun on *umble,* the umbels being the heart, liver, and entrails of the deer, the huntsman's perquisites. When the lord and his household dined, the venison pasty was served on the dais, but the *umbles* were made into a pie for the huntsman and his fellows, who took the lower seats.

Humboldt, Baron **Alexander von** (1769–1854). German naturalist, traveler, and statesman. Like his older contemporary a real *uomo universale.* Spent five years (1799–1804) with Aimée Bonpland on a scientific expedition through South America; wrote on plant distribution; introduced Peruvian guano in Europe; delineated isothermal lines for comparing climates, etc., etc. Chief among his numerous works, written in German or French, is *Kosmos* (1845–1862), a description of the physical universe. He is said to have originated the current designation of Mexico as the "treasure-house of the world." See also Wilhelm von HUMBOLDT, his brother.

Humboldt, Wilhelm von (1767–1835). German philologist and statesman. Brother of Alexander von HUMBOLDT. During the Napoleonic wars, he was the Prussian minister of public instruction. As part of his program for a cultural rebirth of the nation, he became instrumental in the foundation of the University of Berlin (1810). See also under FICHTE. His main work, *Über die Kawisprache auf der Insel Jawa* (*On the Kawi Language of the Island of Java;* 3 vols., 1836–1840) is still studied, mainly on account of the introduction, available as a separate reprint, *On the Difference in the Construction of Language, and its Influence upon the Intellectual Development of the Human Race.*

Humboldt Current. A mass of cold water about 150 miles wide, which flows north from the coast of Chile, bringing cool, moist south and southwest winds. These, meeting with warm air over land, cause heavy fogs along the southern coast of Peru.

Hume, David (1711–1776). Scottish philosopher and historian. His philosophical scepticism, often referred to as Humism, restricts human knowledge to the experience of ideas and impressions, and has been of extraordinary importance in the history of modern metaphysical thinking. Author of many treatises, dissertations, and essays and of a history of England during the reigns of James I and Charles I. His best-known work is *Philosophical Essays Concerning Human Understanding* (1748), later issued as *An Enquiry Concerning Human Understanding.*

Hume, Fergus (1859–1932). Anglo-Australian "story-teller." Writer of detective stories. His *magnum opus,* unreadable today, was *The Mystery of a Hansom Cab* (1886). It received more attention than Conan Doyle's *A Study in Scarlet,* issued a year later. Cf. *Murder for Pleasure* (1941), by Howard Haycraft. It sold a phenomenal number of copies.

Hummel, Abraham Henry (1850–1926). American criminal lawyer known as "Abe." Convicted on a conspiracy charge (1905) and imprisoned; spent last years of his life in obscurity in England. Cf. *Howe and Hummel* (1947), by Richard Rovere.

Hummums, the. Formerly the name of two hotels, the *Old Hummums* and the *New Hummums,* in Covent Garden, London. The word "hummums" is a variant or corruption of *hammam,* "a Turkish bath." The London Hummums were frequented by women of doubtful repute which soon led to their suppression.

humor. As *good humor, ill* or *bad humor,* etc. According to an ancient theory, there are four principal humors in the body: phlegm, blood, choler, and black bile. As any one of these predominates, it determines the temper of the mind and body; hence the expressions sanguine, choleric, phlegmatic, and melancholic humors. A just balance made a good compound called "good humor"; a preponderance of any one of the four made a bad compound called an ill or evil humor. Cf. Ben Jonson's *Every Man Out of His Humor* (*Prologue*).

Humperdinck, Engelbert (1854–1921). German composer. Friend of Richard WAGNER; best known for his fairy opera *Hänsel und Gretel* (1893); composed also incidental music for Shakespeare and Maeterlinck's *Blue Bird.*

Humphrey, to dine with Duke. To have no dinner to go to. Humphrey, Duke of Gloucester, son of Henry IV, the "Good Duke Humphrey," was renowned for his hospitality. At his death it was reported that a monument would be erected to him in St. Paul's, but his body was interred at St. Albans. The tomb of

Sir John Beauchamp (d. 1358), on the south side of the nave of old St. Paul's, was popularly supposed to be that of the Duke, and when the promenaders left for dinner, the poor stay-behinds who had no dinner to go to, or who feared to leave the precincts of the cathedral because, once outside, they could be arrested for debt, used to say to the gay sparks who asked if they were going, that they would "dine with Duke Humphrey" that day.

Humphrey, Master. The hypothetical compiler of the tale entitled *Barnaby Rudge* in MASTER HUMPHREY'S CLOCK, by Charles DICKENS (1840).

Humphry Clinker, The Expedition of. A novel by SMOLLETT (1771). The titular hero, Humphry Clinker, is a poor workhouse lad, put out by the parish as apprentice to a blacksmith, and afterwards employed as an ostler's assistant and extra postilion. When he is dismissed from the stables, he enters the service of Mr. Bramble, a fretful, grumpy, but kind-hearted old gentleman, greatly troubled with gout. Here he falls in love with Winifred Jenkins, Miss Tabitha Bramble's maid, and turns out to be a natural son of Mr. Bramble. Though nominally the hero, Humphry plays a much less important part than the BRAMBLES. The interest centers in the "expedition" of the title, a family tour through England and Scotland. The novel is written in the form of letters from the various characters.

Humpty Dumpty. A little deformed dwarf, "humpty" and "dumpty." It is also applied—in allusion to the old nursery rhyme—to an egg, and to anything that is, or may be, irretrievably shattered.

Humpty Dumpty sat on a wall,
Humpty Dumpty had a great fall,
All the King's horses and all the King's men
Couldn't put Humpty together again.

In James Joyce's FINNEGANS WAKE Humpty Dumpty is interchangeable with Tim FINNEGAN, Lucifer, and mankind.

Hunchback of Notre Dame, see QUASIMODO.

Hunding. In Wagner's opera *Die Walküre,* one of the four music dramas of his RING, the husband of Sieglinde.

hundred.

the Hundred Days. The days between March 20, 1815, when Napoleon reached the Tuileries, after his escape from Elba, and June 28, the date of the second restoration of Louis XVIII. Napoleon left Elba February 26; landed near Cannes March 1, entered Paris March 20, and signed his abdication June 22.

The address of the Count de Chambord, the prefect, begins: "A hundred days, sire, have elapsed since the fatal moment when your Majesty was forced to quit your capital in the midst of tears." This is the origin of the phrase.

the Hundred-eyed. Argus, in Greek and Latin fable. Juno appointed him guardian of Io, but Jupiter caused him to be put to death, whereupon Juno transplanted his eyes into the tail of her peacock.

the Hundred-handed. Three of the sons of Uranus, viz., Aegaeon or Briareus, Kottos, and Gyges or Gyes. After the war between Zeus and the Titans, when the latter were overcome and hurled into Tartarus, the Hundred-handed ones were set to keep watch and ward over them.

Sometimes CERBERUS is so called, because from his three necks sprang writhing snakes instead of hair.

the Hundred Years War. The long series of wars between France and England, beginning in the reign of Edward III, 1337, and ending in that of Henry VI, 1453.

The first battle was a naval action off Sluys, and the last the fight at Castillon. It originated in English claims to the French crown, and resulted in the English being expelled from the whole of France, except Calais.

the Chiltern Hundreds, see CHILTERN.

Huneker, James Gibbons (1860–1921). American critic and author, known for his urbane wit, the richness of his style, and his penetrating essays on contemporary painting, literature, and music. Among the latter are: *Mezzotints in Modern Music* (1899); *Chopin: The Man and His Music* (1900); *Iconoclasts: A Book of Dramatists* (1905); *Egoists: A Book of Supermen* (1909); *Promenades of an Impressionist* (1910); *Ivory Apes and Peacocks* (1915); *Unicorns* (1917); *Variations* (1921). *Old Fogy* (1913) and *Steeplejack* (1921) are books of autobiography, and *Painted Veils* (1921) is a novel dealing with artist life in New York City.

Hungerford, Margaret Wolfe *née* **Hamilton** (1855?–1897). Irish novelist. Best-known among her over thirty novels is *Molly Bawn* (1878). Most of her books were signed **The Duchess.**

hunger strike. The refusal of a prisoner, confined usually for a political misdemeanor, to take any food until he is released or secures some desired concession. This practice seems to have originated in Russia, but was widely employed by suffragette prisoners in England during the early years of the 20th century and later by Irish political prisoners and Mohandas K. ("Mahatma") GANDHI, Indian nationalist leader.

Hung Society. Also known as **Triad Society.** A very large Chinese secret society with an elaborate ritual. Founded in the 17th century and active in political revolts, etc. The triad of the name is "heaven, earth, man."

Huns. A term very generally used with reference to the Germans in World War I, from the tribe of barbarian invaders from western Asia who were a terror to all Europe in the 5th century.

Hunt. *Like Hunt's dog, he would neither go to church nor stay at home.* A Shropshire saying. The story is that one Hunt, a laboring man, kept a mastiff, which, on being shut up while his master went to church, howled and barked so as to disturb the whole congregation. Hunt thereupon thought he would take him to church the next Sunday, but the dog positively refused to enter. The proverb is applied to a self-willed person, who will neither be led nor driven.

Hunt, Frazier (1885–). American journalist. War correspondent in France (1918), etc.

Hunt, Gaillard (1862–1924). American man of letters. Edited the writings of James MADISON (1900–1910) in nine volumes and ten volumes (16–25) of the journals of the Continental Congress (1910–1922). Author of *Life in America One Hundred Years Ago* (1914); etc.

Hunt, Holman (1827–1910). Pre-Raphaelite painter. Member of Order of Merit (1905). Author of *Pre-Raphaelitism and the Pre-Raphaelite Brotherhood* (1905).

Hunt, James Henry Leigh (1784–1859). English journalist, essayist, poet, and political radical, best known for his contemporary reputation and his association with and influence upon the English romantic poets BYRON, SHELLEY, and KEATS. As the result of articles in his periodical THE EXAMINER attacking King George IV, he was imprisoned for two years (1813–1815) and became a hero among the liberals and radicals of the day. Among his verse the best-known are ABOU BEN ADHEM (1834), *The Glove and the Lions* (1836), and *The Story of Rimini* (1816; see FRANCESCA DA RIMINI).

Hunt, Violet (1866–1942). English biographer and novelist. Daughter of the Pre-Raphaelite painter Alfred William Hunt. Formed an alliance with Ford Madox Hueffer (afterward Ford Madox FORD), whose wife refused him a divorce. She and Ford were estranged for many years before his death. Her autobiography, *I Have This To Say* (1926), and her biography, *The Wife of Rossetti* (1932), are excellent source books.

Hunter, Mr. and Mrs. Leo. In Dickens' PICKWICK PAPERS, persons who court the society of any celebrity, and consequently invite Mr. Pickwick and his three friends to an entertainment in their house. Mrs. Leo Hunter is the author of an "Ode to an Expiring Frog," considered by her friends a most masterly performance.

Hunter, Vridar. See FISHER, VARDIS.

Huntington, Archer Milton (1870–). American writer and Hispanic scholar. Son of the railroad builder and millionaire Collis P. Huntington. He himself founded Hispanic Society of America (1904) and gave it the Hispanic Museum. His wife, **Anna Hyatt** (1876–), is a well-known sculptor, represented by bronzes of animals in the Metropolitan Museum in New York, and creator of statues of Joan of Arc, El Cid, etc.

Huntley, Edgar, see EDGAR HUNTLEY.

Huon de Bordeaux. The hero of a medieval French *chanson de geste* of that name, a late prose version of which was translated into English by Lord Berners in the time of Henry VIII.

Huon wishes to go from Syria to Babylon, and learns that the shortest and best way is through a wood sixteen leagues long, and full of fairies; and that few can go that way because King OBERON is sure to encounter them. Whoever speaks to him is lost forever, and if a traveler refuses to answer him, he raises a most horrible storm of wind and rain, and makes the forest seem one great river. Huon proceeds on his way, and finally addresses Oberon, who tells him the history of his birth. They become great friends, and when Oberon goes to Paradise he leaves Huon his successor as lord and king of Mommur. He marries Esclairmond, and was crowned "King of all Faerie."

Hurlothrumbo. A burlesque opera, which in 1729–1730 had an extraordinary run at the Haymarket theater. So great was its popularity that a club called "The Hurlothrumbo Society" was formed. The author was Samuel Johnson (1691–1773), a half-mad dancing master, who put this motto on the title-page when the burlesque was printed:

> Ye sons of fire, read my *Hurlothrumbo*,
> Turn it betwixt your finger and your thumbo,
> And being quite undone, be quite struck dumbo.

The term Hurlothrumbo became proverbial for "absurdity."

Hurricane Nell. In A. G. Simms' historical novel *Eutaw* (1856), a mysterious and tragic woman who possesses a sort of second sight.

Hurst, Fannie (1889–). American novelist and short-story writer, author of best-selling books dealing chiefly with women and their problems in love affairs, domestic life, and public careers. Collections of short stories include *Just Around the Corner* (1914); *Gaslight Sonatas* (1918); *Humoresque* (1919); *The Vertical City* (1922); *Song of Life* (1927); *Procession* (1929); *We Are Ten* (1937). Among her novels are *Star-dust* (1921); *Lum-*

mox (1923); *Appassionata* (1926); *Mannequin* (1926); *A President Is Born* (1928); *Five and Ten* (1929); *Back Street* (1931); *Imitation of Life* (1933); *Anitra's Dance* (1934); *Great Laughter* (1936). Several of her books were dramatized as motion pictures, especially *Humoresque*.

Hurston, Zora Neale (1901–). American Negro novelist. At one time amanuensis for Fannie HURST. Her novels include *Jonah's Gourd Vine* (1934); *Moses, Man of the Mountain* (1939). Her play, *From Sun to Sun*, was produced at the John Golden Theatre in New York. *Dust Tracks on a Road* (1942) is an autobiography.

Hushai. In Dryden's ABSALOM AND ACHITOPHEL, Laurence Hyde, Earl of Rochester (1641–1711). Hushai is David's friend, who opposes the counsels of Achitophel and causes the plot of Absalom to miscarry; so Rochester defeated the schemes of Shaftesbury, and brought to naught the rebellion of the Duke of Monmouth.

Huss, John (1369?–1415). Bohemian religious reformer. Rector of the university of Prague. Condemned and burned at stake for propagating a reform doctrine influenced by WYCLIFFE. His followers, the Hussites, organized a religious and political party and waged a fierce civil war (1419–1434). Their radical wing, the Taborites, became merged with the Bohemian Brethren. The conservatives or Calixtines turned Lutheran or Roman Catholic.

Hussonet. In Flaubert's SENTIMENTAL EDUCATION, an opportunistic journalist and editor, a friend of Frederic Moreau, the hero. At the time of the Revolution of 1848, he is an ardent supporter of radical beliefs, but he rapidly changes with the times and eventually becomes an equally ardent supporter of Napoleon III.

Hutchins, Eveline. In John Dos Passos' trilogy U.S.A. the daughter of a wealthy Chicago clergyman, who goes into the interior decorating business with her friend Eleanor Stoddard, later transferring it to New York, where they join a Bohemian set. The two go to France as Red Cross workers in World War I, Eveline has a brief love affair with a newspaper correspondent named Jerry Burnham, and she and Eleanor quarrel over which one is preferred by J. Ward MOOREHOUSE. Eveline at last manages to trick Paul Johnson, an American soldier, into marrying her. After the war, she and Paul live in GREENWICH VILLAGE, associating with the Bohemians and intellectuals of the time. In THE BIG MONEY Eveline has an unsuccessful love affair and commits suicide.

Hutchins, Robert Maynard (1899–). American educator. President of the University of Chicago (from 1929). Author of *The Higher Learning in America* (1936); etc. His father, **William James Hutchins** (1871–) is especially known as president of Berea College, Ky. (from 1920).

Hutchinson, Anne (1591–1643). American religious liberal, born in England. Preached salvation by personal intuition of divine grace. Tried and convicted as leader of an antinomian faction. Banished from Bay Colony (1637). After having settled near what is now Pelham Manor, N.Y. (1642), she and her family were massacred by Indians (1643) on a split rock near the present Hutchinson Parkway, named in her memory.

Hutchinson, Arthur Stuart Menteth (1879–). English novelist. Author of *If Winter Comes* (1920); *This Freedom* (1922); etc. Belongs to the same general school as Warwick DEEPING, but is a better writer.

Hutchinson, Lucy (1620–1675). English prose writer, known for her biography of her husband, Colonel Hutchinson, an outstanding Puritan leader and soldier during the English Civil War, who was imprisoned by the Stuarts during the Restoration period. The work, entitled *Memoirs of the Life of Colonel Hutchinson,* was written after 1664 and published in 1806. It is considered noteworthy because of its character analysis of its subject, its defense of the Puritan character in general, and its picture of a 17th-century English Puritan household. See also CAVENDISH, MARGARET.

Hutten, Ulrich von (1488–1523). German nobleman, soldier, and humanist. Vigorously defended Luther, disputed with Erasmus. Remarkable both as poet and prose satirist. Crowned poet by emperor Maximilian (1517). Co-author of the EPISTOLAE OBSCURORUM VIRORUM. Early singer of German patriotism. Died in exile on the island of Ufenau near Zurich, Switzerland.

Huxley, Aldous (1894–). English novelist, journalist, and essayist, grandson of Thomas HUXLEY and great-nephew of Matthew ARNOLD, associated with J. Middleton MURRY and Katherine MANSFIELD in editing the ATHENAEUM and a friend of D. H. LAWRENCE. He is best known for his witty, biting satires on the disillusioned and decadent intellectuals and society people in England of the 1920's. Later in his career he became interested in pacifism and Indian mysticism and supernaturalism. In his work of both types the influence of his scientific studies and background is strong.

Collections of Huxley's short stories include: *Limbo* (1920); *Mortal Coils* (1922); *The Little Mexican, And Other Stories* (1924); *Two or Three Graces* (1926); *Brief Candles* (1930). His novels are: *Crome Yellow* (1921); *Antic*

Hay (1923); *Those Barren Leaves* (1925); POINT COUNTER POINT (1928), his best-known novel; BRAVE NEW WORLD (1932); *Eyeless in Gaza* (1936); *After Many a Summer Dies the Swan* (1940). *Grey Eminence* (1942) is an historical study. Among his essays and criticism are: *On the Margin* (1923); *Jesting Pilate* (1923); *Do What You Will* (1929); *The Holy Face, And Other Essays* (1929); *Vulgarity in Literature* (1930); *Music at Night* (1931); *Texts and Pretexts* (1932); *Beyond the Mexique Bay* (1934); *The Olive Tree, And Other Essays* (1936); *An Encyclopedia of Pacifism* (1937); *Ends and Means* (1937). *The Burning Wheel* (1916) and *Jonah* (1917) are books of poetry. Huxley also edited the letters of D. H. Lawrence in 1932. He took up residence in California during the latter 1930's, and has written scenarios for moving pictures.

Julian Sorell Huxley (1887–), his brother, followed the scientific tradition of the family and became a leading English biologist and writer on popular science.

Huxley, Thomas Henry (1825–1895). English biologist and teacher, known for his defense of the theory of evolution held by DARWIN and his lectures and writings popularizing science. His books include: *Man's Place in Nature* (1863); *The Physical Basis of Life* (1868); *Lay Sermons, Addresses, and Reviews* (1870); *Science and Morals* (1886); *Essays upon Some Controverted Questions* (1892); *Ethics and Evolution* (1893). Huxley was called "Darwin's Bulldog" and engaged in a controversy with the English statesman Gladstone on the question of scientific evolutionary theories *vs.* Biblical lore. He was the grandfather of Aldous and Julian HUXLEY.

Huygens, Christian (1629–1695). Dutch mathematician, physicist, astronomer. Constructed improved telescopes; invented the pendulum in clocks; developed the wave theory of light; etc. Fellow, Royal Society of England.

Huysmans, Joris-Karl (1848–1907). French novelist, of Dutch ancestry, known for his neurasthenia, perverse tastes, and attraction, finally conversion, to Catholicism, in all of which he is considered to have been typical of the DECADENTS of his time. His style is marked by vivid and concrete figures, fantastic description, and a gift for portraying the grotesque. His books include *Marthe* (1876); AGAINST THE GRAIN (*A Rebours;* 1884); *Là-bas* (1891); EN ROUTE! (1895); *La Cathédrale* (1898).

Hyacinth. According to Grecian fable, the son of Amyclas, a Spartan king. The lad was beloved by Apollo and Zephyr, and as he preferred the sun-god, Zephyr drove Apollo's quoit at his head, and killed him. The blood became a flower, and the petals are inscribed with the signature Ai, meaning *woe*. See also ADONIS.

Hyatt, Anne. See under HUNTINGTON, Archer.

Hybla Minor and **Major.** In ancient geography, two Sicilian towns. Hybla Minor was noted for its honey. Hence Hyblaean, "honeyed, sweet, etc."

Hyde, Douglas (1860–). Irish historian, poet and folklorist. Most of his writings are in Gaelic. Compiled the incomparable *Love Songs of Connaught* (1894). First president of Eire (1938).

Hyde, Edward. 1st Earl of **Clarendon** (1609–1674). See under CLARENDON PRESS.

Hyde, Mr., see JEKYLL.

Hyde Park. A large park in west central London. A recreative center and favorite place for open-air meetings.

Hydra. A monster of the Lernean marshes, in Argolis. It had nine heads, and one of the twelve labors of Hercules was to kill it. As soon as he struck off one of its heads, two shot up in its place; hence *hydra-headed* is applied to a difficulty which goes on increasing as it is combated.

hydra-headed multitude. The rabble, which not only is many-headed numerically, but seems to grow more numerous the more it is attacked and resisted.

Hygieia. Goddess of health in Greek mythology, and the daughter of AESCULAPIUS. Her symbol was a serpent drinking from a cup in her hand.

Hyksos (*Shepherd Kings*). A line of six or more foreign rulers over Egypt, who reigned for about 250 years between the XIIth and XVIIIth Dynasties, i.e., somewhere about 2000 B. C. It is uncertain whence they came, who they were, what they did, or whither they went; they left little in the way of records or monuments, and practically all that is known of them is the (historically speaking) very unsatisfactory notice gleaned by Josephus from Manetho.

Hylas. In classical mythology a favorite of Hercules whom he accompanied on the Argonautic expedition. While drawing water at a fountain in Mysia, he was drawn down by the water nymphs who had fallen in love with him.

Hymen. Properly, a marriage song of the ancient Greeks; later personified as the god of marriage, represented as a youth carrying a torch and veil—a more mature Eros, or Cupid.

Hymettus. A mountain in Attica, famous for its honey.

Hymir. In Scandinavian mythology, a giant with a frosty beard who personifies the inhospitable sea. He owned the kettle in which the gods brewed their ale, and it was he who took Thor in his boat when that god went to kill the Midgard serpent, and robbed him of his prey.

Hymn of Hate (Hassgesang). A German poem by Ernst LISSAUER, current during World War I and denouncing England by using as a refrain the old phrase, "Gott strafe England" ("God punish England"). Hence the verb "to strafe."

Hyne, Charles John Cutcliffe Wright (1865–1944). English writer. Best-known as creator of the fictional character of Captain Kettle in several series of stories illustrated by Stanley L. Wood and running in *Pearson's Magazine. The Lost Continent* (1900) is a romance of the lost Atlantis.

Hypatia. A historical novel by Charles KINGSLEY (1853), a romance of 5th-century Alexandria. The hero is a young monk named Philammon, who leaves his monastery for a more active struggle with the brilliant pagan life of the great city. He is strongly drawn to Hypatia, a brilliant lecturer on Greek philosophy and a woman of rare spiritual charm. But the fanatical Christians of the city cannot tolerate her teachings, and she is torn to pieces by an angry mob.

hyperbole. The rhetorical figure of speech which consists of exaggeration or extravagance in statement for the purpose of giving effect but not intended to be taken *au pied de la lettre,* as, "the waves were mountains high."

Hyperboreans. A happy people of early Greek legend, who were supposed to dwell on the other side of the spot where the North Wind had its birth, and therefore to enjoy perpetual warmth and sunshine. They were said to be the oldest of the human race, the most virtuous, and the most happy; to dwell for some thousand years under a cloudless sky, in fields yielding double harvests, and in the enjoyment of perpetual spring.

Later fable held that they had not an atmosphere like our own, but one consisting wholly of feathers. Both Herodotus and Pliny mention this fiction, which they say was suggested by the quantity of snow observed to fall in those regions.

Hyperion. In Greek mythology, one of the Titans, son of Uranus and Ge, and father of Helios, Selene and Eos (the Sun, Moon and Dawn). The name is sometimes given by poets to the sun itself. One of the best-known works of Keats is his "poetical fragment" of this name (1820).

Longfellow gave the title to a long poetic romance, *Hyperion, the Wanderer on High* (1839), not concerned, however, with the ancient Titan but with a modern wanderer through many lands. The heroine is Mary ASHBURTON.

Hypermnestra. In Greek legend, the wife of Lynceus and the only one of the fifty daughters of Danaus who did not murder her husband on their bridal night. See DANAÏDES.

hyphenated American. An American citizen of divided allegiance because of foreign birth or parentage; an Irish-American, German-American, etc. The term was popularized during World War I.

Hypnos. In Greek mythology, the god of sleep.

Hypsipyle. In Greek legend, a woman of Lemnos who saved her father Thoas, when all the other men were killed by the women of the island. Cf. the poem of that title by Maurice HEWLETT.

I

Iacchus. A name for BACCHUS.

Iachimo. An Italian libertine who is at the bottom of most of the complications in Shakespeare's CYMBELINE.

Iago. The villain of Shakespeare's tragedy OTHELLO, who deliberately strings together such a mass of circumstantial evidence in proof of Desdemona's love for Cassio, that the Moor kills her out of jealousy.

> The cool malignity of Iago, silent in his resentment, subtle in his designs, and studious at once of his interest and his vengeance, . . . are such proofs of Shakespeare's skill in human nature as it would be vain to seek in any modern writer.—Dr. Johnson.

iambus. An *iambus* or *iamb* is a poetic foot consisting of a short syllable followed by a long one, as betray, confess, be gone. Iambic verse is verse based on iambs. The meter is further designated by the number of poetic feet in the line, as iambic hexameter, pentameter, tetrameter, etc. Some examples follow.

Iambic verse of six feet or hexameter (called the ALEXANDRINE measure)—

> I think the thoughts you think; and if I have the knack
> Of fitting thoughts to words, you peradventure lack,
> Envy me not the chance, yourselves more fortunate!
> Browning, *Fifine at the Fair,* lxxvi.

Iambic verse of five feet or pentameter, the meter of the SONNET of BLANK VERSE and the heroic couplet. See PENTAMETER for a more restricted use.

> The world is still deceived with ornament.
> In law, what plea so tainted and corrupt
> But being seasoned with a gracious voice
> Obscures the show of evil?
> Shakespeare, *Merchant of Venice.*

Iambic verse of four feet (tetrameter) and three feet (trimeter) in alternate lines. This constitutes what is known as BALLAD METER.

> I would begin the music here
> And so my soul should rise
> O for some heavenly notes to bear
> My spirit to the skies.
> Watts, *Horae Lyricae.*

Iambic verse of seven feet or heptameter, a line known as the FOURTEENER.

> But all these things have ceased to be with my desire of life.
> Tennyson, *May Queen.*

Ianthe. A poetic name much in use in the 19th century. The Ianthe to whom Lord BYRON dedicated his *Childe Harold,* was Lady Charlotte Harley, born 1801, and only eleven years old at the time. He borrowed it from U. S. LANDOR, who had thus "etherealized" the middle name of his early sweetheart Sophia *Jane* Swift, who became the Countess de Molandé and died in Paris in 1851. Landor wrote many poems in her praise. SHELLEY gave the name to the maiden to whom Queen Mab appears in his poem of that name.

Iapetus. In classical mythology, son of Uranus and Ge, father of Atlas, Prometheus, Epimetheus, and Menoetius, and ancestor of the human race, hence called *genus Iäpeti,* the progeny of Iapetus.

Iasion. According to a Greek myth, a mortal who was united with Demeter and made her the mother of Plutus. He was killed for his presumption by Zeus' lightning. The myth probably symbolizes the fertilization of the fields.

Ibáñez, Vicente Blasco, see BLASCO IBÁÑEZ, VICENTE.

Ibbetson, Peter, see PETER IBBETSON.

Iberia. Spain; the country of the Iberus, the ancient name of the river Ebro.

Iberia's Pilot. Christopher Columbus (1446?–1507).

Iberville, Pierre le Moyne, Sieur d' (1661–1706). French-Canadian commander and explorer. Born at Montreal. Founded French colony in Louisiana, first at Biloxi, later at Mobile (1698). Died at Havana during preparations for an attack on the coast of North Carolina.

Ibis. A sacred bird of the ancient Egyptians, specially connected with the god Thoth, who in the guise of an ibis escaped the pursuit of Typhon. Its white plumage symbolized the light of the sun, and its black neck the shadow of the moon, its body a heart, and its legs a triangle. It was said that it drank only the purest of water, and that the bird was so fond of Egypt that it would pine to death if transported elsewhere.

ibn-. Arabic prefix meaning "son." Corresponding to Hebrew *ben* ("son"), Scotch and Gaelic *Mac-* ("son"), Irish *O'-* ("descendant of"), etc.

Ibraham. The Abraham of the Koran.

Ibsen, Henrik (1828–1906). Norwegian dramatist, famous for his plays dealing with social problems and urging social reform, which were widely attacked as "immoral" at the time of their first production and which had an important influence on the drama of the 20th century. His works include FRU INGER AT OSTERRAD, THE WARRIORS AT HELGOLAND (1858), and KONGSEMNERNE (1862), historical plays in a romantic vein; LOVE'S COMEDY (1863), BRAND (1866), and PEER GYNT (1867), poetic dramas; THE YOUNG MEN'S LEAGUE (1869); EMPEROR AND GALILEAN (1873); PILLARS OF SOCIETY (1877); A DOLL'S HOUSE (1879); GHOSTS (1881); AN ENEMY OF THE PEOPLE (1882); THE WILD DUCK (1884); ROSMERSHOLM (1886); THE LADY FROM THE SEA (1888); HEDDA GABLER (1890); THE MASTER BUILDER (1892); LITTLE EYOLF (1894); JOHN GABRIEL BORKMAN (1896); WHEN WE DEAD AWAKEN (1899). Ibsen is considered one of the greatest and most important of modern dramatists. He particularly influenced George Bernard SHAW, and was admired by James JOYCE, whose FINNEGANS WAKE contains a number of allusions to the dramatist and his work. Most of Ibsen's problems are dead and buried. His art is alive as ever.

Ibycus. A Greek lyric poet of the 6th century B.C. According to legend, he was murdered with only a passing flock of cranes as witnesses. In the presence of a large crowd one of the murderers betrayed himself, when he saw a flock of cranes pass overhead, by exclaiming: "The cranes of Ibycus!" This phrase signifies hence "unsuspected witnesses to a crime." Cf. SCHILLER's famous ballad, *Die Kraniche des Ibykus.*

Icarius. In Greek legend an Athenian who was taught the cultivation of the vine by Dionysus (Bacchus). He was slain by some peasants who had become intoxicated with wine he had given them, and who thought they had been poisoned. They buried the body under a tree; his daughter Erigone, searching for her father, was directed to the spot by the howling of his dog Maera, and when she discovered the body she hanged herself for grief. Icarius became the constellation *Boötes,* Erigone the constellation *Virgo,* and Maera the star *Procyon,* which rises in July, a little before the dog-star.

Icarus. In Greek mythology, son of DAEDALUS. He flew with his father from Crete; but the sun melted the wax with which his wings were fastened on, and he fell into the sea, hence called the Icarian.

The adjective *Icarian* is used to mean venturesome.

Icebound. A drama by Owen Davis (*Am.,* 1923). The principal characters are the Jordans, hard, selfish New Englanders who can hardly wait until their sharp old mother dies to get her money. She has left it, instead, to Jane Crosby, a girl who has taken care of her for years, with a secret understanding that it is to be held in trust for the black sheep of the family, Ben Jordan, whom Jane loves. The play was awarded the Pulitzer Prize.

Iceland Fisherman, An (*Pêcheur d'Islande*). A novel by Pierre LOTI (1866). The Iceland fishermen live on the coast of Brittany, but make the voyage to Iceland every year during the fishing season. The hero, Sylvestre, takes part in the war between France and China and dies at Singapore on his way home. The charm of the book is considered to be its descriptive passages.

Ichabod. (1) A son of Phinehas, born just after the death of his father and grandfather (1 *Sam.* iv. 21). The name (Heb. I-kabhoth) means "where is the glory?" It is usually popularly translated by "the glory has departed."

(2) A poem by WHITTIER (1850). Whittier said he had in mind Daniel Webster, who had made a speech supporting the Fugitive Slave Law. Later, however, in *The Lost Occasion,* he paid a tribute to Webster's sincerity and genius. The following lines are from *Ichabod:*

> "All else is gone; from those great eyes
> The soul has fled;
> When faith is lost, when honor dies
> The man is dead."

ichthus. Greek for "fish," which in primitive times was used as a symbol of Christ because the word is formed of the initial letters of *I*esous, *CH*ristos, *TH*eou, *U*ios, *S*oter, "Jesus Christ, Son of God, Savior." This notarikon is found on many seals, rings, urns, and tombstones, belonging to the early times of Christianity, and was supposed to be a "charm" of mystical efficacy.

Ickes, Harold LeClair (1874–). American lawyer and politician. Stanch defender of the New Deal. U.S. Secretary of the Interior (1933–1946). Also administrator of public works (1933–1939); etc.

icon. In the Eastern Church, an image or representation of Christ, a saint, or an angel. Icons are sacred and honored with relative worship (kissing, incense, light, etc.) but not with supreme worship or the latria which is due to God alone. They range from elaborate works of art in the church buildings to humble enamel and niello objects carried by the peasantry.

Icon Basilike, see EIKON.

iconoclasts (*Gr.,* image breakers). Reformers who rose in the Eastern Church in the 8th century, and were specially opposed to the employment of pictures, statues, emblems, and all visible representations of sacred objects. The crusade against these things began in 726 with the Emperor Leo III, the Isaurian, and continued for one hundred and twenty years under Constantine Copronymus, Leo the Armenian, Theophilus, and other Byzantine Emperors, who are known as the *Iconoclast Emperors.*

A person who criticizes and seriously questions ideas and attitudes previously accepted as correct, just, and valuable by convention and tradition rather than by independent examination and judgment, is also called an *iconoclast.*

Ida. The name of the titular heroine in Tennyson's poem, THE PRINCESS. There is also a Gilbert and Sullivan opera called *Princess Ida* (1884).

Idaean Mother. Cybele, who had a temple on Mount Ida, in Asia Minor.

Idalian. Pertaining to Idalium, an ancient town in Cyprus, or to Aphrodite to whom the place was consecrated.

idealism. A system of philosophy asserting reality to consist of ideas, or mind, or that only ideas are real. The historical founder of idealism was PLATO, and it was the dominant philosophical system in Europe during the romantic period (see ROMANTICISM), later being carried to the U.S. It was developed by the English philosophers LOCKE, BERKELEY, and HUME, and was brought into full flower by the Germans KANT, FICHTE, SCHELLING, and HEGEL. Later idealists were F. H. BRADLEY, Josiah ROYCE, Charles PEIRCE, and A. N. WHITEHEAD. See also SOLIPSISM; TRANSCENDENTALISM; and MATERIALISM.

In popular usage, *idealism,* being derived from "ideal" rather than from "idea," refers to a belief in the reality of perfection and the perfectibility of the human race; an emphasis on spiritual values, altruism, and the general good, rather than on worldly benefits for the individual; and a tendency to think in terms of what can or what should be, rather than of what is—as "an idealistic reformer." When used in this way, the term usually has a patronizing connotation.

Ides. In the Roman calendar the 15th of March, May, July, and October, and the 13th of all the other months; always eight days after the Nones.

beware the Ides of March. Said as a warning of impending and certain danger. The allusion is the warning received from a soothsayer by Julius Caesar before his assassination:

> Furthermore, there was a certain soothsayer that had given Caesar warning long time afore, to take heed of the day of the Ides of March (which is the fifteenth of the month), for on that day he should be in great danger. That day being come, Caesar going into the Senate-house and speaking merrily unto the soothsayer, told him, "The Ides of March be come": "So be they," softly answered the soothsayer, "but yet are they not past."—Plutarch, *Julius Caesar* (*North's trans.*).

Idiot, The. A novel by Fyodor DOSTOYEVSKY (1868), depicting in Prince MYSHKIN, the epileptic hero, a man of gentle, childlike sincerity in contact with the world. St. Petersburg laughs at him and calls him "the Idiot." His fiancée, Aglaia, resents his magnanimity as lack of pride and is jealous of Nastasia, in whom she fears a dangerous rival. When evil passions break loose and the affair ends tragically for Nastasia, the Prince goes insane.

Idiot, The Inspired, see INSPIRED IDIOT.

Idle Bible, see BIBLE, SPECIALLY NAMED.

Idler, The. A section of the English periodical *The Universal Chronicle, or Weekly Gazette,* to which the English Samuel JOHNSON contributed a series of essays, usually light in character, from 1758 to 1760.

Idomeneus. King of Crete, an ally of the Greeks at Troy. His adventures are related in the *Iliad*. After the city was burnt he made a vow to sacrifice whatever he first encountered, if the gods granted him a safe return to his kingdom. It was his own son that he first met. He offered him up to fulfil his vow, but a plague followed, and the King was banished from Crete as a murderer. See also IPHIGENIA; JEPHTHAH.

Iduna or **Idun.** In Scandinavian mythology, daughter of the dwarf Svald, and wife of Bragi. She was guardian of the golden apples which the gods tasted as often as they wished to renew their youth, and seems to personify the year between March and September, when the sun is north of the equator. Her apples indicate fruits generally. Loki carries her off to Giant-Land, when the Sun descends below the equator, and steals her apples. Iduna makes her escape in the form of a sparrow in March when the Sun rises again above the equator; and both gods and men rejoice in her return.

idyll. A pastoral poem, usually brief, stressing the picturesque phases of country life. The most celebrated idylls of antiquity are those of Theocritus and Vergil. The word is now used to denote such diverse forms of literature as prose tales of country life and Tennyson's poetic *Idylls of the King* (which have a picturesque but not a rustic setting), as well as modern pastorals.

Idylls of the King. A series of poems by TENNYSON (between 1859 and 1872), in twelve books. The titles are—THE COMING OF ARTHUR; GARETH AND LYNETTE; THE MARRIAGE OF GERAINT; GERAINT AND ENID; BALIN AND BALAN; MERLIN AND VIVIEN; LAUNCELOT AND ELAINE; THE HOLY GRAIL; PELLEAS AND ETTARRE; THE LAST TOURNAMENT; GUINEVERE; THE PASSING OF ARTHUR. See also ARTHUR; ARTHURIAN ROMANCE.

Ierne. An ancient name of Ireland or Eire. Cf. also *Erin* and *Hibernia*.

If Winter Comes. A novel by A. S. M. Hutchinson (*Eng.,* 1921). The hero, Mark SABRE, a man of whimsical, affectionate, imaginative temperament, finds life with his unsympathetic wife Mabel a good deal of a trial. With a complete disregard for the conventions but from the best of motives he befriends a girl who is in trouble and is consequently accused of being the father of her illegitimate child. The real offender is the scapegrace son whom his business associate has always idolized; and when the boy's death at the front is reported, Mark knows that he can never bring himself to tell the truth and so clear himself. But in spite of numerous misfortunes, Mark's spring is not far behind; his wife divorces him, the woman he has always loved is suddenly free to marry, and all ends happily. The allusion of the title is to the last line of Shelley's *Ode to the West*

Wind, "If winter comes, can spring be far behind?"

Igerne or **Igraine.** Wife of GORLOIS, Duke of Tintagel, in Cornwall, and mother of King Arthur in Arthurian legend. Tennyson spells the name YGERNE.

Ignaro. Foster-father of ORGOGLIO in Spenser's *Faërie Queene* (I. viii). Whatever question Arthur asks, the old dotard answers that he cannot tell. Spenser says this old man walks one way and looks another, because ignorance is always "wrong-headed."

Ignatius, St., see under SAINT.

Ignatz. See KRAZY KAT.

ignis fatuus. The "will o' the wisp" or "friar's lanthorn" a flame-like phosphorescence flitting over marshy ground caused by the spontaneous combustion of gases from decaying vegetable matter, and deluding people who attempt to follow it; hence, any delusive aim or object, or some Utopian scheme that is utterly impracticable. The name means "a foolish fire"; it is also called "Jack o' Lantern," "spunkie," "walking fire," and "Fair Maid of Ireland."

Igraine, see IGERNE.

I have a Rendezvous With Death. A poem of World War I written by Alan SEEGER.

I.H.S. The Greek ΙΗΣ, meaning ΙΗΣους (Jesus), the long e (H) being mistaken for a capital H, and the dash perverted into a cross. The letters being thus obtained, St. Bernardine of Siena, in 1347, applied them to *Jesus Hominum Salvator* (Jesus, the Savior of men), another application being *In hac salus* (safety in this, i.e., the Cross).

Ike and His Friends. A humorous book by B. P. Shillaber (*Am.,* 1879). Ike is the lively nephew of Mrs. PARTINGTON.

Ikhnaton or **Akhnaton.** Also **Amenhotep** IV. Egyptian king of the XVIIIth Dynasty; reigned ca. 1375–1358 B. C. Established worship of Aten, the sun-god, opposing priests of Amen, and hence sometimes referred to as the "religious revolutionary." His name signifies "splendor of the sun's disk."

Il Cortegiano. Popular title of *Il Libro d'Oro* by Baldassare CASTIGLIONE.

Ilf, Ilya Aronoldovich (1897–1937). Russian humorist. Collaborated with Eugene PETROV, much of their writing appearing in the Moscow satirical magazine *Crocodile* and in PRAVDA. The most noted humorist in post-revolutionary Russia, known as the "Soviet Mark Twain."

Iliad (Gr. *Ilias,* gen. *Iliad-os,* the land of Ilium). The tale of the siege of Troy, or Ilium, an epic poem for centuries attributed to HOMER, in twenty-four books. Menelaus, King of Sparta, receives as his guest Paris (a son of Priam, King of Troy), who runs away with Helen, wife of Menelaus. Menelaus induces the Greeks to lay siege to Troy to avenge the perfidy, and the siege lasts ten years. The poem begins in the tenth year with a quarrel between Agamemnon, King of Mycenae and commander-in-chief of the allied Greeks, and Achilles, the hero who retired from the army in ill temper. A brief synopsis follows:

Book I opens with a pestilence in the Grecian camp. The case is this: Chryses, the priest of Apollo, wishes to ransom his daughter, whom Agamemnon, the Greek commander-in-chief, has kept as a concubine, but Agamemnon refuses to give her up; so the priest prays to Apollo for vengeance, and the god sends a pestilence. A council is now called, Achilles upbraids Agamemnon as the cause of the divine wrath, and Agamemnon replies he will give up the priest's daughter, but will take instead Achilles' concubine. On hearing this, Achilles declares he will no longer fight, and accordingly retires to his tent and sulks there.

II. Jupiter, being induced to take the part of Achilles, now sends to Agamemnon a lying dream, which induces him to believe that he shall take the city at once; but in order to see how the soldiers are affected by the retirement of Achilles, the king calls them to a council of war, asks them if it will not be better to give up the siege and return home. He thinks the soldiers will shout "no" with one voice; but they rush to their ships and would set sail at once if they were not restrained by those privy to the plot.

III. The soldiers are then arrayed for battle. Paris proposes to decide the contest by single combat, and Menelaus accepts the challenge. Paris, being overthrown, is carried off by Venus, and Agamemnon demands that the Trojans shall give up Troy in fulfilment of the compact.

IV. While Agamemnon is speaking, Pandarus draws his bow at Menelaus and wounds him, and the battle becomes general.

V. Pandarus, who had violated the truce, is killed by Diomed.

VI. Hector, the general of the Trojan armies, recommends that the Trojan women in a body supplicate the gods to pardon the sin of Pandarus, and in the meantime he and Paris make a sally from the city gate.

VII. Hector fights with Ajax in single combat, but the combatants are parted by the heralds, who declare it a drawn battle; so they exchange gifts and return to their respective tents.

VIII. The Grecian host, discomfited, retreats; and Hector prepares to assault the enemy's camp.

IX. A deputation is sent to Achilles, but the sulky hero remains obdurate.

X. A night attack is made on the Trojans by Diomed and Ulysses;

XI. And the three Grecian chiefs (Agamemnon, Diomed, and Ulysses) are all wounded.

XII. The Trojans force the gates of the Grecian ramparts.

XIII. A tremendous battle ensues, in which many on both sides are slain.

XIV. While Jupiter is asleep, Neptune interferes in the quarrel in behalf of the Greeks;

XV. But Jupiter rebukes him, and Apollo, taking the side of the Trojans, puts the Greeks to a complete rout. The Trojans, exulting in their success, prepare to set fire to the Grecian camp.

XVI. In this extremity, Patroclus arrays himself in Achilles' armor, and leads the Myrmidons to the fight; but he is slain by Hector.

XVII. Achilles is told of the death of his friend;

XVIII. Resolves to return to the battle;

XIX. And is reconciled to Agamemnon.

XX. A general battle ensues, in which the gods take part.

XXI. The battle rages with great fury, the slaughter is frightful; but the Trojans are routed and retreat into their town, and close the gates.

XXII. Achilles slays Hector before he is able to enter the gates, and the battle is at an end. Nothing now remains but

XXIII. To burn the body of Patroclus, and celebrate the funeral games.

XXIV. Old Priam, going to the tent of Achilles, craves the body of his son Hector; Achilles gives it up, and the poem concludes with the funeral rites of the Trojan hero.

an Iliad of woes. A number of evils falling one after another; there is scarce a calamity in the whole catalogue of human ills that finds not mention in the *Iliad*.

Demosthenes used the phrase (*Ilias kakon*), and it was adopted by Cicero (*Ilias malorum*) in his *Ad Atticum*, viii, 11.

the French Iliad. The *Romance of the Rose* (see under ROSE) has been so called. Similarly, the NIBELUNGENLIED and the LUSIAD have been called respectively the German and Portuguese *Iliad*.

Illidge, Frank. In Aldous Huxley's POINT COUNTER POINT, laboratory assistant to Lord Edward TANTAMOUNT, an ugly little man with red hair who is a Communist and is bitterly conscious of his lower-class origin, hating the rich who patronize him or ignore him in Lord Edward's house.

Illingworth, Lord. A leading character in Oscar Wilde's WOMAN OF NO IMPORTANCE.

Illuminated Doctor, see under DOCTOR.

Ilmarinen. In the Finnish epic poem KALEVALA, a brother of Wanaimonen, the hero. He was a smith and made the heavens of blue steel. One of his wives was the product of his own handicraft, made of gold and silver and brought to life, but she was so cold that whatever came near her was likely to be frozen.

Il Penseroso. A poem by John MILTON, written in 1632. It celebrates the goddess of melancholy, contemplation, solitude, and study—the opposite of its companion poem L'ALLEGRO. The title was thought by the author to mean "The Meditative One," but it has been pointed out that the Italian is incorrect.

Ilsan the Monk or Monte Ilsan. In a German medieval epic called *The Rose Garden at Worms,* a boisterous friar who brings home fifty-two garlands from his successful expedition against Kriemhild's *Rosegarten* and presses these same thorny garlands into the tender flesh of his fellow friars until they consent to pray to Heaven for the forgiveness of his sins.

imagination. In romantic aesthetic theory, the creative function of the intellect, by which separate elements of experience are synthesized in a new whole differing from and transcending any of its original parts. S. T. COLERIDGE was a leading proponent of the theory of imagination, and his two famous poems, THE RIME OF THE ANCIENT MARINER and KUBLA KHAN, are regarded as excellent examples of the working of imagination. See FANCY. For a fuller discussion, consult Coleridge's *Biographia Literaria* and *Coleridge on Imagination,* by I. A. Richards.

imagism. A movement in poetry (ca. 1909–1917), especially flourishing in the U.S. and England, which advocated the use of FREE VERSE, new rhythmic effects, colloquial language, a greater freedom than heretofore in the choice of subject-matter, and the creation of precise, concentrated, sharply delineated images to evoke a unified impression, in which the emotion or association represented and the object in itself are balanced equally in importance. Important single influences on the movement were T. E. HULME and Ezra POUND, the latter especially favoring Greek and Roman classic poetry and the poetry of China, Japan, and the French symbolists (see SYMBOLISM) as models. POUND and later Amy LOWELL were leaders of the imagist movement in America, from time to time compiling anthologies, each of which was entitled *Some Imagist Poets,* of the work of their associates. H. D. and John Gould FLETCHER were other outstanding American imagists; D. H. LAWRENCE, F. S. FLINT and Richard ALDINGTON were prominent in the English movement. See also KAHN, GUSTAVE; OBJECTIVISM.

Imam, see RULERS, TITLES OF.

Imhotep. In Egyptian mythology, the god of learning, protector of scribes. Corresponding to, and identified by the Greeks with their Aesculapius.

Imitation of Christ, The. A famous devotional book written originally in Latin (1417–1421) and attributed to Thomas à Kempis or the Abbé Gerson.

Imlac. In Samuel Johnson's RASSELAS (1759) the son of a rich merchant of Goiama, near the mouth of the Nile. Imlac is a great traveler and a poet, who accompanies Rasselas in his rambles and returns with him to the HAPPY VALLEY.

Immaculate Conception. In the Roman Catholic Church, the dogma that the Virgin Mary "in the first instant of her conception, by a singular privilege and grace granted by God, was preserved free from all stain of original sin." The controversy regarding the Immaculate Conception dates from the twelfth century. It was formally proclaimed by Pope Pius IX (1854) in the bull *Ineffabilis Deus.*

Immanuel. From Hebrew. Literally, "God with us"; an appellation of Christ, also used as a proper name.

Immelmann, Max (1890–1916). German aviator in the first World War who developed the maneuver known as the "Immelmann turn." It is a half loop combined with a half roll and is also known as "reverse turn."

Immoralist, The (L'Immoraliste). A novel by André GIDE (1902), based on details of the author's own biography. The hero goes with his wife to North Africa to recover from an attack of tuberculosis, and while there discovers that his psychological nature is not suited to normal marriage. His wife contracts tuberculosis herself while nursing him and dies, whereupon he goes to live in the native quarter to free himself from the moral laws and conventions of his upbringing and to find satisfaction according to the impulses of his individual psychology.

immortal.

the Immortal. Yông-Tching (1723–1736), third of the Manchu dynasty of China, assumed the title.

the Immortal Tinker. John Bunyan (1628–1688) a tinker by trade.

the Immortals. The forty members of the French Academy; also, the name given to a body of 10,000 foot-soldiers, which constituted the bodyguard of the ancient Persian kings, and to other highly trained troops.

the Immortal Four of Italy. Dante (1265–1321), Petrarch (1304–1374), Ariosto (1474–1533), and Tasso (1544–1595).

the Immortal Three. Homer, Dante and Milton.

Imogen. (1) The heroine of Shakespeare's CYMBELINE.

(2) *Imogen* or *Imogine* is the name of the fair lady in the ballad, ALONZO THE BRAVE AND THE FAIR IMOGEN.

Imoinda. In Mrs. Aphra Behn's novel OROONOKO and Sutherland's tragedy founded upon it, the wife of Oronooko.

imperial. A kind of beard consisting of a pointed tuft of hair on chin and lower lip. It got its name from the French emperor, Napoleon III.

imperialism. Originally the system of government of an emperor or empire. Hence the tendency of a great power to extend its sovereignty for selfish reasons over peoples and regions outside its natural domain.

Imperial Palace. A novel by Arnold BENNETT (1930), dealing with life in a 20th-century "luxury" hotel. See also GRAND HOTEL.

Importance of Being Earnest, The. A well-known comedy by Oscar WILDE, produced in 1899. It is noted for its witty lines, its clever situations, and its satire on the British nobility and clergy. It deals with the aspirations of John Worthing to the hand of Gwendolen Fairfax, daughter of Lady Bracknell, and the objections raised to the proposed marriage because he was found in a hand-bag in Victoria Station and has no information as to who his parents were. Eventually matters are straightened out by the revelation that Worthing is really the son of Lady Bracknell's brother, was left in the hand-bag by the mistake of an absent-minded governess, and is actually named Ernest John Moncrieff, brother to his friend Algernon Moncrieff. He is particularly delighted to discover that his name is Ernest, since it is the one he has been using, in the capacity of guardian to Cecily Cardew, Algernon's sweetheart, as the name of a younger brother whom he has had to help out of "scrapes."

impressionism. A movement in painting, music, and literature in the latter half of the 19th century, originating in France, the aim of which was to portray the effects, or "impressions," of experience upon the consciousness of the artist or an observer with whom he identifies himself, rather than the objective characteristics of things and events.

In *painting,* the work of the impressionist school aroused a great deal of controversy and criticism when it was first exhibited. Its chief subjects were landscapes, and outdoor or semi-outdoor scenes, viewed at varying times of the day, with emphasis on effects of light and color and executed in a hasty, "sketchy" technique intended to bring out the pattern of the whole, as seen by the painter at a particular moment, rather than details and a formal composition. Leading impressionist painters were Sisley, Pissarro, MONET, DEGAS, and RENOIR. The American painters Mary CASSATT and WHISTLER were influenced by and associated with the impressionist school. See also POST-IMPRESSIONISM.

In *music,* impressionism appeared in orchestral pieces which lacked the strict formal organization of the symphony, concerto, and the like, and were intended to evoke a mood in the listener, with associations beyond the basic auditory content of the music. They were marked by great delicacy and striking chromatic effects. DEBUSSY and RAVEL were the leading musical impressionists, and Charles Tomlinson Griffes (1884–1920) was an outstanding American representative of the school. Debussy was influenced by the literary school of SYMBOLISM, and his L'APRÈS-MIDI D'UN FAUNE is an outstanding example of impressionism in music.

In *poetry* and the *novel,* impressionism has a more general application, covering SYMBOLISM, IMAGISM, and related movements, and fiction making use of the STREAM-OF-CONSCIOUSNESS technique, as well as other writing which may not fit into any formal category. RIMBAUD, VERLAINE, MALLARMÉ, G. M. HOPKINS, Carl SANDBURG, Amy LOWELL, EZRA POUND, T. S. ELIOT, Conrad AIKEN, Wallace STEVENS, Marianne MOORE, W. C. WILLIAMS, James JOYCE, Virginia WOOLF, John Dos PASSOS, and Gertrude STEIN may be said to be literary impressionists. See also EXPRESSIONISM.

Impressions of Theophrastus Such, The. A book of essays (1878) by George ELIOT.

Inauguration Day. The day on which the President of the United States is inaugurated. Previous to 1934, it was the 4th of March in every year following a year divisible by four. Through the twentieth amendment, the LAME-DUCK amendment, the date was changed to January 20.

Inca. A member of an ancient tribe of Peruvian Indians. Specifically, a king or royal prince of the ancient Peruvians. The empire of the Incas was founded by Manco Capac about the middle of the 13th century. See RULERS.

> The Inca was a war-chief, elected by the Council to carry out its decision.—Brinton, *The American Race (South American Tribes)*, pt. i, ch. ii, p. 211.

Inchcape Rock, The. A ballad by SOUTHEY concerning a dangerous point east of the Firth of Tay, twelve miles from all land, in the German Sea. Here a warning bell was floated on a buoy by the forethought of an abbot of Aberbrothok. Southey says that Ralph the Rover, in a mischievous freak, cut the bell from the buoy, and it fell into the depths; but on his return voyage his boat ran on the rock, and Ralph was drowned.

Incident of the French Camp. A poem about Napoleon by Robert BROWNING.

Incidents in the Life of My Uncle Arly. A poem by Edward LEAR, parodying Wordsworth's RESOLUTION AND INDEPENDENCE. See also WHITE KNIGHT'S BALLAD, THE.

incunabula (*Lat.*). Literally, a cradle. Works of art or industry of the infant stages in the development of a given field. In the history of bookmaking, books printed before 1500. They are sometimes called cradle books or fifteeners. In this sense the singular "incunabulum" can be used.

Independence Hall. A building on Chestnut Street, Philadelphia, where the Declaration of Independence was adopted (July 4, 1776) and read to the people on **Independence Square.** Independence Hall is now an historical museum.

Index, The. The *Roman Index* contains both the *Index Librorum Prohibitorum* and the *Index Expurgatorius.* The former contains a list of such books as are absolutely forbidden to be read by faithful Catholics. The latter contains such books as are forbidden till certain parts are omitted or amended. The lists are made out by a board of cardinals called the *Congregation of the Index.*

Indian.

Indian file. One after the other, singly. The American Indians, when they go on an expedition, march one by one. The one behind carefully steps in the footprints of the one before, and the last man of the file is supposed to obliterate the footprints. Thus, neither the track nor the number of invaders can be traced.

Indian gift. A gift made with the expectation of its being returned or another made in its place.

Indian summer. The autumnal summer, occurring as a rule in the early part of October. It is often the finest and mildest part of the whole year, especially in North America.

Indians. In American baseball parlance, the Cleveland Americans. See BASEBALL TEAMS.

Indiana. A novel by George SAND (1832), the first to bring her fame. Its heroine, Indiana, is a Creole, who does not love her peevish old husband, Colonel Delmare, but responds to the advances of Raymonde de Ramière, a young and fascinating lover. With the aid of an English cousin, Sir Ralph Brown, she escapes to join Raymonde, but he has married another. She and Sir Ralph leap into a waterfall, on a desperate impulse, but by some miracle are saved.

Indian Summer. A novel by W. D. Howells (1885). In the course of his engagement to the romantic young Imogene Grahame, Theodore Colville, an American journalist of forty living in Florence, becomes acutely conscious that his youth has gone. The pair are saved from each other by Imogene's chaperon, Mrs. Bower, a widow of Colville's own age who consoles him by marrying him herself. Howells considered *Indian Summer* his best book.

One of the novels of Galsworthy's Forsyte Saga is entitled *The Indian Summer of a Forsyte.*

Indigitamenta. In the ancient Roman religion, books containing lists of deities with indications as to how and when they had to be invoked.

indirect discourse. See under direct discourse.

Indo-China, French. In World War II, Japanese troops entered the strategic region of French Indo-China with weak acquiescence of the Vichy Government in the summer of 1940. The upshot of this was the envelopment of Southeast Asia, the attack on Pearl Harbor, the fall of Hongkong, Singapore, etc., in 1941.

Indra. One of the chief deities of Hindu mythology, god of heaven and ruler over thunder, lightning and storm.

In Dubious Battle. A novel by John Steinbeck, published in 1936, dealing with labor organization among migrant fruit-pickers in California. Strikes, violence by the local vigilantes, and the murder of Jim Nolan, a young Communist leader of the workers, are featured. Mac, the leading character, is presented as a veteran Communist organizer who allows nothing to interfere with his service to his cause, not even the death of Jim, his friend.

indulgence. In the Roman Catholic Church, the entire or partial remission of punishment due to sin either in this world or in Purgatory. In the Middle Ages indulgences were of high commercial value, and it was the sale of them that first roused the ire of Luther and prepared the way for the Reformation.

the Declaration of Indulgence. The proclamation of James II in 1687 which annulled religious tests and the penal laws against Roman Catholics and Dissenters. The refusal of certain ecclesiastics to read this in their churches led to the trial of the Seven Bishops.

in extremis (*Lat.*). At the very point of death; *in articulo mortis.*

Inez. One of the leading characters in Meyerbeer's opera L'Africaine.

Inez, Donna. In Byron's Don Juan, mother of Don Juan. She trains her son according to prescribed rules with the strictest propriety, and designs to make him a model of all virtues. Her husband is Don José, whom she worries to death by her prudery and want of sympathy. Donna Inez is a "blue stocking," learned in all the sciences, her favorlte one being "the mathematical."

Infanta. Any princess of the blood royal, except an heiress of the crown, was so called in Spain and Portugal.

Infante. All the sons of the sovereigns of Spain bore this title, as did those of Portugal, except the crown prince, who in Spain was called the Prince of the Asturias.

Infant Phenomenon. The stage name of eight-year-old Ivinetta Crummles in Dickens' Nicholas Nickleby.

inferiority complex. See under Adler, Alfred; Complex.

Inferno, The. The first and most famous of the three parts of Dante's Divine Comedy. It describes his journey through the infernal regions.

in fieri (Lat. *fieri,* "to become, to be done, made, etc."). In the course of accomplishment; on the way.

inflation. Strictly speaking, an undue increase or disproportionate abundance of money and credit in relation to actual business needs. It can be caused, on the one hand, by gold discoveries, unrestrained emission of paper money, and overexpansion of credit, and on the other, by a sudden scarcity of available goods. Loosely, the term is applied to all the economic ills resulting from the discrepancy described. These include a marked rise of price levels.

inflection. Literally, bending. In music, modulation of the voice or change in pitch or tone. In grammar, the change of forms in accordance with the function of words in a sentence pattern. As "me" for "I" and "sees" for "see" in "He sees me."

in forma pauperis (*Lat.*). In the character of a pauper. Persons without money or the means of obtaining it are allowed to sue in the courts *in forma pauperis,* when fees are remitted and the suitor is supplied gratis with the necessary legal advice, counsel, etc.

Information Please. A popular American radio program of the late 1930's and the 1940's, one of the first of the many "quiz programs" of the time and the most literate. It consists of questions on literature, history, music, current events, the theater, motion pictures, and the like, which are sent in by the radio audience and which are to be answered by a "board of experts," among whom are journalists, novelists, musicians, actors and actresses, government officials, and other public figures.

infra-red, ultraviolet. Said of rays "beneath red" and "beyond violet" in the spectrum. They are invisible. Infra-red rays are heat-producing.

Infusoria. A term introduced by the Danish naturalist Otto Frederik Müller (1730–1784) and applied originally to all the microscopic organisms which developed (seemingly from nothing) in an infusion of hay and the like. In modern scientific usage the term is restricted in its application to the highest class of Protozoa.

Inge, William Ralph (1860–). Anglican prelate. Dean of St. Paul's, London (1911–1934), occasionally dubbed "the gloomy Dean." Many books on Christianity.

Ingebjorg. In the ancient LAXDALE SAGA, sister of King Olaf, at whose court KJARTAN stays for awhile. On his departure for his home in Iceland, Ingebjorg gives Kjartan an elaborate coif as a gift for GUDRUN.

Ingelow, Jean (1820–1897). English poet and novelist. Famous for the poem *High Tide on the Coast of Lincolnshire.*

Ingenu, The (L'Ingénu). A satiric romance by VOLTAIRE (1767) in which the titular hero, a Canadian half-breed, representing all the sturdy, simple virtues of "nature" comes to live with his European relatives, who are incurably tainted with the pettiness and vice of "civilization."

ingenuous. Free from equivocation or dissimulation; naïve, guileless. Literally, "freeborn, noble, etc." Still occasionally, though less frequently than in the past, confused with *ingenious,* which means literally "possessed of genius."

Inger. The heroine of Hamsun's GROWTH OF THE SOIL.

Ingersoll, Ralph (1900–). American journalist. Began as a mining engineer. Was vice-president and general manager of Time, Inc., and sponsored radio and cinema productions of "The March of Time" (1935–1936). Editor, PM (which see) (1940–1946). Enlisted as private, U.S. Army (1942). Ended as a Lieutenant Colonel attached to General Bradley's staff in the 12th Army Group. He has written the scathing book (except toward Generals Devers and Bradley) TOP SECRET (1946) about the inside history of World War II. Also author of *The Battle is the Pay-Off* (1943) and a satirical novel, *The Great Ones* (1947).

Ingersoll, Robert Green (1833–1899). American lawyer, orator of the Republican Party, and lecturer, best known for his defense of free-thinking in matters of religion, which won him the sobriquet of "the Great Agnostic." He wrote numerous lectures criticizing the Bible and theology and had a wide influence during his time.

Ingmars, the. A Swedish family whose struggles and adventures are narrated in the short stories that comprise Selma Lagerlöf's JERUSALEM.

Ingoldsby Legends, The. A series of legendary tales in prose and verse, supposed to have been found in the family chest of the Ingoldsby family, and told by Thomas Ingoldsby, the assumed name of the Rev. Richard Harris Barham (1788–1845). THE JACKDAW OF RHEIMS is especially celebrated.

Ingres, Jean Auguste Dominique (1780–1867). French historical painter; leader in the classicistic school. Studied and worked in Paris and Italy.

Iniquity, The. In old English mystery and morality plays, the same as the VICE.

Injun Joe. A villainous character in TOM SAWYER by Mark TWAIN.

Inkle and Yarico. Hero and heroine of a story by Sir Richard STEELE, in the *Spectator* (No. 11). Inkle is a young Englishman who is lost in the Spanish main. He falls in love with Yarico, an Indian maiden, with whom he consorts; but no sooner does a vessel arrive to take him to Barbadoes than he sells Yarico as a slave. Steele found the tale in Ligon's *History of Barbadoes* (1657). It was later worked into a musical drama by George COLMAN called *Inkle and Yarico.*

in medias res (*Lat.*). In the middle of the subject. In novels and epic poetry, the author generally begins *in medias res,* and explains the preceding events as the tale unfolds.

In Memoriam (*Lat.,* "in memory of"). A long poem written between the years 1833 and 1850 by TENNYSON, in memory of his friend Arthur H. HALLAM, who died in 1833. It is considered one of the greatest of English elegies.

Innamorato, Orlando, see ORLANDO.

inner light. Spiritual illumination. Specifically, in Quaker doctrine, a divine presence in the soul of every man, the light of Christ which gives moral guidance, and religious and spiritual assurance to all who are willing to receive it.

Inner Temple and **Middle Temple.** Two groups of buildings on the site of a monastic establishment of the Knights Templars in London, wrecked by Nazi bombs in World War II. The Inner Temple was so called because it was within the precincts of the City. The Middle Temple was situated between the Inner and Outer Temple. The Inner and Middle Temple were occupied by two INNS OF COURT. The Outer Temple was converted into the Exeter Buildings and its name has gone out of use.

Innes, Evelyn, see EVELYN INNES.

Inness, George (1825–1894). American landscape painter. Examples of his work are found in the Chicago Art Institute and the New York Metropolitan Museum of Art. His canvases are noted for their sensitive reproduction of the moods of nature.

Innisfail. Literally, island of destiny. A poetical name for Ireland.

Innocence Abroad. A book of literary biographies by Emily CLARK (1931).

Innocents, Massacre of the. The slaughter of the male children of Bethlehem "from two years old and under," when Jesus was born (*Matt.* ii. 16). This was done at the command of Herod the Great in order to cut off "the babe" who was destined to become "King of the Jews." The Feast of the Holy Innocents commemorating this event is December 28.

In British parliamentary phraseology, the phrase denotes the withdrawal at the close of a session of the bills which time has not rendered it possible to consider and pass.

Innocents Abroad, The. A rollicking burlesque of European travel by Mark TWAIN (1869), satirizing the gullible American traveler who uses his guide book as a Bible and regards the entire Old World with awe and ecstasy.

Inns of Court. The four voluntary societies which have the exclusive right of calling to the English Bar. They are all in London, and are the Inner Temple, the Middle Temple, Lincoln's Inn, and Gray's Inn. Each is governed by a board of benchers.

Ino. In Greek myth, the daughter of Cadmus. She became the sea goddess LEUCOTHEA.

In Ole Virginia. A volume of Southern Negro dialect stories by Thomas Nelson PAGE (1887). It contains *Marse Chan* and MEH LADY among others.

in petto. In the breast; secretly. The expression is originally the Italian adaptation of Latin *in pectore* (same meaning) as applied to cardinals whose appointment by the pope has not been promulgated.

Inquisition. A court commonly called the Holy Office, instituted to inquire into offenses against the Roman Catholic religion, and fully established by Gregory IX in 1235. Torture, as a means of extracting recantations or evidence, was first authorized by Innocent IV in 1252, and those found guilty were handed over to the secular arm to be dealt with according to the secular laws of the land. The Inquisition was only once introduced into England (viz., at the trials of the Templars, who were suppressed in 1308); it was most active in southern Europe, particularly in Spain, where it flourished from 1237 to 1820. It was suppressed in France in 1772.

Insarov, Demetri. The hero of Turgenev's *On the Eve,* a young Bulgarian who has resolved to free his country from the Turks. The heroine is Elena Strashov.

Inside of the Cup, The. A novel by Winston CHURCHILL (1913) dealing with 20th-century religious problems. The hero is John Hodder, the young minister of a wealthy church located in a slum district. The allusion of the title is to the Biblical text "Woe unto you, scribes and Pharisees, hypocrites! for ye cleanse the outside of the cup and of the platter, but within they are full from extortion and excess."

Inspired Idiot. OLIVER GOLDSMITH was so called by Walpole.

Institute of France (*Fr.* **Institut de France**). A national French society, established in 1795 by the Republican Convention "to advance the sciences and arts of research . . . and to prosecute those scientific and literary labors which shall have for their end general utility and the glory of the republic." It is a roof organization and embraces these five academies: *L'Académie française, L'Académie des Inscriptions et Belles-Lettres, L'Académie des Sciences, L'Académie des Beaux Arts,* and *L'Académie des Sciences Morales et Politiques.*

Institutes of the Christian Religion (*Institution Chrétienne*). The principal work of John CALVIN, published in Latin in 1536 and French in 1541. It is a statement of the essential tenets of CALVINISM, and was widely used during the Puritan period.

insulin. A specific for diabetes (discovered in 1923). Its active principle is a hormone found in the pancreas, specifically in the so-called islands of Langerhans (Lat. *insula,* "island"; hence *insulin*). Marketed as a solution made from the pancreas of sheep and oxen.

Insull, Samuel (1859–1938). Public-utility magnate born in London. Overexpansion caused three of his largest American companies to go into receivership. After his indictment he fled from arrest for two years, but was finally tried and acquitted.

interior monologue. A narrative technique widely used in 20th-century fiction, by which action and external event are presented indirectly, through the mental soliloquy of one or more characters, composed of sense impressions, thoughts, memories, and associations aroused by external occurrences but never spoken aloud. It was first used by Edouard DUJARDIN in his WE'LL TO THE WOODS NO MORE (*Les Lauriers sont coupés*) and is best exemplified in THE WAVES by Virginia WOOLF. In general, the interior monologue is identical with the STREAM-OF-CONSCIOUSNESS, although some critics prefer to use both terms, in order to distinguish the more formalized soliloquies, controlled and "edited" in harmony with the desired mood and the situation in question, of Mrs. Woolf and other writers like her, from the more chaotic and realistic flow of thought in the characters of James JOYCE.

interlinear. Between the lines. Said also of texts with an interlinear translation into another language. James Hamilton (1769–1829), a British language teacher, worked with an interlinear method which was widely acclaimed in the U.S. and Great Britain.

interlude. A form of dramatic entertainment originating during the reign of Henry VIII and popular at the Tudor court. The exact nature of an interlude is not known, but it is believed to have been a brief skit between the courses of a long banquet, or an oral dialogue. Court interludes, of which John HEYWOOD was the outstanding author, were usually lively and realistic and devoted chiefly to entertainment. There were also educational interludes, didactic and teaching an edifying moral, usually written in Latin, with type characters and situations, for use in public schools such as Eton. See NICE WANTON. The interlude is considered a transitional form between the miracle and MORALITY PLAYS of the Middle Ages and fully developed Elizabethan drama.

international style, see FUNCTIONALISM.

Interpreter, Mr. The Holy Spirit personified, in Bunyon's PILGRIM'S PROGRESS. He is lord of a house a little way beyond the Wicket Gate. Here CHRISTIAN is kindly entertained and shown many wonderful sights of an allegorical character. Christiana and her party also stop here later.

Intimations of Immortality. Current abridged title of *Intimations of Immortality from Recollections of Early Childhood,* an ode (1807) by WORDSWORTH.

In Time to Come. A play about Woodrow WILSON by Howard Koch and John Huston (1942), the foundation of the moving picture *Woodrow Wilson.*

introvert. In psychological parlance, one whose interest is directed inward, to the inner life of thought or fancy. See also the opposite, EXTROVERT; JUNG, CARL GUSTAV.

inverted commas. Quotation marks. Originally a printers' expression, for in composition single and double English quotation marks could actually be produced by inverting the type of one or two commas.

Invictus (*Lat.,* "unconquered"). The title of a well-known poem, written in a tuberculosis hospital, by HENLEY. Its last lines read:

> It matters not how strait the gate
> How charged with punishment the scroll,
> I am the master of my fate,
> I am the captain of my soul.

Invincible Doctor, see under DOCTOR.

Invincibles, the Irish. A Fenian secret society founded in Dublin in 1881 with the object of doing away with the English "tyranny" and killing the "tyrants." Members of this society were responsible for the Phoenix Park murders in 1882.

Invisible Empire. See under KU KLUX KLAN.

Io. In classic myth, the beautiful daughter of Inachus, king of Argos. Jupiter, who had been flirting with her, changed her into a heifer to conceal her from Juno. Argus, who had a hundred eyes, was charged by Juno to watch the heifer. Mercury, at Jupiter's request, killed Argus, and Juno sent a gadfly to chase the heifer all over the world. On the Nile Io finally recovered her shape and was returned to her family after Jupiter had promised not to pay her any more attentions. Io was by Jupiter the mother of Epaphus, the ancestor of Aegyptus, Damaus, Cepheus, and Phineus. In the allegorical interpretation of mythology, Io is the moon.

Iolcos. A city in Thessaly, the modern Volo, point of embarkation of the ARGONAUTS.

Ion. In classic myth, the ancestor of the Ionians or Athenian Greeks, a son of Apollo and Creusa and grandson of Helen of Troy. Euripides made him the subject of a drama, *Ion* (423 B. C.). He is brought up in the temple at Delphi, much like the Hebrew Samuel. The plot turns on the efforts of Creusa to bring about his death, not knowing that he is her own son.

Thomas M. Talfourd was the author of a tragedy *Ion* (1835), dealing with another Ion, a prince of Argos who sacrifices himself to the gods to end a pestilence.

Iona or **Icolmkill.** A small northern island near Scotland, where St. Columba founded a missionary monastery (563 A. D.).

Ione. The heroine of Bulwer Lytton's LAST DAYS OF POMPEII.

Ionic Order. In architecture, one of the three Greek ORDERS, distinguished by the spiral volutes of its capitals.

IOU, i.e., "I owe you." The memorandum of a debt given by the borrower to the lender. It requires no stamp unless it specifies a day of payment, when it becomes a *bill,* and must be stamped.

Iphigenia. In classic legend, the daughter of Agamemnon and Clytemnestra. One account says that her father, having offended Artemis by killing her favorite stag, vowed to sacrifice to the angry goddess the most beautiful thing that came into his possession in the next twelve months; this was an infant daughter. The father deferred the sacrifice till the fleet of the combined Greeks that was proceeding to Troy reached Aulis and Iphigenia had grown to womanhood. Then Calchas told him that the fleet would be wind-bound till he had fulfilled his vow; accordingly the king prepared to sacrifice his daughter, but Artemis at the last moment snatched her from the altar and carried her to heaven, substituting a hind in her place. Euripides, Aeschylus, and Sophocles all wrote tragedies on Iphigenia. Racine's tragedy *Iphigénie* (*Fr.*, 1674) is considered one of his best. GOETHE also has a tragic drama *Iphigenie auf Tauris* (1787). Glück's two operas, *Iphigenia in Aulis* (1777) and *Iphigenia in Tauris* (1779) deal with the legend.

The similarity of this legend to the Scripture stories of Jephthah's vow, and Abraham's offering of his son Isaac, is noticeable. See also IDOMENEUS.

Ippolito, Don. A Venetian priest who plays a leading rôle in Howells' FOREGONE CONCLUSION.

I.Q. Intelligence Quotient, a term used in connection with the mental tests of 20th-century educational psychology. See SIMON BINET TESTS.

Iras. In Shakespeare's ANTONY AND CLEOPATRA and Dryden's ALL FOR LOVE, a female attendant on Cleopatra. When Cleopatra has arrayed herself with robe and crown, prior to applying the asps, she says to her two female attendants, "Come, take the last warmth of my lips. Farewell, kind Charmian! Iras, farewell!" When she has kissed them, Iras falls down dead, either brokenhearted, or else because she has already applied an asp to her arm, as Charmian did a little later.

Ireland, William Henry (1777–1835). English forger of Shakespearean manuscripts and documents. His blank verse play, "*Vortigern and Rowena,* by William Shakspere," was a complete failure on the stage (1796) and led to the exposure of the fraud. Author of *An Authentic Account of the Shaksperian MSS.*

Irena. In Spenser's FAËRIE QUEENE (Bk. v), the personification of Ireland whose inheritance was withheld by the tyrant GRANTORTO. Sir Artegal (*Justice*) is sent by the Faërie Queene to succor the distressed lady, and, Grantorto being slain, she is restored to her throne and reigns in peace.

Irene. (1) The beautiful dead heroine of a poem by Poe which appeared under that title in 1831 but was later republished as *The Sleeper*.

(2) The heroine of Turgenev's novel SMOKE.

Ireson, Floyd. A New England skipper in Whittier's ballad, *Skipper Ireson's Ride* (1860). According to tradition, he was tarred and feathered by the women of Marblehead for refusing to go to the rescue of a leaking ship. There was a real Skipper Ireson, but according to Samuel Roads' *History and Traditions of Marblehead,* the helpless skipper received unjust blame for the actions of a stubborn and cowardly crew. Whittier wrote to Roads, "I have no doubt that thy version of Skipper Ireson is the correct one."

Ireton, Henry (1611–1651). English Parliamentary cavalry leader. Married Oliver Cromwell's daughter Bridget. Signed the warrant for the execution of King Charles I.

Iris. Goddess of the rainbow, or the rainbow itself. In classic mythology, she is called the messenger of the gods when they intended discord, and the rainbow is the bridge or road let down from heaven for her accommodation. When the gods meant peace they sent Mercury.

Irish.

Irish Agitator. Daniel O'Connell (1775–1847).

Irish apricots. Potatoes.

Irish wedding. When a person has a black eye we sometimes say to him, "You have been to an Irish wedding."

Irish Free State (Saorstat Eireann). Constituted as a self-governing dominion within the British Empire (1922).

Irish Renaissance. Term applied to the movement at the end of the 19th century in Ireland to arouse a consciousness of cultural unity and nationality among the Irish people by reviving the literature of the Celtic past and portraying contemporary life and manners. Among the leaders of this movement were: A. E., painting and poetry; Edwin Martyn (1859–1924), drama and liturgical music; George MOORE, novels and poetry; W. B. YEATS, poetry and drama; Lady Augusta GREGORY, plays and studies and adaptations of traditional legends; and John M. SYNGE, drama. An important step in the accomplishment of the movement's objectives was the establishment of the Abbey Theater in Dublin for the presentation of plays on Irish life and legend; Yeats, Synge, and Lady Gregory were outstanding figures in the promotion of the theater's plans. A number of the plays written for and produced by the Abbey Theater are recognized by critics as among the greatest of the 20th century, and had an important influence on English and American drama. Cf. Mary Colum's *Life and the Dream* (1947).

Iroldo. In Boiardo's *Orlando Innamorato,* the friend of PRASILDO.

iron.

if you have too many irons in the fire, some will burn. If you have more affairs in hand than you can properly attend to, some of them will be neglected and turn out badly.

Iron Age, see AGE.

Blood and Iron, see under BLOOD.

the iron chancellor. The German statesman Bismarck (1815–1898).

the iron city. Pittsburgh. See under CITY.

the Iron Cross. A Prussian military decoration (an iron Maltese cross, edged with silver and bearing the initials "F.W.," i.e., Friedrich Wilhelm, and date 1871), formerly awarded for valor in the field.

the Iron Duke. The Duke of Wellington (1769–1852).

the Iron Emperor. Nicholas I of Russia (1796–1855).

Iron, Ralph, see SCHREINER, OLIVE.

Iron Crown. The old crown of the Lombard Kings indicating sovereignty over Italy. It was actually made of gold but contained a circlet of iron forged, according to tradition, from a nail in the cross of Christ.

Iron Hand, Tonty of the. A co-explorer of LA SALLE, the Italian Henry de Tonti or Tonty (1650–1704), who had one iron hand fixed to an amputation.

Iron Maiden of Nuremberg. A famous instrument of torture, formerly exhibited in the museum of the castle at Nuremberg, consisting of a metal frame in the shape of a human body with spikes inside and a hinged opening to admit the victim. There is no record of its ever having been in use.

Iron Mask. See under MAN.

Ironquill. Pseudonym of Eugene Fitch WARE.

Ironsides. The soldiers that served under Cromwell were so called, especially after the battle of Marston Moor, where they displayed an iron resolution. The name had first been applied only to a special regiment of stalwarts.

Old Ironsides, see under OLD.

Iron Woman, The. A novel by Margaret DELAND (1911), a sequel to *The Awakening of Helena Richie.* The "Iron Woman" is Sarah Maitland, a widow who finds her chief satisfaction in managing the Maitland Iron Works in a competent, masculine fashion. The impulsive marriage of her son Blair to Elizabeth Ferguson while Elizabeth is still engaged to David Richie, Helena's adopted son, brings on bitter feelings between Blair and his mother, and she disinherits him. On his mother's death a check which Mrs. Maitland had intended young Dr. Richie to use for his hospital, goes to Blair, and when Elizabeth learns the truth and fails to persuade him to give it up, she decides to run away with David, whom she has always loved. At this juncture Helena Richie intervenes and prevents the elopement by telling them her own story. Eventually Elizabeth is divorced and marries David, and Helena Richie marries Elizabeth's uncle, Robert Ferguson.

irony (from Gr. *eiron,* "a dissembler"). A dissembling; hence, subtle sarcasm, language having a meaning different from the ostensible one and which will be understood correctly by the initiated. *Socratic irony* is an assumption of ignorance, as a means of leading on and eventually confuting an opponent. *Dramatic irony* is the theatrical device of making a speaker utter words which have a hidden meaning for the audience of which he is himself unconscious. Thus Oedipus, in Sophocles' *Oedipus Tyrannus,* calls down curses on the slayer of Laius, not knowing that they will fall on his own head.

the irony of fate. A strange fatality which has brought about something quite the reverse of what might have been expected.

Iroquois. A confederacy of five (later six) North American Indian tribes, organized in the sixteenth century and known to the English as the *Five* (later *Six*) *Nations.* The name they used for themselves signifies "we of the long house." They also called each other "real men," while the word *Iroquois* is of Algonquin origin (as heard by the French) and means "real adder." The Iroquois were the Mohawk, Oneida, Onondaga, Cayuga, Seneca (and later Tuscarora). Their territory was Central New York. After the revolution many of them went to Canada.

irredenta. From *Italia irredenta,* "unredeemed Italy," the slogan of the Italian political party (founded in 1878) that demanded as part of its platform the incorporation of Trieste, Istria, the Ticino, Nice, Corsica, Malta, and other Italian-speaking territories in the Italian kingdom. In English and other languages *irredenta* came to be used for regions detached from the country of their historical allegiance and for the movement advocating their return. As, the Austrian irredenta in the Italian Tyrol, etc.

Irrefragable Doctor, see under DOCTOR.

Irus. In Greek legend, the beggar of Ithaca, who ran on errands for Penelope's suitors. When Ulysses returned home dressed as a beggar, Irus withstood him, and Ulysses broke his jaw with a blow. So poor was Irus that he gave birth to the proverbs, "As poor as Irus," and "Poorer than Irus" (in French, *plus pauvre qu' Irus*).

Irving, Sir Henry (1838–1905). English actor. Particularly remembered for his Shakespearean rôles and as professionally associated with Ellen TERRY. Eight American tours.

Irving, Washington (1783–1859). American journalist, author, satirist, and man of society, known for his early wit and humor and his later portrayal of the romantic and picturesque in his sketches and histories. His works include: *Letters of Jonathan Oldstyle, Gent.* (1802–1803), a series of satires on New York society published in the *Morning Chronicle;* SALMAGUNDI: OR, THE WHIM-WHAMS AND OPINIONS OF LAUNCELOT LANGSTAFF, ESQ., AND OTHERS (1807–1808), satires on New York revealing Irving's conservative viewpoint; KNICKERBOCKER'S HISTORY OF NEW YORK (1809); THE SKETCH BOOK (1819); BRACEBRIDGE HALL (1822); *Tales of a Traveler* (1824); *History of the Life and Voyages of Christopher Columbus* (1828); THE CONQUEST OF GRANADA (1829); THE ALHAMBRA (1832); *A Tour on the Prairies* (1835); *Astoria* (1836); *The Adventures of Captain Bonneville, U.S.A.* (1837), a biography of a frontiersman; *A Book of the Hudson* (1849), sketches; *Mahomet and His Successors* (1849–1850); and a *Life of George Washington* (1855–1859). Irving was active in politics and diplomacy, serving as an attaché and later minister to Spain, where he did research for his Spanish histories and sketches. He was enthusiastic about European culture and was influenced by the English essayists ADDISON and STEELE and to some extent by Sir Walter SCOTT.

Irwin, Wallace (1876–). American humorist and novelist. *The Love Sonnets of a Hoodlum* (1902) are a remarkable contribution to American vernacular verse. Invented the amusing character of the Japanese schoolboy Hashimura Togo.

Irwin, Will (1873–1948). American journalist and writer, first gaining fame with *The City That Was* (1907), an inspired picture of San Francisco before the Fire. War correspondent, playwright, writer on contemporary affairs, etc. His wife, **Inez Haynes Irwin** (1873–) is a well-known writer of fiction who was awarded the O. Henry memorial prize for the best short story (1924). As Inez Haynes Gillmore, she wrote a feminist novel, *Angel Island* (1914) and the popular *Phoebe and Ernest* stories (1910–1919). She has also written mystery novels.

Isaac. In the Old Testament (*Gen.* xxiv–xxviii), the son of ABRAHAM. As a test of faith his father was commanded to offer up the young Isaac as a burnt offering, but at the last moment was told to slay a ram instead. Isaac was the husband of REBEKAH and the father of JACOB and Esau.

Isaac of York. In Scott's IVANHOE, the father of Rebecca. When he is imprisoned in the dungeon of Front de Boeuf's castle, Front de Boeuf comes to extort money from him, and orders two slaves to chain him to the bars of a slow fire, but the party is disturbed by the sound of a bugle. Ultimately, both the Jew and his daughter leave England and go to live abroad.

Isaacs, Mr., see MR. ISAACS.

Isabel Archer. Chief woman character in James' PORTRAIT OF A LADY.

Isabella. In Arthurian legend, the sister of King Mark of Cornwall, married to King Meliadus of Lionesse. In Ariosto's *Orlando Furioso,* the daughter of a king of Galicia, loved by Zerbino but slain by Rodomont.

Isabella. (1) In Shakespeare's MEASURE FOR MEASURE the sister of Claudio, insulted by the base passion of Angelo, deputy of Vienna in the absence of Duke Vincentio.

(2) Heroine of Meyerbeer's opera ROBERT LE DIABLE.

Isabella I, also known as **the Catholic.** Spanish **Isabel la Católica** (1451–1504). Queen of Castile (1474–1504). Through her marriage with Ferdinand II of Aragon (1469), Castile and Aragon were united and ruled jointly by the two monarchs (with Ferdinand as Ferdinand V). They were granted the title of *Los Reyes católicos.*

Isabella, or the Pot of Basil. A story from Boccaccio turned into verse by Keats (1820).

Isabelle. In Molière's comedy, *L'École des Maris,* one of the two orphan sisters brought up to be model wives. See SGANARELLE.

Isaiah. The greatest of the Hebrew Major Prophets. He prophesied during the period preceding the captivity of Judah. Also, the book of the Old Testament containing his prophecies.

Isaie le Triste, see YSAIE LE TRISTE.

Isak. The hero of Hamsun's GROWTH OF THE SOIL.

Isenbras or **Isumbras, Sir.** A hero of medieval romance. Sir Isenbras is at first proud and presumptuous, but adversity makes him humble and penitent. In this stage he carries two children of a poor woodcutter across a ford on his horse.

Isengrin or **Isgrim.** The wolf, afterwards created Earl of Pitwood, in the beast-epic of *Reynard the Fox* (1498). Isengrin typifies the barons, and Reynard the church; and the gist of the tale is to show how Reynard bamboozles his uncle Wolf.

Iseult, see ISOLT.

Ishbosheth in Dryden's satire of ABSALOM AND ACHITOPHEL, is meant for Richard Cromwell, whose father Oliver is called "Saul." As Ishbosheth is the only surviving son of Saul, so Richard was the only surviving son of Cromwell. As Ishbosheth was accepted king on the death of his father by all except the tribe of Judah (2 *Sam.* iv), so Richard was acknowledged "protector" by all except the royalists. As Ishbosheth reigned only a few months, so Richard, after a few months, retired into private life.

Isherwood, Christopher William Bradshaw- (1904–). English short-story writer and novelist, associated with the group of English writers of Marxist sympathies including W. H. AUDEN, C. DAY LEWIS, and Stephen SPENDER. He is best known for the books on which he collaborated with Auden: THE DOG BENEATH THE SKIN (1935) and *The Ascent of F6* (1936), verse plays; *On the Frontier* (1938), "a melodrama in three acts"; and *Journey to a War* (1939), an account of travels in China during the war with the Japanese. Other works of Isherwood are: *The Memorial: Portrait of a Family* (1932); *The Last of Mr. Norris* (1935); *Sally Bowles* (1937); *Lions and Shadows: An Education in the Twenties* (1938); *Goodbye to Berlin* (1939), a collection of sketches of people and life in Germany at the time of the rise of Nazism; and *Prater Violet* (1945), a novel concerning a German refugee from Nazism. He also translated the *Intimate Journals* of BAUDELAIRE (1930), and *A Penny for the Poor*, by Bertolt BRECHT (1937).

Ishmael. In the Old Testament, the son of Abraham and HAGAR; hence any outcast from society, from the prophecy "And he shall be as a wild ass among men; his hand shall be against every man and every man's hand against him." After the birth of Isaac, Ishmael was cast out of Abraham's household and became the father of a separate people.

Ishtar (Gr. **Astarte**). The Babylonian goddess of love and war, corresponding to the Phoenician ASHTORETH except that while the latter was identified with the moon, Ishtar was more frequently identified with the planet Venus. She was the wife of Bel.

Isidore. In Molière's comedy, LE SICILIEN, OU L'AMOUR PEINTRE, a Greek slave, the concubine of Don Pedre, a Sicilian nobleman. This slave is beloved by ADRASTE a French gentleman, who plots to allure her away.

Isidorian Decretals, see DECRETALS.

Isis. The principal goddess of ancient Egypt, sister and wife of Osiris, and mother of Horus. She was identified with the moon (Osiris being a sungod), and the cow was sacred to her, its horns representing the crescent moon which, in Egypt, appears lying on its back.

Her chief temples were at Amydos, Busiris, and Philae. She is represented as a queen, her head being surmounted by horns and the solar disk or by the double crown. Proclus mentions a statue of her which bore the inscription—

> I am that which is, has been, and shall be. My veil no one has lifted. The fruit I bore was the Sun—

hence, *to lift the veil of Isis* is to pierce to the heart of a great mystery.

She was identified with Io, Aphrodite, and others by the Greeks; with Selene, Ceres, Venus, Juno, etc., by the Romans; and the Phoenicians confused her with Ashtoreth. Her worship as a nature goddess was very popular among the later Greeks and with the Romans of republican times. Milton, in *Paradise Lost* (I. 478), places her among the fallen angels.

See MAGIC FLUTE.

The upper reaches of the Thames River in England are called the Isis.

Islam. The Mohammedan religion, the whole body of Mohammedans, the true Mohammedan faith. The Moslems say every child is born in Islam, and would continue in the true faith if not led astray. The word means *resignation* or *submission to the will of God.*

Islam emphasizes five duties:—
(1) Bearing witness that there is but one God.
(2) Reciting daily prayers.
(3) Giving the appointed and legal alms.
(4) Observing the Ramadan (a month's fast).
(5) Making a pilgrimage to Mecca at least once in a lifetime.

island.

island of Saints. So Ireland was called in the Middle Ages.

island of St. Brandan. The flying island, the supposed retreat of King Rodrigo. So called from St. Brandan, who went in search of the Islands of Paradise in the 6th century. See under SAINT.

island of the Seven Cities. A kind of Utopia, where seven bishops, who quitted Spain during the dominion of the Moors, founded seven cities. The legend says that many have visited the island, but no one has ever quitted it.

Island of Penguins, see PENGUIN ISLAND.

Islands of the Blessed, called by the Greeks "Happy Islands," and by the Romans "Fortunate Islands." They are imaginary islands somewhere in the west, where the favorites of the gods are conveyed at death, and dwell in everlasting joy.

the Island City. Montreal. See under CITY.

Isle of Lanterns. In Rabelais' GARGANTUA AND PANTAGRUEL, an imaginary country, inhabited by pretenders to knowledge, called "Lanternois." See also LANTERN LAND.

Ismene. In Greek legend, daughter of Oedipus and Jocasta. Antigone was buried alive by the order of King Creon, for burying her brother Polynices, slain in combat by his brother Eteocles. Ismene declared that she had aided her sister, and requested to be allowed to share the same punishment.

Ismene and Ismenias. A love story in Greek by Eustathius, in the 12th century. Many of its details have been copied by D'Urfé, Montemayor, and others. Ismene is the "dear and near and true" lady of Ismenias.

Isocrates (436–338 B.C.). Attic orator. Pupil of Socrates. Founded a school and taught some of the greatest future statesmen, orators, and philosophers. Killed himself when Philip of Macedon conquered Greece. Of his orations twenty-one have been preserved.

Isokeha and **Tawiskara.** In Iroquois myth, twin brothers, symbols of light and darkness. Isokeha, "the White One," vanquished his brother Tawiskara, "the Dark One" and became the father of mankind and special protector of the Iroquois.

Isolt, Iseult, Yseult, or **Isolde,** etc. The name of two heroines of Arthurian romance, the more important, *Isolt the Fair,* King Mark's wife, being the lover of TRISTAN, the other, *Isolt of the White Hands,* or *Isolt of Brittany,* being his wife, whom he married after he had been discovered by King Mark and had been obliged to flee.

It is through the treachery of Isolt of the White Hands that Sir Tristan or Tristram dies, and that Isolt the Fair dies in consequence. The story has it that King MARK buried the two in one grave, and planted over it a rose-bush and vine, which so intermingled their branches as they grew up that no man could separate them.

In James Joyce's FINNEGANS WAKE, the wife and daughter of Humphrey C. EARWICKER represent the two Isolts to his Tristan.

Israel (*Heb.,* literally, "contender with God"). In the Old Testament, a name given to JACOB after he wrestled with the angel of the Lord; also, the name given to the Jewish nation descended from him and frequently referred to as the *Children of Israel.*

Israel, in Dryden's ABSALOM AND ACHITOPHEL, stands for England.

Israfil or **Israfel.** The angel of music of the Mohammedans. He possesses the most melodious voice of all God's creatures, and is to sound the Resurrection Trump which will ravish the ears of the saints in paradise. Israfil, Gabriel, and Michael were the three angels that, according to the Koran, warned Abraham of Sodom's destruction. *Israfel* is the title of one of Edgar Allan Poe's poems (1831), and also of a biography of him by Hervey ALLEN.

In Heaven a spirit doth dwell
Whose heart-strings are a lute;
None sing so wildly well
As the angel Israfel,
And the giddy Stars (so legends tell),
Ceasing their hymns, attend the spell
Of his voice, all mute.—Poe, *Israfel.*

Issachar, in Dryden's satire of ABSALOM AND ACHITOPHEL, means Thomas Thynne (1648–1682), of Longleat, known as "Tom of Ten Thousand."

Issachar's ears. Ass's ears. The allusion is to *Gen.* xlix. 14: "Issachar is a strong ass couching down between two burdens."

Is't possible that you, whose ears
Are of the tribe of Issachar's . . .
Should yet be deaf against a noise
So roaring as the public voice?
S. Butler, *Hudibras to Sidrophei.*

Issland. In the NIBELUNGENLIED, the kingdom of Brunhild.

Istar, see ISHTAR.

Isthmian games. Games consisting of chariot races, running, wrestling, boxing, etc., held by the ancient Greeks in the Isthmus of Corinth every alternate spring, the first and third of each Olympiad. Epsom races, and other big sporting events have been called *Isthmian games* in allusion to these.

Italian. For *the Italian Froebel, the Italian Molière,* etc., see FROEBEL, MOLIÈRE.

italic.

Italic type or *italics* (the type in which the letters, instead of being erect—as in Roman—slope from left to right, *thus*) was first used by Aldo Manuzio in printing the Aldine classics. It was called by him "Cursive," a running hand (from Lat. *curro,* "I run"). Virgil was the first author printed in this type (1501). Francesco of Bologna cast it.

The words *italicized* in the ordinary versions of the Bible have no corresponding words in the original. The translators supplied these words to render the sense of the passage more full and clear.

In preparing manuscript for the printer, italics are indicated by underlining.

It Can't Happen Here. A novel by Sinclair LEWIS, published in 1935. It presents a fancied Fascist (see FASCISM) dictatorship in the U.S., set up by Berzelius (Buzz) Windrip, a New England demagogue who is elected to the presidency. Doremus Jessup, editor of a small Vermont newspaper, fights Windrip, although he is arrested for his opposition, and secretly aids the New Underground, a revolutionary, anti-Fascist movement set up in Canada by Walt Trowbridge, Windrip's defeated rival in the presidential election. Eventually there is a war against Mexico, and Jessup takes part in the revolution promoted by Trowbridge. The novel has been dramatized, with the author playing the rôle of Jessup.

Ithunn. In Norse mythology, the wife of Bragi. She was the goddess who kept in Asgard the apples which were eaten by the gods to preserve their eternal youth.

Ithuriel. The angel who, with ZEPHON, was, in Milton's *Paradise Lost,* commissioned by Gabriel to search for Satan, after he had effected his entrance into Paradise. The name is Rabbinical, and means "the discovery of God."

He was armed with a spear, the slightest touch of which exposed deceit. Hence, when Satan squatted like a toad "close to the ear of Eve," Ithuriel made him resume his proper form:—

> Him [i.e., Satan], thus intent Ithuriel with his spear
> Touched lightly; for no falsehood can endure
> Touch of celestial temper, but returns
> Of force to its own likeness.—*Paradise Lost,* iv. 810.

Iturbi, José (1895-). Spanish pianist, conductor, and motion picture actor. Musical director, Rochester Philharmonic Orchestra.

Itzcoatl (1360?–?1440). First emperor of the Aztecs (1427–?1440). Through him Tenochtitlan, the modern Mexico City, was set up as an independent power dominating the lake valley.

Ivan IV Vasilievich. Called **Ivan the Terrible** (1530–1584). Czar of Russia. Conquered Kazan and Astrakhan. Acquired Siberia through conquest by Cossacks (1581). Killed his son Ivan in a fit of anger. At the age of seventeen he assumed the title of Czar of Russia which has since been borne by all Russian monarchs.

Ivan Ilyitch, The Death of. A short novel by TOLSTOY.

Ivanhoe. A novel by Sir Walter SCOTT (1820), a tale of the period following the Norman Conquest. The titular hero is Wilfred, knight of Ivanhoe, the son of Cedric the Saxon, in love with his father's ward Rowena. Cedric, however, wishes her to marry Athelstane, who is descended from the Saxon royal line and may restore the Saxon supremacy. The real heroine is Rebecca the Jewess, daughter of the wealthy Isaac of York and a person of much more character and charm than the mild Rowena. Richard I in the guise of the Black Knight and Robin Hood as Locksley play prominent rôles, and knights and palmers from the Holy Land, fair ladies, conspiracies and counterattacks, a tournament and the burning of a great castle combine to give it a rich and varied color. Ivanhoe does not return Rebecca's love; he marries Rowena. See under REBECCA for Thackeray's sequel.

Ivanovich or **Ivan Ivanovitch.** The national impersonation of the Russians as a people. See also NICKNAMES OF NATIONALITIES.

BROWNING has a poem called *Ivan Ivanovich* in his *Dramatic Idylls* (1879). Ivan Ivanovich, a Russian carpenter, is working at a "huge shipmast trunk," when a sledge dashes up to the workyard with a half-frozen, fainting woman in it, who is recognized by the crowd assembled as "Dmitri's wife." She tells them that on her journey home in the sledge, with her three children, she was overtaken by wolves, and, to save herself, threw the children to the beasts. Ivan Ivanovich takes the law into his own hands, and slays her with an axe as she lies before him. The verdict of the village judge and of the neighbors is in Ivan's favor.

ivory gate, see DREAMS, GATES OF.

ivory shoulder, see PELOPS.

Ivy-Day in the Committee Room. A story by James JOYCE in the collection entitled DUBLINERS. It deals with the meeting of a group of Irish politicians on the birthday of Charles Stewart PARNELL, and the dramatic conflicts between his supporters and the conservatives.

Iwain, see YWAIN.

iwis, ywis. Certainly, truly. Archaic. Cf. German *gewiss,* same meaning. The prefix was occasionally mistaken for the pronoun I, and later poets used the word as follows:

> A certain shape I wist.
> Coleridge.

> Our ship, I wis,
> Shall be of another form than this.
> Longfellow.

> I wis, in all the senate
> There was no heart so bold.
> Macaulay.

I.W.W. The popular designation of the INDUSTRIAL WORKERS OF THE WORLD, a wage-earners' union organized in 1905 which rapidly acquired the reputation of being radical and lawless.

Ixion. In Greek legend, a king of the Lapithae who was bound to a revolving wheel of fire in the infernal regions, either for his impious presumption in trying to imitate the thunder of heaven, or for boasting of the favors supposed to have been conferred on him by Hera, Zeus having sent a cloud to him in the form of Hera, and the cloud having become by him the mother of the CENTAURS.

izzard. An old name of the letter "z." Still used in the phrase, *from A to izzard,* "from alpha to omega, from A to Z." The word has no satisfactory explanation. Possibly from "s hard" (which makes little sense) or from French "et z"—pronounced "ay zed" (which is not much better either).

J

Jabal. In the Old Testament, one of the early descendants of Cain, "the father of such as dwell in tents and have cattle."

Jabberwocky. A well-known ballad by LEWIS CARROLL, found in THROUGH THE LOOKING-GLASS. It contains a number of words coined by the author himself, often of the "PORTMANTEAU" variety, such as "brillig," "slithy," "toves," "gimble," "borogove," "mome," "rath," and "outgrabe." Some critics consider it a burlesque of the word-coinages of Edmund SPENSER. The Jabberwock is a species of dragon.

J'accuse (I accuse). Commonly used as the title of the famous letter addressed by Émile ZOLA to President Faure of France (1898) in denunciation of the DREYFUS affair. In it Zola used the phrase several times for rhetorical emphasis.

Jack.

a good Jack makes a good Jill. A good husband makes a good wife, a good master makes a good servant. Jack, a generic name for man, husband, or master; and Jill for a woman.

Jack of all trades is master of none. One who can turn his hand to anything is not usually an expert in any one branch. *Jack of all trades* is a contemptuous expression.

Jack, Colonel. The hero of Defoe's novel entitled *The History of the Most Remarkable Life and Extraordinary Adventures of the truly Hon. Colonel, Jacque, vulgarly called Colonel Jack.* The colonel (born a gentleman and bred a pickpocket) goes to Virginia, and passes through all the stages of colonial life, from that of "slavey" to that of an owner of slaves and plantations.

Jack-a-Lent. A stuffed figure at which boys threw sticks at Lent in Old England.

> Thou didst stand six weeks the Jack of Lent,
> For boys to hurl, three throws a penny, at thee.
> Ben Jonson.

Jackanapes. A pert, vulgar, apish little fellow; a prig. The word first appears as a derisive nickname for William de la Pole, Duke of Suffolk (murdered in 1450), whose badge was the clog and chain of a tame ape. *Jackanapes* must, however, have been in use before it became a nickname, and it is uncertain whether the *-napes* is connected originally with *ape* or with *Naples, Jackanapes* being a *Jack* (monkey) of (imported from) *Naples,* just as *fustian-a-napes* was fustian from Naples. There is an early 15th-century record of monkeys being sent to England from Italy, and by the 16th century, at all events, *Jackanapes* was in use as a proper name for a tame ape.

Jack and Jill. The well-known nursery rhyme is said to be a relic of a Norse myth, accounting for the dark patches in the moon: the two children are supposed to have been kidnaped by the moon while drawing water, and they are still to be seen with the bucket hanging from a pole resting on their shoulders.

> Jack and Jill went up the hill
> To fetch a pail of water;
> Jack fell down and cracked his crown,
> And Jill came tumbling after.

Jack and the Beanstalk. A nursery tale found among all sorts of races from Icelanders to Zulus. Jack is a very poor lad, sent by his mother to sell a cow, which he parts with to a butcher for a few beans. His mother, in her rage, throws the beans away, but one of them grows during the night as high as the heavens. Jack climbs the stalk, and, by the direction of a fairy, comes to a giant's castle, where he begs food and rest. This he does thrice, and in his three visits steals the giant's red hen, which lays golden eggs, his money-bags, and his harp. As he runs off with the last treasure, the harp cries out, "Master! master!" which wakes the giant, who runs after Jack. But the nimble lad cuts the beanstalk with an axe, and the giant is killed in his fall. As we know it, this story is of Teutonic origin. According to a frequently advanced theory, the "beanstalk" is the ash, Yggdrasil, of the *Eddas,* the giant is All-Father, whose three treasures are a harp—i.e., the wind, bags full of treasures—i.e., the rain, and the red hen which lays golden eggs—that is, the genial sun. "Jack" typifies Man, who avails himself of these treasures and becomes rich.

Jack Brag. A vulgar, pretentious braggart, who gets into aristocratic society, where his vulgarity stands out in strong relief. The character is in Theodore Hook's novel of the same name.

Jack Cade, see CADE.

Jackdaw of Rheims, The. The title of a poem in *The Ingoldsby Legends.* It tells how a jackdaw stole the ring of the cardinal of Rheims and was cursed by him.

Jack Drum, see DRUM.

Jack Frost. Frost personified.

Jack Horner. A commonly accepted explanation of the old nursery rhyme *Little Jack Horner* is that Jack was steward to the Abbot of Glastonbury at the time of the dissolution of the monasteries, and that he, by a subterfuge, became possessed of the deeds of the Manor of Mells, which is in the neighborhood and which is still owned by his descendants of the same name. Some say that these deeds with others were sent to Henry VIII concealed, for safety, in a pasty; that "Jack

Horner" was the bearer; and that on the way he lifted the crust and extracted this "plum."

Little Jack Horner sat in a corner
Eating his Christmas pie
He put in his thumb and pulled out a plum
And said "What a brave boy am I."

Jack-in-the-green. In the May-day games of England, a boy in a frame covered with leaves.

Jack Ketch. A hangman and executioner, notorious for his barbarity, who was appointed about 1663 and died in 1686. As early as 1678 his name had appeared in a ballad, and by 1702 it was associated with the Punch and Judy puppet-play, which had recently been introduced from Italy.

Jack Robinson, Before you can say. Immediately. Grose says that the saying originated from a very volatile gentleman of that name, who used to pay flying visits to his neighbors, and was no sooner announced than he was off again; Halliwell says (*Archaic Dictionary,* 1846):

The following lines from "an old play" are elsewhere given as the original phrase—
A warke it ys as easie to be done
As tys to saye *Jacke! robys on.*

But the "old play" has never been identified, and both these accounts are palpably *ben trovato.* The phrase was in use in the 18th century, and is to be found in Fanny Burney's *Evelina* (1778), II. xxxvii.

Jacks, Lawrence Pearsall (1860–). English philosopher and essayist. Editor of the *Hibbert Journal* (1902). Believer in a living universe and creative evolution. Nearly thirty published works.

Jack Sheppard, see SHEPPARD.

Jack Sprat. A character famed in nursery rhyme.

Jack Sprat could eat no fat,
His wife could eat no lean;
And so betwixt 'em both
They licked the platter clean.

Jackson, Andrew (1767–1845). Seventh president of the United States (1829–1837). Inaugurator of spoils system in government. Despite Jackson's intervention, the cabinet was broken up because its members refused to accept socially Mrs. (Peggy O'Neill) Eaton, wife of the Secretary of War. The charter of the United States Bank was vetoed during Jackson's administration and the national debt completely paid off.

Jackson, Helen Maria Hunt (1831–1885). American poet and novelist, best known for her novel RAMONA (1884). *A Century of Dishonor* (1881) is an account of injustice to the Indians on the part of the U.S. government, and *Mercy Philbrick's Choice* (1876) is a novel considered to deal with the life of Emily DICKINSON. *Saxe Holm* was a pseudonym used by the author early in her career.

Jackson, Holbrook (1874–1948). English essayist, literary historian, editor. With Ralph HODGSON and Claude Lovat FRASER, he published the now famous *Flying Fame* chapbooks and broadsides (1913). His *The Eighteen Nineties* (1913) has been called "the finest history" of that literary and artistic period.

Jackson, Mrs. George. In James T. Farrell's STUDS LONIGAN, a married woman of moderate middle class standing who gambles secretly on horse-racing, loses money, and in a desperate attempt to secure funds to pay her gambling debts, impulsively sells her favors to Studs Lonigan and three of his friends who happen to be in the bookmaker's shop at the same time as she. Studs is attracted to her and later returns alone to visit her but is scornfully rebuffed.

Jackson, Thomas Jonathan (1824–1863). One of the Confederate generals in the American Civil War. Called **Stonewall Jackson** because at the Battle of Bull Run (1861) General Bee of South Carolina, observing his men waver, exclaimed, "Look at Jackson's men; they stand like a stone wall!" Mortally wounded by his own men at the battle of Chancellorsville as he was returning from a reconnaissance.

Jack Straw. The name (or nickname) of one of the leaders in the Peasants' Revolt of 1381. There is an allusion to him in Chaucer's *Nun's Prologue* (1386), and the name soon came to signify a man of straw, a worthless sort of person.

Jack Tar. A common sailor, whose hands and clothes are tarred by the ship tackling. Also explained as short for *tarpaulin. Tar* alone was used for sailor as early as the 17th century. The combination with Jack seems to have been introduced by Dickens.

Jack the Giant-killer. The hero of an old nursery tale, who owes much of his success to his four marvelous possessions—an invisible coat, a cap of wisdom, shoes of swiftness, and a resistless sword. When he puts on his coat, no eye can see him; when he has shoes on, no one can overtake him; his sword will cut through everything; and when his cap is on, he knows everything he needs to know. The story is given by Walter Map (and later by Geoffrey of Monmouth), who obtained it in the early 13th century from a French chronicle. Jack is a "valiant Cornishman," and his first exploit is to kill the giant Cormoran, by digging a deep pit which he films over with grass, etc. The giant falls into the pit, and Jack knocks him on the head with a hatchet. Jack encounters various giants, but outwits them all. See also BLUNDERBORE.

Jack the Ripper. Popular name of an unknown London criminal to whom were attributed a number of gruesome murders (1888–1889) and who appears in *The Lodger* (1913) by Mrs. Belloc Lowndes, which was later made into a moving picture, Vincent Price starring. The picture starring the late Laird Cregar departed widely from the novel.

Jacob. A Biblical patriarch of the book of *Genesis,* whose twelve sons were the founders of the twelve tribes of Israel. As a young man Jacob purchased the birthright of his brother Esau for a mess of pottage and by impersonating his brother, secured from his blind old father Isaac the blessing intended for Esau. He served his mother's brother Laban seven years for Rachel, Laban's daughter, and was given her much less attractive sister Leah instead; whereupon he served another seven years "and they seemed to him but a short while, so great was the love he bore her." Jacob is famed for the shrewdness with which he accumulated wealth while in Laban's service. For his later life, see JOSEPH, BENJAMIN.

Jacob's ladder. The ladder seen by the patriarch Jacob in a vision (*Gen.* xxviii. 12). *Jacob* is, on this account, a cant name for a ladder, and steep and high flights of steps going up cliffs, etc., are often called *Jacob's ladders,* as is a flaw in a stocking where only the woof threads are left, the warp threads giving a ladderlike appearance. There is a garden flower also so called.

Jacob Faithful, or The Adventures of a Waterman. A novel by Captain Marryat (1834). The hero is born on a Thames "lighter" and his first experience with land is at the age of eleven.

Jacobins. (1) The Dominicans were so called in France from the "Rue St. Jacques," Paris, where they first established themselves in 1219.

(2) A political club, originally called the *Club Breton,* formed at Versailles in 1789. On their removal to Paris, they met in the hall of an ex-convent of Jacobins (see above), in the Rue St. Honoré.

Jacobites. The partisans of James II and his heirs after William III superseded him. They engaged in fruitless rebellions in 1715 and 1745. See the FIFTEEN; the FORTY-FIVE; also, WARMING-PANS.

Jacobs, Joseph (1854–1916). Jewish scholar and writer. Author of *Earliest English Version of the Fables of Bidpai* (1888); *The Jews of Angevin England* (1893); etc. Editor, *Jewish Encyclopedia* (1900).

Jacobs, William Wymark (1863–1943). English story writer. A delightful humorist of lusty sea-stories. One great horror story, *The Monkey's Paw,* and a number of plays. *Snug Harbor* (1931) is an omnibus of his stories.

Jacobsen, Jens Peter (1847–1885). Danish poet and novelist. Started his career as a botanist. His creative years began after he retired as a tubercular patient to his native Thisted (1873). His work exerted a very strong influence on the generation of German writers typically represented by Rainer Maria RILKE. *Fru Marie Grubbe* (1876); *Niels Lyhne* (1880). A masterly novella by Jacobsen is *Pesten i Bergamo* (*The Plague in Bergamo;* 1881).

Jacob's Room. A novel by Virginia WOOLF (1922).

Jacob Stahl, see STAHL, JACOB.

Jacopo. In Cooper's BRAVO.

Jacopone da Tody (1230?–1306). Italian Franciscan monk. Author (?), on the basis of earlier material, of *Stabat Mater.*

Jacquard, Joseph Marie (1752–1834). French mechanic and inventor of a loom (1801) that revolutionized the technique of inwoven designs. Later awarded a pension and elected to the Legion of Honor (1819).

Jacquemart, Jules Ferdinand (1837–1880). French etcher, distinguished for a remarkable series representing works of Rembrandt, Hals, Meissonier, etc. At Paris exposition (1878) awarded Grand Médaille for etching.

Jacquerie, la. An insurrection of the peasantry of France in 1358, excited by the oppressions of the privileged classes and Charles the Bad of Navarre, while King Jean II was a prisoner in England. It was so called from *Jacques,* or *Jacques Bonhomme,* the generic name which was often given to the French peasantry. They banded together, fortified themselves and declared war to the death against every gentleman in France, but in six weeks some 12,000 of the insurgents were cut down, and the rebellion suppressed with the greatest determination. See also under GOODMAN JAMES.

Jacques (*Fr.*). (1) A generic name for the poor artisan class in France so called from the *jaque,* a rough kind of waistcoat, sleeved, and coming almost to the knees, that they used to wear. A peasant is also frequently called *Jacques Bonhomme.*

> Jacques, il me faut troubler ton somme;
> Dans le village, un gros huissier
> Rude et court, suivi du messier:
> C'est pour l'impôt, las! mon pauvre homme,
> Lève-toi, Jacques, lève-toi,
> Voici venir l'huissier du roi.
>
> Béranger (1831).

pauvre Jacques (poor Jacques). The absent sweetheart of a love-lorn maiden. Marie Antoinette sent to Switzerland for a lass to attend the dairy of her "Swiss village" in miniature, which she arranged in the Little Trianon (Paris). The lass was heard sighing for *pauvre Jacques,* and her longing made a capital sentimental amusement for the court idlers. The swain was sent for, and the marriage consummated.

Pauvre Jacques, quand j'etais près de toi
Je ne sentais pas ma misère;
Mais à présent que tu vis loin de moi
Je manque de tout sur la terre.
Marquis de Travenet, *Pauvre Jacques.*

(2) The hero of a novel of that name by George SAND. Discovering that his wife is in love with another man, he disappears and kills himself in order to insure their happiness.

Jacquotte. In Balzac's COUNTRY DOCTOR (*Le Médecin de campagne*), the faithful old cook of Dr. Benassis.

Jade Emperor. The chief god of the triad of popular Taoism.

Jadwin, Curtis. The hero of Frank Norris' novel THE PIT.

Jael. In the Old Testament, a woman who offered Sisera, the Canaanite, refuge from the pursuit of Deborah and Barak, and then killed him with a tent-pin.

Jaffar, see GIAFER.

Jaffier. The hero of Otway's tragedy, VENICE PRESERVED.

Jagganath, see JUGGERNAUT.

Jaggers. In Dickens' GREAT EXPECTATIONS, a lawyer of Little Britain, London. He is a burly man, of exceedingly dark complexion, with a large head and large hands; when he speaks to anyone, he throws his fore-finger at him pointedly. A hard, logical man is Mr. Jaggers, who requires an answer to be "yes" or "no," allowing no one to express an opinion, but only to state facts in the fewest possible words. Magwitch appoints him Pip's guardian, and he is Miss Havisham's man of business.

Jahannam. A name of the Mohammedan HELL or of the first of its seven divisions. The word is the same as the Hebrew GEHENNA.

Jairus' daughter. In the New Testament, a child twelve years old who was raised from the dead by Jesus.

Jalna, see under DE LA ROCHE, MAZO.

jalopy. In American slang, a dilapidated automobile or airplane. Possibly from some foreign equivalent of *sloop,* as French *chaloupe.*

James I of England and **VI of Scotland** (1566–1625). He appears in Scott's FORTUNES OF NIGEL (1822) as one of the principal characters. He was called "the English Solomon" and "the Wisest Fool in Christendom" on account of his impractical learning. He was the author of *Essays of a Prentice in the Divine Art of Poesy* (1584), a critical treatise, and *Poetical Exercises at Vacant Hours* (1591), but wrote little after becoming sovereign of England. He failed to live up to the hopes of the English poets that he might become their patron; he is known to have assisted only Ben JONSON. RHYME ROYAL was so named because it was believed James had been the first to use it. For *King James Bible,* see under BIBLE.

James II (1633–1701). King of England, Scotland, Ireland (1685–1688). Son of Charles I and Henrietta Maria. Embraced Roman Catholic faith (probably before 1672). Succeeded to throne at death of his brother, Charles II. Out of fear of a Roman Catholic tyranny the English nobles offered the throne to William of Orange, James's son-in-law. James escaped to France, where he was received by Louis XIV. He later landed in Ireland (1689) but was defeated at the battle of the Boyne (July 1, 1690).

James, Henry (1843–1916). American novelist, considered one of the greatest figures in the history of the novel form, educated in England and Europe and in 1915 naturalized as a British citizen. He is known for his realistic psychological penetration and analysis; his subtle, intricate, and balanced prose style; his attitude of detachment in dealing with his characters and plot; his studies of the American upper middle class, especially as, ingenuous and self-confident in their newly obtained wealth, they are contrasted with the sophisticated and often decadent aristocracy of Europe; and his frequent use of melodrama and the supernatural for purposes of psychological symbolism. See also REVERBERATOR, THE. James preferred to live abroad, finding the brash, materialistic spirit of the U.S. of his time not conducive to his best work. Important influences on James' writing were George ELIOT, HAWTHORNE, FLAUBERT, and TURGENEV.

James' novels include: RODERICK HUDSON (1876); THE AMERICAN (1877); THE EUROPEANS (1878); DAISY MILLER (1879); *An International Episode* (1879); *Confidence* (1880); *Washington Square* (1881); *The Bostonians* (1886); THE PORTRAIT OF A LADY (1881); THE PRINCESS CASAMASSIMA (1886); THE REVERBERATOR (1888); *The Aspern Papers* (1888); *The Tragic Muse* (1890); *The Other House* (1896); *The Spoils of Poynton* (1897); *What Maisie Knew* (1897); *In the Cage* (1898); *The Awkward Age* (1899); *The Sacred Fount* (1901); THE WINGS OF THE DOVE (1902); THE AMBASSADORS (1903); THE GOLDEN BOWL (1904); *The Ivory Tower* (1917) and *The Sense of the Past* (1917), these last two being left incomplete. Among his collections of tales are: *A Passionate Pilgrim, And Other Tales* (1875); *The Madonna of the Future* (1879); *The Author of Beltraffio* (1885); *The Lesson of the Master, And Other Tales* (1892); *The Private Life* (1893); *The Real Thing, And Other Tales* (1893); *Termination* (1895); *Embarrassments* (1896); *The Soft Side*

(1900); *The Better Sort* (1903); The Altar of the Dead (1909); *The Finer Grain* (1910). *The Two Magics* (1898) contains the famous story called The Turn of the Screw. His essays and criticism include: *French Poets and Novelists* (1878); *Hawthorne* (1879); *Partial Portraits* (1888); *The American Scene* (1907); *Views and Reviews* (1908). *Theatricals* (1894–1895) is a collection of four comedies, and *A Small Boy and Others* (1913), *Notes of a Son and Brother* (1914), and *The Middle Years* (1917) are autobiographical works.

Henry James was the brother of William James and the son of **Henry James, Sr.** (1811–1882), a clergyman, author, and lecturer, who rebelled against Calvinism and was strongly influenced by the mystical doctrines of Swedenborg.

James, Jesse Woodson (1847–1882). American outlaw, famous for his railroad and bank robberies in the Middle West during the period following the Civil War. He was popularly regarded as a hero, and after his death several folk-tales and dime novels and a well-known ballad, *Jesse James,* were written about him. A play, *Missouri Legend,* dealing with James's life, was produced in 1938.

James, William (1842–1910). Brother of Henry James. American psychologist and philosopher. One of the founders of pragmatism. Author of *The Principles of Psychology* (1890); *The Will to Believe and Other Essays* (1897); *The Varieties of Religious Experience* (1902); *Pragmatism* (1907); etc.

The *James-Lange theory* of emotion, named after William James and the Danish physician Carl Georg Lange (1834–1900), states characteristically that an emotion, which seems to find expression in certain bodily symptoms, is really not the cause of those symptoms but rather the individual's sensation of them. The "symptoms" are the cause and not the effect of an emotion.

Jameson, Storm (1897–). English novelist. Successful in evoking the Victorian era. A liberal and profound feminist but "as English as Yorkshire pudding."

Jameson Raid. A raid on Johannesburg, South Africa (1895–1896), led by the Englishman Dr. Jameson, that is, Sir Leander Starr Jameson (1853–1917), in an attempt to overthrow the Boer government during the troubles between the Boers and foreigners in the gold mines. Jameson was captured, handed over to the British for trial, but was released shortly and became later prime minister of Cape Colony (1904–1908).

James Shore's Daughter. A novel by Stephen Vincent Benét (1934).

James the Pretender. See under pretender.

Jamestown. The first permanent English settlement in the New World, founded (1607) by Capt. John Smith on the site of the abandoned Spanish settlement of San Miguel (1526), and named after King James I. It was the capital of Virginia until 1698. The first settlers suffered great hardships, especially during the starving years of 1609–1610. Jamestown was burned down in Bacon's Rebellion (1676). Before its restoration in modern times, the only surviving relics were the tower of the church and a number of tombs.

Jamieson, the Honorable Mrs. In Mrs. Gaskell's Cranford, the social arbiter of the little village of Cranford.

Jammes, Francis (1868–1938). French poet and novelist, characterized by his passionate love for nature and, especially since the time of Claudel's influence on him, by his deep Catholic faith. He has been called "the Thoreau of France." It is a fitting symbol that he should be a namesake of St. Francis of Assisi. No one complete book of his has appeared in English.

Jamshid or **Giamschid.** In Persian legend, the fourth king of the Pishdadian Dynasty, i.e., the earliest, who is fabled to have reigned for 700 years and to have had the Deevs, or Genii, as his slaves. He possessed a seven-ringed golden cup, typical of the seven heavens, the seven planets, the seven seas, etc., which was full of the elixir of life; it was hidden by the genii and was said to have been discovered while digging the foundations of Persepolis.

> I know too where the genii hid
> The jewelled cup of their king Jamshid,
> With life's elixir sparkling high.
> Thomas Moore, *Paradise and the Peri.*

> Iram indeed is gone with all his rose
> And Jamshyd's Sev'n-ring'd Cup where no one knows.
> Fitzgerald, *Rubaiyat of Omar Khayyám.*

Jane, Calamity, see Calamity Jane.

Jane Clegg. A drama by St. John Ervine (1911). The heroine, Jane Clegg, comes at last to find life with her scoundrel husband Henry and his doting old mother unendurable.

Jane Eyre. A novel by Charlotte Brontë (1847). In both heroine and hero the author introduced types new to English fiction. Jane Eyre is a shy intense little orphan, never for a moment, either in her unhappy school days or her subsequent career as a governess, displaying those qualities of superficial beauty and charm that had marked the conventional heroine. Jane's lover, Edward Rochester, to whose ward she is governess, is a strange, violent man, bereft of conventional courtesy, a law unto himself. Rochester's moodiness is due to the fact that he is married to an insane wife, whose existence, long kept secret, is revealed on the very day of his projected marriage to Jane. Years afterward the lovers are reunited.

Jane Seymour (1509?–1537). Third queen

of Henry VIII of England. Lady-in-waiting to Catharine of Aragon and to Anne Boleyn, one day after whose execution she married the king. Died a few days after giving birth to Edward VI.

Jane Shore. A tragedy by Nicholas Rowe (1714), based on the life of the historical Jane Shore, the wife of a London merchant who, in 1470, left her husband to become the mistress of Edward IV. After the death of that monarch she was accused of witchcraft by Richard III, who condemned her to wander about in a sheet, holding a taper in her hand, and decreed that anyone who offered her food or shelter should be put to death. Jane continued an outcast for three days; then her husband came to her succor, but he was seized by Gloucester's myrmidons, and Jane Shore died. She is also the heroine of a ballad included in Percy's *Reliques,* and of an anonymous drama earlier than Rowe's.

Janet's Repentance. A story by George Eliot, one of her *Scenes of Clerical Life* (1857). Mr. Tryan, the earnest young Evangelical curate in the town of Mibly, has aroused great opposition. Chief among his opponents are Robert Dempster, a dissipated lawyer, and his beautiful but unhappy wife Janet, both of whom are addicted to drink. Janet meets the curate, becomes interested in his ideals and gradually breaks away from her evil habits.

Janice Meredith. A historical novel by Paul Leicester Ford (1899) dealing with the American Revolution. The plot centers about the love affair of the patriotic Janice Meredith, daughter of a Tory father, and Charles Fownes, whose name is really John Brereton. He is first an indentured servant of Janice's father but later becomes a general in Washington's army. Washington is also a prominent figure.

Janiculum. A hill in Rome on the right bank of the Tiber, opposite the Capitoline and Aventine. On the point nearest the city was a watch tower. It is the highest of the Roman hills (276 feet).

Janissaries or **Janizaries** (Turk. *yenitscheri,* new corps). A celebrated militia of the Ottoman Empire, raised by Orchan in 1326, originally, and for some centuries, compulsorily recruited from the Christian subjects of the Sultan. It was blessed by Hadji Bektash, a saint, who cut off a sleeve of his fur mantle and gave it to the captain. The captain put the sleeve on his head, and from this circumstance arose the fur cap worn by these foot guards. In 1826, having become too formidable to the state, they were abolished after a massacre in which many thousands of the Janissaries perished.

Jannes and **Jambres.** The names under which St. Paul (2 *Tim.* iii, 8) referred to the two magicians of Pharaoh who imitated some of the miracles of Moses (*Exod.* vii). The names are not mentioned in the Old Testament, but they appear in the Targums and other rabbinical writings, where tradition has it that they were sons of Balaam, and that they perished either in the crossing of the Red Sea, or in the tumult after the worship of the golden calf.

Jannings, Emil (1887–). Swiss-born actor of German-American parentage. Stage career with Max Reinhardt at Deutsches Theater in Berlin. Screen début (1916) in Lubitsch films. Very successful in Hollywood (1926–1929) but did not survive advent of "talkies." Returned to stage (1932). Especially remembered for *The Last Laugh* and *The Blue Angel,* with Marlene Dietrich.

Jansenists. A sect of Christians, who held the doctrines of Cornelius Jansen, Bishop of Ypres, in West Flanders. Jansen professed to have formulated the teaching of Augustine (1640) which resembled Calvinism in many respects. He taught the doctrines of "irresistible grace," "original sin," and the "utter helplessness of the natural man to turn to God." Louis XIV took part against them, and they were put down by Pope Clement XI, in 1705, in the famous bull Unigenitus.

Jansoulet. Hero of Daudet's Nabob.

Januarius, St., see under Saint.

January and **May.** The chief characters in *The Merchants Tale,* one of the *Canterbury Tales* of Chaucer (1388). January was an old Lombard baron, some sixty years of age, who married a girl named May. This young wife loved Damyan, a young squire. One day, the old baron found them in close embrace; but May persuaded her husband that his eyes were so dim he had made a mistake, and the old baron, too willing to believe, allowed himself to give credit to the tale.

Janus. The ancient Roman deity who kept the gate of heaven; hence, the guardian of gates and doors. He was represented with two faces, one in front and one behind, and the doors of his temple in Rome were thrown open in times of war and closed in times of peace. At one time, they had to stay open with only one very brief interlude, for 700 years. The name is used allusively both with reference to double-facedness and to war.

Japhet. A name for Iapetus, introduced by Milton in *Paradise Lost.* Also one of the sons of Noah and, according to legend, the father of Histion from whom descended the French, Italian, German, and British peoples.

Jaquenetta. In Shakespeare's LOVE'S LABOUR'S LOST, a country wench courted by Don Adriano de Armado.

Jaques. In Shakespeare's AS YOU LIKE IT, one of the lords attendant on the banished duke in the forest of Arden, a philosophic idler, cynical, sullen and contemplative. He could "suck melancholy out of a song, as a weasel sucks eggs." He has little to do with the plot, but his musings furnish some of Shakespeare's most frequently quoted lines, notably from the familiar soliloquy on the "Seven Ages of Man" (Act II. Sc. 1) beginning—

> All the world's a stage . . .

Jaques-Dalcroze, Émile (1865–). Swiss musician and teacher of EURHYTHMICS. The *Institut Jaques-Dalcroze* at Geneva was founded by him for the teaching of eurhythmics.

Jarley, Mrs. In Dickens' OLD CURIOSITY SHOP a kind-hearted woman, mistress of a traveling wax-work exhibition, containing "one hundred figures the size of life"; the "only stupendous collection of real wax-work in the world"; "the delight of the nobility and gentry, the royal family, and crowned heads of Europe." Mrs. Jarley is kind to Little Nell, and employs her as a decoy-duck to "Jarley's unrivalled collection."

Jarndyce v. Jarndyce. An interminable Chancery suit in Dickens' BLEAK HOUSE. Mr. Jarndyce, the client in the great Chancery suit of "Jarndyce *v.* Jarndyce," and guardian of Esther Summerson, conceals the tenderest heart under a flimsy churlishness of demeanor, and can never endure to be thanked for any of his numberless acts of kindness and charity. If anything goes wrong with him, or if he hears of an unkind action, he will say, "I am sure the wind is in the east"; but if he hears of kindness or goodness, the wind veers round at once, and is "due west."

Jarvie, Bailie Nicol. In Scott's ROB ROY, a magistrate at Glasgow, and kinsman of Rob Roy. He is petulant, conceited, purse-proud, without tact, and intensely prejudiced, but kind-hearted and sincere. Jarvie marries his maid.

Jason. The hero of Greek legend who led the ARGONAUTS in the quest for the Golden Fleece. He was the son of Aeson, king of Iolcus, was brought up by the centaur, Chiron, and when he demanded his kingdom from his uncle, Pelias, who had deprived him of it, he was told he could have it in return for the Golden Fleece. Jason thereupon gathered together the chief heroes of Greece and set sail in the *Argo*. After many tests and trials he, through the help of MEDEA, was successful. He married Medea, but later deserted her, and, according to one account, killed himself with grief, according to another, was crushed to death by the keel of his old ship, *Argo,* while resting beneath it. He is the hero of the Alexandrian epic poem *Argonautica* by Rhodius (222–181 B.C.). William MORRIS made him the hero of a long narrative poem called *The Life and Death of Jason* (1866).

Jas Pagan, see under EARWICKER.

Jastrow, Joseph (1863–1944). American psychologist. Gifted popularizer and author of many books, as *The Life of the Mind* (1938), etc.

Jaurès, Jean Léon (1859–1914). French socialist leader. With Briand, founder and editor of the daily *L'Humanité* (1904). Assassinated by a French chauvinist at the outbreak of World War I. One of the greatest orators in French parliamentary history.

Java Head. A novel by Joseph HERGESHEIMER (1919), a tale of old Salem. Gerrit Ammidon, the big-hearted, unconventional son of a family of New England sea-traders, amazes Salem by bringing home a Chinese wife, Taou Yuen. Much of the novel is a study in contrasting civilizations. Gerrit is loved by Nettie Vollar, a wretched girl whom he has befriended, and when her dissipated uncle, Edward Dunsack, succeeds in his evil schemes of insinuation and traps the unhappy Chinese woman in Nettie's room, Taou Yuen commits suicide. Gerrit and Nettie are later married.

Javert. In Victor Hugo's LES MISERABLES, an officer of police, the impersonation of inexorable law. He pursues the ex-convict Jean Valjean relentlessly, but at the end he commits suicide rather than arrest his prey.

Jay Gould's daughter. The principal figure of a popular American song, the best verse of which, and a famous one, is:

> Jay Gould's daughter said before she died,
> "Fix the blinds so the bums can't ride;
> If ride they must, let 'em ride the rod,
> Let 'em put their trust in the hands of God!"

A certain likeness to the immortal ballad of "Casey Jones" is apparent in its rhythm and in some words.

Jay Hawk. An irregular soldier belonging to a band of anti-slavery guerrillas active before and during the Civil War, particularly in Kansas and Missouri. Kansas is known as the *Jay Hawk State* on this account.

jay walker. One who crosses a city street in the middle of a block instead of at a corner crossing. In some American cities this practice is against the regulations. The term probably comes from the common use of "jay" or "jake" (country-jake) as a stupid person from the country who does not know how to behave in town.

jazz. Syncopated or ragtime music played by a band of very loud, clangy instruments, tremendously popular during the 1920's, especially in the U.S. Jazz music is said to have originated in New Orleans. According to one story, in March, 1916, Bert Kelly's "Jazz Band" (said to be the first so called) was engaged by the Boosters' Club of Chicago, scored an immediate success, and started jazz on its conquering career. The term was soon widely applied to modern life and such expressions as a *jazz* resort, this *jazz* civilization, and the adjective *jazzy* (meaning loud, gaudy, vulgar, exciting to the senses) came into common use.

Another account of the origin of jazz traces it back to the year 1895 when it was heard in New Orleans as the accompaniment to a dance called the "Pasmala."

The word is of uncertain origin. It may have come from an African word for hurry, getting into English by way of Creole, or from Arabic or even Hindustani. The most picturesque story links it up with the abbreviated first name of the Vicksburg singer, *Charles* (that is, *Chas.* or *Chazz*) *Alexander,* whose audience (about 1910) would encourage him at "hot" moments in his songs by the exclamation, "Come on, Jazz!"

jazz age. A term used to designate the period of the 1920's in the U.S., when the crude abandon of JAZZ seemed to express best the spirit of determined unconventionality, gaiety, and dissipation of the American boom era that followed World War I. Such dances as the "BLACK BOTTOM" and "CHARLESTON" went hand in hand with "SPEAKEASIES," "PETTING PARTIES," and the bobbed hair, short skirts, and new freedom of behavior of the "FLAPPER." F. Scott FITZGERALD and John HELD, JR. were outstanding portrayers of the mores of the jazz age. John Dos PASSOS' U.S.A. and James T. Farrell's STUDS LONIGAN take place in part against a background of the period, and present a somewhat more objective picture of it than the work of Fitzgerald and Held. E. E. CUMMINGS and Hart CRANE were among the poets who sought to express the jazz age in their poetry, and in music such composers as George GERSHWIN and Aaron COPLAND tried to raise jazz to the level of serious music. See also GANGSTERS; PROHIBITION; SWING.

Jean. In Maupassant's PIERRE ET JEAN.

Jean-ah Poquelin. A short story by G. W. CABLE in his *Old Creole Days* (1879). The Creole, Jean-ah Poquelin, lives alone in an almost furtive fashion despite his wealth. When an attack of a suspicious mob brings on his death, his only mourner is the leper brother, long since thought dead, to whom he had devoted himself.

Jean Baptiste. See under NICKNAMES OF NATIONALITIES.

Jean Christophe. A novel by Romain ROLLAND (1904–1912) in three very long volumes. *Jean Christophe* is the spiritual biography of a German musician and composer who is forced to escape from his own country and lives for years in Paris. His unhappy childhood, his friendships and loves, his struggles, all the external events and inner vicissitudes of his long life are put before the reader. There is little plot in any strict or artificial sense. Probably the most interesting of Jean Christophe's many relationships with other people are not so much his affairs of passion as his boyhood friendship with Oliver and the platonic devotion to the Italian Countess Grazia that was the inspiration of his later life. Music is the all absorbing interest of the book.

Jean or **Johnny Crapaud.** See under NICKNAMES OF NATIONALITIES.

Jean de Meun. Pseudonym of **Jean Clopinel** (*fl.* ca. 1270). Medieval French poet, known for his completion of the *Romance of the Rose* (see under ROSE), in which he introduces a realistic and middle-class point of view, in contrast to that expressed by Guillaume de LORRIS in the first part of the allegory, and bitingly satirizes women and the evils of society as he saw them.

Jeanie with the Light-brown Hair. A sentimental song by Stephen FOSTER, revived of late years and again popular in the U.S.A. The first verse runs:

> I dream of Jeanie with the light-brown hair
> Borne like a vapor on the summer air.
> I see her tripping where the bright streams play,
> Happy as the daisies that dance on her way.

Jean Jacques. So J. J. ROUSSEAU (1712–1778) is often called.

Jean Paul. J. P. Friedrich RICHTER (1763–1825) is generally so called.

Jeanneret-Gris, Charles Edouard. See LE CORBUSIER.

Jeans, Sir **James Hopwood** (1877–1946). English physicist, astronomer and author. One of the greatest scientists of modern times. Evolved from the study of electrons a theory of supernaturalism. Author of many books, among them excellent popularizations. According to H. L. Mencken, Jeans has "a really extraordinary gift for making the most difficult of scientific concepts understandable." *The Mysterious Universe* (1930); *The New Background of Science* (1933); etc.

Jebusites. In Dryden's ABSALOM AND ACHITOPHEL, the Roman Catholics. England was Roman Catholic before the Reformation, and Jerusalem was called Jebus before the time of David.

> Succeeding times did equal folly call,
> Believing nothing, or believing all.
> The Egyptian rites the Jebusites embraced,
> When gods were recommended by their taste.
> Pt. i. 117–23.

Jeddler, Dr. A character in Dickens' BATTLE OF LIFE, "a great philosopher." The heart and mystery of his philosophy is to look upon the world as a gigantic practical joke, something too absurd to be considered seriously by any rational man. He is kind and generous by nature.

Grace and *Marion Jeddler.* Daughters of the doctor, beautiful, graceful and affectionate. They both fall in love with Alfred Heathfield, but Alfred loves the younger daughter.

Jedwood justice. Putting an obnoxious person to death first, and trying him afterwards. This sort of justice was dealt to moss-troopers. Same as *Jedburgh justice, Jeddart justice.* We have also "Cupar justice" and "Abingdon law."

> Jedwood justice—hang in haste and try at leisure.
> —Scott, *Fair Maid of Perth.* Ch. xxxii.

Jefferies, Richard (1848–1887). English naturalist. Author of the stories *The Gamekeeper at Home* (1877); *Red-Deer* (1884); etc. They are remembered because of their superior descriptions of nature.

Jeffers, John Robinson (1887–). American poet, known for his belief in extreme individualism, tending toward a Nietzschean adulation of the hero (see NIETZSCHE, FRIEDRICH), his opposition to a commercial and mechanical civilization, his attraction to strong, primitive types, and his quasi-mystical preoccupation with sexual abnormality. His work, chiefly narrative and dramatic, shows the influence of Greek drama and Freudian psychology (see also Eugene O'NEILL) and is marked by tragedy and physical violence, the use of psycho-analytical and anthropological symbolism, and a loose, apocalyptic free-verse style. His work includes: *Flagons and Apples* (1912); *Californians* (1916); *Tamar* (1924); ROAN STALLION (1925), his best-known poem; *The Women at Point Sur* (1927); *Cawdor* (1928); *Dear Judas* (1929); *Thurso's Landing* (1932); *Give Your Heart to the Hawks* (1934); *Solstice* (1935); *Such Counsels You Gave to Me* (1937); *Selected Poems* (1939); *Be Angry at the Sun* (1941).

Jefferson, Thomas (1743–1826). Third president of the United States (1801–1809). A gentleman and a scholar of thorough legal and diplomatic training. Drafted the Declaration of Independence, became governor of Virginia (1779–1781), was U.S. minister to France (1785–1789), and founded the Democratic-Republican party as whose candidate he won the presidential election and became the successor of John Adams. As an opponent of the federative party he was bitterly opposed to Alexander Hamilton. During his administration occurred the war with Tripoli, the Louisiana Purchase, the reduction of the national debt, etc. He retired to his seat at Monticello in Virginia and died, as did John Adams, on Independence Day, July 4, 1826.

Jefferson Davis's Birthday. June 3, a holiday in most of the Southern states. See Jefferson DAVIS.

Jefferson's Birthday. April 13, celebrated as a holiday in Alabama and elsewhere. See Thomas JEFFERSON.

Jeffreys, George. 1st Baron **Jeffreys of Wem** (1648–1689). English judge. As chief justice and lord chancellor of England (from 1685), he became notorious for his flagrant injustice. See BLOODY ASSIZES. When James II was overthrown, Jeffreys was imprisoned and died in the Tower.

Jehennam, see JAHANNAM.

Jehoash, see JOASH.

Jehovah, see ELOHISTIC AND JEHOVISTIC SCRIPTURES.

Jehovah's Witnesses. Members of the International Bible Students' Association. See RUSSELLITE.

Jehu. A coachman, especially one who drives at a rattling pace.

> The watchman told, saying, . . . The driving is like the driving of Jehu the son of Nimshi; for he driveth furiously.—*2 Kings* ix. 20.

Jehu overthrew Ahab's son Joram, king of Israel and seized the throne. See JEZEBEL.

Companions of Jehu. The CHOUANS were so called, from a fanciful analogy between their self-imposed task and that appointed to Jehu, on being set over the kingdom of Israel. Jehu was to cut off Ahab and Jezebel, with all their house, and all the priests of Baal. The Chouans were to cut off all who assassinated Louis XVI, and see that his brother (*Jehu*) was placed on the throne. Alexandre DUMAS has a romance entitled *The Companions of Jehu* (1851).

Jellicoe, John Rushworth. 1st Earl **Jellicoe** (1859–1935). British naval commander. During World War I, commander of the grand fleet in battle of JUTLAND. Governor general of New Zealand (1920–1924). Member, Order of Merit (1916).

Jellicot, Old Goody. In Scott's WOODSTOCK, servant at the under-keeper's hut, Woodstock Forest.

Jekyll, Dr. One of the two phases of one man, "the law of his members warring against the law of his mind." Dr. Jekyll is the "would do good," the other, Hyde, is "the evil that is present." The phrase comes from R. L. Stevenson's *The Strange Case of Dr. Jekyll and Mr. Hyde,* first published in 1886. Dr. Jekyll is an honorable man, beloved by all for his philanthropic labors. Mr. Hyde is positively loathsome, lives without restraint, and plunges into all manner of evil. The truth is that Dr. Jekyll has discovered a potion by means of which he can change himself into Mr. Hyde, and another to effect the change back again into Dr. Jekyll. By the time that he finally resolves, in revolt against a murder committed by Hyde, to have no more to do with him, it is too late. He finds himself transformed into Mr. Hyde without taking the potion, and, though he takes double doses of the other potion to keep himself Dr. Jekyll, he often lapses. At last he can procure no more of one of the ingredients of the mixture, and commits suicide.

Jellyby, Mrs. The type of the enthusiastic, unthinking philanthropist who forgets that charity should begin at home. She figures in Dickens' BLEAK HOUSE, and would do anything for the poor fan-makers and flower-girls of Borrioboola-Gha, but she shamefully neglects her own children and would bundle into the street a poor beggar dying of starvation on her step.

je maintiendrai (*Fr.*). Literally, I will maintain. Motto of the Netherlands and of William of Orange. Title of a novel by Marjorie BOWEN (*I Will Maintain*).

Jenkins, Mrs. Winifred. In Smollett's HUMPHRY CLINKER, Miss Tabitha Bramble's maid, noted for her bad spelling, misapplication of words, and ludicrous misnomers. Mrs. Winifred Jenkins is the original of Mrs. Malaprop.

Jenkins's Ear, see WAR OF JENKINS'S EAR.

Jenkinson, Ephraim. In Goldsmith's VICAR OF WAKEFIELD, a green old swindler, whom Dr. Primrose meets in a public tavern. Imposed on by his venerable appearance, apparent devoutness, learned talk about "cosmogony," and still more so by flattering praise of his work on the subject of monogamy, Dr. Primrose sells the swindler his horse, Old Blackberry, for a draft upon Farmer Flamborough. When the draft is presented for payment, the farmer tells the vicar that Ephraim Jenkinson "is the greatest rascal under heaven," and that he is the very rogue who sold Moses Primrose the spectacles. Subsequently Jenkinson becomes a reformed character.

Jenkinson, Mrs. Mountstuart. A clever social dictator in Meredith's novel, THE EGOIST.

Jenkyns, Misses Deborah and Mattie. Two old maid sisters, the chief characters in Mrs. Gaskell's CRANFORD. Their brother *Peter Jenkyns* is also an important character.

Jenner, Edward (1749–1823). English physician. First performed public vaccination on his own son (1796). The practice was accepted in the army and navy and soon spread to other countries.

Jennifer Lorn: A Sedate Extravaganza. An imaginative novel by Elinor WYLIE, published in 1923. It deals with the adventures of the heroine, Jennifer Lorn, in England and colonial India in the 18th century and is a delicate and poetic adaptation of the 18th-century picaresque tradition.

Jennings, Sarah. See under CHURCHILL, JOHN.

Jenny Wren. The sweetheart of Robin Redbreast in the old nursery rhyme. Robin promises Jenny, if she will be his wife, she shall "feed on cherry-pie and drink currant-wine." He says:

> "I'll dress you like a goldfinch,
> Or any peacock gay;
> So, dearest Jen, if you'll be mine,
> Let us appoint the day."

Jenny replies:

> "Cherry-pie is very nice,
> And so is currant wine;
> But I must wear my plain brown gown
> And never go too fine."

Jensen, Johannes Vilhelm (1873–). Danish lyric poet and novelist; representative of a modern school, opposed to that led by Georg BRANDES. His most ambitious work, *The Long Journey,* is a six-volume epic of the Cimbrians, i.e., the Teutonic race, from their emergence in Jutland after the ice age to Christopher Columbus. Jensen was awarded the Nobel prize for literature (1944).

Jenson. A style of type originally cut (about 1470) by the noted Venetian printer Nicholas Jenson (1420–1483).

Jephthah's Daughter. Jephthah was judge of Israel (*Judges* xi) who sacrificed his only daughter because he had vowed to offer up to Jehovah the first thing that met him on his return home from victory over the Ammonites.

Jeremiah. One of the Major Prophets of the Jews, who lived at the time of the conquest of Jerusalem by Nebuchadnezzar, King of Babylon, and the subsequent carrying away of Judah into captivity. His prophecies are to be found in the book of *Jeremiah* and the dirge *Lamentations.*

Jeremiad. A pitiful tale, a tale of woe to produce compassion; so called from *Lamentations* of the prophet Jeremiah.

Jericho. Used in a number of phrases for the sake of giving verbal definition to some altogether indefinite place. The reason for fixing on this particular town is possibly to be found in 2 *Sam.* x. 5, and I *Chron.* xix. 5.

> And the king said, Tarry at Jericho until your beards be grown.

Another derivation is from *Jericho,* the manor of Blackmore, near Chelmsford. Here Henry VIII had a house of pleasure, and when he was absent on some affair of gallantry, the expression in vogue was, *he's gone to Jericho.*

go to Jericho with you. A euphemistic turn of phrase for "Go and hang yourself," or something more offensive still.

gone to Jericho. No one knows where.

I wish you were at Jericho. Anywhere out of my way.

Jeritza, Maria (1887?–). Operatic soprano, chiefly known for her interpretation of Wagnerian rôles and the title-rôle in Puccini's *Tosca.* Also widely acclaimed as a concert singer. Imperial Opera, Vienna (1913) and Metropolitan Opera Company, New York (1921).

Jermyn, Matthew. In George Eliot's FELIX HOLT, an attorney who is in reality the father of Mrs. Transome's son Harold.

Jeroboam. In the Old Testament, the "son of Nebat who made Israel to sin." Under his leadership the ten tribes revolted against Rehoboam, the son of Solomon, and set up a separate state, of which he became king. His name is a byword for wickedness because of the idol-worship he initiated.

Jeroboam. A very large wine bottle or flagon is so called in allusion to this Biblical Jeroboam, the "mighty man of valor" (1 *Kings* xi. 28, xiv. 16). Its capacity is not very definite.

Jerome, A Poor Man. A novel of New England life by Mary E. Wilkins FREEMAN (1897).

Jerome, Jerome Klapka (1859–1927). English humorist and playwright. Best known for his *Three Men in a Boat* (1889), and *The Passing of the Third Floor Back* (1908), a successful modern morality play.

Jerome, St. See under SAINTS.

Jerome Coignard, see COIGNARD.

Jeronimo. The chief character in *The Spanish Tragedy* by Thomas KYD (acted about 1590). On finding his application to the king ill-timed, he says to himself, "Go by, Jeronimo," which tickled the fancy of the audience so that it became for a time a street jest, and was introduced into many contemporary plays, as in Shakespeare's *Taming of the Shrew* (*Induction*), Jonson's *Every Man in his Humour* (I. v), Dekker's *Shoemaker's Holiday* (II. i), etc.

Jerrymandering, see GERRYMANDERING.

Jerusalem. (1) A long, mystical poem by William BLAKE (1804), in which he presents his theory that the world of "imagination" is a world of eternity after death. See entry IMAGINATION for rôle of this function of the intellect in romantic aesthetics.

(2) A collection of stories by Selma LAGERLOF (1901), dealing with an old peasant family, the Ingmars of Ingmarson, and their devotion to the family farm in Sweden. The title refers to a pilgrimage to Jerusalem, for which the land is finally sold at auction by one member of the family, but another Ingmar gives up his fiancée and marries a rich wife to buy it back.

Jerusalem Delivered. An Italian epic poem in twenty books, by Torquato TASSO. It was published in 1581, and was translated into English by Edward Fairfax in 1600. The tale is as follows:

The Crusaders, encamped on the plains of Tortosa, choose Godfrey for their chief, and Alandine, King of Jerusalem, makes preparations of defense. The overtures of Argantes to Godfrey are declined and he declares war in the name of the King of Egypt. When the Christian army reaches Jerusalem, the King of Damascus sends Armida to beguile the Christians; she tells an artful tale by which she draws off several of the most puissant. It is found that Jerusalem can never be taken without the aid of Rinaldo; but Rinaldo has withdrawn from the army, because Godfrey cited him to answer for the death of Girnando, slain in a duel. Godfrey, being informed that the hero is dallying with Armida in the enchanted island, sends to invite him back to the army. He returns, and Jerusalem is taken in a night attack. As for Armida, after setting fire to her palace, she flees into Egypt, and offers to marry any knight who slays Rinaldo; but when she finds the Christian army is successful, she flees from the field. The love of Rinaldo returns; he pursues her and she relents. The poem concludes with the triumphant entry of the Christian army into the Holy City, and their devotions at the tomb of the Redeemer. The two chief episodes are the loves of Olindo and Sophronia, and of Tancred and Corinda.

Jerusalem the Golden. A hymn (published 1858) translated by John Mason NEALE from the Latin of BERNARD OF CLUNY.

Jervis, Mrs. In Richardson's PAMELA, the virtuous housekeeper of young Squire B. Mrs. Jervis protects Pamela when her young master assails her.

Jessamy Bride. The name given by Oliver GOLDSMITH to Mary Horneck when he fell in love with her in 1769. Title of a novel by F. Frankfort Moore.

Jesse. In the Old Testament, the father of David. A *Jesse tree* is a genealogical tree usually represented as a vine or as a large brass candlestick with many branches, tracing the ancestry of Christ, called a "rod out of the stem of Jesse." (*Is.* xi. 1.) Jesse is himself sometimes represented in a recumbent position with the vine rising out of his loins; hence a stained-glass window representing him thus with a tree shooting from him containing the pedigree of Jesus is called a *Jesse window.*

Jesse, Fryniwyd Tennyson. English novelist, dramatist, criminologist. Grandniece of Lord TENNYSON. See also HARWOOD. She evolved the theory that there were "born murderees," i.e., people destined to be murdered. *A Pin to See the Peepshow* (1934) is a novel based on the Thompson-Bywaters murder.

Jessup, Doremus. In Sinclair Lewis' IT CAN'T HAPPEN HERE, editor of a small newspaper in Vermont, honest and liberal in his views but forced into revolutionary action by the oppressions of an American Fascist dictatorship set up by President Berzelius WINDRIP.

Jest, The. A play by Sem BENELLI (1917) in which John and Lionel Barrymore starred. Also made into an opera.

Jesuit. The popular name of members of the "Society of Jesus," founded by St. Ignatius Loyola (see under SAINT) in 1533, who, when asked what name he would give his order, replied, "We are a little battalion of Jesus." The order was founded to combat the Reformation and to propagate the Roman Catholic faith among the heathen, but through its discipline, organization, and methods of secrecy, it soon acquired such political power that it came into conflict with both the civil and religious authorities. It was driven from France in 1594, from England in 1579, from Venice in 1607, from Spain in 1767, from Naples in 1768; in 1773 it was suppressed by Pope Clement XIV, but was revived in 1814.

Owing to the casuistical principles maintained by many of its leaders and attributed to the order as a whole, the name *Jesuit* has acquired a very opprobrious signification both in Protestant and Roman Catholic countries, and a *Jesuit,* or *Jesuitical person* has come to mean (secondarily) a deceiver or prevaricator.

Jesuit Martyrs of North America. Eight French missionaries, the priests Isaac Jogues, John de Brebeuf, Noel Chabanel, Anthony Daniel, Charles Garnier, Gabriel Lalemant, and the laymen René Goupil and John Lalande, whom the Indians martyred in the 17th century in New York and Canada. They were canonized by Pope Pius XI (1930). Cf. the epic poem by the Canadian poet Edwin John Pratt, *Brebeuf and His Brethren.*

Jesus, Lover of My Soul. A hymn by Charles WESLEY. It was first published in the grammatically more orthodox form of *Jesu, Lover of My Soul* (1740).

Jevons, Tasker. The hero of May Sinclair's novel, THE BELFRY, supposed to be a combination of Arnold BENNETT and H. G. WELLS.

Jevons, William Stanley (1835–1882). English economist and logician. He was the son of a nailmaker. Among his numerous books is one on the exhaustion of coal mines (1865).

Jew, the Wandering, see WANDERING JEW.

Jewel Song, The. An aria in the third act of GOUNOD's *Faust.*

Jewett, Sarah Orne (1849–1909). American novelist and short-story writer, known for her local-color stories of Maine. Her works include the following collections of sketches and tales: *Deephaven* (1877); *Old Friends and New* (1879); *Country By-Ways* (1881); *A White Heron, And Other Stories* (1886); *The King of Folly Island, And Other People* (1888); *Strangers and Wayfarers* (1890); *A Native of Winby, And Other Tales* (1893); *The Country of the Pointed Firs* (1896), considered to contain her best work; *The Queen's Twin, And Other Stories* (1899). *A Country Doctor* (1884), *A Marsh Island* (1885), and *The Tory Lover* (1901) are novels. Because of her charming style, her perception, and her sympathetic understanding of her subjects, Sarah Orne Jewett is regarded as one of the best of the LOCAL COLOR writers. She influenced the writing of Willa CATHER. (Cf. the latter's *Not Under Forty*).

Jewish. For the *Jewish Plato,* the *Jewish Socrates,* etc., see PLATO, SOCRATES.

Jewkes, Mrs. A detestable character in Richardson's PAMELA.

Jew of Malta, The. A tragic drama by Christopher MARLOWE (c. 1590), anticipating *The Merchant of Venice* in plot. The Jew of the title is BARABAS.

Jezebel, a painted. A flaunting woman of bold spirit but loose morals; so called from Jezebel, wife of Ahab, king of Israel (see 2 *Kings* ix, 31).

John MASEFIELD has a poetic drama *A King's Daughter,* on the story of Jezebel and Jehu.

Jill. A generic name for a lass, a sweetheart. See also JACK AND JILL.

Jim. In Mark Twain's HUCKLEBERRY FINN, Huck's faithful Negro friend who accompanies him down the river on his raft. In the latter part of the book Jim is imprisoned, and Huck and his pal, Tom Sawyer, outdo themselves in the effort to get him free.

Jim, Lord. Titular hero of Joseph Conrad's LORD JIM.

Jim Bludsoe. A poem by John HAY, one of his PIKE COUNTY BALLADS, relating the heroism of the engineer of a steamboat on the Mississippi. When the vessel catches fire, he beaches it and sacrifices himself to save his passengers. The poem is based on an actual incident; in real life the engineer was Oliver Fairchild.

Jim Crow. A Negro. The expression came from a popular Negro song and dance first introduced by Thomas D. Rice into a play called *The Rifle* by Solon Robinson. The story is that Rice picked up the song and peculiar limping dance by accident from an old Negro in Louisville, Kentucky, in 1828, whom he heard singing—

> Wheel about, turn about
> Do jis so,
> An' ebery time I wheel about
> I jump Jim Crow.

Jim Crow car. A railroad or street car in the southern U.S. for the use of Negroes. In many of the Southern states they are forbidden to sit elsewhere.

Jimmy. In Masefield's WIDOW IN THE BYE STREET.

Jinaglo, John of. A fantasy by Laurence HOUSMAN (1912).

Jingle, Alfred. In Dickens' PICKWICK PAPERS, a strolling actor, who, by his powers of amusing others and his sharp-wittedness, imposes for a time on the members of the Pickwick Club, and is admitted to their intimacy; but being found to be an impostor, he is dropped by them. The generosity of Mr. Pickwick, in rescuing Jingle from the Fleet, reclaims him, and he quits England.

Jingling Geordie. Nickname for George HERIOT. Cf. Scott's *Fortunes of Nigel.*

Jingo. A word from the unmeaning jargon of the 17th-century conjurers (see HOCUS-POCUS), probably substituted for *God,* in the same way as *Gosh, Golly,* etc., are. In Motteux's translation of Rabelais (1694), where the original reads *par Dieu* (Bk. iv. lvi), the English rendering is "By jingo"; but there is a possibility that the word is Basque *Jinko* or *Jainko,* God, and was introduced by sailors.

> Hey, Jingo! What the de'il's the matter?
> Do mermaids swim in Dartford water?
> Swift: *Actaeon or The Original Horn Fair.*

The later meaning of the word, a blustering so-called "patriot" who is itching to go to war on the slightest provocation—a *Chauvinist* in France—is from a music-hall song by G. W. Hunt, which was popular in 1878 when the country was supposed to be on the verge of intervening in the Russo-Turkish War on behalf of the Turks:

> We don't want to fight; but, by Jingo, if we do,
> We've got the ships, we've got the men, and got the money too.

The Russophobes became known as the *Jingoes,* and such policy has been labeled *Jingoism* ever since.

Jiniwin, Mrs. In Dickens' OLD CURIOSITY SHOP, a widow, the mother of Mrs. Quilp. She is a shrewd, ill-tempered old woman, who lives with her son-in-law in Tower Street.

jinn. Demons of Arabian mythology, according to fable created from fire two thousand years before Adam was made of earth, and said to be governed by a race of kings named Suleyman, one of whom "built the pyramids." Their chief abode is the mountain Kaf, and they assume the forms of serpents, dogs, cats, monsters, or even human beings, and become invisible at pleasure. The evil jinn are hideously ugly, but the good are exquisitely beautiful. The word is a plural; its singular is *jinnee.* A Jinnee is the chief character in *The Brass Bottle,* by "F. ANSTEY."

Jinnah, Mohammed Ali (1876–). Head of the Moslems in India. Read law in Lincoln's Inn, London, after going to school in Bombay. Worked for Moslem-Hindu unity in World War I. Governor-General (since 1947) of the Dominion of Pakistan. The name is derived as follows:

> P for Punjab, A for the Afghans of the North-West Frontier, K for Kashmir, S for Sind, Tan from Baluchistan. "Pak" also means "pure" in Urdu, with "stan" means "Land of the Pure."

Jinnistan. The Fairy Land of the Arabs.

Jinny. In Virginia Woolf's THE WAVES a child, pretty, fond of flattery, and "ambitious of distinction," who grows up to be a society beauty loved by many men and afraid of growing old. In the novel she is paired with NEVILLE.

Jip. In Dickens' DAVID COPPERFIELD, the pet dog of David's child wife, Dora.

jitterbug. A devotee of swing music, that is, a bug (not the insect but a slightly crazy enthusiast) who behaves as though he had the jitters (a mixture of gin and bitters).

jive. Swing music or selections in this style. Also, the lingo of swing musicians. JITTERBUGS are "hep to jive."

Jno Citizen, see under EARWICKER.

Jo. In Dickens' BLEAK HOUSE (1852), a poor little outcast, living in one of the back slums of London, called "Tom All Alone's." The little human waif is hounded about from place to place, till he dies of want.

Joad. A family of "OKIES" in John Steinbeck's THE GRAPES OF WRATH. The family includes: *"Grampa"* and *"Granma,"* who die on the way to California; *Uncle John; Pa,* a rather weak and quiet man; *Ma,* strong and courageous, who is the ruler and leader of the family; *Tom,* the hero, who was imprisoned in Oklahoma for killing a man, is involved in further murder in the California fruit-growing region, and later becomes a labor organizer; *Noah,* who leaves the group before they reach California; *Rose of Sharon* (called "Rosasharn") who is pregnant; *Connie,* Rose of Sharon's husband, who runs away when the family comes into difficulties in California; *Al;* and *Ruthie* and *Winfield,* children.

Joad, Cyril Edwin Mitchinson (1891–). English philosopher of considerable individuality: "persuasive, glib, caustic, profound." He has written, among other books, *Common Sense Ethics* (1921); *Common Sense Theology* (1922); *Guide to Philosophy* (1936); *The Testament of Joad* (1937); *Good and Evil* (1943); etc.

Joan, see DARBY AND JOAN.

Joan, Pope. A mythical female pope, fabled in the Middle Ages to have succeeded Leo IV (855). The vulgar tale is that Joan conceived a violent passion for the monk Folda and in order to get admission to him assumed the monastic habit. Being clever and popular, she was elected pope, but was discovered through giving birth to a child during her enthronization. The whole story has long since been exploded.

The name was given to a once popular card-game played with an ordinary pack *minus* the eight of diamonds (called the "Pope Joan"), and a circular revolving tray divided into eight compartments.

Joan of Arc. (Fr. *Jeanne d' Arc.*) A heroine of French history, surnamed *La Pucelle* and known as the Maid of Orleans. She was born in the village of Domrémy, the child of poor country folk. While still a mere girl, she assumed military leadership, raised the English siege of Orleans in 1429 and crowned the Dauphin Charles VII. Shortly afterward she was taken prisoner by the English and burned as a witch.

Joan has been variously represented in literature. In many works, notably in VOLTAIRE's poem *La Pucelle d'Orléans* (1738) and in early English representations she appears in very uncomplimentary character. SCHILLER's famous tragedy, *Die Jungfrau von Orleans* (1801), Mark TWAIN's historical romance, *Personal Recollections of Joan of Arc* (1896) Percy MACKAYE's *Jeanne d'Arc* (1906) Anatole France's *Jeanne d'Arc* (*Fr.*, 1908), and Bernard SHAW's drama, *Saint Joan* (1922), are the most outstanding attempts to present her tragic story in an idealistic vein that is nevertheless true to history.

Job. The personification of poverty and patience, in allusion to the patriarch whose history is given in the Bible. According to the story, which is in the form of a poetic drama (Book of *Job*), the Lord gave Satan permission to test Job. His wealth thereupon vanished, his children died and he was smitten with boils. In spite of his wife's advice to "curse God and die" he remained steadfast, even under the admonitions of his friends, the "three false comforters." He was finally restored to health and prosperity "greater than the first."

In the Koran, Job's wife is said to have been either Rahmeh, daughter of Ephraim, son of Joseph, or Makhir, daughter of Manasses; and the tradition is recorded that Job, at the command of God, struck the earth with his foot from the dunghill where he lay, and instantly there welled up a spring of water with which his wife washed his sores, and they were miraculously healed.

Job's comforter. One who means to sympathize with you in your grief, but says that you brought it on yourself, thus in reality adding weight to your sorrow.

Job's post. A bringer of bad news.

Job's pound. Bridewell prison.

Joblillies. A famous nonsense word. See PANJANDRUM.

> There were present the Picninnies, and the Joblillies, and the Garyulies, and the Grand Panjandrum himself.—Foote, *The Quarterly Review*, xcv. 516, 517.

Jocasta. In classic legend, the mother of OEDIPUS. She plays a prominent rôle in all the tragedies concerning him.

Jocelyn. A narrative poem by Alphonse LAMARTINE (1836). The hero is a priest. As a lad he finds refuge from war in an Alpine cave, where he lives with another boy, who turns out to be a girl named Laurence. Although he loves her, he remains true to his priestly vows and leaves her for a life of self-denying devotion.

Jocelyn, Rose. Heroine of Meredith's novel, EVAN HARRINGTON.

Jock o' Hazeldean. A ballad by SCOTT. Jock is beloved by a "ladye fair." The lady's father wants her to marry Frank, "the chief of Errington and laird of Langley Dale," rich, brave, and gallant; but "aye she let the tears down fa' for Jock o' Hazeldean." At length the wedding morn arrives, the kirk is gaily decked, the priest and bridegroom, with dame and knight, are duly assembled; but no bride can be seen, for she has crossed the border and given her hand to Jock of Hazeldean. This ballad is a modernized version of an ancient ballad entitled *Jock o' Hazelgreen.*

Joconde. A tale by LA FONTAINE (1665), which is a paraphrase of an episode in Ariosto's ORLANDO FURIOSO, where Joconde is known as Giocondo. The hero, a wondrous breaker of hearts, is called to dispute his skill in this art with Astolpho. He discovers first his own, then Astolpho's wife in secret love affairs, but the two heroes can think of no better way to revenge themselves on the sex than by breaking more hearts. The tale was made into a farce by Fagan (1740), and into two comic operas, the first by Deforge (1790), the second by Etienne and Nicolo (1814).

Joconde, la Belle, see MONA LISA.

Jocoseria. Title of a book of lyrics by Robert Browning, including the famous *Never the Time and The Place* (1863). It means "mingled mirth and seriousness," and comes from the adjective "joco-serious."

Joel. One of the Minor Prophets of the Old Testament; also, the book of prophecy called by his name.

Joe Miller. A jestbook or a joke; usually a stale joke. See MILLER, JOSEPH.

Joey. See under GRIMALDI, JOSEPH.

Joffre, Joseph Jacques Césaire (1852–1931). In World War I, commander in chief of the French armies and victor in the decisive battle of the Marne (Sept., 1914) where he stopped the German advance on Paris. Created field marshal and marshal of France (1917).

John, Don. In Shakespeare's comedy, MUCH ADO ABOUT NOTHING, the bastard brother of Don Pedro, prince of Aragon. In order to torment the governor, Don John tries to mar the happiness of his daughter Hero, who is about to be married to Lord Claudio, by false accusation against Hero, but his perfidy is finally unmasked.

John, Friar. A prominent character in Rabelais' GARGANTUA AND PANTAGRUEL, a tall, lean, wide-mouthed, long-nosed friar of Seville, who dispatches his matins with wonderful celerity, and runs through his vigils quicker than any of his fraternity. He swears lustily and is a Trojan to fight:

> a right monk if ever there was any, since the monking world monked a monkery (I, xxvii).

In the original he is called "Friar John *des Entommeures.*" Urquhart mistakenly translated this as "of the Funnels," although "of the Trenchermen" is the best equivalent (from Fr. *entamer,* to broach, to carve, with reference to a hearty appetite). *Entonnoirs* are "funnels," and as this word has been used as slang for the throat, perhaps that accounts for the mistake.

John, Little. A semi-legendary character in the Robin Hood cycle, a big stalwart fellow, first named John Little (or John Nailor), who encountered Robin Hood, and gave him a sound thrashing, after which he was rechristened, and Robin stood godfather. He is introduced by Scott in THE TALISMAN.

> "This infant was called John Little," quoth he;
> "Which name shall be changed anon.
> The words we'll transpose, so wherever he goes,
> His name shall be called Little John."
> Ritson, *Robin Hood,* xxi.

John-a-dreams. A stupid, dreamy fellow, always in a brown study and half asleep.

> "Yet I,
> A dull and muddy-mettled rascal, peak,
> Like John-a-dreams, unpregnant of my cause,
> And can say nothing."
> Shakespeare, *Hamlet,* ii, 2.

John Anderson, my Jo. Burns' well-known poem of this title is founded on an old song.

> But now your brow is bald, John,
> Your locks are like the snow;
> But blessings on your frosty pow
> John Anderson, my jo.

John-a-Nokes and **John-a-Stiles.** Names formerly given, instead of the very impersonal "A and B," to fictitious persons in an imaginary action at law; hence, either name may stand for "just anybody." See also DOE.

> Poets gyve names to men they write of, which argueth a conceite of an actuall truth, and so, not being true, prooves a falshood. And doth the Lawyer lye then, when under the names of *John a stile* and *John a noakes,* hee puts his case?—Sir Philip Sidney, *An Apologie for Poetrie* (1595).

John Bockhold or **Boccold.** See under JOHN OF LEYDON.

John Bull. The national nickname for an Englishman, represented as a bluff, kind-hearted, bull-headed farmer. The character is from Dr. Arbuthnot's satire *The History of John Bull,* which was originally published in 1712 as *Law is a Bottomless Pit. John Bull* is the Englishman, the Frenchman is termed *Lewis Baboon,* the Dutchman *Nicholas Frog,* etc.

> One would think, in personifying itself, a nation would . . . picture something grand, heroic, and imposing, but it is characteristic of the peculiar humour of the English, and of their love for what is blunt, comic and familiar, that they have embodied their national oddities in the figure of a sturdy, corpulent old fellow . . . with red waistcoat, leather breeches, and a stout oaken cudgel . . . [whom they call] John Bull.—Washington Irving.

In the early years of the 19th century there was a scurrilous journal of this name, and in the early years of the 20th (1906) the name was adopted for a British weekly edited by Mr. Horatio Bottomley. Owing to the fact that it forms a convenient vent for all sorts of real and imaginary grievances, the phrase Why not write to *John Bull* about it? is sometimes heard.

George Bernard SHAW has a play entitled *John Bull's Other Island* (1904), concerned with the Irish question.

See also NICKNAMES OF NATIONALITIES.

John Company. The old "Honorable East India Company." It is said that "John" is a perversion of "Hon.," but probably "John Company" is allied to the familiar "John Bull."

John Doe, see DOE.

John Dory. A popular ballad of the 14th century, often referred to in later literature. John Dory was a French pirate, who was taken prisoner by the English.

John Dory is also the name given to a golden yellow fish, the *Zeus faber.*

John Drum's Entertainment. See under DRUM.

John Duns Scotus, see DUNS SCOTUS, JOHN.

John Ferguson. A play by St. John ERVINE (1915). The hero is an old man of sterling character whose children are involved in tragedy which he is powerless to prevent. When his daughter Hannah is betrayed, her brother Andrew murders the offender. Hannah's boastful, cowardly lover, Jimmy Caesar, is accused of the crime, but Andrew confesses and gives himself up to justice. Presented in New York by the Theatre Guild May 13, 1919. It started the Guild on the road to success.

John Gabriel Borkman. A drama by Henrik IBSEN (1896). Bernard Shaw, in his *Dramatic Opinions,* describes the titular hero as "a man of the most energetic imagination whose illusions feed on his misfortunes and whose conception of his own power grows hyperbolical and Napoleonic in his solitude and impotence."

John Gilpin. A humorous ballad by William COWPER, the full title of which reads *The Diverting History of John Gilpin, Showing How He Went further than He Intended and Came Safe Home Again* (1782). Gilpin's wife says to him, "Though we have been married twenty years, we have taken no holiday"; and at her advice the well-to-do linen-draper agrees to make a family party, and dine at the Bell, at Edmonton. Mrs. Gilpin, her sister, and four children go in the chaise, and Gilpin promises to follow on horseback. The horse begins to trot, and then to gallop, and John, being a bad rider, grasps the mane with both his hands. On goes the horse and off flies John Gilpin's cloak, together with his hat and wig. The dogs bark, the children scream, the turnpike-men, thinking he is riding for a wager, fling open their gates. He flies through Edmonton, and never stops till he reaches Ware. Here he heads his horse back toward Edmonton, but is unable to stop until he reaches his original starting place in London. John Gilpin was a Mr. Beyer, of Paternoster Row, who died in 1791, and it was Lady Austin who told the anecdote to the poet.

John Halifax, Gentleman. A novel by Dinah Maria Mulock Craik (1856). The hero is an orphan dependent entirely on his own resources, but he has the inspiration of an autograph in one of his dead father's books, "John Halifax, Gentleman," which sets for him an ideal. His friendship with Phineas Fletcher, his employer's invalid son, and his love for Ursula March, furnish much of the interest of the book. Eventually he wins through to well-deserved success.

John Hancock. An autograph signature. See under HANCOCK, JOHN.

John Long, the carrier, to wait for. To wait a long time; to wait for John, who keeps us a long time.

Johnny Appleseed. Nickname of John Chapman (1775?–1843), a New England eccentric who settled (about 1800 or 1810) in the Ohio valley and made it his business to plant apple seeds all over the countryside and to tend the growing trees. He became the hero of a body of popular legends of great folkloristic interest. Cf. Vachel Lindsay, *In Praise of Johnny Appleseed.*

Johnny Reb. In the U.S. Civil War, a Confederate. Obviously short for *Johnny Rebel.*

John of Austria, Don (1547–1578). Spanish general who won the great naval battle of Lepanto over the Turks (1571). Cf. Chesterton's ballad *Lepanto,* reprinted in Burton E. Stevenson's *The Home Book of Modern Verse.*

John o' Groat's. The story is that John o' Groat (or Jan Groot) came with his two brothers from Holland in the reign of James IV of Scotland, and purchased lands on the extreme northeastern coast of Scotland. In time the o' Groats increased, and there came to be eight families of the name. They met regularly once a year in the house built by the founder, but on one occasion a question of precedency arose, and John o' Groat promised them the next time they came he would contrive to satisfy them all. Accordingly he built an eight-sided room, with a door in each side, and placed an octagonal table therein. This building went ever after with the name of *John o' Groat's House;* its site is the Berubium of Ptolemy, in the vicinity of Duncansby Head.

> Hear, land o'cakes and brither Scots,
> Frae Maidenkirk to Johnny Groat's . . .
> A chield's amang you takin' notes,
> And, faith, he'll prent it.
> Burns, *Captain Grose.*

from John o' Groat's to the land's end. From Dan to Beersheba, from one end of Great Britain to the other.

John Peel. An old English hunting song, beginning:

> Do you ken John Peel, with his coat so gay,
> Do you ken John Peel, when he's far, far away

It is one of the songs echoed throughout FINNEGANS WAKE by James Joyce.

Johns, Orrick (1887–1946). American poet. Winner of *Lyric Year* national poetry prize (1912) with "Second Avenue." *Wild Plum* (1926); *Time of Our Lives, the Story of My Father and Myself* (1937); etc. Co-organizer of first American Writers' Congress and League of American Writers.

Johnson, alias **Ramarrez.** The outlaw hero of THE GIRL OF THE GOLDEN WEST.

Johnson, Andrew (1808–1875). Seventeenth president of the United States (1865–1869). Nominated vice-president by Republicans to placate Democrats. Succeeded to presidency on death of Lincoln. Impeached (1868) but acquitted by a vote of 35 to 19. His friction with the Republican majority in Congress was basically due to his Democratic adherence to the principle of State rights.

Johnson, Edward (1881?–). Canadian-born opera singer. General manager, Metropolitan Opera Association, New York City (from 1935).

Johnson, Esther. See under STELLA.

Johnson, Hewlett (1874–). English churchman. Dean of Canterbury (from 1931). Known as "the Red Dean." Author of *The Socialist Sixth of the World* (1940; American title, *The Soviet Power*).

Johnson, Hugh Samuel (1882–1942). American lawyer and army officer. Administrator, NRA (1933–1934), New York City WPA (1935), etc. Opponent of Roosevelt in third presidential election (1940).

Johnson, James Weldon (1871–1938). American Negro poet and essayist. Editor of Negro anthologies. Vigorous polemic writer for his race. *Selected Poems* (1936). Killed in railroad accident.

Johnson, Paul. In John Dos Passos' U.S.A., a young American soldier in France during World War I who is married by Eveline HUTCHINS as a means of providing herself with security.

Johnson, Owen McMahon (1878–). Son of Robert Underwood JOHNSON. American novelist and short-story writer. Famous for his Lawrenceville school stories. Also author of adult novels and plays.

Johnson, Robert Underwood (1853–1937). American editor, diplomat, poet. Editor in chief, *Century Magazine* (1909–1913). Chiefly responsible for the marble Hall of Fame at New York University in uptown New York City. Director of it (from 1919), and secretary of the American Academy of Arts and Letters.

Johnson, Samuel (1696–1772). American philosopher, the first native disciple of the 18th-century movement of RATIONALISM. He corresponded with Bishop BERKELEY when the British philosopher was visting in America in 1729, and debated with Jonathan Dickinson on CALVINISM, attacking the doctrine of Predestination. Johnson is not considered to have been a thinker of any great value, but he is known for his introduction into America of the leading philosophical ideas circulating in Europe in the early 18th century. His works include: *Introduction to Philosophy* (1731); *A Letter from Aristocles to Authodes Concerning the Sovereignty and Promise of God* (1745); *System of Morality* (1746); *Elementa Philosophica* (1752).

Johnson, Samuel (1709–1784). English poet, critic, and man of letters. the literary dictator of England in the latter half of the 18th century and one of the most famous personalities of his time, known for his eccentricity of behavior, slovenliness of dress and manner, indolence, peevishness, arrogance, and predilection for learning. He wrote essays, philosophical poems, satires according to the Latin tradition, classical tragedies, fiction, and criticism, in a neo-classical style marked by heaviness, awkwardness, excessive Latinity, and complicated generality. Johnson's works include: *London* (1738), a satirical poem; *The Vanity of Human Wishes* (1749), a philosophical poem; *Irene* (1749), a classical tragedy which the actor David Garrick tried in vain to produce; the RAMBLER papers (1750–1752); his *Dictionary* (1755), his most famous work, in some respects an innovation in lexicography but chiefly important because of the picture its subjective definitions give of the personality of the author; RASSELAS, PRINCE OF ABYSSINIA (1759), a didactic novel; the IDLER papers (1758–1760); and *Lives of the Poets* (1779–1781), a series of critical biographies presenting the typical neo-classical theories of the time. In his early youth Johnson was forced to do hack-writing to support himself (1738–1746) and lived on GRUB STREET. He had the strongest influence of any of his contemporaries on the literary thought and style of the latter 18th century, and became famous in later periods through the celebrated biography written by James BOSWELL. See also METAPHYSICAL POETS.

Johnsonese. A complicated, Latinized literary style like that of Samuel Johnson.

> I own I like not Johnson's turgid style,
> That gives an inch th' importance of a mile:
> Casts of manure a waggon-load around,
> To raise a simple daisy from the ground,
> Uplifts the club of Hercules—for what?
> To crush a butterfly or brain a gnat;
> Creates a whirlwind from the earth, to draw
> A goose's feather or exalt a straw.
>
> Dr. John Wolcot, *Peter Pindar* (1816).

Johnson's Circle. A group of literary and professional men associated with Samuel Johnson. Among them were: David GARRICK, the actor; JONES, the philologist; Edmund BURKE, Edward GIBBON, Oliver GOLDSMITH, and Joshua REYNOLDS.

Johnston, Albert Sidney (1803–1862). During U.S. Civil War, famous Confederate general. Defeated Grant in battle at Shiloh Church, but was himself killed in the same action (April 6, 1862).

Johnston, Sir Harry Hamilton (1858–1927). British explorer and writer. "Not only wrote the history of Africa but often made it." *The Gay-Dombeys* (1919), a novel continuing the history of characters in Dickens' *Dombey and Son,* and a long list of other books.

Johnston, Joseph Eggleston (1807–1891). American Confederate general. Lost Vicksburg to Grant (1863). Surrendered to Sherman (1865) at Durham Station, N.C. Author of a *Narrative of Military Operations Directed, during the Late War between the States, by Joseph E. Johnston* (1874). U.S. Commissioner of railroads (1887–1891).

Johnston, Mary (1870–1936). American historical novelist, author of the phenomenally popular *To Have and to Hold* (1900) *Audrey* (1902), the Civil War novels (told from the Confederate point of view) *The Long Roll* (1911) and *Cease Firing* (1912), and mystical novels like *Silver Cross* (1921).

Johnstone, Christie, see CHRISTIE JOHNSTONE.

Johnstown flood. May 31, 1889, in Johnstown, Pa., caused by the bursting of a reservoir. Cost 2,205 lives and a property loss of ten million dollars.

John the Baptist, St., and **John the Beloved Disciple**; see under SAINTS; SALOME.

John Ward, Preacher. A once widely discussed novel by Margaret DELAND (1888), presenting the problem of the married life of an orthodox minister and a wife whose religious tendencies are liberal.

Joinville, Jean de (1224?–1317). French chronicler. Wrote *L'Histoire de Saint Louis* (1305–1309), which is particularly valuable since author and king were connected by ties of personal friendship and both had been on a crusade together.

Jókai, Maurus (1825–1904). Hungarian novelist and dramatist of political propensities. Leader in the revolution of 1848.

Joliet, Louis (1645–1700). Canadian-French explorer. Intended for the priesthood, he became a merchant and is remembered for his trips through the Mississippi valley and the region of the Gulf of St. Lawrence and Hudson Bay.

Jolly Beggars, The. A poem by Robert BURNS, published in 1799, although written in 1785. It is in the form of a cantata and vigorously presents a series of songs by a group of beggars who tell variously of their sorrows, their wretchedness, their cynicism and disillusionments, and their scorn for the church and wealthy nobility. Its realism, satire, and drama have been highly praised by critics, many of whom regard it as Burns' greatest work.

Jolly God, the, see BACCHUS.

Jolly Roger. The black flag of a pirate ship.

Jolyon. See under FORSYTE SAGA.

Jonah. A famous Biblical prophet, said to have been swallowed by a whale. Instructed by Jehovah to go to preach to the great and wicked city of Nineveh, he wilfully took ship in another direction. A great storm arose, and the sailors, after casting lots, threw Jonah into the sea to appease the deity. After the "great fish" had deposited Jonah on dry land, he went to Nineveh and was the cause of widespread repentance in that city. His story is told in the book of *Jonah.*

Jonathan. In the Old Testament, the son of King Saul, famed for his friendship with DAVID.

Jonathan's arrows. They were shot to give warning, and not to hurt. (1 *Sam.* xx. 36.)

Jonathan Oldbuck, see OLDBUCK, JONATHAN.

Jonathan Oldstyle, see OLDSTYLE, JONATHAN.

Jonathan Ploughboy, see PLOUGHBOY, JONATHAN.

Jonathan Wild, see WILD, JONATHAN.

Jones. Everybody's neighbor; the other fellow; Mr. Averageman. He and his family correspond to the *Dubois* in French, to *Meier* and *Müller* in German, etc.

Jones. A gentleman adventurer in Conrad's VICTORY.

Jones, Sir **Henry Arthur** (1851–1929). English playwright, known for his presentation of social relationships and social problems in his plays, several of which were influenced by IBSEN. His works include: *Breaking a Butterfly* (1885); *Saints and Sinners* (1891); MICHAEL AND HIS LOST ANGEL (1896); and *Mrs. Dane's Defense* (1900).

Jones, Howard Mumford (1892–). American educator and poet, playwright, and critic.

Jones, Inigo (1573–1652). English architect. Sometimes referred to as "the English Palladio." Designed stage sets for court masques written by JONSON, HEYWOOD, DAVENANT, etc. Designed queen's home at Greenwich, Lincoln's Inn Chapel, banqueting hall at Whitehall (1619–1622), reconstruction of St. Paul's Cathedral, Covent Garden piazza, etc. In 1646 he was fined for being a favorite of the king and a Catholic. He was painted twice by Vandyck.

Jones, John Paul (1747–1792). An American seaman famed for his exploits in the Revolution. He is the hero of Cooper's novel THE PILOT, and a prominent character in Churchill's RICHARD CARVEL.

Jonson, Ben (1572–1637). English poet and dramatist, once a bricklayer, soldier, and playwright for the Elizabethan theatrical manager Philip Henslowe, later leading author of masques at the court and pensioned under James I and Charles I as the "King's poet," a forerunner of the poet laureateship. Jonson is known for his satire, his classicism, his rigid observance of theoretic principles in his writing, his opposition to the romantic attitude and style of his contemporary playwrights, including Shakespeare, and his use of the theory of "humors." See HUMOR. His plays, chiefly comedies, for which he was most famous in his own time, include: EVERY MAN IN HIS HUMOR (1598); *Every Man Out of His Humor* (1600); *Cynthia's Revels* (1600); *The Poetaster* (1601); *Sejanus* (1603) and *Catiline* (1611), classical tragedies; *Eastward Ho* (1605), in collaboration with MARSTON and CHAPMAN; VOLPONE, OR THE FOX (1606); EPICENE, OR THE SILENT WOMAN (1609); THE ALCHEMIST (1610); BARTHOLOMEW FAIR (1614); *The Devil Is an Ass* (1616); *The Staple of News* (1625); *The New Inn* (1629); *The Magnetic Lady* (1632); and *Tale of a Tub* (1633). Jonson took part in the quarrel among Elizabethan playwrights known as the "War of the Theaters," and in *Cynthia's Revels* and *The Poetaster* attacks his enemies under classical names. His poetry includes odes, epigrams, songs, and letters in verse, and shows the influence of the classics, being polished, restrained, and musical.

Jonson was the first literary dictator (see also DRYDEN, POPE, Samuel JOHNSON) in English literature, and held forth as an acknowledged leader in gatherings of men of letters at the Mermaid Tavern. The faithful members of this group later were called the "tribe of Ben," and the poets they approved as followers of Jonson's poetic principles and practice were known as "sons of Ben." Among the latter are Thomas CAREW, Robert HERRICK, Richard LOVELACE, and Sir John SUCKLING.

Jordan, David Starr (1851–1931). American biologist and educator. President (1891-1913) and chancellor (1913–1916), Stanford University. Author of many books on fishes.

Jordan, Robert. Hero of Ernest Hemingway's FOR WHOM THE BELL TOLLS. He is a young instructor in Spanish at the University of Montana, of sincere liberal convictions, who joins the Spanish Republican army during the civil war of the 1930's. Although he perceives the weaknesses of the Communist command and doubts that he himself will survive the mission, he carries through his assignment to blow up a bridge as a gesture in support of his own belief.

Jordan, Ruth. The heroine of Moody's drama, THE GREAT DIVIDE.

Jordans, The. The New England family of Owen Davis' play, ICEBOUND.

Jormungandr or **Midgardsormen** (i.e., "earth's monster"). The great serpent of Scandinavian mythology, brother of HELA and FENRIS, and son of LOKI, the spirit of evil. It lay at the root of the celestial ash till All-Fader cast it into the ocean; it then grew so large that in time it encompassed the whole world, and was forever biting its own tail.

Jorrocks. A famous amateur sportsman created by Robert Smith Surtees (*Eng.*, 1803–1864). He appeared in *Hunts with Jorrocks from Handley Cross* and in *Jorrocks' Jaunts and Jollities, the Hunting, Shooting, Racing, Driving, Sailing, Eating, Eccentric and Extravagant Exploits of that Renowned Sporting Citizen, Mr. John Jorrocks of St. Botolph Lane and Great Coram Street.*

Josaphat. See under BARLAAM.

José, Don. (1) In Byron's DON JUAN, the father of Don Juan, and husband of Donna Inez. He is henpecked and worried to death by his wife's "proprieties."

(2) A Spanish officer in Bizet's opera CARMEN, in love with Carmen.

Joseph. A Biblical hero of the book of *Genesis.* A younger son and favorite of his father Jacob, he was hated by his ten older brothers, and when the opportunity presented itself, they sold him as a slave to a caravan going to Egypt. There he rose to a position of responsibility with his master Potiphar, but was maligned and thrown into prison on his refusal to respond to the advances of Potiphar's wife. In time he was set free and given rank and honor as a result of his interpretations of the dreams, first of his fellow-prisoners, the chief butler and baker, and later of Pharaoh himself. Pharaoh's dreams of seven lean cattle swallowing up seven fat cattle and seven lean ears of corn devouring seven full ears were said to betoken the coming of famine, and Joseph was therefore installed as food administrator. During the famine his brothers came to Egypt to buy corn and after a dramatic series of events (see BENJAMIN) Joseph revealed his identity and brought about their migration to Egypt.

Thomas MANN wrote a series of elaborately symbolic novels on the *Joseph* story, in which Joseph represents the artist who redeems society by his own vicarious suffering. Included in the series are: *Joseph and His Brothers* (1924); *Young Joseph* (1935); and *Joseph in Egypt* (1938). For a discussion of the symbolism, see *Thomas Mann's Joseph Story,* by Harry Slochower.

a Joseph. One not to be seduced from his continency by the severest temptation is sometimes so called. The reference is to Joseph in Potiphar's house (*Gen.* xxxix). See also BELLEROPHON.

A great-coat used to be known by the same name, in allusion to Joseph, who left his garment, or upper coat, behind him.

Joseph's coat. Either the above, or the "coat of many colors" given Joseph by his father.

Joseph Andrews. A novel by FIELDING (1742). He is a footman who marries a maid-servant. The novel was begun as a burlesque of Richardson's PAMELA, and Joseph Andrews is Pamela's brother. His adventures with the high-born Lady Booby are modeled after those of Pamela and Mr. B., and, like Pamela, Joseph remains virtuous.

> The accounts of Joseph's bravery and good qualities, his voice too musical to halloa to the dogs, his bravery in riding races for the gentlemen of the county, and his constancy in refusing bribes and temptation, have something refreshing in their *naïveté* and freshness, and prepossess one in favour of that handsome young hero.—Thackeray.

Josephine. The heroine of Gilbert and Sullivan's comic opera, H.M.S. PINAFORE.

Joseph of Arimathea. The rich Jew, probably a member of the Sanhedrin, who believed in Christ but feared to confess it, and, after the Crucifixion, begged the body of the Savior and deposited it in his own tomb (see *Matt.* xxvii. 57–60, *Mark* xv. 42). Legend relates that he was imprisoned for forty-two years, during which time he was kept alive miraculously by the Holy Grail (see GRAIL), and that on his release by Vespasian, about 63 A. D., he brought the Grail and the spear with which Longinus wounded the crucified Savior, to Britain, and there founded the abbey of GLASTONBURY, whence he commenced the conversion of Britain.

The origin of these legends is to be found in a group of apocryphal writings of which the *Evangelium Nicodemi* is the chief one. These were worked upon at Glastonbury between the 8th and 11th centuries, and were further embellished by Robert de Boron in the 13th, the latter version (by way of Walter Map) being woven by Malory into his MORTE D'ARTHUR.

George Moore introduces Joseph of Arimathea into his romance, THE BROOK KERITH.

Josephson, Matthew (1899–). American critic and biographer. Started as a literary "expatriate," tried brokerage, wrote biographies of ZOLA and ROUSSEAU, and, with his *The Robber Barons* (1934), switched from literary to economic history. *The Politicos* (1938) followed, and *The President Makers* (1940).

Joseph Prudhomme, see PRUDHOMME, JOSEPH.

Joseph Surface, see SURFACE, JOSEPH.

Josephus, Flavius. Original name **Joseph ben Matthias** (37–?100). Jewish historian and general. Imbued with deep admiration for Rome and its institutions, he managed in his later years to live in the sunshine of the favor of the emperors Vespasian and Titus. This was after the defeat of his people in the revolt of 66 A. D., in which he had taken an active part. Author of a *History of the Jewish War* (7 books in Aramaic and Greek); *Antiquities of the Jews* (in 20 books); etc. Called the "Hebrew Livy."

Joseph Vance, An Ill-Written Autobiography. A novel by William DE MORGAN (1906). The hero's love for his childhood playmate, Lossie Thorpe, is the central interest of the book, but both heroine and hero contract other and in each case quite congenial marriages and are not united until late in life. The irresponsible father of Joseph Vance, now successful, now utterly down-and-out, is a well-drawn character.

Joshua. A Biblical hero whose name is given to the sixth book of the Old Testament. It tells how Joshua, after the death of Moses, led the Israelites into the Promised Land. Forty years before, Joshua had been among the twelve spies appointed to spy out the land of Canaan, and because of his favorable report, maintained in the face of the prevailing discouragement, he was one of the two Israelites of his generation permitted by Jehovah to enter Canaan. He was a valiant fighter and gradually conquered the land. One of his most striking exploits was to command the sun to stand still.

Joshua tree. A treelike yucca of some elevated desert regions in the southwestern United States, often 25 feet high, with short leaves and greenish-white flowers.

Josiah Allen's Wife. Pseudonym of Marietta Holley (1836–1926), American writer of humorous stories chiefly devoted to the adventures of Josiah Allen and Josiah Allen's wife Samantha. *Samantha at the Centennial* (1877) and *Samantha in Europe* are perhaps the best.

Josiana, Lady. The heroine of Victor Hugo's historical romance, THE MAN WHO LAUGHS (*L'Homme qui rit*).

joss (Pidgin English). An idol or house-god of the Chinese; every family has its *joss.* A temple is called a *joss house,* and a *joss-stick* is a stick of scented wood which is burnt as incense in a joss-house.

Josse. A jeweler in Molière's L'AMOUR MÉDECIN. Lucinde, the young daughter of SGANARELLE, pines and falls away, and the anxious father asks his neighbors what they would advise him to do. Josse replies that he woud buy the young lady a beautiful piece of jewelry. Sganarelle's answer is, "You are a jeweler, M. Josse (*Vous êtes orfèvre, Monsieur Josse!*), and are not disinterested in your advice."

Jotham. In Dryden's ABSALOM AND ACHITOPHEL, he represents Saville, Marquis of Halifax. The original Jotham (cf. *Judges* ix. 7) uttered the parable of *The Trees Choosing a King* when the men of Shechem made Abimelech king.

Jötunnheim or **Jötunheim.** Literally, "home of the giants." In Norse mythology, one of the Nine Worlds. It lies in the northwest where the ocean reaches the edge of the universe and is inhabited by the giants. One of the roots of the ash tree Yggdrasill extends into it.

Joubert, Petrus Jacobus, known as **Piet** (1831–1900). Boer farmer, lawyer, soldier and statesman. Commander of Boer forces in several successful engagements with the British during the war waged in opposition to British annexation of the Transvaal (1880–1881). Opponent of KRUGER but forced by ill health to abandon military commandership at outbreak of Boer War (1899).

Jourdain, Monsieur. The type of the bourgeois, placed by wealth in the ranks of gentlemen, who makes himself ridiculous by his endeavors to acquire their accomplishments. The character is from Molière's comedy *Le Bourgeois gentilhomme* (1670). He employs masters of dancing, fencing, and philology. The fun of the drama is provided by the ridiculous remarks he makes, and the awkward figure he cuts as the pupil of these professors. One remark is especially noted: he says he had been talking prose all his life, and never knew it till his professor told him.

Journal of the Plague Year, A. A famous account of the epidemic of bubonic plague in England during the summer and fall of 1665 by Daniel DEFOE (1722). It is fictitious, although it purports to be authentic, and is considered by critics to show greater imagination and dramatic appeal than the original, eyewitness account in the diary of Samuel PEPYS.

Journal to Stella. A private diary kept by Jonathan SWIFT from 1710 to 1713, written partly in cipher and in the form of letters addressed to "STELLA," the woman deeply loved by Swift. It reveals the author intimately in his hopes and anxieties, his social life, political intrigue, associations with his friends, and tenderest emotions. See also PPT.

Jove. Another name of JUPITER, the later being *Jovis pater,* father Jove. The Titans made war against Jove, and tried to dethrone him.

> Not stronger were of old the giant crew,
> Who sought to pull high Jove from regal state.
> Thomson, *Castle of Indolence,* canto I.

Milton, in PARADISE LOST, makes Jove one of the fallen angels (i. 512).

Jowett, Benjamin (1817–1893). English Greek scholar, of great influence through his translations of Plato, Thucydides, and Aristotle. Regius professor at Oxford (1855); master of Balliol (1870–1893); vice-chancellor of Oxford (1882–1886). Tried but acquitted on a charge of heresy because of religious liberalism.

Joyce, James Augustine Aloysius (1882–1941). Irish novelist and poet, regarded as one of the greatest literary talents of the 20th century. Leading influences on his thought and technique, paid tribute by constant echoes and allusions throughout his work, were Henrik IBSEN, the Elizabethan writers, especially Ben JONSON; DANTE ALIGHIERI; the French symbolists (see SYMBOLISM); ARISTOTLE; ST. THOMAS AQUINAS and other scholastic philosophers; the dogma and hagiography of the Roman Catholic Church; the legend, history, and politics of Ireland, especially as epitomized in the figure of Charles Stewart PARNELL; the ODYSSEY; medieval romance, especially the TRISTRAM cycle; Benedetto CROCE; Jonathan SWIFT; Sir James G. FRAZER; Giambattista VICO; Giordano BRUNO; Sigmund FREUD. He is most famous for his experiments in the structure and narrative technique of the novel, in the technique of the "STREAM OF CONSCIOUSNESS," and in language, where his linguistic studies and his interest in philology had an important influence on his numerous innovations.

In his youth Joyce rebelled strongly against what he regarded as the bigotry, narrowness, and insularity of his Irish Roman Catholic background, and was contemptuous of the movement in poetry and the drama known as the IRISH RENAISSANCE. Although he never returned to Ireland after 1912, the subject-matter of all his work is the city of Dublin, its streets, topography, history, and residents, and to a somewhat lesser extent, biographical details of his own childhood and youth. It might be said that Joyce's work is narrower in scope than that of any novelist of his time, but also deeper in its roots and wider in its ramifications. It is marked by humor, tremendous vitality, a robust coarseness sometimes compared to that of CHAUCER, realistic detail and documentation in the painstaking manner of the naturalistic tradition (see NATURALISM), psychological penetration (stream-of-consciousness passages), an understanding treatment of character (see DUBLINERS) and a talent for character creation (see ULYSSES), and a remarkable sensitivity to language, speech, and auditory impressions in general. His works are THE DAY OF THE RABBLEMENT (1901); CHAMBER MUSIC (1907), poetry; DUBLINERS (1914), short stories; EXILES (1915), a play; A PORTRAIT OF THE ARTIST AS A YOUNG MAN (1916); ULYSSES (1922); POMES PENYEACH (1927); FINNEGANS WAKE (1939). Like the great French novelists BALZAC, FLAUBERT, the GONCOURT brothers, and DAUDET, Joyce toiled long hours at his writing and repeatedly revised and polished his work. *Ulysses* required 7 years to complete (1914–1921) and *Finnegans Wake,* which was known until its publication as *Work in Progress,* took 17 years (1922–1939).

Although Joyce suffered from partial blindness during most of his life; was forced to do teaching and clerical work to support himself and his family; saw his books banned by censors or pirated by publishers; was widely misunderstood and denounced as obscene or unintelligible, and in general had one of the most difficult lives in the history of literature, he had the greatest influence on his contemporaries of any novelist in the 20th century and is regarded by serious critics as one of the outstanding writers of modern times. Among leading authors showing the influence of Joyce in style, technique, approach, and vocabulary are Virginia WOOLF, Ernest HEMINGWAY, John Dos PASSOS, William FAULKNER, Thomas WOLFE, and James T. FARRELL. For a fuller discussion of Joyce, cf. the biography by Herbert Gorman and *James Joyce,* by Harry Levin.

Joyeuse. A name given to more than one sword famous in romance, but especially to Charlemagne's, which bore the inscription *Decem praeceptorum custos Carolus,* and was buried with him.

Joyeuse Garde, La or **La Garde Joyeuse** (*Fr.*). Anglicized, **Joyous Gard.** The estate given by King ARTHUR to Sir Launcelot of the Lake for defending the Queen's honor against Sir Mador. It is supposed to have been at or near Berwick-on-Tweed, but the Arthurian topography is very indefinite.

Juan de la Cruz, San, see ST. JOHN OF THE CROSS under SAINTS.

Juárez, Benito Pablo (1806–1872). Mexican statesman of pure Indian blood. Repeatedly (self-styled or by election) president of Mexico for and after the interlude of Maximilian's French-supported puppet emperorship. His name will always remain associated with that of Maximilian whom, after his defeat, he had court-martialed and shot. Cf. WERFEL's drama, *Juarez and Maximilian* (1926).

juba. A characteristic Negro dance, originally of the southern plantations. The nonsense word *juba* occurs repeatedly in the refrain sung by the spectators who also keep time by hand-clapping, stamping, etc., which is known as *patting juba.*

> And our hearts are patting juba
> To the banjo of the spring.
> Richard Hovey, *Stein Song.*

Jubal. In the Old Testament, son of Lamech and Adah, the inventor of the lyre and flute (*Gen.* iv. 19–21). George ELIOT has a narrative poem of that title (1874).

jubilee. In Jewish history, the year of jubilee was every fiftieth year, which was held sacred in commemoration of the deliverance from Egypt. In this year the fields were allowed to lie fallow, land that had passed out of the possession of those to whom it originally belonged was restored to them, and all who had been obliged to let themselves out for hire were released from bondage. The year of jubilee was proclaimed with trumpets of ram's horn, and takes its name from Hebrew *yobel,* "a ram's horn." (Cf. *Lev.* xxv. 11–34, 39–54 and xxvii. 16–24.)

Hence, any fiftieth anniversary, especially one kept with great rejoicings, is called a jubilee, and the name has been applied to other outbursts of joy or seasons of festivity, such as the *Shakespeare Jubilee,* which was held at Stratford-on-Avon in September, 1769, and the *Protestant Jubilee,* celebrated in Germany in 1617 at the centenary of the Reformation.

Judah. In the Old Testament, one of the sons of Jacob; also, the tribe of his descendants. After the death of Solomon, King of Israel, ten tribes seceded under Jeroboam and the remaining kingdom was known thereafter as Judah. Its capital was Jerusalem.

Judas Iscariot. The traitorous disciple who betrayed Jesus to his enemies for thirty pieces of silver. See ACELDAMA. He had kept the bags containing the money for the group during the years of his master's ministry. According to the Biblical narrative, after the crucifixion he was overcome by remorse and hanged himself. DANTE in his *Inferno* places Judas in the mouth of Satan. There is a tradition that he is released from hell once a year to cool himself on an ice floe. In his poem *St. Brandan,* Matthew ARNOLD describes the saint's encounter with the arch-traitor on his annual holiday.

Judas kiss. A deceitful act of courtesy. Judas betrayed his Master with a kiss (*Matt.* xxvi. 49).

> So Judas kissed his Master,
> And cried, "All hail!" whenas he meant *all harm.*
> Shakespeare, III *Henry VI.* v. 7.

Jude the Obscure. A novel by Thomas HARDY (1895), dealing with the mutual love of Jude Fawley and his cousin, Sue Bridehead. They both marry outsiders, but finally secure divorces to live with each other. After some years, young Jude, the son of Jude's former wife Arabella, murders Jude's two younger children and hangs himself to escape from misery. Broken by this tragedy, Sue returns to her husband and Jude to Arabella. Soon afterward Jude dies.

Judges. A book of the Old Testament which contains the history of the Israelites after the death of JOSHUA, when the people were governed by judges. Gideon, Jephthah, Samson, and Deborah are the chief rulers mentioned in *Judges.*

Judgment Day. A novel by James T. FARRELL, published in 1935, the final part of his trilogy STUDS LONIGAN. It deals with Studs' declining health, futile dissipation, love affair with Catherine Banahan, fruitless search for a job, and ultimate death from pneumonia. The climax of the novel is a dramatic death scene against a background of the family's lamentations and quarrels and the Roman Catholic prayers for the dead.

Judith. A legendary Jewish heroine whose story is told in the Apocryphal book of *Judith.* She was a beautiful girl of Bethulia, who, to save her native town, assassinated Holofernes, the general of Nebuchadnezzar. When Judith showed the head of the general to her countrymen, they rushed on the invading army, and put it to a complete rout.

Judson, Edward Zane Carroll (1823–1886). American adventurer and author. Wrote, under the pseudonym of **Ned Buntline,** early dime novels and adventure fiction.

Jugendbewegung (*Ger.,* "Youth Movement"). A collective term applied in Germany to a teen-age movement of opposition to dogmatistic religion, bourgeois parent authority, and conventionalized school, seeking inspiration in folk art, history, and nature, and finding an organizational frame in the boy-scoutlike associations of the *Wandervogel* (Migratory Bird) which date from about 1906. The declining remnants of the youth movement were absorbed by the Hitler youth organization.

Juggernaut or **Jagannath.** A Hindu god, "Lord of the World," having his temple at Puri, in Orissa. The legend, as told in the *Ayeen-Akbery,* is that a learned Brahmin was sent to look out a site for a temple. The Brahmin wandered about for many days, and then saw a crow dive into the water, and, having washed, make obeisance to the element. This was selected as the site of the temple. While the temple was being built, the king, Indica Dhumna, had a prophetic dream, telling him that the true form of Vishnu should be revealed to him in the morning. When the king went to see the temple he beheld a log of wood in the water, and this log he accepted as the realization of his dream, enshrining it in the temple.

Jagannath is regarded as the remover of sin. His image is on view three days in the year. The first day is the *Snanayatra,* or Bathing Festival, when the god is washed; he is then supposed to have a cold for ten days, at the end of which he is again brought out and taken in his car to the nearest temple. A week later the car is pulled back amid the rejoicings of the multitude at his recovery. It was formerly erroneously supposed that on this final day, the *Rathayatra,* fanatical devotees threw themselves beneath the wheels of the enormous, decorated machine, in the idea that they would thus obtain immediate admission to Paradise. Hence, the phrase *the car of Juggernaut* is used of customs, institutions, etc., beneath which people are ruthlessly and unnecessarily crushed.

Juive, La (The Jewess). A tragic opera (1835) in five acts by Jacques HALÉVY, after a text by Eugène Scribe. Eleazar, in *La Juive,* was one of the great rôles of Enrico CARUSO.

jujitsu. Literally, "soft art." A Japanese system of self-defense without weapons, based entirely on the principle that the opponent's own (superior) strength can be used to defeat him. Thus the adept will, for instance, be able to provoke with little force a counteraction which he can guide to dislocate a joint of his opponent's arm, etc. Also called *judo.*

juke box. A type of automatic phonograph, stationed in taverns, restaurants, lunch-rooms, cocktail lounges, etc., which was extremely popular in the U.S. in the late 1930's and early 1940's. Juke boxes were usually brilliantly colored and offered a list of phonograph recordings—principally of popular songs and "SWING" music—from which the customer could make a selection that he would hear after he had inserted a nickel.

Jukes, The. Full title, *The Jukes, a Study in Crime, Pauperism, Disease, and Heredity* (1877). A report of the New York Prison Association by Richard Louis Dugdale (1841–1883). The subjects are the descendants of a group of sisters who lived in New York toward the end of the 18th century. In a sense the study is the criminological precursor of the wave of interest on the part of novelists in the "fall and decline" of entire families. Cf., for instance, Thomas Mann's BUDDENBROOKS.

Julia. (1). In Shakespeare's TWO GENTLEMEN OF VERONA, a lady who disguises herself as a page to gain the love of Proteus.

(2). The heroine of Knowles' drama *The Hunchback* (1832).

Julian. Pertaining to Julius Caesar (100–44 B. C.), particularly with reference to the Calendar (i.e. the "Old Style") instituted by him in 46 B. C. (the *Julian Year,* consisting of 365¼ days), which was in general use in Western Europe till it was corrected by Gregory XIII in 1582, in England till 1752, and much longer in Russia. To allow for the odd quarter day, Caesar ordained that every fourth year should contain 366 days, the additional day being introduced after the 6th of the calends of March, i.e. February 24. Caesar also divided the months into the number of days they contain at present, and July is named in his honor.

Julian, Count. A legendary hero whose tale is told in Scott's VISION OF DON RODERICK, Southey's RODERICK and Landor's COUNT JULIAN. He was a powerful lord of the Spanish Goths. When his daughter Florinda was violated by King Roderick, the Count was so indignant that he invited the Moors to come and push him from the throne, and even turned renegade the better to effect his purpose.

Julian, surnamed **the Apostate** (331–363). Roman emperor. Brought up in the Christian faith. As governor of Spain, Gaul, Britain, resident of Paris. On his accession (361), he publicly announced his apostasy and published an edict of tolerance. Killed in action during a war against Persia.

Julie. The heroine of J. J. ROUSSEAU's novel entitled *Julie, ou la nouvelle Héloïse* (1761). The prototype was the Comtesse d'Houdetot. In the novel the hero is Saint Preux, Julie's tutor, drawn chiefly from Rousseau himself, who bore the same relation to his countess. The two love, but are parted and Julie marries M. de Wolnar. Later Saint Preux returns as the trusted friend of the household and tutor of the children. See also HÉLOÏSE.

Juliet. (1). The heroine of Shakespeare's ROMEO AND JULIET.

(2). In Shakespeare's MEASURE FOR MEASURE, the lady beloved by Claudio.

Juliette. The heroine of George Sand's LEONE LEONI.

Julius Caesar. A historic tragedy by Shakespeare (ca. 1601). The real hero is BRUTUS, but see also CAESAR, JULIUS.

July Revolution. An uprising (July 27–29, 1830) of the people of France against the Bourbon dynasty. The newspapers led the insurrection and after some fighting in barricaded streets, the king, Charles X, abdicated—with the result that the Bourbon-Orléans line succeeded to the throne in the person of the "citizen king" Louis Philippe.

Jumblies, The. Subjects of a nonsense poem by Edward LEAR.

> Far and few; far and few
> Are the lands where the Jumblies live.

Jungle, The. A novel by Upton SINCLAIR (1906) which caused widespread discussion on account of its grim picture of life in the Chicago stockyards. The central figures are Slav immigrants, Jurgis Rudkus and his wife Ona.

Jungle Books. A series of animal stories for children in two volumes by Rudyard KIPLING (1894, 1895). The central figure is the human MOWGLI, brought up in the jungle by Mother Wolf.

Junípero, Father, see SERRA, JUNÍPERO.

Jung, Carl Gustav (1875–). Swiss psychologist and psychiatrist, originally of the Freudian school. His view that the *libido* (energy or driving force) is a will to live rather than a sexual manifestation puts his later work in opposition to the Viennese school. Introduced the now popular terms INTROVERT and EXTRAVERT and advanced psychoanalysis immeasurably by applying it to national myths, legends, etc.

Jungfrau. One of the most magnificent mountains of Switzerland, rising 13,670 feet in the Bernese Alps twelve miles south of Interlaken on the boundary of the cantons of Bern and Valais. First ascended in 1811. It is part of the Jungfrau-Eiger-Mönch group and its contours, especially on postal cards of dubious taste, are often depicted as the outline of a reclining young woman. German *Jungfrau,* "young woman, virgin," but the origin of the name is obscure.

Jumping Frog, The. A story by Mark TWAIN (1865), more formally known as *The Celebrated Jumping Frog of Calaveras County.* It appeared first in the *New York Saturday Press* as *Jim Smiley and His Jumping Frog.*

Junius Letters. A series of anonymous letters, the authorship of which has never been finally settled, which appeared in the London *Public Advertiser* from November 21, 1768, to January 21, 1772, and were directed against Sir William Draper, the Duke of Grafton, and the Ministers generally. The author himself said, "I am the sole depositary of my secret, and it shall die with me." They were probably by Sir Philip Francis (1740–1818) but many other authors have been suggested.

Junker (*Ger.,* from *jung,* "young" and *Herr,* "master, lord"). Originally a young nobleman. Later, any member of the landed aristocracy, especially of Prussia east of the Elbe river. The caricature of the Junker emphasizes his bullying and overbearing attitudes and his reactionary narrow-mindedness. Historically the Junker class has been an important factor in the development of east-Elbian culture and the formation of the Prussian state. Its decline is depicted in Eduard von Keyserling's masterpiece, *Abendliche Häuser* (*Houses at Dusk*).

Junkers, Hugo (1859–1935). German aeronautical engineer. Pioneer in the construction of all-metal airplanes. Developed the Junkers motors which at one time were used by a third of the world's airplanes.

Juno. The "venerable ox-eyed" wife of Jupiter, and queen of heaven, in Roman mythology. She is identified with the Greek Hera, was the special protectress of marriage and of woman, and was represented as a war goddess.

Junonian bird. The peacock, dedicated to the goddess-queen.

junta (*Sp.*). In Spain, a council or legislative assembly other than the Cortes, which may be summoned either for the whole country, for one of its separate parts, or for some special object only. The most famous is that called together by Napoleon in 1808.

I had also audience of the King, to whom I deliver'd two Memorials since, in His Majesty's name of *Great Britain*, that a particular Junta of some of the Council of State and War might be appointed to determine the business.—Howell's *Letters*, Bk. i, sect. iii, 10 (*Madrid*, Jan. 5, 1622).

Junto. In English history, the name given to a faction that included Wharton, Russell, Lord-Keeper Somers, Charles Montague, and several other men of mark, who ruled the Whigs in the reign of William III for nearly twenty years, and exercised a very great influence over the nation. The word is a corruption of JUNTA.

Jupien. In Marcel Proust's REMEMBRANCE OF THINGS PAST, especially in CITIES OF THE PLAIN, a valet, father of Charles MOREL, who as well as his son engages in abnormal relations with Baron de CHARLUS.

Jupiter. The supreme deity of Roman mythology, corresponding to the Greek Zeus (see JOVE), son of Cronus, or Saturn, whom he dethroned, and Rhea. He was the special protector of Rome, and as Jupiter Capitolinus—his temple being on the Capitoline Hill—presided over the Roman games. He determined the course of all human affairs and made known the future to man through signs in the heavens, the flight of birds, etc.

As Jupiter was lord of heaven and prince of light, white was the color sacred to him; hence, among the medieval alchemists, *Jupiter* designated tin. In heraldry Jupiter stands for *azure*, the blue of the heavens.

His statue by PHIDIAS (taken to Constantinople by Theodosius I and there destroyed by fire in 475 A. D.) was one of the Seven Wonders of the World.

Jupiter Scapin. A nickname of Napoleon Bonaparte, given him by the Abbé de Pradt. SCAPIN is a valet famous for his knavish tricks, in Molière's comedy of *Les Fourberies de Scapin.*

Jupiter tonans (the thundering Jupiter). A complimentary nickname given to the London *Times* in the days of its greatness, i.e., about the middle of the 19th century. See THUNDERER.

Jupiter's beard. House leek, supposed to be a charm against evil spirits and lightning; hence, it was at one time grown very generally on the thatch of houses.

Jura. A picturesque range of mountains between France and Switzerland. Highest peaks about 5,000 feet. Famous for its watch home-industry, less so for its cheese. Hence the geological term *Jurassic.*

juramentado (*Span.*) Literally, "one bound by an oath." In the Philippines, a Moro of Mohammedan faith who has bound himself by the oath to sacrifice his life while killing Christians. Hence, *to go juramentado*, "to run amuck."

Jurgen, a Comedy of Justice. A satiric romance by James Branch CABELL (1919), a tale of medieval POICTESME. Jurgen is a middle-aged pawnbroker who is given a year of youth, which he spends adventuring. He visits Heaven and Hell, to say nothing of other mysterious regions in which he toys with and wins the love of Guinevere, of the Lady of the Lake (here called Anaïtis), and of other strange and lovely ladies. He even sees his old love Dorothy la Désirée, and looks, too, upon the immortal Helen of Troy. But he cannot regain his youthful illusions nor his youthful ideals, and in the end he is content to return to his scolding old wife, Dame Lisa.

Jurgen purports to be retold from old chronicles. Its temporary suppression caused it to become widely discussed. See also MANUEL.

jus et norma loquendi (*Lat.*). The right method of speaking and pronouncing established by the custom of each particular nation.

Multa renascentur quae jam cecidere, cadentque
Quae nunc sunt in honore vocabula, si volet usus.
Quem penes arbitrium est, et jus, et norma loquendi.
Horace, *Ars Poetica*, 70.

As translated by Conington:

Yes, words long faded may again revive;
And words may fade now blooming and alive,
If usage wills it so, to whom belongs
The rule and law, the government of tongues.

Jusserand, Jean Jules (1855–1932). French writer, diplomat, and student of English literature and history. Minister at Washington, D.C. (1902–1925). The only non-American ever to head the American Historical Society. In 1917 he received the Pulitzer prize in History for his *With Americans of Past and Present Days.*

Just, the. Among rulers and others who have been given this epithet are:

Aristides, the Athenian (d. 468 B. C.).

Baharam, styled *Shah Endeb*, fifth of the Sassanidae (276–296).

Casimir II, King of Poland (b. 1117, reigned 1177–1194).

Ferdinand I, King of Aragon (b. 1373, reigned 1412–1416).

Harun al Raschid, the most renowned of the Abbasside caliphs, and the hero of several of the *Arabian Nights* stories (b. 765, reigned 786–808).

James II, King of Aragon (1261–1327).

Khosru or Chosroes I of Persia (531–579), called by the Arabs *Molk al Adel* (the Just King).

Pedro I of Portugal (b. 1320, reigned 1357–1367).

juste-milieu (*Fr.*). The just or golden mean. In political parlance said of actions and attitudes characterized by moderation and compromise.

Just So Stories. Children's animal stories by Rudyard KIPLING (1902) explaining questions like why the leopard has spots, etc.

Justice. A drama by John GALSWORTHY (1910). The central character, William Falder, forges a check in order to secure funds to free the woman he loves from her husband's cruelty. He serves out a three years' sentence with good resolution, but his subsequent struggle to live down his past ends in tragedy.

Justinian, the English. Edward I (b. 1239, reigned 1272–1307).

Jutland, Battle of. Greatest naval battle in history (May 31–June 1, 1916) fought in North Sea off Jutland peninsula between the German battle cruiser and High Seas fleet under Admirals von Scheer and von Hipper, respectively, and the British battle-cruiser and Grand fleets under Admirals Beatty and Jellicoe, respectively. The Germans lost 11 out of 110 vessels engaged, with 2,863 officers and men; the British 14 out of 149 vessels, with 6,617 officers and men. The German fleet retired after the battle and left the British in undisputed control of the North Sea. Identical with German Battle of the Skagerak.

Juvenal. Full Latin name **Decimus Junius Juvenalis** (60?–?140). Roman lawyer and satirist of Roman vices under the Empire. Sixteen satires of his are extant.

the English Juvenal. John Oldham (1653–1683).

the Juvenal of painters. William Hogarth (1697–1764).

juveniles. In theatrical parlance, those actors who play young men's parts; in journalistic and book-trade slang, periodicals or books intended for the young.

K

K. The hero of Franz Kafka's THE CASTLE, a land surveyor allegorically in search of divine grace, sometimes compared to John Bunyan's CHRISTIAN. See also Joseph K. below.

K., Joseph. In Franz Kafka's THE TRIAL, a bank assessor who is charged with a crime of which he knows nothing. His attempts to defend himself against the charges and to win a legal trial are interpreted as being symbolic of mankind's quest for divine justice. See also K. above.

ka. In Egyptian mythology, a sort of double which survived after a man's death if a statue of him were made into which it might enter, and sundry other rites were performed; hence, such a statue, placed usually near the mummy in the tomb.

Kaaba (Arabic *kabah,* "a square house"). A shrine at Mecca, said to have been built by Ishmael and Abraham on the spot where Adam first worshiped after his expulsion from Paradise, and where, after being a wanderer on the face of the earth for two hundred years, he received pardon. In the northeast corner is the famous "black stone." See HAJAR AL ASWAD.

Kabul. National capital of Afghanistan on Kabul river. Taken by the British (1839) but liberated again (1842) with losses of 16,000 lives to the conquerors. Since 1880 under an Afghan consul. Cf. Kipling's poem of that title.

Kaddish. In Jewish ritual, the DOXOLOGY recited in the synagogue. So called because of the repeated occurrence of the word (meaning "holy") in the text.

Kadr, Al. The night on which the *Koran* was sent down to Mahomet. Al Kadr is supposed to be the seventh of the last ten nights of Ramadan, or the night between the 23rd and 24th days of the month.

> Verily we sent down the Koran on the night of Al Kadr; and what can make thee comprehend how excellent the night of Al Kadr is?—*Koran,* xcvii.

Kaempffert, Waldemar (1877–). American editor and author. Writer on astronomy, science, inventions, etc.

Kaf, Mount. The huge mountain in the middle of which, according to Mohammedan myth, the earth is sunk, as a night light is placed in a cup. Its foundation is the emerald *Sakhrat,* the reflection of which gives the azure hue to the sky.

from Kaf to Kaf. From one extremity of the earth to the other. The sun was supposed to rise from one of its eminences and to set on the opposite.

Kaffir. Literally, "infidel." An Arabic term of contempt for non-Mohammedans, chiefly in Africa. Hence the name came to be applied in the Western languages to either all or some of the Bantu races in Southern Africa, including the Zulus of Natal. The Kaffirs are among the tallest people in the world. They are intelligent, warlike, and socially well organized.

Kafka, Franz (1883–1924). Bohemian novelist, known for his mysticism, his interest in philosophy and religion, in which he was especially influenced by the CABALA and the works of Sören KIERKEGAARD, and the unique character of his books. These, broadly expressionistic in manner (see EXPRESSIONISM), are marked by an objective narrative technique; an extensive use of philosophical and religious symbolism, bordering on the allegorical; a compact, intense, and closely reasoned style; frequent analytical discussions of logical and theological points; fantastic and nightmarish occurrences sometimes suggesting a comparison with SURREALISM; and moving portrayals of tragic and pathetic men and women of humble status. Kafka's dominating ideas as expressed in his writings are: the fruitlessness of man's trying to understand the laws of God; the necessity for unquestioning submission and obedience to God; and the necessity also for tireless striving on the part of man in order to discover what is required of him by God, although success depends more on his attitude than on his comprehension. Kafka's works, which give an excellent picture of society in Germany and Central Europe immediately before and after World War I, had an important influence on a small group of English and, later, American writers—among them being W. H. AUDEN, Rex WARNER, and Delmore SCHWARTZ—during the 1930's. His published writings include: THE TRIAL (*Der Prozess*), first published in 1924; THE CASTLE (*Das Schloss*), first published in 1926; AMERICA, first published in 1927; *The Great Wall of China* (*Beim Bau der Chinesischen Mauer*), a collection of short stories, first published in 1931; *The Metamorphosis* (*Die Metamorphose;* 1937); and *A Kafka Miscellany* (1940). The first three titles are of unfinished novels; a number of other works remain in manuscript, the author having left instructions that all his writings be destroyed, since he had written them originally with a religious rather than literary aim.

For a discussion of Kafka and his work, consult the critical sections of *A Kafka Miscellany.* See also KLEIST.

Kagawa, Toyohiko (1888–). Japanese social worker and novelist. U.S. university training. Powerful influence in Japanese social life, especially in labor matters. Organized Japanese cooperatives. His autobiographical novel, *Across the Death Line* (1924), sold a quarter of a million copies. Author of more than fifty books. A believer in communism of the early Tolstoyan brand rather than in Marxism.

Kagey, Rudolf (1905–1946). American author of ten mystery stories. Also a writer on philosophy and logic, secretary of the Authors' Guild, and instructor in philosophy and director of the evening division of New York University (from 1928). His writing name was Kurt Steel. He was director of public education for the New York World's Fair (1939).

Kahn, Gustave (1859–1936). French poet of the symbolist group (see SYMBOLISM), with Jules LAFORGUE considered the official originator of modern free verse, especially as practiced in France. His contributions were freedom from observing a definite line-length and the use of assonance, internal rhyme, and the like, as rhythmic devices. Kahn's volumes of poetry include: *Les Palais nomades* (1887); *Chansons d'amant* (1891); *La Pluie et le beau temps* (1895); and *Le Livre d'images* (1897). His later books of verse are regarded as early examples of IMAGISM.

Kahn, Otto Hermann (1867–1934). American banker and patron of music and literature. Chairman, the Metropolitan Opera Company; vice-president, the New York Philharmonic Symphony Orchestra. Assisted the American poet Hart CRANE.

Kailyal. The heroine of Southey's CURSE OF KEHAMA, the lovely and holy daughter of Ladurlad, persecuted relentlessly by Arvalan; but virtue and chastity, in the person of Kailyal, always triumphed over sin and lust.

kailyard. Scottish, "kale *or* cabbage patch." The motto of Ian Maclaren's *Beside the Bonnie Brier Bush* (1894) is, "There is a bonnie brier bush in our kailyard." Hence, *kailyard school* (as introduced by W. E. HENLEY), a group of Scottish writers of the 90's who wrote, partly in dialect, on humble homespun topics. They were, besides Maclaren, J. M. Barrie, S. R. Crockett, etc. Cf. Geo. Douglas (Brown), *The House With the Green Shutters* (1901), written in reaction against them.

Kaiser, see under RULERS, TITLES OF.

Kaiser, Georg (1878–1944). German dramatist. Considered with Ernst TOLLER the outstanding German exponent of EXPRESSIONISM.

Kaiser, Henry J. (1882–). American industrialist. Engaged in enormous projects like San Francisco Bridge (1933), Bonneville Dam (1934), Grand Coulee Dam (1939). During World War II, he developed new methods of construction of ships and cargo planes.

Kalakaua I, David (1836–1891). King of Hawaiian Islands (1874–1891). His ideas of reform aroused political opposition culminating in a revolution (1887). Died in San Francisco.

Kalb, Johann, known as **Baron de Kalb** (1721–1780). German-born army officer. Major general in Continental army (1777–1780); mortally wounded in action (Aug. 16, 1780).

Kaled. In Byron's LARA, Gulnare disguised as a page in the service of Lara.

kalends, see CALENDS.

Kalevala (*Finn.,* from the name of the giant hero *Kaleva*). The national epic of the Finns, compiled from popular songs and oral tradition by the Swedish philologist, Elias Lönnrott (1802–1884), who published his first edition of 12,000 verses in 1835, and a second, containing some 22,900 verses, in 1849. The hero is a great magician, Wäinamöinen, and a large part of the action turns on Sampo, an object that gives one all his wishes.

The epic is influenced by, but by no means dependent upon, Teutonic and Scandinavian mythology, and, to a lesser extent, by Christianity. It is written in unrhymed alliterative trochaic verse, and is the prototype, both in form and content, of Longfellow's HIAWATHA.

Kali. The Hindu goddess after whom Calcutta receives its name, Kali-ghat, the steps of Kali, i.e., those by which her worshipers descended from the bank to the waters of the Ganges. She was the wife of SIVA, the acme of bloodthirstiness, many human sacrifices being made to her. It was to her that the Thugs sacrificed their victims. Her idol is black besmeared with blood; she has red eyes, four arms with blood-stained hands, matted hair, huge fanglike teeth, and a protruding tongue that drips with blood. She wears a necklace of skulls, earrings of corpses, and is girdled with serpents. She is also known as Durga and Parvati.

Kalidasa (fl. 5th century A. D.). Greatest Hindu dramatist and lyric poet, often referred to as the "Shakespeare of India." Author of SAKUNTALA.

Kalinin, Mikhail Ivanovich (1875–1946). Russian statesman. Peasant deputy from Leningrad and president of the Union of Soviet Socialist Republics (from 1923).

Kallas, Aino Julia Maria, *née* **Krohn** (1878–). Finnish-Esthonian novelist. Received several prizes for literature in Finland. John Galsworthy admired her work. *The White Ship* (1924) was well received in England.

Kallen, Horace Meyer (1882–). German-born professor of philosophy at the New School for Social Research, New York City. Author of *A Free Society* (1934), etc.

Kaltenborn, H. V. (1878–). American radio commentator. Original name **Hans von Kaltenborn.**

Kalyb. The "Lady of the Woods," who stole St. George from his nurse, brought him up as her own child, and endowed him with gifts. St. George enclosed her in a rock, where she was torn to pieces by spirits. See SEVEN CHAMPIONS OF CHRISTENDOM, Pt. i.

Kama. The god of young love in Hindu mythology. His wife is Rati (voluptuousness), and he is represented as riding on a sparrow, holding in his hand a bow of flowers and five arrows (i.e., the five senses). He is also known as Kamadeva or Kandarpa.

Kamakura. A town in Japan in the southern part of Honshu, near Yokohama. Noted for a colossal bronze statue of the seated Buddha, known as the Daibutsu. Cf. the poem by KIPLING. Kamakura was the seat of government in late medieval times.

Kamehameha I (1737?–1819). King of Hawaii (1795–1819). Had known Captain Cook. Encouraged foreign trade and suppressed human sacrifice.

Kamenev, Lev Brisovich. Original surname, **Rosenfeld** (1883–1936). Russian Communist leader. With STALIN and ZINOVIEV, member of triumvirate ruling Russia after LENIN's death (1924). Married to TROTSKY's sister. During purge of party after murder of Kirov, executed with Zinoviev.

Kami. A god or divinity in *Shinto,* the native religion of Japan; also, the title given to daimios and governors, about equal to "lord."

kampong. In Malaysia, a group of houses or a compound. *Compound* (in this sense) and *kampong* are the same word.

Kanaka. In Hawaii, Polynesia, etc., a native. From the Hawaiian word for "man."

Kanchanjanga. The third highest mountain in the world (28,176 feet), situated in the Himalayas on the boundary between Nepal and Sikkim.

Kandarpa, see KAMA.

Kandinski, Vassili (1866–1944). Russian postimpressionist painter and designer. With Paul KLEE, founder of new school of abstract painting in Munich (1911); instructor at BAUHAUS (1922–1933). Wrote *The Art of Spiritual Harmony* (1914).

Kane, Elisha Kent (1820–1857). American arctic explorer. Participant in First, head of Second Grinnell Expedition into the arctic (1853–1855) discovering new territory. Wrote *The U.S. Grinnell Expedition in Search of Sir John Franklin* (1853); *The Second Grinnell Expedition* (1856); etc.

Kane, Saul. The drunkard whose conversion is the subject of John Masefield's narrative poem, *The Everlasting Mercy.*

Kang, Younghill (1903–). Korean-American author. Guggenheim fellowship in Europe for two years. Connected with Metropolitan Museum of Art in New York. *The Grass Roof* (1931); *East Goes West* (1937), a novel.

Kansa. In Hindu mythology, the uncle and constant enemy of KRISHNA.

Kansas-Nebraska Act. An act of Congress (1854) for the organization of Kansas and Nebraska territories in the region closed to slavery by the MISSOURI COMPROMISE. Its provision that either territory might become a state "with or without slavery, as their constitutions may prescribe at the time of admission," which violated the Missouri Compromise, angered abolitionists and aggravated the problems leading to the outbreak of the Civil War.

Kant, Immanuel (1724–1804). German philosopher. His system, known as Kantian criticism or Kant's critical philosophy, is formulated in his three major works, *Critique of Pure Reason* (*Kritik der reinen Vernunft;* 1781, 1787); *Critique of Practical Reason* (*Kritik der praktischen Vernunft;* 1788); and *Critique of Judgment* (*Kritik der Urteilskraft;* 1790). His major metaphysical concern was the determination of the limits of human reason; his ethics is summed up in the CATEGORICAL IMPERATIVE. His style is difficult and heavy. It has been said that his system as a whole is as lucid as his individual statements are obscure, in contrast to Hegel, whose system is obscure while his detached statements are clear. Kant's influence on SCHILLER and the philosophers of the Romantic era (FICHTE, SCHELLING, HEGEL, etc.) was considerable. The philosophy of the latter has been characterized as nothing but a desperate attempt to break through the limits of cognition erected by Kant.

In an unexpected upsurge of poetic inspiration, Kant stated that the two fixed poles in his spiritual life were the moral law within and the starred firmament above. He never left his native city of Königsberg; he remained a bachelor all his life; there is a story according to which the people of Königsberg used the phases of his daily routine to set their clocks by.

Kantor, MacKinlay (1904–). American novelist and story writer. His *Long Remember* (1934) is one of the best Civil War novels. The long short-story, *The Voice of Bugle Ann* (1935), has also been very popular.

kaolin. A very pure white clay used as the raw material for porcelain. The word is Chinese, means "high hill," and was originally the name of a place where kaolin was found.

Kapellmeister (*Ger.*). The conductor of a *Kapelle* in the sense of an orchestra in the employ of a prince or a military band. Hence

Kapellmeister music, uninspired music; the kind of music to be expected from a *Kapellmeister* whose duties often included mass composition to order. Nevertheless, men like Haydn and Gluck were *Kapellmeisters.*

Karakoram Range. Formerly also **Mustagh.** A mountain range in the Himalaya with some of the highest peaks in the world. Mount Godwin-Austen, the highest, reaches 28,251 feet. The range is crossed by the Karakoram Pass with a height of 18,550 feet.

Karamazov, Alexey Fyodorovich. Also known as **Alyosha.** In Dostoyevsky's THE BROTHERS KARAMAZOV, the youngest of the three brothers, dreamy, gentle, and "pure in heart," a religious mystic.

Dmitry Fyodorovich Karamazov. Also known as **Mitya.** The eldest of the brothers, of military education, wild, hot-tempered, and extravagant.

Fyodor Pavlovich Karamazov. Father of the three brothers, a crafty, miserly, scheming old sensualist, suggestive of a Dickens character.

Ivan Fyodorovich Karamazov. Also known as **Vanya.** The middle brother, university-educated, interested in philosophy and literature and influenced by the NIHILISM of the time, a typical young Russian intellectual of the latter part of the 19th century.

It has been pointed out that the Karamazov brothers respectively represent three national psychological types of Russia in Dostoyevsky's day: the religious mystic, a holdover from medieval Christianity; the soldier and roisterer, a type almost as old as Russia itself, a spiritual descendant of the ancient heroes of the BYLINY; and the Europeanized intellectual, an heir of the period of ROMANTICISM, differing from the intellectual of France or Germany only in the conflict he feels between the new ideas and attitudes imported from western Europe and the century-old ideas and attitudes of his Russian background. The novel dramatizes this conflict.

karela. The balsam apple, a vine of India, mentioned in Kipling's *Jungle Books.*

> . . . and the karela, the bitter karela shall cover you all.

Karénina, Anna, see ANNA KARÉNINA.

Karlfeldt, Erik Axel (1864–1931). Swedish poet. In 1912 he refused the Nobel prize for poetry arguing that his work was unknown outside of Sweden. He was the only poet who ever did that. The prize was awarded him posthumously in 1931.

karma (*Sans.,* "action, fate"). In Buddhist philosophy, the name given to the results of action, especially the cumulative results of a person's deeds in one stage of his existence as controlling his destiny in the next. Among Theosophists the word has a rather wider meaning, viz., the unbroken sequence of cause and effect; each effect being, in its turn, the cause of a subsequent effect.

Karol, Prince. A character in George Sand's novel, LUCREZIA FLORIANI.

Károlyi, Count Mihály (1875–). Hungarian nobleman and politician. After World War I, prime minister of Hungary and president of the newly organized Hungarian People's Republic (1918–1919). Overthrown by the communists and forced into exile. To U.S. (1925). In his absence, he was tried and convicted of high treason. His lands were confiscated.

Karoon or **Karun.** The Arabic form of *Korah* (*Numb.* xvi.), who, according to the commentators of the Koran, was the most wealthy and most beautiful of all the Israelites. It is said that he built a large palace, which he overlaid with gold, and that the doors of his palace were solid gold. He was the Croesus of the Mohammedans, and guarded his wealth in a labyrinth.

karroo. From Hottentot; literally "red soil." In South Africa, a dry table-land. The *Great* or *Central Karroo* in Cape Province has an elevation of 3,000 to 4,000 feet.

Karsavina, Tamara (1885–). Noted Russian dancer. Successor to Anna PAVLOVA as première danseuse of the Imperial Russian Opera House at St. Petersburg (1910).

Karshish. The narrator in Robert BROWNING's poem, *An Epistle containing the Strange Medical Experience of Karshish.* He gives an account of his meeting with Lazarus after the latter had been brought back alive from the tomb.

Karslake, Cynthia. Heroine of Langdon Mitchell's comedy, THE NEW YORK IDEA.

Kartaphilos, see CARTAPHILUS.

Karttikeya. The Hindu Mars, god of war. He is said to have been born without a mother and to have been fostered by the Pleiades or *Krittikas,* whence he is sometimes called "the son of Krittikas." He is represented riding on a peacock, with a bow in one hand and an arrow in the other, and is known also as *Skanda* and *Kumara.*

Kaswa, al. Mahomet's favorite camel, which fell on its knees in adoration when the prophet delivered the last clause of the Koran to the assembled multitude at Mecca. This is one of the dumb creatures admitted into the Moslem paradise.

Kataev, Valentin Petrovich (1897–). Russian novelist and playwright. "The licensed humorist of the Soviets." His most popular play is *Squaring the Circle* (1936) with a world total of more than 6,000 performances.

Kate Croy. In Henry JAMES' *Wings of the Dove* (1902).

Kate Greenaway dress. From the designs by Kate GRENAWAY. A dress with a long full skirt, short waist and sleeves, a round neck, and usually a sash and ruffled edges.

Kate Hardcastle, see HARDCASTLE.

Katerfelto. A generic name for a quack or charlatan. Gustavus Katerfelto was a celebrated quack who became famous during the influenza epidemic of 1782, when he exhibited in London his solar microscope and created immense excitement by showing the infusoria of muddy water. The doctor used to aver that he was the greatest philosopher since the time of Sir Isaac NEWTON. He was a tall man, dressed in a long, black gown and square cap, and died in 1799.

Katharina. The heroine of Shakespeare's TAMING OF THE SHREW, the elder daughter of Baptista of Padua. She was of such an ungovernable spirit and fiery temper, that she was nicknamed "the shrew."

Katharine, Queen. In Shakespeare's *Henry VIII,* the divorced wife of Henry VIII.

Kathay. China. See CATHAY.

Katherine Walton, or the Rebel of Dorchester. The third novel in W. G. SIMMS' trilogy of the American Revolution (1851). The others are *The Partisan* (1835) and *Mellichampe* (1836). The trilogy deals with the exploits of General Marion's men in the Carolinas, for the most part near Dorchester. The central characters are the Walton family, particularly the intrepid Colonel Walton and his daughter Katherine, who finally marries Singleton, the hero. But far more captivating than these stilted heroic figures is the amusing braggart Captain PORGY. Many of the characters of the trilogy appear also in *The Forayers* (1855) and its sequel *Eutaw* (1856).

Kathleen Mavourneen. A popular song composed by Frederick Nicholls Crouch (1808–1896) with words by a Mrs. Crawford, probably Louisa Crawford (1790–1858).

Kathleen Mavourneen, the gray dawn is breaking,
The horn of the hunter is heard on the hill; . . .
Oh, hast thou forgotten how soon we must sever?
Oh, hast thou forgotten this day we must part?
It may be for years, and it may be for ever!
Oh, why art thou silent, thou voice of my heart?

The line, "It may be for years, and it may be for ever," caused the name of Kathleen Mavourneen to be used as a synonym of "promissory note." See also MAVOURNIN.

Kathrina. A long narrative poem by J. G. HOLLAND (1867).

Katmir or Kratim. In the Koran, the dog of the seven sleepers. It spoke with a human voice, and said to the young men who wanted to drive it out of the cave, "I love those who love God. Go to sleep, masters, and I will keep guard." The dog kept guard over them for 309 years, and neither slept nor ate. At death it was taken up into paradise.

He wouldn't give a bone to Katmir, or *he wouldn't throw a bone to the dog of the seven sleepers* is an Arabic proverb, applied to a very niggardly man.

Katrine, Loch. Lake in the lowlands of Scotland with Ellen's Isle, known from Scott's poem, *The Lady of the Lake.* Also the source of Glasgow's water supply.

Katusha. A name by which Maslova, the heroine of Tolstoi's RESURRECTION, is called.

Katz, H. W. (1906–). German refugee novelist. *The Fishmans* won the Heinrich Heine prize (1938) awarded by a group of German writers in exile including Feuchtwanger, Mann, etc. In 1939 Katz joined the French forces and was awarded the Croix de Guerre with citation. In America since 1941.

Katzenjammer Kids. Mischievous young imps of the American comic supplement, the invention of the cartoonist, Rudolph Dirks.

Kauffman, Reginald Wright (1877–). American author and war correspondent. *What is Socialism?* (1910); etc.

Kauffmann, Angelica. Originally **Marie Angélique Catharine Kauffmann** (1741–1807). Swiss historical and portrait painter. Worked mainly in Italy and London. Twice painted by REYNOLDS.

Kaufman, George S. (1889–). American playwright, author of numerous popular plays and musical comedies written in collaboration with a number of well-known writers including Marc CONNELLY, Ring LARDNER, Edna FERBER, Morrie Ryskind, and Moss HART. Among the best-known works of which he was co-author are: *Merton of the Movies* (1922); *The Royal Family* (1927); *June Moon* (1929); OF THEE I SING (1931); *Once in a Lifetime* (1930); *Dinner at Eight* (1932); *Merrily We Roll Along* (1934); *You Can't Take It With You* (1936), a comedy which won the Pulitzer Prize in 1937; *The American Way* (1939); and *The Man Who Came to Dinner* (1939).

Kaun, Hugo (1863–1932). German composer of operas, symphonies, overtures, etc.

Kauravas, the. The opponents of the Pandavas in the Hindu epic, the MAHABHARATA. They were descended from KURU.

Kautsky, Karl Johann (1854–1938). German champion of Marxism of anti-bolshevist tendencies. Secretary to Friedrich Engels in London (1881). Pacifist during World War I;

adviser of EBERT after the German revolution, etc. Died in exile in Holland.

Kavenaugh, Alice. The heroine of William De Morgan's ALICE-FOR-SHORT.

Kay, Sir. In Arthurian romance, son of Sir Ector and foster-brother of King ARTHUR, who made him his seneschal or steward. He is represented as a rude and boastful knight, the first to attempt an achievement, but very rarely successful. See GARETH.

Kaye-Smith, Sheila (1888–). English novelist. Most of her tales are laid in Sussex. *Joanna Godden* (1921), etc. A Catholic convert.

Keable, Robert (1887–1927). English novelist. *Simon Called Peter* (1921), a perhaps autobiographical portrait of a disillusioned clergyman, was a best seller.

Kean, Edmund (1787–1833). Famous English actor. Unrivaled in his day as a tragedian. The irregularity of his life destroyed his career.

Kearsarge. A wooden corvette of the U.S. Navy that destroyed the *Alabama* of the Confederate States in the only open sea fight of the Civil War outside Cherbourg, France (June 11, 1864). She was wrecked on Roncador reef in the Caribbean (February 2, 1894).

Keats, John (1795–1821). English poet, one of the outstanding representatives of ROMANTICISM in England and associated with Leigh HUNT, as well as being acquainted with HAZLITT, SHELLEY, LAMB, COLERIDGE, and WORDSWORTH. His poetry is marked by youthful exuberance, intense sensuous appeal and pictorial quality, imagination, emotion, a sense of symbolism, and attraction to medieval and supernatural subjects. Vividness in poetic imagery was a more important consideration in Keats's poetry than in that of the other English Romantic poets, and he influenced the Pre-Raphaelites (see PRE-RAPHAELITE BROTHERHOOD), TENNYSON, and the French symbolists (see SYMBOLISM). Among his most famous poems are: ENDYMION (1818); LAMIA, ISABELLA, THE EVE OF ST. AGNES, LA BELLE DAME SANS MERCI, *The Eve of St. Mark*, HYPERION, *Ode to a Nightingale, Ode on a Grecian Urn,* and *Ode on Melancholy,* all published in 1820. Keats himself was strongly influenced by the poetry of Edmund SPENSER. He died of tuberculosis in Italy, although his friends preferred to believe he died of a broken heart because of the harsh criticism of *Endymion* delivered by the reviewers on BLACKWOOD'S MAGAZINE. Shelley's elegy *Adonais* was written in Keats's memory. Amy LOWELL and J. M. MURRY are among 20th century writers who were admirers of Keats and prepared, respectively, a biography and several critical studies concerning him. See also BRAWNE, FANNY.

Keble, John (1792–1866). Anglican clergyman and poet. The OXFORD MOVEMENT of Newman's day took its origin from a sermon he preached at St. Mary's, Oxford (1833). Wrote hymns and seven numbers of *Tracts for the Times.*

Kedar's tents. This world. Kedar was a son of Ishmael (*Gen.* xxv. 15), and was the ancestor of an important tribe of nomadic Arabs. The phrase means houses in the wilderness of this world, and comes from *Ps.* cxx. 5: "Woe is me, that I sojourn in Mesech, that I dwell in the tents of Kedar." Seton Merriman's novel, *In Kedar's Tents* (1897), tells the adventures of a wandering, exiled Irishman who joins the anti-Carlist forces in Spain.

Keeldar, Shirley. The heroine of Charlotte Brontë's SHIRLEY.

Keeley cure. A method of treating alcoholics and drug addicts, developed by the American physician Leslie E. Keeley (1832–1900).

keelhaul. To haul under the keel of a ship. In former times, the keelhauling of sailors was an accepted form of punishment in the Dutch and British navies.

> Some also have an effigy of Judas, which the crew amuse themselves with keelhauling.
>
> R. H. Dana, *Two Years Before the Mast.*

keen. Anglicized form of Irish *caoine.* A lamentation or dirge for the dead.

Keeping Up with Lizzie. A humorous story by Irving BACHELLER (1911). The phrase became synonymous with living beyond one's means or desires in order to make an impression on the neighbors.

Keeping Up with the Joneses. An American comic supplement feature by A. R. Momand.

Kehama. The Hindu rajah of Southey's epic poem, *The Curse of Kehama* (1810). He was the almighty rajah of Earth, and all-powerful in Swerga or Heaven. After a long tyranny, he went to Pandalon (Hell) to claim domination there also. He demanded why the throne of Yamen was supported by only three persons, and was told that he himself must be the fourth. When Kehama drank the amreeta, or draught of immortality, which he thought would bring eternal happiness, he drank immortal death, and was forced to bend his proud neck beneath the throne of Yamen, to become the fourth supporter. LADURLAD was the person subjected to the "curse of Kehama."

Keir Hardie, James, see HARDIE, Keir James.

Keller, Albert Galloway (1874–). Professor of science of society at Yale (from 1907). Author of *Science of Society* (1927; 4 vols.) in which material left by William Graham SUMNER is incorporated; etc.

Keller, Arthur Ignatius (1867–1924). American illustrator and painter. Well-known for magazine work and illustration of editions of Bret Harte, Longfellow, Irving, and others.

Keller, Helen Adams (1880–). American author and lecturer. Blind and deaf through illness at age of 19 months. Educated by Anne Mansfield Macy (1887–1936). *The Story of My Life* (1902); *Helen Keller's Journal* (1938); etc. A great American liberal.

Kellermann, Annette. Australian swimmer. Took up swimming to cure a crippled condition of the legs in childhood. Entered her first swimming competition at fifteen. Won the championship for New South Wales; made several attempts to swim the English Channel (beginning in 1909) and once got three-quarters across. She claimed that no woman had the "brute strength" to do it, a statement which Gertrude Ederle later confuted. Miss Kellermann came to the U.S. in 1910 and went into vaudeville and moving pictures. A spectacular exhibition swimmer, who made popular the one-piece bathing-suit for women.

Kellermann, Bernhard (1879–). German novelist. His *Der Tunnel* (1913) was a German best-seller. It is a technological fantasy (partly symbolic) about a tunnel connecting America with Germany.

Kelley, Ethel M. American writer, born on Cape Cod of Irish-Quaker descent. In her teens associated with Theodore Dreiser in editing *Hampton's Magazine.* A regular contributor to "F.P.A.'s" newspaper column *The Conning Tower.* Author of poems, short stories, several books under pen-names, and of *Beauty and Mary Blair* (1921); *Heart's Blood* (1923); *Wings* (1924); *Home, James* (1927); *Strange Avenue* (1932); etc.

Kellogg, Clara Louise (1842–1916). American dramatic soprano. Organized a company presenting grand opera in English.

Kellogg, Frank Bellings (1856–1937). American statesman. U.S. Secretary of State (1925–1929). With Briand negotiated a multilateral treaty to outlaw war, signed at Paris (1928) by fifteen nations and generally known as the Kellogg Pact. Awarded Nobel peace prize (1929). Judge, Permanent Court of International Justice (from 1930).

Kellogg, Vernon Lyman (1867–1937). American zoologist. Author of *The Animals and Man* (1911); *Nuova, the New Bee* (1921); *Mind and Heredity* (1923), etc.

Kellogg-Briand Pact, see Pact of Paris.

Kelly, Eleanor, *née* **Mercein** (1880–). American novelist and short-story writer for magazines. *Kildares of the Storm* (1916); etc.

Kelly, George Edward (1887–). American playwright. *The Show-Off* (twice filmed) (1924) nearly won the Pulitzer prize; *Craig's Wife* (1925) did win it. The latter, concerning a cold, house-proud woman, was also made into a moving picture. It was revived in New York in 1947.

Kelly, Myra (1875–1910). Irish-born American author. Teacher on New York's East Side (from 1899), an experience which inspired her short stories in *Little Citizens* (1904); etc.

Kelmscott Press. A famous coöperative publishing and printing enterprise established by William Morris on his English country estate in 1891, noted for the beauty of paper, binding, and typography in the books it published. The *Kelmscott Chaucer* is considered the masterpiece among these. See also Hubbard, Elbert.

kelpie or **kelpy.** In Scottish folklore, a spirit of the waters in the form of a horse. It was supposed to take delight in the drowning of travelers, but also occasionally to help millers by keeping the mill-wheel going at night.

Kelvin, 1st Baron. **William Thomson.** Known as **Lord Kelvin** (1824–1907). British mathematician and physician. Employed in laying Atlantic telegraph cables (1857–1858, 1865–1866). Many important inventions. One of the original Members of the Order of Merit (1902).

Kemal Atatürk. Formerly **Kemal Pasha.** Originally **Kemal Mustafa** (1881–1938). Turkish army leader and statesman. First president of Turkish Republic (1923–1938). Under him Turkey became a modern European power. Since 1922, officially named *Ghazi,* "victorious." Since 1934 (by act of the National Assembly) his family name was *Atatürk,* "chief Turk."

Kemble, Charles (1775–1854). English actor, of a noted family of actors. Manager of Covent Garden (from 1822). His daughter **Frances Anne** or **Fanny Kemble** (1809–1893), was a popular leading lady, who resided alternately in England and America and wrote several autobiographical books; a play, *The Star of Seville* (1837); and a collection of notes on Shakespeare.

Kemp, Harry Hibbard (1883–). American poet who worked his way around the world and lived as a tramp. Author of *Tramping on Life* (1922), and books of poetry and plays.

Kemp, William (fl. ca. 1600). English comedian and dancer, especially remembered as having appeared in plays by Shakespeare and Ben Jonson. Cf. *The Companion of a Mile* by Alfred Noyes, telling of Kemp's famous morris dance from Norwich to York.

Kempis, Thomas à. See St. Thomas à Kempis under saints.

Kemp Owyne (Scot. *kemp,* a "champion," "warrior"; from A.S. *cempa*). A medieval Scotch or English ballad, dealing with the transformation of Isabel into a "loathly lady" by her stepmother's magic, and her deliverance by the fortitude and courage of the knight Kemp Owyne. See also Cid.

Ken, Thomas (1637–1711). English prelate and hymn writer. One of the "seven bishops" who petitioned James II not to demand that the clergy should read the second Declaration of Indulgence (1688) and were deprived of their sees as nonjurors. Acquitted of a charge of seditious libel. Author of the hymns *Praise God, from whom all blessings flow; Awake, my soul, and with the sun;* etc.

Kendall, Sergeant (1869–1938). American painter and sculptor. Dean, School of Fine Arts, Yale (1913–1922). *The Seer* and *Psyche* in the Metropolitan Museum of Art in New York City.

Kenelm Chillingly, His Adventures and Opinions. A novel by Bulwer Lytton (1873). The dreamy, introspective hero says of himself, "I do not stand in this world; like a ghost I glide beside it and look on."

Kenelm, St., see under saints.

Kenilworth. A novel by Sir Walter Scott (1821), famous for its portrayal of Queen Elizabeth. Aside from Her Majesty, the chief characters are the Earl of Leicester, who entertains ambitions of becoming king-consort, and his beautiful, unhappy wife, Amy Robsart. She suffers neglect, insult and finally death at his hands.

Kenna. See Kensington Garden.

Kennan, George (1845–1924). American journalist, war-correspondent, magazine-article writer and author of books stemming from his assignments and travels.

Kennaquhair (*Scot.,* "Don't know where"). Any imaginary locality. See also Weissnichtwo.

Kennaston, Felix. Hero of Cabell's Cream of the Jest.

Kennedy, Charles Rann (1871–). Anglo-American playwright and actor. *The Servant in the House* (1908), his first and best-known drama, deals with the theme of a Christ-like figure solving the problems of a modern household. Married to the actress Edith Wynne Matthison (since 1898).

Kennedy, Joseph P. (1888–). American banker and diplomat. Headed Securities Exchange Commission (1934–1935). Ambassador to Great Britain (1937–1940; resigned).

Kennedy, Margaret (1896–). English novelist, best known for *The Constant Nymph* (1924), a popular book later dramatized with success. She also wrote *The Ladies of Lyndon* (1923); *A Long Weekend* (1927); *The Fool of the Family* (1930).

Kennerley, Mitchell (1878–). British-born American publisher (from 1905). Director of the printing house of William Edwin Rudge. First brought out the work of Edna St. Vincent Millay, Arthur Davison Ficke, and other well-known American writers. Frederic W. Goudy, the type designer, named one of his type faces Kennerley.

Kenneth, Sir. In Scott's Talisman, the "Knight of the Leopard," a disguise assumed by David, Earl of Huntingdon, prince royal of Scotland, during his adventures in Palestine in the service of Richard Coeur de Lion.

Kennicott, Carol. The heroine of Main Street, by Sinclair Lewis. She is a woman hungry for culture and an individual life of her own who feels stifled in the vegetable-like atmosphere of the small town where she lives.

kenning. In Anglo-Saxon poetry, a figure of speech by which a descriptive circumlocution is used in place of the common noun; as in "whale-road" or "gannet's bath" for "sea," "wave-traveler" for "ship," and "ash-wood" for "spear." Beowulf contains a number of excellent examples of kennings.

Kensington Garden. A mock-heroic poem by Thomas Tickell (1722) peopling Kensington Gardens, which a few years before had been laid out, with fairies. The gardens were the royal domain of Oberon, and the hero is Albion, son of "Albion's royal blood," who was stolen thence by a fairy named Milkah. He later fell in love with Kenna, daughter of Oberon, and after many adventures and a war caused by Oberon's opposition they were married and "lived happy ever after." See also *Peter Pan in Kensington Gardens* (1906) by J. M. Barrie.

Kent, Earl of. A character in Shakespeare's King Lear. He is banished, but under the assumed name of Caius attends upon the old King Lear when his two elder daughters refuse to entertain him with his suite.

Kent, Rockwell (1882–). American artist and travel writer. Excels in woodcuts and lithography. Thinks of all the arts as by-products of life and is an extreme individualist. In addition to his own books, he has illustrated Voltaire's *Candide,* Melville's *Moby Dick,* Chaucer's *Canterbury Tales,* and many others. *Wilderness* (1920) and *Voyaging* (1924) are two of his best books.

Kentigern, St., see under saints.

Kentish fire. Rapturous applause, or three times three and one more. The expression originated with the protracted cheers given in Kent to the No-Popery orators in 1828–1829. Lord Winchilsea, who proposed the health of the Earl of Roden on August 15, 1834, said: "Let it be given with the 'Kentish Fire.'"

Kenton, Simon (1755–1836). American pioneer and Indian fighter; associated with Daniel BOONE (1775–1778).

Kentons, The. A novel by W. D. HOWELLS (1902). It deals with an Ohio family who roam over England and America in the effort to save their daughter from an unhappy love affair. Of the two Kenton girls, Lottie is lively and carefree; Ellen, a more spiritual type, tormented with a conscience. "From her unselfishness spring all the woes of the Kenton family."

Kentucky Cardinal, A. A novel by James Lane ALLEN (1894). The hero, Adam Moss, is a recluse, in love with nature only, until he falls in love with his charming next-door neighbor Georgianna. She is jealous of his interest in the out-of-doors. At her capricious demand he reluctantly cages a Kentucky cardinal, and to her great remorse the bird dies in a wild effort to regain its freedom. *Aftermath* (1895), a sequel, tells of the short but happy married life of Adam and Georgianna. The latter dies, and Adam is left with a son and his old love, nature.

Kenwigs, Mr. In Dickens' NICHOLAS NICKLEBY, a turner in ivory, and "a monstrous genteel man." He toadies to Mr. Lillyvick, his wife's uncle, from whom he has "expectations."

Mrs. Kenwigs. Wife of the above, considered "quite a lady," as she has an uncle who collects the water-rates and sends her daughter Moleena to a day school.

Kenyon. In Hawthorne's MARBLE FAUN, the New England sculptor who marries Hilda.

Keokuk (fl. 1790–1848). American Indian chief of the Sac tribe. The city of Keokuk on the Mississippi in Iowa was named in his honor for the aid he gave the Americans in the Black Hawk War (1832).

Kepler, Johannes (1571–1630). German scientist and one of the fathers of modern astronomy. Assistant and successor to Tycho BRAHE at Prague. His name is associated with three important laws of planetary motion, known as Kepler's laws. (1) The orbit of a planet is an ellipse. The sun occupies one of the foci. (2) The line drawn from the sun to a planet covers equal areas in equal times. (3) The squares of the times the planets need to revolve around the sun are in the ratio of the cubes of their mean distances from the sun.

Ker, John. 1st Duke of **Roxburgh** or **Roxburghe** (ca. 1680–1741). Beneficiary of the last creation in the Scottish peerage (1707). His grandson, **John Ker,** 3rd Duke of **Roxburgh** (1740–1804), was the famous bibliophile whose superb collection, including many books from Caxton's press, was sold in 1812. The *Roxburghe Club* was formed after the sale. At first meant merely for convivial gatherings, it did some good work in printing rare volumes. The *Roxburghe Ballads* were three rare volumes of broadside ballads contained in the original library.

Ker, William Paton (1855–1923). English authority on medieval literature. His best-known work is *Epic and Romance* (1897).

Kerensky, Aleksandr Feodorovich (1881–). Russian revolutionary leader of moderate policies. After the February revolution of 1917, minister and prime minister of the provisional government. Lost his chance through indecision and fled to Paris after the Bolshevik Revolution (Nov., 1917).

kermis or **kermess.** Literally, "church mass." In the Low Countries, originally a local outdoor festival on the feast day of the patron saint; later a kind of country fair.

kern. In medieval days, a light-armed foot soldier of the militia of Ireland and Scotland. Opposed to *gallowglass,* a heavy-armed foot soldier.

> The merciless Macdonwald . . .
> Of kernes and gallowglasses is supplied.
> Shakespeare, *Macbeth.*

Kern, Jerome David (1885–1945). American composer of songs and music for *Show Boat, Sweet Adeline, The Cat and the Fiddle, Music in the Air, Roberta, Leave It to Jane,* and many other musical comedies. Also composer of music for moving-picture operas. His music was notable for a wistful quality and charming melodic invention. *Ol' Man River, Smoke Gets in Your Eyes, They Wouldn't Believe Me, Kalua,* etc.

Kernahan, Coulson (1858–). English writer on celebrities and poets. *A Book of Strange Sins* (1895). Assisted Frederick Locker-Lampson edit *Lyra Elegantiarum* (1891), a collection of some of the best social and occasional verse. Wrote *Swinburne As I Knew Him* (1919); *Six Famous Living Poets* (1926); etc. His wife, **Mary Jean Hickling,** nee **Gwynne Bettany** (1857–1941), was also a writer.

Kerr, Orpheus C., see ORPHEUS C. KERR PAPERS.

Kerr, Sophie (1880–). American novelist and short-story writer of women's-magazine standards. Expertly amusing and content to skim the surface of things.

Kesten, Hermann (1900–). German-Jewish novelist and playwright. A prolific writer who attacked Hitlerism in vitriolic novels. Resident in America (since 1940). In *The Twins of Nuremberg* (1946), Kesten tries to show that fascists are made, not born.

Kester, Vaughan (1869–1911). American novelist and short-story writer. *The Prodigal Judge* (1911) is his most famous book. His brother, **Paul Kester** (1870–1933), is known as a novelist and playwright.

Ketch, see *Jack Ketch* under JACK.

Kettering, Charles Franklin (1876–). American engineer. Inventor of Delco system of starting, lighting, and ignition for automobiles, of Delco-light for farmhouses, etc. General manager, General Motors Research Corporation (from 1917).

Kettledrummle, Gabriel. In Scott's novel OLD MORTALITY, a Covenanter preacher.

kettle of fish. An old Border name for a kind of *fête champêtre,* or picnic by the riverside, in which newly caught salmon is the chief dish. After water is thickened with salt to the consistency of brine, the salmon is put therein and boiled, and when it is fit for eating, the company partake in gipsy fashion. The discomfort of this sort of picnic probably gave rise to the phrase "a pretty kettle of fish," meaning an awkward state of affairs, a mess, a muddle.

ketuba. From a Hebrew word meaning "document." A Jewish marriage contract. It was instituted as a check to divorce and provides for a payment to be made to the wife after the husband's death or in case of a divorce.

Kevin, St., see under SAINTS.

key. Often used figuratively in the sense of something which affords or prevents an entrance, as follows:

key of art. Alchemy.

key of Christendom. Buda in Hungary, a strategic point of resistance against the Turks.

key of India. Herat in Afghanistan.

key of Russia. Smolensk.

key of Spain. Ciudad Rodrigo.

key of the Gulf. Cuba.

key of the Mediterranean. Gibraltar.

Key, Ellen (1849–1926). Swedish feminist and writer. Author of sociological, literary, and historical works on the feminist movement, child welfare, etc. She has been called "the Pallas of Sweden," which is a tribute to her wisdom and courage.

Key, Francis Scott (1779–1843). American lawyer, author of THE STAR-SPANGLED BANNER.

Key, Sir, see KAY, SIR.

Keyes, Frances Parkinson (1885–). American popular magazine writer and novelist.

Keyne, St., see under SAINTS.

Keynes, John Maynard (1883–1946). English economist, representing Great Britain at BRETTON WOODS. Director of the Bank of England (from 1941). Author of many books notably *The Economic Consequences of the Peace* (1919).

Keyserling, Count **Hermann Alexander** (1880–1946). Estonian social philosopher and mystic of German stock. Deprived of his estates by the Russian Revolution, he founded at Darmstadt the *Schule der Weisheit* (School of Wisdom). His thought was conditioned by contact with many cultures and the direct result of his far-flung travels. He well deserved the epithet of "the wandering philosopher." His final ideal was a synthesis of the western notion of *doing* with that of the oriental *being.* His books include *Reisetagebuch eines Philosophen* (1919) or *Travel Diary of a Philosopher* (1925) and THE BOOK OF MARRIAGE (1926).

Keystone State. Pennsylvania. See under STATES.

Khadijah. Mahomet's first wife, and according to the Koran, one of the four perfect women. The other three are Fatima, the prophet's daughter; Mary, daughter of Imran; and Asia, wife of the Pharaoh drowned in the Red Sea.

khamsin. A hot southerly wind in Egypt, coming from the Sahara. It blows regularly for about fifty days commencing by the middle of March. It frequently carries particles of sand. Hence, a dust storm.

Khan, see RULERS, TITLES OF.

khedive. The title by which, from 1867 to 1914, the ruler of Egypt, as viceroy of the Sultan of Turkey, was known. The word is Turkish (from Persian) and means a prince, or viceroy. See also RULERS, TITLES OF.

Khepera. An Egyptian solar deity represented by the beetle.

Khnemu. An Egyptian ram-headed deity, worshiped especially in the region of the five cataracts of the Nile.

Khufu. First king of the IVth or Memphite dynasty of Egypt. The Greek form of his name is Cheops. See under PYRAMID.

kiblah or keblah. The point towards which Mohammedans turn when they worship, *i.e.*, the KAABA at Mecca; also, the stone or slab (called the *mihrab*) on the interior wall of a mosque indicating this direction.

Kicklebury's on the Rhine, The. "A Christmas Book," by THACKERAY (1851).

Kidd, Captain. A famous pirate about whom many legends have collected. He was finally caught and hanged at Execution Dock, London, in 1701. Many of the stories concern buried treasures supposed to have been left by him at various points. He was the hero of a popular melodrama of a century ago, *Captain Kyd, Or the Wizard of the Sea,* by J. S. Jones (*Am.,* 1830), and was prominent in dime-novel fiction.

Kidnapped. A novel by Robert Louis STEVENSON (1886). The title-page contains the following summary: "Kidnapped; Being Memoirs of the Adventures of David Balfour in the Year 1751—How he was Kidnapped and Cast Away; his Sufferings in a Desert Isle, his Journey in the Wild Highlands; his Acquaintance with Alan Breck Stewart and other notorious Highland Jacobites; with all that he suffered at the hands of his Uncle, Ebenezer Balfour of Shaws, falsely so called." There is a sequel, DAVID BALFOUR.

Kiel Canal. Formerly known as **Kaiser-Wilhelm Canal.** The canal through the Schleswig isthmus, which connects the Baltic with the North Sea and makes of the important German naval base of Kiel a port with free access to the Atlantic. Opened in 1895.

Kieran, John Francis (1892–). American journalist. Well-known for his memory work on "INFORMATION PLEASE" radio forum. Formerly a sports editor.

Kierkegaard, Sören Aabye (1813–1855). Danish philosopher. In contrast to Hegel's objective philosophy, based his system on "faith, knowledge, thought, reality." The "razor-edge decision" of human free will which determines man's personal relation to God is clearly analyzed in *Enten-Eller* (*Either-Or;* 1843). Most of Kierkegaard's books were published under various pseudonyms. The twentieth-century revival of Kierkegaard was initiated by the German philosophers Heidegger and Jaspers and furthered by their (indirect) disciples of the French existentialist movement. See SARTRE. In South America, Kierkegaard plays a rôle almost as important as in Europe. In the U.S., Princeton University Press has become the center of Kierkegaard publicity. W. H. AUDEN acknowledges his debt to Kierkegaard.

Kildare's Holy Fane. Famous for the "Fire of St. Bridget," which was inextinguishable, because the nuns never allowed it to go out. Every twentieth night St. Bridget was fabled to return to mend the fire. Part of the chapel still remains, and is called "The Firehouse."

Kilimanjaro, The Snows of. One of HEMINGWAY's best short stories, the result, like his book, *The Green Hills of Africa* (1935), of a journey to the dark continent. The Kilimanjaro is a volcanic snow-clad peak in East Africa, the highest in the continent (19,780 feet).

Killers, The. A short story by Ernest HEMINGWAY, published in *Men Without Women* (1927), and the most famous of his stories. In a detached and coldly "hardboiled" manner, chiefly through dialogue, it tells of two gunmen, Al and Max, who come to a lunchroom and inquire about Ole Andreson, an ex-prize-fighter, whom they announce they are going to murder for having "double-crossed" them. Nick Adams, a customer in the lunchroom, goes to warn Andreson in his rooming-house, but Andreson says simply, "There isn't anything I can do about it." The story made an excellent moving picture.

Killigrew, Thomas (1612–1683). English playwright and courtier of Charles I and his successors. Remembered chiefly as a wit. Built several theaters, among them the original *Theatre Royal* in Drury Lane (1663).

Kilmansegg, Miss. Heroine of a satirical poem by Thomas HOOD called *Miss Kilmansegg and her Golden Leg* (1828). She is an heiress with great expectations, who has an artificial leg of solid gold.

Kilmer, Alfred Joyce (1886–1918). American poet, chiefly remembered for his poem *Trees* (1914). His best war poem, written at the front in World War I, is *The Peacemaker.* Killed in action on reconnaissance as a sergeant of infantry. His wife, **Aline Kilmer** (1888–1941), daughter of the poet Ada Foster Murray, is remembered as the author of several volumes of verse: *Candles that Burn* (1919); *Vigils* (1921); etc.

Kim. A novel of Indian life by Rudyard KIPLING (1901). The Irish boy hero, Kimball O'Hara, better known as Kim, is an orphan, shifting for himself in Lahore. He attaches himself to a holy man, an old lama from Tibet who is on a quest for the mystic River of the Arrows, and together the pair roam about India. By accident Kim is recognized by his father's Irish regiment and much against his wishes is sent to St. Xavier's College. During the long vacations he still tramps with his beloved lama. His intimate knowledge of India makes him a valuable asset of the English Secret Service, in which he wins renown while still a mere boy.

Kimberley. A town in Cape Colony, Africa, famous for its diamond mines which were first worked in 1871. During the Boer War, it was besieged by the Boers for 123 days.

Kimmel, Husband Edward (1882–). Commander of U.S. Pacific fleet (1941). Relieved after Pearl Harbor. Through his position he would automatically have become the wartime commander in chief of the combined U.S. fleet.

kindhart. A jocular name for a tooth-drawer; so called from a dentist of the name in the reign of Queen Elizabeth.

Kindred, Peter. Titular hero of Robert NATHAN's first novel (1919).

king. For individual kings of legend or fiction, as King Arthur, King Cole, King Horn, etc., see under their respective names. Dramas, etc., beginning with the word *king*, as *King John, King Lear,* are given below under separate entries.

King Cotton. Cotton, the staple of the southern states of America, and one of the chief articles of manufacture in England. The expression was first used by James H. Hammond in the United States Senate in 1858.

King James' Bible, see BIBLE, THE ENGLISH.

King Mob. The crowd.

King of Bark. Christopher III of Scandinavia, so called because he had bark mixed with bread in time of famine.

King of Bath. Richard Nash (1674–1761), generally called Beau Nash, a celebrated master of the ceremonies at Bath for fifty-six years. He was ultimately ruined by gambling.

King of beasts. The lion.

king of the beggars. Bampfylde Moore Carew (1693–1770), a famous English vagabond who was elected King of the Gipsies.

king of birds. The eagle.

King of Dalkey. A burlesque king. Dalkey is a little island to the south of Dublin Bay.

king of the forest. The oak.

king of fresh-water fish. So Izaak Walton called the salmon.

king of the jungle. The tiger.

King of Kings. In the Prayer Book the term, of course, refers to the Deity, but it has been assumed by many Eastern rulers, especially Artaxerxes, first Sassanid king of Persia (ca. 226–240).

king of metals. Gold.

King of Misrule. In medieval and Tudor times, the director of the Christmas-time horseplay and festivities, called also the *Abbot,* or *Lord, of Misrule,* and in Scotland the *Master of Unreason.* At Oxford and Cambridge one of the Masters of Arts superintended both the Christmas and Candlemas sports, for which he was allowed a fee of 40s. A similar "lord" was appointed by the lord mayor of London, the sheriffs, and the chief nobility. Stubbs tells us that these mock dignitaries had from twenty to sixty officers under them, and were furnished with hobby-horses, dragons, and musicians. They first went to church with such a confused noise that no one could hear his own voice. Polydore Vergil says of the Feast of Misrule that it was "derived from the Roman Saturnalia," held in December for five days (17th to 22nd). The Feast of Misrule lasted twelve days.

King of Painters. A title assumed by Parrhasius, the painter, a contemporary of Zeuxis (1400 B.C.).

the Wise King. SOLOMON.

King's English. See under ENGLISH.

King's Evil. Scrofula; so called from a notion which prevailed from the reign of Edward the Confessor to that of Queen Anne that it could be cured by the royal touch. The Jacobites considered that the power did not descend to William III and Anne because the "divine" hereditary right was not fully possessed by them, but the office remained in the Prayer-Book till 1719. Prince Charles Edward, when he claimed to be Prince of Wales, touched a female child for the disease in 1745; but the last person touched in England was Dr. Johnson, in 1712, when only thirty months old, by Queen Anne.

The French kings laid claim to the same divine power from the time of Clovis, 481 A. D.; on Easter Sunday, 1686, Louis XIV touched 1,600 persons, using these words: *le Roi te touche, Dieu te guérisse.*

the king-maker. Richard Neville, Earl of Warwick (1420–1471); so called because, when he sided with Henry VI, Henry was king, but when he sided with Edward IV, Henry was deposed and Edward crowned. He was killed at the battle of Barnet. See LAST OF THE BARONS.

Kings of Brentford, see BRENTFORD.

Kings of Cologne, see MAGI.

King of Preachers. Louis Bourdaloue (1632–1704), the eloquent French Jesuit.

king of the sea. The herring.

king of shreds and patches. In the old mysteries, Vice used to be dressed as a mimic king in a particolored suit. (Cf. Shakespeare, *Hamlet,* iii. 4). The phrase has been applied to hacks who compile books for publishers but supply no originality of thought or matter.

king of terrors. Death.

king of waters. The Amazon River.

King of Wisdom. Omár KHAYYÁM.

King of the World. The Roman Emperor.

the Snow King. So the Austrians called Gustavus Adolphus of Sweden (born 1594, reigned 1611–1632), because, said they, he "was kept together by the cold, but would melt and disappear as he approached a warmer soil."

King, Basil (1859–1928). Canadian-born American novelist. Rector, Christ Church, Cambridge, Mass. (1892–1900). *The Inner Shrine* (1909); *The Street Called Straight* (1912); etc.

King, Charles (1844–1933). American army officer and author. In Spanish-American war as brigadier-general of volunteers. Many novels of army life; also *Campaigning with Crook, Rock of Chickamauga* (1907), etc.

King, Clarence (1842–1901). American geologist. Conducted survey of western Cordilleran region (1866–1877), known as the "survey of the 40th parallel." It has been characterized as a "signal contribution to the material of science."

King, Dr. William. A prominent character in Margaret DELAND's novels and stories of Old Chester, notably THE AWAKENING OF HELENA RICHIE, *Old Chester Tales,* and *Dr. Lavendar's People.* His son, *Sam King,* is an important character in the first-named book.

King, Edward (1612–1637). Friend of MILTON and subject of Milton's elegy, *Lycidas.*

King, Ernest Joseph (1878–). American admiral. Commander in chief, U.S. Atlantic fleet (1940); combined fleet, 1941; Chief of naval operations (1942). See under KIMMEL. Commanded the Tenth Fleet in North Atlantic (1944).

King, Grace Elizabeth (1851–1932). American novelist and short-story writer, known for her studies of Creole life in New Orleans, emphasizing character. These include *Monsieur Motte* (1888); *Earthlings* (1889); *Chevalier Alain de Triton* (1889); *Balcony Stories* (1893); *Tales of Time and Place* (1892); *The Pleasant Ways of St. Medard* (1916). She also wrote biography and history dealing with New Orleans and Louisiana. See LOCAL COLOR.

King, Stoddard (1889–1933). American humorist; author of *What the Queen Said* (1926) in verse; *Listen to the Mocking Bird* (1929); etc. He also wrote the words of the famous song, *There's a Long, Long Trail.*

King Cambyses. The titular hero, a pompous, ranting character, of a tragedy by Thomas Preston (1537–1598). Cf. Shakespeare, 1 *Henry IV,* ii. 4, line 426: "I will do it in King Cambyses' vein." Hence the expression, *King Cambyses' vein,* "rant."

King Charles Spaniel. An English toy spaniel named for King Charles II, but known much earlier.

King Cole. A legendary British king of the third century, described in the nursery rhyme as "a merry old soul" fond of his pipe, fond of his glass, and fond of his "fiddlers three." Robert of Gloucester says he was father of St. HELENA (and consequently grandfather of the Emperor Constantine); and Colchester has been said to have been named after him, though it is more probable that the town is named from Lat. *colonia.* John Masefield wrote a narrative poem entitled *King Cole* (*Eng.* 1921) and E. A. ROBINSON has a King Cole among the characters of his TILBURY TOWN.

King Dagobert and St. Eloi. In a very popular French song, St. Eloi tells King Dagobert that his coat has a hole in it, and the king replies, *"C'est vrai, le tien est bon; prête-le moi."* Next the saint complains of the king's stockings, and Dagobert makes the same answer. Then of his wig and cloak, to which the same answer is returned. After seventeen complaints St. Eloi said, "My king, death is at hand, and it is time to confess," when the king replied, "Why can't you confess, and die instead of me?"

kingdom come. As a slang phrase, death, the grave, execution, the next world.

King John. A tragedy by Shakespeare (ca. 1595). This drama is founded on an earlier play, formerly attributed to Shakespeare, *The First and Second Parts of the Troublesome Raigne of John King of England, etc. As they were sundry times publickly acted by the Queenes Majesties players in the Honourable Citie of London* (1591). The drama covers the whole of King John's reign (1199–1216). The action centers about John's usurpation of the crown from Prince Arthur, the rightful heir, his attempts to injure Arthur (see HUBERT), and the complications caused by the concerted opposition of the Pope and the French Dauphin to John's reign.

Kinglake, Alexander William (1809–1891). English historian; wrote *Eöthen, or Traces of Travel Brought Home from the East* (1844), a classic.

King Lear. A tragedy by Shakespeare (ca. 1605). Lear is the King of Britain, son of Bladud. He has three daughters, and, when four-score years old, wishing to retire from the active duties of sovereignty, resolves to divide his kingdom among them in proportion to their love. The two elder say they love him more than their tongue could express, but Cordelia the youngest says she loves him as it becomes a daughter to love her father. The old king, displeased with her answer, disinherits Cordelia, and divides his kingdom between the other two, with the condition that each alternately, month by month, should give him a home, with a suite of a hundred knights. He spends the first month with his eldest daughter, who shows him scant hospitality. When he passes on to the second, she refuses to entertain so large a suite; whereupon the old man will not enter her house, but spends the night abroad in a storm. When Cordelia, who has married the King of France, hears of this, she brings an army over to dethrone her sisters, but is taken prisoner and dies in jail. In the meantime, the elder sister (Goneril) first poisons her younger sister from jealousy, and afterwards puts an end to her own life. Lear also dies. The story of King Lear is given by Geoffrey of Monmouth in his *Chronicles,* whence HOLINSHED, Shakespeare's immediate source, transcribed it. Spenser introduced the same story into his *Faërie Queene* (II. x).

King Log and King Stork. See under LOG.

king-of-arms. Also **king-at-arms.** The chief heraldic officer of a country. In England there are three kings-of-arms, *Garter* (who regulates arms of peers and of knights of the garter), *Clarenceux* (with jurisdiction south of the Trent), and *Norroy* (with jurisdiction north of the Trent). In addition, there are kings-of-arms for Scotland, Ireland, and Wales. They are placed under the Earl Marshal. Formerly their jurisdiction of armory gave them great authority.

King of Rome. A title given at his birth to Napoléon François Charles Joseph (1811–1832), son of Napoleon I and Marie Louise. Also known as the Duke of Reichstadt and counted in the Napoleonic dynasty as Napoleon II. He is the hero of Edmond ROSTAND's *L'Aiglon* (1900).

King of the Wood. *Rex Nemorensis.* The priest of Diana who must pluck the golden bough and then slay his predecessor in a duel before entering on his office at Aricia on the shores of a lake in the Alban Mountains (now Lago di Nemi), where the goddess had a sacred grove. A discussion of this myth is the opening passage and explains the name of Sir James G. Frazer's GOLDEN BOUGH.

Kings, Books of. Two of the canonical books of the Old Testament. They contain the history of the Hebrew people from the death of David to the Exile. In the Vulgate and Douay Versions, among others, they are called *Third and Fourth Books of Reigns,* the *First and Second Books of Reigns* corresponding to 1 and 2 Samuel.

King's Ankus, The. A story by Rudyard KIPLING in the *Jungle Books.* An *ankus* is an elephant goad with a sharp spike, used by the *mahouts.*

King's or **Queen's Bench.** In English law, formerly the highest court of common law. The sovereign, king or queen, used to sit there in person.

King's English, the. See under ENGLISH.

Kingsford-Smith, Sir **Charles Edward** (1897–1935). Australian aviator. Record flights around Australia and from Australia to England, etc. Lost on way to Singapore.

Kings in Exile. A volume by Alphonse DAUDET (1879) which presents, under thinly veiled disguise, portraits of George of Hanover, Isabella of Spain, Christian of Naples and other deposed sovereigns of the day, who found refuge in Paris.

Kingsley, Charles (1819–1875). English clergyman and novelist, known for his interest in the social reform movements of his time. His novels include *Yeast* (1850); ALTON LOCKE (1850); HYPATIA (1853); WESTWARD HO! (1855); *Two Years Ago* (1857); *Water Babies* (1863), a story for children; and HEREWARD THE WAKE (1865). Other works, of wide variety in subject-matter, are *The Heroes* (1856), a book on Greek mythology for children; *The Saint's Tragedy* (1848), a poetic drama; *Andromeda* (1859), a treatment of the classical myth; *Glaucus, Or The Wonders of the Shore* (1855), a book on natural history; *The Roman and the Teuton* (1864), a series of lectures; *At Last* (1871), an account of travel in the West Indies; *Prose Idylls* (1873); and several collections of sermons. He also contributed to several periodicals, including the *Christian Socialist, Fraser's Magazine,* and *Macmillan's Magazine.* It was in the course of a controversy with Kingsley, which began with a book review published by the latter in *Macmillan's Magazine,* that Cardinal NEWMAN wrote his famous *Apologia Pro Vita Sua.*

Kingsley was called "the Chartist clergyman" and associated with the phrase "MUSCULAR CHRISTIANITY."

Kingsley, Henry (1830–1876). English novelist, best known as the author of *Ravenshoe* (1862). He was the brother of Charles KINGSLEY.

Kingsley, Sidney (1906–). American playwright: *Men in White* (Pulitzer Prize, 1933); *Dead End* (1935); etc. His *The Patriots* (1945), which he wrote while a member of the armed forces, has Alexander Hamilton and Thomas Jefferson as its two leading characters. The New York Drama Critics Circle voted to it its "award for the best play of the season" (Jefferson Day, April 13, 1946).

Kingsmill, Hugh. In full **Hugh Kingsmill Lunn** (1889–). British novelist and biographer. *The Return of William Shakespeare* (1929); *Samuel Johnson* (1933); etc.

King Victor and King Charles Emmanuel. A poetic drama by Robert BROWNING dealing with the abdication of King Victor Amadeus of Sardinia (1665, 1675–1732).

King William's War. The war waged by Great Britain and its American colonies against France and its Indian allies (1689–1697). It is the American phase of the war between the Grand Alliance and Louis XIV and was concluded by the Peace of Ryswick.

kiosk. A Turkish open summer house or pavilion. The term is used in Europe for any pagodalike newsstand, refreshment booth, etc., especially in parks and public places.

Kipling, Rudyard (1865–1936). English poet, novelist, and short-story writer, known for his life-long glorification of British imperialism and his verses and tales of British soldiers in the colonies, as well as animal stories for children, all of which were extremely popular in the latter 19th and early 20th centuries. His technique has been called a combination of romantic outlook and realistic detail. His collections of short-stories include: *Plain Tales from the Hills* (1887); *Soldiers Three* (ca. 1887); *Life's Handicap* (1890); and *The Day's Work* (1898). Among his juvenile books are: *Captains Courageous* (1897); *Stalky and Co.* (1899); the JUNGLE BOOKS (1894 and 1895); JUST SO STORIES (1902); PUCK OF POOK'S HILL (1906). THE LIGHT THAT FAILED (1890) and KIM (1901) are novels, and DEPARTMENTAL DITTIES (1886) and BARRACK-ROOM BALLADS (1892) are two of his best-known volumes of verse; the latter contains the popular Cockney dialect poems *Tommy Atkins, Danny Deever, Fuzzy-Wuzzy, Gunga Din,* and *Mandalay*. See also MULVANEY, TERENCE.

the Canadian Kipling. Robert Service (1874–), author of *Rhymes of a Rolling Stone,* etc., so called.

Kipps. A novel by H. G. WELLS (1905), the story of a draper's apprentice whose sudden acquisition of wealth brings him into another world, to which he makes frantic but usually vain efforts to adapt himself. Kipps is a humorous character, sympathetically drawn.

Kirby, Carinthia Jane. Heroine of Meredith's novel, THE AMAZING MARRIAGE.

Kirchkoff, Gustav Robert (1824–1887). German physicist. With R. W. BUNSEN, discoverer of the method of spectrum analysis (1860).

Kirillov, Alexey Nilich. In Dostoyevsky's THE POSSESSED a member of the band of revolutionaries, half-mad and obsessed with a desire to commit suicide and thereby assert his freedom of will, or "become God." On the occasion when he does kill himself at last, he is persuaded by Pyotr Stepanovich VERHOVENSKY after a violent scene to leave a note confessing to the murder of Ivan SHATOV, whom the revolutionaries have killed through fear of betrayal.

Kirke, Hazel. Heroine of Steele MacKaye's drama, HAZEL KIRKE. Her father, *Dunstan Kirke,* also plays an important rôle.

Kirkland, Caroline Matilda. Pseudonym, Mrs. **Mary Clavers** (1801–1864). Author of pioneer books, *A New Home—Who'll Follow* (1839); *Forest Life* (1842); *Western Clearings* (1845).

Kirkland, John (1901–). American playwright and producer. Stage adaptations of *Frankie and Johnnie* (1928), *Tobacco Road* (1933), etc.

Kirkland, Joseph (1830–1894). American novelist, one of the earliest exponents of realism in the fiction of the U.S., known for his frank and powerful studies of life in the Middle West of his time, largely based on his own experiences. His best known work is ZURY, THE MEANEST MAN IN SPRING COUNTY (1887). Other novels are *The McVeys* (1888), a sequel to *Zury,* and *The Captain of Company K* (1891), dealing realistically with the Civil War. With Edward EGGLESTON, Kirkland is considered to have had a strong influence on Hamlin GARLAND. See also HOWE, EDGAR WATSON; LOCAL COLOR; NATURALISM.

Kirov, Sergei Mironovich (1888–1934). Russian revolutionary leader (since 1905). Assassinated at Leningrad. His death was avenged by the execution of 116 persons convicted of conspiracy to overthrow STALIN and the central government.

Kirkrapine. The "robber of churches" in Spenser's *Faërie Queene* (I, iii. 16–22), the lover of Abessa (Superstition), and the typification of the plundering of the Church by the wealthy clergy. While Una is in the hut of Corceca, Kirkrapine forced his way in and is torn to pieces by her lion, i.e., the Reformation.

Kirkwood, Maurice. A character in O. W. HOLMES' *Mortal Antipathy* (1885). He suffers from a "mortal antipathy" to beautiful women, due to an accident in childhood, but is finally cured by one of them who loves him.

Kirsanov, Arcadi. In Turgenev's FATHERS AND SONS, the friend of Bazarov.

kismet (from Turkish *qismat,* "portion, lot"). Fate, destiny; or the fulfilment of destiny.

Kit-cat Club. A club formed about the beginning of the 18th century by the leading Whigs of the day, and held in the house of Christopher Catt, a pastrycook of Shire Lane, which used to run north from Temple Bar to Carey Street. Its site is now covered by the Law Courts. Christopher Catt's mutton pies, which were eaten at the club, were also called *kit-cats,* and in the *Spectator* (No. IX) we are told that it was from these the club got its name.

> Steele, Addison, Congreve, Garth, Vanbrugh, Manwaring, Stepney, Walpole, and Pulteney were of it; so was Lord Dorset and the present Duke. Manwaring . . . was the ruling man in all conversation . . . Lord Stanhope and the Earl of Essex were also members. . . . Each member gave his [picture].—Pope to Spence.

Sir Godfrey Kneller painted forty-two portraits of the club members for Jacob Tonson, the secretary, whose villa was at Barn Elms, and where latterly the club was held. In order to accommodate the paintings to the height of the club-room, he was obliged to make them three-quarter lengths (28 in. by 36 in.), hence a three-quarter portrait is still called a *kit-cat.*

Kitchen Cabinet. A name used by the opponents of President Andrew Jackson during his term of office in the White House (1829–1833) with reference to his political advisers, especially Francis P. Blair and Amos Kendall, both of whom were connected with *The Globe,* which supported Jackson's policies.

Kitchener, Horatio Herbert. 1st Earl **Kitchener of Khartoum and of Broome** (1850–1916). British soldier. Secretary of state for war (1914); engaged in the organization of Britain's military forces (1914–1916); lost at sea in the sinking of the cruiser *Hampshire* (1916).

kitchen middens. Prehistoric mounds (referred to the Neolithic Age) composed of seashells, bones, kitchen refuse, rude stone implements, and other relics of early man. They were first noticed on the coast of Denmark, but have since been found in the British Isles, North America, etc.

Kite, Sergeant. The title rôle in Farquhar's comedy, *The Recruiting Officer* (1705). He describes his own character thus:

> "I was born a gipsy, and bred among that crew till I was 10 years old; there I learnt *canting* and *lying.* I was bought from my mother by a certain nobleman for three pistoles, who . . . made me his page; there I learnt *impudence* and *pimping.* Being turned off for wearing my lord's linen, and drinking my lady's ratafia, I turned bailiff's follower; there I learnt *bullying* and *swearing.* I at last got into the army, and there I learnt . . . *drinking.* So that . . . the whole sum is: canting, lying, impudence, pimping, bullying, swearing, drinking, and a halberd."

Kitely. In Ben Jonson's drama, Every Man in His Humour, a rich city merchant, extremely jealous of his wife.

Kittredge, George Lyman (1860–1941). American philologist, Harvard professor, and Shakespearean authority. A great teacher, stern but beloved by his students, generations of whom remember him simply as "Kitty." His book on *Chaucer and His Poetry* (1915) has done more than any other work to make clear the greatness of Chaucer to the modern reader. In addition to his numerous books and editions, he prepared the final volume of Professor Francis James Child's *English and Scottish Popular Ballads* (1898).

kiva. A Hopi word, signifying, in Pueblo Indian architecture, a normally circular ceremonial chamber with access and lighting through the roof.

Kjartan. In the Laxdale Saga, a young Icelander in love with the strong-willed heroine Gudrun, who is also passionately in love with him. When Kjartan returns home from the Danish court and learns that Gudrun has married for the third time, his own cousin Bolli being her new husband, he decides to take a wife of his own, Hrefna. During the ensuing feud between the two couples, Kjartan continues to love Gudrun and to defend her against Hrefna's complaints, even when he realizes Gudrun is in the wrong.

K. K. K. The initials of the Ku Klux Klan.

Klaboterman. The kobold of the phantom ship, Carmilhan.

Klabund. Pseudonym of **Alfred Henschke** (1891–1928). German poet and (chiefly historical) novelist. Author of translations and imitations of Chinese literature. Especially remembered for his highly subjective volumes on German and universal literary history (1919, 1921).

Klamm. In Franz Kafka's The Castle an official of the Castle whom the hero K. tries in vain to see.

Klaus, Peter. An old German legendary hero, the prototype of Rip Van Winkle. Klaus was a goat-herd of Sittendorf, who was one day accosted by a young man, who beckoned him to follow. He obeyed, and was led into a deep dell, where he found twelve knights playing skittles, no one of whom uttered a word. Gazing around, he noticed a can of wine, and, drinking some of its contents, was overpowered with sleep. When he awoke, he was amazed at the height of the grass, and when he entered the village everything seemed strange to him. After much perplexity, he discovered he had been asleep for twenty years.

Klee, Paul (1879–1940). Swiss modernist painter. Cofounder with Kandinski and Marc of the Munic school of abstract painting, Blaue Reiter (1911). Also cofounder of the Blue-Four movement (1926).

Klein, Charles (1867–1915). American playwright. Best known for *The Lion and the Mouse* (1905). Collaborated on a number of works with Arthur Hornblow.

Kleist, Bernd Heinrich Wilhelm von (1777–1811). German poet and dramatist, a typical figure of the Romantic period in his country. His dramas, a number of which are of the Sturm und Drang type, include *Die Familie Schroffenstein* (1803); *Der Zerbrochene Krug* (1812), a famous comedy; *Penthesilea* (1808), a tragedy; *Das Käthchen von Heilbronn* (1810); *Die Hermannschaft* (1809), a patriotic play inspired by the author's hate for Napoleon; and *Prinz Friedrich von Homburg.* His tales in particular are highly praised, *Michael Kohlhaas* being considered one of the outstanding works of German fiction. Kleist was also editor for a time of the periodical *Berliner Abendblätter* (1810–1811). It is believed by some critics that he had some influence on the 20th-century novelist Franz KAFKA.

Kleist was sensitive and moody in temperament, and at one time had an attack which brought him close to madness. In 1811, discouraged by the failure of his writings to achieve the success he had hoped for, he first shot Henriette Vogel, a woman with whom he was passionately in love, and then committed suicide.

Kleist, Paul Ludwig Ewald von (1881–). German colonel general in World War II. Commanded panzers through the Ardennes in first rush through France (1940); stormed Southern Russian front (1941); advanced through Ukraine and Don region into Caucasus (1941–1942) until defeats and withdrawals forced by the Russian winter offensive (1942–1943) forced him to evacuate his troops to the Crimea (October, 1943).

klepts (*Gr.*, robbers). The name given to those Greeks who, after the conquest of their country by the Turks in the 15th century, refused to submit and maintained their independence in the mountains. They degenerated —especially after the War of Independence (1821–1828)—into brigands, hence the word is often used for a lawless bandit or brigand.

Klesmer, Herr. In George Eliot's DANIEL DERONDA, a poverty-stricken German musician who teaches Gwendolyn Harleth and attempts to convert her to some of his own high ideals.

klieg light. A kind of bright arc light used in motion pictures and named after the inventors John Kliegl (1869–) and Anton Kliegl (1872–1927), partners of the firm of Kliegl Bros. Hence **klieg eyes,** eyes inflamed and weeping from excessive exposure to intense light.

Klinger, Friedrich Maximilian von (1752–1831). German dramatist and novelist. His *Sturm und Drang* (1776) gave its name to the period of German literature in which young GOETHE received his baptism of fire. The Faust theme, mastered by Goethe in the form of a drama, became in Klinger's version a heavy novel (1791).

Klingsor or **Klingshor, Nicolas.** One of the MINNESINGERS of the 13th century, with whom myth has credited many magic powers. According to tradition he presided over the contest of minnesingers on the WARTBURG. In the opera PARSIFAL, Wagner introduces him as a magician who has given himself over to the task of seducing the Knights of the Grail.

Klondike. A region in the Yukon Territory of Canada. Famous for its gold mines. Cf. the poem by Edwin Arlington Robinson and books by Rex Beach. See also Robert William SERVICE.

Klopstock, Friedrich Gottlieb (1724–1803). German poet, especially remembered for his Miltonian epic *The Messiah* in hexameters (20 cantos).

Kluck, Alexander von (1846–1934). German general. In World War I, commanded right-wing army in the three-pronged invasion of France (1914), directed upon Paris. A hastily organized French army under Maunoury repulsed him, marking the beginning of the French success at the first battle of the Marne. Wounded (1915) and forced to give up his command.

Kneisel, Franz (1865–1926). Rumanian-born violinist. Organizer and leader of famous Kneisel Quartet (début in Boston, 1885).

Kneller, Sir **Godfrey** (1646–1723). German-English portrait painter. Principal painter to William III. Paintings by him of ten reigning monarchs are extant. In his earlier years he seems to have received some instruction from Rembrandt.

Knibbs, Harry Herbert (1874–). Canadian poet and story writer. His *forte* is verse narrative of a popular western nature.

Knickerbocker's History of New York. A mock-serious history of early New York by Washington IRVING (1809) purporting to be written by Diedrich Knickerbocker. It relates, in rollicking burlesque, the old Dutch traditions of colonial days.

Knickerbocker school. A name given to a group of early American authors who were followers of Washington Irving. Chief among them were Fitz-Greene Halleck and Joseph Rodman Drake.

Father Knickerbocker. A personification of New York.

knickerbockers, or *knickers.* Loose-fitting breeches, gathered in at the knee, and worn by boys, cyclists, sportsmen, tourists, etc., and at one time by women as an undergarment. So named from George Cruikshank's illustrations of *Knickerbocker's History of New York,* where the Dutch worthies are drawn with very loose knee-breeches. The name *Knickerbocker* is found among the old Dutch inhabitants of New York a century and more earlier; it probably signified a *baker* of *knickers,* i.e., clay marbles.

knight (A.S. *cniht*). Originally meaning merely a boy or servant, the word came to denote a man of gentle birth who, after serving at court or in the retinue of some lord as a page and esquire, was admitted with appropriate ceremonies to an honorable degree of military rank and given the right to bear arms.

There are nine *Orders of Knighthood* in the

British Empire, viz. (in the following order of precedence) the Garter, the Thistle, St. Patrick, the Bath, the Star of India, St. Michael and St. George, the Indian Empire, the Royal Victorian Order, and the British Empire. After these come the Knights Bachelor, who are members of no Order and who do not constitute an order. *Bachelor* here is Fr. *bas chevalier,* signifying "lower than the knight of an order."

The word *knight* is used in various slang or jocular phrases denoting a member of some trade or profession, follower of some calling or occupation, etc. Thus we have: *knight of the blade,* a roystering bully; *knight of the cleaver,* a butcher; *knight of the cue,* a billiard player; *knight of the needle,* a tailor; *knight of the pestle,* a druggist; *knight of the road,* a footpad or a hobo; *knight of the spigot,* a tapster; *knight of the wheel,* a cyclist; etc.

Knight of La Mancha. Don Quixote de la Mancha, the hero of Cervantes' DON QUIXOTE.

Knight of the Carpet or *Carpet Knight,* see under CARPET.

Knight of the Cloak. Sir Walter Raleigh, who spread his cloak in a mud puddle for Queen Elizabeth to walk upon.

Knight of the Invincible Sword. So Amadis styled himself in the 14th century romance AMADIS OF GAUL. He cleft in twain, at one stroke, two tremendous giants.

Knight of the Lions. The appellation assumed by Don Quixote after his attack upon the van containing two lions sent by the general of Oran as a present to the King of Spain.

Knight of the Rueful Countenance. Don Quixote, so called by Sancho Panza, his squire.

Knight of the Swan. LOHENGRIN.

Knights of Columbus. A fraternal and benevolent association of Roman Catholic men in America, founded at New Haven, Conn., in 1882.

Knights of Labor. A secret organization of American workmen, founded at Philadelphia in 1869, a pioneer in the labor movement in the U.S. Its objects were to regulate wages, the degree of skill to be exacted from workmen, the length of a day's work, and to control strikes. This league decided when a strike was to be made, and when workmen of the union might resume work. See AMERICAN FEDERATION OF LABOR; CONGRESS OF INDUSTRIAL ORGANIZATIONS.

Knights of Malta. First called "Knights of St. John of Jerusalem," otherwise "Knights of Rhodes." The most celebrated religious military order of the Middle Ages.

Knights of the Garter. An order instituted by Edward III of England in 1344. According to Selden, "it exceeds in majesty, honor, and fame, all chivalrous orders in the world." The story is that Joan, Countess of Salisbury, while dancing with the King, let fall her garter, and the gallant Edward, perceiving a smile on the faces of the courtiers, picked it up, bound it round his knee, and exclaimed, *"Honi soit qui mal y pense."* The blue garter and the motto of the order are thus accounted for.

Knights of the Round Table. King ARTHUR's knight were so called, because they sat with him at a round table made by Merlin for King Leodegraunce. See ROUND TABLE.

Knight, Charles Robert (1874–). American painter, illustrator and muralist. Excelled in animals and birds, especially for the American Museum of Natural History in New York, the Field Museum in Chicago, etc.

Knight, Eric (1897–1943). Anglo-American novelist. Created *The Flying Yorkshireman* (1937). Killed in airplane crash on official war mission. His *Lassie Come Home* (1940; juvenile) became a successful moving picture.

Knight, Henry. One of the lovers of Elfride Swancourt in Hardy's PAIR OF BLUE EYES.

Knight, Joseph Philip (1812–1887). English song writer. Best known for *Rocked in the Cradle of the Deep* (1839).

Knight, Laura. English painter of scenes and subjects taken from circus life. Dame of the British Empire (1929).

Knight, Sarah Kemble. Known as **Madam Knight** (1666–1727). American teacher of Boston, known for the diary in which she recorded observations and impressions of a journey made on horseback from Boston to New York in the winter of 1704–1705. Published in 1825, it is considered valuable as a first-hand source of information on the transportation, inn facilities, housing, and manners and speech of the early 18th century in New England.

Knightly, Mr. Hero of Jane Austen's EMMA.

Knight of the Burning Pestle, The. A comedy in ridicule of chivalrous romance, by Beaumont (1611).

Knights, The. A comedy by Aristophanes directed against Cleon, the demagogue (produced, 424 B.C.).

Knight's or **Knighte's Tale.** (In Chaucer's CANTERBURY TALES.) See PALAMON AND ARCITE. The Knight is perhaps best described in the following well-known lines:

A Knight ther was, and that a worthy man. . . .
And though that he were worthy, he was wys,
And of his port as meke as is a mayde.
He never yet no vileinye ne sayde
In al his lyf unto no maner wight,
He was a verray parfit gentil knight.
Chaucer, *Prologue to the Canterbury Tales.*

Knittelvers (*Ger.*). Doggerel. Originally a literal translation of Latin *versus rhopalicus* (club verse) which was technically a verse in which the length of the feet kept increasing by one syllable, but came to be understood as meaning any sort of irregular verse. Rehabilitated by the amazingly effective use GOETHE made of it in *Faust* and other works.

Knoblock, Edward (1874–1945). British playwright, scenarist, novelist. *Kismet* (1911); *Milestones* (1921; with Arnold BENNETT); *Grand Hotel* (1931; from the novel by Vicki BAUM); etc.

Knopf, Alfred A. (1892–). American publisher, New York City. Has brought to America much distinguished European literature and was a pioneer in artistic typography and binding of books.

knout (Russ. *knut,* probably connected with *knot*). A long, hard leather thong or a knotted bunch of thongs formerly used in Russia for corporal punishment on prisoners; hence, a symbolification of supremely autocratic rule.

Knowles, Frederic Laurence (1869–1905). American poet and anthologist.

Knowles, James Sheridan (1784–1862). British playwright. *Virginius* (1820), etc. Author of novels, poems, and other works.

Know-Nothings. A political society in the United States, originally (ca. 1853) secret but later (1855) reorganized without its secret machinery and also known as the American Party. In the beginning its members replied to every question about their society, "I know nothing about it." Their object was to accomplish the repeal of the naturalization laws, and to advocate laws which would have excluded all but natives from holding office. It split on the slavery question and died out soon after 1856.

Knox, Edmund George Valpy (1881–) and **Ronald Arbuthnot Knox** (1888–). First and fourth sons, respectively, of the Rt. Rev. E. A. Knox, D.D. Edmund is the "Evoe" of *Punch,* noted for his humorous verse and parodies. Succeeded Sir Owen Seaman as editor of *Punch* (1932). Ronald was converted to Catholicism (1917), ordained priest (1919), and became the Catholic chaplain at Oxford (1925). He is one of the most influential Catholic apologists in England and a master of witty satire. He also writes erudite detective novels.

Knox, Frank (1874–1944). American newspaper publisher. U.S. secretary of the navy (1940–1944) under F. D. Roosevelt though still affiliated with the Republican party.

Knox, John (1505–1572). Scottish reformer. Twice at Geneva in personal contact with Calvin (1554, 1556–1558). Published six tracts dealing with religion in Scotland. The best-known are his *Blasts of the Trumpet against the Monstrous Regiment of Women* (1st and 2nd, 1558). They were not meant for Queen Elizabeth but offended her deeply. Knox preached throughout Scotland against Mary Queen of Scots, whom he simply called "Jezebel," and against catholicism in general. He was a fanatic of wide influence.

Knox, Philander Chase (1852–1921). American politician. Secretary of state (1909–1913); senator (1917–1921). Identified with "DOLLAR DIPLOMACY." Opposed to American collaboration with the League of Nations.

Knudsen, William S. (1879–). Danish-born American industrialist. Came to U.S. at 20, started as bicycle mechanic and became president of the General Motors Corporation (1937). Codirector with Sidney Hillman, Office of Production Management (1941); director of production, War Department (January 1942).

Kobbé, Gustav (1857–1918). American newspaper writer and author of books on musical subjects. *Wagner's Life and Works* (2 vols.; 1890); *The Complete Opera Book* (1918), etc.

Kober, Arthur (1900–). Austrian-born American humorist and dramatist. Wrote screen plays for moving picture stars, was married for a time to the playwright Lillian Hellman, made famous the Gross family in Bronx dialect in the *New Yorker,* and put them in a play with clerks and stenographers at a summer camp, called *Having Wonderful Time,* which won the Roi Cooper Megrue prize as the best comedy of 1937.

Kobold. A house-spirit in German superstition; similar to Robin Goodfellow, and the Scotch brownie. Also a gnome who works in the mines and forests.

Kobrin, Leon (1873–1946). Russian-born, American-Yiddish dramatist, newspaper man, and novelist of immigrant Jews in teeming American ghettos. His best-known characters are in his first book *Yanka Boila and Other Tales* (1898), popular on the Yiddish stage in dramatized form. Author of the novel *A Lithuanian Village* (1920), and more than thirty plays. His *Children of Nature* was produced by the Moscow Art Theatre.

Koch, Howard. American playwright and scenarist. Radio adaptation (for Orson WELLES) of *War of the Worlds* by H. G. Wells; screen version of *Mission to Moscow* by Joseph Davies; etc.

Koch, Robert (1843–1910). German physician and one of the pioneers of modern bacteriology. Isolated anthrax and tubercle bacillus; identified the bacillus which causes Asiatic cholera; investigated bubonic plague in Bombay (1899) and malaria and sleeping sickness in Africa; etc. Awarded Nobel prize for physiology and medicine (1905).

Koh-i-Nûr (*Pers.*, "mountain of light"). A large diamond which, since 1849, has been among the British Crown Jewels; hence, anything of great worth. It is said to have been known 2,000 years ago, but its authentic history starts in 1304, when it was wrested by the Sultan, Al-eddin, from the Rajah of Malwa. From his line it passed in 1526 to Humaiun, the son of Sultan Baber, and thence to Aurungzebe (d. 1707), the Mogul emperor, who used it for the eye of a peacock in his famous peacock throne at Delhi. In 1739 it passed into the hands of Nadir Shah, who called it the Koh-i-nûr. It next went to the monarchs of Afghanistan, and when Shah Sujah was depossessed he gave it to Runjit Singh, of the Punjab, as the price of his assistance towards the recovery of the throne of Cabul. After his death (1839) it was kept in the treasury at Lahore, and when the Punjab was annexed to the British Crown in 1849 it was, by stipulation, presented to Queen Victoria. At this time it weighed 186 1/16 carats, but after its acquisition it was cut down to 106 1/16 carats. There is a tradition that it always brings ill luck to its possessor.

Koizumi, Yakumo, see HEARN, LAFCADIO.

Ko-Ko. Lord High Executioner in the comic opera THE MIKADO by Gilbert and Sullivan.

Kolchak, Aleksandr Vasilievich (1874–1920). Russian counter-revolutionary leader. During World War I, admiral of the Baltic and (later) Black Sea fleet. After the Revolution he gathered a White army in Siberia (1917). His position grew untenable when a Red army captured Omsk. He retreated to Irkutsk, was captured and shot.

Komroff, Manuel (1890–). American writer. Editor of Nietzsche's *Zarathustra.* His two-volume historical novel, *Coronet* (1929) was a great success.

Konoye, Prince **Fumimaro** (1891–). Japanese statesman. Premier (1937–1939, 1940–1941); foreign minister (1928); etc. Japan's policy in the Chino-Japanese war (1937 ff.) was largely shaped by him.

Koo, Vi Kyuin Wellington (1887–). Chinese statesman, representing his country on the Council of the League of Nations (1932–1934); ambassador to France (1936–1941); ambassador to England (1941); etc. "Wellington" became part of his name through sound association with the original **Wei-chün.**

Korah. In the Bible (*Num.* xvi), a Levite who led a rebellion against Moses and Aaron. His name signifies "ice." His descendants, the Korahites, were temple musicians.

Koran. The sacred book of the Mohammedans. The word means "reading." The variant *Alcoran* has a prefixed article. The substance of the Koran is the uncreated and eternal truth that was revealed to Mohammed. The tradition that the text should be transmitted by word of mouth had to be broken at an early date when the best Koran reciters had fallen in battle. The chapters of the Koran are called suras. There are 114, not numbered but individually named and written in Arabic.

The subject matter of the Koran is, historically speaking, of Jewish and to a lesser extent of Christian origin.

Kornilov, Lavr Georgievich (1870–1918). Russian general of Cossack descent. As commander of the imperial troops in Petrograd, he tried after the Revolution (1917) to establish himself as antibolshevik dictator. Forced to flee to the Caucasus, he organized a Cossack force and was killed in action.

Korolenko, Vladimir Galaktionovich (1853–1921). Russian novelist of advanced social ideas in his day. Master of style. *The Blind Musician* (1888) is one of his greatest novels.

korrigans. Nine fays of Breton folklore, who can predict future events, assume any shape they like, move quickly as thought from place to place, and cure diseases or wounds. They are not more than two feet high, have long flowing hair, which they are fond of combing, dress only with a white veil, are excellent singers, and their favorite haunt is beside some fountain. They flee at the sound of a bell or benediction, and their breath is most deadly.

Koshchei. A deity who appears or is referred to in many of James Branch Cabell's novels of medieval POICTESME, notably in JURGEN, where he is responsible for Jurgen's year of youth, given him because he speaks well of the Devil. Koshchei is usually spoken of as "Koshchei the Deathless, who made things as they are."

kosher. A Hebrew word denoting that which is permitted by or fulfills the requirements of the law; applied usually to food—especially to meat which has been slaughtered and prepared in the prescribed manner. See also TREFFA.

Kossuth, Lajos (1802–1894). Hungarian journalist and patriot. Leader of the Hungarian insurrection (1848–1849), made governor with dictatorial powers. Fled to Turkey when the revolution was crushed. Trip to U.S. (1851–1852); resident of Turkey, London, Turin, where he died.

Kotzebue, August Friedrich Ferdinand von (1761–1819). German writer and dramatist in Russian civil service. Quarreled with Goethe and attacked romantic school. Author of over 200 dramatic works. Killed by a university student for ridiculing the *Burschenschaft* movement. His son **Otto von Kotzebue** (1787–1846) commanded the *Rurik* on the Romanzov expedition to Oceania and the Arctic (1815–1818). See also CHAMISSO.

Koussevitzky, Serge Alexandrovitch (1874–). Russian-born conductor of Boston Symphony Orchestra (from 1924). Organized the Berkshire Music Center for symphonic festivals (1934) and the Berkshire Music School (1940).

K. P. Kitchen police; an army abbreviation much in use during World Wars I and II.

Krafft-Ebing, Baron **Richard von** (1840–1902). German neurologist. *Psychopathia Sexualis* (1886; 17th edition, 1924).

Krag-Jörgensen rifle. A Danish-Norwegian breechloading rifle, used with modifications as the standard arm of the U.S. Army (1892–1898), and named for the inventors O. Krag and E. Jörgensen.

Krag the Kootenay Ram. An animal story by Ernest SETON-THOMPSON.

Krakatoa. Volcanic island in Sunda strait, between Java and Sumatra. The waves caused by the eruption of 1883 killed more than 30,000 persons. The consequent atmospheric phenomena were observed over great portions of the globe.

kraken. A fabulous Scandinavian sea monster.

> Then, like a kraken huge and black,
> She crushed our ribs in her iron grasp!
> Longfellow, *The Cumberland.*

Kralitz Bible, see BIBLE, SPECIALLY NAMED.

Krapp, George Philip (1872–1934). American philologist and professor at Columbia University. His comprehensive two-volume *The English Language in America* (1925) was a pioneering work. H. L. MENCKEN said of Krapp's *Pronunciation of Standard English in America* (1919), "no one can henceforth write about American pronunciation without leaning heavily upon Professor Krapp's work."

Krassnoff, Peter Nikolaevich (1869–). Russian monarchist. After failing in his fight against the Bolsheviki he retired to Batum where he wrote a long saga, *From Double Eagle to Red Flag* (English edition, 1926), which has been described as "too emotional to be historically convincing, too vivid to be dull." Other reminiscences, novels and short stories, followed.

Kratim or **Kratimer.** The dog of the seven sleepers, more correctly called KATMIR.

Krazy Kat. An American comic strip, by George Herriman, featuring a cat and his friend Ignatz, a mouse, as leading characters. It was extremely popular during the period of the 1920's and was used as the basis for a ballet by John Alden CARPENTER.

Krehbiel, Henry Edward (1854–1923). American editor of Grove's *Dictionary of Music,* 2d edition (1904–1910). Author of several books and music critic for the New York *Tribune.*

Kreisler, Fritz (1875–). Austrian violin virtuoso and composer. Resident in U.S. (intermittently, from 1915).

Kremlin, the. A gigantic pile of buildings in Moscow, of every style of architecture: Arabesque, Gothic, Greek, Italian, Chinese, etc., enclosed by battlemented and many-towered walls one and one-half miles in circuit. It was built by two Italians, Marco and Pietro Antonio, for Ivan III in 1485 to 1495, but the Great Palace, as well as many other buildings, dates only from the middle of the 19th century.

The name is a French adaptation of Russian *kreml,* a citadel, and other towns beside Moscow possess kremlins, but none on this scale.

The Kremlin is the seat of the Russian government, and the term is often used as a synonym and personification of Soviet rule.

Kreuger, Ivar (1880–1932). Swedish industrialist and financier. Developed an international match monopoly (hence often referred to as the "match king") and various other financial and industrial schemes. The collapse of his organization (1929) led to the discovery of huge irregularities. Committed suicide in Paris.

Kreutzer, Rodolphe (1766–1831). German-French violinist and composer of much varied work. Beethoven dedicated his *Kreutzer Sonata* to him.

Kreymborg, Alfred (1883–). American playwright, poet and critic. An original creator of great versatility; an inspirer of other poets. Has won verse-play prizes, was once professional chess player, and gives entertainments on the "Mandalute." Edited the poetry magazine *Others* and helped edit the *American Caravan.*

kriegspiel. A game with blocks, pins, flags, etc., representing contending forces, guns, etc., moved about according to rules representing conditions in actual warfare. H. G. Wells adapted it as a floor game.

Kriemhild. The legendary heroine of the NIBELUNGENLIED, a woman of unrivaled beauty, sister of GÜNTHER. She first marries SIEGFRIED, and next Etzel (Attila), king of the Huns. Hagen, the Dane, slays her first husband, and seizes all her treasures. In revenge she invites her brothers and Hagen to visit her in Hungary, where they are all slain as a result of the brawl that ensues when Hagen kills Etzel's young son. Kriemhild herself slays first her brother Gunther, in the hope that this will force Hagen to reveal the whereabouts of the hidden hoard. This being unavailing, she strikes off Hagen's head, and is thereupon hewn to pieces by Hildebrand, one of the knights of Dietrich of Bern. Until the death of Siegfried, Kriemhild is depicted as gentle, modest and lovable, but afterwards she becomes a perfect fury. In the VÖLSUNGA SAGA, Kriemhild is known as Gudrun, and in Wagner's operas of the RING DES NIBELUNGEN, as Gutrune.

Krilenko, Nikolai Vasilievich (1886?–1938). Private secretary to Lenin. People's commissar for justice (1922–1938).

Krishna (the black one). One of the greatest of the Hindu deities, the god of fire, lightning, storms, the heavens, and the sun, usually regarded as the eighth AVATAR of Vishnu. One story relates that Kansa, demon-king of Mathura, having committed great ravages, Brahma prayed to Vishnu to relieve the world of its distress; whereupon Vishnu plucked off two hairs, one white and the other black, and promised they should revenge the wrongs of the demon-king. The black hair became Krishna.

Another myth says that Krishna was the son of Vasudeva and Devaki, and when he was born among the Yadavas at Mathura, between Delhi and Agra, his uncle, King Kansa, who had been warned by heaven that this nephew was to slay him, sought to kill Krishna, who was, however, smuggled away. He was brought up by shepherds, and later killed his uncle and became King of the Yadavas in his stead. He was the Apollo of India and the idol of women. His story is told in the Hindu epic, the MAHABHARATA. See also BHAGAVADGITA.

Kriss Kringle. The Pennsylvania Dutch "Santa Claus." On Christmas Eve, arrayed in a fur cap and strange apparel, he goes to the bedroom of all good children, where he leaves a present in the stocking that is hung up in expectation of his visit. The word is a dialectal variant of High German *Christkindle*, "the little Christ child," and has undergone such radical changes because it is no longer associated with either of its component parts.

Kristin Lavransdatter. A trilogy of novels by Sigrid UNDSET, published as a whole in English in 1929 and dealing with the devout Catholic Norway of the 13th and 14th centuries.

Krock, Arthur (1886–). American journalist. Washington correspondent to the New York *Times* (since 1932). Pulitzer prizes for journalism (1935, 1938).

Kröger, Tonio, see TONIO KRÖGER.

Kroll, Leon (1884–). American painter. Murals for U.S. Department of Justice building, Washington, D.C.; also portraits, still-lifes, landscapes, etc.

Kronborg, Thea. The heroine of Willa Cather's SONG OF THE LARK.

Kronos, see CHRONUS.

Krook. In Dickens' BLEAK HOUSE, proprietor of a rag-and-bone warehouse, where everything seems to be bought and nothing sold. He is a grasping drunkard, who eventually dies of spontaneous combustion. Krook is always attended by a large cat as uncanny as her master, which he calls "Lady Jane."

Kropotkin, Prince **Pëtr Alekseevich** (1842–1921). Russian geographer, and social philosopher. Lived in England and Russia. Visited U.S. (1900). Author of works on anarchism, the terror in Russia, and related subjects. His book, *Memoirs of a Revolutionist* (1899), is the English translation of *Paroles d'un Révolté* (1885), originally written in French.

Kruger, Stephanus Johannes Paulus. Known as **Oom Paul** (1825–1904). South African statesman and president for four terms of the Transvaal (1883–1900). In Europe during Boer War (1899–1902), vainly attempting to get European powers to intervene. Died in Switzerland.

Krupkaya, Nadizhola Konstantinova (1869–1939). Russian social worker. A friend of Lenin and of great influence on Soviet youth.

Krupp. A family of German ironmakers, controlling the greatest ordnance works in Germany. The firm was established at Essen (ca. 1810) by Friedrich Krupp (1787–1826). When Alfred Krupp (1812–1887), Friedrich's son, took over, there were three regularly employed workers; when he died the number had risen to 20,000. At the time of the first World War, Bertha Krupp (1886–) and her husband Gustav Krupp von Bohlen und Halbach were in control of the enterprise. Bertha gave her name to the famous BIG BERTHA.

Krutch, Joseph Wood (1893–). American critic and essayist. Author of an important life of Dr. JOHNSON. Member, National Institute of Arts and Letters.

Kshatriya or **Shatriya.** One of the four great castes of Hinduism. See CASTE.

Kubelík, Jan (1880–1940). Czech-Hungarian violinist and composer. Son of a Czech gardener, married to a Hungarian countess. Several visits to U.S. Owner of the famous "Emperor" Stradivarius.

Kubera or **Kuvera.** In Hindu mythology, the god of wealth. In early legends he is lord of the powers of evil. He was the half-brother of Ravana, the demon-king, who drove him from Ceylon.

Kubla Khan. An unfinished poem by COLERIDGE (1797). The poet said that he composed this fragment from a dream, after reading PURCHAS's *Pilgrimage,* a description of Khan Kubla's palace, and wrote it down on awaking. It begins:

> In Xanadu did Kubla Khan
> A stately pleasure dome decree
> Where Alph, the sacred river, ran
> Through caverns measureless to man
> Down to a sunless sea.

The poem is regarded in some respects as a forerunner of both SYMBOLISM and SURREALISM.

Kublai Khan (1216–1294). Mongol emperor of China and founder of the 20th Chinese dynasty. A grandson of Genghis Khan. Visited by MARCO POLO. Humane ruler in peace; successful in war, but his expeditions to Japan and Java bore no fruit.

Kudrun, see GUDRUN.

Ku Klux Klan. A secret society which originated in 1866 in the Southern part of the United States as a move against the carpetbaggers from the North who took control after the Civil War. It attempted to repress the Negroes through acts of terrorism. The old Ku Klux Klan, officially abolished by the "force bill" passed by Congress in 1871, showed no signs of activity for many years; but it was revived in 1915, and on Dec. 4 of that year was incorporated in the State of Georgia as the *Invisible Empire, Knights of the Ku Klux Klan.* Its avowed aims are to maintain pure Americanism and white supremacy; it is accused by its enemies of being violently opposed to Catholics, Jews, and Negroes. The organization played an active part in the 1928 presidential election, when Alfred E. Smith, a Catholic, was the Democratic candidate.

The name is based on Greek *cyclos,* "circle," wilfully corrupted to achieve an alliterative effect and the striking abbreviation *K.K.K.*

kulak. A wealthy Russian peasant. The word is derived from the Lithuanian term for "fist" and is used as an uncomplimentary term implying readiness to exploit the poorer class and unwillingness to cooperate with the government. Under the Soviets, kulaks were liquidated and exiled in great numbers because they were a hindrance to collective farming.

Kultur (*Ger.*). Literally, "culture." In general use in German for civilization as against barbarism. At the time of the first World War, the word was taken over by a number of languages with the sarcastic connotation of the German imperial system of intellectual, moral, aesthetic, economic, and political progress as characterized by the subordination of the individual to the State.

Kulturkampf. In German history, the long and bitter struggle (Ger. *Kampf*) which took place in the last half of the 19th century between Bismarck and the Vatican, with the idea of ensuring the unity of the new Empire and protecting the authority of its government against outside interference. The phrase was coined by Ferdinand LASSALLE in *Demokratische Studien* ii. 505, but it was popularized by Rudolph Virchow, who said that the struggle involved not merely religion but all human culture.

Kumara (the youthful). A name, or, rather, epithet, of the Hindu war-god KARTTIKEYA.

kumiss. Fermented mare's or camel's milk, not unlike sour buttermilk, in common use as a beverage among the nomads of northern Asia. Some tribes distill from it an intoxicating drink which is known by the same name.

Kummer, Clare. American playwright who first made a hit with the popular song *Dearie.* Wrote popular comedies, as *Good Gracious Annabelle* (1916); etc.

Kun, Béla (1885–). Hungarian journalist and leader of the Communist revolution. His reign of terror (1919) was terminated by a successful counter-revolution. Fled to Russia.

Kundry. In Wagner's opera PARSIFAL, an enchantress who, at the instigation of Klingsor, tempts Amfortas into the sin that brings on his terrible wound.

Kunigunde. The Lady of Kynast, a German castle built over an abyss. She vowed to marry no one who would not ride around the edge of the steep battlements and saw one aspirant after another perish. Finally an unknown knight accomplished the feat and won her heart, but scorned her for her cruelty and rode away. This legend is the subject of two famous German poems by Theodor Körner and Friedrich Rückert.

The name *Kunigunde* is sometimes given to the equally cold-hearted lady love of DE LORGE who threw her glove to the lions to test her lover's devotion. Cf. Schiller's poem, *Der Handschuh.*

Kunz, George Frederick (1856–1930). American expert and writer on gems.

Kuomintang. The three parts of this Chinese term stand for *nationalist, people,* and *party.* The Kuomintang is the republican party that was organized chiefly by Dr. Sun Yat-sen and gained control of most of China in 1926–1927. Opposed by the communists.

Kuprin, Aleksandr Ivanovich (1870–1938). Russian anti-Bolshevik author in exile. Satirical realist in short stories and full-length books. *The Duel* (1905) is his most famous novel. *Yama* (1915), an analysis of the lot of prostitutes in Czarist Russia, was primarily a *succès de scandale.*

Kurma, see under AVATAR.

Kuropatkin, Aleksei Nikolaevich (1848–1921). Russian general. Supreme commander of Russia's Far Eastern forces (1904) but opposed to war with Japan. Defeated at Mukden (1905). Author of a book on the Russo-Japanese war.

Kursaal (*Ger.*). A public hall for visitors at a watering place. Center of social activities with café, bandstand, etc.

Kuru. A noted legendary hero of India, the contests of whose descendants form the subject of the Hindu epic the MAHABHARATA. He was a prince of the lunar race, reigning over the country round Delhi.

Kurusu, Saburo (1888–). Japanese diplomat. Special envoy to U.S. (Nov.–Dec., 1941) during negotiations cut short by attack on Pearl Harbor.

Kuvera, see KUBERA.

Kuyumjian, Dikran, see ARLEN, MICHAEL.

Kwasind. In Longfellow's HIAWATHA, the strongest man that ever lived, the Hercules of the North American Indians. The only weapon which could injure him was the "blue cone of the fir tree," a secret known only to the pygmies or Little-folk. This mischievous race, out of jealousy, determined to kill the strong man, and one day, finding him asleep in a boat, pelted him with fir cones till he died; and now, whenever the tempest rages through the forests, and the branches of the trees creak and groan and split, they say, "Kwasind is gathering in his fire-wood."

> Dear, too, unto Hiawatha
> Was the very strong man Kwasind;
> He the strongest of all mortals.
>
> Longfellow, *Hiawatha,* xv. and xviii

Kyd, Thomas (1557?–?1595). English playwright of the Elizabethan period, one of the "UNIVERSITY WITS." He was extremely well-known in his time and was the author of THE SPANISH TRAGEDY (1594) and *Pompey the Great* (1595). *The Tragedy of Solyman and Perseda* (1599) has also been attributed to him, as has been a lost play on HAMLET written before Shakespeare's version.

Kyffhäuser. A hill in Thuringia in the Harz Mountains, one of the supposed sites of the legendary sleep of Frederick BARBAROSSA. See also BERCHTESGADEN.

Kynast, The Lady of. KUNIGUNDE.

Kyne, Peter Bernard (1880–). American writer of popular fiction. Captain of field artillery in World War I. Created the character of *Cappy Ricks* (1916).

Kyoto. Japanese city on Honshu Island. Capital of the empire for nearly eleven centuries (until 1869). Among its historic buildings is the imperial palace, the Nije Castle, a 13th-century Buddhist temple, etc. It is the locale of the famous annual Cherry Dance.

Kyrie Eleison (*Gr.,* "Lord have mercy"). The short petition used in the liturgies of the Eastern and Western Churches, as a response at the beginning of the Roman Mass and in the Anglican Communion Service; also, the musical setting for this.

Kyushu. One of the five large islands of Japan. Mountainous and volcanic and south of the main island of Honshu. Nagasaki is the chief port.

L

Laban. In the Old Testament, the uncle of JACOB, father of Leah and Rachel. Jacob served him for fourteen years for his two daughters.

labarum. The standard borne before the Roman emperors. It consisted of a gilded spear, with an eagle on the top, while from a cross-staff hung a splendid purple streamer, with a gold fringe, adorned with precious stones. Constantine substituted a crown for the eagle, and inscribed in the midst the mysterious monogram. See CROSS.

labdanum. A dark oleoresin of fragrant smell and bitter taste, derived from the Cistus or rockrose.

> Heap Cassia, Sandal-buds and stripes
> Of labdanum, and aloe-balls.
>
> Browning, song in *Paracelsus,* iv.

Labe, Queen. The Circe of the Arabians, who, by her enchantments, transformed men into horses and other brute beasts. She is introduced into the *Arabian Nights' Entertainments,* where Beder, a prince of Persia, marries her, defeats her plots against him, and turns her into a mare. Being restored to her proper shape by her mother, she turns Beder into an owl, but the Prince ultimately regains his own proper form.

La Belle Dame Sans Merci. See under BELLE.

Labor, American Federation of, see AMERICAN FEDERATION OF LABOR.

Labor Day. A legal holiday set aside in honor of the working class. In many European countries and in the Philippines, it is May 1. In most of the states of the U.S.A., the first Monday in September is celebrated as Labor Day. The custom dates back to about 1882. Colorado was the first state to give it legal force (1887).

labor legislation. Laws designed to regulate employment conditions and safeguard the standard of living of the working class. Labor legislation had its origin in the necessity of enacting laws to regulate the employment of women and children, who were not *sui juris.* It soon extended its scope to safeguard the labor of persons in dangerous occupations, etc., and finally to cover the problems of trade unions and collective bargaining. In the period after the Civil War, liberal State labor legislation was often ruled by the courts to be unconstitutional. In more recent years most of the states managed to adopt laws on industrial compensation, old-age pension, regulation of hours, etc. The power of the federal government to enact labor laws is fairly well established under its power to regulate interstate commerce. Pertinent provisions are contained in the National Industrial Recovery Act (1933) and the Social Security Act (1935). The National Labor Relations Act (Wagner Act; 1935), which created the National Labor Relations Board, was in its day the most advanced form of labor legislation in the United States.

labors of Hercules. See under HERCULES.

Labouchère, Henry du Pré (1831–1912). British journalist and liberal political leader. Gained reputation during the Franco-Prussian war by his *Diary of a Besieged Resident in Paris* (1871). Edited *Truth,* a weekly journal dedicated to the exposure of corruption and sham. As M.P. he inquired courageously into the unsavory affair of the JAMESON RAID. Advocated abolition of the House of Lords, home rule for Ireland, etc. His nickname was "Labby."

La Bruyère, Jean de (1645–1696). French author of the neo-classical period, known for his misanthropy, conservativism, social criticism and satire, as revealed in his most famous work, *Les Caractères* (1688). This is a collection of maxims and character portraits of French social types and individuals of his day, in the manner of THEOPHRASTUS. See CHARACTER WRITERS. It attacks particularly aristocrats, fortune-hunters, and religious heretics.

labyrinth. A Greek word of unknown (but probably Egyptian) origin, denoting a mass of buildings or garden walks, so complicated as to puzzle strangers who are trying to extricate themselves; a maze. The chief labyrinths of antiquity are:

(1) The Egyptian, by Petesuchis or Tithoes, near the Lake Moeris. It had 3,000 apartments, half of which were underground. (1800 B. C.) Pliny, xxxvi, 13; and *Pomponius Mela,* i, 9.

(2) The Cretan, by Daedalus, for imprisoning the Minotaur. The only means of finding a way out of it was by help of a skein of thread. Cf. Virgil, *Aeneid,* v.

(3) The Cretan conduit, which had 1,000 branches or turnings.

(4) The Lemnian, by the architects Smilis, Rholus, and Theodorus. It had 150 columns, so nicely adjusted that a child could turn them. Vestiges of this labyrinth were still in existence in the time of Pliny.

(5) The labyrinth of Clusium, made by Lars Porsena, King of Etruria, for his tomb.

(6) The Samian, by Theodorus (540 B. C.). This is referred to by Pliny; by Herodotus, ii. 145; by Strabo, x; and by Diodorus Siculus, i.

(7) The labyrinth at Woodstock, built by Henry II to protect the Fair Rosamund.

Labyrinthine Ways, The. Title of the first American edition of *The Power and the Glory* (1940) by Graham GREENE. Taken from the poem *The Hound of Heaven* by Francis Thompson:

> I fled Him, down the labyrinthine ways
> Of my own mind.

La Calprenède, Gautier de Costes de (1609–1663). French dramatist and novelist, best known for his historical romances. Outstanding among these are: *Cassandre* (1642–1645), in 10 volumes; *Cléopatre* (1646), twelve volumes; and PHARAMOND, OU L'HISTOIRE DE FRANCE (1661–1663), also in twelve volumes. La Calprenède's romances were very popular in his day and were read in England until the time of RICHARDSON and FIELDING. They are marked by long and complicated plots, full and detailed descriptions, "literary portraits," and frequent Oriental backgrounds.

Lacedaemon. An ancient name of Laconia, also of Sparta, its chief city.

> In lordly Lacedaemon,
> The city of two Kings.
> Macaulay, *The Battle of Lake Regillus.*

La Chaise, François d'Aix de (1624–1709). French Jesuit confessor to Louis XIV. His favorite retreat near Paris became later (1806) the site of a famous cemetery, known as the *cimetière du Père Lachaise.*

Lachesis. The Fate who spins life's thread, working into the woof the events destined to occur. See FATES.

Lachryma Christi. A rich Neapolitan wine. The term means "tear of Christ" and is as little sacrilegious as the name of the Rhine wine *Liebfrauenmilch,* "milk of our Lady, the Virgin Mary"; it is rather evidence of a more naïve and robust spirit of worship of past ages.

Lackaye, Wilton (1862–1932). American actor. Best known for his interpretations of Svengali in *Trilby* and Curtis Jadwine in *The Pit.*

Lackland. Nickname for John, King of England (1167?–1199–1216).

Lack-learning Parliament, see under PARLIAMENTS.

Laconian, Laconic. Pertaining to Laconia or its main city, Sparta. Hence *laconic* (but never *laconian*), "sparing of words," as the Spartans were reputed to be.

Lacretelle, Jacques de (1888–). French novelist. Became famous for *Silbermann* (1923), a story of the persecution of a Jewish boy by his Catholic fellow-students in a Paris lycée. *A Man's Life* (1929) is a profound psychological study which won the Grand Prix of the French Academy. *Les Hauts-Points,* a detailed history of a family through half a century (successive volumes since 1932), is perhaps more ambitious in scope than Proust's *Remembrance of Things Past.*

lacrosse. A game of ball, originated by North American Indians, popular in Canada and, spreading from there, throughout the English-speaking world. It may be described as a kind of hockey which is played with a long-handled racket, the so-called *crosse* (*Fr.,* literally "crozier"). Hence the name.

Lacy, Ernest (1863–1916). American poet, dramatist, and authority on Chatterton. He wrote a poetic drama about Chatterton, *The Bard of Mary Redcliffe,* which was never performed but which Christian Gauss, dean of Princeton, has called "the greatest poetic drama written in the United States." His drama *Chatterton* was staged by Julia Marlowe.

Lacy, Sir Hugo de. One of the chief characters of Scott's novel, THE BETROTHED, constable of Chester, a Crusader.

Sir Damian de Lacy. Nephew of Sir Hugo. He marries Lady Eveline.

Randal de Lacy. Sir Hugo's cousin, introduced in several disguises, as a merchant, a hawk-seller, and a robber-captain.

Ladd, George Trumbull (1842–1921). American professor of philosophy at Bowdoin and Yale. Pioneer in experimental psychology. His books include *Philosophy of Mind* (1895) and *Knowledge, Life and Reality* (1909).

Ladislaw, Will. In George Eliot's MIDDLEMARCH the gay, lovable Bohemian whom Dorothea Brooke marries after Rev. Mr. Casaubon's death. He becomes the editor of a Middlemarch newspaper.

Ladon. The name of the dragon which guarded the apples of the HESPERIDES; also, of one of the dogs of Actaeon.

Ladrone Islands. Marianas. From Spanish *ladrón,* "thief, robber." The *Ladrone Islands* were discovered by Magellan (1521) and so called by him because their inhabitants had stolen from him.

Ladurlad. In Southey's *Curse of Kehama* (see KEHAMA), the father of KAILYAL. He kills Arvalan for attempting to dishonor his daughter, and thereby incurs the "curse of Kehama" (Arvalan's father). The curse is that water shall not wet him or fire consume him, that sleep shall not visit him or death release him, etc. After enduring a time of agony, these curses turn to blessings.

Lady Bountiful. The benevolent lady of a village is so called, from *Lady Bountiful* in THE BEAUX' STRATAGEM, by Farquhar.

Lady chapel. A chapel (in a church) dedicated to the Virgin Mary.

Lady Chatterley's Lover. A famous novel by D. H. LAWRENCE (1928), presenting the author's mystical theories of sex in the story of the wife of an English aristocrat who falls in love with her lodge-keeper and runs away with him. Because of the frankness of language and situation in the book, it was banned in England and America as obscene and thereby won a notorious reputation and a sizable illegal circulation. See also Theodore

DREISER; JURGEN; ULYSSES; THE WELL OF LONELINESS.

Lady from the Sea, The. A drama by Henrik IBSEN (1888), portraying the struggle in the titular heroine, Ellida, between wholesome love for her husband, Dr. Wrangel, and an unhealthy hypnotic infatuation for a strange seaman to whom she had once been engaged and to whose renewed appeals she all but yields. Her husband wins her by his understanding sympathy.

Lady of Babylon or **Lady of Rome.** The Roman Catholic Church, with reference to the scarlet woman described in Revelation.

Lady of Lyons, The. A romantic comedy by BULWER-LYTTON (1838) with the subtitle, *Love and Pride.*

Lady of Shalott, the. A maiden of the Arthurian legends, who falls in love with Sir LAUNCELOT of the Lake, and dies because her love is not returned. TENNYSON wrote a poem on the subject, and the story of ELAINE, "the lily maid of Astolat," is substantially the same.

Lady of the Aroostook, The. A novel by W. D. HOWELLS (1879). The position of the New England heroine, Lydia Blood, as the only feminine passenger to make the trip to Venice on board the freighter Aroostook, gives rise to criticism and gossip, but Lydia bears herself with charming propriety and ends by marrying Staniford, who had been one of the most horrified of her fellow passengers.

Lady of the Lake, The. (1) In the Arthurian legends, Nimuë or VIVIAN, the mistress of Merlin. She lives in the midst of an imaginary lake which apparently prevents access to her, surrounded by knights and damsels. She steals Launcelot in his infancy, and plunges with him into her home lake; hence Launcelot comes to be called *du Lac.* When her *protégé* has grown to manhood, she presents him to King Arthur. It was she who gives Arthur the famous sword EXCALIBUR. James Branch CABELL introduces her into his *Jurgen* as ANAÏTIS. See MORGAN LE FAY.

(2) In Scott's poem of this name (1810), Ellen Douglas, who lives with her father near Loch Katrine.

Lady of the Lamp, see Florence NIGHTINGALE.

Lady or the Tiger, The. A short story by Frank R. Stockton (*Am.,* 1882) much admired for its clever ending which does not solve but only proposes the puzzle of the story. A youth so bold as to love the King's daughter is condemned to open one of two doors. Behind one is a fascinating girl whom he must marry, behind the other a tiger. The King's daughter learns the secret and signals her lover to open one of the two doors—but which?

Lady Teazle, see TEAZLE, LADY.

Lady Windermere's Fan. A drama by Oscar WILDE (1892). Annoyed at her husband's persistent interest in Mrs. Erlynne, a woman of little reputation, Lady Windermere decides to leave him and run away with her lover, Lord Darlington. Mrs. Erlynne, who is in reality Lady Windermere's mother, supposed by her to be dead, finds the note left for Windermere and follows her daughter to Darlington's apartments. When Lord Darlington, Lord Windermere and others come in from the club, Lady Windermere yields to Mrs. Erlynne's persuasions and escapes unnoticed. She has, however, left her fan, and only Mrs. Erlynne's quick-witted and generous assumption of guilt and explanation that she took the fan by mistake, saves her daughter's reputation at the cost of her own. She succeeds nevertheless in her scheme of marrying Lord Augustus Lawton and departs for the Continent.

Laelaps. In classical mythology, the powerful dog given by Diana to Procris who gave it to CEPHALUS. While pursuing a wild boar it was metamorphosed into a stone. The name, which was originally that of one of Actaeon's fifty dogs, means "the hurricane."

Laelius. See under DE AMICITIA.

Laemmle, Carl (1867–1939). German-born American motion-picture producer. Organized and headed Universal Pictures Corporation (until 1936).

Laertes. In Shakespeare's HAMLET, son of POLONIUS, and brother of Ophelia. He is induced by the king to challenge Hamlet to a "friendly" duel, but poisons his rapier. Laertes wounds Hamlet, and in the scuffle which ensues, the combatants change swords, and Hamlet wounds Laertes, so that both die.

La Farge, Christopher (1897–). Brother of Oliver H. P. LA FARGE and son of Christopher Grant La Farge (1862–1938), architect. American poet; author of *Hoxsie Sells his Acres* (a novel in verse; 1934); *Each to the Other* (a novel in verse; 1939); *Poems and Portraits* (1940); etc. President, Authors' Guild. Prose novels include *The Wilsons* (1941), and *The Sudden Guest* (1946).

La Farge, John (1835–1910). American artist. Mural decoration of Trinity Church, Boston; panels in St. Thomas' Church, New York City; *The Ascension* in the Church of the Ascension, New York City; etc. Developed opalescent glass. Specimens of his work in stained glass in Memorial Hall, Harvard, and several churches. Member, American Academy of Arts and Letters.

La Farge, Oliver Hazard Perry (1901–). American anthropologist and novelist, best known for his works of fiction dealing with the American Indians. His novels include: *Laughing Boy* (1929), a novel dealing with Navajo Indian life, winner of the Pulitzer Prize in 1930; *The Sparks Fly Upward* (1931); *Long Pennant* (1933); *The Enemy Gods* (1937). *All the Young Men* (1935) is a collection of short stories, and other works are *Tribes and Temples* (1925, 1927), a book on archaeology in Arizona, Mexico, and Central America, and *As Long as the Grass Shall Grow* (1940), a study of the American Indian. *Raw Material* (1945), is his autobiography. La Farge's grandfather was JOHN LA FARGE.

Lafayette, Marquis **de. Marie Joseph Paul Yves Roch Gilbert du Motier** (1757–1834). French statesman and general. In American service during Revolutionary War (1777–1781), partly on furlough in France (1778–1780) to further the American cause. Revisited U.S. (1784; 1824–1825). Active in French politics. Advocated moderation during Revolution and was forced to flee to Flanders (1792). Back in France (1799), he kept aloof from public affairs till the time of Napoleon's fall. During the Revolution of 1830, he was the Commander of the National Guard.

Lafayette Escadrille. In World War I, prior to American participation, a unit of French aviation consisting entirely of American volunteers. Named in memory of the services performed by the Marquis de LAFAYETTE for the American colonies. The squadron first raised the American flag on the Western front in April, 1917. Thirty German aircraft were shot down before it became part of the U.S. Aviation Service. A similar formation in World War II was the American Eagle Squadron.

Lafeu. In Shakespeare's ALL'S WELL THAT ENDS WELL, an old French lord, sent to conduct Bertram, Count of Rousillon, to the King of France, by whom he is invited to the royal court.

Lafitte, Jean (1780–1826). American pirate and smuggler born in France; known as "the pirate of the gulf." Plundered commerce off the coast of Louisiana. Offered services to Andrew Jackson and commanded detachment at Battle of New Orleans (1815). Pardoned by President Madison.

La Follette, Robert Marion (1855–1925). American liberal statesman Governor of Wisconsin (1900–1906); U.S. Senator (1906–1925). Supported Wilson's reform measures; tried to keep America out of the first World War and opposed American participation in League of Nations and World Court. Fought deflation, domination of big business. Ran for President (1924) on a Progressive ticket and received five million votes. *Autobiography* (1912); *Political Philosophy* (collected writings; 1920). His sons, **Robert Marion La Follette, Jr.** (1895–), succeeding his father as U.S. senator, and **Philip Fox La Follette** (1897–), governor of Wisconsin (1931, 1935, 1937), have continued his liberal policies.

La Fontaine, Jean de (1621–1695). French poet and prose-writer, an associate of BOILEAU, RACINE, and MOLIÈRE, known for his skill at story-telling. His *Fables* (1668–1680), in 18 books, is his most famous work, consisting of animal fables in the tradition of AESOP and the medieval "BEAST EPIC" presented with humor, grace, and satire, and a colorful, flexible verse style. Other works of La Fontaine include *Nouvelles en Vers* (1665), containing a translation of part of Ariosto's ORLANDO FURIOSO and a tale by BOCCACCIO, and *Contes et Nouvelles.* La Fontaine was by nature a vagaband, a dreamer, and a lover of pleasure. He drifted from one patron to another, in the last 20 years of his career choosing only women of the aristocracy.

the Danish Lafontaine. Hans Christian ANDERSEN.

Laforgue, Jules (1860–1887). French symbolist (see SYMBOLISM) poet, with Gustave KAHN considered to have "invented" FREE VERSE in the form in which it came to be best known in the 20th century. Among his outstanding poetry, included in *Oeuvres Complètes* (1902–1903), are *Le Sanglot de la terre, Les Complaintes, L'Imitation de Notre-Dame la Lune, Le Concile féerique. Moralités Legendaires* (1897–1898) consists of tales of Hamlet, Lohengrin, Salome, etc. Laforgue was one of the poets exerting important influence with regard to form, rhythm, subject-matter, and attitude on the early poetry of T. S. ELIOT.

Lagado. In Swift's *Gulliver's Travels* (see GULLIVER, LEMUEL), the capital of BALNIBARBI celebrated for its grand academy of projectors, where the scholars spend their time in such useful projects as making pincushions from softened rocks, extracting sunbeams from cucumbers, and converting ice into gunpowder.

Lagerlöf, Selma (1858–1940). Swedish novelist and short-story writer, known for her romantic tales dealing chiefly with her native land. Among these are: *The Story of Gösta Berling* (see GÖSTA BERLING) (1894); *The Miracles of Antichrist* (1897); *Jerusalem* (1901); *The Emperor of Portugallia* (1914); *Bannlyst* (1918); *Mårbacka* (1922), an account of her family and her home; *Charlotte Löwensköld* (1925); *Anna Svärd* (1928); *A Child's Memoirs* (1930), continuing *Mårbacka; Harvest* (1935), legends, sketches, recollections, etc.; *The Diary of Selma Lagerlöf* (1936). Collections of short stories include: *Invisible Links* (1894); *From a Swedish Homestead* (1899);

The Adventures of Nils (1906–1907); *The Girl from the Marsh Croft* (1908); *Men and Trolls* (1916). In 1909 Selma Lagerlöf won the Nobel Prize for literature, the first woman to do so.

lagniappe. In Louisiana, a gratuity given to customers by tradesmen. Mark Twain uses the form "lanny-yap." The word is a Creole assimilation of Spanish *ñapa* or *yapa,* "tip."

La Grande Chartreuse. Until 1903, chief house of the Carthusians in the mountains near Grenoble, France. It was founded by St. Bruno about 1084. See also CHARTREUSE.

La Grange. A character in Molière's PRÉCIEUSES RIDICULES. He and his friend Du Croisy pay their addresses to two young ladies whose heads have been turned by novels.

Lagrange, Joseph Louis (1736–1813). Famous mathematician. Born in Italy of French ancestry, he became the director of the Berlin Academy of Sciences (1766–1786), settled in Paris (1787) and was made senator and count by Napoleon I. At the age of eighteen he was professor of mathematics at Turin and later organized a society which became the Turin Academy of Sciences.

La Guardia, Fiorello H. (1882–1947). American politician, Mayor of New York City (1934–1946). Chief, U.S. Office of Civilian Defense (1941–1942) and United Nations Rehabilitation and Reconstruction Administration (1945).

La Hogue, Battle of. Naval operations of the English and Dutch fleets against the French off the coast of Normandy (May 19 to 23, 1692), from where Louis XIV attempted to invade England.

lai. A short tale of the Middle Ages as written by MARIE DE FRANCE, utilizing the material of the romances but presenting only one incident or the concise development of a single motif of folk-lore. The name of the form is said to have been taken from the songs (Irish *lôid* or *laid*) to the accompaniment of which Breton minstrels told the stories which were the source of many of Marie's works.

L'Aiglon. Title of a play by Edmond ROSTAND (1900). *L'Aiglon,* that is, the eaglet, is Napoleon's son, the Duke of Reichstadt.

Laing, Alexander Kinnan (1903–). American poet. Graduate of Dartmouth; assistant librarian at Dartmouth (since 1937). *Fools' Errand* (1928) and the discourse on poetry, *Wine and Physic* (1934). Also author and editor of horror and sea stories.

Laird's Jock, Death of the. A tale by Sir Walter SCOTT (1827). The "Laird's Jock" is John Armstrong, the laird of Mangerton. This old warrior, who has been the champion of the Border counties, witnesses a combat between his son and the English champion Foster in which his son is overthrown, and the shock of humiliation causes his death.

Laïs. A courtesan, from the name of two celebrated Greek courtesans. The earlier was the most beautiful woman of Corinth, and lived at the time of the Peloponnesian War. The beauty of Laïs the Second so excited the jealousy of the Thessalonian women that they pricked her to death with their bodkins. She was the contemporary and rival of Phryne and sat to Apelles as a model. Demosthenes tells us that Laïs sold her favors for 10,000 (Attic) drachmae, and adds *tanti non emo poenitere.* (Horace, 1 *Epis.* xvii. l. 36.)

laissez faire (*Fr.,* "let do," that is, "let people and things alone"). The principle of *laissez faire* allows problems to work themselves out without planning and regulations. It is, specifically, the principle of non-interference by Government in commercial affairs. The phrase comes from the motto of the mid-18th century "PHYSIOCRATIC" school of French economists, *Laissez faire, laissez passer* (let do, let pass), who wished to have all customs duties abolished, demanded free circulation for their goods, thus anticipating the later Freetraders. Its authorship is generally credited to Jean Claude Marie Vincent de Gournay (1712–1759). Adam SMITH took *laissez-faire* theories to England, from where they later spread to the U.S. As embodied in the writings of Smith, the principle became one of the bulwarks of capitalist economics.

Lajeunesse, Gabriel. The lover of EVANGELINE in Longfellow's poem of that name.

Lajoie, Napoleon. Known as **Larry** (1875–). Famous American professional baseball player.

Lakamba. The native rajah of Sambir in Conrad's OUTCAST OF THE ISLANDS.

Lake, Simon (1866–). American naval engineer. Builder of the *Argonaut* (1897), the first sea-worthy submarine. Originator of the even-keel principle for submarines and inventor of underwater devices for the location of sunken vessels.

Lake School, the. The name applied in derision by the *Edinburgh Review* to WORDSWORTH, COLERIDGE, and SOUTHEY, who resided in the Lake District of Cumberland and Westmoreland and sought inspiration in the simplicity of nature, and to the poets who followed them.

Charles LAMB, LLOYD, and "Christopher NORTH" are sometimes placed among the *Lake Poets* or *Lakers.*

Lake State. Michigan. See under STATES.

Lakmé. A romantic opera (1883) by the French composer Léo Delibes (1836–1891). The libretto by Gondinet and Gille is based on

THE MARRIAGE OF LOTI and is Oriental in character.

Laksmi or **Lakshmi.** One of the consorts of the Hindu god Vishnu, and mother of KAMA. She is goddess of beauty, wealth and pleasure, and the *Ramayana* describes her as springing, like Venus, from the foam of the sea.

Lalique, René (1860–). French jeweler and glassmaker; manufactured fine but inexpensive glass objects. Lalique glass is decorative, ornamented with flowers, birds, or animals in relief.

Lalla Rookh (tulip cheek). In Thomas Moore's poem of that name (1817), the supposed daughter of Aurungzebe, emperor of Delhi, betrothed to Aliris, Sultan of Lesser Bucharia. On her journey from Delhi to the valley of Cashmere, she is entertained by the young Persian poet Feramorz, who relates the four tales of the romance, and with whom she falls in love. Unbounded is her delight when she discovers that the young poet is the sultan to whom she was betrothed.

The four tales are:

(1) The Veiled Prophet of Khorassan. See under VEILED; MOKANNA.

(2) Paradise and the Peri. See PERI.

(3) The Fire Worshippers. See HAFED.

(4) The Light of the Harem. See NOURMAHAL.

L'Allegro. Literally, the cheerful or merry one. A poem written by John Milton in 1632. It is a pastoral idyl, celebrating a mood of gaiety and contrasting with the author's IL PENSEROSO.

Lalou, René (1889–). French essayist and critic. *La Littérature Française Contemporaine* (1922) is his most important book available in English (*Contemporary French Literature*). He has also interpreted the leading modern writers of the English-speaking world to his countrymen.

Lama, see RULERS, TITLES OF.

La Mancha, The Knight of. Don Quixote de la Mancha, the hero of Cervantes' romance DON QUIXOTE. La Mancha, an old province of Spain, is now a part of Ciudad Real.

Lamarck, Chevalier **de. Jean Baptiste Pierre Antoine de Monet** (1744–1829). French naturalist. Advocate of views on organic evolution which are sometimes (mistakenly) interpreted as representing a preparatory stage of Darwinism. Lamarck held (positively) that an organism reacts to a new or changing environment by fitting developments and not (negatively), as Darwin did, that a new or changing environment permits the survival of the accidentally fittest. Lamarck was connected with the Jardin du Roi and was instrumental in changing its name to Jardin des Plantes. He introduced new principles in the classification of animals and originated the terms vertebrate and invertebrate.

Lamartine, Alphonse de (1790–1869). French poet and statesman of the Romantic period. (See *Romanticism.*) His work is marked by a preoccupation with nature, religion, and love, subjectively presented, and is regarded as the first truly romantic poetry in French literature. Among his books are *Les Premières méditations* (1820); *Les Nouvelles méditations* (1823); *Les Harmonies poétiques et religieuses* (1830); *Jocelyn* (1836), a narrative poem dealing with a priest's love; *La Chute d'un ange* (1838). Lamartine was liberal, tending toward radical, in his political beliefs and, after serving as a deputy for several years and distinguishing himself as an orator, he was a leader in the Revolution of 1848. He became Minister of Foreign Affairs and in many ways was virtually the chief of the Provisional Government, but his power was lost when Louis Napoléon made his famous *coup d'état.* Lamartine died in poverty and obscurity.

lamasery. A Buddhist monastery (or convent) presided over by a lama, corresponding to a Christian abbot.

Lamassu. In Babylonian religion, one of a race of semi-divine beings. The Lamassus were visualized as colossal bulls or lions with human heads. Statues of them flanked the entrances of palaces and public buildings.

lamb. In Christian art, an emblem of the Redeemer, in allusion to *John* i, 29, "Behold the Lamb of God, which taketh away the sin of the world."

It is also the attribute of ST. AGNES, ST. GENEVIÈVE, ST. CATHERINE, and ST. REGINA. JOHN THE BAPTIST either carries a lamb or is accompanied by one. It is introduced symbolically to represent any of the "types" of Christ, as Abraham, Moses, and so on.

Lamb, Lady **Caroline** (1785–1828). English novelist. Married William Lamb (later 2nd Viscount Melbourne), from whom she was separated twenty years later (1825). Her nine-months' intrigue (1813) with Lord Byron is notorious. Her anonymous novel, *Glenarvon* (1816; republished, 1865), contains a caricature of her erstwhile lover.

Lamb, Charles (1775–1834). English essayist of the Romantic period, a schoolmate of COLERIDGE and a friend of the other figures of English romanticism as well. Although he attempted work in the field of the drama and poetry, he was most successful in the personal essay. His writings in this form are known for their humor, whimsy, and faint overtones of pathos. They are contained in the two series entitled *Essays of Elia,* which appeared in *The London Magazine* from 1820 to 1823 and from 1824 to 1825, being collected and published in 1823 and 1833, respectively. Outstanding single essays are: *A Dissertation upon Roast Pig, A Chapter on Ears, Mrs. Battle's Opinions on Whist, Dream-Children,* and *The Superannuated Man.* Other works of Lamb are *The Tale of Rosamund Gray and Old Blind Margaret* (1798), a prose narrative; *John Woodvil* (1802), a dramatic tragedy; *Tales from Shakespeare* (1807), adaptations for children written in collaboration with his sister, Mary Lamb; *The Adventures of Ulysses* (1808), another book for children; *Specimens of English Dramatic Poets Contemporary with Shakespeare* (1808); *Album Verses* (1830), poetry.

Lamb's personal life was marked by frustration and sorrow. Because of a stammer, he was unable to take an examination at his preparatory school to qualify for a university, and so went to work as an accountant for the East India Tea House, where he stayed until 1825. There was a strain of insanity in the family, and Lamb's sister, whom he took care of, had several attacks of madness, during one of which she killed her mother; Lamb himself stayed for a while in a sanatorium.

Lamb, Harold (1892–). American writer of historical studies and biographies including *Genghis Khan* (1927); *Tamerlane* (1928); *The Crusades* (2 vols.; 1930); *The March of the Barbarians* (1940); etc.

Lamber, Juliette, see ADAM, JULIETTE.

Lambeth Palace. The official city residence in London (Lambeth) of the archbishops of Canterbury. It was acquired in 1197, but the oldest parts of the present building do not date back beyond the 13th century.

Lambro. In Byron's DON JUAN, a Greek pirate, father of HAIDÉE. The original of this character was Major Lambro, who was captain (1791) of a Russian piratical squadron, which plundered the islands of the Greek Archipelago and did great damage.

Lamech. In the Old Testament, one of the men of pre-diluvian days.

Lamech's song. "Ye wives of Lamech, hearken unto my speech: for I have slain a man to my wounding, and a young man to my hurt! If Cain shall be avenged sevenfold, truly Lamech seventy and sevenfold."—*Gen.* iv. 23, 24.

> As Lemech grew old, his eyes became dim, and finally all sight was taken from them, and Tubal-cain, his son, led him by the hand when he walked abroad. And it came to pass . . . that he led his father into the fields to hunt, and said to his father: "Lo! yonder is a beast of prey; shoot thine arrow in that direction." Lemech did as his son had spoken, and the arrow struck Cain, who was walking afar off, and killed him. . . . Now when Lemech . . . saw [sic] that he had killed Cain, he trembled exceedingly, . . . and being blind, he saw not his son, but struck the lad's head between his hands, and killed him. . . . And he cried to his wives, Ada and Zillah, "Listen to my voice, ye wives of Lemech. . . . I have slain a man to my hurt, and a child to my wounding!"—*The Talmud,* i.

lame duck. (1) In U.S. political cant, an officeholder who has failed of re-election and therefore cannot bring himself to more than half-hearted interest in his work. Before the adoption of the Twentieth Amendment to the U.S. Constitution (lame-duck amendment; February 6, 1933), congressional terms began on March 4 (not, as afterwards, on January 3). Thus there was a session of Congress between election day and the beginning of the new term, and this was known as the Lame Duck Session.

(2) A stock jobber who will not, or cannot, pay his losses. Also anyone who is unable to discharge his obligations or play his part in the world.

Lamentations of Jeremiah, The. The twenty-fifth book of the Old Testament.

Lamerock or Lamoracke, Sir. In Arthurian romance, one of the knights of the Round Table, son of Sir Pellinore, and brother of Sir PERCIVAL. He had an amour with his own aunt, the wife of King Lot.

lamia. A female phantom, whose name was used by the Greeks and Romans as a bugbear to children. She was a Libyan queen beloved by Jupiter, but robbed of her offspring by the jealous Juno. In consequence she vowed vengeance against all children, whom she delighted to entice and devour.

Witches in the Middle Ages were called *lamioe,* and Keats' poem *Lamia* (1820), which relates how a bride when recognized returns to her original serpent form, represents one of the many superstitions connected with the race. Keats' story came (through BURTON) from Philostratus' *De Vita Apollonii,* Bk. iv. In Burton's rendering, the sage Apollonius, on the wedding night—

> found her out to be a serpent, a lamia . . . When she saw herself descried, she wept, and desired Apollonius to be silent, but he would not be moved, and thereupon she, plate, house, and all that was in it, vanished in an instant; many thousands took notice of this fact, for it was done in the midst of Greece. —*Anatomy of Melancholy,* Pt. iii. sect. ii, memb. i, subsect. i.

laminak. Basque fairies, little folk, who live under ground, and sometimes come into houses down the chimney, in order to change a fairy child for a human one. They bring good luck with them, but insist on great cleanliness, and always give their orders in words the very opposite of their intention. They hate church-bells. Every Basque laminak is named Guillen (William).

Lammas. The elements of the word are "loaf" and "mass." Lammas Day was formerly a harvest festival. In the modern calendar it falls on August 1 which is a quarter day in Scotland and a half-quarter day in England.

Lammle, Alfred. In Dickens' novel, OUR MUTUAL FRIEND (1864), a "mature young gentleman, with too much nose on his face, too much ginger in his whiskers, too much torso in his waistcoat, too much sparkle in his studs, his eyes, his buttons, his talk, his teeth." He marries Miss Akershem, thinking she has money, and she marries him under the same delusion, so the two kept up a fine appearance on nothing at all.

Lamont, Corliss (1902–). American essayist. Son of Thomas W. LAMONT. Author of *The Illusion of Immortality* (1935) which he considers his best work in the field of philosophy. *Man Answers Death* (1936), an anthology of "what the poets of the race have had to say about death." He is a member of the editorial council of *Soviet Russia Today,* has taught philosophy at Columbia, and is chairman of the National Council of American-Soviet Friendship, Inc.

Lamont, Thomas William (1870–1948). American banker. Member of J. P. Morgan & Company; etc. Representative of U.S. treasury on the commission to negotiate peace at Paris (1919) and alternate delegate on the committee of experts on German reparations at Paris (1929).

La Motte-Fouqué, Baron **Friedrich Heinrich Karl de** (1777–1843). German romantic novelist and poet; author of *Undine* (1811) and libretto for Hoffmann's opera of the same title. Descendant of a French family of Huguenots that left France after the revocation of Edict of Nantes.

lampad. Variant of "lamp." Francis Thompson refers to "the lampads seven," meaning the seven lamps which, in *Revelations* 4:5, burning before the throne, are said to be "the seven Spirits of God." The word is used exclusively in references of this kind.

Lamplighter, The. A once-popular novel by Maria S. Cummins (*Am.,* 1854). The heroine, Gertrude, a child of unknown parentage, is brought up by the old lamplighter, Trueman Flint. She is befriended by Emily Graham, a wealthy blind girl, and eventually her father turns out to be Miss Graham's long-lost brother.

lampoon. A personal satire in writing, usually malicious. *The Harvard Lampoon* is the humorous publication of that university. The word *lampoon* is an English assimilation of Old French *lampons,* "let's drink," from *lamper,* "to guzzle," which, in turn, is a nasalized development of English *to lap.* The meaning of the word in modern English is explained by the fact that *lampons* occurred frequently as a refrain in drinking songs of a satirical nature.

Lampson, Robin (1900–). Californian poet. Author of several long narratives in cadence, as *Laughter Out of the Ground* (1935) and *Death Loses a Pair of Wings,* the story of Surgeon General William Crawford Gorgas (1854–1920) and the conquest of yellow fever.

Lancastrian. A member or supporter of the English royal house of Lancaster. See also WARS OF THE ROSES.

Lancelot, see LAUNCELOT.

Lancelot, or The Knight of the Cart (Lancelot, ou le chevalier de la charette). A romance of the Arthurian cycle by CHRÉTIEN DE TROYES. It concerns the capture of GUINEVERE by the mysterious Meleagant, interpreted by scholars as the King of Death, after he has challenged and defeated Sir KAY, and the Queen's ultimate deliverance by the valor of Lancelot, or LAUNCELOT. This is the first romance in which the famous knight appears, and when he is introduced he is known only as The Knight of the Cart because, lacking a horse, he rides for awhile in a cart used to transport criminals. Stock elements of the fairy-tale and COURTLY LOVE traditions are found in this romance, including a sword bridge as one entrance to the land of Meleagant and a "perilous bed," equipped with a set of knives, as one of Launcelot's trials. In addition, Queen Guinevere behaves in a cold and imperious manner to Launcelot when she has an interview with him at her captor's castle, because he hesitated 3 steps before entering the cart and so was not a perfect lover according to the strict code of courtly love. She further asserts her power over the knight by bidding him do his "worst" rather than his best as he fights with Meleagant in a tournament. Scholars regard this romance as an embodiment in part of the classic legend of PLUTO and PROSERPINA.

land.

Land of Beulah (*Is.* lxii. 4). In THE PILGRIM'S PROGRESS, that land of heavenly joy where the pilgrims tarry till they are summoned to enter the Celestial City; the Paradise before the resurrection.

land of bondage. Egypt, from the oppression of the Israelites there.

land of cakes. Scotland, famous for its oatmeal cakes.

Land of Nod. To go to the land of Nod is to go to bed. There are many similar puns, and more in French than in English. Of course, the reference is to *Gen.* iv. 16, "Cain went . . . and dwelt in the land of Nod," which seems to mean "the land of wandering" rather than any definite locality.

Land o' the Leal. The land of the faithful or blessed; a Scotticism for a hypothetical land of happiness, loyalty and virtue, hence heaven, as in Lady Nairn's song—

I'm wearin' awa'
To the land o' the leal.

Gladstone, in one of his Midlothian campaigns, once amused the natives by using the phrase as a complimentary synonym for Scotland itself.

Land of Promise, or *Promised Land.* Canaan, which God promised to give to Abraham for his obedience. See *Ex.* xii. 25, *Deut.* ix. 28, etc.

Land of Steady Habits. A name given to the State of Connecticut, which was the original stronghold of Presbyterianism in America and the home of the notorious BLUE LAWS.

Land, The. A long poem (1926) by Victoria SACKVILLE-WEST, which established her reputation. It deals with the year's cycle of an English farmer, interspersed with lyrics, and was awarded the Hawthornden prize (1927).

landgrave. Corresponding to German *Landgraf.* In medieval times (since the 12th century) a German count (that is, "Graf") to whom jurisdiction over a certain territory was entrusted. Later, the title of certain German princes, as the heads of the non-regnant branches of the family of Hesse.

Landis, Kenesaw Mountain (1866–1944). American jurist and high commissioner for American and National Leagues of Professional Base Ball Clubs and National Association of Professional Base Ball Leagues (from 1920).

Land's End. Granite cliffs some sixty to a hundred feet high in Cornwall, the most westerly extremity of England. In ancient geography, Bolerium.

Land of the Midnight Sun. Norway. In the Arctic and Antarctic there are periods when the sun does not descend below and others when it does not rise above the horizon within the twenty-four hours of the day. At the poles these periods are half a year. They decrease in regions closer to the polar circles beyond which the phenomenon can no longer occur. Northern Norway is the region of the Arctic most frequently visited by travelers from western Europe and the U.S. Hence its common association with the sun shining at midnight for a time in mid-summer. It could similarly be associated with the sun not shining at noon for a time in mid-winter and be called the Land of the Midday Night.

Land of Little Rain. Title of a book about California, the region "between the high Sierras south from Yosemite—east and south beyond Death Valley and on into the Mojave Desert," by Mary Austin (1903).

Landon, Alfred Mossman (1887–). American businessman. Governor of Kansas (1933–1937). Unsuccessful Republican candidate for the presidency (1936).

Landon, Letitia Elizabeth (1802–1838). English poet and novelist. Signed her work **L. E. L.**

Landor, Walter Savage (1775–1864). English poet, literary critic, and prose-writer, known for his interest in the Greek and Latin classics and the severity and intellectual coldness of his lyrics, many of which were written in direct imitation of Latin and Greek models. Among his works are: GEBIR (1797), an Oriental tale in blank verse; COUNT JULIAN (1812), a tragedy; *Imaginary Conversations* (1824–1853), a series of discussions between historical figures on a variety of subjects; *Citation and Examination of William Shakespeare* (1834), literary criticism; *Pericles and Aspasia* (1836), imaginary letters; *Poemata et Inscriptiones* (1847), Latin verse; *The Hellenics* (1847), poems on Greek subjects; *Last Fruit Off an Old Tree* (1853); *Antony and Octavius* (1856), dramatic dialogues; *Heroic Idyls* (1863). ROSE AYLMER is his best-known lyric.

In his youth, Landor was influenced by the revolutionary atmosphere of the time, being forced to leave Oxford because of his opinions and in 1808 going off with a regiment he had raised to fight against Napoleon in Spain. He tried to institute humanitarian reform on his estate in Wales but failed, and for a number of years lived in Italy. His poetry was never popular in his own time.

Landseer, Sir **Edwin Henry** (1802–1873). Famous English animal painter. Drew Sir Walter Scott's dogs with the poet in their midst. His paintings owe their popularity largely to the etchings made of them by his brother **Thomas Landseer** (1795–1880).

Landsknecht (*Ger.,* "servant of the land"). Original form of the French adaptation **lansquenet.** One of the mercenary foot soldiers constituting the German (and French) standing armies from the time of Emperor Maximilian through the 17th century. The *Landsknechte* took their name from the serfs of earlier centuries who owed military service to the lord of their land. They became a colorful class of professional warriors who fought for fighting's sake, for booty and personal loyalty to their leader but never (not even in theory) for ideals and principles. The type has been glorified anachronistically by the German general and author Ernst Jünger.

Landsturm (*Ger.*). In German-speaking countries, originally a call to arms throughout the land. Later, and still in Switzerland, the third line of defense. Similarly **Landwehr** ("defense of the land"), the second line of defense. In Switzerland, the first line of defense is called **Auszug** ("marching out").

Lane, Edward William (1801–1876). English Arabic scholar. Author of a translation of *A Thousand and One Nights* (1838–1840), excellent in its day but superseded by that of Richard BURTON. Compiler of an exhaustive thesaurus of Arabic, an Arabic dictionary, etc.

Lane, John (1854–1925). English publisher. Founded (with Elkin Mathews) the Bodley Head Publishing Co. (1887) and the *Yellow Book* (1894), a magazine famous in its time.

Lang, Andreas (1862–1933) and his cousin **Anton Lang** (1875–1938). Members of a family of potters and woodcarvers of OBERAMMERGAU, Bavaria, who enacted various roles in the Passion Plays of their native village.

Lang, Andrew (1844–1912). Scottish scholar and man of letters. In a controversy with Max Müller he held that literary mythology is the outgrowth of anonymous folklore. Author of volumes of graceful verse, translator (in collaboration) of Homer, and editor of numerous volumes of fairy tales. See *Andrew Lang; a Critical Biography* (1946), by Roger L. Green.

Lang, Cosmo Gordon (1864–1945). Anglican prelate. Archbishop of Canterbury (1928–1942). His opposition to the friendship between Mrs. Wallis Simpson and Edward VIII (1936) was said to be partly responsible for the king's abdication.

Langdon-Davies, John (1897–). British anthropologist and sociologist. A popular lecturer both in England and America. He took the part of the Loyalists in the Spanish Civil War from its beginning in 1936. His *Man and His Universe* (1930) has been very popular.

Langeais, Antoinette de. Titular heroine of Balzac's novel, *The Duchess de Langeais,* usually published as part of *The Thirteen* (*L'Histoire des treize*). She is beloved by Armand, Marquis de Montriveau, whom she holds always at arm's length.

Langham, Edward. An Oxford tutor, shy, morbid but nevertheless likable, in Mrs. Humphry Ward's *Robert Elsmere* (1888). The author explained later that the character was suggested by AMIEL, whose diary she had been engaged in translating.

Langland, William (ca. 1332–ca. 1400). Long-assumed author of PIERS PLOWMAN, conjectured to have been a Benedictine cleric of humble birth in the convent of Malvern, later to have led the greater part of his life as a vagabond in London, and to have had a moderate amount of education. The findings of more recent scholarship, however, tend to discredit the theory that the poem is the work of one man, since there are three separate versions of it and more than one man is referred to as the author during the unfolding of the story.

Langley, Samuel Pierpont (1834–1906). American astronomer and pioneer in theory and construction of mechanically propelled heavier-than-air flying machines. First successful experiment with a model plane on the Potomac (May 6, 1896). His full-sized machines failed in several trials. An airdrome near Norfolk, Virginia, is named in his honor.

Langmuir, Irving (1881–). American research chemist. With Gilbert N. Lewis, originator of the Lewis Langmuir atomic theory. Nobel prize for chemistry (1932).

Langner, Lawrence (1890–). Anglo-American playwright and patent lawyer. Organized the Washington Square Players (1914) and helped found the Theatre Guild. With his wife Armina Marshall, co-author of several American historical comedies, and owner and operator of the Westport County Playhouse, a summer theater in Connecticut.

Langstaff, Launcelot. The pseudonym under which SALMAGUNDI was published (1807), the authors being Washington IRVING, William Irving and J. K. Paulding.

Langton, Stephen (1150?–1228). Archbishop of Canterbury (1207). Refused possession of his see by King John until England was placed under interdict by the Pope (1213). Became the leader of the barons in their contest with the king and was the first subscribing witness to the Magna Carta at Runnymede. Crowned Henry III and demanded of him the full execution of the charter (1223).

Langtry, Lily, *née* **Emily Charlotte Le Breton** (1852–1929). Known as "the Jersey Lily." English actress, famous for her beauty.

langue d'oc. The language of southern France. From the 13th century on, it became customary to group the Romance dialects that had emerged from Vulgar Latin according to their word for "yes." The dialects of the *langue de si* were spoken in Italy; those of the *langue d'oc* and the *langue d'oïl* were spoken in France, south and north of the Loire basin, respectively. Standard modern French developed from a *langue d'oïl* dialect (*oïl* = *oui*).

Languish, Lydia. In Sheridan's comedy THE RIVALS, the heroine, a romantic young lady who is for ever reading sensational novels and molding her behavior on the characters.

Lanier, Sidney (1842–1881). American poet and musician, considered one of the most accomplished poets of the South and the U.S. in the latter part of the 19th century. He tried to achieve in his work the auditory effects of music and experimented with varying metrical patterns and unusual imagery. Much of his poetry shows an affinity with that of the Pre-Raphaelites (see PRE-RAPHAELITE BROTHERHOOD) and A. C. SWINBURNE. Among his works are *Tiger Lilies* (1867), a novel based on his experiences in the Civil War; *Poems* (1877); *St. Augustine in April* (1878); *The Boys' Library of Legend and Chivalry* (1879–1882), a series of adaptations of legends and romances for children; *The Science of English Verse* (1883), a work on prosody; *The English Novel* (1883), criticism; *Poems* (1884); *Music and Poetry* (1898); *Retrospects and Prospects* (1899); *Shakespeare and His Forerunners* (1902), lectures; *Poem Outlines* (1908). His son, **Henry Wysham Lanier,** edited *The Golden Book,* an eclectic magazine.

Lanigan, George Thomas (1845–1886). Canadian-American journalist. Wrote the immortal humorous verses, *Threnody for the Ahkoond of Swat.*

Lankes, Julius J. (1884–). American artist, specializing in wood cuts. Represented in permanent collections of Library of Congress, Toronto Art Gallery, British Museum, Metropolitan Museum in New York, etc.

lanner. A small variety of falcon.

> Oh for a noble falcon-lanner
> To flap each broad wing like a banner.
> Browning, *The Flight of the Duchess.*

Lanner, Josef (1801–1843). Austrian violinist and composer. Creator of the modern Viennese waltz. Leader of an amateur quartet, in which Johann STRAUSS, known as the "Waltz King," played the viola.

Lansing, Robert (1864–1928). American lawyer. Secretary of State under Wilson (1915–1920) at whose request he resigned. Author of *The Peace Negotiations* (1921).

lansquenet, see LANDSKNECHT.

Lantenac, the Marquis de. A character in Victor Hugo's NINETY-THREE.

lantern.

Lantern Land. The land of literary charlatans, pedantic graduates in arts, doctors, professors, prelates, and so on ridiculed as "Lanterns" by RABELAIS (with a side allusion to the divines assembled in conference at the Council of Trent) in his GARGANTUA AND PANTAGRUEL, v. 33. See CITY OF LANTERNS.

Feast of Lanterns. A popular Chinese festival, celebrated at the first full moon of each year. Tradition says that the daughter of a famous mandarin one evening fell into a lake. The father and his neighbors went with lanterns to look for her, and happily she was rescued. In commemoration thereof a festival was ordained, and it grew in time to be the celebrated Feast of Lanterns.

Lanternois. Inhabitants of Rabelais' LANTERN LAND.

Laocoön. In Virgil's AENEID, a son of Priam and priest of Apollo of Troy, famous for the tragic fate of himself and his two sons, who were crushed to death by serpents while he was sacrificing to Poseidon, in consequence of his having offended Apollo. The group representing these three in their death agony, now in the Vatican, was discovered in 1506, on the Esquiline Hill (Rome). It is a single block of marble, and is attributed to Agesandrus, Athenodorus, and Polydorus of the School of Rhodes in the 2nd century B. C. It has been restored.

Lessing called his famous treatise on the limits of poetry and the plastic arts (1766) *Laokoön* because he uses the group as the peg on which to hang his dissertation.

> Since I have, as it were, set out from the Laocoön, and several times return to it, I have wished to give it a share also in the title.—*Preface.*

Irving BABBITT has a book entitled *The New Laokoön* (1910).

Laodamia. In classic myth, the wife of Protesilaus, who was slain before Troy. She begged to be allowed to converse with her dead husband for only three hours, and her request was granted. When the respite was over, she voluntarily accompanied the dead hero to the shades. WORDSWORTH has a poem on the subject (1815).

Laodicean. One indifferent to religion, caring little or nothing about the matter, like the Christians of that church, mentioned in the book of *Revelation* (Ch. iii. 14–18).

Laodicean, A. A novel by Thomas HARDY (1881). The plot centers about the rivalry of Somerset, a young architect, and Captain de Stancy for the hand of Paula Powers, the owner of the Stancy castle. Captain de Stancy's son, who is known as Will Dare, steals Somerset's plans and takes underhanded means of discrediting Somerset in his work on the castle, but is finally exposed.

Laomedon. In classic myth, King of Troy, the father of PRIAM. He is remembered chiefly for the sin of ingratitude committed when he refused to give the rewards he had promised to APOLLO for pasturing his flocks on Mount Ida, to POSEIDON for building the walls of Troy, and to HERCULES for rescuing his daughter Hesiode from the sea-monster sent by Poseidon. Hercules slew him and all his sons but Priam in revenge.

Laon. Hero of Shelley's poem THE REVOLT OF ISLAM.

Lao-tzu, Lao-tse, or **Lao-tsze** (ca. 604–531 B.C.). "The Venerable Philosopher." See under TAOISM.

Lapham, Silas. The hero of Howells' RISE OF SILAS LAPHAM. Mrs. Lapham and the daughters Irene and Penelope are important characters in the same novel.

Lapithae. A people of Thessaly, noted in Greek legend for their defeat of the Centaurs at the marriage-feast of HIPPODAMIA, when the latter were driven out of Pelion. The contest was represented on the Parthenon, the Theseum at Athens, the Temple of Apollo at Basso, and on numberless vases.

Laplace, Marquis **Pierre Simon de** (1749–1827). French astronomer and mathematician. Made discoveries in celestial mechanics and set forth a nebular hypothesis of cosmogony (1796) which is essentially like that advanced by Immanuel KANT.

lapsus linguae (*Lat.*). A slip of the tongue, a mistake in uttering a word, an imprudent word inadvertently spoken. Cf. also the Latin phrases *lapsus calami* (a slip of the pen), and *lapsus memoriae* (a slip of the memory).

Laputa. The flying island inhabited by scientific quacks, and visited by Lemuel GULLIVER in his "travels." These dreamy philosophers are so absorbed in their speculations that they employ attendants, called "flappers," to flap them on the mouth and ears with a blown bladder when their attention is to be called off from "high things" to vulgar mundane matters.

Lara. A narrative poem by BYRON (1814) which continues the tale related in THE CORSAIR.

Larbaud, Valéry (1881–). French critic, novelist, short-story writer, translator, and poet. His books, "few and far between, form a sort of continuous veiled autobiography." Edited the French edition of James JOYCE's *Ulysses*.

Larcom, Lucy (1824–1893). American author and educator. *Poems* (1869). Collaborated with John Greenleaf Whittier in editing anthologies. Her best-known poem is *Poor Lone Hannah*.

Lardner, Ringgold Wilmer (1885–1933). American sports writer, newspaper columnist, and short-story writer, known for his bitterly humorous and satirical stories and sketches of 20th-century American life, told in the characteristic slang and vernacular speech of baseball players, boxers, song-writers, stock-brokers, stenographers, chorus-girls, etc., in order to show the stupidity or viciousness of the people involved. His books include *You Know Me, Al: A Busher's Letters* (1916), dealing with a baseball player; *Bib Ballads* (1915), verse; *Gullible's Travels* (1917); *The Big Town* (1921), a novel; *How to Write Short Stories* (1924); *What of It?* (1925); *The Love Nest* (1926), dramatized by Robert E. SHERWOOD in 1927; *June Moon* (1929), a play, a satire on the song-writers of TIN PAN ALLEY, written with George S. KAUFMAN; *The Story of a Wonder Man* (1927), a satire in the form of an autobiography; *Round Up* (1929); and *First and Last* (1934).

lares and penates. Used as a collective expression for home, and for those personal belongings that distinguish a home. In ancient Rome the *lares* (sing. *lar*) were the household gods, usually deified ancestors or heroes; the *penates* were also guardian deities of the household (and the state), but were more in the nature of personifications of the natural powers, their duty being to bring wealth and plenty rather than to protect and ward off danger. The *lar familiaris* was the spirit of the founder of the house, which never left it, but accompanied his descendants in all their changes.

Largo Caballero, Francisco (1869–1946). Spanish labor leader. Directed the *Unión General de Trabajadores,* the Spanish equivalent of the American C.I.O. Reached the height of his career as a Marxist and revolutionary when he became prime minister and minister of war during the Spanish Civil War. Fled to France after the defeat of the Loyalists and landed in a German concentration camp. Liberated by Russian forces at the end of World War II, he was taken to Paris for surgical treatment and died there in his 76th year.

Lariat, the. In Mark Twain's INNOCENTS ABROAD, one of the party of American tourists in Europe, a willing composer of doggerel verse on all subjects and the self-constituted Lariat (Laureate) of the excursion.

Lark, The. A LITTLE MAGAZINE published (1895–1897) by *Les Jeunes,* a San Francisco group of the nineties led by Gelett BURGESS, whose famous poem *The Purple Cow* first appeared in it. It was somewhat influenced by THE CHAP-BOOK, published by Stone and Kimball in Chicago (1894–1898).

Larned, William Augustus (1872–1926). American tennis player. Seven times national singles champion; six times member of the U.S. Davis Cup team.

La Rochefoucauld, Duc **Francois VI** de (1613–1680). French author, known for his maxims, assembled in *Maximes* (1664–1665), and for his memoirs, published in *Mémoires*

(1662). The latter work describes in a detached manner the author's own political failures, especially in his efforts to destroy the power of Cardinal RICHELIEU over the French royal family. The maxims are observations on life in general, witty, succinct, profound, written in a lucid and concise style.

Lars, a Pastoral of Norway. A narrative poem by Bayard TAYLOR. The hero, a Norwegian peasant, escapes to America after a duel and there adopts the Quaker faith.

Larsen, Hanna Astrup (1873–1946). Translator and editor of *The American-Scandinavian Review,* and literary secretary of the American-Scandinavian Foundation. Editor of about seventy books published by the Foundation. She translated novels by J. P. JACOBSEN and short stories by Steen Blicher. She was the editor of *Norway's Best Short Stories* (1927), *Sweden's Best Stories* (1928) and *Denmark's Best Stories* (1928). She wrote biographies of *Knut Hamsun* (1922) and *Selma Lagerlöf* (1935) and was awarded the Swedish Vasa Medal (1931) and the Royal Danish Medal of Merit (1935).

Larsen, Wolf. The leading character in Jack London's SEA-WOLF.

Lars Porsena, see PORSENA.

larvae. A name among the ancient Romans for malignant spirits and ghosts. The *larva* or ghost of Caligula was often seen (according to Suetonius) in his palace.

> [Fear] sometimes representeth strange apparitions, as their fathers' and grandfathers' ghosts, risen out of their graves, and in their winding-sheets; and to others it sometimes sheweth Larves, Hobgoblins, Robbin-goodfellows, and such other Bug-beares and Chimeraes.—Florio's *Montaigne,* I. xvii.

La Salle, Sieur de. **Robert Cavelier** (1643–1687). French explorer in America. Descended Mississippi River to Gulf of Mexico (1682), claiming the whole valley for France and naming the region Louisiana after the French king, Louis XIV. Murdered by his own men in what is now Texas during a second expedition undertaken to conduct a band of French colonists to the Mississippi.

La Salle Street. A street in the heart of Chicago, on which are located the Stock Exchange and many financial institutions. Chicago's WALL STREET, STATE STREET, or LOMBARD STREET.

Las Casas, Bartolomé de (1474–1566). Spanish Dominican missionary and historian. Arrived at Hispaniola as a planter (1502) and became the first priest ordained in the New World (1510). Preached and labored against Indian slavery and other colonial abuses. The title "protector of the Indians," bestowed on him by Cardinal Ximenes, was well earned. Among his works on America is the important historical source, *Historia General de las Indias,* available in a number of manuscripts until it was finally published in 1875.

lasher. Water rushing through a weir. Hence its pool.

> To bathe in the abandoned lasher . . .
> Matthew Arnold, *The Scholar Gipsy.*

Lasker, Emanuel (1868–1941). German Chess master.

Laski, Harold Joseph (1893–). English political scientist. Adviser to the Labor Government of England (1945). Lectured at universities in Canada and U.S. (1914–1920). Connected with London School of Economics (from 1920). Member of the FABIAN Society and of the Industrial Court (since 1926). Professor of political science in the University of London (since 1926). "Probably no Englishman since Lord Bryce has known American politics, history and law as thoroughly as he does." A convinced Marxist but not a Communist. Has edited the words of Edmund BURKE and John Stuart MILL. Among his many books are *The American Presidency: An Interpretation* (1940); *Strategy of Freedom* (1941); *Reflections on the Revolution of our Time* (1943); etc.

Lasky, Jesse L. (1880–). American motion-picture producer. Head, Jesse L. Lasky Feature Play Co. (from 1914); associate producer, RKO Radio Pictures, Inc.

Lassalle, Ferdinand (1825–1864). German socialist leader. Disciple of Karl MARX (from 1848). Regarded as founder of the German Social Democratic party. Killed in a duel growing out of his love affair with Helene Dönniges, wife of the Rumanian boyar Racowitza. George MEREDITH's novel, *The Tragic Comedians* (1880) is based on this affair.

Lassus, Orlandus de. Also **Orlando di Lasso.** Original name **Roland Delattre** (1530–1594). Flemish composer and choirmaster. More than 2,000 compositions. He understood the instruments of his day—lute, viol, dulcimer, etc.—and did not confine himself to church music. He and PALESTRINA "represent the highest point attained in sixteenth century polyphonic writing." The year of his death coincided with that of Palestrina.

last.

last of the barons. Another name given to Warwick, the Kingmaker. See below for synopsis of Bulwer Lytton's novel of this title.

last of the dandies. Count Alfred d'Orsay (1801–1852).

last of the English. HEREWARD (fl. ca. 1070).

last of the Fathers. St. Bernard, Abbot of Clairvaux (1091–1153).

last of the Goths. Roderick, who was the last of the kings of the Visigoths in Spain and died in 711. SOUTHEY has a tale in blank verse on him.

last of the Greeks. The general, Philopoemen of Arcadia (253–183 B. C.).

last of the knights. The Emperor Maximilian I (1459–1519).

last of the Romans. A title, or sobriquet, given to a number of historical characters, among whom are:

Marcus Junius Brutus (85–42 B. C.), one of the murderers of Caesar.

Caius Cassius Longinus (d. 42 B. C.), so called by Brutus.

Stilicho, the Roman general under Theodosius.

Aetius, the general who defended the Gauls against the Franks and other barbarians, and defeated Attila near Châlons in 451. He was so called by Procopius.

François Joseph Terasse Desbillons (1711–1789), a French Jesuit; so called from the elegance and purity of his Latin.

Pope called CONGREVE *Ultimus Romanorum,* and the same title was conferred on Dr. Johnson, Horace Walpole, and C. J. Fox.

last of the Saxons. King HAROLD (1022–1066), who was defeated and slain at the Battle of Hastings.

last of the Stuarts. Henry, Cardinal of York (1725–1807), the last legitimate male descendant of James I.

last of the Tribunes. Cola di RIENZI (1314–1354), who led the Roman people against the barons.

last of the Troubadours. Jacques Jasmin, of Gascony (1798–1864).

Last Assize. The Last Judgment.

Last Chronicle of Barset, The. A novel by Anthony Trollope, one of his *Chronicles of Barsetshire.* See BARSETSHIRE.

Last Days of Pompeii, The. A historical novel by BULWER LYTTON (1834). The hero, Glaucus, is a noble young Athenian, in love with the beautiful Ione. Her guardian Arbaces, a priest of Isis and the villain of the story, makes every effort to thwart the romance and win Ione for his own evil ends. When the city is destroyed by the eruption of Vesuvius, the blind flower girl, Nydia, who has loved Glaucus passionately but in vain, leads the lovers out of the doomed city. Nydia's bitter despair finally brings her to a tragic end.

Last Leaf, The. A poem by O. W. HOLMES (1833) about an old, old man.

> I know it is a sin
> For me to sit and grin
> At him here
> But the old three-cornered hat
> And the breeches, and all that
> Are so queer.

Last of the Barons, The. A historical novel by Bulwer LYTTON (1843), dealing with the WARS OF THE ROSES. The hero is Richard Neville, Earl of Warwick, known as the Kingmaker. The novel traces his downfall. Sibyll Warner and her father Adam WARNER are important characters.

Last of the Mohicans, The. A historical novel by James Fenimore COOPER (1826), one of the LEATHERSTOCKING series. The action takes place in the dense forests about Fort William Henry during the French and Indian War. "The Last of the Mohicans" is Uncas, the son of CHINGACHGOOK and the pride of his friend HAWKEYE. Uncas is a brave and noble Indian youth who cherishes a hopeless love for Cora Munro, the quadroon daughter of the English commander, and dies in the attempt to rescue her from his Huron enemy Magua. Chingachgook and Hawkeye (the Leatherstocking of the other novels) play a prominent part in the plot, which consists largely of pursuit, escape and capture, and is one of the swiftest-moving of all Cooper's novels. The Yankee psalm-singer, David Gamut, an incongruous figure in the silent woods, adds a touch of humor. The French general Montcalm plays a subordinate part in the action.

Last Puritan, The, A Memoir in the Form of a Novel. A novel by George SANTAYANA (1936), a study of Oliver Alden, descendant of an old and wealthy New England family, who comprises in himself the Puritan characteristics of austerity, single-mindedness, gravity, and conscientious, scrupulous devotion to purpose. He is out of place in the civilization of the 20th century; as a friend of his in the novel says, ". . . In Oliver Puritanism worked itself out to its logical end. He convinced himself, on Puritan grounds, that it was wrong to be a Puritan. . . . He thought it his clear duty to give Puritanism up, but couldn't." Oliver is presented to us in the prologue of the novel supposedly as a former student of the author at Harvard University and one of the young men killed during World War I. (Santayana later stated that he was partly based on W. Cameron Forbes.) In style, subject-matter, and approach, *The Last Puritan* recalls the novels of Henry JAMES.

Last Ride Together, The. Title of a short poem by Robert BROWNING in *Dramatic Romances* (1841–1846).

Last Rose of Summer, 'T is the. Title and first line of a song, generally known from the second act of the opera *Martha* (1847) by Flotow, but written (1813) by Thomas Moore to the tune of an old air.

Latch, William. In George Moore's ESTHER WATERS, the father of Esther's child.

Late Christopher Bean, The. Title of a play (1933) by Sidney HOWARD, adapted from the French.

Late George Apley, The. Title of a Pulitzer Prize-novel (1937) by J. P. MARQUAND.

Lateran. The church or basilica of St. John Lateran. It is the Cathedral church of Rome and as such the highest in the hierarchy of churches in the Catholic world. Adjoining is the Lateran Palace, scene of a number of Church councils known as Lateran Councils. The name goes back to the Roman family Lateranus who owned a palace on the same site until the last owner was put to death by Nero.

Lateran Treaty. A concordat between the Holy See and the Kingdom of Italy (ratified June 8, 1929). It settled a sixty-year-old controversy, establishing the sovereign (Papal) State of Vatican City and stipulating that Catholicism should be the only state religion in Italy.

Lathrop, Dorothy Parsons (1891–). American illustrator and author, with a long list of book illustrations. *Three Mulla-Mulgars* by Walter DE LA MARE (1919); *A Little Boy Lost* by William Henry HUDSON (1920); *Down-Adown-Derry* (1922) and *Crossings* (1923) by Walter De la Mare; *The Princess and Curdie* by George Macdonald (1927); *Hitty: Her First Hundred Years* by Rachel Field (1929); author and illustrator of *The Fairy Circus* (1931); *The Snail Who Ran* (1934); *The Little White Goat* (1933); *The Lost Merry-Go-Round* (1934); *Who Goes There?* (1935); *Bouncing Betsy* (1936); etc.

Lathrop, George Parsons (1851–1898). American journalist and poet; son of a well-known American mural painter. Married Nathaniel Hawthorne's daughter Rose, and wrote *A Study of Hawthorne* (1876).

Latimer, Darsie. Hero of Scott's REDGAUNTLET. He is supposed to be the son of Ralph Latimer, but is really the son of Sir Henry Darsie Redgauntlet, and grandson of Sir Redwald Redgauntlet.

Latimer, Hugh (1485?–1555). English reformer and Protestant martyr. On Mary's accession committed to Tower. Burned at stake for heresy, "at the ditch over against Balliol College" (October 16).

Latin Church, Fathers of the, see under FATHER.

Latini, Brunetto, see BRUNETTO LATINI.

Latin Quarter (*le Quartier Latin*). The University quarter of Paris on the left bank of the Seine. For centuries it has been a center for artists, writers, students, intellectuals, and Bohemians of all varieties and from many lands.

Latinus. Legendary king of the Latini, the ancient inhabitants of Latium. According to Virgil, he opposes Aeneas on his first landing, but subsequently forms an alliance with him, and gives him his daughter, Lavinia, in marriage. Turnus, King of the Rutuli, declares that Lavinia has been betrothed to him. The issue is decided by single combat, and Aeneas, being victor, obtains Lavinia for his wife and becomes by her the ancestor of Romulus, the mythical founder of Rome.

The name Latinus is given to one of the Italian heroes in Tasso's JERUSALEM DELIVERED. He and his five sons are all slain in battle by the Soldan Solyman in a single hour.

Latitudinarians. A Church of England party in the time of Charles II, opposed both to the High Church party and to the Puritans. The term came to be applied to those persons who attach little importance to dogma and what are called orthodox doctrines.

Latmos, Mount. The mountain where Endymion pastured his flocks when Diana fell in love with him.

Latona. The Roman name of the Greek Leto, mother by Jupiter of Apollo and Diana. Milton, in one of his sonnets, refers to the legend that when she knelt by a fountain in Delos with her infants in arms to quench her thirst, some Lycian clowns insulted her and were turned into frogs.

Latour, Jean. In DEATH COMES FOR THE ARCHBISHOP, an aristocratic French bishop who reveals qualities of intellectual distinction, tolerance, and courage.

latria and **dulia.** Greek words adopted by the Roman Catholics. The former is used to express that supreme reverence and adoration which is offered to God alone, and the latter, that secondary reverence and adoration which is offered to saints. *Latria* is from the Greek suffix *-latreia,* worship, as in our ido*latry; dulia* is the reverence of a *doulos* or slave.

Latter-Day Saints, see MORMONISM.

Latzko, Andreas (1876–). Hungarian writer whose best-known book, *Men in War* (1917), is a war novel of pacifist tendencies.

Laud, William (1573–1645). English prelate; son of a clothier, who rose to the rank of Archbishop of Canterbury (1633). Most influential statesman under Charles I, representing absolutism in both Church and State. Sought to root out Presbyterianism in Scotland and Calvinism in England. Provoked riot in St. Giles, Edinburgh, leading to Bishops' Wars and the Long Parliament. Impeached of high treason by the Long Parliament, he was condemned and beheaded.

Lauder, Sir Harry. Real name **Harry MacLennan** (1870–). Scottish singer and composer of songs, internationally popular for rendition of Scottish songs and ballads, such as *I Love a Lassie*.

Laughing Boy. Title of a Pulitzer prize-novel (1930) about a young Navajo silversmith by Oliver LA FARGE.

Laughing Philosopher. Democritus of Abdera (5th century B. C.), who viewed with supreme contempt the feeble powers of man. See WEEPING PHILOSOPHER.

Laughton, Charles (1899–). English character actor on stage and (from 1932) in motion pictures, chiefly in Hollywood. Major rôles in *The Private Life of Henry VIII; The Barretts of Wimpole Street; Ruggles of Red Gap; Mutiny on the Bounty; The Suspect;* etc. Married (1929) Elsa Lanchester, English actress and comedienne.

Launce. In Shakespeare's TWO GENTLEMEN OF VERONA, the clownish servant of Proteus, one of the two "gentlemen of Verona." He is in love with JULIA. Launce is especially famous for soliloquies to his dog Crab, "the sourest-natured dog that lives."

Launcelot or **Lancelot du Lac.** In Arthurian romance, the most famous of the knights of the ROUND TABLE.

Sir Launcelot is the son of King Ban of Brittany, but is stolen in infancy by Vivien, the LADY OF THE LAKE. She plunges with the babe into the lake (whence the cognomen of *du Lac*), and when her *protégé* has grown to man's estate, presents him to King Arthur. Sir Launcelot goes in search of the GRAIL, and twice catches sight of it. Though always represented in the Arthurian romances as the model of chivalry, bravery, and fidelity, Sir Launcelot is the adulterous lover of GUINEVERE, wife of King Arthur, his friend, and it is through this love that the war, which results in the disruption of the Round Table and the death of Arthur, originates.

ELAINE, "the lily maid of Astolat," falls in love with Launcelot; the love is not returned, and she dies. By another Elaine, daughter of King PELLES, he (through a stratagem) unwittingly becomes the father of Sir GALAHAD. At the close of his life the repentant knight becomes a hermit, and dies in the odor of sanctity. Launcelot is an outstanding figure in all the old romances and in Tennyson's IDYLLS OF THE KING. He is the hero of a narrative poem *Lancelot* by E. A. ROBINSON (1920). See also LANCELOT, OR THE KNIGHT OF THE CART.

Launcelot Greaves, The Adventures of Sir. A satiric novel by SMOLLETT (1760), a sort of English *Don Quixote*. The hero, Sir Launcelot Greaves, is a well-bred and noble-minded young English squire of the George II period, half crazed by love. He sets out attended by Captain Crow, an old sea-captain, to detect fraud and right the wrongs of the world. After sundry adventures which give the author opportunity for satiric treatment of English life, he is welcomed back by his Amelia.

Launfal, Sir. In Arthurian romance, one of the Knights of the Round Table. His story is told in a metrical romance written by Thomas Chestre in the reign of Henry VI. He is steward to King Arthur, and falls in love with Tryamour, who gives him an unfailing purse, telling him that if he ever wishes to see her, all he has to do is to retire into a private room, and she will instantly be with him. Sir Launfal attracts much attention at court by his great wealth, but when he tells Gwennere (Guinevere), who solicits his love, that she is not worthy to kiss the feet of his lady love, the Queen accuses him, as Potiphar's wife did Joseph, of insulting her. Thereupon Arthur tells him that, unless he makes good his word by producing this paragon of women, he is to be burned alive. On the day appointed Tryamour arrives, Launfal is justified and set at liberty, and he accompanies his mistress to the isle of Oleron, after which he is never seen again.

Another legend is given in James Russell Lowell's poem *The Vision of Sir Launfal* (1848). On a beautiful day in June the knight (in a dream) goes in search of the Holy Grail, tosses a leper a gold coin, and learns that the leper is Christ.

Laura. The lady of this name immortalized by PETRARCH is generally held to have been Laure de Noves, who was born at Avignon in 1308, was married in 1325 to Hugues de Sede, and died of the plague in 1348, the mother of eleven children. It was Petrarch's first sight of her, in the church of St. Clara Avignon, that, he says, made him a poet.

In Byron's poem BEPPO, a Venetian lady who marries Beppo, is also called Laura. So are, in emulation of Petrarch, many recipients and heroines of lyrical poems. Cf., for instance, Schiller's poems to Laura.

laureate, see POETS LAUREATE.

Laurence, Friar. In Shakespeare's ROMEO AND JULIET, the good friar who promises to marry Romeo and Juliet. He supplies Juliet with the sleeping draught, to enable her to quit her home without arousing scandal or suspicion.

Laurence, William L. (1888–). Lithuanian-born American journalist. Pulitzer prize for reporting the Harvard Tercentenary Conference of Arts and Sciences (1937). Fellow of the American Institute for "distinguished service in the interpretation of science." He reported exclusively the discovery that uranium 235 held the key to the utilization of atomic energy. Wrote the magazine article "The Atom Gives Up" (September 7, 1940). Pulitzer prize (1946) for his general reportage, but more specifically for his eye-witness account of the dropping of an atomic bomb on Nagasaki and ten articles in the New York *Times* on the development, production, and significance of the atomic bomb, reprinted, with additions, in *Dawn Over Zero* (1946).

Laurentian Library. A library that has grown out of the private collection of Cosimo and Lorenzo (that is, Laurentius; hence the name) de' MEDICI. The monks of San Marco in Florence acquired it after the expulsion of the Medici. It was purchased by Pope Leo X, taken to Rome, and enlarged. Pope Clement VII (of the Medici family) returned it to Florence.

Laurie, Annie (1682–1764). Subject of a famous Scottish song (ca. 1700). Daughter of Sir Robert Laurie of Maxwellton, Dumfriesshire. She married Alexander Ferguson. The song was written by the man she rejected, William Douglas. Revised and set to music by Lady John Scott (1855).

Laurier, Sir Wilfrid (1841–1919). Liberal Canadian-French statesman of Catholic parentage. One of the most eloquent Canadian orators of his day. Prime minister of Canada (1896–1911).

Laurin. The dwarf-king in the German folk-legend *Laurin,* or *Der kleine Rosengarten.* He possesses a magic ring, girdle, and cap, and is attacked in his rose garden, which no one may enter on pain of death, by Dietrich of Bern. The poem belongs to the late 13th century, and is attributed to Heinrich von Ofterdingen.

Lautréamont, Le Comte de. Real name **Isidore Lucien Ducasse** (1846–1870). French poet, born in Montevideo, Uruguay, settled in Paris (from ca. 1860), known for the despair, savagery, and violence of his poetry as represented in *Les Chants de Maldoror* (1868–1870). See also RIMBAUD, ARTHUR.

Lautrec, see TOULOUSE-LAUTREC.

Lavaine, Sir. A knight of Arthurian romance, brother of ELAINE, the "lily maid of Astolat." In Tennyson's *Elaine* (*Idylls of the King*), he accompanies Sir LAUNCELOT when he goes, *incognito,* to tilt for the ninth diamond. He is described as young, brave, and a true knight.

Laval, Pierre (1883–executed, October 15, 1945). French politician. Member of Chamber of Deputies (from 1914). In cabinet with various portfolios and as premier (1931–1936). Responsible with Sir Samuel Hoare of Britain for Western non-interference with Mussolini's Ethiopian venture. Since the outbreak of World War II, advocate of a separate French peace with the Axis. After the collapse of France, Laval was taken into the Vichy Government as Vice-Premier, but was removed from office (December 13, 1940) and temporarily interned. Released by German pressure. Shot and seriously wounded (August 27, 1941) by P. Colette who posed as one of the French Volunteers to Combat Bolshevism. Recovered and continued to conspire with the Germans who forced Marshal Pétain to make him chief of government. Announced a policy of complete collaboration with Germany. At the time of the American victory over Germany, Laval fled to Spain by airplane. He was returned to France, taken into custody by the Americans, tried by a French court, and executed by a firing squad.

Lavater, Johann Kaspar (1741–1801). Swiss theologian and author. Through his major work, *Physiognomical Fragments for the Promotion of a Knowledge of Man and of Love of Man* (1775–1778), he became the father of the modern science of characterology. Hampered in his work by the conflict of his Christian faith in free will with the apparent determinism of his physiognomic findings. The importance of his contribution should not be judged on the basis of amusing details as his suggestion that one might obtain an ideal "royal line" by shaving a queen bee in profile or his tirade on the physiognomically obvious inability of a bed bug to experience or inspire love.

La Vallière, Duchesse de. Françoise Louise de la Baume Le Blanc (1644–1710). One of the mistresses of Louis XIV (1661–ca. 1674), replaced by the Marquise de Montespan. She is the heroine of an episode in DUMAS' *The Vicomte de Bragelonne,* often published separately as *Louise de la Vallière* (see under THREE MUSKETEERS), and of Bulwer-Lytton's *Duchess de la Vallière* (1836).

Lavendar, Dr. The best known character of Margaret DELAND's Old Chester novels and stories, a wise and kindly old clergyman who is the close friend of many of his parishioners, a counsellor in time of need. Dr. Lavendar can be stern when he conceives it his duty, but his sincerity and disinterestedness are never in question. He is a prominent character in THE AWAKENING OF HELENA RICHIE, *Old Chester Tales,* and *Dr. Lavendar's People.*

Lavengro: The Scholar, Gipsy, Priest. A famous romance by George BORROW (1851) which with its sequel, *The Romany Rye* (1857), gives a picturesque account of the author's wanderings among the gipsies.

Lavery, Sir John (1856–1941). British artist, chiefly known for his portraits and figures.

Polymnia; A Lady in Black; Spring; Game of Tennis; etc.

Lavinia. Daughter of LATINUS, betrothed to Turnus, King of the Rutuli. When AENEAS landed in Italy, Latinus made an alliance with the Trojan hero, and promised to give him Lavinia as his wife. This brought on a war between Turnus and Aeneas, which was decided by single combat, in which Aeneas was victor.

Shakespeare gives this name to the daughter of TITUS ANDRONICUS in the play of that name.

Palemon and Lavinia. A pair of lovers whose tale is told in Thomson's SEASONS.

Lavoisier, Antoine Laurent (1743–1794). French chemist. One of the founders of modern chemistry. Overthrew the phlogiston theory of combustion by the use in experimentation of scales. His reforms in chemical nomenclature are the basis of the system still in use. Guillotined by order of the Convention.

Lavransdatter, Kristin, see KRISTIN LAVRANSDATTER.

Law, Andrew Bonar (1858–1923). Canadian-born British statesman. M.P. as Unionist member for a Glasgow division (1900). Succeeded A. J. Balfour as leader of the Unionist Party. Colonial Secretary (1915) and Chancellor of the Exchequer (1916–1918). Succeeded Lloyd George as Premier (October 22, 1922), but soon resigned because of ill health.

Law, John (1671–1729). Scottish financier. Condemned to death for having killed one Edward Wilson in a duel (1694), he fled to the continent cultivating various financial schemes including that of the issuance of paper money. He founded the first French bank (Banque Générale; 1716) and organized (1717) the so-called "Mississippi Scheme" or "System" which had control of colonization in Louisiana and soon absorbed the East India and China companies, the African Company, and the mint. It collapsed due to the overissue of paper money and governmental hostility (1720), and Law left the country. He declined Czar Peter's invitation to take charge of Russia's finances, returned to England for a while, and died poor and forgotten in Venice. Law's Louisiana venture, popularly known as the Mississippi Bubble, is alluded to in Goethe's *Faust,* Part II, when Mephistopheles proposes to the Emperor that paper money be issued on all the hidden treasures throughout the country.

Law, William (1686–1761). English devotional writer. Follower of the German mystic Jakob BÖHME. Author of the *Serious Call to a Devout and Holy Life* (1728) which influenced the Evangelical Revival. Especially remembered for his attack on Mandeville's *Fable of the Bees* (1723).

Lawes, Henry (1596–1662). English composer. Suggested to MILTON the subject of *Comus.* His music for it was performed in 1634. Cf. Milton's sonnet *To Mr. H. Lawes, on his Aires,* beginning,

> Harry, whose tuneful and well-measured song . . .

Lawes, Lewis E. (1883–1947). American penologist; warden of Sing Sing Prison, N.Y. (1920–1941). Author of works on prisons and penology, the best-known of which is *20,000 Years in Sing Sing* (1932).

Lawless, Emily (1845–1913). Irish novelist and poet. Author of *Hurrish* (1886) and *Grania* (1892), novels; and *With the Wild Geese* (1902), a volume of verse.

Lawless Parliament, see under PARLIAMENTS.

Law of Moses, see PENTATEUCH.

Law of the Medes and Persians. Used as an expression of the irrevocable. Cf. *Daniel* vi. 15.

Lawrence, David Herbert (1885–1930). English poet, short-story writer, and novelist, known for his lifelong obsession with problems of sexual relations, his attraction to primitive religions and philosophies of nature mysticism and the hero (see also Robinson JEFFERS), his maladjustment to the 20th-century industrial world, his hatred of and attacks upon Puritanism and Anglo-Saxon social conventions, and his constant search for a way of life in which he could put his theories of sex, morals, and society into practice. His writings, of great volume and variety, are uneven in literary value and at their best are marked by intensity of feeling, color and a mystical lyricism in their descriptions of nature, and skill in both satirical and sympathetic portrayals of character. Critics also point out his overfondness for preaching, his ranting and ill-balanced attacks on people and institutions he regarded as his enemies, and his tendency in several of his works to sacrifice character and plot to the exposition of his moral theories.

Lawrence's novels include *The White Peacock* (1911); *The Trespasser* (1912); SONS AND LOVERS (1913), regarded as his masterpiece; THE RAINBOW (1915); *The Lost Girl* (1920); WOMEN IN LOVE (1920); *Aaron's Rod* (1922); *Kangaroo* (1923); *The Boy in the Bush* (1924), in collaboration with M. L. Skinner; *St. Mawr* (1925); *The Plumed Serpent* (1925); LADY CHATTERLEY'S LOVER (1928), probably his best-known work; *The Virgin and the Gipsy* (1930). Books of his poetry, which began in the school of IMAGISM, include *Love Poems and Others* (1913); *Amores* (1916); *Look! We Have Come Through* (1917); *New Poems* (1918); *Tortoises* (1921); *Birds, Beasts, and Flowers* (1923); *Collected Poems* (1928); *Pansies* (1929); *Nettles* (1930); *Last Poems* (1933). Among collections of his short stories are *The Prussian Officer* (1914); *England, My England* (1922); *The Ladybird* (1923), in the U.S. known as *The Captain's Doll; Glad Ghosts* (1926); *The Woman Who Rode Away* (1928); *The Man Who Died* (1929); *The Lovely Lady* (1933); *Love Among the Haystacks* (1933); *Christ in the Tyrol* (1933). Travel-sketches are: *Twilight in Italy* (1916); *The Sea and Sardinia* (1921); *Mornings in Mexico* (1927); *Etruscan Places* (1927). Essays and criticism are represented by *Psychoanalysis and the Unconscious* (1921); *Movements in European History* (1921), written under the pseudonym of Lawrence H. Davidson; *Studies in Classical American Literature* (1923); *Pornography and Obscenity* (1930); *Apocalypse* (1931); *Phoenix: The Posthumous Papers of D. H. Lawrence* (1937). *The Widowing of Mrs. Holroyd* (1914), *Touch and Go* (1920), and *David* (1926) are plays.

Lawrence had an extremely unhappy childhood, having been the son of a Puritan-minded schoolteacher and a coal miner who beat his wife and child when drunk. The author also suffered from tuberculosis during the latter part of his life, saw his books banned as obscene, and was continually disappointed in his quest for a homeland and congenial associates. At one time or another he traveled and lived in Italy, Australia, Ceylon, New Zealand, Tahiti, the French Riviera, Mexico, and the southwestern part of the U.S.; in Taos, New Mexico, an artist's colony, he once dreamed of setting up an ideal social community. Aldous HUXLEY, Katherine MANSFIELD, and J. M. MURRY were close friends of Lawrence, and his admirers included several women who called him "Lorenzo," regarded themselves as his disciples, and engaged in jealous quarrels over his attentions. After his death, a number of books and memoirs, both unfriendly and adulatory, attacking each other, were published about Lawrence by the people who had known him; among these were Murry, Mabel Dodge LUHAN, Dorothy BRETT, and his wife, Frieda von RICHTHOFEN. The characters of Mark and Mary RAMPION in Huxley's POINT COUNTER POINT are believed to have been drawn from Lawrence and Frieda.

More for his personality and his ideas and attitudes than for his actual writing, D. H. Lawrence is considered one of the outstanding literary figures of the 20th century.

Lawrence, Friar, see LAURENCE.

Lawrence, Gertrude. Originally **Gertrud Alexandra Dagmar Lawrence Klasen** (1901–). English actress of Danish-Irish parentage. In U.S. (from 1924) played opposite Noel Coward in his *Private Lives* (1930) and *To-Night at Eight-Thirty* (1936–1937). Leading rôles in *Susan and God* (1935), *Lady in the Dark* (1940); the Theatre Guild production of Shaw's *Pygmalion* (1946); etc. Cf. her autobiography, *A Star Danced* (1945). Married to the theatrical producer Richard S. Aldrich.

Lawrence, James (1781–1813). American naval officer; commanded the *Chesapeake* in an unsuccessful engagement with the British frigate *Shannon* (June 1, 1813) which was blockading Boston harbor. Mortally wounded, he shouted, "Don't give up the ship!" The British captured the *Chesapeake,* but Lawrence's last words became a popular slogan in the U.S. navy.

Lawrence, Josephine (1897?–). American novelist, author of *Head of the Family* (1932); *If I Have Four Apples* (1935); *Sound of Running Feet* (1937); *Bow Down to Wood and Stone* (1938); *No Stone Unturned* (1941); etc. Miss Lawrence calls herself "an old-fashioned conservative," and writes streamlined moral tales. *Years Are So Long* (1934) is considered her best book.

Lawrence, St., see under SAINTS.

lazy as Lawrence, see under SAINTS.

Lawrence, Sir **Thomas** (1769–1830). English portrait painter, known chiefly for his courtly and elegant canvases of contemporary notables, as the countess of Derby (1790); George III (1792); Mrs. SIDDONS; the Princess de Lieven; J. P. Kemble (as Hamlet); etc. Succeeded Sir Joshua REYNOLDS as principal painter to the king.

Lawrence, Thomas Edward (1888–1935). English soldier, archaeologist, and author, famous for his activities in arousing and directing a successful rebellion of the Arabs against the Turks during World War I. A long account of his adventures and his ideas on Arab politics was published as *The Seven Pillars of Wisdom* (1926) in an edition of eight copies for the author's friends; later the book was published in a shorter form as *Revolt in the Desert* (1927) and was a best-seller. Lawrence held several official positions of importance and received a number of honors after the war. He enlisted in the British air force as "Private Shaw" and in 1927 had his name legally changed to T. E. Shaw in order, he said, to avoid the publicity that had attended him as a result of his exploits. It is reported that he chose the name of Shaw because on one occasion he was mistaken for a son of George Bernard SHAW.

Lawson, John Howard (1895–). American playwright, known for his experiments in EXPRESSIONISM in the 1920's and his later plays expressing proletarian sympathies. See PROLETARIAN LITERATURE. His works include *Roger Bloomer* (1923) and *Processional* (1925), examples of expressionism;

Loud Speaker (1927), on American politics; *The International* (1928), dealing with a world-wide revolution of the PROLETARIAT; *Success Story* (1932); *The Pure in Heart* (1934); *Gentlewoman* (1934); *Marching Song* (1937), dealing with a SIT-DOWN STRIKE. Convicted April 19, 1948, of contempt of Congress for refusing to tell House Committee on Un-American Activities whether or not he was a Communist.

Lawson, Robert (1892–). American illustrator. Best known for his collaboration with Munro LEAF as illustrator of *The Story of Ferdinand* (1936).

Lawson, Sam. A shiftless amusing Yankee who tells the stories related in Mrs. Harriet Beecher STOWE's *Old Town Folks*.

Layamon (fl. ca. 1200). English priest. Author of the Middle English chronicle in alliterative verse (with occasional rhymes), THE BRUT.

Lay of the Last Minstrel. A narrative poem by Sir Walter SCOTT (1805). Lady Margaret of Branksome Hall, "the flower of Teviot" is beloved by Baron Henry of Cranstown, but a deadly feud exists between the two families. The poem narrates how he wins both glory in arms and the hand of his fair lady.

Lays of Ancient Rome. A series of ballads of MACAULAY (1842). The chief ballads are *Horatius,* THE BATTLE OF THE LAKE REGILLUS, and *Virginia.*

Lays of the Scottish Cavaliers. Ballads by William Edmonstoune AYTOUN (1848). Ballad-romances in the style of Scott.

Laxdale Saga. An Icelandic saga of the early Middle Ages, dealing chiefly with the willful, selfish, and much-married GUDRUN who falls in love with KJARTAN. While Kjartan is at the court of King Olaf abroad, his cousin Bolli tells Gudrun that he, Kjartan, has become friendly with Olaf's sister Ingebjorg. Out of spite, Gudrun marries Bolli, and when Kjartan returns to Iceland and hears of the marriage, he, also out of spite, marries Hrefna. He gives to Hrefna an ornate coif which Ingebjorg had originally sent with him as a gift for Gudrun, and this causes Gudrun to precipitate a feud between the two families by having the coif stolen. There follows a series of raids and battles in which Kjartan is eventually killed through the machinations of the woman who loved him and whom he loved.

Lazarillo de Tormes. A romance by Diego Hurtado de Mendoza (*Sp.,* 1553), which was the forerunner of a whole school of fiction known as *gusto picaresco,* the style of roguery or picaresque romance.

Lazarus. (1) Any poor beggar; so called from the Lazarus of the parable, who was laid daily at the rich man's gate (*Luke* xvi). Another form of the same word is *lazar,* "a diseased person," from which are derived *lazar house, lazaretto,* "a pest-house," and *lazzarone,* "one of the homeless idlers of Naples."

(2) Another better known Lazarus of the New Testament is the brother of Mary and Martha of Bethany, whom Jesus raised from the dead. In Browning's poem concerning KARSHISH, the speaker, a skeptical Arabic physician, tells of his encounter with Lazarus after his resurrection.

Lazarus, Emma (1849–1887). American poet of Portuguese-Jewish ancestry, early in her career influenced by R. W. EMERSON, best-known for her poetry dealing with Jewish nationalism and the persecution of Jews in Europe at the time. Her books include *Admetus, And Other Poems* (1871), dedicated to Emerson; *Alide* (1874), a romance on the life of GOETHE; *The Spagnoletto* (1876), a tragedy; *Poems and Ballads of Heine* (1881), translations; *Songs of a Semite* (1882); *By the Waters of Babylon* (1887); *Poems* (1889). She was the author of the lines carved on the base of the STATUE OF LIBERTY, entitled *The New Colossus.*

Lazarus Laughed. A drama by Eugene O'NEILL (1927), dealing with Lazarus after his resurrection by Jesus. The man to whom new life has been given goes about preaching a new religion of love and eternal life, symbolized by laughter. He eventually goes to Rome and causes a sensation there, finally being stabbed by Caligula in the great amphitheater of the city but affirming until the last his belief in the triumph of life. Seven masked choruses, symbolizing varying periods of life, are used in this play.

Lazy Susan. A (revolving) muffin stand or turntable for sugar bowl, saltcellar, etc., as used in restaurants.

Lea, Fanny Heaslip (1884–). Popular American novelist and short-story writer. *Quicksands* (1911); *Wild Goose Chase* (1929); *Half Angel* (1932); etc.

Lea, Homer (1876–1912). American soldier and author. Physically handicapped. General in Chinese army (1909); adviser to Sun Yat-Sen (1911–1912). Author of *The Valor of Ignorance* (1909); *The Day of the Saxon* (1912); etc. His warnings about war in the Far East were revived after Japan's attack on Pearl Harbor, notable through the publicity given them by Clare BOOTHE Luce.

Leacock, Stephen Butler (1869–1944). Canadian humorist and professor of political science and economics at McGill University, Montreal (1903–1936). In addition to his professional works, he published studies of Mark Twain and Charles Dickens. His most famous books are his books of humor, as *Literary Lapses* (1910), *Nonsense Novels* (1911), *Moonbeams from the Larger Lunacy* (1915), *Frenzied Fiction* (1917); etc.

leader or **leading article.** A newspaper article in large type by the editor or one of the editorial staff; so called because it takes the lead or chief place in the summary of current topics, or because it is meant to lead public opinion. A short editorial article is called a *leaderette.*

The leading counsel in a case, the senior counsel on a circuit, the first fiddle of an orchestra, the first cornet of a military band, etc., is also called the *leader.*

Leaf, Munro (1905–). American humorist and illustrator of books for children. His best-known book, illustrated by Robert LAWSON, is the best seller *The Story of Ferdinand* (1936). Inventor of the Watchbirds in *A Picture Book of Behavior* (1939), illustrated by himself.

League of Nations. A league with headquarters at Geneva, formed after the close of World War I, largely through the exertions of Woodrow Wilson, President of the United States (1913–1921). The United States, however, never was a member of the League. With this exception the members were the signatories of the Treaty of Peace at Versailles (June 28, 1919), on behalf of the Allies, with certain other States, including Germany and the U.S.S.R.

The territorial integrity and existing political independence of all members was guaranteed by the League, and in cases of dispute between members arbitration, with a time limit, was agreed upon. The League was founded on a Covenant and a Charter of XXVI Articles, the High Contracting Parties agreeing to the Covenant in order to promote International Co-operation and to achieve International Peace and Security, by the acceptance of obligations not to resort to War—

> by the prescription of open, just, and honourable relations between Nations:
> by the firm establishment of the understandings of International Law as the actual rule of conduct among Governments: and
> by the maintenance of justice and a scrupulous regard for all Treaty Obligations in the dealings of Organized Peoples with one another.

The Council of the League consisted of the representatives of the British Empire, France, Italy, and Japan, with four others elected from among the remaining members.

During the 1920's, the League was able to settle a few minor disputes between nations and its contributions in the fields of refugee rehabilitation, public health, and international labor problems became considerable, but it had no power to enforce its policies in cases of war waged by important nations. It failed especially to be effective at the invasion of China by Japan (1937) and of Ethiopia by Italy (1934), as also during the Civil War in Spain (1936–1939). Several nations, including Italy, Japan, and Germany, resigned from the League in the late 1930's. With the beginning of World War II (1939) its membership was lost entirely. It was formally dissolved on April 18, 1946, its material and moral heritage being taken over by the United Nations Organization.

Leah. In the Old Testament, the daughter of LABAN. She is one of the wives of JACOB.

Leahy, William Daniel (1875–). American fleet admiral. Commander of battle force (1936–1937); chief of naval operations (1937–1939); retired (1939). Governor of Puerto Rico (1939–1940); ambassador to France (1941). Chief of staff to President (from July, 1942).

Leander Club. Oldest English open rowing club, dating from the early 19th century.

Léandre. (1) In Molière's *Fourberies de Scapin* (see SCAPIN), the son of Géronte. During the absence of his father, he falls in love with Zerbinette, whom he supposes to be a young gipsy but who is in reality the daughter of Argante, his father's friend. Scapin manages to secure the money for her ransom.

(2) In Molière's MÉDECIN MALGRÉ LUI, the lover of Lucinde.

Leaning Tower. The famous Leaning Tower at Pisa, in Italy, the campanile of the cathedral, is 181 ft. high, 57½ ft. in diameter at the base, and leans about 14 ft. It was begun in 1174, and the sinking commenced during construction.

> The Leaning Tower of Pisa continues to stand because the vertical line drawn through its centre of gravity passes within its base.—Ganot, *Physics.*

leap year. A year of 366 days, i.e., in the Julian and Gregorian calendars any year whose date is exactly divisible by four except those which are divisible by 100 but not by 400. Thus 1900 (though exactly divisible by 4) was not a leap year, but 2000 will be. It is an old saying that during leap year *the ladies may propose, and, if not accepted, claim a silk gown.* Fable has it that the custom was originated by St. Patrick.

Lear, Edward (1812–1888). English painter and writer, known for his LIMERICKS and NONSENSE VERSE, marked by absurd humor, whimsy, and fantasy. *The Owl and the Pussy-Cat* (1871) is his best-known set of verses. See also INCIDENTS IN THE LIFE OF MY UNCLE ARLY.

Lear, King, see KING LEAR.

learned. Coloman, King of Hungary (1095–1114), was called *The Learned.*

the learned blacksmith. Elihu Burritt (1811–1879), the linguist, who was at one time a blacksmith.

the learned painter. Charles Lebrun (1619–1690), so called from the great accuracy of his costumes.

the learned tailor. Henry Wild, of Norwich (1684–1734), who mastered, while he worked at his trade, the Greek, Latin, Hebrew, Chaldaic, Syriac, Persian, and Arabic languages.

the most learned fool in Christendom. James I of England, so called by the Duke of Sully.

Learned Ladies (*Les Femmes savantes*). A comedy by MOLIÈRE (1672). See FEMMES SAVANTES.

Learoyd, John. A Yorkshire private who appears in many of KIPLING's tales with his boon companions Terence Mulvaney and Stanley ORTHERIS. He is particularly prominent in *Greenhow Hill,* which relates the story of his youth.

Leatherstocking. The famous scout whose adventures bind together James Fenimore COOPER's five historical novels known as the *Leatherstocking series.* The novels in their chronological order (not as written but as regards their action) may be briefly summarized as follows. In THE DEERSLAYER (1841) are related the scout's adventures as a youth of twenty in the Lake Otsego settlement. THE LAST OF THE MOHICANS (1826) deals with the exploits of his prime under the name of Hawkeye in the French and Indian War. THE PATHFINDER (1840) narrates how he surrenders the girl he loves to a more successful suitor. In THE PIONEERS (1823) the old scout, here known as Natty Bumppo, is back in his boyhood home in the Otsego region. In THE PRAIRIE (1826) he spends his last days as a trapper in the vast plains west of the Mississippi, to which he has come in despair because of the destruction of the forests.

The character of Leatherstocking was probably drawn in part from Daniel BOONE, the American frontiersman. This "philosopher of the wilderness," Cooper says of Leatherstocking, "was simple-minded, faithful, utterly without fear, and yet prudent. . . . His feelings appeared to possess the freshness and nature of the forest in which he passed so much of his time, and no casuist could have made clearer decisions in matters relating to right and wrong."

Although ignorant of books, the scout is thoroughly versed in all the lore of woodcraft, and no emergency finds him at a loss. He is the immortal type of the American frontiersman, hardy, self-reliant, passionately devoted to the free, open country, which has stamped him as her own. His bitter-hearted retreat before the encroachments of civilization gives him a touch of tragedy that only adds to his stature.

Leavenworth. City in northeastern Kansas, site of a federal penitentiary and of Fort Leavenworth.

Leavenworth Case, The. A mystery novel (1878) by Anna Katharine GREEN.

Leaves of Grass. A volume of poems in free verse by Walt WHITMAN, first issued under this title in 1855, and reissued with additional poems several times during his lifetime.

> I loafe and invite my Soul;
> I lean and loafe at my ease, observing a spear of summer grass.
> Walt Whitman, *Song of Myself.*

Le Beau. In Shakespeare's AS YOU LIKE IT, a courtier attending upon Frederick, the usurper of his brother's throne.

Leblanc, Maurice (1864–1941). French detective-story writer. Creator of the detective Arsène Lupin.

Lebrun, Mme Vigée-, see VIGÉE-LEBRUN, MARIE ANNE ELISABETH.

Lebyadkin, Captain. In Dostoyevsky's THE POSSESSED, an army captain, simultaneously crafty, comically pompous, and proud, who seeks to extort money from Nikolay STAVROGIN, his brother-in-law, for the support of his sister Marya, and also to blackmail Stavrogin. The captain writes poetry to Lizaveta Nikolaevna TUSHIN and, in a manner alternately cringing and insolent, offers to be her protector.

Marya Timofyevna Lebyadkin. The captain's sister, a pathetic crippled idiot, one of the best examples of Dostoyevsky's studies of abnormal psychology. Stavrogin, in part to make a martyr of himself and in part as a weird joke, has married her secretly and continues to treat her, half-ironically, with the utmost gallantry and respect while his family and associates try to decide whether or not an actual marriage has taken place.

Le Charlier, Jean, see GERSON, JEAN.

Lecks, Mrs. One of the elderly New England heroines of F. R. STOCKTON's burlesque *The Casting Away of Mrs. Lecks and Mrs. Aleshine.*

Lecky, William Edward Hartpole (1838–1903). Irish historian and essayist. His most important work is *The History of England in the Eighteenth Century* in 8 volumes (1878–1890). Liberal Unionist M.P. (1895); opposed to home rule.

Leconte de Lisle, Charles Marie René (1818–1894). French poet, born on an island near Madagascar, a leader of the PARNASSIANS. His work deals with the religions, beliefs, and legends of the past, physical types and characteristics of various races and periods of history, and natural science, especially with respect to animals. He was opposed to the excessive subjectivity and emotional exaggeration of the romantic period, and his work is characterized by objectivity, a respect for the teachings of science, vivid descriptions, a precise, austere, and balanced style, cosmic pessimism, and a dislike for the industrial, mechanical civilization in which he lived. His books include *Poèmes antiques* (1852); *Poèmes barbares* (1862); *Histoire populaire du Christianisme* (1871); *Poèmes tragiques* (1884); *L'Apollonide* (1888), a drama; *Les Erinnyes* (1889), a tragedy in verse; *Derniers Poèmes* (1895). He also made translations from classic Greek literature. José-Maria de HEREDIA was a pupil of Leconte de Lisle.

Lecoq, Monsieur. A brilliant French detective, the chief character in the novel, *Monsieur Lecoq* (1869), by Émile Gaboriau (1833–1873) and its sequel *The Honor of the Name,* in *L'Affaire Lerouge* (1866) and *Le Dossier no. 113* (1867).

Le Corbusier. Pseudonym of **Charles Édouard Jeanneret** (1887–). Swiss architect and painter, known for his contributions to FUNCTIONALISM. Among these are the corner window, the glass façade, the use of ferroconcrete in buildings, and the elevated traffic ramp. See also BAUHAUS; WRIGHT, FRANK LLOYD.

Leda. In Greek mythology, the mother by ZEUS (who is fabled to have come to her in the shape of a swan) of two eggs, from one of which came CASTOR and CLYTEMNESTRA, and from the other Pollux and HELEN. The subject of Leda and the Swan has been a favorite with artists. Paul VERONESE, CORREGGIO, and MICHELANGELO have all left paintings of it.

the Leda Bible, see BIBLE, SPECIALLY NAMED.

Ledoux, Louis Vernon (1880–). American poet and critic. President, Ledoux & Co., chemists and assayers. Author of *The Art of Japan* (1927), and volumes of poetry, as *Songs from the Silent Land* (1905), *The Soul's Progress and Other Poems* (1907); etc.

Ledwidge, Francis (1891–1917). Irish poet, killed in first World War in Belgium. *Songs of the Field* (1915); *Songs of Peace* (1916); *Last Songs* (1918).

Lee, Ann (1735–1784). English mystic and founder of the American Shaker Society in Watervliet, N.Y. (1776). Known to her followers in England and America as "Ann the Word" or "Mother Ann."

Lee, Annabel, see ANNABEL LEE.

Lee, Canada (1907–). Negro actor, making his reputation in the dramatization of *Native Son* by Richard WRIGHT (1941), produced by Orson WELLES. He also played in an all-Negro *Macbeth,* in *Stevedore* (1934), *Mamba's Daughters,* and took the part of Caliban in Margaret WEBSTER's production of *The Tempest* (1945). On the screen he appeared in *Lifeboat* by John STEINBECK.

Lee, Gerald Stanley (1862–1944). American Congregational clergyman. Author of *Crowds* (1913), etc. Married **Jennette Barbour Perry** (1860–), professor of English at Smith College.

Lee, Henry. Known as **Light-Horse Harry Lee** (1756–1818). American soldier and statesman. Father of Robert Edward LEE. Cavalry commander in the Revolutionary War. His eulogy of Washington (1799) contains the famous words, "First in war, first in peace, and first in the hearts of his countrymen."

Lee, Robert Edward (1807–1870). American soldier. Son of Henry LEE. Commanded detachment which suppressed uprising at Harpers Ferry at the time of John Brown's raid (1859). At outbreak of Civil War, accepted command of Virginia forces. Turned Federals back at Fredericksburg (1862) and Chancellorsville (1863). Defeated at Gettysburg (1863). Conducted brilliant defensive operations against Grant, but finally, two months after having been made commander in chief of the Confederate armies, was forced to surrender at Appomattox Court House (April 9, 1865).

Lee, Sir **Sidney** (1859–1926). English scholar and man of letters. Associated (from 1883) with *Dictionary of National Biography,* finally (1891–1917) as editor in chief. Commissioned by George V to compile a biography of King Edward VII from original papers. Author of *A Life of William Shakespeare* (1898); *A Life of Queen Victoria* (1902); etc.

Lee, Simon, see SIMON LEE.

Lee, Vernon, see PAGET, VIOLET.

Leech, John (1817–1864). English caricaturist, especially noted for his work on the staff of *Punch* (1841–1864). Started his career as a student of medicine. After Seymour's suicide, Leech's application to become his successor as illustrator of the *Pickwick Papers* was rejected by Dickens (1836).

Leech, Margaret (1893–). American writer. Married (1928) Ralph Pulitzer (1879–1939). Author of *The Back of the Book* (1924); *Tin Wedding* (1926); *Anthony Comstock* (with Heywood Broun; 1927); *Reveille in Washington* (Pulitzer prize in history; 1942); etc.

Leech-Gatherer, The. See RESOLUTION AND INDEPENDENCE.

Lee-Hamilton, Eugene Jacob (1843–1907). English poet and novelist. Half-brother of Violet PAGET with whom he lived in Florence (from 1871). Best known for his *Sonnets of the Wingless Hours* (1894) and his translation of Dante's *Inferno* (1898).

Le Fanu, Joseph Sheridan (1814–1873). Irish novelist, famous for his mystery novel *Uncle Silas* (1864).

Le Fevre. A poor lieutenant, whose story is told by Laurence Sterne in *The Life and Opinions of Tristram Shandy*. See TRISTRAM SHANDY.

left, right, center. In the amphitheater, where the French National Assembly of 1789 convened, the nobles still commanded sufficient respect to be given places of honor to the *right* of the president. The radicals moved naturally as far away from them to the *left* as they could. The moderates found themselves squeezed in between in the *center*. Hence the political connotations of these terms. Carlyle, in *The French Revolution* (1847), was one of the first to speak in English of "the extreme Left." Derivatives like *leftist, leftism,* etc., did not come into general use until after the Russian Revolution (ca. 1920).

Le Gallienne, Eva (1899–). Famous American actress, daughter of the English writer **Richard Le Gallienne** (1866–1947) who enjoyed considerable renown in the nineties. Her name is permanently associated with the Civic Repertory Theater in New York which she founded (1926) and directed, and where she appeared in leading parts in *The Cherry Orchard, Peter Pan, Cradle Song, The Master Builder,* etc. A later venture in repertory, 1946–1947, was not successful.

Legend, Sir Sampson. In Congreve's comedy, LOVE FOR LOVE, a foolish, testy, prejudiced, and obstinate old man. He tries to disinherit his elder son Valentine, for his favorite son Ben, a sailor, and he fancies Angelica is in love with him, when she only intends to fool him. He says, "I know the length of the Emperor of China's foot, have kissed the Great Mogul's slipper, and have rid a-hunting upon an elephant with the Cham of Tartary."

Valentine Legend. The hero of *Love for Love,* in love with Angelica.

Benjamin Legend. Valentine's sailor brother, known as Ben.

Legenda Aurea, see GOLDEN LEGEND.

Legend of Good Women, The. A poem by Geoffrey CHAUCER, written about 1386. It is in the form of a dream-vision. See also BOOK OF THE DUCHESS. The god of love appears to Chaucer in a dream and rebukes him for having aided in giving women a reputation for unfaithfulness by writing TROILUS AND CRISEYDE and translating THE ROMANCE OF THE ROSE. In penance the poet is assigned to write a history of "good" women, or those who have been faithful according to the principles of COURTLY LOVE. See PALINODE. CLEOPATRA, THISBE, DIDO, MEDEA, LUCRECE, ARIADNE, and PHILOMELA are among the women so celebrated, their stories being taken chiefly from Virgil and Ovid.

The Prologue to *The Legend of Good Women,* containing a lyrical tribute to the daisy, is more famous than the narratives. The work is written in decasyllabic, or "heroic," COUPLETS, and is considered to be the first use of this form in English.

Legend of Montrose. A novel by Sir Walter SCOTT (1819), dealing with the struggle between the Royalists and Parliamentarians in the time of Charles I, culminating in the victory of the former in 1645 at Inverlochy under James Graham, Earl of Montrose. The heroine, Annot Lyle, the daughter of a Parliamentarian, is courted by two Royalist lovers and finally chooses one of them, the Earl of Monteith. The Rittmaster, Dugald DALGETTY, one of Scott's most famous characters, appears in this novel.

Legend of Sleepy Hollow. A tale (1819) by Washington IRVING, in *The Sketch Book.* See CRANE, ICHABOD; also SLEEPY HOLLOW.

Léger, Alexis St. Léger. Pseudonym **St.-J. Perse** (1887–). French poet, born on a coral island off Guadeloupe. His nurse was a secret priestess of Shiva. While in China as Secretary of the Diplomatic Corps, his friends were Chinese philosophers. Traveled in the Gobi Desert and the islands of the South Seas. Intimate friend and "right arm" of the French "apostle of peace," Aristide BRIAND. During World War II, his apartment in Paris was looted and five volumes of unpublished poems in manuscript were destroyed. Léger now lives in the U.S.A. His reputation as a poet rests almost entirely on the long poem *Anabase* (1924), translated into English (by T. S. Eliot; 1930), German, Italian, Rumanian, and Russian. It is "a series of images of migration, of conquest of vast spaces in Asiatic wastes," an intense expression of barbaric civilization.

Leginska, Ethel. Pseudonym of **Ethel Liggins** (1890–). English pianist and conductor. First woman to conduct Berlin Philharmonic, New York Symphony, Boston Philharmonic, etc.

Legion Kondor (*Ger.* "Condor Legion"). An organization of trained German airmen, fighting, supposedly as volunteers, against the Loyalists during the Spanish civil war (1936–1939).

Legion of Honor. A French order of distinction and reward (*Légion d'honneur*) instituted by Napoleon (1802) for either military or civil merit, and continued in France in the 19th and 20th centuries.

legitimate drama. Also **legitimate** or, in theatrical cant, **legit.** Drama of literary qualities, as opposed to farce, musical comedy, screen plays, etc.

leg-of-mutton school. So Eckhart called those authors who lauded their patrons in prose or verse, under the hope of gaining a commission, a living, or, at the very least, a dinner for their pains.

Legouis, Émile (1861–1937). French professor of English at the Sorbonne; authority on William Wordsworth. His *Histoire de la Littérature Anglaise* (written with Louis Cazamian; 1924) is available in an English translation (*A History of English Literature;* 1926) and has been acclaimed because of its refreshing conciseness throughout the Anglo-Saxon world.

Legree, Simon. In Harriet Beecher Stowe's UNCLE TOM'S CABIN, a slave-dealer and hideous villain, brutalized by slave-dealing and slave-driving.

Lehár, Franz (1870–). Hungarian composer of operettas. *The Merry Widow* (1905); *The Count of Luxemburg* (1909); *The Yellow Jacket* (1923), etc.

Lehman, Herbert H. (1878–). American banker. Governor of New York (1932–1942). First director of foreign relief and rehabilitation operations (UNRRA), succeeded by Mayor LA GUARDIA.

Lehmann, Lilli (1848–1929). German dramatic coloratura soprano, especially in Wagnerian rôles. Also interpreter of *lieder.*

Lehmann, Lotte (1895–). German concert and operatic soprano. North American début with Chicago Civic Opera Company (1930). Permanent residence in U.S. (since 1938). Author of the novel *Orplid mein Land* (1937), translated as *Eternal Flight* (1938), and an autobiography (1937).

Lehmann, Rosamond (1903–). English novelist. *Dusty Answer* (1927); *Invitation to the Waltz* (1933); *The Ballad and the Source* (1945); etc.

Lehmann, Rudolph Chambers (1856–1929). British journalist and liberal politician. Famous oarsman. On staff of *Punch* (from 1890). Author of *Mr. Punch's Prize Novels* (1893); *Anni Fugaces* (1901); etc. Father of Rosamond LEHMANN.

Leibnitz, Gottfried Wilhelm von (1646–1716). German philosopher and mathematician. Inventor of the differential and integral calculus, his treatise on the subject being published (1684) before Newton's and causing a long controversy. Left no complete and finished exposition of his philosophy. His principal work was published posthumously, *Nouveaux Essais sur l'Entendement Humain.* Ridiculed by Voltaire in *Candide.* Popularly his name remains associated with the ideas of the "monad" and a "pre-established harmony" in the universe.

Leicester, Robert Dudley, Earl of. Hero of Scott's KENILWORTH. See DUDLEY, ROBERT.

Leif Ericson, see ERICSON, LEIF.

Leigh, Amyas. The hero of Charles Kingsley's novel WESTWARD HO, a young man of great bodily strength and amiable but very combative disposition.

Leigh, Augusta. Half-sister of Lord BYRON. His wife, Anne MILLBANKE, hinted that he had had incestuous relations with her. Modern critics are inclined to believe the charge.

Leigh, Aurora, see AURORA LEIGH.

Leigh, Jocelyn. The heroine of Mary Johnston's historical novel TO HAVE AND TO HOLD.

Leighton, Clare (1899–). English woodcutter and wood engraver. Wrote and illustrated *The Farmer's Year* (1933); *Four Hedges* (1935); *County Matters* (1937); etc.

Leighton, Frederick. Baron **Leighton of Stretton** (1830–1896). English painter. Excelled in draughtsmanship and use of classical subjects.

Leila. (1) In Byron's GIAOUR, the beautiful slave of the Caliph Hassan. She falls in love with "the Giaour," flees from the seraglio, is overtaken, and cast into the sea.

(2) In Byron's DON JUAN, the young Turkish child rescued by Don Juan at the siege of Ismail.

Leilah. The Oriental type of female loveliness, chastity, and impassioned affection. Her love for Mejnoun, in Persian romance, is held in much the same light as that of the bride for the bridegroom in Solomon's song, or Cupid and Psyche among the Greeks.

Leipzig. *So-and-so was my Leipzig.* My fall, my irrevocable disaster, my ruin; referring to the Battle of Leipzig (October 1813), in which Napoleon I was defeated and compelled to retreat.

leitmotiv or **leitmotif** (*Ger.,* "leading motive"). In the Wagnerian music drama, a theme consistently reappearing with the reappearance of a given character, problem, thought, etc. Also, a corresponding device in literature. Thomas Mann has used the leitmotiv technique in conscious emulation of Wagner. Cf., for instance, in *The Magic Mountain,* the character of Settembrini, whose appearance is always accompanied by the same brief description of his clothes.

Lejeune, John Archer (1867–1942). American Marine Corps officer. Commanding officer (1920–1929; retired). Superintendent, V.M.I. (1929–1937); lieutenant general (April, 1942).

Leland, Charles Godfrey (1824–1903). American journalist and humorist; notable for

The Breitmann Ballads (collected, 1871), the most famous of these being *Hans Breitmann's Party* (May, 1857). Student of the language and customs of the gipsies. Compiler (with Albert Barrère) of *A Dictionary of Slang* (1889).

Lélia. (1) A novel by GEORGE SAND (1833). The beautiful heroine, Lélia, has forsworn love because of a cruel deception practiced on her. When she is made love to by the idealistic young poet Stenio, she pretends to yield but substitutes in her place her sister Pulcherie, a prostitute who closely resembles her. Shocked at the experience, Stenio plunges into dissipation and finally commits suicide. Magnus, a priest who has been beside himself with love for Lélia, now goes insane and kills her.

(2) A novel by Fogazzaro. See MAIRONI, PIERO.

Lélie. (1) In Molière's L'ÉTOURDI, an inconsequential, light-headed, but gentlemanly coxcomb. (2) In Molière's SGANARELLE, the lover of Célie.

Lely, Sir Peter. Originally **Pieter Van der Faes** (1618–1680). Dutch portrait painter, resident in England (from 1641).

Lemaître, Jules (1853–1914). French critic and author. His essays and reviews were published in the series *Contemporains* (7 vols.; 1885–1899) and *Impressions de Théâtre* (10 vols., 1888–1898). His fame rests on his refreshing skill in conveying unprejudiced impressions not cramped by preconceived theories.

Lemnos. The island where Vulcan fell when Jupiter flung him out of heaven. One myth connected with Lemnos tells how the women of the island, in revenge for their ill-treatment, murdered all the men. The ARGONAUTS found the place an "Adamless Eden." They were received with great favor by the women, and as a result of their few months' stay the island was repopulated, and the queen, Hypsipyle, became the mother of twins by Jason.

lemming. A small furry rodent, the best-known European species being noted for mysterious migrations in enormous numbers at long intervals, when they cover the land like locusts and finally progress into the sea where many are drowned. They have been called "the rats of Norway." Cf. *The Lemmings,* a sonnet by John Masefield.

Lemon, Mark (1809–1870). English novelist, playwright, etc. One of the founders and first editor of *Punch* (1841–1870).

Lemoyne, see BIENVILLE.

Lemprière, John (1765?–1824). English classical scholar. Compiler of the reference work, *Bibliotheca Classica, or Classical Dictionary* (1788), dealing with classical history and mythology.

lemures. The name given by the Romans to the spirits of the dead, especially specters which wandered about at night-time to terrify the living ones.

Lemuria. The name given to a lost land that is supposed to have connected Madagascar with India and Sumatra in prehistoric times. Cf. W. Scott Elliott's *The Lost Lemuria* (1904). See also ATLANTIS.

Lena. The heroine of Conrad's VICTORY.

Lena Rivers. A widely read 19th-century novel by Mary Jane Holmes (*Am.,* 1856).

Lenclos, Anne. Known as **Ninon de Lenclos** (1620–1705). French lady of fashion. Famous for her beauty and wit. Conducted a dazzling salon. The most distinguished men of her day were among her lovers. Mlle. Scudéry drew a portrait of her under the name of Clarisse in *Clélie*.

Lend-Lease Act. An act passed by Congress and approved by President Franklin D. Roosevelt (March 11, 1941) designed to give material aid to the democracies fighting the Axis, with the settlement to wait until later. By it the President was empowered to sell, exchange, or otherwise dispose of any article of defense (through a later amendment also of foodstuffs and industrial products) to any country on any terms and for any purpose he chose. The first lend-lease material went to Britain. In course of time it included planes, ordnance, guns, bombs, ammunition, tanks, watercraft, metals, motor vehicles, petroleum products, machinery, agricultural products (3¾ billions of pounds of food to Britain and Russia in 1942), etc., etc. In February, 1942, the first of twelve mutual aid agreements was signed providing for reverse lend-lease to U.S.A. Victory over Germany and Japan brought an end to the lend-lease program. Total lend-lease aid from March, 1941, to July 1, 1945, was $42,020,779,000. Reciprocal lend-lease aid to U.S. had a dollar value of $5,600,364,000 as of April 1, 1945.

Lenglen, Suzanne (1899–1938). French lawn-tennis player; won world's hard-court (women's) singles championship at Paris (1913); won championships in singles, doubles, mixed doubles of France and England; defaulted in her sole attempt for American singles title (1921); defeated Helen WILLS at Cannes (1926); became professional same year, touring U.S.A., and retired in 1927. An impassioned player. She said of herself: "I just throw dignity to the winds and think of nothing but the game."

Lengyel, Emil (1895–). Hungarian-born professor of history at the Brooklyn Polytechnic Institute (since 1935). Naturalized American citizen (1927). Author of *Hitler* (1932); *Millions of Dictators* (1936); *The Danube* (1939); *Siberia* (1943); etc.

Leni. In Franz Kafka's THE TRIAL, the servant of the hero's advocate. She is a childish, *gamine*-like little creature who tries to gain for the hero, K., assistance in his case.

Leni-Lenape. So the Delaware Indians call themselves. The name signifies in their language "original" or "outstanding men."

Lenin, Nikolai. Original name **Vladimir Ilich Ulyanov** (1870–1924). Russian Communist leader. Engaged in revolutionary activities in Czarist Russia (from 1894). Exiled (1897) to eastern Siberia, where he married and completed his major work on *The Development of Capitalism in Russia* (1899). Edited the revolutionary journal *Iskra* (*The Spark*) from Switzerland (1900). After the Socialist Congress of 1903, which brought about the schism of Mensheviks and BOLSHEVIKS, Lenin became a leader of the Bolsheviks. Encouraged revolution at the time of the Russo-Japanese war. Denounced World War I as imperialistic. Issued a program for the creation of a new Socialist International (1914); laid foundation for Communist International at Socialist Congress in Switzerland (1915). When the Russian front collapsed (1917), Lenin was returned to Russia in a sealed train across Germany. Under his leadership the moderate provisional government of KERENSKY was overthrown and the supreme power in Russia was vested in the Soviets. Lenin became head of the Soviet of People's Commissars and premier upon the establishment of the dictatorship of the proletariat (1918). Accepted peace of Brest-Litovsk with Germany (1918). Defended Russia against counter-revolutionary armies (1918–1921); introduced extensive socialistic reforms which were modified (1921) by the New Economic Policy. Died at Gorki (January 21, 1924). His body was embalmed and placed on permanent exhibition in Moscow. He remains the great modern hero and practically the god of the Union of Soviet Socialist Republics. The name of the city of Petrograd, before 1914 known as St. Petersburg, was changed (1924) in his honor to Leningrad.

Lennie. In John Steinbeck's OF MICE AND MEN, a pathetic half-wit of prodigious strength who is fond of small, soft things but kills what he attempts to caress.

Lenore. (1) The "rare and radiant maiden" of Poe's poem THE RAVEN; the dead love of the narrator. Poe has another poem called *Lenore*.

(2) The heroine of Bürger's ballad of that name (*Ger.*, 1748–1794), in which a spectral lover appears after death to his mistress, and carries her on horseback behind him to the graveyard, where their marriage is celebrated amid a crew of howling goblins. The poem is based on a popular legend.

Lenôtre, André (1613–1700). French landscape architect under Louis XIV, ennobled by the king. Designed, partly in collaboration, the gardens at Versailles, Chantilly, Saint-Cloud, Fontainebleau, etc.; also Kensington Gardens and St. James' Park in London, and the gardens of the Quirinal and the Vatican in Rome.

Lent. The word means originally "the season of spring." Hence, in many Christian churches, the spring period of fasting which prepares the faithful for Easter and is a time of special penitence.

Leodogrance of Camiliard. In Arthurian romance, the father of GUINEVERE, wife of King Arthur. Uther Pendragon once gave him the famous ROUND TABLE, which can seat 150 knights, and when Arthur marries Guinevere, Leodogrance gives him the table and 100 knights as a wedding gift.

Leo Hunter, Mr. and Mrs., see HUNTER.

León, Fray Lui Ponce de. See under PONCE.

Leonard, St. See under SAINTS.

Leonard, William Ellery (1876–1944). American educator and poet. English faculty, University of Wisconsin. Highest achievement, *Two Lives*, an autobiographical story in verse (1925). Also *Sonnets and Poems* (1906); *The Poet of Galilee* (1907); *The Lynching Bee and Other Poems* (1920); *A Son of Earth* (collected verse; 1928); several plays; translations; the prose autobiography, *The Locomotive God* (1927); a posthumous volume of poetry, *A Man Against Time* (1945); etc.

Leonato. In Shakespeare's MUCH ADO ABOUT NOTHING, governor of Messina, father of Hero, and uncle of Beatrice.

Leoncavallo, Ruggiero (1858–1919). Italian operatic composer and librettist. Best known for *I Pagliacci* (1892). His *La Bohème* (1897) is inferior to Puccini's version of the same subject. Other works include *Chatterton* (1896); *Der Roland* (1904); etc.

Leone Leoni. A romance by George SAND (1835), centering about the devotion of the heroine, Juliette, to her faithless and unscrupulous lover, Leone Leoni.

Leonesse, Leonnesse, Leonnais, Leones, Leonnoys, Lyonnoys, etc. A mythical country belonging to Cornwall, supposed to have been sunk under the sea since the time of King ARTHUR. It is very frequently mentioned in the Arthurian romances. See LYONESSE.

Leonidas. The Spartan hero who resisted the Persians at Thermopylae with only three hundred men.

the Leonidas of Modern Greece. Marco Bozzaris, from his courageous feats at Kerpenisi in 1823.

Leonine city. The part of Rome which contains the Vatican. It was fortified by Pope Leo IV. Hence the name.

Leonine verse. So called from Leonius, a canon of the church of St. Victor, in Paris, in the 12th century, who first composed in such verse. It has a rhyme in the middle of the line; as:

> Pepper is black, though it hath a good smack.
> *Est avis in dextra melior quam quattuor extra.*

Léonor. In Molière's *L'École des Maris,* an orphan brought up by ARISTE.

Leonora. (1) In Verdi's opera IL TROVATORE, a princess who falls in love with Manrico.

(2) In Beethoven's opera entitled FIDELIO, the heroine, wife of Fernando Florestan, a state prisoner in Seville. In order to effect her husband's release, she assumes the attire of a man, and the name of Fidelio. For the rest of the tale, see FERDINAND.

(3) In Donizetti's opera LA FAVORITA, Leonora de Guzman was the "favorite" of Alfonso XI of Castile.

(4) For the *Leonora* celebrated for her relation to the Italian poet Tasso, see TASSO AND LEONORA.

Leonov, Leonid Maksimovich (1899–). Russian novelist. Called by Maxim Gorki "one of the chief representatives of the contemporary group of Soviet writers who continue the work of classical Russian literature." He lost one eye in the fighting before Leningrad and was one of the six script writers to contribute to the Soviet war film *This Is the Enemy.*

Leontes. In Shakespeare's WINTER'S TALE, King of Sicily, husband of Hermione.

leopard. So called because it was thought in medieval times to be a cross between the lion (*leo*), or lioness, and the *pard,* which was the name given to a panther that had no white specks on its body.

References to the impossibility of a leopard changing its spots are frequent. The allusion is to *Jeremiah,* xiii. 23.

> Loins make leopards tame.
> Yea; but not change his spots.
> Shakespeare, *Richard II,* i. 1.

In Christian art, the leopard represents that beast spoken of in *Revelation* xiii. 1–8, with seven heads and ten horns; six of the heads bear a nimbus, but the seventh, being "wounded to death," lost its power, and consequently is bare.

> And the beast which I saw was like unto a leopard, and his feet were as the feet of a bear, and his mouth as the mouth of a lion.—*Rev.* xiii, 2.

In heraldry, the leopard is supposed to typify warriors who have performed some bold enterprise with force, courage, promptitude, and activity. The lions in the royal coat of arms of England were formerly called and depicted as leopards, the idea being that no lion would permit another to remain on the same field.

the Knight of the Couching Leopard. Sir Kenneth, or rather, the Earl of Huntingdon, Prince Royal of Scotland, who followed, *incognito,* Richard I to the Crusade, and is the chief character of Scott's TALISMAN.

Leopardi, Conte Giacomo (1798–1837). Italian poet and philologist. Physically handicapped and deeply pessimistic in his work. *Canzoni* (1824); *Versi* (1826); *Canti* (1836); etc.

Leopolita Bible, see BIBLE, NAMED.

Leporello. In Mozart's opera DON GIOVANNI, the valet of Don Giovanni or Don Juan.

leprachaun. The fairy shoemaker of Ireland; so called because he is always seen working at a single shoe (*leith,* half, *brog,* a shoe or brogue). Another of his peculiarities is that he has a purse that never contains more than a single shilling at one time.

> Do you not catch the tiny clamour,
> Busy click of an elfin hammer,
> Voice of the Leprachaun singing shrill,
> As he merrily plies his trade?
> W. B. Yeats, *Fairy and Folk Tales.*

He is also called lubrican, cluricaune, etc. In *The Honest Whore* (Pt. II, III, i) by DEKKER and MIDDLETON, Hippolito speaks of Bryan, the Irish footman, as "your Irish lubrican."

Le Queux, William Tufnell (1864–1927). English novelist, chiefly known for his mystery and detective stories.

Ler, King. The earliest known original of the King in Shakespeare's tragedy KING LEAR, an ocean god of early Irish and British legend. He figures in the romance *The Fate of the Children of Lir* as the father of FIONNUALA. On the death of Fingula, the mother of his daughter, he married the wicked Aoife, who, through spite, transformed the children of Lir into swans, doomed to float on the water for centuries till they hear the first mass-bell ring. This is the subject of one of Thomas MOORE's *Irish Melodies.*

Lermontov, Mikhail Yurievich (1814–1841). Russian poet and novelist. Known as "the poet of the Caucasus," where he was twice sent in exile (once for his impassioned ode to the Czar after the death of Pushkin), and where he was killed in a duel. Some of his best-known poems are *The Demon, Ismail Bey, Hadji Abrek,* and *The Song of the Czar*

Ivan Vasilievich. His best known novel is *A Hero of Our Time* (1839).

Lernean hydra. In Greek mythology, a monster hiding in the swamps of Lerna in Argolis, and killed by HERCULES as one of his twelve labors.

Lerner, Max (1902–). Russian-born American writer and educator. Editor of *The Nation* (1936–1938); professor of political science, Williams College (from 1938). Editorial writer for the New York newspaper *PM*. Author of *It Is Later Than You Think* (1938); *Ideas are Weapons* (1939); *Ideas for the Ice Age* (1941); etc.

le roi le veut (*Fr.*, "the king wills it"). The form of royal assent made by the clerk of the old French *parlement* to bills submitted to the Crown. The dissent is expressed by *le roi s'avisera* (The king will give it his consideration).

Le Roi s'amuse (*Fr.*, "the king takes his pleasure"). Title of a drama by Victor HUGO (1832). It is the source of the libretto of Verdi's opera *Rigoletto* (1851).

Lerouge, Claudine. In Émile Gaboriau's detective novel *L'Affaire Lerouge* (1866) a worthless nurse, whose murder gives the famous detective Monsieur LECOQ an opportunity to use all his skill at unraveling mystery.

Leroux, Gaston (1868–1927). French journalist. Author of detective and mystery stories.

Le Sage, Alain-René (1668–1747). French novelist and dramatist, best known for his famous picaresque romance GIL BLAS (1715). This work is marked by realism, vivid character portraits, and a satirical depiction of the social life of the time of its composition; some critics regard it as the first example of the modern novel of manners. Le Sage also wrote a number of plays in the tradition of MOLIÈRE, the most outstanding of which is *Turcaret* (1709), one of the first cynical studies of money and finance in French literature.

Lesbian. Pertaining to Lesbos, one of the islands of the Greek Archipelago, or to Sappho, the famous poetess of Lesbos, and to the practices of female homosexuality (Lesbianism) attributed to her.

Lesbian kiss. An immodest kiss. The ancient Lesbians were noted for their sensuality.

Lesbian poets. Terpander, Alcaeus, Arion and Sappho, all of Lesbos.

Lesbian rule. A flexible rule used by ancient Greek masons for measuring curved moldings, etc.; hence, figuratively, a pliant and accommodating principle or rule of conduct.

Lescaut, Manon, see MANON LESCAUT.

lese majesty. Also **lèse-majesté** (Fr., from Lat. *laesa majestas,* "hurt or violated majesty"). High treason, a crime against the sovereign.

Leslie, Bonnie, see BONNIE LESLIE.

Leslie, Frank. Original name **Henry Carter** (1821–1880). English-born American engraver and publisher of illustrated journals, as *Frank Leslie's Illustrated Newspaper* (founded in 1855). He died in poverty, but after his death, his wife, **Miriam Florence Leslie,** *née* **Follin** (1836?–1914) legally changed her name to Frank Leslie (1882) and successfully continued his publishing venture.

Leslie, Shane (1885–). Irish journalist and writer.

Lesly, Ludovic, surnamed **le Balafré.** In Scott's QUENTIN DURWARD, an old archer in the Scotch guard of Louis XI of France. He is the uncle of Quentin Durward.

Les Misérables, see MISÉRABLES, LES.

Le Soeur, Meridel. American author. Her *North Star Country* (1945) is a study of the region of Minnesota, Wisconsin, and the western shores of the Great Lakes. She has written many short stories, some of which appeared in the *Best Short Stories* of 1927 and 1932.

Lespinasse, Julie Jeanne Éléonore de (1732–1776). French letter-writer. Companion to the blind Mme. du Deffand (1754–1764), with whom she conducted a sparkling literary *salon.* Friend of D'Alembert, the Marquis de Mora, the Count de Guibert, etc. To Guibert were addressed the *Lettres de Mlle de Lespinasse,* published (1809) by Guibert's widow, giving a picturesque account of contemporary life.

Lesseps, Vicomte **Ferdinand Marie de** (1805–1894). French diplomat and engineer. Originator of the Suez-Canal plan (first conceived in 1832). Received concession from Said Pasha, Viceroy of Egypt (1854), and completed the canal in ten years (1859–1869). Also president of a French company that began work on cutting through the Isthmus of Panama (1881–1888). The scheme collapsed, and Lesseps was condemned for misappropriation of funds. Sentence not carried out.

Lessing, Gotthold Ephraim (1729–1781). German dramatist and critic, best known for his dramas *Minna von Barnhelm* (1763) and NATHAN THE WISE (1779) and his critical treatise entitled LAOKOÖN (1766). For a full statement of Lessing's rôle in the history of modern criticism, cf. Mary Colum, *From These Roots* (1937).

Lessways, Hilda. The heroine of Arnold Bennett's trilogy of novels, CLAYHANGER, *Hilda Lessways* (1911) and *These Twain* (1916).

L'Estrange, Sir **Roger** (1616–1704). English journalist and writer of political pamphlets. Surveyor of printing presses and licenser of the press under Charles II and James II (1663). Issued the *Public Intelligence* and *The News* (1663–1666). Perhaps also projected the *City Mercury* (1675). Edited the *Observator* (1681–1687), in which he attacked the Whigs. Notable linguist and translator.

Lestrigons. A fabulous race of cannibal giants who lived in Sicily. ULYSSES (*Odyss.* x) sent two of his men to request that he might land, but the king of the place ate one for dinner and the other fled. The Lestrigons assembled on the coast and threw stones against Ulysses and his crew; they fled with all speed, but many men were lost. See also POLYPHEMUS.

Lethe (Gr. *letho, latheo, lanthano,* "to cause persons not to know"). In Greek mythology, one of the rivers of HADES, which the souls of all the dead are obliged to taste, that they may forget everything said and done when alive. See STYX.

Lethean dew. Dreamy forgetfulness.

Letters from an American Farmer. A group of essays by Hector St. John de CRÈVECOEUR published in London in 1782. They deal with farm life on the American frontier in the 18th century, partly idealistic in the tradition of J. J. ROUSSEAU and partly realistic, with social life and customs in the American colonies, and with America as a refuge for the persecuted and oppressed peoples of the world.

letters patent. In American law, an open letter under seal of the government, granting some right, privilege or title. Specifically, an instrument issued by the Patent Office giving the patentee for a stated period a monopoly in the manufacture, use, and sale of an article he has patented.

lettre de cachet. See under CACHET.

Leucadia's Rock. A promontory, the south extremity of the island Leucas or Leucadia, in the Ionion Sea. SAPPHO leapt from this rock when she found her love for Phaon unrequited. At the annual festival of Apollo, a criminal was hurled from Leucadia's Rock into the sea; but birds of various sorts were attached to him, in order to break his fall, and if he was not killed, he was set free. The leap from this rock is called "the Lovers' Leap."

Leucothea (the white goddess). So Ino, the mortal daughter of Cadmus and wife of Athamas, was called after she became a sea goddess. Athamas in a fit of madness slew one of her sons; she threw herself into the sea with the other, imploring assistance of the gods, who deified both of them. Her son, Melicertes, then renamed Palemon, was called by the Romans Portunus, or Portumnus, and became the protecting genius of harbors.

Levana. A Roman goddess whose special province it was to watch over new-born babes. Her name was used as the title of an educational treatise by J. P. RICHTER.

Levant, Oscar (1906–). American pianist, formerly one of the experts on the radio program "Information Please." Author of *A Smattering of Ignorance* (1940). Also composer and conductor.

levant and ponent winds. The east wind is the levant, and the west wind the ponent. The former is from Lat. *levare,* "to raise" (sunrise), and the latter from *ponere,* "to set" (sunset).

Levelers. In English history, a body of ultra-Republicans in the time of Charles I and the Commonwealth, who wanted all men to be placed on a level, particularly with respect to their eligibility to office. John Lilburne was one of the leaders of the sect, which was active from 1647 to 1649, when it was suppressed by Cromwell's troops.

In Irish history the name was given to the 18th century agrarian agitators, afterwards called WHITEBOYS. Their first offences were leveling the hedges of enclosed commons; but their program developed into a demand for the general redress of all agrarian grievances.

Lever, Charles James (1806–1872). British novelist, born in Ireland. His song, "The pope he loved a merry life," is an adaptation of the German, "Der Papst lebt herrlich in der Welt," which he knew from the time when he had traveled as a student from Göttingen to Weimar. His novels include *Harry Lorrequer* (1837); *Charles O'Malley* (1841); etc.

lever de rideau (*Fr.,* "curtain-raiser"). A short sketch performed on the stage before "drawing up the curtain" on the real business.

Leverhulme. 1st Viscount (since 1922). **William Hesketh Lever** (1851–1925). English soap manufacturer. Known for his progressive employment practices, as the profit-sharing plan adopted at Port Sunlight, the model industrial city founded by him.

Levering, Albert (1869–1924). American humorist draughtsman. Best known for his work on *Life* magazine, under John Ames Mitchell. Illustrated various books by John Kendrick BANGS.

Leverrier, Urbain Jean Joseph (1811–1877). French astronomer. Determined mathematically, on the basis of previously observed irregularities in the motion of Uranus, the existence and exact position of another planet. It was found by Galle in Berlin (1846) and named Neptune. The same discovery was made independently by the British astronomer J. C. Adams.

Levi. (1) In the Old Testament, one of the sons of the patriarch JACOB, also the tribe of his descendants, known as Levites, the priestly tribe among the Israelites.

(2) In the New Testament, a name for MATTHEW.

Levi, Isaac. In Reade's IT IS NEVER TOO LATE TO MEND, a wise and kindly Jew.

Leviathan (*Hebr.*, "that which gathers itself together in folds." Cf. Is. xxvii, 1). The name given in the Bible to a mythic sea-serpent. The name is also applied to a whale, and to a ship of great size from the reference in *Ps.* civ. 25, 26:

> This great and wide sea, wherein are things creeping innumerable, both small and great beasts. There go the ships: there is that leviathan, whom thou hast made to play therein.

Thomas HOBBES took the name as the title for his famous political treatise on "the Matter, Form, and Power of a Commonwealth Ecclesiastical and Civil" (1651), and applied it to the Commonwealth as a political organism.

the Leviathan of literature. Dr. Johnson (1709–1784).

Levin, Meyer (1905–). American journalist and novelist, known for his studies of American-Jewish and proletarian life, especially in the city of Chicago. His books include *Reporter* (1929); *Frankie and Johnny* (1930); *Yehuda* (1931), concerned with Zionist Palestine of the 20th century; *The New Bridge* (1933), about city tenement-dwellers; *The Old Bunch* (1937), a novel of young people of Jewish parentage growing up in Chicago in the 1920's, realistically presented (see STUDS LONIGAN); *Citizens* (1940), dealing with a steel-strike "massacre." See also HALPER, ALBERT; PROLETARIAN LITERATURE.

Levine, Constantine Dmitrich. A character in Tolstoi's ANNA KARÉNINA, a man of wealth and good birth but of a shy, unworldly disposition. Matthew Arnold expresses the opinion that "in Levine's religious experiences Tolstoi was relating his own."

Levinsky, David, see DAVID LEVINSKY.

Levites. In Jewish history, the descendants of Levi, one of the sons of JACOB. Hence, the body of assistants to the priests in the temple, originally consisting of all male members of the tribe of Levi. Later, the Levites were the learned class, becoming teachers, religious instructors, scribes and judges.

Leviticus. The Greek title of the third book of the Old Testament. It was intended for the Levites, the tribe of the Jewish priesthood, and gives them full instructions about feast-days and sacrifices.

Levy, Benn Wolfe (1900–). English playwright. *Mrs. Moonlight; Art and Mrs. Bottle;* etc.

Lewes, George Henry (1817–1878). English philosophical writer and literary critic, influenced by Auguste COMTE. His connection with Marian Evans (George ELIOT) was regarded by both partners as a marriage. Author of a *Biographical History of Philosophy* (1845–1846); *Aristotle* (1864); *Actors and the Art of Acting* (1875); *Physical Basis of Mind* (1877). First editor, *Fortnightly Review* (1865–1866). His *The Life of Goethe* (1855) has still more than historical interest.

Lewis, Alfred Henry (1858?–1914). American journalist and writer of fiction. Best known for stories about his invented Arizona town Wolfville, as *Wolfville Days* (1902); *Wolfville Folks* (1908); etc.

Lewis, Cecil Day, see DAY-LEWIS, CECIL.

Lewis, Clive Staples. Pseudonym **Clive Hamilton** (1898–). Author of *The Screwtape Letters; Beyond Personality* (1945), and other books on Christianity and Christian behavior, which excel in both wit and depth. *Out of the Silent Planet* (1938) is the first of a trilogy of "fantastic" novels with theological overtones.

Lewis, Dominic Bevan Wyndham (1894–). British journalist and author. *François Villon* (1928); *King Spider: Louis XI of France* (1930); *Emperor of the West, Charles V* (1932); etc. Not identical with the American painter and author Percy Wyndham LEWIS.

Lewis, Mrs. **Ethelreda** (died 1946). English writer. "Discovered" Alfred Aloysius HORN, whose life story *Trader Horn* (1927) she rewrote in part and edited for him. The book sold 170,000 copies.

Lewis, Gilbert Newton (1875–1946). Collaborated with Dr. Ernest O. Lawrence in inventing the CYCLOTRON, and was, with Dr. Irving Langmuir, co-author of the Lewis-Langmuir atomic theory. He developed the valence theory of chemical reaction. Cf. his *Valence and the Structure of Atoms and Molecules* (1923). With Dr. Harold C. Urey, a former student of his, he discovered "heavy water." He won many scientific awards and the Distinguished Service Medal in World War I.

Lewis, Harry Sinclair (1885–). American novelist, famous during the 1920's for his biting satires on the smugness, hypocrisy, bigotry, and vulgarity of American small-town life as he saw it in his time, especially in the Middle West and especially as embodied in the businessman and the Protestant clergyman. The best-known of these novels, in which Lewis is considered to have been influenced by the writings of H. L. MENCKEN, are MAIN STREET (1920); BABBITT (1922); ARROWSMITH (1925); and *Elmer Gantry* (1927), an attack on the hypocrisy of the church. They aroused a great deal of controversy on their first publication, and Lewis was denounced with the same vigor as Mencken. His works of the 1930's, however, considered to be inferior to his best-known books, tended to exalt the attitudes and institutions of the family, the middle-class businessman, and the small town that he had previously satirized; *Work of Art* (1934), praising the success of a small hotel-keeper, and *The Prodigal Parents* (1938), presenting rebellious and radical-minded children in an unsympathetic light, are notable examples of his change of viewpoint. Other works of Lewis are: *Our Mr. Wrenn* (1914); *The Trail of the Hawk* (1915); *The Innocents* (1917); *The Job* (1917); *Mantrap* (1926); *The Man Who Knew Coolidge* (1928); DODSWORTH (1929), dramatized in 1934; *Ann Vickers* (1933); IT CAN'T HAPPEN HERE (1935), dramatized in 1936; *Jayhawker* (1934), a play; *Bethel Merriday* (1940); *Angela Is Twenty-Two* (1940), a play; *Cass Timberlane* (1945) and *Kingsblood Royal* (1947).

In 1926 Lewis was awarded the Pulitzer Prize for *Arrowsmith,* but refused it. In 1930 he won the Nobel prize, being the first American to be so honored, and did not refuse it. His second wife was Dorothy THOMPSON.

Lewis, Isaac Newton (1858–1931). American army officer. Invented among other military devices the Lewis machine gun (1911) and was the originator of the modern artillery corps organization of the U.S. army (1902).

Lewis, Matthew Gregory (1775–1818). English novelist, author of the famous Gothic novel THE MONK (1796). He was known as "Monk Lewis."

Lewis, Meriwether (1774–1809). American explorer closely associated with William Clark on expedition (1804–1806) up Missouri River to source. Sent out by President Jefferson to explore the Louisiana Purchase. Governor of Louisiana Territory (1807–1809). Cf. *Lewis & Clark; Partners in Discovery* (1947), by John BAKELESS.

Lewis, Percy Wyndham (1886–). American-born English painter, essayist, and novelist, not to be confused with the British journalist Dominic Bevan Wyndham LEWIS. First known as the leader of a school of painting called VORTICISM which attracted a great deal of public attention in the period immediately preceding World War I. Later, during the 1920's, he became known for his bitter attacks on contemporary writers and social philosophy. His books include *The Art of Being Ruled* (1925), a long essay; *The Lion and the Fox: A Study of the Rise of the Hero in the Plays of Shakespeare* (1926); *Time and Western Man* (1928); *The Childermass* (1928), a prose "epic" on the judgment of sinners after death; *The Wild Body* (1928), a collection of short stories; *Paleface: The Philosophy of the Melting-Pot* (1929); *The Diabolical Principle* (1930); *Apes of God* (1930), a satirical novel, ranked in novelty by some critics with James Joyce's ULYSSES; *The Snooty Baronet* (1932); *One-Way Song* (1933); *Men Without Art* (1934), criticism; *Blasting and Bombardiering* (1937), an autobiography covering the years 1914–1926; *The Revenge for Love* (1937); *The Mysterious Mr. Bull* (1938). During the 1920's, he also edited for a time the little magazines *Blast* and *The Enemy.*

Lewis' writings are marked by iconoclasm and extreme individuality. Some critics denounced his ideas on social philosophy as Fascist in tendency. In the late 1930's he became the champion of a return to naturalistic, representational painting and attacked the abstract schools of the earlier part of the 20th century, especially the type of work represented by PICASSO.

Lewis Baboon. Louis XIV of France is so called in Arbuthnot's *History of John Bull* (1712). See JOHN BULL. A play upon the word Bourbon.

Lewisohn, Ludwig (1883–). German-born American novelist and critic. His novels include *The Case of Mr. Crump* (1927); *The Island Within* (1928); etc. His critical works are *The Spirit of Modern German Literature* (1916); *The Poets of Modern France* (1918); *Story of American Literature,* first published (1932) as *Expression in America;* etc. Also known as an accomplished translator.

Lexington. A town in Massachusetts, site of the first bloodshed in the American Revolution (April 19, 1775). American militia forced the British to withdraw. The losses were 88 American and 273 British lives.

lex non scripta (*Lat.,* unwritten law). The common law, as distinguished from the statute or written law. Common law does not derive its force from being recorded, and though its several provisions have been compiled and printed, the compilations are not statutes, but simply remembrancers.

lex talionis (*Lat.*) The law of retaliation.

Ley, Robert (1890–1945). German Nazi leader, noted for his rabid anti-Semitism. Ruthlessly ruled German labor front (from 1933). Committed suicide after imprisonment by U.S. forces.

Lhasa. Capital of Tibet and sacred city of the Lamaist Buddhists. Chief public edifices are Buddhist monasteries, some built 1,200 years ago, the most recent being two centuries old. The summer resident of the DALAI LAMA is nearby, accommodating about 7,500 monks. Because of the monks' hostility to visitors other than pilgrims Lhasa is known as the Forbidden City.

On the road to Ihasa,
Himalayan and strange,
I thought I saw them winding
From range to lower range.
Cale Young Rice, *The Pilgrims of Thibet.*

Libbey, Laura Jean (1862–1924). American writer of sentimental novels, as *Lovers Once but Strangers Now; Miss Middleton's Lover; When His Love Grew Cold;* etc.

Libby Prison. Notorious Confederate military prison at Richmond, Virginia, during the American Civil War, converted from a tobacco warehouse. Later reassembled at Chicago as a war museum.

Liber. In Roman mythology, a god of wine. In course of time identified with BACCHUS.

liberal arts. In the Middle Ages, the seven branches of learning: grammar, logic, rhetoric, arithmetic, geometry, music and astronomy. In modern times, the liberal arts include the languages, sciences, philosophy, history, etc. The term is a translation of Latin *artes liberales,* so called not because they were liberal in any modern sense of the word, but because their pursuit was the privilege of the freemen who were called *liberi.*

Liberator, The. The Peruvians so call Simón Bolívar (1783–1830), who established the independence of Peru. Daniel O'Connell (1775–1847) was also so called, because he led the agitation which resulted in the repeal of the Penal Laws and the emancipation of the Irish Roman Catholics.

Liberator of the World. So Benjamin Franklin (1706–1790) has been called.

Liberator, The. (1) Antislavery weekly published in Boston (1831–1865), edited by William Lloyd GARRISON.

(2) For the 20th-century journal of the same name, see under MASSES, THE.

Liberia. Negro republic on the west coast of Africa. 43,000 square miles. A million to a million and a half inhabitants. Greater part of country densely forested. Rubber and palm products. Established by the American Colonization Society for the repatriation of freed slaves (begun ca. 1820), and constituted as an independent republic (1847) with the capital Monrovia, named for President James Monroe of the U.S.

Liberty Bell. The bell, now in Independence Hall, which was rung when the Continental Congress adopted the Declaration of Independence. First cast in London (1752) with the inscription, "Proclaim liberty throughout the land unto all the inhabitants thereof," it was recast (1753) in Philadelphia with the same legend and was cracked in 1835.

liberty cap. The *bonnet rouge* (red bonnet) of the French revolutionists. It is identical with the Roman *pilleus,* the cap that was given to a slave at his manumission, and also with the Phrygian cap, which in Greek art is often characteristic of Orientals.

Liberty Enlightening the World. The colossal statue standing on Bedloe's (or Liberty) Island, at the entrance of New York Harbor, presented to the American people by France in commemoration of the centenary of the American Declaration of Independence, and inaugurated in 1886. It is of bronze, 155 ft. in height, standing on a pedestal 135 ft. high, and represents a woman, draped, and holding a lighted torch in her upraised hand. It is the work of the Alsatian sculptor, Auguste Bartholdi (1834–1904). On its base is carved a sonnet, *The New Colossus,* by Emma LAZARUS.

Liberty Hall. A place of freedom. In Goldsmith's comedy SHE STOOPS TO CONQUER, Squire Hardcastle says to young Marlow and Hastings, when they mistake his house for an "inn," and give themselves airs, "This is Liberty Hall, gentleman; you may do just as you please here."

the Apostle of Liberty, see under APOSTLE.

Libethra. The place in Greece where the nightingales sing most sweetly since it is there that the Muses buried the fragments of ORPHEUS' body.

libido. In psychoanalysis, animal energy as motive force in psychic reaction and behavior. FREUD identifies it as a sexual phenomenon; JUNG conceives of it as an all-inclusive primal urge to live.

Libra (*Lat.,* "the balance"). The seventh sign of the Zodiac (and the name of one of the ancient constellations), which the sun enters about September 22 and leaves about October 22. At this time the day and night being "weighed" would be found equal.

Library of Congress. U.S. national library at Washington, D.C., created by Congress (1800) for its own use but later made available for generally governmental and public service. It is one of the greatest libraries in the world with about 196,000 new acquisitions every year. Its printed library cards are available for use in other institutions. Librarian of Congress (by presidential appointment): Herbert Putnam (1899–1939); Archibald MACLEISH (1939–1945); Luther Harris Evans (1945–).

libretto (*It.,* "little book"). Originally, the booklet in which the text of an opera or any extended choral composition is printed. Now generally, the text itself.

Libya. Africa, or all the north of Africa between Egypt and the Atlantic Ocean. It was the

Greek name for Africa in general. The Romans used the word sometimes as synonymous with Africa, and sometimes for the fringe containing Carthage.

Lichas. In Greek mythology, the friend of HERCULES who brought him Deianira's fatal tunic. He was thrown into the sea by Hercules.

lichwake, formerly **likewake.** Watch over a dead person. From *like,* "body" or "corpse." *A Lykewake Dirge* is an old Scotch ballad.

Lick Observatory. An observatory on Mt. Hamilton, California, East of San José, founded by James Lick (1796–1876), and later transferred to the University of California (1888). In the twenties, when the 100-inch reflector was installed, the English poet Alfred NOYES, who was present, wrote in the "Prologue" to *Watchers of the Sky:*

> This long battle for the light,
> This little victory of the spirit of man
> Doomed to defeat—for what was all we saw
> To that which neither eyes nor soul could see?
> Doomed to defeat and yet unconquerable,
> Climbing its nine miles nearer to the stars.

lictor. In Roman antiquity, an officer attending a magistrate. A dictator had twenty lictors, a consul twelve, a praetor six, etc. The lictor bore the FASCES as the insignia of his office. He cleared the way and enforced due respect for his superior and also arrested offenders and executed condemned criminals.

Liddell, Henry George (1811–1898). English classical scholar, Dean of Christ Church (1855–1891). Author with Robert Scott of the standard *Greek-English Lexicon* (1843; revised 1925 ff.). Also *History of Ancient Rome* (1855). His daughter **Alice Liddell** was the original of ALICE IN WONDERLAND and the child for whom Lewis CARROLL wrote his famous fantasy.

Liddell Hart, Basil Henry (1895–). English military writer. His *The Defence of Britain* (1939) is a book reputed to have influenced British military strategy at the outbreak of World War II. His theory concerning the character the war would assume was proved erroneous. Close friend of T. E. LAWRENCE.

Lido. A reef and sandbank outside the lagoon of Venice. Famous as a fashionable bathing resort on the Adriatic.

lie (A.S. *lyge,* from *leogan,* "to lie"). A falsehood.

a white lie. A conventional lie, such as telling a caller that Mrs. A or Mrs. B is not at home, meaning not "at home" to that particular caller.

the father of Lies. Satan (*John* viii. 44).

the greatest lie. In Heywood's FOUR P's, an INTERLUDE of about 1543, a Palmer, a Pardoner, a Poticary, and a Pedlar dispute as to which can tell the greatest lie. The Palmer says he has never seen a woman out of patience, whereupon the other three P's throw up the sponge, saying such a falsehood cannot possibly be outdone.

the lie circumstantial, direct, etc., see COUNTERCHECK.

to give one the lie. To accuse him to his face of telling a falsehood.

to give the lie to. To show that such and such a statement is false; to belie.

Lie, Jonas (1880–1940). Norwegian-born American painter. President, National Academy of Design (from 1934).

Lie, Trygve (1896–). Secretary general of the United Nations (1945). Formerly Norwegian minister for foreign affairs, and (since 1935) member of the Norwegian cabinet as minister of justice, minister of commerce, and minister of supply.

Lieberman, Elias (1883–). Russian-born American educator and poet. Teacher of English in New York City schools. Author of a volume of verse, *Hand Organ Man* (1930); etc.

Liebknecht, Wilhelm (1826–1900). German journalist and politician. Founder (with the assistance of Karl MARX) of the Social Democratic Labor party (1869). His son **Karl Liebknecht** (1871–1919) was a lawyer and Communist leader in the German Reichstag (1912) who violently opposed Germany's policies before World War I. After the collapse of the second Reich, he became one of the leaders of the Spartacus party and was arrested and murdered (with Rosa LUXEMBURG) during transfer to prison.

Lieschen. In Carlyle's SARTOR RESARTUS, the housekeeper of Diogenes Teufelsdrökh.

Lifar, Serge (1905–). Russian choreographer and ballet master. Friend and student of DIAGHILEV. Author of *Serge Diaghilev: His Life, His Work, His Legend* (1940).

Life. An American magazine, founded in 1883 and known for its humor and its serious editorial campaigns on general issues. It was extremely popular during the 1890's and the early 1900's, Charles Dana GIBSON being one of its outstanding contributors. It lost its foothold during the 1920's and in 1936 was sold in part to the magazine *Judge* and in part to Time, Inc. See LUCE, HENRY. The latter transformed it into a new *Life,* of enlarged size, consisting chiefly of photographs of current news events, with a style and viewpoint similar to those of TIME.

Life, The Battle of, see BATTLE OF LIFE.

Life and Death of Jason. A poem by William MORRIS.

Life and Death of Mr. Badman, The. An allegorical dialogue by John BUNYAN (1680), in which Mr. Wiseman tells of the vicious life and habits and the eventual death of Mr. Badman, using his story to point out the folly of wickedness.

Life-in-Death. A phantom in Coleridge's ANCIENT MARINER who throws dice with Death and wins the Mariner, though his comrades fall to Death's lot.

> Her lips were red, her looks were free
> Her locks were yellow as gold
> The Nightmare Life-in-Death was she,
> Who thicks man's blood with cold.
> Pt. III. 190.

Life in the Iron Mills. A realistic short story of life among factory workers, written by Rebecca H. DAVIS and published in the *Atlantic Monthly* in 1861. It was the first of the author's works to attract attention.

Life on the Mississippi. A book by Mark TWAIN (1883) recording his own youthful adventures as a pilot on the Mississippi River. The second part of the book reports a later trip through the same territory.

Life's Handicap, Being Stories of Mine Own People. A volume of short stories of India by Rudyard KIPLING (1891). It includes several stories in which Terence MULVANEY, Stanley ORTHERIS, and John LEAROYD appear.

Life with Father. See under Clarence Shepard DAY.

Liffey. A river in Ireland on which the city of Dublin is located. In James Joyce's FINNEGANS WAKE it plays an important part, personified as Anna Livia PLURABELLE. See also EARWICKER.

Lifted Veil, The. A story by George ELIOT (1859) dealing with clairvoyance.

Ligea. In classic myth, one of the three SIRENS.

Ligeia. Title and heroine of one of Edgar Allan POE's short stories. The beloved first wife of the narrator comes to him for a moment through the just-dead body of her successor, whom she has haunted into her death. See also LIGEA.

Light, Christina. A beautiful girl with whom the hero is infatuated in Henry James' RODERICK HUDSON. She reappears as the Princess CASAMASSIMA in James' novel of that title (1886; reprinted in 1948).

Light-Horse Harry. A nickname given to General Henry LEE with reference to his quick movements of cavalry in the campaigns of the Revolutionary War.

Lightnin'. A play by Winchell SMITH and Frank BACON (*Am.*, 1918), which owed its success to the homely, lovable character of the hero, Lightnin' Bill Jones. It had 1291 performances.

Light of Asia, The. An exposition of Buddhism in verse by Sir Edwin ARNOLD (1878).

Light that Failed, The. A novel by Rudyard KIPLING (1890). Through his experience as an illustrator in the Sudan, the hero, Dick Heldar, wins both professional success and a firm friend in the war correspondent Torpenhow. He is in love with his foster sister Maisie, now also an artist, but Maisie is shallow and selfish and does not appreciate his devotion. Dick gradually goes blind from a sword cut received in the Sudan, working courageously against time on his painting, *Melancholia.* Although Maisie is summoned by Torpenhow, she heartlessly leaves Dick to his fate, and he carries out his plan of dying at the front. In a later edition a happy ending is provided.

Lightwood, Mortimer. In Dickens' novel OUR MUTUAL FRIEND, a solicitor who conducts the "Harmon murder" case. He is the great friend of Eugene Wrayburn, barrister-at-law, and it is the great ambition of his heart to imitate the *nonchalance* of his friend.

Li Hung-chang (1823–1901). Chinese statesman. Founded Chinese navy. Prime minister (1895–1898); visited Europe and U.S. (1896). Commissioned to restore peace after the Boxer uprising (1900). Often referred to as "the BISMARCK of Asia."

Lilburne, John (ca. 1614–1657). A contentious LEVELER in the Commonwealth who was so rancorous against rank that he could never satisfy himself that any two persons were exactly on the same level; hence the phrase, *if no one else where alive, John would quarrel with Lilburne.*

> Is John departed? and is Lilburne gone?
> Farewell to both—to Lilburne and to John.
> Yet, being gone, take this advice from me.
> Let them not both in one grave buried be.
> Here lay ye John, lay Lilburne thereabout;
> For if they both should meet, they would fall out.
> *Epigrammatic Epitaph.*

Liliencron, Baron **Detlev von** (1844–1909). German poet and novelist. His first volume of verse, *Adjutantenritte* (1883) established him at the age of forty as a leader of the youngest generation of poets (naturalists, impressionists).

Lilienthal, David Eli (1899–). Director (1933–1946) and chairman (1941–1946) of the Tennessee Valley Authority (TVA). Member of American Bar Association. Chairman (since 1946) of U.S. Atomic Energy Commission.

Liliom. A drama by Ferenc MOLNÁR (1909), produced in New York in 1921. The hero is a disreputable but fascinating sideshow barker. One act shows him before the judges of the other world; another, on earth again with a single chance to redeem himself. The play was made into a charming and touching musical under the title *Carousel* in 1944, with music by Richard Rodgers.

Lilith. A Semitic (in origin probably Babylonian) demon supposed to haunt wildernesses in stormy weather, and to be specially dangerous to children and pregnant women. She is referred to in *Is.* xxxiv. 14, as the "screech-owl" (Revised Version, "night monster," and in margin "Lilith") and the Talmudists give the name to a wife that Adam is fabled to have had before Eve, who, refusing to submit to him, left Paradise for a region of the air, and still haunts the night. In Arabic legend, she married the Devil and became the mother of the *Jinn.* Superstitious Jews put in the chambers occupied by their wives four coins inscribed with the names of Adam and Eve and the words "Avaunt thee, Lilith!" GOETHE introduced her in his FAUST, and D. G. ROSSETTI in his *Eden Bower* adapted the Adamitic story, making the Serpent the instrument of Lilith's vengeance.

> It was Lilith, the wife of Adam . . .
> Not a drop of her blood was human,
> But she was made like a soft sweet woman.
> D. G. Rossetti, *Eden Bower.*

Liliuokalani, Lydia Kamekeha (1838–1917). Queen of the Hawaiian Islands, sister of King Kalakaua, after whose death she succeeded to the throne. Deposed (1893). Married to the American governor of Oahu, John O. Dominis.

Lillibulero. A political song, popular during the English revolution of 1688 and still the most savagely thunderous of British marching songs. The music is by Henry PURCELL. The text by Lord Wharton (?) satirizes James II and the Catholics, using the refrain "lillibulero bullen a la" which is said to have been used as a watchword by the Irish Catholics in their massacre of the Protestants (1641). The song was included by Bishop Percy in his *Reliques.*

Lillie, Beatrice (1898–). Canadian-born satirical comedienne. On London stage since 1914; first appearance in New York in 1924, with Gertrude LAWRENCE, in *Charlot's Revue.* Also in moving pictures. In private life, she is Lady Peel.

Lilliput. The country of pigmies (Lilliputians) to whom Lemuel GULLIVER was a giant.

Lilly, William (1602–1681). English astrologer and prophet. Issued prophetic pamphlets and almanacs (1644–1680). Author of *Christian Astrology* (1647); etc. As Sidrophel he is satirized in Butler's *Hudibras.*

Lillyvick. In Dickens' NICHOLAS NICKLEBY, the collector of water-rates, and uncle to Mrs. KENWIGS. Mr. Lillyvick looks on himself as one of the *élite* of society. "If ever an old gentleman made a point of appearing in public shaved close and clean, that old gentleman was Mr. Lillyvick. If ever a collector had borne himself like a collector, and assumed a solemn and portentous dignity, as if he had the whole world on his books, that collector was Mr. Lillyvick."

lily. There is a tradition that the lily sprang from the repentant tears of Eve as she went forth from Paradise.

In Christian art, the lily is an emblem of chastity, innocence, and purity. In pictures of the Annunciation, Gabriel is sometimes represented as carrying a lily-branch, while a vase containing a lily stands before the Virgin, who is kneeling in prayer. St. Joseph holds a lily-branch in his hand, indicating that his wife Mary was a virgin.

lily of France. The device of CLOVIS was three black toads, but the story goes that an aged hermit of Joye-en-valle saw a miraculous light stream one night into his cell, and an angel appeared to him holding an azure shield of wonderful beauty, emblazoned with three gold lilies that shone like stars, which the hermit was commanded to give to Queen Clotilde. She gave it to her royal husband, whose arms were everywhere victorious, and the device was thereupon adopted as the emblem of France. Cf. *Les Petits Bollandistes,* vol. vi, p. 426. Tasso, in his JERUSALEM DELIVERED, terms the French *gigli d'oro* (golden lilies). It is said the people were commonly called *Liliarts,* and the kingdom *Lilium* in the time of Phillippe le Bel, Charles VIII, and Louis XII.

the city of lilies. Florence.

Lily Maid of Astolat, see ELAINE.

Lily of the Valley, The (Le Lys dans la vallée). A novel by BALZAC (1836), the heroine of which is Mme de MORTSAUF.

Limbus (*Lat.,* "border, fringe, edge"). The borders of Hell; the portion assigned by the schoolmen to those departed spirits to whom the benefits of redemption did not apply through no fault of their own. According to DANTE, Limbo is between Hell and that borderland where dwell "the praiseless and the blameless dead."

Limbus Fatuorum. The Paradise of Fools. As fools or idiots are not responsible for their works, the old schoolmen held that they are not punished in Purgatory and cannot be received into Heaven, so they go to a special "Paradise of Fools."

> Then might you see
> Cowls, hoods, and habits, with their wearers tossed
> And fluttered into rags; then relics, beads,
> Indulgences, dispenses, pardons, bulls,
> The sport of winds. All these, upwhirled aloft,
> Into a Limbo large and broad, since called
> The Paradise of Fools.
> Milton, *Paradise Lost,* iii, 489.

See also FOOL'S PARADISE under FOOL.

Limbus of the Moon. Ariosto, in his ORLANDO FURIOSO, xxxiv. 70, says that in the moon are treasured up the precious time misspent in play, all vain efforts, all vows never paid, all counsel thrown away, all desires that lead to nothing, the vanity of titles, flattery, great men's promises, court services, and death-bed alms.

Limbus Patrum. The half-way house between earth and heaven, where the patriarchs and prophets who died before the death of the Redeemer await the Last Day, when they will be received into Heaven. Some hold that this is the "Hell" into which Christ descended after He gave up the ghost on the cross.

Shakespeare uses *limbo patrum* for "quod," jail, confinement.

> I have some of them in limbo patrum, and there they are like to dance these three days.—*Henry VIII,* v. 4.

Limbus Puerorum. The Child's Paradise, for children who die before they are baptized or are responsible for their actions.

Limehouse. Violent and vitriolic abuse of one's political opponents; so called out of compliment to an oratorical display by Mr. Lloyd George at Limehouse, London, on July 30, 1909, when he poured forth scorn and abuse on dukes, landlords, financial magnates, etc., many of whom, in the course of later events, became his best friends. Hence, *Limehousing,* indulging in such abuse.

limerick. A nonsense verse in the meter popularized by Edward LEAR in his *Book of Nonsense* (1846), of which the following is an example:

> There was a young lady of Wilts,
> Who walked up to Scotland on stilts;
> When they said it was shocking
> To show so much stocking,
> She answered, "Then what about kilts?"

The name was not given till much later, and comes from the chorus, "We'll all come up, come up to Limerick," which was interposed after each verse as it was improvised and sung by a convivial party.

In the 20th century, especially in the U.S., the composition of limericks became a popular parlor game, with the products often tending toward the ribald and the off-color.

limey. Short for lime-juicer. In slang, a British sailor. In the British navy the consumption of lime juice was compulsory as a protection against scurvy. Also, an Englishman.

Lin, Leslie Charles Bowyer, see CHARTERIS, LESLIE.

Linacre, Thomas (1460?–1524). English physician and classical scholar; one of the founders of the College of Physicians in London (1518). Among his students were Sir Thomas MORE and ERASMUS. Physician to Henry VIII; ordained priest (1520). Author of a Latin grammar *Rudimenta Grammatica* (1523) for Princess Mary; a Latin translation of GALEN's works; etc. One of the earliest representatives of British humanism.

Lincoln, Abraham (1809–1865). Sixteenth president of the United States. Lincoln appears in a number of historical novels of the Civil War period and previous, notably Edward Eggleston's novel, THE GRAYSONS, which introduces him in his early career, Winston Churchill's CRISIS, Irving Bacheller's *Man for the Ages* (1919) of which he is the hero, and its sequel, *Father Abraham* (1925). John Drinkwater treated Lincoln's life dramatically in his play, *Abraham Lincoln* (*Eng.,* 1918), and Robert E. SHERWOOD also wrote a popular play on the Civil War president, entitled ABE LINCOLN IN ILLINOIS (1938). Biographies by Carl SANDBURG and Edgar Lee MASTERS are well known, and many American poets wrote poems to and concerning Lincoln, most notably Walt WHITMAN in WHEN LILACS LAST IN THE DOORYARD BLOOMED. Other memorable poems concerning Lincoln have been written by Edwin Markham, Edwin Arlington Robinson, James Oppenheim, and John Gould Fletcher.

Lincoln, Joseph Crosby (1870–1944). American novelist, born on Cape Cod, Massachusetts, which furnishes the setting of his novels and short stories. CAP'N ERI (1902); *Shavings* (1918); *Rugged Water* (1924); *The Big Mogul* (1926); *All Alongshore* (1931); *Storm Signals* (1935); etc.

Lincoln Memorial. A memorial erected in Potomac Park, Washington, D.C., dedicated to the memory of Abraham LINCOLN. Construction work began on Lincoln's Birthday, 1914. It is in the general form of a classic Greek temple, having one large enclosed hall of oblong shape which is surrounded by a Doric colonnade, with a large seated statue of Lincoln by Daniel Chester French, within.

Lincoln's Inn. An INN OF COURT in London, taking its name from the 14th-century town house of the Earl of Lincoln which once stood on the site.

Lind, Johanna Maria. Known as **Jenny Lind** or Madame **Jenny Lind-Goldschmidt** (1820–1887). Swedish coloratura soprano called "the Swedish Nightingale." Made her début as Agatha in *Der Freischütz* (1838); introduced to America by P. T. Barnum (1850–1852). Married in Boston (1852) Otto Goldschmidt, German-born composer and pianist; toured continent. Resident in her last years of England; British subject (1859) and professor of singing at the Royal College of Music (1883–1886).

Linda Condon. A novel by Joseph HERGESHEIMER (1919), the story of a child brought up by a devoted but not too respectable mother in the uncongenial atmosphere of fashionable hotels. She becomes a beautiful, self-contained, elusive, fastidious being who fascinates men but can never give them anything of herself. Even when she marries and has a family, she remains essentially aloof. She is the life-long inspiration of a great sculptor, Pleydon, who sees her seldom, but is able through his imagination to glimpse in her elusive spirit the unattainable ideal he is always seeking.

Lindabrides. The heroine of the romance entitled *The Mirror of Knighthood,* one of the books in DON QUIXOTE's library. Lindabrides became later a common name for a loose woman, a courtesan.

Lindau. An old German Socialist in Howells' HAZARD OF NEW FORTUNES. Whittier spoke of him as "that saint of the rather godless sect of dynamiters and atheists—a grand figure."

Lindbergh, Mrs. **Anne Spencer,** *née* **Morrow** (1907–). American poet and essayist. Wife of Charles LINDBERGH. Her best books concern flights taken with her husband. *North to the Orient* (1935); *Listen, the Wind* (1938); etc. Her prose has a distinctly poetic vein. Her sharply criticized essay, *The Wave of the Future* (1940), was influenced by her husband's isolationism, and was regarded in some quarters as an apologia for FASCISM.

Lindbergh, Charles Augustus (1902–). American aviator of Swedish descent. Began his career as airmail pilot. First solo non-stop transatlantic flight from Roosevelt Field, N.Y., to Le Bourget Air Field, Paris (May 20–21, 1927) in monoplane *The Spirit of St. Louis.* Promoted aeronautics, made physiological experiments with Dr. Alexis Carrel in Paris. Awarded Congressional Medal of Honor. Joined "America First," opposing U.S. entry into war in Europe. Contributed to U.S. war effort in the laboratory and on airplane production lines. As a technical observer flew P-38's in a large number of missions against Japan and engaged in combat with Japanese planes. Author of *We* (1926).

Lindon, Mr. and Mrs. Fred. Characters in Clyde Fitch's drama THE TRUTH.

Lindsay, Howard (1889–). American actor and playwright. Collaborated with Russel CROUSE on musical comedies, the stage adaptations of *Life with Father* by Clarence Day, Jr. (1939; with title rôle played by Lindsay); *Arsenic and Old Lace;* and the Pulitzer prize play *State of the Union* (1946).

Lindsay, Nicholas Vachel (1879–1931). American poet, known for the vivid imagery and striking dramatic and auditory effects of his poetry, which he read from the lecture platform with theatrical gestures and intonation, in an effort to cultivate a love of poetry in the populace. His work dealt with American subjects and heroes, patriotism, and a mystic faith in nature and the soil. His books include *The Tree of Laughing Bells* (1905); *Rhymes to be Traded for Bread* (1912); *General William Booth Enters into Heaven, And Other Poems* (1913); *The Congo, And Other Poems* (1914); *The Chinese Nightingale, And Other Poems* (1917), considered to contain his best work; *The Daniel Jazz* (1920); *The Golden Whales of California* (1920); *The Candle in the Cabin* (1926); and *Johnny Appleseed* (1928). He also wrote a number of books of essays on politics, his adventures, and his "gospel of beauty." Among his most famous single poems are GENERAL WILLIAM BOOTH ENTERS INTO HEAVEN, THE CONGO *Abraham Lincoln Walks at Midnight,* and *The Chinese Nightingale.*

Lindsay was a striking personality and lived an adventurous life, during the first years of his career lecturing on temperance and art in the winter and in the summer vagabonding about the country, frequently trading his poems for food and shelter. He was a friend of Edgar Lee MASTERS.

Lindsay, Norman Alfred William (1879–). Australian artist excelling in pen drawings and water color. Also known as a novelist of rebellious irony. Co-sponsor of the Endeavor Press and founder, with his three sons, of the magazine *Vision* (1924). "A sort of healthy, roistering Aubrey Beardsley."

Lindsay, Jack (1900–). Australian novelist and classical scholar. Son of Norman LINDSAY. He is associated with fine presses in London, doing translations from Greek and Latin. He says that in his historical novels he has tried "to stabilize a world-view based subjectively on Freud and objectively on Frazer's *Golden Bough.*" He has also experimented with "mass-declamation poems." A prolific writer and an active anti-Fascist.

Linet, see LYNETTE.

ling. The common heather.

> Where the pewit wheels and dips
> On heights of bracken and ling.
> Sir William Watson, *Ode in May.*

Lingard, Captain. In Conrad's OUTCAST OF THE ISLANDS and *Almayer's Folly* (1895), a powerful white trader, the "Rajah Laut" of an entire district of the Dutch East Indies. He is the hero of another novel, THE RESCUE, which deals with his youth.

lingua franca. A species of Italian mixed with French, Greek, Arabic, etc. spoken especially in medieval times on the coasts of the Mediterranean as an international trade language. Hence, any natural international language of the mixed type, as Pidgin, Sabir, etc. The term means properly "language of the Franks," but it is often associated (erroneously but appropriately) with the idea of free: a language free from national boundaries.

linkboy or linkman. An attendant bearing a link (torch) to light passengers in the streets of a city at night. An institution that disappeared with the introduction of street lighting.

Linkinwater, Tim. In Dickens' *Nicholas* NICKLEBY, confidential clerk to the brothers Cheeryble, a kind-hearted old bachelor, fossilized in ideas, but devoted to his masters almost to idolatry. He is much attached to a blind blackbird called "Dick," which he keeps in a large cage. The bird has lost its voice from old age; but, in Tim's opinion, there is no equal to it in the whole world. The old clerk marries Miss La Creevy, a miniature-painter.

> Punctual as the counting-house dial . . . he performed the minutest actions, and arranged the minutest articles in his little room in a precise and regular order. Paper, pens, ink, ruler, sealing-wax, wafers, . . . Tim's hat, Tim's scrupulously folded gloves, Tim's other coat . . . all had their accustomed inches of space. . . . There was not a more accurate instrument in existence than Tim Linkinwater.—*Nicholas Nickleby,* xxxvii.

Linklater, Eric (1899–). Scottish novelist, best known in U.S. for his novel *Juan in America* (1931).

Lin McLean. A volume of short stories by Owen Wister (*Am.,* 1897), concerning the Wyoming cowboy, Lin McLean.

Linnaeus, Carolus. Swedish form, **Carl von Linné** (1707–1778). Swedish botanist. In his *Systema Naturae* (1735) he outlined what was largely adopted as the *Linnaean classification* or *system* of plants. It is also known as the *sexual system.* It differs from Jussieu's system (1789), by which it was superseded, in that it made no attempt to show the relationship of species and genera. Hence the name *artificial system* as opposed to Jussieu's *natural system.* Linnaeus' *Species Plantarum* (1753) is considered the foundation of modern botanical nomenclature.

Linne, The Heir of. The hero of an old ballad, given in Percy's *Reliques,* which tells how he wastes his substance in riotous living, and, having spent all, sells his estates to John o' the Scales, his steward, reserving only a "poor and lonesome lodge in a lonely glen." When no one will lend or give him money, he retires to the lodge, where there is found dangling a rope with a running noose. He puts it round his neck and springs aloft, but he falls to the ground. When he comes to, he sees two chests of beaten gold and a third full of white money, over which is written—

> Once more, my sonne, I sette thee clere;
> Amend thy life and follies past;
> For but thou amend thee of thy life,
> That rope must be thy end at last.

The heir of Linne now returns to his old hall, where he is refused the loan of 40 pence by his quondam steward. One of the guests tells John o' the Scales he ought to have lent it, as he bought the estate cheap enough. "Cheap call you it?" exclaims John. "Why, he shall have it back for 100 marks less." "Done," says the heir of Linne, and thus recovers his estates.

linotype. A type-setting machine which produces castings (or slugs) representing complete lines of type. Introduced by the German-American inventor Ottmar Mergenthaler (1854–1899). First patent (1884).

Lin Yutang (1895–). Chinese-American author and philologist. Inventor of a system that permits the indexing of material written in Chinese ideographs. Collaborated in the official plan to adopt the Roman alphabet and Roman characters. Author of *My Country and My People* (1936); *The Importance of Living* (1937); *A Leaf in the Storm* (1941); etc. Editor of the anthology *The Wisdom of China and India* (1942).

lion. The king of beasts, an animal that figures perhaps more than any other in legend, symbolism and heraldry.

The lion an emblem of the Resurrection. According to tradition, the lion's whelp is born dead, and remains so for three days, when the father breathes on it and it receives life. Another tradition is that the lion is the only animal of the cat tribe born with its eyes open, and it is said that it sleeps with its eyes open. This is not a fact, but undoubtedly it sleeps watchfully and lightly.

St. Mark the Evangelist is symbolized by a *lion* because he begins his gospel with the scenes of St. John the Baptist and Christ in the wilderness. For the stories of St. Jerome and St. Gerasimus and the lions befriended by them, see under SAINTS. See also ANDROCLES, HERCULES, and UNA for legends of lions.

Ever since 1164, when it was adopted as a device by Philip I, Duke of Flanders, the lion has figured largely and in an amazing variety of positions as an heraldic emblem, and, as a consequence, in public-house signs. The earliest and most important attitude of the heraldic lion is rampant (the device of Scotland), but it is also shown as passant, passant gardant (as in the shield of England), salient, sejant, etc., and even dromant. For these terms, see HERALDRY. The device of Venice is the winged Lion of St. Mark.

In Story and Legend.

Cybele is represented as riding in a chariot drawn by two tame lions.

Pracriti, the goddess of nature among the Hindus, is represented in a similar manner.

Hippomenes and *Atalanta* (fond lovers) were metamorphosed into lions by Cybele.

Hercules is said to have worn over his shoulders the hide of the NEMEAN lion, and the personification of Terror is also arrayed in a lion's hide.

The lions in the arms of England. They are three lions passant gardant, i.e., walking and showing the full face. The first was that of Rollo, Duke of Normandy, and the second represented the country of Maine, which was added to Normandy. These were the two lions borne by William the Conquerer and his descendants. Henry II added a third lion to represent the Duchy of Aquitaine, which came to him through his wife ELEANOR. Any lion not rampant is called a *lion leopardé,* and the French heralds call the lion passant a *leopard;* accordingly Napoleon said to his soldiers, "Let us drive these leopards (the English) into the sea."

Since 1603, the royal arms of Britain have been supported as now by (dexter) the English lion and (sinister) the Scottish UNICORN. Prior to the accession of James I, however, the sinister supporter was a family badge. Edward III, with whom supporters began, had a lion and eagle; Henry IV, an antelope and swan; Henry V, a lion and antelope; Edward IV, a lion and bull; Richard III, a lion and boar; Henry VII, a lion and dragon; Elizabeth, Mary, and Henry VIII, a lion and greyhound.

The lion in the arms of Scotland is derived from the arms of the ancient Earls of Northumberland and Huntingdon, from whom some of the Scotch monarchs were descended. The *tressure* is referred to the reign of Achaius (d. ca. 819), who made a league with Charlemagne, "who did augment his arms with a double trace formed with Floure-delyces, signifying thereby that the lion henceforth should be defended by the ayde of Frenchemen." (Holinshed, *Chronicles.*)

A lion at the feet of crusaders or martyrs, in effigy, signifies that they died for their magnanimity.

the Lion of St. Mark or *of Venice.* A winged lion sejant, holding an open book with the inscription *Pax tibi, Marce, Evangelista Meus.* A swordpoint rises above the book on the dexter side, and the whole is encircled by an aureola.

lions. The lions of a place are sights worth seeing, or the celebrities; so called from the ancient custom of showing strangers, as chief of London sights, the lions at the Tower. Hence, a *lion-hunter* is one who hunts up a celebrity to adorn or give prestige to a party. Mrs. Leo HUNTER, in *Pickwick,* is a good satire on the name and character of a lion-hunter.

lion's mouth. To place one's head in the lion's mouth. To expose oneself needlessly and foolhardily to danger.

lion's share. The larger part: or all, nearly all. In Aesop's *Fables,* several beasts joined the lion in a hunt, but, when the spoil was divided, the lion claimed one quarter in right of his prerogative, one for his superior courage, one for his dam and cubs, "and as for the fourth, let who will dispute it with me." Awed by his frown, the other beasts yielded and silently withdrew.

to beard the lion in his den. Vehemently to contradict one either on some subject he has made his hobby, or on his own premises; to defy personally or face to face.

Lion of God. Ali-Ben-Abou-Thaleb (602–661), the son-in-law of Mahomet, was so called because of his zeal and his great courage. His mother called him at birth *Al Haïdara,* "the Rugged Lion."

Lion of Sweden. General Johan von Baner (1596–1641).

Lion of the North. The Swedish King, Gustavus Adolphus (1594–1632).

lion of the tribe of Judah. A lion is emblem of the tribe of Judah; Christ is so called.

> Judah is a lion's whelp: . . . he couched as a lion, and as an old lion; who shall rouse him up?—*Gen.* xlix. 9.

Lion Rouge. (*Fr.,* "red lion.") Marshal Ney (1769–1815), so called from his red hair.

the Lion's Heart. Richard I of England (1157–1199), called *Coeur de Lion.*

the British Lion. A personification of Great Britain. See under BRITISH.

the Nemean Lion, see NEMEAN.

the Winged Lion. The Lion of St. Mark, the heraldic device of Venice.

Lionel. A leading character in Flotow's opera, MARTHA.

Liones, Lionesse, etc., see LYONESSE.

Li Po or **Li T'ai-po** or **Li Tai-peh** (d. 762 A. D.). Sobriquet "Banished Angel." Probably the greatest Chinese poet of all time. Lived a dissipated life at court and in exile on the road. He was one of a group of eight hard-drinking boon companions, "The Eight Immortals of the Wine Cup." Legend insists that he drowned from a boat when he tried to embrace the moon mirrored in the water.

Lippi, Fra **Filippo** or **Lippo** (1406?–1469). Florentine painter and Carmelite monk. Protégé of Cosimo de' MEDICI. His chief works are the frescoes in Prato cathedral. For Browning's poem on Lippi, see FRA LIPPO LIPPI.

Lippmann, Walter (1889–). American editor and journalist. Column in New York *Herald Tribune* (since 1931). Author of *A Preface to Politics* (1913); *Drift and Mastery* (1914); *The Method of Freedom* (1934); *The New Imperative* (1935); etc.

Lipton, Sir **Thomas Johnstone** (1850–1931). British merchant and yachtsman. Built up a large chain of grocery stores through Great Britain; known in U.S. chiefly for Lipton's Tea. Competed for America's Cup, symbol of international yachting championship, with five yachts (1899, 1901, 1903, 1920, 1930).

They were all named *Shamrock*. Lipton had Irish parents.

Lirriper, Mrs. Heroine of Dickens' tale *Mrs. Lirriper's Lodgings* (1863). It recounts her troubles with her lodgers, and with Miss Wozenham, an opposition lodging-house-keeper. The central point of interest is the adoption of poor Jemmy by Mayor Jackman, and his education at home and in a boarding-school. A sequel, called *Mrs. Lirriper's Legacy,* appeared in 1864.

Lisa. The heroine of a poem by George ELIOT (1859), *How Lisa Loved the King,* which retells a story from Boccaccio's DECAMERON. Because she loves the King, Lisa will have nothing to do with any of her lovers until the King himself, touched by her story sung by a poet for his diversion, searches her out in her bourgeois quarters and urges her to marry the man who loves her.

Lisa, Dame. In Cabell's JURGEN, Jurgen's ill-tempered wife to whom he returns with relief after his year of youth and adventure with fairer ladies is over.

Lisa, Mona, see MONA LISA.

Lismahago, Captain. In Smollett's novel THE EXPEDITION OF HUMPHRY CLINKER, a super-annuated officer on half-pay, who marries Miss Tabitha Bramble for the sake of her £4000. He is a hard-featured, forbidding Scotchman, singular in dress, eccentric in manners, conceited, disputatious, and rude. Though most tenacious in argument, he can yield to Miss Tabitha, whom he wishes to conciliate.

Lissauer, Ernst (1882–1937). German poet and playwright. Internationally remembered for his HYMN OF HATE.

Lister, Joseph. 1st Baron **Lister of Lyme Regis** (1827–1912). English surgeon. Influenced by the discoveries of PASTEUR; he used carbolic acid to prevent septic infection and became the founder of antiseptic surgery. A commercial antiseptic containing benzoic and boric acids is called after him "Listerine."

Liszt, Franz (1811–1886). Hungarian composer and one of the greatest of pianists. A child prodigy, he gave his first public performance at the age of nine. Studied in Vienna (1821–1823) under Czerny and Salieri, in Paris under Reicha. Lived at Geneva (1835–1839) with the Comtesse d'Agoult, by whom he had three children, one of whom was Cosima. See under Richard WAGNER. Court Kapellmeister at Weimar (1848–1859). Entered the Franciscan order at Rome (1865) and was henceforth known as Abbé Liszt. Died at Bayreuth (1886) in the midst of a Wagner festival.

Liszt is considered the creator of the modern style of piano playing. He deeply influenced modern music by his daring innovations in form and harmonic relations. His works include *Hungarian Rhapsodies; Legends* (among them *St. Francis Preaching to the Birds*); 2 concertos for piano and orchestra; the symphonic poems *Dante, Hamlet;* etc.

Literary Guild. See under SUBSCRIPTION BOOK.

litotes. Understatement for the sake of effect, as "a citizen of no mean city." See HYPERBOLE.

littérateur (*Fr.*). Also **litterateur.** A man of letters. One who makes of literature and writing a profession or a job.

Littimer. In Dickens' DAVID COPPERFIELD, the painfully irreproachable valet of STEERFORTH, in whose presence David Copperfield feels always most uncomfortably young. Though as a valet he is propriety in Sunday best, he is nevertheless cunning and deceitful. Steerforth, tired of "Little Em'ly," wishes to marry her to Littimer, but from this lot she is rescued, and emigrates to Australia.

Little.

Little Corporal. Napoleon Bonaparte. So called after the battle of Lodi, in 1796, from his low stature, youthful age, and amazing courage. He was barely 5 ft. 2 in. in height.

Little Englanders. An opprobrious name which became popular about the time of the last Boer War for those who refused to "think imperially," upheld the doctrine that the English should concern themselves with England only, and were opposed to any extension of the Empire.

Little Father. The Czar of Russia was so called.

little gentleman in velvet, i.e., the mole, was a favorite Jacobite toast in the reign of Queen Anne. The reference was to the mole that raised the molehill against which the horse of William III stumbled at Hampton Court. By this accident the King broke his collar-bone, a severe illness ensued, and he died early in 1702.

Little Giant. Stephen A. Douglas (1813–1861) American politician, so called from his small stature and formidable nature.

Little Paris. (1) Brussels; (2) Milan.

Little Parliament. See under PARLIAMENTS.

Little Venice. Arendal, Norway.

Little, Henry. The inventor hero of Charles Reade's PUT YOURSELF IN HIS PLACE.

Little, Thomas. Pseudonym under which Thomas MOORE's *Poetical Works* of 1801 were published. Moore is called by this name in Byron's ENGLISH BARDS AND SCOTCH REVIEWERS.

Little Billee. A comic ballad by THACKERAY, telling how three sailors of Bristol city go to sea, and, having eaten all their food, resolve to make a meal of Little Billee; but the lad eludes his fate.

There was gorging Jack, and guzzling Jimmy,
And the youngest he was little Billee.
Now, when they got as far 's th' equator,
They'd nothing left but one split pea.
To gorging Jack says guzzling Jimmy,
"We've nothing left, us must eat we."

Little Billee or *William Bagot.* The hero of Du Maurier's TRILBY. The author borrowed the nickname from Thackeray's ballad.

Little Boy Blue. The hero of an old nursery rhyme:

Little Boy Blue, come blow your horn
The sheep's in the meadow, the cow's in the corn
Where is the boy who looks after the sheep?
He's under the haystack fast asleep.

Eugene Field (*Am.,* 1850–1895) has a well-known poem, *Little Boy Blue,* commemorating the faithfulness with which the toys of a little boy who has died await his return.

Little Breeches. One of John Hay's PIKE COUNTY BALLADS.

Little Buttercup, see BUTTERCUP.

Little Clay Cart, The (*Sans.* **Mrichchhakatika**). A Sanskrit comedy ascribed to a certain King Sudraka and variously assigned to the 8th to 10th centuries. The hero is Charudatta, an impoverished Brahmin merchant, the heroine the lovely courtesan Vasantasena. The villain of the play, the King's brother-in-law, smothers Vasantasena in a remote garden and accuses Charudatta of the crime, but Vasantasena recovers and appears just in time to save her lover from execution. An important subplot is concerned with a successful conspiracy to overthrow the reigning monarch. GOETHE paraphrased the drama in his poem *The God and the Bayadere,* and it was made the basis of a popular ballet *Le Dieu et la bayadère* which was staged throughout Europe about the year 1830. The drama itself was produced in New York by the Neighborhood Playhouse players in 1924–1925.

Little Dorrit. The heroine and title of a novel by Charles DICKENS (1855). Little Dorrit was born and brought up in the Marshalsea prison, Bermondsey, where her father was confined for debt; and when about fourteen years of age she used to do needlework, to earn a subsistence for herself and her father. The child was idolized by the prisoners, and when she walked out, every man in Bermondsey who passed her touched or took off his hat out of respect to her good works and active benevolence. Her father, coming into a property, was set free at length, and Little Dorrit married Arthur Clennam, the marriage service being celebrated in the Marshalsea, by the prison chaplain.

Little Em'ly. See under PEGGOTTY.

Little Endians. In Swift's *Gulliver's Travels* (see GULLIVER) (*Voyage to Lilliput*) the faction which insists on interpreting the vital direction contained in the 54th chapter of the Blundecral: "All true believers break their eggs at the convenient end," as meaning the *little end,* and wage a destructive war against those who adopted the alternative. See BIG ENDIANS. The godfather of the emperor happens to cut his finger while breaking his egg at the big end, and publishes a decree commanding all his subjects to break them in future at the small end. This leads to a terrible war, and to the publication of many hundreds of large treatises. Today the terms are still used in connection with hostilities or arguments arising out of trifling differences of opinion, etc., especially in matters of doctrine. In Swift's satire the Big Endians typify the Catholics, and the Little Endians the Protestants.

Little Entente, see ENTENTE.

Little Eohippus, The. Title of story by Eugene Manlove RHODES; the "dawn-horse," subject of a humorous poem by Charlotte Perkins Gilman Stetson, "Similar Cases."

Little Eva. In *Uncle Tom's Cabin* by Harriet Beecher Stowe, the daughter of the wealthy Mr. St. Clare. Uncle Tom saves her life; her early death is an important event in the plan of the book.

Little Eyolf. A drama by Henrik IBSEN (1894). Little Eyolf, the crippled son of Mr. and Mrs. Allmers, is lured and tormented by a mysterious old hag known as the Rat-wife, while Allmers, impervious to his son's needs, is writing a book on *Human Responsibility.* Allmers suddenly awakes to his parental responsibility, but his wife feels only jealousy of his devotion to the drowned child as she has of his devotion to the book.

little-go. A preliminary examination of a general nature which all Cambridge undergraduates must pass (unless excused on account of having passed certain other examinations) before proceeding to take any examination for a degree. The *little-go* is almost invariably taken in or before the first term. There is no examination at Oxford corresponding with this, but SMALLS (see also MODS) is much on its level.

Little Lord Fauntleroy. A story by Frances Hodgson BURNETT (1886), illustrated by Reginald BIRCH. The seven-year-old hero, Cedric Errol, is the son of a disinherited English father and an American mother. His title of Lord Fauntleroy he would normally inherit from his grandfather, an English earl, who has, however, never forgiven the boy's father for marrying an American. On the death of the father the boy is summoned to England, leaving his mother, whom he calls "Dearest" in the poverty-stricken quarters where they have been living in New York. He so completely wins the hearts of his English relatives that they are soon persuaded to extend to "Dearest" a cordial welcome. Little Lord Fauntleroy is a striking figure, dressed in black velvet with lace collar and yellow curls, and the phrase passed into common usage as referring either to a certain type of children's clothes or to a beautiful, but spoiled or effeminate small boy. The novel was successfully dramatized.

little magazine. Term applied to a periodical whose aim is the promotion of literary experiment and reform and the encouragement of obscure and hitherto unpublished authors, frequently in accordance with a definite editorial viewpoint in the matter of aesthetics or politics, rather than high sales and financial profit. THE GERM (1850) and THE YELLOW BOOK (1894–1897) foreshadowed the form in England, and *The Bibelot* (1895–1915) and *The Chap-Book* (1894–1898) were the first characteristic representatives of it in the U.S., although the Transcendentalist DIAL (1840–1844) must also be considered a forerunner. The little magazine was most prominent in the U.S. in the years immediately preceding and following World War I and during the 1920's. Outstanding examples were POETRY: A MAGAZINE OF VERSE (1912–); THE LITTLE REVIEW (1914–1929); THE SEVEN ARTS (1916–1917); THE DIAL (1917–1929); *The Frontier* (1920–1939); *The Fugitive* (see FUGITIVES) (1922–1925); *Broom* (1921–1924); *Secession* (1922–1924); TRANSITION (1927–1938); *This Quarter* (1925–1932); HOUND AND HORN (1927–1934); *The Symposium* (1930–1933); STORY (1931–); THE SOUTHERN REVIEW (1935–); *Kenyon Review* (1939–); *Partisan Review* (1934–). English little magazines of the same period were *The Blue Review* (1911–1913); *Signature* (1915); *The transatlantic review* (1924); CRITERION (1922–1939); *Life and Letters Today* (1928–1939); *Horizon* (1940–).

A number of the outstanding writers of the 20th century were first known through their publications in little magazines, including Katherine MANSFIELD, Edgar Lee MASTERS, Sherwood ANDERSON, T. S. ELIOT, Ezra POUND, D. H. LAWRENCE, James JOYCE, Gertrude STEIN, Ernest HEMINGWAY, E. E. CUMMINGS, Hart CRANE, William FAULKNER, Erskine CALDWELL, Wallace STEVENS, Allen TATE, John Crowe RANSOM, Edmund WILSON, Dylan THOMAS. Cf. *The Little Magazine* (1946) by Frederick J. Hoffman and others. See also MARXISM IN LITERATURE; NEW DIRECTIONS.

Little Minister, The. A novel by J. M. BARRIE (1891). The hero, Gavin Dishart, is a young preacher in the Scotch village of Thrums. He struggles in vain against his love for the irresistible upsetting "gypsy" Babbie. The parish is scandalized at the romance; Babbie gives him up to marry her elderly fiancé, Lord Rintoul; but a false rumor of Gavin's death brings them together and on impulse they are married by a gypsy ceremony "over the tongs" in the woods. The two are separated, but after many vicissitudes, the Little Minister regains both his prestige and his bride.

Little Nell. A child character in Dickens' OLD CURIOSITY SHOP whose death scene, like that of LITTLE EVA, has become famous.

Little Orphant Annie. The title and heroine of a well-known dialect poem by James Whitcomb RILEY (1885), which relates how Orphant Annie tells hair-raising tales about the goblins and is finally carried off by them. Later *Little Orphan Annie* became the title of a popular comic strip.

Little Pierre, see PIERRE.

Little Review, The. An American literary periodical, founded in 1914 and considered one of the most outstanding of the LITTLE MAGAZINES. It was published in Chicago, New York, and Paris, under the editorship of Margaret C. Anderson, and championed all the 20th-century experimental movements, publishing the work of the outstanding English, American, and European writers of the period. James Joyce's ULYSSES appeared as a serial in this magazine, and nearly resulted in its suppression. It ceased publication in 1929.

Little Shepherd of Kingdom Come, The. A once popular novel by John Fox, Jr. (*Am.,* 1903) dealing with the life of the Kentucky mountaineers. The hero is Chad Buford, a waif who grows up in the mountains but is later proved a relative of Major Buford of Lexington who had befriended him. During the Civil War he fights in the Union Army and so alienates himself from Major Buford and his daughter Margaret, whom he loves, but after peace is declared, all ends happily.

little theater. A name given to an amateur or semi-professional theatrical group that aims to produce plays as a sort of community venture, with primary emphasis on artistic rather than commercial success; also, the theater of such an organization. The *little theater movement* was a movement to organize such groups throughout the United States, especially strong in the 1920's.

Outstanding little theater groups, a number of which later became professional, included the following: the Moscow Art Theater in Russia (1890); the Abbey Players and the Irish National Theater in Ireland (1899); the Washington Square Players (1915); the PROVINCETOWN PLAYERS (1915); the Theater Guild (1918); the Group Theater (1931); the W.P.A.

THEATER PROJECT (1936). CHEKHOV, YEATS, SYNGE, Sean O'CASEY, Eugene O'NEILL, Paul GREEN, Philip BARRY, Thornton WILDER, and Clifford ODETS are among the authors whose plays became known through little theaters or organizations which were once little theaters. The 47 Workshop (see HARVARD WORKSHOP) was also associated with the little theater movement.

Little Women. A widely read story for young people by Louisa May ALCOTT (1867). The heroine is Jo March, the tomboyish and literary member of the MARCH family, who retires to the attic when "genius burns" and is usually in hot water the rest of the time. Her three sisters, Meg, Beth and Amy, figure almost as prominently. Beth, the good and gentle one of the family, does not live long. Meg marries a young tutor, John Brooke, and reappears in the sequel, *Little Men,* with her twins Daisy and Demi. The fashionable and artistic Amy finally marries Laurie, a high-spirited boy who had long been Jo's boon companion but who failed to persuade her to marry him. Jo herself becomes the wife of a kindly old German professor, Mr. Bhaer; in *Little Men* (1871) she and the professor turn their home into a school for a few boys. *Jo's Boys* (1886) is a second sequel.

Litvinov. The hero of Turgenev's SMOKE.

Litvinov, Maksim Maksimovich (1876–). Russian Communist statesman. Most important mediator between his country and the bourgeois world. People's commissar for foreign affairs (1930–1939), succeeded by MOLOTOV. Russian ambassador to U.S. (1941–1943). Author of *The Bolshevik Revolution.*

Live Oak State. Florida. See under STATES.

Liveright, Horace Brisbin (1886–1933). American publisher and theatrical producer; with Albert Boni headed publishing firm of Boni and Liveright (1918–1936). In theatrical field produced *Hamlet in Modern Dress;* Dreiser's *An American Tragedy; Dracula;* etc.

Livingstone, David (1813–1873). Scottish missionary and explorer in Africa. Discovered Lake Ugami (1849); Zambesi River (1851); Victoria Falls of the Zambesi (1855); Lakes Shirwa and Nyasa (1859); etc., etc. Was rescued from an expedition into cannibal country by Henry M. Stanley (1871), who is reputed to have greeted the exhausted explorer with a bow and the words, "Dr. Livingstone, I presume?" Livingstone died during a second expedition to discover the sources of the Nile. He was buried in Westminster Abbey. Author of *Missionary Travels in South Africa* (1858); *Narrative of an Expedition to the Zambesi* (1865); etc.

Livy. Latin name **Titus Livius** (59 B.C.–17 A.D.). Roman historian, protégé of Emperor Augustus, and greatest prose writer of the AUGUSTAN AGE. Author of *The Annals of the Roman People* (142 books), of which about one third is extant.

the Livy of France. Juan de Mariana (1537–1624).

the Livy of Portugal. João de Barros (1496–1570), the best of the Portuguese historians.

the Russian Livy. Nicholas Karamzin (1765–1826).

Liza. Heroine of Turgenev's *Nest of Nobles* (1858), translated under the title *Liza.* The hero, Fyodor Lavretsky, unhappily mismated with a woman who is false to him, is strongly drawn to Liza, whom he feels is representative of genuine womanhood. When he receives news of his wife's death, they confess their mutual love. His wife, however, is not dead, and wishes him to return to her. The two lovers renounce their happiness and Liza enters a convent.

Liza of Lambeth. The first novel of W. S. MAUGHAM (1897), written in the tradition of NATURALISM and presenting a study of life in the slums of London in the late 19th century, with emphasis on the psychological and physical illnesses of the characters. The book, written while the author was a medical student at St. Thomas Hospital in London, was considered shocking because of its technique and subject matter.

Lizaveta Nikolaevna, see TUSHIN, LIZAVETA NIKOLAEVNA.

LL.D. Doctor of Laws—i.e., both civil and canon. The double L is the plural, as in MSS., the plural of MS. (manuscript), pp., pages, etc.

Llewellyn, Richard. *Nom de plume* of **Richard David Vivian Llewellyn Lloyd** (1907?–). British novelist and playwright of Welsh descent. Author of *How Green Was My Valley* (1940), *None But the Lonely Heart* (1943), novels that were successfully dramatized in motion pictures.

Lloyd George, David (1863–1945). British statesman of Welsh descent. Succeeded Asquith as prime minister (1916–1922) and directed British policies during World War I and in the negotiation of peace terms. Instituted negotiations resulting in the establishment of the Irish Free State. Author of *War Memoirs* (6 vols., 1933–1936) and *The Truth About the Peace Treaty* (2 vols., 1938). Created Earl Lloyd-George of Dwfour (1945).

Lloyd's. An association of underwriters, merchants, shipowners, brokers, etc., principally dealing with ocean-borne commerce, marine insurance, and the publication of shipping intelligence. It was so called because the society was founded (1688) at a coffee-house kept in Lombard Street by one Edward Lloyd. In 1774 the offices, or *Lloyd's Rooms,* were removed to the Royal Exchange, where they still are.

Lloyd's books. Two enormous ledger-like volumes, placed on desks at the entrance (right and left) of Lloyd's Rooms. They give the principal arrivals, and all losses by wrecks, fire, or other accidents at sea. The entries are written in a fine, bold Roman hand, legible to all readers.

Lloyd's List. A periodical, in which the shipping news received at Lloyd's Rooms is published. It has been issued regularly from 1726, and since 1800 as a daily.

Lloyd's Register. A register of ships, British and foreign, published yearly.

Llyr. In the Welsh *Mabinogion,* a mythical king of Britain, father of Bran and BRANWEN. See KING LEAR; LIR.

loan translation. A FOREIGN WORD or phrase naturalized by the translation of all its parts, as English *badlands* from French *mauvaises terres.*

loan word. A FOREIGN WORD partly naturalized, as French *fuselage* in English. See also LOAN TRANSLATION.

Loathly Lady. A stock character of the old romances who is so hideous that everyone is deterred from marrying her. When, however, she at last finds a husband, her ugliness—the effect of enchantment—disappears, and she becomes a model of beauty. Her story—a very common one, in which sometimes the enchanted beauty has to assume the shape of a serpent or some hideous monster—is the feminine counterpart of that of BEAUTY AND THE BEAST.

lob. Archaic. A clown, country bumpkin; a Puckish fairy.

> Farewell, thou lob of spirits . . .
> Shakespeare, *Midsummer Night's Dream.*

Here Puck is spoken to. Hence **lob's pound,** also **cob's pound, hob's pound** (pound = prison), a jail or lock-up. Cf. *Lob-Lie-By-the-Fire,* a book of tales for children (1873) by Juliana Horatia EWING.

Lobaba. In Southey's THALABA THE DESTROYER, one of the sorcerers in the caverns of Domdaniel, "under the roots of the ocean."

lobsters. English soldiers used to be called lobsters because they were "turned red" when enlisted into the service. But the term was originally applied to a troop of horse soldiers in the Great Rebellion, clad in armor which covered them as a shell.

died for want of lobster sauce. Sometimes said of one who dies or suffers severely because of some trifling disappointment, pique, or wounded vanity. At the grand feast given by the great Condé to Louis XIV, at Chantilly, Vatel, the *chef,* was told that the lobsters intended for sauce had not arrived, whereupon he retired to his private room, and, leaning on his sword, ran it through his body, unable to survive such a dire disappointment. A great number of hotels and restaurants in France are named "Le Grand Vatel."

local color. In reference to drama or fiction, the concrete details of natural scenery, architecture, peculiarities of dialect, local customs and traditions, etc., that give an impression of authenticity to a particular setting. Thus an author who wishes to lay the scene of his novel in a certain region may perhaps spend some time in the vicinity or read its history "to soak up local color." Any spot rich in unique traditions that make it different from the rest of the world is said to have "plenty of local color."

During the 19th century in the U.S., a widespread school of local-color writing grew up, emphasizing chiefly individualities of background, dialect, and custom in the various parts of the nation, combined with the standardized humor, sentiment, or melodrama of the time. The *Far West* was depicted by Bret HARTE and Joaquin MILLER; *New England,* by Rose Terry COOKE and Sarah Orne JEWETT; the *Middle West,* by Edward EGGLESTON and John HAY; the *South,* by George Washington CABLE, Lafcadio HEARN, Charles Egbert CRADDOCK, Joel Chandler HARRIS, Thomas Nelson PAGE, and Grace Elizabeth KING. Realism was added to the local color tradition in the portrayals of Middle Western life by Edgar Watson HOWE, Joseph KIRKLAND, Hamlin GARLAND, and the Edgar Lee MASTERS of *Spoon River Anthology.* Among descendants of the early local-color writers in at least part of their work might be listed the following 20th-century authors: *New England,* Mary E. Wilkins FREEMAN, Joseph C. LINCOLN, J. P. MARQUAND, and E. A. ROBINSON; *New York City,* Henry Cuyler BUNNER, O. HENRY, Edith WHARTON, Damon RUNYON, Jerome WEIDMAN, and Arthur KOBER; *Pennsylvania,* Margaret DELAND; the *South,* Kate CHOPIN, Du Bose HEYWARD, Paul GREEN, Julia PETERKIN, William FAULKNER, Erskine CALDWELL, T. S. STRIBLING, Ellen GLASGOW, Elizabeth Madox ROBERTS, and Jesse STUART; *Chicago,* Carl SANDBURG, James T. FARRELL, Ben HECHT, Meyer LEVIN, Albert HALPER, Nelson ALGREN; the *Middle West,* Carl SANDBURG, Sinclair LEWIS, Sherwood ANDERSON, Theodore DREISER, Ruth SUCKOW, Zona GALE, Bess Streeter ALDRICH, Phil STONG, Willa CATHER; the *Southwest,* Mary AUSTIN, Willa CATHER, Oliver LA FARGE; the *Far West,* Gertrude ATHERTON, John STEINBECK, William SAROYAN;

the *Northwest,* H. L. DAVIS and Archie BINNS.

In Great Britain, writers who might be classed in the local-color school include the following: *Ireland,* J. M. SYNGE, Sean O'CASEY, Sean O'FAOLAIN, and Lady GREGORY; *Scotland,* the KAILYARD SCHOOL; *Wessex,* Thomas HARDY; the *Five Towns,* ARNOLD BENNETT; *Shropshire,* A. E. HOUSMAN; *Yorkshire,* Winifred HOLTBY. In all of the novels of James JOYCE the atmosphere of Dublin is vividly present. In France, many of the works of Guy de MAUPASSANT deal with life in Normandy, and Alphonse DAUDET, Frédéric MISTRAL, and Jean GIONO have written of Provence.

local-option law. In the U.S., a law whose enforcement is contingent upon local acceptance by popular vote. The phrase *local option* is commonly applied to regulations of the liquor traffic.

Locarno Pact or **Treaty.** A series of five treaties concluded by Germany with Belgium, France, Great Britain, Italy, Poland and Czechoslovakia (October 1925), negotiated at Locarno in Switzerland with the purpose of guaranteeing peace and the existing territorial boundaries.

Lochaber ax. A long ax head on a pole with a hook on its end used by Scottish Highlanders. Named from the district of Lochaber in Scotland.

Lochiel. The title of the head of the clan Cameron.

> And Cameron, in the shock of steel,
> Die like the offspring of Lochiel.
> Scott, *The Field of Waterloo*

The hero of Campbell's poem, *Lochiel's Warning* (1802) is Donald Cameron, known as *The Gentle Lochiel.* He was one of the Young Pretender's staunchest adherents, and escaped to France with him after Culloden (1746). He took service in the French army, but died two years later.

Lochinvar. A young Highlander, hero of an episode in Scott's poem MARMION. Being in love with a lady at Netherby Hall, he persuaded her to dance one last dance. She was condemned to marry a "laggard in love and a dastard in war," but her young chevalier swung her into his saddle and made off with her, before the "bridegroom" and his servants could recover from their astonishment.

Locke, Alain LeRoy (1886–). American Negro educator and essayist. Rhodes scholar at Oxford University (1907–1910). Ph.D. at Howard (1918). Teacher of philosophy at Howard University (from 1917). Corresponding member of the Académie des Sciences Coloniales, Paris. Author of books on the cultural contributions made by the Negro race and (in collaboration with B. J. Stern) *When Peoples Meet: A Study in Race and Culture Contacts* (1942); etc.

Locke, Alton, see ALTON LOCKE.

Locke, David Ross (1833–1888). Pseudonym **Petroleum V. Nasby.** American journalist, native of Vestal, N.Y. Going to Ohio at the age of nineteen, Locke became editor of the *Jeffersonian* at Findlay. On March 21, 1861, the first of his "Petroleum V. Nasby letters" appeared in that paper, starting a series which continued through 1887 (after 1865 in the Toledo, Ohio, *Blade*). Locke's fame began in the Civil War years. The "V" of his pseudonym stood for "Vesuvius," and he was envisaged as a dissolute country preacher, a Copperhead arguing for the South in an illiterate fashion. He used grotesque spelling and equally grotesque logic, after the fashion of Artemus Ward. It is said that Lincoln read some of the letters to his Cabinet.

Locke, John (1632–1704). English philosopher, known as "the father of English empiricism." Interested in experimental science and philosophy rather than in Aristotelean subtleties. His best-known work, *An Essay Concerning Human Understanding* (1690), took him seventeen years to complete and was the result of a promise given during a talk with friends about morality and religion. to try to determine what questions the understanding of man was qualified to resolve and what others exceeded its powers. Suspected of complicity in the plots of Shaftesbury, whose confidential adviser he had been (from 1667), he went to Holland (1684) but returned during the Revolution. Became adviser on coinage to new government.

Locke, William John (1863–1930). British novelist. Author of *The Morals of Marcus Ordeyne* (1905); *The Beloved Vagabond* (1906); etc.

Locke Amsden, or The Schoolmaster. A once popular novel by D. P. THOMPSON (*Am.,* 1847) portraying the life of the old district school.

Locker-Lampson, Frederick. Before 1885, **Frederick Locker** (1821–1895). English poet; noted for his light verse. *London Lyrics* (1857); editor of *Lyra Elegantiarum* (an anthology of light verse; 1867). Lampson was the maiden name of his second wife.

Lockhart, John Gibson (1794–1854). Scottish editor and novelist. Biographer of BURNS (1828) and his father-in-law, Sir Walter SCOTT (7 vols.; 1837–1838). His sketches of Edinburgh society, *Peter's Letters to his Kinsfolk* (1819), were published under the pseudonym Peter Morris. Translator of *Ancient Spanish Ballads* (1823). At the age of twenty-three he wrote a series of four articles signed "Z," concerning a supposed "Cockney School" of poetry, in which he excoriated John Keats after principally attacking Leigh Hunt. The tone of these articles is ruffianly, but his work on Scott ranks second only to Boswell's *Johnson* among the great biographies in English.

Lockit. The jailer in Gay's BEGGAR'S OPERA. He is an inhuman brute, who refuses to allow Captain MACHEATH any more candles in his cell, and threatens to clap on extra fetters unless he supplies him with more "garnish" (jail fees). Lockit loads his prisoners with fetters in inverse proportion to the fees which they pay ranging "from one guinea to ten."

Lucy Lockit. The daughter of Lockit the jailer, a foolish young woman, who, decoyed by Captain Macheath under the specious promise of marriage, effects his escape from jail. The Captain, however, is recaptured and condemned to death. After being reprieved, he confesses himself married to Polly PEACHUM, and Lucy is left to seek another mate.

> How happy could I be with either [Lucy or Polly]
> Were t'other dear charmer away!
> Gay, *The Beggar's Opera,* ii. 2.

Lockridge, Richard (1898–). American drama critic and novelist. Best known for the adventures of *Mr. and Mrs. North,* begun as a series of stories in the *New Yorker,* and continued in collaboration with his wife. They were used as the basis for a popular radio program. Also author of biography of Edwin BOOTH.

Locksley. In Scott's IVANHOE, a name assumed by Robin Hood, who appears as an archer at the tournament. It is said to have been the name of the village where the outlaw was born.

Locksley Hall. Tennyson's poem of this name (1842) deals with an imaginary place and an imaginary hero. The Lord of Locksley Hall falls in love with his cousin Amy; she marries a rich clown, and he, indignant at this, declares he will wed a savage. He changes his mind, however, and decides, "Better fifty years of Europe than a cycle of Cathay."

In 1886 Tennyson published *Locksley Hall Sixty Years After,* another dramatic poem.

Lockyer, Sir Joseph Norman (1836–1920). British astronomer. Initiated (1866) the spectroscopic observation of sun-spots. Investigated the chemistry of the sun and determined the presence in its atmosphere of an unknown element (1868) which was called helium (from Greek *helios,* "the sun"), a name which it has kept although it was later discovered in the atmosphere of the earth as well.

Locofocos. A trade-name coined in America as that of a self-igniting cigar (patented in New York, 1834), but quickly transferred to lucifer matches, and then to the extreme Radicals, or Equal Rights faction, in America, because, so the story goes, at a meeting in Tammany Hall (1835), when the chairman left his seat, and the lights were suddenly extinguished, with the hope of breaking up the turbulent assembly, those in favor of extreme measures drew from their pockets their *locofocos,* re-lighted the gas, and got their way.

Locrine. Father of Sabrina and eldest son of the mythical Brutus, King of ancient Britain. On the death of his father he became king of Loegria. His story is told in Geoffrey of Monmouth's *British History,* ii. 5.

> Virgin daughter of Locrine,
> Sprung from old Anchises' line.
> Milton, *Comus,* 942–3.

An anonymous tragedy, based on HOLINSHED and GEOFFREY OF MONMOUTH, was published under this name in 1595. As the words "Newly set foorth, overseene and corrected, By *W. S.*" appear on the title-page, it was at one time ascribed to Shakespeare. It has also been ascribed to Marlowe, Greene, and Peele—the weight of evidence being rather in favor of the latter.

locum tenens (*Lat.*). Literally, a lieutenant or place-holder. A substitute or deputy, especially one acting for a doctor or clergyman.

Locusta. One who murders those she professes to nurse, or those whom it is her duty to take care of. The original Locusta was a professional poisoner living in Rome about 54 A. D. She poisoned Claudius and Britannicus, and attempted to destroy Nero. She was put to death in the reign of the Emperor Galba. *Locusta in Scotland* is an essay by William ROUGHEAD.

lodge. In Masonic and similar orders, the meeting place of a local branch or its membership. So called from the lodges which served in the Middle Ages as workshops for groups of (free) masons.

Lodge, Henry Cabot (1850–1924). American legislator and author. U.S. Senator (1893–1924). As chairman of the foreign affairs committee after World War I, he led the opposition to the Peace Treaty and the League of Nations (1919). Author of biographies of Hamilton, Webster, and Washington. His son, **George Cabot Lodge** (1873–1909), was a poet, and his grandson, **Henry Cabot Lodge, Jr.** (1902–), was on the editorial staff of the New York *Herald Tribune* (1924–1936) and U.S. Senator from Massachusetts (1937–1944; 1946–).

Lodge, Sir Oliver Joseph (1851–1940). English physicist and author. Became absorbed in psychical research and published his belief in the possibility of communication between the living and the dead. His writings include

Life and Matter (1905); *The Substance of Faith* (1907); *Man and the Universe* (1908); *The Survival of Man* (1909); *Raymond, or Life and Death* (an account of his communication with his dead son Raymond; 1916); *Relativity* (1925); the autobiography *Past Years* (1931); etc.

Lodge, Thomas (1558–1625). English poet, playwright, and prose-writer of the Elizabethan period, one of the "UNIVERSITY WITS." He was influenced by John LYLY and the style of EUPHUISM. His best-known work, and the one most popular in his own day, is *Rosalynde: Euphues' Golden Legacy* (1590), a pastoral romance, based on *The Tale of Gamelyn* (see GAMELYN) and used by Shakespeare as the source of his AS YOU LIKE IT. Lodge also wrote a number of plays, two of which have survived: *A Looking Glass for London and England* (1594), written with Robert GREENE, and *The Wounds of Civil War* (1594). His poetry includes *Scilla's Metamorphosis* (1589), a mythological poem; *Phillis* (1593), a sonnet-sequence; a large number of lyrics in the Elizabethan miscellany *The Phoenix Nest* (see TOTTEL'S MISCELLANY; 1593); and *A Fig for Momus* (1595), one of the first satires in verse.

Lodge in the course of his lifetime was successively a law student, a soldier, a traveler and adventurer, and, after studying medicine at Avignon and Oxford, a well-known London physician.

Lodovico. In Shakespeare's OTHELLO, kinsman to Brabantio, the father of DESDEMONA.

Lodowick. In Shakespeare's MEASURE FOR MEASURE, the name assumed by the Duke of Vienna when he retired for a while from State affairs and dressed as a friar to watch the carrying out of a law recently enforced against prostitution.

Loeb, James (1867–1933). American banker and philanthropist. Founder (1912) of the Loeb Classical Library, a series of publications of about 300 volumes of Greek and Latin authors, giving the original text and its translation on opposite pages. Founder of Institute of Musical Art (1905) in New York City, later absorbed by the Juilliard Musical Foundation.

Loegria or **Logres.** England is so called by Geoffrey of Monmouth, from LOCRINE, the son of the mythical King Brut.

Loewi, Otto (1873–). See under DALE, HENRY HALLETT.

Lofoten. A group of precipitous islands off the northwest coast of Norway. The MAELSTROM is located at their southwest end.

Lofting, Hugh (1886–1947). British-born American writer and illustrator of children's books, including the "Dr. Dolittle" series, one of which was awarded the Newbery Medal (1922).

Loftus, Cissie. Stage name of **Marie Cecilia McCarthy** (1876–1943). Scottish actress of stage and early motion pictures. Known for her sparkling impersonations of stage and screen stars.

Lofty Jack. In Goldsmith's comedy THE GOODNATURED MAN, a character whose foible is modesty. See also BEAU TIBBS.

Log, King. A *roi fainéant,* a king who rules in peace and quietness, but never makes his power felt. This is in allusion to the fable of the frogs asking for a king. Jupiter first threw them down a log of wood, but they grumbled at so spiritless a king. He then sent them a stork, which devoured them eagerly.

logbook. On board ship, the journal in which the "logs" are entered by the chief mate. It contains also all general transactions pertaining to the ship and its crew, such as the strength and course of the winds, the conduct and misconduct of the men, and, in short, everything worthy of note.

Logi. In Norse mythology, one of Utgard-Loki's men, actually Fire in disguise, who managed in a contest at Utgard to eat more and faster than Loki.

Logris or **Locris.** Same as Locrin or LOCRINE, eldest son of Brut, the mythical king of Britain.

log-rolling. The combination of different interests, on the principle of "Scratch my back; I'll scratch yours." It was applied in politics to the "give and take" principle, by which one party will further certain interests of another in return for assistance given in passing their own measures, and in literary circles to mutual admiration criticism. The mutual admirers are called "log-rollers," and the allusion is to neighbors who assist a new settler to roll away the logs of his clearing.

Lohengrin. A son of Percival or PARSIFAL in German legend, the Knight of the Swan. He appears at the close of Wolfram von Eschenbach's *Parzival* (ca. 1210), and in other German romances, where he is the deliverer of Elsa, a princess of Brabant, who has been dispossessed by Telramund and Ortrud. He arrives at Antwerp in a skiff drawn by a swan, champions Elsa, and becomes her husband on the sole condition that she shall not ask his name or lineage. She is prevailed upon to do so on the marriage-night, and he, by his vows to the Grail, is obliged to disclose his identity, but at the same time disappear. The swan returns for him, and he goes, but not before retransforming the swan into Elsa's brother Gottfried, who, by the wiles of the sorceress Ortrud, had been obliged to assume that form. Richard

WAGNER has an opera based on the subject, composed (words and music) in 1847.

Loki. The god of strife and spirit of evil in Scandinavian mythology, son of the giant Firbauti and Laufey, or Nal, the friend of the enemy of the gods, and father of the Midgard Serpent Fenris, and Hel. It was he who artfully contrived the death of BALDER. He was finally chained to a rock with ten chains, and—according to one legend—will so continue till the Twilight of the Gods appears, when he will break his bonds. The heavens will disappear, the earth will be swallowed up by the sea, fire will consume the elements, and even Odin, with all his kindred deities, shall perish. Another story has it that he was freed at RAGNAROK, and that he and Heimdall fought until both were slain.

Lokman. A fabulous personage, the supposed author of a collection of Arabic fables. The name is founded on *Lugman,* the title of the 31st Surah of the Koran, in which occur the words "We gave to Lugman wisdom." Like AESOP, he is said to have been a slave, noted for his ugliness.

Lola. In Mascagni's opera, CAVALLERIA RUSTICANA, the beautiful young woman for whom TURIDDU leaves his sweetheart SANTUZZA.

Lola Montez, see MONTEZ, LOLA.

Lollards. The early German reformers and the followers of WYCLIF were so called. An ingenious derivation is given by Bailey, who suggests the Latin word *lolium* (darnel), because these reformers were deemed "tares in God's wheat-field," but the name is from Mid. Dut. *lollaerd,* a mutterer, one who mumbles over prayers and hymns.

Gregory XI, in one of his bulls against Wyclif, urged the clergy to extirpate this *lolium.*

Lollius. In Chaucer's TROILUS AND CRISEYDE, claimed by the English poet as the original author of the story, although internal evidence shows that Chaucer's source for the romance was BOCCACCIO. Lollius is also mentioned in Chaucer's *House of Fame.*

Lomax, John Avery (1872–1948). American folklorist; editor of *Cowboy Songs and Other Frontier Ballads* (1910); *Plantation Songs of the Negro* (1916); etc.

Lombard. A banker or money-lender, so called because the first bankers were from Lombardy, and set up in Lombard Street (London), in the Middle Ages. The name Lombard (according to Stow) is a contraction of Longobards. Among the richest of these Longobard merchants was the celebrated Medici family, from whose armorial bearings the insignia of three golden balls has been derived. The Lombard bankers exercised a monopoly in pawnbroking till the reign of Queen Elizabeth.

Lombard fever. Laziness. Pawn-brokers are called Lombard brokers, because they retain the three golden balls of the Lombard money-changers, and lazy folk will pawn anything rather than settle down to steady work.

Lombard Street to a China orange. Long odds. Lombard Street, London, is still the center of great banking and mercantile transactions. To stake the Bank of England against a common orange is to stake what is of untold value against a mere trifle.

Lombroso, Cesare (1836–1907). Italian physician and criminologist; professor of criminal anthropology at Turin. Taught that a criminal is a distinct anthropological type, the product of heredity and degeneracy rather than of social environment.

London, Jack. In full **John Griffith London** (1876–1916). American novelist, journalist, and wanderer, known for his stories of adventure and violence, chiefly laid in the Far North or the South Seas. He was strongly influenced by his conception of the ideas of both MARX and NIETZSCHE, and his work is marked by sympathy with the poor, prophecies of world revolution and a future Socialist state, and emphasis upon the primitive, the powerful, the cruel, and the violent, usually embodied in an animal or a "superman." Among his works are *The Son of the Wolf* (1900); *The Cruise of the Dazzler* (1902); *The People of the Abyss* (1903, on slum conditions in London); *Tales of the Fish Patrol* (1905); THE CALL OF THE WOLF (1904); *The War of the Classes* (1905); a treatise on Socialism; *The Game* (1905), dealing with prize-fighting; *Before Adam* (1907); *White Fang* (1907), about a wild dog; *The Iron Heel* (1907), concerning a revolution and a Utopia; *Martin Eden* (1909), an account of a Socialist author, considered to be partly autobiographical; *Revolution* (1910); *Burning Daylight* (1910), about a gold-miner in Alaska; THE CRUISE OF THE SNARK (1911); *South Sea Tales* (1911); SMOKE BELLEW (1912); *The Abysmal Brute* (1913); *The Valley of the Moon* (1913); JOHN BARLEYCORN (1913), an autobiography; *The Mutiny of the Elsinore* (1914); *The Scarlet Plague* (1915); *Jerry of the Islands* (1917); *The Human Drift* (1917); *On the Makaloa Mat* (1919).

As a boy and youth, London lived a dissolute life on the California waterfront, went to sea, was a tramp for awhile, did menial jobs, and went to Alaska during the Gold Rush. His writing became extremely popular during the early 1900's, and he lived extravagantly on his royalties. He had been a member of the Socialist party, but resigned in 1916, accusing it of lacking "fire and fight." He was twice married.

Lone Ranger, The. Hero of a popular American radio series of "cowboy" dramas of the late 1930's and early 1940's, appealing chiefly to children. The Lone Ranger is a "mysterious masked rider of the plains in the days when the West was young," who canvasses frontier settlements, saving lives, restoring lost husbands and sweethearts, promoting courtships, and in general defeating injustice. He is a combination Robin Hood and Deadwood Dick—quick on the trigger, but beneficent. The Lone Ranger was also a prominent character in the comic strips.

Lone Star State. Texas. See under STATES.

Long, Gabrielle Margaret Vere, *née* **Campbell.** Pseudonyms **Marjorie Bowen, George Runnel Preedy, Joseph Shearing,** etc. (1886–). Prolific English novelist and playwright. Author of many biographical accounts of famous people. Her novels with Dutch and Italian backgrounds are the most successful. Her *General Crack* (1928) made an effective motion picture, starring John Barrymore. Her "Shearing" romances are remarkable, macabre reconstructions of famous crimes.

Long, Haniel (1888–). American journalist, teacher and poet. Organized (1933) a cooperative publishing business, *Writers' Editions,* in Santa Fé, New Mexico. His most famous poem is *Wild Plum.* He has written a book on Walt Whitman.

Long, Huey Pierce (1893–1935). American lawyer and politician. As governor of Louisiana (1928–1931) and U.S. Senator (1931–1935) he acquired the reputation of a miniature replica of Hitler. Assassinated in 1935. His brother, **Earl Kemp Long** (1895–), became governor of Louisiana upon the retirement of governor Richard W. Leche (1939) but was defeated (1940). Reelected governor (1947).

Long, John Luther (1861–1927). American novelist and playwright. Especially remembered for his short story *Madame Butterfly* (*Century Magazine,* January, 1898), which was adapted for the stage by David Belasco and served as the basis for Puccini's opera.

Longaville. In Shakespeare's LOVE'S LABOR'S LOST, a young lord attending on Ferdinand, King of Navarre. He promises to spend three years in study with the King, during which time no woman is to approach the court. No sooner has he signed the compact than he falls in love with MARIA.

Longfellow, Henry Wadsworth (1807–1882). American poet and college professor, extremely popular and almost universally respected during his lifetime. His work is simple, mild, conventional, and kindly, marked by skill in metrics and influenced by the German lyric poets of the romantic period. His works include *Outre-Mer: A Pilgrimage Beyond the Sea* (1834–1835), prose sketches; HYPERION (1839), a romance; *Voices of the Night* (1839), poems; *Ballads and Other Poems* (1842); *Poems on Slavery* (1842), expressing the poet's interest in ABOLITIONISM; *The Spanish Student* (1843), a drama; *The Belfry of Bruges, And Other Poems* (1845); EVANGELINE (1847); *Kavanagh* (1849), a tale in prose, said to be partly autobiographical; *The Seaside and the Fireside* (1849), poems; THE GOLDEN LEGEND (1851); HIAWATHA (1855); THE COURTSHIP OF MILES STANDISH (1858); TALES OF A WAYSIDE INN (1863); *The Masque of Pandora* (1875); *Kéramos* (1878); *Ultima Thule* (1880); *In the Harbor* (1882). Among his best-known single poems are: *A Psalm of Life, The Village Blacksmith, The Wreck of the Hesperus* (see HESPERUS), EXCELSIOR, *The Children's Hour,* and PAUL REVERE'S RIDE.

Longfellow, who was a classmate of HAWTHORNE at Bowdoin College, studied in France, Spain, Germany, and Italy. He was one of the first teachers of modern languages in an American university, teaching for six years at Bowdoin (1829–1835) and for eighteen at Harvard (1836–1854). By the 20th century his verse was known principally among grammar-school pupils.

long house. A communal dwelling of the Iroquois Indians. By extension, in the form *Long House* the name of the Iroquois Confederacy of Five Nations.

Longinus, or **Longius.** The traditional name of the Roman soldier who smote our Lord with his spear at the Crucifixion. In the romance of King ARTHUR, this spear is brought by JOSEPH OF ARIMATHEA to Listenise, when he visits King Pellam, "who was nigh of Joseph's kin." Sir Balim the Savage, being in want of a weapon, seizes this spear, with which he wounds King Pellam. "Three whole countries" are destroyed by that one stroke, and Sir Balim sees "the people thereof lying dead on all sides."

Longinus, Dionysius Cassius (*fl.* 3rd century A.D.). Greek philosopher, to whom is attributed a famous treatise on poetry *On the Sublime,* which exalts a mystic inspiration from without as the chief factor in poetic composition.

Long Meg of Westminster. A noted virago in the reign of Henry VIII, round whose exploits a comedy (since lost) was performed in London in 1594. Her name has been given to several articles of unusual size. Thus, the large blue-black marble in the south cloister of Westminster Abbey, over the grave of Gervasius de Blois, is called *Long Meg of Westminster.* Fuller says the term is applied to things of "hop-pole height, wanting breadth proportionable thereunto," and refers to a great gun in the Tower so called, taken to Westminster in troublous times; and in the *Edinburgh Antiquarian Magazine* (September, 1769) we read of Peter Branan, aged 104, who was 6 ft. 6 in. high, and was commonly called *Long Meg of Westminster.*

Long Parliament. See under PARLIAMENTS.

Long Roll, The. A historical novel of the Civil War by Mary Johnston (*Am.,* 1911). The chief romantic interest is in the love affair of Judith Cary and Richard Cleave, a Confederate officer who is disgraced through a trick of his rival, Maury Stafford, but finally given another trial through the good offices of Stonewall JACKSON.

Longstreet, Augustus Baldwin (1790–1870). American clergyman, educator and humorous writer. Practiced law in Georgia and wrote about the Georgia Crackers, as in *Georgia Scenes* (1835 and 1840). President, University of Mississippi (1849–1856), University of South Carolina (1857–1865).

Longstreet, James (1821–1904). American army officer; in Confederate service (from 1861); lieutenant general in command of a corps under LEE at Gettysburg (July, 1863), where his delayed attack was partly responsible for the defeat of the Confederacy. Surrendered with Lee at Appomattox Court House (April 9, 1865). Cf. his autobiography, *From Manasses to Appomattox* (1896). During the Reconstruction he became a champion of Grant. Held government offices at home and in diplomatic service abroad.

Long Tom. A large field gun of long range. Originally the name of a 42-pound gun on the French man-of-war *Hoche.* It was captured by the British (1798), sold to America, transferred to the General Armstrong which ran the British blockade of New Orleans, and finally had to be abandoned in the Azores. It was rescued, however (1893), and brought back to New York.

Longus (4th or 5th century A. D.). Greek writer, supposed author of DAPHNIS AND CHLOË.

Long Valley, The. A collection of short stories by John STEINBECK (1938).

Lonigan, William, called **Studs.** Hero of James T. Farrell's trilogy STUDS LONIGAN, a youth of moderate pride and ambition in early adolescence, certain that he will accomplish great things in the world when he grows up, who is defeated in life under the combined influence of his family background, his associates, and his economic environment. He is shown throughout the novel as a commonplace young man, repelled by viciousness but unable to avoid drifting into it, dissatisfied by his way of life but unable to escape from it, uncertain of what he wants from life, easily swayed by the preachings of the Roman Catholic Church and the practices of his friends, without being able to think out his problems rationally for himself, occasionally prompted by impulses of decency but unable to carry them through, given to concealing his sense of frustration from himself by identifying himself with the bold and ruthless heroes of the gangster motion pictures he goes to see. He is exceptional in neither sensitivity nor essential viciousness of character, in accordance with the author's plan to make him representative of a class of youth in the U.S. of the 1920's and early 1930's.

Lonsdale, Frederick (1881–). British playwright of sophisticated comedies. His best-known play is *The Last of Mrs. Cheyney* (1925).

Look Homeward, Angel: A Story of the Buried Life. A novel by Thomas WOLFE, autobiographical in character, published in 1929. It describes the childhood and youth of Eugene GANT in the town of Altamont, state of Catawba (said to be Asheville, North Carolina), as he grows up, becomes aware of the relations among his family, meets the eccentric people of the town, goes to college, discovers literature and ideas, has his first love affairs, and at last sets out alone on a mystic and romantic "pilgrimage." OF TIME AND THE RIVER is a sequel to this novel.

Looking Backward 2000–1887. A romance by Edward BELLAMY (1888), describing a Utopian, Communistic Boston in the year 2000. It caused widespread discussion.

Lookout Mountain. See under MISSIONARY RIDGE.

Loomis, Charles Battell (1861–1911). American humorist. Author of *Just Rhymes* (1899); *A Bath in an English Tub* (1907); *A Holiday Touch* (1908); *Just Irish* (1909); etc.

Loop. The "downtown" district of Chicago, the business and theatrical center, so called from the "loop" made by the elevated tracks running in to the center of the city.

Loos, Anita (1893–). American humorous writer, best known for her *Gentlemen Prefer Blondes* (1925), and scenarios for moving pictures.

Lope de Vega, see VEGA, LOPE DE.

L'Oracolo (*Ital.,* **The Oracle**). An opera (1905) by Camillo Zanoni. The libretto is based on the story, *The Cat and the Cherub* (1896) by Chester Bailey Fernald.

Lorbrulgrud. The capital of Brobdingnag in Swift's *Gulliver's Travels.* See GULLIVER, LEMUEL. The word is humorously said to mean "Pride of the Universe."

Lorca, Federigo García (1899–1936). Spanish poet and playwright of Andalusian stock. Deeply indebted to the popular song tradition of his native province. Organized the first *cante hondo* ("deep-song") festival at the Alhambra (1922). Cf. the superb ballads in *Romancero Gitano* (1928). Came to New York (1929–1930) where he was struck by the affinity of Negro spirituals to the *cante hondo*. The result was his *Oda al Rey de Harlem*, available in English in the collection *The Poet in New York* (1940). His career as a dramatist reached a climax with the rural tragedy *Bitter Oleander* (1935), reissued as *Blood Wedding* (1939). García Lorca was a friend of Salvador DALI's. His own drawings remind of Cocteau. He was also an accomplished musician. He was murdered at the start of the Spanish Civil War, and his books were suppressed by the Franco government.

Lord Jim. A novel by Joseph CONRAD (1900), dealing with a man's lifelong efforts to atone for an act of instinctive cowardice. As a young man, Jim is one of the officers of the *Patna* who frantically take to the boats when she hits a derelict in the Red Sea, leaving their eight hundred native passengers, as they suppose, to certain death. After years of wandering from place to place pursued by the disgrace, he wins a measure of satisfaction and self-respect from a busy, useful life among the natives of Patusan, who put complete confidence in *Tuan* Jim (Lord Jim). Finally, however, a gang of intrusive white men whom he has persuaded the natives to allow to go free repay his trust by murdering Dain Maroola, his best friend, the son of Chief Doramin. Lord Jim immediately gives himself up to Doramin and is killed. The story is told by Conrad's favorite character, MARLOW.

Lord of Burleigh, The. A ballad by TENNYSON (1842). In the guise of a village painter the noble-born hero courts and wins a simple country maiden, but when he takes her home to his castle, she feels out of place and pines away and dies.

Lord of Misrule, The. Formerly, the master of revels or officer in charge of courtly entertainment in Great Britain. In Scotland he is called the Abbot of Unreason. Also, the title of a poem by Alfred Noyes.

Lord of the Isles. Donald of Islay, who in 1346 reduced the Hebrides under his sway. The title of *Lord of the Isles* had been borne by others for centuries before, was borne by his (Donald's) successors, and is now one of the titles of the Prince of Wales. Sir Walter SCOTT has a metrical romance entitled *The Lord of the Isles* (1815).

Lord Ormont and His Aminta. A novel by George MEREDITH (1894) based on the career of the Earl of Peterborough, who rendered distinguished service at Valencia but in later life nourished resentment against the government which had recalled him (1707) for high-handedness. He married Anastasia Robinson, the singer, but made no public acknowledgment of the marriage for many years. In the novel the names are changed, and Aminta remedies her equivocal position by eloping with Matthew Weyburn and opening a school in the Alps.

Lord's (cricket ground). Headquarters of the Marylebone Cricket Club in London, named from Thomas Lord. England's most famous cricket ground.

Lord Ullin's Daughter. A ballad by Thomas CAMPBELL (1809). The lady elopes with the Chief of Ulva's Isle, and is pursued by her father with a party of retainers. The lovers reach a ferry, and promise to give the boatman "a silver pound" to row them across Lochgyle. The waters are very rough, and the father reaches the shore just in time to see the boat capsize, and his daughter drowned.

> 'Twas vain; the loud waves lashed the shore,
> Return or aid preventing;
> The waters wild went o'er his child,
> And he was left lamenting.

Lorelei or **Lurlei.** A siren of German legend, who haunted a rock of the same name on the right bank of the Rhine, half-way between Bingen and Coblenz. She combed her hair with a golden comb, and sang a wild song, which enticed fishermen and sailors to destruction on the rocks and rapids. Heinrich HEINE has a well-known poem on the Lorelei.

Lorentz, Pare (1905–). American scenario writer and motion-picture director, famous for his script *The River*.

Lorenz, Adolf (1854–1946). Austrian orthopedic surgeon, widely known for his "bloodless surgery," particularly in the treatment of congenital hip-disease by manipulation and subsequent use of a cast. Visited U.S. more than twenty times.

Lorenzo. (1) A young man in Shakespeare's MERCHANT OF VENICE with whom Jessica, the daughter of the Jew Shylock, elopes.

(2) In Edward YOUNG's *Night Thoughts*, the embodiment of evil and atheism.

(3) The name by which D. H. LAWRENCE was known to his admirers and disciples.

Lorenzo The Magnificent. See under MEDICI.

Loretto, The house of. The Santa Casa, the reputed house of the Virgin Mary at Nazareth. It was "miraculously" translated to Fiume in Dalmatia in 1291, thence to Recanati in 1294, and finally to a plot of land belonging to a certain Lady *Lauretta*, situated in Italy, 3 m. from the Adriatic, and about 14 S.S.E. from Ancona, round which the town of Loretto sprang up. The chapel contains bas-reliefs showing incidents in the life of the Virgin, and a rough image which is traditionally held to have been carved by St. Luke.

> Our house may have traveled through the air, like the house of Loretto, for aught I care.—Goldsmith, *The Good-natured Man*, iv, 1.

Father Malachy's Miracle, by Bruce MARSHALL (1934), is a humorous variation on this legend.

Lorge, De. The hero of a legend retold by SCHILLER in his ballad *The Glove* (*Der Handschuh*) and the subject of poems by Leigh HUNT and BROWNING. According to the tale, De Lorge's lady love threw her glove into the arena of wild beasts, purely to test his devotion. He recovered it, threw it in her face, and scornfully left her. Browning's version presents a unique justification of the motives behind the lady's act. See GLOVE, THE. The tale is to be found in Froissart's *Chronicles*, attributed to the period of Francis I of France.

Lorimer, George Horace (1868–1937). American man of letters. Author of *Letters of a Self-made Merchant to his Son* and *Old Gorgon Graham*, books of rugged individualism. Editor of *Saturday Evening Post* (1899–1936). Cf. *George Horace Lorimer* (1948), by J. W. Tebbel.

Lorna Doone, a Romance of Exmoor. A historical novel by R. D. Blackmore (1869). At the age of fourteen, the young hero, John Ridd, falls into the hands of the robber Doones, a band of high-born Devonshire outlaws. He is saved by Lorna Doone, a mere child, and when he is of age, he sets out to find her again. Because the Doones have killed his father he hates them; he protects Lorna against them and finally marries her.

Lorrain, Claude (1600–1682). French landscape painter and engraver. Original name, **Claude Gellée,** changed after his native province Lorraine. The *Claude Lorraine mirror* is a black, slightly convex mirror, in which landscapes appear changed in fancied resemblance to Lorrain's canvases.

Lorraine, Mrs. Felix. A clever intriguing woman in Disraeli's VIVIAN GREY. This is one of the numerous characters of fiction for whom Lady Caroline Lamb was the model.

Lorrequer, Harry, see HARRY LORREQUER.

Lorris, Guillaume de, see GUILLAUME DE LORRIS.

Lost Chord, The. A poem, once very popular, by Adelaide Ann PROCTER. It begins, "Seated one day at the organ . . ." and was set to music by Sir Arthur SULLIVAN.

Lost Generation. A term used to refer to the generation of men and women who came to maturity during World War I and as a result of their experiences in the war itself and of the social dislocations following it were rootless, disillusioned, and neurotic. Gertrude STEIN is said to have first used the term in a conversation with Ernest HEMINGWAY, whose early novels are considered to typify the attitudes and behavior of the Lost Generation. Malcolm COWLEY has a book on the post-war period entitled *The Lost Generation* (1931). See also FITZGERALD, F. SCOTT; JAZZ AGE; WAR IN LITERATURE.

Lost Lady, A. A novel by Willa CATHER (1923). Concerns graceful, charming, and passionate Marian Forrester, and the course of her life in a new country.

Lost Leader, The. A poem by Robert BROWNING (1845), reproaching a former liberal poet, once admired by the author, for deserting his cause.

> Just for a handful of silver he left us,
> Just for a riband to stick in his coat.

The change made by WORDSWORTH from liberalism to conservatism was the inspiration for the poem.

lost tribes. The members of the ten tribes of the Jews who seceded after the death of Solomon and established the separate kingdom of Israel. In 722 B. C. it was overthrown by Sargon of Assyria; 27,000 Jews were displaced to various parts of the Assyrian Empire and never returned to Palestine. The theory now is that the lost tribes were absorbed by neighboring nations.

Lot. (1) In the Old Testament, the nephew who accompanied ABRAHAM to Canaan and divided the land with him. Lot was one of the inhabitants of the wicked city of SODOM and escaped by the intervention of an angel just before the city was destroyed by fire and brimstone. Lot's wife was turned to a pillar of salt for looking back at the city (*Gen.* xix. 26).

(2) In Arthurian romance, King of Orkney, one of the kings subdued by ARTHUR. Malory makes Lot's wife Margawse or MORGAUSE, but Tennyson in his *Idylls* calls her Bellicent. Lot was the father of GAWAIN, AGRAVAIN, GAHERIS, GARETH, and, according to Tennyson's account, of MODRED.

Lothair. A novel by DISRAELI (1871). The hero, Lothair, is a young English nobleman who, upon coming of age, inherits a great fortune. The plot centers about the struggle between the Anglican Church, the Church of Rome, and the revolutionary societies of Italy to secure his money and support. One of the most interesting characters of the book is the witty Lord ST. ALDEGONDE. A primary cause for the popularity of the book was the interest taken by the English public in identifying the characters who were prominent people under slight disguise, generally supposed to represent the following:

The Oxford Professor, Goldwin Smith.
Grandison, Cardinals Manning and Wiseman.
Lothair, Marquis of Bute.
Catesby, Monseigneur Capel.
The Duke and Duchess, the Duke and Duchess of Abercorn.
The Bishop, Bishop Wilberforce.
Corisande, one of the Ladies Hamilton.

Lothario. (1) A gay libertine, a seducer of women, a debauchee. The character is from Rowe's tragedy *The Fair Penitent* (1703), which is founded on Massinger's *Fatal Dowry* (1632), though Rowe probably got the name from Davenant's *Cruel Brother* (1630), where is a similar character with the same name.

Is this that haughty, gallant, gay Lothario?
Fair Penitent, v. 1.

(2) A character in Cervantes' story THE CURIOUS IMPERTINENT told in *Don Quixote.*

(3) The patron of WILHELM MEISTER in Goethe's *Wilhelm Meister's Lehrjahre.*

Loti, Pierre. Real name **Louis Marie Julien Viaud** (1850–1923). French novelist, known for his exotic tales of the sea and foreign lands, characterized by sensuous and impressionistic description and an attitude of consistent melancholy. Among these works are *Aziyadé* (1879), published anonymously; *Le Mariage de Loti* (THE MARRIAGE OF LOTI; 1880); *Roman d'un Spahi* (1881); *Fleurs d'Ennui* (1882); *Mon Frère Yves* (*My Brother Yves;* 1883); *Pêcheur d'Islande* (AN ICELAND FISHERMAN; 1886); MADAME CHRYSANTHÈME (1887); *Le Roman d'un Enfant* (*A Child's Romance;* 1890); *Fantôme d'Orient* (*A Phantom from the East;* 1892); *Le Livre de la Pitié et de la Mort* (*The Book of Pity and Death;* 1891); *Jérusalem* (1895) and *La Galilée* (1895), dealing with a journey to the Holy Land; *Ramuntcho* (1897); *Madame Prune* (1905); *Les Désenchantées* (*Disenchanted;* 1906); *Un Jeune officier Pauvre* (1923).

In his youth, Loti was a French naval officer and traveled extensively about the world. He was widely celebrated for his writings, and in 1892 was elected to the French Academy, defeating Émile ZOLA. In the days of his success and prosperity, he lived in a palace which contained several halls decorated elaborately and authentically in Gothic, Renaissance, Turkish, Chinese, and 19th-century bourgeois French styles.

Lot Sap Sago, see SAGO.

Lotte. The heroine of Goethe's *Sorrows of Young Werther.* See WERTHER.

lotus. A name given to many plants, e.g., by the Egyptians to various species of water-lily, by the Hindus and Chinese to the Nelumbo (a water-bean, *Nymphaeaceae speciosum*), their "sacred lotus," and by the Greeks to *Zizyphus Lotus,* a north African shrub of the natural order Rhamneae, the fruit of which was used for food.

According to Mahomet a lotus-tree stands in the seventh heaven, on the right hand of the throne of God, and the Egyptians pictured God sitting on a lotus above the watery mud. One of the most familiar of Buddhist prayers begins "Hark the jewel in the lotus." See OM.

The classic myth is that Lotis, a daughter of Neptune, fleeing from Priapus was changed into a tree, which was called Lotus after her. Another story goes that Dryope of Oechalia was one day carrying her infant son, when she plucked a lotus flower for his amusement, and was instantaneously transformed into a lotus.

Lotus-eaters or *Lotophagi.* In Homeric legend, a people who ate of the lotus-tree, the effect of which was to make them forget their friends and homes, and to lose all desire of returning to their native country, their only wish being to live in idleness in Lotus-land (*Odyssey,* ix).

Hence, a *lotus-eater* is one living in ease and luxury. Tennyson wrote one of his best-known poems on this subject.

Loubet, Émile (1838–1929). French statesman and 7th president of the Third French Republic (1899–1906). Sought revision of the DREYFUS case.

Loudon, Joe. The hero of Tarkington's CONQUEST OF CANAAN.

Louis. In Virginia Woolf's THE WAVES, the son of an Australian banker, staying in England for his education; he is proud, vain, and ashamed of being a colonial at the same time that he resents the English children with whom he associates. He does not go to college but goes to work in business and eventually becomes wealthy, although he still retains the feelings of inferiority of his childhood. At one time he and RHODA, drawn together by their personal uncertainties and the sense of isolation they both share, become lovers, but later she leaves him.

Louis de Conte. In Mark Twain's JOAN OF ARC, the friend who tells the story.

Louis XI of France (1423–1483) is introduced by Scott in two of his novels, QUENTIN DURWARD and ANNE OF GEIERSTEIN. In *Quentin Durward,* he appears disguised as Maitre Pierre, a merchant. He is the hero of a drama by Casimir de la Vigne and appears in Hugo's NOTRE DAME DE PARIS and Theodore de Banville's play of *Gringoire.*

Louis XIV. Often called **Louis the Great** or in French **le Grand Monarque** and **le Roi Soleil** (the great monarch, the sun king) (1638–1715). The greatest autocratic monarch of France whose extravagances and wars made his country great and almost bankrupt. Reputed to have summed up his political creed in the phrase, *L'état, c'est moi,* "I am the state." His reign of 73 years was the longest in European history; his court was the indisputable model for almost all the lesser princes in Europe. By revoking the Edict of NANTES he caused thousands of Huguenots to flee France. He had famous mistresses; the end of his reign was made religious by Madame de Maintenon, the best-known of them.

Louis Quatorze. As an adjective, applied to the style of architecture, decorative art, furniture, etc., that prevailed during the reign of Louis XIV. The architecture is cold and regular with richness of interior decoration. The furniture had elaborate carving and gilding, buhlwork inlay and Roman motives in ornamentation with a tendency toward the rococo. Similarly, **Louis Quinze** style (Louis XV, 1715–1774), is characterized in interior ornamentation by an irregular curved line and surface replacing the straight. **Louis Seize** style (Louis XVI, 1774–1793) in architecture is more antique yet lighter. Decoration again takes up the straight line. Interior ornamentation shows the influence of the recently discovered frescoes of Pompeii and Herculaneum and pastoral motives.

Louis Philippe. Known as **Citizen King** or in French **Roi citoyen** (1773–1850). Eldest son of Philippe Égalité; elected King of the French (1830), at the instance of LAFAYETTE, after the deposition of Charles X; was himself deposed after the July Revolution (1848). A partisan of the Revolution in his youth, democratic in the first years of his reign, he became more and more a typical Bourbon and absolutist. Died in exile in Claremont, England.

Louise, the Glee-maiden. In Scott's FAIR MAID OF PERTH.

Louise de la Vallière. A historical romance by Alexandre Dumas which forms a part of his *Vicomte de Bragelonne.* See under THREE MUSKETEERS. It is also a drama by BULWER LYTTON.

Louisiana Purchase. The vast territory (885,000 square miles) purchased (April 30, 1803) by the United States during Jefferson's administration for $15,000,000 from France under the consulate of Bonaparte. It extended from the Mississippi to the Rocky Mountains and from the Gulf of Mexico to British America. See also Meriwether LEWIS.

Lounsbury, Thomas Raynesford (1838–1915). American scholar and educator. His *History of the English Language* (1879) has been called a masterpiece. One of the original members of the American Academy of Arts and Letters, and fellow of the American Academy of Arts and Sciences. Edited Chaucer's minor poems; a biography of J. Fenimore Cooper; wrote a book on Tennyson which was completed after his death by Wilbur L. CROSS; etc.

Loupgarou (*Fr.,* "werewolf"). In Rabelais' GARGANTUA AND PANTAGRUEL, a leader of the giants. When Pantagruel grew angry with him, he picked him up by his ankles and used him like a quarter-staff.

Lourdes. A town on the Gave de Pan in the department Hautes-Pyrénées, France; one of the chief centers of Roman Catholic pilgrimages because of a grotto located there in which the Virgin Mary, according to tradition, appeared (1858) to the local peasant girl Bernadette Soubirous and revealed to her the miraculous properties of a spring. See also *St. Bernadette* under SAINTS. *Lourdes* is the title of a novel by Émile ZOLA (1894). Franz WERFEL made Bernadette Soubirous and her visions the subject of his best-selling novel *The Song of Bernadette* (*Das Lied von Bernadette;* 1942), made into a successful moving picture.

Louvre. The former royal palace of the French kings in Paris. Dagobert is said to have built here a hunting-seat, but the present magnificent pile of buildings was begun by Francis I in 1541. After the French Revolution the greater part of the Louvre was used for the national museum and art gallery.

Louÿs, Pierre (1870–1925). French man of letters. Author of *Les Chansons de Bilitis* (prose poems; 1894); *Aphrodite* (novel; 1896); etc.

Lövberg. A leading character in Ibsen's HEDDA GABLER.

love feast. A banquet in token of love and friendship. Among the early Christians, the love feast (called agape) preceded the Lord's Supper.

Love for Love. A famous comedy by CONGREVE (1695). The heroine, Angelica, the ward of Sir Sampson LEGEND, is courted by her guardian but is in love with his son Valentine and finally agrees to marry him. Angelica is said to represent the famous actress, Mrs. Bracegirdle, to whom Congreve addressed numerous attentions.

Lovel, Lord. Hero of Bayley's song, THE MISTLETOE BOUGH.

Lovelace. The principal male character of Richardson's novel CLARISSA HARLOWE. He is a selfish voluptuary, a man of fashion, whose sole ambition is to seduce young women. He is rich, proud, handsome, brave and gay, a type of the most unscrupulous but polished libertine.

Lovelace, Richard (1618–1658). English poet, with CAREW and SUCKLING classified in the Cavalier group or the "sons of Ben." See

JONSON, BEN. He was known for his grace, his handsome appearance, and his aristocratic gallantry. His poetry includes a number of graceful and facile songs among which *To Althea, from Prison* and *To Lucasta, Going to the Wars* are the best-known. Collections of the poems to "LUCASTA" were published in 1649 and 1659. Lovelace was in the royal army during the Civil War and was imprisoned on two occasions for his connections with the Royalist faction.

Loveless, Edward and **Amanda.** Husband and wife, the chief characters in *Love's Last Shift or the Fool in Fashion* by Colley CIBBER (1695), in its sequel *The Relapse or Virtue in Danger* by Sir John Vanbrugh (1696) and in *A Trip to Scarborough,* an adaptation of *The Relapse* by Sheridan. The plays center about Amanda's successful schemes to win back her husband's roving affections.

Lovell, Charlotte. The "old maid" in Edith WHARTON's short novel of that title published as one of the four parts of her *In Old New York* (1924). Actually a mother but forced for propriety's sake to seem only an old-maid aunt to her daughter Tiny, Charlotte accepts the home offered the two of them by her married cousin, Delia Ralston, but suffers intolerably from her situation.

Love Me Little, Love Me Long. A novel by Charles READE (1859). See DODD, DAVID.

Lover, Samuel (1797–1868). Irish novelist, song writer and painter. His novel *Rory O'More* (1839) was dramatized with the original Tyrone Power (1797–1841) in the leading role. His best-known songs are *Rory O'More, The Four-leaved Shamrock, The Low-Backed Car,* etc.

Lovers' Leap, see LEUCADIA'S ROCK.

Love's Labor's Lost. A comedy by Shakespeare (ca. 1594). Ferdinand, King of Navarre, with three lords named Biron, Dumain, and Longaville, agrees to spend three years in study, during which time no woman is to approach the court. Scarcely have they signed the compact, when the Princess of France, attended by Rosaline, Maria, and Katharine, seeks an interview respecting certain debts said to be due from the King of France to the King of Navarre. The four gentlemen fall in love with the four ladies: the King with the Princess, Biron with Rosaline, Longaville with Maria, and Dumain with Katharine. In order to carry their suits, the four gentlemen, disguised as Muscovites, present themselves before the ladies, but they, being warned of the masquerade, have disguised themselves also, so that each gentleman in every case addresses the wrong lady. However, it is at length arranged that the suits be deferred for twelve months and a day, and if, at the expiration of that time, they remain of the same mind, the matter is to be taken into serious consideration.

Loves of the Angels. The stories of three angels, in verse, by Thomas MOORE (1822). The stories are founded on the Eastern tale of *Harût and Marût,* and the rabbinical fictions of the loves of *Uzziel and Shamchazai.*

(1) The first angel falls in love with Lea, whom he has seen bathing. She returns love for love, but his love is carnal, hers heavenly. He loves the woman, she loves the angel. One day, the angel tells her the spell-word which opens the gates of heaven. She pronounces it, and rises through the air into paradise, while the angel becomes imbruted, being no longer an angel of light, but "of the earth, earthy."

(2) The second angel is Rubi, one of the seraphs. He falls in love with Liris, who asks him to come in all his celestial glory. He does so, and she, rushing into his arms, is burnt to death; but the kiss she gives him becomes a brand on his face forever.

(3) The third angel is Zaraph, who loves Nama. It is Nama's desire to love without control, and to love holily, but as she has fixed her love on a creature, and not on the Creator, both she and Zaraph are doomed to live among the things that perish, until this mortal is swallowed up by immortality, when Nama and Zaraph will be admitted into the realms of everlasting love.

Lovett, Robert Morss (1870–). American educator and author. Professor of English at the University of Chicago (1909–1936). Author (with William Vaughn MOODY) of books on English literature. Government secretary of the Virgin Islands (1939). Member, National Institute of Arts and Letters. Edited *Selected Poems of William Vaughn Moody. All Our Years* (1948), is an autobiography.

Lovey Mary. A novel by Alice Hegan Rice, a sequel to MRS. WIGGS OF THE CABBAGE PATCH.

Low, David (1891–). British cartoonist. Created the character of Colonel BLIMP. His best-known collections of political cartoons are *Europe at War* (1940) and *A Cartoon History of the War* (1941).

Low, Seth (1830–1916). American politician and educator. President of Columbia University (1890–1901). As mayor of New York City (1901–1903) he was a civic reformer.

Low, Will Hicok (1853–1932). American illustrator and painter; friend of Robert Louis STEVENSON. His works include murals and stained glass windows.

Low Countries. Holland, Belgium and sometimes Luxemburg; so called from the point of view of other regions of Central Europe which enjoy higher elevation above sea level.

Lowe, Sir Hudson (1769–1844). British soldier; as governor of St. Helena, custodian of Napoleon Bonaparte (1815–1821).

Lowell, Abbott Lawrence (1856–1943). American political scientist and educator. Brother of Amy LOWELL and Percival LOWELL. President of Harvard University (from 1909), emeritus (from 1933). Author of *Governments and Parties in Continental Europe* (1896); *Conflicts of Principle* (1932); etc.

Lowell, Amy Lawrence (1874–1925). American poet and critic, of a wealthy and distinguished New England family which included James Russell LOWELL in the 19th century. She is known for her association with and leadership of the movement of IMAGISM, in accordance with which she wrote numerous poems in free verse and "POLYPHONIC PROSE," many showing the influence of Chinese and Japanese poetry. Among her books of poetry are *A Dome of Many-Colored Glass* (1912); *Sword-Blades and Poppy-Seeds* (1914); *Men, Women, and Ghosts* (1916); *Can Grande's Castle* (1918); *Pictures of the Floating World* (1919); *Legends* (1921); *Fir-Flower Tablets* (1921), a collection of adaptations and translations of Chinese poetry; *What's O'Clock?* (1925); *East Wind* (1926); *Ballads for Sale* (1927). Her works of criticism include: *Six French Poets* (1915); *Tendencies in Modern American Poetry* (1921); *A Critical Fable* (1922), an imitation of J. R. Lowell's A FABLE FOR CRITICS; and *John Keats* (1925), an exhaustive and sympathetic study of the English poet.

Amy Lowell tended to be celebrated more for her personality than for the artistic value of her work. She was eccentric in behavior, keeping a large troupe of dogs, smoking large black cigars, treating servants and waiters with great arrogance, and using language of extreme frankness. She was interested in painting and sculpture and frequently traveled abroad. A number of the well-known writers of her day attended her literary salons at her home in Brookline, Mass., Sevenels. Cf. *Amy Lowell: a Chronicle* (1935), by S. Foster Damon.

Lowell, James Russell (1819–1891). American literary critic, poet, and humorist, a professor of French and Spanish at Harvard University after the retirement of LONGFELLOW. He was first editor of the ATLANTIC MONTHLY and was also on the editorial staff of the *North American Review,* strongly influencing the taste of his time. His verse is ingenious and clever but is not considered among the best of 19th-century America, and his views were conservative except with respect to ABOLITIONISM and the Union cause during the Civil War, which he strongly advocated. Among his works are A FABLE FOR CRITICS (1848); *The Vision of Sir Launfal* (see LAUNFAL; 1848); BIGLOW PAPERS (1846–1848; 1867); *Fireside Travels* (1864), literary essays; *Among My Books* (1870, 1876); *My Study Windows* (1871); *Latest Literary Essays and Addresses* (1891); *The Old English Dramatists* (1892). He was minister to Spain (1877–1880) and to England (1880–1885). Amy LOWELL was a descendant.

Lowell's wife, **Maria White Lowell** (1821–1853), was an ardent abolitionist in her poetry and her convictions and influenced her husband while she was alive.

Lowell, Orson (1871–). American illustrator with a distinctive style of draughtsmanship. Did much illustration of magazine stories and helped illustrate *The Court of Boyville* by William Allen WHITE; *A Bicycle of Cathay* by Frank R. STOCKTON; etc.

Lowell, Percival (1855–1916). American astronomer. Brother of Amy LOWELL. Founder of Lowell Observatory near Flagstaff, Arizona (1893–1894). Best known for his studies of the planet Mars. By mathematical calculations he determined the existence of a planet X (finally observed, January, 1930, by C. W. Tombaugh and named Pluto). Author of *Mars* (1895); *Mars as the Abode of Life* (1908); *The Genesis of the Planets* (1916); etc.

lower case. The printer's name for the small letters (minuscules) of a font of type, as opposed to the capitals; these are, in a hand-operated type-setter's "case," on a *lower* level than the others.

Lower Depths, The. A drama by Maxim GORKY. The characters are the poor and wretched inmates of a fourth-rate boarding house.

Lowes, John Livingston (1867–). American scholar and educator. Professor of English at Harvard (from 1918). Author of *Convention and Revolt in Poetry* (1919); *The Road to Xanadu* (1927), a unique study of Coleridge; *The Art of Geoffrey Chaucer* (1931); etc. Responsible (with G. L. Kittredge) for analyses of synonyms in *Webster's New International Dictionary.*

Lowestoft. Seaport in Suffolk, England, where high-grade pottery, known as *Lowestoft ware,* was manufactured (1775–1802).

Low Heels and **High Heels.** Two factions in the Lilliput of Swift's *Gulliver's Travels.* See GULLIVER, LEMUEL. The High Heels were opposed to the Emperor, who wore low heels.

Lowndes, Mrs. Belloc. Pen name of **Marie Adelaide Lowndes,** *née* **Belloc** (1868–1947).

English historical novelist and mystery story writer. Sister of Hilaire BELLOC. Her mystery novels include *The Chink in the Armour* (1912); *The Lodger* (1913), a fictionized presentation of the JACK-THE-RIPPER murders; *Who Rides on a Tiger* (1936); etc.

Loyalist. During the American Revolution, one loyal to the British crown; a Tory. In the Spanish Civil War (1936–1939), those who fought for the Spanish Republic against Generalissimo Franco and fascism.

Loyola, St. Ignatius, see under SAINTS.

Lubbe, Marinus van der (1910–1934). Dutch brick mason. Convicted in Germany of implication in the burning of the Reichstag building (February 27, 1933) and guillotined at Leipzig (January 10, 1934). Thought to have been mentally deficient and falsely accused for political purposes.

Lubberland. A burlesque name for a sort of Utopia, the same as COCKAIGNE.

Lubitsch, Ernst (1892–1947). German-born American motion-picture director. Called to U.S. (1922) to direct Mary Pickford. Known for witty and charming society comedies, as *Lady Windermere's Fan; Design for Living; Ninotchka; Cluny Brown;* etc.

Lucan. In full **Marcus Annaeus Lucanus** (39–65 A. D.). Roman poet and prose-writer. Author of *Pharsalia,* an epic in 10 books on the civil war between Caesar and Pompey. No other work of his is extant. First a favorite of NERO, he was forbidden by the jealous emperor to give public recitals. He joined Piso's conspiracy, was denounced and condemned to death but committed suicide.

Lucas, Edward Verrall (1868–1938). English essayist and publisher. On staff of *Punch;* chairman, Methuen & Co. Editor of *Letters of Charles and Mary Lamb* (1935). His best-known novel is *Over Bemerton's* (1908).

Lucasta. The lady of this name to whom Richard LOVELACE sang (1649), is usually supposed to have been Lucy Sacheverell, called by him *lux casta,* i.e., Chaste Lucy or Chaste Light.

Luce, Henry Robinson (1898–). American editor and publisher. Founder of *Time,* a weekly newsmagazine (1923); *Fortune,* a monthly for capitalists (1930); *Life,* a weekly picture magazine (1936). Husband of Clare BOOTHE LUCE.

Lucentio. In Shakespeare's TAMING OF THE SHREW, son of Vicentio of Pisa. He marries Bianca, sister of "the Shrew."

Lucetta. In Shakespeare's TWO GENTLEMEN OF VERONA, the waiting-woman of Julia, the lady-love of Proteus.

Lucia, St. See under SAINTS.

Lucia di Lammermoor. An opera by Donizetti (1835) based on Scott's BRIDE OF LAMMERMOOR. In the opera Lucy Ashton is Lucia, Arthur Bucklaw, Arturo, and Edgar of Ravenswood, Edgardo. Bucklaw does not recover from the wound given him by his bride, as he does in the novel, and Edgardo, instead of being swallowed up in the quicksands, kills himself.

Lucian. The chief character in the *Golden Ass* of Apuleius (2nd century A. D.), a work which is in part an imitation of the *Metamorphoses* by LUCIAN. In the *Golden Ass,* Lucian, changed into an ass, is the personification of the follies and vices of the age.

Lucian (ca. 120–200 A. D.). Greek satirist and humorist, the most brilliant wit of Greek letters under the Roman Empire. A free-thinker, often referred to in his time as "the Blasphemer" and later compared with SWIFT and VOLTAIRE. Author of rhetorical, critical, and biographical works, of romances, dialogues, poems, etc. His *Veracious History,* a mock narrative of travel, is the archetype of books like Swift's *Gulliver's Travels.* His *Dialogues of the Dead* have been called brilliant satires of the living.

Lucifer. The morning star; also a name for SATAN.

proud as Lucifer. Very haughty and overbearing. Lucifer is the name given by Isaiah to Nebuchadnezzar, the proud but ruined king of Babylon: "Take up this proverb against the King of Babylon, and say . . . How art thou fallen, from heaven, O Lucifer, son of the morning!" (*Isa.* xiv. 4, 12). The poets declare that Satan, before he was driven out of heaven for his pride, was called Lucifer. Milton introduces him as the demon of Sinful Pride in his PARADISE LOST.

Lucifera. In Spenser's FAËRIE QUEENE (I. iv), the typification of pride, luxury, and worldliness, and chief of the Seven Deadly Sins. She lives in a splendid palace, only its foundation is of sand; the door stands always open, and she gives welcome to every comer. Her carriage is drawn by six different animals —viz., an ass, swine, goat, camel, wolf, and lion, on each of which rides one of the Sins, Satan himself being coachman. While here, the Red Cross Knight is attacked by SANSJOY, who would have been slain if Duessa had not rescued him.

Lucile. A narrative poem by Robert, Lord Lytton, published (1860) under the pseudonym of Owen MEREDITH. The heroine, Lucile, is beloved by two bitter rivals, the English Lord Alfred Hargrave and the French Duke of Luvois. She loves Alfred, but misunderstanding keeps them apart. Long years after,

Alfred's son and the Duke's niece fall in love, are separated by the old feud but finally reunited through the efforts of Lucile, who has become a nursing nun, under the name of Soeur Seraphine. The book went through more than ninety editions in America.

Lucina. In Roman mythology, the goddess of childbirth; hence, a midwife.

Lucinde. (1) Heroine of Molière's L'AMOUR MÉDECIN (*Love As a Doctor*), the daughter of SGANARELLE. As she has lost her spirit and appetite, her father sends for four physicians, who all differ as to the nature of the malady and the remedy to be applied. Lisette, her waiting-woman, sends in the meantime for Clitandre, the lover of Lucinde, who comes under the guise of a mock doctor. He tells Sganarelle the disease of the young lady must be reached through the imagination, and prescribes the semblance of a marriage. As his assistant is in reality a notary, the mock marriage turns out to be a real one.

(2) Heroine of Molière's MÉDECIN MALGRÉ LUI (*Physician In Spite of Himself*), daughter of Géronte. Her father wants her to marry Horace, but as she is in love with Léandre, she pretends to have lost the power of articulate speech, to avoid a marriage which she abhors. SGANARELLE, the faggot-maker, is introduced as a famous dumb doctor, and soon sees the state of affairs. He takes with him Léandre as an apothecary, and the young lady receives a perfect cure.

Lucio. A character in Shakespeare's MEASURE FOR MEASURE, not absolutely bad, but vicious and dissolute. He is "like a wave of the sea, driven by the wind and tossed," and has no abiding principle.

Lucius. One of the mythical kings of Britain, placed as the great-great-grandson of CYMBELINE, and fabled as the first Christian king. He is supposed to have died about 192.

Luck of Roaring Camp, The. A short story by Bret HARTE in his volume by that name (1870). "The Luck," a baby born into a crude California mining camp where his mother is the only woman, soon makes his influence felt and the miners vie with one another in providing for his welfare. His death is very keenly felt by these rough men.

Lucrece, see LUCRETIA, LUCREZIA.

Lucretia. (1) In Roman legend, the daughter of Spurius Lucretius, prefect of Rome, and wife of Tarquinius Collatinus. She was dishonored by Sextus, the son of Tarquinius Superbus. Having avowed her dishonor in the presence of her father, her husband, and their friends Junius Brutus and Valerius, she stabbed herself. The outcome was an insurrection which changed the magistracy of kings to that of consuls. This subject has been dramatized in French by Ant. Vincent Arnault in a tragedy called *Lucrèce* (1792); and by François Ponsard in 1843; in Italian by Alfieri in *Brutus;* in English by Thomas Heywood, in a tragedy entitled *The Rape of Lucrece* (1630); by Nathaniel Lee, in *Lucius Junius Brutus* (17th century); and by John H. Payne, in *Brutus or The Fall of Tarquin* (1820). Shakespeare selected the same subject for his poem entitled *The Rape of Lucrece* (1594).

(2) The titular heroine of a romance by BULWER LYTTON.

Lucretius. In full **Titus Lucretius Carus** (96?–55 B.C.). Roman philosophical poet. Author of the unfinished *De Rerum Natura* (*On the Nature of Things*), a didactic poem in six books setting forth a complete cosmology on the basis of the philosophy of Democritus and Epicurus. Committed suicide in a fit of insanity induced, according to popular tradition, by a love-potion given him by his wife.

Lucrezia. See under BORGIA.

Lucrine Lake. A lake in Campania, famed in Roman times for its oysters.

Lucullus. (1) A wealthy Roman (110–57 B.C.) noted for his banquets and self-indulgence. On one occasion, when a superb supper had been prepared, being asked who were to be his guests, he replied, "Lucullus will sup to-night with Lucullus."

(2) A false friend in TIMON OF ATHENS referred to as "thou disease of a friend."

Lucy, St. See under SAINTS.

Lucy, Sir **Thomas** (1532–1600). English squire and justice of the peace, who prosecuted Shakespeare, according to Nicholas Rowe (1710), for stealing deer from Charlecote Park (1585). Shakespeare retaliated by caricaturing him as Justice Shallow in *The Merry Wives of Windsor* and 2 *Henry IV*.

Lucy and Colin. A ballad by Thomas Tickell (1720), called by Goldsmith "the best ballad in our language." Colin was betrothed to Lucy, but forsook her for a bride "thrice as rich as she." Lucy was sad, but was present at the wedding; when Colin saw her, "the damps of death bedewed his brow, and he died." Both were buried in one tomb, and many a hind and plighted maid resorted thither, "to deck it with garlands and true-love knots."

Lud. A mythical king of Britain, founder of London. The account of his reign is given in the history of GEOFFREY OF MONMOUTH (1142). He was buried near what is still known as *Ludgate*.

Lud's Town. London; so called from King Lud.

General Lud. Leader of the distressed and

riotous artisans in the manufacturing districts of England, who, in 1811, endeavored to prevent the use of power-looms. His followers were called *Luddites*.

Ludendorff, Erich Friedrich Wilhelm (1865–1937). German general and politician. Responsible with Hindenburg for defeat of Russia in World War I; brought about collapse of Italy at Caporetto (1917). After German defeat fled to Sweden. Took part in Hitler Beer Hall Putsch (1923). In his last years, adulated and influenced by his wife Mathilde Ludendorff, he led various crusades against the Jews, the Catholics, the Masons, the Protestants, etc. He supported Hitler for a while and wound up as a militant pacifist. Author of several books on World War I.

Ludgate. A gate in the old wall of London, west of St. Paul's Cathedral, so-called possibly from the legendary British King LUD, who was supposedly buried near it. Before Newgate was built it was used as a prison and was destroyed in 1760.

Ludlow Strike. A strike of coal miners (beginning in September, 1913) against the Rockefeller-controlled Colorado Fuel and Iron Company. The fatal "Battle of Ludlow" (April, 1914) caused much loss of life. Federal troops were sent and could not be recalled until early the following year. The strikers were forced to return to work without satisfaction of their demands.

Ludovico. A character in Shakespeare's OTHELLO.

Ludwig, Emil. Originally **Emil Ludwig Cohn** (1881–). German writer, especially known for his numerous biographies. *Goethe* (1920); *Napoleon* (1924); *Wilhelm II* (1925); etc. He also wrote *The Nile* (1939), *The Mediterranean* (1942), etc., and (in his younger years) a number of quite effective plays.

Lufbery, Raoul (1885–1918). French-American aviator in World War I; member of Escadrille Lafayette (1916–1918). Seventeen air victories. Killed in combat.

Luftwaffe (*German*, "air weapon"). The German air force in World War II.

Luggnagg. In Swift's *Gulliver's Travels* (see GULLIVER, LEMUEL), an island where people live for ever. Swift shows the evil of such a destiny, unless accompanied with eternal youth. See STRULDBRUGS.

Luhan, Mabel Dodge, *née* **Mabel Ganson** (1879–). American heiress, known for her *salons* in Italy and New York which were attended by the leading artists and writers of the early 20th century, and for her association with such personalities as Lincoln STEFFENS, John REED, Max EASTMAN, Carl VAN VECHTEN, and D. H. LAWRENCE. Lawrence spent some time on her estate in Taos, New Mexico, and her book *Lorenzo in Taos* (1932) is an account of their relations. She also wrote *Winter in Taos* (1935) and an autobiography, *Intimate Memories*, in the following volumes: *Background* (1933); *European Experiences* (1935); *Movers and Shakers* (1936); and *Edge of Taos Desert* (1937). She was married four times, her fourth husband being Tony Luhan, an Indian of the Taos country. She is said to appear as a character in Carl Van Vechten's *Peter Whiffle*, Max Eastman's *Venture*, D. H. Lawrence's *The Woman Who Rode Away*, Gertrude Stein's *A Portrait of Mabel Dodge*, and other novels; she also posed for a number of well-known painters, including Maurice Sterne, her third husband. During the 1920's, she sponsored the movements of CUBISM and Freudian psycho-analysis. See also FREUD, SIGMUND.

Lukas, Paul (1895–). Hungarian-born actor, associated with the Comedy Theatre in Budapest (1918–1927); also in motion pictures. Starred in Lillian Hellman's play *Watch on the Rhine* (1941).

Luke. The mean and hypocritical hero of Massinger's comedy *The City Madam* (1639), the type of the man in whom sudden acquisition of wealth releases his worst qualities.

Luke, Dr., see DR. LUKE OF THE LABRADOR.

Luke, St. See under SAINTS.

Luke Havergal. A poem by Edward Arlington ROBINSON.

Luks, George Benjamin (1867–1933). American painter. Also creator of the comic strip *The Yellow Kid* in the New York *World*.

Lully, Jean Baptiste (1632–1687). French composer born in Italy. Founder of the French grand opera. Court composer to Louis XIV (from 1653). Wrote the music to several of MOLIÈRE's comedy-ballets (1664–1670); created the "Académie Royale de Musique" (1672), now the Grand Opéra, in Paris. His operas, originally staged by himself, include *Alceste* (1674); *Proserpine* (1680); *Amadis de Gaule* (1684); etc. They "held the stage for nearly a century, until GLUCK's grander creations overshadowed them." Many of his ballets and masques were performed by members of the court, including himself and occasionally the king.

Lully, Raymond. In Catalan **Ramón Lull** (1235?–1315). Spanish (Catalan) scholastic and missionary in Mohammedan North Africa. Taught Arabic in the Franciscan monastery at Miramar (1275–1285); author of *Blanquerna*, a novel dealing with a religious Utopia, containing the famous *The Book of the Lover and the Beloved;* a system of logic known as Lully's *Ars Magna;* etc. He was stoned to death near Bougie, North Africa, while preaching the gospel to Mohammedan Arabs.

Lulu Bett, see MISS LULU BETT.

Lumber State. Maine. See under STATES.

Lummis, Charles Fletcher (1859–1928). American author and editor, authority on ethnology and folklore of the Pueblo Indians in New Mexico. Author of books on their life and customs; editor of volumes of Pueblo folk tales and old California Spanish songs.

Lumpenproletariat (*Ger.*, "proletariat of scamps"). A word used in the COMMUNIST MANIFESTO to designate the social scum, "that passively rotting mass thrown off by the lowest layers of old society" which, rather than join in a workers' world would probably become "a bribed tool of reactionary intrigue."

Lumpkin, Grace. American novelist of the proletarian school, author of novels dealing chiefly with sharecroppers and mill-workers in the South. These include *To Make My Bread* (1932), dramatized as *Let Freedom Ring* (1936); *A Sign for Cain* (1935); *The Wedding* (1939). See also PROLETARIAN LITERATURE.

Lumpkin, Tony. In Goldsmith's SHE STOOPS TO CONQUER, a sheepish, mischievous, idle, cunning lout, "with the vices of a man and the follies of a boy," fond of low company, but giving himself the airs of the young squire. He is described (Act I. 2) as "an awkward booby, reared up and spoiled at his mother's apron-string."

Luna, Count of. In Verdi's opera IL TROVATORE, the rival of MANRICO.

Lunacharski, Anatoli Vasilievich (1875–1933). Russian Communist leader and writer. As commissar for education (1917–1929) originator of widespread educational reforms. Author of *Religion and Socialism* (2 vols.; 1911); *Culture and the Working Class* (1919).

lunar month. From new moon to new moon, i.e., the time taken by the moon to revolve round the earth, about 29½ days. Popularly, the lunar month is 28 days. In the Jewish and Mohammedan calendars, the lunar month commences at sunset of the day when the new moon is first seen after sunset, and varies in length, being sometimes 29 and sometimes 30 days.

lunar year. Twelve lunar months, i.e., about 354¾ days.

Lundy's Lane. A road leading westward from a point near Niagara Falls. Known as the site of a battle, *Battle of Lundy's Lane* or *of Bridgewater,* in which (July 25, 1814) inferior American forces first repulsed but then gave way to a British corps of 4,500 men. American losses 852, British, 878.

Lunsford.

> Make children with your tones to run for't,
> As bad as Bloodybones or Lunsford.
>
> Butler, *Hudibras,* iii, 2.

Sir Thomas Lunsford was governor of the Tower, a man of most vindictive temper, and the dread of everyone.

Lunt, Alfred (1893–). Notable American actor. With his wife, Lynn FONTANNE, appeared on the stage in *The Guardsman, Elizabeth the Queen, Design for Living, Taming of the Shrew, Idiot's Delight, Amphitryon, The Sea Gull, O Mistress Mine,* etc.

Lupercal. (1) A grotto near Rome, sacred to Lupercus. See below.

(2) Now generally **Lupercalia.** In ancient Rome, an annual festival held on the spot where Romulus and Remus were suckled by the wolf (*lupus*), on February 15, in honor of Lupercus, the Lycaean Pan (so called because he protected the flocks from wolves). It was on one of these occasions that Antony thrice offered Julius Caesar the crown, and Caesar refused, saying, "Jupiter alone is king of Rome."

> You all did see that on the Lupercal,
> I thrice presented him a kingly crown,
> Which he did thrice refuse.
>
> Shakespeare, *Julius Caesar,* iii, 2.

Lupescu, Magda (1904?–). Rumanian adventuress, whose original name was probably Wolff. Mistress (later wife) of Prince (later King) Carol. Exerted great political influence. Forced to flee with Carol to Spain (1940) and Cuba (1941).

Lupin, Arsène. See under LEBLANC, MAURICE.

Luria. In Browning's tragedy of that title (1846), a noble Moor employed by the Florentines to lead their army against the Pisans. Luria is entirely successful, but meantime the Florentines have distrusted him and summoned him to trial. Overwhelmed by their ingratitude, he ends his life with poison. He was a historical character of the 15th century.

Lusiad, The (*Port.*, **Os Lusíadas**). The Portuguese national epic, written by Luis de Camoëns, and published in 1572. It relates the stories of illustrious actions of the *Lusians,* or Portuguese, of all ages, but deals principally with the exploits of Vasco da Gama and his comrades in their "discovery of India." Gama sailed three times to India. It is the first of these voyages (1497) which is the groundwork of the epic, but its wealth of episode, the constant introduction of mythological "machinery," and the intervention of Bacchus, Venus, and other deities, make it far more than a mere chronicle of a voyage. Bacchus is the guardian power of the Mohammedans, and Venus, or Divine Love, of the Lusians. The fleet first sails to Mozambique, then to Quiloa, then to Melinda in Africa, where the adventurers are hospitably received and provided with a pilot to conduct them to India. In the Indian Ocean, Bacchus tries to destroy the fleet, but the "silver star of Divine Love" calms the sea, and Gama arrives in India in safety.

Lusitania. (1) The ancient name for Portugal.

(2) The name of a passenger ship sunk by a German submarine (May 7, 1915). This event did much to solidify feeling against the German war policy and to make possible the entrance of the United States into World War I.

Luska, Sidney, see Henry HARLAND.

Lutetia (from Lat. *lutum,* "mud"). The ancient name of Paris, which, in Roman times, was merely a collection of mud hovels. Caesar called it *Lutetia Parisiorum* (the mud-town of the Parisii), which gives the present name Paris.

Luther, Martin (1483–1546). German religious reformer. Professor of Biblical exegesis at Wittenberg (1511–1546). Nailed to the churchdoor (October 31, 1517) his ninety-five theses questioning the value of indulgences. Publicly defended his position and went further by denying the supremacy of the Pope. He was excommunicated (1520), his writings were burned publicly, and he retaliated by burning in public the bull of excommunication. Appeared before the Diet of Worms (1521) which put him under the ban of the empire. At this occasion he made the famous statement, "There I take my stand. I can do naught else. So help me God, Amen." Hidden at the Wartburg, he wrote his pamphlet *On Monastic Vows* and translated the New Testament into German (1521; the Old Testament followed, 1532). Returned to Wittenberg and devoted himself to the organization of the new church he had inaugurated. His version of the Bible became the most important factor in the consolidation of the German dialects in a common literary language. His *Tischreden* (*Table-Talk*) are a valuable source of historical and theological detail. He wrote and composed or adapted many hymns, the best-known of which is *Ein feste Burg ist unser Gott* (*A mighty fortress is our God*).

Luther, Seth (*fl.* 1817–1846). Pioneer in American labor reform who attacked child labor in the cotton mills.

lutin. A goblin in the folklore of Normandy; similar to the house-spirits of Germany. The name was formerly *netun,* and is said to come from the Roman sea-god *Neptune.* When the *lutin* assumes the form of a horse ready equipped it is called *le cheval Bayard.*

to lutin. To twist hair into elf-locks. These mischievous urchins are said to tangle the mane of a horse or head of a child so that the hair must be cut off.

Franz Liszt wrote a piano solo, *Ronde des Lutins.*

Lvov, Aleksei Fëdorovich (1794–1870). Russian composer. Commissioned by Czar (1833) to write the music for the Russian national anthem by Vasili Zhukovski. Composer of operas, including *Undine* (1846); etc.

Lycaon. In classical mythology, a king of Arcadia, who, desirous of testing the divine knowledge of Jove, served up human flesh on his table, for which the god changed him into a wolf. His daughter, Callisto, was changed into the constellation the Bear, whence this is sometimes called *Lycaonis Arctos.*

lycanthropy. Literally, wolfmanhood. See WEREWOLF. The term is also used in psychopathology for a form of insanity in which the patient thinks of himself as a wolf.

Lyceum. A gymnasium on the banks of the Ilissus, in Attica, where Aristotle taught philosophy as he paced the walks.

Lycidas. The name under which Milton celebrates the untimely death of Edward King, Fellow of Christ College, Cambridge, who was drowned in his passage from Chester to Ireland, August 10, 1637. He was the son of Sir John King, secretary for Ireland. In Virgil's *Eclogue III,* Lycidas is the name of a shepherd, and Milton borrowed the connotations as well as the name. *Lycidas* is one of the most famous elegies in the English language.

Lycurgus. A legislator, from the legendary Spartan lawgiver of antiquity.

Lydford law. Punish first and try afterwards. Lydford, in the county of Devon, was a fortified town, where were held the courts of the Duchy of Cornwall. Offenders against the statutory laws were confined before trial in a dungeon so loathsome and dreary that the prisoners frequently died before they could be brought to trial.

> I oft have heard of Lydford law,
> How in the morn they hang and draw,
> And sit in judgment later.
>
> A Devonshire Poet.

Lydgate, John (ca. 1370–ca. 1451). English poet, a Benedictine monk of Bury-St. Edmund's, believed to have had as patrons such important figures of the time as Duke Humphrey of Gloucester, Henry VI, and the Earl of Warwick. He was an extremely prolific writer, making use principally of allegorical forms. Among his works are: *The Court of Sapience, The Temple of Glass,* and *The Court of Venus,* all written ca. 1400–1403 and showing the influence of CHAUCER; *Reason and Sensuality* (ca. 1403–1412), dealing with social duties and functions; *Troy Book* (ca. 1420) based on the *Historia Troiana* of GUIDO DELLE COLONNE;

The Story of Thebes (ca. 1420–1422); *The Pilgrimage of the Life of Man* (ca. 1424), a translation of a work by Guillaume de Deguileville; and FALLS OF PRINCES (ca. 1430–1438), based on Boccaccio's *De Casibus Virorum Illustrium.*

Lydgate, Dr. In George Eliot's MIDDLEMARCH, a doctor whose medical ideals gradually became dulled and tainted with a commercial spirit.

Lydian mode. One of the four principal modes of ancient Greek music, a minor scale appropriate to soft pathos.

> Lap me in soft Lydian airs.
> Milton.

See also DORIAN MODE; PHRYGIAN MODE; MYXOLYDIAN MODE.

Lygia. In Sienkiewicz' QUO VADIS, a beautiful Christian maiden who undergoes many trials for her faith.

Lying Traveler, The. So Sir John MANDEVILLE, an explorer of the 14th century, has been called.

Lyly, John (1554?–1606). English poet, dramatist, novelist, and prose-writer of the Elizabethan period, one of the "UNIVERSITY WITS." He was associated with the court of Elizabeth for a number of years and served to popularize there both the balanced, elegant, and artificial prose style called Euphuistic (see EUPHUES) and the dramatic form of comedy, which he refined and intellectualized and raised from its former crude state. Lyly, who has been called a novelist and dramatist of social manners, took his plots from Greek and Roman classic literature and transformed them into charming, ornate allegories of court flirtations and intrigues and the political affairs of the time. His most famous works are the romances *Euphues: The Anatomy of Wit* (1579) and *Euphues and His England* (1580). His plays include *Alexander and Campaspe* (1584); ENDIMION (1579), an allegory of the marriage of Lord Leicester to the Countess of Essex, disapproved by Elizabeth; *Sappho and Phaon* (1584); and *Midas* (ca. 1588).

Lynceus. One of the ARGONAUTS. He was so sharp-sighted that he could see through the earth, and distinguish objects nine miles off.

lynch law. Mob-law, law administered by private persons. The origin of the term is unknown; old editions of Webster's *Dictionary* referred it to James Lynch, a farmer of Piedmont, Virginia, saying that, as Piedmont was seven miles from any law court, the neighbors, in 1686, selected him to pass sentence on offenders for the nonce. Other conjectures father the phrase on a certain James Lynch Fitz-Stephen, said to have been warden of Galway in 1526, and to have passed sentence of death on his own son for murder; on Charles Lynch, a Virginian justice of the peace who was indemnified in 1782 for having imprisoned political opponents on his own responsibility, and on Lynche's Creek, South Carolina, where, in 1786, a body of men known as *Regulators* used to meet and try cases themselves because the regular administration of justice in those parts was lacking.

The term is first recorded in 1817, and is certainly American in origin, though there is an old northern English dialect word *linch,* meaning to beat or maltreat. In the states of the South in the U.S., lynch law came to be widely invoked in the punishment of Negroes accused or suspected of committing crimes. It is occasionally referred to by re-personification as Judge Lynch.

Lynd, Robert (1879–). Irish journalist and man of letters; his wife, **Sylvia Lynd** (1888–), English novelist and poet.

Lynd, Robert Staughton (1892–). American professor of sociology at Columbia University. With his wife wrote comprehensive sociological studies of a typical small Middle Western city (Muncie, Indiana): *Middletown* (1929); *Middletown in Transition* (1937); etc.

Lyndall. The heroine of Olive Schreiner's STORY OF AN AFRICAN FARM.

Lyndon, Barry, see BARRY LYNDON.

Countess Lyndon. The wife of BARRY LYNDON.

Lynette or **Linet.** A heroine of Arthurian romance (the first spelling is Tennyson's, the second Malory's), whose story Tennyson has told in his GARETH AND LYNETTE. Tennyson, however, makes a radical departure from the old romances by marrying Gareth to Lynette instead of her sister Lyonors or Liones.

Tennyson describes Lynette thus:

> A damsel of high lineage; and a brow
> May-blossom; and a cheek of apple-blossom;
> Hawk-eyes; and lightly was her tender nose,
> Tip-tilted like the petal of a flower.

Lyon, Harris Merton (1883–1916). American short-story writer. *Sardonics: Sixteen Sketches* (1908); *Graphics* (1913), sixteen stories published by William Marion REEDY.

Lyon, Rufus. A lovable old Independent clergyman in George Eliot's FELIX HOLT THE RADICAL, said to have been drawn from Rev. Francis Franklin, a Baptist minister, the pastor of the Cow Lane Chapel in Coventry.

> At the first glance, every one thought him a very odd-looking rusty old man; the free-school boys often hooted after him and called him "Revelations"; and to many respectable church people old Lyon's little legs and large head seemed to make Dissent additionally preposterous. But he was too shortsighted to notice those who tittered at him—too absent from the world of small facts and petty impulses in which titterers live.—*Ch. IV.*

Esther Lyon. Rufus Lyon's adopted daughter, the heroine of the novel.

Lyonors or **Liones.** A heroine of Arthurian romance (the first spelling is Tennyson's, the second Malory's) who was held captive in Castle Perilous by several knights until rescued by GARETH. See also LYNETTE.

Lyonnesse. "That sweet land of Lyonnesse"—a tract of land fabled to stretch between the Land's End and the Scilly Isles, now submerged full "forty fathoms under water." ARTHUR came from this mythical country. The battle of Lyonnesse was the "last great battle of the West," and the scene of the final conflict between Arthur and Sir Modred. For variant spellings, see under LEONESSE; LIONES.

Lyons, Eugene (1898–). Russian-born American journalist and author. In his earlier years, in sympathy with the radical labor movement. Mustered world protest (1921–1922) against the conviction of Sacco and Vanzetti. Associated with Soviet news agencies. Became disillusioned with Soviet Russia. Editor *American Mercury* (1939–1944). Author of *Assignment in Utopia* (1937); *Stalin: Czar of All the Russias* (1940); *The Red Decade* (1941); etc. *The Red Decade* was such a "detailed invective" as to bring a law suit against Lyons and his publisher from Corliss LAMONT, settled out of court (1942) to Mr. Lamont's satisfaction. In 1948 he published a flattering biography of Herbert HOOVER.

Lyrical Ballads. A volume of poems by S. T. COLERIDGE and William WORDSWORTH, first published in 1798, in a second edition in 1800, and in a third in 1802. It was the first important publication of the poetry of the new romantic period in English literature, and is considered one of the landmarks of literature. Wordsworth's contributions were his simple poems of country scenes and country people, written in plain language and style, and his TINTERN ABBEY. Coleridge contributed principally *The Rime of the Ancient Mariner.* See ANCIENT MARINER. The second edition of *Lyrical Ballads* contains a preface by Wordsworth explaining his theory of poetry.

Lysander (died 395 B.C.). Spartan naval and military commander.

> Some talk of Alexander
> And some of Hercules,
> Of Hector and Lysander
> And such great names as these.
> *British Grenadiers.*

Lysander. In Shakespeare's MIDSUMMER NIGHT'S DREAM, a young Athenian, in love with Hermia, daughter of Egeus.

Lysistrata. The title and heroine of a comedy by ARISTOPHANES (ca. 415 B.C.), dealing with an effective women's peace organization. In the twenty-first year of the Peloponnesian War Lysistrata persuades the wives of Athens to shut themselves up in the Acropolis away from their husbands until peace shall be concluded. She has the satisfaction of dictating the terms. There is a modern version by Gilbert SELDES.

Lys rouge, Le, see RED LILY.

Lytton, Bulwer, see BULWER LYTTON.

Lytton, Edward Robert Bulwer, Earl of, see MEREDITH, OWEN.

M

Maartens, Maarten. Pen name of **Joost Marius Willem van der Poorten-Schwartz** (1858–1915). Dutch author (in English) of novels and stories chiefly of his native Holland.

Maat. Egyptian goddess of truth, justice, law. Associated with Ra and Thoth. Her symbol is a feather which appears in judgment scenes balanced in the scales against a heart.

Mab (perhaps the Welsh *mab,* "a baby"). In 15th-century English and Welsh legend, Queen of the fairies, an honor later given to Titania. She is described in Shakespeare's ROMEO AND JULIET as the "fairies' midwife"—i.e., employed by the fairies as midwife to deliver man's brain of dreams. Excellent descriptions of Mab are given by Shakespeare (*Romeo and Juliet,* i. 4), by Ben Jonson, by Herrick, and by Drayton in *Nymphidia.*

Queen Mab. A speculative poem by Shelley (1810) written when he was about eighteen. Ianthe falls asleep, visits the court of Queen Mab in her dreams and hears of the scheme of the universe from AHASUERUS, the Wandering Jew.

Mabbott, Thomas Ollive (1898–). American scholar and leading authority on POE.

Mabie, Hamilton Wright (1845?–1916). American editor and critic. Frank Moore COLBY said of him that he "conducted young women into the suburbs of literature and left them there."

Mabinogion. A series of Welsh tales, chiefly related to ARTHUR and the ROUND TABLE. These tales were long inaccessible because of the difficulties in the language, but are now available. Many interesting variations from the legends of Arthur and his court as given in Malory's *Morte d'Arthur,* etc., are to be found in the Welsh version.

Mac. In Dos Passos' U.S.A. See MCCREARY, FAINY.

macabre. See under DANCE OF DEATH.

McAdam, John Loudon (1756–1836). British engineer. Introduced "macadamized" roads.

McAdoo, William Gibbs (1863–1941). U.S. secretary of the treasury (1913–1918). Married Eleanor, daughter of President Wilson. Candidate, Democratic nomination for President (1924); U.S. senator from California (1933–1939).

Macaire, Robert. The typical villain of French comedy; from the play of this name (a sequel to *L'Auberge des Adrets*) by Frédéric Lemaître and Benjamin Antier (1834). Macaire is

> le type de la perversité, de l'impudence, de la friponnerie audacieuse, le héros fanfaron du vol et de l'assassinat.

Macaire is the name of the murderer of Aubrey de Montdidier in a famous old French legend. He is brought to justice by the sagacity of Aubrey's dog, Dragon, the Dog of MONTARGIS, who shows such an aversion to Macaire that suspicion is aroused, and the man and dog are pitted to single combat. The result is fatal to the man, who dies confessing his guilt.

McAllister, Samuel Ward (1827–1895). American socialite. Arbiter of New York and Newport society. Introduced the term "the Four Hundred" for the *crême de la crême* of New York's social register.

Macapa, Maria. In Frank Norris's MCTEAGUE, an insane charwoman who is murdered by ZERKOW through greed.

macaroni (Ital. *maccheróne*). A coxcomb. The word is derived from the Macaroni Club, instituted in London about 1760 by a set of flashy men who had traveled in Italy, and introduced at Almack's subscription table the new-fashioned Italian food, *macaroni.* The Macaronies were the most exquisite fops that ever disgraced the name of man; vicious, insolent, fond of gambling, drinking, and dueling, they were (ca. 1773) the curse of Vauxhall Gardens.

There is a tradition that an American regiment raised in Maryland during the War of Independence was called The Macaronies from its showy uniform. This presumably explains the allusion in the American song, *Yankee Doodle:*

> Yankee Doodle went to town
> A-riding on a pony
> Stuck a feather in his hat
> And called it macaroni.

macaronic Latin. DOG LATIN, modern words with Latin endings, or a mixture of Latin and some modern language. From the Italian *macheroni* (macaroni), originally a medley or mixture of coarse meal, eggs, and cheese. The law pleadings of G. Steevens, as *Daniel* v. *Dishclout* and *Bullum* v. *Boatum,* are excellent examples.

macaronic verse. Verses in which foreign words are ludicrously distorted and jumbled together, as in Porson's lines on the threatened invasion of England by Napoleon or J. A. Morgan's "translation" of Canning's *The Elderly Gentleman,* the first two verses of which are—

> Prope ripam fluvii solus
> A senex silently sat
> Super capitum ecce his wig
> Et wig super, ecce his hat
>
> Blew Zephyrus alte, acerbus,
> Dum elderly gentleman sat;
> Et a capite took up quite torve
> Et in rivum projecit his hat.

It seems to have been originated by Odaxius of Padua (born ca. 1450), but was popularized by his pupil, Teofilo Folengo (Merlinus Coccaius), a Mantuan monk of noble family, who published a book entitled *Liber Macaronicorum,* a poetical rhapsody made up of words of different languages, and treating of "pleasant matters" (1520). A. Cunningham in 1801 published *Delectus Macaronicorum Carminum,* a history of macaronic poetry.

MacArthur, Charles (1895–). American playwright. Married Helen HAYES. Wrote with Ben Hecht *The Front Page* (1928; also adapted for moving picture) and the scenario for *Wuthering Heights.*

MacArthur, Douglas (1880–). Son of American military governor of the Philippines. Lieutenant general and commander of United States forces in the Far East. Promoted general and supreme commander of Allied forces in the Pacific (March 1942). Head of peacetime administration of Japan.

Macassar oil. See under ANTIMACASSAR.

Macaulay, Fannie (1863–1941). American author. *The Lady of the Decoration* (1906); etc. Pseudonym **Frances Little.**

Macaulay, Rose (1889?–). English novelist. The satirical novel *Potterism* (1920) is a sort of English *Babbitt. Told by an Idiot* (1923) and *Staying with Relations* (1930) are two other ironic and amusing books out of many.

Macaulay, Thomas Babington (1800–1859). English statesman, poet, historian, essayist, and biographer, best-known for his *History of England* (1855, 1859), a work extremely popular in his day, marked by a colorful style and vivid presentation. His LAYS OF ANCIENT ROME (1842), narrative poems dealing with Roman heroes, were also very popular with the public. He wrote in addition a number of well-known historical and biographical essays under the guise of book reviews for the *Edinburgh Review* and a series of biographies of literary figures for the *Encyclopaedia Britannica.* Macaulay was the son of a philanthropist, believed in the democratic ballot and other popular Victorian ideas of reform, and was elected a Whig representative in the House of Commons in 1830, 1839, and 1852. He was also legal adviser to the Supreme Council of India, Secretary of War in the English cabinet, and Lord Rector of Glasgow, and in 1857 was made Baron Macaulay of Rothley. Critics usually oppose Macaulay to Thomas CARLYLE, Matthew ARNOLD, and John RUSKIN as an ardent enthusiast for the Victorian age in England, rather than a critic of its policies and values.

Macaulay's schoolboy. An imaginary schoolboy. The phrase "Every schoolboy knows" was so frequently used by T. B. Macaulay to refute and put to shame his opponents that the boy became proverbial.

Macaulay's New Zealander. In Macaulay's essay on von Ranke's *History of the Popes,* a man from "down under" visiting London in the distant future when it is a ruined city.

Macbeth. A tragedy by Shakespeare (ca. 1606), based on an episode in Scottish history as recorded in HOLINSHED's *Chronicles.* The victorious general Macbeth is hailed by three mysterious witches as thane of Glamis, thane of Cawdor (to be) and future King of Scotland. To his companion, Banquo, the witches promise that his children shall be kings. Macbeth is soon made thane of Cawdor, and, urged by his own and Lady Macbeth's ambition, he murders King Duncan, is proclaimed king and accomplishes the murder of Banquo. Banquo's ghost appears at a great banquet unseen by any but Macbeth, and one disaster now follows another. Lady Macbeth, tormented by conscience, walks in her sleep, washing from her hands imaginary blood stains, and finally takes her own life. Macbeth had been promised by the witches that none of woman born should kill him and that he should not die till Birnam Wood removed to Dunsinane. He is finally slain in battle by MACDUFF, who was "from his mother's womb untimely ripped"; as for the moving wood, the soldiers of Macduff, in their march to Dunsinane, are commanded to carry boughs of the forest before them, to conceal their numbers. Duncan's son Malcolm is proclaimed king.

Maccabaeus. The surname given to Judas (the central figure in the struggle for Jewish independence, about 170–160 B. C.), third son of Mattathias, the Hasmonaean, and hence to his family or clan. LONGFELLOW wrote a poem called *Judas Maccabaeus.*

Maccabees, The. The family of Jewish heroes, descended from Mattathias the Hasmonaean (see under MACCABAEUS) and his five sons, John, Simon, Judas, Eleazar and Jonathan, which delivered its race from the persecutions of the Syrian king Antiochus Epiphanes (175–164 B. C.), and established a line of priest-kings which lasted till supplanted by Herod in 40 B. C. Their exploits are told in the two *Books of the Maccabees,* the last books in the Apocrypha.

McCarthy, Justin Huntly (1861–1936). Son of English writer and politician. Playwright, novelist, and historian. Best-known for his novel *If I Were King* (1901; also adapted by him for the stage) which is concerned with François VILLON. His wife was Cissie LOFTUS.

MacCathmhaoil, Seosamh, see CAMPBELL, JOSEPH.

McCauley, Mary. Known as **Mollie Pitcher** (1754?–1832). American Revolutionary heroine. Manned a cannon at the Battle of Monmouth (June 28, 1778).

McChesney, Emma. A breezy, energetic, whole-souled traveling saleswoman in the skirt and petticoat line, the heroine of many stories of business life by Edna FERBER, notably *Personality Plus* (1914). Ethel BARRYMORE played Emma in the author's dramatization, *Our Mrs. McChesney* (1915).

McClellan, George Brinton (1826–1885). American Civil War general. Commanded at Antietam (September 17, 1862). Democratic candidate for President (1864), defeated by Lincoln.

McClintic, Guthrie (1893–). American stage director and producer. Husband of Katharine CORNELL.

McClure, John (1893–). American lyric poet. Editor, *The Stag's Hornbook.*

McClure, Samuel Sidney (1857–). Irish-born American editor and publisher. McClure's Syndicate (1884) was the first newspaper syndicate in the U.S. Founder of *McClure's Magazine* (1893).

MacCool, Finn. Legendary leader of the Irish Fianna in the second and third centuries A. D. See under FENIANS.

McCormack, John (1884–1945). Irish-born American operatic and concert tenor. Metropolitan Opera Company (1909), etc. Well known for his programs of Irish songs.

McCormick, Anne O'Hare. American journalist. Foreign correspondent and columnist for the *New York Times.* First woman to receive a major Pulitzer prize in journalism (1937).

McCormick, Cyrus Hall (1809–1884). American inventor. Invented the McCormick reaper and formed with his brother the McCormick Harvesting Machine Co.

McCrae, John (1872–1918). Canadian physician and poet. His fame rests solidly on the fifteen-line poem, *In Flanders Fields,* written during the second battle of Ypres (April 1915), and first printed in *Punch* (December 8, 1915).

McCreary, Fainy ("Mac"). In John Dos Passos' U.S.A., a young Irish-American who spends his childhood in Chicago and comes under the influence of the Socialist convictions of his uncle, Tim O'Hara. When O'Hara, for whom he has been working, goes into bankruptcy, Fainy gets a job with a traveling book salesman, is cheated, joins with a Socialist friend and travels as a hobo across the country, and arrives in San Francisco, where he becomes editor of an I.W.W. newspaper. He marries and has children but is dissatisfied with his life and eventually leaves his family to take part in the 1914 revolution in Mexico.

McCullers, Carson (1917–). American novelist and short-story writer. Her first novel, *The Heart is a Lonely Hunter* (1940), intended to be an ironic parable of Fascism, tells the story of a deaf-mute in a southern town. *The Member of the Wedding* (1946).

McCumber, Porter James. See under FORDNEY-MCCUMBER TARIFF.

McCutcheon, George Barr (1866–1928). American writer of popular fiction. Famous for his first novel, GRAUSTARK (1901), and for *Brewster's Millions* (1902).

MacDiarmid, Hugh. Pseudonym of **Christopher Murray Grieve** (1892–). Scottish poet of proletarian sympathies, active in labor and nationalist movements in Scotland and as a member of the Socialist, Independent Labor, and, later, Communist parties. His poetry deals with the conditions of the poor in his country, the state of society in his time, and the hope of a future under Socialism; it is written in Scotch dialect and is marked by vigor and often bitterness. His books include *Penny Wheep* (1926); *Albyn, Or Scotland and the Future* (1927); *First Hymn to Lenin, And Other Poems* (1931); *Second Hymn to Lenin, And Other Poems* (1935). See also PROLETARIAN LITERATURE; MARXISM IN LITERATURE.

MacDonagh, Thomas (1878–1916). Irish poet and patriot. Five volumes of poems (1902–1913). Shot with Padraic Pearse and Joseph Plunkett by a British firing squad in Dublin, having been involved in the Irish Easter Rebellion.

Macdonald, Flora (1722–1790). Scottish Jacobite heroine. Aided Prince Charles Edward in his escape after CULLODEN. In U.S. (1774–1779), where her husband, Allan Macdonald, was a brigadier-general in the British army in the American Revolution.

MacDonald, George (1824–1905). Scottish novelist and poet. Best-known for the juvenile *At the Back of the North Wind.*

MacDonald, James Ramsay (1866–1937). British prime minister and secretary for foreign affairs (January 1924). Organized first Labor Ministry in the history of Britain. Defeated (1924). Again prime minister, with second Labor Ministry (1929–1931). Resigned (1937). Author of *Socialism and Society,* etc.

Macdonald, Ranald. The hero of Ralph Connor's MAN FROM GLENGARRY.

McDougall, William (1871–1938). British-born American psychologist; professor at Harvard and Duke Universities. Author of *Body and Mind* (1912); etc.

MacDowell, Edward Alexander (1861–1908). American composer of symphonic poems, piano sonatas, orchestral suites, etc. His widow founded in his memory the MacDowell Colony for musicians, artists and writers at Peterborough, N.H., where a group of talented people congregate every summer for a period of undisturbed production.

MacDowell, Gerty. In James Joyce's ULYSSES, a young girl whose exhibitionism on the beach excites Leopold BLOOM to sexual desire. She corresponds to NAUSICÄA in the *Odyssey.*

Macduff. The thane of Fife in Shakespeare's MACBETH. His castle of Kennoway is surprised by Macbeth, and his wife and babes are "savagely slaughtered." Macduff vows vengeance and joins the army of Siward to dethrone the tyrant. On reaching the royal castle of Dunsinane he attacks Macbeth and slays him.

McEvoy, Joseph Patrick (1895–). American writer for magazines and the theater.

MacFall, Haldane (1860–1928). British novelist, art historian and painter. Best-known for his picaresque West Indian novel *The Wooings of Jezebel Pettyfer* (1897), in the opinion of George Meredith, "one of the finest novels of his generation."

McFee, William (1881–). Anglo-American novelist and essayist. Chief engineer in English merchant marine service. In America (since 1912). *Casuals of the Sea* (1916); *Captain Macedoine's Daughter* (1920); etc. Book reviewer for New York *Sun.*

McFingal. An early American satire in verse by John TRUMBULL. The first canto was published shortly after Lexington and Concord in 1775 and greatly aided the Revolutionary cause. "Great Squire McFingal" is a Scotch-American Tory who exercises his oracular talents at a New England town meeting. After he is tarred and feathered, he repents his sins and prophesies final victory for the Whigs.

> Thus stored with intellectual riches
> Skilled was our Squire in making speeches,
> Where strength of brain united centers
> With strength of lungs surpassing Stentor's.

MacFlecknoe. In Dryden's famous satire so called (1682), he is meant for Thomas Shadwell, who was promoted to the office of poet laureate. The design of Dryden's poem is to represent the inauguration of one dullard as successor of another in the monarchy of nonsense. Flecknoe was an Irish priest and hackney poet of no reputation, and Mac is Celtic for son; *MacFlecknoe,* therefore, means the son of the poet so named. Flecknoe, seeking for a successor to his own dulness, selects Shadwell to bear his mantle:

> Shadwell alone my perfect image bears,
> Mature in dulness from his tender years; . . .
> The rest to some faint meaning make pretence,
> But Shadwell never deviates into sense.
> *MacFlecknoe.*

M'Flimsey, Miss Flora. The heroine of W. A. Butler's humorous poem NOTHING TO WEAR.

MacGill, Patrick (1890–). Irish poet and novelist. Best-known for *Songs of the Dead End.*

Macgowan, Kenneth (1888–). American author and theatrical and moving-picture producer. Dramatic director, Provincetown Players, Greenwich Village Theater, Actors' Theater. Wrote *The Theater of Tomorrow* (1921); etc.

MacGrath, Harold (1871–1932). Popular American fiction writer. *The Man on the Box* (1904) made a successful play.

McGraw, John J. (1875–1934). American professional baseball player. Manager, N.Y. Giants (1902–1932).

Macgregor or **Campbell, Robert** (1671–1734). Known as ROB ROY.

McGuffey, William Holmes (1800–1873). American educator. Best-known for his series of readers (from 1836). More than 120 million copies of *McGuffey's Readers* in various editions have been sold in the United States.

Machado, Manuel (1874–). Spanish librarian and author. Collaborated in plays with his brother, **Antonio Machado Ruiz** (1875–1929), well-known Spanish poet, playwright, and scholar.

Machado y Morales, Gerardo (1871–1939). Fifth president of Cuba. Veteran of Cuban-Spanish war of 1898. Rich agriculturalist and business man. Elected president in 1924; re-elected in 1928. Initiated a large program of public works. Assumed dictatorial powers and was compelled (1933) to flee from popular insurrection.

Macheath, Captain. A highwayman, hero of *The Beggar's Opera,* by John GAY. He is a fine, gay, bold-faced and dissolute ruffian, game to the very last. He is married to Polly PEACHUM, but finds himself dreadfully embarrassed between Polly, his wife, and Lucy LOCKIT to whom he has promised marriage. Betrayed by eight women at a drinking bout, the Captain is lodged in Newgate, but Lucy effects his escape. He is recaptured, tried, and condemned to death; upon being reprieved, he acknowledges Polly to be his wife, and promises to remain constant to her in the future.

Machen, Arthur (1863–1947). Welsh novelist and essayist, noted as master of the ghostly and supernatural. Early London career wretched. His first "romance of the soul," *The Hill of Dreams,* published 10 years after he wrote it, has become practically a classic. His work is "caviar to the general."

Machiavelli, Niccolò (1469–1527). The celebrated Florentine statesman, author of *Il*

Principe, whose name was long used as an epithet or synonym for an unscrupulous politician. Political cunning and overreaching by diplomacy and intrigue came to be known as *Machiavellianism* or *Machiavellism.* The general trend of his treatise, *Il Principe* (*The Prince*) (1513), is to show that rulers may resort to any treachery and artifice to uphold their arbitrary power, and whatever dishonorable acts princes may indulge in are fully set off by the insubordination of their subjects.

In the 20th century, some critics began to react against the traditional conception of Machiavelli, inherited from the Elizabethan period, which presented him as a diabolical villain, and to interpret him instead as an early political idealist, seeking to unify Italy by appealing to the ambitions of the Renaissance princes, especially of the MEDICI family.

Somerset Maugham's novel, *Then and Now* (1946), is based on Machiavelli's comedy, *The Mandrake,* the plot of which is treated by Maugham as an incident in Machiavelli's life.

the Imperial Machiavelli. Tiberius, the Roman emperor (42 B. C.–37 A. D.).

H. G. Wells has a novel called THE NEW MACHIAVELLI.

McHugh, Vincent (1904–). American novelist. Best-known for *Caleb Catlum's America* (1936), a story concerning an imagined American folk-figure. *Victory* (1948).

MacIan, Gilchrist. In Scott's FAIR MAID OF PERTH, chief of the Clan Quhele and father of Ian Eachin M'Ian.

Ian Eachin or *Hector M'Ian.* One of Scott's most famous characters, better known, however, under the name of CONACHAR.

McIlwain, Charles Howard (1871–). American political scientist. Professor at Harvard (since 1916). *The American Revolution* (1923; Pulitzer prize for history); etc.

McIntire, Samuel (1757–1811). American architect, born in Salem, Mass., and noted for his work there and elsewhere in Colonial style. Also remembered as a wood carver.

McIntyre, John Thomas (1871–). American novelist. His *Steps Going Down* (1936) won the $4,000-prize in the All-Nations Prize Novel Competition sponsored by the Literary Guild, Farrar & Rinehart, Warner Brothers, and eleven foreign publishers.

McIntyre, Oscar Odd (1884–1938). American journalist and columnist. His syndicated column *New York Day By Day* appeared in over 300 newspapers.

MacIvor, Fergus. In Scott's WAVERLEY the chief of Glennaquoich, also known as "Vich Ian Vohr."

Flora MacIvor. Sister of Fergus, and the heroine of *Waverley.*

Mackail, John William (1859–1945). British classical scholar. Author of books on Shakespeare and Homer. Father of Angela THIRKELL. His son, Denis Mackail, has written light fiction and a biography of J. M. BARRIE.

McKay, Claude (1890–1948). Distinguished Negro poet and novelist. First of his race to receive the medal of the Institute of Arts and Sciences. Traveled in Russia. His first novel, *Home to Harlem* (1927), was a success. One of the foremost figures in the "Negro Literary Renaissance" of the 1920's. Famous for his poem *If We Must Die.*

McKay, Donald (1810–1880). Boston shipbuilder, famous for his clippers, especially *The Flying Cloud* (1851).

MacKaye, Percy Wallace (1875–). American poet and dramatist. His best-known dramas are *The Canterbury Pilgrims* (1903; see under CANTERBURY TALES); *Fenris the Wolf* (1905; see under FENRIS); *Jeanne d'Arc* (1906; see JOAN OF ARC); SAPPHO AND PHAON (1907); THE SCARECROW (1908); CALIBAN (1916); *This Fine-Pretty World* (1923); etc. See also RIP VAN WINKLE.

Mackaye, Saunders. A prominent character in Kingsley's ALTON LOCKE, said to have been drawn from Thomas CARLYLE.

McKenna, Mr. One of the frequenters of Mr. DOOLEY's saloon.

McKenna, Stephen (1888–). Prolific English novelist. Popular in the United States.

McKenney, Ruth (1911–). American journalist, sociological writer, and humorist. Editor, *New Masses. Industrial Valley* (1939), "the true story of what happened in Akron, Ohio, from 1932 to 1936." Her best-known book is *My Sister Eileen* (1939), successfully adapted as a comedy (1941). The prototype and her husband were killed in an automobile accident in the west shortly before the New York première. Miss McKenney is the wife of Bruce Minton, author of *Men Who Lead Labor.*

Mackenzie, Compton (1882–). English Roman Catholic author descended from a famous family of actors and novelists. Best-known for his second novel, *Carnival* (1912), and the two-volume SINISTER STREET (1913–1914). Acquired the 2 Channel Islands of Herm and Jethou (1914). One of the founders of the National Party in Scotland. Elected Lord Rector of Glasgow University (1931). He was prosecuted (1932) by the Crown for breach of official war secrets in *Greek Memories;* later the ban was withdrawn and the book appeared as *Aegean Memories* (1940). Family name is Compton.

Mackenzie, Henry (1745–1831). Scottish novelist. Known as "The Man of Feeling" (after the title of a novel of his, 1771), and sometimes as "The Addison of the North."

McKinley, William (1843–1901). Twenty-fifth president of the United States (1896–1901). Republican. Political pressure forced his intervention in Cuban insurrection against Spain. Under him the U.S. acquired the Philippines, Puerto Rico, and Guam. Assassinated in Buffalo, N.Y., by the anarchist Leon Czolgosz.

Mackinnon, James (1860–). Scottish historian. *A History of Modern Liberty* (1906–1908, 1941), and books about the Reformation.

MacKinstry, Elizabeth. American illustrator, known for her color work. Illustrated her own *Puck in Pasture* (1925); *Trees* by Joyce Kilmer (1925); *Tall Tales of the Kentucky Mountains* by Percy MacKaye (1926); several books by Rachel Field; *The Night Before Christmas* by C. C. Moore; *Forty Singing Seamen* by Alfred Noyes; *Fairy Tales from Hans Christian Andersen; Peer Gynt* by Henrik Ibsen; a version of *Aladdin and the Wonderful Lamp* (1935); etc.

McLaughlin, Wully. The hero of Margaret Wilson's Able McLaughlins.

McLean, Lin, see Lin McLean.

MacLeish, Archibald (1892–). American poet, influenced successively by a number of figures and movements in the poetry of his lifetime, including T. S. Eliot, Ezra Pound, St.-J. Perse, and the writers of proletarian sympathies. See proletarian literature; Marxism in literature. As an expatriate in France during the 1920's he wrote disillusioned lyrics, considered his best work, expressing a hope for salvation in love and beauty. Later he became preoccupied with the wars and the social customs of ancient, primitive civilizations. After his return to the U.S. he was influenced by the revolutionary and reform movements of the time and criticized in his poetry the society of his day, later coming to affirm faith in the future of America. These later poems, which achieved a measure of popularity, are considered by critics to be inferior to his earlier work, tending to be formularized. Among his works are *Tower of Ivory* (1917); *The Happy Marriage* (1924); *The Pot of Earth* (1925); *Nobodaddy* (1926), a play; *Streets in the Moon* (1926); *The Hamlet of A. MacLeish* (1928); *New Found Land* (1930); Conquistador (1932), winner of the Pulitzer prize in 1932; *Frescoes for Mr. Rockefeller's City* (1933); *Union Pacific* (1934), a ballet; *Panic* (1935), a play; *Public Speech* (1936); *The Fall of the City* (1937) and *Air Raid* (1938), radio plays; *The Land of the Free* (1938); *America Was Promises* (1939).

MacLeish was one of the editors of the magazine Fortune. In 1939 he was appointed U.S. Librarian of Congress, and during the early years of World II he was for a time director of the Office of Facts and Figures, a government information agency. After his official appointments he published essays on public issues, including *The Irresponsibles* (1940), an attack on the disillusioned writers of the 1920's for shirking political responsibility; *The American Cause* (1941); and *A Time to Speak* (1941), a collection of his previous prose writings.

MacLennan, (John) Hugh (1907–). Canadian novelist. *Barometer Rising* (1941); *Two Solitudes* (1945); *The Precipice* (1948).

Macleod, Fiona. Pseudonym of William Sharp.

McLeod, Irene Rutherford (1891–). English poet. Author of *Songs to Save a Soul* (1915); etc.

MacMahon, Comte **Marie Edme Patrice Maurice de** (1808–1893). Marshal of France (1859) and second president of the Third Republic (1873–1879). Successful as commander in three wars, but defeated by the Prussians in the fourth (1870).

MacManus, Seumas (1869–). Irish poet, novelist, and playwright.

McMaster, John Bach (1852–1932). American historian. Taught at Princeton. Wrote *The History of the People of the United States* (8 vols.; 1883–1913).

MacMillan, Donald Baxter (1874–). American arctic explorer. With Peary on expedition to north pole (1908–1909). Organized and led expeditions to Labrador, Greenland, and Baffin Land. Wrote *How Peary Reached the Pole* (1932); etc.

Macmillan, Harold (1894–). Director of Macmillan & Company, publishers, in England. Made resident minister in North Africa (1942). Author of *Reconstruction* (1933); *The Middle Way* (1938); etc.

MacMonnies, Frederick William (1863–1937). American sculptor. Examples of his work in City Hall Park, New York; Boston Public Library; Metropolitan Museum of Art, New York; etc.

MacNeice, Frederick Louis (1907–). Irish-born English poet, associated with W. H. Auden, Stephen Spender, C. Day-Lewis, and Christopher Isherwood during the 1930's, but not as definitely committed to Marxist (see Marxism) sympathies and theories as were the first three members of the group at that time. His poetry is marked by a greater preoccupation with psychological problems than that of his associates, and by a skillful use of the symbols of 20th-century British life in the manner of Auden. Occasionally his work suggests the influence of his studies of Latin and Greek classic literature. His books include *Blind Fireworks* (1929); *Roundabout Way* (1932), published under the pseudonym of Louis Malone; *Out of the Picture* (1937), a play; *Letters from Iceland* (1937), travel sketches in verse, written in collaboration with W. H. Auden; *The Earth Compels* (1938); *I Crossed the Minch* (1938), travel sketches of the Hebrides Islands; *Modern Poetry* (1938), a critical essay; *Autumn Journal* (1939); *Poems, 1925–1940* (1940); *The Poetry of W. B. Yeats* (1941), criticism.

McNeile, Herman Cyril (1888–1937). English writer of crime and adventure fiction, under the pseudonym "Sapper." Creator of Bulldog Drummond, who was later impersonated on the stage by Sir Gerald DU MAURIER in London and by A. E. Matthews in New York.

Macpherson, James (1736–1796). Scotch poet, known for the poems dealing with the epic deeds of ancient Gaelic tribes which he published as translations from old works of OSSIAN collected in the Scotch Highlands, although they were actually a literary hoax. See also CHATTERTON, THOMAS. *Fragments of Ancient Poetry Collected in the Highlands* (1760), FINGAL (1762), and *Tesmara* (1763) aroused a great deal of interest, and the author collected funds from a number of well-known literary figures to make a tour through the Highlands in search of more epic material. The London critics, especially Samuel JOHNSON, soon became suspicious, however, and Macpherson ceased making further Ossianic "discoveries." These pseudo-Gaelic works are actually written in a poetic prose and are marked by rhapsodic nature descriptions and an atmosphere of vague mystery and melancholy. Although critics do not consider them to be of much literary value, they had an important influence on the development of ROMANTICISM in France and Germany as it appeared in such figures as CHATEAUBRIAND, GOETHE, and SCHILLER.

Macpherson's later writing was historical and political, including *Introduction to the History of Great Britain* (1771); *History of Great Britain from the Restoration to the Accession of the House of Hanover* (1775); and *Original Papers, Containing the Secret History of Great Britain* (1775). All three showed a bias against Britain and the ruling house of the time. For a while, the author was secretary to the governor of Florida, in the U.S., and in the last years of his life held a number of comfortable political sinecures at home.

See also CARTHON: A POEM.

Macquart, Nana. The heroine of Zola's *Nana.* Nana's mother Gervaise and other of the Macquarts and their offspring appear in other novels of the ROUGON-MACQUART series, which deals with the complete history of the family.

Macready, William Charles (1793–1873). English tragedian, well known for his interpretation of Shakespearean rôles. Manager, Covent Garden Theatre (1837–1839), producing plays by Shakespeare, Browning, and Bulwer-Lytton; etc.

Macreons. The island of the Macreons in Rabelais' GARGANTUA AND PANTAGRUEL (Bk. IV. ch. xxv), has been taken by some commentators—rather unconvincingly—to be intended for Great Britain. The word is Greek, and means *long-lived.* Rabelais describes a terrible storm at sea (possibly a typification of the persecutions of the Reformers), in which Pantagruel and his fleet are tempest-tossed but contrive to enter one of the harbors of this island, which is so called because no one is put to death there for his religious opinions. It is full of antique ruins, which may be taken as a symbol of decayed Popery and ancient superstitions.

MacSwiney, Terence (1879–1920). Irish nationalist and revolutionary; identified with Sinn Fein from its beginning; leader in Easter Rebellion (1916); elected Lord Mayor of Cork. Died of starvation on hunger strike in Brixton Jail in London (October 25, 1920).

MacSycophant, Sir Pertinax. In Macklin's comedy *The Man of the World* (1764), the hot-headed, ambitious father of Charles Egerton. His love for Scotland is very great, and he is continually quarreling with his family because they do not hold his country in sufficient reverence.

McTeague. A novel by Frank NORRIS (1899), dealing with a dentist, McTeague by name, who is prevented from carrying on his practice by an enemy's having informed the authorities of his lack of a license and diploma. Greed comes to dominate his life, and he murders his wife, Trina, while stealing her savings, which were originally based on a lottery prize. He tries to escape across Death Valley and is pursued by Marcus Schouler, Trina's cousin and the man responsible for his being prohibited from practicing dentistry. The two men fight, and Schouler is killed, but since McTeague is handcuffed to the corpse he is faced with a horrible death from thirst and madness in the desert. A fine silent motion picture, *Greed,* was based on the novel. See also MACAPA, MARIA; ZERKOW.

MacTurk, Captain Mungo or Hector. (1) In Scott's ST. RONAN'S WELL, "the man of peace."

(2) A seaman in stories by Cutcliffe HYNE.

Macy, John Albert (1877–1932). American critic and biographer. Married Anne Sullivan, Helen Keller's companion, and edited Helen Keller's *Story of My Life* (1903). Joined Socialist party (1911). Literary editor, Boston *Her-*

ald (1913–1914) and *The Nation* (1922–1923). Literary adviser to William Morrow & Co. Teacher at the Rand School of Social Science. His best-known book is *The Spirit of American Literature* (1913).

Mad.

Mad as a hatter. The probable origin of this phrase is "Mad as an *adder*" (A.S. *naeddre,* A.S. *atter* being "poison"), but evidence is wanting. It was popularized by Lewis CARROLL (*Alice in Wonderland,* 1865), but was well known earlier, and was used by THACKERAY (*Pendennis,* Ch. x) in 1849.

mad as a March hare, see under HARE.

the Mad Cavalier. Prince Rupert (1619–1682), noted for his rash courage and impatience of control.

the Mad Parliament, see under PARLIAMENTS.

the Mad Poet. Nathaniel Lee (ca. 1653–1692), who was confined for four years in BEDLAM, and wrote some of his best poetry there.

Madame. So the wife of Philippe, Duc d'Orléans, was styled in the reign of Louis XIV; other ladies were only Madame This or That.

Madame la Duchesse. Wife of Henri-Jules de Bourbon, eldest son of Prince de Condé.

Madame la Princesse. Wife of the Prince de Condé, and natural daughter of Louis XIV. See MONSIEUR.

Madame Bovary. A novel by FLAUBERT (1856), tracing with grim, realistic detail the affairs of Emma BOVARY, wife of a good-hearted but stupid village doctor. Unhappy in her marriage, finding her pathetic dreams of romantic love unfulfilled, she has one lover, then another, piles up enormous debts, and, when she can see no other way out, commits suicide. *Madame Bovary* exerted a great influence as one of the first novels of the realistic school, and is considered one of the masterpieces of 19th-century literature.

Madame Butterfly. An opera by Giacomo PUCCINI (1904), based on a drama of the same title by Belasco and Long. The scene is laid in Japan. Lieutenant Pinkerton, U.S.N., contracts a temporary "Japanese marriage" with the gay and affectionate Cho-Cho-San, who thus becomes *Madame Butterfly.* She, on her part, believing the marriage a permanent one, cuts herself off from her religion and her people. Pinkerton is recalled to America and later returns with an American wife. The American consul, Sharpless, has vainly tried to fulfill Pinkerton's request and break the news to the trusting Cho-Cho-San, but she stands the shock bravely, plays her rôle with dignity and agrees to give her child into Mrs. Pinkerton's care. On Mrs. Pinkerton's departure, she kills herself with her father's sword.

Madame Chrysanthème. A novel by Pierre LOTI (1887), dealing with the love life of a French naval officer and a Japanese geisha.

Madame de Treymes. Title of a novelette by Edith WHARTON.

Madame Sand. Title of a comedy by Philip MOELLER (1917).

Madame Sans Gêne. (*Mistress Don't Care.*) A drama by SARDOU and MOREAU (later made into an opera by GIORDANO), with Napoleon as its central character. The heroine is Caterina Hubscher, a spirited French washwoman, and the first act takes place in her laundry before the French Revolution. Nineteen years later the laundress has become the Duchess of Danzig, and she and her bourgeois friends are prominent at Napoleon's court. Of them all, Madame Sans Gêne alone retains and rejoices in her old blunt crudities, and Napoleon finally orders her to divorce her husband and retire from court. With all the old fire and spirit she reminds him of the days of military struggle and triumph which she shared, and flaunts before him his unpaid laundry bill of bygone years, at which the Emperor relents and reinstates her.

The real *Madame Sans Gêne* was Marie Therese Figueur (1774–1861), who fought through all the Napoleonic wars, and later, by her marriage to Marshal Lefebre, became the Duchess of Danzig.

Madame Tussaud's, see TUSSAUD, Mme MARIE GROSHOLTZ.

Mad Anthony. A sobriquet of General Anthony WAYNE.

Madariaga y Rojo, Salvador de (1886–). Spanish publicist and literary critic. Honorary M.A. from Oxford (1928). Professor of Spanish studies at Oxford. A leading authority on English poetry of the romantic school, author of *The Genius of Spain* (1923); *Hernán Cortes: Conqueror of Mexico* (1941); etc.

Madeleine, M. In Hugo's LES MISÉRABLES, the name under which Jean Valjean gains wealth and position.

Madeline. The heroine of Keats' poem, THE EVE OF ST. AGNES (1820).

Madelon. In Molière's PRÉCIEUSES RIDICULES, one of the affected heroines, cousin of CATHOS.

Mademoiselle. The daughter of Philippe, Duc de Chartres, grandson of Philippe, Duc d'Orléans, brother of Louis XIV.

la Grande Mademoiselle. The Duchesse de Montpensier, cousin to Louis XIV, and daughter of Gaston, Duc d'Orléans.

Madero, Francisco Indalecio (1873–1913). Mexican revolutionist and liberal politician. Opposed Díaz, fled to U.S. (November, 1910).

Forced resignation of Díaz and became president (1911–1913). Overthrown by Huerta and shot.

Madge Wildfire, see WILDFIRE, MADGE.

Madison, Cora. The heroine of Booth Tarkington's THE FLIRT.

Madison, Dorothea, *née* **Payne** (1768–1849). Wife of James MADISON, known as **Dolly Madison,** the most famous hostess in Washington while her husband was secretary of state (1801–1809) and president (1809–1817).

Madison, James (1751–1836). Fourth president of the United States (1809–1817). Collaborated with Hamilton and Jay in the series of papers known as *The Federalist* (1787–1788); later, as leader of the Democratic-Republican party, opposed Hamilton's financial policies. With Jefferson drafted the VIRGINIA RESOLUTIONS (1798). As president, declared war (1812) on Great Britain. Cf. *Madison Papers* (3 vols.; 1840).

Madison, John. The hero of Walter's EASIEST WAY.

madman.

Macedonia's madman. Alexander the Great (b. 356, reigned 336–323 B. C.).

the brilliant madman or *madman of the North.* Charles XII of Sweden (b. 1682, reigned 1697–1718).

Mad Mullah. Mohammed ibn Abdullah (died 1920), a Somali dervish and religious agitator against the British (1902–1920).

Madog ab Owain Gwynedd. A legendary Welsh prince, youngest son of Owain Gwynedd, king of North Wales, who died in 1169. According to tradition, he sailed to America, and established a colony on the southern branches of the Missouri. About the same time the Aztecs forsook Aztlan, under the guidance of Yuhidthiton, and founded the empire called Mexico, in honor of Mexitli, their tutelary god. Southey's poem, *Madoc* (1805), harmonizes these two events. In the poem Madog is called "The Perfect Prince," "The Lord of Ocean," and is the very beau-ideal of a hero.

Mador, Sir. In Arthurian legend, the Scottish knight slain in single combat by Sir LAUNCELOT of the Lake in defense of the reputation of Queen Guinevere.

Madras House, The. A play by Harley GRANVILLE-BARKER (*Eng.,* 1910). The Madras House is a great business concern, and the characters are the various members of the family that controls it and the employes to whom it provides a means of livelihood. Philip Madras and his wife, Jessica, the central figures, represent the new generation.

Maecenas. A patron of letters; so called from Gaius Cilnius Maecenas (d. 8 B.C.), a Roman statesman in the reign of Augustus, who kept open house for all men of letters, and was the special friend and patron of Horace and Virgil.

the last English Maecenas. Samuel Rogers (1763–1855), poet and banker.

Maël, Saint, see SAINT MAËL.

Maeldune. The hero of an ancient Irish legend. Cf. Tennyson's poem *The Voyage of Maeldune.*

Maelgan Gwynedd. Uncle of Elphin, whose boasts about his wife and his bards young Elphin countered by boasting about his own wife and his bard TALIESIN. Maelgan caused Elphin to be thrown into a prison until Taliesin helped him to prove the truth of what he had claimed.

Maëlstrom. A whirlpool in the Arctic Ocean near the Lofoten Islands off the west coast of Norway. According to an old tradition, it sucked in all ships within a wide radius. *A Descent into the Maëlstrom* is the title of a famous short story by Edgar Allan POE.

maenads. In Greek mythology, the female attendants of Dionysius. The word means mad or frenzied women. Also called Bacchae.

Maeonides or **the Maeonian Poet.** HOMER, either because he was the son of Maeon, or because he was born in Maeonia (Asia Minor).

Maerlant, Jacob van (1235?–after 1291). Flemish poet. Often called "the father of Dutch poets."

Maestricht. Capital of the province of Limburg, Holland. When Germany invaded the Lowlands in 1940, the capture of Maestricht and the breaking of the Maestricht-Hasselt line exposed all of Belgium.

maestro (*Ital.,* "master"). Term used to refer to a master in any art in which Italians have excelled, especially in music, as a composer, conductor, eminent teacher, etc.

Maeterlinck, Maurice (1862–). Belgian poet and dramatist, in his early career influenced by the school of SYMBOLISM and known for the delicate fantasy, mystery, and dreamy melancholy of his most famous plays, which deal chiefly with historical and legendary material and make wide use of moral and psychological symbolism. Among his works are *La Princesse Maleine* (1889); *Les Aveugles* (*The Sightless;* 1890); ARIANE ET BARBE BLEU; PELLÉAS ET MÉLISANDE (1892), later set to music by Claude DEBUSSY and produced as an opera; *Aglavaine et Sélysette* (1896); SISTER BEATRICE (*Soeur Béatrice;* 1901); MONNA VANNA (1902); THE BLUE BIRD (*L'Oiseau bleu;* 1909), his most famous work; *Mary Magdalene* (see under SAINTS; 1909); *La Mort* (*Death*) (1913); *Les Fiançailles* (*Betrothal*) (1918); *The Burgomaster of Stilemonde* (1918); *The Miracle of St. Anthony* (1919); *The Cloud that*

Lifted (1923); *The Power of the Dead* (1923). Maeterlinck also wrote essays on Shakespeare, and, in later life, a number on nature and death, including *The Life of the Bee* (1901); *Life and Flowers* (1907); *The Life of the Ant* (1930); *Before the Great Silence* (*Avant le Grand silence;* 1934); *La Grande porte* (1939); *L'Autre monde* (1942). He was also interested in astrology and carefully recorded and catalogued his dreams.

Maeviad, see BAVIAD.

Maffia or **Mafia** (*It.*). In Sicily and hence elsewhere, the name of a supposed or real secret society of Italian members prone to acts of violence, such as murder, blackmail, etc. The word *maffia* (of unknown origin) signifies in Sicily hostility to the law implying refusal to bear witness to crimes, etc. See also CAMORRA.

maffick. To celebrate an event, especially an occasion of national rejoicing, with wild and extravagant exuberance. From the uproarious scenes and unrestrained exultation that took place in London on the night of May 18, 1900, when the news of the relief of the South African town of Mafeking (besieged by the Boers since the previous November) became known.

Magda. (1) Heinrich's forsaken wife in Hauptmann's drama THE SUNKEN BELL.

(2) Heroine of *Magda* (*Die Heimat*) by Sudermann (*Ger.,* 1893).

Magdalene. An asylum for the reclaiming of prostitutes; so called from Mary Magdalene or Mary of Magdala, "out of whom He had cast seven devils" (*Mark* xvi. 9). See *St. Mary Magdalene* under SAINTS.

Magellan, Ferdinand. In Portuguese **Fernando de Magalhães** (1480?–1521). Portuguese navigator. Emperor Charles V allowed him to set sail for the Spice Islands (Moluccas) by the western route. Sailed from Spain (September 20, 1519) with five ships, passed through what is now known as the Strait of Magellan (October 21–November 28, 1520), discovered the Philippines, and was killed (April, 1521) by treacherous natives. One of his vessels, the *Concepción* under Juan Sebastián del Cano, completed the circumnavigation of the globe after a voyage of three years.

Maggie: A Girl of the Streets. A novel by Stephen CRANE, published privately in 1893 under the name of Johnston Smith, issued to the public in 1896. It deals with the life of Maggie Johnson, daughter of a brutal father and drunken mother in the slums of New York City. Maggie goes to work in a collar factory, falls in love with Pete, a bartender who is a friend of her brother Jimmie, and is seduced by him. Her mother disowns her, she becomes a prostitute, and in despair she finally kills herself.

Magi (*Lat., pl.* of *magus*). Literally "wise men"; specifically, the Three Wise Men of the East who brought gifts to the infant Savior. Tradition calls them Melchior, Gaspar, and Balthazar, three kings of the East. The first offered *gold,* the emblem of royalty; the second, *frankincense,* in token of divinity; and the third, *myrrh,* in prophetic allusion to the persecution unto death which awaited the "Man of Sorrows."

Melchior means "king of light," Gaspar, or Caspar "the white one," Balthazar, "the lord of treasures."

Medieval legend calls them the Three Kings of Cologne, and the Cathedral there claims their relics. They are commemorated on January 2, 3, and 4, and particularly at the Feast of the Epiphany.

Henry Van Dyke in his story *The Other Wise Man* published in *The Blue Flower* (*Am.,* 1902) tells of a fourth wise man, Artaban, who stopped at crucial moments to respond to appeals for help and so failed to reach his goal. The tale is a modern addition to the old legend.

Among the ancient Medes and Persians the *Magi* were members of a priestly caste credited with great occult powers, and in Camoëns' LUSIAD the term denotes the Indian Brahmins.

Magic. A play by Gilbert K. CHESTERTON (1913).

Magic Flute, The (Die Zauberflöte). An opera by MOZART (1791), with a libretto by Emmanuel Schikaneder. The "flute" was bestowed by the Powers of Darkness, and has the power of inspiring love. Unless purified, love is only lust, but, being purified by the Powers of Light, it subserves the holiest purposes. TAMINO and PAMINA are guided by it through all worldly dangers to the knowledge of Divine Truth, or the mysteries of Isis.

Magic Mountain, The. English translation of **Der Zauberberg,** a symbolic novel by Thomas MANN and the author's most famous work, published in 1924. In it, Hans CASTORP comes to HAUS BERGHOF, a tuberculosis sanatorium in the Swiss Alps, to visit his cousin, Joachim ZIEMSSEN for three weeks, but stays seven years. He comes under the influence of the diseased atmosphere of the sanatorium, which is interpreted as a symbol of pure aestheticism, and falls in love with Clavdia CHAUCHAT, a beautiful and mysterious Russian. SETTEMBRINI, symbolizing humanism and political liberalism, tries to recall to Hans's mind his duty to society and thereby rescue him from the fatal debility of the mountain; he also carries on long and eloquent philosophic arguments with his intellectual opponent, the schoolmaster Leo NAPHTA. Hans, however, is held under the spell of the mountain and Clavdia, his thralldom being symbolized strikingly by a scene in which he wanders alone among the crags, becomes fascinated by the whiteness and silence of the snow, and finds he has lost his way. Mynheer PEEPERKORN, a former Dutch planter, regarded as representing animal sensuality, comes to the sanatorium, and his personality immediately overshadows both Naphta and Settembrini. He tends to influence Hans towards a return to the normal and the human, but, finding himself weakened in physical vigor by oncoming old age, he commits suicide, and his influence is removed. Clavdia leaves the sanatorium soon after this event, and Hans falls into a stupor, interested only in operating a phonograph and listening to its music; this is seen by critics as symbolic of the rôle played by music in the psychological effects of aestheticism. His almost death-like inactivity is broken at last by the outbreak of the European war of 1914–1918, and Hans is suddenly released from the enchantment of the mountain. He leaves the sanatorium and becomes a soldier in the German army—apparently once more a normal, "practical" man, fulfilling what would be generally regarded as his duty to the society in which he lives. He remains a dreamer nonetheless and goes into battle singing Schubert's *Lindenbaum,* the song of which he was most fond at the Berghof. He is shown at the conclusion of the novel as maintaining a balance between the aesthetic and the practical tendencies of his nature, not yielding completely to one or the other, with his dilemma still unresolved.

The Magic Mountain, with James Joyce's ULYSSES and Marcel Proust's REMEMBRANCE OF THINGS PAST, is considered one of the great novels of the 20th century. It contains elaborate symbolism throughout, often bordering on allegory, and there are numerous striking and dramatic scenes and characters against the background of the sanatorium and the mountain, including the Walpurgisnacht revel, weighing-day and X-ray examinations in the clinic, Mynheer Peeperkorn's speech and his suicide, and the séance.

Although it emphasizes political interpretations, an adequate introductory study of *The Magic Mountain* is contained in Harry Slochower's *Three Ways of Modern Man,* on which the above summary is based.

magician.

The Great Magician or *Wizard of the North.* Sir Walter Scott (1771–1832).

Magician of the North. The title assumed by Johann Georg Hamann, of Prussia (1730–1788).

Maginn, William (1793–1842). Irish poet and contributor of prose pieces to various periodicals. Prototype of Captain Shandon in *Pendennis* by Thackeray.

Maginot, André (1877–1932). French politician. Minister of colonies (1917), of war (1922–1924), etc.; advocate of military preparedness. The **Maginot Line,** named in his honor, was a supposedly impregnable defense against Germany, having been erected with a series of forts, etc., at a cost of two million dollars a mile. At the beginning of World War II, the French, feeling safe behind the Maginot Line, intended to fight a comfortable war of attrition. They suffered from what became known as the "Maginot mentality." Neither the line nor the mentality proved fit in the modern warfare of air power and armor.

magliabecchi. A book-worm; from Antonio Magliabecchi (1633–1714), librarian to Cosmo III, Grand Duke of Tuscany. He never forgot what he had once read, and could turn at once to the exact page of any reference.

Magna Charta. The *Great Charter* of English liberty extorted from King John, 1215; called by Spelman—

Augustissimum Anglicarum, liberta tum diploma et sacra anchora.

It contained in its final form thirty-seven clauses, and is directed principally against abuses of the power of the Crown. Among other guarantees it insured that no subject should be kept in prison without trial and judgment by his peers.

Magnalia Christi Americana, or The Ecclesiastical History of New England. A history by Cotton MATHER (1702), one of the first pretentious pieces of literary work in America and an important source book for the period.

Magnanimous, the. (1) Alfonso V of Aragon (b. 1385, reigned 1416–1458).

(2) Chosroes or Khosru, King of Persia, twenty-first of the Sassanides, surnamed *Noushirwan* (the Magnanimous) (531–579).

Magnetic Mountain. A mountain of medieval legend which drew out all the nails of any ship that approached within its influence. It is referred to in MANDEVILLE'S TRAVELS and in many stories, such as the tale of the Third Calender and one of the voyages of Sinbad the Sailor in the *Arabian Nights.* Also the title of a book of poems by Cecil DAY LEWIS (1933).

Magnificat. The hymn of the Virgin (*Luke* i. 46–55) beginning "My soul doth magnify the Lord" (*Magnificat anima mea Dominum*), used as part of the daily service of the Catholic Church since the beginning of the sixth century, and at Evening Prayer in England for over 800 years.

to correct Magnificat before one has learnt Te Deum. To try to do that for which one has no qualifications; to criticize presumptuously.

to sing the Magnificat at matins. To do things at the wrong time, or out of place. The Magnificat belongs to vespers, not to matins.

Magnificent Ambersons, The. A novel by Booth TARKINGTON (1918). The Ambersons for years have been the most prominent family of the "Midland town" in which the story is laid, and the impressive Amberson Mansion, built by Major Amberson, the founder of the family fortune, is the pride of the inhabitants. The story is concerned chiefly with the Major's grandson, George Amberson Minafer, a spoiled young cub whose high and mighty scorn for people he disposes of as "riff-raff" is unendurable to the city that once worshiped at the Amberson shrine. He has, however, an adorer in Lucy Morgan, in spite of the fact that she sees through his pretensions. Eventually George becomes somewhat subdued and adopts a more wholesome attitude toward life. This novel was awarded the Pulitzer prize in 1918 and made into a successful motion-picture, with Orson WELLES directing and producing (1942).

Magnifico, see MEDICI, LORENZO DE'.

Magnitogorsk. A city in the Soviet Union at the source of the Ural River, made into an enormous steel-producing center (1929) as part of STALIN's second Five Year Plan. American engineers were engaged to install the plants.

magnum opus (*Lat.*, "great work"). The chief or most important work of an author or artist.

Magnus. A priest in George Sand's LÉLIA.

Magog. See GOG AND MAGOG.

Magua. A bold and cruel Huron Indian, the enemy of Uncas in Cooper's LAST OF THE MOHICANS. He is known as *le Renard subtil.*

Magwitch, Abel. In Dickens' GREAT EXPECTATIONS, the convict benefactor who arouses Pip's "expectations." When Pip is twenty-three years old, Magwitch who has become a successful sheep-farmer in Australia, returns to England under the assumed name of Provis and makes himself known to Pip. He is tracked down by Orlick and Compeyson, arrested, and condemned to death, and dies in jail.

Mah-abadean Dynasty. The first dynasty of Persian mythology. Mah (the great) Abad and his wife were the only persons left on the earth after the great cycle, and from them the world was peopled. Azer Abad, the fourteenth and last of this dynasty, left the earth because "all flesh had corrupted itself," and a period of anarchy ensued.

Mahabharata. One of the two great epic poems of ancient India, the other being the RAMAYANA, about eight times as long as the *Iliad* and *Odyssey* together. Its main story is the long struggle between the five Pandavas, or sons of Pandu, and the Kauravas, a name applied, from their ancestor Kuru, to the family of Dhritarashtra, Pandu's brother, who refuses to give up the throne to his nephews, the rightful heirs. Of the five Pandavas, the most heroic are Yudhishthira, the eldest, who finally gains the kingdom, and Arjuna, who wins the hand of the lovely Draupadi in open contest and brings her home as the wife of all five brothers. Friendly to the Pandavas and very prominent throughout a large part of the epic is the man-god KRISHNA, an avatar of Vishnu. After the death of Krishna, Yudhishthira tires of his throne and the five Pandavas, accompanied by their loyal wife and dog, start out to seek admission to the heaven of Indra on MOUNT MERU. Only Yudhishthira and the dog succeed in completing the long journey; when the dog is refused admittance, Yudhishthira will not enter. The dog turns out to be the god of justice, and all of the Pandavas eventually gain their just reward in heaven. The epic contains an immense number of episodes, among them the well-known story of Nala and DAMAYANTA.

Mahadeva (*Sans.*, "great god"). A widely used name of SIVA, one of the Hindu Triad.

Mahaffy, Sir John Pentland (1839–1919). Irish classical scholar and professor of ancient history at Dublin (1869–1901). Author of books on life and letters in ancient Greece. Directed defense of Trinity college in Easter Rebellion (1916).

Mahan, Alfred Thayer (1840–1914). United States admiral. Most famous for his work on *The Influence of Sea Power upon History, 1660–1783* (1890).

Maharajah (*Sans.*, "great king"). The title of certain native rulers of India whose territories are very extensive. The wife of a *Maharajah* is a *Maharanee*. See also RULERS, TITLES OF.

mahatma (*Sans.*, "great soul"). Max Müller tells us that

> mahatma is a well known Sanskrit word applied to men who have retired from the world, who, by means of a long ascetic discipline, have subdued the passions of the flesh, and gained a reputation for sanctity and knowledge. That these men are able to perform most startling feats, and to suffer the most terrible tortures, is perfectly true.—*Nineteenth Century*, May, 1893.

By the Esoteric Buddhists and by Theosophists the name is given to one who has reached perfection spiritually, intellectually and physically. As his knowledge is perfect he can produce effects which, to the ordinary man, appear miraculous.

Mahbub Ali. In Kipling's KIM, an Afghan horsedealer who befriends Kim. He is in the "Great Game," that is, the British secret service in India, and plays a prominent rôle in the book.

Mahdi (*Arab.*, "the divinely directed one"). The expected Messiah of the Mohammedans; a title often assumed by leaders of insurrection in the Sudan, especially Mohammed Ahmed (1843–1885), who led the rising of 1883, and who, say some, is not really dead, but sleeps in a cavern near Bagdad, and will return to life in the fullness of time to overthrow Dejal (Antichrist). The SHIAHS or Shiites believe that the Mahdi has lived, and for the most part maintain that he is in hiding and will reappear at the appointed time as ruler of the Moslem world.

mah-jongg. An ancient Chinese game, played by four persons with 144 "tiles," similar to dominoes. The object is to secure by drawing and discarding four complete combinations of tiles.

Mahler, Gustav (1860–1911). Austrian composer and conductor, born in Bohemia. Director, Imperial Opera in Vienna (1897–1907). Conducted in the U.S. (1907–1910). Composed ten symphonies, the last unfinished. His biography, *Gustav Mahler, Memories and Letters* (1946), was written by his widow, Alma Maria Mahler, then the wife of Franz WERFEL. Bruno WALTER has conducted Mahler's symphonies in the U.S. where he has tried to make him popular.

Mahomet or **Mohammed** (*Arab.*, "the praised one"). The titular name of the founder of ISLAM, or Mohammedanism (born at Mecca about 570, died at Medina, 632) which was adopted by him about the time of the Hegira to apply to himself the Messianic prophecies in the Old Testament (*Haggai* ii, 7, and elsewhere). His original name is given both as Kotham and Halabi.

VOLTAIRE was the author of a drama *Mahomet* (1738), an English version of which, by James Miller, called *Mahomet the Imposter,* was produced in 1740. The plot centers about Mahomet's love for the captive Palmira, and he is pictured as making utterly unscrupulous use of his religious authority to dispose of his rivals and secure his own ends.

Mahomet's coffin. Legend used to have it that Mahomet's coffin is suspended in mid-air at Medina without any support. The story probably arose from the rough drawings sold to visitors.

Mahomet's dove. Mahomet had a dove which he fed with wheat out of his ear. When it was hungry it used to light on the prophet's shoulder, and thrust its bill into his ear to find its meal. Mahomet thus induced the Arabs to believe that he was divinely inspired.

> Was Mahomet inspired with a dove?
> Shakespeare, 1 *Henry VI*, i. 2.

Mahomet and the spider, see under SPIDER.

if the mountain will not come to Mahomet, Mahomet must go to the mountain. When Mahomet introduced his system to the Arabs, they asked for miraculous proofs. He then ordered Mount Safa to come to him, and as it did not move, he said, "God is merciful. Had it obeyed my words, it would have fallen on us to our destruction. I will therefore go to the mountain, and thank God that He has had mercy on a stiffnecked generation." The phrase is often used of one who, not being able to get his own way, bows before the inevitable.

Mahon, Christie. The Irish hero of Synge's drama THE PLAYBOY OF THE WESTERN WORLD.

Mahony, Francis Sylvester. Pseudonym **Father Prout** (1804–1866). Irish humorist. Contributed to *Fraser's Magazine* and *Bentley's Miscellany* translations from Horace and various French writers. Best-known for his own poem *The Bells of Shandon.* Member of the Jesuit order until he was expelled (1830) and embarked on his literary career.

Mahoun, Mahound. Names of contempt for Mahomet, a Moslem, a Moor, particularly in romances of the Crusades. The name is sometimes used as a synonym for "the Devil."

mahout. In the East Indies, the keeper and driver of an elephant. He sits on the elephant's neck and guides him with a goad called an ankus. Cf. Kipling's stories, *Toomai of the Elephants* and *The King's Ankus.*

Mahu. One of the fiends whose names Shakespeare got from Harsnett (see HOBBIDIDANCE) and introduced into *King Lear:*

> Five fiends have been in poor Tom at once: of lust, as Obidicut; Hobbididance, prince of dumbness; Mahu, of stealing; Modo, of murder; Flibbertigibbet, of mopping and mowing. (iv. 1.)

Maia. In Greek mythology, originally a mountain nymph in Arcadia who became the mother of Hermes.

maid.

Maid Marian. A female character in the old May games and morris dances, in the former usually being Queen of the May. In the later Robin Hood ballads she became attached to the cycle as the outlaw's sweetheart, probably through the performance of Robin Hood plays at May-Day festivities. The part of Maid Marian both in the games and the dance was frequently taken by a man dressed as a woman.

Maid of Athens. A poem by BYRON, said to refer to Theresa Macri.

Maid of Norway. Queen Margaret of Scotland (1283–1290), so called because she came from Norway.

Maid of Orleans. JOAN OF ARC.

Maid of Perth, see FAIR MAID OF PERTH.

Maid of Saragossa. Augustina Zaragoza, distinguished for her heroism when Saragossa was besieged in 1808 and 1809, and celebrated by BYRON in his *Childe Harold* (I. liv–lvi).

Maid of the Mist. The steamboat on the Niagara River which takes passengers through the spray from the Falls.

Maiden.

Maiden King. Malcolm IV of Scotland. (b. 1141, reigned 1153–1165).

"Malcolm . . . son of the brave and generous Prince Henry . . . was so kind and gentle in his disposition, that he was usually called Malcolm the Maiden."—Scott, *Tales of a Grandfather,* iv.

Maiden or *Virgin Queen.* Elizabeth, Queen of England, who never married. (b. 1533, reigned 1558–1603.)

Maiden Town. Edinburgh. So called (1) because it was never captured by a siege; or (2) because some maiden daughters of a Pictish monarch found a retreat there.

Maid's Tragedy, The. A famous drama by BEAUMONT and FLETCHER (1619). The titular heroine is ASPASIA, the principal character EVADNE.

mailed fist, the. Aggressive military might; from a phrase (Ger. *gepanzerte Faust*) made use of by William II of Germany when bidding adieu to Prince Henry of Prussia as he was starting on his tour to the Far East (December 16, 1897):

Should any one essay to detract from our just rights or to injure us, then up and at him with your mailed fist.

Maimonides or **Rabbi Moses ben Maimon** (1135–1204). Jewish philosopher who attempted to reconcile Rabbinic Judaism with Aristotelianism in its Arabic form.

Main, see SPANISH MAIN.

Maine. An American battleship destroyed by an explosion of undetermined cause in the harbor of Havana (1898). The incident was important in carrying on the Spanish-American War. The slogan, "Remember *The Maine!*", became current. The hulk was raised in 1911.

Mainsail Haul, A. Title of a book of short stories of the sea by John MASEFIELD.

Main Street. A novel by Sinclair LEWIS (1921) which attained such popularity that "Main Street" and "GOPHER PRAIRIE" passed almost immediately into the language as expressions of small town provincialism and prejudice. The heroine, Carol Kennicott, is very much bored with the narrow round of her duties and interests as wife of the doctor of Gopher Prairie, Minn., and finally breaks away to lead her own life. Small town life is very minutely and realistically described. HAWTHORNE had used the phrase "Main Street" previously as the title of a sketch in his *Snow Image* dealing with the history of Salem.

Maintenon, Marquise de. Françoise d'Aubigné (1635–1719). Mistress and second wife of Louis XIV. Exercised strong religious influence over the king in his later years. Founded the Convent of St. Cyr. Originally wife of the poet Scarron (1652).

Main-Travelled Roads. Title of a collection of short stories (1890) by Hamlin GARLAND.

Maironi, Piero. The hero of Antonio FOGAZZARO's novels, *The Sinner* (*Piccolo Mondo Moderno*) and *The Saint* (*Il Santo*). The first novel of this trilogy, *The Patriot* (*Piccolo Mondo Antico;* 1896), is the story of Piero's father, Franco Maironi, one of the patriots who fought for the cause of a United Italy. The struggle between his father's deeply religious nature and his mother's skepticism, as depicted in *The Patriot,* prepares the way for an understanding of Piero's own inner struggle in *The Sinner* and *The Saint.* In *The Sinner* (1901) he has an insane wife, Elisa, and is passionately in love with Jeanne Dessalle, a married woman who is living apart from her worthless husband. Elisa recovers her sanity just before she dies. At the end of the novel Piero renounces his property and all thought of Jeanne; in *The Saint* (1901) she finds him as Benedetto, a lay brother in a Benedictine monastery. The news that her husband has died has little effect on him; he has become the spokesman of a new Christianity which will accept and make use of the findings of modern science. As such he arouses tremendous opposition from within the Catholic Church. Jeanne, whose love can find no other outlet, manages to ward off much of this opposition through her powerful friends. He sends for her on his death bed. A fourth novel, *Leila* (1910) deals primarily with the love affair of the titular heroine and Massimo Alberti, a young doctor and a disciple of Benedetto, "the Saint."

Maisie. The heroine of Kipling's LIGHT THAT FAILED.

Maison Rouge, Chevalier de, see CHEVALIER DE MAISON ROUGE.

Maitland, Sarah. The "IRON WOMAN" in Margaret Deland's novel of that title. Her children, Blair and Nannie Maitland, are also leading characters in the novel.

Major, Charles (1856–1913). American romantic novelist. *When Knighthood Was in Flower* (1898); etc.

Major Barbara. A play by George Bernard SHAW (1907), presenting the theme that poverty is "the worst of crimes." The titular heroine, the granddaughter of an earl, becomes a Salvation Army lass. Undershaft, the other leading character, is the head of a great munitions factory.

Majorca. The largest of the Balearic Islands (Spain) in the Mediterranean. A favorite resort of writers.

make-up. The materials used by an actor for painting his face and otherwise transforming his appearance to suit a character on the stage; the manner in which he is *made up;* hence, in colloquial use, the sum of one's characteristics, idiosyncrasies, etc. In *printing,* the *make-up* is the arrangement of the printed matter in columns, pages, etc.

Making of an American, The. An autobiography by Jacob RIIS (1901), an immigrant of Danish birth who attained distinction in America.

Making of Americans, The. A novel by Gertrude STEIN, written in 1906–1908, published in 1926. It presents the history of the author's own family, extended to represent also the history of everyone in the past, present, and future. It is written in a simpler style than much of the author's later work and is marked by frequent verbal repetition to suggest repetition in time.

Malachi. The last book of the Old Testament, a book of prophecy.

Malade imaginaire, Le (The Imaginary Invalid). A comedy by MOLIÈRE (1673), a satire on the medical profession. The titular rôle is taken by ARGAN.

Malagigi. In Carolingian legend, the Italian form of the name of a great magician, one of Charlemagne's paladins; the same as the French MAUGIS.

Malagrowther, Malachi. The signature of Sir Walter SCOTT to a series of letters contributed in 1826 to the *Edinburgh Weekly Journal* upon the lowest limitation of paper money to £5. They caused an immense sensation, similar to that produced by DRAPIER'S LETTERS, or BURKE'S *Reflections on the French Revolution.*

Malagrowther, Sir Mungo. In Scott's FORTUNES OF NIGEL, a crabbed old courtier, soured by misfortune, and peevish from infirmities. He tries to make everyone as sour and discontented as himself.

Malambruno. A giant in Cervantes' DON QUIXOTE (II. iii. 45); he enchants Antonomasia and her husband, and Don Quixote effects their disenchantment by mounting the wooden horse, Clavigo.

Malaprop, Mrs. (from Fr. *mal à propos,* "out of place.") A famous character in Sheridan's comedy, THE RIVALS, noted for her blunders in the use of words. "As headstrong as an *allegory* on the banks of the Nile," is one of her grotesque misapplications. She has given us the word *malapropism* to denote such mistakes.

Malbecco. A "cankered, crabbed carle" in Spenser's FAËRIE QUEENE (III. x), wealthy, very miserly, and the impersonation of self-inflicted torments. His young wife, Helenore, sets fire to his house and elopes with Sir Paridel, whereupon Malbecco casts himself from a rock, and his ghost is metamorphosed into Jealousy.

Malbrouk or **Marlbrough.** The old French song, *Malbrouk s'en va-t-en guerre* (Marlborough is off to the wars), is said to date from 1709, when the Duke of Marlborough was winning his battles in Flanders, but did not become popular till it was applied to Charles Churchill, third Duke of Marlborough, at the time of his failure against Cherbourg (1758), and was further popularized by its becoming a favorite of Marie Antoinette about 1780, and by its being introduced by BEAUMARCHAIS into *Le Mariage de Figaro* (1784). The air, however (the same as "We won't go home till morning"), is of far older date, was well known in Egypt and the East, and is said to have been sung by the Crusaders. According to a tradition recorded by CHATEAUBRIAND, the air came from the Arabs, and the tale is a legend of Mambron, a crusader.

> Malbrouk s'en va-t-en guerre;
> Mironton, mironton, mirontaine;
> Malbrouk s'en va-t-en guerre,
> Nul sait quand reviendra.
> Il reviendra z'à pâques—
> Mironton, mironton mirontaine . . .
> Ou à la Trinitè.

One of the arias sung by George du Maurier's TRILBY is an elaboration of this song.

Malchus. In the New Testament, the servant of the high priest whose ear was cut off by Peter. Cf. *John* xviii. 10.

Malcolm. In Shakespeare's MACBETH, the eldest son of Duncan, King of Scotland. When Duncan is murdered, the two young princes flee—Malcolm to the English court, and his brother Donalbain to Ireland. Later, when Macduff slays Macbeth in the battle of Dunsinane, the son of Duncan is set on the throne of Scotland, under the name and title of Malcolm III.

Maldon, The Battle of. A poem in Old English dealing with a raid of the Danes on Essex in 991.

Malebolge. The eighth circle of Dante's INFERNO (Canto xviii), containing ten *bolgi* or pits. The name is used figuratively of any cesspool of filth or iniquity.

Malecasta. The impersonation of lust in Spenser's FAËRIE QUEENE, III. i. She is mistress of Castle Joyous.

Maleger. The incarnation of evil passions in Spenser's FAËRIE QUEENE, II. xi. He is "thin as a rake," and cold as a serpent, and attacks the Castle of Temperance with a rabble in twelve troops, typifying the seven deadly sins and the lusts of the five senses. Prince Arthur stabs him again and again, but it is like stabbing a shadow, and finally the Prince calls to mind that every time the carl touches the earth his strength is renewed, so he squeezes all his breath out and tosses the body into a lake. See also ANTAEUS.

Malesherbes, Chrétien Guillaume de Lamoignon de (1721–1794). French statesman, instrumental in securing publication of the *Encyclopédie* (1751–1772). Defended Louis XVI during the French Revolution. Was himself arrested and executed.

Malet, Lucas. Pseudonym of Mary St. Leger KINGSLEY.

Malfi or **Malfy, Duchess of,** see DUCHESS OF MALFI.

Malengin. The typification of guile in Spenser's *Faërie Queene,* V. ix. Being attacked by Sir ARTEGAL and his iron man, he turns himself first into a fox, then to a bush, then to a bird, then to a hedgehog, then to a snake; but Talus is a match for all his deceits and kills him.

Malherbe, François de (1555–1628). French poet and critic of the neo-classical period (see NEO-CLASSICISM), insisting on order, balance, simplicity, clarity, rationality, and "common sense" in poetry, opposed to the PLÉIADES. His most famous poems are *Consolation de Monsieur du Périer sur la mort de sa fille* (1598) and an *Ode* to Marie de Medici (1600). He was official court poet under Henry IV of France, and was literary dictator of France until his death. Mathurin Régnier, his contemporary, said of his poetry, "C'est proser de la rime et rimer de la prose."

Malikites. One of the four sects of SUNNITES.

Malinowski, Bronislaw Kasper (1884–1942). Polish anthropologist; lecturer in England and United States. Author of books on the sexual life of savages.

Mallarmé, Stéphane (1842–1898). French poet and teacher, leader of the school of SYMBOLISM and formulator of its aesthetic theories. Influenced by the work of BAUDELAIRE, POE, VERLAINE, and the PRE-RAPHAELITE BROTHERHOOD, Mallarmé's poetry is marked by elliptical phrases, unusual syntax, and condensed figures, each poem being built about a central symbol, idea, or metaphor and consisting of subordinate images that illustrate and help to develop the idea. THE AFTERNOON OF A FAUN (*L'Après-midi d'un faune*), THE SWAN (*Le Cygne*), HÉRODIADE, and *Le Tombeau d'Edgar Poe* (*The Tomb of Edgar Poe*) are outstanding examples of Mallarmé's method. A volume of *Poems* by him was translated into English by Roger FRY in 1936.

Malleus Maleficarum. The "Hammer of Witches" (1484) published at Cologne, "the text-book of the day on witch-craft."

Mallinger, Sir Hugo. A wealthy aristocrat in George Eliot's DANIEL DERONDA.

Mallock, William Hurrell (1849–1923). English writer, author of *The New Republic* (1877), an elaborate ROMAN À CLEF.

Malmaison. A hamlet near Paris, where the Empress Joséphine had a palace. Also, the title of a poem by Amy LOWELL.

Malmesbury, the Philosopher of. Thomas HOBBES (1588–1679), author of LEVIATHAN, so called from his birthplace.

Malone, Edmund (1741–1812). Irish Shakespearean scholar and literary critic. His conclusions regarding the order in which Shakespeare's plays were written is still for the most part accepted.

Malone, Louis, see MACNEICE, LOUIS.

Malory, Sir **Thomas** (1394?–1471). English author famous for his MORTE D'ARTHUR, completed in 1469 and printed in 1471. Little is known of Malory except his authorship of the famous romance and his escapades in the later years of his life. After having been a soldier in the Hundred Years' War and a member of Parliament (1445), he suddenly (in 1451) made his name notorious by raiding a monastery occupying land that had once belonged to him. When he was captured, he was charged with a number of crimes, including robbery and rape, and imprisoned for the remainder of his life. The *Morte d'Arthur* was written while he was in prison.

Malraux, André (1895–). French novelist, known for his Marxist beliefs (see MARXISM; MARXISM IN LITERATURE; PROLETARIAN LITERATURE) and his novels dealing dramatically with Communists in Europe and Asia in the 1920's and 1930's, considered to be written with greater technical skill and insight into character than most revolutionary fiction of the time. Among his books are *La Tentation de l'Occident* (1926), dealing with Chinese civilization; *The Royal Way* (*La Voie royale;* 1930), on archaeology in Cambodia; *La Condition humaine* (1933), translated in the U.S. as MAN'S FATE and in England as *Storm in Shanghai; Le Temps du Mépris* (1935), translated as *Days of Wrath* in the U.S., set against a background of concentration camps for political prisoners in Nazi Germany (see NAZISM); *L'Espoir* (1937), translated as *Man's Hope* in the U.S. and as *Days of Hope* in England, dealing with the Civil War in Spain (1936–1939).

Malthus, Thomas Robert (1766–1834). English economist. See MALTHUSIAN DOCTRINE.

Malthusian doctrine. A doctrine, promulgated by T. R. Malthus, especially in *An Essay on the Principle of Population* (1798), holding that population increases more than the means of increasing subsistence does, so that in time, if no check is put upon the increase of population, many must starve or all be ill fed. Applied to individual nations, it intimates that something must be done to check the increase of population, as all the land would not suffice to feed its inhabitants. The doctrine became obsolete, when—in the wake of the industrial revolution—the productive power of agriculture assumed undreamed-of dimensions.

Maltravers, Ernest, see ERNEST MALTRAVERS.

Maltz, Albert (1908–). American dramatist and novelist. His short story, *The Happiest Man on Earth,* is a study of unemployment, and won first prize in the 1938 O. Henry Memorial Volume.

Malvin, Roger, see ROGER MALVIN'S FUNERAL.

Malvolio. In Shakespeare's TWELFTH NIGHT, Olivia's steward, against whom Sir Toby Belch and Sir Andrew Aguecheek join MARIA in a trick. Maria forges a letter in the handwriting of OLIVIA, leading Malvolio to suppose that his mistress is in love with him, telling him to dress in yellow stockings and to smile on the lady. Malvolio falls into the trap, and when Olivia shows astonishment at his absurd conduct, he keeps quoting parts of the letter he has received until he is shut up in a dark room as a lunatic.

Mamamouchi. A "spoof" Turkish title or dignity invented by MOLIÈRE in his comedy *Le Bourgeois Gentilhomme,* which M. Jourdain is told has been conferred upon him by the Grand Signior. Hence, the term was sometimes used in England of a mock honor or a fantastic piece of buffoonery.

Mamba's Daughters. See under DU BOSE HEYWARD.

Mambrino. A pagan king of old romance, introduced by Ariosto into ORLANDO FURIOSO. He had a helmet of pure gold which rendered the wearer invulnerable and which was taken possession of by Rinaldo. This is frequently referred to in Cervantes' DON QUIXOTE, and we read that when the barber is caught in a shower and claps his brazen basin on his head, Don Quixote insists that this is the enchanted helmet of the Moorish king.

Mamelukes (Arab. *mamluc,* "a slave"). The slaves brought from the Caucasus to Egypt, and formed into a standing army, who, in 1254, raised one of their body to the supreme power. They reigned over Egypt until 1517, when they were overthrown by the Turkish sultan, Selim I, and the country, though nominally under a Turkish viceroy, was subsequently governed by twenty-four Mameluke beys. In 1811 the Pasha of Egypt, Mohammed Ali, by a wholesale massacre annihilated the Mamelukes.

Mamillius. A young prince of Sicilia in Shakespeare's WINTER'S TALE.

mammet or **maumet.** An idol; hence, a puppet or doll (as in *Romeo and Juliet,* iii. 5, and 1 *Henry IV,* ii. 3). The word is a corruption of *Mahomet.* Mohammedanism being the most prominent non-Christian religion with which Christendom was acquainted before the Reformation, it became a generic word to designate any false faith. Even idolatry is called *mammetry,* and in a 14th century MS. Bible (first edited by A. C. Paues, 1904) 1 *John* v. 21 reads—

> My smale children, kepe ye you from mawmetes and symulacris.

Mammon. The god of this world. The word, in Syriac, means "riches," and it occurs in the Bible (*Matt.* vi. 24, *Luke* xvi. 13): "Ye cannot serve God and mammon." Spenser (*Faërie Queene,* II. vii) and Milton (who identifies him with Vulcan or Mulciber, *Paradise Lost,* i. 738–751) both make Mammon the personification of the evils of wealth and miserliness.

> Mammon led them on—
> Mammon, the least erected Spirit that fell
> From Heaven; for even in Heaven his looks and thoughts
> Were always downward bent, admiring more
> The riches of Heaven's pavement, trodden gold,
> Than aught divine or holy.
>
> *Paradise Lost,* i, 678.

the Mammon of unrighteousness. Money; cf. *Luke* xvi. 9.

Sir Epicure Mammon. A worldly sensualist in Ben Jonson's *Alchemist.*

man. For titles beginning with *man,* see also below under separate entries.

Man Friday. A useful and faithful servant, like the Man Friday in *Robinson Crusoe.*

the Man in the Iron Mask. A mysterious individual held for over forty years as a state prisoner by Louis XIV at Pignerol and other prisons, ultimately dying in the Bastille (November 19, 1703) with his identity still undisclosed. His name was given as "Marchiali" when he was buried. Subsequently many conjectures as to the real identity of Marchiali were advanced. One possibility was General du Bulonde, who, in 1691, raised the siege of Cuneo against the order of Catinat. In 1891

Captain Bazeriès published in *Le Temps* translations of some cipher dispatches, apparently showing that this is the solution; but if it is, it can be only part of it, and Bulonde must have taken the place of some earlier masked prisoner, for *l'homme au masque de fer* was at Pignerol in 1666 and was transferred to the island of St. Marguerite twenty years later, that is well before the siege of Cuneo.

Other persons who have been suggested are:

A twin brother of Louis XIV, or, perhaps, an elder brother, whose father is given both as Cardinal Mazarin and the Duke of Buckingham.

Louis, Duc de Vermandois, natural son of Louis XIV by De la Vallière, who was imprisoned for life because he gave the Dauphin a box on the ears.

Among the less likely names that have been put forward are the Duke of Monmouth; Avedick, an Armenian Patriarch; Fouquet, the disgraced Minister of Finance; the Duc de Beaufort, who disappeared at the siege of Candia in 1669; and Mattioli's secretary, Jean de Gonzague.

Since the private papers of Louis XIV and the correspondence of his minister Louvois and Barbezieux were made available to Franz Funck-Brentano, it has become apparent that the man in the iron mask was Count Girolamo Mattioli, Minister to the Duke of Mantua, a theory now widely accepted. In 1678 he acted treacherously towards Louis in refusing to give up the fortress of Casale—the key of Italy—after signing a treaty promising to do so, and in consequence was lured on to French soil, captured, and imprisoned at Pignerol.

In 1790 the Abbé Soulavie put forth the theory that the mysterious personage was a twin brother of Louis XIV. This supposition was accepted in tragedies on the subject by Zschokke in German and Fournier in French, and in DUMAS' romance *The Iron Mask*, sometimes published separately, but originally a part of his *Vicomte de Bragelonne* (see THREE MUSKETEERS), a conspiracy to substitute the Man in the Iron Mask for his royal brother which is all but successful.

Man in the Moon. See MOON.

Man of Belial. Any wicked man. Shimei so called David (2 *Sam.* xvi. 7). The ungodly are called "children of Belial," or "sons of Belial." The word *belial* means "worthlessness."

Man of Blood. David is so called (2 *Sam.* xvi. 7). The Puritans applied the term to Charles I, because he made war against his Parliament. It is applied to any man of violence.

man of blood and iron. Otto Prince von Bismarck (1815–1898), for many years chancellor of Prussia and Germany, called "man of blood" from his great war policy, and "iron" from his indomitable will.

man of brass. TALUS.

man of December. Napoleon III. He was made President of the French Republic December 11, 1848; made his *coup d'état* December 2, 1851; and was made emperor December 2, 1852. See also MAN OF SEDAN and MAN OF SILENCE below.

Man of Destiny. Napoleon Bonaparte (b. 1761, reigned 1804–1814, d. 1821). He looked on himself as an instrument in the hands of destiny. Bernard SHAW has a play so called (1897), dealing with Napoleon.

man of letters. An author.

man of remnants. A tailor.

Man of Ross. A name given to John Kyrle (1637–1724), a native of Whitehouse in Gloucestershire. He resided the greater part of his life in the village of Ross, Herefordshire, and was famous for his benevolence and for supplying needy parishes with churches.

> Who taught that heaven-directed spire to rise?
> "The Man of Ross," each lisping babe replies.
> Pope, *Moral Essays.*

Man of Sedan. Napoleon III was so called, because he surrendered his sword to William, King of Prussia, after the battle of Sedan (Sept. 2, 1870).

Man of Silence. Napoleon III (b. 1808, reigned 1852–1870, d. 1873).

Man of Sin (2 *Thess.* ii. 3). The Roman Catholics say the Man of Sin is Antichrist. The Puritans applied the term to the Pope of Rome; the Fifth-Monarchy men to Cromwell; many modern theologians apply it to that "wicked one" (identical with the "last horn" of *Dan.* vii.) who is to immediately precede the second advent.

Man of Sorrows. Jesus Christ. Cf. *Is.* liii. 3.

man of straw. A person without capital. It used to be customary for a number of worthless fellows to loiter about the English law courts to become false witness or surety for anyone who would buy their services. Their badge was a straw in their shoes.

man of the sea, see under OLD.

Man of the Third Republic. Napoleon III.

man of the world. One "knowing" in world-craft; no greenhorn. Charles Macklin brought out a comedy (1704), and Henry Mackenzie a novel (1773) with the same title.

man of wax. A model man like one fashioned in wax. Horace speaks of the "waxen arms of Telephus," meaning model arms, or of perfect shape and color, and the nurse says of Romeo, "Why, he's a man of wax" (i. 3), which she explains by saying, "Nay, he's a flower, i' faith a very flower."

man of whipcord. A coachman.

"He would not have suffered the coachman to proceed while the horses were unfit for service. . . . Yet the man of whipcord escaped some severe . . . reproach."—Sir W. Scott, *The Antiquary,* i.

sick man of the East, see under SICK.

Man Against the Sky, The. Book and title poem by Edwin Arlington ROBINSON (1916).

Man and Superman. A comedy by George Bernard SHAW (1903), on the theme that man is the pursued, woman the pursuer. The hero is Jack Tanner. Warned by 'Enery, his chauffeur, he makes every effort but is powerless to escape the schemings of the heroine, Ann Whitfield, the instrument of the Life Force, who marries him in triumph. One act of this play presents DON JUAN in Hell.

manatee. An aquatic, herbivorous mammal. American species in waters of West Indies and near-by coasts from Florida to Yucatán. *The Manatee* is the title of a sensational novel by Nancy Bruff (1945).

Manchester. A manufacturing city of England.

the Manchester of America. Lowell, Mass., from its cotton mills.

the Manchester of Belgium. Ghent.

the Manchester of Japan. Osaka.

the Manchester of Prussia. Elberfeld.

the Manchester poet. Charles Swain (1801–1874).

Manchester Guardian, The. Famous liberal newspaper in England. Founded as a weekly in 1821.

Manchester school. A group of free-trade advocates led by Cobden and Bright, originally meeting at Manchester, England. First so called by DISRAELI in 1848.

Mancini. Family of Roman patricians. The best-known members are **Marie Mancini** (1640?–1714), the early love of Louis XIV, who became a patroness of men of letters, and her sister **Hortense Mancini** (1646?–1699), who had a liaison with Charles II of England. They were nieces of Cardinal Mazarin, who introduced them together with three other sisters to the French court. Hortense took the name and arms of Mazarin.

Manciple's or **Maunciples Tale.** One of Chaucer's CANTERBURY TALES. A manciple is a purveyor of food, a steward, or clerk of the kitchen. (Lat. *manceps, mancipis,* "a buyer, manager.") The tale is as follows: Phoebus had a crow which he taught to speak. It was white as down, and as big as a swan. He had also a wife, whom he dearly loved. One day, when he came home, the crow cried, "Cuckoo, cuckoo, cuckoo!" and Phoebus asked the bird what it meant; whereupon it told the god that his wife was unfaithful to him. Phoebus, in his wrath, seized his bow, and shot his wife through the heart, but to the bird he said, "Curse on thy telltale tongue! never more shall it brew mischief." So he deprived it of the power of speech, and changed its plumage from white to black. Moral—

My sone, bewar and be noon auctour newe,
Of tydyngs, whether they ben fals or trewe;
Wherso thou comest, amongst high or lowe,
Kep wel thy tonge and think upon the crowe.
Canterbury Tales, 17, 291–4.

The basis for this tale can be found in Ovid's *Coronis* in the *Metamorphoses,* ii. 543.

Manco Capak or **Manco Inca** (1500?–1544). Indian sovereign in Peru. Recognized by Pizarro after death of former sovereigns. Assassinated by his followers in the course of an unsuccessful revolt against the Spaniards. Named after **Manco Capak** (11th century), the traditional founder of the Peruvian Inca dynasty.

Mandalay. Title of a very popular poem by Rudyard Kipling, first published in 1892 in *Barrack-Room Ballads.*

By the old Moulmein Pagoda, lookin' eastward to the sea,
There's a Burma girl a-settin', and I know she thinks o' me;
For the wind is in the palm-trees, and the temple-bells they say:
"Come you back, you British soldier; come you back to Mandalay!" . . .

Oh, the road to Mandalay, where the flyin'-fishes play,
An' the dawn comes up like thunder outer China crost the Bay!

Mandane. The heroine of Mlle de Scudéry's romance CYRUS THE GREAT.

mandarin is not a Chinese word, but one given by the Portuguese colonists at Macao to the officials called by the natives *kwan.* It is from Malay and Hindu *mantri,* counsellor, which is related to Sans. *mantra,* counsel (man, to think).

the nine ranks of mandarins in China were distinguished by the button in their cap:—1, ruby; 2, coral; 3, sapphire; 4, an opaque blue stone; 5, crystal; 6, an opaque white shell; 7, wrought gold; 8, plain gold; and 9, silver.

The whole body of Chinese mandarins consists of twenty-seven members. They are appointed for (1) imperial birth; (2) long service; (3) illustrious deeds; (4) knowledge; (5) ability; (6) zeal; (7) nobility; and (8) aristocratic birth.—Gutzlay.

The word is sometimes used derisively for over-pompous officials.

mandate (Lat. *mandatum, mandare,* "to command"). An authoritative charge or command; in law, a contract of bailment by which the mandatory undertakes to perform gratuitously a duty regarding property committed to him. After World War I it was decided by the victorious powers that the former extra-European colonies and possessions of Germany and Turkey should be governed under *mandate* by one or other of the powers. Thus, the German colonies in West Africa and parts of the Turkish possessions became *mandatory spheres* under Great Britain, Syria under France, etc.

Manders, Parson. In Ibsen's GHOSTS, the adviser of Mrs. Alving. He has been called "the consummate flower of conventional morality."

Mandeville, Sir John (ca. 1300–1372). An explorer whose *Travels* (ca. 1357), despite their lack of veracity, or perhaps because of it, are one of the classics of travel literature. Hence, anyone who tells an exaggerated story is a *Sir John Mandeville*.

Mandrabul's offering, from gold to nothing. Mandrabul, having found a gold-mine in Samos, offered to Juno a golden ram for the discovery; the next year he gave a silver one, then a brazen one, and in the fourth year nothing.

mandrake. The root of the mandrake, or mandragora, often divides in two, and presents a rude appearance of a man. In ancient times human figures were cut out of the root, and wonderful virtues ascribed to them, such as the production of fecundity in women (*Gen.* xxx. 14–16). It was also thought that mandrakes could not be uprooted without producing fatal effects, so a cord used to be fixed to the root and round a dog's neck, and the dog, being chased, drew out the mandrake and died. Another fallacy was that a small dose made a person vain of his beauty, and a large one made him an idiot; and yet another, that when the mandrake is uprooted it utters a scream, in explanation of which Thomas Newton, in his *Herball to the Bible,* says, "It is supposed to be a creature having life, engendered under the earth of the seed of some dead person put to death for murder." "Ferdie," by F. Anstey GUTHRIE, is a short story on this theme.

> Shrieks like mandrakes, torn out of the earth.
> Shakespeare, *Romeo and Juliet,* iv. 3.

From the old notion that they excited amorous inclinations, mandrakes were also called *love apples;* hence, Venus is called *Mandragoritis,* and the Emperor Julian, in his epistles, tells Calixenes that he drank its juice nightly as a love-potion.

MACHIAVELLI wrote a comedy with the title *Mandragola* (*Mandrake*).

he has eaten mandrake. Said of a very indolent and sleepy man, from the narcotic and stupefying properties of the plant, well known to the ancients.

Mandricardo. In Boiardo's and Ariosto's ORLANDO poems, the son of Agrican, who laid siege to Albracca because he was in love with Angelica. He was slain by Orlando.

manes, to appease his. To do, when a person is dead, what would have pleased him or was due to him when alive. The spirit or ghost of the dead was by the Romans called his *manes.* It never slept quietly in the grave so long as survivors left its wishes unfulfilled. February 19 was the day when all the living sacrificed to the shades of dead relations and friends—a kind of non-Christian ALL SOULS' DAY.

Manet, Édouard (1832–1883). French painter, originator and leader of IMPRESSIONISM in painting.

Manetho. Egyptian priest and historian of the third century B.C. Wrote in his (Greek) history of Egypt the most accurate annals of that ancient civilization, down to the arrival of Alexander the Great. Only fragments of his work are extant.

Manette, Dr. A character in Dickens' TALE OF TWO CITIES. He has been imprisoned eighteen years, and has gradually lost his memory. After his release he somewhat recovers it, but any train of thought connected with his prison life produces a relapse. While in prison, the doctor made shoes, and whenever the relapse occurs, his desire for cobbling returns.

Lucie Manette. The heroine of the novel, daughter of Dr. Manette. She marries Charles DARNAY.

> Lucie Manette had a forehead with the singular capacity of lifting and knitting itself into an expression that was not quite one of perplexity or wonder or alarm, or merely of bright fixed attention, though it included all the four expressions.—*A Tale of Two Cities,* i. 4.

Manfred. (1) Count Manfred, the hero of Byron's dramatic poem of this name (1817), sells himself to the Prince of Darkness, is wholly without human sympathies, and lives in splendid solitude among the Alps. He once loved the Lady ASTARTE, who dies. Manfred goes to the hall of Arimanes to see her, and is told that he will die the following day. This prophecy is fulfilled.

(2) Prince of Otranto and the central figure in Horace Walpole's CASTLE OF OTRANTO.

Man from Glengarry, The. A novel by Ralph Connor (*Can.,* 1901). The hero, Ranald Macdonald, grows up in a Canadian lumber camp, whose feuds he inherits but learns to overcome. He becomes at last the manager of a great coal and lumber company.

Mangan, James Clarence (1803–1849). Irish poet. *Dark Rosaleen* and the autobiographical ballad *The Nameless One* with its tragic theme are his best-known poems.

Mangin, Charles Marie Emmanuel (1866–1925). French general. Commanded defense of Verdun (1916), and the offensive along Chemin des Dames (1917) which halted the German advance.

Manhattan. The island on which the city of New York was first founded, purchased in 1626 by the Dutch from the Manhattan Indians for $24. It is one of the boroughs of New York City and contains the leading banking and commercial organizations of the city, as well as fashion and art centers, the chief theatrical district of the nation, wealthy residential sections, and such well-known districts as BROADWAY, the BOWERY, GREENWICH VILLAGE, HARLEM, and WALL STREET. Manhattan is usually taken to symbolize the complexity and teeming activity of New York City as a whole.

Manhattan Transfer. A novel by John Dos PASSOS (1925), making early use of a technique later developed and used to great effect in U.S.A. It presents a picture of life in New York City during the 1920's through passages of impressionistic description and the simultaneous stories of several people from varying levels of society. Among these characters are Bud Korpenning, a young man from the country who fails in the city and commits suicide; Joe Harland, a Wall Street gambler, who loses his fortune and becomes a beggar; Jimmy Herf, Harland's nephew, who is a journalist, is divorced by his actress wife, and leaves the city to begin over elsewhere; Ellen Thatcher Ogelthorpe, Jimmy's former wife, who is a successful actress but loses the man she loves and is unable to find happiness; Joe O'Keefe, a labor organizer; Congo Jake, a bootlegger; George Baldwin, a politician; and others.

Mani. The moon, in Scandinavian mythology, the son of Mundilfoeri, taken to heaven by the gods to drive the moon-car. He is followed by a wolf, which, when time is no more, will devour both Mani and his sister Sol.

Mani, Manes, or **Manichaeus.** The founder of Manichaeanism, born in Persia probably about 216, prominent at the court of Sapor I (240–272), but crucified by the Magians in 277.

Manichaeans or **Manichees.** The followers of MANI, who taught that the universe is controlled by two antagonistic powers, viz., light or goodness (identified with God), and darkness, chaos, or evil. The system was the old Babylonian nature-worship modified by Christian and Persian influences, and its own influence on the Christian religion was, even as late as the 13th century, deep and widespread. The headquarters of Manichaeanism were for many centuries at Babylon, and later at Samarkand.

manifest destiny. A slogan used by the politicians in the imperialistic wave that swept the U.S. after the Spanish War. Under pressure of this philosophy of "expansion willed by destiny," the U.S. acquired the Philippines, Puerto Rico, and Cuba. The phrase as such can be traced back at least as far as 1845. Its use at the close of the nineteenth century inspired such poems (not in its favor) as Richard Hovey's *Unmanifest Destiny* and William Vaughn Moody's *On a Soldier Fallen in the Philippines.*

Manilius, Marcus or **Gaius.** Roman poet of the time of the beginning of the Christian era, reputedly the author of the learned astrological poem *Astronomica* in five books. A. E. HOUSMAN was an authority on Manilius.

Man in Black. A character in Goldsmith's *Citizen of the World* (1759), said to be meant for Goldsmith's father. He is a true oddity, with the tongue of a Timon and the heart of an Uncle Toby. He declaims against beggars, but relieves everyone he meets; he ridicules generosity, but would share his last cloak with the needy. Washington IRVING wrote a tale called *The Man in Black*. A clergyman is frequently so called.

manitou. A great spirit of the American Indians. The word is Algonquin, and means either the great good spirit or the great evil spirit. The former they call *Gitche-Manito,* and the latter *Matche-Manito.* The good spirit is symbolized by an egg, and the evil one by a serpent. (Longfellow, *Hiawatha,* xiv.)

Manley, Mary de la Rivière (1663?–1724). English playwright and political pamphleteer of doubtful reputation. Remembered as author of *Secret Memoirs and Manners of Several Persons of Quality of Both Sexes from the New Atalantis,* usually known as *The New Atalantis.* Succeeded Swift as editor of *Examiner* (1711). Author of plays and an autobiography.

Manly. The chief character of Wycherly's PLAIN DEALER (1674), a comedy based to some extent upon Molière's MISANTHROPE. Manly is an honest, surly sea-captain, who thinks everyone a rascal, and believes himself to be no better. "Counterfeit honors," says Manly, "will not be current with me. I weigh the man, not his titles. 'Tis not the king's stamp can make the metal better or heavier."

Mann, Horace (1796–1859). American educator. Introduced new methods and ideas in public-school organization and teaching. Elected to American Hall of Fame (1900). The Horace Mann School in New York City is named in his honor.

Mann, Thomas (1875–). German scholar and novelist, known for his studies of the psychology of the artist and the artist's relation to society, especially the industrial society of the 20th century, and for his extensive use of philosophic symbolism. His writings show a strong influence from 19th-century German romanticism, especially as expressed in the intellectual systems of NIETZSCHE, SCHOPENHAUER, Richard WAGNER, and Sigmund

FREUD. The decadence of the 20th-century world, the artist regarded as an abnormality or a social aberration, and death as a symbol of the aesthetic life, play an important part in Mann's works, which include BUDDENBROOKS (1901); *Fiorenza* (1906), a play; *Royal Highness* (*Königliche Hoheit;* 1909); DEATH IN VENICE (*Der Tod in Venedig;* 1912); *A Man and His Dog* (*Herr und Hund;* 1918); THE MAGIC MOUNTAIN (*Der Zauberberg;* 1924); *Children and Fools* (1928); *Tristan* (1929); MARIO AND THE MAGICIAN (*Mario und der Zauberer;* 1930); TONIO KRÖGER (1931); *Past Masters* (1933), a collection of essays; a series of novels dealing symbolically with the Biblical character of JOSEPH, including *Die Geschichten Jakobs* (1933; translated as *Joseph and His Brothers*), *Young Joseph* (*Der Junge Joseph;* 1934), and *Joseph in Egypt* (*Joseph in Ägypten;* 1936); *Stories of Three Decades* (1936), a collection of short stories from earlier sources; *Freud, Goethe, and Wagner* (1937), critical essays; *The Coming Victory of Democracy* (1938), a lecture on politics delivered on a nation-wide tour of the U.S.; *This Peace* (1938), an essay on European politics of the period following the MUNICH CRISIS; *Lotte in Weimar* (1940), translated as THE BELOVED RETURNS; *This War* (1940), an essay on World War II; *The Transposed Heads* (*Die vertauschten Köpfe;* 1941), a novel on a Hindu theme; *Order of the Day* (1942), a collection of political speeches.

With James JOYCE and Marcel PROUST, Thomas Mann is considered among the greatest novelists of the 20th century. He was awarded the Nobel Prize for literature in 1929. In 1933, after a political disagreement with the National Socialist government of Germany, he decided to stay in Switzerland where he happened to be on a visit. He came to the U.S., where he taught at Princeton University and endorsed a variety of liberal causes; during the 1930's he was a particular favorite among American liberal groups and wrote a number of essays denouncing FASCISM and NAZISM. Later he took up residence in Hollywood.

Heinrich Mann (1871–   ), elder brother of Thomas Mann, liberal in political views at an earlier period than Thomas and long international in his viewpoint, also became known as a novelist, devoting himself especially to a portrayal of social life in Germany before and after World War I.

Erika Mann (1905–   ) and *Klaus Mann* (1906–   ), two of Thomas Mann's children, also fled from Germany to the U.S. and were active in liberal causes and writings attacking Nazism.

Mannerheim, Baron **Carl Gustaf Emil von** (1867–   ). Field Marshal of Finland (1933). Supervised construction of the Mannerheim Line. Commanded Finnish army against Russia (1939). Made alliance with Germany (1941). Armistice with U.S.S.R. and Great Britain (1944). Acting president of Finland (Nov., 1945); resigned for reasons of ill health (March, 1946).

Mannering, Guy, see GUY MANNERING.

Julia Mannering. Heroine of Scott's *Guy Mannering,* the daughter of Guy. She marries Captain Bertram.

Mannering, Mary. Stage name of **Florence Friend** (1876–   ). English actress. Appeared under Daniel Frohman's management. Married James K. Hackett.

Manners, Dorothy. The heroine of Churchill's RICHARD CARVEL.

Mannes, David (1866–   ). American violinist. Brother-in-law of Walter DAMROSCH. Director, David Mannes Music School.

Mannin, Ethel (1900–   ). English novelist and essayist. Joined Independent Labor Party (1932). One of her best-known novels, *Venetian Blinds* (1933), is a study of working class life.

Manning, William Thomas (1866–   ). English-born Protestant Episcopal bishop of New York (1921–1946).

Mannon, Ezra, Christine, Lavinia, Orin. See MOURNING BECOMES ELECTRA.

Mannyng, Robert or **Robert de Brunne** (fl. 1288–1338). English chronicler and poet. Author of *Handlyng Synne* (ca. 1300), a free version of a French original, of great linguistic importance.

Manoa. The fabulous capital of EL DORADO, the houses of which were roofed with gold.

Man of Feeling, The. The title of a novel (1771) by Henry Mackenzie (1745–1831), also used as a nickname for the author. His "man of feeling" is named Harley—a sensitive, bashful, kind-hearted, sentimental hero. It is said that this novel was a particular favorite with Robert BURNS.

Man of Law's Tale or **Mannes Tale of Lawe.** One of Chaucer's CANTERBURY TALES. See also CUNSTANCE. The Man of Law is perhaps best described in the following well-known lines:

> A Sergeant of the Lawe, war and wys. . . .
> No-wher so bisy a man as he ther was,
> And yet he seemed bisier than he was.
> Chaucer, *Prologue to the Canterbury Tales.*

man-of-war bird, see FRIGATE BIRD.

Man on Horseback. General Boulanger (1837–1891); so called because he usually appeared mounted. See BOULANGISM. Hence, any unexpected leader.

Manon Lescaut. A novel by the Abbé PRÉVOST (1731). It is the history of a young man, the Chevalier des Grieux, possessed of many brilliant and some estimable qualities, but, being intoxicated by a fatal attachment to Manon, a girl who prefers luxury to faithful love, he is hurried into the violation of every rule of conduct. The novel is the basis of an opera by PUCCINI entitled *Manon Lescaut* (1893) and Massenet's more frequently performed *Manon*.

Manrico. In Verdi's opera, IL TROVATORE, the supposed son of Azucena the gipsy, but in reality the son of Garzia.

Mansart or **Mansard, François** (1598–1666). French architect. Designer of many buildings in Paris. Credited with invention of the mansard roof, which at any rate owes its general use to him.

Man's Fate. American translation of *La Condition Humaine,* the best-known novel of André MALRAUX (1933). It deals with revolutionary and counter-revolutionary activities in China in 1926 and dramatically portrays the psychology of the revolutionists, who live and die in violence, forcing from each moment as much as they can and eschewing all thought of a personal future, in accordance with their belief that their acts of terrorism and their individual sacrifices will win a better future for society.

Mansfield, Katherine. Pseudonym of **Kathleen,** *née* **Beauchamp, Murry** (1888–1923). British short-story writer, born in New Zealand, a cousin of the novelist ELIZABETH and wife of J. M. MURRY. She is considered one of the most important short-story writers of the 20th century. Her work, influenced by that of Anton CHEKHOV, is marked by psychological penetration, sensitivity of perception, a particular sympathy for and understanding of children, irony and pathos, a subtlety of technique by which the significance of the story is compressed in and often implied by a single incident, and a precise, delicate style at times suggestive of the poetry of IMAGISM. It has been pointed out that the popular type of "sketch" standardized by the magazine THE NEW YORKER is derived in large degree from the work of Katherine Mansfield. Her books of short stories include: *In a German Pension* (1911); *Bliss* (1920); *The Garden Party* (1922); *The Doves' Nest* (1923); *Something Childish* (1924), known in the U.S. as *The Little Girl; The Aloe* (1930). BLISS, THE DOVES' NEST, and THE GARDEN PARTY are among her best-known single stories. *Novels and Novelists* (1930) is a collection of her criticism, and her *Journal* (1927), *Letters* (1929), and *Scrapbook* (1939) were edited by her husband.

Katherine Mansfield was extremely sensitive and at times morbid in temperament and suffered from tuberculosis, from which she eventually died, during the latter years of her life. She never fully recovered from the shock of her brother's death in World War I. She was associated with Murry in editing a number of LITTLE MAGAZINES, including *The Blue Review, Signature* (for which she wrote under the name of Matilda Barry), and the *Athenaeum*. She was also a friend of D. H. LAWRENCE, Aldous HUXLEY, and Virginia WOOLF, and is said to be represented by the characters of Gudrun in Lawrence's WOMEN IN LOVE and Beatrice GILRAY in Huxley's POINT COUNTER POINT.

Mansfield, The Miller of. The old ballad (given in Percy's *Reliques*) tells how Henry II, having lost his way, meets a miller, who takes him home to his cottage. Next morning the courtiers reach the King, and the miller discovers the rank of his guest, who, in merry mood, knights his host as "Sir John Cockle." On St. George's Day, Henry II invites the miller, his wife and son, to a royal banquet, and after being amused by their rustic ways, makes Sir John "overseer of Sherwood Forest, with a salary of £300 a year."

Mansfield, Richard (1854–1907). English actor, born in Berlin. On English stage (1877–1882); on American stage (from 1882). Famous as Cyrano in Rostand's CYRANO DE BERGERAC and the dual rôles in Stevenson's DR. JEKYLL AND MR. HYDE.

Mansfield Park. A novel by Jane AUSTEN (1814). Due to the persuasions of the hateful bullying "Aunt Norris," perhaps the most celebrated character in the book, the heroine, Fanny Price, is adopted into the family of her rich uncle, Sir Thomas Bertram. Here she falls in love with her cousin, Edmund Bertram, a young clergyman. Fanny's life as a poor relation is anything but agreeable; she becomes accustomed to the comforts of life but is constantly patronized and taken advantage of. Edmund is uniformly kind to Fanny, but is irresistibly drawn to Mary Crawford, a girl of decidedly worldly interests who mocks at the church, but nevertheless returns his love. Her brother Harry Crawford makes love to Maria Bertram and, after Maria's marriage, to Fanny, but finally elopes with Maria. This incident causes Edmund to break away from Mary Crawford, and he and Fanny are now happily married.

Manship, Paul (1885–). American sculptor. Bronze statue of Lincoln as a young man in Fort Wayne, Indiana.

Mantalini, Madame. A fashionable milliner in Dickens' NICHOLAS NICKLEBY, near Cavendish Square. Her husband, whose original name was "Muntle," noted for his white teeth, minced oaths, and gorgeous morning gown, is an exquisite man-doll, who lives on his wife's earnings, and ultimately goes to "the demnition bow-wows." Hence a husband supported in luxury by his wife is a *Mantalini*.

Mantegna, Andrea (1431–1506). Italian historical painter and engraver of great influence on Raphael and the entire subsequent development of Italian renaissance art as also on Dürer and Holbein. Decorated the Belvedere Chapel in Rome at the behest of Pope Innocent VIII; executed murals at Padua; etc. Some of his cartoons are in Hampton Court, the Louvre, the National Gallery in London, the Vienna Museum, the Venice Academy, the New York Historical Society collection, and the Metropolitan Museum of New York.

Mantell, Robert Bruce (1854–1928). Scottish-born actor. In American melodramas (from 1884) and later in Shakespearean rôles.

Man that Corrupted Hadleyburg, The. A story by Mark TWAIN (1899), in which greed corrupts an entire town.

Mantle, (Robert) Burns (1873–1948). American journalist and dramatic critic. Editor (from 1919) of *Best Plays and Year Book of the Drama in America*.

Mantle of Fidelity. A curious garment described in the old ballad *The Boy and the Mantle* in PERCY's *Reliques* "which would become no wife that was not leal." Queen GUINEVERE tries it, but it changes from green to red, and red to black, and seems rent into shreds. Sir Kay's lady tries it, but fares no better; others follow, but only Sir Cradock's wife can wear it. The theme is a very common one in old story, and was used by Spenser in the incident of FLORIMEL's girdle.

Mantrap. A novel by Sinclair LEWIS (1926).

Mantuan Bard. See under BARD.

Manu. Literally, "man." In Hindu mythology, one of a class of progenitors of mankind. The seventh Manu, from whom stem all men now living, is comparable to Noah in that he survived the deluge in an ark.

Manuel, Count. The hero of Cabell's FIGURES OF EARTH. In the Preface the author quotes an imaginary historian as commenting, "Where Manuel faces the world, JURGEN considers the universe . . . Dom Manuel is the Achilles of Poictesme as Jurgen is its Ulysses." Manuel is the father of Melicent, the heroine of DOMNEI, of Dorothy la Desirée, beloved by Jurgen in the novel of that title, and of Ettare, the heroine of THE CREAM OF THE JEST, as well as of Emmerich, his successor in POICTESME; through his love affair with ALIANORA he is supposedly the ancestor of the Plantagenet kings of England.

Manutius, Aldus. Italian form **Aldo** or **Teobaldo Manucci** (1450–1515). Italian printer and classical scholar. Credited with twenty-eight editions of classical authors and extensive introductions to each. Brought out the first book printed in Greek letters and was the first to use Italic type. See ALDINE EDITIONS.

Man Who Died Twice, The. Long blank-verse poem by Edwin Arlington ROBINSON (1924).

Man Who Laughs, The (L'Homme qui Rit). A historical romance by Victor HUGO (1869). In childhood the hero, Gwynplaine, was deliberately disfigured by cuts made upward from both sides of his mouth as far as the ears, which left him a monster with a horrible grin. Strangely enough, it is his very deformity that appeals to the fancy of the Duchess Josiana, a wilful, temperamental being who scorns the love of ordinary men and desires "either a god or a monster." Gwynplaine is loved also by the blind Dea whom he found in the snow in her infancy and who has grown up to trust and adore him. Only in her love does he find the wholesome element he needs to withstand Josiana; when she dies, he takes his own life.

Man Who Was, The. One of KIPLING's best-known short stories, published in *Life's Handicap* (1891) and later dramatized. The man is a mere "limp heap of rags" who responds to a number, speaks in disconnected fashion of life in Siberia, and seems vaguely to recognize the regiment of the White Hussars. In the regimental records under date of "Sebastopol 1854," Lt. Austin Limmason is marked missing. The man recognizes his name but lives only a few days.

Man Who Would Be King, The. A short story by Rudyard KIPLING in his volume called *The Phantom Rickshaw* (1889). By natural white man's shrewdness Daniel Dravot sets himself up as god and king in Kafristan, dividing the kingdom with his servant, Peachey Carnehan. A woman discovers that he is human and betrays him. Peachey escapes to tell the tale, but Dravot is killed.

Man with the Hoe, The. The best-known poem of Edwin MARKHAM inspired by MILLET's celebrated painting of that title.

Man Without a Country, The. A story by E. E. HALE (1863), concerning Philip Nolan, an apocryphal U.S. Navy officer involved in the treason of Aaron Burr. His expressed desire never to hear the name of his country again is carried out, and for fifty-five years Nolan goes from one vessel to another in his lonely exile, never permitted to see a newspaper or book containing any reference to the United States or to hear it mentioned in conversation. There is a sequel entitled *Philip Nolan's Friends.* Walter DAMROSCH composed an opera on this subject and with this name.

Manxman, The. A novel by Sir Hall CAINE (1894). A Manxman is a native of the Isle of Man.

Manzoni, Alessandro Francesco Tommaso Antonio (1785–1873). Italian poet, novelist and dramatist of the romantic school. Best-known for his novel *I Promessi Sposi* (1825–1826; translated into English as *The Betrothed Lovers*), a historical study of 17th-century Milan, which Sir Walter Scott called "the best ever written." Giuseppe VERDI honored his memory in his *Manzoni Requiem* (1874).

Maori. Literally, "native, indigenous." One of the aborigines of New Zealand, a brave and warlike people, noted for their poetic nature myths. The Maori were formerly cannibals.

Mao Tse-tung (1893–1940). Chinese scholar and Communist leader. President of the first Chinese Peasants' Union, (1927); took part in the "Long March" (1934–1936). Active in the war against Japan (from 1937).

Map, Walter (1140?–?1209). English medieval author and satirist. Member of the court of Henry II and archdeacon of Oxford (from 1197). Author of *De Nugis Curialium* (*Courtiers' Triflings;* ca. 1182–1192), a satirical notebook of daily events and court gossip. He has been credited with the linking of the Arthurian legends to the stories of the Holy Grail and is reputed to be the author of a lost Latin romance of *Lancelot du Lac* on which later accounts are based. Also an older version of the drinking song, "Meum est propositum in tabernam mori," is attributed to him.

Maqueda. One of the names of the Queen of SHEBA.

maquis. French guerrilla fighters in the underground resistance movement in France during the German occupation in World War II. The word stands properly for the copselike growths of shrubs along the Mediterranean coasts, which are like our chaparral and suggest hiding.

Mar, Helen. Heroine of Jane Porter's SCOTTISH CHIEFS. She is carried off to France but is rescued by Bruce and William Wallace.

Marah, (*Heb.,* "bitter"), **the waters of.** Bitterness of spirit, from the spring into which the powdered dust of the GOLDEN CALF was put as a punishment for the Children of Israel.

maranatha (*Syriac,* "the Lord will come"—i.e., to execute judgment). A word which, with ANATHEMA, occurs in 1 *Cor.* xvi. 22, and has been erroneously taken as a form of anathematizing among the Jews; hence, used for a terrible curse.

Marat, Jean Paul (1743–1793). Swiss-born French politician. At the beginning of the Revolution he published the paper *L'Ami du Peuple* (1798), in which he advocated a republican form of government. With DANTON and ROBESPIERRE he overthrew the Girondists. Assassinated in his bath by Charlotte CORDAY (July 13, 1793).

Marathon. A plain in Attica, northeast of Athens. Site of the Greek victory over the Persians (490 B. C.) which ended Darius' Greek ambitions. According to tradition, the news of the victory was brought back to Athens by a runner whose feat is commemorated in the modern marathon races, usually fixed at 26 miles, 385 yards.

Marble, Alice (1913–). American tennis champion.

Marble Faun, The. A novel by Nathaniel HAWTHORNE (1860). The scene is laid in Rome. The "faun" is Count Donatello, a happy carefree being who resembles the Faun of Praxiteles and who might, the author half suggests, be found to have furry ears if the wind should blow his curls aside. Enraged because the beautiful and mysterious art student, Miriam, is constantly annoyed by a monk named Antonio, who seems to have some evil hold on her, in an impulsive moment Donatello throws Antonio over the Tarpeian rock. The secret knowledge of crime slowly changes the light-hearted Donatello into a wretched victim of conscience, and he finally gives himself up to justice. Meantime another art student, Hilda, who has accidentally witnessed the murder which she can neither reveal nor forget, endures untold torments from her New England conscience and finds it impossible to work until she at last seeks relief in the Catholic confessional. Hilda marries Kenyon, a New England sculptor who has been a spectator of much of the drama, and Miriam disappears.

Marc, Franz. See BLAUE REITER.

Marcella. (1) A fair shepherdess whose story forms an episode in DON QUIXOTE (II. ii. 4, 5). She is "the most beautiful creature ever sent into the world," and every bachelor who sees her falls madly in love with her, but she declines every suit. One of her lovers, Chrysostom, the favorite of the village, dies of disappointed hope, and the shepherds write on his tombstone: "From Chrysostom's fate, learn to abhor Marcella, that common enemy of man, whose beauty and cruelty are both in the extreme."

(2) A novel by Mrs. Humphry WARD (1894). The heroine refuses to marry the young nobleman Aldous Raeburn because of her ardor for social reform, but changes her mind after some years spent in London. In a sequel, *Sir George Tressady* (1896), Aldous Raeburn has become

a prominent statesman. Tressady falls in love with Marcella, but she succeeds in keeping the relationship one of friendship only.

Marcellus. In Shakespeare's HAMLET, an officer of Denmark, to whom the ghost of the murdered King appears before it presents itself to Prince Hamlet.

March, Basil and **Isabel.** Prominent characters in several of the novels of W. D. HOWELLS, notably in THEIR WEDDING JOURNEY, A HAZARD OF NEW FORTUNES and THEIR SILVER WEDDING JOURNEY. According to D. G. Cooke, "Howells has incarnated in them his ideal of the normal male and female." Basil March is an American journalist of pleasant, kindly, unassuming nature with a drily humorous outlook on life. His wife, Isabel, for all her illogical and "contrary" feminine traits and her dangerous love of match-making, is a warm-hearted woman, combining both idealism and common sense. The Marches are sufficiently detached in temper to allow the author to use them, for the most part, as observers and commentators on the life about them, but they assume a somewhat more active rôle in *A Hazard of New Fortunes,* in which Basil goes to New York to become the editor of *Every Other Week.*

March, Fredric (1897–). American actor. Married (since 1927) to the actress **Florence Eldridge** (1901–). Acted in *The Skin of Our Teeth; A Bell for Adano;* also in motion pictures. Received award of Academy of Motion Picture Arts and Sciences (1932).

March, Joseph Moncure (1899–). American poet; author of the "hard-boiled" staccato stories in verse *The Wild Party* (1928) and *The Set-Up* (1928).

March, Meg, Jo, Beth and **Amy.** The four girl heroines of Louisa May Alcott's LITTLE WOMEN.

March, Ursula. The heroine of Craik's JOHN HALIFAX, GENTLEMAN.

March, William. Pseudonym of **William Edward March Campbell** (1894–). American novelist and short-story writer. *Company K* (1933); *Some Like Them Short* (1939); etc.

Marchbanks, Eugene. An ardent young poet in Shaw's CANDIDA.

march. Boundary. Cf. German *Ostmark,* etc. In English history, the *Welsh marches.*

March hare. See under HARE.

Marchioness, the. The half-starved girl-of-all-work in Dickens' OLD CURIOSITY SHOP. As she has no name of her own Dick Swiveller calls her the "Marchioness" when she plays cards with him, because it seems "more real and pleasant" to play with a Marchioness than with a domestic slavey. When Dick Swiveller is turned away and falls sick, the Marchioness nurses him, and he afterwards marries her.

Marcia. Heroine of Addison's drama *Cato* (1713), beloved both by Sempronius and by Juba.

Marck, William de la. In Scott's QUENTIN DURWARD, a French nobleman, called "The Wild Boar of Ardennes" (*Sanglier des Ardennes*).

Marco Bozzaris. A heroic ballad by Fitz-Greene Halleck (*Am.,* 1790–1820) on the last battle of the Greek hero, Bozzaris. It begins:

> At midnight, in his guarded tent
> The Turk was dreaming of the hour
> When Greece, her knee in suppliance bent
> Should tremble at his power.

Marco Millions. A play concerning Marco Polo by Eugene O'NEILL (1928).

Marconi, Marchese **Guglielmo** (1874–1937). Italian electrical engineer and inventor. First successful experiments with wireless telegraphy (1895); erected first wireless station near La Spezia, Italy (1897); sent and received signals across English Channel (1898) and across the Atlantic (1901). Nobel prize for physics (1909; with K. F. Braun).

Marco Polo. See MESSER MARCO POLO; POLO, MARCO.

Marcus Aurelius. Original name **Marcus Annius Verus** (121–180). Roman emperor (161–180) and stoic philosopher. Author (in Greek) of the collection of philosophical precepts *The Meditations of Marcus Antoninus.*

Mardi. An allegorical romance by Herman MELVILLE (1849).

Mardi Gras (*Fr.,* "fat Tuesday"). The last day of the Lent carnival in France, Shrove Tuesday, which is celebrated with all sorts of festivities. In Paris a fat ox used to be paraded through the principal streets, crowned with a fillet, and accompanied by mock priests and a band of tin instruments in imitation of a Roman sacrificial procession. In the U.S., New Orleans is famed for its Mardi Gras celebration.

mare clausum (*Lat.,* "a closed sea"). A sea that is closed by a certain political power or certain political powers to the unrestricted trade of other nations, as the Black Sea; the free and open sea is called *mare liberum.* John SELDEN in 1635 published a treatise with the title *Mare Clausum.*

Mare Nostrum. A novel by Vicente BLASCO IBÁÑEZ (1918). The title means "our sea," a phrase used by Italians of the Mediterranean.

Margaret. The heroine of Goethe's FAUST. Faust first encounters her on her return from church, falls in love with her, and seduces her. Overcome with shame, Margaret destroys the infant to which she gives birth, and is condemned to death. Faust attempts to save her, and, gaining admission to her cell, finds her huddled up on a bed of straw, singing wild snatches of ancient ballads, her reason faded, and her death at hand. Faust tries to persuade the mad girl to flee with him, but in vain. MEPHISTOPHELES, passionless and grim, arrives to hurry them both to their spiritual ruin, but Margaret calls upon the judgment seat of God. When Mephistopheles says, "She is judged," voices from above answer, "Is saved." She ascends to heaven, as Faust disappears with Mephistopheles. Margaret is often called by the pet diminutive Gretchen, and in Gounod's opera, *Faust* (1859), and Boïto's opera, *Mefistofele* (1868), both based on Goethe's *Faust*, she appears as Marguerite.

Margaret, Lady. Heroine of Scott's LAY OF THE LAST MINSTREL.

Margaret, St. See under SAINTS.

Margaret of Anjou (1430–1482). Queen of King Henry VI of England. She appears in Scott's ANNE OF GEIERSTEIN and presents herself, disguised as a mendicant, to Philipson, i.e., the Earl of Oxford.

Margaret of Valois. Known as **Queen Margot** (1553–1615). Daughter of Henry II of France and Catherine de Médicis. Married (1572) Henry of Navarre (later Henry IV of France) just before St. Bartholomew's day. Divorced (1599). Known as much for her beauty and learning as for her loose living. Author of *Mémoires* (first published 1628) and *Lettres*.

Margaret Ogilvy. A biography of his mother by J. M. BARRIE (1896). He calls her by her maiden name, according to the old Scotch custom.

Margause, see MORGAUSE.

Marguerite. Heroine of Gounod's opera *Faust* and Boïto's *Mefistofele;* the same as MARGARET in Goethe's *Faust*.

marguerite des marguerites (the pearl of pearls). So François called his sister, Marguerite de Valois (1492–1549), authoress of the *Heptameron*. She married twice: first, the Duc d'Alençon, and then Henri d'Albret, king of Navarre, and was the mother of Henry IV of France. She is a prominent character in Meyerbeer's opera, THE HUGUENOTS.

Sylvius de la Haye published (1547) a collection of her poems with the title *Marguerites de la marguerite des princesses,* etc.

Margutte. In Pulci's MORGANTE MAGGIORE, a low-minded, vulgar giant, ten feet high, with enormous appetite and of the grossest sensuality. He dies of laughter on seeing a monkey pulling on his boots. Leigh HUNT refers to him as the first unmitigated blackguard in history and the greatest no less than the first.

Maria. (1) In Sterne's SENTIMENTAL JOURNEY, a fair, quick-witted, amiable maiden, whose banns were forbidden by the curate who published them; in consequence of which she lost her reason, and used to sit by the roadside near Moulines, playing vesper hymns to the Virgin all day long.

(2) In Shakespeare's LOVE'S LABOR'S LOST, a lady in attendance on the Princess of France. Longaville, a young lord in the suite of Ferdinand, King of Navarre, asks her to marry him, but she defers her answer for twelve months.

(3) In Shakespeare's TWELFTH NIGHT, the waiting-woman of the Countess Olivia.

(4) In Cervantes' DON QUIXOTE, Sancho Panza's wife, Maria Theresa, is sometimes called Maria and sometimes Theresa.

(5) In Ernest Hemingway's FOR WHOM THE BELL TOLLS, a young Spanish girl accompanying the band of guerrilla soldiers in the mountains who cannot forget her horrifying experiences in the war, during which her mother and father were killed and she herself was raped by the Fascist soldiers. She and Robert JORDAN fall in love, and she is completely devoted to him, responding intensely to his slightest desire.

Maria, Black. See under BLACK.

Maria Chapdelaine. See HÉMON, LOUIS.

María Cristina (1858–1929). Austrian princess, wife of Alfonso XII of Spain, and queen regent (1885–1902) for her son Alfonso XIII. During her regency the Spanish-American War (1898) deprived Spain of her American possessions.

Maria d'Aquino. Object of the love of BOCCACCIO, who first saw her in church and whom she later betrayed. All of his works up to the *Ninfale Fiesolano* were inspired in one way or another by this love affair, and the character of Criseida in IL FILOSTRATO, the source of Chaucer's version of the TROILUS legend, is considered to have been drawn to a great extent from Maria herself. See also FIAMMETTA.

Mariage de Figaro, Le, ou La folle Journée à la Mode. A comedy by Beaumarchais (1784), the story of which is a continuation of THE BARBER OF SEVILLE and forms the basis of Mozart's *Nozze di Figaro*. See FIGARO.

Mariage forcé, Le (The Enforced Marriage). A comedy by MOLIÈRE (1664) in which Louis XIV appeared as a gipsy. The chief character is SGANARELLE.

Mariamne. A Jewish princess, daughter of Alexander and wife of HEROD THE GREAT. Mariamne was the mother of Alexander and Aristobulus, with both of whom she was put to death in a fit of jealousy by Herod, who then fell into a state of morbid madness in which he fancied he saw Mariamne and heard her asking for her sons. This story has been made the subject of several tragedies: Alexandre Hardy's *Mariamne* (1610); Piere Tristan l'Ermite's *Mariamne* (1637); Voltaire's *Mariamne* (1724); and in more modern times, Friedrich Hebbel's *Herodes und Mariamne* (*Ger.*, 1850); and Stephen Phillips' *Herod and Mariamne* (*Engl.*, 1900).

Mariana. In Shakespeare's MEASURE FOR MEASURE, a lovely and lovable lady, married to Angelo, deputy Duke of Vienna, by civil contract, but not by religious rites. After he abandons her, she passes her sorrowful hours "at the moated grange." Thus the Duke says to Isabella,

> Haste you speedily to Angelo. . . . I will presently to St. Luke's. There, at the moated grange, resides the dejected Mariana.—Act iii. sc. 1.

TENNYSON wrote a poem in two parts, *Mariana* and *Mariana in the South* (1830–1832) enlarging upon the woes of the dejected Mariana at the moated grange.

Marianne or **Mary Anne.** The French republic personified. *Mary Anne associations* were secret republican societies in France. The name comes about thus: Ravaillac, the assassin of Henri IV, was honored by the red republicans as "patriot, deliverer, and martyr." This regicide was incited to his deed of blood by reading the celebrated treatise *De rege et regio institutione* by Mariana the Jesuit, published 1599, about ten years previously. As Mariana inspired Ravaillac "to deliver France from her tyrant" the name was attached to the republican party generally. *Marianne* was also a statuette to which the republicans of France paid homage. It symbolized the republic, and was arrayed in a red Phrygian cap. This statuette was sold at earthenware shops, and in republican clubs, enthroned in glory, and sometimes carried in procession to the tune of the MARSEILLAISE.

Marianne. (1) In Goethe's WILHELM MEISTER, an actress with whom Wilhelm is in love.

(2) The heroine of Turgenev's VIRGIN SOIL.

Marianne Dashwood. In Jane Austen's SENSE AND SENSIBILITY.

Maria Theresa. In German **Maria Theresia** (1717–1780). Archduchess of Austria and queen of Hungary and Bohemia; daughter of Emperor Charles VI; married (1736) Francis Stephen, Duke of Lorraine (from 1745 to 1765 Francis I, Holy Roman Emperor). Her claim to the hereditary Hapsburg estates on the basis of the PRAGMATIC SANCTION involved her with France, Prussia and Spain in the War of Austrian Succession (1740–1748), which ended with her losing only Silesia to Frederick the Great of Prussia (1748). She strengthened Austria by financial and other reforms, and sought in vain to recover Silesia in the Seven Years' War (1756–1763). Joseph II, Holy Roman Emperor (1765–1790), and MARIE ANTOINETTE were among her numerous children. Maria Theresa conceived of her duties as a ruler in a spirit of maternal benevolence. Her peoples reacted by conceiving of her as a great empress. Her memory is alive in innumerable songs.

Marie Antoinette (1755–1793). Queen of France, wife of Louis XVI. As daughter of Maria Theresa of Austria, sought Austria's aid against French Revolutionaries, and counseled Louis XVI to attempt the flight from France (1791). Imprisoned with the king and their children, found guilty of treason, and guillotined (October 16, 1793). Her personal charm, her naïve ignorance of practical life, her extravagance, and her frank and courageous honesty contributed to her unpopularity at court and with the masses of the French people. When she was told that a revolution was threatening because the people had no bread, she is said to have replied, "Why don't they eat cake?" On the part she played in the famous necklace affair, see under DIAMOND. She is a much-treated subject in world literature. Cf., e.g., *Marie Antoinette* (1932) by Stefan ZWEIG.

Marie de France (*fl.* ca. 1165). French medieval author, thought to have been a half-sister of King Henry I. She is famous for her LAIS, or short tales of courtly tone, each of which presents a simple situation chosen from classical, romance, or folklore sources, in clear, graceful, and charming style. Her best-known *lais* are *The Lai of Gugemar; The Lai of Yonec; The Lai of Eliduc; The Lai of the Thorn; The Lai of the Nightingale.* Marie also wrote a collection of *Fables and L'Espurgatoire de Saint Patrice,* a French version of ST. PATRICK'S PURGATORY. With HÉLOISE and ROSWITHA she is regarded as one of the few outstanding women writers of the Middle Ages.

Marie de Médicis (1573–1642). Italian princess, second wife of Henry IV of France (from 1600). After his murder, regent for her son Louis XIII (1610–1617). Forced to leave France (1631) by RICHELIEU, against whom she continued plotting until her death.

Marie de Verneuil, see VERNEUIL, MARIE DE.

Marigold, Dr., see DR. MARIGOLD'S PRESCRIPTIONS.

marimba. A kind of XYLOPHONE used in Africa and Central America. Also, a modern concert xylophone developed from it.

Marina. The heroine of an Elizabethan drama, PERICLES, PRINCE OF TYRE, the daughter of Pericles, long mourned by him as dead.

Marinel. In Spenser's *Faërie Queene,* the beloved of FLORIMEL the Fair.

Marinetti, Emilio Filippo Tommaso (1876–1944). Italian poet who founded the futurist movement in literature (1911). Joined the Fascist party (1919). Wrote *Futurismo e Fascismo* (1924); etc.

Marinism. Excessive literary ornateness and affectation. So named from Giambattista Marino (1569–1625), the Neapolitan poet, famous for his whimsical comparisons, pompous and overwrought descriptions, and "CONCEITS."

Marino Faliero. A tragedy by BYRON (1820). Historically, Faliero was the forty-ninth doge of Venice, elected 1354. He joined a conspiracy to overthrow the republic, under the hope and promise of being made a king, but was betrayed by Bertram, one of the conspirators, and was beheaded on the "Giant's Staircase," the place where the doges were wont to take the oath of fidelity. In Byron's tragedy we are told that the patrician, Michel Steno, having behaved indecently to women at a civic banquet, was kicked off the solajo by order of the doge. In revenge he wrote a scurrilous libel against the dogaressa; and the doge joined the conspiracy because he was furious with the Council of Forty for condemning the young patrician to only one month's imprisonment.

Mario and the Magician (Mario und der Zauberer). A novelette by Thomas MANN (1930) which tells of the visit made by a crippled magician to an Italian seaside resort and the tragic events that take place when he hypnotizes a young peasant. The story is considered to be an allegory of the effects of the system of FASCISM on the Italian people.

Marion, Francis (1732?–1795). American Revolutionary general; known as "the Swamp Fox" because of his skill in retreating—Indian fashion—to swamps and forests after quick and effective raids on the British forces. Participated in the battle of Eutaw Springs. See also KATHERINE WALTON.

Marion Delorme. A tragedy by Victor HUGO (1831). The titular heroine, Marion, was a courtesan in the reign of Louis XIII. In the drama, she is shown in the throes of a genuine love for a young man named Didier, who is ignorant of her past. Many complications arise from the interventions of the Marquis de Saverney, a former lover, and the affair ends tragically.

Maritain, Jacques (1882–). French philosopher. Strongly attracted by the philosophy of St. Thomas Aquinas, he became a Roman Catholic (1906) and is recognized as the leading neo-Thomist of the contemporary world. He has played a leading role in the Catholic renaissance in France and has been called "the most interesting living revivalist." After the fall of France (1940) he came to America as professor at the Institute of Medieval Studies in Toronto and visiting professor at Columbia and Princeton.

Marius. Cosette's lover and husband in Hugo's LES MISÉRABLES.

Marius the Epicurean. A philosophic romance by Walter PATER (1885). The hero is a young Roman noble of the time of Marcus Aurelius, and the book records his "sensations and ideas" rather than outward events. Though he makes no formal profession of Christianity, Marius is greatly drawn to it through his friend Cornelius and his own high principles and deeply religious nature. His death is of such a nature that the Christian Church looks upon him as a martyr.

Marivaux, Pierre Carlet de Chamblain de (1688–1763). French novelist and playwright. Best-known for his novel *La Vie de Marianne* (*The Life of Marianne;* 1731–1741) in 11 volumes, in which, as Crébillon describes it, "the characters not only say everything that they have done and everything that they have thought, but everything that they would have liked to think but did not." His peculiar style gave rise to the term "marivaudage," now used chiefly in a derogatory sense.

Marjorie Daw. A celebrated short story by T. B. ALDRICH (1873). To amuse his sick friend, John Flemming, Edward Delaney writes letter after letter about the charms of his neighbor, Marjorie Daw. Flemming recovers and comes to pay court to the lady with surprising consequences. (She proves to be non-existent).

Mark, King. A king of Cornwall in the Arthurian romances, Sir Tristan or TRISTRAM's uncle. He lived at Tintagel, and is principally remembered for his treachery and cowardice, and as the husband of Iseult or Isolde the Fair, who was passionately enamored of his nephew, Tristan.

Mark, St. See under SAINTS.

Markham, Edwin Charles (1852–1940). American poet, best known for his poem *The Man with the Hoe,* published in *The Man with the Hoe, And Other Poems* (1899), which presents in social protest a picture of a farmer made brutal by hard work and was suggested by a painting by MILLET. This poem was extremely popular. *Lincoln, And Other Poems* (1901) is another popular collection of Markham's work, which is not considered by critics to be distinguished by any important literary value.

Markham, Gervase (1568?–1637). English writer on war, horsemanship, forestry, cookery, hawking, etc., and author of poems and plays. Remembered especially for his versified account (1595) of Sir Richard Grenville's heroic naval battle against the Spanish fleet—a theme also treated by TENNYSON—and his continuation of Sir Philip Sidney's *Arcadia* in *The English Arcadia* (1607).

Markheim. A short story by R. L. STEVENSON in his volume, *The Merry Men* (1887), a tale of gradual degeneration and of last-minute repentance. The hero, Markheim, is driven by conscience to confess that he murdered a man for his money in cold blood.

Markievicz, Countess **de. Constance Georgine,** *née* **Gore-Booth** (1876–1927). Irish politician, orator, and leader. Involved in the Irish Easter Rebellion (1916); sentenced to death but later amnestied (1917). Supporter of Eamon de Valera and Minister of Labor in his cabinet; member of Dail Eireann (1922, 1923, 1927).

Markleham, Mrs. In Dickens' DAVID COPPERFIELD, the mother of Annie. Devoted to pleasure, she always maintained that she indulged in it for "Annie's sake." Mrs. Markleham is generally referred to as "the old soldier."

Marko, Prince. In George Meredith's TRAGIC COMEDIANS, a rival of Dr. Alvan for the affections of the heroine Clotilde von Rüdiger.

Marko Kraljevic. Literally, "Marko, son of the king." Serbian national hero, prominent also in Bulgarian and Rumanian folklore, who lived, according to popular tradition, 300 years fighting all the time against foreign oppressors, especially the Turks. Historians give him about sixty years (1335?–1394).

Mark Rutherford, The Autobiography of. A novel by William Hale White ("Reuben Shapcott") (1881) which, with its sequel *Mark Rutherford's Deliverance* (1885), presents the story of an honest, idealistic young minister tormented by intellectual scepticism, his break with the church, and the gradual working out of his ideals in a life of social service.

Marks, Jeannette Augustus (1875–). American poet, playwright, and educator. Established (1916) at Mt. Holyoke the Play and Poetry Shop Talk, a forum for American poets and dramatists. Her Welsh plays have been performed in the United States, Great Britain, and even in Japan.

Marks, Percy (1891–). American novelist and educator. Noted for *The Plastic Age* (1924), a somewhat outspoken novel of college life; etc.

Marlborough, 1st Duke of, see CHURCHILL, JOHN.

Marlbrough, see MALBROUK.

Marley, Jacob. In Dickens' CHRISTMAS CAROL, the partner of SCROOGE, the grasping, cheating "old sinner." He was dead before the story begins, but his ghost contributes to the conversion of Scrooge.

Marlow. The narrator in several of Joseph CONRAD's tales and novels, notably LORD JIM, YOUTH, CHANCE and HEART OF DARKNESS. The reader sees the events of the story through the eyes of this detached yet keenly interested observer and shares his effort to understand what is behind mere externals and his concern over the happiness of the human beings involved.

Marlow, Sir Charles. In Goldsmith's SHE STOOPS TO CONQUER, the kind-hearted old friend of Squire HARDCASTLE.

Young Marlow. Son of Sir Charles. "Among women of reputation and virtue he is the modestest man alive; but his acquaintances give him a very different character among women of another stamp" (Act i. sc. 1). Having mistaken Hardcastle's house for an inn, and Miss HARDCASTLE for the barmaid, he is quite at his ease, and makes love freely. When fairly caught, he discovers that the supposed "inn" is a private house, and the supposed barmaid is the Squire's daughter, but as the ice of his shyness is broken, he has no longer any difficulty in loving according to his station.

Marlowe, Christopher (1564–1593). English poet and playwright, considered the greatest figure in Elizabethan drama before Shakespeare. His contributions to the drama are considered to have been the molding of the BLANK VERSE line, formerly stiff and wooden, into a "mighty line" of eloquence and dignity and dramatic power, and the raising of the conventional, academic tragedy of his time, rigidly held within the limitations of the Senecan form, to a level of serious and emotionally gripping art. His dramas usually lack love scenes and comic interest and are concerned with the overweening ambition and desire and subsequent downfall of a single hero. His dramatic poetry is dignified and passionate, his lyric poetry graceful, musical, and warmly sensuous. His plays are TAMBURLAINE THE GREAT (1587); *The Tragical History of Doctor Faustus* (see FAUST; ca. 1592), the earliest known published version of which is 1604; THE JEW OF MALTA (ca. 1590); EDWARD II (1594); *The Tragedy of Dido* (1594), written with Thomas NASH; and *The Massacre at Paris* (ca. 1600). Marlowe is also believed by some scholars to have written parts of Shakespeare's plays *Titus Andronicus, Henry VI,* and *Edward III*, the last being attributed to Shakespeare. Marlowe's lyric and narrative poetry includes a translation of Ovid's *Amores* (ca. 1597); a paraphrase of Musaeus' HERO AND LEANDER, left unfinished at the time of the English poet's death and completed by George CHAPMAN, being published in 1598; a translation of the first book of Lucan's *Pharsalia*, published in 1600; and the famous Elizabethan lyric *Come Live with Me and Be My Love*.

Marlowe was the son of a shoemaker, a graduate of Cambridge, and a member of the Earl of Nottingham's theatrical company. He had a wild life and was accused of atheism, being arrested in 1593, although some scholars believe he was in some capacity a spy for the Crown. He was killed by a man named Ingram Frisar in a London tavern during a quarrel about a drinking score.

Marlowe, Julia. Stage name of **Sarah Frances Frost** (1866–). American actress, noted for her vivid portrayals of Shakespearean heroines. Starred in dramatic rôles (from 1888). Retired (1924). Her second husband was Edward Hugh SOTHERN. (Her first was Robert Taber.)

Marmion, a Tale of Flodden Field. A romantic narrative poem by Sir Walter SCOTT (1808). Lord Marmion is betrothed to Constance de Beverley, but he jilts her for Lady Clare, an heiress. Lady Clare is in love with Ralph de Wilton, and therefore rejects Marmion's suit and takes refuge from him in the convent of St. Hilda in Whitby. Constance takes the veil in another convent, but after a time she makes her escape, is captured, and is taken back and buried alive in the walls of a deep cell. Eventually Marmion is slain in the battle of Flodden Field, and Lady Clare is released from the convent and marries her old love, Ralph de Wilton.

Marmontel, Jean François (1723–1799). French author of tragedies, librettos for light operas, the philosophical novel *Bélisaire* (1767), the historical novel *Les Incas* (1777), etc. Protégé of Voltaire and contributor to the *Encyclopédie*.

marmoset. A small tropical monkey, not larger than a squirrel.

> Call Tullia's ape a marmosyte
> And Leda's goose a swan.
> Thomas Weelkes, *Avis or Fantastic Spirits* (1608).

Marne. French river. Scene of two important battles in World War I (September 6–10, 1914 and July 15, 1918). For a poetic account of the German defeat at the Marne, cf. G. K. Chesterton's *Ballad of St. Barbara*.

Marneffe, Mme Valére. One of Balzac's most heartless coquettes, a prominent character in his *Cousin Betty*. She is used by her friend Lisbeth FISCHER to bring unhappiness to the relatives whom Lisbeth secretly hates.

Marner, Silas, see SILAS MARNER.

Marnix, Philip van. Baron **Sint Aldegonde** (1538–1598). Flemish writer and statesman, active in the liberation of the Netherlands and the propagation of Protestantism. His *De Byencorf der h. Roomscher Kercke* (*The Beehive of the Holy Church of Rome;* 1569) is a fierce and Rabelaisian attack on Catholicism. Putative author of the Dutch national song *Wilhelmus van Nassouwen*.

Maro. Virgil (70–19 B.C.), whose full name was Publius Virgilius Maro; born on the banks of the rivers Mincio, at the village of Andes, near Mantua.

> Sweet Maro's muse, sunk in inglorious rest,
> Had silent slept amid the Mincian reeds.
> Thomson, *Castle of Indolence*.

Marocco or **Morocco.** The name of BANKS' HORSE.

Marot, Clément (1496?–1544). French poet, known for his light and graceful lyrics. He was the first to introduce the SONNET into the French language, and is considered to have helped end the influence of the medieval RHÉTORIQUEURS on French poetry. His best-known works are *Temple de Cupido* (1515), addressed to Francis I; *Enfer* (1540); and *Saint Cancionnaire* (1542), a translation of a number of Biblical psalms, intended to be sung to popular tunes played on the spinet. The *Saint Cancionnaire* was considered sacrilegious in Roman Catholic France, but was later made a part of the liturgy of the Protestants and became extraordinarily popular. Marot was attached to the court of King FRANCIS I, but because of his Protestant beliefs, half-hearted though they were, he fluctuated in the royal favor, finally being forced to flee to Geneva in 1542.

Marotte. Footman of Gorgibus, in Molière's PRÉCIEUSES RIDICULES, a plain bourgeois, who hates affectation. When the fine ladies of the house try to convert him into a fashionable flunky, and teach him a little grandiloquence, he bluntly tells them he does not understand Latin.

Marpessa. In Greek legend, daughter of Evenus, courted by both Idas and Apollo. When Idas opposed his mortal strength to that of the god and carried her off, Zeus intervened to insure Marpessa the lover of her own choice. Fearing that Apollo would tire of her when she lost her youth, she decided in favor of Idas. Stephen PHILLIPS (1868–1915) wrote a poem called *Marpessa*.

Marphurius. In Molière's MARIAGE FORCÉ, a doctor of the Pyrrhonian school. SGANARELLE consults him about his marriage, but the philosopher replies, "Perhaps; it is possible; it may be so; everything is doubtful," until at last Sganarelle beats him, and Marphurius says he will bring action for assault and battery. "Perhaps," replies Sganarelle; "it is possible; it may be so," etc., using the philosopher's own words.

Marplot. The hero of two comedies by Mrs. CENTLIVRE, *The Busy Body* (1709) and *Marplot in Lisbon* (1711). The character is to some extent based on the heroes in *Sir Martin Marall,* by Dryden, and *Sir Martin Marplot,* by William Cavendish, Duke of Newcastle, both in turn adapted from Molière's *L'Étourdi.* Marplot is a blundering, good-natured, meddlesome young man, very inquisitive, too officious by half, and always bungling whatever he interferes with:

> That unlucky dog Marplot . . . is ever doing mischief, and yet (to give him his due) he never designs it. This is some blundering adventure, wherein he thought to show his friendship, as he calls it.—*The Busy Body,* iii. 5.

Marprelate controversy. The name given to the vituperative paper war (1589), in which Puritan pamphleteers attacked the Church of England under the pseudonym of "Martin Marprelate." Thomas Cooper, Bishop of Winchester, defended the Church; the chief of the "Martinists" were Udall, Throckmorton, Penry, and Barrow.

Marquand, John Phillips (1893–). American novelist, best-known for his satirical studies of upper-class New Englanders struggling to maintain their aristocratic, Puritan standards in the 20th century. These are contained in *The Late George Apley* (1937), awarded the Pulitzer Prize in 1938; *Wickford Point* (1939); and *H. M. Pulham, Esq.* (1941), dramatized as a successful motion picture. Marquand also wrote a number of popular detective stories in which Mr. MOTO is the keen-witted hero. Other books are *The Unspeakable Gentleman* (1922); *Four of a Kind* (1923); *Black Cargo* (1925); *Lord Timothy Dexter* (1925); *Warning Hill* (1930); *Haven's End* (1933); *Ming Yellow* (1935); *No Hero* (1935); *So Little Time* (1944).

Marquette, Jacques. Known as **Père Marquette** (1637–1675). Jesuit missionary in America. Accompanied Jolliet down Wisconsin and Mississippi Rivers and back via Lake Michigan (1673). *Voyage et découverte de quelques pays et nations de l'Amérique Septentrionale* (1681).

Marquis, Donald Robert Perry (1878–1937). American journalist and humorist, known for his columns *The Sun Dial* in the New York *Sun* and *The Lantern* in the New York *Tribune.* Among his best-known humorous and satirical books are THE OLD SOAK (1921), a comedy; ARCHY AND MEHITABEL (1927), and several sequels, a satire on life in the 1920's in terms of a cockroach and a cat; HERMIONE AND HER LITTLE GROUP OF SERIOUS THINKERS (1916); *The Revolt of the Oyster* (1922), *A Variety of People* (1929), and *Chapters for the Orthodox* (1934), collections of stories; *The Old Soak's History of the World* (1924); *The Almost Perfect State* (1927); *Off the Arm* (1930), a novel. He also wrote books of humorous verse and several serious works, including volumes of poetry, dramas, and an autobiographical novel left incomplete at the time of his death, *Sons of the Puritans* (1939). Cf. Christopher Morley's essay in his *Letters of Askance.*

Marriage of Figaro, The. See FIGARO.

Marriage of Heaven and Hell, The. The chief prose work of William BLAKE (1790), which presents his negativistic ideas, including the denial of the right of authority, of eternal punishment for sins, and of matter as reality.

Marriage of Loti, The (Le Mariage de Loti). A novel by Pierre LOTI (1880), first published as *Rarahu,* the name of the Tahitian heroine. The story is the favorite one, with Loti, of a transitory love affair between a European and a beautiful and passionate young native. The pseudonym, Pierre Loti, later adopted by the author, is the name of the hero of this book.

Marriage of the Adriatic. See BRIDE OF THE SEA.

Marriage of William Ashe, The. A political novel by Mrs. Humphry WARD (1905), dealing with the married life of William Ashe and his turbulent, unconventional wife, Kitty. Lady Caroline Lamb is said to have been in some measure the original of Kitty, Lord Melbourne of her devoted husband and Byron of her ardent lover, Geoffrey Cliffe.

Marrow controversy. A memorable struggle in Scotland about 1719 to 1722, between Puritanism and Presbyterianism; so called from Edward Fisher's *Marrow of Modern Divinity* (1644), a book of ultra-evangelical tendency, which was condemned by the General Assembly in 1720.

Marryat, Captain **Frederick** (1792–1848). English novelist of the sea, best known for his *Mr. Midshipman Easy* (1836), *Peter Simple* (1834) and *Masterman Ready* (1841).

Mars. The Roman god of war, identified in certain aspects with the Greek Ares. He was also the patron of husbandmen. Camoëns introduces him in the Portuguese epic, THE LUSIAD, as typifying divine fortitude. As Bacchus, the evil demon, is the guardian power of Mohammedanism, so Mars is the guardian of Christianity.

The planet of this name was so called from early times because of its reddish tinge, and under it, says the *Compost of Ptholomeus,* "is borne theves and robbers . . . nyght walkers and quarell pykers, bosters, mockers, and skoffers; and these men of Mars causeth warre, and murther, and batayle. They wyll be gladly smythes or workers of yron . . . lyers, gret swerers . . . He is red and angry . . . a great walker, and a maker of swordes and knyves, and a sheder of mannes blode . . . and good to be a barboure and a blode letter, and to drawe tethe." Among the alchemists, Mars designated iron.

the Mars of Portugal. Alfonso de Albuquerque, Viceroy of India (1452–1515).

Marsay, Count Henri de. A nobleman who appears in several of the novels of Balzac's COMÉDIE HUMAINE, is involved in numerous love affairs with women of the world, and becomes finally the prime minister of Louis Philippe. He has been described as "one of the finest gentlemen and most utter cads in fiction." He was a member of the CÉNACLE.

Marse Chan. A short story by Thomas Nelson PAGE (1884) in Negro dialect. The narrator is a faithful old Southern slave who tells of the effects of the Civil War on the household to which he is attached.

Marseillaise, La. The hymn of the French Revolution. Claude Joseph Rouget de Lisle (1760–1835), an artillery officer in garrison at Strasburg, composed both the words and the music (April 24, 1792) with the title *Chant de guerre pour l'armée du Rhin.* On July 30, 1792, volunteers from Marseilles entered Paris singing the song, and the Parisians, enchanted with it, called it the *Chant des Marseillais* and later *La Marseillaise.* It has often been made use of by later composers, as for instance by Schumann in his music for Heine's poem, *The Two Grenadiers.*

Marsh, Ngaio (1899–). New Zealand detective-story writer. Her first name is the Maori word for "flowering tree," pronounced Ny-o.

Marsh, "Pink." A city Negro, the hero of George ADE's humorous volume, *Pink Marsh* (1897). "Pink" made his first appearance in the columns of the Chicago *Record.*

Marsh, Reginald (1898–). American painter. His paintings of New York City scenes are noteworthy. Illustrator for New York journals.

Marshal Forwards, see FORWARDS.

Marshall, Archibald (1866–1934). English novelist, publisher, and humorist. Author of the Trollopean "Squire Clinton" series (1909–1915). *Simple Stories* (1927) first appeared in *Punch.*

Marshall, George Catlett (1880–). American army officer. Chief of staff, U.S. army (1939–1945). Served with A.E.F. in France in World War I. Sent to China on special mission by President Truman (1946). Secretary of State (1947–).

Marshall, John (1755–1835). Chief justice, U.S. Supreme Court (1801–1835). His major decisions established principles of constitutional interpretation.

Marshall, Sylvia. The heroine of Dorothy Canfield's BENT TWIG.

Marshalsea. A prison in Southwark, London, long used as a debtors' prison but abolished in 1842. It is described in *Little Dorrit* by Charles Dickens whose father had once been consigned to it. The spelling of the name is a folk-etymological interpretation of marshalcy.

Marsh City. Leningrad. See under CITY.

Marshes of Glynn, The. A poem by Sidney LANIER.

Marsiglio, Marsile, or Marsilius. In Carolingian romance, a Saracen king who with the Christian traitor GANELON plots the attack upon ROLAND, under "the tree on which Judas hanged himself." With a force of 600,000 men, divided into three armies, he attacks the paladin and overthrows him, but is in turn overthrown by CHARLEMAGNE, and hanged on the very tree beneath which he arranged the attack. Of the spellings given above, the first is the Italian, the second the French, and the third the English form.

Marston, John (1575?–1634). English Elizabethan dramatist and satirist. Known for his entertaining comedies, as *The Malcontent* (1604), and his melodramatic tragedies, as *The Wonder of Women, or the Tragedy of Sophonisba* (1606); etc. Ben JONSON ridiculed him as Crispinus in his *Poetaster* (1601) for his overladen melodramatic style.

Marston, Philip Bourke (1850–1887). English poet, blind from early youth. *All in All* (1875) and *Wind Voices* (1883) are collections of his poems. He is the subject of an elegy by Swinburne and of *Philip My King* by Dinah Maria Craik.

Marston Moor. A plain in Yorkshire, England, scene of a decisive battle (July 2, 1644) between the Royalist and Parliamentary and Scotch armies. Prince Rupert, in command of the Royalists, defeated the Scots and was in turn defeated by Oliver Cromwell's picked troops, the Ironsides.

Marsyas. The Phrygian flute-player who challenged Apollo to a contest of skill, and, being beaten by the god, was flayed alive for his presumption. From his blood arose the river so called.

Martano. A braggart in Ariosto's ORLANDO FURIOSO, who decoys Origilla from Gryphon. He is a great coward, and flees from the tournament amid the jeers of the spectators. While Gryphon is asleep he steals his armor, goes to King Norandino to receive the honors due to Gryphon, and then quits Damascus with Origilla. Another knight encounters them and brings them back to Damascus, where Martano is committed to the hangman's mercies.

Martel, Charles, see CHARLES MARTEL.

Martello tower. A circular masonry fort.

> A-top the cracked martello tower.
> Thomas Bailey Aldrich, *An Old Castle.*

The Italian word *martello* means hammer, but in Martello tower it is a plausible misinterpretation of the original *Mortella,* from *Cape Mortella* in Corsica where a Martello tower repulsed an attack by the British fleet in 1794.

Martext, Sir Oliver. A vicar in Shakespeare's comedy of AS YOU LIKE IT.

Martha. (1) A light opera by FLOTOW (1847), libretto by St. Georges and Friedrich. Disguised as servants, Lady Henrietta, a maid of honor to Queen Anne, and her maid Nancy go to a Country Fair and in fun unwittingly bind themselves out to service for a year with two rich farmers, Lionel and Plunkett by name. When the sheriff decrees that the contract is legal, Henrietta takes the name of Martha, but the two are not very successful as servants. After a gay comedy of errors, they escape. Later, when the love-stricken Lionel becomes the Earl of Derby, another Country Fair is staged, the mystery is cleared up, and all ends happily for the two couples.

(2) In Goethe's FAUST, a friend of Margaret. She makes love to Mephistopheles with great worldly shrewdness. She also appears in Gounod's opera *Faust.*

Martha, St. See under SAINTS.

Martial. In full **Marcus Valerius Martialis** (*fl.* first century A. D.). Latin author, born in Spain and a resident of Rome for a large part of his life, famous for his great number of witty and ribald epigrams commenting on Roman *mores* of the time.

Martian, The. A novel written and illustrated by George DU MAURIER (1896).

Martianus Capella or **Marcian** (*fl.* 5th century). Latin author of North Africa, best known for his *De Nuptiis Philologiae et Mercurii* (*Concerning the Marriage of Mercury and Philology*), an allegorical work on the seven liberal arts, which is mentioned by CHAUCER in the *House of Fame* and the *Merchant's Tale.*

Martin, Edward Sanford (1856–1939). American editor and writer. Founder (1883) and first editor of *Life* magazine; also on editorial staff of *Harper's Weekly* (1920–1935); and writer of the "Easy Chair" in *Harper's Magazine* (1920–1935). Author of a book of verse (1890) and books of personal essays.

Martin, Everett Dean (1880–1941). American educator. Author of *The Behavior of Crowds,* etc.

Martin, Helen Reimensnyder (1868–1939). American novelist. Author of novels about the Mennonites.

Martin, St. See under SAINTS.

Martin, Violet Florence. Pseudonym **Martin Ross** (1865–1915). Irish novelist. Wrote in collaboration with her cousin, Edith O. SOMERVILLE. After her death, her cousin continued to publish all her work as by "Somerville and Ross." Best known for *Some Experiences of an Irish R.M.* (1899).

Martin-Bellême, Thérèse. The leading character in Anatole France's RED LILY.

Martin Chuzzlewit. A novel by Charles DICKENS (1843). Because of his love for Mary Graham, the titular hero is forced by his old grandfather to leave home and emigrates to America. He has some sadly disillusioning experiences with real estate in an over-advertised swamp named EDEN, and returns to England with little love for anything American. The hypocrite, PECKSNIFF, is a prominent character, as are the various members of the CHUZZLEWIT family.

Martine. In Molière's *Médécin malgré Lui,* wife of SGANARELLE.

Martineau, Harriet (1802–1876). English author and economist. Deaf from early childhood. Wrote stories illustrating the theories of MALTHUS, Ricardo and MILL (1832). Visited the U.S. (1834) where she supported the Abolitionist movement. Translated Auguste COMTE's *Philosophie Positive* (1853); also wrote two novels, *Deerbrook* (1839), and *The Hour and the Man* (1840), and popular tales for children. Her brother, **James Martineau** (1805–1900) was a Unitarian clergyman and author of philosophical works.

Martin Eden. A novel by Jack LONDON (1909), largely autobiographical.

martinet. A strict disciplinarian; so called from the Marquis of Martinet, a young colonel in the reign of Louis XIV, who remodeled the infantry and was slain at the siege of Doesbourg in 1672. Cf. Voltaire, *Louis XIV.* The French still call a cat-o'-nine-tails a martinet.

Martínez Ruiz, José. Pseudonym **Azorín** (1873–). Spanish essayist, novelist, and playwright. Member of the Spanish Academy.

Martinez Sierra, Gregorio (1881–). Leading Spanish dramatist. Best-known for *Cancíon de Cuna* (*The Cradle Song;* 1911) which was a great success in America. Edited a library of translated World Classics.

Martínez Zuviría, Gustavo Adolfo. Pseudonym **Hugo Wast** (1883–). Argentine author. Royal Spanish Academy prize for *Valle Negro* (*Black Valley;* 1918). Author of a trilogy dealing with the history of Argentine independence. A later novel, *Stone Desert* (1925), won the national prize for literature of $30,000; etc.

Martinus Scriblerus, see SCRIBLERUS, MARTINUS.

Martyn, Edward (1859–1923). Irish critic and playwright. Associated with Lady Gregory, W. B. Yeats, and George Moore in founding Irish Literary Theatre (1914). President of Sinn Fein (1904–1908).

martyr (*Gr.*), simply means a witness, but is applied to one who witnesses a good confession with his blood.

the martyr king. Charles I of England, beheaded January 30, 1649. He was buried at Windsor, and was also called "the White King."

martyr to science. Claude Louis, Count Berthollet (1748–1822), who determined to test in his own person the effects of carbolic acid on the human frame, and died under the experiment.

the first martyr. St. Stephen. See under SAINTS.

the Book of Martyrs, see under ACTS AND MONUMENTS; John FOXE.

Martyrs, Les. A prose epic by CHATEAUBRIAND (1809), dealing with the conversions of the early Christians of the Roman Empire, and their subsequent struggles and martyrdom. The hero is Endore, a young man who travels through the various provinces of the Empire, finding adventure where he goes.

Marvel, Ik. The pseudonym under which Donald Grant Mitchell issued his *Reveries of a Bachelor* and *Dream Life* (*Am.,* 1850–1851).

Marvell, Andrew (1621–1678). English poet, a late representative of the METAPHYSICAL POETS, known for his combination of intellectual CONCEITS with lyric grace. During the rule of the Cromwell government, Marvell was assistant to John MILTON, then Latin Secretary of the Commonwealth, and was first elected to Parliament, after which he held public office until his death. Among his best-known poems are *The Garden, To His Coy Mistress,* and *Bermudas,* in his early manner; *Horatian Ode upon Cromwell's Return from Ireland;* and *The Last Instructions to a Painter,* a verse satire on the Dutch War. In his later years he wrote a number of pamphlets and verse-satires attacking the Restoration government. He was also a defender and admirer of Milton.

Interest in Marvell was revived in the 20th century among English and American poets, largely through the influence of the essays of T. S. ELIOT.

marvellous boy, the. Thomas CHATTERTON (1753–1770), the poet.

> I thought of Chatterton, the marvellous boy,
> The sleepless soul, that perished in his pride.
> Wordsworth, *Resolution and Independence.*

Marwood, Alice. In Dickens' DOMBEY AND SON, daughter of an old woman who calls herself Mrs. Brown. When a mere girl, she was concerned in a burglary and was transported. CARKER, manager in the firm of Dombey and Son, seduces her, and both she and her mother determine on revenge. Alice bears a striking resemblance to Edith, Mr. Dombey's second wife.

Marx, Karl (1818–1883). German political philosopher. Expelled from Prussia (1845), he settled in London and developed his theory of socialism; aided the elder LIEBKNECHT and his associates in founding the German Social Democratic Labor Party (1869). His great work *Das Kapital* (3 vols.; 1867, 1885, 1895) was completed by his collaborator Friedrich ENGELS.

Marxism. The doctrine of philosophical socialism taught by Karl MARX and its modern developments.

Marxism in literature. With the stabilization and prosperity of the Soviet Union, the growth and increasing influence of COMMUNISM and COMMUNIST PARTIES, and the interest in social and economic reform in a period of widespread depression and unemployment, Marxism came to be reflected in the literature of Europe and especially the U.S. during the 1930's. Its most outstanding manifestation was to be found in PROLETARIAN LITERATURE, but a fuller use of its philosophical concepts was made in the fields of criticism and scholarship, where authors of both the past and the present were interpreted in terms of their economic and social backgrounds, systems of technical aesthetics and theories of "ART FOR ART'S SAKE" were attacked, and contemporary authors were estimated according to their treatment of the "class struggle" in their works. In England, leading critics making use of Marxist ideas included Herbert READ, C. DAY LEWIS, and Stephen SPENDER; in the U.S., V. F. CALVERTON, Granville HICKS, Michael Gold, Joseph Freeman, Bernard Smith, and David Daiches. As in proletarian literature, some but by no means all of the critics expressing Marxist ideas were themselves Communists in their political affiliation. The socio-historical method of interpretation, which had a development parallel to Marxism, was applied in their studies of literature by a number of critics and scholars without partisan aims or associations.

In addition to their portrayals of the proletariat, a few poets of the 1930's attempted to embody in their work accurate statements of Marxist theories on history, revolution, and class relationships, which gave their poetry a didactic ring; chief among these were C. DAY LEWIS, W. H. AUDEN, and Hugh MACDIARMID.

Most of the Marxist LITTLE MAGAZINES in the U.S. were organs for proletarian literature, but some were devoted to discussion of the philosophical aspects of Marxism and to the application of its concepts to literature, science, history, and sociology. Included among these and representing opinion of the followers of both TROTSKY and STALIN were *Modern Monthly, Partisan Review, Science and Society,* and *The New International.*

Mary. The mother of Jesus. See under SAINTS.

Little Mary. A euphemism for the stomach; from the play of that name by Sir J. M. BARRIE (1903).

the four Marys. Mary Beaton (or *Bethune*), Mary Livingston (or *Leuson*), Mary Fleming (or *Flemyng*), and Mary Seaton (or *Seyton*); called the "Queen's Marys," that is, the ladies of the same age as Mary, afterwards Queen of Scots, and her companions. Mary Carmichael was not one of the four, although introduced in the well-known ballad.

> Yestre'en the queen had four Marys,
> This night she'll hae but three:
> There was Mary Beaton, and Mary Seaton,
> Mary Carmichael, and me.

Mary, Highland, see HIGHLAND MARY.

Mary, Lovey, see LOVEY MARY.

Marya Timofyevna, see LEBYADKIN, MARYA TIMOFYEVNA.

Mary Barton. A novel by Mrs. GASKELL (1848), dealing with labor problems among the weavers of Manchester.

Mary Magdalene, St. See under SAINTS.

Mary, Mary quite contrary. The heroine of an old nursery rhyme. St. John ERVINE wrote a play entitled *Mary, Mary Quite Contrary* (1923).

> "Mary, Mary quite contrary,
> How does your garden grow,
> With silver bells and cockle shells
> And pretty maids all in a row?"

Mary Olivier. A novel by May SINCLAIR (1919). It is a psychological study of a brilliant, sensitive girl, a member of a family tainted with insanity. Most of her life is devoted to the care of her mother. Intellectual interests, always strong with her, result in her becoming an author in later years. Although she considers marriage out of the question, she finds happiness in a very intense love affair.

Mary Queen of Scots. This ill-fated queen who was executed in 1587, is a prominent character in Scott's ABBOT, which has for its subject her flight to England. She is the heroine of SCHILLER's tragedy *Maria Stuart* (1800), of Swinburne's trilogy of poetic tragedies, CHASTELARD, BOTHWELL and *Mary Stuart,* and of John DRINKWATER's *Mary Stuart* (1921). The Norwegian poet and dramatist Björnstjerne BJÖRNSON made his dramatic reputation with a play entitled *Mary, Queen of Scots.*

Maurice Hewlett's QUEEN'S QUAIR also tells her story. Cf. also Stefan Zweig's biography, *Mary, Queen of Scotland* (1935).

Mary the Virgin, St. See under SAINTS.

Mary I or **Mary Tudor.** Also known as **Bloody Mary** (1516–1558). Victor HUGO wrote a tragedy called *Mary Tudor* (1833), and TENNYSON in 1878 published a play called *Queen Mary,* an epitome of her reign. It centers about her love for Philip of Spain, her marriage, and her hopeless yearning for a son who might inherit the crown of Great Britain and of Spain. Mary Tudor is also the heroine of Charles Major's historical novel, WHEN KNIGHTHOOD WAS IN FLOWER.

Maryland! My Maryland! A well-known song of Civil War times by James R. Randall.

> Thou wilt not cower in the dust, Maryland,
> Thy beaming sword shall never rust, Maryland,
> Remember Carroll's sacred trust,
> Remember Howard's warlike thrust,
> And all thy slumbers with the just,
> Maryland! My Maryland!

Masaniello. A corruption of Tommaso Aniello, a Neapolitan fisherman, who led the revolt of July, 1647. The great grievance was heavy taxation, and the immediate cause of Masaniello's interference was the seizure of his property because his wife had smuggled flour. He obtained a large following, was elected chief of Naples, and for nine days ruled with absolute control; then he was betrayed by his own people, was shot, and his body flung into a ditch. Next day, however, it was reclaimed and interred with a pomp and ceremony never equaled in Naples. AUBER's opera *Masaniello,* or *La Muette de Portici* (1828) takes the story for its groundwork. The libretto is by SCRIBE.

Masaryk, Jan Garrigue (1886–1948). Son of the famous Czechoslovak statesman and philosopher **Tomáš Garrigue Masaryk** (1850–1937). Foreign minister (1940) and vice-premier (1941) of the Czechoslovak provisional government in London. Committed suicide in Prague after Communist coup (1948).

Mascagni, Pietro (1863–1945). Italian composer. Famous for his one-act opera *Cavalleria Rusticana* (1890).

Mascarille. A valet who appears in Molière's PRÉCIEUSES RIDICULES (1659). Molière had already introduced the same name in two other of his comedies, *L'Étourdi* (1653) and *Le Dépit Amoureux* (1654). In his devotion to his master Mascarille will go to any extreme of trickery.

Masefield, John (1878–). English poet, dramatist, novelist, and short-story writer, best known for his popular poems and ballads dealing with the sea. His works include *Salt-water Ballads* (1902); *Ballads* (1903); *A Mainsail Haul* (1905), a collection of short stories; THE TRAGEDY OF NAN (1909), a play; *Multitude and Solitude* (1909), a novel; *Poems and Ballads* (1910); THE EVERLASTING MERCY (1911); THE WIDOW IN THE BYE STREET (1912); DAUBER (1912); *The Daffodil Fields* (1913); REYNARD THE FOX (1919); KING COLE (1921); *The Dream* (1922); *The Midnight Folk* (1927), a novel; *The Coming of Christ* (1928), a drama; *Minnie Maylow's Story, and Other Tales and Scenes* (1931); *The Bird of Dawning* (1933); *The Box of Delights* (1935); *Eggs and Baker* (1936); *Basilissa* (1940), a historical novel; *Conquer* (1941), a historical novel; *Dead Ned* (1938); *Live and Kicking Ned* (1941); *Gautama the Enlightened, And Other Verse* (1941); *In the Mill* (1941), autobiographical; *Natalie Maisie and Pavilastukay: Two Tales in Verse* (1942).

Masefield's work combines romantic and realistic elements and is marked by an extensive later use of the long narrative poem, influenced by his admiration for CHAUCER. He ran away from home at the age of fourteen and spent a number of years wandering about the world. For a time he was in the U.S., serving as a bartender's assistant in New York City and working in a carpet factory in Yonkers, N.Y. In 1930 he was made Poet Laureate of England.

Masham, Lady **Abigail** (d. 1734). Daughter of the London merchant Francis Hill and an aunt of the Duchess of Marlborough. As favorite of Queen Anne, replacing the Duchess of Marlborough, she exercised much influence at court.

Mask, Man in the Iron, see under MAN.

Maskwell. In CONGREVE's comedy, *The Double Dealer* (1694), the titular hero. He pretends to love Lady Touchwood, but it is only to make her a tool. Maskwell pretends friendship for Mellefont merely to throw dust in his eyes respecting his designs to carry off Cynthia, to whom Mellefont is betrothed. Cunning and hypocrisy are his substitutes for wisdom and honesty.

Maslova. The heroine of Tolstoi's RESURRECTION. She is also called Katusha.

masochism. Sexual abnormality in which pleasure is derived from abuse and cruelty suffered at the hands of one's associate. Opposite of SADISM. The word was formed from the name of the Austrian novelist Leopold von Sacher-Masoch (1835–1895), who depicted the abnormality now so called in some of his works (*Venus in Furs,* etc.).

Mason, Alfred Edward Woodley (1865–). English romantic novelist and playwright. Best-known for his novel of contemporary life, *The Four Feathers* (1902). Several of his novels were dramatized, notably *Fire Over England* (1936), which was also successful as a moving picture. In *At the Villa Rose* (1910), Mason introduced the detective M. Hanaud, a Gallic counterpart of Sherlock Holmes.

Mason, Daniel Gregory (1873–). American Professor of Music, Columbia University; composer of symphonies and piano pieces. Member, National Institute of Arts and Letters. His son, Gregory Mason, is a writer and teacher. *September Remember* (1945), under name of "Eliot Taintor"; etc.

Mason, James (1909–). English moving-picture actor. *The Seventh Veil, Odd Man Out,* etc. Mrs. Mason is Pamela Kellino.

Mason, Van Wyck (1897–). American novelist. Historical romances and 14 detective stories which belong to the "Oppenheim tradition."

Mason, Walt (1862–1939). American humorist, writing widely syndicated doggerel in slang.

Mason and Dixon's Line. The southern boundary line which separated the free state of Pennsylvania from what were at one time the slave states of Maryland and Virginia. It lies in 39° 43′ 26″ north latitude, and was fixed by Charles Mason and Jeremiah Dixon, English astronomers and surveyors (1763–1767).

Maspero, Sir **Gaston Camille Charles** (1846–1916). French Egyptologist and author. Chiefly noted for remarkable discoveries at the temple of Karnak. Wrote a number of books on archeology.

Masque of Judgment, The. A drama in verse by William Vaughn MOODY (1900).

Mass. The Eucharistic rite of the Roman Church. See under EUCHARIST.

Massacre of St. Bartholomew. See under BARTHOLOMEW.

Massacre of the Innocents, see INNOCENTS.

Massenet, Jules Émile Frédéric (1842–1912). French composer of oratorios, operas, cantatas, biblical dramas, etc. Best known operas *Manon* and *Thaïs.*

Masses, The. An American weekly magazine founded in New York in 1911 to express a broadly liberal and Socialist viewpoint. It is best known for its issues appearing during the years of World War I, when Max EASTMAN was the editor (beginning in 1912) and such writers as Floyd DELL, Randolph BOURNE, and John REED were also associated with it. Until its publication was suspended by the U.S. government in 1918, its viewpoint was definitely Socialist and pacifist. The magazine *The Liberator* was founded by Eastman almost immediately after the suspension of *The Masses,* and, growing increasingly radical in its opinions, it became associated with the COMMUNIST PARTY in 1922.

New Masses, The. A later form of *The Liberator* (which ceased publication in 1924), founded in 1926. Its editorial viewpoint continued in accordance with the policies of the Communist party, and from time to time it crusaded for American civil liberties, the trade union movement, amelioration of the conditions of Southern sharecroppers, Negro rights, etc. It also contained literary features, and during the 1930's published short stories and poems of a number of the leading proletarian writers of the time, as well as satirical cartoons by such figures as William GROPPER. It ceased publication in 1947.

See also PROLETARIAN LITERATURE.

Massey, Gerald (1828–1907). English poet. A Chartist and Christian Socialist. His career suggested to George Eliot the theme of her novel FELIX HOLT (1866).

Massey, Raymond (1896–). Actor and producer. Best-known for his interpretation of Lincoln on stage and screen.

Massine, Léonide (1896–). Russian-born dancer and choreographer. With Ballet Russe de Monte Carlo company as producer and dancer in Europe and America.

Massinger, Philip (1583–1640). English dramatist of the period of Jacobean drama following Shakespeare. His plays express his ideas on the politics of the time and his advocacy of Roman Catholicism. Among his works are *The Virgin Martyr* (1622), in collaboration with DEKKER; *The Duke of Milan* (1623); *The Bondman* (1624); *The Parliament of Love* (1624); *The Roman Actor* (1629); *The Renegado* (1630); *The Maid of Honor* (1632); A NEW WAY TO PAY OLD DEBTS (1633), a comedy and Massinger's best-known work; *The Emperor of the East* (1632); *The Great Duke of Florence* (1636); *The Guardian* (1655); *The Bashful Lover* (1655); *The City Madam* (1658). He also wrote several plays in collaboration with John Fletcher (see under BEAUMONT) and Nathan Field.

Massingham, Henry William (1860–1924). English journalist. Editor of *The Nation* (1907–1923), which became under him an influential periodical of liberalism. His son, **Harold John Massingham** (1888–) is a prolific writer.

Master, the Old. A character who figures in O. W. HOLMES' *Poet at the Breakfast Table.* The Poet says that "he suspects himself of a three-story intellect, and I don't feel sure that he isn't right."

Master Builder, The. A drama by Henrik IBSEN (1892). Intoxicated by his success as a builder and fearful of the rivalry of younger, better trained men, Halvard Solness "the Master Builder," outdoes himself and falls from the heights of one of his own towers. The tragedy is largely due to the young heroine, Hilda Wangel, who has relentlessly urged him on.

Master Humphrey's Clock. A proposed series of tales by Charles Dickens, purporting to be told by Master Humphrey, an old deformed clockmaker, who appears in OLD CURIOSITY SHOP. This novel and *Barnaby Rudge* were the only two included in the series (1840–1841), and according to its author, *Master Humphrey's Clock* "as originally constructed became one of the lost books of the earth, which, we all know, are far more precious than any that can be read for love or money."

Master Leonard. In medieval demonology, the grand master of the witches' Sabbaths. He had the shape of a goat with three horns and a black human face.

Master of Ballantrae, The. A romance by Robert Louis STEVENSON (1889), the tale of a bitter hatred between two Scotch brothers. In the Stuart uprising of 1745 the elder brother, James, supports the Pretender, while the younger, Henry, is for King George. When James, the Master, does not come back, Alison Graeme, who has been betrothed to him, marries Henry instead. James, however, returns to subject Henry to persecutions of every imaginable sort. Eventually, after years of enmity, the end comes in a lonely American wilderness. The Master has been buried alive by Secundra Dass, his East Indian attendant, to deceive his foes, and Henry finds the Indian digging him up. James is only able to open his eyes, but at this dreadful portent Henry falls dead, and the two brothers are buried together. Much of the tale is told by the old steward of Ballantrae, John MacKellar.

Masters, Edgar Lee (1869–). American poet and author, a lawyer by training, famous for his SPOON RIVER ANTHOLOGY (1915), giving a dramatic and realistic picture of life in the Middle West. See LOCAL COLOR. His later books of poetry, not considered as successful as *Spoon River,* include *Songs and Satires* (1916); *Toward the Gulf* (1918); *Starved Rock* (1919); *Domesday Book* (1920); *The New Spoon River* (1924); *Lee* (1926), *Jack Kelso* (1928), and *Godbey* (1931), dramatic poems; *The Fate of the Jury* (1929), a sequel to *Domesday Book; Lichee Nuts* (1930), pseudo-Chinese philosophy; *Invisible Landscapes* (1935); *The New World* (1937). Among his works in prose are *Mitch Miller* (1920), *Skeeters Kirby* (1923), and *Mirage* (1924), a trilogy of novels; *Children of the Market Place* (1922) and *The Tide of Time* (1937), also novels; *The Tale of Chicago* (1933), a history of the midwestern city; *Lincoln, the Man* (1931), *Vachel Lindsay* (1935), *Walt Whitman* (1937), and *Mark Twain* (1938), biographies; *Across Spoon River* (1936), an autobiography. Masters wrote in the tradition of E. W. Howe, Joseph Kirkland, and Hamlin Garland, depicting the Middle West, and later 20th-century America also, in a realistic, pessimistic, and iconoclastic light. His aims in his best-known poetry were similar to those of Sherwood Anderson in prose.

Mata Hari (died 1917). Danced on French stage. Executed by the French as a spy. There is a word *matahari* in Malayan. It means sun and may have suggested the stage name Mata Hari to **Gertrude Margarete Zelle**, as her real name ran.

Matali. In Hindu mythology, the charioteer of Indra.

materialism. Term applied to those systems of philosophy which assert reality to consist only of matter, opposed to idealism. Materialist systems flourished among the Greeks in the period before Plato (see atomists; milesians), and with the development of the mechanistic science of the late 18th century and the 19th century they came into prominence again. Marxism is the outstanding modern materialist philosophy, although as a system it remained incomplete on the death of Marx. Utilitarianism, pragmatism, and instrumentalism are based on materialist assumptions.

In a popular and less accurate sense, materialism is used to refer to a system of values, on the part of a period of history or a nation, class, or individual, which emphasizes commerce, money, comfort, power, and possessions and minimizes art, culture, ethics, and religion; thus the 20th century is often called a *materialistic* era and the U.S. a *materialistic* nation.

dialectical materialism. See under dialectic.

historical materialism. A concept regarded as the cornerstone of the philosophy of Marxism, best known through its statement in Karl Marx's Communist Manifesto. It maintains that "the history of all hitherto existing society is the history of class struggles"—that is, that historical change takes place with the overthrowing of a previously dominant economic and social class (such as Roman patricians or medieval feudal lords) by a previously subservient class (such as Roman plebeians or medieval serfs), which then become the dominant class (as the merchant bourgeoisie of the Renaissance, whose ancestors were serfs and whose descendants were modern industrial capitalists). On the basis of this assumption, all the institutions and values of a given society or a given period of history—all law, art, culture, ethics, logic and philosophy, politics, social conventions, ideas of freedom, justice, honor, and the like—are considered to be, not eternal, but merely the social reflections of prevailing modes of production, forms of property, and property relations, subject to change with the rise to power of a new economic class. Historical materialism came to play an important rôle in literary and cultural criticism in the 20th century. See Marxism in literature.

Mather, Cotton (1663–1728). American Puritan theologian, son of Increase Mather and grandson of Richard Mather and John Cotton, regarded as the epitome of the New England Puritan spirit. He is known for his vanity and arrogance, his precocity as a child (having entered Harvard at the age of 12), his prodigious learning, and his priggishness, bigotry, and fanaticism. He attempted to tyrannize over all of Massachusetts and held great power in the Second (Congregational) Church in Boston, playing an important part in the famous witchcraft trials of Salem. Attacked by a number of his contemporaries, Mather is considered to represent an effort of the old Puritanism to retain its power in the American colonies at a time when ideas and mores were changing. His works include *The Present State of New England* (1690); *Eleutheria: Or an Idea of the Reformation in England* (1698); *La Fé del Christiano* (1699), a work in Spanish; *Reasonable Religion* (1700); *Le Vrai Patron des saines Paroles* (1704), a work in French; *The Negro Christianized* (1706); *The Good Education of Children* (1708); *Bonifacius (Essays to Do Good)* (1710); *Christian Philosopher* (1721), a philosophical work regarded as tending toward Deism; *An Account . . . of Inoculating the Small-Pox* (1722); *The Angel of Bethesda* (1722), a manual on medicine; *Parentator* (1724), a biography of Increase Mather; *Manductio ad Ministerium* (1726). His most famous works are his Magnalia Christi

AMERICANA (1702) and his works on witchcraft, *Memorable Providences, Relating to Witchcrafts and Possessions* (1689) and *The Wonders of the Invisible World* (1693).

Mather wrote more than 450 volumes on a variety of subjects, had a library of about 2000 books, and spoke seven languages. He was a member of the ROYAL SOCIETY, being elected in 1714, and was influenced by the scientific spirit of his age sufficiently to endorse inoculation for smallpox, for which he was severely criticized in New England.

Mather, Frank Jewett (1868–). American art critic. One of the school of humanism represented by Irving Babbitt and Paul Elmer More.

Mather, Increase (1639–1723). American Puritan theologian, son of Richard Mather and father of Cotton MATHER. He was a well-known preacher in England and Boston, served as president of Harvard College (1685–1701), and took an important part in the famous Salem witchcraft trials. He wrote over 130 books on numerous subjects, the best-known of which are *Cases of Conscience Concerning Evil Spirits* (1693), on the witchcraft trials; *A Brief History of the War with the Indians* (1676); *Life and Death of That Reverend Man of God, Mr. Richard Mather* (1670), a biography of his father; and *An Essay for the Recording of Illustrious Providences* (REMARKABLE PROVIDENCES), (1684). Like his son, he proved himself to be under the influence of the growing scientific spirit of his time by upholding inoculation as a precaution against infection during a smallpox epidemic, and by favoring scientific courses at Harvard.

Richard Mather (1596–1669), his father, was a Puritan preacher in England before coming to New England and was an important leader in the establishment of the Congregational Church in America. He wrote numerous works and was one of the authors of the BAY PSALM BOOK.

Mathew, Father. Theobald Mathew (1790–1856), called *The Apostle of Temperance.* He was an Irish priest, and in his native country the success of his work in behalf of total abstinence was almost miraculous.

> O Father Mathew!
> Whatever path you
> In life pursue
> God grant your Reverence
> May brush off never hence
> Our mountain dew.
>
> W. S. Landor, *An Irishman to Father Mathew.*

Mathewson, Christopher. Known as **Christy Mathewson** (1880–1925). American baseball pitcher for New York Giants (1900–1916); Manager of Cincinnati team (1916–1918).

Matho. In Flaubert's SALAMMBÔ, the leader of the mercenary rebels, in love with *Salammbô.*

Mathurin, St. See under SAINTS.

Matilda. Heroine of Scott's poem ROKEBY, daughter of Rokeby, and niece of Mortham. Matilda is loved by Wilfred, son of Oswald; but she herself loves Redmond, her father's page, who turns out to be Mortham's son.

Matisse, Henri (1869–). French painter and sculptor. Leader of post-impressionism. A number of his works are in the Museum of Modern Art, New York City.

Matiwan. Mother of Occonestoga in Simms' novel THE YEMASSEE.

Matriarch. Woman who rules a family or group. *The Matriarch* is the American title of the novel *Tents of Israel* (1924) by G. B. STERN, one of a series of novels.

Matson, Norman Häghejem (1893–). American novelist and journalist. Best-known for *Flecker's Magic* (1926), which E. M. Forster praised highly. Once married to SUSAN GLASPELL.

Matsuoka, Yosuke (1880–1946). Japanese foreign minister (1940–1941). From the age of 13, American-educated, working his way through school and college. Diplomatic career in Japan (from 1904). Head of Japanese delegation at League of Nations' sessions (1932–1933) when his country was condemned for the "Manchurian incident." As prime minister concluded Tripartite Pact with Germany and Italy (Sept. 27, 1940) and Neutrality Pact with Russia. After Germany's attack on Russia, replaced in reorganization of Japanese cabinet. Died while on trial accused as war criminal.

Matsya, see AVATAR.

Matterhorn. The German name of the mountain in the Pennine Alps, known to the French as *Mont Cervin* and to the Italians as *Monte Silvio;* so called from its peak (*horn*) and the scanty patches of green meadow (*matter*) which hang around its base. Above a glacier-line 11,000 feet high, it rises in an almost inaccessible obelisk of rock to a total elevation of 14,703 feet. It was first scaled in 1865 by Whymper, when four of his party lost their lives.

Figuratively, any danger, desperate situation threatening destruction, or leap in the dark, as "the matrimonial Matterhorn."

Matthew, St., see under SAINTS.

Matthew Parker's Bible, see BIBLE, THE ENGLISH.

Matthews, James Brander (1852–1929). American educator and author. Professor of dramatic literature (1900–1924) at Columbia.

Author of plays, essays, novels, and books on the drama.

Matthiessen, Francis Otto (1902–). American educator and literary critic. Associate professor of history and literature at Harvard University. Interested in progressive labor movement. His *American Renaissance* (1941) is a work of profound literary criticism.

Matthison, Edith Wynne. See under Charles Rann KENNEDY.

Mattie. In Edith Wharton's ETHAN FROME, the cousin of his wife, with whom Ethan falls in love.

Maturin, Charles (1782–1824). English novelist, one of the leading writers of the GOTHIC NOVEL. His works include: *The Fatal Revenge, Or the Family of Montorio* (1807); *The Wild Irish Boy* (1808); *The Milesian Chief* (1811); *Bertram* (1816), a successful tragedy; *Women, Or Pour et Contre* (1818); *Melmoth the Wanderer* (see MELMOTH, SEBASTIAN) (1820), his best-known work; *The Albigenses* (1824).

Maud. A dramatic poem by TENNYSON (1855). Maud is described as a young lady—

Faultily faultless, icily regular, splendidly null.
Tennyson, *Maud,* I. ii.

Maude, Aylmer (1858–1938). English writer, best known as leading translator of Tolstoy.

Maude, Cyril (1862–). English actor and manager. Founded The Playhouse (London, 1907). Married Winifred Emery (1862–1924), actress and descendant of several generations of actors.

Maud Muller. A narrative poem by J. G. WHITTIER (1854). It records a chance meeting between the Judge and Maud, a rustic beauty who laid aside her rake and gave him a drink from the spring. Each married another, in a more suitable station of life, but was tormented by regretful illusions:

For of all sad words of tongue or pen
The saddest are these: "It might have been."

Maufrigneuse, the Duchess of, see CADIGNAN, DIANE DE.

Maugham, William Somerset (1874–). English novelist, short-story writer, and playwright, educated to be a physician. His work is marked by satire, skillful craftsmanship, a frequent ironical detachment on the part of the author, and the use of plots and material of intended popular appeal; his subject-matter is frequently concerned with white people living in the Orient. His novels include LIZA OF LAMBETH (1897); *The Making of a Saint* (1898); *Orientations* (1899); *The Hero* (1901); *Mrs. Craddock* (1902); *Merry-Go-Round* (1904); OF HUMAN BONDAGE (1915), regarded as the best of his works; THE MOON AND SIXPENCE (1919); *The Painted Veil* (1925); *British Agent* (1928), based on the author's experiences as a secret agent for the British government during World War I; CAKES AND ALE (1930); *First Person Singular* (1931); *The Narrow Corner* (1932); *Theater* (1937); *Christmas Holiday* (1939); *The Razor's Edge* (1943); *Then and Now* (1946). On the last, see also under MACHIAVELLI. Among his plays, chiefly comedies and dramas of manners, the most popular and most financially successful of his works, are *A Man of Honor* (1903); *Lady Frederick* (1907); *Penelope* (1909); *Jack Straw* (1912); *Mrs. Dot* (1912); *Caesar's Wife* (1919); *The Circle* (1921); *Our Betters* (1923); *The Letter* (1927); *Rain,* a dramatization by John Colton and Randolph Clemence of Maugham's short story *Miss Thompson; The Constant Wife* (1927); *The Sacred Flame* (1928); *The Breadwinner* (1930); *For Services Rendered* (1932); *Sheppey* (1933). Collections of short stories are: *The Trembling of a Leaf* (1921); *On a Chinese Screen* (1922); *The Casuarina Tree* (1926); *Ah King* (1933); *Cosmopolitans* (1936); *The Mixture as Before* (1940). *Andalusia* (1927), *The Gentleman in the Parlor* (1930), and *Don Fernando* (1935) are travel books. *The Summing Up* (1938) is autobiographical, and *The Hour Before the Dawn* (1942) is a novel dealing with World War II.

Maugis. In Carolingian legend, the French form of the Italian MALAGIGI, one of Charlemagne's paladins, a magician and champion. The French romance of *Maugis d'Aygremont* relates that he was the son of Duke Bevis d'Aygremont, stolen in infancy by a female slave. As the slave rested under a white thorn, a lion and a leopard devoured her, and then killed each other in disputing over the infant. Oriande the fairy, attracted to the spot by the crying of the child, exclaimed, "By the powers above, the child is *mal gist* (badly nursed)" and ever after he was called Mal-gist or Mau-gis. When grown to manhood, he obtained the enchanted horse BAYARD and took from Anthenor, the Saracen, the sword Flamberge. Subsequently he gave both to his cousin Renaud (Rinaldo). His adventures also form a part of *The Four Sons of Aymon.* See AYMON.

Maul. In Bunyan's PILGRIM'S PROGRESS, a giant who spoils young pilgrims with sophistry. He attacks Mr. Greatheart with a club, but Greatheart pierces him under the fifth rib and then cuts off his head.

Maule, Matthew. In Hawthorne's HOUSE OF THE SEVEN GABLES, the man whom old Colonel Pyncheon once had executed for witchcraft in order to confiscate his property.

Mauley, Sir Edward. The real name of the "BLACK DWARF" in Scott's novel of that title. Because of sensitiveness over his physical deformity and cynical disillusionment at having been robbed of his bride by his best friend, he lives alone and acquires the reputation of being in league with the Devil. Gradually, however, he wins many friends through his wisely directed kindness to all who seek his help, and at last he comes out of his retirement and assumes his own name and station.

Maunciple's Tale, see MANCIPLE.

Maundy Thursday. The day before Good Friday is so called from the Latin *dies mandati* ("the day of Christ's great mandate"). After He had washed His disciples' feet, He said, "A new commandment give I unto you, that ye love one another" (*St. John* xiii. 34). In the monasteries it was the custom to wash the feet of as many poor people as there were monks, and for centuries in England the sovereign, as a token of humility, did the same.

Maupassant, Guy de (1850–1893). French novelist and short-story writer, influenced by FLAUBERT and the school of NATURALISM. He is best known for his numerous short stories, dealing chiefly with Norman peasant life, the Franco-Prussian War, the behavior of the *petit-bourgeoisie,* fashionable life in Paris, and the morbid psychological obsessions of the author's own later life. His characteristic stories are usually built around an actual situation or episode from life, either his own or that of someone else. They are distinguished by detachment on the part of the author, swift movement, realistic detail, and a dramatic denouement at the close, frequently producing a "surprise ending." See also O. HENRY. Among his best-known stories are: *The Necklace, En Famille, The Rendezvous,* and *The Umbrella.* His novels include: *Une Vie* (1883), concerning the frustrations of a Norman wife; *Bel-Ami* (1885), dealing with the career of an unscrupulous and ambitious journalist in Paris; PIERRE ET JEAN (1888); *Fort comme la Mort* (1889).

Maupassant held a number of official positions in the French government during much of his career. As a result of overwork he became insane near the end of his life.

See also MOT JUSTE.

Maupin, Mlle de, see MLLE DE MAUPIN.

Mauprat, Adrien de. In BULWER LYTTON's drama *Richelieu* (1838), a colonel and chevalier in the King's army, "the wildest gallant and bravest knight of France." He marries Julie, but the King accuses him of treason for so doing, and sends him to the Bastille. He is released by Cardinal RICHELIEU.

Mauriac, François (1885–). French poet, playwright, and novelist. His series of novels concerning Bordeaux and its countryside, in which—being a Catholic himself—he boldly criticized the petty meanness of old provincial Catholic families, was awarded the *Grand Prix du Roman* of the French Academy (1925). He is regarded as one of the best minds in France.

Maurois, André. Pseudonym of **Émile Salomon Wilhelm Herzog** (1885–). French biographer and novelist. Best known for *The Silence of Colonel Bramble* (1919) which had a great popular and critical success. Has visited the United States several times and lectured at universities. One of the foremost followers of Lytton Strachey in practicing "the new biography." Well known for his life of Shelley entitled *Ariel* (1923).

mausoleum. Originally the name of the tomb of Mausolus, King of Caria, to whom his wife Artemisia erected at Halicarnassus a splendid sepulchral monument (353 B.C.). Parts of this sepulcher, which was one of the seven wonders of the world, are now in the British Museum. The name is now applied to any sepulchral monument of great size or architectural quality.

The chief mausoleums are: that of Augustus; that of Hadrian, i.e., the castle of St. Angelo, at Rome; that erected in France to Henry II by Catherine de Medici; that of St. Peter the Martyr in the church of St. Eustatius, by G. Balduccio in the 14th century; and that erected to the memory of Louis XVI.

Mauthe dog. A ghostly black spaniel that for many years haunted Peel Castle, in the Isle of Man. It used to enter the guard-room as soon as candles were lighted, and leave it at daybreak. While this specter dog was present the soldiers forbore all oaths and profane talk. One day a drunken trooper entered the guard-house alone out of bravado, but lost his speech and died in three days. Scott refers to it in his LAY OF THE LAST MINSTREL, vi stanza, 26, and again in a long note to ch. xv of PEVERIL OF THE PEAK.

mauve decade. Descriptive term applied to the period of the 1890's, especially in the U.S.; "pink trying to be purple." Thomas BEER wrote a social history of the period entitled *The Mauve Decade* (1926).

Mauves, Madame de. Heroine and title of a short story in *A Passionate Pilgrim and Other Tales* by Henry JAMES (1871). The story is a study of the marriage of a young and idealistic American girl and a worthless Frenchman.

Mavering, Dan. The hero of W. D. Howells' APRIL HOPES.

mavournin, mavourneen. Irish (*mo mhurnin*) for "My darling." Erin mavournin = Ireland, my darling; Erin go bragh = Ireland for ever!

Land of my forefathers, Erin go bragh! . . .
Erin mavournin, Erin go bragh!
Campbell, *Exile of Erin.*

See also KATHLEEN MAVOURNEEN.

Mavriky Nikolaevich, see DROZDOV, MAVRIKY NIKOLAEVICH.

mawworm. A hypocritical pretender to sanctity, a pious humbug, from the character of this name in Isaac Bickerstaffe's *The Hypocrite* (1769).

Max. Hero of Weber's opera, DER FREISCHÜTZ, a huntsman, and the best marksman in Germany.

Maxim, Sir Hiram Stevens (1840–1916). American-born inventor. Naturalized British subject (1881). Invented the Maxim machine gun and became a leading industrialist in Britain's munitions manufacture. His brother, **Hudson Maxim** (1853–1927), stayed in America, held numerous patents in connection with explosives, invented a smokeless powder called maximite and a theory of poetry called trotempoetry.

Maximilian. Full name **Ferdinand Maximilian Joseph** (1832–1867). Brother of Emperor Francis Joseph of Austria. Built the beautiful château of Miramar at Trieste. Pressed by Napoleon III, he accepted the imperial crown of Mexico (1863). Upon U.S. insistence, France withdrew its armies from Mexico, making it impossible for Maximilian to resist JUAREZ' attack. Involved in great difficulties. Surrendered at Querétaro (1867), was tried by a Mexican court-martial, condemned and executed (June 19, 1867).

Maxtone Graham, Mrs. Joyce, *née* **Anstruther.** Pseudonym **Jan Struther** (1901–). English poet and novelist. Her book of sketches of family life, *Mrs. Miniver,* was a best seller and a hugely successful moving picture.

Maxwell, James Clerk (1831–1879). Scottish physicist. Noted for his work on electromagnetism.

Maxwell, William Babington (1866–1938). English novelist. Son of the popular Victorian novelist Mary Elizabeth Braddon (1837–1915). Maxwell's second book, *The Ragged Messenger* (1904) was a best seller; it was dramatized and filmed three times. *The Guarded Flame* (1906) consolidated his success. He lived to produce about 40 books. Cf. especially his autobiography, *Time Gathered* (1937).

May. The heroine of *The Merchant's Tale* in Chaucer's *Canterbury Tales.* See JANUARY AND MAY.

May.

May Day. The first day of May. Polydore Virgil says that the Roman youths used to go into the fields and spend the calends of May in dancing and singing in honor of Flora, goddess of fruits and flowers. The English consecrated May Day to Robin Hood and the Maid Marian, because the favorite outlaw died on that day, and villagers used to set up Maypoles around which to dance, elect a May Queen, and spend the day in archery, morris dancing, and other amusements.

Evil May Day, see under EVIL.

May, Phil (1864–1903). English caricaturist, noted for his studies of London characters, as the coster-girl, the street waif, etc. For many years member of the staff of *Punch* (from 1896).

Mayakovsky, Vladimir (1894–1930). Russian futurist poet, regarded by some as *the* poet of revolutionary Russia. He sang "the might of the collective 'Ivan,'" satirized the enemies of the Revolution, and tirelessly served the new order. His most characteristic long poem is *A Cloud in Pants* (1915). Being essentially a violent individualist, a primitive who hated all restraint, his loyalty to the State produced a dichotomy in his temperament that eventually drove him to commit suicide.

Mayerling. A hunting lodge near Vienna. Scene of the tragic deaths of Prince RUDOLF of Hapsburg and Marie Vetsera.

Mayeux. After about 1830 the stock name in French plays for a vain and licentious hunchback, who always has a wide command of slang and wit.

Mayfair. A fashionable district in London, east of Hyde Park, so called from an annual fair formerly (till 1708) held in May in and around Shepherd's Market. Michael ARLEN wrote a short story of that title (1925).

Mayflower. The name of the ship that took the PILGRIM FATHERS from Southampton to Massachusetts in 1620. It is sometimes used in allusion to the snobbery of Americans of good family whose ancestors came over in the *Mayflower.*

Maylie, Rose. In Dickens' OLIVER TWIST, a character who turns out to be Oliver's aunt. Before she marries Henry Maylie, she is Rose Fleming.

Maynard, Theodore (1890–). English poet, author, and lecturer. Naturalized American (1941). Catholic convert (1913). Edited *The Book of Modern Catholic Verse* (1926) and *The Book of Modern Catholic Prose* (1927). Wrote *Exile and Other Poems* (1928); *The Odyssey of Francis Xavier* (1936); *The Story of American Catholicism* (1941); *Orestes Brownson* (1943); etc.

Mayo, Katherine (1867–1940). American journalist. Best-known for her sensational study of child-marriage in India, entitled *Mother India* (1927). See MUKERJI.

Mayo, Robert and **Andrew.** The two brothers in Eugene O'Neill's play BEYOND THE HORIZON.

Mayor of Casterbridge, The. A novel by Thomas HARDY (1886). Michael Henchard, a young hay trusser, while intoxicated at a fair sells his wife and child at auction for five pounds to a man named Newson. Eighteen years afterward when Henchard has become the Mayor of Casterbridge, they reappear, and most of the novel deals with the problems and embitterments of his later life. The girl, Elizabeth Jane, who, he finally learns, is not his own daughter but Newson's, marries his business rival, Farfrae.

mayor of the palace (maire du palais). The superintendent of the household of the king of the Franks and steward of the royal *leudes* (companies) before the accession of the CAROLINGIAN DYNASTY. The position became one of great influence, a "power behind the throne."

May Queen, The. A poem by Tennyson (1842). Alice, the heroine, says:

> I sleep so sound all night, mother, that I shall never wake,
> If you do not call me loud when the day begins to break:
> But I must gather knots of flowers, and buds and garlands gay,
> For I'm to be queen o' the May, mother, I'm to be queen o' the May.

She falls ill and pines away, but before she dies she speaks of the old sweetheart she once despised:

> And say to Robin a kind word, and tell him not to fret;
> There's many a worthier than I, would make him happy yet.
> If I had lived—I cannot tell—I might have been his wife;
> But all these things have ceased to be, with my desire of life.

Mazarin, Jules (1602–1661). French Cardinal and statesman of Italian birth. Succeeded Richelieu as prime minister (1642) and was retained by the queen regent Anne of Austria after the death of Louis XIII (1643–1661). Laid stage for Louis XIV's later successes. Amassed a great fortune. Founded (1642) the Bibliothèque Mazarine. See also under MARY, *the four Marys.*

Mazarin Bible, see BIBLE, SPECIALLY NAMED.

Mazeppa, Ivan (1644–1709). The famous Cossack hetman, hero of Byron's poem *Mazeppa* (1819), was born of a noble Polish family in Podolia, became a page in the court of John Casimir, King of Poland, but intrigued with Theresia, the young wife of a Podolian count, who had the young page lashed naked to a wild horse, and turned adrift. The horse dropped dead in the Ukraine, where Mazeppa was released and cared for by Cossacks and in time became hetman and prince of the Ukraine under Peter the Great of Russia. Byron makes Mazeppa tell his tale to Charles XII of Sweden after the battle of Pultowa, in which he had deserted to Charles and fought against Russia. Mazeppa is the hero of a Russian drama *Pultowa* by PUSHKIN.

Mazikeen or **Shedeem.** A species of beings in Jewish mythology resembling the Arabian JINN, and said to be the agents of magic and enchantment. When Adam fell, says the Talmud, he was excommunicated for 130 years, during which time he begat demons and specters, for, it is written "Adam lived 130 years and begat children in his own image" (*Gen.* v. 3). (*Rabbi Jeremiah ben Eliezar.*)

> And the Mazikeen shall not come nigh thy tents.—*Ps.* xci, 5 (Chaldee version).

swells out like the Mazikeen ass. The allusion is to a Jewish tradition that a servant, whose duty it was to rouse the neighborhood to midnight prayer, one night mounted a stray ass and neglected his duty. As he rode along the ass grew bigger and bigger, till at last it towered as high as the tallest edifice, where it left the man, and where next morning he was found.

Mazzini, Giuseppe (1805–1872). Italian patriot; proposed to unify Italy under a republican form of government. Refused to take seat in Italian parliament under a monarchy. Involved in revolutionary movements, captured (1870) but released.

Mead, Margaret (1901–). American anthropologist. Her major expeditions have each resulted in a book, notably *Coming of Age in Samoa* (1928), etc. Also lecturer in psychology at New York University and visiting lecturer in child study at Vassar College.

Meadows, Mr. In Fanny Burney's novel CECILIA, a young gallant, very much fêted by the ladies and ostensibly very much bored with life.

Meal-Tub Plot. A pretended conspiracy against Protestants, fabricated by Thomas Dangerfield (d. 1685) in 1679, so called because he said that the papers relating to it were concealed in a meal-tub in the house of Mrs. Cellier, a Roman Catholic. She was tried for high treason and acquitted, while Dangerfield was convicted of libel, whipped, and pilloried.

Meander. The modern Menderes river in Asia Minor. It dried up when Phaëthon drove the sun chariot. Its proverbial windings are comparable to the labyrinth of Minos.

Measure for Measure. A comedy by Shakespeare (ca. 1604). The Duke of Vienna pretends to leave the city, deputing his authority to Angelo, while he assumes the disguise of a friar and stays to watch proceedings. Angelo almost immediately sentences CLAUDIO to death for seducing JULIET, but when Claudio's sister Isabel comes to plead for him, Angelo brazenly endeavors to seduce her. The "friar" persuades her to appear to consent to the plan but to send Angelo's deserted fiancée MARIANA to the rendezvous instead. Eventually the Duke assumes authority again and matters are straightened out. The plot of the play is founded on Whetstone's *Promos and Cassandra* (1582), which was taken from the 85th tale in Cinthio's *Hecatommithi* (1565).

Mecca. A long desired goal; the end of a pilgrimage; from Mecca in Arabia, the birthplace of Mahomet and the Holy City to which all pious Mohammedans make the HADJ or pilgrimage at least once in a lifetime.

Meck, Nadezhda Filaretovna von (1831–1894). Widow of a Russian railroad contractor, who helped TSCHAIKOVSKY by getting him commissions for his work and (1877) by making him an annual allowance of £600. They never met but corresponded continuously, she being known as his "beloved friend." Cf. Catherine Drinker Bowen, *Beloved Friend.*

Medal, The. Title of a satirical poem by John DRYDEN (1682), aimed at the Earl of Shaftesbury and the Whigs whose recent triumph had been the occasion for the striking of a medal.

Medamothi. The island at which the fleet of PANTAGRUEL lands on the fourth day of their voyage, and where they buy many choice curiosities, such as the picture of a man's voice, an echo drawn to life, Plato's ideas, the atoms of Epicurus, a sample of Philomela's needlework, and other objects of *vertu* which could be obtained in no other portion of the globe (Rabelais, *Pantagruel,* iv. 3). The word is Greek, and has the same meaning as More's *Utopia* and Butler's *Erewhon,* i.e., "Nowhere."

Medea. In Greek legend, a sorceress, daughter of Aeetes, King of Colchis. She marries JASON, the leader of the ARGONAUTS, whom she aids to obtain the golden fleece, and is the mother of Medus, whom the Greeks regard as the ancestor of the Medes. After being married ten years, Jason repudiates her for Glauce, and Medea, in revenge, sends the bride a poisoned robe, which kills both Glauce and her father. Medea then tears to pieces her two sons, and flees to Athens in a chariot drawn by dragons. The story has been dramatized in Greek, by Euripides; in Latin, by Seneca and by Ovid; in French, by Corneille (*Médée,* 1635), Longepierre (1695), and Legouve (1849); in English, by Glover (1761) and Robinson JEFFERS (1947), starring Judith Anderson.

Medea's kettle or *cauldron.* A means of restoring lost youth. Medea cut an old ram to pieces, threw the pieces into her cauldron, and a young lamb came forth. Jason's father Aeson was then given back his youth. The daughters of PELIAS thought to restore their father to youth in the same way, but Medea refused to utter the magic words, and the old man ceased to live. See also ABSYRTUS.

Médecin malgré Lui, Le (The Physician in Spite of Himself). A comedy by MOLIÈRE (1666). The "enforced doctor" is SGANARELLE, a faggot-maker, who is called in by Géronte to cure his daughter LUCINDE of dumbness.

Medes and Persians, laws of. Unalterable decisions; rules that cannot be modified. The allusion is to *Dan.* vi. 12.

Medici (*Ital.*) or **Médicis** (*Fr.*). Literally, "physicians" or "doctors." Name of an Italian family powerful in Florence and Tuscany especially from the 14th to the 16th century. **Cosimo de' Medici,** called **Cosimo the Elder** (1389–1464), for thirty years patron of literature and fine arts and often surnamed the "father of his country." **Lorenzo de' Medici,** known as **Lorenzo the Magnificent** or in Italian **Il Magnifico** (1449–1492), a polished prose writer and original poet; a tyrannical ruler; especially influential in causing the Tuscan dialect to become the national speech of Italy.

medicine, father of. See under FATHER.

medicine show. A typically American type of entertainment in the early days designed to advertise patent medicines and cure-alls. Medicine shows were given from a traveling wagon. They featured freaks, song-and-dance "artists," and musical numbers. The actors were made up as Indian medicine men. Modern moving picture and radio advertising reflect this influence.

Medill, Joseph (1823–1899). Canadian-born American journalist. Bought interest in Chicago *Tribune* (1855); supported Lincoln for presidency and during his administration gained control of *Tribune.* His grandchildren, Joseph Medill MCCORMICK, Robert Rutherford MCCORMICK, Joseph Medill PATTERSON, and Eleanor Medill PATTERSON, inherited interest in the *Tribune.*

Medina (from Lat. *medium,* "middle, mean"). (1) In Spenser's FAËRIE QUEENE (II. ii.), the typification of "the golden mean." She is the stepsister of Perissa (excess) and Elissa (deficiency), who can never agree upon any subject.

(2) A city in Arabia, the second holy city of the Mohammedans; it was called "Yathrib" before Mahomet fled thither from Mecca, but afterwards Medinat-al-Nabi ("the city of the prophet"), whence its present name.

Medivin, Thomas (1788–1869). British biographer of Shelley; associated with Shelley and Byron in Italy (1821). His *Memoir of Shelley* (1833) was later expanded into *The Life of Shelley* (2 vols.; 1847).

Medmenham Abbey. A ruined Cistercian abbey near Marlow on the Thames. It became the meeting place of the Hell-fire Club, founded by Dashwood, Wilkes, and Bubb Dodington in the 18th century. Its convivialities became orgies and its ritual was a mockery of all religion. For an account of some of its procedures, cf. Johnstone, *Chrysal, or the Adventures of a Guinea,* volume 3, book II.

Medora. In Byron's poem THE CORSAIR, the beloved wife of Conrad, the corsair. When Conrad is taken captive by the pasha Seyd, Medora sits day after day expecting his return. When he does not come back, Medora dies.

Medoro. In Ariosto's ORLANDO FURIOSO, a Moorish youth of extraordinary beauty, but of humble race; page to Agramante. Angelica dresses his wounds, falls in love with him, marries him, and retires with him to Cathay, where, in right of his wife, he becomes king. This event is the cause of Orlando's madness.

Medrawd. In the Welsh *Triads,* the name given to MODRED.

Medusa. The chief of the GORGONS of Greek mythology. Legend says that she was a beautiful maiden, specially famous for her hair, but that she violated the temple of Athene, who thereupon transformed her hair into serpents and made her face so terrible that all who looked on it were turned to stone. PERSEUS, assisted by Athene (who lent him her shield wherein he looked only on the *reflection* of Medusa during his attack), struck off her head, and by its means rescued ANDROMEDA from the monster. Medusa was the mother by Poseidon of Chrysaor and PEGASUS.

Meg Dods, see DODS, MEG.

Megissogwon ("the great Pearl-Feather"). In Longfellow's poem HIAWATHA, a magician, and the Manito of wealth. It was Megissogwon who sent the fiery fever on man, the white fog, and death. This great Pearl-Feather slays the father of Nokomis the grandmother of Hiawatha. Hiawatha all day long fights with the magician without effect. At nightfall the woodpecker tells him to strike at the tuft of hair on the magician's head, the only vulnerable place. Hiawatha accordingly discharges his three remaining arrows at the hair-tuft, and Megissogwon dies.

Meg Merrilies, see MERRILIES, MEG.

Meh Lady. A Negro dialect story of the old South by Thomas Nelson PAGE. Also see MARSE CHAN.

Meier-Graefe, Julius (1867–1935). German art critic. Founded four art magazines. Besides almost 50 books on art and travel he wrote one novel and one volume of short stories.

Meiklejohn, Alexander (1872–). Educator. President, Amherst College (1912–1924). Director, experimental college at the University of Wisconsin (1926–1933). Instructor, School for Social Studies in San Francisco (from 1933).

Meiklewham, Mr. Saunders. In Scott's ST. RONAN'S WELL, one of the Managing Committee of the Spa. He is known as "the man of law."

Meissonier, Jean Louis Ernest (1825–1891). French painter, noted for small meticulous genre pictures, often of military subjects. *Hallebardier; Le Grand Fumeur; Campagne de France; Les Cuirassiers;* etc.

Meister, Wilhelm, see WILHELM MEISTER.

Meistersingers. Burgher poets or minstrels of Germany, who attempted, in the 14th to 16th centuries, to revive the national minstrelsy of the MINNESINGERS, which had fallen into decay. Hans Sachs, the cobbler (1494–1576), was the most celebrated. The original corporation of meistersingers was called the Twelve Wise Masters.

Die Meistersinger von Nürnberg. An opera by Richard WAGNER (1868), in which he satirized his critics. The hand of the fair young Eva Pogner, daughter of the town goldsmith, is promised as the prize for a Nuremberg singing contest. The chief rivals are Beckmesser the town clerk, and a young nobleman, Walter or Walther von Stolzing, who is loved by the lady and has dreamed a beautiful song but is hampered by his ignorance of all the petty artificial rules of the song-*fest.* Walter's cause is championed by Hans Sachs, the cobbler, and with his aid Beckmesser is put to confusion. Walter sings his *Preislied* and scores a triumph.

Mejnoun and Leilah. A Persian love tale, the *Romeo and Juliet* or *Pyramus and Thisbe* of Eastern romance.

Mel, The great. Melchisedec Harrington, the tailor, father of EVAN HARRINGTON in Meredith's novel of that name.

Melaine. A narrative poem by N. P. Willis (*Am.,* 1806–1867). The heroine, Melaine, learns just before her wedding that she has fallen in love with her own brother. The shock causes her death.

Melampus. In Greek legend, a seer who understood the language of birds and beasts. He was the first mortal to practice the art of healing. The introduction into Greece of the worship of Dionysus was ascribed to him.

Melancholy, The Anatomy of, see ANATOMY.

Melanchthon, Philip. Grecized form of German **Schwarzert**, wrongly interpreted as meaning "black earth" (1497–1560). German reformer and scholar. Friend and collaborator of LUTHER. His *Loci Communes Rerum Theologicarum* (1521) is the first major Protestant treatise on theological dogmatism. Drafted the Augsburg Confession (1530) and worked with persistent moderation for the restitution of Christian unity. Noted for his skill in dialectics and exegesis, and his great learning.

Melanchthon's Hellenized name is one instance among many. Oecolampadius corresponds to German Hausschein; Erasmus to Gheraerd; etc. This procedure was in vogue at the time of the re-awakening of interest in Greek at the beginning of the modern era. It has its counterpart in a wealth of Latinized names in the periods preceding and following.

Melba, Mme Nellie. Stage name of **Helen Porter Mitchell** (1861?–1931). Australian operatic soprano. Début as Gilda in *Rigoletto* (1887). First appearance in New York (1893). Prima donna at Royal Opera, Covent Garden, London. Dame of the British Empire (1918).

Melchers, Julius Gari (1860–1932). American painter of genre pictures of Dutch peasant life, religious paintings, and murals.

Melchior. One of the three MAGI.

Melchizedek. Cf. *Gen.* xiv. 18. E. A. Robinson's poem *Two Men* begins:

> Melchizedec, he praised the Lord,
> And gave some wine to Abraham;
> But who can tell what else he did
> Must be more learned than I am.

Meleager. A hero of Greek legend, son of Oeneus of Calydon and Althaea, distinguished for throwing the javelin, for slaying the Calydonian boar, and as one of the ARGONAUTS. It was declared by the Fates that he would die as soon as a piece of wood then on the fire was burnt up, whereupon his mother snatched the log from the fire and extinguished it. After Meleager had slain his maternal uncles, his mother threw the brand on the fire again, and Meleager died.

Melema, Tito. In George Eliot's ROMOLA, the scapegrace husband of Romola.

> [He] made almost every one fond of him for he was young, and clever, and beautiful, and his manners to all were gentle and kind. I believe when I first knew him, he never thought of anything cruel or base. But because he tried to slip away from everything that was unpleasant, and cared for nothing else so much as his own safety, he came at last to commit some of the basest deeds—such as make men infamous. He denied his father, and left him to misery; he betrayed every trust that was reposed in him, that he might keep himself safe and get rich and prosperous.—*Epilogue.*

Meliadus. Father of TRISTRAM in the Arthurian romances, and King of Lyonesse. He was drawn to a chase by the wiles of a fay who was in love with him, and from whose thraldom he was ultimately released by Merlin.

Meliboeus or **Melibee.** The central figure in Chaucer's prose *Tale of Meliboeus,* one of his CANTERBURY TALES, which is a translation of a French rendering of Albertano da Brescia's Latin *Liber Consolationis et Concilii.* Meliboeus is a wealthy young man, married to Prudens. One day, when he has gone "into the fields to play," enemies of his beat his wife and leave his daughter for dead. Meliboeus resolves upon vengeance, but his wife persuades him to call together his enemies, and he tells them he forgives them "to this effect and to this ende, that God of His endeles mercy wole at the tyme of oure deyinge forgive us oure giltes that we have trespased to Him in this wreeched world."

Melicent. The heroine of Cabell's DOMNEI originally published as *The Soul of Melicent.* She is the daughter of Count MANUEL, the hero of *Figures of Earth,* and appears in that romance as a child.

Melicertes. Son of Ino, a sea deity of Greek legend. See LEUCOTHEA. Athamas imagined his wife to be a lioness, and her two sons to be lion's cubs. In his frenzy he slew one of the boys, and drove the other, Melicertes, with his mother into the sea. The mother became a sea goddess, and the boy, under the name of Palaemon, the god of harbors.

Melincourt. A satirical novel by Thomas Love PEACOCK (1817).

Mélisande. (1) See PELLÉAS AND MÉLISANDE; (2) See MELUSINA; (3) See MÉLISSANDE.

Melisendra. In medieval romance, the supposed daughter of Marsilio and Charlemagne, married to his nephew Don Gwyferos. She was taken captive by the Moors, and confined seven years in a dungeon before Gwyferos rescued her. Cf. *Don Quixote* II. ii. 7, where the story is played as a puppet-show.

Melissa. (1) The prophetess in Ariosto's ORLANDO FURIOSO, who lives in Merlin's cave. BRADAMANT gives her the enchanted ring to take to ROGERO, so, assuming the form of Atlantes, she goes to Alcina's island, and not only delivers Rogero, but disenchants all the forms metamorphosed in the island. In Book xix she assumes the form of RODOMONT, and persuades Agramant to break the league which was to settle the contest by single combat. A general battle ensues.

(2) In Spenser's FAËRIE QUEENE (VI. xii), Melissa is Pastorella's handmaid.

Mélissande. The heroine of Rostand's *Far Away Princess* (*La Princesse Lointaine;* 1895), based on a 13th century Provençal romance. Her beauty was far-famed.

Melkarth, in Greek **Melicertes.** Literally, "city king." Chief god of ancient Tyre, a variant of the Canaanite BAAL, later identified with HERCULES.

Mell, Mr. In Dickens' DAVID COPPERFIELD, a poor down-trodden second master at Salem House, assistant to Mr. CREAKLE. The fact that his mother lives in an almshouse brings upon him the sneers of STEERFORTH. Mr. Mell plays the flute with great pleasure.

Mellen, Grenville (1799–1841). American poet, story-teller, and journalist.

Mellichampe: a Legend of the Santee. The second novel in W. G. Simms' trilogy of the American Revolution (1836). The first was *The Partisan,* the third, KATHERINE WALTON.

Mellifluous Doctor. See under DOCTOR.

Melmoth, Sebastian. The name used by Oscar WILDE while the author was living in France following his release from prison. It was signed to both THE BALLAD OF READING GAOL and DE PROFUNDIS. *Melmoth* is the name of a man who sells his soul to the Devil in return for everlasting life in *Melmoth the Wanderer,* a famous novel of terror and mystery by Charles MATURIN, a relative of Wilde's mother, "Speranza."

Melnotte, Claude. Hero of BULWER LYTTON's comedy *The Lady of Lyons* (1838). Though only a gardener's son, he plays the rôle of Prince of Como with such success that he wins the fair Pauline Deschapelles. When she learns the truth she repudiates him, but he wins her back.

Melpomene. In Greek mythology, the Muse of tragedy. See MUSES.

Melting Pot, The. A drama by Israel ZANGWILL (1908). The hero, David Quixano, a young Russian Jew, is the composer of a symphony, *America,* which expresses his idealistic conception of his new country as a great crucible that will dissolve racial prejudices. He is in love with Vera Revendal, a Russian Gentile, but when her father comes over from Russia, he recognizes the officer responsible for the massacre of his father, mother, and sister at Kishenev and leaves her. The performance of his symphony *America* brings him back to his ideals and to the girl he loves.

Melun. In Shakespeare's KING JOHN, a French lord.

Melusina or **Melisande.** The most famous of the *fées* of French romance, looked upon by the houses of Lusignan, Rohan, Luxemburg, and Sassenaye as their ancestor and founder. Having enclosed her father in a high mountain for offending her mother, she is condemned to become every Saturday a serpent from her waist downward. She marries Raymond, Count of Lusignan, and makes her husband vow never to visit her on a Saturday, but the Count hides himself on one of the forbidden days, and sees his wife's transformation. Melusina is now obliged to leave her husband, and is destined to wander about as a specter until the day of doom. In another version of the story, the Count immures her in the dungeon of his castle. See also UNDINE.

A sudden scream is called in French *un cri de Mélusine,* in allusion to the scream of despair uttered by Melusina when she was discovered by her husband; in Poitou, certain gingerbread cakes bearing the impress of a beautiful woman *"bien coiffée,"* with a serpent's tail, made by confectioners for the May fair in the neighborhood of Lusignan, are still called *Mélusines.*

Melville, Herman (1819–1891). American novelist, known for his stories of adventures at sea and in the South Sea Islands, largely autobiographical, which were extremely popular in the early part of his career. These are TYPEE (1846); OMOO (1847); *Mardi* (1849); *Redburn* (1849); and WHITE-JACKET (1850). His most famous book is MOBY DICK (1851), considered one of the greatest novels in the history of American literature and the literature of the world. Melville was strongly influenced by HAWTHORNE, who was a neighbor of his for several years, and his later books were not liked by the public because of their pessimism and symbolism. His work at its best is marked by realism, rich and poetic prose, the use of allegory and symbolism, and an effort to express the philosophical and religious meanings the author felt he had found in the world. His remaining works include PIERRE (1852); *Israel Potter* (1855); *Piazza Tales* (1856), short stories; *The Confidence Man* (1857); *Billy Budd,* written just before the author's death and published in 1924; and the following books of poems: *Clarel* (1876), *Battle-Pieces and Aspects of the War* (1866), *John Marr and Other Sailors* (1888), and *Timoleon* (1891).

Melville, who is considered among the most important of American novelists, spent several years in his early life as a sailor on whaling ships and men-of-war in the U.S. navy and as a laborer or traveler in the South Sea islands. During the last 20 years of his life he was a customs inspector in New York City and allowed his writing to slip. He died in obscurity, and interest in him was not revived until the period following World War I. For a full analysis of Melville and his work, see *American Renaissance,* by F. O. Matthiessen.

Melville, Julia. In Sheridan's comedy THE RIVALS, a ward of Sir Anthony Absolute, in love with Faulkland, who saved her life when she was thrown into the water by the upsetting of a boat.

Melyhalt, Lady. In the old romances, a powerful subject of King ARTHUR, whose domains Galiot invades. She chooses Galiot as her lover.

memento mori (*Lat.*, "remember you must die"). An emblem of mortality, such as a skull; something to put us in mind of the shortness and uncertainty of life.

> I make as good use of it [Bardolph's face] as many a man doth of a death's head or a memento mori.—Shakespeare, *Henry IV*, iii, 3.

Memling, Hans (1430?–1495). Early Flemish painter, celebrated for his treatment of religious subjects. His best work is in the reliquary of St. Ursula in the hospital of St. John at Bruges.

Memnon. The Oriental or Ethiopian prince who, in the Trojan War, went to the assistance of his uncle PRIAM and was slain by ACHILLES. His mother Eos (the Dawn) was inconsolable for his death, and wept for him every morning.

The Greeks called the statue of Amenophis III, in Thebes, that of Memnon. When first struck by the rays of the rising sun, it is said to have produced a sound like the snapping asunder of a cord. Poetically, when Eos kissed her son at daybreak, the hero acknowledged the salutation with a musical murmur. *Memnon* is the title of a novel by VOLTAIRE, the object of which is to show the folly of aspiring to too much wisdom.

Mémoires d'Outre-Tombe. A volume of personal reminiscences by CHATEAUBRIAND (1849–1850), describing the author's youth, recounting his adventures, and presenting vivid character-portraits of outstanding personalities of his time.

Memoirs of a Cavalier. A historical romance by DEFOE (1724).

Memorial Day, see DECORATION DAY.

Memory.

the bard of memory, see under BARD.

Memory Woodfall. William Woodfall (1746–1803) who would attend a debate, and, without notes, report it accurately next morning.

Menalcas. Any shepherd or rustic. The name figures in the *Eclogues* of Virgil and the *Idyls* of Theocritus.

Menander (343?–?291 B.C.). Athenian dramatist; author of more than 100 comedies, characterized by wit, ingenious plots, and great literary style, which survived only in fragmentary form and through adaptations by PLAUTUS and TERENCE.

Men and Women. A collection of poems by Robert BROWNING (1855), including FRA LIPPO LIPPI.

Mencia of Mosquera. Heroine of an episode in Le Sage's GIL BLAS. As a young girl she marries Don Alvaro de Mello. A few days after the marriage, Alvaro happens to quarrel with Don Andrea de Baesa and kill him. He is obliged to flee from Spain, leaving his bride behind, and his property is confiscated. Seven years later, having heard the news of his death, she marries the wealthy Marquis of Guardia. Alvaro, however, appears one day as an under-gardener on the place. She flees with him, only to see him killed by robbers, and returns to the Marquis, only to find him dying.

Mencken, Henry Louis (1880–). American journalist, essayist, and literary critic, for a number of years associated with the Baltimore *Sun*. During the period of the 1920's he was famous for his violent and vitriolic attacks on the hypocrisy, stupidity, and bigotry of much of American life as he saw it at the time, especially the Puritan and Victorian traditions and the bourgeoisie, the latter being termed by him "boobs." See also LEWIS, SINCLAIR; SHAW, GEORGE BERNARD. He began as a contributor to the magazine THE SMART SET in 1908, becoming co-editor with George Jean NATHAN in 1914. In 1924 he and Nathan founded the AMERICAN MERCURY, which became famous for its "debunking" articles and its section entitled AMERICANA. Mencken was violently denounced by the nation's conservative elements, and during World War I, when he was a war correspondent with the German army, was accused of being in the pay of Kaiser Wilhelm II. He had a wide influence on the young American intellectuals of the 1920's, especially students in colleges. He retired in 1933 to devote himself to politics and religion, became a foe of the NEW DEAL, and quickly dropped out of the public eye. Critics credit Mencken for his skill at satire and the vigor and trenchancy of his attacks on the shams and stuffiness of his day, but call attention to his intolerance and frequent crudity and misinformation. He is considered to have been influenced by the writings of Thomas HUXLEY.

Collections of Mencken's essays, through which his views were best known, include *A Book of Burlesques* (1916); *A Little Book in C Major* (1916); *In Defense of Women* (1917); *A Book of Prefaces* (1917, 1924, 1928); *Damn—A Book of Calumny* (1917); THE AMERICAN LANGUAGE (1919, revised in 1936; two *Supplements* 1945, 1948); *Prejudices* (1919, 1920, 1922, 1924, 1926, 1927), his most popular series. Among other works are *Ventures into Verse* (1903), poems; *The Artist* (1912) and *Heliogabalus* (1920), plays; *George*

Bernard Shaw, His Plays (1905); *Philosophy of Friedrich Nietzsche* (1908); *Notes on Democracy* (1926); *James Branch Cabell* (1927), a literary study; *Schimpflexikon* (*Dictionary of Abuse;* 1928), a collection of attacks and adverse criticism of the author, edited by Mencken himself; *A Treatise on the Gods* (1930); *Making a President* (1932, 1936); *A Treatise on Right and Wrong* (1934); and three autobiographical works—*Happy Days, 1880–1892* (1940), *Newspaper Days, 1897–1906* (1941), and *Heathen Days, 1890–1936* (1943).

Mendelism. The theory of heredity promulgated by Gregor Johann Mendel (1822–1884), the Austrian scientist and Abbot of Brunn, showing that the characters of the parents of cross-bred offspring reappear in certain proportions in successive generations according to definite laws. *Mendel's Law* was discovered by him in 1865 through experiments with peas.

Mendelssohn, Felix. In full **Jakob Ludwig Felix Mendelssohn-Bartholdy** (1809–1847). German composer, conductor, and concert pianist; grandson of Moses MENDELSSOHN. First appearance as a concert pianist at the age of nine. Instrumental in re-introduction of BACH by performing (1829) his *Passion According to St. Matthew* for the first time after the composer's death. Conductor at the Gewandhaus in Leipzig (from 1835). Composer of 4 symphonies (among them the famous "Italian" in A major), chamber music, concert overtures, choral works and oratorios; concertos; numerous works for the piano, as his 8 books of *Lieder ohne Worte* (*Songs without Words*); etc.

Mendelssohn, Moses (1729–1786). German Jewish philosopher, known as "the German Socrates." Author of *Abhandlung über die Evidenz in den Metaphysischen Wissenschaften* (1764), an essay which was awarded the Berlin Academy prize over one submitted by KANT; *Jerusalem oder über religiöse Macht und Judentum* (1783), a history of Judaism urging religious tolerance; and especially *Phädon* (1767), a comprehensive collection of evidence to support the belief in the immortality of the soul. He was a close friend of LESSING, whose *Nathan der Weise* is an idealized portrait of him. His daughter **Dorothea** (1763–1839) married Friedrich SCHLEGEL.

Mendès, Catulle (1841–1909). French man of letters; founder of the PARNASSIAN school of poetry, the beginning of which he described in *Légende du Parnasse Contemporain* (1884).

Mendicant Orders or **Begging Friars.** The orders of the Franciscans (*Grey Friars*), Augustines (*Black Friars*), Carmelites (*White Friars*), and Dominicans (*Preaching Friars*).

Menechmians. Persons exactly like each other; so called from the *Menaechmi* of Plautus, the basis of Shakespeare's COMEDY OF ERRORS, in which not only the two Dromios are exactly like each other, but Antipholus of Ephesus is the facsimile of his brother, Antipholus of Syracuse.

Menelaus. In Greek legend, son of Atreus, brother of AGAMEMNON, and husband of HELEN, through whose desertion of him was brought about the Trojan War. He was the King of Sparta or of Lacedaemon. See ILIAD.

Meng-tse. The fourth of the sacred books of China; so called from the name of its author (372?–?287 B.C.), Latinized into Mencius. Confucius or Kung-fu-tse wrote the other three; viz., Ta-heo (*School of Adults*), Chong-yong (*The Golden Mean*), and Lun-yu (*Book of Maxims*).

mother of Meng. A Chinese expression, meaning "an admirable teacher." Meng's father died soon after the birth of the sage, and he was brought up by his mother.

Men in White. A play about the internal workings of a hospital by Sidney KINGSLEY (1933), awarded the Pulitzer prize for 1934.

Menken, Adah Isaacs (1835–1868). American actress of Jewish ancestry, famous for her extravagant personality and wild and fabulous adventures. She was associated at one time or another with a number of the leading literary figures of the day in both the U.S. and Europe, including Walt WHITMAN, Mark TWAIN, Bret HARTE, DICKENS, Charles READE, SWINBURNE, D. G. ROSSETTI, Théophile GAUTIER, and Alexandre DUMAS *père*. She wrote flamboyant romantic poetry on her life, in free verse compared to that of both Walt Whitman and the Bible.

Menninger, Karl Augustus (1893–). American psychiatrist. Founder of the Menninger Clinic; of great influence on psychiatric practice in America. Wrote *The Human Mind* (130; revised, 1937); *Man Against Himself* (1938); *Love Against Hate* (1942); etc.

Mennonites. Followers of Simons Menno (1492–1559), a native of Friesland, who modified the fanatical views of the Anabaptists. The sect still survives, in the United States as well as in Holland and Germany.

Men of Harlech. Welsh national anthem. Anonymous. From the translation by John Oxenford, published with the Welsh version, and music (1873):

> Men of Harlech, march to glory,
> Victory is hov'ring o'er ye,
> Bright-eyed freedom stands before ye,
> Hear ye not her call?
> At your sloth she seems to wonder.
> Rend the sluggish bonds asunder,
> Let the war-cry's deaf'ning thunder
> Ev'ry foe appall.

Menpes, Mortimer (1859–1938). British painter and etcher. Edited *The Menpes Series of Great Masters.* Author of *Whistler as I Knew Him* (1904); etc.

Menshevik. See under BOLSHEVIK.

mental tests. See SIMON BINET TESTS.

mentor. A guide, a wise and faithful counsellor; so called from Mentor, in whose care ULYSSES left his son Telemachus when he embarked for the Trojan War.

Menuhin, Yehudi (1917–). American violin virtuoso. First concert appearance as a child prodigy in 1923. With his sister, the talented pianist **Hephzibah Menuhin** (1920–), in joint sonata recitals (from 1930). As mature artist on the concert stage (from 1937), regarded as one of the finest living violinists.

Men Without Women. A volume of short stories by Ernest HEMINGWAY (1927).

Mephibosheth. In the Old Testament, the lame son of Jonathan to whom David showed great kindness for his dead father's sake.

Mephibosheth in Dryden's ABSALOM AND ACHITOPHEL, Pt. ii, is meant for Samuel Pordage (d. 1691), a poetaster.

Mephistopheles. A manufactured name (possibly from three Greek words meaning "not loving the light") of a devil or familiar spirit which first appears in the late medieval FAUST legend. He is well known as the sneering, jeering, leering tempter in Goethe's *Faust* and in Gounod's opera of the same name and Boïto's opera, *Mefistofele.* He is mentioned by Shakespeare (*Merry Wives,* i. 1) and Fletcher as *Mephostophilus,* and in Marlowe's *Faustus* as *Mephostopilis.*

Mercator, Gerhardus. Latin for **Gerhard Krämer** (1512–1594). Flemish geographer, especially remembered for the system of projection, first used in his map of 1568 and now known as Mercator's projection, in which the meridians are drawn as parallel lines so that only comparatively small areas can be made to appear in correct relative dimensions.

Mercedes. (1) In Dumas' COUNT OF MONTE CRISTO, the Catalan sweetheart of Edmond Dantes.

(2) A drama (1883) by T. B. ALDRICH. The heroine, Mercedes, is a Spanish woman whose native town has been invaded by French soldiers. They are to be poisoned, and to allay their suspicions, she and her child drink the fatal wine with them.

Merchant of Venice, The. A comedy by Shakespeare (ca. 1595). The titular "merchant" is Antonio, from whom his young friend Bassanio, who is in love with Portia, borrows 3,000 ducats to carry on his suit. According to the terms of the will left by Portia's father, the lover who would win her hand and fortune must rightly choose the one of three caskets, of lead, gold and silver, that contains her picture. Bassanio chooses the leaden casket and is successful. In the meantime Antonio has met with ill fortune. He had borrowed the 3,000 ducats for Bassanio from Shylock, the Jew on these conditions: if the loan was repaid within three months, only the principal would be required; if not, the Jew should be at liberty to claim a pound of flesh from Antonio's body. Antonio's ships have not returned as he expected, and the Jew demands the forfeiture. Portia, in the disguise of a doctor of law, conducts the defense and saves Antonio by reminding the Jew that a pound of *flesh* gives him no drop of blood and that he must cut neither more nor less than an exact pound or his life will be forfeited.

The interwoven stories of this comedy are drawn from medieval legends the germs of which are found in the GESTA ROMANORUM. The tale of the bond is ch. xlviii, and that of the caskets is ch. xcix. Much of the plot is also given in the 14th century *Il Pecorone* of Ser Giovanni, but Shakespeare could not read Italian, and since there was no translation in his day it is more than doubtful whether he ever saw or was aware of it.

Merchant's or **Marchantes Tale,** see JANUARY AND MAY.

Mercier, Désiré Joseph (1851–1926). Belgian cardinal (from 1907). Professor of Thomist philosophy at Louvain (1882–1906). Archbishop of Malines and primate of Belgium (1906). Spokesman of Belgians during German occupation of Belgium in World War I. Visited U.S. (1919) to thank America for assistance to Belgium. Worked for unification of Anglican, Protestant Episcopal and Roman churches.

Merciless Parliament. See under PARLIAMENTS.

Mercury. The Roman equivalent of the Greek HERMES, son of Maia and Jupiter, to whom he acted as messenger. He was the god of science and commerce, the patron of travelers and also of rogues, vagabonds and thieves. Hence, the name of the god is used to denote both a messenger and a thief.

Mercury is represented as a young man with winged hat and winged sandals (*talaria*), bearing the CADUCEUS, and sometimes a purse.

Mercury fig (Lat. *Ficus ad Mercurium*). The first fig gathered off a fig-tree was by the Romans devoted to Mercury. The proverbial saying was applied generally to all first fruits or first works.

you cannot make a Mercury of every log. Pythagoras said: *Non ex quovis ligno Mercurius fit.* That is, "Not every mind will answer equally well to be trained into a scholar." The proper wood for a statue of Mercury was box.

Mercutio. In Shakespeare's ROMEO AND JULIET, kinsman of Prince Escalus, and Romeo's friend. He is an airy, sprightly, elegant young nobleman, so full of wit and fancy that Dryden says Shakespeare was obliged to kill him in the third act, lest the poet himself should have been killed by Mercutio.

> Mercutio's wit, gaiety, and courage will always procure him friends that wish him a longer life; but his death is not precipitated—he has lived out the time allotted him in the construction of the play.—Dr. Johnson.
>
> The light and fanciful humor of Mercutio serves to enhance and illustrate the romantic and passionate character of Romeo.—Sir W. Scott, *The Drama.*

Mercy. In Bunyan's PILGRIM'S PROGRESS, a young pilgrim who accompanies Christiana in her walk to Zion. When Mercy reaches the Wicket Gate, she swoons from fear of being refused admittance. Mr. Brisk proposes to her, but, after being told that she is poor, leaves her, and she afterwards marries Matthew, the eldest son of Christian.

Merdle, Mr. In Dickens' LITTLE DORRIT, a banker who is called the "Master Mind of the Age." He becomes insolvent and commits suicide. The great banker is "the greatest forger and greatest thief that ever cheated the gallows."

Meredith, Burgess (1908–). American actor. Started with Eva Le Gallienne's student repertory group (1930). Appeared in Maxwell Anderson's *Winterset; High Tor* (drama critics' award); *Star-Wagon;* etc. Moving-picture début in *Winterset* (1936). Radio actor (since 1937). Vice-President, Actors' Equity Association. His wife is Paulette Goddard.

Meredith, George (1828–1909). English novelist, poet, and essayist, known for his psychological studies of character and his treatment of social problems in his novels. The best-known of these are *The Ordeal of Richard Feverel* (see RICHARD FEVEREL) (1859); EVAN HARRINGTON (1860); SANDRA BELLONI (1864); RHODA FLEMING (1865); BEAUCHAMP'S CAREER (1876); THE EGOIST (1879); THE TRAGIC COMEDIANS (1880); DIANA OF THE CROSSWAYS (1885); LORD ORMONT AND HIS AMINTA (1894); THE AMAZING MARRIAGE (1895). Meredith's poetry is concentrated in meaning and exact in detail, considered in his time as obscure. It deals chiefly with nature subjects and includes the following volumes: *Poems* (1851); MODERN LOVE (1862); *Poems and Lyrics of the Joy of Earth* (1883); *Ballads and Poems of Magic Life* (1887); *A Reading of Earth* (1888); *The Empty Purse, And Other Poems* (1892); *Odes in Contribution to the Song of French History* (1898); *A Reading of Life, With Other Poems* (1901). He contributed essays to various magazines of the time, and his lecture *The Idea of Comedy and the Uses of the Comic Spirit* (1877) was well known.

See also NICOLLS, MARY ELLEN.

Meredith, Janice. Heroine of P. L. Ford's JANICE MEREDITH.

Meredith, Owen. A pseudonym adopted by Edward Robert, first Earl of Lytton (1831–1891), son of the novelist BULWER-LYTTON, the author of LUCILE (1860), etc. He took his pseudonym from the names of two of his ancestors, *Owen* Gwynned ap. Griffith, King of North Wales, and ap. *Meredith* ap. Tudor, great-grandfather of Henry VI of England. Once Meredith was termed "third among living poets." He won the qualified praise of the Brownings and George Meredith. Yet due to his prolixity, posterity remembers him but vaguely as a facile rhymester who drew a malicious parody by Swinburne and judged himself in the lines:

> . . . Genius is master of man,
> Genius does what it must, and talent does what it can.

Merezhkovsky, Dmitry Sergeyevich (1866–1941). Russian poet, novelist, and critic, known for his mystical religious preoccupations and his series of historical novels dealing with religion in the past. The best-known of these is *Christ and Antichrist,* a trilogy consisting of *Julian the Apostate* (1901), *Leonardo da Vinci* (1917), and *Peter and Alexis* (1906). He also wrote studies of such literary figures as MONTAIGNE, FLAUBERT, IBSEN, DOSTOYEVSKY, and TOLSTOY. Merezhkovsky was a violent opponent of the Russian revolution of 1917.

Mergenthaler, Ottmar (1854–1899). German-born American inventor of the first Linotype typesetting machine (patented 1884).

Mérimée, Prosper (1803–1870). French novelist, best known for his picturesque historical novels and his nouvelles, or long short-stories, dealing with fiery passions in plots set against exotic backgrounds, especially Spain. His works include *La Chronique du Règne de Charles IX* (1829), compared by some critics with the novels of Sir Walter SCOTT; *Colomba* (1840); CARMEN (1845); also *La Vénus d'Isle; Le Vase Étrusque;* and *La Double Méprise.* Early in his career he wrote *Théâtre de Clara Gazul* (1825), which included plays imitating the Spanish style. Mérimée was a student of archaeology, and held the position of Inspector-General of historical monuments in France. Later he also became a senator.

Merivale, Philip (1886–1946). English actor. Member of F. R. Benson's Shakespearean Company (1906). First visit to U.S. in *Scarlet Pimpernel* (1910). Played modern and many Shakespearean rôles. Author of *The Wind-*

Over the Water; Knut at Roeskilde; The Peace of Ferrara.

Merle, Madame. A prominent character in Henry James' PORTRAIT OF A LADY.

Merlin. The historical Merlin was a Welsh or British bard, born towards the close of the 5th century, to whom a number of poems have been very doubtfully attributed. He is said to have become bard to King ARTHUR, and to have lost his reason and perished on the banks of the river after a terrible battle between the Britons and their Romanized compatriots about 570.

His story has been mingled with that of the enchanter Merlin of the Arthurian romances, which, however, proceeds on different lines. This Prince of Enchanters is the son of a damsel seduced by a fiend, but is baptized by Blaise and so rescued from the power of Satan. He becomes adept in necromancy, but is beguiled by the enchantress Nimuë, who shuts him up in a rock, and later Vivien, the LADY OF THE LAKE, entangles him in a thornbush by means of spells. There he still sleeps, though his voice may sometimes be heard.

He first appears in Nennius (as Ambrosius). GEOFFREY OF MONMOUTH wrote the *Vita Merlini* (ca. 1145); this was worked upon by Wace and Robert de BORON, and formed the basis of the English prose romance *Merlin,* and of most of the Merlin episodes in the Arthurian cycle. He is prominent in Malory's MORTE D'ARTHUR, in Spenser's FAËRIE QUEENE (III. iii), and Tennyson's IDYLLS OF THE KING. Edwin Arlington ROBINSON made him the subject of a narrative poem (1917). C. S. LEWIS brings him to life in his fantastic novel, *That Hideous Strength* (1946).

the English Merlin. William Lilly (1602–1681), the astrologer, who published two tracts under the name of "Merlinus Anglicus" and was the most famous charlatan of his day.

mermaid. The popular stories of the mermaid, a fabulous marine creature half woman and half fish—allied to the SIREN of classical mythology—probably arose from sailors' accounts of the dugong, a cetacean whose head has a rude approach to the human outline, and the mother of which while suckling her young holds it to her breast with one flipper, as a woman holds her infant in her arm. If disturbed, she suddenly dives under water and tosses up her fishlike tail.

In Elizabethan plays the term is often used for a courtesan. Cf. Massinger's *Old Law,* iv. 1, Shakespeare's *Comedy of Errors,* iii, 2, etc.

the Mermaid Tavern. The famous meeting-place (in Bread Street, Cheapside) of the wits, literary men, and men-about-town in the early 17th century. Among those who met there at somewhat of an early club were Ben JONSON, Sir Walter RALEIGH, BEAUMONT, Fletcher, John SELDEN, and in all probability SHAKESPEARE.

> What things have we seen
> Done at the Mermaid! Heard words that have been
> So nimble, and so full of subtile flame,
> As if that everyone from whence they came
> Had meant to put his whole wit in a jest.
>
> Beaumont, *Lines to Ben Jonson.*

Merman, The Forsaken, see FORSAKEN MERMAN.

Merodach or **Marduk.** A god of Babylon identified with the BAAL of the Old Testament and Apocrypha.

Merope. (1) One of the Pleiades; dimmer than the rest, because, according to Greek legend, she married SISYPHUS, a mortal. She was the mother of GLAUCUS.

(2) In classic myth, the daughter of Oenopion, king of Chios. Her too-eager lover ORION was blinded for his treatment of her.

(3) In classic myth, the mother of Aepytus by Cresphontes, king of Messenia. Her royal husband was murdered by Polyphontes, who possessed himself of both throne and widow, but years later Aepytus returned under pretext of claiming a reward for having murdered Cresphontes' son and avenged his father's death. This legend is the subject of a drama by Euripides, now lost, and dramas in Italian by Maffei (1713) and Alfiero, in French by VOLTAIRE, and in English by Matthew ARNOLD.

Merops' son or a son of Merops. One who thinks he can set the world to rights, but can only set it on fire. The allusion is to PHAETON, son of Merops, who thought himself able to drive the car of Phoebus but, in the attempt, nearly set the world on fire.

Merovingian. Name of the first Frankish dynasty (428–751), succeeded by the Carolingians. Its first important member was CLOVIS.

Merrick, Leonard (1864–1939). English novelist and playwright. Began as an actor. His best-known novel is *Conrad In Quest of His Youth* (1903).

Merriam, Eve (1916–). American poet and writer of fiction. Broadcaster of poetry program *Out of the Ivory Tower* (1942); contributor to *New Yorker; New Republic;* etc.

Merrilies, Meg. One of Scott's most famous characters, a half-crazy sibyl, queen of the gipsies, who appears in GUY MANNERING. She is the nurse of the young Mannering heir before he is kidnaped and recognizes him when he returns as Harry Bertram. Subject of a poem by KEATS.

Merrill, Stuart Fitzrandolph (1863–1915). American-French poet, born near Whitman's birthplace on Long Island. Attended Columbia Law School. Became interested in Single Tax movement and supported the defendants in the Haymarket Riot in Chicago. For this his father disinherited him. Leaving the United States

(1892), he never returned, expressing hatred of his country and settling in Versailles (1913). Died of heart attack during first World War. His poems, all symbolistic and expressionistic, have the romantic dreaminess of the pre-Raphaelites. His best-known book is *Une Voix dans la Foule* (1909), which expresses pity for the suffering of man.

Merriman, Henry Seton. Pseudonym of Hugh Stowell SCOTT.

merry. The original meaning is pleasing, delightful; hence, giving pleasure; hence mirthful, joyous.

The old phrase *Merrie England* (*Merry London,* etc.) merely signified that these places were pleasant and delightful, not necessarily bubbling over with merriment; and so with *the merry month of May.*

Merry Andrew. A buffoon, jester, or attendant on a quack doctor at fairs. Said by Hearne (1735)—with no evidence—to derive from Andrew Borde (d. 1549), physician to Henry VIII, who to his vast learning added great eccentricity. Matthew PRIOR wrote a poem on *Merry Andrew.* Andrew is a common name in old plays for a man-servant, as Abigail is for a waiting-woman.

merry as a Grig (*Greek*), see GRIG.

Merry Monarch. Charles II of England.

Merry del Val, Marqués **Alfonso de** (1864–1943). Spanish diplomat and ambassador to Great Britain (1918–1931). His brother, **Rafael Merry del Val** (1865–1930) was a Roman Catholic prelate, created cardinal (1903) and secretary of the Holy Office (1914–1930).

Merrygreek, Matthew. In the first English comedy, RALPH ROISTER DOISTER by Nicholas Udall, the servant of Ralph Roister Doister.

Merry Mount. See under MORTON, THOMAS.

Merry Wives of Windsor. A comedy by Shakespeare (ca. 1600). The redoubtable Sir John FALSTAFF is shown making ardent love to Mrs. Ford and Mrs. Page, and these "merry wives," by comparing notes, contrive to make a pretty fool of him. Even Ford introduces himself to Falstaff under an assumed name, gets into his confidence concerning the progress of his love affair with Mrs. Ford, and helps along the sport. On one occasion, Falstaff is put into a basket, covered with dirty linen and tossed into the Thames to escape the return of the supposedly irate husband; on another, having hurried into the garments of Old Mother Pratt on Ford's approach, he is beaten black and blue; and still later he is persuaded to disguise himself as Herne the Hunter, wearing a buck's head, and is pinched, and burned by "fairies" who have no mercy on him. There is a subplot dealing with the love affair of Mrs. Page's daughter, "sweet Anne Page."

The overture to Nicolai's opera, *The Merry Wives of Windsor,* is very popular.

Mertoun, Mordaunt. In Scott's PIRATE, the son of the ex-pirate, Basil Mertoun. He marries Brenda Troil.

Meru. The "Olympus" of the Hindus; a fabulous mountain in the center of the world, 80,000 leagues high, the abode of Vishnu, and a perfect paradise.

Merveilleuse (*Fr.,* "marvelous"). The sword of DOOLIN OF MAYENCE. It was so sharp that when placed edge downwards it would cut through a slab of wood without the use of force.

The term is also applied to the dress worn by the fops and ladies of the Directory period in France, who were noted for their extravagance and aping of classical Greek modes.

Merz, Charles (1893–   ). Editor of the *New York Times,* succeeding Dr. John H. Finley (November, 1938). Author of *The Great American Bandwagon* (1928).

Mesa Verde. The book for a native American opera by Christopher LA FARGE (1945), based on the history of a tribe of vanished pueblo Indians in the Southwest.

Meshach. In the Old Testament, one of three Hebrews cast into a fiery furnace. See SHADRACH.

Mesmer, Franz Anton (1734–1815). Austrian physician. Developed the theory of animal magnetism, later known as MESMERISM.

mesmerism. The theory and system of medical treatment developed by F. A. MESMER and called by him *animal magnetism.* It was based essentially on the observation that a living organism influences another and was named by analogy with electric phenomena then in the limelight of public interest. See also KING'S EVIL.

Mesopotamia (*Gr.,* "the land between the rivers," i.e., the Euphrates and Tigris). The territory bounded by Kurdistan on the N. and N.E., the Persian Gulf on the S. and S.E., Persia on the E., and Syria and the Arabian Desert on the W. After World War I—as a consequence of which it was freed from Turkish rule and constituted a separate kingdom—its name was changed to *Irak* or *Iraq.*

the true "Mesopotamia" ring. Something high-sounding and pleasing, but wholly past comprehension. The allusion is to the story of an old woman who told her pastor that she "found great support in that blessed word *Mesopotamia.*"

Message to Garcia, A. A famous inspirational essay by Elbert HUBBARD (1899), recounting Lieutenant Andrew S. Rowan's heroic journey to meet the leader of the Cuban insurgents. Estimated to have reached a circulation of forty million copies.

Messala. In the historical novel BEN HUR by Lew Wallace, Ben Hur's false friend and lifelong enemy.

Messalina. Wife of the Emperor Claudius of Rome, executed by order of her husband in 48 A. D. Her name has become a byword for lasciviousness and incontinency. Catherine II of Russia (1729–1796) has sometimes been called *the modern Messalina.*

Messenger, Angela Marsden. The heroine of Besant's ALL SORTS AND CONDITIONS OF MEN.

Messer Marco Polo. The titular hero of a romance (1921) by Donn BYRNE, dealing with his prolonged adventures at the court of China. See also POLO, MARCO.

Messerschmitt, Wilhelm (1898–). German aircraft designer. Awarded Lilienthal prize for research in aviation (1937).

Messiah, The. (1) An oratorio by HANDEL (1749). The libretto was by Charles Jennens, nicknamed "Soliman the Magnificent."

(2) An epic poem in fifteen books by the German poet KLOPSTOCK, dealing with the life of Christ. The first three books were published in 1748 and the last in 1773.

messiah complex, see under COMPLEX.

Messidor. In the French revolutionary calendar, the harvest month.

Metamorphoses. A series of tales in Latin verse by OVID, chiefly mythological. They are written in hexameters, in fifteen books, beginning with the creation of the world, and ending with the deification of Caesar and the reign of Augustus.

metaphor. From Greek *metaphora;* literally, "a carrying over" and thus basically identical in meaning with Latin *translatio,* "transfer" or "translation." A metaphor is a figure of speech in which a subjective impression or a descriptive comparison is boldly presented as a bit of ulterior but factual truth. In a metaphor the writer would not say, "You *remind me* of a tomb in which my love is buried alive," nor, "You are *like* a coffin," but simply, "Thou art the grave where buried love doth live" (Shakespeare). When a metaphor is accepted as fact, it turns into an element of mythology. Metaphors are evidence of the human ability to visualize the universe as a coherent organism, to see one thing in another, as "the world in a grain of sand" or "heaven in a flower" (Blake).

In a mixed metaphor two or more logically incompatible identifications are brought together. The effect can be absurd as well as sublime. E.g.: "The British lion will never pull in its horns," or, "To take up arms against a sea of troubles."

metaphysical poets. Term generally applied to several English poets of the early 17th century whose poetry is marked by highly complex and greatly compressed meanings, most often concerned with concepts of religion, by complex and long-sustained CONCEITS, by a frequent avoidance of smooth and regular meter in order to achieve dramatic and oratorical effects, and by unusual syntax and an unconventional type of imagery chosen from philosophy, religion and theology, and the arts, crafts, sciences, and ordinary daily life of the period in which the poets lived. These poets, among whom there is wide variation in individual style, represented a reaction against the tradition of the Elizabethan sonnet sequence of the late 16th century, the products of which had become feeble and over-conventionalized as the vogue died out, and a return in some ways to the cruder, more homely type of imagery in poetry of the middle of the 16th century, as well as to the intellectualism of the Middle Ages. The awakening interest in science in the early 17th century is also considered to have had an influence on metaphysical poetry, and its complex conceits, most popularly associated with the school, were paralleled and excelled in "fantastic" character in GONGORISM and MARINISM. Its use of imagery from the trades, professions, arts, and crafts was foreshadowed by practice in Italian and French poetry of the 16th century and by a critical recommendation in the DÉFENSE ET ILLUSTRATION DE LA LANGUE FRANÇAISE of Joachim du Bellay. The most famous of the metaphysical poets are John DONNE, George HERBERT, Thomas TRAHERNE, Richard CRASHAW, Henry VAUGHAN, Francis QUARLES, Andrew MARVELL, Abraham COWLEY, and John CLEVELAND. Donne is considered the greatest among these, and Cowley and Cleveland are regarded as the most culpable in the use of far-fetched conceits; Crashaw and Vaughan have been found to be less characteristic than the rest.

The poets in this loosely associated school were first called "metaphysical" by Samuel JOHNSON in his study of Cowley in his *Lives of the English Poets* (1779–1781), where he condemns them for their excessive use of "learning" in their poetry. The term had been implied, however, in the earlier condemnations of the poets by William DRUMMOND OF HAWTHORNDEN and John DRYDEN. In the 20th century interest in the metaphysical poets was revived, and their work was highly praised by such English and American critics as Sir H. J. C. Grierson, T. S. Eliot, I. A. Richards, William Empson, Allen Tate, John Crowe Ransom, and Cleanth Brooks; Eliot, Richards, and Brooks use metaphysical poetry, especially that of John Donne, as examples in their studies of poetic theory. A number of 20th-century poets came under the influence of the metaphysicals and revealed this influence varyingly in their own work; according to critics, they include ELIOT, Archibald MACLEISH, Louise BOGAN, Horace GREGORY, Elinor WYLIE, Léonie ADAMS, Ruth PITTER, Richard EBERHART, RANSOM, TATE, Hart CRANE, Wallace STEVENS, and R. P. BLACKMUR. In the 19th century, Gerard Manley HOPKINS is regarded as a poet outstandingly showing the influence of the metaphysicals, and the poetry of R. W. EMERSON, Jones VERY, and Emily DICKINSON has also been called metaphysical.

Metastasio. Original name **Pietro Antonio Domenico Bonaventura Trapassi** (1698–1782). Italian poet and dramatist. His works include lyrical dramas, oratorios, poems for cantatas, and operas.

metathesis. In linguistics, the transposition of single sounds or syllables within a word, as "ax" (aks) for "ask" in illiterate speech. Metathesis is a process by which many changes in a language take place, and a number of words in modern English are metathesized forms of the original A.S. or M.E. words. Thus *bird* was once A.S. *brid; wasp,* A.S. *waeps; clasp,* M.E. *clapsen;* etc. The *r* sound is particularly susceptible to transposition in this manner, as in *fresh,* from A.S. *fersc,* and *thresh,* from A.S. *therscan.*

Metchnikoff, Élie (1845–1916). Russian zoologist and bacteriologist. Second director (1895) of the institute founded in Paris by Louis PASTEUR. Nobel prize for physiology and medicine (1908, shared with Paul Ehrlich).

metempsychosis (*Gr.,* from *meta,* "beyond," and *empsychoun,* "to animate"). Transmigration of souls. The doctrine, originating in India and Egypt, that the human soul after death enters into another body, human or animal.

Methodism. The doctrines, etc., originally of a protestant denomination which grew from a loose religious association formed at Oxford University in 1729 by John and Charles WESLEY. The name began as a term of derision applied by the Oxford students to the members of the association because of their methodical habits of study. In course of time, the movement became widely evangelical and broke away from the Church of England. In America it is chiefly represented by the Methodist Episcopal Church.

Methuselah, old as. Very old indeed, almost incredibly old. He is the oldest man mentioned in the Bible, where we are told (*Gen.* v. 27) that he died at the age of 969.

Gelett BURGESS entitled one of his humorous volumes *Maxims of Methuselah* (1907). George Bernard SHAW has a drama entitled BACK TO METHUSELAH.

metonymy. The substitution of one noun for another closely associated with it, usually a part for the whole, or a single attribute for the noun, as "the kettle boils," "the pen is mightier than the sword," "he drank the cup."

meter. Rhythm is the underlying repetitive beat existing in all life, for us notably in the beat of the human heart. It is the foundation of music and of verse. Meter is the measuring out of rhythm. Among the Greeks and Romans it was based on "quantity," that is the succession of short and long syllables according to definite metrical patterns. English verse depends upon accent. The different meters are named for the number of their accents. A trimeter, for instance, is a line of three accents or beats. Modern poetry attempts closeness to casual speech, and hence meter, in free verse, has become either irregular or, in some cases, non-existent.

metric system. The decimal system of measures and weights based on the meter which is a unit of length arbitrarily fixed during the French Revolution as the "natural" unit of one forty-millionth of the circumference of the globe. The standard meter is the distance (at the melting point of ice) between two lines drawn on a bar of platiniridium kept in the pavillon de Breteuil near Sèvres, France.

Metternich, Prince **Klemens Wenzel Nepomuk Lothar von** (1773–1859). Austrian statesman. Lifelong reactionary. By skillful diplomacy kept Austria out of war between France and Russia (1812–1813) but finally joined alliance with Russia against France. The Congress of Vienna (1814–1815) saw the height of his power. Suppressed liberal ideas and revolutionary movements (1815–1830) especially through the Holy Alliance with Russia and Prussia. The "Age of Metternich" (1815–1848) is condemned by some as antiliberal and obscurantistic. It is praised by others as marking the last stand of tradition and evolution against disorder and revolution.

meum and **tuum.** That which belongs to me and that which is another's. *Meum* is Latin for "what is mine," and *tuum* is Latin for "what is thine." If a man is said not to know the difference between *meum* and *tuum,* it is a polite way of saying he is a thief.

Mew, Charlotte (1870–1928). English poet. In 1922, Thomas Hardy, John Masefield, and Walter de la Mare procured for her a Civil List pension of 75 pounds per annum. In 1927 she became desperately ill and finally took her own life. Her work, says Louis Untermeyer, is like "a cameo cut in steel." Within its range it is nearly of the first rank. *The Farmer's Bride* (1916); *The Rambling Sailor* (1929).

Mexico, conquest of. See under CONQUEST.

Mexitl or **Mextli.** The principal god of the ancient Mexicans (whence the name of their country), to whom enormous sacrifices, running into many thousands of human beings, were offered at a time. Also called *Huitzilopochtli.*

Meyer, Kuno (1858–1919). German authority on Celtic philology. Professor of Celtic at the universities of Liverpool and Berlin. Co-founder and director of the Summer School of Irish Learning at Dublin (1903).

Meyerbeer, Jacob. Real name **Jakob Liebmann Beer** (1791–1864). Composer of German birth but generally considered of the French school. His chief operas are ROBERT LE DIABLE, LES HUGUENOTS, LE PROPHÊTE and L'AFRICAINE.

Meyerhofer, Paul. The hero of Sudermann's DAME CARE.

Meynell, Alice (1847–1922). English essayist and poet, a convert to the Roman Catholic religion, whose religious beliefs are reflected in her writings. Volumes of her poetry include *Preludes* (1875); *Poems* (1893); *Later Poems* (1901); *Father of Women* (1918); *Last Poems* (1923). Among her books of essays are *The Rhythm of Life* (1893); *The Color of Life* (1896); *The Children* (1896); *The Spirit of Peace* (1898); *Ceres Runaway* (1910); *The Second Person Singular* (1921). She and her husband, Wilfrid Meynell, editor of the magazine *Merry England,* befriended the poet Francis THOMPSON early in his career when he was living in London in poverty and loneliness. She was also a friend of D. G. ROSSETTI, John RUSKIN, Robert BROWNING, Coventry PATMORE, George MEREDITH, and other leading literary figures of her time, who gathered at the Meynell home. Her daughter, **Viola Meynell,** author of novels and short stories, wrote a *Memoir* on her mother (1929).

Meyrick, Hans. In George Eliot's DANIEL DERONDA, an artist friend of the hero.

Mezentius. A legendary king of the Tyrrhenians, noted for his cruelty and impiety, who put his subjects to death by tying a living man to a dead one. He was driven from his throne by his subjects, and fled to TURNUS, King of the Rutuli. When AENEAS arrived, he fought with Mezentius, and slew both him and his son Lausus.

Micah. One of the Minor Prophets of the Old Testament; also, the name of the book in which his prophecy is recorded.

Micah Clarke. A romance of 17th century England by A. Conan DOYLE (1888), dealing with the MONMOUTH REBELLION.

Micawber, Mr. Wilkins. In Dickens' novel DAVID COPPERFIELD, a great maker of speeches, letter-writer, and projector of bubble schemes sure to lead to fortune but always ending in grief. Notwithstanding his ill success, he never despairs, but feels certain that something will "turn up" to make his fortune. Having failed in every adventure in the old country, he emigrates to Australia, where he becomes a magnate. He is said to have been drawn from Dickens' father. Hence, a *Micawber* came to mean an incurable optimist.

Michael. A narrative poem by WORDSWORTH, telling the story of an honest, hardworking herdsman whose virtues are ill-rewarded by the failure of a nephew and the crime of his only son.

Michael, St. See under SAINTS.

Michael and His Lost Angel. A drama by Henry Arthur JONES (1896), portraying the struggle of the stern and upright young minister, Rev. Michael Faversham, to resist his love for Mrs. Lesdon, a wilful, lovable, irresistible woman who comes suddenly into his life and will not be put out. He sins and forces himself to make public confession, but finds he cannot forget her.

Michael Angelo, see MICHELANGELO.

Michaëlis, Karin (1872–). Danish novelist and short-story writer. Best-known for her novel *The Dangerous Age* (1911), which was widely sold abroad. Author of more than 50 books.

Michaelis, Ulrich. Titular hero of Moody's FAITH HEALER.

Michaelmas Day. September 29, the Festival of St. Michael (see under SAINTS) and All Angels. In England it is one of the quarter-days when rents are due and the day when magistrates are elected. It is customary there to eat goose on Michaelmas Day.

Michel or **Cousin Michael.** Generic name for a German.

Michelangelo. Full Italian name **Michelangelo Buonarrotti** (1475–1564). One of the greatest painters and sculptors of all time. Also an architect and poet of the Italian Renaissance. Pope Julius II had him decorate the ceiling of the Sistine Chapel in Rome (1508–1512). He worked on the façade of San Lorenzo in Florence. He became architect of St. Peter's in Rome. For his friend, the Italian nobleman Tommaso Cavalieri, and for his adored VITTORIA COLONNA he wrote his sonnets and did allegorical drawings. From a single block of marble he carved his huge statue of *David* (Florence Academy). The tomb of Pope Julius II has his famous statue of *Moses.* For Popes Clement VII and Paul III he did a great fresco of *The Last Judgment* in the Sistine Chapel. He wrought many architectural works and made many plans. His work is renowned for its grandeur and extraordinary knowledge of anatomy. He also wrote lyrical and philosophical poems. Next to Leonardo da Vinci he is the greatest figure of the Renaissance.

the Michelangelo of battle scenes. Michelangelo Cerquozzi (1600–1660), a native of Rome, famous for his battle scenes and shipwrecks.

Michelangelo des bamboches. Peter van Laar (1613–1673), the Dutch painter.

Michelangelo of music. Christoph Willibald von Gluck (1714–1787), the German opera composer.

Michelangelo of sculptors. Pierre Puget (1622–1694), the French sculptor. Also, Réné Michael Slodtz (1705–1764).

Michelet, Jules (1798–1874). French historian, known for the vividness and penetration of his accounts of French history, his sympathy for the PROLETARIAT and the ideals of the Revolution of 1789, and his opposition to the Church, the crown, and the bourgeoisie. His great work is *Histoire de France* (1833–1843, 1847–1853, 1855–1867). Michelet came from a background of poverty and secured his education through his own efforts. He lost his position as professor in the Collège de France because of his attacks on the Jesuits, and later, when Napoleon III assumed power, he was also dismissed from his employment in the national archives. His writings attribute great influence to material and physical factors in historical events.

Mickey Mouse. A sprightly, self-confident, and quick-witted mouse, the world-famous hero of a series of animated cartoons by Walt DISNEY. His leading lady is usually *Minnie Mouse*.

Midas. A legendary king of Phrygia who requested of the gods that everything he touched might be turned to gold. His request was granted, but as his food became gold the moment he touched it, he prayed the gods to take their favor back. He was then ordered to bathe in the Pactolus, and the river ever after rolled over golden sands.

Another story about Midas tells that, when appointed a judge to musical contest between Apollo and Pan, he gave judgment in favor of the satyr; whereupon Apollo in contempt gave the king a pair of ass's ears. Midas hid them under his Phrygian cap, but his barber discovered them, and, not daring to mention the matter, dug a hole and relieved his mind by whispering in it, "Midas has ass's ears," then covering it up again. The rushes were ever after murmuring the secret to the winds.

Middle Ages. The period of European history characterized by a FEUDAL social and economic organization and the international dominance of the Roman Catholic Church, with a distinct culture and civilization of its own. It may be said to extend broadly from about 476 (the fall of the Roman Empire) to 1453 (the capture of Constantinople by the Turks). It varies a little with almost every nation; in France it is usually dated from Clovis to Louis XI (481 to 1461); in England, from the Heptarchy to the accession of Henry VII (409 to 1485). The earlier part of this time (to about 1200) is still sometimes referred to as the DARK AGES.

Middle Border, A Son of the. The title of Hamlin GARLAND's autobiography (1917), which deals with life in the Middle West. His *Daughter of the Middle Border* (1921), which treats of the life of his mother and wife and continues his own experiences, was awarded the Pulitzer Prize for biography in 1922.

Middle East. See under EAST.

Middle Kingdom. An old name for China.

Middlemarch: A Study of Provincial Life. A novel by George ELIOT (1872), with a double plot interest. The heroine, Dorothea Brooke, longs to devote herself to some great cause and for a time expects to find it in her marriage to Rev. Mr. Casaubon, a middle-aged scholar. Mr. Casaubon lives only eighteen months after their marriage, but this is a more than sufficient period to disillusion her completely. On his death he leaves her his estate with the express proviso that she is to forfeit it if she marries his young cousin Will Ladislaw, whom she had seen frequently in Rome. In the endeavor to find happiness without Ladislaw, whom she now comes to care for deeply, Dorothea throws herself into the support of the medical reforms advocated by the young Dr. Lydgate. Finally, however, she decides to give up her property and marry Ladislaw. The second plot has to do with the efforts and failure of Dr. Lydgate to live up to his early ideals. Handicapped by financial difficulties into which his marriage to the selfish and ambitious Rosamond Vincy had thrown him and by the criticism and opposition of his medical associates, he drifts gradually into cultivating a wealthy practice at the expense of his medical standards. There is a subplot dealing with the love affair of Rosamond's brother Fred Vincy and Mary Garth, the daughter of Caleb Garth, the builder.

Middlesex. The territory of the Middle Saxons—that is, between Essex, Sussex, and Wessex. In fiction it is best known as the scene of Thomas HARDY's novels. See also WESSEX.

Middleton, Clara. The heroine of Meredith's novel THE EGOIST. Her father, Dr. Middleton, also plays a part in the story.

Middleton, George (1880–). American playwright. Married the daughter of Senator

La Follette (1911). His first play, *The Cavalier,* written with Paul Kester, was produced by Julia Marlowe (1902). *Polly With a Past,* written with Guy Bolton (1917), was a great success and established Ina Claire as a light comedienne. *The Light of the World* (1920) was the first play by an American to be accepted by a French state theater. *These Things are Mine* (1947) is his autobiography.

Middleton, Richard Barham (1882–1911). English poet and short-story writer, descended from Richard Harris Barham, author of the INGOLDSBY LEGENDS. His masters were Ernest Dowson, Swinburne, and Symons. He committed suicide in Brussels. He was "a poet born out of his time." His best work in prose is in his volume of short stories, *The Ghost-Ship and Other Stories* (1912).

Middleton, Sir John. In Jane Austen's novel SENSE AND SENSIBILITY, the great squire of the neighborhood in which the story is laid. He is fairly amiable and loves "collecting parties of young people to eat ham and chicken out of doors," but his wife is "reserved, cold and had nothing to say for herself beyond the most commonplace inquiry or remark."

Middleton, Thomas (1570?–1627). English playwright, known chiefly for his satirical and romantic comedies. Among his works are *A Trick to Catch the Old One* (1608); *The Roaring Girl* (1611), in collaboration with Thomas DEKKER; *A Fair Quarrel* (1617), *The Changeling* (1623), and *The Spanish Gipsy* (1623), all written with William Rowley; *A Game at Chess* (1624), concerning politics, which brought the author into official investigation; *A Chaste Maid in Cheapside* (1630); *The Mayor of Quinborough* (1651); *No Wit, No Help Like a Woman's* (1657); *Women Beware Women* (1657). Middleton, whose plays were very popular in their day, also wrote verse, prose, and a large number of masques for performances on public occasions in London.

Middletown. A famous sociological study of a typical small city of the U.S. during the boom period of the 1920's, written by Robert S. and Helen M. Lynd, American social scientists, and published in 1929. *Middletown in Transition* (1937) is a sequel, presenting a supplementary picture of the same city in the depression era of the 1930's. The actual city in which the study was made was Muncie, Indiana.

Midgard (Literally, "the yard in the middle"). In Scandinavian mythology, the abode of the first pair from whom sprang the human race. It was made of the brow of YMER, and was joined to ASGARD by the rainbow bridge called BIFROST.

Midgard serpent. Also known as **Midgardsorm** ("the worm or serpent of Midgard"). In Norse mythology, with Fenris and Hel, offspring of Loki and the giantess Angerboda. Odin threw the serpent into the sea, where it encircles the earth. At Utgard, THOR almost managed to lift the serpent off the ground [341, 343]. When the twilight of the gods comes, the Midgard serpent will repair to the battlefield of Vigrid. There it will be killed by Thor, but its venom will be vomited over him and he will not survive.

Midlothian, The Heart of, see HEART OF MIDLOTHIAN.

midnight oil. Late hours.

burning the midnight oil. Sitting up late, especially when engaged in literary work.

Midrash. The rabbinical investigation into, and interpretation of, the Old Testament writings, which began when the Temple at Jerusalem was destroyed and was committed to writing in a large number of commentaries between the 2nd and 11th centuries A. D. The three ancient *Midrashim* (*Mechiltha, Sifre,* and *Sifra*—first half of the 2nd century) contain both the HALACHAH and the HAGGADAH.

Midshipman Easy, Mr. Titular hero of a novel (1836) by Captain Frederick MARRYAT.

Midsummer Night's Dream. A drama by Shakespeare (ca. 1595). Plans are on foot for the wedding of THESEUS, Duke of Athens, and the Amazon queen, HIPPOLYTA, whom he has defeated in battle. Egeus, an Athenian, has promised his daughter Hermia to Demetrius, and although Hermia is in love with Lysander, the Duke orders her to obey her father. The two lovers escape to the forest, followed by Demetrius and by Helena, who is in love with Demetrius. Here they are found by OBERON, King of the fairies, his queen, Titania, with whom he is extremely disgruntled, and the merry PUCK. Puck has a magic love-juice that will make the one whose eyelids are anointed fall in love with the first object he sees upon awaking, and as he uses it somewhat indiscriminately, a strange comedy ensues, but eventually Demetrius abandons Hermia to Lysander and devotes himself to Helena. At the Duke's wedding feast, which celebrates three weddings in place of one, BOTTOM THE WEAVER and his group of players present as an interlude the play of PYRAMUS AND THISBE. Shakespeare's comedy is indebted to Chaucer's KNIGHT'S TALE for the Athenian setting, and to Ovid's METAMORPHOSES for the *Pyramus and Thisbe* interlude.

Mifflin, Roger. The bookseller of Christopher MORLEY'S *Parnassus on Wheels* (1917) and *The Haunted Bookshop* (1919).

Miggs, Miss. In Dickens' BARNABY RUDGE, the handmaiden and "comforter" of Mrs. VARDEN, a tall, gaunt young woman, addicted to pattens, slender and shrewish, of a sharp and acid visage. She holds the male sex in utter contempt, but makes a secret exception in favor of Sim TAPPERTIT, who irreverently calls her "scraggy." Miss Miggs always sides with madam against master, pretending that she is a suffering martyr and he an inhuman Nero.

> Miss Miggs, baffled in all her schemes . . . and cast upon a thankless, undeserving world, turned very sharp and sour . . . but the justices of the peace for Middlesex . . . selected her from 124 competitors to the office of turnkey for a county Bridewell, which she held till her decease, more than thirty years afterwards, remaining single all that time.—*Last Chapter.*

Mignon. In Goethe's WILHELM MEISTER, a beautiful, dwarfish, fairy-like Italian girl, in love with Wilhelm, her protector. Full of fervor, full of love, she is overwhelmed by despair at finding her love is not returned, becomes insane, and dies. The opera *Mignon* by Thomas (1866) is based on her story.

Mihajlovic, Draza (1893?–1946). Following German conquest of Yugoslavia (1941) organized an army of guerrillas against German and Italian armies. General (1941) and commander of Free Yugoslavian army (1942). Charged by the later Russian-supported Tito government of Yugoslavia with collaboration with the Germans. Condemned to death and executed (July 17, 1946).

Mikado. See RULERS, TITLES OF.

Mikado, The. A GILBERT and SULLIVAN comic opera (1885). Nanki-Poo, the son of the Mikado, traveling in disguise, falls in love with Yum-Yum, the lovely ward of Ko-Ko. The latter, who is Lord High Executioner but never beheads anyone, is now informed by Pooh-Bah, Lord High Everything Else, that he will lose his office unless there is an execution within a month. Nanki-Poo agrees to be the victim if he may marry Yum-Yum. When the Mikado is told that his son, Nanki-Poo, has been executed, his wrath is fearful, but luckily Ko-Ko's report of the execution was a false one, so all is well.

Mike. A common name for an Irishman. See also PAT.

Milan Decree. A decree made by Napoleon, dated "Milan, Dec. 27th, 1807," declaring "the whole British Empire to be in a state of blockade, and forbidding all countries either from trading with Great Britain or from even using an article of British manufacture."

Milbanke, Anne (1792–1815). Wife of Lord BYRON; a beautiful, wealthy, and rigorously moral woman unsuited to a man of her husband's temperament. The two were separated a year after their marriage, following the birth of a daughter, Ada. It was rumored at the time that the separation was caused by Lady Byron's discovery of an incestuous relationship existing between the poet and his half-sister, Augusta LEIGH. The rumor added to Byron's scandalous reputation.

Mildendo. The metropolis of LILLIPUT in Swift's *Gulliver's Travels* (see GULLIVER, LEMUEL), the wall of which is two and one-half feet in height, and at least eleven inches thick. The city is an exact square; two main streets divide it into four quarters, and the emperor's palace, Belfaborac, is in its center.

Mildmay, Frank, see FRANK MILDMAY.

Miles. In Henry James' THE TURN OF THE SCREW, the little boy of the two suspected children. When the governess first enters employment in the family, her suspicions are aroused by the fact that Miles has been expelled from school and will not confess to her the reason, beyond that it was for "telling things" to the other boys. Miles receives the particular attention of Peter QUINT.

Miles Gloriosus (*Lat.,* "glorious soldier"). A Latin comedy by Plautus. The hero is Captain PYROPOLINICES, a character who furnished the basis for a long line of military braggarts in Continental and English drama. See also BOBADIL; COPPER CAPTAIN; PAROLLES.

Milesian Fables. A Greek collection of witty but obscene short stories by Antonius Diogenes, compiled by Aristides, of Miletus (2nd century B. C.), whence the name. They were translated into Latin by Sisenna about the time of the civil wars of Marius and Sulla, and were greedily read by the luxurious Sybarites, but are no longer extant. Similar stories, however, are still sometimes called *Milesian Tales.*

Milesians. (1) Properly, the inhabitants of Miletus; but the name has been given to the ancient Irish because of the legend that two sons of Milesius, a fabulous king of Spain, conquered the country and repeopled it after exterminating the Firbolgs then living there.

(2) An early school of Greek philosophers, of the period preceding PLATO, who tried to find a unifying principle for the universe in a basic "world-stuff" which maintained its identity throughout all physical change. Water, air, and the "infinite" were suggested. The school was made up of ANAXIMANDER, ANAXIMENES, and THALES.

Miles Standish, see COURTSHIP OF MILES STANDISH.

Milhaud, Darius (1892–). French polytonal composer. In U.S. as conductor and lecturer (1923, 1940). Author of a musical novel (1923) based on Francis JAMMES's *La Brebis Égarée.*

Milholland, Ramsey, see RAMSEY MILHOLLAND.

Milky Way. A great circle of stars entirely surrounding the heavens, apparently so crowded together that they look to the naked eye like a "way" or stream of faint "milky" light; the *Galaxy* or *Via Lactea.*

> A broad and ample road, whose dust is gold
> And pavement stars, as stars to thee appear,
> Seen in the galaxy—that Milky Way,
> Thick, nightly, as a circling zone, thou seest
> Powdered with stars.
> Milton, *Paradise Lost,* vii, 577, etc.

Mill, John Stuart (1806–1873). English philosopher and economist, eldest son of James Mill (1773–1836), Scottish philosopher, historian and economist. At ten John Stuart Mill read Plato and Demosthenes with ease. Champion of utilitarian school of thought before the age of twenty. After a mental crisis, widened his philosophy, infusing idealism. Created impression with his *System of Logic* (1843). Applied economic doctrines to social conditions. His best-known treatises are *On Liberty* (1859); *Thoughts on Parliamentary Reform* (1859); *Representative Government* (1861); *Utilitarianism* (1863); etc. Voted with advanced Radical party and advocated women's suffrage.

Millais, Sir **John Everett** (1829–1896). English painter. Originated with Holman HUNT and D. G. ROSSETTI the Pre-Raphaelite movement (1848). Illustrated Trollope's works and Tennyson's poems. Deviated from Pre-Raphaelite manner. Painted Gladstone, Lord Beaconsfield, Wilkie Collins, Carlyle, John Bright, Irving, Tennyson, etc.

Millamant. In Congreve's comedy THE WAY OF THE WORLD (1700), a brilliant girl, who says she "loves to give pain because cruelty is a proof of power, and when one parts with one's cruelty, one parts with one's power." Beautiful, witty and full of caprice, she arouses the jealousy of women and the adoration of many men, but particularly of Edward MIRABELL.

Millay, Edna St. Vincent (1892–). American poet, one of the best known and financially most successful poets of her time. She became famous during the 1920's for her poems celebrating love and unfaithfulness and the right of women to as much freedom in matters of morals as men, presented with a flippancy and bravado that expressed the spirit of the period. Later she became interested in liberal causes, but her subject-matter changed little. In form her poetry is conventional and shows the influence of the Elizabethan and 17th-century lyricists. Her books of verse include RENASCENCE, AND OTHER POEMS (1917); *A Few Figs from Thistles* (1920); *Second April* (1921); *The Harp Weaver, And Other Poems* (1923), winner of the Pulitzer Prize in 1923; *The Buck in the Snow* (1928); *Fatal Interview* (1931); *Wine from These Grapes* (1934); *Flowers of Evil* (1936), translations of Baudelaire's FLEURS DU MAL; CONVERSATION AT MIDNIGHT (1937); *Huntsman, What Quarry?* (1939); *Make Bright the Arrows* (1940).

Edna St. Vincent Millay for a while early in her career lived in GREENWICH VILLAGE and wrote short stories under the name of Nancy Boyd. She also was associated with the PROVINCETOWN PLAYERS as an actress and playwright. Her verse plays are *Two Slatterns and a King, Moral Interlude,* and *The Lamp and the Bell* (1921); and *The King's Henchman* (1926), produced in 1927 and later presented in operatic form at the Metropolitan Opera House in New York City, with music by Deems TAYLOR. *The Murder of Lidice* (1942) is a radio play in verse.

Mill Boy of the Slashes. Henry Clay (1777–1852), American statesman and orator, was so called from the district in Virginia where he spent his boyhood.

Miller, Mrs. **Alice** nee **Duer** (1874–1942). American novelist, poet, and writer. *The Charm School* (1919) and *Come Out of the Kitchen* (1916) were successfully staged. *Gowns By Roberta* (1933) formed the basis of the musical comedy *Roberta. The White Cliffs* (1940), a long poem about England, was read over the radio by Lynn Fontanne and proved to be a runaway best seller. Her husband, Henry Wise Miller, published an autobiographical account of their life together entitled *All Our Lives* (1945).

Miller, Caroline (1903–). American novelist and short-story writer. Pulitzer prize (1944) for *Lamb In His Bosom,* a story of back-country life in Georgia before the Civil War.

Miller, Daisy, see DAISY MILLER.

Miller, Henry (1891–). American novelist and short-story writer, for a number of years a resident of France. His work, often compared to SURREALIST painting, is marked chiefly by iconoclasm, fantastic wit, and a semi-mystical emphasis on sex. Among his books are *Tropic of Cancer* (1935); *Black Spring* (1939); *Scenario* (1937), "a film with sound," based on *The House of Incest,* a surrealist novel by Anaïs Nin; *Money, And How It Gets That Way* (1938); *Max and the White Phagocytes* (1938), a collection of short stories; *Tropic of Capricorn* (1939); *The Cosmological Eye* (1939), a collection of stories, sketches, and essays; *The World of Sex* (1940); *The Colossus of Maroussi* (1941), on travels in Greece; *The Wisdom of the Heart* (1941), stories and essays. During World War II, Miller took refuge in the U.S. The result of a "lugubrious trip" across the country was *The Air-conditioned Nightmare* (1946).

Miller, Henry John (1860–1926). English-born American actor and theatrical manager. With Charles Frohman's Empire Theater stock company (ca. 1890–1896); opened Princess Theater, New York (1906); manager, director and star of the Henry Miller Theater, New York City (1918–1920). His son, Gilbert Miller, is a well-known manager.

Miller, Joaquin. In full **Cincinnatus Hiner** or **Heine Miller** (1841?–1913). American poet, famous in the latter half of the 19th century for his rhetorical poems of the West, in which he claimed to have lived with the Indians for a time and served variously as a pony-express rider, Indian fighter, horse-thief, etc. He was particularly popular among the English, who called him "the Byron of Oregon." *Pacific Poems* (1870) and *Songs of the Sierras* (1871) attracted the most attention. Other books are *Specimens* (1868); *Joaquin et al* (1869); *Songs of the Sunlands* (1873); *Unwritten History: Life Among the Modocs* (1874), a picturesque autobiography; *The Ship in the Desert* (1875); *The Danites in the Sierras* (1881); and several novels and plays as well as other volumes of verse. Miller's fame died quickly; he spent the latter part of his life traveling to the Orient, Alaska, South Africa, and Central America. Cf. *Americans* (1922), by Stuart P. SHERMAN.

Miller, Joe. A stale jest. A certain John Mottley compiled a book of facetiae in 1739, which he, without permission, entitled *Joe Miller's Jests,* from Joseph Miller (1684–1738), a popular comedian of the day who could neither read nor write.

Millerin, Luise. Heroine of Schiller's drama LOVE AND INTRIGUE (*Kabale und Liebe*), a poor musician's daughter loved by Ferdinand von Walther, son of a German prince. She is persuaded to give him up, writes a compromising letter which is allowed to fall into his hands, and steadfastly continues the deception.

miller of Sans Souci, the. One of the innumerable stories told about FREDERICK THE GREAT of Prussia. When the king had built his new residence of Sans Souci, he felt annoyed by the noise of a near-by mill. The miller refused to sell his property. When the king threatened to seize it, the miller took the matter to court. The judges upheld the miller's rights, and the king accepted the verdict because, even though absolute in his power, he considered himself subject to the laws of the state.

Miller of Trompington, see THE REEVE'S TALE, one of Chaucer's *Canterbury Tales.*

Miller's or **Milleres Tale,** see NICHOLAS.

Millet, Jean François (1814–1875). French genre and landscape painter of the BARBIZON SCHOOL. Most famous for *The Angelus* and *The Man with the Hoe*. The latter inspired Edwin MARKHAM'S poem of that title. *the Millet of literature* or *the Millet without the Angelus.* The English novelist Thomas HARDY.

Millikan, Robert Andrews (1868–). American physicist. Isolated the electron and measured its charge. Investigated cosmic rays, absorption of X rays, etc. Received Nobel prize in physics (1923). His books include *The Electron* (1917); *Protons, Photons, Neutrons and Cosmic Rays* (1935), etc. His *Evolution of Sciences and Religion* (1927) stamps him as an outstanding representative of the modern trend in science which concludes that purely quantitative thinking is confined to unnecessarily narrow limits.

Millin, Mrs. **Sarah Gertrude,** nee **Liebson** (1889–). South African novelist. Her most successful book is *God's Stepchildren* (1924).

Millis, Walter (1899–). American journalist. His first book to attract attention was *The Martial Spirit* (1931), a study of the Spanish-American War of 1898. *The Road to War* (1935) is an extremely critical account of the propaganda influences which preceded America's entry into the first World War.

Mill on the Floss, The. A novel by George ELIOT (1860). The principal characters are Maggie TULLIVER and her brother Tom, who grow up together at Dorlcote Mill, united by a strong bond in spite of their opposing temperaments. Maggie is loved by Philip Wakem, the deformed son of the lawyer responsible for the ruin of Maggie's father, but Tom's opposition makes their relationship impossible. Later she falls in love with Stephen Guest, the handsome and passionate fiancé of her cousin, Lucy Deane. They go off together on impulse, and although Maggie repents before it is too late, her return is misconstrued and her life is made desperately unhappy. Only death unites her with Tom; the two are drowned together in a great flood of the Floss.

Mills, Clark (1913–). American poet. Known for expert translations from the French. His own works include *The Migrants* (introduction by Jules ROMAINS), *A Suite for France, The Circus.*

Mills, Miss. In Dickens' DAVID COPPERFIELD, the bosom friend of DORA, supposed to have been blighted in early life in some love affair. She therefore looks on the happiness of others with a calm, supercilious benignity, and talks of herself as being "in the desert of Sahara."

Milne, Alan Alexander (1882–). English novelist and playwright. His first play was written on the western front in World War I. Famous for his poems and prose concerning Christopher Robin, his young son. His best plays are *Mr. Pim Passes By* (1919), *The Dover Road* (1923), and *The Truth About Blayds* (1923). His detective novel, *The Red House Mystery* (1921), is a minor classic.

Milner, Alfred. 1st Viscount **Milner** (1854–1925). British administrator and governor of the Transvaal and Orange River colonies (1900–1905). Headed mission to Egypt (1919) that recommended recognition of Egyptian independence.

Milo. An athlete of Crotona. It is said that he carried through the stadium at Olympia a heifer four years old, and ate the whole of it afterwards. When old he attempted to tear in two an oak tree, but the parts closed upon his hands, and while held fast he was devoured by wolves.

Miltiades (540?–?489 B.C.). Athenian general at MARATHON.

Milton. A symbolic poem by William BLAKE (1804), in which the poet John MILTON returns to earth from Heaven and alters the message of his works which has encouraged erroneous beliefs among men. Eventually he enters the spirit of Blake himself and begins to preach redemption and forgiveness.

Milton, John (1608–1674). English poet and prose-writer, one of the best-known and most respected figures in English literature. Although he was trained at Cambridge University in the Anglican faith, he became a Puritan in religious and political belief, and his greatest works reflect his Puritan ideas. At its best, his poetry is marked by intense moral preoccupation, dramatic power, lofty eloquence, and an effective use of sonorous, dignified blank verse. His prose is rhetorical and polemical, in the style of the time in which he lived. Milton's poetic works include COMUS (1634), a masque; LYCIDAS (1637), an elegy; L'ALLEGRO and IL PENSEROSO (1632), pastoral poems; PARADISE LOST (1667); PARADISE REGAINED (1671); SAMSON AGONISTES (1671). Among his prose works are *Doctrine and Discipline of Divorce* (1644); AREOPAGITICA (1644); *Eikonoklastes* (1649); *Defensio pro Populo Anglicano* (1651).

Milton was appointed Latin secretary in 1649 by the Puritan government of England, and held this post until the Restoration, when he was arrested and fined, although not imprisoned. He became blind in 1652, and dictated his poetry to his daughters. He was married three times.

See also HORTON PERIOD; MINSHELL, ELIZABETH; POWELL, MARY; WOODCOCK, CATHERINE.

Milton of Germany. Friedrich G. Klopstock (1724–1803), author of THE MESSIAH.

the Anglo-Saxon Milton. Caedmon (*fl.* 675).

Milvain, Jasper. A successful essayist, one of the chief characters in Gissing's NEW GRUB STREET.

Mime. In Wagner's RING, the smith who helps Siegfried attain the golden hoard. He is a dwarf and the brother of ALBERICH. Finally he is slain by Siegfried for his treachery.

Mime of Mick, Nick, and the Maggies, The. In James Joyce's FINNEGANS WAKE, a play a performance of which is announced and prepared for in the dream of H. C. EARWICKER, the hero, but which never takes place. The performance is scheduled for the Feenichts Playhouse, representing PHOENIX PARK. In the language of the hypothetical program, the play has been "adopted from the Ballymooney Bloodriddon Murther by Bluechin Blackdillain (authorways 'Big Storey')"—an allusion to the unspecified crime committed by Earwicker in Phoenix Park—and contains as characters "Glugg," "The Floras," "Izod," "Chuff," "Ann," "Hump," "The Customers," "Saunderson," and "Kate." In the title, "Mick" is considered to represent St. Michael, "Nick," Nicholas of Cusa or the Devil ("Old Nick"), and "the Maggies," Earwicker's wife Maggie and daughter Isobel.

Mimi. Heroine of Puccini's opera, LA BOHÈME.

Mimir. The Scandinavian god of wisdom, a water-demon, and one of the most celebrated of the giants. The Vanir, with whom he was left as a hostage, cut off his head. Odin embalmed it by his magic art, pronounced over it mystic runes, and ever after consulted it on critical occasions. Mimir dwelt under the roof of YGGDRASILL, where was Mimir's Well (*Mimisbrunnr*), in which all wisdom lay concealed, and from which Mimir drank with the horn Giallar. Odin gave one of his eyes to be permitted to drink of its waters, and thereby became the wisest of the gods.

Min. See GUMP, ANDY AND MIN.

Minafer, George Amberson. The central figure in Booth Tarkington's MAGNIFICENT AMBERSONS.

Minerva. The Roman goddess of wisdom and patroness of the arts and trades, fabled to have sprung, with a tremendous battle-cry, fully armed from the head of Jupiter. She is identified with the Greek ATHENE, and was one of the three chief deities, the others being JUPITER and JUNO. She is represented as grave and majestic, clad in a helmet, with drapery over a coat of mail, bearing the AEGIS on her breast. The most famous statue of this goddess was by PHIDIAS, and was anciently one of the seven wonders of the world.

invita Minerva (*Lat.*, "in spite of Minerva"). Against the grain. The phrase is from HORACE's *Ars Poetica*, l. 385—*Tu nihil invita dices faciesve Minerva* (Beware of attempting anything for which nature has not fitted you).

the Minerva Press. A printing establishment in Leadenhall Street, London, famous in the late 18th century for its trashy, ultra-sentimental novels, which were characterized by complicated plots, and the labyrinths of difficulties into which the hero and heroine got involved before they could be married.

Minerva's bird. The owl.

Ming. The second last Chinese dynasty (1368–1644), most notable for its art in porcelain, painting, fabrics, etc. The Manchu dynasty succeeded it.

Minié, Claude Étienne (1814–1879). French army officer who invented an expanding lead bullet known as *Minié ball* and used extensively in the American Civil War.

Minister's Charge, The. A novel by W. D. HOWELLS (1887). Against the judgment of his wife, the "minister" of the title, the Rev. Mr. Sewell, known to readers of THE RISE OF SILAS LAPHAM, encourages Lemuel Barker, a promising young country boy, to come to Boston and try his fortune in the literary field.

Minister's Wooing, The. A historical novel by Harriet BEECHER STOWE (1859), which J. R. LOWELL ranked as her best. The scene is laid in 18th-century Newport. The heroine, Mary Scudder, is in love with James Marvyn, but his failure to profess Christianity keeps them apart. The other suitor for Mary's hand is Dr. Hopkins, the "minister" of the title.

Miniver Cheevy. Title of a famous poem by Edwin Arlington ROBINSON.

Minjekahwun. In Longfellow's HIAWATHA, Hiawatha's mittens, made of deer-skin. When Hiawatha had his mittens on, he could perform Herculean feats of strength.

> He [Hiawatha] had mittens, Minjekahwun,
> Magic mittens made of deer-skin;
> When upon his hands he wore them,
> He could smite the rocks asunder.
> Longfellow, *Hiawatha,* iv.

Minna von Barnhelm. A drama by Gotthold Ephraim LESSING (1767). The heroine, Minna, is an heiress; her fiancé, Major von Tellheim, a Prussian officer in the Seven Years' War, who suddenly suffers disgrace on a false charge of embezzlement. He frees her from their engagement in spite of her wishes, but she wins him back by the subterfuge of pretending to be disinherited on his account, and eventually his honor is cleared.

Minnehaha (Laughing Water). The lovely daughter of the old arrow-maker of the Daco-Tahs, and wife of Hiawatha in Longfellow's poem, HIAWATHA. She dies of famine.

> From the waterfall, he named her,
> Minnehaha, Laughing Water.
> Longfellow, *Hiawatha,* iv.

minnesingers. The lyric poets of 12th- to 14th-century Germany were so called, because the subject of their lyrics was *minne* (love). See COURTLY LOVE. The chief *minnesingers* were Heinrich von Ofterdingen, WOLFRAM VON ESCHENBACH, WALTHER VON DER VOGELWEIDE, and, the earliest, Heinrich von Veldeke. All of them were men of noble birth. They were succeeded by the MEISTERSINGERS.

Minnie. The heroine of Belasco's drama THE GIRL OF THE GOLDEN WEST and PUCCINI's opera of the same title.

Minnigerode, Meade (1887–). American writer of historical novels and sidelights on history.

minor prophets. See under PROPHETS.

Minos. A legendary king and law-giver of Crete, made at death supreme judge of the lower world. All the dead appeared before him to give an account of their stewardship, and to receive the reward of their deeds. He was the husband of PASIPHAE and the owner of the labyrinth constructed by DAEDALUS. From his name we have the adjective *Minoan,* pertaining to Crete; the *Minoan period* is the Cretan bronze age, roughly about 2500–1200 B. C.

Minotaur. A mythical monster with the head of a bull and the body of a man, fabled to have been the offspring of PASIPHAE and a bull that was sent to her by POSEIDON. MINOS kept it in his labyrinth and fed it on human flesh, seven youths and seven maidens being sent as tribute from Athens every year for the purpose. THESEUS, with the aid of ARIADNE, slew this monster.

Minshell, Elizabeth. Third wife of John MILTON, who was only twenty-four years old when she married him in 1663 and lived a number of years after his death.

minstrel.

minstrel of the border. Sir Walter SCOTT (1771–1832); also called "The Border Minstrel."

The Lay of the Last Minstrel, see LAY.

Minstrel show. A musical show, once popular in the United States, employing white singers and dancers in blackface makeup. Dan Emmett was an early minstrel star and Eddie Leonard a late one. Now played chiefly by amateurs.

Minton, Bruce, pseudonym of **Richard Bransten** (1906–). American writer on sociological topics. His *Men Who Lead Labor* (1937) includes essays on John L. LEWIS, Heywood BROUN, etc. His wife is the writer Ruth MCKENNEY.

Minuit, Peter (1580–1638). Dutch colonial official in America. Purchased Manhattan Island from the Indians for trinkets valued at sixty guilders (ca. $24). Lost at sea.

Minute Men. Militia organized in Massachusetts at the time of the American Revolution. A statue of the Minuteman by Daniel Chester FRENCH stands at Concord, Massachusetts.

Miolnir or **Mjolnir** (i.e., lightning). The magic hammer of THOR. It was fashioned by the dwarfs, and Thor used it in peace to bless and in war to shatter. It would never miss whatever it was thrown at, always returned to the owner of its own accord, and became so small when not in use that it could be put into Thor's pocket.

Mirabeau, Comte **de. Honoré Gabriel Victor Riqueti** (1749–1791). French orator and revolutionary leader. Most important figure in first two years of French Revolution. Believed strongly in a limited, or constitutional, monarchy. President, Jacobin Club (1790), National Assembly (1791). Died a natural death.

Mirabell, Edward. In Congreve's comedy *The Way of the World* (1700), the hero, in love with MILLAMANT. He likes her, "with all her faults; nay, liked her for her faults, . . . which were so natural that (in his opinion) they became her."

Mirabella. In Spenser's FAËRIE QUEENE, a scornful but beautiful lady. She is summoned to Cupid's judgment-hall and sentence is passed on her that she should "ride on a mangy jade, accompanied by a fool, till she had saved as many lovers as she had slain." Mirabella is also doomed to carry a leaky bottle which she is to fill with tears, and a torn wallet which she is to fill with repentance, but her tears and her repentance drop out as fast as they are put in, and are trampled under foot by Scorn.

Miraben. Literally, "sister Mira." Name of the Rajput Princess who gave up all worldly possessions to follow Krishna, the Hindu god. It became the Hindu name of Miss Madeleine Slade, daughter of the British admiral, Sir Edmond Slade, when she left England to join Mahatma Mohandas GANDHI (1925). Miss Slade left Gandhi again (1946) after an unfortunate love affair with another of her master's disciples.

Mirabilis Doctor. See under DOCTOR.

miracle plays or **miracles.** The name given to medieval dramatic presentations of the miracles of Christian saints. They developed from the earlier Biblical MYSTERY PLAYS and the term *miracle* is sometimes used to include both. *The Miracle,* a Geddes-Gest-Reinhardt production dealing with a miracle of the Virgin Mary, presented in New York in 1924, was an adaptation of this old form of drama. See also MORALITY PLAYS; INTERLUDE.

Miranda. (1) In Shakespeare's TEMPEST, daughter of Prospero, the exiled duke of Milan, and niece of Antonio, the usurping duke. She is brought up on a desert island, with Ariel, the fairy spirit, and Caliban the monster as her only companions. Ferdinand, son of the King of Naples, is shipwrecked on the island, falls in love with her, and marries her.

(2) A Boston blue stocking in Lowell's FABLE FOR CRITICS (1848), said to be a caricature of Margaret Fuller (1810–1850), one of the New England Transcendentalists. See also ZENOBIA.

Mirandola, see PICO DELLA MIRANDOLA.

Miriam. (1) In the Old Testament, the sister of Moses.

(2) A mysterious and beautiful art student in Rome, a leading character in Hawthorne's MARBLE FAUN.

(3) A poem by J. G. WHITTIER (1870), the story of a Christian maiden and her Moslem lord.

(4) In D. H. Lawrence's SONS AND LOVERS, a shy, quiet, dark, intense farm girl who is the first love of Paul MOREL. A tacit struggle for his complete love takes place between Miriam and Paul's mother. The girl's almost painful intensity of feeling at first fascinates and then irritates Paul, and, by turning to another love, he convinces himself that he is escaping from her. The character is considered to have been based on the girl in Lawrence's own life who first encouraged his writing and submitted several of his early poems to Ford Madox FORD, then editor of *The English Review,* who was very much impressed by them.

Miroir de L'Homme (Speculum Meditantis). A long didactic and allegorical work by John GOWER (ca. 1376–1379), written in Norman French. It concerns the conflict of the seven vices, and their offspring by the Devil, with the seven virtues, and their offspring by Reason, for the possession of the soul of man. It also contains a sermon on the corruptive influence of sin and how it may be overcome, an account of the life of the Virgin, and an analysis of the various "estates" of contemporary medieval society.

Mirouet, Ursula, see URSULA MIROUET.

Mirror for Magistrates, The. A work on the caprices of Fortune, presenting first-person accounts of the rise to power and decline of famous men, chiefly figures in English history. See FORTUNA; also FALLS OF PRINCES; MONK'S TALE. The first edition was published in 1554–1555, but was considered treasonable by Queen Mary. The second edition appeared in 1559, with nineteen tragedies by various authors, including George Ferrers, William Baldwin (the editor), and John SKELTON. The third edition (1563), which is the most famous, contained eight additional tragedies, among them Thomas Churchyard's JANE SHORE, and an *In-*

duction by Thomas SACKVILLE which is regarded by a number of critics as the most important example of English written between the death of Chaucer and the publication of Spenser's SHEPHERD'S CALENDAR. *The Mirror for Magistrates* became very popular, appearing in numerous new editions and imitations, and exerted a wide influence on the poetry of England in the second half of the 16th century.

Mirror of Knighthood. A famous romance of chivalry. It is one of the books in DON QUIXOTE's library, and the curé says to the barber—

"In this same *Mirror of Knighthood* we meet with Rinaldo de Montalban and his companions, with the twelve peers of France, and Turpin the historian. These gentlemen we will condemn only to perpetual exile, as they contain something of the famous Bojardo's invention, whence the Christian poet Ariosto borrowed the groundwork of his ingenious compositions; to whom I should pay little regard if he had not written in his own language [*Italian*]."—Cervantes, *Don Quixote*, I. i. 6.

Mirvan, Captain. In Fanny Burney's novel EVELINA, a sea captain, whose conversation is full of oaths and "unintelligible sea terms."

Misanthrope, The (Le Misanthrope). A comedy by MOLIÈRE (1666). The hero is ALCESTE.

Miscellany, Poetic, see TOTTEL'S MISCELLANY.

Misérables, Les. A romance by Victor HUGO (1862). The central figure is the convict Jean Valjean. For stealing bread for his sister's starving family, he was sentenced to the galleys, and by his numerous attempts to escape lengthened his term to nineteen years. Free at last, he becomes a beggar and is befriended by the Bishop of D———, but repays the Bishop's hospitality by stealing his silver. When he is brought back by the police, the charitable Bishop declares that the silver was a gift, and by this one act changes Jean Valjean's entire life. During the years that follow, the ex-convict prospers and even becomes mayor of his town under the name of M. Madeleine. He is, however, pursued by the detective Javert, a man with a ruthless sense of justice, and finally, when another man is mistakenly arrested in his place, he gives himself up and is sent back to the galleys. Again he escapes. One of his acts of kindness had been to befriend Fantine, an abandoned woman of the streets. She is now dead and he rescues her daughter, little Cosette, from the abusive Thenardiers, with whom she has been living and brings her up as his own child. In time she falls in love with and marries the brave and handsome young Marius. *Les Misérables* is painted on an enormous canvas with innumerable characters and episodes. Chief of the characters not mentioned above is Little Gavroche, an impish young street Arab, who helps defend the barricades and sings a brave defiance to the enemy as he goes to his death in the fray. Among the most famous chapters are the account of the battle of Waterloo and Jean Valjean's exciting flight through the Paris sewers.

Miserere. The fifty-first psalm is so called because its opening words are *Miserere mei Deus* (Have mercy upon me, O God). One of the evening services of Lent is called *miserere,* because this penitential psalm is sung, after which a sermon is delivered. The under side of a folding seat in choir-stalls is called a *miserere,* or, more properly, a *misericord;* when turned up it forms a ledge-seat sufficient to rest the aged in a kneeling position.

misericord. A medieval dagger with a needle-like blade. Used for the "mercy stroke," hence the name.

Mishe-Mokwa. The great bear slain by Mudjekeewis in Longfellow's HIAWATHA.

Mishe-Nahma. In Longfellow's HIAWATHA, the great sturgeon, "king of fishes," subdued by Hiawatha. With this labor, the "great teacher" teaches the Indians how to make oil for the winter. When Hiawatha throws his line for the sturgeon, that king of fishes first persuades a pike to swallow the bait and tries to break the line, but Hiawatha throws it back into the water. Next, a sun-fish is persuaded to try the bait, with the same result. Finally the sturgeon, in anger, swallows Hiawatha and his canoe also, but Hiawatha smites the heart of the sturgeon with his fist, and the king of fishes swims to the shore and dies. Then the sea-gulls open a rift in the dead body, out of which Hiawatha makes his escape.

"I have slain the Mishe-Nahma,
Slain the king of fishes," said he.
Hiawatha, viii.

Mishna (*Heb.,* "repetition or instruction"). The collection of moral precepts, traditions, etc., forming the basis of the TALMUD; the second or oral law. See also GEMARA. It is divided into six parts: (1) agriculture; (2) Sabbaths, fasts, and festivals; (3) marriage and divorce; (4) civil and penal laws; (5) sacrifices; (6) holy persons and things.

Misogonus. The third English comedy by Thomas Rychardes (1560). It is written in rhyming quatrains, and not in couplets like RALPH ROISTER DOISTER and GAMMER GURTON'S NEEDLE.

Misrule, King, Lord or **Abbot of,** see LORD OF MISRULE.

missing link. A popular term for the hypothetical being that is supposed, according to the theory of evolution, to bridge the gap between man and the anthropoid apes. HAECKEL held it to be *Pithecanthropus erectus* but scientists are not agreed, either on this or on the number of "missing links" there may be.

Missionary Ridge. A mountain on the border of Georgia and Tennessee, scene of the last phase of the battle of Chattanooga in the American Civil War (November 25, 1863). The Confederates were forced to withdraw.

Mississippi Bubble. The "South Sea scheme" of France (1717–1720), projected by John Law, a Scotchman. It was so called because the projector was to have the exclusive trade of Louisiana, on the banks of the Mississippi, on condition of his taking on himself the National Debt of France. The scheme was a notorious fiasco. See also SOUTH SEA BUBBLE.

Miss Lulu Bett. A novel by Zona GALE (1920), which in its dramatic version received the Pulitzer Prize as the best American play of 1921. It is a story of the much abused unattractive old-maid sister who is "given a home." She is expected to do all the work, take the worst of everything, and be properly grateful. When Lulu Bett, in a sudden flare of rebellion, runs off with a man and later returns alone, the Deacon family expect her to be more abject than ever, but to their utter bewilderment she has gained an independent outlook that makes it impossible for them to treat her as they did before.

Missouri.

I'm from Missouri. I must be shown; I will have to have proof; I will take nothing on faith. The origin of the phrase is obscure. It has been suggested that it started as a mannerism of a Missouri congressman.

Missouri Compromise. An act passed by the U.S. Congress in 1821 prohibiting slavery north of the Missouri boundary (36° 30′) but admitting Missouri as a slave state.

mistletoe. In Norse mythology, when Baldur's life seemed threatened, all things were asked by FRIGGA to swear an oath that they would do no harm to the god of light and beauty. She passed by the mistletoe which seemed too insignificant. Loki induced blind Hodur to throw a mistletoe at Baldur in playful fun, and Baldur was killed. The Celtic druids sought the mistletoe as a cure-all. It had magic virtues when it grew on oak trees and was plucked on the sixth day of the moon.

Mistletoe, John. A book by Christopher MORLEY, written, as he puts it himself, "to celebrate (or deplore) his own fortieth birthday . . . an early example of what is now a universal passion, the autobiographies of young men."

Mistletoe Bough, The. The song so called is by Thomas Haynes Bayley, who died in 1839. The tale is this: Lord Lovel marries a young lady, a baron's daughter, and on the wedding night the bride proposes that the guests play "hide-and-seek." The bride hides in an old oak chest, and the lid, falling down, shuts her in. Lord Lovel seeks her that night and seeks her next day, but nowhere can he find her. Some years later the old oak chest is sold, and, on being opened, is found to contain the skeleton of the bride. See also GINEVRA.

Mistral, Frédéric (1830–1914). Famous Provençal poet. Best-known member of the FÉLIBRIGE. Shared Nobel prize for literature with José Echegaray y Eizaguirre (1904). Pastoral, lyric, and narrative poems in Provençal.

Mistral, Gabriela (1889–). Famous poet of Chile. Nobel prize for poetry (1945). Cf. *Gabriela Mistral's Anthology* (1942).

Mistress of the Adriatic. Venice.

Mistress of the Seas. Great Britain.

Mistress of the World. Rome.

Mistress Quickly. The wife of Pistol and hostess of the Boar's Head Tavern in Eastcheap in Shakespeare's *Henry IV* and *Henry V*. Also, a servant in *The Merry Wives of Windsor.*

Mitchell, John Ames (1845–1918). Famous American editor (and founder) of the humorous weekly *Life* (1883–1938). He also wrote fantastically imaginative novels, the best-known being *The Last American* (1889) and *Amos Judd* (1895).

Mitchell, Langdon Edwyn. Pseudonym **John Philip Varley** (1862–1935). American playwright and poet. Son of Silas Weir MITCHELL. Author of *Becky Sharp* (a dramatization of Thackeray's *Vanity Fair*); etc.

Mitchell, Margaret (1900–). American novelist, author of the best seller *Gone With The Wind* (1936), which took her 10 years to write. It sold as many as 50,000 copies in a single day—2 million copies by 1939. Translated into 16 languages. Pulitzer prize for fiction in 1937. The moving-picture version (1940) with Vivien Leigh and Clark Gable broke all records. Period is the Civil War.

Mitchell, Ruth Comfort (1882–). American poet and novelist. Her best work is in *Narratives in Verse* (1923).

Mitchell, Silas Weir (1829–1914). American physician, poet, and novelist. Specialized in, and wrote about, nervous disorders. Best-known for his novels *Hugh Wynne, Free Quaker* (1898); *The Adventures of François* (1899); *The Autobiography of a Quack* (1900); etc.

Mitchell, William (1879–1936). American army officer. In command of A.E.F. air forces (1917–1918). Court-martialed for criticism of alleged mismanagement of aviation service (1925) and sentenced to suspension from service. A prophet without honor, he spread a vast influence "like giant wings" over the army air service. Author of *Winged Defense* (1925); *Skyways* (1930); etc.

Mitchison, Mrs. **Naomi Margaret,** *née* **Haldane** (1897–). English novelist, sister of the famous biologist J. B. S. Haldane. Greatly interested in social problems and in politics, but her best work is in the historical novel, dealing mostly with ancient Greece and Rome. She has been called "the most interesting historical novelist now writing." *The Conquered* (1923); *When the Bough Breaks* (1924); etc.

Mite, Sir Matthew. In Samuel Foote's comedy, *The Nabob* (1772), a returned East Indian merchant, dissolute, dogmatical, ashamed of his former acquaintances, hating the aristocracy, yet longing to be acknowledged by them. He squanders his wealth on toadies, dresses his livery servants most gorgeously, and gives his chairmen the most costly exotics to wear in their coats. Sir Matthew is forever astonishing weak minds with his talk about rupees, lacs, jaghires, and so on.

Mitford, Mary Russell (1787–1855). English novelist and dramatist. Her magazine sketches of country life were collected as *Our Village* (5 vols., 1824–1832).

Mithra or **Mithras.** The god of light of the ancient Persians, one of their chief deities and the ruler of the universe; sometimes used as a synonym for the sun. The word means *friend,* and this deity is so called because he befriends man in this life, and protects him against evil spirits after death. He is represented as a young man with a Phrygian cap, a tunic, and a mantle on his left shoulder, in the act of plunging a sword into the neck of a bull. Cf. *Thebais,* i.

Mithridates. King of Pontus (120–63 B. C.), conquered by the Romans. To guard against being poisoned by his enemies, Mithridates had so accustomed his system to poison of various sorts that he found it impossible to end his life by this means even when he wished to do so. He was slain by a Gaul at his own orders. RACINE wrote a French tragedy on the subject, called *Mithridate* (1673). Nathaniel Lee brought out his *Mithridates, King of Pontus* in English about the same time (produced 1678).

Mitre Tavern. A place of resort in the time of Shakespeare. It was in Mitre Court, leading south of Cheapside, and was in existence from before 1475 till the Great Fire (1666), when it was destroyed and not rebuilt. There was another tavern of the same name in Fleet Street. Cf. Barrey's *Ram Alley,* v. 1611.

Mitya, see *Dmitry Fyodorovich Karamazov,* under KARAMAZOV.

Mjolnir, see MIOLNIR.

Mizpah. Title of a poem by TENNYSON.

Mlle de Maupin. A novel by Theophile GAUTIER (1835) described by one critic as "a story of perverted morality beautifully told."

Mlle Modiste. See **Modiste, Mlle.**

Mnemosyne. Goddess of memory and mother by Zeus of the nine Muses of Greek mythology. She was the daughter of Heaven and Earth (Uranus and Ge).

> To the Immortals every one
> A portion was assigned of all that is;
> But chief Mnemosyne did Maia's son
> Clothe in the light of his loud melodies.
> Shelley, *Homer's Hymn to Mercury,* lxxiii.

Mobtown. Baltimore, so called from its reputation for lawlessness. See also under CITY.

Moby Dick. A novel by Herman MELVILLE (1851). Moby Dick is a ferocious white whale, who was known to whalers of the period as Mocha Dick. He is pursued in a fury of revenge by Captain AHAB, whose leg he has bitten off, and under Melville's handling the chase takes on a significance beyond mere externals. Moby Dick becomes a symbol of the terrific forces of the natural universe, or of evil, and Captain Ahab, representing human will, is doomed to disaster, even though Moby Dick is killed at last. See also SCHMAEL; PIP; QUEEQUEG; STARBUCK.

In World War II, the U.S. navy had an experimental rocket engine which was known as Moby Dick.

Mockbeggar. A novel by Everard Meynell, son of Alice MEYNELL.

modern. For *modern Athens, modern Babylon,* etc., see under ATHENS; BABYLON.

Modern Chivalry. A once widely popular satirical novel by Hugh Henry BRACKENRIDGE, published in parts between 1792 and 1805. It is a sort of American DON QUIXOTE in which the hero, Captain Farrago, and his man Teague leave western Pennsylvania to travel about and "observe human nature." Carl Van Doren in *The American Novel* says that as a description of manners in the early days of the Republic the book is unapproached by any other. It satirizes primarily the rule of political upstarts, of which the scalawag Teague is chief; in Part II, when Farrago becomes governor of a backwoods community, the settlers are persuaded to give the vote to beasts as well as men and to make use of a monkey clerk and a hound lawyer. But the book also satirized contemporary life in all phases and was frequently brought up to date in new revisions.

Modern Instance, A. A novel by W. D. HOWELLS (1881), dealing with the courtship, marriage and subsequent misfortunes of Bartley Hubbard and Marcia Gaylord. Marcia's Yankee father, Squire Gaylord, whose newspaper in Equity, Maine, young Hubbard runs for a time, distrusts him from the start and endeavors in vain to protect Marcia from unhappiness. Bartley Hubbard is what Hamlin Garland calls "the modern substitute for a villain"—good-natured but unprincipled, and above all things "smart."

Modernists and Fundamentalists. Names adopted into general usage in 1923 and 1924 for theological radicals and conservatives, respectively, in several of the Protestant churches. The issue of difference centered most conspicuously in the effort of the Presbyterian Fundamentalists to force the withdrawal of Dr. Harry FOSDICK, a Baptist minister of liberal intellectual tendencies, from the pulpit of the First Presbyterian Church in New York City. It was also marked by several heresy trials in various ecclesiastical bodies, by the efforts of William Jennings BRYAN to discredit the theory of evolution on the ground that it was not in accord with Biblical teaching, and by a widespread opposition on the part of the Fundamentalists to the principles of HIGHER CRITICISM. The Fundamentalists were so called because they wished to preserve the "fundamental" principles of Christianity from attack.

Modern Love. A series of fifty sixteen-line poems connected in subject-matter, by George MEREDITH (1862). They present the various thoughts and emotions of a married couple who perceive that their love for each other is dying, the husband occasionally speaking as "I." The sequence is considered to have been based on Meredith's own difficulties in his unfortunate first marriage with Mary Ellen NICOLLS.

Modern Painters. A critical treatise on landscape painting (1843) by John RUSKIN, which aimed to prove the superiority of contemporary artists, especially Turner, over the old masters. Its brilliant style and original ideas established Ruskin's reputation as an art critic.

Moderns. See ANCIENTS AND MODERNS.

Modern Temper, The. An important book by Joseph Wood KRUTCH (1929), a clear statement of the author's "cheerful acceptance in gallant despair of a pragmatic stoicism."

Modest Proposal, A. Full title, *A Modest Proposal for Preventing the Children of Poor People from Being a Burden to their Parents or the Country.* A savagely satirical pamphlet (1729) by Jonathan SWIFT, in which he suggests that the problem of starving children in Ireland be solved by using the children as food for the rich.

Modiste, Mlle. Operetta by Victor HERBERT (1905). Includes famous aria, *Kiss Me Again.*

Modo. The fiend mentioned in KING LEAR (iv. 1) as he who urges to murder. He is one of the five that possessed "Poor Tom." See MAHU.

Modred or **Mordred.** One of the knights of the ROUND TABLE in Arthurian romance, nephew and betrayer of King ARTHUR. He is represented as the treacherous knight. He revolts against the King, whose wife he has seduced, is mortally wounded in the battle of Camlan, in Cornwall, and is buried on the island of Avalon. The accounts of Modred vary considerably. In the older romances, his mother is King Arthur's half sister MORGAUSE (or sometimes Anne) and he is son as well as nephew of Arthur by unconscious incest, but Tennyson departs from this tradition in his *Idylls of the King* where his mother is Bellicent. According to the older versions Arthur is off fighting the Romans, but according to Tennyson, punishing Launcelot, when Modred, whom he has left in charge of the kingdom, raises his fatal revolt. Modred, who hates Launcelot, was at the bottom of the plot to expose his guilty relations with GUINEVERE. With twelve other knights he forced his way into the Queen's chamber when Launcelot was there. The name is spelled Mordred by MALORY in his *Morte d' Arthur;* Modred by Tennyson. In the Welsh MABINOGION Modred appears as Medrawd.

Mods. In Oxford, a contracted form of moderations. The three necessary examinations in Oxford are the Smalls, the Mods, and the Greats. No one can take a class till he has passed the Mods.

modus operandi (*Lat.*). The mode of operation; the way in which a thing is done or should be done.

modus vivendi (*Lat.*, "way of living"). A mutual arrangement whereby persons not at the time being on friendly terms can be induced to live together in harmony. The term may be applied to individuals, to societies, or to peoples.

Moeller, Philip (1880–). American playwright. One of the founders (1914) and directors of the Washington Square Players and the New York Theater Guild. *Madame Sand* (1917); *Molière* (1919); etc.

Mogul.

the Mogul Empire. The Mohammedan-Tartar Empire in India, which began in 1526 with Baber, great-grandson of Timur, or TAMBURLAINE, and split up after the death of Aurungzebe in 1707, the power passing to the British and the Mahrattas. The Emperor was known as the *Great* or *Grand Mogul;* besides those mentioned, Akbar, Jahangir, and Shah Jehan are the most noteworthy.

Mogul cards. The best quality playing-cards were so called because the wrapper, or the "duty card" (cards are subject to excise duty), was decorated with a representation of the Great Mogul. Inferior cards were called "Harrys," "Highlanders," and "Merry Andrews" for a similar reason.

Mohammed, see MAHOMET.

Mohicans, Last of the, see LAST OF THE MOHICANS.

Mohocks. In 18th-century London, ruffians (often aristocrats) who committed outrages in the streets. The name is a variant of Mohawks. See also APACHE.

Mokanna. The "Veiled Prophet of Khorassan," chief figure in the first story told in Moore's LALLA ROOKH (1817). Mokanna is the name given to Hakem ben Haschem, from a silver gauze veil worn by him "to dim the lustre of his face," or rather to hide its extreme ugliness. See under VEILED.

Molesworth, Mary Louisa, *née* **Stewart.** Pseudonym **Ennis Graham** (1839–1921). Scottish writer noted for her children's books.

Moley, Raymond (1886–). American journalist, author, and university professor. Member of the "brain trust" advising President F. D. ROOSEVELT. Contributing editor, *Newsweek* (from 1937). Author of *Lessons in American Citizenship* (10 editions; 1917–1930); *Tribunes of the People* (1932); etc.

Molière. Pseudonym of **Jean Baptiste Poquelin** (1622–1673). French playwright, famous for his satirical comedies holding up to ridicule the follies and pretenses of social types and individuals of his day, and for his studies of character. He was influenced by the Roman comedies of TERENCE and PLAUTUS and the Italian Comedy of Masks. His works include LES ÉTOURDIS (1653); LES PRÉCIEUSES RIDICULES (*The Ridiculous Misses;* 1659); SGANARELLE (1660); L'ÉCOLE DES MARIS (*The School for Husbands;* 1661); L'ÉCOLE DES FEMMES (*The School for Wives;* 1662); TARTUFFE (1664), which was forbidden after its first performance and, revised, was finally presented again in 1669; LE MARIAGE FORCÉ (*The Enforced Marriage;* 1664); DON JUAN, OU LE FESTIN DE PIERRE (1665); L'AMOUR MÉDECIN (*Love As a Doctor;* 1664); LE MISANTHROPE (1666); Le MÉDECIN MALGRÉ LUI (Physician *In Spite of Himself;* 1666); L'AMPHITRYON (1668); L'AVARE (*The Miser*) (1668); GEORGES DANDIN (1668); MONSIEUR DE POURCEAUGNAC (1670); LE BOURGEOIS GENTILHOMME (*The Bourgeois Gentleman;* 1670); LES FOURBERIES DE SCAPIN (*The Knaveries of Scapin;* 1671); LES FEMMES SAVANTES (*The Learned Ladies;* 1672); LE MALADE IMAGINAIRE (*The Imaginary Invalid;* 1673).

Molière started his theatrical career by touring the French provinces with a small company of actors, for whom he wrote comedies. After his fame was established, he received a pension from King Louis XIV, although he was frequently attacked, especially by the clergy, for "indecency." He died of a hemorrhage while acting in the rôle of ARGAN in his last play, *Le Malade imaginaire.*

the Italian Molière. Carlo Goldoni (1707–1793).

the Spanish Molière. Leandro Fernandez Moratin (1760–1828).

Molinier, Olivier. In André Gide's THE COUNTERFEITERS, an adolescent youth, school friend of Bernard PROFITENDIEU and nephew of the narrator Edouard. His parents, **Oscar** and **Pauline Molinier, Vincent,** his elder brother, and **George,** his younger brother, are also characters in the novel.

Moll Flanders. A novel by Daniel DEFOE (1721) written in the form of an autobiography. The heroine is a woman of extraordinary beauty, born in Old Bailey. She is twelve years a harlot, five years a wife, twelve years a thief, and eight years a convict in Virginia; but ultimately she becomes rich, lives honestly, and dies a penitent in the reign of Charles II.

Mollison, James Allan (1905–). British aviator. Holder of numerous aviation records. Author of an autobiography, *Death Cometh Soon or Late;* etc. Wife was the late Amy Johnson, famous aviatrix.

Molloch, May, or **The Maid of the Hairy Arms.** An elf of folklore who mingles in ordinary sports, and will even direct the master of the house how to play dominoes or draughts. Like the White Lady of Avenel, May Molloch is a sort of BANSHEE.

Molly Maguires. An Irish secret society organized in 1843. Stout, active young Irishmen dressed up in women's clothes, blackened faces, and otherwise disguised themselves to surprise those employed to enforce the payment of rents. Their victims were ducked in bog-holes, and many were beaten most unmercifully.

A similar secret society in the mining districts of Pennsylvania was (about 1877) known by the same name. They figure in Sir Arthur Conan Doyle's *The Valley of Fear* (1915), a long Sherlock Holmes story.

Molly Mog. This celebrated beauty was an innkeeper's daughter, at Oakingham, Berks. She was the toast of the gay sparks of the first half of the 18th century, and died unmarried in 1766, at the age of sixty-seven. John GAY has a ballad on this *Fair Maid of the Inn,* in which the "swain" alluded to is Mr. Standen, of Arborfield, who died in 1730. It is said that Molly's sister Sally was the greater beauty. A portrait of Gay still hangs in the inn.

Molly Pitcher, see MCCAULEY, MARY.

Molnár, Ferenc (1878–). Hungarian journalist, novelist, and playwright. Noted figure in Budapest society; war correspondent on German-Austrian front in World War I (1914–1918); came to U.S. (1940) as fugitive from Nazism. Author of the plays LILIOM (1909); *The Guardsman* (1910); *The Play's the Thing* (1925); *No Greater Glory* (1934); etc. His comedies are known for ingenious plots and uncommon themes, with dialogue that "lends to all his work an air of intimacy and familiarity."

Moloch. Any influence which demands from us the sacrifice of what we hold most dear. The allusion is to the god of the Ammonites, to whom children were "made to pass through the fire" in sacrifice (2 *Kings,* xxiii. 10). Milton says he was worshiped in Rabba, in Argob, and Basan, to the stream of utmost Arnon. (*Paradise Lost,* i. 392–398).

Molotov, Vyacheslav Mikhailovich. Surname originally **Skryabin** (1890–). Soviet Russian statesman. Commissar of foreign affairs (1939). Signed Soviet-Nazi non-aggression pact (1939). President at Anglo-Soviet conference in Moscow (1941) and represented the U.S.S.R. at most of the important conferences between England, the United States, and the Soviet Union after the end of World War II.

Moltke, Count **Helmuth von** (1800–1891). Chief of Prussian general staff (1858–1888); reorganized Prussian army (1858–1863); created field marshal (1871). His nephew, **Helmuth von Moltke** (1848–1916), chief of general staff (from 1906) and director of German strategy at the outbreak of World War I, lost the first battle of the Marne (1914) and was succeeded by General von Falkenhayn.

moly. The mythical herb given, according to HOMER, by HERMES to ULYSSES as an antidote against the sorceries of CIRCE.

> Black was the root, but milky white the flower,
> Moly the name, to mortals hard to find.
> Pope's *Odyssey,* x, 365.
>
> That moly
> That Hermes once to wise Ulysses gave.
> Milton, *Comus,* 655.

Mommsen, Theodor (1817–1903). German classical scholar and historian. Active in politics as a liberal and opponent to Bismarck. Best-known as author of the famous *History of Rome* (1854–1856). Nobel prize for literature (1902).

Mommur. The capital of the empire of OBERON, king of the fairies. It is here he held his court.

Momus. The sleepy god of the Greeks, son of Nox (Night), who was always railing and carping. Being asked to pass judgment on the relative merits of Neptune, Vulcan, and Minerva, Momus railed at them all. He said the horns of a bull ought to have been placed in the shoulders, where they would have been of much greater force; as for man, he said Jupiter ought to have made him with a window in his breast, whereby his real thoughts might be revealed. Hence Byron's—

> Were Momus' lattice in our breasts . . .
> *Wegener,* iii. 1.

Hence also, a *Momus* is one who carps at everything.

Monaciello (*Ital.,* "little monk"). A sort of incubus in Neapolitan folklore, described as a thick little man, dressed in a monk's garment and broad-brimmed hat. Those who will follow when he beckons will be led to a spot where a treasure is concealed. Sometimes, however, it is his pleasure to pull the bedclothes off, and sometimes to sit perched on a sleeper.

Mona Lisa. A famous portrait by Leonardo da VINCI also known as *La Belle Joconde.* Mona Lisa was the wife of Francesco de Giocondo. Many popular legends have grown up regarding her enigmatic smile, which is reputed to exercise an uncontrollable fascination over those who do not actively resist it. According to one story, the smile is a forced one, concealing some terrible torment.

Monarque, Le Grand. Louis XIV of France (b. 1638, reigned 1643–1715).

Monastery, The. A novel by Sir Walter SCOTT (1820). The hero is Halbert Glendenning, the heroine Lady Mary Avenel. Much of the plot concerns the effort of the Abbot of St. Mary's Monastery to secure a Bible which belonged to Lady Alice Avenel, but which the mysterious WHITE LADY of the Avenels exercises superhuman power to keep him from obtaining.

Moncada, Matthias de. In Scott's *Surgeon's Daughter,* a merchant, stern and relentless. He arrests his daughter Zilia the day after her confinement of a natural son.

Monck or **Monk, George.** 1st Duke of **Albemarle** (1608–1670). British general. Suppressed the insurrection of the Scottish Royalists for Cromwell (1652) and was made governor of Scotland (1654). Organized the Coldstream Guards (1660). General in Chief of land forces and joint commander of Navy. After the death of both Cromwells, helped restore monarchy and welcomed Charles II. Buried at Westminster Abbey.

Monday.

Black Monday. (1) Easter Monday; (2) The Monday beginning a school term.

Fat Monday. The day before Shrove Tuesday.

Saint Monday. A day of idleness.

Mondriaan, Pieter Cornelis (1872–1945). Dutch ultramodern painter, mostly living in Paris. Collaborated with van Tongerlow and van Doesburg in founding the Dutch "de Stijl" group.

Monet, Claude (1840–1926). French landscape painter, one of the leading figures of impressionism. *Un Déjeuner sur l'Herbe; Gare Saint-Lazare* and *Camille* are among his best-known canvases.

Monflathers, Miss. In Dickens' OLD CURIOSITY SHOP, mistress of a boarding and day establishment, to whom Mrs. Jarley sent Little Nell, to ask her to patronize the wax-work collection. Miss Monflathers received the child with frigid virtue, and said to her, "Don't you think you must be very wicked to be a wax-work child? Don't you know it is very naughty to be a wax child when you might have the proud consciousness of assisting, to the extent of your infant powers, the noble manufactures of your country?"

Mongrel Parliament. See under PARLIAMENTS.

Monime. The heroine of Racine's tragedy of *Mithridate*. See MITHRIDATES.

Monimia. The heroine of Thomas OTWAY's tragedy *The Orphan* (1610), sister of Chamont and ward of Lord Acasto. Monimia is in love with Acasto's son Castalio and privately marries him. Polydore, the brother of Castalio, also loves her, but his love is dishonorable. By treachery, Polydore obtains admission to Monimia's chamber, and passes the bridal night with her, Monimia supposing him to be her husband. When next day she discovers the deceit, she poisons herself. Polydore, learning that Monimia is his brother's wife, provokes a quarrel, runs on his brother's sword, and dies.

Moniplies, Richie. The honest self-willed Scotch servant of Lord Nigel Olifaunt of Glenvarlach in Scott's FORTUNES OF NIGEL.

monism. The philosophical doctrine that ultimate reality is one and uniform, not polar as in *dualism*, or varied as in *pluralism*.

Monitor. So the Romans called the nursery teacher. The *Military Monitor* was an officer to tell young soldiers of the faults committed against the service. The *House Monitor* was a slave to call the family of a morning, etc.

A shallow-draught ironclad warship with a flat deck, sharp stern, and one or more movable turrets, is so called. They were first used in the American Civil War and were so named by the inventor, Captain Ericsson, because they were to be "severe monitors" to the leaders of the Southern rebellion. The conflict between the original *Monitor* and the *Merrimac* decided the supremacy of iron war vessels over those of wood. The battle is an episode in *The Long Roll* (1911), a novel by Mary JOHNSTON.

Monk, The. A novel by Matthew G. LEWIS (1795) which enjoyed a great vogue and earned for its author the nickname of *Monk Lewis*. Ambrosio, the monkish hero, is abbot of the Capuchins of Madrid, and is called "the man of holiness" but Matilda overcomes his virtue. He goes on from bad to worse, until he is condemned to death by the Inquisition. He now bargains with Lucifer for release. He gains his bargain, it is true, but only to be dashed to pieces on a rock.

Monkbarns, The Laird of. See OLDBUCK, JONATHAN.

monkey puzzle. A Chilean evergreen tree of interlaced branches, introduced into England, and spoken of in English novels. (Title of novel by J. D. BERESFORD).

Monk Lewis. See THE MONK.

Monk's or **Monkes Tale, The.** One of Chaucer's CANTERBURY TALES (1388). The subject is the uncertainty of fortune illustrated with seventeen examples:—

From Scripture: Lucifer, Adam, and Samson; Nebuchadnezzar, Belshazzar, Holofernes (from the *Book of Judith*).

Greek and Roman History: Alexander the Great, Julius Caesar and Nero.

Other Histories: Croesus, Hugolin of Pisa, Pedro of Spain, Pierre de Lusignan (King of Cyprus), Visconti (Bernardo), Duke of Milan, and Zenobia.

From Mythology: Hercules.

This tale was based on Boccaccio's *De Casibus Virorum Illustrium*. See also FALLS OF PRINCES; MIRROR FOR MAGISTRATES.

Monmouth, Duke **of. James Scott** (1649–1685). Known also as **James Fitzroy** and **James Crofts,** and as "The Protestant Duke." Natural son of Charles II, born in Holland during Charles' exile, and brought up a Protestant. Acknowledged by Charles and created Duke of Monmouth (1663). Commanded English forces sent to aid France in the Dutch war (1675) and to suppress the Scottish Covenanters (1675–1679). Exiled twice by Charles II, after whose death he returned to claim the British crown in place of James II (1685). Defeated at Sedgemoor and beheaded. See also BLOODY ASSIZES.

Monmouth, the Marquis of. A prominent character in Disraeli's CONINGSBY.

Monna Vanna. A drama by Maurice MAETERLINCK (1902), later made into an opera by Fevrier. The scene is laid in 15th century Pisa. Prinzivalle, at the head of a Florentine army, has laid siege to Pisa and promises relief only if Monna Vanna will spend a night in his tent. To save the city, Monna Vanna persuades her husband Guido Colonna, the commander of the Pisan forces, to agree. Prinzivalle, who has adored Vanna for years, does not harm her and himself returns with her to Pisa, but Guido refuses to believe them and is about to kill Prinzivalle by torture. Vanna then liberates Prinzivalle and escapes with him.

monodrama. A play designed to be acted by a single person.

Monro, Harold Edward (1879–1932). British poet and critic of Scottish descent. Established the magazine *Poetry Review* (1911) and The Poetry Book Shop (1912) in London.

was of more influence as an appreciator of poetry than as a poet, although T. S. Eliot called his work "honest and bitter."

Monroe, Harriet (1861?–1936). American poet and editor. Chiefly known for establishing (1912) and editing to the time of her death *Poetry: a Magazine of Verse,* which exercised great influence in the years prior to World War I, and is still being published, open to every sort of experimental work. Author of *Valeria and other Poems* (1892); *The Columbian Ode* (1892); *You and I* (1914); etc.

Monroe, James (1758–1831). Fifth president of the United States (1817–1825) during the period known as the "era of good feeling." During his presidency Florida was acquired (1819); the MISSOURI COMPROMISE legislation was enacted (1820); the MONROE DOCTRINE was promulgated (1823); etc. He is represented in the American Hall of Fame. The capital of LIBERIA is named after him Monrovia.

Monroe Doctrine. The doctrine first promulgated by James MONROE in 1823, to the effect that the American states are never to entangle themselves in the broils of the Old World, nor to suffer it to interfere in the affairs of the New; and they are to regard any attempt on the part of nations of the Old World to plant their systems of government in any part of North America not at the time in European occupation as dangerous to American peace and safety.

Mons. The story of the "angels of Mons" is a fictional account of supernatural aid being brought to the English at the battle of Mons in World War I, written by Arthur MACHEN in *The Bowmen, and Other Legends of the War* (1915). It found full acceptance with many soldiers as well as civilians.

Monsieur. Philippe, Duke of Orleans and brother of Louis XIV was so called.

Monsieur Veto. Louis XVI of France (1754–1793).

Monsieur Beaucaire. A short story by Booth TARKINGTON (1900). The scene is laid in 18th-century Bath, and the hero is a cousin of Louis XV, Louis Philippe de Valois. Disguised as a barber, on adventure bent, he falls in love with Lady Mary Carlisle and forces his rival, the Duke of Winterset, whom he has caught cheating at cards, to present him as the Duke de Chateaurien. All goes well with his suit until Winterset announces that he is a mere barber, whereupon Lady Mary treats him with the utmost scorn. Shortly after, on an occasion of state, he is greeted as the Duke of Orleans, but her regret is of no avail.

Mons Meg. A large cannon on Edinburgh Castle, dating from the 15th century and supposedly cast at Mons in Flanders. Removed to the Tower of London (1745), but later restored to Edinburgh (1829).

Mont, Michael. In Galsworthy's WHITE MONKEY, the young publisher whom Fleur Forsyte marries.

Montagna, Bartolommeo (1450?–1523). Italian painter who founded the school of Vicenza.

Montagu, Lady **Mary Wortley** (1689–1762). English author, best known for her lively and amusing letters as collected in *Turkish Letters* (1763) and *Letters and Works* (1837). She also wrote *Town Eclogues* (1716) and *Court Poems by a Lady of Quality* (1716), quarreled notoriously with Alexander POPE, and introduced small-pox inoculation into England.

Montague. In Shakespeare's ROMEO AND JULIET the name of the feudal house of Verona to which Romeo belonged.

Lord and *Lady Montague,* Romeo's father and mother, play their part in keeping up the tragic enmity between the houses of Montague and Capulet.

Montague, Charles Edward (1867–1928). British journalist, novelist, and critic. On staff of *Manchester Guardian* as chief editorial writer and brilliant theater critic. His novels and short stories include *A Hind Let Loose* (1910); *The Morning's War* (1913); *Rough Justice* (1926); *Right Off the Map* (1927); etc. *Fiery Particles* (1923) are short stories.

Montaigne, Michel Eyquem de (1533–1595). French author, considered the ideal gentleman-scholar of the later Renaissance, famous for his *Essays* (1582, 1587, 1588), which are the earliest examples of the form of the personal essay and give an excellent picture of the author's temperate, skeptical, inquiring, peace-loving, nature-loving, humanistic personality. They were translated into English by John FLORIO (1603) and became very popular in England. SHAKESPEARE and Francis BACON are considered to have been influenced by them. As a child, Montaigne was given a careful and complete education, which included travel, instruction in languages, and familiarization with music, by his father, who was an outstanding personality of his day. Montaigne himself studied law and was a magistrate for several years until he retired to devote his time to writing. He was twice elected Mayor of Bordeaux, where he lived (1581 and 1583).

Montalembert, Comte **de. Charles Forbes** (1810–1870). French journalist and politician. Cofounder with Lamennais of the journal *L'Avenir* (1830) in which he upheld the interests of the Roman Catholic Church and the clergy.

Montargis, the dog of. A famous dog of legend named Dragon. He belonged to Captain Aubrey de Montdidier, and is especially noted for his fight with the Chevalier Richard MACAIRE. The dog was called Montargis because the encounter was depicted over the chimney of the great hall in the castle of Montargis. It was in the forest of Bondi, close by this castle, where Aubrey was assassinated. Guilbert de Pixerecourt dramatized this tale in his play called *Le Chien de Montargis* (*The Dog of Montargis;* 1814).

Montauran, Marquis de. The hero of Balzac's novel THE CHOUANS, a leader of the Royalists.

Mont Cenis tunnel. A tunnel through a peak in the Alps connecting Turin in Italy with French Savoy. Completed in 1870.

Montcorbier, François de, see VILLON, FRANÇOIS.

Monte Cristo, Count of, see COUNT OF MONTE CRISTO.

Montesinos. A legendary hero, one of Charlemagne's paladins, who received some affront at the French court, and retired to La Mancha, in Spain. Here he lived in a cavern, some sixty feet deep, called "The Cavern of Montesinos." DON QUIXOTE in Cervantes' romance of that title, descends part of the way down this cavern, and falls into a trance, in which he sees Montesinos himself, Durandarte, and Belerma under the spell of Merlin, his own Dulcinea del Toboso enchanted into a country wench, and other visions, which he more than half believes to be realities.

Montespan, Madame de (1641–1707). One of the mistresses of Louis XIV. She and her husband, the Marquis de Montespan, appear in Bulwer Lytton's drama *The Duchess de la Vallière* (1836), and in Sir Arthur Conan Doyle's romance, *The Refugees* (1893).

Montesquieu, Baron **de La Brède et de. Charles de Secondat** (1689–1755). French lawyer, philosopher, and man of letters. Noted for his *Lettres Persanes* (1721) which criticized the society of his time. His *L'Esprit des Lois* (1748) analyzes the relation between human and natural law and has exerted a profound influence on later political thinking in Europe.

Montesquiou-Fezensac, Comte **Robert de** (1855–1921). French literary figure, associated with the movement of SYMBOLISM. He is reputed to have been the original on whom Proust's character of Baron de CHARLUS, Huysmans' DES ESSEINTES, and the Peacock in Rostand's *Chantecler* (see under CHANTICLEER) were based.

Montessori, Maria (1870–). Italian physician and educator. The first Montessori school for children was located in the slum districts of Rome (1907). The Montessori method endeavors to develop the child's initiative and emphasizes sense and muscle training by means of special materials.

Montez, Lola. Stage name of **Marie Dolores Eliza Rosanna Gilbert** (1818?–1861). British dancer who became famous as the mistress of King Louis I of Bavaria (1847–1848). She aroused the antagonism of the Jesuits and was forced to take up dancing again. She spent her last years (from 1856) in New York where she wrote on beauty and helped fallen women.

Montezuma. Emperor of the Aztecs in Mexico in the early 16th century. He is a prominent character in THE FAIR GOD, a historical romance by Lew Wallace. See also under CORTES.

Montgolfier, Joseph Michel (1740–1810), and his brother **Jacques Étienne Montgolfier** (1745–1799). French inventors. Built the first practical balloon, filled with heated air, which made a ten-minute ascent at Annonay (June 5, 1783).

Montgomery, Sir **Bernard Law** (1887–). British army captain in World War I. In World War II he became the commander of the British 8th army in Egypt (August 1942) which drove Rommel's forces from Africa. Commanded the Twenty-first Army Group in Northern France after D-day. On May 4, 1945, he signed the acceptance of German surrender in behalf of the Allied supreme commander-in-chief, General Dwight D. Eisenhower.

Montgomery, Ellen. The child heroine of Susan Warner's WIDE, WIDE WORLD.

Montgomery, Lucy Maud (1874–1942). Canadian writer for young people. Creator of *Anne of Green Gables* (1909).

Montherlant, Henry Millon de (1896–). French writer. Author of poems and novels on sports, bullfighting, etc. His *Les Célibataires* (1934) won the *Grand Prix de Littérature* of the French Academy. The four-volume novel *Les Jeunes filles* (1935–1939) was called by André Gide an eloquent offensive against women.

Montmartre. A Parisian district distinguished for its night life and for its literary and artistic associations. It overlooks the city from the north. Its name is thought to be derived from Mons Martyrum where the patron saint of France, St. Denis, and two companions were beheaded.

Mont-Saint-Michel and Chartres. An historical study by Henry ADAMS privately published in 1904 and given to the public in 1913. It contrasts the two great cathedrals of the Middle Ages, the ROMANESQUE Mont-Saint-Michel and the GOTHIC Chartres, and finds the Dynamo, the symbol of the machine, an integrating force in the industrial 20th century in the way that the Virgin of Chartres, the symbol of medieval Roman Catholicism, was the integrating force of the 13th century. This was one of the first works to celebrate the "medieval synthesis" and to contrast it with 20th-century disintegration. The ideas of T. S. ELIOT are considered to have received impetus from *Mont-Saint-Michel and Chartres.* Its subtitle is "A Study of Thirteenth-Century Unity" as that of THE EDUCATION OF HENRY ADAMS is "A Study of Twentieth-Century Multiplicity."

Monumental City. Baltimore. See under CITY.

Monvel, Louis Maurice Boutet de, see BOUTET DE MONVEL.

Moody, Dwight Lyman (1837–1899). American evangelist. With Ira D. Sankey made tours of Great Britain and the U.S. Founded Northfield Seminary for girls (1879); Mount Hermon School for boys (1881); and the Chicago Bible Institute (1889).

Moody, Helen Wills, see WILLS, HELEN.

Moody, William Vaughn (1869–1910). American poet and playwright, known for the idealism and mysticism of his dramas and lyrics. Among his works are *The Masque of Judgment* (1900), *The Fire Bringer* (1904), and *The Death of Eve* (1912), a trilogy of unproduced verse dramas; THE GREAT DIVIDE (1906, 1909) and THE FAITH HEALER (1909), his best-known plays; *Poems and Plays* (1912).

Mookse and the Gripes, The. In James Joyce's FINNEGANS WAKE, a fable recited during the course of the dream of Humphrey Chimpden EARWICKER and his family. The title is obviously a distortion and parody in dream-language of *The Fox and the Grapes.*

moon. In classical mythology, the moon was known as HECATE before she had risen and after she had set; as ASTARTE when crescent; as DIANA or CYNTHIA (she who "hunts the clouds") when in the open vault of heaven; as PHOEBE when looked upon as the sister of the sun (i.e., PHOEBUS); and was personified as SELENE or LUNA, the lover of the sleeping ENDYMION, i.e., moonlight on the fields.

The moon is called *triform,* because it presents itself to us either *round,* or *waxing* with horns towards the east, or *waning* with horns towards the west.

One legend connected with the moon was that there was treasured everything wasted on earth, such as misspent time and wealth, broken vows, unanswered prayers, fruitless tears, abortive attempts, unfulfilled desires and intentions, etc. In Ariosto's ORLANDO FURIOSO, Astolpho found on his visit to the moon (Bk. xviii and xxxiv. 70) that bribes were hung on gold and silver hooks; princes' favors were kept in bellows; wasted talent was kept in vases, each marked with the proper name, etc.; and in *The Rape of the Lock* (canto v) Pope tells us that when the Lock disappeared—

> Some thought it mounted to the lunar sphere,
> Since all things lost on earth are treasured there,
> There heroes' wits are kept in pond'rous vases,
> And beaux' in snuff-boxes and tweezer-cases.
> There broken vows and death-bed alms are found
> And lovers' hearts with ends of ribbon bound,
> The courtier's promises, and sick man's prayers,
> The smiles of harlots, and the tears of heirs
> Cages for gnats, and chains to yoke a flea,
> Dried butterflies, and tomes of casuistry.

Hence the phrase, *the limbus of the moon.*

I know no more about it than the man in the moon. I know nothing at all about the matter.

it's all moonshine. Bunkum; nonsense; it's a "tale told by an idiot." The light of the moon was formerly held to have very deleterious effects on mental stability.

once in a blue moon. See BLUE MOON.

the Island of the Moon. Madagascar is so named by the natives.

the man in the moon. Some say it is a man leaning on a fork, on which he is carrying a bundle of sticks picked up on a Sunday. The origin of this fable is from *Numb.* xv. 32–36. Some add a dog also; thus the prologue in *Midsummer Night's Dream* says, "This man with lantern, dog, and bush of thorns, presenteth moonshine"; *The Testament of Cressid* says "he stole the bush." Another tradition says that the man is Cain, with his dog and thorn bush, the thorn bush being emblematical of the thorns and briars of the fall, and the dog being the "foul fiend." Some poets make out the "man" to be Endymion, taken to the moon by Diana.

> Now doth Cain with fork of thorns confine
> On either hemisphere, touching the wave
> Beneath the towers of Seville. Yesternight
> The moon was round.
>
> Dante, *Inferno,* xx. (1300).

> Her gite was gray and full of spottis black,
> And on her brest a chorle painted ful even,
> Bering a bush of thornis on his back,
> Which for his theft might clime so ner the heven.
>
> Chaucer.

to aim or *level at the moon.* To be very ambitious; to aim in shooting at the moon.

to cry for the moon. To crave for what is wholly beyond one's reach. The allusion is to foolish children who want the moon for a plaything.

Moon and Sixpence, The. A novel by W. S. MAUGHAM (1919), based closely on the life of the French painter Paul GAUGUIN. It tells of Charles Strickland, a conventional London stock broker, who in middle life becomes interested in painting, changes completely in character, and deserts his wife, family, and business in order to live and paint in Tahiti, where he takes a native mistress and eventually dies of leprosy.

moon-calf. An inanimate, shapeless abortion formerly supposed to be produced prematurely by the cow owing to the malign influence of the moon. Floyd DELL gave the name to a novel (1920), relating the adventures of the very young, very temperamental and introspective hero of the LOST GENERATION, Felix Fay, in Chicago. His story was continued in *The Briary-Bush* (1921).

Mooney, Thomas J. Zechariah (1885–1942). American labor leader. With Warren K. Billings (1894–), convicted of responsibility for a bomb explosion during the Preparedness Parade in San Francisco (July 22, 1916). Death sentence commuted to life imprisonment. Finally pardoned and released (January 7, 1939). The "Mooney Case" was for years a subject of agitation similar to the case of SACCO AND VANZETTI. Cf. the poem by William Ellery LEONARD, *Tom Mooney*.

Moonshine, Bottled, see BOTTLED MOONSHINE.

Moonstone, The. A famous mystery novel (1868), by Wilkie COLLINS.

Moor, Karl. The hero who turns brigand in Schiller's drama THE ROBBERS (1781).

Moore, Clement Clarke (1779–1863). American scholar and poet. Best-known for the ballad *A Visit From St. Nicholas* ("'Twas the night before Christmas") (1822). Also compiled *A Compendious Lexicon of the Hebrew Language* (1809).

Moore, Frank Frankfort (1855–1931). Irish novelist. Best-known for *The Jessamy Bride* (1897), a best seller in its period.

Moore, George (1852–1933). Irish novelist and journalist, in the early years of his career a poet and student of painting in Paris where he was associated with the famous figures of IMPRESSIONISM in painting and SYMBOLISM in poetry. MANET was an intimate friend of his, and in his writing he was influenced by GAUTIER, BAUDELAIRE, VERLAINE, BALZAC, MALLARMÉ, and ZOLA. At first, he could write only in the French language. Later, as a journalist in London, he became known for his realistic novels and his memoirs. Among his works are *Flowers of Passion* (1878) and *Pagan Poems* (1881), books of poetry; *A Modern Lover* (1883); *A Mummer's Wife* (1885); *A Drama in Muslin* (1886); *Confessions of a Young Man* (1888), autobiographical; *Mike Fletcher* (1889); ESTHER WATERS (1894), EVELYN INNES (1898), and *Sister Teresa* (1901), considered his best novels; *Ave* (1911), *Salve* (1914), and *Vale* (1914), constituting an autobiographical trilogy, *Hail and Farewell;* THE BROOK KERITH (1916); *Memoirs of My Dead Life* (1920), reminiscences; *Héloïse* and *Abélard* (1921); *Conversations in Ebury Street* (1924), further reminiscences; *Ulich and Soracha* (1926); *Aphrodite in Aulis* (1930); *A Flood* (1930); *The Passing of the Essenes* (1930), a drama. He also wrote plays and short stories, and essays on art criticism.

Moore, Marianne Craig (1887–). American poet and literary critic, editor of the magazine THE DIAL (1925–1929). Her poetry is of the type called objectivist (see OBJECTIVISM), presenting in each poem an object, scene, person, or bit of information precisely expressed and meticulously delineated. Her work is distinguished by wit, irony, intellectual appeal, and compact, individual metrical patterns. Her books include *Poems* (1921); *Observations* (1924); *The Pangolin, and Other Verse* (1936); *What Are Years?* (1941); etc.

Moore, Merrill (1903–). American psychiatrist and poet, early in his career a member of the group known as FUGITIVES and known for his large quantities of verse, all written in the sonnet form. His books include *The Noise That Time Makes* (1929); *It Is a Good Deal Later Than You Think* (1934); *Six Sides to a Man* (1935); *M* (1938), a volume of 1000 sonnets.

Moore, Thomas (1779–1852). Irish poet of the romantic period, known for his graceful lyrics and his Irish folk-songs, set to traditional tunes of great age, on which he worked for nearly twenty years and published in *Irish Melodies* (1807–1835). LALLA ROOKH (1817) and THE LOVES OF THE ANGELS (1822), narrative poetry with an Oriental setting, were also very popular. Additional writings by Moore include *Poetical Works* (1801), published under the pseudonym of Thomas Little; *The Two-Penny Post Bag* (1813), satires; *The Epicurean* (1827), a novel; pieces dealing with the adventures of the FUDGE FAMILY; a *History of Ireland* (1846); and several biographies, including one of Lord BYRON (1830), a close friend of Moore.

Moore came to be regarded as the national poet of Ireland, and he was, next to Byron, the most popular writer of verse in the English romantic period. Among his most famous single songs are *The Harp That Once Through Tara's Halls, The Minstrel Boy,* and *Believe Me, If All Those Endearing Young Charms.*

Moore, Thomas Sturge (1870–1944). English poet, man of letters, and wood engraver. His verse is severely classical in tone. *Selected Poems* (1934).

Moorehouse, John Ward. In Dos Passos' U.S.A., the son of a station agent in Wilmington, Delaware, who is serious, high-minded, and idealistic as a young man but, through advantageous marriages, fortunate "contacts," and ruthless ambition, rises to the position of successful advertising executive and public relations counselor. He directs Red Cross publicity during World War I and takes part in the

Peace Conference, engages in brief affairs with Eveline HUTCHINS and Eleanor STODDARD, and enables Richard Ellsworth SAVAGE to start on his own rise to power. Moorehouse represents "big business" in the novel.

morality plays or **moralities.** A type of early drama in which the characters are personifications of abstract qualities and the drama itself an allegory. The best-known English morality is EVERYMAN. The Devil and his attendant, The Vice, were prominent characters in most of the moralities. They were at the height of their vogue in the 15th and 16th centuries. See also MYSTERY PLAYS.

Morand, Paul (1888–). French writer and diplomat. Attaché to the French Embassy in England (1913–1916). His best-known books available in English are the short-story collections, *Open All Night* (1922) and *Closed All Night* (1923).

moratorium (Lat. *morari*, "to delay"). A legal permission to defer for a stated time the payment of a bond, debt, or other obligation. This is done to enable the debtor to pull himself round by borrowing money, selling effects, or otherwise raising funds to satisfy obligations. The device was adopted in 1891 in South America during the panic caused by the Baring Brothers' default of some twenty millions sterling, and the word came into popular use during World War I, and afterwards in connection with the inability of Germany to pay to date the stated amount due as reparations under the TREATY OF VERSAILLES.

Moray, Captain Robert. The hero of Gilbert Parker's SEATS OF THE MIGHTY.

Mordecai. In the Old Testament, the uncle of ESTHER, a Jew who saved his people from the plots of Haman through his wise counsel to his niece when she became queen.

Mordred, Sir. The name given to MODRED in Malory's *Morte d'Arthur* and other of the old Arthurian romances.

More, Hannah (1745–1833). English author, reformer, and philanthropist, associated with leading 18th-century literary figures, including Edmund BURKE, Dr. JOHNSON, Horace WALPOLE, and Lady Mary Wortley MONTAGU. Her writings include *Percy* (1777) and *The Fatal Falsehood* (1779), tragedies; *Village Politics* and *Repository Tracts*, religious tracts on reforming the poor; *Thoughts on the Importance of the Manners of the Great* (1788); *Coelebs in Search of a Wife* (1809), a novel; and numerous letters.

More, Paul Elmer (1864–1937). American literary critic and scholar, associated with Irving BABBITT in the movement of HUMANISM. He was opposed to humanitarianism in art and to the literary movements that followed World War I and stressed morality and submission of the individual to society. His works include *The Great Refusal* (1894); *A Century of Indian Epigrams* (1898); *Judgment of Socrates* (1898); the SHELBURNE ESSAYS (1904–1935); *Nietzsche* (1912); *Platonism* (1917); *The Religion of Plato* (1921); *Hellenistic Philosophies* (1923); *The Christ of the New Testament* (1924); *Christ, the Word* (1927); *The Demon of the Absolute* (1928); *The Catholic Faith* (1931); *Pages from an Oxford Diary* (1937), autobiographical.

More was a professor of Sanskrit and the classics at Harvard, Bryn Mawr, and Princeton, and edited THE NATION from 1909 to 1914.

More, Sir Thomas (1478–1535). English statesman, humanist, poet, and author, a friend of ERASMUS, Colet, and other leading scholars of the time. He wrote in both Latin and English, his most famous work being UTOPIA (1516), written in Latin. His English works include a biography of PICO DELLA MIRANDOLA (1510); a *History of Richard III* (1543); *Supplication of Souls* (1529); and *An Apology of Sir Thomas More* (1533).

More held a number of important positions in the government of his time, being a member of Parliament, an envoy on several missions abroad, a court official, and ultimately Lord Chancellor, succeeding Cardinal WOLSEY in 1529. He was also a stanch Catholic, engaging in vigorous controversies with the Protestant heretics of the time, especially William TYNDALE, against whom he wrote a *Dialogue* in English in 1528. Although he had been a friend of King Henry VIII, he would not take an oath to the Act of Supremacy acknowledging the King to be chief authority over the English Church as against the Pope, and for this refusal was beheaded as a traitor.

Moreau, Frederic. The hero of Flaubert's SENTIMENTAL EDUCATION, a satire on the typical romantic hero of the early 19th century. He is an egotistical, ambitious, and sentimental young man who dabbles in the fashionable political movements of the time, which range from revolution to reaction, schemes to achieve entry into Parisian society, deserting his provincial family and friends, and from afar nourishes an unconsummated passion for Mme ARNOUX in the best romantic tradition, although he does not permit it to interfere with the love affairs into which physical desire and worldly ambition lead him. He is neither totally ambitious nor totally absurd, but rather an average upper middle-class young Frenchman of the 19th century who takes the conventions of his time seriously. He has been called a male counterpart, in some degree, of Emma BOVARY.

Morehouse, Ward (1897–). American journalist, playwright, and dramatic critic of N.Y. SUN. Wrote biography of George M. COHAN. See also MOOREHOUSE, JOHN WARD.

Morel, Charles. In Marcel Proust's REMEMBRANCE OF THINGS PAST, an ambitious and unscrupulous young violinist who is the son of JUPIEN and becomes the protégé and lover of BARON DE CHARLUS.

Morel, Paul. The hero of D. H. Lawrence's SONS AND LOVERS, considered to be autobiographical. Because of his fear and hatred of his father, Paul has come during childhood and early adolescence to feel an excessive dependence upon and emotional attachment to his mother, who responds in a similar fashion. The result is that in his first love affairs the youth is tortured by the feeling that he is betraying his mother by loving someone else, and she in her turn is jealous of the affection he extends to other women.

Moreland, Catherine. Heroine of Jane Austen's NORTHANGER ABBEY.

Morell, Rev. James. In Shaw's CANDIDA, the husband of Candida.

Morella. In Poe's tale so called, a woman fascinated with the mystical study of personality. When she dies in childbirth, her spirit, it is implied, passes into her new-born daughter.

Morgan, Charles (1894–). English novelist. Drama critic of London *Times* (since 1926). Winner of the *Femina-Vie Heureuse* Prize (1930) with *Portrait in a Mirror;* the Hawthornden Prize (1933) with *The Fountain;* the James Tait Black Memorial Award (1941) with *The Voyage.* George MOORE appointed him his literary executor. Has written essays under pseudonym "Menander."

Morgan, Harry. The hero of Ernest Hemingway's TO HAVE AND HAVE NOT, a native of Key West, Florida, who, in order to support his wife and family, participates in smuggling and other illegal activities, with fatal results.

Morgan, Sir **Henry** (1635?–1688). British buccaneer. Captured and sacked Porto Bello and ravaged the coast of Cuba, Maracaibo and Gibraltar (1669), Panama City (1671); etc. After the treaty between Spain and England, he was called back to England where he gained the favor of the King. He was appointed lieutenant governor of Jamaica and commander in chief. Cf. the poems, *Morgan Sails the Caribbean* (1934) by Berton Braley, and *The Sack of Old Panama,* by Dana Burnet.

Morgan, James. In Thackeray's novel PENDENNIS, the valet of Major Pendennis. After years of discreet service, he makes a shrewd and bold but futile attempt to blackmail his employer through his knowledge of the past history of Colonel ALTAMONT.

Morgan, John Pierpont (1837–1913). American banker and financier. Formed J. P. Morgan & Co. (1895). Financed government; reorganized railroads; formed United States Steel Corporation (1901). Collected art and rare books. Was president of the Metropolitan Museum of Art in New York; a benefactor of the Cathedral of St. John the Divine, the New York Public Library, etc. His son, **John Pierpont Morgan** (1867–1943), succeeded him as head of the firm of J. P. Morgan & Co., and acted as agent of Allied governments in floating large loans in the U.S. during World War I, etc.

Morgan, Thomas Hunt (1867–1945). American zoologist; discovered the existence of genes which determine heredity. Nobel prize (1933).

Morgan, Wallace (1873–). Well-known magazine illustrator, who, during World War I, was appointed official artist with the American Army and made many drawings for a historical record of the War. Member National Institute of Arts and Letters. Illustrated books by Joseph C. LINCOLN, etc.

Morgan, William (d. 1826). A mechanic of Batavia, New York, said to have been killed by Freemasons for revealing secrets of the order during a furious political issue. When a body, supposedly Morgan's, was found, a naïvely honest worker of Morgan's group doubted its identity in the presence of another leader, who then coined the famous phrase: "A good enough Morgan until after the election."

Morgana. An enchantress, identified with the Lady of the Lake in *Orlando Furioso,* and also with MORGANE LE FAY, the fairy sister of King Arthur.

Morgana, Fata, see FATA MORGANA.

morganatic marriage. A marriage between a man of high (usually royal) rank and a woman of inferior station, by virtue of which she does not acquire the husband's rank, and neither she nor the children of the marriage are entitled to inherit his title or possessions; often called a "left-handed marriage" because the custom is for the man to pledge his troth with his left hand instead of the right. An instance of a morganatic marriage in the British Royal Family is that of George, Duke of Cambridge (1819–1904), cousin of Queen Victoria and uncle of Queen Mary, who married morganatically in 1840. His children took the surname Fitz-George.

The word comes from the medieval Latin phrase *matrimonium ad morganaticam,* the last word representing the O.H. Ger. *morgangeba,* morning-gift. It meant that the children were entitled to nothing of the father's beyond his first, or "morning" gift, i.e., the privilege of being born.

Morgan le Fay. The fairy sister of King ARTHUR; one of the principal characters in Arthurian romance and in Celtic legend generally; also known as *Morgaine* and (especially in ORLANDO FURIOSO) as *Morgana.* See FATA MORGANA.

In Malory's *Morte d'Arthur,* on one occasion Morgan le Fay steals her brother's sword Excalibur, with its scabbard, and sends them to Sir Accolon of Gaul, her paramour, that he may kill Arthur in mortal combat. If this villainy succeeds, Morgan intends to murder her husband, marry Sir Accolon, and "devise to make him king of Britain," but Sir Accolon, during the combat, drops the sword. Arthur, snatching it up, would have slain him had he not craved mercy and confessed the treasonable design. After this, Morgan steals the scabbard and throws it into the lake. Lastly, she tries to murder her brother by means of a poisoned robe, but Arthur tells the messenger to try it on, that he may see it, and when the messenger does so he drops down dead, "being burnt to a coal."

In ORLANDO FURIOSO Morgan le Fay is represented as living at the bottom of a lake, and dispensing her treasures to whom she likes; in ORLANDO INNAMORATO she first appears as "Lady Fortune," but subsequently assumes her witch-like attributes. In the romance of OGIER THE DANE, Morgan le Fay receives Ogier in the Isle of Avalon when he is over one hundred years old, restores him to youth, and becomes his bride.

Morgante Maggiore. A serio-comic romance in verse, by Luigi Pulci (1432–1484) of Florence (1485). The characters had appeared previously in many of the old romances; Morgante is a ferocious giant, converted by Orlando (the real hero) to Christianity. After performing the most wonderful feats he dies at last from the bite of a crab.

Pulci was actually the inventor of this species of poetry, although it is called by the French *bernesque,* from Berni, who greatly excelled in it.

Morgause or **Margawse.** In Arthurian romance, wife of King Lot. Their four sons are Gawain, Agravain, Gaheris, and Gareth, but Morgause has had another son by Arthur, named MODRED. This is the version of the legend given in Malory's MORTE D'ARTHUR, according to which Morgause is also Arthur's half-sister, although at the time of Modred's conception he was unaware of the relationship.

Morgenthau, Henry, Jr. (1891–). American diplomat, son of the German-born American diplomat **Henry Morgenthau** (1856–1946). Governor, Farm Credit Administration (1933); U.S. secretary of the treasury (1934–1945). Remembered also as author of the controversial "Morgenthau Plan" of German de-industrialization after World War II.

Morgiana. In the story of ALI BABA AND THE FORTY THIEVES in the *Arabian Nights,* the clever, faithful, female slave of Ali Baba, who pries into the forty jars, and discovers that every jar but one contains a man. She takes oil from the only one containing it, and, having made it boiling hot, pours enough into each jar to kill the thief concealed there. At last she kills the captain of the gang, and marries her master's son.

Morglay. The sword of Sir BEVIS OF HAMTOUN; also, a generic name for a sword.

Morgue la Faye. The form taken by the name MORGAN LE FAY in *Ogier the Dane.*

Morier, James Justinian (1780?–1849). British diplomat and novelist; known for his *The Adventures of Hajji Baba of Ispahan* (1824) and *The Adventures of Hajji Baba of Ispahan in England* (1828), in which he satirizes Western civilization in the tradition of MONTESQUIEU's *Lettres Persanes.*

Morison, Samuel Eliot (1887–). American historian. Member of the American Commission to Negotiate Peace in Paris (1919). Awarded Jusserand medal and Loubat prize for *Tercentennial History of Harvard University* (5 vols.; 1930–1936). Also, Pulitzer prize for the story of Columbus, *Admiral of the Ocean Sea* (1942).

Morisot, Berthe (1841–1895). French painter; influenced by her brother-in-law Édouard MANET.

Morland, George (1763–1804). English painter with 4,000 canvases to his credit. Specialized in pastoral and rural genre scenes with animals and especially pigs. His masterpiece is *The Interior of a Stable* (1791).

Morley, Christopher Darlington (1890–). American journalist, essayist, novelist, and poet. Connected with *Saturday Review of Literature* (1924–1941). His best novels are *Where the Blue Begins* (1922); *Thunder on the Left* (1925); *Human Being* (1932); and *Kitty Foyle* (1939). He considers that his play *The Trojan Horse,* finished two years before the outbreak of World War II, foreshadowed what was to come. His best poetry is included in the volumes *Parson's Pleasure* (1923); *Toulemonde* (1928); and *The Middle Kingdom* (1945). *John Mistletoe* (1931) is an autobiography. Felix and Frank MORLEY are his brothers.

Morley, Felix Muskett (1894–). President of Haverford College (1940–1945). Editor, *Washington Post* (1933–1940). Pulitzer prize for editorial writing (1936). Author of the Hart, Schaffner and Marx prize essay, *Our Far Eastern Assignment* (1926). Brother of Christopher MORLEY.

Morley, Frank Vigor (1899–). Writer and publisher. London manager, Century Co. (1924–1929); director, Faber and Faber, publishers, London (1929–1939); former director, Harcourt, Brace & Co., New York. Author of *East South East* (1929); *Inversive Geometry* (1933; with F. Morley); *The Wreck of the Active* (1936); *My One Contribution to Chess* (1946); etc. He is a Doctor of Philosophy in Mathematics, and an authority on whaling and Boswell. Brother of Christopher MORLEY.

Morley, Henry (1822–1894). English man of letters. Edited classics in various collections. His magnum opus is *English Writers* (1864–1894), a ten-volume history of English literature down to the death of Shakespeare.

Morley, John. Viscount **Morley of Blackburn** (1838–1923). English statesman and man of letters. Chief secretary for Ireland (1886, 1892–1895); secretary of state for India (1905–1910). Author of books on Edmund Burke, Voltaire, Rousseau, Diderot and the Encyclopaedists, Cobden, Emerson, Cromwell, Gladstone, etc.

Morley, Mrs. The name under which Queen Anne corresponded with "Mrs. Freeman" (the Duchess of Marlborough).

Mormonism. The religious and social system of the Mormons, or Latter-day Saints. It is largely connected in the minds of most people with the practice of polygamy, which became part of the Mormon code in 1852, was very widely indulged in, but later became a diminishing—if not vanished—quantity. Hence the phrase *a regular Mormon,* for a flighty person who cannot keep to one wife or sweetheart.

The fraternity takes its name from *The Book of Mormon, or Golden Bible,* which is supposed to have been written on golden plates by the prophet Mormon at dictation by the angel Moroni. The early leaders were Joseph SMITH (1805–1844) and Brigham YOUNG (1801–1877), under whom the Mormons settled in Utah.

Morning Star of the Reformation. John Wyclif (1324–1384).

Morose. In Ben Jonson's *Epicene or the Silent Woman* (1609), a miserly old man, who hates to hear any voice but his own. His nephew, Sir Dauphine, wants to wring out of him a third of his property. He therefore gets a lad to impersonate "a silent woman," and the phenomenon so delights the old man that he consents to a marriage. No sooner is the ceremony over than the boy-wife assumes the character of a virago of loud and ceaseless tongue. Morose is half mad, and promises to give his nephew a third of his income if he will take this intolerable plague off his hands.

Morpheus. Ovid's name for the son of Sleep, and god of dreams; so called from Gr. *morphe,* "form," because he gives these airy nothings their form and fashion. Hence the name of the narcotic, *morphine* or *morphia.*

Morphy, Paul Charles (1837–1884). American world's chess master (1857–1859). Mentally deranged in later life.

Morrice, Gil or **Childe.** See under CHILDE.

Morris, Clara (1848?–1925). Canadian-American actress of impressive emotionalism. In Augustin Daly's company (1870–1873). Author of *The Life of a Star* (1906), and other books.

Morris, Dinah. A Methodist preacher in George Eliot's ADAM BEDE.

Morris, Gouverneur (1752–1816). American statesman and diplomat. Member of Continental Congress; assistant minister of finance; U.S. minister to France; etc. His diary edited by his great-granddaughter, *A Diary of the French Revolution 1789–1793* (1939) is valuable as a historical source. His great-grandson, **Gouverneur Morris** (1876–), is a popular American writer, among whose best stories are *The Footprint and Other Stories* (1908); *The Voice in the Rice* (1910); *Yellow Men and Gold* (1921) etc.

Morris, Lloyd (1893–). American biographer and playwright. His best-known work is his biography of Hawthorne, *The Rebellious Puritan* (1927); his best play the comedy, *The Damask Cheek* (1943; with John Van Druten). *A Threshold in the Sun* (1943) is his autobiography.

Morris, Sir **Lewis** (1833–1907). Welsh lawyer and writer of English verse. Instrumental in establishing University of Wales (1893); author of *The Epic of Hades* (1876–1877); etc.

Morris, William (1834–1896). English art-lover, poet, and prose-writer, associated with the PRE-RAPHAELITE BROTHERHOOD and the English Socialist movement. His best-known works of poetry, in which he was influenced by the Pre-Raphaelites and by CHAUCER and which deal chiefly with ancient Greek and Norse heroic legends, are *The Defense of Guenevere, And Other Poems* (1858); *The Life and Death of Jason* (1867); THE EARTHLY PARADISE (1868–1870); SIGURD THE VOLSUNG (1876); *Three Northern Love Songs* (1875). He also wrote prose romances, interspersed with lyrics, among which are *The Dream of John Bull* (1888) and *News from Nowhere* (1891), setting forth his Socialist ideas; *The House of the Wolfings* (1889); *The Story of the Glittering Plain* (1890); *The Roots of the Mountains* (1890); *The Wood Beyond the World* (1894); *Child Christopher* (1895); *The Well at the World's End* (1896); *The Water of the Wondrous Isles* (1897); *The Story of the Sundering Flood* (1898).

Morris was greatly interested in painting and architecture in the early part of his career, and in 1861, in order to improve the artistic taste of the Victorian middle class of the time, he helped to found Morris, Marshall, Faulkner & Co., a firm which manufactured furniture, carpets, tapestries, and the like. In 1891 he also founded the KELMSCOTT PRESS. As a Socialist, he helped to establish the Social Democrat Federation in 1883 and was one of its leaders until he left in a secessionist movement. He was disappointed in its policies and attitudes and returned to writing in 1889.

morris dance. A grotesque dance, popular in England in the 15th century and later, in which the dancers usually represented characters from the Robin Hood stories. See MAID MARIAN. It was brought from Spain in the reign of Edward III, and was originally a military dance of the Moors, or Moriscos—hence its name.

Morrison, Arthur (1863–). English novelist, dramatist, and writer of detective stories featuring Martin Hewitt.

Morrow, Mrs. **Honoré Willsie** (1880?–1940). American novelist, biographer, and magazine editor. Wrote three Lincoln novels collected in *Great Captain.*

Morse, Samuel Finley Breese (1791–1872). American artist and inventor. Founder and first president (1826–1842), National Academy of Design. Invented Morse telegraphic code. Sent first message, "What hath God wrought!" over experimental line between Washington and Baltimore, built at a cost of $30,000 voted him by Congress (1843). Statue in Central Park, New York. Member, American Hall of Fame.

Mortality, Old, see OLD MORTALITY.

Morte d'Arthur. A famous volume of Arthurian legends by Sir Thomas MALORY, printed by William CAXTON in 1470. For its significance in the development of the Arthurian cycle, see ARTHUR; ARTHURIAN ROMANCE.

> This book was finished the ninth year of the reign of King Edward IV, by Sir Thomas Malory, knight. Thus endeth this noble and joyous book, entitled *La Morte d'Arthur,* notwithstanding it treateth of the birth, life, and acts of the said king Arthur, and of his noble knights of the Round Table . . . and the achieving of the holy Sancgreall, and in the end the dolorous death and departing out of the world of them all.—*Concluding paragraph.*

Morton, David (1886–). American poet. Professor (from 1926), Amherst College. Author of *Ships in Harbour* (1921), *This Is for You* (1943), and other books of poems.

Morton, Thomas (1590?–?1646). English-born American adventurer. Settled in Quincy, Mass. His maypole and attendant frolics were frowned on by the Pilgrim fathers. He was arrested and sent to England several times. He published abroad *New English Canaan* (1637), a description of New England, for which he was imprisoned (1644–1645) after his return to Boston.

Morton's Fork. Archbishop Morton's plan for increasing the royal revenues, in the time of Henry VII, so arranged that nobody should escape. Those who were rich were forced to contribute on the ground that they could well afford it, and those who lived without display on the ground that their economies must mean that they were saving money.

Mortsauf, Henriette de. The heroine of Balzac's LILY OF THE VALLEY. She is the wife of de Mortsauf, and although she prefers the ardent young Felix de Vandenesse and toys with his love, she remains within the letter of the law.

Morven (a ridge of high hills). A kingdom frequently referred to in the poems of OSSIAN including all the northwest of Scotland; called in Ossian "windy Morven," "resounding Morven," "echoing Morven," "rocky Morven." Fingal is called indifferently "King of Selma" and "King of Morven." Selma was the capital of Morven. Probably this district was Argyllshire extended north and east.

Moryson, Fynes (1566–1630). English traveler, remembered for his account of his travels and experiences in Ireland, *An Itinerary* (1617).

Mosby, John Singleton (1833–1916). American Confederate officer. Author of *Mosby's War Reminiscences, and Stuart's Cavalry Campaigns* (1887); *Stuart's Cavalry in the Gettysburg Campaign* (1908).

Moschus (2nd century B.C.). Bucolic Greek poet.

Mose the Fireboy. The first "tough" character to attain popularity on the American stage. Mose made his appearance in a play by B. A. Baker called *A Glance at New York* (*Am.,* 1848) at a time when the city's volunteer fire companies, with their rowdy social life and exciting rivalries, were very much to the fore. In the play he initiates an out-of-towner into all the mysteries of New York life, including a "ladies' bowling club" where the ladies smoke large cigars. This first play was so popular that Mose in his red shirt and plug hat, with his huge fire hose which he had plenty of opportunity to drag about the stage, became the hero of a whole series of comedies—*New York as It Is, Mysteries and Miseries of New York, Mose in California, Mose in a Muss, Mose's Visit to Philadelphia,* and finally *Mose in China.*

Moses. In the Old Testament (*Exod.* i–*Deut.* xxxiv), the hero under whose leadership the Israelites left Egypt and made their way through the wilderness to the Promised Land.

Because PHARAOH had decreed that all Hebrew boy babies should be killed, Moses' mother put him in a basket and left him in the bulrushes, where he was found and adopted by Pharaoh's daughter. Later he identified himself with his own people and because he killed an abusive Egyptian taskmaster, was forced to flee the country. He returned, called down on Pharaoh's recalcitrant head the Ten Plagues and led the Children of Israel out of Egypt, passing through the Red Sea on dry land. For forty years he led his discontented, rebellious followers through the wilderness and was mediator for them with Jehovah, to whom he talked on Mount Sinai on the occasion of his receiving the TEN COMMANDMENTS. Moses is spoken of in the Bible as the meekest of all men, but on one occasion he impulsively and vaingloriously struck a rock to bring water out of it instead of merely speaking, and for this sin was punished by being forbidden to enter the Promised Land. He was, however, given a glimpse of it from Mount Pisgah, where he died. George ELIOT wrote a poem, *The Death of Moses.*

the horns of Moses' face. Moses is conventionally represented with horns, owing to a blunder in translation. In *Ex.* xxxiv. 29, 30, where we are told that when Moses came down from Mount Sinai "the skin of his face shone," the Hebrew for this *shining* may be translated either as "sent forth *beams*" or "sent forth *horns*"; and the Vulgate took the latter as correct, rendering the passage—*quod cornuta esset facies sua.*

Moses' rod. The divining-rod is sometimes so called, after the rod with which Moses worked wonders before Pharaoh (*Ex.* ii. 2–5).

Moses, Robert (1888–). American state and municipal official. Won wide acclaim for excellent work as New York City park commissioner (from 1934).

Mosher, Thomas Bird (1852–1923). Maine publisher. Founded *The Bibelot* (1895), a little magazine of choice reprints of little-known literary masterpieces. Published a series of aesthetically printed and bound small volumes in exquisite good taste.

Moslem or **Muslim.** A Mohammedan; the pres. part. of Arab. *aslama,* to be safe or at rest, whence ISLAM.

Mosley, Sir **Oswald Ernald** (1896–). English politician. Leader of British Union of Fascists (Blackshirts). Taken into custody (1940) and later released.

Moss, Adam. The hero of J. L. Allen's novels, A KENTUCKY CARDINAL and *Aftermath.*

Mosses from an Old Manse. A collection of tales and sketches by HAWTHORNE (1846). The first sketch, *The Old Manse,* describes the Concord parsonage, the home of the Emerson family, where the Hawthornes lived from 1842 to 1846.

Moth. In Shakespeare's LOVE'S LABOR'S LOST, page to Don Adriano de Armado the fantastical Spaniard. He is cunning, versatile and playful.

mother (Sans. *matr,* Gr. *meter,* Lat. *mater,* A.S. *modor,* Ger. *mutter,* Fr. *mère,* etc.). Properly, a female parent; hence, figuratively, the source or origin of anything, the head or headquarters of a religious or other community, etc.

Mother Ann, Bunch, Goose, Hubbard, Shipton, etc., see these names.

Mother Carey's chickens. Stormy petrels. Mother Carey is *mata cara,* dear mother. The French call these birds *oiseaux de Notre Dame* or *aves Sanctae Mariae.* Cf. Captain Marryat's *Poor Jack,* where the superstition is fully related. Kate Douglas Wiggin used the phrase as the title of a novel (*Am.,* 1911).

Mother Carey's goose. The great black petrel or fulmar of the Pacific.

Mother Carey is plucking her goose. It is snowing. See HULDA. Sailors call falling snow *Mother Carey's chickens.*

Mother Church. The Church considered as the central fact, the head, the last court of appeal in all matters pertaining to conscience or religion. St. John Lateran at Rome is known as the Mother and Head of all Christian Churches. Also, the principal or oldest church in a country or district; the cathedral of a diocese.

mother country. One's native country; or the country whence one's ancestors have come to settle. England is the *mother country* of Australia, New Zealand, Canada, etc. The German term translated into English means *fatherland.*

Mother Earth. When Junius Brutus (after the death of LUCRETIA) formed one of the deputation to Delphi to ask the Oracle which of the three would succeed Tarquin, the response was, "He who should first kiss his mother." Junius instantly threw himself on the ground, exclaiming, "Thus, then, I kiss thee, Mother Earth," and he was elected consul.

mother-of-pearl. The inner iridescent layers of the shells of many bivalve molluscs, especially that of the pearl oyster.

mother-sick. Hysterical. Hysteria in women used to be known as "the mother."

mother-wit. Native wit, a ready reply; the wit which "our mother gave us."

mothers' meeting. A meeting of working-class mothers held periodically in connection with some church or denomination, at which the women can get advice or religious instruction, drink tea, gossip, and sometimes do a little needlework. Hence, the term is applied in slang to any gossiping group of people —men, as well as women.

the Mother of Believers. Among Mohammedans, Ay-e-shah, the second and favorite wife of Mahomet, who was called the "Father of Believers."

mother of Books. Alexandria, from its famous library.

the mother of cities (Arab. *Amu-al-Bulud*). Balkh is so called.

mother of presidents. Virginia, which furnished six presidents of the United States.

mother of southwestern statesmen. Tennessee.

mother of states. Virginia.

mother of the Gracchi, see CORNELIA.

Motherwell, William (1797–1835). Scottish man of letters and antiquary. Known for several collections of ballads and as author of *Poems, Narrative and Lyrical* (1832).

mot juste (*Fr.,* "the correct or exact word"). A term for the expressiveness and meticulousness of style, down to each word of each sentence, which was the goal of Gustave FLAUBERT in writing his novels. His careful polishing and repolishing of his work is famous. Guy de MAUPASSANT, a follower of Flaubert, also was an adherent of the principle of the *mot juste.* The phrase occurs as the title of the French equivalent of Roget's *Thesaurus.* The Dutch Roget is *Het juiste woord.*

Motley, John Lothrop (1814–1877). American historian and diplomat, known for his historical studies of Holland, emphasizing the conflicts between Protestantism and Catholicism, freedom and despotism. These include *The Rise of the Dutch Republic* (1856); *History of the United Netherlands* (1860, 1867); *The Life and Death of John of Barneveld* (1874). Motley was minister to Austria from 1861 to 1867, and to Great Britain from 1869 to 1870, being recalled during the Alabama (see ALABAMA CLAIMS) dispute.

Moto, Mr. A clever Japanese sleuth, hero of a popular series of detective novels by John P. MARQUAND including *Thank You, Mr. Moto* (1936); *Think Fast, Mr. Moto* (1937); *Mr. Moto Is So Sorry* (1938); etc.

Mott, Frank Luther (1886–). American journalist. Author of *A History of American Magazines* (3 vols.; 1930); *American Journalism 1690–1940* (1941); *Golden Multitudes* (1947), etc. Pulitzer prize for American history (1939).

Mott, Lucretia, *née* **Coffin** (1793–1880). American social reformer and Quaker minister. Cooperated with her husband in antislavery activities. Instrumental in calling the first woman's rights convention at Seneca Falls, N.Y. (July 19–20, 1848). See also Elizabeth Cady STANTON.

Motteux, Peter Anthony, originally **Pierre Antoine** (1660?–1718). English playwright and translator who edited book III of Thomas URQUHART's translation of Rabelais and translated books IV and V himself (1693–1708).

Mottram, Ralph Hale (1883–). English novelist. Best-known for *The Spanish Farm,* which won the Hawthornden prize (1924) and sold over 100,000 copies. It was made into a moving picture as *Roses in Picardy.*

Mouldy, Ralph. A recruit in Shakespeare's *2 Henry IV.*

Mou-Mou. A story by TURGENEV. The hero is a lonely serf, a deaf mute, who is compelled by his nervous mistress to drown his one friend in the world, a little dog.

Mount. For *Mount Kaf, Mount Meru, Mount Zion,* etc., see under KAF, MERU, ZION, etc.

mountain.

the Mountain (*la Montagne*). The extreme democratic party in the French Revolution, the members of which were known as *les Montagnards* because they seated themselves on the highest benches of the hall in which the National Convention met. Their opponents, the Girondins, were nicknamed *the Plain.* Their leaders were Danton and Robespierre, Marat, St. André, Legendre, Camille-Desmoulins, Carnot, St. Just, and Collot d'Herbois, the men who introduced the "Reign of Terror." Extreme radicals in France in later times often were called *Montagnards.*

the Old Man of the Mountains, see OLD MAN.

Mountain States. The states of the Rocky Mountain region, specifically, Montana, Idaho, Wyoming, Colorado, New Mexico, Arizona, Utah, Nevada.

Mountbatten, Lord **Louis** (1900–). Great-grandson of Queen Victoria. Head of Commandos in World War II (from March 1942). Director of strategy of successful British invasion of Madagascar (May 1942), etc. His name was adapted (1917) from the original Prince **Louis of Battenberg.**

Mourning Becomes Electra. A trilogy of plays by Eugene O'NEILL, produced in 1931. The separate parts are entitled *Homecoming, The Hunted,* and *The Haunted,* and present an adaptation of the ELECTRA theme of classical literature in terms of a 19th-century New England family. The leading characters are: General Ezra Mannon, returning from the Civil War; Christine, his wife, a beautiful and sensual woman; their daughter Lavinia; Orin, their son; Adam Brant, Ezra's nephew; Peter Niles, a suitor of Lavinia; and Hazel Niles, Peter's sister, loved by Orin. The Mannon family correspond, respectively, to Agamemnon,

Clytemnestra, Electra, and Orestes in the original legend. Christine, assisted by Brant, her lover, poisons her husband. Lavinia, in love with Brant herself, discovers the rôle of her mother in the crime and persuades Orin to join her in a plan of revenge. Orin as a result murders Brant, and Christine commits suicide in grief. Orin and Lavinia travel to the South Seas, but the consciousness of their guilt preys upon them, and on their return home Orin kills himself and Lavinia retires to the lonely Mannon house to imprison herself among recollections of her crime.

Mourt's Relation. *A Relation or Journal of the Beginnings and Proceedings of the English Plantation Settled at Plymouth in New England,* published in 1622 and known as *Mourt's Relation* from the name of the author of its preface. It consists chiefly of letters from various of the colonists to their friends and families in England, and includes a diary kept by William BRADFORD during the voyage of the *Mayflower* and the early settlement of Plymouth.

Mouse Tower, the. A medieval watchtower on the Rhine, near Bingen, so called because of the tradition that Archbishop HATTO was there devoured by mice. The tower, however, was built by Bishop Siegfried, two hundred years after the death of Hatto, as a toll-house for collecting the duties upon all goods which passed by. The German *Maut* means "toll" (mouse is *Maus*), and the similarity of the words together with the great unpopularity of the toll on corn gave rise to the tradition.

moutons; revenons à nos. (*Fr.*). Literally, "let us come back to our sheep," a phrase used to express, "let us return to our subject." It is taken from the 14th century French comedy *La Farce de Maître Pathelin,* or *L'Avocat Pathelin* (line 1282), in which a woolen-draper charges a shepherd with ill-treating his sheep. In telling his story he keeps running away from his subject, and to throw discredit on the defendant's attorney (Pathelin), accuses him of stealing a piece of cloth. The judge must pull him up every moment with, *"Mais, mon ami, revenons à nos moutons."* The phrase is frequently quoted by RABELAIS.

Mouzon. A lawyer in Brieux's RED ROBE, typical of the selfishness and corruption in the French courts.

Mowatt, Anna Cora (1819–1870). Writer and actress. Born in France of American parentage. Her books include plays, cookbooks, novels, books on etiquette, etc. Her best-known play is *Fashion: or Life in New York* (produced, 1845; published, 1850).

Mowcher, Miss. In Dickens' DAVID COPPERFIELD, a benevolent little dwarf, patronized by STEERFORTH. She is full of humor and vulgarity. Her chief occupation is that of hairdressing and her pet saying, "Ain't I volatile?"

Mowgli the Frog. A native baby brought up by Mother Wolf with her cubs, in KIPLING's *Jungle Books* (1894–1895). After a boyhood spent with the animals of the jungle, he finally becomes a man among men.

Mowis. The bridegroom of snow, who, in American Indian tradition, wooed and won a beautiful bride. When morning dawned, Mowis left the wigwam, and melted into the sunshine. The bride hunted for him night and day in the forests, but never saw him again.

Mowrer, Edgar Ansel (1892–). American war correspondent. Pulitzer prize in journalism (1932) for his dispatches collected as *Germany Puts the Clock Back.*

Mowrer, Paul Scott (1887–). American journalist; foreign and war correspondent on staff of Chicago *Daily News* (from 1905). Pulitzer prize for best foreign correspondence (1928).

Moylan, Father. In James T. Farrell's STUDS LONIGAN and TOMMY GALLAGHER'S CRUSADE, a Roman Catholic priest with a wide following who makes demagogic speeches over the radio and conducts a campaign against Jews, Communists, and bankers. He is considered to be based on Father Charles E. COUGHLIN.

Mozart, Wolfgang Amadeus (1756–1791). Austrian composer. His best-known operas are THE MARRIAGE OF FIGARO, DON GIOVANNI and THE MAGIC FLUTE. "Master of melody . . . golden child of music." More than six hundred compositions, mostly published after his death. The exact position of his grave is not known.

M.P. Member of Parliament, but in slang use in England, Member of the Police.

M. Quad. Pseudonym of LEWIS, C. B.

Mr. Britling Sees It Through. A novel by H. G. WELLS (1916), an analysis of the effects of the first two years of World War I on the emotional and intellectual life of Mr. Britling, a man of letters who, when the war opens, is living comfortably with his family in an English country town. His son Hugh dies in the trenches, his old aunt is killed by a bomb, and the likable young German tutor who had left his household is shot in Russia. Out of these and other experiences he endeavors to fashion a philosophy that can be trusted to stand the strain of war.

Mr. Dooley. See DUNNE, FINLEY PETER.

Mr. Fortune's Maggot. A novel by Sylvia Townsend WARNER (1927).

Mr. Gilfil's Love Story. A story by George ELIOT, one of her *Scenes of Clerical Life* (1857). It chronicles the love and short-lived marriage of Maynard Gilfil, a clergyman, and the young Italian, Caterina Sorti. Caterina has fallen passionately in love with Captain Anthony Wybrow and is jealous of his fiancée, Beatrice Asshur. Wybrow is found dead of heart failure by Caterina, who has come with a dagger to meet him, and the shock is so great that, although she recovers enough to give her affection to the faithful Maynard and marry him, she dies a year after the marriage.

Mr. Isaacs. A novel by F. Marion CRAWFORD (1882) concerning a Mohammedan with three wives and the love affair with the English Miss Westonhaugh that stirs him to other ideals. The scene is laid in India.

Mr. Polly, The History of. A novel by H. G. WELLS (1910). The hero is an imaginative, unsuccessful small tradesman who, on sudden impulse, vanishes while his house is on fire and roams about on whimsical adventure.

Mrs. For characters in fiction and drama, as *Mrs. Grundy, Mrs. Gummidge, Mrs. Partington,* etc., see also under surnames.

Mrs. Dalloway. A novel by Virginia WOOLF (1925), describing the events during the course of a day in the life of Clarissa Dalloway, an English society woman. Through means of passages written in modified "INTERIOR MONOLOGUE" form, we see portrayed the personalities of Mrs. Dalloway and the people with whom she comes in contact during her day.

Mrs. Miniver. A best-selling collection of essays and sketches dealing with everyday events in the life of Mrs. Miniver, a middle-class English woman, during the early years of World War II, written by Jan STRUTHER (1940). It was extremely popular in both Great Britain and the U.S. and was adapted as a successful American motion picture.

Mrs. Warren's Profession. A drama by SHAW (1898). In his *George Bernard Shaw,* G. K. Chesterton describes it thus: "The play of *Mrs. Warren's Profession* is concerned with a coarse mother and a cold daughter; the mother drives the ordinary and dirty trade of harlotry; the daughter does not know until the end the atrocious origin of all her own comfort and refinement. The daughter, when the discovery is made, freezes up into an iceberg of contempt . . . the mother explodes into pulverizing cynicism and practicality." See also under DALY, ARNOLD.

Mrs. Wiggs of the Cabbage Patch. A novel of mingled humor and sentiment by Alice Hegan RICE (1901). The "Cabbage Patch" is a straggling group of huts and shanties along the railroad track in a Kentucky town. Here Mrs. Wiggs, the plucky widow of a drunkard, mother of Asia, Australia, Europena, and Jimmy and presiding genius of the Patch, finds ample scope for her talents. A slight love story is interwoven, and the irrepressible Wiggses pride themselves at last on the fact that it is in their cottage that their much admired Miss Lucy Olcott becomes reconciled to her lover, Robert Redding. In *Lovey Mary* (1903), a sequel, "Lovey Mary," who has been brought up in a Home, runs away with a child named Tommy to whom she has become attached. Luck brings her to the Cabbage Patch, where Mrs. Wiggs, resourceful as usual, finds a home for her with the shiftless Miss Hazy, and at the end of the tale the two children are befriended by the well-to-do Mr. and Mrs. Redding whose love story was told in *Mrs. Wiggs.* There was a successful dramatized version of *Mrs. Wiggs* in 1904.

Mr. Waddington of Wyck. A novel by May SINCLAIR (1921), an analytical study, not without humor, of a completely self-centered and conceited person.

MS. (*pl.* MSS.). Manuscript (from Lat. *manusscriptum,* "that which is written by hand"), applied to literary works either in hand-writing or typescript.

Much Ado About Nothing. A comedy by Shakespeare (ca. 1599). There are two main plots. One concerns the love affairs of Beatrice and Benedict, who fall in love as a result of the clever schemes of their friends, each one being told the other is pining away of unrequited passion. The other plot has to do with a conspiracy against Beatrice's gentle cousin, Hero, who is engaged to Claudio of Aragon. Hero's uncle, Don John, from hatred of her father, bribes Hero's waiting maid to impersonate her mistress and keep a rendezvous with him, and then invites Claudio to witness it. Claudio rejects his bride at the altar, but through the good offices of a kindly, understanding priest, the matter is finally cleared up. Many sources have been suggested for the plot, for similar tales were told by Bandello, Ariosto and Spenser, among others.

Muck, Karl (1859–1940). German orchestra conductor. Guest conductor in London (1899), Vienna (1903–1906), Boston (1906–1908), etc. Regular conductor of Boston Symphony Orchestra (1912–1918).

Muckle-Mouth Meg. A humorous poem by Robert BROWNING about an English trespasser across the Scots border who is offered the choice of "Muckle-Mouth Meg" or the gallows. The fearsomely named female turns out to be a winsome girl. James Ballantine (1808–1877) wrote a ballad on the same subject, "Muckle-Mou'd Meg," though in his version the girl's mouth is in reality very large, but Wat Scott, the young man in this case, relents at her tears at the foot of the gibbet. "'Twas better to marry than hang"; and, apparently, all turned out well, for they "lo'ed ither muckle and lang."

muckrakers. Term applied to a group of authors and journalists in the early 1900's, from 1902 to about 1917, who took part in a movement exposing corruption in the business and politics of the U.S. at the time. Leading participants included Lincoln STEFFENS, Ida TARBELL, George CREEL, T. W. LAWSON, Ray Stannard BAKER, Mark SULLIVAN, and Samuel Hopkins ADAMS. A number of magazines and newspapers were devoted to muckraking campaigns, among them being *McClure's, Everybody's, Collier's,* the *Independent, Cosmopolitan,* the New York *World,* and the Kansas City *Star.* THE JUNGLE is a famous muckraking novel. The term *muckraker* was first used by Theodore Roosevelt in a speech in 1906 attacking charges of corruption in the U.S., and referred to a character in PILGRIM'S PROGRESS who spends his time raking muck and never sees the crown above his head.

Mud Cat State. Mississippi. So called for large number of catfish in the Mississippi River. See under STATES.

Mudie, Charles Edward (1818–1890). English publisher. Founder of Mudie's Lending Library in London (1842).

Mudjekeewis. In Longfellow's poem HIAWATHA, the father of Hiawatha, and subsequently potentate of the winds. He gives all the winds but one to his children to rule; the one he reserves is the west wind, which he himself rules over. The dominion of the winds is given to Mudjekeewis because he once slew the great bear called the Mishe-Mokwa.

> Thus was slain the Mishe-Mokwa . . .
> "Honor be to Mudjekeewis!
> Henceforth he shall be the west wind,
> And hereafter, e'en for ever,
> Shall he hold supreme dominion
> Over all the winds of heaven."
>
> *Hiawatha,* ii.

mufti. An Arabic word meaning an official expounder of the Koran and Mohammedan law; but used in English to denote *civil,* as distinguished from *military* or official costume.

Mugello. The giant that, according to medieval romance, was slain by Averardo de Medici, a commander under Charlemagne. The tale is interesting, for it is said that the Medici took the three balls of his mace, now the pawnbrokers' sign (see BALLS), for their device.

mugwump. An Algonquin word meaning a chief; in John Eliot's *Indian Bible* (1663) the word "centurion" in the *Acts* is rendered *mugwump.* It later came to be applied in the U.S. to independent members of the Republican party, who refused to follow the dictum of a caucus, and to all political independents whose party vote could not be relied on.

Muir, Edwin (1887–). Scottish poet and literary critic. His essays contributed to *The Freeman* under the editorship of Van Wyck BROOKS were collected under the title *Latitudes* (1924). He is (with his wife, Willa Muir) one of the best known contemporary translators from the German. His book, *The Structure of the Novel* (1928), postulates that the contemporary realistic novel is comparatively a failure.

Muir, John (1838–1914). Scottish-born American naturalist. Worked principally in Yosemite Valley (1868–1874) and later in Nevada, Utah, and Alaska. Settled in California and campaigned for forest reserves and National Parks, like the Yosemite which was finally established by Congress (1840). Wrote *The Mountains of California* (1849); *Our National Parks* (1901); *The Yosemite* (1912); etc.

Mukerji, Dhan Gopal (1890–1936). East Indian-American novelist. Won the Newbery medal of the American Library Association for the best children's book with *Gay-Neck* (1927). Also wrote an answer to Katherine Mayo's *Mother India,* entitled *A Son of Mother India Answers* (1928), claiming that Miss Mayo exaggerated the situation in India.

Mulciber. Literally, "the softener." A Latin surname of VULCAN.

Mulford, Clarence Edward (1883–). American writer of western stories. Best-known for his *Bar-20* stories concerning a character called Hopalong Cassidy.

Mulla's Bard. See under BARD.

Mullens, Priscilla. Heroine of Longfellow's *The Courtship of Miles Standish.*

Müller, Friedrich Max (1823–1900). German-born British philologist. Devoted himself to comparative study of religions; of very stimulating influence on Oriental studies. See also under BOWWOW THEORY.

Muller, Maud, see MAUD MULLER.

Mulligan, Malachi ("Buck"). In James Joyce's ULYSSES, a vigorous, sardonic, and ebullient Irish medical student, a friend of STEPHEN DEDALUS, with whom Stephen lives in an abandoned tower overlooking the harbor of Dublin. He is said to represent Oliver St. John GOGARTY.

Mulligan of Ballymulligan. An obstreperous Irishman in Thackeray's Christmas book, *Mrs. Perkins' Ball.* He attends the ball and dances a double shuffle jig, to the terror of his partner.

Mulock, Dinah Maria, see CRAIK.

multum in parvo (*Lat.*). Literally, "much in little." Much information condensed into few words or into a small compass.

Mulvaney, Terence. One of Kipling's best-known characters, with his friends Stanley ORTHERIS and John LEAROYD forming a trio, "collectively . . . the worst men in the regiment so far as genial blackguardism goes." They made their first appearance in a short story entitled *The Three Musketeers,* included in PLAIN TALES FROM THE HILLS (1888) and thereafter were moving spirits of many an adventure. E. W. Gosse thus described the trio in *The Century*—

> Mulvaney, the Irish giant, who has been the "grizzled, tender and very wise Ulysses" to successive generations of young and foolish recruits, is a great creation. He is the father of the craft of arms to his associates; he has served with various regiments from Bermuda to Halifax; he is "old in war, scarred, reckless, resourceful, and in his pious hours an unequaled soldier." Learoyd, the second of these friends, is "six and a half feet of slow-moving, heavy-footed Yorkshireman, born on the wolds, bred in the dales, and educated chiefly among the carriers' carts at the back of York railway station." The third is Ortheris, a little man as sharp as a needle, "a fox-terrier of a cockney," an inveterate poacher and dog-stealer.

Mumbo Jumbo. The name given by Europeans (possibly from some lost native word) to a bogy or grotesque idol venerated by certain African tribes; hence, any object of blind and unreasoning worship. Vachel LINDSAY composed a poem entitled, *The Congo,* in which the chant "Mumbo Jumbo will hoodoo you!" is used as a striking refrain.

Mumford, Ethel, *née* **Watts** (1878?–1940). American writer. Best-known for her contributions, with Oliver Herford, to *The Cynics' Calendar* (1905–1910).

Mumford, Lewis (1895–). American social, literary, and art critic, author of several well-known studies of American life and accomplishment in the 19th and 20th centuries. These are *The Story of Utopias* (1922); *Sticks and Stones* (1924), on the reflection of the American spirit through architecture; *The Golden Day* (1926), a study of American literature of the first half of the 19th century; *Herman Melville* (1929), a psychological biography; *The Brown Decades* (1931), on art, engineering, and architecture in the U.S. in the latter part of the 19th century; *Technics and Civilization* (1934); *The Culture of Cities* (1938), on sociology and community planning; *Faith for Living* (1940); *Green Memories* (1947), a biography of his young son, Geddes, killed in World War II.

Münchausen, Baron. A traveler who meets with the most marvelous adventures, the hero of a collection of burlesque stories by the German author Rudolf Erich Raspe, published in English in 1785. The original English title read *Baron Münchausen's Narrative of His Marvellous Travels and Campaigns in Russia.* The name of the author was not definitely known until after his death. The incidents were compiled from various sources, including the adventures of an actual Hieronymus Karl Friedrich von Münchhausen (1720–1797), a German officer in the Russian army, noted for his marvelous stories, Bebel's *Facetiae,* Castiglione's *Cortegiano,* Bildermann's *Utopia,* etc. The book ran through numerous editions. It is unique in its field of high-spirited satire.

Mundy, Talbot (1879–1940). Anglo-American novelist who became deeply interested in East-Indian occult teachings. His romantic novels are popular, as *Rung Ho* (1914); etc.

Muni, Paul. Originally **Paul Weisenfreund** (1895–). Famous moving-picture actor who started as member of the Yiddish Art Theater in New York (1918–1925). Starred in *I am a Fugitive from a Chain Gang; Life of Louis Pasteur* (Motion Picture Academy award, 1936); *The Good Earth; Life of Émile Zola;* etc.

Munich Crisis. A European diplomatic crisis of September 1938, when war was threatened by the demand of Adolf HITLER for the incorporation into Germany of a group of Sudeten Germans living in a region which had been given to Czechoslovakia as part of its national territory by the Treaty of Versailles at the close of World War I. In an effort to prevent war, Neville CHAMBERLAIN Prime Minister of Great Britain, flew to confer with Hitler at BERCHTESGADEN and later made a peace treaty at Munich, Germany, which permitted the annexation of the Sudeten region to Germany in return for a pledge by Hitler that the independence of the remainder of Czechoslovakia would be respected. Chamberlain believed that "peace in our time" had been achieved, but Hitler's pledge was not kept. The Munich agreement indirectly strengthened Hitler for his later aggression against Poland (September 1939), which brought about World War II.

Munin, see MUGINN.

Munkácsy, Mihály von. Real name **Michael Lieb** (1844–1900). Hungarian painter. His *Christ Before Pilate* (1882) became internationally famous.

Munkar and Nakir. Two black angels of Mohammedan mythology who interrogate the dead immediately after burial. The first two questions they ask are, "Who is your Lord?" and "Who is your prophet?" Their voices are like thunder, their aspects hideous. If the scrutiny is satisfactory the soul is gently drawn forth from the lips of the deceased, and the body is left to repose in peace; if not, the body is beaten about the head with clubs half iron and half flame, and the soul is wrenched forth by racking torments.

Munro, Cora. The heroine of Cooper's LAST OF THE MOHICANS. Her sister Alice and her father, the English commander of Fort William Henry, are also prominent characters.

Munro, Hector Hugh (1870–1916). Pseudonym **Saki.** Scottish writer of humorous short stories and novels, including *Reginald, Beasts and Super-Beasts,* and *The Unbearable Bassington.* His work has been praised as having the qualities of champagne, high spirits and fantastic humor. His first book was a serious work, *The Rise of the Russian Empire* (1900). Killed in World War I.

Munro, Neil (1864–1930). Scottish novelist and poet. All of his work Scottish in background. His best novels, *John Splendid* and *Gillian, the Dreamer.* Sir Hugh Walpole called him "one of Scotland's few great novelists." His newspaper work was all written under the pseudonym of "Mr. Incognito."

Munroe, Kirk (1850–1930). Popular American writer of boys' books. Editor of *Harper's Young People.* His most popular story is *The Flamingo Feather* (1887).

Munsey, Frank Andrew (1854–1925). American publisher of magazines and mortician of newspapers. He bought up and killed the New York *Herald, Globe, Mail,* and *Sun.* Among his successes were *Munsey's Magazine* and the *Argosy All-Story Weekly.* He left the bulk of his fortune to the Metropolitan Museum of Art in New York.

Munson, Gorham (1896–). American critic and economist. Founded (1922) and edited (1922–1924) a little review called *Secession,* contributors to which included Waldo Frank, E. E. Cummings, etc. Joined the faculty of New School for Social Research (1927). Edited the social-credit review, *New Democracy* (1933–1939), and organized the American social-credit movement. Van Wyck Brooks has called him "the most important of younger American critics."

Münsterberg, Hugo (1863–1916). German-American psychologist. Taught at Harvard (1892–1895; 1897–1916) superintending the construction of a laboratory especially equipped for experimental psychology. His books on psychology are numerous.

Munthe, Axel Martin Fredrik (1857–). Swedish physician, psychiatrist, and writer. Famous for *The Story of San Michele* (1929) which sold over 200,000 copies in the U.S. The royalties Dr. Munthe used for his bird sanctuaries in Italy and Sweden.

Murasaki, Baroness. Full Japanese name **Murasaki Shikibu** (11th century). Japanese poet. Author of a great novel, translated into English by Arthur Waley as *Genji Monagati, or The Tale of Genji* (2 vols., 1935).

Murat, Joachim (1767?–1815). French general who had risen from the ranks. Aided Napoleon in the *coup d'état* of 1799. He married Napoleon's sister and became marshal of France (1804). Commanded cavalry at Austerlitz (1805), Jena (1806), Eylan and Friedland (1807). Made king of Naples (1809), he became known as the "Dandy King." Joined Napoleon on his return from Elba but was captured and executed. Both his sons came to the United States.

Muratore, Lucien (1878–). French dramatic tenor. Member, Chicago Opera Co. (1913–1915). Married Lina CAVALIERI.

Murder in the Cathedral. A drama in verse by T. S. ELIOT (1935). It deals with the assassination of St. Thomas à Becket (see under SAINTS), and shows him choosing to obey the laws of God rather than of man, even though thereby he loses opportunity for worldly power and insures his murder by the party representing the English king. The conflicts between church and state at the time (1170) are portrayed in the drama, which is considered one of Eliot's best works and was produced on the British and American stage with some artistic success.

Murderers' Bible, see BIBLE, SPECIALLY NAMED.

Murders in the Rue Morgue, The. A story by Edgar Allan POE, published in 1841 and collected in the *Prose Tales of Edgar A. Poe* (1843). It introduced the famous literary detective C. Auguste Dupin.

Murdstone, Edward. In Dickens' DAVID COPPERFIELD, David's stepfather, the second husband of Mrs. Copperfield. His character is "firmness," that is, an unbending self-will, which renders the young life of David intolerably wretched.

Jane Murdstone. Sister of Edward, as hard and heartless as her brother.

Murfree, Mary Noailles, see Charles Egbert CRADDOCK.

Murger, Henri (1822–1861). French writer. Best-known for his *Scènes de la Vie Bohème* (1847–1894), sketches of Bohemian life in Paris.

Murillo, Bartolomé Esteban (1617–1682). Spanish painter of the Andalusian school.

murrain. Plague. Used in Elizabethan invective, as, "a murrain on you!" The word is ultimately related to *murder.*

Murray, Gilbert (1866–). British classical scholar. Considered one of the most notable translators of Greek drama in the world. Also active in encouraging the return of the Greek drama to the English stage.

Murray, Lindley (1745–1826). Scottish-American grammarian, called the "Father of English Grammar." *Grammar of the English Language* (1795).

Murrieta, Joaquín (1832?–1853). A California desperado (1849–1853) who, because of some personal affront or wrong, swore vengeance to all Americans. He led a raiding and marauding gang of horsemen and has been presented in moving pictures in a sort of Robin Hood rôle.

Murry, John Middleton (1889–). English journalist and literary critic, husband of Katherine MANSFIELD and friend of D. H. LAWRENCE, Virginia WOOLF, Henri GAUDIER, and other English and European figures of the artistic world in the period immediately preceding and following World War I. Murry's literary criticism emphasizes mystical, religious, and ethical values in literature and the lives of literary personalities. Among his studies are *Fyodor Dostoyevsky* (1916); *The Evolution of an Intellectual* (1919); *Countries of the Mind* (1922); *Pencillings* (1923); *Discoveries* (1924); *To the Unknown God* (1924); *Keats and Shakespeare* (1925); *Jesus, Man of Genius* (1927); *Things to Come* (1928); *God* (1929); *Studies in Keats* (1930); *Son of Woman* (1931), dealing with D. H. Lawrence. He also wrote poetry and fiction, edited the letters, papers, and journals of Katherine Mansfield after her death, and published a revealing *Autobiography*.

During his career, Murry served as editor of several LITTLE MAGAZINES, including *Rhythm*, later *The Blue Review* (1911), the *Athenaeum* (1919–1921), and *The Adelphi* (1923–1930). He tends to be generally known more through the opinions held of him by other writers than through his own work. It is said that his personality suggested the character of Denis BURLAP in Aldous HUXLEY'S POINT COUNTER POINT.

muscular Christianity. Healthy or strong-minded Christianity, which braces a man to fight the battle of life bravely and manfully. The term was applied to the teachings of Charles KINGSLEY—somewhat to his annoyance.

> It is a school of which Mr. Kingsley is the ablest doctor; and its doctrine has been described fairly and cleverly as "muscular Christianity."—*Edinburgh Review*, Jan., 1858.

Muses. In Greek mythology, the nine daughters of ZEUS and Mnemosyne; originally goddesses of memory only, but later identified with individual arts and sciences. The paintings of Herculaneum show all nine with their respective attributes.

(1) *Calliope,* the epic Muse. Her symbols are a tablet and stylus; sometimes a scroll.

(2) *Clio,* Muse of history. Her symbol is a scroll, or an open chest of books.

(3) *Erato,* Muse of love poetry. Her symbol is a lyre.

(4) *Euterpe,* Muse of lyric poetry, whose symbol is a flute.

(5) *Melpomene,* Muse of tragedy: a tragic mask, the club of Hercules, or a sword. She wears the cothurnus, and her head is wreathed with vine leaves.

(6) *Polyhymnia,* Muse of sacred poetry. She sits pensive, but has no attribute, because deity is not to be represented by any visible symbol.

(7) *Terpsichore.* Muse of choral song and dance. Her symbols are a lyre and the plectrum.

(8) *Thalia.* Muse of comedy and idyllic poetry. Her symbols are a comic mask, a shepherd's staff, or a wreath of ivy.

(9) *Urania,* Muse of astronomy. She carries a staff pointing to a globe.

the Tenth Muse. (1) Marie Lejars de Gournay (1566–1645); (2) Antoinette Deshoulières (1633–1694); (3) Madeleine de Scudéry (1607–1701); (4) Delphine Gay (1804–1855), all French women of letters; (5) Anne Bradstreet, the first American poetess. See under TENTH.

the Scian and the Teian Muse. Simonides and Anacreon.

Musidorus. See PYROCLES AND MUSIDORUS.

Musketeers, The Three, see THREE MUSKETEERS.

Muslim, see MOSLEM.

Musorgski or **Moussorgsky, Modest Petrovich** (1835–1881). Russian composer. His most notable work is the opera *Boris Godunov*. See also under PUSHKIN. It was revised by Rimsky-Korsakov; under the Soviets it was made available in the original version which has been eagerly performed. Musorgski was the instigator of the antiformalist movement and father of folk idiom in Russian music.

Muspelheim. In Scandinavian mythology, the abode of fire which at the beginning of time existed in the south. It was light, warm, and radiant, but was guarded by Surtr with a flaming sword. Sparks were collected therefrom to make the stars.

Musset, Alfred de (1810–1857). French poet and dramatist of the romantic period (see ROMANTICISM), associated with the group of poets led by Victor HUGO. His poetry is passionate in the manner of BYRON, dealing chiefly with the ecstasies and despairs of love, with strong emphasis on the individuality of the author. His plays consist of comedies of manners, called *comédies-proverbes,* because many of the titles were taken from proverbs popular at the time, and fanciful comedies in the style of Shakespeare. Musset's poetic works include *Contes d'Espagne et d'Italie* (1829); *Premières poésies* (1833); *Poésies nouvelles* (1836–1852); *Namuna* and *Rolla* (1833), narrative poems; a series of lyrics (1835) for which he is best known, including *Nuit de mai, Nuit de decembre, Nuit d'août, Nuit* *d'octobre*, and *Souvenir*. Among his plays are *A quoi Revent les jeunes filles; Il Faut qu'une porte soit ouverte ou fermée; Un Caprice; Barberine; Lorenzaccio; On ne badine pas avec l'amour. La Confession d'un enfant du siècle* (1836) is a romance in prose.

Musset was involved in a celebrated love affair with George SAND which ended disastrously and was responsible for the poet's turning to debauchery to forget his sorrows. The affair is reflected in his poetry and plays.

Mussolini, Benito (1883–1945). Fascist dictator of Italy. Began as socialist journalist; editor of *Avanti* (1912); etc. Led Fascists in march on Rome (1922). Summoned by King to form a ministry. Assured Fascist control of government; denounced Versailles Treaty; conquered Ethiopia (1933–1936); withdrew from League of Nations; aided Franco in Spanish war; became ally of Germany in World War II (1940). Died a miserable death by the hands of his own people, with his mistress, after the victory of the Allies.

Mussulman. A Mohammedan, a MOSLEM.

Mut (mother). In Egyptian mythology, the consort of AMMON. She is sometimes called Amaune.

Mutiny on the Bounty. A best-selling novel by Charles NORDHOFF and James Norman HALL (1932), based on the famous 18th-century mutiny on the H.M.S. BOUNTY. Together with the two other novels by the same authors which form a trilogy—*Men Against the Sea* (1934) and *Pitcairn Island* (1934)—it describes how the mate of the ship, Fletcher Christian, and a number of the crew rebel against the cruel Captain Bligh and set him adrift in an open boat with the loyal members of the crew. The mutineers have many adventures at sea following this act and eventually, with a group of Tahitian natives, reach Pitcairn Island and found a colony. *Mutiny on the Bounty* was dramatized as a successful American motion picture.

Mutsuhito (1852–1912). Japanese emperor, the 122nd in direct lineage. During his reign Japan was modernized and made her greatest industrial progress. The position of Japanese women was improved, a constitution was adopted (1889), and the Japanese secured a victory over China (1894) and Russia (1905).

Mute and Jute. In James Joyce's FINNEGANS WAKE, a pair of comic Irishmen. In the first section of the book they carry on an exuberant dialogue in dream-language which contains allusions to places in Ireland and events and characters in Irish history.

Mutt and Jeff. Two American comic-strip characters by "Bud" Fisher.

Mutual Admiration Society. Any club or informal group of friends who laud each other to the skies; sometimes used cynically of writers who sing each other's praises in print. The phrase comes from Oliver Wendell HOLMES' *Autocrat of the Breakfast Table* (1857–1858)

Mutual Friend, Our, see OUR MUTUAL FRIEND.

My Ántonia. A novel by Willa CATHER (1918), dealing with the life of Bohemian immigrant and native American settlers in the frontier farmlands of Nebraska. The heroine, Ántonia Shimerda, is forced to work as a servant on the farms of her neighbors after her father kills himself in despair at his failure to become a farmer. She has an unfortunate love affair and elopes with an Irish railway conductor, but returns home and eventually becomes the patient and strong wife of a Bohemian farmer, Anton Cuzak, the mother of a large family, and a typical woman of the pioneer West. The author says of her:

> She lent herself to immemorial human attitudes which we recognize as universal and true. . . . She had only to stand in the orchard, to put her hand on a little crab tree and look up at the apples, to make you feel the goodness of planting and tending and harvesting at last . . . She was a rich mine of life, like the founders of early races.

Mycerinus. An Egyptian king, son of CHEOPS. He is the hero of a poem by Matthew ARNOLD.

Myers, Frederic William Henry (1843–1901). English poet and essayist. One of the founders of the Society for Psychical Research (1882). Author of the remarkable poem *Saint Paul* (1867); etc.

Myers, Gustavus (1872–1943). American economic historian. Best-known for his *History of the Great American Fortunes* (1910), "a semi-classic of research."

My Friend's Book (*Le Livre de mon ami*). An autobiographical volume by Anatole FRANCE (1885). See also under PIERRE NOZIÈRE.

My Heart and My Flesh. Novel by Elizabeth Madox ROBERTS (1927).

My Heart's in the Highlands. A play by William SAROYAN (1939).

My Lady Nicotine. Tobacco. The phrase is the title of a book by J. M. BARRIE (1890).

My Last Duchess. A dramatic monologue by Robert BROWNING (1842). The speaker is the Renaissance Duke of Ferrara who, while negotiating a marriage with the daughter of a count, indicates to the count's agent a portrait of his former wife, his "last Duchess." As he speaks of her, there is the intimation that, because she did not properly appreciate the honor bestowed upon her by his marrying her, he arranged for her murder.

My Lost Youth. Title of a famous poem by LONGFELLOW.

My Mortal Enemy. Title of a novel by Willa CATHER (1926).

Mynheer Closh. A Dutchman. *Closh* or *Claus* is an abbreviation of Nicholaus, a common name in Holland.

My Novel, Or Varieties in English Life. A novel by BULWER LYTTON (1853), supposedly written by Pisistratus CAXTON.

My Old Kentucky Home. Song by Stephen FOSTER.

Myriel, Monseigneur Bienvenu. In Victor Hugo's LES MISÉRABLES, the charitable Bishop of D. who entertains the convict Jean VALJEAN. When Valjean repays his hospitality by making off with the silver plate and is caught, the Bishop sets him free. His act proves the turning point of Valjean's whole life.

Myrmidons. In classic mythology, a people of Thessaly who followed Achilles to the siege of Troy, and were distinguished for their savage brutality, rude behavior, and thirst for rapine. They were originally ants, turned into human beings by Zeus to populate the island of Oenone.

myrmidons of the law. Bailiffs, sheriffs' officers, and other law menials. Any rough fellow employed to annoy another is the employer's myrmidon.

Myron (5th century B.C.). Greek sculptor. His most celebrated work is the *Discobolus* or *Discus Thrower,* replicas of which are in the Vatican and the British Museum.

Myrrha. (1) The mother of ADONIS, in Greek legend. She is fabled to have had an unnatural love for her own father, and to have been changed into a myrtle tree.

(2) In BYRON's historic drama *Sardanapalus* (1819), an Ionian slave, and the beloved concubine of Sardanapalus, the Assyrian king. She rouses him from his indolence to resist Arbaces the Mede, who aspires to his throne, and when she finds his cause hopeless, induces him to mount a funeral pile, which she fires with her own hand. Then, springing into the flames, she perishes with the tyrant.

myrrophores (*Gr.,* "myrrh bearers"). The three Marys who went to see the sepulcher, bearing myrrh and spices. (*Mark* xvi. 1). In Christian art they are represented as carrying vases of myrrh in their hands.

Myshkin, Prince. The hero of Fyodor Dostoyevsky's THE IDIOT, a gentle, childlike, almost saintly man, an epileptic, who is innocent of the evils and consuming passions of the world in which he moves. He tries to promote charity, understanding, and love among the sinning and tortured persons with whom he comes in contact, but fails tragically, ultimately being reduced by the mental strain and shock of his experiences to the condition of a mumbling idiot. He is considered one of the foremost fictional spokesmen for the ideas by which Dostoyevsky hoped to save the Russia of his day. See also ALEXEY FYODOROVICH KARAMAZOV (*Alyosha*) under KARAMAZOV.

Mysteries, see MYSTERY PLAYS.

Mysteries of Paris, The. A romance by Eugène SUE (1842–1843), giving a many-sided picture of Parisian life.

Mysteries of Udolpho, The. A romance by Mrs. RADCLIFFE (1794), one of the first and perhaps the most famous novel of the so-called "terror school" of English romanticism. See GOTHIC NOVEL. The scene is laid in a grim medieval castle in the Apennines. The heroine, an English girl named Emily St. Aubyn, suffers exciting agonies from a long succession of supposedly supernatural horrors, until at last her lover, the Chevalier de Velancourt, breaks the spell.

Mysterious Stranger, The. A novel by Mark TWAIN (written, 1898; published posthumously, 1916). The scene is laid in 16th-century Austria and the story is told by Theodor Fischer, the center of a group of three friends to whom appears at times the "mysterious stranger." He calls himself Philip Traum but in reality is the nephew of Satan. He is considered a vehicle for much of Mark Twain's own philosophy.

Mystery of Marie Rogêt. A detective story by Edgar Allan POE, suggested by the actual murder case of Mary Cecilia Rogers in New York.

mystery plays or **mysteries.** The name given to medieval dramatic presentations of Biblical stories. Beginning with a simple pageant of the Christmas or Easter story in the church itself, the dramas gradually assumed a secular aspect. At the height of their popularity, from the 13th to the 15th or 16th centuries, they were presented by members of the various trade guilds on movable stages, which sometimes, especially in France, had three stories, representing Heaven, Earth, and Hell. The English Mystery Plays have been preserved in four important cycles—the Townley, York, Chester, and Coventry plays, so called (with the exception of the first named, which were played at Wakefield) from the towns where they were enacted. Extraneous comic elements were frequently introduced, as in the case of the stubborn wife of Noah, who caused much merriment by refusing to enter the Ark. The line between the mysteries and the MIRACLE PLAYS which dealt with the miracles of Christian saints, is not always clearly drawn, and the mysteries are sometimes included in the term "miracle plays."

Mystery, meaning something beyond human comprehension, is (through French) from the Lat. *mysterium* and Gr. *mustes,* from *muein,* to close the eyes or lips. It is from this sense that the plays were called *mysteries,* though, as they were frequently presented by members of some single guild, or *mystery* in the sense of a trade or handicraft, even here the words were confused and opening made for many puns.

Mytyl. Girl, one of the two children who go in search of the BLUE BIRD in Maeterlinck's play of that name. The boy is Tyltyl.

myxolydian mode. One of the four principal modes in ancient Greek music. See also DORIAN MODE; LYDIAN MODE; PHRYGIAN MODE. Myxo-Lydians, in several novels by Angela THIRKELL, are rude, grasping and ungrateful refugees.

N

Naaman. In the Old Testament, a leper, "captain of the host of the king of Syria and . . . a mighty man of valor," cured by the Hebrew prophet Elisha, of whose power he had heard through a captive Israelite maid. See RIMMON.

nabob. Corruption of the Hindu *nawab,* plural of *naib,* a deputy-governor under the Mogul Empire. These men acquired great wealth and lived in splendor; hence, *rich as a nabob* came to be applied in England to a merchant who had attained great wealth in the Indies, and returned to live in his native country.

Nabob, The (Le Nabab). A novel by Alphonse DAUDET (1877). The "Nabob," Jansoulet, returns to Paris from Tunis with a fortune and becomes the prey of all varieties of schemers and parasites. He succeeds in buying his way into the French parliament. The character is said to have an original in François Bravay.

Naboth's vineyard. The possession of another coveted by one able to possess himself of it (1 *Kings* xxi). The Israelite king, AHAB, had Naboth put to death on a false charge in order to obtain a vineyard which Naboth refused to sell.

Nadab. In Dryden's ABSALOM AND ACHITOPHEL, he is meant for Lord Howard of Escrick, a profligate who laid claim to great piety. Nadab offered incense with strange fire, and was slain by the Lord (*Lev.* x. 2); and Lord Howard, while imprisoned in the Tower, is said to have mixed the consecrated wafer with a compound of roasted apples and sugar, called lamb's-wool.

> And canting Nadab let oblivion damn,
> Who made new porridge of the paschal lamb.
> *Absalom and Achitophel,* Pt. i, 538–9.

Nadgett. In Dickens' MARTIN CHUZZLEWIT, a man employed by Montague Tigg, manager of the "Anglo-Bengalee Company," to make private inquiries. He is a dried-up, shriveled old man. Where he lives and how he lives, nobody knows, but he is always seen waiting for someone who never appears.

nadir. An Arabic word, signifying that point in the heavens which is directly opposite to the zenith, i.e., directly under our feet; hence, figuratively, the lowest depths of degradation.

> The seventh century is the nadir of the human mind in Europe.—Hallam, *Hist. Lit. in Midd. Ages,* I, i, 4.

Naglfar. The ship of the Scandinavian giants, in which they will embark on "the last day" to give battle to the gods. It is made of the nails of the dead (O.N. *nagl,* "nail," and *fara,* "to make"), and is piloted by HRYMIR.

naiads. Nymphs of lakes, fountains, rivers, and streams in classical mythology.

> You nymphs, call'd naiads, of the wand'ring brooks,
> With your sedg'd crowns, and ever-harmless looks,
> Leave your crisp channels, and on this green land
> Answer your summons: Juno does command.
> Shakespeare, *Tempest,* iv. 1.

Naidu, Sarojini (1879–). Hindu poet and reformer. Organized flood-relief work in India (1908); lectured in India and U.S. (1928–1929). First Indian woman president of the Indian National Congress (1925). Author of *The Golden Threshold* (1905), *The Bird of Time* (1912), and *The Broken Wing* (1915–1916), books of poetry translated into many languages of India.

Naïla. Ballet, music by DELIBES.

nain rouge (*Fr.,* "red dwarf"). A lutin or house spirit of Normandy, kind to fishermen. There is another called *le petit homme rouge* (the little red man).

Nairne, Caroline, *née* **Oliphant.** Baroness Nairne (1766–1845). Scottish song writer and poet. Her poems were posthumously published as *Lays from Strathearn* (1846). Most famous for the Jacobite song, *Charlie is my Darling,* the humorous ballad *The Laird of Cockpen,* and the sentimental song, *Land o' the Leal.*

Nala. In Hindu legend, a king of Nishadha, and husband of Damayanti, whose story is one of the best known in the MAHABHARATA. Damayanti, through enchantment, falls in love with Nala without ever having seen him. The gods want her for themselves, and employ the unsuspecting Nala as their advocate; she declares that none but Nala shall possess her, whereupon the four gods appear in Nala's shape and Damayanti is obliged to make her choice, which she does—correctly. Nala is then given many magic gifts by the gods. The wedding is celebrated, but later Nala loses his all by gambling, and becomes a wanderer, while Damayanti returns to her father's court. Many tribulations and adventures (in which magic performs a large part) befall the lovers before they are reunited.

Namby Pamby. Nickname of Ambrose PHILIPS.

Nameless City. Ancient Rome.

Namo. In Carolingian legend, the Duke of Bavaria and one of Charlemagne's famous paladins.

Nana. A novel by Zola, one of the ROUGON-MACQUART series.

Nancanou, Mrs. Aurora and Clothilde. A charming Creole mother and equally charming daughter in G. W. Cable's *Grandissimes* (1880).

Nancy. (1) In Dickens' OLIVER TWIST, a poor misguided girl, who loves the villain Bill SIKES. In spite of her surroundings, she still has some good feelings, and tries to prevent a burglary planned by FAGIN and his associates. Bill Sikes, in a fit of passion, strikes her twice upon the face with the butt-end of a pistol, and she falls dead at his feet.

(2) A leading character in Flotow's opera, MARTHA.

Nancy, Miss. An effeminate, foppish youth.

The celebrated actress, "Mrs." Anne Oldfield (see NARCISSA) was nicknamed "Miss Nancy."

Nanki-Poo. In Gilbert and Sullivan's comic opera THE MIKADO, the son of the Mikado.

Nankivell, Frank Arthur (1869–). Australian-born American cartoonist and painter. With *Puck* (1896). Experimented with animated motion pictures in color.

Nanna. Wife of BALDER in Scandinavian mythology. When the blind god HODUR slew her husband, she threw herself upon his funeral pile and was burnt to death.

Nansen, Fridtjof (1861–1930). Norwegian arctic explorer and statesman. Famous for expeditions in his exploring vessel *Fram.* Searched for North Pole and explored north Atlantic Ocean. Chairman, Norwegian Association for League of Nations (1918). Awarded Nobel peace prize (1922). Represented Norway on Disarmament Committee, League of Nations (1927). Author of *Eskimo Life* (1891); *In Night and Ice* (1897); *Through Siberia* (1914); *Russia and Peace* (1923); etc.

To honor Nansen, the certificate provided by the "League of Nations Advisory Commission for Refugees" to White Russians and other persons who had lost their nationalities since World War I was named a *Nansen Passport.*

Nantes, Edict of. In 1598 Henry IV of France issued the Edict of Nantes in which he decreed qualified religious toleration and certain civil rights for the HUGUENOTS. This terminated the religious wars in France. Nearly a century later, in 1685, Louis XIV formally revoked the edict, declaring that all Protestant churches were to be destroyed and forbidding the Protestants to hold religious meetings, etc. The "Revocation of the Edict of Nantes" was followed by terrible persecutions and resulted in a mass exodus of French Huguenots, notably to England, Prussia, Switzerland, and the United States. In all these countries French names of prominent men and women often testify to the superior quality of the human material thus expelled by the "Sun King."

Naomi. In the Old Testament, the mother-in-law of RUTH.

Naphta, Leo. In Thomas Mann's THE MAGIC MOUNTAIN, a teacher of elementary Latin in the Davos school, near the sanatorium; also ill. He is a middle-class Austrian Jew who has become a convert to both the Roman Catholic Jesuit order and the revolutionary Socialism of Karl MARX. He is considered by some commentators to symbolize simultaneously within himself the principles of spiritualism and materialism, political revolution and reaction, and Catholicism, Communism, and Fascism. In the long debates he has with SETTEMBRINI, to whom he is an intellectual antithesis, he upholds mysticism and faith (as against empiricism and reason), philosophic absolutism, the doctrine of ORIGINAL SIN, and the principles of authority and discipline in political and intellectual organization.

Napier, John. Laird of **Merchiston** (1550–1617). Scottish mathematician, famous as the inventor of logarithms. *Mirifici Logarithmorum Canonis Descriptio* (1614).

Napoleon Bonaparte (1769–1821). Napoleon is introduced as a minor character in many of the historical romances that deal with the French Revolution and the period immediately following. He is prominent in Lever's TOM BURKE OF OURS and Conan Doyle's *Uncle Bernac,* and the central figure of Sardou's comedy MADAME SANS GÊNE and Shaw's MAN OF DESTINY.

the Napoleon of oratory. W. E. Gladstone (1809–1898) was so called.

the Napoleon of Peace. Louis Philippe (1773–1850), King of France.

the Little Napoleon. Napoleon III.

Naraka. The Hell of Hindu mythology. It has twenty-eight divisions, in some of which the victims are mangled by ravens and owls; in others they are doomed to swallow cakes boiling hot, or walk over burning sands. Each division has its name; *Rurava* (fearful) is for liars and false witnesses; *Rodha* (obstruction) for those who plunder a town, kill a cow, or strangle a man; *Sukara* (swine) for drunkards and stealers of gold; etc.

Narcissa. (1) In Young's NIGHT THOUGHTS, a reference to Elizabeth Lee, Dr. Young's step-daughter.

(2) In Pope's *Moral Essays, Narcissa* stands for the celebrated actress, Anne Oldfield (1683–1730). When she died her remains lay in state attended by two noblemen. She was buried in Westminster Abbey in a very fine Brussels lace head-dress, a holland shift, with a tucker and double-ruffles of the same lace, new kid gloves, etc.

> "Odious! In woolen? 'Twould a saint provoke!"
> Were the last words that poor Narcissa spoke.
> *Moral Essays,* i. 246.

In woolen is an allusion to a law enacted for the benefit of the wool-trade, that all shrouds were to be made of wool.

Narcisse. In G. W. Cable's DR. SEVIER, a Creole who wishes to be called Papillon, or Butterfly, because, says he gaily, "thass my natu'e. I gatheth honey eve'y day fum eve'y opening floweh, as the baod of Avon wemawked."

narcissism. See under COMPLEX.

Narcissus. The son of CEPHISUS in Greek mythology, a beautiful youth who saw his reflection in a fountain, and thought it the presiding nymph of the place. He gradually pined away for love of this unattainable spirit. According to one version he jumped into the fountain, where he died. The nymphs came to take up the body that they might pay it funeral honors, but found only a flower, which they called by his name. Narcissus was beloved by ECHO and his fate was a punishment from Nemesis for his cruel indifference to her passion.

Nardac. The highest title of honor in the realm of LILLIPUT in Swift's *Gulliver's Travels* (see GULLIVER, LEMUEL). Gulliver receives this distinction for carrying off the whole fleet of the Blefuscudians (see BLEFUSCU).

Narrenschiff. A satire of the late Middle Ages by Sebastian BRANDT, written in Swabian dialect, first published in 1494. It deals with the assembling of fools of all sorts from many countries and their transportation to the Land of Fools. It became very popular in Europe. Alexander BARCLAY translated it and adapted its theme in terms of the English life of his time under the title of *The Ship of Fools*, published in 1509.

Narváez, Pánfilo de (1480?–1528). Spanish soldier and adventurer. Sent to Mexico to arrest Cortes, who captured him and held him imprisoned for two years (1520–1522). Returned to Spain, he secured the governorship of Florida, from where he tried to reach Mexico with a fleet of small ships. Lost at sea in the Gulf of Mexico.

Nasby, Petroleum V. The pseudonym under which David Ross LOCKE published his humorous sketches. First created in 1861, the character of Nasby became immensely popular:

> A type of the backwoods preacher, reformer, workingman, postmaster and chronic office seeker, remarkable for his unswerving fidelity to the simple principles of personal and political selfishness. To him the luxuries of life are a place under the government, a glass of whisky, a clean shirt and a dollar bill. No writer ever achieved popularity more quickly. The letters were published in all the Northern papers. . . . and universally read by the Federal soldiers. —*Cambridge History of American Literature*, Ch. xix.

Nash, Beau. See under BEAU.

Nash, Ogden (1902–). American writer of light verse, known for his sophisticated whimsy and satire, dealing chiefly with the lives and interests of upper-middle-class residents of New York City and its environs. His verse, frequently published in THE NEW YORKER, is usually written in long, rambling, and ill-balanced couplets, with no attempt at meter and strained or over-simplified rhymes, in a burlesque of inferior "serious" poetry. Among his books are *Free Wheeling* (1931); *Hard Lines* (1931); *Happy Days* (1933); *The Primrose Path* (1935); *The Bad Parent's Garden of Verse* (1936); *I'm a Stranger Here Myself* (1938); *The Face Is Familiar* (1940); *Good Intentions* (1942).

Nash or Nashe, Thomas (1567–1601). English prose-writer and dramatist, known for his active participation in the various controversies—religious, literary, and political—of the Elizabethan period, in which he savagely attacked the Puritans, Gabriel HARVEY, and the abuses of the state. Nash's works include *Anatomy of Absurdities* (1589), attacking contemporary literature; *A Countercuff Given to Martin Junior* (1589), *The Return of the Renowned Cavaliero Pasquil of England* (1589), and *The First Part of Pasquils Apology* (1590), written under the pseudonym of "Pasquil" during the Martin MARPRELATE CONTROVERSY; *A Wonderful, Strange, and Miraculous Astrological Prognostication* (1591), defending Richard Harvey, an astrologer and brother of Gabriel; *Pierce Penniless His Supplication to the Devil* (1592); *Strange News of the Intercepting Certain Letters* (1593), attacking Gabriel Harvey, who is denounced further and satirized in *Have with You to Saffron-Walden* (1596); *Christ's Tears Over Jerusalem* (1593); *The Terrors of the Night* (1594); *The Unfortunate Traveler, Or The Life of Jack Wilton* (1594), a romance of adventure, regarded as an important precursor of the English novel; *The Isle of Dogs* (1597), a comedy which resulted in Nash's being imprisoned for a time for having attacked the state; *Lenten Stuff* (1599) and *Summer's Last Will* (1600), also plays. Nash was one of the "UNIVERSITY WITS" and an outstanding personality of his time.

Naso. The "surname" of OVID (Publius Ovidius Naso), the Roman poet, author of METAMORPHOSES. Naso means "nose"; hence HOLOFERNES' pun, "And why Naso, but for smelling out the odoriferous flowers of fancy." Shakespeare, *Love's Labor's Lost*, iv. 2.

Nason, Leonard Hastings (1895–). American novelist. Infantry sergeant in World War I in France; wounded twice; won Purple Heart and Silver Star. Author of entertaining stories of soldiers and sailors, as *Chevrons*

(1926); *The Top Kick* (1928); *Among the Trumpets* (1932); *Approach to Battle* (1941); etc.

Nasr-ed-Din. In Turkish legend, a famous jester, sometimes called the Turkish Tyl EULENSPIEGEL and like Eulenspiegel the reputed hero of many pranks which have been collected in a jest-book and attributed to him. He is said to have died about 1410.

Nasser. The Arabian merchant whose fables were the delight of the Arabs. D'Herbelot tells us that when Mohammed read them the Old Testament stories they cried out with one voice that Nasser's tales were the best; upon which the Prophet gave his malediction on Nasser, and all who read him.

Nast, Thomas (1840–1902). German-born American political cartoonist. On the staff of *Frank Leslie's Illustrated Newspaper* (1855–1859) and staff artist of *Harper's Weekly* (1862–1886). His slashing cartoons of Boss Tweed's Tammany Tiger ring (1869–1872) as vultures were largely responsible for the Ring's collapse. U.S. consul to Guayaquil, Ecuador (1902). He issued *Thomas Nast's Christmas Drawings for the Human Race* (1890). Cf. Allan Franklin's *The Trail of the Tiger: Being an Account of Tammany from 1789* (1928) for reproductions of some of the most effective of Nast's cartoons.

Nastasia. In Dostoyevsky's novel THE IDIOT, a beautiful and passionate girl in love with Prince MYSHKIN.

Nastrond. The worst place of torment in the ancient Scandinavian Hell, where serpents incessantly pour forth venom from the high walls, and where the murderer and the perjurer are doomed to live for ever. The word means, "the strand of the dead," *na,* a dead body, and *strond,* a strand.

Nat, Uncle. The central figure in Herne's drama SHORE ACRES.

Natchez, Les. A romance by CHATEAUBRIAND, written between 1797 and 1800 and based in part on the author's own experiences in America. The Frenchman René, hero of an earlier novel bearing his name, marries Celuta, a devoted Indian girl of the tribe of Natchez, by which René has been adopted after being driven by characteristic romantic disillusionment to seek escape among the American savages. Celuta is torn between love for her husband and traditional duty to her people when it appears that René has betrayed the tribe, although the true traitor is Ondouré. The novel ends tragically and violently for all concerned. See NOBLE SAVAGE.

Nathan. In the Old Testament (2 *Sam.* xii), a prophet who rebuked DAVID for his treachery toward URIAH by telling him the story of the rich man who took his poor neighbor's one ewe lamb, ending with the words, "Thou art the man."

Nathan, George Jean (1882–). Family name originally Naret. American author and literary and dramatic critic, associated with H. L. MENCKEN on the SMART SET (1908–1923) and co-founder with Mencken of THE AMERICAN MERCURY in 1924, acting as an editor until 1930. In the 1920's Nathan, a disciple of James HUNEKER, was virtually literary dictator of New York City, his essays and critical writings being marked by cynicism, an attitude of sophistication, a belief in "ART FOR ART'S SAKE," bitter and violent dislikes, and a variety of dilettante enthusiasms; he and Mencken constituted a pair of scornful commentators on the foibles of their day. Among his books are *Europe After 8:15* (1914), written in collaboration with Mencken and W. H. Wright; *Heliogabalus* (1920), a play, and *The American Credo* (1920), both written with Mencken; *The World in Falseface* (1923); *The Eternal Mystery* (1913); *Mr. George Jean Nathan Presents* (1917); *The Popular Theater* (1918); *The Theater, The Drama, The Girls* (1921); *Materia Critica* (1924); *The Autobiography of an Attitude* (1925); *The New American Credo* (1927); *Art of the Night* (1928); *Testament of a Critic* (1931); *The Avon Flows* (1937), a comedy combining portions of ROMEO AND JULIET, THE TAMING OF THE SHREW, and OTHELLO; *The Morning After the First Night* (1938); *The Bachelor Life* (1941); and a series of yearbooks of the drama. A number of his books are on the theater, and Nathan was among the first critics to see the worth of Eugene O'NEILL's plays.

Nathan, Raoul. An affected and eccentric dramatist who appears in several of the novels of Balzac's COMÉDIE HUMAINE. He indulges in numerous love affairs, notably one with Mme de Vandenesse.

Nathan, Robert (1894–). American author, known for his novelettes marked by whimsical, sentimental, or satirical fantasy. His works include *Peter Kindred* (1919); *Autumn* (1921); *Youth Grows Old* (1922), poems; *The Puppet Master* (1923); *Jonah* (1925), published in England as *The Son of Amittai,* a new version of the Biblical story of Jonah; *The Fiddler in Barly* (1926); *The Woodcutter's House* (1927); *The Bishop's Wife* (1928); *There Is Another Heaven* (1929); *A Cedar Box* (1929), poems; *One More Spring* (1933), presenting a solution for economic depression through Christian love; *Road of Ages* (1935), depicting Jews of all nations and classes in exile in the Gobi Desert; *Journey of Tapiola* (1938), dealing with the adventures of a dog, a rat, and a canary; *Win-*

ter in April (1938); *Portrait of Jennie* (1940), concerned with a painter and a little girl from another world; *They Went On Together* (1941), dealing with war refugees. A number of these were best-sellers, and several were filmed, notably *The Bishop's Wife*.

Nathan the Wise. A drama by Gotthold Ephraim LESSING (1779). The scene is laid in Jerusalem at the time of the Crusades. More important than the plot is the character of the trader, Nathan, a Jew, who has come to look upon all religions as forms of one great truth. A Christian knight woos his adopted daughter Recha, and when the matter is brought to the notice of the Mohammedan Sultan Saladin all three faiths come into the closest of contacts. Nathan's philosophy is aptly illustrated by his story of the father who, possessing one valuable ring and three sons, had two others made exactly like it, so that each son should receive an equal inheritance.

Nathan is said to have a prototype in Moses MENDELSSOHN.

Nathaniel. One of the twelve disciples, of whom Jesus said, "Behold an Israelite indeed in whom is no guile." He was also known as Bartholomew.

Nathaniel, Sir. In Shakespeare's LOVE'S LABOR'S LOST, the grotesque curate of Holofernes. Though grotesque, he is sharp, witty and sententious.

nation.

the nation of gentlemen. So George IV called the Scotch when, in 1822, he visited that country.

a nation of shopkeepers. This phrase, applied to Englishmen by Napoleon in contempt, comes from Adam Smith's *Wealth of Nations* (iv. 7), a book well known to the Emperor. He says—

> To found a great empire for the sole purpose of raising up a people of customers, may at first sight appear a project fit only for a nation of shopkeepers.

a nation of poets and thinkers. So BULWER LYTTON calls Germany in his introduction to ERNEST MALTRAVERS.

the battle of the nations. See under BATTLE.

the hermit nation. See HERMIT.

Nation, Carry Amelia (1846–1911). American temperance agitator, notorious for her wrecking expeditions throughout Kansas. Frequently arrested, fined, and even shot at, but never dismayed.

Nation, The. An American weekly magazine dealing with news, politics, literature, and the arts, founded in 1865 and known for its consistently liberal policies. In the 19th century it crusaded for reforms in the tariff and the civil service system and against corrupt politics, as those of Boss Tweed (see also Thomas NAST), in the 20th century, especially under the editorship of Oswald Garrison VILLARD (1918–1933), it was sympathetic toward the U.S.S.R., upheld Negro rights, civil liberties, and the American trade-union movement, supported the reforms of the NEW DEAL, and attacked FASCISM in Europe, continually warning of its symptoms in the U.S. During World War II, over the protests of Villard, then retired, it was one of the first liberal journals to come out for the entry of the U.S. into the war, although in the early 1930's it had opposed war. A number of leading American literary critics and authors of both the 19th and 20th centuries, as Mark and Carl van Doren, Ludwig Lewisohn, Joseph Wood Krutch, etc., were contributors to *The Nation*.

National Academy of Design. A society of painters, sculptors, and engravers, founded in 1828 in New York City. In 1906 it absorbed the Society of American Artists and affiliated itself with the Metropolitan Museum of Art and Columbia University. It awards annually various medals and prizes, exhibits the work of members, and offers free instruction in the arts.

National Academy of Sciences. Incorporated in 1863, with the approval of President Lincoln, to investigate, experiment and report on any subject within its field that the government or any department of the government should demand of it. It corresponds to the Royal Society in London, has 350 active members and 50 foreign associates.

national anthems. *The national anthems* or principal patriotic songs of the leading nations, either adopted by law or merely established by usage, are:

Austria: In the old Empire, *Gott erhalte Franz den Kaiser, Unsern guten Kaiser Franz* (God protect Franz the Kaiser, Our good Kaiser Franz); air by Haydn.

Belgium: The BRABANCONNE.

British Empire: God Save the King. Words and music have been attributed both to Dr. John Bull (d. 1628) and to Henry Carey, author of *Sally in Our Alley;* also RULE BRITANNIA.

Denmark: The Song of the Danebrog (see *Danebrog*); *Kong Christian stod ved höien Mast, Rög og Damp* (King Christian stood beside the lofty mast, In mist and smoke).

France: The MARSEILLAISE.

Germany: In the former German Empire, *Deutschland Über Alles* (*Germany Over All*), and *Die Wacht am Rhein* (*The Watch*—or *Guard—on the Rhine*).

Holland: Wien Neerlandsch bloed in de aders vloeit, Van vreemde smetten vrij . . . (Let him in whose veins flows the blood of the Netherlands, free from an alien's strain . . .)

Hungary: The Rakoczy March; *Tied*

vagyok, tied hazán! E siv e lélek! (Thine, I am, thine, my fatherland, heart and soul!).

Italy: Mercantini's *Italy has awaked; Si scopron le tombe, si levano i morti* (The tombs are opened, the dead are rising).

Norway: Ja, vi elsker det te Landet som det stiger frem (Yes, we love our country, just as it is).

Russia: In the days of the Empire, *God protect the Tsar;* the air by Lwoff is sung in England to—

> God the All-terrible King who ordainest,
> Great winds thy clarion, lightning thy sword.

Sweden: Du gamla du friska, du fjellhöga Nord, du tysta, du glädjerika skona! (Thou ancient, free, and mountainous North! Thou silent, joyous, and beautiful North!)

Switzerland: Rufst du, mein Vaterland. Sieh uns mit Herz und Hand, All dir geweiht! (Thou call'st, my Fatherland! Behold us, heart and hand, all devoted to thee!)

The United States: THE STAR-SPANGLED BANNER; AMERICA.

In *Wales* the chief patriotic song is *March of the Men of Harlech;* in *Scotland, Scots wha hae wi' Wallace bled!;* and in *Ireland, The Wearing o' the Green, A Nation Once Again,* or *Who Fears to Speak of 'Ninety-eight?*

National Gallery. The British national art gallery on Trafalgar Square, London, founded in 1824. At the beginning of World War II, it had more than 1,200 paintings by English and Continental masters.

National Gallery of Art. The United States national museum, opened in 1941. Its building is the largest building made of marble in the world. It cost fifteen million dollars and houses the collection of paintings given with the building by Andrew MELLON, one-time Secretary of the Treasury, which is worth fifty million dollars. Another collection included, the Kress collection, is worth thirty millions.

National Institute of Arts and Letters. The parent body of the American Academy of Arts and Letters (see under ACADEMY) from which the members of the latter are chosen.

National Union for Social Justice. See COUGHLIN, Father CHARLES E.

native son. An American political phrase for a native-born candidate for office, much used in California.

Native Son. A novel by Richard WRIGHT (1940), dramatized and produced in 1941. It deals with Bigger THOMAS, a Negro raised in the Black Belt slums of Chicago, who is confused and divided in his mind with regard to his attitude toward the society in which he lives, because of his environment and the race prejudice he encounters. He becomes a chauffeur in a wealthy family and is patronized by his employer's daughter, whom, in the throes of mental torture and confusion, he accidentally kills. He goes into hiding, pursued by the police and a mob, and, after murdering his own sweetheart, is finally captured and sentenced to death.

Natoma. An opera by Victor HERBERT (1911). Natoma, the heroine, is an Indian maiden, and the characters are Spanish, Indian and American. The scene is laid in the California of 1820.

Nattier, Jean Marc (1685–1766). French portrait painter who painted the portraits of the principal figures in the court of Peter the Great of Russia (from 1715).

Nat Turner's Insurrection. An insurrection of Negro slaves in Virginia (1831). Its leader, the Negro Nat Turner, believed himself chosen by God to free his people. Some sixty white people were killed. The leading insurrectionists were hanged.

Natty Bumppo, see BUMPPO, NATTY; also LEATHERSTOCKING.

naturalism. A movement in fiction in the 19th and 20th centuries, influenced by the new, mechanistic theories in biological and social science of the 19th century. It aims to portray human society and the lives of the men and women composing it as objectively and as "truthfully" as the subject-matter of science is studied and presented. Its chief characteristics are a selection of setting and subjects from the lower strata of society; an objective and detached method of narration on the part of the author; usually a large number of characters and a hero or heroine who represent the vices and weaknesses of a particular type or group, rather than the more conventional individual, and an idealized leading character involved in purely personal problems or adventures; a fullness and a meticulous accuracy of detail; scholarly care in documentation of the historical background; constant emphasis on the social environment of the characters and their subordinate relation to it; and a pervading, deterministic sense of the control over the actions and destinies of the characters exerted by impersonal social, economic, and biological forces, with the efforts of human free will shown as weak and ineffectual.

Naturalism arose in France, STENDHAL and BALZAC being considered important forerunners of the movement. Its chief leaders were FLAUBERT, the GONCOURT brothers, Alphonse DAUDET, MAUPASSANT, and—the most widely known, most characteristic, and most consciously naturalistic in his work—Émile ZOLA. In England, the novels of George GISSING, Thomas HARDY, and Samuel BUTLER (*The Way of All Flesh*) may be said to show certain affinities with naturalist writings. Somerset MAUGHAM'S LIZA OF LAMBETH is in the tradition of Zola, and James JOYCE's ULYSSES makes use of a number of the principles of naturalism. In the U.S., Stephen CRANE and Frank NORRIS were the first genuine naturalists, although Edgar Watson HOWE and Joseph KIRKLAND in their realistic works were native forerunners of the movement. Other Americans writing to a greater or less degree in the tradition of naturalism include Harold FREDERIC, Jack LONDON, Hamlin GARLAND, Edgar Lee MASTERS (*Spoon River Anthology*), Theodore DREISER, Sherwood ANDERSON, William FAULKNER, Erskine CALDWELL, John Dos PASSOS, and James T. FARRELL. Farrell's STUDS LONIGAN was the outstanding American naturalist novel of the 1930's, with Dos PASSOS' U.S.A. a runner-up. In Europe, the work of GORKY, NEXÖ (*Ditte*), and HAMSUN shows resemblances to naturalism in many respects.

Naturalism had an important influence on the technique of PROLETARIAN LITERATURE. See REALISM. See also DÎNERS MAGNY.

natural selection. Survival of the fittest. The principle that the evolution of species is the result of a constant selection of the fittest individual variants in the struggle for life in nature. It is the backbone of Charles Darwin's theory of evolution. Cf. *On the Origin of Species by Means of Natural Selection, or the Preservation of Favored Races in the Struggle for Life* (1859). Later evolutionists have qualified its importance.

Nature. The first and one of the best-known works of Ralph Waldo EMERSON (1836). According to the *Cambridge History of American Literature,* "appearing the same year the Club was formed [it] may be fittingly considered the philosophical 'constitution' of TRANSCENDENTALISM."

Natwick, Mildred (1911–). Young American actress who first made her reputation acting the part of elderly ladies, once even appearing as the mother of Dame Sybil Thorndike in *The Distaff Side*. One of the original University Players, at West Falmouth, Mass., with James Stewart, Henry Fonda, etc. Has given brilliant performances in Noel COWARD's *Blithe Spirit* and in several motion pictures.

Nausicaä. In Homer's ODYSSEY, daughter of Alcinous, King of the Phaeacians, who conducts ULYSSES to the court of her father when he is shipwrecked on the coast. See also MACDOWELL, GERTY.

Nausithous. In Homer's *Odyssey,* the king of the Phaeacians, who took his people away from the neighborhood of the savage CYCLOPES to the island of Scheria. He was succeeded by his son Alcinoüs, under whose realm ULYSSES stayed with the Phaeacians.

Navigation, the Father of. See under FATHER.

nawab. See RULERS, TITLES OF; also NABOB.

Naxos. The largest island of the Cyclades group in the Aegean Sea. It is celebrated for its wine and appears in legend as Bacchus' favorite island. It was here that THESEUS deserted Ariadne whom Bacchus found, consoled, and married. The island figures prominently in the account of Acetes, the Tyrrhenian mariner, who alone among his fellows did not conspire to abduct Bacchus to Egypt and subsequently became a Bacchanal on Naxos.

Nazareth. The village where Jesus lived as a boy and young man and where He learned the trade of a carpenter.

can any good thing come out of Nazareth? (*John* i. 46). A general insinuation against any family or place of ill repute. A native of Nazareth is called a *Nazarene.* There is also a fanatical American religious sect called Nazarenes.

Nazarite. One separated or set apart to the Lord by a vow. They refrained from strong drink, and allowed their hair to grow. (Heb. *nazar,* to separate. *Numb.* vi. 1–21.)

Nazhivin, Ivan Fedorovich (1874–). Russian novelist. For a while influenced by Tolstoi. Fled to France after the Russian Revolution (1917). Wrote *Rasputin* (1929); *The Dogs* (1931); *According to Thomas* (1931); etc.

Nazimova, Alla (1879–1945). Russian-American actress. Début, in St. Petersburg (1904), in New York (1906), in Ibsen's *Hedda Gabler.* Successful in other Ibsen plays, in Chekhov's CHERRY ORCHARD, O'Neill's MOURNING BECOMES ELECTRA, and also in moving pictures.

Neaera. A name used by HORACE, VIRGIL, and Tibullus as a synonym of "sweetheart."

> To sport with Amaryllis in the shade,
> Or with the tangles of Neaera's hair.
>
> Milton, *Lycidas.*

Neale, John Mason (1818–1866). English hymn writer; famous especially for *Jerusalem the Golden,* a translation of part of Bernard of Cluny's *De Contemptu Mundi.*

Neanderthal. A valley near Bonn, Germany, which gave its name to the Neanderthal Man, a type of prehistoric race of men, of whose skeleton a skull-cap and other bones were found there (1857). The Neanderthal Man indulged in the working of flints on one side only, known as the Mousterian industry, from Moustier in the Dordogne in France. The bones referred to were found in deposits of the Middle Pleistocene period. The Neanderthal Man is said to have come from northern Asia to Europe. He became extinct, and modern man is not his descendant.

Nearer, My God, to Thee. A hymn (1840) written by Sarah Flower Adams (1805–1848).

Nearing, Scott (1883–). American sociologist. Author of *Poverty and Riches* (1916); *Education in Soviet Russia* (1926); etc.

Nebo, Mount, modern **Jebel Neba.** A mountain near the north end of the Dead Sea. In the Old Testament God sent Moses "up to mount Nebo, to see the land, and die. . . . And Moses went up from the plains of Moab unto the mountain of Nebo, to the top of Pisgah, that is over against Jericho." Browning uses *Pisgah-Sights* as the title of a poem, in two parts, about a man viewing his whole life while in the article of death. Cecil Frances Alexander (1818–1895) wrote a poem, *The Burial of Moses,* beginning:

> By Nebo's lonely mountain,
> On this side Jordan's wave,
> In a vale in the land of Moab,
> There lies a lonely grave.

Nebuchadnezzar. The greatest king of Assyria. His reign lasted forty-three years (604–561 B. C.). He restored his country to its former prosperity and importance, practically rebuilt Babylon, restored the temple of Bel, erected a new palace, embanked the Euphrates and probably built the celebrated Hanging Gardens. In the Old Testament narrative he besieges Jerusalem, is victorious and carries the Jews away captive into Babylon. His name became the center of many legends, and the story related in *Daniel* (iv. 29–33) that he was one day walking in the palace of the kingdom of Babylon and said, "Is not this great Babylon that I have built . . . by the might of my power, and for the honor of my majesty?" And "the same hour . . . he was driven from men, and did eat grass as oxen, and his body was wet with the dew of heaven, till his hairs were grown like eagles' feathers, and his nails like birds' claws," is probably an allusion to the suspension of his interest in public affairs, which lasted, as his inscription records, for four years. Nebuchadnezzar was the king who, according to the account in *Daniel,* put the three Hebrews, Shadrach, Meshach and Abednego into the fiery furnace for refusing to bow down to a golden image.

Necessity of Atheism, On the. A pamphlet supporting atheism, written by Percy Bysshe SHELLEY in 1811 and circulated among his fellow-students at Oxford University; for this he was expelled.

Neckan, The. A ballad by Matthew ARNOLD in which a water-spirit of that name marries a human bride whom he carries to his deep-sea home. She soon regrets that Neckan is not a Christian knight, so he comes to earth to be baptized into the Christian faith. A priest says to him, "Sooner shall my staff bud than Neckan go to heaven." The words are scarcely uttered when the staff breaks into buds. "Ah!" says Neckan, "there is mercy everywhere except in the heart of a monk."

Necker, Suzanne, *née* **Curchod** (1739–1794). Wife of the French financier and statesman Jacques Necker (1732–1804), famous before and at the time of the French Revolution as hostess to political and literary leaders. Her daughter was Madame de STAËL.

necking. "Necking" and "petting" were terms that came into vogue among young people in the early 1920's, about the time of F. Scott FITZGERALD's *This Side of Paradise.* They referred to pocket-flask-stimulated caressing that went on in parked cars or dark rooms.

neck-verse. The first verse of *Ps.* li. See MISERERE. "Have mercy upon me, O God, according to Thy loving-kindness: according unto the multitude of Thy tender mercies blot out my transgressions."

> He [a treacherous Italian interpreter] by a fine cunny-catching corrupt translation, made us plainly to confesse, and cry *Miserere,* ere we had need of our necke-verse.—Nash, *The Unfortunate Traveller* (1594).

This verse was so called because it was the trial-verse of those who claimed BENEFIT OF CLERGY, and if they could read it, the ordinary of Newgate said, *"Legit ut clericus,"* and the prisoner *saved his neck,* being only burnt in the hand and set at liberty.

> If a clerk had been taken
> For stealing of bacon,
> For burglary, murder, or rape.
> If he could but rehearse
> (Well prompt) his neck-verse,
> He never could fail to escape.
> *British Apollo* (1710).

nectar (*Gr.*). The drink of the gods of classical mythology. Like their food, *ambrosia,* it conferred immortality.

Ned Bratts. Titular character of one of Robert Browning's *Dramatic Idyls,* in which the poet adapted an episode in John Bunyan's *The Life and Death of Mr. Badman* (1680).

Nedda. The heroine of Leoncavallo's opera I PAGLIACCI.

Ned McCobb's Daughter. An American comedy by Sidney HOWARD (1927).

Negri, Pola (1899–). Polish-born actress, starred in moving pictures in the U.S. (from 1923). First great success in *Passion,* concerning Mme DU BARRY.

Nehemiah. In the Old Testament, a Jew whom Artaxerxes, the Persian king, sent to assist with the rebuilding of Jerusalem after the Babylonian captivity; also the book of the Old Testament called by his name.

Nehru, Jawaharlal (1889–). English-educated Hindu leader, son of the Indian naionalist leader **Pundit Motilal Nehru** (1861–931). Joined Gandhi's movement in 1919. Secretary of National Congress (1929–1939). Second only to Gandhi in influence through-out India. Three times president of the Indian National Congress, succeeding Gandhi as eader of the National Congress Party (1942). Author of *The Unity of India* (collected speeches; 1937–1940). Prime Minister of the Dominion of India (1947–).

Neibelungenlied, see NIBELUNGENLIED.

Neihardt, John Gneisenau (1881–). American poet of Pennsylvania German de-scent. Professor of poetry, University of Ne-braska (from 1923); literary editor, St. Louis *Post-Dispatch* (from 1926). Chiefly known for his epic cycle of the West, five book-length narrative poems, *The Song of Hugh Glass* (1915); *The Song of Three Friends* (1919); *The Song of the Indian Wars* (1925); *The Song of the Messiah* (1936); *The Song of Jed Smith* (1941). They cover "the entire trans-Missouri country from 1882–1890." Neihardt was appointed Poet Laureate of Nebraska by he Nebraska legislature in 1921.

Neilson, William Allan (1869–1946). Professor of English, Harvard University (1906–1917). President, Smith College (1917–1939). Author of *Essentials of Poetry* (1912); *A History of English Literature* (1920). Edi-tor, *Complete Edition of Shakespeare's Works* (1906–1942). Editor-in-chief, Webster's *New International Dictionary,* Second Edition (1934).

Nekayah. In Samuel Johnson's RASSELAS, sister of Rasselas, Prince of Abyssinia.

Nekhludov. The hero of Tolstoi's novel RESURRECTION.

Nell, Little, see LITTLE NELL.

Nellie Bly. Pseudonym of Elizabeth C. SEAMAN.

Nellie the Beautiful Cloak Model. A melo-drama of the early 20th century by Owen DAVIS which, probably because of the obvious nature of its title, is frequently referred to as a type of the American melodramatic play.

Nell Trent, see LITTLE NELL.

Nelson, Horatio. Viscount **Nelson** (1758–1805). British naval hero. Won Battle of Tra-falgar (1805) during which he was fatally wounded. His friendship with Emma Lady Hamilton was the subject of numerous books and plays, notably *Lady Hamilton* by Alexan-dre DUMAS, *Divine Lady* by Mrs. L. Adams BECK, etc.

Nelson, John Byron, Jr. (1912–). American golf champion.

Nelson, Starr (1910–). American woman poet. Author of *Heavenly Body* (1942). Contributor of poems to *Saturday Review of Literature, Voices,* etc.

Neluska. A savage in Meyerbeer's opera L'AFRICAINE.

Nemean. Pertaining to Nemea, the an-cient name of a valley in Argolis, Greece, about ten miles southwest of Corinth.

the Nemean games. One of the four great national festivals of Greece, celebrated at Nemea every alternate year, the second and fourth of each Olympiad. Legend states that they were instituted in memory of Archemo-rus, who died from the bite of a serpent as the expedition of the Seven Against Thebes (see under SEVEN) was passing through the valley. The victor's reward was at first a crown of olive leaves, but subsequently a garland of ivy. Pindar has eleven odes in honor of victors.

the Nemean lion. A terrible lion which kept the people of the valley in constant alarm. The first of the twelve labors of HER-CULES was to slay it. He could make no im-pression on the beast with his club, so he caught it in his arms and squeezed it to death. Hercules ever after wore the skin as a mantle.

Nemesis. The Greek goddess who allotted to men their exact share of good or bad for-tune, and was responsible for seeing that every-one got his due and deserts; the personifica-tion of divine retribution. Hence, retributive justice generally, as *the Nemesis of nations,* the fate which, sooner or later, has overtaken every great nation of the ancient and modern world.

Nemo, Captain. The hero of *Twenty Thousand Leagues Under the Sea* by Jules VERNE (1870).

Nemo, Little. A character invented by the cartoonist Winsor McKay about 1905 in his fantastic colored Sunday newspaper cartoons of the adventures of *Little Nemo in Slum-berland,* with his vis-à-vis, the tough cigar-smoking character Flip. Nemo is a little boy who has wonderful dreams.

neo-classicism. The dominant literary con-vention of the late 17th century and the 18th century, especially in France and England, so called because the poets and critics writing in accordance with it believed they were reviving the virtues of the Roman and Greek classics, especially as exemplified in the works of VIR-GIL and HORACE. Its principles, in accordance with the emphasis on reason and law in the philosophy of the time, were clarity, ration-ality, moderation, dignity, "DECORUM," and loftiness of purpose. Preferred subjects were Greek and Roman mythology and history, and the favored forms were the epigram, the epic poem (modeled on the *Aeneid*), and the verse tragedy. In poetic technique, clarity, balance, symmetry, and order were required, epitomized in the heroic COUPLET. The use of the EPITHET and the popularity of the satire, both personal and social, were notable in England.

Neo-classicism reached its highest development in France, where its leaders were CORNEILLE, RACINE, BOILEAU (the critical arbiter of the age), and BOSSUET; BRUNETIÈRE and NISARD continued to uphold neo-classical standards in the 19th century. The outstanding representatives of neo-classicism in England were DRYDEN, POPE, and JOHNSON. Boileau's *L'Art poëtique* (1674) and Pope's *Essay on Criticism* (1711) are considered the best critical statements of neo-classicism. See also ANCIENTS AND MODERNS; ROMANTICISM.

Neolithic Age (from Gr. *neos,* "new," *lithos,* "a stone"). The later Stone Age of Europe, the earlier being called the Paleolithic (Gr. *palaios,* "ancient"). Stone implements of the Neolithic age are polished, more highly finished, and more various than those of the Paleolithic, and are found in kitchen-middens and tombs with the remains of recent and extinct animals, and sometimes with bronze implements. Neolithic man knew something of agriculture, kept domestic animals, used boats, and caught fish.

neon. A rare atmospheric gas discovered by Sir William RAMSAY (1898). It has been widely used in gas-discharge lamps for advertising signs. It has also proved important in the investigation of isotypes.

Neoplatonism. A philosophical system, founded by Plotinus of Alexandria (204–270), "the last of the great philosophers of antiquity." Early Christian theology took over a great deal of his philosophy, which was exceptionally free from worldliness. Plotinus believed in an eternal world of glory which is a world of thought and imagination. In Rome Plotinus once conceived the idea of making Plato's Republic a reality by building a new city, to be called Platonopolis, in the Campagna. His works were edited by his friend and disciple Porphyry in six divisions of nine books each, called the *Enneads.* Hypatia of Alexandria was one of the most famous exponents of Neoplatonism. Cf. Charles KINGSLEY's novel, *Hypatia.*

Neoptolemus or **Pyrrhus.** Son of ACHILLES; called *Pyrrhus* from his yellow hair, and *Neoptolemus* because he was a new soldier, or one that came late to the siege of Troy. According to Virgil, it was this youth who slew the aged PRIAM. He married Hermione, daughter of HELEN and Menelaus. On his return home he was murdered by ORESTES at Delphi.

neo-Thomism. A 20th-century movement in philosophy to revive the Aristotelian system of St. Thomas Aquinas (see under SAINTS), especially in metaphysics and aesthetics. Mortimer J. ADLER was a leader of the movement in the U.S. and Jacques MARITAIN in France. Neo-Thomists disagreed as to whether Aquinas' Roman Catholic theology should also be adopted.

Nepenthe or **Nepenthes** (Gr. *ne,* "not" *penthos,* "grief"). An Egyptian drug mentioned in the *Odyssey* (iv. 228) that was fabled to drive away care and make persons forget their woes. Polydamna, wife of Thonis, king of Egypt, gave it to Helen, daughter of Jove and Leda.

> Quaff, oh quaff this kind Nepenthe and forget thy lost Lenore.
>
> Poe, *The Raven.*

Nepenthe is the name given to the isle of Capri in SOUTH WIND, novel by Norman DOUGLAS.

Nephelidia. A poem by A. C. SWINBURNE (1880) in which the poet parodies his own peculiar mannerisms—alliteration, assonance, onomatopoeia, anapestic meter, etc. The title means *Cloudlets,* and the poem itself is purposefully reduced to a pattern of sound alone.

Nephelo-Coccygia. See CLOUD-CUCKOO-LAND.

Nephthys. An Egyptian goddess, sister and wife of Set. Both she and Set are associated with the ritual of the dead.

Nepomuk, St. John of (1340?–?1393) The patron saint of Bohemia. As confessor to the queen of King Wenceslaus IV he refused to reveal to the king what the queen had confessed, and the king caused him to be drowned in the river Moldau at Prague. Canonized in 1729.

nepotism. From Italian *nepote,* "nephew." Favoritism shown to relatives, especially as practiced by certain Popes. Alexander VI who bestowed special favors upon his children, is a well-known case in point. Cf. also *The Venetian Glass Nephew* by Elinor WYLIE.

Neptune. The Roman god of the sea, corresponding to the Greek POSEIDON, hence used allusively for the sea itself. Neptune is represented as an elderly man of stately mien bearded, carrying a trident, and sometimes astride a dolphin or a horse.

> . . . great Neptune with this threeforkt mace,
> That rules the Seas, and makes them rise or fall;
> His dewy lockes did drop with brine apace,
> Under his Diademe imperiall.
>
> Spenser, *Faërie Queene,* IV. xi. 11

Nereids. The sea-nymphs of Greek mythology, the fifty daughters of NEREUS and "grey-eyed" Doris. The best known are Amphitrite, Thetis, and Galatea.

Nereus. In classic mythology, father of the water nymphs, a very old prophetic god of great kindliness. The scalp, chin, and breast of Nereus were covered with seaweed instead of hair.

> By hoary Nereus' wrinkled look.
> Milton, *Comus*, 871.

Nerissa. In Shakespeare's MERCHANT OF VENICE, the clever confidential waiting-woman of Portia, the Venetian heiress. Nerissa is the counterfeit of her mistress with a fair share of the lady's elegance and wit. She marries Gratiano.

Nero. Any bloody-minded man, relentless tyrant, or evil-doer of extraordinary savagery; from the depraved and infamous Roman emperor, C. Claudius Nero (54–68 A. D.), who set fire to Rome to see, it is said, "what Troy looked like when it was in flames," and fiddled as he watched the conflagration. He is a prominent character in Sienkiewicz' *Quo Vadis*. Stephen PHILLIPS wrote a poetic drama entitled *Nero*.

Nero of the North. Christian II of Denmark (b. 1480, reigned 1534–1558, d. 1559).

Neroni, Signora Madeleine. In Trollope's *Barchester Towers* (see BARSETSHIRE), a vivid, unconventional coquette, a chronic invalid who from her couch, exercises a strange fascination over the entire prosaic world of Barchester.

Nerthus or **Hertha.** The name given by Tacitus to a German or Scandinavian goddess of fertility, or "Mother Earth," who was worshiped on an island. She roughly corresponds to the classical Cybele, and is probably confused with the Scandinavian god *Njorthr* or NIORD, the protector of sailors and fishermen. *Nerthus* and *Njorthr* alike mean "benefactor." SWINBURNE wrote a poem called *Hertha:*

> Before ever land was,
> Before ever the sea,
> Or soft hair of the grass,
> Or fair limbs of the tree,
> Or the flesh-coloured fruit of my branches,
> I was, and thy soul was in me.
> Swinburne, *Hertha.*

Nesbit, Edith (1858–1924). English novelist and poet, who wrote as "E. Nesbit." She and her husband, Hubert Bland, were FABIAN Socialists. Author of unique stories of magic for children, introducing such "curious and unheard of fairies" as the PSAMMEAD, the Phoenix, and the Mouldiwarp. *The Red House* (1903) is an adult novel.

Nessus, shirt of. A source of misfortune from which there is no escape; a fatal present. The legend is that HERCULES ordered Nessus (the centaur) to carry his wife Dejanira across a river. The centaur attempted to carry her off, and Hercules shot him with a poisoned arrow. Nessus, in revenge, gave Dejanira his tunic, deceitfully telling her that it would preserve her husband's love, and she gave it to her husband, who was devoured by the poison still remaining in it from his own arrow as soon as he put it on. He was at once taken with mortal pains; Dejanira hanged herself from remorse, and the hero threw himself on a funeral pile, and was borne away to Olympus by the gods. See also HARMONIA.

Nestor. In Greek legend, king of Pylos, in Greece; the oldest and most experienced of the chieftains who went to the siege of Troy. Hence the name is frequently applied as an epithet to the oldest and wisest man of a class or company. Samuel Rogers, for instance, who lived to be 92, was called *the Nestor of English poets.* Shakespeare introduces Nestor in TROILUS AND CRESSIDA.

Nestor of the chemical revolution. A term applied by Lavoisier to Dr. Black. (1728–1799.)

Nestor of Europe. Leopold, king of Belgium (b. 1790, reigned 1831–1865).

Nestorians. Followers of Nestorius, patriarch of Constantinople (428–431). He maintained that Christ had two distinct natures, and that Mary was the mother of His human nature, which was the mere shell or husk of the divine. The sect spread in India and the Far East, and remains of the Nestorian Christians, their inscriptions, etc., are still found in China, but the greater part of their churches were destroyed by Timur (see TAMBURLAINE) about 1400.

Nets to Catch the Wind. Title of the first publicly published book of poems by Elinor WYLIE (1921), taken from John Webster's (1580?–?1625) *The Devil's Law Case:*

> Vain the ambitions of kings
> Who seek by trophies and dead things
> To leave a living name behind.
> And weave but nets to catch the wind.

Neuha. Heroine of Byron's poem *The Island,* a native of one of the Society Islands. It was here that the mutineers of the H.M.S. *Bounty* landed. In the poem, when the vessel is sent to capture the mutineers, Neuha conducts her husband Torquil to a secret cave till all danger is over. "And Neuha led her Torquil by the hand" is quoted in PETER IBBETSON, by George DU MAURIER.

Neumann, Alfred (1895–). German novelist and dramatist. A "psychologist historian." Kleist prize in (1926) for *The Devil,* which gained for him an international audience. His play *The Patriot* (1928) was widely produced in Europe and America. *Another Caesar* (1934) and *Gaudy Empire* (1936) are parts of a historical trilogy of the nineteenth century. He lived in Florence, then in France.

Neumann, Robert (1897–). Austrian novelist. His first book, the novel *Flood* (1930), brought him immediate success. The novel *Mammon* (1932; in England, *The Poison Tree,* 1933), a superior study of the armament king Zaharoff, the oil magnate Deterding, etc., caused his books to be banned and burned in Germany. Fled to England.

Neuvillette, Christian de. The handsome but stupid lover of Roxane for whom Cyrano supplies the eloquence in Rostand's CYRANO DE BERGERAC.

never. There are numerous locutions to express this idea; as—

At the coming of the Coqueligrues (*Rabelais: Pantagruel*).
At the Latter Lammas.
On the Greek Calends.
In the reign of Queen Dick.
On St. Tib's Eve.
In a month of five Sundays.
When two Fridays or three Sundays come together.
When Dover and Calais meet.
When Dudman and Ramehead meet.
When the world grows honest.
When the Yellow River runs clear.

Never-Never Land. A sort of fairyland in Barrie's PETER PAN.

Never Too Late To Mend, It Is. A novel by Charles READE (1853), a study of the discovery of gold in Australia and the British convict system. The book is notable for the character of the Jew, Isaac Levi, one of the first serious attempts to portray the Jew in fiction in a favorable light.

Neville. One of the children in Virginia Woolf's THE WAVES, of a retiring, scholarly temperament, who grows up to be an Oxford don. He is paired with JINNY.

Neville, Miss. In Goldsmith's comedy SHE STOOPS TO CONQUER (1773), the friend and *confidante* of Miss HARDCASTLE, a handsome coquettish girl, destined by Mrs. Hardcastle for her son Tony LUMPKIN. But Tony does not care for her, and she dearly loves Mr. Hastings; so Hastings and Tony plot together to outwit madam, and of course win the day.

Neville, Richard. Earl of Warwick (1428–1471). Known as "the Kingmaker" in the Wars of the Roses. He is the subject of the novel *The Last of the Barons* (1843) by BULWER-LYTTON.

Nevins, Allan (1890–). Leading American historian. Editorial writer for New York *Evening Post* (1913–1923) and *Nation* (1913–1918); literary editor, New York *Sun* (1924–1925); etc. Editor, *American Social History Recorded by British Travellers* (1923). Professor of American history, Columbia University (from 1931). *Grover Cleveland: A Study in Courage* (Pulitzer prize; 1933); *Hamilton Fish: The Inner History of the Grant Administration* (Pulitzer prize; 1937); *The Life of John D. Rockefeller* (1940); etc.

Nevinson, Henry Woodd (1856–1941). English journalist and war-correspondent. His three-volume autobiography was condensed as *Fire of Life* (1935) by R. Ellis Roberts, with a preface by John Masefield who said, "No better autobiography has been written in English in the last hundred years . . . [Nevinson] can reflect that he has been a friend to every generous cause that has stirred men's hearts in his time."

New Arabian Nights. A volume of fantastic stories by R. L. STEVENSON (1882). Best-known is *The Suicide Club.*

Newbery, Clare Turlay (1903–). American artist, best known for her drawings of cats. *Mittens* (1936); *Babette* (1937); etc.

Newbery, John (1713–1767). English publisher of newspapers and children's books. Among the contributors to his newspapers were Goldsmith and Dr. Johnson. Goldsmith described him in *The Vicar of Wakefield.* The "Newbery Medal," established by Frederic Melcher, is awarded annually (since 1921) for the best children's book written by an American.

Newbolt, Sir Henry John (1862–1938). English poet. His book of verse, *Admirals All* (1897), contained the now famous poem "Drake's Drum," which drew praise from Robert Bridges. It was followed by *The Island Race* (1898); *The Sailing of the Long Ships* (1902); etc. Edited the *Monthly Review* (1900–1904) with such contributors as Sir Arthur Quiller-Couch, Alice Meynell, Roger Fry, Robert Bridges, W. B. Yeats, etc. His *The Year of Trafalgar* (1905) established him as a naval historian. Official Naval Historian (from 1923). A few of his poems that will live are *He Fell Among Thieves; The Fighting Teméraire; Waggon Hill; Commemoration.*

Newcastle, Margaret Cavendish, Duchess of, see CAVENDISH, MARGARET.

Newcomes, The. *Memoirs of a Most Respectable Family, Edited by Arthur Pendennis, Esq.* A novel by THACKERAY (1855). The plot is loose and complex, dealing with three generations of Newcomes. Chief in interest and one of the most famous characters of all fiction is the lovable Colonel Thomas Newcome, a man of simple, unworldly tastes and the utmost honor. The Colonel's son, Clive, an artist, is in love with his cousin, Ethel Newcome, who, however, desires a more ambitious marriage. In this project Ethel is urged on by her selfish, cold-blooded brother, Barnes Newcome, but his true character is revealed to her when his mistreated wife, Lady Clara, elopes with her quondam lover, Jack Belsize, then Lord Highgate. Clive, despairing of winning Ethel, marries Rosey Mackenzie, with whom he finds he is mismated. When his father, through a bank failure, loses their combined resources, the family live in poverty and the Colonel finally becomes a brother at the Grey Friars to escape the bad temper of Clive's mother-in-law, Mrs. Mackenzie. Rosey dies in the course of time and Clive, who has fallen heir to some money, marries Ethel.

New Deal. Popular and journalistic designation for the governmental program of President Franklin D. ROOSEVELT, established in 1933 to promote economic recovery and social and economic reform. It was derived from the title of a book by Stuart CHASE, *A New Deal* (1932), suggesting a type of liberal reform which could be instituted under the existing government of the U.S.; the phrase was first a campaign slogan of the Democratic Party in the presidential election of 1932, when Roosevelt was overwhelmingly chosen to replace Herbert HOOVER. The term *New Deal* was universally used in referring to the program, the President himself using it, and advocates and administrators of the various new reform policies were called *New Dealers.* See also HOPKINS, HARRY; WALLACE, HENRY A.

Among the agencies set up by the New Deal for the administration of its policies, widely known through the initial letters of their titles, were: AGRICULTURAL ADJUSTMENT ADMINISTRATION (A.A.A.); CIVILIAN CONSERVATION CORPS (C.C.C.); NATIONAL RECOVERY ADMINISTRATION (N.R.A.); TENNESSEE VALLEY AUTHORITY (T.V.A.); WORKS PROGRESS ADMINISTRATION (W.P.A.). Under the New Deal, the 18th Amendment was repealed (see PROHIBITION), the Supreme Court was liberalized, the unemployed were given assistance in the form of work and home "RELIEF," and legislation was passed benefiting the farmer and labor, recognizing trade unions, reducing the number of weekly working hours and setting a minimum on wages, providing for unemployment and old-age insurance, and initiating public control of water-power and electricity. Rearmament was also carried on, and American neutrality in time of war was favored, although with the beginning of World War II this provision was altered to permit assistance to the nations fighting the Axis powers. During World War II, especially after the entrance of the U.S. into the conflict, a number of war agencies with wide powers, similar in organization to the emergency agencies of the depression era, were set up, including: OFFICE OF PRODUCTION MANAGEMENT (O.P.M.), later WAR PRODUCTION BOARD (W.P.B.); OFFICE OF EMERGENCY MANAGEMENT (O.E.M.); OFFICE OF PRICE ADMINISTRATION (O.P.A.); OFFICE OF CIVILIAN DEFENSE (O.C.D.); BOARD OF ECONOMIC WARFARE (B.E.W.); OFFICE OF FACTS AND FIGURES (O.F.F.); OFFICE OF WAR INFORMATION (O.W.I.); etc.

Many conservatives of the 1930's regarded the New Deal as extremely radical. It is referred to in a number of works of fiction, as well as non-fiction, of the period.

Newdigate, Sir **Roger** (1719–1806). English antiquary. Founder of the Newdigate prize at Oxford (21 guineas) for English poetry.

New Directions. A LITTLE MAGAZINE in book form, a collection of American and European *avant-garde* verse, fiction, and criticism published annually, founded in 1936 under the editorship of James LAUGHLIN. It particularly featured surrealist writings (see SURREALISM) and published the work of the outstanding poets and authors of the time.

Newell, Peter Sheaf Hersey (1862–1924). American cartoonist and illustrator. Worked for *Harper's Weekly* and *Harper's Bazaar.* Did popular picture books, *Topsys and Turvys* (1894); *A Shadow Show* (1896); *Peter Newell's Pictures and Rhymes* (1894); *The Hole Book* (1908); *The Slant Book* (1910). Also illustrated John Kendrick BANGS, Frank R. STOCKTON, Guy Wetmore CARRYL, Lewis CARROLL, Carolyn WELLS, etc.

New England: Indian Summer. A work by Van Wyck BROOKS (1940), sequel to THE FLOWERING OF NEW ENGLAND. It gives an atmospheric and impressionistic picture of the authors and literary activity in New England in the years 1865–1915.

New England Nun, A. A short story by Mary E. Wilkins FREEMAN, contained in *A New England Nun, And Other Stories* (1891). It concerns Louisa Ellis and her fiancé Joe Dagget, who has been away for fourteen years of their fifteen-year engagement, acquiring a fortune in Australia. When he returns at last and the date of the wedding is set, Louisa is overcome with consternation at the thought of having to change the neat, orderly, spinsterish ways in which she has lived in peaceful solitude for fourteen years. When she discovers by accident that Joe has become fond of Lily Dyer, a younger woman who has acted as companion to his mother, with great relief she breaks the engagement and returns to her former existence, "like an uncloistered nun."

New England Primer, The. A series of quaint Biblical rhymes illustrated by wood cuts, used in early New England to teach children the alphabet and first processes of reading. The earliest edition was 1727.

New Found Land. A book of poems by Archibald MacLeish (1930). It contains fourteen poems, of which *You, Andrew Marvell* and *Not Marble, Not the Gilded Monuments* are among the best.

Newgate. *Newgate Gaol* was originally merely a few cells over the gate. The first great prison here was built in 1422, and the last in 1770–1783. For centuries it was the prison for London and for the County of Middlesex. It was demolished in 1902, and the Central Criminal Court (opened 1905) erected on its site. From its prominence, *Newgate* came to be applied as a general name for prisons.

the Newgate Calendar. A biographical record of the more notorious criminals confined at Newgate; begun in 1773 and continued at intervals for many years. The term is often used as a comprehensive expression embracing crime of every sort.

I also felt that I had committed every crime in the Newgate Calendar.—Dickens, *Our Mutual Friend,* Ch. xiv.

New Grub Street. A novel by George GISSING (1891), dealing in grimly realistic fashion with the struggles and compromises of the modern literary world. The hero is Edwin Reardon, a novelist whose valiant attempts to maintain the standards of his art in the face of financial pressure are opposed by an unsympathetic wife. In sharp contrast to Reardon is his friend Jasper Milvain, an essayist who adjusts himself easily to current materialistic ideals. In the background are poor scholars, authors and literary hacks of all sorts.

New Hampshire. Title poem of the first Pulitzer Prize volume of verse by Robert FROST (1923). In it he stated that, far from espousing any causes, he chose "to be a plain New Hampshire farmer." He won the Pulitzer prize twice again (1931 and 1937).

New Harmony. One of the various cooperative communities attempted in the U.S. in the 19th century, founded in Indiana by the Rappists (1814) and purchased by Robert OWEN (1825). Here Owen sought to put into practice his theories of communal ownership, but dissensions arose immediately. After ten secessions by ten different groups, the plan was abandoned in 1828. See also BROOK FARM; PANTISOCRACY.

New Home, Who'll Follow? Or Glimpses of Western Life, A. Title of a collection of sketches of the Michigan frontier (1839) written by Caroline Matilda Kirkland under the pen name of Mrs. Mary Clavers.

New Jerusalem. The paradise of Christians, in allusion to *Rev.* xxi.

Newland, Abraham, see ABRAHAM NEWLAND.

New Machiavelli, The. A novel by H. G. WELLS (1911) in the form of an autobiography written by Richard Remington. With an attractive, devoted wife and a brilliant political career before him, Remington leaves England to elope with Isabel Rivers, a "new woman" whose appeal he cannot resist.

Newman, Christopher. The hero of THE AMERICAN by Henry James.

Newman, Ernest (1868–). English music critic of *Manchester Guardian,* Sunday *Times,* etc. Author of *The Life of Richard Wagner* (4 vols.; 1933–1946); *A Musical Critic's Holiday* (1925); etc.

Newman, Frances (1888–1928). American novelist and short-story writer, encouraged by James Branch CABELL. Translator and editor, *The Short Story's Mutations: From Petronius to Paul Morand* (1924). Her first novel, *The Hard-Boiled Virgin* (1926), was banned in Boston. *Dead Lovers are Faithful Lovers* (1927) also caused a sensation. She went nearly blind and dictated her translation of *Tales by Jules Laforgue* (1928). She caught pneumonia and took her own life. She had great erudition and originality. Her letters were published in 1929.

Newman, John Henry (1801–1890). English churchman, lecturer, and author, famous as the leader of the OXFORD MOVEMENT. He took outstanding part in the theological controversies involved in the movement and in 1845, after resigning the position which he had held as Protestant vicar of St. Mary's, was converted to the Roman Catholic Church. In 1846 he was ordained a priest and in 1879 was made a cardinal. Throughout his career he continued to engage in bitter controversies especially with the Protestant clergyman and novelist Charles KINGSLEY and with the Catholic Cardinal Manning. His most famous work, *Apologia pro Vita Sua* (1864), a history of his intellectual development and conversion to Catholicism, was written to refute charges made against him by Kingsley. Among his other works, those in prose being marked by a clear, quiet, and smoothly flowing style, are *Loss and Gain* (1848), a partially autobiographical novel dealing with the Oxford Movement; a collection of religious lyrics published with hymns of other authors in *Lyra Apostolica* (1836); *Dream of Gerontius* (1865), a mystic religious poem; *Grammar of Assent* (1870), analyzing religious belief; *The Idea of a University Defined* (1873), a collection of lectures which had an important influence on later theories of liberal arts education. See also TRACTS FOR THE TIMES.

New Masses. See under MASSES.

New Model. The name given to the Parliamentary army organized (1645) in the English Civil War after the second battle of Newbury. Sir Thomas Fairfax was its head, and it was composed mostly of Puritans officered by Independents.

Newnes, Sir George (1851–1910). English magazine publisher, famous for founding the *Strand Magazine* (1891), in which appeared the first Sherlock Holmes stories by A. Conan DOYLE.

New Netherland. The early name of New York during the days when it was a Dutch colony.

Newnham College. A women's college opened at Cambridge, England, in 1876.

New Republic, The. An American weekly magazine "of opinion," founded in 1914 and known for its consistent liberal policies. It opposed ratification of the Treaty of Versailles at the close of World War I, was sympathetic toward the U.S.S.R., supported Negro rights, civil liberties, the American trade-union movement, and the reforms of the NEW DEAL, and opposed FASCISM. It also had a distinguished literary department, leading authors and critics of the 1920's and 1930's serving as contributors. Malcolm COWLEY and Stark YOUNG were among members of its editorial staff. Henry WALLACE, former vice-president of the U.S., was editor for a time. See also THE NATION.

New Republic, The. A satire on contemporary English society and ideas by William Hurrell MALLOCK (1877). In it many actual persons are disguised by other names, among them Ruskin, Jowett, Arnold, Pater, Huxley, Tyndall, etc.

Newsome, Chad. In Henry James' AMBASSADORS, the son whose lengthy sojourn in Paris caused his mother to send over Lambert Strether as an "ambassador" to bring about his return.

newsreel. In John Dos Passos' U.S.A., a device by which the rapidly changing events in the historical background of the novel are portrayed. It consists of newspaper headlines, advertising slogans, snatches of popular songs, excerpts from speeches, etc., selected to give a quick, impressionistic view of the particular period of time being presented at the moment, and inserted at appropriate locations in the text. See also CAMERA EYE.

Newton, Alfred Edward (1863–1940). Famous American bibliophile. Author of *The Amenities of Book-Collecting and Kindred Affections* (1918); etc. Authority on Dr. JOHNSON, whose silver tea-pot he owned, and first American president of the Johnson Society of Great Britain. His extensive library was sold at auction.

Newton and the Apple. See under APPLE.

New Way to Pay Old Debts. A drama by Philip MASSINGER (1633). Wellborn, the nephew of Sir Giles Overreach, having run through his fortune and gotten into debt, induces Lady Allworth, out of respect and gratitude to his father, to show him favor. This induces Sir Giles to suppose that his nephew is about to marry the wealthy dowager. Feeling convinced that he will then be able to swindle him of all the dowager's property, as he once ousted him out of his paternal estates, Sir Giles pays his nephew's debts, and supplies him liberally with ready money, to bring about the marriage as soon as possible. After he has paid Wellborn's debts, the overreaching old man is compelled, through the treachery of his clerk, to restore the estates also, for the deeds of conveyance are found to be only blank sheets of parchment, the writing having been erased by some chemical acids.

New Yorker, The. An American weekly magazine of comment, fiction, and light verse, founded in 1925 and noted for its whimsical, satirical, and sophisticated humor, of greater subtlety and originality than that current at the time of its first appearance. Although designed primarily to appeal to upper middle-class residents of Manhattan and the metropolitan area and to aspirants to that category, *The New Yorker* became known throughout the U.S. Among its features are book, theater, screen, art, and music reviews; discussions of fashion, sports, and places of entertainment; "The Talk of the Town" and "Notes and Comment," consisting of anecdotes and whimsical comment in the manner of a newspaper "COLUMN"; "Profiles," biographical sketches, chiefly of unusual or little-known personalities of the day; humorous drawings with single-line or no captions; and examples of unconscious humor selected from current books, magazine articles, and newspaper stories, recalling the "AMERICANA" department of Mencken's *American Mercury*. Particularly outstanding is the brief fictional sketch, popularized and standardized by *The New Yorker* and considered to derive ultimately from CHEKHOV through James JOYCE and Katherine MANSFIELD, in which the character or personal drama of an individual, who is often petty and vicious or pathetic and commonplace, is implied through an ordinary incident in his life. Leading American short-story writers and poets appearing in *The New Yorker,* many of them regularly, have included Ogden NASH, E. B. WHITE, Dorothy PARKER, Elinor WYLIE, Conrad AIKEN, Kenneth FEARING, Horace GREGORY, Sally BENSON, Cornelia Otis SKINNER, Robert BENCHLEY, James THURBER, Ruth MCKENNEY, Clarence DAY, Arthur KOBER, Irwin SHAW, James M. CAIN, John CHEEVER, John M. COATES, Kay BOYLE, Nancy HALE. Among its artists have been Peter Arno, O. Soglow, William Steig, Helen Hokinson, Rea Irvin, and James Thurber. Anthologies of drawings, verse, short stories, and "Profiles" have been made from material published in *The New Yorker,* as well as collections of the work of individual authors.

New York Idea, The. A comedy by Langdon Mitchell (*Am.,* 1906), the theme of which is expressed in the sentence, "Marry for whim and leave the rest to the divorce court—that's the New York idea of marriage." Cynthia Karslake, the heroine, finally gives up her second husband to return to her first.

New York Public Library. Founded by the consolidation of the Astor, Lenox and other libraries (1895). The New York Public Library Building at Fifth Avenue and 42nd Street is noted for its guardian lions (of a supercilious cast of countenance). The library has over three million volumes available to the public through an amazingly efficient call system. Numerous local branches.

New York University. Privately endowed, co-educational, non-sectarian. Chartered in 1831. Its sites are on Washington Heights (where the HALL OF FAME is located) and on Washington Square. Its enrollment in 1946–1947 was 59,466, the combined faculties numbering 3,200. It has extension courses and a summer school.

Nexö, Martin Andersen (1869–). Danish proletarian novelist, known for his dramatic and understanding portrayals of working-class life in his own country. His best-known works are PELLE THE CONQUEROR (1906–1910), divided into *Boyhood, Apprenticeship, The Great Struggle,* and *Daybreak;* and *Ditte* (1920), the story of a poor and suffering servant-girl. Other books are *Days in the Sun* (1929), an account of travels in Andalusia; *In God's Land* (1929); and *Under the Open Sky: My Early Years* (1938), an autobiography.

Nexö lived in the slum sections of Copenhagen as a boy, later working as a herd-boy and a shoemaker's apprentice among the people with whose lives his novels deal. He was associated in his later career with international literary organizations of Communist sponsorship, and is considered one of the outstanding proletarian novelists of the first half of the 20th century. See PROLETARIAN LITERATURE.

Ney, Michel (1769–1815). Famous marshal of Napoleon. Although created peer by Louis XVIII, he supported Napoleon after his return from Elba and commanded the Old Guard at Waterloo (June 18, 1815). After the Hundred Days he was condemned for treason and shot (December 7, 1815).

Niafer. In Cabell's FIGURES OF EARTH, the wife of Manuel. When Manuel and Niafer are lovers newly met, Grandfather Death demands one of them, and Manuel lets Niafer go. Afterwards he serves Misery in the shape of a human head made of clay for a term of years to win her back.

Nibelungenlied, The. A Middle High German poem, the greatest monument of early German literature, founded on old Scandinavian legends contained in the VOLSUNGA SAGA and the EDDA, and written in its present form by an anonymous South German of the early part of the 13th century.

Nibelung is a mythical king of a race of Scandinavian dwarfs dwelling in *Nibelheim* (i.e., the home of darkness, or mist). See NIFLHEIM. These *Nibelungs,* or *Nibelungers,* are the possessors of the wonderful "Hoard" of gold and precious stones guarded by the dwarf ALBERICH; their name passes to later holders of the Hoard, Siegfried's following and the Burgundians being in turn called the *Nibelungs.*

SIEGFRIED the hero of the first part of the poem, becomes possessed of the Hoard, and gives it to KRIEMHILD as her marriage portion. After his murder Kriemhild carries it to Worms, where it is seized by HAGEN and GUNTHER. They bury it in the Rhine, intending later to enjoy it, but they are both slain for refusing to reveal its whereabouts, and the Hoard remains for ever in the keeping of the Rhine Maidens.

The first part of the *Nibelungenlied* relates the marriage of Gunther, king of Burgundy, with BRUNHILD; the marriage of Siegfried with Kriemhild, his murder by Hagen, the removal of the "Nibelungen Hoard" to Burgundy, and its seizure and burial in the Rhine by Gunther and Hagen. It contains nineteen lays, divided into 1188 four-line stanzas. The second part tells of the marriage of the widow Kriemhild with King ETZEL (Attila), the visit of the Burgundians to the court of the Hunnish king, and the death of all the principal characters, including Gunther, Hagen, and Kriemhild. This part contains twenty lays.

The Scandinavian version of the legend, the VOLSUNGA SAGA, gives the same story with variations in name and detail. For Wagner's use of this legendary material in his operas, see DER RING DES NIBELUNGEN.

Nibelungenring, Der, see RING DES NIBELUNGEN.

Niblo's Garden. A New York theater, opened as the *Sans Souci* in 1828 at Broadway and Prince Street by the restaurant owner and impresario William Niblo. For 60 years the testing ground of almost all the best actors on the American stage. It first produced the extravaganza *The Black Crook.*

Nicander (fl. 2nd century B.C.). Greek poet and grammarian.

Nicander, Karl August (1799–1839). Swedish poet. Won Swedish Academy award (1827). Made translations of SCHILLER; etc.

Nicene Creed. The creed formulated by the Council of Nicaea (325 A.D.) on the basis of older wordings, specially designed to combat the heresy of Arianus. The modern creeds of the Eastern, Roman, and Anglican Churches are variants of it.

Nice Wanton, A Pretty Interlude Called. An INTERLUDE of the Elizabethan period, published in 1560. It is didactic and allegorical in nature, dealing with education, and is thought to have been modeled on the Dutch moral playlet *Acolastus,* by Gnapaeus, which was performed in Latin in 1528 and translated into English in 1540 by John PALSGRAVE. It presents Nice Wanton, a silly, pampered child who easily falls into temptation and meets a tragic fate. Then the audience is shown in contrast the child of disciplined upbringing and careful education, who spends his time with his books and never once yields to sin. Didactic interludes of this type were often performed for the direct edification of the students in schools such as ETON.

Nic Frog. See NICKNAMES OF NATIONALITIES.

Nicholas. One of the three principal characters of THE MILLER'S TALE, one of Chaucer's CANTERBURY TALES, a poor scholar, who boards with John, a rich old miserly carpenter. The poor scholar falls in love with Alison, his landlord's young wife, who joins him in duping the foolish old man. Nicholas tells John that such a rain would fall on the ensuing Monday as would drown everyone in "less than an hour"; and he persuades the old fool to provide three large tubs, one for himself, one for his wife, and the other for his lodger. In these tubs, says Nicholas, they will be saved; and when the flood abates, they will then be lords and masters of the whole earth. A few hours before the time of the "flood," the old carpenter goes to the top chamber of his house to repeat his *pater nosters.* He falls asleep over his prayers, and is roused by the cry of "Water! water! Help! help!" Supposing the rain had come, he jumps into his tub, and is let down by Nicholas and Alison into the street. A crowd soon gathers, and the people are delighted at the joke and pronounce the old man an idiot and fool.

Nicholas, St., see under SAINTS.

Nicholas Nickleby. The title and chief character of a novel by Charles DICKENS (1838–1839). Nicholas Nickleby is the son of a poor country gentleman, and has to make his own way in the world. He first goes as usher to Mr. SQUEERS, schoolmaster at Dotheboys Hall, in Yorkshire, but leaves in disgust with the tyranny of Squeers and his wife, especially to a poor boy named SMIKE. Smike runs away from the school to follow Nicholas, and remains his humble follower till death. At Portsmouth, Nicholas joins the theatrical company of Mr. CRUMMLES, but leaves the profession for other adventures. He falls in with the brothers CHEERYBLE, who make him their clerk; in this post he rises to success as a merchant, and ultimately marries Madeline BRAY. See also NICKLEBY; NOGGS, NEWMAN.

Nicholas of Cusa (1401–1464). Roman Catholic cardinal and philosopher, born in Cusa, the modern Kues near Trier, Germany, who anticipated Copernicus by holding that the earth revolved about the sun.

Nichols, Anne. American dramatist, whose *Abie's Irish Rose* established a new performance record, running in New York continuously from 1922 to 1927.

Nichols, Robert Malise Bowyer (1893–1944). English poet and dramatist. Held chair of English Literature at the Imperial University of Tokyo, Japan (1921–1924). He once said that a study of Goethe changed his whole development as a man and an artist. He was in opposition to recent theory and practice of poetry in England and the United States. His best-known poems are in *Ardours and Endurances* (1917). His best-known play (with Maurice Browne) is *Wings Over Europe* (1929), in which a youthful scientist, Francis Lightfoot, discovers how to harness atomic energy.

Nicholson, Kenyon (1894–). American playwright. After spending one summer with upper New York State carnivals, wrote *The Barker* (1927) which featured Claudette Colbert and was a hit. His *Sailor Beware* (1933; with Charles Robinson) sold to the moving pictures for $80,000, and was made into a musical comedy, *Nice Goin'* (1939). Associated with the Bucks County Playhouse, New Hope, Pa.

Nicholson, Meredith (1866–1947). Famous Hoosier novelist. He wrote *The Hoosiers* (1900) for the National Studies in American Letters Series. His novels, *The House of a Thousand Candles* (1905) and *Rosalind at Red Gate* (1907) were dramatized by George MIDDLETON. Envoy extraordinary and minister plenipotentiary to Nicaragua (1938–1941).

Nicholson, Sir **William** (1872–). English painter and wood engraver. With James Pryde, his brother-in-law, designed well-known posters signed "Beggarstaff Brothers."

Nicias. A comic character in Machiavelli's comedy *La Mandragola* (*The Mandrake*) whom MACAULAY considered superior to any of the great comic characters of MOLIÈRE.

Nick.

Nick, the Bear. A nickname given to Russia by the English PUNCH.

Old Nick. The Devil. The term was in use in the 17th century, and is perhaps connected with the German *Nickel,* a goblin.

Nick Carter, see CARTER, NICK.

Nick of the Woods. A historical novel by Robert Montgomery BIRD (*Am.,* 1837) dealing with the Kentucky frontier of 1782. It presents the white man who has sworn vengeance as only less bloodthirsty than the ferocious Indians. Bird wished to protest against Cooper's idealization of the American Indian as portrayed in UNCAS.

nicker or nix. In Scandinavian folklore, a water-wraith, or kelpie, inhabiting sea, lake, river, and waterfall. They are sometimes represented as half-child, half-horse, the hoofs being reversed, and sometimes as old men sitting on rocks wringing the water from their hair. The female nicker is a *nixy.*

> Another tribe of water-fairies are the Nixies, who frequently assume the appearance of beautiful maidens.—Dyer, *Folk-lore of Plants,* ch. vii.

Nickleby, Nicholas. See NICHOLAS NICKLEBY.

Mrs. Nickleby. Mother of Nicholas, and a widow. She is an enormous talker, fond of telling long stories with no connection. Mrs. Nickleby is a weak, vain woman, who imagines an idiot neighbor is in love with her because he tosses cabbages and other articles over the garden wall.

> "The original of 'Mrs. Nickleby,'" says John Forster "was the mother of Charles Dickens."—*Life of Dickens,* iii. 8.

Kate Nickleby. Sister of Nicholas; beautiful, pure-minded, and loving. Kate works hard to assist in the expenses of housekeeping, but shuns every attempt of Ralph and others to allure her from the path of virgin innocence. She ultimately marries Frank, the nephew of the CHEERYBLE brothers.

Ralph Nickleby, of Golden Square (London). Uncle to Nicholas and Kate, a hard, grasping money-broker, with no ambition but the love of saving, no spirit beyond the thirst of gold, and no principle except that of fleecing everyone who comes into his power. This villain is the father of SMIKE, and ultimately hangs himself, because he loses money, and sees his schemes one after another burst into thin air.

nicknames of nationalities. Humorous personifications of nations and individual nationals in common use are *Antonio* or *Tony* (Italian); *Brother Jonathan* or *Uncle Sam* (American); *Colin Tampon* (Swiss); *Jean* or *Johnny Crapaud, Jacques Bonhomme* or *Robert Macaire* (French); *Cousin Michael, Michel* or *Fritz* (German); *Ivan Ivanovitch* (Russian); *Jean Baptiste* (Canadian); *John Bull* (English); *Mynheer Closh* or *Nic Frog* (Dutch); *Paddy* (m.), *Biddy* (f.) (Irish); *Sawney* (Scot); etc., etc.

Nickneven. A gigantic malignant hag of Scotch superstition. William DUNBAR has well described this spirit in his *Flyting of Dunbar and Kennedy.*

Nicodemus. In the New Testament (*John* iii. 1, 2), a Pharisee who came to visit Jesus by night. After the crucifixion he brought myrrh and aloes and helped JOSEPH OF ARIMATHAEA with the burial.

Nicodemused into nothing. To have one's prospects in life ruined by a silly name; according to the proverb, "Give a dog a bad name and hang him." It is from Sterne's TRISTRAM SHANDY (vol. i. 19):

> How many Caesars and Pompeys . . . by mere inspiration of the names have been rendered worthy of them; and how many . . . might have done . . . well in the world . . . had they not been Nicodemused into nothing.

Nicolay, John George (1832–1901). German-born private secretary to Abraham Lincoln (1860–1865). Collaborator with John Hay in a Lincoln biography (1890) and in the edition of Lincoln's complete works.

Nicoll, Allardyce (1894–). English writer on the theatre, who succeeded George Pierce BAKER in the Harkness School of the Drama at Yale University. *A History of Restoration Drama* (1923), etc.

Nicolle, Charles Jean Henri (1866–1936). French physician and bacteriologist. Nobel prize for physiology and medicine (1928).

Nicolls, Mary Ellen. Daughter of Thomas Love PEACOCK and first wife of George MEREDITH. She was temperamental, and after ten years of disagreements and quarrels she and Meredith separated. His poetic sequence MODERN LOVE is said to deal with their unfortunate marital experience.

Nicolson, Harold George (1886–). Well-known English biographer who married Victoria SACKVILLE-WEST. A cosmopolitan, he has held various posts in the diplomatic service. Was on staffs of *Evening Standard, Daily Express,* and, as a columnist, *Spectator.* Member of Parliament for National Labour Party. A brilliant but hard-working biographer. *Tennyson* (1923); *Curzon: The Last Phase* (1934); *Dwight Morrow* (1935); *Peacemaking 1919,* (1939); etc.

Niddhögge. The monster serpent of Scandinavian mythology. He lies hid in Niflheim and for ever gnaws the roots of YGGDRASIL, and sucks the corpses of the dead.

Niebuhr, Reinhold (1892–). Professor of applied Christianity at Union Theological Seminary (from 1930). Son of a German-born Evangelical minister. His Gifford Lectures at the University of Edinburgh (1939) were published in book form as *The Nature and Destiny of Man* (1941–1943). Cf. also *Discerning the Signs of the Times* (1946).

Nielsen, Kay (1886–). Danish artist and illustrator living in California. He first illustrated a book of Old French Fairy Tales in 1913. In 1915 appeared his illustrations for *East of the Sun and West of the Moon.* In 1917 he put on a big stage production of the story of Aladdin in Copenhagen. In Hollywood he did the scenic production of *Everyman.*

Niemöller, Martin (1892–). Famous anti-Nazi Protestant minister. Became leader (1933) of opposition to state control of Lutheran Church. Imprisoned in concentration camp (1937). Had been submarine officer in World War I.

Nietzsche, Friedrich Wilhelm (1844–1900). German philosopher and poet. The uncompromising rigor of his ideal conception of man made him despise the rabble, defy Christianity, and postulate the demand for self-education and the training of a race of "supermen." His best-known work is *Also Sprach Zarathustra* (1883 ff.). His influence on the language as well as on the thought of German philosophers and poets of subsequent generations has been marked.

Nieuport, Édouard (1875–1911). French aviator and airplane builder. His biplanes were much used in World War I.

Niflheim. Literally, "mist-home." The region of endless cold and everlasting night of Scandinavian mythology, ruled over by HELA. It consisted of nine worlds, to which were consigned those who die of disease or old age. It existed "from the beginning" in the North, and in its middle was the well Hvergelmir, from which flowed twelve rivers.

Nigel, see FORTUNES OF NIGEL; SIR NIGEL.

Nigger, The. A drama by Edward SHELDON (1909). The hero, Philip Morrow, a proud, ambitious young Southerner with all the prejudices of his caste, learns that he has Negro blood in his own veins.

Nigger Heaven. A novel of Negro life in Harlem by Carl VAN VECHTEN (1926).

Nigger of the Narcissus, The. A sea story by Joseph CONRAD (1898), the tale of a long voyage from Bombay to London. James Wait, "the Nigger of the Narcissus," is dying of tuberculosis, and the violent emotions of this big St. Kitts Negro, who is in terror and revolt over his fate, react upon the entire crew. The Cockney Donkin takes advantage of the situation to stir up feeling against the officers of the ship. There is more atmosphere than plot in this tale.

Night At An Inn, A. A one-act drama of the supernatural by Lord DUNSANY (1916).

Night Before Christmas, The. The popular title by which Clement Clarke Moore's poem, *A Visit from St. Nicholas,* is known. It was published in 1823. For a quotation from this poem, see SANTA CLAUS.

nightingale. For the classic legend, see PHILOMELA. There is a passage in T. S. Eliot's *The Wasteland* which confuses the nightingale with the nightjar:

> . . . yet there the nightingale
> Filled all the desert with inviolable voice
> And still she cried, and still the world pursues,
> "Jug Jug" to dirty ears.

This is unfair. No nightingale ever cried "Jug Jug." The goatsucker does and *nightjar* is another name for it, not *nightingale.*

the Italian nightingale. Angelica Catalani (1782–1842).

the Swedish nightingale. The great operatic singer Jenny LIND (1821–1886). She was a native of Stockholm.

Nightingale, Florence (1820–1910). English nurse and hospital reformer, known as "The Lady with the Lamp." Organized nurses and hospitals in Crimean War and founded institution for training nurses (1860); first woman to receive Order of Merit (1907).

Nightmare Abbey. A novel by Thomas Love PEACOCK (1818), satirizing the leading figures and concepts of ROMANTICISM in England in the author's day. Among the characters, *Mr. Flosky* is considered to represent S. T. Coleridge, *Mr. Cypress,* Lord Byron, and *Scythrop Glowry,* Shelley.

nightmare of Europe. Napoleon Bonaparte (b. 1769, reigned 1804–1814, d. 1821).

Night Must Fall. A melodrama (1936) by the English writer and actor Emlyn WILLIAMS.

Night Over Taos. A three-act play in free verse by Maxwell ANDERSON (1932). The theme is a clash of American frontiersmen with the Mexican patriarchate of Taos in 1847.

Night Thoughts on Life, Death and Immortality. A famous poem by Edward YOUNG, written in nine books in blank verse and published in 1742–1745. Its full title reads *The Complaint; or, Night-Thoughts on Life, Death and Immortality,* but the poem is commonly referred to simply as *Night Thoughts.* It presents the reflections of the poet late at night on "life, death, and immortality," a long soliloquy urging one Lorenzo to turn to virtue, and a vision of the Judgment Day and eternity thereafter, with a description of the magnificence of the starry heavens. The poem, which is said to contain several autobiographical allusions, was very popular in its day. It is one of the outstanding examples of the melancholy "GRAVEYARD SCHOOL" in 18th-century English literature. See also NARCISSA.

Nightwood. A novel by Djuna BARNES (1937). Republished in New Classics Series (1946) with an introduction by T. S. Eliot, in which he says, "To say that *Nightwood* will appeal primarily to readers of poetry does not mean that it is not a novel, but that it is so good a novel that only sensibilities trained on poetry can wholly appreciate it."

Nihilism (from Lat., *nihil,* "nothing"). An extreme form of 19th-century revolutionism, indignantly disclaimed by Karl MARX, which took form in Russia in the 1850's, and was specially active in the 1870's and later, under Bakunin. It aimed at anarchy and the complete overthrow of law, order, and all existing institutions, with the idea of re-forming the world *de novo.* The following was the code of the Nihilists: (1) annihilate the idea of a God, or there can be no freedom; (2) annihilate the idea of right, which is only might; (3) annihilate civilization, property, marriage, morality, and justice; (4) let your own happiness be your only law.

The name was given to them by the novelist Turgenev in his FATHERS AND SONS. Dostoyevsky portrays Nihilism in THE POSSESSED and THE BROTHERS KARAMAZOV.

Nijinsky, Waslav (1890–). Polish-born Russian dancer. Début in Imperial Ballet, St. Petersburg (1907); début in Paris (1909) with Diaghilev's Ballet Russe. Particularly well-known for his dancing in *L'Après-midi d'un faune; Schéhérazade; Spectre de la rose;* etc. Later insane and confined in an asylum.

Niké of Samothrace, see WINGED VICTORY.

Nikitin, Ivan Savvich (1824–1861). Russian lyric poet, well-known for his poem *The Volga Boatman.*

Nile. The Egyptians used to say that the swelling of the Nile was caused by the tears of ISIS. The feast of Isis was celebrated at the anniversary of the death of OSIRIS, when Isis was supposed to mourn for her husband.

The **Battle of the Nile** was fought in Abukir Bay, near Alexandria, Egypt (August 1, 1798). The British fleet under Nelson defeated the French fleet under Brueys. It caused the failure of Napoleon's expedition to Egypt. Nelson earned for himself the epithet of "the hero of the Nile."

Niles, Mrs. **Blair,** *née* **Rice.** American novelist and travel writer. First married to William BEEBE, with whom she went on many expeditions. After their divorce she married the architect Robert Niles, an explorer and photographer by avocation. On a trip with him she gathered material for *Condemned to Devil's Island* (1928), which was a great success, also as a moving picture.

Nilsson, Christine (1843–1921). Swedish operatic soprano and violinist.

nimini-pimini. Affected simplicity. Lady Emily, in General Burgoyne's THE HEIRESS, III. ii. (1786), tells Miss Alscrip the way to acquire the paphian "Mimp" is to stand before a glass and keep pronouncing *nimini-pimini*—"The lips cannot fail to take the right plie." See also PRUNES.

Nimitz, Chester William (1885–). American admiral, commander in chief, U.S. Pacific Fleet (from December, 1941), replacing Admiral KIMMEL.

Nimrod. Any daring or outstanding hunter; from the "mighty hunter before the Lord" (*Gen.* x. 9). Pope says of him, he was "a mighty hunter, and his prey was man" (*Windsor Forest,* 62); so also Milton interprets the phrase (*Paradise Lost,* xii. 24, etc.).

Nimrod Wildfire, see WILDFIRE, COL. NIMROD.

Nina. In Conrad's ALMAYER'S FOLLY, the half-caste daughter of Almayer. She appears as a small child in AN OUTCAST OF THE ISLANDS.

Nina Leeds. Heroine of Eugene O'NEILL's STRANGE INTERLUDE.

nine. From the earliest times the number nine has been regarded as a mystical number of peculiar significance. Deucalion's ark, made by the advice of PROMETHEUS, was tossed about for nine days before it stranded on the top of Mount Parnassus. There were the nine MUSES, frequently referred to as merely "the Nine"—

> Descend, ye Nine! Descend and sing
> The breathing instruments inspire.
> Pope, *Ode on St. Cecilia's Day.*

There were nine *Gallicenae* or virgin priestesses of the ancient Gallic oracle; and Lars Porsena swore by the nine gods—

> Lars Porsena of Clusium
> By the nine gods he swore
> That the great house of Tarquin
> Should suffer wrong no more.
> Macaulay, *Lays of Ancient Rome* (*Horatius,* i).

who were Juno, Minerva, and Tinia (*the three chief*), Vulcan, Mars, Saturn, Hercules, Summanus, and Vedius; while the nine of the Sabines were Hercules, Romulus, Esculapius, Bacchus, Aeneas, Vesta, Santa, Fortuna, and Fides.

There were nine rivers of Hell, or, according to some accounts, the STYX encompassed the infernal regions in nine circles. Milton makes the gates of Hell "thrice three-fold; three folds are brass, three iron, three of adamantine rock." They have nine folds, nine plates, and nine linings. (*Paradise Lost,* ii. 645.)

In the early Ptolemaic system of astronomy, there were nine spheres; hence Milton, in his *Arcades,* speaks of the "celestial syrens' harmony that sit upon the nine enfolded spheres." They are those of the Moon, Mercury, Venus, the Sun, Mars, Jupiter, Saturn, and the Firmament, or that of the fixed stars, and the Crystalline Sphere. In Scandinavian mythology there were nine earths, HEL being the goddess of the ninth; there were nine worlds in NIFLHEIM, and ODIN'S ring dropped eight other rings (nine rings of mystical import) every ninth night.

In folk-tale, nine appears many times. The ABRACADABRA was worn nine days, and then flung into a river; in order to see the fairies one is directed to put "nine grains of wheat on a four-leaved clover"; nine knots are made on black wool as a charm for a sprained ankle; if a servant finds nine green peas in a peascod, she lays it on the lintel of the kitchen door, and the first man that enters in is to be her cavalier; to see nine magpies is most unlucky; a cat has nine lives (see also CAT-O'-NINE-TAILS); and the nine of diamonds is known as the CURSE OF SCOTLAND.

There are nine orders of ANGELS; in heraldry, there are nine marks of cadency and nine different crowns recognized; and among ecclesiastical architects there are nine crosses, viz., altar crosses, processional crosses, roods on lofts, reliquary crosses, consecration crosses, marking crosses, pectoral crosses, spire crosses, and crosses pendent over altars.

a nine days' wonder. Something that causes a great sensation for a few days, and then passes into the limbo of things forgotten. An old proverb is: "A wonder lasts nine days, and then the puppy's eyes are open," alluding to dogs which, like cats, are born blind. As much as to say, the eyes of the public are blind in astonishment for nine days, but then their eyes are open, and they see too much to wonder any longer.

nine-tail bruiser. Prison slang for the CAT-O'-NINE-TAILS.

nine tailors make a man. See TAILORS.

possession is nine points of the law. It is every advantage a person can have short of actual right. The "nine points of the law" have been given as—

(1) A good deal of money; (2) a good deal of patience; (3) a good cause; (4) a good lawyer; (5) a good counsel; (6) good witnesses; (7) a good jury; (8) a good judge; and (9) good luck.

to look nine ways. To squint.

1919. A novel by John Dos PASSOS, the second book in his trilogy U.S.A., published in 1932. It takes the characters introduced in THE 42ND PARALLEL, plus a few additions, through World War I to the armistice and presents a kaleidoscopic picture of the war years. It also contains brief biographical sketches of a number of outstanding personalities of the period, including Theodore ROOSEVELT, J. P. MORGAN, Randolph BOURNE, Joe HILL, John REED, Paxton HIBBEN, Woodrow WILSON, and the UNKNOWN SOLDIER.

Nineteenth Amendment. The woman's suffrage amendment to the United States Constitution (August 26, 1920).

Ninety-Three **(Quartre-vingt-treize.)** A novel by Victor HUGO (1879), dealing with the France of 1793. Marat, Danton, and Robespierre are introduced. The principal characters are the Marquis de Lantenac, a Breton nobleman, his nephew Gauvain, who saves him from danger but loses his life in consequence, and Cimourdean, an ex-priest and ardent republican. Much of the plot is concerned with the safety of three little children who are in constant danger.

Nine Worthies. The nine persons considered in medieval times most worthy. They were Hector, son of Priam; Alexander the Great; Julius Caesar; Joshua, conqueror of Canaan; David, king of Israel; Judas Maccabeus; Arthur, king of Britain; Charlemagne; Godfrey of Bouillon. The list includes three Gentiles, three Jews, and three Christians.

Ninon de Lenclos, see LENCLOS, ANNE.

Ninus. Son of Belus, husband of SEMIRAMIS, and the reputed builder of Nineveh. It is at his tomb that the lovers meet in the Pyramus and Thisbe travesty in Shakespeare's MIDSUMMER NIGHT'S DREAM.

Niobe. The personification of maternal sorrow. According to Grecian fable, Niobe, the daughter of TANTALUS and wife of AMPHION, King of Thebes, was the mother of twelve children, and taunted LATONA because she had only two—APOLLO and DIANA. Latona commanded her children to avenge the insult, and they caused all the sons and daughters of Niobe to die. Niobe was inconsolable, wept herself to death, and was changed into a stone, from which ran water, "like Niobe, all tears" (*Hamlet,* I. 2).

the Niobe of nations. So Byron styles Rome, the "lone mother of dead empires," in his CHILDE HAROLD.

Niord or **Njorthr.** The Scandinavian god of the sea, the protector of seafaring men, he who ruled the winds, calmed the seas, and warded off fire. He was one of the AESIR, and father, by his wife SKADHI, of FREY and FREYA. His home was Noatun, "the place of ships." The name means "benefactor."

Nipper, Susan. A character in Dickens' DOMBEY AND SON, generally called "Spitfire," from her snappish disposition. She is the nurse of Florence Dombey, to whom she is much attached. Susan Nipper marries Mr. TOOTS after he has gotten over his infatuation for Florence.

Nirvana (*Sans.,* "a blowing out, or extinction"). Annihilation, or rather the final deliverance of the soul from transmigration. See BUDDHISM.

Nisan. The first month of the Jewish calendar. It corresponds to March–April.

Nisard, Désiré (1806–1888). French literary critic, known for his opposition to romanticism, his respect for tradition, and his championing of the neo-classical period of the 17th century (see NEO-CLASSICISM) as the period of the greatest achievement in French literature. His *Histoire de la littérature française* (1844–1861) is his best-known work.

Nisus and Euryalus. Two famous friends in Virgil's AENEID, young Trojans who accompany AENEAS from Troy and win great distinction in the war with TURNUS. They enter the enemy's camp at dead of night but are detected by the Rutulians. Euryalus is slain, and Nisus, trying to save his friend, perishes also.

Nitouche, Sainte. A French humorous adaptation of *n'y touche,* applied to one affecting great innocence.

> This kiss upon your fan I press—
> Ah! Sainte Nitouche, you don't refuse it!
> Harrison Robertson, *Two Triolets.*

Niven, Frederick John (1878–1944). Scottish Canadian novelist. Traveler and mountain-climber. *Justice of the Peace* (1914); *Wild Honey* (1927); and many other books.

nix, see NICKER.

Njal. Hero of the Icelandic saga BURNT NJAL, whose friendship for GUNNAR is shaken and almost destroyed by the feud raised between the two families by HALLGERDA, Gunnar's wife.

Njorthr. See NERTHUS; NIORD.

Noah. In the Old Testament (*Gen.* vi–ix), the builder of an Ark in which he and his family lived during the forty days and nights of the Deluge. All varieties of animals were also taken into the ark, two by two. The Ark finally came to rest on Mount Ararat, and Noah and his three sons, Shem, Ham and Japheth, with their families and the various birds and animals came out safely. According to the Biblical narrative, the rainbow was given Noah as a promise that the world should never again be destroyed by flood. See also DEUCALION'S FLOOD.

Noah's Ark. A name given by sailors to a white band of cloud spanning the sky like a rainbow and in shape something like the hull of a ship. If it extends east and west, expect dry weather; if it extends north and south, expect wet. A *Noah's Ark* is also a child's toy.

Noah's wife. According to legend she was unwilling to go into the ark, and the quarrel between the patriarch and his wife forms a prominent feature of *Noah's Flood,* in the Chester and Townley Mysteries. In the Koran, Noah's wife, known as Waila, tries to persuade the people that her husband is out of his mind.

Noah is a play by André OBEY.

Noah an' Jonah an' Cap'n John Smith. Widely-known poem by Don MARQUIS.

Noah's Dove. Title poem of a volume of verse by Laura Benét, sister of Stephen Vincent and William Rose BENÉT.

Noailles, Comtesse **Mathieu de** (1876–1933). Roumanian-born French poet, known for the color and richness, Oriental exoticism, and ecstatic emotional abandon of her poetry, dealing chiefly with nature, love, and death. Her works include *Le Coeur innombrable* (1901); *Les Ebouissements* (1907); *Les Forces eternelles* (1920); *L'Honneur de souffrir* (1929).

Nobel prizes. International prizes established by the will of Alfred Bernard Nobel (1833–1896), the Swedish chemist and inventor of dynamite, etc., to encourage work in the cause of humanity. There are five prizes of large amounts given annually, as follows: (1) for the most noteworthy work in *physics,* (2) in *chemistry,* (3) in *medicine* or *physiology,* (4) in *idealistic literature,* and (5) in the furtherance of *universal peace.*

The following are the winners of the Nobel prizes in literature:

1901—René François Armand Sully PRUDHOMME (*Fr.,* 1839–1907), poet
1902—Theodor MOMMSEN (*Ger.,* 1817–1903), historian
1903—Björnstjerne BJÖRNSON (*Nor.,* 1832–1910), novelist and dramatist
1904—Frédéric MISTRAL (*Fr.,* 1830–1914), poet
José ECHEGARAY (*Span.,* 1833–1916), dramatist
1905—Henryk SIENKIEWICZ (*Pol.,* 1846–1916), novelist
1906—Giosué CARDUCCI (*It.,* 1835–1907), poet
1907—Rudyard KIPLING (*Eng.,* 1865–1936), poet, novelist, short-story writer
1908—Rudolf EUCKEN (*Ger.,* 1846–1926), philosopher
1909—Selma LAGERLÖF (*Swed.,* 1858–1940), novelist
1910—Paul HEYSE (*Ger.,* 1830–1914), dramatist, poet, novelist
1911—Maurice MAETERLINCK (*Bel.,* 1862–), dramatist
1912—Gerhart HAUPTMANN (*Ger.,* 1862–1946), dramatist
1913—Rabindranath TAGORE (*Bengalese,* 1861–1941), poet
1914—none
1915—Romain ROLLAND (*Fr.,* 1866–1945), novelist
1916—Verner von HEIDENSTAM (*Swed.,* 1859–1940), poet
1917—Henrik PONTOPPIDAN (*Dan.,* 1857–1943), novelist and short-story writer
Karl GJELLERUP (*Dan.,* 1857–1919), dramatist, short-story writer, novelist

1918—none
1919—Carl SPITTELER (*Swiss,* 1845–1925), poet
1920—Knut HAMSUN (*Nor.,* 1859–), novelist
1921—Anatole FRANCE (*Fr.,* 1844–1924), novelist and critic
1922—Jacinto BENAVENTE (*Span.,* 1866–1936), dramatist
1923—William Butler YEATS (*Irish,* 1865–1939), poet and dramatist
1924—Ladislaw S. REYMONT (*Pol.,* 1868–1925), novelist
1925—George Bernard SHAW (*Irish,* 1856–), dramatist
1926—Grazia DELEDDA (*It.,* 1875–1936), novelist
1927—Henri BERGSON (*Fr.,* 1859–1941), philosopher
1928—Sigrid UNDSET (*Nor.,* 1882–), novelist
1929—Thomas MANN (*Ger.,* 1875–), novelist
1930—Sinclair LEWIS (*Am.,* 1885–), novelist
1931—Erik Axel KARLFELDT (*Swed.,* 1864–1931), poet
1932—John GALSWORTHY (*Eng.,* 1867–1933), novelist
1933—Ivan BUNIN (*Rus.,* 1870–), novelist and short-story writer
1934—Luigi PIRANDELLO (*It.,* 1867–1936), dramatist
1935—none
1936—Eugene O'NEILL (*Am.,* 1888–), dramatist
1937—Roger Martin DU GARD (*Fr.,* 1886–), novelist
1938—Pearl S. BUCK (*Am.,* 1892–), novelist
1939—Frans Eemil SILLANPÄÄ (*Finn.,* 1888–), novelist
1940—none
1941—none
1942—none
1943—none
1944—Johannes V. JENSEN (*Dan.,* 1873–), novelist
1945—Gabriela MISTRAL (*Chile.,* 1889–).
1946—Hermann HESSE (*Ger.,* 1877–).
1947—André GIDE (*Fr.,* 1869–).

Well-known winners in other fields include Röntgen, Arrhenius, Pavlov, Koch, Metchnikov, Ehrlich, Marie Curie, Carrel, Michelson, Marconi, Bohr, Einstein, Millikan, Compton, Irene Joliot-Curie, Langmuir, Elihu Root, Woodrow Wilson, Frank B. Kellogg, Fridtjof Nansen, and others. (See under those names).

Nobile, Umberto (1885–). Italian arctic explorer and aeronautical engineer. Flew across north pole with Amundsen and Ellsworth (1926); commanded expedition to north pole in dirigible *Italia;* rescued (1928) after wreck of dirigible; resigned as general in flying force (1929). Went to Russia where he spent five years supervising the construction of airships. Taught aeronautics in Chicago for three years. After the fall of Mussolini, returned to Rome and was put up as a candidate on the Communist ticket in the Italian elections for the Constituent Assembly.

noble. An English gold coin (6s 8d in silver), first minted by Edward III. A new issue was called the *angel-noble,* and later the *angel,* because it showed Michael and the dragon on its face. It was last coined by Charles I. It was presented to be "touched" to patients suffering from KING'S EVIL. The *rose-noble* or *ryal* is a gold coin (10s in silver) first minted by Edward IV.

Noble Numbers. Title of a collection of religious poems by Robert HERRICK.

noble savage. The highly idealized, oversentimentalized primitive man admired in the late 18th century and the early romantic period (see ROMANTICISM) for his supposedly simpler, purer, and less inhibited emotional responses and superior intellect. He originated in the writings of J. J. ROUSSEAU and was the ancestor of the persistent convention of PRIMITIVISM in the art and literature of the 19th and 20th centuries. The characteristic concept of the noble savage is considered to be best portrayed in the novels of CHATEAUBRIAND, dealing with the American Indian—*René,* ATALA, and LES NATCHEZ. James Fenimore COOPER'S Indian novels are also written in the convention of the noble savage.

noble science. (1) Fencing; (2) boxing.

Noctes Ambrosianae. A series of papers on literary and topical subjects, in the form of dialogues, contributed to *Blackwood's Magazine* (1822–1835). They were written principally by Professor John Wilson under the pseudonym, "Christopher North." The conversations were supposed to take place in the "blue parlor" of an inn in Edinburgh kept by one Ambrose, and hence were called *Noctes Ambrosianae.* The Ettrick Shepherd, under which name the poet, James HOGG, appears, and Timothy Tickler, who represents the Edinburgh lawyer, Robert Sym, take part with Christopher North in these famous conversations.

Nocturne. A novel by Frank SWINNERTON (1917). The chief characters are two sisters, Jenny and Emmy Blanchard, daughters of a good-for-nothing, paralytic old father to whom Emmy devotes her days. Jenny, who works in a millinery shop, has been passively accepting the attentions of Emmy's quondam suitor Alf, though she cares nothing for him and Emmy does. On the night in which the action of the story takes place, she gives up Alf to Jenny and then yields to the spell of a more romantic lover, Keith, knowing that in the morning he will sail away.

Nod, Land of. See under LAND.

Nodel. In the medieval beast-epic REYNARD THE FOX, the lion, representing the regal element of Germany; Isegrim, the wolf, represents the baronial element; and Reynard, the fox, the Church element.

Nodier, Charles (1780–1844). French poet and short-story writer of the early period of ROMANTICISM, known for his indolent, dilettantish nature, representative of one type of romantic man of letters, and for his tales, marked by sentiment, melancholy, mystery, fantasy, and terror, in the manner of HOFFMAN and the GOTHIC NOVEL. Among these are *Jean Sbogar* (1818); *Smarra* (1820); and TRILBY (1822), considered the source of the title of Du Maurier's novel. Nodier was banished to Switzerland for a number of years during the Napoleonic period, for having opposed the Emperor. He was interested in nature study and philology, was a journalist in France during the period of the Bourbon Restoration, and in 1824 became librarian at the Bibliothèque de l'Arsénal (Arsenal Library). While serving in the latter capacity, he was the leader of a *cénacle* of romantic writers formerly associated with the journal *La Muse française* (1823–1824). He once defined romanticism as *"la liberté régie par le goût"* ("liberty ruled by taste" or "liberty ruled by desire").

noel. In English (also written *nowell*), a Christmas carol, or the shout of joy in a carol; in French *noël*, "Christmas Day." The word is Provençal *nadal*, from Lat. *natalem*, "natal."

> Nowells, nowells, nowells!
> Sing all we may
> Because that Christ, the King,
> Was born this blessed day.—*Old Carol.*

Noggs, Newman. In Dickens' NICHOLAS NICKLEBY, Ralph Nickleby's clerk. He is a tall man of middle age, with two goggle eyes, one of which is fixed, a rubicund nose, a cadaverous face, and a suit of clothes decidedly the worse for wear. He has the gift of distorting and cracking his finger-joints. This kind-hearted, dilapidated fellow "kept his hunter and hounds once," but ran through his fortune. He discovers a plot of old Ralph which he confides to the Cheeryble brothers who frustrate it and then provide for Newman.

Nogi, Maresuke (1849–1912). Japanese general. Captured Port Arthur in the Russo-Japanese War (1905). Defeated Kuropatkin at Mukden. He and his wife committed hara-kiri upon the death of Emperor Meiji (1912).

Nokomis. In Longfellow's HIAWATHA, mother of Wenonah, and grandmother of Hiawatha. Nokomis is the daughter of the Moon. While she is swinging one day, some of her companions, out of jealousy, cut the ropes, and she falls to earth in a meadow. The same night her first child, a daughter, is born, and is called Wenonah. Old Nokomis teaches Hiawatha the legends of her race when he is a mere boy.

Nolan, Philip. The chief figure in *The Man Without a Country* (1863) by Edward Everett HALE; also, as a historical personage, a horse-trader who was killed on the Mexican border (1801). In *The Real Philip Nolan* (1901), Hale explains that *The Man Without a Country* was not based on the historical Philip Nolan, but only his novel *Philip Nolan's Friends* (1876).

Nolan, the. An appellation of Giordano BRUNO, from his birthplace Nola in Italy. In James Joyce's FINNEGANS WAKE, Bruno is sometimes referred to under the title of "Messrs. Browne & Nolan," a Dublin advertising firm.

noli me tangere (*Lat.*, "touch me not"). An allusion to Christ's words after his resurrection. Cf. *John* xx. 17.

Noll or Old Noll. Oliver CROMWELL was so called by the Royalists. Noll is a familiar form of *Oliver*.

Nolte, Vincent (1779–1853?). Merchant and traveler, born in Italy of German parents. In New Orleans during war of 1812; met, in the course of his travels, Napoleon, Queen Victoria, Audubon, Jackson, Cooper, Nicholas Biddle, etc. Wrote *Fifty Years in Both Hemispheres, or, Reminiscences of the Life of a Former Merchant* (translated from the German, 1854). His book inspired Hervey ALLEN's *Anthony Adverse*. He is, himself, a character in it.

nom.

nom de guerre is French for a "war name," but really means an assumed name. It was customary at one time for everyone who entered the French army to assume a name; this was especially the case in the times of chivalry, when knights were known by the device on their shields.

nom de plume. English-French for "pen name," or pseudonym, the name assumed by a writer, cartoonist, etc., who does not choose to give his own to the public; as *Currer Bell* (Charlotte Brontë), *Fiona MacLeod* (William Sharp), *Henry Seton Merriman* (Hugh Stowell Scott), etc. Occasionally, as in the case of *Voltaire* (François Marie Arouet) and *Stendhal* (Marie Henri Beyle), the assumed name quite replaces the true name.

no man's land. The strip of ground between the front-line trenches of opposing armies; a term coined in World War I.

nominalism. In Scholastic philosophy, the doctrine that universal terms, as *animal, house, finger,* etc., are names which correspond to no reality. Only individual animals, houses, etc. are real. Nominalism arose in the eleventh century with Abélard's teacher, Roscellinus, as its main protagonist. The doctrine was held down by the opposition of the realists whose argument that universals must have a corresponding reality tallied better with the theological doctrine of the trinity which the nominalists could not accept until Occam qualified the significance of their tenets as grammatical, not logical.

Nomura, Kichisaburo (1877–). Japanese ambassador to the United States (1940–1941), conducting the negotiations which were interrupted by the Japanese attack on Pearl Harbor (December 7, 1941).

Nonconformists. In England, members of Protestant bodies who do *not conform* to the doctrines of the Church of England (also called *Dissenters* and *Noncons.*); especially the 2000 clergymen who, in 1662, left the Church rather than submit to the conditions of the Act of Uniformity—i.e., "unfeigned assent to all and everything contained in the Book of Common Prayer."

nones. In the ancient Roman calendar, the ninth (Lat. *nonus*) day before the Ides; in the Roman Catholic Church, the office for the ninth hour after sunrise, or 3 p.m.

Nonne Prestes Tale. In Chaucer's *Canterbury Tales.* See CHANTICLEER.

No-Popery Riots. Those of Edinburgh and Glasgow, February 5, 1779. Those of London, occasioned by Lord George Gordon, occurred in 1780.

Nordau, Max Simon (1849–1923). Hungarian-German physician and author. Active Zionist leader favoring Herzl's plans for a Jewish national home in East Africa. Outstanding among his numerous works is DEGENERATION (1892–1893). The name *Nordau* (literally, "a northern meadow") is a witty pseudonym for *Südfeld* (literally, "a southern field").

Nordhoff, Charles Bernard (1887–1947). American novelist, noted chiefly for his collaboration with James Norman Hall on the "Bounty" series of novels, beginning with MUTINY ON THE BOUNTY (1932).

Nordica, Lillian. Pseudonym of **Lillian Norton** (1859–1914). American operatic soprano. Popular in Wagnerian rôles, chiefly with Metropolitan Opera House, Hammerstein's Manhattan Opera Company, and on concert tours.

Norgem in Brickwall. A reference to this locality occurs in a poem by Rudyard Kipling, beginning "King Bess was Harry's Daughter." It says she left her shoe "at Norgem in Brickwall." In E. V. Lucas's *Highways and Byways in Sussex* it is stated that "Brickwall" is "The neighboring seat of the Frewens, the great family of Northiam, for many generations a noble old country mansion, partly Elizabethan and partly Stuart." Coulson Kernahan says, "In a glass case in the hall at Brickwall the silk shoes which Queen Elizabeth left behind her at Norgem (now Northiam) are carefully preserved."

Norma. In Bellini's opera of that name (1831) with a libretto by Romani, a Druidic priestess, secretly married to a Roman proconsul. When she discovers that he is planning to seduce a sister priestess, she gives herself up to vengeance but at the last minute shares the tragic fate she has brought upon him.

Norna of the Fitful Head. In Scott's novel THE PIRATE, a name given to Ulla Troil, who believes herself to be "something pre-eminently powerful, pre-eminently wicked," a person of mysterious supernatural powers. She is the mother of Clement Cleveland, the Pirate, by her lover and seducer, Basil Mertoun (Vaughan).

Norns, the. The three giant goddesses who, in Scandinavian mythology, presided over the fates of both men and gods. Anciently there was only one Norn, *Urdur* (i.e., the power of fate), but later two others were added, and the three became known as *Urdur* (the Past), *Verdandi* (the Present), and *Skuld* (the Future), who determined the fate of men by carving runestaves and with them casting lots. They appeared at the cradle on the birth of a child, and dwelt at the root of YGGDRASIL beside the well Urdar, from which they daily sprinkled Yggdrasil to preserve it from decay. The Three Weird Sisters in MACBETH are probably connected with the Norns; see also FATE.

Norris, Frank. In full **Benjamin Franklin Norris** (1870–1902). American novelist and journalist, known for his naturalistic (see NATURALISM) novels of the U.S. of his day, in which he was strongly influenced by Émile ZOLA. His work is marked by emphasis on the physical, sordid, and violent, and by pessimism and determinism. His works include *Yvernelle: A Tale of Feudal France* (1892); MCTEAGUE (1899); *Blix* (1899); *Moran of the Lady Letty* (1898); *A Man's Woman* (1900); THE OCTOPUS (1901), considered his best novel, which, together with THE PIT (1903) and the unwritten *The Wolf,* was planned as the first part of a trilogy, *The Epic of the*

Wheat; The Responsibilities of a Novelist (1903); *A Deal in Wheat* (1903); *The Joyous Miracle* (1906); *The Third Circle* (1909); *Vandover and the Brute* (1914); *Works* (1928), ten volumes.

In his early youth, Norris studied art in Paris and wrote medieval romances in the manner of FROISSART; *Yvernelle* is one. Later he worked on the staff of *The Wave*, a magazine in San Francisco, and was a correspondent in Cuba for *McClure's Magazine* during the Spanish-American War.

Charles Gilman Norris (1881–1945). Brother of Frank Norris, became known as the author of novels dealing with various social problems of the 20th century, including education, women's rights, and birth control. Among these are *Salt* (1917); *Brass* (1921); *Bread* (1923); *Pig Iron* (1925); *Zelda Marsh* (1927); *Seed* (1930); *Bricks Without Straw* (1938).

Kathleen Thompson Norris (1880–). Wife of Charles G. Norris, wrote numerous sentimental domestic novels which sold widely and were extremely popular throughout the U.S. *Mother* (1911) was her first success. *Certain People of Importance* (1922) is her best novel.

Norris, George William (1861–1944). American statesman. Opposed U.S. entry into World War I. Was instrumental in securing passage of act creating Tennessee Valley Authority (1933). The first TVA-built dam was called the Norris Dam in his honor. Also initiated the Twentieth Amendment known as "the LAME DUCK ACT" (1933).

Norris, Mrs. or **Aunt.** A famous character in Jane Austen's MANSFIELD PARK, a great busybody and a constant trial to Fanny Price.

North, Jessica Nelson (1894–). American poet. Associate editor of *Poetry*. John Reed prize (1927). Wrote critical articles on collections of Art Institute of Chicago. *The Long Leash* (poems; 1928); *Morning in the Land* (novel; 1941); etc.

North, Sterling (1906–). Younger brother of Jessica Nelson NORTH. Novelist and critic. Among his novels is *Night Outlasts the Whippoorwill* (1936). Has also written several juveniles. Literary editor, Chicago *Daily News* and New York *Post*.

North American Review, The. A quarterly review devoted to literature, criticism, and history, founded in Boston (1815) and edited by William Tudor. William Cullen Bryant's *Thanatopsis* and *To a Waterfowl* were first published in it. It later became a monthly, and among its editors were Charles Eliot Norton, James Russell Lowell, Henry Adams, and Henry Cabot Lodge. Emerson, Irving, Longfellow, Parkman, Howells, etc., contributed to it. Its next incarnation, in New York, saw it in the midst of contemporary social and political movements. After World War I it again became a quarterly.

Northanger Abbey. A novel by Jane AUSTEN (1818). Visiting at Bath her friend Mrs. ALLEN, called by one critic "perhaps as good a portrayal of pure inanity as the history of literature can supply," the heroine, Catherine Morland, an attractive young girl under the spell of Mrs. Radcliffe's MYSTERIES OF UDOLPHO, falls in love with Henry Tilney, a young clergyman, and is made love to by the blustering young blackguard, John Thorpe. At the invitation of Henry's father, General Tilney, who believes her wealthy, she visits at Northanger Abbey, where, due to her romantic imagination, she sees mystery and horror on all sides. This situation gives Jane Austen ample opportunity for satire on the Radcliffe school of romantic mystery. Hearing that the report of Catherine's wealth is ill-founded, Henry's dictatorial father abruptly orders her to leave, but Henry follows and persuades her to marry him.

Northcliffe, Viscount, see HARMSWORTH, ALFRED CHARLES.

Northeast Passage. A way from the Atlantic to the Pacific and on to India from Europe eastward round the north extremity of Asia. Often attempted even in the 16th century. Hence Beaumont and Fletcher:

> That everlasting cassock, that has worn
> As many servants out as the North-east Passage
> Has consumed sailors.
>
> *The Woman's Prize*, ii. 2.

After the discovery of America, there was much talk of a **Northwest Passage** through to the East by way of the Atlantic, and explorers were constantly sailing up the bays and rivers of the American coast in hopes of finding such a passage.

North, Christopher or **Kit.** The pseudonym of John Wilson (1785–1854), professor of moral philosophy, Edinburgh. He contributed to *Blackwood's Magazine* most of the NOCTES AMBROSIANAE.

Northern. For *the Northern Herodotus, the Northern Semiramis,* etc., see under HERODOTUS, SEMIRAMIS.

the Northern Bear. Russia has been so called.

the Northern Gate of the Sun. The sign of Cancer, or summer solstice; so called because it marks the northern tropic.

the Northern Lights. The AURORA BOREALIS.

> [The old King goes] up with music
> On cold starry nights
> To sup with the Queen
> Of the gay Northern Lights.
>
> Allingham, *The Fairies.*

the Northern Wagoner. The genius presiding over the Great Bear, or CHARLES' WAIN, which contains seven large stars.

By this the northern wagoner has set
His sevenfold team behind the stedfast star [*the pole-star*]
Spenser, *Faërie Queene,* I, ii, 1.

Dryden calls the Great Bear *the Northern Car,* and similarly the crown in Ariadne has been called *the Northern Crown.*

North of Boston. Title of Robert FROST'S first book of poems (1914).

North Star State. Minnesota. See under STATES.

North to the Orient. A book by Anne LINDBERGH (1935).

Northumberland, Henry Percy, Earl of. In Shakespeare's RICHARD II and 1 and 2 HENRY IV, a powerful and treacherous nobleman.

Northwest Passage. (1) See under NORTHEAST PASSAGE.

(2) Title of a novel (1937) by Kenneth ROBERTS.

Northwest Territory. An American territory northwest of the Ohio River, comprising practically all the land owned as unsettled territory by the thirteen colonies at the time of the Declaration of Independence. It was ceded to the federal government by the various states laying claim to it and later organized into separate units. See WESTERN RESERVE.

Norton, Caroline Elizabeth Sarah (1808–1877). Well-known English author, principally remembered for her poetry. Said to have been George Meredith's model for the heroine of DIANA OF THE CROSSWAYS.

Norton, Charles Eliot (1827–1908). American author and educator. With E. L. Godkin and others founded *The Nation* (1865). Professor at Harvard (1873–1897).

Norton, Grace Fallow (1876–). American poet, *Little Gray Songs From St. Joseph's* (1912); *The Sister of the Wind* (1914); etc.

Norton, Thomas (1532–1584). English lawyer and poet. Staunch defender of anti-Catholicism. Translator of Calvin's *Institutes* (1559). With Thomas SACKVILLE, author of the first English tragedy (in blank verse), *Gorboduc or Ferrex and Porrex* (performed 1561; published 1565).

Norumbega. Early map-makers' name for a region and its chief city vaguely situated on the east coast of North America. On the map of Hieronimus da Verrazano (1592) it reads *Aranbega,* and coincides more or less with Nova Scotia. It was sought in vain in the region of the Penobscot River by Champlain in 1604. WHITTIER wrote a poem *Norembega* dealing with the search for this fabulous city. The word *Norumbega* is possibly of Indian origin.

Norway, Nevil Shute. Pseudonym **Nevil Shute** (1899–). English novelist. *Ordeal* (1939); *Pied Piper* (1941); etc. *Pied Piper* became a successful moving picture.

Nostradamus, Michel (1503–1566). A French astrologer who published an annual *Almanac,* as well as the famous *Centuries* (1555), containing prophecies which, though the book suffered papal condemnation in 1781, still occasion controversy from time to time. His prophecies are couched in most ambiguous language, hence the saying *as good a prophet as Nostradamus*—i.e., so obscure that none can make out your meaning. Interest in the prophecies of Nostradamus was revived at the time of World War II.

Nostromo. A novel by Joseph CONRAD (1904), dealing with a South American revolution. The action is extremely involved and there are many characters. Due largely to the efforts of Charles Gould, head of the Gould concession silver mine in Sulaco, the Occidental Province has been kept free from revolutionary disturbances such as have kept the rest of the republic of Costaguana in a state of chaos. Gould, however, in his devotion to the building of an orderly and prosperous state, has been growing less considerate of his wife, Doña Emilia (who has been called "the most moving figure in all Conrad's books"). Finally revolution strikes the province. The cynical but genuinely patriotic young journalist Decoud dreams of a separate republic, but he is forced to flee, although something much like the secession he planned actually takes place after his death. "Nostromo," from whom the book takes its title, is the nickname of Capatez de Cargadores, a picturesque and powerful Italian who has become "the most reliable, the most useful, the most feared man in Sulaco." When the revolutionists attack Sulaco, he is entrusted with the silver treasure; afterwards it is believed to have been sunk at sea, and Nostromo gradually grows even more prosperous and powerful. At last he is shot by an old lighthouse keeper, the father of Gizelle, the girl he loves and has come to meet.

Notables. An assembly of nobles or notable men, in French history, selected by the king to form a parliament. They were convened in 1626 by Richelieu, and, not again till 1787 (160 years afterwards), when Louis XVI called them together with the view of relieving the nation of some of its pecuniary embarrassments. The last time they ever assembled was November 6, 1788.

Notes and Queries. An English weekly periodical for literary criticism and information; started by W. J. Thoms, in 1849. Its motto is the famous remark of Captain Cuttle, "When found, make a note of." The name came to be given occasionally to similar projects in other fields, as *Notes and Queries on China and Japan, American Notes and Queries,* etc.

Notes of a Son and Brother. An autobiographical account by Henry JAMES (1914), a sequel to *A Small Boy and Others* (1913). The period is the late 1850's to 1870.

Notestein, Wallace (1879–). Sterling professor of English history at Yale (since 1928). Author of *History of English Witchcraft* (1913); *English Folk* (1938); and editor of various scholarly compilations, several in collaboration.

Nothing to Wear. A well-known humorous poem by William Allen BUTLER (1857), relating the sad state of Miss Flora M'FLIMSEY who made three separate journeys to Paris, each spent in "one continuous round of shopping," and yet:

> This same Miss M'Flimsey of Madison Square
> The last time we met was in utter despair
> Because she had nothing whatever to wear!

Notre Dame de Paris. A romance of medieval times by Victor HUGO (1831), centering about the life of the great Parisian cathedral. The principal characters are ESMERALDA, the gypsy dancer in love with Captain PHOEBUS, Claude FROLLO, the hypocritical archdeacon, whose evil passion for Esmeralda causes him to denounce her as a witch, and QUASIMODO, the "Hunchback of Notre Dame," a deformed bellringer, whose devotion saves Esmeralda for a time when she seeks protection from the mob in the belfry of the Cathedral. Esmeralda is finally executed, and Quasimodo throws Frollo from the heights of Notre Dame.

Nott, Henry Junius (1797–1837). Early American humorist of the Southwest. He wrote a picaresque work presumed to be from "the Knapsack of Thomas Singularity, Journeyman Printer." He may be compared with, but does not equal, Augustus Baldwin LONGSTREET.

Nouman, Sidi. Hero of *The History of Sidi Nouman,* one of the tales in the ARABIAN NIGHTS. He is an Arab who marries Amine, a very beautiful woman, who eats her rice with a bodkin. Sidi, wishing to know how his wife can support life and health without more food than she takes in his presence, watches her narrowly, and discovers that she is a ghoul, who goes by stealth every night and feasts on the fresh-buried dead. When Sidi makes this discovery, Amine changes him into a dog. After he is restored to his normal shape, he changes Amine into a mare, which every day he almost rides to death.

Nourmahal (*Arab.,* "the light of the harem"). One of the ladies in the harem of the Caliph Haroun al Raschid, afterwards called Nourjehan (light of the world). The story of her love for Selim and how she regains his lost affections by means of a love-spell is told in Moore's LALLA ROOKH.

Nouvelle Héloïse, Julie ou la. A novel by Jean Jacques ROUSSEAU (1761). It is the story of a wife beset by her former lover.

Novalis. Pseudonym of **Friedrich Leopold von Hardenberg** (1772–1801). German romantic poet and novelist, known for his mystic, religious poems and his celebration of night and death in characteristic romantic symbolism. See ROMANTICISM. His best-known works are *Hymns of Night,* prose poems lamenting the death of Sophie von Kühn; *Heinrich von Ofterdingen* (1799) and *Die Lehrlinge zu Sais* (*The Disciples at Sais*), both unfinished novels. Known in English chiefly through Henry Van Dyke's *The Blue Flower.*

Novarro, Ramon (1899–). Famous moving-picture actor, especially in the days of the "silent" film. Hero of *The Prisoner of Zenda, Scaramouche, Ben Hur, The Student Prince,* etc. In "sound": *Ben Hur, Mata Hari, Laughing Boy,* etc. Made *La Virgen que Forjó una Patria* for the Mexican government as a start in his efforts to build up the moving-picture industry of his native Mexico.

novelist's novelist. Term applied to an author generally admired by other writers, whose works they study in order to improve their own techniques. It has been applied notably to Gustave FLAUBERT, Henry JAMES, and James JOYCE.

novella (*It.*). A short prose narrative, generally with a structural center represented by a surprising event. Developed by Giovanni BOCCACCIO in the DECAMERON (1353, published 1471). The term occurs in Renaissance English before *novel.* See NOVELLE by Matteo Bandello.

Novelle. The German development of the Italian NOVELLA. Particularly cultivated in the romantic and post-romantic periods. Cf. E. K. Bennett, *History of the German Novelle, Goethe to Thomas Mann* (1934).

Novelle (*It.,* **Novellas**). A collection of stories by Matteo Bandello (1554), translated both in French and English. It contains the sources of Shakespeare's *Romeo and Juliet, Much Ado About Nothing,* and *Twelfth Night.*

Novello, Ivor. Originally **Ivor Novello Davies** (1893–). English actor, composer, and film star. Author of the song *Keep the Home Fires Burning,* and musical revues.

Novello, Vincent (1781–1861). English organist who composed sacred music and introduced to England unknown works of Haydn, Mozart, and Palestrina.

Novels by Eminent Hands. A series of parodies by THACKERAY. Among the authors parodied are Fenimore COOPER, DISRAELI, LEVER, BULWER LYTTON, etc.

Novum Organum (*Lat.*, "new instrument," from Gr. *organon*). A philosophical treatise by Francis BACON (1620), written in Latin. It presents Bacon's statement of his inductive method of interpreting nature and organizing knowledge, by which the results of experience are studied and a general conclusion regarding them is then reached; Bacon believed this was the opposite of the procedure of reasoning deductively from a given postulate by means of the SYLLOGISM, which was the universal practice among the scholastic philosophers of his day. The *Novum Organum* also contains an exposition of Bacon's famous concept of the four "Idols," or false images of the mind, which he saw hindering the attainment of true knowledge: (1) *Idols of the Tribe* (*Idola Tribus*), errors originating in human nature itself; (2) *Idols of the Cave* (*Idola Specus*), errors originating in the peculiar psychology of each individual; (3) *Idols of the Market-Place* (*Idola Fori*), errors and confusions of language originating in social and practical intercourse among men; (4) *Idols of the Theater* (*Idola Theatri*), errors originating in formal systems of philosophy, each of which presents a world of its own, like a stage-play.

Now It Can Be Told. Title of a book by Sir Philip GIBBS.

Nowowiejski, Feliks (1877–1946). Polish conductor and composer. Wrote the music for the national hymn of Poland. Paralyzed in a Nazi prison camp during World War II.

Nox. In classic mythology, goddess of night.

Noyades, Les. A ballad by SWINBURNE, relating how Jean Baptiste Carrier, the French Revolutionist, executed many people by drowning at Nantes during the Reign of Terror (1793–1794). Swinburne imagines a thwarted lover bound to the woman he loves and drowning with her.

Noyes, Alexander Dana (1862–1945). American journalist; financial editor, New York *Times* (from 1920). Wrote three volumes covering the financial history of the United States through half a century. In the time of the Great Bull Market before the financial crash of 1928, his was a voice crying in the wilderness against confidence in the "Boom" which preceded the "Bust."

Noyes, Alfred (1880–). English poet, critic and essayist, author chiefly of narrative verse and ballads dealing with English history. He was converted to Roman Catholicism in 1925. His works include *Drake* (1908), an epic poem in blank verse in twelve books; *Tales of the Mermaid Tavern* (1912); *The Watchers of the Sky* (1922), *The Book of Earth* (1925), and *The Last Voyage* (1930), constituting *The Torch-Bearers: An Epic Trilogy of Scientific Discovery; No Other Man* (1940), serialized in America in 1946 and made into a successful moving picture by Frank CAPRA; *If Judgment Comes* (1941); *Orchard's Bay* (1940), poems and essays; *The Edge of the Abyss* (1942), lectures. His best-known single poem is *The Highwayman.*

Noyes, George Rapall (1873–). Teacher at the University of California (since 1901), professor of Slavic languages (1919–1943). Fellow of American Academy of Arts and Sciences. Editor of *Dryden's Poetical Works* (1909); translator—with Leonard Bacon—of *Heroic Ballads of Serbia* (1913), *Masterpieces of the Russian Drama* (1933), etc.

Noyes, John Humphrey (1811–1886). American social reformer. Formed Putney Community in Vermont (1826), expounding the gospel of perfectionism. Forced to flee to the ONEIDA COMMUNITY (1848) and from there to Canada, to escape prosecution for his doctrine of free love and promiscuity. Author of *Bible of Communism* (1848), etc.

n*th*, or n*th* plus one, in University slang, means to the utmost degree. Thus, *Cut to the nth* means wholly unnoticed by a friend. The expression is taken from the index of a mathematical formula, where n stands for any number, and $n + 1$, one more than any number. Hence, *n-dimensional,* having an indefinite number of dimensions, *n-tuple* (on the analogy of *quadruple, quintuple,* etc.), having an indefinite number of duplications.

Nubbles, Kit. In Dickens' OLD CURIOSITY SHOP, the lad employed to wait on LITTLE NELL, and do all sorts of odd jobs at the "curiosity shop" for her grandfather. He generally begins his sentences with "Why then." When the "curiosity shop" is broken up by QUILP, Kit takes service under Mr. Garland, Abel Cottage, Finchley.

> Kit was a shock-headed, shambling, awkward lad with an uncommonly wide mouth, very red cheeks, a turned-up nose, and a most comical expression of face. He stopped short at the door on seeing a stranger, twirled in his hand an old round hat without a vestige of brim, resting himself now on one leg, and now on the other, and looking with a most extraordinary leer. He was evidently the comedy of little Nell's life.—Dickens, *The Old Curiosity Shop,* i.

Nucingen, Frédéric de. A shrewd promoter and financier who appears in many of the novels of Balzac's COMÉDIE HUMAINE, notably *The Firm of Nucingen* (*La Maison Nucingen;* 1838). Aside from his affair with Esther van GOBSECK, his one passion is finance. This wealthy Alsatian Jew is so successful that his favor is sought on all hands and he is admitted into both the peerage and the Legion of Honor.

Madame de Nucingen. Wife of the above, known chiefly as one of the two selfish and ungrateful daughters of Père GORIOT and the mistress of Eugène de RASTIGNAC.

Augusta de Nucingen. Madame de Nucingen's daughter, who marries Eugène de RASTIGNAC.

Nugent, John Charles (1878–1947) and his son, **Elliott Nugent** (1900–). American actors and playwrights.

Numa Pompilius. The legendary second king of Rome (715–672 B.C.). The nymph Egeria favored him with secret interviews and taught the lessons of wisdom and law which he embodied in the institutions of his nation. These include the temple of Janus, the worship of Terminus, the vestal virgins, etc.

Numa Roumestan. A political novel by Alphonse DAUDET (1881), relating the rise to power of the titular hero, a Provençal of sufficient wit, ambition and impudence to win notable success in the field of politics. He is said to have been drawn from GAMBETTA.

number.

number of the beast. 666; a mystical number of unknown meaning but referring to a certain man mentioned by St. John. It is also known as the *Apocalyptic number.*

Let him that hath understanding count the number of the beast; for it is the number of a man; and his number is six hundred threescore and six.—*Rev.* xiii. 18.

golden number. See under GOLDEN.

Numbers. The fourth book of the Old Testament, dealing with the passage of the Jews through the wilderness on their way to the Promised Land.

Nunc Dimittis. The Song of Simeon (*Luke* ii. 29), "Lord, now lettest thou thy servant depart in peace," so called from the opening words of the Latin version, *Nunc dimittis servum tuum, Domine.*

Hence, *to receive one's Nunc dimittis,* to be given permission to go; *to sing one's Nunc dimittis,* to show great delight at departing.

Núñez Cabeza de Vaca, Álvar, see CABEZA DE VACA.

Nungesser, Charles (1892–1927). French military aviator in World War I, believed to have brought down 45 enemy planes. Lost in transatlantic flight.

Nunky. Slang for "Uncle" especially as meaning a pawnbroker; or for "Uncle Sam."

Nunky pays for all. The American Government (see SAM) has to "stand the racket."

Nuns Fret Not at Their Convent's Narrow Room. A sonnet by William WORDSWORTH (1806), celebrating the strict limits and the discipline of the sonnet form in developing the style of a poet.

Nun's Priest's or Nonne Prestes Tale. See CHANTICLEER.

Nurmi, Paavo (1897–). Finnish long distance runner. Olympic winner at Antwerp (1920); Paris (1924); Amsterdam (1928); etc.

Nut-Brown Maid, The. An English ballad (given in Percy's *Reliques*) dating probably from the late 15th century. It tells how the "Not-browne Mayd" is wooed and won by a knight who pretends to be a banished man. After describing the hardships she would have to undergo if she married him, and finding her love true to the test, he reveals himself to be an earl's son, with large hereditary estates in Westmorland.

Nutmeg State. Connecticut. See under STATES.

Nutter House and The Nutter Family, The. Title of a chapter in Thomas Bailey Aldrich's *The Story of a Bad Boy* (1870). The old Aldrich house at Portsmouth, N.H., the original of the Nutter house at Rivermouth, still stands, a wing in the rear being now used as a museum of Aldrich relics.

Nutting, Wallace (1861–1941). American clergyman and antiquarian; author of a series of illustrated books, *Maine Beautiful; Vermont Beautiful;* etc. Painter of water colors.

N.V.A. The National Variety Artists, a club for vaudeville performers. Formerly known as the National Vaudeville Artists.

Nydia. A blind flower girl, one of the leading characters in Bulwer Lytton's LAST DAYS OF POMPEII.

Nym. A corporal in the army under Captain Sir John FALSTAFF, introduced in Shakespeare's drama, *The Merry Wives of Windsor* and in *Henry V,* but not in *Henry IV.*

Nymphidia. A fairy poem by Michael DRAYTON (1627). It is a story told to the poet by Nymphidia, an attendant to Queen Mab. The description of the court, people, and events, all diminutive in scale, is a remarkable performance.

nympholepsy. The frenzy supposed to seize a person after bewitchment by a nymph. Swinburne has a poem called *A Nympholept* in *Astrophel and Other Poems,* containing the great lines:

I dare not sleep for delight of the perfect hour,
Lest God be wroth that his gift should be scorned of man.

O

Oak, Gabriel. A prominent character in Hardy's FAR FROM THE MADDING CROWD.

oakenshaw. An oak grove.

> When winds were in the oakenshaws and all the cauldrons tolled.
>
> A. E. Housman, *The Oracles.*

Oakhurst, John. In Bret HARTE's short stories, notably in *The Luck of Roaring Camp* and *The Outcasts of Poker Flat,* a California gambler who "had the melancholy air and intellectual abstraction of a Hamlet." He kills himself when snowbound and starving.

Oakley, Annie. Real name **Phoebe Anne Oakley Mozee** (1860–1926). Famous markswoman who married the vaudeville actor Frank E. Butler. She became a member of Buffalo Bill's Wild West Show (1885–1902) and starred with rifle and pistol. Among her stunts was shooting holes in tossed-up playing-cards. Hence a punched theatrical pass or any other complimentary ticket came to be called an *Annie Oakley. Annie Get Your Gun,* a long-run musical comedy (1946–) by Irving BERLIN, starring Ethel Merman, was based on her career.

Oakley, Violet (1874–). American mural painter. Designed murals for the Church of the Angels, New York, for the state capitol at Harrisburg, Pa., etc.

Oaks, The. One of the "classic" English horse-races; it was for three-year-old fillies, and was run at Epsom on the Friday after the DERBY. It was named by the twelfth Earl of Derby, who established the race in 1779, from an estate of his near Epsom named "The Oaks."

Oates, Titus (1649–1705). English impostor fomenting agitation against an alleged Popish Plot whereby Roman Catholics were to be pledged to massacre Protestants, and burn London. Finally convicted for charges preferred against the Duke of York, imprisoned, but pardoned (1689) on accession of William and Mary.

Oath of the Tennis Court. An oath taken by the French National Assembly—after it had been prevented by the king from using its normal meeting place and had convened at the tennis court building (June 20, 1789)—never to disband till France had been given a constitution. As this negated the power of the king, the event is often considered the beginning of the French Revolution.

Oaths of Strassburg. Mutual oaths taken by Charles and Ludwig, grandsons of CHARLEMAGNE, at Strassburg in 842 A. D., in which each brother swore, in the presence of the other's army, to defend the other and not make an alliance against him with Lothair, the third brother, against whom both Charles and Ludwig were fighting for control of the Holy Roman Empire. Each brother swore in the dialect of Latin which the other's army was accustomed to speak in its respective part of the Empire, and the Oaths are historically important as the earliest existing specimens of the languages which later became French and German. The dialect spoken by Charles in his oath was the ancestor of modern German; that spoken by Ludwig, the ancestor of modern French.

oats, he has sown his wild. He has left off his gay habits and has become steady.

Obadiah. (1) A Minor Prophet of the Old Testament and the name of the book in which his prophecy is recorded.

(2) A slang name for a Quaker.

(3) A household servant in Sterne's novel TRISTRAM SHANDY. There is also an Obadiah in Fielding's TOM JONES.

obeahism. The belief in and practice of obeah, i.e., a kind of sorcery or witchcraft prevalent in West Africa and formerly in the West Indies. *Obeah* is a native word, and signifies something put into the ground to bring about sickness, death, or other disaster.

Oberholtzer, Ellis Paxson (1868–1936). American historian. Pupil of John Bach MCMASTER, of whom he wrote a *Memoir* in 1933. His *A History of the United States Since the Civil War* (5 vols.; 1917–1936) is not considered entirely unprejudiced, being unfair to the Mormons, the labor movement, etc. Also author of *The Referendum in America* (1893); *Robert Morris, Patriot and Financier* (1903); *Jay Cooke, the Financier of the Civil War* (2 vols.; 1907); *Henry Clay* (1909); etc.

Obermann. A much-heralded novel or psychological study by Etienne de SENANCOUR (1804) which exerted a great influence on the romantic movement of the 19th century. Written in the form of letters, in part describing the author's wanderings in the forest of Fontainebleau and in Switzerland, but in the main confessing his restlessness, disillusionment and torment of mind and soul, the book displays the analytical, introspective trend of 19th and 20th-century fiction.

Oberon. King of the Fairies, husband of Titania. Shakespeare introduces them in his MIDSUMMER NIGHT'S DREAM. The name is probably connected with ALBERICH, the king of the elves.

He first appears in the medieval French romance, HUON DE BORDEAUX, where he is a son of Julius Caesar and MORGAN LE FAY. He is only three feet high, but of angelic face, and is lord and king of Mommur. At his birth the fairies bestow their gifts; one gift is insight into men's thoughts, and another the power of transporting himself to any place instantaneously. In the fullness of time legions of angels convey his soul to Paradise.

In *Midsummer Night's Dream,* Oberon quarrels with his wife Titania about a "changeling" which Oberon wants for a page but Titania refuses to give up. Oberon, in revenge, anoints her eyes in sleep with the extract of "Love in Idleness," the effect of which was to make the sleeper in love with the first object beheld on waking. Titania happens to see a country bumpkin whom PUCK has dressed up with an ass head. Oberon comes upon her while she is fondling the clown, and sprinkles on her an antidote. She is so ashamed of her folly that she readily consents to give up the boy to her spouse for his page. The magic extract is also used to good effect by Puck to straighten out the tangled love affairs of HERMIA and LYSANDER and of HELENA and DEMETRIUS.

Obey, André (1892–). French dramatist. NOAH, etc.

Obidicut. The fiend of lust, and one of the five which possess "poor Tom," in Shakespeare's KING LEAR. See HOBBIDANCE.

Obiter Dicta. Title of a book of essays (1884) by Augustine Birrell. An *obiter dictum* is an incidental and unbinding opinion given by a judge and hence any incidental comment.

objectivism. A term used to designate a type of 20th-century poetry in which material objects are selected, studied, and presented for their own particular value as objects, rather than for their capability in symbolizing an emotion or intellectual concept of the author. See also IMAGISM; SYMBOLISM. The work of William Carlos WILLIAMS, who first used the term, is considered the best example of objectivism; Marianne MOORE and Wallace STEVENS have also been called objectivist poets.

Oblonsky, Prince Stepan Arcadievitch. A character in Tolstoi's ANNA KARÉNINA, better known as Stiva.

Oboler, Arch (1907–). American radio dramatist. His *Alter Ego* (1938) was declared best original radio drama of year.

Obregón, Álvaro (1880–1928). Mexican soldier and politician, commanding army during presidency of Carranza (1915–1920) and Huerta (1920). As president of Mexico (1920–1924), he put down Huerta's revolt (1923–1924). Re-elected (1928) but assassinated.

O'Brien, Edward J. (1890–1941). American editor and anthologist. Principally known for the annual American short-story anthology, *The Best Short Stories* (from 1915).

O'Brien, Fitz-James (1828–1862). American journalist and writer of remarkable short stories of the weird and uncanny, notably *The Diamond Lens, The Wondersmith,* and *What Was It?*

O'Brien, Frederick (1869–1932). Widely-traveled American writer, principally known for *White Shadows in the South Seas* (1919).

Obstinate. In Bunyan's PILGRIM'S PROGRESS, an inhabitant of the City of Destruction, who advises Christian to return to his family, and not run on a wild-goose chase.

obverse. In coins, the side bearing the more important device. In U.S. coins, the side with the date. The opposite of reverse.

O Captain! My Captain! Title of a poem by Walt Whitman, published in *Sequel to Drum-Taps* (1865–1866) and *Leaves of Grass* (1867). It was written as a tribute to Lincoln, shortly after his assassination. Whitman himself preferred his Lincoln tribute *When Lilacs Last in the Dooryard Bloom'd.*

ocarina (*Ital.,* literally, "little goose"). A terracotta wind-instrument with mouthpiece and holes for the fingers, which makes a whistling noise. Its shape is responsible for the name.

O'Casey, Sean (1884–). Irish playwright, associated with the Abbey Theater (see IRISH RENAISSANCE) and known for his plays dealing with Irish urban working-class life. See PROLETARIAN LITERATURE. These emphasize character rather than plot, and are usually performed as comedies, although often intended by the author as tragedies. His works include *The Shadow of a Gunman* (1923); *Kathleen Listens In* (1923); *Juno and the Paycock* (1924), winner of the British Hawthornden prize in 1926; *Nannie's Night Out* (1924); *The Plough and the Stars* (1926); *The Silver Tassie* (1928); WITHIN THE GATES (1933), which reflects the author's admiration for George Bernard SHAW; *Windfalls* (1937), stories, poems, plays; *The Flying Wasp* (1937), drama criticism; *I Knock at the Door* (1939) and *Pictures in the Hallway* (1942), autobiographical; *The Star Turns Red* (1940).

O'Casey was born and raised in the slums of Dublin, not learning to read until he was twelve years old. He worked as a laborer in his early youth, was for a time associated with the Irish Transport Workers Union, taking part in its strike of 1913, and helped organize the Irish Citizen Army during the Irish Revolution of 1916. *The Story of the Citizen Army* (1919) was his first work to be published.

Occam, William of, see OCKHAM.

Occasion. A lame old hag in Spenser's FAËRIE QUEENE (II. iv), mother of Furor, and symbolical of the cause of anger. She is quite bald behind, but Sir GUYON seizes her by the forelock, throws her to the ground, and ultimately vanquishes her.

to improve the occasion. To draw a moral lesson from, or otherwise make good use of, some event which has occurred.

Occleve or **Hoccleve, Thomas** (1370?–1450?). English poet, a late contemporary of CHAUCER, best known for his *De Regimine Principum* (written ca. 1412), a political treatise on the duties of a ruler, addressed to the Prince of Wales; it was a translation into English of a Latin work by Aegidius. Occleve also wrote *La Male Règle* (1406), an autobiographical poem, and other minor works.

Occonestoga. A young Indian who betrays his people in Simms' novel THE YEMASSEE.

Occurrence at Owl Creek Bridge, An. A famous short story by Ambrose BIERCE (1891), describing the execution by hanging of Peyton Farquhar, a Southern plantation owner and civilian during the American Civil War, who has been apprehended while trying to obstruct the building of a Union railroad at Owl Creek Bridge. The hanging takes place at the bridge, and when the trap is pulled and Farquhar falls into the water, he has the delusion, during the last few seconds of his life, that he is swimming underwater and escaping back to his wife and family. The story is considered remarkable for its time in its depiction of the sensations and psychological states of a dying man.

Oceana. A philosophical treatise on the principles of government by James HARRINGTON (1656). See COMMONWEALTHS, IDEAL.

ocean greyhound, see GREYHOUND.

Oceanus. In classic mythology, a TITAN, the god of the salt river which the ancients believed flowed round the earth and father of all river gods and water sprites.

Ochiltree, Edie. One of Scott's most famous characters, a king's bedesman or bluegown in THE ANTIQUARY. Edie is a garrulous, kind-hearted, wandering beggar, who assures Mr. Lovel that the supposed ruins of a Roman camp are no such thing. The old bedesman delights "to daunder down the burnsides and green shaws."

Ochs, Adolph Simon (1858–1935). American publisher of the New York *Times* (1896–1935) as well as the Philadelphia *Times* (1902–1912), Philadelphia *Public Ledger* (1902–1912), and other newspapers.

Ochs von Lerchenau, Baron. In Richard Strauss' opera DER ROSENKAVALIER, a coarse, jovial, amorous country gentleman, who plans to bestow the "favor" of his old name upon the merchant's daughter Sophie Faninal, in return for her considerable dowry. He is considered one of the most vivid caricatures in all opera.

Ockham or **Occam, William of** (1300?–1349?). English scholastic philosopher, known as *Doctor Invincibilis.* Disputed the temporal power of the Pope and, in his *Dialogues,* anticipated the modern idea of civil rule being independent from the church. His nominalistic thesis, that universals are abstractions devoid of concrete reality, practically concluded the scholastic controversy and prepared the way for the philosophy of Francis BACON.

Ockham's razor. *Entia non sunt multiplicanda* (*Lat.,* "entities are not to be multiplied"). With this axiom, which means that all unnecessary facts or constituents in the subject being analyzed are to be eliminated, William of OCKHAM dissected every question as with a razor.

Ocnus, rope of. Profitless labor. Ocnus was always twisting a rope with unwearied diligence, but an ass ate it as fast as it was twisted.

O'Connell, Daniel (1775–1847). Irish leader, often called *the Liberator.* As M.P. (elected, 1828), he took his seat only after the Catholic Emancipation (1829). Lord Mayor of Dublin (1841). His leadership was challenged by the Young-Ireland revolutionaries (1845). He died at Genoa on his way to Rome.

O'Connor, Norreys Jephson (1885–). American poet, author of *Songs of the Celtic Past* (1918); etc.

Octavia (died 11 B.C.). Half-sister of Emperor Augustus and wife of Marc Antony until he divorced her (32 B.C.) when Cleopatra had come into his life. She appears in *Antony and Cleopatra* by Shakespeare, and in *All for Love* by Dryden.

octavo. A book composed of sheets folded so that each leaf is one-eighth of a given size of paper.

Octopus, The. A novel by Frank NORRIS (1901), the first of a trilogy planned to deal with American wheat. The production of wheat in California is the subject of this novel, and the "Octopus" is the Pacific and Southwestern Railroad, a symbol of organized trade strangling the country that feeds it. *The Octopus* was followed by THE PIT.

Octoroon or Life in Louisiana, The. An American drama by Dion BOUCICAULT (1859), based on a novel by M. Reid called *The Quadroon.* It concerns the fortunes of the octoroon Zoë, sold away from the man she loves to become the property of one she despises.

odalisque. In the harem of a Sultan, a female slave or concubine. The word is of Turkish origin and means literally "chambermaid."

ode. A type of lyric, of no set form, originally intended to be set to music. See PINDARIC VERSE. The ode was widely favored among English poets of the 17th, 18th, and early 19th centuries, appearing in the work of such figures as MILTON, DRYDEN, COLLINS, COLERIDGE, WORDSWORTH, SHELLEY, and KEATS.

Ode in Time of Hesitation, An. Title of a poem by William Vaughn MOODY. The subtitle of the poem is, *After seeing at Boston the statue of Robert Gould Shaw, killed while storming Fort Wagner, July 18, 1863, at the head of the first enlisted Negro regiment, the Fifty-fourth Massachusetts.* It is one of the finest odes in American poetry. Written during the Spanish-American War, it is a tribute to Shaw and a plea for the United States (bemused by talk of "MANIFEST DESTINY") to "let the island men go free." Moody was strongly against the annexation of the Philippines by the U.S.

Ode on Intimations of Immortality from Recollections of Early Childhood. A famous poem by William WORDSWORTH (1836), based on the Platonic doctrine of recollection, which asserts that the process usually called learning is actually only a recollection to the adult mind of knowledge lost by each individual at birth; a statement occurs in PLATO's dialogue *Phaedo.* Wordsworth's poem celebrates the child which, "trailing clouds of glory," still retains in infancy memories of the celestial abode from which it has come. Although the mature man has forgotten this knowledge, we are told, he can regain it by heeding his intuition and remembering his own childhood.

Ode Recited at the Commemoration of the Living and Dead Soldiers of Harvard University. By James Russell LOWELL. Privately printed (1865), published in *The Cathedral* (1877). Also known as the *Commemoration Ode.* An irregular Pindaric ode, one of the finest in American poetry.

Oderic. In Ariosto's *Orlando Furioso,* the false knight who, under pretense of escorting ISABELLA, sold her as a slave.

Ode to a Nightingale. A poem by John KEATS (1819), considered one of the poet's greatest compositions. It expresses the emotions of the poet as he listens to the song of a nightingale—his visions of sensuous beauty and his melancholy as he feels the imminence of death.

Perhaps the self-same song that found a path
 Through the sad heart of Ruth, when, sick for home,
She stood in tears amid the alien corn;
 The same that oft-times hath
Charmed magic casements, opening on the foam
 Of perilous seas, in faery lands forlorn.

Ode to the West Wind. One of the best-known poems of Percy Bysshe SHELLEY (1820), written in TERZA RIMA. In it, the poet addresses the strong wind of Autumn—"tameless, and swift, and proud"—and identifies himself with its force.

Scatter, as from an unextinguished hearth
Ashes and sparks, my words among mankind!
Be through my lips to unawakened earth
The trumpet of a prophecy! O Wind,
If Winter comes, can Spring be far behind?

odeon or **odeum.** In classical antiquity, a building devoted to poetic and musical contests (hence the name, from *ode*). The first was built at Athens in the reign of Pericles. Afterwards it was used for public meetings. There were odeons in most Greek cities and in Rome. They were small roofed theaters. Opposite the Luxembourg Gardens in Paris is a theater called *L'Odéon,* built in 1728.

Odets, Clifford (1906–). American playwright, known in the 1930's as an outstanding proletarian author. See PROLETARIAN LITERATURE. His plays, most of which deal with the frustrations and minor tragedies of middle and lower middle-class people living in New York City during the depression era, and which were compared by enthusiastic critics of the time to the plays of CHEKHOV, are marked by striking dialogue semi-colloquial and semi-journalistic in character. These plays include WAITING FOR LEFTY (1935), Odets' best-known work; AWAKE AND SING (1935), considered the author's best work; *Till the Day I Die* (1935), concerned with the Communist underground movement in NAZI Germany; *Paradise Lost* (1935), depicting decline in a middle-class family; *Golden Boy* (1937), dealing with a violinist of Italian parentage who becomes a prize-fighter in order to make money; *Rocket to the Moon* (1938), showing a middle-aged Bronx dentist in the throes of a love affair; *Night Music* (1940); *Clash by Night* (1942); etc.

Odets was at first an actor with the Theater Guild (see LITTLE THEATER) and in 1931 was one of the founders of the Group Theater, which later produced his best-known plays. A number of critics of the 1930's regarded him as the most promising playwright of the time and a possible successor to Eugene O'NEILL. They expressed disappointment, however, in respect to his later works.

Odin. The Scandinavian name of the god called by the Anglo-Saxons Woden, the supreme god of the later Scandinavian pantheon, he having supplanted THOR.

Odin was god of wisdom, poetry, war, and agriculture, and on this latter account Wednesday (*Woden's day*) was considered to be specially favorable for sowing. He was god of the dead also, and presided over the banquets of those slain in battle. See VALHALLA. He became the *All-wise* by drinking from MIMIR's fountain, but purchased the distinction at the cost of one eye, and is usually represented as a one-eyed man wearing a hat and carrying a staff. His remaining eye is the Sun.

The father of Odin was Bör. His brothers are Vili and Ve. His wife is Frigga. His sons are Thor and Balder. His mansion is Gladsheim. His court as war-god is Valhalla. His two black ravens are Hugin (thought) and Munin (memory). His steed is Sleipnir. His ships are Skidbladnir and Naglfar. His spear is Gungnir, which never fails to hit the mark aimed at. His ring is called Draupnir, which every ninth night drops eight other rings of equal value. His throne is Hlidskjalf. His wolves are Geri and Freki. He will be ultimately swallowed up by the Fenris wolf at Ragnarok.

the promise of Odin. The most binding of all oaths to a Norseman. In making it the hand was passed through a massive silver ring kept for the purpose, or through a sacrificial stone, like that called the "Circle of Stennis."

I will bind myself to you . . . by the promise of Odin, the most sacred of our northern rites.—Scott, *The Pirate,* ch. xxii.

Odin's tree. The gallows.

odium theologicum (*Lat.*). The bitter hatred of rival theologians. No wars are so sanguinary as holy wars; no persecutions so relentless as religious persecutions; no hatred is so bitter as theological hatred.

Odle, Mrs. Alan, see RICHARDSON, DOROTHY M.

Odo, Duke. The hero of Edith Wharton's VALLEY OF DECISION.

Odrovir or Odhrevir. The "poet's mead" of the Scandinavian gods. It was made of Kvasir's blood mixed with honey, and all who partook of it became poets. Kvasir was the wisest of all men, and could answer any question put to him. He was fashioned out of the saliva spat into a jar by the AESIR and VANIR on their conclusion of peace, and was slain by the dwarfs Fjalar and Galar.

odor of sanctity. In the Middle Ages it was held that a sweet and delightful odor was given off by the bodies of saintly persons at their death, and also when their bodies, if "translated," were disinterred; hence the phrase, *he died in the odor of sanctity,* i.e., he died a saint.

O'Donnell, Peader (1896–). Irish novelist, militant in Sinn Fein and Irish Republican Army. Professor of English, Trinity College, Dublin. Knows Gaelic well. *The Way it Was with Them* (1927), etc.

ODTAA. Title of a novel by John Masefield (1926). It means "life is simply *one damned thing after another,*" a pronouncement which has been variously ascribed to Frank Ward O'MALLEY and Elbert HUBBARD.

Odyssey. The epic poem attributed to the Greek poet Homer which records the adventures of Odysseus (Ulysses) on his long journey from Troy. The word is an adjective formed out of the hero's name, and means the *things* or *adventures* of Ulysses. Any long journey may be referred to as an odyssey. A brief summary of the epic follows:

Book I. The poem opens in the island of CALYPSO, with a complaint against Neptune and Calypso for preventing the return of Odysseus to Ithaca.

II. TELEMACHUS, the son of Odysseus, starts in search of his father, accompanied by Pallas Athene in the guise of MENTOR.

III. He goes to Pylos, to consult old NESTOR, and

IV. is sent by him to Sparta, where he is told by MENELAUS that Odysseus is detained in the island of Calypso.

V. In the meantime, Odysseus leaves the island, and, being shipwrecked, is cast on the shore of Phaeacia,

VI. where NAUSICAÄ, the king's daughter, finds him asleep, and

VII. takes him to the court of her father ALCINOUS, who

VIII. entertains him hospitably.

IX. At a banquet, Odysseus relates his adventures since he started from Troy. Tells about the Lotus-eaters and the CYCLOPS, with his advenures in the cave of Polyphemus. He tells how

X. the wind-god gave him the winds in a bag. In the island of CIRCE, he says, his crew were changed to swine, but HERMES gave him a herb called moly, which disenchanted them.

XI. He tells the king how he descended into HADES;

XII. gives an account of the sirens; of SCYLLA and CHARYBDIS; and of his being cast on the island of Calypso.

XIII. Alcinous gives Odysseus a ship which conveys him to Ithaca, where he assumes the disguise of a beggar,

XIV. and is lodged in the house of EUMAEUS, a faithful old domestic.

XV. Telemachus, having returned to Ithaca, is lodged in the same house,

XVI. and becomes known to his father.

XVII. Odysseus goes to his palace, is recognized by his dog Argus; but

XVIII. the beggar Irus insults him, and Odysseus breaks his jaw-bone.

XIX. While bathing, the returned monarch is recognized by a scar on his leg;

XX. and when he enters his palace, becomes an eye-witness to the disorders of the court, and to the way in which

XXI. PENELOPE is annoyed by suitors. To excuse herself, Penelope tells her suitors he only shall be her husband who can bend Odysseus' bow. None can do so but the stranger, who bends it with ease. Concealment is no longer possible or desirable.

XXII. He falls on the suitors hip and thigh;
XXIII. is recognized by his wife;
XXIV. visits his old father LAERTES; and the poem ends.

The 20th-century Irish novelist James JOYCE adapted the *Odyssey* as the framework of his famous novel ULYSSES, presenting the epic characters in contemporary Irish metamorphoses of his day.

Oedipus. In classic myth, the son of Laius, King of Thebes, and Jocasta, his wife. In order to evade the prediction of an oracle that this child would slay his father, he was left to die on Mount Cithaeron. A Corinthian shepherd found the babe with his feet bound together (hence his name *Oedipus* or "swollen feet") and he grew to maturity as the adopted son of Polybus, King of Corinth. Again an oracle predicted that he would slay his own father and defile his mother. Thinking Polybus his true father, he set out from Corinth and on his journey met, quarreled with and killed a stranger, who was really Laius. He next solved the famous riddle of the SPHINX and became in consequence King of Thebes, unwittingly marrying Jocasta, his own mother. Later a terrible plague ravaged Thebes, and the oracle declared that only the banishment of the murderer of Laius would bring it to an end. The truth came out at last through the seer TIRESIAS; Jocasta took her own life, and Oedipus put out his eyes and roamed about the earth in misery, attended only by his daughter, the faithful ANTIGONE.

This legend is the basis of a famous trilogy by Sophocles, *Oedipus Tyrannus, Oedipus at Colonus* and *Antigone;* also of tragedies by CORNEILLE (1659) and VOLTAIRE (1718), both entitled *Oedipe,* and of many other tragedies. For the story of the two sons of Oedipus, Eteocles and Polynices, whom he left as rulers of Thebes, see *Seven Against Thebes* under THEBES.

Oedipus complex. See under COMPLEX.

Oemler, Mrs. **Marie,** *née* **Conway** (1879–1932). American novelist and short-story writer, born in Georgia. Her *Slippy McGee* (1917) is an appealing and very popular novel about a crook. Her most ambitious book, *The Holy Lover* (1927), is about John Wesley.

Oenone. In classic myth a nymph of Mount Ida, who had the gift of prophecy, and told her husband Paris that his voyage to Greece would involve him and his country (Troy) in ruin. According to the legend, Paris came back to her beseeching her to heal his severe wounds, but she refused, and changed her mind too late. When the dead body of old Priam's son was laid at her feet, she stabbed herself. This story forms the subject of Tennyson's *Oenone* and *The Death of Oenone* and William Morris' *Death of Paris* (*Earthly Paradise* III).

Oenopian. In classic myth, father of MEROPE, to whom the giant ORION made advances. Oenopian, unwilling to give his daughter to him, put out the giant's eyes in a drunken fit.

Oenslager, Donald Mitchell (1902–). American stage designer, Associate Professor of Drama, Yale University. Author of *Scenery Then and Now.*

O'Faoláin, Séan (1900–). Irish teacher, novelist, and biographer of De Valera. Charter Member, Irish Royal Academy of Letters. Began writing in Gaelic. *A Nest of Simple Folk* (1933); *King of the Beggars: A Life of Daniel O'Connell* (1938); etc.

O'Feeney, Sean, see FORD, JOHN.

Offenbach, Jacques (1819–1880). German-born creator of French burlesque opera. Contributed *opéra bouffe* to theaters in Paris and opened his own theater there. Famous for his *Contes d'Hoffmann* (see TALES OF HOFFMANN), which was finished by Guiraud after his death (1881).

O'Ferrall, Trilby, see TRILBY.

Office of Production Management (O.P.M.), see under WAR PRODUCTION BOARD.

Offitt. In John Hay's THE BREAD-WINNERS, a labor organizer shown as a villain.

offset process. A process in printing where the impression is first made on a cylinder with a rubber surface, and then transferred to the paper, instead of being made directly upon the paper.

Of Human Bondage. A novel by W. Somerset MAUGHAM (1916), semi-autobiographical in content and regarded as the author's best work. It deals with the childhood, adolescence, and early youth of Philip CAREY and his efforts to "find" himself. An orphan raised by an elderly aunt and uncle, Philip is lonely, shy, and sensitive, very much aware of his inferior social position and his club foot, a congenital infirmity. After a period of misery at school, he succeeds in going to Paris to study painting, for which he believes he has a vocation, and comes in contact with a group of art students, painters, writers, and the like—typical BOHEMIANS of early 20th-century Paris. He is impressed by their iconoclasm and their free and careless, if often impecunious and sordid, lives, but he is unable to emulate them. When his art teacher frankly tells him that his work shows "industry and intelligence" but no talent, he decides to give up painting completely rather than become a second-rate artist. He returns to London, where he has an unhappy love affair with MILDRED, a petty, selfish, and vulgar little Cockney waitress. After further misfortunes, he at last enters a London hospital to study medicine and is offered passage as a ship's doctor to the Orient. See also PRICE, FANNY. In 1946 Mr. Maugham presented the sixteen leather-bound exercise books making up the manuscript of *Of Human Bondage* to the Library of Congress "as a way of showing his appreciation to this country, for the hospitality with which he was received here during the war."

O'Flaherty, Liam (1896–). Irish novelist, known for his novels of 20th-century Irish life, especially during the Irish Revolution of 1916. Among his works are *Thy Neighbor's Wife* (1924); *Black Soul* (1924); *The Informer* (1925), his best-known novel, later produced as a highly praised American motion picture; *Mr. Gilhooley* (1926); *The Life of Tim Healey* (1927), biography; *The Assassin* (1928); *A Tourist's Guide to Ireland* (1929); *The House of Gold* (1929); *The Return of the Brute* (1929); *Two Years* (1930); *The Puritan* (1931); *I Went to Russia* (1931), travel; *Skerrett* (1932); *The Martyr* (1933); *Hollywood Cemetery* (1935); *Famine* (1937); *Shame the Devil* (1934), autobiography. Collections of short stories include: *Spring Sowing* (1926); *The Tent* (1926); *The Fairy Goose* (1927); *Red Barbara* (1928); *The Mountain Tavern* (1929); *The Wild Swan* (1932).

O'Flaherty took active part in the Irish Revolution, organizing a regiment of ex-soldiers to fight against the English. After the conclusion of World War I, he vagabonded around the world, working at odd jobs in numerous countries, including the U.S. See also O'CASEY, SEAN; PROLETARIAN LITERATURE.

Of Mice and Men. A novelette by John STEINBECK (1937), dramatized for the theater in 1938 and later for the screen. It deals with the friendship between two migrant laborers in California—Lennie Small, a giant half-wit of tremendous strength, who likes to caress soft things, and George Milton, who acts as Lennie's protector and directs him in feats of strength. The two dream of owning a farm of their own one day. The daughter-in-law of the owner of the farm on which the two are working is a nymphomaniac and decides to try to seduce Lennie. When in response he attempts to stroke her "soft" hair, she becomes frightened and tries to escape, Lennie accidentally breaks her neck with his huge hands. In order to save his friend from an angry lynch mob, George shoots Lennie.

Ofterdingen, Heinrich von, see HEINRICH VON OFTERDINGEN.

Of Thee I Sing. A musical comedy with book by George S. KAUFMAN, Morrie Ryskind, and Ira Gershwin, and music by George GERSHWIN, produced in 1931. It satirizes American party politics, showing a presidential campaign conducted on a platform of Love, with John P. Wintergreen, the party candidate, to choose a bride in an Atlantic City beauty contest if he is successful. It won the Pulitzer prize in 1932.

Of Time and the River: A Legend of Man's Hunger in His Youth. A partially autobiographical novel by Thomas WOLFE (1935), a sequel to LOOK HOMEWARD, ANGEL. In it, Eugene GANT, the hero, continues the pilgrimage of passionate discovery through the world that he began in adolescence in the earlier book. He spends two years as a graduate student at Harvard University, there meeting various scholars, eccentrics, and aesthetes, returns home for the dramatic and terrible death of his father, and takes a job as a teacher of literature in New York City, at the "School for Utility Cultures" (New York University). There he meets more odd characters, has further passionate love affairs, and becomes acquainted with the life of the suburban, socially élite classes. Eventually he goes to Europe, touring France with two girls and a former Harvard friend, Starwick (also drawn from life) whom he discovers to be a homosexual. When he is exhausted financially—and, to some extent, emotionally—Eugene returns to the U.S., ready for more adventures.

Og. King of Bashan; according to rabbinical mythology, an antediluvian giant, saved from the flood by climbing on the roof of the ark. After the passage of the Red Sea, Moses first conquered Sihon, and then advanced against the giant Og (whose bedstead, made of iron, was above fifteen feet long and nearly seven feet broad, *Deut.* iii. 11). The legend says that Og plucked up a mountain to hurl at the Israelites, but he got so entangled with his burden that Moses was able to kill him without much difficulty.

In Dryden's ABSALOM AND ACHITOPHEL, Og stands for Thomas SHADWELL, who was very large and fat. See also MAC FLECKNOE.

Ogden, Charles Kay (1889–). British educator; inventor of BASIC ENGLISH. Coauthor with I. A. Richards of *The Meaning of Meaning* (1923). Author of *The System of Basic English* (1934).

Ogden, Rollo (1856–1937). American journalist. Editor, New York *Evening Post* (1903–1920); New York *Times* (1922–1937).

Ogham or Ogam. The traditional alphabet of the ancient British and Irish peoples, used in writing on wood or stone, supposedly invented by one Ogma.

Ogier the Dane. One of the great heroes of medieval romance; a paladin of Charlemagne, and son of Geoffrey, King of Denmark, of which (as Holger Danske) he is still the national hero. Fairies attended at his birth, and bestowed upon him divers gifts. Among these fairies was MORGAN LE FAY, who, when the knight is a hundred years old, puts him on a ship for Avalon, "hard by the Terrestrial Paradise." On reaching the island he enters the castle, where he finds a horse sitting at a banquet-table. The horse, who was once a mighty prince, conducts him to Morgan le Fay, who gives him a ring which removes all infirmities and restores him to ripe manhood, and a crown which makes him forget his country and past life, and introduces him to King Arthur. Two hundred years roll on, and France is invaded by the Paynims. Morgan le Fay now sends Ogier to defend *"le bon pays de France,"* and when he has routed the invaders she takes him back to Avalon, where he remains until the time for him to reappear on the earth. In a pack of French cards, *Ogier the Dane* is knave of spades. His exploits are related in the *chansons de geste;* he is introduced by Ariosto in ORLANDO FURIOSO, and by William MORRIS in his *Earthly Paradise* (*August*).

Ogilvie, William Henry (1869–). Scottish journalist, author of hunting and sporting verse.

Ogilvy, Margaret, see MARGARET OGILVY.

Ogpu. The Soviet secret service. *O, g, p, u* are the initials of the Russian words for Special Government Political Administration. It succeeded the Cheka in 1922. Also *Gay-Pay-Oo.*

O'Grady, Standish James (1846–1928). Irish pioneer of Celtic renaissance. Author of *History of Ireland: Heroic Period* (1878).

Ogres. In nursery and fairy tales, giants of very malignant disposition, who live on human flesh. The word was first used (and probably invented) by Charles PERRAULT in his *Contes* (1697), and is thought to be made up from *Orcus,* a name of Pluto, the god of Hades.

O'Groat, John, see JOHN O'GROAT.

Ogygia. CALYPSO's island.

O'Hara, Geoffrey (1882–). Canadian composer of songs and operettas, known for *K-K-K-Katy, Wreck of the Julie Plante,* etc.

O'Hara, John Henry (1905–). American journalist, novelist, and short-story writer. Also a screen writer (since 1934) and an original and bitter social commentator. *The Doctor's Son and Other Stories* (1935) contains some of his best work. *Butterfield 8* (1935) is the story of Starr Faithfull, a mysteriously killed New York girl, transposed into fiction. His *Pal Joey* sketches in the *New Yorker* made a successful musical comedy (1941) and a Hollywood moving picture.

O'Hara, Scarlett. The beautiful, fiery-tempered heroine of GONE WITH THE WIND.

O. Henry, see HENRY, O.

O'Higgins, Harvey Jerrold (1876–1929). Canadian-born American novelist and short-story writer. Wrote much of Irish types for the magazines. Collaborated with Judge Ben B. LINDSEY of Denver in the study of city youth, *The Beast and the Jungle* (1910). Wrote several melodramas with Harriet Ford, among them *The Dummy* (1913). Dramatized *Main Street* by Sinclair LEWIS. Adapted Freud's methods in studying character in his stories, notably in *Some Distinguished Americans* (1922). His *From the Life* purports to be stories of people in *Who's Who. Julie Crane* (1924) was his most successful novel.

Ohm, Georg Simon (1787–1854). German physicist for whom the practical unit of electrical resistance is named.

Oh! Susannah. A song by Stephen FOSTER, printed in his *Songs of the Sable Harmonists* (1848). Popular in the California gold rush of 1849.

Oil. A novel (1927) by Upton SINCLAIR, based on the TEAPOT DOME scandal of the HARDING administration.

O.K. From Choktaw Indian *okeh,* "it is so"; from the initials of Obadiah Kelly, the railroad clerk, who initialed the packages he accepted; from *orl korrect,* a faulty spelling for "all correct"; from Middle English *hoacky,* "the last load of a harvest"; etc., etc.

O'Keeffe, Georgia (1887–). American painter of desert scenes and symbolic abstracts. Married to Alfred STIEGLITZ.

O'Kelly, Sheumas (d. 1920). Irish writer and editor of *Sinn Fein.*

Okies. A term applied to dispossessed farm families of the Dust Bowl region of the southwestern part of the U.S., who were forced in the 1930's to abandon their land because of soil erosion and travel elsewhere in search of work, most often going to California as migrant laborers in the fruit orchards. The term had its origin in Oklahoma, the name of the state from which most of the first Dust Bowl refugees came. The JOAD family, in John Steinbeck's THE GRAPES OF WRATH, is the outstanding Okie family in fiction.

Oklahoma! A musical play based on *Green Grow the Lilacs* by Lynn RIGGS, music by Richard RODGERS, libretto by Oscar HAMMERSTEIN. It closed in May 1948 after 2246 performances, an all-time record for musicals.

Okraska, Madame. The central figure of Anne Douglas Sedgwick's TANTE.

Olaf, St., see under SAINTS.

Olaf, King, Saga of, see SAGA OF KING OLAF, THE.

Olcott, Chauncey (1860–1932). American tenor and actor, star in Irish musical dramas. Sang *Mother Machree;* wrote and sang *My Wild Irish Rose;* etc.

old.
Old Abe. Abraham Lincoln (1809–1865).
Old Bendy. The Devil.
Old Bona Fide. Louis XIV of France.
Old Bullion. The American politician, Thomas H. Benton (1782–1858), an advocate of bimetallism.
Old Cap Collier. See COLLIER.
Old Clootie. The Devil.
Old Colony. The eastern part of Massachusetts.
old country. The home country of an immigrant to the United States or the British dominions.
Old Cracow Bible. See BIBLE, SPECIALLY NAMED.
Old Dominion. Virginia. Every Act of Parliament to the Declaration of Independence designated Virginia "the Colony and Dominion of Virginia." Captain John Smith, in his *History of Virginia* (1629), calls this "colony and dominion" *Old Virginia,* in contradistinction to *New England,* and other British settlements.
Old Ephraim. A grizzly bear.
Old Fox. Marshal Soult (1769–1851).
Old Fritz (Ger. *Der alte Fritz*). Frederick the Great (1712–1786).
Old Glorious. William III of England.
Old Harry. (1) The Devil. (2) Henry VIII of England.
Old Hickory. See HICKORY.
Old Line State. Maryland. See STATES.
Old Man Eloquent. (1) Isocrates, so called by Milton; (2) Samuel Taylor Coleridge; (3) John Quincy Adams; (4) W. E. Gladstone.
Old Man of the Mountains (Sheikh-al-Jebal). Hassan ben Sabbah, the founder of the ASSASSINS, who made his stronghold in the mountain fastnesses of Lebanon. He died in 1124, and in 1256 his dynasty, and nearly all the Assassins, were exterminated by the Tartar prince, Hulaku.
Old Man of the Sea. In the *Arabian Nights* story of SINBAD THE SAILOR, the *Old Man of the Sea* climbs on the shoulders of Sinbad, and clings there for many days and nights, much to the discomfort of Sinbad, who finally releases himself by making the Old Man drunk. Hence, any burden, figurative or actual, of which it is impossible to free oneself without the greatest exertions is spoken of as an *Old Man of the Sea.*
Old Nick. The Devil.
Old Noll. Oliver Cromwell (1599–1658).
Old North State. North Carolina.
Old Pretender. See PRETENDER.
Old Public Functionary. James Buchanan (1791–1868), U.S. president.
Old Put. The American Revolutionary general, Israel Putnam (1718–1790).
Old Reliable. The American general, George Henry Thomas (1816–1870).
Old Rough and Ready. See under ROUGH.
Old Scratch. The Devil.
old style—new style. Terms used in chronology, the *old style* being the JULIAN CALENDAR, and the *new style* the GREGORIAN. See also CALENDAR.
old wives' tale. A gossipy or unconvincing story, from Tyndale's translation of 1 *Tim.* iv. 7. George PEELE was the author of a drama called *The Old Wives' Tale* (ca. 1595) and Arnold BENNETT wrote a novel so called.
Old World. So Europe, Asia, and Africa are called when compared with North and South America, or the New World.

Old Bailey. See under BAILEY.

Oldbuck, Jonathan. In Scott's ANTIQUARY, the Laird of Monkbarns, an "antiquary" devoted to the study and accumulation of old coins and medals, etc. He is sarcastic, irritable, and a woman-hater, but kind-hearted and a great humorist. The author said a certain George Constable (1719–1803) was the original of Jonathan Oldbuck.

> An excellent temper, with a slight degree of subacid humour; learning, wit, and drollery, the more poignant that they were a little marked by the peculiarities of an old bachelor; a soundness of thought, rendered more forcible by an occasional quaintness of expression.—these were the qualities in which the creature of my imagination resembled my benevolent and excellent old friend.—Sir Walter Scott.

Oldcastle, Sir **John** (1377?–1417). A historical character, better known as Lord Cobham, the original of Shakespeare's famous FALSTAFF. A play called *Sir John Oldcastle,* now ascribed to Anthony Munday, was printed in 1600 as Shakespeare's work, and in the 1600 quarto edition of 1 and 2 *Henry IV,* there are indications that the name Oldcastle was originally used but later changed to Falstaff.

Old Chester. The scene of most of the novels and short stories of Margaret DELAND, notably the two volumes of short stories, *Old Chester Tales* (1898) and *Around Old Chester* (1915) and the novels, THE AWAKENING OF HELENA RICHIE, THE IRON WOMAN and *An Old Chester Secret* (1920). Mrs. Deland's Old Chester is said to be in many respects a counterpart of Manchester, Pa., where she was born, now a part of Pittsburgh.

Old Contemptibles. The German Kaiser jeered at the small Expeditionary Force England sent to France in 1914 as a "contemptible little army." In typically British fashion the name was immediately adopted.

Old Curiosity Shop, The. A novel by Charles DICKENS (1841). The heroine, Nell Trent, better known as LITTLE NELL, lives with her grandfather, an old man who keeps a "curiosity shop." He adores her, but loses what little he has by gambling, and they roam about the country as beggars until finally Little Nell dies. The book relates also the adventures of a boy named Kit NUBBLES, employed for a time in the curiosity shop. Later, the hunchback, Daniel QUILP, contrives to have him convicted of theft and sentenced to transportation, but he is saved from this fate by the good offices of a girl-of-all-work, nicknamed "the MARCHIONESS."

Oldenburg Horn. A horn long in the possession of the reigning princes of the House of Oldenburg, but now in the collection of the King of Denmark. According to tradition, Count Otto of Oldenburg, in 967, was offered drink in this silver-gilt horn by a "wild woman," at the Osenborg. As he did not like the look of the liquor, he threw it away, and rode off with the horn.

Oldfield, Anne (1683–1730). English eighteenth-century actress. Most successful in *The Fair Penitent* by Rowe and *The Provok'd Husband* by Colley Cibber. Pope called her "Narcissa" in his *Moral Essays.* She liked comedy better than tragedy, and would often say, "I hate to have a Page dragging my Tail about. Why do they not give Porter these parts? She can put on a better Tragedy Face than I can." Buried in Westminster Abbey under Congreve's monument.

Oldfield, Claude Houghton. Pseudonym **Claude Houghton** (1889–). English poet and novelist, best-known for *I Am Jonathan Scrivener* (1934). Metaphysical yet witty.

Old Folks at Home, The (1851). A very popular song by Stephen FOSTER. Also called *Swanee River,* because it begins, "Way down upon the Swanee River . . ."

Old Fortunatus. A comedy by Thomas DEKKER (published, 1600). It involves the legend of the purse of gold which is inexhaustible provided only ten pieces are drawn from it at one time.

Old Glory. A popular name for the flag of the United States of America. The story is that Captain William Driver, master of the brig *Charles Doggett,* before sailing from Salem, Mass., in 1831, received an American flag and spoke of it as Old Glory.

Old Homestead, The. A drama in four acts (1887) by Denman Thompson. Thompson's excellent acting of the leading part (the country boy who makes good in the city and returns to pay off the mortgage on the old farm) made the play a success and caused many imitations of its theme.

Old Ironsides. A poem by O. W. HOLMES (1830) written in protest against an order to destroy the frigate CONSTITUTION. It aroused so much popular concern that the decision was revoked. The poem begins:

> Ay, tear her tattered ensign down,
> Long has it waved on high.

Old Kentucky Home, My. A song by Stephen FOSTER.

Old Lady Shows Her Medals, The. A one-act play by J. M. BARRIE.

Old Maid, The. A novelette (1924) by Edith WHARTON. It is one of the four novelettes in the series *Old New York,* the others being *False Dawn, The Spark,* and *New Year's Day.* Zoë Akins made it into a play (1935) which won the Pulitzer prize.

Old Man's Comforts And How He Gained Them, The. A poem by Robert SOUTHEY (1799), best-known through the parody of it written by Lewis Carroll in his FATHER WILLIAM.

> "You are old, Father William," the young man cried,
> "And life must be hastening away;
> You are cheerful, and love to converse upon death,
> Now tell me the reason, I pray."
> "I am cheerful, young man," Father William replied,
> "Let the cause thy attention engage;
> In the days of my youth I remembered my God!
> And He hath not forgotten my age."
> Southey, *The Old Man's Comforts*

Old Mortality. A novel by Sir Walter SCOTT (1816), a story of the struggle between the Covenanters and the Cavaliers under Claverhouse in 1670–1671. "Old Mortality," who tells the story to the supposed author, Jedediah CLEISHBOTHAM, is an eccentric itinerant whose whole life is given over to cleaning the moss from old gravestones, cutting new inscriptions and erecting new stones for the fallen Covenanters. The original of this character was Robert Paterson (1715–1801).

Old Oaken Bucket, The. An old and popular song by Samuel Woodworth (*Am.,* 1784–1842).

> The old oaken bucket, the moss-covered bucket,
> The iron-bound bucket that hung in the well.

Old Possum. Name assumed by T. S. ELIOT in his whimsical *Old Possum's Book of Practical Cats* (1939).

Old Rowley. Nickname of King Charles II of England in allusion to his numerous amours. There was a stallion in the royal stud famed for the mettle of its progeny. Cf. *"Old Rowley," A Private Life of Charles II* by Dennis Wheatley (1934).

Old Soak, the. A character created by Don MARQUIS who appeared first in the columns of the New York *Evening Sun* and later became the central figure in a humorous volume entitled *The Old Soak* (1921) and in a comedy of the same title.

Old South Church. Affectionately called "Old South," it is a historic landmark in Boston, Mass. It was built in 1729 and became a meeting place for patriots before the Revolution.

Oldstyle, Jonathan, see IRVING, WASHINGTON.

Old Swimmin' Hole and 'Leven More Poems, The. Title of James Whitcomb RILEY's first book of poems in Hoosier dialect (1883), signed "Benj. F. Johnson, of Boone," but with the author's real name in brackets. One of Riley's most popular poems, *When the Frost is On the Punkin* is included.

Oldtown Folks. A novel written and dramatized (1869) by Harriet Beecher STOWE.

Old Uncle Ned. A minstrel show song by Stephen FOSTER. Popular with glee clubs.

Old Uncle Tom Cobbleigh, and all. See WIDDICOMBE FAIR.

Old Vic. Affectionate or brief for *Royal Victoria Hall.* A famous London theater opened as *The Royal Coburg* (May 11, 1818). Re-opened February 6, 1928 as a repertory house, principally devoted to Shakespearean productions.

Old Wives' Tale, The. A novel by Arnold BENNETT (1908). The central figures are two sisters, Constance and Sophia, who come together in their old age, both wives and finally widows. Constance has lived quietly in her native town of Bursley, one of Bennett's FIVE TOWNS, while Sophia has prospered by keeping boarders in Paris. The book gives a realistic picture of middle-class English life. For the allusion of the title, see above under OLD.

Old Woman of Berkeley. A ballad by SOUTHEY, based on an old legend, concerning a woman whose life has been very wicked. On her death-bed she sends for her son who is a monk, and for her daughter who is a nun, and bids them put her in a strong stone coffin, and to fasten the coffin to the ground with strong bands of iron. Fifty priests and fifty choristers are to pray and sing over her for three days, and the bell is to toll without ceasing. The first night passes without much disturbance. The second night, the candles burn blue, and dreadful yells are heard outside the church. But the third night the Devil breaks into the church and carries off the old woman on his black horse.

'ole, a better. See under HOLE.

Olga. In Franz Kafka's THE CASTLE, the daughter of a cobbler of the village of Madeleinegasse and sister of Amalia and BARNABAS. She befriends the hero, K.

Olin, Darius. The hired man hero of Irving Bacheller's DRI AND I.

Olindo. The lover of SOPHRONIA, hero of one of the most famous episodes of Tasso's JERUSALEM DELIVERED.

Oliphant, Laurence (1829–1888). English travel writer and novelist. Under the influence of the American spiritualist prophet Thomas Lake Harris (1867–1881), he wrote the mystical novel *Massolam* (1885). His last work, *Scientific Religion* (1888), he professed to have written under the influence of his deceased wife.

Oliphant, Margaret (1828–1897). Scottish novelist, chiefly known for her books dealing with provincial English society in the 19th century. Among her works are *Passages in the Life of Mrs. Margaret Maitland* (1849); *Chronicles of Carlingford* (1863–1876), including *Salem Chapel* (regarded as her best novel), *The Perpetual Curate, The Rector, Miss Marjoribanks,* and *Phoebe Junior; A Beleaguered City* (1880); *A Little Pilgrim of the Unseen* (1882); *Makers of Florence* (1888); *Makers of Venice* (1889); *Kirsteen* (1892); *Autobiography* (1899).

Olivares, Conde de. Gaspar de Guzmán (1587–1645). Spanish statesman and extravagant courtier. Caused Spain to enter Thirty-Years War against France (1636). Finally exiled (1643).

olive. In ancient Greece the olive was sacred to Pallas Athene, in allusion to the story (see ATHENS) that at the naming of Athens she presented it with an olive tree. It was the symbol of peace, and also an emblem of fecundity, Athenian brides wearing or carrying an olive garland as ours do a wreath of orange blossom. A crown of olive was the highest distinction of a citizen who had deserved well of his country, and was the highest prize in the Olympic Games.

to hold out the olive branch. To make overtures for peace; in allusion to the olive's being an ancient symbol of peace. In some of Numa's medals the king is represented holding an olive twig, indicative of a peaceful reign.

olive branches. A facetious term for children in relation to their parents: the allusion is to "Thy wife shall be as a fruitful vine . . . thy children like olive plants round about thy table" (*Ps.* cxxviii. 3).

Oliver. In Shakespeare's AS YOU LIKE IT, Orlando's older brother. He marries Celia.

Oliver or Oliviero. One of the greatest heroes of Carolingian legend, Charlemagne's favorite paladin, who, with ROLAND, rode by his side. He is the son of Regnier, Duke of Genoa (another of the paladins), and brother of the beautiful Aude. His sword is called *Hauteclaire,* and his horse *Ferrant d' Espagne.* After a life full of notable adventure, Oliver perishes with his great friend Roland in the fatal battle of RONCESVALLES.

a Roland for an Oliver. See ROLAND.

Oliver, John Rathbone (1872–1943). American clergyman and psychiatrist whose novel, *Victim and Victor,* nearly won the Pulitzer prize in 1929. He combined the priest and the psychiatrist in all his work.

Oliver Optic, see OPTIC, OLIVER.

Oliver Twist. A novel by Charles DICKENS (1838). Oliver starts his career in the workhouse, where he distinguishes himself by the unspeakable crime of asking for more gruel. When he is taken out of the workhouse, he is so shamefully treated that he runs away, only to fall into the hands of the Artful DODGER and his master, FAGIN THE JEW, who keep a gang of pickpockets and housebreakers into which Oliver is pressed against his will. In the course of time, however, he is befriended by Mr. Brownlow and received into the house of Mrs. MAYLIE, whose niece Rose proves to be his sister. See also SIKES, BILL; NANCY.

Olivia. In Shakespeare's TWELFTH NIGHT, a rich countess, loved by Orsino, Duke of Illyria. She marries SEBASTIAN.

Olivia Primrose, see PRIMROSE.

Olivier, Edith (1879?–). English novelist and biographer of Huguenot descent. Close friend of David Garnett, Sylvia Townsend Warner, and Elinor Wylie. Her best novels include *The Love Child* (1927); *The Triumphant Footman* (1930); *Dwarf's Blood* (1931); etc. *The Eccentric Life of Alexander Cruden* (U.S. title, *Alexander the Corrector;* 1934) is a study of the compiler of the well-known *Concordance,* who thrice went mad before finishing his work!

Olivier, Sir **Laurence** (1907–). English actor of stage and screen. Début in London (1926) in *The Marvellous History of Saint Bernard,* in America (1929) in *Murder on the Second Floor.* Established his reputation in *Private Lives* (1931) with Noel Coward and Gertrude Lawrence. Associated with the OLD VIC Theatre Company (1937, 1944 ff.). Has proved the amazing versatility of his interpretative genius in classical, Shakespearean, and modern rôles. *Oedipus Rex; Henry IV, Henry V, Romeo and Juliet, Richard III; Wuthering Heights* (screen), *Rebecca* (screen); etc. Knighted in 1947. His screen version of *Henry V,* filmed in Ireland during World War II, is superbly directed and acted.

Olivier, Mary, see MARY OLIVIER.

olla-podrida (*Span.*). A hodgepodge or miscellaneous collection. In the Latin countries an *olla* is a water jar or cooking pot of baked clay and *podrida* means "rotten."

Ollivant, Alfred (1874–1927). English novelist, whose *Bob, Son of Battle* (1898) is one of the world's most famous dog stories, to be compared with the animal stories of Anna Sewell (*Black Beauty*), Marshall Saunders (*Beautiful Joe*), and Albert Payson TERHUNE's *Lad.* Ollivant's amazing juvenile, *Redcoat Captain* (1907), and some of his romances deserve to be better known.

Ol' Man Adam an' His Chillun. A book by Roark Bradford (1928), which suggested to Marc CONNELLY the Pulitzer-prize play THE GREEN PASTURES (1930). The book contains Negro versions of stories in the Old Testament.

Olney. A country parish in England where William COWPER boarded with Mrs. UNWIN, for a time, assisting the local curate in charitable activities in the parish. His *Olney Hymns* (1779) is named for this community.

Olson, Elder (1909–). American poet. *Thing of Sorrow* (1934); *The Cock of Heaven* (1940); etc. Also author of *General Prosody, Rhythmic, Metric, Harmonics* (1938).

Olympiad. Among the ancient Greeks, a period of four years, the interval between the celebrations of the OLYMPIC GAMES. The first Olympiad began in 776 B.C., and the last (the 293rd) in 393 A.D.

Olympian odes. See EPINICIA.

Olympian Zeus or **Jove.** A statue by PHIDIAS, one of the seven wonders of the world. Pausanias (vii. 2) says when the sculptor placed it in the temple at Olympia (433 B.C.), he prayed the god to indicate whether or not he was satisfied with it, and immediately a thunderbolt fell on the floor of the temple without doing the slightest harm.

It was a chryselephantine statue, i.e., made of ivory and gold, and though seated on a throne, was sixty feet in height. The left hand rested on a scepter, and the right palm held a statue of Victory in solid gold. The robes were of gold, and so were the four lions which supported the footstool. The throne was of cedar, embellished with ebony, ivory, gold, and precious stones.

It was removed to Constantinople in the 5th century A.D., and was lost in the great fire of 475.

Olympic games. The greatest of the four sacred festivals of the ancient Greeks, held at Olympia every fourth year, in the month of July. The festival commenced with sacrifices and included racing, wrestling, and all kinds of contests, ending on the fifth day with processions, sacrifices, and banquets to the victors —who were garlanded with olive leaves. In 1895 an international committee met in Paris in the interests of establishing modern *Olympic games* to which various countries should send contestants. The first games of the new series were held at Athens in 1896, and after that date they occurred every four years with the exception of the duration of World War I and II.

Olympus. The home of the gods of ancient Greece, where Zeus held his court, a mountain about 9800 ft. high on the confines of Macedonia and Thessaly. It is used for any pantheon, as "Odin, Thor, Balder, and the rest of the Northern Olympus."

om. Among the Brahmans, the mystic equivalent for the name of the Deity. It was adopted by modern occultists to denote absolute goodness and truth or the spiritual essence.

om mani padme hum (Om, the jewel, is in the lotus: amen). The mystic formula of the Tibetans and northern Buddhists used as a charm and for many religious purposes. They are the first words taught to a child and the last uttered on the death-bed of the pious. The lotus symbolizes universal being, and the jewel the individuality of the utterer.

O'Mahony, John (1816–1877). Irish political leader. Helped organize Irish Republican brotherhood (1858). Headed American Fenians (1858–1866 and 1872–1877).

O'Malley, Grace. See PRANKQUEAN.

Omár Kháyyám. The 11th-century Persian astronomer-poet of Nishapur. He wrote ten works, the chief of which is *The Rubáiyát.* This was translated by Edward FITZGERALD (1859) in a free rather than a literal version.

omega. The last letter of the Greek alphabet. See ALPHA.

Omega Workshops. A communal art enterprise organized by Roger FRY in the early 20th century, based on the experiments of William MORRIS. For a time, Wyndham LEWIS participated in the undertaking.

Omnium, Palliser Plantagenet, Duke of. One of Trollope's best known characters. He first appears in *Can You Forgive Her* (1864) and subsequently plays a leading rôle in the four PARLIAMENTARY NOVELS, *Phineas Finn* (1869), *Phineas Redux* (1874), *The Prime Minister* (1876) and *The Duke's Children* (1880). Although his talents and his high sense of honor and devotion to his country bring him the premiership, the Duke is too typically the shy, proud and reserved English gentleman to win the cordial sympathy that is given to the magnetic young Irishman, Phineas Finn, of the same Parliamentary novels. Lady Glencora, the Duke's wife, is like him, typically English. Trollope said of them—

> I think that Plantagenet Palliser, Duke of Omnium, is a perfect gentleman. If he be not, then I am unable to describe a gentleman. She is by no means a perfect lady; but if she be not all over a woman, then am I not able to describe a woman. I do not think it probable that my name will remain among those who in the next century will be known as the writers of English prose fiction; but if it does, that permanence of success will probably rest on the character of Plantagenet Palliser, Lady Glencora and the Rev. Mr. Crawley.—Trollope, *Autobiography,* 313.

Omnibus Bill. A congressional bill dealing with a number of different subjects. The famous Omnibus Bill of American history was the Compromise of 1850.

Omoo. A romance of the South Seas by Herman MELVILLE (1847) completing the adventures of the voyage recorded in TYPEE. *Omoo* is Polynesian for "rover." The scene is laid largely in Tahiti; and sailors, natives, beach-combers and missionaries are portrayed in lively manner. The book occasioned much criticism because of its treatment of missionaries.

O'More, Rory. Name of three famous Irish rebel chiefs of the 16th and 17th centuries, appearing often in Irish poetry.

Omphale. In classic myth the masculine but attractive Queen of Lydia, to whom HERCULES was bound a slave for three years. He fell in love with her, and led an effeminate life spinning wool, while Omphale wore the lion's skin and was lady paramount. *Le Rouet d'Omphale* (*Omphale's Spinning-Wheel*), is the name of a well-known tone-poem by the composer Camille SAINT-SAËNS.

On American Taxation. A famous speech by Edmund BURKE, delivered in the English Parliament on April 19, 1774, urging that the duty on tea imported into the American colonies be repealed. It was not successful.

On Borrowed Time. An American comedy by Paul Osborn, based on a novel (1937) by Lawrence Watkin.

Once in a Lifetime. An American comedy (1930) by George S. KAUFMAN and Moss HART.

On Conciliation with the American Colonies. A speech by Edmund BURKE, delivered to the English Parliament in March 1775 in an effort to prevent disaffection between Great Britain and the colonies in America by granting them autonomy.

on dit (*Fr.,* "they say"). A rumor, a report, a bit of gossip; as, "There is an *on dit* that he is trying to get a divorce."

Ondt and the Gracehoper, The. In James Joyce's FINNEGANS WAKE, a fable told by Shaun, or Kevin EARWICKER, obviously named for the fable of *The Ant and the Grasshopper.* It is interpreted as an allegory for the conflict between the practical and artistic ways of life.

O'Neale or **O'Neill, Margaret** (1796–1879). Known as Peggy. Second wife of John Henry Eaton (1790–1856), daughter of a Washington innkeeper. When Eaton became Andrew Jackson's Secretary of War, Mrs. Eaton was not accepted socially by the cabinet member's wives, and Eaton was forced to resign (1831). Cf. *That Awful Mrs. Eaton,* a play by Stephen Vincent Benét and John Farrar, and *The Patience of John Morland,* a ROMAN À CLEF by Mary Dillon.

Onegin, Evgeni B. (1883–1919). Russian composer of operas, ballets, choral works, and songs. *Eugen Onegin* is an opera by TCHAIKOVSKY, based on a story by PUSHKIN.

One-Hoss Shay, The. A famous poem by O. W. HOLMES (1858), actually titled *The Deacon's Masterpiece.* The deacon constructed his shay without a "weakest spot," and it lasted a hundred years, but:

> You see, of course, if you're not a dunce
> How it went to pieces all at once,
> All at once and nothing first,
> Just as bubbles do when they burst,
> End of the wonderful one-hoss shay,
> Logic is logic. That's all I say.

Oneida Community. A perfectionist religious society established (1847) in New York State by John Humphrey NOYES, an experiment in practical communism which developed a good school system and metal manufactures. The polygamy, polyandry, and other unconventional practices of the colony aroused the self-righteousness of the general public, and caused its abandonment in 1879. It was later reorganized as a business corporation (1881).

O'Neill, Danny. Hero of a series of novels by James T. FARRELL including *A World I Never Made* (1936); *No Star Is Lost* (1938); *Father and Son* (1940); etc. At the outset, he is brought up in a lower-middle-class Irish Catholic background in Chicago similar to that of Studs LONIGAN, his father being a driver for an express company. He goes to live with more well-to-do relatives, however, and is shown as a quiet little boy with a precocious knowledge of baseball. He grows up to be a sensitive young man, becoming a student at the University of Chicago and rebelling against the life accepted by Studs Lonigan. Danny, who is considered to be based on the author himself, also appears briefly in the Lonigan series, pointed out by representative characters of those novels as a horrible example of non-Catholic education.

O'Neill, Eugene Gladstone (1888–). American playwright, famous for his technical experiments and innovations in the theater, his powerful pessimism, and his grim and moving psychological studies of men and women in the America of his time, sometimes with mystical and religious overtones. His works, which show the influence of classic Greek drama, STRINDBERG, and, possibly, the plays of the Irish nationalist theater (see IRISH RENAISSANCE), include *Provincetown Plays* (1916); *The Long Voyage Home* (1917); *Ile* (1918); *The Moon of the Caribbees* (1918); BEYOND THE HORIZON (1920), winner of the 1920 Pulitzer prize; THE EMPEROR JONES (1921); *The Straw* (1921); THE HAIRY APE (1922); ANNA CHRISTIE (1922), awarded the Pulitzer prize and a gold medal from the National Institute of Arts and Letters; ALL GOD'S CHILLUN GOT WINGS (1924); *Desire Under the Elms* (1924); *Marco Millions* (1924); THE GREAT GOD BROWN (1925); LAZARUS LAUGHED (1926); *Dynamo* (1928); STRANGE INTERLUDE (1928), winner of the 1928 Pulitzer prize; MOURNING BECOMES ELECTRA (1931); *Ah! Wilderness* (1932); *Days Without End* (1933); *The Iceman Cometh* (1946). His plays show a development from realism in his earlier compositions, which many critics consider his best, to symbolism in his later works, drawn from the classic Greek, Elizabethan, and expressionistic (see EXPRESSIONISM) traditions. His subject-matter is usually life on the sea or the waterfront, or decadence and violence in New England.

O'Neill, whose father, James O'Neill was a well-known American actor, best known for his MONTE CRISTO, spent his early youth in restless wandering, working at odd jobs about the country and taking several voyages at sea, which provided him with much material for his plays. He studied in the famous HARVARD 47 Workshop course in playwriting and joined the PROVINCETOWN PLAYERS soon after the organization was founded. His work first attracted attention in productions at the Provincetown Playhouse in GREENWICH VILLAGE. He was one of the founders of the Theater Guild. (See LITTLE THEATER.) He was awarded the Nobel prize for literature in 1936, and is considered by many critics to be the greatest of American dramatists. After the production of *Days Without End* in 1933, he retired to seclusion to write a new cycle of plays on a single theme.

O'Neill, Rose Cecil (1874–1944). American illustrator and author; widely known as the original designer of the kewpies (from Cupids) which made a great commercial success for her as pictures and dolls, etc. Rose O'Neill is less well known for her remarkable poetry, as in *The Master-Mistress* (1922), her paintings and strange drawings, her novels *Garda* (1929) and *The Goblin Woman* (1930). She lived near Westport, Connecticut, in what she called Carabas Castle, and held salons. Once wife of Harry Leon WILSON.

Oneiza. In Southey's THALABA THE DESTROYER, the bride of Thalaba. She dies on the wedding night.

One of Ours. A novel by Willa CATHER (1922). It is the story of Claude Wheeler, a boy who grows up on a Western farm, goes to a Western university and later serves his country overseas in World War I. It was awarded the Pulitzer prize.

one-step. An American ballroom dance, adapted from the TURKEY-TROT, with turns and draw-steps.

Onions, Oliver. Also **George Oliver** (1873–). English novelist; married to the novelist Berta Ruck. A typical Yorkshireman. Clemence Dane called him "a lone wolf of literature." A grim realist and remarkable writer on the supernatural. *Whom God Hath*

Sundered (a trilogy; 1926); *Collected Ghost Stories* (1935); etc.

Only, the (Ger. *der Einzige*). A name given to the German writer, Johann Paul Friedrich RICHTER (1763–1825).

Only the Dead Know Brooklyn. A prose sketch in soliloquy form by Thomas WOLFE, celebrating the streets, neighborhoods, and local points of interest of BROOKLYN. It is written in the supposed dialect of the borough itself.

Only Yesterday. An informal history of the U.S. (1931) in the 1920's, with a sequel, *Since Yesterday* (1940), for the following decade by Frederick Lewis ALLEN. Both volumes are valuable source books for the social historian.

onomatopoeia. Primarily the forming of words to suggest by their sound the object or idea presented (see BOWWOW THEORY), as buzz, hiss, clack, bang, twitter. In poetry, it is used as a device to give by the combination of sounds an effect consonant with the meaning, as Milton's:

Fountains, and ye that warble as ye flow,
Melodious murmurs, warbling tune His praise.

Dryden's *Alexander's Feast,* Tennyson's *Lotus Eaters,* and Swinburne's *Garden of Proserpine* are noteworthy examples of the use of onomatopoeia.

On the Banks of the Wabash Far Away. A popular song in the U.S. at the time of the Spanish-American War. See DREISER, THEODORE.

Onward, Christian Soldiers. A hymn written by Sabine Baring-Gould (1834–1924) and set to music by Sir Arthur Sullivan.

Oom Paul, see KRUGER, JOHANNES PAULUS.

Opal Whiteley, The Story of. An imaginative narrative said to be the production of the child Opal Whiteley, published in the *Atlantic Monthly* (1920) and later in book form. There was a great deal of discussion regarding its authenticity. See also ASHFORD, DAISY.

open.

Open Door. The principle of equal opportunity to all nations in the matter of foreign trade.

Open, Sesame! See SESAME.

open shop. See SHOP.

Open Boat and Other Tales of Adventure, The. Eight short stories by Stephen CRANE (published in book form, 1898). They give, for the most part, Crane's own experiences as a war correspondent.

opéra bouffe (*Fr.*). Farcical comic opera.

Operation Crossroads. The code name given by the military to the atom bomb experiments conducted by the Navy in the Pacific in the summer of 1946. The operations were designed to show whether navies would stand up under atom bombs.

Ophelia. In Shakespeare's HAMLET, the young, beautiful daughter of POLONIUS, Lord Chamberlain to the King of Denmark. Hamlet falls in love with her, but, finding marriage inconsistent with his plans for vengeance, he simulates madness. Ophelia is so wounded by his strange behavior to her that her intellect gives way.

Ophir. The country, in southeastern Arabia, which was the source of the treasure of King Solomon. Cf. *1. Kings* x. 11.

Ophiuchus. A northern constellation south of Hercules, shown on old astronomical charts as a man grasping the Serpent. Also known as "the Serpent-bearer" or "Serpentarius."

Opie, John (1761–1807). English portrait and historical painter, known as "The Cornish Wonder." Did portraits of Dr. Johnson, Burke, Southey, William and Mary Godwin, etc. His second wife **Amelia Opie,** *née* **Alderson** (1769–1853), a novelist and poet, based her novel *Adeline Mowbray* (1804) upon the life-story of Mary Wollstonecraft and became a Quaker and friend of Elizabeth Fry.

O Pioneers! A novel by Willa CATHER (1913), dealing with Swedish settlers in Nebraska. On the death of her father, John Bergson, Alexandra Bergson takes over the care of her family and the management of the farm. The other Bergsons are weak or dull, but Alexandra, energetic and courageous, succeeds in building up a prosperous farm. Her hopes for the future of her younger brother, Emil, are blasted when Emil is killed by a jealous husband of the community, but eventually her loneliness comes to an end with her marriage to Carl Linstrum, who shares her superior qualities.

Opp, Julie. See under FAVERSHAM, WILLIAM.

Oppenheim, Edward Phillips (1866–1946). Author of 100 novels of adventure and political intrigue, besides many short stories and plays. A daily output of 5,000 words, dictated simultaneously into two dictaphones.

Oppenheim, James (1882–1932). American free verse poet and fiction writer. His best poems are collected in *The Sea* (1924). His stories of *Dr. Rast* are his best prose and a reflection of his early experiences as a social worker. In his later years he was exceedingly interested in psychoanalysis. Cf. Horace Gregory's remarkable poem "13 (For J. O.)," in *Poems 1930–40, The Meek Shall Disinherit the Earth.*

Opper, Frederick Burr (1857–1937). American cartoonist and illustrator. On staffs of

Frank Leslie's Magazine, Puck, and New York *Journal.* Created *Happy Hooligan,* the mule *Maud, Alphonse and Gaston,* and other comic-strip characters. Illustrated *Short Sixes* by Henry Cuyler BUNNER; Bill NYE's *Comic History of the United States;* and produced *Puck's Opper Book* (1888), *Happy Hooligan Home Again* and *Maud the Matchless* (30 color comics each; 1907); etc.

oppidan. At Eton, a student who is not a *colleger* but boards in the town or in the house of an assistant master. The word means "townsman." *The Oppidan* is a suppressed novel by Shane LESLIE.

opportunism. A policy of expediency, of seizing the opportunity regardless of abstract or logical principles. The famous opportunists of French history were the followers of GAMBETTA (1838–1882).

Ops. In classic myth, a goddess of plenty, identified with RHEA.

Optic, Oliver. The pen name of William Taylor ADAMS, a prolific writer for boys, author of the *Army and Navy* series, *Starry Flag* series, etc.

optimism. The doctrine that "whatever is, is right," that everything which happens is for the best. It was originally set forth by LEIBNITZ from the postulate of the omnipotence of God, and is cleverly travestied by Voltaire in his CANDIDE, OU L'OPTIMISME, where Dr. Pangloss continually harps on the maxim that "all is for the best in this best of all possible worlds."

oracle (Lat. *oraculum,* from *orare,* "to speak, to pray"). The answer of a god or inspired priest to an inquiry respecting the future; the deity giving responses; the place where the deity could be consulted, etc.; hence, a person whose utterances are regarded as profoundly wise, an infallible, dogmatical person—

> I am Sir Oracle,
> And when I ope my lips let no dog bark.
> Shakespeare, *Merchant of Venice,* i, 1.

In ancient Greece oracles were extremely numerous, and very expensive to those who consulted them. The most famous were the—

Oracle of APOLLO, at Delphi, the priestess of which was called the Pythoness; at Delos, and at Claros.

Oracle of DIANA, at Colchis; of ESCULAPIUS, at Epidaurus, and another in Rome.

Oracle of HERCULES, at Athens, and another at Gades.

Oracle of JUPITER, at Dodona (the most noted); another at Ammon, in Libya; another at Crete.

Oracle of MARS, in Thrace; MINERVA, in Mycenae; PAN, in Arcadia.

Oracle of TRIPHONIUS, in Boeotia, where only men made the responses.

Oracle of VENUS, at Paphos, another at Aphaca, and many others.

In most of the temples women, sitting on a tripod, made the responses, many of which were either ambiguous or so obscure as to be misleading; to this day, our word *oracular* is still used of obscure as well as of authoritative pronouncements.

The difficulty of "making head or tail" of oracles is well illustrated by the following classic examples:

When Croesus consulted the Delphic oracle respecting a projected war, he received for answer, *"Croesus Halyn penetrans magnum, pervertet opum vim"* (When Croesus passes over the river Halys, he will overthrow the strength of an empire). Croesus supposed the oracle meant he would overthrow the enemy's empire, but it was his own that he destroyed.

Pyrrhus, being about to make war against Rome, was told by the oracle: *"Aio te, Aeacide, Romanos vincere posse"* (I say, Pyrrhus, that you the Romans can conquer), which may mean either *You, Pyrrhus, can overthrow the Romans,* or *Pyrrhus, the Romans can overthrow you.*

Another prince, consulting the oracle on a similar occasion, received for answer, *"Ibis redibis nunquam per bella peribis"* (You shall go shall return never you shall perish by the war), the interpretation of which depends on the position of the comma; it may be *You shall return, You shall never perish in the war,* or *You shall return never, you shall perish in the war,* which latter was the fact.

Philip of Macedon sent to ask the oracle of Delphi if his Persian expedition would prove successful, and received for answer—

> The ready victim crowned for death
> Before the altar stands.

Philip took it for granted that the "ready victim" was the King of Persia, but it was Philip himself.

When the Greeks sent to Delphi to know if they would succeed against the Persians, they were told—

> Seed-time and harvest, weeping sires shall tell
> How thousands fought at Salamis and fell.

But whether the Greeks or the Persians were to be "the weeping sires," no indication was given, nor whether the thousands "about to fall" were to be Greeks or Persians.

the Oracle of the Church. St. Bernard of Clairvaux (1091–1153).

the oracle of the Holy Bottle. The oracle to which Rabelais (*Pantagruel,* Bks. iv and v) sends Panurge and a large party to obtain an answer to a question which had been put to sibyl and poet, monk and fool, philosopher and witch, judge and "sort," viz. "whether Panurge shall marry or not?" The oracle is situated at BACBUC, "near Cathay in Upper Egypt," where the "bottle" is kept in an alabaster fount in a magnificent temple. When the party arrives at the sacred spot, the priestess throws something into the fount; whereupon the water begins to bubble, and the word "Drink" issues from the "bottle." So the whole party sets to drinking Falernian wine, and, being inspired with drink, raves with prophetic madness; and so the romance ends. The story has been interpreted as a satire on the Church. The celibacy of the clergy was for long a moot point, and the "Holy Bottle" or cup to the laity was one of the moving causes of the schisms between the Church and its dissenting factions.

to work the oracle. To induce another to favor some plan or to join in some project, generally by maneuvering behind the scenes. Also—in slang—to raise money.

Orage, Alfred Richard (1873–1934). English journalist and psychologist. Lectured on theosophy; founded the Leeds Art Club. Through a large anonymous donation was able to buy the *New Age* and make it a weekly of the Socialist masses. He attracted to it many distinguished contributors, as Shaw, Wells, Belloc, Chesterton, Havelock Ellis, Arnold Bennett, Katherine Mansfield, Richard Aldington, J. C. Squire, etc. When the founding of the *New Statesman* produced a rival in the field, Orage gave up the *New Age* and became a follower of OUSPENSKY and the Russian occultist GURDJIEFF, of whose Fontainebleau colony he became a member. Orage was a remarkably clear expositor of a broad economic philosophy.

orange girls. In the Restoration Theaters, the girls who sold refreshments to the spectators were so called. Nell Gwyn (1650–1687) began her career as one of them.

Orangemen. A name given by Roman Catholics to the Ulster Protestants of Ireland, on account of their allegiance to William III of the House of Orange.

Orator Hunt. Henry Hunt (1773–1835), a violent orator who presided over the meeting in St. Peter's Field, Manchester, at the time of the "Peterloo" massacre (1819). Yeomen and soldiers charged upon the reform meeting, and the news of this outrage so aroused the poet SHELLEY in Italy that he wrote *The Masque of Anarchy*. Orator Hunt was sentenced to two years' imprisonment. Later he became an M.P. (1830–1833), and published his memoirs in 1820.

Orators, The: An English Study. A combined verse and prose work by W. H. AUDEN (1932), in which revolution and the collapse of the British social system of the poet's day are prophesied by means of symbols taken from such characteristic events in English middle-class life as the public school ceremony, the weekend house-party, and the Sunday church service. Outstanding sections of the book are *Address for a Prize-Day,* a parody on the speeches delivered at commemoration exercises at English boys' schools, and *Journal of an Airman,* a collection of diagrams, plans, memoranda, and day-by-day records compiled by an aviator at war, symbolizing the revolutionary, in reference to his campaign against "the enemy," or the English middle class itself.

Orbilian stick, the. A cane or birch rod. Orbilius was the schoolmaster who taught HORACE, and Horace calls him *Plagosus* (the flogger). (*Ep.* ii. 71.)

Orc. In Ariosto's ORLANDO FURIOSO, a great sea monster that devours men and women. ROGERO, on the back of his winged steed Hippogriff, rescues the fair Angelica from the Orc by means of a burnished shield whose brightness is fatal to man and beast. See also PERSEUS AND ANDROMEDA.

Orcades. Poetic name for the Orkney Islands.

Orcus. A Latin name for HADES, the abode of the dead.

Orcutt, William Dana (1870–). American author and book designer. Associated with the Plimpton Press. Designer of Humanistic and Laurentian types. Author of many books, including *Desk Reference Book* (1926); *Master Makers of the Book* (1928); *Dagger and Jewels—The Gorgeous Adventures of Benvenuto Cellini* (1931); *Escape to Laughter* (1942); etc.

Orczy, Baroness **Emmuska** (1865–1947). English novelist and playwright, principally known for *The Scarlet Pimpernel* (1905), dramatized in collaboration with her husband (1905), and filmed by Leslie Howard, James Mason, and other actors.

ordeal (A.S. *ordel,* related to *adoelan,* "to deal, allot, judge"). The ancient Anglo-Saxon and Teutonic practice of referring disputed questions of criminality to supernatural decision, by subjecting the suspected person to physical tests by fire, boiling water, battle, etc.; hence, figuratively, an experience testing endurance, patience, courage, etc.

This method of "trial" was based on the belief that God would defend the right, even by miracle if needful. All ordeals, except the ordeal of battle, were abolished in England by law in the early 13th century.

In *ordeal of battle* the accused person was obliged to fight anyone who charged him with guilt. This ordeal was allowed only to persons of rank.

Ordeal of fire was also for persons of rank only. The accused had to hold in his hand a piece of red-hot iron, or to walk blindfold and barefoot among nine red-hot ploughshares laid at unequal distances. If he escaped uninjured he was accounted innocent, *aliter non.* This might be performed by deputy.

Ordeal of hot water was for the common people. The accused was required to plunge his arm up to the elbow in boiling water, and was pronounced guilty if the skin was injured in the experiment.

Ordeal of cold water was also for the common people. The accused, being bound, was tossed into a river; if he *sank* he was acquitted, but if he *floated* he was accounted guilty. This ordeal remained in use for the trial of witches to comparatively recent times.

In the *ordeal of the bier,* a person suspected of murder was required to touch the corpse; if he was guilty, the "blood of the dead body would start forth afresh."

In that of the *cross,* plaintiff and defendant had to stand with their arms crossed over their breasts, and he who could endure the longest won the suit.

The *ordeal of the Eucharist* was for priests. It was supposed that the elements would choke him, if taken by a guilty man.

Ordeal of Richard Feverel, The. See RICHARD FEVEREL.

orders. In classical architecture, a column with its entablature viewed as a unit fully characteristic of a given style. It is customary to distinguish five orders (three Greek: Doric, Ionic, Corinthian; and two Roman: Tuscan, Composite). The distinctive features of an order affect all its constituent parts: the base, shaft, and capital of the columns as well as the architrave, frieze, and cornice of the entablature.

Oread, pl. **Oreads or Oreades** (from Gr. *oros,* "a mountain"). Nymphs of the mountains.

> The Ocean-nymphs and Hamadryades,
> Oreads and Naiads, with long weedy locks,
> Offered to do her bidding through the seas,
> Under the earth, and in the hollow rocks.
> Shelley, *The Witch of Atlas,* xxii.

O'Reagan, Teague. In Hugh Henry Brackenridge's MODERN CHIVALRY, a Sancho Panza character, servant to Captain John Farrago.

Oregon Trail, The. Originally **The California and Oregon Trail.** A book by Francis PARKMAN (1849). The account of an actual trip taken by the author and his cousin, Quincy Adams Shaw, in 1846.

O'Reilly, John Boyle (1844–1890). Irish born American writer. His novel *Moondyne* (1870) about Australian convict life was based on his own experiences. As a result of his Fenian activities, he had been deported to Australia (1868) but succeeded in escaping to America (1869). On editorial staff of Boston *Pilot* (from 1870), proprietor and editor (1876–1890). Wrote *Songs from Southern Seas* (1873); *Songs, Legends, and Ballads* (1878); etc.

O'Reilly, Persse. In James Joyce's FINNEGANS WAKE, the author, hero, or singer of *The Ballad of Persse O'Reilly,* which is spiritedly delivered in the tavern of H. C. EARWICKER and deals with Earwicker's secret crime in PHOENIX PARK. *Persse O'Reilly* is derived from Fr. *pierce-oreille,* meaning earwig; hence this is another incarnation of Earwicker himself. The name is also believed to contain an allusion to two Irish patriots who were victims of the Easter-Day Massacre during the Revolution of 1916—Pearse and O'Rahilly.

O'Reilly, Private Miles. An Irish private in the Union army during the Civil War, a character created by C. G. Halpine (*Am.,* 1829–1868), whose adventures amused a host of contemporary readers.

C'Rell, Max, see BLOUET, PAUL.

Orenburgsky, Sergey Gusev (1867–). Russian novelist who wrote *The Land of the Fathers* (1905) and *The Land of the Children* (1928), showing on a large scale the life of the middle-class Russian intelligentsia and the effect of the Revolution upon it.

Orestes. In classic myth, the son of AGAMEMNON and CLYTEMNESTRA. When Clytemnestra and her paramour Aegisthus murdered Agamemnon, his sister ELECTRA saved the young Orestes by sending him to Phocis, where he became the fast friend of PYLADES. In course of time he returned to avenge his father's death by killing Aegisthus and Clytemnestra. For the crime of matricide he was seized with madness and pursued from one land to another by the Furies. AESCHYLUS constructed about this legend his great trilogy of the *Agamemnon, Choephori* and *Eumenides,* SOPHOCLES dealt with it in his *Electra,* and EURIPIDES in a drama also entitled *Electra.* In more modern times it forms the subject matter of a tragedy by Alfieri, of VOLTAIRE'S *Oreste* (1750) and of HOFMANNSTHAL'S *Elektra* (*Ger.,* 1874); and an opera, *Elektra,* by Richard STRAUSS, based on the last-named play. See also MOURNING BECOMES ELECTRA.

Orfeo and Heurodis. The tale of ORPHEUS and EURYDICE, with the Gothic machinery of elves or fairies. It exists in a number of ballad versions. Sometimes Eurydice is also called Lady Isabel.

Orgoglio (*Ital.,* "Arrogant Pride, or Man of Sin"). In Spenser's FAËRIE QUEENE (I, vii and viii), a hideous giant as tall as three men, son of Earth and Wind. Finding the Red Cross Knight at the fountain of Idleness, he beats him with a club and makes him his slave. Una, hearing of these mischances, tells King Arthur, who liberates the knight and slays the giant.

He typifies the tyrannical power of the Church of Rome; in slaying him Arthur first cut off his *left arm*—i.e., Bohemia was first cut off from the Church of Rome; then the giant's *right leg*—i.e., England, after which Orgoglio fell to earth, and was easily dispatched.

Orgon. In Molière's TARTUFFE, brother-in-law of Tartuffe. His credulity and faith in Tartuffe, like that of his mother, can scarcely be shaken even by the evidence of his senses. He hopes against hope, and fights every inch of ground in defense of the religious hypocrite.

Oriana. The beloved of Amadis of Gaul, who called himself Beltenebros when he retired to the Poor Rock. (*Amadis de Gaul,* ii. 6.)

The name is also given to the nurseling of a lioness, with whom Esplandian, son of Oriana and Amadis, fell in love, and for whom he underwent all his perils and exploits. She is represented as the fairest, gentlest and most faithful of womankind.

Queen Elizabeth is sometimes called the *peerless Oriana,* especially in the madrigals entitled the *Triumphs of Oriana* (1601). Ben JONSON called Anne, queen of James I, *Oriana.* Mrs. Brooks ATKINSON is named Oriana.

oriflamme (*Fr.,* "flame of gold"). The ancient banner of the kings of France, first used as a national banner in 1119. It was a crimson flag cut into three "vandykes" to represent "tongues of fire," with a silken tassel between each, and was carried on a gilt staff (*un glaive tout doré où est attaché une bannière vermeille*). This celebrated standard was the banner of St. Denis, but when the Counts of Vexin became possessed of the abbey, it passed into their hands. In 1082 Philippe I united Vexin to the crown, and the sacred Oriflamme fell to the king. It was carried to the field after the battle of Agincourt, in 1415. The romance writers say that "mescreans" (infidels) were blinded by merely looking on it. In the *Roman de Garin* the Saracens cry, "If we only set eyes on it we are all dead men," and FROISSART records that it was no sooner unfurled at Rosbecq than the fog cleared away from the French, leaving their enemies in misty darkness.

In the 15th century the Oriflamme was succeeded by the blue standard powdered with fleurs-de-lis, and the last heard of the original Oriflamme is a mention in the inventory of the Abbey of St. Denis dated 1534.

Origen (185?–?254 A.D.). One of the Greek Fathers of the Church. Many works on the Old Testament, etc.

Origin of Species, The. A famous scientific treatise by Charles DARWIN (1859), in which he first promulgated his theory of evolution. The full title is *The Origin of Species by Means of Natural Selection.*

Original Sin. In Roman Catholicism, that corruption which is born with us, and is the inheritance of all the offspring of Adam. As Adam was the federal head of his race, when Adam fell the taint and penalty of his disobedience passed to all his posterity.

Orillo. One of the magicians in Ariosto's ORLANDO FURIOSO (Bk. viii). His life depends —literally—upon a single hair, but he is able, when his head is cut off, to put it on again. Astolpho encountered him, cut off his head, and fled with it. Orillo mounted and gave chase, but meanwhile Astolpho cut the hair from the head, and as soon as that was severed the head died, and the magician's body fell lifeless.

Orinda the Matchless, or the Matchless Orinda. Mrs. Katherine PHILIPS, the poetess and letter-writer. She first adopted the signature "Orinda" in her correspondence with Sir Charles Cotterell, and afterwards used it for general purposes. Her praises were sung by COWLEY, DRYDEN, and others.

Orion. In classic mythology, a giant of great beauty, and a famous hunter, who cleared the island of Chios of wild beasts. While in the island, Orion fell in love with MEROPE, daughter of King Oenopion, but one day, in a drunken fit, he offered her violence. The King put out the giant's eyes and drove him from the island. Orion was told if he would travel eastwards, and expose his sockets to the rising sun, he would recover his sight. Guided by the sound of a Cyclops' hammer, he reached Lemnos, where VULCAN gave him a blacksmith as guide to the abode of the sun. In due time his sight returned to him, and at death he was made a constellation. The lion's skin was an emblem of the wild beasts which he slew in Chios, and the club was the instrument he employed for the purpose.

O'Riordan, Conal Holmes O'Connell (1874–1948). Irish novelist and playwright. Succeeded John Millington SYNGE as director of the Abbey Theatre in 1909. Got Synge's suppressed play, *The Playboy of the Western World* (1907), produced again. Katherine Mansfield praised his novel *Adam of Dublin* (1920). He wrote other novels and plays, from 1891 to 1920 under the pseudonym of **Norreys Connell.**

Oriskany. A village in Oneida County, N.Y., site of one of the bloodiest battles of the American Revolution (August 6, 1777). The Americans under General Herkimer, on their way to the relief of Fort Stanwix and about 800 strong, defeated a British and Indian detachment of about equal strength. General Herkimer was fatally wounded. The battle took place in a wild thunderstorm. On both sides every third man was killed.

Orithyia. In classic mythology, the nymph whom the north wind Boreas loved. She bore him two sons, Zetes and Calais, who became famous as winged warriors in the company of the ARGONAUTS.

Orlando. The hero of Shakespeare's AS YOU LIKE IT, the younger son of Sir Rowland de Boys, in love with ROSALIND.

Orlando. The Italian form of ROLAND, one of the great heroes of medieval romance, and the most celebrated of CHARLEMAGNE's paladins. Under the French form of Roland he is the hero of the so-called CHRONICLE OF TURPIN and the CHANSON DE ROLAND.

As Orlando, he is the hero of a celebrated trilogy of Italian poems written in mock heroic vein. The three poems are: (1) *Morgante Maggiore.* A poem by Luigi Pulci (1488), in which Orlando converts the huge MORGANTE MAGGIORE and is the hero of numerous adventures with giants and magicians.

(2) *Orlando Innamorato* (*Orlando In Love*). A romance in verse by BOIARDO (1495), telling the love of Orlando for the fair Angelica. Boiardo supposes Charlemagne to be warring against the Saracens in France, under the walls of Paris. He represents the city as besieged by two infidel hosts—one under AGRAMANT, Emperor of Africa, and the other under Gradasso, King of Sericana. His hero, Orlando, he supposes (though married at the time to Aldabella) to be in love with Angelica, a fascinating coquette from Cathay who makes her appearance to sow discord in the Christian army. Boiardo died in 1494, not having finished the work, and Ariosto wrote his *Orlando Furioso* as a sequel to it.

(3) *Orlando Furioso* (*Orlando Mad*). An epic poem in forty-five cantos, by ARIOSTO (1515–1533). Orlando's madness is caused by the faithlessness of Angelica. In Paris Rinaldo falls in love with her, and, to prevent mischief, the king places the coquette under the charge of NAMO. But she contrives to escape her keeper, and flees to the island of Ebuda, where Rogero finds her exposed to a sea-monster, and liberates her. In the meantime, Orlando goes in search of his lady and is decoyed into the enchanted castle of Atlantes, but is liberated by Angelica, who again succeeds in effecting her escape to Paris. Here she arrives just after a great battle between the Christians and pagans, and, finding MEDORA, a Moor, wounded, takes care of him, falls in love with him, and elopes with him to Cathay. When Orlando finds himself jilted, he is driven mad with jealousy and rage, or rather, his wits are taken from him for three months and deposited in the moon. ASTOLPHO goes to the moon in Elijah's chariot, and St. John gives him the lost wits in an urn. On reaching France, Astolpho binds the madman, holds the urn to his nose, and the hero is himself again. After this, the siege of Paris by Agramant is continued, and the Christians are wholly successful. The true hero of Ariosto's romance is ROGERO, and not Orlando. In the pagan army are two heroes—Rodomont, called the Mars of Africa, and Rogero. The latter becomes a Christian convert, and the poem ends with a combat between these two, and the overthrow of Rodomont. The concluding lines are:

> Then at full stretch he [Rogero] raised his arm above
> The furious Rodomont, and the weapon drove
> Thrice in his gaping throat—so ends the strife,
> And leaves secure Rogero's fame and life.

About 1589 a play (printed 1594) by Robert GREENE entitled *The History of Orlando Furioso* was produced in England. In this version, Orlando marries Angelica. Rhodes' farce BOMBASTES FURIOSO is a burlesque of Ariosto's romance.

Orlando's ivory horn. Olifant, once the property of Alexander the Great. Its bray could be heard for twenty miles.

Orlando's horse. Brigliadoro ("golden bridle").

Orlando's sword. Durindana or Durandana, which once belonged to Hector.

Orlando; a Biography. A remarkable novel by Virginia WOOLF (1928).

Orleans, The Maid of. JOAN OF ARC.

Orley Farm. A novel (1862) by Anthony TROLLOPE.

orlop. The lowest deck of a vessel.

> Battered chain-gangs of the orlop.
> Kipling, *The Galley-Slave.*

Ormont, Lord. See LORD ORMONT AND HIS AMINTA.

Orosius, Paulus. Spanish priest of the 5th century. Author of a vast medieval textbook of universal history.

Ormulum. A Middle English religious and didactic poem, written in Northeast Midland dialect (ca. 1200). It consists of paraphrases of the gospels and homilies based on them, and was only one-eighth completed although it is almost 10,000 lines in length. Metrically, it is in iambic lines of fifteen syllables. Its unique feature is its orthography, in which the author tried to indicate pronunciation by means of special signs and called attention to a short vowel by doubling the consonant that followed it, as *wordess* for "wordes." The title *Ormulum* is interpreted as a diminutive form of the author's name, Orm.

Ormuzd or **Ahura Mazda.** The principle or angel of light and good, and creator of all things, according to the Magian system. He is in perpetual conflict with AHRIMAN, but in the end will triumph. The Latin form of the name is *Oromasdes.*

Ornithology, Father of. See under FATHER.

Oromasdes. The same as ORMUZD.

Oroonoko, Prince. The hero of a novel by Mrs. Aphra BEHN which was dramatized by Thomas SOUTHERN (1695) under the title *Prince Oroonoko.* Prince Oroonoko was a real character, the grandson of an African king, and the novelist became acquainted with him in Surinam in the West Indies where he had been sold as a slave. Here, in the literary account, Oroonoko meets IMOINDA, his wife, from whom he has been separated, and whom he had believed dead. He heads an uprising of the slaves, whereupon the governor tries to seduce Imoinda. The result is that Imoinda kills herself, and Oroonoko slays first the governor and then himself. This is the ending of the drama; the novel ends in a different but equally tragic manner.

Orozco, José Clemente (1883–). Mexican painter, identified with modernist school. Associated with RIVERA, etc. Did mural paintings in Mexico City.

Orpen, Sir **William Newenham Montague** (1878–1931). British painter, appointed official artist by British Government in World War I.

Orphan Angel, The. A novel by Elinor WYLIE (1926) concerning the hypothetical story of Shelley in America after his rescue from drowning in the Gulf of Spezzia. Highly imaginative, and emphasizing Elinor Wylie's preoccupation with the character of the poet Shelley.

Orpheus. A Thracian poet of Greek legend, son of APOLLO and CALLIOPE, who could move even inanimate things by his music. When his wife Eurydice died, he went into the infernal regions, and so charmed PLUTO that she was released on the condition that Orpheus would not look back until they reached the earth. He was just about to place his foot on the earth when he turned round, and Eurydice vanished from him in an instant.

> Orpheus' self may . . . hear
> Such strains as would have won the ear
> Of Pluto to have quite set free
> His half-regained Eurydice.
> Milton, *L'Allegro,* 145–50.

The prolonged grief of Orpheus at his second loss so enraged the Thracian women that in one of their Bacchanalian orgies they tore him to pieces. The fragments of his body were collected by the Muses and buried at the foot of Mount Olympus, but his head had been thrown into the river Hebrus, whither it was carried into the sea, and so to Lesbos, where it was separately interred. This story is the subject of GLUCK's opera *Orpheus and Eurydice* (*Orfeo;* 1762), the libretto of which is by Calzabigi. BROWNING wrote a poem *Eurydice to Orpheus.*

Orpheus of highwaymen. So John GAY has been called on account of his *Beggar's Opera* (1728).

Orpheus of the 18th century. Handel (1685–1759).

Orpheus of the Green Isle. Furlough O'Carolan (1670–1738).

Orpheus C. Kerr Papers. A series of humorous sketches by Robert Henry Newell which were published in daily newspapers during the Civil War and after (*Am.,* 1862–1868). Orpheus C. Kerr was an insistent "officer-seeker," and the sketches have to do with the affairs of a Mackerel Brigade.

Orphic. Connected with Orpheus, the mysteries associated with his name, or the doctrines ascribed to him, similar to his music in magic power. Thus, Shelley says,

> Language is a perpetual Orphic song,
> Which rules with Daedal harmony a throng
> Of thoughts and forms, which else senseless and shapeless were.
> *Prometheus Unbound,* IV, i, 415.

orrery. A movable model of the solar system. A planetarium.

> In Queen Mab's chariot I ventured on the sea;
> 'Twas like a mammoth hazel-nut, with matchless orrery
> Asparkle on its ceiling—
> William Rose Benét, *Munchausen.*

Orsay, Count **Alfred Guillaume Gabriel d'** (1801–1852). French society leader; friend of Lady Blessington in London.

Orsini, Felice (1819–1858). Italian revolutionist. Known for his attempted assassination of Napoleon III (January 14, 1858). Executed at Paris.

Orsino. In Shakespeare's TWELFTH NIGHT, the Duke of Illyria, in love with OLIVIA. He marries VIOLA.

Orson. Twin brother of Valentine in the old romance, VALENTINE AND ORSON. The twins are born in a wood near Orleans, and Orson (Fr. *ourson,* "a little bear") is carried off by a bear, which suckles him with her cubs. When he grows up he becomes the terror of France, and is called the *Wild Man of the Forest.* He is reclaimed by Valentine, overthrows the Green Knight, and marries Fezon, the daughter of Duke Savary of Aquitaine.

Ortega y Gasset, José (1883–). Spanish essayist and philosopher. Founder of numerous periodicals. In voluntary exile though not a leftist. In America his best-known book is *The Revolt of the Masses* (1932; *La Rebelión de las Masas,* 1930).

Ortheris, Stanley. A Cockney soldier who appears in many of Kipling's stories with his pals, Terence MULVANEY and Jock LEAROYD. He is especially prominent in *Garm—a Hostage, The Madness of Private Ortheris* and *His Private Honour.*

Ortiz, Roberto M. (1886–1942). President of Argentina (1938–1942). In temporary retirement (1940 ff.).

Orton, Arthur (1834–1898). English impostor. Impersonated eldest son of widow of Sir James Tichborne, who had been lost at sea, and convinced Lady Tichborne and others. Brought action against the 12th Baronet and after a trial of 290 days, during which his case collapsed, was committed for perjury (1895).

Orville, Lord. In Fanny Burney's EVELINA, the amiable and devoted lover of Evelina, whom she ultimately marries. He is represented as "handsome, gallant, polite, and ardent—he dressed handsomely."

Osbaldistone, Rashleigh. In Scott's ROB ROY, a pretended scholar who turns out to be a perfidious villain. He is killed by Rob Roy.

Frank Osbaldistone. His brother, who loves and marries Di Vernon.

Osborn, Henry Fairfield (1857–1935). American paleontologist and archaeologist. Curator of vertebrate paleontology, American Museum of Natural History (from 1891). Author of *The Age of Mammals* (1910); *Men of the Old Stone Age* (1915); *Origin and Evolution of Life* (1917); *Evolution and Religion in Education* (1926); etc.

Osborne, Mr. In Thackeray's VANITY FAIR, a hard, money-loving, purse-proud, wealthy London merchant, whose only gospel is that "according to Mammon."

Captain George Osborne. Son of the merchant, selfish, vain, extravagant, and self-indulgent. He has been engaged to Amelia Sedley while her father was in prosperity, and Captain Dobbin induces him to marry her after the father has become a bankrupt. Happily, George falls on the field of Waterloo, or one would never vouch for his conjugal fidelity.

Osborne, Thomas (d. 1767). English bookseller, responsible for getting Samuel RICHARDSON to write in a series of letters the novel *Pamela* (1740). Pope satirized him in the *Dunciad* and Dr. Johnson beat him for his impertinence.

Osborne, Thomas Mott (1859–1926). American prison reformer. Founded Mutual Welfare League under which prisoners of Sing Sing exercised self-government. Warden of Sing Sing Prison (1914–1916). Author of *Within Prison Walls* (1914).

Osbourne, Lloyd (1868–1947). Step-son of Robert Louis Stevenson with whom Stevenson wrote *The Wrong Box* (1889); *The Wrecker* (1892); and *The Ebb Tide* (1894). Author, with his sister Isobel Strong, of *Memories of Vailima* (1902).

O'Shanter, Tam, see TAM O'SHANTER.

Osiris. One of the chief gods of Egyptian mythology; he is judge of the dead, ruler of the kingdom of ghosts, the Creator, the god of the Nile, and the constant foe of his brother (or son) SET, the principle of evil. He was the husband of ISIS, and represents the setting sun. See RA. He was slain, but came to life again and was revenged by HORUS and Thoth.

The name means *many-eyed.* Osiris was usually depicted as a mummy wearing the crown of Upper Egypt, but sometimes also as an ox.

Oslerize. To regard a man as of little use or force him into retirement after he has passed the prime of life. The word was derived from a remark of the distinguished surgeon Dr. (later Sir) William Osler (1849–1919) in his address on leaving Johns Hopkins University for England. In this address, which was seized upon by the press and greatly distorted, he referred to "the comparative uselessness of men over forty years of age" and said that if their discoveries were subtracted from the sum of human achievement, it would make little difference to progress.

Osmond, Gilbert. In Henry James' PORTRAIT OF A LADY, the dilettante whom Isabel ARCHER marries.

Osric. In Shakespeare's HAMLET, a court fop, contemptible for his affectation and finical dandyism. He is made umpire by Claudius, when LAERTES and Hamlet fight their duel.

Ossa. See under PELION.

Ossian (Oisin). The legendary Gaelic bard and warrior of about the end of the 3rd century, son of FINN (Fingal), and reputed author of a group of poems published 1760–1763 by James MACPHERSON, who professed that he had translated them from MSS. collected in the Highlands. A great controversy as to the authenticity of the supposed originals was aroused. It was soon generally agreed that Macpherson, although compiling from ancient sources, was the principal author of the poems as published.

Ostade, Adriaen van (1610–1685). Dutch genre painter and etcher.

Ostend Manifesto. A declaration made in 1854 by the Ministers of the United States in England, France, and Spain, "that Cuba must belong to the United States." It occasioned great discussion.

Ostenso, Martha (1900–). Norwegian-born American author of the prize-winning novel *Wild Geese* (1925), and other novels and poems.

ostracism (from Gr. *ostrakon,* "an earthen vessel"). Black-balling, boycotting, expelling; exclusion from society of common privileges, etc. The word arose from the ancient Greek custom of banishing one whose power was a danger to the state, the voting for which was done by the people recording their votes on tiles or potsherds.

ostrich policy. A short-sighted policy of shutting one's eyes in time of danger, from the habit attributed to the ostrich of hiding its head in the sand when threatened by an enemy.

Ostrog Bible. See BIBLE, SPECIALLY NAMED.

O'Sullivan, Seumas, see STARKEY, JAMES SULLIVAN.

O'Sullivan, Vincent (1872–). American poet and playwright.

Oswald. In Shakespeare's KING LEAR, steward to Goneril, daughter of King Lear.

O tempora! O mores! (*Lat.*, from Cicero's *Pro Rege Deiotaro,* xi, 31). Alas! how times have changed for the worse! Alas! how the morals of the people have degenerated!

Othello. A tragedy by SHAKESPEARE (1604). Othello, a Moor, is commander of the Venetian army and elopes with DESDEMONA. Her father Brabantio accuses him of necromancy, but Desdemona refutes the charge. The Moor, being then sent to drive the Turks from Cyprus, wins a signal victory. On his return, IAGO, Othello's "ancient" (i.e., ensign or lieutenant), plays upon his jealousy and persuades him that Desdemona has been false to him with Cassio. He therefore murders her, and, after learning how he has been duped by Iago, slays himself. This tragedy had its source in a tale in Cinthio's *Hecatommithi* (1565). There is an opera, *Otello,* by VERDI (1887) founded on Shakespeare's play.

Othello's occupation's gone (iii. 3). A phrase sometimes used when one is "laid on the shelf," no longer "the observed of all observers."

> The fiery openness of Othello, magnanimous, guileless, and credulous, boundless in his confidence, ardent in his affection, inflexible in his resolution, and obdurate in his revenge. . . . The gradual progress which Iago makes in the Moor's conviction, and the circumstances which he employs to inflame him, are so artfully natural . . . that we cannot but pity him. —Dr. Johnson.

Other Wise Man, The. A story by Henry Van Dyke. See under MAGI.

Otis, Harrison Gray (1837–1917). American army officer and journalist. Editor of Los Angeles *Times* (from 1882); etc.

Otis, Isabel. The heroine of Gertrude Atherton's ANCESTORS.

Otis, James. Pseudonym of **J. O. Kaler** (1848–1912). Author of many stories for boys, the best-known being *Toby Tyler, or Ten Weeks with a Circus* (1881).

otium cum dignitate (*Lat.*, "leisure with dignity"). Retirement after a person has given up business and has saved enough to live upon in comfort. The words were taken as a motto by CICERO.

Otnit. Hero of a story in the medieval HELDENBUCH (*Book of Heroes*), a legendary emperor of Lombardy, who gains the daughter of a powerful heathen ruler for wife, through the help of ALBERICH the dwarf.

Otranto, Castle of, see CASTLE OF OTRANTO.

O'Trigger, Sir Lucius. In Sheridan's comedy THE RIVALS, a fortune-hunting Irishman, ready to fight everyone, on any matter, at any time.

ottava Rima. A stanza of eight ten-syllabled lines, rhyming *a b a b a b c c,* used by KEATS in his *Isabella,* by BYRON in *Don Juan,* etc. It was originally Italian and was employed by TASSO (the lines were eleven-syllabled), ARIOSTO, and many others. The following example is from *Don Juan:*

> When Nero perished by the justest doom
> Which ever the destroyer yet destroy'd,
> Amidst the roar of liberated Rome
> Of nations freed, and the world overjoy'd,
> Some hands unseen strew'd flowers upon his tomb;
> Perhaps the weakness of a heart not void
> Of feeling for some kindness done, when power
> Had left the wretch an uncorrupted hour.

Ottenberg, Fred. The lover of Thea Kronborg in Willa Cather's SONG OF THE LARK.

Otterbourne, The Ballad of. An early English ballad included in PERCY'S *Reliques.* It relates how the Scots, returning from a raid, attacked the castle of Otterburn in Northumberland (August 19, 1388). Earl Douglas, the Scots' leader, was slain, but his men won the day and Lord Percy, the English leader, was taken prisoner.

Otway, Thomas (1652–1685). English dramatist of the Restoration period, known for his tragedies. His works include *Don Carlos* (1676), written in rhymed verse; *The Orphan* (1680) and VENICE PRESERVED (1682), both written in blank verse; *Alcibiades* (1675); *Titus and Berenice* (1677), adapted from RACINE; *The Cheats of Scapin* (1677), adapted from MOLIÈRE; *Friendship in Fashion* (1678); *The Soldier's Fortune* (1681); *The Atheist* (1684). Otway was an actor for a while, although he was unsuccessful. He died in poverty.

Ouïda. The pseudonym of Louise de la Ramée (1839–1908), author of *Under Two Flags* (1867), etc. The novel was dramatized.

Our American Cousin. A comedy by Tom TAYLOR (1858). The titular hero, Asa Trenchard, who was at first the principal character of this popular play, was gradually superseded in interest by the English swell Lord DUNDREARY who served as entertaining contrast to the "American cousin."

Oumansky, Constantine Alexandrovich (1902–1945). Russian ambassador to United States (1939–1941).

Our Mutual Friend. A novel by Charles DICKENS (1864). The "mutual friend" is John HARMON, friend of Mr. BOFFIN and of the WILFERS. Old John Harmon has cursed his son and sent him adrift as a boy of fourteen, but he leaves him a fortune on condition of his marrying Bella Wilfer. As young Harmon has never met Bella, has not been home for fourteen years, and is reported to have been murdered, he returns under the assumed name of John Rokesmith and acts as secretary to Mr. Boffin, the "golden dustman" who is to have the Harmon money if the conditions laid down in the will are not fulfilled. John and

Bella fall in love, marry, and live for a time on John's earnings. Finally Boffin turns over the fortune, and John Rokesmith becomes again John Harmon.

Oursler, Charles Fulton (1893–). American journalist and author. Editor, *Liberty* Magazine under Bernarr MacFadden.

Our Town. A play by Thornton WILDER (1938), winner of the Pulitzer prize in 1938. It presents a picture of life in a typical New England town, Grover's Corners, New Hampshire, by means of a novel technique. A ubiquitous Stage Manager, a familiar garrulous Yankee character, sits at the side of the stage and talks intimately to the audience as the play unfolds, describing the action and the characters. Act I is entitled "Daily Life," and shows the citizens of the town engaged in their customary pursuits, while Professor Willard and Editor Webb of the local newspaper comment on them objectively. In Act II, "Love and Marriage," Emily, daughter of Editor Webb, and George, son of Dr. Gibbs, fall in love and marry. In Act III, "Death," Emily dies in childbirth and is buried, and the ancient dead in the cemetery speak of their peace and their perception of eternal harmony in the universe.

outcaste. See CASTE.

Outcast of the Islands, An. A novel by Joseph CONRAD (1896). The scene is laid in Sambir, a settlement in the Dutch East Indies. The story has to do with two protégés of Captain LINGARD, the powerful "Rajah Laut" of the district—Almayer, whom he sets up as a trader in Sambir, and Willems, whom, after his dishonesty as a clerk in Macassar, he brings to the same lonely settlement. Willems falls in love with Aïssa, daughter of the scheming, one-eyed native Babalatchi, who hides her until Willems treacherously agrees to pilot Abdulla, a native trader, to the settlement. Once there, his wealth and shrewdness enable him to throttle Almayer's trade. Lingard, when he discovers Willems' treachery, imprisons him in the jungle, and at the moment when his escape seems probable, he is shot by Aïssa with his own revolver. Almayer's later history is told in ALMAYER'S FOLLY.

Outcasts of Poker Flat, The. A story by Bret HARTE (1869), reprinted in *The Luck of Roaring Camp and Other Sketches* (1870).

Outcault, Richard Felton (1863–1928). American cartoonist, originator of comic strips, as *The Yellow Kid* and *Buster Brown.*

Outis (*Gr.,* "nobody"). The name assumed by ODYSSEUS in the cave of POLYPHEMUS. When the monster roars with pain from the loss of his eye, his brother giants ask from a distance who is hurting him. "Nobody," thunders out Polyphemus, and his companions go their way.

Outlook, The. An American weekly (1893–1935), superseding *The Christian Union* (1870–1893) and edited first by Henry Ward Beecher and then by Lyman Abbott. It had among its contributors Theodore Roosevelt, Jacob Riis, the famous Negro educator Booker T. Washington, Hamilton Wright Mabie, and others. The American poet Harold Trowbridge Pulsifer was president of the Outlook Company and managing editor of *The Outlook* from 1923 to 1928, when it was merged with the *Independent.*

Out of the Cradle Endlessly Rocking. A poem by Walt Whitman first published as *A Word Out of the Sea* in *Leaves of Grass* (1860). Whitman gave it its present title in 1871.

Outre-Mer: A Pilgrimage Beyond the Sea. The first prose work of Henry W. LONGFELLOW (1834–1835), modeled after Irving's *Sketch Book.*

Overbury, Sir **Thomas** (1581–1613). English prose-writer, one of the early 17th-century CHARACTER WRITERS. A series of *Characters* by him, faintly mocking and satiric, was published in 1614 with *A Wife,* a poem. Overbury was made a prisoner in the Tower of London and killed by slow poison for having opposed the marriage of a friend, Lord Rochester, who was one of the favorites of King James I.

Overland Monthly, The. A California magazine (1868–1875, 1883–1933) edited during its first two-and-a-half years by Bret Harte, and carrying upon its cover a picture of the California grizzly. Bret Harte contributed to it *The Luck of Roaring Camp, Plain Language from Truthful James,* etc. The *Overland* published such early California writers as Ina Coolbrith, Charles Warren Stoddard, Edward Rowland Sill, and others. Ambrose Bierce with his usual wit called its later incarnation "the warmed-Overland Monthly." Yet good writers contributed to it also in its later phase: George Sterling, Gertrude Atherton, Edwin Markham, Jack London, and others.

Overreach, Sir Giles. An avaricious schemer, the principal character in Massinger's drama A NEW WAY TO PAY OLD DEBTS.

Over Soul, The. An essay by Ralph Waldo EMERSON (1841), in which the author describes his concept of the Oversoul, or a pantheistic unity of the universe which is present in the soul of each individual man and is made known by means of divine revelation, which is generally interpreted as expression of individual genius.

Over the Hill to the Poorhouse. Title of the best-known poem of Will CARLETON.

Over There. Popular American song of World War I, composed by George M. COHAN.

Ovid. In full **Publius Ovidius Naso** (43 B.C.–?17 A.D.). Latin poet in the Augustan age. He wrote *Metamorphoses,* poetic fables based on the principal classical legends, and is considered the model of elegiac poetry. His *Amores, Heroides,* and *Ars Amatoria* or *Ars Amoris,* were widely known in the Middle Ages, influencing the convention of COURTLY LOVE and the English poet CHAUCER, among others.

the French Ovid. Du Bellay (ca. 1525–1560); also called "the Father of Grace and Elegance."

Owain. The hero of a 12th-century legend, *The Descent of Owain,* written by Henry of Saltrey, an English Benedictine monk. Owain (the name is a form of Welsh *Owen*) is an Irish knight of Stephen's court who, by way of penance for a wicked life, enters and passes through St. Patrick's PURGATORY.

Owen, Anne. See PHILIPS, KATHERINE.

Owen, Robert (1771–1858). Welsh pioneer in cooperative industry. His several "Owenite" communities founded in Great Britain and the U.S., including one at NEW HARMONY, Indiana (1825–1828), were all unsuccessful. He spent his fortune on social schemes, devoted all his energies to the propagation of his social doctrines, and toward the end of his life took up spiritualism. His son, **Robert Dale Owen** (1801–1877), edited the New Harmony *Gazette,* became a member of the U.S. House of Representatives (1843–1847), was U.S. minister to Italy (1855–1858), and worked for the emancipation of slaves.

Owen, Ruth, *née* **Bryan,** see ROHDE, RUTH BRYAN.

Owen, Wilfred (1893–1918). English poet, considered the best of the poets who wrote in and about World War I. See WAR IN LITERATURE. Although he enlisted voluntarily, received the Military Cross for bravery in action, and was killed while leading the Artists' Rifles in battle, he hated war fiercely. His poetry expresses savagely the cruelty and horror he saw about him at the battlefront, and shows interesting experiments in form and technique, in which he was encouraged by Siegfried SASSOON, whom he met in an army hospital. His most characteristic poem is DULCE ET DECORUM EST. W. H. AUDEN is considered to have been influenced in form to some degree by Wilfred Owen.

Owl and the Nightingale, The. A Middle English allegorical and didactic debate, in which an owl, considered to represent the clergy, and a nightingale, interpreted as symbolizing the feudal knightly estate, argue, each attacking the other's way of life and defending his own. It is believed that this is an allegorical attack on the medieval nobility, and several contemporary references have been found. There is disagreement among scholars as to the date of composition of *The Owl and the Nightingale,* but it was probably written in the late 12th century or early 13th century. Some think the author was one Nicholas of Guildford, to whom the birds decide to refer their controversy for judgment.

Owlglass, Owlyglass or Howleglass, Tyll. See EULENSPIEGEL, TYL.

Oxenham, John (d. 1575). Sailed with Sir Francis Drake. Was captured by the Spaniards during an expedition of his own and hanged at Lima, Peru. Charles Kingsley introduces him in his novel, *Westward Ho!* (1855).

Oxenham, John. Pseudonym of **William Arthur Dunkerley** (1861?–1941). English poet and novelist. *The Vision Splendid* (1917).

Oxford, Edward de Vere, Earl of (1550–1604). English courtier and poet, one of the favorites of Queen ELIZABETH, regarded as typical of the group of courtly lyric poets of the time which included Sir Philip SIDNEY, Fulke GREVILLE, and Sir Walter RALEIGH. He was known among his contemporaries as somewhat of a fop and introduced Italian styles of dress among the English courtiers; he is considered to be the object of satire in Gabriel HARVEY'S *Speculum Tuscanismi,* dealing with Italianate young Englishmen. Oxford was a patron of a number of Elizabethan actors and writers, John LYLY having served as his secretary and dedicated *Euphues and His England* (1580) to him. Since Oxford, as a nobleman, could not publish his verse as such, scholars have found themselves obliged to search out his poems from among the contributions to the poetic miscellanies (see TOTTEL'S MISCELLANY) of the time. It is believed by some that several of the poems included in *A Hundred Sundry Flowers* (1573) were written by Oxford, and that he was also the editor of the collection. He was one of the jury at the treason trial of Lord ESSEX, and served as Lord Great Chamberlain at the coronation of James I. A certain school of critics contends that he wrote Shakespeare's plays. See also BACON, FRANCIS.

Oxford Movement, the. (1) A High Church movement which originated at Oxford in 1833 under the leadership of Pusey, J. H. NEWMAN (afterwards a cardinal in the Roman Catholic Church), and Keble. It was strongly opposed to anything in the way of LATITUDINARIANISM, and sought to bring back into the service of the Church much of the ritual, ornaments, etc., that had been dispensed with at the time of the Reformation. See TRACTS FOR THE TIMES.

(2) An American evangelist, Frank Nathan Daniel Buchman (1878–), evolved a religion called A First Century Christian Fellowship when directing Christian work at Pennsylvania State College (1909–1915), organized the "Oxford Group Movement" at Oxford, England (1921), and started a campaign in many countries which had to do with what he called "Moral Rearmament" (1939). His cult, often called "Buchmanism" or, in brief, "the Oxford Movement," is in no way related to the original Oxford Movement. The cult specializes in luxurious living and public confession of sexual misdoing.

oxymoron (*Gr.,* "pointedly foolish"). A seeming contradiction for effect; for example, the use of a noun with a qualifying adjective that seems to imply a contrary meaning, as "strenuous idleness," "wise folly," etc.

Oz, The Land of. The setting for the *Wonderful Wizard of Oz* (1900) and other fantastic stories by Lyman Frank BAUM. A mythical kingdom extremely popular with American children. Elaborately filmed in 1939.

Ozark State. Nickname for Missouri.

Ozenfant, Amédée (1886–). French Cubist painter. Collaborated with Le CORBUSIER in writing several books on cubism and modern painting.

Ozymandias. A famous poem by Shelley, first published by Leigh Hunt in his *Examiner* (January, 1818). It is an ironic poem on the vanity and futility of a tyrant's power.

P

P.

The Four P's. A "merry interlude" by John HEYWOOD, published in 1569. The four principal characters are "a Palmer, a Pardoner, a Poticary (apothecary), and a Pedlar." See under FOUR.

the five P's. William Oxberry (1784–1824) was so called, because he was Printer, Poet, Publisher, Publican, and Player.

p, pp, ppp. In musical notation, *p* stands for *piano; pp* for *pianissimo* or *piu piano;* and *ppp* for *pianississimo.* In the same way, *f* stands for *forte; ff* for *fortissimo;* and *fff* for *fortississimo.*

Paassen, Pierre van (1895–). Dutch-born American journalist in Canada and the U.S. His best-selling book is *Days of Our Years* (1939). A fighting journalist and writer. He is that *rara avis,* a Gentile Zionist. Author of *Earth Could Be Fair* (1946).

Pach, Walter (1883–). American artist and art critic. Translator of *The History of Art* by Élie Faure, in 5 vols. Has lectured and written on art extensively.

Pachmann, Vladimir de (1848–1933). Eccentric Russian pianist; known for his interpretations of Chopin whose works he edited. Toured Russia, Europe, and America. Received Beethoven Medal of London Philharmonic (1916).

pacifism. The doctrine professed by those people who, on moral or religious grounds, refuse to participate in activities of organized violence, especially war. During World War I English and American pacifists, among whom a number of well-known writers, artists, and other intellectuals were included, were harshly treated, being fined, imprisoned, and in general socially ostracized by their former friends. William Jennings BRYAN, Woodrow WILSON (at the beginning of his presidential career), Bertrand RUSSELL, and Randolph BOURNE were pacifists at this time. In the twenty years following World War I pacifism grew to be a comparatively influential international movement, especially among youth, and was supported by numerous religious and political organizations, both conservative and radical. Its culmination occurred about the middle of the 1930's, in the annual anti-war "strikes" held at a number of American schools, colleges, and universities, in the Oxford Oath, originating at Oxford University in England, by which students swore not to fight in any war waged by their national governments under any circumstances, and in the passage of legislation by the U.S. Congress to insure American neutrality in time of war. President Franklin D. ROOSEVELT was for a while identified with a speech in which the words "I hate war" occurred. With the rearmament of Germany, however, under Adolf HITLER, the avowed military ambitions of Fascist Italy and Nazi Germany (see FASCISM; NAZISM), and the outbreak of the Spanish Civil War (1936), pacifism began to lose its popularity. An important factor in this change was the new stand of the U.S.S.R. and the national COMMUNIST PARTIES, which had formerly encouraged the pacifist movement but now condemned only an "imperialist war" and advocated the formation of a POPULAR FRONT against Fascism. With the beginning of World War II, pacifism had lost its former influence, although legislation whose passage had been secured in England and the U.S. during the period of the movement's power permitted pacifists who could prove a *bona fide* basis for their beliefs—usually an acceptable religious creed—to become "CONSCIENTIOUS OBJECTORS" and live together in camps at their own expense, exempt from military service but not permitted their former freedom until the end of the war. The QUAKERS have been outstanding among traditional religious pacifists.

See also WAR IN LITERATURE.

pack. See under COVEY.

Packlemerton, Jasper. A personage in Dickens' OLD CURIOSITY SHOP, one of the chief figures in Mrs. JARLEY's wax-work exhibition.

> "Jasper courted and married fourteen wives, and destroyed them all by tickling the soles of their feet when they were asleep. On being brought to the scaffold and asked if he was sorry for what he had done, he replied he was only sorry for having let them off so easy. Let this," said Mrs. Jarley, "be a warning to all young lâdies to be particular in the character of the gentlemen of their choice. Observe, his fingers are curled, as if in the act of tickling, and there is a wink in his eyes."—*The Old Curiosity Shop,* xxviii.

Pacolet. A dwarf in the romance of VALENTINE AND ORSON. He is in the service of Lady Clerimond, and has a winged horse which carries off Valentine, Orson, and Clerimond from the dungeon of Ferragus to King Pepin's palace; afterwards it bears Valentine to the palace of Alexander, Emperor of Constantinople, his father. Hence, a very swift horse, that will carry the rider anywhere, is called a *horse of Pacolet.*

> I fear neither shot nor arrow, nor any horse how swift soever he may be, not though he could outstrip the Pegasus of Perseus or of Pacolet, being assured that I can make good my escape.—Rabelais, *Gargantua,* Bk. ii, 24.

Steele's familiar spirit in the TATLER was named Pacolet after this dwarf.

Pact of Paris. Also known as the **Kellogg-Briand Pact.** A treaty signed (1928) by fifteen nations in an attempt to outlaw war. Another forty-five nations agreed to the provision, in Article I, that the contracting parties of the treaty "condemn recourse to war for the solution of international controversies, and renounce it as an instrument of national policy in their relations with one another."

Pactolus. A small river of Lydia in Asia Minor, a tributary of the Hermus. The fact that it carried gold was explained by the story of Midas whose ability—given him by Bacchus—to turn everything he touched into gold proved fatal when it affected also his food, and was mercifully transferred to the waters of the river. By the time of Augustus the Pactolus had ceased to produce gold.

Paddington, Harry. In THE BEGGAR'S OPERA by John GAY, one of Macheath's gang of thieves. PEACHUM describes him as a "poor, petty-larceny rascal, without the least genius. That fellow," he says, "though he were to live for six months, would never come to the gallows with credit."

paddy, paddywhack. An Irishman; from Patrick (Ir. *Padraig*). In slang both terms are used for a loss of temper, a rage on a small scale; the latter also denotes the gristle in roast meat, or a spanking.

Paderewski, Ignace (1860–1941). Polish pianist, composer, and statesman. Interpreter of Schumann, Chopin, Liszt, Rubinstein, etc. Abandoned music to work for Polish national independence during World War I. Took part in the Peace Conference at Versailles and was elected premier of the new Polish Republic (1919), holding office for 10 months. Resumed public performances in 1922.

Padishah. See under RULERS, TITLES OF.

paean. From *Paian,* in Greek mythology, the physician of the gods or, specifically, Apollo. Hence a paean is a hymn of praise, joy, triumph, etc.; originally as an invocation of Apollo.

Paganini, Nicolò (1782–1840). Italian violinist, unrivaled in virtuosity. Also composed concertos and sonatas for violin, now merely considered brilliant show-pieces. The brilliant *Variations on a Theme of Paganini,* by Sergei RACHMANINOFF, are also the basis of a ballet, *Paganini.*

Page, Curtis Hidden (1870–1946). American educator and poet. Author of *A History of Japanese Poetry* (1923). Translator of Molière and Anatole France.

Page, Mr. In Shakespeare's MERRY WIVES OF WINDSOR, a gentleman living at Windsor. When Sir John FALSTAFF makes love to Mrs. Page, Page himself assumes the name of Brook, to outwit the knight. Sir John tells the supposed Brook his whole "course of wooing," and how nicely he is bamboozling the husband.

Mrs. Page. Wife of Mr. Page, of Windsor. When Sir John Falstaff makes love to her, she joins with Mrs. FORD to dupe him and punish him.

Anne Page. Daughter of the above, in love with Fenton. SLENDER calls her "the sweet Anne Page."

William Page. Anne's brother, a schoolboy.

Page, Thomas Nelson (1853–1922). American novelist and short story writer of the South, a member of the school of LOCAL COLOR, best known for his two short stories MARSE CHAN and MEH LADY in the volume *In Ole Virginia* (1887). He is also the author of *Red Rock* (1898) and *Two Little Confederates* (1888). Many of his stories are in Negro dialect.

Page, Walter Hines (1855–1918). American journalist and diplomat. Partner in Doubleday, Page & Co., publishers (from 1899). Founder and editor of *The World's Work* (1900–1913). U.S. ambassador to Great Britain during World War I (1913–1918). Cf. *The Life and Letters of Walter H. Page* (3 vols., 1922–1925), edited by Burton J. Hendrick.

Paget, Violet. Pseudonym **Vernon Lee** (1856–1935). English novelist and writer on art. Her more than 40 books include fiction, plays, books on psychology, musicology, travel, and art criticism, and controversial books on sociology and politics. Her half-brother was Eugene LEE-HAMILTON.

Pagliacci, I (The Players). An opera by LEONCAVALLO (1892). The characters are traveling players: Nedda, the wife of Canio, the showman; Tonio, a member of the company; and Silvio, a villager who has long been in love with Nedda.

Pain, Barry Eric Odell (1865–1928). English humorist. Popular at the beginning of the century, especially for *Eliza* (1900), a comedy of manners. Also author of parodies and ghost stories.

Paine, Albert Bigelow (1861–1937). American biographer, chiefly known for his gossipy and uncritical *Mark Twain, a Biography* (1921). Children's editor of the New York *Herald;* also on editorial staff of *St. Nicholas Magazine* (1899–1909).

Paine, Ralph Delahaye (1871–1925). American war correspondent and writer of books for boys. He appears in *Wounds in the Rain* by Stephen Crane as "William B. Perkins."

Paine, Thomas (1737–1809). English pamphleteer and political radical, famous for his activities in behalf of the colonies during the American Revolution, as well as in France during the French Revolution. He consistently urged revolt and independence instead of reform, and tried to promote a world revolution. Among his works are *The Case of the Officers of Excise* (1772), a plea for higher wages to excisemen, of whom he had been one; COMMON SENSE (1776); THE AMERICAN CRISIS (1776–1783), a series of pamphlets supporting the American Revolution; *Public Good* (1780); *Dissertations on Government* (1786), an attack on monetary inflation in the American colonies; THE RIGHTS OF MAN (1791–1792); THE AGE OF REASON (1794–1795), for which he was denounced as an atheist. Paine lived a turbulent career, beginning in a variety of humble occupations. He held several official positions in the colonies during the Revolution but made enemies and subsequently lost favor. In England, he was tried for treason and banished. In France, he was made an honorary citizen by the Republican government and was a delegate to the Convention, until the more radical government of the REIGN OF TERROR came into power and imprisoned him as an enemy Englishman. He died ultimately in the U.S. amid poverty and calumny, denounced as a radical, a drunkard, and an atheist and was denied burial in consecrated ground. His remains were lost after being taken to England for reburial. In later years he came to be regarded as an American patriot and an important crusader for democratic rights. *Citizen Tom Paine,* a semi-fictional account of his life by Howard FAST, was withdrawn from libraries of New York City public schools in 1946.

Painlevé, Paul (1863–1933). French mathematician and premier of France (1917, 1925). Author of books about higher mathematics.

Painted Veils. A novel by James Gibbons HUNEKER (1920), concerning artists, critics, and Bohemians in New York.

Painter, William (1540?–1594). English schoolmaster and author of the early Elizabethan period, known for *The Palace of Pleasure* (1566–1567), a collection of prose tales from Herodotus, Plutarch, Tacitus, Livy, Cinthio, and other classic and Italian sources, especially Boccaccio's DECAMERON and Bandello's *Novelle* (1554). *The Palace of Pleasure* supplied the leading poets and playwrights of the day with plots. Shakespeare's ALL'S WELL THAT ENDS WELL and TIMON OF ATHENS were derived from Painter's collection, and an early version of ROMEO AND JULIET is contained in it. Painter was for a while Clerk of Ordnance in the Tower of London.

Pair of Blue Eyes, A. A novel by Thomas HARDY (1873). Elfride Swancourt, the daughter of a rector, is loved by Stephen Smith and starts to elope with him but changes her mind and returns. Later she loves and is loved by Henry Knight, but Mrs. Jethway, a spying neighbor, writes Knight of Elfride's former experience, and the lovers quarrel. Sometime later the two men, each intending to be reconciled with Elfride, meet on a train but arrive only in time for her funeral. She has married, but loving Knight, has pined away and died.

Pakistan. See under Mohammed Ali JINNAH.

Palace of Art, The. An allegorical poem by TENNYSON (1830). Its object is to show that love of art will not alone suffice to make man happy.

Palace of Pleasure, The. See under PAINTER, WILLIAM.

paladin. Properly, an officer of, or one connected with, the palace; usually confined in romance to the Twelve Peers of Charlemagne's court, and hence applied to any renowned hero or knight-errant.

The most noted of Charlemagne's paladins were ORLANDO or Roland (Orlando the Italian, Roland the French form), the favorite nephew of Charlemagne; RINALDO (Renauld) of Montalban, Orlando's cousin; NAMO (Nami), Duke of Bavaria; SALOMON (Solomon), King of Brittany; ASTOLPHO of England; Archbishop TURPIN; FLORISMART; MALAGIGI (Maugis), the magician; GANELON (Gan), the traitor; and OGIER THE DANE. The converted Saracen FIERAMBRAS (Ferumbras) was also prominent. Lists of the twelve paladins vary greatly.

Palamedes. (1) In Greek legend, one of the heroes who fought against Troy. He was the reputed inventor of lighthouses, scales and measures, the discus, dice, etc., and was said to have added four letters to the original alphabet of Cadmus. It was he who detected the assumed madness of ULYSSES by putting the infant TELEMACHUS in the way of the plow the supposed madman was driving; in revenge the latter achieves his death. The phrase, *he is quite a Palamedes,* meaning "an ingenious person," is an allusion to this hero.

(2) In Arthurian romance, Sir Palamedes is a Saracen knight who is overcome in single combat by TRISTRAM. Both love Iseult, the wife of King Mark, and after the lady has been given up by the Saracen, Tristram converts him to the Christian faith, and stands as his godfather at the font.

TASSO introduces a *Palamedes of Lombardy* in his JERUSALEM DELIVERED (III. ii). He joins the Crusaders with his brothers, Achilles and Sforza, and is shot by CLORINDA with an arrow.

Palamon and Arcite. Two young Theban knights of romance whose story (borrowed from Boccaccio's *Le Teseide*) is told by Chaucer in his KNIGHT'S TALE, by Fletcher and (probably) Shakespeare in *The Two Noble Kinsmen* (1634), and elsewhere. Both are in love with Emilia, sister-in-law to the Duke of Athens, in whose hands they are prisoners. In time they secure their liberty, and the Duke appoints a tournament, promising Emilia to the victor. Arcite prays to Mars to grant him victory; Palamon prays to Venus to grant him Emilia. Arcite wins the victory, but, being thrown from his horse, is killed. Palamon, though not the winner, therefore wins the prize for which he prayed and fought.

palanquin or **palankeen.** A large box with wooden shutters, carried by four bearers by means of projecting poles, used in China and East India as a conveyance.

Palatine, The. A ballad by WHITTIER, versifying the New England legend of a ship of that name that was lured on to the rocks of Block Island by false lights, plundered and sent to sea again in flames with its passengers aboard. The story seems to have some basis in the hasty forced landing near that spot of a load of emigrants from the German Palatinate in 1720. According to legend, a phantom burning ship periodically visits the island. This story suggested R. H. DANA's poem *The Buccaneer.*

Pale, the English. The name given in the 15th century to that part of Ireland which had been colonized in the 12th century by Henry II, viz., the districts of Cork, Dublin, Drogheda, Waterford, and Wexford. It was only in these districts that the English law prevailed, hence the phrases, *within the pale* and *outside the pale.* They are often used figuratively of the social conventions. One of Kipling's most successful stories is entitled *Beyond the Pale.*

the Jewish pale of settlement. Under the Czarist rule the Jews of Russia were restricted to fifteen governments or districts of Western Russia.

palefaces. So the American Indians called the European settlers.

Pale Horse, The. Death.

> And I looked, and behold a pale horse: and his name that sat on him was Death, and Hell followed with him.
>
> *Rev.* vi. 8.

Palemon and Lavinia. A poetic version of Boaz and Ruth told by THOMSON in the *Seasons: Autumn* (1730). Palemon is also the name of the hero in FALCONER's narrative poem *The Shipwreck* (1756).

Palestrina. Full name **Giovanni Pierluigi da Palestrina** (1525?–1594). Italian composer of church music in polyphonic style, considered the "absolute ideal of perfection" in music composed in the medieval church modes. Among his works are masses, motets, madrigals, and hymns.

Paley, William (1743–1805). English theologian and philosopher. His most original essay is *Horae Paulinae* (1790), but his *View of the Evidences of Christianity* (1794) is probably his best-known work.

Palgrave, Francis Turner (1824–1897). English poet and critic; best-known for his anthology *The Golden Treasury of the Best Songs and Lyrical Poems in the English Language* (1861; second series, 1897), which has been re-issued in many editions. He was a friend of TENNYSON.

palimpsest. A parchment or tablet which has been used several times, the earlier writing having been erased; also called a *codex rescriptus.* By the use of chemicals, etc., it is often possible to recover the obliterated original text.

palindrome (Gr. *palin dromo,* "to run back again"). A word or line which reads backwards and forwards alike, as *Madam, I'm Adam,* also *Roma tibi subito motibus ibit amor.* They have also been called *Sotadics,* from their reputed inventor, Sotades, a scurrilous Greek poet of the 3rd century B. C.

Probably the longest palindrome in English is

> Dog as a devil deified
> Deified lived as a god;

and others well known are

> Lewd did I live, evil did I dwel,

and Napoleon's famous reputed saying,

> Able was I ere I saw Elba.

The following Greek palindrome is very celebrated:

ΝΙΨΟΝΑΝΟΜΗΜΑΤΑΜΗΜΟΝΑΝΟΨΙΝ,

i.e., "wash my transgressions, not only my face."

palingenesis. A new birth; more especially, METEMPSYCHOSIS.

palinode or **palinody.** A recantation, from the name of the poem in which the Greek poet Stesichorus (608–552 B. C.) expressed his regret for his former bitter satire against HELEN OF TROY and presented a form of the legend allowing for a more favorable interpretation of her character. According to tradition, Stesichorus had been struck blind for his original calumny. Chaucer's LEGEND OF GOOD WOMEN is a palinode.

Palinurus. The pilot of AENEAS. Palinurus, sleeping at the helm, fell into the sea and was drowned. The name is employed as a generic word for a steersman or pilot, and sometimes for a chief minister.

Palisades, The. A steep mass of basalt or trap-rock rising up from the west bank of the Hudson River to a height of almost 500 feet and extending north along the New Jersey side of the river for about eighteen miles.

Palissy, Bernard (ca. 1510–1589). French potter, noted for a distinctive type of rustic pottery; also, author of a book on ceramics.

Palladian style. Georgian designs of architecture. Andrea Palladio (1518–1580) was a sixteenth-century Italian architect, who adapted Roman principles, designing in Venice, among other structures, the church of San Giorgio Maggiore and the palaces on the Grand Canal. Inigo JONES introduced the classicism of Palladio into England in the seventeenth century and Sir John VANBRUGH developed from it in the eighteenth century the English baroque style of architecture.

Palladino, Eusapia (1854–1918). Spiritualistic medium of Italian birth who practiced deceptions upon many noted scientists. She was exposed by Prof. Hugo Münsterberg of Harvard during her séances in the U.S. (1909–1910).

Palladium. Something that affords effectual protection and safety. The Palladium was a colossal wooden statue of Pallas in the city of Troy, said to have fallen from heaven. It was believed that so long as this statue remained within the city, Troy would be safe, but if ever it were removed, the city would fall into the hands of the enemy. The statue was carried away by the Greeks, and the city burnt by them to the ground.

The Scotch had a similar tradition attached to the great stone of Scone, near Perth. Edward I removed it to Westminster, and it is still framed in the Coronation Chair of England.

Pallas. A name of MINERVA, sometimes called *Pallas Athene*.

Pallen, Condé Benoist (1858–1929). American editor and poet; managing editor, *The Catholic Encyclopedia* (1907–1914). Author of *The Philosophy of Literature* (1897); *Death of Sir Launcelot and Other Poems* (1902); *Ghost House* (1928); etc.

pallet. A small bed or one of straw. Related to French *paille*, "straw."

> On your midnight pallet lying,
> Listen, and undo the door.
> A. E. Housman, *A Shropshire Lad* XI.

Pallet. In Smollett's novel of PEREGRINE PICKLE, a painter, "without any reverence for the courtesies of life."

Palliser, Plantagenet. See OMNIUM, DUKE OF.

Pall Mall. This fine thoroughfare in the West End of London has been so called since the early 18th century because it is the place where formerly the game of Palle-malle (Ital. *palla*, "ball," *maglia*, "mallet") was played.

palm.

Palm Sunday. The Sunday next before Easter. So called in memory of Christ's triumphant entry into Jerusalem, when the multitude strewed the way with palm branches and leaves. (*John* xii.)

Sad Palm Sunday. March 29th, 1463, the day of the Battle of Towton, the most fatal of all the battles in the War of the Roses. It is said that over 37,000 Englishmen were slain.

palmy days. Prosperous or happy days, as those were to a victorious gladiator when he went to receive the palm branch as the reward of his prowess.

to bear the palm. To be the best. The allusion is to the Roman custom of giving the victorious gladiator a branch of the palm tree.

to palm off. To pass off fraudulently. The allusion is to jugglers, who conceal in the palm of their hand what they pretend to dispose of in some other way.

palmer. A pilgrim to the Holy Land who was privileged to carry a palm staff, and who spent all his days in visiting holy shrines, living on charity. At the dedication of palmers, prayers and psalms were said over them as they lay prostrate before the altar; they were sprinkled with holy water, and then received the consecrated palm branch, sign of their office.

Palmer, Albert Marshman (1838–1905). American theatrical producer who encouraged many new American playwrights and founded the Actors' Fund of America (1882).

Palmer, Frederick (1873–). American war correspondent in the Greek War (1897); the Russo-Japanese War (1904–1905); the Balkan War (1912); World War I (1914–1916). Among his numerous books are *Going to War in Greece* (1897); *America in France* (1918); *The Man With a Country* (1935); etc. Also known as a novelist.

Palmer, George Herbert (1842–1933). American philosopher and educator associated with Harvard University. The principal value of his work lies in its criticism of human conduct. Author of *The Life of Alice Freeman Palmer* (1908) (biography of his wife); *The Problem of Freedom* (1911); *Autobiography of a Philosopher* (1930); etc.

Palmer, John Leslie. See under BEEDING, FRANCIS.

Palmerin. The hero of a number of 16th-century Spanish romances of chivalry on the lines of *Amadis of Gaul*. The most famous are *Palmerin of Oliva*, and *Palmerin of England*. SOUTHEY published an abridged translation of the latter.

Palmerston, 3rd Viscount. **Henry John Temple** (1784–1865). English statesman. Disciple of Pitt. Prime minister (1855–1865, except from 1858 to 1859). Opposed construction of Suez Canal. Supported policy of neutrality in American Civil War, but intervened successfully in a considerable number of threatening and actual international conflicts in favor of the status quo or the restitution of liberal order. Cf. *Palmerston* (1926), by Philip Guedalla.

Palmetto State. South Carolina. See under STATES.

Palmyra. The Biblical Tadmor, a city east of Syria. After the revolt of its queen ZENOBIA, it was destroyed by the Emperor Aurelian (273 A. D.). Cf. *I Kings* ix. 18.

palsgrave. A count palatine. Cf. German *Pfalzgraf.*

Paltock, Robert (1697–1767). English lawyer and author, principally known for the extraordinary fantastic romance, *The Life and Adventures of Peter Wilkins, a Cornish Man* (1751), which describes a country of flying women.

Pamela or **Virtue Rewarded.** A famous novel by Samuel RICHARDSON (1740) of great significance in the early development of the English novel. The heroine is Pamela Andrews, a simple, unsophisticated country girl, the daughter of two aged parents, and maidservant of a rich young squire, called B, who tries to seduce her. She resists every temptation, and at length marries the young squire and reforms him. Pamela is very modest, bears her affliction with much meekness, and is a model of maidenly prudence and rectitude. The story is told in a series of letters which Pamela sends to her parents.

Sir Philip SIDNEY had used the name Pamela for one of the heroines in his ARCADIA.

Pamina and Tamino. In Mozart's opera THE MAGIC FLUTE (Ger. *Die Zauberflöte;* 1790), the two lovers who were guided by "the magic flute" through all worldly dangers to the knowledge of divine truth or the mysteries of Isis.

Pan (*Gr.,* "all, everything"). The god of pastures, forests, flocks, and herds of Greek mythology; also, the personification of deity displayed in creation and pervading all things. He is represented with the lower part of a goat, and the upper part of a man.

Legend has it that at the time of the Crucifixion, just when the veil of the Temple was rent in twain, a cry swept across the ocean in the hearing of many, "Great Pan is Dead," and that at the same time the responses of the oracles ceased for ever. *The Dead Pan,* a poem by Elizabeth Barrett Browning (1844), is founded on this legend. Pan is also the subject of her poem *A Musical Instrument,* of Robert Browning's *Pan and Luna,* and E. C. Stedman's *Pan in Wall Street* (*Am.,* 1869). See also PETER PAN.

pan-. This prefix came to be widely used in the 19th and 20th centuries, in various compounds implying cooperation of the several units of a race, religion or geographical division. Thus we have:

Pan-Americanism. The movement for political cooperation among the various states of North and South America.

Pan-Germanism. A movement to incorporate the German populations of Austria in Germany and to extend German influence generally. It reached a height before World War I, and was continued by Adolf HITLER.

Pan-Islamism. A movement for the greater cooperation of all Mohammedan peoples, with the goal of ultimate freedom from Western domination. The abolition of the Caliphate in 1923 gave the movement a severe setback.

Pan-Slavism. A movement for the political union of all Slavic peoples and originally for their incorporation into the Russian Empire.

Pan-Turanism. A movement for the cooperation and final political union of all Turkish or Tartar races, with the motto "Turkey for the Turks."

Pan, Uncle. Pandarus, in Christopher MORLEY'S *The Trojan Horse* (1937) is so called.

Panacea (*Gr.,* "all-healing"). In Greek myth, the daughter of Aesculapius, god of medicine. Her name was later applied to any universal cure, for, figuratively, medicine that cures is the daughter or child of the healing art.

In the Middle Ages, the search for the panacea was one of the alchemists' self-imposed tasks. Fable tells of many panaceas, such as the Promethean unguent, which rendered the body invulnerable; Aladdin's ring; the balsam of FIERABRAS; and Prince Ahmed's apple (see under APPLE). See also ACHILLES' SPEAR; MEDEA'S KETTLE.

Pan American Union. The official organization of the 21 republics of the Americas, founded in 1890 as the International Bureau of American Republics, and bearing its present name since 1910. The governing board is constituted of all the diplomatic representatives of the American countries and the Secretary of State of the U.S. Its headquarters are in Washington, D.C.

Panathenaea. A festival in honor of Pallas Athene, the Roman Minerva.

pancake. A thin, flat "cake" made in a frying-pan. It was originally intended to be eaten after dinner to stay the stomachs of those who went to be shriven; hence, SHROVE TUESDAY, a special day for these, came to be called *Pancake Day,* and the Shrovebell the *Pancake Bell.*

pancake turner. In radio "shop talk," the sound technician controlling the playing of double-faced records.

Pancrace. In Molière's MARIAGE FORCÉ, a doctor of the Aristotelian school, who involves himself in constant absurdity in his attempts to apply his cumbersome logical analysis to trivial matters. When his adversary cannot agree, he calls him *"un ignorant, un ignorantissime, ignorantifiant, et ignorantifié."*

Pancras, St. See under SAINTS.

Pandarus. In Greek legend, a Lycian leader, one of the allies of PRIAM in the Trojan War. In the classic story he is depicted as an admirable archer, slain by Diomed, and honored as a hero-god in his own country, but in medieval romance he is represented as such a despicable fellow that the word *pander* is derived from his name. Chaucer in his *Troilus and Criseyde* (see TROILUS), and Shakespeare in his drama of *Troilus and Cressida,* represent him as procuring for Troilus the good graces of Cressida, and in MUCH ADO ABOUT NOTHING, it is said that Troilus "was the first employer of pandars."

> Let all pitiful goers-between be called to the world's end after my name; call them all "Pandars." Let all constant men be "Troiluses," all false women "Cressids."—Shakespeare, *Troilus and Cressida,* Act iii. Sc. 2.

Pandavas, the. The five brothers who are joint heroes of the great Hindu epic, the MAHABHARATA.

pandemonium (*Gr.,* "all the demons"). A wild, unrestrained uproar, a tumultuous assembly, a regular row. The word was first used by MILTON as the name of the principal city in Hell, "the high capital of Satan and his peers."

Pandora. In Greek mythology, the first woman. Prometheus had made an image and stolen fire from heaven to endow it with life. In revenge, JUPITER commanded VULCAN to make a woman, who was named Pandora (i.e., the All-gifted), because each of the gods gave her some power which was to bring about the ruin of man. Jupiter gave her a box which she was to present to him who married her. Prometheus distrusted Jupiter and his gifts, but Epimetheus, his brother, married the beautiful Pandora, and—against advice—accepted the gift of the god. As soon he opened the box all the evils that flesh is heir to flew forth, and have ever since continued to afflict the world. According to some accounts the last thing that flew out was Hope, but others say that Hope alone remained. Some versions blame Pandora's curiosity for the disaster.

Pandora's box. A present which seems valuable, but which is in reality a curse; like that of MIDAS, who found his very food became gold, and so uneatable.

panegyric. A laudatory oration, song, essay, etc.

Pangloss, Dr. (*Gr.,* "all tongues"). The pedantic old tutor to the hero in Voltaire's CANDIDE, OU L'OPTIMISME. His great point is his incurable and misleading optimism; it does him no good and brings him all sorts of misfortune, but to the end he reiterates "All is for the best in this best of all possible worlds." He is said to have been based on the philosopher LEIBNITZ.

Panhandle. In the United States a narrow strip of territory belonging to one State which runs between two others, such as the Texas Panhandle, the Panhandle of Idaho, etc. West Virginia is known as *the Panhandle State.* The allusion is obvious.

Panhard, René (b. 1841). French automotive engineer, the first to mount the internal combustion engine invented by Daimler (1887) on a mobile chassis (1891).

Panic. A verse play by Archibald MACLEISH (1935).

Pan in Wall Street. A famous poem by Edmund Clarence STEDMAN.

Panjandrum, The Grand, "with the little red button a-top." A village boss, who imagines himself the "Magnus Apollo" of his neighbors. The word occurs in the famous farrago of nonsense which the comic dramatist Foote (1721–1777) composed to test old Macklin, who said he had brought his memory to such perfection that he could remember anything by reading it over once. There is more than one version of the test passage; the following is as well authenticated as any:

> So she went into the garden to cut a cabbage-leaf to make an apple-pie, and at the same time a great she-bear came running up the street and popped its head into the shop. "What! no soap?" So he died, and she—very imprudently—married the barber. And there were present the Picninnies, the Joblillies, the Garyulies, and the Grand Panjandrum himself, with the little red button a-top, and they all fell to playing the game of catch-as-catch-can till the gunpowder ran out at the heels of their boots.

It is said that Macklin was so indignant at this nonsense that he refused to repeat a word of it.

Pankhurst, Emmeline (1858–1928). English woman-suffragist; endured several hunger-strikes. Her daughters also supported the suffragist movement, and one of them, **Estelle Sylvia Pankhurst** (1882–   ), published a biography of her mother (1935).

Pan Michael. The third of a Polish historic trilogy by Sienkiewicz. See WITH FIRE AND SWORD.

panniers. A frame of steel, whalebone, or the like, formerly worn by women to expand their skirts at the hips.

Pansy. The *nom de plume* of Mrs. Isabella Alden (b. 1841) whose religious stories for young people, the *Pansy Books* were for a time very popular in America.

Pantagruel. The principal character in RABELAIS' great satire, *Gargantua and Pantag-*

ruel (the first part published in 1533, the last posthumously in 1564), King of the Dipsodes, son of GARGANTUA, and by some identified with Henri II of France. He is the last of the giants, and Rabelais says he got his name from the Greek *panta,* "all," and Arab. *gruel,* "thirsty," because he was born during the drought which lasted thirty and six months, three weeks, four days, thirteen hours, and a little more, in that year of grace noted for having "three Thursdays in one week." He is covered with hair at birth, "like a young bear," and is so strong that though he is chained in his cradle he breaks his bonds into five hundred thousand pieces with one blow of his infant fist. When he grows to manhood he knows all languages, all sciences, and all knowledge of every sort, out-Solomoning Solomon in wisdom. His immortal achievement is his voyage from Utopia in quest of the "ORACLE OF THE HOLY BOTTLE."

Pantagruel's course of study. Pantagruel's father, Gargantua, says in a letter to his son:

"I intend and insist that you learn all languages perfectly; first of all Greek, in Quintilian's method; then Latin, then Hebrew, then Arabic and Chaldee. I wish you to form your style of Greek on the model of Plato, and of Latin on that of Cicero. Let there be no history you have not at your fingers' ends, and study thoroughly cosmography and geography. Of liberal arts, such as geometry, mathematics, and music, I gave you a taste when not above five years old, and I would have you now master them fully. Study astronomy, but not divination and judicial astrology, which I consider mere vanities. As for civil law, I would have thee know the *digests* by heart. You should also have a perfect knowledge of the works of Nature, so that there is no sea, river, or smallest stream, which you do not know for what fish it is noted, whence it proceeds, and whither it directs its course; all fowls of the air, all shrubs and trees whether forest or orchard, all herbs and flowers, all metals and stones, should be mastered by you. Fail not at the same time most carefully to peruse the Talmudists and Cabbalists, and be sure by frequent anatomies to gain a perfect knowledge of that other world called the microcosm, which is man. Master all these in your young days, and let nothing be superficial; as you grow into manhood you must learn chivalry, warfare, and field manoeuvres."—Bk. II. 8.

Pantagruel's tongue. It forms a shelter for a whole army, and his throat and mouth contains whole cities.

Then did they [the army] put themselves in close order, and stood as near to each other as they could and Pantagruel put out his tongue half-way, and covered them all, as a hen doth her chickens.—Bk. II. 32.

Pantagruelian lawsuit. This is a lawsuit between Lord Busqueue and Lord Suckfist, who plead their own cases. The writs, etc., are as much as four asses can carry. After the plaintiff and defendant have stated their cases, Pantagruel gives judgment, and the two suitors are both satisfied, for no one can understand a word of the pleadings, or the tenor of the verdict.

Pantagruelion. The name given by Rabelais to hemp, of which the hangman's rope is made, "because Pantagruel was the inventor of a certain use which it serves for, exceeding hateful to felons, unto whom it is more hurtful than strangle-weed to flax."

Pantagruelism. Coarse and boisterous buffoonery and humor, like that for which Pantagruel is famous.

Pantaloon or **Pantaleone.** Originally, a stock character of Italian comedy, a thin, emaciated old man who always appeared in slippers. In England he became a pantomime character. See also PIERROT.

The sixth age shifts
Into the lean and slippered Pantaloon.
Shakespeare, *As You Like It,* act ii. sc. 7 (1600).

Panter-Downes, Mollie (1906–). Anglo-Irish novelist and journalist, known for her "Letters From England," published weekly in THE NEW YORKER and later collected in book form (1940). Author of *The Shoreless Sea* (1924); etc.

Panthea. In classical history the wife of Abradatus, King of Susa. He joined the Assyrians against CYRUS, and she was taken captive. Cyrus refused to visit her, that he might not be tempted by her beauty, and Abradatus, charmed by this restraint, joined his party. Shortly after he was slain in battle, and Panthea put an end to her life, falling on the body of her husband. XENOPHON'S *Cyropoedia,* in which her history is related, is said to be "the first extant example of a prose love-story in European literature."

pantheism (from Gr. *pan,* "all," and *theos,* "god"). The doctrine that God is everything and everything is God; a monistic theory elaborated by SPINOZA, who, by his doctrine of the Infinite Substance, sought to overcome the opposition between mind and matter, body and soul.

During the romantic period (see ROMANTICISM) and later, WORDSWORTH, SHELLEY, EMERSON, TENNYSON, and others expressed various doctrines of pantheism in their writings.

Pantheon (from Gr. *pan,* "all," and *theos,* "god"). A temple dedicated to all the gods; specifically, that erected at Rome by Agrippa, son-in-law to Augustus. It is circular, nearly 150 ft. in diameter, and of the same total height; since the early 7th century, as Santa Maria Rotunda, it has been used as a Christian Church.

The Pantheon at Paris was originally the church of St. Genevieve, built by Louis XV and finished in 1790. The following year the Convention gave it its present name, and set it apart as the shrine of those Frenchmen whom their country wished to honor.

Pantisocracy. A scheme for an ideal social community in America, planned by S. T. COLERIDGE and Robert SOUTHEY in 1794. The community was to be based on the theories of

Rousseau and Godwin and was to be located on the banks of the Susquehanna River in Pennsylvania. The scheme never materialized because of lack of financial backing.

pantomime. A dumb-show performance. Popular in ancient Rome and 17th- and 18th-century Italy and France. In England, the Christmas pantomime survives as an extravaganza for children put on in a theater with many magical spectacles. The silent motion picture worked essentially with a pantomime technique.

Panurge (from Gr. *pan,* "all," *ergos,* "worker"; the "all-doer," i.e., the rogue, he who will "do anything or anyone"). The roguish companion of Pantagruel, and one of the principal characters in Rabelais' satire of that name. He is a desperate rake, is always in debt, has a dodge for every scheme, knows everything and something more, is a boon companion of the mirthfullest temper and most licentious bias; but he is timid of danger, and a desperate coward. The third, fourth, and fifth (last) books of the satire are taken up with the adventures of Panurge, and the rest in their endeavor to find by divination whether or not he should marry. Besides Pantagruel, Panurge consults lots, dreams, a sibyl, a deaf and dumb man, the old poet Rominagrobis, the chiromancer Herr Trippa, the theologian Hippothadée, the physician Rondibilis, the philosopher Trouillogan, the court fool Triboulet, and, lastly, the oracle of the Holy Bottle. To every one of the very obscure answers Panurge receives, whether it seems to point to "Yes" or to "No," he invariably finds insuperable objections.

Some "commentators" on Rabelais have identified Panurge with John Calvin, others with Cardinal Lorraine; this part of the satire seems to be an echo of the great Reformation controversy on the celibacy of the clergy.

Panza, Sancho, see Sancho Panza.

Paolo and Francesca. See under Francesca da Rimini.

Papen, Franz von (1879–). German diplomat. Military attaché in Washington (1915); recalled to Germany by request of U.S. state department for "improper activities" (1915). Premier of Prussia (1932–1933). Under Hitler, vice-chancellor of Germany (1933–1934). Ambassador, to Austria (1934–1938), and to Turkey (from 1939). One of the group of German nationalists who seconded the Nazi bid for power in the belief that they could exploit the expected revolution for the benefit of their own ideology. Acquitted at Nuremberg Trial (1946).

Paphian. Relating to Venus or rather to Paphos, a city of Cyprus, where Venus was worshiped; a Cyprian; a prostitute.

Paphnutius. The young monk who is the central figure in Thaïs, a romance by Anatole France.

Papimany. In Rabelais' satire Gargantua and Pantagruel (ix, xlv), the country of the Papimanes, i.e., those who are madly devoted to, or have a *mania* for, the Pope; hence, any priest-ridden country.

Papini, Giovanni (1881–). Italian critic and author, at first known for his bitterness and his negative philosophy, but after World War I converted to Roman Catholicism (1920) and transformed into an exponent of mysticism. His best-known work is his *Storia di Cristo* (1921), translated as *The Life of Christ* (1923). Other writings, under their English titles, include *Memoirs of God* (1926); *Prayer to Christ* (1926); *Laborers in the Vineyard* (1930); *Life and Myself* (1930); *Saint Augustine* (1930); *Gog* (1930), an anti-20th-century satire. Among his later works are *Dante Vivo* (1933) and *I Testimoni della Passione* (1937).

Paracelsus. A narrative poem by Robert Browning (1835). The hero is a historical character, a famous Swiss physician (1493–1541), who was said to have delved deeply into alchemy and to have kept a small devil prisoner in the pommel of his sword. His full name was Philippus Aureolus Theophrastus Paracelsus, but his family name was Bombastus. In the poem, Paracelsus, at twenty, thinks knowledge the *summum bonum,* and on the advice of his two friends, Festus and Michal, retires to a seat of learning. Eight years later, dissatisfied, he falls in with Aprile, an Italian poet, and resolves to seek the *summum bonum* in love. Again he fails, and, when dying in a cell in the hospital of St. Sebastian, deserted by all but Festus, he declares the *summum bonum* to be "To see good in evil, and a hope in ill-success."

Paraclete. From Greek. A helper, intercessor, etc. Hence, the Holy Spirit in the sense of "the Comforter."

paradigm. A model, example, or pattern, especially, in grammar, of declension, conjugation, etc., constituting a full survey of all the forms of a noun, verb, or any other word that can be inflected.

paradise. The Greeks borrowed this word from the Persians, among whom it denoted the enclosed and extensive parks and pleasure grounds of the Persian kings. The Septuagint translators adopted it for the garden of Eden, and in the New Testament and by early Christian writers it was applied to Heaven, the abode of the blessed dead. The third part of Dante's Divine Comedy is entitled *Paradise* (*Paradiso*). It describes the poet's journey through the ten spheres of paradise.

An old word, "paradise," which the Hebrews had borrowed from the Persians, and which at first designated the "parks of the Achaemenidae."—Renan, *Life of Jesus,* xi.

a fool's paradise. See FOOL.

paradise of exiles. Italy, from its foreign population, especially during the 19th century.

earthly paradise. See under EARTHLY.

Paradise and the Peri. See under PERI.

Paradise Lost. MILTON's epic poem—considered the greatest epic in any modern language—was published in twelve books in 1667. It tells the story—

Of Man's first disobedience and the fruit
Of that forbidden tree whose mortal taste
Brought death into the World, and all our woe,
With loss of Eden.

SATAN rouses the panic-stricken host of fallen angels with tidings of a rumor current in Heaven of a new world about to be created. He calls a council to deliberate what should be done, and they agree to send him to search for this new world. Satan, passing the gulf between Hell and Heaven and the limbo of Vanity, enters the orb of the Sun (disguised as an angel), and, having obtained the information, goes to Paradise in the form of a cormorant. Seating himself on the Tree of Life, he overhears Adam and Eve talking about the prohibition made by God, and at once resolves upon the nature of his attack. GABRIEL sends two angels to watch over the bower of Paradise, and Satan flees. RAPHAEL is sent to warn Adam of his danger, and tells him the story of Satan's revolt and expulsion from Heaven, and why and how this world was made. After a time Satan returns to Paradise in the form of a mist, and, entering the serpent, induces Eve to eat of the forbidden fruit. Adam eats "that he may perish with the woman whom he loved." Satan returns to Hell to tell his triumph, and MICHAEL is sent to lead the guilty pair out of the Garden.

Milton borrowed largely from the epic of Guillaume du BARTAS entitled *La Semaine* (*The Week of Creation;* 1578), which was translated into almost every European language. He was also indebted to St. Avitus (d. 523), who wrote in Latin hexameters *The Creation, The Fall,* and *The Expulsion from Paradise,* for his description of Paradise (Bk. i), of Satan (Bk. ii), and other parts.

In 1671, *Paradise Regained* (in four books), written by Milton on suggestion of his Quaker friend Thomas Ellwood, was published. The subject is the Temptation. Eve, being tempted, falls, and loses Paradise; Jesus, being tempted, resists, and regains Paradise. The New Testament narrative is followed and enlarged upon.

The American playwright Clifford ODETS named one of his plays *Paradise Lost* (1935).

Paradise of Dainty Devices, The. An English "poetical miscellany" (see TOTTEL'S MISCELLANY) of the Elizabethan period, first published in 1576 and extremely popular, appearing in nine editions from its first date to 1606. Its contents, originally assembled by Richard Edwards, are marked by a greater seriousness than Tottel's.

paradox. A statement or proposition that is obviously contrary to common sense, yet full of significance when viewed from the proper angle. The Christian doctrine of the Trinity is paradoxical. Gilbert K. CHESTERTON and Oscar WILDE, for instance, are masters in the use of paradoxes as rhetorical devices.

Paragot. Hero of W. J. Locke's BELOVED VAGABOND.

Parcae. The Latin name for the Fates. The three were Clotho, Lachesis, and Atropos. Parcae is from Lat. *pars,* "a lot"; and the corresponding Moirae of the Greeks is from Gr. *meros,* "a lot."

Pardoner's or **Pardoneres Tale, The.** One of the stories in Chaucer's CANTERBURY TALES, that of *Death and the Rioters,* which comes from an Oriental source through the Italian *Cento Novelle Antiche.*

Three rioters in a tavern agree to hunt down Death and kill him. As they go their way they meet an old man, who tells them that he has just left him sitting under a tree in the lane close by. Off go the three rioters, but when they come to the tree they find a great treasure, which they agree to divide equally. They cast lots to determine who is to carry it home, and the lot falls to the youngest, who is sent to the village to buy food and wine. While he is gone the two who are left agree to kill him, and so increase their share; but the third buys poison to put into the wine, in order to kill his two *confreres.* On his return with his stores, the two set upon him and slay him, then sit down to drink and be merry together. But, the wine being poisoned, all three rioters find Death under the tree, as the old man predicted.

the pardoner's mitten. Whoever put this mitten on would be sure to thrive in all things.

He that his hondë put in this metayn,
He shal have multiplying of his grayn,
When he hath sowen, be it whete or otes,
So that ye offre pans [pence] or ellës grootes.
Prologue to The Pardoner's Tale.

Paré, Ambroise (1517–1590). French surgeon, often called the father of modern surgery; introduced practice of ligature of arteries in place of cautery in amputations; court physician to Henry II, Francis II, Charles IX, and Henry III.

Paret, Hugh. The hero of Winston Churchill's FAR COUNTRY.

Pareto, Vilfredo (1848–1923). Italian economist and sociologist. Mussolini is said to have recognized him as the father of Fascist theory, his contempt for democracy being well known. He died soon after the establishment of Fascism in Italy. Max Lerner has said, "Pareto's Republic is now a reality: it is Hitler's totalitarian state." But though Pareto detested political liberty, he wished for economic and intellectual liberty.

pariah. A member of a very low caste of Hindus in Southern India, from a native word meaning "a drummer," because it was these who beat the drums at certain festivals. Europeans often extend the term to those of no caste at all; hence it is applied to outcasts generally, the lowest of the low. *The Pariah* is the title of a novel by F. ANSTEY.

Parian. Pertaining to the Greek island of Paros, noted for its marble used in ancient sculpture; hence, of or pertaining to marble or to ancient sculpture.

Paribanou. In the tale of *Prince Ahmed and Paribanou* in the *Arabian Nights,* a fairy who gives Prince Ahmed a tent which will fold into so small a compass that a lady may carry it about as a toy but that, when spread, will cover a whole army.

Paridell. A libertine in Spenser's FAËRIE QUEENE (III. viii, ix, x, IV, ii, v, ix, etc.) typifying the Earl of Westmorland. Pope in his DUNCIAD uses the name for a young gentleman who travels about and seeks adventure, because he is young, rich, and at leisure.

Paris. (1) In Greek legend, the son of PRIAM, King of Troy, and HECUBA; and through his abduction of HELEN the cause of the siege of Troy. Before his birth Hecuba dreamed that she was to bring forth a firebrand, and, as this was interpreted to mean that the unborn child would bring destruction to his house, the infant Paris was exposed on Mount Ida. He was, however, brought up by a shepherd, and grew to perfection of beautiful manhood. When the golden Apple of Discord (see under APPLE) was thrown on the table of the gods, it was Paris who had to judge between the rival claims of Hera (Juno), Aphrodite (Venus), and Athene (Minerva). Each goddess offered him bribes—the first power, the second the most beautiful of women, and the third martial glory. He awarded the Apple and the title of "Fairest" to Aphrodite, who in return assisted him to carry off Helen, for whom he deserted his wife, OENONE, daughter of the river-god, Cebren. At Troy Paris earned the contempt of all by his cowardice, and he was fatally wounded with a poisoned arrow by PHILOCTETES at the taking of the city.

(2) In Shakespeare's ROMEO AND JULIET, a young nobleman, kinsman of Prince Escalus of Verona, and the unsuccessful suitor of his cousin Juliet.

Paris. A gay city is sometimes so called, from Paris, capital of France, which was known for its brilliant social life.

the Paris of Japan. Osaka.

the little Paris. (1) Brussels; (2) Bucharest; (3) the Galleria Vittorio Emanuelo of Milan.

Paris, Matthew (1200?–1259). English historian of the Middle Ages, a monk at the monastery of St. Albans, known for his lively chronicles of the outstanding events in England and Europe of his time. His *Chronica Majora,* beginning with 1235, and his *Historia Minor,* or *Historia Anglorum,* covering the period between 1200 and 1250, are his chief works.

Paris Bound. A light sophisticated comedy by Philip BARRY (1927).

Parisian Wedding, the. The massacre of St. Bartholomew, which took place (Aug. 24, 1572) during the festivities at the marriage of Henri of Navarre and Margaret of France.

> Charles IX, although it was not possible for him to recall to life the countless victims of the Parisian Wedding, was ready to explain those murders.—Motley, *Dutch Republic,* iii, 9.

Parisina. Titular heroine of a poem by BYRON (1816), the wife of Azo, chief of Ferrara. She has been betrothed before her marriage to Hugo, a natural son of Azo, and after Azo takes her for his bride, the attachment of Parisina and Hugo continues and has freer scope for indulgence. One night Azo hears Parisina in her sleep confess her love for Hugo, whereupon he has his son beheaded; though he spares the life of Parisina, no one ever knows what becomes of her. The real Azo was Niccola III of Ferrara, whose story corresponds in the main with that given in the poem.

Parizade, Princess. Heroine of one of the tales of the *Arabian Nights,* the *Story of the Sisters Who Envied Their Younger Sister.* She is most famed for her adventures in search of the Talking Bird, the Singing Tree, and the Yellow or Gold-colored Water. After she finds these treasures, her troubles are at an end. See PRINCE CHERY.

Park, Mungo (1771–1806). English surgeon, traveler, and author, a friend of Sir Walter SCOTT and famous for his *Travels in the Interior of Africa* (1799), an account of an exploratory trip along the Niger River. He was killed in a skirmish with the African natives.

Parker, Dorothy, *née* **Rothschild** (1893–). American journalist, short-story writer, and author of light verse, known for the malice, satire, cynicism, and flippancy of her poems and sketches, many of which were first published in THE NEW YORKER. Her books include *Enough Rope* (1926), *Sunset Gun* (1928), and *Death And Taxes* (1931), verse; *Laments for the Living* (1930) and *After Such*

Pleasures (1933), stories and sketches; *Not So Deep as a Well* (1936), a collection of her verse; *Here Lies* (1939), a collection of her prose. She was a correspondent in Spain during the Spanish Civil War (1936–1939).

Parker, Sir Gilbert (1862–1932). Canadian novelist. His greatest success was *The Seats of the Mighty* (1896), a novel of the American Revolution, which sold more than 100,000 copies. *The Right of Way* (1901) was nearly as successful.

Parker, Henry Taylor (1867–1934). American drama and music critic, for 29 years on the staff of the Boston *Transcript* (1905–1934).

Parker, Horatio William (1863–1919). American composer. Dean of Yale Music School (1904–1919). Wrote two prize-winning operas with Brian Hooker: *Mona* (1911) and *Fairyland* (1915).

Parker, Louis Napoleon (1852–1944). English dramatist and composer, chiefly known for the comedy *Pomander Walk* (1910), the historical play, *Disraeli,* starring George ARLISS, and the drama *Joseph and His Brethren* (1913). His versions of the plays of Edmond ROSTAND were often used.

Parker, Matthew (1504–1575). English prelate. Chaplain to Anne Boleyn (1535); dean of Lincoln (1552); during Mary's reign, deprived of preferments; second Anglican archbishop of Canterbury under Queen Elizabeth (1559). Extremely influential in Anglicanism. Published revised *Bishops' Bible* (1572).

Parker, Theodore (1810–1860). American Unitarian clergyman and transcendentalist (see TRANSCENDENTALISM), known for his emphasis on the role of direct intuition in religion. Because of his unorthodox ideas he was opposed by conservative religionists of his day. He was active in agitation against war, slavery, drunkenness, and the subjugation of women, and gave vigorous assistance to fugitive slaves. His best-known works are *The . . . Question between Mr. Andrews Norton and his Alumni . . .* (1830), written under the pseudonym of Levi Blodgett; *A Discourse of Matters Pertaining to Religion* (1842); and *Letter Touching the Matter of Slavery* (1848). He is the Mr. Power of *Work,* a novel by Louisa M. ALCOTT.

Parkhurst, Charles Henry (1842–1933). American Presbyterian clergyman. Famous for his attacks on political corruption and organized vice (1892) which caused the election of the reform administration of Mayor William L. Strong in New York.

Parkman, Francis (1823–1893). American historian, known for his accounts of the early colonization of America by the French, English, and Spanish, their relations with the American Indians, and their colonial wars with each other. His works include *The Oregon Trail* (1849); *History of the Conspiracy of the Pontiac* (1851); *Vassall Morton* (1856), a novel, considered to be partly autobiographical; *Pioneers of France in the New World* (1865); *The Book of Roses* (1866), a book on horticulture; *The Jesuits in North America in the 17th Century* (1867); *LaSalle and the Discovery of the Great West* (1869); *The Old Régime in Canada* (1874); *Count Frontenac and New France under Louis XIV* (1877); *Montcalm and Wolfe* (1884); *A Half-Century of Conflict* (1892). Parkman wrote under great difficulty, being afflicted during most of his life by weakened eyes and a nervous and mental derangement that prevented him from concentrating on his work.

Park Row. A short street near City Hall, New York, once famous as a newspaper publishing center.

Parley, Peter. The *nom de plume* of the American author, Samuel Griswold Goodrich (1793–1860). His books attained great popularity.

Parleyings with Certain People of Importance in Their Way. A series of poems by Robert BROWNING (1887). The "people" are Bernard de Mandeville, Daniel Bartoli, Christopher Smart, George Bubb Dodington, Francis Furini, Gerard de Lairesse, and Charles Avison. The poems are introduced by a prologue, *Apollo and the Fates,* and concluded by *A Dialogue between John Fust and His Friends.*

Parliamentary Novels. A series of novels of parliamentary life by Anthony TROLLOPE, including PHINEAS FINN, PHINEAS REDUX, *The Prime Minister* (1876), and *The Duke's Children* (1880). The hero is Phineas Finn, a young Irishman, but Plantagenet Palliser, Duke of OMNIUM, plays a prominent role.

Parliament of Fowls, The. A poem in rime-royal by Geoffrey CHAUCER. Probably written between 1372 and 1386.

parliaments.

the Addled Parliament. A parliament held in 1614–1615, so called because it remonstrated with the King for his levying of "benevolences" but passed no act.

the Barebones Parliament. The parliament convened by Cromwell in 1653; so called from Praise-God Barebones, a fanatical leader, who was a prominent member. Also called the *Little Parliament,* because it comprised under 150 members.

the Black Parliament. A parliament held by Henry VIII in Bridewell.

the Club Parliament. See below, PARLIAMENT OF BATS.

the Devil's Parliament. The parliament

convened at Coventry by Henry VI in 1459, which passed attainder on the Duke of York and his supporters.

the Drunken Parliament. A Scotch parliament assembled at Edinburgh, January 1, 1661, the members of which, it was said, were almost perpetually drunk.

the Good Parliament. Edward III's parliament of 1376; so called because of the severity with which it pursued the unpopular party of the Duke of Lancaster.

the Illiterate, Lack-learning or *Lawless Parliament.* Same as THE UNLEARNED PARLIAMENT.

the Little Parliament. Another name for the BAREBONES PARLIAMENT.

the Long Parliament. The parliament that sat twelve years and five months, from November 2, 1640, to April 20, 1653, when it was dissolved by Cromwell. A fragment of it, called "THE RUMP" continued till the Restoration, in 1660.

the Mad Parliament. The parliament which assembled at Oxford in 1258, and broke out into open rebellion against Henry III. It confirmed the Magna Charta, the King was declared deposed, and the government was vested in the hands of twenty-four councillors, with Simon de Montfort at their head.

the Merciless (or *Unmerciful*) *Parliament.* A junto of fourteen tools of Thomas, Duke of Gloucester, which assumed royal prerogatives in 1388, and attempted to depose Richard II.

the Mongrel Parliament (1681), held at Oxford, consisting of Whigs and Tories, by whom the Exclusion Bill was passed.

the Pacific Parliament. A triennial parliament, dissolved August 8, 1713. It signed the treaty of peace at Utrecht, after a war of eleven years.

the Pensioner (or *Pensionary*) *Parliament* (from May 8, 1661, to January 24, 1678 [i.e., 16 years and 260 days]). It was convened by Charles II, and was called "Pensionary" from the many pensions it granted to the adherents of the King.

the Rump Parliament (1659). In the Protectorate; so called because it contained the rump or fag-end of the LONG PARLIAMENT. It was this parliament that voted the trial of Charles I.

the Running Parliament. A Scotch parliament; so called from its constantly being shifted from place to place.

the Unlearned or *Lawless Parliament* (*Parliamentum Indoctum*). The parliament convened by Henry IV at Coventry, in Warwickshire (1404), so called because lawyers were excluded from it.

the Unmerciful Parliament. The parliament of 1388 in the reign of Richard II; so called by the people from its tyrannical proceedings.

the Useless Parliament. The parliament convened by Charles I, on June 18, 1625, adjourned to Oxford, August 1, and dissolved August 12, having done nothing but offend the King.

the Wondermaking Parliament. The same as THE UNMERCIFUL PARLIAMENT.

the Parliament of Bats. A parliament held in 1426 during the regency in the reign of Henry VI; so called because the members, being forbidden by the Duke of Gloucester to wear swords, armed themselves with clubs or bats.

Parliament of Dunces. Another name for the UNLEARNED PARLIAMENT.

Parnassians. A school of French poets, flourishing in the latter part of the 19th century, which opposed the excessive emotionalism and subjectivism of ROMANTICISM and aimed at "Olympian calm" in attitude and meticulous precision in technique. The leader of the school was Charles LECONTE DE LISLE; members included Catulle Mendès, Sully PRUDHOMME, José-Maria de HEREDIA, François Coppée, and Paul VERLAINE. Some critics consider the Parnassian movement the result of the influence of the growing 19th-century scientific and historical objectivity on poetry. LE PARNASSE CONTEMPORAIN (1866, 1871–1876), a collection of the work of the Parnassian poets, gave the school its name.

See also SYMBOLISM.

Parnassus. A mountain near Delphi, Greece, with two summits, one of which was consecrated to Apollo and the Muses, the other to Bacchus. Owing to its connection with the Muses, Parnassus came to be regarded as the seat of poetry and music, and we still use such phrases as *to climb Parnassus,* meaning "to write poetry." Christopher MORLEY called his narrative on migratory book-selling *Parnassus on Wheels* (1917).

the legislator or *Solon of Parnassus.* BOILEAU (1636–1711) was so called by VOLTAIRE, because of his *Art of Poetry.*

Parnell, Charles Stewart (1846–1891). Irish nationalist leader, a Member of Parliament, who constantly agitated for Home Rule for Ireland, winning Gladstone and the Liberal party over to his side and uniting a number of dissident elements in his own country, until his career was brought to an end by charges of crime that were made against him by his enemies and by his being named co-respondent in a divorce suit (1890) initiated by one Captain O'Shea against his wife Kitty. Parnell is known for the devoted partisans and violent enemies that his policies and his personality created among the Irish people. He is referred to frequently throughout the works of James JOYCE, to whom he was an early hero. See IVY DAY IN THE COMMITTEE ROOM; PHOENIX PARK.

parochial. Restricted to a parish: hence narrow and limited in scope or understanding.

To be parochial is to turn away from the great and look at the little.—Thomas Wentworth Higginson, *Margaret Fuller Ossoli*, ix.

parodos. In Greek tragedy, the first choral passage sung as the chorus enters. Ordinarily it is preceded by the prologue.

parody. A satirical imitation of a novel or poem. *A Christmas Garland*, by Max BEERBOHM; *Condensed Novels*, by Bret HARTE, etc.

Parolles. One of the most famous braggarts and cowards of all literature, a follower of Bertram in Shakespeare's ALL'S WELL THAT ENDS WELL. His name signifies mere empty words. In one scene the bully is taken blindfold among his old acquaintances, and he vilifies their characters to their faces in the belief that he is talking to their enemies.

I know him a notorious liar
Think him a great way fool, solely a coward.—Act I. 1.

paronomasia. A pun; a play on words.

Parr, Catherine (1512–1548). The sixth and last wife of Henry VIII of England whom she survived. A kind woman, she tried to lessen the religious persecutions of the time, and acted as mother to Prince Edward and Princesses Elizabeth and Mary.

Parricide, the Beautiful, see CENCI, BEATRICE.

Parrington, Vernon Louis (1871–1929). American literary scholar, best known for his *Main Currents in American Thought* (1927–1930), left incomplete at the time of his death, which was awarded the Pulitzer prize for its first two volumes in 1928. This work is a history of the development of American ideas and their expression in literature, as seen from a liberal viewpoint. It was one of the first critical works to interpret American literature according to economic influences, and had an important effect on scholarship in its field.

Parrish, Anne (1888–). American novelist, noted for her satirical gift. *The Perennial Bachelor* (1925) won the Harper prize. *The Methodist Faun* (1929) displays her delicate talent and humor at their best.

Parrish, Maxfield (1870–). Well-known American book illustrator with a romantic and individual style. Also did murals such as the Old King Cole mural now in the St. Regis Hotel in New York. Noted for the luminous blue of his skies.

Parrott, Ursula (1902–). American novelist, principally known as author of sensational novels such as *Ex-Wife* (1929), etc.

Parry, Sir Charles Hubert Hastings (1848–1918). English composer of symphonies, chamber music, and choral compositions, notably *Blest Pair of Sirens*. Also noted as musicologist and author of *The Evolution of the Art of Music* (1896); etc.

Parsees or Parsis. Ghebers or fire-worshipers; descendants of Persians who fled to India during the Mohammedan persecutions of the 7th and 8th centuries and still adhere to their Zoroastrian religion. The word means *People of Pars*—i.e., Persia.

Parsifal or Parzival. A hero of medieval romance whose story, taken mainly from the 13th-century German epic *Parzival* by WOLFRAM VON ESCHENBACH, forms the subject of Wagner's opera *Parsifal* (1882). In English romance he is known as PERCIVAL, in Welsh as Peredur. According to the German legend, Parzival is the guileless fool who alone can heal the sore wound of Amfortas, guardian of the HOLY GRAIL kept in its temple at Montsalvat (Mont Salvagge) in the mountains of Spain. He grows up in innocence in the forest, becomes one of the knights of the ROUND TABLE at King ARTHUR's court, and takes part in numerous adventures but keeps always his strange innocence. Once as a mere lad he visits Amfortas in his castle but with no results, since he is ignorant of his mission and fails to ask the cause of Amfortas' wound, but when he returns years later, he effects the cure and becomes himself guardian of the Holy Grail. In most versions Amfortas has been wounded by the lance of LONGINUS as a punishment for sin, and in many he must be cured by a touch of that same weapon.

Wagner's opera, based on the old romances, makes the wound of Amfortas a product of his sin with the enchantress KUNDRY whom the evil magician KLINGSOR provided as a temptress for the Knights of the Grail. Kundry, who because she laughed at Christ is compelled to wander about the earth until she expiates her sins (see WANDERING JEW), soon repents and endeavors to find healing balsams for the wound, but in vain. When Parsifal, the guileless fool, appears, Klingsor again forces Kundry to act as temptress, but Parsifal resists her, seizes in mid air the lance hurled at him by the angry Klingsor, and fulfills his mission. Amfortas is cured of his wound, Kundry is baptized, and Parsifal becomes the guardian of the Holy Grail.

Parson.

Parson Adams, see ADAMS.

Parson Runo. A simple-minded clergyman, wholly unacquainted with the world; a Dr. Primrose, in fact. It is a Russian household phrase, having its origin in the singular simplicity of the Lutheran clergy of the Isle of Runo.

Parson Trulliber, see TRULLIBER.

Parsons, Elizabeth (1749–1807). An English impostor, who as a child at the age of eleven started the legend of the "Cock Lane Ghost" and was exposed by Dr. Johnson in *Gentleman's Magazine.*

Parsons, Geoffrey (1879–). American journalist. Chief editorial writer of the New York *Herald Tribune* (from 1924). Pulitzer prize for editorial writing (1942).

Parsons, Thomas William (1819–1892). American poet, chiefly known as interpreter and translator of Dante's *Inferno* (with illustrations by Gustave Doré; 1867). His best-known poems are *On a Bust of Dante* and *Paradisi Gloria.*

Parson's Tale, The. One of the two tales in prose in Chaucer's CANTERBURY TALES. It is a kind of Bunyan's PILGRIM'S PROGRESS, comparing the life of a Christian to a journey from earth to heaven.

The Parson is perhaps best described in the following well-known lines:

> A good man was ther of religioun
> And was a poore Persoun of a toun
> But riche he was of holy thogt and werk
> He was also a lerned man, a clerk
> That Cristes gospel trewely wolde preche . . .
> But Cristes lore and his apostles twelve
> He taughte, and first he folwed it himselve.
> Chaucer, *Prologue to the Canterbury Tales.*

Parthenia. The mistress of Argalus in Sir Philip Sidney's ARCADIA.

Parthenius (fl. 1st century B.C.). Greek grammarian and poet. The only work of his which has come down to us is *Love's Woes,* consisting of 36 love stories.

Parthenon. The great temple at Athens to Athene *Parthenos* (i.e., the Virgin), many of the sculptured friezes and fragments of pediments of which are now in the British Museum among the Elgin Marbles. The Temple was begun by the architect Ictinus about 450 B. C., and the embellishment of it was mainly the work of PHIDIAS, whose colossal chryselephantine statue of Athene was its chief treasure.

Parthenope. An old name for Naples; so called from Parthenope, the siren, who threw herself into the sea out of love for ULYSSES, and was cast up on the bay of Naples.

Parthian shot. The ancient Parthians fought on horseback with the bow, and turned their horses as though for flight after each shot. Hence "Parthian shot" or "Parthian arrow" came to mean something cutting or impressive said on the moment of departure.

Partington, Dame, and her mop. A taunt against those who try to withstand progress. Sydney Smith, speaking on the Lords' rejection of the Reform Bill, October, 1831, compares them to Dame Partington with her mop, trying to push back the Atlantic. "She was excellent," he says, "at a slop or puddle, but should never have meddled with a tempest." The story is that a Mrs. Partington had a cottage on the shore at Sidmouth, Devon. In November, 1824, a heavy gale drove the waves into her house, and the old lady labored with a mop to sop the water up.

Mrs. Partington. A popular character created, perhaps on the suggestion of the above-related incident, by the American humorist B. P. Shillaber. She is the central figure in his *Life and Sayings of Mrs. Partington* (1854), *Partingtonian Patchwork* (1873) and *Ik and His Friends* (1879). One of the characteristic outbursts of this American Mrs. Malaprop is: "I am not so young as I was once, and I don't believe I shall ever be, if I live to the age of Samson, which, heaven knows as well as I do, I don't want to, for I wouldn't be a centurion or an octagon and survive my factories and become idiomatic by any means."

> Her benevolent face, her use of catnip tea, her faith in the almanac, her domestic virtue, and her knowledge of the most significant facts in the life of every person in the village immediately made a large circle of readers recognize the lifelike portrayal of a person known in every American community.—*Cambridge History of American Literature.*

Partisan, The, a Tale of the Revolution. The first novel in W. G. SIMMS' Revolutionary trilogy (1835). The others are *Mellichampe* and KATHERINE WALTON.

Partisan Leader, The. A novel by the Virginia judge, Nathaniel Beverly (*Am.,* 1836), which gained note because of its prediction of the Civil War.

Partisan Review. American literary quarterly, founded in 1934, at first associated with the Communist party and after 1938 characterized by an independent radical editorial viewpoint, broadly sympathetic with Trotskyist Marxism. See MARXISM; TROTSKY, LEON. Its contributors, in the fields of politics, literary criticism, fine arts, fiction, and poetry, included John Dos Passos, James T. FARRELL, T. S. ELIOT, Wallace STEVENS, W. C. WILLIAMS, Edmund WILSON, Dwight MacDonald, and George L. K. Morris.

partlet. The hen in Chaucer's NUN'S PRIEST'S TALE, and in REYNARD THE FOX. A partlet was a ruff worn in the 16th century by women, and the reference is to the frill-like feathers round the neck of certain hens.

> In the barn the tenant cock
> Close to partlet perched on high.
> *Cuningham.*

Sister Partlet with her hooded head, allegorizes the cloistered community of nuns in DRYDEN'S HIND AND PANTHER, where the Roman

Catholic clergy are likened to barnyard fowls.

Parton, James (1822–1891). English-born American biographer. His best-known book is the noteworthy *Life of Horace Greeley* (1855).

Partridge. In Fielding's TOM JONES, the attendant of Tom Jones, faithful, shrewd, and of childlike simplicity. His excitement in the play-house when he goes to see Garrick in *Hamlet* is described in a famous chapter. Partridge has been both barber and schoolmaster before attaching himself to Tom Jones.

Partridge, Bellamy. American biographer and novelist. Author of the best-seller *Country Lawyer* (1939), *Big Family* (1941), and *January Thaw* (1945).

Partridge, Sir **Bernard** (1861–1945). Well-known chief cartoonist of *Punch,* the staff of which he joined in 1891. Originally an actor.

Partridge, William Ordway (1861–1930). American sculptor. Busts of Chief Justice Fuller, Robert Peary, etc.; statues of Grant, Nathan Hale, Horace Greeley. Author of several books on art.

parts of speech. A grammatical class of words of a particular character. The old rhyme by which children used to be taught the parts of speech is:

> Three little words you often see
> Are ARTICLES, *a, an,* and *the.*
> A NOUN's the name of anything;
> As *school* or *garden, hoop* or *swing.*
> ADJECTIVES tell the kind of noun;
> As *great, small, pretty, white,* or *brown.*
> Instead of nouns the PRONOUNS stand;
> *Her* head, *his* face, *our* arms, *your* hand.
> VERBS tell of something being done;
> To *read, count, sing, laugh, jump,* or *run.*
> How things are done the ADVERBS tell;
> As *slowly, quickly, ill,* or *well.*
> CONJUNCTIONS join the words together;
> As, men *and* women, wind *or* weather.
> The PREPOSITION stands before
> A noun, as *in* or *through* a door.
> The INTERJECTION shows surprise;
> As, *oh!* how pretty! *ah!* how wise!
> The whole are called nine parts of speech,
> Which reading, writing, speaking teach.

Parvati. In Hindu mythology, the consort of Siva, better known as Durga or KALI.

Pascal, Blaise (1623–1662). French religious thinker and author, known for his defenses of the religious reform movement of JANSENISM. His writings, a number of which became famous in later centuries, are marked by objectivity, rationality, insight, and a graceful, charming, and often ironic style. His best-known works are *Lettres provinciales* (*Provincial Letters*), issued beginning in 1656, appearing first anonymously and then under the pseudonym of Montalte, in which he attacks the Jesuit opponents of Jansenism; and the PENSÉES (*Thoughts*). Before his conversion to Jansenism, Pascal was greatly interested in science, especially mathematics, having invented a calculating machine, done work in connection with the theory of probability, and, in the opinion of some critics, anticipated the system of calculus.

pasch eggs. Easter eggs, a term still in use in Scotland and certain parts of England.

Pasht. See BUBASTIS.

Pasiphae. In Greek legend, a daughter of the Sun and wife of Minos, King of Crete. She was the mother of ARIADNE, and also (through intercourse with a white bull given by Poseidon to Minos) of the MINOTAUR.

pasque eggs. See PASCH EGGS.

Pasquinade. A lampoon or political squib, having ridicule for its object; so called from Pasquino, an Italian tailor of the 15th century, noted for his caustic wit. Some time after his death, a mutilated statue was dug up, representing Ajax supporting Menelaus, or Menelaus carrying the body of Patroclus, or else a gladiator, and was placed at the end of the Braschi Palace near the Piazza Navoni. As it was not clear what the statue represented, and as it stood opposite Pasquin's house, it came to be called "Pasquin." The Romans affixed their political, religious, and personal satires to it; hence the name. At the other end of Rome was an ancient statue of Mars, called *Marforio,* to which were affixed replies to the Pasquinades.

> Then the procession started, took the way
> From the New Prisons by the Pilgrim's Street
> The street of the Governo, Pasquin's Street,
> (Where was stuck up, 'mid other epigrams,
> A quatrain . . . but of all that, presently!)
> Browning, *The Ring and the Book,* xii, 137.

pass or **common pass.** At the English Universities, an ordinary degree, without honors. A candidate getting this is called a *passman.*

Passage to India. Title of a poem by Walt WHITMAN. E. M. FORSTER wrote a novel entitled *A Passage to India* (1924).

Passamonte, Gines de. In Cervantes' DON QUIXOTE, the galley-slave set free by Don Quixote. He returned the favor by stealing Sancho's wallet and ass. Subsequently he reappeared as a puppet-showman.

Passelyon. A young foundling brought up by Morgan le Fay whose amorous adventures are related in the old romance *Perceforest,* vol. iii.

Passepartout. In Verne's romance AROUND THE WORLD IN EIGHTY DAYS, the French valet who accompanies Phileas Fogg on his hurried world tour.

Passionate Pilgrim, The. A collection of lyric poems (1599), published by William Jaggard, an English printer, with an announcement on the title page that they were "By W. Shakespeare," although only about four of the poems are considered by 20th-century scholars to be of Shakespeare's authorship. Others are by Griffin, Barnfield, Marlowe, and lesser-known writers; the collection is regarded as being properly a "poetical miscellany." See TOTTEL'S MISCELLANY.

The earliest story by Henry JAMES is entitled *The Passionate Pilgrim* (1870 or 1871).

Passion Play (Ger. *Passionsspiel*). A dramatic presentation of the events of Passion Week, i.e., the Passion and Death of Christ, given periodically by the peasants of OBERAMMERGAU, a little village in Bavaria. It was first performed there in 1633; at that time the villagers made a vow to give it at regular intervals if delivered from a ravaging plague. After 1680, the Passion Play has, with some few interruptions, been given every tenth year. It attracts great crowds of spectators, who come from all over the world.

Passions Spin the Plot. A novel by Vardis Fisher (*Am.*, 1933). The title is taken from a sonnet in George Meredith's MODERN LOVE, which supplies also the titles of three other novels by Mr. Fisher, *In Tragic Life* (1932); *We Are Betrayed* (1935); and *No Villain Need Be* (1936).

> In tragic life, God wot,
> No villain need be. Passions spin the plot.
> We are betrayed by what is false within.

Passover. A Jewish festival to commemorate the deliverance of the Israelites, when the angel of death (that slew the first-born of the Egyptians) *passed over* their houses, and spared all who did as Moses commanded them. It is held from the 15th to the 22nd of the first month, Nisan, i.e., about April 13 to 20.

Pasternak, Boris Leonidovich (1890–). Russian poet, author of *Themes and Variations* (1923); *Second Birth* (1932); etc.

Pasteur, Louis (1822–1895). French scientist, famous for his discoveries in applied bacteriology. His most sensational work was concerned with the development of a curative treatment for hydrophobia. Popularly, his name is associated with a process (developed by him and called *pasteurization* in his honor) of destroying pathogenic organisms in milk and other liquids by the application of heat. Pasteur is the titular hero of a drama by Sacha GUITRY. A film, *The Life of Louis Pasteur,* with Paul Muni, received the Motion Picture Academy Award in 1936.

pastiche. A literary or artistic effort that imitates or caricatures the work of another artist or artists. *The Unique Hamlet,* by Vincent STARRETT, is a *pastiche* of a SHERLOCK HOLMES story.

Paston Letters. A series of letters (with wills, leases, and other documents) written by or to members of the Paston family in Norfolk between the years 1424 and 1509. The *Letters* are an invaluable source of information concerning the customs and business methods of the upper middle classes of 15th-century England.

Pastor, Tony (1837–1908). Famous American actor and theatrical manager. Opened in New York "Tony Pastor's Opera House" (1865) and built his own theater, known as Tony Pastor's, on Union Square (1888). Reputed to have started farce-comedy in America. He initiated vaudeville road shows and imported talent from the London music halls.

pastoral poetry. In the strict sense, poetry dealing with the life of actual shepherds and country folk. Many celebrated pastorals, among them Virgil's BUCOLICS, Milton's LYCIDAS, Shelley's ADONAIS, and Arnold's THYRSIS present contemporaries in the guise of shepherds leading a pastoral existence. This convention was also followed in fiction in such romances as Mlle de Scudéry's CYRUS.

Past Recaptured, The. English translation of *Le Temps retrouvé,* the final volume of Marcel Proust's long novel REMEMBRANCE OF THINGS PAST, published in 1928. It carries the narrator and the various characters down to the time of World War I, showing the effect of the war on their lives and thoughts, and presents generalizations by the author on the subject of time and memory, as in SWANN'S WAY, the first volume.

Pat. An Irishman.

Patchen, Kenneth (1911–). American poet, known for the combined bitterness and sentimentality, violence, melodrama, and imagination of his poetry, distinguished by striking imagery and dealing with the injustices and tragedies of 20th-century American life. His books include *Before the Brave* (1936); *First Will and Testament* (1939); *The Journal of Albion Moonlight* (1941; prose); *The Dark Kingdom* (1942); etc.

Patelin. The artful cheat in the 14th-century French comedy *L'Avocat Pathelin.* The French say, *savoir son Patelin* (to know how to bamboozle you). When he wants William Josseaume to sell him cloth on credit, he artfully praises the father of the merchant. One of his remarks, "*revenons à nos moutons* (Let us return to our sheep)" has become a proverbial expression for "let us get back to the subject." See also under MOUTONS.

Pater, Walter Horatio (1839–1894). English critic, essayist, and novelist, known for his emphasis on ideal beauty and the perfection of form in art and literature, and for his graceful, harmonious, and subtle prose style. His works include *Studies in the History of the Renaissance* (1873), a collection of essays; MARIUS THE EPICUREAN (1885), a philosophic novel and his most widely known work;

Imaginary Portraits (1887); *Appreciations* (1889), studies of Shakespeare, Wordsworth, and other writers; *Plato and Platonism* (1893); The Child in the House (1894); *Greek Studies* (1894) and *Gaston de Latour* (1896), posthumously published although left unfinished at the time of his death. Pater, most strongly influenced by Plato and Goethe, was associated with the Pre-Raphaelite Brotherhood and was a leading spokesman for the doctrine of "art for art's sake." He spent most of his life in scholarly seclusion at Oxford University. His essay on the *Monna Lisa* of Leonardo da Vinci is often quoted.

paternoster (*Lat.*, "Our Father"). The Lord's Prayer; from the first two words in the Latin version. Every tenth bead of a rosary is so called, because at that bead the Lord's Prayer is repeated; the name is also given to a certain kind of fishing tackle, in which hooks and weights to sink them are fixed alternately on the line, somewhat in rosary fashion.

a paternoster-while. Quite a short time; the time it takes one to say a paternoster.

Paternoster Row (London) was probably so named from the rosary or paternoster makers. There is mention as early as 1374 of a Richard Russell, a "paternosterer," who dwelt there, and we read of "one Robert Nikke, a paternoster maker and citizen," in the reign of Henry IV. Another suggestion is that it was so called because funeral processions on their way to St. Paul's began their *paternoster* at the beginning of the Row.

Paterson, Mrs. **Isabel (Bowles).** American novelist, wit, and literary columnist. Her novels are chiefly historical. Her book column in the New York *Herald Tribune Books* (now *Weekly Book Review*) has run since 1922.

Paterson, William (1658–1719). Scottish-born British merchant and financier who originated the plan of the Bank of England. Headed the ill-fated and wildly speculative Darien Expedition to colonize the Isthmus of Panama (1698), from which he returned, partially insane, as one of a handful of survivors. Helped promote the Scottish union with England and advocated free trade prior to Adam Smith.

Pathan. A member of the principal race of Afghanistan or of one of the independent Afghan tribes on the northwestern frontier of India. Many Pathans have served the British in the native army and in civil service. There are about four million Indian Pathans.

Pathelin, see Patelin.

pathetic fallacy. A phrase invented by Ruskin to designate the illusion that external objects seem actuated by human feelings, particularly when one is under great emotional strain. Thus when a poet is tormented by grief, he is apt to ascribe to inanimate nature either sympathy or heartless cruelty. Tennyson's In Memoriam, Shelley's Adonais, and other elegies are especially noteworthy for eloquent effects gained by the use of the pathetic fallacy.

Pathfinder. A title given to the American Major-General John Charles Frémont (1813–1890), who conducted four expeditions across the Rocky Mountains.

Pathfinder, The. A historical novel by Cooper (1840), one of the Leatherstocking series. Its setting, in the Lake Ontario region, gives it the scope of a novel of both woodcraft and seamanship. The plot is largely concerned with Leatherstocking's hopeless love for Mabel Dunham, whom he finally surrenders to another lover.

Patience or Bunthorne's Bride. A well-known comic opera by Gilbert and Sullivan (1881). The hero, Bunthorne (a caricature of Oscar Wilde) is pursued by a whole troop of love-sick ladies.

Patience Worth. A mysterious spirit who according to her own account, which was dictated on the ouija board in 1913 to Mrs. John H. Curran of St. Louis, lived in 1649 "across the sea." She is the reputed author of two or three works of fiction, especially one, published under the title *Patience Worth,* which received wide publicity.

Patient Griselda or **Grisildis,** see Griselda.

Patmore, Coventry Kersey Dighton (1823–1896). English poet, a friend of Tennyson, Ruskin, and later G. M. Hopkins, for awhile associated loosely with the Pre-Raphaelite Brotherhood, contributing to The Germ. During the first part of his career his poems were concerned with the love between husbands and wives. After the year 1864, when he was converted to Roman Catholicism, his poetry dealt with mystical and religious subjects. Among his works are *The Betrothal* (1854), *The Espousals* (1856), *Faithful For-ever* (1860), and *The Victories of Love* (1862), all parts of *The Angel in the House,* a planned long poem; *The Unknown Eros* (1877); *Amelia* (1878); *Collected Works* (1886); *Principle in Art* (1889), *Religio Poetae* (1893), and *Rod, Root, and Flower* (1895), prose essays and articles.

Patmos. The island of the Sporades in the Aegean Sea (now called *Patmo* or *Patino*) to which St. John retired—or was exiled (*Rev.* i. 9). Hence the name is used allusively for a place of banishment or solitude.

patriarch (Gr. *patria,* "family," *archein,* "to rule"). The head of a tribe or family who rules by paternal right; applied specially (after *Acts* vii. 8) to the twelve sons of Jacob, and to

Abraham, Isaac, and Jacob and their forefathers. In one passage (*Acts* ii. 29) David also is spoken of as a patriarch.

In the early Church, *patriarch,* first mentioned in the council of Chalcedon, but virtually existing from about the time of the council of Nice, was the title of the highest of Church officers. In the Orthodox Eastern Church the bishops of Constantinople, Alexandria, Antioch, and Jerusalem are patriarchs; and within a religious order the title is given to the founder, as St. Benedict, St. Francis, and St. Dominic.

patrician. Properly speaking, one of the *patres* (fathers) or senators of Rome, and their descendants. As they held for many years all the honors of the state, the word came to signify the magnates or nobility of a nation, the aristocrats.

Patrick, St. See under SAINTS.

Patrick Spens, Sir. A famous early Scotch ballad.

patrin or patteran. The leaves or grass that gypsies throw down along their trail to indicate the way they have gone. A collection of essays by Louise Imogen GUINEY (1897) was called *Patrins.*

Patriot, The (Piccolo mondo antico). A novel by FOGAZZARO (1896), the first of a trilogy. See MAIRONI, PIERO.

Patroclus. The loyal friend of Achilles, in Homer's ILIAD. When Achilles refused to fight in order to annoy Agamemnon, he sent Patroclus in his own armor at the head of the Myrmidons to the battle, and Patroclus was slain by HECTOR.

patronymic. A name formed with an affix which means "the son of," as *Pelides,* son of Peleus; *Johnson,* son of John; *MacDonald,* son of Donald; *Ivanovich,* son of Ivan; etc.

patroons. The name given to the original landed proprietors in what was then the New Netherlands. These colonists retained their feudal privileges up to the time of the Anti-Rent War.

Pattee, Fred Lewis (1863–). American literary critic. Author of *A History of American Literature Since 1870* (1915); *The Development of the American Short Story* (1923); *The New American Literature* (1930); etc.

Patten, Gilbert (1866–1946). Known to many American boys by the name of Burt L. Standish, author of *The Adventures of Frank Merriwell,* a serial carried on through 986 consecutive weeks (1896–1915). Prolific writer. Put together an estimated 40,000,000 words in his lifetime. His *Merriwell* stories reached a total circulation of 125,000,000 copies.

Patterne, Sir Willoughby. "The Egoist" in George Meredith's novel of that name. See EGOIST.

Crossjay Patterne. A young boy, lazy and lovable, in the same novel.

Patterson, Joseph Medill (1879–1946). American journalist. Editor of the New York *Daily News* (from 1925).

Pattie, James Ohio (1804–?1850). A Kentucky-born explorer whose *Personal Narrative* (1831) was edited and partially written by one Timothy Flint. In another book, *The Hunters of Kentucky* by B. Bilson (1847), a great deal of the material was plagiarized.

Pattieson, Mr. Peter. A character who appears in the introduction of THE HEART OF MIDLOTHIAN, by Walter Scott, and again in the introduction of THE BRIDE OF LAMMERMOOR. He is a hypothetical assistant teacher at Gandercleuch, and the feigned author of *Tales of My Landlord,* which Scott pretends were published by Jedediah CLEISHBOTHAM after the death of Pattieson.

Pattison, Mark (1813–1884). English scholar and follower of John Henry NEWMAN. Author, among other books, of a *Life of John Milton* (1879).

Paul, Eden (1865–). With his wife, **Gertrude Mary Paul,** *née* **Davenport,** professionally known as **Cedar Paul,** translator of important European, chiefly Russian, novelists.

Paul, Elliot Harold (1891–). American journalist and novelist, for a number of years a resident of France and Spain and associated with the expatriate group of American writers of the LOST GENERATION. He was one of the editors of the magazine TRANSITION. Among his novels are *Indelible* (1922); *Impromptu* (1923); *Low Run Tide* (1929); *Lava Rock* (1929); *The Amazon* (1930); *The Governor of Massachusetts* (1930); *Concert Pitch* (1938). After his return to the U.S. in the late 1930's, he wrote several best-selling books, including *The Life and Death of a Spanish Town* (1937), an account of life in the Balearic Islands before and during the Spanish Civil War; *The Last Time I Saw Paris* (1942), reminiscences of life in Paris before the defeat of France in World War II; *Linden on the Saugus Branch* (1947); and a number of satirical detective stories.

Paul, Kegan (1828–1902). English publisher of the works of Tennyson, Hardy, Meredith, Stevenson, etc. Was joined (1881) by Alfred Trench and helped form (1889) the house of Keegan Paul, Trench, Trübner & Co., Ltd., which was later incorporated in George Routledge & Sons, Ltd.

Paul, Louis (1901–). American satirical and humorous novelist; author of *The Pumpkin Coach* (1935); etc.

Paul, St. See under SAINTS.

St. Paul the Hermit. See under SAINTS.

robbing Peter to pay Paul. See ROB.

Paul and Virginia. A romance by Bernardin de ST. PIERRE (1788). Paul is the illegitimate child of Margaret, who has retired to Port Louis in the Mauritius to bury herself. He grows up as the playmate of Virginia, the daughter of a French widow, Mme de la Tour, and as they grow in years, their fondness for each other develops into love. When Virginia is fifteen, her mother's aunt adopts her and begs that she be sent to France to finish her education. She is two years in France. As she refuses to marry according to her aunt's wishes, she is disinherited and sent back to her mother. Within a cable's length of the island, a hurricane dashes the ship to pieces, and the dead body of Virginia is thrown upon the shore. Paul is prostrate with grief, and within two months follows her to the grave.

Paul Bunyan, see BUNYAN, PAUL.

Paul Clifford. A novel by BULWER LYTTON (1830). The hero, a youth of unknown parentage, is falsely accused of stealing a watch from a lawyer named Brandon. He escapes from prison, turns highwayman, and is brought to trial in the course of time, before this same Brandon, who is now a judge. Just before he passes the death sentence Judge Brandon learns from a note passed to him that this is his own son. He dies of shock and Clifford escapes to America.

Paulding, James Kirke (1778–1860). Associated with Washington Irving in publishing the humorous magazine *Salmagundi* (1807–1808). U.S. secretary of the navy (1838–1841); author of *A Life of Washington* (1835); etc.

Paulina. In Shakespeare's WINTER'S TALE, the noble-spirited wife of Antigonus, a Sicilian lord, and the friend of Queen Hermione.

> Paulina is clever, generous, strong-minded, and warm-hearted, fearless in asserting the truth, firm in her sense of right, enthusiastic in all her affections, quick in thought, resolute in word, and energetic in action, but heedless, hot-tempered, impatient, loud, bold, voluble, and turbulent of tongue.—Mrs. Jameson.

Paul Pry. An idle, meddlesome fellow, who has no occupation of his own, and is always interfering with other folk's business. The term comes from the hero of John Poole's comedy, *Paul Pry* (1825). He always introduces himself with the apology, "I hope I don't intrude."

Paul Revere's Ride. A narrative poem by LONGFELLOW (1861) telling of the midnight ride of the Revolutionary patriot Paul Revere, to spread the news of an expected British raid.

Paumanok. The Indian name of Long Island which was used by Walt Whitman in his LEAVES OF GRASS.

Pauncefote, Julian. 1st Baron **Pauncefote** (1828–1902). English diplomat. Ambassador to the U.S. (1893). Signed Hay-Pauncefote Treaty (1901) which provided equal passage for all nations through the Panama Canal.

Pau-Puk-Keewis. In Longfellow's HIAWATHA, a cunning mischief-maker, who teaches the North American Indians the game of hazard, and strips them by his winnings of all their possessions. When Hiawatha pursues him, he is changed into a huge beaver, but is slain nevertheless.

> Now in winter, when the snowflakes
> Whirl in eddies round the lodges. . . .
> "There," they cry, "comes Pau-Puk-Keewis;
> He is dancing thro' the village,
> He is gathering in his harvest."
>
> *Hiawatha*, xvii.

Pausanias (2nd century A.D.). Greek traveler and geographer. His accounts of the monuments of ancient Greece before their destruction are of extreme value in research.

Pavlova, Anna (1885–1931). Russian dancer, especially famous for *The Death of the Swan* (a ballet composed for her by FOKINE).

pax (*Lat.*, "peace"). The "kiss of peace," which is given in the Roman Church at High Mass. It is omitted on Maundy Thursday, from horror at the kiss of Judas.

Pax Britannica. The peace imposed by British rule. The phrase is modeled on the Latin *Pax Romana,* the peace existing between the different members of the Roman Empire.

pax vobis (*cum*) (Peace be unto you). The formula used by a bishop instead of "the Lord be with you," wherever this versicle occurs in Divine service. They are the words used by Christ to His Apostles on the first Easter morning.

Paxson, Frederic Logan (1877–). American historian. Pulitzer prize (1924) for *History of the American Frontier.*

Payn, James (1830–1898). English novelist. A voluminous writer of popular novels. Contributed to *Household Words,* edited by Charles Dickens, and was himself the editor of the *Cornhill Magazine* (1883–1896).

Payne, John (1842–1916). English poet and translator. Principally known for his version of the *Arabian Nights* (9 vols.; 1882–1884). See also under BURTON.

Payne, John Howard (1791–1852). American actor and playwright. His plays, *Brutus, or the Fall of Tarquin,* and *Virginius,* were written for the actor Edmund Kean. In his opera *Clari* (1823) occurs the song that assured his fame, *Home, Sweet Home,* which was based on a song he had heard sung by a Sicilian peasant girl.

P.C. The Roman *Patres Conscripti.* See CONSCRIPT FATHERS.

Peabody, George (1795–1869). American philanthropist who founded and endowed a number of institutions and museums in his name at Baltimore, Peabody, Mass., Yale, Harvard, etc. Member, American Hall of Fame (1900).

Peabody, Josephine Preston (1874–1922). American poet and dramatist. Her play, *The Piper,* won the 1910 verse play contest of the Shakespeare Memorial Theatre at Stratford-on-Avon. Her best-known poem is *The Singing Man.*

peace.

peace at any price. Lord Palmerston sneered at the Quaker statesman, John Bright, as a "peace-at-any-price man." The expression was used of an extreme pacifist.

peace in our time. A phrase used by Prime Minister Neville Chamberlain of England in an attempt to justify his appeasement of the demands of Adolf HITLER at the time of the MUNICH CRISIS (1938).

peace with honor. A phrase popularized by Lord Beaconsfield on his return from the Congress of Berlin (1878), when he said:

> Lord Salisbury and myself have brought you back peace—but a peace I hope with honor, which may satisfy our Sovereign and tend to the welfare of the country.

peace without victory. A self-explanatory phrase much in use during World War I.

the Perpetual Peace. The peace concluded June 24, 1502, between England and Scotland, whereby Margaret, daughter of Henry VII, was betrothed to James IV. A few years afterwards the battle of Flodden Field was fought. The name has also been given to other treaties, as that between Austria and Switzerland in 1474, and between France and Switzerland in 1516.

Peace, The. A comedy by ARISTOPHANES (415 B.C.). The hero is TRYGAEUS.

Peachum. In Gay's BEGGAR'S OPERA, a despicable fellow, a patron of a gang of thieves, and receiver of their stolen goods. His house is the resort of thieves, pickpockets, and villains of all sorts. He betrays his comrades when it is for his own benefit, and even procures the arrest of their leader, Captain MACHEATH.

Mrs. Peachum. Wife of Peachum. She recommends her daughter Polly to be "somewhat nice in her deviations from virtue."

Polly Peachum. The daughter of Peachum, a pretty girl, who really loves Captain Macheath, marries him, and remains faithful even when he disclaims her. When the reprieve arrives, the captain confesses his marriage and vows to abide by Polly for the rest of his life. This stage role led three actresses to the peerage: Miss Fenton (Duchess of Bolton), Miss Bolton (Lady Thurlow), and Miss Stephens (Countess of Essex).

peacock.

by the peacock! An obsolete oath which at one time was thought blasphemous. The fabled incorruptibility of the peacock's flesh caused the bird to be adopted as a type of the resurrection.

the peacock's feather. An emblem of vainglory, and in some Eastern countries a mark of rank.

As a literary term, the expression is used of a borrowed ornament of style spatchcocked into the composition; the allusion is to the fable of the jay who decked herself out in peacock's feathers, making herself an object of ridicule.

The peacock's tail is emblem of an Evil Eye, or an ever-vigilant traitor; hence the feathers are considered unlucky, and the superstitious will not have them in the house. The classical legend is that ARGUS, who had 100 eyes, was changed into a peacock by Juno, the eyes forming the beautifully colored disks in the tail.

Peacock, Thomas Love (1785–1866). English novelist, known for his burlesque romances containing eccentric characters (often drawn from life), ridiculous incidents, and interpolated drinking songs of a rousing nature; these books particularly satirize the GOTHIC NOVEL. Among them are HEADLONG HALL (1816); *Melincourt* (1817); *Nightmare Abbey* (1818); *Maid Marian* (1822); *The Misfortunes of Elphin* (1829); CROTCHET CASTLE (1831); *Gryll Grange* (1860). Peacock was a businessman, working for the East India Tea Company. See also LAMB, CHARLES. He was a friend of SHELLEY and the father of the first wife of George MEREDITH.

Peacock Throne. A throne built (1628 to 1635) at Delhi, India, for the Indian ruler, Shah Jehan. Each of its twelve pillars was decorated with two peacocks glittering with gems. A century later (1739), Nadir Shah took it to Persia.

Peale, Rembrandt (1778–1860). American painter. Widely known for his portraits and historical scenes. Painted a portrait of Washington from life (1795). Rembrandt's brothers, Raphael and Titian, were also painters. So was their father, although his name was Charles.

peanut gallery. A name applied to the top gallery in the theater where the cheaper seats are located. The origin of the name came from the practice of eating peanuts and throwing shells on the stage. In other countries the same gallery is called Olympus.

pearl.

to cast pearls before swine. To give what is precious to those who are unable to understand its value: a Biblical phrase (*Matt.* vii. 6).

Pearl, The. A 14th-century mystical allegorical poem, written in Middle English, brought to light only in the latter part of the 19th century but considered one of the best in existence. It laments the death of a child, considered to be the poet's daughter Margaret (from Fr. *Marguerite,* "pearl" or "daisy"), and gives a picture of her happiness in heaven. Symbolism of the pearl and the daisy, both signifying virginity, recurs throughout the poem, as does allusion to the Bible and medieval theology.

Pearl, Little. In Hawthorne's SCARLET LETTER, the elf-like child of Hester Prynne, born out of wedlock.

Pearl Poet, the. Supposed author of THE PEARL, which appears as one of four poems in a late 14th-century manuscript, written in the West Midland dialect and known as MS. Cotton Nero A X. See COTTON, Sir ROBERT BRUCE. The other four poems in the manuscript are *Purity, Patience,* and *Sir Gawain and the Green Knight.* See GAWAIN. Virtually nothing is known of the poet, although scholars agree that the sophisticated form and concept of the poem suggest that he was either attached to the court or subject to its influence. Oscar Cargill believes that the man might have been either one John Don (or Donne) or one John Prat, and that he served as guardian to the small daughter of the Earl of Pembroke, granddaughter to King Henry III, writing the poem *The Pearl* on the death of the child at the age of two, although he himself bore no blood relationship to her. There seems to be further evidence for this theory in the fact that Henry III was very fond of pearls and that the child's mother had been named Margaret.

Pearse, Padraic Henry (1879–1916). Irish poet and patriot. During the Easter Rebellion (1916), commander in chief of the Irish republican forces and president of the provisional government. Shot by a British firing squad. *Collected Works* (1917).

Pearson, Edmund Lester (1880–1937). American librarian, bibliophile and literary criminologist. *Books in Black or Red* (1923); *Studies in Murder* (1924); *Murder at Smutty Nose* (1926); *The Trial of Lizzie Borden* (1937); etc. See also BORDEN, LIZZIE.

Peary, Robert Edwin (1856–1920). American arctic explorer. Reached North Pole on April 6, 1909. Dr. Frederick A. Cook's claim that he had reached the Pole on April 21, 1908, a year before Peary, was later discredited.

Peasant Bard. See under BARD.

Peasant Cantata, see under CANTATA.

Peasants' War, the. The name given to the insurrections of the peasantry of southern Germany in the early 16th century, especially to that of 1524 in Swabia, Franconia, Saxony, and other German states, in consequence of the tyranny and oppression of the nobles. It was ended by the Battle of Frankenhausen (1525), when many thousands of the peasants were slain. In 1502 occurred the rebellion called the *Laced Shoe,* from its cognizance; in 1514, the *League of Poor Conrad;* in 1523, the *Latin War.*

Peaseblossom. A fairy in Shakespeare's MIDSUMMER NIGHT'S DREAM. Other fairies in the play are *Cobweb, Moth,* and *Mustardseed.*

Peattie, Donald Culross (1898–). American botanist and author, best known for his popular books on nature subjects, written in a lyrical prose style. These are *Singing in the Wilderness: A Salute to John James Audubon* (1935); *Almanac for Moderns* (1935); *Green Laurels: The Lives and Achievements of the Great Naturalists* (1936); *A Book of Hours* (1937); *Flowering Earth* (1939). He also wrote scholarly scientific studies, novels, books for children, and an autobiography, *The Road of a Naturalist* (1941). His wife, **Louise Peattie,** *née* **Redfield** (1900–) has written a number of novels.

Peau de Chagrin. A novel by BALZAC, usually translated as THE WILD ASS'S SKIN.

peccavi (*Lat.,* "I have sinned"). An admission of guilt. Hence *to cry peccavi,* "to acknowledge one's guilt."

Peck, George Wilbur (1840–1916). American humorist, well-known for *Peck's Bad Boy and His Pa* (1883) and other Peck's-Bad-Boy stories.

Peck, Harry Thurston (1856–1914). Professor of Latin at Columbia and editor of *The Bookman* (1895–1902). An unusual critic who met with social disaster in 1910, leading to his suicide.

Peck, John Mason (1789–1858). A Baptist preacher in New York State who wrote several books on the West still considered authoritative. *Guide for Emigrants* (1831); *Life of Daniel Boone* (1847); etc.

Peckham, Richard. See under HOLDEN, RAYMOND PECKHAM.

Peckham, Silas. In O. W. Holmes' ELSIE VENNER, a hard-headed New England school teacher who "keeps a young lady's school exactly as he would have kept a hundred head of cattle—for the simple unadorned purpose of making just as much money in just as few years as can be safely done."

Pecksniff. A hypocrite, from the character of that name in Dickens' MARTIN CHUZZLEWIT, who is "architect and land surveyor," at Salisbury. He prates about the beauty of charity and the duty of forgiveness, but is altogether a canting humbug. Ultimately he is so reduced in position that he becomes "a drunken, begging, squalid, letter-writing man," out at elbows, and almost shoeless. Pecksniff's specialty is the "sleek, smiling, drawling abomination of hypocrisy."

If ever man combined within himself all the mild qualities of the lamb with a considerable touch of the dove, and not a dash of the crocodile, or the least possible suggestion of the very mildest seasoning of the serpent, that man was Mr. Pecksniff, "the messenger of peace."—Ch. iv.

Charity and *Mercy Pecksniff.* The two daughters of the "architect and land surveyor." Charity is thin, ill-natured, and a shrew, eventually jilted by a weak young man, who really loves her sister. Mercy Pecksniff, usually called "Merry," is pretty and truehearted. Though flippant and foolish as a girl, she becomes greatly toned down by the troubles of her married life.

Pédauque, Queen. See COIGNARD, JEROME.

Pedlington, Little. An English village typical of all the pettiness and hypocrisy that flourish in small communities; described in John Poole's *Little Pedlington and the Pedlingtonians.* It has no actual existence.

Pèdre, Don. A Sicilian nobleman in Molière's comedy LE SICILIEN OU L'AMOUR PEINTRE, owner of the slave Isidore, loved by Adraste.

Pedro, Dr. A character in Cervantes' DON QUIXOTE, whose full name is Dr. Pedro Rezio de Aguero, court physician in the island of Barataria. He carries a whalebone rod in his hand, and whenever any dish of food is set before SANCHO PANZA, the governor, he touches it with his wand, that it may be instantly removed as unfit for the governor to eat. Partridges are "forbidden by Hippocrates," olla podridas are "most pernicious," rabbits are "a sharp-haired diet," veal may not be touched, but "a few wafers and a thin slice or two of quince" may not be harmful.

The governor, being served with some beef hashed with onions, . . . fell to with more avidity than if he had been set down to Milan godwits, Roman pheasants, Sorrento veal, Moron partridges, or green geese of Lavajos; and turning to Dr. Pedro, he said, "Look you, signor doctor, I want no dainties, . . . for I have been always used to beef, bacon, pork, turnips, and onions."—*Don Quixote,* II. ii, 10, 12.

Pedro, Don. (1) The Prince of Aragon in Shakespeare's MUCH ADO ABOUT NOTHING.

(2) Vasco da Gama's rival in Meyerbeer's opera, *L'Africaine.*

Peebles, Peter. In Scott's REDGAUNTLET, the Scotch plaintiff in the celebrated case of Peebles against Plainstanes that is finally appealed to Parliament. By this time Peter has become so self-important and so utterly goodfor-nothing that he is soon known as "the old scarecrow of Parliament House." He is litigious, hard-hearted and credulous; a liar, and a miserable drunken pauper.

peel. A small castle, tower or fortified residence, common on both sides of the Scottish border in the sixteenth century.

Peel, Sir **Robert** (1788–1850). English statesman. First lord of treasury, chancellor of exchequer, and prime minister (1834–1835). Again first lord of treasury and prime minister (1841). Reorganized Bank of England, initiated reforms in Ireland, supported free trade and emancipation of the Jews. As chief secretary for Ireland (1812–1818) he instituted the Irish constabulary, from which came the nickname "peelers," afterwards also applied to the London police, who are also called "Bobbies."

Peele, George (1558?–1597). English playwright and poet of the Elizabethan period, author of dramas, pageants, lyrics for use in his plays, and verse celebrating various occasions of honor in the lives of noble patrons. His works include the following: plays—*The Arraignment of Paris* (ca. 1581), *The Battle of Alcazar* (1594), *The Old Wives' Tale* (1595), and *The Love of King David and Fair Bethsabe* (1599); poetry—*Polyhymnia* (1590) and *The Honor of the Garter* (1593), the latter addressed to the Earl of Northumberland.

peeler. See under PEEL, Sir ROBERT.

Peeperkorn, Mynheer. In Thomas Mann's THE MAGIC MOUNTAIN, a rich, elderly, retired Dutch coffee-planter from the Dutch East Indies, who comes with Clavdia CHAUCHAT to the HAUS BERGHOF. He immediately overwhelms the other characters of the novel—all sick or half-sick patients at the sanatorium —by his forceful personality and astonishing physical appearance, for he is a great, fat man with white hair, tremendous energy, a huge appetite for food and drink, and a habit of speaking in broken, incoherent sentences, as though his immense strength and passion refuse to be disciplined. Peeperkorn is considered to represent the sensually human element in the novel, and for a while he interests Hans CASTORP in leaving the mountains and returning to "normal" society. The planter is, however, growing old, and one day in the forest, in the presence of a party from the sanatorium, he delivers his final challenge to nature—a mighty speech which no one can hear because the roar of a nearby waterfall drowns out his words. Finding he can no longer live with the intensity of his youth, he commits suicide by means of a symbolic mechanism made of steel, gold, ivory, and rubber, and a poison composed of animal and vegetable substances.

Peeping Tom of Coventry. See GODIVA.

Peep-o'-Day Boys. Irish insurgents of 1784, who prowled at daybreak, searching for arms.

Peer Gynt. A poetic drama by Henrik IBSEN (1867), which takes as its hero the legendary Peer Gynt of Norse folklore. In the drama Peer Gynt possesses a riotous imagination, is a great braggart and egotist, but invariably avoids any issue. In a long series of fantastic adventures that take him over the face of the globe, he proves his true character, and comes back to Norway at last to find Death, the Button Molder, waiting to melt him back to nothing, and Solveig, the faithful love of his youth, also waiting. Peer Gynt's doting, scolding old mother, Ase, is a prominent character, and her death in the third act is one of the most effective scenes of the play. The music written by Edward GRIEG for the play became famous as the *Peer Gynt Suites,* especially the first suite (*Anitra's Dance,* etc.).

Peers. The twelve most illustrious knights or paladins of Charlemagne. Also known as *douzepers.* Their names are not always given alike. In the *Chanson de Roland* they are Roland (or Orlando), Oliver, Ivon, Ivory, Oton, Berengier, Samson, Anseis, Gerin, Gerier, Engelier, and Gerard de Rousillon.

Peers of the Realm. The five orders of Duke, Marquess, Earl, Viscount, and Baron. The word peer is the Latin *pares* (equals), and in feudal times all great vassals were held equal in rank.

the Twelve Peers of Charlemagne. See PALADINS.

Peerybingle, John. In Dickens' CRICKET ON THE HEARTH, a carrier, "lumbering, slow, and honest; heavy, but light of spirit; rough upon the surface, but gentle at the core; dull without, but quick within; stolid, but so good. O mother Nature, give thy children the true poetry of heart that hid itself in this poor carrier's breast, and we can bear to have them talking prose all their life long!"

Mrs. Peerybingle. John's wife, called by her husband "Dot." She is a little chubby, cheery young wife, very fond of her husband and very proud of her baby. She shelters Edward PLUMMER in her cottage for a time, and thereby places herself under a cloud. But the marriage of Edward with May FIELDING clears up the mystery, and John loves his little Dot more fondly than ever.

Peg. In Arbuthnot's satire, *The History of John Bull* (1712), the sister of John Bull; meant for the Scotch Presbyterian Church and the country of Scotland.

> What think you of my sister Peg [Scotland], that faints at the sound of an organ, and yet will dance and frisk at the noise of a bagpipe?—*History of John Bull.*

Pegasus. In classic myth, the winged horse of the Muses, born of the sea foam and the blood of the slaughtered MEDUSA. He was caught by BELLEROPHON, who mounted him and destroyed the CHIMAERA. But when Bellerophon attempted to ascend to heaven, he was thrown from the horse, and Pegasus mounted alone to the skies to become the constellation of the same name. Hence *Pegasus* is used as a synonym for inspiration. According to the legend, when the Muses contended with the daughters of Pieros, Mount Helicon rose heavenward with delight; but Pegasus gave it a kick, stopped its ascent, and brought out of the mountain the soul-inspiring waters of the fountain HIPPOCRENE.

to break Pegasus's neck. To write halting poetry.

Peggotty, Clara. In Dickens' DAVID COPPERFIELD, the servant-girl of Mrs. Copperfield, and the faithful old nurse of David Copperfield. Her name "Clara" is taboo, because it is the name of Mrs. Copperfield. In the course of time Peggotty marries BARKIS, the carrier.

> Being very plump, whenever she made any little exertion after she was dressed, some of the buttons on the back of her gown flew off.—Ch. ii.

Dan'el Peggotty. Brother of David Copperfield's nurse. Dan'el is a Yarmouth fisherman. His nephew, Ham Peggotty, and his brother-in-law's child, "little Em'ly," live with him in a houseboat. Dan'el himself is a bachelor, and a Mrs. Gummidge (widow of his late partner) keeps house for him. Dan'el Peggotty is most tender-hearted, and loves little Em'ly dearly.

Ham Peggotty. Nephew of Dan'el Peggotty of Yarmouth, and son of Joe, Dan'el's brother. Ham is in love with little Em'ly, daughter of Tom (Dan's brother-in-law), but STEERFORTH steps between them and steals Em'ly away. Ham Peggotty is represented as the very beau-ideal of an uneducated, simple-minded, honest and warm-hearted fisherman. He is drowned in his attempt to rescue Steerforth from the sea.

Em'ly Peggotty. Daughter of Dan's brother-in-law Tom, better known as "Little Em'ly." She is engaged to Ham Peggotty, but being fascinated with Steerforth, runs off with him. She is afterwards reclaimed and emigrates to Australia with Dan'el and Mrs. Gummidge.

Peg o' My Heart. A comedy (1912) by J. Hartley Manners, in which the author's wife, Laurette TAYLOR, was a triumphant success as an Irish colleen. A popular song of that title was revived 35 years later with equal success.

Pégoud, Adolphe (1889–1915). French aviator who was the first to fly a plane upside down and loop the loop. He joined the French air corps and destroyed six German planes in World War I. Killed in aerial combat.

Péguy, Charles (1873–1914). French poet, at first a Socialist and an admirer of BERGSON, later a convert to orthodox religion and a French nationalist. His work consists chiefly of long, mystical epics in free verse, notably *Le Mystère de la charité de Jeanne d'Arc* (The *Mystery of the Charity of Joan of Arc*) and *Eve* (1913). Péguy was killed in the Battle of the Marne in World War I.

Peg Woffington. A novel by Charles READE (1853), first brought out as a drama called *Masks and Faces* (1852). Its heroine is the famous Irish actress, Margaret Woffington (1718–1760). In both play and novel, proof of her art is given in two extraordinary impersonations: she first imitates a famous tragic actress of the day so skilfully as to deceive an entire dramatic company, and later substitutes her own face for the face of her portrait which has been painted by James Triplet and is being inspected by a group of critics. The plot centers about the relations of Peg and Ernest Vane, a married man who falls in love with the famous actress during a sojourn in town. When she learns that he is already married and has no serious intentions, she determines on revenge, but renounces her purpose, won over by the naïveté and charm of Mrs. Vane.

peine forte et dure. An old punishment, applied when a prisoner would not confess, and consisting of pressing him to death with heavy weights. The phrase is also used figuratively of great emotional distress, as in Aline Kilmer's line in her poem *The Jest*, in *The Poor King's Daughter*:

> Will he let fall
> Sudden and sure,
> Or make me suffer
> *Peine forte et dure?*

Peirce, Charles Sanders (1839–1914). American physicist and mathematician. Founder through a paper in *Popular Science Monthly* (1878) of pragmatism, which was later developed by William JAMES, and of pragmaticism, which he differentiated from James' system. Regarded by many as the greatest logician of his time.

Peixotto, Ernest Clifford (1869–1940). American painter and illustrator. Illustrated Theodore Roosevelt's *Life of Cromwell* and Henry Cabot Lodge's *Story of the Revolution*, etc.

Peleus. In Greek legend, the King of the Myrmidons and father of ACHILLES by THETIS. He gave his son the famous PELIAN SPEAR.

Pelham. The hero of a novel by BULWER LYTTON, entitled *Pelham, or The Adventures of a Gentleman* (1828).

Pelian spear or Pelias. The huge spear of Achilles, which none but the hero could wield; so called because it was cut from an ash growing on Mount Pelion or beacuse it was given him by his father Peleus. TELEPHUS, King of Mysia, who was wounded in single combat with Achilles, was told by an oracle that only that which had inflicted his wound could heal it, and was finally cured by rust scraped from the famous spear.

Pelias. In Greek mythology, the uncle of JASON, who by arrangement with his twin brother Neleus was to hold the throne of Iolcus only until Jason's majority. He refused to give it up unless Jason secured the GOLDEN FLEECE, and was thus the instigator of the famous Argonautic expedition. After Jason's return, Pelias perished in Medea's cauldron in the hope of regaining his youth as Jason's father AESON had done.

pelican. In Christian art, a symbol of charity; also an emblem of Jesus Christ, by "whose blood we are healed." St. Jerome gives the story of the pelican restoring its young ones destroyed by serpents, and his salvation by the blood of Christ. The old popular fallacy that pelicans fed their young with their blood arose from the fact that when the parent bird is about to feed its brood, it macerates small fish in the large bag attached to its under bill, then pressing the bag against its breast, transfers the macerated food to the mouths of the young. The correct term for the heraldic representation of the bird in this act is *a pelican in her piety, piety* having the classical meaning of filial devotion.

The medieval *Bestiary* tells us that the pelican is very fond of its brood, but when the young ones begin to grow they rebel against the male bird and provoke his anger, so that he kills them; the mother returns to the nest in three days, sits on the dead birds, pours her blood over them and revives them, and they feed on the blood.

> Than sayd the Pellycane,
> When my byrdts be slayne
> With my bloude I them reuyue [revive]
> Scrypture doth record,
> The same dyd our Lord,
> And rose from deth to lyue.
> Skelton, *Armoury of Birdts.*

the Pelican State. Louisiana, which has a pelican in its device.

Pelides. In Greek legend, especially the *Iliad*, ACHILLES, son of Peleus, chief of the Greek warriors at the siege of Troy.

Pelion.

heaping Pelion upon Ossa. Adding difficulty to difficulty, embarrassment to embarrassment, etc. When the giants tried to scale heaven, they placed Mount Pelion upon Mount Ossa, two peaks in Thessaly, for a scaling ladder (*Odyssey*, xi. 315).

Pelle the Conqueror. A novel (1913–1917) by Martin Anderson NEXÖ, dealing with the labor movement. The Danish hero, Pelle, becomes a Union leader, puts through countless struggles, wins his goal, loses again, and is thrown into prison.

Pellean Conqueror. Alexander the Great, born at Pella, in Macedonia.

Pelleas. In Arthurian romance, one of the knights of the Round Table. In *Pelleas and Ettare,* one of Tennyson's IDYLLS OF THE KING, he is pictured as a noble and idealistic youth who is raised to the seventh heaven by the love of Ettare, but suffers a terrible disillusionment when she scorns him for his innocence, and both she and his friend, Sir Gawain, prove the falsest of the false. Sir Pelleas is introduced into the *Faërie Queene* (VI, xii) as going after the "Blatant Beast" when it breaks the chain with which it had been bound by Sir Calidore.

Zona Gale is the author of a book, *The Loves of Pelléas and Étarre* (*Am.*, 1907), the scheme of which is indicated by the words, "In spite of our sad gray hairs, Pelléas and I—"

Pelléas and Mélisande. A drama by Maurice MAETERLINCK, which forms the libretto for the opera of the same title by Claude DEBUSSY (1902). Mélisande is found wandering wretchedly about in the forest by Golaud, a grandson of King Arkel, who marries her and takes her to court, although she will disclose nothing about herself. Her sadness and charm win her first the sympathy and then the love of Pelléas, Golaud's brother. While talking with Pelléas she loses her wedding ring, and at that same moment Golaud meets with an accident, but she nurses him back to health. Golaud's little son Yniold, the child of a former marriage, unwittingly confirms his father's growing suspicions. Finally Pelléas and Mélisande decide to part and meet for a last interview, but the jealous Golaud kills Pelléas, and after the birth of her child, Mélisande dies.

Pellerin. In Flaubert's SENTIMENTAL EDUCATION, an opportunistic painter who, after "experimenting with Syndicalism, homoeopathy, table-turning, Gothic art, and humanitarian painting" becomes a successful photographer under the régime of Napoleon III. ". . . There were pictures of him on all the walls of Paris, with a tiny body and an enormous head."

Pelles, Sir. In Arthurian romance, the father of ELAINE and grandfather of GALAHAD. According to some legends he was "king of the foragn land and nigh cousin of Joseph of Arimathy" and guardian of the Holy Grail, which he kept in his Castle of Corbonec.

Pellinore, Sir. In Arthurian romance one of the knights of the Round Table.

Pelmanism. A system of mind and memory training originated by W. J. Ennever in the closing years of the 19th century, and so called arbitrarily as it seemed to be an easy name to remember. Owing to its success, and its very extensive advertising, the verb *to Pelmanize,* meaning to obtain good results by training the memory, was coined.

Peloponnesian War. The war between Athens and Sparta and their allies (431–404 B.C.). It resulted in the leadership of Greece passing from Athens to Sparta.

Pelops. In Greek legend, son of TANTALUS and father of Atreus and Thyestes. He was King of Pisa in Elis, and was cut to pieces and served as food to the gods. The Morea was called Peloponnesus, the "island of Pelops," from this mythical king.

the ivory shoulder of Pelops. The distinguishing or distinctive mark of anyone. The tale is that Demeter ate the shoulder of Pelops when it was served up by Tantalus; when the gods put the body back into the cauldron to restore it to life, this portion was lacking, whereupon Demeter supplied one of ivory.

Pemberton, Brock (1885–). Well-known American producer who was in partnership with Arthur Hopkins until 1920 and since then has been independent. He has produced plays by Sidney Howard, Pirandello, Maxwell Anderson, Clare Boothe, etc.

pemmican. Dried buffalo meat or venison, pounded into a powder and mixed to a paste which is pressed into small cakes to be easily carried as food on arctic expeditions. Of Indian origin.

Penates. The household gods of the Romans who cared for the welfare of the family. See also LARES.

Pendennis, The History of: *His Fortunes and Misfortunes, His Friends, and His Greatest Enemy.* A novel by THACKERAY (1850), which is admittedly largely autobiographical. The young hero, Arthur Pendennis, known as Pen for short, is spoiled by his mother and by Laura Bell, a distant relative of his own age with whom he grows up. He goes through the University, enters London society, writes a successful novel, becomes editor of the *Pall Mall Gazette,* and meantime is involved in love affairs of varying character with the actress Miss Fotheringay, with Fanny Bolton, a London porter's daughter, and with Blanche Amory, daughter of Lady Clavering. He finally marries Laura, who has always loved him and whom he has grown to love. Pen's uncle, Major Arthur Pendennis, and his friend George Warrington play prominent roles.

Pendragon. A title conferred on several British chiefs in times of great danger, when they were invested with supreme power, especially (in the Arthurian legends) to Uther

Pendragon, father of King Arthur. The word is Welsh *pen,* head and *dragon* (the reference being to the war-chief's dragon standard); it corresponded to the Roman *dux bellorum.*

A legend recorded by GEOFFREY OF MONMOUTH relates that when Aurelius, the British king, was poisoned by Ambron, during the invasion of Pascentius, son of Vortigern, there "appeared a star at Winchester of wonderful magnitude and brightness, darting forth a ray, at the end of which was a globe of fire in form of a dragon, out of whose mouth issued forth two rays, one of which extended to Gaul and the other to Ireland." Uther ordered two golden dragons to be made, one of which he presented to Winchester, and the other he carried with him as his royal standard, whence he received the title "Pendragon."

Penelope. (1) The wife of Ulysses and mother of Telemachus in Homeric legend. She was a model of all the domestic virtues.

the web of Penelope. A work "never ending, still beginning"; never done, but ever in hand. Penelope, according to Homer, was pestered by suitors at Ithaca while ULYSSES was absent at the siege of Troy. To relieve herself of their importunities, she promised to make a choice of one as soon as she had finished weaving a shroud for her father-in-law. Every night she unraveled what she had done in the day, and so deferred making any choice till Ulysses returned and slew the suitors.

(2) The heroine of Kate Douglas WIGGIN's travel narratives, *Penelope's English Experiences* (*Am.,* 1893), *Penelope's Progress* (1898), and *Penelope's Irish Experiences* (1901).

Penelophon. The name of the beggar-maid loved by King COPHETUA as given in the old ballad in Percy's *Reliques.* Shakespeare called her "Zenelophon."

Penelva. A knight whose adventures and exploits form a supplemental part of the Spanish romance entitled AMADIS DE GAUL.

Peneus. A river in Thessaly. Also the name of the god of the river who was the father of DAPHNE.

> Liquid Peneus was flowing,
> And all dark Tempe lay
> In Pelion's shadow. . . .
>
> Shelley, *Hymn of Pan.*

Penfeather, Lady Penelope. In Scott's novel ST. RONAN'S WELL, a patroness at the Spa. She presides over a sort of court there for "painters and poets and philosophers and men of science and lecturers and foreign adventurers."

Penfield, Edward (1866–1925). American illustrator and poster artist. Editor of *Harper's Magazine, Harper's Weekly,* and *Harper's Bazaar* (1890–1901).

Penguin Island (L'Île des pingouins). A volume by Anatole FRANCE (1908), dealing with French history in satiric vein. The old Breton monk Saint Maël lands on an island and in his semi-blindness fails to perceive that the inhabitants whom he baptizes are penguins and not men. They are, however, changed to men in the course of time and he carefully tows the island back to the Breton shore. Its subsequent history is given at some length.

Peninsula State. Florida. See under STATES.

Peninsular War. The war carried on, under the Duke of Wellington, against the French in Portugal and Spain, between 1808 and 1814. It was brought about through the French attack on Spain and Portugal, and, so far as England was concerned, was the most important of the Napoleonic Wars. It resulted in the expulsion of the French from the Peninsula.

Peniston, Darthea. Heroine of Weir Mitchell's HUGH WYNNE.

Penitentes. A religious order in New Mexico which puts on an annual Passion Play in the course of which the practice of self-flagellation is indulged in. The Penitentes are all Catholics, though the practice is condemned by the Church.

Penitential Psalms. The seven psalms expressive of contrition—viz. vi, xxxii, xxxviii, li, cii, cxxx, cxliii. From time immemorial they have all been used at the Ash Wednesday services: the first three at Matins, the 51st at the Commination, and the last three at Evensong.

Penn, William (1644–1718). Famous founder of Pennsylvania. Member of the Society of Friends. Superintended the laying out of Philadelphia.

Pennant, Thomas (1726–1798). British antiquarian, traveler, and naturalist. Author of *British Zoology* (1766) and *History of Quadrupeds* (1781), which were regarded as classics for a long time. In Gilbert White's *Natural History of Selborne* (1789), he appears as a correspondent of the author.

Pennell, Joseph (1857–1926). American etcher. Author of *Pen Drawing and Pen Draftsmen* (1889); *The Life of James McNeill Whistler* (1908); *Joseph Pennell's Pictures of War Work in England* (1917); etc. In the U.S. (1917) he made excellent drawings of industrial war activities.

Pennsylvania Avenue. The avenue from the Capitol to the White House in Washington, D.C.

Pennsylvania Dutch. The descendants of immigrants from southwestern Germany and Switzerland, who settled in Pennsylvania in the seventeenth and eighteenth centuries. Their language is essentially a development from an early south German dialect with more or less fully assimilated English elements. The literature of the Pennsylvania Dutch is folkloristic. Their other forms of folk art are more highly developed.

penny-a-liner. The old name for a contributor to the newspapers who was not on the staff, because he used to be paid a penny a line. As it was to his interest to "pad" as much as possible the word is still used in a contemptuous way for a second-rate writer or newspaper hack; but a man who does this work is now usually called a *linage-man,* a *spaceman,* or simply a *free lance.*

penny dreadful. A morbidly sensational story of the kind at one time printed and sold for a penny. There is also a shilling shocker.

Penny for the Old Guy, A. Subtitle of T. S. Eliot's poem, *The Hollow Men.* It is what the street urchins ask in London on Guy FAWKES Day when they carry around the effigy of Guy Fawkes. The effigy suggests "the hollow men, the stuffed men" of the poem.

Pennys, The Three Black. See THREE BLACK PENNYS.

Howat Penny. One of the "Three Black Pennys," in Hergesheimer's novel of that title.

Penrod. A story by Booth TARKINGTON (1914), relating the escapades of the twelve-year-old Penrod Schofield, a youngster whose active imagination keeps him in hot water at school and at home. *Penrod and Sam* (1916) is a sequel, continuing his adventures and those of his friend Sam Williams.

Penrose, Boies (1860–1921). American politician. Senator from Pennsylvania (1897–1921). In general the opponent of most progressive measures. Republican boss of Pennsylvania succeeding Matthew Quay.

Pensées, Les (Thoughts). A collection of reflections on religion by Blaise PASCAL, found among the effects of the author after his death but published in entirety only in 1844, having been delayed because it was feared to be unorthodox. The collection is considered to consist of the fragments of an *Apology* for Christianity planned by the author. Several well-known quotations are derived from the *Pensées,* including the following: *Le Nez de Cléopatre: s'il eût été plus court, toute la face de la terre aurait été changée* (Cleopatra's nose: if it had been shorter, the whole face of the earth would have been changed); *L'Homme n'est qu'un roseau, le plus faible de la nature, mais c'est un roseau pensant* (Man is only a reed, the frailest in nature, but he is a thinking reed). *The Thinking Reed* is the title of a novel by Rebecca WEST.

Penseroso, Il, see IL PENSEROSO.

pentameter. In prosody, a line of five feet, particularly one of dactyls or spondees, divided by a caesura into two parts of two and a half feet each—the line used in alternation with the HEXAMETER in Latin elegiac verse. The name is sometimes, but less correctly, applied to the English five-foot iambic line.

In the hexameter rises the fountain's silvery column,
In the pentameter aye falling in melody back.
Coleridge, *Example of Elegiac meter.*

Pentapolin. In Cervantes' DON QUIXOTE (I. iii. 4), the drover of a flock of sheep, whom Don Quixote conceives to be the Christian King of the Garamantians and surnames the *Naked Arm,* because he always enters the field with his right arm bare.

Pentapolis. The name given in ancient history to a number of groups or confederations of five cities (Gr., *penta,* "five," *polis,* "city"), especially the Dorian Pentapolis in Asia Minor—Cnidos, Cos, Lindos, Ialysos, and Camiros, and the five cities of Italy in the exarchate of Ravenna—Rimini, Pesaro, Fano, Sinigaglia, and Ancona—which were given by Pepin to the Pope.

Pentateuch (from Gr. *penta,* "five," *teuchos,* "a tool, a book"). The first five books of the Old Testament, supposed to be written by Moses.

the Samaritan Pentateuch. The Hebrew text as preserved by the Samaritans; it is said to date from 400 B.C.

Pentecost (Gr. *pentecoste,* "fiftieth"). The festival held by the Jews on the fiftieth day after the second day of the Passover; the modern Whit Sunday, which commemorates the descent of the Holy Spirit on the Apostles on the Day of Pentecost (*Acts* ii).

Pentelic. Pertaining to Mount Pentelicus near Athens, Greece. The white marble used for the Parthenon came from the quarries of Mount Pentelicus. Hence, Pentelic came to connote the whiteness of marble.

Penthesilea. In classic myth, the Queen of the Amazons, slain by Achilles when she came to the aid of the Trojans after the death of HECTOR. Her beauty and courage won for her a sincere lament from her slayer.

Pentheus. In classic myth, a king of Thebes, who tried to abolish the orgies of Bacchus, but was driven mad by the offended god. In his madness he climbed into a tree to witness the rites, and being descried was torn to pieces by the Bacchantes. See BACCHAE.

Peona. The loyal and tender sister of ENDYMION in Keats' poem of that name. She is not a classical character, but a creation of his own.

People, Yes, The. A free-verse poem by Carl SANDBURG (1936), celebrating the vigor of the American common people and expressing hope for their eventual progress in spite of social injustice and economic inequality. It makes use of colloquial American idiom, speech rhythms, slang, proverbs, and native folk-tales.

People's Commissar. In the U.S.S.R., formerly the head of a commissariat or department of government; now called minister. The Union Council of Ministers, formerly the Union Council of People's Commissars, is the Russian national cabinet.

peplos. The outer garment for women in ancient Greece. It was ample, pinned over the shoulders, and variously draped.

Pepper, George Wharton (1867–). American lawyer. Author among other books of *In the Senate* (1930) and numerous legal treatises.

Pepys, Samuel (1632–1703). English author and Secretary of the Admiralty during the Stuart Restoration (1673–1688), best known for his *Diary* (see DIARY OF SAMUEL PEPYS), written in shorthand between 1660 and 1669 and not deciphered until 1825. He also wrote *Memoirs of the Navy* (1690). Pepys, the son of a tailor, had as a patron Sir Edward Montagu, Earl of Sandwich, and met the outstanding personalities of his day in his official position. After the ascension of William III to the English throne, Pepys lost his secretaryship and was imprisoned for a time for his Stuart sympathies.

per ardua ad astra (*Lat.*). Through hardship to the stars. Motto of the British Royal Air Force (R.A.F.).

per aspera ad astra (*Lat.*). Through difficulties to the stars. The motto of Kansas.

Perceforest, King. A legendary king of Britain, hero of an old romance first printed at Paris in 1528. According to the narrative, he was crowned King of Britain by the shipwrecked Alexander the Great. He was called *Perceforest* because he dared to *pierce,* almost alone, an enchanted *forest,* where women and children were most cruelly treated.

Perchta. A fairy (*the white lady*) of southern Germany, corresponding to HULDA (*the gracious lady*) of Northern Germany. After the introduction of Christianity, when pagan deities were represented as demons, Perchta lost her former character, and became a bogy to frighten children. See also BERTHA, FRAU.

Percival. In Virginia Woolf's THE WAVES, a character who does not appear but acts as a unifying force, since the six leading characters of the novel all admire him and are deeply fond of him, finding in him the type of vigorous, "outward" personality they would like to possess but lack. He is killed by a fall from a horse in India, and his death serves as a symbol of all death.

Percival, James Gates (1795–1856). American poet and geologist, an aspirant to fame as a romantic poet, although he never achieved more than a brief contemporary success. His works include *Poems* (1821); *Clio* (1822–1827); and *The Dream of a Day* (1843). He was eccentric in behavior and paranoiac in temperament, living voluntarily for a time at the New Haven State Hospital. During his lifetime he was a physician, a journalist, and a chemistry instructor, and held the position of state geologist in Connecticut (1835–1842) and Wisconsin (1854–1856).

Percival, Sir. A knight of the Round Table who, according to Malory's MORTE D'ARTHUR (and Tennyson's IDYLLS OF THE KING), finally wins sight of the HOLY GRAIL. He is the son of Sir Pellinore and brother of Sir Lamerocke, and is brought up in innocence in the forest. After his initial experiences at the court of King Arthur, he joins either GAWAIN or GALAHAD in the quest of the Holy Grail. In the English legend, he catches a glimpse of the Grail, but it is Sir Galahad who wins the quest. In German versions, under the name Parzival or PARSIFAL, he is the one who finally is made knight of the Grail.

Percy, Bishop **Thomas** (1729–1811). English scholar and antiquarian, known for his work called *Percy's Reliques of Ancient English Poetry* (1763), a collection of English and Scotch songs, ballads, and metrical romances, some dating from the Middle Ages and some from the period of Charles I. This was the chief source of medieval characters and themes for the poets of the romantic period.

Percy's Reliques, see under PERCY, Bishop THOMAS.

Perdita. In Shakespeare's WINTER'S TALE, the daughter of Leontes and Hermione of Sicily. She is abandoned by order of her father, and put in a vessel which drifts to "the seacoast of Bohemia," where the infant is discovered by a shepherd, who brings her up as his own daughter. In time Florizel, the son and heir of the Bohemian king Polixenes, falls in love with the supposed shepherdess. The match is forbidden by Polixenes, and the young lovers flee to Sicily. Here the story is cleared up, and all ends happily in the restoration of the lost (Fr. *perdu*) Perdita to her parents, and her marriage with Florizel.

Mrs. Mary Robinson, the actress and mistress of George IV when he was Prince of Wales, was specially successful in the part of Perdita, and she assumed this name, the Prince being known as Florizel. Cf. *The Exquisite Perdita* (1926), by L. Adams BECK.

Perdix. The skillful nephew and apprentice of Daedalus. He invented the saw and made the first pair of compasses. When his jealous uncle tried to kill him by pushing him off a high tower, Minerva saved his life by changing him into a partridge. Latin *perdix*, "partridge."

Peredur. A knight of Welsh legend identified with the English PERCIVAL and the German PARSIFAL. He is the son of Evrawc and one of the knights of the Round Table, known as Sir Peredur of the Long Spear. He is for many years called "The Dumb Youth," from a vow he has made to speak to no Christian till Angharad of the Golden Hand loves him better than she loves any other man.

Père Goriot. See GORIOT.

Père Grandet. The miserable miser in Balzac's *Eugénie Grandet* who sacrifices her to his own cupidity.

Peregrine. A well-known poem by Elinor WYLIE, in which she made a staccato meter particularly her own.

> Liar and bragger,
> He had no friend
> Except a dagger
> And a candle end . . .

The feat of rhyming in it is brilliant. It was a favorite poem of F. Scott Fitzgerald's.

Peregrine Pickle, The Adventures of. A novel by Tobias SMOLLETT (1751). Peregrine Pickle is a savage, ungrateful spendthrift, fond of practical jokes, and suffering with evil temper the misfortunes brought about by his own wilfulness.

Perelman, Sidney Joseph (1904–). American humorist, a brilliant parodist, punster, and satirist of advertising clichés. *Dawn Ginsbergh's Revenge* (1929); *Strictly from Hunger* (1937); *Look Who's Talking* (1940); *The Dream Department* (1943); etc.

Pérez de Ayala, Ramón (1880–). Spanish novelist, poet, and critic. Ambassador to London (1931–1936). Author of lyrics and novels.

Pérez Galdós, Benito (1845–1920). Spanish novelist and playwright. Wrote historical romances and novels of contemporary life.

perfectibilism. The doctrine of man's individual and social perfectibility. In Thomas Love Peacock's novel *Headlong Hall* there is a Mr. Foster who is represented as "perfectibilian."

perfectionism. A religious doctrine which was the leading principle of J. H. NOYES' ONEIDA Community. It was a sort of religious utopianism which considered that no sin existed, and that the Kingdom of Heaven was rapidly approaching with complete salvation for everybody.

Pergolesi, Giovanni Battista (1710–1736). Italian composer. He strongly influenced the development of operatic and instrumental music. His music is known for its radiant vitality.

Per Hansa. The hero of *Giants in the Earth* (1927) by O. E. RÖLVAAG.

Peri. Originally, a beautiful but malevolent sprite of Persian myth, one of a class which was responsible for comets, eclipses, failure of crops, etc. In later times it was applied to delicate, gentle, fairy-like beings begotten by fallen spirits who direct with a wand the pure in mind on the way to heaven. These lovely creatures, according to the Koran, are under the sovereignty of EBLIS, and Mahomet was sent for their conversion, as well as for that of man. The name is often applied to any beautiful, fascinating girl.

Paradise and the Peri. The second tale in Moore's LALLA ROOKH. The Peri laments her expulsion from heaven, and is told she will be readmitted if she will bring to the gate of heaven the "gift most dear to the Almighty." After a number of unavailing offerings she brings a guilty old man, who weeps with repentance, and kneels to pray. The Peri offers the Repentant Tear, and the gates fly open.

Pericles, Prince of Tyre. A drama attributed to Shakespeare (ca. 1608), but generally regarded as of doubtful authorship. The hero, Pericles, a wanderer because of the persecutions of Antiochus, Emperor of Greece, long believes that his wife Thaisa and his daughter Marina are dead, but finds the former a priestess of Diana and the latter a celebrated dancer. The action extends over sixteen years.

Pericles and Aspasia. See ASPASIA.

perigee. The point in the moon's orbit nearest to the earth. Opposed to apogee.

> But flourish in our perigee
> And have one Titan at a time.
> Edwin Arlington Robinson, *The Master.*

Perilous Castle. The castle of Lord Douglas was so called in the reign of Edward I, because Douglas destroyed several English garrisons stationed there, and vowed to be revenged on anyone who dared to take possession of it. Sir Walter SCOTT calls it "Castle Dangerous" in his novel so entitled.

In the story of Gareth and Lynette in Arthurian romance, the castle in which Lyonors is held prisoner is called Castle Perilous. See GARETH; LYNETTE.

Perinet. The hero of Rostand's ROMANCERS.

periodic sentence. A sentence in which, for rhetorical effect, the several clauses are so arranged as to suspend the interest until the very last words. See also BALANCED SENTENCE.

Perion. (1) King of Gaul, father of AMADIS OF GAUL. His "exploits and adventures" form part of *Le Roman des Romans.*

(2) The hero of Cabell's romance DOMNEI

peripatetic school. The school or system of philosophy founded by ARISTOTLE who used to walk about (Gr. *peri,* "about," *patain,* "to walk") as he taught his disciples in the covered walk of the lyceum. This colonnade was called the *Peripatos.*

periphrasis. The substitution of an elaborate phrase for a simple word or phrase, as, for example, Wordsworth's "fragrant beverage drawn from China's herb." See also EPITHET.

Perissa. The typification of excessive exuberance of spirits in Spenser's *Faërie Queene* (II, ii). She is the mistress of Sansloy and a step-sister of ELISSA.

> In wine and meats she flowed above the bank,
> And in excess exceeded her own might;
> In sumptuous tire she joyed herself to prank,
> But of her love too lavish.
>
> *Faërie Queene,* II, ii, 36.

Peri Stephanou, see DE CORONA.

peristyle. A range of columns surrounding a court or cloister. In the Roman house it was a large room containing a central open space surrounded by pillars.

Perkins, Frances (1882–). U.S. secretary of labor (1933–1945). Formerly commissioner, N.Y. State Industrial Commission, and chairman, N.Y. State Industrial Board. Author of *The Roosevelt I Knew* (1946).

Perkins, George Walbridge (1862–1920). American financier, partner in J. P. Morgan & Co. (1901–1910). Supported Theodore Roosevelt in the Progressive party (1912).

Perkins, James Breck (1847–1910). American lawyer and author of notable works on French history.

Perkin Warbeck (1474–1499). Walloon pretender to the English crown (1495). Hence any pretender.

Perlmutter. See POTASH AND PERLMUTTER.

Pernelle, Madame. In Molière's TARTUFFE, mother of Orgon, a regular vixen, who interrupts everyone, without waiting to hear what was to have been said to her.

perpetual motion. The term applied to some theoretical force that will move a machine for ever of itself—a mirage which holds attractions for some minds much as did the search for the philosophers' stone, the elixir of life, and the fountain of perpetual youth in less enlightened times.

Perrault, Charles (1628–1703). French author and critic, known for his collection of Mother Goose rhymes, *Contes de ma Mere l'Oye* (1697), and for his leading role in the quarrel between the ANCIENTS AND MODERNS. Outstanding in this connection are his poem *Le Siècle de Louis le Grand* (1687), asserting the superiority of the age of Louis XIV to that of the Roman Emperor Augustus; and *Parallèles des Anciens et des Modernes* (1688–1697), a series of dialogues surveying the arts and pointing out the progress made by the writers of the author's own day over those of the past. Perrault was among the first to celebrate in verse the new inventions of the telescope and microscope and the study of physiology, and to assert a definite principle of progress.

Charles' brother, **Claude Perrault** (1613–1688), was a physician and architect and built the façade of the Louvre; he was satirized by BOILEAU in the latter's *Art Poétique.* **Pierre Perrault** (1608–1680), another brother, translated works from the Italian and in 1678 attacked Boileau and the Ancients in one of his prefaces; he himself was later attacked by RACINE.

Perry, Bliss (1860–). American literary critic, educator, and editor of *Atlantic Monthly* (1899–1909). Professor of English at Harvard (1907–1930). Member, American Academy of Arts and Letters. Author of numerous books, among them studies of *Walt Whitman* (1906); *Whittier* (1907); *Carlyle* (1915); etc.

Perry, Matthew Calbraith (1794–1858). American naval officer, brother of Oliver Hazard PERRY. Famed for opening Japan to U.S. commerce (1854).

Perry, Oliver Hazard (1785–1819). American naval officer. Fought battle of Lake Erie (Sept. 10, 1813). Noted for the words of his brief dispatch to General Harrison, "We have met the enemy and they are ours."

Perry, Ralph Barton (1876–). American philosopher and educator. Pupil and close friend of William JAMES. Author of the Pulitzer prize biography *The Thought and Character of William James* (1935). His own philosophy is an extension of the pragmatism of William James and is known as *neo-realism. The New Realism* (1912); *General Theory of Value* (1926); etc.

Perry, Thomas Sergeant (1845–1928). A friend of William Dean HOWELLS and Henry JAMES to whom, it is said, he introduced the works of Turgenev.

Perse, St.-J., see LÉGER, ALEXIS ST. LÉGER.

Persephone, see PROSERPINE.

Perseus. In Greek legend, the hero son of ZEUS and DANAË. He and his mother were set adrift in a chest, but were rescued through the intervention of Zeus, and he was brought up by King Polydectes, who, wishing to marry his mother, got rid of him by giving him the almost hopeless task of obtaining the head of MEDUSA. He, with the help of the gods, was successful, and with the head (which turned all that looked on it to stone) he rescued ANDROMEDA, and later metamorphosed Polydectes and his guests to stone.

Before his birth, an oracle had foretold that Acrisius, Danaë's father, would be slain by Danaë's son Perseus. This came to pass, for, while taking part in the games at Larissa, Perseus accidentally slew his grandfather with a discus.

Pershing, John Joseph (1860–1948). Commander in chief, American Expeditionary Force (1917–1919); chief of staff, U.S. Army (1921–1924). His *My Experiences in the World War* (1931) was awarded the Pulitzer prize for history.

Persius. In full **Aulus Persius Flaccus** (34–62 A. D.). Roman satiric poet influenced by HORACE. Friend of LUCAN. Author of satires in hexameters, which are mostly "versified lectures on Stoic tenets."

Persuasion. A novel by Jane AUSTEN (1818). The heroine, Anne Elliott, and her lover, Captain Wentworth, have been engaged eight years before the story opens but Anne has broken the engagement in deference to family and friends. Upon his return he finds her "wretchedly altered," but after numerous obstacles have been overcome, the two lovers are happily united. Anne is gentle, sensitive and charming; the author wrote of her, "She is almost too good for me."

Perth, The Fair Maid of. See FAIR MAID.

Pertinax. Pseudonym of the French journalists Charles Gérault (1878–) and André Géraud (1882–). André Géraud adopted the pseudonym later as editor of the *Echo de Paris* (1918).

Pertwee, Roland (1886–). English playwright and novelist. Also a popular writer for magazines and an actor in the companies of H. B. Irving, Charles Hawtrey, etc.

Peru, Conquest of, see CONQUEST OF MEXICO.

Perugino, Il. Real name **Pietro Vannucci** (1446–1523). Umbrian painter of the early Renaissance, teacher of RAPHAEL. His work shows devotional fervor, delicate color, minute delineation and the beginnings of scientific perspective.

Pervigilium Veneris. A famous short Latin poem of love and spring by an anonymous writer, probably of the 2nd century A. D.

Peshkov, Alexey Maximovich, see GORKY, MAXIM.

Pestalozzi, Johann Heinrich (1746–1827). Swiss educational reformer, whose work influenced strongly the methods of education in elementary schools in Europe and America.

Pétain, Henri Philippe (1856–). Commander in chief of French Army under Marshal Foch (1918); marshal of France (1918). After defeat of France by Germany (1940), set up a government at Vichy in unoccupied section of France, under German control. Upon defeat of Germany, tried by a French Tribunal for high treason (1945); death sentence commuted to life imprisonment.

Pétaud.

'tis the court of King Pétaud, where everyone is master. There is no order or discipline at all. This is a French proverb. *Le Roi Pétaud* (Lat. *peto,* "I beg") was the title of the chief who was elected by the fraternity of beggars in medieval France, in whose court all were equal. In his GARGANTUA AND PANTAGRUEL, Rabelais introduces Henry VIII as *Le Roi Pétaud.*

Peter, St. See under SAINTS.

to rob Peter to pay Paul. See under ROB.

Peter Bell. The subject of a "tale in verse" by WORDSWORTH (1798). SHELLEY wrote a burlesque upon it, entitled *Peter Bell the Third.*

Peter Grimm, see RETURN OF PETER GRIMM.

Peter Ibbetson. A novel by George DU MAURIER (1891), a story of a strange, idealistic dream life shared by the hero, Peter Ibbetson, and his childhood friend, Mimsey Seraskier, afterwards Mary, the Duchess of Towers. The external events are few; the two see each other only two or three times after their childhood; Peter spends the greater part of his life in jail as a murderer, and dies in a criminal lunatic asylum. The novel has been dramatized (1917) starring John and Lionel BARRYMORE; filmed; and is the basis of an opera by Deems TAYLOR, with Lucrezia BORI as the Duchess of Towers.

Peterkin, Julia, *née* **Mood** (1880–). American novelist, known for her books dealing sympathetically with the Gullah Negroes of South Carolina. Her works include *Green Thursday* (1924), sketches; *Black April* (1927); *Scarlet Sister Mary* (1928), awarded the Pulitzer prize in 1929; *Bright Skin* (1932); *Roll, Jordan, Roll* (1933), a book of text and photographs.

Peter Pan. A children's drama by J. M. BARRIE (1904). The boy hero, Peter Pan, has run away to Never-Never-Land to escape growing up, and lives in the trees with the fairies. One day he shows the Darling children, Wendy, Michael, and John, how to fly and persuades them to come home with him. Peter has a terrible enemy in the one-handed Captain Hook, leader of a band of Pirates. If the crocodile who bit off the Captain's missing hand had not swallowed an eight-day alarm clock which ticks a loud warning at his approach, he would probably have succeeded in making away with the rest of the Captain. Once the children are captured by the Pirates, but Peter frightens Captain Hook away by pretending to be the ticking crocodile. The Indian princess, Tiger Lily, and Peter's unseen fairy friend, Tinker Bell, protect the children through many adventures. Finally Wendy has to go home, but she promises to come again every spring. A long succession of actresses, notably Maude ADAMS, and including Pauline Chase, Cissie LOFTUS, and Eva Le GALLIENNE, have played Peter.

Peter Parley, see PARLEY, PETER.

Peter Porcupine, see COBBETT, WILLIAM.

Peter Quince at the Clavier. A poem by Wallace STEVENS.

Peter Rugg, the Missing Man. A tale by William Austin (*Am.,* 1824), once widely known. The hero swears a terrible oath that a thunderstorm shall not keep him from reaching home, and is punished by being forced to roam about forever between Boston and Hartford in a phantom chaise with a thunderstorm in his wake. The tale is based on an old New England legend.

Peters, Charles Rollo (1862–1928). American painter.

Peters, Curtis Armoux, Jr., see ARNO, PETER.

Peter Schlemihls wunderbare Geschichte. A tale by Adelbert von CHAMISSO (1814), treating realistically the adventures of a man who gives up his shadow to a gray stranger in return for Fortunatus' purse. Hence *Peter Schlemihl* became a synonym for any person who makes a desperate and senseless bargain. Chamisso derived the name of his hero from Yiddish *schlemihl.* The book can be read as a delightful and fanciful tale but also as a deeply bitter autobiography of a man who feels somehow excluded from normal human relations through no fault of his or of his environment. Chamisso was a Frenchman by birth, a German by education and language.

Petersham, Maud (1889–), and **Petersham, Miska** (1888–). Writers and illustrators of books for children. Illustrators of the *Rootabaga Stories* by Carl Sandburg and of many books by Mabel Scudder La Rue. Among their own books are *Miki; The Ark of Father Noah and Mother Noah;* etc.

Peter Simple. A novel (1834) by Captain MARRYAT.

Peterson, Houston (1897–). American educator. His study of the poetry of Conrad Aiken, *The Melody of Chaos,* was awarded the Butler Medal for 1931. Has edited anthologies of poetry. *Poet to Poet* (1945).

Peter's pence. An annual tribute of a penny paid before the Reformation to the Pope by every English householder who held land of a certain value. The term is now used to denote voluntary contributions by Roman Catholics to the Papal Treasury.

Peter Stirling, see HONORABLE PETER STIRLING.

Peter the Hermit. Also known as **Peter of Amiens** (1050?–?1115). French monk, one of the instigators of the First Crusade (1095), one section of which he led as far as Asia Minor (1096). He is introduced by Tasso in JERUSALEM DELIVERED; and by Scott in his COUNT ROBERT OF PARIS, a novel laid in the time of Rufus. A statue was erected to him at Amiens in 1854.

Petition of Right. An act of Parliament, passed in 1628 and reluctantly assented to by Charles I, providing that no one should be imprisoned without cause shown; that no forced loans or taxes be imposed without Parliamentary grant; that there be no martial law; etc. It is one of the chief documents of the English constitution.

Petitioners and **Abhorrers.** Two political parties in the reign of Charles II. When that monarch was first restored, he used to grant everything he was asked for. After a time this became a great evil, and Charles enjoined his loving subjects to discontinue their practice of "petitioning." Those who agreed with the King and disapproved of petitioning, were called *Abhorrers;* those who were favorable to the objectionable practice were nicknamed *Petitioners.*

Peto. In Shakespeare's 1 and 2 *Henry IV,* lieutenant of "Captain" Sir John Falstaff's regiment.

Petra. The heroine of Björnson's FISHER MAIDEN.

Petrarch. In full **Francesco Petrarca** (1304–1374). Italian poet, scholar, patriot, and humanist, a friend of BOCCACCIO and the son of a Florentine who was exiled from his native city in the same year as DANTE. Petrarch was one of the first great figures of the Renaissance in Italy, studying Latin and Greek literature, writing in Latin and interesting his contemporaries in classical antiquity, showing his patriotism by his writings and his participation in numerous political affairs, and initiating the vogue for the sonnet-sequence in celebration of an unattainable mistress, an adaptation of the medieval COURTLY LOVE tradition, which was ubiquitous in the literature of Italy, France, and England for over 200 years after his death. He is best known for his spiritualized passion for the lady LAURA, which inspired his famous series of poems, called *Canzoniere,* or *Rime in Vita e Morte di Madonna Laura* (*Verses on the Life and Death of My Lady Laura*). He also wrote an *Ode to Italy,* an *Epistle to Posterity, Africa,* an epic-poem in Latin, and numerous other epistles and treatises in Latin.

petrel, the stormy. A small sea-bird (*Procellaria pelagica*), so named, according to tradition, from the Ital. *Petrello,* "little Peter," because during storms it seems to fly patting the water with each foot alternately as though walking on it. The allusion is to St. Peter, who walked on the Lake of Gennesareth. Sailors call these birds "Mother Carey's chickens." The term is used figuratively of one whose coming always portends trouble, one who can be calculated upon to "raise Cain" wherever he goes or whatever he does.

Petrie, Sir **Flinders** (1853–1942). World-renowned English Egyptologist, whose excavations in Egypt and Palestine led to many discoveries in archeology and anthropology. Author of numerous books on ancient civilizations.

Petrified Forest, The. A drama by Robert E. SHERWOOD (1935). The star of the stage and film production was Leslie HOWARD.

Petronius, Gaius or **Titus,** surnamed **Arbiter** (died ca. 66 A. D.). Roman author, called by Tacitus *Arbiter Elegantiarum,* that is "judge of elegance," director of court entertainment under the Emperor Nero. He is known for his *Satyricon,* a fragmentary manuscript in prose and verse which is considered one of the first examples of the novel form and gives a vivid, sardonic, and extremely realistic picture of the luxuries, vices, and social manners of the Imperial Age. One "W. Burnaby" made an English translation of the work about 1700 in the quaint, prolix style of his day. Almost the only historical evidence of Petronius' existence is to be found in the sixteenth book of the *Annals* of Tacitus, where it is reported that he committed suicide to escape being put to death by Nero. He figures in QUO VADIS, by SIENKIEWICZ.

Petrov, Eugene (1903–1942). Russian journalist and humorist. Author, in collaboration with Ilya ILF, of *Diamonds To Sit On* (1930); *Little Golden Calf* (1933); *Little Golden America* (1937). Also with Ilya Ilf, wrote a satirical series of feuilletons which earned them the name of "the Soviet Mark Twains." Killed in the siege of Sevastopol (July 2, 1942).

Petruchio. In Shakespeare's TAMING OF THE SHREW, a gentleman of Verona, who undertakes to tame the haughty Katharina, called "the Shrew." He marries her, and without the least personal chastisement reduces her to lamb-like submission. Being a fine compound of bodily and mental vigor, with plenty of wit, spirit and good-nature, he rules his subordinates dictatorially and shows he will have his own way, whatever the consequences.

Petty, Sir **William** (1623–1687). English political economist and statistician. Author of *Treatises of Taxes and Contributions* (1662, 1667, 1685), which contain the first statement of the economic doctrine that price depends upon the labor invested in production.

Petulengro, Mr. The favorite gipsy character of George Borrow, in his ROMANY RYE.

Peveril of the Peak. The longest of all Walter SCOTT's novels (1823). It contains one hundred and eight characters, besides courtiers, officers, etc. The hero is Julian Peveril, a Cavalier; the heroine is Alice Bridgenorth, daughter of Major Bridgenorth, a Roundhead; the main subject is the "Popish Plot." The novel is crowded with well-known historic characters, among them, Charles II, his brother James, Duke of York, Prince Rupert, Antony Cooper, Earl of Shrewsbury, Lord Rochester, George Villiers, duke of Buckingham, Sir Edmondbury Godfrey, Hudson the dwarf, Colonel Blood, Titus Oates, and Settle the poet. Among the women are the widow of Charles I, the wife of Charles II, and his mistresses, Nell Gwyn and Louise de Kerouaille.

Pew. The blind beggar in TREASURE ISLAND by Robert Louis Stevenson.

Peyrouton, Marcel B. (1888?–). French politician, minister of the interior under PÉTAIN (1940–1941). Appointed governor general in Algiers (1943) by General Giraud.

Pfaff's Beer Cellar. A famous Bohemian resort in New York City during the 1850's, a meeting place of writers such as Walt Whitman, Bayard Taylor, Fitz-James O'Brien, Adah Menken, etc.

Pfister's Bible. See BIBLE, SPECIALLY NAMED.

Phaeacians. In the Odyssey, the inhabitants of the mythical land over which Alcinous was king. His daughter Nausicaä welcomed ODYSSEUS.

Phaedo or **Phaedon** (fl. 4th century B. C.). Greek philosopher, friend and disciple of Socrates. PLATO gave his name to a dialogue which purports to be a record of Socrates' last conversation with his friends. It is mainly concerned with the immortality of the soul.

Phaedra. In classic myth, daughter of MINOS, King of Crete, and wife of THESEUS. She conceived a criminal love for Hippolytus, her step-son, and, being repulsed by him, accused him to her husband of attempting to dishonor her. Hippolytus was put to death, and Phaedra, stricken with remorse, strangled herself. This legend has been the subject of many tragedies, the most famous of which are by EURIPIDES in Greek, SENECA in Latin, and RACINE in French (*Phèdre,* 1677). A French *Phèdre et Hippolyte* by Pradon (1677) and an English *Phaedra and Hippolytus* by Smith (1708) were preferred by some contemporary critics to Racine's *Phèdre,* which is now considered his masterpiece, and was one of the greatest roles of Sarah BERNHARDT.

Phaedria. The typification in Spenser's FAËRIE QUEENE (II, vi) of wantonness. She is handmaid to Acrasia the enchantress, and sails about Idle Lake in a gondola. Seeing Sir Guyon, she ferries him across the lake to the floating island, where Cymochles attacks him. Phaedria interposes, the combatants desist, and the little wanton ferries the knight Temperance over the lake again.

Phaëthon (*Gr.*, "the shining one"). In classical myth, the son of Phoebus, the Sun. He undertook to drive his father's chariot, but was upset and thereby caused Libya to be parched into barren sands, and all Africa to be injured, the inhabitants blackened and vegetation nearly destroyed. He would have set the world on fire had not ZEUS transfixed him with a thunderbolt.

Phaëthon's bird. The swan. Cygnus, son of Apollo, was the friend of Phaëthon and lamented his fate so grievously that Apollo changed him into a swan, and placed him among the constellations.

phalanstery. See under FOURIERISM.

Phantasmagoria. A humorous poem about a ghost in seven "cantos" by Lewis CARROLL (1869).

Phaon or **Phedon.** In Spenser's FAËRIE QUEENE (II, iv), a young man ill-treated by Furor, and rescued by Sir Guyon. He loves Claribel, but Philemon, his friend, persuades him that Claribel is unfaithful, and, to prove his words, makes him see what appears to be Claribel holding an assignation with a groom. Rushing forth, Phaon meets the true Claribel, whom he slays on the spot. When he is tried for the murder, it comes out that the groom was Philemon, and the supposed Claribel her maid. He poisons Philemon, and would have murdered the maid, but she escapes, and while he pursues her he is attacked by Furor. This tale is designed to show the evil of intemperate revenge. In some editions of the poem Phedon is the name, not *Phaon.*

Phaon and Sappho. See SAPPHO.

Pharamond. In the Arthurian romances, a knight of the ROUND TABLE, who is said to have been the first king of France, and to have reigned in the early 5th century. He is the son of Marcomir and father of Clodion.

La Calprenède's novel *Pharamond, ou l'histoire de France,* was published in 1661. William MORRIS made Pharamond the hero of his *Love is Enough, Or the Freeing of Pharamond, A Morality* (1873), which tells how he abdicates his throne to marry a humble maiden.

Pharaoh. The title or generic appellation of the kings in ancient Egypt. The word originally meant "the great house," and its later use arose much in the same way as, in modern times, "the Holy See" for the Pope, or "the Sublime Porte" for the Sultan of Turkey.

None of the Pharaohs mentioned in the Old Testament has been certainly identified, owing to the great obscurity of the references and the almost entire absence of reliable chronological data. There are two who figure prominently in the book of *Genesis:*

(1) The Pharaoh who raised JOSEPH to power because of his interpretation of the dreams predicting seven years of famine, and who later welcomed Joseph's father JACOB and his family into Egypt.

(2) The Pharaoh who "knew not Joseph" and cruelly mistreated the Israelites. MOSES was brought up by his daughter but later violently opposed him (or possibly his successor) and called down upon him the famous Ten Plagues for refusing to let the Children of Israel go out from Egypt. This is the Pharaoh who pursued the Israelites into the Red Sea when the waters were parted for their benefit, and who was drowned as the waters returned.

In Dryden's satire ABSALOM AND ACHITOPHEL, Pharaoh stands for Louis XIV of France.

Pharaoh's chicken or *hen.* The Egyptian vulture, so called from its frequent representation in Egyptian hieroglyphics.

Pharaoh's corn. The grains of wheat sometimes found in mummy cases.

Pharaoh's serpent. A chemical toy consisting of sulpho-cyanide of mercury, which fuses into a serpentine shape when lighted; so called in allusion to the magic serpents of *Exod.* vii. 9–12.

Pharisees (Heb. *perusim,* from *perash,* "to separate"). In the Old Testament, "those who have been set apart," not as a sect but as a school of ascetics who attempted to regulate their lives by the letter of the Law. The opprobrious sense of the word was given it by their enemies, because the Pharisees came to look upon themselves as holier than other men, and refused to hold social intercourse with them. Many of Christ's sayings begin "Woe unto you, Scribes and Pharisees, hypocrites."

Pharos. A lighthouse; so called from the lighthouse—one of the seven wonders of the world—built by Ptolemy Philadelphus in the island of Pharos, off Alexandria, Egypt. It was 450 feet high, and, according to Josephus, could be seen at the distance of 42 miles. Part of it was blown down in 793.

Pharsalia. An epic in Latin hexameters by LUCAN. It tells of the civil war between POMPEY and CAESAR, and of the Battle of Pharsalus (48 B.C.) in which Pompey, with 45,000 legionaries, 7,000 cavalry, and a large number of auxiliaries, was decisively defeated by Caesar, who had only 22,000 legionaries and 1,000 cavalry. Pompey's battle-cry was *Hercules invictus;* that of Caesar, *Venus victrix.*

Phebe. In Shakespeare's AS YOU LIKE IT, a shepherdess beloved by the shepherd Silvius. While ROSALIND is in boy's clothes, Phebe falls in love with the stranger, and makes a proposal of marriage. When Rosalind appears in her true character and gives her hand to Orlando, Phebe is content to accept her old love Silvius.

Phedon. An alternative name of PHAON.

Phèdre. See under PHAEDRA.

Pheidias, see PHIDIAS.

Pheidippides. (1) In Aristophanes' comedy THE CLOUDS, a caricature of Alcibiades.

(2) A Greek runner, famed for his exploits at the time of the battle of Marathon. BROWNING makes him the hero of a poem in his *Dramatic Idylls*.

Phelps, Elizabeth Stuart, see Elizabeth S. WARD.

Phelps, William Lyon (1865–1945). American teacher and popularizer of literature; professor of English at Yale (from 1901). Wrote *Essays on Russian Novelists* (1910); *Some Makers of American Literature* (1923); *As I Like It* (1923), the outgrowth of his book department in *Scribner's Magazine;* and many other books. The influence of his personality on his students was greater still than that of his writings.

Phi Beta Kappa key. The golden watch key which is the badge of the oldest Greek letter society in American colleges and universities. Members are elected according to their excellence in scholarship. The society was founded on December 5, 1776, at William and Mary College, Williamsburg, Va., originally as a secret society. The initials phi, beta, and kappa, inscribed on the key, represent the Greek words for "Philosophy, the guide of life."

Phidias (fl. 5th century B.C.). Greek sculptor of the Periclean age. In charge of all Athenian public works under construction at the time, which included the Parthenon and most of the other great monuments of the city. His Olympian Zeus at Elis and his Athene Parthenos, both colossal CHRYSELEPHANTINE statues, are known from descriptions and more or less doubtful copies. Fragments of his frieze of the Parthenon have survived and hold the supreme place among all existing works of sculpture. Phidias died in prison, apparently under a charge of sacrilege for having represented Pericles and himself on Athene's shield.

philabeg (Scottish). A kilt. The term is used in the first verse of the famous old Scotch Jacobite song:

> Cam' ye by Athol, lad wi' the philabeg,
> Down by the Tummel or banks o' the Garry;
> Saw ye our lads, wi' their bonnets and white cockades,
> Leaving their mountains to follow Prince Charlie?
>
> Follow thee! follow thee! wha wadna follow thee?
> Lang has thou loved and trusted us fairly:
> Charlie, Charlie, wha wadna follow thee,
> King o' the Highland hearts, bonnie Prince Charlie?

Philadelphia Story, The. A comedy (1939) by Philip BARRY.

Philaminte. One of the principal characters of Molière's FEMMES SAVANTES, a "learned lady," wife of Chrysale, the bourgeois, and mother of Armande, Henriette, Ariste, and Bélise.

Philammon. A young monk, one of the two chief characters of Kingsley's HYPATIA.

Philander. A male coquet; so called from Philander, the Dutch knight, who coquettes with Gabrina in Ariosto's ORLANDO FURIOSO. To *philander* is to wanton or make licentious love to a woman.

Philaster or Love Lies a-Bleeding. A tragedy by BEAUMONT AND FLETCHER (1620). The hero, Prince Philaster, is heir to the crown of Sicily, and the plot concerns his love and marriage to Princess Arethusa of Spain. The most appealing character is Euphrasia, a maiden whose devotion to Philaster leads her to enter his service disguised as the page Bellario. Philaster gives his page to Arethusa and then grows jealous of Arethusa's love for the young page.

Philemon and Baucis. Poor cottagers of Phrygia, husband and wife, who, in OVID's story (*Metamorphoses,* iii. 631), entertained Jupiter so hospitably that he promised to grant them whatever request they made. They asked that both might die together, and it was so. Philemon became an oak, Baucis a linden tree, and their branches intertwined at the top.

In the second part of Goethe's FAUST, *Philemon and Baucis* are an old couple who refuse to sell their home at any price. Because theirs is a part of the land that he is redeeming from the sea, Faust, with the aid of Mephistopheles, dispossesses them, and they die of the shock.

Philidor, François André. Real name **François André Danican** (1726–1795). French chess player and composer. Chiefly known in chess circles for "Philidor's Defense" and "Philidor's Legacy." Composed many operas.

Philip, St. See under SAINTS.

Philip, The Adventures of. A novel by W. M. THACKERAY (1862), a sequel to the unfinished SHABBY GENTEEL STORY. The hero, Philip Firmin, is an outspoken young man, in revolt against the underhanded hypocrisy of his father, Dr. George Brandon Firmin, whose sham marriage to Caroline Gann forms the subject of the earlier novel. As a boy he is nursed and befriended by Caroline, now known as Mrs. Brandon, or "the Little Sister," and throughout the book he champions her cause and owes much to her guidance. He is brought up in luxury, but due to his father's scheming, loses all his money and is forced to make a living as an editor. He marries Charlotte Baynes, the daughter of his trustee and guardian, whom his father had tricked to secure his fortune. After numerous difficulties Philip comes into a fortune from Lord Ringwood, a wealthy relative.

Philip and His Wife. A novel by Margaret DELAND (1894) on the theme of married life. Philip Shore is an unsuccessful artist, his wife Cecilia a beautiful heiress. The chief cause of their disagreement is the bringing-up of Molly, their only daughter.

Philip drunk. The phrase, "appeal from Philip drunk to Philip sober," springs from an anecdote which has it that a woman, condemned by Philip of Macedon when he was intoxicated, averred that she would appeal to him when he was sober again.

philippic. A severe scolding; a speech full of acrimonious invective. So called from the original *Philippics,* a group of nine orations by Demosthenes against King Philip of Macedon, designed to rouse the Athenians to resist his encroachments. The orations of Cicero against Antony are an example of philippics in the generic sense.

Philippines, I just came back from the. A nonsense song, appearing in Carl Sandburg's *The American Songbag* under the title *The Horse Named Bill.* Mr. Sandburg says he got the text from Sinclair Lewis, who got the last verse from George Sterling and two other verses from an Englishman. Actually, Sinclair Lewis first heard the song from William Rose Benét, who had got it from Lieutenant Storrs Bowen of the Presidio of San Francisco, except for the last verse in Carl Sandburg's version, which was made up by Sinclair Lewis himself. Mr. Sandburg does not give the refrain of the song, which gave it its original title. It goes:

I just came back from the Philippines.
 I have, I was.
My uncle has a factory there
And they make brushes, and they use 'em for the hair
And the teeth, and the feet, and the eyebrows,
 aaaaaand— the fingers.

The man in the ballad was originally not "so very *sleepy*" when he jumped into the river, but rather "so very *thirsty*."

Philips, Ambrose (1675?–1749). English poet, friend of Addison and Steele. Involved in a long quarrel with Alexander Pope, who adopted for him the nickname **Namby Pamby** originally conferred on him by Henry Carey. Pope thought the name fitted Philips' "eminence in infantile style."

Philips, John (1676–1709). English poet, chiefly known for *The Splendid Shilling* (1701).

Philips, Katherine (1631–1664). English poet and leader of a literary group in Cardigan, Wales. Each member of the group assumed a fictitious name: Mrs. Philips was known as "The Matchless Orinda"; her husband was called Antenor; and Anne Owen, her best friend, was Lucasia. Mrs. Philips' poetry was circulated in manuscript, and was well known in her day.

Philisides. A poetical name of Sir Philip SIDNEY used in his ARCADIA and elsewhere.

Philistines. In the Old Testament, the inveterate enemies of the Israelites against whom Samson, David and other Jewish heroes waged war. In modern usage, the term refers to the ill-behaved and ignorant; persons lacking in liberal culture, or of low and materialistic ideas. This meaning of the word was first used by Matthew ARNOLD, who adapted it from *Philister,* the term applied by students at the German universities to the townspeople, the "outsiders." This usage is said to have arisen at Jena, because, after a "town and gown" row in 1689, which resulted in a number of deaths, the university preacher took for his text "The Philistines be upon thee" (*Judges* xvi).

> The people who believe most that our greatness and welfare are proved by our being very rich, and who most give their lives and thoughts to becoming rich, are just the very people whom we call the Philistines.
> —Matthew Arnold, *Culture and Anarchy* (1869).

James Branch CABELL introduces the country of *Philistia* into his satiric romances, notably JURGEN.

Phillies. In American baseball parlance, the Philadelphia Nationals. See under BASEBALL TEAMS.

Phillips, David Graham (1867–1911). American journalist and novelist, known for his muckraking newspaper and magazine articles (see MUCKRAKERS) and his novels exposing political corruption and dealing with social problems. Among these novels are *The Great God Success* (1901); *Golden Fleece* (1903); *The Master-Rogue* (1903); *The Cost* (1904); *The Deluge* (1905); *The Plum Tree* (1905); *Light-Fingered Gentry* (1907); *The Second Generation* (1907); *The Fashionable Adventures of Joshua Craig* (1909); *The Conflict* (1911); *Old Wives for New* (1908); *The Hungry Heart* (1909); *The Husband's Story* (1910); *George Helm* (1912); *The Price She Paid* (1912); and *Susan Lenox: Her Fall and Rise* (1917), regarded as his best work, a realistic account of the career of a country girl who becomes a prostitute and later a successful actress. Phillips was murdered by a madman in revenge for a fancied slander of his sister in *The Fashionable Adventures of Joshua Craig.*

Phillips, Edward (1630–?1696) and **Phillips, John** (1631–1706). Nephews of John

Milton. The former became tutor to the son of John EVELYN and wrote a popular philological dictionary. The latter attacked Puritanism, wrote in favor of Titus OATES, did translations, and became a literary hack.

Phillips, Henry Wallace (1869–1930). American humorist, writer of Western stories, and creator of the character of the cowhand Red Saunders.

Phillips, Stephen (1868–1915). English poet and dramatist. His first work of poetry, *Poems* (1897), was so fulsomely acclaimed as to make his later under-estimation all the more ironic. His *Paolo and Francesca, Christ in Hades,* etc., are, however, still worth reading.

Phillips, Wendell (1811–1884). Prominent Boston abolitionist and supporter of William Lloyd Garrison.

Phillis. A pastoral name for a maiden in English poetry. See PHYLLIS.

Phillpotts, Eden (1862–). English novelist and playwright. Chiefly known for his long series of Dartmoor novels, which have been compared to Hardy's Wessex novels. Has also written mystery and detective novels, some under the name Harrington Hext.

Philoctetes. In classic myth, the most famous archer in the Trojan War, to whom HERCULES, at death, gave his arrows. He joined the allied Greeks with seven ships, but in the island of Lemnos his foot was bitten by a serpent, ulcerated, and became so offensive that the Greeks left him behind. In the tenth year of the siege ULYSSES commanded that he should be sent for, as an oracle had declared that Troy could not be taken without the arrows of Hercules. Philoctetes accordingly went to Troy, slew PARIS, and Troy fell. The *Philoctetes* of SOPHOCLES is one of the most famous Greek tragedies. The title of *The Wound and the Bow,* by Edmund WILSON, is derived from the legend.

Philomela. In Greek legend, daughter of Pandion, King of Attica. According to one version of the story, Tereus, king of Thrace, brought Philomela to visit his wife, Procne, who was her sister. When he reached the "solitudes of Heleas," he dishonored her, and cut out her tongue that she might not reveal his conduct. Tereus told his wife that Philomela was dead, but Philomela made her story known by weaving it into a peplus, which she sent to Procne. In another version Tereus married Philomela, telling her that Procne was dead, and it was Procne whose tongue was cut out and who wove the tell-tale story. In each case the end is the same. Procne, in revenge cut up her own son Itys, or Itylus, and served the flesh to Tereus. The gods changed all three into birds; Tereus became the hawk, his wife the swallow, and Philomela the nightingale, which is still called Philomel ("lover of song") by the poets. Matthew ARNOLD's *Philomela,* COLERIDGE's *Nightingale,* and SWINBURNE's *Itylus* are among the best-known poems based on the tale.

philosopher. The sages of Greece used to be called *sophoi* ("wise men"), but Pythagoras thought the word too arrogant and adopted the compound *philosophoi* ("lovers of wisdom"), whence "philosopher," one who courts or loves wisdom.

Marcus Aurelius (121–180) was surnamed *the Philosopher* by Justin Martyr, and the name was also conferred on Leo VI, Emperor of the East (d. 911), and Porphyry (d. 305), the neo-Platonic opponent of Christianity.

the philosopher of China. CONFUCIUS (551–479 B.C.). His mother called him *Little Hillock,* from a knob on the top of his head.

the philosopher of Ferney. VOLTAIRE (1694–1778); so called from his château of Ferney, near Geneva.

the philosopher of Malmesbury. Thomas Hobbes (1588–1679) author of *Leviathan.*

the philosopher of Persia. Abou Ebn Sina, of Shiraz (d. 1037).

the philosopher of Samosata. Lucan.

the philosopher of Sans-Souci. Frederick the Great (b. 1712, reigned 1740–1786).

the philosopher of Wimbledon. John Horne Tooke (1736–1812), author of *Diversions of Purley.*

philosophers' stone. The hypothetical substance which, according to the medieval alchemists, would convert all baser metals into gold. Its discovery was the prime object of all the alchemists, and to the wide and unremitting search that went on for it we are indebted for the birth of the science of chemistry, as well as for many inventions. According to one legend, Noah was commanded to hang up the true and genuine philosophers' stone in the ark, to give light to every living creature therein. Another relates that DEUCALION had it in a bag over his shoulder, but threw it away and lost it.

philosopher's or *Diana's tree.* An amalgam of crystallized silver, obtained from mercury in a solution of silver; so called by the alchemists, with whom Diana stood for silver.

Philosophical Inquiry into the Origin of Our Ideas of the Sublime and Beautiful, A. A treatise on esthetics by Edmund BURKE (1756), which defines beauty as a quality arousing emotions of love, through small size, smooth surface, and bright coloring, and the sublime as that which arouses sensations of pain. The work also includes an analysis of the psychological effects of various types of sensuous stimuli which is considered unusual for the time of its composition.

Philosophy of Composition, The. A critical essay by Edgar Allan POE (1846), presenting the poet's method of composition, with an analysis of THE RAVEN in illustration. It contains statements of Poe's well-known critical principles favoring a short over a long poem and designating melancholy as "the most legitimate of all poetical tones." See also POETIC PRINCIPLE, THE.

Philosophy, the father of. See under FATHER.

Philostrate. In Shakespeare's MIDSUMMER NIGHT'S DREAM, master of the revels for Theseus, King of Athens.

Philostratus (170?–245 A. D.). Greek Sophist philosopher at Athens and Rome. He wrote the *Lives of the Sophists.*

Philoxenos of Leucadia. The ancient Greek epicure of whom it is told that he wished he had the neck of a crane, that he might enjoy the taste of his food the longer (Aristotle, *Ethics,* iii. 10).

Phil the Fluter's Ball. An Irish music-hall song, describing the festivities when "Phil the Fluter" holds a ball. There are allusions to it in James Joyce's FINNEGANS WAKE, and echoes of its bouncing rhythm and its onomatopoeia recur throughout the book. See also FINNEGAN, TIM.

Phineas Finn. A novel by Anthony TROLLOPE (1869). The hero is a young Irishman of talent and great personal attractions who goes to London to enter Parliament. There he carries everything before him and indulges in affairs of the heart too numerous to mention. Eventually, however, he gives up politics, marries a poor Irish girl, and goes home to become inspector of poorhouses in Cork County. In the sequel, *Phineas Redux* (1874), his wife dies, and he returns to his Parliamentary career. He reappears in *The Prime Minister* (1876) as Secretary for Ireland and later Lord of the Admiralty. By this time, after several additional love affairs, he has contracted a very happy second marriage. The three are called the *Parliamentary Novels.*

Phineus. In classic myth, a blind soothsayer who was tormented by the harpies. Whenever a meal was set before him, the harpies came and carried it off. The ARGONAUTS delivered him from these pests in return for his information respecting the route they were to take in order to obtain the GOLDEN FLEECE.

Phips, Sir William (1651–1695). American-born colonial governor of Massachusetts (1692–1694), named under a new charter and at the request of Increase Mather. His government was attacked as neglectful. In the biography of Cotton Mather, Phips, who had begun his career as a ship's carpenter, is praised.

Phiz. The pseudonym of Hâblot K. Browne, who illustrated the PICKWICK PAPERS, NICHOLAS NICKLEBY, and most of Cha es DICKENS' works of fiction. He also illustrated the Abbotsford edition of Sir Walter SCOTT's *Waverley Novels.*

Phlegethon (Gr. *phlego,* "to burn"). In classic myth, a river of liquid fire in HADES. It flowed into the river Acheron. For the other rivers, see STYX.

> Fierce Phlegethon,
> Whose waves of torrent fire inflame with rage.
> Milton, *Paradise Lost,* ii.

phlegm. In early physiology, one of the four "humors." It was a cold, moist humor that caused sluggishness. From this the word came to mean coolness of temperament or equanimity.

> They judge with fury, but they write with phlegm
> Alexander Pope.

phlogiston. The principle of inflammability. The German chemists, Georg Ernst Stahl (1660–1734) and Johann Joachim Becher (1635–1682), advanced the phlogiston theory which explained combustion as the freeing and escape of phlogiston. The theory remained in force for about a century, and was then superseded by the modern theory of Lavoisier, which explained combustion as a combination with oxygen. Becher and Stahl trusted their senses in holding that combustion reduces the weight of a burning substance. Lavoisier used scales and demonstrated that the products of combustion show an increase in weight.

Phobos. Greek goddess of panic fear. Hence *phobia,* "fear."

Phocensian despair. Desperation which terminates in victory. In the days of Philip, King of Macedon, the men of Phocis had to defend themselves single-handed against the united forces of all their neighbors, because they presumed to plough a sacred field belonging to DELPHI. The Phocensians suggested that they should make a huge pile, and that all the women and children should join the men in one vast human sacrifice. The pile was made, and everything was ready, but the men of Phocis, before mounting the pile, rushed in desperation on the foe, and obtained a signal victory.

Phoebe of the ringlets. Phoebe Throssel, the heroine of J. M. Barrie's QUALITY STREET.

Phoebus (from Greek *phoibos,* "bright"). An epithet of APOLLO, particularly in his quality as the sun god. The name often stands for the sun personified.

Phoebus, Captain. In Victor Hugo's NOTRE DAME DE PARIS, the betrothed of Fleur de Marie. He entertains a base love for Esmeralda, the beautiful gypsy girl.

phoenix. A fabulous Arabian bird, the only one of its kind, that is said to live a certain number of years, at the close of which it makes in Arabia a nest of spices, sings a melodious dirge, flaps its wings to set fire to the pile, burns itself to ashes, and comes forth with new life, to repeat the former one.

> The enchanted pile of that lonely bird,
> Who sings at the last his own death-lay,
> And in music and perfume dies away.
> Thomas Moore, *Paradise and the Peri.*

It is to this bird that Shakespeare refers in CYMBELINE (i. 7):

> If she be furnished with a mind so rare,
> She is alone the Arabian bird.

The phoenix was adopted as a sign over chemists' shops through the association of this fabulous bird with alchemy. PARACELSUS wrote about it, and several of the alchemists employed it to symbolize their vocation. It is also a symbol of immortality. The men of Lord Louis Mountbatten's Southeastern Asia command wore it as an insigne in World War II. *The Phoenix and the Carpet* (1904), by E. NESBIT, is a romance for children dealing with the theme.

phoenix period or *cycle*. The period between the transformations of the phoenix, generally supposed to be 500 years but sometimes estimated as high as 1500 years.

Phoenix, John. Pseudonym of **George Horatio Derby** (1823–1861). Nicknamed **Squibob.** American journalist and humorist of California, known for his sketches and burlesques published in the San Diego *Herald,* of which he was editor. Collections of his works are *Phoenixiana* (1855) and *The Squibob Papers* (1859).

Phoenix Nest, The. (1) Title of a poetic miscellany (1593), edited by "R. S. of the Inner Temple, gentleman," and containing, among other poems, some by Lodge and Breton.

(2) A literary column given to poetry and talk about writers of the past, conducted by William Rose BENÉT in the *Saturday Review of Literature.*

Phoenix Park. A public park in Dublin, Ireland, situated on the banks of the river LIFFEY. It plays an important part in James Joyce's FINNEGANS WAKE, symbolizing there the Garden of Eden and also serving as the site of the secret crime that troubles the dreams of H. C. EARWICKER. Its latter rôle is believed by Harry Levin to be in memory of the "Phoenix Park murders," in which Charles Stewart PARNELL, Joyce's political hero, was implicated. The action of the first section of *Finnegans Wake* takes place broadly in and around Phoenix Park, which is doubly significant because of its name, the PHOENIX appearing frequently throughout the novel as a symbol of resurrection and recurrence.

Phooka or **Pooka.** A hobgoblin of Irish folklore, a spirit of most malignant disposition, who hurries people to their destruction. He sometimes comes in the form of an eagle, and sometimes in that of a horse, like the Scotch KELPIE. See also PUCK.

Phorcos. "The old man of the sea" of Greek mythology. He was the father of the three GRAIAE, who were gray from their birth, and had but one eye—which was stolen by PERSEUS as one of the means through which he was to obtain the head of MEDUSA—and one tooth common to the three.

Phrygian cap. See LIBERTY CAP.

Phrygian mode. One of the four principal modes in ancient Greek music. It is described as brisk and spirited. See also DORIAN MODE; LYDIAN MODE; MYXOLYDIAN MODE.

Phryne. A famous Athenian courtesan of the 4th century B. C., who acquired so much wealth by her beauty that she offered to rebuild the walls of Thebes if she might put on them this inscription: "Alexander destroyed them, but Phryne the hetaera rebuilt them." She is said to have been the model for Praxiteles' Cnidian Venus, and also for Apelles' picture of Venus rising from the sea.

Phrynicus. The name of two playwrights of Athens. One wrote tragedies (late 6th and early 5th centuries B. C.), the other comedies (late 5th century B. C.).

Phyfe, Duncan (1768–1854). Famous Scottish-born furniture maker, coming to America about 1783. His designs for mahogany chairs, couches, tables, etc., are highly prized. He had a joiner's shop in New York from about 1792 until he retired in 1847.

Phyllis or **Phillis.** A country girl in Virgil's third and fifth *Eclogues.* Hence, a rustic maiden.

physicians, the prince of. See under PRINCE.

Physician's or **Phisicien's Tale.** One of Chaucer's CANTERBURY TALES, having its source in the Roman legend of Appius Claudius and Virginia. See VIRGINIA.

Physick, Philip Syng (1768–1837). American surgeon, often called the "Father of American Surgery." Invented a number of surgical instruments of great value.

physiocrats. A French school of thought in political economy, started by François QUESNAY and Jean Claude Marie Vincent, sieur de Gournay (1712–1759). It systematized principles earlier expounded by R. Cantillon in 1755. The term is of Greek origin and combines the words for "nature" and "to rule." The physiocrats believed that society should be governed in accord with natural order, that individual rights should be limited only insofar as they do not infringe the rights of others, and that government is a necessary evil. They reached the conclusion that only agriculture, with the addition of the production of metals, is truly productive, and that manufactures and commerce are "sterile." TURGOT was the chief practical member of the school. Adam SMITH was influenced by some physiocratic doctrines, and certain tenets of the physiocrats foreran the contentions of Henry GEORGE in America.

Physiologus. A Greek collection, of the second century A. D., of allegories concerning animals and other things in nature. In the fifth century, Latin translations of the *Physiologus* became popular throughout Europe. They constitute the foundation of the bestiaries of the later Middle Ages.

Piatt, John James (1835–1917). American journalist and poet who wrote, with William Dean HOWELLS, *Poems of Two Friends* (1860). His wife, Sarah Morgan, was also a poet.

Piazza Tales, The. Stories by Herman MELVILLE collected in 1856.

pibroch. A war-like kind of bagpipe music used by the Scottish clans.

pica. A size of type; in the point system, equal to twelve points. Used as a unit in measuring widths of columns, etc. The term is probably derived from Latin *pica,* "a pie book," that is, a book containing the rules for the proper church service as used in pre-Reformation England. The pie book seems to have been so called because its color was that of a (mag)pie. The type size chosen for the first printed pie book would explain the transfer of the name to what is now 12-point type.

Picabia, Francis (1878?–). French post-impressionist painter of the cubist and Dadaist groups.

picador. In bull fighting, the horseman with a lance who helps exhaust the strength of the bull before the matador (who alone may do the killing) enters the ring.

picaresque (Sp. *picaresco,* "roguish, knavish"). The term applied to the class of literature that deals sympathetically with the adventures of clever and amusing rogues. The earliest example of the picaresque novel is Mendoza's *Lazarillo de Tormes* (1554). Le Sage's GIL BLAS is perhaps the best known. Thomas NASH's *Jack Wilton* (1594) is the earliest English example, and others are Defoe's MOLL FLANDERS and *Colonel Jack.*

Picasso, Pablo (1881–). Spanish painter, known especially as a leader of post-impressionism and with his friend George Braque as a founder of cubism (1906).

Piccadilly. This well-known London thoroughfare is named from a house that stood near the corner of Sackville Street which, in the early 17th century, was nicknamed *Pickadilly Hall.*

The "piccadille" was originally "the round hem or the several divisions set together about the skirt of a Garment," and was so called because it was pierced (Sp. *picado*) or slashed; thence it came to be applied to the stiff collar that supported the ruff of 17th century gallants.

One early account (1656) says *Pickadilly Hall* was so called because it was the "outmost or *skirt* house of the Suburbs that way"; another—of the same date—because it was built by one Higgins, a tailor, who made his fortune by selling "piccadilles."

piccaninny or piccannin (West India Negro, from Sp. *pequeño,* "small"). A little Negro child of the West Indies and southern part of the United States; also, in South Africa, applied to small Kaffir children, and sometimes to native children in Australia.

Piccard, Auguste (1884–). Swiss physicist. Investigator of atmospheric electricity. Made famous balloon ascents into stratosphere in an air-tight gondola of his own invention at Augsburg, Germany (1931), and Zurich, Switzerland (1932). His twin brother, **Jean Felix Piccard** (1884–), made a stratosphere ascent from the Ford airport at Dearborn, Michigan (1934).

Piccini, Niccolò (1728–1800). Italian opera composer, remembered especially for a feud (1774–1780), in which he did not participate, between his followers, the Piccinists, and the admirers of C. W. Gluck, the GLUCKISTS, who represented the German school of music.

Piccolomini. Famous Italian family, including archbishops, philosophers, soldiers, etc. **Octavio Piccolomini** (1599–1656) was a general in the imperial and Spanish armies during the Thirty Years' War. Cf. Schiller's drama *Die Piccolomini,* second part of the Wallenstein trilogy, in which the poet supplies Octavio with a non-historical son and rival Max.

Pickering, William (1796–1854). English publisher who improved the standard of printing. He adopted the dolphin-and-anchor device of the ALDINE Press and issued the Aldine edition of English Poets in 53 volumes.

Pickett, George Edward (1825–1875). American (Confederate) army officer who made a famous charge at Gettysburg (July 3, 1863) against the Union positions on Cemetery Ridge. He was beaten back with the loss of three-quarters of his division.

Pickford, Mary. Professional name of **Gladys Smith** (1893–). Famous Canadian-born moving-picture actress, usually in rôles of young girls. Wife (1920–1935) of Douglas Fairbanks. First husband Owen Moore (divorced 1920). After divorcing Fairbanks she married Charles ("Buddy") Rogers.

Pickle, Peregrine, see PEREGRINE PICKLE.

Pickthall, Marjorie Lowry Christie (1883–1922). Canadian poet and novelist.

Pickthall, Marmaduke (1875–1936). English novelist. Best-known for his oriental novels, such as *Saïd the Fisherman* (1903) and *Oriental Encounters* (1918).

Pickwick Papers. A novel by Charles DICKENS (1836–1837), more formally entitled *The Posthumous Papers of the Pickwick Club.* Aside from the immortal Sam WELLER, the chief character is Samuel Pickwick, general chairman of the Pickwick Club, a most naïve, benevolent, elderly gentleman, who, as member of a club instituted "for the purpose of investigating the source of the Hampstead ponds," travels about with three members of the club, to whom he acts as guardian and adviser. His misadventures are many, but worst of all is his sad experience with Mrs. BARDELL, which led to a famous trial.

in a Pickwickian sense. Said of words or epithets, usually of a derogatory or insulting kind, that, in the circumstances in which they are employed, are not to be taken as having quite the same force or implication as they naturally would have. The allusion is to the scene in chapter I where Mr. Pickwick accuses Mr. Blotton of acting in "a vile and calumnious manner," whereupon Mr. Blotton retorts by calling Mr. Pickwick "a humbug." It finally is made to appear that both use the offensive words only in a Pickwickian sense, and that each has, in fact, the highest regard and esteem for the other.

Pico della Mirandola, Count **Giovanni** (1463–1494). Italian humanist, philosopher, and author, a member of the Florentine Academy established by the MEDICI family for the study of philosophy. He is known for his neo-Platonic studies and for his work in Hebrew philosophy and the CABBALA, of which he was one of the first Christian scholars. He was condemned for a time by the Pope for certain of his philosophical publications. Sir Thomas MORE translated a number of his writings into English, including an account of his life.

Picon, Mollie (1903–). American Yiddish actress. Began in the Philadelphia Yiddish Arch Street Theater at the age of 5. After going to Europe and becoming famous internationally, she returned to New York in 1922. The Second Avenue Theater is known as Mollie Picon's, and she is part owner of it.

Picrochole. In Rabelais' *Gargantua,* a fire-eater who personifies satirically mankind's quarrelsome nature and lust for conquest. He may represent Charles V or Ferdinand of Aragon.

Picts. An ancient people of Great Britain who occupied parts of the Scottish highlands. They continually warred with the Romans and the Saxons. In Kipling's *Puck of Pook's Hill,* the Picts are described as the Little People, and figure in several of the stories.

Picture of Dorian Gray, The. A fantastic, allegorical novel (1891), by Oscar WILDE. Dorian remains youthful while his portrait grows old and corrupt. See also WILD ASS'S SKIN.

Picus. In classic mythology, a soothsayer and augur; husband of Canens. In his prophetic art he made use of a woodpecker (*picus*), a prophetic bird sacred to Mars. CIRCE fell in love wtih him, and, as he did not respond to her advances, changed him into a woodpecker, whereby he still retained his prophetic power.

Pidgin, Charles Felton (1844–1923). American novelist, best-known for his *Quincy Adams Sawyer* (1900), which is said to have been inspired by the poem *The Courtin'* by James Russell Lowell, and *Blennerhassett* (1901), a novel about Aaron BURR.

pidgin English. A lingua franca which has established itself in the intercourse of Chinese natives with foreigners. It consists essentially of more or less assimilated English words with Chinese grammatical constructions. For instance, the Chinese cannot pronounce *r,* so replace it with *l—te-le* for "three," *solly* for "sorry," etc. In Chinese, between a numeral and its noun there is always inserted a word (called the "classifier") and this, in pidgin English, is replaced by piece—e.g. *one piece knifee, two piece hingkichi* (handkerchiefs). The word *pidgin* is a corruption of *business.*

pieces of eight. The old Spanish silver *peso* (piastre) or dollar of eight reals. It was marked with an 8. In use in the 17th and 18th centuries.

pied-à-terre (*Fr.,* "foot on the ground"). A temporary lodging, a country residence.

> Mr. Harding, however, did not allow himself to be talked over into giving up his own and only *pied-à-terre* in the High Street.—Anthony Trollope, *Barchester Towers.*

pied de la lettre, au (*Fr.,* "to the foot of the letter"). Quite literally—close to the letter.

> A wild enthusiastic young fellow, whose opinions one must not take *au pied de la lettre.*—Thackeray, *Pendennis,* I, xi.

Pied Piper of Hamelin. The legend is that the town of Hamelin (Westphalia) was infested with rats in 1284, that a mysterious Piper, clad in a parti-colored suit, appeared in the town and offered to rid it of the vermin for a certain sum. The townspeople accepted the offer, but, after the Pied Piper had fulfilled his contract, the payment was withheld. On the following St. John's Day he reappeared, and again played his pipe. This time all the children of the town, in place of the rats, followed him; he led them to a mountain cave where all disappeared save two—one blind, the other dumb, or lame; and one legend adds that the children did not perish in the mountain, but were led over it to Transylvania, where they formed a German colony. Robert BROWNING popularized the legend in his children's poem *The Pied Piper*. More recently Josephine Preston PEABODY made it the subject of her poetic drama *The Piper* (1909), which was awarded the Stratford-on-Avon prize.

> To blow the pipe his lips he wrinkled,
> And green and blue his sharp eyes twinkled . . .
> And ere three notes his pipe had uttered . . .
> Out of the houses rats came tumbling—
> Great rats, small rats, lean rats, brawny rats,
> Brown rats, black rats, grey rats, tawny rats,
> And step by step they followed him dancing,
> Till they came to the river Weser.
>
> Browning.

Pierce, Franklin (1804–1869). Fourteenth president of the U.S. Senator (1837–1842), Brigadier General (1847). His friend Nathaniel HAWTHORNE wrote a campaign biography for him and was rewarded after election with the consulship at Liverpool.

Pierian spring. Inspiration, from Pieria where the MUSES were born.

Pierpont, John (1785–1866). American Unitarian clergyman and author. His best-known works are on political subjects. They include *The Anti-Slavery Poems of John Pierpont* (1843). One of his grandsons was J. Pierpont Morgan.

Pierre or the Ambiguities. A novel by Herman MELVILLE (1852), regarded as partially autobiographical. It deals with the love of Pierre Glendinning and his half-sister Isabel, Pierre's murder of his cousin and the brother of Lucy Tartan, his fiancée, when they attempt to interfere with him, and the double suicide of Pierre and Isabel in prison. The "ambiguities" of the subtitle are good and evil, and critics interpret Pierre as a man defeated by his adherence to Christian ideals.

Pierre et Jean. A short novel by Guy de MAUPASSANT (1888), a story of two brothers, one of whom receives an unexpected inheritance. The other brother, by his suspicions, forces his once-adored mother, Madame Roland, to confess that the money comes from a former lover who has left it to his own son.

Pierre Nozière. The second of a series of four autobiographical volumes by Anatole FRANCE (1899). The others are *My Friend's Book* (*Livre de mon ami;* 1885), *Little Pierre* (*Le Petit Pierre;* 1918) and *The Bloom of Life* (*La Vie en fleur;* 1922).

Pierrot (*Fr.* "Little Peter"). A favorite character of pantomime, a sort of clown-lover. He is generally the tallest and thinnest man that can be obtained, has his face and hair covered with white powder or flour, and wears a white gown with very long sleeves and a row of big buttons down the front. Pierrot is the lover of Pierrette, or sometimes of Columbine. From the simple figure of the early pantomime, poets and artists have gradually evolved another, more romantic Pierrot, an artist-lover of soaring imagination who grimly hides his real passions behind a comic mask. Among many others, the French DEBURAU, BAUDELAIRE and GAUTIER, the English Ernest DOWSON and the Canadian Bliss CARMAN have written of this new Pierrot. Ernest Dowson's dramatic fantasy, *The Pierrot of the Minute,* is the best known of several short plays on the subject. An interesting collection of poems on Pierrot (and, incidentally, Pierrette, Columbine, Harlequin and other of the pantomimic characters) is given in *Mon Ami Pierrot, Songs and Fantasie,* compiled by Kendall Banning.

Piers Plowman, The Vision of. A long allegorical and satirical poem in Middle English alliterative verse, written between 1362 and 1399 by probably as many as four or five different authors. On internal evidence the first part was long ascribed to William LANGLAND.

The title should really be *The Vision Concerning Piers the Plowman,* for in the earlier parts Piers typifies the simple, pious English laborer, and in the later, Christ Himself. The poet supposes himself falling asleep on the Malvern Hills, and in his dream sees various visions of an allegorical character, bearing on the vices of the times. The whole poem consists of nearly 15,000 verses, and is divided into twenty parts, each part being called a *passus.*

Pietà. In painting or sculpture, a representation of the Virgin Mary with the dead body of Christ held on her knees, or mourning for him. Michelangelo did a famous *Pietà* of white Carrara marble. He signed his name on the ribbon across the Madonna's gown. Other world-renowned *Pietàs* are by Van Dyck, Andrea del Sarto, Quentin Massys, etc.

Pietro. In Browning's RING AND THE BOOK, the putative father of Pompilia.

Pietro of Abano (1250?–?1316). The greatest Italian philosopher and physician of the 13th century. He was an astrologer, and was persecuted by the INQUISITION as a wizard. Browning wrote a poem called *Pietro of Abano* (1880).

pig.

a pig in a poke. A blind bargain. The French say *acheter chat en poche* ("to buy a cat in a pocket"). The reference is to a common trick in days gone by of trying to palm off on a greenhorn a cat for a sucking-pig. If he opened the sack he "let the cat out of the bag," and the trick was disclosed.

pigs in clover. People who have any amount of money but don't know how to behave themselves as gentlefolk. Also, a game consisting of a box divided into recesses into which one has to roll marbles by tilting the box.

pigeon wing. *To cut a pigeon wing* is an American phrase for "to execute a fancy step in dancing by jumping into the air and clapping the legs together."

Pig Iron. A novel by Charles G. NORRIS (1925).

Pigs in Clover. A novel by "Frank Danby" (Julia Frankau) (1904).

Pigs Is Pigs. The title of a widely-read humorous story by Ellis Parker BUTLER (1906).

Pigwiggen. An elf in Drayton's NYMPHIDIA, in love with QUEEN MAB. He combats the jealous OBERON with great fury.

> Pigwiggen was this Fairy Knight,
> One wond'rous gracious in the sight
> Of fair Queen Mab, which day and night
> He amorously observed.

Pike. A term denoting the crude hardy Westerner in American literature. It came into use with the publication, almost simultaneously in the year 1871, of John HAY's *Pike County Ballads* and Bret HARTE's *East and West Poems,* both of which attempted to express Western life in its own vernacular in ballad form. The best known of Bret Harte's poems are his HEATHEN CHINEE and *Jim Bludsoe;* of Hay's, probably *Little Breeches.*

Pilar. In Ernest Hemingway's FOR WHOM THE BELL TOLLS, a strong and vigorous peasant woman who is the leader of the Spanish Republican guerrilla band in its mountain hideout. She sentimentally encourages MARIA and Robert JORDAN in their love for each other.

Pilate, Pontius. A Roman procurator of Judea in the first half of the 1st century A. D. before whom Jesus was tried. He attempted to persuade the mob of Jesus' innocence, but failing, washed his hands before them with the words, "I am innocent of the blood of this righteous man; see ye to it." Tradition has it that Pontius Pilate's later life was so full of misfortune that, in Caligula's time, he committed suicide in Rome. His body was cast into the Tiber, but evil spirits disturbed the water so much that it was retrieved and taken to Vienna, where it was thrown into the Rhone, eventually coming to rest in the recesses of a lake on Mount Pilatus opposite Lucerne. Another legend states that the suicide occurred so that he might escape the sentence of death passed on him by Tiberius because of his having ordered the crucifixion of Christ; and yet another, that both he and his wife became penitent, embraced Christianity, and died peaceably in the Faith.

Tradition gives the name Claudia Procula, or Procla, to Pilate's wife, and by some she has been identified with the Claudia of 2 *Tim.* iv, 21.

Pilate's voice. A loud, ranting voice. In the old MYSTERIES, all tyrants were made to speak in a rough, ranting manner.

Pilgrim Fathers. The first shipload of settlers in Massachusetts, who set sail in the ship *Mayflower* in 1620; also, by extension of the term, any early Puritan settlers of New England. The *Mayflower* brought English, Scotch and Dutch Puritans, 102 in all.

> Men in the middle of life, austere and grave in deportment . . .
> God had sifted three kingdoms to find the wheat for this planting.
> Longfellow, *Courtship of Miles Standish,* iv. (1858).

Pilgrim's Progress, The. A famous narrative by John BUNYAN (Pt. I, 1678; Pt. II, 1684), supposed to be a dream, and to allegorize the life of a Christian from his conversion to his death. His doubts are giants, his sins a bundle or pack, his Bible a chart, his minister Evangelist, his conversion a flight from the City of Destruction, his struggle with besetting sins a fight with Apollyon, and his death a toilsome passage over a deep stream.

The second part deals with Christiana and her family led by Greatheart through the same road, to join Christian, who had gone before.

pillars of Hercules. Two opposite promontories at the entrance of the Mediterranean, one in Spain and the other in Africa. The tale is that they were bound together till Hercules tore them asunder in order to get to Gades (Cadiz). The ancients called them Calpe and Abyla; we call them Gibraltar and Mount Hacho.

I will follow you even to the pillars of Hercules. To the end of the world. The ancients supposed that these rocks marked the utmost limits of the habitable globe.

Pillars of Society, The. A four-act drama by Henrik IBSEN (1877).

Pilnyak. Pseudonym of **Boris Andreevich Vogau** (1894–). Russian novelist. *The Naked Year* (1922; translated, 1928) has been called the earliest attempt to interpret the Russian Revolution. It was rather scorned by Soviet critics but sold over half a million copies in the Soviet Union alone. *The Volga Falls to the Caspian Sea* (1931) concerns the huge Kolumna dam and the Five-Year Plan, again criticized by Soviet critics for bourgeois leanings. Pilnyak was president of the All Russian Writers Union (1929) and has traveled widely.

Pilot, The. A sea story by James Fenimore COOPER (1823), relating the adventures of the Revolutionary hero John Paul JONES. The sailor Long Tom COFFIN, one of Cooper's most famous characters, appears in this book.

Pilpay or **Bidpay.** The name given as that of the author of *Kalilah and Dimnah* (otherwise known as *The Fables of Pilpay*), which is the 8th century Arabic version of the Sanskrit *Panchatantra.* The word is not a true name, but means "wise man" (Arab. *bidbah*), and was applied to the chief scholar at the court of an Indian prince.

Pilsudski, Józef (1867–1935). Polish general and statesman. In World War I, he offered his army to Austria and fought against the Russians. Worked for Polish independence. Chief of state and first marshal of Poland (1920); dictator (1921); premier (1926–1928, 1930). He was in complete control of Polish policies until the time of his death. Respected by HITLER.

Piltdown man. An extinct manlike primate, reconstructed from the remains of two skulls found early in the 20th century at Piltdown, near Lewes, in Sussex, England. A bone implement was found nearby. Also known as *Dawn man.*

Pimpernel, The Scarlet, see SCARLET PIMPERNEL.

pin.

pin money. A lady's allowance of money for her own personal expenditure. At one time pins were a great expense to a woman, and in 14th- and 15th-century wills there are often special bequests for the express purpose of buying pins.

policy of pin pricks. A policy of petty annoyances. The term came into prominence during the strained relations between England and France in 1898, and is an Anglicization of the very much older French phrase, *un coup d'épingle.*

Pinafore, H.M.S., or The Lass that Loved a Sailor. A comic opera by GILBERT and SULLIVAN (1878). The plot hinges on the fact that Josephine, the daughter of the Captain of *H.M.S. Pinafore,* refuses the advances of the all-important Sir Joseph PORTER because she loves a "common sailor" named Ralph Rackstraw. Finally Little Buttercup, the bumboat woman, confesses to having changed the two babies, Ralph Rackstraw and the Captain, as nurse long years before.

pinball game. In the U.S., a game similar to bagatelle. A tilted board allows the ball, shot up a side alley, to run down through a field of pins which deflect it from point to point, either into certain receptacles or away from them. The game is often used for gambling and has frequently been raided by the police.

Pinch. In Shakespeare's COMEDY OF ERRORS, a schoolmaster and conjurer, who tries to exorcise Antipholus.

Pinch, Tom. In Dickens' MARTIN CHUZZLEWITT, a clerk to Mr. PECKSNIFF, "architect and land surveyor." He is as simple as a child, green as a salad, and honest as truth itself. Tom is very fond of story-books, but far more so of the organ.

Pinchbeck, Christopher (1670?–1732). London maker of watches and toys who invented a copper and zinc alloy resembling gold. Hence **pinchbeck,** "a spurious kind of gold."

Pinchot, Gifford (1867–1946). American political leader. Professor of forestry at Yale (1903–1936). Founder, with his brother **Amos Pinchot,** of the Pinchot School of Forestry at Yale. Governor of Pennsylvania (1923–1927), 1931–1935).

Pinchwife, Mr. In WYCHERLY's comedy *The Country Wife* (1675), the town husband of a raw country girl, unpracticed in the ways of the world, whom he watches with ceaseless anxiety.

Mrs. Pinchwife. The counterpart of Molière's AGNES in his comedy entitled *L'École des femmes,* a young woman wholly unsophisticated in affairs of the heart.

GARRICK changed the title of Wycherly's comedy to *The Country Girl* (1766), and Mrs. Pinchwife's name to Peggy Thrift.

Pinckney, Charles Cotesworth (1746–1825). American statesman who served in the revolution, became a member of the federal convention (1787), and helped to frame the constitution. When he went to France on a special mission, he was refused recognition; his report on the attempts of Talleyrand's agents to obtain bribes from him is known as the "XYZ Correspondence."

Pindar. The Theban poet (ca. 518–442 B.C.) whose lyrics in irregular verse have furnished the word "pindaric."

the British Pindar. Thomas Gray (1716–1771). On his monument in Westminster Abbey are inscribed these lines—

> No more the Grecian muse unrivalled reigns;
> To Britain let the nations homage pay:
> She felt a Homer's fire in Milton's strains,
> A Pindar's rapture in the lyre of Gray.

the French Pindar. (1) Jean Dorat (1507–1588); (2) Ponce Denis Lebrun (1729–1807).

the Italian Pindar. Gabriello Chiabrera (1552–1637).

the Pindar of England. Abraham Cowley (1618–1667) was called by the Duke of Buckingham "The Pindar, Horace, and Virgil of England."

Pindaric verse. Irregular verse; a poem of various meters and of lofty style, in imitation of the odes of Pindar. *Alexander's Feast,* by DRYDEN, and *The Bard,* by GRAY, are representative examples. See also ODE.

Pindar, Peter. Pseudonym of **John Wolcot** (1738–1819).

Pinero, Sir **Arthur Wing** (1855–1934). English playwright, known for his comedies of manners and his "society" dramas. His works include *The Money Spinner* (1881); *The Magistrate* (1885); *The Schoolmistress* (1886); *Dandy Dick* (1887); *Sweet Lavender* (1888); THE SECOND MRS. TANQUERAY (1893); *Lady Bountiful* (1891); *The Cabinet Minister* (1892); *The Weaker Sex* (1894); *The Amazons* (1895); *The Notorious Mrs. Ebbsmith* (1895); *The Princess and the Butterfly* (1898); TRELAWNY OF THE WELLS (1898); THE GAY LORD QUEX (1899); *Iris* (1901); *His House in Order* (1906); *The Thunderbolt* (1908); *Mid-Channel* (1909); *The Widow of Wasdale Head* (1912). His later plays are in a lighter vein, and include *The Enchanted Cottage* (1922), made into a successful motion picture; *Child Man* (1930); *Dr. Harmer's Holidays* (1930); and *A Cold June* (1932).

Pine-Tree State. Maine. See under STATES.

Pink or **Pinks.** Also **Parlor Pink.** In derisive political jargon, partly or mildly Red.

Pinkerton, Allan (1819–1884). Scottish-born head of a widely-known American private detective agency. Organized and conducted secret service for General McClellan (1861–1862). Author of *Criminal Reminiscences and Detective Sketches* (1879); *The Spies of the Rebellion* (1883); *Thirty Years a Detective* (1884); etc.

Pinkerton, Miss. In Thackeray's VANITY FAIR, a majestic lady, tall as a grenadier, and most proper. Miss Pinkerton keeps an academy for young ladies on Chiswick Mall. She is "the Semiramis of Hammersmith, the friend of Dr. Johnson, and the correspondent of Mrs. Chapone." This very distinguished lady "had a Roman nose, and wore a solemn turban." Amelia SEDLEY was educated at her academy, and Rebecca SHARP was a pupil teacher there.

"Pink" Marsh. See MARSH.

Pinkney, Edward Coote (1802–1828). American poet who served in the U.S. Navy (1815–1824). His *Poems* (1825) show a rather imitative lyrical gift.

Pink 'Un, The. English nickname for the popular sports journal, *The Sporting Times.*

pin money. See under PIN.

Pinski, David (1872–). Jewish-American dramatist and editor, born in Russia and writing in Yiddish. His comedy, *The Treasure,* was produced by the Theater Guild in 1920. *King David and His Wives* (1923; a drama) and *The Final Balance* (1928) are among his best works.

Pioneer, The. A monthly literary magazine founded by James Russell Lowell and Robert Carter (1843). It ran through only three issues but published *The Tell-Tale Heart* and *Notes on English Verse* by Edgar Allan Poe, and contributions by Nathaniel Hawthorne, Lowell, Whittier, etc.

Pioneers, The. A historical novel by James Fenimore COOPER (1823), one of the LEATHERSTOCKING series. In this novel, Leatherstocking is an old man in the Otsego settlement of his boyhood days. The action takes place in post-Revolutionary times and shows the corrupting effects of the settlements upon the Indians. Leatherstocking, embittered by the inroads of civilization upon the old freedom of the open country, lives on in lonely rebellion.

Walt WHITMAN wrote a poem *Pioneers! O Pioneers* (1865) and Willa CATHER a novel *O Pioneers* (1913).

Pioneers of France in the New World. A history by Francis PARKMAN (1865).

Piozzi, Hester Lynch, *née* **Salusbury.** Chiefly known as Mrs. **Thrale** (1741–1821). English writer. Well-known for her friendship of twenty years with Dr. Johnson, to whom the Thrales' home was always open. After her first husband's death, she married (1784) the Italian musician Gabriel Piozzi to the great displeasure of Dr. Johnson. Her anecdotes about Dr. Johnson and her correspondence with him approach Boswell's *Life* in interest.

Pip. The hero of Dickens' novel GREAT EXPECTATIONS. Real name, Philip Pirrip.

Pip. In Herman Melville's MOBY DICK, a little Negro cabin-boy, a favorite of Captain AHAB, who goes mad during the wild pursuit of the white whale through storm and disaster.

Pipchin, Mrs. In Dickens' DOMBEY AND SON, an exceedingly "well-connected lady," living at Brighton, where she keeps an establishment for the training of children. Mrs. Pipchin is an ill-favored old woman, with mottled cheeks and gray eyes. She is given to buttered toast and sweetbreads, but keeps her children on the plainest fare and gives them "everything that they didn't like and nothing that they did."

Piper, The. A drama dealing with the theme of the PIED PIPER OF HAMELIN by Josephine Preston PEABODY (1909).

Piper of Hamelin. See PIED PIPER OF HAMELIN.

Pipes, Tom. In Smollett's PEREGRINE PICKLE, a retired boatswain's mate, living with Commodore Trunnion to keep the servants in order. Tom Pipes is noted for his taciturnity.

Pippa Passes. A dramatic poem by Robert BROWNING (1841). Pippa is a very poor child, at work all the year round, except one day, in the silk mills at Asolo in Italy. Her one holiday is New Year's Day, and the drama hinges on her chance appearance "at critical moments in the spiritual life-history of the leading characters in the play." Just at the supreme moment, Pippa passes, singing some refrain, and her voice alters the destinies of the men and women to whom she is unknown. Unconsciously, her own destiny is altered in the end by her last song. The statement of Browning's theme lies in the refrain of Pippa's first song,

God's in His heaven—
All's right with the world!

piracy. The violation of copyright is technically an *infringement*. More currently and picturesquely, an illegal reprint is called a *pirated edition* and the practice of bringing out such editions, *piracy*. The term is often used loosely with reference to the era preceding modern COPYRIGHT conventions, when "pirating" was an honorable and lucrative business.

Piraeus. The port of Athens in Greece, built originally by Themistocles in 493 B. C.

Pirandello, Luigi (1867–1936). Italian playwright and novelist, known for his symbolical and psychological dramas and satires, which were internationally famous during the 1920's and aroused a great deal of controversy because of their alleged "obscurity." SIX CHARACTERS IN SEARCH OF AN AUTHOR (*Sei Personaggi in Cerca d'Autore;* 1921) is his most celebrated play. Others are *Enrico IV* (1922), produced in New York as *The Living Mask; Right You Are If You Think You Are* (*Così È Se Vi Pare;* 1918); *As You Desire Me* (*Come Tu Mi Vuoi;* 1931); *Tonight We Improvise* (*Questa Sera Si Recita a Soggetto;* 1932); *Tutto Per Bene* (1937). His non-theatrical works include *Il Fu Mattia Pascal* (1904), translated into English as *The Late Mattia Pascal, L'Esclusa* (*The Outcast;* 1913), and *Uno, Nessuno, e Centomila* (*One, None, and a Hundred Thousand;* 1926), novels; *Novelle per un Anno* (1932–1937), part of which was translated as *Better Think Twice About It* (1933), *A Character in Distress* (1938), and *The Medals, and Other Stories* (1939), collections of short stories.

Pirandello spent most of his early career as a professor of literature in an Italian girls' school. After his success as a writer for the stage he founded his own theater in Rome and took his own acting company on tours with his plays through Europe.

Piranesi, Giambattista (1720–1778). Italian architect, painter, and engraver. His copperplate engravings have become source material for the investigation of Louis XIV, Adam, and Empire styles of architecture.

Pirate, The. A novel by Sir Walter SCOTT (1822). The action takes place in the wild sea country of the Shetlands, and the chief characters are Minna and Brenda Troil, daughters of old Magnus Troil. Minna becomes infatuated with "the Pirate," Captain Clement Cleveland, a son of Basil Mertoun, who had sailed under the Jolly Roger himself but later repented. His other son, Mordaunt Mertoun, falls in love with Minna's sister Brenda and finally wins the reluctant consent of old Magnus to his suit. See also NORNA.

Pirates, the. In baseball parlance, the Pittsburgh Nationals. See BASEBALL TEAMS.

Pirates of Penzance. A well-known comic opera by GILBERT and SULLIVAN (1879), presenting the capers of a band of pirates, a bevy of girls, and a Major General.

Pirithous. King of the Lapithae in Thessaly, and friend of Theseus. He was the husband of Hippodamia, at whose wedding feast the Centaurs offered violence to the bride, thus causing a great battle.

Pisanio. In Shakespeare's CYMBELINE, servant of Posthumus. Sent to murder Imogen, the wife of Posthumus, he persuades her to escape to Milford Haven in boy's clothes, and sends a bloody napkin to Posthumus, to make him believe that she has been murdered.

Pisgah. The mountain from which Moses saw the Promised Land (*Deut.* iii. 27). See also NEBO.

Pisistratus (d. 527 B.C.). Tyrant of Athens. Presented the city with many splendid buildings. He was a patron of literature, and it was probably during his rule that dramatic contests were first introduced. According to Cicero and Pausanias, Pisistratus was instrumental in one phase of the Homeric literary tradition. The simple interpretation that this signified that "Pisistratus first committed the poems of Homer to writing and reduced them to the order in which we now read them" (F. A. Wolf, *Prolegomena*), is now generally discarded.

Piso's justice. Verbally right, but morally wrong. Seneca tells us that Piso condemned a man on circumstantial evidence for murder, but when the suspect was at the place of execution, the man supposed to have been murdered appeared. The centurion sent the prisoner to Piso, and explained the case to him, whereupon Piso condemned all three to death, saying *fiat justitia* (*Lat.*, "let justice be done"). The condemned man was executed because sentence of death had been passed upon him, the centurion because he had disobeyed orders, and the man supposed to have been murdered because he had been the cause of death to two innocent men, and *fiat justitia ruat coelum* ("let justice be done though the heavens should fall").

Pistol. An unprincipled bully who appears in Shakespeare's MERRY WIVES OF WINDSOR and the two parts of *Henry IV* as the ancient or ensign of Sir John FALSTAFF, and in *Henry V* as his lieutenant. Pistol is married to Mistress Nell Quickly, hostess of the tavern in Eastcheap.

Pit, The. A novel by Frank NORRIS (1903), dealing with the wheat market of Chicago. The hero is Curtis Jadwin, whose winning of Laura Dearborn and subsequent growing prosperity mark him as a successful man. He is ruined in the Pit, but his misfortune wins back for him the love and devotion of his wife. This book is the second of a proposed wheat trilogy. See also OCTOPUS.

Pit and the Pendulum. A famous tale by Edgar Allan POE (1843) concerning the horrors of the INQUISITION.

Pitcairn Island. A Polynesian island colonized by refugee mutineers from the H.M.S. BOUNTY, who were the ancestors of its present natives. Named after the British midshipman Robert Pitcairn (1747?–1770?) who first sighted the island (July 2, 1767) from *H.M.S. Swallow*.

pitchblende. A dark green mineral found in England, Europe, the U.S., and Canada; the chief source of radium and uranium. The word is adapted from German *Pechblende*.

Pitcher, Mollie. See MCCAULEY.

Pithecanthrope. The name given by HAECKEL in 1868 to the hypothetical "MISSING LINK"; from Gr. *pithekos*, "ape," and *anthropos*, "man." Later, *Pithecanthropus* was the generic name given to the remains of the extinct manlike ape discovered in the Pliocene of Java in 1891.

Pithom and Raamses. The treasure cities built for Pharaoh by the Israelites. (*Ex.* i. 11.)

Pitkin, Walter Boughton (1878–). American college professor and author of best-selling books on applied psychology and self-help. The best-known of these are *The Art of Rapid Reading* (1929); *The Psychology of Happiness* (1929); *Life Begins at Forty* (1932); *More Power to You* (1933); *Let's Get What We Want* (1935).

Pitman, Sir Isaac (1813–1897). English inventor of an original system of phonographic shorthand.

Pitt, William, see CHATHAM, LORD.

Pitter, Ruth (1897–). English poet, known for her treatment of conventional lyric subjects—love, death, nature, the English countryside—in intellectual, 20th-century adaptations of earlier models, and her use of forms and imagery which, critics point out, derive from the 17th-century English poets. Her metrical effects have been particularly praised. Her books, for which she was acclaimed as one of the outstanding women poets of her time, include *First Poems* (1920); *First and Second Poems* (1927); *Persephone in Hades* (1931); *A Mad Lady's Garland* (1934); *A Trophy of Arms* (1936); *The Rude Potato* (1941); *The Spirit Watches* (1940); *The Bridge* (1946).

Pitti Palace. Renaissance building in Florence, Italy, which contains one of the finest collections of paintings in the world. It takes its name from Luca Pitti, once head of the Florentine Republic, for whom it was designed (ca. 1440).

Pixie or **Pixy.** A sprite or fairy of folklore, especially in Cornwall and Devon, where some hold them to be the spirits of infants who have died before baptism. The Pixy monarch has his court like OBERON, and sends his subjects on their several tasks. The word is probably Celtic, but its history is unknown.

pixilated. Balmy, daffy. An American word, probably a corruption of *pixy-led*, "led astray by pixies." Popularized by R. Riskin's screen play *Mr. Deeds Goes to Town* (1936), based on a story by C. B. Kelland, but traceable as far back as 1848.

Pizarro. (1) Title and hero of a drama supposedly by Richard Brinsley SHERIDAN (1799). The hero, Francisco Pizarro (1470?–1541), was a Spanish adventurer who made war on Atahualpo (in the drama Ataliba), the Inca of Peru, conquered him (1532) and had him executed for his refusal to accept Christianity. The play was based on a previous drama by Kotzebue entitled *Spaniards in Peru*.

(2) In Beethoven's opera *Fidelio* (1791), the governor of the State prison in which Fernando Florestan is confined.

Placebo (*Lat.*, "I shall please," or "be acceptable"). Vespers for the dead; they are so called because in the old church services this was the opening word of the first antiphon—*Placebo Domino in regione vivorum* ("I will walk before the Lord in the land of the living") (*Ps.* cxvi. 9).

As sycophants and those who wanted to get something out of the relatives of the departed used to make a point of attending this service and singing the *Placebo*, the phrase *to sing Placebo* came to mean "to play the flatterer or sycophant"; and Chaucer, who in the *Merchant's Tale* gives this as a name to a parasite, has—

> Flatereres been the develes chapelleyns that singen evere *Placebo*.—*Parson's Tale*, § 40.

Place in the Sun. See under SUN.

Place-makers Bible. See BIBLE, SPECIALLY NAMED.

plagiarism. Literary or artistic theft. The appropriation of the literary or artistic work of someone else as one's own. Ultimately from Latin *plagium,* "kidnaping."

Plagiary, Sir Fretful. In Sheridan's comedy THE CRITIC, a playwright, whose dramas are mere plagiarisms from "the refuse of obscure volumes." He pretends to be rather pleased with criticism, but is in reality sorely irritated thereby.

Plagued by the Nightingale. A novel by Kay BOYLE (1930).

Plague Year, A Journal of the. A narrative by DEFOE (1722), purporting to be an eyewitness account by a resident of London of the Great Plague of 1664–1665. It is a work of imaginative genius founded on first-hand evidence.

Plain, the. The Girondists were so called in the French Revolutionary National Convention, because they sat on the level floor or plain of the hall. See MOUNTAIN.

Plain Dealer, The. A comedy by William WYCHERLEY (*c*1674). The titular hero is Captain MANLY.

Plain Language from Truthful James. A poem by Bret HARTE, better known as THE HEATHEN CHINEE.

Plain Tales from the Hills. A volume of short stories of life in India by Rudyard KIPLING, first published in Calcutta in 1888. It contains, among others, several stories about the famous trio, Ortheris, Learoyd and MULVANEY.

Planché, James Robinson (1796–1880). English playwright who gained a reputation for his knowledge of costume and heraldry. Produced plays for Mme VESTRIS. Author of works on British costume.

planetarium. A model of the solar system. In the Zeiss planetarium (first produced by the firm of Zeiss in Jena, Germany) the planets and stars are projected in motion onto the ceiling of a large auditorium. There are such Zeiss planetariums in New York City, Philadelphia, Chicago, Pittsburgh, etc.

planets. The heavenly bodies that revolve round the sun in approximately circular orbits; so called from *Gr.* (through *Lat.* and *O. Fr.*) *planasthai,* "to wander," because, to the ancients, they appeared to wander about among the stars instead of having fixed places.

The *primary planets* are Mercury, Venus, the Earth, Mars, Jupiter, Saturn, and Neptune; these are known as the *major planets,* the asteroids between the orbits of Mars and Jupiter being the *minor planets.*

The *secondary planets* are the satellites, or moons, revolving round a primary.

Mercury and Venus are called *inferior planets* because their orbits are nearer to the sun than the earth's; the remaining major planets are *superior planets.*

Only five of the planets were known to the ancients (the earth, of course, not being reckoned), viz., Mercury, Venus, Mars, Jupiter, and Saturn; to these were added the sun and the moon, making seven in all. Among the astrologers and alchemists—

THE SUN (APOLLO)	represented	Gold.
THE MOON (DIANA)	"	Silver.
MERCURY	"	Quicksilver.
VENUS	"	Copper.
MARS	"	Iron.
JUPITER	"	Tin.
SATURN	"	Lead.

In HERALDRY, the arms of royal personages used to be blazoned by the names of planets.

to be born under a lucky or unlucky planet. According to astrology, some planet, at the birth of every individual, presides over his destiny. Some of the planets, like Jupiter, are lucky; others, like Saturn, are unlucky. See HOUSES, ASTROLOGICAL.

Plantagenet (from *planta genista* "broom-plant"). The family cognizance first assumed by Geoffrey, Count of Anjou (d. 1151), during a pilgrimage to the Holy Land, as a symbol of humility. By his wife Matilda, daughter of Henry I of England, he was father of Henry II, the founder of the House of Plantagenet.

the House of Plantagenet. Henry II, and the English kings descended in the direct male line from him, viz.:

Henry II	Edward I
Richard I	Edward II
John	Edward III
Henry III	Richard II

They reigned from 1154 to 1399.

Plantagenet Palliser, see OMNIUM, DUKE OF.

Plantin, Christophe (1520?–1589). Famous French printer who established presses at Antwerp (1555) and later at Leyden and Paris.

Plastic Age, The. A realistic novel of college life by Percy MARKS (1924).

Plato, that is, the broad-shouldered one. Original name **Aristocles** (427?–347 B.C.). Famous Greek philosopher, disciple of SOCRATES and teacher of ARISTOTLE. He was the student and companion of Socrates until the latter's trial and death (399 B.C.). His work is in the form of dialogues in which Socrates interrogates others in his characteristic manner. The dialogues include *Republic* (probably the greatest work of Plato); *Laws; Symposium* (on ideal love, which has given rise to the expression "Platonic love"; see below); *Phaedrus,* etc. *Phaedo* (concerning the immortality of the soul) is supposed to be the last conversation of Socrates before his death.

the English Plato. The Rev. John Norris (1657–1711).

the German Plato. Friedrich Heinrich Jacobi (1743–1819).

the Jewish Plato. Philo Judaeus (*fl.* 20–40 A. D.).

the Puritan Plato. John Howe (1630–1706).

the Plato of the Eighteenth Century. Voltaire (1694–1778).

Plato's year. 25,000 Julian years, in the course of which the heavenly bodies pass through a complete cycle and return to their original positions.

> Cut out more work than can be done
> In Plato's year.
> S. Butler, *Hudibras,* iii. 1 (1678).

Platonic love. A popular term for spiritual love between persons of opposite sexes; the friendship of man and woman, without sexual implications. The phrase is founded on a misinterpretation of a passage towards the end of the *Symposium,* in which Plato is extolling not the non-sexual love of a man for a woman, but the loving interest that Socrates took in young men—which was pure, and therefore noteworthy in the Greece of the period.

Platt, Jim. In Edward Sheldon's play SALVATION NELL, Nell's lover.

Platt, Thomas Collier (1833–1910). American politician, of great influence in the Republican party machine in New York. Politically associated with Roscoe Conkling.

Plattsburg. A village on Lake Champlain in northern New York. Headquarters for the American frontier troops in the War of 1812, when the Battle of Lake Champlain took place. Plattsburg was the site of a training camp for officers during the first World War and was again used for military purposes during the second.

Plautus, Titus Maccius (ca. 254–184 B. C.). Roman comic dramatist, known for his numerous comedies, including *Amphitruo, Bacchides, Menaechmi, Mercator, Miles Gloriosus, Poenulus, Rudens,* etc. SHAKESPEARE, MOLIÈRE, and other English and European playwrights adapted his plays or modeled their own upon his. Little is known of his life, except that he settled in Rome, worked at a variety of menial occupations, and was very poor until finally recognized as a playwright.

Playboy of the Western World, The. A drama by J. M. SYNGE (1907). The Irish protagonist, Christie Mahon, gets his first taste of being a hero when he escapes from home to a distant village under the terrible conviction that he has killed his domineering old father. He is regarded with awe and women vie with one another for his love. But when his father turns up alive and beats him, his glory is gone. When he actually tries to kill the old man, the villagers turn him over to the police. Nevertheless, something has happened; he will never be the timid, shrinking farmer's boy again.

Players, The. A club in New York City founded by Edwin BOOTH (1888), who was president until his death (1893). Originally intended for actors and dramatists, its membership was extended to writers, painters, and sculptors. Its building was designed by Stanford White. Among its later presidents were Joseph Jefferson and John Drew.

Playfair, Sir Nigel (1874–1934). English actor and manager who produced John Drinkwater's *Abraham Lincoln* (1919) and *The Beggar's Opera* by John Gay (1920).

Plays for Puritans, Three. Plays (1901) by George Bernard SHAW collected in one volume. They are *The Devil's Disciple; Caesar and Cleopatra;* and *Captain Brassbound's Conversion.*

Plays, Pleasant and Unpleasant. Seven plays in two volumes by George Bernard SHAW (1898). The pleasant ones are: *Arms and the Man; Candida; The Man of Destiny;* and *You Never Can Tell.* The unpleasant ones are: *Widowers' Houses; The Philanderer;* and *Mrs. Warren's Profession.*

play upon words. See PARONOMASIA.

Playwrights' Company, The. An organization founded in 1938 for the production of plays by its members: S. N. Behrman, Elmer Rice, Robert E. Sherwood, Maxwell Anderson, and Sidney Howard. When Sidney Howard died (1939), the Company established in his honor a memorial award of $1500 annually for the best first play by an American author to be produced in New York. (See under names of members.)

plebiscite. In Roman history, a law enacted by the "comitia" or assembly of tribes; in modern political terminology, the direct vote of the whole body of citizens of a nation on a question phrased in definite terms.

Pleiades. The cluster of stars in the constellation Taurus, especially the seven larger ones out of the great number that compose the cluster; so called by the Greeks, possibly from Gr. *plein,* "to sail," because they considered navigation safe at the return of the Pleiades, and never attempted it after those stars disappeared.

In Greek myth, the *Pleiades* were the seven daughters of Atlas and Pleione. They were transformed into stars, one of which, ELECTRA, is invisible, some said out of shame, because she alone married a human being, while others held that she hides herself from grief over the destruction of the city and royal race of Troy. She is known as "the lost Pleiad."

The name *The Pleiad* has frequently been

given to groups of seven specially illustrious persons, *e.g.*:

(1) The SEVEN WISE MEN OF GREECE, sometimes called the *Philosophical Pleiad*.

(2) *The Pleiad of Alexandria.* A group of seven poets in the 3rd century B. C., viz., Callimachus, Apollonius of Rhodes, Aratus, Philiscus (called *Homer the Younger*), Lycophron, Nicander, and Theocritus.

(3) *Charlemagne's Pleiad.* The group of scholars with which the Emperor surrounded himself, viz., Charlemagne (who, in this circle, was known as David), Alcuin (Albinus), Adelard (Augustine), Angilbert (Homer), Riculfe (Damaeas) Varnefrid, and Eginhard.

(4) *The French Pleiad* (or *Pléiade*) of the 16th century, who wrote poetry in the meters, style, etc., of the ancient Greeks and Romans, and put into practice the principles enunciated in the DÉFENSE ET ILLUSTRATION DE LA LANGUE FRANÇAISE. Of these, RONSARD was the leader, the others being Dorat, Joachim du BELLAY, Remi-Belleau, Jodelle, Baïf, and Ponthus de Thyard.

(5) *The second French Pleiad.* Seven contemporary poets in the reign of Louis XIII, very inferior to the "first Pleiad." They are Rapin, Commire, Larue, Santeuil, Ménage, Dupérier, and Petit.

plein-air (*Fr.*, literally "full-air"). Pertaining to a school of painting started in France (ca. 1865), when certain painters left the falsified light of the studio to paint in the open air. Pissarro, Monet, Renoir, Sisley, later Cézanne, and Manet, started "the invasion of painting by color," outdoor light, the sun's illumination and the tangled reflections in nature, the play of sun and colored shadow.

Pleydell, Mr. Paulus. In Scott's GUY MANNERING, an advocate in Edinburgh, shrewd and witty. He was at one time the sheriff at Ellangowan.

Mr. counsellor Pleydell was a lively, sharp-looking gentleman, with a professional shrewdness in his eye, and, generally speaking, a professional formality in his manner; but this he could slip off on a Saturday evening, when . . . he joined in the ancient pastime of High Jinks.—Sir W. Scott, *Guy Mannering*, xxxix.

Pleydon. A sculptor in Hergesheimer's LINDA CONDON.

Pliable. In Bunyan's PILGRIM'S PROGRESS, one of Christian's neighbors, who accompanies him as far as the Slough of Despond and then turns back.

Pliant, Sir Paul. In Congreve's DOUBLE DEALER (1694), a hen-pecked husband, who dares not even touch a letter addressed to himself till his lady has read it first.

Plimsoll or **Plimsoll's line** or **mark.** The load-line mark painted on the sides of British merchant ships. It indicates how deeply the vessel may be submerged by loading. The name comes from Samuel Plimsoll (1824–1898), who secured an Act of Parliament (1876) to prevent overloading.

Pliny the Elder. In full, **Caius Plinius Secundus** (23–79 A. D.). Latin author, known for his *Historia Naturalis* (*Natural History*), which was regarded as a scientific sourcebook during the Middle Ages. He was one of those who were killed when the city of POMPEII was destroyed.

Pliny the Younger. In full, **Caius Plinius Caecilius Secundus** (b. 61 A. D.), the Elder's nephew, wrote a number of letters to the Emperor Trajan which have been found of value for a picture of the times in which they both lived.

Plomer, William Charles F. (1903–). South African novelist and trader in Zululand. Wrote a biography of Cecil Rhodes.

Plotinus (205?–270 A. D.). See under NEO-PLATONISM.

Plornish, Thomas. In Dickens' LITTLE DORRIT, a plasterer of Bleeding-Heart Yard. He is a smooth-cheeked, fresh-colored, sandy-whiskered man of thirty, long in the legs, yielding at the knees, foolish in the face, flannel-jacketed and lime-whitened. He generally joins in a conversation by echoing the words of the person speaking.

Mrs. Plornish. The plasterer's wife, a young woman, somewhat slatternly in herself and her belongings, and dragged by care and poverty already into wrinkles. She generally begins her sentences with, "Well, not to deceive you."

Ploughboy, Jonathan. A popular Yankee character of the early American stage, one of several such rôles made famous through the acting of James H. HACKETT. Jonathan Ploughboy owed much to the shrewd, homely character of Jonathan (see BROTHER JONATHAN) in Royall Tyler's previous drama THE CONTRAST, but provided much more uproarious fun than that sober-minded citizen. As the center of interest in Woodworth's *Forest Rose* (*Am.*, 1825), a comedy with the subtitle *American Farmers,* he delighted theater-goers for over forty years.

Plowden. *"The case is altered," quoth Plowden.* There is more than one story given by way of accounting for the origin of this old phrase—used by Ben JONSON as the title of one of his comedies (1598). One of them says that Plowden was an unpopular priest, and that he was inveigled by an enemy into attending mass performed by a layman. When impeached for so doing, the cunning priest asked the layman if it was he who officiated. "Yes," said the man. "And are you a priest?" said Plowden. "No," said the man. "Then," said

Plowden, turning to the tribunal, *"the case is altered,* for it is an axiom with the Church, 'No priest, no mass.'"

Another story fathers the phrase on Edmund Plowden (1518–1585), the great lawyer. He was asked what legal remedy there was against some hogs that had trespassed on complainant's ground. "There is very good remedy," began Plowden, but when told that they were his own hogs, said, *"Nay, then, the case is altered."*

Plowman, Piers, see PIERS PLOWMAN.

Plugson of Undershot. Thomas CARLYLE'S typical commercial radical, who in the middle of the 19th century finds that no decent Tory will shake hands with him, but at the close of the century shares a free-competition company with latter-day Tories.

Plumb, Glenn Edward (1866–1922). American lawyer who devised a plan, known as the Plumb Plan, for government ownership of railroads (1919). The plan drew the endorsement of groups of railroad employers, of the American Federation of Labor, and of the Nonpartisan League. It was the subject of debate in Congress, but no practical results were achieved.

Plumed Knight, The. A name given to James G. BLAINE by Robert Ingersoll in the Republican campaign at Cincinnati in 1876.

Plummer, Caleb. In Dickens' CRICKET ON THE HEARTH, a little old toy-maker in the employ of Gruff and Tackleton, toy merchants. He is spare, gray-haired, and very poor. It is his pride "to go as close to Natur' in his toys as he could for the money." Caleb Plummer has a blind daughter, who assists him in toymaking and whom he has brought up in the belief that he himself is young, handsome, and well off, and that the house they live in is sumptuously furnished and quite magnificent.

Bertha Plummer. The blind daughter of the toy-maker. She is in love with Tackleton, the toy merchant, whom she thinks to be a handsome young prince. When she hears that he is about to marry May FIELDING, she falls ill. She is then disillusioned, hears the real facts, and becomes reconciled to the situation.

Edward Plummer. Son of the toy-maker, and brother of the blind girl. He is engaged from boyhood to May Fielding, goes to South America, and returns to marry her. Hearing of her engagement to Tackleton the toy merchant, he assumes the disguise of a deaf old man, to ascertain whether she loves Tackleton or not. In due course of time he marries her himself.

Plunkett. A leading character in Flotow's opera MARTHA.

Plunkett, Joseph Mary (1887–1916). Irish poet and patriot of an old Catholic family. The only collection of his poems published in his lifetime is *The Circle and the Sword* (1911), a book full of Catholic mysticism. After the Easter Rebellion he was shot by a British firing squad at Dublin Castle with his fellow poets Padraic PEARSE and Thomas MACDONAGH.

Plutarch (fl. ca. 66 A. D.). Greek author of forty-six *Parallel Lives* of Greeks and Romans of antiquity. In their classical stylization they are "character studies admirable in their distinctive medium as are the statues of Greek and Roman sculptors."

Pluto. In Roman mythology, the ruler of the infernal regions, son of Saturn, brother of Jupiter and Neptune, and husband of PROSERPINA; hence, the grave, the place where the dead go before they are admitted into Elysium or sent to Tartarus.

plutocrat. One who has influence and power because of his wealth. Plutocracy is government by the wealthy.

Plutus. In Greek mythology, the god of riches. Hence the phrase *rich as Plutus,* and the term *plutocrat,* one who exercises influence or possesses power through his wealth. The legend is that he was blinded by Zeus so that his gifts should be equally distributed and not go only to those who merited them.

Plymouth Rock. The ledge in the harbor of Plymouth, Massachusetts, where the Puritans were first supposed to have landed. As a matter of fact, they landed on Cape Cod at Provincetown (1620).

PM. A tabloid newspaper published daily in New York City, founded in 1940 under the editorship of Ralph INGERSOLL. It was characterized by a departmentalized presentation of the news, a wide use of photographs and illustrations, and a politically liberal, pro-labor editorial policy. Purchased (1945) by Marshall Field. The name was suggested by Lillian HELLMAN, the dramatist. Resold (1948) to Bartley Crum and Joseph S. Barnes, who changed its name to *The New York Star.*

Pocahontas (1595–1617). Daughter of Powhatan, an Indian chief of Virginia. She is said to have rescued Captain John Smith when her father was on the point of killing him. She subsequently married John Rolfe, one of the settlers at Jamestown, was baptized under the name of Rebecca, and in 1616 was brought to England, where she became an object of curiosity and frequent allusion in contemporary literature.

Pocahontas was the subject of a number of dramas, of which the most noteworthy are Barker's *Indian Princess, Or La Belle Sauvage* (*Am.,* 1808); *Pocahontas, Or the Settlers of Virginia,* by G. W. P. Curtis (*Am.,* 1830); *Pocahontas,* by R. D. Owen (*Eng.,* 1838); *The Forest Princess,* by Mrs. C. B. Conner (*Am.,*

1848); and finally a burlesque, *Pocahontas, Or the Gentle Savage,* by John Brougham (*Am.,* 1855).

pocket.

pocket borough. A borough where the influence of the magnate is so powerful as to be able to control the election of any candidate he may choose to support.

pocket veto. A veto by the President of the United States which works automatically if he does not return a bill during session of Congress.

Pocket, Herbert. A cheerful young fellow, friend of Pip in GREAT EXPECTATIONS, by Charles Dickens.

Podsnap. A pompous, self-satisfied man in Dickens' OUR MUTUAL FRIEND, the type of one who is extremely proud of the patronage of his rich acquaintances and is overburdened with stiff-starched etiquette and self-importance. Hence the noun *Podsnappery.*

He always knew exactly what Providence meant. Inferior and less respectable men might fall short of that mark, but Mr. Podsnap was always up to it. And it was very remarkable (and must have been very comfortable) that what Providence meant was invariably what Mr. Podsnap meant.—*Our Mutual Friend,* Bk. I, Ch. ii.

Mrs. Podsnap. "A fine woman for Professor Owen: quantity of bone, neck and nostrils like a rocking-horse, hard features, and majestic head-dress in which Podsnap has hung golden offerings."

Georgiana Podsnap. Daughter of the above, called by her father "the young person." She is a harmless, inoffensive girl, "always trying to hide her elbows."

Poe, Edgar Allan (1809–1849). American poet, critic, and short-story writer, considered one of the most important American authors of the 19th century. His short stories, in which he is said to have been influenced by Charles Brockden BROWN and for which he came to be best known, deal chiefly with mystery, horror, and crime in the tradition of the GOTHIC NOVEL; they are considered to be important forerunners of the typical detective story of the 20th century. His criticism, written under the influence of S. T. COLERIDGE, contains some of the first statements of the literary principles included under the heading of "ART FOR ART'S SAKE." His poetry, in which the influence of TENNYSON has been found, is marked by metrical experiment, pervasive romantic "atmosphere," and occasionally striking and complex imagery not common at the time it was written. Among Poe's works are *Tamerlane* (1827); *Al Aaraaf* (1829); *Poems* (1831); POLITIAN (1837), an unfinished tragedy; *The Narrative of Arthur Gordon Pym* (1838), a novelette; *Tales of the Grotesque and Arabesque* (1840); *Tales* (1845); *The Raven, And Other Poems* (1845); *Eureka* (1848), a poem on metaphysics. His best-known single poems include THE RAVEN, ANNABEL LEE, *To Helen, Israfel, Ulalume, The Bells.* Well-known single tales are THE GOLD BUG, THE BALLOON HOAX, *The Fall of the House of Usher* (see USHER), THE PIT AND THE PENDULUM, *The Murders in the Rue Morgue, MS. Found in a Bottle, The Masque of the Red Death, The Black Cat, The Purloined Letter, The Cask of Amontillado.* THE PHILOSOPHY OF COMPOSITION and THE POETIC PRINCIPLE are his outstanding works of criticism.

Poe did editorial work and hack-writing for a number of newspapers and magazines in Richmond, Baltimore, Philadelphia, and New York, attracting attention through his stories and engaging in critical quarrels with contemporary writers, notably LONGFELLOW, whom he charged with plagiarism. Throughout his career he was erratic and morbid in temperament, a natural tendency to instability being aggravated by poverty and unhappiness in his personal affairs. He died in Baltimore after having been picked up in drunken delirium outside a polling-place, in which it is believed he had served as a repeating voter.

As an artist, Poe came to be regarded more highly abroad than in his own country. His influence appears in the work of ROSSETTI, SWINBURNE, DOWSON, Ambrose BIERCE, Hart CRANE, and, especially, the poets of the French school of SYMBOLISM. BAUDELAIRE introduced Poe's work into France and started a vogue for it. MALLARMÉ made some masterful translations.

poems of chance (*Fr.* **poèmes de chance**). In DADAISM, a type of poetry composed by writing down without alteration the illogical, chance associations of words as they occurred, free of the more conventional limitations of rational and artistic thought processes.

poet (from Gr. *poieo,* "to make"). See also BARD.

Poet of France. Pierre Ronsard (1525–1585).

Poet of Greta Hall. Robert Southey (1774–1843).

Poet of Haslemere. Alfred Lord Tennyson, Poet Laureate (1809–1892).

poet of the poor. Rev. George Crabbe (1754–1832).

prince of poets. Edmund Spenser (1552–1599) is so called on his monument in Westminster Abbey.

prince of Spanish poets. Garcilaso de la Vega (1503–1536) is frequently so called by Cervantes.

Poet's Corner. The southern end of the south transept of Westminster Abbey, said to have been first so called by Oliver GOLDSMITH because it contained the tomb of CHAUCER.

ADDISON had previously (*Spectator,* No. 26, 1711) alluded to it as the "poetical Quarter," in which, he says,

I found there were Poets who had no Monuments, and Monuments which had no Poets.

Besides Chaucer's tomb, it contains that of Spenser, and either the tombs of or monuments to Drayton, Ben Jonson, Shakespeare (a statue), Milton (bust), Samuel Butler, Davenant, Cowley, Prior, Gay, Addison, Thomson, Goldsmith, Dryden, Dr. Johnson, Sheridan, Burns, Southey, Coleridge, Campbell, Macaulay, Longfellow, Dickens, Thackeray, Tennyson, and Browning.

The term *Poet's Corner* is also facetiously applied to the part of a newspaper in which poetical contributions are printed.

Poet Laureate. In England, a court official, appointed by the Prime Minister, whose duty it is (or *was*) to compose odes in honor of the sovereign's birthday and in celebration of State occasions of importance, in return for £200 a year and a butt of sack.

The first Poet Laureate officially recognized as such was Ben Jonson, but in earlier times there had been an occasional *Versificator Regis,* and Chaucer, Skelton, Spenser, and Daniel were called "Laureates" though not appointed to that office. The following is the complete list of Poets Laureate:

Ben Jonson, 1619–1637.
Sir William Davenant, 1660–1668.
John Dryden, 16·0–1688.
Thomas Shadwell, 1688–1692.
Nahum Tate, 1692–1715.
Nicholas Rowe, 1715–1718.
Laurence Eusden, 1718–1730.
Colley Cibber, 1730–1757.
William Whitehead, 1757–1785.
Thomas Warton, 1785–1790.
Henry James Pye, 1790–1813.
Robert Southey, 1813–1843.
William Wordsworth, 1843–1850.
Alfred Tennyson, 1850–1892.
Alfred Austin, 1896–1913.
Robert Bridges, 1913–1930.
John Masefield, 1930–

The term arose from the ancient custom in the universities of presenting a laurel wreath to graduates in rhetoric and poetry. There were at one time "doctors laureate," "bachelors laureate," etc.; in France, in modern times, authors of distinction continued "crowned" by the Academy.

Poetaster, The, or His Arraignment. A satirical comedy by Ben JONSON (acted 1601; published 1602). It was an attack upon DEKKER and MARSTON, with whom Johnson collaborated, however, later on (1603 and 1604).

Poetical Miscellanies. See TOTTEL'S MISCELLANY.

poetic license. A phrase denoting the liberties which it is generally considered allowable for a poet to take with his subject-matter, grammatical construction, etc., in order to conform to the exigencies of rhyme and meter. The phrase is frequently used in humorous fashion to account for many vagaries of poets.

Poetic Principle, The. A lecture by Edgar Allan POE, delivered in 1848–1849 and published in 1850. It favors the short poem over the long, proclaims the primacy of beauty in poetry, condemns the didactic, and pleads for "the poem written solely for the poem's sake." See also ART FOR ART'S SAKE; PHILOSOPHY OF COMPOSITION, THE.

poetics. A treatise on poetry and its theory as an art. Aristotle's *Poetics* analyzes poetic and dramatic laws, defines comedy and tragedy, discusses the laws of composition in a drama and the three UNITIES of time, place, and action. Its principles were more literally adhered to in French than in English poetry.

Poetry: A Magazine of Verse. A monthly magazine devoted to the publication of poetry, founded in 1912 under the editorship of Harriet MONROE, one of the first and most influential of the LITTLE MAGAZINES in the U.S. It published, and often introduced, the work of the leading American and English poets of its time, among them being Vachel LINDSAY, Carl SANDBURG, Amy LOWELL, Ezra POUND, T. S. ELIOT, and Hart CRANE. Pound was for a while the magazine's foreign correspondent.

Pogány, Willy (1882–). Hungarian-born American artist, illustrator, mural painter, stage and costume designer, and moving-picture art director. He has illustrated children's books by Padraic COLUM; *Tales from the Arabian Nights; Gulliver's Travels;* etc.

Poggio Bracciolini, Gian Francesco (1380–1459). Italian humanist, one of the first to uncover and study ancient Latin manuscripts.

Pogner, Eva. The heroine of Wagner's opera DIE MEISTERSINGER.

Pogram, Elijah. In Dickens' DAVID COPPERFIELD, one of the "master minds" of America, and a member of Congress. He is possessed with the idea that there is a settled opposition in the British mind against the institutions of his "free, enlightened country."

pogrom (from Russ. *gromit,* "to thunder, to destroy unmercifully"). An organized massacre, especially those directed against the Jews in Russia in 1905 and later in Poland.

Poictesme. An imaginary country of medieval Europe which is the scene of many of the romances of James Branch CABELL, notably JURGEN, FIGURES OF EARTH, and DOMNEI. In THE CREAM OF THE JEST, the scene is laid partly in a Virginia town and partly in Poictesme. Carl VAN DOREN says of Poictesme:

The Poictesme, which James Branch Cabell has created and gradually populated with a whole dynasty, and its subjects, friends and enemies, lies somewhere on the map of Europe—just where, there are no precise geographers to say. The country was a fief of the wicked King Ferdinand of Castile and Leon, who beheaded his old friend, the rightful count, to make a place for Manuel. At that time, which was 1234, Poictesme was in the hands of the Northmen under Duke Asmund, later expelled. Not too far from Provence, neither was it too far from Albania, both of which Manuel visited on his way to claim his new possession. It had a sea-coast, the cities of Bellegarde and Storisende, in which Manuel ordinarily lived, and many dark woods and twilight heaths and haunted mountains. It engaged in diplomatic relations with France and England, to say nothing of less formal contacts between its rulers and all the countries, real or imagined, of the medieval universe. . . . Though it seems to have seen its great days in the thirteenth century, it was still prosperous as late as the eighteenth. Nothing, indeed, in the matter of geography or history is impossible to Poictesme, for it is, of course, a pure creation.—*Two Heroes of Poictesme* (*Century*, Nov., 1924).

poilu. The popular name for the French private soldier, like the British "Tommy Atkins." It sprang into use during World War I, and means literally "hairy," but had been used much earlier by BALZAC in the sense of "brave."

Poincaré, Raymond (1860–1934). French statesman and writer. Prime minister (1912–1913); president (1913–1920). Strengthened French defenses. Served through World War I. Again prime minister (1922–1924; 1926–1929) and minister of finance (1926–1929). Member of French Academy (1909).

Poins. In Shakespeare's 1 and 2 *Henry IV*, a companion of Sir John FALSTAFF.

Point Counter Point. The best-known novel of Aldous HUXLEY, published in 1928. With sardonic, biting wit and merciless satire, it presents a picture of the lives of British upperclass society and London intellectuals during the 1920's. Frequent allusions to literature, painting, music, and contemporary British politics occur throughout the book, and much scientific information is embodied in its background. The leading characters are as follows: Walter and John BIDLAKE, Marjorie CARLING, Denis BURLAP, Beatrice GILRAY, Philip and Elinor QUARLES, Frank ILLIDGE, Mark and Mary RAMPION, SPANDRELL, Lord Edward TANTAMOUNT, Hilda and Lucy Tantamount, Everard WEBLEY. Several of the characters are considered to represent well-known literary personalities of Huxley's day.

Pointillism, see under SEURAT.

point system. In printers' parlance. See under EM.

Poirier, M. In *Le Gendre de M. Poirier* (*The Son-in-Law of M. Poirier*), a comedy by Emile Augier and Jules Sandeau (*Fr.,* 1855), a Parisian bourgeois who makes a fortune and buys a title for his daughter Antoinette. His dissipated son-in-law, the Marquis de Presles, begins by being extremely scornful of his plebeian wife, but to his own surprise falls in love with her and reforms for her sake.

poisson d'avril (*Fr.,* "April fish"). The French equivalent for our "APRIL FOOL."

Polanyetski, Pan Stanislas. The hero of Sienkiewicz' CHILDREN OF THE SOIL.

Pole, Reginald (1500–1558). English Roman Catholic prelate. Friend of Sir Thomas MORE; opposed the divorce of Henry VIII. Archbishop of Canterbury (from 1556) during the reign of Queen Mary, and largely responsible for the persecutions of Protestants.

Polichinelle. French equivalent of the Italian PUNCHINELLO. A *secret of Polichinelle* is a secret known to everybody.

Polish. For the *Polish Byron, the Polish Franklin,* etc., see under BYRON, FRANKLIN, etc.

Politburo. The controlling body of the Russian Communist party and its foreign propaganda.

Politian: A Tragedy. An unfinished drama in blank verse by Edgar Allan Poe, parts of which were published in *The Southern Literary Messenger* (1835–1836).

Politian. See POLIZIANO.

Poliziano, Angelo (1454–1494). Italian poet and humanist, a member of the Florentine Academy established by the MEDICI family for the study of philosophy. He translated Latin poetry and wrote poetry in Latin and Italian. In English he was known as POLITIAN. Cf. FICINO, MARSILIO; PICO DELLA MIRANDOLA.

Polixene. In Molière's PRÉCIEUSES RIDICULES, the name assumed by Madelon Gorgibus, a shopkeeper's daughter, as far more romantic and genteel than her baptismal name.

Polixenes. Father of FLORIZEL and King of Bohemia in Shakespeare's WINTER'S TALE.

Pollaiuolo, Antonio (1429–1498). Florentine painter, sculptor, and goldsmith. A protégé of the Medicis. His brother, **Pierro Pollaiuolo** (1443–1496), collaborated with him in his painting.

Pollard, Albert Frederick (1869–). English historian; principally known for his work on the early Tudor period, including a life of Thomas CRANMER (1904) and one of Cardinal Wolsey (1929).

Pollente. In Spenser's FAËRIE QUEENE (V. ii), the puissant Saracen, father of Munera, who takes his station on "Bridge Perilous," and attacks everyone who crosses it, bestowing the spoil upon his daughter. He is slain by Sir ARTEGAL. He is supposed to typify Charles IX of France, notorious for the slaughter of Protestants on St. Bartholomew's Eve.

Pollexfen, Sir Hargrave. In Richardson's SIR CHARLES GRANDISON, the villain who attempts to carry off Harriet Byron.

pollice verso (*Lat.,* literally "with turned thumb"). At the gladiatorial games in ancient Rome, the general public condemned a participating gladiator to death by holding out their hands with the thumbs turned down;

hence our phrases, "thumbs down" and, correspondingly, "thumbs up." The newspaper *PM,* in its dramatic criticism, once showed a small drawing of a hand with the thumb turned up or down to denote approval or disapproval of a play.

Pollio, Gaius Asinius (75 B. C.–5 A. D.). Roman soldier and politician, who constructed the first public library in Rome and was a patron of literature. Author of plays and prose works. Only fragments of his orations are extant. To him the poet Virgil addressed his fourth eclogue.

Pollock, Channing (1880–1946). American playwright. He dramatized *The Pit* by Frank NORRIS, in which Wilton LACKAYE was the star. He also wrote one-act plays, essays, novels, and several popular songs, including *My Man* for Fannie BRICE. *The Sign on the Door* (1919) and *The Fool* (1922) were his most successful plays. *Harvest of My Years; an Autobiography* (1943).

Pollock, Sir **Frederick** (1845–1937). Professor of jurisprudence at Oxford University (1883–1903). Many publications on legal subjects. With F. W. Maitland, author of *History of English Law Before the Time of Edward I* (1895). His early work, *Spinoza, his Life and Philosophy* (1880), continues to be praised. Carried on a notable correspondence with Justice Oliver Wendell HOLMES.

Poll Pineapple. The "BUMBOAT WOMAN" of Gilbert's *Bab Ballads.*

Pollux. In classical mythology, the twin brother of CASTOR.

Polly. A ballad-opera by John Gay (published 1729), a sequel to THE BEGGAR'S OPERA. It was not performed till 1777, and then only in an adaptation by Colman the elder, because of government resentment at Gay's satire.

Polly, Aunt. In Mark Twain's TOM SAWYER, Tom's conventional and over-zealous aunt.

Polly, Mr., see MR. POLLY.

Pollyanna. The child heroine of a popular story by that name by Eleanor H. Porter (1868–1920), followed by numerous sequels. As an expert in her favorite "Glad Game" of looking on the bright side of her numerous trials, Pollyanna is a close second to Voltaire's Dr. Pangloss, who believed that "All is for the best in this best of all possible worlds." The name *Pollyanna* became a synonym for a fatuous optimist who makes a business of "making the best of things" for himself and other people.

Polo, Marco (1254?–?1324). Venetian traveler and adventurer. Famous for his journeys through Asia where he traveled as member of the diplomatic staff of Kublai Khan (from 1275). Dictated (1298) an account of his travels, published as *The Book of Marco Polo.* In 1921, Donn BYRNE made him the hero of a romance, MESSER MARCO POLO, dealing with his prolonged adventures at the court of China.

polonium. An element discovered by Mme CURIE in 1898. Named from Poland, Mme Curie's native country. Symbol *Po.* It is also known as *radium F.* It has come into popular notice as a factor in the construction of the atomic bomb.

Polonius. A garrulous old courtier in Shakespeare's HAMLET, typical of the pompous, sententious old man. He is the father of Ophelia, and Lord Chamberlain to the King of Denmark.

poltergeist. From German; literally, "noisy spirit." A violent and mischievous spirit who is responsible for the odd noises one hears in some houses at night, who breaks crockery, and is generally fond of playing practical jokes.

polyandry. That form of polygamy in which the woman enjoys the privilege of a plurality of mates. Contrasted with polygyny. Polyandry is on the whole a practice indicative of a primitive state of civilization. See also ONEIDA.

Polybius (204?–?125 B. C.). Greek historian. Author of a history of Rome from the beginnings of the Punic Wars to the destruction of Carthage (266–146 B. C.) in 40 books, of which five have come down to us.

Polycletus. A sculptor of Sicyon, of the late 5th century B. C., who deduced a canon of the proportions of the several parts of the human body, and made a statue of a Persian bodyguard which was admitted by all to be a model of the human form and was called "The Rule" (the standard).

Polyclites. See under DORYPHORUS.

Polycrates. Tyrant of Samos, so fortunate in all things that AMASIS, King of Egypt, advised him to vary his pleasures by relinquishing something he greatly prized. Whereupon Polycrates threw into the sea a beautiful seal, the most valuable of his jewels. A few days afterwards a fine fish was sent him as a present, and in its belly was found the jewel. Amasis, alarmed at this good fortune, broke off his alliance, declaring that sooner or later this good fortune would fail. Not long afterwards Polycrates was shamefully put to death by Oroetes, who had invited him to his court. On this tale is based SCHILLER's ballad, *The Ring of Polycrates.*

Polydamas. A Grecian athlete of immense size and strength. He killed a fierce lion without weapons, stopped a chariot in full career, lifted a mad bull, and died at last in attempting to stop a falling rock. See also MILO.

Polydore. The name assumed by Guiderius, in Shakespeare's CYMBELINE. See also POLYDORUS.

Polydorus or **Polydore.** In classic myth, the youngest son of Priam and Hecuba. According to HOMER (*Iliad,* xx. 470), he was killed by ACHILLES, but other legends state that he was committed to the care of Polymnestor, King of Thrace, who treacherously slew him.

Polyeucte. A drama by Pierre CORNEILLE (ca. 1641). It deals with the Christian martyr Polyeuctus and his Roman wife, who heeds her duty to her husband, becomes a convert to his religion, and wins others to his belief.

polygamy. The primitive practice of having several wives (polygyny) or husbands (polyandry).

Polyglot Bible. See *Complutensian Polyglot* under BIBLE, SPECIALLY NAMED.

Polyhymnia. The Muse of lyric poetry, and inventor of the lyre. See MUSES.

Polyidus. The soothsayer who advised Bellerophon to procure the horse Pegasus for his conflict with the Chimaera.

Polynices. In classic myth, the brother of Eteocles and joint heir with him to the throne of Thebes after their father Oedipus' exile. The celebrated "Seven against Thebes" expedition was launched by him to force his brother to yield the crown to him. See under THEBES.

Polyolbion. A long poem by Michael DRAYTON (1612, 1622), a topographical description of England interspersed with many legends of early Britain.

Polyphemus. In classic myth, one of the Cyclops, an enormous giant, with only one eye, and that in the middle of his forehead, who lived in Sicily. When ULYSSES landed on the island, this monster made him and twelve of his crew captives; six of them he ate, and then Ulysses contrived to blind him, and escape with the rest of the crew. Polyphemus was in love with Galatea, a sea-nymph who had set her heart on the shepherd Acis; Polyphemus, in a fit of jealousy, crushed him beneath a rock.

the Polyphemus of literature. Dr. Samuel Johnson (1709–1784) has been so called.

polyphonic prose. A type of FREE VERSE resembling prose in its thought sequence and published as a prose passage. Its use is outstanding in the poetry of Amy LOWELL.

polyrhythmic verse. A type of free verse, characterized by a variety of not necessarily integrated rhythms.

Polyxena. In classic myth, a daughter of PRIAM and Hecuba. The early poets say little about her, but according to later legends she is the heroine of a tragic love affair with ACHILLES, the Greek hero.

pomander. A perforated box, often in the shape of an apple, containing a mixture of perfumes expected to guard the bearer against infection. Also, the perfume mixture itself. E. NESBIT gave the title *A Pomander of Verse* to one of her books.

Pombodita. A land of incredible happenings.

pomegranate seed. See PROSERPINE.

Pomes Penyeach. A collection of lyric poems by James JOYCE published in 1927.

Pomona. (1) In Roman mythology, the goddess of fruit trees. She was wooed and won by VERTUMNUS, god of the seasons.

(2) The entertaining servant-maid heroine of F. R. Stockton's novels RUDDER GRANGE, *The Rudder Grangers Abroad* and *Pomona's Travels.*

Pompadour, Marquise de. Jeanne Antoinette Poisson (1721–1764). Mistress of Louis XV. Established as Versailles (1745) and given the estate of Pompadour. Had great influence over the king, especially in internal affairs (1745–1764). Opposed RICHELIEU's foreign policy and was instrumental in bringing on the Seven Years' War which ended in disaster for France.

Pompeii, The Last Days of, see LAST DAYS etc.

Pompey the Great. *Lat.* **Gnaeus Pompeius Magnus** (106–48 B.C.). Roman general and statesman. Organized the First Triumvirate (60) with Julius Caesar and Crassus. Became the champion of the Conservative party. The civil war he instigated led to his decisive defeat in Pharsalus (48) and to his subsequent flight to Egypt where Ptolemy had him murdered. The earliest English tragedy based on the story of Pompey is *Pompey the Great, his faire Corneliaes Tragedy,* a translation into blank verse by Thomas KYD from the French of Garnier. Cf. also *Five Men and Pompey,* the first book of poems by Stephen Vincent BENÉT; also, *Pompey the Great* by John MASEFIELD.

Pompilia. Heroine of Browning's RING AND THE BOOK.

Ponce de León, Juan (1460?–1521). A Spanish explorer, famed for his search for the Fountain of Youth, which, as its name implies, would make those who drank of it young again. His explorations were largely in the vicinity of Florida, where he has left many traces of his name. Most legends located the Fountain of Youth on the island of BIMINI.

Ponce de León, Fray **Luis** (1527–1591). Spanish Augustinian monk, celebrated as a mystic poet. Cf. his life by James Fitzmaurice-Kelly (1921).

Pond, James Burton (1838–1903). American lecture manager. Under his management were Henry Ward Beecher, Mark Twain, Sir Arthur Conan Doyle, Henry M. Stanley, Matthew Arnold, and other well-known literary personages of his day.

Ponderevo, George. The hero of H. G. Wells' TONO-BUNGAY.

ponent wind. The west wind or wind from the sunset. *Levant* is the east wind, or wind from the sunrise.

Pons, Lily (1904–). French operatic coloratura soprano. In U.S. (from 1928). Married to André Kostelanetz, a well-known orchestra leader. Principal rôles are Lakmé, Lucia, Philine.

Pons, Sylvain. Hero of Balzac's COUSIN PONS (*Le Cousin Pons;* 1847), a musical composer and collector of works of art, on which he squanders his substance. He is ugly, lonely, and not over-successful; as he grows older, he becomes a glutton and social parasite. His greatest source of satisfaction is his friendship for the pianist Schmucke, whom he makes his residuary heir.

Pons Asinorum (*Lat.,* "the asses' bridge"). The fifth proposition, Bk. I, of Euclid—the first difficult theorem, which dunces rarely get over without stumbling.

Pontiac (died 1769). American Ottawa Indian chief who led an attack upon the British known as "the Conspiracy of Pontiac." Cf. *History of the Conspiracy of Pontiac* (1851) by Francis PARKMAN.

Pontifex, Ernest. The hero of Samuel Butler's WAY OF ALL FLESH. His father, Theobald, and mother, Christina, are also prominent characters, and were unflattering portraits of Butler's own parents.

Pontoppidan, Henrik (1857–1943). Danish novelist, who shared the Nobel prize (1917) with Karl Gjellerup. Author of *Kingdom of the Dead* (5 parts; 1912–1916); etc.

pony express. The U.S. mail service from St. Joseph, Mo., to Sacramento, Calif., which operated from 1860 until the end of 1861, when it was discontinued owing to the completion of the transcontinental telegraph. It was the first rapid transit system in the Far West and covered its 1,960 miles in as little as 8 days.

Pooh-Bah. Lord High Everything Else, an official in the Gilbert and Sullivan comic opera THE MIKADO.

poohpooh theory. See BOWWOW THEORY.

Pooka, see PHOOKA.

Poole, Ernest (1880–). American novelist. His first book, THE HARBOR (1915), ran through 6 editions in one month. Won the 1918 Pulitzer prize for *His Family* (1917). Other novels of his are *Millions* (1922); *One of Us* (1934); *Giants Gone* (1942); etc. Also a newspaper correspondent and playwright.

Poole, William Frederick (1821–1894). American librarian. At Yale (1848) he started *An Alphabetical Index to Subjects Treated in the . . . Periodicals* (*Poole's Index*), which was the forerunner of the *Readers' Guide to Periodical Literature.*

Poorgrass, Joseph. In Hardy's FAR FROM THE MADDING CROWD, a bashful farmhand who provides the humorous element in the book. In his apology for drunkenness he says he "only suffers from a multiplying eye."

Poor Henry. See HEINRICH VON AUE.

Poor Little Rich Girl. An expression used with reference to the neglect and loneliness which children of the wealthy sometimes suffer; from a comedy of that name by Eleanor GATES.

Poor Relations. A famous humorous essay by Charles LAMB in his *Essays of Elia* (1823).

Poor Richard's Almanack. An almanac first issued in 1733, and annually thereafter for twenty-five years, by Benjamin FRANKLIN under the pseudonym of Richard Saunders. To *Poor Richard* are attributed most of Franklin's famous adages.

Poor Robin. Pseudonym of the author of a series of almanacs published at first (from 1662) with the help of Robert HERRICK. Probably William Winstanley (1628?–1698). A *Poor Robin* came to signify "an almanac."

Poor White. A novel by Sherwood ANDERSON (1920). It concerns Hugh McVey, a shy telegraph operator in Bidwell, Ohio, whose amazing inventions make him a millionaire and transform Bidwell into a boom-town with all the vices and corruptions of industrialism, although Hugh is not aware of these harmful effects of his genius until it is too late.

Pope.

Pope Joan. See JOAN.

Pope of Geneva. John Calvin (1509–1564).

Pope of Philosophy. Aristotle (384–322 B.C.).

Pope, Alexander (1688–1744). English poet, literary dictator of his age and regarded as the English epitome of NEO-CLASSICISM. His poetry is characterized by satire, epigram, didacticism, smoothness and technical finish, invective, biting and malicious wit, and skillful use of the closed or heroic COUPLET. His best-known works are *Pastorals* (1709); ESSAY ON CRITICISM (1711), which made Pope famous and which, he claimed, he wrote when he was only twelve years old; THE RAPE OF THE LOCK (1712); *Windsor Forest* (1713); translations of the *Iliad* (1715–1720) and the *Odyssey* (1725–1726); THE DUNCIAD (1728, 1742); *Moral Essays* (1731–1735); ESSAY ON MAN (1733); EPISTLE TO DR. ARBUTHNOT (1735).

Pope, a Roman Catholic and the son of a linen-draper in London, was unable to attend a public school or a university because of governmental restrictions against Catholics after the Revolution of 1688. A hunchback and cripple as the result of a serious illness in childhood, Pope relieved his sense of rancor in jealous, spiteful, and venomous attacks on his contemporaries; because of this, he was called the "Wicked Wasp of Twickenham," from the name of the London suburb where he lived. He was a Tory in politics and a friend of John GAY and Jonathan SWIFT.

Pope-Figs. Protestants.

Pope-Figland. An island in Rabelais' satire GARGANTUA AND PANTAGRUEL (Bk. IV, ch. 45), inhabited by the Gaillardets (*Fr.,* "gay people"), rich and free, till, being shown the Pope's image, they exclaimed, "A fig for the Pope!" whereupon the whole island was put to the sword, its name changed to Pope-Figland, and the people called Pope-figs.

Pop Goes the Weasel! American folk song, used for fiddling at country square dances.

popinjay. A parrot; also a fop who dresses in bright clothes and chatters like a parrot. There is a popinjay in the poem *The Lang Coortin'* by Lewis CARROLL, appearing in the volume *Rhyme? and Reason?:*

> Then up and spake the popinjay,
> Sae wisely counselled he . . .

The poem is a burlesque of the old Scotch ballads.

Popinot, Jean-Jules. One of the few characters in the novels of the Balzac's COMÉDIE HUMAINE who display any altruistic qualities; a lawyer who "gave free rein to the exercise of charity, a virtue that had become a passion with him."

Popish Plot. A fictitious plot implicating the Duke of York and others in high places, invented by Titus Oates (1678) who alleged that the Catholics were about to massacre the Protestants, burn London, and assassinate the King. Some thirty innocent persons were executed, and Oates obtained great wealth by revealing the supposed plot. Ultimately he was pilloried, whipped, and imprisoned.

Poppaea. The mistress and later the wife of the Roman Emperor Nero. She is a character in Seneca's Latin tragedy *Octavia* and appears in Sienkiewicz' historical novel QUO VADIS.

popular etymology, see FOLK ETYMOLOGY.

Popular Front. A term brought into notice in the later years of the 1930's, during the Spanish Civil War (1936–1939) and again after the beginning of World War II (1939–1945), signifying an alliance between the capitalist democracies (especially the U.S. and Great Britain) and the U.S.S.R. against Nazi Germany, Fascist Italy, and, later, Japan. See NAZISM; FASCISM. The Popular Front became a reality only after the German invasion of the U.S.S.R. in June 1941. The term is also applied to coalitions of certain progressive parties in Spain and France (after 1936), as those which supported the French cabinets of Léon Blum, Camille Chautemps, and Édouard Daladier, and opposed the Spanish insurgents in the early phases of the Civil war.

Populists. In U.S. politics, the members of the People's party, organized (1891) by agricultural and labor groups. William Jennings BRYAN captured their vote as presidential candidate (1896; 1900) through his advocacy of free and unlimited coinage of silver.

Poquelin, Jean-Ah. See JEAN-AH POQUELIN.

Poquelin, Jean-Baptiste, see MOLIÈRE.

Porch, the. A philosophic sect, generally called Stoics (Gr. *stoa,* "a porch"), because Zeno, the founder, gave his lectures in the public ambulatory, *Stoa poecile,* in the agora of Athens.

> The successors of Socrates formed societies which lasted several centuries: the Academy, the Porch, the Garden.—Seeley, *Ecce Homo.*

Porcupiad. See PORCUPINE, PETER and CAREY, MATTHEW.

Porcupine, The. A play by Edwin Arlington ROBINSON (1915).

Porcupine, Peter. The name under which William COBBETT wrote, and was bitterly satirized by Matthew CAREY for his criticisms of America.

Porgy. A very successful Negro folk play (1927) by Du Bose and Dorothy HEYWARD, originally written as a novel. It was made into a combination of grand opera and musical comedy by George GERSHWIN under the title of *Porgy and Bess* (1935).

Porgy, Captain. A once famous comic character appearing in the American Revolutionary series of William Gilmore SIMMS (*The Partisan,* 1835; *Mellichampe,* 1836; *Katherine Walton,* 1851), and in other novels by Simms, notably *Woodcraft* (published first as *The Sword and the Distaff, or Fair, Fat, and Forty,* 1854), of which he is the leading character. This fat, boastful Southern soldier has been called "a prose Falstaff." In the earlier books he serves under Marion and Singleton; in *Woodcraft* he rescues the charming rich widow, Mrs. Eveleigh, from the schemes of McKewn and the attack of Bostwick and pays her ardent but unsuccessful court.

Porkopolis. Chicago, from the meat industry located there.

Porphyro. The hero of Keats' EVE OF ST. AGNES who rescues Madeline from the Baron's castle.

porphyrogene. Born in the purple, said of a child born after its father's accession to the throne. The meaning of the word is linked up with the fact that Greek has the same word for porphyry and purple. In ancient Byzantium, a room lined with porphyry was reserved for the empress. Her children born there were *porphyrogene* or *porphyrogenitic,* which could be taken to mean "born in the porphyry room" or "born in the purple." In *The Haunted Palace* by Edgar Allan Poe, the word porphyrogene occurs in the 3rd stanza. It seems to refer to the kind of room above described where "the ruler of the realm" was sitting.

Porphyry. *Lat.* **Porphyrius.** Original name **Malchus** (232?–?304). Greek scholar and neoplatonic philosopher.

Porrex. In the early English tragedy GORBODUC, the younger son of Gorboduc.

Porsena, Lars. A legendary king of Etruria, who made war on Rome to restore Tarquin to the throne. Lord MACAULAY made this the subject of one of his *Lays of Ancient Rome* (1842).

Porson, Richard (1759–1808). English classical scholar. Regius Professor of Greek at Cambridge (1792). Widely known through his critical *Letters to Archdeacon Travis* (1788–1789), upholding Gibbon's views regarding the genuineness of *1 John* v. 7.

Porte, the Sublime. See SUBLIME PORTE.

Porter, Cole (1892–). American composer of popular songs and music. Best-known songs are *Night and Day, Begin the Béguine, Let's Do It,* etc.

Porter, David (1780–1843). American naval officer, commander in chief of the West Indian squadron against piracy (1823–1825). Court-martialed and suspended from duty for action against the Spanish authorities in Puerto Rico (1825–1826). Resigned from U.S. Navy (1826) and went into Mexican naval service (1826–1829). U.S. minister to Turkey (from 1839); died in Constantinople. *Journal of a Cruise Made to the Pacific Ocean* (1815).

Porter, Mrs. **Eleanor** (1868–1920). American novelist, famous for the sensational success of her book POLLYANNA (1913).

Porter, Gene Stratton (1868–1924). American novelist, author of sentimental romances, the best-known of which are *Freckles* (1904), which sold over two million copies, *A Girl of the Limberlost* (1909), and *The Harvester* (1911).

Porter, Harold Everett. Pseudonym **Holworthy Hall** (1887–1936). American writer, chiefly known for his short stories, and a one-act play, *The Valiant* (with Robert Middlemass).

Porter, Jane (1776–1850). English novelist famous for the popularity of her romances *Thaddeus of Warsaw* (1803) and *The Scottish Chiefs* (1810). The latter was translated into German and Russian.

Porter, Katherine Anne (1894–). American journalist and short-story writer, known for the psychological insight and characterization of her stories. Her books include *Flowering Judas* (1930); *Hacienda* (1934); *Noon Wine* (1937); *Pale Horse, Pale Rider* (1939); *No Safe Harbor* (1941), a novel.

Porter, Noah (1811–1892). American Congregational clergyman and author. Editor in chief of *Webster's American Dictionary of the English Language* (1864) and of *Webster's International Dictionary of the English Language* (1890).

Porter, Sir Joseph, K.C.B. An admiral in the comic opera H.M.S. PINAFORE by GILBERT and SULLIVAN, who "stuck close to his desk and never went to sea" and therefore became in time "ruler of the Queen's navee." He is said to have been drawn in parody of the contemporary First Lord of the Admiralty, William H. Smith, who was a powerful newspaper publisher with few practical qualifications for his task.

Porter, William Sydney, see HENRY, O.

Porteous Riot. At Edinburgh in September, 1736. C. Porteous was captain of the city guard, and, at the execution of a smuggler named Wilson, ordered the guards to fire on the mob, which had become tumultuous. Six persons were killed, and eleven wounded. Porteous was condemned to death, but reprieved, whereupon the mob burst into the jail where he was confined, and, dragging him to the Grassmarket (the usual place of execution), hanged him by torchlight on a barber's pole. Scott introduces the riot in his HEART OF MIDLOTHIAN.

Porthos. One of the famous trio in Dumas' THREE MUSKETEERS, and a prominent character in the sequels, *Twenty Years After* and *The Vicomte de Bragelonne.*

Portia. (1) A rich heiress and "lady barrister" in Shakespeare's MERCHANT OF VENICE, in love with Bassanio. Her name is often used allusively for a female advocate.

(2) In Shakespeare's *Julius Caesar,* the noble wife of Marcus Brutus. She kills herself by "swallowing fire."

portmanteau word. An artificial word made up of parts of others, and expressive of a combination denoted by those parts—such as *squarson,* a "cross" between a *squire* and a *parson.* Lewis CARROLL invented the term in *Through the Looking-Glass,* ch. vi; *slithy,* he says, means *lithe* and *slimy, mimsy* is *flimsy* and *miserable,* etc. It is so called because there are two meanings "packed up" in the one word. In FINNEGANS WAKE James Joyce makes frequent use of portmanteau words.

Portolá, Gaspar de (1723?–?1784). Spanish governor of the Californias who marched 1,000 miles (1769) from Lower to Upper California where he founded San Diego and Monterey. Father Junípero Serra was one of the diarists of the expedition.

Portrait of a Lady, The. A novel by Henry JAMES (1881). The motives that lead Isabel Archer, a romantic New England girl who inherits an English fortune, to refuse other suitors and marry Gilbert Osmond are skilfully analyzed and her subsequent disillusionment traced in its devastating detail. Osmond is a dilettante, an impoverished gentleman living in retirement in Italy with his daughter, Pansy, because his exquisite tastes and sensibilities make him scornful of the crudities of the modern struggle for existence. After Isabel's marriage she discovers that she has only served the purposes of her quasi-friend, Madame Merle, who, as Osmond's mistress and the mother of Pansy, had brought the two together for the sake of Isabel's fortune. Osmond's fine sensibilities are likewise seen to be but the expression of an intensely egocentric, unpleasant nature.

Portrait of a Man with Red Hair. A sadistic novel (1925) by Sir Hugh WALPOLE.

Portrait of the Artist as a Young Man, A. An autobiographical novel by James JOYCE, published in 1915. It portrays the childhood, schooldays, adolescence, and early manhood of Stephen DEDALUS, later one of the leading characters of ULYSSES, touching upon his unhappy experiences at the Jesuit school at Clongowes, the bitter conflicts among the Irish regarding Charles Stewart PARNELL, Stephen's awakening interest in art, metaphysics, and aesthetics, his first love affairs, and his growing rebellion against his bigoted and poverty-stricken family background, the Roman Catholic religion, and his native Ireland itself. This book contains Joyce's first experiments in the technique of STREAM OF CONSCIOUSNESS. See also DOLAN, FATHER; RIORDAN, MRS. DANTE.

Port Royal. A convent about eight miles southwest of Versailles, which in the 17th century became the headquarters of the JANSENISTS and a literary and religious community of great influence. The community was suppressed by Louis XIV in 1660, but later again sprang into prominence and was condemned by a bull of Clement XI in 1708. Two years later the convent, which had been removed to Paris about 1637, was razed to the ground.

Portuguese. For *the Portuguese Cid, the Portuguese Horace,* etc., see under CID, HORACE, etc.

Posa, the Marquis of. A Spanish nobleman in Schiller's DON CARLOS, who, according to Heine, "is at once prophet and soldier and who under a Spanish cloak bears the noblest heart which ever loved and suffered in all Germany." In many ways he typifies Schiller's own ideals.

Poseidon. The god of the sea in Greek mythology, the counterpart of the Roman NEPTUNE. He was the son of Cronus and Rhea, brother of ZEUS and PLUTO, and husband of Amphitrite. It was he who, with Apollo, built the walls of Troy. When the Trojans refused to give him his just reward he began to hate them and took part against them in the Trojan War. Earthquakes were attributed to him, and he was said to have created the first horse.

Positivism. A philosophical movement of the 19th century, developed under the influence of the new discoveries in the science of the period, particularly outstanding in the thought of Auguste COMTE, regarded as its founder. Its chief principles call for the following: a study of the various sciences and an arrangement of them in a "scale of subordination," with those of greater complexity placed near the top of an ascending series; the assignment of sociology, with its study of past history and contemporary society and its attempts to solve persistent social problems, to a position at the summit of hierarchy; and a belief in the progress of mankind toward a superior state of civilization by means of the science of sociology itself. In the later years of his career, Comte, turning toward mysticism, attempted to convert sociology into a literal Religion of Humanity, with a set creed, rituals and ceremonies for private and public use, the worship of great men and women of the past, saints' days, etc. As a church, Positivism lasted in France down through the 20th century, although this development of his philosophy alienated a number of early admirers from the side of Comte. J. S. MILL and G. H. Lewes (see under ELIOT, GEORGE) were among the leading disciples of early Positivism in England. George Eliot's poem *The Choir Invisible* expresses its aspiration. Herbert CROLY, first editor of the NEW REPUBLIC, was the first American child to be christened in the faith.

Possessed, The. A novel by Fyodor DOSTOYEVSKY, published in 1871 as an attack on NIHILISM. It deals with the return of Nikolay STAVROGIN, son of the well-to-do widow Varvara Petrovna Stavrogin, to his home in a small Russian provincial town after years of absence in Moscow and Europe. Pyotr Stepanovich VERHOVENSKY, son of Stepan Trofimovich Verhovensky, a former liberal professor who lives on the estate of Mme Stavrogin, his old friend, also appears. It soon develops that Nikolay and Pyotr Stepanovich, along with SHATOV, a former servant of the household, and KIRILLOV, an engineer, have belonged to a band of revolutionary terrorists. Pyotr Stepanovich is the leader and plans to organize terroristic activities in the neighborhood. Tragedy and death result, with LEBYADKIN, a craftv army captain, and his half-wit sister, Marya Timofyevna, being murdered and burned in their dwelling, Shatov being slain as a suspected traitor, Lizaveta Nikolaevna TUSHIN, a young noblewoman in love with Nikolay, becoming a victim of mob vengeance, and both Kirillov and Nikolay committing suicide.

The novel, which contains a number of scenes bitterly satirizing the revolutionaries at their meetings, was designed by the author to show what he regarded as the horrors of Western revolutionary doctrines as imported into Russia in the 19th century, and to propose, through the mouth of Shatov, Dostoyevsky's own solution for the plight of his country—a return to the Russian Orthodox religion and an awakened spirit of nationalism. The title refers to the Biblical account of the Gadarene swine, the nihilists being regarded as the "swine" into which the social ills of Russia enter and thus are removed.

See also DROZDOV, MAVRIKY NIKOLAEVICH; GAGANOV, ARTEMY PAVLOVICH; KARAMAZINOV.

For a discussion of *The Possessed* and other works by Dostoyevsky, consult *Dostoyevsky: The Making of a Novelist*, by Ernest J. Simmons.

Post, Emily, *née* **Price** (1873?–). American writer and columnist, particularly well-known for her articles on manners and social etiquette. Author of *Etiquette* (1922) which has gone through many editions.

Post, Guy Bates (1875–1946). American actor on New York and London stage. Leading man for Mrs. Fiske (1907–1908).

Post, Melville Davisson (1871–1930). American lawyer, short-story writer, and novelist. Best known for his magazine detective stories about a Virginia squire by name of Uncle Abner. The best of them were afterwards published in book form as *Uncle Abner, Master of Mysteries* (1918).

posteriori, see A POSTERIORI.

postern. A rear or side door for private use.

> As hard to come as for a camel
> To thread the postern of a small needle's eye.
> Shakespeare, *King Richard II.*

Post Exchange. See CANTEEN.

Posthumus, Leonatus. The husband of Imogene in Shakespeare's CYMBELINE.

post-impressionism. A term coined by Roger FRY to denote movements in modern art. The most important post-impressionist painters are Cézanne, Seurat, Gauguin, Van Gogh, Matisse, etc. What these men had in common was that, not content with "outward effects," they strove to grapple with the "form beneath."

Postumus. The friend of the poet HORACE, to whom, in *Ode* 14 of Book 2, he addresses the famous words, *Eheu! fugaces, Postume, Postume, labuntur anni* (*Alas! Postumus, Postumus, the flying years glide by*).

Potash and **Perlmutter.** Joint heroes of a series of popular, humorous stories by Montague Glass (*Am.*, 1877–1934), which formed the basis for a number of comedies, notably *Potash and Perlmutter, Abe and Mawruss,* and *His Honor Abe Potash.* These two typical Jewish business men are partners in the cloak-and-suit trade. Later they go into the motion-picture business.

pot-boiler. Anything done merely for the sake of the money it will bring in—because it will *keep the pot boiling*, i.e., help to provide the means of livelihood; applied specially to work of small merit by artists or literary men.

Potemkin, Grigori Aleksandrovich (1739–1791). Russian field marshal, favorite of Empress Catherine of Russia and influential in her councils.

Potiphar Papers. A series of satires of New York society by G. W. Curtis (*Am.*, 1824–1892) published in 1853, relating the adventures of the newly rich Mr. and Mrs. Potiphar. They were dramatized as *Our Best People* the following year. The most popular character was Mrs. Potiphar's friend and adviser, Rev. Cream CHEESE.

Potiphar's wife. In the Old Testament and the *Koran*, the wife of Joseph's master in Egypt. JOSEPH fled from her advances, leaving his coat behind him, whereupon she accused him of evil and had him cast into prison. Some Arabian commentators have called her Rahil, others Zuleika, and it is this latter name that the 15th century Persian poet gives her in his *Yusuf and Zulaikha.*

Potocka, Countess **Anna,** *née* **Tyczkiewicz** (1776–1867). Polish writer whose *Memoirs* are valuable as historic source material. They cover the period from 1794 to 1820 and give an account of Napoleon's stay in Warsaw (1806–1807).

Pot of Basil, The, see ISABELLA, OR THE POT OF BASIL.

Pot of Earth, The. A long poem by Archibald MacLeish (1925) based on the fertility legend in *The Golden Bough.*

Potomac, Army of the. The principal part of the Union army in the U.S. Civil War. It was engaged under General McClellan in the Peninsular and Antietam Campaigns (1862). Under the command of General Meade it won the victory at Gettysburg (1863) and continued under his leadership during General Grant's operations (1864–1865).

Potter, Paul (1625–1654). Dutch animal painter, best-known for *The Young Bull* in the Museum at The Hague.

Potter, Paul Meredith (1853–1921). English-born American playwright, best-known for his dramatizations of Du Maurier's *Trilby* (1895) and Ouida's *Under Two Flags* (1901).

Potteries. See under Bennett, Arnold.

Potteries, Father of. See under father.

Potterism. A novel by Rose Macaulay (*Eng.,* 1920). The word speedily became a synonym for humbug and hypocrisy.

poulter's measure. In prosody, a meter consisting of alternate Alexandrines and fourteeners, i.e., twelve-syllable and fourteen-syllable lines. The name was given to it by George Gascoigne (1576) because it is said, poulterers—then called *poulters*—used sometimes to give twelve to the dozen and sometimes fourteen. It was a common measure in early Elizabethan times. The following specimen is from a poem by Surrey:

Good ladies, ye that have your pleasures in exile,
Step in your foot, come take a place, and mourn with me a while;
And such as by their lords do set but little price
Let them sit still, it skills them not what chance come on the dice.

Pound, Sir **Dudley** (1877–). British admiral. Fought in the Battle of Jutland (May 31, 1916); commander in chief of the Mediterranean fleet (1936–1939); sea lord of England and chief of naval staff (from 1939).

Pound, Ezra Loomis (1885–). American poet, editor, and literary critic, the most famous of the American expatriate writers of the period before and after World War I, known for his influence on a number of the leading poets of his time. His poetry, beginning in the school of Imagism, of which Pound was one of the founders, is marked by extensive learning, iconoclasm, individualism, the characteristic disillusionment of the Lost Generation, and wide freedom of form. It reflects the author's interest in scholarly research into the past and foreign languages, and includes numerous translations and adaptations of poetry from the ancient Chinese and Japanese, the Latin of the Empire period, medieval Provençal, Middle English, and 19th-century French Symbolism. His best-known work is a project entitled Cantos, consisting of *A Draft of XXX Cantos* (1930), *Eleven New Cantos* (1934), *The Fifth Decad of Cantos* (1937), *Cantos LII–LXXI* (1940). Among other books of poetry are: *A Lume Spento* (1908); *Exultations* (1909); *Provença* (1910); *Ripostes* (1912); *Lustra* (1916); *Quia Pauper Amavi* (1919); *Poems: 1918–1921* (1921); *Personae* (1926); *Selected Poems* (1928). His prose includes: *The Spirit of Romance* (1910); *Noh, Or Accomplishment: A Study of the Classical Stage of Japan* (1916); *Gaudier-Brzeska* (1916), a memoir; *Pavannes and Divisions* (1918); *Instigations* (1920); *Indiscretions* (1923); *The A.B.C. of Reading* (1934); *Make It New* (1935); *Jefferson and/or Mussolini* (1936); *Culture* (1938); *Polite Essays* (1939); *The A.B.C. of Economics* (1939).

Pound contributed steadily to the numerous little magazines of his day, edited the first anthology of Imagist poetry (1914), served as foreign correspondent of Poetry (1912–1919) and London editor of the Little Review (1917–1919), and founded and edited *The Exile* (1927). He was one of the first critics to call attention to the talents of Rabindranath Tagore, T. S. Eliot, James Joyce, and the sculptor Henri Gaudier. Among the poets most influenced by his own work were Eliot, Hart Crane, and Archibald MacLeish.

Pound went to Europe in 1907 and thereafter never lived again in the U.S. After moving from one place to another in London, Venice, Paris, and Provence, he took up residence in Rapallo, on the Italian Riviera, about 1924. He held an official position under Benito Mussolini, whom he professed to admire, and during World War II broadcast the Fascist party line by short wave to America. After Italy's surrender, he was arrested and tried for high treason (1945), but was adjudged insane.

Pound, Roscoe (1870–). American educator, professor at Northwestern, Chicago, Harvard. Dean of Harvard Law School (1916–1936). Author of a number of books on law. His sister, **Louise Pound** (1872–), a folklorist and authority on the English ballad, was senior editor of *American Speech* (1925–1933).

pound of flesh. The whole bargain, the exact terms of the agreement, the bond *literatim et verbatim.* The allusion is to Shylock in Shakespeare's The Merchant of Venice, who bargains with Antonio for a "pound of flesh," but is foiled in his suit by Portia, who says the bond is expressly a pound of flesh, and therefore these conditions would follow: (1) Shylock must cut the exact quantity, neither more nor less than a just pound; and

(2) in so doing he must not shed a drop of blood.

pourboire (*Fr.*). Literally, "for drinking." A small gratuity or tip.

Pourceaugnac, M. de. The hero of a comedy so called by MOLIÈRE (1669). He is a pompous country gentleman, who comes to Paris to marry Julie, daughter of Oronte. Julie loves Erasta, and this young man plays off so many tricks, and devises so many mystifications upon M. de Pourceaugnac, that the latter is willing to give up his suit.

Poussin, Nicolas (1594–1665). French landscape painter of the classical school.

Powder of Sympathy, The. A book of essays by Christopher MORLEY (1923).

Powell, Dawn (1897–). American novelist and dramatist. She has written some film scenarios and has broadcast a *Music and Manners* program. *The Locusts Have No King* (1948) is in her usual satiric vein.

Powell, Mary. First wife of John MILTON, whom she married in 1643 when she was only seventeen years old. She left him within a month after the wedding, and it is believed that his pamphlet *The Doctrine and Discipline of Divorce* was written as a result of this. In 1645 Mary returned to Milton and died at the birth of her fourth child by him in 1652.

Power, Tyrone Edmond (1914–). Direct descendant of the famous Irish comedian **William Grattan Tyrone Power** (1797–1841) and son of the well-known American leading man **Frederick Tyrone Power** (1869–1931) who acted with Mrs. Fiske, Mrs. Leslie Carter, and Julia Marlowe. Tyrone Edmond Power is a widely-known actor of leading parts in motion pictures (from 1935). Before that he played in Katharine Cornell's production of *Romeo and Juliet.*

Powers, Paula. Heroine of Hardy's novel A LAODICEAN.

Powys, John Cowper (1872–). English novelist and critic, whose writings are characterized by a strong and mystic love of nature. Among his novels are *Wood and Stone* (1915); *Rodmoor* (1916); *Ducdame* (1925); *Wolf Solent* (1929); *A Glastonbury Romance* (1932); *Weymouth Sands* (1934); *Jobber Skald* (1935); *Maiden Castle* (1936); *Morwyn, Or The Vengeance of God* (1937); *Owen Glendower* (1940). His essays and criticism include *Visions and Revisions* (1915); *The Religion of a Skeptic* (1925); *In Defense of Sensuality* (1930); *A Philosophy of Solitude* (1933); *Enjoyment of Literature* (1938).

Powys' brothers, **Llewelyn Powys** (1884–1939) and **Theodore Francis Powys** (1875–), were also well-known English writers. Among Llewelyn's books are *Ebony and Ivory* (1922), stories and sketches of life in East Africa; *Skin for Skin* (1925); *Apples Be Ripe* (1930), a novel; *Earth Memories* (1934), *Rats in the Sacristy* (1937), and *A Baker's Dozen* (1941), collections of essays; *Love And Death* (1939), an "imaginary autobiography" (1939). Theodore's works, novels and stories dealing chiefly with evil and tragedy in the Dorset countryside, realistically presented, include *The Left Leg* (1923); *Black Bryony* (1923); *Mockery Cap* (1925); *Mr. Weston's Good Wine* (1928); *The House with the Echo* (1929); *The Two Thieves* (1932).

Poyser, Mrs. One of George Eliot's best-known characters, a farmer's wife in ADAM BEDE whose keen, pungent wit makes her running commentary on the other persons of the story both entertaining and discerning.

P.P., Clerk of this Parish. The hero and pretended author of a famous volume of *Memoirs* written by John ARBUTHNOT as a burlesque on Burnet's *History of My Own Times.* His self-important affectations proved highly amusing and made his name a byword for conceit.

p.p.c. (Fr. *pour prendre congé*). For leave-taking; sometimes written on the address cards of persons about to leave a locality when they pay their farewell visits. In English, *paid parting call.*

Ppt. In Jonathan Swift's *Journal to Stella* (see STELLA), a cryptic abbreviation which is believed to have been a pet name for Stella. It recurs throughout James Joyce's FINNEGANS WAKE, where it serves H. C. EARWICKER as a pet name for his daughter Isobel. See also PRESTO.

Prado. The national museum of painting and scultpure in Madrid, Spain, next to the famous fashionable promenade of the same name. The word means "meadow."

Praed, Winthrop Mackworth (1802–1839). English poet of *vers de société.*

praetor. A Roman magistrate, second in rank to a consul and appointed only from the patrician class.

Praetorian Guard. In Roman history, the imperial body guard. Organized by Augustus on the basis of the older praetorian cohorts, the body guards of praetors. The Praetorian Guard grew more and more powerful and many emperors were hardly more than its puppets. It survived to the time of Constantine.

Pragmatic Sanction. *Sanctio* in Latin means a "decree or ordinance with a penalty attached," or, in other words, a "penal statute." *Pragmaticus* means "relating to state affairs," so that Pragmatic Sanction is a penal statute bearing on some important question of state. The term was first applied by the Romans to those statutes which related to their provinces. The French applied the phrase to certain statutes which limited the jurisdiction of the Pope, but generally it is applied to an ordinance fixing the succession in a certain line.

Pragmatic Sanction of 1713. A statute whereby the succession of the Austrian Empire was made hereditary in the female line, in order to transmit the crown to Maria Theresa, the daughter of Charles VI. This is emphatically *the* Pragmatic Sanction, unless some qualification is added restricting the term to some other instrument.

Pragmatism (from Gr. *pragma,* "deed"). The philosophical doctrine that the only test of the truth of human cognitions or philosophical principles is their practical results, i.e., their workableness. It does not admit "absolute" truth, as all truths change their trueness as their practical utility increases or decreases. The word was introduced in this connection about 1875 by the American logician C. S. PEIRCE, and was popularized by William JAMES, whose *Pragmatism: A New Name for Some Old Ways of Thinking,* lectures delivered at the Lowell Institute and Columbia University (1906–1907) were published in 1907. See also MATERIALISM.

Prairie, The. A historical novel by James Fenimore COOPER (1827), one of the LEATHERSTOCKING series. It relates the story of the last days of Leatherstocking, now an exile whom civilization has driven westward to the great prairies beyond the Mississippi. Here the old scout becomes a trapper, and here, as everywhere, there are captives for him to rescue and numerous adventures for him to undertake. Finally, the old trapper dies in the arms of friends. Much of the action is taken up with the concerns of the rough, crude squatter Ishmael Bush and his family.

prairie schooner. A name given to the covered wagon which crossed the plains in the early days of America.

Prairie State. Illinois. See under STATES.

Prankquean. A name for Grace O'Malley (Graine Ni Maille), an Irish princess of Connaught, who was refused shelter in HOWTH CASTLE one Christmas day while she was on her way home from a visit to Queen Elizabeth. In revenge, she kidnaped the child of the lord of the castle. Her name, in the form "Granuille," later came to be a symbol of Ireland itself, because she had defied Elizabeth.

Critics find an adaptation of this anecdote in James Joyce's FINNEGANS WAKE, in an episode which apparently takes place in the taproom of the tavern of H. C. EARWICKER. Earwicker is here called Jarl van Hoother, or "Earl of Howth," and a riddle asked him by the Prankquean herself ("Why do I am alook alike a poss of porterpease?") is combined with the request of a customer for "a pot of porter, please." Harry Levin thinks this refers to Earwicker's confused emotions regarding his wife and daughter.

Prasildo. In Boiardo's ORLANDO INNAMORATO, a Babylonish nobleman, who falls in love with Tisbina, wife of his friend Iroldo. He is overheard by Tisbina threatening to kill himself, and, in order to divert him from his guilty passion, she promises to return his love on the condition that he perform certain deeds which she thinks to be impossible. However, Prasildo performs them all, and then Tisbina and Iroldo, finding no excuse, take poison to avoid the alternative. Prasildo resolves to do the same, but is told by the apothecary that the "poison" he had supplied was a harmless drink. Prasildo tells his friend, Iroldo quits the country, and Tisbina marries Prasildo. Time passes on, and Prasildo hears that his friend's life is in danger, whereupon he starts forth to rescue him at the hazard of his own life.

Prater. A famous Viennese park on an island formed by the Danube and the Danube Canal. It was opened to the public in 1766 by Emperor Joseph II. The name (like PRADO, derived from Lat. *pradum,* "meadow") is often used for the amusement park which is actually but a small part of the Prater.

Pratt, Silas Gamaliel (1846–1916). American pianist and composer who founded the Pratt Institute of Music and Art in Pittsburgh (1906).

Praxiteles. Famous Greek sculptor of the 4th century B.C. He did the Aphrodite of Cnidus for which the courtesan PHRYNE is said to have posed. The statue of a satyr at the Roman Capitol referred to in the title of *The Marble Faun* by Nathaniel HAWTHORNE is possibly a copy of a statue by Praxiteles.

Prayers of Steel. A free verse poem (1915) by Carl SANDBURG.

prayer wheel. A device used by the Tibetan Buddhists as an aid to, or substitute for, prayer, the use of which is said to be founded on a misinterpretation of the Buddha's instructions to his followers, that they should "turn the wheel of the law"—i.e., preach Buddhism incessantly. The prayer wheel consists of a pasteboard cylinder inscribed with—or containing—the mystic formula OM MANI PADME HUM and other prayers, and each revolution represents one repetition of the prayers.

praying mantis. A grotesque insect that holds its stout anterior legs in a manner suggesting prayer. *The Praying Mantis* is the title of a novel by Edgar JOHNSON.

Preacher, the. Solomon, the reputed author of *Ecclesiastes* in the Old Testament.

the glorious preacher. Saint John Chrysostom (347–407).

the king of preachers. Louis Bourdaloue (1632–1704).

the little preacher. Samuel de Marets (1599-1663), Protestant controversialist.

preadamites. The name given by Isaac de la Peyrère (1655) to a race of men whom he supposed to have existed long before the days of Adam. He held that only the Jews are descended from Adam, and that the Gentiles derive from these "preadamites."

Précieuses Ridicules, Les. A comedy by MOLIÈRE (1659). The chief characters are two girls, who assume the airs of the HOTEL DE RAMBOUILLET, a coterie of savants of both sexes in the 17th century. The members of this society were termed *précieuses,* and the *précieuses ridicules* means a ridiculous aping of their ways and manners.

The plot is, briefly, as follows: Cathos, cousin of Madelon, has been brought up by her Uncle Gorgibus, a plain citizen in the middle rank of life. These two silly girls have had their heads turned by novels, and, thinking their names commonplace, Cathos calls herself Aminte, and her cousin adopts the name of Polixene. Two gentlemen wish to marry them, but the girls consider their manners too unaffected and easy to be "good style," so the gentlemen send their valets to represent the Marquis of Mascarille and the Viscount of Jodelet. The girls are delighted with these "distinguished noblemen," but when the game has gone far enough, the masters enter, and lay bare the trick. The girls are taught a useful lesson, without being involved in any fatal consequences.

Preciosa. The heroine of Longfellow's SPANISH STUDENT.

Preedy, George, see LONG, GABRIELLE MARGARET.

Preface to Morals, A. A philosophical work (1929) by Walter LIPPMANN.

Prejudices. Six series of critical essays (1919–1927) by H. L. MENCKEN.

prelapsarian. In theology, referring to the state of man before his fall. From Latin *lapsus,* "a fall."

Prelude, The. A long autobiographical poem by William WORDSWORTH, showing the growth of a poet's mind by tracing his own life from childhood on. The full text was published only in 1926 through the devotion of E. de Sélincourt. Wordsworth originally dedicated the poem to Coleridge.

Pre-Raphaelite Brotherhood, the. A group of artists and poets formed in London in 1848, consisting originally of Holman HUNT, John Everett MILLAIS, D. G. ROSSETTI, the leader, and Thomas Woolner, later adding James Collinson, Frederick George Stephens, Walter Deverell, and W. M. Rossetti. It had for its objects a closer study of nature than was practiced by those bound by academic dogmas, and the cultivation of the methods and the spirit of the early Italian (the "pre-Raphael") painters. The group was championed by John RUSKIN, but was attacked by many artists and critics.

> . . . a society which unfortunately, or rather unwisely has given itself the name of "Pre-Raphaelite"; unfortunately, because the principles on which its members are working are neither pre- nor post-Raphaelite, but everlasting. They are endeavouring to paint with the highest possible degree of completion, what they see in nature, without reference to conventional or established rules; but by no means to imitate the style of any past epoch.—Ruskin, *Modern Painters,* pt. ii, sect. vi, ch. iii, § 16, *n.*

In poetry, the Pre-Raphaelites championed the medieval ballad, the supernaturalism of Edgar Allan POE, and the concrete, sensuous imagery of John KEATS. They published a LITTLE MAGAZINE called THE GERM, one of the first of such experimental journals, and poets either associated with the movement at one time or another or generally sympathetic with its aims were Christina ROSSETTI, William MORRIS, Coventry PATMORE, and A. C. SWINBURNE. The French Symbolist leader MALLARMÉ is considered to have been influenced to some degree by the Pre-Raphaelites. See also FLESHLY SCHOOL. For a study of the Pre-Raphaelite movement, cf. *Poor Splendid Wings,* by Frances WINWAR.

Presbyterian. Pertaining to one of the Churches of Calvinistic origin, in which, as in the early Christian Church, the presbyters or elders are the medium through which all members of the church govern it. See also FREE KIRK; John KNOX.

Prescott, William Hickling (1796–1859). American historian, known for his colorful and dramatic works in the field of Spanish history, written under the influence of Sir Walter SCOTT and emphasizing the role of powerful individuals, such as CORTÉS and MONTEZUMA, in the events portrayed. His works include *History of Ferdinand and Isabella* (1838); *History of the Conquest of Mexico* (1843), regarded as his greatest accomplishment; *Biographical and Critical Miscellanies* (1845); *History of the Conquest of Peru* (1847); *History of the Reign of Philip the Second,* begun in 1849 and left unfinished at the time of the author's death. Prescott was blind in one eye during most of his life and wrote his studies under great difficulty.

Presidium. In the organization of the soviet system in Russia, every factory or trade or profession chooses members for the local or town soviet. The town or village soviets choose representatives to larger bodies above them. There is an ascending scale of soviets till it reaches a small legislative body known as the Presidium and a ministry known as the Council of Peoples' Commissars, of which Lenin was originally the chief.

Presles, the Marquis de. In *LeGendre de M. Poirier,* a comedy by Augier and Sandeau, the titled son-in-law of the bourgeois M. POIRIER.

press gang. In English history, a detachment of seamen under a naval officer who had the power to seize any sailor in time of emergency and make him serve on board one of the King's ships. When the British tried to impress American seamen it was one of the causes of the War of 1812.

Prester John (i.e., John the Presbyter). A fabulous Christian king and priest, supposed in medieval times to have reigned in the 12th century over a wonderful country somewhere in the heart of Asia. He figures in Ariosto's ORLANDO FURIOSO (Bks. xvii–xix), and has furnished materials for a host of medieval legends, including that of the HOLY GRAIL.

According to Sir John MANDEVILLE he was a lineal descendant of OGIER THE DANE, who penetrated into the north of India with fifteen of his barons, among whom he divided the land. John was made sovereign of Teneduc, and was called *Prester* because he converted the natives. Another tradition says he had seventy kings for his vassals, and was seen by his subjects only three times in a year. So firm was the belief in his existence that the Pope, Alexander III (d. 1181), sent him letters by a special messenger. The messenger never returned.

> The centuries go by, but Prester John endures for ever
> With his music in the mountains and his magic on the sky.
>
> Alfred Noyes, *Forty Singing Seamen.*

Presto. The name frequently applied to himself by Jonathan SWIFT in his JOURNAL TO STELLA. According to his own account (*Journal,* August 1st, 1711) it was given him by the Duchess of Shrewsbury, an Italian. See also PPT.

pretender.

the Old Pretender. James Francis Edward Stuart (1688–1766), son of James II. He is introduced in Thackeray's HENRY ESMOND.

the Young Pretender. Charles Edward Stuart (1720–1788), son of the "Old Pretender." By his friends he was called "the Chevalier" or Bonnie Prince Charlie. Scott introduces him in WAVERLEY and again in REDGAUNTLET, where he appears disguised as Father Buonaventura.

Prettyman, Prince. In the burlesque *Rehearsal* (1621) by the Duke of Buckingham, the lover of Cloris, who, much to his own annoyance, is sometimes a prince and sometimes a fisherman. He is said to be a caricature of Leonidas in Dryden's MARRIAGE À LA MODE.

preview. In motion-picture and theatrical parlance, a performance, sometimes a dress-rehearsal, which is given before an especially invited audience prior to the opening night.

Prévost, Abbé. Full name, **Antoine François Prévost d'Exiles** (1697–1763). French novelist and Benedictine abbé. He conducted a journal, *Le Pour et le Contre* (1733–1740) made translations into French of the English novels of Samuel RICHARDSON, and wrote a number of popular romances with wild plots and exotic backgrounds. His best-known work is MANON LESCAUT (1731). Prévost had a stormy youth, serving as a soldier and escaping twice from the Church before finally settling down as an unattached abbé in Paris.

Prevost, Eugène Marcel (1862–1941). French novelist. Member of the French Academy (1909).

Priam. In Greek legend, King of Troy when that city was sacked by the Greeks, husband of Hecuba, and father of fifty children, among whom were HECTOR, Helenus, PARIS, Deiphobus, Polyxena, TROILUS, CASSANDRA and POLYDORUS. When Hector was slain, the old King went to the tent of ACHILLES and made a successful plea for the body of his dead son. After the gates of Troy were thrown open by the Greeks concealed in the wooden horse, Pyrrhus, the son of Achilles, slew the aged Priam. See also TROJAN WAR.

Priamond. In Spenser's FAËRIE QUEENE (IV. ii), the elder brother of Diamond and Triamond, sons of Agape, a fairy. He is very daring, and fights on foot with battleaxe and spear. He is slain by Cambalo.

Priapus. In Greek mythology, the god of reproductive power and fertility (hence of gardens), and protector of shepherds, fishermen, and farmers. He was the son of DIONYSUS and APHRODITE, and in later times was regarded as the chief deity of lasciviousness and obscenity.

Pribilof Islands. A group of islands in the Bering Sea, discovered (1786) by the Russian sea captain Gerasim Pribylov who gave them his name. They became a fur-seal reservation under the American government in 1868.

Price, Byron (1891–). American newspaper man. During World War II, U.S. director of censorship, appointed (1941) by President Roosevelt.

Price, Fanny. (1) Heroine of Jane Austen's MANSFIELD PARK.

(2) In W. S. Maugham's OF HUMAN BONDAGE, a lonely, unhappy, and bitterly frustrated English spinster, an art student in Paris who doggedly persists in her studies in spite of great poverty and the warnings of her teachers that she has no talent. She finally hangs herself.

Pride, Thomas (died 1658). English Parliamentarian commander. Principally remembered for his conduct of the expulsion of more than 100 Royalist and Presbyterian members from the Long Parliament which was known as *Pride's Purge* (1648).

Pride and Prejudice. A novel by Jane AUSTEN (1813). The story concerns the middle-class household of the Bennets, a family of five daughters. Mr. Bennet, a mild and indolent man, has little but witty cynicisms to oppose to the everlasting scheming of his wife, who is a type of the silly garrulous mother anxious to marry off her daughters. During the first half of the novel, Elizabeth Bennet grows more and more impatient with her suitor, Darcy, whose haughty consciousness of superior birth and uncalled for interference in the love affair of her sister Jane and his friend Bingley win her growing dislike. In the latter half, Bingley renews his suit with Darcy's approval, a boisterous younger sister, Lydia, causes great excitement by eloping with an officer named Wickham, and Darcy himself finally conquers his own pride and Elizabeth's prejudice to their mutual satisfaction. In this novel, which is the best-known of Jane Austen's novels, appear also two of her best-known minor characters, Mr. COLLINS and Lady Catherine de BOURGH.

Pride's Purge. The Long Parliament, not proving itself willing to condemn Charles I, was *purged* of its unruly members by Colonel Pride, who entered the House with two regiments of soldiers (December 6th, 1648), imprisoned sixty members, drove more than one hundred out into the streets, and left only sixty —the "Rump." See under PARLIAMENTS.

Priest, Judge. A well-known character appearing in a number of short stories by Irvin S. COBB. He is a wise and kindly retired Kentucky judge who assists in the solution of numerous problems.

Priestley, John Boynton (1894–). English novelist, playwright, and journalist, best known as the author of *The Good Companions* (1929) and *Angel Pavement* (1930), best-selling novels compared by critics to Dickens' works. Other books are *The Old Dark House* (1928) and *Faraway* (1932), novels; *Dangerous Corner* (1932), a novel, also dramatized as a play; *Four-In-Hand* (1934), stories and essays; *The Doomsday Men* (1938); *Let the People Sing* (1940); *Blackout In Gretley* (1942), dealing with World War II in England. Priestley's plays include *Dangerous Corner* (1932); *Eden End* (1934); *Laburnum Grove* (1934); *Duet in Floodlight* (1935); *Mystery At Greenfingers* (1937); *People At Sea* (1937); *Time and the Conways* (1937); *I Have Been Here Before* (1938). *Midnight on the Desert* (1937) concerns travel in the western U.S.; *Rain Upon Godshill* (1939) is autobiographical.

During the 1930's, Priestley was elected a Member of Parliament and assisted in securing the passage of a liberalized English divorce law. During World War II he delivered radio talks to the U.S. He is interested in theories of time, as shown in *Time and the Conways,* and others.

Priestley, Joseph (1733–1804). English clergyman, chemist, and philosopher. Pursued fruitful investigations into the nature of electrical discharges and discovered what is now called oxygen (1774). His theory of government, as set forth in his *Essay on the First Principles of Government* (1768), stipulates that the happiness of the majority is the great standard of all good government. See also BENTHAM. As a psychologist, he was influenced by HARTLEY to evolve an early theory of association. He spent the last decade of his life in America after his home in Birmingham had been burned by a mob infuriated on account of his sympathies with the French Revolution. A direct descendant was Mrs. BELLOC LOWNDES.

Prig, Betsey. In Dickens' MARTIN CHUZZLEWIT, an old monthly nurse, "the frequent pardner" of Mrs. Gamp. She is equally ignorant, equally vulgar, and equally selfish and brutal towards her patients as is her friend.

> "Betsey," said Mrs. Gamp, filling her own glass, and passing the teapot [*of gin*], "I will now propose a toast: 'My frequent pardner, Betsey Prig.'" "Which, altering the name to Sarah Gamp; I drink," said Mrs. Prig, "with love and tenderness."—*Martin Chuzzlewit,* xlix.

prima facie (*Lat.*). At first view.

Primate. In the Roman Catholic Church, originally a bishop set over other bishops in matters of jurisdiction or as vicar of the Holy See. Later the term became purely an honorary title.

Prime Minister, The. A novel by Anthony TROLLOPE (1876). See OMNIUM, DUKE OF; PHINEAS FINN.

primitivism. Term applied to a persistent tendency in European literature, art, and thought since the 18th century, stimulated by the acquisition of foreign colonies of low cultural development and by new discoveries in scholarship and the social sciences, to attribute superior virtue to primitive, non-European civilizations. J. J. ROUSSEAU was the first notable primitivist, with his doctrine of the "natural man," and the widespread 18th-century veneration of the NOBLE SAVAGE had an important influence on the romantic movement. See ROMANTICISM. The American Indian was a favorite early exemplar of the Noble Savage. Later, primitivism expanded to include among the objects of its enthusiasm the violent, the crude, undeveloped, ignorant, naïve, nonintellectual or sub-intelligent of any kind, such as peasants, children, and idiots.

The following are literary figures of the 18th, 19th, and 20th centuries whose work embodies primitivism in one or another of its aspects: MACPHERSON (pseudo-Ossianic poems); BLAKE (innocence, childhood); WORDSWORTH (peasants, children, idiot boys); CHATEAUBRIAND and James Fenimore COOPER (the American Indian); the GRIMM brothers (fairy tales, legends); Richard WAGNER (pre-Christian religion and myth); Fyodor DOSTOYEVSKY (children, idiots); TOLSTOY (peasants); RIMBAUD (sadism, violence, the occult); HUYSMANS and the DECADENTS (sadism, violence, the cult of sensation); Pierre LOTI (South Sea Islands); W. B. YEATS (myth and legend); Thomas MANN (myth and legend); D. H. LAWRENCE (the mystical rôle of sex, the cult of sensation, primitive religion and ritual); Sherwood ANDERSON and Carl VAN VECHTEN (the American Negro); Ernest HEMINGWAY (violence, cult of sensation); James JOYCE (legend and myth, the subconscious). In psychology, FREUD and JUNG (the subconscious), and in anthropology, Sir J. G. FRAZER (primitive religion, myth, and ritual), are also representatives of primitivism and of the scientific thought which helped to stimulate primitivism. Primitivists in painting include MILLET and van GOGH (peasants); GAUGUIN (Tahitian themes); PICASSO and BRAQUE (African Negro forms); Joan MIRO and Paul KLEE (children's art); Salvador DALI and the surrealists (the subconscious). Henri ROUSSEAU, a naïve, self-taught painter, was a favorite among primitivist art groups in the early part of the 20th century. Igor STRAVINSKY (the primitive ritual of *Le Sacre du printemps*) and the American jazz composers of the 1920's (African and American Negro rhythms) outstandingly represent primitivism in music, and the political movements of NAZISM and FASCISM of the period following World War I are striking examples of primitivism also, seeking a return to the social organization and cultural and religious ideals of the Roman Empire and the early Germanic tribes.

primogeniture. The right of the first-born son to succeed to the patrimony.

Primrose, the Rev. Dr. Charles. The hero of Oliver Goldsmith's famous novel THE VICAR OF WAKEFIELD, a clergyman, rich in heavenly wisdom. He has his little foibles and vanities, but is genuinely devout and kindly, a man whom all his parishioners love.

Mrs. (Deborah) Primrose. The doctor's wife, full of motherly vanity, and desirous to appear *genteel.* She can read without much spelling, prides herself on her housewifery, especially on her gooseberry wine, and is really proud of her excellent husband. She is painted as Venus, and the vicar, in gown and bands, is presenting to her his book on "second marriages," but when completed, the picture is found to be too large for the house.

George Primrose. Son of the vicar. He goes to Amsterdam to teach the Dutch English, but never once calls to mind that he himself must know something of Dutch before this can be done. He becomes Captain Primrose, and marries Miss Wilmot, an heiress.

Moses Primrose. Younger son of the vicar, noted for his greenness and pedantry. Sent to sell a good horse at a fair, he barters it for a gross of green spectacles with copper rims and shagreen cases, of no value at all.

Olivia Primrose. The eldest daughter of the doctor. Pretty, enthusiastic, eager for adventure, she "wished for many lovers," and elopes with Squire Thornhill. Her father finds her at a roadside inn called the Harrow, where she is on the point of being turned out of the house. Subsequently, she is found to be legally married to the Squire.

Sophia Primrose. The second daughter of Dr. Primrose. She is "soft, modest, and alluring." She is twice rescued by Sir William THORNHILL, then disguised as Mr. Burchill, and marries him at last.

Primrose League, The. A British organization of conservatives, founded (1883) in memory of Benjamin DISRAELI whose favorite flower was the primrose.

primum mobile (*Lat.,* "the first moving thing"). In the Ptolemaic system of astronomy, the ninth (later the tenth) sphere, supposed to revolve around the earth from east to west in twenty-four hours, carrying with it all the other SPHERES. Milton refers to it as "that first mov'd" (*Paradise Lost,* III. 483), and Sir Thomas BROWNE (*Religio Medici*) uses the phrase, "Beyond the first movable," meaning outside the material creation. According to PTOLEMY the *primum mobile* was the boundary of creation, above which came the EMPYREAN or seat of God.

The term is figuratively applied to any machine which communicates motion to others, and also to persons and ideas suggestive of complicated systems. Thus, Socrates may be called the *primum mobile* of the Dialectic, Megaric, Cyrenaic, and Cynic systems of philosophy.

prince (Lat. *princeps,* "chief, leader"). A royal title which, in England, is now limited to the sons of the sovereign and their sons. *Princess* is similarly limited to the sovereign's daughters and his sons' (but not daughters') daughters.

Crown Prince. The title of the heir-apparent to the throne in some countries, as Sweden, Denmark, and Japan (formerly also in Germany).

Prince Consort. A prince who is the husband of a reigning Queen, as Albert of Saxe-Coburg-Gotha, husband of Queen Victoria, and the husband of Wilhelmina, Queen of the Netherlands.

Prince Imperial. The title of the heir-apparent in the French Empire of 1852–1870.

Prince of Wales. See WALES.

Prince of Alchemy. Rudolph II, Emperor of Germany, also called The German Hermes Trismegistus.

Prince of Angels. Michael.

Prince of Apostles. St. Peter. See under SAINTS.

Prince of Asturias. The title of the heir-apparent to the Spanish throne.

Prince of Dandies. BEAU BRUMMEL (1778–1840).

Prince of Darkness. Satan (*Eph.* vi. 12).

Prince of Destruction. Timur or Tamerlane (1333–1405).

Prince of Gossips. Samuel Pepys (1632–1703) noted for his gossiping *Diary,* commencing January 1, 1659, and continued for nine years.

Prince of Grammarians. Appolonios of Alexandria (*fl.* 40–30 B. C.), so called by Priscian.

Prince of Hell. Satan.

Prince of Hypocrites. Emperor Tiberius (42 B. C.–37 A. D.).

Prince of Liars. Fernando Mendes Pinto, so called by Cervantes.

Prince of Music. Palestrina (1529–1594).

Prince of Painters. (1) Parhasius (*fl.* 400 B. C.); (2) Apelles (*fl.* 330 B. C.). Both Greek painters.

Prince of Peace. A title given to the Messiah (*Isa.* ix. 6).

Prince of Physicians. Avicenna (980–1037) the Arabian physician.

Prince of Piedmont. The Italian heir-apparent.

Prince of Poets. (1) *Virgil* (70–19 B. C.); (2) Edmund Spenser (1552–1599), so called on his monument.

Prince of Spanish Poetry. Garcilaso de la Vega (1503–1536), so called by Cervantes.

Prince of the Church. A cardinal.

Prince of the Ode. Pierre de Ronsard (1524–1585).

prince of the vegetable kingdom. So Linnaeus calls the palm tree.

Prince, Morton (1854–1929). American neurologist. Founder and editor (1906–1929) of the *Journal of Abnormal Psychology.* Author of several books on the nature of mind and the unconscious.

Prince and the Pauper, The. A historical romance by Mark TWAIN (1882), describing in satirical vein the comedy resulting from a prankish change of garments between Prince Edward, after Edward VI, and his double, Tom Canty the beggar boy. Tom is regarded as the lawful prince, temporarily unbalanced, and only when he is on the point of being crowned king is the mistake cleared up.

Prince Chery or **Cheri.** See CHERY AND FAIR-STAR.

Prince Hohenstiel-Schwangau. A monologue poem by Robert Browning imagined to be spoken by Napoleon III, disguised under the name of the title.

Prince of India, The. A novel by Lew WALLACE (1893) based on the legend of the WANDERING JEW. Here the Jew has assumed the title *Prince of India* and devotes himself to preaching brotherly love. He takes his teaching to both the Mohammedans and the Greek Church, but with little success; then he gives his support to Mohammed, heir to the Turkish Empire. The capture of Constantinople by Mohammed and his marriage to Princess Irene are important incidents. At the conclusion of the novel the Prince, left for dead on the battlefield, starts out with renewed youth on fresh wanderings.

Prince of Parthia. A tragedy by Thomas Godfrey, the first play written by an American and performed by professional actors in America. It was played on April 24, 1767. The scene is laid in Parthia about the 1st century A. D.

Prince Rupert's drops. Also **Rupert's drops or ball or tear.** Delicate pieces of glass made by dropping molten glass into water. They were introduced into England from Germany by Prince RUPERT, the nephew of Charles I, and looked like tears made out of glass.

Prince's Progress, The. An allegorical poem (1866) by Christina ROSSETTI.

Princess, The. A long narrative poem by TENNYSON (1847), especially noted for the songs introduced. It deals with the general subject of the "new woman," and shows the heroine, Ida, as founder of a university to which only women are admitted. The Gilbert and Sullivan comic opera, *Princess Ida* (1884), is "a respectful operatic perversion of Tennyson's *Princess.*"

Princess Casamassima, The. A novel by Henry JAMES (1886), dealing with socialism.

The titular heroine is the Christina Light who appeared in RODERICK HUDSON. Wealthy, beautiful and unhappily married, she seeks an outlet in her espousal of the socialist cause and in her sympathetic association with Hyacinth Robinson, a handsome and ardent young radical.

Princesse de Clèves, La. A novel (1678) by Mme de La Fayette (1634–1693). Its historical importance lies in the fact that it is a brilliant forerunner of the psychological novel.

Princip, Gavrilo (1893?–1918). The Serbian student who assassinated the Austrian Archduke Francis Ferdinand at Sarajevo (June 28, 1914), thereby precipitating the first World War.

Principia. See NEWTON, Sir ISAAC.

Pringle, Henry Fowles (1897–). American journalist and biographer. His *Theodore Roosevelt: A Biography* (1931) won the Pulitzer prize for biography.

Printers' Bible. See BIBLE, SPECIALLY NAMED.

Printing, Father of English. See under FATHER.

Printing House Square. Once the site of the King's printers in London. Now the office of the London *Times.*

Prinzivalle. In Maeterlinck's MONNA VANNA, the Florentine admirer of Vanna.

Prior, Matthew (1664–1721). English poet and diplomat, known chiefly for his epigrams, satires, and "society" verse. His works include *Alma, Or the Progress of the Soul,* a long poem on worldly vanity; *Henry and Emma,* a paraphrase of THE NUT-BROWN MAID; *Solomon on the Vanity of the World* (1718); *Down-Hall* (1723), a ballad on a journey through Essex; *Carmen Saeculare* (1700), an "occasional" piece on William III; *The Secretary,* reminiscences of his experiences in diplomacy; and several prose works, among them being *Essay upon Learning, Essay upon Opinion,* and *Four Dialogues on the Dead.* Prior took part in several important European treaty negotiations of his time, including the Treaty of Ryswick and the Peace of Utrecht.

Prioress's Tale, The. One of Chaucer's CANTERBURY TALES, similar to the story of HUGH OF LINCOLN. A little boy is constantly singing the *Alma redemptoris,* and the Jews capture him on his way to school, kill him, and cast his dead body into a well. His mother, anxious at his absence, goes in search of him, and, coming to the well hears her son's voice singing the *Alma redemptoris.* She tells the provost, who has the Jews executed. The child is drawn up still repeating the same words, and, being asked why he does so, replies that he can never die until his tongue is cut out. The abbot cuts out the tongue, the child instantly gives up the ghost, and the body is buried in a marble tomb. WORDSWORTH has modernized this tale. In his drama THE CANTERBURY PILGRIMS, Percy MACKAYE makes the gentle, lovable Prioress play a prominent role as the rival of the Wife of Bath.

She is perhaps best described in the following lines:

> Ther was also a Nonne, a Prioresse
> That of hir smyling was ful simple and coy
> Hir gretteste ooth was but by seynt Loy
> And she was cleped madame Eglentyne
> Ful wel she song the service divyne
> Entuned in hir nose ful semely
> And Frensh she spak ful faire and fetisly. . . .
> She was so charitable and so pitious
> She wolde wepe, if that she sawe a mous
> Caught in a trappe, if it were deed or bledde.
>
> *Prologue to the Canterbury Tales.*

Priscian. A great grammarian of the fifth century. The Latin phrase, *Diminuere Prisciani caput* (to break Priscian's head), means to "violate the rules of grammar."

Priscilla. (1) The heroine of Longfellow's COURTSHIP OF MILES STANDISH. (2) A delicate little seamstress, one of the chief characters in Hawthorne's BLITHEDALE ROMANCE.

Prisoner of Chillon. See CHILLON.

Prisoner of Zenda, The. A popular romance by Anthony HOPE (1894). The English hero, Rudolf Rassendyll, for three months impersonates King Rudolf of Ruritania, the "Prisoner of Zenda," meantime making every effort to secure the King's release and return to him the throne. His final success in so doing loses for Rassendyll the hand of the Princess Flavia, whom he surrenders to his royal rival, together with the crown.

Prithu. A hero of the Indian *Purânas.* Vena having been slain for his wickedness, and leaving no offspring, the saints rubbed his right arm, and the friction brought forth Prithu. Being told that the earth had suspended for a time its fertility, Prithu went forth to punish it, and the Earth, under the form of a cow, fled at his approach. Unable to escape, she promised that in future "seed-time and harvest should never fail."

Private Papers of Henry Ryecroft, The. A novel by George GISSING (1903), largely autobiographical and dealing with the problems of the struggling author.

Privy Council. The council chosen by the English sovereign originally to administer public affairs, but by the 20th century never summoned as a whole except to proclaim the successor to the Crown on the death of the Sovereign. The business of the Privy Council is now performed by Committees (of which the Cabinet is technically one), such as the Judicial Committee of the Privy Council, and the great departments of State—the Board of Trade, Local Government Board, Board of

Education, etc. All of these are, in theory, merely committees of the Privy Council. Privy Councillors are entitled to the prefix "the Right Honorable" before their names, and rank next after Knights of the Garter, who may be commoners.

Prix Goncourt. A prize, at first of 5000, later of 10,000 francs, awarded every year (since 1903) by the Académie Goncourt in Paris for the most remarkable imaginative work composed during the year by a young French writer. The academy was founded with an endowment bequeathed by Edmond GONCOURT and is composed of ten outstanding French men of letters.

pro and con (*Lat.*). For and against. *Con* is an abbreviation of *contra. The pros and cons* of a matter are all that can be said for or against it.

Proclus (410?–485). Greek Neoplatonic philosopher who defended paganism and opposed Christianity. He issued a brief statement of the principles of Neoplatonism.

Procne. In classic myth the sister of PHILOMELA.

Procopius. A Byzantine historian who was private secretary (527 A.D.) to Belisarius and accompanied him on his campaigns. He wrote histories of the Persian, Vandal, and Gothic wars.

Procris. In classic myth, the jealous wife of CEPHALUS.

unerring as the dart of Procris. When Procris fled from Cephalus out of shame, Diana gave her a dog (Laelaps) that never failed to secure its prey, and a dart which not only never missed aim, but which always returned of its own accord to the shooter.

Procrustes' bed. Procrustes, in Greek legend, was a robber of Attica, who placed all who fell into his hands upon an iron bed. If they were longer than the bed he cut off the redundant part, if shorter, he stretched them till they fitted it. He was slain by THESEUS. Hence, any attempt to reduce men to one standard, one way of thinking, or one way of acting, is called *placing them on Procrustes' bed.*

Procter, Bryan Waller. Pseudonym **Barry Cornwall** (1787–1874). English poet. Friend of Charles Lamb, Leigh Hunt, Hazlitt, Dickens, etc. His daughter **Adelaide Ann Procter** (1825–1864), is remembered for her poem THE LOST CHORD which she wrote under the pseudonym of Mary Berwick.

Procyon. A first-magnitude star in Canis Minor.

Prodigal Son. A repentant sinner from the parable of the Prodigal Son (*Luke* xv.) who "wasted his substance in riotous living" in a far country, but returned to his father's house and was forgiven.

prodigy (Lat. *prodigium*). A portent, prophetic sign.

the Prodigy of France. Guillaume Budé (1467–1540); so called by Erasmus.

the Prodigy of Learning. Samuel Hahnemann (1755–1843), the German founder of homeopathy, was so called by J. Paul RICHTER.

Professor, The. A novel by Charlotte Brontë (written, 1846; published posthumously, 1857), founded on the facts of the author's experiences in teaching school in Brussels.

Professor Bernhardi. A drama by Arthur SCHNITZLER (1862–1931) concerning the public persecution of a distinguished Jewish physician who has refused to let a Catholic priest disturb a charity patient, dying in the hospital in happy ignorance of her impending fate.

Professorenroman (*Ger.*). Literally, "professor's novel." In German literary history a very convenient term applied to novels which are crammed full of reliably correct historical detail but which remain absolutely devoid of literary inspiration.

Professor's House, The. A novel (1925) by Willa CATHER.

Profitendieu, Bernard. In André Gide's THE COUNTERFEITERS, the adolescent hero, a Paris schoolboy who runs away from home when he discovers a letter which appears to be evidence that his birth was illegitimate.

Promised Land, The. An autobiography (1912) by Mary ANTIN.

Profound Doctor. See under DOCTOR.

Progne, see PROCNE.

program music. A type of music the aim of which is to tell a story, either by the imitation of natural sounds or by the suggestion in sound of the actions and situations of a definite plot, or "program." Beethoven's Sixth or *Pastoral Symphony* is an early example of program music, as is the *Symphonie fantastique* of BERLIOZ. The orchestral TONE POEMS of Richard STRAUSS are also representative examples of program music. See also ABSOLUTE MUSIC.

Progress and Poverty. A treatise on economics by Henry GEORGE (1879). In it, the author tries to analyze why there is an increase in poverty with the increasing prosperity of a nation and attributes the cause to private ownership of land and the rising rate of rent in proportion to the rising value of the land. George's proposed solution is his famous "Single Tax," by which only the return from rented land is made subject to taxation.

Progressive party. The first of the American political organizations to have this name was formed during the 1912 presidential campaign by Republicans opposed to the nomination of William Howard Taft. These insurgents nominated Theodore Roosevelt for president and Hiram Johnson for vice-president. Their party was also given the name of the Bull Moose Party, and the platform included approval of woman suffrage and other advanced measures. In 1924 the second Progressive party was organized, nominating Robert La Follette for president and Burton K. Wheeler for vice-president. It was supported by farmer, labor, and socialist groups. It opposed monopoly, and collected 5 million votes, one-sixth of the total votes in the election.

Prohibition. The term by which the national legal curb on the sale of intoxicating liquors, as authorized by the 18th Amendment to the U.S. Constitution (passed 1918, repealed by the 21st Amendment in 1933), was popularly known. During the period that Prohibition was in force nationally there was predominant BOOTLEGGING, racketeering, and crime. See GANGSTERS; SPEAKEASY. Prohibition laws, all the result of agitation by leaders of the temperance movement and the ANTI-SALOON LEAGUE, were passed from time to time by individual states during the 19th century, and some continued after the repeal of the 18th Amendment. A Prohibition party, founded in 1869, regularly entered candidates in national elections.

Prokofiev, Sergei Sergeevich (1891–). Russian composer, noted for the brilliance and boldness of his compositions. His *The Buffoon* was played by Diaghilev's ballet in Paris (1921). *Peter and the Wolf* is also a popular ballet. His CLASSICAL SYMPHONY is more conventional in style.

Prokosch, Frederic (1909–). American poet and novelist, author of poetry marked by rich, sensuous imagery and an atmosphere of decay, and novels dealing chiefly with romantic adventure and unusual, introspective characters portrayed against exotic foreign backgrounds. *The Assassins* (1936), *The Carnival* (1938), and *Death at Sea* (1940) are books of his poetry; his novels include *The Asiatics* (1935), *The Seven Who Fled* (1937), *Night of the Poor* (1939), and *The Idols of the Cave* (1946), a novel of New York and the ballet.

proletarian literature. A type of literature, at the height of its influence during the 1930's, especially in the U.S., which had as its aim a sympathetic portrayal of the lives and sufferings of the PROLETARIAT and an exposure of the injustices and economic inequalities seen by its writers in the society in which they lived, with a view toward inducing amelioration. A presentation of the aims and activities of labor organizers, revolutionaries, and members of the COMMUNIST PARTY, all regarded as representatives of the proletariat, was also an outstanding characteristic of proletarian literature, and a novel or play dealing with the privations of a family of miners, factory-workers, or southern sharecroppers would often conclude with a burst of hope on the part of the characters as they went out to join a labor union or become Communists. But although the leading writers of proletarian literature were often Communists or Communist sympathizers, and the Communist party enthusiastically endorsed and encouraged its production, frequently using it for purposes of PROPAGANDA for the achievement of various of its objects, to a large degree this type of literature represented the sincere response of its authors to an era of economic depression and unemployment and to certain persistent social injustices which they knew from their own experience or observation.

In subject-matter and sympathetic approach to its characters, proletarian literature had its forerunners among the humanitarian novelists of the 19th century, such as Mrs. GASKELL, DICKENS, George ELIOT, Charles KINGSLEY, Victor HUGO, Harriet Beecher STOWE, and Rebecca H. DAVIS, Jack LONDON, and such humanitarian poets as Thomas HOOD, Elizabeth Barrett BROWNING, and Edward MARKHAM. In its social perspective, it was preceded by the naturalists (FLAUBERT, the GONCOURTS, ZOLA) and their American disciples Stephen CRANE and Frank NORRIS, by the MUCKRAKERS, and by such "problem" novelists as W. D. HOWELLS, Robert HERRICK, and D. G. PHILLIPS. Its technique, in turn, is derived from that of the naturalists and the unaffiliated realists, such as KIRKLAND, E. W. HOWE, and Hamlin GARLAND, while the spirit of bitter or idealistic rebellion that animates its most characteristic examples had a precedent among the English and American romantics—Robert BURNS, the early WORDSWORTH, P. B. SHELLEY, EMERSON, THOREAU, and Walt WHITMAN. Whitman's exaltation of the "common man" was continued particularly by American proletarian poets.

In the field of fiction and the theater, proletarian writers include the following: Maxim GORKY, Gerhart HAUPTMANN (in his early career), Sean O'CASEY, Liam O'FLAHERTY, NEXÖ, John Dos PASSOS (in part in U.S.A.), James T. FARRELL (in part in STUDS LONIGAN), BARBUSSE, Erskine CALDWELL, John STEINBECK, André MALRAUX, Clifford ODETS, John Howard LAWSON, Irwin SHAW, Marc BLITZSTEIN, Albert HALPER, Meyer LEVIN, Albert MALTZ, Grace LUMPKIN, Meridel LE SUEUR, Henry ROTH, Richard WRIGHT, Waldo FRANK, and Leane ZUGSMITH. Among proletarian poets are: Carl SANDBURG (in his celebration of the "common man," which preceded the general movement in proletarian literature by a number of years), Bertolt BRECHT, Hugh MACDIARMID, Stephen SPENDER (in part), Kenneth FEARING, Alfred HAYES, Muriel RUKEYSER (in her early work), Horace GREGORY (in part). Characteristic proletarian novels are MAN'S FATE, IN DUBIOUS BATTLE, and GRAPES OF WRATH; WAITING FOR LEFTY and LET FREEDOM RING are characteristic proletarian plays. With the growth of the international ambitions of Nazi Germany and Fascist Italy, anti-Nazi and anti-Fascist works, by such writers as Ralph BATES and Ignazio SILONE, came to be included in the category of proletarian. Leading organs of proletarian literature were the magazines NEW MASSES, THE ANVIL, and PARTISAN REVIEW, the last-named in its early period of publication only. A school of proletarian criticism also developed which sought to advance the notion that literature should concern itself with social and economic injustice and participate actively in the "class struggle," impelling its readers to "action" rather than causing them pleasure or turning them to contemplation. It vigorously condemned theories of "ART FOR ART'S SAKE."

See also MARXISM IN LITERATURE.

proletariat. The lowest class of the community, laborers and wage-earners who are destitute of property. In ancient Rome, the *proletarii* contributed nothing to the state but their *proles*, i.e., offspring; they could hold no office, were ineligible for the army, and were useful only as breeders of the race.

The term came into wide use with the spreading influence of the Socialist and Communist movements in the 19th and 20th centuries, being frequently used in Marxist writings (see MARX, KARL; MARXISM), and was especially known after the successful Russian Revolution of 1917. In Marxist and Communist context it refers particularly to workers in factories.

dictatorship of the proletariat. A period of strict control by the working-class revolutionaries which, according to Marxist doctrine, is to mark the transition from a capitalist society to a state of communal ownership, its political forms "withering away" when its work of expropriating land, factories, resources, capital, etc., from private hands has been completed. The dictatorship of the proletariat in the U.S.S.R. was supposed to have ended within a few years after the revolution, although some critics maintained that a political dictatorship continued as the government of the nation.

Prometheus (*Gr.,* "forethought"). One of the Titans of Greek myth, son of Iapetus and the ocean-nymph Clymene, and famous as a benefactor to man. It is said that ZEUS employed him to make men out of mud and water, and that then, in pity for their state, he stole fire from heaven and gave it to them. For this he was chained by Zeus to Mount Caucasus, where an eagle preyed on his liver all day, the liver being renewed at night. He was eventually released by Hercules, who slew the eagle. It was to counterbalance the gift of fire to mankind that Zeus sent PANDORA to earth with her box of evils.

Prometheus is the subject of a famous trilogy by the Greek dramatist AESCHYLUS (*Prometheus Bound, Prometheus Unbound, Prometheus the Fire Bringer*). One of Shelley's best-known works is his poetic drama *Prometheus Unbound*. William Vaughn MOODY'S drama, *The Fire Bringer* (1904) also deals with Prometheus, and many other poets have sung of him.

Promethean. Capable of producing fire; pertaining to Prometheus. The earliest "safety" matches, made in 1805 by Chancel, a French chemist, who tipped cedar splints with paste of chlorate of potash and sugar, were known as *Prometheans*.

Promethean fire. The vital principle; the fire with which Prometheus quickened into life his clay images. Figuratively, inspiration.

the Promethean unguent. Made from a herb on which some of the blood of Prometheus had fallen. MEDEA gave Jason some of it, and thus rendered his body proof against fire and warlike instruments.

Promised Land or **Land of Promise.** Canaan or Palestine; so called because God promised Abraham, Isaac, and Jacob that their offspring should possess it. (*Gen.* xii. 7, xxvi. 3, xxviii. 13).

The expression is frequently in use with reference to the promise of the BALFOUR DECLARATION that the Jews should have a "homeland" in Palestine.

Promised Land, The. An autobiography by Mary ANTIN (1912), describing her life in Polotsk as the child of a Russian Jew, her emigration to America at the age of ten, and her school days in Boston, where her talents and enthusiasm for America made friends for her and opened many doors of opportunity.

proof. A trial imprint to be corrected and approved before it is finally printed.

galley or *first proof.* Galleys are shallow oblong containers that hold the equivalent of three or four pages of book type. First proofs are practically always taken in galley form—that is, in single column on long strips of paper. Corrections noted on galley proof are made before the type is arranged in pages.

page proof (usually *second proof,* although the proofreader sometimes calls for a second galley proof). After the type has been taken out of the galley and arranged in pages, page proofs are taken, with page numbers, titles or chapter headings, etc.

foundry or *stone proof.* Proofs made after the type pages are locked in the forms for the electrotyping process. They have a black border made by the ink from the metal guards. After the electrotype plates are cast, corrections are very expensive.

author's proof. The proof sent to the author of the manuscript for his corrections and O.K.

clean proof. A proof having very few printers' errors, or a revised proof.

foul or *dirty proof.* A proof after it has been corrected by proofreader or author, or a proof with many printers' errors.

revised proof. Second proof, either galley or page.

press proof. The final proof O.K.'d for the press.

proofreader. One who reads and corrects printers' proofs.

Proof marks for correction of proof:

cap., change to capital letters those trebly underlined.

δ delete, take out.

ital., change to italic letters those underlined.

l.c., change to lower-case letters (small, not caps or s. caps) those underlined.

n.p., or ¶, begin a new paragraph with the word after the bracket [.

press, print off.

Qy., or ?, added by reader to mark something about which he is uncertain.

revise, submit another proof.

rom., change to roman letters those underlined.

run on and a line drawn from the last word of the first paragraph to the first word of the second, no new paragraph.

s. caps., change to small capitals those doubly underlined.

stet, let the canceled word dotted underneath remain.

tr/ transpose as marked.

w.f., wrong font (type face or size), alter.

╳ bad letter, substitute good type.

⋀ the caret mark, insert matter in margin.

□ indent first word.

insert space, or equalize spacing.

ʟ space to be reduced.

ɓ a type inverted, turn.

⌒ remove space, close up.

V to be put under all apos., quotes, and superior letters (as *r* in Mr.) to be added.

⊥ a space to be pushed down.

Γ move to the left.

˥ move to the right.

|| make parallel at the sides.

..... see *stet,* above.

≡ lines to be straightened.

/ a stroke as this to be put after each note in the margin to show that it is concluded, to separate it from others, and to call attention to it.

All corrections are to be made in *ink,* and attention called to them *in the margin,* as otherwise they are likely to be overlooked. All punctuation marks, as full stop, etc., to be enclosed in a circle.

propaganda. A type of literature or journalism which, by means of style and emphasis as well as content, seeks to appeal to the fears, emotions, and prejudices of a certain group of people in such a way as to persuade them to undertake a desired action or to inculcate in them a desired attitude. Commercial advertising, certain types of political oratory, and certain official releases to the newspapers by governments or organizations are outstanding examples of propaganda. The word came to have an opprobrious connotation during the 1920's and 1930's as a result of revelations that the "atrocities" attributed to Germany during the invasion of Belgium in World War I were untrue, although proletarian critics (see PROLETARIAN LITERATURE) defended the use of propaganda in fiction and poetry, claiming that all good literature has been propaganda. A striking and apparently overwhelmingly effective use of propaganda was made during this period by the movements of FASCISM and NAZISM. The science of SEMANTICS made propaganda one of the objects of its study, and at the beginning of World War II an Institute for Propaganda Analysis was founded in the U.S. for the analysis of statements made by the various belligerents and the demonstration of their fallacious or specious reasoning and misleading wording. When the U.S. entered the war, the Institute was disbanded.

Propertius, Sextus (b. ca. 51 B.C.). Latin poet, known for his elegiac verse dealing with the varying phases of ecstasy and disillusionment in love. The 20th-century American poet Ezra POUND was much interested in the work of Propertius.

Prophet, the. The special title of MAHOMET. According to the KORAN, there have been 200,000 prophets, but only six of them brought new laws or dispensations, viz., Adam, Noah, Abraham, Moses, Jesus, and Mahomet.

the Great or *Major Prophets.* Isaiah, Jeremiah, Ezekiel, and Daniel; so called because their writings are more extensive than the prophecies of the other twelve.

the Minor or *Lesser Prophets.* Hosea, Joel, Amos, Obadiah, Micah, Jonah, Nahum, Habakkuk, Zephaniah, Haggai, Zechariah, and the author of Malachi, whose writings are less extensive than those of the four Great Prophets.

Prophète, Le (The Prophet). An opera by MEYERBEER (1849), libretto by SCRIBE. The scene is laid in Holland in 1534–1535, and the central figure is John of Leyden, the fanatical leader of the Anabaptist uprising. The heroine, Bertha, wreaks vengeance against the blood-thirsty Prophet, unconscious of the fact that he is her betrothed, and kills herself on discovery of the truth. The chief dramatic interest lies in the part of Fides, the Prophet's mother, whom he publicly denies because he wishes the people to believe he is of supernatural origin, but who forgives him with true motherly love.

Prophetess, the. A title of Ayeshah, the second and beloved wife of MAHOMET. Like *Sultana,* it is simply a title of honor.

props. In theatrical and motion-picture cant, short for property, the things that are necessary to the action of a play and have to be placed on the stage by the "property man."

prose (Lat. *oratio prosa*—i.e., *proversa,* "straightforward speaking"). The form of man's ordinary language. The term is meaningful only by opposition to the foot-bound form of language which is normally called poetry. The rhythm of artistic prose is not pre-established but emerges from the rhythm of thought.

Monsieur Jourdain, in Molière's *Le Bourgois gentilhomme* suddenly discovers that he has been talking prose for twenty years without knowing it.

Father of English, French, etc., *prose.* See under FATHER.

Proserpina or **Proserpine.** The Roman counterpart of the Greek goddess Persephone, daughter of DEMETER, queen of the infernal regions and wife of PLUTO. As the personification of seasonal changes, she passed six months of the year on Olympus, and six in Hades; while at Olympus she was beneficent, but in HADES she was stern and terrible. Legend has it that, as she was amusing herself in the meadows of Sicily, Pluto seized her and carried her off in his chariot to the infernal regions as his bride. In her terror she dropped some of the lilies she had been gathering, and they turned to daffodils. In Hades she was disconsolate and would eat nothing, but finally tasted a few pomegranate seeds, for which she was compelled to spend a part of each year in the underworld.

In later legend, Proserpina was the goddess of sleep, and in the myth of *Cupid and Psyche,* by Apuleius, after PSYCHE had long wandered about searching for her lost Cupid, she was sent to Proserpina for "the casket of divine beauty," which she was not to open till she came into the light of day. Just as she was about to step on earth, Psyche thought how much more Cupid would love her if she were divinely beautiful; so she opened the casket and found it contained Sleep, which instantly filled all her limbs with drowsiness, and she slept as though it were the sleep of death.

> Thou art more than the day or the morrow, the seasons that laugh or that weep;
> For these give joy and sorrow; but thou, Proserpina, sleep.
>
> Swinburne, *Hymn to Proserpine,* I. 3.

prosody. The science of versification according to syllabic quantity, accent, etc. The systematic study of metrics. All types of metrical feet, patterns of rhyme, kinds of stanzas, etc., come in its domain.

Prosper le Gai. The hero of Maurice Hewlett's FOREST LOVERS.

Prospero. The rightful Duke of Milan in THE TEMPEST, deposed by his brother. Having drifted to a desert island, he practices magic and raises a tempest in which his brother is shipwrecked. Ultimately Prospero breaks his magic wand, and his daughter marries the son of the King of Naples.

Prospice. Latin, "Look forward!" Soon after his wife's death, Robert BROWNING wrote a poem of this title (1864) in which he expressed an optimistic and courageous attitude toward death.

protagonist. The chief person in a drama or novel. Hence also the chief supporter of a given "cause."

Protagoras. Greek philosopher of the 5th century B.C. Known as the first of the Sophists. "Man is the measure of all things: of those which are, that they are; of those which are not, that they are not." Driven from Athens under a charge of atheism. One of Plato's dialogues bears his name. In it Socrates makes the point that virtue is knowledge.

pro tanto (*Lat.*). As an instalment, good enough as far as it goes, but not final; for what it is worth.

pro tempore (*Lat.*). Temporarily; for the time being, until something is permanently settled. It is usually contracted into *pro tem.*

Protesilaus. At the siege of Troy an oracle prophesied that the first Greek to step on land would be killed. Protesilaus took the office upon himself and was promptly slain. After that, his wife, Laodamia, always kept an image of him where she could see it. When her father took it from her, she killed herself.

Proteus. (1) In Greek legend, Neptune's herdsman, an old man and a prophet, famous for his power of assuming different shapes at will. Hence the phrase, *as many shapes as Proteus*—i.e., full of shifts, aliases, disguises, etc., and the adjective *protean,* readily taking on different aspects, ever-changing. Proteus lived in a vast cave, and his custom was to tell over his herds of sea-calves at noon, and then to sleep. There was no way of catching him but by stealing upon him at this time and binding him; otherwise he would elude anyone by a rapid change in shape.

(2) In Shakespeare's Two GENTLEMEN OF VERONA, one of the two titular heroes.

prothalamion. The term coined by SPENSER (from Gr. *thalamos,* "a bridal chamber") as a title for his "Spousall Verse" (1596) in honor of the double marriage of Lady Elizabeth and Lady Katherine Somerset, daughters of the Earl of Worcester, to Henry Gilford and William Peter, Esquires. Hence, a song sung in honor of the bride and bridegroom before the wedding is called a *prothalamion.*

Prothero, George Walter (1848–1922). English historian. Coeditor, *Cambridge Modern History* (1902–1912).

Protocol, Mr. Peter. In Scott's GUY MANNERING, the attorney in Edinburgh employed by Mrs. Margaret Bertram of Singleside.

protomartyr. The first martyr in a given cause. The Christian protomartyr is St. Stephen.

Proudhon, Pierre Joseph (1809–1865). French philosophic anarchist. His most famous work, *What is Property?* (1840), starts out with the answer, "Property is theft!"

Proudie, Bishop and **Mrs.** Two of the best-known characters in Anthony Trollope's *Chronicles of Barsetshire* (see BARSETSHIRE). Dr. Proudie is a hard-working, earnest clergyman, but whether he would ever have risen to the position of bishop without the exertions of the redoubtable Mrs. Proudie is something about which no reader of the novels can be in doubt. That strong-willed and sharp-tongued lady is a born executive and can be trusted with the fortunes of the household and of the diocese as well. Trollope killed her off at last on impulse after overhearing two clergymen say that they would not continue to write novels if they could not create new characters, but he is said to have mourned her loss ever afterward.

Proust, Marcel (1871–1922). French novelist, one of the most famous literary figures of his generation, known for his REMEMBRANCE OF THINGS PAST (*A la Recherche du temps perdu;* 1913–1928), a long novel in seven books. As epitomized here, his work is characterized by psychological penetration, skill in character portraiture, intense introspective analysis, and a complex, delicate, and suggestive style. He was strongly influenced by Henri BERGSON, whose theories of time and memory he embodied in his great work; Anatole FRANCE, Robert de MONTESQUIOU, and John RUSKIN were also admired by Proust. His other works are *Pastiches et Mélanges* (1919), written in his early youth, and *Les Plaisirs et les jours* (1896).

Proust, as a wealthy and popular young man, was well-known in the Parisian world of society that he portrayed in his novels. He suffered from asthma and heart-trouble and spent most of the final ten years of his life in an unventilated bedroom, where he wrote, studied, and received his friends, going out only on rare occasions and then only at night. He was known for his eccentric behavior, his almost morbid hypersensitivity, and his tireless literary drudgery which, according to some reports, ruled him even on his deathbed. See also BALZAC, FLAUBERT, GONCOURT brothers, DAUDET. With James JOYCE and Thomas MANN he is ranked among the greatest novelists of the 20th century.

See also ROMAN-FLEUVE.

Prout, Father. The pseudonym of Francis Mahoney (1805–1866), a humorous writer who contributed the *Prout Papers* to *Fraser's Magazine.* They consisted of a series of dialogues and episodes in the life of a parish priest.

Prouty, Mrs. **Olive Higgins** (1882–). American novelist, best-known for *Stella Dallas* (1922).

Proverbs. A section of the Old Testament written by several authors, formerly thought to include Solomon. In the Douay Version it is called *Book of Proverbs.*

Provincetown Players. An American LITTLE THEATER group, organized in 1915 at Provincetown, Massachusetts. At first, its plays were produced in the "Wharf Theater," formerly a fishing smack. Later it moved to GREENWICH VILLAGE, where its productions attracted critical attention. Among the authors who wrote for the Provincetown Players are Eugene O'NEILL, Edna St. Vincent MILLAY, John REED, Sherwood ANDERSON, Susan GLASPELL, Floyd DELL, Paul GREEN, and E. E. CUMMINGS. The group included among its productions some of the artistically most important plays of its time, and had a strong influence on the commercial drama. It lasted as an association for almost twenty-five years.

Provok'd Wife, The. A comedy (1697) by Sir John VANBRUGH.

Prudhomme, Monsieur. An extremely self-important, self-satisfied person, from *Joseph*

Prudhomme, a character created by Henri Monnier, whose original adventures were enlarged upon and published as *Les Memoires de Joseph Prudhomme* in 1857. He is a "calligraphist and sworn expert in the courts of law," a man of experience and great prudence and practical good sense.

Prudhomme, Sully, see SULLY PRUDHOMME.

Prue and I. A leisurely narrative, or more accurately, a series of essays, by G. W. Curtis (*Am.,* 1856), in which a bookkeeper whose meager salary provides for few luxuries, indulges to the full his bent for "Castles in Spain."

Prufrock, J. Alfred. The protagonist of T. S. ELIOT's long poem *The Love Song of J. Alfred Prufrock* (1917). Mr. Prufrock is a decorous New England bachelor approaching middle age who spends his time attending stuffy and useless social gatherings and associating with stuffy and useless people of the New England upper classes. In the poem, which makes use of the rhythms and the techniques of the Symbolist poets, especially Jules LAFORGUE, Prufrock contemplates the emptiness of his life in ironic despair.

prunella. A woolen or mixed stuff, formerly used for clergymen's gowns and the uppers of shoes.

> Worth makes the man, and want of it the fellow;
> The rest is all but leather or prunella.
> Alexander Pope, *An Essay on Man.*

Prunella is the name of a fantasy by Laurence HOUSMAN, in which the petite American actress Marguerite Clark played.

prunes and prisms. The words which give the lip the right ply of the highly aristocratic mouth, as Mrs. General tells Amy Dorrit in Dickens' LITTLE DORRIT:

> " 'Papa' gives a pretty form to the lips. 'Papa,' 'potatoes,' 'poultry,' 'prunes and prisms.' You will find it serviceable if you say to yourself on entering a room, 'Papa, potatoes, poultry, prunes, and prisms.' "

Prussianism. Prussian militarism; hence, any ruthless theory or practice of the kind popularly associated with Prussia.

Pry, Paul, see PAUL PRY.

Pryce, Richard (1864–1942). Welsh novelist and playwright.

Prynne, Hester. The heroine of Hawthorne's SCARLET LETTER.

Prynne, William (1600–1669). English Puritan pamphleteer who particularly attacked popular amusements and stage plays.

Pryor, Lloyd. In Margaret Deland's AWAKENING OF HELENA RICHIE, Helena's lover.

P.S. (Lat. *post-scriptum*). Written afterwards—i.e., after the letter or book was finished.

Psalmanazar, George (1679?–1763). The name under which an unidentified Frenchman posed as a Formosan in London. He translated the catechism into his "native" language for the bishop of London. After a serious illness (1728) he confessed to his imposture and took up a new career as a hack writer. Dr. Johnson thought highly of him.

Psalmist, the. King David is called "The Sweet Psalmist of Israel" (2 *Sam.* xxiii. 1).

Psalm of Life, A. A didactic poem by Henry Wadsworth LONGFELLOW, in his *Voices of the Night* (1839).

psaltery. An ancient zither-like musical instrument, mentioned in the *Psalms.* Also called a psalterion, as in:

> My fingers thou hast taught to con
> Thy flame-chorded psalterion,
> Till I can translate into mortal wire—
> Till I can translate passing well—
> The heavenly harping harmony
> Melodious, sealed, inaudible,
> Which makes the dulcet psalter of the world's desire.
> Francis Thompson, *Orient Ode.*

The origin of the word is identical with that of *psalter,* which stood for a musical instrument before its meaning was restricted to *Psalter,* "The Book of Psalms."

Psammead. The strange monkey-like creature with snail-like eyes who has the power of granting wishes that usually turn out badly, in *Five Children and It,* THE PHOENIX AND THE CARPET, and *The Story of the Amulet,* by "E. NESBIT."

P's and Q's. The phrase, *Mind your P's and Q's,* means "Be very circumspect in your behavior."

Several explanations have been suggested, but none seems to be wholly satisfactory. One is that it was an admonition to children learning the alphabet—and still more so to printers' apprentices sorting type—because of the similar appearance of these tailed letters; another that in old-time bar-parlors in the accounts that were scored up for beer "P" stood for "pints" and "Q" for "quarts," and of course the customer when settling up would find it necessary "to mind his P's and Q's," or he would pay too much; and yet another—from France—is that in the reign of Louis XIV, when huge wigs were worn, and bows were made with great formality, two things were specially required: a "step" with the feet, and a low bend of the body. In the latter the wig would be very apt to get deranged, and even to fall off. The caution, therefore, of the French dancing-master to his pupils was, "Mind your P's (i.e., *pieds,* feet) and Q's (i.e., *queues,* wigs)."

Psaphon's birds (Lat. *Psaphonis aves*). Puffers, flatterers. Psaphon, in order to attract the attention of the world, reared a multitude of birds, and having taught them to pronounce his name, let them fly.

pschent. The double crown of the Egyptian pharaohs, worn after Upper and Lower Egypt had been united under one rule. The under crown of Upper Egypt was a tall red caplike structure. Over it was the crown of Lower Egypt, made of stiff white linen.

Psellus, Michael Constantine. A Byzantine philosopher and writer of the 11th century; at one time prime minister of Michael VII Ducas. He revived the study of Plato and was influential in the policies of the rulers of his time.

pseudonym. A fictitious name assumed by a writer for purposes of anonymity. Synonyms are: pen name, *nom de plume,* stage name, *nom de théâtre, nom de guerre,* etc. "Mark Twain" is the pseudonym of Samuel L. CLEMENS.

Psycarpax (*Gr.* "granary thief"). In the Greek BATTLE OF THE FROGS AND MICE, the son of Troxartas, the king of the Mice. The Frog-king offers to carry the young prince over a lake, but scarcely has he reached midway, when a water-hydra appears and King Frog, to save himself, dives under water. The mouse, being thus left on the surface, is drowned, and this catastrophe brings about the battle of the Frogs and Mice.

> The soul of great Psycarpax lives in me,
> Of great Troxartas' line.
> Parnell, *Battle of the Frogs and Mice,* i.

Psyche (*Gr.,* "breath"; hence, life, or soul itself). In "the latest-born of the myths," *Cupid and Psyche,* an episode in the *Golden Ass* of Apuleius (2nd century A.D.), a beautiful maiden beloved by Cupid, who visited her every night but left her at sunrise. Cupid bade her never seek to know who he was, but one night curiosity overcame her prudence; she lit the lamp to look at him, a drop of hot oil fell on his shoulder, and he awoke and fled. The abandoned Psyche then wandered far and wide in search of her lover; she became the slave of Venus, who imposed on her heartless tasks and treated her most cruelly; but ultimately she was united to Cupid, and became immortal.

Psychical Research, The Society for. A society founded in England (1882) with Henry Sidgwick as president, then professor of moral philosophy in Cambridge University. The object of the society was to study and investigate supernatural phenomena. A great mass of case histories and statistics was collected, and much progress was made into the knowledge of telepathy, autohypnoses, the subliminal self, etc. F. W. H. Myers, Andrew Lang, and Mrs. Sidgwick were among the earliest members. A. J. Balfour and Professor William James of Harvard, as well as Sir William Crookes, were among its presidents.

psychoanalysis. A 20th-century science attributing the greater part of human activity to motives of the subconscious mind. It endeavors, largely through analysis of the symbolic value of dreams, to bring "suppressed desires" into the sphere of consciousness and to strip them of their power or set them free to work in more normal channels. The prime mover in the field of psychoanalysis was Dr. Sigmund Freud, who identified the *libido,* that is, the prime motive power in living creatures, with the sex urge. Freud's disciple and later rival JUNG rejected such a restriction. Both Freud's and Jung's forms of psychoanalysis are primarily theories advanced to increase our knowledge of the workings of the human mind. Their therapeutic value is secondary. The psychoanalytical system of ADLER's *Individual Psychology* is the work of a doctor, a general practitioner of diseases of the soul, rather than of a philosopher.

psychological tests. See SIMON BINET TESTS.

Ptah. Chief god of Memphis. Worshiped as the molder of the world and the father of gods and men.

Ptolemy. *Latin* **Claudius Ptolemaeus** (2nd century A. D.). Astronomer and geographer of Alexandria, who described in his *Almagest* a new system of astronomy. The Ptolemaic system, as it is called, stipulates that the sun, the planets, and the stars revolve around the earth. It was the generally accepted system until, during the 16th and 17th centuries, it was replaced by the Copernican system. See COPERNICUS.

Ptolemy Philadelphus or **Ptolemy II** (285–246 B. C.). King of Egypt. As a patron of learning he increased the extent of the Alexandrian library begun by his father. Famous men of letters visited Alexandria during his reign. The SEPTUAGINT is said to have been begun at Ptolemy's request. See also MANETHO.

Public Advertiser, The. A London journal (1758–1793), edited by Henry Sampson Woodfall. In it appeared the letters of JUNIUS.

Public Occurrences, Boston, see BOSTON PUBLIC OCCURRENCES.

Public Ledger. A Philadelphia newspaper, founded (1836) as the first penny paper in that city. Purchased (1913) by C. H. K. Curtis.

Public Opinion. Book by Walter LIPPMANN (1922).

public school. In Great Britain, a school either maintained by the community or by private endowment not carried on for profit. Eton, Harrow, Rugby, and Winchester are well-known public schools. In the U.S., an elementary or secondary school maintained by the local government, which requires no tuition fees.

Public Speech. A collection of poems (1936) by Archibald MACLEISH.

Puccini, Giacomo (1858–1924). Italian composer. His principal operas are MANON LESCAUT; LA BOHÈME; LA TOSCA; MADAME

BUTTERFLY; and THE GIRL OF THE GOLDEN WEST.

Pucelle, La. (*Fr.*, "The Maid," i.e., of Orléans). Jeanne d'Arc (1410–1431). Voltaire wrote a mock-heroic, satirical and in part scurrilous, poem with this title. See JOAN OF ARC.

Puck. (1) A mischievous, tricksy sprite of popular folklore, also called ROBIN GOODFELLOW, originally an evil demon, but transformed and popularized in his present form by Shakespeare (MIDSUMMER NIGHT'S DREAM), who shows him as a merry wanderer of the night, "rough, knurly-limbed, faun-faced, and shock-pated, a very Shetlander among the gossamer-winged" fairies around him. The name seems to be connected with *Pooka,* or PHOOKA.

Rudyard KIPLING in his *Puck of Pook's Hill* (1906), a series of tales for children, represents Puck as appearing to two children, Dan and Una, and guiding them through a series of extraordinary adventures, in the course of which they visit many places famed in legend and meet many legendary and historical personages.

(2) An American humorous weekly with colored cartoons (1877–1918). Its most famous editor was Henry Cuyler Bunner (1878–1896). Other notable editors were Harry Leon WILSON (1896–1902), and John Kendrick BANGS (1904–1905).

Puck of Pook's Hill. A book of tales for children by Rudyard KIPLING (1906). See also under PUCK.

Pudd'nhead Wilson. A novel by Mark TWAIN (1894). Pudd'nhead Wilson is the village atheist, and his adventures as an amateur detective form the substance of the book.

pueblo (*Span.*). An Indian village in Arizona, New Mexico, etc., of terraced communal houses built of adobe, sometimes on mesas, with flat-roofed houses reached by trap-doors and ladders and subterranean ceremonial chambers called *kiva.*

puff. An onomatopoeic word, suggestive of the sound made by blowing air from the mouth. As applied to inflated or exaggerated praise, extravagantly worded advertisements, reviews, etc., it dates at least from the early 17th century, and the implication is that such commendation is really as worthless and transitory as a gust of wind.

In Sheridan's *The Critic* (1779), Puff, who, he himself says, is "a practitioner in panegyric, or, to speak more plainly, a professor of the art of puffing" gives a catalogue of puffs:

> Yes, sir,—puffing is of various sorts, the principal are, the puff direct, the puff preliminary, the puff collateral, the puff collusive and the puff oblique, or puff by implication. These all assume, as circumstances require, the various forms of letter to the editor, occasional anecdote, impartial critique, observation from correspondent, or advertisement from the party.—I, ii.

Pugin, Augustus Welby (1812–1852). English architect and designer who was instrumental in reviving Gothic architecture in England in the 19th century.

Pulcherie. In George Sand's LÉLIA, the sister and physical double of Lélia.

Pulci, Luigi. See MORGANTE MAGGIORE.

Pulitzer prizes. Prizes given annually for what is judged to be the best American novel, the best American drama, the best books of biography, history, and (from 1921) poetry, published by American authors, and for the best work done in five distinct fields by American journalists during each year. They are so called from Joseph Pulitzer (1847–1911), American newspaper proprietor and philanthropist, who bequeathed a fund of money for the establishment of the Columbia University School of Journalism, and provided that the annual interest be used for prizes. The first awards were made in 1917.

The following are works of literature awarded the Pulitzer prize:

Novels.

1918—*His Family,* by Ernest Poole
1919—*The Magnificent Ambersons,* by Booth Tarkington
1920—none
1921—*The Age of Innocence,* by Edith Wharton
1922—*Alice Adams,* by Booth Tarkington
1923—*One of Ours,* by Willa Cather
1924—*The Able McLaughlins,* by Margaret Wilson
1925—*So Big,* by Edna Ferber
1926—*Arrowsmith,* by Sinclair Lewis (author declined award)
1927—*Early Autumn,* by Louis Bromfield
1928—*The Bridge of San Luis Rey,* by Thornton Wilder
1929—*Scarlet Sister Mary,* by Julia Peterkin
1930—*Laughing Boy,* by Oliver La Farge
1931—*Years of Grace,* by Margaret Ayer Barnes
1932—*The Good Earth,* by Pearl Buck
1933—*The Store,* by T. S. Stribling
1934—*Lamb in His Bosom,* by Caroline Miller
1935—*Now in November,* by Josephine Johnson
1936—*Honey in the Horn,* by H. L. Davis
1937—*Gone with the Wind,* by Margaret Mitchell
1938—*The Late George Apley,* by J. P. Marquand
1939—*The Yearling,* by Marjorie Kinnan Rawlings

1940—*The Grapes of Wrath,* by John Steinbeck

1941—none

1942—*In This Our Life,* by Ellen Glasgow

1943—*Dragon's Teeth,* by Upton Sinclair

1944—*Journey in the Dark,* by Martin Flavin

1945—*A Bell for Adano,* by John Hersey

1946—No award

1947—*All the King's Men,* by Robert Penn Warren

1948—*Tales of the South Pacific,* by James Albert Michener

Drama.

1918—*Why Marry?* by Jesse L. Williams

1919—none

1920—*Beyond the Horizon,* by Eugene O'Neill

1921—*Miss Lulu Bett,* by Zona Gale

1922—*Anna Christie,* by Eugene O'Neill

1923—*Icebound,* by Owen Davis

1924—*Hell-Bent for Heaven,* by Hatcher Hughes

1925—*They Knew What They Wanted,* by Sidney Howard

1926—*Craig's Wife,* by George Kelly

1927—*In Abraham's Bosom,* by Paul Green

1928—*Strange Interlude,* by Eugene O'Neill

1929—*Street Scene,* by Elmer Rice

1930—*The Green Pastures,* by Marc Connelly

1931—*Alison's House,* by Susan Glaspell

1932—*Of Thee I Sing,* by George S. Kaufman and Morrie Ryskind

1933—*Both Your Houses,* by Maxwell Anderson

1934—*Men in White,* by Sidney Kingsley

1935—*The Old Maid,* by Zoë Akins

1936—*Idiot's Delight,* by Robert E. Sherwood

1937—*You Can't Take It With You,* by George S. Kaufman and Moss Hart

1938—*Our Town,* by Thornton Wilder

1939—*Abe Lincoln in Illinois,* by Robert E. Sherwood

1940—*The Time of Your Life,* by William Saroyan (author declined award)

1941—*There Shall Be No Night,* by Robert E. Sherwood

1942—No award

1943—*The Skin of Our Teeth,* by Thornton Wilder

1944—No award

1945—*Harvey,* by Mary Chase

1946—*State of the Union,* by Russel Crouse and Howard Lindsay

1947—No award

1948—*A Streetcar Named Desire,* by Tennessee Williams

Poetry.

1922—*Collected Poems,* by Edwin Arlington Robinson

1923—*The Harp-Weaver, And Other Poems,* by Edna St. Vincent Millay

1924—*New Hampshire,* by Robert Frost

1925—*The Man Who Died Twice,* by Edwin Arlington Robinson

1926—*What's O'Clock?* by Amy Lowell

1927—*Fiddler's Farewell,* by Leonora Speyer

1928—*Tristram,* by Edwin Arlington Robinson

1929—*John Brown's Body,* by Stephen Vincent Benét

1930—*Selected Poems,* by Conrad Aiken

1931—*Collected Poems,* by Robert Frost

1932—*The Flowering Stone,* by George Dillon

1933—*Conquistador,* by Archibald MacLeish

1934—*Collected Verse,* by Robert Hillyer

1935—*Bright Ambush,* by Audrey Wurdemann

1936—*Strange Holiness,* by Robert Coffin

1937—*A Further Range,* by Robert Frost

1938—*Cold Morning Sky,* by Marya Zaturenska

1939—*Selected Poems,* by John Gould Fletcher

1940—*Collected Poems,* by Mark Van Doren

1941—*Sunderland Capture,* by Leonard Bacon

1942—*The Dust Which is God,* by William Rose Benét

1943—*A Witness Tree,* by Robert Frost

1944—*Western Star,* by Stephen Vincent Benét

1945—*V-Letter and Other Poems,* by Karl Shapiro

1946—No award

1947—*Lord Weary's Castle,* by Robert Lowell

1948—*Age of Anxiety,* by Wystan Hugh Auden

Winners of Pulitzer prizes in the fields of biography and history include Henry Adams' *The Education of Henry Adams;* Hamlin Garland's *A Daughter of the Middle Border;* Michael Pupin's *From Immigrant to Inventor;* Carl Van Doren's *Benjamin Franklin;* Ray Stannard Baker's *Woodrow Wilson;* James Truslow Adams' *The Founding of New England;* John J. Pershing's *My Experiences in the World War;* Herbert Agar's *The People's Choice;* Van Wyck Brooks' *The Flowering of New England;* Frank L. Mott's *A History of American Magazines;* Carl Sandburg's *Abraham Lincoln: The War Years.*

Pullman, George Mortimer (1831–1897). A cabinet maker in Albion, New York, who designed with his friend Ben Field in Chicago the first Pullman car. Organized the Pullman Palace Car Co. (1867).

pulque. A fermented Mexican drink made from the juice of various agaves.

Pumblechook. In Dickens' GREAT EXPECTATIONS, uncle to Joe GARGERY the blacksmith. He is a well-to-do corn-chandler and drives his own chaise-cart. A hard-breathing, middle-aged, slow man is Uncle Pumblechook, with fishy eyes and sandy hair inquisitively on end. He calls Pip, in his facetious way, "sixpen'orth of ha'pence," but when Pip comes into his fortune, Mr. Pumblechook is the most servile of the servile. He ends almost every sentence with, "May I, Mr. Pip?" i.e., "have the honor of shaking hands with you again."

pumpernickel. A coarse rye bread ("brown George") relished in Germany and originally made in Westphalia. Thackeray applied the term as a satirical nickname to petty German princelings ("His Transparency, the Duke of Pumpernickel") who made a great show with the court officials and etiquette, but whose revenue was almost *nil.* The origin of the word is obscure. The charming story which relates that a Napoleonic soldier rejected this coarse bread as only *bon pour Nickel* (good enough for the dog Nickel), whereupon the Germans picked up the phrase and made of it their word *Pumpernickel,* is unfortunately incorrect, for the word can be traced back to the 17th century.

pun. A word-play in which two meanings appear in one word or in two words of identical sound. Used as a rather low form of wit, often in playful humor, but sometimes with deeply serious implications.

> Ask for me tomorrow and you shall find me a grave man.
>
> Shakespeare, *Romeo and Juliet.*

> Eve was nigh Adam;
> Adam was naïve.
>
> Mark A. Neville.

> Sticks float.
> They wood.
>
> Clark Stillman.

Punch. The boy hero of KIPLING's story *Baa Baa Black Sheep* in his volume called *Wee Willie Winkie* (1889).

Punch and Judy. The hero and heroine—and the story—of the popular puppet show, *Punch and Judy,* are of Italian origin, Punch being a contraction of *Punchinello.* In the 18th century the suggestion was made that the name was from a popular and ugly low comedian named Puccio d'Aniello, but nothing definite is known of him, and the conjecture is probably an example of "FOLK ETYMOLOGY." Another suggestion is that the name is derived from that of Pontius Pilate in the old MYSTERY PLAYS.

The show first appeared in England a little before the accession of Queen Anne, and the story is attributed to Silvio Fiorillo, an Italian comedian of the 17th century. Punch, in a fit of jealousy, strangles his infant child, whereupon his wife, Judy, fetches a bludgeon with which she belabors him till he seizes another bludgeon, beats her to death, and flings the two bodies into the street. A passing police officer enters the house; Punch flees, but is arrested by an officer of the Inquisition and shut up in prison, whence he escapes by means of a golden key. The rest is an allegory, showing how the light-hearted Punch triumphs over (1) Ennui, in the shape of a dog, (2) Disease, in the disguise of a doctor, (3) Death, who is beaten to death, and (4) the Devil himself, who is outwitted.

The English satirical humorous weekly paper, PUNCH, OR THE LONDON CHARIVARI, was, of course, named from "Mr. Punch." It first appeared on July 17th, 1841.

Punch's advice to those about to marry. "Don't." This well-known counsel appeared in the *Punch Almanac,* January 1845.

pleased as Punch. Greatly delighted. Our old friend is always singing with self-satisfaction in his naughty ways, and his evident "pleasure" is contagious to the beholders.

Suffolk punch. A short, thick-set carthorse. The term was formerly applied to any short fat man, and is probably the same word as above, though it may be connected with *puncheon,* the large cask.

Punchinello. One of the characters of the old Italian pantomime. See PUNCH AND JUDY and also PIERROT.

Punch the Immortal Liar. A long poem by Conrad AIKEN.

pundit. An East Indian scholar, skilled in Sanskrit and learned in law, divinity, and science. We use the word for a *porcus literarum,* one more stocked with book-lore than deep erudition.

Punic faith (Lat. *Punica fides.*). Treachery, violation of faith, the faith of the Carthaginians. The Latin word *Punicus,* earlier *Poenicus,* meaning a Phoenician, was applied to the Carthaginians, who were of Phoenician descent. The Carthaginians were accused by the Romans of breaking faith with them, a most extraordinary instance of the "pot calling the kettle black"; for whatever infidelity they were guilty of, it could scarcely equal that of their accusers. See also ATTIC FAITH.

Pupin, Michael Idvorsky (1858–1935). Yugoslav-born American physicist and inventor. Extended the range of long-distance telephones; developed a method for short exposures in X-ray photography; etc. Pulitzer prize (1924) for his autobiography, *From Immigrant to Inventor.*

Puranas. Literally, "old stories." A class of Sanskrit works, serving as the Scriptures of Hinduism, and containing the history and legends of the gods.

Purcell, Henry (1659–1695). English composer. Organist at the Chapel Royal (from 1682) and composer in ordinary to the King. His opera *The Fairy Queen* (1693) had a libretto adapted from Shakespeare's *Tempest.*

Purchas, Samuel (1575?–1626). English author and clergyman, known for his editions of voyage literature of Elizabethan times. His outstanding works are *Purchas His Pilgrimage, Or Relations of the World and the Religions Observed in All Ages* (1613); *Purchas His Pilgrim: Microcosmus, Or The Histories of Man* (1619); and *Hakluytus Posthumus, Or Purchas His Pilgrims, Containing a History of the World in Sea Voyages and Land Travel by Englishmen and Others* (1625). The last-named work was compiled in part from material left by HAKLUYT. S. T. COLERIDGE is considered to have made use of the narratives assembled by Purchas in his famous poems *The Rime of the Ancient Mariner* and *Kubla Khan.* Cf. *The Road to Xanadu,* by J. L. Lowes.

Pure, Simon, see SIMON PURE.

Purefoy, Mrs. Mina. In James Joyce's ULYSSES, a woman whose having given birth to a child supplies the basis for the famous Oxen-of-the-Sun scene in the novel. Leopold BLOOM, a friend of Mrs. Purefoy, goes to the maternity hospital to visit her, and while he is there Stephen DEDALUS revels with Buck MULLIGAN in the internes' quarters of the same hospital; eventually Bloom and Stephen meet. This episode is told in a series of parodies on successive literary styles, each representing a particular stage in the development of the English language, to suggest a correspondence with the development of the embryo in the womb. The parodies range from the Bible and the Anglo-Saxon epic through Malory, Shakespeare, and Bunyan to the 19th-century scientific essay, the sentimental novel, and 20th-century Irish slang.

Purgatory. The second part of Dante's DIVINE COMEDY. The doctrine of Purgatory, according to which the souls of the departed suffer for a time till they are *purged* of their sin, is of ancient standing, and was held in a modified form by the Jews, who believed that the soul of the deceased was allowed for twelve months after death to visit its body and the places or persons it especially loved. This intermediate state they called by various names, as "the bosom of Abraham," "the garden of Eden," "upper Gehenna." The outline of this doctrine was annexed by the early Fathers, and was considerably strengthened by certain passages in the New Testament, particularly *Rev.* vi. 9–11, and 1 *Pet.* iii. 18 and 19.

St. Patrick's Purgatory. See under SAINTS.

purge. In the modern sense, in Russia and Germany, the purging of a national party of those opposed to its principles, accomplished by execution or exile. See PRIDE'S PURGE for a bloodless variant in British history.

Puritans. Originally, seceders from the Reformed Church of England in the time of Queen Elizabeth. They are so called because, wishing for a more radical purification of religion, they rejected all human traditions and interference in religious matters, acknowledging the sole authority of the "pure Word of God," without "note or comment." Under Cromwell's leadership they played a major rôle in the history of 17th century England. The PILGRIM FATHERS of New England were Puritans. In both England and America the rigid morals of the Puritans and their stern suppression of various forms of recreation and of art have made the word *Puritanical* synonymous with narrow-minded.

> The Puritan hated bearbaiting, not because it gave pain to the bear, but because it gave pleasure to the spectators. Indeed he generally contrived to enjoy the double pleasure of tormenting both spectators and bear.—Macaulay, *History of England,* Bk. i, ch. ii.

Puritan City. Boston, Mass. See under CITIES.

Puritans, The (I Puritani). An opera by BELLINI (1835), book by Count Pepoli, dealing with the period of CROMWELL. The heroine is Elvira, a Puritan; her lover, Lord Arthur Talbot, a Cavalier. Many circumstances combine to prevent their marrying, but they are united at last.

purple. The imperial color in Rome; hence a mark of dignity and luxury.

purple patches. Highly colored or brilliant passages in a literary work which is, generally speaking, otherwise undistinguished. The allusion is to Horace's *De Arte Poetica,* l. 15:

> Inceptis gravibus plerumque et magna professis,
> Purpureus, late qui splendeat, unus et alter
> Adsuitur pannus.
>
> (Often to weighty enterprises and such as profess great objects, one or two purple patches are sewed on to make a fine display in the distance.)

Purple Cow, The. A quatrain by Gelett BURGESS. It first appeared in the LARK (1895).

> I never saw a PURPLE COW,
> I never HOPE to see one;
> But I can tell you, anyhow,
> I'd rather SEE than BE one.

Some years later, for obvious reasons, he recorded his sentiments with,

> Ah, Yes! I Wrote the PURPLE COW—
> I'm Sorry, now, I Wrote it!
> But I can Tell you Anyhow,
> I'll KILL you if you QUOTE it!

Purple Heart. A military order originally established by George Washington and revived in 1932 to give a mark of distinction to soldiers wounded in the service of their country. The heart has a head of Washington upon it and is worn on a purple ribbon.

Purple Island. An allegorical poem on the human body by Phineas FLETCHER (1633).

Purûravas and Urvasi. A Hindu myth similar to those of Cupid and PSYCHE and Apollo and DAPHNE. King Purûravas fell in love with Urvasi, a heavenly nymph, who consented to become his wife on certain conditions. When these conditions were violated, Urvasi disappeared, and Purûravas, inconsolable, wandered everywhere to find her. Ultimately he succeeded, and they were indissolubly united. There are many versions of the story. One of the best-known is found in Kalidasa's Sanskrit drama, *Vikramormasi.*

Pusey, Edward Bouverie (1800–1882). Anglican theologian. Stood with KEBLE and NEWMAN for a reform of the church and became the leader of the OXFORD MOVEMENT; endeavored to bring about a reunion of the English and Roman churches.

Pushcart at the Curb, A. A collection of poems (1922) by John Dos PASSOS.

Pushkin, Alexander Sergeyevich (1799–1837). Russian poet, dramatist, novelist, and author of tales, the first great author of modern Russia, influenced by the European movement of ROMANTICISM, especially by Lord BYRON. Pushkin's works include *Ruslan and Liudmila* (1820), a long poem; *The Prisoner of the Caucasus* (1825); *The Tzigani* (1827); BORIS GODUNOV (1825), an historical tragedy, dramatized as an opera by MOUSSORGSKY in 1874; *Poltava* (1829); *Eugene Onegin* (1831), a romance in verse, later dramatized as an opera by TCHAIKOVSKY; and a number of tales and lyrics. One tale, *Pique Dame,* has also been made into an opera (music by Tchaikovsky) and a moving picture. Pushkin lived like a characteristic romantic poet, becoming involved in duels and court intrigue, and was a liberal in politics.

Puss in Boots. A famous tale retold from many sources but notably from Charles PERRAULT'S tale *Le Chat botté* (1697). The cat is marvelously accomplished, and by ready wit or ingenious tricks secures a fortune and royal wife for his master, a penniless young miller, who passes under the name of the Marquis de Carabas. In the Italian tale, Puss is called "Constantine's cat."

Putnam, Abbie. See under DESIRE UNDER THE ELMS.

Putnam, George Palmer (1814–1872). American publisher. Founded *Putnam's Monthly Magazine* (1853) and the publishing house of G. P. Putnam & Son (1866). His grandson, **George Palmer Putnam** (1887–), treasurer of G. P. Putnam's Sons, was the husband of Amelia EARHART.

Putnam, Herbert (1861–). Librarian of Congress (1899–1939). Succeeded by Archibald MACLEISH and Luther H. Evans.

Putnam, Israel (1718–1790). American Revolutionary major general who fought in the Battle of Bunker Hill and was in chief command of New York during the defeat in the Battle of Long Island (1776).

Putnam, Mrs. **Nina Wilcox** (1888–). Popular American novelist and short-story writer. *Laughing Through* (1930).

Putnam, Phelps (1894–). American poet. His best-known volumes of verse are *Trinc* (1927) and *The Five Seasons* (1930).

Putsch (*Swiss German*). A small rebellion. Hitler's Beer Hall Putsch (1923) is the most recently famous.

Puttenham, George (d. 1590). English author, known for *Arte of English Poesie* (1589), an early critical treatise, chiefly dealing with rhetorical figures and the classification of types. Sometimes the work is attributed to **Richard Puttenham** (1520?–?1601), George's brother.

putti (*Italian;* singular **putto**). The little nude Cupids or figures resembling Cupids used in decorative painting and sculpture.

Put Yourself in His Place. A novel by Charles READE (1870) dealing with the labor question. The hero is Henry Little, a laborer and inventor who struggles against the jealous antagonism of the trade unions. The title is the favorite saying of the philanthropist, Dr. Amboyne, an important character.

Pwyll. A hero of the Welsh MABINOGION, Prince of Dyfed.

Prince Pwyll's bag. A bag that was impossible to fill.

> Come thou in by thyself, clad in ragged garments, and holding a bag in thy hand, and ask nothing but a bagful of food, and I will cause that in all the meat and liquor that are in these seven cantreves were put into it, it would be no fuller than before.—*The Mabinogion.*

Pye, Henry James (1745–1813). English poet laureate (1790). He wrote patriotic verses and is considered one of the least of the poets laureate.

Pygmalion. A sculptor and king of Cyprus in Greek legend, who, though he hated women, fell in love with his own ivory statue of Aphrodite. At his earnest prayer the goddess gave life to the statue and he married it. The story is told in Ovid's *Metamorphoses,* x, and appeared in English dress in John Marston's *Metamorphosis of Pygmalion's Image* (1598). William MORRIS retold it in

The Earthly Paradise (*August*), and W. S. GILBERT adapted it in his comedy of *Pygmalion and Galatea* (1871), in which the sculptor is a married man. His wife Cynisca is jealous of the animated statue Galatea, which, after considerable trouble, voluntarily returns to its original state.

Bernard SHAW's play, *Pygmalion* (1913), takes its name from this legendary figure. His "Galatea" is a London flower girl who is transformed into a charming woman of the world by three months' labor on the part of a professor of phonetics, and is successfully exhibited in a London drawing-room. The girl's father, Mr. Doolittle, a dustman who eloquently presents the cause of the "undeserving poor" until he is suddenly made respectable by a legacy from a philanthropist, is one of Shaw's most amusing characters.

Pygmies. The name used by Homer and other classical writers for a supposed race of dwarfs said to dwell somewhere in Ethiopia; from Gr. *pugme,* "the length of the arm from elbow to knuckles." Fable has it that every spring the cranes made war on these creatures and devoured them. They used an axe to cut down corn-stalks. When Hercules went to the country, they climbed up his goblet by ladders to drink from it, and while he was asleep two whole armies of them fell upon his right hand, and two upon his left. They were rolled up by Hercules in his lion's skin. It is easy to see how Jonathan SWIFT availed himself of this Grecian legend in his *Gulliver's Travels.* See GULLIVER, LEMUEL.

The term is now applied to certain dwarfish races of Central Africa (whose existence was first demonstrated late in the 19th century), Malaysia, etc.; also to small members of a class, as the *pygmy hippopotamus.*

Pylades and Orestes. Two friends in Homeric legend, whose names have become proverbial for friendship, like those of Damon and Pythias, David and Jonathan. ORESTES was the son, and Pylades the nephew, of AGAMEMNON, after whose murder Orestes was put in the care of Pylades' father Strophius, and the two became fast friends. Pylades assisted Orestes in obtaining vengeance on Aegisthus and Clytemnestra, and afterwards married Electra, his friend's sister.

Pyle, Ernie (1900–1945). American journalist and war correspondent. Killed by Japanese gunfire on Ie, west of Okinawa. His *Here Is Your War* (1943) and *Brave Men* (1944) were immensely popular.

Pyle, Howard (1853–1911). Widely-known American illustrator and author, famous for his pen-and-ink drawings and carefully detailed, colorful and romantic paintings, especially of scenes from American history. Also wrote and illustrated for children, *The Merry Adventures of Robin Hood* (1883); *The Wonder Clock* (1888); *Twilight Land* (1895); etc.

Pym, John (1584–1643). English Parliamentary statesman who decided the fate of Strafford in the time of Charles I, and at the opening of the Civil War led Parliament in refusing peace negotiations.

Pyncheon. The name of the Salem family who built, and lived in, the HOUSE OF THE SEVEN GABLES in Hawthorne's novel of that name.

Colonel Pyncheon. The first Pyncheon, builder of the "House of the Seven Gables," upon whom the wizard Maule pronounced the curse.

Alice Pyncheon. The proud and lovely girl whom the carpenter grandson of Maule hypnotizes and makes subject to his will.

Clifford Pyncheon. The cousin whom Judge Jaffrey Pyncheon allows to suffer thirty years' imprisonment on the false charge of murdering his uncle.

Hepzibah Pyncheon. The gaunt and sallow old maid sister of Clifford, finally forced by poverty to conquer her pride and open a cent-shop.

Judge Jaffrey Pyncheon. The distinguished head of the Pyncheons at the time of the story, a man whose prosperity and eminent reputation are founded on hypocrisy.

Phoebe Pyncheon. The pretty young cousin who lives with Hepzibah and finally marries HOLGRAVE.

Pynson, Richard (d. 1530). Norman printer, settled in London. Successor, with Wynkyn de Worde, to Caxton as king's printer. Introduced Roman type in England. Printed an edition of Chaucer and the SHIP OF FOOLS by Barclay. The modern Pynson Printers in New York take their name from him.

pyramid. A tall structure, built of stone, usually on a square foundation, used as royal tombs in ancient Egypt. There are some seventy pyramids still remaining in Egypt, but those specially called *The* Pyramids are the three largest in the group of eight known as the Pyramids of Gizeh. Of these the largest, the Great Pyramid, is the tomb of Cheops, first king of the 4th Dynasty, about 3000 B. C. It was 480 ft. in height and the length of each base is 755 ft. The Second Pyramid, the tomb of Chephren (also 4th Dynasty) is slightly smaller (472 ft. by 706 ft.); the Third, the tomb of Menkaura, or Mycerinus (4th Dynasty, about 3630 B. C.), is much smaller (215 ft. by 346 ft.). Each contains entrances, with dipping passages leading to various sepulchral chambers.

Pyramid of Mexico. This pyramid is said to have been built in the reign of Montezuma, emperor of Mexico (1466–1520). Its base is double the size of Cheops' pyramid, that is, 1423 feet each side, but its height does not exceed 164 feet. It stands west of Puebla, faces the four cardinal points, was used as a mausoleum, and is usually called the Pyramid of Cholula.

Pyramus. A Babylonian youth in classic story (Ovid's *Metamorphoses,* iv), the lover of Thisbe. Thisbe was to meet him at the white mulberry-tree near the tomb of Ninus, but she, scared by a lion, fled and left her veil, which the lion besmeared with blood. Pyramus, thinking his ladylove had been devoured, slew himself, and Thisbe, coming upon her dead lover soon afterwards, stabbed herself also. The blood of the lovers stained the white fruit of the mulberry-tree into its present color. The "tedious brief scene" and "very tragical mirth" presented by the rustics in Shakespeare's comedy A MIDSUMMER NIGHT'S DREAM is a travesty of this legend.

Pyrocles and Musidorus. The two heroes of Sidney's ARCADIA, famed for their friendship. They have many adventures and are finally shipwrecked in Arcadia, where many more await them.

Pyrocles in Spenser's FAËRIE QUEENE, is the personification of fiery anger.

Pyrrha. The wife of DEUCALION in Greek legend. They were the sole survivors of the deluge sent by Zeus to destroy the whole human race, and repopulated the world by casting stones behind them.

Pyrrhic dance. The famous war-dance of the Greeks; so called from its inventor, Pyrrichos, a Dorian. It was a quick dance, performed in full armor to the flute, and its name is still used for a metrical foot of two short, "dancing" syllables. The *Romaika,* still danced in Greece, is a relic of the ancient Pyrrhic dance.

> Ye have the Pyrrhic dance as yet:
> Where is the Pyrrhic phalanx gone?
> Byron, *The Isles of Greece.*

Pyrrhic victory. A ruinous victory. Pyrrhus, King of Epirus, after his victory over the Romans at Asculum (279 B. C.), when he lost the flower of his army, said to those sent to congratulate him, "One more such victory and Pyrrhus is undone."

Pyrrhonism. Skepticism, or philosophic doubt; so named from Pyrrho (4th cent. B. C.), the founder of the first Greek school of skeptical philosophy. Pyrrho maintained that nothing was capable of proof and admitted the reality of nothing but sensations.

> Blessed be the day I 'scaped the wrangling crew
> From Pyrrho's maze and Epicurus' sty.
> Beattie, *Minstrel.*

Pyrrhus. See NEOPTOLEMUS.

Pythagoras (*fl. ca.* 530 B. C.). The Greek philosopher and mathematician, born at Samos (hence his epithet the "Samian Sage"), to whom was attributed the enunciation of the doctrines of the transmigration of souls and of the harmony of the spheres, and also the proof of the forty-seventh proposition in the first book of Euclid, which is called the *Pythagorean proposition.*

Pythagoras was noted for his manly beauty and long hair. Many legends are related of him, such as that he distinctly recollected previous existences of his own, having been (1) Aethalides, son of Mercury, (2) Euphorbus the Phrygian, son of Panthous, in which form he ran Patroclus through with a lance, leaving Hector to dispatch the hateful friend of Achilles, (3) Hermotimus, the prophet of Clazomenae, and (4) a fisherman. To prove his Phrygian existence he was taken to the temple of Hera, in Argos, and asked to point out the shield of the son of Panthous, which he did without hesitation.

Other legends assert that one of his thighs was of gold, and that he showed it to Abaris, the Hyperborean priest, and exhibited it in the Olympic games; also that Abaris gave him a dart by which he could be carried through the air and with which he expelled pestilence, lulled storms, and performed other wonderful exploits.

Pythia. In Greek legend, a name for the priestess of APOLLO at his famous oracle in DELPHI. The *Pythia* officiated and uttered the words of the oracle.

Pythian games. One of the four great national Greek festivals celebrated every four years at Delphi in honor of Apollo. An earlier name of Delphi was Pytho. The games were instituted by Apollo in commemoration of his slaying of the serpent Python.

Pythias. See DAMON.

Python. The monster serpent hatched from the mud of DEUCALION's deluge, and slain near Delphi by APOLLO.

Q

Q. *To mind one's P's and Q's.* See under P.

Q.E.D. (Lat. *quod erat demonstrandum,* "which was to be demonstrated"). An abbreviation appended to the theorems of Euclid:—Thus have we proved the proposition stated above, as we were required to do.

Q.T., On the strict. With complete secrecy. "Q.T." stands for "quiet."

Quadrilateral. In northern Italy, the four fortresses of Peschiera and Mantua on the Mincio, with Verona, and Legnago on the Adige.

the Prussian Quadrilateral. The fortresses of Luxemburg, Coblentz, Sarrelouis, and Mayence.

quadrivium (Lat. *quadri,* "four," and *via,* "way"). The collective name given by the Schoolmen of the Middle Ages to the four "liberal arts," viz., arithmetic, music, geometry, and astronomy. The *quadrivium* was the "fourfold way" to knowledge; the TRIVIUM the "threefold way" to eloquence; both together comprehended the seven arts or sciences enumerated in the following hexameter:

> Lingua, Tropus, Ratio, Numerus, Tonus, Angulus, Astra.

Quadruple Alliance. An international alliance for offensive or defensive purposes of four powers, especially that of Britain, France, Austria, and Holland in 1718, to prevent Spain from recovering her Italian possessions, and that of Britain, France, Spain, and Portugal in 1834 as a counter-move to the "Holy Alliance" between Russia, Prussia, and Austria. Another is that of 1674, when Germany, Spain, Denmark, and Holland formed an alliance against France to resist the encroachments of Louis XIV.

quaestor. In ancient Rome, an official with the functions of a judge or treasurer.

Quai d'Orsay. The French Foreign Office, from its location in Paris.

Quakers. A familiar name for members of the Society of Friends, an evangelical religious body having no definite creed and no regular ministry, founded by George Fox, 1648–1650. It appears from the founder's *Journal* that they first obtained the appellation (1650) from the following circumstance:—"Justice Bennett, of Derby," says Fox, "was the first to call us Quakers, because I bade him quake and tremble at the word of the Lord."

the Quaker City. Philadelphia. See under CITY.

the Quaker poet. (1) Bernard Barton (*Eng.,* 1784–1849); (2) John Greenleaf Whittier (*Am.,* 1807–1892).

a Quaker's bargain. An offer that must be accepted or rejected without modification.

Quality Street. A drama by J. M. BARRIE (1901). When she sees that her lover, Valentine Brown, finds her very much changed on his return after a long absence, the heroine, Phoebe Throssel, "Phoebe of the ringlets," gaily arrays herself as an imaginary niece Livvy and sets out to conquer him anew.

Quangle Wangle Quee. A creature in Edward LEAR's nonsense poem, *The Quangle Wangle's Hat.*

Quantrill, William Clarke (1837–1865). A guerrilla leader in the Confederate Army. His band operated in Kansas and Missouri (1861–1862).

Quaritch, Bernard (1819–1899). German-born bookseller in London. One of his publications was the extremely valuable *General Catalogue of Old Books and Manuscripts* (12 vols., 1887–1897).

Quarles, Francis (1592–1644). English poet of the Metaphysical school. See METAPHYSICAL POETS. He is known for his religious poetry, marked by an elliptical, colloquial or hortatory style and striking imagery chosen from the everyday pursuits and interests of his time similar to that of George HERBERT. The greatest contemporary popularity was achieved by his EMBLEM books. His works include *A Feast for Worms* (1620); *Argalus and Parthenia* (1629); *Divine Fancies* (1632); *Emblems* (1635); *Hieroglyphics* (1638).

Quarles, Philip. In Aldous Huxley's POINT COUNTER POINT, an English novelist, brother-in-law of Walter BIDLAKE. Quarles is solitary, reserved, analytical, devoted to his work, tending to be cold and devoid of average human weaknesses and sympathies. He is said to represent HUXLEY himself.

Elinor Quarles. Philip's wife, who is unhappy because of the novelist's aloofness.

Quarterly Review, The. An English review, founded by John Murray (1809) as a Tory rival of the *Edinburgh Review.* Sir Walter Scott promoted it and set forth the liberal attitude it should adopt. Famous contributors were Sir Walter Scott (with his favorable review of Jane Austen's *Emma*), Canning, Southey, Rogers, Lord Salisbury, and Gladstone. Croker's review of *Endymion* by John Keats has been said to have hastened Keats's death. Cf. Byron's lines:

> Who killed John Keats?
> 'I,' says the Quarterly,
> So cruel and Tartarly,
> ''Twas one of my feats.'

Quartier Latin, see LATIN QUARTER.

quarto. A book composed of sheets folded twice so that each leaf is one-fourth of a given size of paper.

Quasimodo. The "Hunchback of Notre Dame" in Victor Hugo's novel NOTRE DAME DE PARIS.

quatrain. A stanza of four lines, particularly one of ten-syllable iambic verse. See STANZA.

Quatre-vingt treize. See NINETY-THREE.

quattrocento. The fifteenth century, applied to Italian art or literature. The word means "four hundred."

Quay, Matthew Stanley (1833–1904). Political boss of the state of Pennsylvania (from 1885). U.S. senator (1887–1899, 1901–1904).

Quayle, Gloria. The heroine of Hall Caine's novel THE CHRISTIAN.

Queechy. A once popular novel by Susan WARNER ("Elizabeth Wetherell") (1852). Queechy is the name of the Vermont town where the heroine, Fleda Ringgan, supports herself by making maple sugar after the loss of the money that had provided for her bringing up in Paris. Fleda is a model of all the charms and virtues. She marries Carleton whom she had known in Paris and succeeds in winning him away from his worldly ways.

Queed. A novel by Henry Sydnor HARRISON (*Am.*, 1911). The hero, Queed, is at first a recluse, completely absorbed in a sociological work he is writing, but through his interest in the charming and sympathetic heroine, Sharlee Wayland, becomes a much more normal human being.

queen.

Queen Consort, the wife of a reigning king; *Queen Dowager,* the widow of a deceased king; *Queen Mother,* the mother of a reigning sovereign; also, a queen who is a mother; *Queen Regnant,* a queen who holds the crown in her own right, in contradistinction to a *Queen Consort,* who is queen only because her husband is king.

Queen Anne is dead. A reply made to the teller of stale news.

Queen Dick. Richard Cromwell is sometimes so called. To say a thing occurred *in the reign of Queen Dick* implies it never happened at all.

Queen Quintessence. See QUINTESSENCE.

Queen Mab. See MAB.

Queen of Hearts. Elizabeth, daughter of James I. This unfortunate Queen of Bohemia (1596–1662) was so called in the Low Countries, from her amiable character and engaging manners, even in her lowest estate. Also, a character in Lewis Carroll's ALICE IN WONDERLAND.

Queen of Heaven, with the ancient Phoenicians, was Astarte; Greeks, Hera; Romans, Juno; Trivia, Hecate, Diana, the Egyptian Isis, etc., were all so called; but with the Roman Catholics it is the Virgin Mary.

Queen of Sheba. See SHEBA.

Queen of the Adriatic: Venice. See also BUCENTAUR.

Queen of the East. (1) Antioch, Syria; (2) Batavia, Java; (3) Queen Zenobia of Palmyra, who reigned in the 3rd century.

Queen of the Eastern Archipelago. The island of Java.

Queen of the May. A village lass chosen to preside over the parish sports on May Day. TENNYSON has a poem on the subject.

Queen of the Mississippi Valley. St. Louis.

Queen of the North. Edinburgh.

Queen of the Northern Seas. Elizabeth, who greatly increased the English navy, and was successful against the Spanish Armada, etc.

Queen of the Sciences. Theology.

Queen of the Sea. Tyre.

the Queen's English. Dean Alford wrote a small book on this subject, whence has arisen three or four phrases, such as "clipping the Queen's English," "murdering the Queen's English," etc. Queen's English means grammatical English, as does King's English.

the White Queen. Mary Queen of Scots, from the white mourning she wore for her husband, Lord Darnley; also, one of the remarkable personages of Lewis Carroll's THROUGH THE LOOKING-GLASS.

Queen, Ellery. Pseudonym of Frederic Dannay (1905–) and Manfred B. Lee (1905–), who have also used the pen name of "Barnaby Ross." They are cousins who have been very successful in producing a series of mystery and detective stories, the chief character, the detective, being Ellery Queen. They also publish a monthly magazine of the better type of short mystery stories, *Ellery Queen's Mystery Magazine.*

Queen's Quair, The. A romance (1904) by Maurice HEWLETT, founded on the life of Mary Queen of Scots. The title was suggested by *The Kingis Quair,* a poem composed by James I of Scotland while he was a prisoner in England (1423–1424). *Quair* is an older form of *quire,* "booklet."

Queequeg. In Herman Melville's MOBY DICK, a Polynesian prince who is the comrade of the narrator Ishmael on board the whaling ship. He daily worships a little god which he carries about with him, and occasionally Ishmael joins him.

Quennell, Peter Courtney (1905–). English poet, critic, and biographer; best-known for his books on Byron, Baudelaire and the symbolists, for his *Caroline of England* (1940), and for his highly individual poetry. His parents, **Charles Henry Quennell** (1872–1935) and **Marjorie Quennell,** *née* **Courtney** (1884–), are well-known as the authors of a series of educational books used both in

England and America, including *A History of Everyday Things in England* (4 vols.; 1918–1934), which has sold more than 100,000 copies.

Quentin Durward. A novel by Sir Walter SCOTT (1823), a story of French history. In this novel are introduced Louis XI and his Scottish Guards, Oliver le Dane and Tristan l'Hermite, Cardinal Balue, De la Marck (the "Wild Boar of Ardennes"), Charles the Bold, Philip des Comines, Le Glorieux (the court jester), and other well-known historic characters. The main plot has to do with the love of the gallant young Quentin Durward, a member of the Scottish Guards, and Isabelle, Countess of Croye. The hero saves the King's life in a boar hunt and later wins the hand of the Countess from his rival, the Duke of Orleans.

Quercus, P. E. G. A *nom de plume* used by Christopher MORLEY in his column *The Bowling Green* in *The Saturday Review of Literature*. It was taken from the Latin for "Tall Oaks from Little Acorns Grow" displayed in back of a quick-lunch-counter in Grand Central Station, New York City, which goes back to David Everett's *Lines Written for a School Declamation*.

Quesnay, François (1694–1774). Physician to the King of France. As an economist, contributor to the *Encyclopédie* of articles which were the basis for the theory adopted by the PHYSIOCRATS.

question.

the previous question. The question whether the matter under debate shall be put to the vote or not. In Parliament, and debates generally, when one party wishes that a subject should be shelved, it is customary to "move the previous question"; if this is carried, the original discussion comes to an end, for it has been decided that the matter shall not be put to the vote.

to beg the question. To take for granted something that demands proof; to assume a proposition which, in reality, involves the conclusion. Thus, to say that parallel lines will never meet because they are parallel, is simply to assume as a fact the very thing you profess to prove. The phrase is the common English equivalent of the Latin term, *petitio principii.*

to put the question. To call for a vote; to come to a decision.

Quetzalcoatl. Prior to the Spanish conquest of Mexico, a nature god of various Indian tribes. His symbol was the quetzal or royal bird, which is known abroad as the emblem of Guatemala.

Quex, Lord. The hero of Pinero's comedy THE GAY LORD QUEX.

Quezon y Molina, Manuel Luis (1878–1944). President of the Philippine Senate (1916–1935); president of the Commonwealth of the Philippines (from 1935). After the Japanese conquest of the Philippines he became the head of the Philippine Government in Exile with headquarters first in Australia and then (from May 1942) in the U.S.

Quiberon Bay. An arm of the Bay of Biscay, scene of an historic naval battle (Nov. 20, 1759), in which Admiral Hawke in command of the British fleet defeated the French under Admiral Conflans.

Quick, Herbert (1861–1925). American lawyer and novelist. He became a Single Taxer after reading Henry GEORGE's *Progress and Poverty.* His best-known books are *Vandemark's Folly* (1922) and *The Hawkeye* (1923).

Quickly, Mistress. In Shakespeare's MERRY WIVES OF WINDSOR, servant-of-all-work to Dr. Caius, a French physician. She says, "I wash, wring, brew, bake, scour, dress meat and drink, make the beds, and do all myself." She is the go-between of three suitors for "sweet Anne Page," and with perfect disinterestedness wishes all three to succeed, and does her best to forward the suit of all three, "but speciously of Master Fenton."

Quickly, Mistress Nell. In Shakespeare's 1 and 2 *Henry IV,* hostess of a tavern in East Cheap, frequented by Harry, Prince of Wales, Sir John FALSTAFF, and all their disreputable crew. In *Henry V,* Mistress Quickly is represented as having married Pistol, the "lieutenant of Captain Sir John's army." All three die before the end of the play. Her description of Sir John Falstaff's death (*Henry V* Act ii. Sc. 3) is very graphic. In 2 *Henry IV,* Mistress Quickly arrests Sir John for debt, but, as soon as she hears of his commission, she is quite willing to dismiss the bailiffs, and trust "the honey sweet" old knight again to any amount.

quiddity. The essence of a thing, or that which differentiates it from other things—"the Correggiosity of Correggio," "the Freeness of the Free." Hence it is used of subtle, trifling distinctions, quibbles, or captious argumentation.

quidnunc (*Lat.,* "what now?"). One who is curious to know everything that's going on, or pretends to know it; a self-important newsmonger and gossip. It is the name of the leading character in Murphy's farce *The Upholsterer, Or What News?* (1758).

Quietism. A form of religious mysticism based on the doctrine that the essence of religion consists in the withdrawal of the soul from external objects and in fixing it upon the contemplation of God; especially that professed by the Spanish mystic, Miguel Molinos (1640–1696), who taught the direct relationship between the soul and God. His followers were termed Molinists, or *Quietists.*

Quiller-Couch, Sir Arthur Thomas. Pseudonym **Q** (1863–1944). Cornish writer and scholar, principally known in America as the editor of the *Oxford Book of English Verse* and other collections of poetry in the Oxford series. His best-known novel is *The Splendid Spur* (1889). The background for most of his novels is his native Cornwall.

Quilp, Daniel. In Dickens' OLD CURIOSITY SHOP, a hideous dwarf, cunning, malicious, and a perfect master in tormenting. He lives on Tower Hill, collects rents, advances money to seamen, and keeps a sort of wharf, containing rusty anchors, huge iron rings, piles of rotten wood, and sheets of old copper, calling himself a ship-breaker. He is on the point of being arrested for felony when he is drowned.

He ate hard eggs, shell and all, for his breakfast, devoured gigantic prawns with their heads and tails on, chewed tobacco and water-cresses at the same time, drank scalding hot tea without winking, bit his fork and spoon till they bent again, and performed so many horrifying acts, that one might doubt if he were indeed human.—Ch. v.

Mrs. Betsy Quilp. Wife of the dwarf, a loving, young, timid, obedient and pretty blue-eyed little woman, treated like a dog by her diabolical husband, whom she really loves but more greatly fears.

Quin, James (1693–1766). Irish tragic actor (at Drury Lane, Lincoln's Inn Fields, Covent Garden) of the old school prior to Garrick who displaced him in public favor. He serves as a character in Tobias Smollett's *Humphry Clinker* (1770).

Quinapalus. A kind of "Mrs. Grundy" or "Mrs. Harris" invented by Feste, the Clown in Shakespeare's TWELFTH NIGHT, when he wishes to give some saying the weight of authority. Hence the name is sometimes "dragged in" when one wishes to clench an argument by some supposed quotation.

What says Quinapalus: "Better a witty fool, than a foolish wit."—*Twelfth Night,* i. 5.

Quinbus Flestrin. The man-mountain. So the Lilliputians call GULLIVER in Ch. ii. of *Gulliver's Travels* by Swift. John GAY wrote an ode to this giant.

Quince, Peter. A carpenter, who undertakes the management of the play called PYRAMUS AND THISBE, in Shakespeare's MIDSUMMER NIGHT'S DREAM. He speaks of "laughable tragedy," "lamentable comedy," "tragical mirth," and so on.

quincunx. An order of five items placed in the middle and at each corner of a square. Sir Thomas Browne's *Garden of Cyrus* (1658) is one long discussion of the prevalence of the quincunx throughout the universe. Coleridge's comment upon it was:

. . . quincunxes in heaven above, quincunxes in earth below, quincunxes in the mind of man, quincunxes in tones, in optic nerves, in roots of trees, in leaves, in everything!

Quinn, Arthur Hobson (1875–). American educator and critic. Edited *Representative American Plays* (1917; latest revised edition, 1938). He was one of the founders of the Franklin Inn Club (for writers) in Philadelphia (1902). *Edgar Allan Poe* (1941).

Quinn, Edmond Thomas (1868–1929). American sculptor and painter. He did the bronze statue of Edwin BOOTH as Hamlet which stands before The Players Club in Gramercy Park, New York City.

Quint, Peter. In Henry James' THE TURN OF THE SCREW, the former steward of the estate who is one of the apparitions the governess-narrator believes to return and appear to the children. Quint has particular influence over the boy, MILES.

Quintana, Manuel José (1772–1857). Spanish poet and statesman. His patriotic poems during Spain's war for independence were very popular. He was elected Senator in 1835.

Quintessence, Queen. In Rabelais' GARGANTUA AND PANTAGRUEL (v. 19), the sovereign of Entélechy, the country of speculative science visited by Pantagruel and his companions in their search for "the oracle of the Holy Bottle." See under ORACLE. She is also sometimes known as Queen Whims.

Quintilian. *Latin* **Marcus Fabius Quintilianus** (1st century A. D.). Spanish-born rhetorician and teacher of oratory in Rome (from 68 A. D.). His writings contain a description of the whole educational system of first-century Rome.

Quintus Fixlein. The title and chief character of a romance by Johann Paul Friedrich RICHTER (1796).

Francia, like Quintus Fixlein, had perennial fireproof joys, namely, employments.—Carlyle.

quip modest, the. Sir, it was done to please myself. TOUCHSTONE says (*As You Like It,* v. 4): "If I sent a person word that his beard was not well cut, and he replied he cut it to please himself," he would answer with the quip modest, which is six removes from the lie direct; or, rather, the lie direct in the sixth degree. See also COUNTERCHECK QUARRELSOME.

Quirinus. In Roman legend, a war god, said to be ROMULUS, the founder of Rome, but sometimes identified with MARS.

qui s'excuse, s'accuse (*Fr.*) He who excuses himself, or apologizes, condemns himself.

Quisling, Vidkun (1887–1945). Norwegian official who actively collaborated in the German conquest of Norway (1940) and became head of the State Council under the Nazis. Tried and executed after the German defeat.

His name has become synonymous with "traitor": a *quisling,* also a *quisler.*

Quivira. A mythical city of fabulous treasures, supposed to be located in the present state of Kansas. It was sought by CORONADO and later explorers. Arthur GUITERMAN wrote a poem of that title, which describes Coronado's expedition.

qui vive? (*Fr.*). Literally, *Who lives?* but used as a sentry's challenge and so equivalent to our *Who goes there?*

to be on the qui vive. On the alert; to be quick and sharp; to be on the tiptoe of expectation, like a sentinel.

Quixano, Daniel. A character in Israel Zangwill's THE MELTING POT.

Quixote, Don, see DON QUIXOTE.

Quixotic. Having foolish and impractical ideas of honor, or schemes for the general good, like Don Quixote.

the Quixote of the North. Charles XII of Sweden (1682–1718).

quos ego. A threat of punishment for disobedience. The words, from Virgil's *Aeneid* (i. 135), were uttered by Neptune to the disobedient and rebellious winds, and are sometimes given as an example of aposiopesis, i.e., a stopping short for rhetorical effect. "Whom I—," said Neptune, the "will punish" being left to the imagination.

Quo Vadis. A historical novel by H. SIENKIEWICZ (1895), dealing with the Rome of Nero and the early Christian martyrs. The Roman noble, Petronius, a worthy representative of the dying paganism, is perhaps the most interesting figure, and the struggle between Christianity and paganism supplies the central plot, but the canvas is large. A succession of characters and episodes and, above all, the richly colorful, decadent life of ancient Rome give the novel its chief interest. The beautiful Christian Lygia is the object of unwelcome attentions from Vinicius, one of the Emperor's guards, and when she refuses to yield to his importunities, she is denounced and thrown to the wild beasts of the arena. She escapes and eventually marries Vinicius, whom Peter and Paul have converted to Christianity. Has been filmed, with Charles LAUGHTON as Nero.

q.v. (Lat. *quantum vis*). As much as you like, or *quantum valeat,* as much as is proper.

q.v. (Lat. *quod vide*). Which see.

R

Ra. The principal deity of ancient Egypt, one of the numerous forms of the sun-god, and the supposed ancestor of all the PHARAOHS. He was the creator, the protector of men and the vanquisher of evil; Nut, the sky, was his father, and it was said of him that every night he fought with the serpent Apepi. He is usually represented as hawk-headed and is crowned with the solar disk and ureus. See OSIRIS; AMON.

Rabagas. The title and hero of a comedy by SARDOU (1872), a satirical study of the rise and fall of an unscrupulous politician, said to have been drawn from GAMBETTA.

Rab and his Friends. A famous dog story by Dr. John BROWN (1858). Rab is a dog fond of his master and mistress, and most faithful to them. He is described as "old, gray, brindled, as big as a little Highland bull."

Rabbi Ben Ezra. A famous poem by Robert BROWNING on old age, beginning:—

Grow old along with me,
The best is yet to be,
The last of life, for which the first was made.

The supposed speaker, Rabbi Ben Ezra (Abraham ben Meir ben Ezra or Ibn Ezra), was one of the most distinguished Jewish literati of the Middle Ages (ca. 1090–1168). See also under ADMIRABLE.

Rabble in Arms. A novel (1933) by Kenneth ROBERTS, of the American Revolution.

Rabelais, François (1494?–1553). French scholar, humanist, physician, and satirist, early in his career a member first of the Franciscan order and then of the Benedictine order. He is famous for his robust and outspoken burlesque GARGANTUA AND PANTAGRUEL, satirizing contemporary religion, pedantry, politics, and social institutions, exalting nature, empiricism, and characteristic Renaissance variety and richness, and showing evidence of derivations from numerous source-books of the author's day. This work was published as follows: *Les Grandes et Inestimables Chroniques du Grand et Enorme Géant Gargantus* (1532), a chapbook; *Pantagruel* (1533), later Book II of the work in its best-known form; *La Vie Inestimable du Grand Gargantua, Père de Pantagruel* (1534), later Book I; Book III (1546); Book IV (1552), condemned by the Sorbonne and prohibited from sale; *Isle Sonnante* (1562) and *Le Cinquième et dernier Livre des Faits et Dits Héroïques du Bon Pantagruel* (1564), constituting Book V and considered by some scholars to be of doubtful authenticity, although it is believed that an outline prepared by the author was used for it.

Rabelais took his Master's and Doctor's degrees in medicine and divided his time between his practice as a physician and a second profession of editing and publishing books. His great work contributed in an important degree to the development of the French language, more than 600 words having been added through it to the vocabulary of the modern language of France. Rabelais is considered to have influenced most MONTAIGNE, MOLIÈRE, Blaise PASCAL, Anatole FRANCE, Jonathan SWIFT, and Laurence STERNE.

Rabelaisian. Coarsely and boisterously satirical; grotesque, extravagant, and licentious in language; reminiscent in literary style of Rabelais.

Dean SWIFT, Thomas Amory (d. 1788, author of *John Buncle*), and Laurence STERNE have all been called *the English Rabelais.* MELVILLE, the author of MOBY DICK, is sometimes called *the American Rabelais.*

Rabican. A famous horse of Carolingian legend whose exploits are related in the Italian epics, ORLANDO INNAMORATO and ORLANDO FURIOSO. His first owner is Argalia; later he comes into the possession of RINALDO. Rabican feeds on air alone and is unsurpassed for speed.

Rabinowitz, Solomon. Pseudonym **Shalom** or **Sholem Aleichem** (1859–1916). Yiddish humorist born in Russia; to U.S. (1906).

Rabourdin. In several of BALZAC's novels, notably *The Government Clerks* (*Les Employés*), an official whose honesty and industry, carried to excess, causes his downfall.

Raby, Aurora. In Byron's DON JUAN a rich young English orphan, Catholic in religion, of virgin modesty, "a rose with all its sweetest leaves yet folded." Aurora Raby is introduced in canto XV, and here and there in the two remaining cantos but, as the tale was never finished, it is not possible to divine what part the beautiful and innocent girl was destined by the poet to play.

Rachel. (1) In the Old Testament, daughter of Laban and wife of JACOB, for love of whom he served her father fourteen years.

Rachel weeping for her children "and she would not be comforted, for they were not." An allusion to Herod's Massacre of the INNOCENTS after the birth of Christ. The phrase is an Old Testament quotation introduced in the New Testament narrative.

(2) In Marcel Proust's REMEMBRANCE OF THINGS PAST, an actress, early mistress to Robert SAINT-LOUP.

Rachel, Mlle. Stage name of **Élisa Félix** (1820–1858). French actress, celebrated for her tragic roles, as Camille, Phèdre, Lucrèce, etc.

Rachmaninoff, Sergei Wassilievitch (1873–1943). Distinguished Russian musician; well-known in the U.S. as concert pianist, conductor, and composer. Resident of New York City (from 1918). His music is sombre and romantic. *Prelude in C Sharp Minor* and *Second Piano Concerto* best known to the general public.

Racine, Jean (1639–1699). French dramatist, known for the effective simplicity of his poetic style and his psychological portrayals of the passions of his characters. His works include *La Thébaïde* (1664); *Alexandre* (1665); *Andromaque* (1667); *Les Plaideurs* (1668), his sole comedy; *Britannicus* (1669); *Bérénice* (1670); *Bajazet* (1672); *Mithridate* (1674); *Iphigénie* (see IPHIGENIA; 1674); PHÈDRE (see PHAEDRA; 1677), regarded as the author's masterpiece; ESTHER (1688–1689); *Athalie* (1690), performed privately, called by some critics the author's greatest dramatic poem. The subjects of most of these dramas were derived from the tragedies of Euripides or historical accounts.

Racine was educated in a JANSENIST school and at first intended for the priesthood; the influence of Jansenist doctrines of ORIGINAL SIN combined with the classic Greek concept of FATE has been found in his tragedies. MOLIÈRE, LA FONTAINE, and BOILEAU were his friends in Paris, where his plays suffered through the enmity of partisans of his rivals, among whom was CORNEILLE. Racine retired as a writer for the stage after the production of *Phèdre. Esther* was performed by the schoolgirl daughters of French nobles, and *Athalie* was not produced in Paris until 1716.

Rackham, Arthur (1867–1939). British illustrator, especially of classics for children, as Andersen's *Fairy Tales; The Pied Piper of Hamelin;* etc.

Rackrent, Castle, see CASTLE RACKRENT.

Rackstraw, Ralph. A character in Gilbert and Sullivan's comic opera, PINAFORE.

Rada. Poetic play by Alfred NOYES (1915) originally entitled *A Belgian Christmas Eve.*

Radcliffe, Mrs. **Ann** *née* **Ward** (1764–1823). English novelist, known for her tales of mystery and terror in the convention of the GOTHIC NOVEL. Her works include *The Romance of the Forest* (1791); THE MYSTERIES OF UDOLPHO (1794); *A Sicilian Romance* (1790); *An Italian Romance* (1891); *The Italian* (1797).

Radek, Karl Bernardovich (1885–). Russian Communist politician, one of the leaders of the Communist International (1923). Dismissed from the Party (1925) for being an adherent of Trotsky (re-admitted, 1930). Tried for treason in Moscow (1937) and condemned to 10 years' imprisonment.

Radiguet, Raymond (1903–1923). French poet and novelist. Protégé of Jean COCTEAU, associated with the surrealist movement, though his style is distinctly classicistic. His novels, *The Devil in the Flesh* (*Le Diable au corps;* 1923) and *The Count's Ball* (*Le Bal du Comte d'Orgel;* 1924), are highly regarded.

Radigund. Queen of the Amazons in Spenser's FAËRIE QUEENE (V, iv, 33, etc.), reigning over

> A goodly citty and a mighty one,
> The which of her owne name she called Radegone.

Getting the better of Sir Artegal in a single combat, she compels him to dress in "woman's weeds," and to spin flax. BRITOMART goes to the rescue, cuts off the Amazon's head, and liberates her knight.

Radio City. Popular designation of Rockefeller Center, a group of buildings in New York City specially designed to house the city's leading commercial enterprises, built between 1931 and 1940. The term is derived from the R.C.A. (Radio Corporation of America) Building, which is the center of the group and contains the studios of the National Broadcasting Company. A sunken plaza, landscaped gardens, outdoor sculpture, shops, restaurants, and two theaters are included in the group.

Radisson, Pierre Esprit (1636–?1710). French fur trader and explorer; to Canada (about 1651), where he made trips to the western parts of the country (1657; 1659), possibly reaching the Upper Mississippi. Instrumental in organizing the Hudson Bay Company (chartered, 1670). His description of his voyages were published as *Voyages of Peter Esprit Radisson* (1885).

Radziwill, Princess **Catherine.** Pen name **Count Paul Vassili** (1858–1941). Russian writer. Author of *Behind the Veil of the Russian Court; Confessions of the Czarina; The Taint of the Romanovs;* etc.

Raeburn, Aldous. A leading character in Mrs. Humphry Ward's MARCELLA and its sequel *Sir George Tressady.*

Raeburn, Sir **Henry** (1756–1823). Scottish portrait painter, fashionable in Edinburgh (from 1787), and often referred to as the "Scottish Reynolds."

Raeder, Erich (1876–). German admiral. Commander in chief of German navy (1935–1943); inspector of war fleet (from 1943).

Raemaekers, Louis (1869–). Dutch political cartoonist, famous for his anti-German cartoons appearing during World War I and published in book form as *The Great War in 1916, The Great War in 1917,* and *Cartoon History of the War* (1919).

Raffles. The debonair criminal hero of *The Amateur Cracksman* (1899) and other stories by E. W. HORNUNG, dramatized and filmed.

Raggedy Man. The hero of one of James Whitcomb RILEY's dialect poems, an admirer of the hired girl Lizbeth Ann and her custard pies.

Raghuvansha (*Sansk.*, "the race of Raghu"). One of the great Sanskrit poems ascribed to KALIDASA. It deals with the history of Ramachandra, who also appears in the RAMAYANA.

Raglan, 1st Baron. **Fitzroy James Henry Somerset** (1788–1855). British commander who, in the Crimean War, won the Battle of Alma (1854) but was blamed for the loss of the light brigade at Balaklava. Cf. Tennyson's *The Charge of the Light Brigade.* He was made field marshal for the victory at Inkerman (1854).

Ragnarok. The twilight of the gods, known in German as *Götterdämmerung.* It will result in the destruction of the universe. Loki and his offspring, Hel, Fenris, and the Midgard serpent, will break their bonds and kill, and be killed by, the gods on the battlefield of Vigrid. Ragnarok will be followed by the regeneration of all things. A new earth will arise, and sons of Odin and Thor together with Baldur and Hödur will people it.

Rahab. In the Old Testament (*Josh.* ii.), the woman of Jericho who protected the twelve spies of the Israelites and managed their escape. She and her family alone were saved when the city was later destroyed.

Rahu. The demon that, according to Hindu legend, causes eclipses. He one day quaffed some of the nectar of immortality, but was discovered by the Sun and Moon, who informed against him, and VISHNU cut off his head. As he had already taken some of the nectar into his mouth, the head was immortal, and he ever afterwards hunted the Sun and Moon, which he caught occasionally, causing eclipses.

rail. A garment (Middle English), remaining in the language only in the expression night rail, "night gown."

Railroad City. Indianapolis. See under CITY.

Rail Splitter, the. Abraham LINCOLN was so called because of his early experience as a rail splitter.

Raimond, C. E. Pseudonym of Elizabeth ROBINS.

Rain. A play (1922) by John Colton and Clemence Randolph, based on the short story *Miss Thompson* by W. Somerset MAUGHAM.

Rainbow, The. A novel by D. H. LAWRENCE (1915), dealing with the strong, vital, passionate Brangwen family, farmers and craftsmen of Nottinghamshire. The stories of three generations of the family are told in the novel. Tom Brangwen, a farm youth, marries Lydia Lensky, a Polish lady, widow of a Polish political exile. Anna, Lydia's daughter by her first marriage, grows up as Tom's own child and marries her cousin, Will Brangwen, a strange, strong-willed, morose man with a passion for wood-carving. Ursula, daughter of Anna and Will, in her turn becomes a proud, sensitive, and high-spirited girl who rebels against the confinements of her family background. She falls in love with Anton Skrebentsky, son of a Polish exile who was a friend of her grandmother, and conceives an intense affection for Winifred Inger, her teacher at school, an athletic woman interested in the intellectualism of her time and the woman-suffrage movement. But Winifred eventually marries Tom Brangwen the second, Ursula's uncle, and Anton, an officer in the British army, proves so capricious and undependable that Ursula voluntarily rejects him after a brief love affair. At the end of the book we see her, after having taught in a local school and attended college, about to set out on a life of her own.

Women in Love (1920), a sequel to *The Rainbow,* portrays the love affairs of Ursula and her sister Gudrun (said to have been based on Katherine MANSFIELD) and their lives in the "emancipated" era of the 20th century. *The Rainbow* caused a sensation on its publication, being the first of Lawrence's books to present situations involving sex in frank and honest language. *Women in Love,* even more than its predecessor, is a vehicle for the author's theories of sex.

Rainbow Division. The name of the 42nd Division of the United States Army which was made up of National Guard troops from all over the country. They were the first American troops in combat in World War I. Their insigne was a rainbow on a black field.

Raine, William MacLeod (1871–). English-born American journalist and novelist, especially known for adventure stories of the Wild West.

Raines Law. Named after the American legislator John Raines (1840–1909). As passed in 1896, the law provided that on Sundays liquor should only be sold by licensed hotels having at least ten bedrooms. Saloons, trying to comply with the law, began to fix up the required number of bedrooms, which did not serve to better their reputation. Establishments of this sort were called Raines Law Hotels.

Rainey, Paul J. (1877–1923). American explorer, known for his motion pictures of African wild life.

Rain-in-the-Face. Famous Sioux Indian who was one of the leaders at the battle of the Little Big Horn. He was killed on an Indian reservation in South Dakota. Longfellow wrote a poem, *The Death of Rain-in-the-Face.*

Rais, Gilles de. See RETZ.

raison d'être (*Fr.*). The reason for a thing's existence, its rational ground for being;

as "Once crime were abolished there would be no *raison d'être* for the police."

Raisuli, Ahmed ibn-Muhammed (1875?–1925). A brigand of Morocco who created international incidents by kidnaping the London *Times* correspondent Walter Harris (1904); Perdicaris, an American (1904); and Sir Harry MacLean (1907). The Sultan of Morocco met his ransom demands to avoid war with the powers involved. An American slogan of the time ran "Perdicaris alive or Raisuli dead!"

Rajah (*Sans.*, "king," cognate with Lat. *rex*). The title of an Indian king or prince, given later to tribal chiefs and comparatively minor dignitaries and rulers, and also to Malayan and Japanese chiefs, as Rajah Brooke, of Sarawak. *Maha-rajah* means the "great rajah." See also RULERS, TITLES OF.

Rajput. An Indo-Aryan of a high military caste, specifically, of the ruling caste of Rajputana.

Rake's Progress, The. A famous series of didactic engravings by William HOGARTH (1735), showing the downhill course of a profligate in the 18th century.

rakshas. Evil spirits of Hindu legend, who guard the treasures of Kubera, the god of riches. They haunt cemeteries and devour human beings, and can assume any shape at will; their strength increases as the day declines. Some are hideously ugly, but others, especially the female spirits, allure by their beauty.

Raleigh, Sir Walter (1552?–1618). A famous historical personage of the time of Queen Elizabeth, introduced by Scott in his KENILWORTH. The tradition of Sir Walter laying down his cloak on a miry spot for the Queen to step on, and the Queen's commanding him to wear the "muddy cloak till her pleasure should be further known," is mentioned in Ch. xv.

Raleigh, Sir Walter Alexander (1861–1922). English critic and essayist, especially concerned with the English novel, Wordsworth, Shakespeare, Johnson, etc.

Ralph or **Ralpho.** The squire of HUDIBRAS in Butler's satire of that title. The model was Isaac Robinson, a zealous butcher in Moorfields, always contriving some queer art of church government. He represents the Independent party, and Hudibras the Presbyterian.

Ralph, James (1695?–1762). American writer, who accompanied Benjamin Franklin to London (1724) and established himself there with the Thomsonian blank-verse poems *The Tempest* and *Night* (1727). His ballad opera *The Fashionable Lady* (1730) was the first play by an American produced on a London stage. Franklin refers to him in his own *Autobiography*.

Ralph, Julian (1853–1903). American war correspondent; with the Turkish army in the war against Greece (1897) and with Lord Roberts in South Africa during the South African War (1899).

Ralph Roister Doister. The title of the earliest English comedy, so called from the chief character. It was written by Nicholas Udall about 1533 for performance by the boys at Eton, where he was then headmaster. Ralph is a vain, thoughtless, blustering fellow, who is in pursuit of a rich widow named Custance, but he is baffled in his intention.

Rama. The seventh incarnation of VISHNU. Rama performed many wonderful exploits, such as killing giants, demons and other monsters. He won Sita to wife because he was able to bend the bow of Siva. He is the hero of the great Hindu epic, the RAMAYANA. See also AVATAR.

Ramachandra. See AVATAR.

Ramadan or **Ramazan.** The ninth month of the Mohammedan year, and the Mussulmans' Lent or Holy Month. No food is touched by pious Mohammedans from sunrise to sundown during this period.

> As the Moslem year is calculated on the system of twelve lunar months, Ramazan is liable at times to fall in the hot weather, when abstinence from drinking as well as from food is an extremely uncomfortable and inconvenient obligation. What wonder, then, that the end of the fast is awaited with feverish impatience?—H. M. Batson, *Commentary on Fitzgerald's "Omar,"* st. xc.

Raman, Sir Chandrasekhara Venkata (1888–). Indian physicist and professor at Calcutta University, who was awarded the Nobel prize in physics in 1930. President, Indian Academy of Sciences (1934).

Ramayana (*Sans.*, **"The Deeds of Rama"**). The history of Rama, the great epic poem of ancient India, ranking with the MAHABHARATA. It is ascribed to the poet Valmiki, and, as now known, consists of 24,000 stanzas in seven books. The young hero, Rama, an incarnation of the deity Vishnu (see AVATAR), wins his bride Sita by bending the great bow that had belonged to Rudra, one of the gods. Although heir to the throne of Ayodhya, Rama is exiled for fourteen years through the jealousy of one of his father's wives, who desires the throne for her own son. Sita is now carried off by Ravana, a demon-king of Ceylon, to his capital at Lanka, and a great part of the narrative is concerned with Rama's efforts to win her back. He secures the assistance of Ravana's own brother Vibhishana, and of the great monkey-god, Hanuman, whose monkeys throw up a bridge across the straits. After the rescue of Sita, Rama is welcomed as the monarch of Ayodhya. But both Rama and the people fear that Sita has been defiled by her sojourn with the demon-king, and although she successfully undergoes certain ordeals, Rama sends her away. She wanders into the forest, finds shelter in the hut of Valmiki (the poet to whom the epic is ascribed), and there gives birth to Rama's two sons, whom she brings up to be brave and noble youths. Eventually she is found by Rama and received back as his wife.

Rambler, The. An 18th-century English periodical which was issued from March, 1750, to March, 1752. Dr. Samuel JOHNSON contributed to it a series of essays on literature, manners, and morals.

Rambouillet, Hôtel de. The house in Paris where, about 1615, the Marquise de Rambouillet, disgusted with the immoral and puerile tone of the time, founded the *salon* out of which grew the *Académie Française*. Mme de SÉVIGNÉ, DESCARTES, RICHELIEU, BOSSUET, and LA ROCHEFOUCAULD were among the members. They gradually developed a language of their own, calling common things by uncommon names, and so on; the women were known as *Les précieuses* and the men as *esprits doux*. Preciosity, pedantry and affectation led to the disruption of the coterie which, after having performed a good and lasting service, was finally demolished by the satire of Molière's LES PRÉCIEUSES RIDICULES (1659) and LES FEMMES SAVANTES (1672).

Rameau, Jean Phillipe (1683–1764). French organist and composer; his *Traité de L'Harmonie* (1722) established the modern science of harmony.

Ramée, Marie Louise de la. Pseudonym **Ouida** (1839–1908). English novelist, widely known for her flamboyant romances of fashionable life, including *Under Two Flags* (1867); *Tricotrin* (1869); *Moths* (1880); etc. She also wrote animal stories and children's books, which include *A Dog of Flanders* (1872) and *Bimbi* (1882). Her pseudonym was baby talk for *Louise*.

Ramière, Raymonde de. In George Sand's INDIANA, the young lover of the heroine.

Ramillies. A village in Belgium, scene of one of Marlborough's famous victories over the French (1706). The battle gave its name to various articles and modes of dress, as *Ramillies wig*, etc.

Raminagrobis. Rabelais, in his famous satire GARGANTUA AND PANTAGRUEL (III. xxi) under this name satirizes Guillaume Crétin, a poet in the reigns of Charles VIII, Louis XII, and François I.

In LA FONTAINE's fables, the name is given to the great cat chosen as judge between the weasel and the rabbit.

Ram of the Zodiac. This is the famous Chrysomallon, whose golden fleece was stolen by JASON in his Argonautic expedition. It was transposed to the stars, and made the first sign of the Zodiac.

Ramona. A historical novel by Helen Hunt JACKSON (1884), dealing with Spanish and Indian life in California. The heroine, Ramona, of mixed Scotch and Indian blood, is brought up by a Spanish Señora and jealously loved by her foster brother. She, however, regards him with no more than sisterly affection and finally irrevocably offends the Señora by eloping with a young Temecula Indian, Alessandro. But wherever the couple go, their land is confiscated by the United States government, and they are forced to seek another Indian reservation. Because of his resentment and shame at being forced to submit to such treatment, the proud young Alessandro comes to a tragic end.

Rampion, Mark. In Aldous Huxley's POINT COUNTER POINT, a novelist who, with his wife Mary, lives a simple, vigorous, passionate, and dignified life, devoid of the artificiality, falsehood, repression, and frustration represented by the other characters in the novel. Mark and Mary are the only characters who are presented sympathetically. They are considered to be idealized portraits of D. H. LAWRENCE and his wife Frieda.

Ramsay, Allan (1686–1758). Scottish poet and wigmaker. He became a bookseller and edited old Scottish poems. He was the first to have a circulating library in Scotland. His eldest son, **Allan Ramsay** (1713–1784), was a well-known portrait painter in Edinburgh and London and became court painter to George III.

Ramsay, Sir **William** (1852–1916). Distinguished British chemist who first advanced proof that the emanation of radium produces helium during its atomic disintegration. Won the Nobel prize for chemistry (1904).

Ramsey Milholland. A novel by Booth TARKINGTON, one of his studies of the American boy in his teens. See also PENROD.

Ramus, Petrus. *Lat.* of *Fr.* **Pierre La Ramée** (1515–1572). French philosopher and mathematician; professor of philosophy in the Collège de France (1543). His anti-Aristotelian doctrine of logic, known as *Ramism,* became current in the English universities, principally at Cambridge. Victim of the massacre of St. Bartholomew.

Ramuz, Charles Ferdinand (1878–). Swiss poet and novelist writing in French. Ever since the success of his first work, *Le Petit village* (1903), a prolific writer. His major theme is the conflict of sound and simple souls, children of God and Nature, with the fatal artifices of a complex society. *Aline* (1905); *Le Village dans la montagne* (1909); *Vie de Samuel Belet* (1913); *Terre du ciel* (1918); *La Beauté sur la terre* (*Beauty on Earth;* 1927); etc.

Ran or **Rana.** In Norse mythology, goddess of the sea, and wife of AEGIR. Her name signifies robbery, and it was she who caught seafarers in her net and drew them down to her dwelling beneath the waves.

Rance, Jack. The sheriff of Belasco's GIRL OF THE GOLDEN WEST and Puccini's opera of the same title, based on the play.

Randall, James Ryder (1839–1908). American journalist and song writer, famous for the Civil War song, *Maryland, My Maryland* (1861), sung to the tune of *O Tannenbaum, O Tannenbaum*. His *Poems* were brought out in 1910.

Randolph, John. Known as **John Randolph of Roanoke** (1773–1833). American politician; representative and senator in opposition to Jefferson. A brilliant orator who was against the War of 1812 and against the Missouri Compromise. In his last years he became insane. U.S. minister to Russia (1830).

Randolph, Thomas (1605–1635). English poet and dramatist. A friend of Ben Jonson. His plays and poems were edited by W. C. Hazlitt (1875).

Random, Roderick, see RODERICK RANDOM.

Rands, William Brighty (1823–1882). Often called "The Laureate of the Nursery." Author of many poems and fairy tales for children published under various pseudonyms.

Rand School of Social Science. An educational institution established in New York (1906), giving courses in economics, labor policies, journalism, and other subjects to working people.

Ranee or **Rani.** See RULERS, TITLES OF.

Ranelagh Gardens. A place of public entertainment in Chelsea, London (1742–1804), where fashionable people liked to go and listen to the music of the orchestra in the Rotunda.

Ranievskaia, Madame. The chief character in Chekhov's CHERRY ORCHARD.

Ranjit Singh (1780–1839). Indian maharaja who founded the Sikh kingdom and was known as "the Lion of the Punjab." Loyal to Britain.

Ranke, Leopold von (1795–1886). German historian, especially known for a *History of the Popes* (3 vols.; 1834–1839), which was translated by Mrs. Sarah Austin (1840) and concerning which Lord Macaulay wrote a famous essay.

Rankin, Jeannette (1880–). American woman suffragist and first woman member of the House of Representatives (1917–1919; 1941). Voted against the United States' entering World Wars I and II. Represented Montana.

Ransom, John Crowe (1888–). American poet and literary critic, a member of the group known as FUGITIVES and later of the AGRARIANS. His poetry, broadly showing the influence of the METAPHYSICAL POETS, is marked by irony, intellectualism, criticism of the 20th-century industrial world, and nostalgia for the past, especially the aristocratic society of the South before the Civil War. His literary criticism is devoted chiefly to an attempt to formulate an aesthetic system for poetry by which poety is shown to present a form of knowledge of equal status with scientific knowledge. His books of poetry include *Poems About God* (1919); *Chills and Fever* (1924); *Two Gentlemen in Bonds* (1927). *God Without Thunder* (1930), *The World's Body* (1938), *The New Criticism* (1941), and *Poetics* (1942) are volumes of his criticism. Ransom, after 1914 a professor of English at Vanderbilt University and later at Kenyon College, was among the editors of *The Fugitive* (1922–1925) and *Kenyon Review* (1938). See LITTLE MAGAZINE. He also edited *I'll Take My Stand* (1930), an anthology of writings by the Agrarians. His *Selected Poems* were published in 1945.

Ransome, Arthur (1884–). English writer, chiefly of excellent books for children, notably the *Swallows and Amazons* series.

ranz des vaches. A melody played on a Swiss alpenhorn to call cattle.

Raoul de Nangis. Hero of Meyerbeer's opera THE HUGUENOTS.

Rape of the Lock. A famous poetic satire by Alexander POPE. The first sketch was published in 1712 in two cantos, and the complete work in five cantos in 1714. Lord Petre, in a thoughtless moment of frolic gallantry, cut off a lock of Arabella Fermor's hair, and this liberty gave rise to a bitter feud between the two families, which Pope worked up into the best mock-heroic poem of the language. The heroine, called Belinda, indignantly demands back the ringlet, but after a fruitless charge it is affirmed that, like BERENICE's hair, it has been transported to heaven, and henceforth shall "midst the stars inscribe Belinda's name."

Raphael. (1) One of the principal angels of Jewish angelology. In the book of *Tobit* we are told how he traveled with Tobias into Media and back again, instructing him on the way how to marry Sara and to drive away the wicked spirit. Milton calls him the "sociable spirit," and the "affable archangel" (*Paradise Lost*, vii. 40), and it is he who is sent by God to advise Adam of his danger. Raphael is usually distinguished in art by a pilgrim's staff, or is carrying a fish, in allusion to his aiding Tobias to capture the fish which performed the miraculous cure of his father's eyesight.

(2) The hero of Balzac's novel *Le Peau de chagrin,* usually translated under the title The Wild Ass's Skin.

Raphael. Full Italian name **Raffaello Sanzio** (1483–1520). One of the greatest painters of the Italian Renaissance. Examples of his numerous works are in the Louvre, the Vatican Gallery, the National Gallery in London, etc. He was also an architect and designed the Palazzo Pandolfi in Florence.

the Flemish Raphael. Frans Floris (1520–1570).

the French Raphael. Eustace Lesueur (1617–1655).

the Raphael of Cats. Godefroi Mind, a Swiss painter, famous for his cats (1768–1814).

the Raphael of Holland. Martin van Hemskerck (1498–1574).

Rapp, George (1757–1847). See New Harmony.

Rappaccini's Daughter. A well-known story by Hawthorne in his *Mosses From an Old Manse* (1846). As a curious, cold-blooded experiment, the scientist Rappaccini feeds his daughter Beatrice on poisons, so that she grows up immune to their effect. When, finally, she is given an antidote by a medical man, the wholesome drug is fatal to her. The suggestion for this story is found in the following quotation from Sir Thomas Browne, copied into Hawthorne's *American Notebook:* "A story there passeth of an Indian King that sent unto Alexander a faire woman fed with aconytes and other poisons, with this intent complexionally to destroy him."

rara avis (*Lat.,* "a rare bird"). A phenomenon; a prodigy; something quite out of the common course. It was first applied by Juvenal to the black swan, which, since its discovery in Australia, is quite familiar to us, but was unknown before.

> Rara avis in terris nigroque simillima cygne (a bird rarely seen on the earth, and very like a black swan.)—Juvenal, vi. 165.

Rarahu. The Tahitian heroine and the original title of Pierre Loti's Marriage of Loti (*Le Mariage de Loti*).

Rare Ben. The inscription on the tomb of Ben Jonson, the dramatist, in the Poets' Corner, Westminster Abbey, reads "O rare Ben Jonson." The phrase was first used by Shakespeare.

Rascoe, Burton (1892–). American journalist, reviewer, and dramatic critic. When literary editor of the Chicago *Tribune* he "discovered" James Branch Cabell. Coming to New York, he wrote for the *Herald Tribune* a weekly department of literary gossip widely syndicated under the title of *A Bookman's Daybook.* Afterwards he edited *The Bookman,* was on the Editorial Board of the Literary Guild, and dramatic critic for the *World-Telegram.* His own books include *Titans of Literature* (1932) and the autobiographical *Before I Forget* (1937) and *We Were Interrupted* (1947).

Raskolnikov. The unhappy, introspective, self-willed hero of Dostoyevsky's Crime and Punishment.

Rasmussen, Knud Johan Victor (1879–1933). Danish arctic explorer. Made ethnological expeditions to North Greenland and was the author of *The People of the Polar North* (1908); *Myths and Legends from Greenland* (3 vols.; 1921–1925); *Across Arctic America* (1927); etc.

Raspe, Rudolph Erich (1737–1794). See Münchausen, Baron.

Rasputin, Grigori Efimovich (1871?–1916). A Russian monk who gained ascendancy over the Czar and Czarina. Notorious for his evil life, he was assassinated by a group of Russian nobles on December 31, 1916. Cf. René Fülöp-Miller, *Rasputin, the Holy Devil* (1927).

Rasselas. Prince of Abyssinia, in Dr. Johnson's philosophical romance of that name (1759). He dwells in a secluded "Happy Valley," shut off from all contact with the world or with evil. This paradise is in the valley of Amhara, surrounded by high mountains. It has only one entrance, which is by a cavern under a rock concealed by woods, and closed by iron gates. The prince makes his escape with his sister Nekayah and Imlac, the poet, and wanders about to find out what condition or rank of life is the most happy. After careful investigation, he finds no lot without its drawbacks, and resolves to return to the "Happy Valley."

Rassendyll, Rudolf. The hero of Anthony Hope's Prisoner of Zenda.

Rastignac, Eugène de. One of Balzac's best known characters, appearing in several of the novels of the Comédie Humaine, notably *Father Goriot* (*Le Père Goriot*) and *Cousin Betty* (*La Cousine Bette*). Introduced as a struggling young law student who has come to Paris to make his fortune, Rastignac quickly becomes cynical and determines to conquer society by giving up his ideals and taking advantage of circumstances. By installing himself as the adorer of Madame de Nucingen, the daughter of his poor old fellow-boarder, Père Goriot, and wife of a wealthy financier, he manages to better his fortunes. Later he marries Augusta de Nucingen, the daughter of his former mistress, and in the course of time becomes a prominent statesman, a peer and a millionaire. He is the type of ruthless and cynical ambition. See also Goriot; Lisbeth Fischer.

Rat, the Cat and Lovel, the Dog, The. This line and the following one, "Rule all England under the Hog" refer to RICHARD III and three of his followers named Ratcliffe, Catesby, and Lovell. "The Hog" means the wild boar which figured in the royal arms.

Ratcliffe, Senator. The chief character in DEMOCRACY (1880), a study of the unscrupulous American politician. The novel was published anonymously, but is now known to be the work of Henry ADAMS.

Ratcliffe Highway. A London highway which extended from one end of the place of execution at Wapping along the Thames into the city.

Rathenau, Walther (1867–1922). German-Jewish industrialist and statesman. After World War I he secured the lessening of reparation payments, was foreign minister, and signed the Rapallo Treaty with Russia (1922). He was assassinated by ultra-nationalists.

rationalism. Term applied to a trend in philosophic thinking toward emphasis on the reason and intellect, rather than the emotions and imagination. ARISTOTLE and St. Thomas Aquinas (see under SAINTS) are considered rationalists, and the 18th century was dominated by rationalist philosophy.

Rattlin, Jack. A famous naval character in Smollett's RODERICK RANDOM.

Rat-Wife, The. A hag in Ibsen's LITTLE EYOLF, who is responsible for the death of the child hero.

Rauschning, Hermann (1887–). German political writer, at one time president of the Danzig senate, but soon breaking away from the Nazi party. He came to the U.S. and took out first citizenship papers in 1942. His *The Revolution of Nihilism: A Warning to the West* (1939) conveyed his knowledge of and insight into the machinations of the Nazis in Germany.

Rautendelein. The nymph in Hauptmann's drama THE SUNKEN BELL.

Ravana. A gigantic ten-faced demon of Hindu legend, who was fastened down between heaven and earth for 10,000 years by SIVA's leg, for attempting to move the hill of heaven to Ceylon. He is prominent in the Hindu epic, the RAMAYANA, especially because of his abduction of Rama's wife, Sita.

Ravel, Maurice Joseph (1875–1937). French impressionist composer. Some of his best-known works are the songs *Shéhérazade* (1903); the one-act opera *L'Heure Espagnole* (1910); the ballets *Daphnis et Cloé* (1912) and *Boléro* (1928); etc.

raven. A bird of ill omen; fabled to forebode death and bring infection and bad luck generally. The former notion arises from their following an army under the expectation of finding dead bodies to *raven* on; the latter notion is a mere off-shoot of the former, since it was noted that pestilence kills as fast as the sword.

In Christian art, the raven is an emblem of God's Providence, in allusion to the ravens which fed Elijah.

the fatal raven, consecrated to Odin, the Danish war god, was the emblem on the Danish standard, *Landeyda* (the desolation of the country), and was said to have been woven and embroidered in one noontide by the daughters of Regner Lodbrok, son of Sigurd, that dauntless warrier who chanted his death-song (the *Krakamal*) while being stung to death in a horrible pit filled with deadly serpents. If the Danish arms were destined to defeat, the raven hung his wings; if victory was to attend them, he stood erect and soaring, as if inviting the warriors to follow. See also HUGINN AND MUGINN.

Raven, The. The best known poem of Edgar Allan POE (1845). The poet, trying to forget his lost love Lenore, is visited by a "grim, ungainly, ghastly, gaunt and ominous bird of yore."

> And the Raven, never flitting, still is sitting, *still* is sitting
> On the pallid bust of Pallas just above my chamber door;
> And his eyes have all the seeming of a demon's that is dreaming,
> And the lamp-light o'er him streaming throws his shadow on the floor;
> And my soul from out that shadow that lies floating on the floor
> Shall be lifted—nevermore!

Ravenel, Mrs. **Beatrice,** *née* **Witte** (1870–). American poet of Charleston, S.C. *The Arrow of Lightning* (1926).

Raven-Hill, Leonard (1867–1942). Famous British cartoonist, mainly known for his work for *Punch* (1896–1936).

Ravenshoe. A novel (1861) by Henry KINGSLEY.

Ravenswood, Edgar. The hero of Scott's BRIDE OF LAMMERMOOR and of Donizetti's opera LUCIA DI LAMMERMOOR, founded on the novel. In the novel, Edgar is lost in the quicksands of Kelpie's Flow, but in the opera he kills himself.

Rawlings, Marjorie Kinnan (1896–). American novelist, best known for *The Yearling,* which won the Pulitzer prize for fiction in 1938.

Rawlinson, George (1812–1902). British Orientalist. Author of *The Five Great Monarchies of the Ancient Eastern World* (4 vols.; 1862–1867); etc.

Ray, Man (1890–). American surrealist painter and photographer and author of surrealist moving pictures.

Raymond. In Tasso's JERUSALEM DELIVERED, the Count of Toulouse, equal to Godfrey in the "wisdom of cool debate" (Bk. iii). This Nestor of the Crusaders slays Aladine, King of Jerusalem, and plants the Christian standard upon the tower of David (Bk. xx). He is introduced by Scott in his COUNT ROBERT OF PARIS, a novel of the period of Rufus.

Razumov. The principal character in Conrad's UNDER WESTERN EYES.

Read, Herbert Edward (1893–). English literary and art critic and author, at times sympathetic with both MARXISM and SURREALISM. Among his works are *Collected Poems, 1913–1925* (1926); *Reason and Romanticism* (1926); *English Prose Style* (1928); *Ambush* (1930), short stories; *The Meaning of Art* (1931); *Wordsworth* (1930); *The Anatomy of Art* (1932), on art and aesthetics; *Art Now* (1933), on 20th-century painting and sculpture; *Form in Modern Poetry* (1932); *The Innocent Age* (1933) and *Annals of Innocence and Experience* (1940), reminiscences; *The End of a War* (1933), poems on World War I; *Art and Industry* (1934), on industrial design; *Essential Communism* (1935); *The Green Child* (1935), a novel; *Poems, 1914–1934* (1935); *Art and Society* (1937); *Collected Essays in Literary Criticism* (1938); *Poetry and Anarchism* (1938); *Thirty-Five Poems* (1940); *The Philosophy of Anarchism* (1941).

Read, Opie Percival (1852–1939). American humorist who wrote many novels. *The Jucklins* (1895) is said to have sold over a million copies.

Read, Thomas Buchanan (1822–1872). American poet, famous for the popular poem, *Sheridan's Ride.*

Reade, Charles (1814–1884). English novelist, known for his attempts to deal with social problems in his fiction and to expose social abuses. His novels include PEG WOFFINGTON (1853); CHRISTIE JOHNSTONE and IT IS NEVER TOO LATE TO MEND (1853); *The Course of True Love Never Did Run Smooth* (1857); *The Autobiography of a Thief* and *Jack of All Trades* (1858); LOVE ME LITTLE, LOVE ME LONG (1859); THE CLOISTER AND THE HEARTH (1861), considered his best work; HARD CASH (1863); *Griffith Gaunt* (1866); *Foul Play* (1869); PUT YOURSELF IN HIS PLACE (1870); *A Terrible Temptation* (1871); *The Wandering Heir* (1872); *A Hero and a Martyr* (1874); *A Woman-Hater* (1874). His plays include *Masks and Faces* (1852); *The Courier of Lyons* (1854); *Drink* (1879), based on Zola's L'ASSOMMOIR.

Reader's Digest. A magazine, originally of articles condensed and simplified from printed sources, founded in 1921 in New York City by DeWitt Wallace, who had first tried reducing articles when he was in a hospital recovering from a wound received in the first World War. In course of time the reprint idea was partly abandoned but the "simplist" formula was retained. In 1944 the Reader's Digest sold 11,000,000 copies a month. The British, Spanish, Portuguese, Arabic, Finnish, and Danish editions were the largest selling magazines in the respective countries and languages. Cf. John Bainbridge, *Little Wonder or, The Reader's Digest and How it Grew* (1946).

Reading Gaol, The Ballad of, see BALLAD OF READING GAOL, THE.

Ready-Money Jack. The nickname given to an English yeoman in Washington Irving's BRACEBRIDGE HALL.

Ready-to-Halt. A pilgrim in Pt. II of Bunyan's PILGRIM'S PROGRESS, who journeys on crutches. He joins the party under the charge of Mr. Greatheart, but when he is "sent for," he throws away his crutches, and, lo! a chariot bears him into paradise.

realism. Rather than a definite form of writing in fiction, realism is an inclusive term the interpretation of which varies with both writers and critics. The foundation of realism is an endeavor to depict life in an entirely honest manner, without prejudice or glamor, but in practice this virtue can only be relative. Realism may be said to begin with such early English novelists as Defoe, Fielding and Smollett. It assumed the proportions of a definite literary trend in the nineteenth century. The advance of science and the growth of rationalism in philosophy were contributing factors. In the English writers George Eliot, Trollope, Thackeray, and Dickens we can follow the growth of realistic treatment of contemporary life. In the U.S., Mark Twain and Whitman can be cited as outstanding examples. A school of writing dependent upon "LOCAL COLOR" developed with such writers as Bret Harte, in the West, and Thomas Nelson Page in the South. William Dean Howells and Henry James practiced realism, one in straightforward novels of American life, the other in psychological exploration of Americans abroad. In the early part of the twentieth century the sociological trend can be noted in such writers as Jack London and Upton Sinclair. Later on, Ellen Glasgow in the South, and Willa Cather for the Middle West, contributed a new growth of the realistic spirit. The work of Ernest Hemingway introduced a new realistic style which a great many younger writers have since attempted to copy. John Steinbeck, in such a novel as *The Grapes of Wrath,* has been a prime exemplar of realism. In American poetry one can point to such writers as Carl Sandburg and Edgar Lee Masters, whose *Spoon River Anthology* explores the lives of a whole Middle Western community. In the drama we have the experimental plays of Eugene O'Neill and later Elmer Rice and Clifford Odets. (See under all these names.)

Reardon, Edwin. The hero of Gissing's NEW GRUB STREET.

reason.

it stands to reason. It is logically manifest; this is the Latin *constat* (*constare,* literally, "to stand together").

the Age of Reason. See AGE.

the Goddess of Reason. The central figure in a philosophic religion introduced among the people for worship during the French Revolution. The role was taken by various young women of questionable repute, who, in turns, were enthroned and "worshiped" in the cathedral of Notre Dame. Mary JOHNSTON wrote a poetic drama on this subject.

the woman's reason. "I think so just because I *do* think so." Cf. *Two Gentlemen of Verona,* i. 2.

> First then a woman will, or won't, depend on't;
> If she will do't, she will, and there's an end on't.
> Hill, *Epilogue to "Zara."*

Reaumur. A scale of the thermometer set up by the French physicist René Réaumur (1683–1757). It is graduated so that zero marks the freezing point and 80 degrees the boiling point of water. 4 degrees *R.* (that is, Reaumur) equal 5 degrees *C.* (that is, Celsius or centigrade) or 9 degrees *F* (that is, Fahrenheit).

Rebecca. In Scott's IVANHOE, the real heroine, daughter of Isaac the Jew. She loves Ivanhoe, who has shown great kindness to her and to her father. When Ivanhoe marries Rowena, both Rebecca and her father leave England for a foreign land.

Rebecca and Rowena. A burlesque continuation of Scott's *Ivanhoe* by THACKERAY (1850). Ivanhoe is now a henpecked husband and Rowena makes him promise never to marry a Jewess, but after Rowena's death Rebecca becomes a Christian and she and Ivanhoe finally marry.

Rebecca of Sunnybrook Farm. A story for girls by Kate Douglas Wiggin (*Am.,* 1903). The ten-year-old heroine, Rebecca Randall, leaves her widowed mother and brothers and sisters to go to live with her two old maid aunts, Miranda and Jane. Aunt Miranda, particularly, is a great trial, but Rebecca finds a friend in Emma Jane Perkins and a hero and admirer in Adam Ladd, whom she calls Mr. Aladdin. The book ends with her graduation from Wareham Academy, in Maine. There was a sequel, *New Chronicles of Rebecca,* in 1907, and *Rebecca of Sunnybrook Farm* was successfully dramatized in 1910, with Mabel Taliaferro in the title rôle.

Rebecca's Camel's Bible. See BIBLE, SPECIALLY NAMED.

Rebekah. In the Old Testament, the wife of ISAAC. Isaac's meeting with Rebekah at the well is one of the most celebrated of pastoral love stories. Rebekah became the mother of JACOB and Esau and suggested to the former, who was her favorite, his deception of Isaac and his theft of Esau's blessing.

Rebound. A three-act comedy (1929) by Donald Ogden Stewart.

Récamier, Mme **Jeanne Françoise Julie Adélaïde,** *née* **Bernard** (1777–1849). French beauty and wit, the wife of a Paris banker, whose salon was filled with the most noteworthy people of her time. Her adopted daughter, Mme Lenormand, published her *Souvenirs et correspondence* (1852).

Recessional. A famous poem by Rudyard Kipling (1897) written to celebrate the sixtieth anniversary of the reign of Queen Victoria. A recessional in a church is the hymn sung while the choir is leaving the chancel and proceeding to the robing room.

Recherche du temps perdu, A la, see REMEMBRANCE OF THINGS PAST.

Recio, Marie. Italian singer, for whom the composer BERLIOZ left his wife and whom he later married (1854).

Reclamation Service. A bureau of the Department of the Interior established in 1902 to reclaim desert lands, chiefly in the West, by means of irrigation and the development of electric power.

Reconstruction Finance Corporation (R.F.C.). Established in 1932 to grant emergency relief, by means of loans to financial institutions including banks, insurance companies, etc., and to stimulate agriculture, commerce, and industry. It had as resources nearly four billion dollars in capital.

Recruiting Officer, The. A comedy (1706) by FARQUHAR.

recusant. One who refuses to conform. In English history, a Roman Catholic who refuses to attend the services of the established Church of England. Louise Imogen GUINEY compiled a book of poems by "recusant" Catholic writers under the title of *The Recusant Poets.*

Red. One of the primary colors. In heraldry, it is said to signify magnanimity and fortitude. In ecclesiastical use, it is worn in honor of martyrs on Ash Wednesday and the remaining days of Holy Week, and on Whit-Sunday. In popular folklore, it is the color of magic.

> Red is the colour of magic in every country, and has been so from the very earliest times. The caps of fairies and musicians are well-nigh always red.—Yeats, *Fairy and Folk Tales of the Irish Peasantry,* p. 61.

During the later periods of modern history, it came to be more often symbolical of anarchy and revolution—"Red ruin, and the breaking up of laws" (Tennyson, *Guinevere,* 421). In the French Revolution, the *Red Republicans* were those extremists who never hesitated to dye their hands in blood in order to accomplish their political object, and in modern Russia the *Reds,* with their *Red Army,* played a similar part. In general, red is regarded as the color of liberty.

In the old ballads, *red* was frequently applied to gold ("the gude red gowd"), and this use still survives in thieves' cant, a gold watch being a *red kettle,* and the chain a *red tackle.* One of the names given by the alchemists to the PHILOSOPHERS' STONE was *the red tincture,* because, with its help, they hoped to transmute the base metals to gold.

Red Book. A directory relating to the court, the nobility, and the "Upper Ten" generally. The *Royal Kalendar,* published from 1767 to 1893, was known by this name, as also Webster's *Royal Red Book,* a similar work, first issued in 1847. The name is also given to other special works covered in red, as, e.g., the official parliamentary papers of the old Austro-Hungarian Empire which corresponded to the British "BLUE BOOKS." In New York City, the *Red Book* is that part of the telephone directory that gives names classified according to occupations, trades, etc.

the Red Book of Hergest. A Welsh manuscript of the 14th century, containing the MABINOGION among other things of great interest.

red button. In the Chinese Empire, a mandarin of the first class wore one of these as a badge of honor in his cap. See also PANJANDRUM.

Red Coats. British soldiers, from the color of the uniform formerly universal in line regiments. Red is the color of the royal livery, and it is said that this color was adopted by huntsmen because foxhunting was declared a royal sport by Henry II.

the Red Crescent. The Turkish equivalent of the Red Cross, i.e., the military hospital service.

Red Cross. The badge adopted by all nations (except Mohammedans, who, in its place, use the *Red Crescent*), in accordance with the Geneva Convention of 1864, as that of military ambulance and hospital services, hospital ships, etc. It is a red Greek cross on a white ground, and is also called the *Geneva Cross.* Hence it became the name of various national societies for the relief of the wounded and sick.

red flag. The emblem of anarchy, Bolshevism, Communism, and revolution and rebellion generally. English Communists adopted a "battle hymn" with this title, which was also used as the title of anarchical and revolutionary journals. The red flag was used during the French Revolution as the symbol of insurrection and terrorism, and in the Roman Empire it signified war and a call to arms.

Red Hand. The badge of Ulster, in northern Ireland.

red letter day. A lucky day; a day to be recalled with delight. In almanacs, saints' days and holidays are printed in red ink, other days in black; only the former have special services in the Prayer Book.

> "It's a great piece of luck, ma'am," said Mrs. Belfield, "that you should happen to come here of a holiday! . . . Why, you know, ma'am, to-day is a red-letter day!"—Fanny Burney, *Cecelia,* X, vi.

Red Republicans. Extreme Republicans.

Red Shirts. Revolutionists. The allusion is to the red shirts worn by Garibaldi's followers in the struggle for a united Italy.

Red Sox. In American baseball parlance, the Boston Americans. See under BASEBALL TEAMS.

Red Sultan. Abdul Hamid II (1842–1918) was so called.

red tape. Official formality, or rigid adherence to rules and regulations, carried to excessive lengths; so called because lawyers and government officials tie their papers together with red tape. Charles DICKENS is said to have introduced the expression, but it was the scorn continually poured upon this evil of officialdom by CARLYLE that brought the phrase into popular use.

Red, White, and Blue. The American flag; also, the British flag.

Admiral of the Red. See ADMIRAL.

Red and the Black, The (Le Rouge et le Noir). The most celebrated novel of STENDHAL, published in 1830. It deals with the rise to power of Julien Sorel, a handsome, cold, and intensely egotistical young man who uses his love affairs to serve his ambition and tries to murder his first mistress when she betrays him to her successor in his interest. The title refers to the colors of the military class, represented by Napoleon, the author's hero, and of the clergy, which Stendhal detested. The novel is noted for its psychological analysis and exposition of the character of Sorel.

Red Badge of Courage, The: An Episode of the American Civil War. A novel by Stephen CRANE (1895). It presents a study of the psychological reactions of Henry Fleming, a young soldier, during the Civil War Battle of Chancellorsville, his first experience in combat. He is shown in successive emotional states of patriotic zeal, bravado, fear, shame, near-hysteria, and finally courage. This was one of the first realistic studies of war in literature, written before the author had himself seen a battle. See WAR IN LITERATURE.

Redburn: His First Voyage. A novel (1849) by Herman MELVILLE.

Red Cloud (1822–1909). American Indian Chief, famous leader of Sioux and Cheyenne bands in a war against the whites (1866–1868).

Red Cotton Night-Cap Country, or Turf and Towers. A difficult and rather tedious poem (1873) by Robert BROWNING, the title of which suggested itself to the poet when his friend, Miss Annie Thackeray, called St. Aubin *White* Cotton Night-Cap Country, because the women there wore white caps.

Red Cross, American. See BARTON, CLARA.

Red Cross Knight. In Spenser's FAËRIE QUEENE (Bk. I), a personification of St. George, the patron saint of England. He typifies Christian Holiness, and his adventures are an allegory of the Church of England. The Knight is sent by the Queen to destroy a dragon which is ravaging the kingdom of Una's father. With UNA he is driven into Wandering Wood, where they encounter Error, and pass the night in Hypocrisy's cell. Here he is deluded by a false vision and, in consequence, abandons Una and goes with DUESSA to the palace of Pride. He is persuaded by Duessa to drink of an enchanted fountain, becomes paralyzed, and is taken captive by ORGOGLIO, whereupon Una seeks Arthur's help, and the prince goes to the rescue. He slays Orgoglio, and the Red Cross Knight is taken by Una to the house of Holiness to be healed. On leaving Holiness they journey onward, and as they draw near the end of their quest, the dragon flies at the knight, who has to do battle with it for three whole days before he succeeds in slaying it. The Red Cross Knight and Una are then united in marriage.

Redemption. A drama in two acts by Leo N. TOLSTOI. As performed in 1912, it was an abridgement of *The Living Corpse*.

Redfield, William C. (1789–1857). Founder and first president of the American Association for the Advancement of Science (1848). His grandson, **William Cox Redfield** (1858–1932), was U.S. secretary of commerce (1913–1919).

Redgauntlet. A novel by Sir Walter SCOTT (1824), told in a series of letters. Sir Edward Hugh Redgauntlet, a Jacobite conspirator in favor of the Young Pretender, Charles Edward, is the hero; among others, his niece, Lilias Redgauntlet, is prominently involved. The whole enterprise proves a fiasco, Redgauntlet becomes a prior abroad, and Lilias marries her brother's friend, Allan Fairford, a young advocate.

Red-Haired Man's Wife, The. A poem by James Stephens.

Red-Headed Woman. A novel (1931) by Katharine BRUSH.

Red-Haired Girl, the. In Kipling's LIGHT THAT FAILED, a friend of Maisie's who shares her studio. She is mentioned little, and by no other name, but her hopeless love for Dick Heldar is hinted at in a way that makes her unforgettable.

redingote (*Fr.*, from English "riding coat"). A plain double-breasted outside coat, such as was frequently worn by Napoleon.

Red Jacket. Indian name **Sagoyewatha** (1758?–1830). American Indian chief of the Senecas who was friendly to the whites but did not wish Indian lands ceded to the U.S.

Redlaw, Mr. The principal character of a story by Dickens called *The Haunted Man* (1848).

Red Lily, The (Le Lys rouge). A novel by Anatole FRANCE (1894). When she meets and falls in love with the sculptor, Dechartre, the lovely and accomplished Thérèse Martin-Bellême is already the wife of one man and the mistress of another. In spite of an absorbing love, Dechartre and Thérèse find only wretchedness, and his jealous refusal to listen to her explanations finally brings their affair to an end.

Redman, Ben Ray (1896–). American writer of poetry and criticism. Also translator from the French and author of several detective stories. For eleven years he conducted a book column on the *Herald Tribune* under the title of *Old Wine in New Bottles,* and now conducts a similar department, *New Editions,* in the *Saturday Review of Literature.*

Red Pony, The. A story by John Steinbeck, reprinted in his collection of novelettes, *The Long Valley* (1938).

Red Ridinghood, Little. This celebrated nursery tale is, with slight alterations, common to Sweden, Germany, and France. It comes to us from the French *Le Petit Chaperon Rouge,* in Charles PERRAULT's *Contes des Temps,* and probably originated in Italy. A little girl takes a present to her grandmother, but a wolf has assumed the place of the old woman, and, when the child gets into bed, devours her. The brothers GRIMM have reproduced this tale in German and the *finale,* which tells of the arrival of a huntsman who slits open the wolf and restores little Red Ridinghood and her grandmother to life, is a German addition.

Red Robe, The (La Robe rouge). A drama by Eugene Brieux (*Fr.,* 1900). The lawyers Mouzon and Vagret, in their ambition to win the red robe of a judge (an honor based, in France, on the number of convictions), completely wreck the happiness of the peasant Etchepars, who has been falsely accused of murder, by destroying his wife's good name. Vagret realizes his selfishness in time and loses promotion; Mouzon is promoted, but is stabbed by the peasant's wife, Yanetta.

Red Rock, A Chronicle of the Reconstruction. A historical novel by Thomas Nelson PAGE (1898). It deals with the reconstruction period, when Northern carpet-baggers were influential in the South, and the raids of the KU KLUX KLAN are a prominent feature. Red Rock is the old Gray estate which the hero, Jacquelin Gray, is forced to see in the possession of another man after the Civil War. He gradually wins back the plantation and the love of his old playmate, Blair Cary. His brilliant cousin, Steve Allen, with whom he had thought Blair was in love, marries a Northern girl, Ruth Welch.

Red Rover, The. A sea tale by James Fenimore COOPER (1827) relating the exploits of the pirate "Red Rover." This bold and fearful seaman is finally brought to repent of his evil deeds and to render honest, patriotic service in the American Revolution.

reductio ad absurdum. A proof of inference arising from the demonstration that every other hypothesis involves an absurdity. In common parlance, the phrase has come to signify the opposite: an argument that brings out the absurdity of a contention made.

reduplicated or **ricochet words.** There are probably some hundreds of these words, which usually have an intensifying force, in use in English. The following, from ancient and modern sources, will give some idea of their variety: chit-chat, click-clack, clitter-clatter, dilly-dally, ding-dong, drip-drop, fal-lal, flimflam, fiddle-faddle, flip-flap, flip-flop, handy-pandy, harum-scarum, helter-skelter, heyvekeyve, higgledy-piggledy, hob-nob, hodgepodge, hoity-toity, hubble-bubble, hugger-mugger, hurly-burly, mingle-mangle, mishmash, mixy-maxy, namby-pamby, niddy-noddy, niminy-piminy, nosy-posy, pell-mell, ping-pong, pit-pat, pitter-patter, pribbles and prabbles, randem-tandem, randy-dandy, razzle-dazzle, riff-raff, roly-poly, shilly-shally, slip-slop, slish-slosh, tick-tack, tip-top, tittle-tattle, wibble-wobble, wig-wag, wiggle-waggle, wish-wash, wishy-washy.

Redworth, Thomas. Diana's faithful friend and lover in Meredith's novel DIANA OF THE CROSSWAYS.

reed.

a broken or *bruised reed.* Something not to be trusted for support; a weak adherent. Egypt is called a broken reed, in which Hezekiah could not trust if the Assyrians made war on Jerusalem, "which broken reed if a man leans on, it will go into his hand and pierce it" (See 2 *Kings* xviii. 21; *Is.* vi. 6).

> Lean not on Earth, 'twill pierce thee to the heart;
> A broken reed at best; but oft, a spear.
> Young, *Night Thoughts,* ii.

a reed shaken by the wind. A person blown about by every wind of doctrine, John the Baptist (said Christ) was not a "reed shaken by the wind," but from the very first had a firm belief in the Messiahship of the Son of Mary and this conviction was not shaken by fear or favor. Cf. *Matt.* xi. 7. *Shaken With the Wind* is the title of a novel (1942) by Miriam Allen deFord.

a thinking reed. Man. See PASCAL, BLAISE.

Reed, John (1887–1920). American journalist and author, known for his sympathies with the Socialist movement and his reporting of the Russian Revolution of 1917. He was one of the editors of THE MASSES, wrote and acted for the PROVINCETOWN PLAYERS, of which he was one of the founders, served as a war correspondent in Mexico and Europe, worked for the Bureau of International Revolutionary Propaganda, in connection with which he lectured on the revolution of the BOLSHEVIKS, and helped organize the first American COMMUNIST PARTY. His works include *Insurgent Mexico* (1914), dealing with the revolt of Pancho Villa; *The War in Eastern Europe* (1916); *Red Russia* (1919); and *Ten Days That Shook the World* (1919), his most famous work, a vivid eyewitness account of the Bolshevik revolution, which was later officially approved and came to be used as a textbook in the Russian schools.

Reed came of a wealthy and prominent Oregon family and was somewhat of a playboy before he became interested in Socialism. He was a friend of the Russian revolutionary leaders and was a member of the executive committee of the 1920 congress of the Communist International. After his death at Baku from typhus, he was treated as a Russian hero and buried in the Kremlin.

Reed, Sampson (1800–1880). A Swedenborgian whose *Observations on the Growth of the Mind* (1826) greatly influenced Ralph Waldo EMERSON.

Reed, Thomas Brackett (1839–1902). Speaker of the House of Representatives (1889–1891, 1895–1899); compiled a series of rules known as Reed's Rules (1890) which were an improvement on the former rules as to the powers of the speaker.

Reed, Walter (1851–1902). American army surgeon. He headed a commission, with James Carroll, Jesse Lazear, and Aristides Agramonte, to investigate yellow fever (1900).

As a result of his experiments, the carriers of the disease were identified and the manner of transmission established. The Walter Reed Hospital in Washington, D.C., is named in his honor. Cf. *Yellow Jack,* a play by Sidney HOWARD (1928).

Reedy, William Marion (1862–1920). American editor, whose St. Louis *Sunday Mirror* (from 1893), known as *Reedy's Mirror,* was distinguished by printing the first portions of *The Spoon River Anthology* by Edgar Lee MASTERS under the pseudonym of Webster Ford. Reedy was a great editor; as an encourager of American literature he was a decided influence on his time.

Reese, Lizette Woodworth (1856–1935). American lyrical poet of fine achievement. Thomas B. Mosher of Portland, Me., published Miss Reese's poems in limited editions. Her most famous poem is a sonnet called *Tears.* She was for the greater part of her life a school teacher, teaching at Western High School in Baltimore for 20 years. She published five books of poetry and a book of reminiscences called *A Victorian Village.*

Reeve, Arthur Benjamin (1880–1936). American writer of detective stories who created the character of "scientific detective" Craig Kennedy.

Reeve's Tale, The. One of the "broadest" in Chaucer's CANTERBURY TALES, and fittingly placed in the mouth of one who is neither an ecclesiastic nor one of the "gentles," but an upper servant. The tale occurs frequently in the jest- and story-books of the 16th and 17th centuries. Boccaccio has it in the DECAMERON (*Day* xi, nov. vi), but Chaucer probably took it from Jean de Bove's *fabliau, Gombert et des Deux Clercs.* It concerns Simon Simkin, the Miller of Trompington, known as an arrant thief. Two scholars undertake to see that a sack of corn is ground for "Solar Hall College" without being tampered with, so one stands at the hopper and the other at the trough below. In the meantime, Simon Simkin lets loose the scholars' horse; while they go to catch it, he purloins half a bushel of the flour, which is made into cakes, and substitutes meal in its stead. But the young men have their revenge; they not only make off with the flour, meal, and cakes without payment, but also leave the miller well trounced.

referendum. The submission to the people in general of any act of legislature. In the U.S. about half the states can exercise the referendum as to state matters. In municipal affairs about 300 cities use this principle of action.

Reflections in a Golden Eye. A novel (1941) by Carson MCCULLERS.

Reflections on the French Revolution. A treatise by Edmund BURKE (1790), attacking the leaders and principles of the French Revolution for their violence and excesses, and urging reform rather than rebellion as a means of correcting social and political abuses. This work was, in turn, attacked by Thomas PAINE.

Reformation. In Church history, the movement leading to the various Protestant schisms of the 16th century. The leaders were: in Germany, Martin LUTHER; in France, John CALVIN; in Switzerland, Ulrich ZWINGLI; in Scotland, John KNOX. The Reformation was caused by the need for certain reforms in the church of Rome.

Regan. The second of King Lear's unfilial daughters in Shakespeare's tragedy KING LEAR. She is characterized as "most barbarous, most degenerate." She is married to the Duke of Cornwall.

Regan, Michael. Titular hero of Edward Sheldon's drama THE BOSS.

Regent Street. A street in London containiny many fine shops; it was originally (1813) designed to connect Carlton House, then the residence of the Regent, with Regent's Park.

Regicide. In English history, one of the judges involved in the execution of King Charles I. There were about eighty-four Regicides. Twenty-five were imprisoned for life, ten were executed; others escaped, several of them to the American colonies. At New Haven, Connecticut, a cave on the outskirts of the town, on the West Rock, is still known as "Judges' Cave," named after the Regicides William Goffe and Edward Whalley who hid there in 1661.

Regillus, Lake. A lake near Rome, scene of a battle in which the Romans defeated the Latins (498 B.C.), and concerning which Macaulay wrote one of his ballads.

regius professor. The incumbent of a professorship instituted by a king. The first English regius professorships were founded by Henry VIII (1540) at Cambridge University. Six years later five further regius professorships were established at Oxford University and still others have been added since.

Regler, Gustav (1898–). German novelist who fled to France and was acquainted with André Malraux, André Gide, etc. He joined the International Brigade during the Spanish Civil War and participated in the defense of Madrid. He was wounded and came to America, where he stayed with Ernest Hemingway who wrote a preface for his book, *The Great Crusade* (1940).

Régnier, Henri de (1864–1936). French poet and novelist, at first one of the PARNAS-

SIANS, later a disciple of MALLARMÉ and a member of the school of SYMBOLISM. His poetry is characterized by serenity of mood, semi-mythological subject-matter, and the wide use of free verse, of which Régnier is regarded by some critics as a master. His works include *Poèmes anciens et romanesques* (1890); *Tel qu'en songe* (1892); *Les Jeux rustiques et divins* (1897); *Les Médailles d'Argiles* (1900); *La Sandale Ailée* (1906); *Le Miroir des heures* (1910); *Scènes Mythologiques suivies de petites fables modernes* (1924); *Vestigia Flammae* (1928). Régnier, who was the son-in-law of José-Maria de HEREDIA, was elected to the French Academy in 1911.

Rehan, Ada (1860–1916). Irish-born American actress. Played over 200 parts in the company of Augustin Daly (1879–1899). Especially known for Shakespearean roles.

Rehearsal, The. A famous farce by George Villiers, Duke of Buckingham (1671), designed for a satire on the pretentious "heroic" plays of the time. The chief character, BAYES, is meant for DRYDEN, the Poet Laureate. See also BRENTFORD.

Rehoboam. In the Old Testament (1 *Kings* xii), the son and successor of Solomon. His remark, "My father chastised you with whips, but I will chastise you with scorpions," cost him the allegiance of the greater part of his kingdom. See JEROBOAM.

Reid, Forrest (1876–1946). Irish novelist, biographer and critic. A stylist and student of abnormal psychology. *Spring Song* (1916) and its sequel, *Pirates of the Spring* (1919) are his best novels. Excellent biographies of Walter DE LA MARE and William Butler YEATS.

Reid, Samuel Chester (1783–1861). American naval officer. Commanded privateer *General Armstrong* in War of 1812; in repulsing a British attack at Fayal, 1814, he detained British ships on their way to New Orleans, enabling Jackson to make adequate preparations to save the city. Designed present U.S. flag, with 13 stripes and the addition of a star for each new state. The first one, made by his wife Mary, was hoisted over the Capitol April 12, 1818.

Reid, Thomas Mayne (1818–1883). Irish-born writer of popular fiction who served in the U.S. army during the Mexican War and distinguished himself at the storming of Chapultepec. In London he found the publisher for his adventure stories, among which are *The Rifle Rangers* (1850); *The Scalp Hunters* (1851); *Afloat in the Forest* (1865). *The Quadroon* (1856) was the basis for a successful play, *The Octoroon* (1859), by Dion BOUCICAULT.

Reid, Whitelaw (1837–1912). U.S. ambassador to Great Britain (1905–1912), who had made his reputation as a war correspondent in the Civil War. Editor, New York *Tribune* (1872–1905). His son **Ogden Mills Reid** (1882–1946) also was editor of the New York *Tribune* (1913).

Reigneir. Duke of Anjou and Lorraine and titular king of Naples, introduced in all three parts of Shakespeare's *Henry VI*. The name is more accurately spelled RENÉ and under this form the Duke is a character in Scott's ANNE OF GEIERSTEIN.

Reign of Terror. A term applied to a period of anarchy, bloodshed, and confiscation in the French Revolution. It began after the fall of the Girondists (May 31, 1793), and extended to the overthrow of ROBESPIERRE and his accomplices (July 27, 1794). During this short time thousands of persons were put to death.

Reilley, Weary. In James T. Farrell's STUDS LONIGAN, a vicious, dissipated young braggart, an associate of Studs. Weary Reilley's rape of a girl named Irene at a wild New Year's Eve Party in 1929 is one of the outstanding scenes of sordidness and vice in the novel.

Reinach. Name of three distinguished French brothers: **Joseph Reinach** (1856–1921) was a member of the Chamber of Deputies and conducted a campaign (1897–1906) to prove the innocence of Captain Alfred Dreyfus. **Salomon Reinach** (1858–1932) was an archeologist whose two most notable treatises are *Apollo: A General History of the Plastic Arts* (1904) and *Orpheus: A General History of Religions* (1909). **Théodore Reinach** (1860–1928) was a professor of numismatics.

Reine Pédauque, At the Sign of the. A novel by Anatole FRANCE (1893). The chief character is Jerome COIGNARD.

Reinhardt, Max. Originally **Max Goldmann** (1873–1943). Austrian stage director and producer specializing in mass effects; best known for *Sumurun* (New York, 1912), *The Miracle* (London, 1911), and *Oedipus Rex*. He toured the U.S. in 1923, producing his pageant-play, *The Miracle*. Regularly every year at Salzburg he produced the mystery play *Everyman*. Upon Hitler's coming to power, Reinhardt left the continent, worked in England and America, became a film director in Hollywood, and, in 1937, put on Werfel's *Eternal Road* in New York City.

Réjane. Stage name of **Gabrielle Charlotte Réju** (1856–1920). French actress who in her first year on the stage became a huge success both in vaudeville and at the Odéon. She founded and managed the Théâtre Réjane (1905). She appeared successfully at the Gaiety Theater in London as Catherine in *Mme Sans Gêne* which also had a long run in New York.

Rejected Addresses. A collection of parodies (1812) by James and Horace SMITH.

relief. Popular and journalistic term during the 1930's for governmental assistance given to persons who were unemployed, in the form either of money allotments or jobs provided at public expense. Relief was one of the chief features of the NEW DEAL, the Civilian Conservation Corps, Public Works Administration, and Works Progress Administration providing it through jobs, or "work relief." See also BOONDOGGLING.

Religio Medici. See BROWNE, Sir THOMAS.

Reliques of Ancient English Poetry. See PERCY, Bishop THOMAS.

Remarkable Providences Illustrative of the Earlier Days of American Colonization. A pseudo-scientific work by Increase MATHER (1684). It is a collection of reports of puzzling natural phenomena, unusual happenings, amazing escapes from danger, apparitions, demons, and the like, considered to have been compiled by several hands at an earlier date, to which Mather added comments, speculations, and reports of his own experiences or of authors he had read, in *An Essay for the Recording of Illustrious Providences.* He meant it to be a proof of the existence of the supernatural.

Remarque, Erich Maria. Original surname Krämer (1897–). German novelist, known for his dramatic, realistic accounts of the devastations of World War I and the depression period of the early 1920's among German youth. These are ALL QUIET ON THE WESTERN FRONT, English translation of *Im Westen nichts Neues* (1929), a sensational best-seller in Europe and the U.S., dramatized as a successful American motion picture; *The Road Back* (*Der Weg zurück;* 1931); *Three Comrades* (*Drei Kameraden;* 1937); *Flotsam* (1941). Remarque served in the German army (1915–1918) and held a number of menial jobs in Germany before his success as a novelist. During World War II, he sought refuge in the U.S. and wrote the best-seller *Arch of Triumph* (1946).

Rembrandt van Rijn, Paul (1606–1669). One of the most famous painters in the world. Born in Leiden, he is the principal representative of the Dutch school of painting and distinguished by his handling of light and shadow. He settled in Amsterdam and married a wealthy woman known as Saskia, of whom he painted several portraits. Some of his most famous pictures are *The Anatomy Lesson of Dr. Tulp; The Sortie of the Banning Cocq Company* (known familiarly as *The Night Watch*); *The Syndics;* and many religious and mythological canvases.

Remember the Alamo. A phrase arising from the war between the U.S. and Mexico when a gallant band of insurgent Texans defended to the last the Alamo, a mission building at San Antonio, against the Mexican government troops.

Remember the Maine. A slogan used in the Spanish American War after the destruction of the battleship *Maine* in Havana Harbor.

Remembrance of Things Past. English title for *A la Recherche du temps perdu,* the most famous work of Marcel PROUST. It consists of the following separate books, published 1913–1928: *Du Coté de Chez Swann* (1918), translated as SWANN'S WAY (1923); *A l'Ombre de jeunes Filles en Fleurs* (1918), translated as WITHIN A BUDDING GROVE (1924); *Le Coté de Guermantes* (1920–1921), as THE GUERMANTES WAY (1925); *Sodome et Gomorrhe* (1921–1922), as CITIES OF THE PLAIN (1928); *La Prisonnière* (1923), as THE CAPTIVE (1929); *Albertine disparue* (1926), as THE SWEET CHEAT GONE (1930); *Le Temps Retrouvé* (1928), as THE PAST RECAPTURED (1932). This long novel, an outstanding example of the ROMAN-FLEUVE, presents the author's theories of time and memory, developed under the influence of Henri BERGSON, with respect to the social groups with whom he associated in his youth, in combination with details of the life of the narrator, "Marcel," which are considered to be in part autobiographical.

Three definite groups are treated in *Remembrance of Things Past:* the GUERMANTES family and their friends, representing the aristocracy; Charles SWANN and his friends, representing the established bourgeosie; and the VERDURINS, nouveaux riches, considered vulgar by the Guermantes, and the various artists and intellectuals who come to their weekly salons. In addition to lengthy accounts of social gatherings attended by the narrator in the company of one or another of these groups, and of the personal intrigues in which numerous of their members are involved, the novel describes MARCEL's relations with his family, his love affair with Albertine SIMONET and his adoration from afar of Mme de Guermantes and Gilberte Swann, his preferences in painting, music, literature, and the theater, and numerous examples of introspection during which he analyzes minutely his feelings, motives, memories, and desires with regard to a given situation. The book also gives an amazing portrayal of homosexuality among both men and women.

See also the following: BALBEC; BERGOTTE; BERNARD, NISSIM; BLOCH; BRICHOT, DR.; CAMBREMER, MME DE; CHARLUS, PALAMÈDE, BARON DE; COMBRAY; COTTARD, DR.; FRANÇOISE; EL-

STIR; JUPIEN; MOREL, CHARLES; RACHEL; SAINT-LOUP, ROBERT; SANIETTE; SURGIS, MME DE; VINTEUIL.

Remembrance of Things Past is particularly noted for its social and individual portraiture and its psychological analysis. With THE MAGIC MOUNTAIN and ULYSSES, it is ranked among the greatest novels of the 20th century. The title of the English translation is from a quotation from one of Shakespeare's sonnets:

> When to the sessions of sweet silent thought
> I summon up remembrance of things past . . .

This translation, by Charles SCOTT-MONCRIEFF (except the final volume) is considered one of the most masterly ever made.

Remigius, St. See under SAINTS.

Remington, Frederic Sackrider (1861–1909). American painter who worked on a ranch as a cowboy in the West and was in Cuba during the Spanish-American War (1898) as an artist-correspondent. Best known for his scenes of the American West and his drawing of horses. He wrote and illustrated *Pony Tracks* (1895); *Crooked Trails* (1898); and *The Way of an Indian* (1906).

Remington, Richard. The hero and supposed narrator of Wells' NEW MACHIAVELLI.

Remizov, Aleksei Mikhailovich (1877–). Russian novelist; follower of Gogol and Pushkin. *Collected Works* (8 vols.; 1910–1912).

remora. A sucker-disked fish which attaches itself to larger fish and to vessels, and which, in ancient times, was fabled to be able to check their progress.

Remus, see UNCLE REMUS.

renaissance (*Fr.*, "re-birth"). The term was applied, broadly, to the movement and period of transition between the medieval and modern worlds which, beginning with PETRARCH and the Italian humanists in the 14th century, was immensely stimulated by the fall of Constantinople (1453), resulting in the dissemination of Greek scholarship and Byzantine art, the invention of printing (about the same time), and the discovery of America (1492). In England, this revival first manifested itself in the early years of the 16th century.

Renan, Ernest (1823–1892). French scholar, critic, and author, best known for his *La Vie de Jésus* (*The Life of Jesus;* 1863), a study of Christ as a man which popularized the "HIGHER CRITICISM" of the Bible. Among his other works are *L'Avenir de la Science* (1849), a testament of faith in science and social progress under the guidance of scientist rulers; *Averroès et L'Averroïsme* (1852), on Aristotelianism among the Arabs of the Middle Ages; *Histoire générale des Langues Semitiques* (1855); *Essais de Morale et de Critique* (1859); *Histoire des Origines du Christianisme* (1866–1881), a social, historical, and geographical study of Christianity, of which *La Vie de Jésus* was the first volume; *Histoire du Peuple d'Israël* (1887–1895); *Dialogues Philosophiques* (1876); *Souvenirs d'Enfance et de Jeunesse* (1883), personal reminiscences; *Drames Philosophiques* (1888).

Renan was brought up in poverty and was a student preparing for the priesthood when he lost his faith in orthodox religion under the influence of German philosophy and Semitic philology. His dominant ideas were later skeptical and politically liberal, based on the principle that the various systems of religious, scientific, and historical knowledge have only a relative value, no one system being wholly true. Renan influenced the 19th- and 20th-century conception of religious history and had an important effect on the writings of Anatole FRANCE, Paul BOURGET, and Maurice BARRÈS.

Renascence. A poem by Edna St. Vincent MILLAY, written in octosyllabic couplets and first published in 1912. It describes a mystic experience by the poet, in which she first acquires a cosmic knowledge of sin and suffering and then is given a rebirth of innocence and knowledge of God. This was the first poem to win public acclaim for Millay.

Renault or **Renaud of Montauban** or **Reynold of Montalban.** One of Charlemagne's knights and paladins, better known by his Italian name RINALDO.

René. A romance by CHATEAUBRIAND (1807). Much of the setting is in America, where the hero René tells the story of his restless wanderings to his adopted American Indian father Chactas and the French missionary Father Souel. René is a violently unhappy, morbid, introspective youth, typical of the heroes of the romantic school. See ROMANTICISM. His passion for his sister Amélie and his scorn of civilization are at the root of his misery. LES NATCHEZ is a sequel to *René*.

René, Le bon Roi (1408–1480). Son of Louis II, Duc d'Anjou, Comte de Provence, father of Margaret of Anjou. He was the last minstrel monarch, just, joyous, and debonair; a friend to the chase and the tilt, but still more so to poetry and music. He gave in largesses to knights-errant and minstrels (so says Thiebault) more than he received in revenue. He appears in Scott's ANNE OF GEIERSTEIN and also, under the name of Reignier, in all three parts of Shakespeare's *Henry VI*.

Reni, Guido (1575–1642). Well-known Italian painter whose most famous works include *The Crucifixion of St. Peter; Concert of Angels; Triumph of Phoebus; Massacre of the Innocents; Ecce Homo;* etc.

Renn, Ludwig see VIETH VON GOLSSENAU.

Renoir, Pierre Auguste (1841–1919). French impressionist painter, well-known for harmony of line and brilliance of color. His best canvases include *Lise; Madame Charpentier et ses Enfants* (at the Metropolitan Museum in New York); *Baigneuses;* portraits of Monet, Sisley, Wagner; many nudes; etc.

Repington, Charles à Court (1858–1925). British soldier and military correspondent whose gossipy *Diary* (1920) was much discussed, sometimes unfavorably.

reply churlish. Sir, you are no judge; your opinion has no weight with me. Or, to use TOUCHSTONE's illustration (*As You Like It,* v. 4), "If a courtier tell me my beard is not well cut, and I disable his judgment, I give him the reply churlish, which is the fifth remove from the lie direct, or, rather, the lie direct in the fifth degree." See COUNTERCHECK QUARRELSOME.

Repplier, Agnes (1858–1945). American writer, known for the grace, wit, and learning of her personal essays. Among these are *Books and Men* (1888); *Essays in Miniature* (1892); *Essays in Idleness* (1893); *The Fireside Sphinx* (1901); *Compromises* (1904); *Americans and Others* (1912); *Counter Currents* (1916); *Under Dispute* (1924); *To Think of Tea!* (1932); *In Pursuit of Laughter* (1936). She also wrote biographies of Roman Catholic subjects.

Representative Men. A collection of essays (1850) on Plato, Swedenborg, Montaigne, Napoleon, Goethe, etc., by Ralph Waldo EMERSON.

reproof valiant. Sir, allow me to tell you that is not the truth. This is TOUCHSTONE's fourth remove from the lie direct, or, rather, the lie direct in the fourth degree. See COUNTERCHECK QUARRELSOME.

The reproof valiant, the countercheck quarrelsome, the lie circumstantial, and the lie direct, are not clearly defined by Touchstone. The following, perhaps, will give the distinction required: *That* is not true; How *dare* you utter such a falsehood; *If* you said so, you are a liar; You are a liar, or you lie.

Republic, The. A famous philosophical treatise by PLATO, in which he describes the workings of an imaginary ideal state. See COMMONWEALTHS, IDEAL.

Republican.

Black Republicans, see under BLACK.

Red Republicans, see under RED.

Republican Queen. Sophie Charlotte, wife of Frederick I of Prussia.

republic of letters, the. The world of literature; authors generally and their influence. GOLDSMITH, in *The Citizen of the World, No. 20* (1762), says it "is a very common expression among Europeans"; it is found in Molière's *Mariage forcé,* Sc. vi (1664).

Rescue, The. A novel by Joseph CONRAD (1920). Like THE ARROW OF GOLD, *The Rescue* deals with the snares and pitfalls which a sophisticated woman of the world can throw about a simple-hearted, romantic young man. The hero is Captain Lingard, who appears in his later life as the powerful trader Rajah Laut of some of Conrad's other tales. The last words of the novel, "Steer North," signify his escape from Edith Travers, the dangerous woman he still loves.

Research Magnificent, The. A novel by H. G. WELLS (1915), narrating the life of William Benham and his search for the worthwhile in life.

Reserve Officers' Training Corps (R.O.T.C.). A students' corps, maintained by the War Department in schools and colleges throughout the U.S., pursuing studies of military science and tactics. Its graduates are eligible for commissions in the army or navy reserve.

Resolution and Independence. A poem by William WORDSWORTH (1807), sentimentally portraying the sad lot of an old and crippled leech-gatherer encountered on one of the poet's country walks; from the subject, the poem is also known as *The Leech-Gatherer.* It was parodied by Edward LEAR, in *Incidents in the Life of My Uncle Arly,* and by Lewis CARROLL in *The White Knight's Ballad.*

Respighi, Ottorino (1879–1936). Italian composer, well-known as pianist and conductor in the U.S., having appeared (1926–1935) in Philadelphia, New York, and Chicago. His *Pines of Rome* has often been conducted by Arturo TOSCANINI.

Restaud, Mme de. In Balzac's *Father Goriot* (*Le Père Goriot*), one of the ungrateful daughters of old GORIOT.

Restif de la Bretonne. Literary name of **Nicolas Edmé Restif** (1734–1806). French novelist often labeled as the "Rousseau of the Gutter" or the "Voltaire of Chambermaids."

Restoration. In English history, the period after the time of Cromwell and the Commonwealth, when the Stuart dynasty returned to England in the person of Charles II. It was a very licentious period, marked in the field of English letters by characteristic developments in the drama (DRYDEN and CONGREVE) and a remarkable flourishing of diarists (PEPYS and EVELYN).

Resurrection. A novel by Leo TOLSTOI (1899). The young, noble and light-hearted hero, Nekhludov, is one of the jury to decide upon the case of a girl who has poisoned a merchant for his money. To his horror he recognizes Maslova, whom he has seduced on his aunt's estate years before. Tormented by a sense of responsibility that completely upsets his previous scheme of life, Nekhludov determines to follow her to Siberia and marry her.

The novel deals with the working out of this strange undertaking. Maslova is also known as Katusha.

resurrection men. Grave robbers, body-snatchers. The term was first applied to Burke and Hare, in 1829, who rifled graves to sell the bodies for dissection, and sometimes even murdered people for the same purpose.

Reszke, Jean de. Originally **Jan Mieszislaw** (1850–1925). Polish operatic tenor who sang often in the U.S. toward the end of the 19th century and at the beginning of the 20th. He was best known in *Faust; Romeo and Juliet; Aïda;* and *Benvenuto Cellini.* His brother, **Édouard de Reszke** (1855–1917), was a basso who also toured this country and was successful in Wagnerian roles.

retort courteous, the. Sir, I am not of your opinion; I beg to differ from you; or, to use TOUCHSTONE's illustration (*As You Like It,* v. 4), "If I said his beard was not cut well, he was in the mind it was." The lie seven times removed; or rather, the lie direct in the seventh degree. See COUNTERCHECK QUARRELSOME.

Return of Peter Grimm, The. A drama by David BELASCO (1911). Peter Grimm is an old Dutch nursery man who comes back in the spirit after his death.

Return of the Druses. A tragedy by Robert BROWNING (1841). The Druses, a semi-Mohammedan sect of Syria, attacked by Osman, take refuge in one of the Sporades and place themselves under the protection of the knights of Rhodes. These knights slay their sheiks and oppress the fugitives. In the sheik massacre, Djabal is saved by Maäni, and entertains the idea of revenging his people and leading them back to Syria. To this end he proclaims that he is Hakim, the incarnate god, returned to earth, and soon becomes the leader of the exiled Druses. A plot is formed to murder the prefect of the isle, and to betray the island to Venice, if Venice will supply a convoy for their return. Aneal, a young woman, stabs the prefect, and dies of bitter disappointment when she discovers that Djabal is a mere impostor. Djabal stabs himself when his imposition is made public, but Loys, a Breton count, leads the exiles back to Lebanon.

Return of the Native, The. A novel by Thomas HARDY (1878). Clym Yeobright, tired of city life, returns from Paris to open a school on Egdon Heath, and in spite of the opposition of his mother marries Eustacia Vye, a passionate, pleasure-loving girl who hopes to persuade him to return to Paris. She has been in love with Damon Wildeve, "one in whom no man would have seen anything to admire and in whom no woman would have seen anything to dislike," but Wildeve now marries Clym's cousin Thomasin. Almost immediately Clym's eyesight fails and he becomes, for the time being, a furze cutter. With the idea of becoming reconciled to her son, Mrs. Yeobright takes the long walk over the heath to his cottage, but Eustacia, who is entertaining Wildeve, does not answer the door until after Clym's mother leaves in despair. Overcome with fatigue and suffering, she sinks down and is found by Clym, unconscious and dying from an adder bite. Clym learns enough to blame Eustacia and the couple part. Eustacia meets Wildeve at a midnight rendezvous, but throws herself into a pool, and in attempting to rescue her, Wildeve also drowns. Thomasin later marries Diggory Venn, a reddleman who has long been devoted to her, and Clym becomes an itinerant preacher.

Retz or **Rais,** Baron **de. Gilles de Laval** (1404?–1440). Marshal of France who fought with Joan of Arc against the English; notorious for his cruelty, especially to children. According to some his history begot the tale of *Bluebeard.* See Charles PERRAULT. Retz was finally burned alive.

Reuben. In the Old Testament, the oldest son of the patriarch JACOB; also, the tribe of his descendants. Of Reuben Jacob said, "Unstable as water, thou shalt not excel."

Reunion in Vienna. A comedy (1931) by Robert E. SHERWOOD, starring Alfred LUNT and Lynn FONTANNE.

Reuter, Baron **Paul Julius von.** Original name **Israel Beer Josaphat** (1816–1899). German-English capitalist who established in Aachen (1849) a telegraphic and pigeon post bureau for the collection and transmission of news. This was the beginning of Reuter's News Agency, which later (1851) established its headquarters in London.

Reuterdahl, Henry (1871–1925). Swedish-American painter and illustrator who was a correspondent during the Spanish-American War and was noted for his naval paintings and illustrations. His painting of the *Combat Between the Monitor and the Merrimac* is in the National Gallery of Art in Washington, D.C.

Revendal, Vera. The heroine of Zangwill's MELTING POT. Her father is also a prominent character.

Revenge, The. A poem by TENNYSON (1878). The *Revenge* is a ship under the command of Sir Richard GRENVILLE, anchored at Flores, in the Azores, when a fleet of fifty-three Spanish ships comes in sight.

Revenger's Tragedy, The. A play (1607) by Cyril TOURNEUR.

Reventlow, Count **Ernst zu** (1869–1943). Pan-German journalist. During World War I, he was an ardent supporter of the von Tirpitz policy of unrestricted submarine warfare. He wrote a 3-volume work on the Russo-Japanese War (1904–1906) and a book on *Nationalistic Socialism in the New Germany* (1932).

reverberator. In the best-known novels of Henry JAMES, a character who mediates between the reader and the plot, observing the events that take place in the novel but standing aside from them and thereby serving as someone with whom the reader may identify himself. One of James's novelettes is entitled *The Reverberator* (1888).

Revere, Paul. See PAUL REVERE'S RIDE.

Reveries of a Bachelor. A narrative, or rather a series of essays, which Donald Grant Mitchell published under the pseudonym of Ik Marvel (*Am.*, 1850). There was a sequel entitled *Dream Life* (1851).

Reviewer, The. A small magazine published (1921–1925) at Richmond, Va., to increase interest in Southern literature. It was edited by Emily Clark, assisted by James Branch Cabell and other Southern writers. Its discoveries among Southern writers included Julia Peterkin, Frances Newman, Paul Green and Du Bose Heyward. (See those names.)

Revised Version. See BIBLE, THE ENGLISH.

Revival of Letters. A term applied to the RENAISSANCE in so far as the movement reacted on literature. It really commenced earlier—at the close of the DARK AGES—but it received its chief impulse from the fall of Constantinople (1453) and the consequent dispersal over Europe of Greek manuscripts and Greek scholars. Also referred to as **Revival of Learning.**

Revocation of the Edict of Nantes. See under NANTES.

Revolt of Islam, The. A poem by SHELLEY written in his youth (1818). The hero and heroine, Laon and Cynthia, are united by burning enthusiasm for the cause of liberty as well as by the ties of love. When Othman, the tyrant, seizes Cynthia and commands that Laon be burned alive, Cynthia escapes and perishes with him.

Revolt of the Angels, The (La Révolte des anges). A satiric novel by Anatole FRANCE (1914). A group of angels, tired of life in heaven, seek to amuse themselves in modern Paris and finally join the company of Satan.

Revolutionary calendar. The calendar of the first French republic, dated from the 22 of September, 1792. It was divided into twelve months of thirty days with five additional days (six every fourth year) for celebration. The year began at midnight on the day of the autumnal equinox. Every month was divided into three groups of ten days each. The names of the months were: Vendémiaire (Vintage), from September 22; Brumaire (Fog), from October 22; Frimaire (Sleet), from November 21; Nivôse (Snow), from December 21; Pluviôse (Rain), from January 20; Ventôse (Wind), from February 19; Germinal (Seed), from March 21; Floréal (Blossom), from April 20; Prairial (Pasture), from May 20; Messidor (Harvest), from June 19; Thermidor (Heat), from July 19; Fructidor (Fruit), from August 18.

revue (*Fr.*). A kind of musical comedy concerning current events, expressed in songs, tableaux, skits, etc.

Reymont, Wladyslaw Stanislaw (1868–1925). Polish novelist, chiefly known for his four-volume masterpiece, *The Peasants,* for which he received the Nobel prize for literature (1924).

Reynard. A fox.

Reynard the Fox. A medieval beast-epic, satirizing contemporary life and events in Germany, in which all the characters are animals. The chief of them, Reynard, typifies the church; his uncle, Ysengrim the wolf, the baronial element; and Nobel the lion, the regal. The plot turns on the struggle for supremacy between Reynard and Ysengrim. Reynard uses all his endeavors to victimize everyone, especially his uncle Ysengrim, and generally succeeds.

The germ of the story is found in Aesop's fable, *The Fox and the Lion.* This was built upon by more than one writer, but the *Roman* as we now know it goes back to the work of a Fleming named *Willem,* of the early 13th century, of which a new and enlarged version was written about 1380 by an unknown author. William CAXTON made his translation from a late 15th century Dutch version of this, which was probably by Herman Barkhusen.

Reynard's globe of glass. Reynard, in *Reynard the Fox,* says he has sent this invaluable treasure to her majesty the queen as a present, but it never comes to hand, inasmuch as it has no existence except in the imagination of the fox. It is supposed to reveal what is being done—no matter how far off—and also to afford information on any subject that the person consulting it wishes to know. Hence, *Your gift was like the globe of glass of Master Reynard,* means a great promise, but no performance.

False Reynard. By this name DRYDEN describes the Unitarians in his *Hind and Panther.*

John MASEFIELD is the author of a long narrative poem called Reynard the Fox (1919).

Reynardine. In Reynard the Fox, the eldest of Reynard. He assumes the names of Dr. Pedanto and Crabron. His brothers are Rossel and Reinikin.

Reynaud, Paul (1878–). Premier of France in 1940 when the French were defeated by Germany. The Pétain Government interned him in September. In 1942 he became one of the principal defendants in the war-guilt trials at Riom, which were inconclusive. He was imprisoned in Germany in 1943.

Reynold of Montalban, see RENAULT.

Reynolds, Jeremiah N. (1799?–1858). American author, chiefly remembered as propagator of an extraordinary theory about the construction of the world, originally thought up by a certain Captain J. C. Symmes, Jr. This theory, which assumed polar openings in a world composed of five concentric spheres, influenced Edgar Allan Poe in his story *The Unparalleled Adventure of One Hans Pfaall.* After returning from South America, Reynolds made an impassioned plea to Congress for a polar expedition, and part of his address appears in Poe's *The Narrative of Arthur Gordon Pym.* Reynolds' story of Mocha Dick, a fierce white whale, which was published in the *Knickerbocker Magazine,* is said to have been the source of MOBY DICK by Herman Melville.

Reynolds, Sir Joshua (1723–1792). Famous English portrait painter. At his suggestion the Literary Club was founded in London (1764), its chief members being Dr. Johnson, Garrick, Goldsmith, Burke, Boswell, and Sheridan. He was painter to the king (1784) and did many portraits, one of the most famous being that of the actress Mrs. Siddons as the *Tragic Muse.* His failing eyesight compelled him to stop painting in 1790.

Rezánov, Nikolai Petrovich (1764–1807). Russian organizer of a Russian-American fur trading company (1801), which had a monopoly in the coast of northwest America. His visit to California and his romance are the subject of Gertrude Atherton's novel, *Rezánov* (1906). There is also a poem about Rezánov by Bret Harte in *Concepcion de Arguello.*

Rhadamanthus. In Greek mythology, son of JUPITER and EUROPA. He reigned in the Cyclades with such impartiality, that at death he was made one of the judges of the infernal regions. *Rhadamanthine* means severe.

Rhadames. The hero of Verdi's opera AÏDA.

Rhapsody in Blue. See under BLUES; GERSHWIN, GEORGE.

Rhea. In Greek mythology, wife of CRONUS, her brother, and "Mother of the Gods," i.e., of ZEUS, POSEIDON, HERA, DEMETER, etc. She became identified with the Asiatic CYBELE.

Rheims-Douai Version, the. See BIBLE, THE ENGLISH.

Rheingold, Das (The Rhine Gold). An opera by Richard Wagner, one of the four of the RING DES NIBELUNGEN.

rhetorical question. A question solely for effect, with no answer expected.

Rhétoriqueurs, Les Grands. A group of French poets of the first half of the 16th century, whose work is characterized by elaborate and complicated stanza forms, rhyme schemes, metaphors, alliteration, onomatopoeia, etc., with either lyric or didactic subject-matter. The leading members of the group, which is regarded as representative of the decadence of medieval poetry at the time, were Jean Meschinot (1420–1491), Guillaume Crétin (*fl.* ca. 1520), and Jean Lemaire de Belges (ca. 1473–ca. 1520). The name was derived from *Le Grand et Vrai Art de Pleine rhétorique* (1522), by Pierre Fabri, a treatise supplying the ambitious poet with rules for winning a patron's favor by his verses.

Rhett Butler, see BUTLER, RHETT.

Rhinedaughters. In Wagner's *Ring* (not in actual mythology), the three innocent nymphs Flosshilda, Woglinda, and Wellgunda, set to guard the Nibelungen Hoard in the Rhine.

Rhine Gold, The. See RING DES NIBELUNGEN.

Rhoda. In Virginia Woolf's THE WAVES, one of the six characters whose lives are presented as the novel unfolds. As a child, Rhoda is shy and retiring, conscious of no definite existence or personality of her own, imitating JINNY OR SUSAN in her overt actions. Her sense of isolation and unreality persists when she matures. She has a brief love affair with LOUIS but leaves him.

Rhoda Fleming. A novel by George MEREDITH (1865). The plot concerns the tireless efforts of the titular heroine Rhoda, aided by her lover Robert Armstrong, to set right the affairs of her sister, Dahlia, who has been seduced by Edward Blancove, an irresponsible young nobleman. Rhoda goes in search of Dahlia, obstinately believes in her innocence through a long series of revealing episodes, and when she learns the truth, as obstinately forces her to marry a worthless man under the conviction that her only hope lies in becoming a married woman.

Rhode, John, see STREET, CECIL.

Rhodes, Cecil John (1853–1902). Famous British financier who amalgamated the diamond mines around Kimberley in South Africa under a corporation called the De Beers Consolidated Mines (1888). As prime minister of Cape Colony (1890–1896) he sought to establish a federal South African dominion under Great Britain. He instigated the JAMESON RAID (1895) in pursuit of his imperialistic aims. Its failure compelled him to resign as premier, but in spite of this he is remembered in South

Africa as a great figure. He founded the Rhodes scholarships which have enabled young men from all over the British Empire, from the U.S., and from Germany to study at Oxford University.

Rhodes, Eugene Manlove (1869–1934). American writer of Western stories, called by Bernard De Voto "the novelist of the cattle kingdom." His principal books are *Good Men and True* (1910); *Bransford in Arcadia* (1914); *West is West* (1917); *Beyond the Desert* (1934); and *The Proud Sheriff* (1935). He was a cowboy for 25 years and knew thoroughly the life of which he wrote.

Rhodes, Harrison Garfield (1871–1929). American writer, chiefly noted for his stage version (1915) of the novel *Ruggles of Red Gap* by Harry Leon Wilson.

Rhodes, James Ford (1848–1927). American historian whose nine-volume *History of the United States* (1899–1928) won him the Pulitzer prize for history in 1918.

Rhodes scholarships. See under RHODES, CECIL. Under the provisions of Cecil Rhodes' will, there are 202 Rhodes scholarships: 100 British, 96 American, and 6 German. They are provided for three years, and one-third of their total number is awarded every year. The candidates must be unmarried, between nineteen and twenty-five years of age, and fully matriculated students. Awards are made on a competitive basis.

Rhodopis. Tennyson alludes in *The Princess* to the unfounded tradition that the Greek courtesan Rhodopis built the third pyramid. Even without a pyramid, she was a considerable character in her time. One of the poems of Sappho is directed against her under the name of Doricha.

Rhoecus. A poem by James Russell LOWELL (1843). Rhoecus falls in love with a Dryad, but, because he neglects her messenger, she disappears. The story is from classic mythology.

Rhondda, Viscount. **David Alfred Thomas** (1856–1918). Welsh mine operator. A Gladstonian liberal who was president of the local-government board in Lloyd George's cabinet (1916) and stopped speculation and black-market practices while in office as wartime food controller. Lady Rhondda is a well-known feminist, backer of the Liberal periodical *Time and Tide*, for which E. M. DELAFIELD wrote.

rhyme.

double or *feminine rhyme*. A bisyllabic rhyme, such as tender, slender; ocean, motion. See under FEMININE.

internal rhyme. Rhyme within the line, as—

> We were the first that ever burst into that silent sea.
> Coleridge, *The Ancient Mariner*.

> Once upon a midnight dreary while I pondered weak and weary—
> Poe, *The Raven*.

triple rhyme. Three-syllable rhyme, as—

> Father all glorious,
> O'er all victorious,
> Come and reign over us,
> Ancient of Days.

rhyme royal. A stanza of seven lines of heroic or five-foot iambic verse, rhyming *ababbcc*. It was called the *rhyme royal* from James I of Scotland who was both king and poet, and was also widely known as *Troilus verse* because Chaucer employed it in his TROILUS AND CRISEYDE, the first stanza of which is as follows:

> The double sorwe of Troilus to tellen,
> That was the king Priamus sone of Troye,
> In lovinge, how his aventures fellen
> Fro wo to wele, and after out of joye,
> My purpos is, er that I part fro ye,
> Thesiphone, thou help me for t'endyte
> Thise wóful verse that wepen as I wryte.

Rhymes to be Traded for Bread. An early collection of poems by Vachel LINDSAY actually composed upon his travels through the West, when he was making the experiment of exchanging his rhymes for a night's lodging on the road. Cf. his *Adventures while Preaching the Gospel of Beauty* (1914).

rhyming slang. A kind of slang popular in Great Britain in the early 20th century, in which the word intended was replaced by one that rhymed with it, as "Charley Prescott" for *waistcoat*, or "plates of meat" for *feet*. When the rhyme was a compound word, the rhyming part was almost invariably dropped, leaving one who did not know the idiom somewhat in the dark. Thus Chivy (Chevy) Chase rhymes with "face"; by dropping the "chase," *chivy* remains, and becomes the accepted slang word. Similarly, daisies became *boots*, thus: daisy-roots will rhyme with boots; drop the rhyme and *daisy* remains. By the same process, *sky* is slang for *pocket*, the compound word which gave birth to it being "sky-rocket." "Christmas," a *railway guard*, as "ask the Christmas," is, of course, from "Christmas-card"; and "raspberry," *heart*, is "raspberry-tart."

Rhys, Ernest (1859–1946). Welsh poet and anthologist. Editor of EVERYMAN'S LIBRARY (from 1905). Began his career as a coal-mine worker.

Rialto (From *rivo alto*). A famous island and commercial district in Venice, Italy. Shakespeare mentions it in *The Merchant of Venice*. Also, a marble bridge in Venice built (ca. 1590) across the Grand Canal.

Ribaut, Jean (ca. 1520–1565). French Huguenot navigator who laid claim to the territory of Florida for France in 1562 and wrote an account of his expedition and discovery of the Terra Florida. A modern account of it is to be found in *Pioneers of France in the New World* (1865) by Francis PARKMAN.

Ribbentrop, Joachim von (1893–1946). German national socialist diplomat, who had begun his career as a champagne salesman. Ambassador to Great Britain (1936); minister of foreign affairs (1938). He negotiated the German-Japanese anti-Comintern agreement (1936); the Russo-German non-aggression pact (1939); and the Italo-German-Japanese alliance (1940). Tried at Nuremberg and executed by hanging.

Ricardo, David (1772–1823). Famous English economist. It was the encouragement of James Mill (father of John Stuart MILL) that led to the publication of his *Principles of Political Economy and Taxation* (1817). He developed a theory of rent, property, and wages; and a quantity theory of money. He wrote economic studies, of which particularly one on bullion caused great discussion at the time of its publication.

Riccabocca, Dr. In BULWER LYTTON'S *My Novel,* an Italian philosopher, a close friend of the Caxton family.

rice. The custom of throwing rice after a bride comes from India, rice being, with the Hindus, an emblem of fecundity. The bridegroom throws three handfuls over the bride, and the bride does the same over the groom. Among Americans, the rice is thrown by neighbors and friends.

Rice Christians. Converts to Christianity for worldly benefits, such as a supply of rice to Indians. The term implies a profession of Christianity born of lucre, not faith.

Rice, Mrs. **Alice Caldwell,** *née* **Hegan** (1870–1942). Popular American novelist, chiefly remembered for such books as MRS. WIGGS OF THE CABBAGE PATCH (1901); *Lovey Mary* (1903); etc. Her husband, **Cale Young Rice** (1872–1943), was a well-known American poet who received, however, more praise in England than in his own country; his *Bridging the Years* (1939) is an account of his literary life. He committed suicide after his wife's death.

Rice, Elmer. Original surname **Reizenstein** (1892–). American playwright, known for his use of experimental technique, his realism, and his portrayal of the problems of his time, especially social injustice; his more important plays so characterized alternated with comedy and melodrama of greater commercial appeal. His dramatic works include *On Trial* (1914); THE ADDING MACHINE (1923); *Wake Up, Jonathan* (1928); STREET SCENE (1929); *Cock Robin* (1929), written with Philip BARRY; *Close Harmony* (1929), written with Dorothy PARKER; *The Subway* (1929); *See Naples and Die* (1929); *The Left Bank* (1931); *Counsellor-at-Law* (1931); *Black Sheep* (1932); *We, the People* (1933); *Judgment Day* (1934), dealing with the trials held by the German Nazi government (see NAZISM) for the burning of the Reichstag building; *Between Two Worlds* (1935); *American Landscape* (1938); *Two on an Island* (1940); *Flight to the West* (1941); *Dream Girl* (1946). *A Voyage to Purilia* (1930), is a satire on HOLLYWOOD, and *Imperial City* (1937), dealing with life in New York City, is a novel. Rice first wrote plays for the Morningside Players, a little-theater group (see LITTLE THEATER) in New York.

Rice, Grantland (1880–). Well-known American sports-writer who wrote for years a widely syndicated column called "The Sportlight." His column in the New York *Sun* is called "Setting the Pace." He has also written *Songs of the Stalwart* (1917) and *Songs of the Open* (1924).

Riceyman Steps. A novel by Arnold BENNETT (1923), presenting a study of a miser, a book-seller, who influences his wife to the adoption of his parsimonious habits, starves himself to death, and brings about her death as well.

Rich, John (1682?–1761). A theatrical producer in London forevermore connected with John GAY, because he produced *The Beggar's Opera,* a play that became so successful that it was said to have "made Rich gay and Gay rich."

Rich, Obadiah (1783–1850). London bookseller whose catalogues were found very valuable by such historians as Washington Irving, Prescott, and George Bancroft.

Rich, Penelope, *née* **Devereux** (1562?–1607). Heroine of the sonnets by Sir Philip Sidney, which were collected under the title of *Astrophel and Stella* (1591).

Rich, Richard (fl. 1609–1610). British adventurer, whose *Newes from Virginia,* a well-known ballad based upon his encountering shipwreck in the Bermudas and his adventures in the Virginia Colony, is said to have suggested to Shakespeare certain scenes in *The Tempest.*

Richard I. See RICHARD COEUR DE LION.

Richard II (1367–1400). King of England (1377–1399) of the House of Plantagenet. Son of the Black Prince. As a young man at the time of the Peasants' Revolt under Wat Tyler (1381), he betrayed the people. Finally defeated by Henry of Bolingbroke (the later Henry IV), he was deposed by Parliament and probably killed in prison. He is the subject of a tragedy by Shakespeare.

Richard III (1452–1485). King of England (1483–1485) of the House of York. Known as

"Crouchback." Cf. *Crouchback* by Carola Oman. He was the supposed murderer of the Princes in the Tower, who were the rightful king, Edward V, and his brother, the Duke of York. The story is told in Sir Thomas More's *History of King Richard III*, and is the subject of a famous painting by Sir John Everett Millais (1878). Richard III was finally defeated at Bosworth Field (August, 1485) by the Earl of Richmond, as Henry VII the first of the Tudors. He is the subject of a tragedy by Shakespeare. As Richard Plantagenet, duke of Gloucester, he appears in two parts of Shakespeare's *Henry VI*.

Richard, Poor, see POOR RICHARD.

Richard Carvel. A novel by Winston CHURCHILL (1899), dealing with the Revolutionary period. As a young man in Maryland, Carvel falls in love with Dorothy Manners, but is forced to see her taken to England with a view to contracting a more ambitious marriage. Carvel's subsequent adventures, largely brought on by his uncle's jealousy of his position as heir of the family estates, include kidnaping by pirates, capture by John Paul Jones, a period in the debtor's prison of London, from which he is rescued by Dorothy, life in England, with such men as Horace Walpole and George Fox as his associates, and a series of exciting experiences during the Revolution. He serves with John Paul Jones, who has become his firm friend, is wounded, nursed back to health by Dorothy, and at last wins back his estate and succeeds in making her his wife.

Richard Cœur de Lion or **Richard I** (1157–1199). This king of England appears in three of SCOTT's novels. In *The Betrothed* (1825) he takes part in the siege of the Castle of Garde Doloureuse with his father Henry II. THE TALISMAN shows him crusading in the Holy Land, the enemy and friend of Saladin. In IVANHOE he appears at the tournament disguised as the Black Knight. He is the hero of Maurice Hewlett's RICHARD YEA-AND-NAY.

Richard Feverel, The Ordeal of. A novel by George MEREDITH (1859) with the sub-title *A History of Father and Son*. The plot has to do with the tragic working out of Sir Austin Feverel's self-evolved "system" of education, a system that implies the exclusion of most, if not all, normal interests. His son Richard, who is tutored at home by an uncle, Adrian Feverel, and carefully protected from any stray influences of sex, falls in love, nevertheless, with Lucy Desborough, a farmer's niece whom he happens to meet, and goaded by opposition, marries her before he is twenty. Sir Austin refuses to see Lucy and attempts to punish Richard by maneuvering to keep the two apart, with the result that Richard succumbs to the attractions of a clever woman of the world, while Lucy, in his absence, is annoyed by an aristocratic libertine. Bessie Berry, Richard's old nurse, a person much loved for her good judgment and large heart, finally succeeds in extricating Lucy from her difficulties. In the meantime, the repentant Richard lingers abroad until his Uncle Austin Wentworth, a man of tolerance and understanding, effects a reconciliation between Lucy and Sir Austin. Richard now returns, hears of the insult upon Lucy's honor, challenges his enemy to a duel, is badly wounded and on recovery learns that Lucy has died of brain fever.

Richard Roe. See under John DOE. Also, hero of *Human Being* (1932) by Christopher MORLEY.

Richards, Grant (1872–1948). English publisher and writer. He was the second publisher of A. E. HOUSMAN and wrote *Housman: 1859–1936* (1940) as well as several light novels and *Memories of a Misspent Youth* (1932).

Richards, Ivor Armstrong (1893–). English literary critic, psychologist, and aesthetician, known for his studies and experiments in aesthetic meaning and experience, especially in connection with the science of SEMANTICS, and for his insistence that the ostensible statements in poetry be considered in a different light from the statements involved in scientific exposition or factual information. His works include *The Foundations of Aesthetics* (1922), written with C. K. Ogden and James Wood; *Principles of Literary Criticism* (1924); *Science and Poetry* (1926); *Practical Criticism: A Study of Literary Judgment* (1929); *Mencius on the Mind* (1932), "experiments in multiple definition"; *Coleridge on Imagination* (1934); *The Meaning of Meaning* (1936), written with C. K. Ogden; *The Philosophy of Rhetoric* (1936); *Interpretation in Teaching* (1938); *How to Read a Page* (1942); *The Republic of Plato* (1942), a new version in BASIC ENGLISH. Richards had an important influence on literary criticism in England and the U.S. during the 1920's and 1930's, turning it from individual impressionism and moral and political consideration into more systematic and exact scientific channels.

Richards, Mrs. **Laura Elizabeth,** *née* **Howe** (1850–1943). Daughter of Julia Ward HOWE; author of children's books and a biography of her mother which was awarded the Pulitzer prize for biography in 1917. Cf. *Long, Long Ago* by Alexander WOOLLCOTT.

Richardson, Dorothy M. (1882–). English novelist; a pioneer and outstanding exemplar of the STREAM-OF-CONSCIOUSNESS school. Her novels, grouped under the general title of *Pilgrimage*, are almost entirely concerned with the exploration of the human consciousness.

Richardson, Henry Handel. Pen name of Mrs. **Henrietta Robertson,** *née* **Richardson** (1880?–1946). Australian-born novelist. Her *The Fortunes of Richard Mahony* (1930), a trilogy including *Australia Felix, The Way Home,* and *Ultima Thule,* has been compared to BUDDENBROOKS by Thomas Mann and JEAN-CHRISTOPHE by Romain Rolland.

Richardson, Samuel (1689–1761). English novelist, known for his contributions to the study of character and domestic and social manners in the development of the form of the novel in 18th-century England. His leading works, which influenced later writers of fiction, are PAMELA, OR VIRTUE REWARDED (1740), regarded as the first modern English novel; CLARISSA HARLOWE (1749); and SIR CHARLES GRANDISON (1753). Richardson was a joiner's son, a printer, and, for a while, a village letter-writer, which influenced him in the epistolary technique of his most famous novels. In 1741 he published a collection of prepared letters on various subjects for the use of people unable to write.

Richard Yea-and-Nay, The Life and Death of. A historical romance by Maurice HEWLETT (1900), dealing with the Third Crusade and the love affair of Richard the Lionhearted (see RICHARD COEUR DE LION) and Jehane Saint-Pol. The supposititious author is Abbot Milo, Richard's confessor and friend.

Richelieu, Duc de. Armand Jean du Plessis (1585–1642). A famous French statesman, cardinal, and chief minister of France in the reign of Louis XIII, and often referred to as *Éminence Rouge.* He is a prominent character in Alfred de Vigny's *Cinq Mars* (1826); in Bulwer-Lytton's historical drama *Richelieu, or the Conspiracy* (1838); and in *The Three Musketeers* and other romances by Dumas. See also LA ROCHEFOUCAULD.

Richepin, Jean (1849–1926). French author. *Les Caresses* (poetic drama; 1877); *Les Blasphèmes* (poems; 1884); *Nana Sahib* (drama; 1883); *Le Filibustier* (comedy; 1888); and other works including opera, heroic dramas, and several psychological novels.

Richie, Helena. The heroine of Margaret Deland's AWAKENING OF HELENA RICHIE and an important character in its sequel THE IRON WOMAN. Her adopted son David is prominent in both novels.

Richman, Arthur (1886–1944). American playwright. President, Authors' League of America (1928–1930). Author of *The Awful Truth* (1922); *A Proud Woman* (1927); *The Season Changes* (1936); and other plays.

Richmond. The title **Earl of Richmond** was borne by Henry VII before he became king of England. The phrase, *another Richmond in the field,* has been used to point out the arrival of a new opponent and is taken from the lines in Shakespeare's *King Richard III:*

> I think there be six Richmonds in the field:
> Five have I slain to-day instead of him.

Richmond, Mrs. **Grace Louise,** *née* **Smith** (1866–). American popular romantic novelist known best for *Red Pepper Burns* (1910) and subsequent books in the same vein.

Richter, Conrad (1890–). American novelist of the Southwest and Middle West, whose books, *The Sea of Grass* (1937); *The Trees* (1940); *The Fields* (1946); etc., are regarded as of unusual merit. Louis Bromfield has said that few writers today are sounder in their understanding and treatment of American pioneer life.

Richter, Johann Paul Friedrich, called **Jean Paul** (1763–1825). German novelist of the romantic period (see ROMANTICISM), known for his portrayals of life in simple country villages. His works include *Hesperus* (1792–1794); *Quintus Fixlein* (1796); *Siebenkäs* (1796); *Titan* (1800–1803); *Flegeljahre* (1802–1805).

Richthofen, Frieda von. German wife of D. H. LAWRENCE, who was married to Ernest Weekley, an English lexicographer, when Lawrence fell in love with her and persuaded her to elope with him (1914). The author celebrated his marriage in his writings and claimed that the influence of his wife freed him of the repressions and inhibitions he had acquired under his English Puritan training. *Not I, But the Wind . . .* (1934) is a memoir of Lawrence by his wife, who was the sister of Baron Manfred von Richthofen, a celebrated German aviator during World War I.

Rich Young Ruler. In the New Testament, a young man who had kept all the commandments all his life and wished to know what more he ought to do. When he was told to give his fortune to the poor, "he went away sorrowing, for he had great possessions."

Rickard, George Lewis. Best known as **Tex** (1871–1929). Famous American prizefight promoter (from 1906).

Rickenbacker, Edward Vernon. Known as **Eddie** (1890–). Famous American aviator who began his career as an automobile racer. In World War I, he was credited with 26 personal victories and was awarded the Congressional Medal of Honor. Cf. his *Fighting the Flying Circus* (1919). In World War II, he was active in aviation, having been president and general manager of the Eastern Air Lines. He will be particularly remembered for his account of three weeks on a raft in the Pacific Ocean in *Seven Came Through* (1943).

Rickert, Edith (1871–1938). American educator and creative writer. Her best-known reference books, compiled with John Matthews Manly, are *Contemporary British Literature* (1921) and *Contemporary American Literature* (1922).

Ricketts, Charles (1866–1931). British painter, sculptor, and designer for the stage. Founded the Vale Press (1896). A great friend of the English artist, Charles Shannon.

Rickman, Savage Keith. The hero of May Sinclair's THE DIVINE FIRE.

ricochet words, see REDUPLICATED WORDS.

Ridd, John. The hero of Richard Blackmore's LORNA DOONE.

Riddell, John, see FORD, COREY.

Riddle of the Sands, The. A novel (1903) by Erskine CHILDERS. It is an oddly prophetic book outlining the discovery of a planned German invasion of England. It appeared in America in 1915. A second American edition was published in 1940 at the time of the biggest air raids over London.

Rideout, Henry Milner (1877–1927). Californian writer of novels, short stories and English textbooks.

Rider, Fremont (1885–). American editor of *Monthly Book Review* (1909–1917); *Publishers' Weekly* (1910–1917); *Library Journal* (1914–1917). President, Rider Press (1914–1933), and librarian at Wesleyan University (from 1933).

Riderhood, Rogue. A longshoreman and villain in Dickens' novel OUR MUTUAL FRIEND.

Ridge, Lola (1871–1941). American poet, born in Ireland and raised in Australia, known for her presentations of the sufferings of the poor and downtrodden in a technique showing the influence of IMAGISM. Among her books of poems are *The Ghetto, And Other Poems* (1918); *Sun-Up* (1920); *Red Flag* (1927); *Firehead* (1929), an account of the Crucifixion inspired by the SACCO-VANZETTI CASE; *Dance of Fire* (1935).

Ridicule, Father of. See under FATHER.

Riding, Laura (1901–). American poet, friend of Robert GRAVES, a member of the group known as FUGITIVES and an expatriate in Europe for a number of years. Among her books are *Collected Poems* (1938); *Contemporaries and Snobs* (1928), critical studies; *A Trojan Ending* (1937), a historical novel on the Trojan war; *Lives of Wives* (1939), dealing with outstanding figures of the classical Greek and Roman world from the standpoint of their private lives.

riding rhyme. An early form of the heroic couplet, a rhymed couplet in iambic pentameter. Used by Chaucer, and hence taking its name from the riding of the Canterbury pilgrims. Also used by Lydgate.

Ridley, Nicholas (1500?–1555). A Protestant martyr who denounced Queen Mary and Queen Elizabeth as illegitimate and took up the cause of Lady Jane Grey. He, with Latimer, was burned at the stake.

Ridpath, John Clark (1840–1900). American popular historian. His works include *A Popular History of the United States of America* (1876); *Cyclopedia of Universal History* (4 vols.; 1880–1885); and *Great Races of Mankind* (4 vols.; 1884–1894). He was also editor in chief of the *Ridpath Library of Universal Literature* (25 vols.; 1898).

Riel, Hervé, see HERVÉ RIEL.

Rienzi, Cola di. Real name **Niccolo Gabrini** (1313–1354). Italian patriot, often called the "last of the Romans," who, for a time, restored the old Roman system of government, but failed and went to his death. He is the hero of Bulwer-Lytton's historical romance, *Rienzi, the Last of the Tribunes* (1835) and Wagner's opera *Rienzi* founded on the novel (1841).

Riesenberg, Felix (1879–1939). American author whose father was a sea captain and who followed the sea for a dozen years himself. His first novel, *Under Sail* (1915), celebrates the last of the sailing ships out of Maine. His *East Side, West Side* became a moving picture before the days of the talking film (1927). His non-fiction, too, concerns for the most part the sea.

rift in the lute. A small defect which mars the general result.

> Unfaith in aught is want of faith in all
> It is the little rift within the lute
> That by-and-by will make the music mute,
> And ever widening slowly silence all.
> Tennyson, *Merlin and Vivien: Vivien's Song.*

Rigdon, Sidney (1793–1876). American Mormon leader. From his rewriting of a religious novel may have grown the *Book of Mormon.* See Joseph SMITH. He was excommunicated after Smith's assassination and founded his own church in Pittsburgh.

Rigdum Funnidos. A character in Carey's burlesque of *Chrononhoton-Thologos* (1734).

The name of this character supplied the sobriquet given by Sir Walter SCOTT to John Ballantyne (1774–1821), his publisher, because he was full of fun.

Riggs, Lynn (1899–). American playwright, author of plays dealing with life and characters in Oklahoma and Texas, especially in the framework of folk-themes of that region. These include *Roadside* (1930); *Green Grow the Lilacs* (1931), his best-known play, dramatizing a Western folk-song, basis of the sensationally successful musical play OKLAHOMA!; *Russet Mantle* (1936); *The Cherokee*

Night (1936), on the decline of the Cherokee Indians in Oklahoma.

right. In politics, the *right* is the Conservative party, because in the continental chambers the Conservatives sit on the right-hand side of the Speaker, and the Liberals, Radicals, and Labor on the left.

right as a trivet. Quite right; in an excellent state. The trivet was originally a three-legged stand—a tripod—and the allusion is to its always standing firmly on its three legs.

right foot foremost. It is still considered unlucky to enter a house, or even a room, on the left foot, and in ancient Rome a boy was stationed at the door of a mansion to caution visitors not to cross the threshold with their left foot, which would have been an ill omen.

right-hand man. An invaluable, or confidential, assistant; originally applied to the cavalryman at the right of the line, whose duties were of great responsibility.

right of way. The legal right to make use of a certain passage whether high road, byroad, or private road. Private right of way may be claimed by immemorial usage, special permission, or necessity.

Right of Way, The. A novel (1901) by Sir Gilbert PARKER.

Rights, Declaration of. An instrument submitted to William and Mary and accepted by them (February 13, 1689), setting forth the fundamental principles of the constitution. The chief items are: The Crown cannot levy taxes without the consent of Parliament, nor keep a standing army in times of peace; the Members of Parliament are free to utter their thoughts, and a Parliament is to be convened every year; elections are to be free, trial by jury to be inviolate, the right of petition not to be interfered with, and the Sovereign should take the oath against Transubstantiation and agree not to marry a Roman Catholic.

to rights. In apple-pie order.

to put things to rights. To put every article in its proper place.

Rights of Man, The. A political work by Thomas PAINE (1791–1792), defending the French Revolution against attacks made on it by Edmund BURKE. In it, Paine argues that civil government exists only through a contract with the majority of men for the safeguarding of the individual, and that if man's "natural rights" are interfered with by the government, revolution is permissible. As a result of this tract, Paine found himself forced to flee to France and was tried in England in his absence as a traitor. See also SOCIAL CONTRACT.

Rigoletto. An opera by VERDI (1851) based on Victor HUGO's drama *Le Roi s'amuse* (*The King Amuses Himself*). The opera scene is laid in 16th century Mantua instead of the court of Francis I, and the principal character becomes Rigoletto instead of Triboulet. In the opera, Rigoletto is the jester and attendant of the Duke of Mantua, and it is his daughter Gilda who is finally seduced by the amorous Duke. Rigoletto, who has assisted his master in many adventures of this nature, and indeed unknowingly in this one, vows a horrible vengeance. But the assassins whom he hires agree, in deference to a woman's plea, to save the Duke if a substitute can be found. Gilda, who has overheard, appears in man's attire, and when the jester comes to carry away the body of his victim in a sack, he finds it is his daughter.

Rig-Veda. See VEDA.

Riis, Jacob Augustus (1849–1914). American journalist and reformer, of Danish birth, known for his crusade against slum conditions in New York City. His books, through which he called attention to the social ills of his time, include *How the Other Half Lives* (1890); *The Children of the Poor* (1892); *Nisby's Christmas* (1893); *Out of Mulberry Street* (1898); *A Ten Years' War* (1900); *The Making of an American* (1901), his autobiography and his best-known book; *The Battle with the Slum* (1902); *Peril and Preservation of the Home* (1903). Riis first came to the U.S. as a penniless immigrant, later worked as a police reporter on the N.Y. *Tribune,* his experiences in this capacity serving to interest him in social reform, and was eventually made secretary of the N.Y. Small Parks Commission in 1897. Theodore ROOSEVELT gave him assistance in his work.

Rikki-Tikki-Tavi. A pet mongoose in KIPLING's *The Jungle Book* (1894), who twice saves his boy master from danger and once his master's father and mother.

Riksdag. The Swedish legislature. The word is identical with German *Reichstag.* In English it is normally referred to as the Diet.

Riley, James Whitcomb (1849–1916). The "Hoosier poet," best known for his dialect poems of Indiana, such as *Little Orphant Annie, Waitin' for the Cat to Die, The Raggedy Man,* etc.

Rilke, Rainer Maria (1875–1926). German lyric poet, influenced by BAUDELAIRE and the romantics (see ROMANTICISM), known for his mysticism and his later use of a highly developed system of symbolism. Among English or American translations of his work are the following: *The Notebook of Malte Laurids Brigge* (*Die Aufzeichnungen des Malte Laurids Brigge;* 1922), also translated as *The Journal of My Other Self* (1930); *Translations from the Poetry of Rainer Maria Rilke* (1931); *Stories of God* (*Vom lieben Gott und andere*

Geschichten; 1932), short mystical tales; *The Tale of the Love and Death of Cornet Christopher Rilke* (*Die Weise von Liebe und Tod des Cornets Christopher Rilke;* 1932); *Letters to a Young Poet* (*Briefe an einen jungen Dichter;* 1934); *Poems* (1934); *Requiem, And Other Poems* (1935); *Sonnets to Orpheus* (*Sonette an Orpheus;* Eng., 1936, Am., 1942); *Later Poems* (1938); *Fifty Selected Poems* (1940); *Wartime Letters, 1914–1921* (1940); *Duino Elegies* (*Duineser Elegien;* 1939); *Selections from The Book of Hours* (*Das Stundenbuch,* 1937; 1941); *Letters, 1893–1910* (1945) and *Selected Letters: 1902–1926* (1946).

An intense interest in Rilke's poetry sprang up in England and the U.S. in the 1930's, Stephen SPENDER and Muriel RUKEYSER being among the poets whose work then showed his influence in part. For a study of the poet and his work, consult *Rainer Maria Rilke,* by E. M. Butler.

Rima. The "bird-girl," heroine of W. H. Hudson's GREEN MANSIONS.

Rimbaud, Arthur (1854–1891). French poet, considered an important forerunner of SYMBOLISM and in some respects of SURREALISM. His poetry is characterized by dramatic and imaginative vision, especially in the realm of hallucination, extreme sensibility, the partial use of free verse, the distortion of common meaning and syntax, the use of words for tone-color (as expressed in his famous *Sonnet des Voyelles*), and the grouping of images and associations about a single central metaphor. His best-known works are *Les Illuminations,* prose poems, *Le Bâteau Ivre* (*The Drunken Boat*), and *Une Saison en Enfer* (*A Season in Hell*), a prose-poem, called a "psychological autobiography," describing the pöet's tortured spiritual experiences. Rimbaud was a striking and enigmatic personality, brought up in poverty and strict religious home training by a widowed mother. He was an industrious, quiet, and irreproachably mannered student in a provincial school until the age of fifteen, when suddenly, in savage rebellion, he turned to cruelty, perversion, and dissolute wanderings in Paris, Brussels, and London. He studied occult writings, especially PLATO, the CABBALA, and Buddhist scriptures, to make himself a seer, believing the rôle of poetry to be one of mystic revelation, and deliberately debauched himself in order to reach a transcendent world through sin and suffering and "become God." For awhile he was associated intimately with Paul VERLAINE and had a powerful influence—morally corruptive but aesthetically fruitful—on the older poet. All of Rimbaud's known poetry was written before he was twenty years old; the remainder of his life he spent as a trader in Africa. He came to be regarded by many critics as an authentic genius and had an important influence on a number of 20th-century poets. A translation of *Une Saison en Enfer* by Delmore SCHWARTZ was published in 1940. For a study of his life and works, consult *Arthur Rimbaud,* by Enid Starkie.

Rimini, Francesca di, see FRANCESCA DI RIMINI.

Rimmon. The Babylonian god who presided over storms. Milton, in PARADISE LOST, identifies him with one of the fallen angels:

> Him followed Rimmon, whose delightful seat
> Was fair Damascus, on the fertile bank
> Of Abbana and Pharphar, lucid streams.
> Bk. i, 467

to bow the knee to Rimmon. To palter with one's conscience; to do that which one knows to be wrong so as to save one's face. The allusion is to NAAMAN's obtaining Elisha's permission to worship the god when with his master (2 *Kings,* v. 18).

Rimski-Korsakov, Nikolai Andreevich (1844–1908). Famous Russian composer. Member of the nationalist "Five." Professor of composition at the Conservatory of Music in St. Petersburg (1871). Best known for the symphonic suites *Antar, Russian Easter,* and *Schéhérazade.* His operas, based on Russian legends, include the famous *Le Coq d'or.*

Rinaldi, Dr. In Ernest Hemingway's A FAREWELL TO ARMS, an Italian physician and friend of Frederic HENRY, the hero. Rinaldi, essentially a light-hearted Latin, is cast down by the monotony, horror, and suffering of war that he sees about him in his hospital work.

Rinaldo. One of the great heroes of medieval romance (also called Renault of Montauban, Regnault, Reynold, etc.), a paladin of Charlemagne, cousin of ORLANDO, and one of the four sons of Aymon. He is the owner of the famous horse Bayardo, and is always painted with the characteristics of a borderer; he is valiant, ingenious, rapacious and unscrupulous.

In Ariosto's ORLANDO FURIOSO, he appears as the son of the fourth Marquis d'Este, Lord of Mount Auban or Albano, eldest son of Amon or Aymon, nephew of Charlemagne, and Bradamant's brother. He is the rival of his cousin Orlando for the favor of the fair Angelica, but Angelica detests him. Pulci introduces the same character in his bernesque poem entitled MORGANTE MAGGIORE.

In Tasso's JERUSALEM DELIVERED, Rinaldo is the Achilles of the Christian army, despising gold and power but craving renown. He is the son of Bertoldo and Sophia, and nephew of Guelpho. At the age of fifteen he joins the Crusaders as an adventurer, and, having slain Gernando, is summoned by Godfrey to public trial, but goes into voluntary exile.

Rinehart, Mary Roberts (1876–). American novelist, short-story writer, and playwright, best known for her humorous stories and popular detective novels. These include *The Circular Staircase* (1908); *The Man in Lower Ten* (1909); the numerous *Tish* stories; *The Door* (1930). *My Story* (1931) is an autobiography.

Rinehart, Stanley M., Jr. (1897–). Son of Mary Roberts Rinehart. With his brother, **Frederick Rinehart** (1902–), and John Farrar (1896–), founded the publishing house of Farrar & Rinehart which preceded (to 1945) Rinehart & Co. and Farrar and Straus. **Alan Rinehart,** a writer, is the third son.

Ring and the Book, The. A long poem (20,934 lines), by Robert BROWNING (1872), telling twelve times over, from different points of view, the story of a *cause célèbre* of Italian history (1698). Guido Franceschini, a Florentine nobleman of shattered fortune, marries Pompilia, an heiress, to repair his state. Pompilia is a supposititious child of Pietro, supplied by his wife, Violante, to prevent certain property going to an heir not his own. When the bride discovers the motive of the bridegroom, she reveals to him this fact, and the first trial occurs to settle the said property. The count treats his bride so brutally that she quits his roof under the protection of Caponsacchi, a young priest, and takes refuge in Rome. Guido follows and has them arrested; a trial ensues, and a separation is permitted. Pompilia is sent to a convent and Caponsacchi is suspended for three years. Pompilia's health gives way, and as the birth of a child is expected she is permitted to leave the convent and live with her putative parents. She pleads for a divorce, but, pending the suit, the child is born. The Count, hearing thereof, murders Pietro, Violante, and Pompilia but, being taken red-handed, he is executed.

The poem is a series of dramatic monologues, in which the whole of the evidence is weighed and sifted. The Pope pronounces the final judgment. He names Pompilia "perfect in whiteness," and calls her "my rose I gather for the breast of God." Of Caponsacchi he says

> And surely not so very much apart
> Need I place thee, my warrior-priest.

The title is explained thus: The book is a parchment-covered book Browning picked up in a square in Florence in the Piazza San Lorenzo, containing the records of the Franceschini murder case.

> The story . . . forms a circle of evidence to its one central truth; and this circle was constructed in the manner in which the worker in Etruscan gold prepares the ornament circlet which will be worn as a ring. The pure metal is too soft to bear hammer or file; it must be mixed with alloy to gain the necessary power of resistance. The ring once formed and embossed, the alloy is disengaged, and a pure gold ornament remains.—Mrs. Orr, *Handbook to Browning.*

See also CAPONSACCHI.

Ring des Nibelungen, Der. A series of four music-dramas or operas by Richard WAGNER based on old Scandinavian legends and first performed together at Bayreuth in 1876. Although Wagner's principal source was not the NIBELUNGENLIED but the VOLSUNGA SAGA, the *Nibelungenlied,* the *Elder* and *Younger Eddas* and the *Eckelied* were also drawn upon for material. The interest centers about the magic ring made from the Rhine gold and the curse it brought to all who owned it.

The four operas may be briefly summarized as follows:

(1) *Das Rheingold* (*The Rhine Gold;* 1869). In the bottom of the Rhine is a hoard of gold guarded by the Rhine Maidens. Alberich, the dwarf, forswears love to gain this hoard, which confers boundless power upon its possessor. From it he makes a magic ring. Meantime Wotan, chief of the gods, has given Freya, the goddess of youth and love, to the giants as payment for their labor in building for him the castle Valhalla. Without Freya, everything grows old, even the gods. To get her back, Wotan and Loki steal the ring and the hoard from Alberich and trade them for the goddess. Alberich has put a curse on the ring; and almost immediately the giant Fafner kills his brother Fasolt. As the opera ends, the gods go over the rainbow bridge to Valhalla.

(2) *Die Walküre* (*The Valkyr;* 1870). Wotan is the father of two children, Siegmund and Sieglinde, who grow up on earth in ignorance of each other but who, by the desire of Wotan, are to mate in the interests of the coveted ring. Sieglinde has married Hunding, but when Siegmund comes, she goes with him into the forest. Fricka, Wotan's wife, the goddess of marriage, insists that Siegmund be punished, and Wotan finally yields and commissions the Valkyr Brunhild with the task. In spite of her orders, Brunhild tries to protect Siegmund, but Hunding, finally aided by the angry Wotan, kills him. She succeeds, however, in escaping with Sieglinde, who is about to give birth to the hero Siegfried. Brunhild is punished by being made a mortal woman and is left asleep on a mountain peak, surrounded with flame through which only a hero can pass.

(3) *Siegfried* (1876). Siegfried, since the death of his mother Sieglinde, has been brought up to the trade of the smithy by Mime, the dwarf, whom he has learned to scorn. He remakes his father's sword and slays a dragon who is really the giant Fafner. A drop of the dragon's blood on his tongue makes him understand the language of the birds. Acting on the information they give him, he kills the treacherous Mime, secures the

magic ring and finds Brunhild and marries her.

(4) *Götterdämmerung* (*The Dusk of the Gods;* 1876). Siegfried leaves the magic ring with Brunhild and goes to seek adventure. At the court of Gunther and his sister Gutrune, their half-brother Hagen, son of the dwarf Alberich, gives Siegfried a magic potion that causes him to forget Brunhild and become a suitor for the hand of Gutrune. He even agrees to secure Brunhild for Gunther and does so. Unable to understand his fickleness, Brunhild denounces him and enters into schemes for revenge with the wily Hagen. At a hunting feast, just as Siegfried is remembering his past and calling for Brunhild, he is killed by a thrust in the back from Hagen. The hero's body is burned on a funeral pyre; Brunhild sacrifices herself in the flames; Gunther and Hagen have perished in the struggle for the ring, which now returns to the Rhine Maidens, and Valhalla, with all the gods, is destroyed by fire.

Ringgan, Fleda. The heroine of Susan Warner's QUEECHY.

Ringling. Name of five American brothers who built up their famous circus by acquiring, in addition to their own initial circus (organized in 1884), the Forepaugh-Sells Circus (1906) and the Barnum and Bailey Circus (1907). The eldest was born in 1852; the last one died in 1936.

Rintoul, Lord. In Barrie's LITTLE MINISTER, Babbie's fiancé from whom she wishes to escape.

Rio Bravo. Literally, the fine river. Another name, no longer in current use, of the *Rio Grande.*

Riordan, Mrs. Dante. In James Joyce's A PORTRAIT OF THE ARTIST AS A YOUNG MAN, a pious Irish woman who once studied to be a nun and turns against PARNELL. In an outstanding scene in the novel, Mrs. Riordan, a guest named Mr. Casey, and Simon Dedalus, father of Stephen DEDALUS, the hero, quarrel bitterly about Parnell and the Catholic Church during a Christmas dinner.

R. I. P. (Lat., *requiescat in pace*). "May he (or she) rest in peace"; a symbol used on mourning cards, tombstones, etc.

Ripheus. A Trojan, highly praised for his justice and nobility of character in Virgil's *Aeneid* (II. 426), and one of the two pagans whom DANTE, in his *Paradiso* (xx. 67), admits to heaven.

Ripley, George (1802–1880). Massachusetts transcendentalist who helped to organize and headed Brook Farm (1841–1847). After its failure he continued, with Parke Godwin, editing its organ, *The Harbinger* (1845–1849). He became a distinguished literary critic and edited with Charles A. DANA the *New American Cyclopedia* (16 vols.; 1858–1863).

Ripley, Robert LeRoy (1893–). Began as a sports cartoonist. Creator of "Believe-It-or-Not" cartoons (1918), which were widely syndicated in various parts of the world.

Rip Van Winkle. The creation of Washington IRVING, one of the stories in the *Sketch Book* (1819). It tells how Rip Van Winkle, a Dutch colonist of New York in pre-Revolutionary days, met with a strange man in a ravine of the Catskill Mountains. Rip helps him to carry a keg, and when they reach the destination he sees a number of odd creatures playing nine-pins, but no one utters a word. This is the quaint Dutch crew of Hendrick Hudson. Van Winkle seizes the first opportunity to take a sip at the keg, falls into a stupor, and sleeps for twenty years. On waking, he finds that he is a tottering old man, his wife is dead and buried, his daughter is married, his native village has been remodeled, and America has become independent. The story was dramatized with great success, Rip being one of the notable rôles of Joseph Jefferson. In more recent years Percy MACKAYE wrote the libretto and Reginald de Koven the music for a folk opera *Rip Van Winkle* (1920). See also Peter KLAUS.

Rise of Silas Lapham, The. A novel by W. D. HOWELLS (1885). Silas Lapham is a self-made man whose crudities are in sharp contrast with the culture of the Boston aristocracy whom he would like to see his daughters meet on friendly terms. He has built up a huge fortune; finally he becomes involved in speculations and is ruined, but shows in disaster the sterling qualities of his character. Meantime the Laphams have taken it for granted that Tom Corey, who is a frequent caller, is a suitor for the hand of Irene Lapham, but developments show that it is her sister Penelope whom he loves. Irene also is able to count upon a hidden strength in calamity.

> Silas Lapham is one of the great triumphs of modern fiction. He is a type and yet he is intensely individual . . . Strong, gentle, pushing, pertinacious, bragging, unconsciously scrupulous with the scrupulousness of the New England conscience, provincial, limited in his ideas, and yet not hostile to the light in so far as he can perceive it, Silas Lapham is an American type which has never before been so boldly presented.
>
> Brander Matthews, *London Saturday Review.*

Rise of the Dutch Republic, The. The principal work of the American historian John Lothrop MOTLEY (1856).

Risorgimento. Italian, literally "resurrection." The word is used (1) as a synonym of Italian Renaissance and (2) for the revolutionary movement in Italy at the time of MAZ-

ZINI and GARIBALDI. It was the name of a newspaper founded (1847) by Count Cavour.

Ristori, Adelaide (1822–1906). Famous Italian tragedienne who first visited New York in 1866, and toured the country successfully. Her most notable roles were Francesca da Rimini, Maria Stuart, Medea, Phaedra, and Lady Macbeth.

Rita, Doña. The heroine of Conrad's ARROW OF GOLD.

Ritchey, George Willis (1864–). American astronomer and optical inventor, who designed (1931) and constructed the forty-inch reflecting telescope in the U.S. Naval Observatory in Washington, D.C.

Ritchie, Anne Isabella, *née* **Thackeray** (1837–1919). Eldest daughter of William Makepeace THACKERAY, a novelist in her own right.

Ritchie, David. Hero of Winston Churchill's CROSSING.

Ritchie, Lewis, formerly **L. A. da Costa Ricci** (1886–). British naval paymaster; author, under the pseudonym of Bartimeus, of *Naval Occasions* (1914); *Under Sealed Orders* (1938), etc.

Ritson, Joseph (1752–1803). English antiquary, remembered for his aggressive criticism, as in his attack on STEEVENS' edition of Shakespeare. He published several collections of old English songs. He also produced a valuable *Bibliographia Poetica,* a catalogue of the English poets from the 12th to the 16th centuries.

Rittenhouse, Jessie Belle (1869–). American poet and anthologist, chiefly known for her anthologies of contemporary American verse and an excellent appraisal of newer American poets after the turn of the century, *The Younger American Poets* (1904).

Rivals, The. A comedy by R. B. SHERIDAN (1775). The rivals are Bob ACRES and Ensign BEVERLY (*alias* Captain Absolute), and Lydia LANGUISH is the lady for whom they contend.

Rivera, Diego (1886–). Famous Mexican painter, especially known for his murals. His fresco in Rockefeller Center in New York was removed because it was felt to be too radical in its political allusions. It was repainted in Mexico City.

Rivera y Orbaneja, Miguel Primo de (1870–1930). By a military *coup d'état* he proclaimed a directorate of army and naval officers in Spain (September 12, 1923) and made himself dictator. He later restored the original government and made himself premier. Shortly before his death he resigned.

Rivers, Guy. Hero of Simms' novel GUY RIVERS.

Rives, Amélie. *Princess* **Troubetzkoy** (1863–1945). Popular American novelist and playwright who married Prince Pierre Troubetzkoy of Russia.

Rizal, José (1861–1896). National hero of the Filipinos. The Spanish Government sent him into exile because of his political story *Noli Me Tangere* (1886). In 1896, on his return to the Philippines, he was charged with fomenting revolution and executed. Before his death he wrote the remarkable poem *Mi Ultimo Adiós,* which has been translated by Murat Halstead.

Rizpah. A poem (1880) by Tennyson. Cf. 2 *Sam.* xxi. 8–10.

Rizzio, David (1533?–1566). Italian musician who entered the service of Mary Queen of Scots, became her private foreign secretary, arranged her marriage with Darnley, and finally attained such influence that he was attacked and killed in Queen Mary's apartment at Holyrood Palace in Edinburgh by Darnley, Morton, and Lindsay. Swinburne treats this event in *Mary Stuart: A Tragedy* (1881), and Maurice Hewlett tells of it in THE QUEEN'S QUAIR.

road-hog. See HOG.

Road of Ages. A novel (1935) by Robert Nathan, concerned with the Jewish search for a homeland.

Road to Rome, The. A comedy (1927) by Robert SHERWOOD.

Roads of Destiny. A book of short stories (1909) by O. HENRY.

Roan Stallion. A symbolical narrative by Robinson JEFFERS (1925), dealing with the half-religious love for a beautiful and powerful roan stallion which grows up in the emotions of a California farmer's wife, repelled and disgusted by her brutal husband. Eventually she permits the horse to trample her husband to death, but herself shoots the animal which has been to her the symbol of a beautiful and passionate ideal.

Roaring Girl, The. A comedy by Thomas MIDDLETON and Thomas DEKKER, produced in 1611. The leading character is Moll CUTPURSE, who was a celebrated thief at the time the authors wrote. To win the consent of his father to his marriage with Mary Fitzallard, Sebastian Wentgrave persuades Moll to assist him in a little deception whereby he pretends to be eager to marry the notorious female cutpurse. The play is particularly noted for its realistic atmosphere of Jacobean London.

rob.

to rob Peter to pay Paul. To take away from one person in order to give to another; or merely to shift a debt—to pay it off by incurring another one. Fable has it that the phrase alludes to the fact that on December 17, 1550, the abbey church of St. Peter, Westminster, was advanced to the dignity of a cathedral by letters patent; but ten years later it was joined to the diocese of London again, and many of its estates appropriated to the repairs of St. Paul's Cathedral. But it was a common saying long before this date, and had been used by Wyclif about 1380:

> How should God approve that you rob Peter, and give this robbery to Paul in the name of Christ?—*Select Works*, III, 176.

The hint of the President Viglius to the Duke of Alva when he was seeking to impose ruinous taxation in the Netherlands (1569) was that—

> it was not desirable to rob St. Peter's altar in order to build one to St. Paul.—Motley, *Dutch Republic, III*, v.

roaring forties. In the language of sailors, the part of the ocean between the 40th and 50th degrees of latitude, north or south, where there are usually very strong winds.

Robarts, Lucy. Sister of the vicar in TROLLOPE's *Framley Parsonage*. The author said of her that she was "perhaps the most natural English girl that I ever drew—the most natural, at any rate, of those who have been good girls."

Rev. Mr. Robarts. The vicar of Framley Parsonage, a man of good intentions but weak will, who is overwhelmed by debt.

Robbers, The. A drama by SCHILLER (1781), which, following the publication of Goethe's WERTHER, had a great influence on the romantic movement of the STURM-UND-DRANG period. The hero of the drama is Karl Moor, a young man of good birth and supposedly high motives, who turns robber because of his reaction against a society that will tolerate such injustice as has been shown him by a hypocritical brother.

Robbery under Arms. A novel (1888) by Rolf Boldrewood, pseudonym of Thomas Alexander Browne (1828–1915), who wrote some thirty novels and stories of adventure in Australia.

Robbia, Luca della (1400?–1482). Famous Florentine sculptor, best-known for a series of panels called the *Singing Galleries.* His nephew and pupil, *Andrea della Robbia* (1437–1528), became a terra-cotta sculptor.

Robert Elsmere. A novel by Mrs. Humphry WARD (1888), dealing with 19th century religious problems. The hero is a young clergyman whose intellectual convictions force him to leave the church. His wife Catherine loves him but cannot share his changing faith.

Robert of Gloucester (fl. 1260–1300). English chronicler. Author or co-author of a famous metrical chronicle bringing the history of England down to the latter part of the 13th century.

Robert of Lincoln. A poem by William Cullen BRYANT, on the song of the bobolink.

Robert of Paris, Count, see COUNT ROBERT OF PARIS.

Roberto vincera. During World War II, an Italian slogan. Literally, "Robert will win." Roberto is contracted from *Ro*me, *Ber*lin, *To*kyo.

Roberts, Cecil (1892–). A versatile English writer of short stories, novels, plays, etc. His first novel, *Scissors* (1922), introduced Rupert Brooke and Philip Gibbs as "Ronald Stream" and "Phipps."

Roberts, Sir **Charles George Douglas** (1860–1943). Leading Canadian poet and novelist. Cousin of Bliss CARMAN. His historical romances (*A Sister to Evangeline,* etc.) and animal stories (*The Kindred of the Wild,* etc.) were widely read. Hamlin GARLAND called *The Heart of the Ancient Wood* (1900) a beautifully written and deeply-felt sylvan romance.

Roberts, David. In Galsworthy's STRIFE, the chief spokesman for the strikers.

Roberts, Elizabeth Madox (1886–1941). American novelist, poet, and short-story writer, known for her treatments, humorous, lyrical, and dramatic, of the pioneers and the "poor whites" of Kentucky and the Virginias. Among her works are *The Time of Man* (1926); *My Heart and My Flesh* (1927); *Jingling in the Wind* (1928); *The Great Meadow* (1930), her best-known novel, dealing with the settlement of Kentucky by the pioneers; *A Buried Treasure* (1931); *The Haunted Mirror* (1935) and *Not by Strange Gods* (1941), short-story collections; *He Sent Forth a Raven* (1935); *Black Is My Truelove's Hair* (1938); *In the Great Steep's Garden* (1915), *Under the Tree* (1922), and *Song in the Meadow* (1940), verse.

Roberts, Frederick Sleigh. 1st Earl **Roberts of Kandahar.** Known as **Bobs** or **Bobs Bahadur** (1832–1914). Famous British field marshal who compelled the surrender of the Boers in 1900. He annexed the Transvaal and, after his retirement, devoted himself to the creation of a citizen army. He wrote *The Rise of Wellington* (1895) and *Forty-One Years in India* (1897). Cf. Kipling's poem, *Bobs.*

Roberts, Kenneth Lewis (1885–). American historical novelist. Best known for his *Rabble in Arms* (1933). His *Oliver Wiswell* (1940) is a study of an American Tory at the time of the Revolution. He has a real gift for re-creating a historical period.

Roberts, Morley (1857–1942). English writer of fiction who led a roving life reflected in his books.

Roberts, Owen Josephus (1875–). Associate Justice, U.S. Supreme Court (from 1930).

Robertson, Eileen Arbuthnot. English author. Her best-known novel is *Four Frightened People* (1931), which exemplifies her biting wit and was made into a moving picture.

Robertson, Morgan (1861–1915). A sea-roving American writer, best known for his stories of the sea.

Robertson, William (1721–1793). Scottish historian and king's historiographer. Best known for his *History of the Reign of Emperor Charles V* (1769), which drew the praise of both Gibbon and Voltaire and was an important source for SCHILLER's *Don Carlos.*

Robert the Devil or **Le Diable.** (1) Robert, Duke of Normandy (1028–1035), father of William the Conqueror. He supported the English against CANUTE, and made the pilgrimage to Jerusalem. Many legends grew up regarding his daring and cruelty. The Norman tradition is that his wandering ghost will not be allowed to rest till the Day of Judgment. He is also called *Robert the Magnificent.*

Meyerbeer's opera *Roberto il Diavolo* (1831), founded on this story, shows the struggle in Robert between the virtue inherited from his mother, and the vice imparted by his father. The latter, Bertram, is a sort of arch fiend who invariably appears at the critical moment to lure his son away from duty. In the end, by the aid of his foster-sister Alice, Robert breaks the spell and wins the love of Isabella, princess of Sicily. The libretto is by Scribe and Delavigne.

(2) Robert François Damiens (1715–1757), who attempted to assassinate Louis XV, was also called *Robert le Diable.*

Robeson, Paul (1898–). Celebrated American Negro singer and actor. He has appeared in *The Emperor Jones* (1923), *Porgy and Bess, All God's Chillun Got Wings, Show Boat, Othello,* etc. He has sung Negro spirituals in concert appearances and has gone on concert tours in Europe and in Russia. His political sympathies lie with the latter country.

Robespierre, Maximilien François (1758–1794). Known as "the Sea-Green Incorruptible." A leader in the French Revolution who was practically prime minister of the Committee of Public Safety in the year 1793–1794. To him must be laid the responsibility for most of the REIGN OF TERROR. He was overthrown by the Revolution of the Ninth Thermidor in 1794 and sent to the guillotine. His death ended the Reign of Terror.

Robin. In Shakespeare's MERRY WIVES OF WINDSOR, the page of Sir John FALSTAFF.

Robin, Fanny. In Hardy's FAR FROM THE MADDING CROWD, a former love of Sergeant Troy.

Robin Adair. A famous song written by Lady Caroline Keppel, daughter of the second Earl of Albemarle. She married (after the usual run of true love) Robert Adair, a young Irish surgeon, in 1758. The air was the old Irish tune of "Eileen Aroon," which her lover had sung to her.

Robin and Makyne. An ancient Scottish pastoral. Robin is a shepherd for whom Makyne sighs. She goes to him and tells her love, but Robin turns a deaf ear, and the damsel goes home to weep. After a time the tables are turned, and Robin goes to Makyne to plead for her heart and hand; but the damsel replies,

> The man that will not when he may
> Sall have nocht when he wald.
>
> Percy, *Reliques, etc.,* series ii.

Robin Goodfellow. A "drudging fiend," and merry domestic fairy, famous for mischievous pranks and practical jokes; also known as PUCK, the son of Oberon, and the fairies' jester. The story is that at night-time he will sometimes do little services for the family over which he presides. There is a ballad by this title, attributed to Ben JONSON.

Robin Gray, Auld. See under AULD.

Robin Hood. This traditionary outlaw and hero of English ballads is mentioned by the Scottish historian Fordun, who died about 1386, and also in the *Vision of Piers Plowman,* Bk. V, 402 (see PIERS PLOWMAN), but which of these is the earlier is uncertain. It is doubtful whether he ever lived—the truth probably being that the stories associated with his name crystallized gradually around the personality of some popular local hero of the early 13th century—but the legends are that he was born in 1160 at Locksley, Notts, or, alternatively, that he was the outlawed Earl of Huntingdon, Robert Fitzooth, in disguise. His chief haunt was Sherwood Forest, in Nottinghamshire. Ancient ballads abound with anecdotes of his personal courage, his skill in archery, his generosity and his great popularity. It is said that he robbed the rich, but gave largely to the poor, and that he protected women and children with chivalrous magnanimity. According to tradition, he was treacherously bled to death by a nun, at the command of his kinsman, the prior of Kirkless, in Notts.

Robin Hood's companions in Sherwood Forest and Barnsdale, Yorks, were Little John, Friar Tuck, Will Scarlet, Allen-a-Dale, George-a-Greene and Maid Marian. According to one tradition, Robin Hood and Little John were two heroes defeated with Simon de Montfort at the battle of Evesham.

The first published collection of ballads about the hero was the *Lytel Geste of Robin*

Hood, printed by Wynkyn de WORDE about 1490. The stories about him formed the basis of early dramatic representations and were later amalgamated with the MORRIS DANCES and May-day revels.

a Robin Hood wind. A cold thaw-wind. Tradition runs that Robin Hood used to say he could bear any cold except that which a thaw-wind brought with it.

epitaph of Robin Hood.

> Hear underneath this latil stean,
> Laiz Robert earl of Huntington;
> Nea arcir ver az hie sae geud,
> An pipl kauld him Robin Heud.
> Sich utlaz az he an hiz men
> Vil England nivr si agen.
> *Obit. 24, Kalend Dikembris, 1247.*

Notwithstanding this epitaph, other traditions assert that Robin Hood lived into the reign of Edward III, and died in 1325. One of the ballads relates how Robin Hood took service under Edward II.

Robin Hood and Guy of Gisborne. Robin Hood and Little John, having had a tiff, part company, and Little John falls into the hands of the sheriff of Nottingham, who binds him to a tree. Meanwhile, Robin Hood meets with Guy of Gisborne, sworn to slay the "bold forrester." The two bowmen struggle together, but Guy is slain, and Robin Hood rides till he comes to the tree where Little John is bound. The sheriff mistakes him for Guy of Gisborne, and gives him charge of the prisoner. Robin cuts the cord, hands Guy's bow to Little John, and the two soon put to flight the sheriff and his men. (Percy, *Reliques.*)

to go round Robin Hood's barn. To arrive at the right conclusion by very roundabout methods.

to sell Robin Hood's pennyworth. To sell things at half their value. As Robin Hood stole his wares, he sold them, under their intrinsic value, for just what he could get on the nonce.

An excellent sketch of Robin Hood is given by DRAYTON in his *Polyolbion,* xxvi. Sir Walter SCOTT introduces him in two novels—IVANHOE and THE TALISMAN. In the former he first appears as Locksley the archer, at the tournament. He is also called "Dickon Bend-the-Bow." Ritson, in 1791, published all the ballads, songs, and poems extant on this famous outlaw; and T. L. PEACOCK, in 1822, wrote a romance called *Maid Marian,* on the subject. He is also the hero of a number of dramas and operas, especially a successful light opera by Reginald DE KOREN (*Am.*), and has been played in moving pictures by Douglas FAIRBANKS and Errol Flynn.

Robin of Bagshot. One of the highwaymen in Gay's BEGGAR'S OPERA, noted for the number of his aliases.

Robin Redbreast. The tradition is that when our Lord was on His way to Calvary, a robin picked a thorn out of His crown, and the blood which issued from the wound falling on the bird dyed its breast with red.

Another fable is that the robin covers dead bodies with leaves; this is referred to in Webster's *White Devil,* V, i (1612):

> Call for the robin-red-breast and the wren,
> Since o'er shady groves they hover,
> And with leaves and flowers do cover
> The friendless bodies of unburied men.

And in the ballad *The Babes in the Wood*—

> No burial this pretty pair
> From any man receives,
> Till Robin Redbreast piously
> Did cover them with leaves.

Robins, Elizabeth. Pseudonym **C. E. Raimond** (1862–). American actress and writer who appeared in England in several of Ibsen's plays and in *Paolo and Francesca* by Stephen Phillips. One of her novels, *My Little Sister* (1913), dealing with the white-slave traffic, was a sensational success.

Robins, Raymond (1873–). American social economist who studied conditions in Russia in 1933. His wife, **Margaret Dreier,** also a social economist, was president of the International Congress of Working Women in Vienna in 1923. Brother of Elizabeth ROBINS.

Robinson, Bill (1878–). American Negro buck-and-wing dancer, vaudeville actor, tap-dancer, etc., known as "the soft-shoe king."

Robinson, Boardman (1876–). Painter and illustrator. Well known for his murals and lithographs. He illustrated John Reed's *The War in Eastern Europe* (1916) having accompanied the author on a tour through Russia and the Balkans.

Robinson, Corinne Roosevelt (1861–1933). Sister of president Theodore ROOSEVELT. Known for her social service and Red Cross work, and also as a poet and the biographer of her brother.

Robinson, Edwin Arlington (1869–1935). American poet, known for his narrative poems and his objective psychological portraits of New England characters, many of them representing tragedy and frustration, written usually in blank verse or dramatic monologue form, in the simple imagery and irregular rhythms of everyday speech. The influence of Thomas HARDY and Robert BROWNING has been found in his work. Collections of Robinson's poetry include *The Torrent and the Night Before* (1896); *The Children of the Night* (1897); *Captain Craig* (1902); *The Town Down the River* (1910); *The Man Against the Sky* (1916); *The Three Taverns* (1920); *Collected Poems* (1922), winner of the Pulitzer Prize; *Dionysus in Doubt* (1925);

Sonnets (1928); *Nicodemus* (1932). Among his narrative and dramatic poems are: *Van Zorn* (1914); *The Porcupine* (1915); *Merlin* (1917), *Lancelot* (1920), and *Tristram* (1927, awarded the Pulitzer prize in 1928), a trilogy on themes of ARTHURIAN ROMANCE; *Avon's Harvest* (1921); *Roman Bartholow* (1923); *The Man Who Died Twice* (1924, awarded the 1925 Pulitzer prize); *Cavender's House* (1929); *The Glory of the Nightingales* (1930); *Matthias at the Door* (1931); *Talifer* (1933); *Amaranth* (1934); *King Jasper* (1935). These works are marked by somberness, tragedy, moral conflict, and emphasis on the individual.

Robinson worked at uncongenial occupations in New York City in the early years of his career until Theodore ROOSEVELT became interested in his poetry and secured a position for him in the N.Y. Customs House in 1905. See also TILBURY TOWN.

Robinson, William Heath (1872–1942). English comic illustrator for *The Sketch; The Graphic; Strand Magazine;* etc. Also designer of fantastic sets for London theater productions and illustrator of books. Like Rube GOLDBERG, he was fond of drawing fantastic, involved "gadgets" and machines.

Robinson, Henry Crabb (1775–1867). English diarist and friend of the Lake poets. His diary and general reminiscences are of enormous value for the study of Lamb, Coleridge, Wordsworth, Blake, etc.

Robinson, Horseshoe, see HORSESHOE ROBINSON.

Robinson, Hyacinth. A character in THE PRINCESS CASAMASSIMA by Henry James.

Robinson, Jack. See under JACK.

Robinson, James Harvey (1863–1936). American historian. Some of his works were written in collaboration with Charles A. Beard, J. H. Breasted, etc. *The Mind in the Making* (1921) discusses the relation of intelligence to social reform.

Robinson, Lennox (1886–). Irish dramatist and anthologist. His *The Golden Treasury of Irish Verse* is one of the best collections of Irish poetry extant. His most successful play was *The Whiteheaded Boy* (1916).

Robinson, Mary. Known as **Perdita** (1758–1800). English actress who became famous as Perdita in a production by David Garrick of *The Winter's Tale*. In that rôle she attracted the attention of the Prince of Wales (George IV), whose mistress she became after having received a bond for £20,000 which was never paid. When the prince cast her off, she wrote novels, plays, and poems under the nostalgic pen name of Perdita. Portraits of her exist by Reynolds, Romney, Gainsborough, etc.

Robinson Crusoe. A famous tale by Daniel DEFOE (1719). Robinson Crusoe runs away to sea, is wrecked, and leads for many years a solitary existence on an uninhabited island of the tropics. He relieves the weariness of life by numberless ingenious contrivances. At length he meets a human being, a young native, whom he saves from death on a Friday. He calls him his "Man Friday" and makes him his companion and servant. Defoe founded this story on the adventures of Alexander Selkirk, sailing-master of the privateer *Cinque Ports Galley*, who, at his own request, was left by Captain Stradling on the desolate island of Juan Fernandez off the coast of Chile for four years and four months (1704–1709). He was rescued by Captain Woodes Rogers and brought to England.

Robles Quiñones, José María Gil (1898–). Spanish Catholic political leader of the Acción Popular. Minister of war (1935); fled to Portugal at the outbreak of the Civil War (1936).

Robsart, Amy. One of the principal characters in Scott's KENILWORTH.

Rob Roy (Robert the Red). A nickname given to Robert M'Gregor (1671–1734), a noted Scottish outlaw and freebooter, on account of his red hair. He assumed the name of Campbell about 1716, and was protected by the Duke of Argyle. He may be termed the Robin Hood of Scotland.

Scott's novel *Rob Roy* was published in 1817. The hero of the novel is Frank Osbaldistone, who gets into divers troubles, from which he is rescued by Rob Roy. Rob's last service is to kill Rashleigh Osbaldistone, whereby Frank's great enemy is removed, and Frank then marries Diana Vernon. The following description of Rob Roy may be quoted:

> Rather beneath the middle size than above it, his limbs were formed upon the very strongest model that is consistent with agility. . . . Two points in his person interfered with the rules of symmetry; his shoulders were so broad . . . as to give him the air of being too square in respect to his stature; and his arms, though round, sinewy, and strong, were so very long as to be rather a deformity.—Ch. xxiii.

Robson, Eleanor (1879–). English actress who came to America at a very early age and was a great success in *Merely Mary Ann* (1903–1905). After her marriage to August Belmont, she retired from the stage and has been connected with many public and charitable enterprises, especially the Metropolitan Opera Association.

Robson, May (1865–1942). Australian-born American actress. A member, chiefly in comedy roles, of the company of Daniel Frohman, the Lyceum Theater Company, and Charles Frohman's Company. Also in moving pictures (from 1932).

roc. In the *Arabian Nights,* notably in the story of SINBAD THE SAILOR, a fabulous white bird of enormous size and such strength that it can "truss elephants in its talons," and carry them to its mountain nest, where it devours them.

roc's egg. Something unattainable.

Roch or **Roque, St.** See under SAINTS.

Rochambeau, Comte **de. Jean Baptiste Donatien de Vimeur** (1725–1807). Joined, as commander of a French force, Washington's Continental army (1781); helped besiege Cornwallis at Yorktown and with the French fleet forced his capitulation (1781). Marshal of France (1791).

Roche, Arthur Somers (1883–1935). Popular American magazine writer and novelist.

Rochefoucauld, François de Marsillac, Duc **de la,** see LA ROCHEFOUCAULD.

Rochester, Edward Fairfax. The passionate and headstrong hero of Charlotte Brontë's JANE EYRE, to whom Jane Eyre is eventually married.

Rochester, John Wilmot, Second Earl of (1648–1680). English courtier and poet, a favorite of Charles II, known for his contemporary reputation as a libertine and for the obscene and scurrilous character of his verse. His best-known work is *A Satire Against Mankind* (1675). He was from time to time a patron of a number of poets of his day, including John DRYDEN.

Rock, The. A pageant in verse by T. S. ELIOT (1934), depicting the struggles and difficulties of the Christian Church in a sinful world, and its eventual triumph over all obstacles.

Rock, Captain, see CAPTAIN ROCK.

Rocked in the Cradle of the Deep. A poem by Emma WILLARD. As a song, it is a favorite of bassos profundo. A phrase from this poem was taken by Joan Lowell as the title of her book *The Cradle of the Deep.*

Rockefeller, John Davison (1839–1937). American oil magnate. Established and endowed four charitable corporations: The Rockefeller Foundation, the General Education Board, the Laura Spelman Rockefeller Memorial, and the Rockefeller Institute for Medical Research. His son, **John D. Rockefeller, Jr.** (1874–), has continued his father's business and philanthropic interests. He planned and built the development in New York City known as Rockefeller Center.

Rockefeller Center. See RADIO CITY.

Rockefeller Foundation. See ROCKEFELLER, JOHN D.

Rocket to the Moon. A play (1938) by Clifford ODETS.

Rockminster, Lady. In Thackeray's PENDENNIS, the friend with whom Laura Bell lives after the death of Mrs. Pendennis.

Rockne, Knute (1888–1931). Famous football coach, having formerly been captain of the Notre-Dame football team. Head Coach of Notre Dame (1918–1931). Killed in an airplane accident.

Rockwell, Kiffin Yates (1892–1916). American aviator; one of the original members of the Lafayette Escadrille. Killed in action in France.

Rockwell, Norman (1894–). American illustrator, chiefly known for his covers for the *Saturday Evening Post* and paintings of American youth and village life. During World War II his paintings illustrating the FOUR FREEDOMS were widely circulated.

Rodeheaver, Homer Alvan (1880–). Musical director with Billy SUNDAY in his evangelistic campaigns (1909–1931). Author of *Song Stories of the Sawdust Trail* (1917); *20 Years with Billy Sunday;* etc.

Roderick or **Rodrigo.** A Spanish hero round whom many legends have collected. He was the thirty-fourth and last of the Visigothic kings, came to the throne in 710, and was routed, and probably slain, by the Moors under Tarik in 711.

SOUTHEY took him as the hero of his *Roderick, the Last of the Goths* (1814), where he appears as the son of Theodofred. Witiza, the usurper, puts out the eyes of Theodofred, and murders Favila, a younger brother of Roderick. But Roderick recovers his father's throne and puts out the eyes of the usurper. In an evil moment he now violates Florinda, the daughter of COUNT JULIAN, thus making a powerful enemy. The sons of Witiza, joining with Count Julian, invite the aid of Muza ibn Nozeir, the Arab chief, who sends Tarik into Spain with a large army. Roderick is routed at the Battle of Guadalete, near Xeres de la Frontera (711). He himself disappears from the battlefield, and the Spaniards transform him into a hero who will come again to save his country. One legend relates that he is befriended by a shepherd who is then rewarded with the royal chain and ring. Roderick passes the night in the cell of a hermit, who tells him that by way of penance he must pass certain days in a tomb full of snakes, toads, and lizards. After three days, the hermit goes to see him, and he is unhurt, "becuse the Lord kept His anger against him." The hermit goes home, passes the night in prayer, and goes again to the tomb. There Rodrigo says, "They eat me now, they eat me now, I feel the adder's bite." So his sin is atoned for, and he dies. According to other versions, he does not die but will come again in time of need. After a year of penance, so the story goes, he reappears at the Battle of Covadongo with the old rallying cry "Roderick the Goth! Roderick and victory!" and saves the day, but is seen no more.

SCOTT in his *Vision of Don Roderick* (1811) portrays Roderick descending into an ancient vault near Toledo where he is shown a panoramic vision of Spanish history to the beginning of the 19th century. Walter Savage LANDOR made the Roderick legend the subject of his poetic drama, COUNT JULIAN (1812).

Another famous Spanish hero named Roderigo is the CID.

Roderick Hudson. A novel by Henry JAMES (1876). The titular hero is a talented young American sculptor who goes to study in Rome at the instance of a wealthy benefactor and becomes gradually disillusioned about his art and utterly demoralized by his experience. He neglects his New England fiancée, becomes involved in a love affair with Christina LIGHT and finally leaps over a cliff.

Roderick Random. A novel by SMOLLETT (1748). The titular hero is a young Scotch scapegrace in quest of fortune. At one time he revels in prosperity, at another he is in utter destitution. Roderick is led into many different countries (whose peculiarities are described), and falls into the society of wits, sharpers, courtiers and harlots. Strap, his devoted follower, lends him money in his necessity, but the heartless Roderick wastes the loan, treats Strap as a mere servant, fleeces him at dice, and cuffs him when the game is adverse. At the end of the novel he wins the hand of Narcissa.

Roderigo. (1) The Spanish hero known as the CID. RODERICK is also called *Roderigo*.

(2) In Shakespeare's OTHELLO, a Venetian gentleman in love with Desdemona.

Rodgers, Richard (1902–). American composer. Collaborated with Lorenz (Larry) Hart in many musical comedy successes, Hart supplying the lyrics and Rodgers the music. After Hart's death, Oscar Hammerstein II collaborated with Rodgers.

Rodin. A crafty Jesuit priest in Sue's WANDERING JEW.

Rodin, François Auguste René (1840–1917). French sculptor, whose romantic groups or figures, *Le Baiser, Le Penseur, L'Homme qui marche,* etc., and statues or busts of Victor Hugo, Bernard Shaw, Balzac, etc. are internationally known. It has been said of him that he was not afraid of the impossible problem of showing emotion by motion in static marble.

Rodman, Selden (1909–). American poet. Author of a dramatic narrative poem concerning T. W. Lawrence, *Lawrence: The Last Crusade* (1937); a narrative poem, celebrating the achievements of fliers from Icarus to the pilots of our own time, *The Airmen* (1941); a three-act tragedy in free verse dealing with Toussaint L'Ouverture and Henry Christophe, *The Revolutionists* (1942); etc.

Rodney, George Brydges. 1st Baron **Rodney** (1719–1792). English admiral who captured seven Spanish ships out of eleven off Cape St. Vincent (1780) and defeated de Grasse off Dominica (1782).

Rodó, José Enrique (1872–1917). Uruguayan writer. Author of a famous essay on Rubén Darío (1899). His chief work, *Motives of Proteus* (1909), won him high praise. "The greatest master of Spanish prose," in the opinion of at least one Latin American critic.

Rodogune. A tragedy by CORNEILLE (1645), the author's own favorite, which contrasts to the terrifying events of the main plot the devotion to each other of the two sons of Cleopatre, the heroine. They are both in love with Rodogune, their mother's rival, but each wishes to sacrifice his own happiness for that of his brother.

Rodomont. In Carolingian legend, one of the most notable of the Saracen heroes. He appears in both ORLANDO INNAMORATO and ORLANDO FURIOSO. Rodomont is King of Sarza or Algiers, Ulien's son, and is called the "Mars of Africa." He is commander both of horse and foot in the Saracen army sent against Charlemagne, and may be termed the Achilles of the host. His lady-love is Doralis, Princess of Granada, who runs off with Mandricardo, King of Tartary. At Rogero's wedding-feast, Rodomont rides up to the King of France in full armor, and accuses ROGERO, who has turned Christian, of being a traitor to King Agramant, his master, and a renegade; whereupon Rogero meets him in single combat, and slays him.

Rodrigo. See RODERICK and RODERIGO.

Rodzinski, Artur (1894–). Assistant conductor under STOKOWSKI of the Philadelphia orchestra (1926–1929); conductor of the Los Angeles Philharmonic orchestra (1929–1933) and of the New York Philharmonic orchestra (1943–1946). Frequently at odds with his sponsors.

Roe, Edward Payson (1838–1888). Popular American novelist. His first novel *Barriers Burned Away* (1872) was a great success; his succeeding books followed the same somewhat melodramatic pattern.

Roe, Richard. See under DOE, JOHN.

Roebling, John Augustus (1806–1869). German-born American civil engineer who designed suspension bridges including the one over the Niagara River at Niagara Falls. He made preliminary plans for the Brooklyn Bridge and his son, **Washington Augustus**

Roebling (1837–1926), carried the bridge to completion (1869–1883). Cf. the long poem by Hart CRANE, *The Bridge.*

Roentgen, Wilhelm Konrad (1845–1923). German physicist who discovered X-rays, which are often (in German always) called Roentgen rays (1895). He received the Nobel prize for physics (1901).

Roger.

Roger Bontemps. See BONTEMPS.

the Jolly Roger. The black flag with skull and cross-bones, the favorite ensign of pirates.

Roger de Coverley, Sir. The simple, good, and altogether delightful country squire created by Richard STEELE as the chief character in the club that was supposed to write for the SPECTATOR. He was developed by ADDISON, and it is to the latter that we are indebted for this perfect portrait of a perfect English gentleman. He has left his name to a popular country dance which, he tells us, was invented by his great-grandfather. Coverley is intended for Cowley, near Oxford.

Roger Malvin's Funeral. A well-known story by HAWTHORNE in his *Mosses from an Old Manse* (1846). In a lonely and dangerous spot in the wilderness the young Reuben Bourne leaves his dying father-in-law to save his own life, promising to return. Later, fate has it that he unintentionally kills his own child on the very spot of his broken promise.

Rogero or Ruggiero. One of the principal figures in Carolingian legend, a hero of the Saracen army. In Ariosto's ORLANDO FURIOSO he appears as the brother of Marphisa, and son of Rogero and Galacella. His mother is slain by Agolant and his sons, and he is nursed by a lioness. He is brought up by Atlantes, a magician, who gives him a shield of such dazzling splendor that everyone quails who sets eyes on it, but, holding it unknightly to carry a charmed shield, he throws it into a well. He deserts from the Moorish army to Charlemagne and is baptized, and his marriage with Bradamant, Charlemagne's niece, and election to the crown of Bulgaria conclude the poem.

In Tasso's JERUSALEM DELIVERED, Rogero is brother of Boemond, and son of Roberto Guiscardo, of the Norman race. He is one of the band of adventurers in the crusading army, and is slain by Tisaphernes (Bk. xx).

Rogers, Bruce (1870–). Well-known American printer. With university presses in Cambridge, England, and Cambridge, Mass. Associated with William Edwin RUDGE and Emery Walker, Ltd. in London. Known for his fine book designs.

Rogers, Henry Huddleston (1840–1909). American financier. Chief executive officer of the Standard Oil interests.

Rogers, John (1829–1904). Massachusetts sculptor who made realistic statuettes of plaster or bronze, known as Rogers groups. Each one told a little story through the situation portrayed.

Rogers, Robert (1731–1795). American frontier captain whose rangers became famous in 1756. As a royalist, he was imprisoned at the start of the Revolution, but escaped and organized the Queen's Rangers. He fled to England (1780) where he received a pension from the government.

Rogers, Robert Cameron (1862–1912). American poet, chiefly known for his poem, *The Rosary,* which has been set to music and is sung widely. His son, **Cameron Rogers** (1900–), is a well-known essayist and biographer. *Colonel Bob Ingersoll* (1927), etc.

Rogers, Samuel (1763–1855). English poet and patron of men of letters. A friend of Wordsworth, Scott, and Byron. Noted for his table talk and his records of his conversations with his friends. On the death of Wordsworth he was offered the laureateship of England but declined.

Rogers, Will (1879–1935). American actor and humorist, widely popular in the U.S. for his vaudeville act of talking while swinging a lasso. Active in moving pictures (1929–1935), interpreting characters by Irvin Cobb, George Ade, etc. One of his pictures was made from the famous novel, *David Harum.* He also ran an extremely popular syndicated column on the news of the day. He was killed while flying with Wiley Post in Alaska.

Roget, Peter Mark (1779–1869). English scholar, compiler of the famous *Thesaurus of English Words and Phrases, classified and arranged so as to facilitate the expression of ideas and assist in literary composition* (1852). The book, like Webster's dictionary, has grown through many editions until it became *Roget's International Thesaurus: New Edition: The Complete Book of Synonyms and Antonyms in American and British Usage* (1946).

rogue literature. A type of literature, written in prose, which was popular in the Elizabethan period in England. It dealt realistically and exuberantly with the lives and adventures of thieves, vagabonds, and tricksters in the "underworld" of London or the highways of the rural districts, often expanding from fact to fiction, and is regarded as one of the forerunners of the English novel. Robert GREENE and Thomas DEKKER were the outstanding authors of rogue literature.

Rohde, Ruth *née* **Bryan** (1885–). Daughter of William Jennings BRYAN. U.S. minister to Denmark (1933–1936), the first U.S. woman diplomat.

Röhm, Ernst (1887–1934). Nazi leader who took part in the Hitler Putsch in Munich (1923). He commanded the Brown Shirts and Black Shirts (1931), and became the secretary of state in Bavaria. In the purge of conspiratorial members of the Nazi party (June 1934), Röhm, who had been one of the first supporters and an intimate friend of Hitler, was executed.

Rohmer, Sax. Pen name of **Arthur Sarsfield Ward** (1886–). British writer of widely-read mysteries with rather flamboyant Far Eastern backgrounds. He made popular the character of Fu-Manchu, an imperturbable Oriental who is the villain of many hair-raising adventures.

Roi d'Yvetot, Le. A ballad (1813) by the French poet Béranger about the imaginary country and its king, whose code was pleasure while his actions were those of a contented *bon enfant*. It is a characteristic expression of the state of mind of the French people after the Napoleonic Wars. They were fed up with glory and longed for the delights of petty-bourgeois quietude. Thackeray made a very good translation of the song.

Roisin Dubh. An Irish metaphorical name for Ireland. It means literally, "dark little rose."

Roi Soleil, Le. Literally, "the Sun King." A title adopted by Louis XIV when he took the sun as his emblem.

Roister Doister, Ralph. See RALPH ROISTER DOISTER.

Rokeby. A poem in six cantos by Sir Walter SCOTT (1813), the tale of the love of Wilfrid Wycliffe for Matilda, heiress of the Knight of Rokeby.

Rokesmith, John. A leading character in Dickens' novel, OUR MUTUAL FRIEND. He also appears as John Harmon.

Roland or **Orlando.** The most famous of Charlemagne's paladins, slain at the battle of Roncesvalles (778), called "The Christian Theseus" and "the Achilles of the West." He was Count of Mans and Knight of Blaives, and son of Duke Milo of Aiglant, his mother being Bertha, the sister of Charlemagne. Fable has it that he was eight feet high, and had an open countenance, and he is represented as brave, loyal and simple-minded. On the return of Charlemagne from Spain, Roland, who commanded the rear-guard, fell into the ambuscade at Roncesvalles, in the Pyrenees, and perished with all the flower of Frankish chivalry.

His achievements are recorded in the Chronicle attributed to TURPIN, Archbishop of Rheims, which was not written till the 11th or 12th century, and he is the hero of the *Song of Roland,* Boiardo's ORLANDO INNAMORATO, and Ariosto's ORLANDO FURIOSO. In Pulci's MORGANTE MAGGIORE he is also a principal character, and converts the giant Morgante to Christianity.

In *Orlando Furioso* (*Orlando Mad*), although married to Aldabella, he falls in love with Angelica, daughter of the infidel King of Cathay. She marries Medoro, a Moor, with whom she flees to India, whereupon Orlando goes mad, or rather his wits are taken from him for three months by way of punishment, and deposited in the moon. Astolpho goes to the moon in Elijah's chariot, and St. John gives him an urn containing the lost wits. On reaching earth again, Astolpho first binds the madman, then, holding the urn to his nose, cures Orlando of both his madness and his love.

a Roland for an Oliver. A blow for a blow, tit for tat. The exploits of Roland and Oliver, another of the paladins of Charlemagne, are so similar that it is difficult to keep them distinct. What Roland did Oliver did, and what Oliver did Roland did. At length the two met in single combat, and fought for five consecutive days on an island in the Rhine, but neither gained the least advantage. Shakespeare alludes to this similarity in the phrase, "England all Olivers and Rolands bred" (1 *Henry VI,* i. 2).

The Song (*Chanson*) *of Roland.* The 11th-century *chanson de geste* ascribed to the Norman trouvère Théroulde, or Turoldus, which tells the story of the death of Roland and all the paladins at Roncesvalles, and of Charlemagne's vengeance. When Charlemagne has been six years in Spain he sends GANELON on an embassy to Marsilius, the pagan king of Saragossa. Ganelon, out of jealousy, betrays to Marsilius the route which the Christian army is designed to take on its way home, and the pagan king arrives at Roncesvalles just as Roland is conducting through the pass a rear-guard of 20,000 men. He fights until 100,000 Saracens are slain, and only fifty of his own men alive. At this juncture another army, consisting of 50,000 men, pours down from the mountains. Roland now blows his enchanted horn, and blows so loudly that the veins of his neck burst. Charlemagne hears the blast, but comes too late. Roland dies of his wounds.

The *Song* runs to 4,000 lines, and it was probably parts of this that—as we are told by Wace in the *Roman de Rou*—the Norman minstrel sang to encourage William's soldiers at the battle of Hastings:

> Taillefer, the minstrel-knight, bestrode
> A gallant steed, and swiftly rode
> Before the Duke, and sang the song
> Of Charlemagne, of Roland strong,
>   Of Oliver, and those beside
>   Brave knights at Roncevaux that died.
>
> Arthur S. Way's rendering.

like the blast of Roland's horn. Roland had

a wonderful ivory horn, named Olivant, that he won from the giant Jutmundus. When he was set upon by the Gascons at Roncesvalles, he sounded it to give Charlemagne notice of his danger. At the third blast it cracked in two, but it was so loud that birds fell dead and the whole Saracen army was struck with horror. Charlemagne heard the sound at St. Jean Pied de Port and rushed to the rescue, but arrived too late.

Roland's sword. Durindana, or Durandal, which was fabled to have once belonged to Hector, and which—like the horn—Roland won from the giant Jutmundus. It had in its hilt a thread from the Virgin Mary's cloak, a tooth of St. Peter, one of St. Denis' hairs, and a drop of St. Basil's blood. Legend relates that, to prevent Durandal from falling into the hands of the Saracens after he had received his death-wound, he strove to break it on a rock. Finding it unbreakable he hurled it into a poisoned stream, where it remains for ever.

Roland. In Clyde Fitch's drama THE TRUTH, the father of the heroine.

Roland, Childe, see CHILDE ROLAND.

Roland, Jeanne Manon, *née* **Phlipon** (1754–1793). Famous character in the French Revolution, commonly known as Madame Roland, who was guillotined in 1793. According to tradition, her last words on the scaffold were, "Oh Liberty! What crimes are committed in thy name!"

Roland de Vaux. In *The Bridal of Triermain* (1813) by Sir Walter SCOTT, the Baron of Triermain is so called. The name is also used in *Christabel* by Samuel Taylor COLERIDGE.

Rolfe, Frederick William Serafino Austin Lewis Mary. Pen name **Baron Corvo** (1860–1913). Versatile and eccentric English novelist and historical writer. Brilliantly original, but unbalanced and somewhat of a charlatan. A musician, photographer, and fine swimmer. Cf. his biography by A. J. A. Symons, *The Quest for Corvo* (1934). One of his best books is *Chronicles of the House of Borgia* (1901).

Rolfe, John (1585–1622). See under POCAHONTAS.

Rolland, Henry Augustus (1848–1901). First professor of physics at Johns Hopkins University (1875–1901). Conducted researches on the solar spectrum.

Rolland, Romain (1866–1944). French novelist, known for his idealism, cosmopolitanism, tendency toward hero-worship, and interest in music and the problems of the artistic temperament. His most famous work is JEAN CHRISTOPHE (1904–1912), in ten volumes, considered to be the first true example of the ROMAN-FLEUVE; it consists of *L'Aube* (Dawn), *L'Adolescent* (*Adolescence*), *La Révolte* (*Revolt*), *La Foire sur la Place* (*The Market on 'Change*), *Antoinette, Dans la Maison* (*At Home*), *Les Amies* (*The Friends*), *La Nouvelle Journée* (*The New Day*). Other works of Rolland are COLAS BREUGNON (1919); *Pierre et Luce* (1921), a tragedy of lovers in war; *Clérambault* (1920); *L'Âme Enchantée* (*The Enchanted Soul;* 1922–1934), another cyclical novel, seven volumes, in its English translation divided into *Annette and Sylvie, Summer, Mother and Son, The Death of a World,* and *A World in Birth; Le Jeu de L'Amour et de la Mort* (*The Game of Life and Death;* 1926), a play; *Above the Battle* (*Au Dessus de la Mêlée;* 1916), articles and letters on World War I; *Les Léonides* (1921); *Pâques Fleuries* (*Palm Sunday;* 1926), a play; *Goethe and Beethoven* (1930); *Beethoven: Les Grandes Époques Creatrices* (1928–1937), translated as *Beethoven the Creator; The Revolt of the Machines* (1932); *Quinze Ans de combat* (1935), translated as *I Will Not Rest; Danton* (1936), a drama; *Les Loups* (*The Wolves;* 1937); *Le Quatorze Juillet* (*July 14;* 1936), and *Robespierre* (1939), dramas.

Rolland was much interested in music and from 1904 to 1912 was Professor of the History of Music at the Sorbonne in Paris. During the 1920's he became interested sympathetically in the U.S.S.R.

Rolle, Richard. Known as **the Hermit of Hampole** (1290?–1349). English recluse who wrote religious treatises and the poem *The Pricke of Conscience* in seven books. It is an early protest against certain pretensions of the papacy.

Rolling Stones. A volume of short stories by O. HENRY (1913). The allusion is to the old proverb "A rolling stone gathers no moss," that is, one who roams about and refuses to settle down will never grow wealthy. Robert W. SERVICE entitled a volume of verse *Rhymes of a Rolling Stone* (1912).

Rollins, Carl Purington (1880–). Printer and typographical expert. With the Yale University Press (from 1918) and printer to Yale University (1920–1948). Editor of *The Compleat Collector* in the *Saturday Review of Literature.* Honorary member of the American Institute of Graphic Arts.

Rollins, Hyder Edward (1889–). American educator. Professor at Harvard (since 1926). Editor of *Old English Ballads* (1920); *The Pepys Ballads* (8 vols.; 1929–1932); *England's Helicon* (2 vols.; 1935); and *Shakespeare's Poems* in the *New Variorum Shakespeare* (1938).

Rollo. Called **the Ganger** or **Walker** (860?–?931). Viking leader who received through a treaty territory in France which was the beginning of Normandy. He was the ancestor of Norman dukes and kings.

Rollo Books. A once popular series of books for children by Jacob ABBOTT. The Lucy, Jonas and Franconia books were by the same author. They told of simple adventures in a New England town and countryside and were packed with information and a fair amount of "morals."

Rölvaag, Ole Edvart (1876–1931). Norwegian-American novelist, known for his dramatic and realistic accounts of the life of Norwegian pioneers in the Dakotas, marked particularly by psychological studies of the characters. His works, all written in Norwegian and later translated into English, include *Letters from America* (1912), semi-autobiographical; *Giants in the Earth* (1927), *Peder Victorious* (1929), and *Their Fathers' God* (1931), a trilogy, the author's best-known work; *Pure Gold* (1930); *The Boat of Longing* (1933). Rölvaag himself was an immigrant to the U.S. and from 1907 to his death taught Norwegian at St. Olaf's College in Minnesota.

Romains, Jules. Pseudonym of **Louis Farigoule** (1885–). French novelist and dramatist, known for his fictional modification of the tradition of NATURALISM according to his early theory of UNANIMISM. His best-known work is MEN OF GOOD WILL (*Les Hommes de bonne Volonté*), begun in 1931, a gigantic representative of the ROMAN-FLEUVE. Among his other works are *La Vie Unanime* (1908), a collection of poetry expressing his Unanimist ideas; *Le Bourg Régénéré* (1906); *Mort de Quelqu'un* (1911); *Les Copains; Donogoo-Tonka* (1920), called a *conte cinématographique; Lucienne* (1922), *Le Dieu des corps* translated as *The Body's Rapture* (1928), and *Quand le Navire . . .* (*When the Boat . . . ;* 1929), constituting a trilogy, *Psyché,* on domestic and sexual relations; *Knock, ou Le Triomphe de la Médecine* (*Knock, Or The Triumph of Medicine;* 1923), *Le Dictateur* (*The Dictator;* 1926), *Cromedeyre-le-Vieil* and *Jean Le Maufranc,* plays; *Grâce Encore pour la Terre* (1941); *Une Vue des Choses* (1941); *Salsette Discovers America* (*Salsette Découvre L'Amérique;* 1942).

Roman. Pertaining to Rome, especially ancient Rome, or to the Roman Catholic Church. As a surname or distinctive title the adjective has been applied to:

Giulio Pippi, *Giulio Romano* (1492–1546), the Italian artist.

Adrian van Roomen (1561–1615), the famous mathematician, *Adrianus Romanus.*

Stephen Picart (1631–1721), the French engraver, *Le Romain.*

Jean Dumond (1700–1781), the French painter, *Le Romain.*

Marcus Terentius Varro (116–27 B. C.) was called the *Most Learned of the Romans,* and Rienzi (1313–1354), the Italian patriot and "last of the Tribunes," was known as *Ultimus Romanorum,* the Last of the Romans—an honorific title later applied to Horace Walpole, Charles James Fox, and others.

King of the Romans. The title usually assumed by the sovereign of the Holy Roman Empire previous to his actual coronation in the Holy City. Napoleon's son, afterwards the Duke of Reichstadt, was styled the *King of Rome* at his birth in 1811. See also AIGLON, L'.

Roman birds. Eagles; so called because the ensign of the Roman legion was an eagle.

Roman à clef. Literally, key-novel. *Romans à clef* and *drames à clef* contain one or more characters based on actual persons. Cf. *Literary Characters Drawn From Life* (1936), by Earle Walbridge. *See also* LA CALPRENÈDE; SCUDÉRY.

Roman Bartholow. A narrative poem (1923) by Edwin Arlington ROBINSON.

romance. Applied in linguistics (see below) to the languages, especially Old French, sprung from the Latin spoken in the European provinces of the Roman Empire; hence, as a noun, the word came to mean a medieval tale in Old French or Provençal describing, usually in mixed prose and verse, the marvelous adventures of a hero of chivalry. The transition to the modern meanings—a work of fiction in which the scenes, incidents, etc., are more or less removed from common life and are surrounded by a halo of mystery—or the atmosphere of strangeness and imaginary adventure itself—is simple.

The medieval romances fall into three main groups or *cycles,* viz., the Arthurian, the Charlemagne cycle, and the cycle of Alexander the Great. Nearly, but not quite, all the romances are connected with one or other of these.

Romance languages. Those languages which are the immediate offspring of Latin, as the Italian, Spanish, Portuguese, and French.

Romance. (1) A novel by Joseph Conrad and Ford Madox FORD (1903). The plot is one of complicated intrigue in the Jamaica and Cuba of the early 19th century. The hero, John Kemp, finally marries Seraphina, a Spanish girl.

(2) A drama by Edward SHELDON (1913), presenting the love story of Madame Cavallini, an Italian opera singer.

Romancers, The (Les Romanesques). A drama by Edmund ROSTAND (1894). The plot turns on the attempts of two neighbors to bring about a match between their romance-loving children by providing sufficient obstacles. The high wall between the two places is an important piece of stage setting, now up, now torn down. After some unexpected twists, the romantic young lovers, Perinet and Sylvette, are married at last.

Roman de la Rose. See under ROSE.

Roman des Romans. A French version of AMADIS OF GAUL, greatly extended by Gilbert Saunier and Sieur de Duverdier.

Romanes, George John (1848–1894). British biologist and professor of physiology at the Royal Institution of London. Friend of Charles DARWIN and founder (1891) of the Romanes Lecture at Oxford, which was to be given annually on some scientific or literary topic.

Romanesque. An intermediate style of architecture which existed in Europe between the Roman and the Gothic, during the period approximately from 600 A. D. to 1200 A. D. A form of the Romanesque in England is the Norman architecture.

roman-fleuve (*Fr.*, "river-novel"). French term for the type of lengthy novel, dealing with a given set of characters through a period of years, which came to be characteristic of the fiction of France during the first half of the 20th century. Outstanding examples of the *roman-fleuve* are JEAN CHRISTOPHE, by Romain Rolland; REMEMBRANCE OF THINGS PAST, by Marcel Proust; LES THIBAULT, by Roger Martin du Gard; and MEN OF GOOD WILL, by Jules Romains.

Romanov or Romanoff. The name of the rulers of Russia whose dynasty was ended by the revolution of March 12, 1917. The Romanoff dynasty was founded by Michael Romanov (1598–1645) who became czar in 1613.

Romans, The Epistle to the. One of the books of the New Testament, a letter written by the Apostle PAUL.

Romantic Comedian, The. A novel (1926), by Ellen GLASGOW.

romanticism or the romantic revival. Term applied to the movement in European literature and other arts, which began at the end of the 18th century, emphasizing the imagination and emotions over reason and the intellect and revolting against the conventional strictness of NEO-CLASSICISM. Called "romanticism" because it was ostensibly defended as a return to the freer fancies and methods of ROMANCE, the movement is interpreted by many critics as the response of the artist's psychology to the growing complexity of an increasingly mechanized industrial and scientific civilization, which came into being with the industrial revolution of the mid-18th century. The leading characteristics of romanticism are individualism, nature-worship, PRIMITIVISM, a fondness for the Middle Ages, the Orient, and vanished or alien cultures in general, philosophic IDEALISM, a paradoxical tendency toward both free thought and religious mysticism, revolt against political authority and social convention, the exaltation of physical passion and the encouragement of sexual inconstancy, the cultivation of emotion and sensation for their own sake, and a persistent attraction to the supernatural, the morbid, the melancholy, and the cruel.

The French writer J. J. ROUSSEAU is considered the father of romanticism, although its first manifestation as an organized movement appeared in Germany, in the work of SCHILLER, GOETHE, NOVALIS, KLEIST, and TIECK, early romantic leaders there, and especially in the idealist philosophy of KANT, FICHTE, SCHELLING, and HEGEL. Scattered English forerunners of romanticism in the later 18th century were GRAY, COLLINS, COWPER, BURNS, CHATTERTON, BLAKE, and the GOTHIC NOVEL. The movement was given impetus by the publication of PERCY's *Reliques* and Macpherson's OSSIAN, and was powerfully stimulated by the French Revolution. Under the influence of Rousseau, Percy's *Reliques,* and German idealist doctrines, English romanticism flowered (1798–1832) in the work of WORDSWORTH, COLERIDGE, SHELLEY, BYRON, KEATS, SOUTHEY, CAMPBELL, MOORE, Leigh HUNT, HOOD, BEDDOES, SCOTT, LAMB, HAZLITT, DE QUINCEY, and LANDOR.

In France, Mme de STAËL and CHATEAUBRIAND were forerunners of romanticism after Rousseau, but there was no definite French romantic movement until about 1820, lasting until about 1843. The chief influences were German (GOETHE, SCHILLER, and the TALES OF HOFFMAN) and English (Shakespeare, Macpherson's *Ossian,* Byron, and Scott); the outstanding literary representatives were LAMARTINE, NODIER, BÉRANGER, HUGO, MUSSET, VIGNY, GAUTIER, George SAND, DUMAS *père,* STENDHAL, SAINTE-BEUVE, and MÉRIMÉE. In the U.S., romanticism developed at a later date than in Europe and was less well defined, exhibiting modifications from the peculiar nature of American culture of the time, with a strong emphasis on humanitarianism and reform. Foreign influences were chiefly German idealism, Rousseauistic nature-worship, the Gothic novel, and the historical romance and pseudopopular ballad of Scott. Among American romantic writers were Charles Brockden BROWN, COOPER, IRVING, SIMMS, BRYANT, POE, EMERSON, THOREAU, VERY, HAWTHORNE, MELVILLE, LONGFELLOW, WHITTIER, LOWELL, and WHITMAN. TRANSCENDENTALISM (ca. 1830–1860) is regarded as the clearest example of romanticism in the U.S.

Among the arts other than literature, romanticism is exemplified by BEETHOVEN, BERLIOZ, SCHUBERT, MENDELSSOHN, and SCHUMANN in music, and by DELACROIX, INGRES, COROT, and MILLET in painting.

The romantic movement was arrested in its development in England after 1832, with only a brief revival under the PRE-RAPHAELITE BROTHERHOOD, and in the U.S. it was rapidly absorbed by native tendencies and other influences. In Germany, however, it persisted, continuing especially in the philosophy of SCHOPENHAUER and NIETZSCHE, and in the various works of WAGNER, MANN, Stefan GEORGE, and RILKE. In France, dominant romantic characteristics were developed by BAUDELAIRE and through him passed to the DECADENTS, the Symbolists (see SYMBOLISM), and, ultimately, the surrealists (see SURREALISM).

For a study of the romantic movement and its characteristics, cf. *The Romantic Agony,* by Mario Praz.

Romany. A gypsy; or the gypsy language, the speech of the Roma or Zincali. The word is from Gypsy *rom,* a man, or husband.

Romany rye. One who enters into the gypsy spirit, learns their language, lives with them as one of themselves, etc. *Rye* is gypsy for gentleman. Borrow's book with this title (a sequel to LAVENGRO), was published in 1857.

Rome. The greatest city of the antique world, according to legend founded (753 B.C.) by ROMULUS and named after him; but in all probability so called from Greek *rhoma,* "strength," a suggestion confirmed by its other name *Valentia,* from Latin *valens,* "strong."

Oh, that all Rome had but one head, that I might strike it off at a blow! Caligula, the Roman emperor, is said to have uttered this amiable sentiment.

Rome's best wealth is patriotism. So said Mettius Curtius, when he jumped into the chasm which the soothsayers prophesied would never close till Rome threw therein "its best wealth."

Rome was not built in a day. Achievements of great pith and moment are not accomplished without perseverance and considerable time. It is an old saying, and is to be found in Heywood's *Collection* (1562).

'tis ill sitting at Rome and striving with the Pope. Don't tread on a man's corns when you are living with him or are in close touch with him—especially if he's powerful.

when you go to Rome, do as Rome does. Conform to the manners and customs of those amongst whom you live. St. Monica and her son St. Augustine said to St. Ambrose: "At Rome they fast on Saturday, but not so at Milan; which practice ought to be observed?" To which St. Ambrose replied, "When I am at Milan, I do as they do at Milan; but when I go to Rome, I do as Rome does!" (*Epistle* xxxvi).

Rome saved by geese. See under GOOSE.

Rome Haul. Title of Walter D. EDMONDS' first novel (1929). Its theme is the Erie Canal.

Romeo and Juliet. Shakespeare's tragedy (first published 1597) is founded on the story of the lovers of Verona as told in Arthur Brooke's poem, *The Tragicall Historye of Romeus and Juliet, containing a rare example of love constancie, with the subtill counsels and practices of an old Fryer* (1562), and a story in Painter's *Palace of Pleasure* (1567). The story had appeared earlier, notably in Bandello's *Novelle* (1554). The plot is well known. Romeo, though a despised Montague, attends the great ball of the Capulets and falls in love with Juliet, the daughter of the house. Because of the deadly feud between the Montagues and Capulets, the lovers are married secretly in the cell of Friar Laurence. Romeo now becomes involved, against his will, in a street quarrel between members of the two houses and is banished from Verona. In desperation Juliet, who is about to be married to Paris against her will, takes a sleeping potion given her by the Friar to bring on a semblance of death. Romeo, hearing of her death before the Friar's explanation reaches him, returns and drinks poison at Juliet's tomb. When she wakes up a few moments later to find him dead, she stabs herself. There is an opera *Roméo et Juliette* by Gounod (1867).

Romney, George (1734–1802). English historical and portrait painter.

Romola. A novel by George ELIOT (1863). The scene is laid in medieval Florence, and the great reformer SAVONAROLA is a prominent figure. It is in him and his cause that Romola finds consolation when she is forced to admit the failure of her marriage with the attractive but weak and selfish Tito Melema. Tito has been brought up as the adopted child of the wealthy scholar, Baldassare Calvo, but after a shipwreck in which he is separated from Calvo, he sells his father's gems for his own benefit, turns a deaf ear to letters from his father asking for ransom from slavery, and refuses to acknowledge him when he appears. Although in love with Romola, he goes through a wedding ceremony with the pretty peasant, Tessa, and continues to visit her after his marriage to Romola. The latter gradually learns Tito's true character, and when he sells the library which her father has spent his life collecting and has left to her in trust for the people of Florence, she gives up all hope of happiness with him and spends herself in work for Savonarola's cause. Savonarola is finally brought to trial and condemned. Tito has managed to win favor in both local parties, but he is unmasked at last, pursued by an angry mob, and, at the end of his strength, is choked to death by the embittered Baldassare Calvo. Romola cares for Tessa and her children.

Romulus. With his twin brother Remus the legendary and eponymous founder of Rome. They were sons of Mars and Rhea Silvia, who, because she was a vestal virgin, was condemned to death and her sons exposed. They were, however, suckled by a she-wolf, and eventually set about founding a city but quarreled over the plans, and Remus was slain by his brother in anger. Romulus was later taken to the heavens by his father, Mars, in a fiery chariot, and was worshiped by the Romans under the name of Quirinus.

the second Romulus. Camillus was so called because he saved Rome from the Gauls (365 B.C.).

the third Romulus. Caius Marius, who saved Rome from the Teutons and Cimbri (101 B.C.).

we need no Romulus to account for Rome. We require no hypothetical person to account for a plain fact.

Roncesvalles. A defile in the Pyrenees, famous for the disaster which here befell the rear of Charlemagne's army, on the return march from Saragossa (778). Ganelon betrayed ROLAND to Marsillus, King of the Saracens, and an ambuscade, attacking the Franks, killed every man, including Roland, Oliver, and all the paladins. See *Song of Roland* under ROLAND.

rondeau. A verse-form, best-known in French literature, which usually consists of fifteen lines in three stanzas, with two rhymes only used throughout. The first line of the first stanza serves as a refrain ending the second and third stanzas. The rondeau is used mostly in light or witty verse. A. C. SWINBURNE devised a variation on the rondeau which he called the *roundel* and used frequently in his poetry. See also RONDEL.

rondel. A verse-form composed of three stanzas and two rhymes, with the first two lines of the first stanza usually repeated as the last two lines of the second and third stanzas. Chaucer in his *Parliament of Fowls* uses a "roundel" which employs the first two lines of the first stanza as a refrain at the end of the second stanza, and the whole first stanza of three lines as the refrain of the third stanza:

> Now welcom somer, with thy sonne softe,
> That hast this wintres weder over-shake,
> And driven awey the longe nightes blake!
> Seynt Valentyn, thou art ful hy on-lofte;—
> Thus singen smale foules for thy sake—
> Now welcom somer, with thy sonne softe,
> That has this wintres weders over-shake.
>
> Wel han they cause for to gladen ofte,
> Sith ech of hem recovered hath his make;
> Ful blisful may they singen whan they wake;
> Now welcom somer, with thy sonne softe,
> That hast this wintres weders over-shake,
> And driven awey the longe nightes blake.
>
> Chaucer, *The Parliament of Fowls.*

See also RONDEAU.

Ronin. *The Loyal League of Forty-Seven Ronin, Or The Chushingura.* A famous play of the Japanese marionette theater, first performed in Yedo (Tokyo) in 1748. The story it embodies is a very popular one; it had previously been dramatized on the regular stage and has furnished the inspiration for many of the most famous of Japanese color prints. It is founded on an incident that took place in 1701. A certain Japanese noble is so insulted by his instructor in court etiquette that he draws his weapon within the court precincts. This offense is punishable by death; he is compelled to commit HARA-KIRI, his property is confiscated and his retainers become *ronin* or leaderless men. The play deals with the conspiracy by which forty-seven of these *ronin* secure revenge for their lord's death. Cf. also John Masefield's play *The Faithful.*

Ronsard, Pierre de (1525–1585). French poet, leading member of the PLÉIADE, best known for his light and graceful amorous verse, especially in the form of the sonnet and the ode, which was written during the first period of his career (1550–1560) under the influence of PETRARCH, HORACE, PINDAR, THEOCRITUS, and PROPERTIUS. Between 1560 and 1574, when he was official court poet under Henry II and Charles IX, he wrote elegies and nationalistic and oratorical poetry, and in retirement during the last period of his life turned to melancholy nature poems. Among his works are *Odes* (1550); *Sonnets* (1553); *Bocage Royal* and *Mélanges* (1554); *Hymnes* (1555); *Continuation des Amours* (1555–1556); *Discours des Misères de ce Temps, Continuation du Discours,* and *Remonstrance au Peuple de France* (1562–1563); *Elegies, Mascarades, Bergeries* (1565); *Franciade* (1572), an uncompleted French epic poem; *Sonnets pour Hélène; Dernières Amours; Bocage Royal* (last part).

Ronsard, of noble birth, was a page at the court of Francis I and served in a diplomatic capacity in Scotland and England before an illness left him deaf. While a student at the Collège de Coqueret, he began his long assocation with Joachim du BELLAY. Ronsard was hailed as the greatest French poet of his day and had an important influence on the Elizabethan writers of sonnets.

Roof of the World. The Pamirs, a plateau north of India.

Roosevelt, Anna Eleanor, *née* **Roosevelt** (1884–). Wife of Franklin Delano Roosevelt, prominent in social welfare and widely known through her newspaper column *My Day*. Also author of the autobiography *This is My Story* (1937) and several other books.

Roosevelt, Franklin Delano (1882–1945). Thirty-second president of the U.S. (1933–1945). Still a controversial but doubtless a great figure in modern history.

Roosevelt, Kermit (1889–1943). One of the sons of President Theodore Roosevelt, brother of Theodore Roosevelt, Jr., Archibald Roosevelt, Quentin Roosevelt, and half-brother of Alice Longworth. Accompanied his father on hunting expeditions; wrote *War in the Garden of Eden* (1919); *The Happy Hunting Grounds* (1920); etc. Major in the British army (1939–1941). Transferred to U.S. army and died on active duty in Alaska.

Roosevelt, Nicholas (1893–). American journalist and diplomat. Vice-governor of the Philippines (1930); U.S. minister to Hungary (1930–1933). On staff of New York *Herald Tribune* and New York *Times*. Author of *The Philippines, a Treasure and a Problem* (1926); *A New Birth of Freedom* (1938); etc.

Roosevelt, Quentin (1897–1918). Youngest son of President Theodore Roosevelt. American aviator in World War I, killed in action.

Roosevelt, Theodore (1858–1919). Twenty-sixth president of the U.S. (1901–1909). Author of *Ranch Life and the Hunting Trail* (1888); *The Winning of the West* (4 vols.; 1889–1896); *Life of Oliver Cromwell* (1900); *African Game Trails* (1910).

Roosevelt, Theodore, Jr. (1887–1944). Son of President Theodore Roosevelt. Governor of Puerto Rico (1929–1932); governor general of the Philippines (1932–1933). Brigadier general, World War II; in invasions of North Africa and France, where he died. Author of *Trailing the Giant Panda*.

Root, Elihu (1845–1937). U.S. secretary of war (1895–1904); U.S. secretary of state (1905–1909); U.S. senator from New York (1909–1915). President of the Carnegie Endowment for International Peace, 1910. Awarded the Nobel prize for peace (1912).

Root, George Frederick (1820–1895). American composer and teacher of music. Founded the New York Normal Institute for the training of teachers of music (1853) and is known for a number of popular songs, including *The Battle Cry of Freedom; Tramp, Tramp, Tramp, the Boys are Marching;* etc.

Root, John Wellborn (1850–1891). Chicago architect who pioneered in constructing steel-frame office buildings. Brother-in-law of Harriet MONROE who wrote his biography (1896).

Rootabaga Stories. A book of children's stories (1922) by Carl SANDBURG.

Rope of Ocnus. See OCNUS.

Roque, Louise. In Flaubert's SENTIMENTAL EDUCATION, a country girl, a childhood neighbor of Frederic MOREAU, with whom she is intensely in love in early adolescence. Later she marries his friend DESLAURIERS but leaves him to run off with a singer.

Rory O'More. A novel (1836) and ballad by Samuel Lover.

Rory o' the Hill. The signature adopted in 1880 by the writer of threatening letters to Irish landlords, to those who paid their rents, to those who occupied the farms of ejected tenants, etc. These letters were written under the authority of the "Irish Land League."

Rosa, Salvator (1615–1673). Painter of the Neopolitan school; known chiefly for his landscapes and battle scenes. Also a poet.

Rosa Dartle, see DARTLE, ROSA.

Rosalba. The heroine of Elinor Wylie's *Venetian Glass Nephew* (1925).

Rosalba, Princess. A character in Thackeray's ROSE AND THE RING.

Rosalia or Rosalie, St. See under SAINTS.

Rosalind. (1) The anagrammatic name under which SPENSER introduces his early love, Rosa Daniel (sister of Samuel DANIEL, the poet), into the SHEPHERD'S CALENDAR, he himself figuring as COLIN CLOUT.

(2) In Shakespeare's AS YOU LIKE IT, the daughter of the banished Duke, brought up with Celia in the court of Frederick, the Duke's brother, and usurper of his dominions. After sundry adventures, in the course of which she disguises herself as a youth and Celia as a peasant-girl, she obtains her father's consent to marry her lover, Orlando.

Rosaline. In Shakespeare's ROMEO AND JULIET, the niece of Capulet, with whom Romeo is in love before he sees Juliet. Mercutio calls her "a pale-hearted wench," and Romeo says she does not "grace for grace and love for love allow," like Juliet. Rosaline is frequently mentioned in the first act of the play, but is not one of the *dramatis personae*.

Rosamond, the Fair. Higden, monk of Chester, writing about 1350, says: "She was the fayre daughter of Walter, Lord Clifford, concubine of Henry II, and poisoned by Queen Elinor, 1177 A. D. Henry made for her a house of wonderful working, so that no man or woman might come to her. This house was named Labyrinthus, and was wrought like unto a knot in a garden called a maze. But the queen came to her by a clue of thredde, and so dealt with her that she lived not long after. She was buried at Godstow, in an house of nunnes, with these verses upon her tombe:

His jacet in tumba Rosa mundi, non Rosa munda;
Non redolet, sed olet, quae redolrē solet."

This "evidence," dating nearly 200 years after the supposed event, is all the substantiation we have for the popular legend about the labyrinth, and there is none for the stories that Rosamund Clifford was the mother of William Longsword and Geoffrey, Archbishop of York. She is introduced by SCOTT in two of his novels —*The Talisman* and *Woodstock*—and a subterranean labyrinth in Blenheim Park, near Woodstock, is still pointed out as "Rosamond's Bower."

Jane Clifford was her name, as books aver
Fair Rosamund was but her *nom de guerre.*
Dryden, *Epilogue to Henry II.*

Rosamund. See ROSMONDA.

Rosary, The. A novel (1909) by Florence L. BARCLAY. See also ROGERS, Robert Cameron.

Rosas, Juan Manuel de (1793–1877). Argentine dictator who wielded supreme power over the Argentine provinces and subjugated Uruguay. He was finally defeated and fled to England. Cf. *Rosas,* a poem by John MASEFIELD.

Roscius. A first-rate actor; so called from Quintus Roscius (d. about 62 B.C.), the Roman actor, unrivaled for his grace of action, melody of voice, conception of character, and delivery.

another Roscius. So CAMDEN terms Richard Burbage (d. 1619).

the British Roscius. Thomas Betterton (1635–1710), of whom Cibber says, "He alone was born to speak what only Shakespeare knew to write." The title was also accorded to Garrick.

the Roscius of France. Michel Boyron (1653–1729), generally called Baron.

the Young Roscius. William Henry West Betty (1791–1874).

Roscoe, Sir **Henry Enfield** (1833–1915). English chemist, son of the historian, **William Roscoe** (1753–1831), who, with Bunsen, laid the foundations of photochemistry.

rose. Medieval legend asserts that the first roses appeared miraculously at Bethlehem as the result of the prayers of a "fayre Mayden" who had been falsely accused and was sentenced to death by burning. As Sir John MANDEVILLE tells the tale (*Travels,* ch. vi), after her prayer

sche entered into the Fuyer; and anon was the Fuyer quenched and oute; and the Brondes that weren brennynge, becomen red Roseres; and the Brondes that were not kyndled, becomen white Roseres, fulle of Roses. And these weren the first Roseres and Roses, both white and rede, that evere any Man saughe. And thus was this Mayden saved be the Grace of God.

The *Rose* has been an emblem of England since the time of the Wars of the Roses, a civil contest that lasted thirty years, in which eighty princes of the blood, a large portion of the English nobility, and some 100,000 common soldiers were slain. It was a struggle for the crown between the houses of York (*White* rose) and Lancaster (*Red*). When the parties were united in the person of Henry VII, the united rose was taken as his device.

under the rose (Lat. *sub rosa*). In strict confidence. The origin of the phrase is wrapped in obscurity, but the story is that Cupid gave Harpocrates, the god of silence, a rose, to bribe him not to betray the amours of Venus. Hence the flower became the emblem of silence. In 1526 it was placed over confessionals.

the little black rose. Ireland.

Rose, John Holland (1855–1942). English historian, author of *The Life of Napoleon I* (1902); *The Development of the European Nations* (1923); etc.

Rose, The Romance of the. An early French poem of over 20,000 lines, an elaborate allegory on the Art of Love beneath which can be seen a faithful picture of contemporary life. It was begun by Guillaume de LORRIS in the first half of the 13th century, and continued by Jean de Meung in the second part of the 13th. The poet is accosted by Dame Idleness, who conducts him to the Palace of Pleasure, where he meets Love, accompanied by Sweet-Looks, Riches, Jollity, Courtesy, Liberality, and Youth, who spend their time in dancing, singing, and other amusements. By this retinue the poet is conducted to a bed of roses, where he singles out one and attempts to pluck it, when an arrow from Cupid's bow stretches him fainting on the ground, and he is carried far away from the flower of his choice. As soon as he recovers, he finds himself alone, and resolves to return to his rose. Welcome goes with him, but Danger, Shame-Face, Fear, and Slander obstruct him at every turn. Reason advises him to abandon the pursuit, but this he will not do; whereupon Pity and Liberality aid him in reaching the rose of his choice, and Venus permits him to touch it with his lips. Meanwhile, Slander rouses up Jealousy, who seizes Welcome and casts him into a strong castle, giving the key of the castle door to an old hag. Here the poet is left to mourn over his fate, and the original poem ends.

In the second part—which is much the longer—the same characters appear, but the spirit of the poem is altogether different, the author being interested in life as a whole instead of solely in love, and directing his satire especially against women.

A 15th century English version, the *Romaunt of the Rose,* is often published with CHAUCER's works, and it is probable that the first 1,700 lines or so are by Chaucer.

Rose and the Ring, The. A burlesque fairy tale by THACKERAY (1855). The fun arises from the fact that the magic rose, which belongs to Prince Bulbo of Crim Tartary, and the magic ring worn by Prince Giglio of Paflagonia make their possessors seem both lovely and lovable. So long as she is allowed to wear either the rose or the ring, the Princess Angelica, Giglio's cousin, who has been wrongfully put in his place by her father, appears the most charming of individuals, but the moment she is deprived of them, she becomes the most ill-tempered and ugly. Rosalba, the deposed princess of Crim Tartary, shares with Giglio the favor of the all-powerful Fairy Blackstick, and although at their christenings she gave them each a little misfortune, she stands by them in their difficulties and brings their affairs to a happy ending.

Rose Aylmer. A short lyric by Walter Savage LANDOR (1806) in memory of Rose Aylmer, who had been his companion on his walks about Swansea in Wales. She died in India in 1800.

> Rose Aylmer whom these wakeful eyes
> May weep but never see
> A night of memories and signs
> I consecrate to thee.

Rosecrans, William Starke (1819–1898). American army commander who defeated the Confederates at Murfreesboro (1863) and was, in turn, defeated at Chickamauga in the same year. He commanded the Department of the Missouri (1864) and was U.S. minister to Mexico (1868–1869) and congressman from California (1881–1885).

Rosedale, Simon. A rich but objectionable Jew in Edith Wharton's HOUSE OF MIRTH.

Rose Mary. A ballad by Dante Gabriel ROSSETTI in his *Ballads and Sonnets* (1881). It deals with a magic beryl stone in which only the pure in heart can see the truth.

Rosenbach, Abraham S. Wolf (1876–). American bibliophile and rare book collector. Author of *The Unpublishable Memoirs* (1917); *A Book Hunter's Holiday* (1936); etc.

Rosenberg, Alfred (1893–). German Nazi leader and writer who directed the foreign policy office of the Nazi party in 1933. His most influential book was *Der Mythus des XX. Jahrhunderts* (1930), in which the racial ideology of National Socialism was given the status of a mythology or religion. Tried as a war criminal at Nuremberg.

Rosenberg, Isaac (1890–1918). English poet, killed in action in the first World War. After his death his poems were collected by several literary friends and issued as *Collected Works* (1937).

Rosencrantz and Guildenstern. Time-serving courtiers, willing to betray anyone, and do any "genteel" dirty work to please a king. They are characters in Shakespeare's HAMLET.

Rosenfeld, Paul (1890–1946). American music and art critic. *Musical Portraits* (1920); *Music Chronicle* (1923); *By Way of Art* (1926); *Discoveries of a Music Critic* (1936); etc.

Rosenwald, Julius (1862–1932). American merchant and philanthropist. President, Sears Roebuck & Co. (1910–1925). Created the Julius Rosenwald Fund for the "well-being of mankind." The endowment has built Negro schools in the South and supported Negro education at Howard, Fisk, Atlanta, and Dillard Universities, etc., and was exhausted by 1948.

Rose of Sharon. A flower mentioned in the Old Testament. Also, the name of a character in *The Grapes of Wrath* by John Steinbeck. In the illiterate speech of the Okies it is reduced to *Rosasharn.*

Rose Tavern. A meeting place in Covent Garden which is referred to in eighteenth-century literature.

Rose Theatre. A theater (founded in 1592) in SOUTHWARK where Shakespeare once acted.

Rosetta stone. A stone found in 1799 by M. Boussard, a French officer of engineers, in an excavation made at Fort St. Julien, near Rosetta, in the Nile delta. It has an inscription in three different languages—the hieroglyphic, the demotic, and the Greek. It was erected 195 B. C., in honor of Ptolemy Epiphanes, because he remitted the dues of the sacerdotal body. The great value of this stone is that it furnished the French Egyptologist Jean François Champollion (1790–1832) the key whereby he deciphered the Egyptian hieroglyphics.

Rosicrucian Society. A secret philosophical society of religious reformers, probably founded after 1614, the year of publication of two anonymous pamphlets, probably written by the German Johann Valentin Andreä and describing (no doubt fictitiously) just such a society going back to one Christian Rosenkreuz (hence the name) who would have organized it in 1484. *John Inglesant* by SHORTHOUSE has a good deal of information about the Rosicrucians.

Rosinante or **Rozinante.** In Cervantes' DON QUIXOTE, the steed of Don Quixote. The name implies "that the horse had risen from a mean condition to the highest honor a steed could achieve, for it was once a cart-horse, and rose to become the charger of a knight-errant."

Rosinante was admirably drawn, so lean, lank, meagre, drooping, sharp-backed, and raw-boned, as to excite much curiosity and mirth.—Pt. I. ii. 1.

Rosin Bible. See BIBLE, SPECIALLY NAMED.

Rosmersholm. A drama by Henrik IBSEN (1886). The principal characters are Rosmer, his wife Beata, and Rebecca West, a scheming young woman of ultra-modern ideas. The unhappy Beata commits suicide. Under Rebecca's influence Rosmer has gradually become a free thinker, but when it comes out that Rebecca had planned his wife's misery as a part of her project of setting him free as a leader of men, Rosmer rebels, and he and Rebecca together leap into the mill stream.

Rosmonda or **Rosmunda.** A historical character, the daughter of Cunimond, king of the Gepidae. She was compelled to marry Alboin, King of the Lombards, who put her father to death 567 A. D. Alboin made her drink from the skull of her own father, and Rosmonda induced Perideus, the secretary of Helmichild, her lover, to murder the wretch. She then married Helmichild, fled to Ravenna, and later sought to poison her second husband, that she might marry Longin, the exarch, but Helmichild, apprised of her intention, forced her to drink the mixture she had prepared for him. She is the titular heroine of two Italian tragedies. The first by Rucellai in 1525, dramatizing the first part of her career, was one of the earliest of modern tragedies. The second, by Alfieri in 1783, deals with her later life. SWINBURNE also has a poetic tragedy, *Rosamund, Queen of the Lombards,* dealing with her fate.

Ross. In Shakespeare's MACBETH, a Scotch nobleman who tells Macduff that his castle has been besieged, and his wife and children savagely murdered by Macbeth.

Ross, Betsy (1752–1836). Reputed to have made the first American flag at the special request of George Washington. The Stars and Stripes was adopted as the national emblem by the Continental Congress on June 14, 1777.

Ross, Edward Alsworth (1866–). American sociologist and professor.

Ross, Harold Wallace (1892–). American journalist; editor of THE NEW YORKER (1925–).

Ross, Sir James Clark (1800–1862). Scottish polar explorer for whom are named *Ross Sea, Ross Island,* and other parts of the Antarctic.

Ross Leonard Q., see ROSTEN, L. C.

Ross, Man of. See under MAN.

Ross, Sir Ronald (1857–1932). British physician, director of the Ross Institute and Hospital for Tropical Diseases in London. Awarded the Nobel prize (1902) for physics and medicine. Author of *The Prevention of Malaria* (1910), and other works.

Rossetti, Christina Georgina (1830–1894). English poet of Italian parentage, sister of D. G. and W. M. Rossetti, associated with the PRE-RAPHAELITE BROTHERHOOD and known for her ballads and her mystic religious lyrics, marked by symbolism, vividness of detail, and intensity of feeling. Among her works are *Goblin Market, and Other Poems* (1862); *The Prince's Progress* (1866); *Sing-Song* (1872), a collection of verse for children; *Annus Domini* (1874); *A Pageant* (1881); *Time Flies* (1885), prose and verse; *The Face of the Deep* (1892), an interpretation of the *Apocalypse. Goblin Market,* THE CONVENT THRESHOLD, and MONNA INNOMINATA are her best-known single works.

The father of Christina Rossetti and her brothers was **Gabriele Rossetti,** an Italian scholar exiled from his native land; his children had the advantage of early contact with other distinguished Italian exiles—painters, literary men, and musicians—who were his friends. Christina published her first poems in THE GERM, and frequently served as a model for the Pre-Raphaelite painters. After a serious illness in 1874, she was left an invalid and rarely received visitors or left her home. See also CAYLEY, CHARLES.

Rossetti, Dante Gabriel. In full **Gabriel Charles Dante Rossetti** (1828–1882). English poet and painter of Italian parentage, brother of Christina ROSSETTI. He was the leader of the PRE-RAPHAELITE BROTHERHOOD and became known for his paintings and his lyric poems, the latter being distinguished by richness and vividness of detail, mysticism and fantasy, and the use of a modified ballad form. His books of poetry are *The Early Italian Poets* (1861), translations of the lyrics of Dante ALIGHIERI and of Italian poets preceding and contemporaneous with Dante; *Poems* (1870), a group of poems that was at first buried in the coffin of Elizabeth SIDDALL, Rossetti's wife; *Ballads and Sonnets* (1881). His best-known single works are THE BLESSED DAMOZEL, *Sister Helen, Troy Town,* THE HOUSE OF LIFE. He also made a number of translations from the Italian, German, and French, the most outstanding of which is THE BALLAD OF DEAD LADIES of François VILLON. See also FLESHLY SCHOOL, THE.

William Michael Rossetti (1829–1919), brother of Dante Gabriel, was an art critic and author and one of the original members of the Pre-Raphaelites, serving as an editor of THE GERM. He wrote a translation of Dante (1865), a *Life of Keats* (1887), and memoirs of both his brother (1895) and his sister Christina (1904).

Rossi, Bruno (1905–). Italian physicist, chiefly known for his investigations of cosmic rays.

Rossini, Gioacchino Antonio (1792–1868). Italian composer of the bel-canto school of opera. His best-known works are the operas *The Barber of Seville* (1816) and *William Tell* (1829), and the celebrated *Stabat Mater* (1842).

Rostand, Edmond (1868–1918). French dramatist, known for his wit and satire, his talent for romantic and dramatic scenes, and his attempts to revive the French poetic drama. His works include *Les Musardises* (1890), verse; *Les Romanesques* (THE ROMANCERS; 1894); *La Princesse Lointaine* (*The Faraway Princess;* 1895); *La Samaritaine* (1897); CYRANO DE BERGERAC (1897); L'AIGLON (*The Eaglet;* 1900); *Chantecler* (CHANTICLEER; 1910); *Le Vol de la Marseillaise* (1919), a series of nationalist lyrics; *La Dernière Nuit de Don Juan* (*The Last Night of Don Juan;* 1921).

Rosten, Leo Calvin. Pseudonym **Leonard Q. Ross** (1908–). Polish-born American economist and author, best known for *The Education of H*y*m*a*n K*a*p*l*a*n* (1937), a series of amusing sketches based on his experiences as part-time teacher of English to adult immigrants.

Rosten, Norman (1914–). American poet and writer for the radio. His books are *Return Again, Traveler* (1940); *The Fourth Decade* (1943); *The Big Road* (1946).

Roswitha or **Hrotsvitha** (*fl.* 10th century). A nun in the Benedictine convent of Gandersheim, in Saxony, regarded as Germany's first dramatist, since she tried to combat the influence of the comedies of TERENCE by adapting them as vehicles for the life stories of outstanding saints and virgins. She also wrote a poem celebrating the military deeds of the Emperor Otto I. With HÉLOÏSE and MARIE DE FRANCE, Roswitha is considered one of the three noteworthy women authors of the Middle Ages.

Rota. In full **Sacra Romana Rota.** In the Roman Catholic Church, the supreme court for both ecclesiastical and secular cases.

Rotarian. A member of one of the local clubs of the International Association of Rotary Clubs. The Rotary Club is a friendly association of business and professional men, formed in Chicago (1905), which holds regular meetings and endeavors to promote local civic interests. It was frequently the object of satire in American fiction during the 1920's.

Rothenstein, Sir **William** (1872–1946). Well-known English artist whose *Men and Memories* (2 vols., 1931–1932) and *Since Fifty: More Men and Memories* (1939) are, as Peter Munro Jack put it, "the best record of the characters and the turn of events in the Victorian-Edwardian-Georgian cycle of history." A distinguished painter and teacher of painting, and a draughtsman of great power. Active in an official capacity in both World Wars.

Rothermere, Viscount. See under HARMSWORTH.

Rothschild. A family of internationally known Jewish financiers, whose banking house was established at Frankfort-am-Main near the end of the 18th century. The name is believed to come from the house sign, *zum rothen Schilde,* "at the red shield."

Rotisserie de la Reine Pédauque, La (*At the Sign of the Reine Pédauque*). One of the best-known novels of Anatole FRANCE (1893). The chief character is Jerome COIGNARD.

rotogravure. A method of reproducing photographic illustrations on rotary printing presses. It was invented in Germany and came to the United States about 1912. Used in printing the illustrated supplements of newspapers.

Rotrou, Jean de (1609–1650). French playwright, one of Richelieu's "Five Poets" who jointly produced dramas after the cardinal's plans. Called by Voltaire, "le véritable fondateur du théâtre français." Among his works only *Saint-Genest* (1646) and *Venceslas* (1647) are remembered.

rouge et noir (*Fr.,* "red and black"). (1) A game of chance; so called because of the red and black diamond-shaped compartments on the board. The dealer deals out to *noir* first till the sum of the pips exceeds thirty, then to *rouge* in the same manner. That packet which comes nearest to thirty-one is the winner of the stakes.

(2) The title of a 20th-century ballet set to the music of the First Symphony of SHOSTAKOVICH.

Rouge et le Noir, Le. See RED AND THE BLACK, THE.

Rouget de l'Isle, Claude Joseph (1760–1836). French army officer, composer of the words and music of LA MARSEILLAISE (1792), the French national anthem.

Roughead, William (1870–). Scottish criminologist and authority on the "gentle art of murder." Lillian Hellman's play, *The Children's Hour* (1934), is based upon an essay by Roughead concerning an old Edinburgh scandal. He was the editor of many volumes in the *Notable British Trials* series, and also wrote essays on crime collected in *Rascals Revived* (1940); *Reprobates Reviewed* (1941); etc.

Roughing It. A book by Mark TWAIN (1872), written as an autobiography in which the narrator describes his journey west from Missouri to California and Hawaii.

Rough Riders, The. Name given to the First Volunteer Cavalry serving in Cuba during the Spanish-American War, under Theodore ROOSEVELT and Leonard Wood. The Rough Riders distinguished themselves in their charge up San Juan Hill. Cf. Roosevelt's *The Rough Riders* (1899).

Rough and Ready. So General Zachary Taylor (1784–1850), twelfth president of the United States, was called.

Rougon-Macquart novels. A series of twenty novels by Emile ZOLA (1871–1893), tracing the complete social history of a family of the Second Empire. The Rougon-Macquart family springs from sordid origins. Adelaide Fouqué, the daughter of an insane father, marries a stupid gardener named Rougon, and the pair have a son, Pierre Rougon, who grows up to enter business. In the meantime, after the death of the elder Rougon, Adelaide and a drunken smuggler named Macquart have two illegitimate children, Antoine and Ursule. In time the former becomes as great a drunkard as his father and marries a market woman; the latter marries a good, honest workman named Mouret. So much of the family history is related in the first volume of the series, *La Fortune des Rougons* (*The Rougon Family;* 1871) and in the nineteen succeeding novels the experiences of Adelaide's offspring and their children are followed in some detail.

Of these novels the following are probably the best known:

L'Assommoir (*The Dram Shop;* 1877). This novel first brought Zola his reputation. The central figure is Gervaise, the daughter of Antoine. At the age of fourteen she is driven from home on account of an affair with a lover who, shortly after, deserts her and her two illegitimate children in Paris. She marries Coupeau, a tinsmith, but betters her fortunes only temporarily. The novel traces in detail the poverty and slow demoralization of the family.

Nana (1880). This novel relates the subsequent career of Nana, the daughter of Gervaise, who has grown up in the squalid atmosphere depicted in *L'Assommoir.* Possessed of great physical beauty, she attracts the attention of a theater manager and makes her début on the stage. In spite of her utter lack of ability as an actress, men become so infatuated with her that her success is assured and she enters upon a life of luxury and dissipation. Eventually, however, she dies a horrible death of black smallpox, deserted by her friends.

La Terre (*The Soil;* 1888). This novel of peasant life has as its theme the greed for land. Its climax is the murder of Jean Macquart's wife by her sister.

La Débâcle (*The Downfall;* 1892). This novel treats of the Franco-Prussian War, with the siege of Sedan as its central episode. The hero is Jean Macquart, a young French corporal; the plot concerns his friendship for Maurice Levasson, a private in his company, and his love for Maurice's sister, Henriette Weiss, whom the siege of Sedan leaves a widow. Under pressure of war he kills his friend unknowingly, and in spite of their mutual passion, this incident brings about the separation of the two lovers.

Roumestan, Numa, see NUMA ROUMESTAN.

roundel. See under RONDEAU.

Roundheads. Puritans of the Civil War period; especially Cromwell's soldiers. They are so called because they wore their hair short, while the Royalists wore long hair covering their shoulders.

Round Table, the. The table fabled to have been made by MERLIN at Carduel for Uther Pendragon. Uther gave it to King Leodegraunce, of Cameliard, who gave it to King Arthur when the latter married GUINEVERE, his daughter. It was circular to prevent any jealousy on the score of precedency; it seated 150 knights, and a place was left in it for the HOLY GRAIL. The first reference to it is in Wace's *Roman de Brut* (1155), but the fullest legendary details are from Malory's *Morte d'Arthur,* III. i and ii.

Knights of the Round Table. According to Malory (*Morte d'Arthur,* III. i, ii), there were 150 knights who had "sieges" at the table. King Leodegraunce brought 100 when, at the wedding of his daughter Guinevere, he gave the table to King Arthur. Merlin filled up twenty-eight of the vacant seats, and the King elected Gawain and Tor; the remaining twenty were left for those who might prove worthy.

Of all the knights of King Arthur's court there were, however, always twelve who held positions of the highest honor. The twelve vary in different accounts, but the following names hold the most conspicuous places: (1) Launcelot, (2) Tristram, (3) Lamoracke, the three bravest; (4) Tor, the first made; (5) Galahad, the chaste; (6) Gawain, the courteous; (7) Gareth, the big-handed; (8) Palomides, the Saracen or unbaptized; (9) Kay, the rude and boastful; (10) Mark, the dastard; (11) Modred, the traitor. The twelfth must be selected from one of the following names, all of which are seated with the prince in the frontispiece attached to the *Morte d'Arthur* by Sir Thomas Malory published in 1470: Sirs Acolon, Ballamore Beleobus, Belvoure, Bersunt, Bors, Ector de Maris, Ewain, Floll, Gaheris, Galohalt, Grislet, Lionell, Marhaus, Paginet, Pelleas, Percival, Sagris, Superabilis, and Turquine.

> There Galahad sat with manly grace,
> Yet maiden meekness in his face;
> There Morolt of the iron mace,
> And love-lorn Tristrem there;
> And Dinadam with lively glance,
> And Lanval with the fairy lance,
> And Mordred with his looks askance,
> Brunor and Bevidere.
> Why should I tell of numbers more?
> Sir Cay, Sir Banier, and Sir Bore.
> Sir Caradoc the keen.
> The gentle Gawain's courteous lore,
> Hector de Mares, and Pellinore,
> And Lancelot, that evermore
> Looked stol'n-wise on the queen.
> Scott, *Bridal of Triermain,* ii, 13.

a round table conference. A conference between political parties in which each has equal authority, and at which it is agreed that the questions in dispute shall be settled amicably and with the maximum amount of "give and take" on each side.

The expression came into prominence in connection with a private conference in the house of Sir William Harcourt, January 14, 1887, with the view of reuniting, if possible, the Liberal party, broken up by Gladstone's Irish policy.

Rourke, Constance Mayfield (1885–1941). American biographer who wrote the first article on Paul Bunyan (*New Republic,* 1918) to appear in an American magazine. Her best-known books are *Trumpets of Jubilee* (1927); *Troupers of the Gold Coast* (1928); *Davey Crockett* (1934); *Audubon* (1936); and *The Roots of American Culture* (1942).

Rousseau, Jean Jacques (1712–1778). Swiss-born French author and thinker, one of the most outstanding and most influential personalities of his age. He is considered the most important forerunner of ROMANTICISM, and his life and writings show the characteristics of the typical romantic personality: extreme individualism, bordering on megalomania at times; excessive sensibility; emotional instability and moral irresponsibility; a passionate love of nature; rebellion against the established social and political order; the glorification of feelings over ideas; imagination and intense introspection; an idealization of sensual love; prolific expression of sentiment; and exaltation of the primitive and "natural." See NOBLE SAVAGE; PRIMITIVISM. Among Rousseau's works are his CONFESSIONS (1781–1788), regarded as one of the greatest and most candid of autobiographies; *Julie, ou La Nouvelle Héloïse* (JULIE, OR THE NEW HELOISE; 1761), a novel; *Discours sur les Sciences et les Arts* (1750), asserting that science and art are partially responsible for corrupting mankind; *Discours sur l'Origine et les Fondements de l'Inégalité parmi les Hommes* (1755), celebrating the "natural man" and indicting private property and the political state as the cause of inequality and oppression; THE SOCIAL CONTRACT (*Le Contrat Social;* 1762), his most famous and most influential work; ÉMILE (1762), an "educational romance," regarded as partly fictional and partly autobiographical.

A child prodigy and the son of a watchmaker, Rousseau led an erratic and adventuresome life, having set out from Geneva at the age of sixteen to seek his fortune in France. He was assisted by women of both high and low social estate, became a success in social and intellectual circles in Paris, quarreled with his friends, was exiled from France because of *Émile,* wandered from country to country, and died at last in Paris. William GODWIN and the leaders of the French Revolution of 1789 were among those influenced by his political ideas; LAMARTINE and Alfred de MUSSET were influenced by his style. A contemporary disciple was Bernardin de SAINT-PIERRE.

See also LEVASSEUR, THÉRÈSE; WARENS, MADAME DE.

Rousseau, Philippe (1816–1887). French painter of animals, fruits, and flowers.

Rousseau and Romanticism. A critical work (1919) by Irving BABBITT.

Roussillon, Alice. The heroine of Thompson's ALICE OF OLD VINCENNES.

Roustam or **Rostam,** see RUSTUM.

Routledge, George (1812–1888). English publisher of classics at one shilling each in the *Railway Library* (1848) and *Routledge's Universal Library* (1883).

Roux, Pierre Paul Émile (1853–1933). French physician and bacteriologist; worked with PASTEUR (from 1888); director of the Pasteur Institute (1904–1918).

Rover Boys, The. See under STRATEMEYER, EDWARD.

Rowan, Andrew S. (1857–). Famous for having carried a message to General Garcia, in Cuba, during the Spanish-American War. Author of *How I Carried the Message to Garcia* (1923). See also HUBBARD, ELBERT, and GARCIA.

Rowan, Stephen Clegg (1808–1890). American naval officer in the Civil War; seized Roanoke Island (1862) destroying the Confederate fleet. He commanded the *New Ironsides,* and became a vice-admiral (1870).

Rowe, Nicholas (1674–1718). English poet and dramatist; brought out the first modern edition of Shakespeare's plays from the Fourth Folio (6 vols.; 1709), with biographical matter, an arrangement of acts and scenes, and modernized grammar and spelling. His own plays include *Tamerlane* (1702); *The Fair Penitent* (1703); and *The Tragedy of Jane Shore* (1714). Poet laureate (1715).

Rowena. The nominal heroine of Scott's IVANHOE, a ward of Cedric the Saxon, of Rotherwood. She marries Ivanhoe.

Rowland or **Roland, Childe.** See under CHILDE.

Rowlandson, Mary (1635?–?1678). Wife of an early American settler and minister, who was captured by the Indians and wrote a famous account of her experiences, which was one of the most popular American prose works of the seventeenth century. It has been reprinted many times as an excellent account of the dangers through which the early settlers had to live.

Rowlandson, Thomas (1756–1827). English caricaturist, especially well-known for his series of plates titled *Tours of Dr. Syntax* (1812, 1820, 1821). He also illustrated books by Smollett, Goldsmith, Sterne, etc.

Rowley, Thomas. See CHATTERTON, THOMAS.

Rowley, William (1585?–?1642). English playwright and actor. His works include *A New Wonder* (1632); *All's Lost by Lust* (1633); *A Shoemaker a Gentleman* (1638); *A Fair Quarrel* (1617) and *The Changeling* (1623), written with Thomas MIDDLETON; *Fortune by Land and Sea* (1655), written with Thomas HEYWOOD; *The Thracian Wonder* (1661) and *A Cure for a Cuckold* (1661), written with John WEBSTER. (The dates of the last three plays refer to publication, not performance.) Rowley also collaborated on plays with DEKKER, FORD, and MASSINGER. He acted for a time with Queen Anne's company.

Rowton Houses. Lodging-houses for the poor established in London (1892) in accordance with a scheme originated by Montagu William Lowry Corry, Baron Rowton. Hence the name. A series of poems called *Rowton House Rhymes* appeared in the early 20th century, in *Blackwood's Magazine.*

Roxana. One of the two heroines of Lee's drama *Alexander the Great, Or the Rival Queens.* Her rival was STATIRA.

Roxane. The heroine of Rostand's CYRANO DE BERGERAC.

Roxburghe ballads; Roxburghe Club. See under KER, JOHN.

Royal Exchange. The building in London where all exchange business is conducted. The original Royal Exchange was built by Sir Thomas Gresham in 1566 and was named by Queen Elizabeth.

Royal Society of London for Improving Natural Knowledge, The. An English scientific academy, founded in 1660 for the purpose of studying the whole field of knowledge. Abraham COWLEY and the chemist Robert Boyle had presented plans for such an organization, and among its members were included some of the leading literary, diplomatic, and scientific figures of the day. Samuel PEPYS, who was admitted to the Society in 1665 and later became its president, has a number of references to its meetings and its experiments in his famous diary, and John WINTROP and Cotton and Increase MATHER were the leaders of a group of New England correspondents of the Royal Society. Thomas SPRAT, Bishop of Rochester, was historian of the organization, which sought, among other aims, to improve the English prose style of the time, making it simpler, clearer, and more suited to the needs of scientific exposition than the usual literary style then current. In this connection, an international language of symbols was proposed by Bishop Wilkins, considered to have been the Society's most important member.

The Royal Society was satirized in frequent contemporary works, including Shadwell's *Virtuosi* (1676), Samuel Butler's THE ELEPHANT IN THE MOON, and Jonathan Swift's *Gulliver's Travels* (see GULLIVER, LEMUEL), Book III, *A Voyage to Laputa.* See LAPUTA.

Royall, Charity. The heroine of Edith Wharton's SUMMER. Her guardian, Lawyer Royall, is also an important character.

Royce, Josiah (1855–1916). American philosopher who wished to unite absolute idealism with social realism. His famous theory of the Absolute appeared first in *The Religious Aspect of Philosophy* (1885). Royce believed that it was possible to prove ultimate truths.

Roycroft Press. See HUBBARD, ELBERT.

Royde-Smith, Naomi Gwladys. English novelist. Author of *The Altar-Piece* (1939); *Jane Fairfax* (1940); etc. Also wrote a play, *Private Room* (1934).

Royle, Edwin Milton (1862–1942). American playwright, best-known for his Indian play *The Squaw Man* (1905).

Rozinante, see ROSINANTE.

r's, the three. Reading, writing and arithmetic; or phonetically "readin', ritin', 'n' rithmetic." Hence it means the elementary principles; the fundamentals of education.

R.S.V.P. (Fr. *Répondez s'il vous plaît,* "Answer, if you please.") Letters frequently affixed to an invitation requiring an answer.

Ruach. In Rabelais' GARGANTUA AND PANTAGRUEL, the isle of winds, visited by Pantagruel and his companions on their way to the oracle of the Holy Bottle. The people of this island live on wind, such as flattery, promises and hope. The poorer sort are very ill-fed, but the great are stuffed with huge mill-draughts of the same unsubstantial puffs.

Rubáiyát of Omar Khayyám, The. It was translated by Edward FITZGERALD (1859). The oldest known manuscript, which is in the Bodleian Library, Oxford, is dated from Shiraz, A.H. 865 (1460 A.D.). *Rubai* means "quatrain." See OMAR KHAYYÁM.

Rubempré, Lucien de. A young journalist and poet who appears in a number of the novels of Balzac's COMÉDIE HUMAINE, notably *Scenes from a Courtesan's Life* (*Les Splendeurs et misères des courtesanes*) and *The Last Incarnation of Vautrin* (*La dernière Incarnation de Vautrin*). As a promising young man from the provinces he is introduced by D'Arthez into the Cénacle, a congenial club, but finds the path to success full of difficulties and grows despondent. He is befriended by a Spanish priest who is in reality a noted criminal, Jacques COLLIN. Lucien now falls madly in love with the courtesan, Esther Van Gobseck, is the half unwitting tool of Collin in the affair, and finally is committed to prison for participation in Collin's crimes. Unable to endure the shame and remorse, he hangs himself.

Rubens, Peter Paul (1577–1640). Celebrated Flemish painter. Among his works are *The Descent from the Cross* (in Antwerp Cathedral), *The Rape of the Sabines* (in London), etc.

Rubicon.

to pass the Rubicon. To take some step from which it is not possible to recede.

The Rubicon was a small river separating ancient Italy from Cisalpine Gaul (the province allotted to Julius Caesar). When, in 49 B.C., Caesar crossed this stream, he passed beyond the limits of his own province and became an invader of Italy, thus precipitating the Civil War.

Ruck, Berta (1878–). Prolific English novelist, married to Oliver ONIONS. Her first novel, *His Official Fiancée* (1914), was made into a silent moving picture.

Rudder Grange. A novel by Frank R. STOCKTON (1879). It relates in whimsical fashion the adventures of the maid Pomona, her blood-and-thunder tastes in literature, her honeymoon in a lunatic asylum, and the charms of her entertaining child. The Rudder Grangers, who have as servant the irrepressible Pomona, are happy-go-lucky folk who live now in a canal boat, now in a deserted tavern, now in a tent on the edge of their own estate. Their adventures are continued in *The Rudder Grangers Abroad* (1891) and *Pomona's Travels* (1894).

Ruddymane. The infant son of Sir Mordant, in Spenser's FAËRIE QUEENE (II, i, iii); he is so called because his hand is red with his mother's blood. She stabbed herself because her husband was paralyzed by a draught from an enchanted stream.

Rudge, Barnaby. The hero of Dickens' novel, *Barnaby Rudge* (1841), a half-witted young man, three and twenty years old. He is rather spare, of a fair height and strong make. His hair, of which he has a great profusion, is red, and hangs in disorder about his face and shoulders. His face is pale, his eyes glassy and protruding. His dress is green, clumsily trimmed here and there with gaudy lace. He has a large raven, named Grip, which he carries at his back in a basket, a most knowing imp, which cries out in a hoarse voice, "Halloa!" "I'm a devil!" "Never say die!" "Polly, put the kettle on!"

Barnaby joins the GORDON RIOTERS for the proud pleasure of carrying a flag and wearing a blue bow. He is arrested and condemned to death, but by the influence of Gabriel Varden, the locksmith, the poor half-witted lad is reprieved, and lives the rest of his life with his mother in a cottage and garden near the Maypole.

> Here he lived, tending the poultry and the cattle, working in a garden of his own, and helping every one. He was known to every bird and beast about the place, and had a name for every one. Never was there a lighter-hearted husbandman, a creature more popular with young and old, a blither and more happy soul than Barnaby.—Ch. lxxxii.

Mr. Rudge. The father of Barnaby, supposed to have been murdered the same night as Mr. Haredale, to whom he was steward. The fact is that Rudge himself is the murderer both of Mr. Haredale and also of his faithful servant, to whom the crime was falsely attributed. After the murder, he is seen by many haunting the locality, and is supposed to be a ghost. He joins the Gordon rioters and is sent to Newgate, but makes his escape with the other prisoners when it is burnt down.

Mrs. Mary Rudge. Mother of Barnaby, and very like him, "but where in his face there was wildness and vacancy, in hers there was the patient composure of long effort and quiet resignation."

Rudge, William Edwin (1876–1931). New York printer, distinguished for his book designing; associated with such experts as Goudy, Bruce Rogers, Frederic Warde and W. A. Dwiggins.

Rüdiger. Margrave of Bechelaren, liegeman of King Etzel, and one of the principal characters in the NIBELUNGENLIED. He is sent to Burgundy by King Etzel, to conduct Kriemhild to Hungary if she will consent to marry the Hunnish king. When Gunther and his suite go to pay a visit to Kriemhild, he entertains them all most hospitably, and gives his daughter in marriage to Kriemhild's youngest brother, Giselher. When the broil breaks out in the dining-hall of King Etzel, and Rüdiger is compelled to take part against the Burgundians, he fights with Kriemhild's second brother, Gernot. Rüdiger strikes Gernot "through his helmet," and the Prince strikes the Margrave "through shield and morion," and "down dead dropped both together, each by the other slain."

Rüdiger, Clotilde von. The heroine of Meredith's TRAGIC COMEDIANS.

Rudkis, Jurgis and his wife **Ona Rudkis.** Slav immigrants, the leading characters of Upton Sinclair's novel THE JUNGLE.

Rudolf or **Rudolph** of Hapsburg (1858–1889). Archduke and crown prince of Austria, the only son of Emperor Francis Joseph. His love for the Baroness Marie Vetsera resulted in the tragedy of the hunting lodge of MAYERLING where the couple was found dead. The official explanation was double suicide, but investigation into the cause of death was suppressed.

Rudolph. The poet hero of Puccini's opera LA BOHÈME.

Rudolstadt, Count Albert of. The hero of George Sand's novel CONSUELO.

Rudra (Sans., *rud,* "to weep," and *dra,* "to run"). Father of the tempest gods in the Hindu mythology of the Vedas. The legend says that the boy ran about weeping because he had no name, whereupon Brahma said, "Let thy name be Rud-dra."

Rudy. In James Joyce's ULYSSES, the son of Leopold BLOOM. The child died in infancy a number of years before the time of the action of the novel, but Bloom constantly thinks of him and imagines how he would look if he had lived. Stephen DEDALUS becomes for a while a substitute for the lost son.

Rue de la Paix. A street in Paris on which are situated the most expensive shops.

Rufus. Surname of William II of England (1087–1100). So called because of his fiery complexion.

Rugby. A famous PUBLIC SCHOOL in England, founded in 1567. Its headmaster from 1828 to 1842 was Thomas Arnold, the father of Matthew ARNOLD. The book TOM BROWN'S SCHOOLDAYS by Thomas Hughes concerns the school in the nineteenth century. A poem by Matthew Arnold is called *Rugby Chapel.* The game of Rugby football originated at this school.

Rugg, Peter, see PETER RUGG.

rugged individualism. A well-known American phrase, especially espoused by Herbert HOOVER.

Ruggiero, see ROGERO.

Ruggles family. In Kate Douglas Wiggin's BIRDS' CHRISTMAS CAROL.

Ruggles of Red Gap. A humorous novel (1915) by Harry Leon Wilson, dealing with a British butler in a western pioneer town. Successfully adapted for the screen, starring Charles Laughton.

Ruisdael, Jacob van (1628–1682) and his uncle **Salomon van Ruisdael** (1600?–1670). Dutch landscape painters.

Ruiz, Juan (1283?–?1351). Spanish poet, remembered chiefly for his *Libro de Buen Amor,* a collection of legends, love stories, satire, etc. Also known as the Archpriest of Hita.

Rukeyser, Muriel (1913–). American poet, on first publication acclaimed as among the most promising poets of her generation. Her first work was marked by proletarian sympathies and Marxist convictions (see MARXISM IN LITERATURE; PROLETARIAN LITERATURE), emotional intensity, and an attempted use of 20th-century industrial and scientific symbols in dealing with social injustice and personal problems; critics found here the influence of the British revolutionary poets AUDEN, SPENDER, and DAY LEWIS. Her later work, considered to show the influence of Rainer Maria RILKE, became concerned more extensively with personal emotions and the problem of symbolism, written in a condensed and extremely elliptical style. Her books include *Theory of Flight* (1935), in which symbols from aviation are used; *U. S. 1* (1938), dealing with the exploitation of working-people living along the American highway so named; *A Turning Wind* (1940); *Wake Island* (1942), dealing with a battle during World War II; *Willard Gibbs* (1942), a biography of the American scientist of that name.

Ruksh or **Rakush.** The horse of the Persian hero RUSTUM.

> And Ruksh, his horse,
> Followed him, like a faithful hound, at heel—
> Ruksh, whose renown was noised through all the earth.
> Matthew Arnold, *Sohrab and Rustem.*

Rule, Britannia. A famous national anthem of Great Britain, with words by James THOMSON, author of *The Seasons,* and music by Dr. Arne (1740). It first appeared in a masque entitled *Alfred.*

rulers, titles of. Titles of sovereigns and other rulers may be divided into two classes, viz. (1) designations that correspond more or less to our *King* or *Emperor* (such as *Bey, Mikado, Sultan*), and (2) appellatives that were originally the proper name of some individual ruler (as *Caesar*).

Ameer, Amir. Ruler of Afghanistan, Sind, and other Mohammedan states; also spelled *Emir.*

Archon. Chief of the nine magistrates of ancient Athens. The next in rank was called

Basileus, and the third *Polemarch* (field marshal).

Beglerbeg. See BEY.

Begum. A queen, princess, or lady of high rank in India.

Bey—of Tunis. In Turkey, a bey is usually a superior military officer, though the title is often assumed by those who hold no official position. The governor of a province is known as a *beglar-bey* or *beglerbeg* (lord of lords).

Brenn or *Brenhin* (war-chief) of the ancient Gauls, a dictator appointed by the Druids in times of danger.

Bretwalda (wielder of Britain). A title of some of the Anglo-Saxon kings who held supremacy over the rest; a king of the HEPTARCHY.

Caliph or *Calif* (successor). Successors of Mahomet in temporal and spiritual matters; the office formerly claimed by the Sultan of Turkey. The Turkish National Assembly abolished the Caliphate in 1923.

Cazique or *Cacique*. A native prince of the ancient Peruvians, Cubans, Mexicans, etc.

Chagan. The chief of the Avars.

Cham. See KHAN.

Cral. The despot of ancient Servia.

Czar (from Lat. *Caesar*). The popular title of the former Emperors of Russia (assumed in 1547 by Ivan the Terrible), but officially his only as King of Poland and a few other parts of his Empire. His wife was the *Czarina* or *Czaritza,* his son the *Czarevich,* and his daughter the *Czarevna.* The sovereign of Bulgaria is still officially styled *Czar.*

Dey (Turk. *dai,* "uncle"). In Algiers, before it was annexed to France in 1830; also, the 16th-century rulers of Tunis and Tripoli.

Diwan. The native chief of Palanpur, India.

Doge. The ruler of the old Venetian Republic (697–1797); also of that of Genoa (1339–1797).

Duce, Il (*Ital.,* "the leader"). Title by which Benito MUSSOLINI, Fascist dictator of Italy, was known. See also FÜHRER, DER.

Duke (from Lat. *dux,* "leader"). The ruler of a duchy; formerly in many European countries of sovereign rank.

Elector. A Prince of the Holy Roman Empire (of sovereign rank) entitled to take part in the election of the Emperor.

Emir. The independent chieftain of certain Arabian provinces, as Bokhara, Nejd, etc. It is the same as *Amir.*

Emperor (from Lat. *imperator,* "one who commands"). The paramount ruler of an empire (as India or Japan); especially, in medieval times, the Holy Roman Empire.

Exarch. The title of a viceroy of the Byzantine Emperors, especially the *Exarch* of Ravenna, who was *de facto* governor of Italy.

Führer, Der (*Ger.,* "the leader"). Official title of Adolf HITLER, Nazi dictator of Germany. See also DUCE, IL.

Gaekwar. Formerly the title of the Monarch of the Mahrattas; now that of the native ruler of Baroda under the British (his son being the *Gaekwad*). The word is Marathi for a cowherd.

Hospodar (*Slavic,* "lord, master"). The title borne by the princes of Moldavia and Wallachia before the union of those countries with Roumania.

Imam. A title of the Sultan as spiritual successor of Mahomet; also, of the ruler of Yemen, Arabia. It is also used for certain religious leaders and the Shiites employ it for the expected MAHDI. The word means "teacher" or "guide."

Imperator. See EMPEROR.

Inca. The title of the sovereigns of Peru up to the conquest by Pizarro (1531).

Kaiser. The German form of Lat. *Caesar;* the old title of the Emperor of the Holy Roman Empire, and of the Emperors of Germany and of Austria.

Khan. The chief rulers of Tartar, Mongol, and Turkish tribes, as successors of Genghis Khan (d. 1227). The word means "lord" or "prince."

Khedive. The title conferred in 1867 by the Sultan of Turkey on the viceroy or governor of Egypt. In November, 1914, the Khedive, who had declared himself an adherent of the Central Powers, was deposed and a British Protectorate declared. See VALI.

King. The Anglo-Saxon *cyning,* literally "a man of good birth" (*cyn,* tribe, kin, or race, with the patronymic *-ing*).

Lama. The priest-ruler of Tibet, known as the *Grand Lama* or *Dalai Lama.* Also the ecclesiastical potentate of that country, known as the *Tashai Lama.*

Maharajah (*Hind.,* "the great king"). The title of many of the native rulers of Indian States.

Mikado. The popular title of the hereditary ruler of Japan—officially styled "Emperor." The name (like the Turkish *Sublime Porte*) means "The August Door." See also *Shogun.*

Mogul or *Great Mogul*. The Emperors of Delhi, and rulers of the greater part of India from 1526 to 1857, of the Mongol line founded by Baber.

Mpret. The old title of the Albanian rulers (from Lat. *imperator*), revived in 1913 in favor of Prince William of Wied, whose Mpretship, as a result of the outbreak of World War I, lasted only a few months.

Nawab. The native rulers of Bhopal,

Tonk, Jaora, and some other Indian States.

Padishah (*Pers.*, "protecting lord"). A title of the Sultan of Turkey, the Shah of Persia, and of the former Great Moguls; also, of the King of Great Britain as Emperor of India.

Pendragon. The title assumed by the ancient British overlord.

Polemarch. See ARCHON.

Prince. Formerly in common use as the title of a reigning sovereign, as it still is in a few cases, such as the Prince of Monaco and Prince of Liechtenstein.

Rajah. Hindustani for *king* (see *Maharajah*); specifically the title of the native rulers of Cochin, Ratlam, Tippera, Chamba, Faridkot, Mandi, Pudukota, Rajgarh, Rajpipla, Sailana, and Tehri (Garhwal). See *Rex.*

Ranee or *Rani.* A Hindu queen, the feminine of *Rajah.*

Rex (*regem*). The Latin equivalent of our "king," connected with *regere,* to rule, and with Sanskrit *rajan* (whence *Rajah*), a king.

Sachem, Sagamore. Chieftains of certain tribes of North American Indians.

Satrap. The governor of a province in ancient Persia.

Shah (*Pers.*, "king"). The supreme ruler of Persia and of some other Eastern countries. See PADISHAH.

Sheikh. An Arab chief, or head man of a tribe.

Shogun. The title of the virtual rulers of Japan (representing usurping families who kept the true Emperor in perpetual confinement with some prestige of sovereignty but little power) from about the close of the 12th century to the revolution of 1867–1868. It means "leader of an army," and was originally the title of military governors. He is sometimes also called the *Tycoon.*

Sirdar. The commander-in-chief of the Egyptian army and military governor of Egypt.

Stadtholder. Originally a viceroy in a province of the Netherlands, but later the chief executive officer of the United Provinces.

Sultan (formerly also *Soldan*). The title of the rulers of many Mohammedan States, especially Turkey, before the formation of the new Turkish state.

Tetrarch. The governor of the fourth part of a province in the ancient Roman Empire.

Tycoon. An alternative title of the Japanese *Shogun.* The word is from Chinese and means "great sovereign."

Vali. The title of the governors of Egypt prior to 1867, when the style *Khedive* was granted by the Sultan; also, a Turkish official.

Voivode, or *Vaivode.* Properly (*Russ.*) "the leader of an army." The word was for a time assumed as a title by the Princes of Moldavia and Wallachia, later called *Hospodars.*

The following names have been adopted in varying degrees as royal titles among the peoples mentioned:

Abgarus (The Grand). So the kings of Edessa were styled.

Abimelech (my father the king). The chief ruler of the ancient Philistines.

Attabeg (father prince). Persia, 1118.

Augustus. The title of the reigning Emperor of Rome, when the heir presumptive was styled "Caesar."

Caesar. Proper name adopted by the Roman emperors. See *Kaiser; Czar.*

Candace. Proper name adopted by the queens of Ethiopia.

Cyrus (mighty). Ancient Persia.

Darius, Latin form of *Darawesh* (king). Ancient Persia.

Melech (king). Ancient Semitic tribes.

Pharaoh (light of the world). Ancient Egypt.

Ptolemy. Proper name adopted by Egypt after the death of Alexander.

Sophy or *Sophi.* A former title of the kings of Persia, from Cafi-ud-din, the founder of the ancient dynasty of the Cafi or Cafavi.

Rum, Romanism, and Rebellion. A phrase used to denounce the Democratic party at the time of the Republican candidacy of James G. BLAINE (1884). It was directed specifically against the Irish Catholics and resulted in losing for the Republicans the Irish Catholic vote, which helped Cleveland to win the election.

Rumford, Count, see THOMPSON, BENJAMIN.

Ruml, Beardsley (1894–). American businessman, noted for his pay-as-you-go plan of Federal taxation presented to the U.S. Senate finance committee (1942) and resulting in the adoption of a compromise tax bill (1943).

Rumpelstiltskin or **Rumpelstilzchen.** A passionate little deformed dwarf of German folktale. A miller's daughter is enjoined by a king to spin straw into gold, and the dwarf does it for her, on condition that she give him her first child. The maiden marries the king, and grieves so bitterly when the child is born that the dwarf promises to relent if within three days she can find out his name. Two days are spent in vain guesses, but the third day one of the queen's servants hears a strange voice singing—

> Little dreams my dainty dame
> Rumpelstilzchen is my name.

She tells the queen of this, and the dwarf destroys himself in anger at having lost his bargain.

Rundstedt, Karl Rudolf Gerd von (1875–). German field marshal, who commanded the southern armies against Poland (1939), the center group of armies against

France (1940), and was commander in chief of the German army of occupation in France (from 1942).

runes. Characters in the alphabet used by the early Germanic peoples, especially the Anglo-Saxons and Scandinavians. They were formed by the modification of the Roman alphabet to eliminate horizontal strokes, so that inscriptions might be carved in wood; as new diphthongs arose through sound-changes in the languages, new runes were devised, each of which was named for a common or proper noun beginning with the character in question. The best-known rune is the "thorn" (þ), used throughout Anglo-Saxon and Middle English to represent the *th* sound and so named for the thorn which it resembles. In the poems attributed to CYNEWULF, there are passages containing runes which spell out the author's name.

Runkle, Bertha. American novelist, author of several best-sellers, notably *The Helmet of Navarre* (1901); *The Truth about Tolna* (1906); *The Scarlet Rider* (1913); etc.

Running Footman, The, or **The Sentimental Servant.** A novel (1932) by John Owen (1878–).

Running Parliament. See under PARLIAMENTS.

Runnymede. A name assumed by Benjamin DISRAELI in the *Times.*

Runnymede. An island (Charter Island) in the Thames in Surrey, where King John, on June 15, 1215, was forced to sign the Magna Carta. Cf. Kipling's poem, *The Reeds of Runnymede.* Some say the document was signed in the meadow on the south side of the Thames.

Runyon, Damon (1884–1946). American journalist and popular short-story writer who has interpreted the semi-literate American, in slangy Americanese and with unusual observation. He has been called a master of "the art of anonymity in the first person." After his death by cancer, a large sum was raised for a cancer research foundation to bear his name.

Rupert, Prince. Count Palatine of **Rhine** and Duke of **Bavaria** (1619–1682). Son of Frederick V, Elector Palatine, and Elizabeth, daughter of James I of England. After having played a minor part in the Thirty Years' War, he became cavalry leader for his uncle Charles I during the English Civil War. He distinguished himself by his gallantry and won the nickname of "the Mad Cavalier." Upon surrendering Bristol to Fairfax (1645), his uncle took his offices away from him, but he was later cleared by a court-martial. He commanded the King's fleet (1648–1650), and became admiral of the fleet (1673) and first lord of the admiralty (1673–1679). Besides his warlike exploits he was an artist and experimental scientist. He improved the mezzotint process, made gunpowder experiments, and invented the alloy which is known as *Prince Rupert's* or *Prince's metal.* See also PRINCE RUPERT'S DROPS.

Ruppert, Jacob (1867–1939). American brewer. Owner of the New York Yankees.

R.U.R. A play by Karel ČAPEK, produced in 1923. It deals with an imagined future state in which robots, enslaved to do work for men, revolt against their masters. The initials in the title stand for "Rossum's Universal Robots," the name of the commercial firm which manufactures the mechanical creatures.

Rural Rides. A book of descriptions of the English countryside and of agricultural and social conditions in England by William COBBETT (1830).

Ruritania. The imaginary kingdom in which occurs the action of *The Prisoner of Zenda* (1894) and *Rupert of Hentzau* (1898) by Anthony HOPE.

Rush, Benjamin (1745?–1813). American physician, member of the Continental Congress (1776–1777), and signer of the Declaration of Independence.

Rush, Friar. A legendary house-spirit who originated as a kind of ultra-mischievous and evil-dispositioned Robin Goodfellow in medieval German folk-tales (*Bruder Rausch,* i.e., "intoxication"). His particular duty was to lead monks and friars into wickedness and keep them in it. A prose *History of Friar Rush* appeared in English as early as 1568, and in 1601 Henslowe records a comedy (now lost), *Friar Rush and the Proud Woman of Antwerp,* by Day and Houghton.

Rush, Richard (1780–1859). Son of Benjamin RUSH. Comptroller of the Treasury (1811); attorney general (1814–1817); minister to England (1817–1825); etc. He was prominent in the negotiations which led to the promulgation of the Monroe Doctrine.

Ruskin, John (1819–1900). English painter, art critic, and essayist, associated with the PRE-RAPHAELITE BROTHERHOOD, known for his rebellion against the materialistic standards of Victorian England, his attraction to the Middle Ages, his interest in economic theory and social experimentation, and his rich and eloquent prose style. His works include MODERN PAINTERS (1843–1860); *The Seven Lamps of Architecture* (1849), an attempt to relate artistic value to morality; *The Stones of Venice* (1851–1853), a celebration of Gothic architecture and an attack on "the pestilent art of the Renaissance"; *Unto This Last* (1862), a series of articles on wealth, published in the *Cornhill*

Magazine; Munera Pulveris (1862–1863), a similar series of articles in *Fraser's Magazine*, published in 1873; *Sesame and Lilies* (1863), three lectures; *The Crown of Wild Olive* (1866), a collection of lectures tending toward social and economic interpretations of war, England's future, labor, etc.; *Fors Clavigera* (1871–1884), a series of open letters addressed to English workingmen on a number of subjects; *Praeterita* (1885–1889), an account of the author's early life.

Ruskin was the son of a well-to-do London wine merchant, pampered and isolated in his youth. Like William MORRIS, he tried to reform the prevailing Victorian taste in art, and at Oxford University, where he lectured on art from time to time, he attempted the founding of guilds based on the system in use in the Middle Ages, so that each worker might become a master craftsman. St. George's Guild, The Hinksey Diggers, and other groups were established as the result of Ruskin's efforts. He also led a movement to prevent the railroads from spoiling the natural beauty of the landscape, and advocated state control of the railroad systems in order to accomplish his aim.

See also PATHETIC FALLACY.

Russell, Annie (1869–1936). English-born American actress. Under the management of Charles Frohman (1896). Created the title rôle in *Major Barbara* by George Bernard Shaw (1906). Under her own management (1912–1914).

Russell, Bertrand Arthur William. 3rd Earl **Russell** (1872–). English philosopher and author, known for his studies in logic and mathematics, his essays and lectures on philosophic problems in a semi-popularizing vein, his early advocacy of PACIFISM, and his interest in politics and such social problems as divorce and sexual relations. Among his works are *Principia Mathematica* (1910); *The Problems of Philosophy* (1911); *Mysticism and Logic* (1918); *The Practice and Theory of Bolshevism* (1920); *Analysis of the Mind* (1921); *The A.B.C. of Atoms* (1923); *The A.B.C. of Relativity* (1925); *Skeptical Essays* (1928); *Marriage and Morals* (1929); *The Conquest of Happiness* (1929); *Our Knowledge of the External World* (1929); *Education and the Modern World* (1932); *Freedom versus Organization, 1814–1914* (1934), on European politics; *In Praise of Idleness* (1935), essays; *Religion and Science* (1935); *Power: A New Social Analysis* (1938); *Why I Am Not a Christian* (1940); *An Inquiry into Meaning and Truth* (1940); *Let the People Think* (1941).

Russell's unorthodox opinions involved him in frequent difficulties with English and American authorities. During World War I in England he was fined and imprisoned for his pacifist views. An experimental nursery school conducted by him and his wife beginning in 1927 was severely criticized, and in 1939 an appointment he had received to the mathematics department of the College of the City of New York was withdrawn on the grounds that his teachings were immoral. He later quarreled with Albert Barnes, wealthy art collector of Merion, Pa., at whose Foundation he lectured.

Russell, Charles Edward (1860–1941). American journalist. Repeatedly Socialist candidate for governor and mayor of New York. Pulitzer prize in biography (1928) for *The American Orchestra and Theodore Thomas*. Author of many other books both on Socialistic themes and in the realm of biography and history.

Russell, Charles Taze (1852–1916). American religious leader, known as "Pastor Russell." His followers, the Russellites, became organized into a society called the International Bible Students' Association. He taught that the second coming of Christ had taken place invisibly in 1874 and that forty years later a period of social revolution and chaos would begin, ultimately to be followed by the establishment of Christ's kingdom on earth.

Russell, Elizabeth Mary. Countess **Russell.** *Née* **Mary Annette Beauchamp** (1866–1941). See (3) under ELIZABETH.

Russell, George William, see A. E.

Russell, Irwin (1853–1879). American poet, chiefly known for his poems in Negro dialect. The collected *Poems by Irwin Russell* were published (1888) posthumously with a preface by Joel Chandler HARRIS.

Russell, Lillian. Stage name of **Helen Louise Leonard** (1861–1922). American operatic soprano. She first appeared in Tony PASTOR's Variety Theatre (1880) and sang for over thirty-five years in burlesque and comic opera. Her beauty and figure (of the Gibson Girl type) made her a great popular favorite. She was called the "American Beauty" from a burlesque in which she appeared. She had four husbands in succession. She retired in 1912. Cf. her biography, *Lillian Russell: The Era of Plush* (1940), by Parker Morell.

Russell, William Clark (1844–1911). English novelist. After 8 years in the British merchant service he became a journalist in London and wrote a great many stories of nautical adventure. He also wrote lives of Dampier, Nelson, and Collingwood. *The Wreck of the Grosvenor* (1877).

Russell, Sir William Howard (1820–1907). Well-known English war correspondent. When reporting the Crimean War he coined the phrase, "the thin red line" which he applied to the British Infantry at Balaclava.

Russellite. See under RUSSELL, CHARLES.

Russell's Bookstore. A bookstore in Charlestown, S.C., where, in the 1850's, a number of Southern writers such as TIMROD, SIMMS, and HAYNE used to meet. Their meetings resulted in *Russell's Magazine* (1857–1860), which was edited by Hayne and modeled on *Blackwood's* in Edinburgh.

Russell Square. A residential square in London referred to by Thackeray in describing the wealthy homes of certain people in his novels.

Russian. For *the Russian Byron, the Russian Murat,* etc., see under BYRON, MURAT.

Rustam or **Rustum.** Chief of the Persian mythical heroes, son of Zâl "the Fair," King of India, and regular descendant of Benjamin, the beloved son of Jacob the patriarch. His story is told in the Persian epic SHAH NAMAH. He delivers King Caïcaus from prison, but afterwards falls into disgrace because he refuses to embrace the religious system of ZOROASTER. Caïcaus sends his son Asfendiar (or Isfendiar) to convert him, and, as persuasion avails nothing, the logic of single combat is resorted to. The fight lasts two days, and then Rustam discovers that Asfendiar bears a "charmed life," proof against all wounds. The valor of these two heroes is proverbial, and the Persian romances are full of their deeds of fight. Rustam is also famous for his victory over the white dragon Asdeev. In Matthew ARNOLD's poem *Sohrab* and *Rustum,* Rustum fights with Sohrab, overcomes him, and finds too late he has slain his own son.

Rutgers College. An institution of learning, founded (1766) under the name of Queen's College at New Brunswick, N.J., and renamed Rutgers College (1825) in honor of its benefactor Henry Rutgers (1745–1830). Among its famous former students are the poet Joyce KILMER, who died in action in World War I, and the Negro singer and actor Paul ROBESON, who was an All American football star while in college.

Ruth. Heroine of a love story of the Old Testament told in the book of *Ruth.* She is a Moabitess, and the chief appeal of the idyll lies in her devotion to her Hebrew mother-in-law, Naomi, after the death of her husband, Naomi's son. She accompanies Naomi back to Bethlehem with the words, "Entreat me not to leave thee and to return from following after thee; for whither thou goest, I will go; and where thou lodgest, I will lodge; thy people shall be my people and thy God my God." In Bethlehem she becomes a gleaner in the fields of Boaz, a rich kinsman, and he falls in love with her and marries her.

Ruth, George Herman. Known as **Babe Ruth** (1894–). American professional baseball player, voted the most valuable player in the American League in 1923. In 1927 he made 60 home runs. Retired in 1935.

Rutherford, Ernest. 1st Baron **Rutherford of Nelson** (1871–1937). British physicist who taught at McGill University in Canada and at Manchester, England. In 1919 he succeeded in transmuting chemical elements by artificial means and formulated the theory that the atom is not indivisible but consists of a nucleus round which electrons revolve in planetary orbits. Won the Nobel prize for chemistry (1908).

Rutherford, Mark, see MARK RUTHERFORD.

Rutledge, Ann (1816–1835). Abraham Lincoln's early love; she was the daughter of his landlord at New Salem, Illinois, and died suddenly of malarial fever. The affair has been much written about by novelists and poets.

Ruy Blas. A drama by Victor HUGO (1838), in which a Spanish valet falls in love with a queen.

Ruy Lopez de Sigura. Sixteenth-century Spanish writer on chess (1561). The Ruy Lopez opening is named after him.

Ruysbroeck, Jan van (1293–1381). Flemish mystic, called "the Ecstatic Doctor." Author of mystical works in Flemish and Latin.

Ruyter, Michel Adriaanszoon de (1607–1676). Famous Dutch admiral and naval hero who defeated the English fleet in a four-day battle off Dunkirk in 1666.

Ružička, Leopold (1887–). Swiss chemist, born in Yugoslavia, who won the Nobel prize for his work on the sex hormones (1939). The German chemist Adolph Butenandt declined his share of the prize because the Nazis had prohibited the acceptance of it.

Ryan, Abram Joseph (1839–1886). American Roman Catholic priest, journalist, and author of verse, a chaplain in the Confederate army during the Civil War. *Father Ryan's Poems* were published in 1879, and other volumes appeared in 1880 and 1896. *The Conquered Banner* and *The Sword of Robert Lee* are his best-known single poems.

Ryder, Albert Pinkham (1847–1917). American painter, three of whose imaginative and fantastic paintings hang in the Metropolitan Museum of Art in New York City. He specialized in moonlit marines.

Ryecroft, Henry. Hero of George GISSING's *Private Papers of Henry Ryecroft* (1903), a study of the problems and disillusionments of the literary life.

Rye House Plot. In English history, a conspiracy (1683) to seize the Stuart brothers at

King Ryence shall do me homage on both William Russell and Algernon Sidney, who were implicated in it, were executed.

Ryence, King. A Welsh king of the Arthurian romances, who sends a dwarf to King ARTHUR to say he has overcome eleven kings, all of whom have given him their beards to purfell his mantle. He now requires King Arthur to do likewise. King Arthur answers, "My beard is full young yet for a purfell, but before it is long enough for such a purpose, King Ryence shall do me homage on both his knees." Cf. Percy's *Reliques,* third series, book one.

Rymenhild. The princess beloved by King HORN.

Rymer, Thomas (1641–1713). English archaeologist and critic; author of numerous poems and translations. Criticized Beaumont and Fletcher, and condemned Shakespeare's failure to observe the law of the classical unities in *Othello.*

Ryskind, Morris or **Morrie** (1895–). American playwright, awarded the Pulitzer prize, with George and Ira GERSHWIN, for *Of Thee I Sing* (1931).

Ryti, Rysto Heikki (1889–). President of Finland (1940–1946).

S

Saadi or **Sadi.** Real name **Muslih-ud-Din** (1184?–1291). Persian poet, author of *Gulistan* (*Rose Garden;* 1258) and a collection of lyrics, *Diwan.*

Saavedra Lamas, Carlos (1880–). Argentine lawyer and diplomat; president of the Assembly of the League of Nations (1936); awarded Nobel peace prize (1936).

Saba, Queen of. See SHEBA.

Sabaoth (*Hebrew,* "armies" or "hosts"). In the New Testament, the phrase "the Lord of Sabaoth" is translated by the "Lord of Hosts."

Sabatini, Rafael (1875–). Italian novelist, author of best-selling historical and adventure romances in English, the best-known of which are *Scaramouche* (1921), *Captain Blood* (1922), and *The Sea-Hawk* (1923). He was at the height of his popularity in the early 1920's.

Sabbatical year. One year in seven when all land with the ancient Jews was to lie fallow for twelve months. This law was founded on *Ex.* xxiii. 10, etc.; *Lev.* xxv. 2–7; *Deut.* xv. 1–11. It is used for a missionary's furlough, or a year of vacation from a profession.

Sabines. An ancient Italian people, subjugated by the Romans about 290 B. C. The rape of the Sabine women, an important incident in the legendary history of Rome, was instigated by Romulus who needed wives for his men and solved the problem by telling them to help themselves to Sabine virgins after he had lured the male population away. It is the subject of many paintings, as for instance by Giordano and Rubens.

sabotage. Wilful and malicious destruction of tools, plants, machinery, materials, etc., by discontented workmen or strikers, or by enemy agents in war time. The term came into use after the great French railway strike of 1912, when the strikers cut the shoes (*sabots*) holding the railway lines.

Sabra. The legendary daughter of Ptolemy, King of Egypt, rescued by St. George (see under SAINTS) from the fangs of the dragon and ultimately married to her deliverer. She is represented as pure in mind, saintly in character, a perfect citizen, daughter, and wife. Her three sons, born at one birth, were named Guy, Alexander and David. Sabra died from the "pricks of a thorny brake."

Sabre, Mark. The hero of Hutchinson's IF WINTER COMES. He says of himself that he is "unsatisfactory, because I've got the most infernal habit of seeing things from about twenty points of view."

Sabrina. The Latin name of the river Severn, but in British legend the name of the daughter of LOCRINE and his concubine Estrildis. Locrine's queen, Guendolen, vowed vengeance against Estrildis and her daughter, got an army together, and overthrew her husband. Sabrina fled and jumped into the Severn; NEREUS took pity on her, and made her goddess of the river, which is hence poetically called Sabrina.

> There is a gentle nymph not far from hence,
> That with moist curb sways the smooth Severn stream
> Sabrina is her name, a virgin pure.
>
> Milton, *Comus,* 840

Sacco Benedetto or **San Benito** (*Span.,* "the blessed sack or cloak"). The yellow linen robe with two crosses on it, and painted over with flames and devils, in which persons condemned by the Spanish Inquisition were arrayed when they went to the stake. See AUTO DA FÉ. In the case of those who expressed repentance for their errors, the flames were directed downwards. Penitents who had been taken before the Inquisition had to wear this badge for a stated period. Those worn by Jews, sorcerers, and renegades bore a St. Andrew's cross in red on back and front.

Sacco-Vanzetti Case. A famous court case during the period of the "Red scare" in the early 1920's, in which two Italian-born radicals, Nicola Sacco and Bartolomeo Vanzetti, were arrested, tried, and convicted for murder committed during a payroll robbery by a gang of bandits in South Braintree, Massachusetts (1920). The evidence was considered flimsy, and a world-wide protest was raised on the charge that the two men were the victims of injustice, but they were finally executed in 1927. The case inspired several literary works, including *Justice Denied in Massachusetts* (1927), a poem by Edna St. Vincent Millay; *Boston* (1928), a novel by Upton Sinclair; *Firehead* (1929), a narrative poem by Lola Ridge; and *Winterset* (1935), a play by Maxwell Anderson.

sachem. See under RULERS, TITLES OF.

Sacher-Masoch, Leopold von (1836–1895). German novelist, author of *Das Vermächtnis Kains* (1870–1877); *Die Messalinen Wiens* (1874); etc. From his name is derived the term MASOCHISM, denoting a sexual abnormality (pleasure in being hurt) depicted in some of his novels.

Sacheverell, Henry (1674?–1724). English preacher, whose political sermons attacking the Whig ministry made him the idol of the Tory party. He was impeached and suspended from preaching, but selected to preach the Restoration sermon (1713).

Sachs, Hans. In Wagner's opera THE MEISTERSINGER, the town cobbler, singer, and poet of Nuremberg, the central figure of the opera. Sachs was a real person, who lived

1494–1576, and left behind him thirty-four folio vols. of MS., containing 208 plays, 1700 comic tales, and about 450 lyric poems.

Here Hans Sachs, the cobbler-poet, laureate of the gentle craft,
Wisest of the Twelve Wise Masters, in huge folios sang and laughed.
Longfellow, *Nuremberg*.

sack (from Fr. *sec,* "dry"). Originally a dry wine, later any of a variety of wines from southern Europe, frequently mentioned in Elizabethan drama and the literature of the 17th century; particularly "Sherris sack" is referred to by Shakespeare.

sack, to give one the. To dismiss from further service. At one time, manufacturers who employed those who worked at home put the work to be done in a bag or sack. If, when brought back, the work was satisfactory, the bag or sack was filled again with materials; if not, it was laid empty on the counter, and this indicated that the person would no longer be employed by the firm.

Sackville, Charles. 6th Earl of **Dorset,** 1st Earl of **Middlesex** (1638–1706). English poet and courtier. Friend and patron of poets, including Prior, Wycherly, Dryden, and others. His best-known poem is, "To all you Ladies, now at land," written (1665) in the first Dutch war at sea, the night before an engagement.

Sackville, Thomas. 1st Earl of **Dorset** and Baron **Buckhurst** (1536–1608). English poet and statesman, known for his authorship of the last two acts of the *Tragedy of Gorboduc* (see GORBODUC; 1562), an important work in the history of the English drama, the first three acts of which were written by Thomas Norton, and especially for his *Induction* to the 1563 edition of THE MIRROR FOR MAGISTRATES. The latter piece is the most famous part of the *Mirror,* considered by many critics to be the most outstanding poem written in England between the death of Chaucer and the publication of Spenser's SHEPHERD'S CALENDAR. Sackville followed his *Induction* with an account of the life of Henry, Duke of Buckingham, also included in the 1563 edition.

In later life, Sackville devoted himself to a public career, serving variously as a Member of Parliament, an ambassador, a member of the Privy Council, Lord Treasurer, and Chancellor of Oxford University.

Sackville-West, Edward Charles (1901–). English novelist; nephew of Victoria Mary SACKVILLE-WEST. Author of light and witty novels, as *Piano Quintet* (1925); *The Sun in Capricorn* (1934); etc.

Sackville-West, Victoria Mary (1892–). English novelist, poet, and critic, a descendant of Thomas SACKVILLE and associated with the BLOOMSBURY GROUP. Her works include *Poems of East and West* (1917), *Orchard and Vineyard* (1921), *The Land* (1926), *King's Daughter* (1930), and *Collected Poems* (1933), books of poetry; *Heritage* (1919), *The Dragon in Shallow Waters* (1922), *Challenge* (1923), *Gray Wethers* (1923), *Seducers in Ecuador* (1924), *The Edwardians* (1930), *All Passion Spent* (1931), *Family History* (1932), *The Dark Island* (1934), and *Pepita* (1937), novels; *The Heir* (1922) and *Thirty Clocks Strike the Hour, and Other Stories* (1932), collections of short stories; *Knole and the Sackvilles* (1922), a family history; *Andrew Marvell* (1929), criticism; *St. Joan of Arc* (1936); *Country Notes in Wartime* (1940).

Miss Sackville-West, of a noble Engish family, was brought up in the picturesque Knole Castle, in Kent, an ancestral possession which originally was a gift from Queen Elizabeth to Thomas Sackville; the family background is incorporated in several of the author's works. She married Harold NICOLSON, also a writer, in 1913. *Orlando,* by Virginia WOOLF, is said to be a portrait of Knole Castle and V. Sackville-West herself, who was a close friend of Mrs. Woolf.

sacrament. Originally "a military oath" (Lat. *sacramentum*) taken by the Roman soldiers not to desert their standard, turn their back on the enemy, or abandon their general. The early Christians used the word to signify "a sacred mystery," and hence its application to baptism, the Eucharist, marriage, confirmation, etc.

The five sacraments are Confirmation, Penance, Orders, Matrimony, and Extreme Unction. These are not counted "Sacraments of the Gospel." Cf. *Thirty-nine Articles,* Article XXV.

The seven sacraments are Baptism, Confirmation, the Eucharist, Penance, Orders, Matrimony, and Extreme Unction.

The two sacraments of the Protestant Churches are Baptism and the Lord's Supper.

sacred college. The college of cardinals who elect the Pope from among themselves and form the council of the Pope.

Sacred Fount, The. A novelette by Henry JAMES (1901), dealing with psychological explorations into the lives of the guests at an English house-party.

Sacred Isle or **Holy Island.** Ireland was so called because of its many saints, and Guernsey for its many monks. The island referred to by Thomas MOORE in his *Irish Melodies* (No. II) is Scattery, to which St. Senanus retired, and vowed that no woman should set foot thereon:

"Oh, haste and leave this sacred isle,
Unholy bark, ere morning smile."

Sacred Nine, The. The MUSES.

Sacred Wood, The. A volume of essays (1920) by T. S. ELIOT.

sacring bell. A small hand bell, rung at the Elevation of the Host in the Roman Catholic Mass.

Sacripant. In the Italian epic poems, ORLANDO INNAMORATO by Boiardo and ORLANDO FURIOSO by Ariosto, the Emperor of Circassia, one of the most notable of the Saracens who lays siege to Charlemagne's citadel in Paris. He is the lover and for a time the champion of the fair ANGELICA, but fails to win her.

Sacys Bible. See BIBLE, SPECIALLY NAMED.

Sadducees. A Jewish party which existed about the time of Christ. They denied the existence of spirits and angels, and did not believe in the resurrection of the dead; said to be so called from Sadoc or Zadok (see 2 *Sam.* viii. 17), who is thought to have been a priest or rabbi some three centuries before the birth of Christ. They were opposed to the Pharisees in that they did not accept the oral parts of the Law traditionally handed down from Moses, and as they did not believe in future punishments, they punished offenses severely.

Sad Fortunes of the Reverend Amos Barton. See AMOS BARTON.

sadism. A type of sexual perversion in which pleasure is found in cruelty to, and the suffering of, the object of love; so called from Count (known as Marquis) Donatien de Sade (1740–1814), a French author whose writings first introduced sadistic practices into public knowledge. The term has come to be applied to any delight in the sufferings of others, sex not necessarily being involved. See also MASOCHISM.

Sadleir, Michael (1888–). English author and publisher. Wrote biographies of Sheridan, Trollope, Bulwer, and Lady Blessington, and half a dozen novels. Director of Constable & Co. (1920); member, British delegation to Peace Conference at Paris (1919) and secretariat, League of Nations.

Safa. In Mohammedan myth, the hill in Arabia on which Adam and Eve came together, after having been parted for 200 years, during which they wandered homeless over the face of the earth.

safari. An expedition with carriers, pack animals, etc.; usually a hunting expedition. The word is East African.

Saffron Hill. The abode of ballad singers in London, north of Holborn.

Saga (plural **Sagas**). The Teutonic and Scandinavian mythological and historical traditions, chiefly compiled in the 12th and three following centuries. The most remarkable are those of *Lodbrog, Hervara, Vilkina, Voluspa, Volsunga, Blomsturvalla Ynglinga, Olaf Tryggva-Sonar,* with those of *Jomsvikingia* and of *Knytlinga* (which contain the legendary history of Norway and Denmark), those of *Sturlinga* and *Eryrbiggia* (which contain the legendary history of Iceland), and the collections, the *Heims-Kringla* and *New* or *Younger Edda,* by Snorri Sturluson. See also VÖLSUNGA SAGA; EDDA.

Saga of King Olaf, The. A group of poems by Henry W. LONGFELLOW, using the accounts in the HEIMSKRINGLA which describe the feats of King Olaf of Norway (995–1000).

Sagasta, Práxedes Mateo (1827–1903). Spanish statesman and journalist. Leader of Liberals in the Cortes (1875–1883). Twice prime minister, resigned because of trouble in Cuba, but conducted the government at the time of Spain's war with the U.S. (1897–1899).

sage.

the Sage of Auburn. W. H. Seward (1801–1872), American politician.

the Sage of Chappaqua. Horace Greeley (1811–1872), American editor and statesman.

the Sage of Chelsea. Thomas Carlyle (1795–1881) from his Chelsea residence.

the Sage of Concord. Ralph Waldo Emerson (1803–1882) from his Concord, Mass., home.

the Sage of Monticello. THOMAS JEFFERSON, whose country seat was at Monticello, Va.

the Sage of Samos or *the Samian Sage.* Pythagoras (*fl.* 540–510 B. C.), the Greek philosopher.

Sage Hens. Nickname for inhabitants of Nevada.

Sage-Brush State. Nevada. See STATES.

Sage, Russell (1816–1906). American financier, associated with Jay Gould in stock market operations. His second wife, **Margaret Olivia Sage,** *née* **Slocum** (1828–1918), inherited his fortune with which she founded and endowed the Russell Sage Foundation for improving social and living conditions, the Russell Sage Institute of Pathology, and other philanthropic organizations.

Sagittary. The name given in the medieval romances to the centaur, a mythical monster, half horse and half man, whose eyes sparkled like fire and struck dead like lightning, fabled to have been introduced into the Trojan armies.

> The dreadful Sagittary
> Appals our numbers.
> Shakespeare, *Troilus and Cressida,* v, 5.

The "Sagittary" referred to in *Othello* i, 1:

> Lead to the Sagittary the raised search,
> And there will I be with him,

was probably an inn, but may have been the Arsenal, where, it is said, the statue of an archer is still to be seen.

Sago, Lot Sap. A typical Yankee character who appeared in C. A. Logan's comedy *Yankee Land* (*Am.,* 1834) and later in *Hue and*

Cry (1846). See also JONATHAN PLOUGHBOY; Solomon SWAP; Solon SHINGLE.

Sagramour le Desirus. In Arthurian romance, a knight of the ROUND TABLE.

Sailor King. William IV. of England (b. 1765, reigned 1830–1837) who entered the navy as midshipman in 1779, and was made Lord High Admiral in 1827.

Saint, The (Il Santo). A novel by Antonio FOGAZZARO. See MAIRONI, PIERO.

St. Bartholomew, Massacre of. See under BARTHOLOMEW.

St. Brendan's Voyage. See *St. Brandan* or *Brendan* under SAINTS.

St. Clare, Augustin. In Harriet Beecher Stowe's UNCLE TOM'S CABIN, the kind, indulgent master of Uncle Tom. He is beloved by all his slaves.

Evangeline St. Clare or *Little Eva.* The daughter of Mr. St. Clare, the good angel of the family, adored by Uncle Tom. Her sentimental death scene is famous. For an amusing parody, cf. *Season in the Sun* (1946) by Wolcott Gibbs.

Miss Ophelia St. Clare. Cousin of Augustin. She is a New England Puritan.

St. Cleve, Swithin. One of the chief characters in Hardy's TWO ON A TOWER.

St. Cloud. A suburb of Paris, notable for its palace where many important events in French history took place. Built by Louis XIV (1658) on the site of an older castle, it was bought by Louis XVI for Marie Antoinette, and was later a favorite residence of Napoleon I and Napoleon III. It was badly damaged during the Franco-Prussian War, and afterwards demolished.

Saint-Cyr. A convent school for daughters of the French nobility founded at the village of that name, near Versailles, by Mme de Maintenon. In 1806 it became the famous French military school which corresponded to Sandhurst in England.

St. Denis, Ruth. Real name **Ruth Dennis.** American dancer and teacher of the modern dance. Married Ted Shawn (now separated) and organized the Denishawn School of Dancing. Toured with the Denishawn Dancers in the U.S., England, and the Orient.

Sainte-Beuve, Charles-Augustin (1804–1869). French literary critic and author, successively influenced in his thought by scientific skepticism, physiology and POSITIVISM, ROMANTICISM, Saint-Simonism, liberal Catholicism, Swiss Calvinism, and other intellectual movements of his time. His criticism is sometimes divided into three periods: one, in which he was the spokesman for the romantic school; the second, in which he developed his biographical and psychological approach, studying a literary work through the life and personality of its author; and a third, in which he emphasized historical background and social environment in his studies in a method similar to that of NATURALISM in the novel. His standards of judgment are taste, truth in the portrayal of life, moderation, and artistic unity.

Sainte-Beuve's works include *Vie, Poésies, et Pensées de Joseph Delorme* (*The Life, Poetry, and Thought of Joseph Delorme;* 1829), an autobiographical work, morbid in tone; *Consolations* (1831); *Pensées d'Août* (1837); *Le Livre d'Amour* (1843); *Volupté* (1834), an autobiographical novel in the romantic vein, ending in a conversion of the hero to religion; *Tableau de la Poésie Française au XIVe Siècle* (1828); *Port-Royal* (1840–1860), a study of the JANSENISTS; *Chateaubriand et son Groupe Littéraire; Causeries du Lundi* (1851–1862) and *Nouveaux Lundis* (1863–1870), weekly critical articles; *Portraits Littéraires* (1862–1864); *Portraits Contemporains* (1869–1871).

Sainte-Beuve had a reputation for extreme variability in his friendships, personal loyalties, and intellectual affiliations. *Le Livre d'Amour* celebrates with great frankness the critic's early love-affair with the wife of Victor HUGO and aroused a great deal of scandal on its publication.

St. Elmo or St. Elmo's Fire. The corposant (Port. *corpo santo,* "sacred body"), or corpozant, an electrical luminosity often seen on the masts and rigging of ships on dark, stormy nights. There is no saint of this name, and the suggestions are that "Elmo" is a corruption of St. *Anselm* (of Lucca), St. *Erasmus* (the patron saint of Neapolitan sailors), or of *Helena,* sister of Castor and Pollux, by which twin-name the St. Elmo's Fire is also known.

St. Elmo is the name of the title and hero of a once popular novel by Augusta Jane Evans Wilson (*Am.,* 1866).

Saint-Évremond, Seigneur **de. Charles de Marguetel de Saint-Denis** (1610?–1703). French wit and littérateur, involved in the fall of Fouquet. Attacked Mazarin and fled to England (1661), where he was well received by Charles II and became a member of Hortense MANCINI's London salon. Among his works are critical essays, poems, dialogues, etc., all published after his death.

Saint-Exupéry, Antoine de (1900–1945). French aviator and writer. His books are poetic in style, mostly about flights he made. His work was recognized at once. Awarded the *Prix Fémina-Vie Heureuse* (1931) and the *Grand Prix* of the French Academy (1939). His *Wind, Sand and Stars* (1939) was a best-seller in the U.S.; his children's book, *The Little Prince* (1943), illustrated by himself, is a delightfully wise fairy tale. Killed in an airplane accident.

Saint-Gaudens, Augustus (1848–1907). Irish-born American sculptor. His *Reminiscences,* in two volumes, were published in 1913. Member, American Hall of Fame (1920).

Saint-Germain-en-Laye. French town and castle on the left bank of the Seine, eight miles from Paris, where James II resided during his exile.

Saint-Germain, Treaty of. The peace treaty between Austria and the Allies after World War I (September 10, 1919). Among other provisions, it prohibited *Anschluss* (union with the Reich).

St. Helena. A British-owned island in the South Atlantic where Napoleon was exiled after the battle of Waterloo (1815–1821).

St. James's Park. A public park in London. Charles II modeled it on the gardens of Holland. It served both the Palaces of St. James and of Whitehall. Mention of it is made in the diaries of Pepys and Evelyn.

Saint John Lateran. The cathedral of the Pope in Rome, in which ecclesiastical councils are held. Known as "the mother and head of all churches."

Saint-Just, Louis Antoine Léon de (1767–1794). French revolutionary leader and intimate of ROBESPIERRE. He was active in overthrowing the Girondists and instrumental in bringing on the Reign of Terror. Guillotined together with Robespierre (1794).

St. Leger. A famous English horse-race established by Colonel St. Leger (1776) and second in importance only to the Derby.

St. Louis Blues. See under BLUES.

Saint-Loup, Robert. In Marcel Proust's REMEMBRANCE OF THINGS PAST, the nephew of Baron de CHARLUS and friend of the narrator Marcel. At first he is a morally upright young man, but later, after experience in the army and in aristocratic society, he is unmoved by the most outrageous practices. RACHEL is his mistress; eventually, however, he marries GILBERTE, the daughter of Charles SWANN.

St. Maël. The old Breton monk whom Anatole France in his satire PENGUIN ISLAND portrays as preaching to a congregation of penguins.

Saint-Mihiel. A French town on the Meuse river. In World War I, scene of an American, French, and British offensive (September 12–13, 1918) designed to free the railway lines in that vicinity which the Germans had held since 1914.

St. Nicholas. A monthly magazine for children edited (1873–1905) by Mary Mapes Dodge. Among its contributors were Louisa M. Alcott, Frank R. Stockton, Edward Eggleston, Mark Twain, Kipling, Palmer Cox (the inventor of the Brownies), Howard Pyle, and others.

St. Patrick's Purgatory. See *St. Patrick* under SAINTS.

St. Paul's. Anglican cathedral in London. The original (Gothic) building was destroyed in the Great Fire of 1666. Christopher WREN designed the present St. Paul's (completed in 1701). It has a huge, high dome. Inside are the tombs of Wellington, Nelson and other notables, including the architect. The German bombing of 1940–1941 destroyed the eastern section; the dome was not hurt.

St. Peter's in Rome is the largest church in Christendom. It can accommodate fifty thousand people, and in it most of the important papal functions are held. Donato Bramante laid out the plan in the form of a Greek cross. This was modified but Michelangelo used Bramante's ideas in bringing the plan to completion. The famous dome is Michelangelo's work.

Saint-Pierre, Jacques Henri Bernardin de (1737–1814). French author, a direct follower of J. J. ROUSSEAU, known for his sentimental worship of nature and his doctrine that everything in the universe was created for the special benefit of man. His best-known works are *Études de la Nature* (1784) and PAUL AND VIRGINIA (1788), a novel dealing with Rousseauistic natural education and natural feeling.

St. Pol, Jehane. Heroine of Maurice Hewlett's RICHARD YEA-AND-NAY.

St. Prieux. The *amant* of JULIE, in Rousseau's novel entitled *Julie ou la Nouvelle Héloïse.*

St. Ronan's Well. A novel by Sir Walter SCOTT (1823). The tale is involved, but chiefly concerns Clara Mowbray of St. Ronan's and the two sons of the Earl of Ethrington. One of them is Frank Tyrrel, the son of the Earl's wife, but said to be illegitimate. The other is Valentine, the child of Mrs. Bulmer married in bigamy. Clara is deceived into a private marriage with Valentine, supposing him to be the heir of the title. After it is proved that Frank Tyrrel is not illegitimate, and therefore the true heir, Clara dies, and Valentine is slain in a duel. This novel contains the famous Meg DODS of the Clachan or Mowbray Arms Inn.

saints.

For fictitious names and titles of books beginning with Saint, see under separate entries. See also lists of SAINTS OF SPECIAL COMPETENCIES below. Among the most important saints of Christian tradition are the following:

St. Adrian. The patron saint of the Flemish brewers is represented in art with an anvil and a sword or axe close by it. He had his limbs cut off on a smith's anvil, and was afterwards beheaded.

St. Agatha. A saint who was tortured and martyred in Sicily during the Decian persecution of 251. She is sometimes represented in art with a pair of shears or pincers, and holding a salver on which are her breasts, these having been cut off. The *Veil of St. Agatha* is a miraculous veil belonging to St. Agatha, and deposited in the church of the city of Catania, in Sicily, where the saint suffered martyrdom. It is believed to be a sure defense against the eruptions of Mount Etna.

St. Agnes. A saint martyred in the Diocletian persecution (ca. 303) at the age of 13. She was tied to a stake, but the fire went out, and Aspasius, set to watch the martyrdom, drew his sword, and cut off her head. There is a picture of the incident by Domenichino. St. Agnes is the patron of young virgins. She is commemorated on January 21.

One of KEATS' best known poems is THE EVE OF ST. AGNES.

St. Alexis. Patron saint of hermits and beggars. The story goes that he lived on his father's estate as a hermit till death, but was never recognized. It is given at length in the GESTA ROMANORUM (Tale XV). He is represented in art with a pilgrim's habit and staff. Sometimes he is drawn as if extended on a mat, with a letter in his hand, dying.

St. Ambrose. Bishop of Milan in the 4th century. He is represented in Christian art in the robes of a bishop. His attributes are (1) a *beehive,* in allusion to the legend that a swarm of bees settled on his mouth when he was lying in his cradle; (2) a *scourge,* by which he expelled the Arians from Italy.

St. Andrew. One of the twelve disciples of Jesus; the brother of St. Peter. He is depicted in Christian art as an old man with long white hair and beard, holding the Gospel in his right hand, and leaning on a cross like the letter X, termed St. Andrew's cross. His day is November 30. It is said that he suffered martyrdom in Patrae (70 A. D.).

St. Anne. The mother of the Virgin Mary and wife of St. JOACHIM.

St. Anthony the Great. The patron saint of swineherds. He lived in the 3rd or 4th century, and was the founder of the fraternity of ascetics who lived in the deserts. The story of his temptations by the devil is well known in literature and art. It forms the subject of FLAUBERT's novel, *La Tentation de St. Antoine.* His day is January 17. Not to be confused with *St. Anthony of Padua,* who was a Franciscan of the 13th century, and is commemorated on June 13.

St. Anthony's cross. The tau-cross, T; used as a sacred symbol and in heraldry.

St. Anthony's fire. Erysipelas is so called from the tradition that those who sought the intercession of St. Anthony recovered from the pestilential erysipelas called the *sacred fire,* which proved so fatal in 1089.

St. Anthony's pig. A pet pig, the smallest of the litter, also called the "tantony pig"; in allusion to St. Anthony's being the patron saint of swineherds. The term is also used of a sponger or hanger-on.

St. Augustine (354–430). Bishop of Hippo, and, with St. Ambrose, Jerome, and Gregory the Great, one of the four great Fathers of the Church. Born in Tagaste, Algeria, of a Christian mother and a pagan father, he first sought his salvation in Manichaeism, and led a life of promiscuous pleasure-seeking. He sought to establish himself as a rhetorician first at Tagaste, later at Carthage, Rome and Milan. In Milan, listening to the sermons of Bishop AMBROSE, he was converted to Christianity (386), after which he returned to his hometown. Invited to preach at Hippo Regius, the modern Bona, he so impressed the congregation that he was appointed assistant to the aging bishop, whom he succeeded into the bishopric (395). His most important work, THE CONFESSIONS (397), constitutes the first completely honest self-analysis in the history of literature. See also THE CITY OF GOD (begun 413). His total work is enormous in volume and encyclopedic in scope. He has justly been called the "Christian Aristotle," for it is he who first succeeded in compacting the truths of religion into a system. His theology has been of lasting influence on Christian dogma and philosophy.

St. Augustine (d. 631). First Archbishop of Canterbury; led an expedition of monks to England, landing in Thanet (597). Settled in Canterbury and converted Ethelbert, King of Kent. Pope Gregory gave him authority over the Celtic Churches in Britain. Founded a monastery in Canterbury, and is known as the "Apostle of the English."

St. Barbara. The patron saint of arsenals and powder magazines. Her father delivered her up to Martian, governor of Nicomedia, for being a Christian. After she had been subjected to the most cruel tortures, just as her unnatural father was about to strike off her head, a lightning flash laid him dead at her feet. Hence, St. Barbara is invoked against lightning.

St. Barnabas. A fellow laborer of the Apostle Paul (*Acts* iv. 36–37). According to tradition he was martyred at Salamis. His day is June 11.

St. Bartholomew. One of the twelve disciples of Jesus. The symbol of this saint is a knife, in allusion to the knife with which he was flayed alive. He is commemorated on August 24, and is said to have been martyred in Armenia. See BARTHOLOMEW FAIR.

St. Bernadette of Lourdes. Full name, **Bernadette Soubirous** (1844–1879). French peasant girl, who joined the Sisters of Charity (1866) and took perpetual vows (1878). She claimed to have seen visions of the Virgin Mary who instructed her about the healing powers of the waters at Lourdes, which was subsequently made a shrine. Bernadette is the subject of Franz WERFEL's novel *The Song of Bernadette* (1942), which has been made into a successful motion picture.

St. Bernard of Clairvaux (1091–1153). Great French ecclesiastic, called "Thaumaturgus of the West." Founded the Cistercian monastery of Clairvaux, France, and was its first abbé. Bitterly opposed ABÉLARD's rationalism as heresy. Wrote epistles, sermons, theological treatises. Made Doctor of the Church by Pope Pius VIII. Canonized 1173.

St. Bernard of Menthon (922–1008). Archdeacon of Aorta, who founded the hospices of Great and Little Saint Bernard (ca. 962). He is the patron saint of all mountain climbers.

St. Bernard dog, or *Great St. Bernard.* A large and handsome breed of dog, so called because for many years they have been bred at the Hospice of St. Bernard at the Great St. Bernard Pass, Switzerland, and trained to track travelers lost in the snow.

St. Blaise. Patron saint of wool-combers, because he was torn to pieces with iron wool-combs. He is invoked for diseases of children and cattle.

St. Boniface (680–750). The apostle of Germany, an Anglo-Saxon whose original name was *Winifred* or *Winfrith.* He was made archbishop of Mayence by Pope Gregory III. St. Boniface was murdered in Friesland by some peasants. His day is June 5.

St. Bonaventura. Real name **Giovanni di Fidanza** (1221–1274). Known as "the Seraphic Doctor." Celebrated medieval mystic and writer. General of the Franciscan Order (1257); Bishop of Albano (1273); made a Cardinal. Canonized in 1482, and declared Doctor of the Church in 1587. He appears as a saint in DANTE's *Paradiso.*

St. Brandan or *Brendan.* A semi-legendary Irish saint, said to have died and been buried at Clonfert (at the age of about 94), in 577, where he was abbot over 3,000 monks.

He is best known on account of the very popular medieval story of his voyage in search of the Earthly Paradise, which was supposed to be situated on an island in mid-Atlantic. The voyage lasted for seven years, and the story is crowded with marvelous incidents, the very birds and beasts they encountered being Christians and observing the fasts and festivals of the Church! As late as 1755 St. Brandon's Island, or the Island of San Borandan, was set down in geographical charts as west of the Canary group. According to legend it is the retreat of the Spanish Roderigo or RODERICK and the Portuguese Don Sebastian.

St. Catharine. St. Catharine was a virgin of royal descent in Alexandria (4th century), who publicly confessed the Christian faith at a sacrificial feast appointed by the Emperor Maximinus, a confession for which she was put to death by torture by means of a wheel like that of a chaff-cutter. Hence:

Catharine wheel, a sort of firework; also, a turning head over heels on the hands. Boys in the street, etc., often do so to catch a penny or so from passers-by.

Catharine-wheel window. A wheel-window, sometimes called a rose-window, with radiating divisions.

to braid St. Catharine's tresses. To live a virgin.

St. Cecili, Cecily, or *Cecile.* The heroine of the SECOND NUN'S TALE in Chaucer's CANTERBURY TALES.

St. Cecilia. A Roman lady who underwent martyrdom in the 3rd century. She is the patron saint of the blind, being herself blind; also patroness of musicians, and "inventor of the organ." According to tradition an angel fell in love with her for her musical skill, and used nightly to visit her. Her husband saw the heavenly visitant, who thereupon gave to both a crown of martyrdom which he brought from Paradise. DRYDEN and POPE have written odes in her honor, and both speak of her charming an angel by her musical powers.

St. Christopher. Legend relates that St. Christopher was a giant who one day carried a child over a brook, and said, "Child, thou hast put me in great peril. I can bear no greater burden." To this the child answered, "Marvel thou nothing, for thou hast borne all the world upon thee, and its sins likewise." As Christopher sank beneath his load, the child told the Giant He was Christ, and Christopher resolved to serve Christ and Him only. He died three days afterwards, and was canonized. The Greek and Latin Churches look on him as the protecting saint against floods, fire, and earthquake.

St. Clement. Patron saint of tanners, having himself been a tanner. His day is November 23, and his symbol is an anchor, because he is said to have been martyred by being thrown into the sea with an anchor around his neck.

St. Cosme. Patron of surgeons, born in Arabia. He practiced medicine in Cilicia with his brother St. Damien, and both suffered martyrdom under Diocletian in 303 or 310. Their fête day is December 27. In the 12th century there was a medical society called *Saint Cosme.*

St. Crispin. Crispin and Crispian were two brothers, born at Rome, from which place they traveled to Soissons, in France (ca. 303 A. D.), to propagate the gospel. They worked as shoemakers, so that they might not be chargeable to anyone. The governor of the town ordered them to be beheaded the very year of their arrival, and they were made the tutelary saints of shoemaking. St. Crispin's Day is October 25.

St. Cuthbert. A Scotch monk of the 6th century.

St. Cuthbert's beads. Joints of the articulated stems of encrinites, used for rosaries, so called from the legend that St. Cuthbert sits at night on the rock in Holy Island, forging these "beads." The opposite rock serves him for anvil.

> On a rock of Lindisfarn
> St. Cuthbert sits, and toils to frame
> The sea-born beads that bear his name,
> Sir W. Scott, *Marmion* (1808).

St. Cyprian. Full name **Thascius Caecilius Cyprianus** (ca. 200–258). The first Christian Bishop to suffer martyrdom. Son of a wealthy patrician family, he was converted to Christianity (246), made Bishop of Carthage (248), and there beheaded as a martyr (258). His *Letters* are an important source of information about the early Christian church.

St. David (*fl.* 6th century A. D.). The patron saint of Wales. Legend relates that he was son of Xantus, Prince of Cereticu, now called Cardiganshire; he was brought up a priest, became an ascetic in the Isle of Wight, preached to the Britons, confuted Pelagius, and was preferred to the see of Caerleon or Menevia (i.e., *main aw,* narrow water or firth). Here the saint had received his early education, and when Dyvrig, the archbishop, resigned his see to him, St. David removed the archiepiscopal residence to Menevia, which was henceforth called St. David's. The waters of Bath "owe their warmth and salutary qualities to the benediction of this saint."

St. David's Day, March 1. The leek worn by Welshmen on this day is in memory of a complete victory obtained by them over the Saxons (March 1, 640). This victory is ascribed "to the prayers of St. David," and his judicious adoption of a leek in the cap, that the Britons might readily recognize each other. The Saxons, having no badge, not unfrequently turned their swords against their own supporters.

St. Denys or *Denis.* The apostle to the Gauls and patron saint of France. He is said to have been beheaded at Paris in 272, and, according to tradition, carried his head, after martyrdom, for six miles in his hands and laid it on the spot where stands the cathedral bearing his name. The tale may have taken its rise from an ancient painting of the incident, in which the artist placed the head between the martyr's hands so that the trunk might be recognized.

St. Dominic (1170–1221), who preached with great vehemence against the Albigenses, was called by the Pope "Inquisitor-General," and was canonized by Gregory IX. He is represented with a sparrow at his side, and a dog carrying in its mouth a burning torch. The Devil, it is said, appeared to the saint in the form of a sparrow, and the dog refers to the story that his mother, during her pregnancy, dreamed that she had given birth to a dog, spotted with black and white spots, which lighted the world with a burning torch.

St. Dorothea. A martyr under Diocletian about 303. She is represented with a rose branch in her hand, a wreath of roses on her head, and roses with fruit by her side; sometimes with also an angel carrying a basket with three apples and three roses. The legend is that Theophilus, the judge's secretary, scoffingly said to her, as she was going to execution, "Send me some fruit and roses, Dorothea, when you get to Paradise." Immediately after her execution, while Theophilus was at dinner with a party of companions, a young angel brought to him a basket of apples and roses, saying, "From Dorothea in Paradise," and vanished. Theophilus, of course, was a convert from that moment. The story forms the basis of MASSINGER's tragedy, *The Virgin Martyr* (1622).

St. Dunstan. Archbishop of Canterbury (961), and patron saint of goldsmiths, being himself a noted worker in gold. He is represented in pontifical robes, carrying a pair of pincers in his right hand, the pincers referring to the legend that on one occasion at Glastonbury (his birthplace) he seized the Devil by the nose with a pair of red-hot tongs and refused to release the hateful fiend till he promised never to tempt him again.

St. Dymphna. The tutelar saint of the insane. She is said to have been the daughter of an Irish prince of the 7th century, and was murdered at Gheel, in Belgium, by her own father, because she resisted his incestuous passion. Gheel has long been a center for the treatment of the mentally afflicted.

St. Edmund. See *St. Sebastian* below.

St. Elizabeth of Hungary. Patron saint of queens, being herself a queen. She died in 1231 at the age of 24, and her day is November 19. She gave so bountifully to the poor that she starved her own household. One day her husband met her going out with her apron filled with something heavy, and demanded of her what she was carrying. "Only flowers, my lord," said Elizabeth, and to save the lie God converted the loaves of bread into flowers. She is the heroine of KINGSLEY's dramatic poem *The Saint's Tragedy* (1846).

St. Eloi or *Eligius.* Patron saint of artists and smiths. He was a famous worker in gold and silver, and was made Bishop of Noyon in the reign of Dagobert (6th century). His day is December 1.

St. Eulalie. A virgin martyr born at Barcelona. When she was only twelve the persecution of Diocletian broke out, and she, in the presence of the Roman judge, cast down the idols he had set up. She was martyred February 12, 304, and is the patron saint of Barcelona and of sailors.

Longfellow calls EVANGELINE the "Sunshine of St. Eulalie."

St. Filumena. A saint unknown till 1802, when a grave was discovered in the Catacomb of St. Priscilla on the Salarian Way (leading from Rome to Ancona), with this inscription on tiles: *"lumena paxte cymfi,"* which, being rearranged, makes *Pax tecum Filumena.* Filumena was at once accepted as a saint, and so many wonders were worked by "her" that she has been called *La Thaumaturge du dix-neuvième siècle.* She is commemorated on August 10.

Filomena. Longfellow called Florence Nightingale (1820–1910) *St. Filomena,* not only because Filomena resembles the Latin word for a nightingale, but also because this saint, in Sabatelli's picture, is represented as hovering over a group of sick and maimed, healed by her intercession.

> A Lady with a Lamp shall stand
> In the great history of the land,
> A noble type of good
> Heroic womanhood.
> Nor even shall be wanting here
> The palm, the lily, and the spear,
> The symbols that of yore
> Saint Filomena bore.
> Longfellow, *Santa Filomena.*

St. Florian. Patron saint of Poland. He was martyred by being drowned in the Enns, near Lorch, about 230. He is also the patron of mercers, having been himself of the same craft.

St. Francis. Founder of the Franciscan order (1181?–1226), one of the best loved of all the saints. Poverty was a fundamental principle with St. Francis. He is famed for his love of all living things; the story of his preaching to the birds is particularly well known.

The Wolf of Gubbio by Josephine Preston PEABODY (*Am.,* 1913) is based on the life of St. Francis.

St. Francis' distemper. Impecuniosity; being moneyless. Those of the Order of St. Francis were not allowed to carry any money about them.

St. Francis of Sales. Fr. St. François de Sales (1567–1622). Savoyard noble, bishop of Geneva (1602). Canonized (1665). Patron saint of authors (since 1922).

St. Genevieve (422–512). The sainted patroness of the city of Paris. Her day is January 3, and she is represented in art with the keys of Paris at her girdle, a devil blowing out her candle, and an angel relighting it, or she is shown restoring sight to her blind mother or guarding her father's sheep. She was born at Nanterre, and was influential in averting a threatened attack on Paris by Attila, the Hun.

St. George. The patron saint of England since about the time of the institution of the Order of the Garter (ca. 1348), when he was "adopted" by Edward III. He is commemorated on April 23. St. George had been popular in England from the time of the early Crusades, for he was said to have come to the assistance of the Crusaders at Antioch (1089), and many of the Normans (under Robert, son of William the Conqueror) then took him as their patron.

St. George was probably a Cappadocian who suffered martyrdom under Diocletian in 303. There are various versions of his *Acta,* one saying that he was a tribune and that he was asked to come and subdue a dragon that infested a pond at Silene, Libya, and fed on the dwellers in the neighborhood. St. George came, rescued a princess (Sabra) whom the dragon was about to make its prey, and slew the monster after he had wounded it and the princess had led it home in triumph by her girdle.

That St. George is an historical character is beyond all reasonable doubt; but the somewhat hesitant assertion of GIBBON (*Decline and Fall,* Ch. xxiii) that the patron saint of England was George of Cappadocia, the turbulent Arian bishop of Alexandria, who was torn to pieces by the populace in 360 and revered as a saint by the opponents of Athanasius, has been fully disproved by the Jesuit Papebroch, Milner, and others. He is now believed to have been an official in Diocletian's army, martyred April 23, A. D. 304.

The legend of St. George and the dragon is simply an allegorical expression of the triumph of the Christian hero over evil, which St. John the Divine beheld under the image of a dragon. Similarly, St. Michael, St. Margaret, St. Sylvester, and St. Martha are all depicted as slaying dragons; the Savior and the Virgin as treading them under their feet; St. John the Evangelist as charming a winged dragon from a poisoned chalice given him to drink. BUNYAN avails himself of the same figure when he makes CHRISTIAN prevail against Apolyon.

The legend forms the subject of an old ballad given in Percy's *Reliques*. Spenser introduces St. George into his *Faërie Queene* as the RED CROSS KNIGHT.

St. George was for England, St. Denis was for France. This refers to the war-cries of the two nations—that of England was "St. George!" that of France, "Montjoye St. Denis!"

St. George's cross. Red on a white field.

when St. George goes on horseback, St. Yves goes on foot. In times of war it was supposed that lawyers have nothing to do. St. George is the patron of soldiers, and St. Yves or Yvo, an early French judge and lawyer noted for his incorruptibility and just decrees (d. 1303, canonized 1347), of lawyers.

St. Gertrude. An abbess (d. 664), aunt of Charles Martel's father, Pepin. She founded hospices for pilgrims, and so is a patron saint of travelers, said to harbor souls on the first night of their three days' journey to heaven. She is also the protectress against rats and mice, and is sometimes represented as surrounded by them, or with them running about her distaff as she spins.

St. Giles. Patron saint of cripples. The tradition is that Childeric, king of France, accidentally wounded the hermit in the knee when hunting; and the hermit, that he might better mortify the flesh, refusing to be cured, remained a cripple for life. His day is September 1, and his symbol a hind, in allusion to the "heaven directed hind" which went daily to his cave near the mouth of the Rhone to give him milk. He is sometimes represented as an old man with an arrow in his knee and a hind by his side. Churches dedicated to St. Giles were usually situated in the outskirts of a city, and originally without the walls, cripples and beggars not being permitted to pass the gates.

St. Gudule or *Gudila.* Patron saint of Brussels, daughter of Count Witger, who died 712. She is represented with a lantern, from a tradition that she was one day going to the church at St. Morgelle with a lantern, which went out, but the Holy Virgin lighted it again with her prayers.

St. Helena. Mother of Constantine the Great. She is represented in royal robes, wearing an imperial crown, because she was empress. Sometimes she carries in her hand a model of the Holy Sepulcher, an edifice raised by her in the East; sometimes she bears a large cross, sometimes she also bears the three nails by which the Savior was affixed to the cross. She died about 328, and is commemorated on August 18.

St. Hilda or *Hild* (614–680). English abbess, famous for her wisdom. Founded the monastery at Whitby (657); known also as Abbess of Whiby.

St. Hubert. Patron saint of huntsmen (d. 727). He was the cousin of King Pepin. Hubert was so fond of the chase that he neglected his religious duties for his favorite amusement, till one day a stag bearing a crucifix menaced him with eternal perdition unless he reformed. Upon this warning he entered the cloister and became in time Bishop of Liége and the apostle of Ardennes and Brabant. Those who were descended of his race were supposed to possess the power of curing the bite of mad dogs. In art he is represented as a bishop with a miniature stag resting on the book in his hand, or as a huntsman kneeling to the miraculous crucifix borne by the stag.

St. Ignatius. According to tradition, St. Ignatius was the little child whom Christ set in the midst of His disciples for their example. He was a convert of St. John the Evangelist, was consecrated Bishop of Antioch by St. Peter, and is said to have been thrown to the beasts in the amphitheater by Trajan (ca. 107). He is commemorated on February 1, and is represented in art accompanied by lions, or chained and exposed to them, in allusion to his martyrdom.

St. Ignatius Loyola (1491–1556). The founder of the Society of Jesus (the order of Jesuits). He is depicted in art with the sacred monogram I.H.S. on his breast, or as contemplating it, surrounded by glory in the skies, in allusion to his claim that he had a miraculous knowledge of the mystery of the Trinity vouchsafed to him. He was a son of the Spanish ducal house of Loyola, and after being severely wounded at the siege of Pampeluna (1521) he left the army and dedicated himself to the service of the Virgin. His Order of the Society of Jesus, which he projected in 1534, was confirmed by Paul III in 1540. His *Spiritual Exercises* (*Exercitia;* 1548), a manual of devotions and prayer, is considered a remarkable treatise on applied psychology as an inducement to mystic vision.

St. James. There were two of the twelve disciples of Christ named James.

(1) The Apostle *St. James the Great,* brother of John and son of Zebedee, is the patron saint of Spain. Legend states that after his death in Palestine his body was placed in a boat with sails set, and that next day it reached the Spanish coast; at Padron, near Compostella, they used to show a huge stone as the veritable boat. According to another legend, it was the *relics* of St. James that were miraculously conveyed in Spain in a ship of marble from Jerusalem, where he was a bishop. A knight saw the ship

sailing into port, his horse took fright, and plunged with its rider into the sea. The knight saved himself by "boarding the marble vessel," but his clothes were found to be entirely covered with scallop shells. The saint's body was discovered in 840 by divine revelation to Bishop Theodomirus, and a church was built at Compostella for its shrine. St. James is commemorated on July 25, and is represented in art sometimes with the sword by which he was beheaded and sometimes attired as a pilgrim, with his cloak covered with shells. He is also known as *Santiago,* a variation of St. James (Span. *San Diego*).

(2) *St. James the Less.* His attribute is a fuller's club, in allusion to the instrument by which he was put to death after having been precipitated from the summit of the temple at Jerusalem in 62 A. D. He is commemorated on May 1. *Less* means the shorter of stature.

The Court of St. James's. The British court, to which foreign ambassadors are officially accredited. King George V held drawing-rooms and levées in St. James's Palace, Pall Mall, but Queen Anne, the four Georges, and William IV resided in this palace.

St. Januarius. The patron saint of Naples, a bishop of Benevento who was martyred during the Diocletian persecution, 304. He is commemorated on September 19, and his head and two vials of his blood are preserved in the cathedral at Naples. This congealed blood is said to bubble and liquefy three times a year, on the Saturday before the first Sunday in May, September 19, and December 16; also whenever the head is brought near to the vials.

St. Jerome. (ca. 340–420). A father of the Western Church, and translator of the VULGATE. He is generally represented as an aged man in a cardinal's dress, writing or studying, with a lion seated beside him. Legend has it that while St. Jerome was lecturing one day, a lion entered the schoolroom and lifted up one of its paws. All the disciples fled, but Jerome, seeing that the paw was wounded, drew out of it a thorn and dressed the wound. The lion, out of gratitude, showed a wish to stay with its benefactor. Hence the saint is represented as accompanied by a lion.

St. Joachim. The father of the Virgin Mary. According to legend, he is generally represented as an old man carrying in a basket two turtledoves, in allusion to the offering made for the purification of his daughter. His wife was St. Anne.

St. John, also *St. John the Evangelist* or *the Divine.* One of the twelve, frequently called "the beloved disciple" from his being referred to as "that disciple whom Jesus loved" in the narrative of the *Gospel of St. John* or "Fourth Gospel." He was one of the sons of Zebedee, brother of St. James the Great. His day is December 27, and he is usually represented bearing a chalice from which a serpent issues, in allusion to his driving the poison from a cup presented to him to drink. Tradition says that he took the Virgin Mary to Ephesus after the Crucifixion, that in the persecution of Domitian (96) he was plunged into a cauldron of boiling oil, and was afterwards banished to the isle of Patmos (where he is said to have written the Book of Revelation), but shortly returned to Ephesus, where he died.

St. John of the Cross (*San Juan de la Cruz*). Real name *Juan de Yepis y Álvarez* (1542–1591). Spanish mystic and religious reformer. With St. THERESA, founded the order of the discalced Carmelites, and was imprisoned repeatedly by those Carmelites who opposed the severe reformed rule of the new order. Author of mystical poems, some of which were translated by Arthur SYMONS in *Images of Good and Evil.* Also wrote *The Ascent of Mount Carmel.* Canonized by Pope Benedict XIII (1726).

St. John the Baptist. Patron saint of missionaries, because he was sent "to prepare the way of the Lord." His day is June 24, and he is represented in a coat of sheepskins (in allusion to his life in the desert), either holding a rude wooden cross, with a pennon bearing the words, *Ecce Agnus Dei,* or with a book on which a lamb is seated; or he is shown holding in his right hand a lamb surrounded by a halo, bearing a cross on the right foot. He baptized Jesus in the river Jordan. John the Baptist was a fearless denouncer of the sins of his contemporaries and was thrown into prison, and later beheaded, because he opposed Herod's act of making away with his brother to secure his brother's wife Herodias. For the use of this story in drama and opera, see SALOME.

St. Joseph. Husband of the Virgin Mary, and the reputed father of Jesus. He is the patron saint of carpenters, because he was of that craft. In art, Joseph is represented as an aged man with a budding staff in his hand. His day is March 19.

St. Jude. One of the twelve disciples, also known as Thaddeus. He is represented in art with a club or staff, and a carpenter's square, in allusion to his trade. His day is October 28. According to tradition, he was shot to death by arrows in Armenia.

St. Julian. Patron saint of travelers and of hospitality, looked upon in the Middle Ages as the epicure of saints. Thus, after telling us that the Frankleyn was "Epicurus owne sone," Chaucer says:

> An householdere, and that a greet was he;
> Seint Julian he was in his contree.
> *Canterbury Tales; Prologue,* 339.

In art he is represented as accompanied by a

stag in allusion to his early career as a hunter. He is also shown either receiving the poor and afflicted or ferrying travelers across a river.

St. Kenelm. An English saint, son of Kenwulf, King of Wessex in the early 9th century. He was only seven years old when, by his sister's order, he was murdered at Clente-in-Cowbage, Gloucestershire. The murder, says Roger of Wendover, was miraculously reported at Rome by a white dove, which alighted on the altar of St. Peter's, bearing in its beak a scroll with these words:

> In Clent cow pasture, under a thorn
> Of head bereft, lies Kenelm king-born.

St. Kenelm's day is July 17.

St. Kentigern (ca. 510–601). The patron saint of Glasgow, born of royal parents. He is said to have founded the cathedral at Glasgow, where he died. He is represented with his episcopal cross in one hand, and in the other a salmon and a ring, in allusion to the well-known legend:

> Queen Langoureth had been false to her husband, King Roderich, and had give her lover a ring. The king, aware of the fact, stole upon the knight in sleep, abstracted the ring, threw it into the Clyde, and then asked the queen for it. The queen, in alarm, applied to St. Kentigern, who after praying, went to the Clyde, caught a salmon with the ring in its mouth, handed it to the queen and was thus the means of restoring peace to the royal couple, and of reforming the repentant queen.

The Glasgow arms include the salmon with the ring in its mouth, and also an oak tree, a bell hanging on one of the branches, and a bird at the top of the tree:

> The tree that never grew,
> The bird that never flew,
> The fish that never swam.
> The bell that never rang.

The oak and bell are in allusion to the story that St. Kentigern hung a bell upon an oak to summon the wild natives to worship.

St. Kentigern is also known as "St. Mungo," for *Mungho* (i.e., dearest) was the name by which St. Servan, his first preceptor, called him. His day is January 13.

St. Kevin. An Irish saint of the 6th century, of whom legend relates that, like St. Senanus, he retired to an island where he vowed no woman should ever land. Kathleen tracked him to his retirement, but the saint hurled her from a rock, and her ghost never left the place while he lived. A rock at Glendalough (Wicklow) is shown as the bed of St. Kevin. Moore has a poem on this tradition (*Irish Melodies,* iv).

St. Keyne. A Celtic saint, daughter of Brychan, King of Brecknock in the 5th century. Concerning her well, near Liskeard, Cornwall, it is said that if a bridegroom drinks therefrom before his bride, he will be master of his house, but if the bride gets the first draught, she will rule. SOUTHEY has a ballad, *The Well of St. Keyne* (1798), on this tradition. The man leaves his wife at the porch and runs to the well to get the first draught, but when he returns his wife tells him his labor has been in vain, for she has "taken a bottle to church."

St. Lawrence. The patron saint of curriers, who was broiled to death on a gridiron. He was deacon to Sextus I and was charged with the care of the poor, the orphans, and the widows. In the persecution of Valerian (258), being summoned to deliver up the treasures of the church, he produced the poor, etc., under his charge, and said to the praetor, "These are the church's treasures." He is generally represented as holding a gridiron, and is commemorated on August 10.

The phrase *lazy as Lawrence* is said to take its origin from the story that when being roasted over a slow fire he asked to be turned, "for," said he, "that side is quite done." This expression of Christian fortitude was interpreted by his torturers as evidence of the height of laziness, the martyr being too indolent even to wriggle.

St. Leonard. A Frank at the court of Clovis in the 6th century. He founded the monastery of Noblac, and is the patron saint of prisoners, Clovis having given him permission to release all whom he visited. He is usually represented a deacon, holding chains or broken fetters in his hand.

St. Louis. Louis IX, King of France (b. 1215, reigned 1226–1270).

St. Loyola. See ST. IGNATIUS LOYOLA.

St. Lucia. A virgin martyr, put to death at Syracuse in 304. Her fête-day is December 13. The "thorn" referred to in the phrase *struck on St. Lucia's thorn,* meaning "in torment, perplexed," is in reality the point of a sword, shown in all paintings of the saint, protruding through the neck.

St. Lucy. Patron saint for those afflicted in the eyes. She is supposed to have lived in Syracuse and to have suffered martyrdom there about 303. One legend relates that a nobleman wanted to marry her for the beauty of her eyes, so she tore them out and gave them to him, saying, "Now let me live to God." Hence she is represented in art carrying a palm branch and a platter with two eyes on it. Her day is December 13.

St. Luke. Patron saint of painters and physicians and author of the *Gospel of St. Luke* and the *Acts of the Apostles* in the New Testament. Tradition says he painted a portrait of the Virgin Mary. *Col.* iv. 14. states that he was a physician. His day is October 18. In art he is usually represented with an ox lying near him, and is often shown with painting materials.

as light as St. Luke's bird. Not light at all,

but quite the contrary. St. Luke is generally represented writing, while behind him is an ox, symbolical of sacrifice, St. John the Evangelist, with whom he was generally represented, being accompanied by an eagle. The suggestion of the ox is that St. Luke begins his gospel with the priest sacrificing in the Temple.

St. Margaret. The chosen type of female innocence and meekness, represented as a young woman of great beauty, bearing the martyr's palm and crown, or with the dragon as an attribute. Sometimes she is delineated as coming from the dragon's mouth, for legend says that the monster swallowed her, but on her making the sign of the cross he suffered her to quit his maw. Another legend has it that Olybrius, governor of Antioch, captivated by her beauty, wanted to marry her, and, as she rejected him with scorn, threw her into a dungeon, where the Devil came to her in the form of a dragon. Margaret held up the cross, and the dragon fled.

St. Margaret is the patron saint of the ancient borough of Lynn Regis, and on the corporation seal she is represented as standing on a dragon and wounding it with the cross. The inscription is *"Sub . Margareta . Teritur . Draco . Stat . Cruce . Laeta."* She is commemorated on July 20.

St. Mark. Author of the *Gospel of St. Mark,* the second book of the New Testament. Little is known about his life. He is famed as the patron saint of Venice.

St. Martha. The sister of Lazarus and Mary. When Jesus came to their house, Mary sat at his feet and listened, but Martha "was cumbered about much serving" and complained of her sister to Jesus. She is the patron saint of good housewives and is represented in art in homely costume, bearing at her girdle a bunch of keys and holding a ladle or pot of water in her hand. Like St. Margaret, she is accompanied by a dragon bound, for she is said to have destroyed one that ravaged the neighborhood of Marseilles, but she has not the palm and crown of martyrdom. She is commemorated on July 29, and is patron of Tarascon.

St. Martin. The patron saint of innkeepers and drunkards, usually shown in art as a young mounted soldier dividing his cloak with a beggar. He was born of heathen parents but was converted in Rome, and became Bishop of Tours in 371, dying at Caudes forty years later. His day is November 11, the day of the Roman *Vinalia,* or Feast of Bacchus; hence his purely accidental patronage (as above), and hence also the phrase *Martin drunk.*

The usual illustration of St. Martin is in allusion to the legend that when he was a military tribune stationed at Amiens, he once, in midwinter, divided his cloak with a naked beggar, who craved alms of him before the city gates. At night, the story says, Christ Himself appeared to the soldier, arrayed in this very garment.

Martin drunk. Very intoxicated indeed; a drunken man "sobered" by drinking more. Baxter uses the name as a synonym of a drunkard.

St. Martin's bird. The goose, whose blood was shed "sacrificially" on November 11, in honor of that saint. See below.

St. Martin's heads, jewelry, lace, rings, etc. Cheap, counterfeit articles. When the old collegiate church of St. Martin's le Grand was demolished at the Dissolution of the Monasteries, hucksters established themselves on the site and carried on a considerable trade in artificial jewels, Brummagem ornaments, and cheap ware generally. Hence the use of the saint's name in this connection in Elizabethan and 17th-century writings.

St. Martin's goose. November 11, St. Martin's Day, was at one time the great goose feast of France. The legend is that St. Martin was annoyed by a goose, which he therefore ordered to be killed and served up for dinner. He died from the repast, and the goose was "sacrificed" to him on each anniversary.

St. Martin of Bullions. The St. Swithin of Scotland. His day is July 4, and the saying is that if it rains then, rain may be expected for forty days.

St. Martin's running footman. The Devil, traditionally assigned to St. Martin for such duties on a certain occasion.

St. Mary the Virgin. The mother of Jesus, who was "conceived by the Holy Ghost." Her husband was St. Joseph.

As *the Virgin,* she is represented in art with flowing hair, emblematical of her virginity.

As *Mater Dolorosa,* she is represented as somewhat elderly, clad in mourning, head draped, weeping over the dead body of Christ.

As *Our Lady of Dolours,* she is represented as seated, her breast being pierced with seven swords, emblematic of her seven sorrows.

As *Our Lady of Mercy,* she is represented with arms extended, spreading out her mantle, and gathering sinners beneath it.

As *The glorified Madonna,* she is represented as bearing a crown and scepter, or a ball and cross, dressed in rich robes and surrounded by angels.

Her seven joys. The Annunciation, Visitation, Nativity, Adoration of the Magi, Presentation in the Temple, Finding Christ amongst the Doctors, and the Assumption.

Her seven sorrows. Simeon's Prophecy, the Flight into Egypt, Christ Missed, the Betrayal, the Crucifixion, the Taking Down from the Cross, and the Ascension, when she was left alone.

MAETERLINCK'S *Sister Beatrice* (1901) is a miracle play of the Virgin Mary. *The Miracle,* a spectacular Gest-Geddes-Reinhardt production of 1924 for which the Century Theater in New York was turned into a medieval cathedral, was a dramatic presentation of one of her miracles.

St. Mary Magdalene. Patron saint of penitents, being herself the model penitent of Gospel history. Seven devils were cast out of her by Jesus. In art she is represented either as young and beautiful, with a profusion of hair and holding a box of ointment, or as a penitent, in a sequestered place, reading before a cross or skull. MAETERLINCK has made her the subject of a drama, *Mary Magdalene* (1909).

St. Mathurin. Patron saint in France of idiots and fools. He was a priest of the 3rd century, and was particularly popular in the Middle Ages. His day is November 1.

the malady of St. Mathurin. Folly, stupidity. A French expression.

St. Matthew. Matthew, or Levi, one of the twelve disciples of Jesus, was a publican or collector of tolls paid for goods and passengers coming to Capernaum by the Sea of Galilee. He is the author of the *Gospel of St. Matthew,* the first book of the New Testament. According to tradition Matthew was slain by the sword in Parthia. His day is September 27.

St. Matthias. The apostle chosen by the eleven to supply the place of Judas. He is said to have been first stoned and then beheaded. His day is February 24.

St. Médard. The French "St. Swithin"; his day is June 8.

> Quand il pleut à la Saint-Médard
> Il pleut quarante jours plus tard.

He was Bishop of Noyon and Tournai in the 6th century, and founded the Festival of the Rose at Salency, which was continued even in the 20th century, the most virtuous girl in the parish receiving a crown of roses and a purse of money. Legend says that a sudden shower once fell which wetted everyone to the skin except St. Médard; he remained dry as toast, for an eagle had spread his wings over him, and ever after he was termed *maître de la pluie* (master of the rain).

St. Michael. The great prince of all the angels and leader of the celestial armies.

> And there was war in heaven: Michael and his angels fought against the dragon; and the dragon fought and his angels, and prevailed not.—*Rev.* xii, 7, 8.

> Go, Michael, of celestial armies prince,
> And thou, in military prowess next,
> Gabriel; lead forth to battle these my sons
> Invincible; lead forth my armèd Saints
> By thousands and by millions ranged for fight.
> Milton, *Paradise Lost,* vi, 44.

His day (*St. Michael and All Angels*) is September 29 (see MICHAELMAS), and in the Roman Church he is also commemorated on May 8, in honor of his apparition in 492 to a herdsman of Monte Gargano. In the Middle Ages he was looked on as the presiding spirit of the planet Mercury, and bringer to man of the gift of prudence.

In art St. Michael is depicted as a beautiful young man with severe countenance, winged, and clad in either white garments or armor, bearing a lance and shield, with which he combats a dragon. In the final judgment he is represented with scales, in which he weighs the souls of the risen dead.

St. Nicholas. One of the most popular saints in Christendom, especially in the East. He was the patron saint of Russia, of Aberdeen, of parish clerks, of scholars (who used to be called *clerks*), of pawnbrokers (because of the three bags of gold—transformed to the three gold balls—that he gave to the daughters of a poor man to save them from earning their dowers in a disreputable way), and of little boys (because he once restored to life three little boys who had been cut up and pickled in a salting-tub to serve for bacon). He is invoked by sailors (because he allayed a storm during a voyage to the Holy Land) and against fire. Finally, he is the original of SANTA CLAUS.

Little is known of his life, but he is said to have been Bishop of Myra (Lycia) in the early 4th century. One story relates that he was present at the Council of Nice (325) and there buffeted Arius on the jaw. His day is December 6, and he is represented in episcopal robes with three purses of gold, three gold balls, or three small boys, in allusion to one of the above legends.

St. Olaf. The first Christian king of Norway, slain in battle by his pagan subjects in 1030. He is usually represented in royal attire, bearing the sword or halbert of his martyrdom, and sometimes carrying a loaf of bread, as a rebus on his name, which in Latin is *Holofius* or *Whole-loaf.* According to legend he built the great cathedral at Drontheim.

St. Pancras. One of the patron saints of children, martyred in the Diocletian persecution (304) at Rome at the age of 13. His day is May 12, and he is usually represented as a boy, with a sword in one hand and a palm branch in the other. The first church to be consecrated in England (by St. Augustine, at Canterbury) was dedicated to St. Pancras.

St. Patrick (ca. 373–464). The apostle and patron saint of Ireland (commemorated on March 17) was not an Irishman, but was born at what is now Dumbarton, his father, Calpurnius, a deacon and Roman official, having come from "Bannavem Taberniae," which was probably near the mouth of the Severn. As a boy he was captured in a Pictish raid and sold as a slave in Ireland. He escaped to Gaul about 395, where he studied under St. Martin at Tours before returning to Britain. There he had a supernatural call to preach to the heathen of Ireland, so he was consecrated and in 432 landed at Wicklow. He at first met with strong opposition, but, going north, he converted first the chiefs and people of Ulster, and later those of the rest of Ireland. He founded many churches, including the cathedral and monastery of Armagh, where he held two synods. He is said to have died at Armagh and to have been buried either at Down or Saul. One tradition gives Glastonbury as the place of his death and burial. Downpatrick Cathedral claims his grave.

St. Patrick left his name to numerous places in Great Britain and Ireland, and many legends are told of his miraculous powers—healing the blind, raising the dead, etc. Perhaps the best known tradition is that he cleared Ireland of its vermin.

> The story goes that one old serpent resisted him, but he overcame it by cunning. He made a box, and invited the serpent to enter it. The serpent objected, saying it was too small, but St. Patrick insisted it was quite large enough to be comfortable. After a long contention, the serpent got in to prove it was too small. St. Patrick slammed down the lid and threw the box into the sea.

In commemoration of this, St. Patrick is usually represented banishing the serpents; he is shown with a shamrock leaf, in allusion to the tradition that when explaining the Trinity to the heathen priests on the hill of Tara he used this as a symbol.

St. Patrick's Cross. The same shape as St. Andrew's Cross (X), only different in color, viz. red on a white field.

St. Patrick's Purgatory. A cave in a small island in Lough Derg (between Galway, Clare, and Tipperary). In the Middle Ages it was a favorite resort of pilgrims who believed that it was the entrance to an earthly Purgatory. The legend is that Christ Himself revealed it to St. Patrick and told him that whoever would spend a day and a night therein would witness the torments of Hell and the joys of Heaven. Henry of Saltrey tells how Sir OWAIN visited it, and Fortunatus, of the old legend, was also supposed to be one of the adventurers. It was blocked up by order of the Pope on St. Patrick's Day, 1497, but the interest in it long remained, and the Spanish dramatist CALDERÓN wrote a play on the subject, *El Purgatorio de San Patricio*. See also MARIE DE FRANCE.

St. Paul. The great apostle and missionary of Christianity, author of the principal *Epistles* of the New Testament. As Saul of Tarsus he was originally one of the most bitter persecutors of the early Christians, but he was converted by a vision on the road to Damascus. His great missionary travels, described in the *Acts of the Apostles,* took him "in journeyings often, in peril of rivers, in peril of robbers . . . in perils in the sea, in perils among false brethren." He was finally beheaded at Rome. He is patron saint of preachers and tentmakers (see *Acts* xviii. 3). Originally called Saul, his name, according to tradition, was changed in honor of Sergius Paulus, whom he converted (*Acts* xiii. 6–12).

His symbols are a sword and open book, the former the instrument of his martyrdom, and the latter indicative of the new law propagated by him as the apostle of the Gentiles. He is represented of short stature, with bald head and grey, bushy beard; legend relates that when he was beheaded at Rome (66 A. D.), after having converted one of Nero's favorite concubines, milk instead of blood flowed from his veins. He is commemorated on June 30.

St. Paul the Hermit. The first of the Egyptian hermits. When 113 years old, he was visited by St. Antony, himself over 90. When he died in 341, St. Antony wrapped his body in the cloak given to him by St. Athanasius, and his grave was dug by two lions. His day is January 15, and he is represented as an old man, clothed with palm-leaves and seated under a palm-tree, near which are a river and a loaf of bread.

St. Peter. One of the twelve disciples of Jesus, noted for his impulsive nature. More incidents are related of him in the *Gospels* than of any other disciple. He was first called Simon, but Jesus changed his name and addressed to him the words on which the authority of the Papacy is based "Thou art Peter, and upon this rock (Lat. *petra,* "rock") I will build my church; and the gates of Hades shall not prevail against it; I will give unto thee the keys of the kingdom of Heaven; and whatsoever thou shalt bind on earth shall be bound in heaven; and whatsoever thou shalt loose on earth shall be loosed in Heaven."

At the time of his Master's trial, Peter denied three times that he knew him before the cock crew, as he had been warned that he would. After the crucifixion he became the "Apostle to the Gentiles" and many of his missionary activities are related in the *Acts.* He figures in numerous popular tales as the keeper of the door to Heaven, to whom saints and sinners present themselves for admittance. Peter is the patron saint of fishermen, having been himself a fisherman. His day is June 29, and he is usually represented as an old man, bald, but with a flowing beard, dressed in a white mantle and blue tunic, and holding in his hand a book or scroll. His peculiar symbols are the keys and a sword. Tradition tells that he confuted Simon Magus, who was at Nero's court as a magician, and that in 66 he was crucified with his head downwards at his own request, as he said he was not worthy to suffer the same death as our Lord.

St. Peter's fingers. The fingers of a thief. The allusion is to the fish caught by St. Peter with a piece of money in its mouth. They say that a thief has a fishhook on every finger.

to rob Peter to pay Paul. See ROB.

St. Philip. One of the twelve disciples of Jesus and a missionary of the early church. Tradition has it that he was hanged on a pillar at Hierapolis in Phrygia. His day is May 1.

St. Remigius or *Remy* (438–533). Bishop and confessor, represented as carrying a vessel of holy oil, or in the act of anointing therewith Clovis, who kneels before him. When Clovis presented himself for baptism, Remy said to him, "Sigambrian, henceforward burn what thou hast worshiped, and worship what thou hast burned."

St. Robert. See CISTERCIAN ORDER.

St. Roch or *Roque.* Patron of those afflicted with the plague, because "he worked miracles on the plague-stricken, while he was himself smitten with the same judgment." He is depicted in a pilgrim's habit, lifting his dress to display a plague-spot on his thigh, which an angel is touching that he may cure it. Sometimes he is accompanied by a dog bringing bread in his mouth, in allusion to the legend that a hound brought him bread daily while he was perishing in a forest of pestilence. His feast day, August 16, was formerly celebrated in England as a general harvest-home, and styled "the great August festival."

St. Roch et son chien (St. Roch and his dog). Inseparables, Darby and Joan.

St. Rosalia or *Rosalie.* The patron saint of Palermo, in art depicted in a cave with a cross and skull, or else in the act of receiving a rosary or chaplet of roses from the Virgin. She lived in the 12th century, and is said to have been carried by angels to an inaccessible mountain, where she dwelt for many years in the cleft of a rock, a part of which she wore away with her knees in her devotions. A chapel has been built there, with a marble statue, to commemorate the event.

St. Sebastian. Patron saint of archers, because he was bound to a tree and shot at with arrows. As the arrows stuck in his body, thick as pins in a pincushion, he was also made patron saint of pinmakers. And as he was a centurion, he is patron saint of soldiers.

the English St. Sebastian. St. Edmund, the martyr King of East Anglia (855–870), has been so called. He gave himself up to the Danes in the hope of saving his people, but they scourged him, bound him to a tree, shot arrows at him, and finally cut off his head, which, legend relates, was guarded by a wolf till it was duly interred. The monastery and cathedral of St. Edmundsbury (Bury St. Edmunds) were erected on the place of his burial.

St. Senanus. The saint who fled to the island of Scattery, and resolved that no woman should ever step upon the isle. An angel led St. Canara to the isle, but Senanus refused to admit her. Moore has made this legend the subject of one of his *Irish Melodies, St. Senanus and the Lady* (1814).

St. Severus. Patron saint of fullers, being himself of the same craft.

St. Simeon. Usually depicted as bearing in his arms the infant Jesus, or receiving Him in the Temple. His feast-day is February 18.

St. Simeon Stylites. See STYLITES.

St. Simon (*Zelotes*). One of the twelve disciples of Jesus. He is represented with a saw in his hand, in allusion to the instrument of his martyrdom. He sometimes bears fish in the other hand, in allusion to his occupation as a fishmonger. His feast day is October 28.

St. Stephen. The first Christian martyr—the "protomartyr." He was accused of blasphemy and stoned to death (*Acts* vii. 58). He is commemorated on December 26; the name means "wreath" or "crown" (Gr. *stephanos*).

fed with St. Stephen's bread. Stoned. Of course, the allusion is to the stoning of Stephen.

the Crown of St. Stephen. The crown of Hungary, this St. Stephen being the first king of Hungary (1000–1038). He was a pagan, born at Gran about 969, and was converted to Christianity about 995. During his reign the faith became firmly established in his kingdom. He was canonized by Benedict IX shortly after his death, and is commemorated on September 2.

St. Swithin. If it rains on St. Swithin's day (July 15), *there will be rain for forty days.*

> St. Swithin's day, gif ye do rain, for forty days it will remain;
> St. Swithin's day, an ye be fair, for forty days 'twill rain nae mair.

The legend is that St. Swithin, Bishop of Winchester, who died ca. 862, desired to be buried in the church-*yard* of the minister, that the "sweet rain of heaven might fall upon his grave." At canonization the monks thought to honor the saint by removing his body into the choir, and fixed July 15 for the ceremony, but it rained day after day for forty days, so that the monks saw the saint was averse to their project, and wisely abandoned it.

The St. Swithin of France is St. Gervais and also St. Médard. The rainy saint in Flanders is St. Godelieve.

St. Tammany. See TAMMANY HALL.

St. Teilo. A Welsh saint, who took an active part against the Pelagian heresy. When he died, three cities contended for his body, but happily the multiplication of the dead body into three put an end to the strife.

St. Thecla. The protomartyress of the Eastern martyrologies, as St. Stephen is the protomartyr. All that is known of her is from the *Acts of Paul and Thecla,* pronounced apocryphal by Pope Gelasius. According to the legend she was born of a noble family in Iconium, and was converted by the preaching of St. Paul. Her day is September 23.

St. Theodore. The old patron saint of Venice before St. Mark became the city patron in the 14th century. He was an officer in the Roman army during the reign of Diocletian. After his conversion to Christianity he set fire to the temple of Cybele, and suffered martyrdom for his offense on November 9, 300.

St. Theophilus. A saint of Adana, in Cilicia (6th century). He was driven by slander to sell his soul to the Devil on condition that his character be cleared. The slander was removed, and no tongue wagged against the thin-skinned saint. Theophilus now repented of his bargain, and, after a fast of forty days and forty nights, he was visited by the Virgin, who bade him confess to the bishop. This he did, received absolution, and died within three days of brain fever.

St. Theresa (1515–1582). A Spanish nun who founded a number of convents and monasteries with stricter discipline than the one she had entered. She was famed for her trances and visions. George MOORE has given the name to a modern novel of convent life, a sequel to EVELYN INNES.

St. Thomas. One of the twelve, the disciple of Jesus who doubted (*John* xxi. 25); hence the phrase, *a doubting Thomas,* applied to a skeptic. The story told of him in the Apocryphal *Acts of St. Thomas* is that he was deputed to go as a missionary to India, and, when he refused, Christ appeared and sold him as a slave to an Indian prince who was visiting Jerusalem. He was taken to India, where he baptized the prince and many others, and was finally martyred at Meliapore. His day is December 21.

Another legend has it that Gondoforus, King of the Indies, gave him a large sum of money to build a palace. St. Thomas spent it on the poor, "thus erecting a superb palace in heaven." On account of this he is the patron saint of masons and architects, and his symbol is a builder's square. Still another legend relates that he once saw a huge beam of timber floating on the sea near the coast, and, the king unsuccessfully endeavoring, with men and elephants, to haul it ashore. St. Thomas desired leave to use it in building a church. When his request was granted he dragged it easily ashore with a piece of packthread.

Thomasing. In some rural districts of England the custom still prevails of "Thomasing"—that is, of collecting small sums of money or obtaining drink from the employers of labor on the 21st of December, "St. Thomas's Day."

St. Thomas à Becket. Also *St. Thomas Becket* or *Thomas of London* (1118?–1170). English prelate, archbishop of Canterbury (from 1162) under Henry II against whose lay interference he defended the rights of the Church without compromise. He was forced to flee to France (1164). Papal pressure brought about his reconciliation with the king, but after his return to England (1170), he was murdered in Canterbury Cathedral. Canonized (1172). His shrine was plundered by Henry VIII (1538) and his name erased from the English Church calendar. Chaucer in his CANTERBURY TALES makes a pilgrimage to St. Thomas' shrine the object of the journey he describes. See also MURDER IN THE CATHEDRAL.

St. Thomas à Kempis. Properly *Thomas Hamerken von Kempen* (1380–1471). German ecclesiastic and mystic. Sub-prior of the Augustinian monastery Mt. St. Agnes (1425). He copied many manuscripts, wrote a chronicle of the monastery and original works relating to the secluded life of Christian devotion and benevolence he knew, as well as several biographies and many tracts. He was also most probably the author of the religious classic, *Imitatio Christi.* See IMITATION OF CHRIST.

St. Thomas Aquinas (ca. 1225–1274). Italian scholastic philosopher, known as the Angelic Doctor (*Doctor Angelicus*) and Prince of Scholastics (*Princeps Scholasticorum*). His school companions at Monte Cassino called him the "Dumb Ox." He entered the Dominican order and studied under Albertus Magnus at Cologne where he also began his career as a teacher. He taught (after 1252) at Paris, Rome, Bologna, and elsewhere. Dante, in the Purgatorio, suggests that he was poisoned. His major contribution to the history of human thought is the *Summa Theologiae* which is a systematic survey of catholic theology and assigns to him a rank of honor on a par with Aristotle and Augustine. His philosophy, currently called Thomism, is based on the axiom that knowledge springs from the wells of reason and revelation. See also Jacques MARITAIN; SCHOLASTICISM.

St. Uncumber. Formerly called St. Wilgefortis, a very mystical saint. "Women changed her name" (says Sir Thomas More) "because they reken that for a pecke of oats she will not faile to *uncumber* them of their husbondys." The tradition says that she was one of seven beautiful daughters born to a queen of Portugal. Wishing to lead a single life, she prayed that she might have a beard. The prayer was granted, and she was no more cumbered with lovers; but one of them, a prince of Sicily, was so enraged that he had her crucified.

St. Ursula. Ursula was a legendary Cornish princess, and, as the story says, was going to France with eleven thousand virgins in eleven galleys when they were driven by adverse winds to Cologne, where they were all massacred by the Huns. This extravagant legend is said to have originated in the discovery of an inscription to *Ursula et Undecimilla Virgines,* which could be rendered either "the virgins Ursula and Undecimilla," or "Ursula and her 11,000 (virgins)." *Undecimilla* was probably the name of a handmaid or companion of Ursula. Visitors to Cologne are still shown piles of skulls and human bones heaped in the wall, faced with glass, which the verger asserts are the relics of the 11,000 martyred virgins. The bones exhibited were taken from an old Roman cemetery, across which the wall of Cologne ran, and which was exposed to view after the siege in 1106.

St. Valentine. A priest of Rome who was imprisoned for succoring persecuted Christians. He became a convert himself, and although he restored the sight of his jailer's blind daughter he was martyred by being clubbed to death (February 14, 269).

St. Valentine's day. February 14, the day when, according to every ancient tradition, the birds choose their mates for the year. Chaucer refers to this (*Parliament of Foules,* 309), as also does Shakespeare:

> Good morrow, friends! St. Valentine is past;
> Begin these wood-birds but to couple now?
> *Midsummer Night's Dream,* iv, 1.

It was an old custom in England to draw lots for lovers on this day, the person being drawn being the drawer's *valentine,* and being given a present, sometimes of an expensive kind, but oftener of a pair of gloves. Later it came to be frequently represented by a greeting card of a sentimental, humorous, or merely vulgar character. This custom is said to have had its origin in a pagan practice connected with the worship of Juno on or about this day.

St. Veronica. A late medieval legend says that a maiden handed her handkerchief to our Lord on His way to Calvary. He wiped the sweat from His brow, returned the handkerchief to the owner, and went on. The handkerchief was found to bear a perfect likeness of the Savior, and was called *Vera-Icon* (true likeness); the maiden became *St. Veronica,* and is commemorated on February 4. Milan Cathedral, St. Sylvester's at Rome, and St. Bartholomew's at Genoa all lay claim to the handkerchief.

St. Vincent. A deacon of Saragossa, martyred in the Dacian persecution (304) and commemorated on January 22. He is a patron saint of drunkards, for no apparent reason; an old rhyme says:

> If on St. Vincent's Day the sky is clear
> More wine than water will crown the year.

St. Vitus. A Sicilian youth who was martyred with Modestus, his tutor, and Crescentia, his nurse, during the Diocletian persecution (303). All three are commemorated on June 15.

St. Vitus' dance. In Germany it was believed in the 16th century that good health for a year could be secured by anyone who danced before a statue of St. Vitus on his feast day. This dancing developed almost into a mania, and came to be confused with chorea, which was subsequently known as *St. Vitus' dance,* the saint being invoked against it.

St. Wilfrid. A noble of Northumbria, who became Abbot of Ripon in 661, and in 705 Bishop of Hexham. It was he who at the Synod of Whitby (664) succeeded in substituting the Roman uses and their observation of Easter in England for the Celtic. For many centuries his banner was carried to the wars.

St. Wilfrid's Needle. A narrow passage in the crypt of Ripon cathedral, built by Odo, Archbishop of Canterbury, and said to have been used to try whether young women were virgins or not, none but virgins being able to squeeze through.

St. William of Norwich. The celebrated child said to have been crucified by the Jews in 1137. He is represented as a child crowned with thorns, crucified, holding a hammer and nails in his hands, or wounded in his side with a knife. Cf. Drayton's *Polyolbion,* song xxiv.

St. Winifred. Patron saint of virgins, because she was beheaded by Prince Caradoc for refusing to marry him. She was Welsh by birth, and the legend says that her head falling on the ground originated the famous healing well of St. Winifred in Flintshire. She is usually drawn like St. Denis, carrying her head in her hand. Holywell, in Wales, is St. Winifred's Well, celebrated for its "miraculous" virtues.

St. Wulstan. A Saxon Bishop of Worcester, who received his see from Edward the Confessor, and died in 1075. He fought against William the Conqueror, and when ordered to resign his see, he planted his crozier in the shrine of the Confessor, declaring if any of his accusers could draw it out he would resign. As no one could do so but St. Wulstan himself, his innocence was admitted.

saints of special competencies.

saints for diseases and ills. These saints, who either ward off ills or help to relieve them, are invoked by those who rely on their power:

Ague. St. Pernel and St. Petronella cure.
Bad Dreams. St. Christopher protects from.

Blear Eyes. St. Otilic and St. Clare cure.
Blindness. St. Thomas à Becket cures.
Boils and Blains. St. Roque and St. Cosme cure.
Chastity. St. Susan protects.
Children. St. Germayne. But unless the mothers bring a white loaf and a pot of good ale, Sir Thomas More says, "he wyll not once loke at them."
Children's Diseases (All.) St. Blaise heals; and all cattle diseases.
Colic. St. Erasmus relieves.
Dancing Mania. St. Vitus cures.
Defilement. St. Susan preserves from.
Discovery of Lost Goods. St. Ethelbert and St. Elian.
Diseases Generally. St. Roque, "because he had a sore"; and St. Sebastian, "because he was martered with arrowes."—Sir T. More.
Doubts. St. Catherine resolves.
Dying. St. Barbara relieves.
Epilepsy. St. Valentine cures; St. Cornelius.
Fire. St. Agatha protects from it, but St. Florian is invoked if it has already broken out.
Flood, Fire and Earthquake. St. Christopher saves from.
Gout. St. Wolfgang.
Gripes. St. Erasmus cures.
Idiocy. St. Gildas is the guardian angel of idiots.
Infamy. St. Susan protects from.
Infection. St. Roque protects from.
Leprosy. St. Lazarus the beggar.
Madness. St. Dymphna and St. Fillan cure.
Mice and Rats. St. Gertrude and St. Huldrick ward them off.
Night Alarms. St. Christopher protects from.
Palsy. St. Cornelius.
Plague. St. Roque, they say, in this case is better than the "good bishop of Marseilles."
Quinsy. St. Blaise.
Riches. St. Anne and St. Vincent help those who seek them.
Small-Pox. St. Martin of Tours.
Sore Throats. St. Blaise, who (when he was put to death prayed if any person suffering from a sore throat invoked him, that he might be God's instrument to effect a perfect cure.—Simeon Metaphrastes, *Life of St. Blaise.*
Storms and Tempests. St. Barbara.
Sudden Death. St. Martin saves from.
Tooth-ache. St. Appolonia, because before she was burned alive, all her teeth were pulled out; St. Blaise.
Vermin Destroyers. St. Gertrude and St. Huldrick.

local saints and patrons. The following are the patron saints of the cities, nations, or places set down:

Aberdeen. St. Nicholas.
Abyssinia. St. Frumentius.
Alexandria. St. Mark, who founded the church there.
Antioch. St. Margaret.
Ardennes (The). St. Hubert. He is called "The Apostle of the Ardennes."
Armenia. St. Gregory of Armenia.
Bath. St. David (430–544), from whose benediction the waters of Bath received their warmth and medicinal qualities.
Beauvais. St. Lucian, called "The Apostle of Beauvais."
Belgium. St. Boniface.
Bohemia. St. Wenceslaus; St. John Nepomuk.
Brussels. The Virgin Mary; St. Gudule, who died 712.
Cagliari (in Sardinia). St. Efisio or St. Ephesus.
Cappadocia. St. Matthias.
Carthage. St. Perpetua.
Cologne. St. Ursula.
Corfu. St. Spiridion (4th century).
Cremona. St. Margaret.
Denmark. St. Anscharius and St. Canute.
Dumfries. St. Michael.
Edinburgh. St. Giles.
England. St. George.
Ethiopia. St. Frumentius.
Flanders. St. Peter.
Florence. St. John the Baptist.
Forts. St. Barbara.
France. St. Denys. St. Remy (439–535) is called "The Great Apostle of the French."
Franconia. St. Kilian.
Friesland. St. Wilbrod or Willibrod, called "The Apostle of the Frisians."
Gaul. St. Irenæus and St. Martin. St. Denys is called "The Apostle of the Gauls."
Genoa. St. George of Cappadocia.
Gentiles. St. Paul was "The Apostle of the Gentiles."
Georgia. St. Nino.
Germany. St. Boniface, "Apostle of the Germans," and St. Martin.
Glasgow. St. Mungo, also called Kentigern.
Highlanders. St. Columb.
Hills. St. Barbara.
Holland. The Virgin Mary.
Hungary. St. Louis; Mary of Aquisgrana (*Aix-la-Chapelle*); and St. Anastasius.
Ireland. St. Patrick.
Italy. St. Anthony.
Lapland. St. Nicholas.
Lichfield. St. Chad, who lived there.
Liége. St. Albert.
Lisbon. St. Vincent.
London. St. Paul and St. Michael.
Milan. St. Ambrose, Bishop of Milan.
Moscow. St. Nicholas.
Mountains. St. Barbara.
Naples. St. Januarius and St. Thomas Aquinas.
Netherlands. St. Amand.
North. St. Ansgar and Bernard Gilpin.
Norway. St. Anscharius, called "The Apostle of the North," and St. Olaus, called also St. Ansgar.
Oxford. St. Frideswide.
Padua. St. Justina and St. Anthony.
Paris. St. Genevieve.
Picts. St. Ninian and St. Columb.
Pisa. San Ranieri and St. Efeso.
Poitiers. St. Hilary.
Poland. St. Hedviga and St. Stanislaus.
Portugal. St. Sebastian.
Prussia. St. Andrew and St. Albert.
Rochester. St. Paulinus.
Rome. St. Peter and St. Paul.
Russia. St. Nicholas, St. Andrew, St. George, and the Virgin Mary.
Saragossa. St. Vincent, where he was born.
Sardinia. Mary the Virgin.
Scotland. St. Andrew.
Sicily. St. Agatha, where she was born.
Silesia. St. Hedviga, also called Avoye.
Slavi. St. Cyril, called "The Apostle of the Slavi."
Spain. St. James the Greater.
Sweden. St. Anscharius, St. John, and St. Eric IX.
Switzerland. St. Gall.
United States. St. Tammany.
Valleys. St. Agatha.
Venice. St. Mark, who was buried there; St. Pantaleon and St. Lawrence Justiniani.
Vienna. St. Stephen.
Vineyards. St. Urban.
Wales. St. David.
Yorkshire. St. Paulinus.

specialist saints for tradesmen, children, wives, idiots, students, etc.:

Archers. St. Sebastian, because he was shot by them.
Armorers. St. George of Cappadocia.
Artists and the *Arts.* St. Agatha; but St. Luke is the patron of painters, having been himself one.
Bakers. St. Winifred, who followed the trade.
Barbers. St. Louis.
Barren Women. St. Margaret befriends them.
Beggars. St. Giles. Hence the outskirts of cities are often called "St. Giles."
Bishops, etc. St. Timothy and St. Titus (1 *Tim.* iii. 1; *Titus* i. 7.).
Blacksmiths. St. Peter.
Blind Folk. St. Thomas à Becket, and St. Lucy, who was deprived of her eyes by Paschasius.
Booksellers. St. John Port Latin.
Brewers. St. Florian.
Brides. St. Nicholas, because he threw three stockings, filled with wedding portions, into the chamber window of three virgins, that they might marry their sweethearts, and not live a life of sin for the sake of earning a living.
Brush-Makers. St. Anthony.
Burglars. St. Dismas, the penitent thief.
Candle and Lamp Makers. St. Lucy and St. Lucian.

Cannoneers. St. Barbara, because she is generally represented in a fort or tower.
Captives. St. Barbara and St. Leonard.
Carpenters. St. Joseph, who was a carpenter.
Carpet-Weavers. St. Paul.
Children. St. Felicitas and St. Nicholas. The latter saint restored to life some children who were murdered by an innkeeper of Myra and pickled in a pork-tub.
Cloth-Weavers. St. John.
Cobblers. St. Crispin, who worked at the trade.
Cripples. St. Giles, because he refused to be cured of an accidental lameness, that he might mortify his flesh.
Dancers. St. Vitus.
Divines. St. Thomas Aquinas.
Doctors. St. Cosme, who was a surgeon in Cilicia.
Drunkards. St. Martin, because St. Martin's Day (November 11) happened to be the day of the Vinalia, or feast of Bacchus. St. Urban protects.
Ferrymen. St. Christopher, who was a ferryman.
Fisherman. St. Peter, who was a fisherman.
Fools. St. Mathurin, because the Greek word *matin* or *maté* means "folly."
Freemen. St. John.
Fullers. St. Sever, because the place so called, on the Adour, is or was famous for its tanneries and fulleries.
Goldsmiths. St. Eloy, who was a goldsmith.
Hatters. St. William, the son of a hatter.
Hogs and *Swineherds.* St. Anthony.
Horses. Sir Thomas More says, "St. Ley we make a horse leche, and must let our horse rather renne vnshod and marre his hoofe than to shooe him on his daye."—*Works,* 194. St. Stephen's Day "we must let al our horses bloud with a knife, because St. Stephen was killed with stones."
Housewives. St. Osyth, St. Martha, the sister of Lazarus.
Huntsmen. St. Hubert, who lived in the Ardennes, a famous hunting forest; and St. Eustace.
Idiots. St. Gildas restores them to their right senses.
Infants. St. Felicitas and St. Nicholas.
Insane. St. Dymphna.
Learned Men. St. Catharine, noted for her learning.
Locksmiths. St. Peter, because he holds the keys of heaven.
Madmen. St. Dymphna and St. Fillan.
Maidens. The Virgin Mary.
Mariners. St. Christopher, who was a ferryman; and St. Nicholas, who was once in danger of shipwreck, and who, on one occasion, lulled a tempest for some pilgrims on their way to the Holy Land.
Mercers. St. Florian, the son of a mercer.
Millers. St. Arnold, the son of a miller.
Miners. St. Barbara.
Mothers. The Virgin Mary; St. Margaret, for those who wish to be so.
Musicians. St. Cecilia.
Netmakers. St. James and St. John (*Matt.* iv. 21).
Nurses. St. Agatha.
Painters. St. Luke, who was a painter.
Parish Clerks. St. Nicholas.
Parsons. St. Thomas Aquinas, doctor of theology at Paris.
Physicians. St. Cosme, who was a surgeon; St. Luke (*Col.* iv. 14.
Pilgrims. St. Julian, St. Raphael, St. James of Compostella.
Pinmakers. St. Sebastian, whose body was as full of arrows in his martyrdom as a pincushion is of pins.
Poor Folks. St. Giles, who affected indigence, thinking "poverty and suffering" a service acceptable to God.
Portrait-Painters and *Photographers.* St. Veronica, who had a handkerchief with the face of Jesus photographed on it.
Potters. St. Gore, who was a potter.
Prisoners. St. Sebastian and St. Leonard.
Sages. St. Cosme, St. Damian, and St. Catharine.
Sailors. St. Nicholas and St. Christopher.
Scholars. St. Catharine.
School Children. St. Nicholas and St. Gregory.
Seamen. St. Nicholas, who once was in danger of shipwreck; and St. Christopher, who was a ferryman.
Shepherds and their *Flocks.* St. Windeline, who kept sheep, like David.
Shoemakers. St. Crispin, who made shoes.
Silversmiths. St. Eloy, who worked in gold and silver.
Soothsayers, etc. St. Agabus (*Acts* xxi. 10).
Spectacle-Makers. St. Fridolin.
Sportsmen. St. Hubert.
Statuaries. St. Veronica.
Stonemasons. St. Peter (*John* i. 42).
Students. St. Catharine, noted for her great learning.
Surgeons. St. Cosme, who practiced medicine.
Sweethearts. St. Valentine.
Swineherds and Swine. St. Anthony.
Tailors. St. Goodman, who was a tailor.
Tanners. St. Clement, the son of a tanner.
Tax-Collectors. St. Matthew (*Matt.* ix, 9).
Tentmakers. St. Paul and St. Aquila, who were tentmakers (*Acts* xviii. 3).
Thieves (against). St. Dismas, the penitent thief; St. Ethelbert, St. Elian, St. Vincent, and St. Vinden who caused stolen goods to be restored.
Tinners. St. Pieran, who crossed over the sea to Ireland on a millstone.
Travelers. St. Raphael.
Upholsterers. St. Paul.
Vintners and *Vineyards.* St. Urban.
Virgins. St. Winifred and St. Nicholas.
Weavers. St. Stephen.
Wheelwrights. St. Boniface, the son of a wheelwright.
Wigmakers. St. Louis.
Wise Men. St. Cosme, St. Damian, and St. Catharine.
Woolcombers and *Staplers.* St. Blaise, who was torn to pieces by "combes of yren."

Saint-Saëns, Charles Camille (1835–1921). French organist, pianist, and composer of operas, symphonies, chamber music, choral works, etc. His works include the opera *Samson et Dalila,* and the humorous suite *Le Carnaval des Animaux,* as well as two well-known piano concertos.

Saintsbury, George Edward Bateman (1845–1933). Distinguished English literary critic and writer on the history of English and French literature. Among his works are *Short History of French Literature* (1882); *Essays in English Literature* (1895); *A History of Criticism and Literary Taste in Europe* (1900–1904); *A History of English Prosody* (1906–1921); *The English Novel* (1913); *A History of the French Novel* (1917–1919); *Notes on a Cellar-Book* (1920); and many volumes of essays.

Saint-Simon, Comte de. **Claude Henri de Rouvroy** (1760–1825). French philosopher and social reformer. His social doctrines were developed by his disciples into a system called Saint-Simonianism, which demands that all property be owned by the state, the worker sharing in it according to the amount and quality of his work.

Saint-Simon, Duc de. Louis de Rouvroy (1675–1755). French courtier and author, known for his aristocratic conservativism and for his *Memoirs,* which give a vivid and candid picture of life and personalities at the fashionable court of Louis XIV, to which Saint-Simon was attached for a number of years. He was unsympathetic to the age in which he lived and at court was always preoccupied with questions of etiquette, costume, and ceremony. The *Memoirs* were written during the last thirty years of Saint-Simon's life, which were spent in retirement. The manuscript was published in a degree of completeness only in the romantic period.

St. Valentine's day. February 14. See *St. Valentine* under SAINTS.

St. Vitus Dance. See *St. Vitus* under SAINTS.

Sakhalin. A mountainous island off the coast of Siberia, the northern half belonging to Russia, the southern half to Japan.

Sakhrat. A sacred stone of Mohammedan fable, one grain of which endows the possessor with miraculous powers. It is of an emerald color and its reflection makes the sky blue. See KAF.

Saki, see MUNRO, HECTOR HUGH.

Saktism. A Hindu religious cult, originating about the 5th century A. D., based on the worship of the active producing principle (Prakriti) as manifested in the goddess consort of Siva (Durga, Kali, or Parvati), the female energy, or *Sakti,* of the primordial male. The rites of these worshipers of Sakti are in many cases mere orgies of lust.

Sakuntala. The heroine of Kalidasa's Sanskrit drama *Sakuntala,* translated into English (1789) by Sir William Jones. She is the daughter of a sage, Viswamita, and Menakâ, a water-nymph, and is brought up by a hermit. One day King Dushyanta comes to the hermitage during a hunt, and persuades her to marry him; later, giving her a ring, he returns to his throne. In due course a son is born, and Sakuntala sets out with him to find his father. On the way, while bathing, she loses the ring, and the King does not recognize her, owing to enchantment. Subsequently the ring is found by a fisherman in a fish he has caught, the King recognizes his wife, she is publicly proclaimed his Queen, and Bhârata, his son and heir, becomes the founder of the glorious race of the Bhâratas. The drama had considerable importance in the romantic movement of the early 19th century.

Sakya-Muni. One of the names of Gautama Siddartha, the BUDDHA, founder of Buddhism.

Sakyasinha (*Sansk.,* "the lion"). Epithet applied to Buddha.

Sala, George Augustus Henry (1828–1895). English journalist who contributed for some five years a weekly article or story to *Household Words.* Dickens sent him to Russia as correspondent during the Crimean War. Later he wrote a column for the *Illustrated London News;* for the Sunday *Times;* etc. He established and edited *Temple Bar* (1860) and published in it his best novel, *The Strange Adventures of Captain Dangerous.*

salad days. Days of green youth, while the blood is still cool.

> [*Those were*] my salad days!
> When I was green in judgment, cold in blood.
> Shakespeare, *Antony and Cleopatra,* act i. sc. 5.

Saladin (1137–1193). A famous Saracen sultan, ruler over Syria and Egypt. Scott introduces him in THE TALISMAN, first disguised as Sheerkohf, Emir of Kurdistan, and subsequently as Adonbec el Hakim, the physician. He is the enemy but also the warm friend of RICHARD COEUR DE LION, "as noble adversaries ever love each other." He also appears in Scott's *Betrothed.* In Tasso's Italian epic, JERUSALEM DELIVERED, Saladin figures as Sultan Aladine.

Salamanca, the Bachelor of. See under BACHELOR.

Salamander. A sort of lizard, fabled to live in fire, which, however, it quenches by the chill of its body. Pliny tells us that he tried the experiment once but the creature was soon burnt to a powder. (*Natural History,* x. 67; xxix. 4.)

Salamis. An island off the coast of Greece, famous for the naval victory won by the Greeks over the Persians (480 B. C.) in the bay between it and Attica.

Salammbô. A historical romance by FLAUBERT (1862), treating of the struggle of the city of Carthage against a band of mercenaries who have revolted, under unjust treatment, and stolen the Zaimph, or sacred veil, that guards the safety of the city. Their leader Matho is in love with the Carthaginian maiden Salammbô, daughter of Hamilcar Barca, the famous general of the First Punic War. Urged by patriotic motives, Salammbô enters Matho's tent at night and succeeds in bringing away the Zaimph. The mercenaries are vanquished, Matho is killed in horrible fashion by being forced to run the gauntlet, and Salammbô dies also.

Salandra, Antonio (1853–1931). Prime minister of Italy (1914–1916) at the beginning of World War I; declared war on Austria (1915). Italian defeats forced him to resign (1916). Representative at Paris Peace Conference (1919). Opposed Fascist regime of MUSSOLINI.

Salanio. In Shakespeare's MERCHANT OF VENICE, a friend of Antonio and Bassanio.

Salarino. In Shakespeare's MERCHANT OF VENICE, a friend of Antonio and Bassanio.

Salathiel. One of the names given to the WANDERING JEW. The original Salathiel ben Sadi was a mysterious Jew of 16th century Venice to whom the old legend became attached. The Rev. George Croly gave this name to a romance published in 1829 and republished in 1900 under the title *Tarry Thou Till I Come.*

Salazar y Torres, Agustín de (1642–1675). Spanish poet and playwright, chiefly known for his comedies, especially *Segunda Celestina.*

Salem witchcraft. A hysterical persecution of witches and wizards in Salem, Massachusetts, in 1692. Hundreds of persons were arrested, many were brought to trial, nineteen were hanged and one pressed to death. The subject was successfully dramatized in *Witchcraft or the Martyrs of Salem* by Cornelius Mathews (1817–1889). See also GILES COREY; MATHER, COTTON and INCREASE; SEWALL, SAMUEL; and cf. Charles W. Upham, *Salem Witchcraft;* also *Narratives of the Witchcraft Cases (1648–1706)* in *Original Narratives of Early American History,* edited by J. Franklyn Jameson.

Salic Law. A famous law, established by CLOVIS, limiting succession to the throne, land, etc., to heirs male to the exclusion of females, chiefly because certain military duties were connected with the holding of lands. In the early 14th century it became the fundamental law of the French monarchy, and the claim of Edward III to the French throne, based on his interpretation of the law, resulted in the Hundred Years War. It was, also, through the operation of the Salic Law that the Crowns of Hanover and England were separated when Queen Victoria came to the throne in 1837.

Saliens, the. In ancient Rome, a college of twelve priests of Mars traditionally instituted by Numa. The tale is that a shield fell from heaven, and the nymph Egeria predicted that wherever it was preserved the people would be the dominant people of the earth. To prevent its being surreptitiously taken away, Numa had eleven others made exactly like it, and appointed twelve priests as guardians. Every year these young patricians promenaded the city, singing and dancing, and they finished the day with a most sumptuous banquet, with the result that *saliares coena* became proverbial for a most sumptuous feast. The word *saliens* means dancing.

Salisbury, Earl of. William Longsword, natural son of Henry II, and Jane Clifford, "The Fair Rosamond." He appears in Shakespeare's KING JOHN, and in Scott's TALISMAN.

Salisbury Plain. High ground in Wiltshire, England, site of the group of stones known as STONEHENGE.

Sallust. In full **Gaius Sallustius Crispus** (86–34 B.C.). Roman historian. His *History of the Jugurthine War* and *Conspiracy of Catiline* are extant.

Sally Brass. See under BRASS, SAMPSON.

Sally in our Alley. A famous popular ballad in seven stanzas, by Henry CAREY (1737):

> Of all the girls that are so smart
> There's none like pretty Sally;
> She is the darling of my heart,
> And she lives in our alley.

Sally Lunn. A teacake named after the woman who made and sold them in Bath, England.

Salmagundi. A mixture of minced veal, chicken, or turkey, anchovies or pickled herrings, and onions, all chopped together, and served with lemon-juice and oil. The word appeared in the 17th century; its origin is unknown, but fable has it that it was the name of one of the ladies attached to the suite of Marie de Medici, wife of Henri IV of France, who either invented or popularized the dish.

In 1807–1808 Washington IRVING published a humorous periodical consisting of a series of satires on New York life, known as the *Salmagundi Papers.* J. K. Paulding contributed a few of the papers. Their avowed purpose was "simply to instruct the young, reform the old, correct the town, and castigate the age."

Salmasius, Claudius. Latinized form of *Claude de Saumaise* (1588–1653). French scholar; taught at Leyden at the time of Charles II's exile at The Hague. Charles had him draw up a document in defense of Charles I and against the Regicides. This document, the *Defensio Regia pro Carolo I* (1649), caused John Milton's rebuttal, *Pro Populo Anglicano Defensio* (1650).

Salminen, Sally (1906–). Finnish novelist writing in Swedish. Her first novel, *Katrina* (1936), was based on her experiences while she held a job as general house servant.

Salmoneus. A legendary king of Elis, noted for his arrogance and impiety. He wished to be called a god, and to receive divine honor from his subjects. To imitate JOVE's thunder he used to drive his chariot over a brazen bridge, and darted burning torches on every side to imitate lightning, for which impiety the king of gods and men hurled a thunderbolt at him, and sent him to the infernal regions.

Salome. The daughter of Herodias and Herod Philip. Herodias divorced her husband and married his brother, Herod Antipater, governor of Judea. For his denunciation of this marriage, the prophet John the Baptist was thrown into prison. According to the New Testament narrative, Salome so pleased Herod by her dancing at his birthday feast that he promised her anything to the half of his kingdom. She followed her mother's advice and demanded the head of John the Baptist on a platter. According to medieval legend, Herodias had been in love with John; and in modern treatments of the story, Hermann SUDERMANN in his tragedy, *The Fires of St. John* (1897), and Oscar WILDE in *Salomé* (1894), make Salome also infatuated with the prophet and Herod infatuated with Salome. The opera *Salome* (1905) by Richard STRAUSS is based on Wilde's play. FLAUBERT has a short narrative called *Herodias, the Story of Salomé* (1887).

salt.

the salt of the earth. Properly, the elect; the perfect, or those approaching perfection (see *Matt.* v. 13); now, however, often used of the high and mighty ones, those with great power or even merely great wealth. Also, a man or woman of admirable qualities.

to eat a man's salt. To partake of his hospitality. Among the Arabs, to eat a man's salt was a sacred bond between the host and guest. No one who has eaten of another's salt should speak ill of him or do him an ill turn.

to sit above the salt. In a place of distinction. Formerly the family *saler* (salt cellar) was of massive silver, and placed in the middle of the table. Persons of distinction sat *above* the "saler"—i.e., between it and the head of the table; dependents and inferior guests sat below.

true to his salt. Faithful to his employers. Here salt means salary or interests.

to row up Salt River. To go against the stream, to suffer a political defeat.

There is a small stream called the Salt River in Kentucky, noted for its tortuous course and numerous bars. The phrase is applied to one who has the task of propelling the boat up the stream; but in political slang it is applied to those who are "rowed up." Inman.

Salteena, Mr. The hero of *The Young Visiters,* an imaginative narrative written by the nine-year-old Daisy ASHFORD.

Salten, Felix. Pen name of **Felix Salzmann** (1869–1944). Austrian novelist. Best-known for his charming animal story *Bambi* (1928), which was a best-seller in the U.S., and was made into a feature-length animated cartoon by Walt DISNEY.

Salter, Sir **James Arthur** (1881–). English economist, best known for a book published in America during the depression, *Recovery: The Second Effort* (1932). Held important offices in the League of Nations. Professor at Oxford (since 1934).

Saltonstall, Leverett (1892–). Governor of Massachusetts 1939–1944. Now Senator from Massachusetts.

Saltus, Edgar Evertson (1855–1921). American novelist whose exotic first novel, *Mr. Incoul's Misadventure* (1877), contains astonishing descriptions of a bull fight and of the Paris Opera. Among his other works are *The Peace That Kills* (1889); *Vanity Square* (1906); *The Monster* (1912); etc. His *Imperial Purple* (1892) was a favorite of President Warren G. HARDING.

Salus. In Roman myth, the goddess of health and good fortune. She became identified with the Greek HYGIEIA, the daughter of AESCULAPIUS.

Salvation Army. A religious and charitable organization which grew out of the *Christian Mission* in Whitechapel in London, established by the Methodist evangelist William BOOTH in 1865. The name *Salvation Army,* together with the pseudo- or semi-militaristic setup it implies, was adopted in 1878 and goes back to a chance use of the phrase by Booth in reference to the work of his adherents. For a satirical treatment of the Salvation Army, its officers, its conversions, etc., cf. the play *Major Barbara* (1905) by G. B. SHAW.

Salvation Nell. A drama by Edward SHELDON (1908), starring Mrs. Minnie Maddern FISKE. The scene is laid in the New York slums, and the heroine, Nell Saunders, is a scrubwoman. Her lover, Jim Platt, is involved in a brawl and sent to prison for eight years. Nell resists the temptation to go on the streets and becomes an officer of the Salvation Army. When Jim gets out of prison, he is eager for excitement and crime, but she wins him to a better life.

Salvation Yeo. The name of a character in *Westward Ho!* (1855) by Charles KINGSLEY.

Salvini, Tommaso (1829–1916). Famous Italian tragedian who played the title role in *Othello* with Edwin Booth as Iago (1886).

Sam.

to stand Sam. To pay the reckoning. The phrase is said to be an Americanism, and to have arisen from the letters U.S. on the knapsacks of the soldiers. The government of "Uncle Sam" has to pay, or "stand Sam" for all; hence also the phrase *Nunky pays for all.*

Uncle Sam. The personification of the government, or the people, of the United States—a facetious adaptation of the initials. Fable has it that the inspectors of Elbert Anderson's store on the Hudson were Ebenezer Wilson and his uncle Samuel Wilson, who went by the name of "Uncle Sam." The stores were marked E.A.—U.S. (*Elbert Anderson, United States*), and one of the employers, being asked the meaning, said U.S. stood for "Uncle Sam." The joke took, and in the Revolutionary War the men carried it with them, and it became stereotyped. Another account places the store at Troy, N.Y., and dates the legend from the War of 1812.

upon my Sam or *Sammy.* A humorous form of asseveration; also, *'pon my sacred Sam!*

Sam, Penrod and. See PENROD.

Samael or **Sammael.** The prince of demons in Rabbinical legend, who, in the guise of a serpent, tempted Eve; also called the angel of death.

Samaritan, a good. A philanthropist, one who attends upon the poor to aid them and give them relief (*Luke* x. 30–37).

Samarkand apple. See under APPLE.

Sambo (Span. *zambo,* "bow-legged," from Lat. *scambus*). A pet name given to anyone of Negro race; also, more specifically, applied to the male offspring of a Negro and mulatto. The first Negro character by this name to attain popularity on the American stage was a Sambo in Murdock's *Triumph of Love* (1795).

Little Black Sambo (1900), by Helen Bannerman, is a popular American children's book.

Sambourne, Edward Linley (1844–1910). Famous English illustrator and chief cartoonist of *Punch* (1900–1910). Also illustrator of *Water Babies* (1885) by Charles KINGSLEY.

Sam Hill. A mythical individual of American origin frequently referred to in such phrases as *fight like Sam Hill, swear like Sam Hill.* According to F. J. Wilstach, author of *A Dictionary of Similes,* the expression *what in Sam Hill* occurred at least as early as 1839 (in the Elmira, N.Y., *Republican*) and seems to have been well established in usage at that time. This date excludes a theory that Sam Hill was Sam Hall, the murderous chimney-sweep of an English song popular in 1848–1849. Mr. Wilstach is inclined to derive the fighting, swearing Sam Hill from the demon SAMAEL and to see in references to him a satisfactory Puritan substitute for profanity. A simpler and not therefore necessarily less probable explanation considers the name a playful euphemism for "hell."

Samhin. "Fire of peace." One of the two great festivals observed by the druids, the other being Beltane, "fire of God." Samhin was held on Halloweve.

Samian.

Samian Hera. Hera, wife of Zeus, was born at Samos. She was worshiped in Egypt as well as in Greece.

the Samian letter. The letter **Y**, used by PYTHAGORAS as an emblem of the path of virtue and of vice. Virtue is like the stem of the letter. Once deviated from, the further the lines are extended the wider the divergence becomes.

> When reason, doubtful like the Samian letter,
> Points him two ways, the narrower the better.
> Pope, *The Dunciad,* iv. (1742).

> Et tibi quae Samios diduxit litera ramos.
> Percius, *Satires.*

the Samian Sage. Pythagoras, so called because he was born at Samos.

Samiasa. In Byron's HEAVEN AND EARTH, a seraph, in love with Aholibamah the granddaughter of Cain. When the Flood comes, the seraph carries off his *innamorata* to another planet.

Sammael, see SAMAEL.

Sammy. An American soldier. See SAM.

Sampford ghost, the. A kind of exaggerated "COCK LANE GHOST," or Poltergeist, which haunted Sampford Peverell for about three years in the first decade of the 19th century. Besides the usual knockings, the inmates were beaten; in one instance a powerful "unattached arm" flung a folio Greek Testament from a bed into the middle of a room. The Rev. Charles Caleb Colton (credited as the author of these freaks) offered £100 to anyone who could explain the matter except on supernatural grounds. No one, however, claimed the reward. Colton died in 1832.

samphire. A kind of plant common on the European seacoast. The word is of French origin and is a corruption of *Saint Pierre,* "Saint Peter." Shakespeare used it in a famous passage:

> . . . half-way down
> Hangs one that gathers samphire, dreadful trade!
> *King Lear* IV, vi.

Sämpo. See KALEVALA.

Sampson, Dr. A Scotch physician in Charles Reade's novel HARD CASH.

Sampson, Dominie. One of Scott's most famous characters in GUY MANNERING, tutor to Harry Bertram, son of the laird of Ellangowan. His favorite exclamation is "Prodigious!" Sir Walter describes him as "a poor, modest, humble scholar, who had won his way through the classics, but fallen to the leeward in the voyage of life."

Sampson, William Thomas (1840–1902). American admiral. During the Spanish-American War, commander in chief of the North Atlantic squadron which destroyed the Spanish fleet under Cervera upon its attempt to escape from the harbor of Santiago de Cuba (July 3, 1898). The subsequent controversy as to the credit for the victory involved W. S. SCHLEY.

Sam Slick, see SLICK, SAM.

Samson. In the Old Testament (*Judges* xiii–xvi), a hero whose prodigious strength was dependent upon the fact that his hair had never been cut. He was famed for many remarkable feats by which he routed his enemies, the Philistines. Finally he became infatuated with a Philistine woman named Delilah who wormed out of him his secret and delivered him over to his enemies. His eyes were put out and he was forced to grind meal in the prison-house. When, at the great feast of the Philistine god Dagon, he was brought in to make sport for the people, he prayed to Jehovah so fervently that his strength returned and he was able to pull down the two great pillars that supported the entire edifice. He and all who were present were killed.

MILTON made Samson the hero of his sacred drama *Samson Agonistes* (1671). The opera *Samson et Dalila* by SAINT-SAËNS (1877) also follows the Biblical story.

Samson's crown. An achievement of great renown, which costs the life of the doer thereof.

Samuel. In the Old Testament, a judge and prophet of early Israel. The books 1 and 2 *Samuel* are named after him. He was consecrated to the temple service by his mother HANNAH and as a mere child was communicated with by Jehovah in the night. After a long life as priest and leader, Samuel was forced to yield to the people's demand for a king and established Saul on the throne. He also anointed DAVID as future king.

Samuel, Sir Herbert Louis. 1st Viscount Samuel (1870–). Consistently liberal British politician who became chairman of the Liberal party in 1926. He was home secretary in 1931 but resigned the next year. From 1920 to 1925 he was first high commissioner to Palestine.

Samuel Slick, see SLICK, SAMUEL.

samurai (*Japanese,* "guard"). Title of the feudal warriors of Japan.

Sam Weller, see WELLER, SAM.

San Benito. See SACCO BENEDETTO.

Sanborn, John Pitts (1879–1941). Well-known music editor of the New York *Globe* (1905–1923), the *Evening Mail* (1924) and *World-Telegram* (1931). He edited, with Emil Hilb, *The Metropolitan Book of the Opera* (1937). Author of *Prima Donna—A Novel of the Opera* (1929).

Sancho Panza. The squire of DON QUIXOTE in Cervantes' romance, who becomes governor of Barataria; a short, pot-bellied rustic, full of common sense, but without a grain of "spirituality." He rides upon an ass, Dapple, and is famous for his proverbs. Panza, in Spanish, means *paunch.*

a Sancho Panza. A rough and ready, sharp and humorous justice of the peace. In allusion to Sancho, as judge in the isle of Barataria.

Sancho Panza's wife, called Teresa, Pt. II. i, 5; Maria, Pt. II. iv, 7; Juana, Pt. I. 7; and Joan, Pt. I. 21.

Sanctuary. A novel by William FAULKNER (1931), concerning the experiences of Temple Drake, an Alabama débutante, when she falls into the hands of a gang of BOOTLEGGERS. The girl is horribly raped by Popeye, the degenerate leader of the gang, is sent by him to a brothel in Memphis, and is finally rescued and taken by her father to live abroad, although her mind has been affected by her sufferings. A henchman of Popeye is tried, convicted, and lynched for a murder committed by the leader, and Popeye, in his turn, is eventually executed for a killing for which he has not been responsible.

The novel created a sensation and was dramatized in a modified motion-picture version. The author stated in his preface to the Modern Library edition that he made it deliberately sensational so that it would have a successful sale.

sanctum sanctorum (*Lat.,* "holy of holies"). A private room into which no one uninvited enters; properly the Holy of Holies in the Jewish Temple, a small chamber into which none but the high priest may enter, and that only on the Great Day of Atonement. A man's private house is his sanctuary; his own special private room in that house is the sanctuary of the sanctuary, or the *sanctum sanctorum.*

Sanctus. A passage in the liturgy of the Catholic Church, named from the first word in the Latin text and translated in the Episcopal Book of Common Prayer as "Holy, Holy, Holy, Lord God of Sabaoth." The bell, sounded at the Sanctus by the server at the Mass, is called the Sanctus bell.

Sand, George. Pseudonym of **Amantine Lucile Aurore Dupin** (1804–1876). French novelist, known for her numerous love affairs and her numerous emotional novels. Her work has been divided into three periods: (1) novels of passion, free love, and woman's suffering (1832–1836); (2) socialistic and humanitarian novels (1840–1848); (3) studies of nature and rustic manners (1848–1860). Her books include INDIANA (1832); LÉLIA (1833); *Valentine* (1832); *Mauprat* (1837); CONSUELO (1844); *La Mare au Diable* (1847); *François le Champi* (1846); *La Petite Fadette* (1848); *Nanon* (1872); etc.

Mme Sand, regarded as one of the founders of the social or "problem" novel, was at first unhappily married to the Baron Dudevant and had two children to whom she was sincerely devoted throughout her stormy later career. She was influenced by J. J. ROUSSEAU, traveled abroad, and was for a while interested in the Socialist doctrines of 1848. The most celebrated of her love affairs, on which she is considered to have drawn freely for use in her novels, were with Alfred de MUSSET and Frédéric CHOPIN. Her pseudonym "Sand" is said to have been derived from the name of Jules Sandeau, who helped her on her literary career.

Sandabar or **Sindibad.** Names given to a medieval collection of tales that are very much the same as those in the Greek *Syntipas the Philosopher* and the Arabic *Romance of the Seven Viziers* (known in Western Europe as *The Seven Sages* [*Wise Masters*], and derived from the *Fables of Bidpai.* These names do not, in all probability, stand for the author or compiler, but result from Hebrew mistransliterations of the Arabic equivalent of *Bidpai* or *Pilpay.*

Sandalphon. One of the three angels of Rabbinical legend who receive the prayers of the faithful, and weave them into crowns.

> And he gathers the prayers as he stands,
> And they change into flowers in his hands,
> Into garlands of purple and red.
> Longfellow, *Sandalphon.*

Sandburg, Carl (1878–). American poet and journalist of Swedish ancestry, known for his free-verse poems written under the influence of Walt WHITMAN and celebrating industrial and agricultural America, American geography and landscape, figures in American history, and the American common people, frequently making use of contemporary American slang and colloquialisms. His works, many of which fall into the category of PROLETARIAN LITERATURE, include *In Reckless Ecstasy* (1904); CHICAGO POEMS (1916), which served to establish his reputation; *Cornhuskers* (1918); *Smoke and Steel* (1920); *Slabs of the Sunburnt West* (1922); *Selected Poems* (1926); THE AMERICAN SONGBAG (1927), a collection of folk-ballads; *Good Morning, America* (1928); *Early Moon* (1930); THE PEOPLE, YES (1937); *Rootabaga Stories* (1922), *Rootabaga Pigeons* (1923), *The Rootabaga Country* (1929), and *Potato Face* (1930), all books for children; ABRAHAM LINCOLN, a lengthy biography consisting of *The Prairie Years* (1926; two vols.) and *The War Years* (1939; four vols.), winner of the 1940 Pulitzer prize; *Storm over the Land* (1942), material concerning the Civil War, condensed from the Lincoln biography; and other prose works, such as *The Chicago Race Riots* (1919), *Steichen the Photographer* (1929), and *Mary Lincoln, Wife and Widow* (1932), written with Paul Angle.

Sandburg worked at a variety of odd jobs in his youth, traveled as a hobo to the West, served in the Spanish-American War, worked his way through college, and was an advertising writer, a newspaper reporter, a correspondent in Sweden and Norway, and an editorial writer for the Chicago *Daily News.* Early in his career he evinced Socialist sympathies, and his poetry had an important influence on a number of proletarian poets of the 1930's. His only novel is *Remembrance* (1948).

Sandford and Merton. The schoolboy heroes of Thomas Day's old-fashioned children's tale of this name (published in three parts, 1783–1789). "Master" Tommy Merton is rich, selfish, untruthful, and generally objectionable; Harry Sandford, the farmer's son, is depicted as being the reverse in every respect.

Sandhurst. A parish in Berkshire, England, seat of the Royal Military College which corresponds to Saint-Cyr in France and to West Point in the United States.

sandman. An elf or brownie of folklore who puts wakeful children to sleep at night by throwing sand in their eyes. One of the Andersen fairy tales is called *The Sandman.* See also DUSTMAN.

Sandoz, Mari (1901–). American novelist and biographer. Best known for the study of her father, a remarkable old American pioneer, in *Old Jules* (1935).

Sandra Belloni. A novel by George MEREDITH (1864) relating the adventures of the Italian titular heroine, a musical genius hemmed in and thwarted by her position in a group of thoroughly unsympathetic people. In the sequel *Vittoria* (1866) the heroine leaves her old life and under the name Vittoria wins great renown as a public singer. The action of *Vittoria* takes place during the Revolution of 1848. The earlier novel was first published under the title of *Emilia.*

Sandy Hook. A peninsula with a beacon at its northern tip, which guides vessels into New York Harbor. Fort Hancock is at the end of the peninsula which is also the location of an ordnance proving-ground.

Sandys, Frederick (1829–1904). English artist, associated with the Pre-Raphaelite group. He caricatured Millais and is known especially for his portraits in crayon of Tennyson, Matthew Arnold, Browning, etc.

San Francisco earthquake. An earthquake thought to have been the most severe in the history of the U.S. (April 18, 1906) and affecting a long stretch of the California coast; it wrecked many buildings in San Francisco and started a series of fires which got beyond control. The property loss was estimated at two hundred million dollars and many thousands of people were made homeless.

Sanger. A well-known poem by John REED dealing with an attempt on the part of a peacemaker to interfere in a battle between primitive tribes.

Sanger, Margaret, *née* Higgins (1883–). New York leader of the movement for birth control and author of several books on the subject.

Sanger's Circus. In Margaret KENNEDY's *The Constant Nymph* (1924), Albert Sanger, an eccentric musician, has around him a remarkable family of children both legitimate and illegitimate, all talented, and known collectively as Sanger's Circus. There was a famous English circus proprietor, John Sanger (1816–1889), later known as Lord John Sanger.

Sangster, Margaret Elizabeth (1838–1912). Editor of *Harper's Bazaar* (1889–1899), also a novelist and verse writer. Her granddaughter, of the same name (1894–), has been contributing editor of the *Christian Herald* (from 1913) and is the author of many novels and poems.

Sangraal or **Sancgreal.** See GRAIL, HOLY.

Sangrado, Dr. A name often applied to an ignorant or "fossilized" medical practitioner, from the humbug in Le Sage's GIL BLAS, a tall, meager, pale man, of very solemn appearance, who weighs every word he utters, and gives an emphasis to his sage dicta. "His reasoning was geometrical, and his opinions angular." He prescribes warm water and bleeding for every ailment, for his great theory is that "It is a gross error to suppose that blood is necessary for life." Gil Blas becomes his servant and pupil, and is allowed to drink any quantity of water, but to eat only sparingly of beans, peas, and stewed apples.

> Other physicians make the healing art consist in the knowledge of a thousand different sciences, but I go a shorter way to work, and spare the trouble of studying pharmacy, anatomy, botany, and physic. Know, then, that all which is required is to bleed the patients copiously, and make them drink warm water.—Le Sage, *Gil Blas,* ii. 2.

Sanhedrin or **Sanhedrim** (Gr. *syn,* "together," *hedra,* "a seat," i.e., a sitting together). The supreme council of the Jews, consisting of seventy priests and elders, and a president who, under the Romans, was the high priest. It took its rise soon after the exile from the municipal council of Jerusalem, and was in existence till about 425 A. D., when Theodosius the Younger forbade the Jews to build synagogues. All questions of the "Law" were dogmatically settled by the Sanhedrin, and those who refused obedience were excommunicated.

In Dryden's ABSALOM AND ACHITOPHEL, the *Sanhedrim* stands for the English Parliament:

> The Sanhedrim long time as chief he ruled,
> Their reason guided, and their passion cooled.

Saniette. In Marcel Proust's REMEMBRANCE OF THINGS PAST, a pianist who is the constant butt of practical jokes at the artistic *soirées* held at the home of the VERDURINS.

San Jacinto, Battle of. The battle (April 21, 1836), that decided the independence of Texas. It ended with the defeat and capture by Sam HOUSTON of the Mexican general Santa Anna.

Sankey, Ira David (1840–1908). American evangelist and writer of hymns associated with Dwight L. Moody. The series of *Gospel Hymns* (1875–1891) is his best-known compilation.

Sanscara. The ten essential rites of Hindus of the first three castes: (1) at the conception of a child; (2) at the quickening; (3) at birth; (4) at naming; (5) carrying the child out to see the moon; (6) giving him food to eat; (7) the ceremony of tonsure; (8) investiture with the string; (9) the close of his studies; (10) the ceremony of "marriage," when he is qualified to perform the sacrifices ordained.

sans-culotte (*Fr.,* "without knee breeches," perhaps because they wore trousers instead). A name given by the aristocratic section during the French Revolution to the extremists of the working-classes, the favorite leader of which was Henriot; hence *sansculottism,* the principles, etc., of "red republicans."

Sansfoy, Sansjoy, Sansloy. Three Saracen brothers in Spenser's FAËRIE QUEENE (Bks. I and II), who cared for neither God nor man. The first (Faithless) typifies infidelity and unbelief, and is slain by the Red Cross Knight. The second (Joyless) typifies spiritual misery; he fights the Red Cross Knight but is saved by DUESSA, and carried in the car of Night to the infernal regions, where he is healed of his wounds by Aesculapius. The third (Lawless), having torn off the disguise of ARCHIMAGO and wounded the lion, carries off UNA into the wilderness. Her shrieks arouse the fauns and satyrs, who come to her rescue, and Sansloy flees. The reference is probably to the reign of Queen Mary, when the Reformation was held captive, and the lion was wounded by the "Falselaw of God."

The three were sons of Aveugle (Spiritual Blindness).

Sans Gêne, Madame, see MADAME SANS GÊNE.

Sanson, Charles Henri (1740–1795). Official executioner of Paris. He executed Louis XVI. His son and colleague executed Marie Antoinette.

Sansovino, Andrea. Real name **Andrea Contucci** (1460–1529). Italian sculptor whose works include the tombs of several cardinals. His pupil, **Jacopo Sansovino,** real name **Jacopo Tatti** (1486–1570), became Venetian state architect.

Sans Souci (*Fr.,* "free and easy, void of care"). The name given to the palace built by Frederick the Great near Potsdam (1747).

the Philosopher of Sans-Souci. Frederick the Great (b. 1712, reigned 1740–1786).

Santa Anna, Antonio López de (1795?–1876). President of Mexico (1833–1835) who attempted to crush the Texan Revolution and seized the Alamo (1836) but was defeated and captured at SAN JACINTO by Sam Houston. Later on he was made dictator of Mexico, deposed, recalled, and made provisional president. He commanded an army against the U.S. (1846–1847) and was defeated by General Scott.

Santa Claus or **Santa Klaus.** The patron saint of children and bearer of gifts at Christmas. His name is a corruption of the Dutch form of St. Nicholas. His feast-day is December 6, and the vigil is still held in some places, but for the most part his name is now associated with Christmastide. The old custom used to be for someone, on December 5, to assume the costume of a bishop and distribute small gifts to "good children." The present custom is to put toys and other presents into a stocking late on Christmas Eve, when the children are asleep. When they wake on Christmas morning, they find in the stocking, hung by the mantelpiece, the gifts left by Santa Claus. According to modern tradition Santa Claus lives at the North Pole and comes driving down over the snow in his famous sleigh, driven by eight reindeer. Clement Clarke Moore's familiar poem for children, *A Visit from Saint Nicholas,* better known as *The Night before Christmas,* gives this picture of him:

As I drew in my head and was turning around
Down the chimney St. Nicholas came with a bound.
He was dressed all in fur, from his head to his foot,
And his clothes were all tarnished with ashes and soot;
A bundle of toys he had flung on his back,
And he looked like a pedlar just opening his pack.
His eyes—how they twinkled! his dimples how merry!
His cheeks were like roses, his nose like a cherry!
His droll little mouth was drawn up like a bow
And the beard of his chin was as white as the snow. . . .
He was chubby and plump, a right jolly old elf.
And I laughed when I saw him in spite of myself.

Santa Fé Trail. An early route to Santa Fé, New Mexico, from Independence, Missouri, opened (1821) by William Becknell, who has been called the "Father of the Santa Fé Trail." When the Atchison, Topeka, and Santa Fé Railroad was built (1868), the old trail and its stage line (from 1850) were no longer useful. Its place is now taken by a modern automobile highway.

Santa Fé Trail, The. A humoresque poem by Vachel LINDSAY, especially notable for the sound effects introduced in it.

Santa Sophia. The great metropolitan cathedral of the Orthodox Greek Church at Constantinople. It was built by Justinian (532–537), but since the capture of the city by the Turks (1453) has been used as a mosque. It was not dedicated to a saint named Sophia, but to the "Logos," or Second Person of the Trinity, called *Hagia Sophia* (Sacred Wisdom).

Santayana, George (1863–). Spanish-born American philosopher and author, known for his cosmopolitan viewpoint, his philosophic skepticism and MATERIALISM, his interest in the systems of PLATO and ARISTOTLE, and his fondness for the Greek and Roman classical ideals of beauty. Among his works, written in a style that has been compared to that of Walter PATER, are *The Sense of Beauty* (1896); *The Life of Reason* (1905–1906); *Soliloquies in England* (1922); *Skepticism and Animal Faith* (1923); *Dialogues in Limbo* (1925); *Platonism and the Spiritual Life* (1927); *The Realm of Essence* (1928); *The Realm of Matter* (1930); *The Genteel Tradition at Bay* (1931), a study of the decline of the New England traditions of CALVINISM and TRANSCENDENTALISM; THE LAST PURITAN (1936), a novel; *The Realm of Truth* (1937); *The Realm of Spirit* (1940). Santayana was educated at Harvard University and taught philosophy there for a number of years (1889–1912). He also studied and lived in Germany, France, and England.

Santee, Ross (1889–). American illustrator, chiefly known for his pictures of cowboys, range riders, men and horses, etc. Has written *Cowboy* (1928); *The Pooch* (1931); *Sleepy Black* (1933); etc.

Santiago. St. James, the patron saint of Spain. See under SAINTS.

Sant' Ilario. One of the novels of F. Marion Crawford's SARACINESCA series.

Santos-Dumont, Alberto (1873–1932). Brazilian aeronaut in France whose airship won a prize (1901) for making the first flight from St.-Cloud around the Eiffel Tower and back. He also experimented with an airplane of a box-kite type (1906) and a monoplane (1909).

Santuzza. A peasant girl, the heroine of Mascagni's opera CAVALLERIA RUSTICANA.

Sanutee. Father of Occonestoga in Simms' novel THE YEMASSEE.

Sapho. (1) Title and heroine of a famous novel by Alphonse DAUDET (1884), describing the adventures of a typical French courtesan.

(2) Mlle de SCUDÉRY, the French novelist and poet, went by this name among her own circle. See also SAPPHO.

Sapphics. A four-lined verse-form of classical lyric poetry, named after the Greek poetess Sappho, who employed it, the fourth line being an Adonic. There must be a caesura at the fifth foot of each of the first three lines, which run thus:

— ◡|— —|—||◡ ◡|— ◡|— ◡

The Adonic is—

— ◡ ◡|— ◡ *or* — —

The first and third stanzas of the famous *Ode* of Horace, *Integer Vitae* (i, 22), may be translated thus, preserving the meter:

He of sound life, who ne'er with sinners wendeth,
Needs no Moorish bow, such as malice bendeth,
Nor with poisoned darts life from harm defendeth,
Fuscus believe me.
Once I, unarmed, was in a forest roaming,
Singing love lays, when i' the secret gloaming
Rushed a huge wolf, which though in fury foaming,
Did not aggrieve me.

E. C. B.

Probably the best example of Sapphics in English is Canning's *Needy Knife-Grinder.*

Sapphira. A female liar (*Acts* v. 1). See ANANIAS.

Sappho (*fl.* ca. 600 B.C.). The famous Greek poetess of Lesbos, known as the "tenth Muse." She is fabled to have thrown herself into the sea from the Leucadian promontory because her advances had been rejected by the beautiful youth Phaon.

The subject has frequently been treated in literature, notably in LYLY's comedy *Sappho and Phaon* (1584) and Percy MACKAYE's poetic drama *Sappho and Phaon* (1907). Sara TEASDALE has a poem entitled *Sappho.*

POPE used the name in his *Moral Essays* (II) for Lady Mary Wortley MONTAGU. See also ATOSSA; SAPHO. It has also been given to a number of woman poets of varying powers, among whom are the following:

the English Sappho. Mrs. Mary D. Robinson (1758–1800).

the French Sappho. Mlle Scudéry (1607–1701).

the Scotch Sappho. Catherine Cockburn (1679–1749).

the American Sappho. Mrs. Sarah Wentworth Morton (1759–1846) was so called. Her chief narrative poem was *Ouabi or The Virtues of Nature* (1790).

the Sappho of Toulouse. Clémence Isaure (ca. 1450–1500). She composed an *Ode to Spring.*

Saorstat Eireann. See IRISH FREE STATE.

Saracinesca. A novel by F. Marion CRAWFORD (1887), the first of a series dealing with the life of the Saracinesca family in Rome. The dominating figure of the four novels is old Prince Saracinesca, the head of the house. The first novel centers about the courtship and marriage of his son Giovanni Saracinesca and the noble Corona d'Astrardente; the second, *Sant' Ilario* (1889), treats of the jealousy with which the young husband all but wrecks their marriage. In *Don Orsino* (1892), the hero is their eldest son Orsino, who becomes involved in building schemes, and in *Corleone* (1896), Orsino and his brother Ippolito, a priest, meet with various adventures in their conflict with a gang of Sicilian bandits.

Saragossa, The Maid of. Augustina, a young Spanish girl (d. 1857) noted for her bravery in the defense of Saragossa against the French (1808). She was only twenty-two when she mounted the battery in the place of her lover who had just been shot.

Sarah or **Sarai.** In the Old Testament (*Gen.* xii–xxiii), the wife of ABRAHAM and mother of ISAAC. After Isaac's birth, which occurred in her old age in accordance with Jehovah's promise to make of Abraham a great nation, her name was changed from Sarai to Sarah. See also HAGAR.

Sarajevo. A town in Yugoslavia. Formerly the capital of Bosnia. It was here that in 1914 the Archduke Francis Ferdinand was assassinated, an event which was the immediate cause of World War I. See also PRINCIP, GAVRILO.

Sarasvati. A sacred river in the Punjab, personified by the ancient Hindus as the wife of BRAHMA and goddess of the fine arts. The river loses itself in the sands, but was fabled to become united with the Ganges and Jumna.

Sarazen, Gene (1901–). Professional American championship golfer.

Sardanapalus. The Greek name of Asurbanipal (mentioned in *Ezra* iv. 10, as *Asenappar*), King of Assyria in the 7th century B.C. BYRON, in his poetic drama of this name (1821), makes him a voluptuous tyrant whose effeminacy leads Arbaces, the Mede, to conspire against him. Myrra, his favorite concubine, rouses him to appear at the head of his armies. He wins three successive battles, but is then defeated, and is induced by Myrra to place himself on a funeral pile. She sets fire to it, and, jumping into the flames, perishes with her master.

The name is applied to any luxurious, extravagant, self-willed tyrant.

Sardis, The Great Stone of. A story by Frank R. STOCKTON. Sardis was a city in Asia Minor.

Sardou, Victorien (1831–1908). French playwright. He was the most successful dramatist and master of stage technique of his day, writing comedies and historical dramas, many of the latter for Sarah BERNHARDT (*Tosca, Fédora, Théodora,* etc.), and two plays for Henry IRVING.

Sarett, Lew (1888–). American poet. A guide and forest ranger and later university teacher. His poetry concerns the American Indian. Levinson prize of *Poetry: A Magazine of Verse* (1922) and prize of the Poetry Society of America (1925).

Sarg, Tony (1882–1942). German-born American illustrator and marionette showman. Created "Tony Sarg's Marionettes" (1915). Illustrated *Tony Sarg's Animal Book* (1925); *Tony Sarg's Wonder Zoo* (1927); etc.

Sargasso Sea. A part of the North Atlantic Ocean which derives its name from the great amount of seaweed (gulfweed or Sargassum) floating in it.

Sargent, John Singer (1856–1925). Famous American painter. Chiefly known for his portraits. His mural decorations for the Boston Public Library are well known. In the Metropolitan Museum of Art of New York City are his *Gitana, Hermit, The Wyndham Sisters,* and portraits of W. M. Chase and Henry Marquand.

Sarnoff, David (1891–). Well-known radio executive. President (from 1930), Radio Corporation of America.

Saroyan, William (1908–). American short-story writer, novelist, and playwright of Armenian parentage, known for his impressionistic stories and sketches exalting his own emotions, personal freedom even amid poverty, romantic aspiration, America, kindness and brotherly love, men and women of all types, and life in general. He attracted a wider audience through his plays, which lack conventional dramatic form and plot and deal with the same themes as his sketches, making use of whimsical, fantastic, and sentimental incidents and a variety of picturesque characters. Saroyan's fiction includes *The Daring Young Man on the Flying Trapeze* (1934); *Inhale and Exhale* (1936); *Three Times Three* (1936); *Little Children* (1937); *A Native American* (1938); *The Trouble with Tigers* (1938); *Love, Here Is My Hat* (1938); *Peace, It's Wonderful* (1939); *My Name Is Aram* (1940); *The Adventures of Wesley Jackson* (1946). Among his plays are *My Heart's in the Highlands* (1939); *The Time of Your Life* (1939); *Love's Old Sweet Song* (1940); *The Beautiful People* (1941); *Hello Out There* (1942).

Saroyan attracted particular public notice by the combined naïveté, eccentricity, and outrageous self-confidence of his pronouncements on his own works. *The Time of Your Life* was awarded the Pulitzer prize of 1940, but the author declined it. His reception in other countries, notably France, has been lukewarm.

Sarpedon. In Homer's ILIAD, a favorite of the gods, who assisted Priam when Troy was besieged by the allied Greeks. When ACHILLES refused to fight, Sarpedon made great havoc in battle, but was slain by PATROCLUS.

Sarras. In the Grail legend, the country to which Joseph of Arimathea went from Jerusalem.

sarsen stones. Also **druid stones.** Erosion-resisting blocks of stone on the chalk downs of England; in popular tradition, thought to be remnants of old pagan monuments. The word *sarsen* is a corruption of "Saracen." Cf. John Masefield, *Reynard the Fox:*

> The wind of the downland charmed his bones
> So off he went for the Sarsen Stones.

Sarsfield, Patrick (d. 1693). Irish Jacobite who assisted James II in the reorganization of Irish forces into a Roman Catholic army. He fled with James II to France, returned with him to Ireland, fought at the Battle of the Boyne, and compelled William III to raise the siege of Limerick. He died in action in the service of France.

Sarto, Andrea del. Family name **Vannucchi** (1486–1531). Florentine artist, called "the Faultless Painter," and celebrated for his coloring and his command of chiaroscuro. His frescoes from the life of St. John the Baptist are in Florence, and other examples of his work can be seen in the Pitti Palace, the Uffizi Gallery, the National Gallery in London, etc. Cf. the poem by Robert Browning, *Andrea del Sarto.*

Sartor Resartus. A philosophical satire by Thomas CARLYLE (first published in *Fraser's Magazine,* 1833–1834). This book, the title of which means "The Tailor Re-Tailored," purports to be the author's review of a German work on the philosophy of clothes, written by one Diogenes Teufelsdröckh, an eccentric old professor of Things in General at Weissnichtwo (Know Not Where). Together with philosophic passages supposedly translated from the original German and running comments by the English editor, there is interwoven a narrative of the life of this old German, which is frequently considered to have some autobiographical interest. The inner life is traced in some detail; the external events are few. Teufelsdröckh is left as a baby on the doorstep of Andreas and Gretchen Futteral, simple, kindly farmer folk who bring him up as their own son. Of a restless, sensitive, impressionable temperament, he passes as a young man through one painfully disillusioning experience after another. He attends the University, studies law, falls headlong in love with the Rose Goddess, Blumine, who makes him "immortal with a kiss," but discards him for a more eligible suitor. In his despair at the collapse of his ideals and aspirations he spends years in restless wandering before he comes at last to the steadying conviction that "here, in this poor, miserable, hampered, despicable Actual, wherein thou even now standest, here or nowhere is thy Ideal; work it out therefrom; and working, believe, live, be free."

Sassanides. A powerful Persian dynasty, ruling about 225–641 A. D.; so named because Ardeshir, the founder, was son of Sassan, a lineal descendant of XERXES.

Sassenach. Gaelic or Irish for Saxon; hence English.

Sassoon. Name of a wealthy family of English merchants and financeers of Spanish-Jewish origin, rising to note in India in the 19th century. Sir **Philip Sassoon** (1888–1939), was an art connoisseur, secretary to Sir Douglas Haig during World War I, under-secretary of state for air, etc. The literary member of the family is Siegfried SASSOON.

Sassoon, Siegfried (1886–). English poet of Anglo-Jewish ancestry, known for his lyrics and his poems exposing the horrors of war and satirizing the English upper classes. These volumes include *The Old Huntsman* (1917); COUNTER-ATTACK (1918); *Picture Show* (1920); *Recreations* (1923); *Satirical Poems* (1926); *The Heart's Journey* (1928); *Poems of Pinchbeck Lyre* (1931); *Vigils* (1935); *The World of Youth* (1942). His first book of verse, *Poems,* was published in 1902, and seven others were privately printed between 1911 and 1916. In later years he wrote his autobiography, consisting of *Memoirs of a Fox-Hunting Man* (1928), at first published anonymously, *Memoirs of an Infantry Officer* (1930), and *The Old Century and Seven More Years* (1938). *Sherston's Progress* (1936) is a sequel to the *Infantry Officer* memoirs.

In his youth Sassoon led a pleasant existence in a well-to-do family, interested chiefly in fox-hunting. During World War I he was wounded twice in battle, won the Military Cross and Distinguished Service Cross for bravery, and received the rank of captain; he hated the war bitterly, nevertheless. It is said that once, in disgust, he threw his Military Cross into the sea and refused to go on fighting, but he was considered insane and sent to a sanatorium before being returned to active duty. Sassoon was a friend of Wilfred OWEN and encouraged the latter in his writing.

See also PACIFISM; WAR IN LITERATURE.

Satan. One of the most popular names for the chief of devils. According to the Talmud, Satan was once an archangel but was cast out of heaven. In medieval mythology, he holds the fifth rank of the nine demoniacal orders. Milton, in his PARADISE LOST and *Paradise Regained,* follows the tradition of his expulsion from heaven and makes him monarch of Hell. His chief lords are Beëlzebub, Moloch, Chemos, Thammuz, Dagon, Rimmon and Belial. His standard-bearer is Azazel.

> He [Satan], above the rest
> In shape and gesture proudly eminent,
> Stood like a tower. His form had not yet lost
> All her original brightness; nor appeared
> Less than archangel ruined, and the excess
> Of glory obscured . . . but his face
> Deep scars of thunder had intrenched, and care
> Sat on his faded cheek . . . cruel his eye, but cast
> Signs of remorse.
>
> Milton, *Paradise Lost,* i. 589, etc.

In legendary lore, Satan is drawn with horns and a tail, saucer eyes, and claws; but Milton makes him a proud, selfish, ambitious chief, of gigantic size, beautiful, daring, and commanding. Satan declares his opinion that "'tis better to reign in Hell than serve in Heaven."

Satanic school. A name given to a group of writers in the early part of the 19th century, who were said to show a scorn for all moral rules, and the generally received dogmas of the Christian religion. The most eminent English writers of this school were BULWER LYTTON, BYRON, MOORE, and SHELLEY. Of French writers, the leaders were Paul de KOCK, ROUSSEAU, George SAND, and Victor HUGO. The term was first used by Southey in the preface of his *Vision of Judgment* (1822).

> Immoral writers . . . men of diseased hearts and depraved imaginations, who (forming a system of opinions to suit their own unhappy course of conduct) have rebelled against the holiest ordinances of human society, and hating revelation which they try in vain to disbelieve, labour to make others as miserable as themselves by infecting them with a moral virus that eats into their soul. The school which they have set up may properly be called "The Satanic School."—Southey, *Vision of Judgment* (preface, 1822).

Satanism. Devil-worship. Its origin is obscure as the recesses of the human soul. During the reign of Louis XVI, it was prevalent in France.

Satie, Erik (1865–1925). French ultramodern composer.

Satire, Father of. (Also French, Roman satire.) See under FATHER.

satrap. See RULERS, TITLES OF.

Satsuma. One of the early powerful clans in Japan. *Satsuma ware* is a brand of china.

Saturday Club. A dinner club in Boston, later called *Magazine Club* or *Atlantic Club.* After the foundation of the *Atlantic Monthly* (1857) it included such prominent figures as Emerson, Lowell, Longfellow, Holmes, etc.

Saturday Evening Post, The. An American weekly magazine of fiction and non-fiction, founded in 1821 (not, as it claims, by Benjamin Franklin in 1728). After 1900 it developed into a magazine of tremendous circulation through the adaptation of its contents to the literary standards and general outlook of the average middle-class American reader. Its editorial viewpoint was conservative and sympathetic to the businessman, attacking radicalism and the increase of governmental regulation, and it became the leading medium for advertising of its time. Its standardized short stories in the fields of mystery, adventure, humor, local color, and sentimental romance came to be regarded as typical of 20th-century American commercial fiction. Its greatest editor was GEORGE HORACE LORIMER (1899–1937).

Saturday Review of Literature, The. A weekly journal of book reviews featuring a number of different departments on drama, book publishing, revival of interest in old books, etc. Begun (1920) as an offshoot of the book review of the New York *Evening Post* under the title of *The Literary Review,* its first editor was Henry Seidel CANBY, who made it an independent publication in 1923. Original members of the staff were Amy Loveman, William Rose BENÉT, and Christopher MORLEY. The present editor is Norman COUSINS.

Saturn. A Roman deity, identified with the Greek CRONUS. He devoured all his children except Jupiter (air), Neptune (water), and Pluto (the grave). These Time cannot consume. The reign of Saturn was celebrated by the poets as a Golden Age. According to the old alchemists and astrologers, Saturn typified lead, and was a very evil planet to be born under. "The children of the sayd Saturne shall be great jangeleres and chyders . . . and they will never forgyve tyll they be revenged of theyr quarell." (*Compost of Ptholomeus.*)

Saturn's tree. An alchemist's name for the tree of Diana, or PHILOSOPHER'S TREE.

Saturnalia. A time of unrestrained disorder and misrule. With the Romans it was the festival of Saturn, and was celebrated the 17th, 18th, and 19th of December. During its continuance no public business could be transacted, the law courts were closed, the schools kept holiday, and no war could be commenced and no malefactor punished. Under the empire the festival was extended to seven days.

Satyrane. A blunt but noble knight in Spenser's FAËRIE QUEENE, son of Thyamis (Passion) and a satyr. He typifies natural chivalry, and has been taken as representing Sir John Perrot (d. 1592), Lord Deputy of Ireland, in the political world, and as Martin LUTHER in the religious. His deliverance of UNA from the satyrs (I. vi) has been supposed to mean that Truth, being driven from the cities, takes refuge in caves, where for a time it lies concealed. At length Sir Satyrane (Luther) rescues Una (Truth) from bondage; but no sooner is this the case than she falls in with ARCHIMAGO, showing how very difficult it was at the Reformation to separate Truth from Error.

Satyricon. See PETRONIUS.

Satyrs. In Greek legend, a race of immortal goat-men who dwelt in the woodlands. The most famous satyr was SILENUS.

Saul. In the Old Testament (1 *Sam.* ix-xv), the first King of Israel. He is remembered for his battles against the Philistines (in one of which he and his son Jonathan were finally slain), but even more for his relations with DAVID, whose harp-playing calmed his moods of despair, but whose friendship with Jonathan and general popularity aroused his envy and persecution.

Saul in Dryden's satire of ABSALOM AND ACHITOPHEL, is meant for Oliver Cromwell. As Saul persecuted David and drove him from Jerusalem, so Cromwell persecuted Charles II and drove him from England.

BROWNING has a poem *Saul* in the form of a dramatic monologue, with David as the speaker.

is Saul also among the prophets? An expression of astonishment or skepticism in reference to one who leaves the ranks of one party or cause and aligns himself with another. The allusion is to 1 *Sam.* x. 12.

Saul of Tarsus. See St. Paul under SAINTS.

Saunders, Hilary Aidan St. George. See under BEEDING, FRANCIS.

Saunders, Marshall (1861–1947). Canadian (woman) author of *Beautiful Joe* (1894), one of the world's most famous dog stories.

Saunders, Nell. The heroine of Sheldon's play SALVATION NELL.

Saunders, Richard. Benjamin Franklin's pen name under which he wrote the maxims in *Poor Richard's Almanac* (1732).

Saurat, Denis (1890–). French writer who has contributed to the *New Age* and shown a remarkable grasp of English. A. R. ORAGE wrote a preface to his *The Three Conventions: Metaphysical Dialogues* (1926).

Savage, Augusta Christine. American Negro sculptress, best known for her studies of Negro heads. One of the four women sculptors commissioned to do work for the World's Fair in New York (1939).

Savage, Henry Wilson (1859–1927). American theatrical producer who built the Castle Square Theatre in Boston. He produced *The Girl of the Golden West, The Chocolate Soldier,* etc.

Savage, Philip Henry (1868–1899). A Boston poet mentioned by Richard Hovey in *Songs from Vagabondia* (1894). His *Poems* were published in 1898.

Savage, Richard (1697?–1743). English poet; a friend of Dr. JOHNSON who wrote his biography in *The Lives of the Poets.* Some of his plays were acted in Drury Lane. In one of them, *Sir Thomas Overbury* (1723), he himself played the title rôle. He had an adventurous life and died in prison for debt.

Savage, Richard Ellsworth. In John Dos Passos' U.S.A., the son of a "good" New Jersey family, poor but genteel. Through a benefaction he goes to Harvard and becomes an aesthete; during World War I he serves as an ambulance driver in France and later as an officer in the U.S. army, rising to the rank of captain. He has a love affair with Anne TRENT but refuses to marry her when she becomes pregnant because he fears the marriage would injure his career in the employ of J. Ward MOOREHOUSE. He works with Moorehouse at the Peace Conference in 1919 and later, during the 1920's, becomes prosperous through his association with Moorehouse's public relations agency, eventually succeeding his employer.

saveloy. A kind of dry sausage referred to in English novels. From French *cervelas.*

Savery, William (1721–1787). American cabinet maker, examples of whose furniture are in the Palmer collection of the Metropolitan Museum of Art in New York City.

Savior.

Savior of Rome. C. Marius was so called after the overthrow of the Cimbri, July 30, 101 B.C.

Savior of the Nations. So the Duke of Wellington (1769–1852) was termed after the overthrow of Bonaparte.

Savonarola, Fra **Girolamo** (1452–1498). A famous preacher and reformer of medieval Florence. He is a leading character in George Eliot's ROMOLA, and appears in Harriet Beecher STOWE's *Agnes of Sorrento* (1862).

savory. In England, a course served at the end of dinner, as an anchovy or cheese, etc., but not a sweet.

Savoy, The. A precinct and parish of London between the Strand and the Thames, where once stood the famous Savoy Palace, the London residence of John of Gaunt, where Chaucer, the poet, was married. It was burned by the rebels under Wat Tyler, and rebuilt as a hospital. When Waterloo Bridge was built, the remains of the palace were all swept away. The Savoy Hotel and Theatre (1881) stand near the Strand, and the latter gave its name to the operas of Gilbert and Sullivan which were called the *Savoy Operas.* The Company that produced them was managed by D'Oyly Carte and any member of his company was called a Savoyard.

Savoyard, Vicar. A priest in Rousseau's educational romance EMILE, who remains in the church in spite of his unorthodox views. His "Confessions" are an important part of the book.

sawbuck. American slang for a ten-dollar bill, so called because the X on the bill resembled a sawhorse. The term has been shortened into buck which is used for a dollar bill.

sawdust trail. Western woodsmen, to find their way home, were in the habit of laying trails of sawdust. One of them, at a revivalist meeting of Billy SUNDAY's (who used a layer of sawdust instead of the floor he could not afford) felt reminded of the sawdust trails in the woods and coined the phrase, "they're hitting the sawdust trail," meaning "they come up to repent and confess."

Sawin, Birdofredum. One of the Yankee characters created by James Russell Lowell in his BIGLOW PAPERS.

Sawney. Nickname for Scotchman. The word is a corruption of Sandie which is a contracted form of Alexander.

Sawyer, Bob. In Dickens' PICKWICK PAPERS, a dissipated, struggling young medical practitioner, who tries to establish a practice at Bristol, but without success. Sam WELLER calls him "Mr. Sawbones."

Sawyer, Ruth (1880–). American writer of juveniles. Awarded the Newbery Medal (1937) for her *Roller Skates.*

Sawyer, Tom, see TOM SAWYER.

Saxe, John Godfrey (1816–1887). American wit and author of excellent light and comic verse. For six years he edited the weekly *The Burlington Sentinel* and contributed to the *Knickerbocker Magazine.*

Saxe, Marshal or **Marshal de.** Comte **Hermann Maurice de** (1696–1750). Famous Marshal of France who served under Marlborough and Prince Eugene. He was victor at Fontenoy (1745) and was created Marshal General (1747). He was a natural son of Augustus II of Saxony.

Saxo Grammaticus (*fl.* 13th century). Danish scholar and historian, whose *Gesta Danorum,* a record of the history and deeds of the Danish people, written in Latin, contains an early version of the legend of HAMLET.

Saxon, Lyle (1891–1946). American writer from Louisiana. His best-known books are *Father Mississippi* (1927); *Fabulous New Orleans* (1928); *Old Louisiana* (1929); and *Children of Strangers* (1937).

Sayers, Dorothy Leigh (1893–). Considered one of the leading detective story writers in England. The hero of many of her stories is Lord Peter Wimsey. She has utilized many different settings and her earlier stories display great dexterity and vitality. Her early book of poems, *Catholic Tales* (1919), is a rarity and has much spirit. She has edited three superlative *Omnibuses of Crime.* Her introduction to the first has become a bible for many students of the art she practices.

Sayers, Tom (1826–1865). Famous English pugilist who became champion of England in 1857.

Sayre, Francis Bowes (1885–). American administrator. Married Jessie Woodrow Wilson, a daughter of President Wilson. Assistant secretary of state (1933–1939); high commissioner of the Philippines (1939–1942); deputy director of foreign relief under Herbert Lehman (1942); etc.

Scaevola, Gaius Mucius. According to Roman legend, a youth named Gaius Mucius Scaevola attempted to assassinate Lars Porsena when the latter besieged Rome (509 B.C.). Captured and asked for details of the plot he refused to confess and in order to show that any attempt to force him to talk by torture would be vain, he thrust his right hand into the fire, holding it there until it was completely consumed. Lars Porsena thereupon released him and negotiated peace with Rome.

Scala, della. A noble Italian family who ruled Verona. **Cane Grande della Scala or Can Grande** (1291–1329) was the patron of DANTE while he was in exile from Florence. Cf. Amy Lowell, *Can Grande's Castle.*

Scala, La. An opera house in Milan, inaugurated in 1778. It still is one of the largest in the world.

scalds or skalds. Court poets and chroniclers of the ancient Scandinavians. They resided at court, were attached to the royal suite, and attended the king in all his wars. They also acted as ambassadors between hostile tribes, and their persons were held sacred. These bards celebrated in song the gods, the kings of Norway, and national heroes.

Scaliger, Joseph Justus (1540–1609). The greatest scholar of the Renaissance. He has been called "the founder of historical criticism."

Scaliger, Julius Caesar. Originally **Della Scala** (1484–1558). Italian humanist, philosopher and practicing physician. Among his numerous works are commentaries on Aristotle, Hippocrates, Theophrastes, and others.

Scamander or **Xanthos.** A river near the ancient city of Troy. It figures largely in the accounts of the Trojan War. It is the modern *Mendere.*

Scanderbeg. Turkish **Iskender Bey.** Real name **George Castriota** (1403?–1468). Albanian national hero, known as "the Albanian Alexander." Cf. Longfellow's poem *Scanderbeg.*

Scanlan, Lucy. In James T. Farrell's STUDS LONIGAN, a young Irish-American girl of Chicago, one of the first loves of Studs.

scansion. A term in prosody, denoting the division of lines of poetry into their metrical feet and naming of the meter by analysis of the kind and number of feet. Metrical lines of two, three, four, five and six feet are called dimeter, trimeter, tetrameter, pentameter and hexameter, respectively. The principal varieties of metrical foot are:

Iambus. A short syllable followed by a long, as perceive.

Trochee. A long syllable followed by a short, as number.

Spondee. Two equally accented syllables, as footfall.

Anapest. Two short syllables followed by a long, as colonnade.

Dactyl. A long syllable followed by two shorts, as metrical.

For examples, see under those entries; also under special terms as ALEXANDRINE, BALLAD METER, BLANK VERSE, ELEGIAC STANZA, FEMININE ENDING, FOURTEENER, HEROIC COUPLET AND VERSE, HEXAMETER, OTTAVA RIMA, PENTAMETER, PINDARIC VERSE, RHYME ROYAL, SONNET, SPENSERIAN STANZA, TERZA RIMA.

COLERIDGE wrote the following lines to illustrate for his small son Derwent the principal varieties of metrical feet:

Trochee | trips from | long to | short;
From long to long in solemn sort
Slow Spon | dee stalks; | strong foot, | yet ill | able
Ever to | come up with | Dactyl tri | syllable
Iamb | ics march | from short | to long;
With a leap | and a bound | the swift An | apests
throng.

scapegoat. Part of the ancient ritual among the Hebrews for the Day of Atonement laid down by Mosaic law (see *Lev.* xvi) was as follows: Two goats were brought to the altar of the tabernacle and the high priest cast lots, one for the Lord, and the other for AZAZEL. The Lord's goat was sacrificed; the other was the *scapegoat.* After the high priest, by confession, had transferred his own sins and the sins of the people to it, it was taken to the wilderness and suffered to escape.

the scapegoat of the family. One made to bear the blame of the rest of the family; one always chidden and found fault with, whoever may be in the wrong.

Scapin. A famous character in MOLIÈRE'S comedy *Les Fourberies de Scapin* (1671). He is a clever and intrepid valet whose roguery provides the interest of the drama. As Scapino, this lively rascal had long been one of the stock characters of the Italian stage. In Molière's comedy he is the valet of Léandre, son of Seignior Géronte. Léandre falls in love with Zerbinette, supposed to be a gypsy, but in reality the daughter of Seignior Argante, stolen by the gypsies in early childhood. Her brother Octave falls in love with Hyacinthe, whom he supposes to be Hyacinthe Pandolphe of Tarentum, but turns out to be Hyacinthe Géronte, the sister of Léandre. Now the gypsies demand a large sum as the ransom of Zerbinette, and Octave requires sufficient money for his marriage with Hyacinthe. Scapin obtains both these sums from the fathers under false pretenses. At the end of the comedy he is brought in on a litter, with his head bound as if on the point of death. He begs forgiveness, which he readily obtains; whereupon the "sick man" jumps from the litter to join the banqueters.

OTWAY made an English version of this play, called *The Cheats of Scapin* (1677), in which Léandre is Anglicized into "Leander," Géronte is called "Gripe," and his friend Argante, father of Zerbinette, is called "Thrifty" father of "Lucia."

Scaramuccia (*It.*). French **Scaramouche,** English **Scaramouch.** Literally, "skirmish." A stock character of the Italian COMMEDIA DELL' ARTE. He took the place of the older *Capitan* when the Spaniards lost their influence in Italy and developed into an archetype of boastfulness and cowardice. He was introduced in

France by Tiberio FIORELLI about 1640 and reached England soon after 1670. Rafael SABATINI gave the name *Scaramouche* to a historical romance (1921) dealing with the French Revolution.

Scarborough, Dorothy (1877–1935). American novelist and folk-lorist. Her doctoral dissertation, *The Supernatural in Modern English Fiction* (1917), is still authoritative. Her anonymous novel *The Wind* (1925), with a tragic theme, became a moving-picture vehicle for Lillian GISH. She wrote several books on collecting Southern folk songs. Her course in short-story writing at Columbia was very successful.

Scarborough warning. A warning given too late to be taken advantage of. Fuller says the allusion is to an event which occurred in 1557, when Thomas Stafford seized upon Scarborough Castle, before the townsmen had any notice of his approach.

Scarecrow, The. A "tragedy of the ludicrous" by Percy MACKAYE (1908), based on Hawthorne's *Feathertop,* a tale of a scarecrow brought to life. Goody Rickby and Dickon, "a Yankee improvisation of the Prince of Darkness" are responsible for the scarecrow, who appears as Lord Ravensbane, Marquis of Oxford, Baron of Wittenberg, Elector of Worms, and Count of Cordova. As such, he wins the love of Rachel Merton until she looks in the mirror and to her horror sees only a scarecrow. An impressive silent moving-picture version, called *Puritan Passions,* had in its cast Glenn Hunter (as the Scarecrow), Osgood Perkins and Eliot Cabot.

Scarlatti, Alessandro (1659–1725). Italian composer who is regarded as the founder of modern opera. He left over 100 operas, instrumental pieces and other works. His son, **Domenico Scarlatti** (1683–1757) was an organist and composer, especially known for his sonatas for the harpsichord, many of which are popular in adaptations for the piano.

Scarlet, Scadlock, or **Scathelocke, Will.** One of the companions of Robin Hood.

> "Take thy good bowe in thy hande," said Robyn,
> "Let Moche wend with the [*thee*],
> And so shall Wyllyam Scathelocke,
> And no man abyde with me."
> Ritson, *Robin Hood Ballads,* i. 1 (1520).

> The tinker looking him about,
> Robin his horn did blow;
> Then came unto him little John
> And William Scadlock too.
> *Ibid.,* ii. 7 (1656).

> And there of him they made a
> Good yeoman Robin Hood,
> Scarlet and Little John,
> And Little John, hey ho!
> *Ibid.,* appendix 2 (1790).

Scarlet Letter, The. A novel by Nathaniel HAWTHORNE (1850). The "scarlet letter" is an embroidered A which Hester Prynne is forced to wear on her breast as she stands in the public pillory holding her illegitimate child. Although publicly urged to do so by the young minister, Arthur Dimmesdale, Hester refuses to reveal the name of her companion in sin. She is seen thus, in the pillory, by her husband, Master Prynne, an English physician who sent her on to Boston two years previously and who has just landed. He is a cold, keen-witted overstudious man who urged Hester into her loveless marriage when she was very young. He suspects Dimmesdale, assumes the name of Roger Chillingworth, and becomes the clergyman's physician, taking a diabolical revenge, when his suspicions are confirmed, by subjecting his victim to the most cruel and prolonged mental torments. It is implied that he discovers a "scarlet letter" burned in Dimmesdale's flesh. Hester's pity for Dimmesdale's sufferings and her maternal love for the elfish and wilful little Pearl give her strength; when the minister finally conquers his hypocritical cowardice and mounts the pillory to make public confession, she takes her place by his side. He dies in her arms the same day.

Scarlet Pimpernel, The. A novel of the French Revolution (1905) by Baroness ORCZY, which was dramatized and made into a successful moving picture.

Scarlet Sister Mary. A novel (1928) about the Gullah Negroes by Julia Peterkin. It won the 1929 Pulitzer prize and was made into a play in 1930, featuring Ethel BARRYMORE.

Scarlet Woman or **Scarlet Whore.** The woman seen by St. John in his vision "arrayed in purple and scarlet color," sitting "upon a scarlet colored beast, full of names of blasphemy, having seven heads and ten horns," "drunken with the blood of the saints, and with the blood of the martyrs," upon whose forehead was written, *"Mystery, Babylon the Great, the Mother of Harlots and Abominations of the Earth"* (*Rev.* xvii. 1–6). The author was probably referring to Rome, which, at the time he was writing, was "drunken with the blood of the saints." Some controversial Protestants have applied the words to the Church of Rome, and some Roman Catholics, to the Protestant churches generally.

Scarlett, Sylvia. The heroine of Compton Mackenzie's *Sylvia Scarlett* and *Sylvia and Michael.* See SINISTER STREET.

Scarlett O'Hara, see O'HARA, SCARLETT.

Scarpia, Baron. A leading character, Chief of Police, in Puccini's opera LA TOSCA.

Scarron, Paul (1610–1660). French novelist, known for his realism and satire, notably evinced in *Le Roman Comique* (1651), a fictional account of the adventures of a company of wandering comedy-players, believed by some scholars to have been based on the troupe headed by MOLIÈRE. This work has been praised for its vigorous, swiftly moving narrative and its lifelike characterizations. Scarron, deformed in body, was notorious in his day for his loose morals. His wife, Françoise d'Aubigné, later became Mme de Maintenon, one of the most influential women in the history of France.

Scenes of Clerical Life. Three stories by George Eliot (1857). They are (1) *The Sad Fortunes of the Reverend Amos Barton* (see Amos Barton); (2) Mr. Gilfil's Love Story; (3) Janet's Repentance.

Schacabac. In the Arabian Nights, "the hare-lipped," a man reduced to the point of starvation, invited to a feast by the rich Barmecide.

Schacht, Horace Greeley Hjalmar (1877–). Well-known German financier. President of the Reichsbank (1923–1930; 1933–1939). He took part in the Dawes Committee discussions and the Reparations Commission's deliberations and acted as minister of national economy (1934–1937). Under Hitler, he earned the nickname of "the financial wizard of the Third Reich."

Schaff, Morris (1840–1929). American army officer who wrote *Spirit of Old West Point* (1907); *Sunset of the Confederacy* (1912); etc.

Schahriah. In the Arabian Nights, the Sultan for whose pleasure the tales are told. Since his own wife proves unfaithful, and his brother's wife too, Schahriah imagines that no woman is virtuous. He resolves, therefore, to marry a fresh wife every night, and to have her strangled at daybreak. Scheherazade, the Vizier's daughter, marries him in spite of his vow, and contrives, an hour before daybreak, to begin a story to her sister in the Sultan's hearing, always breaking off before the story is finished. The Sultan gets interested in these tales, and, after a thousand and one nights, revokes his decree, bestows on Scheherazade his affection, and calls her the "liberator of her sex."

Schauffler, Robert Haven (1879–). American poet and musical biographer. His best-known poem, which deals with American immigrants, has the ironical title *Scum o' the Earth* (1912). He has written essays and lives of Brahms and Beethoven, and has edited *The Poetry Cure* (1927), an original kind of anthology, with music and pictures. His second wife (now divorced) was the writer Margaret Widdemer.

Scheff, Fritzi (1882?–). Viennese actress and singer. She joined the Metropolitan Opera Company in New York (1902) and became extremely popular in comic opera (1903–1913) and vaudeville. In the early 1930's she sang in New York in revivals of several operettas by Victor Herbert.

Scheherazade. The mouthpiece of the tales related in the Arabian Nights, daughter of the Grand Vizier of the Indies and wife of the Sultan Schahriah. Also title of a famous orchestral suite by Rimsky-Korsakov, and a Fokine ballet which is danced to its music.

Scheidemann, Philipp (1865–1939). German printer who became a political leader. After Kaiser Wilhelm had fled to Holland (1918), Scheidemann proclaimed the German Republic and was elected its first prime minister. He resigned when the National Assembly accepted the Treaty of Versailles (1919). Upon the rise of the Nazi Party, he went into exile and died in Denmark.

Schelhorn's Bible. See Bible, specially named.

Schelling, Ernest Henry (1876–1939). Well-known American composer, pianist, and conductor, brother of Felix Emanuel Schelling. Conductor of the Young People's Symphony concerts in New York (from 1922) and other cities; conductor, Baltimore Symphony Orchestra (1936–1938). Best-known composition, *A Victory Ball*, for piano and orchestra, suggested by a post-World War I poem by Alfred Noyes.

Schelling, Felix Emanuel (1858–1945). John Welsh Centennial Professor of English Literature at the University of Pennsylvania from 1893 until 1929, when a chair was founded in his name. Authority on Elizabethan literature and the Tudor period. He wrote criticism and edited many of the plays of Shakespeare as well as other Elizabethan dramas and poetry.

Schelling, Friedrich Wilhelm Joseph von (1775–1854). German philosopher of the era of romanticism. His philosophy is essentially an attempt to break the limitations of human cognition as formulated in Kant's criticism by faith in the power of "intellectual intuition."

Scherman, Harry (1887–). Originator of the Book-of-the-Month Club and its head. Also a writer on economic subjects, notably *The Promises Men Live By* (1938).

Schiaparelli, Elsa. Well-known French dress designer, who established a salon in Paris about 1927 and came to the U.S. in 1939.

Schiaparelli, Giovanni Virginio (1835–1901). Italian astronomer and director of the Milan observatory. He made important discoveries concerning comets, falling stars, etc., and introduced the term "canal" for the markings on Mars (1877).

Schickele, René (1883–1940). Alsatian novelist, poet, and playwright of French-German parentage writing in German. His play, *Hans im Schnakenloch* (*Hans in the Mosquito Hole;* 1914), when performed in 1916, was suppressed in Germany because of its pacifist trend and in France because it was considered "a piece of German war propaganda." Outstanding among his works is the trilogy *Das Erbe am Rhein.* The *leitmotiv* of all his novels is the tragic plight of a European for whom the war of nations spells fratricide.

Schicklgruber, see HITLER, ADOLF.

Schieffelin, Dr. **William Jay** (1866–). American chemist. A philanthropist who has worked actively for Negro education for a half-century. Trustee at Hampton Institute (from 1896); chairman of the board of trustees of Tuskegee Institute, Alabama (until 1946); etc. Also associated with civic activities in New York, The Citizens' Union, etc.

Schilda. The German GOTHAM, a city which acquired such a reputation for wisdom that the inhabitants (*Schildbürger*) were forced to pretend to be fools in order to be left in peace. The legends concerning their folly were collected in *The History of the Schildburgers* (16th century). One of their characteristic acts was to build a house without windows and try to carry sunlight in.

Schildkraut, Rudolph (1862–1930). German actor, associated also with moving pictures in Hollywood. His son, **Joseph Schildkraut** (1896–), is well known for his acting the title role of *Liliom* and playing in *Peer Gynt* and in Eva Le Gallienne's Repertory Theatre, also as a film actor.

Schiller, Johann Christoph Friedrich von (1759–1805). German poet, dramatist, historian, and philosopher of the romantic period (see ROMANTICISM), known for his lyrical and philosophical poems and ballads and his historical dramas. His works include THE ROBBERS (*Die Räuber;* 1781) DON CARLOS (1787); WALLENSTEIN (1799), consisting of *Wallenstein's Camp, The Piccolomini,* and *Wallenstein's Death; Maria Stuart* (see MARY QUEEN OF SCOTS; 1800); *Die Jungfrau von Orleans* (*The Maid of Orleans;* 1801); *Die Braut von Messina* (1803); WILHELM TELL (1804); *Philosophical Letters* (1786), on questions of philosophy; *Revolt in the Netherlands* (1788) and *The Thirty Years War* (1789–1793), history. In his later career Schiller was professor of history at the University of Jena.

Schlegel, August Wilhelm von (1767–1845). German poet, scholar, and critic of the romantic period (see ROMANTICISM), known for his translations and studies of Shakespeare, whose plays he helped to introduce and popularize in Germany. His critical works include *Lectures on Belles-Lettres and Art* (1801–1803) and *Lectures on Dramatic Art and Literature* (1808). August Wilhelm, who had an important influence on Mme de STAËL and the English authors CARLYLE and COLERIDGE, edited the literary journal *Athenaeum,* which he helped to found in 1798, and was a professor at the University of Bonn. See also FROZEN MUSIC.

Friedrich von Schlegel (1772–1829), brother of August Wilhelm, was also a critic and poet and a leading spokesman for the typical theories and ideas of romanticism. His writings include *Lucinde* (1799), a fragmentary novel on the subject of free love; *Alarkos* (1802), a tragedy; *History of Ancient and Modern Literature* (1815); and *Language and Wisdom of the Indians* (1808). He was particularly known for his irony and his melancholy temperament.

The two brothers are important figures in the launching of romantic criticism and romantic standards of aesthetics, philosophy, and individual conduct, as well as founders of the sciences of comparative mythology and philology; in connection with philology, both did work in Indian languages. Their wives, Caroline, *née* Böhmer and Dorothea, *née* MENDELSSOHN, were both women of brilliant minds and literary talent; Dorothea and Friedrich were together converted to Roman Catholicism in 1808. The father and the uncle of Friedrich and August Wilhelm, **Johann Elias Schlegel** (1718–1749) and **Johann Adolf Schlegel** (1721–1793), respectively, were well-known men of letters of their own time. Johann Elias was a critic and playwright, an early admirer of Shakespeare; Johann Adolf was a publicist and critic.

Schleicher, Kurt von (1882-1934). German general. Chancellor of Germany (1932, 1933), succeeded by HITLER. He was killed during the Nazi purge (June 30, 1934).

Schlemihl, Peter, see PETER SCHLEMIHLS WUNDERBARE GESCHICHTE.

Schlesinger, Arthur Meier (1888–). American historian. Co-editor of the valuable 12-volume *History of American Life* (1927 ff.). His *Colonial Merchants of the American Revolution, 1763–1776* (1918) won a prize given by the American Historical Association. His son, **Arthur Meier Schlesinger, Jr.,** has, in *The Age of Jackson* (1945), produced a valuable historical work which relates that period closely to the present. It won the Pulitzer prize for history.

Schley, Winfield Scott (1839–1911). American naval officer. Second to Admiral SAMPSON in command of the naval force blockading Santiago de Cuba (1898). One of the central figures in the controversy as to whom credit should be given for the American victory.

Schliemann, Heinrich (1822–1890). German archeologist, principally known for his excavations of sites mentioned in Homer. In Asia Minor he excavated what he believed to be the ruins of ancient Troy. He also wrote a number of books on ancient Troy, Mycenae, etc.

Schmitt, Bernadotte Everly (1886–). American historian. Since 1929 Dr. Schmitt has edited *The Journal of Modern History*. His *The Coming of the War: 1914* was awarded a prize by the American Historical Association (1930) and the Pulitzer prize for History (1931).

Schmitt, Gladys (1909–). American novelist whose *David the King* (1946) was the selection of two book clubs, the Literary Guild and the Religious Book Club.

Schnabel, Artur (1882–). Celebrated Austrian pianist and futuristic composer, considered the most authoritative living interpreter of Beethoven's piano works.

schnauzer. A German terrier with rough hair, looking somewhat like an airedale. The word means snarler. The breed has been known, without noteworthy changes, for 500 years.

Schneider, Isidor (1896–). American poet, novelist, and editor. His first book, *Dr. Transit* (1926), was a fantastic novel with a scientist hero. *The Temptation of Anthony and Other Poems* (1927) was his first volume of verse. *The Judas Time* (1947) is a polemic novel directed against Communists who leave the party.

Schnitzler, Arthur (1862–1931). Austrian novelist and playwright, best known for his witty psychological studies of Viennese amours, many of which were considered immoral on their first introduction to the public. *Das Märchen* (*The Tale;* 1893), ANATOL (1893), *Liebelei* (1895; translated into English as *Flirtation*), and *Reigen* (1900), are his best-known plays. English translations of other works include *Comedies of Words* (1917), *Intermezzo, Countess Mizzie,* and *The Lonely Way* (1926), and PROFESSOR BERNHARDI (1928), all plays; *Viennese Idylls* (1913), *Bertha Garlan* (1918), *The Shepherd's Pipe, And Other Stories* (1922), *Dr. Graesler* (1923), *Beatrice* (1926), *Rhapsody* (1927), and *Daybreak* (1928), novels and stories.

Schnitzler, of a well-known medical family, was a leading physician and a specialist in laryngology before turning to writing.

Schofield, Penrod, see PENROD.

Scholar Gipsy, The. A poem by Matthew ARNOLD (1853). According to an old story current in Oxford, a student of that University, who years before wandered off to learn the gypsy traditions, still roams about. Arnold makes this lonely wanderer, whose life he regards as enviable in many ways, the hero of his poem.

scholasticism. The philosophy and doctrines of the "Schoolmen" of the Middle Ages (9th to 16th centuries) which were based on the logical works of Aristotle and the teachings of the Christian Fathers. It was an attempt to give a rational basis to Christianity, but the methods of the Scholastics degenerated into mere verbal subtleties, academic disputations, and quibblings, till, at the time of the Renaissance, the remnants were only fit to be swept away before the current of new learning that broke upon the world.

See also NOMINALISM, REALISM; *St. Thomas Aquinas* under SAINTS; SIC ET NON.

Schomberg. An innkeeper in Conrad's VICTORY.

Schönberg, Arnold (1874–). Austrian composer, identified with the ultra-modern school of music, writing on a 12-tone system. On the faculty of the University of Southern California (since 1933).

Schönberg-Cotta Family, The Chronicles of the. A historical romance by Mrs. Elizabeth Charles (1865), dealing with the period of the Reformation. Martin LUTHER is a prominent character.

Schoolcraft, Henry Rowe (1793–1864). American ethnologist. Indian agent at Sault Sainte Marie and superintendent of Indian affairs. Longfellow got his basic information for HIAWATHA from Schoolcraft's volumes on the history and conditions of the Indian tribes of the U.S.

School for Scandal, The. A comedy by R. B. SHERIDAN (1777). The principal characters are Lord and Lady TEAZLE, Joseph SURFACE, Charles and Sir Oliver Surface.

School for Wives. See L'ÉCOLE DES FEMMES; AGNES.

Schoolmaster, The. A celebrated treatise by Roger ASCHAM (1570), expressing the ideas of the author on the education of English youths of his time. It opposes foreign schooling, especially in Italy, favors the incorporation of athletics into the curriculum, and attacks English meters in verse, although it defends the use of English prose.

schoolmaster.

the schoolmaster is abroad. Education is spreading, and it will bear fruit. Lord Brougham said, in a speech (Jan. 29, 1828) on the general diffusion of education, and of intelligence arising therefrom, "Let the soldier be abroad, if he will; he can do nothing in this age. There is another personage abroad . . . the schoolmaster is abroad; and I trust to him, armed with his primer, against the soldier in full military array."

Schoolmen. The theologians of the Middle Ages, who lectured in the cloisters or cathedral schools founded by Charlemagne and his successors. They followed Aristotle and the Fathers (see SCHOLASTICISM), but attempted to reduce every subject to a system. For the names of the principal Schoolmen, see under DOCTOR.

Star-Spangled Banner, The. The national anthem of the United States, written by Francis Scott Key in 1814 during the War of 1812. During the British bombardment of Fort McHenry, the gateway to the Baltimore defenses, Key was aboard a British man-of-war, detained on a mission to obtain the exchange of an American prisoner. The bombardment lasted throughout the night from September 13 to 14. The poem was written, or rather scribbled on the back of an envelope, when, after a long night of anxious waiting, "by the dawn's early light," Key could see that the stars and stripes were still flying over the fort.

O! say can you see by the dawn's early light
What so proudly we hailed at the twilight's last gleaming,
Whose bright stars and broad stripes through the perilous fight
O'er the ramparts we watched were so gallantly streaming.
And the rockets' red glare, the bombs bursting in air
Gave proof through the night that our flag was still there.
O! say does the star-spangled banner yet wave
O'er the land of the free and the home of the brave?

The text was printed on handbills and distributed freely. It appeared also in the Baltimore *American* (September 21, 1814) and was sung to the tune of *To Anacreon in Heaven,* composed (most probably) by the English musical antiquary John Stafford Smith (1750–1836).

Schoolmistress, The. A poem by William SHENSTONE (1742), written in Spenserian stanzas. It presents a picture of a village school of the author's time and of the elderly mistress who teaches and punishes her pupils.

School of Abuse, The. A Puritan treatise by Stephen Gosson (*Eng.,* 1554–1624), written in 1579, attacking poets, actors, and playwrights on moral grounds. It was dedicated without authorization to Sir Philip SIDNEY, who answered it in his famous APOLOGY FOR POETRY.

Schopenhauer, Arthur (1788–1860). German philosopher, universally known as the chief expounder of philosophical pessimism. The title of his major work, *Die Welt als Wille und Vorstellung* (*The World as Will and Idea;* 1819), epitomizes his philosophical system. His earliest published essay, *On the Fourfold Root of the Principle of Sufficient Reason* (1813) has the rare distinction of being a doctoral dissertation of lasting importance.

Schopfer, Jean. Pseudonym **Claude Anet** (1868–1931). Swiss-French author, on his mother's side of English ancestry. He specialized in the exotic and has been called "a contemporary of Pierre Loti."

Schreiber, Georges (1904–). Belgian-born American painter, represented in the Metropolitan and Whitney Museums in New York City.

Schreiner, Olive Emilie Albertina (1855–1920). English author, born in Cape Colony, South Africa, known for her books dealing with her native country. Her best-known work is THE STORY OF AN AFRICAN FARM (1883), semi-autobiographical, published under the pseudonym of Ralph Iron. Other books by her include *Dreams* (1891), short stories; *Trooper Peter Halket of Mashonaland* (1897); *Woman and Labor* (1911), on the employment of women; *Stories, Dreams, and Allegories* (1923); *Thoughts on South Africa* (1923); *Letters, 1876–1920* (1924); *From Man to Man* (1926), a novel, left incomplete on the author's death; *Undine* (1928).

Schrim'nir. The boar, cooked nightly for the heroes of Valhalla, becoming whole every morning.

Schubert, Franz Peter (1797–1828). Famous Austrian composer who began writing at the age of fourteen. In his short life he composed some 600 songs and is recognized as one of the greatest writers of lieder in the history of music. Among his most popular songs are the *Erlking* (written at the age of eighteen), *Who is Sylvia?,* and *Hark, Hark, the Lark.* Outstanding among his other works is the *Unfinished Symphony* in B minor.

Schuman, Frederick Lewis (1904–). American writer on governmental questions. Professor of political science at Williams College (since 1936). Author of *Night Over Europe* (1941); *Design for Power* (1942); etc.

Schumann, Elizabeth (1891–). German operatic soprano and interpreter of lieder. Début (1910) in Hamburg; member of State Opera, Vienna (1919–1937). American début (1914) at Metropolitan Opera House, New York, as Sophie in *Der Rosenkavalier.* Member of faculty, Curtis Institute of Music, Philadelphia (from 1938).

Schumann, Robert Alexander (1810–1856). German composer, pianist and music critic; characteristic representative and leader of the romantic school. Among his works are highly imaginative cycles of lieder based on poems by Heine (*Dichterliebe*), Chamisso (*Frauenliebe und -leben*), and others, four symphonies; etc. His wife, **Clara Schumann,** *née* **Wieck** (1819–1896), was a fine pianist and a masterly interpreter of her husband's works. For an account of the celebrated relationship between Robert and Clara Schumann as composer and interpreter, husband and wife, cf. Clara Schumann, *Schumanns Jugendbriefe* (1885) and F. G. Jansen, *Robert Schumanns Briefe* (1904).

Schumann-Heink, Ernestine (1861–1936). Famous operatic contralto who sang often with the Metropolitan Opera Company in New York, appearing last when she was 64 years old. She was also known as a singer on the concert stage, specializing in German *lieder*.

Schurman, Jacob Gould (1854–1942). President of Cornell University (1892–1920). President of the first U.S. Philippine commission (1899). Ambassador to China (1921–1925) and Germany (1925–1930).

Schurz, Carl (1829–1906). German liberal involved in the revolution of 1848, who came to America (1852) where he rose to prominence in the Republican Party. Fought in the Civil War as brigadier general of volunteers. Engaged in the second Battle of Bull Run, Gettysburg, etc. Became major general, was senator from Missouri (1869–1875) and Secretary of the Interior (1877–1881). Also editor of the New York *Evening Post* and (1892–1898) editorial writer for *Harper's Weekly*. He is the author of a *Life of Henry Clay* (2 vols.; 1887).

Schuschnigg, Kurt von (1897–). Chancellor of Austria (from 1934), minister of public security (from 1937), and leader of the "Patriotic Front" (1936–1938). When the Nazis overran Austria, he was arrested and put into a concentration camp. After his liberation (end of World War II), he went to northern Italy.

Schuster, Max Lincoln (1897–). American publisher. With Richard Leo Simon, he founded (1924) the firm of Simon and Schuster, book publishers. Edited (1940) *A Treasury of the World's Great Letters*.

Schütz, Heinrich. Sometimes called **Sagittarius** (1585–1672). German composer of church music, choral works, etc., and, especially, of the first German opera, *Dafne* (1627).

Schütze, Gladys Henrietta. Pseudonym **Henrietta Leslie** (1881–). English novelist and playwright. She has written more than twenty novels, the best known of which is *Mrs. Fischer's War* (1931).

Schwartz, Delmore (1913–). American poet, short-story writer, and critic, especially influenced by W. H. AUDEN and Franz KAFKA. His works represent the interests and trends in "advanced" American writing during the latter 1930's. Books by him include *In Dreams Begin Responsibilities* (1938), consisting of a story, poems, and verse drama; *A Season in Hell* (1939), a translation of *Une Saison en enfer*, by Arthur RIMBAUD; *Shenandoah* (1941), narrative verse; *The Imitation of Life*, critical essays.

Schwartz, Joost Marius Willem van der Poorten, see Maarten MAARTENS.

Schweidler, Mary. The heroine of Meinhold's AMBER WITCH.

Schweinitz, George Edmund de (1858–1938). American ophthalmologist. Well-known for his work on the prevention of blindness. Author of *Diseases of the Eye* (1892), etc.

Schweitzer, Albert (1875–). French clergyman, physician, philosopher, organist, and musicologist, especially known for his devoted work as a missionary physician in French Equatorial Africa, and as an authority on J. S. BACH's life and works.

Scian Muse. See under MUSE.

science.

Christian Science, also called simply *Science.* The religion promulgated by Mary Baker EDDY. It is based upon a belief in the unreality of evil and the power of mind over disease and unhappiness, which are regarded as evil illusions. *Science and Health* is the devotional book written by Mrs. Eddy which contains the principles of the faith.

the Dismal Science. Economics; a name given to it by CARLYLE:

> The social science—not a "gay science," but a rueful—which finds the secret of this Universe in "supply and demand" . . . what we might call, by way of eminence, the *dismal science.*—*On the Nigger Question* (1849).

the Gay Science. Poetry; more exactly TROUBADOUR poetry.

the Noble Science. Boxing, or fencing; the "noble art of self-defence."

the Seven Sciences. A medieval term for the whole group of studies, viz., Grammar, Logic, and Rhetoric (the *Trivium*), with Arithmetic, Music, Geometry, and Astronomy (the *Quadrivium*).

scientia scientiarum (*Lat.*). The science of sciences, that is, philosophy or metaphysics.

Scio, now called **Chios.** One of the seven cities which claimed to be the birthplace of HOMER; hence he is sometimes called "Scio's Blind Old Bard." The seven cities referred to make an hexameter verse:

> Smyrna, Chios, Colophon, Salamis, Rhodos, Argos, Athenae; *or*
> Smyrna, Chios, Colophon, Ithaca, Pylos, Argos, *Athenae.*
>
> *A Greek Epigram.*

Scipio Africanus, Publius Cornelius (237–183 B.C.). Known also as "Scipio the Elder." Roman general and politician. His successful invasion of Carthage caused the Carthaginians to recall Hannibal from Italy. Scipio decisively defeated Hannibal in the battle of Zama (202).

Sciron. A robber of Greek legend, slain by THESEUS. He infested the parts about Megara, and forced travelers over the rocks into the sea, where they were devoured by a sea monster. It was from these cliffs (known as the *Scironian rocks*) that INO cast herself into the Corinthian bay.

Scobellum. A very fruitful land mentioned in the *Seven Champions of Christendom* iii. 10 (see under SEVEN), whose inhabitants "exceeded the cannibals for cruelty, the Persians for pride, the Egyptians for luxury, the Cretans for lying, the Germans for drunkenness, and all nations together for a generality of vices." To punish them, the gods changed the drunkards into swine, the lecherous into goats, the proud into peacocks, scolds into magpies, idle women into milch-cows, jesters into monkeys, misers into moles, etc. Eventually four of the Champions restored them to their normal forms by quenching the fire of the Golden Cave.

Scogan's Jests. A popular jest-book in the 16th century, said by Andrew Boorde (who published it) to be the work of one John Scogan, reputed to have been court fool to Edward IV. He is referred to (anachronously) by Justice Shallow in 2 *Henry IV*, iii. 2, and must not be confused with Henry Scogan (d. 1407), the poet-disciple of Chaucer to whom Ben Jonson alludes:

> Scogan? What was he?
> Oh, a fine gentleman, and a master of arts
> Of Henry the Fourth's times, that made disguises
> For the king's sons, and writ in ballad royal
> Daintily well.
>
> *The Fortunate Isles* (1624).

Scollard, Clinton (1860–1932). Minor poet. Professor of English at Hamilton College, Clinton, N.Y. (1888–1896; 1911–1912). *The Singing Heart* (1934). Husband of Jessie RITTENHOUSE.

Scopes trial. A famous American court trial at Dayton, Tennessee, in July, 1925, at which J. T. Scopes, a public-school teacher, was tried on the charge of teaching Darwinian evolution (see DARWIN, CHARLES) in violation of a state law forbidding such instruction. The famous lawyer Clarence DARROW defended Scopes, but William Jennings BRYAN, who handled the prosecution, succeeded in winning a conviction. The case was notorious in its day, attracting the attention of liberals and civil liberties groups, who vigorously attacked the law. The conviction was later reversed by the Tennessee supreme court.

Scot or **Scott, Michael** (1175?–?1234). Scottish schoolman of legendary fame as a wizard and magician. Mentioned by Dante in the *Inferno*. Cf. also Sir Walter Scott, *The Lay of the Last Minstrel*.

Scotch or **Scottish.** For such designations as *the Scottish Anacreon, the Scottish Iliad*, etc., see under ANACREON, ILIAD.

Scotia. Scotland; sometimes called "Scotia Minor." The Venerable BEDE tells us that Scotland was called Caledonia till 258 A. D., when it was invaded by a tribe from Ireland and its name changed to Scotia.

Scotism. The theological system of John DUNS SCOTUS.

Scotland Yard. The headquarters of the London Metropolitan Police, whence all public orders to the force proceed. The original *Scotland Yard* was a short street near Trafalgar Square, so called from a palace on the spot, given by King Edgar (about 970) to Kenneth II of Scotland when he came to London to pay homage and subsequently used by the Scottish kings when visiting England. *New Scotland Yard*, as it is officially called, is close by, on the Thames Embankment near Westmininster Bridge.

Scots, Wha Hae. A patriotic poem by Robert BURNS (1793), celebrating the victory of Robert BRUCE over the English King Edward II at the Battle of Bannockburn in 1314, and hailing liberty and independence for the Scotch nation. It is believed that Burns was strongly influenced in the writing of this poem by the French Revolution.

Scott, Clement William (1841–1904). English dramatic critic, known for his picturesque style. Also author of sentimental verse and adaptations of French plays.

Scott, Dred (1795?–1858). American Negro, known as the central figure in a famous pronouncement by the U.S. Supreme Court, the DRED SCOTT DECISION.

Scott, Duncan Campbell (1862–1947). Canadian poet. *The Magic House and Other Poems* (1893); *Lundy's Lane* (1916); *Beauty and Life* (1921); etc.

Scott, Evelyn (1893–). American novelist. Her best-known books are *The Wave* (1929) and the autobiography, *Escapade* (1923). Author of several books of poems. Her husband is John METCALFE.

Scott, Geoffrey (1885–1929). English critic and writer on Humanism; author of *The Portrait of Zélide* (1925) and editor of Boswell's private papers (1928–1932).

Scott, Michael (1789–1835). Scotch novelist. Author of *Tom Cringle's Log* and *The Cruise of the Midge*, both published in 1836.

Scott, Robert Falcon (1868–1912). Famous English antarctic explorer who perished with his party on the return trip from reaching the South Pole (January 18, 1912). The searching party found his records and diaries. His son, **Peter Markham Scott** (1909–), is an artist who specializes in the painting of birds.

Scott, Sir Walter (1771–1832). Scotch poet and novelist of the romantic period (see ROMANTICISM), known for his historical novels, narrative poems and ballads on medieval themes and incidents in Scotch history. He was influenced in his choice of subject-matter by German ballads in the medieval manner and by the GOTHIC NOVEL, and in his turn had an important influence on the school of the historical novel that developed in the 19th century in England, France, and the U.S. Scott's novels, for which he is most famous, are marked by vividness of detail, adventure, and a colorful re-creation of the past. In the field of poetry, his works include THE EVE OF SAINT JOHN (1799), a celebrated ballad; *Minstrelsy of the Scottish Border* (1802–1803), a collection of ancient Scotch ballads and legends; THE LAY OF THE LAST MINSTREL (1805); MARMION (1808); THE LADY OF THE LAKE (1810); *The Vision of Don Roderick* (see RODERICK; 1811); ROKEBY (1813). The best-known of his novels and tales include the following:

WAVERLEY (1814); GUY MANNERING (1815); THE ANTIQUARY (1816); OLD MORTALITY (1816); THE BLACK DWARF (1816); THE HEART OF MIDLOTHIAN (1818); ROB ROY (1817); THE BRIDE OF LAMMERMOOR (1819); THE LEGEND OF MONTROSE (1819); IVANHOE (1819); THE MONASTERY (1820); THE ABBOT (1820); KENILWORTH (1821); THE PIRATE (1821); THE FORTUNES OF NIGEL (1822); PEVERIL OF THE PEAK (1823); QUENTIN DURWARD (1823); ST. RONAN'S WELL (1823); REDGAUNTLET (1824); THE BETROTHED (1825); THE TALISMAN (1825); WOODSTOCK (1826); THE HIGHLAND WIDOW (1827); THE TWO DROVERS (1827); THE SURGEON'S DAUGHTER (1827); THE FAIR MAID OF PERTH (1828); ANNE OF GEIERSTEIN (1829); COUNT ROBERT OF PARIS (1832); CASTLE DANGEROUS (1832); THE DEATH OF THE LAIRD'S JOCK (1827); TALES OF A GRANDFATHER (1828–1830).

Scott also wrote several dramatic works, a number of studies in biography and in the history, legends, and antiquities of Scotland, and miscellaneous essays, including articles in the *Encyclopaedia Britannica.*

The novelist came of a family related to the old Scotch clan of Buccleuch, and in childhood was ill with infantile paralysis. In his maturity he was socially ambitious and built the mansion of Abbotsford on the banks of the Tweed. He also was a partner in the publishing business with two brothers named Ballantyne, issuing, among other things, the *Quarterly Review,* a periodical rivaling the *Edinburgh Review;* in the later years of his life much of his writing was done in order to pay the debts of this firm, which went into bankruptcy about 1825.

Scott was known to the readers of his day as "The Wizard of the North."

the Southern Scott or *the Scott of Italy.* ARIOSTO is so called by Lord Byron.

the Walter Scott of Belgium. Hendrick Conscience (19th century).

the Swiss Walter Scott. Zschokke (1771–1848).

Scott, William Bell (1811–1890). Scotch poet and painter, friend of Rossetti and Swinburne. One of his best-known poems is *The Witch's Ballad.*

Scott, Winfield (1786–1866). General in chief of the U.S. Army (1841). Commanded in the Mexican War. Captured Vera Cruz (March 1847); defeated the Mexicans at Cerro Gordo, Chapultepec, etc., and occupied Mexico City (September 1847). Whig candidate for president (1852); defeated by Franklin PIERCE.

Scotti, Antonio (1866–1936). Italian operatic basso, with Metropolitan Opera Company of New York (1899–1933). Most famous rôle: Scarpia in *Tosca.*

Scottish Chaucerians. Term applied to a group of Scotch poets in the late 15th and early 16th centuries who wrote in the tradition of Geoffrey CHAUCER. They are considered by critics to have written the best lyric poetry of their time. Gawain DOUGLAS, William DUNBAR, and Robert HENRYSON were the leaders of the Scottish Chaucerians.

Scottish Chiefs, The. A novel by Jane PORTER (1810). The scene is laid in the Scotland of 1296 and thereafter, and Robert Bruce and William Wallace are prominent characters.

Scott-Moncrieff, Charles Kenneth Michael (1889–1930). Scottish translator of Marcel Proust, Pirandello, and Stendhal into English. Also author of *Austria's Peace Offer* (1921).

Scottsboro Case. A notorious court case (1931), involving nine young Negroes accused of rape on an Alabama freight-train, which enlisted the interest of all liberals. Four of the defendants were convicted and sentenced to life imprisonment. The charges against the others were dropped. The case served as the subject of several plays, as *Scottsboro Limited* (1932) by Langston HUGHES, and *They Shall Not Die* (1934) by John Wexley.

Scotus Erigena, John, see ERIGENA, JOHN SCOTUS.

Scotus, John Duns, see DUNS, JOHN.

scourge.

the scourge of God (Lat. *flagellum Dei*). Attila (d. 453), King of the Huns, so called by medieval writers because of the widespread havoc and destruction caused by his armies. The term was also applied to Genseric, King of the Vandals (d. 477), and to Timur Tamerlane (see TAMBURLAINE), the Tartar.

the Scourge of Princes. Pietro ARETINO.

the Scourge of Scotland. Edward I of England.

the Scourge of Christians. Noureddin-Mahmud of Damascus (1116–1174).

scrap of paper, a. A phrase popularized in the early days of World War I, with reference to an international treaty. It is said to have been first used by the German Chancellor, Herr von Bethman-Hollweg, on August 4, 1914, in a conversation with the British ambassador in which he declared a treaty obligation was, in this emergency, a mere *scrap of paper.*

Scriabin or **Scriabine, Alexander** (1872–1915). Russian composer of mystic and impressionistic leanings. Visited the U.S. (1907). Best known for his tone poems, *Le Poème de l'Extase* and *Le Poème du Feu*.

Scribe, Augustin Eugène (1791–1861). French playwright. Among the best of his more than 350 plays, including many opera and comic-opera librettos, are *My Uncle Caesar* (1821); *Valérie* (1822); *The Money Marriage* (1827); etc.

Scriblerus, Martinus. The hero of a merciless satire on the false taste in literature current in the time of Pope, for the most part written by John ARBUTHNOT, and published in 1741. Its full title was *Memoirs of the Extraordinary Life, Works and Discoveries of Martinus Scriblerus.* Cornelius Scriblerus, the father of Martin, is a pedant, who entertains all sorts of absurd notions about the education of his son. Martin grows up a man of capacity, but although he has read everything, his judgment is vile and his taste atrocious. POPE, SWIFT, and Arbuthnot founded a *Scriblerus Club* with the object of pillorying all literary incompetence, and these *Memoirs* were the first of a proposed series of satires on current topics.

Scripps. Name of a family of American newspaper publishers. **Robert Paine Scripps** (1895–1938) was the editorial director of the Scripps-McRae newspapers and, after the merger with the Howard interests under Roy Wilson Howard (1925), associate editorial director of the Scripps-Howard chain.

Scriptores Decem. A collection of ten ancient chronicles on English history, edited by Sir Roger TWYSDEN and John SELDEN (1652). The ten chroniclers are Simeon of Durham, John of Hexham, Richard of Hexham, Ailred of Rieval, Ralph de Diceto (Archdeacon of London), John Brompton of Jorval, Gervase of Canterbury, Thomas Stubbs, William Thorn of Canterbury, and Henry Knighton of Leicester.

A similar collection of five chronicles was published by Thomas GALE (1691) as *Scriptores Quinque.*

Scrooge, Ebenezer. The principal character in Dickens' CHRISTMAS CAROL, partner, executor, and heir of old Jacob Marley, stockbroker. When first introduced, he is "a squeezing, grasping, covetous old hunks, sharp and hard as a flint," without one particle of sympathy, loving no one, and by none beloved. One Christmas Day, Ebenezer Scrooge sees three ghosts: The Ghost of Christmas Past, the Ghost of Christmas Present, and the Ghost of Christmas to Come. The first takes him back to his young life, shows him what Christmas was to him when a schoolboy, and when he was an apprentice; reminds him of his courting of a young girl, whom he forsook as he grew rich; and shows him that sweetheart of his young days married to another and the mother of a happy family. The second ghost shows him the joyous home of his clerk, Bob Cratchit, who has nine people to keep on 15*s*. a week, and yet can find wherewithal to make merry on this day; it also shows him the family of his nephew, and of others. The third ghost shows him what would be his lot if he died as he then was, the prey of harpies, the jest of his friends on 'Change, the world's uncared-for waif. These visions wholly change his nature, and he becomes benevolent and cheerful, loving all, and by all beloved.

Scudamore, Sir. The lover of Amoret in Spenser's FAËRIE QUEENE (Bk. iv), and finally wedded to her. The name means "Shield of Love."

Scudder, Horace Elisha (1838–1902). American writer. Editor of *Riverside Magazine for Young People* (1867–1870) and of the *Atlantic Monthly* (1890–1898). Author of *Dream Children* (1864), biographies of Noah Webster (1882), Bayard Taylor (1884), George Washington (1890), James Russell Lowell (1901), etc.

Scudder, Janet (1873–1940). American sculptor. Her *Frog Fountain* is in the Metropolitan Museum of Art in New York.

Scudder, Vida Dutton (1861–). American educator; professor of English at Wellesley College (1910–1927). Author of *Social Ideals in English Letters* (1898); *The Disciple of a Saint* (1907); *Socialism and Character* (1912); and *The Franciscan Adventure* (1931).

Scudéry or **Scudéri, Madeleine de.** Known as **Sapho.** (1608–1701). French author of fiction, famous for her exaggerated, sentimental romances of historical times, the first ROMANS À CLEF, on which she collaborated with her brother George. The best-known of these works are *Ibrahim, ou l'Illustre Bassa* (1641); *Artamène, ou le Grand Cyrus* (see under CYRUS; 1648–1653); *Clélie, Histoire Romaine* (1654–1660), in ten volumes. George de Scudéry was associated with the Hôtel de RAMBOUILLET and Madeleine held elaborate gatherings at which competitions in *précieux* gallantry were carried on. Under the Scudérys, the sentimental romance is considered to have reached its apex, but was already the subject of attack in the authors' day. It is satirized in Molière's LES PRÉCIEUSES RIDICULES.

Scyld. In legendary history, the king of Denmark preceding BEOWULF. The Anglo-Saxon epic poem *Beowulf* (6th century) begins with the death of Scyld.

> At his appointed time, Scyld deceased, very decrepit, and went into the peace of the Lord. They . . . bore him to the sea-shore as he himself requested. . . . There on the beach stood the ring-powered ship, the vehicle of the noble . . . ready to set out. They laid

down the dear prince, the distributor of rings, in the bosom of the ship, the mighty one beside the mast . . . they set up a golden ensign high overhead . . . they gave him to the deep. Sad was their spirit, mournful their mood.—*Beowulf* (*Kemble version*).

Scylla. In Greek legend the name (1) of a daughter of King Nisus of Megara and (2) of a sea monster.

The daughter of Nisus promised to deliver Megara into the hands of her lover Minos and, to effect this, cut off a golden hair on her father's head while he was asleep. Minos despised her for this treachery, and Scylla threw herself from a rock into the sea. At death she was changed into a lark, and Nisus into a hawk.

The sea monster dwelt on the rock Scylla, opposite CHARYBDIS, on the Italian side of the Straits of Messina. HOMER says that she had twelve feet, and six heads, each on a long neck and each armed with three rows of pointed teeth, and that she barked like a dog. He makes her a daughter of Crataeis, but later accounts say that she was a nymph who, because she was beloved by GLAUCUS, was changed by the jealous CIRCE into a hideous monster.

between Scylla and Charybdis. Between two equal difficulties; between the Devil and the deep sea.

to fall from Scylla into Charybdis—out of the frying-pan into the fire.

Scythrop Glowry. A character in Peacock's novel NIGHTMARE ABBEY, generally admitted to be a caricature of the poet SHELLEY.

Sea, Old Man of the. See under OLD.

Seabrook, William Buehler (1886–1945). American writer. A great traveler, best known for *The Magic Island* (1929); *Asylum* (1935); *An Analysis of Magic and Witchcraft* (1945).

Seabury, Samuel (1729–1796). American clergyman; loyalist during the American Revolution; first bishop of the Protestant Episcopal Church in America. His great-great-grandson, **Samuel Seabury** (1873–), a lawyer, justice of the N.Y. Supreme Court (1906–1914); associate judge, N.Y. Court of Appeals (1914–1916); etc.

sea deities. In classical myth, besides the fifty NEREIDS, the Oceanides (daughters of Oceanus), the SIRENS, etc., there were a number of deities presiding over, or connected with, the sea. The chief of these are:

Amphitrite, wife of Poseidon, queen goddess of the sea.

Glaucus, a fisherman of Boeotia, afterwards a marine deity.

Ino, who threw herself from a rock into the sea, and was made a sea-goddess.

Neptune, king of the ocean.

Nereus and his wife *Doris.* Their palace was at the bottom of the Mediterranean; his hair was seaweed.

Oceanus and his wife *Tethys* (daughter of Uranus and Ge). Oceanus was god of the ocean which formed a boundary round the world.

Portumnus, the protector of harbors.

Poseidon, the Greek Neptune.

Proteus, who assumed every variety of shape.

Thetis, a daughter of Nereus and mother of Achilles.

Triton, son of Poseidon.

Seafarer, The. An Anglo-Saxon poem of the early 8th century, expressing the conflicting feelings of weariness of and longing for the sea apparently experienced by a veteran voyager. It vividly describes both the hardships and the fascinations of life at sea.

Seaman, Elizabeth, *née* **Cochrane.** Pseudonym **Nellie Bly** (1867–1922). American journalist who undertook several sensational assignments. She had herself committed to the insane ward at Blackwell's Island to prepare an article about the treatment of the insane. It resulted in a book, *Ten Days in a Madhouse* (1888). Her most famous feat, however, was a round-the-world trip in the record time of 72 days, 6 hours, 11 minutes. Its result was again a book, *Nellie Bly's Book: Around the World in Seventy-Two Days* (1890).

Seaman, Sir **Owen** (1861–1936). Famous editor of *Punch* (1906–1932). Author of *The Battle of the Bays* (1896), parodies of Tennyson, Rossetti, Kipling, and others; *Borrowed Plumes* (1902); *Interludes of an Editor* (1929); etc.

sea power. A term made popular by the writings of Admiral MAHAN.

Sears, Edmund Hamilton (1810–1876). American Unitarian clergyman, famous as the author of the Christmas hymn *It Came Upon a Midnight Clear.*

seas.

the four seas. The seas surrounding Great Britain, on the north, south, east, and west.

the high seas. The open sea, the "main"; especially that part of the sea beyond "the three-mile limit," which forms a free highway to all nations.

the seven seas. The Arctic, Antarctic, North Pacific, South Pacific, North Atlantic, South Atlantic, and Indian oceans.

Seasons, The. A famous descriptive poem in blank verse by James THOMSON, in four parts—*Winter* (1726), *Summer* (1727), *Spring* (1728), *Autumn* (1730). The poem contains the love episodes of CELADON and AMELIA, DAMON and MUSIDORA, and LAVINIA and PALEMON.

Seats of the Mighty. A historical novel by Gilbert PARKER (1896). The scene is laid in Quebec. Captain Robert Moray and his enemy Doltaire are rivals for the hand of Alixe Duvarney. The former is a prisoner during the greater part of the novel, but he escapes at last, and all ends well for him.

Seaver, Edwin (1900–). American novelist; also known for his book reviews for *The New Republic, The Nation, The Freeman,* etc. He helped found *The New Masses,* and was editor in chief of *Soviet Russia Today* and literary editor of *The Daily Worker*. Publicity Director of the Book-of-the-Month Club.

Seawell, Molly Elliot (1860–1916). American novelist of the romantic school, best-known for her historical novels dealing with French life, as *The Sprightly Romance of Marsac* (1896); etc.

Sea-Wolf, The. A novel by Jack LONDON (1904). The Sea Wolf is a brutal captain, "Wolf Larsen." Humphrey Van Weyden and Maude Brewster, each a pick-up from a wreck, are in his power, but after many horrible adventures, succeed in escaping to happiness with each other.

Sebastian. (1) In Shakespeare's TWELFTH NIGHT a young gentleman of Messaline, brother to Viola. They are twins, and so much alike that they cannot be distinguished except by their dress.

(2) Brother of Alonso, King of Naples, in Shakespeare's comedy THE TEMPEST.

(3) Villain of Grant ALLEN's "novel of detection and pursuit," *Hilda Wade*.

Sebastian, Don. King of Portugal, a mighty hero who was finally defeated by the Moors and fell in the battle of Alcazarquebir in 1578. Popular legend has it that he will some day return to earth to make Brazil a great kingdom. He was very popular, and for twenty years and more after his death impostors claiming his identity appeared. He is the hero of DRYDEN's *Don Sebastian* (1690).

Sebastian, St. See under SAINTS.

Seccombe, Thomas (1866–1923). English critic and biographer; on editorial staff of *Dictionary of National Biography* (1891–1901). Author of *The Age of Johnson* (1900); etc.

second. For such designations as *the Second Charlemagne, the Second Washington,* etc., see under CHARLEMAGNE, WASHINGTON.

Second Coming. A poem by William Vaughn MOODY, dealing with the belief in the second coming of Christ.

Second Empire. The reign of Emperor Napoleon III of France (1852–1870).

Second Mrs. Tanqueray, The. A drama by A. W. PINERO (1893). Paula, "the second Mrs. Tanqueray," is a woman with a past, and in spite of Aubrey Tanqueray's hopes and efforts, is not very cordially accepted by his friends, nor can she win the affection of his nineteen-year-old daughter Ellean. Ellean goes to Paris with one of her mother's friends and there becomes engaged to Captain Ardale. Paula, who has formerly been Ardale's mistress, feels duty bound to break off the match. Ellean now confesses in her anger that she has guessed from the beginning what sort of woman Paula was and has shunned her on that account. Paula, in despair, kills herself.

Second Nun's Tale, The. One of Chaucer's CANTERBURY TALES, the story of St. Cecile or Cecily, the daughter of noble Roman parents, and a Christian. One day, she tells her husband Valerian she has "an aungel . . . that with gret love, wher so I wake or slepe, is redy ay my body for to kepe." Valerian asks to see this angel, and Cecile tells him he must first go to St. Urban, and, being purged by him "fro synne, than schul ye se that aungel." Valerain is accordingly "cristened" by St. Urban, returns home, and finds the angel with two crowns, brought directly from Paradise. One he gives to Cecile and one to Valerian, saying that "bothe with the palme of martirdom schullen come unto God's blisful feste." Valerian suffers martyrdom first; then Almachius, the Roman prefect, commands his officers to "brenne Cecile in a bath of flammes red." She remains in the bath all day and night, yet "sat she cold, and felte of it no woe." Then they strike her three blows upon the neck, but they cannot smite her head off. She lingers on for three whole days, preaching and teaching, and then dies. St. Urban buries her body secretly by night, and her house he converts into a church, which he calls the church of Cecile.

Second Shepherd's Play, The (Secunda Pagina Pastorum). A medieval English MIRACLE PLAY, written at the end of the 14th century or the beginning of the 15th century and considered to have been from the hand of THE WAKEFIELD MASTER. It deals with the Nativity in a vein of rollicking, farcical, almost burlesque realism, in terms of country life in Yorkshire at the time of the play's composition. It was called the *"Second" Shepherd's Play* because in the manuscript in which it is preserved it follows a *"Prima" Pagina Pastorum*. The manuscript contains a total of thirty-two plays, one-third of which are believed to have been written by The Wakefield Master.

second sight. The power of seeing things invisible to others; the power of foreseeing future events by means of shadows thrown before them.

Secret Agent, The. A novel by Joseph CONRAD (1907), dealing with the London underworld and suggested by a mysterious explosion in Greenwich Park. Verloc "the secret agent" has been living for years as an ostensible anarchist paid to spy upon his comrades. Fearful of losing his job, and goaded by his employers into producing concrete evidence that will rouse public feeling against anarchistic organizations, he persuades Stevie, his stupid, trusting brother-in-law, to blow up Greenwich Observatory. Stevie is killed with his own bomb, and Verloc's wife, Winnie, whose whole life has been devoted to her brother, turns upon Verloc and murders him. The novel was filmed by Alfred HITCHCOCK as *The Woman Alone.*

Sedan. A city on the Meuse river in France, of great strategic importance and hence historical interest. The most famous battle of Sedan (September 1, 1870) caused the surrender to the Germans of an army of one hundred thousand men under the direct command of Napoleon III. In World War I, Sedan was an important point during the advance of the Germans into France. In 1940, it was the gateway through which the German army, skirting the MAGINOT LINE, poured westward.

Sedan, The Man of. See under MAN.

Sedgemoor. A place in Somerset, England, which (in 1685) was the scene of a battle between Royal troops and the Duke of MONMOUTH who had landed in England to lay claim to the crown as an illegitimate son of Charles II. Monmouth was defeated.

Sedgwick, Anne Douglas (1873–1935). Distinguished American writer. Her ninth novel, *Tante* (1911), was dramatized for Ethel Barrymore. She lived mostly in Paris and "thought out her stories in French." Of this *The Little French Girl* (1924) shows considerable traces.

Sedgwick, Ellery (1872–). Editor of the *Atlantic Monthly* (1908–1938). His brother, **Henry Dwight Sedgwick** (1861–), is the author of many books of essays.

Sedley, Amelia. One of the principal characters of Thackeray's VANITY FAIR, the school friend of the heroine BECKY SHARP. Amelia's fortunes form the second and contrasting plot of the novel, and Amelia's gentle, affectionate but not too clever personality is the more lovable by contrast with that of her friend. She was said by Thackeray to have been drawn from three women—Mrs. Brookfield, his mother, and his wife.

Joseph Sedley. Amelia's brother, a collector, of Boggley Wollah; a fat, sensual, conceited dandy. Becky Sharp sets her cap for him but fails to capture him. He flees from Brussels on the day of the battle between Napoleon and Wellington, and returns to Calcutta, where he brags of his brave deeds and makes it appear that he was Wellington's right hand; on the strength of his tale he obtains the sobriquet of "Waterloo Sedley." He later comes back to England and falls into Becky's clutches after her separation from Rawdon CRAWLEY.

Mr. Sedley. Amelia's father, a wealthy London stock-broker, brought to ruin by the fall of the Funds just prior to the battle of Waterloo. The old merchant then tries to earn a meager pittance by selling wine, coals, or lottery-tickets by commission, but his bad wine and cheap coals find few customers.

Mrs. Sedley. Wife of Mr. Sedley, a homely, kind-hearted, motherly woman in her prosperous days, but soured by adversity, and quick to take offense.

Sedley, Sir Charles (1639?–1701). English writer of the RESTORATION, notorious for his wit and profligacy. Author of tragedies, comedies, *vers de société,* and songs, as *Phyllis is My Only Joy.* His daughter, **Catherine Sedley** (1657–1717), became a mistress of King James II.

sedulous.

to play the sedulous ape to. To study the style of another, and model one's own on his as faithfully and meticulously as possible; said, usually with more or less contempt, of literary men. The phrase is taken from R. L. STEVENSON, who, in his essay, *A College Magazine* (*Memories and Portraits*), said that he had—

> played the sedulous ape to Hazlitt, to Lamb, to Wordsworth, to Sir Thomas Browne, to Defoe, to Hawthorne, to Montaigne, to Baudelaire, and to Obermann. . . . That, like it or not, is the way to learn to write.

See, Thomas Jefferson Jackson (1866–). American astronomer, in charge of the U.S. Naval Observatory (1899–1902), and (from 1903) of the naval observatory at Mare Island, California.

Seeger, Alan (1888–1916). American poet, killed in action in World War I (July 4, 1916). His collected poems were published shortly after his death with an introduction by William Archer. He is best known for his poem *I Have a Rendezvous With Death,* which has been extensively anthologized.

Seelig, Dr. A Jewish physician, the leading character in the play AS A MAN THINKS by Augustus Thomas.

Seghers, Anna. Pen name of **Netty Radványi,** *née* **Reiling** (1900–). German novelist. Author of the Book-of-the-Month Club novel, *The Seventh Cross* (1942), written while her husband was in a French concentration camp. Lived as a refugee in Paris; to U.S. after the fall of France.

Segrais, Jean Regnault de (1624–1701). French poet; collaborated with the Duchesse de Montpensier on several romances and himself wrote poetry (*Athis,* 1653) and the novel *Bérénice* (1648–1651).

Seian Horse. See under HORSE.

Seicento. The 16th and 17th centuries of Italian notables, the period of bad taste and degenerate art. The degraded art is termed *Seicentista,* and the notables of the period the *Seicentisti.* The style of writing was inflated and bombastic, and that of art was what is termed "rococo." The chief poet was Giovanni Battista Marino (1569–1625), the chief painter Caravaggio (1569–1609), the chief sculptor Bernini (1593–1680), and the chief architect Borromini (1599–1667).

Seidel, Emil (1864–). Mayor of Milwaukee (1910–1912), the first Socialist mayor in a large American city.

Seitz, Don Carlos (1862–1935). An American journalist who wrote biographies of *Horace Greeley* (1926); *Joseph Pulitzer* (1927); and *The James Gordon Bennetts* (1928).

Sejanus His Fall. A Roman tragedy (1603) by Ben JONSON, who frequently wrote dramas based on classical themes.

selah. A Hebrew word occurring often in the *Psalms* (and three times in *Habakkuk* iii), indicating some musical or liturgical direction, such as a pause, a repetition, or the end of a section.

Selden, John (1584–1654). English lawyer, scholar, and prose writer, known for his treatises, many of which were written in Latin and dealt with questions of law. Among his works are *De Diis Syris* (1617), a study of Oriental religion; *History of Tithes* (1618), which was suppressed after publication because the English clergy objected to it; *Marmora Arundeliana* (1624); *De Successionibus* (1631); *Mare Clausum* (1635); *De Jure Naturali* (1940); *Judicature in Parliament* (1640); *Privileges of Baronage* (1642); *Fleta* (1647); *On the Nativity of Christ* (1661); *Table Talk* (1689).

Selden, of humble birth, was an outstanding lawyer of his day and became especially known for his collection of Oriental manuscripts, which he willed to the Bodleian Library.

Seldes, George (1890–). American journalist and writer; brother of Gilbert SELDES. Author of *You Can't Print That!* (1929); *The Truth Behind the News* (1929); *Sawdust Caesar* (1932), a biography of MUSSOLINI; *The Vatican and the Modern World* (1933); *Lords of the Press* (1938); etc. Editor of a weekly bulletin of "inside" news, *In Fact,* which has a circulation of over 100,000 copies.

Seldes, Gilbert Vivian (1893–). American journalist and critic. Best-known for his volume, *The Seven Lively Arts* (1924). Translated and adapted *Lysistrata* by Aristophanes for the American stage (1930). Also author of murder mysteries written under the pen name Foster Johns.

Selene. The moon goddess of Greek mythology, daughter of Hyperion and Thea, and roughly corresponding to the Roman DIANA, the chaste huntress. Selene had fifty daughters by ENDYMION, and several by ZEUS, one of whom was called "The Dew." Diana is represented with bow and arrow, running after the stag; but Selene is usually shown in a chariot drawn by two white horses, with wings on her shoulders and a scepter in her hand.

Seleucidae. The dynasty of Seleucus Nicator, one of ALEXANDER's generals (ca. 358–280 B.C.), who in 312 conquered Babylon and succeeded to a part of Alexander's vast empire. The monarchy consisted of Syria, a part of Asia Minor, and all the eastern provinces, and the line of the Selucids reigned till about 64 B.C.

Self-Denying Ordinance, the. The name given to an Act passed by the Long Parliament (1644), by which the members bound themselves not to accept certain posts, particularly commands in the army. The name was given also to an arrangement made respecting British naval promotions and retirements in 1870. It is sometimes used in a general sense, with obvious meaning.

self-determination. The theory in political economy that every nation, no matter how small or weak, has the right to decide upon its own form of government and to manage its own internal affairs. This principle was one of the political ideals and war aims of Woodrow WILSON, and there was an attempt to embody it in the European settlement provided for in the Treaty of VERSAILLES at the close of World War I.

Self-Reliance. An essay by Ralph Waldo EMERSON which was published (1841) in his first series of essays.

Selika. In Meyerbeer's opera L'AFRICAINE a native queen.

Selim. (1) The hero of Byron's poem THE BRIDE OF ABYDOS.

(2) The hero of the tale *The Light of the Harem* in Moore's LALLA ROOKH, in reality the Mogul emperor Jehangir. The story deals with his relations with his wife NOURMAHAL, "the Light of the Harem."

Selincourt, Hugh de (1878–). English novelist and playwright. *One Little Boy* (1923); etc.

Seljuks. A Perso-Turkish dynasty of eleven emperors over a large part of Asia, which lasted 138 years (1056–1194). It was founded by Togrul Beg, a descendant of Seljuk, chief of a small tribe which gained possession of Bokara.

Selkirk, Alexander (1676–1723). A Scotch sailor whose narrative of his actual experience as a castaway suggested Defoe's ROBINSON CRUSOE. He is the subject of a well-known poem by COWPER, which begins:

I am monarch of all I survey,
My right there is none to dispute.

Sellenger's round. An English country dance popular in the sixteenth century. The name is a corruption of St. Léger.

Sellers, Col. Mulberry. The principal character in THE GILDED AGE, a novel by Mark Twain and Charles Dudley Warner, which was later successfully dramatized (1876).

Sellers, Isaiah (1802?–1864). Mississippi steamboat pilot who used the pseudonym Mark Twain for his contributions to the New Orleans *Daily Picayune* before it was taken over and made famous by Samuel L. Clemens.

Sellwood, Emily. Wife of Lord TENNYSON, to whom she was married in 1850.

Selvaggio. The father of Sir Industry, and the hero of Thomson's CASTLE OF INDOLENCE:

In Fairy-land there lived a knight of old,
Of features stern, Selvaggio well y-clept;
A rough, unpolished man, robust and bold,
But wondrous poor. He neither sowed nor reaped;
Ne stores in summer for cold winter heaped.
In hunting all his days away he wore—
Now scorched by June, now in November steeped,
Now pinched by biting January sore,
He still in woods pursued the libbard and the boar.
ii. 5.

Selznick, David Oliver (1902–). American moving-picture producer; organized Selznick International Pictures (1935–1936) and produced *Little Lord Fauntleroy; The Garden of Allah; The Prisoner of Zenda; Tom Sawyer; Gone With the Wind;* etc.

Semaine, La. An epic poem by Guillaume du BARTAS (1578), celebrating from the Protestant point of view the Biblical theme of the Creation, based on *Genesis.* The work was extremely popular in its day, going through twenty editions in five years and being translated into Latin, Spanish, Italian, English, and German. Milton's PARADISE LOST is said to have been inspired in part by *La Semaine,* which was translated into English by Joshua SYLVESTER. In 1584 du Bartas began issuing *La Seconde Semaine,* which was intended to carry the epic down to the Last Judgment; it was never completed, however.

semantics. The science of meanings and their relation to the words, or "signs," which represent them in language; a branch of SEMEIOTICS. Semantics came into particular prominence during the 1930's in England and the U.S. in connection with the analysis of PROPAGANDA and the study of poetic imagery and diction. Leading studies of semantics at this time were *The Meaning of Meaning* (1936), by C. K. Ogden and I. A. RICHARDS; *The Tyranny of Words* (1938), by Stuart Chase: *The Theory of Meaning and Truth* (1940), by Bertrand Russell; *Language in Action* (1941), by S. I. Hayakawa; *An Introduction to Semantics* (1942), by Rudolf Carnap.

Sembrich, Marcella. Stage name of **Praxede Marcelline Kochańska** (1858–1935). Operatic soprano. American début as Lucia with the Metropolitan Opera Company in New York (1883); also on the concert stage.

Semele. In Greek mythology, the daughter of Cadmus and Harmonia. By ZEUS she was the mother of DIONYSUS, and was slain by lightning when he granted her request to appear before her as the God of Thunder.

Seminoles. A tribe of Florida Indians mingled with Negro ex-slaves. They fought against the U.S. in the War of 1812. There were two Seminole Wars (1817–1818 and 1835–1842). In the first the Seminoles were put down by Andrew Jackson. The second war arose in the course of the partially successful execution of a plan to remove the Seminoles to the West.

semeiotics. The science, or theory, of signs, dealing with the various elements, processes, and relationships involved in the representation of meanings, objects, associations, etc., in language and expression in general. SEMANTICS is the best-known branch of semeiotics. For an introduction to semeiotics, cf. *Foundations for the Theory of Signs,* by Charles W. Morris, in the *Encyclopaedia of Unified Science,* I, 2; and *Aesthetics and the Theory of Signs,* by the same author, *Journal of Unified Science,* VIII, 1–3 (1939).

Semiramis. In legendary history, Queen of Assyria, wife of NINUS. She survived her husband, and the glory of her subsequent reign stands out so prominently that she quite eclipses all other monarchs of ancient Assyria. She is said to have built the city of Babylon and its famous hanging gardens. After a reign of forty-two years, she resigned the crown to her son Ninyas, and took her flight to heaven in the form of a dove. Semiramis was the daughter of Derceto the fish-goddess and a Syrian youth. Her mother abandoned her in infancy, but she was nursed by doves until some shepherds found her. She is the heroine of Calderón's drama *The Daughter of the Air,* of Voltaire's tragedy *Sémiramis,* and Rossini's opera *Sémiramide,* based on Voltaire's drama. The overture to this opera is very popular.

Semiramis of the North. (1) Margaret of Denmark, Sweden, and Norway (1353–1412); (2) Catherine II of Russia (1729–1796).

Semitic. Pertaining to the descendants of Shem (see *Gen.* x), viz. the Hebrews, Arabs, Assyrians, Aramaeans, etc., nowadays applied in popular use to the Jews, who, when the speaker means to be contemptuous, are often spoken of as *the Semites.*

the Semitic languages. Ancient Assyrian and Chaldee, Aramaean, Syriac, Arabic, Hebrew, Samaritan, Ethiopic, and old Phoenician. The great characteristic of this family of languages is that the roots of words consist of three consonants.

Sénancour, Étienne Pivert de (1770–1846). French man of letters, follower of Rousseau. Best-known for his pessimistic novel *Obermann* (1804) and as the author of *Observations sur le Génie du Christianisme* (1816).

Senanus, St. See under SAINTS.

Sender, Ramón José (1901–). Spanish novelist who served during the Civil War as a brigade commander in the republican army (until 1937). In André Malraux's novel, *Man's Hope* (1939), he appears as "Manuel." He has written *The War In Spain* (1937); *Man's Place* (1940); etc.

Seneca, Lucius Annaeus (4 B. C.–65 A. D.). Latin philosopher and dramatist, a member of the school of STOICISM, known for the rhetorical tragedies called by his name. These include *Hercules, Troades, Phoenissae, Medea, Phaedra, Agamemnon, Oedipus,* and *Thyestes.* Marked by violence, bloodshed, bombast, and characters of little individuality or differentiation, they had an important influence on the tragic drama of Italy, France, and especially Elizabethan England.

Seneca was a tutor of NERO and, when the latter succeeded to the throne of emperor, became an important imperial official, building up a great fortune. When he lost favor, his fortune was confiscated and he committed suicide at Nero's command. His *Naturales Questiones* was used as a textbook of physical science during the Middle Ages.

the Christian Seneca. Joseph Hall (1574–1656), Bishop of Exeter and Norwich.

Sénécal. In Flaubert's SENTIMENTAL EDUCATION, a radical of Syndicalist views who, after the failure of the Revolution of 1848 and the successful *coup d'état* of Napoleon III, becomes a police officer under the Emperor. In his official capacity he kills the naïve DUSSARDIER in a street riot.

senescent. Growing old or aging.

> And now, as the night was senescent,
> And star-dials pointed to morn . . .
> Edgar Allan Poe, *Ulalume.*

Sennacherib. An Assyrian king whose siege of Jerusalem in the days of Hezekiah is dramatically described in 2 *Kings.* In the night "the angel of Jehovah went forth and smote in the camp of the Assyrians a hundred fourscore and five thousand; and when men rose early in the morning, behold these were all dead bodies. So Sennacherib, King of Assyria, departed." BYRON has made this episode the subject of a famous lyric, *The Destruction of Sennacherib,* beginning:

> The Assyrian came down like a wolf on the fold
> And his cohorts were gleaming with purple and gold.

sense.

scared out of my seven senses. According to ancient teaching, the soul of man, or his "inward holy body," is compounded of the seven properties which are under the influence of the seven planets. Fire animates, earth gives the sense of feeling, water gives speech, air gives taste, mist gives sight, flowers give hearing, the south wind gives smelling; hence the seven senses are animation, feeling, speech, taste, sight, hearing, and smelling (see *Ecclus.* xvii. 5).

Sense and Sensibility. A novel by Jane AUSTEN (1811), in which two sisters, Elinor and Marianne, represent "sense" and "sensibility" respectively. Each is deserted by the young man from whom she has been led to expect an offer of matrimony. Elinor is discretion itself, but Marianne, with the foolishly romantic notions of youth, is not content to let well enough alone. Elinor's lover, Edward Ferrars, who has felt honor bound to marry Lucy Steele, a girl of inferior social antecedents, is disinherited, and returns to Elinor when Lucy shifts her interest to his younger brother, the new heir. On the other hand, the dashing John Willoughby, whom Marianne follows to London, furnishes her little but disillusionment, and she finally marries the middle-aged Colonel Brandon.

Sensitive Plant, The. A poem (1820) by Percy Bysshe SHELLEY.

Senta. The heroine of Wagner's opera THE FLYING DUTCHMAN.

Sentences, Master of the. The Schoolman Peter Lombard (d. 1160), an Italian theologian and bishop of Paris, author of *The Four Books of Sentences* (*Sententiarum libri* iv), a compilation from the Fathers of the leading arguments pro and con, bearing on hairsplitting theological questions of the Middle Ages.

The medieval graduates in theology, of the second order, whose duty it was to lecture on the *Sentences,* were called *Sententiatory Bachelors.*

Sentimental Education, The (L'Education Sentimentale). A novel by Gustave FLAUBERT (1869), presenting a satirical picture of life among French dilettantes, intellectuals, and revolutionaries at the time of the Revolution of 1848. The hero, Fréderic MOREAU, is a young man from the provinces who has studied law and wishes to install himself in Paris as a dilettante in the arts and a young man of fashion and affairs, patterning his life according to the modes and principles of his time, in which the influence of the romantic period (see ROMANTICISM) is still strong. He falls in love with Mme ARNOUX, the beautiful and chaste wife of a crude and mercenary art dealer, and suffers from unrequited passion in the best romantic tradition. He sets out on an unsuccessful campaign to win Mme Arnoux as his mistress, but does not allow his passion to interfere with his taking Rosanette BRON as a temporary mistress, seeking a career in society, and eventually becoming the lover of Mme DAMBREUSE, wife of a prominent banker, in the hope of securing a fortune on the death of Dambreuse. As Fréderic's fortunes advance, Mme Arnoux's decline, her husband undertaking and failing in a variety of businesses, each of which is more humble than the one preceding it. Eventually M. Dambreuse dies, but his estate is far less than was anticipated. Fréderic, engaged to marry Mme Dambreuse, forfeits even the reduced inheritance by leaving her, in a sentimental gesture of fidelity to his old love, when the widow, in jealous spite, insists on buying at a creditor's sale of Mme Arnoux's household effects a small box that once belonged to the latter.

After this, Fréderic continues to be disillusioned in his attempts to apply in the changing life of his time the romantic principles he absorbed from his reading as an adolescent. In an ironic conclusion, Mme Arnoux, now old and a widow, at last comes to him and offers herself, but Fréderic, no longer in bondage to his early passion or fearing another and more profound disillusionment, refuses to accept her offer, whereupon she leaves, admiring him for his chivalry.

The action of the novel takes place against a background of the Revolution of 1848 and the establishment of the Second Empire, with careful documentation of the various incidents and events mentioned. Notable portrayals are the assorted artists, intellectuals, liberals, and radicals who are Fréderic's friends. Before the Revolution, they are all for the revival of the principles of 1789, but after Napoleon's successful *coup* they opportunistically become reactionary politically and support the Empire. See also DESLAURIERS; DUSSARDIER; HUSSONET; PELLERIN; ROQUE, LOUISE; VATNAZ, CLÉMENCE; SÉNÉCAL.

Sentimental Journey, A. A famous volume by Laurence STERNE (1768). It was intended to be a collection of sentimental sketches of a tour through Italy in 1764, but the author died soon after completing Part I.

Sentimental Tommy. A novel by J. M. BARRIE (1896), which, together with its sequel *Tommy and Grizel* (1900), relates the story of Thomas Sandys. Tommy is blessed, or cursed, with an over-supply of imagination, and, in whichever of many moods he may happen to be, he sees himself always as a hero playing a hero's part. His talent for writing leads him to adopt the career of author. The loyal Grizel adores but cannot understand him, nor can he, in spite of his spasmodic efforts, succeed in being the faithful lover and husband that she deserves. He meets an accidental death by hanging.

Sentry, Captain. One of the members of the club under whose auspices the SPECTATOR was professedly issued.

Sephardic Jews or **Sephardim.** Jews from Sepharadh, a region of vague identity, later associated with Spain. See also ASHKENAZIM.

sepoy. The Anglicized form of Hindu and Persian *sipahi*, "a soldier," from *sipah*, "army," denoting a native East Indian soldier trained and disciplined in the British manner, especially one in the British Indian Army.

September.

September Bible. See BIBLE, SPECIALLY NAMED.

September Massacres. An indiscriminate slaughter, during the French Revolution, of Loyalists confined in the Abbaye and other prisons, lasting from September 2 to 5, 1792. As many as 8000 persons fell, among whom was the Princesse de Lamballe.

September Morn. French painting of a nude girl which achieved some notoriety in 1917.

Septimius Felton. An unfinished novel by HAWTHORNE, published in 1871 after his death.

Septuagint. A Greek version of the Old Testament and Apocrypha, so called because it was traditionally said to have been made by seventy-two Palestinian Jews in the 3rd century B.C., at the command of Ptolemy Philadelphus. They worked on the island of Pharos and completed the translation in seventy-two days.

This tradition applies, however, only to the Pentateuch; Greek translations of the other books were added by later writers, some, perhaps, being as late as the Christian era. The name Septuagint is frequently printed LXX—"for short."

Serafin, Tullio (1878–). Italian operatic conductor, who succeeded Toscanini as conductor of La SCALA, Milan (1908). Conductor with the Metropolitan Opera Company, New York (1924–1935); guest conductor of the Philadelphia Symphony Orchestra (1929–1930).

Seraglio. The former palace of the Sultan of Turkey at Constantinople, situated on the Golden Horn, and enclosed by walls seven miles and a half in circuit. The chief entrance was *the Sublime Gate* (see *Sublime Porte*);

the chief of the large edifices was the *Harem*, or "sacred spot," which contained numerous houses formerly in use, one for each of the Sultan's wives, and others for his concubines.

seraphic.

the Seraphic Doctor. See under DOCTOR.

the Seraphic saint. St. Francis d'Assisi (1182–1226). See under SAINTS.

seraphim. The highest order of angels in medieval angelology, so named from the seraphim of *Is.* vi. 2. The word is probably the same as *saraph,* "a serpent," from *saraph,* "to burn" (in allusion to its bite); and this connection with burning suggested to early Christian interpreters that the seraphim were specially distinguished by the ardency of their zeal and love. Elizabeth Barrett BROWNING wrote a poem titled *The Seraphim* (1838).

Serapis. An Egyptian deity, combining the attributes of Apis and Osiris. The temples of Serapis were called Serapea. The most famous Serapeum, at Memphis, was the burial place of the sacred bull Apis.

Serbonian Bog. A great morass, now covered with shifting sand, between the isthmus of Suez, the Mediterranean, and the delta of the Nile, that in Strabo's time was a lake stated by him to be 200 stadia long and 50 broad, and by Pliny to be 150 miles in length. TYPHON was said to dwell at the bottom of it; hence its other name, *Typhon's Breathing Hole.* The term is used figuratively of a mess from which there is no way of extricating oneself.

Serendipity. A happy coinage by Horace WALPOLE to denote the faculty of making lucky and unexpected "finds" by accident. In a letter to Mann (January 28, 1754) he says that he formed it on the title of a fairy story, *The Three Princes of Serendip,* because the princes—"were always making discoveries, by accidents and sagacity, of things they were not in quest of."

Serendip is an ancient name of Ceylon.

Serkin, Rudolf (1903–). Bohemian-born Austrian concert pianist, residing in the U.S. Regarded as one of the finest interpreters of Beethoven's piano works.

Sermon on the Mount. Matt. v–vii.

serpentine verses. Verses ending with the same word with which they begin. The following are examples:

Crescit amor nummi, quantum ipsa pecunia crescit.
(Greater grows the love of pelf, as pelf itself grows greater.)

Ambo florentes ætatibus, Arcades ambo.
(Both in the spring of life, Arcadians both.)

The allusion is to the old representations of snakes with their tails in their mouths, which was emblematic of eternity—no beginning and no end.

Serra, Junípero (1713–1784). Spanish Franciscan missionary who worked among the Indians in Mexico City. He led other Franciscans into Upper California (1769), founding nine missions on the coast of California. He converted some six thousand Indians, teaching them to cultivate the mission lands.

Serrano Suñer, Ramón (1901–). Spanish politician, fanatical supporter of his brother-in-law, Francisco FRANCO. Minister of foreign affairs (1940–1942), and head of the Junta Politica.

Servant in the House, The. A drama by Charles Rann KENNEDY (1907). In the guise of a new butler, Manson, the Bishop of Benares, comes into the troubled household of his brother, a vicar, and brings with him peace and a spirit of brotherhood. The vicar's drunkard brother Robert, a plumber, and his daughter Mary, who has been brought up in ignorance of her father, are important characters.

Servetus, Michael. Original Spanish name **Miguel Serveto** (1511–1553). Spanish physician and controversialist. Credited by some with the discovery of the circulation of the blood. See HARVEY. Opposed the church doctrine of the Trinity with the early essay *De Trinitatis Erroribus* (1531) and with *Christianismi Restitutio* (1553), which caused his apprehension by the Inquisition. After a lengthy trial, he was burned at the stake as a heretic upon the instigation of John CALVIN, the "pope of Geneva."

Service, Robert William (1874–). English-born Canadian author, sometimes called "the Canadian Kipling," best known for his poems and ballads of frontier life in the Far North, several of which have become genuine folk property. Among them are *Songs of a Sourdough* (1907); *Ballads of a Cheechako* (1907); *The Spell of the Yukon* (1908); *Bar-Room Ballads* (1940). Other books of verse include *Rhymes of a Rolling Stone* (1913); *Rhymes of a Red Cross Man* (1916); *Ballads of a Bohemian* (1920); *The Trail of '98* (1910) and *The Poisoned Paradise* (1922), novels. *The Shooting of Dan McGrew* is his best-known ballad. His autobiography was published as *Ploughman of the Moon* (1945), and *Harper of Heaven* (1948).

Sesame, Open. The "pass-word" at which the door of the robbers' cave flew open in the tale of *The Forty Thieves* (*Arabian Nights*); hence, a key to a mystery, or anything that acts like magic in obtaining a favor, admission, recognition, etc.

Sesame is an East Indian annual herb, with an oily seed which is used as a food, a laxative, etc. In Egypt the natives eat sesame cakes, and the Jews frequently add the seed to their bread.

Sesame and Lilies. The title of a collection of lectures on reading, education of women, and the mysteries of life and art by John RUSKIN (1865).

Sesha. In the mythology of India, the serpent king who supports the world on his head.

Sesphra. In Cabell's FIGURES OF EARTH, a limping figure modeled by MANUEL and given life by the magic of Queen Freydis, who reappears later to tempt Manuel to leave his wife and child and visit strange lands. He is called *Sesphra of the Dreams,* and Carl Van Doren has pointed out that his name is "phrases" transposed.

sesquipedalian. Literally, "a foot and a half in length." Applied, usually with a humorous intent, to very long words.

sesterce. A Roman coin equal to one quarter of a denarius, first issued in the third century B. C.

sestet. A stanza of six lines, especially the last six lines of the Italian SONNET.

sestiad. One of the six parts or cantos of a poem. The term was first used by Marlowe and Chapman in *Hero and Leander,* where it served with a corresponding number to designate the beginning of each new section. It has nothing to do with six (as *sestina* for instance has) but was originally derived from the place name Sestos (residence of Hero) after the model of *Iliad.*

sestina. A poem of six verses in which the final words of the first stanza appear in inverted order in all the others. Invented by Arnaud DANIEL; adopted by DANTE and PETRARCH and, through the medium of French models, by SWINBURNE.

Sestius or **Sextius, Publius.** Roman politician; instrumental in bringing about the recall of Cicero from exile (57 B. C.) after having helped him to crush the conspiracy of Catiline. He was defended by Cicero (56 B. C.) when he was accused of using illegal force as a tribune. During the civil war, he supported Pompey, but later joined Caesar.

Sestos. An ancient city on the European side of the HELLESPONT, where Hero dwelled in the legend of HERO AND LEANDER. See also ABYDOS.

Set. The Egyptian original of the Greek TYPHON, the god of evil, brother (or son) of OSIRIS, and his deadly enemy. He is represented as having the body of a man and the head of some unidentified mythological beast with pointed muzzle and high square ears.

Setebos. A savage god, spoken of in Shakespeare's TEMPEST as the deity worshiped by Sycorax, mother of CALIBAN, and described in some of the old books of travel among native tribes, notably Eden's *History of Travaile* (1577). Robert BROWNING wrote a poem with the title *Caliban upon Setebos.*

Seton, Ernest Thompson (1860–1946). Famous American writer on natural history. His best-known book is *Wild Animals I Have Known* (1898), illustrated by himself, as were most of his other works.

Settala, Lucio. The young sculptor in D'Annunzio's drama LA GIOCONDA.

Settembrini, Ludovico. In Thomas Mann's THE MAGIC MOUNTAIN, an Italian, one of the patients at the HAUS BERGHOF, who becomes a friend of Hans CASTORP. Settembrini is considered to represent the tradition of humanism, classicism, and political liberalism or republicanism, emphasizing form, reason, social morality, and education. Speaking eloquently, he tries to save Castorp from yielding to the insidious influence of the Magic Mountain, symbol of sterile aestheticism. Leo NAPHTA is Settembrini's intellectual foil, and the two argue ceaselessly, finally fighting a duel, after which Naphta commits suicide.

Settle, Elkanah (1648–1724). English playwright, chiefly remembered as a butt of ridicule for DRYDEN and POPE. His bombastic plays so annoyed Dryden that he pilloried him as Doeg in *Absalom and Achitophel* (1682).

Seurat, Georges (1859–1891). French painter of pointillistic canvases, with Paul Signac one of the founders of neo-impressionism. His style is best exemplified by *Île de la Grand-Jatte.*

Seuss, Dr., see GEISEL, THEODOR SEUSS.

seven. A mystic or sacred number; it is composed of four and three, which, among the Pythagoreans, were, and from time immemorial have been, accounted lucky numbers. Among the Babylonians, Egyptians, and other ancient peoples, there were seven sacred planets. The Hebrew verb *to swear* means literally "to come under the influence of seven things"; thus seven ewe lambs figure in the oath between Abraham and Abimelech at Beersheba (*Gen.* xxi. 28), and Herodotus (III. viii) describes an Arabian oath in which seven stones are smeared with blood.

There are seven days in Creation, seven days in the week, seven graces, seven divisions in the Lord's Prayer, and seven ages in the life of man; climacteric years are seven and nine with their multiples by odd numbers; and the seventh son of a seventh son was held notable.

Among the Hebrews, every seventh year was sabbatical, and seven times seven years was the jubilee. The three great Jewish feasts lasted seven days, and between the first and second were seven weeks. Levitical purifications lasted seven days; Baalam would have seven altars, and sacrificed on them seven bullocks and seven rams; Naaman was commanded to dip seven times in Jordan; Elijah sent his servant seven times to look out for rain; ten times seven Israelites went to Egypt, the exile lasted the same number of years, and there were ten times seven elders. Pharaoh in his dream saw seven kine and seven ears of corn; Jacob served seven years for each of his wives; seven priests with seven trumpets marched round Jericho once every day, but seven times on the seventh day; Samson's wedding feast lasted seven days, on the seventh he told his bride the riddle, he was bound with seven withes, and seven locks of his hair were shorn; Nebuchadnezzar was a beast for seven years; etc.

In the Apocalypse, we have seven churches of Asia, seven candlesticks, seven stars, seven trumpets, seven spirits before the throne of God, seven horns, seven vials, seven plagues, a seven-headed monster, and the Lamb with seven eyes.

The old astrologers and alchemists recognized seven planets, each having its own "heaven"—

> The bodies seven, eek, lo hem heer anoon;
> Sol gold is, and Luna silver we threpe,
> Mars yren, Mercurie quyksilver we clepe;
> Saturnus leed, and Jubitur is tyn;
> And Venus coper, by my fader kyn.
>
> Chaucer, *Prol. of the Canon's Yeoman's Tale.*

And from this very ancient belief sprang the theory that man was composed of seven substances, and has seven natures. See under SENSE.

the Seven. Used of groups of seven people, especially (1) the "men of honest report" chosen by the Apostles to be the first Deacons (*Acts* vi. 5), viz., Stephen, Philip, Prochorus, Nicanor, Timon, Parmenas and Nicolas; (2) the Seven Bishops or (3) the Seven Sages of Greece.

Seven against Thebes. The seven Argive heroes (Adrastus, Polynices, Tydeus, Amphiaraus, Capaneus, Hippomedon and Parthenopaeus), who, according to Greek legend, made war on Thebes with the object of restoring Polynices (son of OEDIPUS), who had been expelled by his brother Eteocles. See also THEBES.

Seven Bishops. Archbishop Sancroft, and Bishops Lloyd, Turner, Kew, White, Lake, and Trelawney, who refused to read James II's Declaration of Indulgence (1688), and were in consequence imprisoned for nonconforming.

seven bodies in alchemy. The Sun is gold, the Moon silver, Mars iron, Mercury quicksilver, Saturn lead, Jupiter tin, and Venus copper. Cf. the quotation from Chaucer above.

Seven Champions. The medieval designation of the national patron saints of England, Scotland, Wales, Ireland, France, Spain, and Italy. In 1596 Richard Johnson published a chap-book, *The Famous History of the Seven Champions of Christendom.* In this he relates that *St. George* of England was seven years imprisoned by the Almidor, the black king of Morocco; *St. Denys* of France lived seven years in the form of a hart; *St. James* of Spain was seven years dumb out of love for a fair Jewess; *St. Anthony* of Italy, with the other champions, was enchanted into a deep sleep in the Black Castle, and was released by St. George's three sons, who quenched the seven lamps by water from the enchanted fountain; *St. Andrew* of Scotland delivered six ladies who had lived seven years under the form of white swans; *St. Patrick* of Ireland was immured in a cell where he scratched his grave with his own nails; and *St. David* of Wales slept seven years in the enchanted garden of Ormandine, and was redeemed by St. George.

Seven Churches of Asia. Those mentioned in *Rev.* i. 11, viz.:

(1) Ephesus, founded by St. Paul, 57, in a ruinous state in the time of Justinian.

(2) Smyrna. Polycarp was its first bishop.

(3) Pergamus, renowned for its library.

(4) Thyatira, now called Ak-hissar ("the White Castle").

(5) Sardis, now Sart, a small village.

(6) Philadelphia, now called Allah Shehr (*City of God*), a small town.

(7) Laodicea, now a deserted place called Eski-hissar ("the Old Castle").

seven cities warred for Homer being dead. See HOMER.

the Island of the Seven Cities. A kind of "Dixie land" of Spanish fable, where seven bishops, who quitted Spain during the dominion of the Moors, founded seven cities. The legend says that many have visited the island, but no one has ever left it.

Seven Gifts of the Spirit. Wisdom, Understanding, Counsel, Power or Fortitude, Knowledge, Righteousness, and Godly Fear.

Seven Gods of Luck. In Japanese folklore, Benten, goddess of love, Bishamon, god of war, Daikoku, of wealth, Ebisu, of self-effacement, Fukurokujin and Jurojin, gods of longevity, and Hstei, god of generosity. These are really popular conceptions of the seven Buddhist *Devas* who preside over human happiness and welfare.

Seven Heavens. See HEAVEN.

Seven-Hilled City. In Latin *Urbs Septicollis;* ancient Rome, built on seven hills, surrounded by Servius Tullius with a line of fortifications. The seven hills are the Palatinus, the Capitolinus, the Quirinalis, the Caelius, the Aventinus, the Viminalis, and the Esquilinus.

Seven Joys. See *St. Mary* under SAINTS.

Seven Lamps of Architecture. A volume by RUSKIN (1849). The seven lamps are Sacrifice, Truth, Power, Beauty, Life, Memory, and Obedience.

seven mortal sins. Pride, wrath, envy, lust, gluttony, avarice and sloth.

seven names of God. The ancient Hebrews had many names for the Deity and the Seven over which the scribes had to exercise particular care were—El, Elohim, Adonai, YHWH (i.e., our *Jehovah*), Ehyeh-Asher-Ehyeh, Shaddai, and Zebaot. In medieval times God was sometimes called simply, *The Seven.*

Now lord, for thy naymes sevyn, that made both moyn and starnys,
Well mo then I can neven thi will, lord, of me tharnys.
Towneley Mysteries, xiii, 191 (about 1460).

seven sciences. See SCIENCE.

seven seas. The Arctic and Antarctic, North and South Pacific, North and South Atlantic, and the Indian oceans. KIPLING called a volume of his poems *The Seven Seas* (1896).

Seven Sisters. An old name of the PLEIADES; also given to a set of seven cannon, cast by one Robert Borthwick and used at Flodden (1513)—

And these were Borthwick's "Sisters Seven,"
And culverins which France had given;
Ill omened gift! The guns remain
The conqueror's spoil on Flodden plain.
Scott, *Marmion,* iv.

Seven Sleepers. Seven noble youths of Ephesus, according to the legend, who fled in the Decian persecution (250) to a cave in Mount Celion. After 230 years, or, according to some versions, 309 years, they awoke, but soon died, and their bodies were taken to Marseilles in a large stone coffin, still shown in Victor's church. Their names are Constantine, Dionysius, John, Maximian, Malchus, Martinian, and Serapion. This fable took its rise from misapprehension of the words, "They fell asleep in the Lord"—i.e., died. According to the Koran, the Sleepers had a dog named KATMIR who kept watch over them (Ch. xviii).

Seven Sorrows. See St. Mary under SAINTS.

seven times Christ spoke on the cross. (1) "Father, forgive them; for they know not what they do"; (2) "To-day shalt thou be with Me in paradise"; (3) "Woman, behold thy son!" etc.; (4) "My God, My God, why hast Thou forsaken Me?" (5) "I thirst"; (6) "It is finished" (7) "Father, into Thy hands I commend My spirit."

Seven Virtues. Faith, hope, charity, prudence, justice, fortitude, and temperance. The first three are called "the holy virtues."

Seven Weeks' War. That between Austria and Prussia, in 1866, for the supremacy of Germany. The war was declared by Austria, June 17, and the Peace of Presburg (giving Prussia the victory) was signed August 20.

Seven Wise Masters. A collection of Oriental tales supposed to be told by his advisers to an Eastern king to show the evils of hasty punishment, with his answers to them. Lucien, the son of the King (who, in some versions, is named Dolopathos), is falsely accused to him by one of his queens. By consulting the stars the Prince discovers that his life is in danger, but that all will be well if he remains silent for seven days. The "Wise Masters" now take up the matter; each one in turn tells the King a tale to illustrate the evils of ill-considered punishment, and as each tale ends the King resolves to relent; but the Queen at night persuades him to carry out his sentence. The seven days being passed, the Prince tells a tale which embodies the whole truth, whereupon the King sentences the Queen to death. This collection of tales is known as SANDABAR'S PARABLES.

seven wonders of the world. See under WONDER.

Seven Years' War. The third period of the War of the Austrian Succession, between Maria Theresa of Austria and Friedrich II of Prussia. It began in 1756, and terminated in 1763. At the close of the war, Silesia was handed over to Prussia.

Seven Arts, The. An American monthly periodical of literature and opinion, one of the best-known of the LITTLE MAGAZINES of the early 20th century, founded in 1916 and published until October, 1917. Its aim was to provide a vehicle for the expression of ideas and forms to which the conservative journals of the day were closed, and it failed as a financial venture because of its pacifist views. See PACIFISM. Van Wyck BROOKS and Waldo FRANK were among its editors, and its contributors included Sherwood ANDERSON, John REED, John Dos PASSOS, Randolph BOURNE, Theodore DREISER, and H. L. MENCKEN.

Seven Dials. A region in London, named after a column topped by seven dials which formerly occupied the center of a square in which seven streets converged. Seven Dials was at one time a very squalid neighborhood frequented by disreputable characters.

Seventeen. A story by Booth TARKINGTON (1916). Its hero is William Sylvanus Baxter, known as "Willie" at home and "Silly Bill" at school. He is smitten by the charms of Lola Pratt, a stranger in town whose chief accomplishment is talking baby talk to her pet dog Flopit and to her numerous admirers. Willie calls upon Lola in his father's dress suit with awful but amusing consequences. The story has been dramatized and made into a motion picture.

Severn. The second longest river in England. Its name corresponds to the Latin Sabrina. According to legend, the name is derived from Sabra, who, together with her mother Estrildis, was thrown into the river by Queen Guendolen.

Severn, Joseph (1793–1879). English painter, chiefly remembered as a friend of John KEATS whom he accompanied to Italy (1820), and attended on Keats's deathbed.

Severus, St. See under SAINTS.

Sevier, John (1745–1815). American frontiersman, Indian fighter, and first governor of Tennessee (1796–1801; 1803–1809); a character in *The Crossing* (1904) by the novelist Winston CHURCHILL.

Sévigné, Marquise **de.** *Née* **Marie de Rabutin-Chantal** (1626–1696). French author and social leader, famous for her letters, *Lettres de Mme de Sévigné,* written to her daughter, Mme de Grignan, and to an intimate circle of friends, dealing with life at court, life in the city, the countryside, her domestic affairs, and her reading. They are marked by wit, imagination, intelligence, learning, and sincerity.

Sèvres. A town near Paris, famous for its porcelain.

Sewall, Samuel (1652–1730). English-born American statesman of early New England, known for his liberal views and for his *Diary,* written between 1674 and 1729, which gives a lively and vivid picture of life and personalities in the Boston of his day and has been compared to the similar and more famous work of Samuel PEPYS. Among his other writings are *The Revolution in New England Justified* (1691), which seeks to justify the deposition of the dictatorial English governor Andros; *The Selling of Joseph* (1700), an attack on slavery; and *A Memorial Relating to the Kennebec Indians* (1721), a humanitarian appeal with regard to the settlers' treatment of the Indians.

Sewall held a number of political offices in the colony of Massachusetts, serving as a deputy to the general court, a member of the Council, and eventually Chief Justice of the superior court. He was one of the judges at the SALEM WITCHCRAFT trials, but later repented publicly in church while his confession was read to the congregation. He is considered an excellent representative of the rising merchant class of New England of his time.

Sewanee Review. A literary quarterly published by the University of the South at Sewanee, Tennessee. It was established by W. P. TRENT in 1892 and is the oldest quarterly of its kind in the United States.

Seward, Anna (1747–1809). English poet who was known as "the Swan of Lichfield." She helped Boswell from her knowledge of Dr. Johnson. She bequeathed her poems to Sir Walter Scott, who published three volumes of them (1810) with a memoir. Cf. *The Singing Swan,* by Margaret Ashmun.

Seward, William Henry (1801–1872). Governor of New York (1839–1843) and U.S. senator (1849–1861). He denounced the DRED SCOTT DECISION and remarked that the issue of slavery was an "irrepressible conflict between North and South." He supported the "squatter sovereignty" plan of Douglas. Lincoln made him Secretary of State (1861). At the time of Lincoln's assassination, an attempt was made to assassinate Seward also, but he recovered and continued as Secretary of State under Andrew Johnson (until 1869). He negotiated the purchase of Alaska from Russia (1867), at one time spoken of as "Seward's folly."

Sewell, Anna (1820–1878). English author whose novel *Black Beauty* (1877) is one of the most famous horse stories in literature.

Sewell, Rev. David. A minister who plays a leading part in Howells' MINISTER'S CHARGE and appears also in THE RISE OF SILAS LAPHAM.

sextette. A group of six, especially of singers, as the Sextette from LUCIA, the *Floradora* Sextette, etc.

Seyd. In Byron's CORSAIR, Pasha of the Morea, assassinated by Gulnare, his favorite concubine.

Seymour, Mrs. **Beatrice Kean.** English novelist; author of a trilogy about a domestic servant, and other novels, uneven in treatment.

Seymour, Charles (1885–). Son of a professor of Greek at Yale, himself president of Yale (since 1937). Author of *The Diplomatic Background of the War* (1916); *The Intimate Papers of Colonel House* (4 vols.; 1926–1928); etc.

Seymour, Horatio (1810–1886). Governor of New York (1853–1855; 1863–1865). Helped to stop the Draft Riots in New York (1863); was Democratic candidate for president (1868); and helped Governor Tilden drive Boss Tweed from power.

Seyss-Inquart, Artur von (1892–). Austrian minister of the interior in the SCHUSCHNIGG cabinet. Chancellor and minister of defense after the German occupation (1938). He was appointed by Hitler governor of the Ostmark (Austria; 1938), deputy governor of occupied German territory in Poland (1939), and German high commissioner of the Netherlands (1940).

Seyton, Catherine. Heroine of Scott's novel THE ABBOT, a maid of honor in the court of Queen Mary.

Sforza. Name of a celebrated Italian family that ruled Milan. A descendant is the Italian statesman, Count **Carlo Sforza** (1873–), a leader of anti-Fascism in Italy (since 1922), who finally came to the U.S. (1940) and is the author of a number of books, including *The Real Italians* (1942); he returned to Italy after the victory of the United Nations.

Sganarelle. In the comedies of MOLIÈRE, a favorite name for the cowardly, domineering or unpleasant character:

(1) *Sganarelle, ou Le Cocu imaginaire* (1660). This is a farce hinging on the complexities brought about by Sganarelle's confiscation of a gentleman's miniature which he thinks has been dropped by his wife. In reality it is the portrait of Lélie which his sweetheart Clélie has lost.

(2) *L'École des maris* (1661). In this comedy Sganarelle and his older brother Ariste are the guardians of two young orphans, Isabelle and Leonor. The conceited and domineering Sganarelle expects to marry Isabelle but makes her lead such a dull, strict life in the meantime that she dupes him and marries Valère instead.

(3) *Le Mariage forcé* (1664). Here Sganarelle, a rich man of sixty-four, promises marriage to Dorimene, a girl under twenty, but decides at the last minute to draw back from the alliance. Dorimene's brother beats him ruthlessly until he consents to go to the altar.

(4) *L'Amour médecin* (1664). Sganarelle is the father of LUCINDE in this play.

(5) *Don Juan* (1665). Here Sganarelle is Don Juan's rather foolish, cowardly valet.

(6) *Le Médecin malgré lui* (1666). In this final play, of which *Le Cocu imaginaire* is logically the sequel, Sganarelle is a faggot maker. Martine, his wife, to get even with him for striking her, tells some inquirers that he is a noted doctor but so eccentric that he will deny it until they beat him well. He is taken to the house of Lucinde, who is apparently dumb, but the shrewd Sganarelle sees through her pretense and brings her lover Léandre in the guise of an apothecary.

Shabby Genteel Story, A. An unfinished tale by THACKERAY usually printed as a sort of prologue to THE ADVENTURES OF PHILIP, which continues the story. The heroine, Caroline Gann, is tricked into a sham wedding by a man named George Brandon.

Shacabac, see SCHACABAC.

Shackleton, Sir **Ernest Henry** (1874–1922). English explorer: Accompanied Robert F. SCOTT (1901) and nearly reached the South Pole in an expedition of his own (1909). In 1918–1919, he organized the winter equipment of the British North-Russian Expeditionary Force. He wrote accounts of his expeditions in *Heart of the Antarctic* (1909) and *South* (1919).

Shadow, The Man Without a. See under PETER SCHLEMIHLS WUNDERBARE GESCHICHTE.

Shadow-of-a-Leaf. A kind of elf who figures in several poems and a poetic drama by Alfred NOYES. He is used as a symbol of spiritual things.

Shadows on the Rock. A novel by Willa CATHER (1931), dealing with life in the French settlement of Quebec in the 18th century. The characters include Bishop Laval; Monseigneur de Saint-Vallier; Mother Juschereau and her nuns; Euclide Auclair, an apothecary; Cécile Auclair, Euclide's daughter; Pierre Charron, a fur-trader; and Jacques, a friendless boy brought up by the Auclairs. Cécile and Charron eventually marry.

Shadrach, Meshach, and **Abednego.** Three Hebrews (*Dan.* iii, 22) who, because of their refusal to worship a golden image, were cast, by the command of NEBUCHADNEZZAR, into a fiery furnace. They received no injury, although the furnace was made so hot that the heat thereof "slew those men" that took them to the furnace.

Shadwell, Thomas (1642?–1692). English poet and playwright. His works include *Sullen Lovers* (1668), based on *Les Fâcheux,* by MOLIÈRE, *Timon of Athens* (1678), *The Squire of Alsatia* (1688), *Epsom Wells* (1673), and *Bury Fair* (1689), all plays; *The Enchanted Island* (1673), an opera based on Shakespeare's THE TEMPEST; *The Medal of John Bayes* (1682) and a translation of the *Tenth Satire* of Juvenal (1687), satires.

Shadwell is best known for his literary feud with John DRYDEN, during which the two poets exchanged satires directed against each other. MACFLECKNOE was directed by Dryden against Shadwell, and in the second part of ABSALOM AND ACHITOPHEL Shadwell again is attacked under the name of Og.

Shaflites. One of the four sects of the SUNNITES; so called from Al-Shafei (d. 819), a descendant of MAHOMET. See also SHIITES.

Shafter, William R. (1835–1906). American major general of volunteers in the Spanish-American War (1898). Received the surrender of the city of Santiago de Cuba (July 17, 1898).

Shaftesbury, Anthony Ashley Cooper, 1st Earl of **Shaftesbury** (1621–1683). A supporter of King Charles I in the English Civil War. After the Restoration he became a member of the CABAL. He was also chancellor, a fomenter of the Popish plot, and a supporter of the Duke of Monmouth. He has been made famous by Dryden as the character Achitophel in *Absalom and Achitophel.*

Shafton, Sir Piercie. In Scott's MONASTERY, a fashionable cavalier, grandson of old Overstitch, the tailor of Holderness. Sir Piercie talks in the pedantic style of the Elizabethan courtiers and is noted for his affectations.

Shah. See RULERS, TITLES OF.

Shah Namah. The famous Persian epic of FIRDAUSI, the most ancient in modern Persian. Rusten or RUSTAM is the Achilles, Feridun the model king, Zohak the cruel and impious tyrant, Kavah (the blacksmith) the intrepid patriot who marches against Zohak, displaying his apron as a banner.

Rusten's horse is called Rakush; the prophetic bird is Simurgh; Rusten's mother is Rudabeh. Her child (Rusten) is cut out of her side, and the wound is healed by milk and honey applied with a feather of the prophetic bird Simurgh. Rusten requires the milk of ten wet-nurses, and when a mere youth kills an elephant with a blow of his mace.

Shakers. A sect of Second Adventists, founded in the 18th century in England by a secession from the Quakers, and transplanted in America by Ann Lee (1736–1784), or "Mother Ann," as she is generally known. Their official name is "The United Society of Believers in Christ's Second Appearing" or "The Millennial Church"; their popular name was given them in derision at their contortions during the religious dances of which their public form of worship chiefly consists.

Shakespeare, William (1564–1616). English poet and dramatist of the Elizabethan and early Jacobean period, probably the most widely known author in all English literature. His plays, the plots of most of which were derived from traditional medieval legend, contemporary chronicles, classic literature, and existent dramas of his own day, are distinguished by a more profound understanding and conception of character than is found in the work of other Elizabethan playwrights and by superior poetry of great delicacy, sensitivity, variety, and dramatic appropriateness. His lyric and narrative poetry is closer to the conventional product of his time but, especially in his SONNETS and the songs from his plays, it is often marked by a combination of imagination, precision, and deep and sincere emotion that is lacking in similar work of his contemporaries.

The following is a list of the accepted canon of Shakespeare's thirty-seven plays, arranged in the classification sometimes used, and followed by the dates generally agreed upon, by 20th-century scholars:

Experiment.

LOVE'S LABOR'S LOST (ca. 1590)
THE COMEDY OF ERRORS (ca. 1591)
TWO GENTLEMEN OF VERONA (ca. 1592)
KING HENRY VI, Parts 1, 2, and 3 (1592?)
THE TRAGEDY OF KING RICHARD III (ca. 1593)
ROMEO AND JULIET (ca. 1593)

Development.

TITUS ANDRONICUS (1594)
THE TRAGEDY OF KING RICHARD II (ca. 1594)
A MIDSUMMER NIGHT'S DREAM (ca. 1594)
THE LIFE AND DEATH OF KING JOHN (ca. 1594)
THE MERCHANT OF VENICE (ca. 1595)
THE TAMING OF THE SHREW (ca. 1596)
KING HENRY IV, Part 1 (1597?)
KING HENRY IV, Part 2 (1598?)
THE LIFE OF KING HENRY V (1599)
THE MERRY WIVES OF WINDSOR (1599?)
MUCH ADO ABOUT NOTHING (ca. 1599)
JULIUS CAESAR (1599)
AS YOU LIKE IT (ca. 1600)
TWELFTH NIGHT (1600?)

Tragedies.

ALL'S WELL THAT ENDS WELL (ca. 1602)
TROILUS AND CRESSIDA (ca. 1602)
HAMLET (ca. 1602)
MEASURE FOR MEASURE (ca. 1604)
OTHELLO, THE MOOR OF VENICE (ca. 1604)
KING LEAR (1605?)
MACBETH (1606?)
ANTONY AND CLEOPATRA (1607?)
CORIOLANUS (ca. 1608)
TIMON OF ATHENS (ca. 1608)
PERICLES, PRINCE OF TYRE (ca. 1608)

Romances.

CYMBELINE (1610?)
THE WINTER'S TALE (1610?)
THE TEMPEST (1611?)
THE FAMOUS HISTORY OF THE LIFE OF KING HENRY VIII (ca. 1611)

The most famous of these are *Hamlet, Romeo and Juliet, Macbeth, Othello, King Lear, A Midsummer Night's Dream, Julius Caesar,* and *As You Like It.* Shakespeare's nondramatic works are *Venus and Adonis* (1593), *The Rape of Lucrece* (1594), and his *Sonnets* (1609).

Beyond the fact that his birthplace was Stratford-on-Avon, that his father at one time was a butcher, that he was a player with the Lord Chamberlain's company, and that he lived for awhile as a country gentleman after his success in the theater, very little is known of Shakespeare's life; as a result, numerous writers have speculated on it and tried to find biographical significance in his works, especially his Sonnets. See W. H. There are also a great many curious theories ascribing Shakespeare's plays to other authors, notably BACON.

He was popular in his own day and much admired by his contemporaries, but during the later 17th century and the 18th century his value as a poet and dramatist was minimized. In the period of ROMANTICISM interest in him and his works was revived in the criticism of S. T. COLERIDGE, Charles LAMB, and William HAZLITT, and later Shakespearean enthusiasm grew to the point of adulation, with Germany and other European countries adopting the playwright as one of their own authors.

See also FIRST FOLIO; PASSIONATE PILGRIM, THE.

the Shakespeare of divines. Jeremy Taylor (1613–1667).

the Shakespeare of eloquence. So Barnave characterized the Comte de Mirabeau (1749–1791).

the Shakespeare of prose fiction. DISRAELI so called Richardson, the novelist (1689–1761).

the German Shakespeare. Kotzebue (1761–1819) has been so styled.

the Spanish Shakespeare. Calderón (1600–1681).

shako. A stiff military head-dress, as the high bearskin head-dress of the British foot guards and the hats of the officers of the Cadet Corps at West Point.

Shaler, Nathaniel Southgate (1841–1906). American geologist, dean of the Lawrence Scientific School at Harvard (1891–1906).

Shallow, Justice Robert. A character who appears in Shakespeare's 2 *Henry IV* and *Henry V* and, more prominently, in THE MERRY WIVES OF WINDSOR; a weak-minded country justice, cousin to SLENDER. He is a great braggart, and especially fond of boasting of the mad pranks of his younger days, many of them imaginary. It is said that Justice Shallow is a satirical portrait of Sir Thomas Lucy of Charlecote, who prosecuted Shakespeare for deer-stalking.

Shamanism. A primitive form of religion; those who practice it believe that the world and all events are governed by good and evil spirits who can be propitiated or bought off only through the intervention of a witch-doctor, or *Shaman.* The word is Slavonic; it comes from the Samoyeds and other Siberian peoples, but is now applied to Red Indian and other primitive worship.

Shand, John and *Maggie.* The principal characters of Barrie's play WHAT EVERY WOMAN KNOWS.

Shandon, Captain. A famous character in *The History of Pendennis* (1849–1850) by THACKERAY.

Shandy, Tristram. The hero of Sterne's novel TRISTRAM SHANDY. Tristram's father, Walter Shandy, his mother, Elizabeth Shandy, and his Uncle Toby, more formally known as Captain Tobias Shandy, are also prominent characters. *Shandean* means characteristic of the Shandy family or of the book.

Shangri-La. In James HILTON's popular novel *Lost Horizon,* a mythical land of eternal youth supposedly situated somewhere in the interior of Tibet. During World War II the term became widely known for a time (1942) as the supposed base of an American air bombing raid on Japan, President Franklin D. ROOSEVELT facetiously announcing it as such to the press.

Shannon. A river in Ireland.

dipped in the Shannon. One who has been dipped in the Shannon loses all bashfulness; at least, so they say.

Shannon, Charles (1863–1937). English painter and lithographer, friend of Charles RICKETTS.

Shannon, Fred Albert (1893–). American historian. Received both an award from the American Historical Association and the Pulitzer prize for his doctoral thesis, *The Organization and Administration of the Union Army 1861–1865* (1928).

shanty songs (from Fr. *chanter,* "to sing"). Songs sung by sailors at work, to ensure united action; also called *chanties.* They are in sets, each of which has a different cadence adapted to the work at hand. Thus, in sheeting topsails, weighing anchor, etc., one of the most popular of the shanty songs runs thus:

> I'm bound away, this very day,
> I'm bound for the Rio Grande.
> Ho, you, Rio!
> Then fare you well, my bonny blue bell,
> I'm bound for the Rio Grande.

Shan Van Voght. This famous song (composed 1798) has been called the Irish *Marseillaise.* The title of it is a corruption of *Ant-sean bhean bhocht* (the poor old woman—i.e., Ireland). The last verse is:

> Will Ireland then be free?
> Said the Shan Van Voght. (*repeat*)
> Yes, Ireland shall be free
> From the centre to the sea,
> Hurrah for liberty!
> Said the Shan Van Voght.

Shapcott, Reuben. A pseudonym adopted by William Hale White (1829–1913), author of MARK RUTHERFORD.

Shapes of Clay. A volume of poems (1903) by Ambrose BIERCE.

Shapley, Harlow (1885–). American astronomer. Most of his writing is highly technical, but he can also write engagingly for the general public. Among his works are *The Stars* (1927); *A Source Book on Astronomy* (with H. E. Howarth; 1929); *Flights From Chaos* (1930); etc.

Sharp, Becky. See under BECKY SHARP.

Sharp, Margery (1905–). English writer whose best-selling novel has been *The Nutmeg Tree* (1937). She has contributed successfully to many popular magazines, and is the author of *Cluny Brown* (1945); and *Britannia Mews* (1946), deft, humorous novels.

Sharp, William. Pen name **Fiona Macleod** (1856?–1905). Scottish man of letters; promoter of the Celtic revival. Wrote under his own name several volumes of poetry and a number of biographies; as Fiona Macleod wrote *Pharais* (1894); *The Sin-Eater* (1895); *The Immortal Hour* (1900; a drama); etc. The identity of Sharp and Macleod was revealed only posthumously.

Shatov, Ivan. In Dostoyevsky's THE POSSESSED, a former peasant on the estate of Varvara Petrovna STAVROGIN, simple, earnest, confused, honest. He has been a member of the revolutionary band headed by Nikolay Stavrogin and Pyotr Stepanovich VERHOVENSKY, very much under the influence of Stavrogin, but he reforms and plans to start his life over. He is eventually murdered at the behest of Verhovensky for fear he will betray the band. Shatov, in the expression of his views on the salvation of Russia through religion and Christian love, is considered to serve as a mouthpiece of the author.

Darya Pavlovna Shatova. Ivan's sister, also a character in the novel. She is a servant in the household of Varvara Petrovna, a simple, meek, devoted, faithful-hearted girl who is in love with Nikolay Stavrogin and is instantly ready to do anything he asks. Before his suicide he asks her to come away with him and without a word she prepares to do so.

Marya Ignatyevna Shatova. Ivan's wife, once involved in a love affair with Nikolay Stavrogin. On the evening of Ivan's murder she gives birth to a child which, although it makes her husband deliriously happy, is suggested to be Stavrogin's.

Shatriya. One of the four great castes of Hinduism. See CASTE.

Shaun. See *Kevin Earwicker,* under EARWICKER.

Shavian. A word applied to anything resembling the thought or humor of George Bernard SHAW.

Shaving of Shagpat, The. A whimsical oriental tale by George MEREDITH (1856), narrating the adventures of Shibli Bagarag who in due course of time becomes a barber and shaves Shagpat.

Shaw, Albert (1857–1947). Founder and editor (1891–1937) of the *American Review of Reviews.* Editor of the *Literary Digest* (1937–1939). Author of a number of books, including *Abraham Lincoln* (2 vols.; 1929).

Shaw, Anna Howard (1847–1919). English-born American woman suffrage leader. President of the National American Woman Suffrage Association (1904–1915).

Shaw, George Bernard (1856–). Irish dramatist, critic, essayist, and lecturer, one of the most celebrated and most discussed authors of the last decade of the 19th century and the first three decades of the 20th century. His writings, influenced by the ideas of IBSEN and NIETZSCHE and the theories of biological science and Fabian Socialism of the period of the author's prime, are characterized by fantasy, wit, satire, iconoclasm, and social perspective. The chief objects of his satirical attacks are social conventions, marriage and infidelity, orthodox religion and morality, social snobbery, philanthropy, social aristocracy, hypocrisy, and, especially, the politics and diplomacy of Great Britain.

Shaw's first works, written between 1879 and 1883, were novels, including *Immaturity, The Irrational Knot, Cashel Byron's Profession, An Unsocial Socialist,* and *Love Among the Artists.* Among his plays, the prefaces to the published versions of which became famous in their own right, are the following: *Plays: Pleasant and Unpleasant* (1898), two volumes containing ARMS AND THE MAN, CANDIDA, THE MAN OF DESTINY, *You Never Can Tell, Widowers' Houses, The Philanderer,* and MRS. WARREN'S PROFESSION; *Three Plays for Puritans* (1900), containing *The Devil's Disciple, Caesar and Cleopatra* (see CAESAR, CAIUS JULIUS), and CAPTAIN BRASSBOUND'S CONVERSION; MAN AND SUPERMAN (1903); JOHN BULL'S OTHER ISLAND (1904); MAJOR BARBARA (1905); *The Doctor's Dilemma* (1906); *Getting Married* (1908); PYGMALION (1912); ANDROCLES AND THE LION (1913); HEARTBREAK HOUSE (1919); BACK TO METHUSELAH (1921); *Saint Joan* (1923); *The Apple Cart* (1929); *Too True to Be Good* (1932); *On the Rocks* (1934); *The Simpleton of the Unexpected Isles, The Six of Calais,* and *The Millionairess* (1934); *Geneva* (1938), *In Good King Charles's Golden Days* (1939).

Other works of Shaw include *Fabian Essays* (1889), a collection edited by him; a number of political and economic treatises written according to Fabian views; *Dramatic Opinions and Essays* (1907); *The Quintessence of Ibsenism* (1891); *The Sanity of Art* (1895); *The Intelligent Woman's Guide to Socialism and Capitalism* (1928); *Music in London, 1890–1894* (1932); *The Adventures of the Black Girl in Her Search for God* (1932), a fictional satire compared by critics to Voltaire's CANDIDE; *American Boobs* (1933), a lecture delivered in the U.S., also published in the same year under the title *The Future of Political*

Science in America; Prefaces (1934); *Short Stories, Scraps, and Shavings* (1934).

Shaw, of a Protestant family of English descent, left school at the age of fourteen and was thenceforth self-educated. In 1885 he became a London newspaper critic, reviewing music and the drama until 1898. In 1884 he joined the Fabian Society and thereafter upheld the Fabian brand of Socialism. A vegetarian, the author early in his career became known for his eccentricity, biting wit, and persistent revolt against commonly accepted conventions and institutions, later extending his reputation by making deliberately shocking statements in public and to the press. He was very popular in the U.S., although he was as outspoken in his criticism of the Americans as of the British; at a public lecture in New York (1933) he once addressed his audience as "boobs."

Shaw, Henry Wheeler, see BILLINGS, JOSH.

Shaw, Irwin (1913–). American playwright and short-story writer, known for his early plays, proletarian (see PROLETARIAN LITERATURE) in character, and his short stories of contemporary New York life, published chiefly in THE NEW YORKER and often dealing ironically with the frustrations of 20th-century American life. His plays are BURY THE DEAD (1936), a sensational anti-war play, a rewritten version of *Miracle at Verdun* (1931), by Hans Chlumberg; *Siege* (1937); *The Gentle People* (1939); and *Retreat to Pleasure* (1940). Collections of his short stories are *Sailor Off the Bremen* (1939) and *Welcome to the City* (1942). Shaw, who was once a semi-professional football player, began his career as a script writer for a radio broadcasting company and later wrote motion-picture scenarios in Hollywood.

Shaw, Robert Gould (1837–1863). In the American Civil War, commander of the first regiment of colored troops from a free state (the 54th Massachusetts). Killed at the head of his troops in the assault on Fort Wagner, S.C. (July 18, 1863). On Boston Common stands a monument to his memory and that of his men by Augustus SAINT-GAUDENS, which is the subject of the famous *Ode in Time of Hesitation* by William Vaughn MOODY.

Shawe, Isabella. Wife of W. M. THACKERAY, to whom she was married in 1836. In 1840 she became insane.

Shay, Frank (1888–). American book dealer, proprietor of Frank Shay's Book Shop in New York and Provincetown on Cape Cod. He has compiled and edited many books on the theater and collections of popular songs, as *Iron Men and Wooden Ships* (1923); *My Pious Friends and Drunken Companions* (1927); etc.

Shays's Rebellion. In 1786–1787, Daniel Shays (1747–1825), who had been a captain in the Revolutionary Army, led an uprising of Western Massachusetts farmers against the foreclosure of mortgages on their property. He was seeking to prevent their imprisonment for indebtedness due to the very high land taxes levied after the Revolution. *The Duke of Stockbridge* (1900), a novel by Edward BELLAMY, sets forth this episode.

She. A romance by Rider HAGGARD (*Eng.*, 1887). "She," or Ayesha, is an African sorceress whom death apparently cannot touch. The young English hero, Leo Vincey, sets out to avenge her murder of his ancestor, an ancient priest of Isis.

Shea, John Dawson Gilmary (1824–1892). American historian, specializing in the early history of the exploration of the Mississippi Valley. He also wrote a four-volume *History of the Catholic Church in the United States* (1886–1892).

Shearing, Joseph, see LONG, GABRIELLE.

Sheba, the Queen of. The queen who visited Solomon (1 *Kings* x) is known to the Arabs as Balkis, Queen of Saba (*Koran*, Ch. xxvii), ruler over the Sabeans, or sometimes as Maquedà. According to the Biblical story, she came "to prove him with hard questions" but when she had seen all his wisdom and glory "there was no more spirit in her." In one version of the story she is so favorably impressed that she becomes his wife and gives birth to a son who is the founder of the Abyssinian dynasty.

She Bible. See BIBLE, SPECIALLY NAMED.

Sheean, James Vincent (1899–). American journalist and foreign correspondent, best known for *Personal History* (1935), a best-selling autobiographical work including accounts of adventure and comment on political affairs in Europe. Other books by him are *An American Among the Riffi* (1926), dealing with the Riff War in northern Africa; *The New Persia* (1927); *The Anatomy of Virtue* (1927), *Gog and Magog* (1930), and *The Tide* (1933), essays; *Sanfelice* (1936) and *A Day of Battle* (1938), historical novels; *The Pieces of a Fan* (1937), short stories; *Not Peace But a Sword* (1939), a denunciation of FASCISM; *An International Incident* (1940), a comedy. Sheean spent a number of years in Europe, Africa, and China, reporting for the Chicago *Tribune* and the newspaper syndicates the various wars, revolutions, and political crises of the 1920's. See also GUNTHER, JOHN.

Sheeler, Charles (1883–). American painter who had been a photographer and was influenced by the French modernists. He has developed a distinct style of his own and has chosen the industrial scene in America as his specialty.

Sheen, Mgr. Fulton J. (1895–). Roman Catholic prelate born in Illinois; member of the faculty of the Catholic University of America (since 1926). Preacher and lecturer and author of many books on religion. Converter to the Roman Catholic faith of Heywood BROUN, Henry Ford II, the Communist editor Louis Budenz, and Congresswoman Clare BOOTHE LUCE.

Sheffield, John. 3rd Earl of **Mulgrave.** 1st Duke of **Buckingham and Normanby** (1648–1721). English political leader and poet, patron and friend of Dryden and Pope. His *Essay on Satire,* which was published anonymously and attributed to Dryden, resulted in the latter's being attacked by some thugs engaged by ROCHESTER.

sheikh. A title of respect among the Arabs (like the Ital. *signore,* Fr. *sieur,* Span. *señor,* etc.); properly, the head of a Bedouin clan, family, or tribe, or the headman of an Arab village.

Sheil, Richard Lalor (1791–1851). Irish dramatist and politician. Helped bring about Catholic emancipation in Ireland (granted, 1829) and fought for repeal of the union of Great Britain and Ireland. After the defeat of the repeal, he agreed to serve under the Melbourne Ministry, and was the first Roman Catholic to be privy councilor.

Shelburne Essays. A series of essays by Paul Elmer MORE, published in fourteen volumes (1904–1921) and reflecting the attitude of the NEW HUMANISTS.

Shelby, Mr. In Harriet Beecher Stowe's UNCLE TOM'S CABIN, Tom's first master. Being in commercial difficulties, he is obliged to sell his faithful slave. His son George afterwards tries to buy Uncle Tom back again, but finds that he has been whipped to death by the villain Legree.

Sheldon, Charles Monroe (1857–1946). American clergyman, author of *In His Steps* (1896), which is said to be the greatest all-time best-seller next to the Bible and Shakespeare. A flaw in the copyright was one reason for its enormous sale.

Sheldon, Edward Brewster (1886–1946). American playwright, author of plays on a variety of subjects, the best-known of which were melodramas related loosely to the social problems with which a large part of American literature in the early 20th century was preoccupied. His works include SALVATION NELL (1908); THE NIGGER (1909); THE BOSS (1911); *Princess Zim-Zim* (1911); *Egypt* (1912); *The High Road* (1912); ROMANCE (1913); *The Song of Songs* (1914), adapted from the novel of the same title by Herman SUDERMANN; *Bewitched* (1924), written with Sidney HOWARD; *Lulu Belle* (1926), written with Charles MACARTHUR; *Dishonored Lady* (1930), written with Margaret Ayer BARNES. He was bedridden and blind for years, but kept up activities in the theater. He had an enormous circle of friends and correspondents, and is the original of a character in *The Ides of March* (1948), a novel of ancient Rome by Thornton WILDER.

shell.

shell shock. An acute neurasthenic condition, due to a shock to the system caused by the explosion of a shell or bomb at close quarters.

shellback. Nautical slang for an old and seasoned sailor, an "old salt."

to retire into one's shell. To become reticent and uncommunicative, to withdraw oneself from society in a forbidding way. The allusion is to the tortoise, which, once it has "gone into its shell," is quite inaccessible.

Shelley, Percy Bysshe (1792–1822). English poet of the period of ROMANTICISM, known for his extreme emotional and physical sensitivity, his vivid imagination, his rebellion against authority of all kinds, and the PANTHEISM, idealistic and visionary aspiration, and musical quality of his poetry. His works include *Queen Mab* (see MAB; 1813); *Alastor* (1816); THE REVOLT OF ISLAM (1818); *Prometheus Unbound* (see PROMETHEUS; 1819); *The Cenci* (see CENCI, BEATRICE; 1819); *The Witch of Atlas* (1820); ADONAIS (1821). His best-known single poems are *Hymn to Intellectual Beauty, The Sensitive Plant, Mutability, The Indian Serenade, To Night, Ozymandias,* THE CLOUD, ODE TO THE WEST WIND, *To a Skylark,* and *Stanzas Written in Dejection.* He had an important influence on BROWNING and SWINBURNE.

Shelley, who is in many ways considered a typical romantic poet, was childlike, naïvely self-centered and irresponsible, and amoral in character. As early as his schooldays he became known for his excessive sensibility and his rebellious spirit, being called "Mad Shelley" and "Shelley the Atheist." See NECESSITY OF ATHEISM, ON THE. He was married twice, on both occasions after an unconventional elopement, and had a number of attachments with other women of his acquaintance, seeking in them an ideal spiritual mate. In 1817 the English court removed from his custody his two children by his first marriage with Harriet WESTBROOK, and, heart-broken, the poet left England for Italy, where he did his best work. See also BYRON, a close friend of Shelley. He was drowned in a storm at sea in the Adriatic, and his body was cremated. *The Orphan Angel,* a novel by Elinor WYLIE, tells a fanciful story of Shelley's adventures in the America of his day, after he has been rescued from the sea by an American whaling vessel in the storm which in fact caused his death.

See also CLAIRMONT, CLAIRE; VIVIANI, EMILIA; WILLIAMS, JANE.

Mary Wollstonecraft Shelley, *née* **Godwin** (1797–1851) was Shelley's second wife and the daughter of William GODWIN. She and the poet met through Shelley's admiration for her father's writings, fell in love at once, and in 1814 eloped to Europe, greatly arousing the wrath of Godwin. After the death of Harriet Westbrook in 1816, Mary legally became Mrs. Shelley. She was herself an author, writing in the convention of the GOTHIC NOVEL. FRANKENSTEIN, *Or The Modern Prometheus* (1818) is her best-known work. Other romances are *Valperga* (1823); *The Last Man* (1826); *Lodore* (1835).

Shem. (1) In the Old Testament, one of the three sons of NOAH. His supposed descendants are called SEMITIC from his name.

(2) (In *Finnegans Wake.*) See *Jerry Earwicker,* under EARWICKER.

Shenandoah. A popular drama by Bronson HOWARD (1888) dealing with the Civil War. The Union officer, Lt. Kerchival West, and Gertrude Ellinham, a loyal Southern beauty, are estranged by the war, but after a series of exciting incidents, they are reunited at last. *Shenandoah* is also the title of a narrative poem by Delmore SCHWARTZ (1941).

Shenstone, William (1714–1763). English poet, known for his pastoral verse, including songs, odes, ballads, elegies, and the like. His best-known work is THE SCHOOLMISTRESS (1742). He also wrote *Essays on Men and Manners* in prose.

Sheol. See HADES.

Shepard, Odell (1884–). American essayist and poet, winner of the Pulitzer prize for *Pedlar's Progress: The Life of Bronson Alcott* (1937).

shepherd.

the Shepherd Kings. See HYKSOS.

the Shepherd Lord. Henry, tenth Lord Clifford (d. 1523), sent by his mother to be brought up by a shepherd, in order to save him from the fury of the Yorkists. At the accession of Henry VII he was restored to all his rights and seigniories. There are many legends concerning him. His story is told by WORDSWORTH in *The Song for the Feast of Brougham Castle.*

Shepherd of the Ocean. Spenser's name for Sir Walter RALEIGH.

Shepherd's Calendar, The. Twelve eclogues in various meters by Edmund SPENSER (1579), one for each month. The theme of the poem is the lament of Colin Clout (Spenser himself) because Rosalind does not return his love. His friend Hobbinol (Gabriel HARVEY) is introduced to exhort him to greater cheerfulness. Rosalind is generally considered to have been meant for Rose Daniel, sister of the poet Samuel DANIEL.

Sheppard, Jack (1701–1724). A notorious highwayman, son of a carpenter in Smithfield, and noted for his two escapes from Newgate in 1724. He was hanged at Tyburn the same year. Daniel DEFOE made *Jack Sheppard* the hero of a romance in 1724, and W. H. AINSWORTH in 1839.

Sheraton. A light style of furniture perfected about 1800 by Thomas Sheraton (1751–1806), a designer of furniture who gave drawing lessons in London but never had a shop of his own.

Sheridan, Bibbs. The hero of Booth Tarkington's TURMOIL. His father and his brothers, Jim and Roscoe, are important characters.

Sheridan, Mrs. **Clare Consuelo** (1885–). English sculptor, journalist, and novelist, first cousin of Winston Churchill. Interviewed, for the New York *World,* Mussolini, Mustafa Kemal, Primo de Rivera, and others. Author of a number of lively travel books. She is supposedly portrayed in *Biography* (1933), a comedy by S. N. Behrman.

Sheridan, Philip Henry (1831–1888). Famous American general in the Civil War. When his army was endangered at Cedar Creek while he was in conference with General Grant at Winchester, he made a famous ride (October 19, 1864), to turn the tide of defeat into victory. The ride is celebrated in SHERIDAN'S RIDE by Thomas Buchanan Read. Cf. *Personal Memoirs of P. H. Sheridan* (2 vols.; 1888).

Sheridan, Richard Brinsley (1751–1816). Irish-born English playwright, known for his satirical comedies of manners in the general vein of the Restoration period, although critics point out in his works a moral tone lacking in the English drama of the 17th century. His plays include THE RIVALS (1775); *St. Patrick's Day* (1775); *The Duenna* (1775), an operetta; *A Trip to Scarborough* (1777), an adaptation of *The Relapse,* by Sir John VANBRUGH (1697); THE SCHOOL FOR SCANDAL (1777); THE CRITIC (1779). Sheridan was of an extravagant and high-spirited temperament, engaging in frequent duels in his youth and ostentatiously spending his money. After his success in the theater he fulfilled his ambition to enter politics and became successively Member of Parliament, Under-Secretary of State for Foreign Affairs, and Secretary of the Treasury. He spoke against Warren Hastings during the latter's seven-year trial for impeachment and through this won the friendship of the soon-to-be King George IV.

See LINLEY, ELIZABETH ANN.

Sheridan's Ride. A narrative poem by Thomas Buchanan READ (1865) in honor of General Sheridan's horse:

> By the flash of his eye and the red nostrils' play
> He seemed to the whole great army to say,
> "I have brought you, Sheridan, all the way
> From Winchester, down to save the day."

Sherlock Holmes, see HOLMES, SHERLOCK.

Sherman, Frank Dempster (1860–1916). American educator and author of much pleasing light verse.

Sherman, Stuart Pratt (1881–1926). American critic. Professor at the University of Illinois (1911–1924). Co-editor of Volumes I and II of the *Cambridge History of American Literature.* Editor of *Books* of the New York *Herald Tribune* (from 1924). He became one of the liveliest literary commentators in the country, though at first an austere critic.

Sherman, William Tecumseh (1820–1891). Great Union general in the American Civil War. After having captured Atlanta, Georgia (1864), he had the civilian population leave the city, burned it, and began the famous "March to the Sea," in order to cut the communications of the South. He so devastated the country in this and his subsequent march through North and South Carolina, as to make his name anathema in the South for a long time to come. He is supposed to have coined the famous phrase, "War is hell." His memoirs appeared in 1875.

Sherriff, Robert Cedric (1896–). English playwright and novelist. His *Journey's End* (1929), a play about World War I, originally written for the Kingston Rowing Club, achieved production through the London Stage Society and, to the author's surprise, became a great success in America.

Sherwood, Robert Emmet (1896–). American playwright, author of a number of comedies and dramas, several of the most successful embodying the varieties of idealism popular at the time of their composition. Among his plays are *The Road to Rome* (1927); *The Love Nest* (1927); *The Queen's Husband* (1928); *Waterloo Bridge* (1930); *This Is New York* (1930); *Reunion in Vienna* (1931), dealing with a group of Hapsburg exiles; *The Petrified Forest* (1935), concerned with individual frustration; *Idiot's Delight* (1936), an anti-war play, awarded the Pulitzer prize; *Tovarich* (1936), dealing with a group of Russian exiled nobility; ABE LINCOLN IN ILLINOIS (1938), awarded the Pulitzer prize; *There Shall Be No Night* (1940), a sympathetic portrayal of the Finnish war with Russia (1939–1940), awarded the Pulitzer prize of 1941.

Sherwood during his career was an editor, a dramatic critic, and a writer for the motion pictures, published a novel, *The Virtuous Knight* (1931), and in World War II held an official position with the U.S. government, on occasion assisting in the preparation of the public speeches of President Franklin D. ROOSEVELT. Biographer of Harry HOPKINS.

She Stoops to Conquer. A famous comedy by Oliver GOLDSMITH (1773). Miss Hardcastle, knowing how bashful young Marlow is before ladies, *stoops* to the manners and condition of a barmaid, with whom he feels quite at his ease, and by this artifice wins the man of her choice. This comedy owes its existence to an incident which actually occurred to its author. When he was sixteen years of age, a wag residing at Ardagh directed him, when passing through that village, to Squire Fetherstone's house as the village inn. The mistake was not discovered for some time, and then no one enjoyed it more heartily than Goldsmith himself. See HARDCASTLE; MARLOW, Sir CHARLES; LUMPKIN, TONY.

Sheva. Hero of Cumberland's comedy *The Jew* (1776), an idealized Jewish figure, "the widow's friend, the orphan's father, the poor man's protector and the universal dispenser of charity; but he ever shrank to let his left hand know what his right hand did."

She-Wolf of France. (1) Isabella (1295–1358) wife of Edward II and paramour of Mortimer. It is said that she murdered the King, her husband, by burning out his bowels with a red-hot poker.

(2) Margaret, queen of Henry VI, so called in Shakespeare's 3 *Henry VI.* i. 4.

shibboleth. The password of a secret society; the secret by which those of a party know each other; also, a worn-out or discredited doctrine. The Ephraimites could not pronounce *sh,* so when they were fleeing from Jephthah and the Gileadites (*Judges* xii. 1–16) they were caught at the ford on the Jordan because Jephthah caused all the fugitives to say the word *shibboleth* (which means "a stream in flood"), which all the Ephraimites pronounced as *sibboleth.*

Shiel, Matthew Phipps (1865–1947). Eccentric English novelist with a touch of genius. His best book is thought to be *The Purple Cloud* (1901); his *The Lord of the Sea* (1924) is also widely known. He has been called "gorgeously mad."

Shigalov. In Dostoyevsky's THE POSSESSED, a burlesque portrait of a revolutionary theoretician, who proposes the division of mankind into two unequal parts, so that "one-tenth enjoys absolute liberty and unbounded power over the other nine-tenths."

Shiites or **Shiahs** (Arab. *shiah,* "a sect"). Those Mohammedans who regard Ali as the first rightful Imam or Caliph (rejecting the three Sunni Caliphs), and do not consider the Sunna, or oral law, of any authority, but look upon it as apocryphal. There are numerous Shiite sects, all of them regarded as heretical by the orthodox SUNNITES. Because of the Shiite doctrine of the MAHDI, a twelfth imam who is supposedly living in concealment through the centuries, but is expected to appear to rule Islam, the Shiites have had a political as well as a religious influence on the development of Mohammedanism.

Shillaber, Benjamin Penhallow (1814–1890). American humorist, chiefly remembered as the author of *The Life and Sayings of Mrs. Partington* (1854).

Shiloh. A locality in Tennessee. Site of a famous battle of the United States Civil War (April 6–7, 1862), when the Southern forces surprised the Union army under Grant and Buell but were nevertheless forced to abandon the battle field.

Shimerda, Ántonia. The strong, vital, patient, and persevering pioneer heroine of Willa Cather's MY ÁNTONIA.

Shingle, Solon. A shrewd old country teamster in J. S. Jones' comedy, *The People's Lawyer* (*Am.*, 1839), one of the most popular comic characters of the early American stage. In an important court scene he causes great mirth by waking up from a nap under the impression that the prisoner is being tried for stealing his "apple sarse." See also SAGO, LOT SAP; JONATAN PLOUGHBOY; SWAP, SOLOMON.

Shinn, Everett (1873–). American artist and magazine illustrator, who has done murals for several New York theaters.

Shinto. The ethnic cult of the Japanese. Its basic tenet is reverence for the spirits of nature and the heroes of the race. It has a religious pattern but is not felt to be incompatible with adherence to either Buddhism or Christianity. The word *Shinto* means literally "the way of the gods."

ship.

Ship of State. The nation; an expression first used by MACHIAVELLI in his political treatise *The Prince.*

ship of the desert. The camel or dromedary employed in "voyages" through the sand-seas of the African deserts.

when my ship comes home. When my fortune is made. The allusion is to the argosies returning from foreign parts laden with rich freights and enriching the merchants who sent them forth.

Ships that Pass in the Night. People who come into one's horizon for a short time and then disappear. This phrase was the title of a novel by Beatrice HARRADEN (1893), but had been used previously by LONGFELLOW in *Evangeline.*

ship-money. A tax formerly levied in time of war on ports and seaboard counties for the maintenance of the English Navy.

Shipman, Samuel (1833–1937). American dramatist who wrote, with Aaron Hoffmann, *Friendly Enemies.*

Shipman's Tale, The. One of Chaucer's CANTERBURY TALES, also called "The merchant's wife and the monk." The monk (Dan Johan) is on most intimate terms with the merchant, and when the merchant is about to leave his home in Florence on business, the wife borrows a hundred francs of the monk. As the monk has not the money at hand, he borrows the loan from the merchant. When the merchant comes home, the monk asserts that he has paid back the loan to the wife. The wife tells her husband that the monk has made her a present of the money, which she has spent. The merchant, plainly seeing there is no redress, says no more about the matter, and allows it to drop.

Ship of Fools. Sebastian BRANT's *Das Narrenschiff* (1494), an allegorical satire lashing the weaknesses and vices of his time and thus becoming an effective preparation for the Protestant Reformation, was imitated throughout Europe. In English letters there are Alexander BARCLAY's *Ship of Fools* (1509); *Cocke Lorelles Bote* (ca. 1515); and others.

Shipton, Mother. This so-called prophetess is first heard of in a tract of 1641, in which she is said to have lived in the reign of Henry VIII, and to have foretold the death of Wolsey, Cromwell, Lord Percy, etc. In 1677 the pamphleteering publisher, Richard Head, brought out a *Life and Death of Mother Shipton,* and in 1862 Charles Hindley brought out a new edition in which she was credited with having predicted steam-engines, the telegraph, and other modern inventions, as well as the end of the world in 1881. Of course she, like the immortal Mrs. Harris, is immortal only because "there is no sich a person." Bret HARTE calls one of the characters in his *Outcasts of Poker Flat* Mother Shipton.

Shirburne Ballads, The. In the early years of the twentieth century these ballads were edited from a collection of English ballads in manuscript dating back to the early seventeenth century.

Shirer, William Lawrence (1904–). Well-known American journalist, war correspondent, and radio commentator. Representative of the Columbia Broadcasting System in Europe (1937–1940). Author of BERLIN DIARY (1941).

Shires, Helen. In James T. Farrell's STUDS LONIGAN, a playmate of the boy Studs, a tomboy who is acutely unhappy and wishes she were male.

Shirley. A novel by Charlotte BRONTË (1849). The heroine, Shirley Keeldar, was in the main drawn from Charlotte's sister, Emily Brontë, author of WUTHERING HEIGHTS.

Shirley, James (1596–1666). English poet and playwright. His plays include *Love's Cruelty* (1631), *The Maid's Revenge* (1626), *The Traitor* (1631), and *The Cardinal* (1641), tragedies; *Changes, Or Love in a Maze* (1632), *Hyde Park* (1632), *The Gamester* (1633), *The Coronation* (1635), *The Lady of Pleasure* (1635), *The Imposture* (1640), and *The Sisters* (1642), all comedies. *Narcissus* (published as *Echo* in 1618) is a narrative poem, and *The Contention of Ajax and Ulysses* (1659) a dramatic entertainment.

In his early career Shirley was a schoolmaster and a converted Roman Catholic; after the Civil War he became a schoolmaster again. His death came as an aftermath of the Great Fire of London in 1666.

shirt-sleeve diplomacy. An informal kind of diplomatic interchange so called because the participants would sit in their shirt sleeves.

shoal. See under COVEY.

shoe.

we all know where the shoe pinches. We each of us know our own special troubles.

if the shoe fits you, put it on. If the matter applies to your case, take it to heart.

Shoemaker's Holiday, The. A play by Thomas DEKKER (1599), dealing farcically with the antics of the craftsmen and tradesmen of Elizabethan London. The shoemaker and hero of the comedy is Simon EYRE, and Dekker took the material for his work from the story of Eyre contained in *The Gentle Craft,* by Thomas DELONEY.

Shogun. The title of the actual ruler of Japan from the 12th century to the modernization of the country in 1868. The Shoguns were hereditary commanders-in-chief (the word means "army leader"), and took the place of the Mikados, whom they kept in a state of perpetual imprisonment with, however, some show of prestige. See also RULERS, TITLES OF.

Sholem Aleichem, see RABINOWITZ.

Sholokhov, Mikhail Aleksandrovich (1905–). Well-known popular Soviet novelist. Best known in America for his novels, *And Quiet Flows the Don* (1934) and *The Don Flows Home to the Sea* (1941).

Shooting of Dan McGrew, The. A famous poem by Robert W. SERVICE. It inspired an equally famous parody by Edward Paramore, Jr., *The Hermit of Sharktooth Shoal.*

shop.

closed shop. The system of employing only laborers belonging to a union in any given industry, and refusing employment to those who will not become union members.

open shop. The system of admitting non-union as well as union laborers to employment in an industry.

Nation of Shopkeepers. See NATION.

Shore Acres. A drama of rural American life by James A. HERNE (*Am.,* 1892), first produced as *The Hawthornes.* The chief character, an old New England farmer known as Uncle Nat, insured the success of the play.

Shore, Jane, see JANE SHORE.

Shore, Philip. The hero of Margaret Deland's novel PHILIP AND HIS WIFE.

Shoreditch. A London district that got its name, according to the story, from the ditch in which JANE SHORE died of starvation.

Shore's Wife. A tragedy by Thomas CHURCHYARD, appearing in THE MIRROR FOR MAGISTRATES (1563). See JANE SHORE.

Shorey, Paul (1857–1934). American classical scholar and professor of Greek at the University of Chicago. Internationally recognized authority on Plato.

Shorter, Clement King (1857–1926). English editor and critic, especially remembered for his many book columns. He also edited the Brontës, George Borrow, Samuel Johnson, etc. His first wife was **Dora Sigerson** (1866–1913), the well-known Irish poet.

Shorthouse, Joseph Henry (1834–1903). English novelist, author of *John Inglesant* (1881), an historical High Church novel.

Short-Lived Administration, The. The English administration formed February 12, 1746, by William Pulteney. It lasted only two days.

Short Sixes: Stories to be Read while the Candle Burns. A book of short stories (1891) by Henry Cuyler BUNNER.

Shostakovich, Dimitri Dimitrievich (1906–). Celebrated Russian composer whose symphonies include the famous Fifth, which commemorates the 20th anniversary of the October Revolution (1937), and the Seventh, which deals with the Battle of Leningrad (1942). He has written operas, ballets, and compositions for the piano.

Shotwell, James Thomson (1874–). Canadian-American historian and editor of Quaker parentage. Professor at Columbia (since 1908). Assistant general editor of the *Encyclopedia Britannica* in London (1904–1905); member of the International Labor Legislation Commission to the Versailles Peace Conference and of the International Labor Conference (1919); etc. Editor of a huge *Economic and Social History of the World War* (150 vols.; since 1919). Author of *What*

Germany Forgot (1940) and other contemporary studies.

Show Boat. A novel (1926) by Edna FERBER; later made into an operetta by Miss Ferber and Jerome KERN and produced by Florenz Ziegfeld (1927). In the 19th century, the show-boats on the Mississippi River were floating theaters where troupes of players gave variety shows, melodramas, etc.

Shrapnel, Dr. A radical agitator in George Meredith's novel BEAUCHAMP'S CAREER.

Shriner. A member of the *Ancient Arabic Order of Nobles of the Mystic Shrine,* a fraternal organization in the U.S., established (1872) by a comedy actor as a branch of a society supposedly founded in Arabia in 646 A. D. by a son-in-law of Mohammed.

Shropshire Lad, A. The title of a well-known volume of lyrics by A. E. HOUSMAN (1896).

Shrovetide. The three days just before the opening of Lent, when people went to confession and afterwards indulged in all sorts of sports and merry-making.

Shrove Tuesday. The day before Ash Wednesday; "Pancake Day." It used to be the great "Derby Day" of cockfighting in England.

> Or martyr beat, like Shrovetide cocks, with bats.
> Peter Pindar, *Subjects for Painters.*

Shunammite woman. In the Old Testament, a woman whose son was overcome by sunstroke and later brought back to life by the Prophet ELISHA. She is known by no other name.

Shuster, George Nauman (1894–). American educator and Roman Catholic writer. Author of *The Catholic Spirit in Modern English Literature* (1922); etc. Editorial writer and managing editor of *The Commonweal.* President of Hunter College (1940).

Shute, Henry A. (1856–1943). American humorist, author of *The Real Diary of a Real Boy* (1902), the hero of which is called Plupy Shute.

Shute, Nevil, see NORWAY, NEVIL SHUTE.

Shylock. A grasping, stony-hearted Jewish moneylender; in allusion to the Jew in Shakespeare's MERCHANT OF VENICE:

> A stony adversary, an inhuman wretch
> Uncapable of pity, void and empty
> From any dram of mercy.
> iv, 1.

The character of Shylock has been subject to varying interpretations on the stage and in critical analysis. The modern tendency has been to make him a great tragic figure, appealing deeply to the sympathies of the audience, but it seems more likely that Shakespeare's Sherlock was a conception half way between the previous type of monster Jew in drama and this modern conception.

Siamese twins. Yoke-fellows, inseparables; so called from the original pair, Eng and Chang, who were born of Chinese parents about 1814 and discovered at Mekong, Siam, in 1829, and were subsequently exhibited as freaks. Their bodies were united by a band of flesh, stretching from breast-bone to breast-bone. They married two sisters, had offspring, and died within three hours of each other on January 17, 1874.

Other so-called Siamese twins were: Barnum's "Orissa twins," born at Orissa, Bengal, and joined by a band of cartilage at the waist only; "Millie-Christine," two joined South Carolina Negresses who appeared all over the world as the "Two-headed Nightingale"; and Josepha and Roza Blazek, natives of Bohemia, who were joined by a cartilaginous ligament above the waist. They died practically simultaneously in Chicago (1922), Josepha leaving a son aged twelve.

Sibelius, Jean (1865–). Finnish composer of symphonies, choral works, etc. Best known for such tone poems as *The Swan of Tuonela, Finlandia,* etc.

Sibley, Hiram (1807–1888). American businessman who with Ezra Cornell organized the Western Union Telegraph Company, joined in the incorporation of Cornell University, to which he contributed benefactions. He also helped found the Sibley College of Mechanical Engineering at Cornell.

sibyl. A prophetess of classical legend, who was supposed to prophesy under the inspiration of a deity. The name is now applied to any prophetess or woman fortune-teller. There were a number of sibyls, and they had their seats in widely separate parts of the world—Greece, Italy, Babylonia, Egypt, etc.

Plato mentions only one, viz., the *Erythraean*—identified with Amalthea, the *Cumaean Sibyl,* who was consulted by AENEAS before his descent into HADES and who sold the SIBYLLINE BOOKS to Tarquin; Martianus Capella speaks of two, the *Erythraean* and the *Phrygian;* Aelian of four, the *Erythraean, Samian, Egyptian,* and *Sardian;* Varro tells us there were ten viz., the *Cumaean,* the *Delphic, Egyptian, Erythraean, Hellespontine, Libyan, Persian, Phrygian, Samian* and *Tiburtine.*

> How know we but that she may be an eleventh Sibyl or a second Cassandra?—Rabelais, *Gargantua and Pantagruel,* iii. 16.

The medieval monks "adopted" the sibyls, as they did so much of pagan myth; they made them twelve, and gave to each a separate prophecy and distinct emblem:

(1) The *Libyan:* "The day shall come when

men shall see the King of all living things." Emblem: a lighted taper.

(2) The *Samian:* "The Rich One shall be born of a pure virgin." Emblem: a rose.

(3) The *Cuman:* "Jesus Christ shall come from heaven, and live and reign in poverty on earth." Emblem: a crown.

(4) The *Cumaean:* "God shall be born of a pure virgin, and hold converse with sinners." Emblem: a cradle.

(5) The *Erythraean:* "Jesus Christ, Son of God, the Savior." Emblem: a horn.

(6) The *Persian:* "Satan shall be overcome by a true prophet." Emblem: a dragon under the sibyl's feet, and a lantern.

(7) The *Tiburtine:* "The Highest shall descend from heaven, and a virgin be shown in the valleys of the deserts." Emblem: a dove.

(8) The *Delphic:* "The Prophet born of the virgin shall be crowned with thorns." Emblem: a crown of thorns.

(9) The *Phrygian:* "Our Lord shall rise again." Emblem: a banner and a cross.

(10) The *European:* "A virgin and her Son shall flee into Egypt." Emblem: a sword.

(11) The *Agrippine:* "Jesus Christ shall be outraged and scourged." Emblem: a whip.

(12) The *Hellespontic:* "Jesus Christ shall suffer shame upon the cross." Emblem: a cross.

Sibylline books, the. A collection of oracles of mysterious origin, preserved in ancient Rome, and consulted by the Senate in times of emergency or disaster. According to LIVY there were originally nine; these were offered in sale by Amalthaea, the Sibyl of Cumae, in Aeolia, to TARQUIN, the offer was rejected, and she burned three of them. After twelve months, she offered the remaining six at the same price. Again being refused, she burned three more, and after a similar interval asked the same price for the three left. The sum demanded was then given, and Amalthaea never appeared again.

The three books were preserved in a stone chest underground in the temple of Jupiter Capitolinus, and committed to the charge of custodians chosen in the same manner as the high priests. The number of custodians was at first two, then ten, and ultimately fifteen. AUGUSTUS had some 2,000 of the verses destroyed as spurious, and placed the rest in two gilt cases, under the base of the statue of Apollo, in the temple on the Palatine Hill but the whole perished when the city was burnt in the reign of NERO.

A Greek collection in eight books of poetical utterances relating to Jesus Christ, compiled in the 2nd century, is entitled *Oracula Sibylina,* or the *Sibylline Books.*

sic (*Lat.,* "thus, so"). A word used by reviewers, quoters, etc., after a doubtful word or phrase, or a misspelling, to indicate that it is here printed exactly as in the original and to call attention to the fact that it is wrong in some way.

Sic et Non (Yes and No). A well-known work by Pierre ABÉLARD, in which he listed a series of questions fundamental to theology and opposite each question cited the varying and contradictory answers and opinions found in the writings of leading theologians and ecclesiastical authorities. This work, given its title because some of the answers supported and some denied each question, was important in the controversy between NOMINALISM and REALISM and is held to give evidence of Abélard's empirical and critical turn of mind.

Sicilian Vespers. The massacre of the French in Sicily, which began at the hour of vespers on Easter Monday in 1282. The term is used proverbially of any treacherous and bloody attack.

Sicilien, Le, ou L'Amour peintre. A comedy by MOLIÈRE (1667). For the plot, see ADRASTE.

Sickert, Walter Richard (1860–1942). German-born British painter and etcher. Among his best-known canvases are *Noctes Ambrosianae; Baccarat at Dieppe;* etc.

Sickles, Daniel Edgar (1825–1914). American army officer. Major general in the U.S. Civil War, he fought at Chancellorsville and Gettysburg and was U.S. minister to Spain (1869–1873). Through his efforts Central Park was obtained for New York City. He was acquitted of shooting and killing the son of Francis Scott KEY for his attentions to Mrs. Sickles. The authorities considered him of unsound mind at the time of the shooting.

Sick Man of the East, the. The Turkish empire. It was Nicholas of Russia who gave this name to the moribund empire.

> We have on our hands a sick man, a very sick man. It would be a great misfortune if one of these days he should happen to die before the necessary arrangements are made. . . . The man is certainly dying, and we must not allow such an event to take us by surprise. —Nicholas of Russia, to Sir George Seymour, British *chargé d'affaires* (Jan. 11, 1844).

Siddall, Elizabeth Eleanor (d. 1862). Wife of D. G. ROSSETTI who both before and after her marriage posed for his paintings and served as an inspiration for his poetry, notably THE BLESSED DAMOZEL. Of the frail, lily-like beauty admired by the Pre-Raphaelites, she died in 1862, two years after her marriage, and Rossetti was beside himself with grief. He buried with her in her coffin the sole copy of a manuscript of poems dealing with their love and marriage, but in 1869 the manuscript was recovered and published. THE HOUSE OF LIFE was contained in the collection.

Siddartha. The family name of the BUDDHA.

Siddons, Sarah, *née* **Kemble** (1755–1831). English tragic actress. Appeared first as Portia (1775) at Drury Lane. She became the leading actress of her time in Shakespearean parts. Her greatest rôle was Lady Macbeth. There is a famous portrait of her as the *Tragic Muse* by Sir Joshua REYNOLDS.

Sidgwick, Ethel (1877–). Distinguished English novelist, somewhat akin in her outlook on life to Henry James though a good deal less profound. She has never been a popular writer, and her work is rather light, but always entertaining.

Sidi Nouman, see NOUMAN.

Sidney, Algernon (1622–1683). English Republican leader who, fighting on the Parliamentary side in the Civil War, was wounded at Marston Moor (1644). After the Restoration he was pardoned by Charles II, but upon his return to England he supported the Duke of Monmouth. In connection with the Rye House Plot he was convicted of treason and executed.

Sidney, Sir **Philip** (1554–1586). English poet, scholar, soldier, and courtier, regarded as the perfect example of the Renaissance gentleman. Among his writings, which were not intended for publication but were circulated privately among his friends, are *An Apology for Poetry* (1580), one of the notable examples of literary criticism in the history of literature; *Arcadia* (1590), a famous pastoral romance in prose; and *Astrophel and Stella* (1591; see STELLA), one of the earliest and best of the Elizabethan SONNET sequences. Sidney came of a noble family, traveled extensively in France, Italy, and Germany, and was the most outstanding and most admired of Queen Elizabeth's courtiers. With his uncle, the Earl of Leicester, he took part in a military expedition to the Low Countries and was killed at Zutphen. According to a traditional story, as he was dying he refused a cup of water and passed it to another wounded man, whose need, said Sidney, was greater than his own.

Sidonia. A high-minded and generous Jew in Disraeli's CONINGSBY.

Sidonian tincture. Purple dye, Tyrian purple. The Tyrians and Sidonians were world-famed for their purple dye.

Siebel. Marguerite's rejected lover, in the opera of FAUST by Gounod (1859).

Siege of Corinth, The. A poetical version of the siege which took place in 1715, written by Lord BYRON in 1816.

Siege of Rhodes, The. The first English opera (1656), written by Sir William Davenant, with music in the prologue by Henry Lawes and "recitation music" by Dr. Charles Coleman and George Hudson.

Siege Perilous, the. The ROUND TABLE of Arthurian romance contains sieges for 150 knights, but three of them are "reserved." Of these, two are posts of honor, but the third is reserved for him who is destined to achieve the quest of the Holy GRAIL. This seat is called "perilous," because if anyone sits therein except he for whom it is reserved, it will be his death. Every seat of the table bears the name of its rightful occupant in letters of gold, and the name on the "Siege Perilous" found under the cloth at the appointed time is Sir GALAHAD, son of Sir LAUNCELOT and ELAINE.

> Said Merlin, "There shall no man sit in the two void places but they that shall be of most worship. But in the *Siege Perilous* there shall no man sit but one, and if any other be so hardy as to do it, he shall be destroyed."—Pt. i. 48.

> Then the old man made Sir Galahad unarm; and he put on him a coat of red sandel, with a mantle upon his shoulder furred with fine ermines, . . . and he brought him unto the Siege Perilous, when he sat beside Sir Launcelot. And the good old man lifted up the cloth, and found there these words written: "THE SIEGE OF SIR GALAHAD."—Malory, *Morte d'Arthur,* iii. 32.

Siegfried. Hero of the first part of the old German epic THE NIBELUNGENLIED and of Wagner's opera *Siegfried,* one of the four music-dramas of his RING DES NIBELUNGEN. In the old poem Siegfried is the youngest son of Siegmund and Sieglinde, king and queen of the Netherlands and is a young warrior of peerless strength and beauty, invulnerable except in one spot between his shoulders. He vanquishes the Nibelungs and carries away their immense hoard of gold and precious stones. He wooes and wins KRIEMHILD, the sister of GUNTHER, king of Burgundy, but is treacherously killed by Hagen, while stooping for a draught of water after a hunting expedition. For his part in the wooing of Brunhild of Issland on behalf of Gunther, see BRUNHILD.

Siegfried has a cape or cloak which renders him invisible, the gift of the dwarf Alberich; and his sword, called Balmung, was forged by WIELAND, blacksmith of the Teutonic gods.

Horny or *Horned Siegfried.* Siegfried, so called because, when he slays the dragon, he bathes in its blood, and becomes covered with a horny hide which is invulnerable. A linden leaf happens to fall on his back between his shoulder-blades, and as the blood does not touch this spot, it remains vulnerable.

In Wagner's handling of the old legends, which he took from Icelandic rather than German sources, the story of Siegfried undergoes many changes and assumes new significance. In the Scandinavian VÖLSUNGA SAGA, Siegfried appears as Sigurd, and the narrative shows many interesting variations from the Teutonic legend.

Siegfried, André (1875–). French writer on political science, known for his studies of the nations of Europe and America in the period between World Wars I and II. His works include *L'Angleterre d'Aujourd'hui* (1924), translated as *Post-War Britain; America Comes of Age* (1927), translation of *Les États-Unis d'Aujourd'hui,* his best-known book in the U.S.; *France: A Study in Nationality* (1930); *La Crise Britannique* (*England's Crisis;* 1931); *Amérique Latine* (1934); *La Crise de l'Europe* (*Europe's Crisis;* 1935); *Canada* (1937); *Suez and Panama* (1940).

Siegfried Line. In World War II, the line of defense in Germany opposed to the Maginot Line in France. The first penetration of the Siegfried Line was made by the U.S. First Army on October 5, 1944. During the "phony" period of the war, the British had a song which began, "We'll hang our wash on the Siegfried Line . . ."

Sieglind or **Sieglinde.** In Scandinavian and Teutonic legend, the wife of SIEGMUND and mother of the hero SIEGFRIED. She is the heroine of Wagner's opera *Die Walküre,* one of the four music dramas of the RING DES NIBELUNGEN.

Siegmund. In Scandinavian and Teutonic legend, husband of SIEGLINDE and father of the hero SIEGFRIED. In the *Nibelungenlied,* he is King of the Netherlands. He is the hero of Wagner's opera *Die Walküre,* one of the four music dramas of his RING DES NIBELUNGEN, in which his story assumes a different guise from that of the old epic.

Sienkiewicz, Henryk (1846–1916). The best-known Polish novelist. *With Fire and Sword* (1884); *Quo Vadis* (1896); *The Crusaders* (4 vols.; 1900). Nobel prize for literature (1905).

Sieveking, Lance (1896–). English playwright, known especially for his radio plays. He was the first to produce a television play (BBC).

Sif. Wife of the old Norse god, THOR, famous for the beauty of her hair. Loki cut it off while she was asleep, but she obtained from the dwarfs a new fell of golden hair equal to that which he had taken.

Sigismonda. The heroine of DRYDEN'S *Sigismonda and Guiscardo* in his *Tales from Boccaccio* (1700). In the original tale in the DECAMERON IV. 1, the heroine is called Ghismonda. She is the daughter of Tancred, King of Salerno. She falls in love with Guiscardo, her father's squire, reveals to him her love, and marries him in a cavern attached to the palace. Tancred discovers them in each other's embrace and gives secret orders to waylay the bridegroom and strangle him. He then goes to Sigismonda, and reproves her for her degrading choice, which she boldly justifies. Next day she receives a human heart in a gold casket, knows instinctively that it is Guiscardo's, and poisons herself. She lives just long enough to request that she may be buried in the same grave as her young husband; and Tancred,

> Too late repenting of his cruel deed,
> One common sepulchre for both decreed;
> Intombed the wretched pair in royal state,
> And on their monument inscribed their fate.
> *Sigismonda and Guiscardo*

Sigourney, Lydia Howard (1791–1865). American writer who was very popular and produced more than sixty moral volumes.

Sigsbee, Charles Dwight (1845–1923). American naval officer, who commanded the U.S. battleship *Maine* when it was blown up in the Harbor of Havana (February 15, 1898). He became rear admiral in 1903.

Siguna. Wife of LOKI in old Norse myth. She nurses him in his cavern, but sometimes, as she carries off the poison which the serpents gorge, a portion drops on the god, and his writhings cause earthquakes.

Sigurd. The name under which the SIEGFRIED of the *Nibelungenlied* appears in the Scandinavian version of the legend, the VÖLSUNGA SAGA.

Sijil, Al. In Mohammedan tradition, the recording angel.

> On that day we will roll up the heavens as the angel Al Sijil rolleth up the scroll wherein every man's actions are recorded.—*Koran,* xxi.

Sikes, Bill. The type of a ruffianly housebreaker of the lowest grade; from the brute of that name in Dickens' OLIVER TWIST. The only rudiment of a redeeming feature he possesses is a kind of affection for his dog. His murder of NANCY is a horrible but celebrated incident in the novel.

Sikh (Hindu *sikh,* "disciple"). The Sikhs were originally a religious (monotheistic) body like the Mohammedans, founded in the Punjab in the 16th century. They soon became a military community, and in 1764 formally assumed national independence. From 1849 to 1947 the Sikhs were ruled by the British. They are famed as police of the British empire.

Sikorsky, Igor I. (1889–). Russian-born American engineer who built and flew the first multimotored airplane (1913). He organized several corporations to build airplanes and eventually merged them into the United Aircraft Manufacturing Corporation.

Silas. In the New Testament, the companion of PAUL on his second missionary journey.

Silas Marner, or the Weaver of Raveloe. A short novel by George ELIOT (1861) which the author says "is intended to set in a strong light the remedial influences of pure, natural, human relations." Silas is a lonely, embittered hand-loom weaver who long ago was accused of a theft of which his best friend was guilty, and so robbed of the girl he loved. He has no friends in Raveloe, the village to which he has come, and cares only to add a little more gold to the pile in his humble cottage. In close succession two strange events occur: he is robbed of his gold, and finds by chance a little yellow-haired baby girl whom no one claims. Gradually he is brought back into a more wholesome, normal life through his love for little Eppie. In the meantime much of the story is concerned with the affairs of the two sons of Squire Cass, Dunstan and Godfrey. Dunstan, who is a wild reckless fellow, always in debt, disappears. Godfrey marries the girl of his choice, Nancy Lammeter. At last, after sixteen years, Silas' lost gold is found, together with the skeleton of Dunstan Cass. Godfrey now confesses that Eppie is his child by a secret marriage with a dissipated woman who had died the night Eppie was found, and asks to be allowed to take his daughter home. Eppie, however, refuses to leave her foster-father Silas, and marries a village boy whom she has always known.

Silence. In Shakespeare's 2 *Henry IV,* a country justice of asinine dullness when sober, but when in his cups of most uproarious mirth. He is in the commission of the peace with his cousin Robert SHALLOW.

Silenus. In classic myth, son of PAN, chief of the sileni, or older satyrs. Silenus was the foster father of BACCHUS the wine-god, and is described as a jovial old toper, with bald head, pug nose, and pimply face.

> Old Silenus, bloated, drunken,
> Led by his inebriate satyrs.
> Longfellow, *Drinking Song.*

Silhouette, Étienne de (1709–1767). French controller general of finances (1759). His rigid economies were ridiculed by certain members of the nobility who applied his name sarcastically to everything deemed by them ostentatiously cheap and eventually in more restricted use to portraits in outline in which the painter's expensive art is replaced by plain black. Hence, *silhouette.*

Sill, Edward Rowland (1841–1887). American poet and essayist. Professor of English at the University of California (1874–1882). One of his most famous poems is *The Fool's Prayer.*

Sillanpää, Frans Eemil (1888–). Finnish novelist. Winner of the Nobel prize for literature (1939) while his country was at war with the Soviet Union. His books are very popular in Sweden.

Silliman, Benjamin (1816–1885). The son of a Yale professor of chemistry (**Benjamin Silliman,** 1779–1864), he became his father's assistant and later on, with John P. Norton, helped establish a school of applied chemistry at Yale, which became the Sheffield Scientific School. Both he and his father were original members of the National Academy of Sciences (1863).

Silly Billy Thompson. The name by which David DODD, hero of Charles Reade's HARD CASH is known while he is out of his mind.

Silone, Ignazio (1900–). Italian novelist and short-story writer, known for his fiction dealing with the resistance of Italian peasants to the inroads made by the Fascist government of Italy (see FASCISM) into the pattern of their lives. His books include FONTAMARA (1934); *Mr. Aristotle* (1935), a collection of short stories; *Bread and Wine* (*Pane e Vino;* 1937); *The School for Dictators* (*La Scuola dei Dittatori;* 1938).

Silurist, the. Henry VAUGHAN, who was so called because he came from South Wales whose inhabitants were known by the ancients as the Silures.

Silva, Don Ruy Gomez de. In Hugo's HERNANI and Verdi's opera *Ernani,* an old Spanish grandee, to whom Elvira is betrothed; but she detests him, and loves the outlaw Hernani.

Silva, Duke. A Spanish commander, hero of George Eliot's narrative poem THE SPANISH GYPSY.

silver.

Silver Age. See under AGES.

Silver-Fork school. A name given to a class of English novelists who gave undue importance to etiquette and the externals of social intercourse. The most distinguished are Lady Blessington (1789–1849); Theodore Hook (1716–1796); Lord Lytton (1804–1873); Mrs. Trollope (1790–1863); and Lord Beaconsfield (1804–1881). (See under these names.)

born with a silver spoon in your mouth. Born to good luck. The allusion is to the silver spoons given as prizes and at christenings. The lucky man is born with the prize in his mouth, and does not need to wait for it or to earn it.

silver wedding. See WEDDING.

Silver, John. The famous one-legged pirate of Stevenson's TREASURE ISLAND.

Silverado Squatters, The. A book (1883) by Robert Louis STEVENSON, in which he describes a trip to California taken by him with his wife and stepson.

Silver Cord, The. A play (1926) by Sidney HOWARD. The plot concerns a widowed mother whose love for her sons almost destroys their lives owing to her interference in their marriages.

Silver Stallion, The. A romantic novel (1926) by James Branch Cabell.

Silver Star Medal. In the U.S., an award for gallantry in action in war. First issued in 1932, it ranks next to the Distinguished Service Cross.

Silvia. (1) In Shakespeare's Two GENTLEMEN OF VERONA, daughter of the duke of Milan, and the lady-love of Valentine, one of the heroes of the play.

(2) The forsaken wife in D'Annunzio's drama LA GIOCONDA.

Silvio. A character in Leoncavallo's opera I PAGLIACCI.

Simenon, Georges. Pen name of **Georges Sim** (1903–). Franco-Belgian mystery story writer. His Inspector Maigret is as well known in France and Belgium as SHERLOCK HOLMES is in England and America.

Simeon, St. See under SAINTS.

St. Simeon Stylites. See STYLITES.

simile. A figure of speech in which things of different categories are compared with a resulting stress on the element of resemblance. Often constructed with "like" or "as." For instance: "Her hair is like silk." But not: "Her hair is like mine."

Simla. Hill station in the Punjab, British India. Summer capital of the Government of India. The scene of some of the early stories of Rudyard KIPLING, particularly those concerning Mrs. Hauksbee.

Simms, William Gilmore (1806–1870). American novelist, known for his romances dealing with Indians and frontier life and the Revolutionary War in South Carolina. These include GUY RIVERS (1834); THE YEMASSEE (L835), *Richard Hurdis* (1838), *Border Beagles* (1840), *Beauchampe* (1842), *Charlemont* (1856), *The Cassique of Kiawah* (1859), and others, all constituting the series known as the *Border Romances; The Partisan* (1835), *Mellichampe* (1836), and KATHERINE WALTON (1851), a trilogy, the outstanding volumes in the series called the *Revolutionary Romances,* which also contains *The Kinsmen* (1841; later issued as *The Scout,* 1854), *The Sword and the Distaff* (1853; later appearing as *Woodcraft,* 1854), *The Forayers* (1855), and *Eutaw* (1856).

Simms' novels, which have been compared to those of James Fenimore COOPER, are characterized by melodrama, chiefly aristocratic heroes and heroines, and a consistent bias in favor of the society, culture, and politics of South Carolina, in keeping with the author's intense admiration for his native state.

Simnel, Lambert (1477?–?1534). English impostor who pretended to be the Earl of Warwick and was crowned (1487) in Dublin, Ireland, as Edward VI. Entering England with an army, he was defeated by Henry VII and finally became a turnspit in the kitchens of the King.

Simon. In the New Testament: (1) the original name of the disciple PETER; (2) a Pharisee who entertained Jesus and criticized him for forgiving the sins of a woman of the streets who anointed his feet; (3) a sorcerer of Samaria, also called Simon Magus, rebuked by Peter because he attempted to buy the power of the Holy Spirit.

Simon, André Louis (1877–). French authority on wine. Author of a number of books on wine and cooking.

Simon, St. (Zelotes). See under SAINTS.

Simon Binet tests. A series of psychological tests to determine the "mental age" and I.Q. (intelligence quotient, or ratio with respect to the normal average) of individuals, particularly of retarded school children, devised by the French psychologists, Drs. Simon and Binet, after exhaustive experiments in the schools of Paris. Adaptations of the Simon Binet tests came to be widely used in educational work in the United States and formed the basis of examinations for admission to some universities, notably Columbia. Individual sets of *mental tests* (or *psychological tests*) are usually known by the name of their originator, as *Terman tests.* The whole subject of mental testing was popularized in connection with tests used for admission to the various branches of the United States armed forces during World War I.

Simonds, Frank Herbert (1878–1936). American newspaper editor with the New York *Evening Sun* (1913–1914) and the New York *Tribune* (1915–1918). His editorial on the anniversary of the sinking of the *Lusitania* won the Pulitzer prize for the year's ablest editorial in 1917. He wrote a five-volume history of World War I which constitutes a valuable record.

Simonides of Ceos. Greek poet of the late sixth century B. C. Remembered particularly for his odes, elegies, epigrams, etc. His work exists only in fragments.

Simon Lee. A poem by WORDSWORTH. The poet helps old Simon with the root of a tree and incidentally tells the simple story of his life.

Simon Legree, see LEGREE, SIMON.

Simonov, Konstantine (1915–). Soviet writer of short stories, plays, poetry, and a remarkable novel, *Days and Nights* (1945), concerning the defense of Stalingrad, which was also made into a motion picture. One of Russia's outstanding war correspondents. His play, *Russian People,* won the Stalin prize in 1942. His works have sold several million copies and are read in twenty-one languages.

Simon Pure. The real man, the authentic article, etc. In Mrs. Centlivre's *Bold Stroke for a Wife* (1718), a Colonel Feignwell passes himself off for Simon Pure, and wins the heart of Miss Lovely. No sooner does he get the assent of her guardian, than the Quaker shows himself, and proves, beyond a doubt, he is the "real Simon Pure."

Simonson, Lee (1888–). American scenic designer, one of the founders and directors of the Theater Guild, who made the sets for such Guild productions as *Liliom, Goat Song, Back to Methuselah* and *Amphitryon.* His *Poems* were published in 1946. He also wrote *The Stage is Set* (1932).

Simple Cobbler of Agawam, The. A tract by Nathaniel WARD, published in England in 1647, violently denouncing religious toleration, the denial of civil liberties, and the extreme fashions of women in London and New England in the author's day. The vitriolic style has been compared to that of the Elizabethan pamphlet writers such as GREENE and NASH, and the work is considered an example of Puritan satire. Agawam was an early name for Ipswich, Massachusetts.

Simple Life, the. A mode of living in which the object is to eliminate as far as possible all luxuries and extraneous aids to happiness, etc., returning to the simplicity of life as imagined by the pastoral poets. The phrase was taken as the title of a book by Charles Wagner (1901), a Lutheran preacher in Paris who was brought up in the pastoral surroundings of the Vosges, and was much popularized by President Theodore ROOSEVELT, who publicly announced that the book contained "such wholesome sound doctrine that I wish it could be used as a tract throughout our country." See also PRIMITIVISM.

Simple Simon. A simpleton, a gullible booby; from the character in the well-known anonymous nursery tale who "met a pie-man."

Simplicissimus. (1) Titular hero of a German novel (1669) by Hans Jakob Christoffel von Grimmelshausen (1621–1676). It is a picaresque story with the Thirty Years' War as its background but the nuclear theme is the arduous development of the simple soul of the hero toward resigned wisdom. As a panorama of contemporary events, also as a psychological study, the book has no peer in German seventeenth-century literature. It is the *Parsifal* (Wolfram von Eschenbach), *Wilhelm Meister* (Goethe), and *Jean-Christophe* (Romain Rolland) of its age.

(2) Hence, the name of a satirical weekly, a sort of PUNCH and NEW YORKER in one package, founded (1896) by Thomas T. Heine in Munich. Its last pre-Nazi editor was Franz Schoenberger whose *Confessions of a European Intellectual* (1946) were well received in America.

Sims, William Sowden (1858–1936). American naval officer. Commanded American naval operations in European waters (1917–1919). In a long report (1920) he severely criticized the U.S. Navy Department for its management of naval operations. With Burton J. Hendrick he wrote *Victory at Sea,* which won the Pulitzer prize for history in 1920.

simurgh. In Eastern legend, a huge bird who has seen the destruction of the world three times and has all the knowledge of the ages. He is perhaps identical with the ROC.

Sin. According to MILTON, she is twin-keeper with Death of the gates of Hell. She sprang full-grown from the head of Satan:

> . . . Woman to the waist, and fair,
> But ending foul in many a scaly fold
> Voluminous and vast, a serpent armed
> With mortal sting.
>
> *Paradise Lost,* ii, 650–653.

Original Sin. That corruption which is born with us, and is the inheritance of all the offspring of Adam. As Adam was the federal head of his race, when Adam fell, the taint and penalty of his disobedience passed to all his posterity.

the Man of Sin (2 *Thess.* ii. 3). Generally held to signify the ANTICHRIST, but applied by the old Puritans to the Pope of Rome, by the Fifth Monarchy men to Cromwell, and by many 19th-century theologians to that "wicked one" (identical with the "last horn" of *Dan.* vii) who is immediately to precede the second advent.

the seven deadly sins. Pride, Wrath, Envy, Lust, Gluttony, Avarice, and Sloth. They are dramatized in Dante's INFERNO.

to earn the wages of sin. To be hanged, or condemned to death.

> The wages of sin is death.—*Rom.* vi. 23.
> I believe some of you will be hanged unless you change a good deal. It's cold blood and bad blood that runs in your veins, and you'll come to earn the wages of sin.—Boldrewood, *Robbery under Arms,* ii.

to sin one's mercies. To be ungrateful for the gifts of Providence.

Sinbad or **Sindbad, the Sailor.** A famous story in the *Arabian Nights.* Sinbad is a merchant of Bagdad who acquires great wealth. He goes on seven voyages, which he describes to a poor discontented porter named Hindbad, to show him that wealth must be obtained by enterprise and personal exertion.

First Voyage. Being becalmed in the Indian Ocean, he and some others of the crew visit what they suppose to be an island, but which is in reality a huge whale asleep. They light a fire on the whale, and the heat wakes the creature, which instantly dives under water. Sinbad is picked up by some merchants, and in due time returns home.

Second Voyage. Sinbad is left, during sleep, on a desert island, and discovers a roc's egg, "fifty paces in circumference." He fastens himself to the claw of the bird and is deposited in the valley of diamonds. Next day, some merchants come to the top of the crags and throw into the valley huge joints of raw meat, to which the diamonds stick, and when the eagles pick up the meat, the merchants scare them from their nests and carry off the diamonds. Sinbad then fastens himself to a piece of meat, is carried by an eagle to its nest, and being rescued by the merchants, returns home laden with diamonds.

Third Voyage is the encounter with the Cyclops. See POLYPHEMUS.

Fourth Voyage. Sinbad marries a lady of rank in a strange island on which he is cast; when his wife dies, he is buried alive with the dead body, according to the custom of the land. He makes his way out of the catacomb and returns to Bagdad, greatly enriched by valuables rifled from the dead bodies.

Fifth Voyage. The ship in which he sails is dashed to pieces by huge stones let down from the talons of two angry rocs. Sinbad swims to a desert island, where he throws stones at the monkeys, and the monkeys throw back cocoanuts. On this island Sinbad encounters and kills the OLD MAN OF THE SEA.

Sixth Voyage. Sinbad visits the island of Serendip (or Ceylon) and climbs to the top of the mountain "where Adam was placed on his expulsion from Paradise."

Seventh Voyage. He is attacked by corsairs, sold to slavery, and employed in shooting from a tree at elephants. He discovers a tract of hill country completely covered with elephants' tusks, communicates his discovery to his master, obtains his liberty, and returns home.

Sinclair, May (1870?–1947). Distinguished and popular English novelist, a keen psychologist and experimenter in method. *The Divine Fire* (1904); *Mary Olivier* (1919); *Anne Severn and the Fieldings* (1922); etc. Also successful in the writing of uncanny stories. Her *The Dark Night* (1924) is a novel in verse.

Sinclair, Upton Beall (1878–). American novelist and miscellaneous author, known for his affiliation with Socialism and his numerous writings, both fiction and non-fiction, dealing with social problems, pacifism, political corruption, perversions of justice, economic inequality, and the like. His novels include *King Midas* (1901); *The Journal of Arthur Stirling* (1903); *Manassas* (1904); THE JUNGLE (1906); *The Metropolis* (1908); *King Coal* (1917); *Jimmie Higgins* (1919); *100%: The Story of a Patriot* (1920); *Oil!* (1927); *Boston* (1928), dealing with the SACCO-VANZETTI case; *Mountain City* (1930); *World's End* (1940), *Between Two Worlds* (1941) (hero, Lanny Budd) dealing with World War I, the peace conference, and the post-war period, etc. Among his other works are *The Profits of Religion* (1918); THE BRASS CHECK (1919); *The Goose-Step* (1923) and *The Goslings* (1924), dealing with American education; *American Outpost* (1932), an autobiography; *Upton Sinclair Presents William Fox* (1933); *The Flivver King* (1937); and numerous pamphlets, children's books, plays, short stories, and studies on a variety of subjects.

Sinclair, the descendant of a once-prominent Southern family, engaged in numerous sensational and experimental ventures during his career, including the founding of the cooperative HELICON HOME COLONY, the organization of a traveling theater for the performance of Socialist dramas, a period of residence at a single-tax (see PROGRESS AND POVERTY) colony, four unsuccessful campaigns for election to public office, and the launching of the EPIC plan during the depression era of the 1930's. His Lanny Budd novels, eight of them by 1947, were called by John Farrelly "a daydream at a newsreel."

See also MUCKRAKERS.

Sindia or **Scindia.** The name of an Indian dynasty. One Sindia was a ruler who drove out the Sikhs in the eighteenth century and later ones were Maharajas who sometimes were on the side of the British and sometimes against them. They took part in the Mahratta War and the Sepoy Rebellion. Kipling's poem *With Scindia to Delhi,* one of his best (and least-known) ballads, tells how this chief, or such a chief, attempted a romantic rescue after a battle. The story is supposedly told by a Mahratta trooper.

sin eating. A kind of atonement in which the sins of the dead person are taken over by a hireling who eats food handed him over the body of the deceased. This strange practice was once fairly usual through England and Scotland. William SHARP, under the pen name Fiona Macleod, wrote a book called *The Sin-eater* (1895).

sine die (*Lat.*). No time being fixed; indefinitely in regard to time. When a proposal is deferred *sine die,* it is deferred without fixing a day for its reconsideration, which is virtually "for ever."

sine qua non (*Lat.*). An indispensable condition. Lat. *Sine qua non potest esse* or *fieri,* "That without which [the thing] cannot be, *or* be done."

Singer, Israel Joshua (1893–1944). Yiddish novelist born in Poland whose best-known book is *The Brothers Ashkenazi* (1936), a novel which has been translated into English, Danish, Swedish, and Dutch. The Yiddish Art Theatre in New York produced it as a play.

Singing Tree. In one of the stories of the *Arabian Nights,* a tree whose leaves were so musical that every leaf sang in concert. See PARIZADE.

There is a *Singing Apple* in Countess d'Aulnoy's fairy story *Prince Chery and Fair-Star.* See CHERY.

Single Hound, The. The title of a book of poems by Emily DICKINSON, edited and published (1914) by her niece, Martha Dickinson Bianchi. It takes its title from the first poem which runs:

> Adventure must unto itself
> The Soul condemned to be;
> Attended by a Single Hound—
> Its own Identity.

single tax. A tax on land values only, to be substituted, according to its advocates, for all other forms of state tax, because increasing land values are due to other causes than individual enterprise and ought therefore to accrue not to individuals but to the public. The single tax theory is associated with the American economist, Henry GEORGE. See also PROGRESS AND POVERTY.

Singleton. The hero of W. G. SIMMS' trilogy of the American Revolution. See KATHERINE WALTON.

Singleton, Captain. The hero of a novel by D. DEFOE, called *The Adventures of Captain Singleton* (1720).

Singmaster, Elsie (1879–). American novelist, short story writer, and writer for young people, specializing in stories about the Pennsylvania Dutch.

Sing Sing. New York state prison at Ossining on the Hudson (founded in 1826). Also the former name of Ossining itself which was changed when the prison's fame began to make it unpleasant for anyone to be connected with Sing Sing.

Singular Doctor. See under DOCTOR.

Sinis. A Corinthian robber of Greek legend, known as *the Pine-Bender,* because he used to fasten his victims to two pine-trees bent towards the earth, and then leave them to be rent asunder by the rebound. He was eventually captured by THESEUS and put to death in this same way.

Sinister Street. The best known volume of a series of novels by Compton MACKENZIE. It relates the early life of Michael and Stella Fane, the illegitimate children of well-born, upper-class parents. *Sinister Street,* published in two volumes in England, appeared in America as *Youth's Encounter* (1913) and *Sinister Street* (1914) respectively. In *Guy and Pauline* (Am. title, *Plashers Mead,* 1915), an episode in Michael's life at Oxford is told. *Sylvia Scarlett* (1918) relates the early life of the titular heroine and Michael Fane's unsuccessful effort to persuade her to marry him, but in the succeeding volume, *Sylvia and Michael* (1919) the couple are married.

Sinjohn, John. Pseudonym under which John GALSWORTHY published his first two novels, *Jocelyn and Villa Rubein.*

sinking fund. The money set aside for the payment of a national debt.

Sinner, The (*Piccolo Mondo Moderno*). A novel by FOGAZZARO. See MAIRONI, PIERO.

Sinn Fein (Ourselves Alone). The name given to the extreme home rule party in Ireland in the 20th century. It grew out of previous nationalistic agitation and with the Easter rebellion of 1916 became more powerful.

Sinon. The Greek who induced the Trojans to receive the wooden horse. (Virgil: *Aeneid,* ii, 102, etc.) Anyone deceiving to betray is called "a Sinon." Dante, in his INFERNO, places Sinon, with Potiphar's wife, Nimrod, and the rebellious giants, in the tenth pit of MALEBOLGE.

Sirat, Al (*Arab.,* "the path"). An imaginary bridge between earth and the Mohammedan paradise, not so wide as a spider's thread. Sinners fall over into the abyss below.

Sir Charles Grandison. A novel by Samuel RICHARDSON (1753), the love story of Sir Charles and Harriet Byron. The hero is an ideal 18th-century gentleman with so many virtues and charms as to make his tale somewhat monotonous.

Sirdar. See under RULERS, TITLES OF.

siren (*Gr.* sirenes, "entanglers"). One of the mythical monsters, half woman and half bird, said by Greek poets (see ODYSSEY, xii) to entice seamen by the sweetness of their song to such a degree that the listeners forgot everything and died of hunger; hence applied to any dangerous, alluring woman. ULYSSES escaped their blandishments by filling his companions' ears with wax and lashing himself to the mast of his ship.

In Homeric mythology, there were but two sirens; later writers name three, viz., Parthenope, Ligea, and Leucosia, and the number was still further augmented by later writers.

Sir George Tressady. A sequel (1896) to Mrs. Humphry Ward's MARCELLA.

Siris. A treatise by George BERKELEY (1744), containing a recommendation and a list of the uses of tar-water in healing the body, as well as a somewhat mystical philosophy.

Sir Nigel. Historical romance (1906) by A. Conan DOYLE. *The White Company* is its sequel.

Sir Patrick Spens, see SPENS, SIR PATRICK.

Sir Thopas, see THOPAS.

Sisera. In the Old Testament (*Judges* iv–v), a Canaanite captain defeated by Barak and DEBORAH. He was killed in his sleep in the tent of JAEL where he had taken refuge after his defeat.

Sisler, George Harold (1893–). First baseman of the St. Louis baseball team in the American League (from 1915).

Sisley, Alfred (1830–1899). English impressionist landscape painter, born in Paris; associated with MANET.

Sismondi, Jean Charles Léonard Simonde de (1773–1842). Swiss historian, author of the famous *History of the Italian Republics in the Middle Ages* (16 vols.; 1803–1818).

Sister Anne, see ANNE; SISTER.

Sister Beatrice. A drama by Maurice MAETERLINCK (1901), a miracle play of the Virgin Mary.

Sister Carrie. A novel by Theodore DREISER (1900), a study of the demoralized life of an actress. The book was widely discussed because of its suppression.

Sister Helen. A poem (1870) by Dante Gabriel ROSSETTI, about the destruction of a false lover by melting a waxen image representing him.

Sistine Chapel. The papal private chapel in the Vatican, built in 1473 by Pope Sixtus IV. Its walls are decorated with paintings by Perugino, Botticelli, Ghirlandajo, and others, and especially the world-famous frescoes by Michelangelo, the *Creation*, the *Deluge*, and the *Last Judgment*.

Sistine Madonna or **Madonna di San Sisto.** A famous representation of the Virgin and Child painted by RAPHAEL (1518) for the church of San Sisto at Piacenza, Italy. It shows the Virgin Mary holding the Child among clouds, surrounded by cherubs, with St. Barbara and Pope Sixtus II (whence the name) kneeling adoringly on either side. It was the pride of the Royal Gallery at Dresden. When Crabb ROBINSON saw it, he exclaimed: "After this, I find it hard to believe in the immaculate conception."

Sisyphus. A legendary king of Corinth, crafty and avaricious, said to be the son of Aeolus, or—according to later legend, which also makes him the father of ULYSSES—of Autolycus. His task in the world of shades is to roll a huge stone up a hill till it reaches the top; as the stone constantly rolls back, his work is incessant; hence "a labor of Sisyphus" or "Sisyphean toil" is an endless, heart-breaking job.

> With useless endeavour,
> Forever, forever,
> Is Sisyphus rolling
> His stone up the mountain!

Longfellow, *Masque of Pandora* (*Chorus of the Eumenides*).

sit-down strike. A type of industrial strike whereby the workers, most often in factories, refuse to continue work or leave the premises until their demands are granted. The sit-down strike was a weapon of great effectiveness and wide use by labor, particularly in the U.S., in the latter 1930's. The Play *Marching Song* (1937), by John Howard LAWSON, deals with a sit-down strike.

Sitting Bull (1834?–1890). American Sioux Indian chief and leader in the Sioux war (1876–1877). Was present at the Little Big Horn when General Custer and his forces were wiped out (June 25, 1876). Again became active in an Indian uprising (1890) and was finally arrested and shot by Indian guards. He figures prominently in many legends of the American frontier.

Sita. In Hindu mythology, the wife of RAMA or Vishnu incarnate, carried off by the giant Ravana. She was not born, but arose from a furrow when her father Janaka, King of Mithila, was ploughing. The word means "furrow." She is the heroine of the Hindu epic, the RAMAYANA, which is largely concerned with her faithfulness under misfortune.

Sitwell, Edith (1887–). English poet and prose writer, known for the irony, wit, and originality of rhythm and imagery of her poetry, much of which is satire and burlesque of an intellectual character. Her collections of verse include *The Mother, And Other Poems* (1915); *Clowns' Houses* (1918); *Wooden Pegasus* (1920); *Façade* (1922), later set to music in a suite by William Walton; *Bucolic Comedies* (1923); *Sleeping Beauty* (1924); *Troy Park* (1925); *Rustic Elegies* (1927); *Gold Coast Customs, And Other Poems* (1930); *Five Variations on a Theme* (1933); *Poems New and Old* (1940); *Street Songs* (1942). Among her prose works are *Alexander Pope* (1930), a critical study; *Bath* (1932), a social history; *The English Eccentrics* (1933), essays and "characters" (see CHARACTER WRITERS); *Aspects of Modern Poetry* (1934), criticism; *Victoria of England* (1936); *I Live Under a Black Sun* (1937), a novel on Jonathan SWIFT; and *Fanfare for Elizabeth* (1946), a sympathetic biography of Elizabeth of England.

Edith Sitwell's brother, **Osbert Sitwell** (1892–), also became known for his satirical poems, short stories, novels, and plays. Among his works are *20th-Century Harlequinade* (1916); *Argonaut and Juggernaut* (1919); *Who Killed Cock Robin?* (1921); *Triple Fugue, And Other Stories* (1924); *England Reclaimed* (1927); *The Man Who Lost Himself* (1929); *Dumb Animal, And Other Stories* (1930); *Dickens* (1932); *Brighton* (1935), a social history, written with Margaret

Barton; *Escape with Me!* (1939), on travel in the Orient; *Mrs. Kimber* (1937), verse; *A Place of One's Own* (1941); and three remarkable volumes of autobiography, *Left Hand, Right Hand* (1945); *The Scarlet Tree* (1946); and *Great Morning!* (1947).

Another brother, **Sacheverell Sitwell** (1900–), came to be best known for his lyric poetry and art criticism, his works including *Southern Baroque Art* (1924); *All Summer in a Day* (1926), an "autobiographical fantasia"; *German Baroque Art* (1927); *Doctor Donne and Gargantua* (1930), a narrative poem; *Canons of Giant Art: Twenty Torsos in Heroic Landscapes* (1933); *Conversation Pieces* (1936), on English domestic portraits; *Mauretania* (1940), on travel in Morocco; *Primitive Scenes and Festivals* (1942), on religious ceremonies.

The Sitwells, of noble Norman and English ancestry, spent their childhood at Renishaw Park, a family estate built in 1625.

Siva or **Shiva.** The third person of the Hindu trinity, or *Trimurti,* representing the destructive principle in life and also, as in Hindu philosophy restoration is involved in destruction, the reproductive or renovating power. The other members of the trinity are BRAHMA and VISHNU. Siva is a great worker of miracles through meditation and penance, and hence is a favorite deity with the ascetics. He is a god of the fine arts, and of dancing. Siva, one only of his many names, means "the Blessed One." He is also known as Mahadeva, "the Great God." His consort is KALI.

Six Characters in Search of an Author (Sei Personaggi in Cerca d'Autore). A play by Luigi PIRANDELLO (1921), the best-known of the author's works. The action takes place on an unprepared stage, where a company of actors is being assembled for a rehearsal. Six persons appear, announce that they are the incomplete, unused creations of the author's imagination, and demand that they be permitted to perform the drama that was never written for them but is implied in their lives. The life stories of all six characters are then presented.

Sixes and Sevens. A volume of short stories by O. HENRY (1911). The phrase *at sixes and sevens* means "in disorder, all awry."

Six Hundred. See CHARGE OF THE LIGHT BRIGADE.

Six Nations. A confederation of North American Indians formed by the union of the FIVE NATIONS with the Tuscaroras.

Sixteen-string Jack. The almost affectionate nickname of a famous highwayman whose real name was John Rann and who is referred to in Boswell's *Johnson.* He was renowned for his affectation of fine clothes. His nickname was an allusion to the many "strings" or ribbons he wore at his knees. He was hanged in 1774.

Sixteen to One. A political slogan associated with the name of the American politician William Jennings BRYAN, referring to the ratio of silver to gold advocated in his free-silver campaigns. His free coinage policy was first outlined in a speech of Aug. 16, 1893, and was kept prominently before the public for a number of years. See also POPULISTS.

sizar. An undergraduate of Cambridge, or of Trinity College, Dublin, who receives a grant from his college to assist in paying his expenses. Formerly sizars were expected to undertake certain menial duties now performed by college servants; the name is taken to show that one so assisted received his *sizes* or *sizings* free.

sizings. At Cambridge, the allowance of food provided by the college for undergraduates at a meal; a pound loaf, two inches of butter, and a pot of milk used to be the "sizings" for breakfast; meat was provided for dinner, but any extras had to be *sized* for. The word is a contraction of *assize,* a statute to regulate the size or weight of articles sold.

> A size is a portion of bread or drinke; it is a farthing which schollers in Cambridge have at the buttery. It is noted with the letter S.—Minshien, *Ductor* (1617).

S.J. The Society of Jesus; denoting that the priest after whose name they are placed is a Jesuit.

Skanda. Another name for the KARTTIKEYA of Hindu mythology.

Skeggs, Miss Carolina Wilhelmina Amelia. In Goldsmith's VICAR OF WAKEFIELD, the companion of "Lady Blarney." These are two flash women introduced by Squire THORNHILL to the PRIMROSE family, with the view of beguiling the two eldest daughters, who are both very beautiful. Sir William Thornhill thwarts their infamous purpose.

skeleton at the feast. PLUTARCH says that in Egyptian banquets toward the close a servant brought in a skeleton, and cried aloud to the guests, "Look on this! Eat, drink, and be merry; for tomorrow you die!" Herodotus says the skeleton was a wooden one, about eighteen inches in length.

> The stranger feasted at his board;
> But, like the skeleton at the feast,
> That warning timepiece never ceased:
> "For ever—Never! Never—For ever!"
> Longfellow, *The Old Clock on the Stairs.*

Skeleton in Armor, The. A narrative poem by LONGFELLOW (1842). It was suggested by the discovery of a skeleton near Fall River, Mass., supposed to be the remains of a Scandinavian warrior and sea-rover who had come to America in the 10th century or thereabouts.

Skelton, John (*ca.* 1460–1529). English poet, known for his satire, his humorous and realistic verse, and his use of short, "breathless" lines and irregular rhyme-scheme, called "Skeltonic meter." His surviving works include *A Garland of Laurel,* an allegorical poem, dealing with the crowning of Skelton himself as a great poet; *Philip Sparrow,* a lyric mourning the death of a sparrow, the pet of a young girl; COLIN CLOUT, a satire on the abuses of the Church; *The Bowge of Court,* a satire in allegory on life at the English court; *Magnificence,* a MORALITY PLAY; *The Tunning of Elinor Rumming,* a coarse and humorous work, giving a realistic picture of contemporary "low life"; *Why Come Ye Not to Court?* and *Speak, Parrot,* satires on Cardinal Wolsey. Skelton received the title of Poet Laureate from both Oxford and Cambridge Universities and held an unofficial position as Laureate under Henry VIII, to whom he had served as tutor. He was ordained a priest but spent most of his time at court, making enemies by his outspokenness. As a result of the hostility between him and Cardinal Wolsey, he was forced to seek refuge with the Abbot of Westminster, with whom he stayed virtually as a prisoner until his death.

Skelton is considered a poet of the transition between England of the Middle Ages and the Elizabethan period, writing in the tradition of CHAUCER, GOWER, and LYDGATE and the medieval Latin poets. Interest in his work was revived in the 20th century by Robert GRAVES, and Skeltonic meter is parodied in the early verse of W. H. AUDEN.

Sketch Book, The. A volume of tales and sketches by Washington IRVING (1819), dealing with old traditions of the Hudson valley and with life in England as seen by an American observer. The book contains the famous LEGEND OF SLEEPY HOLLOW, RIP VAN WINKLE and THE SPECTER BRIDEGROOM.

Sketches by Boz. The title of a collection of stories by Charles DICKENS (1835–1836).

Skewton, The Hon. Mrs. In Dickens' DOMBEY AND SON, mother of Edith, Mr. Dombey's second wife.

Skidbladnir. The miraculous ship which the elves gave to Frey and which had room for all the gods although it could be folded together and put into a side pocket.

Skimpole, Harold. In Dickens' BLEAK HOUSE, an amateur artist, always sponging on his friends. Under a plausible light-hearted manner, he is intensely selfish, but Mr. JARNDYCE looks on him as a mere child, and believes in him implicitly. It was said that the character was drawn from Leigh HUNT, who was much offended.

Skin of Our Teeth, The. A play (1942) by Thornton WILDER. Unconventional in structure, it gives a panoramic picture of George Antrobus (Man), his family, and their maid Sabina (the Eternal Temptress), who manage to survive the world upheavals from pre-historic times until the present. The rôle of Sabina was created by the actress Tallulah BANKHEAD.

Skinner, Constance Lindsay (1882–1939). American novelist and historian, born in British Columbia. She contributed *Adventures in Oregon* and *Pioneers of the Old Southwest* to the *Chronicles of America* series.

Skinner, Otis (1858–1942). Famous American actor. His daughter, **Cornelia Otis Skinner** (1901–), is a well-known monologist and actress, and also the author, with Emily Kimbrough, of *Our Hearts Were Young and Gay* (1942), which was made into a successful moving picture. She has written several other books.

Skipper Ireson's Ride. A ballad (1828) by John Greenleaf WHITTIER, founded upon an actual episode in the history of the fishing village of Marblehead, Massachusetts. The historical Ireson, however, did not desert his wrecked ship.

Skirnir. Frey's messenger, who won the god's magic sword by getting him Gerda for his wife.

Skrymir. A great giant of Scandinavian mythology. The god THOR, traveling through the country of the giants, once spent the night in a shelter which turned out to be the thumb of Skrymir's glove. Skrymir joined him on his journey and carried the wallet of provisions, but at the end of the day fell asleep at the foot of an oak tree. Irritated because he could not open the knots with which the giant had tied up the wallet, Thor hit him a terrible blow on the forehead with his famous hammer, but the giant merely asked if an oak leaf had fallen on him. After sundry other incidents of like nature, Skrymir, who was also known as Utgard-Loki, confessed that he had made use of magic illusions to maintain his superiority over Thor.

Skuld. In Norse mythology, one of the three Norns or Fates. She represents the future, her name being related to the word *shall.*

Skylark, To a. A famous lyric (1820) by Percy Bysshe SHELLEY.

skyscraper. Popular term for the type of exceptionally tall building, erected on a relatively small area of ground, which was notable in the U.S., and especially in New York City, in the 1920's and early 1930's, each new building surpassing its predecessors in height.

Among the best-known skyscrapers of the time were the Woolworth Building, the Chrysler Building, and the Empire State Building, the last-named being the tallest. A ballet by the American composer John Alden CARPENTER is entitled *Skyscrapers* (1924).

Slabs of the Sunburnt West. A book of poems (1922) by Carl SANDBURG.

Sladen, Douglas Brooke Wheelton (1856–). English writer; first professor of history in the University of Sydney, Australia (1879); editor of *Who's Who* (1897–1899); etc.

Slawkenbergius, Hafen. An imaginary author, distinguished for the great length of his nose. In the *Life and Opinions of Tristram Shandy* (see TRISTRAM SHANDY), Slawkenbergius is referred to as a great authority on all lore connected with noses, and a curious tale is introduced from his hypothetical works about a man with an enormously long nose.

Slaygood, Giant. In Bunyan's PILGRIM'S PROGRESS, master of a gang of thieves which infests the King's highway. Mr. Greatheart slays him, and rescues Feeblemind from his grasp in a duel.

Sleary. In Dickens' HARD TIMES, the kind-hearted proprietor of the circus at Coketown; a stout man, with one eye fixed and one loose, a voice like the efforts of a broken pair of bellows, a flabby skin, and muddled head. He is never sober and never drunk.

Josephine Sleary. Daughter of the circus proprietor, a pretty girl of eighteen, who was tied on a horse at the age of two years and made a will at twelve. This will she carries about with her, and in it she indicates her desire to be drawn to the grave by two piebald ponies.

Sleeper, the. Epimenides, the Greek poet, is said to have fallen asleep in a cave when a boy, and not to have waked for fifty-seven years, when he found himself possessed of all wisdom.

In medieval legend stories of those who have gone to sleep and have been—or are to be—awakened after many years are very numerous. Such legends cluster around the names of King Arthur, Charlemagne, and Barbarossa. Cf. also the stories of Endymion, the Seven Sleepers of Ephesus, Tannhäuser, Ogier the Dane, Rip Van Winkle, Peter Klaus, Sebastian, Roderick, Thomas of Erceldoune, and the Mohammedan Mahdi.

sleeping.

sleeping partner. A partner in a business who takes no active share in running it beyond supplying capital.

sleeping sickness. A West African disease caused by a parasite, *Trypanosoma Gambiense.* characterized by fever and great sleepiness, and almost invariably terminating fatally. The disease known in the U.S., which shows similar symptoms and the cause of which is unknown, is also called *sleeping illness* or *sleepy sickness* as a means of distinction; its scientific name is *Encephalitis lethargica.*

Sleeping Beauty, The. This charming nursery tale comes originally from the French *La Belle au Bois Dormante,* by Charles PERRAULT. The Princess is shut up by enchantment in a castle where she sleeps a hundred years, during which an impenetrable wood springs up around the castle. Ultimately she is disenchanted by a young Prince, who marries her. See also BRUNHILD.

Sleepy Hollow, The Legend of. One of the best known tales in Washington Irving's SKETCH BOOK. It relates how Ichabod Crane, the gawky, superstitious country schoolmaster of Sleepy Hollow, is frightened out of his wits by a mysterious headless horseman, the "Galloping Hessian of the Hollow." Ichabod is never seen in the neighborhood again, and the fair and wealthy Katrina Van Tassel marries his rival Brom Van Brunt, a "burly, roaring, roystering blade," known far and wide as Brom Bones. A musical comedy based on the story was produced in New York in 1948.

Irving's grave is in the old Sleepy Hollow churchyard near Tarrytown, N.Y.

Sleipnir. In Scandinavian mythology, ODIN's grey horse, which had eight legs, and could carry his master over the sea as well as land.

Slender. In Shakespeare's MERRY WIVES OF WINDSOR, one of the suitors of "sweet Anne Page." His servant's name is Simple. Slender is a country lout, cousin of Justice SHALLOW.

> Slender is a perfect satire . . . on the brilliant youth of the provinces . . . before the introduction of newspapers and turnpike roads; awkward and boobyish among civil people, but at home in rude sports, and proud of exploits at which the town would laugh.—Hallam.

Slick, Sam. A Yankee of the Yankees, hero of Thomas Chandler Haliburton's volume, *The Clockmaker or the Sayings and Doings of Samuel Slick of Slickville,* first published as a series of letters in the *Nova Scotian* (1835). Sam is a shrewd, ingenious New England clock peddler; he knows a bargain when he sees one and does not scruple to take advantage of the slower-witted Nova Scotians among whom he peddles his wares. So popular were the adventures of Sam Slick that he reappeared in a number of volumes and was finally sent abroad in *The Attaché, or Sam Slick in England* (1843–1844).

Slim Princess, The. A parody by George ADE (1907) burlesquing the romantic novel of the day.

Sloan, John (1871–). American painter; member of a group of American artists called "The Eight," including, besides Sloan, William Glackens, George Luks, Arthur Davies, Everett Shinn, Maurice Prendergast and Ernest Lawson. His book *Gist of Art* (1939) is based upon his lectures.

Sloane, Sir **Hans** (1660–1753). British physician and naturalist. He followed Sir Isaac Newton as President of the Royal Society (1727–1741) and bequeathed to England a very valuable library of 50,000 volumes, having received by bequest the collection of the naturalist William Courten. The library was the foundation of the collection of the British Museum.

Sloane, William Milligan (1850–1928). American historian, best-known for his *Life of Napoleon Bonaparte* (1894–1896).

Slogger Williams. In Thomas Hughes' TOM BROWN'S SCHOOL DAYS, a bully whom Tom finally vanquishes.

Slop, Dr. In Sterne's TRISTRAM SHANDY, a choleric, enthusiastic, and bigoted physician. He breaks down Tristram's nose, and crushes Uncle Toby's fingers to a jelly in attempting to demonstrate the use and virtues of a newly invented pair of obstetrical forceps. The nickname was later given by Wm. Hone to Sir John Stoddart (d. 1856), a choleric physician who assailed Napoleon most virulently in *The Times* (1812–1816).

Slope, Obadiah. In Trollope's *Barchester Towers* (see BARSETSHIRE), a crafty schemer who pits his strength against Mrs. PROUDIE in the effort to control the policies of Bishop Proudie.

Slosson, Edwin Emery (1865–1929). American chemist and science popularizer. *Creative Chemistry* (1919); *Easy Lessons in Einstein* (1920); etc.

Slote, Hon. Bardwell. In B. E. Woolf's comedy *The Mighty Dollar* (*Am.,* 1875), an American politician, Congressman from the Cohosh district. He is a farcical character typifying all the crudities and evils of politics at its worst.

Slough of Despond, the. A period or fit of great depression from the deep bog in Bunyan's PILGRIM'S PROGRESS which CHRISTIAN must pass on his way to the Wicket Gate. Neighbor Pliable will not attempt to pass it, and turns back. While Christian is floundering in the slough, Help comes to his aid:

> The name of the slough was Despond. Here they wallowed for a time, and Christian, because of the burden that was on his back, began to sink into the mire. This miry slough is such a place as cannot be mended. It is the descent whither the scum and filth that attends conviction of sin doth continually run, and therefore is it called the Slough of Despond; for still, as the sinner is awakened about his lost condition there arise in his soul many fears and doubts and discouraging apprehensions, which all of them get together, and settle in this place, and this is the reason of the badness of this ground.

Slowboy, Tilly. In Dickens' CRICKET ON THE HEARTH, nurse and general help of Mr. and Mrs. PEERYBINGLE. She "was of a spare and straight shape, insomuch that her garments appeared to be in constant danger of sliding off her shoulders. Her costume was remarkable for its very partial development, and always afforded glimpses at the back of a pair of dead-green stays." Tilly is very fond of the baby, but has a surprising talent for getting it into difficulties, bringing its head in perpetual contact with doors, dressers, stair-rails, bedposts, and so on.

Sludge, Gammer. In Scott's KENILWORTH, the landlady of Erasmus Holiday, the schoolmaster in White Horse Vale.

Dickie Sludge or "Flibbertigibbet." Her dwarf grandson, "a queer, shambling ill-made urchin."

Sludge, Mr. Hero of Browning's dramatic monologue *Mr. Sludge the Medium* in his *Dramatis Personae* (1864), a Yankee spiritualist, who speaks in justification of his impostor trade. The poem arose out of Browning's strong aversion to the American spiritualist Daniel D. Home.

Slumkey, Samuel. In Dickens' PICKWICK PAPERS, the "blue" candidate for the representation of the borough of Eatanswill in Parliament. His opponent is Horatio Fizkin, who represents the "buff" interest.

Sly, Christopher. A keeper of bears and a tinker, son of a peddler, and a sad, drunken sot in the Induction of Shakespeare's TAMING OF THE SHREW. Shakespeare mentions him as a well-known character of Wincot, a hamlet near Stratford-on-Avon, and it is more than probable that in him we have an actual portrait of a contemporary.

Sly is found dead drunk by a lord, who commands his servants to put him to bed, and on his waking to attend upon him like a lord and bamboozle him into the belief that he is a great man. The play is performed for his delectation. The same trick was played by the Caliph Haroun al Raschid on Abou Hassan, the rich merchant, in *The Sleeper Awakened* (*Arabian Nights*), and by Philippe the Good, Duke of Burgundy, on his marriage with Eleanor, as given in Burton's *Anatomy of Melancholy* (Pt. II, sec. 2, num. 4).

small beer. Properly, beer of only slight alcoholic strength; hence, trivialities; persons or things of small consequence.

Small Boy and Others, A (1913) by Henry James. An autobiographical work which tells of the life of Henry and William James in their early years. A continuation of it is *Notes of a Son and Brother* (1914).

Small Endians. See LITTLE ENDIANS.

smalls. The undergraduates' name at Oxford for Responsions, i.e., the first of the three examinations for the B.A. degree; about corresponding to the Cambridge Little-go.

Small Souls. The first of a series of novels by the Dutch author, Louis Couperus (1863–1923), dealing with the Van Lowe family, a large and diverse group, many of them united by little except the custom of pleasing old Granny Lowe by spending Sunday evenings together at her home. The other novels of the series are *The Later Life, The Twilight of the Souls,* and *Dr. Adrian.* Constance Van Lowe causes a great scandal by her love affair, which ruins the career of the brilliant young diplomat Van Welcke, and the first books deal with the married life of this unhappy couple, who are held together only by their intense love for their small son Adrian. *The Twilight of the Souls* is the story of Gerritt Van Lowe, an apparently healthy, normal member of the family, with a pleasant, domestic wife and large brood of children, who, however, gradually goes to pieces under the influence of a morbid, neurotic fear. Among the other characters who appear throughout the novels are Ernest Van Lowe, a sensitive dilettante, who is as obviously morbid as his brother Gerritt was secretly so; Paul, the foppish idler (whom some critics consider a spokesman for the author's ideas) and the devoted old-maid sister and aunt, who gives herself unstintingly, yet nourishes a bitter resentment at being so made use of. *Dr. Adrian* tells of the career of Adrian Van Welcke, who becomes a physician with a strange power of healing.

Smart, Christopher (1722–1771). English poet. His best-known poem is the sonorous *Song to David* (1763), which was written while he was confined in an asylum.

Smart Set, The. American magazine of wit, satire, and literature, founded in 1890 as a periodical for the amusement of members of New York society, but best known for its issues between 1914 and 1924 under the editorship of H. L. MENCKEN and George Jean NATHAN. During this period it served as a vehicle for the views of Mencken and Nathan, becoming particularly celebrated for its satirical attacks on the average American middle-class standards of the day. It published the works of such leading 20th-century authors as D. H. LAWRENCE, James JOYCE, George MOORE, and Ford Madox FORD, all of whom it introduced to the American magazine public, Eugene O'NEILL, Waldo FRANK, F. Scott FITZGERALD, and Lewis MUMFORD. In 1924 *The Smart Set* was acquired by W. R. HEARST, and its policies were changed. It ceased publication in 1930.

Smattering of Ignorance, A. A book (1940) by Oscar LEVANT, dealing with music.

Smectymnuus. The title of a celebrated pamphlet containing an attack upon Episcopacy (1641). The title is composed of the initial letters of the five writers, SM (Stephen Marshall), EC (Edmund Calamy), TY (Thomas Young), MN (Matthew Newcomen), UUS (William Spurstow). Sometimes one U is omitted. MILTON published *An Apoloy for Smectymnus* the following year.

Smedley, Agnes (1890–). American journalist. As a correspondent for German and Italian left-wing newspapers, she went to China and has tried to interpret Chinese Communism to the world. Her books, written from the Communist position, have been *Red Flood over China* (1934); *China Fights Back* (1938); *Battle Hymn of China* (1943); etc.

Smedley, William Thomas (1858–1920). Well-known American magazine and book illustrator of the '90s. Illustrated books by Thomas Nelson Page, John Kendrick Bangs, William Dean Howells, etc.

Smerdyakov. In THE BROTHERS KARAMAZOV, the weak-witted, illegitimate fourth son, who is held as a servant to his father. The cynical, Nihilistic ideas of Ivan have an unfortunate influence on Smerdyakov, leading him eventually to commit patricide.

Smetana, Bedřich (1824–1884). Bohemian composer and conductor. His opera, *The Bartered Bride* (1866), won international acclaim as virtually *the* national opera of Czechoslovakia. His symphonic poem *The Moldau,* from the cycle *My Fatherland,* is a very popular concert piece.

Smike. In Dickens' NICHOLAS NICKLEBY, a poor half-starved, half-witted boy, the son of Ralph Nickleby. Nicholas Nickleby takes pity on him at DOTHEBOYS HALL and when he leaves, Smike runs away to join his friend. Nicholas thereafter takes care of the poor half-witted creature till he dies.

Smiles, Samuel (1812–1904). Popular Scottish writer. His *Self-Help* (1859) was a considerable success. Also author of a series of biographies of industrial leaders.

Smiley, Jim. The principal character in Mark Twain's *Jim Smiley and His Jumping Frog.* See JUMPING FROG.

Smith, Adam (1723–1790). Scottish economist. His major work, *Inquiry into the Nature and Causes of the Wealth of Nations* (1776), has always been considered to have laid the foundation of the science of political economy. He was also a member of the London literary club which included Dr. Johnson, Garrick, Reynolds, etc.

Smith, Alexander (1830–1867). Scottish poet and author of a book of essays, *Dreamthorp* (1863).

Smith, Alfred Emanuel (1873–1944). Famous American political leader. Governor of New York (1919–1920; 1923–1928); Democratic candidate for President (1928). He was president of Empire State Inc., and manager of the Empire State Building in New York. Cf. his autobiography, *Up to Now* (1929).

Smith, Arthur Cosslett (1852–1926). American author of exquisitely written short stories, collected in two books, *The Monk and The Dancer* (1900) and *The Turquoise Cup and the Desert* (1903). He was a Rochester lawyer who wrote only by avocation and all too little.

Smith, Benjamin Eli (1857–1913). American lexicographer. Managing editor (1882–1894) and editor-in-chief (from 1894) of *The Century Dictionary and Cyclopedia, The Century Cyclopedia of Names,* and *The Century Atlas.*

Smith, Chard Powers (1894–). American poet and novelist. Most successful in his novels *Artillery of Time* (1939) and *Ladies Day* (1941).

Smith, Charles Henry (1826–1903). American humorist of the South who took the pen name of **Bill Arp.** His dialect stories in the lingo of the Georgia "cracker" are said to have influenced Joel Chandler Harris.

Smith, David Stanley (1877–). American music educator and composer. Dean of the Yale school of music (1920–1940). Conductor of the New Haven Symphony Orchestra (from 1919).

Smith, Dodie. English playwright. Author of *Autumn Crocus* (1930) and *Dear Octopus* (1938), two plays which were produced in New York with some success. Up to 1935 she used the pen name **C. L. Anthony.**

Smith, Lady **Eleanor Furneaux** (1902–1945). English novelist, daughter of the first Earl of Birkenhead. Best known for *Red Wagon* (1930); *Flamenco* (1931); and her autobiography *Life's a Circus* (1939). She had gypsy blood and wrote about gypsies, as in *Tzigane, or Romany* (1935), and belonged to several societies concerned with gypsy history and customs.

Smith, Ellison DuRant (1864–1944). Commonly known as "Cotton Ed Smith." U.S. Senator (1909–1944).

Smith, Ernest Bramah. Pen name **Ernest Bramah** (1869–1942). English detective-story writer. Widely known for the suave and witty Kai Lung books: *The Wallet of Kai Lung* (1900); *Kai Lung's Golden Hours* (1922); etc. He invented the blind detective Max Carrados.

Smith, Francis Hopkinson (1838–1915). American artist, engineer, and writer of charming stories, novelettes, and novels, notably *Colonel Carter of Carterville* (1891).

Smith, George (1789–1846). Scotch founder of the English publishing house of Smith, Elder & Co. His son, **George Smith** (1824–1901), published the early works of John Ruskin; *Jane Eyre* by Charlotte Brontë; *Henry Esmond* by Thackeray; the works of Robert Browning and Matthew Arnold; the *Dictionary of National Biography;* etc. and founded the *Cornhill Magazine* of which Thackeray was an editor.

Smith, Goldwin (1823–1910). British historian active in politics as an anti-imperialist and opponent of the Boer War. Regius professor of history at Oxford (1858–1866). Disraeli made him a character in his novel *Lothair* (1870).

Smith, Harry Bache (1860–1936). Popular American librettist. Author of the books for comic operas by Reginald De Koven, Victor Herbert, Irving Berlin, and Jerome Kern.

Smith, James (1737?–?1814). Author of *Life and Travels* (1799), one of the best source books on pioneer life in the Ohio Valley.

Smith, James (1775–1839) and his brother **Horatio** or **Horace Smith** (1779–1849). English humorists. Joint authors of *Rejected Addresses* (1812), which is a classic of parody. Its victims include Wordsworth, Southey, Coleridge, Scott, Byron, etc.

Smith, Jedediah Strong (1798–1831). A fur-trader and Western explorer whose explorations to South California are embodied in *The Ashley and Smith Explorations* by H. C. Dale (1918). In his novel, *The Splendid Wayfaring* (1920), John G. Neihardt has made him the chief figure. Cf. also *The Song of Jed Smith* (1941), the last book in Neihardt's epic cycle of the West.

Smith, Jessie Willcox (died 1935). American painter of children and illustrator of books for children.

Smith, John (1580–1631). One of the most widely known early English colonists in America. He came to Jamestown, Virginia, in 1607 and was on the governing council of the colony. The legend of his being rescued from death by Pocahontas, the daughter of Powhatan, is based on his own story and has become a favorite in American history. He explored the coast of New England and was finally captured by the French in 1615.

Smith, Johnston. Pseudonym under which Stephen Crane published his novel Maggie: A Girl of the Streets.

Smith, Joseph (1805–1844). Founder of the Mormon Church (1830). He asserted that he had received the Book of Mormon mystically from an angel in 1827 and governed the Mormon Colony in Nauvoo, Illinois, despotically. Having authorized polygamy, he was arrested and put into jail by non-Mormons (1844) and became the victim of mob violence. His son, **Joseph Smith** (1832–1914), opposed polygamy, moved to Iowa, increased the membership of the church to over 70,000 and made the headquarters of his own sect in Independence, Missouri. His nephew, **Joseph Fielding Smith** (1838–1918), went with the Mormons under Brigham YOUNG to Utah (1848) and became president of the Mormon Church there.

Smith, Justin Harvey (1857–1930). American historian who won the Pulitzer prize in 1920 for *The War With Mexico* (2 vols.; 1919).

Smith, Logan Pearsall (1865–1946). Anglo-American essayist. Born in New Jersey, he lived in London most of his mature life and became, like Henry James, an expatriate. His brief, incisive, witty essays, *Trivia* (1902) and *More Trivia* (1921), have been collected with other essays into one volume as *All Trivia* (1934).

Smith, Preserved (1880–1941). American professor of history at Cornell (1922–1941). *A History of Modern Culture* (2 vols.; 1930–1934) is his largest work. He is especially known for his studies of Luther (1911) and ERASMUS (1923). Max EASTMAN, in *Enjoyment of Living* (1948), calls him "a thin dark mild shy edge of a man."

Smith, Roswell (1829–1892). American publisher. Originally associated with Charles Scribner, he founded the Century Company (1881) and continued the old *Scribner's Monthly* under the new name of *Century Magazine*. He published *The Century Dictionary and Cyclopedia* (1891).

Smith, Samuel Francis (1808–1895). American clergyman born in Boston, who wrote *America* (*My Country, 'tis of Thee*), first published in 1832.

Smith, Seba (1792–1868). American satirist. Author of a series of letters by "Major Jack Downing," a supposed Yankee peddler. A first series appeared in the Portland *Courier* (1829), another in the Washington *Daily National Intelligence* (1847). The homespun humor of the letters is of the general type that was later made famous by Mr. DOOLEY and Will ROGERS.

Smith, Sidney (1877–1935). Well-known American cartoonist who worked for the Chicago *Tribune* (1911–1935) and created the characters of "The Gumps."

Smith, Stephen. A character in Hardy's PAIR OF BLUE EYES.

Smith, Sydney (1771–1845). Famous London clergyman and wit. Daniel Webster struck him like "a steam engine in trousers." His query, "Who reads an American book?" attracted unfavorable attention.

Smith, Thorne (1892–1934). Fantastic American novelist, whose ribald books, *The Night Life of the Gods* (1931); *Turnabout* (1931); *Topper Takes a Trip* (1932); etc., have had great popularity. Several of them have been made into successful moving pictures featuring Roland Young and others.

Smith, Sir **William** (1813–1893). English classical and Biblical lexicographer, compiler of dictionaries of antiquities, biography, and geography. Editor of *Quarterly Review* (1867–1893).

Smith, Winchell (1871–1933). American playwright whose dramatization of George Barr McCutcheon's *Brewster's Millions* (1906) was an enormous success. His play, *Lightnin'* (1918), written with Frank Bacon, had a run of 1291 performances.

Smithfield. A famous market and district in London. In the time of Queen Mary it was the place for burning heretics at the stake.

Smith of Nottingham. Applied to conceited persons who imagine that no one is able to compete with themselves. Ray, in his *Collection of Proverbs,* has the following couplet:

> The little Smith of Nottingham
> Who doth the work that no man can.

Smithson, James (1765–1829). British scientist who bequeathed over £100,000 to the United States, by means of which was founded in Washington, D.C., the Smithsonian Institution (established by Act of Congress in 1846).

Smoke. A novel by TURGENEV (1867). The unscrupulous heroine, Irene, cannot resist the temptation of reviving the smoldering fires in the heart of Litvinov, a former lover, whom she has refused and now sees betrothed to another. She suceeds in ruining his life, but wilfully draws back at the last minute from the very plan she has urged.

Smoke and Steel. A well-known book of poems (1920) by Carl SANDBURG.

Smoke Bellew. A tale of adventures in the Klondike by Jack LONDON (1912).

Smoky City. Pittsburgh. See under CITY.

Smollett, Tobias George (1721–1771). Scotch-born English novelist and surgeon, known for his satirical picaresque novels. His works include RODERICK RANDOM (1748); PEREGRINE PICKLE (1751); *Ferdinand, Count Fathom* (see FATHOM; 1753); *Sir Launcelot Greaves* (see LAUNCELOT; 1760); *The Expedition of Humphry Clinker* (see HUMPHRY; 1771); *The Tears of Scotland* (1746), a poem;

a translation of DON QUIXOTE (1753); *History of England* (1757); *The Reprisal* (1757), a farce; *Travels in France and Italy* (1766), essays; *The Adventures of an Atom* (1769), a satire on English public affairs. Early in his career Smollett served as surgeon's mate with the British West Indian naval squadron and lived for a number of years on the island of Jamaica. During his last years he resided in Italy, where he died.

Smoot, Reed (1862–1941). American politician and Mormon leader. See HAWLEY-SMOOT TARIFF.

Smuts, Jan Christian (1870–). Famous Boer leader in the Boer War, who, during World War I, organized the South African forces. Prime minister of the Union of South Africa (1919–1924; 1939–1948). He was most influential in World War II, and was made field marshal in 1941.

Snagsby, Mr. In Dickens' BLEAK HOUSE, the law-stationer in Cook's Court, Cursitor Street. He is a very mild specimen of humanity in terrible awe of his termagant wife, whom he calls euphemistically his "little woman." He precedes most of his remarks by the words, "Not to put too fine a point upon it."

Snaith, John Collis (1876–1936). English novelist of light fiction who first received notice for his *Broke of Covenden* (1904).

Snake, Mr. In Sheridan's SCHOOL FOR SCANDAL, a traitorous ally of Lady SNEERWELL, who has the effrontery to say to her, "You paid me extremely liberally for propagating the lie, but unfortunately I have been offered double to speak the truth." He says,

> Ah, sir, consider, I live by the baseness of my character; and if it were once known that I have been betrayed into an honest action, I shall lose every friend I have in the world. v. 3.

snark. The imaginary animal invented by Lewis CARROLL as the subject of his mock heroic poem, *The Hunting of the Snark* (1876). It is most elusive and gives endless trouble, and when eventually the hunters think they have tracked it down their quarry proves to be but a Boojum. The name (a PORTMANTEAU WORD of *snake* and *shark*) has hence sometimes been given to the quests of dreamers and visionaries.

It was one of D. G. ROSSETTI'S beliefs that in *The Hunting of the Snark* Lewis Carroll was caricaturing him and "pulling his leg."

Jack LONDON wrote a travel book called *The Cruise of the Snark* (1911).

Sneak, Jerry. In FOOTE'S comedy *The Mayor of Garratt* (1763), a hen-pecked pinmaker; a paltry, pitiful, prying sneak. If ever he summons up a little manliness, his wife begins to cry, and Jerry is instantly softened. He has become a type of the hen-pecked husband.

Mrs. Sneak. Wife of Jerry, a domineering tartar of a woman, who keeps her lord and master well under her thumb. She is the daughter of Sir Jacob Jollup.

Jerry Sneak Russell. So Samuel Russell the actor (1766–1845) was called, because of his inimitable representation of "Jerry Sneak."

Sneerwell, Lady. In Sheridan's SCHOOL FOR SCANDAL, a scandalmonger, the widow of a City knight. Mr. Snake says, "Every one allows that Lady Sneerwell can do more with a word or a look than many can with the most labored detail, even when they happen to have a little truth on their side to support it." She herself admits:

> Wounded myself, in the early part of my life, by the envenomed tongue of slander, I confess I have since known no pleasure equal to the reducing of others to the level of my own reputation. i. 1.

snickersnee. From "snick and snee." A knife; originally, "a combat with knives." Cf. Thackeray's ballad, *Little Billee:*

> While Jack pulled out his snickersnee. . . .

Snobs, Book of. See under BOOK.

Snodgrass, Augustus. In Dickens' PICKWICK PAPERS, an M.P.C., i.e., Member of the Pickwick Club, a poetical young man, who travels about with Mr. Pickwick, "to inquire into the source of the Hampstead ponds." He marries Miss Wardle.

Snorri Sturluson (1178–1241). Icelandic historian and head of the highest court of Iceland. He is the author of the famous poetic chronicle of Norse mythology known as the *Heimskringla* and also of the *Prose Edda.* See EDDA.

Snout, Tom. In Shakespeare's MIDSUMMER NIGHT'S DREAM, the tinker, who takes part in the "tragedy" of PYRAMUS AND THISBE, played before the Duke and Duchess of Athens "on their wedding day at night." Next to Peter QUINCE and Nick BOTTOM the weaver, Snout is by far the most self-important man of the troupe. He plays the part of the Wall that separates the two lovers.

Snow, Edgar Parks (1905–). American writer on China. Correspondent for several New York and London newspapers and contributor to the *Saturday Evening Post.* He traveled with the Chinese Red Army for five months in 1936. Author of *Red Star Over China* (1937); *The Political Battle of Asia* (1941); etc.

Snow, Wilbert (1884–). American poet, chiefly writing of Maine which is his native state.

Snow-Bound: A Winter Idyl. A famous long poem (1866) by John Greenleaf WHITTIER.

Snowe, Lucy. The heroine of Charlotte BRONTË's novel *Villette* (1853).

Snow-Image, The, and Other Twice Told Tales. A book of short stories (1851) by Nathaniel HAWTHORNE. It contains *The Great Stone Face* and other well-known stories.

Snow King. See under KING.

Snubbin, Sergeant. In Dickens' PICKWICK PAPERS, a lawyer retained by Mr. Perker for the defense in the famous case of "Bardell *v.* Pickwick." His clerk is named Mallard, and his junior Phunky, "an infant barrister," very much looked down upon by his senior.

Snug. In Shakespeare's MIDSUMMER NIGHT'S DREAM, the joiner, who takes part in the "lamentable comedy" of PYRAMUS AND THISBE, played before the Duke and Duchess of Athens "on their wedding day at night." His role is the "lion's part." He asks the manager Peter QUINCE if he has the "lion's part written out, for," says he, "I am slow of memory." Being told he can do it extempore, for it consists of nothing but roaring, he consents to undertake it.

soap or **soft soap.** Flattery, especially of an oily, unctuous kind.

soap opera. Trade and journalistic term for a type of American daytime radio dramatic serial, at the height of its popularity in the latter years of the 1930's; so called because most of the serials were broadcast to advertise laundry soap of various brands. The typical soap opera, appealing to an audience made up almost exclusively of housewives listening as they did their household tasks, consisted of a succession of complex melodramatic and sentimental adventures within a single family, the action being centered about a young, beautiful, and resourceful woman who at the same time was usually also a wife and mother. Among the best-known serials of recent years were *The Goldbergs; John's Other Wife; Just Plain Bill; The Man I Married; The Road of Life; The O'Neills; Life Can Be Beautiful; Joyce Jordan, Girl Interne; Young Dr. Malone; Portia Faces Life; Stella Dallas; Young Widder Brown; Amanda of Honeymoon Hill; Big Sister; Ma Perkins;* etc. In 1948 the NEW YORKER ran some acid articles on them by James THURBER.

Soapy Sam. A nickname applied to Samuel Wilberforce (1805–1873), bishop of Oxford and Winchester, who had unctuous manners.

So Big. A novel (1924) by Edna FERBER.

Sobersides. A grave, steady-going, serious-minded person.

Sobrino. In Ariosto's ORLANDO FURIOSO, one of the most valiant of the Saracen army, called "The Sage." He counsels Agramant to entrust the fate of the war to a single combat, stipulating that the nation whose champion is worsted should be tributary to the other. ROGERO is chosen for the pagan champion, and RINALDO for the Christian army. When Rogero is overthrown, Agramant breaks the compact. Sobrino is greatly displeased, and soon afterwards receives the rite of Christian baptism.

sob stuff. A U.S. slang expression describing newspaper, film, or other stories of a highly sentimental kind. *Sob Sisters* are "human interest" reporters.

Social Contract, The (Le Contrat social). Chief work of J. J. ROUSSEAU (1762), a treatise on the origins and organization of government and the rights of citizens. In keeping with many works on political science of the time, it bases its arguments on the theory that the origin of government first lay in a mutual contract between the citizens and the rulers for the general good of the community. The main principles set forth by the treatise are the equality of all citizens before the law; the merging of the interests of the individual with those of the state; the popular state as the "infallible" expression of the general will, although the despotic state is not; and hence the necessity of the individual's surrendering certain of his private rights for the good of the popular state, or the community, although if a tyrannical monarch requires the surrender of individual rights, the "contract" is considered void. Some critics assert that the injustices of collectivism and "democratic despotism" during the French Revolution and later in the 19th and 20th centuries were in part derived from this work of Rousseau's.

socialism. Basically the philosophy of socialism involves the creation of a coöperative society and a more equitable distribution of wealth. There have always been attempts to outline the perfect society. This was the subject of PLATO's *Republic* and of Sir Thomas MORE's UTOPIA. Many names and many experiments are connected with the name of socialism. Some have been utopian and some more scientifically managed, as for instance, the experiments of Robert OWEN in England. In 1847 MARX and ENGELS issued the *Communist Manifesto* which laid down certain very definite principles concerning socialism. There are today various kinds of socialists. One of the best-known groups has been the Fabian Society in England to which belonged George Bernard Shaw, Sidney Webb and others.

Social Justice. See COUGHLIN, FATHER.

Society for Pure English (S.P.E.). Founded (1913) by a committee of which Robert Bridges, Sir Walter Raleigh and Logan Pearsall Smith were members with the object to direct popular taste and education in the development of the English language.

Society of Friends, see QUAKERS.

Socinus, Faustus (1539–1604). Italian theologian who developed the doctrine of his uncle **Laelius Socinus** (1525–1562) into the anti-Trinitarian (unitarian) system known as Socinianism. Condemned by the Inquisition (1559). Organized his followers into a church at the Synod of Brześć (1587) in Poland.

Socrates (*ca.* 469–399 B. C.). The great Greek philosopher, who was born and died at Athens. He used to call himself "the midwife of men's thoughts," and out of his intellectual school sprang those of Plato and the Dialectic system, Euclid and the Megaric, Aristippus and the Cyrenaic, Antisthenes and the Cynic. Cicero said of him that "he brought down philosophy from the heavens to earth." He was condemned to death for the corruption of youth by introducing new gods (thus being guilty of impiety) and drank hemlock in prison, surrounded by his disciples. Socrates is caricatured in Aristophanes' comedy THE CLOUDS.

Socratic irony. Leading on your opponent in an argument by simulating ignorance, so that he "ties himself in knots" and eventually falls an easy prey—a form of procedure used with great effect by Socrates.

the Socratic method. The method of conducting an argument, imparting information, etc., by means of question and answer.

the English Socrates. Dr. Samuel JOHNSON, so called by Boswell.

the Jewish Socrates. Moses Mendelssohn (1729–1786).

Soddy, Frederick (1877–). English chemist who developed with Rutherford the theory of the atomic disintegration of radioactive elements. He was awarded the Nobel prize for chemistry in 1921.

Sodom and Gomorrah. In the Old Testament, two cities of the plains that were destroyed with fire and brimstone from heaven because of their wickedness. Abraham persuaded Jehovah to spare Sodom if ten righteous men could be found there, but this condition was not fulfilled. LOT and his wife and daughters were the only inhabitants who escaped from the doomed city, and Lot's wife, looking back, became a pillar of salt. See also CITIES OF THE PLAIN.

Sodome et Gomorrhe. See CITIES OF THE PLAIN.

Sofronia. A young Christian of Jerusalem, the heroine of an episode in Tasso's JERUSALEM DELIVERED. Aladine, King of Jerusalem, steals from a Christian church an image of the Virgin, being told by a magician that it is a palladium, and if it is set up in a mosque, the Virgin will forsake the Christian army and favor the Mohammedan. The image is accordingly set up in a mosque, but during the night is carried off by someone. Aladine, greatly enraged, orders the instant execution of all his Christian subjects, but to prevent this massacre, Sofronia accuses herself of the offense. Her lover Olindo, hearing that Sofronia is sentenced to death, presents himself before the King and says that he and not Sofronia is the real offender; whereupon the King orders both to instant execution. But CLORINDA, the Amazon, obtains their pardon, and Sofronia leaves the stake to join Olindo at the altar of matrimony.

Soglow, Otto (1900–). American humorous artist. Famous for his series, *The Little King* (1933), which first appeared in the NEW YORKER. He has illustrated books of verse by Ogden NASH, and others, including several of his own.

Sohrab and Rustum. A narrative poem in blank verse by Matthew ARNOLD (1853), dealing with the legendary Persian hero RUSTUM and his son Sohrab. The two meet in single combat, in ignorance of their relationship, and Sohrab is slain. See also CARTHON.

soi-disant (*Fr.*). Self-styled, would-be; generally used of pretenders, as "a *soi-disant* gentleman," i.e., a snob.

Sokolnikov, Grigori (1888–). Russian Communist politician. Escaped from exile in Siberia and lived abroad (1907–1917); member of the Russian delegation negotiating with Germany the treaty of Brest-Litovsk (1918); ambassador to Britain (1929–1932). Arrested and imprisoned because of his affiliation with Trotsky (1937).

Sokoloff, Nikolai (1886–). Well-known Russian-born violinist and orchestra leader. He conducted the Cleveland Symphony Orchestra (1918–1933).

soldier of fortune. A man who lives by his wits; *chevalier d'industrie*. Referring to those men in medieval times who let themselves for hire into any army. *Soldiers of Fortune* is the title of a novel of adventure by Richard Harding DAVIS (1897), dealing with a revolution in a South American republic. The hero is Robert Clay, a young engineer, general manager of the Valencia Mining Company in Olancho. The novel was dramatized in 1902.

solano.

ask no favor during the solano. A popular Spanish proverb, meaning, "ask no favor during a time of trouble or adversity." The *solano* (from Lat. *solanus*, "sun") of Spain is a southeast wind, extremely hot, and loaded with fine dust; it produces giddiness and irritation.

Soldan or **Sowdan.** A corruption of sultan, meaning in medieval romance the Saracen king; but, with the usual inaccuracy of these medieval sources, we have the Soldan of Egypt, the Soudan of Persia, the Sowdan of Babylon, etc., all represented as accompanied by grim Saracens to torment Christians.

In Spenser's FAËRIE QUEENE (V. viii), the Soldan typifies Philip II of Spain who used all his power to bribe and seduce the subjects of Elizabeth, here figuring as Queen Mercilla.

Sir Artegal demands of the Soldan the release of the damsel "held as wrongful prisoner," and the Soldan "swearing and banning most blasphemously," mounts his "high chariot," and prepares to maintain his cause. Prince Arthur encounters him "on the green," and after a severe combat uncovers his shield, at sight of which the Soldan and all his followers take to flight. The "swearing and banning" typify the excommunications thundered out against Elizabeth; the "high chariot" is the Spanish Armada; the "green" is the sea; the "uncovering of the shield" indicates that the Armada was put to flight, not by man's might, but by the power of God.

Soldiers Three, and Other Stories. A volume of short stories of life in India by Rudyard KIPLING (1888). The "soldiers three" are the famous trio, Ortheris, Learoyd, and Mulvaney. See also THE THREE MUSKETEERS.

solecism. A deviation from correct idiom or grammar; from the Greek *soloikos,* "speaking incorrectly," so named from Soloi, a town in Cilicia, the Attic colonists of which spoke a debased form of Greek.

The word is also applied to any impropriety or breach of good manners.

solemn.

Solemn Doctor. See under DOCTOR.

the Solemn League and Covenant. A league entered into by the General Assembly of the Church of Scotland, the Westminster Assembly of English Divines, and the English Parliament in 1643, for the establishment of Presbyterianism and suppression of Roman Catholicism in both countries. Charles II swore to the Scots that he would abide by it, and therefore they crowned him in 1651 at Dunbar; but at the Restoration he not only rejected the Covenant, but had it burnt by the common hangman.

Solid South. An expression denoting the political unity of the American states south of Mason and Dixon's line, which in any general election, can be counted upon in advance to go Democratic.

Solinus. In Shakespeare's COMEDY OF ERRORS, the Duke of Ephesus. He is obliged to pass the sentence of the law on Aegeon, a Syracusian merchant who has dared to set foot in Ephesus. When, however, the Duke discovers that the man who has saved his life, and whom he best loves, is the son of Aegeon, he releases his prisoner, who thereupon settles in Ephesus.

solipsism. A philosophical doctrine, a development of the theories of IDEALISM, which maintains that, since we have knowledge only of our own ideas, or mental states, only our ideas, or mental states, can be held to exist. David HUME was the leading solipsist in the history of philosophy, and John LOCKE and George BERKELEY were forerunners of the doctrine.

Solness, Halvard. Titular hero of Ibsen's MASTER BUILDER.

Sologub, Fëdor (1863–1927). Russian symbolist novelist and dramatist. His tales have been called "a curious blend of Chekhov and Poe."

Solomine. In Turgenev's VIRGIN SOIL, a manufacturer whose practical reforms are in sharp contrast to the schemes of the idealistic young nihilists. See NIHILISM.

Solomon. The wisest and most magnificent of the kings of Israel, son of DAVID and BATHSHEBA. Aside from his wise choice of "an understanding heart," he is perhaps most celebrated for his building of the famous temple that bore his name and his entertainment of the Queen of SHEBA. The Biblical narrative (I *Kings* ii-xi) relates that "he had seven hundred wives, princesses, and three hundred concubines; and his wives turned away his heart." Nevertheless "King Solomon exceeded all the kings of the earth in riches and in wisdom." The glory of his reign gave rise to innumerable legends, many of which are related in the Talmud and the Koran.

the English Solomon. James I (reigned 1603–1625), whom Sully called "the wisest fool in Christendom."

the second Solomon. (1) Henry VII of England; (2) James I.

the Solomon of France. Charles V. (1364–1380) called *le Sage.*

Solomon's carpet. See CARPET, THE MAGIC.

Solomon's ring. Rabbinical fable has it that Solomon wore a ring with a gem that told him all he desired to know.

Solomon Daisy, see DAISY, SOLOMON.

Solomon Eagle. In *Old St. Paul's* by Harrison AINSWORTH, a fanatic who runs through the streets of London at the time of the Plague calling on people to repent. Sir John SQUIRE used the name as a pen name for his literary column in *The London Mercury.*

Solomon Gundy. See SWAP, SOLOMON.

Solomon Swap, see SWAP, SOLOMON.

Solon. A wiseacre or sage; from the great lawgiver of ancient Athens (d. ca. 560 B.C.), one of the Seven Sages of Greece.

the Solon of Parnassus. So Voltaire called BOILEAU, in allusion to his *Art of Poetry.*

Solon Shingle, see SHINGLE, SOLON.

solstice (from Lat. *sol,* "sun," and *sistit,* "stands"). The summer solstice is June 21; the winter solstice is December 22; so called because on or about these dates the sun reaches its extreme northern and southern points in the ecliptic and appears to stand still before it turns back on its apparent course.

Solvay, Ernest (1838–1922). Belgian industrial chemist who invented the Solvay process for manufacturing soda from common salt.

Solveig. In Ibsen's PEER GYNT, the young girl who leaves her family for love of Peer. She remains faithful to him, and welcomes him home long years afterwards.

Solyman. In Tasso's JERUSALEM DELIVERED, King of the Turks, whose capital is Nice. Being driven from his kingdom, he flees to Egypt and is there appointed leader of the Arabs (Bk. ix). He and Argantes are by far the most doughty of the pagan knights. Solyman is slain by RINALDO (Bk. xx), and Argantes by TANCRED.

Soma. An intoxicating drink anciently made, with mystic rites and incantations, from the juice of some Indian plant by the priests, and drunk by the Brahmins as well as offered as libations to their gods. It was fabled to have been brought from heaven by a falcon, or by the daughters of the Sun, and it was itself personified as a god. Soma is one of the most important of the old Vedic deities, a sort of Hindu Bacchus. All of the 114 hymns in the ninth book of the Rig Veda are invocations in his honor. In later mythology, Soma represented the moon, which was supposed to be gradually drunk up by the gods and then filled up again.

to drink the Soma. To become immortal, or as a god.

Somehow Good. A novel (1908) by William DE MORGAN.

Somers, John. Baron **Somers** (1651–1716). English statesman, influential with William III. During the latter's absence in Holland, member of the council of regency. Helped settle the terms of the union with Scotland (1707).

Somerset. Hero of Thomas Hardy's novel A LAODICEAN.

Somerville, Edith Anna Œnone (1861–). Irish novelist who collaborated with her cousin, **Violet L. Martin,** on *Some Experiences of an Irish R. M.* (1899) and similar humorous books.

somewhere in France, Britain, Africa, etc. An uncertain locality; the address used for overseas soldiers in World Wars I and II, when more exact information as to their whereabouts seemed unwise.

Somnus. In classic myth, the god of Sleep, the son of Night (*Nox*) and the brother of Death (*Mors*).

Sompnour's Tale. See SUMMONER'S or SUMPNOR'S TALE.

son.

son of Belial. One of a wicked disposition; a companion of the wicked. (*Judges* xix. 22.)

> Now the sons of Eli were sons of Belial, they knew not the Lord.—1 *Samuel* ii, 12.

son of Heaven. An epithet of the Emperor of China which was called the *Celestial Empire.*

son of perdition. Judas Iscariot (*John* xvii. 12); Antichrist (2 *Thess.* ii. 3).

Son of the Last Man. Charles II of England, in allusion to the belief of the Puritans that his father Charles I was the last English king who should reign.

son of the morning. A traveler. This is an Oriental phrase, alluding to the custom of rising early in the morning to avoid the mid-day heat, when on one's travels.

sons of Phidias. Sculptors.

sons of Thunder or *Boanerges.* James and John, sons of Zebedee. (*Mark* iii. 17.)

Song of Myself. The best known and probably most characteristic poem of Walt WHITMAN. It begins:

> I celebrate and sing myself
> And what I assume, you shall assume,
> For every atom belonging to me as good as belongs to you.
> I loafe and invite my soul
> I lean and loafe at my ease, observing a spear of summer grass.

Song of Roland (Chanson de Roland). See under ROLAND.

Song of Solomon. One of the books of the Old Testament, a love idyll, sometimes interpreted as an allegory of the union between Christ and his Church.

Song of Songs, The (Das Hohe Lied). A novel by Hermann SUDERMANN (1908), tracing the gradual degeneration of the heroine Lily Czepanek, a girl of great gifts but little moral fiber.

Song of the Chattahoochee, The. A poem (1883) by Sidney Lanier.

Song of the Indian Wars, The. A narrative poem (1925) by John G. Neihardt. It is one of the best historical descriptions of the wars with the Plains Indians, and a part of the author's *Epic Cycle of the West.*

Song of the Lark, The. A novel by Willa CATHER (1915), dealing with the career of Thea Kronborg, a Colorado girl, the daughter of a Swedish clergyman, who has a talent for music. She goes to Chicago to study, has an unhappy love affair with Fred Ottenburg, a wealthy young man who cannot obtain a divorce to marry her, spends ten years in further study in Europe and in performance, and eventually becomes a soprano at the Metropolitan Opera House in New York City, famous for her Wagnerian rôles. Thea is to some extent drawn from the famous Wagnerian singer, Olive Fremstad.

Song of the Shirt. A famous poem by T. Hood (1843). It begins,

With fingers weary and worn,
With eyelids heavy and red,
A woman sat in unwomanly rags,
Plying her needle and thread.
Stitch, stitch, stitch!
In poverty, hunger, and dirt,
And still with a voice of dolorous pitch
She sang "The song of the shirt."

Songs and Sonnets. See Tottel's Miscellany.

Songs before Sunrise (1871). See under Swinburne, A.

Songs from Vagabondia. A book of poems (1891) by Bliss Carman and Richard Hovey. Their fresh out-of-door quality and their celebration of the free spirit made them popular with youth at the turn of the century.

Songs of Innocence (1789) and **Songs of Experience** (1794). See Blake, William.

Songs of the Sierras. A book of poems (1871) by Joaquin Miller.

Song to David. See under Christopher Smart.

Sonia. The heroine of Dostoyevsky's Crime and Punishment.

Sonnambula, La (The Sleepwalker). An opera by Bellini (1831), book by Romani. The "sleepwalker" is Amina, the miller's daughter. She is betrothed to Elvino, a rich young farmer, but the night before the wedding is discovered in the bed of Count Rodolpho. This very ugly circumstance makes the farmer break off the match and promise marriage to Lisa, the innkeeper's daughter. The Count now interferes, and assures Elvino that the miller's daughter is a sleepwalker. While they are still talking she is seen walking on the edge of the mill-roof while the huge mill-wheel is turning rapidly. She then crosses a crazy old bridge and comes into the midst of the assembly, wakes up and runs into the arms of her lover. Elvino, convinced of her innocence, marries her, and Lisa is resigned to Alessio, whose paramour she has been.

Sonnenschein, Edward Adolf (1851–1929). Well-known English grammarian whose brother **William Swan** (1855–1931) was an established publisher in London.

sonnet. A poetic form of fourteen heroic lines, that is, fourteen lines of five-foot iambic verse. There are two main types of sonnet—(1) the Shakespearean sonnet in which the lines are grouped in three quatrains (with six alternating rhymes) followed by a detached rhymed couplet, which is apt to be epigrammatic; (2) the Italian form illustrated by Milton, Wordsworth, Keats, etc., in which the fourteen lines are divided into an octave of two rhyme-sounds arranged *abba abba* and a sestet of two additional rhyme-sounds that may be variously arranged. The latter form tends to divide the thought into two opposing or complementary phases of the same idea.

The two types of sonnet are illustrated below—

Shall I compare thee to a summer's day?
Thou art more lovely and more temperate:
Rough winds do shake the darling buds of May,
And summer's lease hath all too short a date:

Sometime too hot the eye of heaven shines,
And often is his gold complexion dimm'd:
And every fair from fair sometime declines,
By chance, or nature's changing course, untrimm'd.

But thy eternal summer shall not fade
Nor lose possession of that fair thou owest;
Nor shall Death brag thou wanderest in his shade,
When in eternal lines to time thou growest:

So long as men can breathe, or eyes can see,
So long lives this, and this gives life to thee.

Shakespeare, *To His Love.*

Much have I travell'd in the realms of gold
And many goodly states and kingdoms seen;
Round many western islands have I been
Which bards in fealty to Apollo hold.
Oft of one wide expanse had I been told
That deep-brow'd Homer ruled as his demesne:
Yet did I never breathe its pure serene
Till I heard Chapman speak out loud and bold:

—Then felt I like some watcher of the skies
When a new planet swims into his ken;
Or like stout Cortez, when with eagle eyes
He stared at the Pacific—and all his men
Look'd at each other with a wild surmise—
Silent, upon a peak in Darien.

Keats, *On First Looking into Chapman's Homer.*

The first celebrated user of the sonnet form was Petrarch. It was introduced into French by Clément Marot and into English by Wyatt and Surrey. During the latter half of the 16th century in England sonnet sequences, singing usually of an unkind or unapproachable lady and disappointed passion in the Petrarchan tradition, were a widespread literary fad. Leading authors of sonnet sequences at this time were Thomas Watson, Sir Philip Sidney, Samuel Daniel, Michael Drayton, Edmund Spenser, Henry Constable, Barnabe Barnes, Thomas Lodge, Giles Fletcher, and William Shakespeare. The conceit was a marked feature of these sonnets, many of which showed wide irregularity of form. After the Elizabethan period the sonnet was used infrequently until the age of romanticism, when it again became popular. Outstanding 20th-century poets making use of the sonnet form include J. M. Hopkins, E. R. Robinson, Edna St. Vincent Millay, Elinor Wylie, and Merrill Moore. E. E. Cummings, W. H. Auden, and Stephen Spender used an irregular form of the sonnet for satirical and special effects. Cf. *The Book of Sonnet Sequences* (1929), by Houston Peterson.

Sonnets from the Portuguese. A collection of sonnets by Elizabeth Barrett BROWNING (1850), expressing the poet's love for her husband, Robert BROWNING, and presented to him as a gift. The title refers to a pet name, "little Portuguese," frequently applied by Browning to his wife because of her dark complexion.

Sonnets of a Portrait Painter. A book of poems (1914) by Arthur Davison FICKE.

Son of Royal Langbrith, The. A novel (1904) by William Dean HOWELLS.

Son of the Middle Border, A. An autobiographical book (1917) by Hamlin Garland. It first appeared serially and had the sequels *A Daughter of the Middle Border* (1921) and *Trail Makers of the Middle Border* (1926). The second volume was awarded a Pulitzer prize.

Son of the Wolf, The. A book of short stories (1900) by Jack London concerning white men in the Klondike.

Sons and Lovers. A novel, autobiographical in character, by D. H. LAWRENCE (1913), dealing with the family background, childhood, adolescence, and young manhood of Paul MOREL, sensitive and talented son of an English coal miner in Nottinghamshire. Gertrude Coppard Morel, his mother, the daughter of a proud and Puritanical family, herself an educated, intelligent, and highly moral woman, first married Walter Morel, a handsome, sensual, ignorant, brutal, and self-willed miner, in the heat of physical attraction. Later, when she realizes the essential distance between them, she hates and then feels indifferent toward her husband, turning for love and affection to her children—William, Annie, Paul, and Arthur; because of his extreme sensitivity, she is particularly drawn to Paul. The novel is concerned chiefly with Paul's painful introduction to the commercial world, his discovery of books and art, his growing discontent with his background of poverty and gloom, and his love affairs with MIRIAM and later with Clara DAWES. Because of the strong bond of love between him and his mother, he is never able to give his affection wholly to either of the women, although both love him passionately, and there is a constant conflict between them and Mrs. Morel. With the death of the older woman from cancer, Paul decides to set out on an independent life of his own and rejects both Miriam and Clara.

Sons and Lovers, attacked on its first publication because of its frankness in dealing with sexual matters, is considered to be Lawrence's best novel and has been highly praised for its portrayal of English mining life and its vivid and moving characterizations.

Sophia Western. The name of the heroine of *Tom Jones* (1749) by Henry FIELDING.

sophist, sophistry, sophism, sophisticator, etc. Before the time of PYTHAGORAS the sages of Greece were called *sophists* (wise men). Pythagoras out of modesty called himself a *philosopher* (a wisdom-lover). A century later Protagoras of Abdera resumed the title, and a set of quibblers appeared in Athens who professed to answer any question on any subject, and took up the title discarded by the Wise Samian. From this moment *sophos* and all its family of words were applied to "wisdom falsely so called," and *philosophos* to the "modest search after truth."

Sophocles (495–406 B.C.). Greek dramatist, known for the human appeal of his tragedies in contrast to the predominantly heroic qualities of those of EURIPIDES. His best known works are OEDIPUS TYRANNUS; OEDIPUS AT COLONUS; ANTIGONE; ELECTRA; TRACHINIAE; AJAX; and PHILOCTETES.

Sophonisba. In Roman legendary history, daughter of the Carthaginian general Hasdrubal and, like her brother HANNIBAL, reared to detest Rome. She was affianced to Masinissa, king of the Numidians, but was given by her father in marriage to Syphax. Scipio insisted that this marriage should be annulled, but the Numidian sent her a bowl of poison, which she drank without hesitation. This subject and that of Cleopatra have furnished more dramas than any other whatsoever. For example, we have in French dramas by J. Mairet, *Sophonisbe* (1630); Pierre Corneille (1663); and Voltaire. In Italian: Trissino (1514); Alfieri (1749–1803). In English: John Marston, *The Wonder of Women, or the Tragedy of Sophonisba* (1605); Nathaniel Lee, *Sophonisba or Hannibal's Overthrow* (1676) and Thomson, *Sophonisba* (1729). In Thomson's tragedy occurs the line, "Oh Sophonisba! Sophonisba oh!" which was parodied by "Oh Jemmy Thomson! Jemmy Thomson oh!"

Sophronia. The heroine of Boccaccio's tale *Titus and Gisippus,* in the DECAMERON, x. 8.

Sophy. See RULERS, TITLES OF.

Sopwith, Thomas (1888–). British aviator who founded the Sopwith Aviation Company and built certain types of planes that were used in World War I.

Sorbonne. The institution of theology, science, and literature in Paris founded by Robert de Sorbon, canon of Cambrai, in 1252. In 1808 the buildings, erected by Richelieu in the 17th century, were given to the University, and since 1821 it has been called the *Académie universitaire de Paris.*

Sordello (d. ca. 1255). A Provençal troubador, mentioned a number of times by DANTE in the *Purgatorio,* now remembered because of BROWNING's poem of this name (1840). It details, in a setting which shows the restless condition of northern Italy in the early 13th century, the conflict of a poet about the best way of making his influence felt, whether personally or by the power of song. Browning said:

The historical decoration was purposely of no more importance than a background requires; and my stress lay on the incidents in the development of a soul; little else is worth study. I, at least, always thought so.

Tennyson's reference to *Sordello* is well known. He said he had done his best with it, but there were only two lines he understood—the first and the last—and they were both untrue. These are:

Who will, may hear Sordello's story told.
Who would has heard Sordello's story told.

Sorel, Agnes (ca. 1422–1450). Mistress of Charles VII of France (1444–1450); a power behind the throne, supposed to have been poisoned by the dauphin (Louis XI).

Sorel, Albert (1842–1906). French historian, author of books on Europe and the French Revolution, etc.

Sorel, Cecile (1873–). French actress, a star of the COMÉDIE FRANÇAISE.

Sorel, Julien. The leading character in Stendhal's realistic novel *Le Rouge et le Noir* (THE RED AND THE BLACK). He is actuated by the most ruthless sort of selfish ambition, adopts the "black" of the church instead of military "red" (the two opposing parties of the state religion) purely for its material advantages, and badly abuses the women who love him. The novel has had a great influence on the modern realistic and psychological school of fiction.

Sorley, Charles Hamilton (1895–1915). Scottish poet killed in the first World War. *Marlborough and Other Poems* (1916). His letters were published in 1919.

Sorokin, Pitirim Alexandrovich (1889–). American sociologist born in Russia. Professor of sociology, St. Petersburg (1912–1922), University of Minnesota (1924–1930), and Harvard (from 1930). Has written books.

Sorolla y Bastida, Joaquín (1863–1923). Spanish painter, popular in America. His canvases are flooded with sunlight. He won the Grand Prix at the Paris Exposition in 1900. Some of his portraits, including one of the South American novelist, Blasco Ibáñez, are in the New York Hispanic Society.

Sorrel, Hetty. One of the principal characters in George Eliot's ADAM BEDE.

Sorrows of Werther. See WERTHER.

Sorti, Caterina. The Italian heroine of George Eliot's MR. GILFIL'S LOVE STORY.

Sortini. In Franz Kafka's THE CASTLE, an official of the Castle who sends AMALIA an insolent command to present herself to him for his pleasure at the inn. When she defiantly refuses, he punishes her whole family in revenge.

S. O. S. The arbitrary code signal used by Marconi wireless operators on board ship to summon the assistance of any vessels within call; hence, an urgent appeal for help.

The letters have been held to stand for *save our souls* or *save our ship,* but they were adopted merely for convenience, being 3 dots, 3 dashes, and 3 dots, . . . – – – . . .

During World War I, the school attached to headquarters for the training of snipers was known as *the S O S section.*

Sosia. The living double of another, as the brothers Antipholus and brothers Dromio in the COMEDY OF ERRORS, and the Corsican brothers in the drama so called. Sosia is a servant of AMPHITRYON, in Plautus' comedy so called. It is Mercury who assumes the double of Sosia, till Sosia doubts his own identity. Both DRYDEN and MOLIÈRE have adapted this play to the modern stage.

Sotadics or **Sotadic verse.** One that reads backwards and forwards the same, as "llewd did I live, evil I did dwell." So called from Sotades, the inventor. These verses are also called *palindromic.*

Sotheby's. The center of the sale of rare books in London. It is located in New Bond Street.

Sothern, Edward Hugh (1859–1933). American actor. Originally leading man in the company of Daniel Frohman which presented Shakespearean drama (1904–1907 and 1909–1916) with Julia MARLOWE, whom he married.

Soule, George (1887–). American writer on economic subjects. On the staff (editor from 1923) of the *New Republic.* Author of *A Planned Society* (1932); *The Future of Liberty* (1936); *The Strength of Nations* (1942); etc.

Soulsby, Sister. See THE DAMNATION OF THERON WARE.

Soul's Tragedy, A. A drama (1846), half verse and half prose, by Robert Browning, dealing with a sixteenth-century Italian story.

Soult, Nicolas Jean de Dieu. Duke of **Dalmatia** (1769–1851). Marshal of France under Napoleon (1804). Fought in many Napoleonic campaigns and aided Napoleon upon his return from Elba. He was recalled to France after living in exile and again made a marshal in 1820. Minister of war (1830–1834; 1840–1844).

Sound and the Fury, The. A novel by William FAULKNER (1929), dealing with the degenerate Compson family, once distinguished Southern aristocrats in Jefferson, Mississippi. The characters are Benjy, the 33-year-old son, an idiot, unable to speak; Candace, the daughter, a nymphomaniac; Jason, another son, selfish and mean-spirited; Quentin, the youngest son, sensitive and intelligent, a student at Harvard University; the drunken father and neurotic mother; and Dilsey and Luster, mother and son, the Negro servants. During the course of the novel, Candace is seduced and leaves an illegitimate child, Quentin commits suicide through grief at his sister's disgrace, Benjy is castrated by Jason when he attempts to attack a child, and Candace's daughter, grown up, elopes with a performer in a traveling carnival.

The story is told through three separate types of STREAM OF CONSCIOUSNESS, representing Benjy, Jason, and Quentin, respectively, each appropriate in style to the character whose point of view is presented. The final part of the story is told objectively.

Soupault, Philippe (1897–). French poet and writer of fiction and biography. He has written the lives of Henri Rousseau, Baudelaire and Blake.

sour grapes. Things despised because they are beyond our reach. Many men of low degree call titles and dignities *sour grapes* and men of no parts turn up their noses at literary honors. The phrase is from Aesop's fable called *The Fox and the Grapes.*

sour grapeism. An assumed contempt or indifference to the unattainable.

Sousa, John Philip (1854–1932). American bandmaster and composer of famous marches, among the best known of which are *Stars and Stripes Forever* (1897) and *El Capitan* from his comic opera of that name (1896). Known as the "March King."

South, Marty. In Thomas Hardy's WOODLANDERS (1887) the daughter of John South, secretly in love with Giles Winterborne but to no avail. Though she has little to do with the plot, she is considered one of the best of Hardy's women characters.

Southampton, Henry Wriothesley. 3rd Earl of **Southampton** (1573–1624). Patron of Shakespeare and other Elizabethan poets. Shakespeare's *Venus and Adonis* and *Rape of Lucrece* are dedicated to him. He took part in Essex's rebellion and was released from prison by James I. He helped to equip an expedition to Virginia in 1605.

Southcott, Joanna (1750–1814). An English farmer's daughter in Devonshire who became a religious fanatic and prophesied that she would give birth to Shiloh, the second Messiah. This name was, incidentally, Hogg's nickname for Shelley. The Southcott prophecy was made in 1802 when Shelley, in a different part of England, was ten years old.

Southern and Western Monthly Magazine and Review, The. A combination literary review and popular magazine published (1845) in Charleston, South Carolina, and edited by William Gilmore SIMMS, who was also its principal contributor. It was absorbed by the SOUTHERN LITERARY MESSENGER.

Southern Literary Journal and Monthly Magazine (1835–1838). A Southern periodical published in Charleston, S.C., and contributed to by William Gilmore Simms. Its object was to deal with the advance of Southern culture. It was a champion of the cause of slavery.

Southern Literary Messenger (1834–1864). Founded at Richmond, Virginia, this magazine is famous because of the contributions made to it by Edgar Allan POE as one of its editors (to 1837). He published in it many reviews and some of his poems, essays, and stories.

Southern Review, The. An American literary quarterly, founded in 1935 at Louisiana State University, the third magazine in the South to bear such a title. Under the editorship of Cleanth BROOKS and Robert Penn WARREN it came to be one of the most distinguished of the LITTLE MAGAZINES of the 1930's, printing articles on literary criticism, philosophy, and politics of a more scholarly nature than those in similar journals of the time, as well as stories and poems by outstanding 20th-century authors. Kenneth BURKE, Katherine Anne PORTER, J. C. RANSOM, and Allen TATE were among its regular contributors. *The Southern Review* ceased publication in 1942 through lack of funds, a condition brought about by World War II.

Southey, Robert (1774–1843). English poet of the romantic movement (see ROMANTICISM), an important leader in his day but considered by 20th-century critics to have been of mediocre talent. He wrote a great deal of verse and prose, including a number of epic poems the most outstanding of which are THALABA THE DESTROYER (1800); *The Curse of Kehama* (see KEHAMA; 1810); and RODERICK, THE LAST OF THE GOTHS (1814). He also wrote ballads, such as *The Battle of Blenheim;* didactic poems, such as THE OLD MAN'S COMFORTS; and history and biography, such as his *Life of Nelson* (1813). In his youth, Southey joined with S. T. COLERIDGE in the scheme of PANTISOCRACY and married Sarah FRICKER, whose sister married Coleridge. He soon became a conservative and was attacked in satire by Lord BYRON. Southey was Poet Laureate (1813–1843). In the last years of his life his mind gave way as a result of overwork.

south sea scheme or **bubble.** A stock-jobbing scheme devised by Sir John Blunt, a lawyer, in 1710, and floated by the Earl of Oxford in the following year. The object of the company was to buy up the national debt, and to be allowed the sole privilege of trading in the South Seas. Spain refused to give trading facilities, so the money was used in other speculative ventures and, by careful "rigging" of the market, £100 shares were run up to over ten times that sum. The bubble burst in 1720 and ruined thousands. The term is applied to any hollow scheme which has a splendid promise, but whose collapse will be sudden and ruinous. See also MISSISSIPPI BUBBLE.

Southwark. A borough in London. The name comes from "south work" applied to the southern end of London Bridge. Southwark was noted in Shakespeare's time as the center of theatrical life. There were located the Globe Theatre, The Hope and The Rose.

Southwell, Robert (ca. 1561–1595). English Roman Catholic poet and Jesuit, author of mystical and religious verse, published as *Maeoniae* (1595) and *St. Peter's Complaint* (1595). His best-known lyric is *The Burning Babe.* Southwell was ordained a priest in Rome in 1584 and insisted on going to England, although it was legally treason for an English priest ordained after 1557 to remain in England for more than forty days. In 1592 he was arrested and imprisoned; after repeated questioning and torture he was hanged.

South Wind. A satirical novel by Norman DOUGLAS (1917), the action of which takes place on a volcanic island in the Mediterranean Sea called Nepenthe. The leading character is an English bishop of the Anglican Church who visits the island and is brought in contact with a strange group of blackmailers, drunkards, wantons, hedonists, and others who would under other circumstances be beyond the pale of the churchman's society. Under the influence of the insidious south wind of the region, the native wine, the relics of the island's pagan past, and the subtle attacks on conventional English moral and intellectual standards that are made in conversation by the various skeptics with whom he talks, the bishop begins to find his own former beliefs and convictions undermined. Eventually he reaches the point of silently condoning a murder, committed when his sister-in-law pushes a blackmailer off a cliff. The novel is marked by many passages of brilliant and witty conversation on a variety of topics, covering ethics, politics, asceticism, the condition of the 20th-century world, art, and the geology, mythology, and antiquities of the island.

Southwold, Stephen (1887–). English novelist and writer of juveniles, best-known under his pen name of **Neil Bell,** although he has written many books under his own name.

Southworth, Emma Dorothy Eliza, *née* **Nevitte** (1819–1899). American novelist known as Mrs. E. D. E. N. Southworth. Author of many melodramatic novels of large sales, notably *The Hidden Hand* (1859).

Sowdan, see SOLDAN.

Sowerby, James (1757–1822). English artist who illustrated botanical and conchological works.

Sowerby, Katherine Githa. English playwright, author of *Rutherford & Son* (1912); etc.

Sowerby, Leo (1895–). American composer. Won the first fellowship awarded by the American Academy of Rome, and has twice won the award of the Society for the Publication of American Music. He is a member of the National Institute of Arts and Letters. His *The Canticle of the Sun* won the Pulitzer prize for music (1946).

Soyer, Raphael (1899–). Russian-born American painter, best-known for his paintings of slum people of New York.

Spaeth, Sigmund (1885–). American musicologist and "tune detective." His works on music are of a popular kind. He has collected many old popular songs in *Read 'Em and Weep—the Songs You Forgot to Remember* (1926); *Weep Some More, My Lady* (1927); etc. Chairman of the National Committee for American Music (1939).

Spalding, Albert Goodwill (1850–1915). American professional baseball player and businessman who founded a famous sporting goods establishment which issues various athletic guides. His son, **Albert Spalding** (1888–), is a well-known American violinist and composer.

Spandrell. In Aldous Huxley's POINT COUNTER POINT, a sensualist, lazy, debauched, devoid of moral scruples, believing in nothing, seeking to spite his mother for her second marriage. His only interest he finds in corrupting, outraging, and humiliating the women who fall in love with him, leading them skillfully into the most depraved of practices and then gradually making them aware of their shame. Thoroughly bored and disgusted by living, he is eventually killed by the British Freemen, a Fascist group, for the murder of their leader, Everard WEBLEY.

Spanish. For *the Spanish Molière, the Spanish Shakespeare,* etc., see under MOLIÈRE, SHAKESPEARE.

Spanish Bayonet. A novel (1926) by Stephen Vincent BENÉT.

Spanish Fryar, The. A drama by John DRYDEN (1681). It contains two plots, wholly independent of each other. The serious element is this: Leonora, the usurping Queen of Aragon, is promised in marriage to Duke Bertran, a prince of the blood, but is in love with Torrismond, general of the army, who turns out to be the son and heir of King Sancho, supposed to be dead. Sancho is restored to his throne, and Leonora marries Torrismond. The comic element is the illicit love of Colonel Lorenzo for Elvira, the wife of Gomez, a rich old banker. Dominick (the Spanish Friar) helps on this scandalous amour, but it turns out that Lorenzo and Elvira are brother and sister.

Spanish Fury, the. The historical name for the attack upon Antwerp by the Spaniards, November 4, 1576, which resulted in the pillage and burning of the place and a terrible massacre of the inhabitants.

Spanish Gipsy, The. A poem by George ELIOT (1868), relating the tragic love story of Fedalma, a gypsy brought up as a noble Spanish girl, and Duke Silva, the commander of the Spanish fort. The couple are engaged, but when Fedalma's father Zarca recognizes her and reveals her parentage, she believes it her duty to give up her lover and join her people. Silva, on the other hand, deserts his post and resolves to become a gypsy. During his absence the post falls, and Silva in desperation stabs Zarca. The lovers then part forever, Fedalma to lead the gypsies to Africa, Silva to seek pardon at Rome.

Spanish Lady, The. A ballad contained in Percy's *Reliques,* ii. 23. A Spanish lady falls in love with Captain Popham, whose prisoner she is, but as he is already married, her love is of no avail.

Spanish Main, the. Properly the northern coast of South America, going westward from the mouth of the Orinoco to the Isthmus of Panama, or a bit farther; the *main*-land bordering the Caribbean Sea, called by the Spanish conquerors *Tierra Firme.* The term is often applied, however, to the curving chain of islands forming the northern and eastern boundaries of the Caribbean Sea, beginning from Mosquito, near the isthmus, and including Jamaica, Santo Domingo, the Leeward Islands, and the Windward Islands, to the coast of Venezuela in South America.

Spanish Student, The. A dramatic poem by LONGFELLOW (1845). The heroine is Preciosa, a gypsy girl who is threatened with the vengeance of the Inquisition.

Spanish Tragedy, The. A tragedy by Thomas KYD (1594), one of the best known of the old plays that piled up bloody horrors. Horatio, son of Hieronimo, is murdered while he is sitting in an arbor with Belimperia. Balthazar, the rival of Horatio, commits the murder, assisted by Belimperia's brother Lorenzo. The murderers hang the dead body on a tree in the garden, where Hieronimo, roused by the cries of Belimperia, discovers it, and goes raving mad.

Spanker, Lady Gay. A gay horsewoman and huntress in the comedy *London Assurance,* by D. BOUCICAULT (1841).

> Dazzle and Lady Gay Spanker "act themselves," and will never be dropped out of the list of acting plays.—Percy Fitzgerald.

Sparabella. In John GAY's *Pastoral* III (1714), a shepherdess in love with D'Urfey, but D'Urfey loves CLUMSILIS, "the fairest shepherd wooed the foulest lass." Sparabella resolves to kill herself; but how? Shall she cut her windpipe with a penknife? "No," she says, "squeaking pigs die so." Shall she suspend herself to a tree? "No," she says, "dogs die in that fashion." Shall she drown herself in the pool? "No," she says, "scolding queans die so." And while in doubt how to kill herself, the sun goes down, and

> The prudent maiden deemed it then too late,
> And till tomorrow came deferred her fate.

Spargo, John (1876–). British-born American socialist leader and writer. He resigned from the Socialist party in 1917 because of its attitude concerning World War I. He founded, with Samuel GOMPERS, the American Alliance for Labor and Democracy and the Nationalist party (both 1917). Author of many sociological books.

Sparkish. In Garrick's *Country Girl* (1766) and WYCHERLY's *Country Wife* (1675) of which the former is an adaptation, "the prince of coxcombs," a fashionable fool, and "a cuckold before marriage." Sparkish is engaged to Alithea Moody, but introduces to her his friend Harcourt, allows him to make love to her before his face, and, of course, is jilted.

Spark Plug. See BARNEY GOOGLE.

Sparks, Jared (1789–1866). American historian, pioneer in the study of American history. Editor of the *North American Review* (1817–1818; 1824–1830). He became the first professor of history in any American university (Harvard, 1839–1849). President of Harvard (1849–1853). He contributed to the *Library of American Biography,* which he edited (1834–1838).

Sparrowgrass Papers. A series of humorous sketches by Frederick S. Cozzens (*Am.,* 1856). The supposititious author is Samson Sparrowgrass, a young married man from the city who, with his wife, sets up housekeeping in the then suburban village of Yonkers, N.Y.

Spartacist. A member of an extreme group of German socialists (dissolved 1919) under the leadership of Karl LIEBKNECHT, who had used as his pseudonym the name of the famous Roman slave and gladiator SPARTACUS.

Spartacus (died 71 B.C.). Roman slave and gladiator; leader of an insurrection of slaves (73–71 B.C.), he routed several armies but was defeated and killed by Crassus.

Spartan. The inhabitants of ancient Sparta, one of the leading city-states of Greece, were noted for their frugality, courage and stern discipline; hence, one who can bear pain unflinchingly is termed a *Spartan,* a very frugal diet is *Spartan fare,* etc. It was a Spartan mother who, on handing her son the shield he was to carry into battle, said that he must come back either with it or on it.

Spartan dog. A blood-hound; a bloodthirsty man.

Spasmodic School, the. A name applied by Professor Aytoun to certain authors of the 19th century, whose writings were distinguished by forced conceits and unnatural style. The most noted are BAILEY (author of *Festus*), Gerald MASSEY, Alexander SMITH and Sydney DOBELL.

Spaulding, Elbridge Gerry (1809–1897). American banker and legislator, known as the "Father of Greenbacks." He organized the Farmers' and Mechanics' National Bank in Buffalo (1864).

speakeasy. Popular term for a restaurant or cabaret where liquor was illegally sold during the PROHIBITION era of the 1920's in the U.S. It was so called because admittance was surrounded by an air of secrecy and adventure, although police surveillance of speakeasies became quite lax.

Speaker. The title of the presiding officer and official spokesman of the British House of Commons, the United States House of Representatives, and of some other legislative assemblies.

to catch the Speaker's eye. The rule is that the member whose rising to address the House is first observed by the Speaker is allowed precedence.

Speaker, Tristram E. Known as **Tris** (1888–). American professional baseball player.

Spearman, Frank Hamilton (1859–1937). Popular American writer whose story of an outlaw, *Whispering Smith,* was a best seller in 1906, and was twice made into a silent moving picture. He spent his latter years writing for the moving pictures, and was well known as a writer of "horse operas." He has been compared to Owen WISTER and Eugene Manlove RHODES.

Specimen Days and Collect. A partial autobiography (1882) by Walt Whitman. Contains his recollections of his early life and notes on his hospital work during the Civil War.

Spectator, The. A famous series of essays by Joseph ADDISON and Richard STEELE (March, 1711–December, 1712). In these essays the *Spectator,* a shy, observing gentleman who has settled in London, gives a picture of the social life of the times. The concerns of the mythical *Spectator Club,* which had as its members Sir Roger de COVERLEY, Will HONEYCOMB, Sir Andrew FREEPORT and Captain SENTRY, add a narrative interest to the essays.

Specter Bridegroom, The. A well known tale in Irving's SKETCH BOOK. It relates how Sir Herman von Starkenfaust, arriving at the castle of the Katzenellenbogen with the sad tidings of the death of his friend, the expected bridegroom, is prevented from telling his news, falls in love, and plays the role of a specter, until he has gained possession of the bride.

Speculum Humanae Salvationis (*The Mirror of Human Salvation*). A kind of extended *Biblia Pauperum* telling pictorially the Bible story from the fall of Lucifer to the Redemption of Man, with explanations of each picture in Latin rhymes. MS copies of the 12th century are known, but its chief interest is that it was one of the earliest of printed books, the earliest edition known being that of 1467.

Speculum Meditantis, see MIROIR DE L'HOMME.

Spedding, James (1808–1881). English editor of *Works, Life, and Letters of Francis Bacon* (14 vols.; 1857–1874) and author of *Life and Times of Bacon* (1878). Refuted Macaulay's essay on Bacon.

Spee, Count **Maximilian von** (1861–1914). German admiral and strategist. Defeated the British in 1914 off the coast of Chile but his fleet was destroyed off the Falkland Islands about a month later by another British fleet. He went down on his flagship *Scharnhorst.* His name was given to a German warship which was defeated by the English and scuttled by her own men in the harbor of Montevideo in 1939.

Speed. In Shakespeare's Two GENTLEMEN OF VERONA, an inveterate punster and the clownish servant of Valentine, one of the two "gentlemen of Verona."

Speer, Robert Elliott (1867–). American religious leader and writer.

Speicher, Eugene Edward (1883–). Well-known American portrait painter, member of the National Institute of Arts and Letters. His portrait of *Katharine Cornell as Candida* is in the Whitney Museum of Modern Art in New York City.

Spellman, Francis Joseph (1889–). American Roman Catholic archbishop of New York (1939). Created cardinal (1946).

Spelvin, George. A mythical actor; a name used by an actor who plays two or more parts in one play.

Spencer, Claire (1899–). Scottish-American novelist. Her first novel, *Gallows' Orchard* (1930), is still her best-known.

Spencer, Herbert (1820–1903). English philosopher and social scientist, known for his application of the scientific doctrines of evolution (see DARWIN, CHARLES) to philosophy and ethics, with a central principle called Force the agent of all change, form, and organization in the universe. His ethics was derived also from UTILITARIANISM and emphasized the individual. In education, he scorned study of the liberal arts and advocated that science be the chief subject of instruction. Spencer's works include *Social Statics* (1851); *Principles of Psychology* (1855); *Program of a System of Synthetic Philosophy* (1860); *Education: Intellectual, Moral, and Physical* (1861); *First Principles* (1862); *Principles of Biology* (1864–1867); *Principles of Sociology* (1876–1896); *The Classification of the Sciences* (1864); *The Study of Sociology* (1873); *Principles of Ethics* (1879–1893); *The Man versus the State* (1884); *Factors of Organic Evolution* (1887); *Autobiography* (1904).

Spender, Stephen Harold (1909–). English poet, with C. DAY LEWIS and W. H. AUDEN a member of the leading group of British Marxist poets (see MARXISM IN LITERATURE) in the early 1930's. His poetry, regarded by critics as more personal, lyrical, and romantic in tone than that of his associates, deals chiefly with his own emotional reactions as he contemplates unemployment, poverty, suffering, or injustice, or visualizes amelioration in a Socialist state; much of it is characterized by imagery appropriate to an industrial and mechanical civilization. Among his works are *Poems* (1933); *Vienna* (1934), a long poem; *The Destructive Element* (1935), a book of criticism; *The Burning Cactus* (1936), stories; *Trial of a Judge* (1938), a poetic drama; *Forward from Liberalism* (1937), on politics and poetry; *The New Realism* (1939), criticism; *The Still Center* (1939), poems; *The Backward Sun* (1940), a novel; *Ruins and Visions* (1942), poetry.

Spengler, Oswald (1880–1936). German philosopher whose major work, *The Decline of the West* (1918–1922), was translated into many languages and caused great controversy in the U.S. It constitutes a deterministic morphology of history and predicts a phase of "Caesarism" in the further development of Western civilization. Spengler's attitude became very popular with the Nazi government, but he refused to enter into their persecution of the Jews. Being independently wealthy, he managed to exist in Germany, somewhat under a cloud, till the end of his life.

Spenlow, Dora. In Dickens' DAVID COPPERFIELD, a pretty, warm-hearted little doll of a woman, with no practical views of the duties of life or the value of money. She is the "child-wife" of David Copperfield, and loves to sit by him and hold his pens while he writes. She dies, and David then marries Agnes WICKFIELD. Dora's great pet is a dog called "Jip," which dies at the same time as its mistress.

Mr. Spenlow. The father of Dora. He is a proctor, to whom David Copperfield is articled. Mr. Spenlow is killed in a carriage accident.

Misses Lavinia and *Clarissa Spenlow.* Two spinster aunts of Dora Spenlow, with whom she lives after the death of her father:

> They were not unlike birds altogether, having a sharp, brisk, sudden manner, and a little, short, spruce way of adjusting themselves, like canaries.—*David Copperfield*, xli, (1849).

Spens, Sir Patrick. A Scotch hero, sent in the winter-time on a mission to Norway. His ship, in its home passage, was wrecked against the Papa Strongsay, and everyone on board was lost. The incident has furnished the subject of a famous old Scotch ballad.

Spenser, Edmund (1552–1599). English poet of the Elizabethan age, known for the misty, languid quality of his poetry, its imaginative appeal, use of allegory, individual diction involving the use of archaic and coined words, and subtlety of sound effects through the combination of alliteration, assonance, onomatopoeia, etc., with controlled rhythm and meter. His works include THE SHEPHERD'S CALENDAR (1579), a pastoral and allegorical poem; THE FAËRIE QUEENE (1590, 1596), his most famous work, left incomplete at the time of his death; *Complaints* (1591), containing *The Ruins of Time, The Tears of the Muses, Virgil's Gnat, Prosopopoeia, Or Mother Hubberd's Tale* (see HUBBERD, MOTHER), *Muiopotmos, Or The Tale of the Butterfly,* and other shorter poems; *Daphnaida* (1591), an elegy on the death of the daughter of Henry, Lord Howard; COLIN CLOUT'S COME HOME AGAIN (1595), an allegorical attack on artistic taste at Elizabeth's court; *Astrophel* (1595), an elegy on the death of Sir Philip SIDNEY; AMORETTI, a sonnet sequence; *Epithalamion* (1595), a poem celebrating his own marriage to Elizabeth BOYLE, considered his best lyric work; FOUR HYMNS TO LOVE AND BEAUTY (1596); *Prothalamion* (1596), a poem celebrating the double wedding of the two daughters of the Earl of Worcester; *A View of the Present State of Ireland,* a prose defense of the repressive policy of Lord Grey de Wilton in Ireland, not published until 1633.

Spenser was in the service of the Earl of Leicester at Elizabeth's court and became a close friend of Sir Philip Sidney, to whom he dedicated *The Shepherd's Calendar,* and of Gabriel HARVEY. In 1580 he went to Ireland as secretary to Lord Grey de Wilton, Lord Deputy of Ireland, and was later granted an estate, Kilcolman Castle, in Munster, where he wrote *The Faërie Queene*. In 1598 he was appointed Sheriff of Cork, but in an Irish rebellion soon afterwards Kilcolman Castle was burned, and Spenser and his family were forced to flee to England.

Spenser admired CHAUCER greatly, and the Chaucerian influence is evident in much of his work. Because of a certain austerity and "coldness" which some critics find in his own poetry, and because of its predominant formal perfection, Spenser is sometimes called a "poet's poet." John KEATS was an especially enthusiastic admirer of *The Faërie Queene* in his early career.

See also ROSALIND.

Spenserian meter. The meter devised by SPENSER, founded on the Italian *ottava rima,* for his FAËRIE QUEENE. It is a stanza of nine iambic lines, all of ten syllables except the last, which is an Alexandrine. Only three different rhymes are admitted into a stanza, and these are disposed: a b a b b c b c c.

The stanza was used by THOMSON (*Castle of Indolence*), SHENSTONE (*Schoolmistress*), BYRON (*Childe Harold*), etc.

The first stanza of Spenser's Faërie Queene follows. Lines 1 and 3 rhyme; lines 2, 4, 5, 7 rhyme; lines 6, 8, 9 rhyme; thus:

A gentle Knight was pricking on the plaine,
Ycladd in mightie armes and silver shielde,
Wherein old dints of deepe woundes did remaine,
The cruell markes of many a bloody fielde;
Yet armes till that time did he never wield,
His angry steede did chide his foming bit,
As much disdayning to the curbe to yield:
Full jolly knight he seemed and faire did sitt,
As one for knightly guists and fierce encounters fit.

Sperry, Elmer Ambrose (1860–1930). American electrical engineer whose most famous inventions were gyroscopic compasses and stabilizers for ships and airplanes. Founder of the Sperry Gyroscope Company (1910).

Spewack, Mrs. **Bella,** *née* **Cohen** (1899–) and her husband, **Samuel Spewack** (1899–). American playwrights, journalists, and short-story writers. They excel in comedy, as *Clear All Wires!* (1932); *Spring Song* (1934); *Boy Meets Girl* (1935); etc.

Speyer, James (1861–1941). Well-known American banker. Senior partner of Speyer & Company (from 1899). His brother, **Edgar Speyer** (1862–1932), married the American poet Leonora SPEYER.

Speyer, Leonora, *née* **Von Stosch** (1872–). American poet and violinist. Married the banker Edgar SPEYER (1902). Awarded Pulitzer prize for poetry (1927) for *Fiddler's Farewell.* Honorary Vice President of the Poetry Society of America. Teacher of poetry at Columbia University, and winner of numerous other poetry prizes.

spheres. In the Ptolemaic system of astronomy, the earth, as the center of the universe, was supposed to be surrounded by nine spheres of invisible space, the first seven carrying the "planets" as then known, viz., (1) Diana or the Moon, (2) Mercury, (3) Venus, (4) Apollo or the Sun, (5) Mars, (6) Jupiter, and (7) Saturn. The eighth, the Starry Sphere, carried the fixed stars, and the ninth, the Crystalline Sphere, was added by Hipparchus in the 2nd century B. C. to account for the precession of the equinoxes. Finally, in the Middle Ages, was added a tenth sphere, the *Primum Mobile,* a solid barrier which enclosed the universe and shut it off from Nothingness and the Empyrean. These last two spheres carried neither star nor planet.

They pass the planets seven, and pass the fixed [starry sphere],
And that crystal'line sphere . . . and that First-Moved.
Milton, *Paradise Lost,* iii. 482.

the music or *harmony, of the spheres.* PYTHAGORAS, having ascertained that the pitch of notes depends on the rapidity of vibrations, and also that the planets move at different rates of motion, concluded that the planets must make sounds in their motion according to their different rates; and that, as all things in nature are harmoniously made, the different sounds must harmonize. In this originated the old theory of the "harmony of the spheres." KEPLER has a treatise on the subject.

sphinx. A monster of ancient mythology. In Greece it is represented as having the head of a woman, the body of a lion, and winged; in Egypt, as a wingless lion with the head and breast of a man.

The Grecian Sphinx was generally said to be a daughter of TYPHON and CHIMAERA. She infested Thebes, setting the inhabitants a riddle and devouring all those who could not solve it. The riddle was—

What goes on four feet, on two feet, and three,
But the more feet it goes on the weaker it be?

It was at length solved by OEDIPUS with the answer that it was a man, who as an infant crawls upon all-fours, in manhood goes erect on his two feet, and in old age supports his tottering legs with a staff. On hearing this correct answer the Sphinx slew herself, and Thebes was delivered.

The Egyptian sphinx is a typification of Ra, the sun god. The colossal statue of the reclining monster was old in the days of Cheops, when the Great Pyramid, near which it lies, was built. It is hewn out of the solid rock; its length is 140 feet, and its head 30 feet from crown to chin.

EMERSON has a poem entitled *The Sphinx* (1841), and Oscar WILDE also wrote one.

spider.

Bruce and the spider. In 1305 Robert

BRUCE was crowned at Scone king of Scotland, but, being attacked by the English, retreated to Ireland, and all supposed him to be dead. While lying *perdu* in the little island of Rathlin he one day noticed a spider try six times to fix its web on a beam in the ceiling. "Now shall this spider," said Bruce, "teach me what I am to do, for I also have failed six times." The spider made a seventh effort and succeeded, whereupon Bruce left the island (1307), collected 300 followers, landed at Carrick, and at midnight surprised the English garrison in Turnberry Castle. He next overthrew the Earl of Gloucester, and in two years made himself master of well-nigh all Scotland, which Edward III declared in 1328 to be an independent kingdom. Sir Walter SCOTT tells us (*Tales of a Grandfather*) that in remembrance of this incident it has always been deemed a foul crime in Scotland for any of the name of Bruce to injure a spider.

Frederick the Great and the spider. While Frederick II was at Sans Souci, he one day went into his anteroom, as usual, to drink a cup of chocolate, but set his cup down to fetch his handkerchief from his bedroom. On his return he found a great spider had fallen from the ceiling into his cup. He called for fresh chocolate, and next moment heard the report of a pistol. The cook had been suborned to poison the chocolate, and, supposing his treachery had been found out, shot himself. On the ceiling of the room in Sans Souci a spider has been painted (according to tradition) in remembrance of this story.

Mahomet and the spider. When Mahomet fled from Mecca he hid in a certain cave, with the Koreishites close upon him. Suddenly an acacia in full leaf sprang up at the mouth of the cave, a wood-pigeon had its nest in the branches, and a spider had woven its net between the tree and the cave. When the Koreishites saw this, they felt persuaded that no one could have entered recently, and went on.

Spingarn, Joel Elias (1875–1939). American educator and critic. His *History of Literary Criticism in the Renaissance* (1899) was translated into Italian and led to his acquaintance with Benedetto CROCE. One of the founders of Harcourt, Brace & Co. (1919) and its literary adviser (till 1932). Edited its *European Library. Creative Criticism* (1917); *Poems* (1924). The Spingarn Medal (due to his activity in the National Association for the Advancement of Colored People, of which he became president) is awarded for the highest accomplishment by an American Negro during the previous year or years.

Spinoza, Baruch (1632–1677). Famous Dutch philosopher of Portuguese-Jewish parents. He is regarded today as the most eminent expounder of the doctrine of pantheism. He kept aloof from academic obligations by making a living as a grinder of lenses.

Spire, André (1868–). French writer active in Zionism and in the movement for a Jewish Home in Palestine.

spirituals. The generic name for the religious folk songs of the Negro, sung at campmeetings, in churches, etc. These natural and unhampered expressions of deep religious faith and imaginative ecstasy constitute the finest examples of native American music. Some familiar titles are *Swing Low, Sweet Chariot; Golden Slippers; Play on Your Harp, Little David; Joshua Fit de Battle ob Jericho; Sometimes I feel like a Motherless Child;* etc. Marian Anderson, Dorothy Maynor, Paul Robeson, and Roland Hayes are some of the outstanding interpreters of Negro Spirituals on the concert stage.

Spitalfields. A district in London. The name, literally "hospital fields," is explained by the fact that the district was formerly owned by the Hospital of St. Mary. The silk industry of England was established here after the Huguenots had been driven from France in the reign of Louis XIV.

Spitteler, Carl (1845–1924). Swiss poet and novelist. Awarded the Nobel prize (1919) for his epic *Olympischer Frühling* (*Olympian Spring*) and other works. Romain Rolland has called him "the greatest German poet since Goethe."

Spode, Josiah (1754–1827). English Staffordshire potter who made a type of porcelain which is still known as spode or spode ware.

Spofford, Harriet Elizabeth, *née* **Prescott** (1835–1921). American novelist and poet, well-known at the end of the 19th century.

Spoils of Poynton, The. One of the best novels (1897) of Henry JAMES, in which a great art and furniture collection in private hands is used to upset the lives of people connected with it.

spoils system. The system of distributing political offices as rewards for service rendered to a particular political party. It was introduced into American politics by Andrew JACKSON (1767–1845) during his presidential term and is said to have received its designation from the statement made by W. L. Marcy in the Senate, January, 1832, "To the victors belong the spoils of the enemy." Civil Service reforms gradually mitigated the evils of the system.

spondee. In prosody, a poetic foot of two equally accented syllables, used to vary regular meters. *Compound, context, footfall, amen,* are spondaic words. The use of the spondee in iambic verse is illustrated in the following line from Ben Jonson:

Slow, slow, | fresh fount, | keep time | with my | salt tears.

sponge.

throw up the sponge. Give up; confess oneself beaten. The metaphor is from boxing matches, for when a second tossed a sponge into the ring it was a sign that his man was beaten.

to sponge on a man. To live on him like a parasite, sucking up all he has as a dry sponge will suck up water.

a sponger. A mean parasite who is always accepting the hospitality of those who will give it and never makes any adequate return.

Sponge, Mr. The hero of a hunting novel, *Mr. Sponge's Sporting Tour* (1853), by R. SURTEES, illustrated by John Leech.

Spooner, William Archibald (1844–1930). Dean and later warden of New College, Oxford. Acquired a (probably exaggerated) reputation for his "spoonerisms," witty or unwitting transpositions of sounds, technically known as metathesis. "I'll sew you to a sheet." —"There is a roaring pain."—"The tons of soil."—Spoonerisms form part of Joyce's technique in FINNEGANS WAKE and have been used by the American humorist, "Colonel Stoopnagle" in *My Tale is Twisted* (1946) ("Little Slack Bambo," etc.).

Spoon River. The middle western American town whose life is laid bare in Edgar Lee MASTERS' *Spoon River Anthology*, a volume of free verse which created a great sensation on its appearance in 1916. The men and women of Spoon River make their own epitaphs in a series of short monologues uttered from the cemetery where they lie buried. The spirit of the book is relentlessly realistic. *The New Spoon River* appeared in 1924.

Sporus. A favorite of Emperor Nero. The name was applied by Pope to Lord Hervey, and implied effeminacy.

S.P.Q.R. (*Senatus Populusque Romanus*, "the Roman Senate and People"). Letters inscribed on the standards of ancient Rome.

Sprat, Jack. See JACK.

Sprat, Thomas, Bishop of Rochester (1635–1713). English clergyman and author, best known for his history of the ROYAL SOCIETY (1667).

Spratling, William P. (1900–). American illustrator, chiefly known for his drawings of New Orleans and Louisiana. He also did *Little Mexico* with a foreword by Diego Rivera.

spread eagle. The "eagle displayed" of heraldry, *i.e.*, an eagle with legs and wings extended, the wings being elevated. It is the device of the United States, and was hence humorously adopted as emblematic of bombast, hyperbole, and extravagant boasting. *Spread-Eagleism* in a United States citizen is very much the counterpart of the more aggressive and bombastic forms of JINGOISM in the Britisher.

spread-eagle oratory. "A compound of exaggeration, effrontery, bombast, and extravagance, mixed with metaphors, platitudes, threats, and irreverent appeals flung at the Almighty" (*North American Review*, November, 1858).

In the navy a man was said to be *spread-eagled* when he was lashed to the rigging with outstretched arms and legs for flogging.

Spreckels, Claus (1828–1908). German-born American sugar manufacturer. Known in San Francisco as the "Sugar King." In the sugar business (from 1863) he secured a virtual monopoly. His oldest son, **John Diedrich Spreckels** (1853–1926), founded J. D. Spreckels & Brothers Company, shipping and commission merchants.

Sprigg, Christopher St. John. Pseudonym **Christopher Caudwell** (1907–1937). English writer of excellent detective stories. Also a writer on aviation and on poetry. He was killed in action in Spain, having joined the British Battalion of the International Brigade.

Spring, Howard (1889–). British novelist. Author of *My Son, My Son!* (1938); *Heaven Lies About Us* (1939); *Fame is the Spur* (1940), a ROMAN À CLEF about Ramsay MACDONALD; *In the Meantime* (1942); etc.

Springfield Republican, The. A famous Massachusetts newspaper, founded (1824) as a weekly by Samuel Bowles. It supported Abraham Lincoln during the Civil War and subsequently attacked the administration of Grant. The paper has always remained in the hands of the Bowles family.

Spring-Rice, Sir **Cecil Arthur** (1859–1918). British diplomat. Ambassador to the U.S. (1913–1918).

sprung rhythm. A type of poetic rhythm associated in modern times chiefly with the work of Gerard Manley HOPKINS. Its basic unit is a metrical foot usually of from one to four syllables, with any number of weak, or slack, syllables being used for special effects. It has one stress per foot, falling on the only syllable, if there is but one, or on the first syllable, so that each line may contain a variety of the kinds of metrical feet. Sprung rhythm may have rests, as in music, and may add as many as three slack syllables to each foot without their being taken into account in scansion. It is a characteristic of sprung rhythm for scansion to continue through a whole stanza without a break, as though it were all written in one line. Robert BRIDGES in his notes to the 1918 edition of Hopkins' *Poems* points out that sprung rhythm is the natural rhythm of English speech and written prose, and that it was used in Latin and Greek verse and in English verse up to the Elizabethan period.

Spy, The. A novel by J. F. COOPER (1821), laid in Revolutionary times. It relates the adventures of "the spy" Harvey Birch, a peddler who endures unjust suspicions of being in league with the British. He makes constant use of these suspicions to advance his real purpose of securing enemy information for the ears of Washington, who is represented in the novel as a rather solemn and formal character called Harper.

square.

to square the circle. To attempt an impossibility. The allusion is to the impossibility of exactly determining the precise ratio between the diameter and the circumference of a circle, and thus constructing a circle of the same area as a given square. The ratio is 3.14159 . . . The next decimals would be 26537, but the numbers would go on *ad infinitum*.

Square, Mr. A "philosopher," in Fielding's novel called *The History of Tom Jones, a Foundling*. See TOM JONES.

squatter sovereignty. In U.S. history, the principle that squatters in regions not set up as territories or states had the right to make their own laws.

Squeers, Mr. Wackford. In Dickens' NICHOLAS NICKLEBY, a vulgar, conceited, ignorant schoolmaster of DOTHEBOYS HALL, Yorkshire. He steals the boys' pocket money, clothes his son in their best suits, half starves them, and teaches them next to nothing. Ultimately, he is transported for purloining a deed.

Mrs. Squeers. Wife of Mr. Wackford, a raw-boned, harsh, heartless virago, without one spark of womanly feeling for the boys put under her charge. Played by Dame Sybil THORNDIKE in the British-made film (1947).

Miss Fanny Squeers. Daughter of the schoolmaster, "not tall like her mother, but short like her father. From the former she inherited a voice of hoarse quality, and from the latter a remarkable expression of the right eye." Miss Fanny falls in love with Nicholas Nickleby, but hates him and spites him because he is insensible of the soft impeachment.

Master Wackford Squeers. Son of the schoolmaster, a spoiled boy, who is dressed in the best clothes of the scholars. He is overbearing, self-willed, and passionate.

The person who suggested the character of Squeers was a Mr. Shaw of Bowes. He married a Miss Laidman. The satire ruined the school, and was the death both of Mr. and Mrs. Shaw.—*Notes and Queries*, October 25, 1873.

Squibob, see DERBY, GEORGE.

Squire, Sir John Collings (1884–). English poet and editor. Founder (1919) and editor (to 1934) of the London *Mercury*. Author of many books of poetry and a number of books of parodies. He collaborated in the writing of the play *Berkeley Square* (1929) with J. L. BALDERSTON.

Squire of Dames, the. In Spenser's FAËRIE QUEENE, a young knight, in love with Columbell, who assigns him a year's service before she will consent to become his bride. The "Squire" is to travel for twelve months, to rescue distressed ladies, and bring pledges of his exploits to Columbell. At the end of the year he places three hundred pledges in her hands, but instead of rewarding him by becoming his bride, she sets him another task, viz., to travel about the world on foot and not present himself again till he can bring her pledges from three hundred damsels that they will live in chastity all their lives. The Squire tells Columbell that in three years he has found only three persons who would take the pledge, and only one of these, he says a rustic cottager, took it from a "principle of virtue"; the other two (a nun and a courtesan) promised to do so, but did not voluntarily join the "virgin martyrs." The "Squire of Dames" turns out to be BRITOMART. This story is imitated from *The Host's Tale*, in *Orlando Furioso*, xxviii.

Squire's or **Squyeres Tale.** One of Chaucer's CANTERBURY TALES. See CAMBUSCAN. The Squire is perhaps best described in the following well-known lines:

With him [the Knight] ther was his sone a yong Squyer,
A lovyere and a lusty bacheler
With lokkes crulle, as they were leyd in press,
Of twenty yeer of age he was, I gesse . .
Singinge he was, or floyting al the day
He was as fresh as is the month of May.
Prologue to the Canterbury Tales.

Squirt. The apothecary's boy, in Garth's *Dispensary;* hence, any apprentice lad or errand-boy.

Stabat Mater (*Lat.*, "The Mother was standing"). The celebrated Latin hymn reciting the Seven Sorrows of the Virgin at the Cross, so called from its opening words, forming part of the service during Passion week, in the Roman Catholic Church. It was composed by Jacobus de Benedictis, a Franciscan of the 13th century, and has been set to music by Pergolesi, Rossini, Haydn, etc.

Stackpole, Henrietta. In THE PORTRAIT OF A LADY by Henry James, an American newspaper correspondent in Europe, the sincere and likable friend of the heroine, Isabel Archer.

Stacpoole, Henry de Vere Stacpoole (1863–). British physician and author of a number of popular novels, including *The Blue Lagoon.*

Staël, Mme de. *Née* **Germaine Necker** (1766–1817). French author of Swiss parentage, daughter of the French Minister of Finance and wife of Baron de Staël-Holstein, ambassador to France from Sweden. She is known for her celebrated salons, which were attended by the leading literary and political figures of the day, for her sensibility and kindness in personal relations, her talent for conversation, her vigorous mind, and her influence on the movement of ROMANTICISM in France. Among her works are *Lettres sur les Écrits et le Caractère de Jean Jacques Rousseau* (1788); *De l'Influence des Passions* (1796); *Essai sur les Fictions; Delphine* (1802) and CORINNE (1807), called by some critics the first "modern" novels in their view of French society, anticipating the works of George SAND; *De la Littérature* (1800), criticism, in which she was among the first to break away from neo-Classical principles and which caused a sensation on its publication; *De l'Allemagne* (1813), a study of German literature, which introduced German romanticism into France and was at first suppressed on orders by Napoleon; and *Considérations sur la Révolution Française* (1818).

Mme de Staël had an eventful career, being exiled from France after the Revolution of 1789, allowed to return in 1795, and banished again later by Napoleon, of whom she was an outspoken critic. She had several disappointing love affairs, the chief of which involved the Don Juan-like Swiss novelist Benjamin CONSTANT; CHATEAUBRIAND and she were rivals in the literary world. Her influence has been found in LAMARTINE, Victor HUGO, and Charles NODIER in poetry and criticism; Cousin, Ticknor, and Prescott in the study of the German language; and Guizot, Villemain, and Cousin in the study of English and German literature.

staff of life, the. Bread, which is the *support* of life. Shakespeare says, "The boy was the very staff of my age." The allusion is to a staff which supports the feeble in walking.

Stafford, Wendell Philips (1861–). American associate justice of the supreme court of the district of Columbia. Also poet laureate of Vermont.

Stagirite or **Stagyrite.** Aristotle, who was born at Stagira, in Macedon (4th century B.C.).

Stagirius. A young monk to whom St. Chrysostom addressed three books, and of whom those books give an account. Matthew ARNOLD has a prayer in verse supposed to be uttered by Stagirius.

Stahl, Georg Ernst (1660–1734). German chemist who, with Johann Joachim BECHER, originated the PHLOGISTON theory.

Stahl, Jacob. An architect, hero of a trilogy of novels by J. D. BERESFORD, entitled *The Early History of Jacob Stahl* (1911), *A Candidate for Truth* (1912), and *The Invisible Event* (1915).

Stalin, Josef. Real name **Iosif Vissarionovich Dzhugashvili** (1879–). Russian dictator. Son of a shoemaker. Expelled from theological seminary for Marxist propaganda. Active in revolutionary politics (from 1896). Imprisoned during World War I. After Lenin's death (1924), eliminated real and potential opponents and initiated three "Five-Year plans" (1928, 1934, 1937). Concluded a non-aggression pact with Germany (1939), annexed parts of German-defeated Poland, and took Russia into a war against Finland (1939–1940). Created marshal of the Soviet Union (1943) after his country's victorious participation in World War II. As a politician and great statesman, Stalin has demonstrated again the truism that a straight line is often the longest way from one point to another.

Stalky and Co. A boys' story by Rudyard KIPLING (1899), narrating the adventures of three schoolboys, Arthur Corkran, otherwise known as "Your Uncle Stalky," the Irish McTurk, and Beetle. Beetle is usually taken to be Kipling himself. McTurk is George Charles BERESFORD (d. 1938) and Stalky is Major General Lionel Charles DUNSTERVILLE (1866–1946).

Stallings, Laurence (1894–). American journalist, playwright, and author, best known for WHAT PRICE GLORY? (1924), a play on which he collaborated with Maxwell ANDERSON, and for *The First World War* (1933), a book of photographs and text presenting the horrors of World War I which was sensationally successful, the first representative of a type of journalism which had a wide vogue in the 1930's. Other works of Stallings are *Plumes* (1924), a novel; *First Flight* (1925) and *The Buccaneer* (1925), further plays written with Maxwell Anderson; *Deep River* (1926) and *Rainbow* (1928), operettas, for which he wrote book and lyrics; *A Farewell to Arms* (1930), a dramatic version of the novel of the same title by Ernest HEMINGWAY; and a number of motion-picture scenarios.

Stamp, Josiah Charles. 1st Baron **Stamp** (1880–1941). British economist who helped draft the DAWES Plan (1924) and the Young Plan (1929). Director of the Bank of England.

Stamp Act. A revenue act which requires that all legal documents, newspapers, almanacs, and commercial papers of all kinds carry stamps showing the tax paid on them. The American colonies rebelled against such an act, known as Grenville's Stamp Act, passed by the British Parliament in 1765. Samuel Adams,

James Otis, and others were spokesmen against it. In the fall of 1765, a congress was convened in New York, known as the Stamp Act Congress, which petitioned the king to repeal the act. The request was granted the next year.

Standing Fishes Bible. See BIBLE, SPECIALLY NAMED.

Standish, Miles. See THE COURTSHIP OF MILES STANDISH.

Stanford, Leland (1824–1893). Governor of California (1861–1863). Helped to promote and finance the Central Pacific Railroad. President and director, Central Pacific (1863–1893) and Southern Pacific (1885–1890). U.S. Senator. Founder (1891) of Leland Stanford Junior University, now Stanford University, at Palo Alto, California.

Stanhope, Lady **Hester Lucy** (1776–1839). A famous Englishwoman who lived in the Orient and became during her lifetime almost a legend. She is described in Kinglake's *Eöthen* (1844).

Stanley, Sir **Henry Morton** (1841–1904). Famous explorer, chiefly remembered for his expedition into Central Africa to find David LIVINGSTONE. The expedition was commissioned by James Gordon Bennett of the New York *Herald*. Stanley reached Livingstone in November 1871, greeting him with the now famous words, "Dr. Livingstone, I presume?" He published a number of books including *Through the Dark Continent* (2 vols.; 1878); *The Congo and the Founding of its Free State* (2 vols.; 1885); *In Darkest Africa* (2 vols.; 1890); etc.

Stannard, Henrietta Eliza Vaughan, *née* **Palmer.** Pen names **Violet Whyte** and **John Strange Winter** (1856–1911). English author of short stories and novels.

Stanton, Elizabeth Cady (1815–1902). American leader of woman suffrage. First president of the National Woman Suffrage Association (1869–1890). *History of Woman Suffrage* (3 vols.; 1881–1886), with Susan B. ANTHONY and Matilda J. Gage.

Stanton, Frank Lebby (1857–1927). Southern poet. As staff member of the Atlanta *Constitution,* he ran one of the first daily columns, *Just From Georgia.* Published several volumes of poems and has sometimes been called the "Poet Laureate of Georgia."

stanza. In prosody, an arrangement or group of rhymed lines in a certain order, repeated throughout a poetical composition. Among the best-known stanza forms are the following:

(*a*) Four-line stanzas:
(1) BALLAD METER.
(2) ELEGIAC METER.
(3) iambic tetrameter rhyming *abba,* as in Tennyson's *In Memoriam:*

> Fair ship that from the Italian shore
> Sailest the placid ocean-plains
> With my lost Arthur's loved remains,
> Spread thy full wings and waft him o'er.

(4) The quatrain of FitzGerald's *Omar Kháyyám,* five-foot iambic verse rhyming *aaba:*

> Ah Love! could thou and I with Fate conspire
> To grasp this sorry Scheme of things entire,
> Would we not shatter it to bits—and then
> Re-mould it nearer to the Heart's Desire!

(*b*) RHYME ROYAL.
(*c*) OTTAVA RIMA.
(*d*) the SPENSERIAN STANZA.
(*e*) TERZA RIMA.

Stapledon, William Olaf (1886–). English philosopher and novelist whose *Last and First Men* (1931) is an extraordinary imaginative leap into the future of our world. He considers his *Star Maker* (1937) the best of his novels.

star. Figuratively applied to a specially prominent person on the stage, concert platform, etc.; hence *star part,* the part taken by a leading actor, *star turn,* etc.

The stars were said by the old astrologers to have almost omnipotent influence on the lives and destinies of man. (Cf. *Judges* v. 20—"The stars in their courses fought against Sisera"). To this old belief is due a number of phrases still common, as *Bless my stars! You may thank your lucky stars; star-crossed* (not favored by the stars, unfortunate); *to be born under an evil star,* etc.

his star is in the ascendant. He is in luck's way; said of a person to whom some good fortune has fallen and who is very prosperous. According to astrology, those leading stars which are above the horizon at a person's birth influence his life and fortune. When those stars are in the ascendant, he is strong, healthy, and lucky, but when they are in the descendant below the horizon, his stars do not shine on him; he is in the shade and subject to ill-fortune. See also HOUSES, ASTROLOGICAL.

the star of the North. Gustavus Adolphus of Sweden (1594–1632).

Stars and Bars. The flag of the Confederacy formed by the Southern states during the American Civil War. It has a horizontal bar of white between two red bars and a blue field with seven white stars.

Stars and Stripes or *the Star-Spangled Banner.* The flag of the United States. The stripes are emblematic of the original thirteen States, and the stars—of which there are now forty-eight—of the States including those that have since been admitted into the Union.

The first flag of the U.S., raised by Washington June 2, 1776, consisted of thirteen stripes, alternately red and white, with a blue canton emblazoned with the crosses of St. George and St. Andrew. On June 14, 1777, Congress ordered that the canton should have thirteen white stars in a blue field. In 1794, after the admission of Vermont and Kentucky, the stripes and stars were increased to fifteen.

starboard and **larboard.** Star (Anglo-Saxon *steor*) is "rudder," bord is "side," meaning the right side of ship (looking forwards). Larboard, for the left-hand side is now obsolete, and "port" is used instead. The word was earlier *leereboord* (Anglo-Saxon *loere,* "empty"), that side being clear as the steersman stood on the star (*steer*) board.

Starbuck. In Herman Melville's MOBY DICK, chief mate to Captain AHAB. He is an honest and prudent man who tries to dissuade the Captain from his mad chase of the whale.

Star Chamber. A room in the Palace of Westminster whose ceiling had upon it gilt stars. Sittings of a very arbitrary and tyrannical court were held here under the early Stuarts. "Court of star chamber" or "star-chamber proceedings" are phrases still applied to any tyrannical tribunal.

Stareleigh, Justice. In Dickens' PICKWICK PAPERS, a stout, pudgy little judge, very deaf, and very irascible, who, in the absence of the chief justice, sits in judgment on the trial of "Bardell *v.* Pickwick." See BARDELL, MRS.

Star in a Stone-boat, A. A poem by Robert FROST, the first in the volume *New Hampshire.* In New England, a stone-boat is a kind of sledge used to drag stones for building walls, etc.

Stark, Harold Raynsford (1880–). U.S. admiral. Chief of naval operations (1939); replaced by Admiral King and transferred to London as commander of the U.S. naval forces in European waters (1942).

Stark, John (1728–1822). Army officer in the American Revolution. Won the battle of Bennington (August 16, 1777). Member of the court-martial which tried and sentenced Major André.

Starkenfaust, Herman von. Titular hero of Irving's SPECTER BRIDEGROOM.

Starkey, James Sullivan. Pseudonym **Seumas O'Sullivan** (1879–). Irish poet. Founded the Theater of Ireland (1905) and the *Dublin Magazine* (1923). Author of a number of volumes of poetry and essays. One of the first members of the Irish Academy of Letters.

Starr, David. Hero of Bayard TAYLOR's tragedy *The Prophet* (1874), a study of a man who gradually comes to believe that he has a divine mission. The character is said to have been suggested by Joseph SMITH, the founder of Mormonism.

Starrett, Vincent (1886–). Canadian-born American writer on books. He has also written entertaining verse and some mystery fiction and is an authority on the private life of Sherlock Holmes. *Bookman's Holiday* (1942); *Autolycus in Limbo* (poems; 1943); *Murder in Peking* (1946); etc.

Starvation Dundas. Henry Dundas, 1st Lord Melville. According to Horace Walpole, he was so called because he introduced the word *starvation* into the language in a speech on American affairs (1775).

Starveling, Robin. In Shakespeare's MIDSUMMER NIGHT'S DREAM, the tailor cast for the part of "Thisbe's mother," in the drama played before Duke Theseus on "his wedding day at night." See PYRAMUS. Starveling has nothing to say in the drama.

Stassen, Harold Edward (1902–). Governor of Minnesota (1938–1943), resigning to enter the U.S. Navy. Vigorous campaigner for Republican presidential nomination, 1948.

State Fair. The first novel (1932) by Phil STONG. It has been filmed twice.

states. The following are some of the best known designations of American states:

Antelope State. Nebraska.

Badger State. Wisconsin. This name is said to have been given the state because the mining pioneers lived in the ground like badgers. There is a badger on the state coat of arms.

Battle-born State. Nevada, so called because it was admitted into the Union during the Civil War.

Bay State. Massachusetts, so called from the name of the original colony, Massachusetts Bay.

Bayou State. Mississippi. A bayou is a creek, or sluggish and marshy overflow of a river or lake. The word may be of native American origin, but is probably a corruption of Fr. *boyau,* gut.

Bear State. Arkansas, so called from the number of bears formerly within its bounds.

Big Bend State. Tennessee, from the Indian name Tennessee, meaning "River of the Big Bend."

Blue Grass State. Kentucky.

Blue Law State. Connecticut. See BLUE LAWS.

Bonanza State. Nevada. See BONANZA.

Border States. The five "slave" states (Delaware, Maryland, Virginia, Kentucky, and Missouri) which lay next to the "free states" were so called in the American Civil War.

Border Eagle State. Mississippi, from the border eagle in its coat of arms.

Buckeye State. Ohio, so called from its numerous buckeye or horse-chestnut trees. An inhabitant of the state is known as a *Buckeye.*

Bullion State. Missouri, so called from its Congressman, Thomas Hart Benton, who was known as "Old Bullion."

Centennial State. Colorado, from the date of its admission into the Union in 1876, one hundred years after the Declaration of Independence.

Cockade State. Maryland, from the cockades worn by Maryland Revolutionary troops.

Confederate States. The eleven States which seceded from the Union in the Civil War (1861–1865): Georgia, North and South Carolina, Virginia, Tennessee, Alabama, Louisiana, Arkansas, Mississippi, Florida, Texas. They were all readmitted into the Union between 1866 and 1870.

Corn-Cracker State. Kentucky. According to one derivation, the name comes from its corn-cracker birds. *Crackers* or *Corn Crackers* are Southern "poor whites."

Cotton Plantation State. Alabama.

Cracker State. Georgia. *Crackers* are "poor whites."

Creole State. Louisiana, from its large percentage of Creoles, or persons of French (or sometimes Spanish) descent.

Equality State. Wyoming, because it was the first to grant woman suffrage.

Empire State. New York. The name *Empire* was given to the state and city by George Washington, 1784, in reply to an address by the New York Common Council.

Empire State of the South. Georgia.

Everglade State. Florida, so called from its everglades or tracts of marshy flat land.

Excelsior State. New York is so called from its motto *Excelsior*.

Federal States. The name given to those northern states which combined to resist the eleven southern or Confederate states.

Freestone State. Connecticut, from the freestone in its limits.

Garden State. Kansas and New Jersey have been so called from their agricultural interests.

Golden State. California; so called from its gold "diggings."

Granite State. New Hampshire is so called, because the mountainous parts are chiefly granite.

Green Mountain State. Vermont.

Gulf States. Alabama, Florida, Mississippi, Louisiana and Texas, on the Gulf of Mexico.

Hawk Eye State. Iowa, from the name of the Indian chief who opposed the early settlers.

Hoosier State. Indiana, said to be named from Husher, a bully who hushed those opposed to him.

Jay Hawk State. Kansas. See JAY HAWK.

Keystone State. Pennsylvania, so called from its position and importance.

Lake State. Michigan, which touches Lake Michigan, Lake Huron, Lake Erie, Lake Superior, and Lake St. Clair.

Live Oak State. Florida, from its numbers of live oaks.

Lone Star State. Texas, from its coat of arms which displays a single star.

Lumber State. Maine.

North Star State. Minnesota, from its motto *L'Etoile du Nord* (The North Star).

Nutmeg State. Connecticut, from the shrewdness of its inhabitants, who are supposed to produce wooden nutmegs and other frauds.

Old Line State. Maryland, which is separated from Pennsylvania by the Mason and Dixon line.

Old North State. North Carolina.

Palmetto State. South Carolina. The palmetto tree is a prominent feature of the state coat of arms.

Panhandle State. West Virginia. See PANHANDLE.

Pelican State. Louisiana, from the pelican in its coat of arms.

Peninsular State. Florida, so called because of its shape.

Pine Tree State. Maine, which has forests of these trees and bears a pine-tree on its coat of arms.

Prairie State. Illinois, from its vast prairies.

Sage-Brush State. Nevada. The inhabitants are called *Sage Hens.*

Thirteen States. The original thirteen colonies that united to form the United States of America. They are Connecticut, Delaware, Georgia, Maryland, Massachusetts, New Hampshire, New Jersey, New York, North Carolina, Pennsylvania, Rhode Island, South Carolina and Virginia.

Sucker State. Illinois was so called from the "suckers" who worked in the lead diggings of Wisconsin but returned to Illinois for the winter.

Turpentine State. North Carolina, because of the turpentine it produces.

Wolverine State. Michigan, from the wolverines of its pioneer days.

Land of Steady Habits. Connecticut, which is also called the Blue Law State.

Sunset Land. Arizona.

The following are the dates of admission of the various states into the Union:

Alabama (December 14, 1819); Arizona (February 14, 1912); Arkansas (June 15, 1836); California (September 9, 1850); Colorado (August 1, 18 6); Connecticut (January 9, 1788); Delaware (December 7, 1787); Florida (March 3, 1845); Georgia (January 2, 1788); Idaho (July 3, 1890); Illinois (December 3, 1818); Indiana (December 11, 1816); Iowa (December 28, 1846); Kansas (January 29, 1861); Kentucky (June 1, 1792); Louisiana (April 8, 1812); Maine (March 15, 1820); Maryland (April 28, 1788); Massachusetts (February 6, 1788); Michigan (January 26, 1837); Minnesota (May 11, 1858); Mississippi

(December 10, 1817); Missouri (August 10, 1821); Montana (November 8, 1889); Nebraska (February 9, 1867); Nevada (October 31, 1864); New Hampshire (June 21, 1788); New Jersey (December 18, 1787); New Mexico (January 6, 1912); New York (July 26, 1788); North Carolina (November 21, 1789); North Dakota (November 2, 1889); Ohio (March 1, 1803); Oklahoma (November 16, 1907); Oregon (February 14, 1859); Pennsylvania (December 12, 1787); Rhode Island (May 29, 1790); South Carolina (May 23, 1788); South Dakota (November 2, 1889); Tennessee (June 1, 1796); Texas (December 29, 1845); Utah (January 4, 1896); Vermont (March 4, 1791); Virginia (June 25, 1788); Washington (November 11, 1889); West Virginia (June 20, 1863); Wisconsin (May 29, 1848); Wyoming (July 10, 1890).

Stationers' Hall. In London, the hall of the guild of stationers, i.e., booksellers and publishers. For nearly three hundred years the guild regulated the publication of books in England. From 1842 to 1911 proceedings against copyright infringement were possible only in the case of books registered at Stationers' Hall.

stations.

the fourteen stations of the Catholic Church. These are generally called "Stations of the Cross," and the whole series is known as the *via Calvaria* or *via Crucis.* Each station represents, by fresco, picture, or otherwise, some incident in the passage of Christ from the judgment hall to CALVARY, and at each prayers are offered up in memory of the event represented. They are as follows:

(1) The condemnation to death.
(2) Christ is made to bear His cross.
(3) His first fall under the cross.
(4) The meeting with the Virgin.
(5) Simon the Cyrenean helps to carry the cross.
(6) Veronica wipes the sacred face.
(7) The second fall.
(8) Christ speaks to the daughters of Jerusalem.
(9) The third fall.
(10) Christ is stripped of His garments.
(11) The nailing to the cross.
(12) The giving up of the Spirit.
(13) Christ is taken down from the cross.
(14) The deposition in the sepulcher.

Statira. A historical character, daughter of Darius and first wife of ALEXANDER. She and Roxana, the Bactrian, his second wife, are the joint heroines of Lee's drama, *Alexander the Great, Or The Rival Queens* (1678). Statira is finally murdered by her rival.

Miss Boutwell was the original "Statira" of Lee's *Alexander,* and once, when playing with Mrs. Barry [1678] she was in danger of receiving on the stage her death-blow. It happened thus: Before the curtain drew up, the two queens, "Statira" and "Roxana" had a real rivalship about a lace veil, allotted to Miss Boutwell by the manager. This so enraged Mrs. Barry that, in "stabbing 'Statira,'" she actually thrust her dagger through her rival's stays, a quarter of an inch or more into the flesh.—Campbell, *Life of Mrs. Siddons.*

Statue and the Bust, The. A poem (1855) by Robert BROWNING.

Staunton, the Rev. In Scott's HEART OF MIDLOTHIAN, rector of Willingham, and father of George Staunton.

George Staunton. Son of the Rev. Staunton. He appears first as "Geordie Robertson," a felon; in the Porteous mob he assumes the guise of "Madge Wildfire." George Staunton is the seducer of Effie DEANS. Ultimately he comes to the title of baronet, marries Effie, and is shot by a gypsy boy called "The Whistler," who proves to be his own natural son.

Lady Staunton. Effie Deans after her marriage with Sir George. On the death of her husband, she retires to a convent on the Continent.

Stavisky, Serge Alexandre (1886?–1934). A remarkable Russian-born French swindler who managed to sell 40,000,000 francs' worth of worthless bonds to the French working people. The discovery of his huge fraud (December, 1933) resulted in the downfall of two ministries. A trial which ended in January 1936 led to the conviction of nine people. Stavisky's sudden death was probably suicide. Cf. *An American in Paris* (1940), by Janet Flanner.

Stavrogin, Nikolay Vsyevolodovich. In Dostoyevsky's THE POSSESSED, a young Russian of the upper classes, mysterious, magnetic, and erratic in personality, an atheist and adherent of NIHILISM in thought. He has lived abroad for a number of years in debauchery and crime in which Marya Timofyevna LEBYADKIN and the wife of Ivan SHATOV have been involved. During this time he has become associated with Pyotr Stepanovich VERHOVENSKY in the leadership of a band of revolutionary terrorists whom he brings to his native village, but he is unable to believe in their aims. He tries to turn to religion, but he is unable to believe in that, either, and he cannot love, although Lizaveta Nikolaevna TUSHIN gives herself to him. Simultaneously admired and hated by virtually all the other characters, Nikolay is unhappy and plans to start anew elsewhere in the company of Shatov's sister, the devoted Darya, but instead commits suicide.

Varvara Petrovna Stavrogin, Nikolay's mother, is also a leading character in the novel. She is a vigorous and direct woman, temperamental and domineering, who maintains a devoted but stormy friendship with Stepan Trofimovich VERHOVENSKY, who lives on her estate, and for a time is the patroness of a proposed magazine to be issued by the revolutionary band. This character is said to have been based on a real person, A. O. Smirnova-Rosset, a Russian woman of wealth who was a friend of PUSHKIN and GOGOL in the early part of the 19th century.

Stead, Christina Ellen (1902–). Australian-born American novelist. According to Rebecca West, "one of the few people really original we have produced since the [First World] War." *The Salzburg Tales* (1934); *Seven Poor Men of Sydney* (1935); *House of All Nations* (1938); *The Man Who Loved Children* (1940); etc.

Stead, William Thomas (1849–1912). English journalist. Founded the English *Review of Reviews* (1890) and introduced American methods of journalism into England. Advocated international peace and friendship with Russia and was interested in psychic research. He perished with the *Titanic.*

Steady Habits, the Land of. Connecticut is so called, from the supposedly puritanical character of its people.

Stealthy School of Criticism. A term coined by Dante Gabriel ROSSETTI in allusion to criticism published under a pseudonym. It was first used in a letter to the *Athenaeum,* December 16, 1871, with reference to a pseudonymous attack on THE FLESHLY SCHOOL OF POETRY published in the *Contemporary Review* of that year.

Stedman, Edmund Clarence (1833–1908). American critic and poet of the GENTEEL TRADITION, best known for his studies and anthologies of American and English literature, his verse not being regarded highly by 20th-century critics. His works include *Poems, Lyrical and Idyllic* (1860); *Alice of Monmouth: An Idyll of the Great War* (1863); *The Blameless Prince* (1869); *Poetical Works* (1873); *Victorian Poets* (1875); *Commemorative Ode on Hawthorne* (1877); *Poets of America* (1885); *The Nature and Elements of Poetry* (1892); and *A Library of American Literature* (1887–1890), *A Victorian Anthology* (1895), and *An American Anthology* (1900), all of which he edited. His best-known poem is *Pan in Wall Street.* Stedman was a journalist in his early career but spent most of his life as a successful New York stock broker.

Steed, Henry Wickham (1871–). Well-known English journalist. Foreign correspondent for the London *Times* in Berlin, Rome, Vienna; foreign editor (1914–1919) and editor of the *Times* (1919–1922).

Steel, Mrs. **Flora Annie** (1847–1929). English novelist, best known for *On the Face of the Waters* (1896), which deals with the Sepoy Mutiny in India.

Steel, Kurt, see KAGEY, RUDOLF.

Steele, Richard (1672–1729). Irish-born English playwright and essayist, known for his writings in the periodicals THE TATLER and THE SPECTATOR in association with Joseph ADDISON. Steele took the initiative in the founding of these two journalistic enterprises, serving as the first editor of *The Tatler* under the name of Isaac BICKERSTAFF, originally conceiving the character of Sir Roger de COVERLEY, and contributing most of the essays published in *The Tatler.* Other works by Steele are THE CHRISTIAN HERO (1701), a pamphlet; *The Funeral* (1701), *The Lying Lover* (1703), *The Tender Husband* (1705), and *The Conscious Lovers* (1772), all plays. Steele was the more journalistic of the two essayists.

Steele, Wilbur Daniel (1886–). American novelist, playwright, and, especially, short-story writer. Has won several awards. A number of his stories are concerned with the Portuguese of Cape Cod.

Steen, Marguerite. English novelist. Began as an actress and was launched on her writing career by Ellen TERRY. Her two most successful novels are *Matador* (1934) and *The Sun Is My Undoing* (1941), a long historical novel concerned with the slave trade.

steenkirk cravats. After the battle of Steenkerke (1692), when the French defeated the English, these neck scarves became fashionable in England and were supposed to imitate the hasty dress of the French officers who were surprised in the battle.

Steer, P. Wilson (1860–1942). English painter, known for his landscapes. Member of the Order of Merit (1931).

Steerforth. In Dickens' DAVID COPPERFIELD, David's hero at school, who later leads little Em'ly astray. When tired of his toy, he proposes that she marry his valet. Steerforth is shipwrecked off the coast of Yarmouth, and Ham PEGOTTY, who tries to rescue him, is drowned with him.

Steevens, George (1736–1800). Shakespearean scholar who prepared several editions of Shakespeare (1766; 1773; 1785; 1793). His work was criticized harshly by Joseph Ritson (1752–1803) in the *Quip Modest* (1788). Detected CHATTERTON'S and IRELAND'S forgeries.

Stefánsson, Vilhjálmur (1879–). Canadian-born American arctic explorer and writer. One of his most interesting books is *The Standardization of Error* (1927), in which he explodes many myths and superstitions concerning the arctic. He has also written *My Life With the Eskimo* (1913); *Hunters of the Great North* (1922); *Unsolved Mysteries of the Arctic* (1938); etc.

Steffens, Joseph Lincoln (1866–1936). American journalist and author, the best-known of the MUCKRAKERS, associated with the leading liberal and radical movements of his day. His works include *The Shame of the Cities* (1904); *The Struggle for Self-Government* (1906); *Upbuilders* (1909); *The Least of These* (1910); *Moses in Red* (1926); *Autobiography* (1931), perhaps the most popular of his works, describing the personalities and movements with which he came in contact and giving an account of the development of his own ideas; *Lincoln Steffens Speaking* (1936), a posthumous collection of miscellaneous articles and essays; and a collection of his *Letters* (1938). Steffens was on the editorial staffs of *McClure's,* the *American Magazine,* and *Every-*

body's, the leading periodicals of the muckraking movement, and later traveled in Europe.

Stegner, Wallace Earle (1909–). Iowa novelist whose first book, *Remembering Laughter* (1937), won the Little, Brown novelette contest. One of the most promising novelists of the Middle West.

Steichen, Edward (1879–). Noted American photographer, who commanded the photographic division of the air service during World War I. He is well known as a pioneer in experimental photography. Also a painter.

Stein, Gertrude (1874–1946). American poet, novelist, and author of miscellaneous prose, for a number of years one of the leading expatriate American residents of Paris and the subject of wide literary controversy during the 1920's. Her unique and celebrated style, in the development of which she is considered to have been influenced by the psychological theories of William JAMES and 20th-century French painting, is characterized by a use of words for their associations and their sound rather than solely for their literal meaning, an intricate system of repetition and variation on a single verbal theme, an avoidance of conventional punctuation and syntax, an emphasis on the presentation of impressions and a particular state of mind rather than the telling of a story, and concreteness and extreme simplicity in diction, with preference for the commonplace and the monosyllabic. All these elements combine to produce an appealing pattern of sound, occasional flashes of beauty, and frequent vivid, striking images, in a total effect of wit, humor, gaiety, and sensuous immediacy. Sherwood ANDERSON and Ernest HEMINGWAY are considered to have been influenced by the Stein style. John Chamberlain once remarked that "Steinese" style is like "the Chinese water torture; it never stops and it is always the same."

Gertrude Stein's works include THREE LIVES (1909), a novel; *Tender Buttons* (1914), poetry; *Geography and Plays* (1922); THE MAKING OF AMERICANS (1925), a novel; *Composition as Explanation* (1926), lectures; *Useful Knowledge* (1928); *Acquaintance with Description* (1929); *Ten Portraits* (1930); *Lucy Church Amiably* (1930), a novel; *Before the Flowers of Friendship Faded* (1931); *How to Write* (1931); *Operas and Plays* (1932); *A Long Gay Book* (1932); *Matisse, Picasso, and Gertrude Stein* (1932); THE AUTOBIOGRAPHY OF ALICE B. TOKLAS (1933); FOUR SAINTS IN THREE ACTS (1934), an opera, music for which was written by Virgil THOMSON; *Portraits and Prayers* (1934); *Narration* (1935), lectures; *Lectures in America* (1935); *Geographical History of America* (1936); *Everybody's Autobiography* (1937); *Picasso* (1938); *The World Is Round* (1939), a book for children; *Paris France* (1940), a study of Parisian life before World War II; *Ida* (1941), a novel; *Brewsie and Willy* (1946).

Gertrude Stein, who came of a wealthy family, studied psychology under William James at Radcliffe College and received an M.D. degree from Johns Hopkins Medical School in 1902. In that year she went abroad, where, except for a lecture tour in America in 1935, she stayed until the defeat of France in World War II. In Paris she became the center of a group of outstanding painters and writers of the period, being especially interested in such artists as MATISSE, PICASSO and Juan Gris. Her brother, **Leo Stein** (1872–1947), was a leading art critic.

See also IMPRESSIONISM; STREAM OF CONSCIOUSNESS.

Steinach, Eugen (1861–). Austrian physiologist and biologist, well known for his experiments in rejuvenation by gland grafting.

Steinbeck, John Ernst (1902–). American novelist and short-story writer of proletarian sympathies (see PROLETARIAN LITERATURE), known for his realistic studies of life among the depressed economic classes of the U.S., especially the itinerant farm laborers of California, written in alternation with fictional attempts at symbolism and romantic mysticism. Critics call attention to the strong strain of sentimentalism in even his most somberly realistic works. Among Steinbeck's books are *Cup of Gold* (1929); *The Pastures of Heaven* (1932), short stories; *To a God Unknown* (1933); *Tortilla Flat* (1935); IN DUBIOUS BATTLE (1936); OF MICE AND MEN (1937); *The Long Valley* (1938), a collection of short stories; THE GRAPES OF WRATH (1939); winner of the Pulitzer prize in 1940; *The Moon Is Down* (1942), dealing with life in a German-occupied country of Europe during World War II; *Sea of Cortez* (1941), on marine animals near Panama, written with E. F. Rickerts; *Bombs Away* (1942), an account of the training of a bomber crew in World War II; *The Wayward Bus* (1947).

Steinbock, Wenceslas. A talented young Polish sculptor, the protégé of Cousin Betty (see Lisbeth FISCHER) in Balzac's novel of that title.

Steinitz, William (1836–1900). Chess world champion (1866–1894). Defeated by Emanuel LASKER. Born in Prague, he became a naturalized American citizen (1884).

Steinlen, Théophile Alexandre (1859–1923). French artist. Well known for his posters and lithographs, also as illustrator of books and as a contributor to French journals.

Steinmetz, Charles Proteus (1865–1923). German-born American electrical engineer who was an inventive genius. Consulting engineer of the General Electric Company (from 1893). Patented over 100 inventions and wrote *Light and Illumination* (1909); *Engineering Mathematics* (1910); *America and the New Epoch* (1916); etc. He was a passionate smoker of cheap cigars. The "no-smoking" sign which he found in his G.E. office induced him to walk out the very first day of his connection with the company, leaving behind the famous note: "NO SMOKING—NO STEINMETZ." The rule was rescinded.

Steinway. A family of piano manufacturers. **Heinrich Engelhard Steinweg** (1797–1871), German piano manufacturer, founded a factory in New York (1853) and had his name legally changed (1864) to **Henry Engelhard Steinway.** One of his sons, **William Steinway** (1835–1896), planned the first subway in New York. The tunnel under the East River from 42nd Street to Long Island City is called in his honor "Steinway Tunnel."

Stekel, Wilhelm (1868–1940). Viennese psychiatrist who psychoanalyzed over 10,000 people. Disciple of FREUD. Author of *Frigidity in Women.*

Stelio. The young poet hero of D'Annunzio's FLAME OF LIFE (*Il Fuoco*).

Stella. (1) The Lady Penelope Devereux, the object of Sir Philip SIDNEY's affection celebrated in his sonnet series ASTROPHEL AND STELLA. She married Lord Rich, and later became a widow in Sidney's lifetime.

(2) Miss Esther Johnson was so called by Jonathan SWIFT, to whom it is believed she was privately married in 1706. Esther is first converted into the Greek *aster,* which, in Latin, becomes *stella,* "a star." Swift's *Journal to Stella* is a volume of letters and accounts of his friends, his social activities, and general day-by-day doings, which he addressed to Miss Johnson in a cryptic language, deciphered and published a number of years after his death. See also PPT; PRESTO.

Stella, Joseph (1880–). Italian-born American painter of industrial workers. *Brooklyn Bridge; Tree of My Life; Factory;* etc.

Stendhal. Pseudonym of **Henri Beyle** (1783–1842). French novelist, known as one of the first outstanding authors of the psychological novel in France, represented by his studies, considered to be partly autobiographical, of the proud and egotistic nature involved in love and war. His chief works are *De l'Amour* (1822), a series of notes on the effects of four types of love on a variety of temperaments; *Armance* (1827); *Le Rouge et le Noir* (THE RED AND THE BLACK; 1830), regarded as one of the most important works in the development of the 19th-century novel; *La Chartreuse de Parme* (1839). He also wrote *Racine et Shakespeare* (1823), criticism, and *Histoire de la Peinture en Italie.*

Stendhal, who participated in several campaigns of the Napoleonic Wars and thought of both Byron and Napoleon as his heroes, disliked France and lived for a number of years in Italy. His books were not widely read during his lifetime, but later in the 19th century he was hailed as a precursor of BALZAC in his studies of the strong-willed, self-made man, and he influenced BOURGET, TAINE, and ZOLA, among others. Cf. *Stendhal,* by Matthew JOSEPHSON (1946).

Stenio. In George Sand's LÉLIA, the young poet-lover of Lélia.

Steno, Michel. In Byron's MARINO FALIERO, THE DOGE OF VENICE, the man whose insult to the young Dogaressa causes Marino Faliero to conspire against the tribunal.

stentor, the voice of a. A very loud voice. Stentor was a Greek herald in the Trojan War. According to HOMER, his voice was as loud as that of fifty men combined; hence *stentorian,* "loud voiced."

Stephano. A drunken butler in Shakespeare's *The Tempest.*

Stephen, Sir **Leslie** (1832–1904). English philosopher who married the younger daughter of Thackeray and became the father of Virginia WOOLF, *née* Stephen. He was the first editor of the *Dictionary of National Biography.* His most interesting book is *English Literature and Society in the Eighteenth Century* (1904). He is said to have been the original of Vernon Whitford in *The Egoist* by George Meredith. His daughter Vanessa married the English art critic Clive BELL. The Bells and the Woolfs were the principal members of the so-called Bloomsbury group.

Stephen, James Kenneth. Known as **J. K. S.** (1859–1892). English author of excellent light verse, collected in the volumes *Lapsus Calami* and *Quo Musa Tendis.*

> When there stands a muzzled stripling
> Mute, beside a muzzled bore,
> When the Rudyards cease from kipling
> And the Haggards ride no more.

Stephen, St. See under SAINTS.

Stephens, Henry Morse (1857–1919). Scottish historian who came to the U.S. in 1894. Professor at Cornell University (until 1902) and head of the history department at the University of California (until 1919). Widely known as a teacher and founder and first editor (1895–1905) of the *American Historical Review.*

Stephens, James (1882–). Irish poet and fiction-writer, best known for his whimsical tales and adaptations from ancient Irish legend. His poetry includes *Insurrections*

(1909); *The Hill of Vision* (1912); *Songs from the Clay* (1915); *The Rocky Road to Dublin* (1915): *The Adventures of Seumas Beg* (1915); *Green Branches* (1916); *Reincarnations* (1918); *A Poetry Recital* (1925); *Outcast* (1929); *Theme and Variations* (1930); *Strict Joy* (1931); *Kings and the Moon* (1938). Among Stephens' prose fiction are *The Crock of Gold* (1912), his best-known work; *The Charwoman's Daughter* (1912); *The Demi-Gods* (1914); *Irish Fairy Tales* (1920); *Deirdre* (1923); *In the Land of Youth* (1924); *Here Are Ladies* (1913) and *Etched in Moonlight* (1928), collections of short stories.

Stephens, Robert Neilson (1867–1906). American playwright and historical novelist. In 1896, E. H. Sothern appeared in his *An Enemy to the King*. His best novel is *Captain Ravenshaw* (1901).

Stephenson, George (1781–1848). English inventor and founder of railways.

Stepnyak, Sergei Mikhailovich. Pseudonym of **Sergei Mikhailovich Kravchinski** (1852–1895). Russian writer. As a member of the Nihilist party, he stabbed General Mezentsev (1878) and vindicated his act in *Life for Life*. In exile in Switzerland, Italy, and London. Author of *Underground Russia* (1882); *The Career of a Nihilist* (1889); *King Stork and King Log* (1895).

Stepping Heavenward. A pious and popular novel (1869) by Elizabeth Payson Prentiss (1818–1878).

Sterling, George (1869–1926). Leading California poet who has been called the "last classic bohemian." *A Wine of Wizardry* (1907) attracted attention by its inventiveness and glittering imagery. For the Bohemian Club in San Francisco he wrote one of his best longer works, the play *Truth* (1923). A few of his sonnets and several lyrics have given signs of permanence. His books are numerous. A very generous man to other writers, he finally, in a mood of depression, took his own life.

Sterling, John (1806–1844). British essayist and poet. He formed a literary group (1838), the Sterling Club, including such members as Carlyle, Tennyson, John Stuart Mill, Sir Francis Palgrave, etc. Carlyle wrote a *Life of Sterling* (1851).

Stern, Gladys Bronwyn (1890–). English novelist, of Jewish parentage, known for the wit and satire of her writings. Her works include *Pantomime* (1914); *See-Saw* (1914); *Twos and Threes* (1916); *Grand Chain* (1917); *A Marrying Man* (1918); *Children of No Man's Land* (1919; published in the U.S. as *Debatable Ground*), *Tents of Israel* (1924; published in the U.S. as *The Matriarch*, her best-known work), and *A Deputy Was King* (1926), a trilogy on Jewish life; *Larry Munro* (1920); *The Room* (1922); *The Back Seat* (1923); *Thunderstorm* (1925); *Bouquet* (1927); *Debonair* (1928), dramatized for the theater in 1930; *Petruchio* (1929); *Mosaic* (1930); *The Rueful Mating* (1932); *Long-Lost Father* (1932); *Oleander River* (1937); *Long Story Short* (1939), a collection of short stories; *The Woman in the Hall* (1939); *A Lion in the Garden* (1940); *The Young Matriarch* (1942); *The Reasonable Shores* (1946). Her three-volume autobiography makes excellent reading: *Monogram* (1936); *Another Part of the Forest* (1941); *Trumpet Voluntary* (1944).

Sterne, Laurence (1713–1768). English novelist and clergyman, known for his whimsy, humor, eccentricity, and extreme individuality of style as embodied in *Tristram Shandy*, his most famous work, compared by some critics to Burton's ANATOMY OF MELANCHOLY and James Joyce's FINNEGANS WAKE. His works include TRISTRAM SHANDY (1759–1767), attacked by Samuel RICHARDSON, Horace WALPOLE, Oliver GOLDSMITH, Dr. JOHNSON, and other leading literary figures of the time for its lack of conformity to current standards of morality and literary form; *Sermons* (1767–1769); A SENTIMENTAL JOURNEY (1768); *Letters of Yorick to Eliza* (see ELIZA; 1775).

Sterne, the son of a subaltern in the British army, was impoverished during most of his life and had a persistent weakness for the ladies of his acquaintance. His first wife died of insanity. See also BRAMINE AND BRAMIN; JENNY.

Sterner, Albert (1863–). American painter and illustrator. Member, National Institute of Arts and Letters. Studio in New York (since 1885).

Sternhold and Hopkins. The old metrical, largely doggerel, version of the Psalms that used to be bound up with the Book of Common Prayer and sung in churches. They were mainly the work of Thomas Sternhold (d. 1549), and John Hopkins (d. 1570). The completed version appeared in 1562. It was ridiculed by Dryden in ABSALOM AND ACHITOPHEL.

stet (*Lat.*, "let it stand"). An author's or editor's direction to the printer to cancel a correction previously made in a manuscript, proof, etc.

Stettinius, Edward Riley, Jr. (1900–). American industrialist and politician; chairman, War Resources Board (1939–1940); lend-lease administrator and special assistant to President F. D. Roosevelt (1941–1943); undersecretary of state (1943–1944); secretary of state (1944–1945). Conducted the conference of the United Nations at San Francisco; delegate to the United Nations Security Council. Author of *Lend-Lease: Weapon for Victory.*

Steuben, Baron **Friedrich Wilhelm Ludolf Gerhard Augustin von** (1730–1794). Famous Prussian officer who served under Frederick the Great and, being recommended to Washington by Benjamin Franklin, became inspector general of the Continental army in America. He became a naturalized American citizen (1783) and settled in New York (1784–1794). Author of *Regulations for the Order and Discipline of the Troops of the United States* (1778–1779).

Stevedore. A play (1934) by Paul Peters and George Sklar, dealing with racial conflicts in the South.

Stevens, Albert William (1886–). American aerial photographer who has made balloon ascensions into the stratosphere, notably with Captain Anderson (1935).

Stevens, James Floyd (1892–). American writer of folk stories who had been a wandering laborer in the West. His books include *Paul Bunyan* (1925); *Brawnyman* (1926); *Homer in the Sagebrush* (1928); etc.

Stevens, John (1749–1838). American engineer, instrumental in the passage of the first American patent laws (1740). His steamboat *Phoenix* (1808), built very shortly after Robert Fulton's *Clermont,* traveled from New York to Philadelphia and was the first seagoing steamboat in the world.

Stevens, Thaddeus (1792–1868). American legislator and member of the House of Representatives (1849–1853; 1859–1868); opposed slavery; proposed the impeachment of President Andrew JOHNSON and managed the trial.

Stevens, Wallace (1879–). American poet, author of poetry of the type called objectivist (see OBJECTIVISM) which is characterized by wit, irony, polish, and sophistication, most often presenting a picture through the sound and associations of words and the careful building up of striking, exotic imagery. His poems deal chiefly, in an ironic fashion, with frustration in 20th-century society and nostalgia for a vanished past and, increasingly in his later work, with aesthetic problems, such as the role of the creative imagination in artistic composition, the relation of the artist to the external world, and the value of the simple, immediate content of sensuous experience. His books of poetry are *Harmonium* (1923 and 1931); *Ideas of Order* (1935); *Owl's Clover* (1936); *The Man with the Blue Guitar* (1937); *Parts of a World* (1942); *Notes Toward a Supreme Fiction* (1942).

Stevens was educated at Harvard University, went into law practice, and eventually became a vice-president of the Hartford Accident and Indemnity Company, writing his poetry in his spare time.

Stevenson, Burton Egbert (1872–). American writer and anthologist. Best known for his *The Home Book of Verse* (1912); *The Home Book of Verse for Young Folks* (1915); *The Home Book of Modern Verse* (1925); and *The Home Book of Quotations, Classical and Modern* (1934; revised and enlarged, 1937). He is also a writer of mystery stories.

Stevenson, John Hall- (1718–1785). English poet and friend of Laurence Sterne. He is the original of Eugenius in *Tristram Shandy.* Wrote (1769) a continuation of Sterne's *The Sentimental Journey.*

Stevenson, Robert Louis Balfour (1850–1894). Scotch novelist, essayist, and poet, known for his tales of fantasy and adventure and his romantic essays in the personal vein. His fiction includes *The New Arabian Nights* (1882), fantastic tales; TREASURE ISLAND (1883); *The Strange Case of Dr. Jekyll and Mr. Hyde* (see DR. JEKYLL AND MR. HYDE; 1886); KIDNAPPED (1886); THE MASTER OF BALLANTRAE (1889); *The Wrecker* (1892); *Catriona* (called in the U.S. *David Balfour*; 1893), a sequel to *Kidnapped.* Among his volumes of essays are *An Inland Voyage* (1878); *Travels with a Donkey in the Cevennes* (1879); *The Amateur Emigrant; The Silverado Squatters* (1883); *Familiar Studies of Men and Books* (1881); *Virginibus Puerisque* (1881). *A Child's Garden of Verses* (1885) and *Underwoods* (1887) are books of poetry, and he collaborated with W. E. HENLEY on the following dramas: *Deacon Brodie* (1882), *Beau Austin* (1890), and *Admiral Guinea* (1897). *A Lodging for the Night, Markheim,* and *The Sire de Maletroit's Door* are among his best-known short stories.

Stevenson, although seriously ill all his life with tuberculosis, lived adventurously, vagabonding through Belgium, France, California, and the Pacific islands. He spent his last years in Samoa (see VAILIMA), known among the natives as **Tusitala,** "teller of tales." He died while working on *Weir of Hermiston,* an unfinished novel which promised to be one of his best.

See also OSBOURNE, MRS. FANNY.

Stevie. In Conrad's SECRET AGENT, the brother of Winnie Verloc.

Stewart, Alan Breck. In Stevenson's KIDNAPPED and its sequel *David Balfour,* Balfour's Jacobite friend.

Stewart, Alfred Walter. Pseudonym **John Jervis Connington** (1880–). Irish professor of chemistry and writer of detective fiction.

Stewart or Stuart, Prince **Charles Edward.** See under PRETENDER.

Stewart, Donald Ogden (1894–). American author and actor. His early books, *Aunt Polly's Story of Mankind* (1923); *Mr.*

and Mrs. Haddock Abroad (1924); etc., were humorous. His play, *Rebound* (1930), in which he also acted, was written in the manner of Philip BARRY. His second wife is Ella Winter, the widow of Lincoln STEFFENS.

Stewart or **Stuart, Mary.** See MARY QUEEN OF SCOTS.

Stewart, Walking, see WALKING STEWART.

Steyne, Marquis of. In Thackeray's VANITY FAIR, the Earl of Gaunt and of Gaunt Castle, a viscount, baron, knight of the Garter and of numerous other orders. He has honors and titles enough to make him a great man, but his life is not a highly moral one, and his conduct with BECKY SHARP, when she is the wife of Colonel Rawdon CRAWLEY, gives rise to a great scandal. His lordship survives the ill report, but Becky is obliged to live abroad.

stichomythy. Dramatic dialogue of lively repartees in alternate verse lines. Cultivated by the Greeks. Shakespeare uses it in *Richard III*, as for instance in the lines:

King: Wrong not her birth, she is a royal princess.
Queen: To save her life, I'll say she is not so.
King: Her life is safest only in her birth.
Queen: And only in that safety died her brothers.

stick, the big. See under BIG.

Stickit Minister, The. A short story (1893) by S. R. CROCKETT. The word stickit means "stuck," that is, "having failed."

Stickney, Trumbull (1874–1904). American poet. *Dramatic Verses* (1902) and *The Poems of Trumbull Stickney* (1905). The latter were edited by George Cabot Lodge, William Vaughn Moody, and J. E. Lodge. Conrad Aiken and Alfred Kreymborg have included selections from his work in their anthologies. Van Wyck Brooks and Edmund Wilson have spoken of him as a writer of achievement.

Stiegel, Henry William (1729–1785). Famous German-born American glassmaker. Collections of Stiegel ware are in the Metropolitan Museum of Art, New York, and in the Pennsylvania Museum of Art, Philadelphia. He is remembered as "Baron von Stiegel" throughout Pennsylvania Dutchland.

Stieglitz, Alfred (1864–1946). American photographer, who experimented with three-color work (1890–1893). Editor and publisher, *Camera Work* (from 1903). Husband of Georgia O'KEEFFE.

Stiggins, Rev. Mr. In THE PICKWICK PAPERS by Charles Dickens, Mrs. Weller's spiritual adviser who lectures on temperance but loves pineapple rum.

Stiles, Ezra (1727–1795). American clergyman and scholar. President of Yale College (1778–1795). His *Literary Diary* was published at the beginning of the twentieth century in three volumes.

Still, James (1906–). American poet, novelist, and short-story writer, who exploits in his work the Alabama hills. His story, *Bat Flight,* won an award in the *O. Henry Memorial* volume of 1939.

Still, John (1543–1608). Reputed author of the early English comedy, GAMMER GURTON'S NEEDLE.

stilo novo (*Lat.,* "in the new style"). Newfangled notions. When the calendar was reformed by Gregory XIII (1582), letters used to be dated *stilo novo,* which grew in time to be a cant phrase for any innovation.

Stimson, Frederic Jesup. Pen name **J. S. of Dale** (1855–1943). American diplomat. Ambassador to several South American countries. He wrote a number of novels (best-known, *King Noanett,* 1896) and works on the Constitution of the U.S.

Stimson, Henry Lewis (1867–). American statesman. Unsuccessful candidate for governor of New York (1910). Secretary of war in the cabinet of President Taft (1911–1913); governor-general of the Philippines (1927); secretary of state in the cabinet of President Hoover (1928–1933). President Roosevelt appointed him secretary of war and made him a member of the Defense Board in World War II. His term of office extended into the administration of President Truman. *On Active Service in Peace and War* (1948).

Stinnes, Hugo (1870–1924). German industrialist, advocate of the "vertical trust," who controlled mining operations, shipping, and many kinds of commercial business. Elected to the Reichstag (1920). At the time of his death he was seeking to combine the most varied industries in one large trust.

Stirling, Peter. See HONORABLE PETER STIRLING.

Stirling-Maxwell, Sir **William** (1818–1878). Scottish historian. *The Cloister Life of the Emperor Charles V* (1852); *Don John of Austria* (1883); etc.

stirrup cup. A farewell cup of wine.

With a stirrup-cup each to the lily of women that loves him.
Louise Imogen Guiney, *The Wild Ride.*

Stiva. In Tolstoi's ANNA KARÉNINA, the name by which the happy-go-lucky, improvident Prince Stepan Arcadyevich OBLONSKY is best known to his friends.

Stock, Frederick August (1872–1942). German-born American orchestra conductor and composer; succeeded Theodore Thomas as director of the Chicago Symphony Orchestra (1905). General music director for the Century of Progress exposition in Chicago (1933).

Stockton, Francis Richard (1834–1902). American humorist and novelist whose best-known novel is RUDDER GRANGE (1879). His most famous short story is THE LADY OR THE TIGER? (1882). His juveniles are inimitable, the best being *The Bee Man of Orn and Other Fanciful Tales* (1887).

Stoddard, Charles Warren (1843–1909). American writer and traveler. *In the Footprints of the Padres* (1902); *The Island of Tranquil Delight* (1904); etc. He was an early member of the Bohemian Club in San Francisco.

Stoddard, Eleanor. In John Dos Passos' U.S.A., the daughter of an humble clerk in a Chicago meat-packing company who hates her lower-middle-class environment and has aspirations toward culture and social "refinement." She works in a Chicago department store and attends art school until she meets Eveline HUTCHINS with whom she opens an interior decorating shop and goes to New York and then to France during World War I. Although she finds sex repulsive, she has a love affair with J. Ward MOOREHOUSE.

Stoddard, Lothrop (1883–). American writer on national and European affairs; *The Revolt Against Civilization* (1922); *Racial Realities in Europe* (1924); *Europe and Our Money* (1932); etc.

Stoddard, Richard Henry (1825–1903). American critic and poet of the GENTEEL TRADITION, author of sentimental poems, not regarded by 20th-century critics as artistically valuable, dealing chiefly with nature, the Orient, and literary subjects. His works include *Footprints* (1848); *Poems* (1852); *Songs of Summer* (1857); *The King's Bell* (1862); *Abraham Lincoln* (1865); *The Book of the East* (1871); *Poems* (1880); *The Lion's Cub* (1890); *Recollections Personal and Literary* (1903). Stoddard, who was born in poverty and at first worked in an iron mill, became in the latter part of the 19th century the center of a New York literary group which included E. C. STEDMAN and Bayard TAYLOR.

Stoessel, Albert (1894–1943). American violinist and choral and symphonic conductor; conducted the New York Oratorio Society (from 1921). Died with the baton in his hand.

Stoicism. The system of the Stoics, a school of Greek philosophers founded by Zeno, about 308 B. C. The Stoics held that virtue was the highest good, and that the passions and appetites should be rigidly subdued. It was so called because Zeno gave his lectures in the *Stoa Poikile,* the Painted Porch of Athens.

Stoke Poges. A village in Buckinghamshire, England. The poet Thomas GRAY is buried in St. Giles churchyard at Stoke Poges. It is that churchyard which is believed to have been the one referred to in his famous *Elegy.*

Stoker, Bram, i.e., **Abraham** (1847–1912). British writer, best known for *Dracula* (1897), a wild tale of vampires and werewolves which was later on made into a moving picture with Bela Lugosi. His other principal novel, *The Jewel of Seven Stars,* was dedicated to Constance and Elinor Hoyt (Elinor WYLIE), whom he had met as young girls in London. Business manager (27 years) for Sir Henry IRVING.

Stokes, Anson Phelps (1838–1913). American financier who helped found the Metropolitan Museum of Art in New York City. One of his sons, **Anson Phelps Stokes** (1874–), was secretary of Yale University (1899–1921). Another son, **Harold Phelps Stokes** (1887–), was on the staff of the N.Y. *Evening Post* (1911–1923) and secretary to Herbert Hoover (1924–1926), later on the editorial staff of the N.Y. *Times.* Still another son, **James Graham Phelps Stokes** (1872–), joined the Socialist party (1907), withdrawing ten years later and becoming secretary-treasurer of the Social Democratic League of America. His first wife, **Rose Harriet Pastor** (1879–1933), was a political radical of Russo-Polish birth.

Stokowski, Leopold (1882–). Famous orchestra conductor, born in London. Conductor of the Cincinnati Symphony Orchestra (1909–1912) and of the Philadelphia Symphony Orchestra (1912–1941); etc. He has appeared in several moving pictures and has made symphonic transcriptions of Bach.

Stolypin, Pëtr Arkadevich (1863–1911). Russian statesman; premier of Russia (1906), pursuing a liberal policy. He was assassinated.

Stolzing, Walter von. The successful contestant in Wagner's opera DIE MEISTERSINGER.

stone.

a rolling stone. See ROLLING.

to leave no stone unturned. To spare no trouble, time, expense, etc., in endeavoring to accomplish your aim. After the defeat of Mardonius at Plataea (477 B. C.), a report was current that the Persian general had left great treasures in his tent. Polycrates the Theban sought long but found them not. The Oracle of Delphi, being consulted, told him "to leave no stone unturned," and the treasures were discovered.

Stone, Grace Zaring (1896–). American novelist, author of the following books: *The Heaven and Earth of Doña Elena* (1929); *The Bitter Tea of General Yen* (1930), dealing with revolution in China; *The Almond Tree* (1931); *The Cold Journey* (1934); *Escape* (1939), sensationally successful, dealing with Nazi Germany (see NAZISM) and written under the pseudonym of **Ethel Vance** in order to protect a daughter living in Czechoslovakia; *Reprisal* (1942), dealing with German-occupied France during World War II, also written under the name of Ethel Vance.

Stone, Harlan Fiske (1872–1946). Dean of the Columbia Law School (1910–1923); etc. As chief justice of the U.S. Supreme Court (from 1941), an outspoken member of its liberal wing.

Stone, Irving. Originally **Irving Tennenbaum** (1903–). American biographer. Fascinated with the life of Vincent Van Gogh, he produced a biography of him under the title of *Lust for Life* (1934). He has written a biography of Jack London, *Sailor on Horseback* (1938); another of Clarence Darrow (1941); and interesting accounts of the unsuccessful candidates for the U.S. presidency in *They Also Ran* (1943).

Stone, Jabez. See THE DEVIL AND DANIEL WEBSTER.

Stone, Lucy. Mrs. **Henry Brown Blackwell** (1818–1893). American woman suffragist, best known for her insistence upon retaining her maiden name as a married woman. She lectured against slavery, in favor of women's rights, and helped form the American Woman Suffrage Association (1869). With her husband she edited the *Woman's Journal* (1872–1893).

Stone, Melville Elijah (1848–1929). American journalist. Founded the first one-cent daily in Chicago, the Chicago *Daily News* (1875); general manager of the Associated Press of Illinois (1893–1900) and of the Associated Press, Inc. (1900–1923).

Stone Age. The era in which human culture seems to have begun. It is characterized by the use of stone weapons and implements, and is followed by the Bronze Age.

Stonehenge. The great prehistoric (Neolithic or early Bronze Age) monument on Salisbury Plain, originally consisting of two concentric circles of upright stones, enclosing two rows of smaller stones, and a central block of blue marble, 18 feet by 4 feet, known as the Altar Stone. Many theories as to its original purpose and original builders have been propounded. It was probably used, if not built by the Druids, and from its plotting, which, it is certain, had an astronomical basis, it is thought to have been the temple of a sun god and to have been built about 1680 B. C.

The *-henge* of the name seems to refer to something hanging (A.S. *hengen*) in, or supported in, the air, viz., the huge transverse stones; but GEOFFREY OF MONMOUTH connects it with HENGIST, and says that Stonehenge was erected by MERLIN to perpetuate the treachery of Hengist in falling upon Vortigern and putting him and his 400 attendants to the sword. Aurelius Ambrosius asked Merlin to devise a memento of this event, whereupon the magician transplanted from Killaraus, in Ireland, the "Giant's Dance," stones which had been brought thither from Africa by a race of giants and all of which possessed magic properties.

Stone Mountain. A village in De Kalb County, Georgia, noted for an isolated granite dome with a precipitous northern face which is ornamented with relief figures of leaders of the Confederacy, including Robert E. LEE on his famous horse Traveller.

Stones of Venice. A treatise (1851–1853) by John RUSKIN in praise of Gothic art.

Stonewall Jackson, see JACKSON, THOMAS JONATHAN.

Stong, Philip Duffield (1899–). American journalist and novelist, known for his novels, chiefly humorous in character, dealing with life in rural Iowa. These include *State Fair* (1932); *Stranger's Return* (1933); *Village Tale* (1934); *The Farmer in the Dell* (1935); *Weekend* (1935); *Career* (1936); *Buckskin Breeches* (1937); *The Long Lane* (1939); *Ivanhoe Keeler* (1939); *Miss Edeson* (1941). Books of non-fiction are *Horses and Americans* (1939); *Hawkeyes* (1940); *If School Keeps* (1940), autobiographical. Stong also wrote books for boys and motion-picture scenarios.

Stony Point. North of New York City on the west shore of the Hudson, forever associated with "Mad Anthony" WAYNE who retook it from the British at the point of the bayonet on the night of July 15, 1779. The British won it back three days later but abandoned it in the autumn.

Stopes, Marie Carmichael (1880–). English paleobotanist, author, and advocate of birth control. Founder, Mothers' Clinic for Constructive Birth Control (1921); president, Society for Constructive Birth Control and Racial Progress. Author of *Married Love* (1918); *Sex and the Young* (1926); *Sex and Religion* (1929); and a volume of verse, *Songs for Young Lovers* (1939).

Stork, Charles Wharton (1881–). American poet and well-known translator of Scandinavian poetry. Founded the poetry magazine, *Contemporary Verse.*

Stork, King. A tyrant that devours his subjects, and makes them submissive with fear and trembling. The allusion is to the fable of *The Frogs desiring a King.* See LOG, KING.

Storm, Hans Otto (1895–1941). Short-story writer and novelist; killed accidentally while working in San Francisco as engineer for a telegraph company. His only novel, *Count Ten* (1940), reveals the clear mind of the engineer.

Storm, John. Hero of Hall Caine's novel THE CHRISTIAN.

Storm, Theodor (1817–1888). German author, excelling in the NOVELLE, as *Immensee* (1852); *Pole Poppenspäler* (1874); *Der Schimmelreiter* (1888); etc. His lyrical poems combine the charm of a waning romanticism with the directness of early realism.

Storm and Strain period. See STURM UND DRANG.

Stormfield, Captain. The hero of Mark Twain's *Captain Stormfield's Visit to Heaven.*

stormy petrel. See PETREL.

stornello verses. Verses in which certain words are harped on and turned about and about. They are common among the Tuscan peasants. The word is from Italian *tornare*, "to return."

I'll tell him the *white*, and the *green*, and the *red*,
Mean our country has flung the vile yoke from her head;
I'll tell him the *green*, and the *red*, and the *white*,
Would look well by his side as a sword-knot so bright;
I'll tell him the *red*, and the *white*, and the *green*,
Is the prize that we play for, a prize we will win.
Notes and Queries.

Story. American monthly magazine, founded in 1931 in Vienna, Austria, by Martha Foley and Whit Burnett, one of the best-known of the LITTLE MAGAZINES of the time. Its original aim was to provide a vehicle for short stories by unknown authors for which there was no market in popular and conservative magazines. For awhile it was published on the island of Mallorca, and in 1933 began to be issued from New York. With commercial success, its standards altered.

Story, Isaac. Pseudonym **Peter Quince** (1774–1803). American poet, known for his satirical and witty occasional verse collected as *A Parnassian Shop, Opened in the Pindaric Stile; by Peter Quince, Esq.* (1801).

Story, Joseph (1779–1845). Professor of Law at Harvard (1829–1845) and author of a famous series of commentaries on law. His son, **William Wetmore Story** (1819–1905), a sculptor and man of letters, was an intimate friend of many leading literary figures of England and America. Cf. the biography by Henry JAMES.

Storyella as She Is Syung. An excerpt from James Joyce's FINNEGANS WAKE, published separately in early form in 1938.

Story of a Bad Boy, The. A largely autobiographical story by Thomas Bailey ALDRICH (1870) which relates the pranks and adventures of its hero, Tom Bailey, in the quaint old New England town called Rivermouth in the story, in reality Portsmouth, N.H.

Story of a Country Town, The. A novel by E. W. HOWE (1883), depicting the life of Fairview and the Twin Mounds in the plains of Kansas. Joe Erring is the central figure of this story, which was one of the first to show the life of the Middle West in a spirit of grim realism.

Story of an African Farm, The. A novel by Olive SCHREINER (1883), published under the pseudonym of Ralph Iron. Most of the action takes place on a Boer farm in South Africa. The principal characters are the childhood playmates, Waldo, the son of the kindly, pious German overseer, Em, the good-hearted step-daughter of Tant' Sannie, owner of the farm, and Lyndall, Em's talented orphan cousin. Lyndall becomes a woman of great beauty and power, but her life is unhappy. She comes between Em and her lover, has a child by a man whom she refuses to marry, and dies soon after. Waldo, who has always loved her, outlives her only a short while.

Story Teller's Story, A. One of the most interesting books by Sherwood ANDERSON, an autobiographical account of his life as a writer (1924).

Stothard, Thomas (1755–1834). English illustrator and engraver who did illustrations for *Pilgrim's Progress; Don Quixote; Robinson Crusoe; Gulliver's Travels;* etc.

stoup. A flagon or drinking vessel, used in the expression "a stoup of wine."

And surely ye'll be your pint-stowp,
And surely I'll be mine . . .
Robert Burns, *Auld Lang Syne.*

Stout, Rex Todhunter (1886–). American detective-story writer who created the phlegmatic detective Nero Wolfe, a huge fat man addicted to beer and orchids.

Stover, Dink. The hero of Owen Johnson's VARMINT (1910) and its sequels, *The Tennessee Shad* (1911) and *Stover at Yale* (1911).

Stow, John (1525?–1605). English historian and antiquary. He published *The Woorkes of Geffrey Chaucer* (1561); *The Annales of England* (1580); and *A Survey of London* (1598, 1603), a standard work on Old London.

Stowe, Harriet Beecher (1811–1896). American novelist, daughter of Lyman BEECHER, best known for UNCLE TOM'S CABIN (1852), the most famous example of anti-slavery literature in 19th-century U.S. Her other works include *A Key to Uncle Tom's Cabin* (1853), a collection of factual material on slavery to justify the charges implied by her novel; *Sunny Memories of Foreign Lands* (1854), an account of a tour to England; *Dred: A Tale of the Great Dismal Swamp* (1856), a second fictional attack on slavery; *The Minister's Wooing* (1859), *Pearl of Orr's Island* (1862), *Oldtown Folks* (1869), *Sam Lawson's Oldtown Fireside Stories* (1871), and *Poganuc People* (1878), local-color stories and novels of New England; *Agnes of Sorrento* (1862), an historical novel; *Pink and*

White Tyranny (1871); *My Wife and I* (1871), on woman suffrage; *We and Our Neighbors* (1875).

Mrs. Stowe was brought up in an atmosphere of strict CALVINISM, against which she later rebelled. She achieved unfavorable notoriety in England by the publication of *Lady Byron Vindicated* (1870), a book charging Lord BYRON with incest, written after her acquaintance with the poet's widow. Cf. *Crusader in Crinoline* (1941), by Forrest Wilson.

Strabo (63 B. C.?–?24 A. D.). Greek geographer, whose name means, literally, "squint-eyed." His *Geography* (17 books) describes the earth as a globe, fixed in the center of the universe, its habitable portion resembling a military cloak, extending from Ireland to Ceylon.

Strachey, Evelyn John St. Loe (1901–). English lecturer and author on subjects in politics and social science, related to Lytton STRACHEY, known for his Marxist sympathies and beliefs during the 1930's. See MARXISM IN LITERATURE. His writings include *Revolution by Reason* (1925); *The Workers' Control in the Russian Mining Industry* (1928); THE COMING STRUGGLE FOR POWER (1932); *The Menace of Fascism* (1933); *The Nature of the Capitalist Crisis* (1935); *The Theory and Practice of Socialism* (1936); *What Are We to Do?* (1938); *A Faith to Fight For* (1941), on World War II; *Digging for Mrs. Miller* (1941), on Strachey's experiences as an air-raid warden in World War II.

Strachey was elected a Member of Parliament for the Labor Party in Birmingham in 1929 and attracted attention through his writings and lectures. In 1935, when he came to the U.S. for a lecture tour, he was denied entrance into the country on the charge that he was a Communist, and became the subject of heated controversy in the press. Minister of Food, 1946– .

Strachey, Giles Lytton (1880–1932). English biographer, a member of the BLOOMSBURY GROUP and a relative of John STRACHEY, known for his vivid, ironic, realistic, and "humanizing" portraits and studies of famous historical figures. Among his works are *Eminent Victorians* (1918); *Queen Victoria* (1921), which established his reputation; *Books and Characters* (1922); *Pope* (1926); *Elizabeth and Essex* (1928), his best-known biography; *Portraits in Miniature* (1931).

Strad, Stradivarius. A colloquial name for a violin made by the famous violin maker Antonio Stradivarius (1644–1737) of Cremona. George Eliot has a poem called *Stradivarius* (1874).

strafe (Ger. *strafen*, "to punish"). A term introduced into English during World War I and revived during World War II. During the former, one of the favorite slogans of the Germans was *Gott strafe England,* and *strafing* meant usually a heavy bombardment, a sharp action, etc. During the second war, the term was particularly used with reference to the operations of aircraft, which flew low over columns of enemy soldiers, supply trains, or armored vehicles, or even groups of fleeing refugees, and showered them with machine-gun bullets at close range. See also HYMN OF HATE.

Strafford. A historical tragedy by Robert BROWNING (1837). This drama contains portraits of Charles I, the Earl of Strafford, Hampden, John Pym, Sir Harry Vane, etc. The subject of the drama is the attainder and execution of Wentworth, Earl of Strafford.

Strafford, Sir **Thomas Wentworth.** 1st Earl of **Strafford** and 1st Baron **Raby** (1593–1641). English statesman, favorite and chief adviser of Charles I. Lord Lieutenant of Ireland (1640) and leader of an army against the invading Scots (1640). Accused of treason by John Pym, tried and executed (1641). He is the central figure of Browning's drama STRAFFORD.

Strange Case of Lucile Cléry, see CLÉRY, LUCILE: A WOMAN OF INTRIGUE.

Strange Case of Miss Annie Spragg, The. A novel by Louis BROMFIELD (1928), dealing with the lives and personalities of a group of unusual characters as they are revealed through the events arising from the mysterious death of an American spinster living abroad.

Strange Interlude. A drama by Eugene O'NEILL (1928), consisting of two parts and nine acts and dealing with the psychological conflicts and entanglements in the life of Nina Leeds, the heroine. Nina is a passionate, neurotic woman, married to Sam Evans, an unimpressive businessman, and in love with Dr. Darrell, by whom she has a child, Gordon. Gordon prefers Sam to Darrell and, growing up, marries against his mother's wishes. Nina is left to marry Charles Marsden, a novelist who has long loved her but has been abnormally dependent upon his mother. On its first production, the play caused a sensation by its attempted use of the technique of STREAM OF CONSCIOUSNESS, by which the characters speak in asides to reveal their true thoughts, in contrast to what they are saying in their ostensible conversation.

Strap, Hugh. In Smollett's RODERICK RANDOM, a simple, generous, and disinterested adherent of Roderick Random. His generosity and fidelity, however, meet with but a base return from the heartless libertine.

Straparola, Giovanni Francesco (died ca. 1557). Italian writer of *novelle* and stories. His collection, *Tredici Piacevoli Notti* (*Facetious Nights;* 1550–1553), served as source to Shakespeare; Molière, La Fontaine, and others.

Strassburg Oaths. See OATHS OF STRASSBURG.

Strasser, Otto Johan Maximilian (1897–). German writer. Joined the Nazi party (1925) but turned anti-Nazi prompted by his belief in what has been called "national communist" political tenets (1930). As an expatriate (from 1933) in Vienna, Prague, Zurich, Paris, Canada, actively engaged in combating Nazism. Author of *Hitler and I* (1940); *History in My Time* (1941); *Flight from Terror* (1942; in collaboration with Michael Stern); etc. His less fortunate brother **Gregor Strasser** (1892–1934) was assassinated by the Nazis whose ranks he had left together with Otto.

Stratemeyer, Edward. Pseudonym **Arthur M. Winfield** (1862–1930). American writer of books for boys, especially the famous series *The Rover Boys* (1899–1926).

Stratton Porter, Gene, see PORTER, GENE STRATTON.

Strauss, Johann (1825–1899). Known as the "Waltz-King." Austrian composer and conductor; succeeded to the leadership of the orchestra of his father, **Johann Strauss** (1804–1849). Among the best-known operettas of the younger Strauss are *Die Fledermaus* (1874) and *Eine Nacht in Venedig* (1883). His most famous waltzes are *The Blue Danube; Artists' Life; Tales From the Vienna Woods; Roses From the South,* etc.

Strauss, Richard (1864–). German conductor and composer, regarded as leader of the new romantic school. His most famous opera is DER ROSENKAVALIER (1911); his best-known tone poems are *Don Juan* (1889); *Tod und Verklärung* (1891); *Till Eulenspiegels Lustige Streiche* (1895); and *Don Quixote* (1897). His opera SALOMÉ, produced with Olive Fremstad in New York, Jan. 22, 1907, created a sensation.

Stravinsky, Igor Fëdorovich (1882–). Russian composer of the futurist group. Lived in France (from 1910) and in the U.S. Among his best-known works are ballets, as *The Firebird; Petrouchka; The Rites of Spring;* etc., a string quartet, and many works for piano.

straw.

the last straw. The only hope left, the last penny; the ultimate insult, offense, or stroke of ill fortune; in allusion to the old proverb, "'tis the last straw that breaks the camel's back."

to catch at a straw. A forlorn hope. A drowning man will catch at a straw.

to make bricks without straw. To attempt to do something without the proper and necessary materials. The allusion is to the exaction of the Egyptian taskmasters mentioned in *Exod.* v. 6–14.

to pick straws. To show fatigue or weariness, as birds pick up straws to make their nests or bed.

Straw, Jack, see JACK STRAW.

Strawberry Hill. Horace WALPOLE's estate at Twickenham, Surrey, England. It was here that he established his private printing press (1757–1789).

stream of consciousness. Term applied to the uninterrupted flow of sensations, thoughts, memories, associations, etc., in the consciousness of an individual at a given time, according to early 20th-century theories of psychology; the phrase itself is said to be one used by William JAMES. It is best known as a literary technique by which character and events are presented through the mental images, thoughts, and emotional reactions of a person or persons in the story or novel. The first notable use of the stream-of-consciousness technique is considered to be in *We'll to the Woods No More* (*Les Lauriers sont coupés*), by Edouard DUJARDIN, although Dujardin's method is closer to that of the INTERIOR MONOLOGUE as exemplified in the novels of Virginia WOOLF, especially in THE WAVES. The interior monologue differs from stream of consciousness proper in that the recital of the thoughts, sensations, feelings, and the like of the character involved is edited in accordance with a desired mood, pattern of sound or rhythm, or exactitude of narration. The steady flow of the thought-processes of Stephen DEDALUS and Leopold and Molly BLOOM in James Joyce's ULYSSES is the most famous and most representative of the true stream-of-consciousness style. Edgar Allan POE, Herman MELVILLE, and Henry JAMES are considered to have been early forerunners of this technique, as are even some portions of Laurence Sterne's TRISTRAM SHANDY. Followers of Joyce whose writings make use of stream of consciousness with more or less modification according to their particular material and aims include: Virginia WOOLF, Sherwood ANDERSON, Ernest HEMINGWAY, Conrad AIKEN, Gertrude STEIN, John Dos PASSOS, William FAULKNER (see THE SOUND AND THE FURY), James T. FARRELL, W. C. WILLIAMS, and Thomas WOLFE. STRANGE INTERLUDE, by Eugene O'NEILL, is an attempt to apply stream-of-consciousness technique to the stage, and the method was also used, with more success, in radio plays.

Street, Cecil John Charles (1884–). British writer. Under the pen name of **John Rhode,** author of the Dr. Priestley detective stories.

Street, Julian (1879–1947). American writer of entertaining fiction and books on food and drink.

Street and Walker. "In the employ of Messrs. Street and Walker" is a jocular phrase sometimes applied to a person out of employment, a gentleman without means, whose employment is walking about the streets.

street Arabs. Children of the houseless poor; street children. So called because, like the Arabs, they are nomads or wanderers with no settled home.

Streetcar Named Desire, A. A play (1947) of lower-class New Orleans by Tennessee WILLIAMS. Won Pulitzer prize.

Streeter, Edward (1891–). American humorist, widely known during World War I as the author of *Dere Mable: Love Letters of a Rookie* (1918). His son, **Paul Streeter**, is an editor and novelist under the name of "Paul."

Street Scene. A drama by Elmer RICE (1929), awarded the Pulitzer prize. It deals with the events in the lives of the Kaplans and the Maurrants, two families, respectively Jewish and Irish, who live in a tenement neighborhood of New York City. Samuel Kaplan and Rose Maurrant are in love; when Frank Maurrant, Rose's father, kills both her mother and her mother's lover, the girl resolves to protect her brother from the evil influence of their environment. Produced (1946) as an opera by Kurt Weill.

Streicher, Julius (1885–1946). Nazi journalist and politician. Rabid and obscene anti-Semite (from 1919). Took part in Hitler's beer-hall Putsch (1923). After Hitler's usurpation of power, chief of Franconia. Father of the Nuremberg laws. Tried at Nuremberg, found guilty, and hanged.

Streit, Clarence Kirshman (1896–). American publicist who created a sensation with his book *Union Now* (1939), in which he advocated the establishment of an "Inter-Democracy Federal Union."

Strenia. The goddess who presided over the New Year festivities in ancient Rome. Tatius, the legendary Sabine king, entered Rome on New Year's Day, and received from some augurs palms cut from the sacred grove, dedicated to her. After his seizure of the city, he ordained that January 1 should be celebrated by gifts to be called *strenae,* consisting of figs, dates, and honey. The French word *étrenne,* "a New Year's gift," is derived from the name of this goddess.

Strenuous Life, The. Title of a collection of essays by Theodore ROOSEVELT (1900).

Strephon. The shepherd, in Sir Philip Sidney's ARCADIA, who makes love to the beautiful Urania. It is a stock name for a lover, Chloe being usually the corresponding lady.

Stresemann, Gustav (1878–1929). German chancellor (1923) and minister of foreign affairs (1923–1929). Negotiated the Locarno Pact; secured the admission of Germany to the League of Nations on an equal footing with the other large nations; sponsored the adoption of the Dawes and Young Plans on the part of Germany; etc. Shared with Aristide Briand the Nobel prize for peace (1926).

Strether, Lambert. The leading character in Henry James' novel THE AMBASSADORS.

Stribling, Thomas Sigismund (1881–). American novelist, known for his realistic studies of crime, injustice, ignorance, poverty, and economic domination in the South, especially in Alabama of the 20th century. His works include *Birthright* (1922); *Fombombo* (1923) and *Red Sand* (1924), adventure novels; *Teeftallow* (1926), dramatized on the stage as *Rope* (1928); *Bright Metal* (1928); *Strange Moon* (1929); *Clues of the Caribbees* (1929), a collection of detective stories; *Backwater* (1930); *The Forge* (1931), *The Store* (1932; winner of the 1933 Pulitzer prize), and *Unfinished Cathedral* (1934), a trilogy; *The Sound Wagon* (1935); *These Bars of Flesh* (1938), a satire on Columbia University, progressive education, etc.

stricken deer. Term applied to William COWPER by himself and often used as an epithet for the poet. It occurs in Book III of his poem THE TASK:

> I was a stricken deer that left the herd
> Long since.

The reference is to Cowper's attacks of insanity and his morbid religious obsession of guilt. Title of biography of Cowper by Lord David CECIL.

Strickland, Agnes (1796–1874). English historian, principally known for her *Lives of the Queens of England* (12 vols.; 1840–1848); *Lives of the Queens of Scotland and English Princesses* (8 vols.; 1850–1859), both written in collaboration with her sister **Elizabeth Strickland** (1794–1875).

Strife. A drama by John GALSWORTHY (1909), dealing with the struggle between capital and labor. The chief protagonist of the former is John Anthony, head of the Trengartha Tin Plate Works, and of the latter, David Roberts, spokesman for the strikers at the works.

Strindberg, Johann August (1849–1912). Swedish novelist and dramatist, known for his pessimistic and realistic works influenced by the school of NATURALISM and the theories of NIETZSCHE. *Tschandala* and *By the Open Sea* are his best-known novels. His plays include *Master Olaf; The Thunderstorm; The Bridal Crown; Advent; The Confession of a Fool; The Father, Countess Julia,* and *The Creditors,* a trilogy and his best-known dramatic works; *Fair Haven and Foul Strand; Lucky Pehr; Motherlove; Easter; Comrades; Facing Death; The Outlaw; The Road to Damascus; Pariah; The Red Room; The Son of a Servant.*

string.

always harping on one string. Always talking on one subject; always repeating the same thing. The allusion is to the ancient harpers; some, like Paganini, played on one string to show their skill, but more would have endorsed the Apothecary's apology "My poverty, and not my will, consents."

to have two strings to one's bow. To have a second plan in reserve if the first should fail.

Stringer, Arthur John Arbuthnott (1874–). American writer, born in Canada. Literary editor of the magazine *Success,* he has written a great variety of books and some poetry, his best in Irish dialect.

Strode, Hudson (1893–). American educator and traveler. Wrote *The Story of Bermuda* (1932); *The Pageant of Cuba* (1934); *South by Thunderbird* (1937); etc. He also compiled an anthology of English lyric poetry (1938).

Stromkarl. A Norwegian musical spirit. Arndt informs us that the Stromkarl has eleven different musical measures, to ten of which people may dance, but the eleventh belongs to the night spirit, his host. If anyone plays it, tables and benches, cups and cans, old men and women, blind and lame, babies in their cradles, and the sick in their beds, begin to dance.

Strong, Anna Louise (1885–). American journalist who organized (1930) the first English newspaper in Russia. She is known as an arresting speaker and contributor of many articles to magazines. Author of *I Change Worlds: The Remaking of an American* (1935); *One-Fifth of Mankind* (1938); *My Native Land* (1940); etc.

Strong, Austin (1881–). American dramatist, son of Isobel Strong who was sister-in-law to Robert Louis STEVENSON. One of his best-known productions is *The Drums of Oude* (1906). *Seventh Heaven* (1922) was popular on stage and screen.

Strong, Dr. In Dickens' DAVID COPPERFIELD, a benevolent old schoolmaster, to whose school David Copperfield is sent while he is living with Mr. WICKFIELD. The old doctor dotes on his young wife Annie, and supports her scapegrace cousin Jack Maldon.

Strong, Leonard Alfred George (1896–). English poet and fiction writer whose *The Lowery Road* (1924) and *Selected Poems* (1931) displayed an original talent. He has also made from year to year a selection of the best magazine verse.

strophe. From the Greek, literally "a turn." Originally, that part of an ode which was sung by the Greek dramatic chorus as it moved in one direction. Followed by an "antistrophe" when the chorus reversed the direction of its movement. Hence, in prosody, a stanza.

Strothmann, Fred (1879–). Humorous illustrator, best known for his illustrations of Mark Twain's *Extracts from Adam's Diary* and *Editorial Wild Oats.*

Struldbrugs. Wretched inhabitants of LUGGNAGG in Swift's GULLIVER'S TRAVELS, who have the privilege of immortality without those of eternal vigor, strength, and intellect.

> Many persons think that the picture of the Stulbrugs (*sic*) was intended to wean us from a love of life . . . but I am certain that the dean never had any such thing in view.—*Paley's Natural Theology* (Lord Brougham's note, Bk. i, p. 140).

Strunsky, Simeon (1879–1948). American journalist, editorial writer, and essayist, who contributed a regular daily column to the New York *Times,* called *Topics of the Times.* His books include *Belshazzar Court* (1914); *Professor Latimer's Progress* (1918); *The Living Tradition* (1939); and *No Mean City* (1944).

Struther, Jan, see MAXTONE GRAHAM, Mrs. JOYCE.

Strutt, Joseph (1749–1802). English antiquary and engraver. Author of *A Complete View of the Dress and Habits of the People of England* (2 vols.; 1796–1799) and *The Sports and Pastimes of the People of England* (1801). Sir Walter Scott finished a novel partly written by Strutt.

Strutt, Lord. In Arbuthnot's *History of John Bull* (1712), a caricature of the King of Spain, originally Charles II (who died without issue), but also applied to his successor Philippe Duc d'Anson, called "Philip Lord Strutt."

> I need not tell you of the great quarrels that happened in our neighbourhood since the death of the late lord Strutt; how the parson [cardinal Portocarero] . . . got him to settle his estate upon his cousin Philip Baboon [Bourbon], to the great disappointment of his cousin squire South [Charles of Austria].—*History of John Bull,* i.

Stryver, Bully. In Dickens' TALE OF TWO CITIES, counsel for the defense in Darnay's trial. He is more formally known as C. J. Stryver.

> He was stout, loud, red, bluff, and free from any drawback of delicacy; had a pushing way of shouldering himself (morally and physically) into companies and conversations, that argued well for his shouldering his way on in life.—ii. 24.

Stuart, Mary, see MARY QUEEN OF SCOTS.

Prince Charles Edward Stuart. See under PRETENDER.

Stuart, Francis (1902–). Irish novelist and poet, member of the Irish Academy of

Letters. *Pigeon Irish* (1932); *The Coloured Dome* (1932); *The Great Squire* (1939); etc.

Stuart, Gilbert Charles (1755–1828). American painter; studied in London and had a studio there (1776–1787). He gained fame as a portrait painter and was considered the peer of Romney, Gainsborough and Reynolds.

Stuart, Henry Longan (1875–1928). Anglo-American Roman Catholic journalist; writer for *The Freeman* and associated with Michael Williams on *The Commonweal*. His novel *Weeping Cross: an Unworldly Story* (1908) has been highly praised.

Stuart, James Ewell Brown, known as **Jeb** (1833–1864). Confederate commander and general of cavalry. His absence from the Battle of Gettysburg is said to have contributed to the defeat of the South.

Stuart, Jesse Hilton (1907–). American poet, novelist, and short-story writer, known for his books dealing with the mountain region of Kentucky and its people, his poetry having been compared by some critics to that of Robert BURNS. Among his works are *Man with a Bull-Tongue Plow* (1934), a collection of sonnets; *Head o' W-Hollow* (1936) and *Men of the Mountains* (1941), short stories; *Beyond Dark Hills* (1938), autobiographical; *Trees of Heaven* (1940), a novel.

Stuart, Ruth, *née* **McEnery** (1849–1917). American writer on Southern life.

Stuart Little. Title of a children's book by E. B. WHITE (1945) concerning a mouse born into a New York family.

Stubbs or Stubbes, Philip (fl. ca. 1583–1591). English Puritan who violently denounced the evils of his time in *The Anatomie of Abuses* (1583). Thomas NASH answered with *The Anatomie of Absurdities* (1589).

Stubbs, William (1825–1901). English historian; regius professor of modern history at Oxford (1866–1884). Chief work, *The Constitutional History of England* (3 vols.; 1874–1878).

Stuck, Franz von (1863–1928). German painter and sculptor. His illustrations for the comic paper *Fliegende Blätter* became widely known. His paintings and sculptures have religious or allegorical subjects.

Studs Lonigan. A trilogy by James T. FARRELL, consisting of YOUNG LONIGAN (1932), THE YOUNG MANHOOD OF STUDS LONIGAN (1934), and JUDGMENT DAY (1935). In relentless naturalistic style (see NATURALISM) it presents the boyhood, adolescence, early manhood, and finally death of William (Studs) Lonigan, the son of lower-middle-class Irish Catholic parents in Chicago. Although Studs as a boy displays sparks of vigor, spirit, and ambition, the combined influences of his social and economic environment, his swaggering and vicious associates, the general moral laxness and extravagance of the JAZZ AGE, and his narrow family, educational, and religious background, serve to aggravate his weaknesses and guide him into a life of futile dissipation and vice, which he recognizes as unsatisfactory but from which he is unable to escape. The language of the streets, the monotony and crudity of the thought processes of Studs and his associates, and their numerous sordid sexual adventures are all frankly and faithfully reproduced, and there is extensive documentation in the depiction of the social background in the U.S. during the period between Woodrow Wilson's renomination to the presidency and the first years of the depression era of the 1930's. A STREAM-OF-CONSCIOUSNESS portrayal of Studs' thoughts and feelings, by which a complete characterization of him is given, is a notable feature of this work. See also the following names of subordinate characters: BANAHAN, CATHERINE; COHEN, DAVEY; JACKSON, MRS. GEORGE; IRIS; MOYLAN, FATHER; REILLEY, WEARY; SCANLAN, LUCY; SHIRES, HELEN.

Studs Lonigan, which the author describes as a study of "spiritual poverty," rather than one of squalid tenement living or of the criminal underworld, as some readers erroneously considered it, aroused much controversy on its publication, one group of detractors denouncing it on the grounds of obscenity and immorality, and another group dismissing it as mere sociological reporting, devoid of literary merit. Some critics, however, have ranked it with John Dos Passos' U.S.A. as one of the greatest of American novels and one of the best portrayals of life in the U.S. in the 20th century.

Stuka. See under DIVE BOMBER.

Stukely, Will, see STUTLY, WILL.

Sturgis, Russell (1836–1909). American architect and writer on art; editor in chief of *A Dictionary of Architecture and Building* (3 vols.; 1901–1902); author of the first two volumes of A. Sturgis and A. L. Frothingham, *A History of Architecture* (4 vols.; 1906–1915).

Sturluson, Snorri, see SNORRI STURLUSON.

Sturm und Drang (*Ger.,* "storm and stress"). The name given to the intellectual awakening of Germany toward the close of the 18th century, closely allied with the general movement of ROMANTICISM. It was so called from a drama of that name by Friedrich Maximilian von KLINGER (1752–1831). GOETHE's *Götz von Berlichingen* and *Sorrows of Werther,* SCHILLER's *Robbers,* Klinger's tragedies, LESSING's criticisms, and the mania for SHAKESPEARE and OSSIAN, were characteristic of the trend of the times. It was a typical "youth movement," not essentially different from other extravagant rebellions of "the younger generation," and important only because several of its representatives grew up to assume world-wide importance as Germany's greatest poets and dramatists.

Stutly, Will. In the Robin Hood legends, a companion of Little John, sometimes called **Will Stukely.** In the morris-dance on May-day, Little John occupied the right hand side of Robin Hood, and Will Stutly the left. His rescue from the sheriff of Nottingham by Robin Hood, forms the subject of one of the Robin Hood ballads.

> When Robin Hood in the greenwood lived,
> Under the greenwood tree,
> Tidings there came to him with speed,
> Tidings for certaintie,
> That Will Stutly surprizéd was,
> And eke in prison lay;
> Three varlets that the sheriff hired,
> Did likely him betray.
> *Robin Hood's Rescuing Will Stutly,* iv. 15.

Stuyvesant, Peter (1592–1672). Dutch director-general of New Netherland (1647–1664) until he had to surrender the colony to Great Britain. He appears in the *History of New York* by Washington Irving as "Peter, the Headstrong." Legend has it that his false leg was made of silver. His farm, *Bouwerij* (literally, "farm"), included the region of the Bowery in New York City.

stylites or pillar saints. A class of early and medieval ascetics, chiefly of Syria, who took up their abode on the top of a pillar, from which they never descended. The most celebrated are Simeon Stylites, of Syria, and Daniel the Stylite of Constantinople. Simeon (d. 596) spent sixty-eight years on different pillars, each loftier and narrower than the preceding, the last being 66 feet high. Daniel (d. 494) lived thirty-three years on a pillar, and was not unfrequently nearly blown from it by the storms from Thrace. This form of asceticism was still in vogue as late as the 12th century. TENNYSON has a poem *St. Simeon Stylites:*

> I, Simeon of the Pillar by surname,
> Stylites among men—I, Simeon,
> The watcher on the column till the end.

Styx. The river of Hate (Gr. *stugein,* "to hate"), that, according to classical mythology, flowed nine times round the infernal regions.

The fables about the Styx are of Egyptian origin. Thus Isis collected the various parts of OSIRIS (murdered by Typhon) and buried them in secrecy on the banks of the Styx. CHARON the ferryman of the Styx, as Diodorus informs us, is an Egyptian word for a "ferryman."

The five rivers of Hell are the Styx, Acheron, Cocytus, Phlegethon and Lethe.

> Abhorred Styx, the flood of deadly hate;
> Sad Acheron, of sorrow, black and deep;
> Cocytus, named of lamentation loud,
> Heard on the rueful stream; fierce Phlegethon,
> Whose waves of torrent fire inflame with rage.
> Far off from these, a slow and silent stream,
> Lethe, the river of oblivion, rolls.
> Milton, *Paradise Lost,* ii. 577, etc. (1665).

Dante, in his DIVINE COMEDY, places the rivers in different circles of the Inferno. Thus, he makes the Acheron divide the border-land from Limbo. The former realm is for the "praiseless and the blameless dead"; Limbo is for the unbaptized. He places the Stygian Lake of "inky hue" in the fifth circle, the realm of those who put no restraint on their anger. The fire-stream of Phlegethon he fixes to the eighth steep, the "Hell of burning, where it snows flakes of fire," and where blasphemers are confined. He places "the frozen river" of Cocytus in the tenth pit of Malebolge, a region of thick-ribbed ice, the lowest depth of Hell, where JUDAS and LUCIFER are imprisoned. Lethe, he says, is no river of Hell at all, but it is the one wish of all the infernals to get to it, that they may drink its water and forget their torments. It being, however, in "Purgatory," they can never get near it.

John Kendrick Bangs has a humorous narrative entitled *A Houseboat on the Styx* (*Am.,* 1895).

Suárez, Francisco (1548–1617). Spanish scholastic philosopher, considered the chief theologian of the Jesuits. He was a distinguished commentator upon St. Thomas Aquinas.

subject and object. In metaphysics, the *subject* is the ego, the mind, the conscious self, the substance or substratum to which attributes must be referred; the *object* is external as distinct from the ego, a thing or idea brought before the consciousness. Hence *subjective criticism, art,* etc., is that which proceeds from the individual mind and is consequently individualistic, fanciful, imaginative, while *objective criticism* is that which is based on knowledge of the externals.

subject-object. The immediate object of thought as distinguished from the material thing of which one is thinking.

subjectivism. Generalized term for those schools of philosophy holding that only the thinking mind, the conscious self, is real. See IDEALISM; SOLIPSISM.

Sublette, William Lewis (1799?–1845). American soldier who led fur-trading expeditions into the Rocky Mountains (1828, 1832) and to Santa Fé (1831). A part of the Oregon Trail was known as "Sublette's trace."

Sublime Porte. The central office of the former Ottoman Government in Constantinople; hence, the Government or the Empire itself. The term is French in origin, *sublime* signifying "lofty" or "high and mighty." Constantinople has twelve gates, and near one of these is a building with a lofty gateway called "Bab-i-humajun," in which was the official residence of the vizier, and the offices of all the chief ministers of state, whence all the imperial edicts were issued.

submerged or **submerged tenth, the.** The PROLETARIAT, sunken or submerged in poverty; the gutter-class; the waifs and strays of society.

subscription book. A book manufactured after the requisite number of customers have promised by their "subscription" to purchase it. Benjamin Franklin organized the first subscription library in the U.S. It contained Keill, *Astronomy;* Defoe, *Complete English Tradesman;* L'Hospital, *Conic Sections;* Bayle, *Critical Dictionary;* Montaigne, *Essays;* Hayes, *Fluxions;* Sidney, *Government;* Defoe, *Gulliver's Travels;* Homer, *Iliad and Odyssey;* Pufendorf, *Jurisprudence;* Xenophon, *Memorabilia;* Gravesand, *Natural Philosophy;* Newton, *Principia;* Dryden, *Virgil.*

The numerous book clubs of today are financed by a similar plan: subscribers agree to take a certain number of selections during the year. The Book-of-the-Month Club and The Literary Guild, both founded in 1926, each have over a million subscribers. Other clubs include The Book League, The Non-Fiction Book Club, The Religious Book Club, The Dollar Book Club, The Book Find Club, etc. The literary value of the selections of the two largest clubs has often been questioned.

Subtle. In Ben Jonson's comedy THE ALCHEMIST, the "alchemist," an artful quack who pretends to be on the eve of discovering the PHILOSOPHER'S STONE. Sir Epicure Mammon, a rich knight, is his principal dupe, but by no means his only one.

Subtle Doctor. See under DOCTOR.

Succoth (Heb. *sukkoth,* "booths"). The Jewish name for the Feast of TABERNACLES.

succubus. A lascivious demon in female form. From Latin *sub,* "under" and *cubare,* "to lie down." The *succubus* lies under, the *incubus* over.

Such, Theophrastus, see THEOPHRASTUS SUCH.

Sucker State. Illinois. See under STATES.

Suckfist, Lord. In Rabelais' GARGANTUA AND PANTAGRUEL, II. 11–13, the defendant in the great Pantagruelian lawsuit, known as "Lord Busqueue *v.* Lord Suckfist," in which the plaintiff and defendant plead in person. After hearing the case, the bench declares, "We have not understood one single circumstance of the matter on either side." But PANTAGRUEL gives judgment, and as plaintiff and defendant leave the court each fully persuaded that the verdict is in his own favor, they are both highly satisfied, "a thing without parallel in the annals of the law."

Suckling, Sir **John** (1609–1642). English poet, courtier, and soldier, a member of the Cavalier school, or the "sons of Ben" (see JONSON, BEN), although he was influenced to some extent in superficial effects by John DONNE. Suckling was known in his day for his wit, his gaiety, his love of gaining, and his boisterous exhibitionism. His writings include *Aglaura* (1637), a play; an *Account of Religion by Reason,* a prose tract; *Fragmenta Aurea* (1646) and *The Last Remains* (1659), collections of verse. The best known of his numerous lyrics and songs is that beginning "Why so pale and wan, fond lover?"

Suckling took part in several military campaigns and was implicated in the plot to rescue STRAFFORD from the Tower of London in 1641, fleeing to France to escape apprehension. Some accounts say that he committed suicide; others, that he was killed in revenge by a servant.

Suckow, Ruth (1892–). American novelist and short-story writer, known for her studies, generally realistic, of life in Iowa. Her works include *Country People* (1924); *The Odyssey of a Nice Girl* (1925); *Iowa Interiors* (1926), short stories; *The Bonney Family* (1928); *Cora* (1929); *The Kramer Girls* (1930); *Children and Other People* (1931), short stories; *The Folks* (1934); *Carry-Over* (1936), a partial collection of her previous work; *New Hope* (1942).

Sudermann, Hermann (1857–1928). German dramatist and novelist. His novels include DAME CARE (*Frau Sorge;* 1888); THE SONG OF SONGS (*Das Hohe Lied;* 1908); *Regina, Or the Sins of the Fathers,* a translation of *Der Katzensteg* (1898); *The Wish* (*Der Wunsch;* 1895); *The Mad Professor* (*Der Tolle Professor;* 1926). Among his plays are *Heimat* (1893), translated as MAGDA; *Fritzchen* (1896); *The Vale of Content* (*Das Glück im Winkel;* 1896); *The Fires of St. John* (*Johannisfeuer;* 1897; see SALOMÉ); *The Joy of Living* (1902), a translation of *Es lebe das Leben; The Undying Past* (1906), a translation of *Es war; Honor* (1915). Other works include *Geschwister* (1899), *The Indian Lily* (1895–1896), and *The Excursion to Tilsit* (1930), collections of short stories; *The Book of My Youth* (1923).

Sudra. One of the four great CASTES of Hinduism.

Sue, Eugène (1804–1859). French novelist, known for his sensational and popular romances in the manner of DUMAS *père. Les Mystères de Paris* (1843) and THE WANDERING JEW (*Le Juif errant;* 1849) are his best-known works. Sue was an army doctor in his early years and began his literary career by writing sea-tales based on his own experiences.

Suetonius. In full **Gaius Suetonius Tranquillus.** Roman biographer and historian. Private secretary to Emperor Hadrian (ca. 119–121). The work by which he is remembered is *Lives of the Caesars.*

Sufi. Member of a Mohammedan sect of mystics, mentioned, for instance, in *Omar Kháyyám.* The literal meaning of the word is "clad in wool."

Sugimoto, Mme **Etsu Inagaki** (1874–). Japanese autobiographer and novelist. Best known for *A Daughter of the Samurai* (1925).

Suggs, Captain Simon. A rapscallion character created by the Alabama humorist J. J. Hooper in his *Adventures of Captain Simon Suggs* (*Am.,* 1846). The character was admired by THACKERAY. In his *Flush Times of Alabama and Mississippi* (*Am.,* 1853) another Southern humorist, J. G. Baldwin, introduced Simon Suggs, Jr., Esquire, "a good trader and the mean boy of the school."

sui generis (*Lat.,* "of its own kind"). Having a distinct character of its own; unlike anything else.

sui juris (*Lat.*). Of one's own right; the state of being able to exercise one's legal rights, i.e., freedom from legal disability.

Suleiman I. Known as **the Magnificent** (1496?–1566). Famous Turkish ruler who encouraged the arts and sciences.

Sulgrave Manor. An estate in Northamptonshire, England, where the ancestors of George Washington lived. In 1914 it was made a monument by the Sulgrave Institution.

Sulla, Lucius Cornelius. Surnamed **Felix** (138–78 B.C.). Roman general, dictator, and reformer. Took part in various campaigns and was elected consul (88). During the civil war between him and Marius (88–82), he led for the first time an army of Romans against Rome (88 B.C.). Appointed dictator (81). Reorganized the senate and the judiciary of Rome and was the first in Roman history to use the weapon of proscription.

Sullen, Squire. In Farquhar's comedy THE BEAUX' STRATAGEM, the son of Lady Bountiful by her first husband. He marries the sister of Sir Charles Freeman, but after fourteen months they mutually agree to a divorce, for in no one single point is there any compatibility between them. The Squire is sullen, the lady sprightly; he cannot drink tea with her, and she cannot drink ale with him; he hates ombre and picquet, she hates cock-fighting and racing; he will not dance, and she will not hunt. When Squire Sullen separates from his wife, he is obliged to return the £20,000 which he received with her as a dowry.

Sullivan, Sir **Arthur Seymour** (1842–1900). English composer, well-known for his collaboration with W. S. GILBERT in the Gilbert and Sullivan operas. Also an organist and composer of sacred music and serious opera. Outside of comic opera his best-known compositions are songs, as *The Lost Chord* and the hymn *Onward, Christian Soldiers.*

Sullivan, Frank (1892–). Widely popular American humorist. Has conducted columns in the New York *World* and *PM,* contributing also to the NEW YORKER. His books include *The Life and Times of Martha Hepplethwaite* (1926); *Innocent Bystanding* (1928); *Sullivan at Bay* (1939); etc.

Sullivan, John Lawrence (1858–1918). American heavyweight prizefighter.

Sullivan, John William (1886–1937). English scientific popularizer. *Aspects of Science* (1923) is his most successful book. *Three Men Discuss Relativity* (1926) is an endeavor to popularize Einstein's theory for the ordinary reader. The three men are Einstein, Aldous Huxley, and the author himself.

Sullivan, Mark (1874–). American editor and journalist. Best known for his contemporary history, *Our Times—The United States* (6 vols.; 1900–1925); *The Education of an American* (1938) (autobiography); etc.

Sully, Duc **de. Maximilien de Béthune.** Baron de **Rosny** (1560–1641). French statesman; minister of finance and holder of other high offices under Henry IV. Forced to resign at Henry's death (1610). His *Mémoires* (1638) are a valuable historical source.

Sully, Thomas (1783–1872). English-born American painter. Painting of Lafayette hangs in Independence Hall, Philadelphia. Total production, 2,600 works.

Sully Prudhomme, René François Armand (1839–1907). French poet of the group known as PARNASSIANS, one of the most representative poets of his age. His work is characterized by sensibility, melancholy, a conflict between scientific doubt and religious faith, and delicacy of treatment. His works include *Stances et Poèmes* (1865); *Les Solitudes* (1869); *Les Vaines Tendresses* (1875); *La Justice* (1878) and *Le Bonheur* (1888), moral allegories; *Les Epaves* (1908). He wrote a number of sonnets. *La Vase Brisé* (*The Broken Vase*) is his best-known poem. Sully Prudhomme was honored during his lifetime, being elected to the French Academy in 1881. First Nobel prize for literature (1901).

Sulphite. See BROMIDE AND SULPHITE.

Sultan. See RULERS, TITLES OF.

Sulzberger, Cyrus Lindauer (1858–1932). American merchant and philanthropist. His son, **Arthur Hays Sulzberger** (1891–), became president and director of the New York Times Co., and publisher of the New York *Times.*

Summer. A novel by Edith WHARTON (1917), the story of Charity Royall, the child of a degenerate backwoods community, brought up in a small town by Lawyer Royall, a middle-aged relative. After a brief "summer" of love with an attractive young stranger, she is deserted and returns in despair to her birthplace in the hills. But when Lawyer Royall follows and offers to marry her, although she has both feared and despised him, she consents.

Summer, Will. Jester of Henry VIII, said to have been a model for the fools in Shakespeare.

> I think it was Will Summers
> Who once was Shakespeare's fool.
> Alfred Noyes, *The Lord of Misrule.*

Summerall, Charles Pelot (1867–). Chief of staff of the U.S. army (1926–1930).

Summers, Montague. In full **Alphonsus Joseph-Mary Augustus Montague Summers** (1880–). English priest who has written brilliantly on the Restoration, particularly in the realm of the theater and drama. His *The History of Witchcraft and Demonology* (1927) and *The Geography of Witchcraft* (1928) are two of the most important reference books on this weird subject.

Summerson, Esther. The heroine of Dickens' BLEAK HOUSE, a gentle, lovable girl called by those who know and love her "Dame Durden" or "Dame Trot." She turns out to be the illegitimate child of Lady Dedlock and Captain Hawdon. Eventually she marries Allan Woodcourt, a surgeon.

Summoner's, Sumpnor's or **Somnour's Tale, The.** One of Chaucer's CANTERBURY TALES, told by the summoner, a packman or peddler. After some introductory raillery regarding the begging habits of friars, the tale is told of a certain king who commands his officer to take to execution a man charged with murder. On the way they encounter the man supposed to be murdered, and the officer leads back the accused. The king, instead of discharging the innocent man, commands all three to be put to death—the officer, for disobeying orders; the accused, because the king commanded him to be executed; and the man supposed to have been murdered, because he is the cause of death to the other two.

summum bonum (*Lat.,* "the highest good"). The chief excellence; the highest attainable good.

Sumner, Charles (1811–1874). The first American statesman of distinction to urge Negro emancipation (1861). He was prominent in impeaching President Johnson and opposed the re-election of President Grant in 1872. *The Works of Charles Sumner* (15 vols.; 1870–1883). In a poem in his memory Longfellow wrote:

> Like Winkelried he took
> Into his manly breast
> The sheaf of hostile spears, and broke
> A path for the oppressed.

Sumner, William Graham (1840–1910). American teacher of sociology. He was a strong opponent of government interference in business and advocated an imperialistic policy on the part of the U.S. He wrote many books on finance and some biographies. *Folkways* (1907) is his best-known book. His *Science of Society* was completed by A. G. Keller (4 vols.; 1927).

sumptuary laws. Laws to limit the expenses of food and dress, or any luxury. The Romans had their *leges sumptuarii,* and they have been enacted in many states at various times.

Sumter, Fort. A fort in Charleston Harbor in South Carolina where the first engagement of the United States Civil War took place.

sun. The source of light and heat, and consequently of life, to the whole world; hence, regarded as a deity and worshiped as such by all primitive peoples and having a leading place in all mythologies. *Shamash* was the principal sun god of the Assyrians, *Merodach* of the Chaldees, *Ormuzd* of the Persians, *Ra* of the Egyptians, *Tezcatlipoca* of the Mexicans, and *Helios* (known to the Romans as *Sol*) of the Greeks. Helios drove his chariot daily across the heavens, rising from the sea at dawn and sinking into it in the west at sunset. The Scandinavian sun god *Sunna,* who was in constant dread of being devoured by the wolf Fenris (a symbol of eclipses), was similarly borne through the sky. *Apollo* was also a sun god of the Greeks, but he was the personification not of the sun itself but of its all-pervading light and life-giving qualities.

a place in the sun. A favorable position that allows room for development; a share in what one has a natural right to. The phrase was popularized by William II of Germany during the crisis of 1911. In his speech at Hamburg (August 27) he spoke of the German nation taking steps that would make them—

> sure that no one can dispute with us the place in the sun that is our due.

The phrase had been used by PASCAL some two hundred years before.

out of God's blessing into the warm sun. One of Ray's proverbs, meaning from good to less good. When the king says to HAMLET, "How is it that the clouds still hang on you?" the prince answers, "No, my lord, I am too much i' the sun," meaning, "I have lost God's blessing for too much of the sun"—i.e., this far inferior state.

the City of the Sun. See CITY.

the sun of Austerlitz. When Napoleon fought the Russians and Austrians at Austerlitz (December 2, 1805), a brilliant sun suddenly burst through and scattered the mists, thus enabling him to gain an overwhelming victory. Napoleon ever after looked upon this as a special omen from Heaven.

the Sun of Righteousness. Jesus Christ. (*Mal.* iv. 2.)

Sun. A New York newspaper, founded as a penny paper (the former price of papers having been six cents) under the name of the *Daily Sun* (No. 1, September 23, 1833). It was written, edited, and set up by Benjamin Henry Day, a journeyman printer, whose son invented the Ben DAY process and whose grandson was Clarence DAY, Jr., the author of *Life With Father.* During the Civil War, the price of the *Sun* became two cents. It was sold (1838) to Moses Y. Beach and later (1868) to Charles Anderson DANA. William Mackay Laffan (1848–1909) became its publisher in 1884. He made of it the *Evening Sun* (1887), with Charles Anderson Dana and his son Paul (1852–1930) as editors (till 1903). Edward P. Mitchell (editor, 1903–1920) continued the Dana policy of personal journalism and the development of individually written stories. Under him Frank Ward O'Malley (with the paper from 1906 to 1920), established his reputation as a brilliant reporter. When Munsey bought the *Sun* and failed in his attempt to merge it with the *Tribune,* the *Evening Sun* absorbed the New York *Globe* and continued, while the morning *Sun* ceased publication. Some remarkable names in journalism, associated with the old *Sun,* have been Julian Ralph (1875–1895); Arthur Brisbane (1883); Samuel Hopkins Adams (1891–1900); Will Irwin (1904–1906); Don Marquis (1912–1922); etc. (See under these names.)

Sun Also Rises, The. A novel by Ernest HEMINGWAY (1926), dealing with Lady Brett Ashley, an Englishwoman divorcing her husband, and a group of typical representatives of the LOST GENERATION who travel with her through Spain. These include Michael Campbell, whom Brett plans to marry; Jake Barnes, an American journalist; Bill Gorton, friend of Jake; a Greek nobleman; and Robert Cohn, a novelist and an American Jew. Cohn is in love with Brett but is scorned; Brett and Jake love each other but are frustrated because of a wound Jake received during World War I; Brett falls in love with Pedro Romero, a Spanish bullfighter, but decides to go back to Michael.

Sunday, William Ashley. Normally called **Billy Sunday** (1863–1935). Famous American evangelist who had been a professional baseball player. He carried on very vocal evangelistic work for some years at the end of the nineteenth century and the early part of the twentieth. He became a Presbyterian Minister in 1903. Cf. Carl Sandburg's poem, *To a Contemporary Bunk-Shooter.*

Sunken Bell, The (Die versunkene Glocke). A drama by Gerhart HAUPTMANN (1896). As Heinrich the artist is taking it home, the wonderful bell which he has made crashes down the mountain into a lake. Stunned by his loss, Heinrich is found by Rautendelein, a lovely nymph, and stays with her in the mountains. His deserted wife, Magda, finally throws herself into the lake and rings the sunken bell. Heinrich goes home but finds Magda gone, and by the time he returns to the mountain, Rautendelein has married the Frog King, so Heinrich drinks the goblet of death. RESPIGHI wrote an opera entitled *La Campana Sommersa,* based on the play.

Sunna (*Arab.,* "custom, divine law"). Properly, the sayings and example of MAHOMET and his immediate followers in so far as they conform to the KORAN; hence, applied to the collections of legal and moral traditions attributed to the Prophet, supplementary to the Koran as the Hebrew MISHNA is to the Pentateuch.

Sunnites. The orthodox and conservative body of Moslems, who consider the SUNNA as authentic as the Koran itself and acknowledge the first four caliphs to be the rightful successors of Mahomet. They form by far the largest section of Mohammedans, and are divided into four sects, viz., Hanbalites, Hanafites, Malikites, and Shafiites. See also SHIITES.

Sunset Land. Arizona. See under STATES.

Sunthin' in the Pastoral Line. A famous dialect poem in THE BIGLOW PAPERS (1848) by James Russell LOWELL.

Sun-Up. A play by Lula VOLLMER which was produced, 1923; published, 1925. Also the title of a long autobiographical poem by Lola RIDGE (1920).

Sun Yat-sen (1866–1925). Chinese statesman, called in China the "father of the Revolution." He brought about the revolution against the Manchus (1911), founded the Kuomintang and was elected provisional president of the Chinese Republic. He retired in favor of Yüan Shih-k'ai who became president of all China. He disagreed with Yüan and was elected president of Southern China (1921). Under the influence of the Communist doctrines of Mikhail Borodin, he fought against General Ts'ao K'un (1923) and gained more influence in the north. He died of cancer. A large mausoleum was built in his honor at Nanking.

super. In theatrical parlance, "supers" are supernumeraries, or persons employed to make up crowds, processions, dancing or singing choirs, messengers, etc., where little or no speaking is needed.

Superbas. In American baseball parlance, former name for the Brooklyn Nationals. See under BASEBALL TEAMS.

superman. A hypothetical superior human being of high intellectual and moral attainments, fancied as evolved from the normally existing type. The term (*Übermensch*) was invented by the German philosopher NIETZSCHE, and popularized in England by G. B. Shaw's play *Man and Superman* (1903).

The wide popularity of the term gave rise to many compounds, such as *super-woman, super-critic, super-tramp, super-dreadnought,* and *super-tax.*

In the U.S. during the 1930's, *Superman* became known as the name of the hero of a popular comic-strip series, a man of fabulous strength, skill, and ingenuity, constantly outwitting criminals, spies, and villains of all sorts. One of his common feats was flying through the air unaided.

Supplehouse. An ambitious politician in Trollope's novel FRAMLEY PARSONAGE. He has been shelved in a minor position and, remembering the praise bestowed upon him years before, torments himself with the question, "How can a man born to save a nation and to lead a people be content to fill the chair of an under-secretary?"

Suppliants, The. The earliest of the surviving plays of AESCHYLUS (462 B.C.). It is a tragedy concerning the daughters of Danaüs.

supply.

the law of supply and demand. The economic statement that the competition of buyers and sellers tends to make such changes in price that the demand for any article in a given market will become equal to the supply. In other words, if the demand exceeds the supply, the price rises, operating so as to reduce the demand and so enable the supply to meet it, and *vice versa.*

suppressed desires. A term much in use in PSYCHOANALYSIS to indicate inhibitions. According to the Freudians (see Sigmund FREUD), suppressed desires, usually sexual, are at the root of most neurotic conditions, and if these desires can be brought from the realm of the subconscious into consciousness and given some normal outlet, the difficulty will tend to be dissolved. Susan GLASPELL used the phrase as the title of an amusing one-act play in which the silly heroine fancies she has a terrible suppressed desire and gets herself involved in all sorts of absurdities when she tries to give it outlet.

Sura. Any one ethical revelation; thus each chapter of the KORAN is a Sura.

> Hypocrites are apprehensive lest a Sura should be revealed respecting them, to declare unto them that which is in their hearts.—*Koran*, ix.

Surface, Sir Oliver. In R. B. Sheridan's SCHOOL FOR SCANDAL, the rich uncle of Joseph and Charles Surface. He appears under the assumed name of Premium Stanley.

Charles Surface. A reformed scapegrace, and the accepted lover of Maria, the rich ward of Sir Peter TEAZLE.

Joseph Surface. Elder brother of Charles, an artful, malicious, but sentimental knave so plausible in speech and manner as to pass for a "youthful miracle of prudence, good sense, and benevolence." His attentions to Maria and Lady Teazle furnish the chief interest of the plot.

Surgeon's Daughter, The. A novel by Sir Walter SCOTT, laid in the time of George II and III, and published in 1827. The heroine is Menie Gray, daughter of Dr. Gideon Gray of Middlemas. Adam Hartley, the doctor's apprentice, loves her, but Menie herself has given her heart to Richard Middlemas. It so falls out that Richard Middlemas goes to India. Adam Hartley also goes to India, and, as Dr. Hartley, rises high in his profession. One day, being sent for to visit a sick fakir, he sees Menie Gray under the wing of Mme Montreville. Her father has died, and she has come to India, under Madame's escort, to marry Richard, but Richard entraps the girl for a concubine in the harem of Tippoo Saib. When Dr. Hartley hears of this scandalous treachery, he tells Hyder Ali, the father of Tippoo Saib. He and his son are so disgusted at the villainy that they condemn Richard Middlemas to be trampled to death by a trained elephant, and liberate Menie, who returns to her native country under the escort of Dr. Hartley.

Surgery, the Father of French. See under FATHER.

Surgis, Mme de. In Marcel Proust's REMEMBRANCE OF THINGS PAST, the mistress of the Duc de GUERMANTES.

Surratt, Mary E. (1820–1865). Keeper of the boardinghouse in Washington, D.C., where John Wilkes Booth and his gang met to plot against Lincoln. Hanged for complicity in Lincoln's assassination. Cf. *The Story of Mary Surratt* (1947), a play by John Patrick.

surrealism. A movement in literature and painting, succeeding DADAISM and founded in Paris in 1924, with the aim of achieving effects of "super"-realism through the juxtaposition and combination of verbal images and physical objects ordinarily considered incongruous. The Freudian concept of the unconscious (see FREUD, SIGMUND) plays an important role in theoretical surrealism, it being claimed as the origin of the arrangements of incongruities which produce these effects. André BRETON, leader and most representative poet of the movement, in his *Manifeste du surréalisme* (*Surrealist Manifesto;* 1924), defines surrealism as "pure psychological automatism . . . thought's dictation, in the absence of all control exercised by the reason and outside all aesthetic or moral preoccupations." Later, however, some surrealists claimed to be able to control the operations of the unconscious in the production of particular effects and the selection and combination of particular elements in their work.

Unique among 20th-century revolutionary movements in art and literature, surrealism centered its particular revolution in its subject-matter, making use of extremely conventional style and technique. In poetry, it is a descendant of SYMBOLISM with its emphasis on isolated images and individual associations. Literary forerunners claimed by the surrealists themselves include the writers of the GOTHIC NOVEL; the Marquis de Sade (see SADISM); S. T. COLERIDGE (in his poem *Kubla Khan* and in his theories of IMAGINATION); Lewis CARROLL; Lautreamont; RIMBAUD; Alfred Jarry; Guillaume Apollinaire; and Franz KAFKA. Early literary leaders of surrealism and spokesmen for the entire movement were Breton, Louis ARAGON (who later abandoned surrealism for conventional fiction in the tradition of BALZAC), Tristan Tzara, Philippe Soupault, Georges Hugnet, Jean COCTEAU, and Salvador DALI. Later the following, some of whom show in their work rather an affinity with, than an exact conformity to, the principles of surrealism, were also included among outstanding representatives of the movement: David GASCOYNE, Hugh Sykes DAVIES, and Dylan Thomas (*Eng.*); Henry MILLER and Charles Henri FORD (*Am.*); Federico Garcia Lorca and Anaïs Nin (*Span.*); St.-J. PERSE and Paul ELUARD (*Fr.*); Ivan GOLL (*Swiss*).

In painting, surrealism had as its forerunners various examples of fantastic, double-image, and *trompe-l'oeil* (*Fr.,* "deceive-the-eye") art throughout the ages. Giorgio di CHIRICO was the first important painter of surrealism proper, but Salvador DALI became the most famous, supplanting Chirico as leader. Other surrealist painters include René Magritte, Yves Tanguy, Max Ernst, and Frida Kahlo. In addition, the surrealists claimed affinities with their work in the painting or sculpture of the following, although the artists named were known chiefly for their experiments in new forms: Pablo PICASSO, Marcel DUCHAMP, Constantin Brancusi, Francis Picabia, Hans Arp, Paul KLEE, Joan Miro, André Masson, and Pavel Tchelitchew. It was customary for surrealist poets to paint pictures and for surrealist painters to write poems, the difference in content being so slight that an effective interchange was possible.

Surrealism in the first years after its founding claimed that it was a representative of COMMUNISM in art, but it was vigorously disavowed by the Communist leaders. The movement gained relatively few disciples in the U.S., but the publicized exploits of Dali in New York brought surrealism to the attention of a portion of the American general public, which came to find amusement in the superficially comic incongruities of surrealist work. The methods of surrealism came to be used with modification in American advertising, especially fashion advertising and window display in retail shops.

The Blood of a Poet (*Le Sang d'un poète*), written and produced by Jean COCTEAU, was a surrealist motion picture of the early 1930's. For a discussion of surrealism and its aims and techniques, consult *Surrealism,* edited by Herbert Read.

Surrey, Henry Howard, Earl of (1517?–1547). English poet and courtier, a descendant both of Edward the Confessor and Edward III, attached to the retinue of Henry VIII. With Sir Thomas WYATT, his friend, he was an early leader in bringing the influences and forms of Italian and French lyric verse to England, and inaugurated the poetic movement of the Elizabethan and Jacobean periods. He is considered to have introduced blank verse into English, in his translations of Virgil's *Aeneid,* although iambic pentameter had been used by CHAUCER. The translation of Virgil and a number of other poems by Surrey were published in TOTTEL'S MISCELLANY, and the poet was the only contributor mentioned by name on the title-page of that work.

Surrey was proud and headstrong and was imprisoned several times for quarreling with other courtiers. He was eventually arrested and beheaded on a charge of treason by Henry VIII.

Surtees, Robert Smith (1805–1864). English novelist and sports writer. Author of the humorous sketches *Jorrocks' Jaunts and Jollities* (1838), which suggested the original plan of the PICKWICK PAPERS; the novel *Handley Cross* (1843); etc. He was a grandfather of Lord GORT.

Surtur. In Scandinavian mythology, a formidable giant, who is to set fire to the universe at RAGNAROK, with flames collected from Muspelheim.

Survey Graphic. Originally, **The Survey** (1897–). A liberal illustrated magazine, designed to interpret social conditions, founded by the New York Charity Organization Society.

survival of the fittest. A concept of the Darwinian theory of evolution (see DARWIN, CHARLES) in which it is held that the biological species best adapted to its environment will be the one to survive and perpetuate itself in its offspring. A popular misconception of this idea was that the species surviving was the one able to overcome its rivals in a literal, tooth-and-nail struggle. The phrase itself is said to have been coined by Herbert SPENCER in a study on Darwinian natural selection.

Surya. In Hindu mythology, god of the sun. In the older legends he presides over the gods of the sky, sharing the government of nature with Agni, lord of the gods of the earth, and Indra, lord of the gods of the air.

Susan. In Virginia Woolf's THE WAVES, the dependable, domestic member of the group of characters with whose lives the novel is concerned. When she grows up she marries a farmer and lives in the country with her children and her garden. She is in love with BERNARD.

Susan Lenox: Her Fall and Rise. A posthumous novel (2 vols.; 1908) by David Graham Phillips. Its extremely realistic picture of an unfortunate woman who finally achieves a certain amount of security created a sensation. It may be considered one of the best realistic novels of the early twentieth century.

Susanna and the Elders. A favorite subject among Renaissance and later artists. The *Story of Susanna,* one of the books of the Old Testament Apocrypha, tells how Susanna was accused of adultery by certain Jewish elders who had unsuccessfully attempted her chastity, how her innocence was proved by DANIEL, and the Elders put to death.

Suskind. In Cabell's FIGURES OF EARTH, a fairy mistress who is sometimes friendly to the young swineherd Manuel in the twilight and reappears years afterwards to great Manuel, the ruler of POICTESME. "It was she alone who knew the secret of preserving that dissatisfaction which is divine." Manuel does away with her when she lays a charm on his young daughter MELICENT.

Sutras. Ancient Hindu aphoristic manuals giving the rules of systems of philosophy, grammar, etc., and directions concerning religious ritual and ceremonial customs. They form a link between the Vedic and later Sanskrit literature, and are so called from Sansk. *sutra,* "a thread," the aphorisms being, as it were, threaded together.

Sutro, Alfred (1863–1933). British playwright and translator of MAETERLINCK. His best play was *The Walls of Jericho* (1904).

suttee (from Sans. *sati,* "a virtuous wife"). The Hindu custom of burning the widow on the funeral pyre of her deceased husband; also, the widow so put to death. In theory the practice, which lasted for some 2000 years, was optional, but public opinion and the very severe form of ostracism the defaulting widow had to endure gave her practically no choice. The practice was declared illegal in British India in 1829.

Sutter, John Augustus (1803–1880). Swiss pioneer in California who established the colony of New Helvetia where Sacramento now stands. When his partner, James W. Marshall, discovered gold on their property, the '49 gold rush ensued and Sutter lost his workmen, sheep, and cattle, and his land was overrun by squatters. He became bankrupt but was pensioned by the state of California. Cf. *Sutter's Gold* by Blaise Cendrars, translated by John Dos Passos.

Suydam, Edward Howard (1885–). American illustrator, successful with pictures of American cities. Illustrated several books by Lyle SAXON.

Suzuki. The servant of MADAME BUTTERFLY, in Puccini's opera of that title.

Svärd, Lotta. A Finnish woman of the latter part of the eighteenth century who became the subject of many legends. Having lost her husband in the wars, she is said to have served the army as a sutler. In modern Finland a woman's organization is called The Lotta Svärd Organization. *Lotta Svärd* is also the title of a poem by Runeberg.

Svengali. In Du Maurier's TRILBY, an Austrian Jew who controls Trilby's stage singing through his hypnotic power.

swan.

swan song. The song fabled to be sung by swans at the point of death; hence, the last work of a poet, composer, etc. The fable that the swan sings beautifully just before it dies is very ancient, though baseless. Swans do not "sing" at all, in the ordinary sense of the term.

a black swan. A curiosity, a RARA AVIS.

all your swans are geese. All your fine promises or expectations have proved fallacious. "Hope told a flattering tale." The converse, *All your geese are swans,* means all your children are paragons, and whatever you do is in your own eyes superlative work.

Leda and the swan. See LEDA.

the Knight of the Swan. LOHENGRIN.

the Swan of Avon. Shakespeare; so called by Ben JONSON in allusion to his birthplace, Stratford-on-Avon. *Swan,* as applied to poets (because Apollo was fabled to have been changed into a swan), is of very old standing; thus, VIRGIL was known as *the Mantuan Swan,* HOMER *the Swan of Meander,* etc., and Anna SEWARD (1747–1809) was rather absurdly named *the Swan of Lichfield.*

Swan, The. A poem by Stéphane MALLARMÉ, considered his most representative. In it, the swan serves as the symbol of the cold and sterile poet, set apart from the life of ordinary men, and there are images of whiteness, snow, ice, etc., throughout the poem. See HÉRODIADE; also SYMBOLISM.

Swancourt, Elfride. Heroine of Hardy's PAIR OF BLUE EYES.

Swanhild. An old Norse legendary heroine, daughter of SIGURD and GUDRUN. She is falsely accused of adultery with the son of the king who is wooing her, and the king has his son hanged and Swanhild trampled to death by horses.

Swann, Charles. A leading character in Marcel Proust's REMEMBRANCE OF THINGS PAST, a bourgeois of Jewish parentage, cultured, intelligent, and sensitive, who is a friend of the parents of the narrator MARCEL. For a time he is one of the few characters of personal and intellectual integrity in the novel, proudly ignoring the social ostracism that he is subjected to because he is a DREYFUSARD. Eventually, however, in his later years, he is reduced to petty snobbery like many of the other characters.

Swann's wife **Odette** is a beautiful woman with social aspirations who finds her entry into the world of society difficult because she was once a courtesan. Their daughter **Gilberte** also plays an important role in the action of the novel.

Swann's Way. English translation of *Du Côté de chez Swann* (1918), published in 1923, Book I of Marcel Proust's REMEMBRANCE OF THINGS PAST and best-known volume of the series. It introduces the author's theories of time and memory and gives an appealing picture of the childhood of the narrator MARCEL in the village of COMBRAY. The title refers to one of the two paths by which Marcel and his parents could reach their home after having been out for a stroll—the path leading past the house of Charles SWANN. See also THE GUERMANTES WAY.

Swap, Solomon. A famous Yankee character of the early American stage. He had a much-fêted but checkered career. James H. HACKETT, the actor, whose reputation was made in such native American rôles as JONATHAN PLOUGHBOY, adapted Colman's play *Who Wants a Guinea,* making the French Cockney, Solomon Gundy, over into the Yankee Solomon Swap by translating freely into New England vernacular. The play was so successful that he took it to England, but there Solomon became Jonathan. Later George Handell Hill appeared as Solomon Swap and when he was restrained by injunction, revived the old name and played as Solomon Gundy. See also SAGO, LOT SAP; SHINGLE, SOLON.

Swaraj. The extreme home rule party in India. The Sanskrit word *swaraj* signifies "political independence."

swarm. See under COVEY.

swastika. A symbol shaped like a Greek cross with the ends of the arms turned at right angles. It is very ancient and has been found as far back as the Age of Bronze. The Sanskrit word *swastika* signifies "well-being." The same symbol is found in various civilizations under a variety of names. As the *Hakenkreuz* it became the symbol of the Nazi party in Germany.

Swedenborg, Emanuel (1688–1772). Famous Swedish scientist and philosopher. He had a seat in the House of Peers. He published philosophical books that influenced Blake and Coleridge, had visions, and engaged in spiritualistic research. He wrote interpretations of Holy Writ and theological works. His followers organized a society known as the New Jerusalem Church.

Swedenborgians. Followers of Emanuel SWEDENBORG, called by themselves "the New Jerusalem Church" (*Rev.* xxi. 2). Their views of salvation, inspiration of Scripture, and a future state, differ widely from those of other Christians, and they believe the Trinity to be centered in the person of Jesus Christ (*Col.* ii. 9).

Swedish Nightingale, the. See NIGHTINGALE.

Sweeney.

tell that to Sweeney! An exclamation of skepticism or disbelief.

Sweeney. In a number of poems by T. S. ELIOT, a satirical figure, symbolic of the sensual, brutal, and materialistic man of the 20th century. Eliot wrote a play entitled *Sweeney Agonistes.*

Sweet, Henry (1845–1912). English philologist, regarded as the founder of modern phonetics.

Sweet Adeline. A well-known sentimental song (1903) by Richard Gerard and Harry Armstrong. It has been sung in all American colleges and in quartet arrangements all over the country, especially by men in their cups.

Sweet Cheat Gone, The. English translation (1930) of *Albertine Disparue* (1926), Book VI of Marcel Proust's REMEMBRANCE OF THINGS PAST. It deals mainly with the intricate analyses of his grief made by the narrator

MARCEL after he learns of the death by accident of his mistress ALBERTINE. The reader is not shown the death itself, and the details and announcement of it are very briefly given.

sweetness and light. A favorite phrase with Matthew ARNOLD. "Culture," he says, "is the passion for sweetness and light, and (what is more) the passion for making them prevail" (Preface to *Literature and Dogma*). The phrase was used by SWIFT (*Battle of the Books,* 1697) in an imaginary fable by Aesop as to the merits of the bee (the Ancients) and the spider (the Moderns). It concludes:

> The difference is that instead of dirt and poison, we have rather chose to fill our hives with honey and wax, thus furnishing mankind with the two noblest of things, which are *sweetness* and *light*.

See also ANCIENTS AND MODERNS.

Sweet Singer of Israel. King DAVID, who wrote some of the *Psalms*.

Sweet Singer of Michigan, The. A collection of poems (1928) by Julia A. Moore, *née* Davis (1878–1920), who was known as "the sweet singer of Michigan." The unconscious humor of her output is superb. Her *Sketch of Lord Byron's Life* opens with the deathless lines:

> "Lord Byron" was an Englishman
> A poet I believe,
> His first works in old England
> Was poorly received.
> Perhaps it was Lord Byron's fault
> And perhaps it was not.
> His life was full of misfortunes,
> Ah, strange was his lot.

Swift, Jonathan (1667–1745). English poet and satirist, born in Dublin, Ireland, of an English father, known for his proud and sensitive temperament, which made him furiously intolerant of the stupidities and vices of mankind, and for his brilliant and biting satire written on the controversial issues of his time. His works include THE BATTLE OF THE BOOKS (1697), written in connection with the literary controversy between the ANCIENTS AND MODERNS; THE TALE OF A TUB (1704); DRAPIER'S LETTERS (1724), an attack on a currency scandal in Ireland; *Gulliver's Travels* (see GULLIVER, LEMUEL; 1726), his most celebrated work; A MODEST PROPOSAL (1729). His *Journal to Stella* (see STELLA) was written in a cryptic language for his private interest but was deciphered and published after a number of years, becoming one of the best-known of his works.

Swift spent an unhappy and humiliating childhood in Ireland among his Irish relatives, and was similarly unhappy and disillusioned during most of his life. He became a member of the clergy of the Church of England, associated with the English Tory leaders and made the acquaintance of POPE, ADDISON, and STEELE, and for a while, during the reign of Queen Anne, held a position of power in England through his pamphlets and essays. In 1713 he was appointed Dean of St. Patrick's Cathedral in Dublin but lost his power on the death of the Queen the following year. His relations with both Stella and VANESSA ended tragically, and during the final years of his life he was insane. Swift, who is regarded as one of the most brilliant minds in English literature, is frequently mentioned throughout James Joyce's FINNEGANS WAKE.

swim.

in the swim. In a favorable position in society of any kind; a racing-man who is "in the swim" is one who mixes with the class from which he can get the best "tips," and similarly with a diplomat, stockbroker, or a society lady. It is an angler's phrase. A lot of fish gathered together is called a *swim,* and when an angler can pitch his hook in such a place he is said to be "in a good swim."

> Cottontree, who knows nearly everybody in the swim of European society . . . informs him that Lucy Annerley is the daughter of Sir Jonas Stevens.—Gunter, *Mr. Potter of Texas,* III, xiv.

to do something—"sink or swim." To do it no matter what happens. In the good old times convicted witches were thrown into the water to "sink or swim." If they sank they were drowned; if they swam it was clear proof they were in league with the Evil One, so it did not much matter, one way or the other.

to swim with the stream. To allow one's actions and principles to be guided solely by the force of public opinion.

Swinburne, Algernon Charles (1837–1909). English poet, associated with the PRE-RAPHAELITE BROTHERHOOD, known for his rebellion against Victorian social conventions and religion, his active sympathies with the movements and leaders of political revolution of his time, and the pagan spirit and amazing musical effects of his poetry. He was an intense admirer of P. B. SHELLEY and Victor HUGO, and was influenced in his own poetry by Greek legend and Roman classic literature, medieval romance, and Elizabethan drama. Among his poetic works are ATALANTA IN CALYDON (1865), a drama in classical Greek form; *The Queen Mother, Rosamund—Two Plays* (1860); *Poems and Ballads: First Series* (1866), lyrics dealing chiefly with sensual love, which caused a sensation on its first publication; *A Song of Italy* (1867) and *Songs before Sunrise* (1876), on the cause of Italian union and independence; *Poems and Ballads: Second Series* (1878); *Songs of the Springtides* (1880) and *Studies in Song* (1880), concerned mostly with the sea; *Tristram of Lyonesse* (1882), a narrative poem on the legend of TRISTAN AND ISEULT; *Poems and Ballads: Third Series* (1889); CHASTELARD (1865), *Bothwell: A Tragedy* (1874), and *Mary Stuart* (1881), a trilogy of verse dramas on MARY QUEEN OF SCOTS; MARINO FALIERO (1885), a tragedy on the same theme used by BYRON; *Astrophel* (1894); *A Tale of Balin* (1896); *A Channel Passage* (1904); *The Duke of Gandia* (1908). *Essays and Studies* (1875), *Miscellanies* (1886), and several sketches in the *Encyclopaedia Britannica* are works of criticism.

In his early career, Swinburne's behavior was eccentric, violent, and dissipated, intended to shock the respectable people of his age. After an illness resulting from his excesses, he was taken into the home of Theodore Watts-Dunton, a literary critic, and stayed there the rest of his life. Some critics believe that Watts-Dunton stifled Swinburne's talent by "reforming" him, curbing his rebellion and forcing him to be docile and conventional. The poet's later work is not considered to be of as high a quality as his earlier. Cf. Max BEERBOHM's classic essay "No. 2, The Pines," describing a visit to the couple.

Among Swinburne's best-known single lyrics are *Hymn to Artemis, Hymn to Prosperpine, The Garden of Proserpine,* and *Hertha* (see NERTHUS). See also NEPHELIDIA.

A study of Swinburne's life and poetry is contained in *Poor Splendid Wings,* by Frances WINWAR, and a biography was written by Edmund GOSSE.

swing.

I don't care if I swing for him! A remark of one very revengefully inclined; implying that the speaker will even go to the length of murdering the enemy, and getting hanged (swung) in consequence.

Swing, Captain. The name assumed by certain persons who, about 1830, sent threatening letters to farmers who employed mechanical means, such as threshing machines, to save labor. "Captain Swing" was an entirely imaginary person—like the famous Mrs. Harris—but three so-called *Lives* of him appeared in 1830 and 1831.

Swing, Raymond Gram (1887–). American journalist and radio news commentator.

swing music, see JAZZ.

Swinnerton, Frank Arthur (1884–). English novelist and critic, whose works, known for their good-humored satire, include *The Merry Heart* (1909); *The Young Idea* (1910); *The Casement* (1911); *George Gissing* (1912), *R. L. Stevenson* (1914), and *The Georgian Scene* (1935), critical studies; *The Chaste Wife* (1916); NOCTURNE (1917), his best-known novel; *September* (1919); *Coquette* (1921); *Young Felix* (1923); *Summer Storm* (1926); *A Brood of Ducklings* (1928); *Sketch of a Sinner* (1929); *The Georgian House* (1932); *Elizabeth* (1934); *Swinnerton: An Autobiography* (1936); *Harvest Comedy* (1937); *The Two Wives* (1939); *The Fortunate Lady* (1941); *Thankless Child* (1942).

Swiss admiral, a. A poseur, because there is no Swiss navy.

Swiss Family Robinson, or Adventures in a Desert Island. A story for young people by J. R. Wyss (*Swiss,* 1813) relating the adventures of a Swiss clergyman, his wife and four sons, who are wrecked on a desert island.

Swithin, St. See under SAINTS.

Swiveller, Mr. Dick. In Dickens' OLD CURIOSITY SHOP, a dirty, smart young man, living in apartments near Drury Lane. His language is extremely flowery, and interlarded with quotations. "What's the odds," says Mr. Swiveller *à propos* of nothing, "so long as the fire of the soul is kindled at the taper of conwiviality and the wing of friendship never moults a feather?" He is forever humming some dismal air. He says *min* for "man," *forgit, jine;* calls wine or spirits "the rosy," sleep "the balmy," and generally shouts in conversation, as if making a speech from the chair of the "Glorious Apollers" of which he is perpetual "grand." Mr. Swiveller looks amiably upon Miss Sophy WACKLES, of Chelsea. QUILP introduces him as clerk to Mr. Samson Brass, solicitor, Bevis Marks. By Quilp's request, he is afterwards turned away and falls sick of a fever, through which he is nursed by the MARCHIONESS, a poor house-drab whom he marries. By his Aunt Rebecca he is left an annuity of £125.

Swope, Herbert Bayard (1882–). American journalist who was awarded the Pulitzer prize for his work as a war-correspondent with the German armies for the New York *World* (1914–1916). He was a correspondent at the Paris Peace Conference, and executive director of the New York *World* through its most brilliant period (1920–1929).

sword.

sword and cloak plays. See under CLOAK.

the sword of Damocles. See DAMOCLES.

the Sword of God. Khaled ibn al Waled (d. 642), the Mohammedan conqueror of Syria, was so called for his prowess at the battle of Muta.

the Sword of Rome. Marcellus Fabius, also called "The Shield of Rome" (time of Hannibal's invasion).

Famous swords. In the days of chivalry, a knight's horse and sword were his most treasured and carefully kept possessions, and his sword as well as his horse had its own name. The old romances, especially those of the Charlemagne and Arthurian cycles, are full of these names. Below we give a list of the more noteworthy.

Angurvadal (Stream of Anguish), Frithiof's sword.
Ar'ondight, the sword of Launcelot of the Lake.
Azoth, the sword of Paracelsus (Browning's *Paracelsus,* Bk. v).
Balisarda, Rogero's sword, made by a sorceress.
Balmung, one of the swords of Siegfried, made by Wieland.
Caliburn, another name of *Excalibur.*
Chrysaor (sword, as good as gold), Artegal's sword (Spenser's *Faërie Queene*).
Colada, the Cid's sword.
Corrougue, Otuel's sword.
Courtain (the Short Sword), one of the swords of Ogier the Dane; *Sauvagine* was the other, and they both took Munifican three years to make.
Curtana, the blunted sword of Edward the Confessor.
Durandan, Durandal, or *Durandana* (the Inflexible), Orlando's sword.
Excalibur, the sword of King Arthur. (*Ex cal*[*ce*]*liber*[*are*], to liberate from the stone.)
Flamberge or *Floberge* (the Flame-Cutter), the name of one of Charlemagne's swords, and also that of Rinaldo's and Maugis or Maligigi's.
Glorious, Oliver's sword, which hacked to pieces the nine swords made by Ansias, Galas, and Munifican.
Gram (Grief), one of the swords of Siegfried.
Greysteel, the sword of Koll the Thrall.
Haute-Claire (Very Bright); both Closamont's and Oliver's swords were so called.
Joyeuse (Joyous), one of Charlemagne's swords; it took Gallas three years to make.
Merveilleuse (the Marvellous), Doolin's sword.
Mimung, the sword that Wittich lent Siegfried.
Morglay (Big Glaive), Sir Bevis's sword.
Nagelring (Nail-Ring), Dietrich's sword.
Philippan. The sword of Antony, one of the triumvirs.
Quern-biter (a Foot-Breadth); both Haco I, and Thoralf Skolinson had a sword so called.
Sanglamore (the Big Bloody Glaive), Braggadochio's sword (Spenser's *Faërie Queene*).
Sauvagine (the Relentless): see *Courtain* above.
Schrit or *Schritt* (? the Lopper), Biterolf's sword.
Tizona (the Poker), King Bucar's sword. See CID.
Tranchera (the Trenchant), Agricane's sword.
Waske, Iring's sword.
Welsung, both Dietlieb and Sintram had a sword so called.
Zuflagar, Ali's sword.

Sword of Castruccio Castracani, The. A poem by Elizabeth Barrett BROWNING. The hero is Victor Emmanuel II, who, as the liberator of Italy, claims the famous sword referred to in the title.

Sybarite. A self-indulgent person; a wanton. The inhabitants of Sybaris, in South Italy, were proverbial for their luxurious living and self-indulgence. A tale is told by SENECA of a Sybarite who complained that he could not rest comfortably at night, and, being asked why, replied that he found a rose-leaf doubled under him, and it hurt him.

Fable has it that the Sybarites taught their horses to dance to the pipe. When the Crotonians marched against Sybaris, they played on their pipes, whereupon all the Sybarite horses began to dance, disorder soon prevailed in the ranks, and the victory was quick and easy.

Sycorax. In Shakespeare's TEMPEST, a foul witch, the mistress of ARIEL the fairy spirit, by whom for some offense he is imprisoned in the rift of a cloven pine tree. After he has been kept there for twelve years, he is liberated by Prospero, the rightful Duke of Milan and father of MIRANDA. Sycorax was the mother of CALIBAN.

syllepsis. A construction or figure of speech in which a word governs two or more others in the same sentence, while it agrees with only one of them; as, "my lady laughs for joy and I for woe." The sense of "laughs" goes with "my lady" and with "I." The form goes only with "my lady."

syllogism. In deductive reasoning, a scheme of logic consisting of a major premise, a minor premise, and a conclusion, as: gold is valuable; this coin is of gold; therefore this coin is valuable.

sylphs. Elemental spirits of air; so named in the Middle Ages by the Rosicrucians and Cabalists, from the Greek *silphe,* some kind of beetle, or a grub that turns into a butterfly. See also SALAMANDER.

Any mortal who has preserved inviolate chastity may enjoy intimate familiarity with these gentle spirits, and deceased virgins were said to become sylphs, "and sport and flutter in the fields of air."

> Whoever, fair and chaste,
> Rejects mankind, is by some sylph embraced.
> Pope, *Rape of the Lock,* i.

Sylvander. In Robert Burns' correspondence with Mrs. Maclehose, the name taken by Burns, while Mrs. Maclehose was called Clarinda. The correspondence was published in 1802, later withdrawn, and republished in 1845.

Sylvester, Joshua (1563–1618). English poet, best known for his translations of the pastorals of Aeneas SILVIUS and of LA SEMAINE of Guillaume du Bartas, which appeared in English as *Divine Weeks and Works* (1605–1607).

Sylvestre. The hero of Pierre Loti's ISLAND FISHERMAN (*Pêcheur d'Islande*).

Sylvette. The heroine of Rostand's ROMANCERS.

Sylvia: or, the May Queen. A long poem (1827) by George Darley.

Sylvia Scarlett. A novel by Compton Mackenzie. See SINISTER STREET.

symbolism. A movement in French literature, at the height of its importance between the years 1870 and 1886. Revolting against realism and influenced by the English Pre-Raphaelites (see PRE-RAPHAELITE BROTHERHOOD) and by the music of WAGNER, it sought to achieve in poetry the effects of music, making use of clustered images and metaphors suggesting or symbolizing the basic idea or emotion of each poem. Forerunners of symbolism were BAUDELAIRE, RIMBAUD, and VERLAINE, all of whom had an important influence on the movement; its leader and theorist was Stéphane MALLARMÉ. Other members of the symbolist school were Gustave KAHN, Henri de REGNIER, Jules LAFORGUE, Tristan CORBIÈRE,

Francis JAMMES, Stuart MERRILL, Francis VIELÉ-GRIFFIN, Rene GHIL, Jean MOREAS, Albert SAMAIN, Georges Rodenbach, Maurice MAETERLINCK, Marcel SCHWOB. Comte Robert de MONTESQUIOU was also associated with the movement, and LAUTRÉAMONT and VILLIERS DE L'ISLE ADAM are sometimes classed as symbolists. George MOORE, Arthur SYMONS, and W. B. YEATS were strongly influenced by symbolism in their early careers, and T. S. ELIOT and James JOYCE are considered to have made adaptations of the symbolist technique in the development of their own individual styles. The movement also had an important influence on the development of IMAGISM, OBJECTIVISM, and SURREALISM. See also IMPRESSIONISM.

Symonds, John Addington (1840–1893). English historian, scholar, and translator, best known for his *History of the Renaissance in Italy* (1875–1886), a study, often consisting of a series of impressionistic essays on separate subjects under the main heading, of the politics, culture, art, and literature of Italy in the 15th and 16th centuries. He also translated the Autobiography of Benvenuto CELLINI (1888) and did other translations, notably of the Greek poets and the Italian Renaissance poets. In addition, he wrote verse and literary criticism.

Symons, Arthur (1865–1945). English poet, critic, editor, and miscellaneous author, strongly influenced in his early career by BAUDELAIRE, VERLAINE, and the French symbolists (see SYMBOLISM), a leader of the symbolist movement in England in the latter 19th century. His works include *Days and Nights* (1889), *Silhouettes* (1892), *London Nights* (1895), and *Poems* (1901), books of poetry; *The Symbolist Movement in Literature* (1899); *Studies in Prose and Verse* (1904); *Studies in Seven Arts* (1906); *The Romantic Movement in English Poetry* (1909); *Color Studies in Paris* (1918); *Charles Baudelaire* (1921); *Dramatis Personae* (1926); *A Study of Thomas Hardy* (1927); *Studies in Strange Souls* (1929); *Confessions* (1930), autobiographical; *A Study of Walter Pater* (1932).

Symons displayed in himself all the neurasthenic characteristics of the French DECADENTS whom he admired. He suffered from a number of spells of amnesia in his early life, and in 1908, while in Italy, he had an attack of temporary madness, described in his *Confessions.*

sympathetic powder. In alchemy it was believed that if this powder were merely applied to blood taken from a wound, it would cure the wound. The title *Powder of Sympathy* has been used for a book by Christopher MORLEY.

Symphonie Fantastique. A musical composition by Hector BERLIOZ (1853), one of the first examples of PROGRAM MUSIC. It purports to tell in music the story of a typical romantic hero (see ROMANTICISM) who has a tragic love affair with an actress, commits murder, and is executed.

Symphony, The. A poem (1875) by Sidney LANIER in which the sounds of the instruments of an orchestra are illustrated in words. Lanier was a musician of considerable talent.

Symphony, the Father of. See under FATHER.

Symplegades. Literally, "striking together." In the story of the Argonauts, two movable rocks at the entrance of the Bosporus into the Black Sea. Phineus advised the Argonauts on how to pass the Symplegades.

Symposium (Gr. *syn,* "together," and *posis,* "drink"). Properly, a drinking together; hence, a convivial meeting for social and intellectual entertainment, and also a discussion upon a subject, and the collected opinions of different authorities printed and published in a review, etc. *The Symposium* is the title given to a dialogue by PLATO, and another by Xenophon, in which the conversation of Socrates and others is recorded.

synaesthesia (Gr. *syn,* "with or together," *aisthesis,* "perception"). Medical term for a tendency to confuse the senses, as, for example, interpreting taste in terms of color or sound in terms of visual shapes. In certain types of poetry of the 19th and 20th centuries, especially of the symbolists and their forerunners and disciples, this is an extremely effective device for the presentation of vivid imagery and the expression of intense and unusual experiences. POE, RIMBAUD, and Hart CRANE were outstanding users of synaesthesia in their poetry, and Rimbaud's *Sonnet of the Vowels,* expressing the sounds of the common vowels in terms of color, is an excellent example of the device.

syndicalism. The doctrine in economics that all the workers in any industry should have a share in the control and in the profits arising from it, and that to compass this end the workers in the different trades should federate and enforce their demands by sympathetic strikes. The word was first used about 1907, and was coined from the French *chambre syndicale* (*syndic,* "a delegate"), "a trade union."

synecdoche. The figure of speech which consists of putting a part for the whole, the whole for the part, a more comprehensive for a less comprehensive term, or *vice versa.* Thus, *a hundred bayonets* (for *a hundred soldiers*); *the town was starving* (for *the people in the town*).

Synge, John Millington (1871–1909). Irish dramatist, associated with the literary movement of the IRISH RENAISSANCE, known for his realistic and poetic comedies and dramas of Irish peasant life, considered among the most distinguished plays of the 20th century. His works include *The Shadow of the Glen* (1903); *Riders to the Sea* (1904); *The Well of the Saints* (1905); THE PLAYBOY OF THE WESTERN WORLD (1907); *The Tinker's Wedding* (1907); *Deirdre of the Sorrows* (1910). *The Aran Islands* (1907) is a description of life in that desolate group of islands.

Synia. In Scandinavian mythology, the portress of VALHALLA.

Synoptic Gospels, the. Those of Matthew, Mark, and Luke; so called because, taken together and apart from that of John, they form a *synopsis* (*Gr.*, "a seeing together"), i.e., a general view, or conspectus, of the life and sayings of Christ; hence, the *Synoptic Problem,* the questions as to the origin and relationship of these three.

Syntax, Doctor. The pious, henpecked clergyman, very simple-minded but of excellent taste and scholarship, created by William Combe (1741–1823) to accompany a series of colored comic illustrations by Rowlandson. His adventures are told in eight-syllabled verse in the *Three Tours of Dr. Syntax* (1812, 1820, and 1821).

syren. See SIREN.

Syrinx. An Arcadian nymph of Greek legend. On being pursued by PAN she took refuge in the river Ladon, and prayed to be changed into a reed. The prayer was granted, and of the reed Pan made his pipes. Hence the name is given to the *Pan-pipe,* or reed mouth-organ, and also to the vocal organ of birds.

T

T.

it fits to a T. Exactly. The allusion is to work that mechanics square with a *T-square,* a ruler with a cross-piece at one end, especially useful in making right angles, and in obtaining perpendiculars and parallel lines.

marked with a T. Identified as a felon. Persons convicted of felony, and admitted to the benefit of clergy, were formerly branded on the thumb with the letter T (*thief*).

Tabard, the. The inn in Southwark from which Chaucer in his CANTERBURY TALES supposes his Pilgrims to start for Canterbury.

Tabarin. *He's a Tabarin*—a merry Andrew. Tabarin was the fellow of Mondor, a famous vendor of quack medicines in the reign of Charles IX.

Tabernacles, Feast of. A Jewish festival lasting eight days and beginning on the 15th Tishri (toward the end of September), kept in remembrance of the sojourn in the wilderness; also, the Feast of Ingathering. It was formerly a time of great rejoicing.

table d'hôte. See À LA CARTE.

taboo (Maori *tapu*). A custom among the South Sea Islanders of prohibiting the use of certain persons, places, animals, things, etc., or the utterance of certain names and words; it signifies that which is banned, interdicted, or "devoted" in a religious sense. Thus, a temple is *taboo* and so is he who violates a temple. Not only so, but everyone and everything connected with what is taboo becomes taboo also; Captain Cook was *taboo* because some of his sailors took rails from a Hawaiian temple to supply themselves with fuel, and, being "devoted," he was slain.

With us, a person who is ostracized, or an action, custom, etc., that is altogether forbidden by society, is said to be *taboo,* or *tabooed.*

Tabouis, Geneviève (1892–). One of the most brilliant of French journalists. A niece of the well-known politician Jules Cambon, she has been a free-lance correspondent, especially in the field of international politics. Author of *They Called Me Cassandra* (1941).

tabula rasa (*Lat.,* "a scraped tablet"). A clean slate—literally and figuratively—on which anything can be written. Thus we say that the mind of a person who has been badly taught must become a *tabula rasa* before he can learn anything properly.

Tacitus, Cornelius (55?–?117 A. D.). Roman politician and historian, whose most ambitious work is a history of the reigns of emperors Galba, Otho, Vitellius, Vespasian, Titus, and Domitian. His *Germania* is a celebrated ethnographical work on the early Germans.

Tad, see DORGAN, THOMAS ALOYSIUS.

Tadpole and Taper, see TAPER AND TADPOLE.

Tadzio. See under DEATH IN VENICE.

Taffy. A Welshman. So called from *David,* a very common name in Wales. Familiarly *Davy,* it becomes in Welsh *Taffid, Taffy.*

Taft, Lorado (1860–1936). Prominent American sculptor who influenced Middle-Western sculpture. His heroic statue of Black Hawk is in Oregon, Illinois. His bust of Frances E. WILLARD is in the American Hall of Fame. He did several memorable fountains in Washington, D.C., and Chicago, notably the Great Lakes group, and the Fountain of Time.

Taft, William Howard (1857–1930). Twenty-seventh president of the United States (1909–1913). His upholding of the Payne-Aldrich Tariff Act in 1909 and his dismissal of Gifford Pinchot did not add to his popularity. He lost the support of Theodore Roosevelt who had backed him for the presidency and did not receive a second term election. Chief justice of the U.S. Supreme Court (1921–1930). Cf. *The Life and Times of William Howard Taft* by Henry F. Pringle (1939). His son **Robert Alphonso Taft** (1889–) is a U.S. senator from Ohio (from 1939).

tag. A well-known children's game.

tag day. A day on which contributions to some particular charity are solicited and tags given to all who contribute.

tag, rag, and bobtail. The *vulgus ignobile;* all sorts and conditions of riffraff. Shakespeare uses *tag* of the rabble—

> Will you hence
> Before the tag return? whose rage doth rend
> Like interrupted waters.
>
> *Coriolanus,* iii, 1.

Rag and *bobtail* were extensions.

> Midsummer's day moreover was the first of Bedford Fair;
> With Bedford Town's tag-rag and bobtail a-browsing there.
>
> Browning, *Ned Brats.*

Tag, der (*Ger.,* "the day"). An expression said to have been common in German military circles before World War I as referring to the day when Germany would strike at her enemies. *Der Tag* was frequently proposed as a toast, to be drunk. In 1914 J. M. BARRIE gave the name to a play.

Tagalog. A member of one of the most numerous races of the Philippines, mainly of central Luzon. Also, the language of the Tagalogs.

Tages. In Etruscan mythology, a mysterious boy with the wisdom of an old man who was ploughed up, or who sprang from, the ground at Tarquinii. He is said to have been the grandson of JUPITER and to have instructed the Etruscans in the arts of augury. The latter wrote down his teaching in twelve books, which were known as "the books of Tages," or "the Acherontian books."

Taggard, Genevieve (1894–). American poet, critic, and editor, resident in Hawaii during much of her childhood and youth. Her books of poetry include *For Eager Lovers* (1922); *Hawaiian Hilltop* (1924); *Words for the Chisel* (1926); *Traveling Standing Still* (1928); *Not Mine to Finish* (1934); *Poems, 1928–1938* (1938), *Long View* (1942). She also wrote *The Life and Mind of Emily Dickinson* (1930), a critical study, and edited the following: *May Days* (1925), an anthology of verse from THE MASSES and *The Liberator; Circumference: Varieties of Metaphysical Verse* (1930); and *Ten Introductions* (1934), a collection of modern verse.

Taggart, Thomas (1856–1929). Well-known American politician who helped to get Woodrow Wilson nominated for the presidency in 1912. He was Senator from Indiana in 1916.

Taglioni. A gifted Italian family of ballet dancers of which the father, **Filippo Taglioni** (1777–1871), was a ballet master and composer, notably of *Les Sylphides.* His daughter, son and granddaughter also performed and composed for the ballet.

Tagore, Sir **Rabindranath.** Written also **Ravindranatha Thakura** (1861–1941). Hindu poet, painter, and author, known for his lyrics and songs on nature, childhood, and Oriental subjects and for his religious mysticism. English translations of his work include *Gitanjali* (1913); *The Crescent Moon* (1913); *One Hundred Poems of Kabir* (1914); *Chitra* (1916), a play; *The Gardener* (1917); *Lectures on Personality* (1917); *Red Oleanders* (1925); *Fireflies* (1928); *The Religion of Man* (1931), on his ideas of God; *Broken Ties, And Other Stories* (1925); *The Child* (1931); *The Golden Boat* (1932); *Collected Poems and Plays* (1936).

Tagore, awarded the Nobel prize for literature in 1913, was active in instituting social and educational reforms in India. In 1915 he was knighted, but in 1919 he resigned the honor in protest against British repressive measures in his native country.

Taillefer (d. 1066). Norman troubador who is said to have ridden ahead of the invading Norman army in 1066 singing of Charlemagne and Roland. He was killed at the Battle of Hastings.

tailor.

nine tailors make a man. An old expression of contempt at the expense of tailors signifying that a tailor is so much more feeble than anyone else that it would take nine of them to make a man of average stature and strength. As a fact, the occupation of a tailor, and the cramped position in which he works, are not conducive to good physique; but *tailor* is probably a facetious transformation of *teller,* a *teller* being a stroke on the bell at a funeral, three being given for a child, six for a woman, and *nine* for a *man.* Cf. *The Nine Tailors,* by Dorothy SAYERS.

the three tailors of Tooley Street. Canning says that three tailors of Tooley Street, Southwark, addressed a petition of grievances to the House of Commons, beginning—"We, the people of England." Hence the phrase is used of any pettifogging coterie that fancies it represents the *vox populi.*

Taine, Hippolyte (1828–1893). French philosopher and literary critic, influenced in part by HEGEL, COMTE, and the English Utilitarians. See UTILITARIANISM. He is known for his emphasis on the rôle of scientific determinism in literature and history, especially as exemplified in hereditary and environmental influences, among the latter of which even climate and atmosphere were included. His methods are considered to be associated with those of NATURALISM. His works include the following: *La Philosophie de l'Art* (1865–1869); *Histoire de la Littérature Anglaise* (1864 and later); *Nouveaux Essais* (1865); *Origines de la France contemporaine* (1875–1894). Taine's two most famous doctrines are the doctrine of the *faculté maîtresse,* or dominant trait, from which the critic hoped to be able to deduce an author's career "geometrically"; and the theory of *race, milieu, et moment,* the three forces respectively signifying biological inheritance, environment, and the configuration of tradition, precedent, and dominant literary trend at the time of an author's appearance.

Taiping, see TAEPING.

Taj Mahal. The famous mausoleum in Agra, India, built by Shah Jahan in memory of his favorite sultana, Mumtaz Mahal. It is of white marble, and is so beautiful that it is called "A Poem in Marble," and "The Marble Queen of Sorrow."

Takeda Izumo (1688–1756). Japanese dramatist. Author of *The Story of the Forty-Seven Ronins* and manager of a famous theater in Osaka.

Talbot, John. "The English Achilles," first Earl of Shrewsbury (1373–1453). He is a character in Shakespeare's I *Henry VI:*

> Is this the Talbot, so much feared abroad,
> That with his name the mothers still their babes?
> Act ii. Sc. 3.

Talbot, Lord Arthur. The hero of Bellini's opera I PURITANI, a Cavalier who wins the love of Elvira, daughter of Lord Walton.

talbotype. See under DAGUERREOTYPE.

talent (from Gr. *talanton,* "a balance"). Ability, aptitude, a "gift" for something or other. The word is borrowed from the parable in *Matt.* xxv, and was originally the name of a weight and piece of money in Assyria, Greece, Rome, etc.

the Ministry of All the Talents. The name ironically given to Grenville's coalition of 1806. It included Fox, Erskine, Fitzwilliam, Ellenborough and Sidmouth. The term has also been applied—ironically—to later coalitions.

Tale of a Tub. A religious satire by Dean SWIFT (1704). Its object is to ridicule the Roman Catholics under the name of Peter, and the Presbyterians under the name of Jack (Calvin). The Church of England is represented by Martin (Luther). Ben JONSON wrote a comedy of this title (produced 1633), and the expression is sometimes used as synonymous with a cock-and-bull story.

Tale of Two Cities, A. A novel of the French Revolution by Charles DICKENS (1859). The two cities are London and Paris. The plot hinges on the physical likeness of Charles Darnay and Sidney Carton, both of whom are in love with Lucie MANETTE. Lucie loves Darnay, and Sydney Carton, who is a dissipated ne'er-do-well, never pleads his devotion, but it leads him to go to the guillotine in place of Darnay for the sake of Lucie's happiness.

Tales from Shakespeare. Prose stories (1807) made from Shakespeare's plays by Charles and Mary LAMB and addressed to children.

Tales of a Grandfather. A set of stories in three series, by Sir Walter SCOTT, told to his small grandson, "Hugh Littlejohn." These tales are supposed to be taken from Scotch chronicles, and embrace the most prominent and graphic incidents of Scotch history: Series I, to the amalgamation of the two crowns in James I; series II, to the union of the two Parliaments in the reign of Queen Anne; series III, to the death of Charles Edward, the Young Pretender.

Tales of a Wayside Inn. Stories in verse by Henry W. LONGFELLOW (1863), supposed to be told at the Red Horse Inn, Sudbury, Massachusetts.

Tales of Hoffman. A light opera by OFFENBACH (1881), based on three tales by the German author, E. T. A. HOFFMAN. The successive acts deal with the love affairs and other adventures of the poet Hoffman which he recalls over the wine in a Nuremberg tavern.

Tales of My Landlord. The general title for certain of Sir Walter SCOTT's novels, tales supposed to be told by the landlord of the Wallace Inn, in the parish of Gandercleuch, "edited and arranged by Jedediah Cleishbotham, schoolmaster and parish clerk" of the same parish, but in reality corrected and arranged by his usher, Peter or Patrick Pattison, who lived to complete five of the novels, but died before the last two were issued. These novels are arranged thus: Series I, *The Black Dwarf* and *Old Mortality;* Series II, *Heart of Midlothian;* Series III, *Bride of Lammermoor* and *Legend of Montrose;* Posthumous, *Count Robert of Paris* and *Castle Dangerous.* Cf. *Black Dwarf,* introduction.

Tales of Soldiers and Civilians. In later editions, **In the Midst of Life.** A book of stories (1891) by Ambrose BIERCE. It contains several of his best stories, as *A Horseman in the Sky* and *An Occurrence at Owl Creek Bridge.*

Tales of the Genii. These tales, by James Ridley (1765), are said to be from the Persian, and are ascribed to Horam, son of Asmar.

Talfourd, Sir **Thomas** (1795–1854). A friend of Charles Lamb, who published Lamb's *Letters* (1837) and *Memorials* (1848). He also wrote the tragedy *Ion* (1835).

Taliesin (*fl.* 550). The earliest and greatest but perhaps legendary Welsh bard. More poetry has been ascribed to him than he can possibly have written. He is mentioned in the *Idylls of the King* by Tennyson and is prominent in *The Misfortunes of Elphin* by Thomas Love Peacock. The architect Frank Lloyd WRIGHT has given the name *Taliesin* to his residence in Wisconsin.

Talifer. A poem in blank verse (1933) by Edwin Arlington Robinson. It is a story of jealousy and potential murder.

talisman (Ar. *tilasman,* from late Gr. *telesma,* "mystery"). A charm or magical figure or word, such as the ABRAXAS, which is cut on metal or stone, under the influence of certain planets; it is supposed to be sympathetic, and to receive an influence from the planets which it communicates to the wearer.

In Arabia, a talisman consisting of a piece of paper, on which are written the names of the Seven Sleepers (see under SEVEN) and their dog, to protect a house from ghosts and demons, is still used. In order to free any place of vermin, a talisman consisting of the figure of the obnoxious animal is made in wax or consecrated metal, in a planetary hour.

> He swore that you had robbed his house,
> And stole his talismanic louse.
>
> Butler, *Hudibras,* pt. iii, 1.

Talisman, The. A novel by Sir Walter SCOTT (1825), relating the adventures of Sir Kenneth, Prince Royal of Scotland, as a knight in disguise in the Holy Land under RICHARD COEUR DE LION. Richard and his noble enemy, SALADIN, are leading characters. Hearing of Richard's illness, Saladin assumes the disguise of the physician Adonbec al Hakim and gives his patient a healing drink of spring water into which he has dipped his "talisman." At the end of the novel, Sir Kenneth marries his kinswoman, Lady Edith Plantagenet.

Talking Bird. A marvelous bird in one of the stories of the *Arabian Nights*. See PARIZADE.

There is a Green Bird of similar nature in Countess d'Aulnoy's fairy tale, *Prince Chery and Fair-Star*. See CHERY.

Talleyrand-Périgord, Charles Maurice de (1754–1838). French statesman, commonly known as **Talleyrand.** Minister of foreign affairs (1797–1807), created grand chamberlain (1804) by Napoleon. He opposed Napoleon's Russian and Spanish policies, and after Napoleon's fall he helped restore the Bourbons. Louis XVIII made him minister of foreign affairs (1814) and prime minister (1815). He represented France at the Congress of Vienna (1815) where his diplomatic tact succeeded in maintaining his country's territorial integrity. He was forced to resign after Napoleon's defeat at Waterloo. In 1830 he became ambassador to Great Britain and helped form the Quadruple Alliance (1834). Cf. his *Mémoires* (1891).

Talma, François Joseph (1763–1826). Famous French actor who scored his first great success in the anti-royalist drama *Charles IX* (1789). Established the Théâtre de la République under the patronage of Desmoulins and Danton. Napoleon and later on Louis XVIII were among his admirers.

Talmage, Thomas de Witt (1832–1902). Brilliant American preacher in the Dutch Reformed Church. Editor of *The Christian Herald* (1892–1902).

Talmud, the (*Heb.*, "instruction"). The body of Jewish civil and religious law not contained in, but largely derived from, the PENTATEUCH. The name was originally applied only to the GEMARA, but it now usually includes also the MISHNA.

When the *Talmud* is spoken of without any qualification, the reference is to the *Babylonian Talmud*, one of the two recensions of the Gemara, the other being the *Palestinian Talmud*, which is of only about a fourth the volume of the *Babylonian*, and is considered by Jews of less authority. The *Babylonian* codification dates from the 5th or 6th century, the *Palestinian* (or *Jerusalem*) from about a century earlier.

Talus. In Greek mythology, a man of brass, made by Hephaestus (Vulcan), the guardian of Crete. Whenever he caught a stranger on the island he made himself redhot and embraced him to death.

He is introduced by Spenser into the FAËRIE QUEENE (Bk. v) as the "yron man" attendant upon Sir Artegal, and representing executive power—"swift as a swallow, and as lion strong."

> His name was Talus made of yron mould
> Immoveable, resistless, without end;
> Who in his hand an yron flale did hould.
> With which he thresht out falshood, and did truths unfould. V, i, 12.

Tamar. In the Old Testament, the daughter-in-law of Judah. In Landor's poem GEBIR, the brother of Gebir. Also, the heroine of the poem *Tamar* by Robinson JEFFERS.

Tamerlane or Tamburlaine (1336?–1405). Names under which the Tartar conqueror Timur, or Timur Lenk, i.e., "Timur the Lame" is immortalized in Elizabethan drama. He had his capital at Samarkand, was ruler of vast territories in central Asia and a great part of India, and died while preparing to invade China. *Tamburlaine the Great* (acted in 1587), a blank verse tragedy, was MARLOWE's first play. In it Tamburlaine is a terrible, bloodthirsty, inhuman villain and the action consists of one atrocity after another. In Rowe's play, *Tamerlane* (1702), the warrior appears as a calm, philosophic prince, out of compliment to William III. There is a poem called *Tamerlane* by Edgar Allan POE.

Taming of the Shrew, The. Shakespeare's play (first printed in the 1623 Folio) was a rewriting of an anonymous comedy printed in 1594 with the title *A pleasaunt conceited Historie called The Taming of a Shrew. As it hath beene sundry times acted by the right honourable the Earle of Pembroke his servants.* The "Shrew" is Katharina, a maiden of such violent whims and tempers that it seems unlikely she will find a husband. Her father, Baptista, refuses to allow her lovable younger sister Bianca to marry any of her numerous suitors until Katharina is off his hands. Finally Petruchio appears, marries Katharina in short order, and by his own abrupt highhandedness "tames" her to such good effect that he wins a bet with two other men on a test of their wives' obedience. Meantime Lucentio, through the ruse of becoming Bianca's tutor while his servant Tranio assumes his name and clothes and presses his suit with her father, has succeeded in winning her hand. This entire play is enacted for the benefit of Christopher Sly, a drunken tinker who, in the induction, is shown in a nobleman's castle where he is fooled into thinking he is a nobleman himself.

Tam Lin. A figure in a famous old ballad in which he is taken prisoner by the queen of the fairies.

Tammany Hall. The headquarters (formerly on Union Square) of the controlling organization of the Democratic Party in New York City and State; hence, the party itself, and, as this has been the political target for so-called party abuses, the term "Tammany" is figuratively employed for municipal malpractice.

Tammany was the name of a 17th century Delaware chief, and the patriotic, anti-British leagues of pre-Revolutionary days adopted the name "St. Tammany" to ridicule the titles of loyalist organizations—Societies of St. George, St. Andrew, and so on. After the Revolution these leagues became anti-aristocratic clubs, but all soon died a natural death except "Tammany Society, No. 1," which was that of New York. This flourished, and was converted into a political machine by Aaron BURR in his conflict with Alexander HAMILTON (ca. 1798), and in 1800 played a prominent part in the election of JEFFERSON to the presidency.

Tamora. Queen of the Goths, in love with Aaron the Moor in the play TITUS ANDRONICUS, attributed to Shakespeare.

Tam O'Shanter. A narrative poem by Robert BURNS (1791). It was founded on a legend that no sort of bogie could pass the middle of a running stream. Tam sees a hellish legion dancing in Alloway Kirk (near Ayr), and being excited cries out, "Weel done, Cutty Sark!" Immediately the lights are extinguished, and Tam rides for his life to reach the river Doon. He has himself passed the mid-stream, but his horse's tail has not reached that magic line, so Cutty Sark catches hold of it and pulls it off.

> Think, ye may buy the joys owre dear—
> Remember Tam-o'-Shanter's mare.

Tampico. A Mexican seaport on the Gulf. On April 10, 1914 some sailors from an American warship were arrested here. The incident resulted, shortly after that, in the Americans taking Vera Cruz.

Tancred (d. 1112). One of the chief heroes of the First Crusade, and a leading character in Tasso's JERUSALEM DELIVERED. He was the son of Eudes (Otho) and Emma (sister of Robert Guiscard); Boemond or Bohemond was his cousin. In the epic he is the greatest of all the Christian warriors except RINALDO, and shows a generous contempt of danger. His one fault is "woman's love," and that woman Clorinda, a pagan (Bk. i), whom he unwittingly slays in a night attack, and whose death he laments with great lamentation (Bk. xii). Being wounded, he is nursed by Erminia, who is in love with him (Bk. xix).

There is an opera *Tancred* by Rossini (1813).

Tancred, or the New Crusade. A novel by DISRAELI (1847). Tancred is a young and high-born visionary who leaves the social circles of 19th century London to travel in the East. In the Holy Land he experiences the "great Asian mystery" which is to work regeneration for the West.

Taney, Roger Brooke (1777–1864). U.S. secretary of the treasury (1833–1834). Became chief justice of the Supreme Court following John MARSHALL. He is remembered for his association with the DRED SCOTT DECISION (1857).

T'ang. The name of an eminent Chinese dynasty whose rule (618 A. D.–907 A. D.) coincides with the Age of the Arts in China.

Tanglewood Tales. A book of tales retold for children from classic mythology by Nathaniel HAWTHORNE (1853). It forms a companion volume to his *Wonder-Book*.

tank. The heavily armored military motor fort, running on "caterpillar" wheels, enclosed, and with room in the interior for quick-firing guns and several men, was so called by the U.S. War Office before it made its first appearance to prevent information as to its real nature leaking out to the enemy. Telegrams, etc., with inquiries about *tanks* would cause no suspicion if they fell into enemy hands. Tanks were invented during World War I, and were first used in the British attack on the German lines at Flers, September 15, 1916.

tanka. The classic form of Japanese poetry, fixed centuries ago in the standard arrangement of five lines (with 5, 7, 5, 7, 7 syllables). It reduces, through the strict limits of its form, all poetic raw material to the concentrated essence of one static event, image, mood, etc. An example by Saigo Hoshi reads:

> Ima zo shiru
> omoi-ide-yo to
> chigirishi wa
> wasuremu tote no
> nasake narikeri.

> Now indeed I know
> That when we said, "remember,"
> And we swore it so,
> It was in "we will forget"
> That our thoughts most truly met.

See also HOKKU.

Tanner, Henry Ossawa (1859–1937). American Negro painter. One of his paintings is in the Metropolitan Museum of Art in New York City.

Tanner, Jack or John. The hero of Shaw's comedy MAN AND SUPERMAN, played by Robert LORAINE and Maurice EVANS in the United States.

Tanner of Tamworth, The. Hero of a ballad in Percy's *Reliques,* the man who mistakes Edward IV for a highwayman. After some little altercation, they change horses, the King giving his hunter for the tanner's cob, worth about four shillings. As soon as the tanner mounts the King's horse, it throws him, and the tanner gladly pays down a sum of money to get his old cob back again. King Edward now blows his hunting-horn, and the courtiers gather round him. "I *hope* [i.e., *ex-*

pect] I shall be hanged for this," cries the tanner, but the King gives him the manor of Plumpton Park, with 300 marks a year.

Tannhäuser. A lyrical poet, or Minnesinger, of Germany, who flourished in the second half of the 13th century. He led a wandering life, and is said even to have visited the Far East; this fact, together with his *Buszlied* (*Song of Repentance*), and the general character of his poems, probably gave rise to a legend about him which first appeared in a 16th century German ballad. This relates how he spends a voluptuous year wth Venus, in the Venusberg, a magic land reached through a subterranean cave. At last he obtains leave to visit the upper world, and goes to Pope Urban for absolution. "No," says His Holiness, "you can no more hope for mercy than this dry staff can be expected to bud again." Tannhäuser departs in despair, but on the third day the papal staff bursts into blossom. The Pope sends in every direction for Tannhäuser, but the knight is nowhere to be found, for, mercy having been refused, he has returned to end his days in the arms of Venus.

In Wagner's opera *Tannhäuser* (1845), the hero returns from the Venusberg to the court of the Landgrave of Thuringia, where the pure and beautiful Elizabeth, the Landgrave's niece, has remained true to him. At a great singing tourney his friend Wolfram von Eschenbach sings of spiritual love, but Tannhäuser, who has promised Venus to sing her praises, bursts out in a wild, unholy song which brings upon him the condemnation of the entire court. Elizabeth awaits the result of his repentant pilgrimage, but when he is not among the returning pilgrims, she dies. His arrival and the news of the budding staff come too late.

Tanqueray, Paula, Aubrey and **Ellean.** The leading characters in Pinero's Second Mrs. Tanqueray.

Tantalus. In Greek mythology, the son of Zeus and Pluto (daughter of Himantes). He was a Lydian king, highly honored and prosperous, but, because he divulged to mortals the secrets of the gods, he was plunged up to the chin in a river of Hades, a tree hung with clusters of fruit being just above his head. As every time he tried to drink the waters receded from him, and as the fruit was just out of reach, he suffered agony from thirst, hunger, and unfulfilled anticipation.

Hence our verb, *to tantalize,* to excite a hope and disappoint it; and hence the name *tantalus* applied to a lock-up spirit chest in which the bottles are quite visible but quite un-get-at-able without the key.

Tantamount, Lord Edward. In Aldous Huxley's Point Counter Point, a celebrated biologist, innocent and child-like in character, interested only in the experiments carried on in his laboratory and oblivious to all else that is happening in his family and in the world outside.

Hilda Tantamount, Lord Edward's wife, is a beautiful woman, fond of entertaining celebrities at her home, bored by her husband's preoccupation with science. She is the mistress of John Bidlake.

Lucy Tantamount, the daughter of Hilda and Lord Edward, is the typical heroine of society novels of the 1920's—beautiful, independent, faithless, promiscuous in morals, and fatally attractive to the men she meets. Walter Bidlake falls in love with her, neglecting his mistress Marjorie Carling to seek her favor.

Tante. A novel by Anne Douglas Sedgwick (1911). *Tante* is the great pianist, Madame Okraska. The novel is the story of the love affair and marriage of Tante's ward Karen Woodruff and Gregory Jardin, a wealthy young lawyer. Tante's jealousy and thirst for admiration finally bring disillusionment to her hitherto adoring young charge.

Tantivy Towers. A book of light verse by A. P. Herbert. The word *tantivy* means "rapid gallop."

tantony pig. The smallest pig of a litter, which, according to the old proverb, will follow its owner anywhere; so called in honor of St. Anthony, who was the patron saint of swineherds and is frequently represented with a little pig at his side.

Tantony is also applied to a small church bell—or to any hand-bell—for there is usually a bell round the neck of St. Anthony's pig or attached to the Tau-cross he carries. See *St. Antony* under saints.

Tantras, The. Sanskrit religious writings, forming the Bible of the Shaktas, a Hindu sect, the adherents of which worship the divine power in its female aspect. The Tantras consist of magical formulas for the most part in the form of dialogues between Siva and his wife, and treat of the creation and ultimate destruction of the world, divine worship, the attainment of superhuman power, and final union with the Supreme Spirit. They are of comparatively recent date (6th or 7th century A. D.). *Tantra* is Sanskrit for thread, or warp, and hence is used of groundwork, order, or doctrine of religion.

Taoism. One of the three great religious systems of China, Confucianism and Buddhism being the others, founded by the philosopher Lao-tsze (ca. 604–523 B. C.), and based on the *Tao Tê Ching* (*Book of Reason and Virtue*), reputed to be by him.

Taou Yen. In Hergesheimer's Java Head, Gerrit Ammidon's Chinese wife.

Taper and Tadpole. Political tools used by powerful interests to carry out petty, underhanded schemes; so called from two characters introduced by Disraeli in his political novels CONINGSBY and SYBIL.

tapis, on the. On the carpet, under consideration, now being ventilated; an English-French phrase, referring to the *tapis* or cloth with which the table of the council chamber is covered, and on which are laid the motions before the House.

Tapley, Mark. Martin's servant and companion in Dickens' MARTIN CHUZZLEWIT, often taken as the type of one who is invariably cheerful. His ambition is "to come out jolly" under the most unfavorable circumstances. Greatly attached to Martin Chuzzlewit, he leaves his comfortable situation at the Blue Dragon to accompany him to America, and in "Eden" has ample opportunities of "being jolly" so far as wretchedness can make him so. On his return to England he marries Mrs. Lupin, and thus becomes landlord of the Blue Dragon.

Tappertit, Sim or **Simon.** In Dickens' BARNABY RUDGE, the apprentice of Gabriel VARDEN, locksmith. An old-fashioned, thin-faced, sleek-haired, sharp-nosed, small-eyed little fellow is Mr. Sim Tappertit, about five feet high, but thoroughly convinced in his own mind that he is both good-looking and above the middle size—in fact, rather tall than otherwise. Mr. Tappertit has an ambitious soul and admires his master's daughter, Dolly, but is forced to see his rival, Joe Willet, successful. He finally marries the widow of a rag-and-bone collector.

Taprobane. An old name for the island of Ceylon. In the *Adventures of Sir John Maundeville* it is referred to as containing golden hills.

tar or **Jack Tar.** A sailor; probably an abbreviation of *tarpaulin,* of which sailors' caps and overalls were made. Tarpaulins are tarred cloths, and are commonly used on board ship to keep articles from the sea-spray, etc.

Tara, the Hill of. In Meath, Ireland. Here the kings, the clergy, the princes, and the bards used to assemble in a large hall, to consult on matters of public importance.

> The harp that once thro' Tara's halls
> The soul of music shed,
> Now hangs as mute on Tara's walls
> As if that soul were fled.
> Moore, *Irish Melodies.*

Tara's Psaltery or *Psalter of Tara.* The great national register or chronicles of Ireland, read to the assembled princes when they met in Tara's Hall in public conference.

Tarakee. A hero of Brahminical legend and miracle of ascetic devotion. He is fabled to have lived 1100 years, and spent each century in some astounding mortification.

tarantula. A large and hairy venomous spider (so called from *Taranto,* Lat. *Tarentum,* a town in Apulia, Italy, where they abound), whose bite was formerly supposed to be the cause of the dancing mania hence known as *tarantism.* This was an hysterical disease, common, epidemically, in southern Europe from the 15th to the 17th centuries. From the same insect the *tarantella* gets its name. This is a very quick Neapolitan dance (or its music) for one couple, and is said to have been based on the gyrations practiced by those whom the tarantula had poisoned.

Taras Bulba. A historical novel by GOGOL (1839), dealing with the career of Taras Bulba, a violent 15th century Cossack. He kills one of his sons, Andrii, who has turned traitor for the sake of a sweetheart; another, Ostap, is captured and tortured to death before his eyes. He now launches forth on a terrible career of revenge with the cry "A mass for Ostap" accompanying his mad depredations and slaughters. At last he is captured and dies.

Tar Baby. In one of the best-known stories in UNCLE REMUS by Joel Chandler HARRIS, a tar doll set up by the roadside whose unresponsiveness irritates Brer Rabbit to such a pitch that he strikes him, first with one paw, then with another, until he himself is stuck tight.

Tarbell, Edmund C. (1862–1938). American impressionistic painter.

Tarbell, Ida M. (1857–1944). American journalist, chiefly known for her exposés in *McClure's Magazine* (1894–1906). Her *History of the Standard Oil Company* is one of the best accounts of a monopoly. She was associate editor of the *American Magazine* (1906–1915). She wrote a life of Napoleon, a life of Abraham Lincoln and several other books on Lincoln; her autobiography, *All in the Day's Work,* was published in 1939.

Tarde, Gabriel (1843–1904). French philosopher and criminologist. *The Laws of Imitation* (1903); *Underground Man* (1905); etc.

Tardieu, André (1876–1945). French high commissioner in the U.S. (1917–1918). At the Paris Peace Conference (1918–1919) he supported the attitude of CLEMENCEAU. He is credited with having written a large part of the Peace Treaty. Premier of France (1929–1930; 1932).

Tarheels. Inhabitants of South Carolina, so called from the tar produced there. See also under STATES.

Tarkington, Newton Booth (1869–1946). American novelist and short-story writer, known for his popular books dealing with middle-class American life, chiefly in the Middle West, in a semi-realistic vein. Among his works are MONSIEUR BEAUCAIRE (1900), an historical romance; THE GENTLEMAN FROM INDIANA (1899); THE CONQUEST OF CANAAN (1905); THE MAN FROM HOME (1908), a play; *The Flirt* (1913); PENROD (1914), *Penrod and Sam* (1916), *Penrod Jashber* (1929), and *Little Orvie* (1934), humorous books about small boys; SEVENTEEN (1916) and *Ramsey Milholland* (1919), humorous books about adolescents; THE TURMOIL (1915), THE MAGNIFICENT AMBERSONS (1918), and *The Midlander* (1923), published as a trilogy entitled *Growth* (1927); CLARENCE (1919), a comedy; ALICE ADAMS (1921); *The Plutocrat* (1927); *The World Does Move* (1928), an autobiography; *Claire Ambler* (1928); *Mirthful Haven* (1931); *Mary's Neck* (1932); *Wanton Mally* (1932); *Presenting Lily Mars* (1933); *The Lorenzo Bunch* (1936); *The Fighting Littles* (1941); *The Heritage of Hatcher Ide* (1941). Both *The Magnificent Ambersons* and *Alice Adams* were winners of the Pulitzer prize.

In 1943 he received, as the first man, the Howells Medal of the American Academy of Arts and Letters for "general distinction in the field of literature."

Tarlton, Richard (?–1588). Popular Elizabethan comedian, a favorite of Queen Elizabeth, and praised by contemporary authors.

Tarpa, Spurius Metius. A famous critic of the Augustan age. He sat in the temple of Apollo with four colleagues to judge the merit of theatrical pieces before they were produced in public.

Tarpaulin Muster, A. A collection of short stories of the sea (1907) by John MASEFIELD. The title comes from a phrase used of the pooling of funds by sailors, which was originally done by throwing money into a tarpaulin.

Tarpeian Rock. An ancient rock or peak (now no longer in existence) of the Capitoline Hill, Rome; so called from Tarpeia, a vestal virgin, the daughter of Spurius Tarpeius, governor of the citadel, who, according to the legend, agreed to open the gates to the Sabines if they would give her "what they wore on their arms" (meaning their bracelets). The Sabines, "keeping their promise to the ear," crushed her to death with their shields, and her body was hurled from the "Tarpeian Rock." Subsequently, traitors were cast down this rock and so killed.

Tarquin. (1) The family name of a legendary line of early Roman kings. Tarquinius Priscus, the fifth king of Rome, is dated 617–578 B.C. His son, Tarquinius Superbus, was the seventh (and last) king of Rome, and it was his son, Tarquinius Sextus, who committed the rape on Lucrece, in revenge for which the Tarquins were expelled from Rome and a Republic established. For the use of this legend in drama see LUCRETIA.

(2) The name of a "recreant knight" figuring in the Arthurian cycle. A ballad given in Percy's *Reliques* tells how Sir LAUNCELOT meets a lady who asks him to deliver certain Knights of the Round Table from Tarquin's power. Coming to a river, he sees a copper basin suspended from a tree, and strikes it so hard that it breaks. This brings out Tarquin, and a furious encounter takes place in which the latter is slain. Sir Launcelot liberates "threescore knights and four, all of the Table Round." See also YVAIN.

Tarsus. A town in Turkey, the birthplace of St. Paul who was called Saul of Tarsus before his conversion. It is believed to have been founded by Sardanapalus. Alexander the Great conquered it and under Pompey it was part of a Roman province.

Tartar, to catch a. See under CATCH.

Tartarin. A famous comic character created by Alphonse DAUDET, the hero of his *Aventures prodigeuses de Tartarin de Tarascon* (1872) and *Tartarin sur les Alpes* (1885). This typical French southerner, a prodigious braggart, bubbling over with good spirits and with exaggerated tales of his prowess as a sportsman, is the hero of his native Tarascon. Finally, however, even Tarascon is eager for proof; so he sets out on adventure bent and at Algiers shoots an old, tame, blind lion that becomes so fierce and dreadful in the telling of the tale as to insure Tartarin's reputation forever more.

Tartarus. The infernal regions of classical mythology, used as equivalent to HADES by later writers, but by HOMER placed as far beneath Hades as Hades is beneath the earth. It was here that ZEUS confined the TITANS. See also *Hell*.

Tartini, Giuseppe (1692–1770). Italian violinist and composer of many concertos and sonatas. His *Devil's Trill* is a favorite showpiece.

Tartuffe. The chief character and title of a comedy by MOLIÈRE (1664). Tartuffe is a religious hypocrite and impostor, who uses "religion" as the means of gaining money, covering deceit, and promoting self-indulgence. He is taken up by one ORGON, a man of property, who promises him his daughter in marriage, but when his character is exposed, he is not only turned out of the house but is lodged in jail for felony. It is thought that *Tartuffe* is a caricature of Père la Chaise, the confessor of Louis XIV, who was very fond of truffles (Fr. *tartuffes*), and that this suggested the name to the dramatist. Isaac BICKERSTAFF adapted Molière's comedy to the English stage, under the title of *The Hypocrite* (1768). Tartuffe he calls "Dr. Cantwell," and Orgon "Sir John Lambert."

Tarzan. Hero of an extremely popular series of adventure stories by Edgar Rice BURROUGHS in the early 20th century, later dramatized in American motion pictures and featured in a syndicated comic-strip serial. Tarzan is a white boy who has been raised among the animals in the African jungle and is able to understand and control them as though he were one of them. He possesses great physical strength and skill, and is able to outwit countless enemies in his innumerable adventures. He is usually played in motion pictures by Johnny Weissmuller.

Task, The. Chief poem by William COWPER (1785), its purpose being, according to a statement by the author himself, "to discountenance the modern enthusiasm after a London life, and to recommend rural ease and leisure as friendly to the cause of piety and virtue." In its six books (*The Sofa, The Time-Piece, The Garden,* etc.) it deals with a number of subjects in which the author was interested, especially nature, rural life, animals, simple, hard-working people, and social reform. In its recollections of the inspiring and healing qualities of nature, it is considered a forerunner of some of the poetry of William WORDSWORTH. The title refers to the origin of the poem in the suggestion of Lady AUSTEN that Cowper write a poem concerning her parlor sofa. The author complied and, as he himself says, "having much leisure, connected another subject with it; and, pursuing the train of thought to which my situation and turn of mind led me, brought forth at length, instead of the trifle which I at first intended, a serious affair—a volume!"

Tasker Jevons. The English title of May Sinclair's novel THE BELFRY and the name of its hero.

Tasman, Abel J. (1602–1659). Dutch navigator who went to the South Seas and discovered what he called Van Diemen's Land after the governor of the Dutch East Indies. It is the modern Tasmania.

Tasso, Torquato (1544–1595). Italian poet, author of JERUSALEM DELIVERED. After the publication of his great epic, Tasso lived in the court of Ferrara and, according to legend, conceived a violent passion for Leonora, one of the Duke's sisters, but fled in 1577 to Naples. After an absence of two years, he returned to his patron, the Duke of Ferrara. For seven years (1579–1586), he was imprisoned as a lunatic. He is the hero of Goethe's drama *Tasso* (1789) and of Byron's poem *The Lament of Tasso* (1817).

Tate, Allen John Orley (1899–). American poet, novelist, and critic, associated with the AGRARIANS and the FUGITIVES, known for the satire and complexity of his poetry, influenced by the English METAPHYSICAL POETS, and for the emphasis placed in his criticism on rationalism, tradition, and the scientific approach to the interpretation of poetry and poetic imagery. Much of his subject-matter in general is concerned with the South and the sectional interests of the South. His works include biographies of Stonewall Jackson (1928) and Jefferson Davis (1929); *Mr. Pope, And Other Poems* (1928); *Three Poems* (1930); *Poems: 1928–1931* (1932); *The Mediterranean, And Other Poems* (1936); *Selected Poems* (1937); contributions to *I'll Take My Stand* (1930), *The Critique of Humanism* (1930), and *Who Owns America?* (1936), all symposia; *Reactionary Essays on Poetry and Ideas* (1936) and *Reason in Madness* (1941), criticism; *The Fathers* (1938), a novel. *Ode to the Confederate Dead* is his best-known poem.

Tate, Sir Henry (1819–1899). English philanthropist. He built the Tate Gallery in London as a gallery for modern paintings (opened in 1897). Today it is the National Gallery of British Art.

Tate, Nahum (1652–1715). British playwright and poet who was commissioned by Dryden to write a second part of *Absalom and Achitophel* (1682). He was poet laureate (1692) and helped Nicholas Brady write the *New Version of the Psalms of David* in metrical form (1696). His hymn, *While Shepherds Watched Their Flocks by Night,* is well known. Pope satirized him in the *Dunciad.*

Tatler, The. A famous series of essays started by Richard STEELE in 1709, and continued to 1711. ADDISON was also a contributor. *The Tatler* was succeeded by THE SPECTATOR.

Tatlock, John Strong Perry (1876–1948). Well-known Chaucer scholar who compiled with Arthur G. Kennedy a *Concordance to Chaucer* (1927). He taught at the University of California.

Tattersall, Richard (1724–1795). Famous English horseman. Tattersall's horse-auction headquarters in London (1766) are known all over the world. The word *tattersall* is used in various languages as a synonym of "horse market."

Tattle. In Congreve's comedy LOVE FOR LOVE, a man who ruins characters by innuendo, and so denies a scandal as to confirm it. He is a mixture of "lying, foppery, vanity, cowardice, brag, licentiousness, and ugliness, but a professed beau" (Act i.). Tattle is entrapped into marriage with Mrs. Frail.

Tattycoram. The name of a foundling in *Little Dorrit* by Charles Dickens.

Tauchnitz, Christian Bernhard (1816–1895). German publisher, member of a family of printers and publishers. Especially known for the "Tauchnitz Edition" (started 1841) of a *Collection of British and American Authors.* The Tauchnitz volumes were English-language editions for sale on the Continent, not legally to be taken into American or British territory.

Taurus (*Lat.*, "the bull"). The second zodiacal constellation, and the second sign of the Zodiac, which the sun enters about April 21.

Taussig, Frank William (1859–1940). American economist and educator at Harvard (1882–1935). Author of a number of books on tariff, trade, etc. Chairman of the U.S. Tariff Commission (1917–1919).

Tawiskara. See ISOKEHA.

Tawney, Richard Henry (1880–). English Labourite economist. Author of *The Acquisitive Society* (1920); *The British Labour Movement* (1925); *Religion and the Rise of Capitalism* (1926); etc.

Taylor, Bayard (1825–1878). American poet, prose-writer, and journalist, known for his popular essays, lectures, and sentimental poems of romance and adventure; an exponent of the GENTEEL TRADITION. Among his accounts of travel and adventure are *Views Afoot* (1846); *El Dorado* (1850); *A Journey to Central Africa* (1854); *The Lands of the Saracen* (1855); *A Visit to India, China, and Japan, in the Year 1853* (1855); *Northern Travel* (1858); *Travels in Greece and Russia* (1859); *At Home and Abroad* (1860). His verse includes *Ximena* (1844); *Rhymes of Travel, Ballads and Poems* (1849); *A Book of Romances, Lyrics, and Songs* (1852); *Poems of the Orient* (1855); *Lars: A Pastoral of Norway* (1863); *Home Pastorals, Ballads, and Lyrics* (1875); *The Echo Club, And Other Literary Diversions* (1876); *Poetical Works* (1880). He also wrote such fiction as: *Hannah Thurston* (1863); *John Godfrey's Fortunes* (1864); *The Story of Kennett* (1866); *Joseph and His Friend* (1870).

During his early career Taylor traveled widely in Europe, Asia, and Africa, writing of his journeys for American newspapers and making lecture tours. His best work is considered to be his translation of Goethe's FAUST (1870–1871), as a result of which in 1878 he was appointed minister to Germany, where he died soon after his arrival.

Taylor, Bert Leston (1866–1921). Known as **B.L.T.** American columnist, associated for years with the Chicago *Tribune.*

Taylor, Joseph Deems (1885–). American composer and music commentator for the Columbia Broadcasting System. He has edited *A Treasury of Gilbert and Sullivan* and composed the operas *The King's Henchman* (libretto by Edna St. Vincent MILLAY; 1927) and *Peter Ibbetson* (after DU MAURIER; 1931); besides tone-poems and songs. Member, National Institute of Arts and Letters.

Taylor, Frank Walter (1874–1921). American illustrator and painter.

Taylor, Henry Osborn (1856–1941). American writer on the ancient world. *The Mediaeval Mind* (2 vols.; 1911); etc.

Taylor, Jeremy (1613–1667). English clergyman and author. His best known works are *Holy Living* and *Holy Dying* (1650–1651) and his collections of sermons.

Taylor, John (1580–1653). English author, known as "the Water Poet" because he worked for a number of years as a collector of revenue on wines on ships traversing the Thames, and was also at another time a sculler on the river. He wrote a vast number of pamphlets and verses on a variety of subjects; the titles of some of these include *A Kicksey-Winsey, Or A Lerry Come-Twang; A Very Merry Wherry-Ferry Voyage; The Virtue of a Jail, and Necessity of Hanging.* Taylor was known for his eccentric exploits, one of which was sailing on the Thames in a boat made of brown paper.

Taylor, John (1808–1887). Leader in the Mormon Church who took the side of Brigham Young and accompanied him to Utah. After Young's death (1877) he became acting head of the church. Accepted polygamy and was forced to hide from arrest by the government (1884).

Taylor, Laurette (1887–1947). Distinguished American actress who made her original success in *Peg O' My Heart* (1912). See also WILLIAMS, TENNESSEE.

Taylor, Meadows (1808–1876). English administrator in India, who wrote, among other novels on life and manners in India, *Confessions of a Thug* (1839).

Taylor, Norman (1883–). American writer on botany and curator at the Brooklyn Botanic Garden (1911–1929).

Taylor, Mrs. **Rachel Annand** (1876–). Scottish romantic poet. *The Hours of Fiammetta: a Sonnet Sequence* (1909) and *The End of Fiammetta* (1923) are her most outstanding books of poems. *Leonardo the Florentine* (1927) is a poetically-written life of Leonardo da Vinci.

Taylor, Thomas (1758–1835). English student of Greek philosophy. He did a number of translations but was without formal scholarly education. Called "Taylor the Platonist."

Taylor, Tom (1817–1880). Prolific English dramatist. One of his more than a hundred plays, *Our American Cousin* (1858), was a success in America. In it, E. A. Sothern created the character of Lord Dundreary.

Taylor, William (1765–1836). English man of letters, known as William Taylor of Norwich, whose chief function it was to bring to English readers the poetry and drama of Germany in translation. One of his most valuable works is *Historic Survey of German Poetry* (3 vols.; 1828–1830).

Taylor, Zachary (1784–1850). Twelfth president of the United States (1849–July 9, 1850), nicknamed "Old Rough-and-Ready." He was famous as an Indian fighter, and, as commander of the army of the Rio Grande, ended the war in northern Mexico by his important victory over Santa Anna at Buena Vista (February, 1847).

Tchaikovsky, Pëtr Ilich (1840–1893). Famous Russian composer among whose best-known works are the *Fifth Symphony in E Minor;* the *Fourth Symphony in F Minor;* various symphonic poems, as *Francesca da Rimini;* overtures; operas; ballet music; etc. His *Symphonie Pathétique* (sixth) and his piano and violin concertos are extremely popular. See also Nadezhda von MECK.

Tchekhov, see CHEKHOV.

Teach, Edward, known as **Blackbeard** (died 1718). English pirate who cruised the Spanish Main, having originally been a privateer during the War of Spanish Succession. Famous in pirate stories. Killed in action.

Teague. (1). A contemptuous name for an Irishman (from the Irish personal name), rarely used nowadays but common in the 17th and 18th centuries.

(2). Captain Farrago's "man" in Brackenridge's early American novel, MODERN CHIVALRY.

Teapot Dome. The name of an oil field in connection with which several men in official position in the United States were involved in graft proceedings in 1924.

Tearsheet, Doll. In Shakespeare's II *Henry IV,* a common courtesan.

Teasdale, Sara (1884–1933). American lyric poet, known for the mood-evoking quality of her poetry, which is included in the following books: *Sonnets to Duse* (1907); *Helen of Troy* (1911); *Rivers to the Sea* (1915); *Love Songs* (1917); *Flame and Shadow* (1920); *Dark of the Moon* (1926); *Strange Victory* (1933). She committed suicide in her home in New York.

Teazle, Sir Peter. In Sheridan's SCHOOL FOR SCANDAL a man who, in old age, marries a country girl who is lively and fond of pleasure. Sir Peter is forever nagging at her for her inferior birth and rustic ways, but secretly loves her and admires her *naïveté.* He says to Rowley, "I am the sweetest-tempered man alive, and hate a teasing temper, and so I tell her ladyship a hundred times a day."

Lady Teazle. The heroine of *A School for Scandal,* a lively, innocent, country maiden who marries Sir Peter, old enough to be her grandfather. Planted in London in the whirl of the season, she enters a liaison with Joseph Surface, but, being saved from disgrace, repents and reforms.

Tecumseh (1768?–1813). American Shawnee Indian chief. He was a partner of the British in the War of 1812. His brother, known as "the Prophet," lost his prestige after the battle of Tippecanoe when he was defeated by William Henry Harrison (1811).

Tedder, Sir **Arthur William** (1890–). British air chief marshal, whose efforts helped to drive General Rommel out of Africa. He was allied air commander in chief in the Mediterranean, and air adviser to General EISENHOWER.

Teddy bear. A toy bear, named for President "Teddy" Roosevelt because of his love of big game hunting.

Tegnér, Esaias (1783–1846). Leading Swedish poet. Among his works are *Axel* (1822) and *Frithjofs Saga* (1825). Cf. Longfellow's English hexameter version of *The Children of the Lord's Supper.*

Teian Muse, the. See under MUSE.

Teilo, St. See under SAINTS.

Teixeira de Mattos, Alexander Louis (1865–1921). English writer, notable for his translations of Dutch, Belgian, and French writers, especially Maeterlinck, Fabre, etc.

telamones. Large, sculptured male figures (see ATLANTES; CARYATIDS) serving as architectural columns or pilasters; so called from the Greek legendary hero Telamon (father of AJAX), who took part in the Calydonian hunt and the expedition of the Argonauts.

Tel-el-Amarna. Ruins of an Egyptian city built in the fourteenth century B. C. by the great liberal Egyptian ruler Akhenaton. About three hundred clay tablets, representing the diplomatic correspondence between the king of Egypt and the kings of Babylon and Assyria, written in cuneiform characters, were discovered in Tel-el-Amarna (1887). The ruins were further examined by Sir Flinders PETRIE (1891–1892).

Telemachus. In classic legend, the only son of ULYSSES and PENELOPE. As a babe he was thrown in front of his father's plow as a test of that hero's pretended madness. When Ulysses had been absent from home nearly twenty years, Telemachus went to Pylos and Sparta to gain information about him. NESTOR received him hospitably at Pylos, and sent him to Sparta, where MENELAUS told him the prophecy of Proteus concerning Ulysses. Telemachus then returned home, where he found his father and assisted him in slaying the suitors. Telemachus was accompanied in his voyage by Athene, the goddess of wisdom, under the form of Mentor, one of his father's friends. He is the hero of *Les Aventures de Télémaque* (1699), a French prose epic by FÉNELON. This once widely read poem is based on the old legends but adds many incidents, notably Telemachus' love affair with the nymph CALYPSO, who had been so violently enamored of his father. See also Stephen DEDALUS.

Telephus. In Greek legend, King of Mysia. He was wounded in single combat with ACHILLES and was told by an oracle that only that which had inflicted the wound could heal it. Disguised as a beggar he made his way to the hall of AGAMEMNON and succeeded in persuading ULYSSES to scrape some rust from Achilles' famous PELIAN SPEAR and with it cure him of his wound. AESCHYLUS and EURIPIDES both wrote dramas on *Telephus*.

Telford, Thomas (1757–1834). Scottish civil engineer who built, among many works, the Caledonian Canal, many miles of roads and twenty bridges in the north of Scotland, improved Scottish harbors, and constructed the Gotha canal between the Baltic Sea and North Sea. He was a friend of Thomas Campbell and Robert Southey.

Tell, William, see WILLIAM TELL.

Teller, Edward (1908–). German-educated scientist, born in Hungary, working at the Los Alamos atomic bomb laboratory in New Mexico.

Telling the Bees. A poem by WHITTIER (1858) based on the old custom of "telling the bees" of a death in the family.

Tellus. An ancient goddess of Rome, the symbol of fertility.

Temora. One of the principal poems of OSSIAN, in eight books, so called from the royal residence of the kings of Connaught. Cairbar has usurped the throne, having killed Cormac, a distant relative of FINGAL, and Fingal raises an army to dethrone the usurper. The poem begins from this point with an invitation from Cairbar to Oscar, son of Ossian, to a banquet. Oscar accepts the invitation, but during the feast a quarrel is hatched in which Cairbar and Oscar fall by each other's spears. When Fingal arrives a battle ensues in which Fillan, son of Fingal, the Achilles of the Caledonian army, and Cathmor, brother of Cairbar, the bravest of the Irish army, are both slain. Victory crowns the army of Fingal, and Ferad-Artho, the rightful heir, is restored to the throne of Connaught.

Tempe. A valley in Greece, between Mount Olympus and Mount Ossa. The word was employed by the Greek and Roman poets as a synonym for any valley noted for its cool shades, singing birds, and romantic scenery.

Tempest, The. A drama by SHAKESPEARE (ca. 1611). Prospero and his daughter Miranda live on a desert island, enchanted by SYCORAX, who is dead. The only other inhabitants are CALIBAN, the son of Sycorax, a strange misshapen thing like a gorilla, and ARIEL, a sprite who has been imprisoned by Sycorax for twelve years in the rift of a pine tree, from which Prospero sets him free. One day Prospero sees a ship off the island and raises a tempest to wreck it. By this means, his brother Antonio, Prince Ferdinand, and the King of Naples are brought to the island. Now, it must be known that Prospero was once Duke of Milan, but his brother Antonio, aided by the King of Naples, usurped the throne and set Prospero and Miranda adrift in a small boat, which was wind-driven to the desert island. The outcome of the affair is that Ferdinand (son of the King of Naples) and Miranda fall in love with each other, Antonio asks forgiveness of his brother, Prospero is restored to his dukedom, and the whole party is conducted by Ariel with prosperous breezes back to Italy.

Tempest, Lady Betty. In Goldsmith's CITIZEN OF THE WORLD, a lady with beauty, fortune, and family, whose head is turned by plays and romances. Having rejected many offers because the suitors do not come up to her ideal, she is gradually left in the cold until she becomes company only for aunts and cousins, a wallflower in ballrooms, and in society generally "a piece of fashionable lumber."

Tempest, Marie (1866–1942). English actress known in her early years for her musical comedy rôles. She became a theater manager (1911), having visited the United States and starred under Charles Frohman, and produced plays by Arnold Bennett, Henry Arthur Jones, and others.

Templars or **Knights Templars.** A famous order of knighthood founded at the beginning of the 12th century for service in the Holy Land. They used to call themselves the "Poor Soldiers of the Holy City." Their habit was a long white mantle, to which subsequently was added a red cross on the left shoulder. Their war-cry was *Bauseant* (an old French name for a black and white horse), from their banner, which was striped black and white, and charged with a red cross. Their seal showed two knights riding on one horse, the story being that the first Master was so poor that he had to share a horse with one of his followers. The Order afterwards became very wealthy and so powerful that its suppression (effected in 1312) was necessary for the peace of Europe.

temple.

the Temple. The site, in London, between Fleet Street and the Thames, formerly occupied by the buildings of the Knights Templars (see TEMPLARS), of which the Temple Church, dating from 1185, was the last to remain standing. Since 1346 the Temple has been in the possession of doctors and students of the law, who, since 1609, have formed the two Inns of Court known as the *Inner* and *Middle Temples*. They were thoroughly wrecked by Nazi bombs in World War II.

Temple Bar. The old Fleet Street gateway into the City of London, formerly situated close to the entrance into the Temple, on the spot now marked by the monument known as the "Griffin." It was built by Wren in 1670, and was removed and re-erected in private grounds at Theobalds Park, Cheshunt, Herts, in 1878. It was long used for the exhibition of the heads of traitors and conspirators, and was hence sometimes called "the City Golgotha."

Temple of Solomon. The central place of Jewish worship, erected by Solomon and his Tyrian workmen (probably on Phoenician models) on Mount Moriah, Jerusalem, about 1006 B. C. It was destroyed at the siege of Jerusalem by Nebuchadnezzar (588 B. C.), and some 70 years later the *Temple of Zerubbabel* was completed on its site. In 20 B. C. Herod the Great began the building of the last Temple—that of the New Testament—which was utterly destroyed during the siege of Jerusalem by Vespasian and Titus in 70 A. D. For many centuries the site has been covered by the splendid Mohammedan mosque, Haram esh Sherif.

Temple, Charlotte. Heroine of Susannah Rowson's novel CHARLOTTE TEMPLE.

Temple, Sir **William** (1628–1699). English diplomat and statesman. At his estate at Moor Park in Surrey, Jonathan SWIFT worked as his secretary (1689) helping him with his Memoirs. His best-known essay, *Of Ancient and Modern Learning,* started a controversy between Richard Bentley (1662–1742) and Charles Boyle, the editor of a series of epistles which he and Sir William were satisfied had been written by the Sicilian tyrant Phalaris. Bentley showed them to be spurious. This wrangle brought forth Swift's famous *The Battle of the Books* (1704).

Templeton, Fay (1865–1939). American actress who appeared as a child in *East Lynne* (1868). She joined Weber and Fields (1905), played with George M. Cohan, and was also a star in vaudeville.

Templeton, Laurence. The pseudonym under which Sir Walter Scott published his IVANHOE. The preface is initialed L. T., and the dedication is to the Rev. Dr. Dryasdust.

Templois. In medieval legend, the guardians of the Holy GRAIL or San graal.

Temps retrouvé, Le, see THE PAST RECAPTURED.

ten.

the Ten Commandments. See under COMMANDMENTS.

Ten Perfections. In Buddhism, the virtues a candidate for Buddhahood must show in the purest form: charity, good conduct, equanimity, energy, concentration in trance, discrimination, use of convenient means, resolution, strength, and intelligence.

the Ten Thousand. See ANABASIS.

Ten Tribes of Israel. The Lost Tribes.

the upper ten. See under UPPER.

Ten Days that Shook the World. The story of the Russian Revolution as told by John REED (1919).

tendo Achillis. See under ACHILLES.

Teniers, David. Known as "the Elder" (1582–1649). Flemish historical painter. His son **David Teniers,** known as "the Younger" (1610–1690), was a landscape and portrait painter.

Tennessee Shad, The. A boys' story by Owen JOHNSON named from a boon companion of Dink Stover's. See VARMINT.

Tennessee's Partner. A mining camp story by Bret HARTE (1869). Tennessee is a villain caught at wife-stealing and highway robbery, but his loyal partner, though his own wife is involved, does everything in his power to bribe the self-appointed court in Tennessee's favor with "$1700 in coarse gold and a watch." His efforts are in vain, and Tennessee is hanged.

Tenniel, Sir **John** (1820–1914). Cartoonist on the staff of *Punch* (1850–1901). He is best known as the illustrator of *Alice's Adventures in Wonderland* (1865) and *Through the Looking-Glass* (1872) by Lewis CARROLL.

Ten Nights in a Bar Room. A once widely read temperance narrative by T. S. Arthur (*Am.,* 1855).

Tennyson, Alfred, Lord (1809–1892). English poet, considered the most representative of the Victorian age in England, appointed poet laureate in 1850. Tennyson, in his early career influenced by the English romantic poets (see ROMANTICISM), especially John KEATS, is known for his faithful reflection in his poetry of the artistic and cultural tastes and the intellectual and moral values of his time and of the dominant Victorian social class, as well as for the characteristic response of his time and class to the encroachments of science in the domain of religious faith. He was the favorite target for the attacks of English and American poets of the late 19th and early 20th centuries who rebelled against Victorian standards, denouncing him for sentimentality, insipidity, over-ornateness, and narrow patriotism. Later in the 20th century critics began to praise Tennyson for the metrical skill and distinguished imagery of some of his brief lyrics, regarded as unimportant in his own day.

Tennyson's works include the following: *Poems by Two Brothers* (1827), early verse by his brothers and himself; *Poems, Chiefly Lyrical* (1830); *Poems* (1832); *Poems* (1842); LOCKSLEY HALL (1842); THE PRINCESS (1847); IN MEMORIAM (1850); *Ode on the Death of the Duke of Wellington* (1852); MAUD (1855); IDYLLS OF THE KING (1859–1872); *Enoch Arden* (1864), a sentimental verse narrative; *Queen Mary* (1875), *Harold* (1876), and *Becket* (1884), historical tragedies in verse; *Tiresias, And Other Poems* (1885); *Locksley Hall Sixty Years After* (1886); *Demeter, And Other Poems* (1889); *The Death of Oenone* (1892). Among his best-known single poems are *The Lady of Shalott; The Lotos-Eaters; Ulysses; Break, Break, Break; Sweet and Low; Tears, Idle Tears; The Charge of the Light Brigade; The Brook; Come into the Garden, Maud; Northern Farmer,* a dialect poem; *The Higher Pantheism;* and *Crossing the Bar.* Cf. *Tennyson* (1923), by Harold NICOLSON.

Tennyson was immensely popular and successful throughout his entire later career. The one shadow in his life was the early death of his friend Arthur Henry HALLAM, which plunged him into a conflict between faith and doubt.

Tenochtitlan. The capital of the Aztec empire. It occupied the site of the modern Mexico City.

tenson. A contention in verse between rival TROUBADORS; a metrical dialogue consisting of smart repartees, usually on women and love. A subdivision of the troubadors' love lyrics also had the same name.

tenth.

the Tenth Muse. See below; also under MUSE.

the Submerged Tenth. See SUBMERGED.

Tenth Muse Lately Sprung up in America, The. The first volume of American poetry. It was published in London in 1650, and its author, Anne BRADSTREET, the daughter of one New England governor and wife of another, became known as the *Tenth Muse.* Her verse, which is very ambitious in scope, includes the *Four Elements, Four Constitutions, Four Ages of Man, Four Seasons* and *Four Monarchies;* also a *Dialogue between Old England and New.*

Ten Thousand a Year. See under WARREN, SAMUEL.

Tenting on the Old Camp Ground. A famous Civil-War song written by Walter Kittredge (1834–1905).

Terah. In the Old Testament, the father of ABRAHAM. He died on the way from Ur of Chaldees to Canaan.

teraphim. Household gods of the Jews and other Semitic peoples.

Terborch, Gerard (1584–1662; 1617–1681). Two Dutch painters, father and son.

tercet. Three verses that follow each other and are rhymed together or have a rhyme scheme that interlaces with the preceding and/or following ones. The second part of a sonnet often consists of two tercets.

Terence (ca. 190–159 B. C.). Latin dramatist, famous for his comedies.

Tereus. See PHILOMELA.

Terhune, Albert Payson (1872–1942). Celebrated writer of dog stories. His mother, **Mary Virginia Terhune,** *née* **Hawes,** pseudonym **Marion Harland** (1830–1922), was responsible for books on various subjects, including twenty-five-odd novels.

Termagant. The name given by the Crusaders, and by the authors of medieval romances, to an idol or deity that the Saracens were popularly supposed to worship. He was introduced into the MORALITY PLAYS as a most violent and turbulent person in long, flowing Eastern robes, a dress that led to his acceptance as a woman, whence the name came to be applied to a shrewish, violently abusive virago.

outdoing Termagant (*Hamlet,* iii. 2). In old drama the degree of rant was the measure of villainy. Termagant and HEROD, being considered the *beau-ideal* of all that is bad, were represented as settling everything by club law, and bawling so as to "split the ears of the groundlings."

that beats Termagant. Your ranting, raging pomposity, or exaggeration, surpasses that of Termagant of the old moralities.

Terminus. The Roman god of bounds. A boundary stone with a bust of the god is called a *terminus.*

Terpander. Greek musician of the seventh century B. C. who established at Sparta the first Greek school of music.

Terpsichore. One of the nine MUSES of ancient Greece, the Muse of dancing and the dramatic chorus, and later of lyric poetry. She is usually represented seated, holding a lyre. Hence the adjective *Terpsichorean,* "pertaining to dancing."

terra firma. (*Lat.,* "firm earth"). Dry land, in opposition to water; the continents as distinguished from islands. The Venetians so called the mainland of Italy under their sway, and the continental parts of America belonging to Spain were also called by the same term.

Terre, La (The Soil). A novel by Emile ZOLA, one of the ROUGON-MACQUART series, dealing with the French peasantry.

terror.

the Terror or *the Reign of Terror.* The period in the French Revolution between the fall of the Girondists and the overthrow of ROBESPIERRE. It lasted 420 days, from May 31, 1793, to July 27, 1794. The name is also applied to similar cataclysms in the history of other nations, such as the Russian Revolution (the *Red Terror,* March–September, 1917).

Terror of France. John TALBOT, first Earl of Shrewsbury (1373–1453).

> Is this the Talbot, so much feared abroad,
> That with his name the mothers still their babes?
> Shakespeare, 1 *Henry VI.* Act ii. Sc. 3 (1589).

Terror of the World. Attila, King of the Huns (5th century).

Terry, Ellen (1847–1928). Distinguished English actress. Mother of Edward Gordon CRAIG. She was the leading lady of Sir Henry IRVING in plays of Shakespeare. In the United States, England, and Australia, she lectured on Shakespearean subjects (1910–1915). Dame Grand Cross, Order of British Empire (1925).

Terry, Phyllis Neilson (1892–). English actress, daughter of Ellen TERRY's brother Fred. Played many Shakespearean parts in England, the U.S., and Canada.

tertium quid (*Lat.*). A third party which shall be nameless; a third thing resulting from the combination of two things, but different from both. Fable has it that the expression originated with PYTHAGORAS, who, defining bipeds, said—

> Sunt *bipes* homo, et avis, et tertium quid.
> A man is a biped, so is a bird, and a third thing (which shall be nameless).

Iamblichus says this third thing was Pythagoras himself.

In chemistry, when two substances chemically unite, the new substance is called a *tertium quid,* as a neutral salt produced by the mixture of an acid and alkali.

terza rima. An Italian verse-form in TERCETS, the second line rhyming with the first and third of the succeeding triplet. In the first triplet lines 1 and 3 rhyme, and in the last there is an extra line, rhyming with its second. Dante's DIVINE COMEDY is in this meter. It was introduced into England by Sir Thomas WYATT in the 16th century, and was largely employed by SHELLEY, as also by BYRON in *The Prophecy of Dante.*

Tesla, Nikola (1856–1943). American inventor in the field of electricity. Robert Underwood Johnson, the American poet and editor, Tesla's best friend, wrote a poem, *In Tesla's Laboratory,* that contains the line:

> Thoughts to unlock the fettering chains of things.

Tess of the D'Urbervilles. A novel by Thomas HARDY (1891). Tess Durbeyfield, urged by her dissipated father Jack and the necessities of a poverty-stricken household, takes service with the wealthy Mrs. D'Urberville, a supposed connection. Here Alex, the son of the house, makes love to Tess and takes advantage of her against her will. After the death of her child, Tess hires herself out on a farm where she meets and falls in love with Angel Clare, a rector's son who wishes to be a farmer. The couple, after their marriage, relate the story of their past lives, and Angel, although he expects forgiveness for his own past, is horrified at his wife's story and goes abroad, refusing to live with her. After a time Alex D'Urberville, who has become converted, persuades Tess to return to him in the belief that Angel will not come back and that she will be able to help her needy family. When Angel does return, but learning the situation, leaves again, she turns upon Alex and stabs him. She and Angel try to escape justice, but she is arrested and sentenced to death.

Tessa. In George Eliot's ROMOLA, the pretty Tuscan peasant girl whom Tito marries in addition to marrying Romola.

Tesserarian Art (from Lat. *tessera,* "a die"). The art of gambling.

Test Act. An Act of Parliament directed against Roman Catholics and Nonconformists, especially that of 1673, which decreed that all holders of public offices must take the Oaths of Allegiance and Supremacy, receive the Church of England sacrament, renounce the doctrine of Transubstantiation, etc. It was repealed in 1828. Hence *to take the test* means to comply with the requirements of the Test Act.

tête-à-tête (*Fr.,* "head to head"). A confidential conversation, a "heart to heart talk."

Tethys. A sea goddess of the ancient Greeks, wife of Oceanus; hence, the sea itself. Tethys was the daughter of Heaven and Earth and mother of the river gods.

Tetrachordon. The title of one of MILTON's books about marriage and divorce. The word means "the four strings" by which the author means the four chief places in Scripture which bear on the subject of marriage.

Tetrarch. See RULERS, TITLES OF.

Tetrazzini, Luisa (1874–1940). Coloratura soprano born in Italy, who appeared in London (1907) and New York (1908) and toured the U.S. (1910–1913).

Teucer. In the ILIAD, the son of Telamon, and step-brother of Telamon Ajax. He went with the allied Greeks to the siege of Troy, and on his return was banished by his father for not avenging on ULYSSES the death of his brother. He was the best archer among the Greeks.

Teufelsdröckh, Herr Diogenes. The imaginary author of Carlyle's SARTOR RESARTUS, an eccentric German professor and philosopher.

Tezcatlipoca. The chief god of Aztec myth, the life-giver. His name, meaning "Fiery Mirror," comes from his great mirror-shield which reflects all the deeds of mankind.

Thackeray, William Makepeace (1811–1863). English novelist and journalist, known for his satirical and moralistic studies of upper- and middle-class English life, especially in the Victorian age. His works include *The Yellowplush Correspondence* (see YELLOWPLUSH, MR. C. J.; 1837); *The Tremendous Adventures of Major Gahagan* (1838–1839); CATHERINE (1839–1840); A SHABBY GENTEEL STORY (1840); *The Paris Sketch-Book* (1841); *The Great Hoggarty Diamond* (1841); THE FITZ-BOODLE PAPERS (1842–1843); *Men's Wives* (1843); JEAMES'S DIARY (1845); *Mr. Punch's Prize Novelists* (1847); *The Snobs of England* (1847), later THE BOOK OF SNOBS; VANITY FAIR (1847–1848), his best-known work; PENDENNIS (1848–1850); REBECCA AND ROWENA (1850); HENRY ESMOND (1852); THE NEWCOMES (1853–1855); *The English Humorists of the 18th Century* (1851) and *The Four Georges* (1855–1856), lectures delivered on a tour of America; *Christmas Books* (1857), containing *Mrs. Perkins' Ball* and THE ROSE AND THE RING, among other tales; THE VIRGINIANS (1857–1859), a sequel to HENRY ESMOND; *Lovel the Widower* (1860); *The Adventures of Philip* (see PHILIP; 1862); and *Denis Duval* (1864), left unfinished at the author's death. Thackeray also wrote a number of ballads, satirical and otherwise. See also TITMARSH, MICHAEL ANGELO.

Thackeray was born in India and early in his career studied law and then drawing. He worked on newspapers in Paris and London, and virtually all of his works were published serially in *Fraser's Magazine* or in *Punch;* in 1859 he became editor of *The Cornhill Magazine.* The insanity of his wife, Isabella Shawe, in 1840 is considered to have influenced the character of his work in some part.

Thaddeus. The hero of Balfe's opera THE BOHEMIAN GIRL.

Thaddeus of Warsaw. The hero and title of a novel by Jane PORTER (1803), dealing with the period of the partition of Poland.

Thaïs. A novel by Anatole FRANCE (1890). The action takes place in the Egypt of the early Christian era. Thaïs is a beautiful courtesan of Alexandria whom the ardent young monk Paphnutius longs to convert. Stirred by his strange appeal, she follows him through the desert and enters a nunnery, but Paphnutius, now torn by earthly love, is wretched without her. He goes at last to her deathbed and finds her lost in spiritual visions, which he cannot share. In MASSENET's opera *Thaïs* (1894) based on this romance, the monk is called Athanael.

Thaïs is also the name of the Athenian courtesan who, it is said, induced Alexander the Great, when excited with wine, to set fire to the palace of the Persian kings at Persepolis.

> The king seized a flambeau with zeal to destroy;
> Thais led the way to light him to his prey,
> And, like another Helen, fired another Troy.
> Dryden, *Alexander's Feast.*

Thaïsa. The wife of Pericles in the drama PERICLES, PRINCE OF TYRE, attributed in part to Shakespeare.

Thakura, Ravindranatha, see TAGORE, Sir RABINDRANATH.

Thalaba. A famous character of Eastern myth, the hero of SOUTHEY's long narrative poem *Thalaba the Destroyer* (1801). Thalaba, the orphaned son of Hodeirah and Zeinab (Zenobia), is the unceasing enemy of the evil spirits of DOMDANIEL, who have slain his eight brothers and sisters because it is decreed by fate that one of the race will be their destruction. Three great magicians, Abdaldar, Lobaba, and Mohareb, in turn, work their evil designs upon him, each in peculiarly insidious fashion, but he thwarts them all and escapes, bearing with him the magic ring of Abdaldar, which gives him power over all spirits. His next adventure is in the "paradise of pleasure" where he successfully resists temptation, rescues the lovely Bedouin maid Oneiza from the clutches of Aloadin, and marries her, only to see her die on the bridal night. Distracted at this calamity, he falls into the clutches of Maimuna, an old woman who lures him to wind her fine spinning thread round his wrists and so put himself in her power. When he is at last set free, he is threatened anew, this time by the sorcerer Okba, but is saved by Okba's daughter Laila, who dies in his defense. Her spirit becomes his protecting angel in the guise of a green bird, and he achieves at last the destruction of Domdaniel and is received into Heaven.

Thales (ca. 624–546 B.C.). Early Greek philosopher of the school of MILESIANS, regarded by some as the founder of Greek philosophy. He was also a political leader, a civil engineer, a mathematician (as such introducing to the Greeks certain propositions in geometry learned from the Egyptians), and an astronomer, accurately predicting an eclipse of the sun that occurred in 585 B.C. His important philosophic theory was that water is the primary substance in the universe, entering into all change and transformation.

Thalestris. A queen of the AMAZONS, who went with 300 women to meet Alexander the Great, under the hope of raising a race of Alexanders; hence, any bold heroic woman.

Thalia. (1) One of the MUSES, generally regarded as the patroness of comedy. She was supposed by some, also, to preside over husbandry and planting, and is represented holding a comic mask and a shepherd's crook. (2) One of the GRACES.

Thälmann, Ernst (1886–). German Communist leader of the Red Front group. He was arrested and imprisoned by the Nazis in 1933.

Thames.

he'll never set the Thames on fire. He'll never make any figure in the world; never plant his footsteps on the sands of time. The popular explanation is that the word *Thames* is a pun on the word *temse,* a corn-sieve, and that the parallel French locution *He will never set the Seine on fire* is a pun on *seine,* a dragnet. These solutions, however, are very questionable owing to the existence of similar, but older phrases, such as *To set the Rhine on fire.*

Thammuz or **Tammuz.** The Syrian and Phoenician name of ADONIS. His death occurs on the banks of the river Adonis, and in summer-time the waters always become reddened with the hunter's blood. In *Ezek.* viii. 14, reference is made to the heathen "women weeping for Tammuz."

> Thammuz came next behind,
> Whose annual wound on Lebanon allured
> The Syrian damsels to lament his fate
> In amorous ditties all a summer's day,
> While smooth Adonis from his native rock
> Ran purple to the sea, supposed with blood
> Of Thammuz yearly wounded.
> Milton, *Paradise Lost,* iii. 446.

Thamyris. A Thracian bard mentioned by HOMER (*Iliad,* ii. 595). He challenged the Muses to a trial of skill, and, being overcome in the contest, was deprived by them of his sight and power of song. He is represented with a broken lyre in his hand.

> Blind Thamyris and blind Mæon'ides [Homer]
> And Tiresias and Phineus, prophets old.
> Milton, *Paradise Lost,* iii. 35.

Thanatopsis. The best known poem of William Cullen BRYANT, written in 1817 when he was only eighteen. Its theme is death.

Thanatos. In Greek mythology, Death represented as a person. Sleep (Hypnos) was his twin brother.

Thane, Elswyth. American novelist, author of the historical novels, *The Tudor Wench* (1933) and *Young Mr. Disraeli* (1935), which were both made into plays. In 1927 she married the well-known naturalist, William Beebe.

Thanet, Octave. Pseudonym of **Alice French** (1850–1934). American novelist and short-story writer of the LOCAL-COLOR school, known for her treatment of labor and social problems in her fiction, the scene of much of which is laid in the industrial Middle West. Her books include *Knitters in the Sun* (1887); *Expiation* (1890); *Otto the Knight* (1891); *Stories of a Western Town* (1892); *The Missionary Sheriff* (1897); *The Heart of Toil* (1898); *A Slave to Duty, And Other Women* (1898); *The Captured Dream* (1899); *The Man of the Hour* (1905); *The Lion's Share* (1907); *By Inheritance* (1910); *Stories That End Well* (1911); *A Step on the Stair* (1913); *And the Captain Answered* (1917).

Thanksgiving Day. An American holiday, first observed by the PILGRIM FATHERS in gratitude for the harvest after the severe trials of their first year in America. Tradition requires that roast turkey be served at Thanksgiving dinner. It is appointed or recommended annually by the Federal and State executives, normally as the last Thursday in November.

Thatcher, Becky. The little girl in *The Adventures of Tom Sawyer* by Mark Twain, who is lost with Tom in the cave.

Thaukt. The old hag who alone refused to weep for Baldur and thus prevented his return from Hel which could be accomplished only by the unanimous demand of all beings and things. She was suspected of being Loki in disguise.

Thaumast. In Rabelais' GARGANTUA AND PANTAGRUEL, an English pundit who goes to Paris, attracted by the rumor of the great wisdom of Pantagruel. He arranges a disputation with that prince to be carried on solely in pantomime, without the utterance of a single word. PANURGE undertakes the disputation for the prince, and Pantagruel is appointed arbiter. Many a knotty point in magic, alchemy, the Cabbala, geomancy, astrology, and philosophy are argued out by signs alone, and the Englishman freely confesses himself fully satisfied, for "Panurge had told him even more than he had asked."

Thaumaturgus (*Gr.,* a conjurer or wonder-worker). A miracle-worker; applied to saints and others who are reputed to have performed miracles, especially:

Apollonius of Tyana, Cappadocia (3–98 A. D.).

St. Bernard of Clairvaux, "the Thaumaturgus of the West" (1091–1153).

St. Filumena.

St. Francis of Assisi, founder of the Franciscan order (1182–1226).

Gregory (d. ca. 270), Bishop of Neo-Caesarea, in Cappadocia, called emphatically "Thaumaturgus," from the numerous miracles he is reported to have performed.

Plotinus (d. ca. 270), and several other neo-Platonists.

Simon Magus, of Samaria, called "the Great Power of God" (*Acts* viii. 10).

St. Vincent de Paul, founder of the "Sisters of Charity" (1576–1660).

Thayer, Abbott (1849–1921). American painter whose *Caritas* is in the Boston Museum of Fine Arts.

Thayer, Tiffany Ellsworth (1902–). American writer of fantastic, sensational and frequently bawdy fiction. He has a number of pen-names and has written *Thirteen Men* (1930); *Thirteen Women* (1932); *Tiffany Thayer's Three Musketeers* (1939); etc.

Thayer, William Roscoe (1859–1923). American author, chiefly known for his books on Italian history. He also wrote a life of John HAY (1915) and *Theodore Roosevelt: An Intimate Biography* (1919).

Theagenes and Charicleia, The Loves of. A love story, in Greek, by Heliodorus, Bishop of Trikka (4th century), largely borrowed from by subsequent novelists, and especially by Mlle de SCUDÉRY, TASSO, Guarini, and D'Urfé. The two lovers are carried off by pirates and left near the mouth of the Nile.

Theale, Milly. In Henry James' WINGS OF A DOVE, the American heiress whom Merton Densher marries because he knows she cannot live long.

Theater Guild, The. An organization developed as a little theater group from the Washington Square Players (1918). It finally built its own theater (1925) which cost a million dollars. It has specialized in giving the plays of George Bernard Shaw and Eugene O'Neill as well as reviving old plays and giving plays by newer American authors.

Theatre Arts Magazine. A quarterly (founded 1916) superseded (1924) by **Theatre Arts Monthly.** Under new management (1947–). Now edited by Charles MACARTHUR.

Theban Bard, Eagle or Lyre. See under BARD.

Theebaw's Queen. In Kipling's *Mandalay,* the Queen of Burma, wife of Theebaw, the last king of Burma (1878–1885).

Thebes, called *The Hundred-Gated,* was not Thebes of Boeotia, but the chief town of the Thebaid, on the Nile in Upper Egypt, said to have extended over twenty-three miles of land. HOMER says out of each gate the Thebans could send forth 200 war-chariots.

> The world's great empress on the Egyptian plain,
> That spreads her conquests o'er a thousand states,
> And pours her heroes through a hundred gates,
> Two hundred horsemen and two hundred cars
> From each wide portal issuing to the wars.
>
> Pope, *Iliad,* i.

It is here that the vocal statue of MEMNON stood, and here too are the tombs of the kings, the temple of Karnak, and large numbers of sculptures, sphinxes, etc. The village of Luxor now marks the spot.

the Seven against Thebes. An expedition in Greek legend fabled to have taken place against Thebes, Boeotia, before the Trojan War. The Seven were the Argive chiefs Adrastus, Polynices, Tydeus, Amphiaraus, Hippomedon, Capaneus, and Parthenopaeus.

When OEDIPUS abdicated, his two sons agreed to reign alternate years, but at the expiration of the first year, the elder, Eteocles, refused to give up the throne, whereupon Polynices, the younger brother, induced the six chiefs to espouse his cause. The allied army laid siege to Thebes, but without success, and all the heroes perished except Adrastus. Subsequently, seven sons of the chiefs resolved to avenge their fathers' deaths, marched against the city, took it, and placed Terpander, one of their number, on the throne. These are known as the *Epigoni* (*Gr.,* "descendants"). The Greek tragic poets AESCHYLUS and EURIPIDES dramatized the legend.

Thecla, St. See under SAINTS.

Their Wedding Journey. A novel by W. D. HOWELLS (1871), dealing with the adventures of Basil and Isabel MARCH on their honeymoon trip to Niagara, the St. Lawrence, Montreal and Quebec. The plot interest is secondary to description. A later edition contains the additional *Niagara Revisited Twelve Years After,* and the sequel *Their Silver Wedding Journey* (1899) takes the couple on a prolonged trip through Europe.

Thekla. Daughter of Wallenstein in Schiller's historic drama WALLENSTEIN.

Thélème, Abbey of. In Rabelais' GARGANTUA AND PANTAGRUEL, the abbey given by Grangousier to Friar John for the aid he rendered in the battle against Picrochole, King of Lerné. The abbey is stored with everything that contributes to sensual indulgence and enjoyment. It is the very reverse of a convent or monastery. No religious hypocrites, no pettifogging attorneys, no usurers are admitted within it; it is filled with gallant ladies and gentlemen, faithful expounders of the Scriptures, everyone able to contribute to its recreations and general festivity. Their only law: *"Fay ce que Vouldras"* ("Do what you wish").

Walter BESANT and James Rice wrote a novel called *The Monks of Thelema* (*Eng.,* 1878), in which the hero, Alan Dunlop, tries to establish a 19th century Abbey of Thelema in England.

Themis. In Greek mythology, the goddess of justice and law.

Themistocles (527?–?460 B.C.). Greek general who commanded the fleet of Athens at Salamis (480 B.C.) when it defeated the Persians. Accused of treason and exiled, he spent the last years of his life in Persia where he received a royal pension.

Theobald, Lewis (1688–1744). English playwright and critic. He issued a book on Shakespeare criticizing Pope's edition. In rejoinder Pope put him into his *Dunciad.*

Theocritus. A Greek bucolic poet of the 3rd century B.C., regarded as the founder of pastoral poetry. His extant work consists of about 30 poems, termed *idyls,* and a few epigrams.

the Portuguese Theocritus. Saadi di Miranda (1495–1551).

the Scotch Theocritus. Allan Ramsay (1685–1758), author of *The Gentle Shepherd.*

the Sicilian Theocritus. Giovanni Meli of Palermo (1740–1815), immortalized by his eclogues and idyls.

Theodora. In Disraeli's LOTHAIR, an American supporter of Garibaldi's cause who exerts a great influence on the hero.

Theodore, St. See under SAINTS.

Theodore and Honoria. A poem by DRYDEN retold from Boccaccio's DECAMERON (Day v. 8). "The more he loved, the more she disdained," until finally one day she sees in a vision the ghost of Guido CAVALCANTI hunting with two mastiffs a damsel who has scorned his love and is doomed to be torn to pieces by the dogs and restored to life again every Friday.

Theodoric. A king of the East Goths known as **Theodoric the Great** (d. 526), who became celebrated in German legend as Dietrich of Bern and also has a place in the Norse romances and the NIBELUNGENLIED. He invaded Italy about 490, and three years later slew Odoacer and became sole ruler.

Theodorus, Master. In Rabelais' GARGANTUA AND PANTAGRUEL, a learned physician, employed by Ponocrates to cure Gargantua of his vicious habits. The doctor accordingly "purged him canonically with Anticyrian hellebore, cleansed from his brain all perverse habits, and made him forget everything he had learned of his other preceptors."

Theognis. Greek gnomic poet of the sixth century B. C.

Theon. A satirical poet of ancient Rome, noted for his mordant writings. Hence, *Theon's tooth,* the bite of an ill-natured or carping critic. *Dente Theonino circumrodi* (Horace: *Ep.* i, 18, 82), to be nastily aspersed.

Theophilus, St. See under SAINTS.

Theophrastus (390–287 B. C.). Greek philosopher and scientist. Disciple of Aristotle and his successor as head of the Peripatetic school. Among his works are a *History of Plants* and a *Theoretical Botany.* His real name was Tyrtamus. "Theophrastus" means "divine speaker" and was applied by Aristotle. Known for his studies of personality types.

Theophrastus Such, Impressions of. A volume of character sketches and satires by George ELIOT (1879) written in the character of a whimsical, elderly bachelor.

Theory of the Leisure Class, The. A provocative and influential book (1899) by Thorstein VEBLEN.

Theosophy (*Gr.,* "the wisdom of God"). The name adopted by the *Theosophical Society* (founded in 1875 by Mme BLAVATSKY, Mrs. BESANT, Col. Olcott, and others) to define their religious or philosophical system, which aims at the knowledge of God by means of intuition and contemplative illumination, or by direct communion. *Esoteric Buddhism* is another name for it; its adherents claim that the doctrines of the great world religions are merely the exoteric expression of their own esoteric traditions.

The name was formerly applied to the philosophical system of BOEHME.

> The Theosophist is a man who, whatever be his race, creed, or condition, aspires to reach this height of wisdom and beatitude by self-development.—Olcott, *Theosophy,* p. 144 (1885).

Theotocopuli, Domenico, see GRECO, EL.

Theresa, St. See under SAINTS; also EVELYN INNES.

There's a Long, Long Trail. A song, extremely popular with the American troops in World War I, which was written as a Yale college song (1913) by Stoddard King and Zo Elliott.

Thérèse de Lisieux (1873–1897). French Carmelite nun, known as "the Little Flower of Jesus," who was canonized (1925) as Saint Thérèse, the Little Flower.

Thermidor (from Gr. *thermē,* "heat," and *doron,* "gift"). The eleventh month of the French Republican calendar, containing thirty days beginning July 19.

Thermidorians. The milder French Revolutionists, who took part in the *coup d'état* which effected the fall of Robespierre, on Thermidor 9 of the second Republican year (July 27, 1794), thus bringing the REIGN OF TERROR to a close.

Thermopylae. When Xerxes invaded Greece (480 B. C.), Leonidas was sent with three hundred Spartans, as a forlorn hope, to defend the pass leading from Thessaly into Locris. They resisted for three successive days the repeated attacks of the most brave and courageous of Xerxes' army. The Persians, however, discovered a path over the mountains and fell on Leonidas in the rear, and the defenders were cut to pieces.

Thersites. In Greek legend, a deformed, scurrilous officer in the Greek army at the siege of Troy. He was always railing at the chiefs; hence, the name is applied to any dastardly, malevolent, impudent railer against the powers that be. ACHILLES felled him to the earth with his fist and killed him.

> He squinted, halted, gibbous was behind,
> And pinched before, and on his tapering head
> Grew patches only of the flimsiest down.
> . . . Him Greece had sent to Troy.
> The miscreant, who shamed his country most.
> *Homer's Iliad (Cowper),* Bk. ii.

In Shakespeare's TROILUS AND CRESSIDA he is "a slave whose gall coins slanders like a mint."

Thesaurus. See ROGET, PETER MARK.

Theseus. The chief hero of Attica in ancient Greek legend; son of AEGEUS, and the center of innumerable exploits. He was brought up by his mother Aethra, but when he became strong enough to lift the stone under which his father's sword was hidden, he was sent to the court of Athens, where, in spite of the efforts of his father's wife MEDEA, he was recognized as heir to the throne. Among his deeds were the slaying of PROCRUSTES, the capture of the Marathonian bull, the slaying of the MINOTAUR with the aid of ARIADNE whom he subsequently deserted in Naxos, his war against the Amazons, his part in the Argonautic expedition, and the Calydonian hunt.

There are numerous versions of his war against the Amazons. He married the Amazonian queen who opposed him, known as either Antiope or Hippolyta (according to some accounts there were two sisters of these names) and took her home with him. After the death of this queen, he married PHAEDRA whose ill-fated infatuation with her stepson Hippolytus has formed the subject of many tragedies in which Theseus plays a part. In his old age he became unpopular with his people and was foully murdered by Lycomedes in Scyros where he had taken refuge.

According to medieval legend, Theseus' title was Duke of Athens and his Duchess was Hippolyta. Under this title he plays a part in Chaucer's *Knight's Tale* and Shakespeare's MIDSUMMER NIGHT'S DREAM. In the *Knight's Tale,* he marries Hippolyta, and as he returns home with his bride and Emily, her sister, he is accosted by a crowd of female suppliants who complain of Creon, King of Thebes. The Duke forthwith sets out for Thebes, slays Creon, and takes the city by assault. Many captives fall into his hands, among them the two knights PALAMON and ARCITE.

Thespian.

Thespian Maids. The nine MUSES. They are so called from Thespia in Boeotia, near Mount Helicon, often called *Thespia Rupes.*

Thespians. Actors; so called from Thespis, an Attic poet of the 6th century B.C., reputed to be the father of Greek tragedy.

Thespio. A Muse.

Thespis. See THESPIAN.

Thestylis. A stock poetic name for a rustic maiden; from a young female slave of that name in the *Idyls* of THEOCRITUS.

Thetis. The chief of the NEREIDS of Greek legend. By PELEUS she was the mother of ACHILLES.

Thetis' hair-stone. A fancy-name given to pieces of rock-crystal enclosing hair-like filaments.

They Knew What They Wanted. A play (1924) by Sidney HOWARD. It won the Pulitzer prize (1925) and was made into a moving picture.

They Shall Not Die. A play (1934) concerning the SCOTTSBORO Case by John WEXLEY.

They Stoop to Folly: A Comedy of Morals. A novel (1929) by Ellen GLASGOW.

Thialfi. Thor's servant, who accompanied Loki and his master to Utgard, the abode of the giant Utgard-Loki. There he lost a foot race to Hugi, one of Utgard-Loki's men, who actually was Thought in disguise.

Thibaults, Les. A long novel by Roger Martin DU GARD (1922–1936), published in ten volumes. It presents the history of a French family named Thibault up to the beginning of World War I. It is marked by meticulous documentation in the manner of NATURALISM and gives a full picture of the social and historical background of the period portrayed. *The World of the Thibaults* (1941) completes the story. See also ROMAN-FLEUVE.

Thibault, Jacques Anatole François, see Anatole FRANCE.

Thief, the Penitent. For the name usually given to the penitent thief on the Cross and his unrepentant fellow, see DISMAS.

Thiers, Louis Adolphe (1797–1877). French statesman and historical writer. He was a leader of the Liberals (1863–1870) against Napoleon III. He negotiated the peace treaty with Germany (1871), disposed of the Paris Commune, and was elected first president (1871–1873) of the Third Republic.

Thiess, Frank (1890–). German novelist and dramatist some of whose work has been translated into English. His *Farewell to Paradise* (1929) has been the most successful.

thing-in-itself, see DING AN SICH.

third estate. The third of the social classes, or "estates," according to political theory of medieval and feudal times. It comprised peasants, serfs, yeomen, and the early BOURGEOISIE, the nobles and clergy constituting the first two estates. In France the third estate was known as *tiers état* and was not emancipated until the Revolution of 1789. See ESTATES OF THE REALM.

third floor back, the. A room in a lodging or boarding house. Jerome K. JEROME has a play called *The Passing of the Third Floor Back* (1910), "an idle fancy" presenting the effect of Christ's coming into such a room as a stranger.

Third Reich. The official name of Germany during the dictatorship of Adolf HITLER. It implies that the medieval empire which broke up in 1806 was the first and the empire of Bismarck (1870–1918) the second Reich. The term has absorbed a good deal of medieval mysticism in which a "third realm" was understood to be the millennium.

Thirkell, Mrs. **Angela** (1890–). English novelist, daughter of the noted Latin scholar J. W. MACKAIL and niece of the painter Edward BURNE-JONES. Rudyard KIPLING was a cousin of hers. A light touch and gentle irony are her chief characteristics.

thirteen. It is said that the origin of the superstition that sitting down thirteen at dinner is unlucky is that, at a banquet in Valhalla, Loki once intruded, making thirteen guests, and Balder was slain. In Christian countries the superstition was confirmed by the Last Supper of Christ and His twelve apostles, but it antedates Christianity.

The Italians never use the number in their lotteries; in Paris no house bears it, and persons, called *quatorzièmes,* are available to make a fourteenth at dinner parties. Sailors strongly object to leaving port on the 13th of any month, especially if it happens to be a Friday, and they always start on their thirteenth voyage with apprehension.

thirteen colonies or *states.* See STATES.

thirty.

The Thirty. So the Spartan senate established by Lycurgus was called.

thirty tyrants. See TYRANT.

Thirty Years War. A series of wars between the Catholics and Protestants of Germany in the 17th century, in which France, Sweden, and other peoples participated from time to time. It began in Bohemia in 1618, and ended in 1648 with the Peace of Westphalia.

Thirty-Nine Articles, The. The articles of faith of the Church of England, the acceptance of which is obligatory on its clergy. They were originally issued in 1551 as forty-two, but in 1563 were modified and reduced to their present number. They received parliamentary authority in 1571.

Thirty-Six Line Bible. See BIBLE, SPECIALLY NAMED.

Thisbe. See PYRAMUS.

This Side of Paradise. A novel (1920) by F. Scott FITZGERALD.

Thomas, Albert Ellsworth (1872–1947). American playwright of great skill, particularly in light comedy. *No More Ladies* (1934) is one of his fifteen-odd plays.

Thomas, Augustus (1857–1934). American playwright who first achieved success by a stage adaptation (1887) of the novel *Editha's Burglar* by Mrs. F. H. BURNETT. His best-known popular play is *The Witching Hour.*

Thomas, Bigger. Hero of Richard Wright's NATIVE SON, a Negro raised in the slums of Chicago's Black Belt. Bewildered and resentful in the face of the poverty in which he has grown up and the racial discrimination he encounters, he is impelled in spite of himself to crime.

Thomas, Brandon (1849–1914). British playwright, best known in America for his comedy *Charley's Aunt* (1892) which has been many times revived.

Thomas, Dylan (1914–). English poet, born in Wales, known for the distinctive character of his verse and prose, in which typical qualities of SURREALISM are combined with elements of traditional Celtic fantasy in conjuring up strange and haunting experiences. It has been pointed out that Thomas' work lacks the more obvious and sensational incongruities of French surrealism, concentrating on lyric mood. His books include *Twenty-Five Poems* (1936); *The Map of Love* (1939), verse and prose; *The World I Breathe* (1939), prose and poetry; *Portrait of the Artist as a Young Dog* (1940), autobiographical sketches.

Thomas, Edith Matilda (1854–1925). American poet, well known at the turn of the century. Her last book was *The Flower from the Ashes* (1915).

Thomas, Edward (1878–1917). English poet who did hack work for the *Manchester Guardian.* He met Robert Frost in England and was much influenced by him. He is the subject of two books by his widow Helen Thomas which are very moving accounts of their relationship. He was killed at Arras in World War I.

Thomas, Lowell (1892–). Well-known American radio commentator and author of a number of books of travel and contemporary comment.

Thomas, Norman (1884–). Head of the Socialist Party in the U.S. Socialist candidate for president (1928, 1932, 1936, 1940, 1944, 1948). Author of several books on contemporary affairs.

Thomas, St. (called *Doubting Thomas*). See under SAINTS.

Thomas, Theodore (1835–1905). German-born American orchestra conductor. He organized an orchestra which bore his name and gave symphony concerts famous in their day. At one time he was leader of the New York Philharmonic Symphony Orchestra.

Thomashefsky, Boris (1864–1939). Yiddish actor and producer, born in Russia, who started the Yiddish theater in the United States. He established the National Theater in New York and translated the plays of Shakespeare into Yiddish.

Thomason, John William (1893–1944). American marine officer, illustrator, and writer. *Fixed Bayonets* (1926); *Red Pants and Other Stories* (1927); *Jeb Stuart* (1930); etc.

Thomas the Rhymer or **Thomas of Ercildoune.** A poet of the 13th century who has been made the subject of popular legend. Sir Walter SCOTT calls him "the Merlin of Scotland" and makes use of old predictions attributed to him in both *Castle Dangerous* and THE BRIDE OF LAMMERMOOR. He was said to have spent three years in Fairyland with the Fairy Queen, whom he met under the Eildon Tree, after which he became prophet and magician as well as poet. Legend has it that he did not die, but went to Fairyland and will some day return. The so-called *Prophecies of Thomas the Rhymer* were published by the Early English Text Society in 1875.

Thomism. See under AQUINAS, ST. THOMAS.

Thompson, Benjamin. Count **Rumford** (1753–1814). American-born adventurer, created count of the Holy Roman Empire by the elector of Bavaria. He was made Bavarian minister to Great Britain, and helped organize the Royal Academy. He lived chiefly in Paris. His biography, *Count Rumford of Massachusetts* (1935), has been written by his descendant James Alden Thompson.

Thompson, Denman (1833–1911). American actor who wrote the famous play, *The Old Homestead,* which was first presented in Boston (1886).

Thompson, Dorothy (1894–). American journalist, at one time the wife of Sinclair LEWIS, known for her syndicated newspaper column *On the Record,* dealing with politics and foreign affairs and expressing semi-liberal views. During the 1920's she was a foreign correspondent in Europe. *The New Russia* (1928); *I Saw Hitler* (1932); *Dorothy Thompson's Political Guide* (1938); and *Let the Record Speak* (1939).

Thompson, Edward John (1886–). English poet and novelist, author of some thirty books on East Indian and British subjects, often on the unpopular side. Storm Jameson has praised his writing.

Thompson, Francis (1859–1907). English Roman Catholic poet, known for his mystical religious poetry frequently presenting ecstatic visions of Heaven. In color and imagery his work shows the influence of KEATS and SHELLEY, and in spirit and tone it is akin to the poetry of the METAPHYSICAL POETS. Thompson's books include *Poems* (1893); *Sister Songs* (1895); *New Poems* (1897), considered to have been written under the influence of Coventry PATMORE; and *Health and Holiness* (1905), a prose treatise. His most famous poem is THE HOUND OF HEAVEN.

Thompson studied medicine at one time in his early youth, but never received a degree. He was extremely impractical and was unable to make a living for himself. When he was lonely, ill, and in poverty in London he was taken into the home of Wilfrid and Alice MEYNELL, who befriended him and encouraged him in his writing. He was always in poor health and died of tuberculosis.

Thompson, Maurice (1844–1901). American poet and novelist, best known for the popular romance *Alice of Old Vincennes* (1900).

Thompson, Sylvia (1902–). English novelist best known for *The Hounds of Spring* (1925).

Thompson, Will Henry (1848–?). American Confederate soldier and writer, best known for his long poem about the Civil War, *High Tide at Gettysburg* (1888).

Thomson, Hugh (1860–1920). English illustrator, well known for his pictures for *The Vicar of Wakefield; Cranford; Vanity Fair;* etc.

Thomson, James (1700–1748). English poet, known as a forerunner of ROMANTICISM in a period when NEO-CLASSICISM held sway in literature. His best-known works are THE SEASONS, consisting of *Winter* (1726), *Summer* (1727), *Spring* (1728), and *Autumn* (1730), and THE CASTLE OF INDOLENCE (1748), an imitation of the style of Edmund SPENSER. These poems are marked by love of nature, humanitarianism, fantasy, and sensuous imagery, all romantic qualities unique at the time of composition. Thomson is considered to be one of the founders of the tradition of nature poetry in English literature, and to have helped (in *The Seasons*) to reintroduce blank verse as a medium of poetic expression and to establish the tradition of MILTON as an important influence in English poetry. Thomson also wrote *Sophonisba,* a tragedy; *Liberty* (1734), a long poem, which he considered his best work; and the famous *Rule, Britannia.*

Thomson, James (1834–1882). English poet, known for his savage melancholy, political radicalism, and atheism, best expressed in his most famous poem, THE CITY OF DREADFUL NIGHT (1880). He also wrote *Vane's Story, Weddah, and Om-el-Bonain, And Other Poems* (1881); *Insomnia* (1882); and critical prose studies of Ben Jonson, William Blake, and other English writers. The well-known short poem *Give a Man a Horse He Can Ride* (1865), later set to music, was of his authorship. He was a great admirer of both P. B. SHELLEY and NOVALIS, whose names he combined into **Bysshe Vanolis,** a pseudonym he frequently used, signing his work with the initials **B.V.**

Thomson had an extremely unhappy life,

his father being paralyzed when the poet was a young child and his mother being the victim of a melancholy religious mania. For a time he was an army instructor in Ireland; then he became a radical journalist and held a number of other jobs of a miscellaneous nature. His death came as the result of excessive dissipation. See also BRADLAUGH, CHARLES; WELLER, MATILDA.

Thomson, Sir John Arthur (1861–1933). Scottish biologist who has written popular books on science, notably *The Outline of Science* (1922). William Beebe thinks that he is "the most capable compiler of scientific literature in the world."

Thomson, Virgil (1896–). American composer and critic. An intimate friend of Gertrude STEIN, he wrote the music for her opera *Four Saints in Three Acts* (1934). Music critic of the New York *Herald Tribune*. *The State of Music* (1939). *The Musical Scene* (1945); *The Art of Judging Music* (1948).

Thomson, William. 1st Baron **Kelvin** (1824–1907). British mathematician and physicist who made lasting contributions to thermodynamics and electricity. In 1866 he was instrumental in the laying of a trans-Atlantic cable.

Thopas, Rime of Sir. A burlesque on contemporary metrical romances, told as Chaucer's own tale in the CANTERBURY TALES. Sir Thopas is a native of Poperyng in Flanders, a capital sportsman, archer, wrestler and runner. The beginning of his adventures is told in minute, interminable detail. He resolves to marry no one but an elf queen, and sets out for Fairyland. On his way he meets the three-headed giant Olifaunt, who challenges him to single combat. The knight gets permission to go back for his armor, and promises to meet the giant next day. Here mine host interrupts the narrative as intolerable nonsense, and the "rime" is left unfinished.

Thor. In Norse mythology, after Odin, the second principal god. He is the son of Odin and Earth, the god of thunder, and owns as his most precious possessions a hammer, a belt of strength, and a pair of iron gloves. The giant who built the residence for the gods was paid by Thor with his mallet. When this hammer had fallen into the possession of the giant Thrym, Thor recovered it by dressing himself in Freya's clothes, pretending to be the fair goddess whom the giant wanted to be his bride in exchange for the hammer. During a visit to Jotunheim Thor almost lifted the Midgard serpent off the earth; he almost conquered Elli, old age; and almost emptied a drinking horn which was connected with the ocean. At Ragnarok Thor will kill the Midgard serpent but die from its venom.

Thoreau, Henry David (1817–1862). American poet, prose-writer, and naturalist, a member of the school of TRANSCENDENTALISM, chiefly influenced by the philosophic ideas of R. W. EMERSON. Thoreau is known for his extreme individualism, his love of nature, his primitivistic preference for simple, even austere living (see PRIMITIVISM), his tendencies toward mysticism, and his revolt against the demands of society and government. His works include *A Week on the Concord and Merrimack Rivers* (1849); WALDEN (1854), his most famous book; *Excursions* (1863); *The Maine Woods* (1864); *Cape Cod* (1865); *A Yankee in Canada* (1866); *Early Spring in Massachusetts* (1881), *Summer* (1884), *Winter* (1888), and *Autumn* (1892), selections from his massive *Journal*, which was published in its entirety, fourteen volumes, in 1906; *Letters* (1894); *Poems of Nature* (1895). *Civil Disobedience* (1849) and *Life Without Principle* (1863), are his best-known single essays, summarizing his ideas on the individual and society.

Thoreau was extremely eccentric, independent, and individualistic in his behavior. He spent several years in a little hut in the countryside near the village of Concord, Massachusetts, writing and observing nature; on one occasion he spent a day in jail for refusing to pay his poll-tax, because he disapproved of the war with Mexico then in process, regarding it merely as an expedition to seize land. In his later years he traveled in New England and Canada, lectured, especially in connection with the abolitionist movement, wrote in his journal, and worked on a study of the Indians which was never completed. He died of tuberculosis.

Thorfinn Karlsefni (*fl.* 1002–1007). Icelandic explorer who searched for Vineland, which was later discovered by Leif Ericsson.

thorn.

a thorn in the flesh. A source of constant irritation, annoyance, or affliction; said of objectionable and parasitical acquaintances, obnoxious conditions, of a "skeleton in the cupboard," etc. The expression was first used by St. Paul in one of his *Epistles*. There was a sect of the PHARISEES which used to insert thorns in the borders of their gaberdines to prick their legs in walking and make them bleed.

the Crown of Thorns. That with which Jesus was crowned in mockery (*Matt.* xxvii. 29); hence, sometimes used of a very special affliction with which one is unjustly burdened.

Thornbury, George Walter (1828–1876). English writer; in his time a well-known contributor to the magazines edited by Charles Dickens. Cf. also his history of London, *Old and New London* (1872, 1876).

Thorndike, Ashley Horace (1871–1933). American educator; authority on the Elizabethan drama and Shakespeare. His brother, **Edward Lee Thorndike** (1874–), is a well-known psychologist; another brother, **Lynn Thorndike** (1882–), is a historian, especially known for his books on medical history.

Thorndike, Dame **Sybil** (1882–). English actress and theatrical manager. She toured Egypt, Palestine, Australia, and New Zealand in the 1930's. Dame of the British Empire (1931). Her brother, Russell Thorndike, is an actor and writer.

Thorndyke, Dr. A scientific detective, in stories by R. Austin FREEMAN.

Thorne, Dr. In Trollope's *Chronicles of Barsetshire* (see BARSETSHIRE), notably in *Dr. Thorne,* a kindly physician of the village of Greshambury. The heroine of the novel is his niece, Mary Thorne, a lovable girl, typically English in her charms and virtues, who finally marries Frank GRESHAM.

Thornhill, Sir William. The whimsical landlord of the VICAR OF WAKEFIELD in Goldsmith's novel of that name. After traveling through Europe on foot, he returns disguised as MR. BURCHELL. Twice he rescues Sophia PRIMROSE: once when she is thrown from her horse into a deep stream, and once when she is abducted by his nephew, Squire Thornhill. Ultimately he marries her.

Squire Thornhill. Nephew of Sir William Thornhill. He enjoys a large fortune, but is entirely dependent on his uncle. He is a sad libertine, who abducts both the daughters of Dr. Primrose and casts the old Vicar into jail for not paying the rent after the entire loss of his house, money, furniture, and books by fire. He tries to impose upon Olivia Primrose by a false marriage but is caught in his own trap, for the marriage proves to be entirely legal.

Thornton, John. The dog Buck's master in Jack London's novel, THE CALL OF THE WILD.

Thorold, Earl of Tresham. The chief character in Browning's BLOT ON THE 'SCUTCHEON.

Thorpe, John. A young blusterer in Jane Austen's NORTHANGER ABBEY.

Thorpe, Lossie. The heroine of De Morgan's JOSEPH VANCE.

Thorpe, Rose Hartwick (1850–1939). American writer. In 1867 she contributed to a Detroit newspaper the well-known ballad *Curfew Must not Ring Tonight.*

Thorpe, Thomas Bangs (1815–1878). Early American artist and pioneer in the American "tall tale," notably in *The Big Bear of Arkansas* (1841). He was a friend of Zachary Taylor and wrote *The Taylor Anecdote Book* (1848). His *The Bee-Hunter* (1854) was translated and read abroad.

Thorvaldsen, Bertel (1768–1844). Danish sculptor famous for his statue of the *Lion of Lucerne.*

Thoth. A prominent god of Egyptian mythology, identified by the Greeks and Romans with HERMES or MERCURY. He is represented with the head of an ibis on a human body. He is the inventor of the arts and sciences, music and astronomy, speech and letters. Sometimes he is shown holding in his hand the heart and tongue of RA, the sun-god, to imply that he controls the intelligence of that great deity.

Thoughtless, Miss Betty. The heroine of a novel of that name by Mrs. Heywood (1697–1758), a virtuous, sensible, and amiable young lady, utterly regardless of the conventionalities of society, and wholly ignorant of etiquette. She is consequently forever involved in petty scrapes most mortifying to her sensitive mind. Even her lover is alarmed at her *gaucherie,* and deliberates whether such a partner for life is desirable. Mrs. Heywood's novel is said to have suggested the more important *Evelina* of Fanny BURNEY.

Thousand and One Nights. See ARABIAN NIGHTS.

Thrale, Mrs., later **Mrs. Piozzi.** A famous friend of Samuel JOHNSON, who spent much time at her home and regarded her highly. After his death she published anecdotes about him, as well as her correspondence with him.

Thraso. A boastful captain in the comedy *Eunuchus* (*The Eunuch*) by TERENCE, said to have been the inspiration for similar characters in Elizabethan drama. See BOBADIL; PAROLLES; COPPER CAPTAIN, etc.

Thrasybulus. Athenian general who aided Alcibiades in his victories over the Spartans (411–410 B.C.). He was exiled from Athens; upon his return he helped institute a more democratic form of government. In 389 B.C. he commanded the fleet against the Spartans and was killed in battle.

Threadneedle Street. The street in the City of London leading from Bishopsgate to the Bank of England.

the Old Lady of Threadneedle Street. The Bank of England, which stands in this street. The term dates from the late 18th century, and there is a caricature by Gilray, dated May 22, 1797, entitled *The Old Lady in Threadneedle Street in Danger,* which refers to the temporary stopping of cash payments, February 26, 1797, and to the issue of one pound banknotes on March 4 the same year.

three. The philosopher PYTHAGORAS calls three the perfect number, expressive of "beginning, middle, and end," wherefore he makes it a symbol of Deity.

A Trinity is by no means confined to the Christian creed. The Hindu Trimurti consists of Brahma, the Creator, Vishnu, the Preserver, and Siva, the Destroyer. The world was supposed by the ancients to be under the rule of three gods, viz. Jupiter (heaven), Neptune (sea), and Pluto (Hades). Jove is represented with three-forked lightning, Neptune with a trident, and Pluto with a three-headed dog. The Fates are three, the Furies three, the Graces three, the Harpies three, the Sibylline books three times three (of which only three survived); the fountain from which Hylas drew water was presided over by three nymphs; the Muses were three times three; the pythoness sat on a three-legged stool, or tripod; and in Scandinavian mythology we hear of "the Mysterious Three," viz., "Har" (the Mighty), the "Like-Mighty," and the "Third Person," who sat on three thrones above the rainbow.

Man is threefold (body, soul, and spirit); the world is threefold (earth, sea, and air); the enemies of man are threefold (the world, the flesh, and the Devil); the Christian graces are threefold (Faith, Hope, and Charity); the kingdoms of nature are threefold (mineral, vegetable, and animal); the cardinal colors are three in number (red, yellow, and blue), etc. See NINE, which is three times three.

three acres and a cow. See ACRE.

three ages of man. See AGES.

three estates of the realm. See ESTATE.

Three guardsmen. See THREE MUSKETEERS.

Three Kings of Cologne. See COLOGNE; MAGI.

three-mile limit. An expression referring to the three-mile expanse of water out from any shore, the jurisdiction over which, according to international law, belongs to the country owning the mainland. The phrase was widely used in connection with the VOLSTEAD ACT which could not be enforced by the United States beyond the *three-mile limit;* hence, the use of liquor was lawful beyond that point.

three r's. See under R.

three tailors of Tooley Street. See TAILOR.

Three Unities, see UNITIES.

Three Bears, The. See GOLDILOCKS.

Three Black Pennys, The. A novel by Joseph HERGESHEIMER (1917), telling the story of several generations of Pennys. The Pennys are a family of Pennsylvania iron founders, for the most part sober and respectable but with a queer wild strain in the blood that manifests itself in an occasional dark-skinned, passionate "Black Penny." The last of the "Black Pennys," Howat, is a modern dilettante.

Three Lives. The first published work of Gertrude STEIN (1909), consisting of three sympathetic character studies of women in lowly circumstances. *The Good Anna* deals with Anna Federner, a kindly, devoted housekeeper; *The Gentle Lena* tells of the wretched married life of a German servant-girl; *Melanctha* is concerned with an intelligent, partially white Negro girl who finds only unhappiness among the Negroes with whom she grows up. The style in which *Three Lives* is written is extremely simple and concrete, suggesting the author's later experiments.

Three Men in a Boat. A story by Jerome K. JEROME.

Three Men on a Horse. A comedy (1935) by John Cecil Holm and George Abbott.

Three Musketeers, The (*Les Trois Mousquetaires*). A famous historical romance by Alexandre DUMAS (1844), which, together with its sequels, *Twenty Years After* (*Vingt Ans après;* 1845) and *The Vicomte de Bragelonne* (1848) covers the period of 1625 to 1665 in French history. The central figure, D'Artagnan, was a historical personage (1623–1673); his three friends also have counterparts in history, even to their names, and much of the material for the novels is drawn from D'Artagnan's *Memoirs.* Few characters of fiction are so widely beloved as this gay and high-spirited young Gascon, whose arrival in Paris on a raw-boned yellow pony with but three crowns to his name is the opening chapter of a whirlwind of adventures. He is determined to become one of Louis XIII's guardsmen, and before his first day in Paris is over, he has involved himself in duels with Athos, Porthos and Aramis, three of the most renowned fighters of that renowned corps. As an upshot he is welcomed into the congenial fellowship of the "three Musketeers"; and the fortunes and misfortunes, narrow escapes and amazing exploits of these four fast friends form the subject matter of the novels. The trilogy follows the career of D'Artagnan (Charles de Baatz, Seigneur d'Artagnan) through to his death as Comte d'Artagnan, commander of the Musketeers and marshal of France. Of the four friends, Athos is always the gallant gentleman, Porthos the physical giant, good-hearted but not too clever, Aramis the schemer and politician with leanings toward the church, and D'Artagnan first and foremost the soldier, quick-witted, quick-tempered, brave and lovable.

In *Twenty Years After,* a romance which deals with the uprising against Cardinal Mazarin known as the Fronde, the old friends are on opposing sides. D'Artagnan and Porthos, as guardsmen, support the powers that be; Athos and Aramis (who have retired from the corps, the former to a country-seat, the latter to a monastery) join the intrigue. *The Vicomte de Bragelonne,* the last of the trilogy, deals with the reign of Louis XIV and includes portions frequently published as separate novels, notably *Louise de la Vallière* and *The Man in the Iron Mask*. The Vicomte de Bragelonne is a son of Athos, in love with Louise de la Vallière, who becomes the mistress of the King. In this novel Aramis is general of the Jesuits, and the main plot concerns itself with his schemings for power. He it is who discovers the existence of the mysterious individual later known as the "Man in the Iron Mask" (see under MAN) and almost succeeds in kidnaping Louis XIV and setting this twin brother and physical double on the throne in his place.

Rudyard KIPLING has a story entitled *The Three Musketeers* in his *Plain Tales from the Hills,* opening with the sentence "MULVANEY, ORTHERIS, LEAROYD are privates in the B Company of a Line Regiment and personal friends of mine. Collectively I think, but am not certain, they are the worst men in the regiment so far as genial blackguardism goes." This trio appears in many other of Kipling's tales.

Three Sisters, The. A drama in four acts (1900) by Anton CHEKHOV concerning three sisters who spend a dull existence in the country and long to go to a big city.

Three Soldiers. A novel by John Dos PASSOS (1921), dealing with three representative soldiers in the American army during World War I: Dan Fuselli, an Italian-American; Chrisfield, a farmboy from Indiana; and John Andrews, a sensitive musician who longs to be a composer. Fuselli does not mind life in the army, being interested only in advancement, but Chrisfield and Andrews are extremely unhappy and resentful of its regimentation of their lives. The latter two desert, and Andrews spends some time in the French countryside composing a symphony before he is apprehended.

Three Wise Fools. A comedy (1918) by Austin STRONG.

Threshers. Members of an Irish political organization instituted in 1806 by Catholics in opposition to the ORANGEMEN. One object was to resist the payment of tithes. Their threats and warnings were signed "Captain Thresher."

Throckmorton, Cleon (1897–). American stage designer (since 1917), originally a painter. He has done designs for Eugene O'Neill plays; for *Porgy;* Sidney Howard's *The Silver Cord;* etc.

Throgmorton Street. In England the financial world at large, or the Stock Exchange, which is situated in this narrow London street. It was so named from Sir Nicholas Throckmorton (d. 1571), head of the ancient Warwickshire family and ambassador to France in the reign of Queen Elizabeth.

Through the Looking-Glass. Sequel (1872) to ALICE'S ADVENTURES IN WONDERLAND, by LEWIS CARROLL.

Through the Wheat. A war novel (1923) by Thomas BOYD.

Thrums. The town immortalized by Sir James BARRIE under this name in his *Window in Thrums* (1889) and other volumes is Kirriemuir, Forfarshire.

Thrym or **Thrymr.** In Scandinavian mythology, a giant who stole THOR'S hammer Mjolnir and refused to return it unless he was given the goddess FREYA. Thor put on Freya's garments and presented himself as a veiled bride accompanied by LOKI as handmaid. When Thrym expressed surprise at his bride's tremendous appetite, Loki explained that she had been so impatient to see her lover that she had not touched food for eight days. The hammer was now brought and the supposed Freya seized it and killed Thrym and all his company.

Thucydides (471?–?400 B.C.). Greek historian, considered the greatest historian of ancient times. His famous *History of the Peloponnesian War* was written in exile (423–403 B.C.).

thug. Originally, a member of a religious body of northern India, worshipers of KALI, who could be propitiated only by human victims who had been strangled, hence, the thugs became a professional fraternity of stranglers, and supported themselves by the plunder obtained from those they strangled. Their native name is *p'hansigars* ("stranglers"); that of *thug* ("cheat") was given them in 1810. Their methods were rigorously suppressed under British rule, and were practically extinct by 1840. The word is used for any ruffian.

Thule. The name given by the ancients to an island, or point of land, six days' sail north of Britain, and considered by them to be the extreme northern limit of the world. The name is first found in the account by Polybius (ca. 150 B.C.) of the voyage made by Pytheas in the late 4th century B.C. Pliny says, "It is an island in the Northern Ocean discovered by Pytheas, after sailing six days from the Orcades." Others, like CAMDEN, consider it to be Shetland, in which opinion they agree with Marinus, and the descriptions of Ptolemy and Tacitus; still others assert that it was some part of the coast of Norway. The etymology of the name is unknown.

Ultima Thule. The end of the world; the last extremity.

> Tibi serviat Ultima Thule.
> Virgil, *Georgics,* i, 30.

Title of a novel by Henry Handel RICHARDSON.

Thulstrup, Thure (1848–1930). Widely known American illustrator. In the 1880's he contributed many historical pictures to *Frank Leslie's Illustrated Weekly* and *Harper's Weekly*.

Thumb, Tom, see TOM THUMB.

Thummim. See under URIM.

thunder.

the Sons of Thunder. See under SON.

to steal one's thunder. To forestall him; or to adopt his own special methods as one's own. The phrase comes from the anecdote of John Dennis (d. 1734), the critic, who invented a very effective way of producing stage thunder for use in a play of his. The play was refused a hearing, but, to the author's extreme annoyance, they "stole his thunder" for *Macbeth*.

the Thunderer. A name facetiously applied to *The Times* (London) in the mid-19th century, in allusion to an article by the editor, Edward Sterling (d. 1847), beginning:

> We thundered forth the other day on the subject of social and political reform.—*The Times.*

Thundering Legion. A famous Roman legion of the 2nd century, said to be so called from the thunderstorm which aided in their defeat of the Marcomanni.

Thundertentronckh, Arminius von. A pseudonym under which Matthew ARNOLD wrote a number of satiric essays, chiefly for *The Pall Mall Gazette*. They were brought out in book form under the title *Friendship's Garland*.

Thurber, James Grover (1894–). American author and cartoonist, known for the irony, satire, and fantastic, whimsical humor of his drawings and prose sketches of 20th-century American life as published chiefly in THE NEW YORKER. His books include *Is Sex Necessary?* (1929), written with E. B. WHITE; *The Owl in the Attic, And Other Perplexities* (1931); *The Seal in the Bedroom, And Other Predicaments* (1932); *My Life and Hard Times* (1933); *The Middle-Aged Man on the Flying Trapeze* (1935); *Let Your Mind Alone* (1937); *The Last Flower* (1939); *My World—And Welcome to It* (1942); *The Male Animal* (1940), a comedy; *The White Deer* (1945), a fairy tale.

Thurio. In Shakespeare's TWO GENTLEMEN OF VERONA, a foolish rival of Valentine for the love of Silvia, daughter of the Duke of Milan.

Thursday, Black. See under BLACK.

Thurso's Landing. A book of poems (1932) by Robinson JEFFERS.

Thurston, Ernest Temple (1879–1933). Once a husband of Katherine Cecil THURSTON, he was a graceful writer of many books and plays, some of them whimsical and some naturalistic, his sentimental romances being the most popular, the *Richard Furlong* trilogy the best written.

Thurston, Hannah, see HANNAH THURSTON.

Thurston, Mrs. **Katherine Cecil** (1875–1911). English novelist whose greatest popular success was *John Chilcote, M.P.* (1904) which was dramatized by her husband, Ernest Temple THURSTON, as *The Masquerader* (1905). There have been several moving-picture versions of it.

Thus Spake Zarathustra (*Also sprach Zarathustra*). A noted philosophical treatise by Friedrich NIETZSCHE (1883–1891), which develops his doctrine of the SUPERMAN and the supremacy of power. Zarathustra refers to the Persian seer ZOROASTER who is used as a mouthpiece for Nietzsche's theories.

Thwackum, Parson Roger. A famous character in Fielding's novel *The History of Tom Jones, a Foundling* (see TOM JONES), a clergyman and pedagogue. He has a terrific temper and is over-given to looking after his own interests, but is a man of parts and of some principle.

Thwaites, Reuben Gold (1853–1913). American historian, chiefly known for his enormous editorial work, *Jesuit Relations and Allied Documents* (73 vols.; 1896–1901). He also edited many early travel journals.

Thyestes. In classic myth, a son of Pelops who seduced the wife of his brother ATREUS.

Thyestean banquet. A cannibal feast. Thyestes was given his own son to eat at a banquet served up to him by his brother Atreus.

Thyestean revenge. Blood for blood; tit for tat of bloody vengeance.

Thyrsis. (1) A herdsman introduced in the *Idyls* of THEOCRITUS, and in VIRGIL's *Eclogue*, vii. Any shepherd or rustic is so called.

> Hard by, a cottage chimney smokes
> From betwixt two aged oaks,
> Where Corydon and Thyrsis, met,
> Are at their savoury dinner set.
> Milton, *L'Allegro* (1638).

(2) A monody on his friend Arthur Henry Clough by Matthew ARNOLD.

thyrsus. A long pole with an ornamental head of ivy, vine leaves, or a fir cone, carried by BACCHUS and by his votaries at the celebration of his rites. It was emblematic of revelry and drunkenness.

Tibbett, Lawrence (1896–). American baritone who made his début on the concert stage in 1917 and in opera at the Metropolitan Opera House in New York City in 1923. He has sung in many operas and also on the air and in moving pictures.

Tibbs, Beau. A famous character in Goldsmith's CITIZEN OF THE WORLD, a poor, clever, dashing young spark, who has the happy art of fancying he knows all the *haut monde,* and that all the *monde* knows him; that his garret is the choicest spot in London for its commanding view of the Thames; that his wife is a lady of distinguished airs; and that his infant daughter will marry a peer. He takes off his hat to every man and woman of fashion, and pretends that dukes, lords, duchesses, and ladies address him simply as Ned.

> "I was asked to dine yesterday," he says, "at the Duchess of Piccadilly's. My Lord Mudler was there. 'Ned,' said he, 'I'll hold gold to silver I can tell you where you were poaching last night . . . I hope, Ned, it will improve your fortune.' 'Fortune, my Lord? five hundred a year at least—great secret—let it go no further.' My Lord took me down in his chariot to his country seat yesterday, and we had a *tête-à-tête* dinner in the country." "I fancy you told us just now you dined yesterday at the Duchess's in town." "Did I so" replied he coolly. "To be sure, egad! now I do remember—yes, I had two dinners yesterday."—*Letter liv.*

Tiberinus. In Roman myth, the god of the River Tiber.

Tibullus, Albius (54?–?18 B. C.). Roman elegiac poet. Only two books of his verse have come down to us.

Tichborne Claimant. See ORTON, ARTHUR.

Tickell, Thomas (1686–1740). English poet who contributed to Dr. Johnson's *Guardian* and to the *Spectator*. The fact that he published a partial translation of *The Iliad* caused a famous quarrel between Addison and Pope. He collected and edited the works of Addison (1721).

Tickler, Timothy. One of the group whose conversations form the subject matter of the NOCTES AMBROSIANAE by Christopher North (John Wilson). He is said to be an ideal portrait of Robert Sym, a lawyer of Edinburgh (1750–1844).

Ticknor, George (1791–1871). American historian, scholar, and author, known for his pioneer work in the study and teaching of modern European languages in the U.S. He studied and traveled in Europe and was the first Smith Professor of French and Spanish at Harvard University. His leading work is *History of Spanish Literature* (1849, 1872).

Tieck, Johann Ludwig (1773–1853). Voluminous German writer of the romantic school.

Tiepolo, Giovanni Battista (1696–1770). Italian master of the Venetian school. He did many frescoes, some of which are in Italy, some in the Royal Palace at Würzburg and the Royal Palace at Madrid.

Tietjens, Eunice (1884–1944). American author, who was for 25 years on the staff of *Poetry: A Magazine of Verse*. She wrote several books of above-average poems, novels, and some juveniles. Her autobiography, *The World at My Shoulder* (1938), is very interesting.

Tiffany, Louis Comfort (1848–1933). American painter and stained-glass artist, son of the internationally established American jeweler **Charles Lewis Tiffany** (1812–1902). He developed a process for manufacturing opalescent glass and established a foundation for art students at Oyster Bay, Long Island.

Tiffany, Mrs. The leading character in the comedy FASHION by Mrs. Mowatt Ritchie.

Tiffet, Mahetable. See CRÈVECOEUR, HECTOR ST. JOHN DE.

tiffin. An old Northern English dialect word for a small draught of liquor. It was introduced into India, where it acquired its modern meaning of a lunch or light meal between breakfast and dinner. The word is almost solely used by Anglo-Indians, but it is in no way an Indian word.

Tiger, the. The nickname of the French statesman Georges CLEMENCEAU (b. 1841). A *tiger* is also a final yell in a round of cheering.

Tiger, The. A famous poem by William BLAKE, contained in his *Songs of Experience* (1794), celebrating the mystery and triumph of the creation of life. The first stanza is as follows:

> Tiger! Tiger! burning bright
> In the forests of the night,
> What immortal hand or eye
> Could frame thy fearful symmetry?

Tiger Lily. An Indian princess in Barrie's PETER PAN.

Tighe, Mary (1772–1810). Irish poet. Her poem *Psyche* (1805) greatly attracted John Keats.

til. A Portuguese DIACRITICAL MARK, in appearance and origin identical with the Spanish TILDE, used over various vowels to indicate their nasalization.

Tilburina. In Sheridan's comedy THE CRITIC, a character in Mr. Puff's tragic drama, *The Spanish Armada,* which is being rehearsed. Tilburina is a gushing, romantic girl in love with Whiskerandos. She is the daughter of the governor of Tilbury Fort, "a plain matter-of-fact man" whose temperament is in sharp contrast with that of his emotional daughter.

Tilbury Town. An imaginary town created and populated by the poems of Edwin Arlington ROBINSON. It exists presumably in New England. Among the best-known characters are Richard Cory, a fine gentleman who shoots himself, to everyone's surprise; Miniver Cheevy, the town drunkard; the mysterious "man Flammonde from God knows where"; and Old King Cole, whose three sons have proved utterly worthless.

tilde. A Spanish DIACRITICAL MARK, used over the letter *n* (as in *cañon*) to indicate its palatalization. It has evolved from the dash placed by medieval scribes over various letters as a substitute for a following *m* or *n*. The word signifies "title."

Tilden, Samuel Jones (1814–1886). Governor of New York (1875–1876). As Democratic candidate for president (1876), he received more popular votes than the Republican candidate Rutherford B. HAYES, a state of affairs which resulted in the creation of an electoral commission (1877) to examine the contested returns in certain states. The committee reported in favor of Hayes, who was elected by one electoral vote, Tilden always believing that he had been wronged. The fortune that he bequeathed was used to establish a free public library in the City of New York.

Tilden, William Tatem (1893–). American tennis champion of the world (1920–1925) and member of the Davis Cup Team (from 1920).

Tilly, Count of. **Johan Tserclaes** (1559–1632). Flemish field marshal in the Thirty Years' War. He replaced Wallenstein in command of the Imperial forces (1630). In taking Magdeburg, his army committed great atrocities. He was defeated by Gustavus II in two engagements and mortally wounded in the second.

Tilney, Henry. The hero of Jane Austen's NORTHANGER ABBEY. His father, General Tilney, is also a prominent character.

Tim, Tiny, see TINY TIM.

Timaeus. Pythagorean philosopher in Plato's Dialogue named from him. The dialogue is concerned with a theory of the universe and has in it the story of the lost Atlantis.

Time. An American weekly magazine of news, current events, and domestic and foreign affairs, founded in 1923 and known particularly for its compressed, idiomatic, and occasionally fantastic style, making use of word-coinages, epithets, and unusual sentence structure. *Time* became the nucleus of Time, Inc., the publishing enterprise of Henry R. LUCE. It expanded to include *The March of Time,* a radio program and motion-picture newsreel feature.

Time of Man, The. A novel (1926) by Elizabeth Madox ROBERTS.

Times. A New York newspaper, founded in 1851 by Henry Jarvis Raymond (1820–1869) and George Jones (1816–1891) with Whig backers. Raymond, who had helped found the Republican party in 1856, and supported Lincoln during the Civil War, was its editor from 1851 to 1869. After Raymond's death, during the '70s, it led in the attack on the Tweed Ring. It declined during the early '90s, till it was bought by Adolph Ochs, who built it up again and revived its motto, "All the News That's Fit to Print." During two World Wars its war reportage has been of high standard. The family of Adolph Ochs carries on the paper, with Arthur Hays Sulzberger as its publisher. The Times is conservative in editorial tone, though politically independent. It is a morning paper with a large Sunday edition, including the excellent Sunday *Magazine* and *Book Review.*

Times, The. The London *Times* (so named since 1788) was founded by John Walter as *The Daily Universal Register* (1785). There have been many famous editors of the *Times;* its contributors in the early period included George BORROW, Leigh HUNT, DISRAELI, etc.

Timias. Prince Arthur's squire in Spenser's FAËRIE QUEENE, typifying Sir Walter Raleigh. See AMORET.

Timoleon (d. ca. 337 B.C.). The liberator of Syracuse and other cities in Sicily. He is mentioned by James THOMSON in *The Seasons.*

Timon of Athens. An Athenian misanthrope of the late 5th century B.C. and the principal figure in SHAKESPEARE's play so called. The play, which was acted about 1608 and printed in 1623, is not all Shakespeare's work. The drama begins with the joyous life of Timon, and his hospitable extravagance; then it launches into his pecuniary embarrassment, and the discovery that his professed friends will not help him. The play ends with his flight into the woods, his misanthropy, and his death. Aside from the hero, the two most important characters are Flavius, his faithful steward, and Alcibiades, the Athenian captain. Timon finds a hidden treasure in the woods, but so great is his disillusionment and hatred of mankind that he has no desire to make use of it. He gives a part of it to Flavius and another part to Alcibiades to enable him to launch an expedition against Athens.

MACAULAY uses the expression to *out-Timon Timon*—i.e., to be more misanthropical than even Timon.

Timon's banquet. A banquet at which nothing is served; a banquet of lukewarm water. Timon gave such a feast to bid farewell to his friends and express his scorn for them.

Timoshenko, Semën K. (1895–). Russian soldier. Created marshal of the Red Army and people's commissar for defense (1940). He was commander in chief on the southwestern front and directed the defense of Stalingrad and the Caucasus (1941–1942). He also directed the Winter offensive on the northwestern front (1942–1943).

Timotheus (446–357 B.C.). Renowned Greek musician and poet, referred to in *Alexander's Feast* by John DRYDEN.

Timothy. In the New Testament, one of the early Christians, a convert and associate of PAUL; also, either of the two New Testament *Epistles* to Timothy written by Paul.

Timothy Titcomb, see TITCOMB, TIMOTHY.

Timrod, Henry (1828–1867). American poet and journalist, a member of the CHARLESTON SCHOOL, known for his intensely emotional poems, in classic form, celebrating the South and the Confederacy during the Civil War. His *Collected Verse* was published in 1873; his best-known poems are *The Cotton Boll* and *Ethnogenesis.* He was called "the Laureate of the Confederacy."

tin. Money. A depreciating synonym for silver, called by alchemists "Jupiter."

the little tin god. Pettiness in power, from the use of this expression in one of Kipling's *Departmental Ditties* (1886).

Tin Lizzie. A nickname widely bestowed upon the earlier model (T) FORD automobile.

Tingley, Katherine Augusta (1847–1929). American theosophist who helped found the Universal Brotherhood (superseding the Theosophical Society), of which she became the head at Point Loma, California.

Tinker, Chauncey Brewster (1876–). Emily Sanford Professor of English Literature and Sterling Professor at Yale University. His *Young Boswell* (1922) achieved almost the renown of a best seller. In 1924 he published an authoritative edition of the *Letters of James Boswell.*

Tinker, Edward Larocque (1881–). American man of letters, several of whose studies on the Louisiana French were crowned by the French Academy. Contributor to the New York *Times Book Review.* Mr. Tinker is also a lawyer and banker as well as an expert printer, and the owner of an outstanding collection on Lafcadio HEARN.

tinker, the immortal or the inspired. John BUNYAN.

Tinker Bell. An unseen fairy in Barrie's PETER PAN.

Tin Pan Alley. Popular and journalistic term applied to the section of New York City in which the writers and publishers of popular songs were located; later, by extension, applied to the industry as a whole. Tin Pan Alley was at first located in the district around 14th Street, but later moved uptown. George GERSHWIN and Irving BERLIN were among the leading composers of Tin Pan Alley.

Tintagel Castle. Residence of King Mark of Cornwall.

Tinto, Dick. An artist who appears in two of Scott's novels. He is introduced as a lad in the BRIDE OF LAMMERMOOR and later in ST. RONAN'S WELL, as touching up the signboard of Meg Dods.

Tintoretto. Real name **Jacopo Robusti** (1518–1594). Italian painter called *Il Furioso,* from the extreme rapidity with which he painted. His canvases exhibit his endeavor to combine Michelangelo's power of design with Titian's coloring.

Tiny Tim. Bob Cratchit's little lame son in Dickens' CHRISTMAS CAROL.

Tiphany. The name given in the old romances to the mother of the Magi. Of course it is a corruption of EPIPHANY.

Tiphys. In Greek legend, the name of the pilot of the *Argo,* the vessel of the Argonauts.

Tippecanoe and Tyler too. Campaign slogan of the Whig Party in the presidential campaign of 1840. William Henry HARRISON, the candidate for President was nicknamed "Tippecanoe" from his victory over the Indians at Tippecanoe, Indiana, in the War of 1812. His running mate was John TYLER, who became President when Harrison died one month after his inauguration.

Tirante the White. The hero and title of a famous romance of chivalry. Cervantes describes it thus in his DON QUIXOTE:

> "Let me see that book," said the curé; "we shall find in it a fund of amusement. Here we shall find that famous knight don Kyrie Elyson of Montalban. and Thomas his brother, with the knight Fonseca, the battle which Detriantê fought with Alano, the stratagems of the Widow Tranquil, the amour of the empress with her 'squire, and the witticisms of lady Brillianta. This is one of the most amusing books ever written."

Tiresias. A Theban of Greek legend, who by accident saw ATHENA bathing, and was therefore struck with blindness by her splashing water in his face. She afterwards repented, and, as she could not restore his sight, conferred on him the power of soothsaying and of understanding the language of birds, and gave him a staff with which he could walk as safely as if he had his sight. He found death at last by drinking from the well of Tilphosa. There are several versions of this legend. See also OEDIPUS.

Tirpitz, Alfred von (1849–1930). German admiral who created the navy of the Second Reich and was responsible for unrestricted submarine warfare during World War I. Also remembered for his remarkable beard.

Tisiphone. One of the three FURIES. Covered with a bloody robe, she sits day and night at hell-gate, armed with a whip. Tibullus says her head is coifed with serpents in lieu of hair.

Tish. An intrepid old maid, the heroine of Mary Roberts RINEHART's *Adventures of Letitia Carberry* and of numerous short stories. She has two companions in adventure, Lizzie and Aggie (who has hay fever).

Tissot, James Joseph (1836–1902). French painter and illustrator whose three hundred water-color paintings of the life of Christ (based on sketches made in the Holy Land) were exhibited in 1894.

Titan, The. See COWPERWOOD, FRANK.

Titanic. White Star liner which held the record of size and speed but struck an iceberg south of Newfoundland on its maiden voyage to New York (April 15, 1912). It sank within two and a half hours. More than 1,500 lives were lost. This greatest maritime disaster in times of peace has challenged the imagination of poets and novelists. Cf., for instance, *The Titanic,* a narrative poem by E. J. PRATT, and *Parti de Liverpool,* a novel by André Peisson.

Titania. Queen of the fairies and wife of OBERON. She appears in Shakespeare's MIDSUMMER NIGHT'S DREAM.

Titans. Primordial beings of Greek mythology, of enormous size and strength, and typical of lawlessness and the power of force. There were twelve, six male (Oceanus, Coeus, Crius, Hyperion, Japetus, and Cronus) and six female (Theia, Rhea, Themis, Mnemosyne, Phoebe, and Tethys), children of Uranus and Ge (Heaven and Earth). Legends vary, but one states that Cronus swallowed the rest of them, and that when liberated by ZEUS (son of Cronus), they dethroned and emasculated their father Uranus. Thereupon they made war on Zeus, who, after defeating them, imprisoned them all—Oceanus alone excepted—in TARTARUS.

By Virgil and Ovid the sun was sometimes surnamed *Titan.*

Titcomb, Timothy. The pseudonym under which J. G. HOLLAND wrote some of his early books, notably the *Titcomb Papers,* a series of sketches with a didactic flavor.

Tite Barnacle, see BARNACLE.

Tithonus. A beautiful Trojan of Greek legend, son of Laomedon, and beloved by Eos (Aurora). At his prayer the goddess granted him immortality, but as he had forgotten to ask for youth and vigor he grew old, and life became insupportable. He now prayed Eos to remove him from the world; this, however, she could not do, but she changed him into a grasshopper. TENNYSON has a poem entitled *Tithonus.*

Tithorea. One of the two chief summits of PARNASSUS. It was dedicated to BACCHUS, the other (Lycorea) being dedicated to the MUSES and APOLLO.

Titian. *Ital.* **Tiziano Vecelli** (1477–1576). One of the great painters of all time. He is known as the chief of the Venetian school. As painter to the Venetian state, he did many portraits, frescoes, religious pictures, etc., and became later court painter to Charles V. He is known for his remarkable color and the magnificence of his rendering of flesh and costume. Titian red is a red-yellow of high saturation, valued as rare and beautiful in women's hair.

the French Titian. Jacques Blanchard (1600–1638).

the Portuguese Titian. Alonzo Sanchez Coello (1515–1599).

Titmarsh, Michael Angelo. A pseudonym under which THACKERAY published some of his less important work.

Titorelli. In Franz Kafka's THE TRIAL, a lawyer, the advocate of the hero, K., who receives his client in bed and is unwilling to give him any help.

Titurel. A legendary character who appears in many of the narratives concerning the Holy GRAIL and is the titular hero of a 13th century romance by WOLFRAM VON ESCHENBACH, to which Albert of Scharfenberg later added *Young Titurel.* This valiant and holy knight was the first guardian of the Grail, the father of Frimurtel, who succeeded him as guardian and the grandfather of AMFORTAS.

Titus. (1) An alternative name of the Penitent Thief used in Longfellow's *Golden Legend.*

(2) In Roman legendary history, the son of Lucius Junius BRUTUS. His father condemned him to death for supporting the Tarquins.

Titus Andronicus. A drama published among the plays of SHAKESPEARE and formerly attributed to him (ca. 1589). It is a tragedy of pre-Shakespearean type, full of bloody horrors. The plot turns on the ingratitude of Saturninus, who has become Emperor of Rome through the good offices of Titus Andronicus. Saturninus marries not Titus' daughter Lavinia, to whom he had been betrothed, but Tamora, Queen of the Goths, one of the captives whom the conquering Titus has brought home. She and her lover, Aaron the Moor, accomplish the dishonor and horrible mutilation of Lavinia and the execution of Lavinia's two brothers. Titus now gives himself up to vengeance and one atrocity follows another until all the principal characters are killed. There were several plays on this same subject extant in Shakespeare's time.

Tityrus. A poetical surname for a shepherd; from its use in Greek idyls and Virgil's first *Eclogue.* In the SHEPHERD'S CALENDAR (*Feb., June,* and *Dec.*) Spenser calls CHAUCER by this name.

Tityus. A gigantic son of ZEUS and Ge in Greek mythology whose body covered nine acres of land. He tried to defile LATONA, but APOLLO cast him into TARTARUS, where a vulture fed on his liver, which grew again as fast as it was devoured. See also PROMETHEUS. He was the father of EUROPA.

Tiu. In Scandinavian mythology, the son of ODIN and younger brother of THOR. The wolf Fenris bit off his hand.

Tizona. One of the favorite swords of the CID, taken by him from King Bucar. His other favorite sword was Colada. Tizona was buried with him.

Tlascalan. Indian of a Mexican tribe remembered for having finally joined Cortez against the Aztecs.

T. N. T. An abbreviation of trinitrotoluene, a highly explosive substance.

Tobacco Road. A novel by Erskine CALDWELL (1932), dealing with the impoverished and degenerate Lester family in the cotton region of Georgia. The family includes Jeeter and his wife Ada; Jeeter's aged mother; Dude, the swaggering, 16-year-old son; Ellie May, one of the daughters, afflicted with a hare-lip; and Pearl, the second daughter, who at the age of twelve has been married to Lov Benson, a railroad worker. The family is starving but Jeeter, knowing and caring only for farming, insists on staying on his land. In the course of the story, Dude marries Sister Bessie, a woman preacher, who gives him an automobile with which he accidentally kills his grandmother; Pearl runs away from her husband and Ellie May takes her place; and the farmhouse catches fire, Jeeter and Ada being burned to death. *Tobacco Road* was dramatized as a phenomenally successful play in 1933. It had 3,182 performances.

Tobermory. A story about a talking cat by SAKI.

Tobit. The principal character of the *Book of Tobit,* a romance included in the Old Testament Apocrypha. While sleeping outside the wall of his courtyard he was blinded by sparrows "muting warm dung into his eyes." His son Tobias was attacked on the Tigris by a fish, which leapt out of the water and which he caught at the bidding of the angel Raphael, his mentor. Tobias afterwards married Sara, seven of whose betrothed lovers had been successively carried off by the evil spirit Asmodeus, who was driven by the angel Azarias to the extremity of Egypt, bound. Tobit was cured of his blindness by applying to his eyes the gall of the fish which had tried to devour his son.

Toboso. The village home of DON QUIXOTE's lady-love, whom he renamed DULCINEA. It is a few miles east of Ciudad Real.

Toby. (1) The name of the dog who figures in the old PUNCH AND JUDY puppet-show.

(2) The companion of Melville in his TYPEE.

Uncle Toby. The name by which Captain SHANDY, the uncle of TRISTRAM SHANDY in Sterne's novel of that name, is best known. Also, a small jug or pitcher shaped like a pot-bellied man.

Tocqueville, Count **Alexis Charles Henri Maurice Clérel de** (1805–1859). French historian, known for his studies of the nature and operation of democracy, with the view of advancing the rule of the people and at the same time controlling its undesirable tendencies. His best-known works are *Démocratie en Amérique* (*Democracy in America;* 1835–1839), called the first impartial and systematic study of American institutions; and *L'Ancien Régime et la Revolution* (*The Old Régime and the Revolution;* 1856), a history of the French Revolution of 1789, left unfinished at the time of his death. Tocqueville held a number of official positions in the French government, at one time serving on a special mission to the U.S. He was later a deputy and, for awhile, a minister under Napoleon III, retiring from the latter position after the *coup d'état* of December 2, 1851.

Todd, Mabel Loomis (1858–1932). American poet and author of travel books, best known as editor of the *Poems of Emily Dickinson* (3 series; 1890–1896), partly in collaboration with Colonel Thomas Wentworth Higginson, and *Letters of Emily Dickinson* (1894); all with accurate and fascinating introductions. Editorial work on *Bolts of Melody: New Poems of Emily Dickinson* (1945) was completed by Mrs. Todd's daughter, Mrs. Millicent Todd Bingham, who is also the author of *Ancestors' Brocades: The Literary Debut of Emily Dickinson,* the story of the internecine strife over Emily's literary remains.

Todd, Mary (1818–1882) The wife of Abraham Lincoln whom he married November 4, 1842. She came from Springfield, Illinois. In 1870 she was pensioned by Congress; in 1875 she was adjudged insane.

Todgers, Mrs. In Dickens' MARTIN CHUZZLEWIT, proprietress of a "commercial boarding-house"; weighed down with the overwhelming cares of "sauces, gravy," and the wherewithal of providing for her lodgers. Mrs. Todgers has a "soft heart" for Mr. PECKSNIFF, widower, and being really kind-hearted, befriends poor Mercy Pecksniff in her miserable married life with her brutal husband Jonas Chuzzlewit.

Todhunter, John (1839–1916). Irish writer who practiced medicine in Dublin and wrote poetry and dramas.

Tofana. An old woman of Naples (d. 1730) immortalized by her invention of a tasteless and colorless poison, called by her the *Manna of St. Nicola of Bari,* but better known as *Aqua Tofana.* More than 600 persons fell victim to this insidious drug. It was said to be used particularly by young wives who wished to get rid of their husbands.

toga. The usual outer dress of a Roman citizen when appearing in public; the Romans were hence the *gens togata* or the *togaed people.* The toga consisted of single piece of undyed woolen cloth, cut almost in a semicircle and worn in a flowing fashion round the shoulders and body.

toga picta. The toga embroidered with golden stars that was worn by the emperor on special occasions, by a victorious general at his "triumph," etc.

toga praetexta. The toga with a purple border that was worn by children, by those engaged in sacred rites, magistrates, etc.

toga virilis. The toga worn by men (*Lat. virilis,* "manly"), assumed by boys when they had reached fifteen years of age.

Togo, Hashimura. A character in a series of dialect sketches about a San Francisco Japanese school-boy by Wallace IRWIN.

To Have and Have Not. A novel by Ernest HEMINGWAY (1937), dealing with the efforts of Harry MORGAN, a native of Key West, Florida, to earn a living for himself and his family. He has operated a boat for rental to fishing parties, but during the depression era of the 1930's he turns to the smuggling of Chinese immigrants and then of illegal liquor. While assisting a gang of bank-robbers to escape, he is shot and dies murmuring that ". . . one man alone ain't got—no chance."

To Have and to Hold. A historical novel by Mary JOHNSTON (1899). The scene is laid in 17th century Virginia. Ralph Percy, the hero, takes a bride by chance from a shipload sent from England and learns that his wife is not a domestic servant, as he supposed, but the King's ward, Jocelyn Leigh, who has taken this means of avoiding a marriage with Lord Carnal to which the King has urged her. Carnal pursues her to Virginia and a long series of exciting adventures follows, but he admits his defeat at last and takes poison.

To Helen. A poem by Edgar Allan POE.

Toilers of the Sea (Les Travailleurs de la mer). A novel by Victor HUGO (1866). Much of the action centers about the steamboat *La Durande* and its trips between the Isle of Guernsey and St. Malo, and there is a deal of smuggling and exciting adventure. The heroine is Deruchette and the real hero Gilliatt.

Toinette. In Molière's MALADE IMAGINAIRE, a confidential female servant of ARGAN, the *malade imaginaire.* She is *"adroite, soigneuse, diligente, et surtout fidèle,"* but fond of contradicting and always calling into action her master's irritable temper. In order to cure him, she pretends to be a traveling physician of about ninety years of age, although she has not seen twenty-six summers, and in the capacity of a Galen, declares M. Argan is suffering from lungs, recommends that one arm should be cut off, and one eye taken out to strengthen the remaining one.

Tojo, Hideki (1885–). Japanese minister of war in the Konoye cabinet (1940–1941); prime minister (1941–1945). Tried by U.S. for war guilt, spring, 1948.

Toki. The William TELL of Danish legend. His story is told by SAXO GRAMMATICUS.

Toklas, Alice B. See AUTOBIOGRAPHY OF ALICE B. TOKLAS; STEIN, GERTRUDE.

tolbooth. A tollhouse. Hence, in Scotland, a town hall and also a prison. The Tolbooth in Edinburgh is the center of Sir Walter Scott's HEART OF MIDLOTHIAN.

Toledo. A sword made at Toledo in Spain, which long before and after the Middle Ages was specially famous for its fine blades.

Toller, Ernst (1893–1939). German playwright and poet, of Jewish parentage, known for his revolutionary sympathies. His plays, many of which make use of the techniques of EXPRESSIONISM, marked by fervent humanitarianism and indignation at injustice, deal with the miseries of working people in an industrial civilization, the horror and brutality of war, and the eventual political revolt of the oppressed classes. Toller's dramatic works include *Die Wandlung* (1919); *Man and the Masses* (*Masse-Mensch;* 1921), his best-known play; *The Machine Wreckers* (*Maschinenstürmer;* 1922); *Der entfesselte Wotan* (1923); *Hinkemann* (1924); *Hoppla, wir leben!* (1927), written in a panoramic technique compared to that of John Dos PASSOS; *Feuer aus Kesseln* (1930); *Nie wieder Friede!* (*No More Peace!;* 1937); *Pastor Hall* (1939). Other works are *Gedichte der Gefangenen* (1923); *Vormorgen* (1924), and *Das Schwalbenbuch* (*The Swallow-Book;* 1924), books of poetry; *Quer durch* (1930), translated as *Which World—Which Way?,* an account of travel in Russia and America; *Look through the Bars* (1937), a collection of letters from prison.

Toller fought in the German army during the early years of World War I but later helped to organize labor strikes in Germany as a means of stopping the war. He was elected president of the Bavarian Soviet Republic, set up as a result of revolution, but he was imprisoned for five years when the revolution was suppressed; his best-known works were written during his term in prison. When the National Socialist government (see NAZISM) came to power in Germany in 1933, Toller's books were burned and he was deprived of citizenship. He came to the U.S. as a refugee and was active in the anti-Fascist movements of the 1930's. In despair, he committed suicide in New York.

Tolosa.

he has got the gold of Tolosa. A Latin proverb meaning, "ill-gotten wealth will do no good." It is derived from the account of Caepio, who, on his march to Gallia Narbonensis, stole from Toulouse (Tolosa) the gold and silver consecrated by the Cimbrian Druids to their gods. In the battle which ensued (106 B. C.) both Caepio and his brother consul were defeated by the Cimbrians and Teutons, and 112,000 Romans were left dead on the field.

Tolstoi, Count Aleksei Nikolaevich (1882?–). Russian novelist and playwright. Distantly related to the great TOLSTOI and also, through his mother, to TURGENEV. One of the most notable novelists of the Soviet Union. His novel *Darkness and Dawn* (1936) has been highly praised. His play, *The Path to Victory* (1938), brings Lenin and Stalin on the stage. His greatest work is a fictionized biography *Peter the Great* (1930). It has appeared in two parts over a period of five years and was made into a moving picture.

Tolstoi, Count Leo. Full Russian name **Lev Nikolaevich Tolstoi** (1828–1910). Russian novelist, playwright, short-story writer, and essayist, known for his psychological studies of character and his panoramic pictures of Russian life in the 19th century, and later for his PRIMITIVISM and religious mysticism. Among his works are WAR AND PEACE (1865–1872), his most famous novel; ANNA KARÉNINA (1875–1876); *The Death of Ivan Ilyich* (1884); *The Power of Darkness* (1886), a play; *The Kreutzer Sonata* (1889); *What Is Art?* (1898), an analysis of art according to its emotional appeal; RESURRECTION (1899). Others include *Childhood, Boyhood, and Youth, My Religion,* and *My Confession,* autobiographical and introspective; *The Cossacks; Sebastopol; Master and Man; What Is to Be Done?; The Kingdom of God Is Within You.*

Tolstoi came of a wealthy and noble family, but eventually became discontented, developing a system of thought which emphasized simplicity, faith, love, and the Christian brotherhood of man, and deplored man-made institutions such as governments, churches, and creeds. He forswore literature and art, made an effort to renounce his material possessions, and endeavored to live as a peasant in the country. He died in a railway station after having fled from an unhappy domestic background to take refuge in a monastery.

Tom.

long Tom. A familiar name for any gun of great length; especially the naval 4.7's used on land in the second Boer War.

Peeping Tom of Coventry. See GODIVA.

Uncle Tom. See UNCLE TOM'S CABIN.

Tom and Jerry. Types of the roistering young man about town; from Pierce Egan's *Life in London, Or The Day and Night Scenes of Jerry Hawthorn, Esq., and his Elegant Friend Corinthian Tom* (1821).

Tom, Dick, and Harry. A set of nobodies; persons of no note; persons unworthy of notice. "Brown, Jones, and Robinson" are other men; they are the vulgar rich, who give themselves airs, especially abroad, and look with scorn on all foreign manners and customs which differ from their own.

Tom Tug. A waterman.

Tom, Uncle. See UNCLE TOM'S CABIN.

To Mary in Heaven. A poem by Robert BURNS (1789), written on the anniversary of the death of Mary CAMPBELL, one of the poet's sweethearts.

Tom Brown's Schooldays. A famous book for boys by Thomas HUGHES (1857) portraying life in an English public school. When Tom enters Rugby, he is a shy, homesick chap, but he is soon drawn into the life of the school and develops robust, manly qualities. A sequel, *Tom Brown at Oxford,* appeared in 1861.

Tom Burke of Ours. A historical novel by Charles LEVER (1844). The witty, brave, resourceful Irish hero is involved in numerous conspiracies and other adventuresome affairs, both in the British Isles and in France where he is a commissioned officer. Napoleon is a prominent character in the novel. He gives Tom his commission, and on one occasion Tom saves his life.

Tom Grogan. A novel by F. Hopkinson Smith (*Am.,* 1896). The heroine, Tom Grogan, is a plucky Irish widow who adopts her husband's name and business as stevedore on Staten Island, in order to make a living for herself and her two children. She runs counter to the labor unions and has a hard fight, but comes out on top.

Tom Jones. More completely, *The History of Tom Jones, a Foundling.* A novel by FIELDING (1749) which, as one of the first of English novels, exerted a great influence upon the development of fiction. Its hero, Tom Jones, is not overheroic; he is perhaps a model of generosity, and manly spirit, but mixed with dissipation. Lord Byron calls him "an accomplished blackguard" (*Don Juan,* xiii. 110, 1824). See also ALLWORTHY.

> A hero with a flawed reputation, a hero sponging for a guinea, a hero who cannot pay his landlady, and is obliged to let his honor out to hire, is absurd, and the claim of Tom Jones to heroic rank is quite untenable.—Thackeray.

Tomlinson, Henry (1873–). English novelist whose *The Sea and The Jungle* (1912) established his reputation as a writer of real literature. His *Gallions Reach* won the *Fémina-Vie Heureuse* prize (1927). He has been compared in certain ways to Joseph CONRAD.

Tommy or **Tommy Atkins.** A British private soldier, as a Jack Tar is a British sailor. At one time all recruits were served out with manuals in which were to be entered the name, age, date of enlistment, length of service, wounds, medals, and so on of the holder.

With each book was sent a specimen form showing how the one in the manual should be filled in, and the hypothetical name selected, instead of the lawyers' *John Doe* or *Richard Roe,* was *Thomas Atkins.* The nickname was popularized by KIPLING.

For it's Tommy this, and Tommy that, and "Tommy, wait outside";
But it's "Special train for Atkins" when the trooper's on the tide.

Tommy (Barrack-Room Ballads.)

Tommy, Sentimental, see SENTIMENTAL TOMMY.

Tommy and Grizel. A novel by J. M. BARRIE (1900), a sequel to SENTIMENTAL TOMMY.

Tommy Gallagher's Crusade. A short novel by James T. FARRELL (1939), presenting a study of the development of a Fascist attitude (see FASCISM) in the mind of Tommy Gallagher, an ill-educated Irish-American youth, unemployed, who listens to the anti-Semitic harangues of Father MOYLAN, a demagogic Roman Catholic radio priest. Under the influence of the priest's arguments, Tommy gradually comes to focus his bitterness and resentment at his own failure on the Jewish race. As the novel closes, Tommy is shown reflecting that once Adolf HITLER was in a position like his own.

Tom o' Bedlam. A mendicant who levies charity on the plea of insanity. In the 16th and 17th centuries applications for admission to BEDLAM became so numerous that many inmates were dismissed half cured. These "ticket-of-leave men" wandered about chanting mad songs, and dressed in fantastic dresses, to excite pity. Posing as these harmless "innocents," a set of sturdy rogues appeared, called ABRAM MEN, who shammed lunacy, and committed great depredations.

Tom Sawyer, The Adventures of. A famous story by Mark TWAIN (1876) which, together with its sequel HUCKLEBERRY FINN, retails the adventures of the "bad boy" of a little Missouri town. Tom Sawyer's maneuvers to outwit his ultra-conventional Aunt Polly, his sworn friendship for the disreputable Huck Finn, his prize collection of Sunday School tickets, the memorable exploits of the whitewashing of the fence and the appearance of Huck and Tom at their own funeral, to mention only a few of his escapades, have endeared him to thousands of readers. The two books referred to above were followed by *Tom Sawyer Abroad* (1894) and *Tom Sawyer Detective* (1896).

Tom the Piper's Son. The thievish hero of an old nursery rhyme. *Tom the Piper* was one of the characters in the old MORRIS DANCE.

Tom Thumb. Any dwarfish or insignificant person is so called; from the pigmy hero of the old nursery tale, popular in the 16th century. *The History of Tom Thumb* was published by R. Johnson in 1621 and a similar tale by PERRAULT (*Le Petit Poucet*), in 1630. The American midget Charles Sherwood Stratton (1838–1883) exhibited at sideshows by P. T. BARNUM, was popularly called "General Tom Thumb."

Tom Tiddler's ground. A children's game in which one child stands on one side of a line drawn on the ground and the others run across shouting "Here we are on Tom Tiddler's ground picking up gold and silver." They are then pursued by the child who is "it" and the first one caught takes his place.

Tom Titivil. The name of the devil in many of the old MORALITY PLAYS.

Tone, Wolfe (1763–1798). Famous Irish revolutionist who founded the United Irishmen with Thomas Russell and Napper Tandy (Napper Tandy is mentioned in the beginning of the famous Irish song *The Wearing of the Green*). Tone negotiated for a landing of the French in Ireland but the fleet gathered together was scattered by a storm in 1796. The British captured him with a small French squadron off Lough Swilly in 1798. Tone finally committed suicide. One of his descendants is the moving-picture actor Franchot Tone.

tong (Chinese **t'ang,** literally "hall"). A Chinese secret association or society. See also CHINATOWN.

Tonio. A character in Leoncavallo's opera I PAGLIACCI.

Tonio Kröger. A short novel (NOVELLE) by Thomas MANN, considered by many the author's masterpiece because of its concise treatment of the perennial Mann problem of the conflict between the artist and the bourgeois.

Tono-Bungay. A novel by H. G. WELLS (1909). The hero, George Ponderevo, throws in his fortunes with his uncle, inventor of the patent medicine "Tono-Bungay," which brings them both an immense fortune.

Tonson, Jacob (1656?–1736). English publisher. He held the copyright of *Paradise Lost* and published Dryden, Addison and editions of Shakespeare and Beaumont and Fletcher. He also brought out a famous *Miscellany* which Dryden edited and which included poetry by Pope, Swift, etc. Secretary of the Kit-cat Club.

Tonty, Henry de (1650–1704). Companion of La Salle in exploring the Mississippi valley (1678–1683) who also helped the Louisiana colony in its early days (1700–1704). Known as "Tonty of the Iron Hand."

Tooke, Horne (1736–1812). English radical and student, called the "philosopher of

Wimbledon." He wrote on the etymology of English words, including excursions into metaphysics and politics, while he was being imprisoned for opinions which included his championship of the Americans in the Revolution.

Toomer, Jean (1894–). American Negro writer and lecturer. Author of *Cane* (1923); *Essentials* (1931); and *Portage Potential* (1932). A friend of Zona GALE and husband of the novelist Margery Latimer.

Toonerville Trolley. A popular comic supplement feature illustrating the foibles of human nature as seen on a trolley car in the small town of Toonerville, the creation of the American cartoonist Fontaine Fox. The trolley was commercialized as a child's toy during the 1920's.

Tophet. A valley just to the south of Jerusalem, at the southeast of GEHENNA, where children were made to "pass through the fire to MOLOCH." Josiah threw dead bodies, ordure, and other unclean things there, to prevent all further application of the place to religious use (2 *Kings* xxiii. 10), and here Sennacherib's army was destroyed (*Is.* xxx. 31–3). A perpetual fire was kept burning in it to consume the dead bodies, bones, filth, etc., deposited there, and hence it was taken as symbolical of Sheol or Hell. The name is Hebrew, and may mean "a place to be spat upon," or it may be connected with *toph,* a drum, in allusion to the drowning of the murdered children's cries by the beating of drums.

Toplady, Augustus Montague (1740–1778). English clergyman and controversialist, chiefly remembered for his hymn *Rock of Ages* (1775).

Topper. A ribald novel (1926) by Thorne SMITH, later made into a moving picture.

Top Secret. A personal record (1946) by Ralph INGERSOLL about World War II. In it, the author criticizes Generals Montgomery and Eisenhower, and British policy in general, but gives graphic accounts of the invasion of Europe.

Topsy. The Negro slave girl in UNCLE TOM'S CABIN by Harriet Beecher Stowe.

Torah. The name of the first five books of Hebrew law; the Pentateuch.

Toralva. The licentiate in DON QUIXOTE (II. iii. 5), who is conveyed on a cane through the air, with his eyes shut. In the space of twelve hours he arrives at Rome and alights on the tower of Nona, whence, looking down, he witnesses the death of the Constable de Bourbon. Next morning he arrives at Madrid and relates the whole affair. During his flight the Devil bids him open his eyes, and he finds himself so near the moon that he can almost touch it with his finger.

Torch-bearers, The. A play (1922—revised 1938) by George KELLY which is a satire on the little-theater movement.

To-Remain Bible. See BIBLE, SPECIALLY NAMED.

Tormes, Lazarillo de, see LAZARILLO DE TORMES.

Torquato, i.e., **Torquato Tasso,** see TASSO.

Torquemada, Tomás de (1420?–1498). Spanish Dominican monk, appointed by Ferdinand and Isabella the first inquisitor general for all the Spanish possessions and made grand inquisitor by Pope Innocent VIII (1487). Notorious for his cruelty and severity.

Torre, Sir. In Tennyson's IDYLLS OF THE KING, the brother of ELAINE, the lily maid of Astolat.

Torrence, Ridgely (1875–). American poet and playwright, one of the first to write plays of and for the American Negro, as *Plays for a Negro Theater* (1919; including *Granny Maumee; The Rider of Dreams;* and *Simon the Cyrenian*). His poems, *Hesperides* (1925), republished with few additions as *Poems* (1941), make of him an American A. E. Housman.

Torricelli, Evangelista (1608–1647). Italian physicist and mathematician, who invented (1643) the Torricellian Tube, the earliest mercurial barometer.

Torrigiano, Pietro (1472–1522). Florentine sculptor, patronized by Lorenzo the Magnificent. Cellini reports that he once broke Michelangelo's nose in a quarrel.

Tortilla Flat. A novel (1935) by John STEINBECK concerning the halfbreeds in Monterey. Made into a play by Jack Kirkland (1937). Tortillas are Mexican corn cakes.

tory. A word of Irish origin, meaning "pursuer." It was first applied to Irish outlaws, later became a nickname of those opposed to excluding the Duke of York (who became James II and was a Roman Catholic) from succeeding to the Crown. In this way it became the name of one of the great English parties. After 1689 the English tories inclined toward the Stuarts, but after George III came to the throne, their policy became one of upholding church and state and of opposing liberalism. Today "tory" has given place in English politics to "conservative." In a U.S. source of 1777, a tory is defined as "a thing whose head is in England, whose body is in America, and whose neck ought to be stretched."

Tosca, La. An opera by PUCCINI (1900) based on the drama by SARDOU. Tosca, an Italian singer, unable to endure the strain when her lover, the painter, Mario Cavaradossi, who has concealed a dangerous political prisoner, is tortured, reveals the whereabouts of the prisoner to Scarpia, chief of police. Scarpia promises to save Cavaradossi by a mock execution if Tosca will give herself to him. She agrees, but stabs him at the last moment. The execution is, however, a real one, and Tosca leaps from a battlement to her death.

Toscanini, Arturo (1867–). Italian-born operatic and symphonic conductor. He conducted at La Scala in Milan (1898–1907; 1921–1931) and for the Metropolitan Opera Company (1907–1921). He has conducted for the Philharmonic-Symphony Orchestra and at the Bayreuth and Salzburg Festivals. He organized (1937) and conducted the symphony orchestra of the National Broadcasting Company.

Tosti, Sir Francesco Paolo (1847–1916). Italian-born composer and singing teacher to the British royal family (1880). His best-known song is *Good-bye.*

Tostig. Earl of **Northumbria** (died 1066). Saxon ruler, the brother of King Harold of England. Outlawed, he made a pact with Harold Haardraade of Norway and invaded the north of England (1066); defeated and slain by King Harold at Stamford Bridge, just prior to the southern invasion of England by William the Conqueror.

totem. A North American Indian (Algonquin) word for some natural object, usually an animal, taken as the emblem of a person or clan on account of a supposed relationship. Totemism, which is common among primitive peoples, has a distinct value in preventing intermarriage among near relations, for if persons bearing the same totem (as, for instance, in the case of brothers and sisters) intermarry the punishment is death. Another custom is that one is not allowed to kill or eat the animal borne as one's totem.

totem pole. The post standing before a dwelling on which grotesque and, frequently, brilliantly colored representations of the totem were carved or hung. It was often of great size, and sometimes so broad at the base that an archway was cut through it.

Tottel's Miscellany. Popular title for *Songs and Sonnets,* a "miscellany," or collection of poems by various authors, published in its first edition by Richard Tottel in England in 1557. It contained 310 poems, chiefly lyrics, although epigrams, epitaphs, elegies, satires, pastorals, and narrative verse were included also; original work and translations of Latin, Italian, and French poems were represented, as well as the first English SONNETS and possibly the first published genuine English BLANK VERSE. Among the poets appearing in the collection were John HEYWOOD, Sir Thomas WYATT, the Earl of SURREY, Nicholas Grimald, CHAUCER, and a number of "Uncertain Authors." *Tottel's Miscellany* was immensely popular, going through at least eight editions in thirty years, and a number of imitations of it were issued during the latter part of the 16th century, although they were all considered to be inferior to the original. The titles of these later miscellanies include *Pleasant Sonnets and Stories* (1566); *A Hundred Sundry Flowers* (1573); *The Paradise of Dainty Devices* (1576); *Flowers of Epigrams* (1578); *A Gorgeous Gallery of Gallant Inventions* (1578); *The Forest of Fancy* (1579); THE PHOENIX NEST (1593); THE PASSIONATE PILGRIM (1599); *Breton's Bower of Delights* (1591); *The Arbor of Amorous Devices* (1597); *England's Parnassus* (1600); *England's Helicon* (1600); *A Poetical Rhapsody* (1602). A number of these drew some of their selections from *Songs and Sonnets* and *The Paradise of Dainty Devices.*

The poetical miscellany grew out of the "commonplace book," in which the poetry lover of the days before widespread printing would copy down verses that pleased him when he heard them read or saw them in manuscript. There was also a classical model for them in the GREEK ANTHOLOGY.

Tottenham in Boots. A popular toast in Ireland in 1731. Mr. Tottenham gave the casting vote which threw out a Government bill very obnoxious to the Irish, on the subject of the Irish Parliament. He had come from the country, and rushed into the House without changing his boots, just in time to give his vote, which prevented the bill from passing by a majority of one.

Touchstone. The witty clown of Shakespeare's AS YOU LIKE IT. His famous speech is "the seven degrees of affront": (1) the retort courteous, (2) the quip modest, (3) the reply churlish, (4) the reproof valiant, (5) the countercheck quarrelsome, (6) the lie circumstantial, and (7) the lie direct (Act. v. sc. 4). See COUNTERCHECK, etc.

Toulouse-Lautrec. In full **Henri Marie Raymond de Toulouse-Lautrec Monfa** (1864–1901). French painter, designer of posters, and lithographer. His paintings have been frequently exhibited in America. His subjects are taken mostly from the life of the *demi-monde* of Paris. Physically misshapen, he indulged in periodic dissipation. Cf. *Toulouse-Lautrec,* by Gerstle Mack.

Tour, the Grand. A journey through France, Switzerland, Italy, and home by Germany, made by most of the young British aristocrats as the finish of their education. Those who went merely to France or Germany were simply tourists.

tour de force (*Fr.*). A feat of strength or skill.

Tourgée, Albion Winegar (1838–1905). American lawyer and novelist, known for his depiction, realistic in background and detail, of the Reconstruction period in the South after the Civil War. His works include *'Toinette* (1874), reissued in 1881 as *A Royal Gentleman; Figs and Thistles* (1879); *A Fool's Errand* (1879); *Bricks without Straw* (1880); *John Eax and Mamelon* (1882); *Hot Plowshares* (1883); *Button's Inn* (1887); *With Gauge and Swallow* (1889); *Pactolus Prime* (1890); *The Mortgage on the Hiproof House* (1896). These are particularly marked by an understanding of the problems of the Negro.

Tourgée fought in the Northern army during the Civil War, and later went to North Carolina as a carpetbagger. As a judge in the superior court of the state he helped to break up the KU KLUX KLAN, and much of the material in his books was based on first-hand experience.

tournament (O. Fr. *torneiement,* from Lat. *tornare,* "to turn"). A tilt of knights, the chief art of the game being so to maneuver or *turn* your horse as to avoid the adversary's blow.

Tournament of Tottenham, The. A comic romance, given in Percy's *Reliques.* A number of clowns are introduced, practicing warlike games and making vows like knights of high degree. They ride tilt on cart-horses, fight with ploughshares and flails, and wear for armor wooden bowls and saucepan-lids.

Tourneur or **Turnour** or **Turner, Cyril** (1575?–1626). Elizabethan dramatist who wrote *The Revenger's Tragedy* (?1607) and *The Atheist's Tragedy* (?1611). His *Plays and Poems* were edited (1878) by John Churton COLLINS and later (1930) by Allardyce NICOLL. Tourneur's work has tragic intensity.

Toussaint L'Ouverture. The Negro hero who freed San Domingo from French rule (1791). He died in captivity in France. He is the central figure of a historical novel, *The Hour and the Man* (1840), by Harriet Martineau. *Black Majesty* (1928) by John W. Vandercook in his biography, and Selden Rodman, in *The Revolutionists,* has written in drama form the story of him and HENRY CHRISTOPHE.

Tovarich. A comedy (1934) adapted by Robert E. SHERWOOD from the French of Jacques DEVAL. The word means "comrade" and is used in Communist Russia as a greeting and form of address.

Tower Beyond Tragedy, The. A play in free verse which appeared in *Tamar and Other Poems* (1924) by Robinson JEFFERS. It is one of the best English modernizations of a Greek tragic theme.

Tower Hill. An elevation near the Tower of London, the site of the execution of traitors. Among famous figures executed there were Sir Thomas More, the Earl of Surrey, Strafford, and Archbishop Laud.

Tower of Babel. See under BABEL.

Tower of London. William the Conqueror and the monarchs that followed him built the various buildings included in the name Tower of London, which stand by the Thames. The Tower has been a prison for many distinguished persons including kings and queens. It is said that the last person sent to the Tower was Sir F. Burdett in 1810.

Towers, Duchess of. A character in PETER IBBETSON by George DU MAURIER.

town and gown. The two sections of a university town, composed of those who are not attached to the university and those who are; hence, *a town and gown row,* a collision, often leading to a fight, between the students and non-gownsmen. See also PHILISTINES.

Towne, Charles Hanson (1877–). American editor and poet. Editor of *Harper's Bazaar* (1926–1931) and writer of a column for the New York *American* (1931–1937). Two of his best-known poems are *Youth* and *Manhattan.*

Towneley Mysteries or **Plays.** One of the important cycles of English MYSTERY PLAYS. They are also known as the Wakefield Mysteries because they were probably acted at the fairs of Widkirk, near Wakefield. They have a more popular, lively and even jocular tone than the plays of the other cycles. See also WAKEFIELD MASTER.

Town Mouse and Country Mouse. An old fable of a mouse in the city who invites a country mouse to dinner in its fine house. The country mouse, however, prefers its own home in the woods. This fable has been told by Horace and La Fontaine. Cf. the poem for children, *The City Mouse and The Garden Mouse,* by Christina Rossetti.

Townsend, Edward Waterman (1855–1942). American journalist, legislator, and writer, well-known for creating the fictional character *Chimmie Fadden.*

Townsend, Robert Etheridge. The hero of Cabell's CORDS OF VANITY.

Townshend, Charles (1725–1767). English statesman. He introduced taxes on glass, paper, and tea against which the American colonies revolted, thus bringing on the American Revolution against England.

Tox, Miss Lucretia. In Dickens' DOMBEY AND SON, the bosom friend of Mr. Dombey's married sister (Mrs. Chick). Miss Lucretia is a faded lady, "as if she had not been made in fast colors," and is washed out. She "ambled through life without any opinions, and never abandoned herself to unavailing regrets." Miss Tox greatly admires Mr. Dombey and entertains a forlorn hope that she may be selected by him to take the place of his deceased wife.

Toynbee, Arnold Joseph (1889–). English historian and educator at the University of London. His greatest work is *A Study of History* (6 vols.; 1934–1939), an exhaustive study of six principal civilizations, which, in a condensed version, became a best-seller in 1947. His yearly *Survey of International Affairs* (1920–1923) has been continued by other editors.

Tozer, Leora. In Sinclair Lewis' ARROWSMITH, a North Dakota farm girl who has been working as a nurse in a local hospital and who becomes the wife of Martin Arrowsmith. She is loyally devoted to her husband, assisting him in his scientific experiments and helping him in his career as a physician. She dies of tropical fever while working with Arrowsmith in administering serum to afflicted natives on an island in the West Indies.

Tractarians. The authors of the TRACTS FOR THE TIMES, which enunciated the principles of the OXFORD MOVEMENT, also called the *Tractarian Movement;* also, their followers. Hence the term is applied to High Churchmen generally.

Tracts for the Times. A series of papers on theological and liturgical subjects, published at Oxford (hence sometimes called *The Oxford Tracts*) between 1833 and 1841. They were launched by the Rev. J. H. NEWMAN (afterwards Cardinal Newman) with the object of arresting "the advance of Liberalism in religious thought," and reviving "the true conception of the relation of the Church of England to the Catholic Church at large." The authors, who used the first seven letters of the alphabet as signatures to their contributions, were:

A. Rev. John Keble, M.A., author of the *Christian Year,* fellow of Oriel, and Professor of Poetry at Oxford.
B. Rev. Isaac Williams, Fellow of Trinity; author of *The Cathedral, and other Poems.*
C. Rev. E. B. Pusey, D.D., Regius Professor of Hebrew, and Canon of Christ Church.
D. Rev. John Henry Newman, D.D., Fellow of Oriel.
E. Rev. Thomas Keble.
F. Sir John Provost, Bart.
G. Rev. R. F. Wilson, of Oriel.

The series came to an end (at the request of the Bishop of Oxford) with Newman's *Tract No. XC,* "On Certain Passages in the XXXIX Articles"; later many of the Tractarians entered the Roman Catholic Church.

Traddles, Tommie. In Dickens' DAVID COPPERFIELD, a simple, honest young man, who believes in everybody and everything. Though constantly failing, he is never depressed. He has the habit of brushing his hair up on end, which gives him a look of surprise. Tom Traddles marries one of the "ten daughters of a poor curate."

> At the Creakle's school, when I was miserable, he [Traddles] would lay his head on the desk for a little while, and then, cheering up, would draw skeletons all over his slate.—*David Copperfield,* vii.

Tradition and the Individual Talent. An essay by T. S. ELIOT, published in *The Sacred Wood* (1920), in which the author asserts that a poet cannot write significant poetry in the 20th century unless he has a knowledge and understanding of the poetry written in the past, so that he may surrender himself to his art and to the specific work he has to do, thus liberating himself from the bondage of purely personal expression.

Trafalgar, Battle of. A naval battle (October 21, 1805) off Cape Trafalgar on the southwest coast of Spain between the British and the combined French and Spanish fleets. Fifteen French and Spanish ships were either captured or destroyed by the British who did not lose a single vessel. The brilliant victory was marred by the death in action of Lord NELSON, the commander of the British fleet.

Trafalgar Square. A famous square in London, named after Nelson's victory. A tall column in the middle of the square bears a statue of him (designed, 1829).

tragedy (literally, a goat-song from *Gr. tragos,* "goat," *ode,* "song"). HORACE (*Ars Poetica,* 220) says it was called "goat-song" because the winner at choral competitions received a goat as a prize, but the explanation has no authority. Another derivation is from the satyr-like chorus.

It was ARISTOTLE (in his *Poetics*) who said that tragedy should move one "by pity and terror":

> The plot ought to be so constructed that, even without the aid of the eye, he who hears the tale told will thrill with horror and melt to pity at what takes place. —xix (*Butcher*).

the Father of Tragedy. See under FATHER.

Tragedy of Nan, The. A poetic drama by John MASEFIELD (1909). The heroine is Nan Hardwick.

Tragic Comedians, The. A novel by George MEREDITH (1880), dealing with the tragic love affair of the brilliant young Jewish Hungarian leader of the German Republican Socialists, Ferdinand Lassalle (1825–1864) to whom Meredith has given the name Sigismund Alvan. The heroine (Helene von Dönniges) is called Clotilde von Rüdiger. The novel is said by Meredith to follow "the bare railway line of their story." Alvan is killed in a duel by his rival, Prince Marko, who was in real life Yanko von Racowitza.

Traherne, Thomas (1636–1674). English poet, one of the later METAPHYSICAL POETS, known for the emphasis placed in his poetry on what he regarded as the direct and untutored apprehension of truth on the part of children. His work is marked by simple diction and a vivid presentation of the common things of everyday life as the vehicles of mystic revelation. Traherne was not discovered as a poet until the 20th century, his manuscripts at first having been ascribed to Henry VAUGHAN. He is considered to be one of the most important poets of his age and to throw an important light on the mysticism of such poets as Vaughan and William BLAKE. His *Poetical Works* and *Poems of Felicity* were published in 1903 and 1910, respectively; *Centuries of Meditations,* prose, was published in 1908.

Traill, Henry Duff (1842–1900). English journalist and biographer. Editor of a history of England, *Social England* (1893–1897), contributed to by various hands. He was also the author of satiric verse, fantasies, a biography of Sir John Franklin, and an especially notable biography of William III.

Trail of the Lonesome Pine, The. A novel (1908) by John Fox, Jr., made into a play by Eugene Walter (1912). Also title of a popular song.

Train, Arthur (1875–1946). American novelist, short-story writer, and criminologist. President, National Institute of Arts and Letters. Creator of the famous character of Ephraim Tutt, unquestionably the best known of American lawyers, "more real, more typically true to the legal personality than life itself." The Tutt stories appeared for many years in the *Saturday Evening Post* and were afterwards collected in book form. *Mr. Tutt's Case Book* (1937) is required reading in several law schools.

Traitor's Gate. The name of the gate by the river through which prisoners entered the TOWER OF LONDON.

Trajan. In Latin **Marcus Ulpius Trajanus** (52?–117 A. D.). Roman emperor, appointed by his predecessor Nerva (97). It is said that Trajan, although unbaptized, was delivered from Hell in answer to the prayers of St. Gregory. He is one of the two pagans said to have been admitted to Heaven. See also RIPHEUS.

> There was storied on the rock
> The exalted glory of the Roman prince,
> Whose mighty worth moved Gregory to earn
> His mighty conquest—Trajan the emperor.
> Dante, *Purgatory,* xi (1308).

Tramecksan and **Slamecksan.** The High Heels and Low Heels, the two great political factions of Lilliput, in Swift's *Gulliver's Travels* (see GULLIVER, LEMUEL). The High Heels are the Tories, and the Low Heels the Radicals, and "the animosity of these two factions runs so high that they will neither eat, nor drink, nor speak to each other." The king was a Tramecksan, but the heir-apparent a Slamecksan.

Tramp, Tramp, Tramp. A famous song of the Civil War written by George Frederick Root (1820–1895), imitating the sound of the marching feet of the infantry. Cf. Rudyard Kipling's famous poem, *Boots.*

Tramp Abroad, A. A humorous book by Mark TWAIN (1880), the description of a walking trip through the Black Forest and the Alps.

Tranio. A slave in the *Mostellaria,* a comedy by PLAUTUS. He is a clever rogue who from that time on became a sort of stock character in Roman comedy.

transcendentalism. A New England school of literature and philosophy taking its point of departure from the philosophy of Kant's CRITIQUE OF PURE REASON and affirming the importance of phenomena that transcend the experience of the senses. The Transcendental Club, a group of congenial New Englanders who met from time to time from the year 1836 on, included Ralph Waldo EMERSON, Amos Bronson ALCOTT, Theodore PARKER, Margaret FULLER, Henry THOREAU, Nathaniel HAWTHORNE and William Henry CHANNING. According to the *Cambridge History of American Literature,* Emerson's *Nature* "appearing the same year the club was formed may be fittingly considered the philosophical constitution of Transcendentalism." THOREAU and Jones VERY were also associated with the movement, which had THE DIAL as its literary organ.

Transfiguration, Mount of. A mountain top where Jesus went with his disciples Peter and James and John "and he was transfigured before them; and his face did shine as the sun, and his garments became white as the light." Cf. *Matt.* xvii. 1–9.

Trasimenus, Lake. Latin name of the modern Lago Trasimeno or Lago di Perugia in Etruria, Italy. It was the scene of a famous battle (217 B. C.) in the Second Punic War. The Carthagenians and Gauls under Hannibal almost completely destroyed a large Roman army under the consul Flaminius.

Transition. A monthly literary magazine, one of the most famous of the LITTLE MAGAZINES of the 1920's, founded in Paris in 1927 with Elliot PAUL and Eugene Jolas as editors. Its purpose was to encourage experimental writing, especially that giving free play to the imagination. Gertrude STEIN, E. E. CUMMINGS, Ernest HEMINGWAY, and a number of European authors and others of the American expatriate groups were among those whose work appeared in its pages. Several sections of James Joyce's *Finnegans Wake,* then known only as WORK IN PROGRESS, were first published in *Transition,* and the editors and writers of the *Transition* group were among the few persons who knew Joyce's complete plan for his work. The magazine ceased publication in 1930, but was revived in 1940 in the U.S. by Jolas.

Transome, Harold. A leading character in George Eliot's FELIX HOLT.

Mrs. Transome. The mother of Harold Transome.

> Mrs. Transome, whose imperious will had availed little to ward off the great evils of her life, found the opiate for her discontent in the exertion of her will about smaller things. She was not cruel, and she could not enjoy thoroughly what she called the old woman's pleasure of tormenting; but she liked every little sign of power her lot had left her. She liked that a tenant should stand bareheaded below her as she sat on horseback. She liked to insist that work done without her orders should be undone from beginning to end.—*Ch.* I.

Trapbois, Old. In Scott's FORTUNES OF NIGEL, a miser in Alsatia. Even in his extreme age, "he was believed to understand the plucking of a pigeon better than any man in Alsatia."

Martha Trapbois. The miser's daughter, a cold, decisive, masculine woman, who marries Richie MONIPLIES.

Trapper, The. Natty Bumppo or LEATHERSTOCKING is so called in Cooper's novel, *The Prairie.*

Traprock, Captain, see CHAPPELL, GEORGE S.

Traubel, Horace L. (1858–1919). A devoted friend and literary executor of Walt Whitman. His *With Walt Whitman in Camden* (3 vols.; 1906–1914) is a record of their conversations. His *Chants Communal* (1904), a sort of prose verse, and still more his *Optimos* (1914), shows strongly Whitman's influence. Eugene Debs called him the "master democrat of his time." His notes on Whitman are valuable source material.

Traum, Philip. The "MYSTERIOUS STRANGER" in Mark Twain's novel of that title.

Traveller, The. A poem (1764) by Oliver GOLDSMITH. Dr. Johnson is said to have added nine lines to it.

Travels in . . . Remote Regions. See Lemuel GULLIVER.

Travels with a Donkey. A record of travel by foot in the Cévennes (1879) by Robert Louis STEVENSON.

Travers, Edith. Heroine of Conrad's RESCUE.

Travers, Pamela (1906–). Australian author. Her books concerning the mythical nurse Mary Poppins are delightful stories for children.

Traviata, La (The Castaway). An opera by VERDI (1853), based on the romance and drama *La Dame aux Camélias* by Alexandre Dumas *fils,* better known in America as CAMILLE. In the opera the demi-mondaine heroine is Violetta Valery and the man whom she loves but gives up because of his father's protests is called Alfred Germont. The libretto is by Piavé.

Treacle Bible. See BIBLE, SPECIALLY NAMED.

Treasure Island. A romance by Robert Louis STEVENSON (1883), a tale of mutiny, piracy and buried treasure. The one-legged pirate, John Silver, sails as sea-cook of the *Hispaniola,* but appears in his true colors later when he heads the mutiny and runs up the black flag, the Jolly Roger.

Trecentisti. The Italian worthies of the *Trecento* (13th and 14th centuries). They were DANTE, PETRARCH, BOCCACCIO, and others of less note.

tree. The cross on which Jesus was crucified is frequently spoken of in hymns and poetry as *the tree.* See *Acts* v. 30: ". . . Jesus, whom ye slew and hanged on a tree"; 1 *Pet.* ii. 24: "Who his own self bare our sins in his own body on the tree." The gallows is also called *the tree,* TYBURN TREE, *the fatal tree,* etc.

the tree of Buddha or *of Wisdom.* The bo-tree, famous as the scene of Buddha's meditation and enlightenment.

the tree of Diana. See PHILOSOPHER'S TREE.

the tree of liberty. A post or tree set up by the people hung with flags and devices, and crowned with a cap of liberty. In the United States poplars and other trees were planted during the War of Independence, "as symbols of growing freedom." The Jacobins in Paris planted their first trees of liberty in 1790, and used to decorate them with tricolored ribbons, circles to indicate unity, triangles to signify equality, and Caps of Liberty. Trees of liberty were also planted by the Italians in the revolution of 1848.

the Tree of Life and *the Tree of Knowledge.* Forbidden trees in the Garden of Eden (*Gen.* ii. 9), the former conferring immortality, the latter, knowledge of good and evil, upon those who ate their fruit. Adam and Eve were cast out of the Garden for eating the fruit of the Tree of Knowledge.

Tree Grows in Brooklyn, A. A novel by Betty Smith (*Am.* 1943), which sold 2,500,000 copies. Brooklyn is a borough of New York City; the tree was an ailanthus.

Tree, Sir **Herbert Beerbohm** (1853–1917). English manager and actor, brother of Max BEERBOHM. Manager (1887–1897) of the Haymarket Theater in London; acted in plays by Ibsen, Wilde, Maeterlinck, and Shakespeare. He tried to revive the poetic drama with the plays of Stephen Phillips.

trefa meat. Meat prohibited to the Jews as food because it has not been slaughtered in the orthodox manner; the opposite of *kosher* meat. It is so called from a Hebrew word signifying "that which is torn."

Tregeagle. A fabulous giant of Dosmary Pool, Bodmin Downs (Cornwall), whose allotted task is to bale out the water with a limpet-shell. When the wintry blast howls over the downs, the people say it is the giant roaring.

Treitschke, Heinrich von (1834–1896). German historian, who supported the Hohenzollerns and increased anti-British sentiment in Germany. His writings glorify the state, and advocate colonial expansion. Author of *Deutsche Geschichte im XIX. Jahrhundert* (5 vols.; 1879–1894).

Trelawney, Edward John (1792–1881). English adventurer and traveler. Friend and companion of Shelley, at whose death he was present (1822), and of Lord Byron, whom he accompanied to Greece. Author of *Adventures of a Younger Son* (1831) and *Recollections of the Last Days of Shelley and Byron* (1858).

Trelawny of the Wells. A comedy of stage life by PINERO (1898). The actress heroine, Rose Trelawny, becomes engaged to a young aristocrat, but breaks her engagement to return to the stage. Nothing daunted, her lover follows and becomes an actor.

Tremont. The original name of Boston, Massachusetts, sometimes used in reference to old Boston.

Tremouille, Louis de la (1460–1525). French general who commanded the army of Charles VII and acted with ferocity toward his prisoners after he had defeated the Duke of Orleans.

Trench, Frederick Herbert (1865–1923). Irish-born British poet. His *New Poems* (1907) contain the long narrative poem *Apollo and the Seaman* and other poems of distinction. This book established his reputation. He also wrote for the theater and produced, at the Haymarket, *King Lear* and *The Blue Bird*. He spent his last years in Italy.

Trench, Richard Chenevix (1807–1886). Anglican Archbishop of Dublin (1863–1884). Noted philologist, author of *On the Study of Words* (1851); *English Past and Present* (1855); etc. Active in the Philological Society, which supported his scheme for the beginning of the Oxford *New English Dictionary*.

Trenchard, Asa. Titular hero of Tom Taylor's play OUR AMERICAN COUSIN.

Trenck, Baron **Franz von der** (1711–1749). Austrian soldier. Commanded a regiment of Croat peasants who became widely known for their plundering propensities. He joined the army of Maria Theresa and was court-martialed and imprisoned. His cousin, Baron **Friedrich von der Trenck** (1726–1794), was a military adventurer in the army of Frederick the Great. He was twice imprisoned and finally executed by Robespierre.

Trent, Anne. In John Dos Passos' U.S.A., a a young Texas girl, affectionately known as "Daughter" among her family; a tomboy, fond of riding and swimming, imbued with enthusiasm but emotionally naïve and inexperienced. She visits New York for awhile in an effort to forget her disappointment at the marriage of a man she is in love with to another woman, is bewildered and repelled by the unfamiliar city atmosphere, and is briefly involved with Ben COMPTON in a labor strike in New Jersey. Afer the death of one of her brothers in an airplane accident, she goes to France during World War I as a relief worker, stopping off on her way to the Near East. In Paris she meets and has a love affair with Richard Ellsworth SAVAGE; when she becomes pregnant, however, he refuses to marry her. In desperation, she takes an airplane ride with a French aviator and is killed in a crash.

Trent, Nell. See LITTLE NELL.

Trent, William Peterfield (1862–1939). Professor of English Literature at Columbia University (1900–1929); author of *A History of American Literature 1607–1865* (1903). Founder of the *Sewanee Review*.

Trent Affair. An international incident which occurred during the Civil War (1861), when Captain Wilkes removed from the British steamer *Trent* the Confederate commissioners MASON and SLIDELL who were incarcerated in Boston. They were released (January, 1862) and allowed to go to Europe, due to the attitude of Secretary of State Seward, who feared Great Britain might come into the war on the side of the Confederacy.

Trent's Last Case (1913). A famous mystery novel by E. C. BENTLEY.

Tresham, Thorold Lord. One of the chief characters in Browning's BLOT ON THE 'SCUTCHEON.

Tressady, Sir George. A leading character in Mrs. Humphry Ward's novel of that title, a sequel to MARCELLA.

Trevelyan, Sir George Otto (1838–1928). English historian and statesman. He wrote and edited *The Life and Letters of Lord Macaulay* (1876). A well-known work of his is *The American Revolution* (6 vols.; 1899–1914). His third son, **George Macaulay Trevelyan** (1876–), also a historian, was regius professor of modern history at Cambridge (1927–1940). He is the author of *British History in the Nineteenth Century, 1782–1901* (1922); *History of England* (1926); and *England Under Queen Anne* (3 vols.; 1930–1934).

Trevena, John. Pen name of **Ernest George Henham** (1870–). Canadian poet and novelist.

Trevisa, John de (1326–1412). English translator. Fellow at Oxford (1362–1379). His English version (1387) of Higden's *Polychronicon* is one of the most vigorous examples of early English prose.

triads. Three subjects more or less connected treated as a group, as: *the Creation, Redemption, and Resurrection; Brahma, Vishnu, and Siva; Alexander the Great, Julius Caesar, and Napoleon; Law, Physic, and Divinity.*

The Welsh *Triads* are collections of historic facts, mythological traditions, moral maxims, or rules of poetry disposed in groups of three for mnemonic purposes.

Trial, The (Der Prozess). A novel by Franz KAFKA, published in 1925. It deals with the sudden and mystifying arrest of Joseph K., a bank assessor in a German city, for a crime which he is unaware of having committed. He is never told what charges have been leveled against him, and he is unable to discover the nature or the source of the authority of the secret law court which has condemned him and is located in a ramshackle building in the tenement district of the city. The bank assessor tries to defend himself and frantically seeks help from anyone who appears to have influence with the mysterious authorities. Through LENI, a little servant, he secures an interview with his advocate, TITORELLI, but receives no help, and Leni in a moment of sympathy advises him to confess and throw himself on the mercy of the court. His guilt is already assumed, and he learns there are only two alternatives for the mitigation of punishment left open to an accused man. One is indefinite postponement of the case; the other is a temporary release involving possible re-arrest at any time. Joseph K. is unable to win either of these, largely because he attempts to resist the authority of the court. Eventually he is apprehended by two agents of the mysterious organization and murdered by them.

Like Kafka's other famous novel, THE CASTLE, which is regarded in some respects as a companion work, *The Trial* is considered to be a symbolic presentation of the relation between mankind and divine authority. The tyrannical, brutal, inefficient, and insanely irrational system of law courts that condemns Joseph K. is interpreted as the average human misapprehension of the revealed laws of God, for which neither God nor the original form of the laws, but rather man's own imperfect understanding, is responsible. If a man insists on following his own human and faulty conceptions of reason and right in the face of divine retribution (as in *The Trial*) or in the pursuit of divine grace (as in *The Castle*), his fate is certain. It has been pointed out that in both novels the non-intellectuals—the peasants, the tenement dwellers, the courtroom attendants, the amoral slum-girls—are in a secure position with respect to the official bureaucracies because they obey commands unquestioningly, while K. and Joseph K., the heroes, men of some intellect and education who try to impose their own standards on the situations in which they find themselves, are continually frustrated in their aims and doomed to punishment.

The Trial, the most widely known and most influential of Kafka's works, has been highly praised for its moving characterization of Joseph K. in his vain struggle against a power he cannot understand, and for its effective creation of an atmosphere of nightmare horror.

Trial by Jury. A one-act operetta (1875) by W. S. GILBERT with music by Sir Arthur SULLIVAN.

Triamond. Son of the fairy Agape, and brother to Diamond and Priamond, in Spenser's FAËRIE QUEENE (Bk. iv). He is a champion of friendship, and wins the prize on the second day of the tournament after being overcome by SATYRANE (IV. iv). He was the husband of Canace.

Triboulet. A nickname given to Francis Hotman, court fool of Louis XII. This worthy is introduced by Rabelais in GARGANTUA AND PANTAGRUEL and by Victor HUGO in his tragedy *Le Roi s'amuse*. In Verdi's opera based on the latter he appears as RIGOLETTO.

Tribune and **Herald Tribune.** A New York newspaper, founded by Horace GREELEY in 1841. He merged his earlier *New Yorker* with the *Tribune* in the same year. He supported Free Soil and anti-slavery, and the administration in the Civil War, and advocated universal amnesty and suffrage after the war. He edited the paper till his death, when Whitelaw Reid took over. Under him and his son, Ogden Mills Reid, the *Tribune* was the country's most powerful Republican newspaper. In 1924 the *Tribune* bought the New York *Herald* and became the *Herald Tribune.* Its large Sunday edition is distinguished by its literary supplement, *Books,* edited by Irita Van Doren, now called the *Weekly Book Review.* It holds a yearly *Herald Tribune* Forum of public opinion, which is of value. Its chief columnist is Walter Lippmann. It is one of the best morning papers in the U.S.

Tribunes, last of the. Cola di RIENZI, who assumed the title of "Tribune of liberty, peace, and justice." Rienzi is the hero of one of BULWER LYTTON's novels.

tricolor. A flag of three broad strips of different colors, especially the national standard of France, blue, white, and red. The first flag of the Republicans was *green.* The tricolor was adopted July 11, when the people were disgusted with the king for dismissing Necker. The popular tale is that the insurgents in 1789 had adopted for their flag the two colors, *red and blue,* but that Lafayette persuaded them to add the Bourbon *white,* to show that they bore no hostility to the king.

tricoteuses (*Fr.,* "the knitters"). Parisian women who, during the French Revolution, used to attend the meetings of the Convention and, while they went on with their *tricotant* (knitting), encouraged the leaders in their bloodthirsty excesses. They gained for themselves the additional title *furies of the guillotine.* Cf. also Dickens' TALE OF TWO CITIES.

trigon. The junction of three signs. The zodiac is partitioned into four trigons, named respectively after the four elements: the *watery* trigon, Cancer, Scorpio and Pisces; the *fiery,* Aries, Leo and Sagittarius; the *earthy,* Taurus, Virgo, and Capricornus; and the *airy,* Gemini, Libra and Aquarius.

Trilby. A novel by George DU MAURIER, in eight parts (1894). The heroine is Trilby O'Ferrall, and the hero, "Little Billee," or William Bagot. When the novel opens, Trilby is about seventeen, earning her living as an artist's model. She becomes intimate with three art-students in Paris: a big Yorkshire Englishman called Taffy, the Laird of Cockpen, a Scotchman, and Little Billee, an English artist. They all fall in love with Trilby, but Little Billee proposes marriage, and, after nineteen refusals, Trilby accepts his proposal. His mother now speeds from Devonshire and induces Trilby to break off the match. Trilby falls into the hands of an Hungarian musician, who assumes the name of Svengali. He teaches her singing, under mesmeric influence, and when under this influence she is the best vocalist that ever lived. But when she appears before the British public, Svengali, who is sitting in the stage-box, dies suddenly of heart-disease, and Trilby loses her voice entirely. She now languishes, and soon dies, beloved by everyone.

Charles NODIER, in 1822, published a novelette of the same name, but this Trilby was a male spirit who attached itself to a fisherman, fell in love with his wife, and performed for her all kinds of household services.

Trim, Corporal. In Sterne's TRISTRAM SHANDY, Uncle Toby's orderly.

> Trim, instead of being the opposite, is . . . the duplicate of Uncle Toby . . . yet . . . is the character of the common soldier nicely discriminated from that of the officer. His whole carriage bears traces of the drill-yard, which are wanting in the superior. Under the name of a servant, he is in reality a companion, and a delightful mixture of familiarity . . . and respect . . . It is enough to say that Trim was worthy to walk behind his master.—Elwin, editor of the *Quarterly Review.*

Trimalchio. The vulgar and ostentatious multi-millionaire of PETRONIUS ARBITER'S *Satyricon* (1st century A. D.); the subject of allusion on account of the colossal and extravagant banquet that he gave.

Trimurti. (*Sanskrit,* "having three forms"). In Hindu mythology, the threefold impersonation of the Supreme Spirit: Brahma, the creator; Vishnu, the preserver; Siva, the destroyer.

Trinculo. A jester in Shakespeare's TEMPEST.

Trinity. The three Persons in one God as the Christian God the Father, God the Son, and God the Holy Ghost.

> And in this Trinity none is afore or after other; none is greater, or less than another; but the whole three Persons are co-eternal together and co-equal.—*The Athanasian Creed.*

Tertullian (160–240) introduced the word into Christian theology. Almost every mythology has a three-fold deity. See THREE; also TRIMURTI.

Trinity College. The largest of the colleges at Cambridge University in England. It has a library designed by Sir Christopher Wren and has had as masters and scholars many distinguished literary figures.

Trinovant, see TROYNOVANT.

Tripitaka (Pali *tipitaka,* "the three baskets"). The three classes into which the sacred writings of the Buddhists are divided, viz., the *Sutrapitaka* (Basket of Aphorisms or Discourses) or *Sutras,* the *Vinayapitaka* (Basket of Disciplinary Directions), and *Abidhammapitaka* (Basket of Metaphysics).

Triple Alliance. A treaty entered into by England, Sweden, and Holland against Louis XIV in 1668. It ended in the treaty of Aix-la-Chapelle.

A treaty between England, France, and Holland against Spain in 1717. In the following year it was joined by Austria, and became a *Quadruple Alliance.*

Triple Entente. See ENTENTE.

tripos (Gr. *treis,* "three," *pous,* "foot"). A Cambridge term, meaning the *three* honor classes in which the best men are grouped at the final examination, whether of Mathematics, Law, Theology, or Natural Science, etc. The word is often applied to the voluntary classical examination, so called because the champion in the old university disputations held during the admission of graduates to their degrees used to sit on a *three-legged* stool.

Triptolemus. A Greek hero and demi-god, worshiped chiefly at Eleusis as the giver to man of grain and the first instructor in agriculture.

triptych. See under DIPTYCH.

Trismegistus (*Gr.,* "thrice great"). A name given to HERMES, the Egyptian philosopher, or Thoth, counselor of Osiris, to whom is attributed a host of inventions, among others the art of writing in hieroglyphics, the first code of Egyptian laws, harmony, astrology, the lute and lyre, magic, and all mysterious sciences.

Trissotin. In Molière's FEMMES SAVANTES an affected poet and *bel esprit.* Philaminte, a *femme savante,* wishes him to marry her daughter Henriette, but Henriette is in love with Clitandre. The difficulty is soon solved by the announcement that Henriette's father is on the verge of bankruptcy, whereupon Trissotin makes his bow and retires. Trissotin is said to have been meant for the Abbé Cotin, who affected to be poet, gallant, and preacher. His dramatic name was "Tricotin."

Tristan or **Sir Tristram, Tristrem** or **Tristam.** A hero of medieval romance whose exploits, though originally unconnected with it, became attached to the Arthurian cycle, he himself being named as one of the Knights of the ROUND TABLE. There are many versions of his story, which is, roughly, that he is cured of a wound by ISOLT, Iseult, or Isolde (Ysolde), daughter of the king of Ireland, and on his return to Cornwall tells his uncle, KING MARK, of the beautiful princess. Mark sends him to solicit her hand in marriage, and is accepted. Tristan escorts her to England, but on the way they both unknowingly partake of a magic potion and become irretrievably enamored of each other. Isolt marries the King, and on his discovering her with Tristan, the latter flees to Brittany, where, according to some versions, he marries another Isolt—Isolt of Brittany, or of the White Hands. He then goes on his adventures, and, being wounded, learns that he can be cured only by his first Isolt. A messenger is dispatched to Cornwall, and is ordered to hoist a white sail if he brings her back. The vessel comes in sight with a white sail displayed, but Isolt of the White Hands, out of jealousy, tells her husband that the sail is *black,* and Tristan expires.

This version of the story forms the basis of Wagner's opera *Tristan und Isolde* (1865). There are other accounts of his death. Thus Malory's MORTE D' ARTHUR says:

> When by means of a treaty sir Tristram brought again La Beale Isond unto king Mark, from Joyous Guard, the false traitor king Mark slew the noble knight as he sat harping before his lady, La Beale Isond, with a sharp-ground glaive, which he thrust into him from behind his back.—Pt. iii. 147 (1470).

Tennyson in his IDYLLS OF THE KING has it that Sir Tristram, dallying with his aunt, hung a ruby carcanet round her throat, and, as he kissed her neck—

> Out of the dark, just as the lips had touched,
> Behind him rose a shadow and a shriek—
> "Mark's way!" said Mark, and clove him thro' the brain.
>
> *Idylls: The Last Tournament.*

The story of Tristan is of Celtic origin. It was the subject of many medieval romances, notably versions by Thomas and Béroul, a French poem by CHRÉTIEN DE TROYES (now lost), and a German poem by Gottfried von Strassburg based on that of Chrétien and later continued by Ulrich von Thurheim and Heinrich von Freiburg.

Aside from Tennyson's *Last Tournament* (*Idylls of the King*) and Wagner's opera, *Tristan und Isolde,* referred to above, in modern literature it forms the subject of Matthew ARNOLD'S *Tristram and Iseult* and SWINBURNE'S *Tristan of Lyonesse.*

Sir Tristram's book. Any book of venery, hunting or hawking is so called. Tristan was famed as the originator of many hunting terms and feats.

Tristram. A poem in blank verse (1927), one of a trilogy on King Arthur, by Edwin Arlington ROBINSON. It was awarded the Pulitzer prize for poetry.

Tristram Shandy. A famous novel by Laurence STERNE (1760–1767), more formally entitled *The Life and Opinions of Tristram Shandy.* Tristram's father, Water Shandy, is a metaphysical Don Quixote in his way, full of superstitions and idle conceits. He believes in long noses and propitious names, but his son's nose is crushed, and his name becomes *Tristram* intead of *Trismegistus.* Tristram's Uncle Toby, wounded at the siege of Namur and forced to retire on half pay, is benevolent and generous, simple as a child, brave as a lion, and gallant as a courtier. His modesty with Widow Wadman and his military tastes are especially noteworthy. HAZLITT said of My Uncle Toby that he is "one of the finest compliments ever paid to human nature." He is said to be drawn from Sterne's father. Tristram's mother is the *beau-ideal* of nonentity (described by Scott as a "good lady of the pococurante school"); and of Tristram himself, we hear almost more of him before he was born than after he burst upon an astonished world.

Triton. In classic myth, son of NEPTUNE, represented as a fish with a human head. It is this sea god that makes the roaring of the ocean by blowing through his shell.

a Triton among the minnows. The sun among inferior lights.

Triumph of the Egg, The. A book of impressions from American life in stories and poems by Sherwood ANDERSON (1921).

Trivia. John GAY's name for his invented goddess of streets and ways. His burlesque in three books so entitled (1716) is a mine of information on the outdoor life of Queen Anne's time.

> Thou, Trivia, aid my song.
> Through spacious streets conduct thy bard along . . .
> To pave thy realm, and smooth the broken ways
> Earth from her womb a flinty tribute pays.
> *Trivia*, Bk. i.

Diana was called *Trivia* by the Latins in reference to her guardianship over all *trivia* or places where three roads came together. *Trivia* is also the plural of TRIVIUM.

Trivia is also the title of a collection of short humorous sketches by Logan Pearsall SMITH.

trivium (Lat. *tres,* "three," *via,* "a road"). The three roads to learning in the Middle Ages, i.e., Grammar, Rhetoric, and Logic, forming the lower division of the seven liberal arts. See QUADRIVIUM.

trochee. In prosody, a poetic foot consisting of a long syllable followed by a short one, as hateful, legal, holy. Trochaic verse is verse based on trochees. The meter is further designated by the number of poetic feet in the line, as trochaic trimeter, tetrameter, etc. The latter is the most common trochaic meter, exemplified by the following lines:

> Tell me not in mournful numbers
> Life is but an empty dream
> For the soul is dead that slumbers
> And things are not what they seem.
> Longfellow, *Psalm of Life.*

trochilus. A small Egyptian bird fabled by the ancients to enter with impunity the mouth of the crocodile and to pick its teeth, especially of a leech which greatly tormented the creature. Allusions to it are common in 16th- and 17th-century authors.

> Not half so bold
> The puny bird that dares, with teasing hum,
> Within the crocodile's stretched jaws to come.
> Thomas Moore, *Lalla Rookh,* Pt. i.

troglodytes (from Gr. *trogle,* "cave," and *duein,* "to go into"). A people of Ethiopia, southeast of Egypt, so called because they lived in cave dwellings, remains of which are still to be seen along the banks of the Nile. Hence the term is applied to other cave-dwellers, and, figuratively, to those who live in seclusion. There were troglodytes of Syria and Arabia also, according to Strabo, and Pliny asserts that they fed on serpents.

Troil, Magnus. In Scott's PIRATE, the old udaller of Zetland.

Brenda Troil. The udaller's younger daughter, who marries Mordaunt Mertoun.

Minna Troil. The udaller's eldest daughter, in love with the Pirate.

Ulla Troil. See NORNA OF THE FITFUL HEAD.

Troilus. In classic myth, the prince of chivalry, one of the sons of PRIAM, killed by ACHILLES in the siege of Troy (Homer's *Iliad*).

The loves of Troilus and Cressida, celebrated by SHAKESPEARE and CHAUCER, form no part of the old classic tale. Their story appeared for the first time in DARES PHRYGIUS and DIETYS CRETENSIS, then about the 12th century in BENOÎT DE ST.-MAURE, and in the 13th century in GUIDO DELLE COLONNE. Later it passed to BOCCACCIO, whose *Il Filostrato* (1344)—where PANDARUS first appears—was the basis of Chaucer's *Troilus and Criseyde.* Shakespeare's drama by the same name, *Troilus and Cressida* (ca. 1609) follows the general outline of Chaucer's narrative. Cressida or Cressid, daughter of Calchas, a Grecian priest, is beloved by Troilus. They vow eternal fidelity to each other, and as pledges of their vow Troilus gives the maiden a sleeve, and Cressid gives the Trojan prince a glove. Hardly has the vow been made when an exchange of prisoners is agreed to. Diomed gives up three Trojan princes, and is to receive Cressid in lieu thereof. Cressid vows to remain constant, and Troilus swears to rescue her. She is led off to the Grecian's tent, and soon gives all her affections to Diomed, and even bids him wear the sleeve that Troilus gave her in token of his love. Hence Cressida has become a byword for infidelity.

> As false
> As air, as water, wind, or sandy earth,
> As fox to lamb, as wolf to heifer's calf,
> Pard to the hind, or step-dame to her son;
> "Yea," let them say, to stick the heart of falsehood
> "As false as Cressid."
> Shakespeare, *Troilus and Cressida,* iii. 2.

as true as Troilus. Troilus is meant by Shakespeare to be the type of constancy, and Cressida the type of female inconstancy.

> After all comparisons of truth . . .
> "As true as Troilus" shall crown up the verse.
> And sanctify the numbers.
> *Troilus and Cressida,* iii. 2.

Troilus verse. Another name for RHYME ROYAL.

Trojan, a regular. A fine fellow, with good courage and plenty of spirit; what the French call a *brave homme.* The Trojans in Homer's ILIAD and Virgil's AENEID are described as truthful, brave, patriotic and confiding.

Trojan Horse, The. A "political parable" in prose and verse (1937) by Christopher MORLEY. Made into a play by the author.

Trojan War. The legendary war sung by Homer in the ILIAD as having been waged for ten years by the confederated Greeks against the men of Troy and their allies, in consequence of PARIS, son of Priam, the Trojan king, having carried off HELEN, wife of MENELAUS, King of Lacedemon (or of Sparta). The last year of the siege is the subject of the *Iliad;* the burning of Troy and the flight of Aeneas is told by Virgil in his AENEID.

There is no doubt whatever that the story of the siege of Troy has some historical basis, but when it took place is purely a matter of conjecture. Many dates, ranging from the 11th to the 14th centuries B. C., have been assigned to it.

Trojan Women, The. A Greek tragedy (415 B. C.) by EURIPIDES dealing with the destruction of Troy.

Trollope, Anthony (1815–1882). English novelist, known for his simple, natural and semi-realistic stories of English Victorian life. His best-known novels are those included in two series, called *Chronicles of Barsetshire* (see BARSETSHIRE) and PARLIAMENTARY NOVELS. The first series consists of *The Warden* (1855); *Barchester Towers* (1857); *Doctor Thorne* (1858); *Framley Parsonage* (1861); *The Small House at Allington* (1864); *The Last Chronicle of Barset* (1867). Included in the second series are PHINEAS FINN (1869); *Phineas Redux* (1874); *The Prime Minister* (1876); *The Duke's Children* (see OMNIUM, DUKE OF; 1880). Among other works by Trollope are *The Macdermots of Ballycloran* (1847); *The Kellys and the O'Kellys* (1848); *The Belton Estate* (1865); THE CLAVERINGS (1867); THE EUSTACE DIAMONDS (1873); *Ayala's Angel* (1881); *Dr. Wortle's School* (1881); numerous travel books; a study of W. M. Thackeray (1879); and an *Autobiography* (1883). Cf. *The Trollopes* (1945), by Lucy and Richard Stebbins.

Trollope, Frances, *née* **Milton** (1780–1863). English novelist, mother of Anthony TROLLOPE. She visited America and wrote the rather unkind book, *Domestic Manners of the Americans* (1832). Author of many novels, among them *The Vicar of Wrexhill* (1837); *The Widow Barnaby* (1839); and *The Widow Married* (1840).

trolls. Dwarfs of Northern mythology, living in underground caverns or beneath hills; they are represented as stumpy, misshapen, and humpbacked, inclined to thieving, and fond of carrying off children and substituting their own. These hill people, as they are called, are especially averse to noise, from a recollection of the time when THOR used to be forever flinging his hammer after them. The Troll King is a character in Ibsen's PEER GYNT.

trope. A figure of speech. A word or phrase used out of its ordinary usage in such a way as to give life to an idea. The most important types of trope are METAPHOR, METONYMY, SYNECDOCHE, IRONY.

Trophonius. An architect, celebrated in Greek legend as the builder of the temple of APOLLO at Delphi. After his death he was deified and had an oracle in a cave near Lebadeia, Boeotia, which was so awe-inspiring that those who entered and consulted the oracle never smiled again. Hence a melancholy or habitually terrified man was said to have *visited the cave of Trophonius.*

Tropic of Cancer and **Tropic of Capricorn.** Two books (1931 and 1939) by Henry MILLER.

Trotsky, Leon. Real name **Leib Davydovich Bronstein** (1877–1940). Russian Communist leader associated with Lenin. After the Soviet Revolution he became people's commissar for foreign affairs (1917). After Lenin's death (1924), Stalin defeated him in securing control of the Communist party. He was expelled from the party (1927), being charged with subversive activities, and banished from Russia (1929). He lived in Mexico (1937–1940) where he was murdered. Author of *The Defense of Terrorism* (1921); *Literature and Revolution* (1925); *My Life* (1930; with Max Eastman); *History of the Russian Revolution* (3 vols.; 1932); etc.

Trotter, Job. In Dickens' PICKWICK PAPERS, servant to Alfred JINGLE. He is a sly, canting rascal, who has, however, the virtue of fidelity to his master. Mr. Pickwick's generosity touches his heart, and he shows sincere gratitude to his benefactor.

Trotwood, Miss Betsey. In Dickens' DAVID COPPERFIELD, great-aunt of David Copperfield. Her *bête noir* is donkeys. A dozen times a day she rushes on the green before her house to drive off the donkeys and donkey-boys. She effectively conceals her tenderness of heart under a snappish austerity of manner. In her younger days she married a handsome man, who ill-used her and ran away, but sponges on her for money till he dies. Miss Betsey takes the runaway David Copperfield in, defends him with spirit against the MURDSTONES and becomes most devoted to him.

Troubadors or **Troubadours.** Minstrels of the south of France in the 11th, 12th, and 13th centuries; so called from the Provençal verb *trobar,* "to find" or "invent" (cf. "poet," which means "a maker.") They wrote in the *langue d'oc,* principally on love and chivalry according to the conventions of COURTLY LOVE. Leading troubador poets were Bernart de VENTADOUR, Bertran de BORN, Geoffrey Rudel, Peire Vidal, Guiraut de Bornelh, and Guilhelm de Cabestanh.

See also TROUVÈRES.

Troubetzkoy, Princess. **Amélie Rives** (1863–1945). American popular romantic novelist, married to the portrait painter Prince Pierre Troubetzkoy. Her play, *The Young Elizabeth,* was awarded a prize in 1937. Her first novel, *The Quick or the Dead* (1888), was a sensation.

Trouillogan's advice. None at all; "yes and no." In Rabelais' GARGANTUA AND PANTAGRUEL, when Pantagruel asks the philosopher Trouillogan whether PANURGE should marry or not, the reply is "Yes." "What say you?" asks the prince. "What you have heard," answers

Trouillogan. "What have I heard?" says Pantagruel. "What I have spoken," rejoins the sage. "Good," says the prince; "but tell me plainly, shall Panurge marry or let it alone?" "Neither," answers the oracle. "How?" says the prince; "that cannot be." "Then both," says Trouillogan.

Trouvères. The troubadors of the north of France, in the 12th, 13th, and 14th centuries, so called from Fr. *trouver,* "to find or invent." See TROUBADORS. Their work comprises chiefly narrative poems.

Trovatore, Il (The Troubador). An opera by VERDI (1853) based on a Spanish drama by Gatteerez. The scene is laid in 15th century Biscay and Aragon. The heroine, Leonora, is in love with Manrico, a troubador, who has been brought up by the gypsy Azucena as her son but is in reality the kidnaped brother of the Count di Luna, who is also a suitor for the hand of Leonora. The Count captures Azucena, and Manrico is also made prisoner in an attempt to rescue her. Leonora now offers herself to the Count in return for the life of Manrico, but drinks poison and dies. Manrico, who has refused to leave her, is forthwith executed, and a moment afterwards the dying gypsy tells the horrified Count that he has caused the death of his own brother.

Trowbridge, John Townsend. Pseudonym **Paul Creyton** (1827–1916). American writer of books for boys. Among his verse is one famous ballad, *Darius Green and His Flying Machine.*

Trowbridge, Walt. In Sinclair Lewis' IT CAN'T HAPPEN HERE, a former U.S. Senator, opponent of Buzz WINDRIP in the presidential election. When he is defeated and Windrip begins to set up a Fascist dictatorship, Trowbridge takes refuge in Canada and initiates an underground revolutionary movement.

Troxartas (*Gr.,* "bread-eater"). King of the mice in THE BATTLE OF THE FROGS AND MICE, and father of Psycarpax, who is drowned.

> Fix their council . . .
> Where great Troxartas crowned in glory reigns . . .
> Psycarpax' father, father now no more!
> *Battle of the Frogs and Mice,* Bk. i. (Parnell).

Troy.

the Siege of Troy. See ILIAD; HELEN; TROJAN WAR; etc.

Troy town. A Cornish expression for a labyrinth of streets, a regular maze. *Troy* was formerly used figuratively of any scene of disorder or confusion; a room with its furniture all higgledy-piggledy, for instance, would be called a *Troy fair.*

Troy, Sergeant. A character in Hardy's FAR FROM THE MADDING CROWD.

Troynovant. The name given by the early chroniclers to London, anciently the city of the Trinobantes; a corruption of *Trinovant.* As *Troynovant* was assumed to mean *The New Troy,* the name gave rise to the tradition that BRUTE, a Trojan refugee (from whom was derived the name *Britain*) came to England and founded London.

Truce of God. In 1041 the Church attempted to limit private war, and decreed that there should be no hostilities between Lent and Advent or from the Thursday to the next Monday at the time of great festivals. This *Truce of God* was confirmed by the Lateran Council in 1179, and was agreed to by England, France, Italy, and other countries, but little attention was ever paid to it.

Trudeau, Edward Livingston (1848–1915). American doctor who established the Adirondack Cottage Sanatorium, now the Trudeau Sanatorium, where for the first time in America open-air treatment was tried for tuberculosis. He also established at Saranac, New York, the first laboratory for the study of tuberculosis (1894).

Trueman, Adam. A farmer in Mrs. Mowatt Ritchie's comedy FASHION.

Trulliber, Parson. In Fielding's JOSEPH ANDREWS, a fat clergyman, ignorant, selfish, and slothful. He is pictured in sharp contrast to the Parson ADAMS of the same novel.

Truman, Harry S. (1884–). Thirty-third president of the United States, succeeding to the presidency on the sudden death of Franklin D. Roosevelt (April 12, 1945). Formerly vice-president of the U.S. and U.S. senator from Missouri.

Trumbull, John (1750–1831). American poet, a member of the HARTFORD WITS, known as the author of satires and bombastic patriotic poems in the neo-Classical style. See NEO-CLASSICISM. His works include *The Progress of Dullness* (1772–1773), a satire on the methods of contemporary education; *An Elegy on the Times* (1774), a patriotic piece; MCFINGAL (1782), an anti-British satire, extremely popular in its time; essays in the style of THE SPECTATOR; several anonymous revolutionary essays; and a number of incidental poems. He also collaborated with Joel BARLOW and other members of the Hartford school on THE ANARCHIAD.

Trumbull, considered the most popular of the Hartford Wits, came of an outstanding Connecticut family and began his career as a child prodigy. He learned to read and write at the age of two, passed the Yale entrance examinations at the age of seven, and entered the college at thirteen. During the period just before the Revolution he studied law in the office of John Adams in Boston and took part in the political agitation of the time. Later he was a representative in the state legislature of Connecticut and a judge in the superior and supreme courts. He died of tuberculosis.

Trumbull, Jonathan (1710–1785). Early American statesman; governor of Connecticut (1769–1784) and a great supporter of the American Revolution. Washington's nickname for him, "Brother Jonathan," has become a stock phrase to denote the typical American.

trumpet.

the Feast of Trumpets. A Jewish festival, held on the first two days of Tisri (about mid-September to mid-October), the beginning of the ecclesiastical year, at which the blowing of trumpets formed a prominent part of the ritual.

trunk hose. Short padded breeches reaching about half way down the thigh. Often slashed to show lining. Sixteenth and early seventeenth-century dress for men.

Trunnion, Commodore Hawser. In Smollett's ADVENTURES OF PEREGRINE PICKLE, a one-eyed naval veteran, who has retired from the service in consequence of injuries received in engagements but still keeps garrison in his own house, which is defended with drawbridge and ditch. He sleeps in a hammock and makes his servants sleep in hammocks, as on board ship, takes his turn on watch, and indulges his naval tastes in various other ways. Lieutenant Jack Hatchway is his companion. When he goes to be married, he rides on a hunter which he steers like a ship, according to the compass, tacking about, that he may not "go right in the wind's eye." See also WEMMICK.

Truth, The. A drama by Clyde FITCH (1906). The heroine, Mrs. Warder, accused by her husband of a love affair with Fred Lindon of which the jealous Mrs. Lindon has informed him, tells so many lies to protect herself that she loses all chance of making him believe the truth, that the affair is a harmless flirtation. She goes home to her father, Roland, but a few moments after she has been blaming him for bringing her up to tell lies as a matter of course, he sends for Warder on the pretext that she is sick. Warder learns she has been perfectly well and is more infuriated than ever, until she says she has learned to hate lies, whether she tells them or not, and begs to be taken back.

Truth about Blayds, The. A play (1922) by A. A. MILNE, about a literary impostor.

Truthful James. An imaginary character who is the narrator in a number of Bret HARTE's poems, notably *The Society on the Stanislaw* and THE HEATHEN CHINEE. The latter was first published under the title *Plain Language from Truthful James.*

Tryamour, Sir. The hero of an old metrical novel and the model of all knightly virtues.

Tryan, Rev. Edgar. In George Eliot's JANET'S REPENTANCE the curate who is responsible for Janet Dempster's regeneration.

Tryanon. Daughter of the fairy king who lived on the island of Oléron. "She was as white as lily in May," and married Sir Launfal, King Arthur's steward, whom she carried off to "Oliroun her jolif isle," and, as the romance says—

> Since saw him in this land no man,
> Ne no more of him tell I n'can
> For soothë without lie.
> Thomas Chester, *Sir Launfal* (15th cent.).

Trygaeus. The hero of the Greek comedy *The Peace* by ARISTOPHANES (415 B. C.). This comedy was produced in the midst of the Peloponnesian war. The hero rides a dung-beetle to Olympus in search of Peace and finds that she has been thrown down a well. The gods are all away, so he rescues her and brings her back to Athens.

Tsung-Li Yamen. The former department for foreign affairs in China, through which, from its establishment in 1861 until 1901, foreign ministers addressed their communications to the Emperor and the Government.

Tuatha De Danann. A legendary race of super-human heroes which invaded Ireland, overthrew the Firbolgs and Fomors, and were themselves overthrown by the Milesians, who later worshiped them as gods.

Tub, Tale of a. See TALE OF A TUB.

Tubal. In Shakespeare's MERCHANT OF VENICE, a wealthy Jew, the friend of SHYLOCK.

Tubalcain. In the Old Testament, the first "forger of every cutting instrument of brass and iron."

Tuck, Friar. Chaplain and steward of Robin Hood, introduced by Scott in IVANHOE. He is a pudgy, paunchy, humorous, self-indulgent, and combative clerical Falstaff. His costume consists of a russet habit of the Franciscan order, a red corded girdle with gold tassel, red stockings, and a wallet. The name was probably given him because his dress is *tucked* by a girdle at the waist; thus Chaucer says, "Tucked he was, as is a frere about."

> In this our spacious isle I think there is not one
> But he hath heard some talk of Hood and Little John;
> Of Tuck, the merry friar, which many a sermon made
> In praise of Robin Hood, his outlaws, and their trade.
> Drayton, *Polyolbion,* xxvi. 311–16.

Tucker, Luther (1802–1873). American journalist, associated with the magazine *The Country Gentleman* (1853–1873).

Tucker, Sophie (1884–). American vaudeville actress and singer, who began at Tony Pastor's, joined the Ziegfeld *Follies* (1909) and later the Shubert *Gaieties* and the Earl Carroll *Vanities.* She has also been successful in London and New York cabarets.

Tuckerman, Frederick Goddard (1821–1873). American poet, rediscovered by Witter BYNNER, who edited *The Sonnets of Frederick Goddard Tuckerman* (1931).

Tuckerman, Henry Theodore (1813–1871). American essayist and poet. He wrote sonnets in the Petrarchan manner and the stiffness of his writing gave origin to the word "tuckermanity."

Tudor, Antony (1909–). American dancer and choreographer. His most famous ballets are *Lilac Garden* (1936) to Chausson's *Poème,* and *Pillar of Fire* (1942), to SCHOENBERG'S *Verklaerte Nacht.*

tuft. A nobleman or fellow commoner at Oxford, so called because he wears a gold tuft or tassel on his college cap.

tuft-hunter. A nobleman's toady.

tug of war. A rural sport in which a number of men, divided into two bands, lay hold of a strong rope and pull against each other till one side has tugged the other over the dividing line.

when Greek meets Greek then is the tug of war. See GREEK.

Tugwell, Rexford Guy (1891–). American economist. Acted as adviser to President Franklin D. Roosevelt. Governor of Puerto Rico (1941–1946). Author of *Industry's Coming of Age* (1927); *Battle for Democracy* (1935); etc.

Tuileries. One of the oldest palaces in Paris. It has superb gardens which were laid out by Louis XIV. The original palace, begun by Catherine de Médicis, is no longer in existence. The name means "brickyard" and is explained by the previous use of the site it occupies.

Tukhachevski, Mikhail Nikolaevich (1893–1937). Soviet general. In World War I, fought against Kolchak and Denikin. Marshal of the Soviet Union; accused of treason and executed (1937).

Tulliver, Maggie. The heroine of George Eliot's MILL ON THE FLOSS:

> Maggie, in her brown frock, with her eyes reddened and her heavy hair pushed back, looking from the bed where her father lay, to the dull walls of this sad chamber which was the centre of her world, was a creature full of eager, passionate longings for all that was beautiful and glad; thirsty for all knowledge; with an ear straining after dreamy music that died away and would not come near to her; with a blind unconscious yearning for something that would link together the wonderful impressions of this mysterious life, and give her soul a sense of home in it—Bk. 3. v.
>
> When Maggie was not angry, she was as dependent on kind or cold words as a daisy on sunshine or the cloud; the need of being loved would always subdue her.—Bk. 6. iv.

Tom Tulliver. Maggie's beloved brother.

> Tom never did the same sort of foolish things as Maggie, having a wonderful, instinctive discernment of what would turn to his advantage or disadvantage; and so it happened that though he was much more wilful and inflexible than Maggie, his mother hardly ever called him naughty. But if Tom did make a mistake of that sort, he espoused it, and stood by it; he "didn't mind" . . . If Tom Tulliver whipped a gate, he was convinced, not that the whipping of gates by all boys was a justifiable art, but that he, Tom Tulliver, was justifiable in whipping that particular gate, and he wasn't going to be sorry.—Bk. 1. vii.

Tullus Hostilius. Legendary Roman king (673–641 B.C.). His period was distinguished by war between the Horatii and the Curiatii.

Tully. Marcus Tullius CICERO 106–43 B.C.), the great Roman orator.

Tully, Jim (1891–1947). Popular American novelist. *Emmet Lawler* (1922); *Beggars of Life* (1924); *Jarnegan* (1925); *Circus Parade* (1927); *Blood on the Moon* (1931); *A Hollywood Decameron* (1937); *Biddy Brogan's Boy* (1942); etc.

Tully, Richard Walton (1877–1945). California dramatist. Co-author, with David Belasco, of *The Rose of the Rancho* (1906). His play *The Bird of Paradise* (1912) was made into a musical comedy (1930).

Tumbledown Dick. Anything that will not stand firmly. "Dick" is Richard Cromwell (1626–1712), the Protector's son, who was but a tottering wall at best.

Tumulty, Joseph Patrick (1879–). Private secretary to Woodrow Wilson as Governor of New Jersey (1910–1913) and President of the U.S. (1913–1921). Author of *Woodrow Wilson as I Know Him* (1921).

Tunney, Gene (1898–). American heavyweight champion. In World War II, in charge of physical training for the U.S. Navy.

Tunning of Elynour Rumming, The. A poem by John SKELTON which describes low life in England with a Hogarthian touch.

Tupman, Tracy. In Dickens' PICKWICK PAPERS, an M. P. C. (Member of the Pickwick Club), a sleek, fat young man, of very amorous disposition. He falls in love with every pretty girl he sees, and is consequently always getting into trouble.

Tupper, Martin Farquhar (1810–1889). English versifier whose *Proverbial Philosophy* (1838) was very popular and attained international vogue.

tu quoque (*Lat.,* "you too"). A retort implying that the one addressed is in the same boat as the speaker—that his case is no better and no worse.

the tu quoque style of argument. Personal invective; the argument of personal application; *argumentum ad hominem.*

Turberville, George (1540?–?1610). A pioneer in English blank verse. He wrote metrical letters on Russia which appear in Hakluyt's *Voyages.* He also translated from Ovid, and wrote on falconry.

Turcaret. One who has become rich by hook or by crook, and, having nothing else to show, makes a great display of his wealth;

from the hero of the comedy of the same name (1709) by LE SAGE.

Turenne, Vicomte **de. Henri de la Tour d'Auvergne** (1611–1675). French soldier. Napoleon called him the greatest military leader. He served through the Thirty Years' War and helped to hasten its end. He commanded armies under Louis XIV, and, through the king's influence, abandoned his original faith and became a Catholic (1668). He was killed in action, fighting against the Empire.

Turgenev, Ivan Sergeëvich (1818–1883). Russian novelist and poet, known for the realism and local color of his portrayals of life in 19th-century Russia, especially the conflicts between young, Westernized intellectuals and their conservative fathers. He is considered to have fixed the type of introspective, nihilist hero (see NIHILISM) in Russian fiction, and is believed to have influenced George SAND, FLAUBERT, and Henry JAMES in the technique of the novel. His works include *A Sportsman's Sketches* (1847–1851); *Rudin* (1856); *A Nest of Gentlefolk* or *A Nest of Nobles,* also known as LIZA (1859); FATHERS AND SONS (1862); *On the Eve* (1860); SMOKE (1867); VIRGIN SOIL (1876). Among other titles are *The Gamekeeper at Home; A Lear of the Steppes; Torrents of Spring; Clara Milch; Dream Tales and Prose Poems.*

Turgenev traveled a good deal in western Europe and was influenced by the ideas and techniques he encountered there. He was interested in the attempts of his time to westernize Russia, although his art had greater attractions for him than participation in active politics. He took a brief part in the movement to free the serfs, and was exiled to his country estate for calling GOGOL "a great man" in one of his articles. Nationalistic authors, most notably DOSTOYEVSKY, scorned Turgenev for his European ways and ideas, and the character of KARMAZINOV in *The Possessed* is considered to be a satirical portrait of the novelist.

Turgot, Anne Robert Jacques. Baron **de l'Aulne** (1727–1781). French statesman who is considered one of the founders of political economy. As finance minister under Louis XVI (1774–1776) he abolished some feudal privileges.

Turiddu. The hero of Mascagni's opera CAVALLERIA RUSTICANA.

Turk. Applied to barbarous, savage, cruel men, because these qualities have been for centuries attributed to Turks; also to mischievous and unruly children, as *You little Turk.*

the Young Turks. See under YOUNG.

Turk Gregory. Falstaff's *ne plus ultra* of military valor—a humorous combination of the Sultan with Gregory VII (Hildebrand), probably the strongest of all the Popes.

Turkey in the Straw. A frontier song, probably written about 1815. Its first name was *Zip Coon.* It was popular in the 1830s.

Turmoil, The. A novel by Booth TARKINGTON (1915). The hero is Bibbs Sheridan, the sensitive and despised poet son of a father who has been largely responsible for the industrial development of a western city. Bibbs hates machinery and has a nervous breakdown from his father's effort to have him learn the business from the bottom up. His two older brothers, Jim and Roscoe, both ambitious, practical young men, nevertheless fail to make good as their father's successors, and Bibbs proves the mainstay of the family. He loves and marries his neighbor, Mary Vertrees.

Turner, Charles Tennyson (1808–1879). Older brother of Sir Alfred TENNYSON. Author of several volumes of poetry.

Turner, Frederick Jackson (1861–1932). American historian. His best works are: *The Frontier in American History* (1920) and *The Significance of Sections in American History* (1932), which won the Pulitzer Prize for history (1933). His last book on the United States was uncompleted at his death.

Turner, Joseph Mallord William (1775–1851). English painter known for his watercolors and his brilliant effects of light. John Ruskin praised him in *Modern Painters* (1843).

Turner, Walter James Redfern (1889–). English writer. Music critic for the London *Daily Express* (from 1923) and author of many books of poems, novels, and essays on music and life, notably a biography of Mozart. Several of his shorter poems have been much anthologized.

Turn of the Screw, The. A tale by Henry JAMES (1898), told from the viewpoint of the leading character, a spinster governess in love with her employer, who goes to an isolated English estate to take charge of Miles and Flora, two attractive and precocious children. She sees what she believes are the ghosts of Miss Jessel and Peter Quint, respectively the former governess and steward of the estate, and concludes that these two are exerting an evil influence over the children. She tries to convince the housekeeper of the danger she perceives, and struggles to impose her influence on the children and win them from the apparitions. At the climax of the story she enters into direct conflict with the children, with the result that Flora seems to turn into a witch before her eyes and Miles dies of fright.

There have been conflicting interpretations of this famous tale, but the one most favored is that the appearance of the ghosts is merely hallucination on the part of the governess, whose frustrated desire takes the form of an attempt to exert over the children the power she cannot win over their father.

Turnus. In Virgil's AENEID, a prince betrothed to Lavinia, the daughter of the King of Latium. When Aeneas lands in Italy after the Trojan War and becomes a suitor for the hand of Lavinia, the two fight and Turnus is killed.

Turpentine State. North Carolina. See STATES.

Turpin, Archbishop. A famous figure of medieval legend, by most accounts one of the paladins of Charlemagne's court. In historical reality he was a contemporary of CHARLEMAGNE, Archbishop of Rheims from 753 to 794, on whom has been fathered a French chronicle history, written in Latin in the first half of the 11th century. The probable author was a canon of Barcelona. This chronicle, known as the pseudo-Turpin, was a most important link in the growth of the Carolingian legend and was largely drawn upon for the Italian epic poems ORLANDO INNAMORATO and ORLANDO FURIOSO. It relates the expedition of Charlemagne to Spain in 777, and his return to France after subduing Navarre and Aragon. The chronicle says he invested Pampeluna for three months without being able to take it; he then tried what prayer could do, and the walls fell down of their own accord, like those of Jericho. Those Saracens who consented to become Christians were spared; the rest were put to the sword. Charlemagne then visited the sarcophagus of James, and Turpin baptized most of the neighborhood. The King crossed the Pyrenees, but the rear commanded by ROLAND was attacked by 50,000 Saracens, and none escaped.

Turpin, Dick. A noted highwayman executed at York in 1739. Many legends and ballads have him as their central figure. Harrison AINSWORTH, in his once widely read novel *Rookwood* (1834), introduced the incident of Turpin's famous ride from London to York in a single night on his steed Black Bess. The horse was exhausted and died upon arrival.

Turveydrop, Mr. In Dickens' BLEAK HOUSE, a selfish, self-indulgent, conceited dancing-master, who imposes on the world by his majestic appearance and elaborate toilette. He lives on the earnings of his son (named Prince, after the Prince Regent), who reveres him as a perfect model of "deportment."

Tuscan Poet, the. Ludovico ARIOSTO (1474–1533), born at Reggio, in Modena, noted for his epic poem ORLANDO FURIOSO.

Tushin, Lizaveta Nikolaevna. In Dostoyevsky's THE POSSESSED, a young Russian woman, a neighbor of Varvara Petrovna STAVROGIN. Lizaveta Nikolaevna is a proud, passionate, independent young woman, divided by conflicting emotions. For a time she is fascinated by the revolutionary band and its plans for a publication, and especially by Nikolay Stavrogin. She resolves to try to save Nikolay from himself by teaching him truly to love, and spends the night with him. When she discovers that his nature is dead to all genuine, selfless emotions, she denounces him and leaves in a state of desperate excitement. At the scene of the fire and the murder of the LEBYADKINS she is killed by an enfuriated mob. Like many of Dostoyevsky's heroines, Lizaveta Nikolaevna is believed to have been based on the character of Polina Suslova, a proud, passionate woman of keen intellect with whom the author once was unhappily in love.

Tusitala, see STEVENSON, ROBERT LOUIS.

Tuskegee Normal and Industrial Institute. A college for Negroes founded by Booker T. Washington (1881). It has an endowment of seven million dollars and owns two thousand acres in Alabama.

Tussaud, Madame (1760–1850). Swiss originator of a famous collection of wax figures of leaders and victims of the French Revolution, called Madame Tussaud's Exhibition. It was established in Baker Street, London (1833); a supplement to it was a Chamber of Horrors which contained implements and other relics of criminals.

Tusser, Thomas (ca. 1524–1580). English poet, known for his advice on domestic and farm problems, resembling later farmers' almanacs but written throughout in verse, which were very popular in their day among the farmers and housewives of England. His works in this vein include *A Hundred Good Points of Husbandry* (1557); *A Hundred Good Points of Housewifery* (1570); and *Five Hundred Points of Good Husbandry, United to as Many of Good Housewifery* (1573). Religious verse and moral maxims were also included among information on crops, soil cultivation, weather, and the like. Tusser, once a pupil of Nicholas UDALL, was for a time a musician at court, but later retired to the country as a farmer. He died eventually in a debtor's prison.

Tutankh-Amen. An Egyptian king (ca. 1350 B.C.), whose tomb was unearthed in the Valley of the Kings near Luxor by Howard Carter and Lord Carnarvon in 1923.

Tutivillus. The demon of medieval legend who collects all the words skipped over or mutilated by priests in the performance of the services. These literary scraps or shreds he deposits in that pit which is said to be paved with "good intentions" never brought to effect.

tutorial system. The manner of education in English universities where the students study under a particular tutor who instructs them as to university requirements and oversees and directs their reading. This system has also been introduced into certain American universities, especially Harvard.

Tutt, Mr. See Arthur TRAIN.

Twachtman, John Henry (1853–1902). Leading American painter of the impressionist school.

Twa Dogs, The. A poem by Robert BURNS, a dialogue between Caesar, a gentleman's dog, and Luath, a ploughman's collie.

Twain, Mark. Pseudonym of **Samuel Langhorne Clemens** (1835–1910). American humorist, journalist, and author, best known for his humorous stories of American frontier life in the 19th century, written at first under the influence of Bret HARTE, with whom he was for a time associated. His works include *The Adventures of Thomas Jefferson Snodgrass* (1856); *The Celebrated Jumping Frog of Calaveras County* (see JUMPING FROG; 1865), his first work to attract attention, reissued in *The Celebrated Jumping Frog of Calaveras County, And Other Sketches* (1867); THE INNOCENTS ABROAD (1869); *Roughing It* (1872); THE GILDED AGE (1873), a novel written with Charles Dudley Warner; *The Adventures of Tom Sawyer* (see TOM SAWYER; 1876), with its sequel *The Adventures of Huckleberry Finn* (see HUCKLEBERRY FINN; 1884) the most famous of Twain's books; *A Tramp Abroad* (1880), an account of European travel; LIFE ON THE MISSISSIPPI (1883); THE PRINCE AND THE PAUPER (1882); A CONNECTICUT YANKEE IN KING ARTHUR'S COURT (1889); *The American Claimant* (1890); PUDD'NHEAD WILSON (1894); *Tom Sawyer Abroad* (1894) and *Tom Sawyer, Detective* (1896), late sequels to the earlier *Sawyer* books; *Personal Recollections of Joan of Arc* (see JOAN OF ARC; 1896); *Following the Equator* (1897), an account of a lecture tour of the world; THE MAN THAT CORRUPTED HADLEYBURG (1899); *What Is Man?* (1906); *Christian Science* (1907); *Captain Stormfield's Visit to Heaven* (1909); THE MYSTERIOUS STRANGER (1916); *Mark Twain's Letters* (1917); *Mark Twain's Autobiography* (1924). *Tom Sawyer* and *Huckleberry Finn* are considered his best work, marked, as are his most representative humorous sketches, by vigor, high-spirited exaggeration, and native colloquial idiom.

Clemens was born in Missouri and in his early youth held a number of odd jobs, working as a printer and as apprentice to a pilot on a steamboat on the Mississippi River. His pseudonym had its origin in this latter job, "mark twain," meaning "two fathoms deep," being a phrase used in taking soundings on the river boats. At the time of the Civil War he went to Nevada and California, where he met Artemus WARD and Harte, worked on frontier newspapers, and first attracted attention by his writing. He soon became extremely popular, and was also praised by serious critics of the day. After 1894, when he suffered a financial failure, his work began to show a pessimistic, misanthropic quality. Some critics, notably Van Wyck BROOKS in *The Ordeal of Mark Twain,* have attributed this to the frustration of Twain's genuine creative talents by the conservative, Puritanical influence of his wife, Olivia Langdon, and her friends. The author himself directed that some of his works be published only after his death, feeling that they were too pessimistic for the public of his own lifetime.

'Twas the Night Before Christmas. A very popular poem (1823), originally called *A Visit from St. Nicholas,* by Clement Clarke Moore.

Tweed, William Marcy (1823–1878). American politician and head of Tammany Hall. The "Tweed Ring" of politicians swindled the treasury of New York City out of millions. Samuel J. TILDEN was chairman of the Democratic State committee which effected its destruction. Thomas NAST, drawing his remarkable cartoons for *Harper's Weekly,* was a great force in helping to destroy it, and so was the New York *Times* in 1870. Cf. *"Boss" Tweed* (1927), by Denis Tilden Lynch.

Tweedledum and **Tweedledee.** Names invented by John Byrom (d. 1763) to satirize two quarreling schools of musicians between whom the real difference was negligible. Hence, used of people whose persons—or opinions—are "as like as two peas."

> Some say compared to Bononcini
> That Mynheer Handel's but a ninny;
> Others aver that he to Handel
> Is scarcely fit to hold a candle.
> Strange all this difference should be
> 'Twixt Tweedledum and Tweedledee.
>
> J. Byrom.

The Duke of Marlborough and most of the nobility took the side of G. B. Bononcini (d. about 1752), but the Prince of Wales, with POPE and ARBUTHNOT, was for Handel. See also GLUCKISTS.

Lewis CARROLL introduced Tweedledum and Tweedledee into his *Through the Looking-Glass,* the sequel to *Alice in Wonderland,* with entertaining effect. They sing the famous ditty of *The Walrus and the Carpenter.*

Tweedsmuir, 1st Baron, see BUCHAN, JOHN.

Tweedy, Marion. Maiden name of Molly BLOOM, in James Joyce's ULYSSES.

Twelfth Night. January 5, the eve of Twelfth Day, or the Feast of the Epiphany, twelve days after Christmas, January 6. Formerly this was a time of great merrymaking, and the games that took place were, with little doubt, a survival of the old Roman *Saturnalia,* which was held in the same season.

Twelfth Night, or What You Will. A comedy by SHAKESPEARE (ca. 1600). The plot hinges on the physical likeness between Sebastian and his twin sister, Viola. They are shipwrecked off the coast of Illyria, and Viola, separated from her brother, in order to support herself dresses like a man and becomes the page of Duke Orsino.

The Duke cherishes a hopeless passion for the Countess Olivia, but she, instead of returning his devotion, falls in love with his handsome page. Eventually Olivia marries Sebastian, whom she first mistakes for the page, and the Duke, on learning Viola's sex, consoles himself by making her the Duchess of Illyria. The interest in *Twelfth Night* depends largely on the famous comic characters of MALVOLIO, Sir Andrew AGUECHEEK, Sir Toby BELCH and MARIA. The play was called *Twelfth Night,* doubtless, because it was written to be acted at the Twelfth Night festivities. The plot was taken, through various secondary sources, from an Italian *novella* of Bandello.

twelve.

the Twelve. All the prelates of the Roman Catholic Church. Of course the allusion is to the Twelve Apostles.

The Pope identifies himself with the "Master," and addresses those 700 prelates as the "Twelve."—*The Times,* December 11, 1869.

the Twelve Apostles. See APOSTLES.

the Twelve Disciples. See APOSTLES.

the Twelve Knights of the Round Table. See ROUND TABLE.

the Twelve Paladins. See PALADINS.

the Twelve Tables. The earliest code of Roman law, compiled by the Decemviri, and engraved on twelve bronze tablets (Livy, iii, 57; Diodorus, xii, 56).

the Twelve Wise Masters. See MEISTERSINGERS.

Twelve-Pound Look, The. A comedy (1910) by J. M. BARRIE.

Twenty Thousand Leagues Under the Sea. A romance (1870) by Jules VERNE, remarkable for its prediction of submarines.

Twenty Years After (Vingt Ans après). A historical romance by Alexandre DUMAS (1845), a sequel to THE THREE MUSKETEERS.

Twice-told Tales. A collection of short stories (1837) by Nathaniel HAWTHORNE.

Twichell, Joseph Hopkins (1838–1918). American clergyman and friend of Mrs. Stowe, Charles Dudley Warner and Mark Twain. He suggested to Mark Twain that he write *Life on the Mississippi.* In Mark Twain's *A Tramp Abroad,* Twichell appears as Harris.

Twickenham, The Bard of. See under BARD.

Twickenham, the Wicked Wasp of. See POPE, ALEXANDER.

Twilight of the Gods. See RAGNAROK.

Twin Cities. Minneapolis and St. Paul. See under CITY.

Twist, Oliver, see OLIVER TWIST.

Twitcher, Jemmy. A cunning, treacherous highwayman in Gay's BEGGAR'S OPERA.

Two Gentlemen of Verona, The. A comedy by Shakespeare (ca. 1592), the plot of which is taken from the *Diana* of Montemayor (16th century). The "two gentlemen" are Proteus and Valentine, close friends at first, but later rivals for the hand of Silvia, daughter of the Duke of Milan, who is, however, betrothed to Thurio. Proteus forgets his old love Julia, plays his friend false, and brings about his banishment. When Valentine is thus forced to leave the court, he becomes a bandit and in the course of time Silvia falls into his hands. A party from the court comes to the rescue, including Thurio and Proteus, the latter attended by a page who is really his old love, Julia, in disguise. Valentine's conduct is so manly that the Duke freely bestows his daughter upon him, and the repentant Proteus contents himself with marrying Julia.

Two Little Confederates. A boys' story of the Civil War by Thomas Nelson Page (*Am.,* 1888). The scene is laid in Virginia and the heroes are two Southern boys too young to enlist.

Two Noble Kinsmen, The. A drama (1634) by John Fletcher and William Shakespeare. It was reprinted, without Shakespeare being mentioned, in a second folio edition of Beaumont and Fletcher's plays (1679). It is still unknown how great a part Shakespeare played in its authorship. The story is taken from the *Knightes Tale* by Chaucer.

Two on a Tower. A novel by Thomas HARDY (1882), dealing with the mutual love of the young astronomer Swithin St. Cleve and Lady Viviette Constantine. An early secret marriage between them is set aside by later developments, and when St. Cleve finally returns from South Africa to the familiar observatory tower to propose marriage, Viviette falls dead in his arms.

Two Orphans, The. A French play (1875) by D'Ennery and Cormon very popular as a melodrama in the late nineteenth century. D. W. GRIFFITH directed Lillian and Dorothy GISH in a silent motion picture called *Orphans of the Storm.*

Two-Shoes, Goody. See under GOODY.

Two Years Before the Mast. A famous narrative by Richard Henry DANA (1840) giving an account of his voyage around Cape Horn to California as a young sailor of twenty-two.

Tybalt. In Shakespeare's ROMEO AND JULIET, a fiery young nobleman of Verona, Lady

Capulet's nephew and Juliet's cousin. He is slain in combat by Romeo. The name had been given to the *cat* in the beast-epic called REYNARD THE FOX; hence MERCUTIO calls him "ratcatcher" (Act III. Sc. 1), and when Tybalt demands of him, "What wouldst thou have with me?" Mercutio replies, "Good king of cats, nothing but one of your nine lives."

Tyburn Tree, the. A gallows; so called because criminals were at one time hung on the elm trees which grew on the banks of the Tyburn. Hence also the expressions a *Tyburn face,* or criminal appearance; a *Tyburn tippet* or halter; and *to preach at Tyburn Cross,* meaning to be hanged.

Tyburnia. The Portman and Grosvenor Squares district of London, described by THACKERAY as "the elegant, the prosperous, the polite Tyburnia, the most respectable district of the habitable globe."

tycoon. From Chinese, "high prince." A title taken by some of the Tokugawa Shoguns of Japan (1603–1868). The shogun was the first of the daimios who, in turn, were vassals of the crown. Today the term is used as a designation of a magnate of industry in the U.S. or elsewhere, especially by the newsmagazine TIME. Cf. *The Last Tycoon* (1941) by F. Scott Fitzgerald.

Tydeus. In classic myth, one of the "SEVEN AGAINST THEBES."

Tyler, John (1790–1862). Tenth president of the United States (1841–1845). Vice president at the time of President William Henry Harrison's death (April 4, 1841). During the Tyler administration Texas was annexed to the Union.

Tyler, Moses Coit (1835–1900). Professor of American history at Cornell University (1881–1900). He helped to found the American Historical Association (1884) and wrote several weighty books on early American literature.

Tyler, Royall (1757–1826). American lawyer and playwright, best known as the author of THE CONTRAST (1787), the second native American play and the first American comedy. Other works by Tyler are *May-Day in Town, Or New York in an Uproar* (1787), a satirical opera; *The Georgia Spec, Or Land in the Moon* (1797), another satirical comedy; *The Chestnut Tree* (1824), a long poem on American life of the author's time; THE ALGERINE CAPTIVE (1797), a picaresque and satirical novel; *Yankee in London* (1809), a series of letters supposedly by an American living in London; and several unpublished, unproduced plays, including three Biblical dramas in blank verse. Tyler eventually became chief justice of the Vermont supreme court.

Tyler's Insurrection, also called **The Peasants' Revolt.** An armed rebellion of peasants in southern England in 1381, led by Wat Tyler (an Essex man), in consequence of discontent aroused by the Statute of Laborers, and the heavy taxation, especially a poll-tax of three groats to defray the expenses of a war with France. Wat Tyler was slain by the Lord Mayor at Smithfield, the revolt was crushed, and many of the rebels executed. He is the hero of a poem by Southey called *Wat Tyler.* See also VOX CLAMANTIS.

Tyll Owlyglass or **Howleglass.** The English name of the German *Tyll Eulenspiegel,* a figure of popular legend whose pranks were first written down in low Dutch by Thomas Mürner (1483). Tyll is a mechanic of Brunswick, who runs from pillar to post as charlatan, physician, lansquenet, fool, valet, artist, and Jack-of-all-trades.

> To few mortals has it been granted to earn such a place in universal history as Tyll Eulenspiegel. Now, after five centuries, Tyll's native village is pointed out with pride to the traveller, and his tombstone . . . still stands . . . at Mollen, near Lubeck, where, since 1350 [sic], his once nimble bones have been at rest.—Carlyle.

Tyltyl. One of the two children who go in search of the BLUE BIRD in Maeterlinck's play of that title.

Tynan, Katharine (1861–1931). Irish poet and voluminous writer of fiction who was a friend of Alice MEYNELL. She wrote as a Catholic; her work is very Celtic.

Tyndale, William (died 1536). English Protestant preacher, known for his translation of the Bible into English, first printed at Cologne in 1525. He sent copies of his translation into England for distribution, but they were condemned by the Roman Catholic bishops and burned. Tyndale also wrote pamphlets supporting the single authority of the Bible and the king over the power of the Church and the Pope, and for awhile was favored by King Henry VIII, although he soon lost this favor when he disapproved of the King's divorce. He carried on a vigorous controversy with Sir Thomas MORE, and in 1536 was strangled and burned at the stake in Antwerp as a heretic.

Tyndale's Bible. See BIBLE, THE ENGLISH.

Tyndall, John (1820–1893). British popularizer of science. Collaborated with Huxley in Switzerland, and lectured in the United States (1872–1873). He made various investigations of heat and light and wrote a number of treatises on scientific subjects.

Typee. A romance of the South Seas by Herman MELVILLE (1846) recording the adventures of a whaling voyage in the Pacific. *Typee* (Taipi) is a valley in one of the Marquesas where Melville was kept captive by the natives. The book gives a vivid picture of a civilized man in contact with the exotic, dreamlike life of the tropics. Its popularity was revived by the South Sea furor of the 1920's.

types. The following are the sizes most generally used in book-printing—

14 Point: Reader's Encyclopedia.
12 Point: Reader's Encyclopedia.
10 Point: Reader's Encyclopedia.
8 Point: Reader's Encyclopedia.
6 Point: Reader's Encyclopedia.
5 Point: Reader's Encyclopedia

14 Point: Reader's Encyclopedia.
12 Point: Reader's Encyclopedia.
10 Point: Reader's Encyclopedia.
8 Point: Reader's Encyclopedia.
6 Point: Reader's Encyclopedia.

Typhoeus. A giant of Greek mythology, with a hundred heads, fearful eyes, and a most terrible voice. He was the father of the HARPIES. Zeus killed him with a thunderbolt, and he lies buried under Mount Etna.

Typhon. A fire-breathing monster, the father of the Sphinx, the Chimaera, and other monsters. He is often identified with Typhoeus, a son of Tartarus and Gaea, who begot the unfavorable winds or, according to other stories, is himself one of them. As a hundred-headed giant he warred against the gods and was banished by Jupiter to Tartarus under Mount Aetna. Typhon is also the name used by the Greeks for the Egyptian Set, the god of evil, who killed his brother (or father) Osiris.

Typhoon. A well-known short story (1903) by Joseph Conrad.

typographical signs. ´ An acute accent. In Greek, it indicates a rise in the voice; in French, vowel quality; in Spanish, stress; in Bohemian and Hungarian, a long vowel.

` A grave accent. In Greek, indicating a fall of the voice; in French, vowel quality, or sometimes a differentiation (as in *la, là*); and in English, that the accented syllable is to be pronounced (as in *blessèd*).

^ A circumflex; in French, usually indicating that an *s* has been dropped (as *être* for older *estre*), and that the marked vowel is long.

¸ under the letter *c* in French, is called a *cedilla,* and indicates that the *c* (ç) is to be pronounced as *s*. It represents the Greek *zeta* (*z*), which formerly followed the *c* to indicate an *s* sound.

¨ over the second of two vowels, as in *reëstablish,* denotes that each vowel is to be sounded and is called the *diaeresis,* in French, *trema.* In German it is the *umlaut* or *zweipunkt* (*two dots*) and denotes a change in the vowel sound, a following vowel (usually *i*) having been dropped.

° over a vowel, is the Scandinavian form of the *umlaut* or *zweipunkt.*

~ The *tilde,* used in Spanish, over the *n* (as *Oñoro*) to show that it is pronounced *ny.*

& And; the Tironian Sign, or Ampersand.

? The note of interrogation, or query mark; said to have been formed from the first and last letters of Lat. *Quaestio* (question), which were contracted to Qo.

! The note of exclamation; representing the Latin *Io* (joy), written vertically Io.

' The apostrophe; indicating that a letter (or figure) has been omitted, as *don't, I'm; the rebellion of* '98 (for 1798); also marking the possessive case (*John's book*), and plurals of letters and figures, as in *too many I's, half a dozen 8's.*

*, †, ‡, The asterisk, dagger (or obelisk), and double dagger; used as reference marks, etc. Another reference mark is ⁂ or * * *, the asterism.

§ The section mark; said to represent the old long initial *s*'s (ſ ſ) of Lat. *signum sectionis,* sign of a section.

☞ An index-hand, to call attention to a statement.

¶ A blind P (a modification of the initial letter of *paragraph*), marks a new paragraph.

( ) Called parentheses, and

[ ] Called brackets, separate some explanatory or collateral matter from the real sequence.

See also PROOF.

Tyr. In Norse mythology, the god of battle, one-handed since the day when he put his hand in Fenris's mouth as a pledge which the other gods did not redeem.

tyrant. In ancient Greece the *tyrant* was merely the absolute ruler, the *despot,* of a state, and at first the word had no implication of cruelty or what we call *tyranny.* Many of the Greek tyrants were excellent rulers, as Pisistratus and Pericles, of Athens; Periander, of Corinth; Dionysius the Younger, Gelon, and his brother Hiero, of Syracuse; Phidion, of Argos, Polycrates, of Samos; etc. The word *tyrannos* soon, however, obtained much the same meaning as it has with us.

a tyrant's vein. A ranting, bullying manner. In the old MORALITIES the tyrants were made to rant, and the loudness of their rant matched the villainy of their dispositions.

the Thirty Tyrants. The thirty magistrates appointed by Sparta over Athens, at the termination of the Peloponnesian war. This "reign of terror," after one year's continuance, was overthrown by Thrasybulus (403 B.C.).

In the Roman empire, those military usurpers who endeavored, in the reigns of Valerian and Gallienus (253–268), to make themselves independent princes, are also called *the Thirty Tyrants*. The number must be taken with great latitude, as only nineteen are given, and their resemblance to those of Athens is extremely fanciful.

Tyrian purple. A famous crimson or purple dye used by the Greeks and Romans.

Tyrtaeus. A lame schoolmaster and elegiac poet of Athens who is said so to have inspired the Spartans by his songs that they defeated the Messenians (7th century B. C.). The name has hence been given to many martial poets who have urged on their countrymen to deeds of arms and victory.

Tyrwhitt, Thomas (1730–1786). English scholar. His chief claim to fame is that, although at first he believed that the Rowley Poems were authentic, he then exposed the fact that they were actually written by Thomas CHATTERTON.

Tzara, Tristan (1896–). Rumanian-born poet and leader of the DADA movement in French literature. He edited the magazine *Dada* (1916–1920) and was a surrealist in 1930.

U

Ubaldini, Ruggiero. Ghibelline leader and archbishop of Pisa who imprisoned and starved to death (1288) Ugolino della Gherardesca and his sons and grandsons. He appears in the *Inferno* of Dante, Canto xxxiii.

Uberti, Farinata Degli. A noble Florentine, leader of the GHIBELLINE faction. Dante represents him, in his INFERNO, as lying in a fiery tomb not to be closed till the Last Judgment.

Ubique. A poem about the Royal Artillery by Rudyard Kipling. The word is Latin and means "everywhere."

Udall, Nicholas (1505–1556). English playwright and schoolmaster, known as the author of the earliest extant English comedy, RALPH ROISTER DOISTER (1553). Udall was headmaster of both Eton and Westminster schools, translated plays from the Latin of Terence, and wrote other plays in Latin on theological subjects. He once taught Thomas TUSSER.

Udolpho, The Mysteries of. See MYSTERIES OF UDOLPHO.

Uffizi. Great art gallery in Florence, Italy, established by the Medicis in the 15th century.

Ugly Duchess, The. Historical novel (1928), by Lion FEUCHTWANGER. The Duchess was the model for the Duchess in ALICE IN WONDERLAND.

Ugly Duckling, The. One of ANDERSEN's *Fairy Tales,* the story of a swan hatched among ducklings and mocked at as an ungainly member of the brood, until finally it becomes apparent that he is a swan.

Ugolino. A GHIBELLINE, Ugolino della Gherardesca, Count of Pisa, who, about 1270, deserted his party and with the hope of usurping supreme power in Pisa, formed an alliance with Giovanni Visconti, the head of the GUELPHS. The plot failed; Giovanni died, and Ugolino joined the Florentines and forced the Pisans to restore his territories. In 1284 Genoa made war against Pisa, and the Count again treacherously deserted the Pisans, causing their total overthrow. At length a conspiracy was formed against him, and in 1288 he was cast with his two sons and two grandsons into the tower of Gualandi, where all starved to death. Dante, in his INFERNO, has made the sad tale immortal.

Uhland, Johann Ludwig (1787–1862). German poet, playwright, essayist, and literary historian. Especially known for his ballads and songs.

ukase. In the former Russian Empire an edict either proceeding from the senate or direct from the emperor. Hence it came to mean a rigid order or official decree of any kind.

Ulalume. A poem by Edgar Allan POE (1847), in memory of his "lost Ulalume."

Ulania. In the Charlemagne romances, the Queen of Perduta or Islanda. She sent a golden shield to CHARLEMAGNE, which he was to give to his bravest paladin, and whoever could win it from him was to claim the hand of Ulania in marriage. Cf. *Orlando Furioso,* Bk. xv.

ulema. The learned classes in Mohammedan countries, interpreters of the *Koran* and the law, from whose numbers are chosen the mollahs, imams, muftis, cadis, etc. (ministers of religion, doctors of law, and administrators of justice). *Ulema* is the plural of *ulim,* "a wise man." The body is under the presidency of the Sheikh-ul-Islam.

Ulrica. In Scott's IVANHOE, daughter of the late thane of Torquilstone, *alias* Dame Urfried, an old sibyl at Torquilstone Castle. Also, in Verdi's opera LA FORZA DEL DESTINO, a witch who predicts the peril that is to befall the two lovers.

Ulster. The northernmost province of Ireland, which was forfeited to the Crown in James I's reign in consequence of the rebellions of Tyrconnel and Tyrone, and colonized (1609–1612) by English and Scottish settlers, who were forbidden to sell land to any Irishman. Since then the Ulstermen (see also ORANGEMEN) have been intensely English and anti-Irish in sentiment and action and have refused on any terms to coalesce with the original inhabitants, who have ever been anti-British.

The long loose overcoat known as an *ulster* is so called because it was originally made of Ulster frieze.

the Red, or *Bloody, Hand of Ulster.* The badge of Ulster, a sinister hand, erect, open, and couped at the wrist, gules. Legend has it that in an ancient expedition to Ireland it was given out that whoever first touched the shore should possess the territory which he touched; O'Neill, seeing another boat likely to outstrip his own, cut off his left hand and threw it on the coast. From this O'Neill the princes of Ulster were descended, and the motto of the O'Neills is to this day *Lamh dearg Eirin,* "red hand of Erin."

Ultima Thule. See under THULE.

ultramontane party. The extreme Popish party in the Church of Rome. *Ultramontane* opinions or tendencies are those which favor the high "Catholic" party. *Ultramontane* (beyond the mountains, i.e., the Alps) means Italy or the old Papal States. The term was first used by the French to distinguish those who look upon the Pope as the fountain of all power in the Church from the Gallican school, which maintained the right of self-government by national churches.

ultraviolet. See under INFRA-RED.

ultra vires (Law Lat. *ultra,* "beyond," *vires,* pl. of *vis,* "strength"). In excess of the power possessed; transcending authority.

Ulyanov, Vladimir Ilyich, see LENIN, NIKOLAY.

Ulysses. The Roman name of the Greek Odysseus, hero of Homer's ODYSSEY and a prominent character in the ILIAD. He is called Ulysses in most English poetry, including translations of Homer. TENNYSON wrote a poem *Ulysses* (1842), in which the hero in his old age speaks of his still active longing for adventure. Stephen PHILLIPS made him the subject of a poetic drama, *Ulysses.* He is a character in *The World's Desire,* by HAGGARD and LANG.

Ulysses. A novel by James JOYCE, published in Paris in 1922. Making the first major use of the technique of STREAM-OF-CONSCIOUSNESS and employing other unique technical devices, such as excerpts from newspaper headlines, a series of questions and answers, parodies on a variety of literary styles, the dialogue form of a play, etc., *Ulysses* presents a record of the events taking place in the lives of the three leading characters on an average day in Dublin, Ireland (June 16, 1904). A general parallel between the events in the novel and those presented in the ODYSSEY is maintained throughout, with the leading characters, Leopold BLOOM, his wife Molly, and Stephen DEDALUS, corresponding to the classic characters of ULYSSES, PENELOPE, and TELEMACHUS, respectively. The theme of the novel in general is the quest of the average 20th-century man (Bloom) for a son in whom he can place his trust and his hope, and the simultaneous quest of the disinherited 20th-century artist (Dedalus) for a father who will give him encouragement and a sense of continuity with mankind. Both men are lonely, Bloom's child, Rudy, having died in infancy, and Stephen having cast off his family and his Roman Catholic Irish heritage as bigoted and provincial.

The following is an outline of the separate episodes making up the novel, an indication of the Homeric parallels involved, and the approximate time of day at which each takes place:

I *8 A.M.* Stephen Dedalus is seen as he rises from sleep in the old tower on the shores of Dublin Bay where he lives with Buck Mulligan and an English student named Haines. (Stephen as Telemachus.)

II *10 A.M.* Stephen, teaching a class of boys in Mr. Deasy's school, is unhappy and unable to keep his mind on his work. Later he talks with Mr. Deasy, who asks him to try to arrange the publication of a letter on hoof-and-mouth disease. (Stephen as Nestor.)

III *11 A.M.* Stephen takes a walk along the beach, and his personality and his attitude of mind are presented by the flow of his thoughts as he watches the waves, brooding on his spiritual isolation and the death of his mother. (Stephen as Proteus.)

IV *8 A.M.* Leopold Bloom rises, prepares his wife's breakfast, reflects on a variety of subjects, and brings Molly her morning mail, among which is a letter from her lover, Blazes Boylan. (Calypso incident.)

V *10 A.M.* Bloom goes to a post office, where he receives a love-letter from Martha Clifford, a typist with whom he is having a love affair and who addresses him as Henry Flower. Bloom next stops in at a church to hear music, calls at a drug store, or chemist's shop, to buy some lemon soap for his wife, and then goes to a public bath, for awhile reveling in sensuous enjoyment of the water and its warmth. (Episode of the Lotus Eaters.)

VI *11 A.M.* Bloom attends the funeral of a former friend, Paddy Dignam, riding with Simon Dedalus, Stephen's father, and a group of other Dubliners. Bloom reflects at random on the subject of death, and the others ride sedately in silence or make strained remarks. After the funeral a collection is taken up for Dignam's widow. (Ulysses' voyage to Hades.)

VII *12 Noon.* Bloom visits a newspaper office, where he discusses politics and makes arrangements for the placing of an advertisement. A little while after he has left, Stephen comes into the same office and invites those present to join him in a tavern as his guests, he having resigned from his job with Mr. Deasy and for the moment feeling affluent in the possession of a check for his back salary. (Aeolus episode.)

VIII *1 P.M.* Bloom walks through the streets of Dublin, noticing the people about him in the streets, such celebrities as A.E., the poet, being included among them. Bloom at last goes into the "pub" of Davy Byrne and lunches on a sandwich and wine. (Episode of the Lestrygonians.)

IX *2 P.M.* Stephen, Buck Mulligan, and Haines engage in a heated literary discussion in a public library, arguing chiefly about Shakespeare; Stephen advances theories of his own regarding *Hamlet* and Shakespeare's private life. Bloom enters the library also and passes the group of young men on his way to a newspaper file. (Episode of Scylla and Charybdis.)

X *3 P.M.* Bloom, Stephen, Simon Dedalus, Stephen's sister Dilly, and a number of other persons stroll through the streets of Dublin, and the sights and sounds of the city are presented impressionistically in eighteen scenes. The episode concludes with a street parade by the Viceroy of Ireland and his retinue on their way to a charity bazaar. (Episode of the Wandering Rocks.)

XI *4 P.M.* Bloom goes to the Ormand Hotel, where he has a meal and meets Stephen's father and uncle. Later he writes a love letter, while at about the same time Molly Bloom and her lover, Blazes, are enjoying a rendezvous together. (Episode of the Sirens.)

XII *5 P.M.* Bloom enters a bar in search of Martin Cunningham, with whom he plans to discuss arrangements for the payment of the insurance due Mrs. Dignam. He becomes involved in a political quarrel with the drunken Michael Cusack, who soon begins to express anti-Semitic sentiments. Pursued by Cusack's dog, Bloom makes his escape in a cab. (Cyclops episode.)

XIII *8 P.M.* Tired after walking about, Bloom sits down on the beach to rest. He becomes interested in watching a girl, Gerty MacDowell, who is playing with some children, and her exhibitionism causes him to become sexually excited. When Gerty leaves the scene, Bloom muses on his courtship of Molly in his youth. (Nausicäa episode.)

XIV *10 P.M.* Bloom goes to a maternity hospital to visit Mina Purefoy, who has just borne a child; here occurs the famous parody of various literary styles in an implied analogy between the development of the language and the development of the embryo in the womb. Stephen is also at the hospital, drinking and reveling with Buck Mulligan in the internes' quarters, and at last he and Bloom meet. Bloom feels a fatherly interest in the young man, who is rapidly becoming drunk, and decides to follow and watch out for him when the group sets out for nocturnal adventures in the disreputable sections of Dublin. (Oxen of the Sun episode.)

XV *12 Midnight.* In the brothel run by Bella Cohen, to which Bloom has followed Stephen, there occurs the scene called by some critics the WITCHES' SABBATH or *Walpurgisnacht* eipsode. Demonic hallucinations and apparitions appear before Bloom and Stephen, mixing with the drunken revelry of the brothel, all presented in a bewildering variety of literary styles and forms. Stephen at last thinks he sees the ghost of his mother, for whose death he feels responsible, and in a fury he breaks the chandelier with his walking-stick and flees. Outside the house he becomes involved in a fight with two English soldiers, Privates Carr and Compton. He is beaten into unconsciousness, and Bloom rescues him, believing he sees the ghost of his dead son in Stephen. (Circe episode.)

XVI *1 A.M.* Stephen, recovered, goes into a cabman's shelter with Bloom, and the two drink coffee and converse with some stevedores and a sailor who tells them fantastic yarns. (Eumaeus episode.)

XVII *2 A.M.* Stephen goes with Bloom to the older man's home in Eccles Street, and in the kitchen the two drink cocoa and discuss a variety of subjects, such as music, philosophy, astronomy, the future of the Jewish and Irish peoples, and the like. Notable is a recital of pertinent facts in the lives of Bloom and Stephen and details of the physical scene in which they are placed, presented in the form of a catechism. (Ithaca episode.)

XVIII *Later in the night.* Stephen at last goes home, and Bloom retires to bed, where he tells his wife what has happened to him during the day. The novel concludes with its most famous passage—a stream-of-consciousness monologue by Molly Bloom as she lies in bed, thinking of her husband, her lover, her daughter, sex and her own sexual experiences, her childhood, girlhood, and married life, and finally her first youthful acceptance of love and her affirmation of life. (Molly as Penelope.)

(For most of names mentioned above, see separate entries. See also COFFEY, FATHER; O'CONNELL, JOHN; PARNELL, JOHN STEWART. The outline given above is based mainly on the one published in *This Generation,* by George K. Anderson and Eda Lou Walton.)

Ulysses, which required seven years to write, is Joyce's most famous work and was the center of sensational controversy on its first publication. It began as a serial in THE LITTLE REVIEW in New York in 1918 and was regularly presented there until American authorities forbade it in 1920. It was prohibited from sale in a number of places on the charge of obscenity, and was legally admitted into the U.S. only after a long battle in the courts ending in 1934. The novel was also frequently attacked as being utterly unintelligible, until the many imitations and adaptations of its so-called "obscure" forms and techniques in novels and short stories during the 1920's and 1930's made its method generally recognizable and its content more readily understandable than on its first appearance.

With THE MAGIC MOUNTAIN and REMEMBRANCE OF THINGS PAST, *Ulysses* is ranked as one of the greatest novels of the 20th century and also as one of the greatest novels of all time. It has been highly praised for its characterizations of Bloom, Molly, and Stephen, for the vivid realism of its depiction of life in the city of Dublin, for the originality of its techniques and methods, its many passages of lyric and dramatic power, and its success in raising the events of an ordinary day and the thoughts and feelings of an average man to the level of significance of a literary epic.

For a study of *Ulysses,* cf. *James Joyce's Ulysses,* by Stuart Gilbert, and *James Joyce,* by Harry Levin.

umlaut. The transformation of a vowel under the influence of another originally present in the following syllable. Loosely also the DIACRITICAL MARK used in German to differentiate umlauted vowels, as *ä, ö, ü.* The two dots are the remnants of a small *e* formerly placed over the vowel as a substitute for the older DIGRAPHS *ae, oe, ue* still occurring in proper names, as *Goethe,* etc.

Una. The heroine of the first book of Spenser's FAËRIE QUEENE, typifying Truth (*Una,* the One). With the RED CROSS KNIGHT as her champion she sets forth to relieve her royal parents, who are being besieged by a dragon, but is soon parted from her knight, and is met by a lion, who afterwards attends her. She sleeps in the hut of Superstition, and next morning meets Archimago (Hypocrisy) dressed as her knight. As they journey together, SANSLOY meets them, exposes Archimago, kills the lion, and carries off Una to a wild forest. She is rescued by fauns and satyrs who attempt to worship her, but, being restrained, pay adoration to her donkey; she is delivered by Sir SATYRANE and is told by Archimago that the Red Cross Knight is dead, but subsequently hears that he is the captive of ORGOGLIO. She goes to King ARTHUR for aid, and the King slays Orgoglio and rescues the knight, whom Una takes to the house of Holiness, where he is carefully nursed. He eventually slays the dragon whose destruction was the original quest, and Una then leads him to Eden, where their marriage takes place. She is taken to represent Protestantism and Queen Elizabeth as well as abstract truth, and in this connection is strongly contrasted with DUESSA.

Unamuno y Jugo, Miguel de (1864–1936). Spanish scholar, novelist, poet, and essayist, known for his mystical and philosophical preoccupations and his denunciation of 20th-century materialism. English translations of his works include *The Tragic Sense of Life* (1921), a translation of *Del Sentimiento Trágico de la Vida* (1913), his best-known work; *Essays and Soliloquies* (1925); *The Life of Don Quixote and Sancho* (1927); *The Agony of Christianity* (1928); *Mist* (1928); *Three Exemplary Novels and a Prologue* (1930).

As a result of his vehement criticism of the military dictatorship established at the time by Primo de Rivera, Unamuno was exiled from Spain in 1924. When an amnesty was granted him later, he refused to return to his native country, preferring to live thereafter in France.

unanimism. A French school of thought in the early 20th century (ca. 1907), based on the theory that the group is of prime importance and that the individual, especially the poet, can attain power and significance only by merging himself with a social aggregation of one kind or another, he himself being far less important than the collective whole. Georges DUHAMEL and Jules ROMAINS were among the literary men associated with the school. In 1908 Romains published a volume of poetry entitled *La Vie unanime,* and the unanimist influence is considered to be found in the collective emphasis of his MEN OF GOOD WILL.

Uncas. "The Last of the Mohicans" in Cooper's novel of that title. Cooper has frequently been accused of over-idealizing the American Indian in his portrayal of this noble and valiant young warrior. The historical Uncas (1588?–?1683) was constantly engaged in warfare with other Indians and the English, who finally forced him to surrender and to leave his sons in their hands as an earnest of his remaining neutral in King Philip's War.

uncial. A style of writing used in old manuscripts from the third century B. C. to the tenth A. D. Uncials are rounded capitals.

Uncle Remus, His Songs and His Sayings. A famous book of folk tales by Joel Chandler HARRIS (1880). They "are told night after night to a little boy by an old Negro who has nothing but pleasant memories of the discipline of slavery, and who has all the prejudices of caste and pride of family that were the natural results of the system." The characters are animals, chief among them being Brer Rabbit and Brer Fox.

Uncle Sam. See under SAM; NICKNAMES.

Uncle Sam's heel. Florida.

Uncle Sam's ice box. Alaska.

Uncle Silas. A famous mystery novel (1864) by J. Sheridan LEFANU.

Uncle Toby. In Sterne's TRISTRAM SHANDY, the lovable uncle of the hero.

Uncle Tom's Cabin, or Life Among the Lowly. A novel by Harriet Beecher STOWE (1851), which did much to arouse anti-slavery sentiment before the Civil War. The chief figure is the faithful old slave Uncle Tom. Sold by the Shelbys from his old home in Kentucky, where he leaves his wife Chloe, he lives for a time with the easy-going, good-tempered Augustine St. Clare, to whose gentle little daughter Eva he is devotedly attached. In the ST. CLARE household are also the Yankee old maid, Miss Ophelia, and the immortal TOPSY, an amusing black "limb of mischief." After the death of LITTLE EVA and her father, Uncle Tom is sold to the brutal Simon LEGREE, by whom he is treated with such harshness that when George Shelby, the son of his former master, finds him, he is dying. Among the slaves represented is Eliza, whose escape from the bloodhounds, with her boy Harry, by crossing the Ohio River on cakes of ice, is a familiar incident. Her husband, George Harris, follows her along the UNDERGROUND RAILWAY.

Uncle Vanya. A drama in four acts (1897) by Anton CHEKHOV. One of his best-known plays, which has been several times produced on Broadway.

Uncommercial Traveller, The. Twenty-eight miscellaneous papers published by DICKENS in *All the Year Round,* and reproduced in 1860.

Uncumber, St. See under SAINTS.

Under Fire: The Story of a Squad. A translation of *Le Feu,* the best-known novel of Henri BARBUSSE (1916) and one of the earliest books inspired by World War I, giving a bitter, realistic, and denunciatory picture of war. It deals with the experiences of a squad of lower-class French soldiers in combat, showing them undergoing physical tortures, hating their officers, quarreling among themselves, and living in a general atmosphere of filth, horror, and human debasement. The novel was widely heralded on publication, and had an important influence on the war literature of the time. See also WAR IN LITERATURE.

Underground Railway or Railroad, the. A term used in the United States as the embodiment of the various ways by which slaves from the southern states made their escape either to the north or to Canada before slavery was abolished.

Underhill, Evelyn (1875–1941). English mystical writer and poet. *Mysticism* (1911).

Underhill, Updike. Hero of Tyler's ALGERINE CAPTIVE.

Undershaft. A manufacturer of munitions in Shaw's MAJOR BARBARA.

Under the Greenwood Tree. A novel by Thomas HARDY (1872), depicting country life. The heroine, Fancy Day, is loved by Farmer Shiner, by the young vicar, Arthur Maybold, and by Dick Dewy. She chooses the latter, and all ends happily.

Under the Jackstaff. A book of stories by Chester Bailey FERNALD.

Under Western Eyes. A novel by Joseph CONRAD (1911), dealing with anarchistic intrigue in Russia. The revolutionary Haldin, having just killed an official with a bomb, appeals to his fellow student Razumov for help. Razumov is ambitious to enter government service, believes in law and order, and dreads the thought of becoming involved in revolutionary action. Leaving the trusting Haldin asleep in his rooms, he goes out and denounces him to the police. Later he is sent to Geneva as a government spy and meets Nathalie, Haldin's sister, who, knowing nothing of his defection, receives him into the revolutionary circle there as Haldin's benefactor. Tormented by the love that springs up between himself and Nathalie, Razumov forces himself to confess to a roomful of revolutionists. His ear drums are broken in the commotion, and the following morning he is run over by a tram car.

Underwoods. The title of a collection of poems (1640) by Ben JONSON. Robert Louis STEVENSON adopted the title for a book of his own poems (1887).

Undine. A fairy romance by De La Motte FOUQUÉ (1814). The heroine, Undine, is a water-sylph, who is in early childhood changed for the young child of a fisherman living on a peninsula near an enchanted forest. One day, Sir Huldbrand takes shelter in the fisherman's hut, falls in love with Undine, and marries her. Being thus united to a man, the sylph receives a soul. Not long after the wedding, Sir Huldbrand falls in love with Bertalda, the fisherman's real daughter. Undine is spirited away by her angry kinsfolk, and the knight marries his new love. On the wedding day she calls for a drink from the old well, and Undine is forced to arise with the waters and bring about the death of her knight.

Undiscovered Country, The. A novel by W. D. HOWELLS (1880), dealing with spiritualism. Dr. Boynton, a country physician who has become a fanatical devoté of the occult, brings up his high-strung daughter Egeria as a medium. She is torn between filial affection and repulsion at the quackery her duties involve, until finally her health gives way under the strain. Much of the action takes place in a SHAKER community.

Undset, Sigrid (1882–). Norwegian novelist, awarded the Nobel prize for literature in 1928, best known for her novels dealing with life in the Scandinavian countries during the Middle Ages, presented according to the technique and viewpoint embodied in the 20th-century realistic and psychological novel. Her novels of the modern era are chiefly concerned with social and psychological problems, solved according to the views of the Roman Catholic Church. Among her works are *Fru Marta Oulie* (1907); *Den Lykkelige Alder* (*The Happy Age;* 1908); *Jenny* (1911); *Poor Souls* (1912), a collection of short stories; *Spring* (1914); KRISTIN LAVRANSDATTER, her most famous novel, a trilogy consisting of *Kransen* (1920; translated as *The Bridal Wreath*), *Husfrue* (1921; translated as *The Mistress of Husaby*), and *Korset* (1922; translated as *The Cross*); *Olaf Audunsson I Hestviken,* a tetralogy, translated as *The Master* *of Hestviken* and consisting of *The Axe* (1928), *The Snake Pit* (1929), *In the Wilderness* (1929), and *The Son Avenger* (1930); *The Wild Orchid* (1931), a translation of *Gymnadenia; The Burning Bush* (*Den Braendende Busk*; 1932); *Ida Elisabeth* (1932); *Christmas and Twelfth Night* (1932), essays; *The Longest Years* (1935), childhood recollections; *Stages on the Road* (1934), a study of several Catholic authors; *Sagas of Saints* (1934), on early Norwegian saints; *Gunnar's Daughter* (1936), a translation of *Fortaellingen om Viga-Ljot og Vigdis; Images in a Mirror* (1938), a translation of *Fru Hjelde; The Faithful Wife* (1937), a translation of *Den Trofaste Husfru; Madame Dorthea* (1939); *Happy Times in Norway* (1942), reminiscences; *Return to the Future* (1942).

Sigrid Undset was the daughter of a university professor and acquired her fondness for the Middle Ages through assisting her father in his research when she was a child. She was converted to the Roman Catholic Church in 1924, and after her success as a novelist she took up residence in a restored house dating from the year 1000 and surrounded herself with medieval Norse furnishings and art objects; she even dressed habitually in the gown of a Norse matron of the Middle Ages. When Norway was invaded by the Germans in 1940, during World War II, she was forced to flee and came to the U.S. as a refugee.

unearned increment. Increase in the value of property because of external causes, such as public improvements, rather than any effort on the part of the owner.

Unfortunate Traveller, The, or the Life of Jack Wilton. A picaresque story (1594) by Thomas NASH.

unicorn (from Lat. *unum cornu,* "one horn"). A mythical and heraldic animal, represented by medieval writers as having the legs of a buck, the tail of a lion, the head and body of a horse, and a single horn, white at the base, black in the middle, and red at the tip, in the middle of its forehead. The body is white, the head red, and eyes blue. The oldest author that describes it is Ctesias (400 B.C.). The medieval notions concerning it are well summarized in the following extract:

> The unicorn has but one horn in the middle of its forehead. It is the only animal that ventures to attack the elephant; and so sharp is the nail of its foot, that with one blow it can rip the belly of that beast. Hunters can catch the unicorn only by placing a young virgin in his haunts. No sooner does he see the damsel, than he runs towards her, and lies down at her feet, and so suffers himself to be captured by the hunters. The unicorn represents Jesus Christ, who took on Him our nature in the virgin's womb, was betrayed to the Jews, and delivered into the hands of Pontius Pilate. Its one horn signifies the Gospel of Truth.—*Le Bestiaire Divin de Guillaume, Clerc de Normandie* (13th century).

The supporters of the old royal arms of Scotland are two unicorns. When James VI of Scotland came to reign over England (1603) he brought one of the unicorns with him, and with it supplanted the red dragon which, as representing Wales, was one of the supporters of the English shield, the other being the lion. ARIOSTO refers to the arms of Scotland thus:

> Yon lion placed two unicorns between
> That rampant with a silver sword is seen.
> Is for the king of Scotland's banner known.
> *Hoole's Translation,* Bk. iii.

The animosity which existed between the lion and the unicorn referred to by Spenser in his FAËRIE QUEENE (II. v)—

> Like as a lyon, whose imperiall powre
> A prowd rebellious unicorn defyes—

is allegorical of that which once existed between England and Scotland. A battle between the Lion and the Unicorn is an episode in THROUGH THE LOOKING-GLASS, by Lewis CARROLL.

union.

the Union. A short term for *the United States of America,* and (in England) a familiar euphemism for the workhouse, i.e., the house maintained for the destitute by the Poor Law *Union.*

the Act of Union. Specifically, the Act of 1706 declaring that on and after May 1, 1707, England and Scotland should have a united parliament. The two countries had, of course, been united under one sovereign since 1603. The term is also applied to the Act of 1536 incorporating Wales with England, and to that of 1800, which united the kingdoms of Great Britain and Ireland on and after January 1, 1801.

the Union Rose. The combined emblematic rose of the Houses of York and Lancaster, the petals of which are white and red; white representing York, and red representing Lancaster. See also under ROSE.

union is strength. The wise saw of Periander, tyrant of Corinth (665–585 B.C.).

Union Jack. The national banner of Great Britain and Ireland. It consists of three united crosses—that of St. George for England, the saltire of St. Andrew for Scotland (added by James I), and the cross of St. Patrick for Ireland (added at the Union in 1801).

Union Magazine, The. A magazine (1847–1852), chiefly remembered because in it were first published Poe's poems *To Helen* and *The Bells,* his essay *The Poetic Principle,* and stories by William G. SIMMS.

Unitarian. One who denies the Trinity and holds that God is one in person and substance. Specifically, a member of the Unitarian Church which was formed in 1773 by Theophilus Lindsay upon seceding from the Church of England.

United Kingdom. The name adopted on January 1, 1801, when Great Britain and Ireland were united.

unities, the. The three dramatic unities, viz., the rules governing the so-called "classical" drama, are founded on Renaissance interpretations of passages in Aristotle's *Poetics,* and are hence sometimes styled the *Aristotelean unities.* Their principles are that in drama there should be (1) unity of action; (2) unity of time, and (3) unity of place. Aristotle lays stress on (1), meaning that an organic unity, or a logical connection between the successive incidents, is necessary; but (2) was deduced by Castelvetro, the 16th century Italian scholar and critic, from the passage in the *Poetics* where Aristotle, in comparing epic poetry and tragedy, says that the former has no limits in time but the latter "endeavors, as far as possible, to confine itself to a single revolution of the sun, or but slightly to exceed this limit." Having thus arrived at the unity of time, (3) the unity of place followed almost perforce.

The theory of the three unities was formulated in Italy nearly a century before it was taken up in France, where it became, after much argument, the corner-stone of the literary drama. Its first modern offspring was *La Sophonisbe* (1629) by Mairet, though it was not till CORNEILLE's triumph with *Le Cid* (1636) that the convention of the three unities can be said to have been finally adopted. The principle had little success in England, despite the later championship of DRYDEN (cf. his *Essay on Dramatic Poesy*), ADDISON (as exemplified in his *Cato*), and others. Ben JONSON's *The Alchemist* (1610) is perhaps the best example of the small class of English plays in which the unities of place and time have been purposely adhered to. In France, on the other hand, the three unities were much more strictly observed, and not until the momentous performance of Victor Hugo's HERNANI did the old classical theories really give way to those of the modern romantic movement. See ROMANTICISM.

Universal Doctor. See under DOCTOR.

University Wits. Term applied to a group of brilliant young English writers of the later years of the 16th century, in the reign of Queen Elizabeth, who had received their training at the universities of Oxford and Cambridge. Among these, chiefly playwrights and pamphleteers, the latter known for their polemics and their contributions to the "ROGUE LITERATURE" of the day, were Robert GREENE, Gabriel HARVEY, Thomas LODGE, John LYLY, Christopher MARLOWE, and Thomas NASH.

Unknown, the Great. Sir Walter SCOTT, so called (first by his publisher, James Ballantyne) because the WAVERLEY NOVELS were published anonymously.

Unlearned Parliament. See under PARLIAMENTS.

Unleavened Bread. A novel (1900) by Robert GRANT. It was made into a play by the author and Leo DITRICHSTEIN (1901).

Unmerciful Parliament. See under PARLIAMENTS.

Unpopular Review, The. A quarterly (1914–1921) which had as contributors Paul Elmer MORE, Dorothy Canfield FISHER, Mary AUSTIN and Amy LOWELL. In 1919 it changed its name to *The Unpartisan Review.*

Unrighteous Bible. See BIBLE, SPECIALLY NAMED.

Unruh, Fritz von (1885–). German dramatist, poet, and novelist. Between World Wars I and II, the most powerful exponent of the principle that art must serve and must be the vehicle of an inspired message. The leitmotiv of his work is (negatively) hatred of war and militarism and (positively) emphasis on the value of the free and responsible individual human soul. *The Way of Sacrifice* (1916) and *The End Is Not Yet* (1947). Now living in U.S.

Unter den Linden. A famous avenue of linden trees in Berlin, now destroyed.

Untermeyer, Louis (1885–). American poet and anthologist. Widely known for his collections of American and British poetry which have gone into all the schools of the country. His own poetry and parodies have been collected in several volumes. He is a fine lyric writer and as a parodist has few equals today. In his early years he was a contributing editor of THE LIBERATOR and THE SEVEN ARTS. His translations of Heine are among the best of our time. Cf. his autobiography, *From Another World* (1939).

Untermeyer, Samuel (1858–1940). Famous American lawyer who acted as council for a Congressional Committee that investigated the Pujo money-trust. He was head of the board which made the income tax laws and the laws concerning excess profits in World War I.

Unto This Last. Four essays (1860–1862) by John RUSKIN, dealing with employment and wages and published in the *Cornhill Magazine.* They caused such disturbance that they were discontinued by the editor THACKERAY. Although at the time Ruskin's ideas were thought to be chimaerical, today practically every reform he advised has been adopted.

unwashed. The first application of the term, *the great unwashed,* to the mob has been attributed to Edmund BURKE and also to Brougham—perhaps to others, too. CARLYLE has, "Man has been set against man, Washed against Unwashed." (*French Revolution,* II. ii. 4).

Unwin, Mrs. **Mary.** Friend and benefactor of William COWPER, who boarded with her. A poem, *To Mary,* and *Sonnet to Mrs. Unwin,* both written in 1793, indicate the poet's gratitude to her. Her jealousy over the relation of another of Cowper's friends, Lady AUSTEN, to the poem THE TASK resulted in the destruction of the second friendship.

Unwin, Thomas Fisher (1848–1935). English publisher. He founded the publishing firm of T. Fisher Unwin (1882) and was joint founder of the first council of the English Publishers Association. He has been called the discoverer of Joseph CONRAD.

Upanishads. The oldest speculative literature of the Hindus, a collection of treatises on the nature of man and the universe, forming part of the Vedic writings, the earliest dating from about the 6th century B. C. The name is Sanskrit, and means "a sitting down (at another's feet)," hence "a confidential talk," "esoteric doctrine."

Updike, Daniel Berkeley (1860–1941). American printer who established the Merrymount Press in Boston (1893). He helped to improve typography in the United States and wrote the authoritative *Printing Types* (1922).

Up, Guards, and at them! Traditionally the words of the Duke of Wellington ordering the attack in the last part of the Battle of Waterloo.

Upham, Charles Wentworth (1802–1875). Minister in Salem, Mass., known for his books on Salem witchcraft.

upper ten, the. The aristocracy, the cream of society, short for *the upper ten thousand.* The term was first used by N. P. WILLIS in speaking of the fashionables of New York, who at that time were not more than ten thousand in number.

Upson, Arthur (1877–1908). American poet and poetic dramatist. His *Octaves in an Oxford Garden* is a very rare achievement.

Upstream. The autobiography (1922) of Ludwig LEWISOHN.

uraeus. The image of the sacred asp on the headdress of Egyptian rulers.

Urania. The Muse of astronomy in Greek mythology, usually represented pointing at a celestial globe with a staff. Milton (*Paradise Lost* vii. 1–20) makes her the spirit of the loftiest poetry, and calls her "heavenly born" (the name means "the heavenly one") and "sister of Wisdom."

Uranus. In Greek mythology, the personification of Heaven; son and husband of GE (the earth), and father of the TITANS, the CYCLOPS, the FURIES, etc. He hated his children and confined them in TARTARUS, but they broke out and his son Cronus dethroned him. The planet Uranus was discovered in 1781 by Herschell and was named by him *Georgium Sidus* in honor of George III.

Urban, Joseph (1872–1933). Famous Austrian-born stage designer who did many sets for large productions at the Metropolitan Opera House and for the Ziegfeld Follies.

Urbino. The Dukes of Urbino were important figures in Italy in the time of the Renaissance. They were warriors and one of them was prefect to Rome. Their surname was della Rovere. Their history, *Memoirs,* was written by James Dennistown and edited by Edward Hutton.

Urdur or **Urdhr.** The most famous of the three NORNS of Scandinavian mythology.

Urfé, Honoré d' (1568–1626). French noble, author of the pastoral *Astrée* (1608–1624) which was extremely popular and influential. It foreran other romances of the same type by LA CALPRENÈDE, Mlle de SCUDÉRY, etc.

Urfried, Dame. In Scott's IVANHOE, an old sibyl at Torquilstone Castle, *alias* Ulrica, daughter of the late thane of Torquilstone.

Urgan. A mortal born and christened, but stolen by the king of the fairies and brought up in elf-land (Scott's LADY OF THE LAKE, iv. 12). It is decreed that if a woman signs his brow thrice with a cross he should recover his mortal form. Alice Brand does this, and the hideous elf becomes "the fairest knight in all Scotland," in whom she recognizes her brother Ethert.

Urganda. A potent fairy in the *Amadis of Gaul* and other romances of the Carolingian cycle.

Uriah the Hittite. In the Old Testament, a captain in David's army and the husband of Bathsheba, whom David loved. At David's orders he was sent into the most dangerous part of the battle line, where he was killed, and David then took Bathsheba as his wife.

letter of Uriah (2 *Sam.* xi. 15). A treacherous letter, importing friendship but in reality a death-warrant. See also BELLEROPHON.

Uriel. One of the seven archangels of rabbinical angelology, sent by God to answer the questions of Esdras (2 *Esdras,* iv.). In Milton's *Paradise Lost* (iii. 690) he is the "Regent of the Sun," and "sharpest-sighted spirit of all in heaven." Longfellow, in the *Golden Legend,* makes RAPHAEL the angel of the Sun, and Uriel the minister of Mars. The name means "Flame of God," or "Angel of Light."

Urim and Thummim. Two objects of uncertain form and material used in the early forms of ancient Hebrew worship, probably in connection with divination and obtaining oracular answers from Jehovah. They are mentioned in *Ex.* xxviii. 30; 1 *Sam.* xxviii. 6; *Deut.* xxxiii. 8; *Ezra* ii. 63, etc., but fell out of use in post-exilic times, evidently through the Jews developing a higher conception of the Deity.

Urizen. In Blake's mystical poems, the figure of Jehovah but also a symbol of man in bondage. It is not impossible that the name was suggested to Blake through association with "reason."

Urn Burial or Hydriotaphia. An essay (1658) by Sir Thomas BROWNE based on the unearthing of urns in Norfolk.

Urquhart, Sir **Thomas** (1611–1660). Scottish author, chiefly known for his free translation of RABELAIS which is a masterpiece (1653–1693). It was completed by Peter Anthony MOTTEUX (1708). One of Urquhart's treatises contains a famous account of The Admirable CRICHTON.

Ursa Major. The Great Bear, Big Dipper, or Charles' Wain, the most conspicuous of the northern constellations. See CALLISTO.

Boswell's father used to call Dr. JOHNSON *Ursa Major.*

Ursa Minor. The Little Bear; the northern constellation known as CYNOSURE or "Dog's tail," from its circular sweep.

Ursula, St. See under SAINTS.

Ursule Mirouet. A novel by BALZAC (1841), unique among his novels in that it contains only virtuous women. It concerns the schemes of joint heirs to a fortune and the social success of the titular heroine, a woman with a beautiful singing voice. It is said that Balzac wrote this novel for his young nieces.

Urth. One of the three Norns (Fates) in Norse mythology. In the earliest conception Urth was the only Norn and her name was often identified with Death or Hel. When two additional Norns were added [Verthandi, Skuld], Urth came to represent the past.

Urvasi. See PURAVAVAS AND URVASI.

U.S.A. A trilogy by John Dos PASSOS (1938), consisting of THE 42ND PARALLEL (1930), 1919 (1932), and THE BIG MONEY (1936). The novel gives a panoramic picture of life and events in the U.S. in the period just preceding World War I, the period of the war and the armistice settlement, and the boom era of the 1920's, ending with the first years of the depression. Four distinctive devices are used: the NEWSREEL (objective); the CAMERA EYE (subjective); a series of impressionistic biographical sketches of representative politicians, newspapermen, scholars, writers, radicals, captains of industry, scientists, and other public figures of the time; and the life stories, told in episodic fashion and a simple, plain, almost callously impersonal style, of a group of fictional characters representing various geographical sections of the country, social classes, and psychological temperaments. These characters are Fainy McCREARY, Joe WILLIAMS and his sister Janey, J. Ward MOOREHOUSE, Eleanor STODDARD, Eveline HUTCHINS, Charley ANDERSON, Richard Ellsworth SAVAGE, Anne TRENT, Ben COMPTON, Mary FRENCH, and Margo DOWLING.

The pervading tone of *U.S.A.* is one of inevitable sociological and economic determinism, with greed, exploitation, opportunism, dishonesty, and vice triumphing and the various characters finding they have no control over their lives. Those who try to resist their times and those who simply drift along with the times are alike defeated; the only persons who emerge victorious are those who put aside all scruples and take advantage of the opportunities offered by the times for material success. American radicals and radical movements also play an important rôle in the novel, with the more sincere radicals sometimes succeeding in preserving a measure of personal integrity.

With James T. FARRELL'S STUDS LONIGAN, *U.S.A.* is regarded as one of the most important novels of American life in the 20th century. It has been praised by critics for the breadth of its scope and its social perspective, the skill of its individual characterization, the originality and effectiveness of its techniques, and the vividness and realism of its portrayal of an eventful period in American history.

Useless Parliament. See under PARLIAMENTS.

Usher, see FALL OF THE HOUSE OF USHER, THE.

Usk. Celtic for "water." A river in South Wales and Monmouthshire, England. On it is situated Caerleon, the traditional seat of King Arthur's court.

Ussher, James (1581–1656). Archbishop of Armagh. A distinguished Irish scholar who wrote a Latin history of the world. He had a remarkable library and left his books and manuscripts to Trinity College in Dublin. Among them is the famous BOOK OF KELLS.

Ute. Queen of Burgundy, mother of Kriemhild and Gunther in the NIBELUNGENLIED.

Utgard (*Old Norse,* "outer ward"). The circle of rocks that hemmed in the ocean which was supposed by the ancient Scandinavians to encompass the world, and to be the haunt of the giants.

Utgard-Loki. In Norse mythology, the chief of the giants. Disguised as Skrymir he conducted Thor, Thialfi, and Loki to Tötunheim. There fire, disguised as Logi, ate faster than Loki; thought, disguised as Hugi, ran faster than Thialfi; old age, disguised as Elli, was stronger than Thor; etc. When Utgard-Loki had told Thor about his tricks, he escaped the god's wrath by vanishing.

Uther. A legendary king, or PENDRAGON, of the Britons. By an adulterous amour with Igerna (wife of Gorlois, Duke of Cornwall) he became the father of ARTHUR, who succeeded him.

uti possidetis (*Lat.,* "as you at present possess them"). The principle in international law that the belligerents are to retain possession of all the places taken by them before the treaty commenced.

utilitarianism. The ethical doctrine that actions are right in proportion to their usefulness or as they tend to promote happiness; the doctrine that the end and criterion of public action is "the greatest happiness of the greatest number."

John Stuart MILL coined the word, but Jeremy BENTHAM, the official founder of the school, employed the word "utility" to signify the doctrine which makes "the happiness of man" the one and only measure of right and wrong.

Utopia (Gr. *ou,* "not," *topos,* "a place"). Nowhere, the name given by Sir Thomas MORE to the imaginary island in his political romance of the same name (1516), where everything is perfect—the laws, the morals, the politics, etc., and in which the evils of existing laws, etc., are shown by contrast. See COMMONWEALTHS, IDEAL; and WEISSNICHTWO.

Rabelais in his GARGANTUA AND PANTAGRUEL (Bk. II. ch. xxiv), sends Pantagruel and his companions to Utopia, where they find the citizens of its capital, Amaurot, most hospitable. They reach the island by doubling the Cape of Good Hope, and sailing with a "Tramontane Wind" past Meden, Uti, Uden, Gelasim, the Islands of the Fairies, and along the Kingdom of Achoria.

This fictional island has given us the adjective *utopian,* applied to any highly desirable but quite impracticable scheme.

Utrillo, Maurice (1883–). French painter, known for his pictures of Paris streets, cathedrals, etc.

Uz. The home of JOB.

Uzziel. One of the principal angels of rabbinical angelology, the name meaning "Strength of God." He was next in command to Gabriel, and in Milton's *Paradise Lost* (iv. 782) is commanded by Gabriel to "coast the south with strictest watch."

V

Vachell, Horace Annesley (1861–). English novelist. Author of popular books about an antique dealer named "Quinney," the first of which was made into a play (1915). *The Hill* (1905), a novel of life at Harrow, is one of the most popular of British school stories.

vade mecum. A portable manual or handbook. The phrase is Latin and means "go with me."

Vagabondia, Songs from. A book of poems (1891) by Richard HOVEY and Bliss CARMAN. It was followed by several sequels, *More Songs from Vagabondia* (1898) and *Last Songs from Vagabondia* (1901). They are slightly self-conscious "songs of the open road."

Vagret. A lawyer in Brieux's RED ROBE. Like his colleague Mouzon, he puts his personal ambition first and justice second, but unlike him, repents before it is too late.

Vailima. The mountain home of R. L. STEVENSON in Samoa, where he lived during the last years of his life. A collection of his letters was called *Vailima* Letters.

Vaillant, Father Joseph. In DEATH COMES FOR THE ARCHBISHOP, a kindly, simple, and energetic priest who is the devoted friend of the Bishop, Jean LATOUR.

Vaishnava. One of the great sects of reformed Brahmins who worship Vishnu as supreme among the Hindu gods. Their sacred books are known as the *Vaishnava Puranas.*

Vaisya. The third of the four chief Hindu castes, or a member of it, from a Sanskrit word meaning "a settler." See also CASTE.

vae victis! A Latin phrase meaning "woe to the vanquished!" It is ascribed to the Gaul Brennus, who conquered Rome in 390 B. C.

Valclusa. The famous retreat of PETRARCH (father of Italian poetry) and his mistress LAURA, a lady of Avignon.

Vale. See AVE.

Valentine. (1) In Shakespeare's TWO GENTLEMEN OF VERONA, one of the titular heroes. Valentine marries Silvia, daughter of the Duke of Milan.

(2) In Goethe's FAUST and Gounod's opera of the same name, brother of MARGARET. Maddened by the seduction of his sister, he attacks Faust during a serenade, and is stabbed by MEPHISTOPHELES. He dies reproaching his sister.

(3) Heroine of Meyerbeer's opera THE HUGUENOTS.

Valentine, St. See under SAINTS.

Valentine and Orson. An old French romance, connected with the ALEXANDER cycle. The heroes, from whom the romance is named, are the twin sons of Bellisant, sister of King Pepin, and Alexander, and were born in a forest near Orleans. ORSON is carried off by a bear and becomes a wild man. While the mother is searching for him, Valentine is carried off by his uncle, the King. Each has many adventures, but all ends happily, and Valentine marries Clerimond, sister of the Green Knight.

Valentine Day. See under SAINTS.

Valentine Legend. In Congreve's *Love for Love.* See LEGEND, VALENTINE.

Valentino, Rudolph (1895–1926). Moving-picture actor in the silent films, born in Italy, extremely popular in America for his romantic acting. His funeral in New York nearly caused a riot.

Valera, Eamon de, see DE VALERA.

Valère. One of the principal characters in Molière's *L'Avare,* in love with HARPAGON's daughter Elise.

Valerian or Valirian. A martyr whose story is told in the SECOND NUN'S TALE, one of Chaucer's CANTERBURY TALES.

Valérie Marneffe, Mme. (In Balzac's *Cousin Betty.*) See MARNEFFE, MME VALERIE.

Valéry, Paul Ambroise (1871–1945). French poet and critic, in his early career a protégé of Pierre Louÿs and at first influenced by the school of SYMBOLISM. His interest later turned to philosophy, mathematics, science, and economics, and he professed himself to be attracted to poetry only as a mental exercise. Following Leonardo da VINCI, whom he admired, he developed a kind of mathematical metaphysic to guide him in his thought and his art. Valéry is known for his personal aloofness, his emphasis on the importance of the intellectual classes in shaping and controlling society, and the precision, extreme condensation, and abstruseness of theme of his poetry, which was regarded by many contemporary critics as artificial and obscure. His books of poetry include *La Jeune Parque* (1917), considered his best work; *Odes* (1920); *L'Album des Vers anciens* (1920); *Charmes* (1922); *Fragments du Narcisse* (1922); *Poésies* (1923). He is generally best known for his series of literary and philosophical essays consisting of *Variété* (1924), *Variété II* (1930), *Variété III* (1936), and *Variété IV* (1938); these were translated into English. Other works include *L'Idée Fixe* (1934); *Moralités* (1932); *Pièces sur l'Art* (1936); *Poésie et Pensée abstraite* (1939) and *La Politique de l'Esprit* (1941), lectures.

Paul Valéry was elected to the French Academy in 1925, succeeding Anatole FRANCE, about whom he delivered a slighting address on his induction, although it was customary for the new member to laud his predecessor. Declaring that he was a businessman rather than a Bohemian, Valéry made a point of keeping his works inaccessible in order to increase their value, insisting that they be published only in limited and distinctive editions.

Valery, Violetta. Heroine of Verdi's opera LA TRAVIATA.

Valhalla. Literally, the hall of the slain. One of the mansions of Asgard, built (in Wagner's *Ring*) for Odin (or Wotan) by the giants who were paid, in place of the goddess Freya at first agreed upon, with the treasure of the Nibelungs. In Valhalla Odin feasts with heroes fallen bravely in battle on mead and boar's meat. It is a hall with 540 gates from which the warriors go out each morning to return at night for another banquet with the Valkyries as servitors.

Vali. The "silent god" and guardian of justice among the ancient Scandinavians. He was the second son of ODIN, and avenged the death of BALDER by slaying his murderer, Hoder. He was one of the few who were to survive the catastrophe of the Twilight of the Gods, for justice must not be banished from the earth.

Valiant-for-Truth. In Bunyan's PILGRIM'S PROGRESS, a brave Christian, who fights three foes at once. His sword is "a right Jerusalem blade," so he prevails but is wounded in the encounter. He joins Christiana's party in their journey to the Celestial City.

Valjean, Jean. The hero of Victor Hugo's LES MISÉRABLES.

Valkyries, the (*Old Norse,* "the choosers of the slain"). The twelve nymphs of Valhalla, who, mounted on swift horses, and holding drawn swords, rushed into the *mêlée* of battle and selected those destined to death. These heroes they conducted to VALHALLA, where they waited upon them and served them with mead and ale in the skulls of the vanquished. The chief were Mista, Sangrida, and Hilda.

In Wagner's RING DES NIBELUNGEN, Brunhild is the favorite Valkyrie and the heroine of the opera *The Valkyrie* (*Die Walküre*). She also appears in SIEGFRIED and GÖTTERDÄMMERUNG.

Valla, Lorenzo (1406–1457). Italian HUMANIST, known for his study and criticism of history. His notable contribution was the revelation that the so-called Donation of Constantine (see DECRETALS) was a forgery.

Valladolid, the Doctor of. (In Le Sage's *Gil Blas.*) See under SANGRADO.

Vallandigham, Clement Laird (1820–1871). American politician. During the Civil War he was a leading spirit among the COPPERHEADS. He had previously favored a compromise between the North and the South, but, being a strong supporter of states' rights, he held Lincoln responsible for the War. Lincoln banished him to the Confederacy.

Valle Inclán, Ramón María del (1870–1936). Spanish poet, playwright, and novelist. Author of a series of historical novels dealing with nineteenth-century Spain. Curator of National Arts and director of the School of Art in Rome during the Spanish republic. He was an eccentric and a bohemian.

Vallejo, Mariano Guadelupe (1808–1890). In California's struggle against Mexico (1836), Vallejo was a prominent fighter for California. A town in California, close to the Mare Island Navy Yard, bears his name.

Vallette, Marguerite. Pseudonym **Rachilde** (1860?–). French writer, wife of Alfred Vallette, the founder of the "Mercure de France," and author of novels dealing with abnormal psychology.

Valley Forge. A play in free verse (1934) by Maxwell Anderson.

Valley of Decision, The. A novel by Edith WHARTON (1902), the story of an Italian principality of the late eighteenth century. The hero, Odo Valsecca, suddenly becomes Duke of Pianura through several unexpected deaths in the line, and although he loves Fulvia Vivaldi, the daughter of a revolutionary theorist, she sends him from her "to serve liberty on a throne." But the people are not ready for the liberties he wishes to give them, and the way is difficult. Years pass. By the time public opinion changes, Duke Odo has returned to the conservative views of the class to which he was born, and is accordingly banished from his kingdom.

Also title of a popular novel by Marcia DAVENPORT.

Valley of Humiliation. In Bunyan's PILGRIM'S PROGRESS, the place where Christian encounters APOLLYON and puts him to flight.

Valley of the Moon, The. A novel (1913) by Jack LONDON.

Valley of the Shadow of Death. In Bunyan's PILGRIM'S PROGRESS, a "wilderness, a land of deserts and of pits, a land of drought, and of the shadow of death" (*Jer.* ii. 6). "The light there is darkness, and the way full of traps . . . to catch the unwary." Christian must pass through it after his encounter with Apollyon.

> Though I walk through the valley of the shadow of death, I will fear no evil; for Thou art with me; Thy rod and Thy staff they comfort me.—*Ps.* xxiii. 4.

Vallon, Annette. A young French woman with whom William WORDSWORTH had a brief love affair while he was visiting France in 1792. A daughter, Caroline, was born, and Wordsworth corresponded for a time with Annette. It is believed that the poet went to France and had a meeting with the mother and child about 1802 shortly before his marriage to Mary Hutchinson. The affair was kept a secret by the Wordsworth family and was discovered only in the 20th century.

Valois. The name of the French royal house (1328–1589) which preceded the Bourbons.

Valunder. In *Frithiof's Saga,* a Scandinavian form of WAYLAND.

Vamen or **Vamena.** One of the avatars of VISHNU. A dwarf asked Bali, the giant monarch of India, to permit him to measure out three paces to build a hut upon. The kind monarch smiled at the request, and bade the dwarf measure out what he required. The first pace compassed the whole earth, the second the whole heavens, and the third all pandalon, or Hell. Bali now saw that the dwarf was no other than Vishnu, the second person of the Hindu triad.

vampire. A fabulous being, supposed to be the ghost of a heretic, excommunicated person, or criminal, that returns to the world at night in the guise of a monstrous bat and sucks the blood of sleeping persons who, usually, become vampires themselves.

The word is applied to one who preys upon his fellows—a "bloodsucker." In the early 20th century, *vampire,* or *vamp,* meant a *femme fatale,* a beautiful but heartless woman who lures men to moral destruction. KIPLING has a well-known poem called *The Vampire,* beginning:

> A fool there was and he made his prayer
> (Even as you and I!)
> To a rag and a bone and a hank of hair
> (We called her the woman who did not care)
> But the fool he called her his lady fair—
> (Even as you and I!)

See also *Dracula,* by Bram STOKER.

Van Bibber. The hero of a volume of short stories by Richard Harding DAVIS, called *Van Bibber and Others* (1892). He is a favorite of New York society but equally at home in more Bohemian quarters, a likable young chap with a faculty for getting himself into, and other people out of, surprising situations.

Vanbrugh, Sir **John** (1664–1726). English playwright of the Restoration period, son of a refugee from the Spanish persecutions in Belgium, known for his successful comedies. His plays include *The Relapse, Or Virtue in Danger* (1697); *The Provoked Wife* (1697); *The Confederacy* (1705); *The Provoked Husband* (1728). Vanbrugh was also an architect and designed a number of buildings in England, including Blenheim Palace, the residence of the Duke of Marlborough.

Vanbrugh, Dame **Irene** (1872–). English actress who married Dion BOUCICAULT. She was associated with Sir Herbert Beerbohm TREE, George Alexander, etc., played many famous parts and toured extensively.

Van Brunt, Brom. Ichabod Crane's rival in Irving's *Legend of Sleepy Hollow.* See SLEEPY HOLLOW; also BROM BONES.

Van Buren, Martin (1782–1862). Eighth President of the United States (1837–1841). A great party leader but not a great legislator.

Vance, Ethel, see STONE, GRACE ZARING.

Vance, Joseph, see JOSEPH VANCE.

Vance, Louis Joseph (1879–1933). American writer of popular novels and short stories.

Vance, Philo. The sophisticated detective in the detective stories of S. S. Van Dine. See Willard Huntington WRIGHT.

Vancouver, George (1758?–1798). English explorer who has given his name to the city of Vancouver in British Columbia. He wrote *Voyage of Discovery to the North Pacific Ocean, and Round the World* (3 vols.; 1798).

Vandals. A Teutonic race from the Baltic, allied to the *Wends,* i.e., "Wanderers," which in the 5th century A. D. ravaged Gaul and, under Genseric, captured Rome and despoiled it of its treasures of art, literature, and civilization generally. Hence, the name is applied to those who wilfully or ignorantly destroy works of art, etc.

Vandemark's Folly. A novel (1922) by Herbert Quick. It forms a trilogy with *The Hawkeye* (1923) and *The Invisible Woman* (1924).

Vanderbilt, a. A very rich man, from the wealthy American family of that name.

Vanderbilt, Cornelius. Known as Commodore **Vanderbilt** (1794–1877). One of the outstanding capitalists of the United States. He began by running a ferry between Staten Island and New York. He ran a line of steamships from San Francisco to the Nicaraguan Coast and crushed William WALKER, the filibuster, who fought him for control of the company. In his late years Vanderbilt entered railroading, got control of the New York Central, and finally left a hundred million dollars to his son **William H. Vanderbilt** (1821–1885) to whom is attributed the famous saying, "the public be damned!"

Vandercook, John W. (1902–). Author and news commentator for the National Broadcasting Company. *Black Majesty* (1928); *Murder in Trinidad* (1933); etc.

Vanderdecken, Philip. See under FLYING DUTCHMAN.

Van der Meersch, Maxence (1907–). French novelist. His *Invasion* (1937) is one of the best pacifist novels in existence. *Hath Not the Potter* won the Goncourt prize in 1937.

Van Dine, S. S. Pen name of Willard Huntington WRIGHT.

Van Doren, Carl Clinton (1885–). American literary critic, editor, and author, literary editor of The Nation from 1919 to 1922 and an editor of the *Cambridge History of American Literature*. His books include *The American Novel* (1921, 1940); *Contemporary American Novelists: 1900–1920* (1922); *James Branch Cabell* (1925); *Swift* (1930); *Sinclair Lewis* (1933); *Three Worlds* (1936), an autobiography; *Benjamin Franklin* (1938), winner of the 1939 Pulitzer prize for biography.

His brother, **Mark Albert Van Doren** (1894–), also became known as a literary critic and editor, as well as a poet, and was literary editor of *The Nation* from 1924 to 1928. His works include *Spring Thunder* (1924), *Now the Sky* (1928), *Jonathan Gentry* (1931), *Collected Poems* (1939, winner of the 1940 Pulitzer prize), and *Our Lady Peace* (1942), all books of poetry; *The Transients* (1935) and *Windless Cabins* (1940), novels; and a number of critical studies and anthologies.

Vandover and the Brute. A novel by Frank Norris, written 1894–1895, published in 1914 after the author's death by his brother Charles G. Norris. Crude in some respects, it shows the power which Norris brought to his later work.

Van Druten, John William (1901–). English playwright of partially Dutch extraction, whose plays have been very successful in America (he is now an American citizen). *Young Woodley* (1928); *There's Always Juliet* (1931); *Flowers of the Forest* (1936); *Old Acquaintance* (1941); *The Voice of the Turtle* (1945); etc.

Vandyke, Sir **Anthony** (1599–1641). Great Flemish painter who studied under Rubens. Court painter to James I and Charles I, by whom he was knighted (1632). His paintings include many portraits of the royal family and some religious canvases.

the Vandyke of sculpture. Antoine Coysevox (1640–1720).

the English Vandyke. William Dobson (1610–1647).

the French Vandyke. Hyacinth Rigaud y Ros (1659–1743).

van Dyke, Henry (1852–1933). Professor of English at Princeton and Presbyterian minister. Author of many books, usually moralistic in tone, including essays, stories and poems.

Vane, Ernest. In Reade's Peg Woffington, a married man, in love with Peg.

Vane, Sir **Henry** (1613–1662). Governor of Massachusetts (1636–1637) who took the side of Anne Hutchinson when the Massachusetts Colony was divided upon her case. He returned to England and was on the side of the Puritans, sitting on the council although he did not take part in the execution of the king. He appears in Nathaniel Hawthorne's *Howe's Masquerade.*

Vane, Lady Isabel. The heroine of Mrs. Wood's East Lynne.

Vane, Sutton (1888–). English playwright. His *Outward Bound* (1923), written at the age of 26, remains one of the most interesting plays dealing with experiences beyond death.

Vanessa. Dean Swift's name for his friend and correspondent, Esther Vanhomrigh (1690–1723), made by compounding *Van,* the first syllable of her surname, with *Essa,* the pet form of Esther. Swift called himself *Cadenus,* an anagram on *Decanus* (Lat. for *Dean*). He wrote a poem *Cadenus and Vanessa,* declining to marry the lady. See also Stella.

Vanir. The nature-gods of the old Scandinavians, who presided over the ocean, air, earth, streams, etc.; opposed to, and generally at war with, the Aesir. Niörd, the water-god, was the chief; his son was Frey; his daughter Freya (the Scandinavian Venus); his wife Skadi; and his home Noatun.

Vanity Fair. In Bunyan's Pilgrim's Progress, a fair established by Beelzebub, Apollyon, and Legion, in the town of Vanity, and lasting all the year round. Here are sold houses, lands, trades, places, honors, preferments, titles, countries, kingdoms, lusts, pleasures, and delights of all sorts.

Vanity Fair, a Novel without a Hero. A novel by Thackeray (1848) of which he wrote while in the process of composing it: "What I want to make is a set of people living without God in the world (only that is a cant phrase), greedy, pompous men, perfectly self-satisfied for the most part, and at ease about their superior virtue. Dobbin and poor Briggs are the only two people with real humility as yet. Amelia's is to come."

The two boarding school friends, Amelia Sedley and Becky Sharp are in marked contrast throughout the novel. Becky Sharp, clever, scheming, determined to get on in the world, first plays her cards to win Amelia's rich and stupid brother, Joseph Sedley but failing that, secretly marries Rawdon Crawley, a younger son of Sir Pitt Crawley, at whose house Becky is governess. Rawdon is, however, disinherited. The undaunted Becky endeavors to live at the height of fashion on a small income and succeeds with the help of Lord Steyne. Finally Rawdon suspects his wife's relations with Steyne, discovers the truth and departs to become the governor of Coventry Island, leaving their son to the care of Sir Pitt Crawley. Becky is completely ostracized and forced to live by her wits on the Continent. Meantime Amelia, loved by George Osborne and William Dobbin, has married the former, but he is killed in the Battle of Waterloo. Because of her poverty, she is forced to give her son, Georgy, into the care of his grandfather, Mr. Osborne, who will, however, have nothing to do with her. On Mr. Osborne's death, Georgy is left a fortune. Amelia and her brother, traveling on the Continent, now meet Becky Sharp, and she gradually regains her old influence over Joseph Sedley. The faithful Dobbin, having loved Amelia through thick and thin, is at last rewarded with her hand.

Vanity Fair. An American magazine, founded in 1868 and for a time edited by Frank HARRIS, best known in its incarnation during the period 1913–1936. Then, under the editorship of Frank Crowninshield, it presented news of society, examples of the work of leading American and European authors, articles on music and the arts, satire, and reproductions of paintings of the most advanced 20th-century schools, all appealing to a sophisticated and cosmopolitan audience. In 1936 it was incorporated with the fashion magazine *Vogue* and lost its previous identity. An American humorous magazine of the 19th century (1859–1863) was also called *Vanity Fair.*

Van Loon, Hendrik Willem (1882–1945). Dutch-born American journalist and miscellaneous author, known for his best-selling books popularizing historical, scientific, and cultural subjects, written in a sentimental and lightly "familiar" vein, with illustrations of his own. His publications include *The Fall of the Dutch Republic* (1913); *The Rise of the Dutch Kingdom* (1915); *The Golden Book of Dutch Navigators* (1916); *A Short History of Discovery* (1918); *Ancient Man* (1920); *The Story of Mankind* (1921); *The Story of the Bible* (1923); *Tolerance* (1925); *America* (1927); *Man, the Miracle-Maker* (1928); *R. v. R.* (1930), on the painter Rembrandt; *Van Loon's Geography* (1932); *Ships and How They Sailed the Seven Seas* (1935); *The Arts* (1937); *The Story of the Pacific* (1940); *Van Loon's Lives* (1942).

Van Lowe. The name of the large and diverse Dutch family who appear in a tetralogy of novels by Louis COUPERUS, the first of which is SMALL SOULS.

Vanna. Monna, see MONNA VANNA.

Vanoc. The son of MERLIN, one of Arthur's Round Table knights.

Vanolis, Bysshe. Pseudonym of the Victorian James THOMSON.

van Paassen, Pierre (1895–). Dutch-Canadian journalist. During World War II, his *Days of Our Years* (1939) became a best seller. He is a fighter with a deep hatred of fascism.

Van Rensselaer, Kiliaen (1595–1644). Dutch dealer in precious stones in Amsterdam, who helped to found the Dutch West India Company (1621). Dealing through an agent, he bought from the Indians in America large lands which are at present the counties of Albany, Columbia and Rensselaer in New York State. His descendants in America constitute one of the oldest American families.

Van Tassel, Katrina. The Dutch maiden beloved of Ichabod Crane in Irving's *Legend of Sleepy Hollow*. See SLEEPY HOLLOW.

Van Twiller, Wouter (1580?–1656?). Nephew of Kiliaen VAN RENSSELAER; governor of the colony of New Netherland (1633–1637). In the *History of New York* by Washington Irving he is satirized as "Walter the Doubter."

Van Tyne, Claude Halstead (1869–1930). American historian who won posthumously the Pulitzer prize for history for *The War of Independence: American Phase* (1929).

Van Vechten, Carl (1880–). American critic and novelist, best known for his witty, satirical, and sophisticated novels of life among New York society people and aesthetes of the 1920's. His books include *Peter Whiffle* (1922); *The Blind Bow-Boy* (1923); *Firecrackers* (1925); *Red* (1925) and *Excavations* (1926), collections of his criticism; *The Tattooed Countess* (1924); NIGGER HEAVEN (1926); *Spider Boy* (1928); *Parties* (1930); *Sacred and Profane Memories* (1932), autobiographical essays. Van Vechten was a music and dramatic critic in New York for a number of years. In the 1930's he became interested in photography.

Van Winkle, Rip, see RIP VAN WINKLE.

Vanya. (In *The Brothers Karamazov.*) See *Ivan Fyodorovich Karamazov,* under KARAMAZOV.

Vanzetti, Bartolomeo (1888–1927). With Nicola SACCO he was arrested for the murder of a shoe-factory paymaster at South Braintree, Massachusetts, on April 15, 1920. He was tried and convicted on July 14, 1921. The case was appealed, and soon great doubt of the guilt of Sacco and Vanzetti was entertained. The protest in their favor was world-wide. A special committee, appointed to examine the case, confirmed the findings of the court. The two men were electrocuted on August 23, 1927. Many of the writers of America both protested in their favor and wrote concerning their case.

Van Zorn. A play (1914) by Edwin Arlington ROBINSON.

Varden, Gabriel. In Dickens' BARNABY RUDGE, a locksmith; he is a round, red-faced, sturdy yeoman, with a double chin, and a voice husky with good living, good sleeping, good humor, and good health. During the GORDON RIOTS, Gabriel refuses to pick the lock of Newgate prison, though at the imminent risk of his life.

Mrs. Varden (*Martha*). The locksmith's wife, and mother of Dolly, a woman of "uncertain temper" and a "martyr." When too ill-disposed to rise, Mrs. Varden orders up "the little black teapot of strong mixed tea, a couple of rounds of hot buttered toast, a dish of beef and ham cut thin without skin, and the *Protestant Manual* in two octavo volumes. Whenever Mrs. Varden was most devout, she was always the most ill-tempered."

Dolly Varden. The locksmith's daughter; a pretty, laughing girl, with a roguish face, lit up by a lovely pair of sparkling eyes, the very impersonation of good humor and blooming beauty. She marries Joe WILLET, and conducts with him the Maypole Inn, as never a country inn was conducted before. They prosper and have a large and happy family. Dolly dresses in the Watteau style, and Watteau gowns and hats were for a time, about 1875, called "Dolly Vardens." The name was frequently in use in fashions of a later period also.

Vardon, Harry (1870–1937). Famous golf player. He won the British open championship six times.

Varieties of Religious Experience, The. A book (1902) by William JAMES. The material in it was originally given as a series of lectures at the University of Edinburgh (1901–1902).

Variety. Theatrical trade journal (1873–) written in the lingo of Broadway but containing all the news of theatrical events throughout the year. In 1933 it instituted a Hollywood supplement.

variorum. An edition with notes by different persons. A good example is the *Variorum Shakespeare* (1871–1930) edited originally by Horace Howard Furness.

Varmint, The. The first of three volumes by Owen JOHNSON (1878–) concerning the school and college life of Dink Stover. *The Varmint* (1910) and *The Tennessee Shad* (1911) relate his prep-school adventures in hilarious fashion, and *Stover at Yale* (1911), a more pretentious novel, treats seriously the social problems of modern college life.

varnishing day. The day set aside for painters, who are exhibiting in a gallery, to varnish or put finishing touches on their work. Sometimes this is the day when the art critics are asked to attend.

Varro, Marcus Terentius (116–27 B.C.). Roman scholar, called by Quintilian "the most learned of the Romans." He arranged the library in Rome at the direction of Julius Caesar and was appointed superintendent of another library by Augustus.

Varuna. In the early Hindu mythology of the Rig Veda, lord of the universe; with INDRA the greatest of the gods of the Vedic hymns. He is invoked as the night sky and his double, Mitra, as the day sky; in the later Vedic period his power is more and more confined to this one aspect of nature. Finally, however, in the post-Vedic period, Varuna becomes the Hindu Neptune, represented as an old man riding on a sea monster with a club in one hand and a rope in the other.

Vasantasena. Heroine of the old Sanskrit drama known as THE LITTLE CLAY CART.

Vasari, Giorgio (1511–1574). Italian painter, famous especially for writing the valued source book, *Lives of the Most Excellent Architects, Painters and Sculptors* (1550 and 1568). Considered the founder of modern art criticism.

Vasco da Gama, see GAMA, VASCO DA.

Vashti. In the Old Testament, the Queen of King Ahasuerus before the days of Esther. When the heart of the King was merry with wine, he commanded his chamberlains to bring Vashti, the Queen, into the banquet-hall, to show the guests her beauty, but she refused to obey the insulting order, and the King, being wroth, divorced her. (*Esth.* i. 10, 19.)

> O Vashti, noble Vashti! Summoned out,
> She kept her state, and left the drunken king
> To brawl at Shushan underneath the palms.
> Tennyson, *The Princess*, iii. (1830).

Vassar College. A college for women at Poughkeepsie, N.Y. (founded 1861). Among its contributions to literature have been the work of Adelaide CRAPSEY, Edna St. Vincent MILLAY, and Constance ROURKE.

Vatel, François (died 1671). A famous chef who was the steward of the French finance minister Fouquet. He is said to have committed suicide because the fish had not arrived in time for one of the banquets given by the Prince de Condé.

Vathek. The hero of W. BECKFORD's oriental romance of the same name (1786). The ninth caliph of the Abbasside dynasty, he is a haughty, effeminate monarch, induced by a malignant genius to commit all sorts of crimes. He abjures his faith, and offers allegiance to Eblis, under the hope of obtaining the throne of the pre-Adamite sultans. This he gains, only to find that it is a place of torture and that he is doomed to remain in it for ever.

Vathek's daughter. A red-and-yellow mixture given him by an emissary of Eblis, which instantaneously restored the exhausted body, and filled it with delight.

Vatican. The palace of the Pope; so called because it stands on the *Vaticanus Mons* (Vatican Hill) of ancient Rome, which got its name through being the headquarters of the *vaticinatores,* or soothsayers. Hence it is used to mean the Papacy, or the Catholic Church.

Vatnaz, Clémence. In Flaubert's SENTIMENTAL EDUCATION, a spiteful old maid, associated with the radicals of 1848, for a time the mistress of DUSSARDIER. She is particularly inimical toward Rosanette BRON, whose property she on one occasion has sold at public auction.

Vauban, Marquis **de. Sébastien Le Prestre** (1633–1707). French marshal who was also a great military engineer. He introduced a special system of siege approach and invented the socket bayonet.

vaudeville. A light entertainment consisting of a succession of acts, also called *variety*. The name comes from Vau-de-Vire (in Normandy, France) where the kind of song originally designated as "vaudeville" was common. In 1865, when Tony Pastor opened his Opera House in New York, he introduced this kind of entertainment. The Keiths took it up later on. In 1885, there grew up a system of continuous vaudeville, running two shows a day, from eleven in the morning till eleven at night. Some famous vaudeville producers are Oscar Hammerstein, Alexander Pantages, and Marcus Loew. The Palace Theater in New York was formerly the principal home of vaudeville. Sarah BERNHARDT and many lesser stars played in vaudeville. Killed by talking pictures, it may be revived by television.

Vaughan, Henry (1622–1695). Welsh-born English poet, a later member of the METAPHYSICAL POETS, professing himself to be a disciple of George HERBERT. He is known for his mystical poetry, emphasizing the manifestations of God in nature. His published works are *Silex Scintillans* (1650 and 1655) and *Thalia Rediviva* (1678). His best-known poem is THE WORLD. Vaughan fought in the Civil War, studied medicine, and spent a long career as a country doctor in Wales.

Vaughan, Hilda (1892–). Welsh novelist who can claim to be descended collaterally from the poet Henry Vaughan. She married Charles MORGAN. Her novels of Welsh life are notable for their knowledge of the people.

Vaughan Williams, Ralph (1872–). English composer; president of the English Folksong Society. His *A London Symphony* (1918) has been called "the most significant work composed by an Englishman."

Vauquer, Maison (Vauquer House). The cheap, fourth-rate boarding house described in detail in Balzac's *Father Goriot* (*Le Père Goriot*) and famed as the dwelling-place of many of the characters of his *Comédie Humaine*. See GORIOT.

Vautrin. One of the names under which the criminal Jacques COLLIN appears in Balzac's novels.

Vaux, Thomas. 2nd Baron **Vaux of Harrowden** (1510–1556). English poet who contributed to TOTTEL'S MISCELLANY and wrote a song which Shakespeare adapted as the song of one of the grave-diggers in *Hamlet.*

Vauxhall Gardens. A famous place of entertainment in London, laid out in the middle of the seventeenth century as New Spring Gardens. Many writers of the time went to Vauxhall Gardens, among them Samuel Pepys. In *The Spectator* they are visited by Sir Roger de Coverley. Closed in 1859.

Vavasour, Mr. A character in Disraeli's TANCRED who "saw something good in everybody and everything . . . liked to know everybody who was known and to see everything which ought to be seen. His life was a gyration of energetic curiosity, an insatiable whirl of social celebrity."

Ve. Brother of ODIN and Vili, in Scandinavian mythology. He was one of the three deities who took part in the creation of the world; and he and Vili slew YMIR and drowned the whole race of frost-giants in his blood.

Veal, Mrs. An imaginary person, who, according to Daniel DEFOE, appeared, the day after her death, to Mrs. Bargrave of Canterbury, on September 8, 1705. This cock-and-bull story was affixed by Defoe to Drelincourt's book of *Consolations against the Fears of Death,* in order to increase the sale of the book, and such is the matter-of-fact style of the narrative that most readers thought the fiction was a fact. It was later published separately as *The True Relation of the Apparition of One Mrs. Veal.*

Veblen, Thorstein Bunde (1857–1929). Liberal American sociologist and author. His chief works, which contain many acute criticisms of established social and economic institutions, include *The Theory of the Leisure Class* (1899); *The Theory of Business Enterprise* (1904); and *The Vested Interests and the State of the Industrial Arts* (1919); etc. Veblen was born in Wisconsin of Norwegian parents. He concluded his long career as a teacher at the New School for Social Research in New York (from 1919).

Vecelli. The family name of TITIAN.

Veck, Toby. In Dickens' Christmas tale, *The Chimes,* a ticket-porter, nicknamed "Trotty" who runs on errands. One New Year's Eve he eats tripe for dinner and has a nightmare, in which he fancies he has mounted up to the steeple of a neighboring church, and that goblins issue out of the bells, giving reality to his hopes and fears. He is roused from his sleep by the sound of bells ringing in the new year.

Vedas or **Vedams.** The four sacred books of the Brahmins, comprising (1) the *Rig* or *Rish Veda* (2) *Yajur Veda;* (3) the *Sama Veda;* and (4) *the Atharva Veda.* The first consists of prayers and hymns in verse, the second of prayers in prose, the third of prayers for chanting, and the fourth of formulas for consecration, imprecation, expiation, etc.

The word *Veda* means knowledge.

Vedder, Elihu (1836–1923). American painter and illustrator. His best murals are in the Library of Congress, Washington, D.C. His best illustrations were done for an edition of the *Rubáiyát of Omar Khayyám*.

Vega, Garcilaso de la, see GARCILASO DE LA VEGA.

Vega, Lope de (1562–1635). Founder of the Spanish national drama, author of some two thousand plays. Created the comic character, "El Gracioso."

Veiled Prophet of Khorassan, the. Hakim ben Allah, surnamed *Mokanna* or "The Veiled," founder of an Arabic sect in the 8th century. He wore a veil to conceal his face, which had been greatly disfigured in battle. He gave out that he had been Adam, Noah, Abraham, and Moses. When the Sultan Mahadi marched against him, he poisoned all his followers at a banquet, and then threw himself into a cask containing a burning acid, which entirely destroyed him. Thomas MOORE has made this the subject of a poetical tale in his LALLA ROOKH, *The Veiled Prophet of Khorassan:*

There, on that throne, . . . sat the prophet-chief,
The great Mokanna. O'er his features hung
The veil, the silver veil, which he had flung
In mercy there, to hide from mortal sight
His dazzling brow, till man could bear its light.

. . . .

" 'Tis time these features were uncurtained [*now*],
This brow, whose light—oh, rare celestial light!—
Hath been reserved to bless thy favoured sight . . .
Turn now and look; then wonder, if thou wilt,
That I should hate, should take revenge, by guilt,
Upon the hand whose mischief or whose mirth
Sent me thus maimed and monstrous upon earth . . .
Here—judge if hell, with all its power to damn,
Can add one curse to the foul thing I am!"
He raised the veil; the maid turned slowly round,
Looked at him, shrieked, and sunk upon the ground.

Veiller, Bayard (1869–1943). American dramatist. Author of several popular plays, particularly *The Thirteenth Chair* (1922) and *The Trial of Mary Dugan* (1928). *The Fun I've Had* (1941) is his autobiography.

Velásquez, Diego Rodríguez de Silva y (1599–1660). One of the greatest painters of Spain. Court painter to Philip IV (1623). He painted many portraits of the court, as well as of court jesters and dwarves. He also did many religious and mythological paintings. He became a close friend of RUBENS.

Venable, William Henry (1836–1920). Teacher, poet, and author of *Beginnings of Literary Culture in the Ohio Valley*.

Vendée, La. During the French Revolution this department in the west of France became the scene of civil war. The irregular bands which roamed the countryside were called Chouans after the name of one of their leaders, or possibly after a kind of owl whose cry they imitated to call their people together. Balzac wrote a novel, LES CHOUANS (1829).

vendetta. A blood feud of the kind originating in Sicily, Sardinia and especially in Corsica in the eighteenth century. "Feuding" among the mountaineers of Kentucky in the United States is a form of vendetta.

Veneering, Mr. and Mrs. A newly rich couple in Dickens' novel OUR MUTUAL FRIEND:

Mr. and Mrs. Veneering were bran-new people, in a bran-new house, in a bran-new quarter of London. Everything about the Veneerings was spick and span new. All their furniture was new, all their friends were new, all their servants were new, their plate was new, their carriage was new, their harness was new, their horses were new, their pictures were new, they themselves were new, they were as newly married as was lawfully compatible with their having a bran-new baby.

In the Veneering establishment, from the hall chairs with the new coat of arms, to the grand pianoforte with the new action, and upstairs again to the new fire-escape, all things were in a state of high varnish and polish.—ii. (1864).

The Veneerings (1922) by Sir Harry JOHNSTON, is a novel in which these people are characters.

Venetian Glass Nephew, The. A fantastic novel (1925) by Elinor WYLIE.

venial sin. One that may be pardoned; one that does not forfeit grace. In the Catholic Church sins are of two sorts, *mortal* and *venial* (Lat. *venia,* "grace, pardon"). Cf. *Matt.* xii. 31.

Venice.

Venice of the East. Bangkok, capital of Burma.

Venice of the North. Stockholm, Sweden. Sometimes Amsterdam is so called.

Venice of the West. Glasgow.

Venice glass. The drinking-glasses of the Middle Ages, made at Venice, were said to break into shivers if poison were put into them. *Venice glass,* from its excellency, became a synonym for perfection.

Venice Preserved. A famous tragedy by OTWAY (1682). A conspiracy is formed by Renault, a Frenchman, Elliot, an Englishman, Bedamar, Pierre, and others, to murder the Venetian senate. Jaffier is induced by his friend Pierre to join the conspirators, and gives Belvidera, his wife, as hostage of his good faith. As Renault most grossly insults the lady, Jaffier takes her away and she persuades her husband to reveal the plot to her father Priuli, one of the threatened senators, under the promise of a general amnesty. The senate violates the promise made by Priuli, and commands all the conspirators except Jaffier to be broken on the wheel. Jaffier, to save his friend Pierre from torture, stabs him, and then himself. Belvidera goes mad and dies.

veni, vidi, vici (*Lat.,* "I came, I saw, I conquered"). According to Plutarch it was thus that Julius Caesar announced to his friend Amintius his victory at Zela (47 B. C.), in Asia Minor, over Pharnaces, son of Mithridates, who had rendered aid to Pompey. Suetonius, however, says that the words were displayed before his title after his victories in Pontus, and does not ascribe them to Caesar himself. They are often used as an example of laconism, extreme concision.

Venizelos, Eleutherios (1864–1936). Greek statesman who forced the abdication of King Constantine (1917) and brought Greece into World War I on the side of the Allies. He took part in the Peace Conference at Paris (1919), advocated a republic in Greece, was several times premier, and finally (1935), having opposed the government, was forced into exile. King George II, after his return to the throne (1935), granted him an amnesty.

Venn, Diggory. A reddleman in Hardy's RETURN OF THE NATIVE.

Venner, Elsie. The heroine of O. W. Holmes' novel ELSIE VENNER.

Venner, Uncle. An old village character in Hawthorne's HOUSE OF THE SEVEN GABLES.

Venus. In Roman mythology, the goddess of beauty and love. Originally of minor importance, she became through identification with the Greek Aphrodite one of the major characters in classical myths. She was the daughter of Jupiter and Dione. According to another view (influenced by association with the Greek term *aphros,* "foam") she had sprung from the foam of the sea at Cyprus. Jupiter gave her in wedlock to Vulcan. She was the mother, by Vulcan, of Eros and Anteros; by Mars, of Harmonia; by Anchises, of Aeneas; etc. She wore a magic girdle which enabled its wearer to arouse love in others. She plays an important part in many legends and stories: she gave beauty as a gift to Pandora, the first woman; she fell in love with Adonis and after his death changed his blood into the anemone; she first objected and finally consented to her son Cupid's (Eros') love for Psyche; she had Atalanta and Hippomenes changed into lions; she consoled Ariadne and gave her Bacchus as her husband; she competed against Juno and Minerva for the apple of discord and was given the prize by Paris; she destined Helen, the wife of Menelaus, for Paris and caused thus the Trojan war; she sided with the Trojans against the Greeks and enlisted the help of her admirer Mars; etc., etc.

Her name is given to the second planet from the sun, and in astrology "signifie the white men or browne . . . joyfull, laughter, liberall, pleasers, dauncers, entertayners of women, players, perfumers, musitions, messengers of love."

In Camoëns' epic poem THE LUSIAD, Uranian Venus is the impersonation of divine love and the presiding deity of the Lusians. The Isle of Venus is a paradise created for the Lusian heroes. Here Uranian Venus gives Vasco da Gama the empire of the sea.

In Wagner's opera TANNHÄUSER, Venus is goddess of love and illicit delights and entertains the hero in her magic grotto beneath the Venusberg.

Venus and Adonis. A long poem by Shakespeare. For the myth it treats of, see ADONIS.

There are several famous statues of Venus, notably the VENUS DE' MEDICI and the *Venus of Milo* (ca. 400 B. C.).

Venus de' Medici. A statue in Parian marble of Venus holding both hands before her body. Found in Hadrian's villa at Tivoli and brought to Florence by Cosmo de' Medici III about 1680. It is in the Uffizi Gallery. The signature of Cleomenes (ca. 200 B. C.) is considered a forgery. The statue is clearly a Greco-Roman work.

Venus, Mr. In Dickens' novel OUR MUTUAL FRIEND, a man skilled in the preserving of birds and animals and the articulating of human bones. With Silas WEGG he plans to blackmail Mr. BOFFIN, but changes his mind and confesses the plot.

Venusberg. In German legend and in Wagner's opera TANNHÄUSER, a place of fatal delights presided over by Venus, goddess of love. Here Tannhäuser tarries, and when Pope Urban refuses to grant him absolution, he returns there. William MORRIS has a poem *The Hill of Venus* in his *Earthly Paradise* (1870), retelling the old legend with a modern setting.

verbatim et literatim (*Lat.*). Accurately rendered, "word for word and letter for letter."

verb. sap. (Lat. *verbum sapienti,* "a word to the wise"). A hint is sufficient to any wise man; a threat implying if the hint is not taken I will expose you.

verb. sat. (Lat. *verbum satienti,* "a word is enough"). Similar to the above. A word to the wise is enough.

Vercel, Roger (1894–). French novelist. His *Captain Conan* (1934) won him the Goncourt prize; *The Tides of Mont St. Michel* (1938) was popular in America.

Vercingetorix. Gallic chief who fought against Julius Caesar. Executed in Rome. Cf. Book VII of Caesar's *Commentaries.*

Verdant Green. A novel of Oxford undergraduate life by Cuthbert BEDE (1860). The hero, as his name implies, is a young man of infinite simplicity who goes to college and is played upon by all the practical jokers of *alma mater.* After he has bought his knowledge by experience, he uses it to play pranks on juveniles greener than himself. Verdant Green's spectacles win for him the nickname of "Giglamps."

Verdi, Giuseppe (1813–1901). Italian composer. Especially known for his operas, as ERNANI (1844); RIGOLETTO (1851); IL TROVATORE (1853); LA TRAVIATA (1853); LA FORZA DEL DESTINO (1862); AÏDA (1871); OTELLO (1887); and FALSTAFF (1893).

Verdurin, M. and Mme. In Marcel Proust's REMEMBRANCE OF THINGS PAST, a newly-rich couple of insignificant social background, scorned by the aristocratic GUERMANTES group. They hold regular *soirées* to which they invite literary, artistic, and musical celebrities and gradually win away some of the prized guests who attend the Guermantes gatherings.

Vere, Edward de, Earl of **Oxford.** See OXFORD, EDWARD DE VERE, EARL OF.

Vereshchagin, Vasili (1842–1904). Russian artist, famous for his realistic war pictures. Served in the Russo-Turkish and Russo-Japanese Wars. Killed in action.

Verges. In Shakespeare's MUCH ADO ABOUT NOTHING, an old-fashioned constable and night-watch, noted for his blundering simplicity.

Verhaeren, Émile (1855–1916). Famous Belgian poet who came to particular notice during World War I. His books translated into English include *Poems* (1899); *Belgium's Agony* (1915); *Plays* (1916); *Five Tales* (1924); etc.

Verhovensky, Pyotr Stepanovich. In Dostoyevsky's THE POSSESSED, the cold, ruthless leader of the band of revolutionary terrorists, a man utterly devoid of conscience. He has been impressed by Nikolay STAVROGIN, but has himself taken over command of the revolutionaries and feels no scruples in devising the most brutal schemes to carry out his terrorist aims. Verhovensky was intended by the author to represent the typical nihilist (see NIHILISM) of the 19th century in Russia, and is believed to have been based on an actual radical leader, Nechaev, who introduced the system of Bakunin into Russia. Critics point out, however, that Verhovensky's ideas are anarchistic and despotic and are not characteristic of the ideas of Marxian Socialism (see MARXISM) which Dostoyevsky believed he was attacking. Pyotr Stepanovich has been called a typical "self-willed" Dostoyevskian hero, similar to RASKOLNIKOV.

Stepan Trofimovich Verhovensky, the father of Pyotr Stepanovich, is a former professor of history and a political liberal, in his youth regarded as a dangerous radical by the authorities. Living on the estate of Varvara Petrovna Stavrogin, with whom he has frequent passionate quarrels, Stepan Trofinovich is a gentle, innocent, and sentimental academician, an admirer of Western European ideas. He is horrified when he discovers how his own theories have been distorted in the hands of the nihilists. This character is said to have been based on an actual personage also, one T. N. Granovsky, a professor of history at the University of Moscow in the 1840's.

Verisopht, Lord Frederick. In Dickens' NICHOLAS NICKLEBY, a weak and silly nobleman, but far less vicious than his bear-leader, Sir Mulberry HAWK. He drawls in his speech, and is altogether "very soft."

Verlaine, Paul (1844–1896). French poet, an immediate forerunner of SYMBOLISM in France, known for the grace, delicacy, and musical suggestiveness of his characteristic lyrics. Among his books are *Poèmes Saturniens* (1866), a volume in the style of the PARNASSIANS; *Fêtes Galantes* (1869), written in a Watteau-like, 18th-century mood; *La Bonne Chanson* (1870), a celebration of the poet's joy at his coming marriage; *Romances sans Paroles* (1874); *Sagesse* (1881), containing poems of religious sentiment; *Jadis et Naguère* (1884).

Verlaine was extremely erratic in personality and behavior, living a Bohemian life which took him from cafés to hospitals and prisons, and alternating between sensuality and mysticism. He loved his wife, but after their separation he engaged in liaisons of a perverted nature, the most notorious of which was with Arthur RIMBAUD. Rimbaud is considered to have had a morally corrupting influence on Verlaine but to have assisted the older man in developing a new conception of poetry. Verlaine was converted to Catholicism during the 1870's.

Verloc. "The SECRET AGENT" in Conrad's novel of that title. His wife **Winnie Verloc** plays an important part in the action.

Vermeer, Jan. Known as **Jan van der Meer van Delft** (1632–1675). One of the most distinguished Dutch painters. Of his paintings about forty are known. His treatment of life is an outstanding characteristic.

Vermont. A land-locked New England state with a turbulent early history. See also GREEN MOUNTAIN BOYS.

Verne, Jules (1828–1905). French writer of quasi-scientific romances which in some ways have proved prophetic of the advance of science. His books have always been popular with young people. *A Voyage to the Center of the Earth* (1864); TWENTY THOUSAND LEAGUES UNDER THE SEA (1870), etc.

Verneuil, Marie de. In Balzac's novel THE CHOUANS (*Les Chouans*), a beautiful Republican spy whose love for the Royalist chief whom it is her duty to betray, involves both in tragedy.

Vernier, Pierre (1580–1637). French mathematician who invented the double sliding scale, known as *vernier,* which is used for determining distances and angles.

Vernon, Diana. In Scott's ROB ROY, niece of Sir Hildebrand Osbaldistone. She has great beauty, sparkling talents, an excellent disposition, high birth, and is an enthusiastic adherent of the exiled king. She marries Frank Osbaldistone.

Sir Frederick Vernon. Father of Diana, a political intriguer, called "His Excellency the Earl of Beauchamp." He first appears as Father Vaughan.

Vernon, Dorothy, see DOROTHY VERNON.

Vernon, Mme de. The mother of Matilda in Mme de Staël's DELPHINE, a cool-headed intriguing egotist frequently considered a portrait of TALLEYRAND in female guise.

Veronese, Paolo (1528–1588). Italian painter of the Venetian school, called the "Painter of Pageants." Frescoes of his are in the Library of St. Mark in Venice.

Veronica, St. See under SAINTS.

Verrazano, Giovanni da (1485?–?1528). Italian navigator who found the mouth of the Hudson River (1524).

Verrill, Alpheus Hyatt (1871–). American naturalist and explorer, the son of **Addison Emery Verrill** (1864–1907), zoologist and professor at Yale. In Central America, he discovered important evidence of a prehistoric culture. As an avocation he has written a number of adventure books for boys.

Verrinder, Mrs. The old woman in De Morgan's ALICE-FOR-SHORT, who suddenly recovers her memory, lost sixty years before.

Verrocchio, Andrea del (1435–1488). Florentine sculptor and painter; with the exception of Donatello, the chief sculptor of the Tuscan school. His best-known work is the equestrian statue of Colleoni.

Versailles. A town near Paris, noted for its park and palace built by Louis XVI, now used as a museum. Among the treaties concluded at Versailles is that terminating the Franco-Prussian War (1870–1871) and, especially, the one which was to lay the foundation of a durable peace between the Allies and Germany after World War I (June 28, 1919). The U.S. Senate refused to ratify it and it had to be supplemented by a separate treaty concluded at Berlin (August 25, 1921).

the German Versailles. Cassel; so called from its gardens, conservatories, fountains, and colossal statue of Hercules.

the Versailles of Poland. The palace, etc., of the counts of Braniski, taken over by the Municipality of Bialystok.

vers de société (*Fr.,* "society verse"). Light poetry of a witty or fanciful kind, generally with a slight vein of social satire running through it.

vers libre, see FREE VERSE.

versus rhopalicus. See under KNITTELVERS.

Verthandi. In Norse mythology, one of the three Norns or Fates. She represents the present, her name being related to German *werden,* "to grow, become."

Vertrees, Mary. The heroine of Tarkington's TURMOIL.

Vertumnus. In Roman mythology, the god of the seasons, who married POMONA. He courted her unsuccessfully in many guises until finally he appeared as an old woman and pled his own cause under cover of giving good advice.

Verulamium. Roman town near the modern St. Albans in England. From it Sir Francis BACON took his title of Baron Verulam.

Vervain, Florida. Heroine of W. D. Howells' FOREGONE CONCLUSION.

Verver, Maggie. The heroine of Henry James' novel THE GOLDEN BOWL. Her millionaire father, **Adam Verver,** is also an important character.

Very, Jones (1813–1880). American poet and Greek scholar, known for his sonnets and lyrics celebrating ecstatic religious visions of a mystic nature. He was associated with the movement of TRANSCENDENTALISM and was befriended and encouraged by R. W. EMERSON, who believed in the value of his poetry. His work has been found to show stylistic imitations of CHATEAUBRIAND, MONTAIGNE, and the 17th-century English religious writers, especially the METAPHYSICAL POETS, but most often it is written in the couplets of Milton's L'ALLEGRO. Published works by Very are *Essays and Poems* (1839), which Emerson helped to edit; *Poems* (1883); *Poems and Essays* (1886). At one time Very was declared insane and committed to an asylum. After his release he served for awhile as a clergyman in small New England churches, although he was not ordained.

Vesalius, Andreas (1514–1564). Belgian anatomist. He was the first in modern times to dissect the human body. The Inquisition condemned him to death but his sentence was commuted to a pilgrimage to Jerusalem; on his return from there he was shipwrecked. His *De Humani Corporis Fabrica* is a treatise in seven books about the structure of the human body.

Vespasian (9–79 A.D.). Roman emperor chosen by his soldiers. He began the Colosseum. His name is immortalized by the *vespasiennes* (public toilets) in Paris.

Vespucci, Amerigo (1451–1512). Italian navigator. Although he did not reach the American continent until June 16, 1497, he has given his name to it. "Amerigo" is the Italian form of "Emmerich." Vespucci's letters are available in translation through the Hakluyt Society (1894).

Vesta. The virgin goddess of the hearth of Roman mythology, corresponding to the Greek HESTIA, one of the twelve great Olympians. She was custodian of the sacred fire brought by AENEAS from Troy, which was never permitted to go out lest a national calamity should follow. See VESTALS.

Vestal, Stanley (1887–). Legal name by his stepfather, not used by him in his work, **Walter Stanley Campbell.** Author of ballads, novels, biography, history. Authority on the old southwest. *Fandango: Ballads of the Old West* (1927); *Kit Carson* (1928); *The Old Santa Fé Trail* (1939); etc.

Vestals. The six spotless virgins who tended the sacred fire brought by AENEAS from Troy and preserved by the state in a sanctuary in the Forum at Rome. They were subjected to very severe discipline, and in the event of losing their virginity were buried alive. Other duties of the Vestal Virgins were to prepare from the first fruits of the May harvest the sacrificial meal for the Lupercalia, the Vestalia, and the Ides of September.

The word *vestal* has been figuratively applied to any woman of spotless chastity.

Véto, M. et Mme. Louis XVI and Marie Antoinette, so called during the French Revolution because the king had been allowed a veto on the resolutions of the National Assembly. The name is used in the revolutionary song, *La Carmagnole.*

Vetsera, Baroness Marie. See RUDOLF, MAYERLING.

V for Victory. A slogan devised in 1941 by the British propaganda offices as a rallying cry for the citizens of European countries which had been occupied by German troops during World War II. It was represented by three distinctive symbols: the capital letter V of the Roman alphabet; three dots and a dash (. . . –), the signal for the letter V in Morse telegraphic code, known and used internationally; and the opening bar of the first movement of Beethoven's *Fifth Symphony,* which resembles the Morse signal rhythmically. It was hoped that the slogan and its symbols would serve as a signal to arouse the populations of the conquered nations to revolt against the Germans, but the latter vitiated this movement by adopting the idea and using it as their own, asserting that a "V for Victory" meant victory in the war for Germany. In isolated uprisings against the German armies of occupation, however, V's would be found scrawled on walls, or on risk of death a peasant might tap out three dots and a dash on a table-top. In the U.S. the letter V and the Morse signal supplied a popular design for costume jewelry and printed fabrics and was once used in a whiskey advertisement.

Via Crucis. A historical novel by F. Marion CRAWFORD (1898), dealing with the Second Crusade. The English hero, Gilbert Ward, is beloved by beautiful Queen Eleanor of France, but remains true to his early love, Beatrix de Curboil.

Via Dolorosa. The way which Jesus took to the Hall of Judgment, from the Mount of Olives to Golgotha, about a mile in length.

Viaud, Louis Marie Julien, see LOTI, PIERRE.

Vibart, Peter. The hero of Farnol's BROAD HIGHWAY.

Vibert, Jehan (1840–1902). French painter who was a very exact draftsman but not distinguished for his color. He did a great many "story paintings," among them *The Grasshopper and the Ant* (1875).

Vicar of Bray. A semi-legendary vicar of Bray, Berkshire, who, between 1520 and 1560, was twice a Papist and twice a Protestant in successive reigns. His name has been given as Symonds, Alleyne, and Pendleton, and his date transferred to the time of Charles II. Historically nothing is known of him. The well-known song is said to have been written in Restoration times by an officer in Colonel Fuller's regiment. The song begins: "In good King Charles's golden days," I was a zealous high-churchman and continues "When royal James obtained the crown," I found the Church of Rome would fit my constitution. "When William was our king declared," I swore to him allegiance. "When gracious Anne became our queen," I became a Tory. "When George, in pudding-time came o'er," I became a Whig. And "George my lawful king shall be—until the times do alter."

Vicar of Christ. A title given to the Pope, in allusion to his claim of being the representative of Christ on earth.

Vicar of Wakefield, The. A novel by Oliver GOLDSMITH (1766), a story of the Vicar, Dr. PRIMROSE, and his six children. Like Job, the Vicar undergoes a series of terrible trials through no fault of his own, and like Job also, is eventually restored to prosperity. See THORNHILL.

Vice. In Old English MORALITIES, a buffoon who usually wore a cap with ass's ears. He was a boon companion of the Devil.

Vicente, Gil (1470–1540). Portuguese poet who has been mentioned with CAMOËNS as one of the leading poets of his country.

Vice-Versâ. A fantastic novel (1882) by F. ANSTEY. It tells of the transformation of a father into his son and of the schoolboy son into his father. Cf. *Turnabout* (1931) by Thorne SMITH, in which a husband and wife exchange bodies.

Vichy Government. The emergency government set up at the famous health resort, Vichy, in France after the defeat of that nation by Germany during World War II (June, 1940). It was headed by Marshal PÉTAIN, an octogenarian veteran of World War I, and dictatorial powers were granted its members. The Vichy government was accused of "collaborating" with, and giving aid in the form of men and weapons to, the German government during the later years of the war.

Vicksburg. A town on the Mississippi. During the American Civil War, Grant besieged the Confederate forces in Vicksburg for a month and a half. Its surrender (July 4, 1863) gave the Federals control of the Mississippi River.

Vicomte de Bragelonne, The. The third of a trilogy of historical novels by Alexandre DUMAS. See THREE MUSKETEERS.

Victor, Orville James (1827–1910). American publisher. In 1860 he originated the idea of a melodramatic kind of adventure story which would sell as cheaply as ten cents. He got together a group of writers to turn out the first "dime novels."

Victor and Cazire. The pen names under which Percy Bysshe SHELLEY and his sister Elizabeth published a book of poetry in 1810.

Victoria (1819–1901). Queen of Great Britain (1837–1901). Her long reign included the industrial revolution and gave her name to a great period in English literature. Cf. *Queen Victoria* (1921), by Lytton STRACHEY.

Victory. A novel by Joseph CONRAD (1915). Convinced by his pessimistic father that life is not to be trusted, Axel Heyst makes every effort to preserve a complete detachment and wanders about the South Seas, a lonely, impersonal figure. His few impulsive acts of friendship bear fruit that only confirms his theories. Finally, however, he rescues a poor, unhappy girl named Lena from a wandering theatrical troupe and carries her off from their insults and abuse to his lonely island. The innkeeper Schomberg, a vulgar brute who had been infatuated with the girl, hates Heyst and sets the fantastic, unscrupulous gentleman adventurer Jones, with his followers, Ricardo and Pedro, on his track in the belief that there is treasure on the island. A dramatic struggle ensues and the affair ends fatally, but Lena and Heyst achieve a sort of "Victory" in spite of the tragic outcome.

Vidar. One of the Aesir of Scandinavian mythology, a son of ODIN. He avenges his father's death by slaying FENRIS at RAGNAROK.

Vidocq, François Eugène (1775–1857). Chief of detectives in Paris (1809–1827; 1832). He himself organized a robbery and then investigated it as a police officer. Lecoq, in some of the stories by Émile GABORIAU, is evidently based on Vidocq. George Sanders played Vidocq in a moving picture (1946) called "A Scandal in Paris."

Vielé, Egbert Ludovicus. Changed to **Francis Vielé-Griffin** (1863–1937). French poet, born in Virginia, where his father was Federal military governor in the Civil War. He was of Huguenot ancestry, went to France at the age of nine, and never returned to the U.S. He married a French wife, and became associated with the symbolist school. France considers him one of her great poets; he would have become a member of the French Academy had he not insisted on not giving up his American citizenship. His brother, **Herman Knickerbocker Vielé** (1856–1908), was a painter and novelist writing in English, and lived in the United States. *The Last of the Knickerbockers* is his best novel.

Vienna, Congress of. The congress (1814–1815) held by the powers of Europe after Napoleon's first abdication to settle the question of new boundaries. France kept the frontiers she had had in 1792; Prussia's territory was much increased; Poland was made into a new kingdom under the Czars; etc.

Vieth von Golssenau, Arnold. Pseudonym **Ludwig Renn** (1899–). German novelist, well known in the United States for several books about war. In 1936 he was chief of staff of the Eleventh International Brigade in the Loyalist Army in Spain. *Warfare: The Relation of War to Society* (1939).

Vigée-Lebrun, Marie Anne Élisabeth (1755–1842). French portrait painter. One of her best-known pictures is Lady Hamilton as a bacchante. She also did over twenty portraits of Marie Antoinette.

vigilance committee. An unofficial group organized to maintain law and order and suppress crime. The term first came into use at the time of the California gold fever in the mid-19th century. The members of such committees were called *vigilantes* (Spanish for "vigilants"). Accounts of their activities in literature can be found in Bret Harte's *The Outcasts of Poker Flat;* Frank Norris' *The Octopus;* and John Steinbeck's *In Dubious Battle.*

vignette. A design, usually at the head of a chapter or as a tailpiece, which decorates the pages of a book. The word comes from the French word for vine, the decoration often having a design of vine leaves.

Vigny, Alfred de (1797–1863). French poet, playwright, and novelist of the romantic period (see ROMANTICISM), known for the emphasis placed in his poetry on the "inner life" of man and on the role of the poet as a lonely martyr to his art. Vigny is considered to have been among the first poets to express the latter concept and also to adopt the scientific view of the non-human and unalterable character of natural law. His poetry is marked by melancholy, pessimism, stern pride and an attitude of Stoicism, frequent primitive and historical coloring, a simple, classical technique. Among his works are the following: *Poèmes* (1822), *Poèmes Antiques et modernes* (1826), and *Les Destinées* (1864), volumes of poetry; *La Maréchale d'Ancre, Quitte pour la Peur,* and *Chatterton* (1835), dramas, the last-named being considered by some critics to be the best play of French romanticism; *Servitude et Grandeur militaires* (1835), short stories; *Cinq Mars* (1826), the first important example of the historical novel in France; and *Journal d'un Poète* (1867).

Vigny, of a noble family, was disillusioned by the low regard in which nobility was held in his day and by the failure of his term of military service to make a military career attractive to him. After an unhappy love affair with an actress, he broke with his former associates in the romantic movement and retired to intellectual, social, and artistic solitude. It was in connection with this retreat from the active world that Vigny became the first writer about whom the phrase "IVORY TOWER," almost a cliché in later criticism, was used.

Vigrid. In Norse mythology, the battlefield where at Ragnarok Loki and his kin will kill, and be killed by, the gods and where the world will be devastated.

Viking. A Norse pirate of about the 8th to 10th centuries A. D.; probably so called from Icel. *vig.* war, cognate with Lat. *vincere,* to conquer. The word is not connected with *king.* There were *sea-kings,* sometimes, but erroneously, called "vikings," connected with royal blood, and having small dominions on the coast, who were often *vikingr* or vikings, but the reverse is not true that every *viking* or pirate was a sea-king. IBSEN has a drama called *The Vikings* (1861).

Vildrac, Charles (1882–). French dramatist and poet, real name Charles Messager. His one-act play, *Steamship Tenacity,* translated by Sidney HOWARD, was produced in New York.

Vili. In Norse mythology, one of the brothers of Odin. With Ve, the third brother, they slew Ymir and formed the world out of his body. When the first man and the first woman were made, Vili gave them reason and motion.

Villa, Francisco. Known as **Pancho Villa.** Real name **Doroteo Arango** (1877–1923). Mexican brigand and revolutionist, considered by some a champion of the people. In 1914 he held Mexico City and became dictator. He was thought to have raided across the border into New Mexico, as a consequence of which President Wilson sent General PERSHING to capture him. President CARRANZA of Mexico resented American intervention and Pershing's troops were withdrawn. Villa was assassinated (1923). John REED had accompanied him as a correspondent in the early stages of his uprising. His report upon him and his activities was published as *Insurgent Mexico* (1914).

Village, the, see GREENWICH VILLAGE.

Village, The. A long poem by George CRABBE (1783), written in answer to Goldsmith's *The Deserted Village* (see AUBURN), which Crabbe considered too sentimental to be a true picture of rural life. *The Village* describes in realistic terms the hardships, evils, sordidness, and misery of the lives of country-dwellers of the day, with a strong humanitarian note.

I grant indeed that fields and flocks have charms
For him that grazes or for him that farms;
But when amid such pleasing scenes I trace
The poor laborious natives of the place,
And see the mid-day sun, with fervid ray,
On their bare heads and dewy temples play;
While some, with feebler heads, and fainter hearts
Deplore their fortune, yet sustain their parts:
Then shall I dare these real ills to hide,
In tinsel trappings of poetic pride?

Village Blacksmith, The. A well-known poem by LONGFELLOW (1841), beginning:

Under a spreading chestnut tree
The village smithy stands:
The smith, a mighty man is he
With large and sinewy hands
And the muscles of his brawny arms
Are strong as iron bands.

Villa-Lobos, Hector (1884–). Foremost composer of Brazil. Superintendent of musical and artistic education. He has edited a book of folksongs, *Alma do Brasil.*

villanelle. A poem of five three-line stanzas followed by a quatrain and having only two rhymes. In the stanzas following the first, the first and third lines of the first stanza are repeated in alternation as refrains. They are the final two lines of the concluding quatrain.

Villard, Oswald Garrison (1872–). Prominent liberal American journalist. Editorial writer and owner of the New York *Evening Post* (1897–1918). He bought *The Nation* (1908) and edited it (till 1932). His mother was a daughter of William Lloyd Garrison; from her he inherited his fighting spirit in behalf of liberalism. He has written

John Brown: a Biography (1910); *Newspapers and Newspaper Men* (1923); his autobiography, *Fighting Years* (1939); etc.

Villari, Pasquale (1827–1917). Italian historian, known especially for his histories of SAVONAROLA and MACHIAVELLI.

Ville d'Is. The city of Ys on the coast of Brittany, ruled over by King Gradlon. The legend is that it sank into the sea in the fifth century A. D. because of the wickedness of the king's daughter. Norman Douglas, in his fantastic novel *They Went* (1921), gives an account of the princess's treatment of her lovers.

Villehardouin, Geoffroi de (ca. 1150–1218). French noble. He was at the conquest of Constantinople and wrote an eyewitness account of the Fourth Crusade in his *Chronicles*. His book has been called "the first great literary work in French prose."

Villette. A novel (1853) by Charlotte BRONTË. "Villette" is the city of Brussels.

Villiers, Alan John (1903–). Australian sailor and writer about the sea. One of his most exciting books is *Grain Race* (1933).

Villiers de L'Isle-Adam, Jean Marie Mathias Philippe Auguste, Comte de (1828–1889). French novelist and short-story writer, associated with the DECADENTS, known for his fantastic and macabre tales. Among his works are *La Révolte* (1870), a drama; *Le Nouveau-Monde* (1880), also a drama; *Le Secret de l'Echafaud* (1888); *Chez les Passants* (1890); *Axël* (1890), a novel; *Histoire souveraines* (1899); *Oeuvres complètes* (1922–1926). *Contes cruels* is his best-known collection of tales, and among separate titles are *Isis, Claire Lenoir, L'Eve future, Tribulat Bonhomet, L'Amour suprême, Morgane, Elën.*

Villon, François. Real name perhaps either **François de Montcorbier or François des Loges** (1431–?). French poet of the late Middle Ages, widely celebrated by 19th-century romantic novelists and poets and known for the vigor and imagination, the realism, pathos, technical skill, and expressive lyric power of his verse. Well-known single poems by him are his *Petit Testament, Grand Testament, Ballade des Pendus, Ballade des Dames du temps jadis* (famous in English in its translation by D. G. ROSSETTI), and *Ballade pour Prier Nostre Dame*. Villon came of a poor family with well-to-do relatives, from one of whom he took the name by which he is best known. He held both Bachelor's and Master's degrees from the Sorbonne and spent most of his time in student brawls in the LATIN QUARTER. He was arrested several times for complicity in murders and robberies, and in 1462 was sentenced to be hanged. Later his punishment was changed to a banishment of ten years, and immediately thereafter the poet disappeared; no further record exists of him. Victor HUGO and R. L. STEVENSON are among the writers who celebrated his exploits, many of which were imaginative inventions. *The Vagabond King*, a popular 20th-century operetta, deals with a highly fictitious episode in his career. Justin Huntly MCCARTHY's *If I Were King* and *Needles and Pins* portray Villon as a prominent character, and Stevenson depicts him in his *Lodging for the Night*.

Vincent, St. See under SAINTS.

Vincentio. In Shakespeare's MEASURE FOR MEASURE, the Duke of Vienna. He delegates his office to Angelo and leaves Vienna for a time, under the pretense of going on a distant journey; but, by assuming a monk's hood, he observes *incognito* the conduct of his officers.

Vincy, Rosamond. In George Eliot's MIDDLEMARCH, a vivacious, attractive girl who marries Dr. Lydgate and whose selfishness and extravagance corrupt his ideals.

Fred Vincy. Rosamond's brother, in love with Mary Garth.

Vinicius. In Sienkiewicz' QUO VADIS, the lover of Lygia.

Vinland. The name given in the old Norse sagas to a portion of the coast of North America discovered by wanderers from Denmark or Iceland about the opening of the 11th century. The tradition seems to have a solid foundation. The land touched at was probably New Jersey, and got its old name because of some small grapevines found growing there.

Vinson, Frederick M. (1890–). Director of economic stabilization (1943); Secretary of the Treasury in President Truman's cabinet 1945; now Chief Justice.

Vinteuil. In Marcel Proust's REMEMBRANCE OF THINGS PAST, a composer, considered to have been based on the French composer SAINT-SAËNS. A particular phrase in one of Vinteuil's sonatas has a peculiar fascination for the narrator of the novel, MARCEL, and he recalls it under a variety of circumstances. See ELSTIR; BERGOTTE.

Vintry. A ward on the Thames in London where wine was landed by the merchants of Bordeaux.

Viola. The heroine of Shakespeare's TWELFTH NIGHT, sister of Sebastian. She marries Orsino, the Duke.

Violante. In Browning's RING AND THE BOOK, wife of Pietro and putative mother of Pompilia. Violante provides this suppositious child partly to please old Pietro, and partly to cheat the rightful heirs.

Viollet-le-Duc, Eugène Emmanuel (1814–1879). Famous French architect, who led the Gothic revival and whose dictionaries of architecture are still invaluable. He wrote of French architecture from the eleventh to the sixteenth century. His restorations, which affect also several cathedrals, are somewhat romantic.

Vionnet, Madame de. In Henry James' AMBASSADORS, the French woman to whom Chad NEWSOME is devoted.

Virgil. Full name **Publius Virgilius Maro** (70–19 B. C.). The greatest poet of ancient Rome, born near Mantua (hence called *the Mantuan Swan*), a master of epic, didactic and idyllic poetry. His chief works are the AENEID, the *Eclogues* or *Bucolics,* and the *Georgics.*

In the Middle Ages, Virgil came to be represented as a magician and enchanter, and it is this traditional character that furnishes DANTE with his conception of making Virgil, as the personification of human wisdom, his guide through the infernal regions in his *Divine Comedy.*

the Christian Virgil. Marco Girolamo Vida (d. 1566), an Italian Latin poet.

the Virgil and Horace of the Christians. So Bentley calls the Spanish poet, Aurelius Clemens Prudentius (*fl.* ca. 400 A. D.).

the Virgil of our dramatic authors. Ben Jonson (1572–1637), was so called by Dryden.

> Shakespeare was the Homer or father of our dramatic poets; Jonson was the Virgil, and pattern of elaborate writing. I admire rare Ben, but I love Shakespeare.

the Virgil of the French drama. Jean Racine (1639–1699) was so called by Sir Walter Scott.

the English Virgil. Alfred, Lord Tennyson (1809–1892).

the Virgil of Prose. Robert Louis Stevenson (1850–1894).

Virgilia. In CORIOLANUS, Virgilia is made by Shakespeare the wife of Coriolanus, and Volumnia his mother; but historically Volumnia was his wife and Veturia his mother.

Virgin. One of the ancient constellations (*Virgo*), and a sign of the Zodiac. (August 23 to September 23). The constellation is the metamorphosization of ASTRAEA, goddess of justice, who was the last of the deities to quit our earth. See ICARIUS.

The word *virgin* is used to indicate that an article has never been used, tried, or brought into cultivation; as *paper of virgin whiteness,* paper that is unwritten, or unprinted, upon; a *virgin fortress,* one that has never been captured; a *virgin forest,* one that man has never attempted to tame or make use of.

Virginia. (1) In Roman legend, a young Roman plebeian of great beauty, decoyed by Appius Claudius, one of the decemvirs, and claimed as his slave. Her father, Virginius, being told of it, hastened to the Forum, and arrived at the moment when Virginia was about to be delivered up to Appius. He seized a butcher's knife, stabbed his daughter to the heart, rushed from the Forum, and raised a revolt.

This legend has been the subject of a host of tragedies: In French, by Mairet (1628), by Leclerc (1645), by Campistron (1683), by La Beaumelle (1760), by Chabanon (1769), by Laharpe (1786), by Leblanc du Guillet (1786), by Guiraud (1827), by Latour St. Ybars (1845), etc.; in Italian, by Alfieri (1783); in German, by Ephraim Gotthold Lessing (18th century); in English, by John Webster, entitled *Appius and Virginia* (1654); by Miss Brooke (1760); J. S. Knowles (1820), *Virginius.* It is the subject of one of MACAULAY's lays (1842), supposed to be sung in the forum on the day when Sextus and Licinus were elected tribunes for the fifth time, and it forms the subject of the *Physician's* (or *Doctor of Physic's*) *Tale* in Chaucer's CANTERBURY TALES.

(2) The heroine of Bernardin de St. Pierre's romance PAUL AND VIRGINIA.

Virginian, The. A novel by Owen Wister (*Am.,* 1902) portraying cowboy life in Wyoming. The cowboy hero, "the Virginian," wins the love of Molly Wood, a school teacher from the East. The dramatization of the novel was successful, and it has been filmed several times.

Virginians, The. A novel by THACKERAY (1857), a sequel to HENRY ESMOND, relating the story of George and Harry Warrington, the twin grandsons of Colonel Esmond. The novel takes the two brothers, of differing tastes and temperaments, through boyhood in America, through various experiences in England, where they are favorites of their wicked old aunt, Baroness Bernstein (the Beatrix of *Henry Esmond*) and through the American Revolution, in which Harry fights on the side of his friend, George Washington, and George on the British side.

Virginia Quarterly Review, The. A liberal journal (founded in 1925), which, although it is published at the University of Virginia, is not an organ of that institution nor primarily a Southern magazine. Its many contributors have included such names as Robert FROST, Sherwood ANDERSON, Thomas WOLFE, T. S. ELIOT, etc.

Virginia reel. See under COVERLEY, SIR ROGER DE.

Virginibus Puerisque (*Lat.,* "for girls and boys"). A well-known essay by Robert Louis STEVENSON (1881).

Virginius. See VIRGINIA.

Virgin Queen, the. Queen Elizabeth; also called (by Shakespeare) "the fair Vestal."

Virgin Soil. A novel by TURGENEV (1876). The hero, Neshdanov, and his sweetheart,

Marianne, with whom he elopes, are NIHILISTS and eagerly desire to work for the freedom of the peasants. But when his ideals fail him and his work comes to seem futile, Neshdanov commits suicide, advising Marianne to marry his practical-minded employer Solomine.

Virtues, The Seven. See under SEVEN.

Visconti. The name of a powerful Italian family. It supplied for more than a century (1311–1447) the ruling dukes of Milan. Cf. *The Viper of Milan* (1906) by Marjorie BOWEN.

Vishnu. The Preserver; the second member of the Hindu trinity (see TRIMURTI). He has had nine incarnations, or AVATARS, and there is one, Kalki, still to come, during which Vishnu will at the end of four ages destroy sin, the sinful, and all the enemies of the world. He is usually represented as four-armed and carrying a club, a shell, a discus, and a lotus; a bow and sword are slung at his side, and on his breast is a peculiar mark called the *Shrivatsa*. The sect that holds him supreme is known as the VAISHNAVA. He has millions of worshippers, especially under his avatars as RAMA and KRISHNA.

vis inertiae (*Lat.,* "the power of inactivity"). That property of matter which makes it resist any change. Thus it is hard to set in motion what is still, or to stop what is in motion. Figuratively, it applies to that unwillingness of change which makes men "rather bear the ills they have than fly to others they know not of."

Vision of Columbus, The. See COLUMBIAD, THE.

Vision of Judgment, The. A satirical poem by Lord BYRON (1822), parodying an earlier poem by SOUTHEY, *A Vision of Judgment* (1821), in the preface of which Byron himself was attacked for "lewdness and impiety." Byron's poem ridicules Southey and treats with irreverent humor the subject of the earlier work, the entry of King George III, recently dead, into Heaven. The publisher of *The Vision of Judgment* was fined as a result of this satirical treatment of the former king's death.

Vision of Piers Plowman. See PIERS PLOWMAN.

Vision of Sir Launfal, The. A long poem (1848) by James Russell LOWELL. See also under LAUNFAL, SIR.

Vita Nuova, La (*It.,* **The New Life**). A famous work by DANTE Alighieri, written about 1291. In prose, lyric poems, and sonnets, it celebrates the intensely spiritual love of Dante for his lady BEATRICE, whom he worshiped from afar until her death. *La Vita Nuova* is one of the notable landmarks in the tradition which extended from the medieval convention of COURTLY LOVE and the TROUBADOR poets of Provence, through the Italian school of DOLCE STIL NUOVO and the SONNETS of PETRARCH, to the sonnet sequences of Elizabethan England.

Vitellius, Aulus (15–69 A.D.). Roman general, proclaimed emperor (January–December 69) by his troops. Opposed by VESPASIAN. Defeated and killed.

Vitruvius, Pollio Marcus (*fl. ca.* 40 B.C.). Roman architect, author of *De Architectura* (10 books), the only classical work on architecture which has come down to us.

Vittoria. A novel by George MEREDITH (1866). See SANDRA BELLONI.

Vittoria Corombona. Subtitle of *The White Devil* (ca. 1610) by John WEBSTER.

Vitus, St. See under SAINTS.

Vivaldi, Fulvia. The heroine of Edith Wharton's VALLEY OF DECISION.

viva voce (*Lat.,* "with the living voice"). Orally; by word of mouth. A *viva voce* examination is one in which the respondent answers by word of mouth.

Vivian Grey. A novel by DISRAELI (1827), chiefly concerning an intrigue which the very young, gay and talented Vivian Grey persuades the Marquess of Carabas to support against his own government. Although Vivian manages to control the Marquess through his stupidity and vanity, the plot fails because of a woman's double-dealing, and the young hero is involved in a duel, kills his opponent, and is compelled to go abroad, where he meets with sundry adventures which conclude the book. An intriguer of the intriguers, now in support of Vivian, now against him, is the clever and ruthless Mrs. Felix Lorraine, who ends by attempting to poison him. The character of Mrs. Lorraine is said to have been drawn, in part, from Lady Caroline LAMB, and Vivian Grey has usually been regarded, whether rightly or not, as a self-portrait.

Viviani, Emilia. An Italian woman, one of the many to whom P. B. SHELLEY enjoyed "Platonic" attachment during his career.

Vivien. An enchantress of the Arthurian romances, called also *Nimuë* and, because she lived in a palace in the middle of a magic lake, usually identified with *the Lady of the Lake*. It was here that she brought up LAUNCELOT, hence called *Launcelot of the Lake*. King Arthur's famous sword Excalibur was her gift. She is MERLIN's mistress, and at last causes his downfall by entrapping him in a hawthorn bush from which it is impossible for her to release him or for him to free himself. The motive of this act varies in different versions of the legend, from curiosity to sheer malice.

In Tennyson's IDYLLS she appears as a wily wanton who "hated all the knights." She tries to seduce "the blameless king," and does seduce Merlin, who, "overtalked and overworn, told her his secret charm":

> The which if any wrought on anyone
> With woven paces and with waving arms,
> The man so wrought on ever seemed to lie
> Closed in the four walls of a hollow tower,
> From which was no escape for evermore.
> *Vivien*

Having obtained this secret, the wanton "put forth the charm," and in the hollow oak lay Merlin as one dead, "lost to life, and use and name, and fame."

Vizetelly, Frank Horace (1864–1938). American lexicographer; editor (1914–1938) of Funk & Wagnalls *Standard Dictionary;* author of many books on the English language.

Vlaminck, Maurice de (1876–). French painter, identified with the Fauvists.

Vogel, Henriette. See KLEIST, BERND HEINRICH WILHELM VON.

Vogelweide, Walther von der, see WALTHER VON DER VOGELWEIDE.

Vogler, Abt. See ABT VOGLER.

Voisin, Gabriel (1880–). French pioneer manufacturer of airplanes.

Volapük. A language intended for universal use, invented about 1879 by Johann Martin Schleyer (1831–1912), a German priest of Konstanz, Baden. The name is formed by combining two of his manufactured words, *vol,* "the world," and *pük,* speech. Volapük is an ingeniously simplified form of English, containing no sound or sound combination which Schleyer believed would present difficulties for some ethnic group somewhere in the world.

Volkov, Fëdor Grigorievich (1729–1763). Russian actor who organized (1755) the first company of actors in his country and, by command of the Czarina, established the Moscow Theater (1756).

Vollar, Nettie. A leading character in Hergesheimer's JAVA HEAD.

Vollmer, Lula. American dramatist from North Carolina. Author of *Sunup* (1923); *The Shame Woman* (1923); etc.; radio serials; and short stories.

Volpone or The Fox. A comedy by Ben JONSON (1606). Volpone, a rich Venetian nobleman, without children, pretends to be dying, in order to draw gifts from those who pay court to him under the expectation of becoming his heirs. Mosca, his knavish confederate, persuades each in turn that he is named for the inheritance, and by this means exacts many a costly present. At the end, Volpone is betrayed, his property forfeited, and he is sentenced to lie in the worst hospital in all Venice.

Volscius, Prince. In the Duke of Buckingham's comedy *The Rehearsal* (1671), a military hero, who falls in love with the fair Parthenope and disputes with Prince Prettyman upon the superiority of his sweetheart to Cloris, whom Prince Prettyman sighs for.

> Why, this is worse than Prince Volscius in love!—Sir W. Scott.
>
> Oh, be merry, by all means. Prince Volscius in love! Ha, ha, ha!—Congreve, *The Double Dealer* (1694).

Volstead Act. An act passed by the United States Congress on October 28, 1919, providing for enforcement of the Eighteenth Amendment (national prohibition), through the Commissioner of Internal Revenue. See also PROHIBITION.

Völsunga Saga. The Scandinavian prose form of the German epic poem, the NIBELUNGENLIED. The general outlines of the two stories are the same, but names and details vary. The hero, Sigurd (see SIEGFRIED) is brought up by Regin the Smith and at his instigation kills the dragon Fafner. He rides through flames to the sleeping Valkyr maiden Brynhild (see BRUNHILD), marries her, leaves her in search of adventure, and under the influence of a love-potion given him in the hall of the Nibelungs, marries Gudrun (the KRIEMHILD of the *Nibelungenlied*) and aids her brother Gunnar (see GUNTHER) to secure Brynhild as his wife. In jealous fury Brynhild persuades Gudrun's brother Guttorm to kill Sigurd, and then dies herself on his funeral pyre. Gudrun now marries Atli (the Attila of history and the ETZEL of the *Nibelungenlied*), and when she has secured vengeance on her enemies, sets fire to the house and kills Atli.

William MORRIS retold the *Völsunga Saga* in his poetic *Lay of the Völsung and the Fall of the Niblung* (1877) and Wagner drew largely upon it for the four operas of his RING DES NIBELUNGEN.

Volta, Count **Alessandro** (1745–1827). Italian physicist; pioneered in electricity. The electrical unit *volt* is named after him.

Voltaire. Pseudonym of **François Marie Arouet** (1694–1778). French poet, dramatist, satirist, historian, and philosopher, famous for his skepticism, his enmity to organized religion, fanaticism, intolerance, and superstition (attacked under the slogan *Écrasons l'infâme!*), his biting wit and his prejudices, his personal vigor in spite of chronic ill health, his clever and swiftly moving philosophic tales, and his contributions to the objective study of history. His dramatic works, chiefly neo-classical in form, include *Oedipe* (1718); *Zaïre* (see ZARA; 1732); *Alzire* (1736); *Mahomet, ou le Fanatisme* (1742); *Mérope* (1743); *Sémiramis* (1748); *L'Orphelin de la Chine.* Among his polemic and philosophic writings are *Lettres sur les Anglais,* attacking what he regarded as Shakespeare's faulty dramatic construction and poor taste, while praising other aspects of English life and thought; *Lettres Philosophiques* (1734); *Traité de Métaphysique; Epitre à Uranie* and *Discours en Vers sur l'Homme* (1738), philosophical poems; *Poème sur le Désastre de Lisbonne; Poème sur la Loi naturelle; Traité sur la Tolérance; Dictionnaire Philosophique Portatif* (1764); *Sermon des Cinquante; Le Philosophe ignorant* (1766). Of his historical works, the greatest are considered to be *Histoire de Charles XII* (1731); *Le Siècle de Louis XIV* (1751); *Essai sur les Moeurs et l'Esprit des Nations* (1753–1756), regarded as the first history of civilization; *Le Pyrrhonisme de l'Histoire* (1768). The best-known of his philosophic tales, which became the most popular of his works in later times, are *Le Monde Comme il va;* ZADIG (1748); *Micromegas* (1752), often compared to *Gulliver's Travels* (see GULLIVER, LEMUEL); *L'Ingénu* (1757); CANDIDE (1759), the most famous of all his works. Outstanding among his poetry are *La Henriade* (1728–1730), an epic on the period of Henry IV; *Le Temple de Goût* (1733), a satire believed to have been inspired by Pope's DUNCIAD; and *La Pucelle* (1762), a burlesque on Joan of Arc. He also wrote numerous light and witty verses on a variety of occasions.

Voltaire, one of the most famous and influential figures in the history of thought, lived a turbulent life, constantly being arrested and exiled because of his unorthodox ideas, displeasing to political and religious authority of his time, and his merciless satire. He first made his reputation as a dramatist, but after being beaten and imprisoned by an offended noble, he went to England for a time. There he came under the influence of POPE and SWIFT, whom he met, of the ideas of NEWTON and LOCKE, and of English political ideals; as a result of this visit, he introduced the plays of Shakespeare into France on his return, although in time he came to regard Shakespeare's influence on the drama as deplorable. Later Voltaire was banished again from France because of his *Lettres Philosophiques* and took refuge first with Mme du CHÂTELET at CIREY and then in Holland. After a correspondence with Frederick the Great, the author was invited to Prussia, where he stayed at the monarch's court for three years until, in 1753, the two men became estranged. Then Voltaire retired to FERNEY, and for nearly all the rest of his life he lived there at ease, writing treatises which violently denounced the cases of intolerance and injustice that came to his attention, quarreling with J. J. ROUSSEAU, the Roman Catholic Church, and CALVINISM, and winning fame all over Europe. When he returned once more to Paris, just before his death, he was honored as a great man and entertained so sumptuously that it is said he died of exhaustion. In 1791, after the French Revolution, on which he had an important influence, his ashes were placed in the Pantheon.

The name *Voltaire* is simply an anagram of Arouet L. I. (*le jeune*).

the German Voltaire. Johann Wolfgang von Goethe (1749–1838); Christoph Martin Wieland (1733–1813).

the Polish Voltaire. Ignatius Krasicki (1774–1801).

Volund. A Scandinavian form of WAYLAND.

Voluntaries. A poem by Ralph Waldo EMERSON, first published (1863) in the *Atlantic Monthly.* It was written in honor of Colonel Robert G. Shaw who led a Negro regiment in the Civil War. See also ODE IN TIME OF HESITATION.

Vonnoh, Robert William (1858–1933). American portrait painter. His wife, **Bessie Potter Vonnoh** (1872–), is a well-known American sculptor and member of the National Institute of Arts and Letters.

Voodoo or **Voodooism.** A degraded system of magic and witchcraft which includes snake-worship and, in its extreme forms, human sacrifices and cannibalism, said to be a relic of African barbarism and still practiced by Creoles and Negroes in Haiti and other parts of the West Indies and southern American states.

> "BLOOD" screamed the whistles and the fifes of the warriors,
> "BLOOD" screamed the skull-faced lean witch-doctors,
> "Whirl ye the deadly voo-doo rattle."
> Vachel Lindsay, *The Congo.*

The name is thought to have been first given to it by missionaries from Fr. *Vaudois,* a Waldensian, as these were accused of sorcery; but Sir Richard Burton derived it from *vodun,* a dialect form of Ashanti *obosum,* a fetish or tutelary spirit.

Voroshilov, Kliment Efremovich (1881–). Russian soldier. Having commanded a Soviet army at the end of World War I, he reorganized the Russian general staff and developed the tanks and planes of the Soviet forces. In 1941, at the beginning of Russia's war with Germany, he commanded on the Leningrad front and, with ZHUKOV, broke the siege of Leningrad (1943).

Vorse, Mary Heaton. American liberal writer. *Men and Steel* (1921); *Labor's New Millions* (1938); *Time and the Town* (1942); etc.

Vortex, The. A play (1925) by Noel COWARD, about a neurotic son and mother.

Vox Clamantis. A long poem in Latin, partly in allegory, by John Gower, written about 1382, dealing mainly with the Peasants' Revolt of 1381. The rebellious peasants are presented in terms of animals and monsters, including asses, oxen, dogs, and swine, who rise against the nobles, capture London, and are finally put down. This is all told vividly as a dream experienced by the poet; the remainder of the poem is concerned with a discussion of the evils and corruptions of society at the time, in which the faults and duties of the knights, the peasants, the craftsmen and merchants, the lawyers, and finally the King himself, are considered in turn.

vox populi vox Dei (*Lat.*). The voice of the people is the voice of God.

Voyage of Bran, The. An early Irish tale, considered to have been written in the 7th century, dealing with a voyage made by the hero Bran, son of Febal, to the "Happy Otherworld," located on an island far out in the ocean. Bran and his band have a number of adventures on their way to the island, including a sojourn in the Land of Women. When the travelers finally reach Ireland again, they find they have been forgotten. See also Earthly Paradise, The; *St. Brendan,* under saints.

Voynich, Ethel Lillian Boole (1864–). English novelist and translator from the Russian. Her best-known novel is *The Gadfly* (1897).

Voysey Inheritance, The. A drama (1905) by Harley Granville-Barker, concerning financial ethics.

Vronski, Count. In Tolstoi's Anna Karénina, the young officer who becomes Anna's lover.

Vulcan. A son of Jupiter and Juno, god of fire and the working of metals, and patron of handicraftsmen in Roman mythology, identified with the Greek Hephaestus, and called also Mulciber, i.e., "the softener."

His workshop was on Mount Etna, where the Cyclops assisted him in forging thunderbolts for Jove. It is said that he took the part of Juno against Jupiter, and Jupiter hurled him out of heaven. He was nine days in falling, and at last was picked up, half dead and with one leg broken, by the fishermen of the island of Lemnos. It was he who, with the stroke of an axe, delivered Minerva from the head of Jupiter. Venus was his wife, and in consequence of her amour with Mars he came to be regarded as the special patron of cuckolds.

Vulcan's badge. The badge of cuckoldom.

Vulgar Errors. The title of the best-known treatise by Sir Thomas Browne, published in 1646.

Vulgate, the. The Latin translation of the Bible, made about 385–405 by St. Jerome (see under saints), still used, with some modifications, as the authorized version by Roman Catholics.

Vulpius, Christiane. Mistress of Goethe from 1789 to 1806, in the latter year finally becoming his wife. She bore the poet four children.

V. V.'s Eyes. A novel by Henry Sydnor Harrison (*Am.,* 1913). The hero, known as "V.V.," is an utterly unworldly social reformer, and the heroine is a frivolous and selfish society girl who through his influence becomes interested in more worth-while things.

Vye, Eustacia. Heroine of Hardy's Return of the Native.

W

Waals, Johannes Diderik van der (1837–1923). Dutch physicist, awarded the Nobel prize for physics in 1910.

Wace. Often erroneously **Robert Wace.** Anglo-Norman poet of the twelfth century. He wrote two verse chronicles in Norman French, *Roman de Brut* and *Roman de Rou.*

Wacht am Rhein, Die (The Watch on the Rhine). A German national song, written (1840) by Max Schneckenburger, set to music by Karl Wilhelm (1854).

Wackles, Mrs. and **the Misses.** In Dickens' OLD CURIOSITY SHOP, keepers of a "Ladies' Seminary at Chelsea." English grammar, composition, geography and the use of dumb-bells are taught by Miss Melissa Wackles; writing, arithmetic, dancing, music and general fascination by Miss Sophy Wackles; needlework, marking, and samplery by Miss Jane Wackles; corporal punishment and domestic duties by Mrs. Wackles.

Waddell, Helen (1889–). Irish scholar and student of medieval literature. She has translated Latin and Chinese lyrics and is the author of *The Wandering Scholars* (1927); the novel *Peter Abelard* (1933); and *The Desert Fathers* (1936).

Waddington, Mr. The hero of May Sinclair's novel MR. WADDINGTON OF WYCK.

Wade, Miss. In Dickens' LITTLE DORRIT, a handsome young woman who looks at every act of kindness, benevolence, and charity with a jaundiced eye and attributes it to a vile motive. Twice she is loved—in one case she jilted her lover, in the other she was herself jilted. The man in the latter case was Henry Gowan, who has married Pet, the daughter of Mr. Meagles, and in consequence of this marriage Miss Wade hates Gowan, his wife, the Meagleses, and all their friends. She entices Tattycoram away from Mr. Meagles, and the two young women live together for a time, nursing their hatred of man to keep it warm.

Wadman, Widow. In Sterne's TRISTRAM SHANDY, a comely widow, who wishes to secure UNCLE TOBY for her second husband. Among other wiles, she pretends to have something in her eye, and gets Uncle Toby to look at it. As the kind-hearted hero of Namur does so, the gentle widow gradually places her face nearer and nearer the Captain's mouth, in the hope that he will kiss and propose.

wager of battle, trial of battle. The settling of any form of dispute by personal combat. The custom goes back to early Teutonic times. William the Conqueror gave it legal status in England where it was not officially abolished before 1818.

Wagg, Mr. A literary man in Thackeray's PENDENNIS, a professional humorist.

Wagnalls, Adam Willis (1843–1924). American publisher, one of the original founders and president of the publishing house of Funk & Wagnalls Co.

Wagner. The faithful servant and constant companion of FAUST, in Marlowe's drama called *The Life and Death of Dr. Faustus* (1589), in Goethe's *Faust* (1798) and in Gounod's opera *Faust* (1859).

> Wagner is a type of the pedant. He sacrifices himself to books as Faust does to knowledge . . . the dust of folios is his element, parchment the source of his inspiration. . . . He is one of those who, in the presence of Niagara, would vex you with questions about arrow-headed inscriptions . . . or the origin of the Pelasgi.—Lewes.

Wagner, Richard (1813–1883). German musician and author. His major works, though often called operas, were designed as *Gesammtkunstwerke* ("works of all-arts-in-one") with poetry, music, dance, etc., collaborating under the authorship of one creative genius. Posterity has decided that Wagner was (first) a great musician, (second) a second-rate poet, and (third) a man of various avocations. His "music dramas" (the term is his) stress characterization and continuity of action, they work with LEITMOTIVS and endless melodies, and abandon the bravura and stilted artifice of the operatic tradition. The subject matter of most of his works is drawn from Teutonic and German mythology or history. Wagner has been both praised and attacked as an exponent of heroic or tin-and-brass nationalism. Nietzsche, who had admired him greatly, came to despise him ferociously. For the performance of his works he founded the Festspielhaus (completed 1876), at Bayreuth.

His major work is DER RING DES NIBELUNGEN, based on the *Nibelungenlied,* the *Völsunga Saga,* and the *Edda,* and comprising an introduction, *Das Rheingold* (1st performance, 1869), and 3 parts: *Die Walküre* (1st performance, 1870); *Siegfried* (1st performance, 1876); and *Götterdämmerung* (1st performance, 1876). His only comedy, *Die Meistersinger von Nürnberg* (1st performance, 1868), is a flawless masterpiece. It is performed, in Europe as well as in the U.S., more often than any of his other works.

His wife, **Cosima Wagner,** *née* **Liszt** (1837–1930), a daughter of Franz LISZT, was instrumental in securing funds for the establishment of the Bayreuther Festspielhaus. Their son, **Siegfried Wagner** (1869–1930), also a musician, was conductor of his father's works at Bayreuth.

Wagner, Robert Ferdinand (1877–). German-born lawyer and legislator in the U.S. Justice of the supreme court of New York (1919–1926); U.S. senator (from 1927). He sponsored the Wagner Act (1935) which created the National Labor Relations Board. His consistently progressive legislation has made him an admired champion of labor.

Wagon Boy, the. The American orator and politician, Thomas Corwin (1794–1865) was so called from his youthful experience of bringing a wagon-load of supplies to General W. H. Harrison during a war against the Indians.

Wahabites. A Mohammedan sect, whose object is to bring back the doctrines and observances of Islam to the literal precepts of the *Koran;* so called from the founder, Ibn Abdul Wahab (died 1787).

Wailing Wall. A famous place in Jerusalem where, according to tradition, the orthodox Jews gathered to lament the fall of the Jewish nation. At times the wall, which is near the temple of Solomon, now the Mosque of Omar, has been the scene of rioting between the Jews and the Mohammedans.

Wain. Short for **Charles'** or **Charles's Wain,** that is, the wagon of Charlemagne. The constellation *Dipper* or *Ursa Major.* Also called *Bear.*

Wainamöinen. The hero of the KALEVALA, the Orpheus of Finnish mythology.

Wainwright, Jonathan Mayhew (1792–1854). Protestant Episcopal clergyman and bishop of New York (1852). His son, **Jonathan Mayhew Wainwright** (1821–1863), a naval officer in the Civil War, fought with Farragut and Porter on the Mississippi. His grandson, **Jonathan Mayhew Wainwright** (1883–), an officer in the U.S. army, commanded the northern front in the Philippines after the Japanese invasion (December, 1941); he followed MacArthur as commander in chief, and was made lieutenant general (1942); he defended Bataan and Corregidor until compelled to surrender (May, 1942). Cf. *General Wainwright's Story* by General Jonathan M. Wainwright, edited by Robert Considine (1946).

Wait, James. The "nigger" of Conrad's NIGGER OF THE NARCISSUS.

Waiting for Lefty. A play by Clifford ODETS (1935), dealing with a meeting of a cab-drivers' union at which it is to be decided whether or not a strike is to be called. While the members wait for the arrival of Lefty Costello, a particularly popular taximan, the background of the labor difficulties is presented in dramatic form, in terms of injustice and frustration in the lives of the drivers. Eventually word arrives that Lefty has been killed, and the members of the committee, infuriated, vote to call the strike. *Waiting for Lefty* was one of the best-known of the proletarian plays of the 1930's. See PROLETARIAN LITERATURE.

Wakefield Master, the. Conjectural author of the leading works in the TOWNELEY cycle of mystery and miracle plays, thought to have been a man of humble birth, though well educated, and probably a secular priest, flourishing about the middle of the 15th century; so called because internal evidence in the plays suggests they were performed by the local guilds of Wakefield, in southern Yorkshire. The plays attributed to the Wakefield Master include *Noah, Herod, The Way of the Cross,* and the *First* and SECOND SHEPHERD'S PLAY. Because of their humor, the unknown author has been called by some scholars the "first great comic dramatist in English literature."

Wakem, Philip. In George Eliot's MILL ON THE FLOSS, a brilliant but sensitive cripple, in love with Maggie TULLIVER.

Wald, Lillian D. (1867–1940). American social worker. Founded Henry Street Settlement in New York City (1893) with the world's first public school nursing system (1902) and obtained playgrounds for children in New York slums. Vice-president, American Association for Labor Legislation. Author of *The House on Henry Street* (1915); *Windows on Henry Street* (1935); etc.

Waldegrave, Henry. The hero of Campbell's GERTRUDE OF WYOMING.

Walden, or Life in the Woods. The chief work of Henry THOREAU (1854). It is a volume telling of his simple, healthy, hermit-like life on the shores of Walden Pond, where he built himself a hut, cultivated a garden and lived for years on an annual outlay of eight dollars. The book is noted for its nature descriptions.

Waldensians or **Waldenses** (also called the **Vaudois).** Followers of Peter Waldo of Lyons, who began a reform movement in the Church about 1170. They threw off the authority of the Pope, bishops, and all clergy, appointed lay-preachers (women among them), rejected infant baptism and many other rites, and made themselves so obnoxious to the ecclesiastical powers that they met with considerable persecution. This they survived, and their descendants in doctrine still exist, principally in the Alpine valleys of Dauphiné, Provence, and Piedmont.

Waldo. The hero of Olive Schreiner's STORY OF AN AFRICAN FARM.

Waldseemüller or **Waltzemüller, Martin.** Called himself (in pseudo-Greek) **Hylacomylus** or **Ilacomilus** (1470?–?1518). German cartographer. In his map of the world in 12 sheets, *Cosmographiae Introductio* (1507), he was the first to use the term *America* for the New World. See also VESPUCCI.

Wales, The Prince of. The popular story is that the title arose thus: When Edward I subdued Wales, he promised the Welsh, if they would lay down their arms, that he would give them a native prince who could not speak a word of English. His queen (Eleanor) having given birth to a son in Wales, the new-born child was entitled Edward, Prince of Wales, and ever since then the eldest son of the British sovereign has retained the title. The facts, however, are that Edward I obtained the submission of the Welsh in 1276; his eldest son, afterwards Edward II, was born at Carnarvon in 1284, and it was not till 1301 that he was created Prince of Wales.

Waley, Arthur David. Original surname **Schloss.** Assistant curator of prints and drawings in the British Museum and translator from the Chinese and Japanese. With his English version (1925 ff.) of Lady MURASAKI's *Tale of Genji* he made accessible to Western readers "the oldest novel [and one of the finest] in the world."

Walhalla, see VALHALLA.

Walker.

Hookey Walker! A derisive exclamation meaning *Nonsense! Incredible!* used when hearing a "tall story" or some statement that cannot be trusted. The legend is that John Walker was an outdoor clerk at Longman, Clementi and Company's, Cheapside, and was noted for his eagle nose, which gained him the nickname of *Old Hookey.* His office was to keep the workmen to their work, or report them to the principals. Of course it was the interest of the employees to throw discredit on Walker's reports, and the poor old man was so badgered and ridiculed that the firm found it politic to abolish the office.

to go by Walker's bus. To walk. Similar expressions are, "To go by the Marrowbone stage," "To ride Shanks' pony."

Walker, John Brisben (1847–1931). American publisher and journalist. Owner and editor (1889–1905) of the *Cosmopolitan Magazine.*

Walker, Mary Edward (1832–1919). American doctor. Practiced medicine in New York; served with the Union army (1861–1865); practiced in Washington, D.C. (from 1865). She habitually wore male attire and championed woman's rights vociferously.

Walker, Stuart (1888–1941). American playwright and producer of plays; originated the "Portmanteau Theater" and wrote 2 series of *Portmanteau Plays* (1917; 1919). Producer at Paramount (from 1936).

Walker, William (1824–1860). American pirate and filibuster, who made himself president of a republic in Southern California. He landed in Nicaragua and proclaimed himself president (1856). He got into trouble with Cornelius VANDERBILT (1857), who caused a coalition of Central American powers to oust him (1857). He fled to the U.S., but was arrested, turned over to the authorities of Honduras, and shot. Before that he had written a good book on *The War in Nicaragua* (1860).

Walking Stewart. The nickname of John Stewart (d. 1822), an English traveler, who traveled on foot through Hindustan, Persia, Nubia, Abyssinia, the Arabian Desert, Europe, and the United States. He is described as

> a most interesting man, . . . eloquent in conversation, contemplative . . . and crazy beyond all reach of helebore, . . . yet sublime and divinely benignant in his visionariness. This man, as a pedestrian traveler, had seen more of the earth's surface . . . than any man before or since.—De Quincey.

Walküre, Die (The Valkyrie). One of the four operas of Wagner's RING DES NIBELUNGEN.

Wallace, Alfred Russel (1823–1913). English naturalist and traveler. His independent formulation of a theory of evolution by natural selection is his most important contribution to science. His paper, *On the Tendency of Varieties to Depart Indefinitely from the Original Type,* was read before the Linnaean Society the same day as Darwin's paper (July 1, 1858). Among his other writings is a valuable description of a trip to the Amazon, *Travels on the Amazon and the Rio Negro* (1853).

Wallace, Edgar (1875–1932). English writer of sensational fiction and plays. *Sanders of the River* (1930); *On the Spot* (1931).

Wallace, Henry Agard (1888–). U.S. secretary of agriculture (1933–1940) and vice-president of the U.S. (1941–1945). Head of the Economic Defense Board and of the Priorities Board (from 1941) and secretary of commerce (from 1945). Among the books he has written are *Agricultural Prices* (1920); *New Frontiers* (1934); *Technology, Corporations, and the General Welfare* (1937); *The American Choice* (1940); *Sixty Million Jobs* (1945); etc. Editor of the NEW REPUBLIC (1946–1947). Candidate for president (1948), leading his own Third party.

Wallace, Lewis. Known as **Lew Wallace** (1827–1905). American lawyer, army officer, and novelist; author of best-selling romances, including THE FAIR GOD (1873); BEN HUR; *A Tale of the Christ* (1880); and THE PRINCE OF INDIA (1893).

Wallace, Sir **William** (1272?–1305). Known as "the Hammer and Scourge of England." One of the national heroes of Scotland, associated with Robert BRUCE.

Wallack, Henry John (1790–1870). English actor and head of a famous English theatrical family. His nephew, **Lester Wallack** (1820–1888), was a dramatist and actor, who became manager of Wallack's Theater in New York City (1861–1887). His *Memories of Fifty*

Years (1889) are important source material for the theater historian.

Wallas, Graham (1858–1932). English economist and teacher. *The Great Society* (1914); *The Art of Thought* (1926); etc. Among his disciples in the U.S. is Walter LIPPMANN.

Wallenstein. A historic drama by SCHILLER (1799–1800), in three divisions: *Wallenstein's Camp,* the prologue; *The Piccolomini* in five acts; and *Wallenstein's Death* in five acts. The hero is Count Albrecht von Wallenstein (1583–1634), commander of the forces of the German emperor during the Thirty Years' War.

Waller, Edmund (1606–1687). English poet, known for the smoothness and harmony of his verse, which was highly praised by John DRYDEN. Volumes of his poems were published in 1645, 1664, 1668, and 1686. During the Civil War, Waller participated in a Royalist plot and was fined and banished from England as a result, later being allowed to return, however. During the Commonwealth he wrote a panegyric on Oliver CROMWELL, and in the Restoration period he wrote verse celebrating Charles II.

wallflowers. At a dance or party, girls who have no partners and who sit or stand near the walls.

Wallingford, Get-Rich-Quick. An engaging schemer and promoter who was the hero of many stories by George Randolph CHESTER; hence, any clever, unscrupulous schemer.

Wall Street. A term for American business and moneyed interests, from the street in New York City where the financial operations of the country are centered.

Waln, Nora (1895–). American writer. Her book on Germany, *Reaching for the Stars* (1939), was based on personal experiences. Her previous publication, *The House of Exile* (1933) was similarly the fruit of her sojourn in China.

Walpole, Horace. 4th Earl of **Orford** (1717–1797). English politician and author, best known for his CASTLE OF OTRANTO (1764), one of the outstanding examples of the Gothic novel. His letters, several volumes of which were published after his death, are also well known, and other works by him include *Anecdotes of Painting in England* (1762–1771); *Catalogue of Engravers in England* (1763); and *Historic Doubts on Richard III* (1768). Walpole traveled a good deal in France and Italy, and was a Member of Parliament from 1741 to 1767. At Strawberry Hill, in Twickenham, he took up residence in a house made to resemble "a little Gothic castle" and set up a printing press on which he printed several of his own works. He was the son of Sir Robert WALPOLE.

Walpole, Sir **Hugh Seymour** (1884–1941). English novelist, born in New Zealand, author of best-selling novels dealing chiefly with middle- and upper-class English life. His books include *The Wooden Horse* (1909); *Maradick at Forty* (1910); *Mr. Perrin and Mr. Traill* (1911); *The Prelude to Adventure* (1912); *Fortitude* (1913), his best-known work; *The Duchess of Wrexe* (1914); *The Golden Scarecrow* (1915); *The Dark Forest* (1916); *The Green Mirror* (1918); *The Secret City* (1919); *Jeremy* (1919), *Jeremy and Hamlet* (1923), and *Jeremy at Crale* (1927); *The Captives* (1920); *The Thirteen Travelers* (1921); *The Cathedral* (1922); *The Young Enchanted* (1922); *The Old Ladies* (1924); *Portrait of a Man with Red Hair* (1925); *Harmer John* (1926); *Wintersmoon* (1928); *The Silver Thorn* (1928); *Farthing Hall* (1929), written with J. B. PRIESTLEY; *Hans Frost* (1929); *Rogue Herries* (1930), *Judith Paris* (1931), *The Fortress* (1932), and *Vanessa* (1933), a historical tetralogy; *Above the Dark Tumult* (1931); *All Souls' Night* (1933), a collection of stories; *Captain Nicholas* (1934); *The Inquisitor* (1935); *A Prayer for My Son* (1936); *John Cornelius* (1937); *The Joyful Delaneys* (1938); *The Haxtons* (1939), a play; *The Sea Tower* (1939); *Roman Fountain* (1940); *The Bright Pavilions* (1940); *The Blind Man's House* (1941); *The Killer and the Slain* (1942); *Katherine Christian* (1943), an unfinished novel.

Walpole, Sir **Robert.** 1st Earl of **Orford** (1676–1745). A leader of the Whig party in England. Secretary of war (1708–1710); treasurer of the navy (1710–1711); twice prime minister and chancellor of the exchequer. He stood for peace between France, England, and Spain. He studied especially finance and commerce, and laid the basis for free trade. Father of Horace WALPOLE.

Walpurgis Night (*Ger.* **Walpurgisnacht).** The night preceding May 1, the feast of St. Walburga (710?–777), an English missionary nun who aided St. Boniface in Germany. According to German legend, Walpurgis Night is the time of the WITCHES' SABBATH on the Brocken in the Harz Mountains. In Goethe's *Faust* there is a famous Walpurgis Night.

Walsh, Maurice (1879–). Irish novelist. His *The Key Above the Door* (1923) sold a hundred thousand copies.

Walsh, Thomas (1871–1928). American poet who studied under Brander MATTHEWS and George Edward WOODBERRY. *The Prison Ships and Other Poems* (1909); *The Pilgrim Kings: Greco, Goya and Other Poems of Spain* (1915); *Gardens Overseas and Other Poems* (1918); *Don Folquet and Other Poems* (1920). Walsh was a great lover of old Spanish literature and compiled, in English, a well-known

Hispanic Anthology. Also *The Catholic Anthology*.

Walsingham, Sir **Francis** (1530?–1590). English statesman; secretary of state (1573–1590) to Queen Elizabeth. He had Mary Queen of Scots convicted and executed, and warned Queen Elizabeth about the Spanish Armada. His son-in-law was Sir Philip SIDNEY.

Walter, André. An autobiographical character of André GIDE, the hero of Gide's first work, *Les Cahiers d'André Walter* (*The Notebooks of André Walter;* 1891). This book tells in early fictional form the story presented in the author's autobiography, *Si le Grain ne Meurt,* translated as *If It Die,* and again in L'IMMORALISTE. *The Notebooks* is purportedly the posthumously published journal of André, who loves his cousin Emmanuèle, although she is already married and has no suspicion of the emotions she has inspired. André's mother dies, warning the youth to be resigned to the frustration of his love, Emmanuèle, too, dies, and André, stricken with brain fever as a result of his sorrow, finally goes to his grave also. Gide later repudiated the book "except as a testimony of the troubled mysticism of my youth."

Walter, Bruno. Original surname **Schlesinger** (1876–). Famous conductor of opera and symphony in Vienna, Munich, and Berlin. He became guest conductor in New York (1922–1926; 1932–1935), and also in London. Resident of the U.S. (since 1939) as guest conductor of the New York Philharmonic, the Metropolitan Opera Company, the National Broadcasting Company, etc.

Walter, Eugene (1874–1941). American dramatist. His best-known plays are *Paid in Full* and *The Easiest Way* (both 1908). He also made plays of several of the novels of John Fox Jr., as *The Trail of the Lonesome Pine* (1912) and *The Little Shepherd of Kingdom Come* (1916).

Walter, John (1739–1812). English journalist and publisher. He purchased the patents of an invention (called "logotype") which permitted typesetting in units of words rather than of letters. His newspaper, *The Daily Universal Register* (founded in 1785), became the London *Times* (1788).

Walter, Lucy. Known as Mrs. **Barlow** (1630?–1658). Mistress of Charles II (1648–1651) and mother by him of the Duke of MONMOUTH.

Walter of Evesham or **Walter Odington** (*fl.* 1230). English Benedictine monk. Author of *De Speculatione Musices,* an important compendium of musical theory of the Middle Ages.

Walter or **Walther von Stolzing.** In Wagner's opera, DIE MEISTERSINGER, the successful suitor of Eva Pogner.

Walters or **Waters, Childe,** see CHILDE WATERS.

Walther von der Vogelweide (1170?–?1230). Middle High German lyric poet and MINNESINGER, attached to the Viennese court and later leading the life of a wandering minstrel. He is considered the greatest German poet of the Middle Ages, principally because he succeeded in either breaking the petrified forms of the lyrical (Provençal) tradition or filling them with a passionately personal content. He is the first medieval poet whose work is not limited to conventional love lyrics but serves also as a vehicle for the author's political ideals and gives expression to his religious fervor. The German national song, *Deutschland Deutschland über alles,* is a rather sorry nineteenth-century adaptation of a song about love of country and friendship by Walter von der Vogelweide. He appears as contestant for the singer crown at the Wartburg in Wagner's opera TANNHÄUSER.

Walton, Eda Lou. American poet and critic. Author of *Dawn Boy: Blackfeet and Navajo Songs* (1926); *Jane Matthew and Other Poems* (1931); etc. Joint editor with George Anderson Kumler of *This Generation: A Selection of British and American Literature from 1914 to the Present,* to which each editor contributed a historical and critical essay.

Walton, Izaak (1593–1683). English prose-writer, best known for *The Compleat Angler* (1653), a discourse on the quiet pleasures of fishing, presented in the form of a conference among Piscator, the fisherman (or the author himself), Venator, the hunter, and Auceps, the falconer, during a five-day period of fishing. It is written in a simple, quiet, naïve style, and combines odd bits of learning with its pastoral wisdom. Walton followed the trade of ironmonger but in his youth was a close friend of John DONNE and BEN JONSON. He wrote a number of biographies of outstanding literary figures of his ages, his subjects including DONNE (1640), Sir Henry WOTTON (1651), Richard HOOKER (1665), George HERBERT (1670), and Robert Sanderson (1678).

Walton, Katherine. Heroine of W. G. Simms' novel KATHERINE WALTON and a leading character in his Revolutionary trilogy. **Colonel Walton** is a prominent figure in the same books.

Waltzing Matilda. An Australian song about a "swagman" or wanderer, very popular during World War II. Lines originally written by A. B. Paterson (1864–1941) and appearing in his *Collected Verse*.

Wamba. In Scott's IVANHOE, "the son of Witless," the jester of Cedric the Saxon of Rotherwood.

Wanderer, The. An Anglo-Saxon dramatic lyric of the early 8th century, expressing the lament of a warrior or bard who has lost his lord, his tribesmen, and his kinsmen in a defeat in battle and wanders about in search of a new tribal court to which he may attach himself, recalling at random as he does so the pleasures of his lost home and the sorrows he has recently suffered.

Wandering Jew, the. The central figure of a widespread medieval legend which tells how a Jew who refused to allow Christ to rest at his door while He was bearing His cross to Calvary, was condemned to wander over the face of the earth till the end of the world. The usual form of the legend says that he was Ahasuerus, a cobbler. The craftsman pushed him away, saying, "Get off! Away with you, away!" Our Lord replied, "Truly I go away, and that quickly, but tarry thou till I come."

Another tradition has it that the Wandering Jew was Kartaphilos (Cartaphilus); the doorkeper of the judgment hall in the service of Pontius Pilate. He struck our Lord as he led Him forth, saying, "Go on faster, Jesus"; whereupon the Man of Sorrows replied, "I am going, but thou shalt tarry till I come again" (*Chronicle of St. Albans Abbey;* 1228). The same *Chronicle,* continued by Matthew Paris, tells us that Kartaphilos was baptized by Ananias, and received the name of Joseph. At the end of every hundred years he falls into a trance, and wakes up a young man about thirty.

In German legend, he is associated with John Buttadaeus, seen at Antwerp in the 13th century, again in the 15th, and a third time in the 16th. His last appearance was in 1774 at Brussels. In the French version, he is named Isaac Laquedem or Lakedion. Another story has it that he was Salathiel ben Sadi, who appeared and disappeared towards the close of the 16th century, at Venice, in so sudden a manner as to attract the notice of all Europe; and another connects him with the WILD HUNTSMAN.

There is a ballad in Percy's *Reliques* called *The Wandering Jew;* and poems by Béranger and Quintet entitled *Ahasuerus,* and by Caroline Norton entitled *The Undying One,* deal with the legend. SHELLEY introduces Ahasuerus into *Queen Mab, The Revolt of Islam;* and his prose tale *The Assassin.*

In prose fiction, the Jew is the subject of Croly's *Salathiel* (1827) reprinted in 1900 as *Tarry Thou till I Come,* of Lew Wallace's PRINCE OF INDIA, and of the more famous romance by Eugene Sue entitled *The Wandering Jew* (*Le Juif errant;* 1845). In the latter, Ahasuerus and his half-sister Herodias, both eternal wanderers, find their chief interest in guiding the affairs of their descendants. The romance is episodic, but the principal events take place in the Paris of 1832 and the plot centers about the struggle between the Protestants and Catholics to control a large sum of money invested for seven heirs of Count Rennepont, a descendant of Herodias. The Jesuits, led by a shrewd and energetic little priest named Rodin, succeed in bringing six of the seven heirs to disaster and presenting the seventh, Gabriel Rennepont, a young Jesuit priest, as the only claimant for the inheritance, but their schemes are finally thwarted.

Wandering Willie. In Scott's REDGAUNTLET, the blind fiddler who tells the tale about Sir Robert Redgauntlet and his son Sir John.

Wandering Wood. The wood in Bk. i of Spenser's FAËRIE QUEENE, in which the RED CROSS KNIGHT and UNA stray. Una tries to persuade him to leave the wood, but he is self-willed. Error, in the form of a serpent, attacks him, but the knight severs her head from her body. The idea is that when Piety will not listen to Una or Truth, it is sure to get into *Wandering Wood,* where Error will attack it; but if it then listens to Truth it will slay Error.

Wantley, The Dragon of. An old story, preserved in PERCY'S *Reliques,* tells of this monster, which is slain by More of More Hall. He procures a suit of armor studded with spikes and kicks the Dragon in the mouth, where alone it is vulnerable. Percy says the Dragon is an overgrown, rascally attorney, who cheated some children of their estate, and was made to disgorge by one named More, who went against him, "armed with the spikes of the law," after which the attorney died of vexation. Wantley is Wharncliffe in Yorkshire.

war.

war baby. The child of a war bride, particularly an illegitimate child. The term was also applied to stocks in such commodities as airplanes, steel, chemicals, etc., which boomed in wartime.

war bride. A woman who marries a soldier in time of war or threatening war; also, a woman who becomes the mother of a soldier's child without the formality of marriage.

War and Peace. The most famous novel of Leo TOLSTOI (1865–1872), dealing with Russia and France at the time of Napoleon Bonaparte, giving an epic picture of the invasion of Russia by Napoleon and his army, and presenting the author's theories of history. During World War II, when Germany's invasion of Russia was an important feature in the news, *War and Peace* enjoyed renewed popularity in England and the U.S.

Warbeck, Perkin, see PERKIN WARBECK.

Warburg, James Paul (1896–). New York banker, descended from a family of German bankers. Financial adviser to the World Economic Conference in London (1933) and author of *The Money Muddle* (1934) and *Hell Bent for Election* (1935).

Warburton, Bartholomew Eliot George (1810–1852). Irish writer; author of *Memoirs of Prince Rupert and the Cavaliers* (1849) and other historical novels.

Warburton, William (1698–1779). English theologian. Friend of Alexander Pope and instrumental in persuading Pope to add a fourth book to his *Dunciad*. He was also Pope's literary executor (1744) and brought out an edition of his work (1751). His edition of Shakespeare (1747) was criticized severely for want of literary judgment. He was defeated in a literary controversy by Robert Lowth (1765) who attacked his arrogance and lack of scholarship.

Ward, Aaron Montgomery (1843–1913). American businessman whose firm, established with George Thorne, developed into the mail-order house of Montgomery Ward & Co.

Ward, Sir Adolphus William (1837–1924). English historian. Contributed largely to the *Dictionary of National Biography;* was editor of *Cambridge Modern History* (1902–1912) and co-editor of *Cambridge History of English Literature* (1907–1916).

Ward, Artemus. The *nom de plume* of the popular American humorist, Charles Farrar BROWNE. *Artemus Ward* was a wandering showman whom Browne created and whose story he retailed in the first person in the Cleveland *Plain Dealer* until his amusing adventures, his vagaries in spelling, and his shrewd observations on human nature made him a household character.

Ward, Edward (1667-1731). English satirist and keeper of a tavern. On making a trip to New England he wrote an unflattering account of the country and its people (1699). Author of *The London Spy* (1698–1709). Pope pilloried him in his *Dunciad*. Cf. the excellent account of his life and time, *Ned Ward of Grub Street* (1946) by Howard William Troyer.

Ward, Elizabeth Stuart Phelps (1844–1911). American emotional novelist, whose *The Gates Ajar* (1868) was an enormously popular book. Her other novels include *The Madonna of the Tubs* (1886); *A Singular Life* (1894); *Within the Gates* (1901); *Though Life Do Us Part* (1908); and many others.

Ward, Henry Augustus (1834–1906). American naturalist. His collection of specimens was exhibited at the Chicago World's Fair (1893) and forms the basis of the collection of the Field Museum of Natural History in Chicago.

Ward, Mrs. Humphry. In full **Mary Augusta Ward** (1851–1920). English author of popular novels, interested also in philanthropy, social work, and religious polemics. Her best-known books include ROBERT ELSMERE (1888); *The History of David Grieve* (1892); MARCELLA (1894) and its sequel *Sir George Tressady* (1896); THE MARRIAGE OF WILLIAM ASHE (1905); and *The Case of Richard Meynell* (1911). Many of her books were ROMANS À CLEF; for instance *Lady Rose's Daughter* (1903), based on the relations between Mme du DEFFAND and Julie de L'Espinasse.

Ward, Gilbert. The hero of Crawford's historical romance VIA CRUCIS.

Ward, John, see JOHN WARD, PREACHER.

Ward, John Quincy Adams (1830–1910). American sculptor; president of the National Academy of Design (1874).

Ward, Lynd (1905–). American illustrator, noted for his novels in woodcuts, as *God's Man* (1929); *Prelude to A Million Years* (1933); *Madman's Drum* (1930); etc., and his illustrations to books by a variety of authors, both old and new.

Ward, Nathaniel (1578?–1652). New England Puritan clergyman, born in England but forced to leave during the period of Puritan persecution. He is known for two works: *The Body of Liberties* (1641), a code of laws for Massachusetts in the preparation of which Ward figured most prominently, ranked by some critics with Magna Carta and the Bill of Rights in its recognition of fundamental human rights; and THE SIMPLE COBBLER OF AGAWAM (1647). Ward returned to England at about the time of publication of the latter work.

Ward, Wilfrid Philip (1856–1916). English Roman Catholic writer on religion and author of biographies of Cardinals Wiseman and Newman.

Warden, The. A novel by Anthony TROLLOPE, one of his *Chronicles of Barsetshire*. See BARSETSHIRE.

Warder, Becky. The heroine of Clyde Fitch's drama THE TRUTH. Her husband, **Tom Warder,** is the other leading character.

Wardle, Mr. In Dickens' PICKWICK PAPERS, an old country gentleman, who attends some of the meetings of "The Pickwick Club," and feels a liking for Mr. Pickwick and his three friends, whom he occasionally entertained at his house.

Miss Isabella Wardle. Daughter of Mr. Wardle. She marries Augustus Snodgrass, M.P.C.

Miss Emily Wardle. Daughter of Mr. Wardle. She marries Mr. Trundle.

Wardour Street English. A phrase coined in 1888 in disapprobation of a translation of the ODYSSEY by William MORRIS, with particular reference to the affected use of archaic words and phrases. Wardour Street was known for its pseudo-antique furniture.

Ware, Eugene Fitch. Pen name **Ironquill** (1841–1911). American lawyer and poet. *The Rhymes of Ironquill* is the title of his collected poems.

Warens, Mme de. The first benefactress of J. J. ROUSSEAU, whom she took under her protection and installed as her companion at Chambéry in the early years of his career.

Warfield, David (1866–). Popular American actor. He was a favorite of David BELASCO and appeared in Charles Klein's *The Auctioneer* (1901) and *The Music Master* (1904). His greatest success was in *The Return of Peter Grimm* (1911).

Waring. A poem by Robert BROWNING. Waring has been identified with Alfred Domett, a young poet who left England, settled in New Zealand and distinguished himself in politics. The poem, which was suggested by his sudden departure, analyzes the possible motives of such an act. It begins:—

> What's become of Waring,
> Since he gave us all the slip?

war in literature. From the beginning of history war has been an important subject for literature, inspiring in the ancient and medieval eras such epic works as Homer's ILIAD, THE SONG OF ROLAND, and Tasso's JERUSALEM DELIVERED. In modern times, however, with an increase in the size of armies and the invention of murderous weapons, war began to lose its purely adventurous character, with individual combat as its focal point, and writers began at about the middle of the 19th century to interpret it in terms of its destruction and its effect on the individual soldier, who had become only a cipher in the vast battle-plans of generals. Stephen Crane's THE RED BADGE OF COURAGE was one of the first books to treat war realistically, preceded by Tolstoi's WAR AND PEACE and ZOLA's and MAUPASSANT's fictional studies of the Franco-Prussian War. World War I (1914–1918), the most destructive war in history up to its time, caused great social and psychological dislocations and gave rise to a new literary genre which presented a frank and detailed picture of the horrors and brutalities of warfare and the sufferings, both physical and psychological, of the common soldier, and vigorously denounced the whole institution of war. Among the literary works inspired by World War I are the following: LILULI, a play, and CLERAMBAULT, a semi-autobiographical study, by Romain Rolland; HEARTBREAK HOUSE, by G. B. Shaw; UNDER FIRE and *Clarté,* by Henri Barbusse; JEREMIAH, by Stefan Zweig; *Die Wandlung* and *Hinkemann,* by Ernst TOLLER; books of poetry by Siegfried SASSOON and Wilfred OWEN; *Men in War,* by Andreas Latzko; *Le Lâche* (*The Coward*), a play by H. R. Lenormand; *The Unknown,* by W. S. MAUGHAM; THE ENORMOUS ROOM, by E. E. Cummings; *One Man's Initiation* and THREE SOLDIERS, by John Dos Passos; WHAT PRICE GLORY? a play by Laurence Stallings and Maxwell Anderson; A FAREWELL TO ARMS, by Ernest Hemingway; JOURNEY'S END, a play by R. C. Sherriff; *The Case of Sergeant Grischa,* by Arnold ZWEIG; ALL QUIET ON THE WESTERN FRONT, by Erich Maria Remarque; *Testament of Youth,* by Vera Brittain; Dos Passos' U.S.A. and Louis-Ferdinand Céline's *Journey to the End of Night* deal in part with the war. These works were very popular during the 1920's and early 1930's, figuring prominently in the pacifist (see PACIFISM) and social reform movements of the time. The literary works inspired by the Spanish Civil War (1936–1939) and the early years of World War II (1939–1943), such as FOR WHOM THE BELL TOLLS, by Ernest Hemingway, THERE SHALL BE NO NIGHT, a play by Robert E. Sherwood, THE MOON IS DOWN, by John Steinbeck, and ALL NIGHT LONG, by Erskine Caldwell, were concerned with isolated events and periods of the war and made no attempt to consider it as a whole or analyze its psychological effects. In the U.S., the most frequent and most popular type of book on World War II at first was the humorous account of life in the army camps, like Marion Hargrove's *See Here, Private Hargrove.*

War is Kind. A volume of free verse (1899) by Stephen CRANE.

Warman, Cy (1855–1914). American journalist and author of stories about railroads. He also published two volumes of poetry, *Mountain Melodies* (1892) and *Songs of Cy Warman* (1911).

Warming-pans. Nickname of the JACOBITES. It is said that Mary d'Este, the wife of James II, never had a living child, but that on one occasion a child, introduced to her bedroom in a warming-pan, was substituted for her dead infant. This "warming-pan child" was the PRETENDER.

Warne, Frederick (1825–1901). English publisher of the *Chandos Classics* (from 1868); Frances Hodgson BURNETT; and Beatrix POTTER.

Warner. In Bulwer Lytton's LAST OF THE BARONS, a man whose scientific experiments caused him to be regarded as a magician in league with the Devil. His daughter **Sybil** is a prominent character.

Warner, Anne Richmond. Mrs. **Anne Warner French** (1869–1913). American writer, whose stories of "Susan Clegg" were very popular.

Warner, Charles Dudley (1829–1900). American essayist and editor. Co-editor of the *Library of the World's Best Literature* (30 vols.; 1896–1897). He and Mark Twain collaborated in writing *The Gilded Age* (1873). His books of familiar essays include *My Summer in a Garden* (1871); *On Horseback* (1888); and *Fashions in Literature* (1902). *Being a Boy* (1878) is a classic record of New England boyhood.

Warner, Harry Morris (1881–), **Samuel Louis Warner** (1887–1927), **Albert Warner,** and **Jack L. Warner.** Original surname **Eichelbaum.** Four brothers, sons of immigrants from Russia, associated with the moving-picture industry as exhibitors (since 1903) and producers (since 1912). They incorporated their business as Warner Brothers Pictures (1923), Harry M. Warner being president. Pioneers in the field of the talking picture.

Warner, Olin Levi (1844–1896). American sculptor, whose work is represented in the Metropolitan Museum of Art, New York City, in the State Capitol, Hartford, Connecticut, etc. His best-known sculptures are the idyllic figures *Twilight, Dancing Nymph,* and *Cupid and Psyche.*

Warner, Rex (1905–). English novelist, associated with the school of SPENDER, AUDEN, DAY LEWIS, ISHERWOOD, and MACNEICE during the 1930's, known for his fantastic, symbolic and allegorical novels in the style of Franz KAFKA. His books include *The Wild Goose Chase* (1937); *Poems* (1938); *The Professor* (1938); *The Aerodrome* (1941).

Warner, Susan Bogert. Pen name **Elizabeth Wetherell** (1819–1885). American author of novels for children, the most popular being THE WIDE, WIDE WORLD (1851) and QUEECHY (1852).

Warner, Sylvia Townsend (1893–). English poet and novelist, known for the whimsical and satirical fantasy of her work. Among her books are *The Espalier* (1925), *Time Importuned* (1928), *Opus 7* (1931), *Rainbow* (1932), and *Whether a Dove or a Seagull* (1933), poetry; *Lolly Willowes* (1926); *Mr. Fortune's Maggot* (1927); *The True Heart* (1929); *Elinor Barley* (1930); *The Salutation* (1932), novelettes; *After the Death of Don Juan* (1938); *The Cat's Cradle Book* (1940), stories.

War of Jenkins's Ear. In the struggle for sea power between England and Spain, a war (1739–1741) which was declared by Sir Robert WALPOLE when the English master mariner Robert Jenkins declared that a Spanish captain, upon boarding his vessel, had cut off his ear. The conflict was absorbed in the War of the Austrian Succession.

War of Nerves, see BATTLE OF NERVES.

War of the Worlds, The. A fantastic novel (1898) by H. G. Wells, describing an invasion of England by warriors from Mars. A radio dramatization (1938) by Orson WELLES caused widespread panic in the United States.

Warren, Charles (1868–). American lawyer and author who won the Pulitzer prize for history (1923) for *The Supreme Court in United States History* (1922).

Warren, Mercy, *née* **Otis** (1728–1814). Early American writer, friend of the best-known public figures in her time, including John and Samuel Adams, Thomas Jefferson and Elbridge Gerry. Author of *History of the Rise, Progress, and Termination of the American Revolution* (3 vols.; 1805).

Warren, Mrs. The principal character in Shaw's drama MRS. WARREN'S PROFESSION.

Vivie Warren. Mrs. Warren's daughter.

Warren, Robert Penn (1905–). American poet and literary critic, a member of the FUGITIVES and the AGRARIANS, editor of THE SOUTHERN REVIEW. His books, like those of Allen TATE mainly concerned with the regional interests of the South, include *John Brown* (1929), a biography; *Pondy Woods, And Other Poems* (1930); *Thirty-Six Poems* (1935); contributions to *I'll Take My Stand* (1930) and *Who Owns America?* (1936); *Night Rider* (1939), a novel; *Eleven Poems on the Same Theme* (1942); *All the King's Men* (1946) a novel about a Southern dictator which won the Pulitzer prize.

Warren, Samuel (1807–1877). English lawyer and writer on law. His novel, *Ten Thousand A Year* (1839), describes in detail the machinations of a minor law firm through which the draper's assistant Tittlebat Titmouse suddenly inherits a large fortune.

Warren, Whitney (1864?–1943). American architect. Designed the Grand Central Station, the Ritz-Carlton Hotel, the bronze gates of the Cathedral of St. John the Divine, all in New York City. He was the architect chosen after World War I to restore the famous Louvain Library in Belgium and the Cathedral of Rheims.

Warrington, George and **Henry.** The twin heroes of Thackeray's novel THE VIRGINIANS. They are sons of **Madam Rachel Esmond Warrington** (known as Madam Esmond) and grandsons of HENRY ESMOND, the hero of Thackeray's novel of that name.

Warrior Queen, the, see BOADICEA.

Wars of the Roses. See under ROSE.

Wartburg. *Battle of Wartburg* or *War of Wartburg* (*Wartburgkrieg*). In medieval romance, a famous tournament of song held probably between 1204 and 1208 at Wartburg Castle near Eisenach under the auspices of

Hermann, Margrave of Thuringia, a patron of song. In the tournament Heinrich von Ofterdingen pits his skill against Wolfram von Eschenbach, Walter von der Vogelweide and other celebrated Minnesingers (see those names, also *Klingsor; Minnesingers*). Many supernatural elements have been woven into the legend. See TANNHÄUSER.

Warton, Thomas (1728–1790). English literary historian, critic, and poet laureate (from 1785). His *History of English Poetry* (3 vols.; 1774–1781), extending to the end of the Elizabethan age, is a scholarly work of great importance.

Warwick, Diana. Heroine of Meredith's novel DIANA OF THE CROSSWAYS.

Warwick, Earl of. "The King-maker." See NEVILLE, RICHARD.

Wash, The. A broad estuary on the east coast of England between Norfolk and Lincoln. Four rivers flow through it; in it are two anchorages for ships.

Washington, Booker Taliaferro (1856–1915). American Negro educator, born as a slave in Virginia. Struggled for and obtained his education at Hampton Institute (1872–1875). Appointed (1881) head of the Tuskegee Institute for the practical training of Negroes. Recognized as a national leader in the education of the Negro people. Author of *Up From Slavery* (1901); *The Story of the Negro* (1909); etc. In 1946, a bust and tablet in his honor were unveiled at the Hall of Fame, New York City.

Washington, George (1732–1799). First president of the United States (1789–1797) and "Father of his Country." He is introduced into Thackeray's VIRGINIANS and Ford's JANICE MEREDITH; Cooper portrays him under the name of HARPER in his *Spy;* and Hugh Wynne, in Weir Mitchell's novel of that name, is for a time a member of Washington's staff. Percy MACKAYE has made Washington the hero of a "ballad play" entitled *Washington, the Man Who Made Us* (1919). In 1920 it was produced in Washington, D.C., under the title *George Washington.*

Washington of Colombia. Simon BOLÍVAR (1785–1831).

the Second Washington. The American statesman Henry CLAY (1777–1852).

bird of Washington. See under BIRD.

Washington Square. A novel (1881) by Henry JAMES. Dramatized as *The Heiress* and produced in New York (1947).

Washington Square Players, The. A LITTLE THEATER group, established in 1915, the cradle of the THEATER GUILD.

Wassermann, August Paul von (1866–1925). German bacteriologist and department head at the Koch Institute for Infectious Diseases (1906). Discovered (1906) the bio-chemical reaction (Wassermann test) which serves as a test for syphilis.

Wassermann, Jakob (1873–1934). German novelist, resident of Austria. Principally concerned with the problems of psychoanalysis and the question of the Jews in the diaspora, his novels have depth of feeling and insight into the human soul. His writings include *Die Juden von Zirndorff* (1897), *Caspar Hauser* (1909), *Christian Wahnschaffe* (1919), *Der Fall Maurizius* (1928), all novels; *Bula Matari* (1932), a biography of Stanley; and numerous essays and short stories.

Wast, Hugo, see MARTÍNEZ ZUVIRÍA, GUSTAVO.

Waste Land, The. A long poem by T. S. ELIOT (1922), his most famous work. Suggested by a reading of *From Ritual to Romance,* by Jessie L. Weston, a study of the themes of medieval romances and legends, its basic symbolism is that on which the GRAIL legend is believed by many scholars to have been founded. The waste land is a sterile area, blighted by a curse, where crops do not grow, the Fisher King is sexually impotent, and release from the spell can be secured only by a knight's coming to the castle and asking the meaning of the various symbols it contains. In Eliot's poem, physical and sexual sterility are made to symbolize what the author regarded as the spiritual sterility of the 20th century, and two kinds of life and death (life without spiritual meaning, which is a species of death, and redemptive death, which gives eternal life) are contrasted. The author's unique method in the poem is a play on these contrasts by means of quotations from and allusions to a variety of literary and religious works of the past, identified in several pages of notes inserted at the end of the book.

The following is an approximate prose summary of the four separate parts of *The Waste Land,* based on the analysis of the poem by Cleanth Brooks in his *Modern Poetry and the Tradition:*

I. *The Burial of the Dead.* The introductory theme is that of the attractiveness of death, with April and Springtime shown as cruel rather than as joy-bringing because they waken dead lives to an awareness of their emptiness. This is presented through the reveries of a protagonist, mixed with a conversation in the Hofgarten. Allusions are made to passages in *Ezekiel* and *Ecclesiastes,* dealing with a Biblical waste land, and to Wagner's TRISTAN UND ISOLDE in the form of an excerpt from a sailor's song of simple, happy, and naïve love, which is, as shown by another snatch of song from the same opera, absent from the Waste Land. The protagonist then is seen having his fortune told by Madame Sosostris, who consults a pack of Tarot cards, the figures on which are: a Drowned Phoenician Sailor (representing the fertility gods of pagan myth, who were sacrificed to bring fertility to the soil); a Man with Three Staves (representing the Fisher King); Belladonna, the Lady of the Rocks (representing the woman of the Waste Land); a Wheel; and a One-Eyed Merchant (see third section). The protagonist is warned to beware of death by water. (See fourth section.) References are made to a nightmare city mentioned by BAUDELAIRE and to Dante's Limbo (see LIMBUS; the Waste Land again, or the absence of either good or evil in a secular, industrial and commercial world). Twentieth-century London is identified with Dante's Hell, and the protagonist sees a friend he recognizes, a man named Stetson, who represents both the reader and the author. A reference (from John WEBSTER) to a dog digging up a corpse is interpreted by Brooks as signifying modern natural science, humanitarianism, etc., which "dig up," or analyze and banish, the supernatural, thereby preventing a rebirth of life.

II. *A Game of Chess.* A man and woman are seen playing chess in a room filled with rich carvings and paintings; this is considered to symbolize the 20th-century man surrounded by a rich tradition but occupying himself with empty abstractions. References are made to the legend of PHILOMELA (lust as characteristic of a secular society) and to Ariel's song ("Those are pearls that were his eyes," etc.) from THE TEMPEST (death by water as rebirth). The title of this part is from *Women Beware Women,* by Thomas MIDDLETON, in which a chess game is used to keep a widow occupied while her daughter-in-law is being raped (rape again signifying secularization). In contrast to the first scene, the closing scene takes place in a sordid London pub, where two Cockney women are discussing love and abortion (symbol of sterility again), with a quotation from Ophelia's speech in HAMLET.

III. *The Fire Sermon.* This part shows a river scene in London as presented in Spenser's PROTHALAMION, contrasted with the ugliness of a similar scene on the 20th-century Thames. The protagonist is fishing (representing the Fisher King), and there is an allusion to the poem *To His Coy Mistress,* by Andrew MARVELL, combined with the sound of automobile horns in London and references to the ribald ballad of "Mrs. Porter and her daughter" who "washed their feet in soda water"; this dissolves into the sound of children singing at the ceremony of foot-washing in Wagner's Parsifal. After a recapitulation of the symbols of the nightingale and the unreal city, Mr. Eugenides, a merchant from Smyrna (the One-Eyed Merchant of the fortune-teller's cards) appears, signifying the degradation of the prophet and the seer in a secular world, and invites the protagonist to "a weekend at the Metropole" (actually a homosexual orgy). The scene then shifts to a cheap London furnished room, where a typist is seduced by a carbuncular youth, no passion being evidenced by either party; an allusion to Goldsmith's "When lovely woman stoops to folly" is used as an ironic comment on the incident. Across the Thames the protagonist hears the music from the typist's gramophone, and three river-nymphs (comparable to the three Rhine-Daughters in Wagner's *Götterdämmerung*) sing songs on: the sordid modern river; the Elizabethan river of Spenser's poem, with allusions to Elizabeth and Leicester sailing on a barge and to Cleopatra's barge; and the Waste Land again, with reference to Dante's *Purgatory.* The section ends with quotations from St. Augustine (see under SAINTS) and BUDDHA.

IV. *Death by Water.* This section contrasts in symbolism with *The Fire Sermon.* It presents first a description of hooded figures crossing the Waste Land (representing the general decay of Eastern Europe, where the fertility cults originated) in a nightmare picture of the collapse of civilization. There is a reference to the visit to the Perilous Chapel in the Grail legend (a female sexual symbol), and the sound of thunder which recurs throughout this section signifies the coming of rain, hence baptism or redemption. After allusions to and quotations from Dante's *Purgatory,* THE SPANISH TRAGEDY, *The Tempest,* and Sanskrit prayers, the protagonist finally resolves to claim the tradition he has inherited and restore it. The poem ends with the Sanskrit benediction *Shantih, Shantih, Shantih,* equivalent to the "peace that passeth understanding."

On its first publication, *The Waste Land* was attacked as unintelligible, and later, especially among proletarian critics (see PROLETARIAN LITERATURE), a favorite interpretation was that it was an expression of gigantic despair and disillusionment, articulating the feelings of the generation that had lived through World War I; there was also considerable censure of Eliot's technique of using a "patchwork" of quotations and literary allusions. Other critics have pointed out, however, that the poem expresses more than a superficial disillusionment, actually bringing the problem to a resolution at the conclusion, and that the contrasts between the past and the author's present have a symbolic as well as a literal significance, with the quotations and allusions serving as a means of compression. The poem is regarded as the most important single poetic work of the 20th century and had a wide influence on younger poets.

Watchful Waiting. A phrase used by President Woodrow WILSON to characterize the policy of the United States toward Mexico during 1915, when it was asserted that every effort consonant with the protection of American "interests" was made to keep peace with that country.

water.

to water stock. To add extra shares and nominal capital without adding real capital.

the Father of Waters. See under FATHER.

Water Babies, The, A Fairy Tale for a Land-Baby. A fantasy (1863) by Charles KINGSLEY, concerning a small chimney-sweep named Tom who falls into the river.

Waterfowl, To a. A lyric poem (1815) by William Cullen BRYANT.

Waterloo. The phrase, *he met his Waterloo,* is used with the meaning, "He had a final and crushing defeat," in allusion, of course, to the decisive defeat inflicted on Napoleon by Wellington at Waterloo in 1815.

Waterloo Bridge. A play (1930) by Robert E. SHERWOOD, made into a successful moving picture. The scene is London.

Water-Poet, The, see TAYLOR, JOHN.

Waters, Childe, see CHILDE WATERS.

Waters, Esther. See ESTHER WATERS.

Water Witch, The. A romance (1830) by James Fenimore COOPER. It was several times made into a play.

Watkin, Lawrence Edward (1901–). American writer, chiefly known for his fantastic novel *On Borrowed Time* (1937), made into a play by Paul Osborn. Also author of the novels *Geese in the Forum* (1940); *The Gentleman from England* (1941); etc.

Watling Street. One of the great Roman roads in England. It ran apparently from Dover past London, where it crossed the Thames at Westminster, and across England to Chester.

Watson, Henry Brereton Marriott (1863–1921). English novelist and writer of adventure stories.

Watson, John. Pseudonym **Ian Maclaren** (1850–1907). Scottish author and minister, whose novel, *Beside the Bonnie Brier Bush* (1894), was extremely popular both in England and America. He belonged to the KAILYARD school of novelists. His son, Frederick Watson, has written books on witchcraft and other topics, some of them under the pseudonym "Ian Ferguson."

Watson, John Broadus (1878–). American psychologist; known as the principal exponent of BEHAVIORISM. Among his books are *Behaviorism* (1925; revised, 1931); *Ways of Behaviorism* (1928); etc.

Watson, Thomas (1557?–1592). Early English poet. Translated into English a collection of Italian madrigals (1590) and wrote a book of sonnets, *Tears of Fancy* (1593), whose influence can be traced in Shakespeare's work.

Watson, Sir **William** (1858–1935). English poet. His volumes of sonnets, *The Purple East* (1896) and *The Year of Shame* (1896), vigorously expressed his political opinions. *Collected Poems* (1898; 1906).

Watteau, Jean Antoine (1684–1721). Fashionable French painter, known for his charming genre pictures of aristocratic pastoral scenes.

Watterson, Henry (1840–1921). American journalist and politician, called "Marse Henry." Editor of the Louisville, Kentucky, *Courier-Journal* (1868–1918). He was bitter against Theodore Roosevelt, supported Wilson and the cause of the Allies in World War I, but opposed America's entry into the League of Nations. Pulitzer prize for journalism (1917) for his war editorials. Cf. his autobiography, *Marse Henry* (1919).

Watts, George Frederic (1817–1904). English painter, especially known for his series of about three hundred portraits of distinguished people of his time, including Garibaldi, Thiers, Guizot, etc. Also treated allegorical and symbolical subjects, as *Life's Illusions* (1849); *Love and Death* (1877); *Sic Transit* (1892); etc. Husband of Ellen TERRY.

Watts, Isaac (1674–1748). English clergyman and religious poet. Known especially for his hymns, as *O God, our help in ages past; There is a land of pure delight;* etc.

Watts-Dunton, Walter Theodore (1832–1914). English man of letters, with whom SWINBURNE spent the latter part of his life at Putney. *Aylwin* (1898), a gypsy novel, had fictional portraits of D. G. ROSSETTI, etc.

Wat Tyler, see TYLER, WAT.

Waugh, Evelyn Arthur St. John (1903–). English novelist, known for his biting satires on life among the aesthetes and society people of London, especially during the 1920's. See also HUXLEY, ALDOUS. His books include *Rossetti: A Critical Biography* (1928); *Decline and Fall* (1929); *Vile Bodies* (1930); *A Bachelor Abroad* (1930; published in England as *Labels*), on travel; *Black Mischief* (1932); *A Handful of Dust* (1934); *Edmund Campion* (1935); *Mr. Loveday's Little Outing, And Other Sad Stories* (1936); *Scoop* (1938); *Mexico: An Object Lesson* (1939), a social and political study; *Put Out More Flags* (1942); *Brideshead Revisited* (1944); *The Loved One* (1948).

His brother, **Alec Waugh.** In full **Alexander Raban Waugh** (1898–), is also a novelist and miscellaneous author, best known for *The Loom of Youth* (1917), a novel frankly depicting life in an English boys' school, and *The Prisoners of Mainz* (1919), a semi-autobiographical work based on his experiences in a German prison camp during World War I. Other books, many dealing with travel, include: *The Lonely Unicorn* (1922); *Love in These Days* (1926); *Portrait of a Celibate* (1929); *Hot Countries* (1930); *Tropic Seed* (1932); *Playing with Fire* (1933); *The Balliols* (1934); *Jill Somerset* (1936); *Eight Short Stories* (1937); *Going Their Own Ways* (1938); *No Truce with Time* (1941).

Wave, The. A novel (1929) by Evelyn SCOTT dealing with the Civil War.

Wavell, Sir **Archibald Percival** (1883–). British officer who fought first in the South African War (1901) and was with ALLENBY in India (1917–1920). He was in command of the Middle East at the beginning of World War II and organized the British offensive in Egypt (1940–1941). He was sent to India as the commander of all the forces of the United Nations (January, 1942). In 1945 he compiled an excellent anthology of poetry, *Other Men's Flowers*.

Waverley. The first of Sir Walter SCOTT's historical novels, published in 1814. The chief characters are Prince Charles Edward, the Chevalier; the noble old Baron of Bradwardine; the simple faithful clansman Evan Dhu; and the poor fool Davie Gelatley, with his fragments of song and scattered gleams of fancy. The hero is Captain Edward Waverley of Waverley Honor. He is first a captain in the royal army; then resigns his commission, and proposes marriage to Flora M'Ivor, but is not accepted. Fergus M'Ivor (Flora's brother) introduces him to Prince Charles Edward. He becomes a rebel, enters the service of the Prince, and in the Battle of Prestonpans saves the life of Colonel Talbot. When the Pretender's cause collapses, the Colonel, out of gratitude, obtains a pardon for young Waverley, who then marries Rose Bradwardine, and quietly settles down in Waverley Honor.

Waverley Novels, the. All the novels of Sir Walter SCOTT are included under this term; but not the three tales called *Aunt Margaret's Mirror, The Laird's Jock,* and *The Tapestried Chamber*.

Waves, The. A novel by Virginia WOOLF (1931), regarded by some critics as her masterpiece, dealing with the psychological development and personal relationships of a group of six English children, with the rise and fall of the waves of the sea and the ascent and decline of the sun in the sky serving to symbolize the growth of the characters' personalities and the progress of their lives. As children, BERNARD, SUSAN, NEVILLE, JINNY, RHODA, and LOUIS live in the same house, which has a large garden extending down to the seashore, and take their lessons from the same governess; through their relationships with each other in study and play they become aware of their own particular personalities. Becoming older, they separate to go to various schools and colleges, later meeting in a London restaurant after their various graduations. Then they scatter again, pursuing diverse careers but each following out the psychological pattern that was established in his or her childhood, until their final reunion in middle age at Hampton Court. See also PERCIVAL.

The narration of *The Waves* takes two forms: lyrical passages on the sea and rich and colorful descriptions of the sunlight, air, and physical background of each scene; and a series of formalized monologues in which each character in turn speaks of his impressions, his feelings, and the events in his life, with individual differences of personality expressed only by differences in imagery.

way.

the way of all flesh. Death. See also below.

the Way of the Cross. A series of pictures in a church (see STATIONS OF THE CROSS) representing Christ's progress to Calvary; also, the devotions suited to them.

Way Down East. A play (1898) by Lottie Blair Parker. For many years it was one of the most popular melodramas in the United States.

Wayland. A wonderful and invisible smith of English legend, the English form of the Scandinavian *Volund* or *Volunder,* a supernatural smith and king of the elves. In *Frithiof's Saga,* Volund forges the armor of Thorsten, Frithiof's father, particularly a golden arm-ring which descends to Frithiof as one of his most precious possessions. According to the legend, King Nidud or Nidung of Sweden cut the sinews of his feet and cast him into prison to avail himself of his workmanship, but the smith made his escape in a feather boat. Scott introduces Wayland, or Wayland Smith, into KENILWORTH (Ch. xiii), where we are told that he lived in a cromlech near Lambourn, Berks (since called *Wayland Smith's Cave*), and that, if a traveler tied up his horse there, left sixpence for a fee, and retired from sight, he would find the horse shod on his return. KIPLING has a tale of *Weland's Sword* in his PUCK OF POOK'S HILL.

Wayne, Anthony (1745–1796). American general in the Revolution, nicknamed Mad Anthony, famous for a night attack on STONY POINT on the Hudson (July, 1779). Another (mad) Anthony Wayne is the principal character in Morrison Wood's novel, *The Devil is a Lonely Man* (1946).

Waynflete, Lady Cicely. Heroine of Shaw's comedy CAPTAIN BRASSBOUND'S CONVERSION.

Way of All Flesh, The. A novel by Samuel BUTLER, published posthumously in 1903. The hero, Ernest, is the son of Theobald Pontifex, an English clergyman. Few Christian clergymen have been set forth in fiction in such unsympathetic vein as this pious bully, nor is his sanctimonious wife Christina, docile to his every wish, much more lovable. The novel is said to be largely autobiographical but the picture it presents cannot be regarded as other than a keenly satiric criticism of English family life in the middle classes. Ernest's school and university days are not over-happy. He struggles with the problem of orthodoxy, goes to live in the slums, is thrown into prison for impulsive advances to a respectable girl, marries the extremely vulgar Ellen, who had been his mother's maid, but finally wins through to a fair measure of self-respect and genuine success.

Way of the World, The. A comedy by William CONGREVE (1700), called by SWINBURNE "the unequalled and unapproached masterpiece of English comedy." The heroine is MILLAMANT, the hero Edward Mirabell.

W.C.T.U. The Woman's Christian Temperance Union, an organization formed in the interests of universal prohibition of the sale of alcoholic beverages. See PROHIBITION.

Wealth of Nations, The. A famous economic treatise on the nature and causes of national wealth by Adam SMITH (1776).

We are Coming, Father Abraham, Three Hundred Thousand More. This poem appeared in the New York *Evening Post* in July 1862. It was written by James Sloan Gibbons (1810–1892), who was an Abolitionist. The poem was a result of President Lincoln's call for new troops. Stephen Foster made one of the settings for the song and it became a great favorite in the North.

Wearing of the Green, The. An Irish revolutionary song (1798).

Weaver, John Van Alstyn (1893–1938). American author. His use of the vernacular in poetry was lauded by H. L. Mencken. Author of books of verse, as *In American* (1921); *More In American* (1925); co-author, with George Abbott, of the successful play *Love 'Em and Leave 'Em* (1926). After 1928, Mr. Weaver wrote for the moving pictures. In his novel, *Joy-Girl* (1932), he indulged in biting satire against Hollywood.

Weavers, The. A drama in five acts (1893) by Gerhart HAUPTMANN.

Web and the Rock, The. A novel (1939) by Thomas WOLFE.

Webb, Charles Henry. Pseudonym **John Paul** (1834–1905). American journalist, founder and first editor of the *Californian* (1864–1866), in which magazine he published Bret Harte and Mark Twain.

Webb, Mary (1881–1927). English novelist whose *Precious Bane* won the Femina-Vie Heureuse prize for 1924–1925. After her death her five novels were reprinted with introductions by Stanley Baldwin, John Buchan, Chesterton, and others. She wrote of Shropshire, where she was born.

Webb, Sidney James. 1st Baron **Passfield** (1859–1947) and **Beatrice Webb,** *née* **Potter** (1858–1943). English economists, the main founders of the FABIAN SOCIETY. They followed and wrote of the British Labour Movement for fifty years. They have to their credit a large number of books, including *Soviet Communism: A New Civilization* (2 vols.; 1935). Cf. *Beatrice Webb* (1945) by Margaret COLE.

Weber, Karl Maria von (1786–1826). German composer of popular romantic operas. His best-known work is *Der Freischütz* (1821), based on the old legend of the hunter whose bullets, charmed by the devil, cannot miss. Weber employed the LEITMOTIV technique which was later developed by Richard WAGNER.

Weber, Max (1881–). Russian-born American painter who has lectured on the history of art and has written cubist poems and essays on art.

Weber and Fields. Stage name of **Joseph Weber** (1867–1942) and **Lew Fields** (1867–1941), a famous team of vaudeville comedians, who established their own theater, put on many burlesques, and later went into the moving pictures and the radio.

Webley, Everard. In Aldous Huxley's POINT COUNTER POINT, the founder and leader of the Brotherhood of British Freemen, an English semi-Fascist (see FASCISM) organization. He is eventually killed, and the members of his band avenge his death. This character is considered to be based on Sir Oswald Mosley, the actual leader of a similar British Fascist movement during the 1920's and 1930's.

Webster, Daniel (1782–1852). Famous American politician and orator. Secretary of state (1841–1843; 1850–1852) and U.S. senator (1827–1841; 1845–1850). He protected the vested interests of New England and took a middle-of-the-road stand concerning slavery. John Greenleaf Whittier attacked him in a poem *Ichabod*. His writings and speeches have been collected into eighteen volumes. A fantastic story which uses him as an arbitrator is THE DEVIL AND DANIEL WEBSTER by Stephen Vincent Benét (1939). Cf. *Daniel Webster* (1930), by Claude M. Fuess.

Webster, Henry Kitchell (1875–1932). Popular American novelist who wrote for the *Saturday Evening Post, McClure's* and other magazines. One of his best remembered novels, *Calumet "K"* (1901), was written in collaboration with Samuel Merwin.

Webster, Jean (1876–1916). American novelist and writer of short stories. Best known for *Daddy-Long-Legs* (1912) which the author made into a play and which became a silent picture for Mary Pickford. She also wrote a popular book for young people, *When Patty Went to College* (1903). It is said that the heroine of these entertaining stories was really the poet Adelaide Crapsey.

Webster, John (1580?–1625?). English playwright of the Elizabethan era, best known for his tragedies of violence. His works include *Christmas Comes But Once a Year* (1602); *Westward Hoe* and *Northward Hoe* (1607), on which he collaborated with Thomas Dekker; *The White Devil* (ca. 1608); *Appius and Virginia* (ca. 1609); The Duchess of Malfi (ca. 1618); *The Devil's Law Case* (1623); *A Cure for a Cuckold* (1661), written with Rowley. *The White Devil* and *The Duchess of Malfi* are his best-known works. He also collaborated with Heywood, Tourneur, etc.

Webster, Margaret (1905–). Anglo-American theatrical director and producer. In her début as an actress she played with John Barrymore in *Hamlet* in London. She is noted for having directed the presentations of Shakespeare starring Maurice Evans (1937–1939). Daughter of the late Ben Webster and Dame May Whitty.

Webster, Noah (1758–1843). Great American lexicographer and author. He was a teacher, lecturer, journalist, lawyer, etc. In politics he was an ardent partisan of Federalism. While a resident at Amherst, he was president of the Amherst Academy (1820–1821) and helped found Amherst College. His first lexicographical publication was designed as a school book. It was the word-book part, commonly known as *Webster's Spelling Book* or *Blue-Backed Speller* (1782–1783), of a three-volume *Grammatical Institute of the English Language,* of which parts II and III were a grammar and a reader (1784, 1785). The speller was used in all schools and sold in the course of a century some sixty million copies. Webster's first real dictionary was the *Compendious Dictionary of the English Language* (1806). Much more important was *An American Dictionary of the English Language* (2 vols.; 1828. Second edition, prepared with his son, William Greenleaf Webster, 1840), which is the foundation of all modern Websters.

Wedderburn, May. The heroine of Jessie Fothergill's First Violin.

wedding anniversaries. Fanciful names have been given to many wedding anniversaries, the popular idea being that they designate the nature of the gifts suitable for the occasion. The following list is fairly complete, but of these very few except the twenty-fifth and fiftieth are ever observed.

First	Cotton Wedding.
Second	Paper Wedding.
Third	Leather Wedding.
Fifth	Wooden Wedding.
Seventh	Woolen Wedding.
Tenth	Tin Wedding.
Twelfth	Silk and Fine Linen Wedding.
Fifteenth	Crystal Wedding.
Twentieth	China Wedding.
Twenty-fifth	Silver Wedding.
Thirtieth	Pearl Wedding.
Fortieth	Ruby Wedding.
Fiftieth	Golden Wedding.
Seventy-fifth	Diamond Wedding.

The *sixtieth* anniversary is often reckoned the "Diamond Wedding" in place of the *seventy-fifth;* as the *sixtieth* year of Queen Victoria's reign was her "Diamond Jubilee."

Wedding Journey, Their. See Their Wedding Journey.

Wedekind, Frank (1864–1918). German playwright whose first play, *Spring's Awakening* (1891), caused a sensation. *Earth Spirit* (1895) established his reputation. His work was regarded by some as too daring and he was sometimes in trouble with the authorities. He was spoken of as the father of expressionism in Germany.

Wedgwood, Josiah (1730–1795). English potter of Stoke-on-Trent, who perfected a kind of glazed earthenware which still bears his name.

Weed, Thurlow (1797–1882). American journalist and Republican leader. He helped to nominate Harrison, Clay, Taylor, Scott. His name is connected with those of Seward and Greeley as one of the dominating figures in New York State politics. Lincoln sent him on a mission abroad (1861).

Weekley, Ernest (1865–). English etymologist. *The Romance of Words* (1912); *The Romance of Names* (1914); *An Etymological Dictionary of Modern English* (1921); etc. He says that his opinions frequently differ with those of the *Oxford English Dictionary* but that *Webster's Dictionary* has done him the honor of utilizing his work on etymology quite extensively.

Week on the Concord and Merrimack Rivers, A. An account (1849) by Henry Thoreau of a trip he had taken (1839) in a small boat to the White Mountains.

Weeks, Edward A., Jr. (1898–). Editor of the *Atlantic Monthly.* Author of *This Trade of Writing* (1935). Reviewer and lecturer on books and authors.

Wee Macgreegor. The little Scotch lad in a book of the same title by J. J. Bell (1902) who talks in dialect. The book was dramatized (1912).

Weems, Mason Locke (1759–1825). American clergyman and author, known as "Parson Weems." He was a book agent and wrote himself a short biography of George Washington (1800). In its fifth edition (1806) occurs the earliest known version of the cherry-tree story.

weeping.

to go by weeping cross. To repent, to grieve. In ancient times, weeping crosses were crosses beneath which penitents offered their devotions. *Weeping Cross* (1908), by Henry Longan STUART, is an historical novel of Puritan New England.

the Weeping Philosopher. Heraclitus (*fl.* ca. 500 B.C.), so called because he grieved at the folly of man.

the Weeping Saint. St. Swithin (see under SAINTS), so called from the tradition of forty days' rain if it rains on July 15, his name day.

Wee Willie Winkie, And Other Stories. A volume by Rudyard KIPLING (1889). The story that gives the title to the book tells how six-year-old Percival William Williams, the young son of a British officer on duty in India, rescues the fiancée of his friend and hero, Lieutenant Brandis, and so "entered into his manhood." The name *Wee Willie Winkie* is an allusion to the familiar character of nursery rhyme who went about in his nightgown.

Wegg, Silas. In Dickens' novel, OUR MUTUAL FRIEND, a one-legged man who keeps a fruit stand. Mr. BOFFIN hires him to read *The Decline and Fall of the Roman Empire* aloud every evening, a task that is somewhat beyond his powers. Wegg is a shrewd rascal and hopes to blackmail Boffin, but fails in the attempt.

Weidman, Charles Edward (1901–). Well-known member of the Denishawn Dancers (1921–1927), later forming his own dance group with Doris Humphrey.

Weidman, Jerome (1913–). New York metropolitan author of realistic propensities. *I Can Get It for You Wholesale* (1937); *What's In It for Me?* (1938); *The Horse That Could Whistle "Dixie"* (short stories; 1939); *Too Early to Tell* (1946), etc.

Weir, Julian Alden (1852–1919). American painter, especially of historical pictures. He was influenced in Paris by the methods of the impressionists. His best paintings have an atmospheric quality and a delicate lighting which makes them particularly interesting.

Weird Sisters, the. The FATES.

Weir of Hermiston. An unfinished novel (1896) by Robert Louis STEVENSON. It has in it some of his finest work.

Weissnichtwo. Nowhere. The word is German for "I know not where," and was coined by Carlyle in his SARTOR RESARTUS. It is the name of the place where Diogenes Teufelsdrökh holds his professorship of Things in General. See also KENNAQUHAIR; UTOPIA.

Weld, Theodore Dwight (1803–1895). American abolitionist. His tract, *American Slavery As It Is* (1839), was, according to Mrs. Harriet Beecher Stowe herself, the inspiration of her famous book *Uncle Tom's Cabin.*

Weld, Thomas (1595–1661). English Puritan and minister at Roxbury, Mass. Together with John Eliot and Richard Mather he compiled the *Bay Psalm Book* (1640).

Weller, Matilda. Young woman with whom the Victorian James THOMSON was in love in his youth. Her death in 1853 left him gloomy and deeply despairing.

Weller, Samuel. Probably the most popular of all Dickens' characters, the center of comic interest in THE PICKWICK PAPERS, boots at the White Hart, and afterwards servant to Mr. Pickwick, to whom he becomes devotedly attached. Rather than leave his master when he is sent to the Fleet, Sam Weller gets his father to arrest him for debt. His fun, his shrewdness, his comparisons, his archness, and his cunning on behalf of his master are unparalleled.

Tony Weller. Father of Sam, a coachman of the old school, who drives a coach between London and Dorking. Naturally portly in size, he becomes far more so in his great-coat of many capes. Tony wears top-boots, and his hat has a low crown and broad brim. On the stagebox he is a king, elsewhere he is a mere greenhorn. He marries a widow, landlady of the Marquis of Granby, and his constant advice to his son is, "Sam, beware of widders."

Welles, Gideon (1802–1878). Secretary of the navy under Lincoln, who helped to found the Republican party. He wrote *Lincoln and Seward* (1874), but it is his three-volume *Diary* (published in 1911) which is of the most historical value.

Welles, Orson (1915–). American actor and producer. As one of the directors of the New York Federal Theater, he put on *Dr. Faustus* and a Negro *Macbeth.* In 1937 he founded the Mercury Theater and adapted Shakespeare's *Julius Caesar* which he put on with no scenery and in modern dress. In 1938 his presentation of a radio adaptation by Howard Koch of H. G. Wells' THE WAR OF THE WORLDS caused a panic since people thought that the Martians had actually come to earth. Later on Welles made a remarkable moving picture, *Citizen Kane* (1941), obviously modeled on the life and career of William Randolph HEARST. His partner in his theatrical ventures was John Houseman.

Wellgunda. In Wagner's *Ring* (not in actual mythology), one of the three Rhine-daughters guarding the Nibelungen Hoard.

Wellington, 1st Duke of. **Arthur Wellesley** (1769–1852). Famous English commander and statesman, known as "the Iron Duke." He was chief in command, after the death of Sir John Moore, in the Peninsular War (1808); represented England at the Congress of Vienna (1814–1815); and defeated Napoleon at Waterloo. From 1828 to 1830 he was prime minister of England. Although he opposed reform, he later supported Robert Peel in his corn-law legislation. He was a popular idol in England.

Wellman, Walter (1858–1934). American explorer who tried to fly in a dirigible, first over the North Pole (1906–1907; 1909) and then across the Atlantic (1910). He failed in both, but broke the world's records for time and distance in an airship by flying 1,008 miles in 72 hours. He wrote *The Aerial Age* (1911).

Well of the Saints, The. A tragedy (1905) by J. M. SYNGE.

Wells, Charles Jeremiah. Pseudonym **H. L. Howard** (1799?–1879). English poet who was a friend of Keats and Hazlitt and wrote a drama in verse which Rossetti praised and Swinburne reviewed.

Wells, Herbert George (1866–1946). English novelist and journalist, known for his popular fantasies on pseudo-scientific themes, his satires on the English life of his day, his popularized accounts of history and science, and his outspoken social and political theories. His works include *Select Conversations with an Uncle* (1895); *The Island of Dr. Moreau* (1896); *The Time Machine* (1895); *The Invisible Man* (1897); *Thirty Strange Stories* (1897); *The War of the Worlds* (1898); *Tales of Space and Time* (1899); *Love and Mr. Lewisham* (1899); *When the Sleeper Wakes* (1899); *The Sea Lady* (1902); *A Modern Utopia* (1904); *Twelve Stories and a Dream* (1905); KIPPS (1905); *The Misery of Boots* (1907); TONO-BUNGAY (1908); *The War in the Air* (1908); ANN VERONICA (1909); *New Worlds for Old* (1908); *The History of Mr. Polly* (see MR. POLLY; 1910); THE NEW MACHIAVELLI (1910); *Marriage* (1912); *The Passionate Friends* (1913); THE WIFE OF SIR ISAAC HARMAN (1914); THE RESEARCH MAGNIFICENT (1915); MR. BRITLING SEES IT THROUGH (1916); *War and the Future* (1917); *The Soul of a Bishop* (1917); *The Undying Fire* (1919); *The Outline of History* (1920); *The Salvaging of Civilization* (1921); *Men Like Gods* (1923); *A Short History of the World* (1925); *Mr. Blettsworthy on Rampole Island* (1928); *The Open Conspiracy: Blue Prints for a World Revolution* (1928); *The King Who Was a King* (1929); *The Autocracy of Mr. Parham* (1930); *The Way to World Peace* (1930); *The Work, Wealth, and Happiness of Mankind* (1931); *The Shape of Things to Come* (1933); *The Anatomy of Frustration* (1936); *Star-Begotten* (1937); *Man's Mind and Behavior* (1937); *Apropos of Dolores* (1938); *The Brothers* (1938); *All Aboard for Ararat* (1940); *Babes in the Darkling Wood* (1940); *The New World Order* (1940); *Phoenix: A Summary of the Inescapable Conditions of World Reorganization* (1942); *You Can't Be Too Careful* (1942).

Wells was the son of a small shopkeeper and was himself apprenticed to dry-goods dealers and druggists before going to college. In his early career he taught and was a student of biology and sociology, subjects which greatly influenced his writings and his ideas. He aroused much controversy by his criticisms of 20th-century society and his sensational predictions of the future, such as tanks, air warfare, and the atomic bomb.

Welsbach, Aloys Auer von (1813–1869). Austrian printer. Director of the Imperial Press in Vienna. His son, **Carl Auer von Welsbach** (1858–1929), was a chemist and invented the Welsbach burner and mantle.

Welsh.

the Welsh ambassador. The cuckoo. The bird announces the migration of Welsh laborers into England for summer employment.

Welsh main. Same as a "battle royal."

Welsh mortgage. A pledge of land in which no day is fixed for redemption.

Welsh rabbit. Cheese melted and spread over buttered toast. "Rarebit" is incorrect.

We'll to the Woods No More. English translation (1938) of Édouard Dujardin's novel *Les Lauriers sont Coupés* (1888), considered the first example in fiction of an intended INTERIOR MONOLOGUE. Daniel Prince, a young Frenchman, is in love with an actress, Leah d'Arsay, and pretends to himself to be satisfied with a merely "Platonic" relationship, although he actually wishes to make her his mistress. She allows him to believe that she is about to grant him her favors, but after she has secured a sum of money from him she skillfully puts him off. He therefore resolves in sorrow never to see her again.

The story is told through the thoughts and impressions of the hero as he walks in the street, meets friends, sits in a restaurant, rides in a carriage, and visits Leah. James JOYCE is said to have read this book about 1901 and to have been partly influenced by it while writing ULYSSES. Dujardin himself claimed to have been influenced in his technique by Richard

Wagner's device of the musical *Leitmotiv,* by the dramatic monologue of Robert BROWNING, and by the psychological monologue of DOSTOYEVSKY.

Welsh, Jane. Wife of Thomas CARLYLE, to whom she was married in 1826. She herself was known as an intelligent and charming woman, and many critics consider that she was sacrificed by Carlyle to his own ambitions.

Welty, Eudora (1909–). Mississippi writer who has won one Guggenheim and three O. Henry Memorial awards. Her books of short stories are *A Curtain of Green* (1941) and *The Wide Net* (1943). Her first novel, *Delta Wedding* (1946), appeared originally as a serial in the *Atlantic Monthly.*

Wemmick. In Dickens' GREAT EXPECTATIONS, the cashier of Mr. Jaggers the lawyer. Mr. Wemmick wears his hat on the back of his head and looks straight before him, as if nothing is worth looking at. Mr. Wemmick at home and Mr. Wemmick in his office are two distinct beings. At home, he is "his own engineer, his own carpenter, his own plumber, his own gardener, his own Jack-of-all-trades," has fortified his little wooden house like Commodore TRUNNION and calls it his "castle." His father, eighty-two years of age, lives with him, and is known as "The Aged." The old man is very deaf, but heats the poker with delight to fire off the nine-o'clock signal, and chuckles with joy because he can hear the bang. The house has a "real flagstaff," and a plank which crosses a ditch some four feet wide and two feet deep is the drawbridge. At nine o'clock P.M. Greenwich time the gun (called "The Stinger") is fired.

Wendell, Barrett (1855–1921). One of the most distinguished (and eccentric) professors of Harvard University who wrote an excellent study of Cotton Mather and a widely known *Literary History of America* (1900).

Wendy. In Barrie's PETER PAN.

Wenham. In Thackeray's VANITY FAIR, a sort of general manager to the Marquis of STEYNE, a very disagreeable character.

Wenner-Gren, Axel (1881–). Swedish industrialist, owner of the largest wood-pulp company in Sweden and the Bofors munitions works. He established and endowed certain foundations for scientific research in Sweden as well as the Axel Wenner-Gren Foundation for Nordic Co-operation and Research.

Wenonah. In Longfellow's HIAWATHA, mother of Hiawatha and daughter of NOKOMIS. Nokomis is swinging in the moon when some of her companions, out of jealousy, cut the ropes, and she falls to earth "like a falling star." That night is born her first child, a daughter, whom she names Wenonah. In due time Wenonah is wooed and won by Mudjekeewis (the West Wind), and becomes the mother of Hiawatha. The false West Wind deserts her, and the young mother dies.

> Fair Nokomis bore a daughter,
> And she called her name Wenonah.
> *Hiawatha,* iii.

Wentworth, Austin. Richard's helpful and sympathetic uncle in Meredith's novel RICHARD FEVEREL.

Wentworth, Captain. Hero of Jane Austen's novel PERSUASION.

Werfel, Franz (1890–1945). Austrian poet, novelist, and playwright, born at Prague of Jewish parents, best known for his works expressing a semi-mystical belief in the brotherhood of man, the most outstanding being the best-selling novels *The Forty Days of Musa Dagh* (*Die Vierzig Tage des Musa Dagh;* 1934), concerning an Armenian siege during World War I, and *The Song of Bernadette* (*Das Lied von Bernadette;* 1942), the life of a French saint. Other works include *Weltfreund* (1911), *Wir Sind* (1913), and *Einander* (1915), books of poetry; *Verdi* (1924); *The Man Who Conquered Death* (1927), a translation of *Der Tod das Kleinbürgers; Paulus unter den Juden* (*Paul Among the Jews;* 1928), a tragedy; *Goat Song* (*Bockgesang;* 1926), a play; *Juarez and Maximilian* (1926), a play; *Class Reunion* (1929), a translation of *Der Abituriententag; The Pure in Heart* (1932), a translation of *Barbara, oder die Frömmigkeit* (1929); *The Pascarella Family* (1932), a translation of *Die Geschwister von Neapel; The Eternal Road* (*Der Weg der Verheissung;* 1936), a Biblical pageant; *Hearken unto the Voice* (*Höret die Stimme;* 1938); *Embezzled Heaven* (*Der Veruntreute Himmel;* 1940).

Werfel was in France during World War II when that country was invaded by the German army (1940), and he took refuge in the church of St. Bernadette. It is said that he vowed to dedicate a literary work to the saint if he should make his escape. He eventually escaped to the U.S., and the successful *Song of Bernadette* was announced to have been inspired by his experience. His last work, *The Star of the Unborn* (1945), is a vast and fantastic panorama of the experiences of F. W. (= Franz Werfel) in a distant future when only the Jews and the Catholics from among our denominations will have survived.

wergild or, in the *Ger.* form, **Wergeld** (*wer,* "man," and *gild,* "payment"). Among the early Germanic tribes of Europe, a fine imposed on the accused man or his family in reparation for a murder. The nature and amount of the fine varied according to the manner of murder, the political or social position of the victim, or his relative value to the community. Thus, the wergild of a man in the service of the king was higher than that for an ordinary freeman; the fine for the killing of a pregnant woman or a woman who had begun to bear children would be greater than that for one who had ceased bearing children; churchmen usually carried the highest wergild of all; etc. A later and socially more advanced form of wergild, payable not to the kin of the murdered but to the king, was called *bloodwite* (blood fine). The practice of exacting wergild was abandoned when Roman law substituted the principle of public justice for that of reparation and revenge. See also GUNNAR.

Werle, Gregers. A character in Ibsen's WILD DUCK.

Werner. The hero of Byron's drama *Werner or the Inheritance* (1821), retold from *Kruitzner or the German's Tale* in Harriet Lee's *Canterbury Tales.* In a moment of temptation, Kruitzner, or Werner as he calls himself, steals a rouleau of gold from Count Stralenheim, who has unjust possession of his inheritance and has persecuted him for years. Upon hearing his father confess his crime, Ulric, Werner's son, secretly murders the Count. Werner secures his inheritance, but when he learns that his son was the assassin, he sends him away with a curse.

Werner, Alice (1859–1935). English philologist, an expert in certain African tongues and author of books on the races, legends, and languages of Central and Southern Africa. She also wrote stories and poems.

Werner, Morris Robert (1897–). American writer. Author of lively studies of outstanding American characters and institutions. *Barnum* (1923); *Brigham Young* (1925); *Tammany Hall* (1928); *Bryan* (1929); etc.

Werrenrath, Reinald (1883–). American baritone who made his début at the Metropolitan Opera House in New York in 1919.

Werther. The sentimental hero of GOETHE's romance *The Sorrows of Werther* (1774). He is a young German student of poetic fancy and sensitive disposition who is so overcome by his unrequited love for Lotte that he takes his life. In the novel, Lotte is the betrothed and later the wife of Werther's friend Albert. Werther is admittedly drawn from Goethe himself, and Albert from his friend Kestner, who married Charlotte BUFF (Lotte) with whom Goethe was in love.

> *Werther,* infusing itself into the core and whole spirit of literature, gave birth to a race of sentimentalists, who raged and wailed in every part of the world till better light dawned on them, or at any rate till exhausted nature laid itself to sleep, and it was discovered that lamenting was an unproductive labour.—Carlyle.

Wertherism. Spleen, morbid sentimentality, romantic melancholy and disgust of life, in allusion to the romantic desperation of the hero in Goethe's *The Sorrows of Werther.*

werwolf. A "man-wolf" (A.S. *wer,* "man"), i.e., a man who, according to medieval superstition, was turned—or could at will turn himself—into a wolf (the *loup-garou* of France). This creature had the appetite of a wolf, and roamed about at night devouring infants and sometimes exhuming corpses. Its skin was proof against shot or steel, unless the weapon had been blessed in a chapel dedicated to St. Hubert.

This superstition was once common to almost all Europe, and still lingers in Brittany, Limousin, Auvergne, Servia, Wallachia, and White Russia. In the 15th century a council of theologians, convoked by the Emperor Sigismund, gravely decided that the werwolf was a reality.

OVID tells the story of Lycaon, King of Arcadia, turned into a wolf because he tested the divinity of Jupiter by serving up to him a "hash of human flesh"; Herodotus describes the Neuri as having the power of assuming once a year the shape of wolves; Pliny relates that one of the family of ANTAEUS was chosen annually, by lot, to be transformed into a wolf, in which shape he continued for nine years; and St. Patrick, we are told, converted Vereticus, King of Wales, into a wolf. Cf. "The Wolf of Salem," a short story written and illustrated by Howard PYLE, and *Dracula,* by Bram STOKER.

Wescott, Glenway (1901–). American novelist and poet, known for his writings about his native Middle West from the point of view of an expatriate of the 1920's acquainted with life in Europe. Among his books are *The Bitterns* (1920), a collection of poems; *The Apple of the Eye* (1924); *Natives of the Rock* (1926), poetry; *The Grandmothers* (1928), his best-known work, a study in the form of American family portraits; *Like a Lover* (1926); *Goodbye, Wisconsin* (1928), short stories; *The Babe's Bed* (1930); *A Calendar of Saints for Unbelievers* (1932); *Fear and Trembling* (1932); *The Pilgrim Hawk* (1940); *Apartment in Athens* (1945).

Wesley, Charles (1707–1788) and **John Wesley** (1703–1791). Two brothers, Charles founding the METHODIST society to which his brother and George WHITEFIELD belonged. Charles composed many hymns and left a *Journal* (1849). John was a tremendous preacher, traveling on horseback all over the country in England. He also published many collections of hymns and his prose *Works* (1771–1774). He was, further, the author of a *Journal* which was published in a standard edition (1909–1911). It is a very human document. His *Life,* written by Robert Southey, is said to be one of the best of biographies.

Wessex, the novelist of. Thomas HARDY, the author of *Tess of the D'Urbervilles, The Return of the Native, Wessex Tales, etc.* The scenes of most of his novels are laid in the Wessex country, once a kingdom of ancient England known as Wessex, but now called Dorsetshire. In recent editions of his work a map of the Wessex territory is included.

Wesson, Daniel Baird (1825–1906). American inventor. With Horace Smith invented a repeating action for firearms (1854) and organized for its manufacture the Smith & Wesson Co. in Springfield, Mass. (1857).

west.

the West End. The fashionable quarter of London, lying between Charing Cross and the western boundary of Hyde Park.

to go west. Of persons, to die; of things, to be lost, rendered useless, never obtained, as *My chance of promotion has gone west.* The phrase came into very wide use during World War I. Previously the expression *go west* had frequently been used in the United States as an equivalent of "Strike out for yourself" from Horace GREELEY's much quoted advice "Go west, young man, go west," that is, "go to the western states where frontier conditions still mean unusual opportunity."

West, Benjamin (1738–1820). Popular American painter who was historical painter to King George III (1772) and a friend of Sir Joshua Reynolds. He painted heroic canvases, which the American portrait painter John Singleton Copley called "ten-acre" pictures. His best-known works include *The Death of General Wolfe; Penn's Treaty with the Indians;* etc.

West, Lt. Kerchival. The hero of Bronson Howard's drama SHENANDOAH.

West, Mae (1893–). American actress on stage and screen, excelling in "sexy" plays, the best of which was *Diamond Lil.* Although melodrama, it was a real picture of life in the New York Tenderloin. A *Mae West,* in World War II slang, was an inflatable life-belt for aviators.

West, Nathanael (1906?–1940). American novelist, principally known for his story of newspaper life, *Miss Lonelyhearts* (1933). His *The Day of the Locust* (1939) deals with minor characters in Hollywood. He married the late Eileen McKenney, the heroine of *My Sister Eileen* by Ruth MCKENNEY.

West, Rebecca. An important character in Ibsen's drama ROSMERSHOLM.

West, Rebecca. Pseudonym of **Cecily Isabel Fairfield** (1892–). English novelist and critic, best known for her fictional psychological studies. Her books include *Henry James* (1916), criticism; *The Return of the Soldier* (1918); *The Judge* (1922); *The Strange Necessity* (1928), essays; *Harriet Hume* (1928); *D. H. Lawrence* (1930), criticism; *War Nurse* (1930), published under the pseudonym of **Corinne Andrews;** *Ending in Earnest* (1931), essays; *Arnold Bennett Himself* (1935); *St. Augustine* (1933); *A Letter to a Grandfather* (1933); *The Harsh Voice* (1935), four short novels; *The Thinking Reed* (1936), a novel; *Black Lamb and Grey Falcon* (1941), on travel in Jugoslavia; *The Meaning of Treason* (1947). She chose her pseudonym from the name of the heroine of Ibsen's ROSMERSHOLM because in her early career she had acted the rôle of Rebecca West.

West, V. Sackville-, see SACKVILLE-WEST, V.

Westbrook, Harriet (1794?–1816). The first wife of P. B. SHELLEY, whom she met after his expulsion from Oxford. He tried to convert her to atheism, urged her to rebel against the "tyranny" of her father, a retired innkeeper, and eloped with her to Edinburgh, where they were married in 1811. The couple wandered about the British Isles for a time, supported by their fathers, but their marriage was not happy, and in 1814 Shelley left Harriet to elope with Mary Godwin. Harriet thereafter drifted from love affair to love affair of her own, finally committing suicide in 1816.

Westcott, Edward Noyes (1846–1898). American banker and novelist. His *David Harum, A Story of American Life* (1898), was very popular, also as a play and film.

Westermarck, Edward Alexander (1862–1939). Finnish philosopher who wrote among other books *The Origin and Development of the Moral Ideas* (2 vols.; 1906–1908). *The History of Human Marriage* (1891) is his best-known work.

Western, Squire. In Fielding's TOM JONES, a jovial, fox-hunting country gentleman, supremely ignorant of booklearning, very prejudiced, selfish, irascible, and countrified, but shrewd, good-natured and fond of his daughter Sophia.

Sophia Western. The heroine of TOM JONES, daughter of Squire Western. She becomes engaged to Tom Jones, the foundling.

Western Reserve. A tract of land of 3,666,921 acres near Lake Erie which was "reserved" by the State of Connecticut when the states ceded their western lands to the federal government after the Revolution (see NORTHWEST TERRITORY). Connecticut gave up jurisdiction over the Western Reserve in 1800, but kept the title to the soil and sold it to individual purchasers.

Westinghouse, George (1846–1914). American inventor of air brakes and automatic railroad signals. Founder of the Westinghouse Electric Company and holder of some 400 patents.

West Point. The United States military academy at West Point, N.Y., on the Hudson River, where all regular officers of the U.S. army are trained.

West-Running Brook. The fifth book of poems (1928) by Robert FROST.

Westward Ho! A historical novel (1855) by Charles KINGSLEY, more fully entitled *Westward Ho! or The Voyages and Adventures of Sir Amyas Leigh in the Reign of Queen Elizabeth.* There had previously been a comedy, *Westward Ho!* by WEBSTER and DEKKER (1607).

We, the People. A tragedy of social protest (1933) by Elmer RICE.

Wetherell, Elizabeth. The pseudonym adopted by Susan Warner, author of THE WIDE, WIDE WORLD and QUEECHY.

Wetjen, Albert Richard (1900–1948). Anglo-American writer of sea stories. *Captains All* (1924), *Way for a Sailor!* (1928), *In the Wake of the Shark* (1939), etc.

Wexley, John (1907–). American playwright and actor, author of *The Last Mile* (1930), which concerns the last days of a prisoner condemned to death; *Steel* (1931), dealing with the labor situation; and *They Shall Not Die* (1934), which was built around the famous SCOTTSBORO Trial.

Weyburn, Matthew. Aminta's lover in Meredith's LORD ORMONT AND HIS AMINTA.

Weygand, Maxime (1867–). French soldier. Chief of the general staff under Foch (1914–1923). Chief of army general staff (1930). Commander in chief in Near East (1939). He was put in command of the forces of France during the 1940 retreat but was unsuccessful in stemming the German tide. He was made military commander in North Africa in 1940 by the Vichy régime and was governor general of Algeria in 1941. Toward the end of the same year he resigned both the posts.

Weygandt, Cornelius (1871–). American historian who helped to make the new Irish drama known in America. He has written *Irish Plays and Playwrights* (1913) and other books.

Weyler y Nicolau, Valeriano. Marquis of **Tenerife** (1838–1930). The Spanish military commander in Cuba who was recalled (1898) because of American protest against his ruthless policy. As minister of war he was equally ruthless in suppressing the riots in Catalonia (1909).

Weyman, Stanley John (1855–1928). Popular English novelist whose chief talent was for historical novels of an exciting character. He wrote *The House of the Wolf* (1890); *Under the Red Robe* (1894); *Count Hannibal* (1901); etc. Some were dramatized.

W. H. Initials representing the person to whom the sonnets of SHAKESPEARE were dedicated by the publisher. The identity of this person, called "the onlie begetter" of the sonnets, is not known, although William, Lord Herbert (later the Earl of Pembroke) and Henry Wriothesley, Earl of Southampton, Shakespeare's early patron, to whom *Venus and Adonis* (1593) and *The Rape of Lucrece* (1594) were addressed by the poet, have both been suggested as likely candidates.

Whalley, Edward (died 1675?). One of the regicides who signed the death warrant of King Charles I. At the time of the Restoration he fled to America and hid in New England. An avenue in New Haven, Connecticut, is named after him, Whalley Avenue.

Wharf Theatre. See PROVINCETOWN PLAYERS.

Wharton, Anne Hollingsworth (1845–1928). American writer whose books on American colonial customs are valuable works of reference.

Wharton, Edith Newbold Jones (1862–1937). American novelist and short-story writer, strongly influenced by Henry JAMES, best known for her studies of the tragedies and ironies in the lives of members of middle-class and aristocratic New York society in the 19th century. Her work is marked by penetrating psychological characterization, a preoccupation with moral problems, and a strict adherence to artistic form; in addition to that of James, the influence of Gustave FLAUBERT, George ELIOT, Paul BOURGET, and Marcel PROUST has been found in her books. Her works include *The Greater Inclination* (1899), short stories; *The Touchstone* (1900); *Crucial Instances* (1901), short stories; THE VALLEY OF DECISION (1902); *Sanctuary* (1903); *Italian Backgrounds* (1905); THE HOUSE OF MIRTH (1905); *Madame de Treymes* (1907); *The Fruit of the Tree* (1907); *The Hermit and the Wild Woman* (1908), short stories; *Artemis to Actaeon* (1909), poetry; *Tales of Men and Ghosts* (1910); ETHAN FROME (1911); *The Reef* (1912); THE CUSTOM OF THE COUNTRY (1913); *Fighting France* (1915), on World War I; XINGU, *and Other Stories* (1916); SUMMER (1917); *French Ways and Their Meaning* (1919); *The Marne* (1918); *In Morocco* (1920); THE AGE OF INNOCENCE (1920), awarded the 1921 Pulitzer prize; *Glimpses of the Moon* (1922); *A Son at the Front* (1923); *Old New York* (1924), consisting of *False Dawn, The Old Maid, The Spark,* and *New Year's Day,* all novelettes; *The Writing of*

Fiction (1925); *The Mother's Recompense* (1925); *Here and Beyond* (1926), short stories; *Twilight Sleep* (1927); *The Children* (1928); *Hudson River Bracketed* (1929), to which *The Gods Arrive* (1932) is a sequel; *Certain People* (1930), *Human Nature* (1933), The *World Over* (1936), and *Ghosts* (1937), more volumes of short stories; *A Backward Glance* (1934), an autobiography; *The Buccaneers* (1938), an uncompleted novel. THE HOUSE OF MIRTH, THE OLD MAID (a Pulitzer prize-winning play), and ETHAN FROME were successfully dramatized.

Wharton, Philip. Duke of Wharton (1698–1731). Satirized by Alexander Pope in *Moral Essays*. He was a son of **Thomas Wharton** (1648–1715) who wrote the doggerel ballad LILLIBURLERO.

What Every Woman Knows. A drama by J. M. BARRIE (1908). The heroine, Maggie Wylie, is a plain but wise little woman with a humorous charm all her own. The whimsical first act shows John Shand, a student who acts as railway porter in summer, breaking into a house for the experience of investigating the library, and Maggie's affectionate father and brother, who regret that she has "no charm" offering this intruding student enough money to complete his education if he will ask Maggie to marry him five years later. In due course of time he does marry her and, with her encouragement and help, enters Parliament. When he reveals a desire to elope with the fascinating Lady Sybil Lazenby, Maggie manages to give him such a surfeit of that lady's company as to bring him back to her cured.

What Maisie Knew. A novel (1897) by Henry JAMES, about a precocious small girl.

What Price Glory? A play by Maxwell ANDERSON and Laurence STALLINGS, produced in 1924, one of the first realistic American depictions of World War I. It deals with the rivalry of Captain Flagg and Sergeant Quirt, two members of a company of U.S. Marines in France in 1918, for the favors of Charmaine, a French girl. The play caused a sensation on its first production by its frank presentation of the profanity and brutality of the professional soldiers and the wearying ugliness of war. *What Price Glory?* was later dramatized as a motion picture, and "Captain Flagg and Sergeant Quirt" were adopted as the names of a military comedy team featured on the screen and on radio programs.

whaup. The European curlew. A famous poem by Robert Louis STEVENSON in answer to one by Samuel Rutherford CROCKETT centers about this bird which flies over the Scottish moors.

> Blows the wind to-day, and the sun and the rain are flying,
> Blows the wind on the moors to-day and now,
> Where about the graves of the martyrs the whaups are crying,
> My heart remembers how!

Wheatley, Gladys. In John Dos Passos' U.S.A., especially THE BIG MONEY, a Middle Western heiress whom Charley Anderson marries. She is repelled by the grossness of his attentions, rapidly becomes estranged from him, and eventually divorces him. His unhappy marriage contributes to Charley's hopelessness and his predilection for gambling and drinking.

Wheatley, Phyllis or **Phillis** (1753?–1784). Negro poet, the first woman writer of her race in the U.S. In 1761 she was brought to America from Africa and purchased as a slave by John Wheatley, a Boston merchant. As a child she showed unusual intelligence and was given an education and accorded special favors. She became famous in her day, being received in aristocratic society in London before the Revolution and being praised for her poetry by many intellectual and political figures of the day, including George Washington. *Poems on Various Subjects* (1773) is a representative book of her verse, consisting chiefly of occasional poems written in the characteristic manner of 18th century, considered to be of little literary value.

Wheeler, Burton Kendall (1882–). American politician, who ran for vice-president (1924) on the La Follette ticket. Prior to America's entry into the war, he was known as one of the leading isolationists.

Wheeler, Claude. The hero of Willa Cather's ONE OF OURS.

Wheeler, Joseph (1836–1906). American army officer and politician. A major general of volunteers in the Spanish-American War, he commanded a cavalry division in the army of General Shafter. He was at San Juan Hill and commanded a brigade in the Philippines. Retired with the rank of brigadier general (1900).

Wheelock, Eleazar (1711–1779). American educator and clergyman; first president of Dartmouth College (1769–1779).

Wheelock, John Hall (1886–). American poet and editor. His *Collected Poems* (1936) contain work that won its place in American poetry for its lyrical quality and sincerity.

Wheelwright, John (1897–1940) American poet, son of Boston's last civic architect. Deeply interested in social progress; founder of the John Reed Club at Harvard. Published a magazine, *Poems for a Dime*, for the workers. Author of *Rock and Shell* (1933); *Mirrors of Venus* (1938); *Political Self-Portrait* (1940). Wrote religious narratives, his favorite character being Thomas, the doubting apostle, also lyrics, satires, epigrams, and a novel in sonnets.

A vivid intellectual figure in Boston and Cambridge, where he died in a street accident.

When Johnny Comes Marching Home. A marching song of the Civil War, composed (1863) by the bandmaster P. S. Gilmore. Roy HARRIS's overture, *When Johnny Comes Marching Home* (1934), is based on it.

When Knighthood Was in Flower. A popular historical novel by Charles Major (*Am.*, 1898). The scene is laid in 16th-century England. The heroine is Mary Tudor, sister of Henry VIII, and the story concerns her love affair and marriage with Charles Brandon, a commoner. This novel was dramatized with great success, and Julia MARLOWE as Mary.

When Lilacs Last in the Dooryard Bloom'd. One of the best-known poems by Walt WHITMAN, an elegy on the death of Abraham Lincoln, published in *Sequel to Drum-Taps* (1865–1866) and LEAVES OF GRASS (1867). It presents a lament by the poet as he witnesses the funeral procession of the dead president, and makes use of three recurring symbols: a lilac branch, signifying love; "the drooping star in the west," representing Lincoln; and a singing thrush, symbolizing the poet himself.

Where the Blue Begins. A fantasy (1922), whose characters are all dogs, by Christopher MORLEY.

Whibley, Charles (1859–1930). English scholar and critic, associated with William Ernest HENLEY on the *Scots Observer*. He instituted the *Tudor Translations* (1892) and contributed to *Blackwood's* and the *Spectator*.

Whiffle, Captain. In Smollett's RODERICK RANDOM, a loathsome fop, "radiant in silk lace and diamond buckles."

Whiffle, Peter. Dilettante hero of the novel (1922), by Carl VAN VECHTEN.

Whig. An abbreviation of Whiggamore (*whig*, "to drive, and *a mare*). The name was first given to the COVENANTERS in the western part of Scotland, who sprang up about 1648. In 1679 it became a name for those who did not wish James II to succeed to the throne of England, and after that it was applied to one of the two chief political parties. In the latter part of the 19th century gave place to "liberal."

Whilomville Stories. Thirteen short stories (1900) by Stephen CRANE dealing with childhood in a small New York town.

Whims, Queen. In Rabelais' GARGANTUA AND PANTAGRUEL, the monarch of Whimdom, a country of whims, fancies, and literary speculations. Her subjects are alchemists, astrologers, fortune-tellers, rhymers, projectors, schoolmen, and so forth. The best way of reaching this empire is "to trust to the whirlwind and the current." When Pantagruel's ship runs aground, it is towed off by 7,000,000 drums quite easily.

Whipple, Clay. One of the chief characters in THE WITCHING HOUR by Augustus Thomas.

Whipple, Edwin Percy (1819–1886). American lecturer and critic. His work on foreign literature is more authoritative than the rest.

Whisky Insurrection, the. A popular outbreak in Western Pennsylvania, in 1794, resulting from an attempt to enforce an excise law passed in 1791, imposing duties on domestic distilled liquors.

Whistler, James Abbott McNeill (1834–1903). Famous American painter who settled in England (1863). He was of an imperious and quarrelsome nature and published *The Gentle Art of Making Enemies* (1890). He used pastel shades and signed his paintings with a butterfly. His portrait of his mother is his most famous work. Cf. his *Life* by Joseph and Elizabeth Robins PENNELL (1908).

Whistler, Laurence (1912–). English poet who received the gold medal presented by the King of England for the best volume of poetry published in England in 1934.

Whistler, Rex John (1905–1944). English painter who did murals for the Tate Gallery in London and illustrated *Gulliver's Travels; Desert Island;* etc. He also did stage settings, as for *Victoria Regina,* by Laurence HOUSMAN.

white denotes purity, simplicity, and candor; innocence, truth, and hope. See *colors, symbolism of.*

The ancient Druids, and indeed the priests generally of antiquity, used to wear white vestments, as do the clergy of the Established Church of England when they officiate in any sacred service. The Magi also wore white robes.

The head of OSIRIS, in ancient Egypt, was adorned with a white tiara; all his ornaments were white and his priests were clad in white.

The priests of JUPITER, and the Flamen Dialis of Rome, were clothed in white, and wore white hats. The victims offered to Jupiter wore white. The Roman festivals were marked with white chalk, and at the death of a Caesar the national mourning was white; white horses were sacrificed to the sun, white oxen were selected for sacrifice by the Druids, and white elephants are held sacred in Siam.

The Persians affirm that the divinities are habited in white.

white collar. A phrase usually used as an adjective to denote the brain worker—professional classes, office clerks, etc., usually with reference to meager salaries paid to such workers, who must nevertheless dress neatly.

White Cross Knights. The Knights Hospitallers. The Knights Templars wore a *red* cross.

white crow. A *rara avis;* a rare occurrence.

White Elephant. The sacred animal of Siam. Siam was known as *the Land of the White Elephant,* and its ruler as the *King of the White Elephant. To have a white elephant to keep* is to have an expensive and unprofitable dignity to support, or a pet article to take care of. The King of Siam used to make a present of a white elephant to such of his courtiers as he wished to ruin. On account of their sacred nature they necessitated great expense and brought no practical returns.

to show the white feather. To show cowardice; a phrase from the cockpit. No gamecock has a white feather; it indicates a cross-breed in birds.

white flag. The flag of surrender.

White Friars. The Carmelites, from their garb.

White House. The presidential mansion in the United States, at Washington; figuratively, the Presidency.

White Ladies. A species of *fée* in many countries, the appearance of whom generally forbodes death in the house. See also BANSHEE. The belief is a relic of old Teutonic mythology, and the White Ladies represent Holda, or Berchta, the goddess who received the souls of maidens and young children.

German legend says that when the castle of Neuhaus, Bohemia, was being built, a *White Lady* appeared to the workmen and promised them a sweet soup and carp on the completion of the castle. In remembrance thereof, these dainties were for long given to the poor of Bohemia on Maundy Thursday. She is also said to have been heard to speak on two occasions, once in December, 1628, when she said, "I wait for judgment!" and once at Neuhaus, when she said to the princes, " 'Tis ten o'clock." The first recorded instance of this apparition was in the 16th century, and the name given to the lady is Bertha von Rosenberg. She last appeared, it is said, in 1879, just prior to the death of Prince Waldemar. She carries a bunch of keys at her side, and is always dressed in white.

In Normandy, the White Ladies lurk in ravines, fords, bridges, and other narrow passes, and ask the passenger to dance. If they receive a courteous answer, well; but if a refusal, they seize the churl and fling him into a ditch, where thorns and briers may serve to teach him gentleness of manners. The most famous of these ladies is *La Dame d'Aprigny,* who used to occupy the site of the present Rue St. Quentin, at Bayeux, and *La Dame Abonde.*

> One kind of these the Italians *Fata* name;
> The French call *Fée;* we *Sybils;* and the same
> Others *White Dames,* and those that them have seen,
> *Night Ladies* some, of which Habundia's queen.
>
> *Hierarchie,* viii, p. 507.

The most celebrated in Britain is the *White Lady of Avenel,* introduced by Scott into THE MONASTERY. See AVENEL.

White League. A name of the KU KLUX KLAN.

white lie. An excusable or pardonable untruth; a misstatement made either with no ulterior motive or "with the best intentions."

White Man's Burden, the. Euphemism for the type of imperialism predominant in Europe and America, especially Great Britain, at the end of the 19th century and the beginning of the 20th century, justified by many of its supporters as a moral duty devolving upon the "superior" white nations to guide and develop the "backward" peoples in their newly acquired colonies. The term is from the title of a poem by Rudyard KIPLING (1899) which is considered to be an excellent expression of the attitude of conservative British imperialists and the author himself at the time of its composition. The first stanza is as follows:

> Take up the White Man's burden—
> Send forth the best ye breed—
> Go bind your sons to exile
> To serve your captives' need;
> To wait in heavy harness
> On fluttered folk and wild—
> Your new-caught, sullen peoples,
> Half-devil and half-child.

White Man's Grave. Sierra Leone, in Africa, from its unhealthful conditions.

White Paper. An official publication of the English government of less scope than a BLUE BOOK.

White Queen. See under QUEEN.

White Rose. The House of York, whose emblem it was. See under ROSE.

white slave. A prostitute. The *white slave trade* is traffic in prostitutes.

White Sox. In American baseball parlance, the Chicago Nationals. See BASEBALL TEAMS.

white stone. Days marked with a white stone are days of pleasure, days to be remembered with gratification. The Romans used a white stone or piece of chalk to mark their lucky days with on the calendar. Those that were unlucky they marked with black charcoal. See RED-LETTER DAY.

White, Andrew Dickson (1832–1918). American diplomat and educator. President of Cornell University (1867–1885). Minister to Germany (1879–1881) and Russia (1892–1894); etc. He wrote a number of books, including his *Autobiography* (1905).

White, Bouck (1874–). American Congregationalist minister who became a Socialist. He was sentenced to prison because of his politics. He wrote among other works *Letters from Prison* (1915) and *The Free City* (1919).

White, Edward Lucas (1866–1934). American novelist and short-story writer whose greatest success was *Andivius Hedulio* (1921), a very vivid novel of ancient Rome. His weird stories in *Lukundoo* (1927) are outstanding.

White, Gilbert (1720–1793). English naturalist and curate, born in Hampshire. His *A Natural History and Antiquities of Selborne* (1789) is still worth reading.

White, Henry Kirke (1785–1806). English poet, chiefly known because of a memoir which the poet Robert Southey wrote of him in 1807. Byron thought highly of his work, but nothing much has come down to us except one or two hymns.

White, Horace (1834–1916). Famous American editor who championed civil service reform. His most memorable book is *Money and Banking: Illustrated by American History* (1895).

White, Joseph Blanco (1775–1841). British theological writer, best remembered for one poem, a sonnet on *Night and Death* (1828).

Why do we, then, shun Death with anxious strife?
If Light can thus deceive, wherefore not Life?

White, Stewart Edward (1873–1946). American novelist and travel writer. He wrote many stories of California, and his earlier books include *The Blazed Trail* (1902); *Conjuror's House* (1903); *The Silent Places* (1904); etc. After the death of his wife, he wrote of the other world, believing that he had received psychic communications. One of the best of these books is *The Unobstructed Universe* (1940).

White, Terence Hanbury (1906–). English writer of fantasies of the Arthurian Cycle. *The Sword in the Stone* (1938); *The Witch in the Wood* (1939); *The Ill-Made Knight* (1940); *Mistress Masham's Repose* (1946). His eulogy of England, *England Have My Bones* (1937), is beautiful prose.

White, William Allen (1868–1946). Famous American editor who bought the Emporia *Gazette* in 1895 and edited it for many years with so original a touch that it became one of the quoted papers in America. His son, **William L. White** (1900–), author of *They Were Expendable* and other books, has taken over his post after having become well-known in the newspaper field as a roving editor and newspaper correspondent. William Allen White was known as a liberal Republican. His *The Court of Boyville* (1899) is one of the best accounts of boyhood in the old America. He also wrote *In Our Town* (1906), novels, biographies, and essays.

White, William Hale. Pen name **Mark Rutherford** (1831–1913). English novelist and translator.

Whiteboys. A secret agrarian association organized in Ireland about the year 1760, so called because they wore white shirts in their nightly expeditions. In 1787 a new association appeared, the members of which called themselves "Right-Boys." The Whiteboys were originally called Levelers from their throwing down fences and leveling enclosures.

Whitechapel. A quarter in the East End of London inhabited by the poorer classes, alien Jews, etc. *To play Whitechapel* (at cards) is to play in a mean, unsportsmanlike way; a *Whitechapel cart* is a light, two-wheeled spring cart, as used by small tradesmen for delivering goods; a *Whitechapel shave* is no shave at all, but rubbing powder over the bristles instead, "for the sake of appearance."

White Company, The. A historical romance by A. Conan DOYLE (1891), dealing with the 14th century. The hero is Alleyne Edricson, one of the White Company of Saxon bowmen led by Sir Nigel Loring under the Black Prince. He wins both honor and the hand of Sir Nigel's daughter.

White Devil, The. A tragedy (1608; published, 1612) by John WEBSTER. It contains one dirge which has become a classic.

Whitehall. A street in London on which are situated the chief government offices of the British Empire; hence, the governmental administration of the Empire.

White Hart Inn. An inn in Southwark, London, mentioned by Shakespeare in the second part of *Henry VI* as being Jack Cade's headquarters. It was there also that Mr. Pickwick in Dickens' PICKWICK PAPERS met with Sam Weller.

Whitehead, Alfred North (1861–1947). Leading English mathematician and philosopher tending toward mysticism. Fellow of the Royal Society and of the British Academy; president of the Mathematical Association and winner of several prizes and medals. His tenets have been compared to those of JEANS, MILLIKAN, and EDDINGTON. He is best known to the general reader through his *Science and the Modern World* (1925), a book excelling in clarity of style.

White Hoods. A popular party in Ghent, mentioned in *Philip van Artevelde* (1834), a historical drama in blank verse by Sir Henry TAYLOR.

White Horse, the. An historic figure of a horse which is incised on the chalk downs in Berkshire. It is supposed to be the white horse which was the emblem of the Saxons. It is 374 feet long. Since 1736 it has been given periodic scrubbings. *The Ballad of the White Horse* by G. K. Chesterton (1911) makes it symbolic of the struggle between the Saxons under King Alfred and the invading Norsemen and also of Christianity battling against paganism.

Whiteing, Richard (1840–1928). English journalist and writer of fiction. His best novel, *No. 5 John Street* (1899), is the story of a tenement in London.

White-Jacket or The World in a Man-of-War. A novel by Herman MELVILLE (1850), considered to be semi-autobiographical in character, dealing with life aboard the U.S. frigate *Neversink* (said to stand for the American man-of-war *United States,* on which the author himself served in his youth) during a three-year cruise. Its chief interest is its depiction of the character of the various officers and men on the ship. Its revelation of the severe punishments and other abuses suffered by the men on board American naval vessels of the time led to the enactment of reforms. The title refers to a white pea-jacket worn by the narrator, his distinguishing mark among the crew; on one occasion it blows over his head during a storm, blinds him, and causes him to fall into the sea, in which he is nearly drowned.

White Knight's Ballad, The. A poem by Lewis CARROLL, appearing in *Through the Looking-Glass.* It is a parody on Wordsworth's RESOLUTION AND INDEPENDENCE. See also INCIDENTS IN THE LIFE OF MY UNCLE ARLY.

Whiteley, Opal, see OPAL WHITELEY.

White's Chocolate House. In London, opened by Francis White (1697). It was a popular resort of the wits of the early eighteenth century and is mentioned in the *Tatler.*

White Ship, The. A poem (1881) by Dante Gabriel ROSSETTI, appearing in *Ballads and Sonnets.*

White Wings. A dramatic fantasy (1927) by Philip BARRY, about New York street-cleaners.

Whitfield, Ann. The heroine of Shaw's comedy MAN AND SUPERMAN.

Whitford, Vernon. A leading character in Meredith's novel THE EGOIST.

Whitman, Marcus (1802–1847). American pioneer, famous for a seven-month ride from Oregon to the East (1842–1843). He wished to consolidate his position as a missionary and collected many emigrants who went back with him to Oregon. Disease came to his mission in the Far West and he and his wife were killed in an Indian uprising. They are the principal characters in *We Must March* (1925), a novel by Honoré Willsie MORROW.

Whitman, Sarah Helen (1803–1878). American poet who became engaged (1848) to Edgar Allan Poe. The second of his poems called *To Helen* was written for her. Poe's *Last Letters* to her appeared in 1909.

Whitman, Walter, known as **Walt Whitman** (1819–1892). American poet, known for the intense individualism of his poetry, his use of FREE VERSE, and his mystical celebration of America, democracy, and the common man. His poetry, unique among the American verse of his time, is marked by exuberance of spirit, sometimes extravagant rhetoric, extreme love of the sensuous in what some critics have interpreted as a tendency toward homosexuality, a worship of the superior individual, romantic identification of the individual poet with nature and the universe, stress on mystical paradox and conflict, a glorification of democratic equality and the American pioneers, and frequent vivid passages giving a realistic picture of American life in the poet's age, especially in New York City. In his work critics have found evidence of a number of diverse influences, including those of SHAKESPEARE, the BIBLE, contemporary oratory, OSSIAN, SCOTT, Italian opera, HOMER, GOETHE, the philosophy of HEGEL, the NIBELUNGENLIED, DANTE, CARLYLE, the TRANSCENDENTALISTS, and especially EMERSON. His works include *Leaves of Grass* (1855), new and revised editions of poems under the same title being issued in 1856, 1860, 1867, 1871, 1876, 1881–1882, 1884, 1889, 1891–1892, 1897, 1900, and so on; *Drum-Taps* (1865); *Sequel to Drum-Taps* (1865–1866); *Democratic Vistas* (1871), a volume of prose; *Passage to India* (1871); *As a Strong Bird on Pinions Free, And Other Poems* (1872); *Memoranda during the War* (1875), prose; *Two Rivulets* (1876); *Specimen Days and Collect* (1882–1883); *November Boughs* (1888); *Good-Bye, My Fancy* (1891); *Calamus* (1897); *The Wound-Dresser* (1898); *Notes and Fragments* (1899); *The Complete Writings* (1902), ten volumes; *An American Primer* (1904); *The Gathering of the Forces* (1920), a collection of prose writings published in the Brooklyn *Eagle; The Uncollected Poetry and Prose* (1921); *Leaves of Grass* (1926), an inclusive edition; *The Half-Breed, And Other Stories* (1927), a collection of his short stories; *I Sit and Look Out* (1932), a collection of prose writings published in various newspapers. His first work was *Franklin Evans, or The Inebriate* (1842), a temperance novel. Famous single poems are SONG OF MYSELF; *There Was a Child Went Forth; Crossing Brooklyn Ferry; Out of the Cradle Endlessly Rocking; I Hear America Singing; Pioneers! O Pioneers!; Vigil Strange I Kept on the Field One Night; When I Heard the Learned Astronomer;* WHEN LILACS LAST IN THE DOORYARD BLOOM'D; *Once I Pass'd Through a Populous City;* O CAPTAIN! MY CAPTAIN!; *The Base of all Metaphysics.*

Whitman, who had very little formal education, taught in a school on Long Island, worked on various newspapers in New York City, Brooklyn, and New Orleans, and lived somewhat as a Bohemian in his youth, being particularly fond of encouraging the growth of colorful legends about himself. During the Civil War he served as a nurse in the army hospitals in Washington, and later worked as a clerk in the Department of the Interior. He suffered a paralytic stroke in 1873 and spent the remainder of his life in retirement. When his work first appeared in the U.S., it shocked the general public; it is said that he lost his government clerkship because the Secretary of the Interior regarded *Leaves of Grass* as immoral. Whitman was first recognized as an important literary figure in England and France, by such authors as William ROSSETTI, Robert Louis STEVENSON, J. A. SYMONDS, and A. C. SWINBURNE; his free verse influenced the *vers-libre* movement in French poetry. By the 20th century he was regarded as one of the most important writers in the history of American literature and had a strong influence on a number of 20th-century American poets, especially Carl SANDBURG, and the proletarian poets (see PROLETARIAN LITERATURE) of the 1930's. For a study of Walt Whitman and his poetry, cf. *American Renaissance,* by F. O. MATTHIESSEN.

Whitney, Eli (1765–1825). American inventor of the cotton gin (patented 1794).

Whitney, Gertrude Vanderbilt (1877?–1942). The daughter of Cornelius Vanderbilt who married Harry Payne Whitney. She was well-known as a sculptor. She carved a fountain in the Pan-American building and did the memorial of the *Titanic* in Washington. In 1931 she opened the Whitney Museum of American Art in New York City.

Whittier, John Greenleaf (1807–1892). American poet, known for his portrayals of everyday life in rural New England, written largely under the influence of Robert BURNS, and for his poems expressing his humanitarian and politically liberal convictions, especially in connection with the anti-slavery movement. His works include *Legends of New England in Prose and Verse* (1831); *Moll Pitcher* (1832); *Mogg Megone* (1836), a prose account of Indian life in the days of the colonies; *Poems Written During the Progress of the Abolition Question* (1838); *Lays of My Home, And Other Poems* (1843); *Voices of Freedom* (1846), anti-slavery poems; *Leaves from Margaret Smith's Journal in the Province of Massachusetts Bay, 1678–1679* (1849), a prose romance based on records of the SALEM WITCHCRAFT trials; *Poems* (1849); *Songs of Labor* (1850); *Old Portraits and Modern Sketches* (1850) and *Literary Recreations and Miscellanies* (1854), collections of prose; *The Chapel of the Hermits* (1853); *The Panorama, And Other Poems* (1856); *Home Ballads, Poems, and Lyrics* (1860); *In War Time, And Other Poems* (1864); *Snow-Bound* (1866), his best-known poem, dealing with a heavy snowfall in the countryside of New England, presented in an idyllic vein; *The Tent on the Beach* (1867), narrative verse; *Among the Hills* (1869); *Miriam, And Other Poems* (1871); *Hazel Blossoms* (1875); *The Vision of Echard* (1878); *St. Gregory's Guest* (1886); *At Sundown* (1890). Well-known single poems are THE BAREFOOT BOY, MAUD MULLER, ICHABOD, *Skipper Ireson's Ride,* and *Telling the Bees.* Whittier, called "the Quaker Poet," was a fervent and active Abolitionist during a large part of his career.

Whittington, Dick. A poor orphan country lad, who heard that London was "paved with gold," and went there to get a living. When he was reduced to the starving point, a kind merchant gave him employment in his family, to help the cook, but the cook so ill-treated him that he ran away. Sitting to rest himself on the roadside, he heard Bow Bells, and they seemed to him to say, "Turn again, Whittington, thrice lord mayor of London"; so he returned to his master. By-and-by the master allowed him, with the other servants, to put in an adventure in a ship bound for Morocco. Richard had nothing but a cat, which, however, he sent. Now it happened that the King of Morocco was troubled by mice, which Whittington's cat destroyed, and this so pleased His Highness that he bought the mouser at a fabulous price. Dick commenced business with this money, soon rose to great wealth, married his master's daughter, was knighted, and thrice elected lord mayor of London—in 1398, 1406, and 1419. Such is the tale. Some persons assert that Whittington's "cat" was a brig built on the Norwegian model, with narrow stern, projecting quarters, and deep waist. Others think the word *achat,* "barter," furnishes the right solution.

Beneath this stone lies Whittington,
  Sir Richard rightly named,
Who three times Lord Mayor served in London,
  In which he ne'er was blamed.
He rose from indigence to wealth
  By industry and that,
For lo! he scorned to gain by stealth
  What he got by a cat.
Epitaph (destroyed by the fire of London).

Whit Sunday. White Sunday, the seventh Sunday after Easter, to commemorate the descent of the Holy Ghost on the day of Pentecost. In the primitive church the newly baptized wore *white* from Easter to Pentecost, and were called *albati* (white-robed). The last of the Sundays, which was also the chief festival, was called emphatically *Dominica in Albis* (Sunday in White).

An old idea is that it is the *Wit* or *Wisdom* Sunday, the day when the Apostles were filled with wisdom by the Holy Ghost.

This day Wit-sonday is cald,
For wisdom and wit sevene fald,
Was zonen to the Apostles as this day.
Cambr. Univer. MSS., Dd. i, 1, p. 234.

We ought to kepe this our Witsonday bicause the law of God was then of the Holy Wyght or Ghost deliured gostly vnto vs.—Taverner (1540).

This day is called Wytsonday because the Holy Ghost brought wytte and wysdom into Christis disciples . . . and filled them full of ghostly wytte.—*In die Pentecostis* (printed by Wynkyn de Worde).

Whitty, Dame **May** (1865–1948). English actress, noted on stage and screen. *Night Must Fall, The Lady Vanishes,* etc. See also Margaret WEBSTER.

Who's Who. A volume of abbreviated biographies of prominent persons. Both an English and an American *Who's Who* are issued annually and biennially, respectively.

Whymper, Edward (1840–1911). Pioneer alpinist who was successful in climbing the Matterhorn (1865). He wrote several books on his exploits in the Alps and the Andes. He also excelled in wood engraving and was a book illustrator.

Whyte-Melville, George John (1821–1878). British novelist of the hunting field and a great writer. He wrote also *Riding Recollections* (1875) and some poetry. The Australian poet Adam Lindsay Gordon was a great admirer of his.

Wickard, Claude Raymond (1893–). U. S. secretary of agriculture (1940–1945). Made administrator of food production and distribution (1942).

Wicked Wasp of Twickenham. See POPE, ALEXANDER.

Wickersham, George Woodward (1858–1936). Attorney general of the United States (1909–1913) and president of the International Arbitral Tribunal under the Young plan (1932–1936).

Wicker-Work Woman, The. A novel by Anatole France. See under BERGERET.

Wicket Gate, The. In Bunyan's PILGRIM'S PROGRESS, the entrance to the road which leads to the Celestial City. Over the door is written, "Knock, and it shall be opened unto you."

Wickfield, Mr. In Dickens' DAVID COPPERFIELD, a lawyer, father of Agnes. The "umble" Uriah HEEP is his clerk.

Agnes Wickfield. Daughter of Mr. Wickfield; the second wife of David Copperfield. She is considered one of Dickens' most womanly (and colorless) characters.

Wickham, Anna (1884–). English poet of slender output but powerful originality. *The Contemplative Quarry* (1920) is probably her best book. Recognition has been slow in coming to her.

Widdemer, Margaret (1880?–). American poet and popular novelist. Her best poetry is contained in *Cross-Currents* (1921). Her novels are sentimental but manifest a shrewd insight into life.

Widdicombe Fair. A popular English song, the words and the tune probably originating at the end of the eighteenth century.

Tom Pearse, Tom Pearse, lend me your grey mare,
All along, down along, out along, lee.
For I want for to go to Widdicombe Fair . . .

Widener, Harry Elkins (1885–1912). American book collector, lost on *Titanic.* Widener Memorial Library, opened June 1915 at HARVARD, was given by his mother.

Widener, Peter (1834–1915). American financier and collector who left his collection of paintings, porcelains, antiques, etc., to the city of Philadelphia and built and endowed the Widener Memorial Industrial Training School for Crippled Children (1906).

Wide, Wide World, The. A once popular story for girls by Susan WARNER ("Elizabeth Wetherell"; 1851). The heroine, Ellen Montgomery, is left for a time in the care of Miss Fortune Emerson, a relative whose sharp tongue and Puritanical principles almost prove too much for Ellen. With the aid of the sympathetic Miss Alice Humphreys and a conscience such as the child heroines of the 19th century possessed, she manages to remain a model child.

widow.

the widow's cruse. A small supply of anything which, by good management, is made to go a long way and to be apparently inexhaustible; in allusion to the miracle of the cruse of oil in 2 *Kings,* iv.

the Widow of Windsor. Queen Victoria.

a California widow. A woman who lives apart from her husband; so called from the wives left behind at the time of the California gold rush.

a grass widow. A woman living apart from her husband in a state of separation but not divorce; possibly from *grace widow,* a widow by grace of courtesy.

According to another account, the word has nothing to do with *grace* widow, and the modern use seems to have originated among Anglo-Indians about the middle of the 19th century, from the practice of European husbands of sending their wives, during the hot season, to the hills—where grass is plentiful—while they worked in the sweltering plains below. Still another suggestion is that the phrase arose in America, during the gold mania in California. A man would not unfrequently put his wife and children to board with some family while he went to the "diggins." This he called "putting his wife to grass," as a horse is put to grass when not wanted or unfit for work.

Widow in the Bye Street, The. A narrative poem by John MASEFIELD (1912), the story of a devoted mother and her son, Jimmy, who, when the girl he loves is faithless, kills her lover.

Widsith. One of the oldest English poems (seventh century?) in the Exeter Book. It concerns a wandering minstrel and his travels.

Wieland. Another form of Volund or WAYLAND SMITH.

Wieland, Christoph Martin (1733–1813). German writer of romances and ironic tales in verse. He translated eleven plays by Shakespeare into German prose. His long epic *Oberon* was translated into English by John Quincy Adams while U.S. minister in Berlin (1797–1801).

Wieland, or The Transformation. A novel by Charles Brockden BROWN (1798), dealing with mysterious events in the household of the Wielands, the family of a German mystic who has settled in Pennsylvania. The heroine and narrator is Clara Wieland, who falls in love with one Carwin, a fascinating stranger. Suddenly mysterious voices are heard about the house at night which terrify Clara. The voices tell Clara's lover, Henry Pleyel, that she has been unfaithful to him, whereupon he leaves and returns to Germany, where he marries a former fiancée whom he has believed dead. Clara's brother, the younger Wieland, goes mad as a result of hearing the strange voices, murders his wife and children, and is put in an insane asylum. Eventually, however, Carwin confesses that he has produced the voices through ventriloquism and by the same skill is able to rescue Clara from her brother when the madman escapes from the asylum and tries to kill the girl. At the conclusion of the novel Wieland commits suicide, Carwin starts out again on his travels, and Clara marries Pleyel when his former wife dies. *Wieland* is notable as the first American example of the GOTHIC NOVEL.

Wiese, Kurt (1887–). Well-known American illustrator of children's books.

Wife-Hater's Bible. See BIBLE, SPECIALLY NAMED.

Wife of Bath. One of the famous group of pilgrims of Chaucer's CANTERBURY TALES, who made the journey from Southwark to the shrine of THOMAS À BECKET in Canterbury. She is a bold, jovial woman, somewhat deaf, who has traveled over Europe and the Holy Land and has been married no less than five times. John GAY wrote a comedy called *The Wife of Bath* in 1713, and Percy MacKaye in his CANTERBURY PILGRIMS gives her a prominent rôle. She is described by Chaucer as follows:

A good Wyf was ther of bisyde Bathe,
But she was som-del deef, and that was scathe . . .
Bold was his face, and fair, and reed of hewe.
She was a worthy womman al hir lyve,
Housbondes at chirche-dore she hadde fyve.
Withouten other company in youthe.
But therof nedeth not to speke as nouthe . . .
At Rome she hadde been, and at Boloigne,
In Galice, at seint Jame and at Cologne
In felawschip wel coude she laughe and carpe.
Prologue to the Canterbury Tales.

The Wife of Bath's Tale. The story told by the Wife of Bath centers about the old query, "What does a woman like best?" A knight of King Arthur's court, condemned to lose his life if he does not find the answer, hunts far and near, and finally agrees to marry a poor, old, ugly woman who tells him, in return, that what a woman likes best is to have her own sweet way. She then throws off her mask and appears young, beautiful and rich. The tale was taken from Gower's *Confessio Amantis.*

Wife of Sir Isaac Harman, The. A novel by H. G. WELLS (1914). The petted doll wife of the wealthy and domineering Sir Isaac longs for a more active life than he allows her, and gradually comes to take satisfaction in building and managing hostels for working people.

Wiggin, Kate Douglas (1856–1923). Widely popular American writer of children's books and novels. Best known for her *The Birds' Christmas Carol* (1887) and REBECCA OF SUNNYBROOK FARM (1903).

Wigglesworth, Michael (1631–1705). Puritan clergyman and author of early New England, best known for his long poem THE DAY OF DOOM (1662), extremely popular, republished in the U.S. as late as 1867. He also wrote *Meat Out of the Eater, Or Meditations Concerning the Necessity, End, and Usefulness of Afflictions unto God's Children* (1669), a theological poem almost as popular in its day as *The Day of Doom; God's Controversy with New England, Written in the Time of the Great Drought, Anno 1662, by a Lover of New England's Prosperity,* first published in 1871; and a number of shorter poems on theological subjects, such as *Death, Expected and Welcomed* and *A Farewell to the World.* Wigglesworth, both minister and physician at Malden, Massachusetts, during most of career, was a characteristic Puritan of his time, but, unlike the MATHERS, he did not take part in the SALEM WITCHCRAFT trials, instead ordering public repentance and humiliation of those who did participate in the trials.

Wiggs, Mrs., see MRS. WIGGS.

Wight, Isle of. An island off the southern coast of England. Notable in literature as the residence of Lord TENNYSON in the latter part of his life.

Wilcox, Ella Wheeler (1850–1919). American verse-writer, known for her numerous books of lush, sentimental, and platitudinous poetry, extremely popular in her day and considered characteristic of the general literary taste of the time. *Poems of Passion* (1883) is one of her best-known volumes.

wild.

a wild-cat scheme. A rash and hazardous financial venture; a speculation in which one would have about as much chance of making a profit as of catching a wild-cat in the woods.

a wild-goose chase. A hunt after a nest. This chase has two defects: first, it is very hard to catch the goose, and, secondly, it is of very little worth when it is caught. *To lead one on a wild-goose chase* is therefore to beguile one with false hopes, or put one on the pursuit of something not practicable, or at any rate not worth the chase. Rex WARNER wrote an allegorical novel entitled *The Wild Goose Chase* (1937).

the Wild Huntsman. A spectral hunter of medieval legend who, with a pack of spectral dogs, frequents certain forests and occasionally appears to mortals. One account has it that he was a Jew who would not suffer Jesus to drink out of a horse-trough, but pointed to some water in a hoof-print as good enough for "such an enemy of Moses."

The Germans locate him in the Black Forest; the French in the Forest of Fontainebleau, and confuse him with St. Hubert; and in England he has become HERNE THE HUNTER, once a keeper in Windsor Forest, who "walks" in winter time, about midnight, and blasts trees and cattle.

wild oats, he is sowing his. Indulging the buoyant folly of youth; living in youthful dissipation. The idea is that the mind is a field of good oats, but these pranks are wild oats or weeds sown amongst the good seed, choking it for a time, but soon to die out and give place to genuine grain.

Wild, Jonathan (1682–1725). A famous criminal, hanged at Tyburn for housebreaking. Tales of his six wives and of his gang of subordinates have become popular legend. Daniel DEFOE made *Jonathan Wild* the subject of a romance (1725). FIELDING did the same in 1743, calling his novel *The History of Jonathan Wild the Great.* In these romances he is a coward, traitor, hypocrite, and tyrant, unrelieved by human feeling and never betrayed into a kind or good action. The character is historic, but the adventures are in a measure fictitious.

Wildair, Sir Harry. The hero of a comedy so called by George FARQUHAR (1701). The same character had been introduced in the *Constant Couple* (1700), by the same author. Sir Harry is a gay profligate, not altogether selfish and abandoned, but very free and of easy morals. This was Wilks' and Peg Woffington's great part.

Wild Ass's Skin, The (Le Peau de chagrin). A novel by BALZAC (1830). The hero, Raphael, receives from an old man a piece of magic skin which will insure the gratification of every desire, but will diminish with each wish granted, and with it goes the life of the possessor. Raphael cries "A short life and a merry one" and proceeds to enjoy life to the full. But the skin shrinks steadily and in spite of his frantic attempts to find some scientific means of stretching it, he is forced to yield to the inevitable and dies a young man. See FEDORA; AQUILINA.

Wild Duck, The. A drama by Henrik IBSEN (1884). The heroine, Hedwig, a sensitive and charming girl, is supposedly the daughter of Hjalmer Ekdal and his wife Gina, the former mistress of the elder Ekdal's wealthy partner Werle. Werle's son, Gregors, who believes that truth is always better than illusion, tells Hedwig of her illegitimate origin, and she kills herself.

Wilde, Oscar Fingal O'Flahertie Wills (1856–1900). Irish-born English playwright, poet, and prose-writer, known for his eccentricity and affectation of behavior and the brilliant wit and paradox of his society comedies. During his undergraduate years at Oxford he became the leader of an English aesthetic movement, given impetus by the PRE-RAPHAELITE BROTHERHOOD and the theories of Walter PATER, which advocated "ART FOR ART'S SAKE" and sought to cultivate the hyperaesthetic characteristics of the contemporary DECADENTS in France. Wilde's works include *Poems* (1881); *The Happy Prince, And Other Tales* (1888), a collection of fairy tales and allegories; THE PICTURE OF DORIAN GRAY (1891), a novel in the form of a moral allegory; *The House of Pomegranates* (1892), another group of fairy stories; *Intentions* (1892), a collection of reviews and critical studies; *Poems* (1892); LADY WINDERMERE'S FAN (1892), *A* WOMAN OF NO IMPORTANCE (1893), *Salomé* (1893), *An Ideal Husband* (1895), and THE IMPORTANCE OF BEING EARNEST (1895), all plays; THE BALLAD OF READING GAOL (1898); and DE PROFUNDIS (1905). The last two works were signed **Sebastian Melmoth.**

Wilde was the son of a well-known Irish surgeon and an eccentric poetess, Jane Francisca Elgee, who wrote under the name of Speranza. He attracted a deal of attention and ridicule during the period of his active aestheticism, when he wore his hair long, dressed eccentrically, and carried flowers in his hands while lecturing; the Gilbert and Sullivan opera PATIENCE (1881) was a burlesque of the "art for art's sake" movement led by him. His plays were very successful and are considered by some critics to be in part forerunners of the similarly witty comedies of George Bernard SHAW. Wilde's career was wrecked when he brought a suit for libel against the Marquis of Queensberry, lost, and, as a result of evidence revealed at the trial, was sentenced to a prison term of two years at Reading Gaol on a charge of abnormal sexual vice. After his release from prison, he spent his last years in Paris in bitterness and despair.

Wilde, Percival (1887-). American playwright, at his best in the one-act play. His numerous plays for the Little Theater have been acted all over the world.

Wilder. In Cooper's RED ROVER, a name assumed by Henry Ark.

Wilder, Thornton Niven (1897-). American novelist and playwright, known for his sophisticated and ironic novels and later for his successful plays marked by touches of fantasy and experiments in theatrical technique. Among his novels are *The Cabala* (1926); THE BRIDGE OF SAN LUIS REY (1927), a best-seller, awarded the Pulitzer prize; *The Woman of Andros* (1930); *Heaven's My Destination* (1935). His plays include *The Trumpet Shall Sound* (1926); *The Angel That Troubled the Waters* (1928) and *The Long Christmas Dinner* (1931), collections of one-act plays; OUR TOWN (1938), awarded the Pulitzer prize; and THE SKIN OF OUR TEETH (1942), dealing with the hardships and fortitude of mankind through the ages, also a Pulitzer prize play. *The Ides of March* (1948) is a pseudo-historical novel about Julius CAESAR.

Wilderness, Battle of the. A famous action in the U.S. Civil War when Grant tried to dislodge Lee from his position in Eastern Virginia (1864).

Wildeve, Damon. One of the chief characters in Hardy's RETURN OF THE NATIVE.

Tenant of Wildfell Hall, The. A novel (1848) by Anne BRONTË, published under the pen-name of Acton BELL.

Wildfire, Col. Nimrod. A popular character of the early American stage, a Kentucky frontiersman who comes on to New York and by his brusque, direct methods straightens out innumerable difficulties for his city friends. He first appeared in James K. Paulding's *Lion of the West* (1831) and later in Bayle Bernard's comedy entitled *A Kentuckian's Trip to New York in 1815*. He introduces his intended wife, Miss Patty Snap of Salt Licks, to New York acquaintances with the comment, "There's no back out in her breed, for she can lick her weight in wild cats, and she shot a bear at nine years old."

Wildfire, Madge. In Scott's HEART OF MIDLOTHIAN, the insane daughter of old Meg Murdochson, the gypsy thief. Madge was seduced when a girl, and this, with the murder of her infant, turned her brain. COLERIDGE called her the most original character ever created by Scott.

Wild Geese. Jacobite exiles who left Ireland for France after the surrender of Limerick (1691).

Wild Hunt. In European, especially German, folklore, a nocturnal chase of spectral hunters, led by the *Wild Huntsman* who may have to be interpreted as Odin or Woden.

Wilding, Anthony. Called **Tony Wilding** (1883–1915). Famous tennis player from New Zealand. Killed in action in World War I.

Wiley, Harvey (1844–1930). American chemist, famous for leading the campaign against the adulteration of food. He got the Food and Drugs Act passed by Congress (1906) and helped to have it administered effectively. He directed a bureau of foods and health for *Good Housekeeping* (1912–1930) and wrote several books on foods and the Food Law.

Wilfer, Reginald. In Dickens' novel OUR MUTUAL FRIEND, a character called by his wife R.W., and by his fellow-clerks Rumty. He is clerk in the drug-house of Chicksey, Stobbles, and Veneering. In person, Mr. Wilfer resembles an overgrown cherub; in manner, he is shy and retiring.

> Mr. Reginald Wilfer was a poor clerk, so poor indeed that he had never yet attained the modest object of his ambition, which was to wear a complete new suit of clothes, hat and boots included, at one time. His black hat was brown before he could afford a coat; his pantaloons were white at the seams and knees before he could buy a pair of boots; his boots had worn out before he could treat himself to new pantaloons; and by the time he worked round to the hat again, that shining modern article roofed in an ancient ruin of various periods.—Ch. iv.

Mrs. Wilfer. Wife of Mr. Reginald, a most majestic woman, tall and angular. She wears gloves and a pocket-handkerchief tied under her chin. A patronizing, condescending woman is Mrs. Wilfer, with a mighty idea of her own importance. "Viper!" "Ingrate!" and such epithets are household words with her.

Bella Wilfer. Daughter of Mr. and Mrs. Wilfer, a wayward, playful, affectionate, spoilt beauty, "giddy from the want of some sustaining purpose, and capricious because she was always fluttering among little things." Bella Wilfer marries John HARMON (John Rokesmith), the secretary of Mr. Boffin "the golden dustman."

Lavinia Wilfer. Youngest sister of Bella, and called "The Irrepressible." Lavinia is a tart, pert girl, but succeeds in catching George Sampson in the toils of wedlock.

Wilfrid. The hero of Scott's narrative poem ROKEBY, son of Oswald Wycliffe; in love with Matilda, heiress of Rokeby's knight. After various villainies, Oswald forces from Matilda a promise to marry Wilfrid. Wilfrid thanks her for the promise, and falls dead at her feet.

Wilfrid, St. See under SAINTS.

Wilhelmina (1880–). Queen of the Netherlands (1890–1948). During World War II she lived in England. Abdicated in favor of her daughter Juliana.

Wilhelm Meister. A novel by GOETHE, or rather two novels, *Wilhelm Meister's Apprenticeship* (*Lehrjahre;* 1795–1796) and its sequel, *Wilhelm Meister's Wanderings* (*Wanderjahre;* 1821–1829). The hero, the son of a well-to-do German merchant, leaves his comfortable bourgeois surroundings to roam about with a company of strolling players, whose Bohemian life has great attractions for him. He falls in love with Marianne, one of the group, and the lovers have a child named Felix, but Wilhelm leaves both mother and son in a foolish mood of jealousy. He rescues Mignon, a charming elflike Italian girl, from some abusive rope dancers, and his kindness awakens in her a passionate love that he does not return and that brings about her death. In the course of time Wilhelm becomes disillusioned with stage life and settles down into a more conventional existence. He assumes the responsibilities of a father toward young Felix and eventually marries a lady of position and becomes proprietor of an estate. See also Mignon.

Wilhelm Tell, see WILLIAM TELL.

Wilhelmstrasse. The street of the German Foreign Office; hence, the Foreign Office.

Wilkes, Charles (1798–1877). American naval officer, known for stopping the British mail steamer TRENT and taking from her by force the two Confederate commissioners Mason and Slidell (1861).

Wilkes, John (1727–1797). A dissipated writer who joined a fraternity called the Mad Monks of Medmenham Abbey. In writing for *The North Briton,* a paper he had founded in 1762, he attacked the government, and his political periodical was suppressed. He was a Member of Parliament later on, but, although re-elected, he was twice suspended for libel. He was a great favorite with the London mob, and was instrumental in securing certain rights for the people.

Wilkie, Sir **David** (1785–1841). Scottish portrait and historical painter.

Wilkins, Sir **George Hubert** (1888–). Famous polar explorer born in Australia. He took part in the arctic expedition of STEFANSSON (1913–1917), in the British Imperial Antarctic Expedition (1920–1921), and SHACKLETON's expedition (1921–1922). He led an expedition of his own for the British Museum to Australia and other islands and commanded several arctic and antarctic expeditions thereafter. With Lincoln Ellsworth he made the Nautilus Arctic Submarine Expedition (1931). He has written *Flying the Arctic* (1928); *Undiscovered Australia* (1928); *Under the North Pole* (1931); etc.

Wilkins, Mary E., see FREEMAN, MARY.

Wilkins, Peter. Hero of *Voyages of Peter Wilkins* by Robert Paltock (ca. 1750).

Wilkinson, Ellen Cicely (1891–1947). English woman politician active in the labor and suffragist movements. Member of Parliament for Labor (1924–1931; 1935 ff.); parliamentary secretary to the ministry of home security (1940 ff.); minister of education in the Labor Government (1945).

Wilkinson, Sir **John Gardner** (1797–1875). English Egyptologist who wrote *Manners and Customs of the Ancient Egyptians* (1837–1841) and investigated Egyptian hieroglyphics.

Willard, Emma (1787–1870). American pioneer in the education of women. In 1814 she opened a seminary in Vermont for women and in 1821 founded another in Troy, New York. This latter school is still in existence and was a college some sixteen years before the women's college was established at Mount Holyoke. A book of verse which Miss Willard published contained one famous poem, *Rocked in the Cradle of the Deep,* which was set to music by Joseph P. Knight.

Willard, Frances (1839–1898). A leader of the temperance movement and president (1879) of the Women's Christian Temperance Union. She helped to organize the Prohibition party and wrote *Glimpses of Fifty Years* (1889).

Willard, Jess (1883–). American heavyweight champion (1915). Defeated by Jack DEMPSEY.

Willebrandt, Mabel Walker (1889–). As an attorney she defended some two thousand cases involving women in the courts of Los Angeles. She was assistant attorney general of the United States (1921–1929).

Willems. The chief character of Conrad's OUTCAST OF THE ISLANDS.

Willet, John. In Dickens' BARNABY RUDGE, landlord of the Maypole Inn. John Willet is one of the most dogged and positive fellows in existence, always sure that he is right, and that everyone who differs from him is wrong. He ultimately resigns the Maypole to his son Joe, and retires to a cottage in Chigwell, with a small garden.

Joe Willet. Son of the landlord, a broad-shouldered, strapping young fellow of twenty. Being bullied and browbeaten by his father, he runs away and enlists as a soldier, loses his right arm in America, and is dismissed from service. He returns to England, marries Dolly

VARDEN, and becomes landlord of the Maypole, where he prospers and has a large family.

William IV (1765–1837). King of Great Britain and Ireland. His nicknames were "the Sailor-King" and "Silly Billy." He was the third son of George III. His successor was his niece Victoria.

William and Margaret. A ballad (1723) by David Mallet (1705?–1765). It appears in Percy's *Reliques.*

William Ashe. See MARRIAGE OF WILLIAM ASHE.

William of Cloudesley. One of three famous archers. See ADAM BELL.

William of Malmesbury (1095?–1142?). English historian of the Anglo-Norman period, educated at the abbey of Malmesbury, where he served as librarian. He is known for his chronicles, reflecting sympathy with the Norman rulers and the Church. Best-known is *Chronicle of the Kings of England,* finished about 1128, dealing with the history of England from the settlement of the Anglo-Saxons to the contemporary period of the reign of Henry I. William also wrote *Chronicle of the Popes* (1125), and a number of saints' lives and miracle tales. In his later years his patron was Robert of Gloucester, son of Henry I.

William of Newburgh (1136–1198?). English historian, "the father of historical criticism," who wrote in Latin a *History of English Affairs,* covering the period from the Conquest to nearly the beginning of the 13th century.

William of Norwich, St. See under SAINTS.

Williams, Anna. A friend of Samuel JOHNSON, a talented and intelligent woman, mentioned frequently in Boswell's *Life of Johnson.*

Williams, Ben Ames (1889–). American novelist, author of some thirty books. His first book was *All the Brothers Were Valiant* (1919). He is a good story teller, and most of his stories are laid in the state of Maine. *House Divided* (1947) is an immensely long novel of the Civil War.

Williams, Bert. See COON SONGS.

Williams, Caleb, see CALEB WILLIAMS.

Williams, Eleazar (1789?–1858). American missionary among the Indians. He claimed (1839) to be the son of Louis XVI, the lost dauphin of France. He wrote on Indian subjects and knew several Indian languages. Subject of a romance, *Lazarre* (1901), by Mary Hartwell CATHERWOOD.

Williams, Emlyn (1905–). Welsh stage and screen actor and playwright. His plays include *A Murder Has Been Arranged* (1930); *Night Must Fall* (1935); *The Corn is Green* (1938); etc.

Williams, Gluyas (1888–). American cartoonist drawing for the NEW YORKER, *Collier's,* etc. He has illustrated the works of Robert Benchley.

Williams, Jane. One of the ladies with whom P. B. SHELLEY formed a "Platonic" attachment in Italy during the later years of his career. Her husband was drowned with Shelley when the two were caught in a sudden storm on the Adriatic, where they were sailing in a small boat.

Williams, Joe. In John Dos Passos' U.S.A., a young man from Washington, D.C., who enlists in the U.S. Navy. During World War I he becomes disgusted with his life as a sailor, deserts, and joins the merchant marine. He marries, but his wife is unfaithful, and he returns to sea.

Janey, Joe's sister, is also a character in the novel. She has a brief love affair with Jerry BURNHAM, goes to work for G. H. BARROW, and then becomes the secretary of J. W. MOOREHOUSE. Moorehouse's attentions to Eleanor STODDARD and Eveline HUTCHINS arouse her jealousy.

Williams, Michael (1878–). Editor of *The Commonweal,* known as a liberal Catholic. His *The Book of the High Romance* (1918) is one of his best. He was born in Halifax, Nova Scotia, but has for many years lived and worked in the United States.

Williams, Oscar (1900–). American poet who has compiled a number of anthologies of the work of his contemporaries, including *A Little Treasury of Modern Poetry* (1946). Among his books of poems is *That's All That Matters* (1945).

Williams, Roger (ca. 1603–1683). English-born New England Protestant clergyman, known for his individualistic views on religion, politics, and democracy in political and ecclesiastical government. Progressing in belief from the Anglicans through the Separatists and Baptists to the Seekers, he was expelled from Massachusetts for establishing a democratic organization in his church at Salem, and founded the colony of Rhode Island. He was a friend of both Milton and Cromwell in England, took part in the English Civil War, and engaged in a vigorous pamphlet controversy with the Puritan John COTTON. His works include *A Key into the Language of America* (1643), a study of Indian languages; *Queries of Highest Consideration* (1643), a plea addressed to the English Parliament against the establishment of a national church; *Mr. Cotton's Letter Lately Printed, Examined, and Answered* (1644); THE BLOODY TENENT OF PERSECUTION (1644), his most famous work; *The Bloody Tenent Yet More Bloody* (1652); *The Hireling Ministry None of Christ's* (1652); *George Foxe Digged Out of His Burrows* (1676).

Williams befriended the Indians and established a democratic government in Rhode Island, permitting complete religious toleration, although he did attack the views of the Quakers and engaged in a bitter dispute with them. He is considered one of the most important crusaders for democratic rights in the American colonies in the period before the Revolution.

Williams, Tennessee (Thomas Lanier) (1914–). American dramatist. *The Glass Menagerie* (1945), starring Laurette TAYLOR; *A Streetcar Named Desire* (1947), which won the Pulitzer prize.

Williams, Valentine (1883–1947). English writer of popular mystery stories. He also wrote and acted in four radio plays for NBC.

Williams, William Carlos (1883–). American poet, early in his career a disciple of the school of IMAGISM and later an exponent of OBJECTIVISM, known for his vivid, realistic, and precise recording in his poetry of isolated, fleeting, and easily overlooked details of experience, chosen most often from a background of daily, commonplace living in the urban sections of the 20th-century U.S.; his accuracy in reproducing American speech rhythms has also been highly praised. Because of his human and humanitarian sympathies and his understanding of the proletarian and lower-middle-class Americans who supply the subject-matter of most of his poetry and prose, Williams was often ranked among the proletarian writers of the 1930's. See PROLETARIAN LITERATURE. His works include *Poems* (1909), *The Tempers* (1913), *Kora in Hell* (1920), *Al Que Quiere!* (1917), *Improvisations* (1920), *Sour Grapes* (1921), *Spring and All* (1922), *Collected Poems* (1934), *An Early Martyr* (1935), *Adam and Eve and the City* (1936), *The Complete Collected Poems* (1938), and *The Broken Span* (1941), all verse; *The Great American Novel* (1923) and *In the American Grain* (1925), criticism; *A Voyage to Pagany* (1928), *White Mule* (1937), and *In the Money* (1940), novels, the last two part of a planned trilogy; *The Knife of the Times* (1932), and *Life Along the Passaic River* (1938), collections of short stories.

Williams, of English and Puerto Rican parentage, studied medicine in the U.S. and Europe and throughout his career was a practicing physician in the factory region of New Jersey, working among the people about whom he wrote in his spare time. In his youth, while in Europe, he became a friend of the poets Ezra POUND and "H. D." (Hilda DOOLITTLE).

Williams-Ellis, Mrs. **Amabel** (1894–). English novelist, the sister of John STRACHEY and the cousin of Lytton STRACHEY. Her children are said to have been the originals from which Richard Hughes drew the children in his *The Innocent Voyage*. Her best-known novel is *The Big Firm* (1938).

Williamson, Henry (1897–). English writer, best known for his books on nature. His *Tarka the Otter* was awarded the Hawthornden Prize (1927). *The Gold Falcon; or The Haggard of Love* (1933), a brilliantly-written ROMAN À CLEF (New York scene), was published anonymously.

William Tell. The legendary national hero of Switzerland, whose deeds are based on a Teutonic myth of widespread occurrence in northern Europe.

Fable has it that Tell was the champion of the Swiss in the War of Independence against the Emperor Albert I (slain 1308). Tell refused to salute the cap of Gessler, the imperial governor, and for this act of independence was sentenced to shoot with his bow and arrow an apple from the head of his own son. Tell succeeded in this dangerous skill-trial, but in his agitation dropped an arrow from his robe. The governor insolently demanded what the second arrow was for, and Tell fearlessly replied, "To shoot you with, had I failed in the task imposed upon me." Gessler now ordered him to be carried in chains across the lake and cast into Küssnacht castle, a prey "to the reptiles that lodged there." He was, however, rescued by the peasantry, and having shot Gessler, freed his country from the Austrian yoke.

This legend is the subject of Lemierre's tragedy *Guillaume Tell* (1766), Schiller's *Wilhelm Tell* (1804), Knowles' *William Tell* (1840) and Rossini's opera, *William Tell* (1829).

SAXO GRAMMATICUS tells nearly the same story respecting the Danish Toki, who killed Harald, and similar tales are told of the Scandinavian Egil and King Nidung, of Adam Bell, Clym of the Clough, William of Cloudesley and Henry IV, Olaf and Eindridi, etc.

William Wilson. A story (1839) by Edgar Allan POE in *Tales of the Grotesque and Arabesque*.

Willis, Nathaniel Parker (1806–1867). American poet and prose writer of the KNICKERBOCKER SCHOOL.

Willkie, Wendell (1892–1944). President of the Commonwealth and Southern Corporation (1933–1940). Republican nominee for president of the United States (1940); defeated by Roosevelt. Made a famous tour of the Middle East, Russia, and China (1942), recorded by him in the book *One World* (1943).

Will o' the Wisp. See IGNIS FATUUS.

Willoughby, John. In Jane Austen's SENSE AND SENSIBILITY, the fascinating young lover who escapes from Marianne Dashwood's affections.

willow pattern. A favorite design for blue china plates, imitating, but not copying, the Chinese style of porcelain decoration, introduced into England by Thomas Turner of Caughley about 1780, when the craze for things Chinese was at its height.

To the right is a mandarin's country seat, two stories high to show the rank and wealth of the possessor; in the foreground a pavilion, in the background an orange-tree, and to the right of the pavilion a peach-tree in full bearing. The estate is enclosed by a wooden fence, and a river crossed by a bridge, at one end of which is the famous willow-tree and at the other the gardener's humble cottage. At the top of the pattern (left-hand side) is an island. The three figures on the bridge are the mandarin and the lovers, the latter also being shown in a boat on the river.

The willow pattern does not illustrate any Chinese story or legend, and is not Chinese in origin, but the following is the tale that has been built round it:

A wealthy mandarin had an only daughter named Li-chi, who fell in love with Chang, a young man living on the island shown, who had been her father's secretary. The father overheard them one day making vows of love under the orange-tree, and sternly forbade the unequal match; but the lovers contrived to elope, lay concealed for a while in the gardener's cottage, and thence escaped in a boat to the island. The enraged mandarin pursued them with a whip, and would have beaten them to death had not the gods rewarded their fidelity by changing them both into turtle-doves. And all this occurred "when the willow begins to shed its leaves."

Will's. A famous coffee-house of Queen Anne's time that stood at the corner of Bow Street and Russell Street, Covent Garden, sometimes referred to as "Russell Street Coffee House," and "The Wits' Coffee House." It was the meeting-place of the wits and literary men of the day, and was well known to ADDISON, who established his servant, Button, in another coffee house, which eventually, as *Button's,* became the headquarters of the Whig *literati,* as Will's had been of the Tory.

Will to Believe, The, and Other Essays in Popular Philosophy. A collection of ten essays with a preface (1896) by William JAMES.

Willy-Nicky Correspondence. The name popularly given to a series of telegrams between Kaiser Wilhelm of Germany and Czar Nicholas of Russia, sent in 1904 and 1907.

Wilmot. There are three of the name in *Fatal Curiosity* (1736), a tragedy by George Lillo, viz., old Wilmot, his wife Agnes, and their son, young Wilmot, supposed to have perished at sea. The young man, however, is not drowned, but goes to India, makes his fortune, and returns, unknown to any one of his friends. He goes in disguise to his parents, and deposits with them a casket. Curiosity induces Agnes to open it, and when she sees that it contains jewels, she and her husband resolve to murder the owner and appropriate the contents of the casket. No sooner have they committed the fatal deed than they discover it is their own son whom they have killed; whereupon the old man stabs first his wife and then himself.

Wilmot, John, Second Earl of Rochester. See ROCHESTER.

Wilmot, Miss Arabella. In Goldsmith's VICAR OF WAKEFIELD, a clergyman's daughter, beloved by George Primrose, eldest son of the vicar of Wakefield, whom she marries.

Wilmot Proviso. A famous clause introduced by David Wilmot as an amendment to a bill before the United States Congress of 1846, providing for the prohibition of slavery in all territory to be acquired from Mexico.

Wilson, Charles Morrow (1905–). American writer. *Meriwether Lewis* (1934); *Roots of America* (1936); etc.

Wilson, Charles Thomson Rees (1869–). Scottish physicist who, with A. H. Compton, was awarded the Nobel prize for physics in 1927.

Wilson, Edmund (1895–). American literary critic and author, known for his interest in social questions, approached from a Marxist (see MARXISM) viewpoint, and for his personal and psychological studies of leading 20th-century literary figures. His books of criticism include *Discordant Encounters* (1926); *Axel's Castle* (1931); *The Triple Thinkers* (1938); *The Boys in the Back Room* (1941); *The Wound and the Bow* (1941). Among other works are *I Thought of Daisy* (1929), a novel; *Poets, Farewell!* (1929), poetry; *The American Jitters: A Year of the Slump* (1932), social studies; *Travels in Two Democracies* (1936), on the U.S. and Russia; *This Room and This Gin and These Sandwiches* (1937), a collection of plays; *To the Finland Station* (1940), studies of the leading figures in the development of the theories of COMMUNISM in the 19th and 20th centuries; *Notebooks of Night* (1942), poems and essays; *Memoirs of Hecate County* (1946), a collection of satirical sketches, arousing vigorous controversy.

Wilson, Edward Arthur (1886–). American illustrator with a particular liking for the sea. A few of the books illustrated by him are *Iron Men and Wooden Ships,* edited by Frank Shay (1924); *The Magnificent Idler* by Cameron Rogers (1926); *James Shore's Daughter* by Stephen Vincent Benét (1935); etc. Mr. Wilson has also written as well as illustrated *The Pirate's Treasure* (1926).

Wilson, Harry Leon (1867–1939). American novelist and playwright, widely known for his *Bunker Bean* (1913); RUGGLES OF RED GAP (1915); and MERTON OF THE MOVIES (1922). The last two were made into successful moving pictures. Mr. Wilson was at one time married to Rose O'NEILL. His *Ma Pettingill* is a notable humorous creation.

Wilson, John (1595–1674). English composer and lutist. Musician to Kings Charles I and Charles II. He may be the prototype of Jack Willson who appears in a stage direction in *Much Ado About Nothing,* in the folio edition (1623), where it is indicated that he sings the song *Sigh No More, Ladies.*

Wilson, John. Pseudonym **Christopher North** (1785–1854). Scottish author who contributed to *Blackwood's Magazine* most of the *Noctes Ambrosianae.* He was one of the first to appreciate Wordsworth's genius.

Wilson, Margaret (1882–). American novelist. Her first novel, *The Able McLaughlins,* won the Harper prize (1923) and the Pulitzer prize (1924). She has written other interesting American novels.

Wilson, Romer (1891–1930). English novelist known for such novels as *Dragon's Blood* (1926) and *Latter-Day Symphony* (1927). She also wrote a play and a life of Emily Brontë (1928). Wife of Edward J. O'Brien.

Wilson, William (1801–1860). Scottish bookdealer and poet who came to the U.S. in 1833. His collected poetry was published after his death (1869). His son, **James Grant Wilson** (1832–1914), was a bookdealer who helped John Fiske to edit Appletons' *Cyclopaedia of American Biography* in six volumes (1886–1889) and wrote on General Grant, Fitz-Greene Halleck, and *The Poets and Poetry of Scotland.*

Wilson, Thomas Woodrow (1856–1924). Twenty-eighth president of the U.S. (1913–1921). Took America into World War I "to make the world safe for democracy," and died from his efforts to establish an effectual League of Nations. Wrote *A History of the American People* (5 vols., 1902), etc.

Wiman, Dwight Deere (1895–). American theatrical producer, at first producing jointly with William A. Brady, Jr., and then independently. He has had numerous successes.

Wimble, Will. A character in Addison's Spectator, simple, good-natured, and officious. Will Wimble in the flesh was said to be Thomas Morecroft of Dublin.

Wimbledon. A town in Surrey, England. Chiefly known for being the headquarters of the All-English Lawn Tennis Club, where the international matches for the Davis Cup have sometimes been played.

Winant, John Gilbert (1889–1947). Governor of New Hampshire (1925–1926; 1931–1934); chairman of the Social Security Board (1935–1937); United States ambassador to Great Britain (1941–1945). Suicide by shooting. *Letter from Grosvenor Square* (1947).

Winchell, Walter (1897–). At one time in vaudeville. A well-known columnist for the New York *Mirror* (since 1929) and radio commentator on the *Jergens Journal.* He is a gossip writer of the more flamboyant sort having a "style" of his own.

Winchilsea, Anne Finch, Countess of (1661–1720). A friend of Alexander Pope. To Wordsworth some of her verse seemed pleasing. In one of her longer poems a couplet containing the words "Aromatick pain" in relation to a flower may have been the original of the famous phrase by Pope, "Die of a rose in aromatic pain."

Winckelman, Johann Joachim (1717–1768). German classical scholar who influenced Goethe through his understanding of Greek art. Walter Pater wrote an essay on him. He was the son of a German shoemaker. It was mainly through him that the conception of a Greek ideal of Apollonic calm and noble grandeur (*edle Einfalt, stille Grösse*) came to be generally accepted. It was Nietzsche who instilled into it the proper dose of Dionysian fury.

Windermere, Lady. See Lady Windermere's Fan.

windmills.

to fight with windmills. To face imaginary adversaries, combat chimeras. The allusion is to the adventure of Don Quixote, who, when riding through the plains of Montiel, approaches thirty or forty windmills, which he declares to Sancho Panza "were giants, two leagues in length or more." Striking his spurs into Rosinante, with his lance in rest, he drives at one of the "monsters dreadful as Typhoeus." The lance lodges in the sail, and the latter lifts both man and beast into the air. When the valiant knight and his steed fall they are both much injured, and Don Quixote declares that the enchanter Freston, "who carried off his library with all the books therein," had changed the giants into windmills "out of malice."

to have windmills in your head. To be full of fancies; to have "bees in your bonnet." Sancho Panza says—

> Did I not tell your worship they were windmills? and who could have thought otherwise, except such as had windmills in their head?—*Don Quixote:* Bk. i, Ch. viii.

Windrip, Berzelius (Buzz). In Sinclair Lewis' It Can't Happen Here, a demagogic Vermont politician who, on his election to the presidency, sets up a Fascist dictatorship in the U.S., ruling by means of his gang, called the Minute Men. Windrip is eventually ousted from power by Lee Saranson, a former friend of his.

Windsor. The name of the royal family of Great Britain since 1917, replacing the original

Hanover. Windsor Castle was a royal residence for some time, and Windsor Forest is the title and subject of a well-known poem by Alexander Pope. "The Widow of Windsor" is a name applied to Queen Victoria by Kipling in a poem of that name in his *Barrack-Room Ballads.*

Windy City. Chicago. See under CITY.

Windy McPherson's Son. A novel by Sherwood ANDERSON (1916). The hero, Sam McPherson, grows up to hate his squalid home in Caxton, Iowa, where his father, a drunken boaster, is a completely dominating force.

Wine from These Grapes. One of the later books of poems (1934) by Edna St. Vincent MILLAY.

Wine of the Puritans, The. The first book of criticism (1909) by Van Wyck BROOKS.

Wine of Wizardry, A. A fantastic poem (1907) by George STERLING; depicting visions seen in a goblet of wine.

Winesburg, Ohio. A collection of short stories by Sherwood ANDERSON, published in 1919, his best-known work. The stories are psychological portraits of a group of residents of Winesburg, Ohio, a typical American small town of the period, who do not fit into the average pattern of life in the community. The stories are presented as they are noted by George Willard, a reporter. See also SPOON RIVER.

Wingfield-Stratford, Esmé Cecil (1882–). British author. *Facing Reality* (1922); *The History of British Civilization* (1933); *New Minds for Old* (1935); *The Foundations of British Patriotism* (1939); *Crusade for Civilization* (1940); *Churchill: the Making of a Hero* (1942); etc.

Wings of the Dove, The. A novel by Henry JAMES (1902). Kate Croy is secretly engaged to Merton Densher, but allows her wealthy aunt to plan her marriage to Lord Mark. When she discovers that her friend Milly Theale, an American heiress, is in love with Densher and also that Milly has not long to live, she encourages Densher to marry Milly. Lord Mark's discovery and malicious revelation of Densher's and Kate's engagement brings on Milly's death. She leaves Densher her money but he refuses to accept it, and as Kate will not marry him unless he does, their romance is at an end.

Winifred, St. See under SAINTS.

Winkelried, Arnold von. A national hero of Switzerland. In the battle of Sempach (1386) he rushed upon the pikes of the Austrians and gathered them together so that they pierced his own body. This effected a gap in the enemy lines through which the Swiss gained a victory. James Montgomery wrote his famous poem, *The Patriot's Pass-Word,* about this heroic event.

Winkie, Wee Willie. See WEE WILLIE WINKIE.

Winkle, Nathaniel. In Dickens' PICKWICK PAPERS, an M.P.C., that is, Member of the Pickwick Club, a young sportsman, considered by his companions to be a dead shot, a hunter, skater, etc. All these acquirements are, however, wholly imaginary. He marries Arabella Allen.

Winkle, Rip Van, see RIP VAN WINKLE.

Winner Take Nothing. A book of short stories (1933) by Ernest HEMINGWAY.

Winning of Barbara Worth, The. A novel (1911) by Harold Bell WRIGHT.

Winning of the West, The. A four volume historical study (1889–1896) by Theodore ROOSEVELT.

Winslow, Ola Elizabeth (1885?–). American teacher and biographer who received the Pulitzer prize in 1941 for her *Jonathan Edwards.*

Winslow, Thyra Samter (1893–). Popular American short-story writer, writing both of Arkansas, her native state, and of theater life in New York.

Winsor, Kathleen (1919–). Author of *Forever Amber* (1944), a best-selling historical novel (Restoration period) with a pronounced emphasis on sex.

Winter, John Keith (1906–). English novelist and dramatist who is well-known for his novel and play *The Rats of Norway* (1932). *The Shining Hour* (1934) was popular in the United States.

Winter, John Strange. One of the pen-names of **Henrietta Eliza Stannard** (1856–1911). She had written military stories under the pen-name of **Violet Whyte** and she took the name of John Strange Winter from one of these early stories. A book of hers called *Bootles' Baby* (1885) sold two million copies in two years.

Winter, William (1836–1917). Dramatic critic of the New York *Tribune* (1865–1909). At one time considered the chief critic of New York. He wrote theatrical reminiscences of the old New York theater in *Other Days* (1908) and *Old Friends* (1909). His *Shakespeare on the Stage* (2 vols.; 1911, 1915), which examines the various interpretations by famous actors of different parts in the plays of Shakespeare, is of value.

Winterblossom, Mr. Philip. In Scott's novel, ST. RONAN'S WELL, "the man of taste," on the managing committee at the Spa.

Winterich, John Tracy (1891–). American bibliophile who, during World War I, was on the staff of *Stars and Stripes* and received the Purple Heart Medal. After the war he was for fifteen years managing editor of the *American Legion Monthly,* joined *PM* in 1940, worked for the Bureau of Public Relations, and became managing editor of *The Saturday Review of Literature.* He is an authority on first editions and book collecting. *Twenty-three Books* (1939); *Another Day, Another Dollar* (autobiographical; 1947), etc.

Winters, Arthur Yvor (1900–). American literary critic and poet, known for the classical orientation of both his verse and critical studies, in the latter of which he attacks the "advanced" and "experimental" writers of the 20th century. His works include *The Immobile Wind* (1921), *The Bare Hills* (1927), *The Proof* (1930), *The Journey* (1931), *Before Disaster* (1934), and *Poems* (1940), all books of poetry; *Primitivism and Decadence* (1937) and *Maule's Curse* (1938), criticism.

Winterset. A verse drama by Maxwell ANDERSON (1935), based on the SACCO-VANZETTI case. It deals with the attempts of Mio, the son of Romagna, an Italian radical who was executed for a murder he did not commit, to avenge the death of his father. A wanderer about the country, he comes to New York, meets and falls in love with Miriamne, a similarly lonely young girl, and at least meets the actual murderer for whose crime Romagna suffered—a gangster named Trock. Mio is shot by Trock's gang, and Miriamne too is killed. Filmed, with Burgess Meredith.

Winter's Tale, The. One of the last of SHAKESPEARE's plays (produced 1611; printed 1623). It is founded on Greene's *Pandosto, The Triumph of Time* (1588), which was written round an actual incident that occurred in the Bohemian and Polish courts in the late 14th century.

In the play Polixenes, King of Bohemia, is invited to Sicily by King Leontes, and unwittingly excites the jealousy of his friend because he prolongs his stay at the entreaty of Queen Hermione. Leontes orders Camillo to poison the royal guest, but instead of doing so, Camillo flees with him to Bohemia. The King now casts Hermione into prison and orders her infant daughter exposed on a desert shore which turns out to be "the seacoast of Bohemia." In time Florizel, the son and heir of Polixenes, falls in love with Perdita, the lost daughter of Leontes. Polixenes forbids the match, and the young lovers, under the charge of Camillo, flee to Sicily. Polixenes follows the fugitives, the mystery of Perdita is cleared up, the lovers are married and the two kings resume their friendship. Hermione, whom Leontes had long believed dead, is introduced as a statue that turns into the living Queen.

Winthrop, John (1588–1649). Governor of the Massachusetts Bay Colony. He did not believe in democracy, bringing biblical proof to bear that there was no warrant for it as there was "no such government in Israel." He stirred up the people of New England and was impeached by the colonists. He made, however, a speech on liberty which satisfied them, and was re-elected Governor every year. His *Journal,* partly published in 1790, appeared in full as *The History of New England* (2 vols.; 1825–1826). He is portrayed in THE SCARLET LETTER by Nathaniel Hawthorne and in other novels.

Winthrop, Theodore (1828–1861). Connecticut novelist who was killed in the Civil War. His books were published after his death. One of his best is a description of a journey to the Northwest and later to Panama, *The Canoe and the Saddle* (1863).

Winwar, Frances. Translated from the original **Francesca Vinciguerra** (1900–). Italian-born American biographer and novelist. Her *Poor Splendid Wings* (1933) won the Atlantic prize. This was followed by *The Romantic Rebels* (1935), concerning Keats, Shelley, and Byron; *Oscar Wilde and the Yellow 'Nineties* (1940); and *The Life of the Heart* (1946), about George Sand and her times. Her work, though highly colored, is usually accurate. Her style has great vigor and life.

Wireless. A famous short story by Rudyard KIPLING.

Wisdom Tooth, The. A fantasy (1926) by Marc CONNELLY.

Wise, John (1652–1725). American clergyman of New England, known for his opposition to the strict Calvinist doctrine of the "elect" (see CALVINISM) and for his espousal of the cause of democracy and equality a number of years before the American Revolution. His two famous works are *The Church's Quarrel Espoused* (1710), an attack in satire on a proposal by the MATHERS to set up a centralized control of the New England churches; and *A Vindication of the Government of New England Churches* (1717), an assertion of the doctrine of the natural rights of mankind, which Wise was the first American to employ in a plea for political democracy. In 1687 he attracted attention by leading his congregation in a refusal to pay taxes imposed on them by Governor Andros, and was arrested and imprisoned. His writings were widely read in the days of the Revolution.

Wise, Stephen Samuel (1872–). American rabbi, born in Budapest, one of the founders of the Zionist Organization of America. He founded also the liberal Jewish Institute of Religion. He drafted pioneer child-labor and juvenile court laws for the State of Oregon. As president of the American and World Jewish Congress he has done much for the relief of war victims.

Wise, Thomas James (1859–1937). English bibliographer who also indulged himself in literary forgery. Cf. Wilfred Partington, *Forging Ahead: The True Story of the Upward Progress of Thomas James Wise* (1939).

Wistar, Caspar (1761–1818). Famous Philadelphia physician, son of a German glass manufacturer. He taught at the University of Pennsylvania and wrote one of the first American textbooks on anatomy. The plant wistaria was named after him in 1818. His grandnephew founded the Wistar Institute of Anatomy and Biology. His grandniece, **Sarah Wister** (1761–1804), is the author of a valuable *Journal of Life in Philadelphia.* One of her descendants was Owen WISTER.

Wister, Owen (1860–1938). American novelist whose best-known book is THE VIRGINIAN (1902), which has several times been made into a moving picture. He wrote of the West, Wyoming in particular, which he had known much as Theodore Roosevelt knew it in his early days. See also under WISTAR.

witch (A.S. *wiccian,* "to practice sorcery"). A sorceress. The typical witch is usually pictured as an old hag. There are many celebrated witches of history and legend, beginning perhaps with the *Witch of Endor,* who according to the Biblical narrative, called up the prophet Samuel from the dead to answer King Saul's questions concerning the fateful battle in which he would meet his death. The most famous witches in literature are the Three Weird Sisters whose prophecies concerning MACBETH started him on his ambitious and tragic course. One of Shelley's well known poems is entitled *The Witch of Atlas.*

Pope Innocent VIII issued the celebrated bull *Summis Desiderantes* in 1484, directing inquisitors and others to put to death all practicers of witchcraft and other diabolical arts, and it has been computed that as many as nine millions of persons suffered death for witchcraft since that date. In the U.S., witches in Salem, Mass., were hanged or pressed to death. No witch was ever burned, in spite of frequent assertions to that effect.

witches' Sabbath. The muster at nighttime of witches and demons to concoct mischief. The witch first anointed her feet and shoulders with the fat of a murdered babe, then mounting a broomstick, distaff, or rake, made her exit by the chimney, and rode through the air to the place of rendezvous. The assembled witches feasted together, and concluded with a dance, in which they all turned their backs to each other. James JOYCE's ULYSSES and Thomas MANN's MAGIC MOUNTAIN contain scenes based on the tradition of the witches' Sabbath. Hawthorne's *Young Goodman Brown* is a famous short story about a New England witches' Sabbath.

Witching Hour, The. A play by Augustus THOMAS (*Am.,* 1907), dealing with the occult. Because of his mysterious powers, Jack Brookfield, a professional gambler who is always in luck, is able to clear the young Clay Whipple from a murder charge. Clay, who is guilty of accidental but not intentional manslaughter, is in love with Jack's niece, Viola Campbell. In order to free him, Jack brings to light—through hypnotic powers only—a serious and authentic charge against Frank Hardmuth, the assistant district attorney. At the end of the play Jack gives up gambling and everything connected with the occult.

witenagemot. A yearly meeting of all the freemen of a tribe or of a state among the Norse conquerors of Britain. It became a court for the trial of principal offenses and for the election of rulers. With the conquest of England by William the Conqueror in 1066 this assemblage went out of existence.

Wither, George (1588–1667). English poet, a friend of William BROWNE, with whom he was associated in the small group of poets at the beginning of the 17th century, who wrote in the pastoral style of Edmund SPENSER. His verse publications include *The Shepherd's Pipe* (1614), a collection of eclogues to which Browne and John Davies of Hereford also contributed; *Shepherd's Hunting* (1615); *Fidelia* (1615); *Fair Virtue* (1622). He also wrote *Abuses Stript and Whipt,* a book of satires for the publication of which he was sentenced to prison, several volumes of hymns and psalms, and a number of pamphlets on questions of religious and political controversy of the time. Wither was of strong Puritan sympathies and during the Civil War was a captain in the Parliamentary army. It is said that on one occasion he was saved from hanging by the Royalists by the plea by Sir John DENHAM that "whilst [Wither] lived, he [Denham] should not be the worst poet in England."

Witherspoon. A brave and loyal scout in Simms' MELLICHAMPE, considered one of his few well-rounded characters.

With Fire and Sword. The first of a trilogy of historic novels (1890–1893) by SIENKIEWICZ, dealing with the history of Poland from 1648 to the time of Yan III. *With Fire and Sword* has as its subject the struggle between Russia and Poland. In the second novel, *The Deluge,* the subjects treated are the settlement of the Teutonic Knights in Prussia, the union of Lithuania and Poland with Russia brought about by the marriage of a Lithuanian prince and Polish princess, and the conflict between Poland and Sweden in 1665. *Pan Michael,* the third novel of the series, continues and concludes the history of Poland as a separate nation of former centuries.

Within a Budding Grove. The second book of Marcel Proust's REMEMBRANCE OF THINGS PAST, an English translation (1924) of *A l'Ombre de Jeunes Filles en Fleurs* (1918). It describes a period spent by the narrator MARCEL in his adolescence at the seashore resort of Balbec, where for the first time he meets ALBERTINE, one of a group of young girls there.

Within the Gates. A drama by Sean O'CASEY (1933), the action of which takes place in a London park. A Bishop, wishing to learn more of the common people, comes to the park with his sister and meets a variety of the persons who usually inhabit its precincts, including Two Park Chair Attendants, an Atheist, a Policewoman, a Young Man in Plus-Fours, two Nursemaids, a Guardsman, two Evangelists, a Young Whore, a Young Salvation Army Officer, a group of Down-and-Outs, and others. The Bishop hears of their bitternesses and their dreams, their frustrations, their weaknesses, and their unhappinesses, and eventually the Young Whore is revealed to be his own daughter by a youthful affair with a woman of inferior social station. The girl dies, affirming her faith in life, and the Bishop is overcome with shame at the realization of his past smugness and his own sin. There are numerous references to social injustice, poverty, morality, and religion throughout, and frequent songs and chants by single characters and a chorus.

Wititterly, Mr. Henry. In Dickens' NICHOLAS NICKLEBY, an important gentleman, thirty-eight years of age, of rather plebeian countenance, with very light hair. He boasts everlastingly of his grand friends.

Mrs. Wititterly (Julia). Wife of Mr. Wititterly of Cadogan Place, Sloane Street, London; a faded lady living in a faded house. She calls her page Alphonse, "although he has the face and figure of Bill." Mrs. Wititterly toadies to the aristocracy, and, like her husband, boasts of her grand connections and friends.

Witkowski. See under HARDEN, MAXIMILIAN.

Witla, Eugene. The hero of Dreiser's novel THE 'GENIUS.'

Witte, Count **Sergei Yulievich** (1849–1915). Russian statesman; negotiated the Treaty of Portsmouth which ended the Russo-Japanese War (1905). He was the first constitutional premier of Russia (1905–1906). He resigned and was made a member of the council of the empire.

Wittlin, Józef (1896–). Polish poet and novelist, who escaped from his native country (1939) to the U.S. His novel, *Salt of the Earth* (1925), was given the prize of the Polish Academy.

Witwould, Sir Wilful. In Congreve's WAY OF THE WORLD, a country bumpkin of Shropshire, half-brother of Anthony Witwould, and nephew of Lady Wishfort. He is a mixture of bashfulness and obstinacy, but when in his cups he is as loving as the monster in the TEMPEST. He is "a superannuated old bachelor," who is willing to marry MILLAMANT, but as the young lady prefers Edward Mirabell he is equally willing to resign her to him. His favorite phrase is, "Wilful will do it."

Anthony Witwould. Half-brother to Sir Wilful. "He has good nature and does not want wit."

Witzleben, Karl August Friedrich von (1773–1839). German army officer and writer of historical romances. His *Collected Works* (1829–1843) number 108 volumes.

wizard.

the Wizard of Menlo Park. Thomas A. EDISON (1847–1931), American inventor.

the Wizard of the North. Sir Walter SCOTT.

Wodehouse, Pelham Grenville (1881–). English humorist, known for his numerous popular stories and novels dealing with the adventures of a set of whimsical comic characters drawn chiefly from the British upper classes; among the best-known of these are Psmith, a young man-about-town; Jeeves, a perfect butler; and Mr. Mulliner, a middle-aged Englishman. Some of Wodehouse's books include *Leave It to Psmith* (1923); *The Inimitable Jeeves* (1924); *Meet Mr. Mulliner* (1927); *Money for Nothing* (1928); *Mr. Mulliner Speaking* (1929); *Summer Lightning* (1929); *Very Good, Jeeves* (1930); *Big Money* (1931); *The Adventures of Sally* (1935); *The Code of the Woosters* (1937); *The Crime Wave at Blandings* (1938); *Uncle Fred in the Springtime* (1939); *Eggs, Beans, and Crumpets* (1940), a collection of short stories; *Quick Service* (1940). He also wrote plays and musical comedies.

During World War II Wodehouse was accused of "collaborating" with Germany when he broadcast to England from Berlin as a prisoner of war.

Woden. The Anglo-Saxon form of ODIN, chief of the Scandinavian gods.

Wodzinska, Marie. Woman with whom the composer CHOPIN was vainly in love. She married someone else, and he never forgot his grief at her betrayal.

Woeful Countenance, Knight of the. See under KNIGHT.

Woestijne, Karel van de (1878–1929). Belgian poet; samples of his work have been translated in *Contemporary Flemish Poetry*, edited by J. Bithell; *Harvest of the Lowlands*, edited by Jan Greshoff; and in *Heart of Europe*, edited by Klaus Mann and Hermann Kesten.

Woffington, Peg or Margaret. See PEG WOFFINGTON.

Woglinda. In Wagner's *Ring* (not in actual mythology), one of the three Rhinedaughters guarding the Nibelungen Hoard.

Wojciechowski, Titus. Boyhood friend of the composer CHOPIN and object of a strong emotional attachment by the latter when they both were young.

Wolcot, John. Pseudonym **Peter Pindar** (1738–1819). English physician, who attended the governor of Jamaica (1767–1769). He gave up the medical profession for literature and published a mock-heroic poem and several vulgar but amusing satires, one on Boswell among them.

wolf.

to cry "Wolf!" To give a false alarm. The allusion is to the well known fable of the shepherd lad who used to cry "Wolf!" merely to make fun of the neighbors, but when at last the wolf came no one would believe him.

to keep the wolf from the door. To ward off starvation. We say of a ravenous person "He has a wolf in his stomach," and one who eats voraciously is said *to wolf* his food.

Wolf, Friedrich August (1759–1824). German philologist and Homeric scholar. His theory, that Homer's *Iliad* and *Odyssey* were the work of not one man but of several writers, was expounded in his *Prolegomena ad Homerum* (1795). His scholarly editions of Plato, Homer, Cicero and others are still sound.

Wolf, Henry (1852–1916). Alsatian-born American wood engraver who illustrated the works of Edwin A. ABBEY, Joseph PENNELL, Howard PYLE, etc. He also did reproductions of paintings by INNES and SARGENT.

Wolf Larsen. The ship captain in *The Sea-Wolf* (1904) a novel by Jack LONDON.

Wolfe, Charles (1791–1823). Irish writer, author of the famous poem *The Burial of Sir John Moore.*

Wolfe, James (1727–1759). British general who defeated Montcalm in the battle of the Plains of Abraham at Quebec. Both Wolfe and Montcalm were fatally wounded. In *The Virginians* by Thackeray and in *Montcalm and Wolfe* by Francis Parkman, Wolfe is a prominent character.

Wolfe, Humbert (1885–1940). English poet, distinguished for his satire *Lampoons* (1925). His *Requiem* (1927) was widely read.

Wolfe, Reginald. Pseudonym of Thomas Frognall DIBDIN.

Wolfe, Thomas Clayton (1900–1938). American novelist, known for the intense individualism, extreme exuberance of spirit, frequently extravagant rhetoric, and mystical celebration of youth, sex, and America which characterize his writings. His work, virtually all of which is autobiographical or semi-autobiographical in character, has been criticized as over-written in many places and naïve in its inordinate subjective emphasis, and has been found to show the influence of Theodore DREISER, Sinclair LEWIS, and especially James JOYCE. His books include LOOK HOMEWARD, ANGEL (1929) and its sequel OF TIME AND THE RIVER (1935); *From Death to Morning* (1935), stories; *The Story of a Novel* (1936), criticism of his own work; *The Face of a Nation* (1939), a collection of excerpts from his various novels; *The Web and the Rock* (1939) and its sequel *You Can't Go Home Again* (1940), posthumously published novels resembling his first two novels. Critical opinion at the time of Wolfe's death was divided on the value and promise of his work.

Wolfert's Roost and Miscellanies. A book of stories and sketches (1855) by Washington IRVING.

Wolff, Mary Evaline. Sister **Mary Madeleva** (1887–). American poet. Among her students at St. Mary's in Ogden, Utah, were Bernard DEVOTO and Phyllis MCGINLEY. She has written a number of books of poems and some essays.

Wolf-Ferrari, Ermanno (1876–). Italian composer of operas, best known for *The Jewels of the Madonna* (*I Gioielli della Madonna*).

Wolfram von Eschenbach (1170?–?1220). A medieval poet, one of the MINNESINGERS and the author of the romance *Parzeval* (see PARSIFAL) and an early version of the TRISTAN legend. He was the opponent of Heinrich von Ofterdingen in the famous singer contest on the WARTBURG. In his opera TANNHÄUSER Wagner makes him play a prominent role as the generous opponent of Tannhäuser and admirer of Elizabeth.

Wolfville. A book of stories (1897) by Alfred Henry LEWIS, about a Western town.

Wolheim, Louis (1881–1931). American actor, best known for his role of Captain Flagg in WHAT PRICE GLORY. See ANDERSON, MAXWELL.

Wolle, John Frederick (1863–1933). American musician, who founded and conducted the famous Bach Choir in Bethlehem, Pennsylvania.

Wollstonecraft, Mary (1759–1797). English author, best known for her *Vindication of* *the Rights of Woman* (1792), an argument for equality for women. She was at various times a teacher, a governess, and a worker in a London publishing house. In 1797 she married William GODWIN and died when their daughter Mary, later Mary Wollstonecraft SHELLEY, was born.

Wolseley, Garnet Joseph. 1st Viscount **Wolseley** (1833–1913). Commander in chief of the British Army (1895–1899). Led the Nile expedition (1884) which did not arrive in time to relieve General Gordon at Khartoum.

Wolsey, Thomas (1475?–1530). English cardinal (1515) and lord chancellor (1515–1529) to Henry VIII. Because of the delay, caused by his opposition, in King Henry's divorce from Catherine of Aragon, he was deprived of his offices and accused of treason (1530). Shakespeare gives a moving account of Wolsey's dismissal in *Henry VIII*.

Wolverine State. Michigan. See STATES.

Woman in White, The. A mystery novel by Wilkie COLLINS (1860). The plot hinges on the resemblance of Laura Fairlie, an English heiress, to Anne Catherick, a mysterious "woman in white" confined in a lunatic asylum. In order to secure Laura's money the unscrupulous Sir Percival Glyde thrusts her into the asylum in place of the dying Anne, but this villainy is finally exposed by her faithful lover, Walter Hartright. Count Fosco is a subsidiary villain. Filmed in 1948.

Woman of Andros, The. A short novel (1930) by Thornton WILDER.

Woman of No Importance, A. A drama by Oscar WILDE (1893). The chief characters are Gerald Arbuthnot, his mother, and Lord Illingworth, a nobleman who has offered to make George his secretary. Mrs. Arbuthnot tries in vain to persuade George to refuse the offer. Only later, when he is about to attack Illingworth for kissing his fiancée Hester, does his mother confess that the nobleman is his father, who had seduced her as "a woman of no importance."

Woman of Thirty, A (*La Femme de trente ans*). A novel by BALZAC (1834). The titular heroine is Julie D'AIGLEMONT.

Woman's Home Companion, The. A monthly magazine, founded (1886) in Cleveland, Ohio, as *The Ladies' Home Companion.* It has published many popular women writers and has helped the American housewife to keep up with current events in a comfortably diluted fashion.

Woman's Reason, A. A novel by W. D. HOWELLS (1883), dealing with the struggles of Helen Harkness to conquer her pride and ignorance upon being left without financial resources, and learn how to make a living. Her lover, Robert Fenton, goes to China when she refuses to marry him, but in the end the pair are reunited.

woman suffrage. Advocated as early as ca. 1850 both in England and the U.S. The first American national convention of women interested in woman suffrage was held at Worcester, Mass., the leaders of the movement being Susan B. ANTHONY, Lucy STONE, Anna SHAW, Mrs. STANTON, Carrie Chapman CATT and others. The territory of Wyoming was the first to adopt woman suffrage (1869). Thirty states voted for it in 1919. The Nineteenth Amendment (passed August, 1920), made of it a law. In England, John Stuart Mill and his wife were early advocates of woman suffrage. Mrs. Emmeline Pankhurst was a militant leader. Since World War I, woman suffrage has become widespread in Europe; since World War II it has been extended to the women of Japan.

Woman Who Did, The. A novel (1895) by Grant ALLEN. Its views were advanced, and it was considered very daring at the time of its publication.

wombat. A small Marsupial which looks like a small bear. It is mentioned in *Goblin Market* by Christina Rossetti; her brother Dante Gabriel Rossetti had one as a pet.

Women at Point Sur, The. A free verse poem (1927) by Robinson JEFFERS.

wonder.

a nine days' wonder. Something that causes a sensational astonishment for a few days, and is then placed in the limbo of "things forgot"; three days' amazement, three days' discussion of details, and three days of subsidence.

> For whan men han wel cried, than let hem roune!
> For wonder last but nine night nevere in toune!
> Chaucer, *Troilus and Criseyde,* iv, 587.

The Seven Wonders of the World.

Of Antiquity:

(1) The Pyramids of Egypt.
(2) The Gardens of Semiramis at Babylon.
(3) The statue of Zeus at Olympia, the work of Phidias.
(4) The Temple of Diana at Ephesus.
(5) The Mausoleum at Halicarnassus.
(6) The Colossus at Rhodes.
(7) The Pharos of Egypt, the Walls of Babylon or the Palace of Cyrus.

Of the Middle Ages:

(1) The Coliseum of Rome.
(2) The Catacombs of Alexandria.
(3) The Great Wall of China.
(4) Stonehenge.
(5) The Leaning Tower of Pisa.
(6) The Porcelain Tower of Nankin.
(7) The Mosque of St. Sophia at Constantinople.

The palace of the Escurial has sometimes been called the *eighth wonder,* a name which has also been given to a number of works of great mechanical ingenuity, such as the dome of Chosroes in Madain, St. Peter's of Rome, the Menai suspension bridge, the Eddystone lighthouse, the Suez Canal, the railway over Mont Cenis, the Atlantic cable, etc.

the Wonder of the World. The title given to Otto III, Emperor of the Holy Roman Empire (983–1002), on account of his brilliant intellectual endowments. The Emperor Frederick II (1215–1250) was also so called.

the Wonderful or *Wondermaking Parliament.* See PARLIAMENTS.

Wonderful Doctor. See under DOCTOR.

Wonder-Book for Girls and Boys. A book of mythological tales retold for children by Nathaniel HAWTHORNE (1852).

Wonderful One-Hoss Shay, see DEACON'S MASTERPIECE, THE.

Wonderful Magician, The (El Mágico Prodigioso). A drama by CALDERON (1637), treating of the martyrdom of Saint Cyprian and Saint Justina in Antioch (290 A. D.). The "wonderful magician" is a demon whose ingenious attempts to lead Cyprian astray comprise the plot.

Wonders of the Invisible World. An account of the SALEM WITCHCRAFT trials by Cotton MATHER (1693). It purports to give evidence against the various victims of the trials and discusses witchcraft in general.

Wood, Anthony or **Anthony à** (1632–1695). English antiquary and authority on Oxford. Author of a Latin history of Oxford University (1674) and of a biographical dictionary of famous Oxford graduates from 1500, the *Athenae Oxonienses* (1691–1692).

Wood, Babes in the. See CHILDREN IN THE WOOD.

Wood, Charles Erskine Scott (1852–1944). American poet, known for his verse expressing his humanitarian and radical sympathies, often mystical in vein. His best-known works are *The Poet in the Desert* (1915), a poetic dialogue on social injustice, and *Heavenly Discourse* (1927), a satire on war, injustice, and other social evils, published in THE MASSES during World War I. He also wrote *Masque of Love* (1904); *Maia* (1918); *Circe* (1919); *Poems from the Ranges* (1929); *Too Much Government* (1931); *Earthly Discourse* (1937). In his early life, Wood served in the U.S. Army in the West, becoming acquainted with the language and lore of the Indians. Later he became a lawyer; he did not begin writing until he was past sixty.

Wood, Clement (1888–). American poet, novelist, and writer of miscellaneous books, including *Hunters of Heaven* (1929), a discourse on American poetry and *The Complete Rhyming Dictionary and Poet's Craft Book* (1936). He and his wife have also compiled books on games and various anthologies of prose and poetry.

Wood, Fernando (1812–1881). American politician of Tammany Hall. Mayor of New York (1855–1858; 1861; 1862); member of Congress (1863–1865; 1865–1881).

Wood, Grant (1892–1944). American painter, known for his stark pictures of the Middle West, as *American Gothic, Daughters of the Revolution,* etc. He has been called America's "painter of the soil."

Wood, Mrs. **Henry,** née **Ellen Price** (1814–1887). English novelist, best known for *East Lynne* (1861).

Wood, Leonard (1860–1927). American army surgeon, who led Roosevelt's Rough Riders in the Spanish American War. In 1899 he was military governor of Cuba and after that of the Philippines, where his administration was not popular. He was later chief of staff of the army.

Woodberry, George Edward (1855–1930). American poet, remembered as an inspiring teacher of literature at Columbia University (1891–1904). The Woodberry Society, formed (1911) by some of his ex-students, brought out a special edition of his work. His poetry is of a transcendental character, with a Swinburnian flow of rhythm.

Woodcock, Catherine. Second wife of John MILTON, who married the poet in 1656 without ever having been seen by him, and died in childbirth in 1658.

Woodcraft. A novel by W. G. SIMMS (1854) published first as *The Sword and the Distaff, or Fair, Fat and Forty* (1853) continuing the adventures of Captain PORGY, a comic character in Simms' Revolutionary trilogy.

wooden.

the wooden horse. See under HORSE.

wooden walls. Ships made of wood. When Xerxes invaded Greece (480 B. C.), the Greeks sent to ask the Delphic oracle for advice and were told to seek safety in their wooden walls. The British navy has been called *the wooden walls of England.*

wooden wedding. See WEDDING.

Woodhouse, Emma. Heroine of Jane Austen's EMMA. Emma's father, **Mr. Woodhouse,** is a character in the same novel.

Woodhull, Victoria Claflin, see CLAFLIN, VICTORIA.

Woodlanders, The. A novel (1887) by Thomas HARDY.

Woodman, Spare That Tree. A well-known poem by George P. Morris (*Am.,* 1802–1864), beginning—

Woodman, spare that tree!
Touch not a single bough!
In youth it sheltered me
And I'll protect it now.

woodmote. See under FORTY DAYS COURT.

Woodrow, Mrs. **Wilson,** née **Nancy Mann Waddell** (1870–1935). American novelist. *The Bird of Time* (1907); *Burned Evidence* (1925); etc.

Woodstock. A novel by Sir Walter SCOTT (1826). The novel is concerned with the disguises and escapes of Charles II during the Commonwealth, and ends with the death of Cromwell and the triumphant entry of the King into London. It is called *Woodstock* from the Lee family, the head of which, Sir Henry Lee, was head-ranger of Woodstock. His daughter Alice marries Everard, a Cromwellite, and his servant, Phoebe Mayflower, marries Joceline Joliffe, under-keeper of Woodstock forest. Among the subsidiary characters are Shakespeare, Milton, Ben Jonson, Davenant the poet, "Fair Rosamond," Prince Rupert, General Monk, Cromwell's daughter, and many other persons of historic interest.

Woods of Westermain, The. A poem by George MEREDITH, appearing (1883) in *Poems and Lyrics of the Joy of Earth.*

Woodville, Elizabeth, Lady Grey. Queen of Edward IV of England, introduced in Shakespeare's RICHARD III.

Woodward, William E. (1874–). American writer, best known for his biographies of George Washington (1926) and General Grant (1928). His *A New American History* (1936), telling many unusual and interesting things concerning early American life, sold well. *Gift of Life* (1947) is autobiography.

Woolf, Adeline Virginia, *née* **Stephen** (1882–1941). English novelist and critic, a member of the BLOOMSBURY GROUP, known for the delicacy and sensitivity of her style, the penetration of her psychological studies, especially of mature women of the English upper classes, her skill in evoking mood in her writing, the intensity of her preoccupation with time, experience, and relationships, and her experiments in the use of the techniques of INTERIOR MONOLOGUE and STREAM OF CONSCIOUSNESS. Among her works are *The Voyage Out* (1915); *Night and Day* (1919); *Monday or Tuesday* (1921); *Jacob's Room* (1922); MRS. DALLOWAY (1925); *The Common Reader* (1925), criticism; *To the Lighthouse* (1927); *Orlando* (1928), said to have been based on the personality of V. SACKVILLE-WEST; *A Room of One's Own* (1929), essays on women; *Beau Brummell* (1930); *The Second Common Reader* (1932), criticism; THE WAVES (1931), regarded as her best work; *A Letter to a Young Poet* (1932), poetry; *Flush, a Biography* (1933), on the spaniel pet of E. B. BROWNING; THE YEARS (1937); *Three Guineas* (1938), essays on the problems of peace; *Roger Fry* (1940), a biography; *Between the Acts* (1941); *The Death of the Moth, And Other Essays* (1942).

Virginia Woolf, considered one of the most important novelists of the 20th century, was the daughter of Sir Leslie STEPHEN, a well-known biographer and literary critic, and was related to a number of the most distinguished scholarly families in England, such as the DARWINS, the SYMONDSES, and the STRACHEYS. She was raised in an atmosphere of literature and learning, receiving her education at home and as a young girl made the acquaintance of numerous outstanding authors of the day. The Bloomsbury Group had its inception in the gatherings of a group of former Cambridge University students and their friends which were held at the home of Virginia and her sister Vanessa. The novelist and her husband, Leonard WOOLF, an author, editor, and literary critic, together founded the Hogarth Press, a successful publishing house, known for its limited editions of the works of a number of leading 20th-century English writers, which began as a single hand-press. Depressed at the vision of the world about her at war (World War II), Mrs. Woolf committed suicide by drowning in 1941. For a study of her work, cf. *Virginia Woolf,* by David Daiches.

Woolf, Leonard Sidney (1880–). English publicist and writer, husband of Virginia WOOLF. Editor on the *International Review; Contemporary Review; Political Quarterly,* and a contributor to the *New Statesman;* literary editor of the *Nation* (1923–1930). In 1917 he and his wife founded the Hogarth Press.

Woollcott, Alexander Humphreys (1887–1943). American literary and dramatic critic and journalist, best known for his whimsical and sentimental essays and radio talks expressing his opinions on a variety of subjects, including popular comedians and forgotten murder cases. His books include *Shouts and Murmurs* (1922); *Enchanted Aisles* (1924); *Going to Pieces* (1928); and *While Rome Burns* (1934). He at one time wrote a column for THE NEW YORKER, made lecture tours, and acted on the stage and screen. A notable appearance was in *The Man Who Came to Dinner* (1939), a satirical comedy by George S. Kaufman and Moss Hart, in which Woollcott played the leading role, portraying a character suggested by his own personality. His death came as the result of a heart-attack while he was making a radio broadcast. His biography, *A. Woollcott, His Life and his World,* by Samuel Hopkins Adams, was published in 1945. Attempts at Woollcottian characterizations of Woollcott include: "He had the memory of a pachyderm and a pianola's loyalty to the same tune."—"He can be described as the man who couldn't write fiction but who did."—"He was as fascinated by mortals as he was indifferent to the immortals."

Woolley, Mary Emma (1863–1947). American eduactor; president of Mt. Holyoke College (1900–1937). President Hoover appointed her U.S. delegate to the Disarmament Conference (1933).

Woolman, John (1720–1772). A Pennsylvania Quaker whose *Journal* (1774) has a place among the classics of autobiography.

Woolner, Thomas (1825–1892). English sculptor and poet; member of the Pre-Raphaelites and contributor to *The Germ.* His statue of John Stuart Mill stands on the Thames embankment in London.

Woolsack, the. The office of the Lord Chancellor of England, whose seat in the House of Lords is called the *woolsack*. It is a large square bag of wool, without back or arms, covered with red cloth. In the reign of Queen Elizabeth an Act of Parliament was passed to prevent the exportation of wool, and that this source of the national wealth might be kept constantly in mind woolsacks were placed in the House of Peers as seats for the judges. Hence the Lord Chancellor, who presides in the House of Lords, is said to "sit on the woolsack," or to be "appointed to the woolsack."

Woolson, Constance Fenimore (1840–1894). New England writer, grand-niece of James Fenimore COOPER. *Anne* (1883); *For the Major* (1883); *East Angels* (1886); etc.

Worcester, Joseph Emerson (1784–1865). American lexicographer. He published (1860) the first illustrated *Dictionary of the English language.*

Worde, Wynkyn de. Real name **Jan van Wynkyn** (d. 1534?). English printer and stationer, born in Alsace and early in his career an apprentice to William CAXTON. He published a number of well-known books of the time, including the fourth edition (1498) of Chaucer's *Canterbury Tales.*

word square. See under CROSSWORD PUZZLE.

Wordsworth, William (1770–1850). English poet, with his friend S. T. COLERIDGE one of the early leaders of ROMANTICISM in England, known for his worship of nature, his humanitarianism, his early sympathy with democratic liberalism, his interest in the lives, daily pursuits, and common speech of lowly people, and his Platonistically tinged pantheism. He was particularly interested in instituting a reform in poetic diction which would employ "a selection of language really used by men," as he proposes in his famous *Preface* to LYRICAL BALLADS, and many of his best-known poems make use of what the poet regarded as this "real" language. In later times these came to be considered sentimental and almost comically prosaic, failing in their objective.

Wordsworth's most ambitious works are *The Prelude* (published in 1850) and the uncompleted *The Recluse,* long poems autobiographical in character, and *The Excursion* (1814), a long "philosophical" poem. *An Evening Walk* and *Descriptive Sketches* were his earliest works, published in 1793; the bulk of his best-known poetry is contained in *Lyrical Ballads* (1798), which he published jointly with Coleridge. Among well-known shorter poems of Wordsworth's are *Alice Fell;* MICHAEL; SIMON LEE; the LUCY poems; RESOLUTION AND INDEPENDENCE; *The Solitary Reaper;* PETER BELL; *The Idiot Boy; I Wandered Lonely as a Cloud; Elegiac Stanzas; Nuns Fret Not; The World Is Too Much With Us; Tintern Abbey;* ODE ON INTIMATIONS OF IMMORTALITY.

In his early youth, Wordsworth was influenced by the ideas of J. J. ROUSSEAU and William GODWIN and was an enthusiast for the French Revolution. He stayed in France for a while in 1792 and had a love affair with Annette VALLON, evidence of which was uncovered only in the 20th century. As he grew older, he became increasingly conservative in his political views and orthodox in his religion, living peacefully in the Lake Country of northern England. In 1843 he was appointed Poet Laureate, succeeding Robert SOUTHEY.

See also HUTCHINSON, MARY; CAROLINE.

Dorothy Wordsworth (1771–1855), William's sister, was the devoted and constant companion of the poet during most of his life, accompanying him and Coleridge on their tour of Germany just after the publication of *Lyrical Ballads* and keeping house for him while he wrote. She had a keen mind and eye and was credited by her brother with the improvement of his observation of nature on their regular walks. Her journals and letters became widely known on their publication in the 20th century. Best edition is by Ernest de Selincourt (1942).

Work, Henry Clay (1832–1884). American song writer, author of the temperance song,

> Father, dear father, come home with me now,
> The clock in the steeple strikes one . . .

Work in Progress. Title under which James Joyce's FINNEGANS WAKE was known until its publication. From time to time the following sections of the work were published separately in the magazine TRANSITION or in book form: *Anna Livia Plurabelle; Tales Told by Shem and Shaun; Haveth Childers Everywhere; The Mime of Mick, Nick, and the Maggies; Storiella As She Is Syung.*

Works and Days. A long poem by HESIOD. It is a sort of "farmer's almanac" of ancient

Greece, and contains directions and advice concerning labor on the farm.

World. A New York newspaper, founded in 1866 as a religious penny daily. Bought by Joseph PULITZER in 1883, it became a crusading newspaper. OUTCAULT started in it a colored comic strip called *Hogan's Alley,* featuring the *Yellow Kid,* a name which is said to have given rise to the phrase "yellow journalism." During the Spanish-American War the paper was as sensational as the HEARST papers. In 1887 Pulitzer had founded the *Evening World.* From 1911, his son, Ralph Pulitzer, became the head of the Press Publishing Co., publishers of the New York *World* and the New York *Evening World.* Now the *World's* most brilliant period began. It accumulated as columnists Walter LIPPMANN, Franklin P. ADAMS, Heywood BROUN, etc., and Alexander WOOLLCOTT as dramatic critic. The passing of the *World* in 1931 was a newspaper tragedy. It was sold to the Scripps-Howard chain, combined with the New York *Telegram,* and was transformed into an evening paper, the *World-Telegram.* The *World Almanac and Book of Facts,* now published by this paper for the Washington *Daily News* was originated in 1886.

World, The. A famous mystic poem by Henry VAUGHAN (1650), which begins:

> I saw Eternity the other night,
> Like a great ring of pure and endless light,
> All calm, as it was bright.

World Court. The Permanent Court of International Justice which was opened at The Hague (February 15, 1922) by the League of Nations. It had fifteen judges who served for nine years. The court sat on all cases which states or members of the League brought before it and also on other matters provided for in international treaties and conventions. Before World War II, Germany, Italy, and Japan had handed in their resignations. At the outbreak of World War II, the World Court ceased.

World I Never Made, A. A novel (1936) by James T. FARRELL. It is the first of a series of novels concerning Danny O'NEILL.

Worldly Wiseman, Mr. In Bunyan's PILGRIM'S PROGRESS, one who tries to persuade Christian that it is very bad policy to continue his journey toward the Celestial City.

World's Columbian Exposition. To celebrate the four hundreth anniversary of the discovery of America, this exposition was held in Chicago, Illinois, in 1893.

World's Work. A magazine established (1900) by Walter Hines Page, who was also its first editor (to 1913). It discussed national and international affairs. It was merged (1932) with the *Review of Reviews.*

Worm, William. In Hardy's PAIR OF BLUE EYES, a "poor, wambling creature," the out-of-door man of the vicar.

Wormeley, Katharine Prescott (1830–1908). English writer and translator, living in the U.S. (from 1848). Principally known for her translations of Balzac, Dumas, Molière, Sainte-Beuve, etc.

Worthies, the Nine. Nine heroes—three from the Bible, three from the classics, and three from romance—who were frequently bracketed together as in the burlesque Pageant of the Nine Worthies in Shakespeare's LOVE'S LABOR'S LOST. They are: Joshua, David,. and Judas Maccabaeus; Hector, Alexander, and Julius Caesar; Arthur, Charlemagne, and Godfrey of Bouillon.

> Nine worthies were they called, of different rites—
> Three Jews, three pagans, and three Christian knights
> Dryden, *The Flower and the Leaf.*

the Nine Worthies of London. A kind of chronicle-history in mixed verse and prose of nine prominent citizens of London, published in 1592 by Richard Johnson, author also of *The Seven Champions of Christendom.* His "Worthies" are:

Sir William Walworth, who stabbed Wat TYLER, the rebel, and was twice Lord Mayor (1374, 1380).

Sir Henry Pritchard, who (in 1356), feasted Edward III (with 5,000 followers), Edward the Black Prince, John, King of Austria, the King of Cyprus, and David, King of Scotland.

Sir William Sevenoke, who fought with the Dauphin of France and built twenty almshouses and a free school (1418).

Sir Thomas White, merchant tailor, who, in 1553, kept the citizens loyal to Queen Mary during Wyatt's rebellion.

Sir John Bonham, entrusted with a valuable cargo for the Danish market, and made commander of the army raised to stop the progress of the great Solyman.

Christopher Croker. Famous at the siege of Bordeaux, and companion of the Black Prince when he helped Don Pedro to the throne of Castile.

Sir John Hawkwood. One of the Black Prince's knights, and immortalized in Italian history as Giovanni Acuti Cavaliero.

Sir Hugh Caverley. Famous for ridding Poland of a monstrous bear.

Sir Henry Maleverer, generally called Henry of Cornhill, who lived in the reign of Henry IV. He was a crusader, and became the guardian of "Jacob's well."

The names of Sir Richard Whittington and Sir Thomas Gresham are "conspicuous by their absence."

Wotan. The Old High German form of ODIN, chief of the Scandinavian gods. This is the form used in the operas of Wagner's RING

DES NIBELUNGEN, in which Wotan the Mighty plays a leading rôle.

Wotton, Sir **Henry** (1568–1639). English diplomat and poet. Ambassador to Venice (1604–1624); provost of Eton (1624–1639); etc. His poetry contains some famous lyrics. Izaak WALTON wrote his *Life* (1670). Logan Pearsall Smith edited his *Life and Letters* (1907).

W.P.A. See WORKS PROGRESS ADMINISTRATION.

W.P.B. See WAR PRODUCTION BOARD.

Wrangel, Dr. The hero of Ibsen's drama THE LADY FROM THE SEA.

Wrangel, Baron **Ferdinand Petrovich von** (1794–1870). Russian explorer, who commanded an expedition to the polar regions (1820) and was made governor general of Alaska (1829–1834). He was against the sale of Alaska to the U.S. Wrangel Island was named in his honor.

Wrangel, Baron **Pëtr Nikolaevich** (1878–1928). Russian Czarist general, allied with Denikin, who lost Sevastopol (1920). Fled to Yugoslavia. Settled (1926) in Brussels where he died as an engineer.

wrangler. The Cambridge term for one who has obtained a place in the highest class of the mathematical tripos. The first man used to be termed the *senior wrangler,* and the rest were arranged according to respective merit, but since 1909 this arrangement has been dropped and no one now can claim the title of *senior wrangler.*

Wrayburn, Eugene. In Dickens' novel OUR MUTUAL FRIEND, barrister-at-law; an indolent, idle, moody, whimsical young man, who loves Lizzie Hexam. After he is nearly killed by Bradley Headstone, he reforms, and marries Lizzie, who saved his life.

Wreck of the Hesperus, The. A famous ballad by Henry W. LONGFELLOW, published (1841) in *Ballads and Other Poems.*

Wren, Jenny. A character in Dickens' novel OUR MUTUAL FRIEND, whose real name is Fanny Cleaver. She is a dolls' dressmaker, and the friend of Lizzie Hexam, who at one time lodged with her. Jenny is a little, deformed girl, with a sharp shrewd face, and beautiful golden hair. She supports herself and her drunken father, whom she reproves as a mother might reprove a child. "Oh," she cries to him, pointing her little finger, "you bad old boy! Oh, you naughty, wicked creature! What do you mean by it?"

Wren, Percival Christopher (1885–1941). English novelist, soldier, and traveler, for many years a British government official in India. He is best known for his popular adventure novels and stories dealing with life in the French Foreign Legion, based on his own experiences in that organization. These include *The Wages of Virtue* (1916); *Stepsons of France* (1917), a collection of short stories; *Beau Geste* (1924), his best-known book, a best-seller, later dramatized on stage and screen; *Beau Sabreur* (1926), *Beau Ideal* (1928), and *Good Gestes* (1929), sequels to *Beau Geste; Soldiers of Misfortune* (1929) and its sequel, *Valiant Dust* (1931); *Beggars' Horses* (1934); *The Desert Heritage* (1935); *Cardboard Castle* (1938); *The Dark Woman* (1943).

Wren, Sir **Christopher** (1632–1723). The most famous of England's architects. He submitted plans for rebuilding London after the Great Fire (1666) and reconstructed St. Paul's Cathedral (1675–1716). He designed fifty-two churches and many other buildings in London as well as the additions to Kensington and Hampton Court Palace. He is buried in St. Paul's Cathedral.

Wright, Frank Lloyd (1869–). Distinguished American architect; exponent of the theory that "form should follow function," and creator of a strikingly individualistic style, closely followed and studied by young architects all over the globe. Some of his notable works include his own residence "Taliesin" in Spring Green, Wisconsin (1911); the Imperial Hotel at Tokyo, Japan (1916); the Millard House at Pasadena, California (1927); and private homes in and near Chicago. Author of *Experimenting with Human Lives* (1923); *Modern Architecture* (1931); etc.

Wright, Harold Bell (1872–1944). American Christian-Church minister (1897–1908) and novelist, whose *The Shepherd of the Hills* (1907) was a best seller. His *The Winning of Barbara Worth* (1911) sold over a million and a half copies. His novels have a strong religious bias, and castigate the fashionable world.

Wright, Mabel Osgood (1859–1934). American writer of nature books, as *Birdcraft,* a field book of New England birds (1895); *The Flowers and Ferns in Their Haunts* (1901); etc.

Wright, Richard (1908–). American Negro novelist and short-story writer, known for his fictional studies of race problems and of the position of the Negro in the U.S. in the 20th century. *Uncle Tom's Children* (1938 and 1940), a collection of short stories, and NATIVE SON (1940), a novel later dramatized for the theater, are among his published works. On the publication of *Native Son,* Wright was hailed by a number of critics as an extremely promising American author.

Wright, Richardson Little (1886–). American author, principally known as editor of *House and Garden* magazine and a writer on gardening in America. He has also published some books on peculiar American habits, as *Hawkers and Walkers in Early America* (1927) and *Grandfather Was Queer* (1939).

Wright, Sidney Fowler (1874–). English writer, most successful in America with his fantastic novels *Deluge: A Romance* (1928); *The Island of Captain Sparrow* (1928); *Dawn* (1929); and *Elfwin, A Romance of History* (1930).

Wright, Wilbur (1867–1912), and **Orville Wright** (1871–1948). American pioneers in aviation. They began experimenting with gliders at Kitty Hawk, N.C. Their first flight in an airplane with engine was made on December 17, 1903. France first recognized them in 1908, and in 1909 the United States Army adopted their plane. In the same year they founded the Wright Aeroplane Company. Cf. *The Wright Brothers* by Fred C. Kelly.

Wright, Willard Huntington. Pseudonym **S. S. Van Dine** (1888–1939). American art critic, writer of detective stories, and compiler of a chronological anthology of great detective stories. He created the detective Philo Vance who attained great popularity.

Writing on the Wall. See under HANDWRITING.

Wronski, Count Alexis. See VRONSKY.

Wulstan, St. See under SAINTS.

Wurdemann, Audrey May (1911–). American poet. She is a descendant on her mother's side of Harriet WESTBROOK, a great-great-grand-daughter of SHELLEY, and the wife of Joseph AUSLANDER. She was born in Seattle, Washington, and was the protégé of George STERLING. She won the Pulitzer prize for poetry with *Bright Ambush* (1935), the youngest poet ever to receive the prize.

Wuthering Heights. A novel by Emily BRONTË (1847). The hero is a strange, uncouth, passionate creature named Heathcliff, who grows up with Hindley and Catherine Earnshaw in their lonely moorland home. His very love is terrifying, and when Catherine, though she returns his love, marries Edgar Linton, his thwarted passion finds outlet against the Lintons and Earnshaws of his own and the succeeding generation.

Wuyck's Bible. See BIBLE, SPECIALLY NAMED.

Wyatt or **Wyat, Sir Thomas** (1503?–1542). English poet, known for his production of the first sonnets in English in his translations of PETRARCH and for his popularization of other Italian and French verse-forms among the English writers of the 16th century. Wyatt was influenced by Serafino dell' Aquila, Pietro Aretino, Luigi Alamanni, Sannazaro, and other French and Italian poets of the time. His own poetry is characterized by extreme irregularity of rhythm, which 19th-century scholars regarded as evidence of crudity of technique. In the 20th century, however, critics began to point out that this irregularity was important in the total effect of the poems, comparing it with the dramatic rhythm of John DONNE; they also praised the vigor and authentic intensity of feeling embodied in Wyatt's best poems. His work appeared in several anthologies of his time, as *Seven Penitential Psalms* (1549), a collection of religious poetry in imitation of a similar undertaking by Aretino; *The Court of Venus* (1542); and TOTTEL'S MISCELLANY (1557).

Wyatt held a number of official positions under Henry VIII, including those of member of the Privy Council, ambassador to Spain, Member of Parliament, and Commander of the Fleet. During his career he was twice imprisoned: once at the time of the fall of Anne Boleyn, whose lover he was suspected of being; and again in 1541, during his ambassadorship to Spain, when he was charged with treason, although he was later able to clear himself. It was during an official trip to Italy in 1527 that he became acquainted with the work of the Italian love-poets. He was a friend of the Earl of SURREY and had a strong influence on the writing of the younger man; together, Wyatt and Surrey are credited as the founders of the school of English lyric poetry which flourished during the remainder of the 16th century and into the 17th.

Wycherley, William (1640–1716). English playwright of the Restoration period, known for his savage satire, his cynicism, and his realism, often censured for his licentiousness. His plays include *Love in a Wood, or St. James's Park* (1671); *The Gentleman Dancing-Master* (1671); *The Country Wife* (1673), his best-known work; *The Plain Dealer* (see MANLY; 1674), published in 1677.

Wycliffite. A LOLLARD, a follower of John Wyclif (d. 1384), the religious reformer, called "The Morning Star of the Reformation." He denied transubstantiation, condemned monasticism, and taught that all ecclesiastical and secular authority is derived from God and is forfeited by one who is living in mortal sin.

Wyclif's Bible. See BIBLE, THE ENGLISH.

Wyeth, Nathaniel (1802–1856). A merchant of Boston who is a character in *Adventures of Captain Bonneville* by Washington Irving. Wyeth made several expeditions to Oregon and in 1899 his *Correspondence and Journals* were published. He is an ancestor of the American painter Newell Convers WYETH.

Wyeth, Newell Convers (1882–1945). American illustrator and painter, widely known for his illustrations in color to the novels of Robert Louis Stevenson, to Robin Hood, the Odyssey, etc. In all, he illustrated some seventy juvenile classics. He also did murals for the National Episcopal Cathedral in Washington, D.C.; the Hubbard Memorial Building of the National Geographic Society; the Metropolitan Life Insurance Co. Building in New York City; etc. Killed in an automobile accident at a railroad crossing.

Wykehamist. Any member, past or present, of Winchester College in England, from the founder William of Wykeham (1324–1404). Some of the most famous Wykehamists have been Sir Henry Wotton, Sir Thomas Browne, William Collins, Sidney Smith, Anthony Trollope, and Lionel Johnson. (See these names).

Wylie, Elinor Morton, *née* **Hoyt** (1885–1928). American poet, known for the precise and vivid imagery of her lyrics and the intensity and subtle analysis of emotions in her later love poems. Her poetry, in general influenced by medieval Scotch and English ballads and the English Elizabethan and METAPHYSICAL POETS, is considered among the best written by women in the 20th century. Her prose, less well known than her verse, is marked by fantasy, wit and irony, skill in the drawing of character, and extreme delicacy and precision of style. Her books include *Nets to Catch the Wind* (1921), *Black Armor* (1923), *Trivial Breath* (1928), and *Angels and Earthly Creatures* (1928), poetry; *Jennifer Lorn* (1923), *The Venetian Glass Nephew* (1925), *The Orphan Angel* (1926), and *Mr. Hodge and Mr. Hazard* (1928), novels; *Collected Poems* (1932); *Collected Prose* (1933). Her reputation rests mainly on *Angels and Earthly Creatures*. P. B. SHELLEY was her literary idol. Her third husband was William Rose BENÉT.

Wylie, Ida Alexa Ross (1885–). British writer who has written over two hundred short stories and over fifteen novels. One of her best novels is *Towards Morning* (1920). Her writing concerning Germany is based on an eight years' stay there. *My Life with George* (1940) is autobiography.

Wylie, Maggie. The heroine of Barrie's play WHAT EVERY WOMAN KNOWS.

Wylie, Philip (1902–). American writer of popular fiction and biting satire, as *A Generation of Vipers* (1944). His stories of big game fishing have appeared in *The Saturday Evening Post*. The most peculiar of his works is *Finnley Wren* (1934). Frequently attacks "Moms," or excessively maternal American women.

Wyndham, George (1863–1913). English aristocrat who pursued a distinguished political career and as Secretary of Ireland (1900) was instrumental in getting the Wyndham Land Act passed which benefited both the tenants and the landlords. As a writer he was a friend of Wilfred Blunt, Chesterton, and Henley. He wrote a few essays concerning romantic literature, and edited North's version of Plutarch's *Lives* (1895–1896) and Shakespeare's poems (1898).

Wynn, Ed. Real name **Isaiah Edwin Leopold** (1886–). American comedian who was the first to put on the air the entire production of a musical comedy. Over the radio he became famous as "the Fire Chief." His nickname in musical comedy has been "the Perfect Fool." His son, Keenan Wynn, is a well-known film comedian.

Wynne, Hugh, see HUGH WYNNE.

Wyoming Massacre. The massacre in the famous Wyoming valley of a Susquehanna branch where Wilkes-Barré is situated, of American settlers by Iroquois fighting on the side of the Tories (July, 1778). A narrative poem by the English poet Thomas Campbell (1809), *Gertrude of Wyoming*, tells of this event in a vein of exaggeration.

X

Xanadu. A city mentioned by COLERIDGE in his KUBLA KHAN.

Xanthus (*Gr.*, "reddish yellow"). Achilles' wonderful horse, brother of Balios, Achilles' other horse, and offspring of Zephyrus and the harpy Podarge. Being chid by his master for leaving Patroclus on the field of battle, Xanthus turned his head reproachfully, and told ACHILLES that he also would soon be numbered with the dead, not from any fault of his horse, but by the decree of inexorable destiny (*Iliad*, xix). Cf. *Numb.* xxii. 28–30. *Xanthus* is also the ancient name of the Scamander and of a city on its banks.

Xantippe. Wife of the philosopher SOCRATES. Her bad temper shown toward her husband has rendered her name proverbial for a conjugal scold.

> Be she as foul as was Florentius' love,
> As old as Sibyl, and as curst and shrewd
> As Socrates' Xanthippe, or a worse,
> She moves me not.
> Shakespeare, *Taming of the Shrew.* i. 2.

Xavier, St. Francis (1506–1552). Jesuit missionary, the "Apostle of the Indies." As a student in Paris he became a friend of Ignatius of Loyola and helped him establish the Society of Jesus (1534). He worked in Japan for several years and founded a mission in China. Canonized, together with his master and friend, in 1622.

Xenophon (445–391 B.C.). Greek historian, famous for his ANABASIS.

Xerxes. A Greek way of writing the Persian *Ksathra* or *Kshatra.* Xerxes I, the great Xerxes, is identical with the AHASUERUS of the Bible.

When Xerxes invaded Greece, he constructed a pontoon bridge across the Dardanelles, which was swept away by the force of the waves. This so enraged the Persian despot that he "inflicted three hundred lashes on the rebellious sea, and cast chains of iron across it." This story is probably a Greek myth, founded on the peculiar construction of Xerxes' second bridge, which consisted of three hundred boats, lashed by iron chains to two ships serving as supporters. Another story told of him is that when he reviewed his enormous army before starting for Greece, he wept at the thought of the slaughter about to take place. "Of all this multitude, who shall say how many will return?"

Xingu and Other Stories. A collection of eight stories (1916) by Edith WHARTON. Xingu is a river in Brazil.

X Y Z Correspondence. To arbitrate with France over an alliance, President Adams sent PINCKNEY, John MARSHALL, and Elbridge GERRY abroad on a special mission (1797). In their correspondence with Washington they reported that three French agents (referred to as X, Y, and Z; hence the phrase X Y Z Correspondence) had attempted to bribe them. The disclosure of the correspondence (1798) caused considerable excitement in both countries involved.

Y

Yahoo. Swift's name, in GULLIVER'S TRAVELS, for brutes with human forms and vicious propensities. They are subject to the *Houyhnhnms,* the horses with human reason. Hence the word is applied to coarse, brutish or degraded persons.

Yahweh, see JEHOVAH.

Yama. The god of the dead in Hindu mythology, the Hindu PLUTO. The story is that he was the first mortal to die and so was made a god. He is of a green color, four-armed, with eyes inflamed, and sits on a buffalo.

Yamamoto, Isoroku (1884–1943). Japanese admiral. Commander in chief of the 1st fleet (from 1939) and of the combined fleet (from 1941). Killed in action.

Yamashita, Tomoyuki (1885–1946). Japanese general. Conducted the Malayan campaign and received the surrender of Singapore (1942); commanded the Japanese campaign in the Philippines, capturing Bataan and Corregidor (1942). In 1945 he was found guilty of war crimes by a military court sitting in Manila, sentenced to death, and executed the following spring.

Yanetta. In Brieux's RED ROBE, the wife of Etchepars, the accused peasant.

Yank. The "HAIRY APE" in Eugene O'Neill's drama of that title.

Yank. The magazine of the G.I.s during World War II.

Yankee. Properly, a New Englander or one of New England stock, but extended to mean, first, an inhabitant of the Northern as apart from the Southern United States, and later to comprise all United States citizens. In the South, often referred to as "Damyankees."

It is generally taken to be a North American Indian corruption of *English* (or of Fr. *Anglais*). The story is that in 1713 one Jonathan Hastings, a farmer of Cambridge, Massachusetts, used the word as a puffing epithet, meaning genuine, what cannot be surpassed, etc.; as, a "Yankee horse," "Yankee cider," and so on. The students at Harvard, catching up the term, called Hastings, "Yankee Jonathan." It soon spread, and became the jocose pet name of the New Englander.

Yankee Doodle. A quasi-national air of the United States, the doggerel words of which are said to have been written by Dr. Shuckburgh, a surgeon in Lord Amherst's army during the French and Indian war of 1755.

The origin of the tune is disputed. Some say that it comes from a medieval church service, others that it was composed in England in Cromwell's time, others that it was played by the Hessian troops during the American Revolution and adopted by the revolutionaries in mockery. A Dutch origin has also been suggested. The first verse reads:

> Yankee Doodle went to town
> A-riding on a pony,
> Stuck a feather in his hat
> And called it macaroni.

Yankees. In American baseball parlance, the nickname of the New York Americans. See under BASEBALL TEAMS.

Yarico. See INKLE AND YARICO.

Yarmolinsky, Avrahm (1890–). Russian-born chief of the Slavonic division in the New York Public Library (since 1918); author of many books on Russian literature. He and his wife, Babette DEUTSCH, have translated together *Modern Russian Poetry* (1921) and *Contemporary German Poetry* (1923).

Yarrow. *The Braes of Yarrow* is the title of an old Scotch ballad. The Yarrow is a river in Scotland. Scott and Hogg have celebrated its legends, and Wordsworth wrote a poem called *Yarrow Revisited* (1835).

Yates, Edmund Hodgson (1831–1894). English writer whose differences with Thackeray (1858) caused his dismissal from the Garrick Club. This in turn caused a long quarrel between Charles Dickens and Thackeray, which the latter, toward the end of his life, took measures to terminate. As editor of the society weekly *The World,* Yates incurred the wrath of Lord Lonsdale and was imprisoned for libel (1885).

Yazoo Frauds. In 1795, the four *Yazoo Companies* bribed the state legislature of Georgia in order to get large grants of land near the Yazoo River. Royall Tyler wrote a satirical play on this episode called *The Georgia Spec: or Land in the Moon* (1797).

Ybarra, Thomas Russell (1880–). American journalist and humorist, son of a Venezuelan general. Well-known especially for his autobiography, *Young Man of Caracas* (1941).

Yeamans, Anne (1835–1912). American actress, noted for her interpretation of Irish roles. She appeared for years with the comedians Harrigan and Hart.

Years, The. A novel by Virginia WOOLF (1937), dealing with the fortunes of an upper middle-class English family, the Pargiters, from 1880 to the 1930's. There is no formal plot, but rather a series of episodes representative of the development of the family, taking place in 1880–1891, 1907, 1908, 1910, 1911, 1913, 1914, 1917, and "the present day," and constituting a recurring cycle. The book contains numerous atmospheric descriptions of London which have been highly praised by critics.

Yeats, William Butler (1865–1939). Irish poet and dramatist, leader of the movement of the IRISH RENAISSANCE. Influenced by the PRE-RAPHAELITES, William BLAKE, SHELLEY, French SYMBOLISM, MAETERLINCK, and Hindu occultism, he is known for his poems and plays dealing with mystic and Celtic legendary themes, and for the highly developed symbolism of his later poetry. Among his books of poetry are *The Wanderings of Oisin* (1889); *The Wind Among the Reeds* (1899); *In the Seven Woods* (1903); *The Green Helmet* (1910); *The Wild Swans of Coole* (1919); *The Tower* (1928); *The Winding Stair* (1929); *A Full Moon in March* (1935); *The King of the Great Clock Tower* (1934); *Wheels and Butterflies* (1934). His dramatic works include: *The Countess Kathleen* (1892); *The Land of Heart's Desire* (1894); *The Shadowy Waters* (1900); *Cathleen ni Houlihan* (1902); *The Hour Glass* (1903); *The King's Threshold* (1904); *Deirdre* (1907); *Four Plays for Dancers* (1921); *Plays in Prose and Verse* (1923); *The Herne's Egg* (1938); *Last Poems and Two Plays* (1939). Miscellaneous prose works include *John Sherman* (1891), *The Celtic Twilight* (1893), *The Secret Rose* (1897), and *Stories of Red Hanrahan* (1904), collections of stories, tales, and sketches; *Ideas of Good and Evil* (1903), *Per Amica Silentia Lunae* (1918), *The Cutting of an Agate* (1919), *Essays* (1924 and 1937), and *On the Boiler* (1939), all books of essays; *A Vision* (1925), on spiritualism; *Letters to the New Island* (1934), criticism; *Autobiography* (1938), consisting of *Reveries over Childhood and Youth* (1915), *The Trembling of the Veil* (1922), and *Dramatis Personae* (1935); *If I Were Four and Twenty* (1940).

Yeats was the son of John Butler Yeats, a well-known Irish landscape painter, and he himself studied painting for three years. Early in his career he was associated with a group of English "Decadent" poets including DOWSON, HENLEY, and Arthur SYMONS and Lionel Johnson, members of the Rhymers' Club; he was invited to come to London, the headquarters of the group, by Oscar WILDE. Yeats is credited with having been the prime mover in the Irish literary revival of the end of the 19th century, persuading Lady GREGORY, George MOORE, and John M. SYNGE to write about their native country and helping to found both the Irish Literary Society (in London and Dublin) and the Irish Literary Theater, which became the celebrated Abbey Theater. He did not approve of the realism of the plays of Sean O'CASEY which the Abbey Theater later sponsored, however. Yeats was honored widely as one of the most important poets of the 20th century, being elected a senator of the Irish Free State in 1922 and in 1923 being awarded the Nobel prize for literature. In appearance and behavior he was eccentric, foppish, dreamy, melancholy, and absent-minded, being subject to hallucinations and trance-like states since youth. He was a fervent believer in spiritualism, and his wife, Georgie Lees, was a medium who held daily séances.

See also GONNE, MAUD.

For a study of Yeats's poetry, cf. *The Poetry of W. B. Yeats,* by Louis MacNeice; for a vivid personal portrait, *Life and the Dream,* by Mary COLUM.

Yeats-Brown, Francis (1886–1944). English writer who served in the British army in India. He combined love of adventure with a decidedly mystical turn of mind. He is known in America especially as the author of *Lives of a Bengal Lancer* (1930).

yellow (A.S. *geolo,* connected with Gr. *chloros,* "green," and with *gall,* the yellowish fluid secreted by the bile). Indicating in symbolism, jealousy, inconstancy, and adultery. In France the doors of traitors used to be daubed with yellow. In some countries the law ordained that Jews must be clothed in yellow, because they betrayed our Lord; hence Judas, in medieval pictures, is arrayed in yellow. In Spain the vestments of the executioner were either red or yellow—the former to denote bloodshedding; the latter treason.

In heraldry and in ecclesiastical symbolism yellow is frequently used in place of gold.

Yellow Book. Official documents, government reports, etc., in France are known as *Yellow Books,* from the color of their cover. See also SPENGLER, Oswald; BLUE BOOK.

Yellow Dwarf. An ugly and ferocious dwarf prominent in an old fairy tale that appeared first in a French version by Countess d'Aulnoy (1650–1705).

yellow hose. A sign of jealousy. To *wear yellow* or *wear yellow hose* means to be jealous.

Yellow Jack. Yellow fever; also, a flag indicative of contagious disease on shipboard.

yellow journalism. See YELLOW PRESS below.

the Yellow Peril. A scare, originally raised in Germany in the late nineties of the 19th century, that the yellow races of China and Japan would in a very few years have increased in population to such an extent that incursions upon the territories occupied by the white races—followed by massacres and every conceivable horror—were inevitable.

the yellow press. Sensational and jingoist newspapers or journalism. The name arose in the United States about 1898 in consequence of scaring articles on the "yellow peril." Other accounts say the allusion was originally to the color of paper used by cheap newspapers.

Yellow Water. See PARIZADE.

yellow-back. A cheap novel, particularly one of a sensational kind; so called because of the yellow paper board bindings originally used.

Yellow Book, The. An English illustrated quarterly literary journal, published between 1894 and 1897, featuring the work of artists and writers associated with the late Victorian "aesthetic" movement which was inspired in turn by the work of the French DECADENTS. Aubrey BEARDSLEY and Max BEERBOHM were among the contributors. In the 1890's the term "yellow book" came to have a connotation of decadence and super-aestheticism. See also LITTLE MAGAZINE.

Yellow Jacket, The. A Chinese play (1912) by George C. Hazelton and J. Harry Benrimo.

Yellowley, Mr. Triptolemus. In Scott's PIRATE, an experimental agriculturist of Stourburgh or Harfra who follows his calling with the utmost enthusiasm.

Yellowplush, Memoirs of Mr. C. J. A satire by THACKERAY (1838) in which Yellowplush narrates the adventures and opinions of his various masters.

Yemassee, The. A historical novel by William Gilmore SIMMS (1835), dealing with the insurrection of the Yemassee Indians in 1715. The hero is Charles Craven, Governor of Carolina, depicted under the name of Gabriel Harrison. The young Indian Occonestoga becomes a victim of drink and betrays his people to the whites, whereupon his father Sanutee accuses him, and his mother Matiwan kills her son to save him from disgrace.

Yeobright, Clym. Hero of Hardy's RETURN OF THE NATIVE.

Yeoman's Tale. (In Chaucer's *Canterbury Tales*). See CANON YEOMAN'S TALE.

Yeomen of the Guard, The. A comic opera (1888) by Gilbert and Sullivan. The yeomen of the guard are the oldest military corps in England, having been instituted in 1485. They still wear fifteenth-century costumes, guard the Tower of London, and are familiarly known as "Beefeaters."

Yerkes, Charles T. (1837–1905). American financier who secured control of the street-railway system in Chicago through not too scrupulous methods. Popular opinion became so strong that he left the United States. In England he formed a syndicate to build the London underground railway. At Lake Geneva in Wisconsin stands the Yerkes Observatory which he gave to the University of Chicago in 1892. See also DREISER, THEODORE.

Yezierska, Anzia (1885–). Russian-born American author, known for her fictional accounts of life in factories and sweatshops in New York City, based on her own experiences. Her books include *Hungry Hearts* (1920); *Salome of the Tenements* (1922); *Children of Loneliness* (1923); *Bread Givers* (1925); *Arrogant Beggars* (1927); *All I Could Never Be* (1932).

Ygerne or Igerne. In Arthurian romance, the mother of ARTHUR, wife of GORLOIS, lord of Tintagel Castle, in Cornwall. King Uther tries to seduce her, but Ygerne resents the insult, whereupon Uther and Gorlois fight, and the latter is slain. Uther then besieges Tintagel Castle, takes it, and compels Ygerne to become his wife. Nine months afterwards, Uther dies, and on the same day Arthur is born.

> Then Uther, in his wrath and heat, besieged
> Ygerne within Tintagil . . . and entered in . . .
> Enforced she was to wed him in her tears,
> And with a shameful swiftness.
> Tennyson, *Coming of Arthur*.

Yggdrasill or Ygdrasil. Literally, the horse of Yggr or Odin. In Norse mythology, the "Tree of the Universe," which sprang from the body of Ymir. It is an ash tree and has three roots. One extends to Niflheim with the well Hvergelmir where lies the dragon Nithhogg gnawing away its substance. The second extends to Totunnheim and the well of Mimir, which is the source of all wisdom. The third extends to Asgard. By it lies the well Urtharbrunn whose waters the Norns use to preserve Yggdrasill from decay. The squirrel Ratatosk runs up and down the trunk carrying strife. Four harts feed on Yggdrasill's foliage. An eagle and a hawk are sitting in its branches.

Yiddish (from Ger. *jüdisch,* "Jewish"). A language spoken by Jewish ethnic groups in Germany, eastern Europe, the U.S., and elsewhere. It is a development from Rhenish-German dialects (as spoken by fourteenth- and fifteenth-century Jews coming from the Rhineland and settling in Eastern Europe) under the influence of Hebrew and various Slavonic languages. Its literature is considerable. It is written in Hebrew characters.

Y.M.C.A. The Young Men's Christian Association, an international organization with a social and religious program in the interests of men.

Ymir. The primeval being of Scandinavian mythology, the giant from whose body the world was created. He was nourished by the four milky streams which flowed from the cow Audhumla.

One account has it that while he slept a man and woman grew out of his left arm, and sons from his feet. Thus was generated the race of the frost-giants. Another legend relates that when ODIN and his two brothers slew Ymir, and threw his carcass into the *Ginnungagap* (Abyss of Abysses), his blood formed the waters and the ocean, his bones the mountains, his teeth the rocks, his skull the heavens, his brains the clouds, his hair plants of every kind, and his eyebrows the wall of defense against the giants.

yoga. A mental discipline practiced among the Brahmins. It puts particular emphasis on meditation and has an elaborate system of physical and psychological rules of procedure. The Sanskrit word yoga means "union" or "concentration." One who practices yoga is called a *yogi.*

Yom Kippur. The Jewish Day of Atonement. It falls on the tenth day of the Hebrew month Tishri.

Yonge, Charlotte Mary (1823–1901). English novelist chiefly remembered for *The Heir of Redclyffe* (1853) and a historical romance, *The Dove in the Eagle's Nest* (1866).

Yonghy-Bonghy-Bò. In the nonsense poem *The Courtship of the Yonghy-Bonghy-Bò* by Edward LEAR:

> On the coast of Coromandel
> Where the early pumpkins blow,
> In the middle of the woods
> Lived the Yonghy-Bonghy-Bò.

Yorick. The King of Denmark's deceased jester, "a fellow of infinite jest and most excellent fancy," whose skull is apostrophized by HAMLET (Act v. 1). In TRISTRAM SHANDY, Sterne introduces a clergyman of that name, said to be meant for himself.

York, Alvin C. (1887–). American hero of World War I. In the battle of the Argonne (October 8, 1918) he captured single-handed a German machine-gun nest and some ninety men. After the war he received as reward a Tennessee farm. At his request a York Foundation was established to support primary schools in the mountains of Tennessee.

York Mysteries or Plays. One of the important series of English MYSTERY PLAYS, so called because they were acted at York.

Yorktown. The capital of York County, Virginia, noted for the surrender of Cornwallis in the American Revolution (October 19, 1781).

You and I. A play (1923) by Philip Barry, written when he was still studying at the 47 Workshop of George Pierce Baker at Harvard. It was his first play to be produced.

You Can't Take It With You. A comedy (1936) by Moss HART and George KAUFMAN which won the Pulitzer prize for drama in 1937. It concerned an eccentric family.

You Have Seen Their Faces. A book of photographs and descriptive text by Erskine CALDWELL and Margaret BOURKE-WHITE (1937), dealing with life among the Southern sharecroppers, with *The First World War* of Laurence STALLINGS one of the first books successfully combining the photographic and journalistic techniques.

You Know Me, Al: A Busher's Letters. The first collection of short stories (1916) by Ring LARDNER, dealing with a baseball rookie and written in his language.

Youmans, Edward Livingston (1821–1887). American author. Founded the *Popular Science Monthly* (1872) and was instrumental in the establishment of the *International Scientific Series* (1871). He was a great admirer of Herbert SPENCER and gave him much publicity in the U.S.

Youmans, Vincent (1899–1946). Well-known American musician who composed many light operas, including *Hit the Deck* (1927), and the catchy tunes *Tea for Two; Without a Song; Hallelujah;* etc.

You Never Can Tell. A comedy (1899) by George Bernard SHAW.

young. Used as an epithet in the names of political parties who strive to sweep away abuses and introduce reforms.

Young Communist League. An organization for young men and women of student age, preparing them for membership in the Communist party (see COMMUNIST PARTIES), in the U.S. and England as well as in the U.S.S.R.

Young England. A group of young aristocrats of the Conservative party (1833–1846) headed by DISRAELI and Lord John Manners. They wore white waistcoats, gave largely to the poor, and attempted to revive the courtly manners of the past. They are vividly portrayed in Disraeli's novels, notably CONINGSBY, OR THE NEW GENERATION.

Young Germany. A school headed by HEINE in the mid 19th century, whose aim was to liberate politics, religion, and manners from the old conventional trammels.

Young Hickory. See HICKORY.

Young Ireland. The Irish politicians and agitators (at first led by O'Connell) who effected the rising of 1848.

Young Italy. A league of Italian refugees who associated themselves with the French republican party called the *Charbonnerie démocratique.* It was organized at Marseilles by Mazzini about 1834, and its chief object was to diffuse republican principles.

Young Turks. The reform party in Turkey which gained control through the Revolution of 1909.

the Young Adventurer. See under PRETENDER.

The Young Pretender. See PRETENDER.

Young, Alexander (1800–1854). An antiquarian in Massachusetts who reprinted valuable source material as *Chronicles of the Pilgrim Fathers* (1841) and *Chronicles of the First Planters of the Colony of Massachusetts Bay* (1846).

Young, Andrew (1807–1889). Scottish schoolmaster remembered only for his hymn, *There is a Happy Land* (1838).

Young, Art (1866–1944). Well-known American cartoonist. His series on the Inferno (up-to-date) was widely popular. The best of his work was collected as *The Best of Art Young* (1936). He wrote two autobiographical books both of which are pungent with American life: *On My Way* (1928) and *Art Young: His Life and Times* (1939).

Young, Arthur (1741–1820). English agricultural theorist and author. His *Travels in France* (1792) describe conditions in France shortly before the French Revolution.

Young, Brigham (1801–1877). Leader of the American Mormons to whose faith he was converted in 1832. Under him the Mormons migrated to Utah. He was the first governor of the Territory of Utah (1849–1857). His championship of polygamy brought him into conflict with the government and President Buchanan removed him from office. An indictment against him (1871) did not lead to his conviction.

Young, Edward (1683–1765). English poet and playwright, best known for his NIGHT THOUGHTS ON LIFE, DEATH, AND IMMORTALITY (1742–1745), regarded as an important representative of the sentimental and reflective preromantic verse of the 18th century. His other works include *Busiris* (1719) and *The Revenge* (1721; see ZANGA), dramatic tragedies; *The Universal Passion* (1725–1728), a series of satires; *The Brothers* (1753), another tragedy; and *Resignation* (1762), a long poem. Young in his youth hoped for a career as a lawyer but was disappointed, spending most of his life as a country clergyman instead.

Young, Ella (1865–). Irish poet and writer living in California (since 1926). She is the author of *Celtic Wonder Tales* (1923); *Unicorn with Silver Shoes* (1932); and the autobiography, *Flowering Dusk* (1945).

Young, Felix. A character in Henry James' novel THE EUROPEANS.

Young, Francis Brett (1884–). English novelist. Author of numerous books, including the verse epic of England, *The Island* (1946).

Young, Mahonri (1877–). American artist chiefly known as a sculptor.

Young, Owen D. (1874–). Chairman of the board of the General Electric Company (1922–1939; 1942 ff.). With Charles G. Dawes he represented the United States at the Reparations Conference in 1924 and helped inaugurate the Dawes plan. In 1929, as chairman of the Reparations Conference, he was instrumental in preparing the Young Plan.

Young, Rodger W. (1918–1943). Posthumously awarded the Congressional Medal of Honor for gallantry in the battle at Munda, New Georgia, in the Pacific in World War II. He was a member of Company B, 148th Infantry, was born in Ohio, and his name has been made famous by *The Ballad of Rodger Young* by Frank Lesser which has become one of the great songs of the U.S. Infantry.

Younghusband, Sir Francis Edward (1863–1942). British explorer who led an expedition to the forbidden city of Lhasa (1904). He has written of India, Tibet, and Mt. Everest. He also became interested in the mysticism of the East and wrote several books about it.

Young, Stark (1881–). Well-known American dramatic critic for the New York *Times* and the *New Republic.* He has written several novels, of which *So Red the Rose* (1934) is the best-known.

Young Lonigan: A Boyhood in Chicago Streets. A novel by James T. FARRELL (1932), the first volume in his trilogy STUDS LONIGAN. This book introduces the hero, Studs, as a boy of fifteen, graduating from a Roman Catholic grammar school and starting out on the typical career of his class and time, dreaming of becoming a "great guy" and taking care to conform to the pattern of conduct set for him by his associates. Notable events are his initiation into the mysteries of sex, in which he is assisted by Iris, a morally promiscuous adolescent girl of the neighborhood, and his first sentimental attachment, of which another girl, Lucy Scanlan, is the object.

Young Man, Adventures of a. A novel by John Dos PASSOS (1938), presented in a modification of the technique used in the objective narrative portions of U.S.A. It tells of the life and "adventures" of Glenn Spotswood, a young man of sensitivity, sincerity, and a strong sense of justice, whose father, once an instructor at Columbia University, lost his academic position because of his pacifist views during World War I. As a student in the western part of the U.S., Glenn comes in contact with radical and union activities and soon, at the suggestion of Mike Gulick, a young Columbia instructor, and Mike's wife Marice, he comes to New York and completes his education at the university where his father once taught. He meets Boris Spingarn, a Brooklyn Jewish student who is a Communist, and Boris' wife, Gladys Funaroff, and becomes more closely associated with the radical groups of the late 1920's and early 1930's. After his graduation from college, he engages in union organizational work, notably among the Kentucky coal miners, has brief love affairs with Gladys, Marice, and a Kentucky mountain girl named Wheatly, and quarrels with the Communist leaders, wishing to carry through on individual cases and assist distressed workers, while the leaders prefer to think first of general party policy and strategy. Disillusioned with the American radicals and financially embarrassed, Glenn volunteers to go to Spain as an ambulance driver in the Civil War. There he meets several of the Communist leaders whom he knew in the U.S. They are suspicious of him because of his past "opposition" and have him arrested as a Trotskyist spy, accused of plotting an uprising of the Spanish Republicans against the Communists in Barcelona. Eventually, while obeying a command to carry water to the firing-line to relieve a couple of machine-gunners, Glenn is killed.

Young Manhood of Studs Lonigan, The. A novel by James T. FARRELL (1934), the second volume of his trilogy STUDS LONIGAN. In this book the career of Studs is carried through the period of the 1920's, during which he works as a house painter with his father and participates in the vices and dissipations of the time. The activities and experiences of Studs' friends and associates parallel his. The culmination of the novel is a wild New Year's Eve party at which a girl named Irene is raped by Weary Reilley, one of Studs' companions.

Youth and the Bright Medusa. A collection of stories (1920) by Willa CATHER, dealing with the lives of artists. Includes *Paul's Case,* story of a neurotic boy, often reprinted.

Youth's Companion, The. A magazine founded in Boston (1827) by Nathaniel WILLIS. It was planned as an instructive magazine for children, was sold in 1857 and became a magazine for adults as well as for children. In 1929 it was combined with *The American Boy.* Mrs. Stowe, Lord Tennyson, John G. Whittier, Hardy, Kipling, Howells, Stevenson, Jules Verne, Roosevelt, Wilson, and Jack London were among its contributors.

Youwarkee. In Patlock's romance *Peter Wilkins* (1750), the name of the gawrey, or flying woman, that Peter Wilkins marries. She introduces the seaman to Nosmnbdsgrsutt, the land of flying men and women.

Yriarte, Charles (1833–1898). French author and editor whose specialty was the Italian Renaissance. He wrote histories of Venice and Florence, and several biographies.

Ysaie le Triste. In medieval romance, the son of TRISTAN AND ISOLT, born after Tristan's death. He is the hero of a French romance called by his name. The fairies give him, among many other gifts of great value, the ugly, witty, resourceful dwarf Tronc, who accompanies him on numerous adventures. On the eventful day that brings the tale to a climax, his son Mark marries a Saracen princess Orimonda, Ysaie at last marries Mark's mother, Martha, his true love, and Tronc becomes as handsome as he had been ugly and King of Fairyland under the name Aubrun. See also ALBERICH; OBERON.

Ysaye, Eugène (1858–1931). Belgian concert violinist, well-known in the U.S.

Ysengrim, Ysengrimus, Isengrin, or Isgrim (Ger. *Isegrimm,* "a wolf, a surly fellow"). The wolf, afterwards created Earl of Pitwood, in the beast epic of REYNARD THE FOX. Ysengrim typifies the barons, and Reynard the Church; the gist of the tale is the way Reynard tricks his uncle Wolf.

Ysolde, Ysoude, Yseult, etc. See ISOLT.

Yudhishthira. One of the five Pandavas, a hero of the great Hindu epic, the MAHABHARATA.

Yule, Sir Henry (1820–1889). British Orientalist whose glossary of Anglo-Indian words and phrases is a valuable reference book.

Yum-Yum. The heroine of the Gilbert and Sullivan comic opera THE MIKADO.

Yvain, ou le Chevalier au Lion. A medieval romance by CHRÉTIEN DE TROYES, dealing with the adventures of the knight Yvain. Following the directions of a giant, he arrives at a well, finds a golden basin near it, and splashes water from the basin on a stone slab. Immediately a great storm arises and a mysterious knight comes forth to combat, from which Yvain emerges the victor. Yvain next comes to a castle, entrance to which is made possible by the assistance of a lady named Lunette, who shows him how to make himself invisible. While hidden in a room in the castle, he hears the widow of the slain knight weeping for her lost husband, and he falls in love with her. Lunette convinces the widow, Laudine, that since the magic well must be defended, it is most desirable that the man chosen as the new defender and husband be the one who vanquished the first knight. The argument is successful, and eventually Yvain marries Laudine. The remainder of the romance is concerned with his numerous other adventures, during which he rescues a lion from a serpent and thereby acquires the animal as a mascot.

Yvetôt, King of. The lord of a town in Normandy. The tale is that Clotaire, son of CLOVIS, having slain the lord of Yvetôt before the high altar of Soissons, made atonement to the heirs by conferring on them the title of king. BÉRANGER in his famous song *Le Roi d'Yvetôt,* which popularized the name, says this potentate is little known in history but his character and habits were not peculiar.

"He rose late, went to bed early, slept without caring for glory, made four meals a day, lived in a thatched house, wore a cotton night-cap instead of a crown, rode on an ass, and his only law was 'charity begins at home' ":

Il était un roi d'Yvetot
  Peu connu dans l'histoire;
Se levant tard, se couchant tôt,
  Dormant fort bien sans gloire,
Et couronné par Jeanneton
D'un simple bonnet de coton.
      Dit on:
Oh! oh! oh! oh! Ah! ah! ah! ah!
Quel bon petit roi c'etait; là! là! là!

Ywain. One of the knights of the Round Table; identical with the Owain (or Owen) ap Urien of the Welsh bards and the MABINOGION. He is the hero of Chrétien de Troyes' YVAIN, OU LE CHEVALIER AU LION (12th century), which appears as a 14th century English metrical romance, *Ywain and Gawain.*

Y.W.C.A. The Young Women's Christian Association, an international organization with purposes similar to that of the Y.M.C.A.

Z

Zaba or **Saba, The Queen of.** See SHEBA, QUEEN OF.

Zacchaeus. In the New Testament, a little man who climbed up into a sycamore tree to see Jesus pass. He was a rich publican and later entertained Jesus at his house.

Zadig. The hero and title of a novel by VOLTAIRE (1748). Zadig is a wealthy young Babylonian who longs to devote himself to altruistic reform. In spite of all his talent and virtue, his schemes go awry, and conventional society stubbornly refuses to be reformed. The full title *Zadig or Destiny* would seem to imply that the object of the novel is to show that the events of life are beyond human control.

method of Zadig. Drawing inferences from close observation. A man who had lost his camel asked Zadig if he had seen it. Zadig replied, "You mean a camel with one eye, and defective teeth, I suppose? No, I have not seen it, but it has strayed towards the west." Being asked how he knew these things if he had not seen the beast, "Well enough," he replied. "I knew it had but one eye, because it cropped the grass only on one side of the road. I knew it had lost some of its teeth, because the grass was not bitten clean off. I knew it had strayed westward, by its footprints."

Zadkiel. The name of an angel in Jewish theology. It was taken as a pseudonym by William LILLY and by Richard James Morrison, who wrote the *Herald of Astrology* (1831), afterward called *Zadkiel's Almanac.*

Zaharoff, Sir **Basil** (1850–1936). One of the great mysterious figures of munitions-making. The web of his interests in Europe gave him a sinister power. In the universities of Paris, Petrograd, and Oxford, he established chairs of literature and aeronautics.

Zaïre. See ZARA.

Zal. A semi-divinity of Persian myth, father of RUSTAM, the Hercules of Persia. He was the son of Sam Neriman, and was exposed on Mount Elburz because he was born with white hair, and therefore supposed to be the offspring of a deer. He was brought up by the wonderful bird Seemurgh, and when claimed by his father, received from the foster-bird a feather to give him insight into futurity.

> Let Zal and Rustum bluster as they will.
> FitzGerald, *Rubáiyát of Omar Kháyyám.*

Zanga. A famous stage rôle in Young's tragedy *The Revenge* (1721), a Moor, servant of Don Alonzo. The Moor hates Alonzo for two reasons, because Alonzo killed his father, and because he struck him on the cheek; and although Alonzo has used every endeavor to conciliate Zanga the revengeful Moor nurses his hate and keeps it warm. The revenge he wreaks is to poison the friendship which existed between Alonzo and Don Carlos by accusations against the Don, and to embitter the love of Alonzo for Leonora, his wife. Alonzo, out of jealousy, has his friend killed, and Leonora makes away with herself. Zanga now tells his dupe he has been imposed upon, and Alonzo, mad with grief, stabs himself. Zanga, content with the mischief he has done, is taken away to execution.

Zangwill, Israel (1864–1926). English novelist and playwright, of Jewish parentage, best known for his studies of Jewish life in England and the U.S. His plays include *Children of the Ghetto* (1899), published as a novel in 1892 (see GHETTO); *The Moment Before* (1900); *Merely Mary Ann* (1903), published as a novel in 1893; *Nurse Marjorie* (1906); THE MELTING POT (1908), his most famous work; *The War God* (1911); *Plaster Saints* (1914); *Too Much Money* (1918); *The Cockpit* (1921); *The Forcing House* (1922); *We Moderns* (1923). Among his other works are *The Premier and the Painter* (1888), *The Mantle of Elijah* (1900), and *Jinny the Carrier* (1919), novels; *Ghetto Tragedies* (1893), *The King of Schnorrers* (1894), and *Ghetto Comedies* (1907), collections of short stories. *The Big Bow Mystery* (1891), was one of the first "locked room" mystery stories. Filmed (1947).

Because of his outspokenness and his championing of unpopular ideas, Zangwill constantly put himself in public disfavor.

Zanoni. A novel by BULWER LYTTON (1842). The hero, Zanoni, manages by the aid of spirits to produce precious metals and to prolong his own life for many centuries, but he finally gives up his supernatural powers to marry an opera singer.

Zanuck, Darryl (1902–). Moving-picture producer associated with Fox Films and Twentieth Century Pictures. In World War II he was in charge of making educational pictures for the U.S. Army Signal Corps and the official pictures of the campaign in North Africa.

Zany or **Zani.** The buffoon who mimicked the clown in the old theatrical entertainments; hence a simpleton, one who "acts the goat." The name is the Italian *zanni,* "a buffoon," fem. of *Giovanni* (i.e., *John*), our *Jane.*

Zara (in French, **Zaïre**). The heroine and title of a tragedy by VOLTAIRE (1732). Zara is the daughter of Lusignan d'Outremer, King of Jerusalem and brother of Nerestan. Twenty years ago these two children have been taken captives and Zara, a mere infant, was brought up in the seraglio. Osman, the Sultan, falls in love with her, and promises to make her his sultana, but at a critical moment her brother Nerestan returns from France to ransom all Christian captives. Osman, ignorant of the stranger's relation to his beloved, becomes suspicious, surprises her on her way to a rendezvous and stabs her. When he learns the truth, he kills himself.

Zarathustra. See THUS SPAKE ZARATHUSTRA.

Zarca. In George Eliot's narrative poem THE SPANISH GIPSY, the father of the gypsy heroine.

Zaturenska, Marya (1902–). American poet born in Russia. She is married to the poet and critic Horace GREGORY. In 1938 she won the Pulitzer prize for poetry. Her books include *Cold Morning Sky* (1937) and *The Listening Landscape* (1941).

Zauderberg, Der, see MAGIC MOUNTAIN, THE.

Zauberflöte, Die, see MAGIC FLUTE.

Zebedee, Sons of, see BOANERGES.

Zechariah. One of the Minor Prophets of the Hebrews; also the book of the Old Testament called by his name.

Zedekiah. In the Old Testament, the king of Judah that Nebuchadnezzar, King of Babylon, set up in Jerusalem after the conquest. He rebelled against Babylon and was carried into captivity.

Zeebrugge. A seaport in Belgium some six miles north of Bruges. In the spring of 1918 the long stone pier of Zeebrugge was captured by the British and several ships were sunk to block the canal from which the submarines came out.

Zeeman, Pieter (1865–). Dutch physicist who, with H. A. Lorentz, received the Nobel prize for physics in 1902.

Zeitgeist (Ger. *Zeit,* "time," *Geist,* "spirit"). The spirit of the time; the moral or intellectual tendency characteristic of the period.

Zeitlin, Jacob (1883–1937). Russian-born professor at the University of Illinois (from 1925). Editor of Petrarch's *Life of Solitude* (1924) and of *Seventeenth Century Essays* (1926). He also compiled anthologies and translated Montaigne.

Zélide. Pseudonym of **Isabelle de Charrière,** *née* **Isabella van Tuyll** (1740–1805). Dutch woman author of breeding and beauty. One of her friends was James BOSWELL who tried to marry her. She became a very close intellectual friend of Benjamin Constant. Cf. *Portrait of Zélide* by Geoffrey SCOTT and *Four Tales by Zélide,* translated by Sybil Scott, with an introduction by Geoffrey Scott (both 1925).

Zemstvo. The elected local district and provincial administrative assembly in Russia under the old Empire. Theoretically it had large powers and was democratic; but it was always under the thumb of the great landowners, and all its decrees were subject to the approval of the Governor.

Zenda, Prisoner of, see PRISONER OF ZENDA.

Zend-Avesta. The sacred writings of Zoroaster (or Zarathustra) that formed the basis of the religion that prevailed in Persia from the 6th century B.C. to the 7th century A.D. *Avesta* means the text, and *Zend* its interpretation into a more modern and intelligible language; hence the latter name has been given to the ancient Iranian language in which the *Zend-Avesta* is written.

> The sacred writings of the Parsis have usually been called *Zend-Avesta* by Europeans: but this is, without doubt, an inversion of the proper order of the words, as the Pahlavi books always style them "Avisták-va-Zand" (text and commentary).—Haug, *Essays on the Parsis,* Essay iii, p. 19.

Zenelophon. In Shakespeare's LOVE'S LABOR'S LOST, the beggar-girl who marries King Cophetua of Africa. She is more generally called Penelophon.

Zenger, John Peter (1697–1746). German-born printer who came to America in 1710. In his trial for seditious libel (1734–1735) he was defended by Andrew Hamilton, and was acquitted. The decision in this case is believed to have established freedom of the press in America.

Zeena. In Edith Wharton's ETHAN FROME, Ethan's sickly, self-centered wife.

zenith, nadir (*Arabic*). *Zenith* is the point of the heavens immediately over the head of the spectator. *Nadir* is the opposite point, immediately beneath the spectator's feet. Hence, *to go from the zenith of prosperity to the nadir* means to fall from the height of fortune to the depths of poverty.

Zenith. A typical Midwestern American city of the 1920's, the scene of Sinclair Lewis' BABBITT and part of the same author's DODSWORTH.

Zenobia. A beautiful and intellectually brilliant woman in Hawthorne's BLITHEDALE ROMANCE who drowns herself for love of Hollingsworth. She is said to have been drawn, in part at least, from Margaret Fuller.

There is a historical Zenobia, Queen of Palmyra, who is sometimes included in a list of "the nine worthy women" of the world.

Zenocrate. The name of the wife of Tamburlaine in *Tamburlaine* (1587) by Christopher Marlowe.

> Now walk the angels on the walls of heaven,
> As sentinels to warn th' immortal souls,
> To entertain divine Zenocrate.

Zephon. A guardian angel of Paradise in Milton's PARADISE LOST (Bk. iv). With Ithuriel he is dispatched by Gabriel to find Satan, after his flight from Hell.

Zephyr. The west wind in classical mythology, son of AEOLUS and AURORA, and lover of FLORA; hence, any soft, gentle wind.

Zeppelin, Count **Ferdinand von** (1838–1917). German aeronautical pioneer, who produced at Friedrichshafen on Lake Constance the first rigid airship (1900) known as *Zeppelin*. His airships were famous in World War I and in the early days of transatlantic flying.

Zerbino. In Ariosto's ORLANDO FURIOSO, a famous knight, son of the king of Scotland, and intimate friend of Orlando.

Zerkow. In Frank Norris's MCTEAGUE, a junk dealer who marries Maria MACAPA through greed, goes mad and kills her, and commits suicide.

Zero. The name of a Japanese airplane in World War II.

Zero, Mr. Accountant-hero of Elmer Rice's play THE ADDING MACHINE.

Zetes. In classic mythology, a winged warrior, son of BOREAS and Orithyia. He and his brother Calais went on the ARGONAUTIC EXPEDITION and fought against the HARPIES whom they drove from Thrace.

zeugma. A figure of speech in which one word is used to modify several others with only one of which it makes sense. "The fragrance of flowers and the blue sky . . ."

Zeus. The Grecian JUPITER. The word means the "living one" (Sans., *Djaus,* "heaven"); it was once applied to the blue firmament, the upper sky, the arch of light, but in Homeric mythology, Zeus is king of gods and men; the conscious embodiment of the central authority and administrative intelligence which holds states together; the supreme ruler; the fountain of justice, and final arbiter of disputes.

Zeuxis. A Grecian painter who is said to have painted some grapes so well that the birds came and pecked at them. The story goes on to relate that Zeuxis' rival Parrhasius placed a canvas of his next to the grapes, and when the spectators demanded that he remove the curtain concealing his work, it developed that the curtain was a painted one.

Zeyn Alasnam, Prince. See ALASNAM.

Zhukov, Grigori K. (1895?–). Russian general. Commander in chief on the central front in Russia (1941). It was he who planned and directed the offensive of the Red Army which broke the sieges of Stalingrad and Leningrad (October 1942–January 1943). He was made a marshal of the Soviet Union (January 1943).

Ziegfeld, Florenz (1867–1932). American showman who introduced with his *The Follies of 1907* a new type of stage entertainment, the *revue,* consisting of a medley of skits and light pieces with allusions to and re-enactments of the events of the past year, but the chief attractions of which were stage effects and pretty girls scantily clad. The *Follies* reached their height of popularity in the 1920's when they were imitated by other revues calling themselves *The Scandals, The Vanities,* etc.

Ziemssen, Joachim. In Thomas Mann's MAGIC MOUNTAIN, the cousin of Hans CASTORP and a patient at the HAUS BERGHOF. Joachim is a Prussian soldier, doggedly loyal to the principles of discipline and duty as he has learned them, and he pleads with Hans to stop his fatal speculation on aesthetic and metaphysical matters. Joachim is restless at the sanatorium and leaves as soon as he can to return to his duty in the army. In a short time, however, he contracts a throat disease and is forced to come back to the Berghof, where he dies, "a soldier, and honorable."

Zilboorg, Gregory (1890–). Russian-born psychiatrist practicing in New York City (since 1931). Among his books are *The Medical Man and the Witch During the Renaissance* (1935) and *Mind, Medicine and Man* (1943).

Zimbalist, Efrem (1889–). Russian-born concert violinist and composer. He married (1914) the well-known opera singer Alma GLUCK.

Zimmern, Sir **Alfred** (1879–). Professor of International relations at Oxford, England (since 1930). *The Greek Commonwealth* (1911); *Europe in Convalescence* (1922); *The Prospects of Democracy* (1929); etc.

Zimri. In Dryden's satire of ABSALOM AND ACHITOPHEL, the second Duke of Buckingham. As Zimri conspires against Asa, King of Judah (*1 Kings* xvi. 9.), so the Duke of Buckingham "formed parties and joined factions."

> Some of the chiefs were princes in the land:
> In the first rank of these did Zimri stand,—
> A man so various that he seemed to be
> Not one, but all mankind's epitomé;
> Stiff in opinion, always in the wrong,
> Was everything by turns, and nothing long.
> Pt. i. 545–550.

Zineura. In Boccaccio's DECAMERON (Day II, Nov. 9), a character who later suggested the "Imogen" of Shakespeare's CYMBELINE. She assumes male attire with the name of Sicurano da Finale.

Zinoviev, Grigori Evseevich. Real name **Hirsch Apfelbaum** (1883–1936). Russian Communist leader. Exiled with Lenin, he returned to Russia in 1917. In 1919 he was president of the Third International. After the death of Lenin (1924), he, Kamenev and Stalin ruled Russia together. Involved in a conspiracy against Stalin, was expelled from office. Having been re-admitted to the party, he was accused of being involved in the murder of Kirov (1934) and executed.

Zinzendorf, Count **Nikolaus Ludwig von** (1700–1760). Reorganizer of a persecuted sect known as the Bohemian Brethren, which became the Moravian Brethren. He established the Moravians in Pennsylvania where they still flourish in Bethlehem, Nazareth, Philadelphia, Lancaster, etc.

Zionism. The movement for colonizing the Jews in their old home, Palestine, the Land of Zion.

Zipangi, see CIPANGO.

Zobeide. A lady of Bagdad, whose history is related in the THREE CALENDERS, one of the tales of the *Arabian Nights*. The Caliph Haroun al Raschid marries her.

zodiac (Gr. *zodiakos,* "pertaining to animals"; from *zoon,* "an animal"). The imaginary belt or zone in the heavens, extending about eight degrees each side of the ecliptic, which the sun traverses every year.

signs of the zodiac. The zodiac was divided by the ancients into twelve equal parts, proceeding from west to east, each part of thirty degrees, and distinguished by a sign; these originally corresponded to the zodiacal constellations bearing the same names, but now, through the precession of the equinoxes, they coincide with the constellations bearing the names next in order.

Beginning with "Aries," we have first six on the north side and six on the south side of the equator; beginning with "Capricornus," we have six *ascending* and then six *descending* signs—i.e., six which ascend higher and higher towards the north, and six which descend lower and lower towards the south. The six northern signs are: *Aries* (the ram), *Taurus* (the bull), *Gemini* (the twins), spring signs; *Cancer* (the crab), *Leo* (the lion), *Virgo* (the virgin), summer signs. The six southern are: *Libra* (the balance), *Scorpio* (the scorpion), *Sagittarius* (the archer), autumn signs; *Capricornus* (the goat), *Aquarius* (the water-bearer), and *Pisces* (the fishes), winter signs.

Zoë. The name of three empresses of the Eastern Roman Empire; of the chief female character in the blank-verse narrative *King Jasper* (1935) by Edwin Arlington Robinson; and of the heroine of Boucicault's drama THE OCTOROON.

Zoilism. Harsh, ill-tempered criticism; so called from ZOILUS.

Zoilus. A Greek rhetorician of the 4th century B. C., a literary Thersites, shrewd, witty, and spiteful, nicknamed *Homeromastix* (Homer's Scourge), because he mercilessly assailed the epics of Homer, and called the companions of Ulysses in the island of Circe "weeping porkers" (*choiridia klaionta*). He also flew at Plato, Isocrates, and other high game.

Zola, Émile (1840–1902). French novelist, son of an Italian father, known for his leadership of the school of NATURALISM. His works, marked by scrupulous accuracy of background, speech, and psychological traits, and a determinism of character by heredity and environment which has been compared to that of TAINE, include *Thérèse Raquin* (1867); *Les Soirées de Medan* (1880), stories of the Franco-Prussian War, regarded as a manifesto of Zola's group of naturalist writers (Maupassant, Huysmans, Paul Alexis, Céard, Hennique); *Le Roman Expérimentale* (1880) and *Les Romanciers Naturalistes* (1881), books of criticism, explaining his method and his theories; the novels in the ROUGON-MACQUART series (1871–1893); the *Trois Villes* series (1894–1897); the *Quatre Evangiles* series (1897–), which was left incomplete at the author's death; and J'ACCUSE (1898).

Zola was a clerk in a publishing house in the early part of his career, and later became a journalist. He spent most of his life as a recluse (cf. Balzac, Daudet, Flaubert, Goncourt brothers), writing his numerous novels, for the background of which he studied factual monographs and prepared actual dossiers for the characters, as though for real people. His work was attacked for immorality, exaggeration, and lack of taste, and caused much controversy in its day. Zola himself had strong humanitarian sympathies, especially favoring the working class; in 1898 he aroused official wrath by his defense of Dreyfus (see DREYFUSARD), and was sentenced to imprisonment, being obliged to seek refuge in England. He died of accidental asphyxiation.

Zophar the Naamathite. In the Old Testament, one of the three "false comforters" who came to comfort and admonish JOB in his distress.

Zophiel. In Milton's PARADISE LOST, an angel "of cherubim the swiftest wing." The word means "God's spy." Zophiel brings word to the heavenly host that the rebel crew are preparing a second and fiercer attack.

Zorach, William (1887–). An American sculptor born in Lithuania.

Zorn, Anders (1860–1920). Distinguished Swedish painter and sculptor.

Zoroaster or **Zarathustra.** Founder of the Perso-Iranian national religion, flourished early in the first millennium B. C. Zoroastrianism was dominant in Western Asia from about

550 B. C. to about 650 A. D., and is still held by many thousands in Persia and India. It is fundamentally a dualistic system in which the course of the universe is understood as a relentless war of Ormazd, the principle of light and goodness, against Ahriman and his evil spirits. In the end Ormazd will prevail, partly through the help of man whom he created to strengthen his forces. The sacred literature of Zoroastrianism is the Zend-Avesta.

Zouaves. French soldiers, originally mercenaries, of a body of infantry organized in 1831. They assumed an Arab costume. In the American Civil War several regiments of volunteer Federal troops were called Zouaves and wore a costume somewhat like that of their French namesakes.

Zsigmondy, Richard (1865–1929). German chemist who was awarded the Nobel prize for chemistry in 1926.

Zugsmith, Leane (1903–). American novelist and short-story writer. *All Victories Are Alike* (1929); *A Time to Remember* (1936); *The Summer Soldier* (1938); etc.

Zukor, Adolph (1873–). Hungarian-born moving-picture magnate, who began his career in the hardware, upholstery, and fur businesses.

Zuleika. (1) In legend the name traditionally ascribed to Potiphar's wife (*Gen.* xxxix. 7.) whose advances were resisted by the virtuous JOSEPH. Their story is told in the Persian *Yúsuf and Zulaikha* by Nureddin Jami (1414–1492). Zuleika is a very common name in Persian poetry.

(2) The heroine of Byron's BRIDE OF ABYDOS.

> Never was a faultless character more delicately or more justly delineated than that of Lord Byron's "Zuleika." Her piety, her intelligence, her strict sense of duty, and her undeviating love of truth appear to have been originally blended in her mind rather than inculcated by education. She is always natural, always attractive, always affectionate; and it must be admitted that her affections are not unworthily bestowed.—G. Ellis.

Zuleika Dobson. A fantastic novel (1911) by Max BEERBOHM, about OXFORD UNIVERSITY.

Zuloaga, Ignacio (1870–). One of the most vivid painters of Spain, portraying many Spanish types such as bullfighters, gypsies, etc.

Zuñis. Indians of the Zuñi pueblo. The ethnologist Frank H. Cushing (1857–1900) has lived among them and explored the original site of their "Seven Cities of Cibola" which Coronado (ca. 1540) tried to discover for the sake of the treasures supposedly hidden there. Cf. also Cushing's *Outlines of Zuñi Creation Myths* (1896) and *Zuñi Folk Tales* (1901).

Zurbarán, Francisco de (1598?–?1664). Court painter to Philip IV of Spain; known especially for his religious paintings.

Zurich Bible. See BIBLE, SPECIALLY NAMED.

Zweig, Arnold (1887–). German novelist and short-story writer, best known for *The Case of Sergeant Grischa* (*Streit um den Sergeanten Grischa;* 1927), a sensational novel dealing with events in World War I. Other books by Zweig include *Claudia* (1930); *Young Woman of 1914* (1932); *Education before Verdun* (1936); *Insulted and Exiled* (1937), on the treatment of German Jews under NAZISM; *The Crowning of a King* (1938).

Zweig, Stefan (1881–1942). Austrian playwright, author, and biographer, of Jewish parentage, best known for his psychological portraits of literary and historical figures. See also LUDWIG, EMIL. Among his works are *Paul Verlaine* (1913); *Emile Verhaeren* (1914); *Jeremiah* (1917), an allegorical play attacking war; *Romain Rolland* (1921); *Passion and Pain* (1925); *Invisible Collection* (1926); *Conflicts* (1927), three psychological novelettes; *Adepts in Self-Portraiture* (1928), on Casanova, Stendhal, and Tolstoi; *Three Masters* (1930), on Balzac, Dickens, and Dostoyevsky; *Joseph Fouché* (1930); *Mental Healers* (1932), on Franz Mesmer, Mary Baker Eddy, and Sigmund Freud; *Marie Antoinette* (1932); *Kaleidoscope* (1934), stories; *Mary, Queen of Scotland and the Isles* (1935); *The Right to Heresy* (1936); *Conqueror of the Seas* (1938), on Magellan; *The Tide of Fortune* (1940); *Brazil, Land of the Future* (1941); etc. As an expatriate in Brazil, Stefan Zweig took his own life. His autobiography appeared under the title of *The World of Yesterday* (1942). Cf. also *Stefan Zweig* by Friderike Zweig (1946).

Zwingli, Ulrich (1484–1531). Swiss religious reformer. His sermons as rector at the Great Minster in Zurich (1519 ff.) started the Reformation in Switzerland.

PAGE

10 **Adonai.** *For* TETRAGRAMMATON *read* ELOHIM.

19 **Albion.** For *Perfide Albion* read *Albion Perfide.*

20 **Aldebaran.** *Line 3, for* Aldebaran *read* Aldeborn.

20 **Aldine editions.** *For* Minutius *read* Manutius.

22 **Algonquin.** *Omit* CASE AND WAYWARD INN.

26 **Al Raschid, Haroun.** *Following this, substitute:* Caliph of Bagdad, adventures form basis of ARABIAN NIGHTS.

29 **American Caravan.** *Line 3 for* Lewis MUMFORD and Van Wyck BROOKS, *read* Alfred KREYMBORG and Paul ROSENFELD.

33 **Ancient Mariner, Rime of the.** *For* Arctic *read* Antarctic.

38 **Anselm, St.** *Following this, substitute:* 1033-1109. Theologian.

38 **Antigone.** Last line, for *Suppliants* read *Phoenissae.*

49 **art for art's sake.** *Last line, omit* see also LITERARY THEORY.

51 **Arundel.** *Following this, substitute:* Novel by Kenneth ROBERTS.

53 *For* **Asquith,** see OXFORD AND ASQUITH, Lord *substitute:* **Asquith, Herbert Henry,** 1st Earl of Oxford and Asquith (1852-1928). Prime minister (1908-1916). Parliament Act, HOME RULE Bill for Ireland, Welsh Disestablishment Act.

73 **bar.** a bar sinister. *Last line, for* BENCH *read* BEND.

80 **baseball teams.** *Transfer* White Sox *to* American League *and* Cubs *to* National League.

Basic English. *For* F. A. Richards *read* I. A. Richards.

84 **Baviad, The.** *For* Moeviad *read* Maeviad.

84 **Bayeux tapestry.** *For* tapestry *read* embroidery.

94-95 **Benedick** and **Benedict.** *Substitute for these entries:*

Benedick. A sworn bachelor in Shakespeare's MUCH ADO ABOUT NOTHING who marries Beatrice.

Benedict. (1) Probably corrupted from BENEDICK. A confirmed bachelor caught in the snares of matrimony. (2) Formerly a bachelor of marriageable age, not necessarily pledged to celibacy, from St. Benedict, who was a most uncompromising stickler for celibacy.

PAGE

95 *After* **Benes** *insert:* **Benét, Laura** (1884-). Poet and biographer for young people. Among her many books are *Is Morning Sure?* (poems, 1948) and books on SHELLEY, Emily DICKINSON, IRVING, and THACKERAY.

100 **Berners, Isopel.** *For* A Gypsy girl in *read* Heroine of.

107 **Bicorne.** *For* CHICHEVACHE *read* CHICHIVACHE.

113 Black Jack (2). *Insert Pershing's death date* 1948.

115 **Blancheflor.** For *Il Filocopo* read *Il Filocolo.*

117 **Blixen, Karen Dinesen.** *Following this, substitute:* Baroness. Pseudonym **Isak Dinesen** (1883-). *Seven Gothic Tales* (1934), *Winter's Tales* (1942), etc.

125 **Bois de Boulogne.** *For* Anteuil *read* Auteuil.

126 *After* **bolero,** *insert:* **Boleyn, Anne** (1507-1536) HENRY VIII's second queen. Secretly married 1533. Mother of Queen ELIZABETH. Beheaded for unfaithfulness.

129 **Booth, William.** *For* GENERAL BOOTH ENTERS HEAVEN *read* GENERAL WILLIAM BOOTH ENTERS INTO HEAVEN.

132 **Boulle.** *For* buhlework *read* buhlwork.

135 **Boy Scouts.** *Line 3, for* now *read* later.

138 **Bramble, Matthew.** For EXPEDITION OF HUMPHREY CLINKER read *Expedition of* HUMPHREY CLINKER.

139 **Brant, Sebastian.** For *Navrenschiff* read *Narrenschiff.*

146 **Brooks, Cleanth.** *Line 4, for* Allan TATE, *read* Allen TATE.

149 **Browning, Robert.** *Line 17, for* single poems *read* poetic drama. *After* A BLOT IN THE 'SCUTCHEON *insert* His better known poems are.

149 **Brozovich, Josip.** *Substitute for this entry:* **Broz, Josip.** Marshal Tito of Yugoslavia.

149 **Bruce.** *Line 2, for* 1314 *read* 1306.

151 **B. S. degree.** *Line 4, for* A.B. *read* ARTS.

155 **Bureau of Internal Revenue.** *Line 3, for* leveled *read* levied.

157 **burning ghat.** *Following this, substitute:* Hindu cremation place.

160 **Byrne, Donn.** *Line 2, for* Donn Byrne *read* Donn-Byrne. *Line 4, for*

PAGE

1920 *read* 1921. *Line 6, substitute:* See DONN-BYRNE, Brian Oswald.

160 **Byron, George Noel Gordon.** *Line 21, for* FALIERI *read* FALIERO. *Last line in column, for* MILLBANKE *read* MILBANKE.

162 **Cadman, Charles Wakefield.** *Correct death date to* 1946.

163 **Caesar, Caius Julius.** *Line 35, for* See under city *read* Rome.

167 **Caliburn.** *For* EXCALIBAR *read* EXCALIBUR.

167 **Calliope.** *For* See also KALLYOPE *read* Also a musical instrument made up of whistles.

170 **Cameron, Margaret.** *Following this, substitute* (1867-). American writer; *A Sporting Chance* (1926), etc.

172 **Candide.** *For* Cunagonde *read* CUNEGONDE.

177 **Capote, Truman.** *Correct birth date to* 1924.

180 **carmagnole** (2). *Throughout refrain, for* sou *read* son.

181 **Carnal, Grandma Called It.** *Following this, substitute:* A book of reminiscences by Bertha Foster Damon.

185 **Casey Jones.** *Substitute for this entry:* The prototype of this character of American folk song is said to have been the renowned engineer of the "Cannonball" on the Illinois Central Railroad, John Luther Jones, who was killed in a train wreck in Mississippi during the early 1900's. To a Negro engine wiper, Wallace Saunders, is attributed the ballad, known for its serio-comic ending. In the ballad the wreck occurred on Reno Hill, on the road to San Francisco. The town of Cayce, Kentucky, near which Jones was born, may have supplied his famous nickname. A play entitled *Casey Jones* was produced by the Group Theatre in New York.

187 **Castlemaine.** *Following this, substitute:* See Duchess of Cleveland.

187 **Castruccio Castracino's sword.** *For last name read* Castracani.

195 **Champion of England.** *After first sentence, substitute:* The office of champion had existed under the Dukes of Normandy in the family of the lords of Fontenay. Sir John Dymoke, who was the first to perform this office in England at the coronation of Richard II in 1377, was the husband of Margaret de Ludlow, heiress of Philip Marmion, who claimed descent from the lords of Fontenay. The office continued in the Dymoke family. After the coronation of George IV the office was allowed to lapse when the estate passed to a collateral branch of the family.

PAGE

198 **Charles I** and **Charles II** of England. *Following this, substitute:* Stuart kings, 1625-1649 and 1660-1685.

201 **Chauchat.** *For* Claudia *read* Clavdia.

203 **Chesterton, Gilbert Keith.** *Line 2 should read:* English journalist, poet, author of biography.

210 *Top of column 1, continuing entry on* **Christian Science**, *substitute for last two sentences:* The name Christian Science is said to have been first used by P. P. Quimby, a physician and mesmerist, of whom Mrs. Eddy was once a patient. It is claimed that the religion has no connection with this former usage. The official name of the church is Church of Christ, Scientist.

210 **Christians Only.** *For* Brown *read* Broun.

211 **Churchill, Winston Leonard Spencer.** *Line 12, omit* because of his Conservative policies.

216 **Clan-na-Gael.** *Line 1, for* Fenian *read* secret. *Line 3 should read:* successor to the Fenian Brotherhood (1856).

216 **Clarissa Harlowe.** Line 3, for *The History of Clarissa Harlowe* read *Clarissa; or the History of a Young Lady.*

219 **Cleveland, Duchess of.** *Following this, substitute:* (1641-1709). Mistress of Charles II (1660-1674).

221 **Clovis.** *For last sentence, substitute:* The dynasty lasted until 751.

246 **Countess Kathleen, The.** *Read* Cathleen.

248 **Cousins, Norman.** *Correct birth date to* 1912.

262 **cumulative story.** *Substitute for this entry:* In universal folklore there is a particular kind of story that assumes a human understanding in related creatures and objects, whereby all interact upon each other in a sequence of cause and effect. The nursery tale "Titty Mouse and Tatty Mouse" is an example. Titty Mouse is scalded to death and Tatty sits down and weeps. The stool asks why Tatty weeps, and decides to hop. The broom sweeps. The door asks why. "Titty's dead," says

PAGE

the broom, "and Tatty weeps, and the stool hops, and so I sweep." "Then," says the door, "I'll jar." And so it goes —the window creaks, the walnut tree sheds its leaves, a bird moults its feathers—until an old man on a ladder breaks his neck, whereupon the walnut tree falls down and upsets the house, the house knocks out the window, the window knocks down the door, the door upsets the broom, the broom upsets the stool, and poor little Tatty Mouse is buried beneath the ruins.

273 *Column 1, line 24 from bottom, for* was a friend of *read* antedates both.

294 **Dial, The.** (2). *Line 3, for* 1916 *read* 1918. *Line 5, for* under the editorship *read* with the literary aid.

309 *Column 1, line 28 from bottom, for* sermons *read* Devotions.

329 **Eastman, Max Forrester.** *Line 4, for* founded *read* was a founder of. *Line 5, for* 1913 *read* 1912.

332 **Eddy, Mary Morse Baker.** *After* Founder of the Church of Christ, Scientist (1879) *substitute:* Influenced by Dr. P. P. Quimby. Mrs. Eddy's teachings took a religious bent, and Dr. Quimby's son later repudiated any connection between Dr. Quimby and Christian Science. The Christian Science Church is strongly opposed to mesmerism and similar forms of autosuggestion. Mrs. Eddy also wrote *Science and Health, with Key to the Scriptures* and founded the Christian Science Publishing Society.

335 **Elaine.** *Line 4, for* King PELEAS *read* King PELLES.

337 **Eliot, Thomas Stearns.** Line 9, for ALFRED J. PRUFROCK read *J. Alfred Prufrock.*

338 *Ibid. After paragraph 1, last line, insert:* He received the Nobel Prize for literature in 1948. *Next paragraph, line 9, omit* (see OBJECTIVE CORRELATIVE).

338 **Eliza.** *Last line, omit* See also BRAHMINE AND BRAHMIN.

340 **Elsted, Thea.** *For* Elsted *read* Elvsted.

352 **Euclid.** *Quotation should read* Euclid alone has looked on beauty bare.

358 **expressionism.** *Lines 9-10, omit* OBJECTIVE CORRELATIVE.

367 *After* **Fasolt,** *insert:* **Fast, Howard** (1914-) American author. Principal works: *Citizen Tom Paine* (1943); *Freedom Road* (1944).

PAGE

367 **Fastolfe, Sir John.** *After first sentence, substitute:* This is not "Sir John Falstaff" but the lieutenant general of the Duke of Bedford and a Knight of the Garter. Caused loss of important battle by fleeing while in the vanguard.

368 Father of French Surgery. *For* Ambrose *read* Ambroise.

375 *Column 1, line 8, omit* See ANCIENTS AND MODERNS.

378 **Fidelio.** *For* LEONORE *read* LEONORA.

381 **Finn.** *Line 5, for* GRAINME *read* GRAINNE.

387 *After* **Flaccus, Quintus Horatius,** *insert:* **Flack, Marjorie** (1897-). Picture stories for the young, and a pioneer in entertaining REALISM for children. The *Angus* books, *Ask Mr. Bear* (1932), *The Story About Ping* (1933), *Walter the Lazy Mouse* (1937), *The Restless Robin* (1937), *The Boats on the River* (1946). In private life Mrs. William Rose BENET.

394 **Forbes, Esther.** *Next to last line, for* Metro-Goldwyn-Meyer *read* Metro-Goldwyn-Mayer.

396 **Forsyte Saga.** *Paragraph 2, line 3, for* the eldest *read* James, one. *Line 8, for* uncle *read* cousin. *Line 14, for* run off together *read* fall in love.

405 **freedom of the press.** *Substitute for this entry:* The right to publish without governmental censorship.

412 **Führer principle.** *Line 6, for* DUCE *read* FASCISM.

423 *Omit* **Gasoline Alley.** See SKEEZIX.

424 **Gaunt, John of.** *Substitute for this entry:* (1340-1399). Fourth son of Edward III. Soldier; patron of Chaucer.

424 **Gautama.** *Line 1, for* family *read* personal. *Line 2, for* personal *read* family.

428 **geopolitics.** *Lines 4-5, for* see HAUSHOFER *read* Crystallized by Karl Haushofer (1869-1946).

449 **Gothland, The Queen of.** *For* Herbert FRENCH *read* Herbert TRENCH.

450 **Gourmont, Rémy de.** *Last line, omit* See also BARNEY, NATALIE.

455 *Column 2,* Great Captain. *For* See CAPITANO, EL GRAN *read* See under CAPTAIN.

455 *Column 2,* Great Commoner. *Substitute for this entry:* William Pitt, the Elder (Earl of Chatham) (1708-1778).

PAGE

456 **Greek.** *Omit* See also under DOUBLE DUTCH.

461 **Griffith, David.** *For* (1880-) *read* (1875-1948).

466 **Guido delle Colonne.** *Line 5, for* ST. MORE *read* SAINTE-MAURE.

466 **Guiney, Louise Imogen.** *Line 5, for* Sir Edmund GROSSE *read* Sir Edmund GOSSE.

467 **Gulbrannsen, Trygve.** *Read* Gulbranssen.

468 **Gunga Din.** *Quotation, line 5 for* spores *read* spots.

474 **Hall, Holwortly.** *Read* Holworthy.

486 **Hay, John Milton.** *Line 8, for* BLUDSOE *read* BLUDSO.

494 **Henrietta, Anne.** Line 6, for *Fluster* read *Flush.*

496 *Column 1, Lines 16-18, substitute:* A collection of American short stories published annually by Doubleday & Company and edited by Herschel Brickell.

505 *After* **Hillquit, Morris,** *insert:* **Hillyer, Robert Silliman** (1895-). Boylston Professor, Harvard 1937-1945. *Collected Verse* (1933) awarded PULITZER prize 1934. Poet, critic, and novelist, National Institute of Arts and Letters.

522 **Howlegas.** *For both page head and entry, read* Howleglass.

522 **How They Brought the Good News from Ghent.** *Add* to Aix.

532 **Ianthe.** *Line 6, for* U. S. LANDOR *read* W. S. LANDOR.

542 **Interlude.** *Line14, omit* See NICE WANTON.

542 **Interpreter, Mr.** *Line 2, for* Bunyon *read* Bunyan.

542 **Invincibles, the Irish.** *For* A Fenian *read* An Irish.

557 **Jehoash.** *For* see JOASH *read* One of the kings of JUDAH.

558 **Jennings, Sarah.** *For* See under CHURCHILL, JOHN *read* Duchess of Marlborough. See ATOSSA.

560 **Jesse, Fryniwyd Tennyson.** *Line 3, omit* See also HARWOOD.

560 **Jim Bludsoe.** *Read* BLUDSO.

579 **Kate Greenaway dress.** *Line 2, for* Kate GRENAWAY read Catherine GREENAWAY.

580 **Keats, John.** *Column 1, last line, omit* See also BRAWNE, FANNY.

592 **Knight of the Burning Pestle.** *Last line, for* Beaumont (1611) *read* BEAUMONT AND FLETCHER (1609).

PAGE

596 **Krupkaya,** etc. *Substitute for this entry:* Krupskaya, Nadezhda Konstantinovna (1869-1939). Russian social worker and wife of LENIN. Wrote *Memories of Lenin.*

623 **Leigh, Augusta.** *For* MILLBANKE *read* MILBANKE.

625 **Leonesse.** *Last line, for* LYONESSE *read* LYONNESSE.

626 **Leonora** (2). *Last line, for* FERDINAND *read* FIDELIO.

626 **Leopard.** *Quotation, first word, for* loins *read* lions.

627 **Leslie, Bonnie.** *Read* Lesley.

647 **London, Jack.** *Line 17, first word for* WOLF *read* WILD.

648 **Long, Gabrielle.** *Add* See Cléry, L.

653 **Lovberg.** *Read* Lovborg.

654 *After* **Lovell, Charlotte,** *insert:* Loveman, Amy (1881-). Associate editor, *Saturday Review of Literature;* head of editorial department, Book-of-the-Month Club; author of *I'm Looking for a Book* (1936); co-author of *Saturday Papers* (1921) and *Designed for Reading* (1934). C. L. Skinner Award (1946).

662 **Lytton, Bulwer.** *Substitute for this entry:* **Lytton, Edward George Earle Lytton Bulwer-Lytton,** 1st Baron (1803-1873). English novelist, short-story writer, poet, and playwright. His best-known novels are THE LAST DAYS OF POMPEII; EUGENE ARAM; RIENZI; ERNEST MALTRAVERS; THE LAST OF THE BARONS; HAROLD, THE LAST OF THE SAXON KINGS; KENELM CHILLINGLY; and THE CAXTONS. His dramas are THE LADY OF LYONS; RICHELIEU; and *Money.* His poem *The New Timon* jeered at Tennyson who successfully replied to it.

687 **Mao Tse-tung.** *Remove death date* 1940. *Add* Leader of drive against Nationalists.

689 **marguerite des marguerites.** *Line 6, for* mother *read* grandmother.

697 **Martyn, Edward.** *Line 4, for* 1914 *read* 1899.

699 **Mason, Daniel Gregory.** *Line 5, for* son *read* nephew.

700 **Masses, The.** *Line 2, for* 1911 *read* 1912. *For* when Max EASTMAN was the editor *read* Max EASTMAN was one of the founders. *Line 10, for* 1918 *read* 1917.

708 **Medivin, Thomas.** *Read* Medwin. *Entry should come after* Medusa, *and*